—THIRD—

BARNHART

DICTIONARY

OF

NEW

ENGLISH

THIRD

BARNHART

DICTIONARY

OF

NEW

ENGLISH

ROBERT K. BARNHART

SOL STEINMETZ

WITH

CLARENCE L. BARNHART

THE H.W. WILSON COMPANY. 1990

First Printing

Library of Congress Cataloging-in-Publication Data

The Third Barnhart dictionary of new English / [edited by] Robert K.
    Barnhart, Sol Steinmetz with Clarence L. Barnhart.
        p.   cm.
        Rev. ed. of: The Second Barnhart dictionary of new English.
    c1980.
        ISBN 0-8242-0796-3
        1. Words, New—English—Dictionaries. 2. English lan-
    guage—Dictionaries. I. Barnhart, Robert K. II. Steinmetz,
    Sol.   III. Barnhart, Clarence Lewis, 1900–   . IV. Sec-
    ond Barnhart dictionary of new English. V. Title: Barnhart dic-
    tionary of new English.
    PE1630.B3   1990
    423—dc20   90-33483
                                                                    CIP

TABLE OF CONTENTS

PREFACE

As English is used more and more throughout the world, users everywhere need a dictionary that explains important new words and meanings. Unabridged dictionaries are issued infrequently; except for the longer *World Book Dictionary*, standard desk dictionaries have scant space for new entries and almost none at all for quotations showing the new words in use. *The Third Barnhart Dictionary of New English*, in recording the words and meanings not entered or fully explained in standard dictionaries, is a supplement to current dictionaries of the English language.

Like the first and second Dictionaries of New English, this volume "is a lexical index of the new words of the past decade, a record of the most recent terms required and created by our scientific investigations, our technical and cultural activities, and our social and personal lives. Each entry has one or more quotations of a length sufficient to help convey the meaning and flavor of the term; and pronunciations, etymologies, and usage notes are added in many cases to assist the understanding of a word and its use. By 'New English' we mean those terms and meanings which have come into the common or working vocabulary of the English-speaking world . . . ." So wrote Clarence Barnhart in the preface to the first *Barnhart Dictionary of New English*.

In *The Third Barnhart Dictionary of New English* we have continued that record of the development of English by including the new words and meanings of the past ten years. In addition many of the entries found in the two earlier books of this series (both now out of print) are also included to provide a revised and expanded record of new words and meanings introduced into English during the past three decades.

We have had an unusual opportunity to review the original research in the first and second Dictionaries of New English and revise our conclusions according to new findings, from our own work and against the background of others, chiefly of our friend and fellow editor Dr. Robert Burchfield.

We have gained insight about language development from many who are now monitoring the development of English: those in various academic fields, and in particular Dr. John Algeo, who took up the study from Professor I. Willis Russell; my father Clarence Barnhart and brother David; and Dr. Burchfield along with the editors of various so-called commercial dictionaries. Not only have techniques of monitoring English become more sophisticated, but the choice of sources which we use and the commentary which is provided have been refined by watching each other.

Since we started compiling for publication the accumulated evidence in our files, many individuals and dictionary houses have contributed through their publications to make a more complete contemporary record of the English language. Not only have we witnessed the completion of the revision of the *Oxford English Dictionary* and ourselves made a modest contribution to that body of evidence, but we, and all students of language, have also been privileged to draw on the work of Merriam Webster as well as the analysis of Dr. Algeo, the wide-ranging weekly commentary of William Safire, expressed opinions of such language conservators as John Simon, Edwin Newman, and James Kilpatrick, and the reflections of scholars who make a measured examination of the present-day development of English as found, for instance, in the detailed tabulations of Dr. Garland Cannon and others.

These people and many, many others have contributed either directly or indirectly to making this third edition of our Dictionary of New English. Among them it is also appropriate to cite Dr. Frederic Cassidy, whose *Dictionary of Regional American English* has contributed much information useful to our work.

Our particular interest in new English began with Clarence Barnhart in the 1930's working with Sir William Craigie at the University of Chicago. However, the Dictionaries of New English spring from other seeds as well: from the early collecting of contributors to *American Speech,* from the work of Atcheson Hench, and more directly from Marjorie Taylor's *The Language of World War II* (1944) and the work of Paul Berg (1953)—and also from the tradition of John Florio's *A World of Words* (1598) and John Kersey's revision (1706) of Phillips' Dictionary. The Dictionaries of New English have generated other works, such as Merriam Webster's *6,000 Words* (1976), culminating in *12,000 Words* (1986), which is a noteworthy departure from the tradition, begun as early as 1913, of simple "Addenda" to the Unabridged. The experience of monitoring and collecting the language over forty years and reflecting on it has influenced much of our work including that in *The Barnhart Dictionary of Etymology* in which fundamental ideas about the development of English are evident in our views of back formation, functional shift, the processes of blending, and the influence of analogy as it affects internal change in English.

The great problems of financing an independent research operation to produce a book of this type are ever-present. Some of them have been relieved by The H.W. Wilson Company in the capacity of publisher and in their Editor of General Publications, Mr. Bruce Carrick, who has given strong and sympathetic support to the project. In spite of the fact that the burden of the production costs was lifted from our shoulders, it is still necessary to maintain the underlying research of reading, measuring, evaluating, and editing the raw material. It is almost impossible to convey the load such efforts put on our time and energy, except to express the relief in being able to share the editorial burden with a dedicated editorial staff that has contributed so much to the completion of *The Third Barnhart Dictionary of New English.*

It is the hope of the editors that the publication of this edition will mark the beginning of a long association with the publisher in which we may make our continuing research available to those interested in the development of English.

Robert K. Barnhart

COMBINED EDITORIAL ADVISORY COMMITTEES
(Dictionaries of New English)

JOHN ALGEO

Professor of English, University of Georgia.

Editor, *American Speech*, from 1969 to 1981.

Author (with Thomas Pyles) of *The Origins and Development of the English Language* (third edition 1982).

Co-editor of "Among the New Words" department in *American Speech*.

FRANCES NEEL CHENEY

Professor Emeritus, School of Library Science, George Peabody College for Teachers.

Author of *Fundamental Reference Sources*, 1971 (second edition 1980).

RUDOLF FILIPOVIĆ

Professor Emeritus of English and Director, Institute of Linguistics, University of Zagreb, Yugoslavia.

Editor-in-chief of *Studia Romanica et Anglica Zagrabiensia* and *Strani jezici* [Foreign Languages] (Zagreb).

Co-editor of *Suvremena lingvistika* (Zagreb) and *Filološki pregled* (Beograd).

Editor and co-author of *English-Croatian Dictionary*.

Editor of Langenscheidt's *English-Croatian and Croatian-English Dictionary*.

GUY JEAN FORGUE

Ancien Elève de l'E.N.S., agrégé d'anglais, Professor of American English at Sorbonne Nouvelle (France).

Editor of *Letters of H. L. Mencken* and *Collection USA*.

Author of *H. L. Mencken: l'Homme, l'Oeuvre, l'Influence; Poems of E. Dickinson* (translated), 1969; (with Raven I. McDavid, Jr.) *La Langue des Américains*, 1972, and *Les Mots Américains*, 1976.

Contributor to many scholarly and literary reviews.

HANS GALINSKY

Professor Emeritus of English and American Studies, formerly Dean, Fachbereich Philology II, Johannes Gutenberg-Universität, Mainz, Germany.

Past Vice-President of *Deutsche Gesellschaft für Amerikastudien*.

Co-editor of *Amerikastudien*.

Author of *Die Sprache des Amerikaners, Amerikanisches und Britisches Englisch, Amerikanisch-deutsche Sprach- und Literaturbeziehungen, Regionalismus und Einheitsstreben in den Vereinigten Staaten*, and *Das Amerikanische Englisch: Ein kritischer Forschungsbericht* (1919–1945); co-author of *Amerikanismen der deutschen Gegenwartssprache*.

REASON A. GOODWIN

Consulting Editor (Pronunciation) of *The World Book Dictionary*.

Formerly, Assistant Professor in Modern Languages, University of Louisville; Research Associate in Slavic Linguistics at the University of Chicago.

Pronunciation Editor of *New Century Cyclopedia of Names* and Editor (with George V. Bobrinskoy) of *Three Short Stories* by Ivan S. Turgenev and *The Provincial Lady* by Ivan S. Turgenev. Author of *"New Supplement"* to *March's Thesaurus-Dictionary* and *Troika*. (Deceased)

SHIRÔ HATTORI

Professor Emeritus of Linguistics, University of Tokyo, Japan. Councilor of the Linguistic Society of Japan; member of the Board of Directors of the English Language Education Council, Inc.; Honorary Member of the Linguistic Society of America.

Editor of *An Ainu Dialect Dictionary.*

Author of *Phonetics, Phonology and Orthography, The Genealogy of Japanese, Methods in Linguistics, A Study in the Basic Vocabulary of English;* co-editor of *An Introduction to the Languages of the World.*

BERTIL MALMBERG

Professor of Linguistics, University of Lund, Sweden.

Editor of *Studia Linguistica; IRAL.*

Author of *La Phonétique; Phonetics; New Trends in Linguistics; Structural Linguistics and Human Communication; Estudios de fonética hispanica; Phonétique générale et romane; Linguistique générale et romane,* and *Manuel de phonétique générale.*

YUTAKA MATSUDA

Professor of English, Kwansei Gakuin University, Nishinomiya, Japan.

Author of *The American Impact on British English,* 1975, *Aspects of English Usage,* 1977, and *Cross-Over Languages: English and Japanese, Japanese and English,* 1986.

ANGUS McINTOSH

Professor Emeritus of English and Director, Middle English Dialect Project, University of Edinburgh, Edinburgh, Scotland.

Author of *Introduction to a Survey of Scottish Dialects;* co-author of *Patterns of English.*

LADISLAS ORSZÁGH

Chairman of the Lexicographical Committee of the Hungarian Academy of Sciences; formerly Professor of English at the University of Debrecen, Hungary.

General Editor of *Angol-Magyar Szótár: Magyar-Angol Szótár* [English-Hungarian and Hungarian-English Dictionary]. (Deceased)

I. WILLIS RUSSELL

Professor Emeritus of English, University of Alabama.

Chairman of the Research Committee on New Words of the American Dialect Society.

Co-editor of "Among the New Words" department in *American Speech.* (Deceased)

MATTHEW H. SCARGILL

Professor Emeritus of Linguistics and Department Head, University of Victoria, Canada.

Director of Lexicographical Centre for Canadian English.

Co-editor of *Dictionary of Canadian English* series and *A Dictionary of Canadianisms on Historical Principles.*

Author of *An English Handbook* and *Modern Canadian English Usage.*

COMBINED EDITORIAL STAFF

Consulting Editors

John Algeo (General Critical Review)
Arthur Delbridge (Australian English)
Brian Foster (British English)
Robert A. Fowkes (General Critical Review)
Reason A. Goodwin (Linguistics, Pronunciation, and Etymology)
I. Willis Russell (American English)
M. H. Scargill (Canadian English)
Anthony Wharton (British English)

Senior General Editor

Cynthia A. Barnhart

General Editors

David K. Barnhart
Gerard M. Dalgish
Frances M. Halsey
Robert F. Ilson
Ruth Gardner McClare

Senior Associate Editor

Anne-Luise Bartling

Associate Editors

David F. Barnhart
Deirdre Dempsey
Rowena S. Fenstermacher
Catherine E. McEniry

Senior Assistant Editor

Shirley Abramson

Assistant Editors

Paula Alvary
Katherine E. Barnhart
Rebecca L. Barnhart
Maria Bastone
Jane A. Boland
Helen V. Graus

Chief Office Assistant

Albert S. Crocco

Office Assistants

Leroy J. Brightman
John Carter
Lynda Dalgish
Elizabeth E. Fristrom
Julia Galas
Albert L. Gunther
Dolores L. Hannigan
Rosemary E. Keppel
Gloria D. Linden
Virginia L. Spellman
Marion A. Towne

COMBINED READING STAFF

R. A. Auty
John R. Barnhart
Michael G. Barnhart
Dawn Borgeson
Elizabeth Breslin
Ruth B. Cavin
Barbara M. Collins

Sonja H. Coryat
Dannydelle W. Dandridge
Valerie Dean
Marie E. Farenga
Sylvian Hamilton
Jane Knight
Elva G. Knox
Janet McKeel

Benjamin B. Normark
Andrea B. Olsen
Virginia M. Rowe
Robin Smith
Theresa B. Strelec
George S. Waldo
Richard L. Wright

EXPLANATORY NOTES

The Third Barnhart Dictionary of New English is a supplement to existing general purpose, English-language dictionaries. As such it closely follows the style of current dictionaries, which makes the framework of this dictionary a familiar one that is easy to use. However, there are some departures from traditional dictionary content that deserve explanation.

Special Notes

Editorial comments and related information about usage, word formation, cultural or historical facts, and the like, are provided in notes. They describe changing fashions in current English, based on evidence from our files. This departure from the traditional dictionary practice includes notes such as those listed under *adperson*, *a.k.a.*, *dingbat*, *prioritize*, *fulsome*, *man²*, *human rights*, *person*, etc., when it seems appropriate to give the user some of the contemporary information available from an editorial reading of our files.

The special notes appear at the end of entries, following the date or the etymology, and are indicated by the sign (▶); some expanded notes immediately follow the entry word and also have the ▶ to mark them.

Arrangement of Entries

1) Many derivative forms of main-entry words are listed in boldface type directly under the entries to which they are related, as **psychobiographer** and **psychobiographical** under the main entry **psychobiography**. Although these subentries have citations, they are not defined, because, like the run-on entries in standard dictionaries, the meaning is easily derived from the main entry. The grouping also serves to unlock their function by showing that their relationship to the head word is more a grammatical than a semantic one. Moreover, grouping related entries explains subtle elements of development of the language.

2) Derivatives and compounds are entered separately whenever they cannot be satisfactorily explained by a combination of the prefix, suffix, or combining form with the root word. New affixes (as in *-aholic*) and new meanings of affixes and combining forms (as *petro-*) are recorded under the affix or combining form. Unusually active affixes and combining forms are entered and examples of their use and productivity are given. The user should look first under the affix or combining form. If the word is not given there, it may have a specialized meaning or be unusually frequent and the user should consult the proper alphabetical order of the main entries.

3) Variant spellings appear as entries only if they are very common; normally only the most frequent spelling is given because of the great variation found in the spelling of new words. Thus, the spellings *Mujjaheddin*, *Mujahedeen*, and *Mujahidin* are not listed as variants under the entry **Mujahedin**, though variant forms may be given in a quotation.

4) The names of popular new products and services that are known to be registered trademarks are capitalized and described as trademarks in this book. Variant spellings of trademarks that occur very frequently are also recorded, but they

should not be regarded as indications of the legal status of a trademark (that is, as to whether it is becoming a generic term).

Dating of Entries and Definitions

1) Every main entry in this dictionary has the year of its earliest appearance in our files or in other sources as far as the editors could ascertain. The year is given in boldface within brackets at the end of an entry or a definition, but before subentries and usage notes, or at the beginning of an etymology.

> **blowback**. . . . [**1975** for def. 1; **1978** for def. 2]
> **bullhorn**, *v.t.* . . . . [**1970**, verb use of the noun (1955)]
> **Chisanbop**. . . . [**1976**, from Korean . . .]
> **displaced homemaker**. . . . [**1978**]
> **bag**, *n.* 1 . . . [**1962**] 2 . . . [**1967**] 3 . . . [**1963**]

While the date supplied should provide some idea about when a word or meaning became current, it is not necessarily the earliest attestation and serves only as a guide to the word's appearance in the general language. In many cases an example can probably be found that antedates the year cited here, for the usage predominant at any given time has often been nurtured in an earlier decade or an even longer period of time.

Sometimes a word or meaning exists for a long time in isolation among the members of a particular group or within a specialized field of activity or in use restricted to its coiner, before it comes into general currency. Whenever we have evidence that discloses such a fact, two dates are provided: the first is the year of the earliest available quotation for the term; the second date is the year the term begins to be frequently recorded, indicating its probable emergence into the mainstream of the language as indicated by appearance in popular sources.

> **cluster headache**. . . . [**1953, 1972**]
> **lacto-ovo-vegetarian**. . . . [**1952, 1975** . . .]
> **layering** . . . [**1971**, coined in 1950 by Bonny Cashin, born 1915, an American fashion designer]
> **biorheology**. . . . [**1969**, coined in 1948 by A. L. Copley from *bio-* of biology + *rheology* (1931) . . .]

2) In some instances the original meaning or root form of an entry is given a date. This date serves to explain the relationship between the new formation and the older established form and to show the gradual change in form and meaning that occurs in the language.

> **carpool** or **car-pool**, *v.i.* . . . . [**1966**, verb use of *car pool* (1940's)]
> **ban**, *v.t.* . . . . [**1966**, specialized sense of *ban* to forbid, prohibit (OED 1816)]
> **senior citizenship**. . . . [**1972**, from *senior citizen* (1938) + *-ship*]
> **back-to-basics**. . . .[**1975**, from the phrase *back to (the) basics*; the phrase *the basics* is an Americanism (1950's) meaning the fundamentals or elementary principles]

3) To confirm or establish information about the chronology of English vocabulary the editors consulted various well-known historical dictionaries, including *The Oxford English Dictionary* (OED), the four volumes of *A Supplement to the Oxford English Dictionary* (OEDS, now sometimes augmented by more information in the second edition OED2), *The Century Dictionary and Encyclopedia* (CD) and its supplement (CDS), the *Dictionary of Americanisms* (DA), *A Dictionary of American English* (DAE), *A Dictionary of Canadianisms on Historical Principles*, the *Middle English Dictionary*, *The Stanford Dictionary of Anglicised Words and Phrases*, *A Dictionary of Australian Colloquialisms*, *A Dictionary of South African English*, the *Dictionary of Jamaican English*, the *Dictionary of American Slang* (DAS), the *Dictionary of Bahamian English* (DBE), and the *Australian National Dictionary* (AND).

Pronunciation

1) The pronunciation of hard or unfamiliar words is given in parentheses after the entry word.

Usually only one pronunciation is provided despite the possibility of variants, except in the case of loanwords where the foreign pronunciation may be accompanied by an Anglicized form. The pronunciation we provide is that most likely to be heard in the United States but does not preclude other pronunciations in the English-speaking world.

2) The pronunciation key, given in full at the end of these Explanatory Notes, is composed of symbols in a phonemic adaptation of the International Phonetic Alphabet. The letter *y*, however, is an exception which we use to represent what in English is spelled with *y* in *yes* and *you* and *yarn* (for IPA *y*, a non-English vowel sound, we use Y).

In indicating the pronunciation of vowels and diphthongs we have chosen, at points of difference, to represent "American" rather than "British" speech. Thus although the key contains (ɔ) to represent an "aw"-type of "British" pronunciation of the *o* in *hot*, we use the (ɑ) which represents an "ah"-type vowel that is preponderant in America.

Prefixes, Suffixes, and Combining Forms

Derivatives and compounds are entered separately whenever they cannot be explained with the root word. New affixes (as **acousto-**) and new meanings of affixes and combining forms (as **anti-** or **a-**) are recorded under the affix or combining form, though unusually active affixes and combining forms (*re-*, *un-*, *-er*, etc.) that are long established in English make even a representative sampling beyond our resources.

Such affixes and combining forms as **astro-**, **bio-**, **cosmo-**, **immuno-**, **-ian**, **-in**, **-manship**, and **-ville** are entered separately, and examples of their use and productivity are given. The user should look first under the affix or combining form. If not given there, the word may have a specialized meaning of the affix or be unusually frequent, or there may be some interesting information about the word containing the affix that warrants separate entry. Thus, **anticodon** is difficult to explain as a combination of *anti- + codon*. We therefore give it separate entry:

> **anticodon**, *n.* a group of three chemical bases that form a unit in transfer RNA and serve to bind a specific amino acid to a corresponding group (called a codon) in messenger RNA.

Abbreviations, Acronyms, and Shortened or Clipped Words

These three types of entries are replacements of longer words or phrases. Abbreviations are not treated as words but assumed to be pronounced letter by letter; acronyms and clipped words are treated as regular words. The three types are illustrated by the following entries:

> **ASP**, abbreviation of AMERICAN SELLING PRICE.
> **ASP** (æsp), *n.* acronym for *Anglo-Saxon Protestant.* Compare WASP.
> **deli** ('deli:), *n. U.S.* short for *delicatessen.*

Symbols are letters chosen arbitrarily or by some system to represent a thing, a process, or some phenomenon. They are indicated in the following manner:

> **BZ**, a symbol for an incapacitating gas whose effects include disorientation, drowsiness, and hallucination. Compare CS, GB, VX.

Attributive Nouns

Nouns that are sometimes used in an attributive position are labeled after the definition as either (also used attributively) or (often used attributively), or, if frequently found, are given a separate definition number:

> **docking**, *n.* the joining of orbiting spacecraft (also used attributively). *Rendezvous and docking in orbit is a difficult operation; even with men in charge. The first Gemini attempt nearly ended in disaster.* Science Journal 1/68, p10 *The simple task of clamping Agena's tether to Gemini's docking bar is an exhausting struggle.* Time 9/30/66, p54
> **flagship**, *n.* **1** the chief or leading item of a group or collection . . . . **2** Attributive use: *Although the* Beacon *was the first Copley newspaper . . . the flagship paper . . .*

However, we use quotations freely with the noun in attributive position without feeling that it is necessary always to specify this use after the definition. Note, for instance, *C-and-W repertoire* in the quotation under **C&W** or **C-and-W**.

Speech Area Labels

The labels *U.S.* and *British* (occasionally *Canadian* and *Australian*) signal that a term is associated primarily with a particular region and that a term so labeled is most likely to be heard and used within that area without being spotted as out of place.

Where it is felt to be useful, equivalent or corresponding British and American terms are contrasted in definitions, as under **postcode** and **zip code**.

Foreign-language Labels

This book notes the occurrence in English contexts of a number of words and phrases from other languages (for example, **gauchiste** and **furor colligendi**). They may be used freely in English contexts as travelers' local color ("close by is a *hamam* or bath") or may name institutions or events of other lands. Such foreign words and phrases reflect contact with other languages and cultures. A certain amount of French or of other languages may be used with literary swank or flourish or to fill some niche where an English word seems to be lacking (such a word is *aficionado*, which has become so far Englished as sometimes to be respelled with two *ff*'s like *affection*). For these words we use language labels, such as *French, German*, or *Russian*, to indicate that the writer or speaker is consciously using a word known to be foreign instead of using an English equivalent (e.g. *crise de confiance* instead of *crisis of confidence*), as distinguished especially from a foreign word that has no English equivalent and is therefore a genuine loanword (e.g. *aikido*). To be sure, this distinction cannot be made with absolute certainty or maintained with ironclad consistency, and the reader will find numerous borderline cases in this book where a "foreign" word could have been treated either with or without a label.

Usage Labels

With the single exception of the label *Slang*, usage labels such as *Colloquial, Formal, Rare, Nonce*, and the like are not used because evidence is generally lacking, and these labels can only be a marking of a particular context at this point. One of the striking things about the creations of slang, however, is their range over practically all segments of the vocabulary, some even tampering with grammatical relations: *a together person, tell it like it is*. This is in large measure a result of the drive for novelty, freshness of expression, even a defiance of what is established.

The labels *Transferred sense* and *figurative* are given in cases where the basic or concrete sense of a new term has been transferred to analogical or figurative uses. For example:

> **body count**, 1 a count of the enemy killed in a military operation. Compare KILL RATIO. 2 *Transferred sense*. a a count of those killed in a particular way. b any count or tally of individuals.
>
> **equal time**, *U.S.* 1 an equal amount of free air time given, usually at the same hour of another day, to an opposing political candidate, party, group, or citizen, to broadcast their views over radio or television. Compare FAIRNESS DOCTRINE. 2 *Transferred sense*. an equal opportunity to reply to any charge or opposing view.
>
> **recycle**, *v.t.* 1 to put (wastes, garbage, etc.) through a cycle of purification . . . 2 *Figurative*. to put to a new or different use. *Most housewives bent on recycling their talents* . . .

Definitions

The editors have tried to keep the definitions simple, generally relying on carefully selected quotations to supply details and complex explanations that in standard dictionaries would be covered in the definition. Wherever a quotation supplies the actual meaning, no definition is given and the reader is instructed to "See the quotation for the meaning":

> **Reuben sandwich.** See the quotation for the meaning. . . . *the Reuben sandwich . . . has become wildly popular in most areas of the United States . . . It is a combination of corned beef, Swiss cheese and sauerkraut served hot.* NY Times 10/10/67, p50 [**1956**, said to be named after Arnold *Reuben*, 1883–1970, an American restaurant owner]

Occasionally readers are directed to read the quotation for additional facts that they may need in order to round out their understanding of the term's meaning:

> **flake²**, *n. U.S. Slang.* an arrest to meet a quota or to satisfy pressure for police action. See the quotation for details. *"An accommodation collar,"* he [Patrolman William R. Phillips] *said, is an arrest, to satisfy superior officers, that is presented in court with such weak evidence that acquittal is assured. "A flake," however, is the arrest, on known false evidence, of a person for something he did not do.* NY Times 10/20/71, p36 [**1971**, probably so called from the flimsiness of the evidence submitted]

Definitions of entries having several meanings are listed in the order of what our evidence shows to be their greatest frequency. However, where the frequency of the various meanings appears to be evenly divided, or in some cases where starting with the earliest meaning will show an interesting semantic development, the earliest meaning or the one closest to the earliest is given first:

> **man¹**, *n.* **the Man**, *U.S. Slang.* **1** the white man; white society personified. *The Man systematically killed your language, killed your culture, tried to kill your soul, tried to blot you out . . . .* Time 4/6/70, p71 **2** the police. *". . . I catches up with one fella in an alley after he put my TV in a truck. He keeps denyin' what I seen him do with my own eyes, so I blasts him and takes him bleedin' down to the Man."* Maclean's 12/67, p27 **3** the Establishment in general; the system. *"Kent and Cambodia were made to order for radicals. Something like Dowdell's death was made for them: 'The pigs got Tiger. You can't trust the Man. Come on with us.' I can hear them now."* Harper's 12/70, p59

Function and Order of the Quotations

Every definition is followed by one or more quotations selected to perform several functions: 1) to show the word's use in an actual context and a natural environment; 2) to furnish additional details about the meaning or connotation of the word that the definition cannot properly supply; and 3) to call attention to the range of use through several quotations from different sources, times, and places. The order of the quotations is not necessarily chronological and no attempt is made to give the earliest quotation available. The emphasis is placed instead on the utility of the quotations. A quotation from 1970 may precede a quotation from 1967; a quotation from a British or Canadian source may precede one from a U.S. source; quotations from U.S. and British or Canadian or Australian sources are often given to show usage in different areas.

Etymologies

Etymologies, giving the source or history of words, are added in brackets at the end of many entries. But only those words whose forms or meanings call for some explanation are given etymologies. The usual type of etymology, such as is found in standard dictionaries, needs no explanation here; it is common practice to etymologize such terms as *aikido* (a Japanese loanword), *Cold Duck* (a German loan translation), *cloxacillin* (a technical term made up of Latin elements), *glasphalt* (a blend of *glass* and *asphalt*), *eutrophicate* (a back formation of *eutrophication*), and the like. For the special purposes of this book, however, the editors availed themselves of the etymological brackets to insert information that concerns changes in the meaning and use of words that are already part of the language. Thus, shifts in the function of words are noted in the etymologies. Examples are:

> **litterbug**, *v.i.* . . . . [**1968**, verb use of *litterbug, n.* (OEDS 1947)]
> **geriatric**, *n.* . . . . [**1974**, noun use of the adjective]

Likewise, extensions of meanings are sometimes noted in the etymological notes whenever restrictive labels before definitions are not applicable. Examples are:

> **launching pad**, a place from which something starts; springboard. . . .
> [**1959**, figurative sense of the term for a rocket- or missile-launching platform (1951)]
> **track record**, the record of performance made by a person, business, etc., in a particular field or endeavor. . . .
> [**1965**, figurative sense from the racing term (1940's) for the record of speed set by a horse at a particular distance and track]
> **lifer**, *n. U.S. Military Slang.* a career officer or soldier. . . .
> [**1964**, extended from the original meaning of a person sentenced to prison for life (attested since the early 1800's)]

This use of the etymological brackets permits brief, formulaic notation of numerous changes in the function and meaning of older words.

Cross References

In addition to the usual cross references given in dictionaries from one variant spelling or form to another, or from a derived form to the root form, or from an entry giving information that supplements the first entry, we relate one scientific or technical term to correlative terms where possible. Thus, under **abscisic acid** we call attention to **brassin** and **cytokinin**:

> **abscisic acid** (æb'sisik), an organic substance that inhibits plant growth. *Abbreviation:* ABA Also called DORMIN. Compare BRASSIN, CYTOKININ.
>
> **brassin** ('bræsən), *n.* a plant hormone that stimulates the division, elongation, and lateral enlargement of plant cells. Compare ABSCISIC ACID, CYTOKININ, KINETIN.
>
> **cytokinin** (ˌsɑitou'kɑinən), *n.* a plant hormone that directs the differentiation of cells into the roots and shoots of young plants. Compare ABSCISIC ACID, BRASSIN, KINETIN.

PRONUNCIATION KEY

A. Vowels and Diphthongs

æ   a in *hat* (hæt)

ɑ   o in American *hot* (hɑt)
ɑː a in *father* ('fɑːðər)
ɑi i in *nice* (nɑis)
ɑu ou in *out* (ɑut)

e   e in *set* (set)
ei a in *gate* (geit)

i   i in *hit* (hit)
iː ee in *feet* (fiːt)

ɔ   o in British *hot* (hɔt)
ɔː aw in *raw* (rɔː)
ɔi oi in *oil* (ɔil)

ou o in *go* (gou)
u   oo in *book* (buk)
uː oo in *boot* (buːt)

ə   u in *cup* (kəp), a in *ago* (ə'gou)

B. Accented Vowels with R

ɑr ar in *part* (pɑrt)
er ar in *care* (ker)
ir ear in *hear* (hir)

ɔr or in *lord* (lɔrd)
ur oor in *poor* (pur)
ər ir in *bird* (bərd)

C. Syllabic Consonants

əl le in *little* ('litəl)
əm m in *prism* ('prizəm)

ən on in *prison* ('prizən)
ər ar in *altar* ('ɔːltər)

D. Consonants
(1) Ordinary Letter Values

b   in *bed*
d   in *did*
f   in *fat*
g   in *go*
h   in *had*
k   in *kit*
l   in *leg*
m   in *man*

n   in *not*
p   in *pig*
r   in *run*
s   in *sad*
t   in *tan*
v   in *vat*
w   in *wet*
y   in *yes*

z in *zoo*

(2) Special Symbols

ʃ	sh in *she* (ʃiː)	ð	th in *then* (ðen)
tʃ	ch in *chin* (tʃin)	ʒ	s in *measure* ('meʒər)
ŋ	ng in *sing* (siŋ)	dʒ	j in *join* (dʒɔin)
θ	th in *thin* (θin)		

E. Foreign Sounds

Foreign words are for the most part pronounced with the nearest equivalents in English sounds. For example, the close *e* of a French word such as *né* is represented by *ei* as in English *nay* (nei). The following symbols, however, are used for some specifically foreign sounds:

a	a in French *patte* (pat)	y	u in French *du* (dy)
œ	eu in French *heure* (œr)	~	over a vowel letter, nasal
x	ch in German *ach* (ɑːx)		vowel, as in French *sans* (sɑ̃),
			vin (vɛ̃), *bon* (bɔ̃), *un* (œ̃),
			Portuguese *são* (sɑ̃u)

F. Accents

ˈ primary stress, as in bəˈluːn (*balloon*)

ˌ secondary stress, as in ˈeləˌveitər (*elevator*)

THIRD

BARNHART

DICTIONARY

OF

NEW

ENGLISH

A

a-, *prefix.* now freely added to verbs to yield predicate adjectives with rather more vivid effect than the participle in *-ing*, and especially to verbs that denote some picturable activity, motion, or sensation. Examples —**asquish** *adj.* squishing. . . . *the corridor outside the Congressman's office was asquish with trod-upon fruit.* Time 7/4/69, p12 —**awhir,** *adj.* whirring. . . . *the sapphire skies are astir and awhir with rising warplanes.* NY Times 5/16/70, p24 In addition, this usage has been extended to make a vivid replacement for the past participial form in *-ed* in the predicate (or following the noun to which it applies), as in —**aclutter,** *adj.* cluttered. *New York City, already aclutter with candidates for mayor.* Time 7/2/65, p18 —**aglaze,** *adj.* glazed. *Her lips drew back in a snarl, her eyes were dark and aglaze.* Atlantic 7/67, p44

A, a symbol used in Great Britain to designate motion pictures that are unrestricted for showing to adult audiences but may not be suitable for showing to children under 14, and therefore require parental discretion and guidance. The approximate U.S. equivalent symbol is PG. *At the Paris Pullman, Ravi Shankar is being lionised in Raga (A).* Observer (London) 3/31/74, p36 **[1970]** ►See G for a usage note.

AA, a symbol used in Great Britain to designate motion pictures to which persons under 14 are not admitted unless accompanied by an adult. The approximate U.S. equivalent symbol is R. *The committee recommends acceptance of the British Board of Film Censors' four new categories of U, A, AA and X.* Times (London) 5/15/70, p4 **[1970; probably from Accompanied by Adult]**

A. & R. man, one who supervises artists and repertory, especially for a phonograph-record company. *"Just a few friends— artistes, A. & R. men, managers, agents, writers like yourself. . ."* Punch 9/30/64, p485 **[1953;** *A. & R.,* abbreviation of *Artists and Repertory*]

ABA (ˌeiˌbiːˈei), abbreviation of ABSCISIC ACID. **[1968]**

ABC or **A.B.C.,** abbreviation of *Advance Booking Charter,* a type of low-cost air fare available to passengers booking flights a definite length of time before the date of departure (often used attributively). Compare APEX, OTC, SUPER SAVER. See also AFFINITY GROUP. *Air travel also registered substantial gains in 1977, stimulated by the continuing popularity of "alphabet fares," such as the OTC (one-stop tour charter), and the ABC (advanced booking charter).* Americana Annual 1978, p506 **[1972]**

ABD (ˌeiˌbiːˈdiː), abbreviation of *All But Dissertation* (applied to a doctoral candidate who has the necessary credits for a Ph.D. degree but has not written the dissertation). *Ph.D. . . . preferred. ABD's considered, less than ABD will be considered for a one-year temporary appointment only.* Advertisement by University of Southern Maine, NY Times 4/15/79, pE11 **[1963]**

Abgrenzung (*Anglicized* ˈabgrenˌtsuŋ; *German* ˈapgrentsuŋ), *n.* a policy of total separation of East Germany from West Germany. . . . *the word on every official lip was* abgrenzung. *It means demarcation or separation, and is the label attached to the policy of deepening the division between the two Germanies, and banishing forever all hope of reunification.* Times (London) 5/3/72, p16 **[1972,** from German, literally, demarcation]

abortionism, *n.* the support or advocacy of abortion-on-demand. *First, abortion foes must point out that abortionism is indeed an "ism," a creed quite as specific and aggressive as any creed its proponents denounce, demanding not only tolerance but legitimation.* National Review 1/23/76, p31 **[1976,**

from *abortion* + *-ism*] ►This term is chiefly used by antiabortionists. See also the note under RIGHT-TO-LIFE.

abortionist, *n.* a person who supports or advocates abortion-on-demand. Compare ANTIABORTIONIST and PROABORTIONIST. *Marxist vocabulary has spread into all political nooks and crannies. Ecologists as well as abortionists envision "revolution."* National Review 2/20/76, p157 **[1976,** from *abortion* + *-ist*] ►This term is chiefly used by antiabortionists. Its earlier meaning (recorded since 1872) is a person who induces illegal abortions.

abortion-on-demand, *n.* the right of a pregnant woman to have an abortion at any time during pregnancy. *Abortion-on-demand after the first six or seven months of fetal existence has been effected by the Court through its denial of personhood to the viable fetus, on the one hand, and through its broad definition of health, on the other.* National Review 3/2/73, p261 **[1973]**

abortion pill, a synthetic steroid in the form of a tablet, taken orally to end a pregnancy by blocking the action of progesterone and thereby preventing the fertilized egg from becoming implanted in the uterus. *The revolutionary new abortion pill, RU 486, is. . . considered by the medical profession to be a far better means of abortion than surgical procedures. . .* NY Times 3/26/89, pE18 **[1987]**

abscisic acid (æbˈsisik), an organic substance that inhibits plant growth. *Abbreviation:* ABA Also called DORMIN. Compare BRASSIN, CYTOKININ. *The first of the new approaches makes use of a natural plant hormone, abscisic acid or ABA, normally involved in the process of leaf fall and plant dormancy.* New Scientist 12/10/70, p427 **[1968,** from the *abscission* or separation of parts of a plant from the stem]

abscisin (æbˈsisən), *n.* any of a group of organic substances that regulate plant growth. *Abscisins . . . have the ability to accelerate abscission, senescence, and the onset of dormancy; they also retard the growth of plants and inhibit germination.* McGraw-Hill Yearbook of Science and Technology 1968, p93 **[1962,** from *abscission* + the suffix *-in*]

absolute address, the specific location where information is stored in a digital computer. . . . *all symbols used for problem variables will be converted into specific memory location numbers, or "absolute addresses."* Van Court Hare, Jr., Introduction to Programming, A BASIC Approach, 1970, p100 **[1960]**

absurd, *n.* the absurd or the Absurd, a literary and philosophical term descriptive of the absurdity or pointlessness of the human condition from an existential point of view and associated with the works of Albert Camus, Jean Paul Sartre, Eugene Ionesco, Samuel Beckett, and Edward Albee. *Mr. Esslin defines his own influential catchphrase in four long essays on Beckett, Adamov, Ionesco and Genet; then spreads into an informative and international catalogue of related playwrights (Pinter, Frisch, Grass, etc.); and settles into a solid discussion of the tradition and significance of the Absurd.* Times (London) 4/20/68, p23 —**adj.** of or relating to the absurd. *The "absurd" theatre of Ionesco and Beckett. . .* New Yorker 11/28/64, p65 **[1954,** from French *l'absurde*; coined by Camus]

absurdism, *n.* concern with the absurd in literature and drama. *The three parts into which his novel is divided and marked off by distinct shifts in style—from straight, clean narrative, which he is good at, to earthy mysticism, and finally to absurdism.* New Yorker 3/9/68, p154 **[1954,** from French *absurdisme*; coined by Camus]

1

absurdist, *n.* a playwright or other writer who stresses the absurd in his or her work. See also THEATER OF THE ABSURD. *Like the Absurdists (the avant-garde of the late 1950's and early 1960's), Artaud rejected the theatre of realism.* Britannica Book of the Year 1969, p728 —*adj.* characteristic of absurdists or of the theater of the absurd. *There is a lot of witty, high elegant and absurdist dialogue and some terrible puns.* NY Times 4/12/68, p50 **[1960,** from *absurd*ism + *-ist*]

Acapulco gold, a strong variety of Mexican marijuana.... *no one knows whether Acapulco Gold is really obtained from a special variety of Cannabis... or whether it is just any marihuana a dealer can get a high price for.* Science Journal 9/69, p38 **[1967;** so called because it is grown near Acapulco, Mexico and because of the plant's golden color]

accelerogram , *n.* a record or graph of the acceleration of tremors occurring in an earthquake. *Synthetic accelerograms were constructed on a computer . . .in order to determine experimentally how an earthquake generated observed ground shaking.* Scientific American 12/77, p78 **[1973,** from *accelerate* + connecting *-o-* + *-gram,* derived from *accelerograph* (1954), instrument producing such a record]

acceptable, *adj.* capable of being tolerated; bearable. *DDT is eaten by Americans at only 10 per cent of the rate recommended by the WHO* [World Health Organization] *as a maximum acceptable daily intake.* New Scientist and Science Journal 9/23/71, p681 **[1969,** extended from the original (OED *c*1386) meaning "worthy or sure of being accepted"]

access[1] *v.t.* **1** to obtain access to; reach. *Users can access the European Space Agency's system at Frascati, near Rome, by dialling an Orpington telephone number.* New Scientist 9/14/78, p790 **2** to retrieve (data) from a computer storage unit or device.... *dynamic file access, the ability of a program to access a remote data set as if it were local with no special planning.* McGraw-Hill Yearbook of Science and Technology 1973, p157 **[1970** def. 1, verb use of the noun (OED 1382) meaning "entrance" or "admission"; **1973** def. 2, verb use of noun (1950) used in computer technology]

access[2], *n. British.* **a** the temporary release of programming by a radio or television station in order to allow an independent group to use the broadcasting facilities. *For purposes of our discussion. . .'access involves temporary abdication of programme management by a broadcasting organisation, in order that an organisation or group might broadcast messages, subject only to the laws of the land.'* Listener 9/19/74, p35 **b** *Attributive use.* —**access channel:** *But I see nothing inconsistent in supporting the idea of a third and quite different force in broadcasting, designed from the outset to accommodate independent contributions and provide a public service in the fullest sense. It must be ten years since some of us first proposed an accommodation of 'access' channel.* Listener 12/25/76, p848 —**access television:** *Access television is the term used for letting various minority and pressure groups, like one-parent families, black immigrants, people who want to stop black immigrants, old soldiers who feel they have been robbed of pensions, vegetarians, Vegans, even transvestites, into the studio to do their own thing.* Times (London) 5/31/76, p7 **[1974]**

access program, 1 *U.S.* a television program shown by a network affiliate during specified hours each week. See ACCESS TIME. *An analysis published in Broadcasting concluded that on the whole, the most successful "access programs"—those bought or produced by the stations for these periods—usually were updated versions of former network hits, such as "The Lawrence Welk Show" and "Hee-Haw."* Britannica Book of the Year 1973, p664 **2** *British.* a radio or television program designed for use by independent groups. See ACCESS[2]. *Nevertheless, it was recognized that access programmes did present real problems for many existing broadcasting organizations.* Listener 9/19/74, p357 **[1973** for def. 1; **1974** for def. 2]

access speed, the speed with which information is retrieved from a computer memory. *Matsushita's 4-megabit DRAM chip . . . provides an access speed of 60 billionth of a second.* Japan Times Weekly 3/21/87, p7 **[1987]**

access time, *U.S.* a period of time set aside by a network to show programs of affiliates, educational programs, and the like. *Some critics have blasted the station for canceling its 7:30-8 pm "access time" programs, including an investigative reporting series, a 60 Minutes-style magazine-format show, a "hot seat" interview program, and* The Young Reporters *with news and analysis by public-school kids.* TV Guide 7/31/76, p25 **[1976;** perhaps influenced by the earlier computer term *access time* the time it takes to access data stored in a computer (OEDS 1950)]. See ACCESS PROGRAM, def. 1.

accommodationist, *adj. U.S.* favoring accommodation or compromise, especially with the white establishment. *It was extremely easy for Randolph and Owen to dismiss the genuine conservatives, those protectors of Booker T. Washington's accommodationist legacy, who had counselled "first your country, then your rights."* New Yorker 12/2/72, p99 **[1970,** from *accommodation* + *-ist*]

accountability, *n. U.S. Education.* the holding of schools and teachers accountable for student performance by allocating school funds or teachers' salaries on the basis of the test scores of students. *Volume Three deals with the fundamental concern of productivity—or how to get a more effective performance out of teachers for less money; and with its corollary, accountability—or how to arrange the relationship between schools and parents so that the parents can be sure they are getting what they want for the taxes they are paying.* NY Times 10/22/72, p9 **[1972,** specialized sense of the noun (OED 1794) meaning the state of being held accountable or responsible]

accretion disk, a disk of gases or other interstellar matter around a black hole, neutron star, or other celestial body, formed by the gravitational attraction of the interstellar matter to the celestial body. *This formation, called an accretion disk, may be very important in some stellar birth sequences. In our own solar system . . . the planets and asteroids formed from the accretion disk as the sun grew in the embryo core.* World Book Science Annual 1979 (1978), p66 **[1976]**

AC/DC or **AC-DC,** *adj. Slang.* **1** capable of being sexually involved with either sex; attracted to both sexes; bisexual. *This is not just the look-alike, dress-alike unisex of Rolling Stone Mick Jagger and wife Bianca; AC-DC sexuality has jumped out of the closet and into the dinner party.* Newsweek 8/27/73, p56 **2** *Figurative use.* fluctuating between opposites; indecisive, ambivalent, or nonaligned. *The fact that the politically A.C.-D.C. Moynihan should be thought of as having a chance of becoming the Democratic senatorial nominee has much to do with the Democrats' eagerness not to make another mess of things.* New Yorker 6/7/76, p109 **[1971;** this slang use, however, is older although it is recorded only in Wentworth and Flexner's *Dictionary of American Slang* (1960) with this note: "Some jocular use *c*1940." *AC/DC* and *AC-DC* are from the abbreviation of *Alternating Current/ Direct Current.*]

ACD solution, a substance used to prevent coagulation of whole blood stored in blood banks. *Using current technology, whole blood can now be preserved for three weeks or more. A popular formulation was and still is the so-called ACD solution (dextrose-citric acid-sodium citrate), which permits a refrigerated shelf life of 21 days.* 1975 Collier's Encyclopedia Year Book, p67 **[1974,** *ACD* abbreviation of *acid citrate dextrose*]

ace, *v.t.* Often, **ace out.** *U.S.* **1** *College Slang.* to get a high or the highest grade in (a test or course). *The dramatic device that gives* The Paper Chase *its unity and tension is the question of whether Hart will get his grades, whether he will ace-out Kingsfield's course.* Time 10/29/73, p98 **2** *Informal.* to get the better of; come out on top of; defeat; outdo. *Boeing Co. aces out General Dynamics for the first big defense deal of the 1980's, the $4 billion cruise missile contract. . .* Time 4/7/80, p2 **[1970,** extended from the earlier (1920's) sports meaning "to score an ace" against an opponent (in tennis, golf, etc.); influenced by the fact that *A* is both the highest-grade and the letter that appears on the ace in a deck of playing cards]

acetaminophen (ˌæsətəˈminəfən), *n.* a crystalline drug used against pain or fever instead of aspirin in cases of hemorrhagic, sinus, or asthmatic disorders. *Formula:* $C_8H_9NO_2$ *Acetamino-*

phen . . . does not possess the antiinflammatory properties of aspirin and so is not very effective for arthritis patients. It does work for headache, menstrual cramps, and muscle aches. Joe Graedon, The People's Pharmacy, 1976, p67 [**1961**, from *acetic* + *amino* + *phenol*]

Aché (a:'tʃei), *n.* a member of a nomadic hunting tribe of South American Indians living like Stone Age people in the jungles of eastern Paraguay. Compare TASADAY and YANOMAMA. *The Achés . . . subsist on honey, insects, fish and any animals they can reach with seven-foot bows and arrows.* NY Times 1/27/74, pD2 [**1974**]

A chromosome, any one of the set of chromosomes characteristic of a species. *The designation B indicates a supernumerary chromosome, in contrast to the A chromosomes, the representatives of the normal complement.* Nature 1/22/76, p174 [**1976**]

acid, *n. Slang.* the hallucinogenic drug LSD. *I really felt I was through with drugs, at least acid and speed for sure. I am not going to get into that kind of thing again.* Atlantic 3/69, p44 [**1966**, from lysergic *acid* diethylamide, full name of LSD]

acidhead, *n. Slang.* a user or addict of the hallucinogenic drug LSD. *Reality was to be fled: Peter [Fonda] became the acidhead of the house. "In those days, it wasn't an illegal drug," he says. "It was pure, non-chromosome-breaking, non-habit-forming, non-dangerous. So I dropped 500 micrograms and never came back."* Time 2/16/70, p60 *I asked a constable . . . if he could tell me where to go to watch the acid-heads taking a trip.* Punch 9/6/67, p339 [**1966**, from *acid*, a slang term for LSD + *head*, a slang term for drug addict. See ACID, HEAD.]

acid precipitation, precipitation (such as rain or snow) of high acidity (rated on the pH scale as 5.6 or even less) resulting from the emission into the atmosphere of pollutants. Compare ACID RAIN. *Some experts fear that acid precipitation could lead to a 15 percent reduction in timber yields in the next 20 years.* U.S. News & World Report 11/19/79, p66 [**1978**]

acid rain, rain containing a high concentration of acidity, resulting from the emission into the atmosphere of pollutants, primarily sulfur and nitrogen oxides, which form sulfuric and nitric acid in raindrops. Compare ACID PRECIPITATION. *Scandinavian and American researchers suspect that acid rains have killed fish in many lakes in both regions.* NY Times 5/23/75, p76 *It dissolves concrete, rusts cars, kills fish and stunts tree growth by up to 60%. And it comes disguised in gently falling rain. Academics have been fighting over it and businessmen have been suing because of it.* It *is acid rain, the latest environmental shocker, an ecological time bomb on a short fuse that can't be ignored.* Maclean's 7/11/77, p17 [**1975**]

acid rock, a type of rock 'n' roll music with sound and lyrics suggestive of drug-taking or psychedelic experiences. *Significantly, The Band's [a rock group's] music is quiet . . . .But for those who take to them—musicians, college kids who have grown tired of the predictable blast-furnace intensity of acid rock, and an ever-growing segment of the young—The Band stirs amazement and glee.* Time 1/12/70, p38 [**1967**]

acid trip, *Slang.* a hallucinatory experience resulting from taking LSD. Compare BAD TRIP. *Like Western-lovers grooving on scalping scenes . . . this audience was digging the Youngun equivalents: acid trips, nude body paintings, pot smoking, . . . the works, man.* Atlantic 12/68, p146 [**1967**]

acneigenic (ækni:ə'dʒenik), *adj.* causing or producing acne. *The acneigenic potential of a chemical appears to be directly related to its overall toxicity. The importance of this fact is the implication that chloracne in an experimental animal can provide a very important screening test for systemic (not only skin) toxicity.* New Scientist 4/13/78, p79 [**1978**, for *acne* + connecting -*i*- + -*genic*, combining form meaning "producing" (ultimately from Greek *genēs* born + English -*ic*)]

acoustical hologram, the pattern formed in acoustical holography. *By "illuminating" an object with pure tones of sound instead of with a beam of coherent light one can create acoustical holograms that become three-dimensional pictures when viewed by laser light.* Scientific American 10/69, p36 [**1968**]

acoustical holography, a method of holography in which high-frequency sound waves instead of light waves are used to make a pattern or picture of an object. See also HOLOGRAPHY. . . . *acoustical holography could explore for oil and mineral deposits at depths of several miles.* Time 11/10/67, p41 [**1967**]

acoustic coupler or **acoustic data coupler,** a device for transmitting data over telephone circuits without making an electrical connection. *Each client will get a portable teletype and a thing called an "acoustic data coupler" that allows the teletype to send messages to a computer over any old telephone.* NY Times 6/26/68, p70 [**1968**]

acoustic microscope, a microscope in which the object being studied is scanned with sound waves and its image is reconstructed with light waves. *The actual and potential applications of high-resolution acoustic microscopes range from fine-scale materials analysis to the study of biological tissues and organs.* Scientific American 7/78, p80 [**1976**] —**acoustic microscopy:** *The single British research group working on acoustic microscopy, based at University College London, has hailed as a "significant advance" the development in the US of the first acoustic microscope that can "see" objects as sharply as a conventional optical microscope.* New Scientist 11/16/78, p523

acoustic perfume or **acoustical perfume,** another term for WHITE NOISE. *When the noises to be overcome are only mildly offensive or not too great in volume, they can sometimes be masked by an overlay of pleasant sound, which thus has a function similar to that so gallantly fulfilled by perfume through the ages—hence the name, "acoustic perfume."* 1968 Collier's Encyclopedia Year Book, p25 [**1966**]

acousto- (ə'ku:stou-), a new combining form, now used chiefly in technical writing, meaning "of or involving sound or acoustic waves" or "acoustic and _____." —**acousto-electric,** *adj.: Acousto-electric oscillators may also be useful for measuring changes in applied stress.* New Scientist 5/23/68, p402 —**acousto-electronic,** *adj.: Compression and expansion filters could be laid down on a single acousto-electronic strip.* Science Journal 5/70, p44 —**acousto-optic,** *adj.: . . . an acousto-optic modulator which switches the beam on and off.* Advertisement by Bell Labs, Scientific American 10/70, p199 —**acousto-optical,** *adj.: The acousto-optical unit serves the same purpose as the electronic interface which joins measuring equipment to a computer.* New Scientist 5/21/70, p376

acoustoelectronics, *n.* a branch of electronics dealing with the conversion of electrical signals into acoustic waves. *ACOUSTO-ELECTRONICS is based on converting an electrical signal into a flow of Rayleigh waves, acoustic waves travelling along a solid surface.* Science Journal 5/70, p42 [**1970**]

acoustooptics, *n.* a branch of physics dealing with the generation of light waves by means of ultrahigh-frequency sound waves. *Practical applications of acoustooptics are showing up in many areas where laser light may be used to gain or transmit information . . . An example is the manufacture of integrated optics (similar to integrated circuits in electronics) for transmission of information.* Science News 12/9/72, p381 [**1972**, from *acousto-* acoustic + *optics*]

ACP, abbreviation of *African, Caribbean, and Pacific Associables,* an organization of over 40 Third World countries formed for purposes of trading as a group with the European Economic Community and other nations of Europe, North America, etc. *Jamaica's Minister of Trade, who led the ACP group, emphasized that a guaranteed market for sugar in Europe was an essential part of the group's trading strategy.* Annual Register of World Events in 1974, p381 [**1974**]

acquire, *v.t.* (of a robot, computer, etc.) to find, take up, and hold. *Machine vision is . . . capable of locating an object within a certain known area and of describing the identity, position, and orientation of that object. This information can be passed to the computer controlling the robot, which is then able to acquire the object.* McGraw-Hill Yearbook of Science and Technology 1980, p11 [**1980**]

acquired immune deficiency syndrome, the full name of AIDS. *The American Red Cross says it will inform homosexual males, Haitian immigrants, drug users and others considered at high risk of carrying a dangerous disease, acquired immune deficiency syndrome, that they should not donate blood.* NY Times 3/7/83, pB7 **[1982]**

acritarch ('ækrə'tark), *n.* an oceanic one-celled fossil organism of unknown classification. *H. Tappan recently suggested that quantitative and qualitative changes in the oceanic phytoplankton are indicated by its fossil record. In Figure. 1 bluegreen algae, green algae, acritarchs . . . , dinoflagellates, and euglenids are represented as fossils by their highly resistant organic walls.* McGraw-Hill Yearbook of Science and Technology 1972, p215 **[1963,** from Greek *ákritos* indistinguishable + *arché* beginning]

acrolect ('ækrə,lekt), *n. Linguistics.* the dialect that has most prestige among the speakers of a language, usually the standard dialect. Compare BASILECT. *ACROLECT . . . is used for the collection of linguistic features of most prestige among a given community of speakers.* J.L. Dillard, Black English, 1972, p299 **[1964,** coined by the American linguist William A. Stewart from *acro-* highest (part) + dia*lect*]

acronym, *v.t.* to make an acronym of; designate by an acronym. *Nitrogen oxide, acronymed NOx, is another of the plant's noxious by-products . . .* Saturday Review 6/3/72, p30 **[1967,** verb use of the noun]

acrosin ('ækrəsən), *n.* a spermatic enzyme. *On the cap, or acrosome, of a spermatozoon, there is an enzyme called acrosin, which chews through the protective layers around an ovum with an action rather like the protein-digesting enzyme trypsin.* New Scientist 1/14/71, p54 **[1971]**

acrylic, *n.* **1** a paint made with an acrylic resin as the vehicle, used especially in art. *The painterly manner of abstraction, so widespread in the 1950s, changed to the hard-edged manner, with its dry, flat surfaces, usually painted in acrylic.* Saturday Review 11/4/72, p55 **2** a painting done with acrylics. *Byron Burford—Acrylics on paper, some portraying carnival and circus life. Starts Saturday, March 1.* New Yorker 3/3/75, p10 **[1972,** noun use of the adjective (as in *acrylic resin*, 1936)]

act, *n.* **1 get one's act together,** *U.S. Slang.* to get organized; eliminate differences, inconsistencies, etc.; plan or work systematically. *There is no great battle crying to be fought over refugee policy reform. It merely requires that the administration get its act together and the legislators bargain out their differing emphases . . .* Manchester Guardian Weekly (Washington Post section) 4/9/78, p16 *There I was, . . . weeping, feeling like a miserable, self-indulgent, neurotic, middle-aged woman who couldn't get her act together.* Eleanor Coppola, NY Times Magazine 8/5/79, p40 **2 hard** (or **tough**) **act to follow,** something or someone that cannot be surpassed or outdone. *"You're a hard act to follow."* Cartoon legend, New Yorker 3/24/80, p48 *(In curtailed form):* The Rise of Theodore Roosevelt *takes its subject up to the presidency; a second volume will follow. Morris has set himself a tough act, for Volume I does more than evoke the irrepressible Rough Rider.* Time 4/9/79, p81 **[1978,** apparently from show-business usage]

actigraph or **actograph** ('æktə,græf), *n.* any device which records changes in the activity of a substance, organism, etc. *The presence of . . . isotopic methylmercury was established . . . by scanning the chromatographic sheets in an actigraph.* Nature 2/5/75, p. 463 *Single crabs are placed in plastic boxes . . . and as the incarcerated crab moves between ends of this improvised actograph the box teeters, closing a microswitch that causes a deflection of a pen on a chart recorder.* Scientific American 2/75, p70 **[1975,** probably from *act* or *activitiy* + connecting *-i-* or *-o-* + *-graph* instrument that records]

actinin ('æktənin), *n.* a protein forming part of the complex of actin and myosin in muscle tissue. *The other proteins are not so well understood, but it is quite possible that the small proteins found in association with the active part of myosin, like troponin, regulate its movement. Another kind of function may be illustrated by actinin, which may help to maintain the regular architecture of the myofibrils.* New Scientist 1/27/72, p199 **[1972,** from *actin* + *-in*]

action, *n.* in various slang expressions: **1 a piece of the action,** a part or share in something. *And last year mink breeders from Scandinavia to California were falling over themselves to buy a piece of the action . . .* Maclean's 6/4/66, p1 **2 where the action is,** the place of greatest activity, development, etc. Compare WHERE IT'S AT under WHERE, *adv. . . . it is clear today that the early years of a child's life are critically important in the development of learning processes and capacity. "In many ways," he observed, "that's where the action is."* NY Times 12/24/67, pA40 **[1966]**

action level, the level of concentration at which a toxic or other unwanted substance in a food in the United States is considered hazardous enough to public health to warrant government action to prevent the sale of the food. Also called DEFECT ACTION LEVEL. See also ACCEPTABLE and ADI. *In Washington, a spokesman for the Food and Drug Administration said that last May the agency established an "action level" of 0.1 part per million for Mirex in fish. Fish containing that level or more will be seized if shipped in interstate commerce.* NY Times 9/2/76, p64 **[1976]**

action replay, *British.* a videotape playback of a highlight of a sports event or the like. The corresponding U.S. term is INSTANT REPLAY. *To see only the action replays of the Royal Wedding, that long-drawn-out Match of the Day, was no doubt to miss the cumulative effect of an occasion.* Listener 11/22/73, p720 **[1973]**

activator RNA, a form of ribonucleic acid believed to carry information used to activate the genes. *In either case the RNA transcribed from the integrator genes is designated activator RNA, since it bears information used for gene activation.* McGraw-Hill Yearbook of Science and Technology 1973, p204 **[1970]**

active euthanasia, the killing of a person who is incurably ill or injured, especially by the administration of a drug or other treatment that causes or hastens death. Also called POSITIVE EUTHANASIA. *As an adviser of the Euthanasia Council, Van Dusen . . . supported explicitly only the right to die without being kept alive by heroic measures—a view that Pope Pius XII held. This is called "passive" euthanasia, which in law and morality is treated totally differently from active euthanasia, or "mercy killing."* Time 3/10/75, p84 **[1975** ►When the term *euthanasia* is used without a preceding modifier it usually means active euthanasia. See EUTHANASIA.

active site, the site on the surface of an enzyme at which its catalytic action takes place. *Although chemical methods alone had suggested the probable location of the active site, only the structure of the molecule could explain the specificity of the enzymes.* Scientific American 7/74, p78 **[1963]**

active transport, the movement of a substance across a cell membrane by means of chemical energy. Active transport is always in a direction opposite to that of diffusion. *The transmission of nerve pulses, heart function, and kidney processes are coupled to a process known as active transport—the movement of sodium and potassium ions across cell membranes.* 1972 Britannica Yearbook of Science and the Future, p340 **[1963]**

actualize, *v.t.* to fulfill the potentials of. *Society Schooling is based on the premise that human beings actualize themselves through work . . .* Saturday Review 6/24/72, p45 —*v.i.* to fulfill one's potential. *The professionals, she found, were a ludicrously earnest lot. . . Their jargon was tiresome—they were always "resonating," "actualizing," "peaking," or having "gut reactions."* Time 7/27/70, p74 **[1970;** original meaning (1810) is "to make actual"] —**actualizer**, *n.: In regard to comments about our leaders practicing TM, I would prefer seeing some actualizers in managerial positions . . .* Psychology Today 7/74, p8

acupinch ('æk'yə,pintʃ), *n.* a method of relieving a muscle cramp by pinching the upper lip just under the nose for 20 or 30 seconds. *Can a stiff upper lip conquer a leg cramp? A quick pinch of the upper lip—a technique known as Acupinch—has* *proved to be up to 90-percent effective in relieving serious and recurrent muscle cramps in the legs and feet.* Reader's Digest 1/83, p19 [**1980**]

acupressure (ˈækyəˌpreʃər), *n*. **1** another name for SHIATSU. *Batja Cates . . . is really a foot magician. Her foot massage is based on some of the same principles as acupressure—that certain parts of the body carry life energy, and each energy line is related to the function of the body.* Sunday News (New York) 6/3/79, p43 **2** the use of finger pressure to diagnose medical conditions. *The advantages of diagnosis by way of acupressure are obvious, a probing finger on the outside of the body as compared, for example, to opening up the body to see what's wrong. One of the new alternative medical centers . . . reports considerable success in diagnosing otherwise inexplicable complaints with acupressure.* Stephen A. Applebaum, Out In Inner Space, 1979, p 117 [**1977**, extended meaning of "a method of arresting surgical hemorrhage by pressure" (OED 1859), ultimately from Latin *acū* with a needle + English *pressure*]

acupuncture, *v.t.* to treat or anesthetize by inserting fine needles into specific parts of the body. *According to police findings, the two quack herb doctors acupunctured Chong Pyong-Chon, first daughter of Mrs. Park Okrye, 31. The girl died of heart failure one hour after the therapy Saturday.* Korea Times 2/13/73, p4 [**1972**, verb use of the noun] ►Although the noun *acupuncture* first entered English in the late 1600's (the date of the OED quotation is 1684), it then referred only to medical practice in far-off China; thus it did not attain widespread currency until its expanded use in the 1970's. In the 1960's Chinese doctors used acupuncture as an anesthetic in performing major surgery. In the 1970's the American medical profession became interested in the anesthetic qualities of acupuncture and the term attained widespread currency in the language.
   In addition to *acupuncturist* (1952), two other derivative terms have appeared: *acupunctural* (of or relating to acupuncture, 1971), and *acupunctured* (treated or anesthetized by acupuncture, 1972). *Surgeons are now so confident about the effects of acupunctural anaesthesia that they begin by the clock, without testing to check whether the operational area is numbed.* Sunday Times (London) 10/3/71, p5 *As American doctors verified that Chinese doctors were doing lung and other major surgery on acupunctured awake patients, some scientists became intensely curious about the wonders of the ancient practice.* Encyclopedia Science Supplement (Grolier) 1972, p237

acute-care, *adj. U.S.* designated or designed for the care and treatment of patients with diseases of relatively short duration; equipped to treat nonchronic diseases. *Citing a "drastically eroded" financial situation, the head of the city's Health and Hospitals Corporation has recommended reducing from 15 to 11 the number of acute-care municipal hospitals.* NY Times 1/21/76, p1 [**1976**]

ACV, abbreviation of AIR CUSHION VEHICLE. *The ACV . . . derives support from an entrapped bubble of air between the vehicle and the ground or water surface. . .* World Book Science Annual 1968, p379 [**1963**]

acyclovir (ˌeiˈsɑikləˌvir), *n*. an antiviral drug used to treat genital herpes and other herpes infections. *Formula:* $C_8H_{11}N_5O_3$ *Acyclovir interferes with the herpes virus's DNA polymerase enzyme, thus inhibiting viral DNA replication but not healthy cells' DNA replication.* Science News 4/10/82, p247 [**1982**, from *a-* not + *cyclo-* cyclic + *virus*]

AD, abbreviation of *Alzheimer's disease* (a degenerative disorder of the brain similar to senility but often found at an early age). *Insights into the molecular biological mechanisms in selective neuronal vulnerability may ultimately lead to the development of treatments that relieve or prevent the degenerative process of AD.* Science 3/11/83, p1189 [**1983**. The name of the disease is attested since 1912. It was named after Alois *Alzheimer*, 1864-1915, a German pathologist who first described it.]

A/D, abbreviation of *analog-to digital* (conversion in computers). See the quotation under COMPANDING. Compare D/A. [**1972**]

Ada or **ADA** (ˈeidə), *n*. a computer language combining the codes of a variety of other computer languages. *In terms of utilization power, however, ADA, a newly developed programming language, promises to be dominant in the next decade. The language is the culmination of five years of work by the U.S. Department of Defense to devise a common high-order language to meet its varied requirements.* 1981 Collier's Encyclopedia Yearbook, p203 [**1979**, named after Augusta *Ada* Byron, 1815-1852, daughter of Lord Byron, who worked with the British mathematician and inventor Charles Babbage (1792-1871) on an early computer]

adaptor, *n. Molecular Biology.* a molecule of RNA (ribonucleic acid) that binds amino acids to their correct positions on messenger RNA templates during protein synthesis. *The DNA unfolds when it replicates, and each single strand is free to pick up a complementary partner. The information is carried in a "code" contained in the order of these bases. Three sequential bases constitute a "word," and it is this word that is read by the ribosomes, which do the hooking up of the molecules in the cell to make the proteins. The concept of such a ribosome "adaptor" is also largely due to Crick.* NY Times Book Review 4/8/79, p34 [**1963**]

ADC, abbreviation of *advanced developing country.* Compare MDC. See also DEVELOPING. *Although the U.S. had already written off $500 million in debts owed by 15 of the poorest nations, ADCs like South Korea, Singapore and Brazil have feared that any further write-off would make them appear to be poor credit risks and that international lenders might push up interest rates or hold back on future loans.* Time 6/18/79, p57 [**1979**]

added value, the value or cost increase added to a community at each stage of its production and distribution. It forms the basis of the *added-value tax* or *value-added tax* (abbreviated VAT) that is ultimately passed on to the consumer (often used attributively). See ZERO-RATE. *For food and materials generally, and for substitute sources of energy like nuclear and solar power, the early prospect was one not of definite exhaustion but rather of steadily rising marginal cost. In short, the price of food, materials and energy, in terms of manufactured products or 'added value', would be bound to rise.* Annual Register of World Events in 1974, p4 *The international division of labour is speeding up, and unless Europe acts now, it will be left with only a few high added-value industries and a few small subcontractors.* Manchester Guardian Weekly (Le Monde section) 1/18/75, p 12 [**1974**, abstracted from *added-value tax*]

added-value tax, another name for VAT. *To replace that revenue, the "added-value tax," which is France's equivalent of a sales tax, will rise on almost everything.* Time 12/6/68, p56 [**1968**]

add-on, *n. U.S.* **1** an attachment that extends the usefulness, power, or application of a device. *Attachments to the color television receiver which provide the capability of screening taped material, whether homegrown or rented, will be the consumer's prime demand. These sophisticated television "add-ons," known in the industry as electronic video recording and playback equipment . . .* 1973 Collier's Encyclopedia Year Book, p274 **2** *Figurative use. Finally, literature and philosophy are assigned the role of add-ons—intellectual adornments that have nothing to do with "genuine" education.* Saturday Review 12/78, p15 —**adj.** that is added on. *When the "add-on" price starts to fall to just a few pounds . . . then Prestel could be in business.* New Scientist 1/25/79, p242 [**1973**, from the verb phrase *add on*]

address, *v.t.* to indicate or find (the location of a piece of stored information) in a computer. . . . *the hardware is amazingly cheap—and the size of control task is limited only by the amount of memory which can be addressed (a 10 bit address handles 1024 program steps).* New Scientist 1/15/76, p120 [**1976**, verb use of *address*, *n*. (OEDS 1951) the location of a piece of information in a computer memory; see also AD-

DRESSABLE, *adj.* (1963) just below] —**addressable,** *adj.: The past year represents a milestone in demonstrating the practical feasibility of electron beam addressable memory systems (EBAM systems).* McGraw-Hill Yearbook of Science and Technology 1976, p146

adenylate (ə'denə,leit), *v.t.* to convert (a substance, as messenger RNA) to adenylic acid (a constituent of many coenzymes important in muscle contraction and sugar metabolism). *The NIH* [National Institute of Health] *workers conclude that the maternal mRNA in the unfertilized egg is unadenylated or partially adenylated.* New Scientist 12/14/72, p623 [**1972,** from *adenyl* substance derived from adenine + *-ate* verb suffix meaning to cause to become] —**adenylation,** *n: The longevity of the latent messages in the unfertilized egg implies that adenylation of a genetic message can occur well before its translation.* Nature 12/8/72, p334

adenylate cyclase (,ædə'nilit 'sai,kleis), another name for ADE-NYL CYCLASE. *The enzyme in membrane fractions responsible for converting ATP to cyclic AMP was named adenyl cyclase. (It is now referred to as adenylyl cyclase or adenylate cyclase.)* 1974 Britannica Yearbook of Science and the Future, p382 [**1973**]

adenyl cyclase ('ædə,nil 'sai,kleis), an enzyme that manufactures CYCLIC AMP. *Sutherland and his co-workers had established that cyclic AMP is produced from adenosine triphosphate (ATP) by an enzyme, adenyl cyclase, located at the surface of cells.* Scientific American 10/70, p48 [**1967**]

adenylyl cyclase (,ædə'nilil 'sai,kleis), an enzyme located in the membrane of the cell wall responsible for converting ATP (the substance that supplies the energy needed for muscle contraction) to cyclic AMP (a regulatory agent in many cellular processes). *Many tissues contain membrane-bound adenylyl cyclases, which are activated only by specific hormones. Kidney tubules contain one which responds to antidiuretic hormone; heart muscle contains one which is activated by glucagon; and thyroid tissue contains one which is activated by the thyroid-stimulating hormone.* Britannica Book of the Year 1976, p471 [**1972**]

ad hocery (æd 'hakəri:), Also spelled **ad hoccery** and **ad hockery.** *Slang.* decisions, policy, rules, etc., made ad hoc. *That deficiency of "ad hocery"—former Bureau of the Budget Director Charles Schulze's term—may be seen quite clearly in the lawyers' desire to judicialize human affairs.* Saturday Review 8/3/68, p40 *Apart from the network of swap agreements ("ad hoccery" as Mr Callaghan called it when he was Chancellor) it is the only concrete result of the years of wrangling over monetary reform.* Manchester Guardian Weekly 1/16/69, p22 *So, in what one BP operational researcher has called "a mixture of machines and ad-hockery", the company arrived at an essentially circum-African solution, relying heavily on Iran.* New Scientist 6/13/68, p558 [**1961**]

ad-hocracy, *n. Slang.* rule by ad hoc committees. *Some have said that the company's egalitarian, flexible structure approximates the futurist Alvin Toffler's notion of an "ad-hocracy."* NY Times Magazine 1/4/81, p45 [**1970,** blend of *ad hoc* and *-cracy* rule of or by]

ADI, abbreviation of *acceptable daily intake.* See ACTION LEVEL. *The scientific component involves two disciplines: firstly, physical chemistry to determine quantitatively the migrants into the food; second, biological medicine to determine their ADI (acceptable daily intake—the maximum amount that can safely be ingested by humans). Provided the migration is below the ADI for each migrant there is no toxic hazard.* New Scientist 12/18/75, p732 [**1969**]

Adidas (ə'di:dəz), *n.* a trademark for athletic equipment, especially footwear and garments. *Also used attributively. We triple-tied our Adidas at the Staten Island staging area—Fort Wadsworth, alongside the approach to the bridge, and prepared to report on the marathon by joining it and going the classic distance.* New Yorker 11/6/78, p35 [**1975,** named for *Adi Dassler,* German manufacturer who in 1948 founded the company that produces them] ►The trademark is spelled in lower-case, as *adidas,* but in common usage it is written with an initial capital.

adjustment center, *U.S.* a part of a prison where intractable and often mentally deranged inmates are kept in solitary confinement. *In the world of prisons notable advances have also been made recently in prettying-up the nomenclature. Guards are now "correctional officers"; solitary confinement punishment cells, "adjustment centers"; prisons, "therapeutic correctional communities"; convicts, "clients of the Department of Corrections."* NY Times 9/5/73, p41 [**1973**]

adjuvant therapy, treatment of disease involving the use of substances that enhance the action of drugs, especially drugs that stimulate the production of antibodies. *A procedure becoming known as the "extended simple" mastectomy is being done in some medical centers. This procedure is actually a modified radical mastectomy, with the removal of fewer nodes. If cancer is found in any, some kind of adjuvant therapy is begun immediately.* New York Post 2/3/79, p14 [**1976**]

admass, *adj. British.* of or relating to high-pressure advertising and publicity over the mass media to stimulate sales, with detrimental influence on the culture of society. *Mr. Platter . . . offers no well-defined, radical alternative to the admass society he dislikes.* Times (London) 9/18/70, p6 *Hancock makes the most of limited opportunities in scripts designed apparently to hit the widest admass audience of benevolent credulity.* Punch 2/13/63, p246 [**1955,** coined by J. B. Priestley from *advertisement* + *mass:* "Economics I do not pretend to understand, and sometimes I suspect that nobody does. But I understand people, and I know that the system I christened *Admass,* which we borrowed from America and did not improve, and constant inflation have made people unhappy." J. B. Priestley, Punch 7/18/62, p77]

adopt, *v.* **adopt out,** *U.S.* to give up for adoption. *My husband said he would let me decide whether I wanted to keep the baby or adopt it out. I first decided to adopt it out, but at the last minute I changed my mind and kept it.* Louisville Courier Journal 4/21/71 (page not known) [**1970**] ►The preposition *out* in this verb phrase serves to reverse the meaning of *adopt* (to take a child and bring up as one's own), perhaps on the pattern of *rent out* to pay for the use of, *rent out* to receive payment for the use of, and others.

adperson, *n.* a person who is in the advertising business, such as a copywriter, agent, or executive. *Actually, advertising isn't one of those "what do you want to be when you grow up" professions. It's something most adpersons fall into, for one reason or another, like flunking out of dental school.* NY Times Magazine 1/25/76, p52 [**1976,** from *ad* advertisement + -PERSON] ►For the plural, the form *adpeople* also occurs, as in the following quotation. *Perhaps adpeople harbor an unconscious combination of dissatisfaction, foolishness and guilt about their jobs which must be compensated by awards and high salaries.* NY Times Magazine 2/15/76, p42

adrenalin or **adrenaline,** *n. Figurative.* something that stirs to action; a stimulant; stimulus. *A cheap and plentiful supply of money is adrenalin for the stock market.* NY Times Magazine 2/22/76, p28 [**1964,** from *adrenalin(e),* a hormone that speeds up the heartbeat; *Adrenalin* is a trademark in the United States for the synthetic hormone epinephrine]

adrenalize, *v.t.* to stir up; stimulate; excite. *On the evening of April 25th, 1972, 18 miles north of Eureka, in Arcata, the home of Humboldt State University, an adrenalized SRO crowd jammed into a college auditorium to hear America's most renowned Marxist.* Rolling Stone 5/24/73, p44 [**1966,** from ADRENALIN + *-ize* (verb suffix)]

adrenodoxin (ə,drenə'daksən), *n.* a protein containing iron that takes part in the transfer of electrons within animal cells; a proteinlike ferredoxin produced by the adrenal glands. *A number of animal proteins have properties similar to those of plant ferredoxins—for example, adrenodoxin from adrenal glands—so we have included them as "honorary ferredoxins."* New Scientist and Science Journal 9/23/71, p697 [**1971,** from *adreno-* adrenal (gland) + ferre*doxin*]

adriamycin (ˌeidriːəˈmaisən), *n.* an antibiotic derived from a species of streptomyces or produced synthetically, used as an anticancer drug. *Formula:* $C_{27}H_{29}NO_{11}$ Compare DAUNOMYCIN. *The all-out therapy involves simultaneous use of three highly toxic drugs—Cytoxan, adriamycin and vincristine— and radiation to the tumor in the chest and to the brain, where lung cancers commonly spread.* NY Times 3/27/76, p20 [**1973**, from Italian *adriamicina,* from *Adriàtico* Adriatic + *-micina* -mycin (ultimately from Greek *mýkēs* fungus)]

adult, *adj. Especially U.S.* of or dealing with sexual or erotic subjects; pornographic (used as a euphemism). Compare XRATED. See also EUPHEMISMS. *Officials in a few cities, including Las Vegas and Oklahoma City, have proposed creation of special "adult business districts" patterned after Boston's socalled "combat zone," a neighborhood of adult book stores, strip-tease establishments and pornographic movie theaters.* NY Times 11/28/76, pA1 *The governor of California could be seen emerging from a restaurant in the middle of one of the gaudier blocks of strip shows, massage parlors and "adult" entertainments in this city.* Manchester Guardian Weekly (Washington Post section) 7/10/77, p17 [**1972**, abstracted from such phrases as "for adults only" and "restricted to adults" in reference to pornographic motion pictures]

adultism, *n.* prejudice or discrimination against younger people as a group. *The novel is written in the first person, out of the consciousness of Fielding Pierce, would-be Congressman, a young lad of 34, and is thereby restricted by the awareness of a 34-year-old, which is not, cannot be, no matter how longsuffering, perspicacious and knowledgeable our hero is presented as being—and he is—all that aware. (If this is adultism, I apologize.)* NY Times Book Review 5/18/86, p11 [**1986**] ▶The suffix *-ism* (along with the related noun and adjective suffix *-ist*) has been increasingly used in the pejorative sense of "prejudice or discrimination against a particular group based on the unjustified belief in the superiority of one's own group." The trend apparently began with the appearance of SEXISM, and was followed by such coinages as AGEISM, CLASSISM, HEIGHTISM, and SPECIESISM. For more on this development, see Adrienne Lehrer, "A Note On the Semantics of *-IST* and *-ISM*' in *American Speech* 63, p2 (Summer 1988).

advance, *U.S. n.* the making of arrangements ahead of time for the reception of a visiting political candidate. *In political campaigning, "bad advance" means that a Presidential candidate flies into a key city, lands at the wrong airport, and rides in a closed car down back streets to a huge stadium, where he addresses a lonely handful of party workers over a broken mike while the press is still looking for him at the other airport.* New Yorker 6/12/71, p30 —*v.i.* to prepare for a candidate's visit; do the work of an advance man. *Campaigning does not often go as smoothly as this, but when an extraordinary man named Jerry Bruno was "advancing" for John Kennedy, Robert Kennedy, Lyndon Johnson, and others, it sometimes came close.* New Yorker 6/12/71, p30 —*v.t.* to prepare for a candidate's reception in (a place); do the work of an advance man. *In 1957, Bruno went to work for John Kennedy—"organizing Wisconsin"—and during the 1960 Presidential campaign and the Kennedy Administration he "advanced" thirty-four cities.* New Yorker 6/12/71, p30 [**1971**, shortened from *advance man* (1958) an assistant to a political candidate who makes arrangements ahead of time for meetings, demonstrations of support, etc.]

advantage law or **advantage rule,** a rule in rugby under which play may not, at the discretion of the referee, be stopped for an infraction if stopping the play may cause a disadvantage to the team not guilty of the offense. *For the last half-hour—the French referee, André Cuny, whose ideas of the advantage law had not always coincided with those of Wales, was operating with a torn calf muscle, by remote control.* Times (London) 2/9/76, p8 [**1969**, *advantage rule*]

adversarial, *adj. British.* of, involving, or as if opponents in a legal contest; adversary. *There is no suggestion that the magistrates acted in any way improperly; but this only casts a stronger doubt on the system under which juvenile courts have to reach their decisions—the adversarial system of plaintiff and*

defendant. Times (London) 11/2/76, p13 [**1967**] ▶In the U.S., *adversary* is the standard adjective used in legal and judicial contexts: *the adversary system of justice, adversary hearings, adversary proceedings. Adversarial occurs only in British citations in our file.*

advocacy, *n.* Often used attributively in referring to the promoting or advocating of a highly personal, partisan, or activist point of view or policy. —**advocacy advertising:** *It also argues for media access for people who want to counter the so-called "advocacy advertising" of such companies as Imperial Oil, which has flooded the country with commercials telling Canadians about "the big, tough expensive job of developing petroleum."* Maclean's 5/15/78, p60 —**advocacy journalism:** *"Reflections on Joan Little" by Mark Pinsky depicted rather graphically how advocacy journalism has turned reporting into show biz and made a mockery of the public's right to know.* Columbia Journalism Review, May/June 76, p54 Compare NEW JOURNALISM. —**advocacy journalist:** *Advocacy journalists claim derivative constitutional legitimacy from a reading of the First Amendment which stretches liberty into license.* Harper's 10/74, p47 —**advocacy planning:** *Robert Goodman's After the Planners (75p) rejects even the modern philosophy of advocacy planning, only recently emerging on the British scene, for planning by the small community for the small community, in other words a return to Greek-type democracy.* Manchester Guardian Weekly 9/30/72, p23 [**1967**]

aeon, *n. Geology and Astronomy.* one billion years. *You are correct about the "indefinite-period" definition in dictionaries, but "aeon" is being increasingly used by earth and planetary scientists as a convenient short synonym for "billion years."* Science News 8/26/72, p130 [**1972**, specialized meaning of *aeon* (1647) "an immeasurable period of time"]

aequorin (iˈkwɔrən), *n.* a luminescent substance secreted by the jellyfish *Aequorea aequorea,* used in the optical examination of events occurring within cells. *The protein, which they named aequorin, emits a beautiful bluish light, and the agent that causes it to do so is the calcium ion.* Scientific American 4/70, p90 [**1965**]

aeroacoustic, *adj.* of or relating to aeroacoustics. *Extensive acoustic treatment alone may not provide sufficient noise reduction in some situations, and thus a coordinated aeroacoustic approach is needed.* McGraw-Hill Yearbook of Science and Technology 1976, p98 [**1966**]

aeroacoustics, *n.* the study of sound propagation in the air and its effect on the environment. *Aero-acoustics Expert William Meecham of the U.C.L.A. School of Engineering and Applied Science reports that people who reside within a 3-mile radius of Los Angeles International Airport have a 19% higher death rate than people who live six miles away. Most of the difference was in stress-related disease.* Time 9/18/78, p104 [**1966**, from *aero-* combining form meaning air + *acoustics*]

aeroallergen, *n.* a substance in the air that causes or induces an allergy; an airborne allergen. *Advances in Environmental Sciences, Vol. 1. . . . Deals with the application of science and technology to the control and improvement of environmental quality, in specific areas such as oxides of nitrogen, biodegradable detergents, and aeroallergens and public health.* Science News 3/14/70, p279 [**1970**]

aerobic, *adj.* **1** of or relating to aerobics. *The cardinal requirement of aerobic exercise is that it must tax the person's capacity, to the point where he is breathing hard and his heart is pounding at 130 beats per minute or more.* Time 3/8/71, p30 *Then dropping the medical jargon, she said, "Aerobic dancing is jogging, calisthenics, and jazz dancing to music, in that order."* Review-Press Reporter (Bronxville, N.Y.) 8/2/79, p3 **2** of, relating to, or improving the body's consumption or use of oxygen. *Doctors look on aerobic capacity as a critical guide to fitness.* Times (London) 3/6/76, p14 [**1971**, back formation from *aerobics*]

aerobics, *n.* a system of building up physical fitness, developed by Kenneth H. Cooper, an American physician, by correlating oxygen consumption and pulse rate with various exercises (also used attributively). *. . . . I had in the meantime switched to Aer-*

obics, and my lungs and heart were correspondingly mightier.
New Yorker 1/25/69, p28 *An aerobics fan must attain a week-ly score of at least 30 points on Cooper's scale.* Time 3/8/71, p30 [**1968**, from the adjective *aerobic,* applied to organisms that thrive only in the presence of oxygen; ultimately from Greek *aér* air + *bíos* life]

aerobody, n. a lighter-than-air aircraft; an airship or any similar flying vehicle. *Miller . . . reminded the group as a whole that they were to refer to the aircraft as an aerobody. He said, "I'm very anxious that we preserve this semantic thing. This is not an airplane. We consider 'aerobody' to be a generic description we have coined."* New Yorker 2/10/73, p43 *The Pentagon is also stepping up research on a new advanced ICBM and is even looking into the possibility of basing them on zeppelins called "aerobodies."* Newsweek 4/22/74, p53 [**1973**, from *aero-* air + *body*]

aerograph, v.i. to create a painting or design by using an air-brush. *. . . acid-etched gilding to hand-enamelling and ground-laying to aerographing—all executed by hand skills which few firms in the world today (outside Crown Derby, Doulton, Spode, Wedgwood, Worcester) can call upon.* Times (London) 10/12/70, p11 [**1970**, verb use of noun *aerograph* (1898) airbrush]

aeronomy (er'anəmi:), n. a science dealing with the upper at-mosphere of the earth or other body in space. *The "Eltanin"* [research vessel] *had traveled in some of the coldest weather and roughest waters in the world, providing . . . observations on physical and chemical oceanography, aeronomy, meteorol-ogy, marine geology, geophysics, and ornithology.* Britannica Book of the Year 1968, p95 [**1961**, from *aero-* atmosphere + *-nomy,* as in *astronomy*]

aerophobe, n. a person with an abnormal fear of flying. *An or-ganization, Scoff, the Society for the Conquest of Flight Fear, has been formed in London. . . . Scoffers may eventually wear Scoff badges and use Scoff luggage labels. This way the air-lines staff would recognize that they were dealing with fragile human cargo, and aerophobes would also recognize each other and give mutual support.* Auckland Star, New Zealand 2/17/73, p14 [**1966**, from *aero-* air + *-phobe* one who fears or has an aversion to, ultimately from Greek *phóbos* fear]

aerophobia, n. *Biology.* movement of an organism or part of an organism away from oxygen or air. *Some bacteria swim toward molecules of food, a process called chemotaxis. Some that re-quire oxygen for growth migrate toward oxygen (aerotaxis), while bacteria to which oxygen is toxic migrate away from it (aerophobia).* World Book Science Annual 1977, p309 [**1976**, from *aero-* air + *-phobia* fear of]
▶ The earlier sense (since 1775) of this term is that of an abnor-mal fear of air or gases, especially drafts.

aeroshell, n. a protective metallic shell equipped with small thrusters, used for decelerating a spacecraft for a soft landing. *When it reaches an altitude of about eight hundred thousand feet, the lander, inside a sort of pod called an aeroshell, should enter the Martian atmosphere.* New Yorker 6/28/76, p30 *Physical characteristics of the atmosphere will be mea-sured during the landing phase by sensors located on the aero-shell and within the lander.* New Scientist 8/7/75, p314 [**1966**, from *aero-* air + *shell*]

aerosolic, adj. of, having to do with, or like a fine spray of colloi-dal particles. *The oxygen isotopic ratio of the tracer mineral quartz has been used by R. N. Clayton and associates to identi-fy the global distribution of long-range aerosolic dusts carried by winds.* McGraw-Hill Yearbook of Science and Technology 1975, p112 [**1973**]

Af (æf), n. a derogatory name for a black African in Zimbabwe and South Africa. Compare HOUTIE. *A common feature of the conversation with whites was the use of pejoratives to refer to blacks. . . . In English-speaking households, the word "na-tives," or "Afs" were common.* NY Times 6/22/76, p13 [**1976**, shortened from *African*]

AF, abbreviation of AUTOFOCUS. *Auto-focus cameras were first offered to us in the mid-1970's when the Konica C45AF was in-*

troduced as the first one to hit the market (AF stands for auto-focus and is part of the model designation of many subsequent cameras that offer this feature). NY Times 5/24/81, pD32 [**1981**]

Afar triangle ('a:far), an extensive, lava-covered triangular re-gion in northeastern Ethiopia, at the juncture of the Red Sea and the Gulf of Aden. It is regarded by some geologists as evi-dence of continuing continental drift as a focal point about which new oceans may form. *If we suppose that the Afar trian-gle is a part of the Red Sea, the coast of Arabia matches very well the contour of the "coastline" of the part of the African continent from which it is assumed to be separating.* Scientific American 2/70, p32 [**1969**, from *Afar,* another name of the Danakil, a Hamitic people of northeastern Ethiopia and the ad-jacent Djibouti (the former Territory of Afars and Issas)]

affinity card, a credit card issued at special rates to members of an affinity group. *The affinity card . . . is a Visa or Master-Card that a university, union, club, or some other group issues to its members.* Washington Post 9/21/86, pD1 [**1986**]

affinity group, any formally organized group, such as a club, church, union, or other organization. *The change, approved in September, allows the vacationer to choose between dozens of destinations at a price that includes air fare, hotel room, ground transport, taxes and tips. And no longer does the travel-er have to belong to a so-called affinity group, such as a club or union, to qualify for the reduced rates.* Time 1/19/76, p62 [**1971**]

affirm, adj. U.S. Informal. affirmative; correct (used especially in replies). *"You think Main Bus B is good, don't you?" Swigert asked anxiously. Brand answered, "That's affirm. We think it is, but we want to check it out anyway."* New Yorker 11/11/72, p129 [**1971**, short for *affirmative*]

affirmative action, 1 U.S. any plan or program designed to com-bat the effects of discrimination against minorities, women, the elderly, etc., by increasing their representation in employment and other areas (often used attributively). *. . . a proposed "af-firmative action" plan to assure fair representation for women, youths and racial minorities at national conventions.* St. Pe-tersburg Times 11/29/74, p19A *"Affirmative action" includes a whole range of special steps. . . . These include compensatory and remedial training, expanded recruitment, validation of tests and criteria for jobs or university admission and related measures to help the disadvantaged realize their potentials and provide equal opportunity for all.* NY Times 9/13/77, p32 **2** any action taken to improve past performance or eliminate grievances. *Once again under fire for its lack of affirmative ac-tion, the Federal Trade Commission strove this year to demon-strate the range of its powers. FTC Chairman Lewis A. Engman announced on February 19 that the agency was adopting new policies to open itself to "greater public scrutiny."* 1975 Col-lier's Encyclopedia Year Book, p199 [**1965**]

Afghanistanism, n. undue emphasis on things happening in re-mote foreign places, to the neglect of important domestic af-fairs. *Afghanistanism (also a recurring disease in journalism) is a malady that encourages pontification on problems far dis-tant while conveniently ignoring the home front.* Maclean's 6/28/76, p52 [**1966**, from *Afghanistan,* the country in south-western Asia (used as an example of a distant place) + *-ism*]

aflatoxin, n. a poisonous substance secreted by some strains of a common mold, *Aspergillus flavus,* found especially on pea-nuts, cottonseed, and corn. Aflatoxin is thought to cause certain cancers in animals as well as abnormalities in human chromo-somes. *The discovery of the toxicity of peanuts contaminated with aflatoxin led food technologists throughout the world to give careful consideration to the occurrence of other toxicants in foods. . . .* Britannica Book of the Year 1969, p346 [**1962**, from *Aspergillus flavus* + *toxin*]

AFP, abbreviation of ALPHAFETOPROTEIN. *Others had shown that AFP was the only protein in amniotic fluid produced just by the fetus and not also by the mother. With this knowledge, Dr. Brock, a biochemist, developed a theory that high levels of AFP would be present in cases of neural tube defects because* *more AFP would leak from the malformed fetus into the amniotic fluid.* NY Times 9/11/77, pA26 **[1973]**

African-American, *n.* a black American of African ancestry; an Afro-American. *The movement the Rev. Jesse Jackson is spearheading to officially declare us African-Americans.* Washington Post 1/16/89, pA20 **[1973,** adj., patterned after *Italian-American, German-American,* etc.]

Africanized bee or **Africanized honeybee,** another term for KILLER BEE (def. 2). *Africanized bees . . . pour out of their hive by the thousands to attack any person or animal who disturbs them.* World Book Science Annual 1987, p214 *Dr. Rinderer and other scientists prefer to use the term Africanized or African honeybees, to describe the insect's origin as well as to distance the issue from pulp fiction.* NY Times 8/4/87, pC1 **[1986]**

Afro, *n.* a bushy way of arranging the hair, originally fashioned on an African style. Also shortened to 'FRO. *Michael, with the loveliest, fullest, twelve-year-old Afro you'll hope to see, has the history of the group down pat. . . .* Time 6/14/71, p48 —**adj.** *It* [a shop] *has posters of Rap, Stokely, Eldridge, and Malcolm along with dashikis, clenched fists and afro combs.* NY Times 6/11/71, p35 *The girl was rather light-skinned, with an Afro hair-do cut like a loaf of bread; she spoke to Bech in a voice from which all traces of Dixie had been clipped.* John Updike, Bech: A Book, 1970, p113 —**adv.** or **predicate adj.** *Since last June, Laura has been wearing her hair Afro, "My God, yes, black is beautiful," says Laura.* Time 4/6/70, p46 **[1968]**

Afro-Americanese, *n.* another name for BLACK ENGLISH. *The language is Afro-Americanese, and the point is a plague o' both your houses—although Mr. Killens understandably hopes Whitey's plague will be a bit worse.* Atlantic 2/71, p129 **[1971]**

Afro-Americanism, *n.* American Black culture. *The rush is on. Come and get it: Afro-Americanism, black studies, the Negro heritage. From Harvard to Ocean Hill, from Duke to Madison Avenue, they are trying, as they say, to restore the Negro to his rightful place in American history and culture . . .* Harper's 5/69, p37 **[1969]**

Afro-American studies, a program of courses, especially in a college or university, dealing with African and American Black history, culture, and contemporary affairs. Also called BLACK STUDIES. *Black students argue that the goal of Harvard's Afro-American studies should be to build up the black liberationist mentality and teach specific skills that can aid its cause.* Time 1/26/70, p44 **[1970]**

Afro-beat, *n.* a form of popular music combining elements of highlife (West African jazz), calypso, and American jazz. *Westerners first hearing Fela's Afro-beat music find it an acquired taste. The numbers seem too long, often lasting 20 minutes or more, with the brief snatches of lyrics in pidgin English, the lingua franca of the lower classes.* NY Times Magazine 7/24/77, p11 **[1974]**

Afroed ('æfroud), *adj.* wearing an Afro. *In Manhattan. . . . Afroed young blacks and a scattering of long-haired whites demonstrated in Angela's* [Angela Davis's] *support . . .* Time 10/26/70, p28 **[1970]**

Afroism ('æfrou͟izəm), *n.* interest in and devotion to black African culture and the expansion of black African power. Compare NEGRITUDE. *Afroism is still alive. Stokely Carmichael lives in Dar-es-Salaam, dashikis still sell, and the Afro hair style is ever more popular. But this cultural nostalgia is rather like long hair on white students—a matter of fashion and radical chic.* Manchester Guardian Weekly 5/22/71, p16 **[1971]**

Afro-Latin, *adj.* of, based on, or combining African and Latin American music. *Soul music again experienced a strong year, owing largely to the success of such Motown artists as the Temptations, the Jackson Five, and Stevie Wonder. If there were any major musical developments in this style, they were those which were Afro-Latin in general sound.* 1971 Collier's Encyclopedia Year Book, p362 **[1967]** ►This term is used generically to describe the class of dance music that includes the

1940's Afro-Cuban (mambo, conga, etc.), the Brazilian samba, and the more recent SALSA.

Afro-rock, *n.* modern African music incorporating much of the style of traditional rock music. *Afro-rock is a term frequently used in contemporary African music. Manu Dibango, Osibisa, Fela Anikulapo-Kuti, and Victor Uwaifor are internationally famous in this new brand of African soul music.* Times (London) 1/18/77, pII **[1977]**

Afro-Saxon, *n.* a black man who is part of the white establishment or is in favor of working within the white establishment. *Many West Indians maintain that black power against black governments makes little sense. But militants dismiss their present leaders as "Afro-Saxons" and press for revolutionary change.* Time 5/4/70, p48 —**adj.** consisting of Afro-Saxons; having the outlook or attitude of Afro-Saxons. *As in Bermuda, Jamaica, and elsewhere in the English-speaking West Indies, dissident black citizens continued to rally round extremist banners to oppose their own elected, so-called "Afro-Saxon" governments.* Britannica Book of the Year 1971, p162 **[1970,** patterned after *Anglo-Saxon*]

afterheat, *n.* the residual heat produced by a nuclear reactor (often used attributively). *"The failures analyzed in this article occurred in the afterheat system of the Oak Ridge Research Reactor and therefore it is worthwhile to note that it has been determined that at its present operating power of 30 MW, the ORR requires no forced convection afterheat removal."* Atlantic 6/71, p36 **[1969]**

agarose ('ɑːgəˌrous), *n.* a polysaccharide carbohydrate that is the main constituent of agar, the solid medium used for bacterial cultures. *Insulin does not enter the cells which it affects. This has been dramatically demonstrated by experiments in which hormone effects are produced by insulin attached to beads of agarose, which certainly cannot penetrate the cell membrane.* New Scientist and Science Journal 9/30/71, p739 **[1971,** from *agar* + *-ose* suffix used in names of types of sugar, as in *sucrose, glucose,* and *fructose*]

age-date, *v.t., v.i.* to determine scientifically the age of archaeological or geological materials. *A new age-dating method, using the elements samarium and neodymium, was successfully applied to lunar rocks. The results suggest that a major melting and chemical separation of the moon was going on about 4.4 billion years ago.* Encyclopedia Science Supplement (Grolier) 1977/1978, p345 —**n.** a specimen's age obtained by scientific dating. Compare AMINO-ACID DATING, IODINE-XENON DATING, RUBIDIUM-STRONTIUM DATING, THERMOLUMINESCENT DATING. *The dark material has been distributed to scientists, and the age-dates may be available in time for the Fourth Lunar Science Conference, March 5-8 at Houston.* Science News 2/24/73, p117 **[1966]**

ageism ('eidʒizəm), *n.* discrimination against old or elderly people, as in employment and housing. See GERONTOPHOBIA, GRAY POWER. *Ageism has been called the ultimate prejudice, the last discrimination, the cruelest rejection.* Ronald Gross et al., The New Old 1978, p89 **[1970,** coined by Robert N. Butler, an American gerontologist, on the pattern of *sexism*]

ageist ('eidʒist), *adj.* discriminating against old or elderly people; practicing ageism. *She called him "a sexist, ageist pig . . ."* Newsweek 5/6/74, p24 **[1974]**

agenbite of inwit (əˈgenˌbait əv 'inˌwit), *Especially British.* remorse of conscience. [Malcolm] *Muggeridge is haunted (so he intimates) by plastic grass, the possibility that dawn will be photographed as though it were dusk. What agenbite of inwit must seize the old gentleman as they lard him with make-up prior to committing him to the arms of his camera.* Times (London) 4/17/72, p14 **[1967]** ►This is an archaism and a literary term revived in the 1960's. It was used earlier in *Ulysses* (1922) by James Joyce, who adapted it from the title of a Middle English (1340) manuscript, *Ayenbite of Inwyte* meaning "The Remorse of Conscience." *Ayenbite* (the components mean "again-bite") is a loan translation of the Latin source of *remorse* and *inwit* is a loan translation of the Latin source of *conscience.*

Agent Blue, Agent Orange, Agent Purple, Agent White, the names of four herbicidal spraying materials having great toxicity, used especially for purposes of defoliation and crop destruction, especially during the Vietnam war. *On another front it was reported by the Washington Post that more than a million gallons of Agent Orange (the most powerful defoliant used in Vietnam and banned since April, 1970) was being shipped back to the United States. . . . This move still leaves the less toxic Agent White and Agent Blue at the disposal of United States and South Vietnam forces.* New Scientist 1/6/72, p36 [**1970**, so called from the color of the code stripe of each of the herbicides on their containers]

Age of Aquarius, an epoch of the world described by astrologers as marking the advent of freedom in all areas of life, the rule of brotherhood on earth, and the conquest of outer space. See also AQUARIAN. *. . . the Senate's minority leader . . . warned his colleagues that "Clearly the temper of this Age of Aquarius calls for less bureaucratic omphaloskepsis* [meditation while contemplating one's navel]." NY Times 1/19/70, p46 [**1970**; the expression was popularized in a song of the same title in the musical *Hair,* which opened in New York City in 1967.]

age pigment, an aggregate of fluorescent brown compounds of proteins, lipids, and carbohydrates that become concentrated in some cells as a person or animal grows old. *Highly insoluble particles accumulate in some cells as a function of age. These particles, often referred to as "age pigment," may occupy as much as 30% of the space inside an old cell.* 1972 Britannica Yearbook of Science and the Future, p83 [**1962**]

age-specific, *adj.* limited in action or effect to a definite age group. *Fig. 1 shows the age-specific death rates from carcinoma of the cervix in England and Wales, and this clearly shows the importance of using our resources on women over thirty-five, especially those who have not yet been tested.* Nature 7/21/72, p137 [**1963**]

aggiornamento (ə‚dʒɔrnəˈmentou), *n.* the policy of updating or modernizing Roman Catholic doctrines and institutions, adopted as one of the goals of the Second Vatican *Auto-focus cameras were first offered to us in the mid-1970's Without mentioning any of these activities, the Pontiff made it clear that the idea of aggiornamento, or updating, projected by the late Pope John in calling the Council could not be distorted to cover change.* NY Times 4/26/68, p38 [**1962**, from Italian *aggiornamento,* literally, a bringing up to date, from *aggiornare* to bring up to date, from *a-* to + *giorno* day]

aggro, *n. British Slang.* **1** aggressiveness. *He* [John Kenneth Galbraith] *enjoyed the status and glamour of high duty . . . yet is enraged by the crude aggro, the administration's most frequent posture . . .* Punch 11/12/69, p801 **2** aggression. Also spelled AGRO. *Ardrey enters the debate quite specifically when dealing with violence and aggression. The latter, he implies, is a term which includes the striving of plants and animals to grow. . . . Thus to Ardrey life itself is no more than one long aggro . . .* Science Journal 1/71, p94 [**1969**]

AGI, abbreviation of *adjusted gross income. Surrey contended the Treasury distorts its reports by computing the tax rates paid by the rich on their "adjusted gross income" (AGI) and not their actual income, often far higher.* Honolulu Star-Bulletin 2/5/73, p2 [**1972**]

agnosic (æɡˈnousik), *adj.* unable to recognize familiar objects because of brain damage. *He sees faces, figures, objects around him: he sees them clearly, yet is unable to recognise them. They too have lost their meaning: he has become 'mentally blind'—agnosic.* Listener 6/28/73, p872 [**1973**, derivative of *agnosia* (1900), from New Latin, from Greek *agnōsía,* from *a-* without + *gnôsis* knowledge or recognition]

agora (‚ɑːɡouˈrɑː), *n., pl.* **agorot** (‚ɑːɡouˈrɔt). a monetary unit of Israel equal to 1/100 of a shekel. *A further landmark in the saga of Israel's runaway inflation was achieved this week with the disclosure that the Israeli pound is now officially worth less than one agora was in September 1951, the date when the country's cost of living index first began to be measured. (100 agorot*

= *£1 Israeli).* Times (London) 2/20/80, p19 [**1960**, from Modern Hebrew, from Hebrew, a unit of weight]

agravic, *adj.* having zero gravity; characterized by an absence of gravitational pull. *Theoretically, absolute agravic conditions in the true sense of the word do not exist in the universe.* US Air Force Glossary of Standardized Terms, Department of the Air Force, Washington, Vol. 1, 1/2/76, p2 [**1965**, from *a-* not, without + *gravity* + *-ic*]

agri-, a combining form meaning "of or involving agriculture; agricultural," abstracted from *agriculture* (ultimately from Latin *ager* field). The first term in the group was *agri-horticultural* (1912). However, the appearance of *agribusiness* (1955) was the source of the present growth in *agri-* as a word element. In current usage the combining form tends to overlap or become interchangeable with the earlier *agro-* (from Greek), so that one may find *agrobusiness* as well as *agribusiness, agrichemical* as well as *agrochemical,* and so on. Below are some examples of terms using the new form. —**agri-argument,** *n.: This convoluted agri-argument comes out in a volume issued this weekend, in time for the Labour party conference next week.* Sunday Times (London) 10/3/71, p72 —**agribiz,** *n.: Take my advice, kid. Forget about show biz and go back to agribiz.* Cartoon legend by W. Miller, New Yorker 11/22/76, p49 —**agribusinessman,** *n.: As for being a peanut farmer, Carter is actually a wealthy agribusinessman, whose income comes from warehousing and shelling other farmers' peanuts and from commodities trading.* Harper's 3/76, p80 —**agrichemical,** *adj.: As a result, while the agrichemical giants stick with their profitable poisons, the few smaller companies that have taken a chance on the third-generation insecticides complain that the E.P.A. regulation is driving them out of the business.* NY Times Magazine 11/28/76, p53 —**agri-corporation,** *n.: Hutterites control only about one per cent of the province's arable land—but other farmers still resent, envy and fear the sect, partly because its frugal, communal lifestyle finances efficient, modern, prosperous, expansionist agri-corporations.* Maclean's 12/25/78, p22 —**agricrime,** *n.: . . . Agricrime has become so bad in the state of California that the annual loss in crops and machinery is estimated at $30 million.* Time 10/3/77, p27 —**agri-industrial,** *adj.: Our "green ripe" tomatoes are the latest results of agri-industrial improvement.* NY Times 5/14/76, pC22 —**agrindustry,** *n.: Then there are crop and orchard wastes, food-processing wastes, wastes from forestry, pulp and paper production textiles, tanneries, and a host of "agrindustries."* Encyclopedia Science Supplement (Grolier), 1972, p208 —**agripower,** *n.: Butz publicly emphasizes that the United States cannot and should not use what he, at the same time, frankly calls "agripower" as a weapon . . .* NY Times Magazine 6/13/76, p53

agro, *n. British Slang.* another spelling of AGGRO. *The skinheads live for "agro" (causing "aggravation") and "bovver" (street fighting).* Time 6/8/70, p37 [**1970**]

Agro-boy, *n. British Slang.* another name for SKINHEAD. *In the lower depths the Agro-boys have already emerged to present a caricature of working-class conservatism and prejudice.* George Melly, Revolt Into Style, 1970, p251 [**1969**]

agrobusiness, *n.* the coordination or relation of business techniques and methods of farm production and distribution; agriculture treated as a business. *In his recent book on the Agrobusiness Gerard Garreau claimed that "the real power of the cereal companies does not only derive from agreements on prices, but sometimes takes on a political dimension."* Times (London) 3/7/78, pII [**1971**, variant of earlier *agribusiness*]

agrochemical, *adj.* of or involving both agriculture and chemistry. *Amid the loud and often outrageous claims being made in the United States by the organic school of farming on the one hand, and the agrochemical businesses on the other, it is refreshing to come across a group of people (where else but in England?) who for the past thirty-four years have been calmly and quietly studying the soil-plant-animal cycle and the effect of different agricultural methods on this cycle.* Natural History 11/72, p16 [**1963**]

agroecological, *adj.* of or involving both agriculture and ecology. *Every agroecological milieu has its own problems, and new ones keep appearing. For example, during the southwest monsoon period in India, many soil nutrients are lost because of leaching.* Britannica Book of the Year 1975, p11 **[1975]**

agroecosystem, *n.* the system of ecological relationships existing in agriculture; an agricultural ecosystem. *Ecological accounting of energy inputs and outputs of an agroecosystem provides greater understanding of the interrelations and mechanisms underlying various crop production alternatives.* Science 2/14/75, p561 **[1970]**

agro-industry, *n.* an agricultural industry. *Barbara Ward recommends creating rural agricultural centers that would provide the "agro-industries" necessary to employ the peasants left jobless by the Green Revolution—warehouses, fertilizer plants, facilities to manufacture silos and other storage units, work forces for loading and shipping.* Time 7/13/70, p27 **[1970]**

agrotechnician, *n.* a specialist in the technology of agriculture. *Since 1961, Nestlé agrotechnicians, veterinary specialists and agronomists have been hard at work, creating, with the farmer, a modern milk-producing district in this region.* Times (London) 4/8/76, pIII **[1976]**

agrotechnology, *n.* the tools, machines, and techniques used in modern agriculture to increase production; the technology of agriculture. *The importance of efforts to import foreign agrotechnology is apparent in Peking's recent decision to increase its allocations of foreign currency funds to local production units to buy equipment from abroad.* Times (London) 9/29/78, pIII **[1973]** —**agrotechnologist**, *n.: The beauty of our country paths is that they are an organic and continually evolving part of the countryside, not a blueprint by recreational planners, agrotechnologists or, for that matter, ramblers.* Times (London) 7/6/73, p17

AGS (ˌeiˌdʒiːˈes), abbreviation of *abort guidance system* (for use when the primary guidance system of a spacecraft fails to function properly). *And to cap it off, minutes after liftoff from the moon, the secondary guidance and navigation system called AGS (Abort Guidance System) went out.* Science News 2/13/71, p111 **[1969]**

aha reaction, *Psychology.* the sudden achievement of insight or illumination, especially in creative thinking. *He had been studying that sudden insight into the solution of a problem that psychologists sometimes call the "Aha" reaction. Great turning points in science often hinge on these mysterious intuitive leaps.* Scientific American 10/77, p18 *What goes on in a person's mind when he or she solves an important problem with a single flash of insight? How does somebody come up with a short, elegant solution to a seemingly difficult problem? Psychologists call these hunches* aha! *reactions. They have no relationship to general intelligence, but they are closely connected to creativity in science, business, and everyday activity.* Science News 12/23-30/78, p434 **[1977]** ►This term has apparently replaced the earlier phrases *aha experience* (1958) and *ah-ah experience* (1947), used by psychologists, especially of the Gestalt school, to designate the moment of revelation or discovery when one exclaims "aha!" or, as Archimedes is reputed to have done, "eureka!" Variant current expressions are *aha phenomenon* and *aha process.*

AHH, abbreviation of *aryl hydrocarbon hydroxylase*, an enzyme that converts the cancer-producing chemicals in tobacco smoke and in polluted air into their active form within the lungs. *Researchers . . . have come up with an experimental blood test that, by measuring an enzyme called aryl hydrocarbon hydroxylase (AHH), seems to distinguish cigarette smokers whose hereditary makeup makes them prone to develop lung cancer from those resistant to developing cancer.* Encyclopedia Science Supplement (Grolier) 1974, p251 **[1973]**

Ahmadiyya or **Ahmadiyyah** (*Anglicized* ɑːmɑːˈdiːyə), *n.* an Islamic missionary sect of India and Pakistan, whose members are active in many countries (often used attributively). *Riots erupted in Pakistan in June between adherents of the Ahmadiyya sect, said to number over 300,000, and other Muslims.*

The Ahmadiyya's claim that their founder . . . was a prophet, offended orthodox Muslims who believe prophecy terminated with Muhammad. Americana Annual 1975, p485 **[1910; 1970,** from Arabic, from the name of the founder Mirza Ghulam Ahmad, 1839-1908]

-aholic (-əˈhɔːlik), a combining form meaning "one addicted to, obsessed with, having a compulsive need of or for, or particularly fond of (something specified or a specified activity)." Examples: —**beefaholic**, *n.: More people, it seems, are joining with Los Angeles housewife Anne Brone. "We've cut way down on our beef," she said last week. "We used to be 'beefaholics.'"* Newsweek 9/24/73, p98 —**bookaholic**, *n.: For a bookaholic, life without plenty of books lying around the house is like a day without orange juice.* Tuscaloosa News (Alabama) 7/10/77, p3C —**footballaholic**, *n.: Until Thanksgiving Day, I had considered myself just another enthusiastic fan of pro football, not an abuser, a footballaholic.* Washington Post 12/2/74, p25 —**golfaholic**, *n.: Donald Goldstein . . . probably knows more manufacturers personally than Porter and other club craftsmen. Goldstein, you see, is a "golfaholic."* Southern Living 5/71, p29 —**hashaholic**, *n.: The U.S. Army hospital in Wurzburg, West Germany, had an "accessible, defined population" of 36,000 G.I.s, . . . 16,000 of these had used hash at least once. The drug was more readily available than marijuana, and thousands of men were on it consistently enough to be dubbed "hashaholics" by their buddies.* Time 7/24/72, p53 —**spendaholic**, *n.: With the Christmas gift season bringing out the latent spend-aholic in the most sober of budget-watchers, credit crises are as commonplace as holiday hangovers.* NY Times 12/20/78, pC1 —**sweetaholic**, *n.: Though a svelte 5 feet 8 inches and 119 pounds Kim admits to being a "sweetaholic" who dieted resolutely before winning the beauty pageant in Charleston, S.C., then "pigged out" on pecan pie a la mode.* Newsweek 5/30/77, p53 —**wheataholic**, *n.: "I am a wheataholic. Other people dream of whisky. I dream of hot bread."* TV Guide 5/12/73, p20 —**wordaholic**, *n.: Only by tracking bromides can wordaholics impose any kind of constraints and make our excellent lingo vogueword free.* NY Times Magazine 7/23/78, p23 **[1971,** abstracted from WORKAHOLIC] See also the variants -HOLIC and -OHOLIC.

AI¹ (ˈeiˈai), abbreviation of ARTIFICIAL INTELLIGENCE. *The effort to get machines to learn, see, hear, deduce, and intuit—to achieve what is called "Artificial Intelligence," or AI—has received little popular attention, presumably, at least in part, because of this conviction that AI is already a fact.* Atlantic 8/74, p40 **[1971]**

AI² (ˈeiˈai), abbreviation of AMNESTY INTERNATIONAL. *Amnesty International (AI) was founded in 1961 by Peter Benenson, a London lawyer . . . The organization, which now has 170,000 members in 107 nations, works for the release of any prisoner who has been jailed for political or religious reasons.* Britannica Book of the Year 1978, p114 **[1975]**

AIDS (eidz), *n.* a virus disease that attacks and breaks down the body's immune system, leading to fatal infection and often to a form of cancer. Full name, ACQUIRED IMMUNE DEFICIENCY SYNDROME. *Research at New York University Medical School has described components of AIDS that resemble autoimmune diseases. "While AIDS involves a shut-down of cellular immunity, some B cell functions [such as antibody production] certainly are increased," says Jan T. Vilcek. He has discovered an abnormal form of alfa-interferon, a natural disease-fighting substance, in 17 out of 34 homosexual AIDS patients with Kaposi's sarcoma, a cancer that frequently develops in the course of AIDS.* Science News 3/26/83, p197 **[1982,** from *a*(cquired) *i*(mmune) *d*(eficiency) *s*(yndrome)]

AIDS-related complex or **AIDS-related condition,** any of various viral conditions related to AIDS, usually characterized by enlarged lymph nodes and sometimes by sporadic fever, diarrhea, weight loss, and weakness. *While some individuals will develop the full-blown syndrome, others will simply manifest the flulike symptoms of AIDS-related complex (ARC).* Time 11/5/84, p91 *Most AIDS-related conditions are mild, but some* *are severe and others have progressed to AIDS.* World Book Science Annual 1987, p123 [**1984**]

AIDS virus, the retrovirus that causes AIDS by invading and destroying the T cells that help to regulate the immune system. The virus's technical name is HIV. *In early 1985, researchers developed a blood test that detects antibodies to the AIDS virus.* World Book Health & Medical Annual 1987, p229 [**1986**]

aikido (ɑi'ki:dou), *n.* a Japanese method of self-defense consisting of a series of holds and throws that involve strong powers of concentration and a harmonious coordination of body movements. *To avoid the danger of developing a fighting mental attitude, there are no competitive matches in the art of aikido and kyudo.* 1970 Compton Yearbook, p445 [**1968**, from Japanese *aikidō,* from *ai* together + *ki* spirit + *dō* art]

AIM (,ei,ai'em), abbreviation of *American Indian Movement,* a militant American Indian civil-rights organization in the U.S. and Canada, founded in 1968, that seeks the restoration of property and other rights granted by treaties. See NATIVE AMERICAN. . . . *the AIM has mounted forays into several of the towns in the area and it has had a certain success. In Sturgis, for instance, it was agreed that the Indian charged with murder should be given $15,000 bail.* Times (London) 2/20/73, p6 *Pronouncing the state* [North Dakota] *"a zone of war," the AIM urged Indians who plan to visit the area to bring along "gas masks, first aid kits, and self-defense equipment."* National Review 5/24/74, p568 [**1972**]

airbag, *n.* a sturdy plastic bag stored in an automobile dashboard and designed to inflate immediately upon collision to form a protective cushion. *Both these cars also have air-bags instead of safety belts.* Sunday Times (London) 4/25/71, p1 . . . *Volvo engineers are a little worried that the airbag, for instance, will be imposed on them before their own very detailed examination of its value and feasibility has been completed.* Manchester Guardian Weekly 9/5/70, p16 [**1964**]

air bearing, a bearing in which a shaft or other moving part is supported by the pressure of thin jets of air. *If air bearings were to be widely used in industry, this would make a tremendous difference to the noise level in factories.* Times (London) 3/29/68, p25 *Air bearings can be connected to any convenient source of compressed air and usually require little pressure.* Time 11/22/68, p63 [**1963**]

airborne soccer, *U.S.* a game similar to soccer, in which a Frisbee is substituted for the ball by two teams of seven players. Compare FRISBEE GOLF. *There are well-developed games like Guts, where teams of five, 15 yards apart, engage in an all-out, 100 m.p.h., flying disk war. The Ultimate game, airborne soccer, boasts an intercollegiate league of 52 schools.* NY Times Magazine 7/18/76, p47 [**1976**]

air bridge, **1** a closed passageway connecting two buildings above the ground. *But even in the partial model of Arcosanti, one can see Soleri's architectural intent. Air bridges connect units. Roof gardens spread on top of truss systems into which residences are fitted.* Saturday Review 2/12/72, p39 **2** a closed movable passageway used to allow direct access from a passenger terminal to an aircraft. *The original passenger terminal, called the beehive because of its shape, was connected by a tunnel to the station. . . . Access to the aircraft from the beehive was through canvas tunnels, the forerunners of today's movable air bridges.* Times (London) 5/17/76, p12 [**1965**] ►An earlier (1939) meaning of this term is a link or passage formed between two or more distant points by aircraft.

air broker, *British.* a person who arranges charter flights for the transport of cargo. *Without doubt the exchange came into air broking as adjunct to its shipbroking, many of the leading air brokers being in fact subsidiaries of shipping companies. For them the exchange is almost a captive market.* Times (London) 4/22/76, pIII [**1972**, patterned on earlier (OED 1816) *ship broker*]

airbus, *n.* a jet aircraft designed to carry passengers on short to medium-range flights. *As air traffic grows thicker, collisions become more likely. The advent of very large passenger-carrying aircraft—the Boeing 747 and later the "airbus" types*

brings with it the frightening possibility of almost a thousand people dying in a single collision. New Scientist 12/10/70, p144 [**1967**]

Aircav, *n.* a unit of the U.S. armed forces conveyed by aircraft to combat areas. *By now the Aircav, too, has realigned its forces after the first days of hectic seizing of opportunity.* Times (London) 5/18/70, p6 [**1965**, short for *Air cavalry*]

air-cushion or **air-cushioned**, *adj.* supported above the ground or water by a cushion of air produced by propellers or fans. *Air-cushion landing devices for large aircraft have passed their first demonstration trials.* Science News 1/31/76, p73 *Among the alternatives are air-cushioned transport, attractive magnetic levitation and repulsive magnetic levitation.* Scientific American 10/73, p17 [**1963**]

air cushion vehicle, *U.S. and Canada.* a vehicle that travels above the ground or water on a cushion of air produced by propellers or fans. The equivalent term in Great Britain is HOVERCRAFT. The abbreviation, ACV, is probably more frequently used in the United States than *air cushion vehicle.* Also called GROUND EFFECT MACHINE. *A flexible rubber "skirt" around the edge of an air cushion vehicle (ACV) traps air pulled down between the water's surface and the bottom of the ACV by two huge fans.* Science News 6/4/66, p445 [**1963**]

air dam, a device that reduces air resistance, increases stability, or otherwise improves the performance of an automobile, aircraft, or other vehicle moving through the air. *The car is six inches longer than the other Escorts, thanks to its streamlined nose, which has an integral air dam and has been fitted to cut drag and front-end lift.* Times (London) 2/5/76, p27 *The top face* [of the kite] *is described as spanned by a novel aerodynamic surface called an air dam, which operates to stabilize the flight while greatly increasing the lift.* NY Times 4/10/76, p41 [**1974**]

airdash, *v.i.* to rush by airplane; fly quickly or in a rush. *Governor B. K. Nehru, who airdashed to Shillong yesterday, flew back to Imphal today and had his final round of discussions with the persons concerned at the political and administrative levels.* Hindustan Times Weekly 3/25/73, p1 [**1973**] ►The term appears to have originated and be used chiefly in India.

air gun, another name for AQUAPULSE GUN. *Much mapping of ocean topography today is done with sound impulses. One quite useful device is the "air gun," a compressed-air cylinder that is towed submerged behind a ship. It sends out low-frequency sound waves by means of explosions set off at regular intervals.* Encyclopedia Science Supplement (Grolier) 1973, p185 [**1970**] ►The earlier meanings of *air gun* are an air rifle or air pistol, an airbrush, and an air hammer.

air hall, *British.* a large collapsible plastic dome used especially to enclose outdoor swimming pools, tennis courts, or other athletic grounds. Compare AIR STRUCTURE, BUBBLE². *They stress the value of air halls ("balloon" courts), which can permit play in bad weather and . . . are relatively cheap compared with permanent structures.* Times (London) 11/14/70, p12 [**1969**]

airhead, *n. Slang.* a stupid person; blockhead. *One of the many airheads who move torpidly through the $40-million mistake known as* Raise the Titanic *says in a throat-clutching voice: "A ship that big down that deep!?!?"* Macleans's 8/11/80, p54 [**1980**]

airhouse, *n.* an inflated plastic structure used especially to shelter building operations. *For the desired outdoor memorial purpose, the heavier, self-sealing fabric used for inflatable airhouses might provide the puncture-proofing needed to deflect the penknives of schoolboys and the bullets of symbolic assassins.* New Scientist and Science Journal 4/8/71, p71 [**1965**]

airlock module, an airtight compartment in a space station where the atmospheric pressure, temperature, and electrical power of the station are controlled and adjusted for various activities. *Abbreviation:* AM *When three astronauts of the third crew came aboard, they floated headfirst out of the conical command-and-service module; through the docking adapter . . . through a hatch into the airlock module; through another* hatch . . . and finally on into the cavernous workshop. New Yorker 8/30/76, p35 [**1971**]

air miss, an official designation for a narrow escape from collision by two aircraft flying too close to each other. *Yesterday's incident, with at least half a mile separating the two aircraft, falls into the category of an "air miss" rather than a "near miss," one of the dozen or so reported by pilots over Britain every month.* Times (London) 2/6/70, p4 [**1960**]

airmobile, *adj. U.S.* consisting of or relating to troops moved to combat zones by helicopters. *In an effort to bolster its mobility and firepower in Vietnam, the Army has decided to convert a paratroop division into an airmobile division.* NY Times 5/10/68, p12 *More pilots were necessary because the Army was making greater use of airmobile tactics in Vietnam. Since the beginning of the Vietnam buildup, more than 1,000 Army units have been activated.* 1967 Compton Yearbook, p124 [**1965**]

air pirate, a person who hijacks an aircraft. Also called SKYJACK-ER. *They [terrorists] include all air pirates and all who attack and murder the occupants of school buses and all unarmed civilians.* Times (London) 9/11/70, p11 [**1970**]

airplay, *n.* the broadcasting of a phonograph record. *The "underground" promotion man for the record company knew that reviews influenced FM airplay and availability in stores.* Harper's 1/74, p35 *The singer seems quite at home on 'Mr. Bojangles' as on Bob Marley's 'Stir it up' and all tracks, with perhaps the exception of a terrible arrangement of 'Only You,' deserve wide airplay.* Week-end Star (Kingston) 9/7/73, p18 [**1973**]

airspace, *n.* radio frequency channels; airways. *But the black reality is that the Marine Offences Act forbids British firms to use pirate airspace.* Sunday Times (London) 6/20/71, p15 [**1967**] ►The older meanings are (1) a space filled with air (1893) and (2) the space above an area of country (1911).

air structure, **1** an experimental or temporary structure supported by jets or cushions of air. Compare AIR HALL. *Other institutions exploring the growing field of air-structures included Harvard, the University of Minnesota, LaVerne (Calif.) College, and South Dakota State University.* Britannica Book of the Year 1974, p95 **2** another name for BUBBLE². *The new Murray Hill Racquet Club with its bubble of air structure atop the old East Side Airlines Terminal building at 320 East 38th Street, is one of the latest of some 25 commercial tennis clubs, the majority of them in bubbles, that have opened in and near Manhattan alone.* NY Times 1/2/77, pH1 [**1967**]

a.k.a. or **a/k/a** or **AKA** (ˌeiˌkeiˈei), *Especially U.S.* abbreviation of *also known as. The Russian Embassy, a.k.a. the Little Kremlin, had nothing to do with the Soviets. It was a big ol' house on West Avenue in Austin, rented for a couple of sessions in the late 1950s by a group of madcap liberal House members.* Atlantic 3/75, p54 *"The Last Testament of Lucky Luciano" begins on Nov. 23, 1897, and ends on Jan. 6, 1962, the dates when Salvatore Lucania (a/k/a Lucky Luciano) was born, and when he died.* NY Times Book Review 3/23/75, p4 *Now, with a style as gawky and loose as disco is poised and pent up, New Wave music (aka Punk) challenges the mindless complacency of an era in which both René Simard and Joe Clark have won followers.* Maclean's 11/13/78, p78 [**1971**] ►The abbreviation a.k.a. has long been used in law and business and especially by police departments in the United States in place of *alias*, which denotes a false or assumed name, whereas a.k.a. merely indicates another name which may or may not be used by someone to conceal his or her identity. The abbreviation became widespread in American English in the early 1970's and from the beginning was applied to variant names of all people and things. In *The Underground Dictionary* edited by Eugene E. Landy (1971), *a.k.a.* is used to indicate a cross reference from one word to a synonymous word or words, e.g., "**leave**, *v.* Depart. *a.k.a.* blow, cut, cut out, . . . split, slide, splurge, take off, walk."

ALA-dehydratase (ˌeiɛlˌei diˈhaidrəˌteis), *n.* an enzyme important in the synthesis of heme (the nonprotein part of hemoglobin). *Dr Hernberg found that lead affected the functioning of*

an enzyme involved in haem synthesis, and called, for short, ALA-dehydratase.* Sunday Times (London) 4/25/71, p13 [**1970**, *ALA* abbreviation of *aminolevulinic acid*]

alap (ɑːˈlɑːp), *n.* the first movement in the performance of a typical raga, the traditional Hindu musical form. Compare JOR, GAT. *. . . he* [Ravi Shankar] *broke off his alap (or rhythmless introductory section) in order to bow to applause before beginning the gath proper, which is something that would not happen in India.* New Yorker 9/21/68, p138 *Its alap (the uncadenced statement of* raga's *emotive and melodic potential with which its elaboration is always preceded) was played with apt indifference to gushing phraseology.* Times (London) 5/27/68, p14 [**1966**, from Sanskrit *alāp*]

alarm bells, a signal of danger or warning that causes apprehension. *Upon my departure a few months later I thought it right—for a variety of reasons—to sound the alarm bells ringing and this I attempted to do within the columns of your paper.* Times (London) 2/18/70, p9 *To be sure, everybody connected with the scheme avoids with horror this kind of language, and some of my informants will be provoked with me for using terms which could touch off alarm bells on Capitol Hill.* Harper's 11/70, p22 [**1963**] ►*Alarm bell* or *alarum bell* was the term used from at least the time of Shakespeare (cf. Henry IV, Part II: III, i, 17) to Poe's day (cf. The Bells) to designate "the tocsin of burghs in olden times" (*Oxford English Dictionary*).

albatross¹, *n.* a heavy burden, as of debt, responsibility, guilt, etc. (often in the phrase *an albatross around one's neck*). *What was hailed as the biggest breakthrough for Rolls-Royce in March 1968, has become an albatross around the company's neck.* Manchester Guardian Weekly 11/21/70, p22 [**1936; 1963**, in allusion to the albatross in Coleridge's *The Rime of the Ancient Mariner*]

albatross², *n. British.* a hole in golf played in three strokes less than par. *An albatross is a rare bird in golf—probably even rarer than a hole in one—and today one was achieved by Harnett, of Portmarnock, who holed his second shot to the 12th with a brassie, winning the hole but losing the match.* Times (London) 6/2/70, p13 [**1937; 1965**, patterned after *eagle, birdie*]

albomycin (ˌælbouˈmaisən), *n.* an iron-containing antibiotic derived from a species of actinomycetes and used against bacteria that are resistant to penicillin. *Thus albomycin contains ferrichrome, a material normally used by bacteria as a source of iron, and is conveniently taken into the cell via the ferrichrome uptake system.* New Scientist 3/15/73, p590 [**1973**, apparently from Latin *albus* white + *-mycin* (from Greek *mýkēs* fungus), as in *actinomycin*]

ALCM, abbreviation of *air-launched cruise missile.* Compare SLCM. See CRUISE MISSILE. *If the new B-1's are not built, the Air Force has a less dramatic option with the development of a nuclear armed ALCM . . . which could be carried aboard the current B-52 bomber force.* Americana Annual 1976, p384 [**1975**]

aleatoric (ˌeiliːəˈtɔrik), *adj.* (of a musical composition) performed so that the outcome is dependent on chance. Also, ALEATORY. *There is a certain amount of aleatoric, or chance, music here and there, but the structure of the work is entirely tonal, or perhaps one should say "modal," because of the frequent use of Oriental scales.* New Yorker 11/9/68, p213 *. . . Mr. Kay's partly aleatoric score, which he himself conducted, has a brightness yet power that is just right.* NY Times 2/29/68, p28 [**1961**, from Latin *āleātōrius* dependent on chance (from *āleātor* gambler, player with dice) + English *-ic*]

aleatorism (ˌeiliːˈætəˌrizəm), *n.* dependence on chance in the performance of music. *Although the overall forms of the time settings are fixed, the score makes use of a device known as controlled aleatorism.* Listener 4/18/68, p513 *Its characteristically controlled aleatorism produced a broadly conceived structure, in which the musical tension and weight of the simple block sections were so judged as to produce a most satisfying formal direction.* Times (London) 3/2/68, p19 [**1966**]

aleatory ('eili:ə,tɔri:), *adj.* another word for ALEATORIC. *Mr. Joachim's "Contrastes" is not music at all. It is a collection of sound effects, and it has aleatory passages. (All aleatory—or "anything goes"—music is a bore.)* New Yorker 2/10/68, p109 [**1961**]

Aleutian disease, a viral disease of mink noted for its similarity to various human diseases of connective tissue. *In Aleutian disease of mink, for example, there is a marked host response to the presence of the virus; indeed, the proliferation of certain cells and proteins (plasma cells and γ-globulins) of the immunological systems is one of the main problems in the progress of the disease.* New Scientist 3/15/73, p602 [**1966**, from the *Aleutian* Islands]

Alexbow, *n.* the trademark for a device that breaks arctic sea ice upward and throws it clear on each side. *Early in 1970 the Canadian federal government decided to spend an additional Can$500,000 on the further development of the "Alexbow," a Canadian-designed ice plow that would lift ice out of a ship's path rather than crushing it.* Britannica Book of the Year 1971, p103 [**1968**, from Scott Al*exander, the Canadian inventor of the device + *bow* (from its shape)]

alfafoetoprotein (,ælfə,fi:tou'prouti:n), *n. British.* variant of ALPHAFETOPROTEIN. *David Brock of the Western General Hospital, Edinburgh, works on alfafoetoprotein, an a-globulin formed in the unborn child from the age of six weeks.* New Scientist 1/18/73, p121 [**1973**]

Al Fatah (,ɑ:l fɑ:'tɑ:), the largest guerrilla group in the Palestine Liberation Organization (PLO). Also shortened to FATAH. *The publication said the main guerrilla group, Al Fatah, had been making contact with other groups to rally them around the new program, which will be introduced in the Palestinian legislature in exile, known as the National Council.* NY Times 3/1/76, p4 [**1966**, from Arabic, literally, the conquest; *Fatah* is also an acronym in reverse for *Harakat Tahrir Filastin* Palestine Liberation Movement]

Alf Garnett, *British.* a type of working class British man who often reacts to social pressures in a bigoted and self-righteous manner. Compare ARCHIE BUNKER, OCKER. *Beneath that veneer, presumably, lie dark and hideous passions: Lord Hunt worries that "the Alf Garnetts" may become the decisive voice in our society.* Sunday Times (London) 1/25/70, p11 [**1968**, from the name of a television character created by the English actor Warren Mitchell in Johnny Spealght's BBC comedy series "Till Death Us Do Part" (1967)]

Alfisol ('ælfə,sɔ:l), *n.* (in U.S. soil taxonomy) any of a group of soils which are usually moist and are characterized by an iron-rich surface layer. *This time-related variation is exhibited as horizontal variability in most localities. Alfisols on glaciated land surfaces 20,000 years old, for example, are commonly associated with Entisols a few hundred years old on floodplains.* McGraw-Hill Yearbook of Science and Technology 1976, p367 [**1972**, probably from *Alfa* (variant of *alpha* the first of a series) + connecting –*i*– + –*sol* (from Latin *solum* soil)]

Alfvén wave (ɑ:l'vein), *Physics.* a wave propagated within plasma as it interacts with a magnetic field. *Alfvén is credited with opening the whole field of magnetohydrodynamics, which is the study of electrically conductive gases, called plasma, in a magnetic field, and with the discovery of Alfvén waves.* 1971 Collier's Encyclopedia Year Book (1970), p380 [**1963**, named after Hannes O. *Alfvén,* born 1908, Swedish physicist]

algatron ('ælgə,trɑn), *n.* a laboratory structure in which algae are grown under controlled climatic conditions. *The system involves both photosynthetic algae and nonphotosynthetic bacterial components cultured in spin-type reactors (algatrons).* New Scientist and Science Journal 8/26/71, p469 [**1967**, from *alga* + –*tron* an instrument or device, as in *cyclotron*]

ALGOL or **Algol** ('æl,gɑl, -,gɔ:l), *n.* acronym for *Algorithmic Language*, a computer language using algebraic notation. Compare BASIC, COBOL, FORTRAN. *The school-children were helped by three circumstances; they were young, they were using Algol—a powerful programming language—and they had a clear understanding of the problems they were solving.* New Scientist 1/5/67, p36 [**1959**]

algolagniac (,ælgə'lægni:æk), *n.* a person who gets sexual pleasure from inflicting or experiencing pain; a sadomasochist. *Readings in continental decadent literature of the* fin de siècle: *among others, a model esthete and satanist from France (Huysmans), a hair-fetishist from Belgium (Rodenbach), a senile satyr from Holland (Couperus), some algolagniacs from Denmark (Jacobsen, Bang).* New Yorker 3/29/76, p61 [**1976**, derivative of *algolagnia* (1901) sadomasochism, from Greek *álgos* pain + *lagneía* lust]

algolagniaphile (,ælgə'lægni:ə,fail), *n.* another name for ALGOLAGNIAC. *The dazzlingly literate personal ads have launched at least three marriages and countless friendships through such entreaties as "couple seek avid algolagniaphile [a sado-masochist], female 30s, to complete harmonious ménage à trois."* Newsweek 10/29/73, p70 [**1973**, from *algolagnia* + –*phile* lover of]

alimony drone, *U.S.* (*usually used disparagingly*). a divorced woman who chooses not to remarry in order to continue receiving alimony. *There are rules, decisions, and statutes instructing the judge that wives should not be permitted to become "alimony drones"—self-indulgent, indolent parasites.* Saturday Review 7/29/72, p34 *Alimony drone is an indolent divorcee living on alimony.* New York Post 2/26/75 (page not known) [**1972**]

aliterate (ei'litərit), *n.* a person who shows no interest in reading or literature. *These are the "aliterates," people who know how to read but just don't bother.* Newsday 2/27/86, p29 —*adj.* showing no interest in reading or literature. *The student body there consisted of boys who hated books, boys who had gotten into trouble. "They were not only illiterate," Fader says, "they were a-literate."* Saturday Review 6/25/66, p10 [**1966**, from *a*- not + il*literate*]

allatectomy (,ælə'tektəmi:), *n.* removal of an insect's corpus allatum (gland that secretes various hormones) in experiments on molting, metamorphosis, etc. *Allatectomy of the treated fifth instar larvae reversed the effects of the prior treatment with juvenile hormone.* Nature 6/23/72, p458 [**1968**, from corpus al*latum* + –*ectomy* surgical removal (from Greek *ektomé* a cutting out)] —**allatectomize**, *v.t.: Our results, however, do not entirely rule out the possibility that some JHA might have some intrinsic hormone activity. The fact that various compounds have been reported to produce juvenile hormone activity in allatectomized insects, has been put forward in support of this contention.* Science 8/17/73, p673

all-at-once-ness, *n.* the condition in which many things happen or are experienced at the same time. *Instead of "the alphabet and print technology," which fostered fragmentation, mechanization, specialization, detachment and privacy, we now have an "electric technology," which fosters unification, involvement, "all-at-once-ness" and a lack of goals.* NY Times 5/26/68, p72 *The all-at-once-ness of the "field approach" to problems is rapidly replacing the fixed, visual approach of applied or "resolute" knowledge.* Saturday Review 4/15/67, p46 [**1966**]

Allen charge, *U.S. Law.* a charge or instruction to a hung jury in which the judge urges dissenting jurors to reconsider their views in deference to the majority and do their utmost to reach a verdict. Also called DYNAMITE CHARGE. *To many laymen the Allen charge may seem innocuous—an attempt to balance the defendant's right to a hung jury, if the jurors cannot agree, against the judicial system's need to dispose of cases on the docket. But seasoned criminal lawyers feel that its use almost invariably leads to a conviction.* NY Times 10/8/72, pD6 [**1967** (but cf. *Black's Law Dictionary*, 1951), after the case of *Allen* vs. *United States* (1897) in which the charge was first used]

allogeneic, *adj.* genetically different. Compare XENOGENEIC. *Glands cultured for 4 weeks have survived for more than 40 days in allogeneic recipients.* McGraw-Hill Yearbook of Science and Technology 1976, p108 *The cells, taken either from the patient himself (autologous cells) or from a similar case (allogeneic cells), are first killed and treated in various ways to* enhance their immunogenic power. Lucien Israel, Conquering Cancer, 1978, p118 [**1965**, from *allo-* other + *–geneic*, as in *syngeneic*]

allograft, *n.* a graft of tissue taken from another individual's body. Compare XENOGRAFT. *Skin loss from burns and extensive traumatic avulsions were treated in 41 infants and children (New Orleans, La.) by temporary cutaneous allografts of adult cadaver or fetal origin.* Britannica Book of the Year 1970, p520 . . . *earthworms* (Eisenia foetida typica) *from one geographical region rejected first-set allografts from worms of other regions.* New Scientist 11/20/69, p391 [**1967**, from *allo–* other + *graft*]

allopurinol (ˌælouˈpyurəˌnɔːl), *n.* a drug that prevents the formation of uric acid in the blood. *Allopurinol, originally regarded as a drug that specifically inhibits the enzyme xanthine oxidase, inhibits other liver enzymes as well, Dr. Vesell reports. The drug is taken by thousands of patients with gout.* Science News 7/11/70, p37 [**1965**, from *allo–* other + *purine* + *-ol* (chemical suffix)]

allosteric, *adj.* involving a change in the shape of an enzyme at a site other than the catalytic site. . . . *allosteric effects can make big differences to enzyme activity in the direction both of stimulation and inhibition.* New Scientist 1/22/70, p155 [**1964**, from *allo–* other + *ster–* solid + *-ic*]

allostery, *n.* allosteric condition or effect. *The enzymes that make up the metabolism of the living cell change their shape as they work . . . Though the theory was propounded some time ago, this is the first direct evidence of the phenomenon, known as allostery.* 1970 Collier's Encyclopedia Year Book, p138 [**1966**]

allotype, *n.* a variant genetic trait that produces antibodies in an individual when tissue is introduced from another individual having another variation of the trait. *In the rabbit there are several separate genetic markers, called allotypes, which are the characteristics manifested by inheritable amino acid sequence differences at various positions on both light and heavy polypeptide chains.* 1971 Britannica Yearbook of Science and the Future, p266 [**1970**, from *allo-* other + *type*] ►An older meaning of this term in biology is that of a specimen having the opposite sex of the specimen on which a description of the species is based.

allozyme, *n.* an enzyme that varies genetically from one group or species to another. *A further area of present interest is the existence of certain pairs of species which show only very slight genetic difference as measured by allozymes. These cases may represent pairs of newly formed species.* Nature 2/5/76, p359 [**1976**, from *allo-* other + *-zyme* enzyme]

all-play-all, *n. British.* a tournament in which every contestant plays every other contestant. The equivalent U.S. term is *round robin.* Often used attributively. *There is still the feeling, in many people's minds, that a genuine international tournament is one played on the all-play-all principle, with the further notion that such a system lends itself least to the strokes of luck which can occur in events held on the Swiss system.* Times (London) 5/21/77, p9 [**1968**]

all-terrain vehicle, a light-weight, rugged motor vehicle for travel over rough terrain. *Abbreviation:* ATV *Proliferating from Maine to California, they* [off-road vehicles] *now include 200,000 dune buggies, 2,000,000 trail bikes, 1,100,000 snowmobiles and, newest of all, 25,000 all-terrain vehicles (ATV's).* Time 11/23/70, p41 [**1969**]

Almanach de Gotha, the royalty of Europe. *This week, with half the Almanach de Gotha joined by Neil Armstrong, sacrificial lamb of modern capitalism, and Bob Hope, the US Army's court jester, ECY* [European Conservation Year] *in Britain has come officially to an end.* New Scientist 12/10/70, p463 [**1963**, generic use of the name of a statistical publication which lists in detail the genealogies of the European royal families, published since the 1700's, originally in Gotha, Germany]

alphaendorphin, *n.* a pain-suppressing hormone produced in the pituitary gland. *Roger Guillemin of the Salk Institute went on to isolate two other peptides, as well as beta-endorphin it-*

self, *from a mixture of hypothalamus and pituitary tissue from pigs. One of them, named alpha-endorphin, has a sequence corresponding to amino acids 61 through 76 of beta-lipotropin, and it has analgesic and tranquilizing effects in animals.* Scientific American 3/77, p55 [**1976**, from *alpha-* first of a series + ENDORPHIN]

alphafetoprotein (ˌælfəˌfiːtəˈproutiːn), *n.* a glycoprotein abundant in the blood serum of fetuses. Its presence in high concentrations in the blood of an adult indicates pregnancy or certain kinds of cancer; higher concentrations than normal for pregnancy indicate a birth defect in the fetus. See CARCINOEMBRYONIC ANTIGEN. *A study in 19 centres in Britain has shown that a blood test for alphafetoprotein (AFP) can indicate with considerable accuracy if a pregnant woman is carrying a foetus affected by spina bifida or anencephaly (absence of most of the brain).* New Scientist 6/30/77, p759 [**1973**, from *alpha* first of a series + FETOPROTEIN]

alphagalactosidase (ˌælfəgəˌlæktəˈsaideis), *n.* a form of galactosidase, an enzyme that metabolizes fat. The abnormal function of alphagalactosidase is believed to be responsible for FABRY'S DISEASE. *Testing skin cells from a Fabry's patient, the investigators found them deficient in activity of a specific enzyme called alphagalactosidase.* Science News 10/17/70, p312 [**1970**, from *alpha* first of a series + *galactosidase*]

alpha-helical, *adj.* consisting of a single spiral or coil. *Myoglobin is made up of straight runs of alpha-helix from one side of the molecule to the other, so that about three quarters of the whole chain is in the alpha-helical form.* New Scientist 10/26/67, p219 [**1963**]

alpha helix, the single spiral or coil structure of certain protein molecules. Compare DOUBLE HELIX. *It seemed almost unbelievable that the RNA structure was solved, that the answer was incredibly exciting, and that our names would be associated with the double helix as* [Linus] *Pauling's was with the alpha-helix.* James D. Watson, The Double Helix, 1968, p112 [**1955**]

alphametic (ˌælfəˈmetik), *n.* a type of mathematical puzzle in which an arithmetical problem is presented with letters instead of numerals, each letter standing for a particular but different digit. *This cryptarithm (or alphametic, as many puzzlists prefer to call them) is an old one of unknown origin . . .* Scientific American 2/70, p112 [**1963**, from *alpha*bet + arith*metic*]

alpha₁-antitrypsin, *n.* a protein of human blood serum that normally inhibits the action of the enzyme trypsin. A deficiency of $alpha_1$-antitrypsin is believed to indicate a predisposition to emphysema and other lung disorders. *Much of the literature on $alpha_1$-antitrypsin argues the need for the identification of deficient individuals so they can be warned that they are at unusually high risk and should modify their surroundings accordingly.* New Scientist 9/2/76, p486 [**1976**, from *alpha* first of a series + the number *1* + *anti-* against + *trypsin*]

alpha receptor, a site or structure in a cell at which the stimulus of certain adrenergic (adrenaline-producing) agents elicits a usually excitatory response. *Stimulation of the alpha-receptors produced a stimulation of the associated muscles: the lungs worked harder to get more oxygen or the blood vessels expanded to increase circulation. Stimulation of the beta-receptors had the opposite effect, of slowing down activity.* Times (London) 3/19/73, p3 [**1963**, shortened from *alpha-adrenergic receptor*]

alphascope, *n.* a device on a computer which displays words and symbols on a screen. *An alphascope is basically a keyboard, on which the operator types to communicate with the computer, and a CRT* [cathode-ray tube] *screen on which the computer replies.* Science Journal 10/70, p67 [**1969**, from *alphanumeric* (using both letters and numbers) + *-scope* instrument for viewing]

Alpine or **alpine**, *adj.* of or designating ski races that include downhill, slalom, and giant slalom events. Compare NORDIC. *None of the men Alpine skiers was able to come close to matching Mittermaier's combination of Olympic and World Cup dominance.* 1976 Collier's Encyclopedia Year Book, p524 *With training techniques and equipment ever more sophisticated and timing more exact, alpine skiing today resembles Formula One auto racing: runs get faster and the risks bigger.* Time 2/2/76, p64 [**1973**, so called from these events having originated in the Alps]

Alpinist or **alpinist,** *n.* a skier who takes part in Alpine competition; an Alpine skier. *Cindy Nelson, 20, is the only American alpinist given much chance to win a medal. But the favorite in Cindy's best event, the downhill, will probably be Austrian Brigitte Totschnig.* Time 2/2/76, p64 [**1976**, from ALPINE + -*ist*] ▶ The original meaning of *Alpinist* (1880's) is a person devoted to the climbing of high mountains.

also-runner, *n.* an unsuccessful participant in any competition. *The luck of the nonseeding put into practice this fall brought Yale to Brown at the very start of the League program, and Brown, an also-runner for so many seasons, is something else these days.* . . . New Yorker 9/27/76, p79 [**1965,** variant of *also-ran* (1890's)]

altered state of consciousness, any state of mind that differs from the normal mental state of a conscious person. *Abbreviation:* ASC *Other cultures have long had techniques for arriving at altered states of consciousness—through such means as chanting, whirling, fasting, breathing exercises, and flagellation.* Science 3/9/73, p983 *It is beginning to be thought that telepathy, clairvoyance, mystical transports, and other altered states of consciousness may be latent in most, if not all, of us, along with psychic powers and dominions not demonstrated.* New Yorker 1/5/76, p30 [**1972**]

alternative or **alternate,** *adj.* being or representing an alternative to established or conventional institutions, values, ideas, etc. *Which is not to say that Durham does not have its pockets of "alternative" behaviour. There is a beleaguered minority of self-conscious radicals, of "hairies" and "politicos"—as I now and then heard them called—and the Students' Union bookshop seemed to be aiming many of its wares in their direction.* Times Literary Supplement 2/18/72, p183 *In late 1969, Theodore Roszak published his book "The Making of a Counter-Culture" which talked of the youth movement as an alternative society and as a valid culture with its own art, its own music, and its own vocabulary* . . . Manchester Guardian Weekly 4/3/71, p6 *The so-called alternate theater made a tremendous contribution to the variety of the season.* 1976 Collier's Encyclopedia Year Book, p544 [**1970**]

alternative birthing, any of various methods of childbirth in which the delivery is performed at home or in a homelike setting, usually without the use of obstetric instruments or strong sedating drugs. See LEBOYER. *Illinois Masonic's alternative birthing center is a small, completely independent unit with two bedrooms, a nurses' station with rolltop desk, and a small lounge where family and friends can wait.* Time 4/24/78, p60 *The "alternative birthing" movement continued to spread . . . More women declined to have their babies under sterile, technologically sophisticated hospital conditions.* Americana Annual 1979, p321 [**1978**]

alternative energy or **alternate energy,** power and heat derived from sources other than fossil fuels (petroleum, coal, natural gas) or nuclear fission. *The institute's work will cover four general areas of research: a survey of existing energy resources, including an assessment of alternative (renewable) energy sources such as solar energy, geothermal energy, bio-gas, and wind power.* New Scientist 3/24/77, p687 *It seems that while there are many committed to alternate energy, and particularly to wind power, the state of technology is not very healthy and both funds and expertise for research are severely limited.* Maclean's 12/4/78, p14 [**1975**]

alternative school, any school that differs from conventional schools in organization, purpose, and teaching methods, formed because of dissatisfaction with the existing educational system. Compare FREE SCHOOL, STREET ACADEMY. *The two most controversial of these "alternative schools," financed with $3.6 million in federal funds, are Black House, a high school staffed by blacks for blacks only, and Casa de la Raza, a kindergarten-through-high school, the walls of which are*

decorated with Cuban posters lauding the NLF and such homilies as "All Power Comes from the Barrel of a Gun." National Review 3/16/73, p310 [**1972**]

alternative technology, technology that uses small-scale, inexpensive tools that are simple to use and methods which conserve natural resources and protect the environment from exploitation and destruction. *Abbreviation:* AT Compare APPROPRIATE TECHNOLOGY, INTERMEDIATE TECHNOLOGY. *The 'alternative technology' movement in industrially advanced societies is struggling to recover some of the self-sufficient technology of an earlier generation.* Nature 1/29/76, p258 [**1973**]

altruism, *n.* instinctive cooperation or self-sacrificing behavior among animals; animal behavior that seems analogous to human altruism. See SOCIOBIOLOGY. *The weirdest aspect of the behavior of social animals, beyond scientific understanding, is their ceaseless giving away of things. They carry food to each other all day long, they shelter and protect each other, and on occasion they drop dead for each other. The trait seems to be genetically determined, and the biologists have already made up a technical term, borrowed from an old word, now part of the professional jargon:* altruism. NY Times Magazine 7/4/76, p109 *In sociobiology, altruism . . . is what happens when a predator breaks into a nest of termites or ants. Members of the colony's "soldier caste" instinctively rush to place themselves between the intruder and the rest of the colony.* Encyclopedia Science Supplement (Grolier) 1976, p46 [**1975**] —**altruistic,** *adj.: Dolphin society provides examples of altruistic behavior. The drawing depicts an observed incident in which a harpooned dolphin . . . was supported by companions at the sea surface so that it could breathe.* Picture legend, Encyclopedia Science Supplement (Grolier) 1976, p46 —**altruistically,** *adv.: Harry Power of the University of Michigan reported that one way to measure the frequency of true altruism was to give bluebirds the choice of behaving altruistically or selfishly toward the offspring of other bluebirds.* 1977 Britannica Yearbook of Science and the Future, p347

AM, abbreviation of AIRLOCK MODULE. *The workshop, AM and MDA* [multiple docking adapter] *combined provide 12,763 cubic feet of space, about four times larger than the Salyut station and equivalent to a well organized three-bedroom house with a lot of closet and storage space.* Science News 5/5/73, p293 [**1973**]

amantadine (ə'mæntə,di:n), *n.* Full name, **amantadine hydrochloride.** a synthetic chemical that inhibits the penetration of viruses into cells. Amantadine is used against Asian influenza and is reported to be effective against Parkinson's disease, though it is not a vaccine nor an antibiotic. . . . *amantadine releases catecholamines, neurohormones, from storage sites in peripheral nerve tissue. "We think that amantadine may have the same action within the central nervous system," they report. These hormones, particularly dopamine, play an intimate role in the tremors experienced by patients with Parkinson's disease.* Science News 7/25/70, p63 *The drug is amantadine hydrochloride. It was tried out on 37 patients and one of the points emphasized is that for all practical purposes side or toxic effects were absent.* Times (London) 2/6/70, p4 [**1964,** formed by alteration (influenced by *amine*) of *adamantane,* an organic compound]

amaretto (,æmə'retou), *n.* an Italian liqueur with an almond taste. *"The Amaretto we use is only 40 proof so with the cream it is not exactly like putting martinis down."* NY Times 2/23/78, p31 [**1978**, from Italian, originally a cake or macaroon made from bitter almonds, from *amaro* bitter]

ambient air standard, the maximum concentration of an air pollutant considered tolerable for human beings in the outdoor air of a particular area. Compare POLLUTANT STANDARDS INDEX. *EPA Acting Administrator Robert Fri said . . . only four cities would probably have trouble meeting ambient air standards for nitrogen dioxide: Los Angeles, Chicago, Salt Lake City and Metropolitan New York.* Science News 6/16/73, p387 [**1973**]

ambisextrous, *adj.* sexually attracted to or involved with both sexes; bisexual. *In 1736 she* [Lady Mary Wortley Montague] *ran off to Venice with a dreamily beautiful but coldly ambisex-*

trous adventurer, to whom she wrote 26 stormy love letters that appear for the first time in these volumes. Time 3/11/66, p67 [**1958**, from *ambi-* both + -*sextrous*, by analogy with or as a pun on *ambidextrous*]

ambisexual, *n.* a bisexual person. . . . *populating his hotel with football rowdies, ambisexuals and couples on their second honeymoon.* Times (London) 8/19/76, p5 [**1976**]

ambisonic, *adj.* of or having to do with ambisonics. *Ambisonic master recordings are made in the full four-channel format. But the few which have so far been made available as discs or broadcasts have used three channels or less.* New Scientist 3/20/80, p929 [**1973**]

ambisonics, *n.* high-fidelity sound reproduction that stimulates electronically the directional qualities of the sound waves which it reproduces. Compare SURROUND-SOUND. *The new concept, called "ambisonics," aims at giving the listener the experience not only of the spatial positioning of the performers, but also of the directional qualities of the reverberant sound—the quality that adds the atmosphere and realism of a live performance.* New Scientist 12/20/73, p843 [**1973**, from *ambi-* around + English *sonics*]

amelia (ei'mi:lɪə), *n.* a congenital absence of the arms or legs. *Dr. McBride had acknowledged to the committee that his original statement about Imipramine was incorrect in relation to two of three cases of birth defects originally cited by him. The one that was correct was a case of amelia (total absence of arms).* Times (London) 3/9/72, p7 [**1967**, from New Latin, from *a-* without + Greek *mélos* limb] ▶Although this term has long been used in medicine, it has only recently appeared in popular writing as a result of the interest generated by this and similar conditions caused by various drugs taken during pregnancy, such as thalidomide.

Amerasian, *adj.* of mixed American and Asian descent. . . . *this book* [For Spacious Skies by Pearl S. Buck] *deals with the author's concern and efforts to help the Amerasian children of U.S. servicemen in Korea, Japan, Okinawa and Vietnam.* Science News 8/27/66, p140 —*n.* a person of mixed American and Asian descent. *Among the Thais, they are referred to as red-haired babies. Among the sociologists concerned with the problem, they are called Amerasians.* NY Times 4/30/68, p6 [**1965**, from *American* + *Asian*, patterned after *Eurasian* of mixed European and Asian descent]

Amer–English, *n.* American English. Also AMERO–ENGLISH. *One of the glories of the English language is that it welcomes in and naturalizes its vocabulary from every other tongue. It combines and adopts useful words from Anglo-Saxon and Teutonic roots alongside Latin, French, Greek, Hindi, Australian, Amer-English, and anything else that comes to tongue, with majestic disinterestedness.* Times (London) 5/20/76, p18 [**1976**, from *American* + *English*, patterned after *Amerasian* and *Amerindian* (OEDS 1900)]

American Dream, 1 a widely used catchphrase for the ideals of democracy, equality, and freedom upon which the United States was founded. *The Hornell Farm that Hicks painted about 1848 is nothing less than the American dream made tangible. Human beings are there in the background. Portraits of cattle and horses fill the foreground.* Manchester Guardian Weekly 9/19/68, p21 **2** the American way of life; American culture or society. . . . *black people have all too often found the American dream a nightmare.* Atlantic 4/69, p81 [**1967**] ▶The term may have been popularized by its use as the title of various literary works, notably *The American Dream* (1961), a play by Edward Albee, and *An American Dream* (1965) by Norman Mailer.

Americanologist, *n.* an expert on the American government and its policies. Compare KREMLINOLOGIST. *The most important one, titled "Questions calling for a Practical Answer," was written by Georgy Arbatov, director of Moscow's U.S.A. Research Institute and widely regarded as the Kremlin's foremost Americanologist.* Time 8/23/71, p10 [**1965**]

Americanophobe, *n.* a person who hates the United States. . . . *neither hippies nor militant students, neither war resisters nor*

Americanophobes, whatever view one may take of their acts or goals, resemble the old intelligentsia in its heyday . . . Listener 5/2/68, p565 [**1967**]

American Selling Price, the price charged by American manufacturers for a product, used to determine the amount of duty to be paid on a similar product imported into the United States, instead of basing the duty on the actual cost of the product to an importer. *The Administration, ignoring chemical industry pleas that it be retained, urged the repeal of the American Selling Price (ASP), a method of customs valuation that has protected U.S. dyestuff producers since the 1920s.* 1970 World Book Year Book, p267 [**1966**]

American Sign Language, a system of communication by manual signs used by the deaf in North America. It is considered by some linguists to possess most of the range of morphological and syntactic processes found in natural languages. *Abbreviation:* ASL Also called AMESLAN. *What we see on these two dozen close-ups of Mary Beth and a couple of friends are formal words of signing, or American Sign Language (what a few bright chimpanzees such as Washoe have been learning lately, by the way).* Scientific American 12/74, p148 [**1965**; cf. *A Dictionary of American Sign Language on Linguistic Principles*, 1965, by William Stokoe, Jr. and others]

Amero–English, *n.* a variant of AMER–ENGLISH. *The impingement of "franglais," or more precisely, Amero-English, into French cultural life is still a thorn in the side of French science authorities.* New Scientist 6/14/73, p702 [**1973**, from *American* + connecting -*o-* + *English*]

Ameslan ('æməs,læn), *n.* acronym for AMERICAN SIGN LANGUAGE. *Finger spelling is not a language but rather a means of transposing any alphabetized language such as English into a gestural mode. Ameslan is a language, and it is the primary means of communication for deaf people in North America.* Eugene Linden, Apes, Men, and Language, 1974, p18 *There are also indications that female chimps versed in Ameslan automatically teach it to their young, beginning almost immediately after birth.* Maclean's 3/21/77, p68 [**1974**]

Ames test, a test for detecting cancer-producing substances by measuring their relative ability to cause a mutation. *At present, there are two ways to prevent cancer. The first is to try—with the help of the Ames test, for example—to eliminate mutagenic agents from everything that can be ingested or breathed in.* Lucien Israel, Conquering Cancer, 1978, p53 *Because of the mutation/virus-intrusion assumption, the hunt for industrial carcinogens has settled upon substances that cause mutations among laboratory organisms. The most recently developed method is the "Ames test,". . . which uses a highly specialized strain of bacteria that is very susceptible to mutations to measure mutagenic effect.* Harper's 8/78, p57 [**1976**, named after Bruce *Ames*, an American biochemist]

amino-acid dating, a method of dating geological or archaeological specimens of organic origin by measuring the proportion of the two different forms of an amino acid in a specimen. Compare IODINE-XENON DATING, RUBIDIUM-STRONTIUM DATING, THERMOLUMINESCENT DATING. See also AGE-DATE. *Barraco is also investigating a new method of establishing the date of death of the mummified bodies. The new method, called amino-acid dating, not only may prove more accurate than radiocarbon dating, but also requires much smaller samples of tissue and wrappings. Amino acids are small protein units found in equal amounts as d- and l-forms in the living body. After death, however, the d-form slowly but constantly changes to the l-form. The amount of change is proportionate to the time the person has been dead.* World Book Science Annual 1977, p93 [**1972**]

amitriptyline or **amitriptylene** (,æmə'triptəli:n), *n.* an antidepressant drug used especially to treat nonpsychotic depression, marketed under the trademark Elavil. *Formula:* $C_{20}H_{23}N$ *Drugs such as amitriptyline and chlorpromazine, as well as electroshock treatment (ECT), also suppress REM sleep, but there is no rebound following their termination and these drugs are not addictive.* McGraw-Hill Yearbook of Science and Technology 1971, p171 *She was placed on probation after* *being found not guilty of administering a noxious dose of amitriptylene in her baby's medicine so as to endanger her life but admitted giving doses to the baby while in hospital.* Times (London) 7/21/76, p2 [**1964**, from *amino* + altered form of *trypt*amine, a substance in nerve tissue + meth*yl* + -*ine* or -*ene* (chemical suffixes)]

amitrole ('æmə,troul), *n.* a highly toxic herbicide used especially against poison ivy. *Formula:* $C_2H_4N_4$ *The phenoxy herbicides (2,4-D and 2,4,5-T), aminotriazole (amitrole), and picloram are frequently used in forestry.* McGraw-Hill Yearbook of Science and Technology 1974, p330 [**1963**, contraction of *aminotriazole* (1950's)]

Amnesty International, an independent international organization that investigates violations of human rights by governments and works for the release of persons imprisoned for political or religious reasons. *Abbreviation:* AI See HUMAN RIGHTS. *Amnesty International, the widely respected human rights organization headquartered in London, estimates that in the last decade torture has been officially practiced in 60 countries; last year alone there were more than 40 violating states.* Time 8/16/76, p31 *The West German branch of Amnesty International Friday called for an investigation into what is described as the inhuman torture of political prisoners in Turkey.* Athens News 4/1-2/72, p3 [**1961**] ▶The organization became widely known in the early 1970's and in 1977 was awarded the Nobel Peace Prize. It was founded in 1961 by Peter Benenson, an English lawyer.

amniocentesis (,æmni:ousen'ti:sis), *n.* the insertion of a hypodermic needle into the amniotic sac to withdraw fluid for analysis of the embryo's cells. *Averting the birth of children with sexlinked disorders demands the identification of female carriers. At present the technique known as amniocentesis is used to withdraw a small number of cells from the amniotic fluid in order to type the embryo, and an abortion is induced if necessary.* Scientific American 12/70, p53 [**1966**, from *amnion* the membrane enveloping the fetus + *centesis* surgical puncture (from Greek *kéntēsis* a pricking)]

amniography, *n.* the process of taking an X-ray photograph of the amnion to locate defects in a fetus. . . . *amniography . . . entailed X-raying a pregnant woman to procure pictures of the amniotic fluid in the womb and of the condition of the placenta . . .* 1970 Compton Yearbook, p339 [**1967**, from *amnion* the membrane enveloping the fetus + -*graphy* process of recording]

amnioscope, *n.* an instrument for examining the fetus within the amnion. *Several researchers . . . are trying to develop a "fetal amnioscope" that . . . would enable the doctor to view the fetus directly and take a sample of fetal blood and fetal skin, permitting a faster and more accurate diagnosis of more disorders than can now be diagnosed from amniotic fluid cells.* NY Times 6/3/71, p53 [**1966**, from *amnion* the membrane enveloping the fetus + -*scope* instrument for viewing]

amnioscopy, *n.* examination with an amnioscope. *In some clinical centres, amnioscopy is performed on patients at high risk in the latter weeks of pregnancy.* New Scientist 4/9/70, p66 [**1967**]

amotivational, *adj.* characterized by a lack of motivation; unmotivated. *The topic, known to psychologists as the amotivational syndrome, refers to general apathy, mental confusion and lack of goals among college students that often led to the student's dropping out.* NY Times 1/28/76, p25 [**1969**, from *a-* not + *motivational*]

amoxycillin or **amoxicillin** (ə,mɑksə'silin), *n.* an oral penicillin effective against a large variety of bacteria, introduced into the United States from Great Britain in 1975. *Formula:* $C_{16}H_{19}N_3O_5S$ *A newer antibiotic in the family is beginning to take over the running. Amoxycillin has been sold on the Continent only during the past two years.* Sunday Times (London) 5/4/75, p63 [**1971**, from *amino-hydroxy*phenyl (part of its chemical name) + penic*illin*]

AMPase (,ei,em'pi:,eis), *n.* an enzyme thought to be involved in the transport of ions across cell membranes. *In a very neat ex-*

periment James Gurd, also of NIMR [National Institute of Medical Research], *London, has shown the enzyme AMPase to be present on some walls of liver cells and absent from others.* New Scientist and Science Journal 3/4/71, p467 [**1971**, from *AMP* (abbreviation of *adenosine monophosphate*, a compound of adenosine, a constituent of nucleic acid, and one phosphate group) + -*ase* enzyme]

amphipathic or **amphipath**, *adj.* variants of AMPHIPHILIC. *Amphipath molecules, as the Greek derivation implies, are those in which one part of the molecule has an affinity for water and the other part has a greater affinity for itself than for water.* New Scientist 1/14/71, p63 *A membrane can be disrupted by a high concentration of a detergent, which is an amphipathic molecule that forms the small droplets called micelles.* Scientific American 1/79, p53 [**1971**, from *amphi-* both + -*pathic* affected by]

amphiphile, *n.* an amphiphilic compound. *Phospholipids are amphiphiles, and amphiphiles are known to form lyotropic liquid crystals with water.* McGraw-Hill Yearbook of Science and Technology 1971, p259 [**1971**, back formation from *amphiphilic*]

amphiphilic, *adj.* having or showing two different affinities (as for water and fat). *Some molecules, such as fatty acids and phospholipids, have a long hydrophobic tail and a hydrophilic head group, and are known as amphiphilic molecules.* McGraw-Hill Yearbook of Science and Technology 1976, p26 [**1971**, from *amphi-* both + -*philic* liking]

ampicillin, *n.* a type of penicillin that is more active against various bacteria and more resistant to the enzyme which destroys penicillin (penicillinase) than ordinary penicillin. Compare CLOXACILLIN, OXACILLIN. *One of these drugs is ampicillin . . . which acts against* P. aeruginosa, S. aureus *and other microorganisms that, in one of the great epics of self-defense in the natural world, came to dominate as mutant strains producing the enzyme penicillinase.* Science News 8/22/70, p164 [**1963**, from its chemical name *amino* benzyl *penicillin*]

Amtrak, *n.* U.S. a government-controlled public corporation, officially known as the National Railroad Passenger Corporation, created in 1970 to run the essential rail passenger service linking major cities which private enterprise is unable to provide. *Amtrak announces two kinds of savings for New York train travelers . . . We're making the trains worth traveling again.* Advertisement by Amtrak, NY Times 5/31/72, p19 *A new system of rail passenger service is now being launched, called Amtrak, but on the principle that, being partly public and thus a form of socialism and thus wicked, it should be so bad as to discourage people from using it.* Sunday Times (London) 11/7/71, p92 [**1971**, irregular shortening of *American Track*]

anabolic, *n.* short for ANABOLIC STEROID. *Anabolics are supposed to be used for sick cases, where there is some body-wasting disease, and I suppose it led to the belief that they had the effect of producing extra muscle.* Cape Times 4/7/73, p5 [**1965**]

anabolic steroid, any of a group of synthetic hormones that increase the size and strength of muscles, often used by athletes during training. Also called MUSCLE PILL. *Earlier in the year the IOC* [International Olympic Committee] *added anabolic steroids, the so-called body-building drugs, to the list of prohibited substances at the Olympic Games.* Britannica Book of the Year 1975, p636 *The East Germans are suspected of feeding strength-building anabolic steroids to their athletes like so much Wiener schnitzel. Three weeks before the Olympics, the pill-taking stops; no traces are ever discovered in the now routine urine sampling.* Maclean's 7/76, p32 [**1967**, from *anabolic* increasing constructive metabolism, and *steroid* any of a class of compounds including the primary sex hormones]

analogue, *n.* **1** a person's counterpart; one's opposite number. *The precise request transmitted to British Foreign Minister Douglas-Home July 8 by his Irish analogue, Patrick Hillery, is that London order its North Ireland satellite, the Stormont regime of Belfast, to cancel certain Protestant parades . . .* NY Times 7/10/70, p32 **2a** a synthetic chemical substance that is similar in function to a natural chemical. *Fourteen prosta-glandins occur naturally in human tissues of the lung, liver, uterus, and gastrointestinal tract, and chemists have synthe-sized hundreds of similar molecules called analogues.* 1975 World Book Year Book, p232 **b** a synthetic substance used as a substitute for meat, fish, and other foods. *And they're tinker-ing with analogues of scallops, prawns, and, one gets the im-pression, a good many other products that they're not yet willing to talk about publicly.* New Scientist 8/2/73, p277 [**1970,** extended from the earlier meaning of an analogous word, thing, or situation]

anarcho-, a chiefly British combining form used in noun and ad-jective compounds and meaning "anarchist" or "anarchist and." Following are some recently coined compounds. **—anar-cho-authoritarianism,** *n.: What Berlin does not ask himself, however, is whether the rigid totalitarianism of a few decades ago—and we might raise the same question about the fluid an-archo-authoritarianism of today—is a phase in a prolonged crisis of Western civilization. . .* Harper's 8/70, p94 **—anarcho-liberal,** *n.: Tito himself said recently that "both dog-matists and anarcho-liberals" have been acting against the basic principles of the party . . .* Manchester Guardian Weekly 2/7/70, p7 **—anarcho-pacifist,** *n.: Anarcho-pacifists with strong lunatic leanings, their anti-imperialist non-violent pro-testing has, over the years, grown gradually more militant.* Punch 12/17/69, p996 **—anarcho-revolutionary,** *adj.: The Greek Foreign Minister, Mr. Pipinelis, claimed in Athens yes-terday that "an international anarcho-revolutionary move-ment," which had infiltrated Western parliamentary, political and intellectual circles, was instigating the world-wide cam-paign against Greece.* Sunday Times (London) 12/21/69, p6 **—anarcho-situationist,** *n.: . . . While the National Assembly in Paris was debating education policy last week, Nanterre was trying to elect a council. The anarcho-situationists stopped the voting by rampaging through the polling station.* Times (Lon-don) 4/20/70, p9 **—anarcho-socialist,** *adj.: The traditional cen-tres of anarcho-socialist revolt in Barcelona and the coalmines of Asturias have now given way to the industrial workers in the Basque provinces.* Manchester Guardian Weekly 12/5/70, p13

anchor¹, *n.* U.S. and Canadian. the newscaster who coordinates a television or radio broadcast or program; anchorperson. The approximate British equivalent is PRESENTER. See also CO-ANCHOR. *In the fall, NBC moved David Brinkley to Washing-ton, as permanent anchor there for the news of the nation's capital.* Americana Annual 1978, p482 **—v.t., v.i.** to serve as an-chor (of). *On Sundays, she* [Deanna Lawrence] *anchors the six-and eleven-o'clock news for Channel 13. Her ambition is sim-ple and straightforward—"to anchor in the top-ten market."* The New Yorker 4/11/77, p104 [**1974,** shortened from *anchor-man* (1956) to eliminate the suggestion of sexism, perhaps by analogy with *chair* for *chairman* or *chairwoman*]

anchor², *n.* U.S. and Canadian. a department store, convention center or other project large enough to make a shopping or business area around it safe for investment. *Regional centres compete on the basis of high fashion stores, top-of-the-line de-partment stores which are attractive "anchors," along with the artificial allure of a carefully architected, Muzak-filled, tem-perature-controlled suburban package of downtown shopping.* Maclean's 11/1/76, p63 [**1976**]

anchorperson, *n.* another name for ANCHOR¹. See -PERSON. *Many stations, in their fierce fights for local-news rating su-premacy, have placed more importance on importing young and beautiful "anchorpersons"—who know little of their new communities—than on the content of the news itself.* TV Guide 8/14/76, pA-2 *Help Wanted M/F Anchorperson for CBC Na-tional News. Must be neat, articulate and willing to read other people's words.* Maclean's 10/4/76, p77 [**1973,** replacement of *anchorman* (1956) to eliminate the suggestion of sexism]

anchorwoman, *n.* U.S. a female ANCHOR¹. *"Hi, people! This is Patty Smith, anchorwoman for Eliot Hendron, who, as you may not know, has been overwhelmed by the events of the last half hour."* John Cheever, Falconer, 1975, p187 [**1974,** pat-

terned after *anchorman* (1956) to counter the suggestion of sexism]

Andean Group, a free-trade association formed in 1969 by Bo-livia, Chile, Colombia, Ecuador, and Peru, and joined in 1973 by Venezuela. *The increasing cohesion of the Andean group is the most remarkable and heartening development in South America during the past decade.* NY Times 11/19/79, pA26 [**1972,** because the *Andes* Mountains run through these countries]

androcentrism, *n.* emphasis on the male sex or the male role; concentration on males to the exclusion of females. *Even if the Christian tradition has largely been as androcentric as Aristot-le, it has not been entirely so, not by any means. And, whatever Professor Mascall says, androcentrism of the kind he expresses is now no more morally tolerable than racial discrimination or slavery.* Times Literary Supplement 11/17/72, p1399 [**1972,** from *androcentric, adj.* (OEDS 1903) + *-ism*]

androgenize (æn'drədʒə,naiz), *v.t.* to strengthen the male char-acteristics of, especially through the injection of male hor-mones. *But genetic females can be virilised by giving them male hormones, androgens, during foetal development. These androgenised females show rates of rough and tumble play and mounting comparable to normal males.* New Scientist 9/16/76, p591 [**1970,** from *androgen* male sex hormone + *-ize*] **—androgenization,** *n.: The feminizing treatment is successful if the male rats were castrated at birth. The early androgeniza-tion has permanent effects.* Science Journal 6/70, p72

androgynous, *adj.* not distinguishable as to sex in appearance, behavior, etc.; having the roles or characteristics of both sexes. *She has adopted the term "androgynous" to refer to people who freely cross sex-role barriers. Using a questionnaire she devel-oped, Bem found that about half of the 1,500 students she test-ed conformed to the traditional sex roles. Another 35 per cent were androgynous, and the remaining 15 per cent were "cross-sex typed"—that is, feminine men or masculine women.* Ency-clopedia Science Supplement (Grolier) 1976, p31 *For beneath the clothing that symbolizes the new woman lies the new body. This is jogged, Jacuzzi-bathed, exercised, and dieted to the point of looking androgynous.* New Yorker 6/19/78, p65 [**1962,** extended from the original (OED 1651) sense of "being both male and female; hermaphrodite," from Latin *an-drogynus,* ultimately from Greek *anēr, andrós* man + *gynē* woman] ►The term in popular usage is generally synonymous with *unisex* and *unisexual* (1968).

andrology (æn'drɑlədʒi:), *n.* the study of diseases of the male sex, especially disorders of the male reproductive system. *An-other measure of the field's growing importance: emergence of the new medical specialty of andrology. Though still in its in-fancy, andrology is concerned with male fertility problems in much the same way that gynecology has treated disorders of the female reproductive system.* Wall Street Journal 9/1/75, p1 [**1975,** from Greek *anēr, andrós* man + English *-logy* study of]

Andromeda strain, any strain of bacteria, viruses, or other mi-croorganisms whose accidental release from a laboratory might have catastrophic effects because of its unknown biochemical makeup. See RECOMBINANT DNA RESEARCH. *Molecular biolo-gists called for an historic temporary ban on research such as . . . combining animal, viral and bacterial DNA, fearing that it might lead to the creation of uncontrollable "Andromeda strains," or biological warfare agents.* Science News 12/21-28/74, p402 *He* [Bernard Davis, a Harvard Medical School mi-crobiologist] *insists that those who worry about infections are totally ignorant of medicine's long history of safely handling highly contagious bacteria and viruses . . . He adds: "Those who claim we are letting loose an Andromeda strain are either hysterics or are trying to wreck a whole new field of research."* Time 4/16/77, p33 [**1971,** from *The Andromeda Strain,* a sci-ence fiction novel (1969) by the American author Michael Crichton, born 1942, in which an unknown type of bacteria picked up in outer space escapes accidentally from a returning space probe, killing the population of a town and threatening to contaminate the world]

androstenedione (ˌændrəˌsti:n'dɑioun), *n.* a hormone that promotes male secondary characteristics, produced by the testes, ovaries, and adrenal glands. . . . *when the female monkey's adrenals—the principal secretors of the male hormone androstenedione—are removed, her sexual receptivity is greatly reduced.* Scientific American 8/72, p46 [**1972,** derived from *androsterone* (1930's) an androgenic steroid (male sex hormone)]

Anectine ('ænekti:n), *n.* the trademark of a derivative of curare, used as a muscle relaxant. *Dr. Arthur Nugent is particularly quotable on aversion therapy with Anectine, a curare derivative: 'Even the toughest inmates have come to fear and hate the drug. I don't blame them. I wouldn't have one treatment myself for the world.'* Listener 2/20/75, p250 [**1973**]

angel dust, *Slang.* a potent depressant drug, phencyclidine or PCP, used as a narcotic, especially when mixed with a barbiturate or when sprinkled on marijuana, mint leaves, or parsley and smoked. *Angel dust goes by dozens of street names, some of them indicating the form in which it is sold and others as trade names coined by individual street sellers. Peace pills, white powder, superjoint, busy bee, hog elephant tranquilizer, crystal, and green tea are some of the more popular names.* Daily News (New York) 2/23/78, p5 [**1971**]

angiogenin (ˌændʒi:ou'dʒenin *or* ˌændʒi:'ajənin), *n.* a protein that promotes the growth of new blood vessels, discovered in human cancer tissue. *Artificially administered angiogenin could be of great benefit to the victims of heart disease by causing new blood vessels to grow in the heart.* 1986 World Book Year Book, p226 [**1986**]

angiokeratoma (ˌændʒi:ouˌkerə'toumə), *n., pl.* **-mas, -mata.** a small vascular tumor on the skin. *Fabry's disease . . . can give rise to a characteristic skin lesion, angiokeratoma, and the patients may die in middle age of a cerebral artery hemorrhage or renal failure.* Science 8/11/72, p527 [**1970,** from *angio-* vessel, vascular (from Greek *angeîon*) + *keratoma* a callus (from Greek *kéras, -atos* horn + New Latin *-oma* growth, tumor)]

Anglo or **anglo,** *n., pl.* **-glos. 1** *Canadian.* a Canadian of English descent; an English-speaking Canadian. Compare FRANCO. *Some Anglos still insult the French by telling them to "speak white." Throughout Quebec, as well as in "English Canada," economic tradition identifies the Anglos as the businessmen and bankers and the French as the laborers and small shopkeepers.* Saturday Review 10/72, p61 **2** *British.* an Englishman, especially as distinguished from someone who is Scottish, Welsh, or Irish. *He* [Sean O'Casey] *was more completely Irish than many of those who built the first fame of the dramatic renaissance—most of them tended to have a touch of the Anglo about them.* Manchester Guardian Weekly 9/24/64, p14 **3** an English-speaking person. *The Eritreans threw each other an amused glance, to find us Anglos disagreeing.* Harper's 7/78, p52 —*adj.* **1** *Canadian.* English-speaking. *I was oblivious at the time, as were most of my Anglo classmates, as was the community in general . . .* Maclean's 1/74, p58 **2** *British.* or of or for Englishmen. *The Anglo view nevertheless needs its spokesman.* Times (London) 1/8/72, p14 [**1959** for noun def. 1, abstracted from *Anglo-Canadian,* probably by influence of ANGLOPHONE (English-speaking); **1964** for noun def. 2, abstracted from the combining form *Anglo-*] ►In the U.S. *Anglo* has been long used, especially in the Southwest, for a non-Hispanic white American.

Anglophone or **anglophone,** *n.* an English-speaking native or inhabitant of a country in which English is only one of two or more official languages (often used attributively). Compare FRANCOPHONE. *It is because our fizzy Canadian cocktail has intoxicating qualities, because a dazzling future lies in wait for francophones and anglophones (or as international expert John Holmes said wittily, anglo-saxophones)—it is precisely for these reasons that we should hold together, along with the valuable New Canadians.* Saturday Night (Canada) 10/67, p19 *The second fact is that "the Westminster model," so assiduously bequeathed by Britain to the now independent Anglophone states in Africa, has proved to be neither suitable for African conditions nor acceptable to Africans.* Times (London)

1/25/72, p15 [**1964,** from French *anglophone,* from *anglo-* English + *-phone* speech (from Greek *phōnē* voice, speech)]

Anglophonic, *adj.* of an Anglophone; attuned to English. Compare FRANCOPHONIC. *Humorous as Michael Bentine occasionally is, you need an Anglophonic ear and a history book to understand much of what is going on.* Maclean's 8/68, p58 [**1968**]

angries, *n.pl.* angry opponents or protesters against some social or political condition. *To demonstrate their disgust and alienation from sexist society, the angries picket the Miss America contest, burn brassières, and dump into "freedom trashcans" such symbols of female "oppression" as lingerie, false eyelashes and steno pads.* Time 11/21/69, p56 *Expectations are wrongly aroused by the conventional form of his* [David Mercer's] *plays and by the fact that his young angries do, as it happens, talk like real-life students.* Listener 8/8/68, p162 [**1957,** originally *Angries,* shortened from *Angry Young Men,* name of a group of young British writers of the 1950's, including John Osborne, Kingsley Amis, John Braine, and Alan Sillitoe, whose works were marked by anger at social inequities]

Anik, *n.* any of a group of communications satellites launched by Canada to provide television, radio, and telephone services to the country. *The Canadians have established a trio of spacecraft, called Aniks, for their own use. These spacecraft have brought telephone and television service to remote sections of Canada.* Encyclopedia Science Supplement (Grolier) 1977/1978, p332 [**1972,** from the Eskimo word for "brother"; the name was proposed by a Montreal girl in a nationwide contest]

animal liberation or **animal lib,** a militant movement seeking to protect animals from abuse and exploitation. See ANIMAL RIGHTS, SPECIESISM. *A group called Animal Liberation Front . . . sneaked into the hospital the night before and rescued five animals they said were being used in cruel and inhumane experiments.* New York Post 3/16/79, p12 *From that struggle alone, we could never deduce so much more than has since happened—all the other "liberations" that nobody saw coming, even as recently as a decade ago. Women's lib, men's lib, gay lib, gray lib, . . . even animal lib.* Theodore Roszak, Person/Planet, 1978, p67 [**1978**]

animal park, *U.S.* a large park designed for the display of wild animals in which the settings resemble the natural environment of wildlife. Also called SAFARI PARK, especially in Great Britain. *William Conway of the Bronx Zoo thinks some of the animal parks in this country are badly managed. "They don't know how to take care of the animals," he maintains.* Encyclopedia Science Supplement (Grolier) 1973, p91 [**1972**]

animal rights, the fair treatment of animals on ethical or moral grounds; protection from abuse and exploitation sought for or extended to animals. See SPECIESISM. *The thinking of researchers is also beginning to be affected by the growing movement for animal rights . . . as a natural extension of contemporary movements promoting civil rights, women's rights, homosexual rights, human rights and children's rights.* NY Times Magazine 12/31/78, p20 [**1978**] —**animal rightser:** *Although the new Animal Welfare Act is promulgating minimum standards for the physical well-being of laboratory animals, little attention is being paid to what one animal rightser calls their "social, emotional, and behavioral" needs.* Science 1/6/78, p37

anisomycin (ˌænɑisə'mɑisin), *n.* an antibiotic related to streptomycin, used against various pathogenic fungi in plants, and in medicine against the disease-producing parasitic flagellate trichomonad. *Formula:* $C_{14}H_{19}NO_4$ *To investigate the role of protein synthesis . . . one group of reserpine culture ganglia was maintained for 48 h in the presence of anisomycin, a specific blocker of peptide bond formation.* Nature 1/11/74, p113 [**1968,** from *aniso-* unlike + *-mycin,* as in *streptomycin*]

anneal, *v.t., v.i. Molecular Biology.* to link up or reconnect complementary sequences of (DNA or RNA molecules). Compare SPLICE. See also RECOMBINANT DNA RESEARCH. *The DNA from SV40 virions was also separated into single strands by heating, and the resulting single strands were then "annealed" with the cellular DNA at a lower temperature.* Scientific American 2/78, p121 [**1967**, extended sense of the term meaning to temper glass or metals by heating and gradual cooling]

annihilate, *v.t.* to cause (a nuclear particle and an antiparticle) to collide and thereby change to another form of energy. *When a proton-antiproton pair is annihilated, mesons are emitted. These mesons rapidly decay to electrons, massless neutrinos and X rays.* Encyclopedia Science Supplement (Grolier) 1967, p281 —*v.i.* to be annihilated. *When an electron and a positron meet they annihilate to form a photon, which is as near to being a pure bundle of energy as there is.* Science News 7/13/68, p44 [**1960**]

anodynin (ˌænəˈdɑinin), *n.* a hormonelike substance that relieves pain. *Last summer, other scientists isolated two more analgesic chemicals in the bloodstreams of animal species; one was named anodynin, from anodyne, or medicine to relieve pain; it has pain-killing properties as potent as enkephalin and beta-endorphin.* NY Times Magazine 1/30/77, p52 [**1976**, from *anodyne* + *-in* (chemical suffix)]

anointing of the sick, (in the Roman Catholic Church) a new name for the sacrament of extreme unction. See RITE OF RECONCILIATION. *Extreme Unction suggests that the person to be anointed is indeed* in extremis, *while Anointing of the Sick has a more soothing, perhaps euphemistic, quality.* American Speech, Summer 1979, p84 [**1963**]

anomalon, *n. Nuclear Physics.* a hypothetical fragment of a nucleus traveling an unusually short distance after colliding with a target nucleus. *Anomalons is the name given theoretical fragments of projectile nuclei that travel an unusually (anomalously) short distance after colliding with a target nucleus. Scientists from Juadavpur University in Calcutta have found evidence of such behavior in alpha particles derived from carbon-12 atoms.* Encyclopedia Science Supplement (Grolier) 1986, p288 [**1986**]

anoretic or **anorectic,** *n.* variant of ANOREXIC. *Records at Toronto's Hospital for Sick Children, for example, show that in 1965 only one anoretic was treated; in 1974, the last year for which figures are available, 20 were admitted.* Maclean's 2/23/76, p46 *The full-blown anoretic has totally rejected this fatness, together with the biological and reproductive maturity that it heralds.* Times (London) 11/29/77, p20 [**1965**, noun use of the adjective (early 1900's) meaning "causing a loss of appetite," from *anorexia*; see ANOREXIC] ►An earlier and related meaning of *anoretic* is "an appetite-suppressing drug."

anorexic (ˌænəˈreksik), *adj.* suffering from anorexia; lacking appetite; avoiding food, especially from emotional stress. *In a recent case study an anorexic girl saw herself as emaciated, introverted, unsociable and unhappy—the very opposite of being sexually attractive.* Times (London) 9/7/78, p18 —*n.* an anorexic person. See BULIMAREXIA. *Anorexics tend to sleep fitfully, and when they awake, they experience naturally occurring trancelike periods; it is on these periods that the therapist builds.* Scientific American 4/76, p81 [**1974**, from *anorexia* an abnormal lack or loss of appetite (from Greek *anorexiā*) + *-ic*]

anorgastic (ˌænɔrˈgæstik), *adj.* unable to attain orgasm. Compare NONORGASMIC. *Almost all anorgastic women can be taught to respond and revalue themselves to their good.* Listener 4/26/73, p550 [**1973**, from *an-* not + *orgastic*]

anovulation (ˌænˌɑvyəˈleiʃən), *n.* stoppage or suppression of ovulation. *Exposure of newborn female rats to exogenous estrogens or androgens induces permanent sterility with polycystic ovaries, anovulation, persistent vaginal estrus, and absence of female mating behavior.* Science 11/10/72, p582 [**1963**, from *an-* without + *ovulation*]

answer, *n.* someone or something that corresponds (to another); counterpart; equivalent. *Poles have long thrilled to the heroics of Captain Klos, Warsaw's answer to James Bond, who consistently traps West German agents.* Time 11/30/70, p22 *Calling a magazine Success doesn't necessarily make it one, either. At last report, Canada's answer to Playboy and Penthouse was close to folding.* Maclean's 4/74, p94 [**1966**, extended meaning of "a gesture or act done in return"]

answering machine, a tape-recording device that responds to a telephone call with a recorded message and records a message from the caller. *Her husband abandons her and raids all their bank accounts before informing her of his desertion—by leaving a message on her answering machine.* Time 8/4/80, p42 [**1972**, probably shortened from *telephone answering machine*]

antenna, *n.* a strong sense of perception. *His* [Kafka's] *antennae for truth were uncanny.* New Yorker 7/15/72, p76 *He was a pre-Watergate friend of Woodward's, a trusted and experienced Executive Branch official with "extremely sensitive" antennae that seemed to pick up every murmur of fresh conspiracy at the capital's power center.* Time 4/22/74, p55 [**1963**, figurative use of the term for a feeler or aerial]

antenna chlorophyll, a group of chlorophyll molecules that collect light energy and convert it into electronic energy in photosynthesis. *Although many questions remain to be answered, these models . . . for antenna chlorophyll are sufficiently explicit to provide a working basis for current developments of biomimetic systems for the conversion and utilization of solar energy for chemical purposes.* McGraw-Hill Yearbook of Science and Technology 1977, p338 [**1976**, so called from its receiving light waves the way a radio antenna receives radio waves]

anteosaur (ˈæntiːəˌsɔr), *n.* a carnivorous mammalian reptile of the Permian period; a therapsid or theriodont. *Because skull length/body length ratios are fairly constant in primitive mammal-like reptiles, body weight for the smaller genera can be estimated by comparing the cube of the skull length to the cube of the skull length of an anteosaur (taken as 1,000 kg).* Nature 7/14/72, p82 [**1972**, from New Latin *Anteosaurus*, the genus name, probably from *ante-* before + connecting *-o-* .+ *-saurus* lizard (from Greek *saûros*)]

Anthony dollar, a one-dollar coin with raised inner borders, made of copper and nickel and bearing a likeness of the American suffragist leader, Susan B. Anthony (1820-1906), first issued in July, 1979. *The Anthony dollar, they say, looks and feels too much like a quarter.* People Weekly 9/17/79, p96 [**1979**]

anthropozoology, *n.* the study of man as a member of the animal kingdom; the zoology of man. *The two big bookstalls in Trastevere go in for porn and fladge, modulating through books of Nazi atrocities to the anthropozoology of Desmond Morris . . .* Times Literary Supplement 8/4/72, p916 [**1972**, from *anthropo-* man + *zoology*]

anti-, *prefix.* 1 of or belonging to the hypothetical world consisting of antimatter (the counterpart of ordinary matter). See also the main entries ANTIDEUTERIUM, ANTIHELIUM. —**antinucleus,** *n.: The laws of nature as presently understood predict antinuclei of arbitrary complexity. Nevertheless, because antimatter annihilates rapidly with matter, its creation in the matter environment of Earth is something of a feat, possible only with particle accelerators.* McGraw-Hill Yearbook of Science and Technology 1967, p106 —**antiquark,** *n.: In theory, there are three quarks and three antiquarks, and all the so-called elementary particles, of which there are a hundred or more, consist of pairs or trios drawn from among the basic six.* Science News Yearbook 1970, p242 **2** that which rejects or reverses the traditional characteristics of _____, a use chiefly abstracted from the terms *antihero* and *antinovel.* —**anticommunity,** *n.: America is one vast, terrifying anticommunity. The great organizations to which most people give their working day and the apartments and suburbs to which they return at night are equally places of loneliness and alienation.* The New Yorker 9/26/70, p42 —**antientertainment,** *n.: There have been some pretty unsparing anti-entertainments just lately.* Sunday Times (London) 3/23/69, p59 —**antimemoir,** *n.: If antimemoirs are written to tell "what survives," what puts a thumb to the shaping of a man's destiny, a hateful childhood would seem to be one of those influences.* Saturday Review 11/16/68, p45 —**antimusic,** *n.: Their occasionally inspired flashes of innovation and experimentalism were dragged down too often, however, with repetition, painful dissonance and screaming antimusic.* NY Times 7/12/68, p16 —**antinovelist,** *n.: . . . Latin-American novelists . . . have succeeded the French an-*

tinovelists at the top of that duty-reading list, fiction department, which we never quite get around to. Atlantic 6/69,
p101 —**antiplay**, n.: The antihero, the antiplay and the anti-
theatre production . . . seems to set up an antiaudience . . .
Manchester Guardian Weekly 12/5/68, p19 —**antipoet**, n.: Basically, however, he [Thomas Merton] is a modern antipoet.
Time 1/24/69, p72 —**antitheater**, n.: The greatest strength of
surreal "antitheater" is, in point of fact, intensely theatrical:
visual images that slice faster than pain can follow to the deepest resources of the imagination. Time 2/16/70, p64

antiabortion, adj. opposed to or prohibiting induced abortions,
especially abortion-on-demand. Also called ANTI-CHOICE.
Compare PRO-LIFE, RIGHT-TO-LIFE. See also ABORTION. The
antiabortion movement, making its case for the fetus, and
hence for the family, does not have bright prospects. It is arguing for the obligations of the family at a time when the family
is a declining American institution. NY Times Magazine
3/28/76, p9 [**1966**] —**antiabortionism**, n.: I think it is a mistake
to tie antiabortionism too closely to sex-is-for-procreation. National Review 2/6/76, p64 —**antiabortionist**, n.: His [Edward J.
Golden's] program moved into high gear in January 1972,
when busloads of antiabortionists began rolling into Albany,
heavily laden with sensational literature. Harper's 3/74,
p27 Compare ABORTIONIST, PROABORTIONIST.

anti-antibody, n. an antibody that attacks other antibodies, especially antibodies produced by injected lymph cells. Perhaps
part of the viral DNA becomes incorporated into the white
cell's DNA and subsequently proteins are made upon the instructions of the viral DNA. This would mean that, when such
a white cell makes antibodies, the antibodies would have an
abnormal structure which would itself provoke the production
of "anti-antibodies," causing a chain reaction, inflammation
and damage to the joint. New Scientist 10/5/78, p9 [**1972**]

antiatom, n. counterpart of any atom in antimatter. Symmetry
between matter and antimatter is one of the basic principles of
particle physics. To every particle there corresponds an antiparticle . . . It is possible to build up antiatoms, and a certain
poem went so far as to conjure up antiworlds in which Professor Edward Teller met his opposite, Professor Edward Antitel-
ler. Science News 3/31/73, p211 [**1967**]

antiauthority, adj. opposed to or rejecting authority; hostile to
the officials or government of a country, state, etc. Though
today's terrorists have comparable anti-authority aims, their
motivations are by no means uniform. The New Yorker
6/12/78, p38 [**1967**] ►A similar term, antiauthoritarian,
meaning "opposed to authoritarianism" has been in use since
the 1930's.

antibusing, adj. U.S. opposed to the busing of students to
achieve a racial balance in schools. As chairman of an education subcommittee, [Walter] Mondale stayed with his position
in favor of busing ("as one constitutional tool") right through
the worst of the antibusing furor. NY Times Magazine 6/5/77,
p44 [**1969**, from anti- opposed to + BUSING] —**antibuser**, n.:
Conventional-minded political reporters are indignant when
voters hesitate between [George] McGovern and George Wallace or describe themselves as hawks and antibusers and then
vote for McGovern. NY Times Magazine 7/30/72, p11

anticharm, n. the counterpart of charm in antimatter. Theory
says the psi's contain both charm and anticharm, since they are
made of a charmed quark and an anticharmed antiquark. Science News 6/5,12/76, p356 [**1974**] —**anticharmed**, adj.: The
new particle found at Fermilab appeared to be an anticharmed
antibaryon of 2.26 GeV mass. 1977 Collier's Encyclopedia
Yearbook, p444

anti-choice or **antichoice**, another name for ANTIABORTION.
Masquerading under the misnomer 'Right to Life,' antichoice
forces seek not just to deny women access to safe, legal abortions but to deny all people the right to behave in what they
consider responsible ways. NY Times Magazine 3/30/80,
p44 [**1980**]

anticodon, n. a group of three chemical bases that form a unit
in transfer RNA and serve to bind a specific amino acid to a corresponding group (called a codon) in messenger RNA. Each

type of amino acid is transported to the ribosome by a particular form of "transfer" RNA (tRNA), which carries an anticodon
that can form a temporary bond with one of the codons in messenger RNA. Scientific American 10/66, p55 [**1964**]

anti-Confucian, adj. (in Communist China) of or relating to criticism of the teachings of Confucius which are considered backward-looking and reactionary. Compare CONFUCIAN. See also
CAPITALIST ROADER and GANG OF FOUR. In China another
anti-Confucian campaign early in the year was . . . linked
with the disgraced Lin Piao, so that 'Confucius and Lin Piao
were like two cucumbers on the same root.' A new edition of the
Analects of Confucius criticized him as a 'forefather of all reactionaries.' Annual Register of World Events in 1974,
p388 [**1974**] —**anti-Confucianism**, n.: Professor [Merle] Goldman . . . points out that the recent anti-Confucianism has
brought back a number of old writings that the regime had cast
aside. New Yorker 3/8/76, p28

antideuterium, n. the counterpart of deuterium in antimatter.
The first real antinucleus to be found was antideuterium, or
antihydrogen 2, in 1966. Science News 2/28/70, p218 [**1970**]

antideuteron, n. the counterpart of the nucleus of deuterium in
antimatter. Soviet nuclear physicists . . . extended their experiments to study the interactions of protons with antideuterons
and of deuterons with antiprotons. New Scientist 6/18/70,
p567 [**1964**]

antidrug, adj. opposed to the use of narcotics. . . . smuggling
has become more risky in Florida, where antidrug enforcement
efforts have been stepped up and tough new laws against marijuana smuggling include minimum mandatory sentences of
up to 15 years in jail. Time 12/29/80, p16 [**1967**]

anti-European, adj. **1** opposed to the social, cultural, or economic unification of western Europe. M. Pflimlin, who was the last
Prime Minister of the Fourth Republic, left the Government in
1962 in protest against an anti-European speech by de Gaulle.
Times (London) 4/13/70, p4 **2** opposed to Great Britain's entry
into the European Common Market. The formidable leader of
anti-European feeling in the Conservative Party and in the
country will clearly be Mr. Enoch Powell. New Yorker 7/4/70,
p62 —**n.** a person who is anti-European. Compare PRO-
EUROPEAN. See also EUROPEANIST. If Mr. Aitken is right, the
anti-Europeans are in for a nasty shock one of these days, when
they suddenly realize they have got it all wrong, and have left
it too late to concoct a different argument. Times (London)
2/24/70, p4 [**1960**]

antifeedant (ˌænti'fi:dənt), n. **1** a chemical substance that repels
plant-eating insects. Antifeedants may be especially advantageous because they control plant-eating insects indirectly
through starvation while leaving parasites, predators, and insect pollinators unharmed. 1979 Britannica Yearbook of Science and the Future, p281 **2** Attributive use: Recently . . .
they have isolated several "anti-feedant" compounds that appear to dull an insect's taste nerves so that it stops eating and
dies. Harper's 8/78, p47 [**1972**, from anti- + feed + -ant (noun
suffix)]

antifemale, adj. antagonistic or hostile to all women. According
to the complaint by the National Organization of Women, the
station not only discriminates against women in employment
practices but is antifemale in its basic approach, from programming to commercials. Time 5/29/72, p57 [**1966**]

antifeminism, n. opposition to the beliefs and practices of feminists. Los Angeles's Ballance, who refers to all women as "fil-
lies," or "chicklets" and who calls fat women "porkers" and
"lardos," has stirred controversy because of the frank sex talk
he provides and because of his alleged antifeminism.
Newsweek 9/4/72, p90 [**1972**] —**antifeminist**, n.: The antifeminist today, as well as yesterday, holds that the physiological and psychological differences between the sexes determine
the roles they play—and prefer to play—as well as their condition in society. Britannica Book of the Year 1973, p25

antiform, adj. rejecting the traditional or prepared materials
used in making works of art. See also CONCEPTUAL ART.
. . . the decade . . . wound up in a conscious rejection of both

new and old art materials in preference for the earth, rocks, animal matter, and raw substances (strips of felt, rubber, and copper sheets, lead pellets) of the anti-form movement. New Yorker 2/21/70, p84 **[1968]**

antigenic determinant, the part of an antigen which causes a reaction in the immune system, especially an epitope. *First, they discovered that the immune system reacts to only a small part of a microbe—the antigen. Later, they found that the immune system actually reacts only to small pieces of the antigen. These pieces are called* antigenic determinants. *Scientists then reasoned that it should be possible to make vaccines consisting of synthetic antigenic determinants rather than natural whole antigens.* World Book Science Annual 1986, p147 **[1985]**

antihelium, *n*. the counterpart of helium in antimatter. *Soviet physicists have reported the creation and detection of nuclei of anti-helium, thus strengthening the hypothesis that the universe is composed symmetrically of ordinary matter and antimatter.* Times (London) 2/23/70, p5 **[1970]**

antilymphocytic serum or **antilymphocyte serum**, a substance consisting of antibodies against lymphocytes, used for preventing rejection of transplanted tissue. *It seems that if other immunosuppressive drugs are used without antilymphocytic serums, the normal regulatory mechanisms that keep latent viruses suppressed may be upset and the viruses may be activated.* Times (London) 2/6/73, p16 *Clarke and coworkers have speculated whether antidonor gamma globulin, consisting of many antibodies including human antilymphocyte serum, might prevent the formation of immune antibodies to a skin or organ graft.* McGraw-Hill Yearbook of Science and Technology 1970, p128 **[1965]**

anti-Marketeer, *n*. an opponent of Great Britain's entry into the European Common Market. See also ANTI-EUROPEAN. . . . *the two speeches clearly reflect the growing self-confidence of the anti-Marketeers in the Government since the publication of the White Paper giving revised estimates of the cost of entry.* Manchester Guardian Weekly 4/4/70, p8 **[1962, from *anti-* + Common *Marketeer*]**

antinatalism, *n*. limitation of the population by controlling the birth rate. Compare PRONATALISM. *If the introduction of shifts in social institutions had some advantages in addition to antinatalism—for instance, greater freedom for women, a value in its own right—these could be taken as offsetting some other, possibly harmful, consequences.* Science 2/4/72, p492 **[1972, from *anti-* against + *natality* birth rate + *-ism*]** —**antinatalist**, *adj*.: *"Although lip service was paid to the idea that the rate of population growth was not sufficiently high, in fact the actual consequences of much Soviet legislation were then anti-natalist." A liberalized abortion law adopted in 1955, for example, was of major importance in reducing the birthrate.* Scientific American 1/73, p46

antineoplaston, *n*. a substance that inhibits the growth or spread of tumors, especially cancerous ones. *One protein inhibited growth of all three types. The other three were more specific, inhibiting the growth of a specific type of cancer. The researchers dubbed the proteins "antineoplastons," since "neoplasm" means tumor.* Science News 4/24/76, p260 **[1976, from *antineoplastic* (1954), from *anti-* + *neoplastic* of tumors, from *neoplasm* (1860's) a tumor; form influenced by Greek *plastón*, *plastós* molded]**

antinoise, *n*. a sound used to eliminate noise by having its wavelength neutralize the wavelength of the noise. *Digisonix . . . can send antinoise into a fan duct, canceling sounds that would otherwise spread throughout a factory or building.* NY Times 6/30/87, pC9 **[1979]**

antinuclear, *adj*. opposed to the use of nuclear energy. *Members of the congressional Joint Committee have referred to the environmentalists as "anti-nuclear."* New Scientist 11/23/72, p450 *Demonstrations by the Clamshell Alliance, a coalition of antinuclear groups, stopped construction of the controversial Seabrook nuclear power plant in New Hampshire several times.* 1979 World Book Year Book, p315 —**n**. an opponent of the use of nuclear energy. *At present the AEC [Atomic Energy Commission] seems convinced that those who oppose its natural* predilection for nuclear energy are, as one high AEC official said, the "arch-antinuclears."* Atlantic 4/71, p34 **[1971, extended from the original (1957) sense of "opposed to nuclear weapons"]**

antinuke, *adj*., *n*. *Informal*. variant of ANTINUCLEAR. *Last year voters in Ohio, California, Oregon, Colorado, Washington, Arizona and Montana rejected propositions to curb nuclear power. But the anti-nukes have won some fights too.* Time 3/21/77, p73 **[1977, shortened and altered from *antinuclear*, on the pattern of *nuke* (1959) a nuclear weapon or nuclear power plant]** —**antinuker**, *n*.: *When actress-activist Jane Fonda took centre stage recently and trooped her political colors before 90,000 anti-nukers on Washington's Capitol Hill, the impact registered on everyone from a 70-year-old lady dressed as a mushroom to U.S. President Jimmy Carter.* Maclean's 6/18/79, p35

anti-object art, another name for POST-OBJECT ART. *The most spectacular exhibition of anti-object art was Earth, Air, Fire, Water: Elements of Art at the Boston Museum of Fine Arts. It presented 50 artists, who created burning fires, falling waters, and moving air.* Americana Annual 1972, p113 **[1970]**

antipollutionist, *n*. a person who advocates strong measures to prevent or reduce environmental pollution. Compare ENVIRONMENTALIST. *Anti-pollutionists and conservationists should surely be as much concerned with prevention as with cure.* Times (London) 4/8/70, p26 **[1970]**

antipoverty, *n*. *U.S.* a program to combat poverty, especially such a program sponsored by the government. *At a time when the Federal budget is being drastically cut in every area from antipoverty to crime control, the House of Representatives has passed an expanded highway construction bill . . .* NY Times 7/21/68, pD13 **[1964]**

antipsychiatry, *n*. a movement within psychiatry that rejects the conventional concepts and practices of the field, especially the concept of mental illness whereby patients are treated medically to the exclusion of other methods. Compare LAINGIAN. [Gregory] *Bateson saw schizophrenia as a special strategy that a person invents to survive a "double bind" or "can't win" situation. With the publication of the double-bind theory in 1956, Bateson was hailed as the father of antipsychiatry, a controversial movement that holds that the medical model is not applicable to mental illness.* NY Times Magazine 2/29/76, p32 **[1967]** —**antipsychiatrist**, *n*.: *He [Peter Breggin] is a good example of the kind of antipsychiatrist who is especially common in the United States and increasingly vocal in Britain, who is unwilling to admit that any patient should be protected against his own impulses, or hospitalised or treated against his will.* New Scientist 7/27/72, p190

antirejection, *adj*. designed to combat immunological rejection, especially in transplant surgery. . . . *anti-rejection drugs aggravate diabetes.* Washington Post 11/26/84, pA1 **[1984]**

anti-roman (ãti:rɔˈmã), *n*. another name for NOUVEAU ROMAN (a type of experimental novel developed chiefly in France in the 1960's). . . . *there is a new avant-garde and a new aesthetic—based on, say, John Cage, William Burroughs, Samuel Beckett, the concrete poets, the novelists of the anti-roman . . .* Listener 9/19/68, p374 **[1965, from French]**

antisatellite, *adj*. designed to seek out and destroy an artificial satellite. *The Soviets might choose also to respond to SDI satellites with orbiting antisatellite weapons that are less complex than the SDI satellites. This might require the United States to deploy its own antisatellite satellites first, driving a race to control specific regions of space, according to the report.* Science News 6/18/88, p390 **[1963]**

antiscience, *adj*. of or relating to those who oppose scientific research pursued at the expense of humanitarian interests and values. . . . *Dr. Philip Handler, president of the National Academy of Sciences, sees a real threat in an antiscience and antitechnology bias he says is developing.* Science News 5/2/70, p432 **[1967]**

antisense, *adj*. *Genetics*. that does not code for a genetic product but serves only to preserve the coding sequence. Compare

MISSENSE, NONSENSE. *Antisense transcription has been described in bacteria* [and] *in higher forms of life.* Scientific American 6/87, p26 [**1987**]

antisexist, *adj.* opposed to sexism or sexual discrimination. *Last week, in a preliminary demonstration, feminists brandished anti-sexist placards beneath the Statue of Liberty.* Time 8/24/70, p12 [**1970**]

antisickling, *adj.* counteracting or inhibiting the sickling of red blood cells characteristic of sickle cell anemia. *The investigators then injected DBA into mice and found that it had no acute effects. In view of this discovery, and DBA's antisickling ability, they conclude that it might well be an effective and safe sickle cell drug.* Science News 1/10/76, p22 [**1976**]

antismog, *adj.* designed to prevent, reduce, or eliminate smog. *Anti-smog equipment fitted to cars in the United States has reduced hydrocarbon emissions by 80 per cent.* Times (London) 3/10/70, p5 [**1957**]

antismoking, *adj.* seeking to stop or curb the smoking of tobacco. *Countries with an investment in tobacco as a cash crop are hardly likely to enthuse about anti-smoking programmes.* New Scientist 3/23/78, p779 [**1962**]

antitail, *n.* a small spikelike part of a comet's tail that, unlike the main tail, appears to be pointing toward the sun. See DUST TAIL, GAS TAIL. *The view of the comet from the Earth shows how the anomalous "anti-tail" is explained by a perspective generated view of the tail's large dust particles. Comet Kohoutek also showed an anti-tail, first detected by the Skylab astronauts and later photographed at many observatories, but here the theory has been abundantly confirmed by infrared work.* New Scientist 4/17/75, p122 [**1968**]

antitechnology, *n.* **1** in opposition to technological research and development, especially when pursued at the expense of humanitarian interests and values. *The second prominent figure to unfurl the banner of antitechnology was Lewis Mumford. His conversion was particularly significant since for many years he had been known and respected as the leading historian of technology.* Harper's 11/75, p53 **2** attributive use: *The antitechnology chorus, which includes many accredited scientists, is voicing concern in behalf of the "common man."* Encyclopedia Science Supplement (Grolier) 1970, p332 [**1967**] —**antitechnological**, *adj.*: *Quite aware of the strong antitechnological sentiments within the art world, Tuchman and his associates wisely chose a limited number of entries from some of the biggest names in the American art world: Roy Lichtenstein, Claes Oldenburg, Robert Rauschenberg, Tony Smith, and Andy Warhol.* 1973 Britannica Yearbook of Science and the Future, p350 —**antitechnologist**, *n.: The risk of nuclear accident is sufficient justification in his view not to proceed with nuclear power plants. The risk of producing lethal bacteria is sufficient reason to stop DNA research. Mr. Rompler supports the antitechnologists because they can name the risk.* Harper's 4/78, p7

antiterrorist or **antiterrorism**, *adj.* designed to combat terrorists or terrorism. *The opposition Christian Democratic Party also unveiled a legislative package of new antiterrorist measures that would ban forced feeding of prisoners on hunger strikes, simplify identity checks on suspects, widen the legal definition of terrorists and speed up court trials.* Royal Gazette (Bermuda) 5/28/73, p6 *According to an American source, a British antiterrorist expert has also gone to Italy where he, and a liaison man from a similar West German unit, are helping the Italians develop their own antiterrorism teams.* NY Times 5/7/78, pD1 [**1964; 1967**] ▶The synonymous terms *counterterrorist* and *counterterrorism* have been used chiefly as nouns, originally (1950's) in the context of the Algerian revolt against France.

antiviral, *n.* a substance that destroys or inhibits the action of viruses. *At present, the list of known antivirals is short, though potential agents are under study.* Science News 11/1/69, p414 [**1966**, noun use of the adjective *antiviral* (1934)]

Anturane ('æntə,rein), *n.* a trademark for a drug that stimulates the excretion of uric acid, used to treat gout and experimentally to prevent the formation of blood clots. *Formula:*

$C_{23}H_{20}N_2O_3S$ *Patients who began using the antigout drug Anturane (sulfinpyrazone) four to five weeks after their first heart attack had a death rate of 4.9 percent a year compared with 9.5 percent a year for patients taking a placebo.* Science News 2/18/78, p101 [**1968**, probably from *ant-* (variant of *anti-* against) + *ur*ic acid + -*ane* (chemical suffix)]

anxiolytic (æŋ,zaiə'litik), *n.* a drug used to relieve anxiety; a tranquilizer. *Physicians no less than patients, says Dr. Shapiro, have always been, and still are, subject to fads and fashions in medicines, and the anxiolytics are today's "in" drugs.* NY Times Magazine 2/1/76, p2 —*adj.* used or tending to relieve anxiety; tranquilizing. *In their letter, the doctors point out that big cash savings could be made by prescribing meditation rather than anxiolytic, hypotensive and antidepressant drugs and sleeping pills.* Times (London) 8/31/78, p1 [**1976**, from *anxiety* + connecting -*o*- + -*lytic* dissolving, as in *hydrolytic*]

ANZAM or **Anzam** ('ænzæm), *n.* acronym for *Australia, New Zealand, and Malaysia. ANZAM joins Australia and New Zealand with Britain to defend Malaysia.* NY Times 7/15/70, p38 [**1965**]

ANZUK ('ænzək), *n.* acronym for *Australia, New Zealand and United Kingdom. The infantry battalion stationed in Singapore as part of the ANZUK (Australia-New Zealand-U.K.) forces was brought home, although air squadrons in Malaysia—fulfilling a need that country could not meet—remained.* Britannica Book of the Year 1976, p155 [**1972**]

ao dai ('ɑ:ou 'dɑi), the traditional women's dress in Vietnam, consisting of a long, high-necked tunic split to the waist on either side and worn over wide pajamalike trousers. *Sut On looks around her and knows that she will never be: a lithe Annamese girl, pretty in an ao dai. Her bones are too broad, her legs are too heavy, and even if she ever put on an ao dai and got accustomed to the material, just above it her face would be a dead giveaway—she will always look Chinese.* Harper's 7/70, p81 *Pretty Saigon girls in ao dais posed for their boy friends' cameras before the city's monuments.* Time 2/16/70, p19 [**1963**, from Vietnamese]

AONB or **A.O.N.B.**, *British.* abbreviation of *Area of Outstanding Natural Beauty*, a scenic area under national protection. *Both the national parks and the AONBs receive substantial exchequer grants for carparks and lavatories, and the main difference between them is that the AONBs are not subject to even the minimal national control that is exercised in the national parks.* New Scientist 9/27/73, p731 [**1970**]

A-1 protein, a protein found in the myelin of people with multiple sclerosis, believed to contribute to the onset of the disease. *He* [E. H. Eylar] *and his colleagues found that protein taken from the brains of multiple sclerosis patients, a so-called A-1 protein, and injected into experimental animals, sensitized the animals' lymphocytes (immune cells).* Science News 10/16/76, p250 [**1970**]

apamin ('eipəmin), *n.* a polypeptide, derived from bee venom, that is destructive of nervous tissue, used experimentally in neurology and medicine. *Apamin is the smallest neurotoxic polypeptide known, and it is the only one whose interaction with the spinal cord is well established.* Science 7/28/72, p317 [**1972**, from Latin *api*s bee + English *amino* acid]

apartheid (ə'pɑrt,heit), *n.* separateness; exclusiveness. . . . *they* [those who loved movies] *looked for the true nature of cinema in what cinema can do that the other arts can't—in artistic apartheid.* New Yorker 1/13/68, p90 *Their* [children with high IQ's] *very brightness sets them apart from their fellows; that measure of apartheid can inflict lasting psychological damage, even turn them into delinquents instead of dons.* Punch 3/22/67, p109 [**1958**, extended sense of the term for racial segregation (1947), from Afrikaans, in which the word's literal sense is also "separateness"]

aparthotel, *n. British.* a building with furnished apartments which are sold to individuals as investors but which are rented and serviced as hotel suites when the owners are away. *Melia was the first hotel group to use the aparthotel system for the 1,000-room luxury Castilla Hotel in Madrid.* Times (London)

9/13/76, p21 [**1972**, from *apart*ment + *hotel*] ►This type of building differs from an *apartment hotel* (known since the early 1900's) in that the units of the latter are rented to the permanent residents, not sold as investments.

ape, *n.* **go ape,** *Chiefly U.S. Slang.* to lose self-control; go wild with enthusiasm, excitement, etc. *Then when the guys found out it was true, they just went ape.* Time 8/9/68, p42 *When they get away from their customary urban environment, many of "The Summer People," as the locals call their clientele, tend to go ape.* Punch 1/24/68, p118 [**1963**]

ape hanger, *U.S. Slang.* a very high handlebar on a motorcycle or bicycle. *Tyke bike . . . has a solid wood frame and seat, four rubber-tired wheels, and the swooping handlebars known among the motorcycle avant-garde as ape hangers.* New Yorker 12/11/65, p164 [**1965**]

aperture card, a key-punch card with an opening to hold a microfilm frame or frames, used in data processing, documentation, and the like. *The microfilm copies of patents offered to the public and for examiners' use will be stored in the form of aperture cards, which have space for eight images each.* Science News 7/23/66, p57 *Aperture cards are mainly used in the engineering department and are basically an 80 column card holding one 35mm frame of the original drawing.* Times (London) 9/14/77, p15 [**1966**]

aperture synthesis, (in radio astronomy) a method of detecting signals by combining the reception of several small antennas. Compare VLBI. See also SYNTHETIC-APERTURE RADAR. *One of the most powerful techniques radioastronomers use is that of "aperture synthesis." They take two receiving aerials and make simultaneous observations of one source while varying their separation. From the results they obtain they can build up an effective signal equivalent to that which would be produced by one large aerial as big as their widest separation.* New Scientist 2/12/70, p296 [**1965**]

aperturismo (ɑ:ˌpertuˈriːsmou), *n.* the opening of the political process in Spain after Francoism. *Which is the real Spain—the Spain of the future? Is it Franco's surviving State apparatus, with the attached political lobby known as the "Bunker," which still meets for lunch at the Madrid Jockey Club, shaking its head at all this rampant "aperturismo?"* Manchester Guardian Weekly 2/29/76, p9 [**1975**, from Spanish, from *apertura* opening] ►In the early 1960's *aperturismo* was borrowed from Italian in the sense of an opening of Catholic thinking to new trends in ecumenical and political relations. The term was short-lived, however, as the word *aggiornamento,* used in a similar sense, gained currency and replaced it.

APEX or **Apex** (ˈeiˌpeks), *n.* acronym for *A*dvance *p*urchase *ex*cursion, a system of low-cost air fares for reservations paid in advance made for travel abroad of several weeks' duration (usually from 22 to 45 days). Compare ABC, OTC, SUPER SAVER. *Apex fares have been in force on the North Atlantic routes for the past two years and have been a great success. To book for the European version passengers will have to commit themselves a month before travel and stay at their destinations not less than two weeks (one week in the case of Greece) and not more than three months.* Times (London) 1/14/77, p4 [**1971**]

apoapsis (ˌæpouˈæpsis), *n.* the point in the orbit around a heavenly body farthest from the center of the body. . . . *its* [faster-orbiting vehicle's] *companion, in a 50° orbit with apoapsis 20,500 miles and periapsis 530 miles, undertakes the scrutiny of selected areas of Mars* . . . New Scientist and Science Journal 5/6/71, p305 [**1971**, from *apo-* off, away + *apsis* orbit]

apocalypticist or **apocalyptician,** *n.* one who foresees or warns of imminent catastrophe. Also called DOOMSDAYER. *The parallel thought among many apocalypticists, then, runs like this: Why bother with efforts to do away with poverty and war? Of course, one should be personally moral and humane, but he or she should do this apart from politics. Human engineering will not bring progress or paradise. God will intervene and then all will be well.* Americana Annual 1973, p18 *You might be taken to task for writing that Enoch Powell has a 'hang-up' about race, but you would probably get away with calling him an 'apocalyptician' (i.e. one who predicts devastating calamities),*

though both expressions are American and of recent origin. Listener 1/15/76, p45 [**1973**] ►The older, related term *apocalyptist* (early 1800's) means a writer of an apocalyptic work.

apocynthion, *n.* another name for APOLUNE. *The terms "pericynthion" and "apocynthion" were selected about ten years ago by some people at MSC* [Manned Spacecraft Center, Houston] *who did not want to mix Latin and Greek terms; however, even today only about 20% of MSC uses the term "pericynthion" and the majority of the Aerospace industries use the terms "perilune" and "apolune."* The New Yorker 10/11/69, p91 [**1960**, from *apo-* off + Latin *Cynthia* goddess of the moon + *-on*]

apodization, *n.* **1** *Optics.* a method of controlling the overlap between adjacent images by modifying the amplitude of the aperture. *Apodization to correct for line shape distortions introduced by truncation of the input signals.* Science 10/27/72, p365 **2** *Electronics.* a method of varying the overlap between adjacent electrodes in an electric filter. *A popular method of achieving this* [alteration of the amplitude-frequency response], *due to ease of design and relative insensitivity to fabrication errors, has been apodization of the input IDT* [interdigital transducer]. McGraw-Hill Yearbook of Science and Technology 1975, p190 [**1971**, probably from *aperture* peri*odization*]

Apollo asteroid, any one of a group of asteroids whose paths cross the orbit of the earth. *In the initial excitement of the study of a newly discovered object, such as the unique Apollo asteroid 1976AA, some confusion and contradictory conclusions are likely to appear.* Science News 2/28/76, p131 [**1971**, from the name of the first of these asteroids, discovered by the German astronomer Karl Reinmuth at the Heidelberg Observatory in 1932 and named by him Apollo]

apolune, *n.* the point in a lunar orbit farthest from the center of the moon. Also called APOCYNTHION. Compare PERILUNE. *Within minutes, Intrepid was successfully inserted into a low lunar orbit with an apolune (high point) of about 50 miles.* Time 11/28/69, p35 [**1967**, from *apo-* off + French *lune* moon]

apple, *n. U.S. Slang.* **1** a derogatory name for an American Indian who is part of or cooperates with the white establishment. *In the surging of Indian militancy, the most outspoken group is the American Indian Movement, leaders of last November's occupation of the BIA* [Bureau of Indian Affairs] *building in Washington, as well as the Wounded Knee takeover. The group's tactics enrage more conservative Indians, whom AIM refers to as "apples" —red on the outside, white on the inside.* Time 3/19/73, p18 Also called UNCLE TOMAHAWK. **2** a citizens band radio operator. See also EARS and note under CBer. *Because of overcrowding, many a CB enthusiast (called an "apple") is strapping an illegal linear amplifier ("boots") on to his transceiver ("ears") which is limited by the Federal Communications Commission ("Big Daddy" in the US) to an output power of no more than five watts.* New Scientist 6/30/77, p764 [**1971** for def. 1; **1975** for def. 2]

apple-pie, *adj.* having or showing traditional American values and traits. *Could the Cuban vision of life, as reflected in these films, be so appealing that it would corrupt and endanger apple-pie America?* Saturday Review 6/17/72, p50 [H. Ross] *Perot also has mounted a million-dollar-plus ad campaign that trades frankly on the appeal of his Horatio Alger career and apple-pie patriotism.* Time 6/4/73, p84 [**1963**, from the notion that apple pie is an old-fashioned, characteristically American food]

appliance garage, *U.S.* a kitchen cabinet designed to hold appliances such as food processors, blenders, and toasters. *A popular way to conceal appliances, but still keep them handy is the appliance garage . . . Appliance garages keep counter tops neat and uncluttered.* Rodale Home Design, Rodale Press 1986, p68 [**1986**]

applications satellite, an artificial satellite used for some specific purpose, such as communications, meteorology, air traffic control, or navigation. *Despite an increasing tendency to think in terms of applications satellites, the European Space Re-*

search Organisation is still maintaining a viable scientific programme. New Scientist 5/10/73, p327 [**1970**]

appropriate technology, a form of technology that uses methods and devices suited to particular circumstances and conditions, such as the lack of capital and abundance of labor in developing countries or the energy shortage and depletion of natural resources in developed countries. *Abbreviation:* AT Also called SOFT TECHNOLOGY. Compare ALTERNATIVE TECHNOLOGY, INTERMEDIATE TECHNOLOGY. See also NEW ALCHEMIST. *The technology produced within that value system fails the basic criteria of appropriate technology—that it must address the area of greatest need, must promote self-reliance on the part of those for whom it is designed, and must be environmentally sound.* Science 1/11/80, p159 [**1973**] ►*Appropriate technology is used principally by environmentalists and ecologists to designate the kind of technology that relies on human or animal labor, solar power, windmills, and other sources of energy that do not harm the environment and are compatible with decentralization, instead of on large, centralized machinery that is costly to install and operate. The term may be viewed as a broadening of the concept of* INTERMEDIATE TECHNOLOGY *to emphasize its applicability to developed as well as developing countries. It was first used by the British economist E. F. Schumacher in his influential book* Small Is Beautiful: Economics as if People Mattered, *published in 1973.* —**appropriate technologist:** *John Todd, who, as founder of the New Alchemy Institute on Cape Cod, ranks with Brand as a leading appropriate technologist, says, "My impression is that his understanding of human society and phenomena within it operates in a slightly different time frame from most people's."* Psychology Today 11/78, p74

après- (ɑːˈpreɪ-), a combining form meaning "after or following some (specified) activity" (used usually before a noun, often to form a phrase functioning as an adjective). —**après-film:** *Kissinger, who was holding court next to the lobster souffle at an après-film party in the German embassy here, was buttonholed by Washington Post reporter Bob Woodward . . .* Women's Wear Daily 2/6-13/76, p4 —**après-40:** *So what if you're après-40 or even more. There are advantages to everything.* Advertisement, Harper's 11/74, p88 —**après-game:** *Frequently, this budget also includes weekly après-game libations . . . J. Walter Thompson, for instance, allots $1,100 for its team.* NY Times 8/31/77, p19 —**après-sun:** *The sun also dries you: Skin care après-sun.* Advertisement, Harper's Bazaar 5/74, p39 —**après-surgery:** *With the subject of mastectomy no longer discussed in guarded whispers, help has come for problems après-surgery.* Ladies' Home Journal 2/76, p42 —**après-swim:** *In bikinis and après-swim wrappers, the poolside lollers gather at midday.* Saturday Review 10/24/70, p38 —**après-tennis:** *An entire fashion industry was springing up for après-tennis, . . .* Newsweek 4/21/75, p58 [**1963**, abstracted from *après-ski* (1958), from French, literally, after-ski]

Ap star (ˈeɪˈpiː), a star of spectral type A having a peculiarity in its spectrum. *Readers will recall that Ap stars have spectra revealing a bewildering array of rare elements not present on other stars and huge excesses of certain more common elements.* New Scientist and Science Journal 4/8/71, p73 [**1968**, *Ap,* from *A* (the spectral type) + *p* (for *peculiar*)]

APT, abbreviation for: **1** advanced passenger train (a train capable of speeds up to 150 miles per hour). *The APT, now under construction, will be powered by British Layland gas turbine engines and will cruise at over 240 km/h on today's track.* Science Journal 4/70, p59 [**1967**] **2** automatic picture transmission (by weather satellites equipped with television cameras). *More than 150 stations in 45 countries have been receiving and using APT pictures since ESSA II was launched.* World Book Science Annual 1967, p157 [**1963**] **3** automatically programmed tool (a means of operating or controlling machinery by computers). Compare NC. *APT is a generic name for what is actually a family of programming systems with varying capabilities which run on various types and sizes of computers.* McGraw-Hill Yearbook of Science and Technology 1968, p63 [**1959**]

aquafarm, *n.* an artificial pond, lake, stream, etc., used for raising fish, oysters, and other aquatic animals. *The Lummi [Indi-*

an] tribe of Washington State, a sea-oriented people along Puget Sound, are using federal funds and considerable hard labor to develop the most advanced aquafarm in the U.S. Time 2/9/70, p19 [**1970**]

aquakinetics, *n.* a system of training infants and young children to remain afloat in deep water. *"Understand, aquakinetics is purely a survival program for babies at risk,"* Dr. [John] *Schieffelin stressed. "The children float; they do not learn to propel themselves through water. When they grow older, these same children will have to be taught to swim."* NY Times 6/27/75, p43 [**1975**, from *aqua* water + *kinetics* motion (of bodies)]

aquanaut, *n.* a skin diver or other person who engages in underwater exploration and research, often living for extended periods of time inside a habitat, submarine, or other underwater vessel. Also called OCEANAUT. Compare HYDRONAUT. *Five teams of aquanauts will work 12 days each on the sea floor off the coast of California in Sealab III, breathing an atmosphere that is 92.4% helium.* Americana Annual 1969, p512 [**1964**, from *aqua* water + *-naut,* as in *astronaut*]

aquanautics, *n.* underwater exploration and research using scuba diving and its equipment. *Finally, recognizing the growing importance of such research, the University of California at Berkeley has just approved the country's first full-credit "aquanautics" course.* Science News 4/7/73, p222 [**1973**, from *aquanaut* + *-ics*]

aquaplaning, *n.* another name for HYDROPLANING. *Aquaplaning (sliding on a film of water, ice or slush) is a serious problem because the conditions under which it occurs are not readily recognizable and cannot be dealt with entirely from the aircraft side.* Times (London) 7/1/65, p8 [**1963**]

Aquapulse gun, the trademark for a compressed-air device used in undersea exploration to measure shock waves reflected off the ocean bottom as an indicator of rock structures beneath the surface. *The ship also tows four rubber-walled Aquapulse guns, two on each side of the ship. Shock waves are produced by exploding a mixture of propane and oxygen inside the Aquapulse guns.* World Book Science Annual 1976, p18 [**1976**] Also called AIR GUN.

Aquarian, *adj.* of, relating to, or characteristic of the AGE OF AQUARIUS. *'If only we can find ourselves, seek out our own deeper human personality, we may usher in the Aquarian Age in a world of living nature instead of empty destruction.'* Sunday Times (London) 3/26/72, p10 —*n.* a person born under the sign of Aquarius, January 20-February 18. *Presumably a Taurian heaving erasers at an Aquarian may have his cosmic reasons.* Time 10/18/71, p41 [**1933; 1970**]

aquatel, *n.* British. See the quotation for the meaning. *An aquatel consists of a fleet of houseboats moored at a marina which provides restaurants, shops, car parking, a laundry and similar amenities.* Times (London) 4/14/70, p19 [**1970**, blend of *aquatic* and *hotel,* patterned after *motel* (blend of *motor* and *hotel*), and perhaps *boatel* (blend of *boat* and *motel*)]

ara-A (ˈær əˈeɪ), *n.* a drug derived from arabinose and adenine, used against viral infections, especially those causing encephalitis, hepatitis, and influenza. *Formula:* $C_{10}H_{13}N_5O_4 \cdot H_2O$ Also called VIDARABINE. *Agents which interfere with viral metabolism are also likely to injure host cells. It is this fact which is the primary obstacle to the development of selective antiviral agents, and which makes the apparent efficacy of ara-A so remarkable.* Science News 10/15/77, p243 [**1975**, from *arabinose* + Adenine]

Arabist, *n.* a supporter of Arab interests and aspirations. *The Ambassador, who is a career Foreign Service officer but not an Arabist, has made a special point of meeting many Israeli politicians and journalists, and he has conveyed an impression of genuine interest, concern and sympathy.* NY Times Magazine 7/17/77, p40 [**1970**, extended meaning of "a student of Arabic language and literature" (OED 1847)]

aramid, *n.* the generic name for KEVLAR. *Tires belted with fiberglass or aramid—a synthetic fiber that is stronger than steel—cost about 75 per cent as much as steel-belted ones.*

World Book Science Annual 1982, p352 [**1979**, from *a*romatic + *amide*]

arb, *n. U.S. Informal.* short for *arbitrager. The arbs sometimes play a role in a defensive restructuring when the company wants to get its share price up.* Economist 11/22/86, p78 [**1986**]

arbo, *adj.* (of diseases) transmitted by arthropods, such as mosquitoes. *Dr. Prince suggested that the material that had been found in the blood may be part of a member of the arbo family of viruses, some of whose members are known to cause several forms of encephalitis, a type of inflammation of the brain.* NY Times 7/28/68, p34 [**1968**, contraction of *a*rthropod-*bo*rne]

arbovirus, *n.* an arthropod-borne virus that causes such diseases as yellow fever, dengue, and equine encephalitis. *Arthropods, especially mosquitoes and ticks, are of vast importance for the transmission of the members of a large family of viruses, the arboviruses.* New Scientist 3/18/65, p729 [**1957**, contraction of *a*rthropod-*borne* virus]

ARC (ɑrk), *n.* acronym for AIDS-RELATED COMPLEX. *There is a spectrum to the syndrome—some people are infected and have no signs of the disease, and some have "pre-AIDS" or AIDS-related complex (ARC), a collection of symptoms that isn't quite full-blown AIDS.* Science News 4/27/85, p260 [**1985**]

archaebacteria, *n.pl.* a group of microorganisms genetically distinct both from bacteria and from plant and animal cells, that are believed to have evolved before bacteria. They ingest carbon dioxide and hydrogen and emit methane, thriving in a warm, oxygen-free environment. Also called (individually) METHANOGEN. See THIRD KINGDOM. *One of the oldest known forms of life, which developed between three and a half and four billion years ago—the earth and Mars originated four and a half billion years ago—are . . . archaebacteria, which are neither plant nor animal but are ancestral to both, and which inhabit such anaerobic spots as the mud beneath deep hot springs in Yellowstone National Park; they die when they are exposed to oxygen.* New Yorker 2/5/79, p52 [**1977**, coined by Carl R. Woese, an American biophysicist, from *archae-* ancient (ultimately from Greek *archē* beginning) + *bacteria*]

archaeoastronomy or **archeoastronomy**, *n.* the study of the astronomical beliefs and practices of ancient civilizations. Also called ASTROARCHAEOLOGY. *Archaeoastronomy has become a "growth science" in the last few years. Prehistoric arrangements of stones with astronomical significance, such as Britain's famous Stonehenge, have now been more or less firmly identified in many parts of both the Old and New Worlds. Now two archeologists have located what they believe is the first astronomical monument in Africa, near Lake Turkana in northwestern Kenya.* NY Times 5/21/78, pD7 [**1972**, from *archaeo-* ancient + *astronomy*] —**archaeoastronomer**, *n.: Some archeoastronomers believe the complex monument also was used to reckon lunar movements. The most hotly debated claim for Stonehenge is that it was used to predict lunar eclipses.* NY Times 2/19/78, pD9 —**archaeoastronomical**, *adj.: Nineteen basalt pillars at a megalithic site in northwestern Kenya are aligned towards the 300 BC rising directions of seven star formations of significance in the Cushitic calendar still used in the area today. This is the first archaeoastronomical site in sub-Saharan Africa and implies that a prehistoric calendar based on astronomical observations was in use in eastern Africa 2300 years ago.* New Scientist 6/22/78, p825

archaeomagnetism or **archeomagnetism**, *n.* the magnetism remaining in archaeological or geological specimens, used especially as a means of determining the age of a specimen and the location of the earth's magnetic poles in antiquity. *M.J. Aitken and G.H. Weaver . . . have deduced approximate declinations from the magnetic field "frozen" into pottery kilns of known age (archaeomagnetism).* New Scientist 1/3/74, p13 [**1964**, from *archaeo-* ancient + *magnetism*] —**archaeomagnetic**, *adj.: The same archaeomagnetic analyses also yielded fairly precise estimates of the strength of the prevailing Earth's magnetic field at the time of firing for two of the artifacts.* Times (London) 7/1/76, p18

archaeometry or **archeometry** (ˌɑrkiˈɑmə-tri:), *n.* the science of dating archaeological specimens, as by carbon dating or archaeomagnetism. See AGE-DATE. *But the new UC experiments confirm that the timber came from a tree that was chopped down around A.D. 700, UCLA archaeologist Rainer Berger reported last week at a symposium on archaeometry and archaeological prospection at the University of Pennsylvania Museum in Philadelphia.* Science News 3/26/77, p198 [**1965**, from *archaeo-* ancient + *metry* measurement] —**archaeometrist**, *n.: It would appear that there is a hard core of "archeometrists" with a drifting satellite of scientists dabbling in archeology and archeologists dabbling in science.* Science 3/3/72, p976

Archie Bunker, *U.S. and Canadian.* **1** a type of working-class man who habitually reacts to social pressures in a bigoted and self-righteous manner. Compare ALF GARNETT, OCKER. *Our cities would lead us to believe that apartment buildings should be very high and as predictable as Archie Bunker's prejudices.* Maclean's 3/74, p34 **2** Attributive use: *A self-employed iron worker with a self-described "Archie Bunker" perception of the world, Mr. Lambiase is described by Democrats as one of the most effective political leaders in the city.* NY Times 6/5/76, p12 [**1972**, from the name of a television character played by the American actor Carroll O'Connor in the comedy series *All in the Family* (modeled on the British comedy series *Till Death Us Do Part* and first shown on CBS in January 1971)]

Archie Bunkerism, *U.S.* an inept or illiterate expression used by an Archie Bunker (or the television character of that name). Shortened form, BUNKERISM. *There has never been a grandfather figure quite like Senator Sam Ervin . . . His apt biblical allusions, his dropped g's and regionalisms ("Yo' thinkin'. . . Yewnited States") are a happy antidote to Archie Bunkerisms.* Time 6/25/73, p15 [**1972**]

Archipelago, *n.* short for GULAG ARCHIPELAGO. *Leningrad is a colder, more imperious city than Moscow. Literary trials are more frequent there (just last year Vladimir Marazim was on his way to the Archipelago—and now, thanks to a humane solution, he is in Paris, working for the new magazine* Continent). NY Review of Books 2/19/76, p8 [**1976**]

architectural barrier, any feature of a building or other construction that prevents or hinders access or use by physically handicapped people. *"Architectural barriers" can be curbs which are too high for a person in a wheelchair to negotiate by himself, steps leading into a building, light switches too high for him to reach, restrooms without handrails, base-plug electrical outlets—the list could go on and on.* Tuscaloosa News (Alabama) 5/20/76, pA1 [**1963**] ►The U.S. *Architectural Barriers Act* of 1968 ruled that "All government buildings designed, constructed, altered or leased by the Federal government and supported financially, wholly or in part with Federal funds must be barrier-free."

archmonetarist, *n.* an extreme monetarist; an ardent supporter of monetarism. *The archmonetarists, led by Professor Milton Friedman . . . believe that changes in growth of money supply operate on the economy with such a long time lag that it is quite impossible for the authorities to know at any one moment what their policy should be.* Manchester Guardian Weekly 5/9/70, p22 [**1970**, from *arch-* extreme, preeminent + *monetarist*]

archosaur, *n.* a prehistoric reptile that was the ancestor of the dinosaurs, pterosaurs (flying reptiles), and crocodilians. *Not only is there no evidence for dinosaurs having sustained speed capability, there is no need to postulate such a thing. Living archosaurs, the crocodiles and their allies, have an astonishing turn of speed in short bursts, which seems to suffice very well indeed for their needs.* Sunday Times (London) 12/7/75, p13 [**1969**, from New Latin *Archosauria* the class of such reptiles, from Greek *árchōn* ruler + *saûros* lizard]

arc of crisis, a politically unstable area extending in a curve from the Indian subcontinent west to Turkey and south through the Arabian peninsula and northeastern Africa. Also called CRESCENT OF CRISIS. *In an Administration that was intending to give top priority to the Third World, we have Iran* *in anti-American chaos, that whole arc of crisis more and more hostile to the U.S.* Time 1/14/80, p18 [**1980**]

arcology, *n.* a completely integrated planned city or environment within a single structure. *Because the diameter of an arcology is short, walking, bicycling, escalator, elevator, moving sidewalk, pneumatic or electric vehicle transport make automobiles unnecessary except for travel outside the arcology—eliminating another prime source of pollution.* Encyclopedia Science Supplement (Grolier) 1971, p287 [**1969**, coined by the American architect Paolo Soleri from *arc*hitectural *ecology* to designate the concept of creating a balance between architecture and the environment, especially in his book *Arcology: The City in the Image of Man,* 1969]

area code, *U.S. and Canada.* a three-digit number used to telephone long distance directly by dialing this number plus the local telephone number. Compare *British* STD. *The area code for the whole state of Montana is 406. If you use the area code when you call Long Distance, your call goes through faster and easier.* Advertisement by AT&T (Bell System), New Yorker 3/18/67, p197 [**1964**]

area navigation, a system of aircraft navigation that uses airborne computers to receive and process the signals from ground radio beacons to calculate the position of the aircraft in flight. *Area navigation means that a pilot knows where he is at any time in the course of a flight, and is thus able to take whatever route to his destination is the most direct, least congested, or safest, according to instructions from control.* New Scientist 5/28/70, p412 [**1970**]

arginaemia (ˌɑrdʒəˈniːmiːə), *n.* an inherited metabolic disorder in which a person lacking the necessary enzyme (arginase) is unable to metabolize the amino acid arginine. *Arginaemia . . . manifests itself as very high blood levels or arginine and presumably results from a deficiency in cellular mechanisms for breaking down the amino acid.* New Scientist 1/29/70, p194 [**1970**, from *argin*ine + *-aemia* disorder of the blood (from Greek *haîma* blood)]

arguable, *adj.* capable of being shown or proven by argument; demonstrable. *It is arguable that the most influential English writer of the last 150 years is Charles Darwin and the most influential book "The Origin of Species."* NY Times Book Review 10/5/86, p1 [**1964**, extended from the sense of questionable, debatable (OED 1883) by influence of *arguably* as may be shown by argument (OEDS 1890)]

Arica, *n.* a system of consciousness-raising and self-realization, originally developed in Chile (often used attributively). *Arica, a nationwide spiritual organization, searches for "the Essential Self" through, among other things, Egyptian gymnastics and African dances.* Time 10/13/75, p72 [**1973**, named for the city in northern Chile where the first institute using this system was established]

Aridisol (əˈridəˌsɔːl), *n.* (in U.S. soil taxonomy) any of the group of soils of the world's desert regions, characterized by accumulations of calcium carbonate, magnesium, and soluble salts. *Similar to Mollisols in losses of nutrient elements during formation are the Aridisols, Inceptisols of cold or dry regions, and Vertisols. If anything, losses from these soils are smaller than from Mollisols. Collectively these broad groups and the Mollisols occupy 40% of the land surface of the Earth.* McGraw-Hill Yearbook of Science and Technology 1972, p374 [**1972**, from *arid* + connecting *-i-* + *-sol* (from Latin *solum* soil)]

ark, *n.* a structure resembling a greenhouse built over several connected ponds, forming a self-sufficient food-producing system, which may be used as an alternative to conventional agriculture. See NEW ALCHEMIST. *One ark is under construction on Cape Cod. It is a good deal larger than the other buildings, more dramatic and more futuristic looking, mainly because of its long concave panels of reinforced fiberglass·which are designed to capture the low-angle rays of the morning and late-afternoon sun.* NY Times Magazine 8/8/76, p38 [**1975**, so called in allusion to Noah's *ark,* because of the large variety of life forms grown in it and because it is regarded as a means of survival if conventional agriculture should fail]

ARM (ɑrm), *n. U.S.* acronym for *adjustable rate mortgage* (a mortgage with an interest rate that changes periodically during the term of the loan). *The terms range from the obvious to the arcane. Only a greenhorn would assume an IRA (Individual Retirement Account) refers to Irish radicals, or an ARM (Adjustable Rate Mortgage) refers to a limb.* Wall Street Journal 11/24/81 (page not known) [**1981**]

armalcolite, *n.* a lunar mineral composed of iron, magnesium, and titanium, found in lunar rocks brought back to earth by the crew of Apollo 11. *A new mineral discovered on the Moon by the Apollo 11 mission has been identified for the first time on Earth also in a sample found in a diamond-bearing pipe at Kimberley earlier this year, it was disclosed here today. The mineral is known as armalcolite.* Times (London) 9/28/73, p7 [**1971**, from Neil *Arm*strong, Edwin *Al*drin, and Michael *Co*llins, the Apollo 11 astronauts + *-ite,* suffix for a mineral or rock substance]

armpit, *n. U.S. Slang.* an unattractive and undesirable place. *She [Sally Quinn] is an amateur, of considerable intelligence and charm, but still an amateur, with no real notion of who might be out there in the armpit of America, grunting at what she says.* NY Times 8/19/73, p15 *I am a sophomore at Ball State University. We have a saying around here that sums it up in one sentence. Muncie is the armpit of Indiana.* Time 11/13/78, pK3 [**1973**]

arm-twist, *v.i., v.t.* to use pressure to influence (someone). *He [Presidential Assistant Robert S. Strauss] is factual, and if that doesn't work he charms, and if that doesn't work he arm-twists.* New Yorker 5/7/79, p50 *By contrast, the last Democratic President was a master builder of support; Lyndon B. Johnson used to nudge, charm, cajole, seduce, arm-twist, and, if necessary, bludgeon Congress to win approval for his Great Society.* NY Times 6/17/79, pE4 [**1979**, back formation from *arm-twisting,* noun (1948)]

aromatotherapy, *n.* treatment of the skin by the application of oils, essences, resins and other fragrant substances extracted from herbs and fruits. *Starting at 18 with a nose job by Sir Archibald McIndoe (no less) the Princess has undergone hypnosis, cell implants . . . silicone injections, an eyelid lift, aromatotherapy, yoga and gymnastics.* Times (London) 2/22/73, p11 [**1973**, from *aromat*ic + connecting *-o-* + *therapy*]

arp or **Arp,** *n.* short for ARP SYNTHESIZER. *The traditional conflict between engineering excellence and artistic spontaneity has been decided in the engineer's favor. The new jargon is Vu-meters and equalizers, moogs, arps, decibels, phasing, pan-podding, dolby and de-dolby.* Harper's 9/72, p40 [**1972**]

Arp synthesizer or **ARP synthesizer,** the trademark for an electronic device for generating a large variety of musical sounds, used in producing electronic music. Often shortened to ARP or ARP. *Shortly afterward, he found the technical direction he wanted his music to take in the Arp Moog synthesizers, machines which can electronically produce any sound desired . . . He didn't sacrifice the emotional content of his music, but the Arp and Moog did offer him the dimension he wanted.* NY Times Magazine 2/23/75, p26 [**1972**]

array, *n.* any arrangement or assemblage of elements forming a complete unit. Compare PACKAGE. *. . . millions watched on television as Aldrin removed the unit from the bay of the Eagle, carried it out about 60 feet from the craft and set the array on the lunar surface.* Scientific American 3/70, p43 *The array consists of two lines of seismic detectors, each nearly nine km long, and each having 11 equally spaced instruments, with a common time base.* New Scientist 2/6/64, p362 [**1964**]

arrière-garde (*Anglicized* ˌæriˈerˈgɑrd; *French* aryerˈgard), *n.* the group of intellectuals who follow conventional trends or ideas, especially in the arts; those who are behind the avant-garde. Also called DERRIERE-GARDE. *For the arrière-garde there appears this week an agreeably readable first novel by Peter Prince called* Play Things, *which records the misadventures of a timid young man in charge of an adventure playground in a tough area.* Listener 9/7/72, p312 —*adj.* of or relating to the arrière-garde. *On other scores as well, this contemporary composition has certain arrière-garde characteris-*

tics, its most obvious antecedent being Schoenberg's *Pierrot Lunaire.* New Scientist 8/16/73, p407 [**1962** for noun, from French, literally, rear guard; **1966** for adj.]

arrogance of power, a catchphrase used to attack or impugn the policies of a country, etc., as being due to the arrogance that comes from having too much power. *It is high time, I suggest, that we Americans quit deluding ourselves that we are not as other men, that our nation, the most powerful in history, possesses some unique immunity to the corruption and arrogance of power.* NY Times 9/26/70, p28 [**1970**, coined by U.S. Senator William Fulbright in the 1960's and used by him as the title of a book, 1967, in which he questions the validity of American intervention in the affairs of foreign countries]

arrow of time, the direction in which time flows, considered as the continuity or sequence of events from past to future, or in some theories from future to past, as in explaining time in relation to black holes in the universe. Compare TIME-SYMMETRIC, TIME WARP. *The "Arrow of Time" has been much discussed by philosophers and by some scientists, and various manifestations, which have also been offered as explanations of this directionality, are to be noted in the world around us.* Nature 10/13/72, p387 *The most provocative predictions concerning the future of the universe relate to the arrow of time. From our lifelong observations we are so convinced that time always flows in the same direction that it becomes very difficult to conceive of any other situation. Yet every physicist knows that, on the atomic level, a sequence of events can flow with equal ease in either direction.* Walter Sullivan, Black Holes, 1979, p225 [**1972**]

art deco or **Art Deco**, a style of decorative design characterized by ornateness, asymmetry, geometrical forms, and bold colors. The style was popular in the 1920's and 1930's and was successfully revived in the late 1960's (also used attributively). *Bentley-Farrell-Burnett Designs . . . produced the vivid Art Deco-style placards you see in the windows of Achille Serre shops.* Manchester Guardian Weekly 1/31/70, p17 *He* [Henry Geldzahler, curator of contemporary arts at the Metropolitan Museum in New York City] *collects art deco objects as well as modern paintings, secretly yearns to go to Hollywood.* Time 10/24/69, p62 [**1967**, from French *Art Déco*, shortened from (*Exposition Internationale des*) *Arts Décoratifs* (International Exposition of) Decorative Arts, the title of an exhibition held in Paris in 1925]

arte povera (ˈɑrtei ˈpɑvərə), a form of art in which the work itself is not viewed or exhibited directly but presented at second hand through photographs, maps, drawings, or descriptive language. *Artists working under the various labels of conceptual art, antiform art, process art, software, earthworks, and arte povera have rejected the object in favor of the environment. They are concerned with space, time, and change, with man's needs, with natural forces, and with the way things relate to each other.* 1971 Collier's Encyclopedia Year Book, p112 [**1970**, from Italian, literally, impoverished art]

arthrotropic, *adj.* tending to cause disease of the joints. *Animal models indicate that a variety of known microorganisms, including bacteria or their cell walls, mycoplasma, and viruses are arthrotropic and can induce acute and chronic arthritis.* McGraw-Hill Yearbook of Science and Technology 1975, p109 [**1974**, from *arthro-* joint (from Greek *árthron*) + -*tropic* tending toward (from Greek *tropé* a turn)]

article, *v.i. Canadian.* to work or train as an articled clerk (*in*, *with*, or *for* a professional firm). *He went to law school, worked hard enough to graduate in the top third of his class, and articled with the Halifax law firm of Rutledge, McKeigan, Craig and Downie.* Maclean's 3/22/76, p30 [**1974**] ▶ In British (and less commonly American) usage this verb is used only as a transitive: *to article someone* (literally, to bind a person by articles of apprenticeship) *to an attorney; to be articled to an accounting firm.* The Canadian usage was not recorded until the early 1970's.

artificial blood, a chemical substance used as a substitute for natural blood, especially a mixture of fluorocarbons that can carry large amounts of oxygen. See PERFLUOROCHEMICAL. *The*

chemical solution used as artificial blood can keep patients alive by carrying oxygen to the body's cells and carrying away carbon dioxide, the waste product of metabolism.* Daily News (New York) 11/21/79, p2 [**1975**]

artificial gene, a chemically synthesized copy of a gene made by joining specific sequences of nucleotides (compounds that determine the structure of genes). Compare RECOMBINANT. *The first wholly artificial gene with the potential for functioning inside a living cell has been synthesized by Nobel laureate Har Gobind Khorana and his associates at the Massachusetts Institute of Technology, Cambridge.* Science 9/28/73, p1235 [**1973**]

artificial intelligence, **1** the means by which computers, robots, and other automatic devices perform tasks which normally require human intelligence, such as solving problems, making fine distinctions, playing games, and the like; machine intelligence. *Abbreviation:* AI *Mathematicians and engineers at the Massachusetts Institute of Technology Artificial Intelligence laboratory have combined a computer, a television camera and a mechanical arm into a system with enough artificial intelligence to recognize blocks of various sizes, colors and shapes, and to assemble them into structures without step-by-step instructions from an operator.* Science News 8/4/73, p76 **2** the field of science which studies and develops these means. *Asked to say what artificial intelligence has to show for its first fifteen years, any practitioner is bound to say "Terry Winograd's program."* Nature 11/10/72, p112 [**1966**]

artificial sight or **artificial vision**, the ability of a blind person to perceive objects by electrical stimulation of the visual cortex. See BRAILLE CELL, CORTICAL BRAILLE. *A team of researchers at the University of Utah and the University of Western Ontario reported that artificial sight had been electrically stimulated in two blind patients, one of whom had been blind for 28 years.* 1975 Collier's Encyclopedia Year Book, p228 *In 1974, a team of electronic and medical researchers . . . demonstrated that electrical stimulation of the cortex of the brain could produce light pulses, known as phosphenes, which might be the basis of artificial vision for the blind.* World Book Science Annual 1977, p272 [**1974**]

artificial skin, a substance made from carbohydrates reinforced with the protein fiber of cattle or other animals, used in medicine as a substitute for human skin. *Artificial skin designed and constructed from animal tissue by Boston engineers and surgeons offers hope of new treatment for thousands of persons who suffer from burns each year.* NY Times 1/3/76, p35 [**1976**]

artmobile, *n. U.S.* a trailer truck fitted out to exhibit paintings and sculptures as it travels from place to place. *It* [The Virginia Museum of Fine Arts] *was the first museum to establish an artmobile . . .* NY Times 12/4/67, p65 [**1963**, patterned after *bookmobile* a traveling library]

art rock, a form of rock music that uses elements of traditional or classical music, especially in the style of instrumentation. Compare PROGRESSIVE ROCK. *Ever since that group recorded "Sergeant Pepper" in 1967, there have been many excursions into art-rock, the fusion of conservatoire style in instrumentation with the electronics and idioms of pop.* Times (London) 12/5/72, p14 [**1972**]

artsy, *adj.* **1** having a dilettante interest in art. *But the school I went to was not artsy. Mostly it taught kids to be commercial artists . . .* Listener 12/14/67, p784 **2** overly decorated; too elaborate in design. *Book adaptations and artsy photographic portfolios are mixed with nonfiction articles that seem to have a very limited audience indeed.* Time 4/26/71, p36 [**1963**, shortened from *artsy-craftsy* (OEDS 1902), but influenced in meaning by *arty* (OEDS 1901)]

art trouvé (ˈar truːˈvei). *French.* found art (art not fashioned by the artist but taken as found and adapted for its artistic value or effect). *What it is in fact producing is* art trouvé. *In this idiom one looks within a certain subject area (for instance driftwood on a beach) and picks out those shapes which are evocative . . . The dilemma with* art trouvé *is that the ordinary eye may see nothing unless it looks long enough and it is un-*

likely to look long enough unless it sees something. Science Journal 3/70, p81 **[1970]**

Arvin or **ARVN** ('ɑrvən), *n.* **1** acronym for *Army of the Republic of (South) Vietnam. The operation seems to have greatly boosted the morale of the South Vietnamese army (Arvin), which now has a total strength of more than 1.1 million men, the fourth largest army in the world.* New Scientist 12/17/70, p501 **2** a member of the Arvin. *I was watching, in microcosm, the sort of war the Americans wage in Vietnam, and the kind of fighting for which they have generally helped to train the Arvins (regular soldiers, as opposed to regional and popular forces, in the Army of the Republic of Vietnam).* Manchester Guardian Weekly 5/29/69, p5 **[1965]**

ASAT ('ei,sæt), *n.* a type of hunter-killer satellite that is designed to track an orbiting satellite and explode near it, spraying the satellite with metal-piercing fragments. *ASAT . . . has a parabolic "dish" antenna that homes in on the target satellite and gets the ASAT—actually a space bomb—close to the target, where it detonates. The ASAT goes off like a super hand grenade.* Time 10/17/77, p10 **[1977**, from Anti-*Sat*ellite inter*cep*tor**]**

asbestos cancer, cancer of the lungs or of some other organs, caused by long-term exposure to asbestos fibers found in many household products and in emissions from factories, mines, etc. *The increasing use of asbestos and the many years' delay between exposure and development of cancer suggests that the incidence of "asbestos cancer" in workers outside the industry may be increasing.* Times (London) 3/18/77, p21 **[1976]** ►This is a newly identified disease, unrelated to *asbestosis* (1920's), a lung disease of workers caused by extensive inhalation of asbestos particles.

asbestotic, *adj.* affected by or showing asbestosis (chronic congestion of the lungs caused by inhaling asbestos particles). *They then reported to the committee, that among these employees they had found only eight whose X-rays could be diagnosed as asbestotic.* New Yorker 11/19/73, p120 **[1973]**

ASC, abbreviation of ALTERED STATE OF CONSCIOUSNESS. *Experiences of ecstasy, mystical union, other "dimensions," rapture, beauty, space-and-time transcendence, and transpersonal knowledge, all common in ASC's, are simply not treated adequately in conventional scientific approaches.* Science 6/16/72, p1203 **[1972]**

ASCII ('æs,kiː), *n.* a standard code for representing letters, numbers, and other characters in transmitting data among various types of computers and data-processing equipment. *ASCII . . . is just an agreed-upon way for computers to read letters, numbers, and other keyboard symbols like # and $.* Ms. magazine 6/89, p35 **[1970**, acronym for *American Standard Code for Information Interchange***]**

ASEAN or **Asean** ('ɑːsiːən), *n.* acronym for *Association of South East Asian Nations,* an organization for economic and cultural cooperation between Indonesia, Malaysia, the Philippines, Singapore, and Thailand, formed in Bangkok on August 8, 1967. *With Thailand's fertile rice bowl and Indonesia's developing oil resources . . . the ASEAN countries now provide perhaps the greatest new potential for profitable partnership with the industrial nations.* NY Times 4/30/78, p19 **[1967]** ►*ASEAN* gained new importance after the 23-year old SEATO (Southeast Asia Treaty Organization) was formally dissolved on June 30, 1977.

aseasonal, *adj.* not seasonal; readily adapting to different seasons of the year. *In addition to being more responsive to fertilizer, the new strains are aseasonal, that is, not very sensitive to daylength (photoperiod) . . . The aseasonality and early maturity of new strains are opening new possibilities for multiple cropping and year-round farming.* McGraw-Hill Yearbook of Science and Technology 1972, p221 **[1964**, from *a-* not + *seasonal* **]**

ashram ('ɑː,ʃræm), *n. U.S.* a hippie retreat. *"So like it would be really groovy to see a meeting going on between people like you two . . . or a guy named Mike Bowen, who's going to start an indigenous psychedelic ashram . . ."* New Yorker 8/24/68,

p40 **[1966**, extended sense of the Hindu term for a hermitage, monastery, or religious retreat**]**

Asiadollar, *n.* **1** a United States dollar deposited in Asian banks and used in various money markets of Asia. *The Singapore market in Asiadollars is now said to total some $US 3,000m.* Times (London) 5/8/73, pII **2** Attributive use: *U.S. companies flock to buy Asiadollar CDs.* Business Week 4/10/78, p82 **[1973**, patterned on *Eurodollar* (1960)**]**

ask, *v.i.* **ask out**, *U.S.* to retire, withdraw, or resign; bow out. *Apprised of his* [Headmaster Wilfred O'Leary's] *tough ways as principal of Roslindale High, six teachers asked out even before he arrived.* Time 1/8/68, p33 **[1968]**

ASL, abbreviation of AMERICAN SIGN LANGUAGE. *ASL is a system of communication developed for deaf people and used extensively throughout North America. It is a set of hand gestures that corresponds to individual words.* Encyclopedia Science Supplement (Grolier) 1974, p42 **[1969]**

as-maintained, *adj. U.S.* according to the standard weights and measures maintained by the National Bureau of Standards or a similar organization. *Currents and voltages are almost always measured in terms of as-maintained units and converted to absolute units based on the measured value of the conversion factor.* Scientific American 10/70, p68 **[1970]**

ASP[1], abbreviation of AMERICAN SELLING PRICE. *Abolition of the ASP was one of the conditions agreed during the Kennedy Round trade negotiations . . .* Manchester Guardian Weekly 7/25/70, p23 **[1965]**

ASP[2] (æsp), *n.* acronym for *Anglo-Saxon Protestant.* Compare WASP. *"What makes you think she's different from any other ASP (Anglo-Saxon Protestant)?"* Manchester Guardian Weekly 3/19/64, p13 *John Lindsay's parents were descended from pure-blooded WASPs (White Anglo-Saxon Protestants)—though, as Lindsay is fond of pointing out, "If you are really hip, the correct term is ASP; all Anglo-Saxons are white, so why be redundant?"* Time 11/12/65, p21 **[1964]**

asparaginase (,æspə'rædʒə,neis), *n.* a bacterial enzyme that breaks down the amino acid asparagine, obtained chiefly from sewage bacteria and used to treat certain types of leukemia. *Chad was now also supposed to begin series of injections of a fifth drug, asparaginase, which kills leukemic cells by starving them of an essential amino acid. Asparaginase is used in leukemia chemotherapy to "consolidate" remissions induced by vincristine and prednisone.* NY Times Magazine 12/10/78, p167 **[1964**, from *asparagine* + *-ase* (suffix meaning enzyme)**]**

aspartame, *n.* an artificial sweetener, about 200 times as sweet as sugar, containing 4 calories a gram. *Formula:* $C_{14}H_{18}N_2O_5$ *Since cyclamates were banned nearly five years ago, researchers have worked diligently to find an artificial sweetener that is both safe and free of saccharin's bitter aftertaste. And last week the U.S. Food and Drug Administration announced approval of such a substance: a synthetic product known chemically as aspartame.* Newsweek 8/5/74, p73 **[1973**, from *aspar*tic acid + *p*henyl*al*anine *me*thyl *e*ster, the chemical constituents of the substance**]**

asphalt cloud, a mass of asphalt particles ejected by an antiballistic missile to consume the heat shields of enemy missiles. *In the asphalt-cloud technique, the ABM disperses millions of particles in the path of enemy missiles. When the rockets plunge into the atmosphere, the highly combustible bits of asphalt that they have picked up ignite from frictional heat: the asphalt burns so rapidly and creates such great temperatures that the heat shields on the ICBMs are all but consumed. Then the missiles either burn up or are so deformed that they veer off course.* Time 10/12/70, p33 **[1970]**

aspherics, *n.pl.* lenses whose polished surfaces are not spherical, used especially in television and film cameras; aspheric lenses. *Among the top quality lenses introduced in 1975 were many zooms and ultra-wide focal lengths. Light in weight, their compact design was made possible by incorporating lenses varying slightly from sphericity (aspherics) in the Canon lenses and solid catadioptric design (combining lenses and mirrors) in the Vivitar series I.* Americana Annual 1976, p449 [**1969**, from *aspheric* (1920's) *adj.*, not spherical + *-s*, plural suffix]

assemblage, *n.* **1** an artistic work made from bits and pieces of cloth, wood, metal, scraps, and other fragmentary objects. *As colored images, the canvases of Frankenthaler, Louis, and Olitski are arresting, especially as one comes upon them after two or three roomfuls of assemblages.* New Yorker 7/29/67, p78 **2** the technique or art of making assemblages. *Dada has contributed to every new technique employed in this century that it did not actually invent—collage, which is everywhere; its extension, assemblage, which includes junk sculpture, "found" objects and a hundred cousins; the "environment" as well as the Happening; kinetic sculpture, whether motorized or not, and on and on.* NY Times Magazine 3/24/68, p30 [**1961**]

assemblagist, *n.* a person who makes assemblages. *One of the first artists to look appreciatively at these molds was Alfonso Ossorio, an obsessive assemblagist who produces gaudy conglomerations out of the found objects that he squirrels away against the day when he may need them.* Time 12/19/69, p36 [**1969**]

assembler language or **assembly language,** another name for COMPILER LANGUAGE. *The makers offer a library of programs to go with it* [a desk computer], *including . . . an assembler language, and a general mathematics library.* New Scientist 1/11/68, p79 *Manufacturers today are expected to supply . . . a fairly simple assembly language which makes it possible to instruct the machine without recourse to its own confusing language of zeros and ones . . .* Times (London) 1/7/65, p14 [**1965**]

assertiveness training, a method of training submissive individuals to behave with confidence, often by assuming an aggressive attitude. Also rarely, **assertive** or **assertion training.** *Talking to people about the purposes of the group, showing them how assertiveness training can be personally advantageous, and taking the initiative to see that things run relatively smoothly—all these are highly assertive behaviors.* Spencer A. Rathus and Jeffrey S. Nevid, BT: Behavior Therapy, 1977, p126 [**1975**]

asset stripping, *British.* the use of a company's assets or resources by a parent company to finance other enterprises, such as the purchase of a company. *The firm proposals in the Government paper reflect . . . public and political pressure on the Government to stamp out "asset-stripping," the practice by which financiers take over companies and merely sell off their assets, sometimes creating unemployment.* Manchester Guardian Weekly 8/4/73, p9 [**1972**] —**asset stripper:** *So, too, in the Government's view, do certain members of what has been called the British school of asset strippers. It would be perfectly possible to defend most asset stripping on the basis that it is concerned with taking over badly run companies, slimming them down, realizing unused assets and injecting new management. The Government, however, has largely accepted the general view that it is often inhuman and has unacceptable social side-effects.* Times (London) 1/2/73, p15

associable, *adj.* belonging to a cooperative economic or trade association of several countries. *Moves toward closer relations with Cuba and a number of African nations continued, and Kingston was the venue for the meeting in July between the ACP (Africa, Caribbean, and Pacific) . . . associable states and the EEC.* Britannica Book of the Year 1975, p418 —**n.** an associable country or state. Compare ASSOCIATE. *Not only are some of the associables from the Caribbean and the Pacific but the African states, since independence, have tended to divide along Francophone and Anglophone lines.* Times (London) 7/25/73, p16 [**1973**, extended sense of the adjective meaning "capable of being associated" (OED 1855)] ►This term was adopted to avoid confusion with *associated* as applied to a state or nation. An associated (or associate) state is a former protectorate that retains economic or political association with the country that once governed it (as for example the members of the French Community). An associable state is a member of an economic association of small, usually underdeveloped, countries.

associate, *n.* a former colony or protectorate that has attained partial independence, as by gaining control of its domestic affairs, but is bound politically or economically to the former colonial power, especially in international relations; an associated state. *A referendum in Sikkim gave preponderant support to these changes and New Delhi accepted them, even though it had earlier agreed to the protectorate's enjoying the status of "an associate."* Annual Register of World Events in 1975, p253 [**1967**, noun use of the adjective (1953) as applied to a state] ►See ASSOCIABLE.

associated gas, natural gas found in conjunction with petroleum. Compare DISSOLVED GAS. *Every oil reservoir is, in fact, a gas reservoir as well. Gas that is found with oil is known as "associated gas."* Encyclopedia Science Supplement (Grolier) 1975, p182 [**1972**]

associative memory or **associative storage,** a computer memory whose data locations are made accessible by its contents; content-addressable memory. . . . *associative memories can be rated by their storage density (bits stored per unit of silicon area) and search throughout (bits searched per unit of time per unit of silicon area).* Byte 4/85, p193 [**1985**]

astigmatic, *n.* a person having astigmatism. *People with good eyesight can see lines in the vertical and horizontal planes with equal clarity. But when astigmatics were tested, it was found that the acuity of horizontal or vertical lines corresponded to the nature and the degree of the astigmatism, in spite of the fact that all of them wore correcting lenses.* Times (London) 4/7/72, p16 [**1972**, noun use of the adjective (OED 1849)]

as-told-to, *adj. U.S.* written by a professional writer in collaboration with the subject of the book or article. . . . *he wrote an as-told-to account of the visit, but the book won immediate and widespread denunciation as a fake, because "Adam's description of Timbuctoo was of a dull, filthy and exceedingly unattractive town."* Saturday Review 11/30/68, p52 [**1958**]

astration, *n.* the formation of new stars. *All in all, it's a large observational scheme . . . And it may show how details of star formation ("astration," to use the newly coined word) and chemical changes affect progress along the line.* Science News 11/6/76, p300 [**1976**, from *astro-* star + *formation*]

astro-. A new meaning of this combining form, abstracted from or fashioned on *astronaut*, is "of or having to do with outer space, space travel, etc." Compare COSMO-. The following are some examples of compounds formed with *astro-* in this sense.
—**astrobug,** *n.*: *A spacecraft with a crew of 10 million tiny "astrobugs" was launched from Cape Kennedy today in America's second biosatellite experiment.* Times (London) 9/8/67, p1
—**astrodog,** *n.*: *The astrodog stands up on its house, levels an indignant paw at the boy's retreating figure and barks. "Report that man to mission control!"* 1970 World Book Year Book, p147 —**astromouse,** *n.*: *"You've heard of astrobugs—this is astromouse," Dr. Reynolds said. "He is a desert mouse of the Southwest, a pocket mouse, and has a lot of capabilities for space research."* NY Times 1/7/67, p8 —**astrophotographer,** *n.*: *The Apollo 12 team of Charles Conrad and Alan Bean took similar pictures at their landing site. In spite of the excellence of modern color film, however, the true color of the moonscape still eluded the astrophotographers.* 1970 World Book Year Book, p460

astroarcheology or **astroarchaeology,** *n.* another name for ARCHAEOASTRONOMY. *The sheer volume of new evidence is fostering a widening interest in the astronomy of the ancients. Investigation of these matters, a field called archaeoastronomy by many and astroarchaeology by a few, is emerging as a legitimate activity in science.* NY Times 2/19/78, pD9 [**1973**, from *astro-* star + *archaeology*]

astrobleme, *n.* a scar left on the earth's surface by a meteorite. *Most shatter-coned astroblemes are of moderate size, a few miles across, but two of Precambrian age attain diameters of a few tens of miles across—the Sudbury structure in Canada and the Vredefort Ring of South Africa.* New Scientist 11/28/68, p502 [**1961**, from *astro-* star + Greek *bléma* a shot of a missile, or a wound from such a shot]

astrochemistry, *n.* the study of the chemical composition of heavenly bodies and the regions of outer space. *Now that astronomers have shown for certain that complex molecules do exist deep in space, it is interesting to consider the range of chemical reactions that may start up inside cosmic gas clouds. The occurrence of the vast clouds of molecules in the Milky Way has thus opened up a new science—astrochemistry.* New Scientist 5/3/73, p262 [**1973,** patterned after *astrobiology, astrobotany,* and *astrogeology*]

astrochronologist, *n.* a student of the history and evolution of stars and galaxies. *The new breed of astrochronologists use techniques similar to the familiar potassium-argon radioactive dating method employed by geophysicists.* New Scientist and Science Journal 6/17/71, p668 [**1971**]

astrodynamics, *n.* the study of the action of force on bodies in outer space. . . . *there are not many books which deal with this particular subject matter (aside, that is, from the astrodynamics content), and despite these reservations, it should prove particularly useful to students.* New Scientist 1/2/69, p37 [**1955**]

astrogeology, *n.* the study of the physical features and composition of heavenly bodies. *Progress in the field of astrogeology continued with information recorded from unmanned space vehicles. Surveyor 3, after its landing on April 19 in the Ocean of Storms, provided new information about the lunar surface.* 1968 Collier's Encyclopedia Year Book, p263 [**1962**]

astrospace, *n.* the space beyond the nearby planets; space among the stars. *There exists . . . a variety of mobile machines with arms which can either move limited distances or are completely free moving. A variety of these crawling anthropoids emerged from the experimental applications in nuclear power to astrospace and aerospace propulsion.* Science Journal 10/68, p59 [**1968**]

AstroTurf, *n.* the trademark of an artificial surface for lawns and playing fields, made of a green, grasslike nylon material backed with vinyl. *The outfielders . . . are wonderfully fast afoot, an essential attribute on Candlestick's slick AstroTurf, which now covers the whole infield except for dirt cutouts around the mound and bases.* New Yorker 6/19/71, p75 *Putting, however, is primitive: the player must move to an Astroturf green and aim at a real hole.* Time 4/30/73, p83 [**1966,** from *Astro*dome, an indoor ball park in Houston, Texas where this surface was first used + *turf*]

asymptopia, *n. Nuclear Physics.* a hypothetical region of the electromagnetic spectrum characterized by extremely high energies at which the forces of certain particles and their antiparticles asymptotically approach constant values or equality. *Such fantastic power could finally bring experimenters to that wonderland of high-energy physics that . . . S.J. Lindenbaum calls "asymptopia": the far-out region on the energy scale where all the complex events inside the atom—and hence the very nature of matter—comes within reach of man's understanding.* Time 1/10/72, p46 *On the basis of recent research it appeared that this high-energy realm, dubbed "asymptopia," must either lie at a yet higher energy than particle accelerators now achieve or indeed may not exist at all.* 1975 Britannica Yearbook of Science and the Future, p310 [**1969,** blend of *asymptote* (line which continually approaches a given curve without meeting it) and *utopia* ideal place]

AT, abbreviation of: **1** ALTERNATIVE TECHNOLOGY. *In essence, Alternative Technology (AT) is trying to recreate the freedom, togetherness, and rugged self-sufficiency of the best 19th-century American homesteading communities.* World Book Science Annual 1975, p207 **2** APPROPRIATE TECHNOLOGY. *The U.S. government has established the National Center for Appropriate Technology in Butte, Montana, with $3.3 million to research and disseminate AT information.* Psychology Today 11/78, p70 [**1974** for def. 1; **1976** for def. 2]

-athon, a combining form meaning "marathon" (applied to any prolonged or extended activity, event, etc., of a specified kind, usually involving endurance). **—Bachathon,** *n.: Rosalyn Tureck first performed the complete Preludes and Fugues of Bach's "Well-Tempered Clavier," along with the Goldberg Variations,* in six concerts at Town Hall, in 1937 . . . *She is commemorating the fortieth anniversary of this "Bach-athon" in a repeat performance this autumn.* New Yorker 10/10/77, p36 **—bikeathon,** *n.: The Calgary and District International Development Society hopes to raise between $30,000 and $40,000 with the 72-mile "bike-a-thon" May 6.* The Province (Vancouver) 4/14/73, p54 **—space-athon,** *n.: Half a year away from earth is hard to imagine, let alone accomplish, but now the Soviets in their latest space-athon have done it.* New York Post 8/24/79, p22 **—workathon,** *n.: Their performance was a workathon of sweaty energy in which the drama of male-female encounter was inflated to cartoon scale.* NY Times 8/30/77, p35 [**1972**] ►This form has previously appeared in only three widely-established terms: *walkathon* (1932), *talkathon* (1948), and *telethon* (1952), all from *marathon* (OEDS *exten.* 1908). It has lately become productive, influenced probably by the popularity of telethons. The form *-athon* is used after a consonant-final root, while *-thon* follows a vowel (as in *telethon*). Another example of *-thon* is: *The event at the Manhattan Center Saturday night was billed as a "disco-thon"—a competition among local free-lance discotheque disk jockeys.* NY Times 8/16/76, p35

Atlanticism, *n.* a policy of close political cooperation between the countries of western Europe and North America. *"M Pompidou increasingly abandons the positive aspects of General de Gaulle's policy in order to draw closer to the United States and slide towards Atlanticism—something which is contrary to the interest and independence of France."* Times (London) 1/13/72, p6 [**1964,** from the *Atlantic* Pact, which formed the basis of NATO (North *Atlantic* Treaty Organization) + *-ism*]

Atlanticist, *n.* a supporter of close cooperation between western Europe and North America. *Jean Lecanuet, the conservative candidate who entered the political scene as an "Atlanticist" a little over a year ago, has found that he cannot rouse any audiences by promising to save the Atlantic alliance and restore U.S. French friendship.* NY Times 3/5/67, p3 [**1963**]

ATM or **A.T.M.,** abbreviation for automatic teller machine (an electronic machine that dispenses cash, records deposits, etc.). *Remote banking has continued to expand and many customers have become accustomed to automatic teller machines (ATMs), but still only about one third of U.S. bank customers make use of the machines.* Americana Annual 1987, p131 [**1983**]

atmospherics, *n.pl.* atmosphere or ambiance especially created to stimulate optimism, confidence, etc., in order to achieve some desired result. *[Henry] Kissinger frequently stage-manages negotiations to produce the right kind of "atmospherics."* Time 4/1/74, p28 *These people keep in touch with one another and with the press . . . They supply some of the atmospherics that influence events and fill the air of an election.* New Yorker 5/24/76, p120 [**1963**]

atmospherium, *n.* a room or building like a planetarium for simulating atmospheric or meteorological phenomena. . . . *capped with a hyperbolic paraboloid roof, the Atmospherium creates thunderstorms from tiny clouds in a matter of minutes.* Saturday Review 11/4/67, p54 [**1963,** from *atmosphere* + *-ium,* as in *planetarium*]

atomarium, *n.* a room or building in which devices showing the structure and use of atoms are exhibited. *Following the pattern of the atomarium in Stockholm, Sweden, this booklet* [The Cranbrook Atomarium] *describes the demonstrations of the new museum displays at Cranbrook which explain some of the phenomena of atomic and nuclear physics.* Science News Letter 12/26/64, p407 [**1964,** from *atom* + *-arium,* as in *planetarium*]

ATPase (ˌeiˌtiːˈpiːˌeis), *n.* an enzyme that breaks down adenosine triphosphate (ATP), the substance that supplies the energy needed for muscle contraction, sugar metabolism, etc. *As the amino acid passes through the cell membrane, it may stimulate ATPase. ATPase in turn splits a molecule of ATP just inside the cell, in the cytoplasm.* Science News 1/20/73, p44 [**1961,** from *ATP* + *-ase* (suffix meaning enzyme)]

atrazin or **atrazine**, *n.* a moderately toxic chemical widely used as a weed killer. *Some species might even become resistant to sprays, although the only example so far appears to be a United States groundsel reported to be undeterred by simazin and atrazin.* Times (London) 11/23/70, p13 [**1963**, from *amino* + *triazine* (chemical compound with a ring of three carbon atoms)]

attack dog, *U.S.* a dog trained to attack on command in order to assist police or soldiers in their duty or to protect individuals against thieves, muggers, etc. *Policemen with attack dogs ordered the students into a fleet of trucks after a crowd of about 1,500—a number equal to the university's entire enrollment—gathered on the campus for a memorial meeting.* NY Times 9/16/77, pA1 [**1970**]

attendance teacher, *U.S.* an official charged with finding and returning truants and other absentee students to school. *They used to be called truant officers, and the cartoonists always depicted them snagging youthful hookey players with butterfly nets or long hooks and then dragging them off to school . . . Today, they are called attendance teachers, and they do not use butterfly nets or hooks and insist they never did.* NY Times 6/7/76, p34 [**1972**]

atto-, a prefix meaning one quintillionth of any standard unit in the international meter-kilogram-second system of measurements (SI UNIT). *The General Conference* [on Weights and Measures] *has approved 14 such prefixes, ranging from "atto" (10⁻¹⁸) to "tera" (10¹²).* Scientific American 7/70, p23 [**1963**, from Danish *atten* eighteen]

attosecond, *n.* one quintillionth of a second. *They habitually think in terms of microseconds or nanoseconds—millionths or billionths of a second. And, though they do not often have occasion to work with attoseconds, they are unblinkingly aware of them.* New Yorker 8/27/73, p50 [**1973**, from *atto-* + *second*]

attrit, *v.t. U.S. Military use.* to wear down by attrition; weaken by harassment or abuse. *Wear him down. Wear the Cong down, and he'll quit. Put him through the meat grinder. Attrit him. He is hurting, said the American commander in mid-1967.* Atlantic 1/69, p40 [**1969**, back formation from *attrition*]

attrition, *v.t.* Usually, **attrition out.** *U.S.* to reduce the number of (jobs or workers) by not hiring people to fill positions made vacant by retirement, transfer, etc. *No legislature was going to allow ninety thousand city employees to be laid off, or even, in the union phrase, "attritioned out."* New Yorker 5/15/71, p121 [**1971**, verb use of the noun]

ATV, abbreviation of ALL-TERRAIN VEHICLE. *Such rudimentary rules are virtually unenforceable, and marauders on ATVs or snowmobiles occasionally strip hunters' shacks or loot vacation homes.* Time 11/23/70, p41 [**1970**]

A₂, *n.* the virus responsible for Asian flu. See also HONG KONG FLU. *A severe bout of A₂ years earlier left some persons' systems ready to react instantly and forcibly against any related virus.* Time 1/31/69, p36 [**1965**]

Aubrey hole, any one of the 56 equally spaced holes which form the outermost ring of the Stonehenge circle. [Gerald S.] *Hawkins has suggested that the Aubrey holes at Stonehenge were used to count the years of a 56-year cycle, important in the motion of the Moon and the occurrence of eclipses . . . We suggest also that the Aubrey holes, if they were used as counters at all, were used to count intervals of 56 months rather than 56 years.* Nature 10/27/72, p511 [**1959**, named for John *Aubrey*, 1626-97, an English antiquary, and author of *Brief Lives*, who discovered the holes]

audible, *n. U.S. Football.* a play called out by the quarterback at the line of scrimmage to replace the play called in the huddle or to execute a play without a huddle when time is about to run out. *"There are times when I can see myself standing behind the Baltimore Colts' offensive line, calling audibles to pick up a blitz."* Time 8/23/71, p44 [**1967**, noun use of the adjective]

audiocassette, *n.* a cassette containing a sound recording; audiotape cassette. *The total number of records, compact disks (CD's), audiocassettes, and eight-track tapes sold in the first half of 1986 dropped about 6.9 percent from the same period in 1985.* 1987 World Book Year Book, p440 [**1980**]

audiodontics, *n.* the study of the relationship of teeth to hearing. *Elsewhere, researchers in audiodontics had an explanation for the curious habit of Beethoven's of holding one end of a drumstick in his mouth and pressing the other end against the piano frame. He was listening with his teeth.* New Scientist 1/3/74, p26 [**1973**, from *audio-* sound, hearing + *-odontics* study or treatment of the teeth]

audiolingual, *adj.* involving the use of hearing and speech instead of written or printed material. *. . . . the new thrust has been on conversational skills and on the method of oral rather than written communication initially. Electronic language laboratories have been widely installed to facilitate this audiolingual approach.* Americana Annual 1970, p264 [**1957**]

audio pollution, another name for SOUND POLLUTION. *Traffic noise is man's most widespread form of audio pollution, and year by year the problem is becoming more acute. Schools, recreational areas, and even homes are subjected to this irritating invasion.* McGraw-Hill Yearbook of Science and Technology 1975, p282 [**1975**]

audiotactile, *adj.* of or relating to both hearing and touch. *The hospital was partly audio-tactile, the patient being obliged to address his pleas to wall-tubes sieve-ended like the speaking grills in confessional boxes, and then wait for the answers to boom back at him from the ceiling like flight announcements.* Harper's 2/68, p41 [**1967**, patterned after *audiovisual*]

audiotape, *n.* a sound tape recording as distinguished from a videotape. *Consider the technological possibilities we now possess. We have television, audiotapes, records, newspapers, magazines, encyclopedias, movie films—and computers to run them all.* Saturday Review 5/11/68, p51 [**1963**]

audiotyping, *n.* typing which is done from tape recordings as distinguished from written material. *In the area of audiotyping, the work recently done by I.B.M. in establishing certain comparable output norms, which grapple with the many variables involved, may be of interest to people who want to make a low cost measurement of the productivity of their typing services, present and potential.* Times (London) 6/26/68, p27 [**1962**]

audiovisuals, *n.pl.* instructional materials involving the use of both sounds and pictures; audiovisual material or equipment. *The curriculum has begun to draw fire, mainly because of the realistic audio-visuals.* NY Times 1/9/72, pD7 [**1972**, noun use of the adjective *audiovisual*]

audit, *v.t.* make an energy audit of. *The purpose of the program, a Honeywell official says, "is to help a building owner save money on energy conservation possibilities" without having to make all the complex decisions. "Honeywell," he says, "would audit a building, identify conservation possibilities, install the equipment, and monitor its operation."* Christian Science Monitor 4/9/80, p3 [**1980**, from (energy) *audit*]

audit trail, a record of the passage of data in a computer or data processing machine from one step to the next, used especially to trace data from a final output or report back to the original or source items. *Another barrier that the computer criminal or unauthorized user of a computer system has to cope with is that of the computer's audit trail—the internal monitoring system that can record all significant actions of the users and is supposed to provide means of detecting and tracing unauthorized attempts to gain entry.* New Yorker 8/29/77, p60 [**1970**, so called from its original use in computerized accounting systems as the means by which auditors can trace transactions backward and forward]

augmentor, *n.* a type of robot that serves as an extension or replacement of a person in performing excessively hard or dangerous work. Compare MAN AMPLIFIER, TELEOPERATOR. *The augmentors are designed to take over or aid in actual labor, such as handling objects that are too big, too small, too far away, too heavy or too dangerous for men . . . General Electric has a family of other augmentor robots, including O-man,* which hangs from a crane and can lift two and a half tons . . . Science News 3/9/68, p238 [**1968**]

aulacogen (ɔ:ˈlækədʒən), *n. Geology.* a narrow rift valley filled with sediment, associated with plate tectonics as an early fracture of a protocontinent. *Aulacogens can now be recognized as failed arms of three-armed rift systems. When the two successful arms opened to form an ocean, the failed arm remained as a rift valley running inland from the new seacoast. The rift became a feature of the drainage pattern of the continent, accumulating a thick deposit of sediments.* Scientific American 8/76, p56 [**1972,** from Russian *aulakogen,* coined by the Soviet geologist Nicholas S. Shatsky from Greek *aulákos* furrow + *-genḗs* born]

Auntie, *n. British.* a nickname for the B.B.C. (British Broadcasting Corporation). Compare BEEB. *Vintage Years is essentially a delightful collage of anecdotes recounted by two men who were working for Auntie when so many of the fabled BBC events occurred.* Times (London) 11/16/72, p11 [**1963,** chiefly (and originally) in reference to its supposedly strait-laced and conservative outlook]

Aunt Jane, *U.S. (Black English) Slang.* See the quotation for the meaning. . . . *black Christians must relearn the whole-hearted involvement with religion that typifies the churches' "Aunt Janes"[1] . . .* [Footnote] [1]*Affectionate black-church term for the amen-saying, clapping, lustily singing black-church "sister." Women make up a strong majority of most black congregations.* Time 4/6/70, p71 [**1970**]

Aunt Tabby, *U.S. Slang, used disparagingly.* another name for AUNT THOMASINA. *The new feminism parallels the black movement in many ways. Both are encumbered for example, by a huge fifth column—for blacks, the Uncle Toms: for women, Aunt Tabbies, also known as Doris Days.* Time 11/21/69, p58 [**1969**]

Aunt Thomasina, *U.S. Slang, used disparagingly.* a woman who does not support the cause of Women's Liberation. Also called AUNT TABBY, AUNT TOM. *Accommodators and temporizers within the Women's Lib movement were spoken of as Aunt Thomasinas.* Atlantic 3/70, p112 [**1964,** patterned after *Uncle Tom*]

Aunt Tom, *Slang, used disparagingly.* **1** a black woman with a servile attitude toward whites; a female Uncle Tom. *Because Imogene seems to be something of an Aunt Tom in involuntary servitude, the part might draw protests from some black groups—even though Imogene manages to escape her situation near the end.* Sunday Post-Herald (Hongkong) 5/20/73, p28 **2** a woman who does not support the cause of Women's Liberation. Also called AUNT THOMASINA. *In a radio debate, Women's Libber Betty Friedan told anti-libber Phyllis Schlafly, "I consider you a traitor to your sex, an Aunt Tom."* National Review 5/25/73, p564 [**1968,** patterned after *Uncle Tom*]

au pair (ˌou ˈpɛr), *British.* **1** a foreign girl who does housework, tutoring, etc., for a family without pay in exchange for food and board (often used attributively). *Don't worry, it's probably the au pair registering her annoyance at the lack of food in the refrigerator.* Cartoon legend, Listener 2/1/68, p139 *The original idea of the* au pair *girl was German: a 'house-daughter' she was to be, living as one of the family, morally protected and not asked to do much more than arrange the flowers and take the children to the park.* Observer Supplement (London) 11/22/64 (page not known) **2** to be an au pair. *Mr. Letica's subjects were three Yugoslav girls who are brushing up their English, au pairing or toiling among our bureaucrats . . .* Punch 8/13/69, p278 [**1960,** noun and verb use of the earlier adjective (recorded in the OEDS with a 1928 citation from the *Sunday Express*), from French *au pair,* literally, on equal terms]

auralize, *v.t.* to hear mentally; imagine the sound of. *If you can imagine the kind of sound produced by Dietrich Fischer-Dieskau and Hermann Prey in the same cast, then you can also auralize the comparable efforts of Gundula Janowitz and Tatiana Troyanos.* Saturday Review 11/4/72, p68 [**1972,** patterned after *visualize*]

Aussie, *n. Informal.* an Australian terrier. *"It hurts me so much to realize there is antagonism among those who profess to care deeply for our breed," her letter adds. "I have tried desperately to promote good will. Our Aussies are so full of loving good spirits—why can't their owners measure up to them?"* New Yorker 1/26/76, p63 [**1976,** by shortening and alteration] ►The earlier meanings of *Aussie,* "an Australian," "of or from Australia," and "Australia," have been used since World War I.

austral (ɑuˈstrɑ:l), *n.* the monetary unit of Argentina since 1986, equal to 100 centavos. *On June 14, Alfonsín announced . . . the creation of a new currency, the austral, to replace the Argentine peso.* World Book Year Book 1986, p195 [**1986,** from American Spanish (Argentina), from Spanish *austral* southern, from Latin *austrālis*]

Australia antigen, a substance found in the blood of persons infected with serum hepatitis (an acute virus inflammation of the liver). *Serum hepatitis is frequently transmitted to patients receiving transfusions of blood from individuals who may be unknowing carriers of the so-called Australia antigen associated with the hepatitis virus.* Science News 12/19/70, p456 [**1966**]

auteur (ouˈtœr), *n.* a motion-picture director whose films have a distinctive personal style. *Familiar though we are with the axiom that European* auteurs *produce unmistakably personal visions, we have seen Hollywood movies, even the movies of our most "distinctive" directors, as committee efforts.* New Yorker 7/27/68, p41 *Joseph McGrath is undoubtedly, in the cult phraseology of the moment, an auteur.* Times (London) 11/21/68, p16 [**1963,** from French *auteur,* literally, author]

auteurism (ouˈtœrˌizəm), *n.* personal style in directing films; movie direction by auteurs. *The rising popularity of foreign movies, in which directors exert more of a personal influence, at times, than in Hollywood films, gave* auteurism *a mighty shot in the arm.* Saturday Review 12/28/68, p22 [**1968**]

auteurship (ouˈtœrˌʃip), *n.* film direction by an auteur. *For many film critics the thumbprint of style signifies* auteurship, *whether left at the scene of a crime or upon a good achievement.* American Scholar, Autumn 1972, p630 . . . *the Production Designers are not far behind the Film Editors in their claim to a share in the* auteur*ship of recent movies, and with good reason.* New Yorker 3/10/80, p77 [**1972**]

authentification, *n.* confirmation; ratification. *You know about the black briefcase, don't you? Inside are the Emergency War Order (EWO) authentification codes, which are changed frequently and are supposed to ensure that only the President, their possessor, can authorize a thermonuclear missile or bomber launch.* Harper's 3/78, p86 [**1970,** altered from earlier *authentication,* probably by influence of *verification, certification, ratification,* etc.]

autistic, *n.* a person, usually a child, suffering from autism (a pathological condition characterized by self-absorption and lack of contact with reality). *Thanks to the relentless lobbying of the National Society for Autistic Children in Albany, N.Y.— composed largely of parents—more than 30 states have passed laws providing special education for autistics in the last four years.* Newsweek 4/8/74, p52 [**1968,** noun use of the adjective (1912)]

autoaggressive disease, another name for AUTOIMMUNE DISEASE. . . . *the "autoimmune" diseases (which we now call autoaggressive) result from a breakdown in the central system that, in health, regulates normal growth beyond an early stage of embryogenesis.* New Scientist 2/12/70, p9 [**1968**]

autoanalyzer, *n.* any of various devices or systems for the automatic analysis of the chemical constituents in a substance, process, etc. (also used attributively). *Mr. P. D. Faint and Mr. G. H. King, of Technicon Instruments Ltd., in a paper on the results of an autoanalyser study of between 30 and 40 tablets from each of seven pills made by six manufacturers, say they show the need for a single tablet assay.* Times (London) 4/24/70, p4 *Dr. Ralph E. Thiers of the Duke University Medical Center . . . demonstrated a 12-channel blood-testing instrument called an Autoanalyzer . . .* Science News 10/1/66, p245 [**1960,** from *AutoAnalyzer,* a trade name for a device invented in 1950 by Dr. Leonard T. Skeggs of Cleveland]

autocide[1], *n.* self-destruction. *The surest method of eradicating a species is to destroy its ability to reproduce . . . The relatively small amount of information already available has suggested a number of approaches to preventing the reproduction of the insect and bringing about the autocide of disease-carrying species.* Scientific American 4/68, p108 [**1968,** from *auto-* self + *-cide* killing, as in *homicide*]

autocide[2], *n.* suicide committed by crashing one's car. *No one can know for sure, but more and more police and traffic experts suspect that "autocide," as one expert calls it, is an important cause of traffic deaths.* Time 3/10/67, p19 [**1964,** contraction of *auto*mobile sui*cide*]

▶This term is not entirely new. It was coined forty years ago with another but similar meaning and apparently had a very short-lived existence: *The National Safety Council of the United States of America, which is said to have been searching for a suitable term to cover "motor-vehicle fatalities," may think that it has found a very nice one in the selected word "autocide," but the choice is not one that will please the purists . . . it sins against the rule that two languages should not be mixed up in the same word—the first two syllables are of Greek extraction and the last one comes from Latin.* Baltimore Sun 10/21/31, p14

autocross, *n.* an automobile competition to test driving skill and speed. *With the local autocross schedule for the winter months decidedly on the lean side, five Northern California autocross drivers slipped across the border to enter the final Southern California Championship Slalom (their name for autocross).* San Francisco Chronicle 12/19/63, p54 [**1963,** from *auto-* automobile + *cross* (as in *moto-cross* a motorcycle race)]

auto-destruction art or **auto-destructive art,** a form of art in which the art object, usually a mechanical device, destroys or obliterates itself. See also MACHINE ART. *Happenings, "impossible art," auto-destruction art, multi-media events are alternative pursuits that can engage an artist's inventive powers . . .* Manchester Guardian Weekly 1/10/70, p20 *A manifesto by Gustav Metzger relates auto-destructive sculptures to auto-destructive tendencies in contemporary society: "Auto-destructive art is the transformation of technology into public art."* New Yorker 10/21/67, p197 [**1967**]

autofocus, *Photography. adj.* that can focus automatically. *Autofocus cameras were first offered to us in the mid-1970's . . .* NY Times 5/24/81, pD32 —*n.* automatic focusing of a camera lens. *Abbreviation:* AF *Automatic focusing, also called autofocus, is beginning to creep from the rangefinders into the SLRs. On the Pentax ME-F ($300) and the Canon AE-1 ($220), tiny lights in the viewfinder tell you when the picture is in focus.* Money 5/82, p129 [**1978**]

autogenic training, 1 a method for learning to induce physiological changes, such as raising or lowering the temperature, in one's own body. *Somewhat reminiscent of both yoga and self-hypnosis, autogenic training involved learning to control blood flow. Even blood sugar and white cell count are affected by the exercises, according to later studies. Autogenic training became a major factor in European medicine and psychotherapy.* Marilyn Ferguson, The Brain Revolution, 1973, p34 **2** another name for BIOFEEDBACK TRAINING. *Autogenic training . . . involved detecting the variable to be controlled, displaying information about it on a dial or with a light or sound, and then letting the subject practice controlling it. The procedure has been used experimentally in treating high blood pressure and migraine headaches.* 1973 Britannica Yearbook of Science and the Future, p78 [**1964,** from *auto-* self + *-genic* producing]

autogestion, *n.* the management of factories, farms, etc., by committees of workers. *In certain cases, they even go so far as to discuss autogestion, that is to say, the pure and simple confiscation of the firm by its workers.* Times (London) 5/29/68, p11 [**1965,** from French, literally, self-management]

autoimmune disease, any of a class of diseases caused when the body forms antibodies against some of its own cells and tissues. See also the quotation under AUTOAGGRESSIVE DISEASE. *There*

is even the possibility that under certain abnormal conditions the body may form antibodies against some of its own components. It forms an immunity against itself, so to speak, producing a variety of disorders that are classified as autoimmune diseases. Encyclopedia Science Supplement (Grolier) 1967, p185 *Lupus erythematosus [a disease of the skin and connective tissues] is the most perfect example of an autoimmune disease.* Science News 3/7/70, p257 [**1961**]

autoinjector, *n.* a small hypodermic syringe containing a dose of medicine for self-administration, especially such a syringe containing an antidote for nerve gas. *Autoinjectors containing doses of atropine/oxime mixtures are available or on standard issue in a number of armed forces.* New Scientist 9/20/73, p673 [**1968**]

autoland, *n.* the automatic landing of an aircraft by means of electronic devices. *Only when the experts were satisfied was the aircraft cleared for autoland on a normal line service.* Times (London) 9/4/72, pVI [**1963,** from *auto*matic *land*ing]
▶This is more often called *instrument landing* in the United States, and *blind landing* in Great Britain.

autologous, *adj.* (of blood) donated by a person and preserved for one's own future use. *If you're facing elective surgery, you might want to consider putting aside a supply of your own blood. Self-donated (autologous) transfusions prevent your contracting an infectious disease, such as AIDS or hepatitis.* Woman's Day 5/5/87, p24 [**1987,** from earlier use (1920's) meaning transplanted from one's own body, as skin or marrow]

automatic teller, another name for CASHPOINT. *Bankers big and small are rushing to install automatic tellers in their branches.* Time 9/7/81, p56 [**1979**]

autoregulation, *n.* the self-regulation or automatic adjustment of an organ, ecological system, etc., to changing conditions. *G. Wesley Hatfield, microbiologist at the University of California at Irvine, received the 1975 Eli Lilly and Company Award in Microbiology and Immunology . . . for research on the autoregulation of gene expression.* World Book Science Annual 1976, p389 [**1970,** from *auto-* self + *regulation*] —**autoregulative,** *adj.: The particles are large aggregates of molecules, many of which are not therefore accessible to the other reactants. The surfaces of such large particles show special properties: they adsorb ions, double electrical layers form around them, they often function in catalysis. Their "autoregulative properties" were attributed to "the surface field around the particle."* Robert Olby, The Path to the Double Helix, 1974, p7

autoshape, *v.i. Behavioral Psychology.* to respond to a stimulus without the normal pattern of conditioning. *In the present experiment, we assessed the effects of initial treatments by measuring resistance to the powerful autoshaping procedure. If noncontingent food delivery produces a helplessness-like effect, then subjects so treated should autoshape slower than controls not given this treatment.* Science 12/1/72, p1003 [**1972,** from *auto-* self + *shape, v.*]

auto-timer, *n.* a device that turns on a stove burner or an oven at a preset time, making it possible to cook food while one is away. *For instance you can now buy auto-timers which make it possible to come home to a hot supper . . . hot plates which have a pan-sensing device to prevent liquid boiling over . . .* Times (London) 3/12/70, p8 [**1967**]

auto-train, *n.* **1** a train equipped to transport passengers and their automobiles between designated locations. *Each year millions of Northeasterners solve the paramount·vacation question (WHERE TO GO) by opting for Florida, only to face the second (HOW TO GET THERE). The problem is compounded by the multiplicity of choices: private car, bus, rail, auto-train, plane.* NY Times 1/25/76, pJ1 **2 Auto-Train,** *U.S.* the trademark of a rail service using such trains. *The successful operations of Auto-Train Corp., which hauls family automobiles in special cars while the riders sit, eat, sleep, and are entertained in lounge cars, were given another boost by the introduction of new tri-level auto carriers, each of which carried 12 cars instead of the 8 on the bi-level carriers.* 1976 Britannica Yearbook of Science and the Future, p411 [**1964**, from *auto* automobile + *train*]

autotransfusion, *n.* a method of blood transfusion in which blood from a surgical patient is collected in a reservoir and returned to the patient's body during surgery. *The objections of some religious sects to blood transfusions were being overcome by perfection of the technique of autotransfusion. Hundreds of U.S. hospitals had the equipment to collect blood as it was lost, filter and process it, then return it to the body after corrective measures had been taken.* Britannica Book of the Year 1975, p345 [**1963**, from *auto-* self + *transfusion*]

avalanchine (ˌævəˈlæntʃiːn), *adj.* like an avalanche; huge; torrential; overpowering. *On top of the avalanchine sums of money it consumes in exchange for little tangible reward, the land speed record is a hobby involving risks that grow all the more prohibitive as the speeds inch higher.* Harper's 7/74, p68 [**1973**, from *avalanche* + *-ine*, a suffix forming adjectives from nouns; possibly a revival as *avalanchine* is recorded in the OED with one quotation (*c*1860)]

avalanchologist, *n.* an expert in the study of avalanches. . . . *Avalanchologist André Roche and other institute scientists now classify avalanches in two basic groups.* Time 3/9/70, p34 [**1970**]

avalement (əˈvælmənt), *n.* a skiing technique for accelerating on downhill turns. *Nobody else has quite mastered his [Jean-Claude Killy's]* avalement *technique of accelerating on the downhill turns—rocking back on his haunches and thrusting his skis so far forward that he seems certain to fall.* Time 2/9/68, p34 *Avalement is now accepted as the key to faster skiing, providing one has the strength of thigh* . . . Times (London) 12/23/70, p11 [**1968**, from French, literally, a lowering, from *avaler* to go downhill]

avaluative, *adj.* not susceptible to evaluation. *Evasion-responsive academics call facts "supportive," techniques "innovative" and theories "avaluative." If proof is less than total, it may be said to have the "ring of authenticity."* NY Times 1/10/70, p33 [**1970**, from *a-* not + *valuative*]

aversion therapy, a therapy against a harmful habit or addiction by inducing an aversion to it. Compare BEHAVIOR THERAPY. *Russell's experiment is another application of what psychologists call aversion therapy . . . A heroin addict, for instance, is given a drug (Scoline) that seriously impairs his ability to breathe. Just before the drug takes effect, he gets his usual dose of heroin. After several such harrowing experiences, he presumably kicks his habit.* Time 3/2/70, p58 *The medicine was aversion therapy—a highly controversial method of punishing a patient to change his behaviour.* Sunday Times (London) 5/9/71, p8 [**1956**]

avgolemono (ˌævgouˈlemənou), *n.* **1** a chicken soup made with eggs and lemon, introduced from Greece. *Lunch one day was artichoke fritters . . .; dinner was avgolemono, then veal.* Times (London) 1/1/72, p12 **2** a sauce made with eggs and lemon, used in various Greek dishes. *Before the pineapple there had been sole cooked with grapes, avgolemono.* New Yorker 11/12/73, p45 [**1966**, from Modern Greek *avgolémono*, from *avgó* egg + *lemóni* lemon]

aviaphobia or **aviophobia** (ˌeiviːəˈfoubiːə), *n.* an abnormal fear of flying. Compare AEROPHOBE. *The spate of recent air accidents . . . has grounded those who suffer from aviaphobia.* Washington Times 1/10/89, pE2 *Aviophobia . . . is believed to cost the airline industry up to $1.5 billion a year.* Americana Annual 1987, p71 [**1986**, from *aviation* + *phobia*]

aviator glasses or **aviators**, *n.pl.* wide, metal-rimmed eyeglasses, often tinted, with lenses that curve downwards. *Dick wears silver aviator glasses and flared jeans and cowboy boots of black tooled leather.* New Yorker 6/20/77, p28 *Kathy Lingg breaks out her old wire-rimmed aviators and goes instantly incognito.* NY Times Magazine 9/23/79, p101 [**1972**]

A Victoria, a virulent strain of the influenza virus, first identified in 1975 in Victoria, Australia. See INFLUENZA A, B, C. *A vaccine against A-Victoria flu virus was made available to Americans at the same time a swine flu vaccine was, and the A-Victoria strain did strike. Thus, if a swine flu epidemic had also occurred, the vaccines might well have saved millions of lives.* Science News 5/21/77, p324 [**1975**]

AWACS or **Awacs** (ˈeiwæks), *n.* acronym for *Airborne Warning and Control System*, a system of the U.S. Air Force for the early detection of enemy bombers that utilizes aircraft with special radar equipment. *The major effort at NATO for the last year has been to get European allies to agree to buy the system, known by its initials, AWACS, to give Europeans a longer time—15 minutes instead of 3—to detect a Soviet aerial strike.* NY Times 12/9/76, p5 [**1970**]

awesome, *adj. U.S. and Canadian Slang.* used admiringly, especially by teenagers, of something fine, excellent, pleasing, etc. Compare OUTRAGEOUS. *Dave gives the ball such prodigious wallops that TV commentators resort to the newest big word in the sports world—"awesome."* Maclean's 7/30/79, p35 [**1979**]

axe, *n. U.S. Slang.* any musical instrument. *The fogeys didn't know an "axe" (a guitar) from a hole in the ground.* Time 2/14/69, p43 . . . *musicians occasionally refer to their instruments as "axes".* . . . New Yorker 6/28/69, p76 [**1968**, perhaps originally applied to a saxophone, whose short form, *sax*, rhymes with *axe*, and whose shape may have suggested that of an axe. Later it was chiefly applied to a guitar or other stringed instrument, and eventually extended to any instrument used by rock 'n' roll bands.]

axion, *n.* a hypothetical subatomic particle with neutral charge and zero spin, and a mass of less than one-thousandth of a proton. Compare INSTANTON. *Other candidates for dark matter include theoretical particles, such as axions, photinos, gravitons, and quarks, which particle physicists have predicted on the basis of complex theories known as grand unified theories.* World Book Science Annual 1986, p230 [**1978**, perhaps from Greek *áxios* worthy + English *-on* elementary unit or particle; for a possible semantic connection, see the etymology of CHARM]

axotomy (ækˈsɑtəmiː), *n.* microsurgery performed on the axon of a nerve cell. *Axotomy, or section of a nerve cell axon, induces anatomical as well as biochemical changes in the soma of neurons, especially those connected with the periphery.* Science 9/22/72, p1116 [**1972**, from *axon* + *-tomy* a cutting]

ayatollah (ˌɑːyəˈtoulə), *n.* a religious leader of the Shiite sect of Islam in Iran. Also spelled **ayatullah.** *Among the Shiites in Iran, religious leaders carry doctrine down to the grass roots. First, there are the ayatollahs, like Khomeini, about 1,200 of them in the Shiite world, who serve as all-purpose father figures—as collectors and distributors of funds, as confessors, spiritual counselors, legal advisers, teachers and even as marriage counselors . . . Ayatollahs reach the populace through a network of about 180,000 mullahs, who, in effect, serve as field officers in the Shiite setup. These mullahs can spread the word to every one of Iran's 35 million people.* Daily News (New York) 2/4/79, p41 [**1963**, from Arabic *āyatollāh*, literally, sign of God]
►The term has become widely known since January, 1979, through the name of Ayatollah Ruholla Khomeini, the Shiite leader who rose to power in Iran after the deposition of the Shah. *Ayatollah* is commonly used as a capitalized title before the name or preceded by *the*, as in: *The campaign against the government was orchestrated largely by the exiled religious leader Ayatollah Ruholla Khomeini.* Americana Annual 1979, p262 *Those who know the Ayatullah expect that eventually he will settle in the Shi'ite holy city of Qum and resume a life of teaching and prayer.* Time 2/12/79, p39

Azania (əˈzeiniːə), *n.* the name given to South Africa by African nationalists. Compare ZIMBABWE. *It has become pretty obvious to us that these are crucial years in the history of Azania. The winds of liberation which have been sweeping down the face of Africa have reached our very borders.* NY Times 9/18/77, pD1 [**1976**, from the name of an Iron Age civilization that flourished in southern Africa from about A.D. 500 to about 1500] —**Azanian**, *n.: Representative [Charles C.] Diggs sometimes refers to South Africa by the name its indigenous would-be liberationists have given it—"Azania"—and he . . . began* to take the somewhat softer position that it might be all right for American companies already in South Africa to remain there, provided they share their profits with the majority of the South African people—which was, of course, black Azanians. New Yorker 5/14/79, p133

azidothymidine (ˌæzɑidouˈθɑimədin), *n.* an antiviral drug used in the treatment of AIDS. Also called ZIDOVUDINE. *While azidothymidine (trade name AZT) is the first drug shown to benefit AIDS victims, researchers . . . emphasized that it is not a cure.* Science News 9/27/86, p196 [**1986**]

AZT (ˌeiˌziːˈtiː), *n.* a trademark for AZIDOTHYMIDINE. *AZT appeared to extend the life of some AIDS patients.* 1987 World Book Year Book, p293 [**1986**, abbreviation of *azidothymidine*]

Aztec two-step, another name for MEXICALI REVENGE. *South of the border, it is* turista *or "the Aztec two-step." By any name, traveler's diarrhea, a debilitating digestive upset caused by a change in the system's bacterial population, is a synonym for misery that can spoil a trip and jeopardize the victim's health.* Time 5/22/72, p104 [**1970**]

B

Baathism or **Ba'athism** ('baː,θizəm), *n.* principles of the Baath political party of Syria and Iraq, promoting socialism and Arab nationalism. *Baathism, the ideological driving force for the regime, might win an appeal in an area which will undoubtedly suffer a series of political traumas in the coming years.* Times (London) 4/3/70, pX [**1963**, from *Baath* or *Ba'ath* (name of the party, literally, Renaissance) and *Baathist, adj., n.,* both 1955]

Baba ('baː,baː), *n.* **1** the title of a Hindu spiritual guide or guru. *After Nityananda died, in 1961, Muktananda began to let a few disciples live with him. "There were no special activities in those days," one of them told me. "We spent hours sitting with Baba, or helping him in the garden. In the afternoons he let us chant a little and we meditated on a porch outside his room."* Harper's 5/77, p86 **2** Often spelled **baba**, any guru or spiritual guide. *With the meditation melange has come a plethora of practitioners: experimental psychologists, mind researchers, masters, swamis, priestesses, gurus, babas and lamas.* New York Post 2/26/77, p23 [**1967**, from Hindi *bābā* (literally) father]

baboonery, *n.* a place where baboons are kept. *I found that, in addition to the baboonery in Texas, there are, among other things, . . . seven large Primate Centers under the auspices of the National Institutes of Health.* New Yorker 4/17/71, p48 [**1971**] ►An earlier meaning "a collection or colony of baboons," is given in the OED with a citation dated 1613. The usual meaning of this word since the 19th century is "baboonish condition or behavior."

baby-battering, *n.* the act or practice of inflicting harmful physical abuse on an infant or small child, usually by a parent. Compare CHILD BATTERING. See also BATTERED CHILD SYNDROME and CHILD ABUSE. *Baby-battering claims the lives of six children every week in England and Wales, and leaves 3,000 a year severely injured. A further 40,000 children suffer mild or moderate damage, but 400 every year suffer injuries causing chronic brain damage.* Times (London) 6/16/77, p4 [**1972**] —**baby-batterer:** *But "just the other night I screamed and screamed at him maybe for ten minutes without stopping. I shook him real hard and chucked him down in his cot and that made him cry all the more.". . . This is the stuff of which baby-batterers are made.* Times Literary Supplement 6/30/72, p742

baby boom, 1 the sudden great increase in the U.S. birth rate following World War II, especially between 1947 and 1961 (used chiefly in reference to the generation that came of age and joined the work force in the 1970's). *People who were born in the baby boom that started in the late forties and were educated in the late sixties are moving in a self-contained lump through American society, like a rat moving through the body of a python.* New Yorker 4/10/78, p120 **2** any great increase in a population's birth rate. *The Nazis encouraged a baby boom; Zero Population Growthers champion a baby bust. The philosophies of control underlying the goals of both groups are identical—and identically odious.* Saturday Review 4/8/72, p16 [**1941; 1967;** *boom* a sudden increase of activity, rapid growth or expansion (OED 1879)] ►Although historically the United States baby boom occurred in the late 1940's, the term *baby boom* became current during the 1970's according to the data in our files.

baby boomer, a person born in a baby boom; member of a baby-boom generation. Also called BOOM BABY. *We accept as normal the gross and permanent depletion of our oil and natural gas, diminished research in agriculture, an unemployable body of baby boomers, inner cities in decay.* Manchester Guardian Weekly (Washington Post section) 5/15/77, p17 [**1974**]

baby bust, a sudden decline in the birth rate. *The aging of the U.S. population is partly a result of the "baby bust" of the 1970's. Very low levels of fertility persisted during 1977, but the rates have begun to climb slightly. For the year ending June 30, 1978, the general fertility rate (the number of births per 1,000 women of childbearing age) was projected at 66.1, compared to 65.3 in 1976-1977.* 1978 Collier's Encyclopedia Year Book, p453 [**1971**, patterned on BABY BOOM]

BAC ('biː,ei'siː:), abbreviation of *blood alcohol concentration. In each sex, the highest BAC's were found in the 45- to 65-age groups.* Science News 3/18/72, p186 [**1964**]

BACAT (bæ'kæt), *n.* acronym for *barge aboard catamaran. The British Waterways Board was becoming heavily involved with Denmark in the development of a new barge-carrying vessel, designed largely for the European system. Known as the BACAT (barge aboard catamaran), it was to carry 18 450-ton barges designed for the European waterway system or, alternatively, 10 European barges and 3 of the larger 850-ton barges built under U.S. patents.* Britannica Book of the Year 1974, p690 [**1973**]

bachelorette, *n.* an unmarried girl or woman who lives independently. *Articles now offer tips on housework for the woman who hates housework, and describe the delights open to the "bachelorette" who has left her family and is in no hurry to get married.* Saturday Night (Canada) 11/65, p35 [**1961**, from *bachelor + -ette* (feminine suffix)]

back burner, on the back burner, in a secondary place; postponed as subordinate. Compare FRONT BURNER. *The first of the High Energy Astronomy Observatory satellites . . . resumed development earlier this year after being put on the back burner by NASA in January 1973.* Science News 8/10/74, p88 —**adj.** secondary; subordinate. *Integration has become a back-burner issue, by choice or hard political realism. The upfront concern now is to improve economic and social conditions for blacks in the urban ghettos and the rural backwaters—where most blacks are.* Newsweek 2/19/73, p33 [**1966; 1973**]

backcast, *v.t., v.i.* to describe something or some time in the past without having seen or experienced it, especially to reconstruct (past events) on the basis of study or other evidence. Compare HINDCAST. *If a model that is shown to be an adequate representation of a given historical period then cannot "backcast" that period, Meadows says, very reasonably, that testing by backcasting cannot then be judged significant.* New Scientist 3/8/73, p533 [**1961**, patterned after *forecast*]

back channel, U.S. a secret, clandestine, or irregular means of communicating. *The United States SALT delegation . . . didn't know that Nixon's national security adviser had set up a "back channel" and was making a deal or two on his own with the Russians.* NY Times Magazine 2/13/77, p23 [**1973**] ►The use derives from diplomatic jargon, in which reference is to channels other than the normal official diplomatic channels.

backcourtman, *n.* a basketball player who plays the backcourt and brings the ball out into the offensive zone. *Archibald also became the first guard to score more than 1,000 field goals—he had 1,028—and the first backcourtman in 17 years to lead the league in minutes played, with a total of 3,681.* 1974 Collier's Encyclopedia Year Book, p491 [**1967**, from *backcourt + man*]

back end, that part of the fuel cycle of a nuclear reactor in which the used fuel is reprocessed to separate usable uranium and plutonium from radioactive waste. *The Government has planned . . . a system for recycling plutonium fuel, and so put into effect a commercially operable breeder-reactor program* that would produce fuel as it generates power—the so-called "back end" of the fuel cycle. New Yorker 2/9/76, p48 [**1976**]

Backfire, n. or **Backfire bomber**, a supersonic intercontinental warplane developed by the Soviet Union, officially known as the Tupolev V-G (after Andrei N. Tupolev, 1888-1972, Soviet aircraft designer). *The first 25 long-range bombers known in the West as Backfires, swing-wing, Mach 2 aircraft capable of attacking targets anywhere in the United States, have been delivered to the Soviet Air Force.* NY Times 4/19/76, p7 *The problem is that weapons such as the new Soviet mobile medium-range missile, the SS-20, and the Backfire bomber do not fit into either the SALT talks, which deal with U.S. and Soviet strategic weapons, or the troop reduction talks, which deal mostly with conventional weapons.* Manchester Guardian Weekly (Washington Post section) 10/8/78, p15 [**1975**, from the NATO code name of this bomber]

backgrounder, n. *U.S.* a meeting or a memorandum for journalists in which a government official explains the background of a government action or policy. *Immediately after the White House briefing, Congressman Ford called in some reporters for a "backgrounder," in other words, a report to them as to what has happened for background purposes. A "backgrounder" permits newspapermen to publish information given them though without attribution to the source.* Tuscaloosa News 8/5/65, p4 [**1957**]

backlash, n. **1** *U.S.* a reaction of antagonism by whites to the pressure for racial integration exerted by the black civil-rights movement (often used attributively). Also called WHITE BACK-LASH. *Reaction had set in, of course, call it backlash or frontlash.* Harper's 1/67, p33 *If the potential backlash voter is a mixture, so are his motives. Some simply resent growing violence in the streets . . . Some feel threatened by Negroes moving into their neighborhoods, and their response is visceral.* NY Times 10/23/66, pD2 **2** any antagonistic reaction. *The law required the use of the French language in addition to English . . . It aroused a sensational, though temporary, backlash of English-speaking opinion, concentrated in Westmorland county, where the Canadian Loyalist Association has its headquarters.* Americana Annual 1970, p494 —v.i. to produce an antagonistic reaction. *What evidence is there that the public want to be matey with the famous instead of awestruck? The Wilson-Heath image of the clever Little Man is backlashing.* Punch 9/3/69, p392 [**1957**]

backmutate, v.i. *Genetics.* to mutate back to the original form. *. . . of all the mutations studied by Yanofsky it is the only one not to back-mutate or revert to "wild type."* Scientific American 10/66, p59 [**1964**, back formation from *back mutation* (1914)]

back-of-the-book, adj. *U.S.* of or relating to printed or broadcast material of general interest, such as developments in science, the arts, and education, as opposed to current world or national events. *The second major area of departure for ABC news is in so-called "back-of-the-book" stories: features, essays and interviews that focus on areas apart from the "official" hard news of press conferences, statistics and catastrophes.* NY Times Magazine 2/13/77, p34 [**1968**]

back-of-the-envelope or **back-of-an-envelope**, adj. quickly and easily determined; not requiring elaborate calculations. *But recycling has little to do with the problem I was raising, which is how one provides the capital stock of metals that would be required for cars in use. A simple back-of-the-envelope sum illustrates the problem.* New Scientist 12/6/73, p727 *The calculations themselves, Levine says, are easy. Back-of-an-envelope stuff. Thus it's a little strange, but apparently true, he says, that they've never before been published.* Science News 6/11/77, p380 [**1971**]

backproject, v.t. to project (an image) on the back of a translucent screen for viewing from the front. *A projector, the first designed specifically for shipboard installations, . . . backprojects a full-scale 42- × 36-inch colored image of a chart onto the underside of its transparent top.* Science News 10/22/66, p335 —n. a backprojected image. *Eva Schwartz's sets—light, ground-row [low, flat scenery] pieces against street*

back-projects encased in a vast gilt picture-frame—are witty and practical. Times (London) 4/28/70, p7 [**1961**]

backscatter, v.t. *Physics.* to scatter (rays or particles) backward by deflection. *Researchers . . . worked out a simple, nondestructive technique for measuring the strength of egg shells. They measure the number of beta-particles from a ruthenium-rhodium radioactive source, back-scattered by the egg shell.* New Scientist 5/21/70, p382 [**1958**, verb use of *backscatter, n.*, the scattering of rays or particles by an obstacle]

backstroke, v.i. to swim lying on one's back. *The '40s collage includes . . . . a likeable fantasy of America's post-war dreams—Esther Williams bathing beauties backstroking across the dry stage.* Time 3/18/74, p66 [**1970**, verb use of *backstroke, n.*] —**backstroker**, n.: *The American men won eight of their 15 swimming events, and they did it even though two of their stars—breast-stroker John Hencken of Santa Clara, Calif., and backstroker John Naber of Menlo Park, Calif.—passed up the meet.* 1976 World Book Year Book, p478

back-to-basics, adj. *Especially U.S.* of, characterized by, or advocating a return to the basic principles of religion, education, etc. *Disappointing test results have intensified the back-to-basics movement in education, which stresses reading, writing, and math in the lower grades.* Americana Annual 1976, p221 *Frank Freed and his daughter, Dolly, are advocates of a back-to-basics lifestyle that cost them less than $1,500 last year—total.* Today (New York) 6/12/79, pB3 [**1975**, from the phrase *back to (the) basics;* the phrase *the basics* is an Americanism (1950's) meaning the fundamentals or elementary principles]

bacteriocin (bæk,tiri:'ousən), n. any antibiotic effective against the same or closely related bacteria from which it is derived. *For example, the killing effects of certain bacteriocins on bacteria . . . may involve transmission and amplification of localized events over the entire surface of a membrane.* Science 2/18/72, p729 [**1967**, from *bacterio-* bacteria + *colicin,* a substance of this kind]

bacteriorhodopsin (bæk,tiri:ourou'dɑpsən), n. a protein capable of converting light energy into a useful form of cellular energy, found in the bacterium *Halobacterium halobium.* Other than the chlorophyll-based photosynthesis of plants, this is the only known cellular system that converts light to life-sustaining energy. *Walther Stoeckenius and colleagues discovered a purple, light-absorbing pigment protein similar in structure to rhodopsin, the visual pigment in animal retinas. They named the protein "bacteriorhodopsin." This membrane pigment can capture light energy, store it chemically, and use it to drive metabolic processes. This finding may shed light on the evolution of vision and provide a harnessable system for large-scale energy production.* Americana Annual 1977, p117 [**1976**, from *bacterio-* bacteria + *rhodopsin* visual purple (from Greek *rhódon* rose + *ópsis* sight + English *-in*)]

bad, adj. *U.S. Slang, Chiefly (and originally) Black English.* good; admirable; excellent. *"Our differences are complementary. Bullins is a bad dude. There's no better playwright in the American theatre today."* New Yorker 6/16/73, p52 *It was, said the "baddest" heavyweight champion of the world, "like being in the middle of a rainbow knowing that at the end there's a pot of money waiting."* NY Times 1/26/79, pA11 [**1971**] ► The use of *bad* (and of its usual superlative *baddest*) to mean "good" surfaced about 1970, although it was fairly common among black jazzmen during the 1950's (See Robert S. Gold, *A Jazz Lexicon,* 1964). The impetus behind the usage was probably a wish to defy the conventional expression of approval and to conceal the intended meaning from outsiders, either nonblacks or nonjazzmen. Clarence Major, in his *Dictionary of Afro-American Slang* (1970), defines *bad* as "a simple reversal of the white standard, the very best." However, the Africanist David Dalby tentatively traces the usage back to an African origin, citing the frequent use of negative terms to describe positive extremes in various African languages. (See "The African Element in American English" by David Dalby, in *Rappin' and Stylin' Out,* ed. Thomas Kochman, 1972, p. 170.) Whatever its origins, the usage entered the mainstream of general American slang, and in *The Underground Dic-*

tionary (1971), Eugene E. Landy states (without reference to blacks) that it "Can be either positive or negative—e.g. A *bad* scene can mean an unfortunate experience or a very good experience."

bad actor, *U.S.* a chemical, plant, etc. found or thought to be harmful. *In addition to desirable nutrients, the sludge contains some "bad actors"—heavy metals like chromium and nickel that could accumulate to levels toxic to plants, and elements like arsenic, mercury and cadmium that are potentially toxic to man and animals.* NY Times 7/9/76, pA9 *Bad actors in the pea family (Fabaceae) include the rosary pea (Abrus precatorius), one of the most poisonous plants known.* Encyclopedia Science Supplement (Grolier) 1979, p85 [**1976**, extended sense of the U.S. slang term (1940's) for a mean, troublesome person or animal]

bad-mouth, *v.t. U.S. Slang.* to malign; slander. *Black American expressions like "be with it," "do your thing" and "bad-mouth" (to talk badly about someone) are word for word translations from phrases used widely in West African languages, including Mandingo.* NY Times 11/10/70, p47 *Then the spurned client goes around bad-mouthing Lawyer Burnett: 'Don't hire Burnett because the son-of-a-bitch won't sue. He's bought off.'* Harper's 7/69, p72 [**1941**, U.S. dialect; **1965**]

bad news, *U.S.* something or someone disturbing, troublesome, or undesirable. . . . *"I knew the kid was bad news first morning I met him, sipping Angie's coffee."* New Yorker 4/10/71, p148 [**1970**]

bad trip, *Slang.* a frightening experience involving hallucinations, pain, etc., caused by taking a psychedelic drug, especially LSD. Compare ACID TRIP. Also called BUMMER. *Kids on bad trips were treated by volunteer physicians, and were urged over a makeshift public-address system to "bring a few joints [marijuana cigarettes] for the doctors."* Time 8/10/70, p11 [**1967**]

bag, *n. U.S. Slang.* **1** one's principal interest or habit. *Black Studies is not my bag. But doesn't it approach the ridiculous to say or imply that black students are "proposing to study black history in isolation from the mainstream of American history?"* Harper's 4/70, p6 [**1962**] **2** a situation, matter, or problem. *"Let's take his pants down," I said to Bobby. He looked at me. "God damn phraseology," I said. "We're in another bag now, baby. Get his pants off him, and see if you can tell how bad he's hurt . . ."* Atlantic 2/70, p98 [**1967**] **3** a portion of a narcotic drug or the envelope containing it. *In the argot of the drug world, it is "paraphernalia": the necessary accouterments to merchandising heroin. The small glassine envelopes or "bags," used to package heroin, are paraphernalia. So, too, are the legal, harmless powders used to dilute the drug, usually quinine, dextrose, lactose or mannite.* Time 7/20/70, p15 *A typical bag of heroin purchased on the street ordinarily contains only from 0% to 5% heroin.* Americana Annual 1970, p486 [**1963**]

bagelino, *n. U.S.* a cross between a bagel and a pretzel, usually covered with sesame seeds. *For those who follow the fashions in sidewalk vending, frozen yogurt and bagelinos made their debut last year.* NY Times 5/25/83, pC9 [**1983**, from *bagel* + *-ino* (diminutive, from Italian), as in *bambino*]

baggie, *n.* **1** a plastic bag used to store food or to hold trash. *"We're talking about using big baggies that look like sausages, and we'd move them 1,200 miles," said Chris G. Tofalli, a Grace spokesman. "We've taken a little ribbing about it."* NY Times 3/13/83, pE3 **2 Baggie.** a trademark for such a bag. *In fact, if you are an average gold hoarder—30 oz. in 1 oz. bullion coins is a common holding—there's probably no harm in dropping your hoard into a Baggie and stuffing it in your safe-deposit box.* Business Week 11/8/82, p136 [**1975**]

baggys, *n.pl U.S.* baggy shorts, such as boxers wear, used by male surfers. Compare JAMS (def. 2). . . . *among their boyfriends "baggys" (loose-fitting swim trunks) were de rigueur.* NY Times 8/10/65, p31 [**1963**]

bag job, *U.S. Slang.* an illegal search for evidence of espionage. *He [J. Edgar Hoover] also banned what intelligence called "surreptitious entry"—meaning burglary—and a companion*

tactic, the *"bag job,"* in which agents enter a home or office and examine or copy documents, personal papers or notebooks. *In the past, numerous spies—notably Rudolf Abel—have been exposed by bag jobs.* Time 10/25/71, p31 [**1971**]

bag lady, *U.S.* short for SHOPPING BAG LADY. *In truth, bag ladies have a great deal of pride and dignity in spite of their disarray. They have chosen the agony of doorway life rather than the far worse agony of being forced to beg and grovel on their knees for assistance from city agencies supposedly designed to help people in trouble, but which in fact destroy them.* New York Post 2/5/79, p22 [**1975**]

bagman, *n. Canadian Slang.* a person who directs finances in a political campaign. *A confidential memo from the party's chief bagman, Toronto lawyer Patrick Vernon, indicated the PCs* [Progressive Conservatives] *will have to somehow find a way eventually to pay off a further $400,000 still owing on old loans.* Maclean's 2/23/76, p17 [**1976**, probably transferred from the U.S. Slang sense of a person who collects and distributes graft or protection money]

Bahasa Malay or **Bahasa Malaysia** (bɑːˈhɑːsə), the Malay dialect adopted as the official language of Malaysia. *In response to demands for increased special concessions to Malaysians, the Malay Chinese Association (MCA) finally agreed to accept Bahasa Malay as the national language.* 1972 World Book Year Book, p422 *These are the two points Malaysia's education and language authorities have continually to bear in mind in effecting the change from English to Bahasa Malaysia (modern Malay) as the main medium of instruction.* Times (London) 8/31/77, pVI [**1969**, from Malay *bahasa* language, from Sanskrit *bhāṣā*]

bailout, *n.* an emergency rescue or relief, especially through financial aid. *Very soon we may have the Securities Investor Protection Corporation, but a bailout with government funds does not supply a satisfactory long-term solution. A tighter pattern of rules and enforcement is sorely needed.* NY Times 12/21/70, p35 [**1970**, from the verb phrase *bail out* to help out or rescue] ▶*Bailout* is recorded only in the sense of bailing out or parachuting from an aircraft in an emergency.

bait-and-switch, *adj. U.S.* designed to induce customers to purchase a more expensive item than the one advertised at a much lower price. *The Competition Act also makes it a criminal offence to engage in misleading advertising, unfair pyramid selling, bait-and-switch selling (plain switch selling in Britain) . . .* Sunday Times (London) 7/11/71, p40 [**1965**]

Baker-Nunn camera, a large telescopic camera for photographing orbiting satellites as part of an optical network for tracking satellites. *Anderle's paper, in particular, discusses the reduction of observations of satellites by worldwide networks of Baker-Nunn cameras . . .* Science 4/12/68, p177 [**1964**, named after James Gilbert *Baker* and Joseph *Nunn*, American inventors of optical instruments who designed the camera, first used in 1957]

bakkie (ˈbaːkiː), *n.* (in South Africa) a small, light van with an open back, used especially by farmers. *Another nasty moment came between Jamestown and Sterkspruit when the "bakkie" had a puncture and it seemed to take us ages to change the wheel.* NY Times 1/8/78, pD19 [**1971**, from Afrikaans, from *bak* container + *-kie* (diminutive suffix)]

BAL (ˌbiːˌeiˈel), abbreviation of *blood alcohol level. A person of Prefontaine's slight build would have his "driving impaired" if his BAL was in the range of .05 to .07 per cent. He would have reached that low level of intoxication by drinking either three shots of liquor or three glasses of beer within a 2-hour period.* Manchester Guardian Weekly (Washington Post section) 8/15/76, p16 [**1976**]

balance of terror, **1** distribution of nuclear power among nations, serving as a deterrent to the use of nuclear weapons. *To achieve a more stable balance of terror at existing nuclear levels, the negotiators at Moscow signed two nuclear arms pacts, one limiting the installation of antiballistic missiles to two locations in each country, the other freezing offensive weapons at current levels for five years, ensuring numerical su-*

periority for Soviet missiles. 1973 Collier's Encyclopedia Year Book, p588 **2** the ability of a group to exert a dominant influence through the use of brute power. *By "a healthy atmosphere" they [teachers] seemed to mean a balance of terror, with unruly students held in check by the spectre of paddles stockpiled in the principal's office.* New Yorker 5/30/77, p27 **[1955]** ►In the sense of definition 1, this term first appeared in the 1950's as the atomic-age analogue of the much earlier (1701) military-political term *balance of power*, though the mere fact of distribution seems to have overshadowed the older concept of "parity" associated with *balance of power*.

Balance of terror was only sporadically used until the mid-1960's, when nuclear armament became a matter of stockpiling weapons and developing sophisticated missile delivery systems, and atomic bombs began to proliferate among smaller nations. In the following early quotation, the attribution of the term to Churchill is erroneous; the phrase he used in his famous "Iron Curtain" speech of 1946 was "balance of power," which he described as precarious unless security was achieved through U.S.-British cooperation. *Even without any system of international control whatsoever, the danger of nuclear weapons being used is not very great, because of the risk involved for the aggressor in attempting a total knockout blow. But this kind of security—was it Churchill who first called it a "balance of terror"?—is not likely to appeal to mankind indefinitely.* Bulletin of the Atomic Scientists 12/55, p359

balancing act, an act or endeavor requiring careful balancing of opposite forces; a precarious action or undertaking. *In a prodigious balancing act Bob Fosse, the choreographer-director, keeps the period—Berlin, 1931—at a cool distance. We see the decadence as garish and sleazy, yet we also see the animal energy in it—everything seems to become sexualized.* New Yorker, 2/4/80, p20 **[1968, used in allusion to a circus act]**

balatik or **balatic**, *n.* a trap for wild game used in the Philippines. *We checked three balatiks and four deadfall monkey traps, all empty. No one seemed surprised. Animal kills obviously, were rare, and meat no more than a luxury.* National Geographic Magazine 8/72, p245 *The* balatic, *which is known to probably all Filipino peoples, is without question the most effective trap for obtaining wild pigs and deer; it is a bow device that shoots an arrow across the paths of pigs and deer when they have struck a trip cord.* Encyclopedia Science Supplement (Grolier) 1972, p303 **[1972, from the native name]**

ball¹, *n.* **run with the ball,** U.S. Informal. to take up and carry forward an enterprise, venture, or the like. *A 5-year federally funded American FPC [fish protein concentrate] program in Washington State recently ended when Congress declined to extend the experimental period. Even so, the technology developed has not been wasted, says Dr. Bruce Stillings of the National Marine Fisheries Service. Federal approval may still be forthcoming at a later date, and "private industry might choose to run with the ball," he says.* Encyclopedia Science Supplement (Grolier) 1973, p111 **[1971, figurative use of the sports term (especially in U.S. football) meaning to advance in an attempt to score]**

ball², *v.i., v.t.* U.S. Slang *(vulgar use).* to have sexual intercourse (with). *"What's different now," said a Haight [Haight-Ashbury] section of San Francisco] dope peddler, "is that speed's better than it used to be. There's not so much amphetamine poisoning and you can ball on it, which you could never do before . . .* Manchester Guardian Weekly 5/2/70, p16 *Its [the book's] tone is True Romance, with pulpish purple passages such as "the two of us were in love with, and occasionally balling the same silver-tongued devil of a man."* Atlantic 9/73, p108 **[1969** (but used in jazz circles since the 1950's, extended sense of *ball, v.,* to have a ball, have a good time (1940's), probably influenced by *ball, n.,* vulgar slang for a testis (used since the 1300's)]

ball game, U.S. Slang. **1** a center or field of action. *"Most of the news in the papers we [television news broadcasters] cannot cover and we will never be able to. When it comes to covering the news in any kind of detailed way, we are just almost not in the ball game."* Saturday Review 10/10/70, p55 **[1963] 2** a state of affairs; situation. . . . *if an invasion took place the Chinese might enter the war. If this were to happen, some official*

of our government would no doubt announce that we were in a "whole new ballgame," which would mean that none of the policies or promises made in the past were binding any longer, including the prohibition against the use of nuclear weapons. New Yorker 3/13/71, p30 **[1967]**

ball of wax, U.S. Slang. sort of thing; matter of interest. Compare **the whole ball of wax** under WAX. *"It's pretty much a business operation," says airline analyst Raymond Neidl. "If he glitzes it up too much, the average guy will say, 'That's not my ball of wax.'"* Time 10/24/88, p73 **[1969]** ►See the note under YARD.

balloon, *n.* **like a lead balloon,** without the slightest effect. *So Nixon said it. And then went on to say, what nobody has ever quarreled with, that the time had come 'to move mankind from an era of confrontation into an era of negotiation'. A short pause for loud and prolonged cheers. I don't know whether they came, but even this magnificent cliché fell on the ears of Marshal Tito like a lead balloon.* Listener 10/8/70, p475 **[1970]**

balloon astronomy, the collection of astronomical data from photographs, etc., taken at high altitude through a telescope attached to a balloon. *Martin Schwarzschild, "father of balloon astronomy," was awarded the 1967 Albert A. Michelson Award by Case Institute of Technology of Case-Western Reserve University, Cleveland, O . . . He was cited for "leadership in the theory of stellar evolution, and for pioneering application of balloon-borne telescopes for observations of the sun, stars, and planets."* 1969 Britannica Yearbook of Science and the Future, p257 **[1965]**

balloon pump, a device consisting of a balloon and a synchronizing pump that is attached to the line connecting the heart-lung machine and the aorta, used to convert the continuous flow of blood from the machine to a pulsating flow. *In 1975, Dr. David Bregman of Columbia-Presbyterian Medical Center in New York City reported having developed an external balloon pump which avoids the risks inherent in placing the balloon in the aorta . . . As a result, the body is better supplied with blood while the patient is on the pump.* World Book Science Annual 1977, p304 **[1976; the device has been in use since 1967]**

ballotini (ˌbæləˈtiːniː), *n.pl.* tiny particles or beads of glass, used in industry as a grinding medium and for other purposes. *In the US especially, experiments using cullet in the manufacture of road surfaces (glasphalt), tiles, ballotini (reflective glass beads in paints for road signs), and glass reinforced plastics have been reasonably successful.* New Scientist 11/29/73, p627 **[1965,** probably from Italian *ballottini,* plural of *ballottino,* diminutive of *ballotta* small ball, from *balla* ball]

ball park, U.S. the general or approximate area of an estimate (usually in the phrase **in the ball park**). *Dr. Henry C. Huntley, director of the U.S. Public Health Service's Division of Emergency Health Services, emphasizes that "We can save lives with adequately equipped ambulances and properly trained personnel. It may be 50,000 or 75,000, but a figure of 60,000 is in the right ball park."* Saturday Review 5/13/72, p59 **[1960,** transferred use of the term for a baseball field]

ball-park figure, U.S. a rough estimate; an approximate figure. *Some ball-park figures on two-year leases: up to $250 monthly for a full-size luxury car, $80 to $90 for a compact.* Woman's Day 7/73, p80 *"If you recall, I didn't give you an 'estimate.' I gave you a 'ballpark figure.'"* New Yorker 4/10/78, p33 **[1967;** see BALL PARK]

ballsy, *adj.* U.S. Slang. cockily aggressive; robust; tough. *But [Gordon] Parks insists that Shaft—"a ballsy guy, to hell with everybody, he goes out and does his thing"—was an important symbol for the black community.* Time 4/10/72, p53 *Jane [Fonda]. Dressed à la chinoise. Still, a star. The only star they have. But it's wrong: The ballsy, broad voice seems hesitant and confused.* National Review 11/23/73, p1303 **[1959,** from *balls, n.pl.,* vulgar slang for testes]

ballute, *n.* a combination balloon and parachute used for deceleration. *The attraction of the Woomera range is that recovery* *can be made on land. After being decelerated by 'ballute', a type of drag balloon, the test model would be soft-landed either by parachute or an extensible rotor.* Science Journal 12/70, p10 [**1960,** from *balloon* + parach*ute*]

Balmer lines, *Physics.* lines of hydrogen in the visible region of the spectrum. *Balmer lines in the visible portion of the hydrogen spectrum indicate that the principal constituent of the interstellar medium is hydrogen. The lines are produced when the single electron of the hydrogen atom cascades down to the second energy level of the atom.* Scientific American 8/72, p53 [**1965,** named after Johann *Balmer,* 1825-1898, a Swiss physicist, who in 1885 worked out a formula by which the wavelength of any of these lines may be calculated. This term has largely replaced the earlier *Balmer series.*]

ban , in South Africa: *v.t.* to bar from writing or speaking publicly or engaging in political activity (applied to any person or organization officially regarded as a threat to law and order, especially under the Internal Security Act of 1977). *A person who is banned cannot meet with more than one person at a time except for his immediate family. He cannot write anything for publication and he cannot be quoted, publicly or in print, even after he is dead.* NY Times 10/27/77, pA8 **—n.** an act of banning or the condition of being banned. *Woods now has time, lots of time. He is forbidden to write at all, even in a private diary. The government is watching: as part of the ban, the Woodses have been informed that their home, their phones, even their two cars are bugged. Plainclothesmen keep their house under surveillance.* Time 11/7/77, p38 [**1966,** specialized sense of *ban* to forbid, prohibit (OED 1816)] **—banning,** *n.: The death in detention of the black activist, Steven Biko, in September 1977 brought an outraged international response to which the authorities reacted with widespread banning and detentions on October 19.* Manchester Guardian Weekly 10/1/78, p8

Banaban (ˈbɑːnəbən), *n.* a native or inhabitant of Ocean Island, an atoll in the western Pacific noted for its rich phosphate deposits. It is one of the Gilbert Islands. *The Banabans have not accepted a £6.5 millions offer from the British Government in compensation for exploitation of their Pacific island and are preparing for a new fight. They will continue to fight both for higher compensation and the independence of their island.* Manchester Guardian Weekly 6/5/77, p4 **—adj.** of or relating to these people or their island. *The British government announced an exgratia payment of U.S. $11 million to the 2,500 Banabans now living on Rabi Island, in Fiji, as a final settlement of Banaban claims.* Americana Annual 1978, p383 [**1967,** from the original name of the atoll]

Banach space (ˈbɑːnɑːx), *Mathematics.* a geometric configuration of space, used in function analysis to show varying relationships among interdependent values. Compare HILBERT SPACE. *Specialists in the field of Banach spaces were gratified by the solution of one of the oldest problems in the subject. These spaces had been invented by the Polish mathematician S. Banach as a vehicle for the study of functional analysis.* Britannica Book of the Year 1972, p447 [**1963,** named after Stefan *Banach,* 1892-1945, a Polish mathematician who devised an algebra of such spaces]

banalization, *n.* the act of making banal; reduction of something to the trite or ordinary. *Surely, the most serious trivialization and banalization of the Third is Test Match Special, which next week once again forces adult interests off the air in favour of schoolboy stuff.* Times (London) 6/5/72, p15 [**1968,** from *banalize* + *-ation*]

banalize, *v.t.* to make banal; reduce to something commonplace or ordinary. *The great and good traditional virtues have been eroded: love, generosity, self-denial, truthfulness, honesty, loyalty, friendship, kindness to children. That many of these traits have been banalized by advertising seems incidental.* Scientific American 5/64, p140 [**1949; 1960**]

banana, *adj.* denoting or belonging to any small country, especially in Central America, whose entire economy is based on the export of a single agricultural commodity, such as bananas or other fruit. *If we didn't get into the Common Market, I think*

that, try as we might, we would sink into the state of a third-rate banana country. Listener 5/18/72, p652 *The CIA began by handing out bribes to tropical politicians and banana generals in the Fifties.* Harper's 11/73, p78 [**1971,** abstracted from *banana republic* (1935)] **—n.** *U.S. Slang.* a derogatory name for an Oriental who is part of the white establishment or is in favor of working within the white establishment. *In the San Francisco Bay area, with a large population of Japanese-Americans and many militants, young protesters have picketed S. I. Hayakawa, the president of San Francisco State College who is a steadfast believer in assimilation, calling him a "banana"—yellow on the outside, white inside—the equivalent of the blacks' epithet "Oreo."* Wall Street Journal 8/8/72, p9 [**1972**]

banana belt, *U.S. Slang.* a winter resort whose climate is considered comparatively mild. *Skiers enjoying the sport at some of the giant-sized areas in New England and upper New York have cause to thank this southern Catskill Mountain country—often joshingly referred to as "The Banana Belt." For it was in this Sullivan County region that machine-made snow was first produced on a practical basis.* NY Times 1/6/77, p34 [**1963** (originally applied on Baffin Island to mainland North America), because the region (*belt*) is considered warm enough to grow *bananas*]

bananas, *adj.* **go bananas,** *U.S. Slang.* to go crazy. . . . *Liza* [Liza Minnelli] *moved into the sheltered regimented Barbizon Hotel for Women. Liza says: "I went bananas!"* Time 3/9/70, p43 [**1964**]

banana seat, a kind of long, upward-curving seat on a child's bicycle. *"High-rise" handlebars, which force a small child to steer with elbows at chinlevel, and the long, narrow "banana" seats, which invite additional passengers, are major contributors to instability—and may cause additional accidents.* Reader's Digest 8/74 (page not known) [**1972**]

band, *v.t.* British, *Education.* to group (pupils) according to level of their scholastic ability to achieve distribution in enrollment. *The Inner London Education Authority's system of "banding" children being transferred from primary to secondary school, may be made illegal under the Education Bill. Children are "banded" as above average, average and below average.* Times (London) 1/31/76, p1 [**1976,** back formation from *banding* (1970)] **—banding,** *n.: Banding is a form of selection used in some areas to ensure an even spread of abilities in the intake of comprehensive schools . . . but the amendment does not permit the introduction of any new banding arrangements.* Times (London) 11/23/76, p2

band-aid, *adj. U.S.* patched up or put together hastily; serving as a stop-gap; temporary. *The American feeling is probably that quick "fire brigade" action is not enough and better and better economic coordination might prevent the need for such heavy reliance on financial "band-aid" solutions.* Times (London) 4/20/70, p19 [**1968,** generic use of *Band-Aid,* trade name for a prepared adhesive bandage]

B & D or **B and D,** abbreviation of *bondage and discipline* (or *domination*). *One of the things that fascinated me about these ads is that through them there runs, like a litany, the statement "No S. & M. or B. & D."* NY Times Magazine 6/4/72, pF19 . . . *among the 120 contributors is history professor Edward Shorter . . . telling us that B and D (bondage and domination) are now In.* Maclean's 10/1/79, p64 [**1970**]

bandgap, *n. Physics.* a difference between two allowed bands of electron energy; an energy range of electrons over which no quantum states are allowed. *Depending on the magnitude of the bandgaps . . . a solid may be an insulator, semiconductor, or metal. For a solid to exhibit the properties of a semiconductor or an insulator, bandgaps must exist in all directions of electron motion.* 1978 Britannica Yearbook of Science and the Future, p387 [**1962,** from electron *band* + *gap*]

bandh (bɑːnd), *n.* (in India) a general suspension of work and business as an act of protest. Compare GHERAO. *Life was at a standstill in West Bengal today as people stayed away from work in response to a call by leftist parties for a 24-hour bandh*

. . . Times (London) 7/15/70, p6 [**1966,** from Hindi *bāndh* a stop]

bandhnu ('bɑːndnuː), *n.* tie-dyeing (in which parts of the fabric are tied off so that they will not be colored). *The art is almost as old as India—where it is called bandhnu. It is as new as the boutiques that blossom along Sunset Strip and Madison Avenue—where it is called tie-dyeing.* Time 1/26/70, p40 [**1970,** from Hindi *bāndhnū,* from *bāndhnā* to tie]

banger, *n. Slang.* a noisy, old vehicle. *The Illustrated One, at ease astride his ancient Harley two-stroke banger . . .* New Yorker 3/14/70, p33 *A system that allows him to pass his test one day in a 10-year-old "banger" and climb straight into a 150 mph Jaguar the next is the height of dangerous folly.* Sunday Times (London) 2/5/67, p17 [**1962**]

Bangladeshi (ˌbæŋgləˈdeʃiː), *n., pl.* **-deshis** or **-deshi.** a native of Bangladesh, formerly the province of East Pakistan, and since 1971 an independent nation. *There are also 1,600 Pakistanis, who earn a basic £14.69 a month and 1,000 Bangladeshi, earning £16.73 a month.* Times (London) 5/9/73, p2 *Such predictions, of course, are almost timeless, too. Bangladeshis made them themselves a decade ago—protesting against Pakistani domination.* Manchester Guardian Weekly 11/9/74, p5 —*adj.* of Bangladesh or its people. *Pakistan returned the Bangladeshi civilians who had been detained in Pakistan after the war.* Annual Register of World Events in 1974, p296 [**1971,** from Bengali *Bangla Desh,* Bengal Nation]

bang stick, a weapon used by a diver against an attacking shark or other marine animal. It consists of a stick loaded at the end with an explosive charge that fires on impact. *"Suddenly five or six huge grey sharks came churning up from the bottom and several more raced in from the shallows," recalls Alan Emery, a marine scientist . . . "I really thought my time was up because the guy riding shotgun for me panicked and took off. And he took the bang stick (a weapon with a magnum shell at the end which explodes when poked broadside into a shark)."* Maclean's 1/22/79, p39 [**1976**]

banjax, *v.t. Slang.* to hit, beat, or overcome. *Ha-ha, so she ups and banjaxed the old man one night with a broken spade handle, and robbed him of his four rattling pennies in a tin and made off out of the clutter.* New Yorker 10/28/72, p40 *O'Toole brought with him a new, free "version" of the play which translates it verbally from Czarist Russia to the Ireland of Brendan Behan. "Well, I'm banjaxed!" cries Vanya on learning that his monstrous brother-in-law plans to sell the family estate from under the family.* Maclean's 10/9/78, p70 [**1939; 1970,** apparently from dialectal Irish; origin uncertain]

bankable, *adj.* certain to produce box-office success and profits. *At 37, Pacino has become a "bankable" superstar, whose commitment to a project means that a film will be made and will be guaranteed a certain success.* NY Times Magazine 6/5/77, p21 [**1958,** extended from the earlier sense (OEDS 1818) of acceptable at or by a bank; influenced by the requirement of some banks that filmmakers include a famous star in any film venture to be financially backed by them] —**bankability,** *n.: In the secret and all-powerful Q Ratings that are researched for TV networks to determine a performer's appeal—and ultimately his bankability in a series—Rich Little . . . calibrated right up there in third spot.* Maclean's 2/9/76, p32

bank card, a credit card issued by a bank. *Development of existing bank cards—including both cheque guarantee cards and credit cards as we know them today—will play a major role in the advance towards a "cashless and chequeless society."* New Scientist 7/23/70, p181 [**1967**]

barb, *n. U.S. Informal.* short for *barbiturate. But there is no question that "barbs" are reaching the very young—in high school, junior high and even earlier. Several reasons are given. Barbs are cheaper than heroin—only $1 for five pills in most places—and not as detectable as marijuana, the smell of which is known to most school teachers.* NY Times 6/4/72, pD7 [**1972**]

barbie, *n. Informal.* short for *barbecue. "Aussiephilia" . . . began in 1983 with Australia's victory in the America's Cup yacht races and the Australian Tourist Commission's entrancing campaign in which Paul Hogan made "G'day, mate" and "Put another shrimp on the barbie" part of the American vernacular.* New York Magazine 3/21/88, p26 [**1976**]

Barcelona chair, a stainless steel chair with leather cushions and usually without arms. Compare EAMES CHAIR. *The furniture, simple and usually entirely machine made, ranges from the modern classics—the Barcelona chair, the Wassily chair, the Eames lounge chair and ottoman—to inexpensive, down-to-earth pieces such as the director's chair, some of the bentwood styles, and cubes and cylinders in place of small tables.* 1974 Collier's Encyclopedia Year Book, p294 [**1965,** originally exhibited in *Barcelona* in 1929 by Ludwig Mies van der Rohe, its designer]

bar code, **1** a code of lines and numbers printed on a packaged product for identification by an optical scanner. Compare UNIVERSAL PRODUCT CODE. *Large bar code labels—like the one shown here—will soon be appearing on nearly all supermarket items as part of an attempt to speed the changeover to electronic cash registers. With the labels, the shop assistant simply passes a handheld scanner over the code and the price of the item is automatically pulled out of a minicomputer memory.* New Scientist 5/24/73, p498 **2** Also, **bar-code,** *v.* to furnish with such a code. *The Council of Periodical Distributors has asked mass market publishers to . . . "bar code" their books, so that distributors will be able to provide sales and returns information to publishers with greater speed.* Publishers Weekly 4/10/78, p36 [**1973**] —**bar-coded,** *adj.: By using a series of "light pens" (similar to those already used in retail outlets) bar-coded information on labels attached to pathology specimens and, later, on X-ray details can all be read into the machine without any additional work.* Times (London) 6/8/76, p11

bare, *adj.* **go bare,** *U.S.* to carry no insurance against claims of malpractice, product liability, etc. *An increasing number of companies are "going bare," dropping coverage altogether.* Time 2/20/78, p65 *So absurd has the situation become that some doctors are opting out, transferring all their assets to their wives and "going bare," that is stating that there is no point in sueing them because they have neither insurance nor personal assets.* Manchester Guardian Weekly 2/26/78, p19 [**1976**]

barefoot, *adv. U.S. Slang.* within legal limits of CB (citizens band) radio transmission power. Compare APPLE, def. 2. *"While a lot of people like to use linear amplifiers . . . I run as 'barefoot' as they come," said Gary. "Let's face it, anyone can blast out by using 500 to 1000 watts of power, but as far as I can see, when you 'walk all over' everybody, you're destroying their right to talk."* "Personal Comment on Linears," CB Guide, 5/76, p69 [**1976,** so called because BOOTS is CB slang for an illegal linear amplifier that boosts transmission power, hence *barefoot* without such an amplifier]

barefoot doctor, a worker trained as a medical auxiliary and sent to rural areas to perform services such as assisting at childbirth, dispensing medication, and administering first aid. Also (officially translated) PRIMARY HEALTH WORKER. Compare RED GUARD DOCTOR. *The October 1974 issue of the* Chinese Medical Journal *reports that a million "barefoot doctors"—that is, doctors' assistants—have been sent into China's rural areas.* Science News 3/1/75, p141 *The World Health Organisation has pioneered experiments in many countries with health structures based on the primary health worker, better known as the barefoot doctor.* Manchester Guardian Weekly 1/1/78, p9 [**1970,** translation of Chinese *chijiao yisheng*]
►The term referred originally to Chinese medical auxiliaries and derives from the fact that many of them were peasants trained during the slack farming season under an expanded rural health program; peasants trained for other services were referred to as *barefoot specialists,* as in the following early quotation: *Specialists were put to work on improving seed strains and treating plant diseases. One important feature of these activities was that urban specialists were used not only to per-*

form tasks but also to train farmers in the basic skills. These semitrained personnel, or "barefoot specialists," then played a central role in implementing the rural development programs. 1971 Collier's Encyclopedia Year Book, p169

barf, *v.i. U.S. Slang.* to vomit. *One of the guards hooted above the noise of the plane engines, "Hang on, sweethearts!" Then he leaned over to me and said. "Hope none of 'em barfs." I asked if they would be allowed to remove their sacks if they became sick.* Atlantic 1/68, p30 [**1960,** probably imitative of the sound of retching]

bargaining chip, something that can be used to gain an advantage or bring about a concession. *Hitherto the revenue-sharing proposals have helped the U.S. in its role as purported world leader; moreover, they are a bargaining chip in dealing with some developing countries who, under revenue sharing, would stand to benefit.* Science 1/25/74, p292 *One side has argued that we should proceed to develop weapons that could be used as "bargaining chips" in negotiations, and it cites the antiballistic-missile treaty as a successful example of this approach.* New Yorker 4/4/77, p102 [**1965**] Also shortened to CHIP. ▶The use became prominent during the SALT I negotiations in which various details of the arms programs of the superpowers served as bargaining chips. The phrase derives from gambling chips, used in counting points or to represent money. See DETENTE.

bargello (bar'dʒɛlou), *n., pl.* **-loes;** *v.,* **-loed, -loing.** *n.* an upright stitch used in needlework to produce zigzag or oblique lines. *The store also sells material for bargello, an Italian geometric pattern, and crewel embroidery material will be added.* The News (Mexico City) (Supplement) Week ending 4/28/73, p1-C *—v.i., v.t.* to use this stitch; make such stitches on canvas. *To demonstrate his find, he opened a desk drawer and pulled out a canvas that was in the midst of being bargelloed; it was attached to a smooth birch easel that seemed to have its leg folded beneath it.* Harper's 3/74, p99 [**1972,** named for *Bargello,* a museum of sculpture in Florence, Italy]

bariatrician, *n.* a specialist in bariatrics. *One East Coast bariatrician orders his pills in batches of between 500,000 and 1,000,000* . . . Punch 2/1/67, p153 [**1967**]

bariatrics, *n.* the medical treatment of overweight people. . . . *the booming business of weight-doctoring (called bariatrics by its practitioners) is endangering the health of the country because the drugs used may have nasty side-effects.* Punch 2/1/67, p153 [**1967,** from *bar-* weight (from Greek *báros*) + *-iatrics,* as in *geriatrics*]

bar mitzvah, to confirm (a 13-year-old Jewish boy) in the Synagogue. *". . . I'd just been bar mitzvahed when I went off with my brother to pitch snake oil on the Pennsylvania carnival circuit."* Time 5/4/70, p74 [**1963,** verb use of the noun phrase. The verb exists only in English; the original Hebrew (or Yiddish) term does not function as a verb.]

barnburner, *n. U.S. Slang.* a noteworthy condition, situation, or event. *"We had so many requests for reservations by would-be visitors to the People's Republic that we expected it would develop into a real 'barnburner,'" said Mr. Gilmer.* NY Times 1/25/76, pC24 [**1934; 1960;** originally dialectal; later, a term in the game of bridge]

barococo (bə,roukə'kou), *adj.* combining the baroque and rococo styles; grotesquely elaborate. *He* [Hal Prince, a producer] *discovered what came to be the show's essential conception in Eliot Elisofon's picture of Gloria Swanson amid the ruins of Manhattan's Roxy Theater, a barococo movie palace that was demolished in 1960.* Time 5/3/71, p33 [**1962,** blend of *baroque* and *rococo*]

baroquerie, *n.* **1** baroque quality or character. . . . *complaints about his* [the violinist Ricci's] *almost total lack of fashionable baroquerie (no trills, no double-dotting) become mere quibbles.* Sunday Times (London) 1/12/69, p56 **2** something baroque. *In an altogether different vein is what Mr. Gordon calls a "beautiful and nutty" country Chippendale chair, which is full of serpentine curves and baroqueries and still has its original coat*

of paint—a flamboyant turquoise. New Yorker 12/2/67, p182 [**1967,** from French]

barotolerance, *n.* the ability to withstand high pressure. *Compared with the elaborate food-finding and gathering capabilities developed in highly evolved organisms, the bacteria's only way of adapting to the environmental conditions of the deep sea appears to be their acquisition of psychrotolerance* [tolerance of cold] *and barotolerance.* Scientific American 6/77, p52 [**1977,** from *baro-* pressure + *tolerance*]

Barr body, a darkly staining piece of chromatin found in the cell nuclei of females, especially female mammals. *Tremendous advances have been made in biochemistry, genetics and endocrinology in recent years. For example, the presence of the Barr body in a slide of cells taken from a simple smear of buccal tissue allows positive identification of a genetic female* . . . New Scientist 11/21/74, p582 [**1963,** named after Murray L. *Barr,* born 1908, a Canadian anatomist who discovered it]

baryonium, *n.* a short-lived hypothetical elementary particle composed of two quarks and two antiquarks. Compare CHARMONIUM. See also QUARK. *A recent experiment at CERN, Geneva, has shown that there is a candidate for such a meson with a mass of 2·6 GeV* . . . *All of these experiments concern the annihilation of protons by their antiparticles, antiprotons, and it is in just this type of reaction that physicists believed baryonium states would be most clearly seen.* New Scientist 3/24/77, p698 [**1977,** from *baryon* a heavy elementary particle (1953) + *-ium* (suffix for chemical elements)]

base, *n.* **touch base with,** *U.S. Informal.* to get in touch with; contact. *[He] quickly outraged White House staffers by choosing his top assistants without touching base with the President.* Time 6/17/74, p89 [**1966**]

baseload, *n. British.* the minimum amount of goods, services, etc. needed or produced to stay in business. *British Shipbuilders, the recently formed state shipbuilding organization, has secured a useful baseload of orders in the course of this year but is anxious to extend this.* Times (London) 9/27/77, p19 [**1976,** transferred sense of the term for the quantity of electric power that a power plant must produce to satisfy ordinary or minimum needs]

base pair, a combination of two of the four compounds (adenine, cytosine, guanine, and thymine) which make up the molecules DNA (deoxyribonucleic acid, the main carrier of genetic information in living cells). *A mutation can affect the chemistry of the hereditary material—the DNA and RNA . . . in various ways. For example, it can alter the sequence of the base pairs that constitute the triplet code alphabet of the hereditary language. It can also entail the loss of a base pair, resulting in a "misreading" of an entire "line" of the hereditary text.* Scientific American 1/71, p87 [**1968**]

–basher, a combining form added to nouns and meaning "one who attacks or abuses," as in: **—child-basher:** *President Houphouët-Boigny of Ivory Coast, the consummate Francophile, solved France's embarrassing dilemma by granting asylum to His Majesty the child-basher.* Harper's 5/80, p39 **—police basher:** *If the Police Federation care seriously about the role of the police in the eighties, they should abandon their Pavlovian response of dismissing any who criticise as "police bashers", and seek to understand just why the consensus is breaking down.* Manchester Guardian Weekly 4/27/80, p10 [**1963,** from *bash* to strike hard, beat + *-er*]

–bashing, a combining form added to nouns and meaning "attacking," "abusing," as in: **—bureaucrat-bashing:** *As issues, immigration and welfare are out, balanced budgets and bureaucrat-bashing are in.* Maclean's 4/3/78, p24 **—dissident-bashing:** *But now, through a convergence of circumstances, the issue has again been raised, and there is a better-than-ever possibility that Soviet dissident-bashing may evoke a serious response from the American scientific community.* Manchester Guardian Weekly (Washington Post section) 1/22/78, p15 **—Republican-bashing:** *The America he sprang from, the America of a small town drug store in South Dakota, somehow sustained him in the worst moments. So did his sheer pleasure in Republican-bashing. He kept after Richard Nixon—Brand X,* *he would call him.* NY Times 1/15/78, pD5 —**union-bashing:** *We must get away from the idea that every time you disagree with the trade unions it is union-bashing or being tough.* Times (London) 10/11/77, p5 [**1966**, from *bashing* a beating, gerund of *bash* to strike hard, beat]

basho (ˈbɑːʃou), *n. sing.* or *pl.* a fifteen-match tournament in sumo wrestling. See also OZEKI and YOKOZUNA. *Kitanoumi's growing dominance of the sport was strikingly evident when he won both the March and September* basho *with perfect 15-0 records. Wajima won the opening Hatsu* basho *in January (12-3).* Britannica Book of the Year 1978, p255 [**1976**, from Japanese, matches, tournament]

BASIC or **Basic** (ˈbeisik), *n.* acronym for *Beginners All-purpose Symbolic Instruction Code,* a computer language using common English terms in program construction. Compare ALGOL, COBOL, FORTRAN. *BASIC for Beginners is a readable self-instruction for the beginning student of the computer language BASIC, widely used at time-sharing teletypewriter terminals, particularly in schools and colleges.* Scientific American 12/70, p126 [**1964**]

basilect, *n. Linguistics.* a speech variety or dialect that has least prestige among speakers of a language. Compare ACROLECT. *In the American Black community where prestige language still involves the adaptation toward white norms, Black children are the principal speakers of basilect. A sentence like* We don't suppose to go *is more nearly basilect than* We ain't supposed to go *and is more characteristic of younger speakers, even though the second sentence would not be called Standard English by most Americans.* J. L. Dillard, Black English, 1972, p299 [**1964**, coined by the American linguist William A. Stewart from *basi-* lowest part, base + dia*lect*]

basket, *n.* **1** a group of related issues, especially ones for discussion in a negotiation or conference; package. *"Experts" from the same 35 governments will meet in Geneva this September to try to work out practical ways to put the principles of Helsinki into effect . . . Their work will be broken down into four clusters of issues that have come to be called "baskets."* Newsweek 7/16/73, p39 **2** any set, grouping, or collection of things. *The main alternative to the dollar before the ministers is a switch of oil pricing to the average of a "basket" of currencies. The economics department of OPEC headquarters in Geneva has prepared a study of four alternative baskets, based on combinations of four to 15 different currencies—excluding the dollar and OPEC's own currencies. Payment itself would remain in dollars whichever new pricing system was adopted. The switch would effectively increase crude oil prices, for each of the four alternative baskets would bring higher rates per barrel.* Manchester Guardian Weekly 5/14/78, p7 [**1973**, translation of French *corbeille*]

basket case, *U.S. Slang.* **1** a person in an extremely nervous condition; one incapable of functioning normally because of nervous strain; a nervous wreck. *"Still, I think the great distances of this country are a deterrent to long drives,"* [Harold] *Graham went on. "Dad's a basket case by the time he gets out to Yellowstone from the East."* Saturday Review 1/22/72, p16 **2** anyone or anything reduced to an extremely helpless or weakened condition. *Country-by-country investigations, even of the so-called basket cases like Bangladesh, led us to believe that in fact there may well be no country without adequate agricultural resources to feed its population.* Manchester Guardian Weekly (Washington Post section) 5/22/77, p16 [**1967**, figurative and transferred senses of the term (c. 1919) for a person who has lost both arms and both legs]

basse couture (bɑːs kuːˈtYr), women's fashions below the standards of high-fashion designers. *Runners-up were such alleged exemplars of* basse couture *as Princess Anne, Raquel Welch, Tennis Champ Billie Jean King, Jacqueline Onassis . . . Elke Sommer, Sarah Miles, the Andrews Sisters and Liv Ullmann.* Time 1/14/74, p27 [**1965**, from French *basse* low + *couture* sewing; a facetious usage on the model of *haute couture,* probably coined in English]

batch-process, *v.t., v.i.* to process as a single unit or batch in automatic data processing. *Imperial College, London, has about 150 schools using its IBM 7090 computer, with punched cards as the input method. A simple type of punch is used to code the cards, and the cards are batch-processed as part of the normal work of the college's Centre for Computing and Automation.* Times (London) 3/17/72, p19 [**1972**, back formation from *batch processing*] —**batch processor:** *Because the central computer is used as a batch processor, the limitations, costs, and complications of time sharing are avoided.* Science 7/5/68, p26

batch processing, a form of automatic data processing in which all related operations are grouped in a batch before any of them is executed. *Batch processing exhibits significant importance when applied to the lengthy complex mathematical calculations required for many theoretical problems.* McGraw-Hill Yearbook of Science and Technology 1971, p60 [**1966**]

bath, *n.* **take a bath,** *U.S. Slang.* to take a loss; suffer a reversal. *"The people who put up the money for the festival are going to take a big bath . . . But your welfare is a hell of a lot more important, and the music, than a dollar."* New Yorker 4/11/70, p161 *In a lifetime of betting, Martin has made his share of mistakes. "In the 1970 World Series," he concedes, "I picked Cincinnati as six to five favorites over Baltimore. We took a bath on that."* Time 1/14/74, p36 [**1970**]

baton-charge, *v.t., v.i. British.* to attack with drawn truncheon. *The police and troops baton-charged, and running battles with the demonstrators took place over a wide area.* Times (London) 4/4/77, p1 [**1976**, verb use of *baton charge* (1890's)]

batrachotoxin (bəˌtreikəˈtaksən), *n.* a very toxic substance extracted from the skin secretion of a species of frog common in Colombia, used in toxicology and medical research. *Studies of tetrodotoxin stimulated the use of various other chemicals as tools. They include tetraethylammonium, DDT, batrachotoxin, scorpion venoms, and saxitoxin.* McGraw-Hill Yearbook of Science and Technology 1971, p130 [**1965**, from Greek *bátrachos* frog + English *toxin*]

battered child syndrome or **battered baby syndrome,** a condition of severe bruises or other injuries exhibited by a small child, usually under four years of age. Allegedly caused by accident, they actually result from beatings or other extreme punishment administered usually by parents. *One of my correspondents . . . is working with a psychiatric clinic charged with investigating families in which "the battered child syndrome" has produced a beaten child.* Atlantic 3/70, p124 *The battered baby syndrome . . . what no one formerly realised was that the battering had been done on purpose by loving parents.* Punch 4/5/67, p489 [**1962**]

baud, *n.* a unit of speed in communications equal to one binary digit per second. *The new machine at Shell Centre will provide a considerable increase in capacity, and the leased lines forming the communication links will handle 4,800 bauds (bits per second) in the near future compared with 1,200 and 2,400 at present.* Times (London) 7/19/68, p19 [**1968**, originally a unit in telegraphy (one dot per second), named after J. M. E. Baudot; see BAUDOT CODE]

Baudot code (bɔːˈdou), a code for transmitting data in which five or six binary digits of equal length represent one character. *Even a four-letter word could take up a million bits in a high-resolution photograph. At the other extreme a simple, non-redundant, two-level Baudot code can be used to represent the same four-letter word in only 24 bits.* Scientific American 9/71, p186 [**1970**, originally a telegraph and teletype code for transmitting data along five-channel lines, named after J.M.E. Baudot, 1845-1903, a French inventor]

Bavister's medium, a culture medium in which egg cells undergo fertilization in the laboratory. See EXTERNAL FERTILIZATION. *The oöcytes would be ready for fertilization three or four hours after aspiration. The eggs were placed in Bavister's medium, and sperm were added to reach a concentration of from one to two million per milliliter.* Scientific American 12/70, p51 [**1970**, named after B. D. *Bavister,* a British biologist, who devised it in 1970 at the University of Cambridge]

Bayesian (ˈbeizi:ən), *adj.* of or relating to a method of calculating probabilities from individual samples with known characteristics rather than from frequency-distribution data and other empirical evidence. *Each day, the central computer uses Bayesian statistics to do a forward projection and calculates the probability that each of the input numbers is not merely a random fluctuation but stands for a change in slope or a step function.* New Scientist 2/15/73, p363 —*n.* a follower or adherent of Bayesian statistics. *The basic rift between Bayesians and non-Bayesians, which goes right to the bottom of the discussion on scientific truth and statistical method, is not given the importance it deserves, and Ramsey's work is nowhere mentioned.* Nature 8/18/72: p417 [**1965**, from Thomas *Bayes*, 1702-1761, an English mathematician, who devised a famous theorem (known as *Bayes' theorem* or *principle*) which introduced the concept of inverse probability, i.e. probability derived from a given sample by inductive reasoning]

bazaari (bəˈzɑːri:), *n.* an Iranian merchant or shop owner. *He went on, "The merchants of the bazaars worked hand and glove with the mullahs. They were the two most conservative elements in the cities. The bazaaris usually rented land from the religious foundations and made the foundations big gifts. But both the bazaaris and the foundations have been outmoded by recent developments."* New Yorker 12/18/78, p142 [**1978**, from Persian *bāzāri*, from *bāzār* market, bazaar] ►This term became current during the revolution of 1978-79, in which the bazaaris played a major role by uniting with the mullahs or religious leaders against the Shah. See AYATOLLAH.

BCD, abbreviation of BINARY CODED DECIMAL. *Convey has also developed a binary coded decimal (BCD) to binary converter to make counts of blood flow after a radioactive substance has been injected into the blood.* Science Journal 6/70, p21 [**1965**]

B cell or **B-cell,** *n.* a lymph cell that secretes antibodies against most infectious bacteria. Also called B LYMPHOCYTE. Compare T CELL. *These proliferate so as to manufacture antibodies, circulating substances capable of recognizing and neutralizing—or at least attaching themselves to—the particular antigen and that antigen only. Thereafter, B cells with a memory will remain on the alert throughout the life of the organism, ready to start proliferating immediately if the same antigen appears again.* Lucien Israel, Conquering Cancer, 1978, p19 [**1970**, originally from *B*(*ursa of Fabricius*), an organ of chickens in which the cell was discovered + *cell*; later, when applied to mammals, from *b*one-derived + *cell*]

B chromosome, an extra chromosome that appears in some members of a species. Compare A CHROMOSOME. *B chromosomes occur in many species of animals and plants. They are heterochromatic, do not pair with A chromosomes, and have no simple Mendelian effects upon the phenotype. They have been observed, however, to have very sharp clinal distributions which suggests a greater tolerance of B chromosomes under more favourable environmental conditions.* Nature 1/22/76, p174 [**1976**]

beachball, *n.* a compact sealed sphere designed to enclose an astronaut during an emergency transfer from an orbiting spacecraft to a rescue vehicle. Also called PERSONAL RESCUE ENCLOSURE. *The beachballs are nothing if not cramped. The user must step through the zippered opening, tuck into a near-fetal position and close himself into a sphere only 34 inches in diameter, broken only by a single, tiny, plastic porthole. Someone outside the beachball plugs the sealed container into the shuttle's oxygen supply while transfer preparations are being completed.* Science News 5/22/76, p327 [**1976**]

beam weapon, a weapon that fires particle beams or laser beams, especially against nuclear missiles. Compare ENHANCED RADIATION WEAPON. Also called DIRECTED-ENERGY WEAPON. *The first* [question] *is whether it is possible to develop a beam weapon powerful and accurate enough to neutralize fleets of attacking missiles on land or at sea.* NY Times 12/4/78, pD11 [**1977**] —**beam weaponry:** *The whole intention of beam weaponry would be to destroy or disrupt the electronics and guidance systems of incoming missiles, triggering self-*

destruction before they arrived anywhere near their original target area. Manchester Guardian Weekly 5/8/77, p6

beamwidth, *n.* the angular width of a radio or radar beam. *The aerial provides modest resolution, particularly in the 1.3 to 9 MHz band, and has a mid-band beamwidth of about 40°.* Science Journal 3/70, p71 [**1960**]

beanbag chair or **beanbag,** *n.* a chair filled with pellets that takes on the shape of the person sitting on it. *To get more height, the Detrichs used all low furniture—beanbag chairs in the living room and a legless sofa in the den.* Newsweek 1/22/73, p77 *Trevor Baxter's gay Bishop, reclining on a beanbag while oozing appreciation of Simon and Garfunkel, and executing a sumptuous return to episcopal protocol, is as hilarious as ever.* Times (London) 7/25/77, p9 [**1969**, from its supposed resemblance to the small bag of dried beans used for throwing in children's games]

bean counter, a person who keeps account of business or other records, or who enumerates statistics. *Businessmen hang lively monikers on each other's specialties. A bean counter is, as aspiring bookkeepers know, an accountant . . ..* NY Times 6/29/80, p6 [**1980**]—**bean-counting,** *adj.: To avoid "bean-counting" disputes over troop numbers . . . NATO ministers agreed to seek more verifiable limits.* Time 12/19/88, p25

beard, *n. U.S. Slang.* a person who wears a beard, especially a college student, teacher, or other intellectual. *The only beards to be found upstate are on the 45-odd huge State University campuses that gradually are pushing the Adirondack Mountains back into Canada . . .* NY Times 6/6/70, p30 *In the San Francisco area, where last year almost 60,000 housewives, hippies, businessmen and beards marched, only 15,000 zealots turned out . . .* Time 5/3/68, p21 [**1963**]

beatout, *n. Baseball.* a play in which a batter makes a base hit by outrunning the throw of an infielder to first base. *Yankees finished road segment of schedule by drawing 1,427,000, that's largest in 10 years . . . Bladt's second-inning beatout in opener ended zip for 12 at plate for him.* NY Daily News 9/22/75, p53 [**1975**, from the verb phrase *beat out*]

beautiful, *adj.* fashionable; elegant. *At a Washington party the other night, a party jampacked with beautiful men and interesting women, I learned that the I.R.S. is planning to issue, more or less immediately, revised Form 1040s for 1976.* New Yorker 1/19/76, p21 [**1973**, abstracted from BEAUTIFUL PEOPLE] —*interj.* Used as a general term of admiration or approval. *The control room is full of young women in blue jeans, and the steady flow of conversation includes many (sometimes too many) explosions of "Wow! Beautiful! Far out!" and "Too much!"* Maclean's 4/74, p16 [**1966**] ►Although *beautiful* has been applied for centuries in informal usage to anything that one likes or admires ("a beautiful argument," "a beautiful incision"), during the late 1960's it became very common as a replacement of a variety of adjectives such as "simple," "easy," "nice," "friendly," "charming," and the like. For example in the phrase *Beautiful People* it has the meaning "fashionable" and in such catch phrases as *black is beautiful, small is beautiful* it means "of high quality or worth." Its use as an exclamation or interjection parallels the use of "wonderful," "great," and other words of approval to express a pleasurable emotion rather than to describe something that gives pleasure.

beautiful people or **Beautiful People,** the wealthy, fashionable people of high society and the arts who set the trend in beauty and elegance. *Abbreviation:* BP *"The establishment yearns for the days of the Kennedys . . . The shuttle society—artists, nobles, the beautiful people—used to make a pilgrimage down here* [Washington D.C.] *to do its bit nightly."* Manchester Guardian Weekly 7/18/70, p24 *". . . we don't like all these Beautiful People who think they're so great because they got an invitation* [to an exhibition of John Lennon's lithographs]. *They're the ones who are exploiting our culture."* New Yorker 2/21/70, p29 [**1964**]

beautility (byuːˈtɪləti:), *n.* the combined qualities of beauty and utility. *The best new word that fills a gap in the language was minted by architectural writer Ada Louise Huxtable to de-*

scribe a happy marriage of form and function: "beautility." NY Times 10/15/73, p37 [**1973**, blend of *beauty* and *utility*]

beauty, *n. Nuclear Physics.* the property of a type of quark called BOTTOM QUARK. *Now that there is an upsilon-prime (and there may yet be other members of the family) studies of the spectroscopy of beauty may begin. The difference in mass between the upsilon and the upsilon-prime gives some information about the force between beauty and antibeauty; a more numerous group would help even more.* Science News 9/16/78, p196 [**1977**, named on the model of CHARM]

beauty contest, *U.S. Informal.* a primary election contest in which the actual selection of delegates to the nominating convention is determined by party caucuses rather than votes. Compare CATTLE SHOW. *In Illinois, Anderson's popularity in the "beauty contest" voting does not automatically translate into actual delegates, since those delegates are being chosen "blind," i.e., from lists of names with no indication of who supports which candidate.* Time 3/24/80, p16 [**1964**, transferred from the sense of a competition of women for a prize awarded to the most beautiful contestant (OEDS 1899)]

beaver, *v.i. British.* to work like a beaver; work hard. *Between 1952 and 1963 Mr [Anthony] Barber was beavering around in the lower reaches of Government office. He was successively Parliamentary Private Secretary to the Air Ministry, a Government Whip, Lord Commissioner of the Treasury . . . and later Financial Secretary to the Treasury.* Manchester Guardian Weekly 10/17/70, p11 [**1960**, verb use of the noun]

beclomethasone (ˌbeklou'meθəsoun), *n.* a steroid compound used as an inhalant in the treatment of asthma. *Formula:* $C_{28}H_{37}ClO_7$. *Beclomethasone, a cortisonelike compound marketed in England in 1972, was immediately recognized as a significant advance in the treatment of asthma, for it can be delivered directly to the lungs, thereby eliminating the deleterious side effects . . . that occurred when cortisone was swallowed in tablet form and distributed throughout the body.* NY Times Magazine 3/20/77, p70 [**1972**, short for the pharmaceutical name *beclomethasone dipropionate*]

becquerel (ˌbekə'rel *or* ˌbek'rel), *n.* the international unit of radioactivity, equal to one disintegration per second. It is intended to replace the *curie. Among the SI's [Système International] derived units with special names are those for . . . radioactivity (the becquerel, or spontaneous nuclear transitions per second) and absorbed dose of radiation (the gray, or joules per kilogram).* Scientific American 3/76, p60A [**1975**, named for Antoine H. *Becquerel*, 1852-1908, French physicist]

bed of nails, *British.* an extremely difficult or uncomfortable position or situation. *But the famous Government-union compact might just emerge from the economic furnace on one condition: that the Chancellor can find a way of producing a socially just Budget. Mr. Healey had drawn the real bed of nails this time.* Manchester Guardian Weekly 3/9/74, p12 [**1966**, originally used by Ray Gunter, born 1909, British government official, in describing the Ministry of Labour soon after he became its head in the Labour government of Harold Wilson; patterned after *bed of roses* (OED 1806, from the nail-studded bed fakirs lie on]

bedsonia, *n., pl.* **-nias, -niae** (-ni:i:). an intracellular parasitic microorganism that causes trachoma and various other diseases. *Certainly the resemblance that the smaller elements of mycoplasmas and bedsonias bear to true viruses is close enough for them to have been confused on many occasions.* New Scientist 2/8/73, p298 [**1964**, New Latin, from Samuel Phillips *Bedson,* 1886-1969, a British virologist]

bedspace, *n.* the space for beds or the number of beds in a hotel, hospital, dormitory, etc. *Christian Action has established an emergency accommodation bureau for foreigners in a borrowed builders' hut in the courtyard of St. Martin-in-the-Fields, Trafalgar Square. It is finding bedspace for a steady stream of stranded visitors.* Times (London) 8/11/70, p3 *A computer lists available bedspace at the hospital nearest the patient's home.* NY Times 3/13/68, p35 [**1966**]

Beeb, *n. British.* a nickname for the British Broadcasting Corporation. Compare AUNTIE. *The Beeb is to be congratulated on this new venture, and for making available through the SBC [School Broadcasting Council] at this early stage films and tapes of some of the programmes for groups of teachers to inspect.* New Scientist 2/6/75, p338 [**1967**, from the pronunciation of *BB* in *BBC,* abbreviation of British Broadcasting Corporation]

beedie or **beedi** ('bi:di:), *n.* (in India) a small cigarette rolled by hand and tied with thread. *Beedi rollers usually work at home for one of a few large employers. But in this village, the rollers began to sell their beedies at nearby markets. By holding out against the landlords, these peasants had become a major talking point in other villages. The beedies were marketed partly as a form of public support for the struggle.* New Scientist 6/9/77, p594 [**1974**, from Hindi]

beefalo ('bi:fə.lou), *n.* any of a breed of beef cattle developed in the United States by crossbreeding domestic cattle and buffaloes. Compare YAKOW. *This, uh, beefalo, a cow-and-buffalo hybrid, shuffled into a Manhattan parking lot, where its California developer proclaimed the beige beauty's virtue: protein-rich meat, low feeding cost (it grazes), high fertility rate, fast maturation.* 1976 Collier's Encyclopedia Year Book, p111 [**1974**, blend of *beef* (cattle) and *buffalo*]

beefish ('bi:.fiʃ), *n.* a mixture of ground beef and minced fish, used for making hamburgers, etc. *Beefish is just one product involving minced fish that is starting on the long path to the market. Researchers in the Fishery Services Pacific Fishery Products Technology Center in Seattle not only have made a preliminary effort to incorporate the product into hot dogs, but have also managed to lose its fish taste . . .* New Scientist 3/21/74, p763 [**1974**, blend of *beef* and *fish*]

beef Wellington, a roasted filet of beef covered with pâté de foie gras and baked in a pastry crust. *Writing, for example, of the beef Wellington served in a restaurant he is surveying, Mr. Britchky pauses to observe that "filet mignon, wrapped in pâté and pastry, and served in a brown sauce flavored with a deglazing of beef" is "really a silly dish."* New Yorker 12/16/72, p105 [**1965**, probably named for the Duke of *Wellington*]

beehive, *n.* a woman's hair style in which the hair is shaped like a conical, coiled beehive. *The beehives and butch cuts [crew cuts] were bobbing in merriment now, David Rabie's being perhaps the only grim face in the room, but then he was counting empty tables.* Harper's 9/70, p55 *". . . I am also one of the top hairdressers in the world. Seventy-five dollars an hour! I created the beehive hairdo."* New Yorker 8/22/70, p31 [**1960**]

beehived, *adj.* wearing the hair in the beehive style. *The door swung and a little beehived girl ducked under my arm into the cold air.* James Dickey, Deliverance, 1970, p16 [**1970**]

beer bust, *U.S. Slang.* a party at which beer is the main beverage. *Later in the month, 500 members frolicked as guests of the bank at a barbecue and beer bust.* Time 8/22/69, p53 [**1963**]

bee's knees, *U.S.* a cocktail made with lemon juice and gin and sweetened with honey. See the quotation for the etymology. *The definite comment on the subject seems to have come from a cerebral and resourceful acquaintance, also from Washington, D.C., who notes that, "Besides being the name of a cocktail invented at the Savoy Hotel in London, 'the bee's knees' was a slang expression of the 20's meaning something like 'super' or 'smashing'. According to H.L. Mencken's 'The American Language,' the expression was coined by Tad Dorgan, the cartoonist, who also originated 'the cat's pajamas,' 'the snake's hips' and similar absurd superlatives."* NY Times 3/10/75, p33 [**1975**]

before-tax, *adj.* gained or received before taxes are paid. Also called PRETAX. *Before-tax book profits of U.S. corporations declined in the fourth quarter of 1969 to a seasonally adjusted annual rate of $91,500 m. [thousand] (£38.100m.) . . .* Times (London) 3/19/70, p23 *"When I pay talent or buy feature film," said an executive of a competing TV station, "I've got to* *use after-tax dollars. They use before-tax dollars."* Harper's 10/67, p71 [**1956**]

beggar-my-neighbor or **beggar-thy-neighbor**, *adj.* based on or involving a gain of advantage by the losses of another. *It would not be an exaggeration to say that we stand on the brink of the first major outbreak of trade war since the beggar-my-neighbor catastrophes of the inter-war period.* Times (London) 4/29/70, p13 *The last time such beggar-thy-neighbor policies became common, during the 1930s, they contributed mightily to the century's worst economic depression.* Times 5/16/69, p74 [**1958**, from the card game *beggar-my-neighbor*, which is won by capturing all of one's opponent's cards]

behavioralism, *n.* the principles and methods of sociology, psychology, anthropology, and other social sciences that study human behavior. *Anglo-American political scientists have been anxious to become, so to speak, the natural scientists of the political; they have learnt from writers such as R.K. Merton and T.S. Kuhn that the natural sciences progress under the domination of paradigms, beliefs held by the scientific community about what it is they are, at bottom, investigating, and how it is to be uncovered. But "behavioralism" was never within striking distance of being such a paradigm, for, while a paradigm does dictate to a considerable extent the methodology we can intelligibly adopt, the converse does not hold.* Times Literary Supplement 2/4/72, p115 [**1963**, from *behavioral* (science) + *-ism*]
▶*Behavioralism* should not be confused with *behaviorism*, which is psychological study by investigation and analysis of objective acts of behavior. —**behavioralist**, *n., adj.*: *The old guard are, for example, variously described as institutional, descriptive, historical, philosophical, empirical, theoretical; the Essex school as behavioralist and post-behavioralist, statistical, quantitative, analytical, theoretical. . .* Times (London) 4/14/70, p12

behavior mod, short for BEHAVIOR MODIFICATION. *The heart of behavior mod lies in correct use of positive reinforcement, simply because this most closely approximates normal human behavior.* Time 4/1/74, p5 *BT is often equated with behavior modification—"Behavior Mod"—and criticized as a tool for behavior control.* Spencer A. Rathus and Jeffrey S. Nevid, "BT: Behavior Therapy," 1977, p301 [**1974**]

behavior modification, the modification of habits and patterns of behavior by psychological methods such as reinforcement therapy (the use of rewards to reinforce normal responses), aversion therapy (inducing an aversion to harmful habits), the use of teaching machines to facilitate learning, and the like (often used attributively). See SKINNERISM. *Unlike Freudian psychoanalysis, which probes into the life history of the individual and requires hundreds of hours of patient-therapist interaction, behavior modification seeks to change responses and symptoms at the time they occur.* Americana Annual 1971, p562 [He] *feels the behavior-modification process is misunderstood by the public. "They see salivating dogs, shocks, clockwork oranges. They misunderstand the process."* Science News 3/16/74, p181 [**1971**] —**behavior modifier**: *Leading behavior modifiers may be surprised to find Gesell [Institute] people with at least one foot in their camp.* Family Circle 6/72, p2

behavior therapy, a form of psychological therapy in which a patient is conditioned to replace old habits or patterns of behavior with new ones. Compare AVERSION THERAPY. *The scientists, convinced of the errors of Freud, maintain that therapies based on conditioning and learning theory— grouped under the umbrella term "behaviour therapy"—are much more effective and practical than in-depth, "arty" therapy which lays bare the patient's soul.* New Scientist 12/24/70, p541 *Unlike psycho-analysis, which may go on for years, behavior therapy is often completed in fewer than 30 sessions— and it claims success in 85% of its cases.* Time 8/2/71, p50 [**1959**]

be-in, *n.* an informal gathering, usually in a park or other public place, for the purpose of being together and doing whatever one likes. *What, the Judge wanted to know, was a "be-in." With great sweetness and delicacy, Ginsberg explained it was "a gathering of young people imbued with a new planetary life-*

style." Manchester Guardian Weekly 12/20/69, p4 [**1967**, see -IN]

béké (beiˈkei), *n. French Creole.* a white settler. *Martinique still has its white aristocracy, the békés.* Times (London) 9/7/70, pIII *"There are many rich families here* [in Guadeloupe], *very rich. They are the* békés, *the white planters."* Atlantic 12/65, p120 [**1965**]

Belizean or **Belizian** (biˈliːziːən), *adj.* of or relating to Belize (since 1973 the official name of the Central American country formerly known as British Honduras). *The Mexicans have made it clear that they . . . support Belizean independence.* Times (London) 11/1/78, p6 *The Belizian problem will not go away. Guatemala will continue with its threats. Britain may soon be forced to end its defense treaty without solving the problem. Understandably, the Belizians do not want to fall under the authoritarian right-wing Guatemalan rule.* Maclean's 8/22/77, p38 —*n.* a native or inhabitant of Belize. *The Belizeans, a proud and friendly race of English-speaking creoles, want the British out too, but they want the military protection only Britain can give.* Manchester Guardian Weekly 10/12/74, p9 [**1959** *Belize Times*; **1973**, from *Belize*, name of the capital of British Honduras until 1970, from Maya *beliz* muddy water, in reference to the river of that name, supposed to be muddy in the rainy season]

belle époque (beleiˈpɔːk), **1** typical of the turn of the century. *In the U.S., the style is called either* Belle Époque (*after turn-of-the-century coiffures*), *or "Oscar's hairdo" (after Designer Oscar de la Renta, who put topknots on all the models at his spring collections last month).* Time 12/5/69, p56 [**1960**] **2** the era of the turn of the century. *Though his collection is not all of motoring, here we find a record of that* belle époque, *with goggled, face-masked and windswept drivers, snapshots of mud-caked, thundering races in French villages, Jenatzy in the last Gordon Bennett Cup race, strange pedal-carts and adventures awheel in a 35 h.p. Peugeot . . .* Times (London) 9/27/67, p13 [**1954**, from French *la Belle Époque*, name given to the period 1880-1905, literally, the Beautiful Era]

bell lap, the final lap of a race, signaled by the sounding of a bell. *As the race got under way,* [Dave] *Wottle ran dead last for 500 meters, but was finally inspired by the sight of the favorite, Russia's Yevgeny Arzhanov, beginning his furious kick on the bell lap.* Time 9/18/72, p58 [**1972**, originally (about 1960) used in bicycle races]

bells, *n.pl.* bell-bottom trousers. *Having purchased a pair of red velvet bells for thirty dollars and finding them not to his liking after wearing them for a day (wrong size, wrong color), he returned to Sekhmet, on St. Marks Place, to make an exchange.* New Yorker 3/21/70, p39 [**1970**]

bellyhold, *n.* the hold for cargo beneath the passenger cabin in the fuselage of an aircraft. *A further problem will be that in spite of increase of cargo in pure freighter aircraft, the bulk will continue to be flown in the bellyholds of passenger aircraft.* Times (London) 6/2/70, pIII [**1968**]

belly up, *Slang, chiefly figurative.* **1** to fall down flat; collapse; drop dead. *The feed-lot operators are moaning too, because a consumer rebellion against beef and soaring costs of fattening cattle threaten to trim their profits to the bone. Says an official of the Colorado Cattlemen's Association: "A lot of boys are going to belly up."* Time 3/18/74, p78 **2** flattened out; collapsed, dead (often in the phrase *go belly up*). *As the oxygen in the service module was what the astronauts were breathing, it had already crossed Liebergot's mind that the astronauts could be what he called "belly up" in a matter of hours.* New Yorker 11/11/72, p80 *If New York can go belly-up, why not any city in the nation?* Manchester Guardian Weekly (Washington Post section) 10/11/75, p17 [**1968**]

belted-bias tire, an automobile tire with a belt of cord fabric or metal around its circumference beneath the tread. Also called BIAS-BELTED TIRE. Compare RADIAL-PLY TIRE. *In the United States, sales of the belted bias tire both to motorists and to automobile manufacturers began to rise rapidly in 1968. The tire, composed of the body of a conventional tire with a belt around* the circumference of the carcass—was introduced in 1966. 1969 Compton Yearbook, p400 [**1968**]

beltway bandit, *U.S. Slang.* a business or any of its consultants or experts, often former government employees, hired by a corporation to help secure government contracts. *There are more than 1,000 firms in the advising business in the Washington area alone, and for years they have been known as the Beltway Bandits since so many are clustered along the highway that circles the city.* Time 4/14/80, p35 [**1980**]

benchmark, *n.* a computer program, problem, or routine used as a standard for evaluating the performance of a computer (often used attributively). *After a lengthy period of 'bench mark' testing—carrying out paper and simulation tests to determine which computer was best suited to its needs—and amidst considerable speculation, the Met Office's choice of the largest IBM machine, the giant new 360/195, was announced in January.* Science Journal 2/70, p11 [**1970**]

bench-press, *n.* a weightlifting exercise or competitive event in which the lifter lies on the back on a bench and lifts a barbell or similar weight above the chest until the arms are straight. *He currently holds the Canadian record for the bench-press, with a lift of 292¼ pounds.* The Province (Vancouver) 6/9/73, p13 —*v.t.* to lift (a weight) by performing a bench press. *His arms drop lower, and his surprising strength of torso (he can bench-press 180 pounds) churns him into another gear.* Sports Illustrated 7/9/73, p31 [**1965**]

bench scientist, a scientist who works in a laboratory; research scientist. *"Bench scientist" is the term used by higher echelon administrators in USDA* [U.S. Dept. of Agriculture] *to refer to active scientists—by whom the term is generally much resented.* Science 1/17/75, p150 [**1970**]

benign neglect, the deliberate disregard of a bad situation presumably in order to avoid tensions or provocations that might make the situation worse. *The United States government continued its policy of "benign neglect" towards Latin America throughout the year, even abandoning the efforts made earlier to seek a new treaty governing the future of the Panama Canal Zone.* Manchester Guardian Weekly 1/2/77, p13 [**1971**] ►The usage arose in 1970 from a memorandum of a Presidential counselor, suggesting that "the issue of race could benefit from a period of 'benign neglect'."

According to *Time* (March 16, 1970, p 26), the phrase was "first used in 1839 by the Earl of Durham, Governor General of Canada; in a report to Parliament he praised the Whiggish policy of 'benign neglect' toward Canada, which had helped, he said, move that country toward self-government."

During the 1970's, *benign neglect* was frequently used in other contexts: *Black composers and women composers share a heritage of musical subjugation—of malign as well as benign neglect.* NY Times 6/27/71, p31 *How we do, and at the same time, do not, think about our children's books, is best reflected by that infuriating form of benign neglect, the roundup review.* Harper's 1/77, p85

Beninese (bəni:'ni:z), *n.* a native or inhabitant of Benin (country in western Africa called, until 1975, Dahomey). *The most recent in a series of decrees restricting foreign input to Benin came from the Ministry of Information and National Orientation. Henceforth, all Beninese are prohibited from visiting foreign embassies in Cotonou without written Ministry permission.* Manchester Guardian Weekly 4/4/76, p17 [**1875**, name of a people; **1976**]

Benioff zone ('beni:af), a region beneath the earth's surface associated with volcanic activity, deep earthquakes, and tectonic plate margins. *Inclined earthquake zones, called Benioff zones, underlie active volcanic chains and have a variety of complex shapes.* Scientific American 5/72, p51 [**1968**, named after (Victor) Hugo *Benioff*, 1899-1968, an American seismologist]

Benlate, *n.* trademark for BENOMYL. *The fungicide used is a solution of Benlate in lactic acid which is injected through holes half an inch in diameter in the trunk near ground level; the best dose appears to be about 15 grams to the foot circumference.* Times (London) 11/20/72, p5 [**1969**]

Bennery or **Bennism**, *n. British.* the policy of extending state ownership and intervention in private industry. *In practice, "Bennery" might be taken to imply a commitment to nationalization and state intervention, plus worker participation in management, or outright worker control that went further than the government's declared program.* Britannica Book of the Year 1975, p112 *Three desperate problems beset Labour when this year began. The problem of Europe and splitting in two; the problem of an incomes policy, and splitting in two; the problem of Bennism, petrified industry, rampant trades unionism, and splitting in two.* Manchester Guardian Weekly 1/4/76, p6 [**1975**, from Anthony Neil Wedgwood *Benn*, born 1925, Britain's secretary of state for industry in 1974 + -*ery* or -*ism*, noun suffixes]

Bennett, *n.* Also called **Bennett's Comet**. a comet first sighted in Pretoria, South Africa in December 1969, characterized by a surrounding cloud of hydrogen ten times larger than the sun. Compare TAGO-SATO-KOSAKA. *Comet Bennett, discovered on Dec. 28, 1969, by John C. Bennett at Pretoria, S.Af., became one of the most spectacular comets in many years. It revolves around the sun once every 17 centuries in an extremely elongated ellipse whose plane is practically perpendicular to that of the earth's orbit.* 1971 Britannica Yearbook of Science and the Future, p137 *Bennett's Comet . . . was seen from many parts of Britain at daybreak yesterday.* Times (London) 3/28/70, p1 [**1970**]

benomyl ('benə,mil), *n.* a fungicide used to control diseases of flowers, fruits, vegetables, and lawn grass. It is related to thiobendazole. *Formula:* $C_{14}H_{18}N_4O_3$ *Hope of curing elm trees infected with Dutch elm disease fungus (DED) was raised by two developments: a pressure technique for injecting mature trees with liquids containing chemicals and a water-soluble form of the fungicide benomyl that inhibits the disease without damaging the tree.* 1974 Britannica Yearbook of Science and the Future, p160 [**1970**, from *benzomethyl*, part of the chemical name]

Bentley compound, one of a group of chemicals with extremely potent narcotic effects, used especially to incapacitate wild animals. . . . *drugs known as the Bentley compounds which, although difficult to isolate, are ten thousand times as powerful as heroin. Some Government scientists, fearing that the Bentley compounds would replace heroin, suggested growing the bracteatum on Air Force bases surrounded by barbed wire and guard dogs.* Sunday Times Magazine (London) 3/9/75, p17 [**1966**, named for K. W. *Bentley*, a British chemist who synthesized the compounds in the early 1960's]

benzodiazepine (,benzoudaɪ'æzə,pi:n), *n.* the chemical substance that is the source of various widely used tranquilizing drugs such as Valium (diazepam) and Librium (chlordiazepoxide). *When researchers demonstrated binding of opium drugs to specific sites on brain cell membranes, the race was on to discover natural substances that would also bind and suppress pain. Enkephalins and endorphins were soon identified. Now Danish biochemists Richard F. Squires and Claus Braestrup report in the April 21 Nature specific binding for another important group of drugs, called benzodiazepines, which include antianxiety medicines and hypnotics, seem to attach to receptors on rat brain cell membranes.* Science News 5/21/77, p332 [**1972**, from *benzo-* benzene + *di-* two + -*az-* nitrogen + *ep-, epi-* besides + -*ine* (chemical suffix)]

berimbau (bə'rimbau), *n.* a stringed musical instrument of Brazil. It usually has one metal string. *Facing each other in the circle are two Brazilians, Purple Shirt No. 5 and Breaker-of-Iron, both rhythmically undulating while a* berimbau *quavers.* Time 5/1/72, p84 [**1967**, from Brazilian Portuguese, perhaps from an African language]

Berlin Wall, a barrier preventing communication, especially the free flow of information. *A significant call to demolish the "Berlin walls" that have divided Christians over the centuries was issued by Léon Josef Cardinal Suenens.* Britannica Book of the Year 1972, p600 *This insider considers it conceivable, though unlikely, that Nixon was so isolated by his Berlin Wall of Ehrlichman and Haldeman that he did not know about ei-*

ther the espionage plans or the later concealment. Time 7/2/73, p16 [**1968,** from the name of the 26-mile long wall dividing East and West Berlin, built in 1961 by the East Germans but recently demolished as a result of the growing movement to absorb Eastern European countries into the general framework of Europe.]

Bermuda Triangle, an area of the North Atlantic in which disappearances of airplanes and ships have been popularly attributed to mysterious forces. Also called DEVIL'S TRIANGLE. *There have been about half a dozen successful books on the Bermuda Triangle, some of them going high in the best-seller lists. Although they all tell basically the same stories, they advocate different solutions: the missing craft have been carried off by unidentified flying objects (presumably so the extraterrestrials can check on how well mankind is faring on the long road to civilisation); they have been sucked under the sea by an erratic laser-power source from the lost civilisation of Atlantis; they have encountered a time-space warp and been carried into another dimension.* Listener 2/19/76, p199 [**1975,** so called from the triangle formed by the points between Florida, Bermuda, and Puerto Rico comprising this area; popularized in the book *The Bermuda Triangle* (1974), by Charles Berlitz]

Berufsverbot (bə'ru:fsvər,bout), *n., pl.* **-bote** (-,boute). the West German policy of prohibiting anyone suspected of radical political tendencies from employment in the civil service. *Literally a prohibition against engaging in one's profession, Berufsverbot is the popular term given to procedures designed to screen out applicants for public-sector jobs if they advocate the destruction of the constitution.* Harper's 8/78, p5 [**1976,** from German *Berufs* (genitive of) vocation + *Verbot* prohibition]

best-case, *adj.* designed to include or provide for the most favorable conditions or circumstances possible. *Research with recombinant DNA may provide major new social benefits of uncertain magnitude: more effective and cheaper pharmaceutical products; better understanding of the causes of cancer; more abundant food crops, even new approaches to the energy problem. These and other possible outcomes are envisioned in "best-case scenarios" for the future application of recombinant-DNA technology.* Scientific American 7/77, p22 [**1977,** patterned after WORST-CASE]

beta–adrenergic (,beitə,ædrə'nərdʒik), *adj.* of or relating to beta receptors; BETA-BLOCKING. *New uses for the beta-adrenergic drug propranolol continue to be reported. The drug is already in established use for preventing certain cardiac arrhythmias, treating hypertension, and slowing the heart rate in hyperthyroidism.* 1974 Collier's Encyclopedia Year Book, p348 [**1969,** from *beta* (*receptor*) + *adrenergic* producing or activated by adrenalin (from *adren*aline + Greek *érgon* work + English -*ic*)]

beta-blocking, *adj.* (of a drug) preventing or inhibiting the absorption of adrenalin in heart and blood vessel cells by blocking the cells' beta receptors. *Recent experience with the beta-blocking drug practolol confirms that the surveillance of patients undergoing novel therapy leaves much to be desired. Indeed, the authors of the paper recommending registered release cite beta-blocking agents as one area in which the new scheme should be tried out.* New Scientist 1/13/77, p59 [**1966**] —**beta-blocker,** *n.: A majority of the treated men got a "beta-blocker," a kind of drug known to reduce the incidence of sudden death in heart-attack patients.* NY Times 1/29/78, pD18

betaendorphin (,beitəen'dɔrfin), *n.* a pain-suppressing hormone produced in the pituitary gland. Compare ALPHAENDORPHIN. *The substance is beta-endorphin classed as a hormone, tested by medical researchers as a painkiller and hailed as "the brain's own opiate." Actually it originates in the pituitary gland but seems to exert its effects in the brain.* Time 1/23/78, p98 [**1976,** from *beta-* second in a series + ENDORPHIN]

beta-lipotropin, *n.* a form of the pituitary hormone lipotropin that contains 91 amino acids, sequences of which include various endorphins and enkephalins. *Opiatelike proteins in the brain that relieve pain and that alter various mental states and behaviors have been exciting medical researchers recently. Called enkephalins and endorphins, they all derive from a*

larger parent protein—beta-lipotropin. Science News 7/23/77, p58 [**1976,** from *beta-* second in a series + LIPOTROPIN]

beta receptor, a site or structure in a cell at which the stimulus of certain adrenalin-producing agents elicits a usually inhibitory response. Compare ALPHA RECEPTOR. *Stimulation of the alpha-receptors produced by a stimulation of the associated muscles; the lungs worked harder to get more oxygen or the blood vessels expanded to increase circulation. Stimulation of the beta-receptors had the opposite effect, of slowing down activity.* Times (London) 3/19/73, p3 [**1963**]

bête blanche (,bet 'blãʃ), a slight cause of aversion; minor irritation or nuisance. *No doubt the South African Communist Party, the author's special bête noire (or, as he makes it appear, bête blanche) has often made an ass of itself, and at no times more egregiously than when dancing to Moscow's tune.* Times Literary Supplement 5/26/72, p598 [**1967,** from French, literally, white beast, patterned after *bête noire*]

BFT, abbreviation of BIOFEEDBACK TRAINING. *Many researchers contributed to the discovery of BFT, and physiologist Dr. Barbara Brown is perhaps foremost among them. While other researchers in the early 1960s were still experimenting with rats and rabbits, Brown explored BFT techniques with human subjects.* Newsweek 10/14/74, p76 [**1971**]

bi (bai), *adj. Slang.* sexually attracted to or involved with both sexes; bisexual. *He looked at Mick Jagger and shouted to a henchman: "Hey, Dave, this guy is bi."* Manchester Guardian Weekly 1/23/71, p21 [**1966**]

Biafran (bi:'æfrən *or* bai'æfrən), *adj.* of or having to do with Biafra, the eastern region of Nigeria which was an independent republic of the Ibo people between 1967 and 1970. *The crime wave is linked to high unemployment, especially in the East-central State, where thousands of demobilized former Biafran soldiers roam the streets with firearms secured during and after the civil war.* 1972 Collier's Encyclopedia Year Book, p387 —**n.** a native or inhabitant of Biafra. *Nevertheless, in spite of these setbacks and strong rumours that their money is running out and food is getting short, surrender by the Biafrans remains unlikely.* Times (London) 3/23/68, p5 [**1967;** the secessionist region was named after the Bight of *Biafra* (since 1975 called the Bight of Bonny), a part of the Gulf of Guinea]

bialy ('byɑ:li:), *n., pl.* **bialys** or **bialy.** *U.S.* an onion roll. [Allen] *Ginsberg's stepmother, Edith, was in the kitchen fixing a big breakfast of bagels, bialy, lox, cream cheese, and scrambled eggs* . . . New Yorker 8/24/68, p63 [**1966,** shortened from Yiddish *bialstoker,* named after *Białystok,* the Polish city where the type of roll originated]

bias-belted tire, another term for BELTED-BIAS TIRE. *The addition of bias belted tires to GM cars cost the buyer approximately $29.* 1970 Compton Yearbook, p139 [**1970**]

biathlete, *n.* an athlete who competes in a biathlon. . . . *Denver looked a dead duck, threatening us, as had Grenoble four years ago, with long journeys into the mountains in pursuit of skier, bobber, tobogganist and biathlete.* Times (London) 1/29/72, p16 [**1972,** blend of *biathlon* and *athlete*]

biathlon, *n.* a sports event combining a contest in cross-country skiing and rifle shooting. *The world biathlon championships (skiing and shooting), still held annually although the other Nordic events were biennial, took place at Altenberg, E. Ger., on February 19.* Britannica Book of the Year 1968, p692 [**1958,** from *bi-* two + Greek *áthlon* contest]

Bible-thump, *v.i. Slang.* to act like a preacher; evangelize. *The Defenders [a television series] may bible-thump a bit in an all-American way, but . . . never refuses a fence.* Punch 6/29/66, p963 . . . *the Bible-thumping gospeller Aimee Semple McPherson.* Times (London) 4/28/70, p12 [**1965,** back formation from *Bible-thumper* (1920's)]

bicommunal, *adj.* composed of two national communities. *Under the proposed formula, Cyprus would become a bicommunal and (effectively) federal republic—independent, sovereign, integral and, if so desired, non-aligned—to consist of two constituent regions, one inhabited predominantly by Greek*

Cypriots, the other predominantly by Turkish Cypriots. Times (London) 11/22/78, p8 [**1977**, from *bi-* two + *communal*]

bicycle kick, *Soccer.* a kick made with both feet off the ground and moving the legs as if pedaling a bicycle. *Kidd's bicycle kick just on half-time was a rare challenge for the Bristol goalkeeper.* Times (London) 2/18/78, p6 [**1965**] —**bicycle-kick**, *v.i.:* McGrath nodded it to Gabriel and Gabriel with his back to goal bicycle-kicked over his own blond head.* Sunday Times (London) 9/5/71, p23

bicycle motocross, a children's sport of racing stripped-down bicycles with knobby tires over indoor or outdoor tracks featuring dirt mounds, tight turns, and the like. *Bicycle motocross gets its name from conventional motocross racing in which grown-ups propel lightweight motorcycles over rugged courses . . . In bicycle motocross, kids do roughly the same thing—but on bicycles, and without motors.* Wall Street Journal 3/7/86, p21 [**1986**]

bidialectal, *adj.* using or able to use two dialects of a language. *The public schools continue to vacillate between the old line, "Talk American, boy, American," and the more cosmopolitan line, "Are our er um Black students ahh bilingual or um bidialectal?"* NY Times Book Review 9/3/72, p16 [**1954**, from *bi-* two + *dialectal;* patterned after *bilingual*] —**bidialectalism**, *n.: The purpose of this study* [Bi-Dialectalism: a Policy Analysis] *is to examine bidialectalism as an educational policy.* Newsletter of the American Dialect Society, Vol. 6, No. 3, 11/74, p35 —**bidialectalist**, *n.: The bidialectalists have grossly overestimated the power of the schools to influence "adolescent culture"; and when bidialectal projects also fail, that failure will be taken as . . . evidence that black children are stupid.* American Speech 48, 3-4 (1973), p262

bidonville, *n.* a shantytown, or settlement of makeshift houses, often built from tin cans cut and hammered flat. . . . *the ruination that the market economy has brought to Appalachia or in the bidonvilles of underdeveloped nations exposed to the full blast of the capitalist process.* New Yorker 10/8/79, p126 [**1955**, from French, from *bidon* a tin can for liquids + *ville* town]

bierkeller (ˈbirˌkelər), *n.* a German-style beer hall. *The opening of Bierkellers in London and elsewhere, where litres of strong German draught beers can be obtained at around 10s. a time (one litre is usually enough), has helped.* Times (London) 3/12/70, pVIII [**1967**, formed in English from German *Bier* beer + *Keller* cellar]

bifunctional, *adj.* having two distinct functions. *The two hormones share the same bifunctional physiological action in that they both promote bodily growth and stimulate mammary development and milk secretion, as well as have similar immunological responses.* 1973 Britannica Yearbook of Science and the Future, p214 [**1968**, from *bi-* two + *functional*]

big, *adj.* **be big on**, *Slang.* to be enthusiastic about; be a great fan or admirer of. *"I'm very big on* [Goldwater],*" the New Nelse* [Nelson Rockefeller] *has been saying. "We have been good friends over the years—with a few unfortunate hiatuses."* National Review 5/23/75, p544 *She said, "I have just been to Macy's. I have been going to Macy's every day for the last two weeks. I am very big on Macy's."* New Yorker 5/16/77, p36 [**1968**]

Big Apple, **1** a nickname for New York City. *All of them are well aware of the negative aspects of life in New York. They are familiar with the pits in the Big Apple.* Women's Wear Daily 3/23/73, p21 **2 big apple**, the most important part; focus; chief concern. *When you are this way you do not care much how a woman works, sex being peripheral to your life, and you think that your own heavings and gruntings are sufficient unto themselves. They are not, but when the big apple in your life is yourself you never get to know it.* Harper's 7/70, p65 [**1970**] ►The term *Big Apple* was originally used by U.S. jazzmen in the late 1920's and the 1930's to refer to any big city, especially a big northern city, and particularly New York City. Around 1937 the *Big Apple* became the name of a popular jazz dance. The derivation of the term is uncertain. The possible origin is suggested in *Dan Burley's Original Handbook of Harlem Jive*

(1944), which defines *apple* as "the earth, the universe, this planet. Any place that's large."

Big Bang, a cosmic explosion of densely packed gaseous matter which may have occurred from 10 to 15 billion years ago and constituted the origin of the universe (also used attributively). Compare INFLATIONARY. *According to existing ideas, after the Big Bang took place the galaxies were flung outward like shrapnel moving away from each other in straight lines.* Science Journal 10/70, p10 [**1950; 1957**]

Big Banger, a supporter of the theory that the universe originated with the Big Bang. Compare STEADY-STATER. *Galaxies take something like 10 billion years to evolve, he* [Professor Fred Hoyle] *says, which is comparable to the age Big Bangers give to the universe.* New Scientist 6/20/68, p621 [**1966**]

big beat, *U.S. Slang.* rock 'n' roll (also used attributively). *You can blow your mind to the big beat uptown. Cool it in a candlelit cavern downtown.* Advertisement, Harper's 5/68, p22 [**1958**]

big bucks, *U.S. Slang.* a large amount of money. *We cannot sit around and let New Jersey or Connecticut or who knows where establish alternative tourist facilities. That is our big industry. Four hundred thousand jobs. That is big bucks.* NY Times 4/15/79, pE6 [**1970; 1979**]

big C, *Informal.* cancer. *John Wayne . . . whose cancerous left lung was removed in 1964, accepted the news with true grit. "I've licked the Big C before," he said.* Time 1/29/79, p69 [**1968**]

big dress, a wide, loose, flowing dress, made in the style of the Big Look. Also called DROOP. *One "big dress," for example, was adored for its color (which was copper and looked good with her red hair), but rejected for its voluminousness, which she* [Julie Harris] *found overwhelmed her small frame.* NY Times Magazine 3/30/75, p56 [**1975**]

bigemony (ˈbaiˈdʒemənɪ:), *n.* predominant influence or authority of two nations over the others in a group. Compare HEGEMONY. *Bigemony . . . generally refers to the condominium exercised by the two superpowers, but inside the Nato camp, too, there are signs of a bigemony of sorts emerging, based on a Bonn-Washington axis.* Times (London) 12/14/76, p14 [**1976**, from *bi-* two + hegemony]

big enchilada, *U.S. Slang.* a very important or influential person; bigwig. See ENCHILADA. . . . *most of the big enchiladas of the used-car business in those days ended up broke.* NY Times Magazine 3/2/75, p34 [**1974**] ►This phrase became popular during the Watergate affair when the White House tapes revealed a reference by H. R. Haldeman to the then Attorney General John Mitchell as "the big enchilada."

Bigfoot, *n.* another name for SASQUATCH. *Bigfoot . . . is periodically spotted galumphing across the face of North America . . . leaving behind only (big) footprints.* Discover 10/80, p6 [**1972**]

Big Look or **big look**, a fashion in women's clothes introduced in 1974, characterized by loose, broad, voluminous designs. Compare LAYERED LOOK. *The Big Look differed from the midi in that it brought the fabric flowing in immense yardages about the body. It meant very little inner construction, very few seams. Linings, interfacings, and even turned-under hems were practically eliminated. As a result, the clothes could be piled on top of each other in layers without making the wearer look enormous.* 1975 World Book Year Book, p328 [**1974**]

big one, *U.S. Slang.* one thousand dollars or a thousand-dollar bill. *"A guide to the Language and Customs of Sports Betting": Big one—$1,000 bet.* NY Times 1/19/75, pE3 [**1958**]

Big Science, scientific research involving large capital investment. *As an alternative to annexation or satellization, there is the choice of* competition. *This demands that European businesses, particularly those in the area of "Big Science," become fully competitive on the global market.* Harper's 7/68, p39 [**1961**]

biker, *n. U.S.* a motorcyclist, especially one belonging to a motorcycle gang. *The image of the biker as delinquent will take a long time to eradicate. "You meet the nicest people on a Honda," proclaims the Japanese firm that has cornered nearly 50% of the bike market in the U.S.; but the general belief is that you still meet the nastiest ones on a chopper* [motorcycle]. Time 2/8/71, p35 [**1968**, extended from the earlier sense of a bicyclist (OEDS 1883)]

bikeway, *n. U.S.* a road on which only bicycles are permitted. *Block has suggested that ramps and bikeways be built to keep pedaling students from running down their pedestrian counterparts.* Tuscaloosa News 10/27/70, p11 [**1965**]

bikie, *n. Especially Australian Slang.* a motorcyclist, especially one belonging to a motorcycle gang; biker. *More than 30 "bikies" were taken into custody last night four miles south of Feilding after police swooped on an old farmhouse.* Auckland Star (New Zealand) 4/21/73, p2 [**1967**, from *bike* motorcycle + *-ie* (diminutive suffix)]

bilateral, *n.* a conference or discussion involving only two sides. *. . . the so-called "Bonn bilaterals," meaning West Germany's talks with East Germany, Russia and Poland.* NY Times 4/3/70, p36 [**1964**, noun use of *bilateral, adj.*]

bilayer, *n.* a biological structure consisting of two layers each of the thickness of one molecule. *The phospholipid bilayer, now confirmed as the basic molecular arrangement in membranes, may also be the structural basis of the low density lipoproteins in human blood serum.* Nature 11/3/72, p10 [**1968**, from *bi-* two + *layer*; patterned after *monolayer* (1933)]

bilevel, *adj.* having two levels. *Inside the deceptively simple brick house, with a stunning bilevel addition done in exposed rough beams with vaulted ceiling, Gini Johnson is preparing wild rice and peas and loins of pork and beef.* Atlantic 12/70, p90 —*n.* a structure or vehicle with two levels, especially a house with a bilevel ground floor. *Part of a sample spiel: "Look at what the Lions from Leo* [a local real estate company] *have this week! This lovely Georgian bi-level on a sprawling treed lot!. . ."* Time 12/4/72, p45 [**1970**, from *bi-* two + *level*]

billi-bi (ˈbili ˌbiː), *n.* a soup made of fresh mussels, cream, and white wine. *Tuck into a tasty billi-bi soup with its house eccentricity—a couple of empty mussel shells riding the edge of the bowl like earrings.* New York Magazine 3/21/88, p86 [**1967**, from French, named after *Billy B.* Leeds, an American businessman who was a frequenter of Maxim's, in Paris, where the soup was served]

binary coded decimal, a system of coding numbers in binary units in which each decimal digit is represented by four binary digits. *Example:* 234 is represented in binary coded decimal by 0010 0011 0100. *The United States Supreme Court in 1972 decided the Benson case (from Bell Labs) in which a patent for converting BCD (Binary coded decimal) to pure binary utilizing reentrant shift register was denied.* Computers and People, Sept./Oct. 1981, p7 [**1960**]

binary weapon or **binary nerve gas**, a nerve gas consisting of two comparatively nontoxic chemicals that become lethal when mixed in a projectile fired at a target. *The US's current obsession with chemical weapons produced by reacting two agents (binary weapons) is based largely upon environmental considerations. The final product agents in a binary reaction are not necessarily more toxic than VX—indeed some are less.* New Scientist 10/12/78, p101 [**1974**]

bindin (ˈbaindin), *n.* a protein in the sperm cells of sea urchins that binds to receptor sites of eggs. *In the sequence of events that make up fertilization, bindin may do more than glue sperm to eggs. It may also signal the sperm and egg membranes to merge so that genetic material can pass from the sperm into the egg. "Bindin is at the proper place at the proper time."* Science News 11/26/77, p356 [**1977**, from *bind, v.* + *-in* (chemical suffix)]

binocs, *n.pl.* short for *binoculars. No binocs, no bird book. Asher had forgotten his binoculars . . .* New Yorker 11/7/70, p42 [**1966**]

bio-, a prefix with the sense "biological; relating to living things," *bio-* has been used in the past chiefly to form terms in the natural sciences, but recent usage has extended its application to less scientific and more socially oriented contexts, as in *biodestructible, bio-parent, biopolitics, biohazard.* —**biocontamination**, *n.: . . . NASA takes seriously its responsibilities with regard to bio-contamination of the planet!* New Scientist and Science Journal 5/6/71, p305 —**biocybernetics**, *n.: Perhaps the most extraordinary paper at the AAAS meeting came from Manfred Clynes, head of the Biocybernetics Laboratories at Rockland State Hospital, New York State. Clynes, over the last few years, has developed a way of fitting differential equations to emotions such as love and anger.* New Scientist 12/31/70, p580 —**biodestructible**, *adj.: "Mr. Merton, is this biodestructible or residually permanently inert?"* New Yorker 8/1/70, p32 —**biodeterioration**, *n.: Some recent work by two researchers, John Mills and Dr Howard Eggins, at the Biodeterioration Information Centre of the University of Aston, shows that some common fungi will thrive on polythene* [a plastic] *that has been oxidized beforehand.* New Scientist 8/20/70, p379 —**bioexperiment**, *n.: The next project of any kind with bioexperiments aboard will be Skylab in 1972, and those will involve only pocket mice and drosophila flies.* Science News 7/4/70, p7 —**biogeology**, *n.: Preston Cloud and Aharon Gibor ("The Oxygen Cycle") are respectively professor of biogeology and professor of biology at the University of California at Santa Barbara.* Scientific American 9/70, p33 —**bio-parent**, *n.: Bio-parents permitted frequent visits. Telephone contact allowed. Child may spend summer vacation with bio-parents.* Times (London) 9/26/70, p15 —**biopolitical**, *adj.: There may be a biogeographical significance in its* [blossoming blackthorn's] *breaking earlier in this location, but I would not attribute a "biopolitical" turn to it!* Times (London) 4/25/70, p9 —**bioproductivity**, *n.: And their influence—the inflow of the rivers with a mean annual discharge of 1900m³/sec alone accounts for almost 1/3 of the fresh-water entering the Mediterranean—has become one of the major factors governing bioproductivity of the North Adriatic.* New Scientist and Science Journal 7/15/71, p145 See also the entries below.

bioaccumulation, *n.* the accumulation of toxic chemicals in living things. Compare BIOMAGNIFICATION. *There were signs of outright sabotage of certain scientific programs that had been undertaken to measure the possible bioaccumulation of dioxin in the Seveso environment.* New Yorker 9/4/78, p62 [**1975**] —**bioaccumulative**, *adj.: Perhaps most worrisome: PCBs are bio-accumulative, increasing in concentration as they move up nature's food chain.* Maclean's 2/9/76, p55

bioacoustics, *n.* the study of sounds produced by or affecting living organisms. *It is a marginal comfort to know that the relatively new science of bioacoustics must deal with similar problems in the sounds made by other animals to each other.* Harper's 2/73, p98 [**1964**] —**bioacoustic** or **bioacoustical**, *adj.: Brough goes on to explain his "bioacoustic" method, in which a starling's taped "distress call" is broadcast over loudspeakers at a roost.* Natural History 8/75, p44 *Particularly outstanding is the paper by Tandy and Keith on African Bufo, including a wealth of biological and bioacoustical data, and the study of the mechanisms of vocalization.* Science 2/9/73, p559

bioactive, *adj.* having an effect on living matter. . . . *Bioactive ceramics have been used to plug and bridge bone defects, close surgical skull openings and to implant artificial-tooth roots that later bind to the jaw as bone tissue grows into the ceramic's pores.* Science News 3/18/78, p168 [**1974**] —**bioactivity**, *n.: The bioactivity of the drugs correlates with their ability to reach this metastable conformation.* New Scientist 11/21/74, p561

bioavailability, *n.* the extent to which a drug or nutrient is absorbed and made available at its point of action in the body. Compare PHARMACOKINETICS. *Dietary fiber may decrease the bioavailability of certain essential nutrients. Continued ingestion of fiber-rich foods or of individual components of fiber can result in decreased absorption and reduced blood levels of* *calcium, magnesium, iron, and zinc.* McGraw-Hill Yearbook of Science and Technology 1978, p175 [**1970**]

bioceramic, *n.* a ceramic substance implanted to help promote the regrowth of missing bone. Compare BIOGLASS. *A team at the College of Engineering at Clemson University, South Carolina, is using porous calcium aluminate, titania and porcelain implants to provide a matrix for bone ingrowth. The team . . . has found that these "bioceramics" are well tolerated by various body tissues when implanted in dogs and man.* New Scientist 3/30/72, p692 [**1972**]

biochemistry, *n.* biochemical composition or characteristics. *The virus has developed the capacity to change its biochemistry, thus guaranteeing a fresh crop of victims every time a change occurs.* NY Times Magazine 1/11/76, p13 [**1967**, extended sense of the term (1880's) for the science dealing with biochemical processes]

biochip, *n.* a microcircuit whose components consist of organic molecules instead of electronic circuits. *Some molecules that could be used are so small that a three-dimensional biochip occupying 1 cubic centimeter (0.06 cubic inch) could be crowded with an astonishing million billion molecular switches.* World Book Science Annual 1988, p209 [**1983**]

biocidal, *adj.* destroying life or living things. *Of the approximately 800 biocidal compounds used as pesticides, many . . . are degraded to elementary materials that can be recycled.* McGraw-Hill Yearbook of Science and Technology 1971, p319 [**1968**]

biocide, *n.* destruction of life. Compare ECOCIDE. *We are gradually committing biocide—killing every living thing on the earth including ourselves . . .* Scientific American 9/70, p262 [**1963**, from *bio-* + *-cide* killing, as in *genocide*]

biocompatible, *adj.* being biologically compatible; not causing rejection. See BIOMATERIAL. *Thin films and thin-film technology constitute another obvious field of application which includes many different subjects ranging from superconductivity . . . to biocompatible coatings, dry batteries, printing, and others.* Science 9/8/72, p849 [**1972**] —**biocompatibility,** *n.: A new class of polymer with remarkable biocompatibility and high permeability to oxygen was employed successfully in experimental lung-support systems.* 1977 Britannica Yearbook of Science and the Future, p278

bioconversion, *n.* the use of biological materials and processes to convert a compound, waste material, solar energy, etc. to a new form. *Eventually the direct conversion of solar radiation to electricity by means of photovoltaic cells or its bioconversion to wood, methane, or other fuels on a large scale may become economically feasible.* Science 9/22/72, p1088 [**1969**]

biocrat, *n.* a scientist or technician who represents the interests of the biological sciences or their allied professions. *Unfortunately, between the two* [private citizens and lawmakers] *there is a bureaucratic monolith of biocrats and administrators, and the channels of communication, though theoretically present, are tortuous and fraught with obstacles.* New Scientist and Science Journal 3/18/71, p602 [**1970**, from *bio-* + *-crat*, as in *bureaucrat*]

biodegradability, *n.* susceptibility to biodegradation; proneness to decomposition by biological agents, especially bacteria. *Starch is another substance tried and found wanting by industry because, when modified to perform the functions of phosphates, it loses its biodegradability and so could build up in the environment.* Science 12/27/69, p592 [**1961**]

biodegradable, *adj.* that can be decomposed by biological agents, especially bacteria. Compare SOFT. *Oxygen-demanding wastes are biodegradable by using oxygen that is naturally present in the water or artificially supplied in treatment processes.* McGraw-Hill Yearbook of Science and Technology 1968, p23 [**1961**]

biodegradation, *n.* the decomposition of a substance through the action of biological agents, especially bacteria. *Recent advances in biodegradation of plastics . . . offer startling contrast to the previous general belief in the immutability of plastics exposed to possible bacterial attack . . .* New Scientist 9/24/70, p648 [**1960**]

biodegrade, *v.i.* to undergo biodegradation. *Some petroleum compounds that do biodegrade do so over "a much longer time than anticipated,"* says [R.E.] *Kallio, citing recent work at the University of Illinois.* Science News 10/30/71, p293 —*v.t.* to cause to biodegrade. *This detergent can be broken down (biodegraded) about 80% by the oxygen-breathing bacteria.* Science News 12/16/63, p109 [**1963**]

bioelectronics, *n.* the application of the biological sciences to the study and development of electronic systems or processes, as in the creation of biochips. *Bioelectronics incorporates the development of functional neuronal interfaces which permit contiguity between neural tissue and . . . computing technology.* McGraw-Hill Yearbook of Science and Technology 1989, p55 [**1969**]

bioenergy, *n.* energy obtained from biomass (often used attributively). *Fortunately the other inexhaustible sources of energy such as solar radiation, windpower, bioenergy, tidal power, wave-power and geothermal energy present potential sources that can be exploited more quickly and with more certainty than the fusion reactors.* Times (London) 10/24/78, p26 *The cumulative impact of stretching agriculture, bioenergy production and hydroelectric power to their natural limits would transform the face of the earth in the decades to come.* Scientific American 9/80, p131 [**1978**, from *bio*mass + *energy*. An earlier meaning of this term is the energy expended by a living organism or organisms.]

bioengineer, *n.* an expert in bioengineering. *Professor Andrew A. Frank, a University of Wisconsin bioengineer, who has completed a four-legged walking machine, is now working on a two-legged version which will simulate normal leg action.* New Scientist 9/3/70, p473 [**1960**]

bioengineering, *n.* the application of the technology of engineering to problems of medicine, especially in the creation of more responsive artificial limbs. *The Boston arm is just one of many remarkable devices being developed by a partnership between technology and medicine in a new field called biomedical engineering or bioengineering.* World Book Science Annual 1969, p99 [**1960**]

bioenvironmental, *adj.* of, relating to, or involving the interaction between living things and the environment. *His main plea is for greater use of bioenvironmental controls such as rotation and intercropping, which have been replaced by continuous monocultures, susceptible to pest outbreaks.* New Scientist 5/31/73, p531 [**1965**]

bioethical, *adj.* of or relating to the ethical problems arising in biological research and experimentation. *By whatever name, bioethical questions have always troubled us—but perceptions of them change. Today, because the new medicine has made them so much more visible, bioethical questions are being examined more carefully, more extensively, and under a number of broad rubrics.* Harper's 8/78, p21 [**1974**]

bioethics, *n.* the study of the ethical problems involved in biological research with organ transplantation, genetic engineering, artificial insemination, etc. *Andre Helligers, professor of obstetrics and gynecology and director of the newly established Kennedy Institute for Human Reproduction and Bioethics at Georgetown University in Washington, said his guess is that "operations like the one at Georgetown will become institutionalized and more wide spread."* Science News 10/30/71, p294 [**1971**]

biofeedback, *n.* the control or alteration of a person's own body processes by monitoring them on machines that measure blood pressure, record brain waves, etc. *Most of these* [advertisements] *claim that biofeedback can give control over the mind comparable to the inner peace sought by masters of yoga, but at a more mundane level there have also been reports in medical journals of the use of biofeedback in the treatment of physical disorders such as raised blood pressure.* Times (London) 10/14/74, p18 [**1971**]

biofeedback training, a method of training people to control or alter processes of their bodies, such as blood pressure, heart rate, or muscle tension; training in biofeedback. *Abbreviation:* BFT. Also called AUTOGENIC TRAINING. *Biofeedback training enables a patient to become aware of muscle tension and to learn to control it. A therapist places electrodes on the patient's forehead and connects them to a gauge that indicates the extent of muscle contraction or relaxation. A temperature-registering device on the fingers is connected to a visual temperature gauge.* 1978 World Book Year Book, p103 **[1971]**

biofuel, *n.* a fuel composed of material that was once living matter, such as coal. *New alchemist Richard Merrill is the coeditor of* Energy Primer, *a do-it-yourself guide to renewable forms of energy such as solar, wind, water, and biofuels.* Science 2/28/75, p729 **[1975]**

biogas, *n.* gas that is a mixture of methane and carbon dioxide, produced for use as fuel by bacterial action on organic waste matter. Compare SYNGAS. *Some countries faced with fuel shortages, notably India, built bio-gas plants to convert sewage and animal wastes to fertilizer and methane, a fuel gas.* Americana Annual 1974, p166 *Biogas burns in a slightly modified methane burner with a sufficiently hot flame for cooking.* World Book Science Annual 1976, p209 **[1974]**

biogasification, *n.* the production of biogas. *Biogasification, which is "perhaps the most important technology for converting biological material to more useful forms of fuel," should be vigorously pursued.* New Scientist 7/24/75, p219 **[1975]**

biogeocoenology (ˌbaiouˌdʒiːousiˈnɑlədʒiː), *n.* the study of ecosystems. *The publication in 1968 of an English translation of* Fundamentals of Forest Biogeocoenology *brought to the West a new insight into Soviet conservation activities.* Britannica Book of the Year 1969, p227 **[1968**, from Russian *biogeotsenologiya,* from *biogeotsenoz* biogeocoenose + -*logiya* -logy]

biogeocoenose (ˌbaiouˌdʒiːousiˈnouz), *n.* any ecological community and its environment viewed as a unit; ecosystem. *Chapters two to six take in turn various components of forest biogeocoenoses—the atmosphere; a phytocoenose; animal life; microorganisms; soil.* New Scientist 8/22/68, p398 **[1968**, from Russian *biogeotsenoz*]

bioglass, *n.* a calcium and phosphorous biomaterial similar to window glass, used in medicine. Compare BIOCERAMIC. *Bioglass has been used successfully to fuse living bone to artificial hip joints in sheep, leg bones in dogs, teeth and jawbones in baboons and middle ears in cats.* Science News 6/19/76, p392 **[1976]**

biohazard, *n.* a biological hazard, especially one resulting from experimental research (also used attributively). . . . *two flags drooped from a pole: a yellow quarantine flag and, above it, a red-white-and-blue banner—an international biohazard flag.* New Yorker 1/3/70, p40 **[1970]**

biohazardous, *adj.* of or relating to danger, risk, or harm resulting from biological research. Compare BIOSAFETY. *The committee was to assess the advisability and need for life scientists at Princeton to participate in such potentially biohazardous work. The possible dangers of this research had to be considered in terms of its effect on the campus and the community.* World Book Science Annual 1978, p43 **[1975]**

bioinorganic, *adj.* of or having to do with inorganic processes in biochemistry. Compare BIOORGANIC. *This book would seem to represent required reading for anyone professionally interested in bioinorganic chemistry, but biochemists and coordination chemists generally would gain much from it.* Nature 9/15/72, p177 **[1972]**

bioinstrumentation, *n.* the use and development of measuring and monitoring instruments for transmission of data about life processes. *So far, space biology has resulted in a multitude of unpublicized spin-offs such as bio-instrumentation and miniaturization now in use in hospitals and research laboratories across the nation.* Science News 9/9/72, p174 **[1964]**

biological clock, a biological mechanism that governs the rhythmic or cyclic activities of organisms. Compare BODY CLOCK. *The daily activity cycle is just one of many rhythms in man that are regulated by biological clocks.* World Book Science Annual 1968, p113 **[1957]**

biological magnification, another name for BIOMAGNIFICATION. *A process called biological magnification contributed to the ospreys' decline.* World Book Science Annual 1973, p52 **[1973]**

biomagnification, *n.* the progressive concentration of toxic chemicals with each new link in the food chain. Compare BIOACCUMULATION. *As far as damage to aquatic life is concerned, for example, Mr. Edmund M. Sweeney, the public hearing examiner, finds that . . . "the theory of biomagnification would seem to be adequately demonstrated in the case of fish, giving rise to concern over use of pesticides with a persistence such as DDT."* Nature 6/23/72, p423 **[1972]** —**biomagnify**, *v.i.*: *Probably the best news is that arsenic residues from soil and water do not biomagnify in the food chain.* Science News 9/21/74, p184

biomass, *n.* plant material used as a source of energy. *The process by which vegetable material or "biomass" as it is technically known is transformed into alcohol fuel is simple. Brazilians have been converting sugar cane into alcohol by fermentation since colonial days, and ethyl alcohol was mixed with gas as early as the 1930s.* Manchester Guardian Weekly (Washington Post section) 9/10/78, p15 **[1977**, extended from the original (1930's) sense of the total mass or weight of living material in a unit of area]

biomaterial, *n.* biocompatible fabric, plastic, or other material used to replace natural tissue or to construct artificial organs. *Drugs influencing these mechanisms, such as anticoagulants, are widely used to delay or limit thrombus formation in the presence of a biomaterial.* New Scientist 12/2/76, p526 **[1972]**

biomathematician, *n.* a specialist in the mathematical study of biological processes, especially in simulation of such processes by means of computers or mathematical models. . . . *biomathematicians have made computer models of systems in the human body, including the respiratory, nervous and circulatory systems.* Encyclopedia Science Supplement (Grolier) 1970, p115 **[1969]**

biomedical engineering, another name for BIOENGINEERING. *To these two principal pursuits, the modern biomedical engineer would also add a third: an application of the management techniques developed largely within the engineering industry. Thus, in its complete form, biomedical engineering is seen as involving a break with the traditional organization of medicine so that the new technology can be exploited unhampered by a system based upon the methodology of a previous era of medicine.* Science Journal 6/69, p48 **[1962]**

biomedicine, *n.* the biological and medical study of man's tolerance to environmental stresses, especially in space travel. *The role of science—particularly biomedicine—[should] be upgraded as a mission objective to help justify the substantial cost of space exploration.* Science News 1/10/70, p37 **[1963]**

bionic (baiˈɑnik), *adj.* **1** of or relating to bionics. *In building a submarine, designers wish to determine the most efficient shape for the hull. The bionic approach to this problem consists of studying organisms that exhibit the desired characteristic of moving through water with the least amount of resistance.* Encyclopedia Science Supplement (Grolier) 1970, p115 **2** consisting of electronic or mechanical components that replace or augment anatomical structures and thereby supposedly produce extraordinary strength, powers, and abilities. *The Steve Austin doll seems to offer more opportunity for adventure. He has a "bionic eye" with a lens that offers a wide-angle view of the world when you look through a hole in the back of his head; a "bionic grip" that can be closed to grasp a girder (supplied with the doll); and a "bionic arm" . . . that can be raised and lowered.* Consumer Reports 11/77, p638 **3** *Figurative.* having extraordinary strength or ability; extremely powerful. *His awed colleagues in the federal Liberal caucus call Jamieson "the bionic mouth" in tribute to his oratorical skills, and to* *spend some time with him is to realize that this Newfie jokester is a raconteur without peer in Canadian public life.* Maclean's 12/12/77, p41 [**1970**, from *bio-* + *-onic*, as in *electronic;* def. 2 was made popular by the television hero known as the *bionic man* whose electronic and mechanical components give him extraordinary strength and powers] —**bionically,** *adv.: Horrorstricken, I watched last night as the perfect housewife cleaned house bionically . . . in less time than it takes to tell.* Times (London) 7/2/76, p11

bionicist (bai'anəsist), *n.* an expert in bionics. *Bionicists attempt to solve technical problems by the application of mechanical and electrical mechanisms comparable to those found in nature.* Encyclopedia Science Supplement (Grolier) 1970, p114 [**1970**]

bionics (bai'aniks), *n.* the science of applying the formations of various biological structures to problems of engineering in electronics, computer programming, construction, etc. *We have said that bionics is a relatively new science. After all the very word "bionics" did not exist before 1959. It was derived from the Greek word "bion" meaning living and "ics" meaning like. In other words the goal of the programme is to make . . . self-organizing machines, intelligent machines or learning machines.* New Scientist 3/10/66, p626 [**1960**]

bioorganic, *adj.* of or having to do with organic processes in biochemistry. Compare BIOINORGANIC. *One area of bioorganic research focused on the molecular changes wrought by enzymes on small organic substrates.* 1978 Britannica Yearbook of Science and the Future, p274 [**1972**]

biophilia, *n.* love of life as a human instinct. *Biophilia and necrophilia are in many ways similar to Freud's concept of the life instinct and the death instinct. There is, however, an essential difference. For Freud, both tendencies are normal parts of the biological equipment of man, while in the view presented here, this holds true only for biophilia.* NY Times Magazine 2/27/72, p84 [**1968**, from *bio-* + *-philia* love of, patterned after *necrophilia*] —**biophilic,** *adj.: MacCoby, an ardent McCarthy supporter, runs an intensely biophilic household— interviews with him tend to be punctuated by rousing nursery rhymes for the benefit of the children.* Sunday Times (London) 7/21/68, p10

biopolymer, *n.* a protein, nucleic acid, steroid, or other biological polymer. *It has been established in the past several years that many biopolymers can behave as transducers in that they exhibit electric potentials when deformed mechanically. These biological transducers comprise collagen, keratin, elastin, dentin, and cellulose and include, as well, many polycrystalline organic materials such as polypeptides and amino acid crystals.* McGraw-Hill Yearbook of Science and Technology 1974, p136 [**1966**]

biopsy, *v.t.* to perform a biopsy on. *Howard Jones and his colleagues at Baltimore searched the notes of known cases of cervical carcinoma in an attempt to find any whose cervix had been biopsied in the past.* Nature 7/21/72, p135 [**1964**, verb use of the noun]

bioregion, *n.* a place or area as defined by the biological systems in it. *According to Mrs. Salzman, the Island's East End is a self-sufficient bioregion that is being damaged by exploitative development.* NY Times 12/30/84 (page not known) [**1978**]

bioregionalism, *n.* activity in behalf of the preservation of a bioregion. *Bio-regionalism has its roots in the ecology and appropriate-technology movements. While most of these activities are located in the countryside, they can be seen too in such urban projects as gardens, co-ops, recycling centers, and new ways of using abandoned land and buildings.* North Country Anvil, Summer-Fall, 1984, p9 [**1983**, blend of *bioregion* and *regionalism* (OED 1881)]

bioremediation, *n.* the use of microorganisms to clean up toxic waste sites and polluted water. *A major obstacle to the development of bioremediation, some say, has been a thicket of Government regulations limiting the release of genetically altered*

organisms into the environment. NY Times 5/23/89, pC1 [**1989**]

bioresmethrin (ˌbaiourez'mi:θrin *or* ˌbaiourez'meθrin), *n.* variant of RESMETHRIN. *One of these compounds, bioresmethrin . . . has the highest selectivity ratio known for any insecticide chemical; it is 32,000 times more toxic (on a milligram per kilogram basis) to houseflies when applied topically than to rats when given orally.* Science 3/23/73, p1235 [**1971**]

biorheology (ˌbaiouri:'alədʒi:), *n.* the study of the flow and deformation of blood, mucus, and other fluids in animals and plants. *The author* [Elementary Rheology] *. . . gives a brief history of the subject, an account of the main lines of work, definitions of terms used, and short chapters on topical subjects such as haemorheology, aspects of biorheology, and psychorheology.* Science Journal 4/69, p85 [**1969**, coined in 1948 by A.L. Copley from *bio-* of biology + *rheology* (1931) science dealing with flow and deformation of matter, ultimately from Greek *rheós* a flowing] —**biorheologist,** *n.: In addition to the efforts of manufacturers to optimize the design of their units by reducing shear stress and turbulence, two approaches are receiving the attention of biorheologists.* McGraw-Hill Yearbook of Science and Technology 1973, p72

biorhythm, *n.* rhythmical or cyclic changes occurring in the functions or activities of organs and organisms. Compare CIRCADIAN RHYTHM. *Several universities are currently completing studies validating three long-term cyclical patterns called "biorhythms": a 23-day physical cycle, a 28-day emotional cycle (unrelated to the menstrual cycle).* NY Times 4/24/66, pF12 [**1960**]

biorhythmic, *adj.* of or involving a biorhythm. *Biorhythms are physical, emotional and mental elements, all cyclical, that are said to determine, or at least play a large role in a person's behavior and performance at a given time. The biorhythmic forecast is determined by date of birth.* NY Times 9/10/77, p19 [**1966**] —**biorhythmicist,** *n.: Although there has been no rational explanation so far for the claims of biorhythmicists, variations of the concept have been put to practical use in at least two countries.* Time 1/10/72, p48 —**biorhythmicity,** *n.: . . . the study of sleep is, among other things, the study of biorhythmicity.* McGraw-Hill Yearbook of Science and Technology 1977, p147

biosafety, *n.* safety in biological research (often used attributively). Compare BIOHAZARDOUS. *And to further make the point about a significant change in the attitude in the Administration, the name of the local groups designated to oversee the way research is carried out has been switched through 180 degrees from biohazard committees to biosafety committees.* New Scientist 9/7/78, p674 [**1977**]

biosatellite, *n.* an artificial satellite carrying living plants or animals for space-environment research. *The subject was a pigtail macaque monkey named Bonnie, launched from Cape Kennedy in a 1,550-pound capsule, Biosatellite 3.* Science News Yearbook 1970, p60 [**1957**]

bioscience, *n.* the branch or body of science dealing with biological phenomena outside the earth's atmosphere, including biomedicine, exobiology, etc. *In addition to biomedical studies of man in space, NASA is also looking at biological experiments. Although there are four such experiments on Skylab— pocket mice, human tissue, vinegar flies and potatoes—and much ground-based research, the new bioscience program has not yet been formalized. The first era of bioscience ended with the death of the monkey Bonnie after its eight-day space voyage and the remaining biosatellites were canceled.* Science News 8/1/70, p93 [**1963**]

bioscientific, *adj.* of or relating to bioscience. *While not specifying the cost of expanded bioscientific research, the . . . panel compared it to the cost of aborting a single Apollo mission for medical reasons and judged it to be worth the cost.* Science News 12/13/69, p561 [**1969**]

bioscientist, *n.* an expert in bioscience. *Bioscientists studying the effect of the space environment, or more properly the absence of the Earth's environment, on living systems usually* *need to recover the organisms for examination in the laboratory.* McGraw-Hill Yearbook of Science and Technology 1968, p363 [**1959**]

bioshield, *n.* a protective device encasing a spacecraft during and after its sterilization with a heat cycle prior to launch. *Last summer, the two Viking landers were baked for eighty hours, at a peak heat of two hundred and thirty-three degrees Fahrenheit, inside containers called "bioshields," which were not removed until the two craft were safely on their way toward Mars.* New Yorker 6/21/76, p60 [**1976**]

biosonar, *n.* the use of sonarlike impulses by an animal to facilitate movement without harm through its surroundings. *Dr. Griffin's book,* Listening in the Dark, *is the most complete treatise on biosonar to be found in current literature, and his work on bats has been the basis for much of the work today.* McGraw-Hill Yearbook of Science and Technology 1966, p13 [**1963**]

biotechnology, *n.* the use of microorganisms as catalytic agents to produce useful materials or facilitate industrial processes. *The term biotechnology is unfortunately ambivalent, and is confused further by the widespread use of synonyms like "biochemical engineering," "microbial technology" and "fermentation technology." But the meaning that is most widely accepted is that it is the industrial processing of materials by microorganisms and other biological agents to provide desirable products and services. It incorporates fermentation and enzyme technology, water and waste treatment, and some aspects of food technology.* New Scientist 6/7/79, p808 [**1972,** specialized sense of the term meaning originally (1940's) the area of technology dealing with the relation between people and machines]

biotelemetric, *adj.* of or used in biotelemetry. *At the present time, the weight of a practical biotelemetric transmitter is approximately 9-15 g* [grams] *per channel of information, and the transmitting distances range up to 20 mi.* McGraw-Hill Yearbook of Science and Technology 1969, p115 [**1967**]

biotelemetry, *n.* the monitoring of vital functions of a person or animal and the transmission of the data to a distant point for readings by electronic instruments. Also called ECO-TELEMETRY. *Biotelemetry is being used to monitor human response to environmental stress (exercise, heat, cold, space flight), critical illness (myocardial infarction, postsurgery), birth (fetal heart sounds), during surgery and its associated anesthesia, and any situation in which the elimination of encumbering wires or the direct connection of the subject to a recorder is desirable.* McGraw-Hill Yearbook of Science and Technology 1971, p130 [**1966**]

biotoxic, *adj.* relating to or consisting of poisons produced by animals and plants. *In the case of man, painful experience rather than instinct has taught him to respect biotoxic substances.* 1977 Britannica Yearbook of Science and the Future, p223 [**1972,** from *biotoxin* (1959), from *bio-* biological + *toxin* poison] —**biotoxicity**, *n.: The considerable biotoxicity of copper waste obviates any chance of proper restoration at a feasible cost.* New Scientist 11/30/72, p491

biotransformation, *n.* chemical transformation of a compound through biological action. *Biotransformation of mercury in association with microorganisms has been observed in at least three other species; the bacterium* Pseudomonas *K-62 strain transformed some organo-mercury compounds to the free metal; inorganic or phenylmercury was methylated by bacteria in natural sediments; and* Neurospora crassa *is able to methylate inorganic mercury through a different metabolic pathway.* Nature 11/3/72, p44 [**1969**]

biowarfare, *n.* biological warfare. *In the event he* [Mike Gaze] *wrote to the director of Porton, saying that biowarfare was not his thing. Once in the Army, he applied for a job doing physiological research on environmental topics.* New Scientist 10/12/72, p93 [**1966**]

Bircher, *n. U.S.* a member of the John Birch Society, an extreme conservative and anticommunist group formed in 1958. Also called BIRCHITE, JOHN BIRCHER. *George Thayer here* [in The

Farther Shores of Politics] *presents a Baedeker of the outer marches of politics in the United States today—the neo-Nazis, the Klansmen and other racists; the Birchers, the Black Nationalists, the Communists, the pacifists and many more.* NY Times Book Review 3/10/68, p12 [**1961,** from the John *Birch* Society (named after John *Birch,* a U.S. Air Force captain killed by the Chinese Communists in 1945)]

Birchism, *n. U.S.* extreme conservatism in politics. . . . *the Dallas* [Texas] *environment . . . is so accepting of rightist politics that Birchism can become a simple habit.* Science News 2/21/70, p197 [**1963**]

Birchite, *U.S. n.* another name for BIRCHER. *As long as* [Governor George] *Wallace's percentages were down around 5 percent, his strength in the North was for the most part limited to Birchites . . .* Atlantic 11/68, p12 —**adj.** characteristic of Birchers; extremely conservative. *The Intermountain Observer, a weekly with a statewide circulation . . . provides an urgently needed contrast to the generally conservative (and often Birchite) tone of the Idaho press.* Harper's 12/68, p25 [**1961**]

bird, *n.* **1** any flying craft, such as an airplane, rocket, or space vehicle. *The fuselage is 280 feet long, compared with the 318 feet to which its predecessor grew as engineers drew in more seats and bigger fuel tanks to try and keep the increasingly expensive bird profitable.* Science News 11/2/68, p440 [**1933; 1953**] **2** *U.S. Slang.* the eagle as an insigne of military rank. *Every few months there is a new colonel's list . . . and over morning coffee, the man and his wife read down it to see who won:* my God, that bastard made it. *And checking over the career to see what it was that had gotten bird for him.* Atlantic 10/70, p93 [**1969**]

birdcage, *n. U.S. Slang.* the congested airspace of an airport or air terminal. . . . *one of the busy "birdcages" near New York, Chicago, and Los Angeles.* Time 8/17/81, p18 [**1978**]

bird strike, a collision between an aircraft and a flock of birds. *"Bird strikes" are a problem to jets all over the world. Last month in Sydney a Boeing 707 with 136 passengers had to make a crash landing after colliding with a flock of gulls at take-off.* Sunday Times (London) 1/4/70, p5 [**1962**]

birr, *n. pl. and sing.* the monetary unit of Ethiopia that replaced the Ethiopian dollar in 1976. *The Ethiopian birr, divided into 100 cents, is the unit of currency; it is based on 5·52 grains of fine gold. It consists of notes of* [various] *denominations, and bronze 1-, 5-, 10-, and 25-cent coins.* The Statesman's Year-Book 1977-78, p916 [**1977,** probably from Amharic]

birth, *adj.* related by birth or blood, not by adoption or the like; biological. *A small but apparently growing number of adults. . ., even as they enter middle age, have started looking for their biological parents, or their "birth parents" as some prefer it.* NY Times 1/30/77, pD8 [**1977**]

birth pill, an oral contraceptive in pill form. *David Moreau yesterday announced his resignation as managing director of Syntax Pharmaceuticals, the British end of the birth-pill company.* Times (London) 6/16/70, p25 [**1965,** short for *birth-control pill*]

bistatic radar, a system of radar used in astronomy and space sciences. *The conclusion is drawn from studies by bistatic radar—using a sender and receiver in different locations. The sender in this case was the lunar orbiter Explorer 35; the receiver was Stanford's 150-foot radio antenna.* Science News 8/31/68, p213 [**1963**]

bit, *n. Slang.* a typical or standard practice, procedure, or way of acting; a familiar set of actions or things. *So I did the Palm Springs bit, I did the Las Vegas bit, I did the golfing bit.* NY Times 6/30/71, p24 *I'm wearing the uniform: the button-down shirt, the V-neck, the stay-presseds, the penny-loafers, the whole bit.* New Yorker 4/20/68, p178 [**1955,** originally the theater sense of an act, routine, or other piece of stage business]

Bitter coil, an electric coil for the generation of a strong magnetic field in a fusion reactor. *It is possible that the reactor will incorporate elements of the "Bitter coil" that has enabled the Alcator of the Massachusetts Institute of Technology to pro-*

duce extremely powerful magnetic fields. NY Times 3/22/76, p38 [**1968,** named after Francis *Bitter,* an American physicist]

biuniqueness (ˌbaiyuˈniːknis), *n. Linguistics.* the principle of one-to-one correspondence between phonemic and phonetic representations. *The principle of bi-uniqueness forces the inventor of writing to practice a kind of economy of symbols, so that if he can't* hear *a distinction between some class of utterance-pairs, he can't* write *one, and if he* does *consistently hear a distinction, he must write it or fail the read-back test.* Fred W. Householder, Linguistic Speculations, 1971, p148 [**1959; 1971,** from *bi-* two + *uniqueness*]

black[1], *adj., n.* ▶As a label of racial identity, *black* was revived in the late 1960's by the American civil-rights movement and so successfully popularized in the following years that it virtually removed from circulation the formerly standard label *Negro.* However, as late as 1967 a new encyclopedic reference book dealing with black history and culture was entitled *The Negro Almanac* and used the label Negro throughout.

Historically, *black* and *Negro* were used interchangeably, e.g., "He noticed the approach of the black . . . with a smile of contempt" (James Fenimore Cooper, *The Spy,* 1821). It was chiefly during the twentieth century that *negro* was capitalized (*Negro*), and *black* went out of fashion among whites, as it was considered an insult to refer to the color of a black person's skin. Thus *Negro* became the accepted label and standard spelling, though a number of old and new euphemisms, e.g., "colored" (DAE 1780), "Afro-American" (DA 1853), and "nonwhite" (OEDS 1921), were used until the 1960's. The newest term of preference among some black leaders is AFRICAN-AMERICAN.

The revival of *black* probably succeeded in part because black leaders promoted the label, using it in slogans emphasizing pride in being black (BLACK POWER, *Black is* BEAUTIFUL), and in designating concepts intended to raise the consciousness of blacks (BLACK NATIONALISM).

black[2], *n. British.* Usually, **the black,** an instance or policy of boycotting by trade unions. *Mr. Bernie Steer, one of their* [Transport and General Workers' Union] *leaders, told me after yesterday's meeting: "The black is there, it stays there, it will be extended. Nothing this meeting has decided will alter that. If the black is going to be lifted the Government will have to see us and accept our arguments."* Times (London) 5/5/72, p1 [**1968,** noun use of *black, adj.* (1956) applied to work boycotted by trade unions, short for *blackleg, adj.* (1800's) of or relating to work done against the rules of a trade or other group]

black advance, *U.S.* the practice of following a political candidate's scheduled appearances for disruptive purposes. Compare DIRTY TRICKS. *More likely to last, but in a technical rather than general vocabulary, are locutions like "plumbers" (to plug the leaks of news) or "black advance," (to disrupt a political opposition's rallies).* NY Times 8/15/74, p33 [**1974,** so called in reference to the candidate's *advance,* or travel arrangements during a campaign]

black art, art produced by blacks or dealing with black culture, especially in the United States. *Except in certain picturesque aspects, black art is not distinct from majority art; the complaint is that it has been insufficiently incorporated in the national tradition.* New Yorker 8/22/77, p84 [**1968**]

black-bag job, illegal entry by a Federal law-enforcement agent to obtain information. *People also feared that the FBI-controlled system would encourage the growth of a national police force complete with shades of 1984 and gestapo tactics. So-called "black bag" jobs, wiretapping, and other misdeeds committed by FBI agents in the past and only recently revealed by Congressional committees have justified that fear in the hearts of many Americans.* New Scientist 9/23/76, p649 [**1976,** variant of earlier (1971) *bag job*]

black belt, 1 the highest degree of proficiency in judo or karate. *Morris—stocky, balding and 45, with a black belt in judo—is similarly inclined to realize Walter Mitty fantasies.* Maclean's 4/68, p1 **2** a person awarded this degree. Compare BROWN BELT. *A new series of Karate Classes will begin on*

Monday, July 20th, under the direction of Patti-Lee Ivens, a Black Belt. New Yorker 7/11/70, p23 [**1954**]

blackboard jungle, 1 a school in which a condition of disorder and lawlessness exists. *New schools may be built, new curricula devised, and the teacher-pupil ratio cut in half, but if the children who attend these schools come from lower-class homes, the schools will be turned into blackboard jungles and those who graduate from them, or drop out of them, will in most cases be functionally illiterate.* NY Times 10/12/70, p37 **2** a condition of disorder and lawlessness in schools. *There should be welfare officers in the schools to deal with the "blackboard jungle."* Times (London) 4/2/70, p4 [**1955,** from *The Blackboard Jungle,* title of a novel, 1954, about juvenile delinquents in a New York City vocational school, by the American writer Evan Hunter, born 1926; released as a motion picture with the same title in 1955]

black box, 1 any unknown system, especially one considered solely in terms of input and output without an understanding of its workings. *"To some programmers it* [an electronic computer] *might as well be a hamster on a treadmill generating the output. The computer—for many purposes—may be thought of as a black box."* Atlantic 3/70, p66 **2** any electronic device for automatic control that can be installed or removed as a unit. *Black boxes are devices, usually a resistor in a series, which, when attached to home phones, allow all incoming calls to be made without charge to one's caller.* Daily Telegraph Magazine (London) 3/17/72, p18 [**1956,** originally an electronic unit, often housed in a black-colored box, which was put into an aircraft for use in radar detection, monitoring of flight conditions, etc.]

black capitalism, *U.S.* the ownership and management of private businesses by black entrepreneurs. *Still, black capitalism has had its disappointments for both sides. Several ambitious, white-supported projects have failed. Black leaders acknowledge that Negroes who want to be their own bosses should be given more aid, but some doubt that black-owned businesses will employ enough people or generate enough wealth to help significantly in lifting the ghetto masses toward economic equality.* Time 7/20/70, p65 [**1968**]

black caucus or **Black Caucus,** *U.S.* a group of black civil rights advocates, especially at a national political convention or in Congress. *Five years ago, the Congressional Black Caucus held its first fund-raising event here—a well-attended dinner, the proceeds of which were used to establish and operate a caucus office. . .* NY Times 9/29/75, p20 [**1967**]

black comedy, a form of comedy whose humor derives from absurd, grotesque, or morbid situations. Also called DARK COMEDY. *Hal Prince's "Something for Everyone"* [is] *a Bavarian black comedy about a handsome young man (Michael York) who transforms the lives of a family of down-at-heel aristocrats by seducing them all.* Manchester Guardian Weekly 11/14/70, p20 [**1963,** translation of French *comédie noire*]

black consciousness, a political movement in South Africa that stresses the common cultural heritage and destiny of blacks in their struggle against apartheid (also used attributively). *The white authorities have been alert to the dangers, for them, of the development of black consciousness, which quickly won more popularity at black schools and universities than militant left-wing ideologies.* Times (London) 8/24/76, p4 *With one exception all of the banned organisations are part of the black consciousness movement.* Manchester Guardian Weekly 10/30/77, p7 [**1976**] ▶The name of this movement was adopted from the phrase frequently used in the 1960's in reference to the growing self-awareness of black Americans. *Adult Negroes have tried to erase their blackness by dressing, thinking and living "white," an approach that is giving way to the new black-consciousness that says "black is beautiful."* NY Times 7/3/68, p71

Black English, a dialect of English spoken by many American blacks. Black English originated in the South but is now also used in northern cities. It is distinguished by special pronunciation, intonations, vocabulary, and also grammatical or syntactic structure (as by the use of additional present-tense forms: I work, I am working, I be working, I a-working, I be a-working). Also called AFRO-AMERICANESE. *"Black English" is. . .remarkably rich in nuances.* Time 4/6/70, p98 *Present research by linguists has focused on Black English both as a system in itself and as a variety of English which systematically differs from Standard English. Some of the differences between Standard English and Black English, though seemingly small, have important consequences for the communication of a message.* Walter A. Wolfram and Ralph W. Fasold, Teaching Black Children to Read, 1969, p139 **[1969]**

black-flag, *v.t.* to signal (a racing-car driver) to leave the course. *Another drama near the end of the race surrounded Jean-Pierre Beltoise, winner at Monaco earlier in the season. . . In what looked like a secure sixth place, he was black-flagged to lap 12 for a trifling fault on his car.* Manchester Guardian Weekly 8/5/72, p24 **[1963,** so called from the black flag waved for this purpose]

black hole, a hypothetical body in space into which massive stars and other heavenly objects that have condensed to a certain radius collapse under the influence of gravity. Also called COLLAPSAR. See also ERGOSPHERE, SCHWARTZSCHILD RADIUS. *It* [a dying star] *may contract forever, approaching but never reaching a radius of a few kilometers and a density exceeding 10^{16} grams per cubic centimeter. It is then one of the "black holes" predicted by the general theory of relativity: objects so compact that even light cannot escape their gravitational pull. The black hole is the destiny of all stars whose terminal mass considerably exceeds the mass of the sun. No black hole has ever been observed, but then it is not clear by which of its properties an astronomer might observe it.* Scientific American 2/71, p24 **[1968]**

black humor, a form of humor in literature based on absurd, grotesque, or morbid situations. Also called DARK COMEDY or BLACKNESS. *. . .as fictionalised reportage it has a compelling quality because Ford's revulsion and black humor come through so strongly.* Punch 1/3/68, p32 **[1964]**

black humorist, a writer of black humor. *Kurt Vonnegut was mourning the follies of the world with laughter long before the term "black humorist" had been coined.* Time 4/11/69, p68 **[1964]**

black knight, *U.S. Finance.* a company that makes a tender offer to forcibly gain control of another company. *But that didn't mean he had to sell to Lance, the hostile "black knight." He figured he could do what Microdot did when that manufacturer of electrical connectors was under siege by General Cable. Microdot went out and found Northwest Industries, who played the role of a "white knight" (or "sweetheart"), a company that "rescues" the "target company" from the embrace of an "unfriendly suitor" with a much better offer.* Milton Moskowitz, Michael Katz, and Robert Levening, Everybody's Business, 1982, p835 **[1982]**

black lung, 1 a disease that afflicts coal miners. Compare BROWN LUNG DISEASE. *Black lung is a form of pneumoconiosis, a chronic lung inflammation caused by inhaling coal dust over long periods of time.* Britannica Book of the Year 1970, p509 **2** Used figuratively: *"That city room is an outhouse,"* Jimmy Breslin says. *"You can get black lung just by working on the rewrite desk for a week."* Harper's 9/69, p95 **[1968]**

black mist, (in Japan) corrupt or scandalous business or political practices. *Opposition-party politicians, whose leverage is now much greater than it was, are determined to get to the bottom of all these matters—"black mist" affairs, they are called—and the continuing American investigations may help them.* New Yorker 1/23/78, p55 **[1966,** translation of Japanese *kuroi kiri* black mist or fog (that obscures the vision); so called from the intentional cover-up often practiced in such cases]

black money, *U.S. Slang.* income from an illegal source, not reported to the government for tax purposes. *The way this works is beautifully simple. Lansky's couriers take the Mafia's "black money"—profits from illegal activities—to secret bank accounts in Switzerland, where the money is "washed clean in*

the snow of the Alps," as the joke goes. Atlantic 7/70, p65 **[1964]**

Black Muslim, a member of an American religious movement of blacks practicing a form of the Islamic religion and originally calling for the separation of the black and white races. Also shortened to MUSLIM. *America's so-called Black Muslims were once generally regarded by Sunni Muslims as followers of a new heresy. By adopting orthodox beliefs and discarding a rule that limited membership to black Americans, the World Community of Islam in the West, as the movement is now known, has been accepted as being part of the true faith.* Time 4/16/79, p52 **[1960,** said to have been coined by C.E. Lincoln, an American writer, in 1956]

black nationalism, *U.S.* the movement for identifying all black people as a nation or a group separate from the influence of white people. *Nor does the theme* [change in Harlem]. *In one form or another, it has nearly always been black nationalism—from the West Indian brand of Marcus Garvey and his followers to the more militant brand of Charles (Morriss) 37X Kenyatta. . .* New Yorker 1/7/67, p20 **[1964]**

black nationalist, *U.S.* a supporter or advocate of black nationalism. *George Thayer here* [in The Farther Shores of Politics] *presents a Baedeker of the outer marches of politics in the United States today—the neo-Nazis, the Klansmen and other racists; the Birchers, the Black Nationalists, the Communists, the pacifists and many more.* NY Times Book Review 3/10/68, p12 **[1963]**

blackness, *n.* **1** another term for NEGRITUDE or NEGRONESS. *"Talking Black" was essentially an exploration of the new consciousness of blackness as a positive concept among Negroes.* NY Times 6/27/68, p87 **2** another term for BLACK HUMOR. *Nonetheless, the strongest critics of blackness are found among humorists, many of whom believe that humor that does not make people laugh is not humor at all.* Time 3/4/66, p26 **[1966]**

Black Panther, a member of the *Black Panther Party,* an organization of black Americans seeking to establish black power in the United States by extreme militancy. *Abbreviation:* BP Also shortened to PANTHER. *Six Black Panthers—including Eldridge Cleaver—pleaded not guilty Tuesday to attempted murder and assault charges stemming from a gun battle with policemen in West Oakland. . .* NY Times 9/19/68, p48 **[1966]**

Black Paper, *British.* an authoritative document that criticizes or censures an existing policy, practice, institution, etc. Compare GREEN PAPER. *Yet, as spending on education rises, so, too, does public concern or bafflement about its aims and method, as shown in the acrimonious debate initiated by the Black Papers on education.* Times (London) 12/30/70, p7 **[1969,** patterned after *White Paper,* an official policy report by the British government]

black power, *U.S.* power of black Americans to establish their rights by collective action. It is a slogan used by the black civil-rights movement, and was especially popular in the 1960's. Compare BROWN POWER, RED POWER, FLOWER POWER. *The term "Black Power" has meant different things to different people since it was chanted by Negroes during the Mississippi march of last June. To some it has meant only that Negroes should organize themselves politically as other minorities have in the past. To others it has had disturbing connotations of black racism—even black violence against whites.* NY Times 8/7/66, p2 *A more serious issue is posed by the slogan "Black Power." No matter how often it is defined, this slogan means anti-white power. In a racially pluralistic society, "Black Power" has to mean that every other ethnic group is the antagonist. It has to mean "going it alone." It has to mean separatism.* Roy Wilkins, in a Circular Letter from the National Association for the Advancement of Colored People, 11/25/66 **[1966]**

Black Radio, (in psychological warfare) radio broadcasts by one side that are disguised as broadcasts by the other. *Black Radio daily 30-minute programs repeated once, purports to be the voice of dissident elements in North Vietnam.* NY Times 6/13/71, pD37 **[1962]**

blacksploitation, *n.* variant spelling of BLAXPLOITATION. . . . *the black glistening giants of blacksploitation films. On all sides, these larger- and simpler-than-life figures are at play, and their play hypnotizes us.* Saturday Review 12/78, p35 [**1974**]

black spot, an area in South Africa inhabited by blacks in midst of land inhabited by whites. *Driefontein is a village under a death sentence. Pretoria has decreed that the people in it and all other black communities must be trucked to "homelands," the 14 percent of South Africa set aside for black occupation. Half a million blacks have already been swept off such "black spots" as Driefontein to the homelands to join three times that number of people displaced from "white" South Africa by other policies designed to promote territorial apartheid.* NY Times 3/6/83, p9 [**1973**]

black studies, another name for AFRO-AMERICAN STUDIES. *In this city, Negro high school students in an integrated high school struck, demonstrated and caused various difficulties because there were no "black studies" offered in the curriculum.* Time 3/30/70, p2 [**1968**]

black theater, plays written, directed and produced by blacks and using the black community as their reference. *Nor is he [Ed Bullins] likely to be friendly toward anyone who disparages black theatre—to which he is passionately devoted—or the work of any playwright he admires.* New Yorker 6/16/73, p40 [**1970**]

bladelette or **bladelet** ('bleid,let), *n.* a small piece of stone chipped to form a sharp edge, used as a weapon during the Stone Age. *Late in the Upper Paleolithic and during the ensuing Mesolithic, it became the fashion to make smaller and smaller bladelettes. Commonly inserted as "side blades" into lateral grooves in antler and bone projectile points, such "microblades" lacerated the flesh of wounded game animals and thus promoted free bleeding and rapid death.* Britannica Book of the Year 1969, p101 [**1964**, from *blade* + *-lette, -let* (diminutive suffixes)]

blahs, *n.pl.* Usually in the phrase **the blahs.** *U.S. Slang.* a fit of ill humor or vague bodily discomfort or uneasiness; the sulks or, sometimes, the blues. *The* Columbia News, *a rural Georgia weekly, observed: "As long as there have been sweaty, hot summers, there have been cases of the blahs. We all get them, but somehow they seem worse this year."* Time 7/27/70, p9 [**1969**]

blast, *n. Slang.* **1** a party. *The girls were looking for campus clothes and the first item on their list was pants to wear to "beer blasts and dances."* NY Times 9/6/68, p46 **2** a good time; great fun. *And Meyer himself had a blast. An entirely unpretentious man. . .he had dreaded this confrontation with sophisticated, distinguished Yale.* Harper's 7/70, p37 [**1958** for def. 1; **1966** for def. 2.]

blaxploitation, *n. U.S.* the exploitation of interest in blacks by making movies and plays with black actors, especially for black audiences (often used attributively). Also spelled BLACKSPLOITATION. *We must come to understand that all the "violence" in the "blaxploitation" films only serves to create another form of escapism.* Harper's 6/76, p24 [**1972**, blend of *black* and *exploitation*]

bleeper, *n.* an electronic device to generate electronic telephone signals. See BLUE BOX. *Because many countries have their own sets of tones, the international phone phreak will need a set of bleepers. One presented in evidence at the trial was very elaborate, being capable of simulating seven different signalling systems.* New Scientist 12/13/73, p757 [**1964**, from *bleep* (1953) + *-er*]

bleomycin (,bli:ou'maisən), *n.* any of a group of antibiotics derived from a species of soil bacteria (*Streptomyces verticillus*), used in treating cancers of the skin, tongue, and lungs. *One of the newest drugs is an antibiotic, bleomycin, which has had early success in treating some heretofore resistant forms of cancer.* 1973 Britannica Yearbook of Science and the Future, p89 [**1970**, from *bleo-* (of uncertain origin) + *-mycin*, as in *streptomycin* (from Greek *mýkēs* fungus)]

blepharoplasty ('blefərou,plæsti:), *n.* a cosmetic surgery to remove the excess fat and skin from the lower eyelids that cause bags under the eyes, crow's-feet, etc. Also called EYELIFT. Compare RHYTIDECTOMY. *How did Senator William Proxmire (D., Wis.) get two black eyes?. . .The most likely explanation was blepharoplasty—plastic surgery to remove bags under the eyes.* Time 2/21/72, p44 [**1971**, from Greek *blépharon* + *-plastia* a molding] ▶This term was recorded in 19th-century dictionaries in the sense of "the operation of making a new eyelid from a piece of skin transplanted from an adjacent part" (*Century Dictionary*, 1889) and "the operation of supplying any deficiency caused by wound or lesion of the eyelid" (OED, 1882). In recent years, with the increasing use of cosmetic surgery, the term has been revived with a new sense.

blindside, *v.t.* **1** to hit (a player) on his unguarded or blind side. Compare CHEAP SHOT. *That great sportsman Mike Curtis ("The Beasts of Baltimore," January issue) took the cheapest shot of all time when he slammed into (blindside, as these brave gladiators say) an overexuberant spectator who ran onto the field in a recent Baltimore-Miami game.* Atlantic 3/72, p28 **2** *Figurative use.* to deal an unexpected blow. *At one point, Oregon's Tom McCall asked a question most of his colleagues were thinking—whether those Republicans who stand with the President [Nixon] were going to be "blindsided by any more bombs."* Newsweek 12/3/73, p33 [**1968**]

blind trust, a trust which manages the financial holdings of a person who assumes public office in order to avoid possible conflicts of interest between the person's public duties and business interests. *On Jan. 20, 1977, the day he became President, Mr. Carter's 62 percent interest in the business was transferred to a "blind trust" administered by. . .an Atlanta lawyer and confidant of Mr. Carter's. The White House has said that the trust buffers Mr. Carter from direct knowledge or control over the business.* NY Times 1/18/79, pA1 [**1969**]

blip, *v.t.* to replace (a censored word, expression, or remark on a videotape) with one or more sounds like "blip." . . . *Johnny Carson with Judy Brown, a model on whose back he wrote a check to see if it would be cashed. Some of his nightly quips are "blipped" from tape before air time.* NY Times 4/29/68, p86 —*n.* a brief expression; a note. *That a consulting firm had been called in—no matter one of the best—also registered a blip of concern.* Atlantic 4/71, p42 [**1965** for verb; **1971** for noun]

bliss out, *U.S. Slang.* to experience or fill with intense bliss; become or make ecstatic. *Initiates learn to see a dazzling white light, hear celestial music, feel ecstatic vibrations . . .The process is called "blissing out."* Newsweek 11/19/73, p157 *Davis displayed the nonstop, glowing smile and the glazed eyes of one who is "blissed out."* New Yorker 4/8/74, p32 [**1973**, verb use of *bliss, n.*, apparently patterned after *freak out;* a term popularized by followers of the Hindu guru, Maharaj Ji]

blissout, *n. U.S. Slang.* a thoroughly blissful state; rapturous or ecstatic condition. *At the end of the week, she wins something like the Academy Award, except it's at a ceremony where she is the only one being honored, and her girl friends and boy friends are all there, gathered round, to be happy for her. This blissout is the movie every actress must at some point have dreamed of making.* New Yorker 12/20/76, p117 [**1974**, noun use of BLISS OUT]

blitzer, *n. U.S. Football.* a player who moves in quickly to block a ball passer. *"He's done it all," said Sherman. "He's blocked well, picked up blitzers, caught the ball and has been a very quick runner with a good cut."* NY Times 9/6/68, p51 [**1964**, from *blitz, v.,* to charge a ball passer + *-er*]

BL Lacertae ('bi:el lə'sərti:), or **BL Lac,** any of a group of compact celestial bodies that are the sources of intense radiation but lack clearly defined emission lines in their spectra. *In the past few years still another class of objects has been added to this catalogue of astronomical prodigies: the BL Lacertae objects. The first of them was discovered less than 10 years ago, and about 30 more are known today.* Scientific American 8/77, p32 [**1970**, so called because the first such object discovered (in 1929) was identified as a variable star in the constellation *La-*

certa (the Lizard); *BL* designating the nineteenth such variable star]

block association, *U.S.* an organization formed by residents of a city block or other small area to protect and promote their interests. *New York City has 39,000 blocks and about 10,000 block associations, many active and some dormant . . .Block associations have been responsible for organizing a whole range of activities from cleaning up garbage-strewn lots to organizing street fairs and block parties.* Daily News (New York) 5/27/79, pMB1 [**1972**]

blockbust, *v.t.* to cause white property owners to sell (their houses, etc.) hastily and usually at a loss by making them fear that black people are about to move into the neighborhood. *. . . speculators . . .have just begun to appear on the Concourse* [Grand Concourse, an avenue in the Bronx, New York]. *"They've started to blockbust some buildings here," said an aide to Representative James H. Scheuer, who represents the area.* NY Times 7/21/66, p29 [**1966**, back formation from *blockbusting*]

blockbuster[1], *n.* a speculator who engages in blockbusting. *The block-buster induces panic selling to himself and then resells to incoming Negroes who are driven by the severe housing need to pay exorbitant prices.* Times (London) 11/2/67, p4 [**1963**, from *blockbust*ing + *-er*]

blockbuster[2], *n.* a highly promoted best-selling book, especially a novel. *The upshot was that the blockbuster book was monopolizing a larger share of the reader dollar; this held true in paperback also, giving rise to a situation in which a massmarket house without a blockbuster on its list was hurting. As one editor summed it up, "Fiction these days is either big or dead."* 1975 Collier's Encyclopedia Year Book, p153 [**1974**, extended from the earlier sense of a motion picture produced at lavish cost (1956), itself a figurative extension of the original and literal sense of an aerial bomb able to destroy an entire block of buildings (OEDS 1942)]

blockbusting, *n.* the act or practice of causing residents of a white neighborhood to sell their property hastily and usually at a loss, from fear that undesirable people, especially black people, are about to move into the neighborhood and that property value will decline (often used attributively). *During and right after the war, the Hough area, farther eastward, with its bigger and better homes and many apartment buildings, opened to blacks through a combination of block busting and white flight.* NY Times 6/1/71, p28 [**1962**, from *block* a city area + *busting* breaking up]

block club, *U.S.* a group of city dwellers organized to protect the block or area in which they live. *"Block clubs" have been organized in some white areas adjoining Chicago's South Side ghetto. Suspicious of interlopers, the clubs keep track of autos passing through the streets. They also follow up on arrests and prosecution of offenders.* Time 10/4/68, p21 [**1968**]

blocker, *n.* a drug or chemical that inhibits the action of a substance or part of the body. *Methadone was dispensed by 450 clinics nationwide as a chemical blocker and antagonist of heroin.* 1973 Britannica Yearbook of Science and the Future, p272 [**1973**]

block grant, *U.S.* a fixed grant of money made by the Federal Government to the states. *The President. . .would also consolidate 59 specific Federal programs into four so-called "block grants" to the states for health, education, child nutrition and social services for the poor, disabled and elderly. The states would no longer be required to add their own funds for these purposes.* NY Times 1/25/76, pD1 [**1975**] ► The term has been used in Great Britain since the turn of the century for a fixed grant made by the Exchequer to local authorities.

block release, (in Great Britain and on the Continent) a system of temporarily releasing industrial personnel from their jobs to enable them to attend a more advanced course of study. *The School of Management Studies at the St. Helen's College of Technology, is recognized as one of the major non-university schools of management sciences in the country, and provides*

specifically for block-release students. . . Times (London) 2/11/70, pVII [**1962**]

blood, *n.* *Black English.* a fellow black person. Compare BROTHER. *". . . I put it around Christmas because I know that's when a lot of bloods would be partying!"* M. Ron Karenga, Washington Post 5/9/78, pB1 [**1967**]

blood-CSF barrier, a selective impermeability of the capillaries in the central nervous system that prevents most harmful substances in the blood from reaching the cerebrospinal fluid (CSF). *In summary, all the proteins tested, with the exception of lysozyme, have been found in foetal CSF in concentrations much higher than those detected in CSF from normal adult subjects. These results, therefore, support the suggestion that the human blood-CSF barrier is not fully developed during foetal life.* Nature 1/15/76, p140 [**1976**] ► *Blood-brain barrier* (1952) was the first of these body-defense systems to be recognized. *The blood-brain barrier is a mechanism which screens substances passing from the blood vessels into the brain.* Science News 2/7/53, p88

Bloody Maria, *U.S.* an alcoholic drink made with tequila and tomato juice. *Though a few diehards still down tequila the traditional way—straight, with a lick of salt and a wedge of lime—most gringos prefer cocktail variations like the Margarita, made with lime juice and triple sec. Other Aztec Oles!: T'n'T (with tonic); Bloody Maria or Mexican Mary (substituting tequila for vodka).* Time 1/26/76, p62 [**1976**, patterned after earlier (1950's) *Bloody Mary*, a drink of vodka and tomato juice]

blow, *v.t.* *Slang.* **1** to smoke or inhale (a narcotic drug). *For the whole of the voyage they were "popping pills and blowing marijuana."* Times (London) 3/17/70, p1 *It was common knowledge that Jimi* [Hendrix] *blew every kind of dope invented. . .* NY Times 10/27/70, p45 **2 blow away,** to kill or destroy. *The man sees six teen-age blacks sweeping toward him like a pack of wolves. . .They reek of the peppermint smell of angel dust, and they are looking for somebody to blow away, like this turkey.* Time 5/7/79, p6 [**1969** for def. 1; **1979** for def. 2]

blowback, *n.* **1** the enlargement of an image that has been reduced to a microscopic size. *Figure 4 shows three blowbacks from laser-machined frames. The original document in each case was an 8.5 × 11 in. (216 × 279 mm) page which was scanned in raster fashion, with 2000 lines from the top of the page to the bottom.* McGraw-Hill Yearbook of Science and Technology, 1976, p233 **2** false or misleading information that is spread in a foreign country by intelligence agents but that unexpectedly circulates back to the country of origin. *Everyone was especially concerned that American officials had sometimes fallen victim to blowback, and one witness, who had formerly been on the staff of the C.I.A., described efforts he had made on several occasions to apprise policymakers that they had been taken in by their own government.* New Yorker 2/27/78, p26 [**1975** for def. 1; **1978** for def. 2]

blowdown, *n.* the sudden, forceful rupture of a cooling pipe in a nuclear reactor, especially in a power plant. Compare MELTDOWN. *In nuclear parlance, "blow-down" is synonymous with catastrophe, as it signifies loss of coolant with the nuclear reactor continuing to produce heat with nothing to carry it away.* New Scientist 6/22/78, p828 [**1978**, extended sense of the earlier term for a device to let off steam or gas]

blow-dry, *v.t.* **1** to dry or style (the hair) with a BLOW DRYER. *Where hairstylists once painstakingly set hair in curlers or rollers, they now, as often as not, simply cut and briskly blow-dry a breezy new style.* Consumer Reports 11/77, p626 **2** to blow-dry the hair of. *A bevy of bobbed, permed, blow-dried and finger-teased models paraded to popular songs.* Times (London) 2/6/76, p14 —*adj.* dried or styled by blow-drying. *The blow-dry hairdo placed more emphasis than ever on a good haircut and on hair that was in good condition.* 1971 Collier's Encyclopedia Year Book, p234 —*n.* an act or instance of blow-drying. *Staff benefits include having your hair baked set (only horrids like me would clamour for a blow-dry).* Times (London) 1/27/77, p11 [**1969**]

blow dryer, a hand-held hairdryer that blows and directs warmed air, used for drying and styling the hair. *The notion that styling one's hair should require a minimum of time and effort has caught on with women and men alike, and using a blow dryer has become a unisex morning ritual.* Consumer Reports 11/77, p626 **[1969]**

blowout, *n.* an abnormal swelling of a blood vessel; aneurysm. *Only decades later, after a deceptively quiet lull, does syphilis kill by causing a blowout of the aorta, the main artery leading from the heart, among other ways.* NY Times 3/13/76, p49 **[1974]**

blue box, a device attached to a telephone to generate electronic impulses that circumvent operator assistance and a record of the call. It is used by PHONE PHREAKS. *The blue-box— which can actually be any color, but was christened after the first one found—beeps electronic imitations of Bell signals so that users can "seize" lines to make free calls all over the world.* Newsweek 2/17/75, p79 **[1975]**

blue-eyed, *adj.* **1** *U.S. (especially Black English) Slang.* white; Caucasian. *"Blue-eyed soul brother" or "blue-eyed soul sister" is used to label whites who understand and appreciate black culture, and whose actions toward black people are without the reservation, strangeness, and racism that characterize the actions of many white people.* Rappin' and Stylin' Out, edited by Thomas Kochman, 1972, p145 **2** *Canadian Slang.* of English extraction; Anglo-Saxon. *Canadian poetry, too, is being pulled apart by regional interests. . .Recently, anthologies of West Coast, Montreal English, Maritime, and practically everything but blue-eyed poets have been published.* Maclean's 1/15/79, p51 **[1968 for def. 1; 1976 for def. 2]**

blue-eyed devil, *U.S. Slang.* a derogatory name for a white person. *Blue-eyed devils or Devils. . .is usually used in a collective sense and is usually pluralized. . .The adjective "blue-eyed" clarifies to whom "devil" is applied. This label for white people was first used by the Muslim leaders Elijah Muhammed and Malcolm X.* Rappin' and Stylin' Out, edited by Thomas Kochman, 1972, p142 **[1972]**

blue flu, *U.S.* an organized absence of policemen or firemen from work on the pretext of sickness, to influence contract negotiations or to protest working conditions. Compare YELLOW FLU. *City dwellers have learned recently about the "blue flu" that often afflicts police officers who are suspicious of proposed changes.* Atlantic 5/72, p67 **[1968, so called from the blue color of police and fire uniforms]**

bluegrass, *n. U.S.* traditional country music, especially of the southern United States. Compare COUNTRY-AND-WESTERN. *The biggest impact is being made on folk* [music] *fans by a special kind of country music—bluegrass. Bluegrass occupies the intellectual wing of country music.* Maclean's 6/6/64, p26 *After two hours someone suggests it is time for a musical interlude. A bluegrass trio appears from nowhere.* Listener 10/3/68, p428 **[1960, named after the Bluegrass Boys, a band that specialized in this type of music in the 1940's and 1950's, from the Bluegrass State, a nickname of the state of Kentucky]**

blue helmet, a member of the international military peacekeeping force of the United Nations, whose uniform includes a blue helmet. *"However, the United Nations Secretary General, on the advice of a high official of the organization, of American nationality, decided to recall the Blue Helmets. . ."* Times (London) 2/19/70, p10 **[1965]**

blue movie, a pornographic motion picture. *Since there is absolutely no censorship for the Festival, the bluest of blue movies can be seen in Cannes during the first half of May.* Harper's 9/70, p33 **[1965, from blue smutty (OED 1864)]**

blue-rinse or **blue-rinsed**, *adj. Especially U.S.* consisting of or typified by elderly women who are carefully groomed and socially active. *He also goes traipsing across the United States. . . reciting poems to the blue-rinsed brigade.* Manchester Guardian Weekly 8/1/70, p16 *. . .an unlikely coalition of affluent communities, led by embattled suburban matrons known as*

"the blue rinse set." New Yorker 1/3/77, p46 **[1964, so called from the frequently blue-rinsed gray hair of such women]**

blue shift, a shift of the light in a celestial body towards the blue end of the spectrum, indicating movement of the light source towards the observer. *During the collapse, the Doppler effect which, in our present universe, gives rise to a red shift would be reversed and any radiation produced would have been amplified by a blue shift. Now, shift the spectrum of any radiation to the blue and in effect you raise its associated temperature, so the state of maximum density could have been very hot.* Listener 5/25/72, p682 **[1965, patterned after *red shift* (1931)]** —**blue-shift**, *v.t.: In the switchback universe, however, the divisions are quite clear. Even better, the background radiation is a necessary feature of the universe. During the contracting phase of each cycle, starlight and other radiation is blueshifted to an ever-increasing degree, eventually being scrambled up in the fireball between cycles.* New Scientist 11/9/72, p318

▶Blue shifts are rare phenomena and remain largely theoretical; almost all extragalactic objects show the red shift. In 1978, however, an object (designated SS433) was discovered in or on the fringes of the Milky Way simultaneously flying toward and away from the earth at very high speeds—that is, exhibiting alternately a red shift and a blue shift. Since the motion toward the earth was estimated to be as fast as 20,000 miles a second, this was regarded as the largeset blue shift ever observed.

blues rock, a blend of the blues and rock music. *Commander Cody and His Lost Planet Airmen perform some earthy (despite their name) blues-rock and country-rock.* New Yorker 3/10/75, p6 **[1974]**

blue straggler, any of a group of blue stars somewhat to the left of the top of the main sequence. *Perhaps the most puzzling stars to explain are the "blue stragglers," a small number of stars that seemingly refuse to turn off the main sequence. Actually they may represent a brief transitional stage between the red-giant and horizontal-branch phases.* Scientific American 7/70, p33 **[1970]**

blusher, *n.* a cosmetic to give the skin a rosy color. *Blushers were used liberally to give the face a shining quality. Generally more makeup was used to achieve a less made-up look.* 1971 Collier's Encyclopedia Year Book, p234 **[1965]**

blush wine, a table wine slightly paler and drier than a rosé. *He [Ray Spencer] thinks of blush wines as "yuppie rosés." Either rosé will become known as the darker part of a broad blush-wine spectrum or the blush wines will be seen as a pale vanguard in the war of the rosés. We'll sip and see.* NY Times Magazine 9/21/86, p22 **[1984]**

B lymphocyte, another name for B CELL. *The lymphocytes involved in immunity are of two quite distinct classes. The first of these, the so-called B lymphocytes, are those that mature into cells that actually manufacture antibodies. But they cannot do so without the help of the second lymphocyte class, known as T cells.* New Scientist 5/25/72, p432 **[1972]**

BMEWS (bi:'myu:z), *n.* acronym for *Ballistic Missile Early Warning System* (which provides warning against a surprise attack by ICBM's, or intercontinental ballistic missiles). *FOBS would therefore not be detected by the West's ballistic missile early warning systems (BMEWS) as soon as would ICBM's* [intercontinental ballistic missiles]. Britannica Book of the Year 1968, p272 **[1959]**

BMX, abbreviation of BICYCLE MOTOCROSS. *In BMX, youngsters ride small, knobby-tired, stripped-down bicycles along dirt trails full of bumps and turns.* NY Times 4/12/86, pB1 **[1986]**

boa, *n.* a proposed system of jointly floated currencies whose exchange rates are allowed to fluctuate against each other within limits that are wider than in the SNAKE. *Members of the boa arrangement would place part of their reserves in such a fund and in return receive drawing rights on the assets of the fund which could be used to settle debts incurred. . .* Times

(London) 6/13/78 (page not known) [**1978**, patterned after SNAKE]

boarder baby, *U.S.* an infant or young child who is kept indefinitely in a hospital because the parents are not able or legally permitted to assume custody. Compare HEROIN BABY. . . . *A good example of a boarder baby would be a child born addicted to drugs as a result of his or her mother's addiction.* NY Times 12/7/76, p40 [**1976**]

boatel, *n.* a hotel at a small-boat basin or marina for use by boat owners or passengers. Compare AQUATEL. *Another major enterprise being promoted in France was a 100-mile wall of resorts, towns, motels, and boatels along the Mediterranean coast, roughly from Nimes to Perpignan.* Britannica Book of the Year 1966, p103 [**1957**, blend of *boat* and *motel*]

boat people, refugees, especially from Asia, who emigrate in boats to any country that will allow them to enter. *The 25,000 people whose entry was authorized last June, . . . include many of the 3,500 Vietnamese on board the cargo ship Hai Hong, which was turned away by the Malaysians, as well as 15,000 other boat people who have been given temporary refuge in such countries as Malaysia, Indonesia and Thailand.* Times (London) 11/30/78, p7 [**1977**]

bodhran (ˈbaðræn), *n.* an Irish drum. *Apart from the violin, traditional Irish instruments include a small flute, the "tin whistle," a goatskin drum called a bodhran, the pipes and of course the small Irish harp.* NY Times 10/28/77, pC17 [**1976**, from Irish *bodhrán* a deaf person, from *bodhar* deaf]

body art, a form of art in which the body of the artist or another person is decorated or used in other ways for some aesthetic effect, and often recorded photographically. *Painting, declared obsolete by '60s pundits, spurned outright by conceptualists who turned to film, video, earth works and body art—how could Snow, a role model for the upwardly modern, revert to such a retardataire medium?* Maclean's 12/11/78, p4 [**1971**] —**body artist**: *Like the art and language group, body artists are disinterested in and despairing of the traditional formal concerns of abstract art.* Americana Annual 1975, p104

body bag, a rubberized, zippered sack for holding and transporting a corpse. *They dragged him down the stairs and put him in a body bag. It's like a straight jacket.* Harper's 2/74, p64 [**1967**]

body-builder, *n.* a person who develops his or her body by systematic weightlifting exercises. *In Heads, a girl torn between a brainy weed and a moronic body-builder solves things by exchanging their heads with the help of an axe . . .* Times (London) 3/4/70, p13 [**1963**]

body burden, radioactive or other toxic material absorbed in the body. *Lead, too, is under close scrutiny. It has always been one of the "body burdens"—a favorite scientific phrase—that all of us carry around with us, because it settles in our bones.* New Yorker 4/13/68, p107 [**1959**]

body clock, an internal mechanism of the body supposed to regulate physical and mental functions in rhythm with normal daily activities. Swift transition through several time zones during jet flight disturbs the body clock. Compare BIOLOGICAL CLOCK. See also CIRCADIAN RHYTHM. *Dr. Underwood and Dr. Menaker can offer no explanation of how light reaches the clock, but they believe that other animals may possess similar systems for keeping the body clock on time without the use of their eyes.* Times (London) 10/21/70, p13 [**1965**]

body count, **1** a count of the enemy killed in a military operation. Compare KILL RATIO. *American policy at the highest staff levels was to seek to inflate the actual numbers of indigenous guerrilla forces . . . with higher and higher body counts as the war dragged on in the delta.* NY Times 6/3/71, p38 **2** *Transferred sense.* **a** a count of those killed in a particular way. *Dr. Richard H. Seiden, associate professor of behavioral sciences at Berkeley, qualifies the bridge* [Golden Gate] *as "the No. 1 location for death by suicide in the entire Western World" . . . The claim may be accurate, but the Golden Gate is one of the few major U.S. spans that keeps a body count.* Time 8/24/70, p40 **b** any count or tally of individuals. *State*

and Federal aid programs that are based on live body counts will provide less support to the cities and increase their support to the suburbs, unless such programs are changed. NY Times 9/11/70, p40 [**1967**]

body dancing, another name for TOUCH DANCING. *We never called it "body-dancing"; it was just a delicious way for males and females to move together on any smooth public or private floor large enough for a small band and free movement.* Newsweek 12/10/73, p16 [**1973**]

body-jewel, *n.* an ornament worn on the body instead of on clothing. *Accessories were often called body-jewels and were chain-mail type networks of linked metals, chainbelts, . . . snake rings, snake bracelets and arm bracelets, and slave footstraps.* 1970 World Book Year Book, p342 [**1970**]

body language, the unconscious gestures and postures of the body as a form of communication. *The basic movements of body language—Dr.* [Ray] *Birdwhistell calls it "kinesics" from the Greek "kine," to move—are still being described, a task that may take another generation or two. . . . This doesn't mean students of body language can't read body movements, to a limited extent, even at this stage of research.* Encyclopedia Science Supplement (Grolier) 1971, p99 [**1968**]

body mike, *U.S.* a microphone worn on the body usually around the neck. *Mr. Cryer and Miss Towers appear to sing well, although, with the now ubiquitous and damnable amplification of sound with stage-apron and body mikes, we hear not their real voices but their canned ones.* New Yorker 1/23/71, p66 [**1971**]

body paint, a paint or cosmetic preparation for coloring, decorating, or painting designs or figures on parts of the body. . . . *an enterprising firm has brought to the market a range of 12 brilliant body paints which are quick-drying, harmless to the pelt, and removable with soap and water.* New Scientist 1/1/70, p5 [**1968**]

body scanner, a CAT scanner used to diagnose abnormalities of the body. Compare BRAIN SCANNER. *The body scanner took large numbers of low-dosage pictures from different angles, processed the results in a computer, and fed them out as detailed three-dimensional pictures of organs such as the lungs, pancreas, kidneys and other internal structures 'seen' from any required angle.* Annual Register of World Events in 1975, p356 [**1975**] —**body scanning**: *"In diagnosing disease,"* Dr. Cooper points out, *"total body scanning machines are probably the biggest breakthrough in radiology since the invention of the X-ray tube."* Family Weekly 4/4/78, p4

bodyshell, *n.* the outer shell or frame of a motor vehicle. *The derby is a two-door saloon version of the Polo, sharing virtually the same mechanical specification and layout but offering a "three-box" bodyshell, with separate boot, in place of the two-box hatchback.* Times (London) 1/19/78, p29 [**1976**]

body shirt, a tight-fitting shirt or blouse, especially one which is snapped or sewn between the legs. *For those ladies who want their tattoos only temporarily, and without pain, there are Lyle Tuttle-designed body shirts which can be worn when desired, and removed at will.* Bangkok Post 3/18/73, p14 [**1970**] —**body-shirted**, *adj.*: *One of the body-shirted pretty young women came up to Mr. White and said she was going to Macy's to buy some candles.* New Yorker 8/28/71, p20

body shop, *U.S. Slang.* **1** a place of prostitution. *I found your article on the body shops* [Dec. 15] *disheartening. It seems ludicrous for law enforcement officers to devote so much effort to cracking down on a harmless exercise the prostitutes and their clients have been pursuing for thousands of years. It would seem more sensible merely to tax these operations at a fairly high rate.* Time 1/5/76, p4 **2** a business firm that provides people needed for such purposes as filling a hall, staging a demonstration, etc. *Not all consultants are consulting firms . . . Others are employees of concerns known in the trade as "body shops," suppliers of a phantom work force in an era of mandatory Federal personnel ceilings.* NY Times 12/5/77, p32 [**1975**, specialized use of the term for an automobile body repair shop]

body stocking, a woman's tight-fitting, one-piece undergarment of stockinglike material, that usually covers most of the body. . . . *quite diaphanous and quite long dresses of black silk-and-nylon with a faint floral silk-screen print are just $95, and in this instance the only requisite is a body stocking beneath.* New Yorker 4/25/70, p106 [**1965**]

bodysuit, *n.* a woman's tight-fitting, one-piece garment covering the torso, used informally for outer wear or in combination with skirts or slacks. *Warner's, the "grandaddy of the bodysuit family," brought out "You-Curve," a bodysuit in stretch tricot net with three matching panties in different leg lengths, all with stocking locks.* Britannica Book of the Year 1970, p344 [**1970**]

boiloff, *n.* a loss of liquid rocket fuel by vaporizing when the temperature reaches the boiling point (often used attributively). *One reason for choosing this propellant mixture is its relatively high boiling point and therefore long-term storage capability in space without the boil-off which occurs with a liquified gas, such as oxygen or hydrogen.* Americana Annual 1963, p619 [**1963**]

Bok globule (bak), any of a class of interstellar dust clouds that are compact, opaque, and regular in form, thought to be the precursor of stars. *Lacking an internal energy source, Bok globules are among the coldest objects in interstellar space: most are only about 10 degrees Kelvin (10 degrees Celsius above absolute zero). Hence they are nearly ideal subjects for comparison with theoretical cloud models, the highly simplified representations of essential cloud physics that astrophysicists construct to test their understanding of interstellar processes.* Scientific American 6/77, p67 [**1977**, named after Bart J. *Bok*, a Dutch-American astronomer who first suggested their importance in 1947]

bolo tie or **bola tie**, a cord or leather necktie with a decorative clasp, worn in the western United States. Also shortened to **bolo.** *The attorney in Las Vegas, a young chap in a fancy office, wearing a bolo tie and expensive boots, said right away that Earl C. had a case.* Atlantic 12/70, p79 *The* [Arizona] *state legislature passed 208 bills during the first session, ranging from the significant (establishment of state kindergartens) to the innocuous (recognizing the bola tie as the official state neckware).* 1972 Collier's Encyclopedia Year Book, p122 [**1964**, probably from its resemblance to the *bola*, a weapon used by South American cowboys]

bolt-on, *adj.* designed to be bolted on. . . . *the labour content of a Continental car repair bill usually is lower, due to the common use of bolt-on outer panels.* Times (London) 2/14/70, p18 [**1963**]

bomb[1], *n.* the **Bomb**, nuclear weapons and the potential threat they impose. *From the somber afternoon of the nuclear age, two physicists, father and son, look back at its dawn. The elder had helped to build the Bomb. The younger has been blighted by it.* Time 8/24/70, p64 [**1963**]

bomb[2], *v.t. U.S.* to hit (a baseball) a long distance. . . . *Hal McRae . . . bombed the first pitch thrown to him to left field for a two-run homer.* NY Times 3/19/68, p57 [**1964**, probably from *bomb*, n., U.S. term for a long pass in football]

bomb[3], *v.i. U.S. and Canadian Slang.* to flop; fail. *Yet big-name stage shows and acts (Camelot, My Fair Lady, Jack Benny) almost consistently bomb at the box office wherever they play in Edmonton.* Maclean's 3/68, p19 [**1963**]

bomb[4], *n. British Slang.* a fortune. *Let's say I'd put my granny's savings in it, not to make a bomb, but as a secure blue chip for a steady income and long-term capital growth.* Times (London) 9/14/70, p8 [**1958**]

bombed, *adj. Slang.* intoxicated, especially by alcohol or drugs. *"I've come into work bombed on sleepers a couple of times (they make you go round like you're drunk); the boss warned me."* Times (London) 8/18/70, p6 *Usually, when an editor says he*

got bombed last night, he means he had too much to drink. Time 12/5/69, p62 [**1968**]

bomblet, *n.* a small bomb. *There's no wasteful overkill to bomblets—just a nice, uniform distribution of energy.* New Yorker 1/9/71, p55 [**1964**]

BOMFOG or **bomfog**, *n. U.S. Slang.* pompous rhetoric. *Political Consultant David Garth believes that a national primary would lead to what "Nelson Rockefeller used to call BOMFOG—the brotherhood of man and the fatherhood of God—and never get into issues."* Time 1/28/80, p27 [**1976**, coined by Nelson A. Rockefeller, 1908-1979, in reference to the phrase supposedly often used by preachers]

bond, *v.* to establish strong emotional or social ties with another or others. *"I just won't be with the baby right after the birth, because that's when you bond and I don't want to do that."* NY Times Magazine 3/29/87, p35 . . . *female* [reproductive] *success is best accomplished through mating and bonding with just one male.* 1982 Britannica Yearbook of Science and the Future, p247 [**1970**; cf. MALE BONDING] —**bonding**, *n.: The room was full of bikers and bikers' lawyers. A colorful crowd. There was a lot of bonding.* New Yorker 6/8/87, p38

bondage, *n.* **1** a form of sadomasochism especially involving the tying up or shackling of a person, a sexual partner. Compare B & D. . . . *the hunt for the Tate-LaBianca killers led the state authorities to draw up a list of recent unsolved murders in which bondage, mutilation, or excessive stabbing had occurred.* Harper's 5/74, p68 **2** Attributive use: *Sex manuals, starting with Alex Comfort's* The Joy of Sex, *which approves of "bondage games," now treat "loving" S-M as just another sexual variation.* Time 5/4/81, p73 [**1970**]

bong, *n.* a pipe for smoking marijuana or hashish. *A bong is a long, vertical pipe with a large smoke chamber and a hole that creates a carburetor effect, enabling you to draw cool air in on top of the hot smoke.* NY Times Magazine 3/21/76, p21 [**1976**, of uncertain origin]

bonkers, *adj. Slang.* crazy. . . . *she has a choice of feeling guilty and sane or civic-minded and bonkers.* New Yorker 9/14/68, p105 *I'd had a bad mental time. I wasn't going bonkers, but I'd had a lot of overstrain and overwork, and I was sick of being under the London critical eye.* Listener 8/31/67, p272 [**1957**, originally British slang, meaning tipsy, slightly drunk]

boo, *n. U.S. Slang.* marijuana (also used attributively). *Is the traditional boola-boola of Yale being replaced by plain boo, which, translated from the underground argot, means marijuana?* NY Times 2/28/67, p39 [**1966**]

boobird, *n. U.S. Slang.* a sports fan who boos members of the team he roots for when they play poorly *Orr deserves better, but could be pardoned for doubting he'll get it. He has heard the boobirds of Maple Leaf Gardens. He has seen the anticipatory glint in the vulture's eye every time the knee went.* Maclean's 2/21/77, p44 [**1977**]

boob tube, Usually in the phrase **the boob tube.** *U.S. Slang.* television. Compare TUBE. See also THE BOX. *What chance does a child have to develop a taste for books if he never has a minute to himself when the boob-tube isn't blaring forth or he himself is not being whisked off to Scouts or dancing lessons?* Saturday Review 10/10/70, p21 [**1964**]

boogaloo (ˌbu:gəˈlu:), *n.* a dance in two-beat rhythm in which dancers move with shuffling feet, swiveling from side to side and rotating their shoulders and hips. *"I thought Roger was going to bed." "Maybe but I think he just wanted to get rid of the civilians. You can't tell—we might go out and do the Boogaloo."* New Yorker 3/1/69, p39 —*v.i.* to dance the boogaloo. *Today, however, a ballerina may have to arch on point in one sequence, boogaloo in another, then writhe on the floor like a snake . . .* Time 3/15/68, p30 [**1966**, probably influenced by *boogie-woogie*]

boogie or **boogey** *n.* **1** a very fast and lively form of rock'n'roll based on the blues. *"Hip Shake" is a simple Slim Harpo boogie, spotlighting effective mantric guitar and clattering percus-*

sion. *"Casino Boogie" slows it down, with rolling electric piano (Nicky Hopkins, sessionman supreme), and Richard effectively adding an occasional second part of Jagger's lead vocal.* Times (London) 5/25/72, p12 **2** *Slang.* another name for DISCO. *The popularity of roller skating . . . has meant an economic transfusion for older establishments that flourished when skaters skated to sedate tunes like "Skaters' Waltz" instead of the throbbing boogie of such songs as "Stayin Alive" and "I Will Survive."* States-Item (New Orleans) 5/18/79, pC1 —v.i. *Slang.* to dance uninhibitedly, especially to disco music. *Says Cleveland Promoter Jules Belkin, "They are up on the seats boogieing and running around the hall."* Time 6/24/74, p83 [**1972**, extended sense of *boogie* (1941) a style of playing blues on the piano]

boom baby, *U.S.* Usually *pl.*, **boom babies.** a person born during a BABY BOOM. Also called BABY BOOMER. *The boom babies provide a strong core readership within what is sometimes called "the upper half of the eighteen-to-thirty-five market" not just because of their numbers but also because of their habits.* New Yorker 4/10/78, p120 [**1973**]

boom carpet, the area affected by a sonic boom. *Of those who have been asked* [their opinion of Concorde] *in a Government-sponsored survey, as residents of the so-called boom carpet, many will only have experienced a minor boom such as is felt when one is several miles away from the flight path.* Times (London) 5/31/72, p20 [**1966**]

boom corridor, a restricted route for supersonic aircraft. *BOAC would like to operate Concorde with only one stop—at Lagos, West Africa. The most efficient way of doing this would be to establish a "boom corridor" through the sparsely-populated deserts and jungles of Morocco, the Spanish Sahara, Mauritania, and Mali, then, after crossing the Gulf of Guinea, through Angola and Botswana.* Manchester Guardian Weekly 1/6/73, p8 [**1972**]

boomy, *adj. U.S.* growing vigorously; prosperous. *At home, the company's business is not nearly so boomy. Bob Fluor blames federal fumbling. "We expect little or no refinery work here until we get some kind of energy policy," he says.* Time 1/5/76, p75 [**1960**, from *boom* a sudden or rapid growth in business]

boonies, *n.pl. U.S. Slang.* a remote rural area; boondocks. *Then a young woman with the voice of a nineteen-forties chanteuse in some night spot out in the boonies sang "The Star-Spangled Banner."* New Yorker 2/4/80, p28 [**1965**, short for *boondocks* (1944), from Tagalog *bundók* mountain]

boot, *n.* **1** a steel brace with a lock that can be clamped to one of the wheels of a parked automobile to prevent it from being moved. *The French Book program . . . calls for independent contractors with lists of scofflaw license plates to roam the streets, immobilizing violators' cars by attaching the "boot" to the back wheel. The car is then impounded and the owner advised that it can be retrieved only after the payment of all fines.* NY Times 5/25/80, pD7 **2** the initial starting point of a computer, where the operating system is brought into the main memory and takes over control. *The program also executes what is called a checksum on the . . . boot sector, the place where the instructions that start the operation of the computer are located.* NY Times 5/30/89, pC1 [**1980**; def. 2 is a shortening of *bootstrap* (1956)] —v. **to boot** (up). —v.t. **1** to load (a program) in a computer. . . . *the user simply boots it up—hits the buttons that load the program into the machine's memory—and gets ready to fly.* NY Times 7/2/85, pC5 **2** to use a small set of basic instructions in computer programming to develop additional instructions until the complete program is assembled. . . . *I was booting DOS before down-loading . . . and the system crashed.* A. Hedberg, Money 3/82, p71 —v.i. to be loaded into a computer; become ready for operation. *It boots up and loads the directory. . . .in less than 4 seconds.* Global Computer Supplies, Spring 1989, p14 [**1962**, **1965** (OEDS), from *bootstrapping*]

bootleg turn, an abrupt turning around of an automobile by using the emergency brake to lock the rear wheels and spinning the steering wheel in a sharp turn. *To offset the added weight, which brings the total up to some 4,500 lbs., he equips*

the car with a high-powered engine (400 h.p. or more) and an especially strong, road-hugging suspension system. The result: an auto that can absorb considerable punishment and still execute bootleg turns and high-speed escapes.* Time 7/10/78, p55 [**1975**]

boots, *n.pl. U.S. Slang.* an illegal linear amplifier connected to a citizens band radio to boost transmission. *Because of overcrowding, many a CB enthusiast (called an "apple") is strapping an illegal linear amplifier ("boots") on to his transceiver ("ears") which is limited by the Federal Communications Commission ("Big Daddy" in the US) to an output power of no more than five watts.* New Scientist 6/30/77, p764 [**1977**]

bootstrap, *v.t.* **bootstrap oneself,** to get into or out of something by one's own effort. *Somehow we have to bootstrap ourselves to a thriving export trade and the consequent favourable balance of payments.* New Scientist 11/30/67, p525 [**1966**, verb use of the noun, chiefly in the idiom *pull, raise, or lift oneself by one's bootstraps,* or as an adjective, as in the phrase *a bootstrap operation*] —n. a theory in particle physics which holds that all nuclear particles are composed of each other, as distinguished from the theory that all particles are built out of a limited number of elementary particles, such as the quark. *Interdependence is the core of Chew's thinking. The simple fact that all particles are related should be enough to determine everything. If we study hard enough, Chew maintains, we will find that the masses and electric charges of all particles, and the strengths of the forces between them, are exactly what they are because no other arrangement would be logically and mathematically self-consistent. This theory is known as the bootstrap, because it suggests that physics can pull itself by its bootstraps. Assume nothing, prove everything.* World Book Science Annual 1975, p92 [**1966**]

born-again, *adj. Especially U.S.* **1** of or having to do with personal conversion and renewed commitment to Christ as the way to salvation; evangelical; revivalistic. *I worried that the Carters' born-again religion came dangerously close to fanaticism. It didn't seem wise or prudent for a candidate to speak so often of Christ and Christianity.* New York Post 11/5/76, p36 **2** *Figurative.* marked by a rebirth or renewal (as of interest, freshness, or youth); resurgent. *On their way to gourmandise, a curious thing has happened to born-again American cooks: they have rediscovered the glorious raw ingredients and inimitable provincial dishes of their own country.* Time 12/19/77, p56 **3 born again,** *Especially U.S.* converted through a personal renewed commitment to Christ as savior. *Speaking or singing in tongues—messages transmitted via an unknown language—is a regular event for the "born again"—people who have welcomed Jesus into their hearts.* Maclean's 11/15/76, p74 [**1976**, from the phrase in the Gospel of John (3:3 and 3:7): "Jesus answered and said . . . Except a man be born again, he cannot see the kingdom of God . . . Marvel not that I said unto thee, Ye must be born again."]

BOSS (bɔ:s *or* bɑs), *n.* the secret intelligence organization of South Africa. *The group is convinced that there have been between eight and 20 BOSS agents working in Britain.* Manchester Guardian Weekly 11/27/71, p9 [**1969**, acronym for *Bureau of State Security*]

Boston arm, a type of artificial arm developed in Boston, Massachusetts. *Doctors and engineers unveiled today what they called the "Boston arm," an electronically operated artificial limb that an amputee flexes simply by willing it to flex, as is done with a natural arm.* NY Times 9/13/68, p1 [**1968**]

Botswanian or **Botswanan**, *n.* a native or inhabitant of Botswana, a country in southern Africa (the former Bechuanaland), independent since 1966. *He hopes that the school's target of 250 pupils will eventually comprise a majority of Botswanians.* Times (London) 5/9/70, p8 —adj. of Botswana or its people. *The Botswanan Government has said that cattle were slaughtered by veterinary officers to prevent the spread of foot and mouth disease.* Times (London) 5/27/77, p9 [**1967**]

bottleneck, *n. U.S.* a style of guitar playing in which a piece of glass, metal, etc., is used to press down on the strings to produce a gliding sound. *But she draws gasps from the crowd when she* *lets herself go on the guitar—bottleneck, slide, funky, chords overlapping . . .* Newsweek 11/6/72, p66 [**1966,** from the use of the broken neck of a bottle for this purpose]

bottleneck inflation, *Economics.* a rise in prices without an increase in the aggregate demand for goods. Compare HESIFLATION, SLUMPFLATION. *They have even coined a new phrase— "bottleneck inflation"—to describe the 17 per cent rise in wholesale prices and 13 per cent in consumer prices officially expected in the six months to the end of March.* Manchester Guardian Weekly 12/8/73, p1 [**1970**]

bottomless, *adj.* **1** (especially of entertainers) completely naked; nude. *The court decided that state liquor authorities had the power to withhold liquor licenses from places that featured bottomless dancers or erotic films.* Time 6/25/73, p72 **2** featuring naked dancers or performers. *It is a piece of ethnocentrism to assume that Saturday night is the night all Americans go out on the town—movies, plays, ballet, opera, bottomless bars and the like.* NY Times Magazine 3/12/72, p32 [**1972,** patterned after *topless*]

bottom line, Usually, **the bottom line. 1a** the last line in a profit and loss statement, showing the financial condition of a company or other organization. *His only interest is in the bottom line. He doesn't know or care about books or art or music or even his own wife—only about the bottom line.* Harper's Bazaar 10/72, p105 **b** *Figurative.* the main point; gist; summary. *And the bottom line of the lesson is simple: Throw away your analysts, your figures, and your chart board—get yourself a dart board.* Saturday Review 12/18/73, p13 **c** *Figurative.* the chief quality; basic characteristic. *In his new play, Seascape, Edward Albee seems drained of almost all vitality—theatrical, intellectual, artistic. And vitality was always Albee's bottom line, the one quality that even his detractors admitted he possessed.* Newsweek 2/10/75, p75 **2** Also used attributively: *What came after was bottom-line architectural pragmatism and the city as setting for social tragedy rather than a brave new world.* NY Times Magazine 1/26/75, p41 [**1970**] ►This term is said to have been used as far back as the 1930's in the New York financial district.

bottomonium (ˌbatəˈmouni:əm), *n. Nuclear Physics.* a hypothetical subatomic particle consisting of a bottom quark and its antiparticle. Compare TOPONIUM. *It had been assumed from their first discovery that the upsilons contained bottom quarks, namely that they were so-called "bottomonium," a series of structures built of a bottom quark and a bottom antiquark, each one with slightly more energy than the one below it in the series.* Science News 7/26/80, p53 [**1980,** from BOTTOM (QUARK) + *-onium,* as in CHARMONIUM]

bottom quark, a quark that has three times the mass of a charmed quark. Compare TOP QUARK. See also QUARK. *The upsilon, formed of a bottom quark and a bottom antiquark, is 10 times more massive than the proton.* NY Times 2/13/79, pC2 [**1977**]

bou-bou (ˈbu: bu:), *n.* a long, shapeless garment worn by men and women in Mali, Senegal, and some other parts of Africa. Also spelled BUBU. *. . . the Moslem from the north swishing along in the bou-bou sells plastic bags to the tall Mauretanian who wears the turban and has the look of Arabia etched on his face.* Saturday Review 10/31/70, p45 [**1963,** from a native name in Africa]

Boulwarism (ˈbu:lwəˌrizəm), *n.* a method of collective bargaining. *. . . "Boulwarism," named after Lemuel Boulware, G.E.'s [General Electric's] labor relations chief in the 1950's . . . calls for management to make and stick to an initial "firm, fair" offer to employees and to attempt to convince workers of the offer's merits by conducting vigorous "employee marketing" campaigns.* Time 2/9/70, p71 [**1963**]

boutique farm, a farm that specializes in raising exotic crops and livestock. *Elsewhere around the country, boutique farms are producing game birds, ducks and free-range chickens (which are allowed to roam and forage for natural food to add flavor and improve texture).* Time 8/26/85, p54 [**1980**] —**boutique farmer:** *The old Georgetown Market a block away on M street will also reopen this spring as a sort of boutique farmers*

market for the aubergine and alfalfa sprouts crowd. Washington Post 1/31/80, pE9

boutiquier (bu:ti:ˈkyei), *n.* the owner of a boutique. *Adolfo . . . was an important boutiquier when other custom milliners ventured no farther hors d'oeuvre* [outside the (chief) work] *than an occasional scarf or handbag.* New Yorker 10/18/69, p158 [**1966,** from French]

bovver, *British Slang. n.* street fighting, especially by gangs of rowdies. *During the 1870s his* [Lionel Jeffries', character actor] *grandfather, Charles Jeffries, ran an East End gang called the Skeleton Army whose specialty was bovver at Salvation Army meetings.* Times (London) 4/29/70, p12 —*v.i.* to engage in street fighting. *Skinheads don't bovver with the West Indians, probably because they are tough.* Time 6/8/70, p38 [**1970,** probably from the Cockney pronunciation of *bother* meaning "disturbance"]

bovver boot, *British Slang.* a type of heavy hob-nailed and steel-toed shoe designed for kicking and causing injury, typically worn by rowdies in street fighting. Also called CHERRY RED. *. . . the skinhead had kicked Miss Singer in the shins with his bovver boots.* New Scientist 9/17/70, p600 *His* [William McIlvanney, poet] *language is often as clumsy and ugly as his material; his metaphors can be used with the indiscriminateness of bovver boots.* Times (London) 5/2/70, pIV [**1970**]

bowhunt, *v.i., v.t.* to hunt game with a bow and arrow. *I had finally done what I was beginning to believe was impossible— I'd killed a groundhog with a bow! That episode took place only a few years ago. Since then I have bowhunted chucks at every opportunity.* Outdoor Life 3/71, p211 [**1968**]

bow shock, or **bowshock** (bau), *n.* a shock wave caused by the interaction of solar wind with a planet's magnetic field. See SHOCK FRONT. *About 5 million miles (8 million kilometers) from Jupiter, Pioneer detected a major change in the solar wind as the spacecraft passed through an interplanetary shock wave, or bowshock, caused by the planet.* World Book Science Annual 1975, p246 [**1970,** so called from the resemblance of the planetary phenomenon to the wave produced by the bow of a ship]

bow thruster (bau), a propeller in a ship's bow, operated by remote control. *The liner was manoeuvred by use of a bow thruster, which forces jets of water through tubes underwater to turn the nose of the ship.* Times (London) 2/6/70, p1 [**1963**]

bow wave (bau), another name for BOW SHOCK. *One of the most striking discoveries is that the upper atmosphere of Mars ends in a region of ions that forms a kind of bow wave like that of the earth. This is interpreted as a shock front caused by the interaction of the Martian atmosphere and the solar wind.* Science News 6/30/73, p420 [**1972,** extended sense of *bow wave* (1877)]

box[1], *n. British.* short for BOX JUNCTION. *Do not enter box, runs the injunction, unless your exit is clear.* Times (London) 5/5/70, p11 [**1970**]

box[2], *n.* **1** Usually in the phrase **the box,** *Slang.* television. Compare TUBE. See also BOOB TUBE. *Last week I saw Dr* [Billy] *Graham on the box, stating his firm belief in the actual and the physical return . . . of his Lord Jesus Christ . . .* New Scientist 12/10/70, p457 [**1964**] **2** *U.S.* a large, portable radio, often combined with a cassette stereo system. Also called GHETTO BLASTER. *Up at Crazy Eddie's off Fordham Road . . . they have 40 different kinds of boxes on display—cacophony to go, at prices better than $300 a box.* NY Times 8/14/79, pB3 [**1979**]

box junction, *British.* a road intersection that may not be crossed by a vehicle, even if the lights are in its favor, unless the exit is clear of traffic. *Bradford police have temporarily stopped prosecuting motorists for breaches of the box junction regulations, it was stated today.* Times (London) 11/9/72, p3 [**1965,** so called from the boxlike grid of yellow lines painted on the road surface at such an intersection, introduced in Great Britain in 1963]

boychik or **boychick,** *n. U.S. Slang.* boy; kid; young fellow. *The Allen persona—the urban boychik as social misfit—is, of* *course, an act, a put-on, no more the real performer than Chaplin's tramp or Jack Benny's miser.* Time 7/3/72, p58 [**1965**, from American Yiddish *boytshik* (literally) little boy, from English *boy* + Yiddish diminutive suffix *-tshik* (from Russian *-chik*)]

BP, 1 abbreviation of BEAUTIFUL PEOPLE. *Papers were regularly filled with features and with candid-camera shots of BPs going in and out of smart restaurants.* Time 9/14/70, p79 **2** abbreviation of BLACK PANTHER. *Gregory gave her the number of Black Panther HQ, and the BPs sent over a bodyguard.* New Yorker 8/28/71, p37 [**1968** for def. 1; **1971** for def. 2]

B particle, a hypothetical elementary particle that is the unit particle of the NEUTRAL CURRENT. *The B particle is the electrically neutral counterpart of the W particles and with them it forms a triplet of the same mass.* Science News 10/9/71, p253 [**1969**, perhaps from *boson particle*]

bpi, abbreviation of *bits* (or *bytes*) *per inch,* a unit of measure for memory capacity in databanks. *Developments in peripheral equipment included almost simultaneous announcements by IBM and Storage Technology Corp. of magnetic-tape systems with data stored at 6,250 bits per linear inch of tape (bpi).* Britannica Book of the Year 1974, p204 [**1974**]

bps, abbreviation of *bits* (or *bytes*) *per second.* See BPI. *Speech is transmitted at a rate measured in "bits-per-second" (bps). Most modern telephone systems operate at 64,000 bps, which is extremely wasteful.* Times (London) 7/20/78, p4 [**1972**]

b quark, short for BOTTOM QUARK. *Evidence for the b was first found in the upsilon particles discovered about two years ago. The upsilons are examples of what is called hidden beauty. They are made of a b quark and an anti-b quark, and therefore in a sense they are subject to internal cancellation.* Science News 9/22/79, p196 [**1978**]

bra burner, *Slang.* a derogatory term for a militant feminist or Women's Liberationist. *The young girl with the nonassertive mother may . . . believe that assertive women are "women's libbers," "bra burners," "commies," or "sluts."* Spencer A. Rathus and Jeffrey S. Nevid, BT: Behavior Therapy, 1977, p86 [**1972**]

bracket creep, *Economics.* the condition of being taxed on income at an increasingly higher rate as one's income increases, usually because of inflation. *The Republicans also propose indexing taxes to the inflation rate to eliminate bracket creep; this would end the automatic tax increase that occurs when someone gets a pay raise that only keeps up with inflation.* Time 8/25/80, p28 [**1979**]

bradykinin (ˌbrædiˈkainən), *n.* a protein substance that causes dilation of small blood vessels and is believed to produce some of the signs of inflammation, such as swelling and pain. Compare NEUROKININ. *It is a peptide—a short chain made up of nine amino acids which is produced when proteins in the blood plasma are broken down by certain enzymes. Bradykinin was first discovered in snake venom in 1949.* New Scientist 6/10/65, p698 [**1959**, from *brady-* slow (from Greek *bradýs*) + *kinin* any of various proteins involved in dilation and contraction of tissue, from Greek *kīneîn* to move]

braille cell, a group of phosphenes (luminous rings of the visual cortex) forming a unit of perception in experiments in which a blind person's cortex is electrically stimulated to enable perception of braille symbols without touching them. See CORTICAL BRAILLE. *The number and spatial distribution of phosphenes is inadequate for presentation of 26 ordinary letters. Consequently . . . six non-interacting phosphenes were selected to form a 'braille cell.'* Nature 1/15/76, p111 [**1976**]

brain box, *Informal.* an electronic computer. *But then someone plugged the brainbox in, and $18,000-a-month worth of Hewlitt-Packard 21-MX and associated software revealed that it didn't work.* Maclean's 10/2/78, p43 [**1966**]

brain dead, showing brain death. See DEATH. *But because Karen was not "brain dead," few lawyers were surprised when*

Judge Robert Muir ruled against any "pulling of the plug." Time 4/12/76, p50 [**1976**]

brain death, death of the cerebral cortex; final cessation of electrical activity in the brain, as evidenced by flat tracings on an electroencephalograph. Also called CEREBRAL DEATH. . . . *a special Harvard University committee has recommended that brain death, or irreversible coma, be considered a definition of death and has drawn up a set of guidelines for determining when there is no discernible activity in the central nervous system.* Scientific American 9/68, p85 [**1968**]

brain drain, the emigration of scientists, scholars, etc., to countries that offer better job opportunities. *Eleven foreign-born American scholars—sociologists, physicians, literary critics—assess the brain drain, its causes and its effect upon American learning.* Science News 9/21/68, p296 [**1963**]

brain-drain, *v.i.* to emigrate to a country where better jobs are offered to scientists, scholars, etc. *Twice a year he* [William Cooper] *goes to the US and Canada, seeing scientists who have brain-drained westwards and want to come back.* Manchester Guardian Weekly 4/10/71, p21 **—v.t.** to cause to brain-drain. *The institute has recruited a large portion of its faculty from the growing reservoir of "brain-drained" Indian scientists in the West, even paying the cost of resettling them and their families.* NY Times 1/12/68, p69 [**1965**]

brain drainer, a scientist, scholar, etc., who emigrates to another country for a better job. . . . *the general attitude towards the brain drainers is more one of supplying them with information about jobs available.* Science Journal 1/69, p13 [**1965**]

brain gain, an increase in a country's professional and skilled work force resulting from the immigration of foreign scientists, scholars, etc., seeking better job opportunities. *The United States remains the most popular destination, drawing almost half the annual total, or 2,684 last year . . . For the recipient countries the emmigrants produce the opposite of the brain drain, a brain gain.* NY Times 11/7/77, p12 [**1966**, patterned after BRAIN DRAIN]

brain hormone, any of various hormones produced in the hypothalamic region of the brain, such as LRF, TRF, and somatostatin, especially hormones that act upon the pituitary gland to cause release of various factors or hormones. *Enkephalin is composed of a string of five amino acids, the building blocks of proteins. The particular string that comprises one form of enkephalin is also found in a string of 91 amino acids that comprise the brain hormone known as betalipotropin.* Times (London) 9/18/76, p14 [**1975**]

brain life, the capacity of the brain or central nervous system to function as shown by neurobiological tests. *Scientists and physicians should accept "brain life" as a definition for the beginning of human life just as they have accepted "brain death"—complete absence of detectable brain waves—as the leading indicator of death.* New York Daily News 5/9/75, p14 [**1975**, patterned after BRAIN DEATH]

brain scan, an X-ray picture or examination made by a BRAIN SCANNER. *They also propose . . . that boxers should be compelled to go to hospital for a brain-scan after being knocked out.* Times (London) 8/19/78, p6 [**1975**]

brain scanner, a CAT scanner used to diagnose abnormalities in the brain. Compare BODY SCANNER, CAT SCANNER. *At many hospitals, brain scanners are running 10 and 12 hours a day, six days a week, and there are still long waiting lists of patients.* Wall Street Journal 12/10/75, p1 [**1975**]

braless (ˈbrɑːlis), *adj.* favoring the discard of brassieres as a symbol of women's liberation. Compare TOPLESS. *"Miss Loren* [Sophia Loren], *what are your views on the braless movement?"* New Yorker 10/3/70, p31 [**1962**]

Brand X, an unidentified item serving as a foil to show the comparative superiority of another item. *Once it* [ego] *has achieved righteousness, it is ready to sign up for holy war and to kill all who remain confused or who have developed a sort of righteousness (Brand X) that varies in any detail (or only in nomenclature) from the one, true Eternal Verity brand label. Sat-*

urday Review 1/22/72, p25 [**1970**, from the practice in advertisements of referring to a competing product as "brand X"]

brassin (ˌbræsən), *n.* a plant hormone that stimulates the division, elongation, and lateral enlargement of plant cells. Compare ABSCISIC ACID, CYTOKININ, KINETIN. *Isolated recently by investigators at the Department of Agriculture research establishment in Beltsville, Md., the brassins . . . take their name from the genus* Brassica, *a group of plants that includes the oilseed producer rape, whose abundant pollen is the source of the new hormones.* Scientific American 9/70, p91 [**1970**]

Brayton engine, an engine that utilizes a gas turbine to generate mechanical power. *A Brayton engine uses a high-speed rotating turbine instead of pistons to compress its working fluid.* World Book Science Annual 1978, p97 [**1977**, named after G.B. *Brayton*, an American engineer who invented it in the 1800's]

bread, *n. Slang.* money. *"Anyway, she could get to New York on five hundred, couldn't she?" "Sure," shrugged Gary . . . This chick wasn't running away, he flashed, not with that kind of bread.* Atlantic 6/70, p74 [**1952**]

breadboarding, *n.* the construction of an experimental system, such as an electronic circuit, on a flat surface specially equipped to lay out experimental models and circuitry. *The components were interconnected with metal or plastic tubing to form a fluidic device. This approach is suitable for constructing experimental circuits, breadboarding, and developing new fluidic concepts.* McGraw-Hill Yearbook of Science and Technology 1968, p14 [**1958**]

break, *n. U.S.* **1** access to a radio channel by a citizens band radio operator. *I'll be trying to call Gene when he's on the way home in his car, and I just won't be able to get a break—I just can't get on the air.* Family Circle 8/76, p20 **2** Also used as an interjection: *We heard a driver call a passing truck: "Break, Channel 10. I'm calling that blue truck with Ohio plates, westbound. I am eastbound. What's ahead?"* Parade 11/16/75, p27 [**1975**, from *break* interruption]

break-bulk, *adj.* of or relating to the breaking down of carload shipments into smaller shipments for various destinations. *Many shippers have expressed concern over the rapid trend to container shipping and the ousting of ordinary tonnage for break-bulk consignments.* NY Times 6/24/68, p74 [**1966**]

break-dance, *v.i.* to engage in break dancing. *Children were break-dancing . . . on the beach to tapes of his music.* New Yorker 9/24/86, p92 [**1986**]

break dancing, *U.S.* a style of dancing, often competitive, in which the dancers wriggle, spin on their backs, and perform other acrobatics. *Break dancing . . . is the first new dance phenomenon in the cities in more than a decade, and it seems to be picking up new steam after coming and going for the last two years.* New York Daily News 9/23/83, p18 [**1983**]

breaker, *n. U.S.* **1** a citizens band radio operator requesting the use of a channel. *You get in on the conversation by picking up your microphone, pressing the send-button and asking for a "break," as: "Breaker 19, breaker 19." Usually someone will respond, "Go ahead, breaker," and you're on the air.* NY Times Magazine 4/25/76, p28 **2** Also used as an interjection: *"I'm on the truck's CB all the time," he tells CB Guide. "It seems as soon as I say 'Breaker, breaker, this is Sonny Pruitt,' I'm never at a loss for someone to chat with."* CB Guide 5/76, p21 [**1963**, from *break (in)* to interrupt + *-er*]

breathalyse, *v.t., v.i. British.* to subject or submit to a test of intoxication, usually by means of a breathalyser. . . . *the breathalyser test . . . meant blowing into a plastic bag; if the crystals in a connected tube turned green it was prima facie evidence of too much alcohol in the system.* Annual Register of World Events in 1967, p46 [**1960**, from *Breathalyser*, a trade name formed from *breath* + anal*yse* + *-er*]

breathhold diving, underwater diving without the use of breathing apparatus, especially a form of diving used by seals, dolphins, etc., in which the breath is held underwater for regular periods, during which the heart rate and brain waves slow

down markedly. *The adaptation to breathhold diving of marine animals is probably an especially well developed instance of a very general asphyxial defence mechanism common to all vertebrates from fish to man.* Science Journal 4/70, p72 [**1966**]

breath test, *British.* a test of intoxication, usually by means of a breathalyser. *Its opponents argue that the breath test cannot be accurate because of the distortion of alcohol in the mouth.* Manchester Guardian Weekly 11/22/69, p12 [**1966**]

breath-test, *v.t. British.* to breathalyse. *In Britain last year, of 73,455 motorists breath-tested by police, 29,586 were found to be negative.* Manchester Guardian Weekly 6/19/71, p5 [**1960**]

Brezhnev Doctrine, the doctrine that the USSR has the right to intervene in the affairs of other Communist countries in defense of Communism. *In May, Leonid I. Brezhnev, general secretary of the Soviet Communist Party, himself went to Prague to sign the treaty, which legitimized the presence of Soviet troops in Czechoslovakia. The treaty also incorporated the essence of the so-called Brezhnev doctrine.* Britannica Book of the Year 1971, p239 [**1968**]

bricolage (briːkouˈlɑːʒ), *n.* the use of ready-made tools or other objects for a variety of purposes. *Thank You Hide, 1970, is a fair example of Wiley's* [the artist William T. Wiley] *bricolage, with its rusty pickax snagged, like an unwanted anchor, on a knotted line from an improvised fishing pole, its ragged sheet of ox hide . . .* Time 1/17/72, p38 [**1964**, from French, puttering around, doing odd jobs; originally, the act or skill of causing a ball (as in tennis or billiards) to rebound; see BRICOLEUR]

bricoleur (briːkouˈlœr), *n.* a person who makes use of ready-made tools or other objects for a variety of purposes. *Two years ago several graduate students in related fields made a five-year commitment to launch something called the Bricoleur Association. According to Claude Lévi-Strauss, the* bricoleur's *"universe of instruments is closed and rules of his game are always to make do with 'whatever is at hand.'"* Harper's 9/74, p87 [**1974**, from French, putterer, handyman, from *bricoler* to do odd jobs, from *bricole* an odd job; originally, the rebound or ricochet of a ball]

bridgebuilder, *n.* a person who strives to resolve differences between opposing persons, parties, systems, etc. *Initially he* [Halvard Lange] *followed* [Trygve] *Lie's line, that of bridgebuilder between East and West, but the deterioration in the international climate made this an attitude difficult to sustain.* Times (London) 5/21/70, p10 [**1967**]

brigatisti (ˌbriːɡaˈtiːstiː), *n.pl.* members of the RED BRIGADES. *The Communists, in the organization's view, had sold out; the aim of the* brigatisti, *much like that of 19th century anarchists, was to purify society by overthrowing all existing institutions. But the Red Brigades seem to have no coherent vision of what would replace them.* Time 3/27/78, p43 [**1978**, from Italian, from *Brigate (Rosse)* Red Brigades + *-isti*, plural of *-ista* -ist]

Brillouin scattering (briːyəˈwæ), *Physics.* the scattering of light by phonons (units of sound or vibration in crystals). *The formula for Brillouin scattering makes it possible to measure the velocity of sound at various wavelengths in any liquid and thus to study important properties of materials.* Scientific American 9/68, p124 [**1965**, named after Louis Marcel *Brillouin*, 1880?–1948, a French physicist who described it in 1922]

broad-brush, *adj.* not detailed; incomplete or imperfect; rough. *Government economists . . . have taken several routes to arrive at admittedly broad-brush estimates that air pollution costs U.S. citizens between $14,000,000,000 and $18,000,000,000 a year in direct economic loss.* Encyclopedia Science Supplement (Grolier) 1970, p181 [**1960**]

broadcast journalism, the gathering, editing, and reporting of news for radio and television. Compare ELECTRONIC JOURNALISM, PRINT JOURNALISM. *Some powerful broadcasters want the Government totally out of broadcast journalism, and they cite the 1974 landmark First Amendment case that applies to newspapers—Tornillo v. The Miami Herald, in which the Supreme Court decided "it has yet to be demonstrated how Government regulation in this crucial* [editing] *process can be exercised consistent with First Amendment guarantees of a free press."* NY

Times Magazine 3/30/75, p48 [**1968**] —**broadcast journalist:** *The Shadow in the Cave bears the mark of these years—witness his definition of the broadcast journalist as "a eunuch in the harem of ideas."* Manchester Guardian Weekly 11/17/73, p23

broadcast satellite, an artificial satellite designed to receive and transmit television signals. *Broadcast satellites are expected to provide both developed and less-developed countries with further means of transmitting their own television programs and setting up both medical and educational consulting services in sparsely settled areas or regions where lines of microwave towers would be expensive to establish and maintain, as in India or the Canadian arctic.* NY Times 1/30/76, p11 [**1970**]

broederbond ('brü:dər,bȯnd), *n.* a secret fraternity, especially one formed for some unsavory or evil purpose. *These people don't all know each other. It's not as though there are some sinister, trans-Canada broederbond pulling it all together. But they all know about each other, which sometimes amounts to the same thing.* Macleans 3/74, p56 [**1974**, transferred sense of *Broederbond* (1953) the name of a secret society of Afrikaners organized in 1938 to maintain white supremacy in South Africa, from Afrikaans *broederbond* brotherhood]

bromocriptine or **bromocryptine,** *n.* a drug that inhibits excessive secretion of the pituitary hormone prolactin, used especially in the treatment of acromegaly and of infertility in women and men. *Formula:* $C_{32}H_{40}BrN_5O_5$ *In one report . . . bromocryptine increased sexual libido and restored spermatogenesis and sexual potency in seven male patients.* Science News 8/13/77, p105 [**1976**, shortened from *bromoergocryptine,* from *bromo-* bromide + *ergo*t + *crypt* small tubular gland (a reference to the pituitary gland) + *-ine* (chemical suffix)]

Brompton cocktail or **Brompton mixture,** a preparation of narcotics used to relieve pain caused by cancer. *Heroin is thought to be better than other narcotics for treating some cases of cancer pain. The so-called Brompton cocktail, which can include both heroin and cocaine, is valuable in treating nausea and other symptoms.* NY Times 2/26/78, pD7 [**1978**, named after the *Brompton* Chest Hospital, where it was apparently first used]

Brønsted acid or **Brönsted acid** ('brœnsted), an acid that can yield a proton (hydrogen ion) to another substance. *It has recently become possible to determine the acidities of a variety of Brønsted acids in the gas phase and, thus, in the absence of solvent.* McGraw-Hill Yearbook of Science and Technology 1975, p89 [**1967**, named after J.N. *Brønsted,* a Danish chemist who in 1923-24 defined acids and bases in terms of proton transfer]

bronzer, *n.* a cream or lotion used to give a bronze or tan color to the skin. *Some moisturizers are also bronzers . . . A man is much better off using a bronzer instead of a tanning booth during the winter months because of the skin hazards of ultraviolet radiation.* NY Times Magazine 9/7/80, p92 [**1980**]

broomball, *n.* a game similar to ice hockey in which a volleyball is propelled over the ice with brooms. *This year (January 28 to February 6) the carnival's main event will be the seventh annual 500-mile snowmobile race from Winnipeg to St. Paul. There will also be speed skating, curling, sports car racing and slow-pitch softball on ice, broomball, chess, ski jumping, and the country's oldest hot-air balloon race.* Saturday Review 1/29/72, p55 [**1972**] ▶This game is well-known in Canada and the *Dictionary of Canadianisms on Historical Principles* (1967) attests the use of the term since 1933. The game became known outside Canada in the early 1970's.

brother, *n. Black English.* **1** a fellow black; soul brother. Compare BLOOD. *"I'm now at the position Booker T. Washington was about sixty or seventy years ago,"* [Hosea] *Williams said. "I say to my brothers, 'Cast down your buckets where you are'—and that means there in the slums and ghettos."* Harper's 1/70, p29 **2** any black man. *With his sudden visibility on the battlefield, the Negro has achieved the most genuine integration and the fullest participation in policies that America has yet granted. "And,"* it was pointed out during the soul session,

"the brother is dying in order to participate—again." NY Times 5/1/68, p1 [**1967**]

brown bag, brown paper bag containing a bottle of liquor. *He* [Lyndon Johnson] *alienated kennel clubs by lifting beagles as if they were brown bags in a dry county.* NY Times 11/13/67, p66 [**1967**]

brown-bag, *v.t., v.i. U.S. Slang.* **1** to bring one's own (liquor or food) to a restaurant, club, etc., usually in a brown paper bag. Originally the term was applied to the practice of providing one's own liquor in states prohibiting its sale in public establishments. *The . . . Russians brown-bagged their own caviar and vodka.* Time 2/8/71, p6 *Brown-bagging is the genteel disguise adopted by a patron to furnish his own liquor when he dines at the local restaurant.* Saturday Review 6/17/67, p14 **2** to bring one's lunch to work. *Brown-bag it above the Atlantic? Well, why not? You wouldn't be the first. Charles A. Lindbergh took five sandwiches along on his lonely flight.* NY Times 9/4/77, p26 [**1960; 1967**] —**brown-bagging,** *n.: Brown-bagging is the genteel disguise adopted by a patron to furnish his own liquor when he dines at the local restaurant.* Saturday Review 6/17/67, p14 —**brown-bagger,** *n.: First they were the original brown-baggers, the school kids toting their odorous but lovingly prepared peanut butter sandwiches to class.* NY Times 3/5/76, p18

brown belt, 1 a degree of proficiency in judo or karate next below the black belt. *Mr. Trudeau, when he officially takes the post after Mr. Pearson retires later this month, will be the first Prime Minister in Canada to hold a brown belt in karate.* NY Times 4/8/68, p8 **2** a person awarded this degree. *Winners in the form divisions were Toyotaro Miyazaki of Jackson Heights, Queens, black belt; Larry Pomilio of North Miami Beach, Fla., brown belt . . .* NY Times 4/1/68, p66 [**1967**]

Brown Berets, 1 an organization of Mexican Americans seeking political power and greater economic opportunity in the United States. *They have formed the Brown Berets, modeled on the Black Panthers.* Time 7/4/69, p16 **2** the berets worn by its members. . . . *The "Brown Berets", the headgear of the extremist wing of the Mexican-Americans, is a copy of the emblem of the Black Panthers.* Times (London) 3/11/70, p11 [**1969**, name patterned after the *Green Berets,* a guerrilla-fighting unit of the U.S. Army in Indochina]

Brown Book, an annual report on Great Britain's petroleum reserves, explorations, requirements, etc., published by the British Department of Energy since 1974. . . . *this year's "Brown Book" showing yet another rise in the region's estimated reserves . . .* New Scientist 4/28/77, p79 [**1974**, from the *brown* color of its cover]

brown fat, a tissue containing deposits of fat whose oxidation is a major source of heat in animals, and especially in man. *The human baby has brown fat tissue between the shoulder blades, around the neck, behind the breast-bone and around the kidneys—all positions duplicated by the rabbit.* Science Journal 6/70, p90 [**1963**]

brownie point or **Brownie point,** *Especially U.S. Informal.* credit earned by a person for doing the proper or expected thing. *TV station managers realize that the Federal Communications Commission regards full news coverage as part of the price of a ticket to ride the public airwaves. At license-renewal time, stations discover that such brownie points count more than Nielsen numbers with the FCC.* Newsweek 12/10/73, p78 [**1972**, probably from earlier slang *brownie* (1960) a person who tries to curry favor with a superior, from *brown-nose* (1939) to curry favor]

brown lung disease, a disease that affects workers in cotton mills. Compare BLACK LUNG. *Meanwhile, pressure was being exerted in Washington to make the condition ("brown lung disease") compensable under the workmen's compensation acts.* Britannica Book of the Year 1971, p492 [**1970**]

Brown Power, a slogan used by Mexican Americans, modeled on the term BLACK POWER. Compare RED POWER. *Being a member of the Mexican-American minority group, which lately talks of "Brown Power," I have one question to ask of Harvey*

Wheeler. Would he also advocate having a brown Congress for my particular minority group and eventually perhaps a red Congress for the American Indians? Saturday Review 6/8/68, p35 **[1968]**

brown sugar, *Especially U.S. Slang.* a grainy, low-grade variety of heroin made in southeastern Asia. Compare MEXICAN BROWN. *The Asian heroin is coarser—hense its nickname "brown sugar"—and is only 35 to 65 percent pure. It has been known to contain caffeine or even strychnine.* NY Times Magazine 1/9/77, p16 **[1976]**

brown thumb, *U.S.* **1** lack of ability or success in making plants grow. Compare WET THUMB. *The Gardener's Catalogue, by Tom Riker and Harvey Rottenberg. (Morrow, $6.95) How to find what you need to turn a brown thumb into a green one.* Advertisement, NY Times Book Review 2/16/75, p29 **2** someone who dries flowers and leaves. *Traditionally, drying flowers and leaves has been an autumn activity, but now most brownthumbs go picking all year round.* Newsweek 3/10/75, p39 **[1975, patterned after** *green thumb* **(1943)]**

brutalist, *adj.* of a style of architecture that emphasizes massiveness and the suggestion of brute strength by exposing concrete in large, chunky masses. *Breuer, whose recent work included New York City's almost windowless brutalist Whitney Museum of American Art, was involved with plans for a monumental new wing for the Cleveland (O.) Museum of Art.* Britannica Book of the Year 1969, p105 **—n.** an architect of the brutalist school. *The Brutalists also have done much to advocate new forms of mass housing.* Sunday Times (London) 5/7/67, p54 **[1966]**

BSA, abbreviation of *bovine serum albumin.* See the quotation. *BSA is a protein derived from the blood of cattle and is a common substance for experimental use in laboratory experiments in biology.* Science News 5/18/74, p324 **[1968]**

BT, abbreviation of BEHAVIOR THERAPY. *BT is often equated with behavior modification . . . and criticized as a tool for behavior control.* S.A. Rathus and J.F. Nevid, "BT: Behavior Therapy," 1977, p301 **[1974]**

bubble[1], *n.* short for MAGNETIC BUBBLE. *NASA has developed a solid-state data recorder with no mechanical moving parts at all. The device is based on tiny magnetic domains, called "bubbles," which exist in specially prepared garnet chips. With the aid of a magnetic film, applied in a precise pattern on the chips' surfaces, these bubbles can be controlled in such a way as to perform logic functions.* Science News 12/7/74, p362 **[1970]**

bubble[2], *n. U.S.* a domelike structure used to enclose a tennis court, swimming pool, etc., to protect it from bad weather. Also called AIR STRUCTURE. Compare AIR HALL. *Plastic bubbles and other indoor facilities have gone up by the hundred, transforming tennis into a year-round game even in the northern stretches of the country.* New Yorker 10/7/72, p116 **[1971]**

bubble domain, another name for a MAGNETIC BUBBLE. *Thousands of bubble domains can be generated in a square inch of material. They can also be made to move around in the material. These two properties give them a high potential for application in computer memories and similar devices.* Science News 5/8/71, p318 **[1971]**

bubble-gummer, *n.* a performer of BUBBLE-GUM MUSIC. *You've got some nerve calling the Osmonds bubble-gummers (MUSIC, Sept. 3)!* Newsweek 9/24/73, p17 **[1973]**

bubble-gum music, rock music with simple, repetitive lyrics. *Older rock fans dismiss the stuff as "bubble gum music," but Micky Dolenz, one of the Monkees, the prepackaged group who capitalized on subteens in the sixties, defends the genre as "first-grade music for kids in first grade."* Atlantic 10/73, p64 **[1968, so called from the popularity of bubble gum among children who usually make up the audience for this type of music]**

bubbleheaded, *adj. U.S. Slang.* silly; flighty; light-headed. *Who would have expected the Swiss director Alain Tanner and his co-writer, John Berger, to turn out a bubbleheaded political comedy?* New Yorker 10/18/76, p75 *He is making love to his wife (a porky and bubbleheaded blonde played delightfully by Andréa Ferréol). . .* Time 11/6/78, p88 **[1966]**

bubble memory, a computer memory that stores data in magnetic bubbles. *Bubble memories are inherently serial in organization, so that access time depends on the number of storage locations in a serial path and on the maximum shifting rate.* Scientific American 9/77, p140 **[1973]**

bubbletop, *n.* **1** a dome-shaped transparent umbrella; BUBBLE UMBRELLA. *The biggest news in umbrellas since Mary Poppins sailed away with hers is the bubble-top. Made of transparent vinyl that bottles the wearer in his own waterproof demi-jar.* Time 5/24/71, p37 **2** a transparent, dome-shaped cover or roof of an automobile, especially one that is bulletproof and used on cars of public officials for parades and the like. *But the late President [John F. Kennedy] would in all probability be alive today if the people on the Dallas streets had seen him through a bubbletop . . .* New Yorker 6/15/68, p92 **[1956]**

bubble umbrella, a dome-shaped transparent umbrella; BUBBLETOP. *She is a sartorial contrast to the local Puerto Rican women: belted raincoat, stockings, high heels. She is carrying a book, a newspaper, a pocketbook, and a bubble umbrella.* New Yorker 9/23/72, p29 **[1972]**

bubu, *n.* another spelling of BOU-BOU. *Inside the Centennial Ballroom, a babel of people in long white Moslem robes and colored bubus (tribal gowns) mingled with those in formal tie and tails wearing rows of medals.* Time 1/17/69, p28 **[1967]**

buckminsterfullerene (ˌbəkminstərˌfuləˈriːn), *n. Chemistry.* a highly stable molecule consisting of sixty carbon atoms ' arranged as interlocking pentagons and hexagons. *Scientists suspect that buckminsterfullerene has unusual properties that could lead to the development of new lubricants and catalysts.* World Book Science Annual 1987, p242 **[1986, from the name of** *Buckminster Fuller,* **1895-1983, an American designer who developed the geodesic dome, which this molecule resembles + -ene]**

buckwheat braid, *U.S.* a short braid or pigtail, often tied with a ribbon. *Now a growing number of soul brothers are sporting buckwheat braids in as many variations as there are African nations, where the style is traditional.* Time 12/24/73, p84 **[1971]**

budo (ˈbuːdou), *n.* the martial arts, such as judo and karate. *Budo has many different forms. Kendo is a sword-fighting technique; kyudo, a type of archery.* 1970 Compton Yearbook, p445 **[1964, from Japanese** *budō***]**

bufadienolide (ˌbyuːfəˌdaiˈen əlaid), *n.* any of a group of physiologically active steroid hormones that includes bufalin. *The bufadienolides [are] a closely related family of steroids found in both toad venoms and in many plants, and potentially of great importance in the therapy of heart disease and cancer.* New Scientist 6/8/70, p272 **[1970, from** *bufa*lin + *di-* double + *-ene* hydrocarbon + *-ol* alcohol or phenol + *-ide* chemical compound]

bufalin (ˈbyuːfəlin), *n.* a steroid compound derived from the venom of toads, used in the treatment of heart disease. *The cardiac action of bufalin, for example, has been found about equal to digitoxigenin (from digitalis), and in terms of local anesthetic potency is about 90 times more active than cocaine.* 1975 Britannica Yearbook of Science and the Future, p209 **[1970, from** *Bufo* genus of toads + *-alin,* as in *digitalin***]**

build-down, *n.* a reduction of nuclear armament by eliminating existing weapons for new ones produced. *This plan, referred to as a "build down," was offered originally by Senators William S. Cohen, Republican of Maine, and Sam Nunn, Democrat of Georgia, then endorsed by other Senators and Congressmen. Under their proposal, every time a new land-based warhead was deployed, two older ones would have to be destroyed.* NY Times 10/3/83, pA1 **—v.t.** to reduce (armaments) by a builddown. *President Reagan will announce today that he'll offer to "build-down" the USA's nuclear weapons when deadlocked strategic arms talks with the Soviets resume Thursday in Gene-*

va. USA Today 10/4/83, p1 [**1983**, formed to contrast with *build-up* (OEDS 1943)]

building sickness, another name for SICK BUILDING SYN-DROME. *Pure hypochondria? Surveys show that building sickness is far more common in air-conditioned than in naturally ventilated buildings.* Economist 2/8/86, p77 [**1986**]

bulimarexia (byu:‚limə'reksi:ə), *n.* a psychological disorder in which a person alternates between an abnormal craving and an aversion to food, found especially among young women. *Women suffering from bulimarexia alternately gorge themselves with food and then empty themselves, whether by fasting, vomiting, or through self-induced diarrhea. The resemblance to anorexia is plain. Anorexic women also usually break off their harsh fasting with an eating binge. But the distinguishing feature of bulimarexia is its* regular *binges, its orgies of eating followed by ritual purifications, over and over again.* Psychology Today 3/77, p50 [**1976**, from *bulim*ia insatiable appetite + connecting -*a*- + ano*rexia* abnormal aversion to food]

bulimic, *n.* a person affected with an abnormal craving for food. *Some bulimics employ extreme diets, constant exercise, or laxatives to lose weight.* Science News 10/31/87, p278 [**1986**, noun use of the adjective (OED 1854)]

bulk buy club, *British.* a club formed to save its members money by buying goods in bulk rather than in normal sizes and packages. *Where a full time post office, shop or garage cannot be sustained, we need combined or part time services. If it really is not possible to run a commercial service then there should be consumer cooperatives or bulk buy clubs operating perhaps in village halls.* Times (London) 9/19/78, p17 [**1977**]

bulldagger, *n. U.S. Slang.* a female homosexual who acts as a male. Compare BUTCH. *She was extra ugly. There was a rumor that Saralee was a bulldagger. I don't know if that was true or not but she was certainly rough enough to be a man.* Louise Meriwether, Daddy Was a Number Runner, 1970, p25 [**1969**, alteration (probably influenced by *dagger*) of *bulldyke* a "male" dyke or lesbian]

bulletin board, a computer service that displays information, messages, and news to subscribers and often allows them to communicate directly with each other. *There are no consumer-oriented electronic information services in Japan, similar to the Source and Compuserve in the United States. There are few electronic bulletin boards.* NY Times 8/10/84, pD3 [**1975**]

bullet train, a high-speed passenger train of Japan. Japanese name, SHINKANSEN. *Japan's 125 m.p.h. "bullet train" between Tokyo and Osaka is the technological wonder of the Eastern world.* Time 7/6/70, p59 [**1966**]

bullhorn, *v.t. U.S.* **1** to address or announce over a loudspeaker. *Glick at last bullhorned the request to guards not ten feet from him, through the wire.* Harper's 7/72, p63 **2** Figurative use: *While this message of preventive medicine is being bullhorned into one ear, there is a steady muttering of dissent going into the other. It is not clear if the dissent is widespread.* NY Times 10/7/76, p19 [**1970**, verb use of the noun (1955)]

bullshot, *n.* a mixed alcoholic drink consisting usually of beef broth and vodka. *The bullshots—beef consommé, vodka, Worcester sauce and lime—appeared with astonishing speed.* Punch 1/9/74, p37 [**1956**]

Bumiputra or **bumiputra** (‚bu:mi'pu:trə), *n.* a member of the indigenous or native people of Malaysia; a Malay, as distinguished from an ethnic Chinese of Malaysia (often used attributively). See BUMIPUTRAIZATION. *The New Economic Policy . . . promised that the Government's eventual aim was to take care of all the country's poor but the policy orientation for the next five years was concentrated almost totally on the Bumiputras.* Times (London) 8/31/76, pI [**1972**, from Malay, literally, sons of the soil]

bumiputraization (‚bu:mi‚pu:trəai'zeiʃən), *n.* government policy in Malaysia to give preferential treatment to Malays in business, education, language, etc., to compensate for former discrimination by the economically dominant Chinese. *Gov-ernment officials maintain that bumiputraization—which is clearly a code word for discrimination—is designed to redress the balance. In recent years, and particularly this year, there have been a number of changes openly designed to hold back the Chinese and advance the Malays.* NY Times 7/18/76, pA2 [**1976**, from BUMIPUTRA + -*ization*]

bummer, *n. U.S. Slang.* **1** a disappointment. *But, except for the big hits, the newer kinds of movies don't satisfy anybody . . . all the films released this summer have been box-office bummers.* New Yorker 10/3/70, p76 **2** another term for BAD TRIP. *The worst bummer of all time was recorded by Robert Louis Stevenson. It seems that the good Dr. Jekyll tripped out on a mysterious powder and ended up as the nefarious Mr. Hyde.* Science News 4/17/71, p264 [**1969**]

bum out, *U.S. Slang.* to disgust, annoy, or vex. *"They're really good," the cocktail waitress, Debbie, a slim, pretty woman in an embroidered cowboy shirt, said to Joann. "Most of the bands they get in here are so bad they really bum me out, but these guys are good."* Atlantic 1/84, p60 [**1980**]

bump, *n.* Usually **the bump**, a rock'n'roll dance. See the quotation for details. *Instead of the Twist, hipsters nowadays prefer such contemporary contortions as the Puerto Rican Hustle . . . and, of course, the Bump, where partners bump each other back to back, belly to belly.* Newsweek 3/24/75, p89 —**v.i.** to dance the bump. *There is no shortage here of glittering clubs in which to hustle, walk, bump or samba the night away.* NY Times 1/3/76, p10 [**1975**]

bumper sticker, a sticker bearing a printed slogan for display on an automobile bumper. . . . *the two political bumper stickers available at the bookstore of the Ernest L. Wilkinson student center say "I'm Proud to Be an American" and "I'm a Member of the Silent Majority."* New Yorker 3/21/70, p122 [**1960**]

bumper strip, *U.S.* another name for BUMPER STICKER. *Many Texans are bitter over the Sooners' recruiting forays into their state. A bumper strip seen often around Austin in recent years reads. "O.U., The Best Texas Money Can Buy," as if U.T., whose athletic facilities are better than those of most European countries, were lacking in that commodity.* NY Times Magazine 1/1/78, p20 [**1961**]

bumpout, *n. U.S.* an addition that increases the space of a room in an office, apartment, or house without adding significantly to the outside dimension of a structure. *The word "bumpout" can't be found in Webster's New World Dictionary but . . . No matter. It's very commonly used by architects, builders, space planners and practically everyone else involved in remodeling to describe a simple outward expansion of space.* NY Times 4/12/87, p24W [**1987**]

BUN, abbreviation of *blood urea nitrogen* (nitrogen in the form of urea found in the blood). *In principle, an artificial kidney is simply a device that leads the blood outside the body and past a cellophanelike membrane. On the other side of the membrane is a briny solution resembling blood—clean blood. Impelled by osmotic pressure, excess water, BUN, sodium, potassium and other wastes sneak through the membrane from the blood into the briny solution. Thus purified, the blood then flows back into the body.* NY Times Magazine 3/7/76, p46 [**1976**]

bungarotoxin (‚bəngərou'taksən), *n.* a nerve poison, isolated from a snake venom, which blocks the action on muscle tissue of the chemical that transmits nerve impulses (acetylcholine). It is used especially to identify acetylcholine receptors. *Using radioactive bungarotoxin (which binds specifically to ACh [acetylcholine] receptor sites), Nirenberg is able to count the number of receptors in the clusters; it turns out that there are in the region of 9000 per sq.m—this figure is very close to that for receptor concentration in "mature" synapses.* New Scientist 3/1/73, p471 [**1971**, from New Latin *Bungar*us (*mueticinctus*) the banded krait, a snake from Taiwan producing the venom + English connecting -*o*- + *toxin*]

bunker, *adj.* characterized by or adopting a strongly defensive stance in the face of a threat; last-ditch. *The reactionary regime* *has already receded into a bunker mentality.* Time 9/14/81, p41 [**1974**]

Bunker, *n.* Usually, **the Bunker,** a nickname for the coalition of ultra-conservative politicians and government officials of the regime of Francisco Franco (1892-1975); Francoist loyalists as a group. Compare FRANQUISTA. *The reactionary right, the "Bunker," was admittedly still a force to be reckoned with, but many of its members were also shareholders and beneficiaries of* desarrollo *(economic development).* Britannica Book of the Year 1977, p627 [**1976**, from Spanish (*el*) *Bunker,* from English *bunker,* in allusion to the group's entrenched position in government]

Bunkerism, *n. U.S.* short for ARCHIE BUNKERISM. *Besides the song, the album (Atlantic Records) contains excerpts from a dozen shows, a litany of the Bunkerisms that have won All in the Family the respect of rednecks and the laughter of liberals.* Time 1/17/72, p47 [**1972**]

bunny, *n. Slang.* a pretty girl or young woman who appeals to men as a pet or plaything. *Tired of being used only as secretaries and bed bunnies, the female members of Germany's student S.D.S.* [Students for a Democratic Society] *staged a walkout—but not before hurling invective and rotten tomatoes at the organization's male chauvinists.* Time 8/17/70, p25 [**1965**, from the *Bunnies,* nightclub waitresses at Playboy Clubs, dressed in scanty uniforms with fluffy tails and long ears to suggest a bunny (rabbit)]

burakumin ('bur ə ku‚min), *n.pl.* (in Japan) people living in small villages or their descendants, long treated as an inferior caste, although officially granted equality in the 1860's. *He considers the Japanese minority known as the Burakumin an encouraging example of what can happen when caste barriers fall. In ancient times, the Burakumin ranked as subhuman, and they are still outcasts in many respects. But the gap in achievement disappears when Burakumin move to the United States, where Americans treat them exactly like other Japanese immigrants.* NY Times 3/12/78, pD7 [**1967**, from Japanese, from *buraku* village, hamlet]

Burkitt's lymphoma, a cancer of the lymphatic system especially prevalent among children in central Africa, and associated with the Epstein-Barr virus. *Burkitt's lymphoma is the most likely human cancer to be virus-induced.* New Scientist 11/12/70, p313 [**1964**, named after Denis P. *Burkitt,* born 1911, a British surgeon at Mulago Hospital in Kampala, Uganda, who first identified the disease in 1957]

burn, *n.* the firing of a rocket engine or a retrorocket to produce thrust. *A "perfect burn" pulled them out of lunar orbit and towards a splashdown in the Pacific.* Manchester Guardian Weekly 7/24/69, p3 [**1962**] —*v.t.* to fire (a rocket engine or retrorocket). *Armstrong had to burn the engines for another 70 seconds to reach a smoother landing site about 4 miles away.* Americana Annual 1970, p22 [**1970**] —*v.i.* to undergo a burn; be fired. *The engine had to burn for more than seven minutes in order to produce a final velocity of 4,128 miles . . . per hour.* Americana Annual 1970, p26 [**1965**]

burn artist, *U.S. Slang.* a person who sells fake or inferior goods, especially narcotics. *"Who do you have on Haight Street today?" he* [a San Francisco dope peddler] *said disgustedly . . . "You have burn artists (fraudulent dope peddlers), rip-offs (thieves), and snitchers (police spies)."* Manchester Guardian Weekly 5/2/70, p16 [**1970**]

burn bag, *U.S.* a receptacle for secret documents to be officially destroyed by burning. *The most explosive testimony came from Yeoman First Class Charles E. Radford, a clerk who had been assigned to Kissinger's National Security Council staff. In a 23-page statement, Radford admitted rifling White House "burn bags" and briefcases in search of top-secret memos meant only for Kissinger and President Nixon.* Newsweek 3/4/74, p20 [**1973**] ►Though this term has long been used in intelligence work, it became current in 1973 in connection with the Watergate investigations.

burn-bag, *v.t. U.S.* to put in a burn bag. *Sen. Edward M. Kennedy pointedly asked what Kelley would do if he were ap-*

proached with a pitch to stump or gumshoe for the President or to burn-bag evidence in a case that might embarrass the White House ("I would refuse," he said). Newsweek 7/2/73, p21 [**1973**]

burnout, *n.* extinction of energy, motivation, or incentive. *Then there is the project's team approach, which is usually used only as a teaching method; in this instance, aside from pooling brainpower, it serves to prevent the sort of burnout that afflicts so many doctors and other health professionals.* NY Times Magazine 6/21/87, p18 [**1975**, figurative use of term meaning a burning out of an engine, etc.]

burns, *n.pl. U.S. Slang.* sideburns. *Sandy* [a male character in the movie "Carnal Knowledge"] *is a superannuated swinger, complete with stash, burns and a 17-year-old hippie on his arm.* Time 7/5/71, p55 [**1971**]

Bürolandschaft ('bYrou‚la:ntʃa:ft), *n.* Also Anglicized as **burolandschaft.** a style of interior decoration for offices, in which functional dividers, such as screens or plants, replace walls and work units are arranged to allow for flexibility in the use of space (often used attributively). *Plants play an important part in the open office-landscape concept (Bürolandschaft), which developed in Germany and has become widely influential.* Americana Annual 1973, p358 *As an exercise in international architecture this . . . burolandschaft interior will win acclaim, maybe even affection.* Manchester Guardian Weekly 10/13/73, p18 *The open-plan use of a large, unpartitioned office floor . . . is the antithesis of true Burolandschaft.* Times (London) 9/15/77 (page not known) [**1968**, from German, literally, office landscape]

burrito (bə'ri:tou), *n.* a flour tortilla rolled around a spicy mixture of beef, cheese, and refried beans. *Even the drive-in Dairy Queen offers tacos, enchiladas, and burritos along with its standard shakes, burgers, and fries.* New Yorker 12/4/78, p59 [**1971**, from Mexican Spanish, literally, little burro]

bursectomize, *v.t.* to subject to a bursectomy. *We used this approach to obtain information on the relative sensitivity of IgA development to bursectomy. Fifteen chick embryos were bursectomized at 1-day intervals beginning on day 16 of incubation.* Science 1/26/73, p399 [**1973**]

bursectomy (bər'sektəmi:), *n.* removal of a bursa (lubricating sac) of the body by surgery or hormone injection. *A small portion of chicks subjected to this "hormonal bursectomy," however, are tolerant of foreign skin, an anomaly first noted by Noel L. Warner and Aleksander Szenberg of the Walter and Eliza Hall Institute of Medical Research in Melbourne.* Scientific American 11/74, p60 [**1968**, from *burs*a + *-ectomy* surgical removal]

burst, *n.* a sudden, short emission of X rays, gamma rays, etc., occurring at intervals. *MXB 1730-335 emits X-ray bursts at intervals ranging from a few seconds to several minutes. The more intense a particular burst, the longer the interval before the next one.* 1976 Collier's Encyclopedia Year Book, p149 [**1976**]

burster, *n.* another name for X-RAY BURSTER. *Most of the bursters are located within the galactic disk and are concentrated toward the galactic center. Three slow bursters have been found, however, to lie in globular clusters that were previously known to contain persistent X-ray stars. The single rapid burster lies in the direction of a previously unknown globular cluster that is nearly hidden by interstellar dust.* Scientific American 10/77, p42 [**1976**]

bus, *n.* **1** one of the stages of a rocket or missile. *Alternatively, MIRVs are carried on a low-thrust final stage called a bus which has a single guidance system.* New Scientist and Science Journal 2/11/71, p292 **2** a spacecraft that carries one or more detachable craft or vehicles. *The cluster of probes, making the trip from earth mounted on a single, cylindrical "bus," includes one large probe and three small ones (plus the bus itself, which is also instrumented). The large probe, carrying the atmospheric-composition experiments, will separate from the bus 24 days before reaching the planet and head for a planned* *entry near the day-side equator.* Science News 8/12/78, p100 [**1962** for def. 1; **1968** for def. 2]

businesspeak, *n.* commercial jargon. *While they got on with their day to day job as "medical managers," they saw the Department of Health in its efforts to reorganise NHS administration, produce document after document written in almost unintelligible businesspeak.* New Scientist 4/13/72, p94 [**1971**, blend of *business* and -SPEAK]

busing, *n.* U.S. the transportation of students by buses to schools outside their neighborhoods to achieve a racial balance in schools. Also called CROSSBUSING. Compare ANTIBUSING. *The studies suggest that* on the average *busing probably increases black students' test scores, but that there are plenty of exceptions.* Harper's 2/73, p40 *The Berkeley school system, one of the first to begin busing, has more white students than when integration began, but Berkeley does not seem to have inspired nearby school districts.* Science 1/25/74, p341 [**1964**, from gerund of *bus*, *v.* (1950's) to transport by bus]

bust, *Slang.* —*v.t.* **1** to arrest. *I have never been busted for pot, my hair doesn't brush my shoulders, and you won't catch me nude in the park. I am so straight, in fact, that I actually have a job.* Time 8/17/70, p38 [**1964**] **2** to make a raid on. *Galahad . . . says they* [the police] *have "busted" or raided his apartment "about 30 times" in the last two and one-half months.* NY Times 6/1/67, p39 [**1963**] —*n.* an arrest or raid. *They* [people at the Woodstock Music Festival] *asked for volunteers to pick up garbage, and they made announcements warning those leaving to be careful on the way out—not to take grass* [marijuana] *with them, because of busts on the highway, and so on.* New Yorker 8/30/69, p21 [**1968**]

bustier (bYs'tyei, bu:s-), *n.* a strapless top or dress. *Evening clothes were romantically Edwardian, with well-defined silhouettes. Tightly fitted bodices in the form of bustiers or corselets narrowed to nipped-in waists over bouffant skirts.* Americana Annual 1980, p218 [**1979**, from French *bustier* strapless brassiere, from *buste* bust]

busulfan (byu:'səlfən), *n.* a highly toxic white, crystalline substance, used in medicine to destroy certain leukemic cells or tumors and in agriculture as a chemical sterilant. *Formula:* $C_6H_{14}O_6S_2$ *A major step toward integrating several control procedures for eradicating the boll weevil, a cotton pest, has been made with the discovery of a chemosterilant. Busulfan makes male boll weevils sexually sterile with little or no damage to the weevil.* Americana Annual 1973, p73 [**1968**, from the chemical constituents *bu*tanediol dimethane *sulf*onate + -*an*]

busway, *n.* a road, or lane of a road, set aside for buses. *Ninety per cent of commuters who travel by road come in buses running on special 'busways' that give the vehicle complete priority over all others from garage to terminus.* Listener 6/14/73, p785 [**1963**, patterned after *motorway, bikeway*, etc.]

Butazolidin (ˌbyu:tə'zouləˌdin), *n.* a trademark for phenylbutazone, an anti-inflammatory and pain-killing drug with no stimulating side effects. *Formula:* $C_{19}H_{20}N_2O_2$ Also shortened to BUTE or Bute. *The Blazers team physician once suggested treatment with cortisone and Butazolidin, anti-inflammatory analgesics regularly used by athletes.* Newsweek 3/31/75, p74 [**1966**]

butch, *Slang. adj.* **1** (of a female homosexual) assuming a masculine role. *She was never interested in boys sexually and perhaps one of the secrets of the success in our relationship is that she is completely butch and I am completely feminine.* Sunday Times (London) 1/25/70, p60 **2** (of a female) having a masculine appearance. *The rather butch nun holding the baby is actually a boy Picasso knew who was dressed up to add to the picture a religious note; and the doctor is Picasso's father.* Manchester Guardian Weekly 1/9/71, p21 —*n.* a female homosexual who acts as a male. *In the 1960's he* [a male homosexual] *may be the catty hair-dresser or the lisping, limp-wristed interior decorator. His lesbian counterpart is the "butch," the girl who is aggressively masculine to the point of trying to look like a man.* Time 10/31/69, p39 [**1954**, probably from *butch*, U.S.

slang term for a tough-looking youth, from *Butch*, a common nickname for a boy]

butcher-block, *adj.* made or designed like a butcher's chopping block, usually with thick strips of laminated maple. *The kitchen has white cabinets, butcher-block counters and dining table.* NY Times Magazine 2/23/75, p64 [**1967**]

Bute or **bute** (byu:t), *n.* short for BUTAZOLIDIN. *"Bute" does not by itself, make a horse run faster—or slower—but by relieving pain it allows an afflicted horse to perform at its best. The most famous case involving "bute" occurred in the 1969 Kentucky Derby, when Dancer's Image finished first and had his purse taken away . . .* NY Times 3/10/76, p29 [**1968**]

butt-end, *v.i. Ice Hockey.* to jab an opponent with the end of the handle of a hockey stick. *Henderson and Esposito became virtuosos, and ultimately managed to save the series. But others fell back on the NHL way of doing things: punch, elbow, slash, butt-end, charge and otherwise mangle.* Maclean's 9/74, p70 [**1974**, verb use of earlier noun (1963)]

butterfly, *v.i., v.t.* to move from one thing to the next much as a butterfly seems to fly aimlessly from one resting spot to the next; flutter or flit. *Every year sees the appearance of fictional contrivances that pause briefly as larvae in book form before butterflying their way onto the screen.* Time 4/27/70, p98 *If you are not committed to your job, you can take all this lightly and butterfly away to the next one.* Times (London) 12/29/70, p15 [**1968**, verb use of the noun]

buttlegger, *n.* U.S. a person who engages in the illegal transportation and sale of cigarettes on which no cigarette tax has been paid. *A triple combination of greed is the basic element in buttlegging. Racketeers are making millions by spiriting low-tax cigarets bought in tobacco-happy North Carolina into New York, where taxes are high. New York State gathers in $325 million a year in cigaret taxes, despite the losses to the buttleggers, and doesn't want to lose that.* Herald Statesman (Yonkers, N.Y.) 10/13/73, p6 [**1962**, from *butt* (U.S. slang term for a cigarette) + boot*legger*] —**buttlegging**, *n.:* U.S. *Attorney Whitney North Seymour Jr. discusses lucrative buttlegging business at recent press conference.* Sunday News (New York) 3/19/72, p146

button, *n.* **press** or **push (someone's) button** or **buttons**, *U.S. Slang.* to manipulate by getting a planned reaction out of (someone). *"Now if her voice sent me into orbit, when I talked to this other one it was nuclear fusion. We talked everyday for a week. She was pushing all my buttons, she knew my weaknesses . . . What she said to me, I couldn't sleep at night because of that . . . "* Spy (The New York Monthly) 3/88, p92 [**1988**]

button-down or **buttoned-down**, *adj.* U.S. conventional or conservative; without imagination or initiative. *The dominant mood at 57th Street and Park Avenue is . . . one of low-key, button-down professionalism, an atmosphere that permits the languid inquisitiveness of a college seminar, yet requires also the relentless intensity of a Madison Avenue firm with a big client to merchandise and only a few months in which to do it.* NY Times 6/24/68, p16 *Suburbia is something more than the stereotype of buttoned-down WASP commuters and wives who slurp "tee many martoonis" at the country club.* Time 7/6/70, p6 —*n.* a person who has conventional ideas or who lacks initiative. . . . *an anglo button-down in a beer joint . . .* Maclean's 5/26/80, p56 *Like McGovern's bell-bottoms, Nixon's button-downs were essentially ideologues, with tunnel vision that always leads ideologues to muck things up.* Newsweek 4/9/73, p120 [**1963**, from the *button-down* shirt collars thought of as worn by conservative professionals and businessmen]

button man, *U.S. Underworld Slang.* a low-ranking member of the Mafia who does the dirty work. Also called SOLDIER. *Mafia bosses, who had built careful layers of insulation around themselves—never dealing directly with button men, trusting only a few close lieutenants—found their protective covering being stripped away.* Time 7/12/71, p18 [**1967**]

butut ('bu:tu:t *or* bu'tu:t), *n.* a unit of money of Gambia, equal to 1/100 of a dalasi. *A new decimal currency became effective* on July 1. *The dalasi, which was divided into 100 bututs, replaced the Gambian pound; it was pegged at four former Gambian shillings. The move did not involve devaluation.* 1972 Collier's Encyclopedia Year Book, p254 [**1971**]

butyl nitrite, variant of ISOBUTYL NITRITE. *Inhaling butyl nitrite is said to induce a warm feeling, giddiness, flushing of the skin and a "rush" as the blood vessels dilate, the heartbeat quickens and blood rushes to the brain.* New York Post 8/22/79, p3 [**1979**]

buyback, *adj.* of or involving an oil company's purchase of oil it has produced but that is claimed by the government of an oil-producing country as its share of the total amount obtained from its resources. See DOWNSTREAM, POSTED PRICE. *But "it is the Arabs" who are forcing up prices with their takeovers of foreign oil companies and buy-back arrangements.* Time 5/27/74, p66 —*n.* the purchase of something the buyer has produced or previously owned or had a share in. *Calling . . . a conglomerate, "perhaps the most successful practitioner of the art of blotting up excess shares and raising per-share earnings," The Advisor pointed out that the company began buy-backs in 1972 at $20 a share.* NY Times 9/13/77, p44 [**1973** for adj., specialized use of earlier (1954) sense "of buying back, re-purchasing;" **1963** for noun]

buydown, *n. U.S.* a subsidy by a builder or real-estate developer that lowers a buyer's monthly mortgage payments for a specified period. *If you're offered a buy-down consider these questions: How much will your payments increase after the end of the builder's subsidy, and will your income be able to cover that increase? Is the subsidy a part of your contract with the lender or is it provided separately by the builder?* Consumer Reports 1/84, p16 [**1979**]

buy-in, *n. U.S.* a procedure on the stock exchange in which a broker who does not receive a purchased security by a specified date may buy it elsewhere. *A buy-in occurs when a broker fails to receive from another broker securities he has purchased for a customer and he enters another order in the open market for the shares so that he can deliver them. Any resulting loss is charged to the nondelivering broker and his customer.* NY Times 8/3/68, p29 [**1968**]

buy-off, *n. U.S.* **1** the act of purchasing all rights to a product or service. *The Bendix engineers at last developed a sort of enlarged screwdriver, which went through several different phases of production and was almost "finalized," Mr. Micocci says, when NASA "gave it the buy-off"—that is, bought it but didn't use it.* New Yorker 4/12/69, p106 **2** one whose service is or has been paid up in full. *[Jack] Aaron's and other principal actors' pay is based on the number of times the commercials are shown on national networks in successive 13-week cycles. The first time the spot is shown, the principal actor receives $136 (supporting actors—those who do not speak on camera—are sometimes referred to as "buy-offs" because they accept a flat fee).* NY Times Magazine 5/21/72, p50 [**1969,** from the verb phrase *buy off*]

buyout, *n.* the purchase of an entire company or of the entire stock of a product. *Under a new dairy program, producers were offered a "buyout" option, by which some could retire their entire dairy herds.* Americana Annual 1987, p94 [**1971,** from the verb phrase *buy out*]

buzkashi, *n.,* or **buz kashi,** the national sport of Afghanistan, involving competitive riding on horses for the possession of a dead goat. *Grab the goat and ride, Omar! sport known as* buz-kashi. Sports Illustrated 5/17/71, p58 *The players in the game of Buz Kashi do not form teams. The object of the game is not to prove one group better than another, but to find a champion. There are famous champions from the past, and they are remembered.* Listener 5/17/73, p647 [**1968,** from Pashto, literally, goat snatching]

buzz word, or **buzzword,** *n.* a term in the jargon of business, government, technology, etc., used especially to appear up-to-date or knowledgeable. *"Guideline" has become something of a Democratic economists' buzz word, and the . . . White House prefers "yardstick."* Time 11/22/71, p36 *Today the swing is towards buzz-words from business rather than technology, as witness the anonymous author of the preface to Catalyst Handbook. He calls catalysts "these chemical entrepreneurs".* New Scientist 9/10/70, p545 [**1970**]

b.y., abbreviation of *billion years. The Cobalt Beds of Canada, which are thought to be 2.2 b.y. old.* New Scientist 5/8/69, p287 [**1969**]

b.y.o.b., abbreviation of *bring your own booze* (or *bottle). The dance was held in the game room of the rec center—where else? Music was provided by a local group called the Mixed Bag, admission was $1 per person. b.y.o.b.* Saturday Review 6/24/72, p18 [**1972**]

bypass, *n.* a natural or artificial canal introduced to provide an alternate passage or pathway for circulation, digestion, etc. *The DeBakey bypass, a spherical plastic chamber the size of an apple, skirts the heart's left ventricle, through which blood is normally pumped, and offers a parallel route.* Science News Yearbook 1970, p84 —*v.t.* to replace by means of a bypass. *Wu and his colleagues were particularly impressed by a new operation developed here for treating coronary disease. At Montefiore, he looked on while Dr. George Robinson bypassed a clogged coronary artery in a 33-year-old man with a section of vein taken from the patient's leg.* Newsweek 11/6/72, p80 [**1957**]

byr, abbreviation of *billion years. Liquid water first appeared on our planet around 3.8 Byr ago, so this particular ecological niche seems to have been relatively stable for a very long time.* New Scientist 10/26/78, p287 [**1976**]

byte (bait), *n.* a unit of information consisting of a group of eight consecutive binary digits, used especially as a measure of the size of the memory unit in a digital computer. *The B3500 system, which utilizes a combination of tape and disk storage, will provide a data memory bank of some 100m.* [million] *bytes as well as a 40m. byte disk file, and 2m. bytes of system memory.* Times (London) 2/3/70, p23 *The model 195's fast main core storage—with a capacity of up to four million bytes (a byte is eight binary digits, or bits)—provides approximately the storage needed to handle all the computer instructions for a space mission, from launch to recovery.* New Scientist 9/4/69, p478 [**1964,** probably alteration of earlier (1948) *bit* binary digit, with influence of *bite, n.*]

Byzantine, *adj.* characterized by much scheming and intrigue; Machiavellian. *In spite of the protests of Aleksandr Solzhenitsyn, the celebrated Russian novelist, the often Byzantine struggle to publish his works in America and Europe continues unabated.* Times (London) 10/3/68, p10 *Was French party politics, with its Byzantine maneuvers and its feuding factions, really en route to a transformation?* NY Times 1/2/66, pD3 [**1960,** in allusion to the political scheming of the Byzantine emperors after Justinian]

BZ, a symbol for an incapacitating gas whose effects include disorientation, drowsiness, and hallucination. Compare CS, GB, VX. *"Can you imagine the public outcry if you used something like BZ* [an Army-developed hallucinogen] *to put down a prison riot and some of that gas drifted over the walls and into a nearby town?" asks an Army chemical-warfare expert.* Newsweek 10/18/71, p39 [**1970**]

C

cable, *n.* short for CABLE TELEVISION. *According to Diane Martin: "The variety available on cable today is already astounding—six hundred programs a week in New York seen only on cable."* New Yorker 3/15/76, p26 [**1972**]

cablecast, *n.* a telecast by cable television. *Shuey also helped develop and produce a series of cablecasts to acquaint Kansas voters with the candidates during the 1974 primary and general elections.* News Release of the National Cable Television Association, Washington, D.C., 4/14/75 —*v.i.* to telecast by cable television. *Subscription cablecasting of sports is not permitted within two years of the sports event telecast live on a regular basis on a Grade A . . . signal in the system community, or within two years of the specific sports event telecast in the community when it occurred.* Britannica Book of the Year 1973, p656 [**1968**, from *cable* (television) + tele*cast*] —cablecaster, *n.: The FCC decided . . . that cablecasters can bring in up to two additional channels from beyond normal reception range.* Popular Science 4/72, p34

cablecasting, *n.* telecasting by cable television. Also called NARROWCASTING. *From everybody's standpoint, the best thing in the franchise is a requirement that the two companies keep abreast of current developments in the art of cablecasting.* TV Guide 4/10/71, p39 [**1968**]

cable-ready, *adj.* designed or able to be plugged into a cable television system. *Make sure the VCR is cable-ready and can be hooked up directly to the cable.* NY Times 11/27/86, pC3 [**1986**]

cable television or cable TV, a system for transmitting television programs by coaxial cable to individual subscribers. *Abbreviation:* CATV Also called CABLEVISION. *Cable television was originally introduced in the area in 1962 to provide better reception because Shooters Hill to the south consistently interfered with Television pictures.* Times (London) 1/21/72, p2 . . . *cable TV offers, technologically, a chance for great variety in programming.* New Yorker 4/25/70, p138 [**1963**]

cablevision, *n.* another name for CABLE TELEVISION. *"Cablevision is a system which, to put the matter bluntly, contains possibilities of discrimination against sections of the population."* Times (London) 9/8/73, p14 [**1971**, from *cable* tele*vision*]

cabtrack, *n.* a proposed automatic taxicab, consisting of an electrically powered car shuttling around an elevated loop track. *Cabtracks have the potential to bring most city destinations within three minutes walk of a station, but they would have to be threaded through the structure of London with great care.* New Scientist 7/27/72, p206 [**1971**]

CAD, 1 abbreviation of *computer-aided design*. Compare CAI, CAM, CAP¹. *CAD is generally a matter of entering design information into the memory of a computer whose output is linked with a CRT display which can present human operators with graphical portrayals of a part's shape of plotted parametric performance.* Science Journal 5/70, p43 [**1968**] 2 abbreviation of *coronary artery disease*. *CAD [is] the leading cause of death among American adults. CAD, a progressive narrowing of the blood vessels that carry blood to the heart muscle, can lead to heart attacks and other problems.* The 1989 World Book Health & Medical Annual, p371 [**1987**]

café coronary, a condition resembling coronary thrombosis, caused by choking on food. See HEIMLICH MANEUVER. *The stricken woman was a victim of "food inhalation," an often fatal accident that is so often misdiagnosed as a heart attack that it has come to be called the café coronary.* Time 10/22/73, p68 [**1973**]

café théâtre (kɑˌfeiteiˈɑːtrə), a cafe where lectures and theatrical presentations are given. Compare DINNER THEATER. *Besides its teaching activities, the institute has a library of 60,000 books and a large modern auditorium where M. Zavriew presents new French films and plays—he introduced Parisian café-théâtre to London—and invites lecturers as diverse as M Jean-Louis Barrault and M Claude Lévi-Strauss.* Times (London) 2/11/76, p13 [**1972**, from French]

cage, *n.* a sheer or lacy outer dress worn over a slip or a dress. *The trade, which invents words and meanings faster than Variety does, now calls many of these dresses "cages"—that is to say, there is a fairly close-fitting slip underneath the yards and yards of floating fabric.* New Yorker 3/19/66, p184 [**1965**]

CAI, abbreviation of *computer-assisted instruction*. Compare CAD, CAM, CAP¹. *Although computer-assisted instruction, or C.A.I. varies in purpose and capability, the operative word is "interactive"—the student, through a keyboard, in effect carries on a dialogue with the machine as he performs its programmed exercises.* NY Times 6/13/76, pD9 [**1967**]

cake, *n.* a whole with reference to the parts into which it may be divided, especially parts to be shared, spent, or the like. See the note below. *President Julius Nyerere of Tanzania . . . called for a new kind of African Socialism, acknowledging its beginnings in poverty, intended to raise the life of those at the bottom a little and hold down those at the top, giving all a more equal share of the cake.* NY Times 1/5/70, p36 [**1957**] ►An older synonym of this word is *pie. Pie* refers to the familiar graph known as a *pie chart*, which is a circle divided into sectors resembling the slices of a pie.

calcitonin (ˌkælsəˈtounən), *n.* a hormone that regulates the amount of calcium in the blood. Also called THYROCALCITONIN. *Copp, on the basis of experiments similar to Sanderson's, concluded that the agent must be a hormone that he named calcitonin, signifying that it participated in regulating the tone, or concentration, of calcium in the blood.* Scientific American 10/70, p42 [**1962**, from *calci*um + *ton*e + -*in* (chemical suffix)]

calculus, *n.* an act or instance of calculating; a calculation. . . . *give them a stake in the status quo and create, as Henry Kissinger used to say, "a calculus of risks and benefits that will induce the Soviet Union to behave."* NY Times Magazine 1/27/80, p45 [**1965**, generalized from the sense of an advanced mathematical system of calculation dealing with changing quantities (OED 1672)]

calefaction, *n.* another name for THERMAL POLLUTION. *The release of waste heat into the environment is called thermal pollution or calefaction.* New Scientist and Science Journal 8/26/71, p456 [**1970**, extended sense of *calefaction* a heating or being heated, ultimately from Latin *calefacere* to make warm]

Californicate or Californiate, *v.t.* to disfigure or ravage the landscape of (a state, scenic area, etc.) by urbanization and industrialization. *Whether . . . "the region is none the worse for that," visitors to the ziggurats beside the Var or road travellers on the same, now Californiated route from Cannes to Grasse, may question; but Nice remains totally, and traditionally, French.* Times (London) 9/1/77, p11 [**1972**, blend of *California* and *fornicate*, in allusion to uncontrolled development of southern California] —Californication, *n.: Legislators, scientists and citizens are now openly concerned about the threat of "Californication"—the haphazard, mindless development that has* *already gobbled up most of Southern California.* Time 8/21/72, p15

call-back, *n.* the recall of a product by its manufacturer for the purpose of correcting previously undetected defects. *Last month alone, automakers announced at least six call-backs involving more than 180,000 cars and trucks.* Time 6/2/67, p50 **[1967]**

calligram or **calligramme**, *n.* a poem whose lines are arranged to form a picture appropriate to the poem's subject. Compare CONCRETE POEM. *"A leading French graphic designer" has put together more than 1,000 diverse and fascinating illustrations around the theme of the symbol turned real . . . There are two large divisions: the letters of the alphabet drawn to have meaning beyond the symbolic, and "calligrams" (as Apollinaire named his "lyrical ideograms," the written word given visual form).* Scientific American 7/71, p121 **[1965,** from French *calligramme,* from *calli-* beautiful + *-gramme* writing]

call-in, *n.* U.S. a radio or television program which broadcasts telephone calls, comments, or questions made by listeners to the studio (often used attributively). Also called PHONE-IN. Compare HOT LINE (def. 3). *. . . the complaints in some cities were encouraged by newspaper editorials and call-in radio shows.* Saturday Review 1/6/68, p85 **[1966;** see -IN]

caló (kɑ:'lou), *n.* a variety of Mexican Spanish containing many slang expressions and English words, spoken by Chicano youths in the southwestern United States. *A lot of articles and letters are written in caló, a cholo slang that combines Spanish and English, or in Chicano rhetoric left over from the movement of the late sixties.* New Yorker 7/10/78, p72 **[1975,** from Mexican Spanish *Caló* the argot of the Mexican underworld; see *El Lenguaje de los Chicanos,* Center for Applied Linguistics, 1975, pp xiv, 191]

calzone (kæl'zouni: *or* kæl'zoun), *n.* a dome-shaped baked pie filled usually with cheese. *I went partway down into the valley and stopped at a pizzeria called the Capri, where I had a calzone.* New Yorker 11/13/78, p117 **[1976,** from Italian, from dialectal *calisoni* a kind of dumpling or patty, influenced in form by Italian *calzoni* trousers]

CAM, abbreviation for *computer-aided manufacture.* Compare CAD, CAI, CAP[1]. *In CAM, the final description of the product that the computer decides upon is fed, in computer code, to a machine tool which shapes the finished object.* New Scientist 2/7/80, p383 **[1970]**

Cambodianize, *v.t.* to put conduct of (the war in Cambodia) under Cambodian control. *We can well imagine the Vietnamese telling the United States that they will leave Cambodia just as soon as they have "Cambodianized" the war there.* New Yorker 5/30/70, p21 **[1970,** patterned after *Vietnamize]*

camcorder, *n.* a videocassette recorder combined with a TV camera. *There are two types of camcorders to consider, VHS and 8mm, which has replaced the older Beta format. Both will record for up to two hours on one cassette and then put an excellent picture on your TV.* Business Week 3/24/86, p143 **[1985,** from *camera* + *(tape)* re*corder]*

Camelot, *n.* a time or place of glamorous doings, in allusion to King Arthur's court and applied especially to the Kennedy administration and Washington, 1961-1963. *At several Cambridge dinner parties one heard faculty-types discuss . . . institutional politics, their glory days in Washington when Camelot reigned, their books or research or career frustrations.* Harper's 10/70, p102 **[1970]**

camel's nose, U.S. a small or superficial part of something very large, especially something difficult or unpleasant to deal with. *Even this amount, the authors of the study . . . contend, "represents merely the camel's nose of the modernization program planned for the Aerospace Defense Command (ADC)."* Scientific American 6/73, p39 **[1965,** abstracted from the metaphorical phrase *to let the camel's nose into the tent*]

cameo, *adj.* miniature; on a small scale. *They were gathered in a spacious downstairs den, along a massive table of food—a cameo panorama of the whole Arab world: sober Lebanese*

businessmen, a dour Palestinian with a moist handshake who introduced himself somberly by his "underground name," a silent Syrian with the fierce profile of a scimitar . . . Harper's 10/70, p60 **—n.** a cameo role or performance in a film, play, etc. *Marvellous cameo of elderly mayor from Frederic March, goodish small-town atmospheres but very simplistic moralising from Ralph Nelson, the director.* Manchester Guardian Weekly 10/10/70, p21 **[1955]**

camo ('kæmou), *adj.* having the colors of military camouflage, especially on clothing. *So those lovable mercenaries at Brigade Quartermaster came up with nonfragile implements and carrier—the Notesaf Tablet Holder, of nylon packcloth, black, green, or camo, which stays robustly on duty in a rear pocket.* Whole Earth Review 3/22/86, p116 **—n.** a garment or other item with a camouflage pattern. *Wool will keep you warm and allow you to stalk quietly. I never wear camouflage clothing. Most camo is made of denim or canvas material and is very loud in the woods.* Outdoor Life 12/85, p46 **[1985]**

camp, *n.* anything so exaggerated, banal, mediocre, or outmoded that it is considered clever or amusing because of its unsophisticated artistic quality. Compare HIGH CAMP, LOW CAMP. *. . . "the essence of Camp is its love of the unnatural: of artifice and exaggeration. And Camp is esoteric—something of a private code, a badge of identity even, among small urban cliques."* Harper's 11/65, p64 **[1954]** **—adj.** amusing or clever for its exaggerated, banal, outmoded, or mediocre artistic quality; campy. *Everyone is supposed to murmur respectfully how brilliant Oscar Wilde's comedies still are, but personally they seem to me horribly dated; camp art carried beyond the boundaries of triviality into oblivion.* NY Times 7/6/68, p9 **[1952]** **—v.i., v.t.** to act in a campy manner. **—camp around:** *The man who steals the show, if not the bank's money, is David Warner of England's Royal Shakespeare Company, who swoops and camps around in the perfect comic caricature of the decadent nobleman.* Time 11/23/70, p105 **—camp it up:** *Mr.* [Richard] *Burton has the edge; Mr.* [Rex] *Harrison camps it up rather too much.* Punch 10/29/69, p719 **[1959]**

►The term *camp,* used since at least the 1940's as a private code word in sophisticated theatrical and literary circles, was popularized by the American writer Susan Sontag in the 1960's, chiefly through her essay *Notes on 'Camp,'* which appeared in the fall 1964 issue of *Partisan Review.*

camper, *n.* a vehicle equipped with a stove, bunks, and often bathroom facilities for travel and camping out. *Many campers are separate boxlike units placed on the bed of a pickup truck. Though Mrs. Savoie has been tenting for years, she now takes to the road with her husband, seven children and 69-year-old mother-in-law in their converted bus. "With our camper," she explains happily, "everything is built right in. We just add food and clothes and take off."* Time 6/9/67, p43 **[1965]**

camptothecin (ˌkæmptou'θi:sən), *n.* an extract from a tree in China long used there in treating cancer, or a synthetic chemical identical to it. *Information about new drugs or new ways to exploit tried and tested drugs . . . is always welcome and no doubt the suppliers of camptothecin can look forward to a boom in demand as a result of what Abelson and Pentman have to say in* Nature New Biology *next Wednesday (May 31).* Nature 5/26/72, p195 **[1966,** from New Latin *Camptotheca (acuminata)* the species of tree + English *-in* (chemical suffix)]

campy, *adj.* characteristic of camp; amusing or clever because of exaggerated, banal, old-fashioned, unsophisticated, or mediocre quality. *It seemed to me that Lawrence Kornfield's staging overemphasized the campy elements and at the same time underplayed the very special verbal stylishness of the piece.* NY Times 3/25/68, p53 **[1959]**

can, *n.* **carry the can**, Slang. to take the blame or responsibility. *Now . . . senior military men want to lay down new rules, a new definition of the role of the Army. No more Vietnams, where the armed forces carry the can for civilian stupidities.* Atlantic 11/70, p71 **[1959]**

can-carrier, *n.* Slang. one who carries the responsibility for an undertaking. *As secretary of MCC* [Marylebone Cricket Club] *for the past nine years, and of the Cricket Council, Griffith has* been cast as spokesman, can-carrier, and in some quarters as chief villain. Manchester Guardian Weekly 5/22/71, p14 [**1971**]

cancer stick, *Slang.* a cigarette. *First of all we spend about £30 million each year on importing the stinking weed. Admittedly, we recover a useful chunk of this money by exporting manufactured cancer sticks, principally to the natives of Kuwait, Aden and Hong Kong, who have been brought up to appreciate English blends.* New Scientist 4/2/70, p23 [**1959**]

can-do, *adj. U.S.* eager to get things done; diligent and enthusiastic. *She [Liz Carpenter] applied the same forthright approach to selling a first family. Nothing was too good for the client. LBJ [Lyndon B. Johnson] obviously thought of her as a "can-do" lady in the jargon of that administration, and once told a friend: "Liz would charge hell with a bucket of water."* Manchester Guardian Weekly 12/12/70, p16 [**1963**]

CANDU (ˈkændu:), *n.* the type of nuclear reactor used in Canada. It uses heavy water as both the moderator and the coolant. *Different types of nuclear reactors rely on slightly different technologies. Some use ordinary water under pressure to transport the heat. Others, such as Canada's "CANDU" reactors, rely on "heavy water"—in which ordinary hydrogen is replaced by a heavier form called deuterium.* 1987 Collier's Encyclopedia Year Book, p524 [**1963**, acronym for *CANada Deuterium oxide-Uranium*]

C & W or **C-and-W**, abbreviation of COUNTRY-AND-WESTERN. *Tommy Common Sings Country Classics: . . . Common has a C-and-W repertoire that can't miss, a pleasant twang-free voice, and enough steel-guitar accompaniment to make the whole thing authentic.* Maclean's 9/68, p88 [**1964**]

candyfloss, *n. British.* flimsy or insubstantial ideas, proposals, projects, etc. *We must look more closely at what the Tories will do in the longer run. The cuts in themselves do not perhaps tell us very much. Some clearing up of the candyfloss of the Wilsonian Government is perfectly sensible.* Manchester Guardian Weekly 11/14/70, p10 [**1961**, figurative sense of the British term for cotton candy]

cannabinoid, *n.* any of the chemical compounds, such as TETRAHYDROCANNABINOL, found in cannabis or marijuana. *After a fatal traffic accident in Britain, the blood plasma of the dead driver was found to contain very high levels of the active cannabinoids present in marijuana smoke, as measured by a new, highly accurate radioimmunoassay method.* Britannica Book of the Year 1977, p259 [**1971**]

canoe slalom, a white-water sport in which a canoeist must maneuver his craft through gates similar to a slalom course in skiing. *"They mess around with canoe slalom," says Kynoch, with a canny glint in his voice, "which as you know, is another new event in the Olympics."* Sunday Times (London) 11/7/71, p30 [**1970**]

can of worms, *U.S. Slang.* a complicated and unsolved problem. *The whole area of screen acting is probably going to be a big can of worms in the next few years.* New Yorker 10/4/69, p148 [**1955**]

CAP¹, abbreviation of *computer-aided production.* Compare CAD, CAI, CAM. *But the logical extension of CAD is into the field of general industrial manufacturing, so that CAD can become CAP—computer aided production.* Science Journal 5/70, p44 [**1968**]

CAP², abbreviation of *Common Agricultural Policy*, a program of price supports for agricultural products of members of the European Community. *By means of variable import duties, CAP penalizes the sale of American farm products except those items that Europe does not produce at all.* Newsweek 2/12/73, p39 [**1967**]

cap, *n.* **1** *British.* a contraceptive diaphragm. *The sincerity of the Pope's trenchwork is unquestioned. Nor were his alternative options easy: if the cap, the pill, and the loop had suddenly been legitimised, numerous sacrificially obedient Catholics in many countries would have been distressed.* Manchester Guardian Weekly 8/1/68, p1 **2** *U.S.* an upper limit on increases

in cost; ceiling. *Edward F. King [is] founder of an organization that wants to put a cap on state spending.* Time 10/2/78, p34 [**1968** for def. 1; **1976** for def. 2]

Capcom (ˈkæpkɑm), *n.* acronym for *Capsule Communicator* (the person at a space flight center who communicates with the astronauts during a space flight). *Their pulse rates rose to around a hundred and fifty (anywhere from sixty to ninety is normal), and Dr. Hawkins urged the Capsule Communicator, or CapCom, who was talking to the astronauts by radio, to get them to take things easier.* New Yorker 4/17/71, p136 [**1968**]

capital-intensive, *adj.* requiring great expenditure of capital to increase productivity or earnings. Compare LABOR-INTENSIVE. *The [Cuban] authorities complain of being desperately short of manpower, and where possible capital-intensive techniques are being introduced.* Manchester Guardian Weekly 10/31/71, p7 [**1959**]

capitalist road, the policies and objectives of capitalist roaders. *In a message broadcast through loudspeakers, he [Peking's Mayor] charged that the riots were aimed at Chairman Mao Tse-tung and the Central Committee of the Chinese Communist Party and that behind them were persons who supported the "capitalist road."* NY Times 4/6/76, p1 [**1976**, loan translation from Chinese]

capitalist roader, a Chinese communist accused of promoting capitalistic methods of production. Compare CONFUCIANIST. See also CODE WORD. *The underlying theme of the power struggle known as the Cultural Revolution was Mao's attacks on "capitalist roaders" who introduced an incentive system in the early 1960's.* Sunday Post-Herald (Hongkong) 6/24/73, p19 [**1967**, loan translation from Chinese]

capital transfer tax, *British.* a government tax imposed on money or property transferred from one person to another, especially by inheritance. *Abbreviation:* CTT *Now comes the new squirearchy: the bowler-hatted money managers from the City, eased into landed power with the help of capital transfer tax and the inexorable demise of the wealthy owner-farmer.* Listener 6/8/78, p718 [**1974**]

caplet, *n.* a coated medicinal tablet shaped like a capsule. *He [James E. Burke] saved—if not actually improved— J & J's [Johnson & Johnson's] image in the wake of the Tylenol scare and, in the process, just may have developed a new market for the caplet that could restore J & J's market share and perhaps far more.* Forbes 4/7/86, p141 [**1979**, from *cap*sule + tab*let*]

capo (ˈkæpou), *n. U.S. Underworld Slang.* the head of one of the units or branches of the Mafia. *Subpoenas have been served in the last few days upon Carlo Gambino, head of one of the major Mafia "families," several of his "capos" (captains) and officers of one or more locals . . .* NY Times 5/7/68, p18 [**1963**, from Italian *capo* head, from Latin *caput*]

capo di (tutti) capi (ˈkɑːpou di: ˈtuːti ˈkɑːpiː), *n.* **1** a Mafia overlord. *The death last fall of New York Don Carlo Gambino, who as capo di tutti capi had brought a measure of peace to the nation's Mafia families through guile, diplomacy and strong-arm discipline . . .* Time 5/16/77, p32 **2** Figurative use: *At 7:25 on a warm evening in August, Jean-Pierre Rampal, capo di Capi of flutists the world over, is looking down at the stage of Avery Fisher Hall from the private Green Room to the right above it.* NY Times Magazine 2/22/76, p30 [**1972**, from Italian, literally, head of (all) heads]

capoeira (ˌkɑːpəˈweirə), *n.* a Brazilian dance of African origin, combining elements of folk dancing and self-defense. *African traditions still survive, like the capoeira, an intricate dance/fight routine rather like a graceful karate, which men practise in the market place.* Times (London) 5/3/76, pXIII [**1967**, from Portuguese, literally, coop for capons, fortification]

caporegime (ˌkæpouriˈʒiːm), *n. U.S. Underworld Slang.* a member of the Mafia next below a capo in rank and serving as his lieutenant. Compare CAPO, BUTTONMAN. *Inside the hospital, caporegimes and "button men," or soldiers, the lowest-ranking Mafia family members, prowled the corridors near Colombo's* *room.* Time 7/12/71, p14 [**1967**, from Italian *caporegime* head of regime]

capper, *n. U.S. Slang.* end; ending; climax. *Another friend, who knows Hollywood well, thought it was the end of an era. "It's the capper to drugs. People were at the point where they were taking anything. It was insane. But they won't go back now. Booze and pot, but no more of the big brutal stuff."* Harper's 11/70, p55 [**1968**, from *cap, v.,* to crown, climax + the suffix *-er*]

Capri pants (kə'pri:), *U.S.* tight-fitting women's trousers, worn informally. Also shortened to CAPRIS. *This imaginative state [California] that popularized freeways, supermarkets, swimming pools, drive-ins, backyard barbecues, the bare midriff, house trailers, Capri pants, hot rods, sports shirts, split-level houses and tract living has a former B-movie actor in the Governor's chair at Sacramento . . .* NY Times 6/2/68, pA1 [**1956**, named for the island of *Capri,* in the Bay of Naples, Italy, where the fashion of wearing such pants may have originated]

Capris (kə'pri:z), *n.pl. U.S.* short for CAPRI PANTS. *"They [granny dresses] are a good change from Capris and a top for parties,"* says 20-year-old Gail Eckles. Time 10/8/65, p44 [**1962**]

capsid, *n.* the protein shell surrounding the core of a virus particle. Compare NUCLEOCAPSID. See also ENCAPSIDATE. *In the virus particle, DNA occurs associated with two or three arginine-rich (basic) proteins. This nucleoprotein complex forms the core of the virus particle and is surrounded by a shell (capsid) which has the strict symmetrical shape of an icosahedron.* McGraw-Hill Yearbook of Science and Technology 1971, p89 [**1963**, from French *capside,* from Latin *capsa* box + French *-ide* -id (suffix meaning structure, body)]

capsomere ('kæpsə,mir), *n.* one of the identical units that make up a capsid. *J.T. Finch and A. Klug examined single crystals of poliovirus by x-ray diffraction and concluded that the virion had icosahedral (5:3:2) symmetry, and that the capsid was therefore likely to be composed of 60* n *asymmetric structural units ("capsomeres").* McGraw-Hill Yearbook of Science and Technology 1972, p116 [**1961**, from French *capsomère,* from *caps*ide + connecting *-o-* + *mère* (from Greek *méros* part)]

capture, *n.* retrieval of information stored in a computer memory bank. . . . *the credit card holder can be replaced with a document holder or a roll of paper tape, for other data capture purposes.* New Scientist 1/27/72, p207 [**1972**]

caravan park, *British.* an area where holidayers may park their caravans or house trailers. The equivalent U.S. term is *trailer park. Between the hotels and a group of chalets there is accommodation for 580 visitors. Plans for further expansion, including . . . a caravan park, will increase this capacity to 1,080 by 1971.* Manchester Guardian Weekly 11/29/69, p10 [**1962**]

carbaryl ('karbə,ril), *n.* an insecticide having a wide range of applications, used as a substitute for DDT. It is a carbamate compound with a short period of toxicity. *Formula:* $C_{12}H_{11}O_2N$ *The death of bees in enormous numbers is the result of a recent switch by canning companies, who are the largest vegetable growers, from DDT to an insecticide thought more benign, carbaryl.* Science News 10/31/70, p349 [**1964**, from *carb*amate + *aryl* an aromatic hydrocarbon radical]

carbecue, *n.* a device for disposing of a junked car by rotating it over fire. *Another is the "carbecue," a machine that turns an old automobile body into a solid lump of metal by pressure and heat.* NY Times 1/2/68, p39 [**1968**, from *car* + bar*becue*]

carbenicillin (kar,benə'silin), *n.* a type of penicillin effective against various gram-negative bacteria. *Formula:* $C_{17}H_{18}N_2O_6S$ *Pfizer's J. B. Roerig Division of the British-owned Beecham Pharmaceuticals . . . announced they were in the market with carbenicillin, a new antibiotic effective against* Pseudomonas aeruginosa, *a bacterium looming with new importance in human disease . . . Carbenicillin has "little or no toxicity even in very high dosage."* Science News 8/22/70, p164 [**1968**, contraction of *car*boxy*benzylpenicillin,* its chemical name]

carbenoxolone (,karbə'naksəloun), *n.* a drug that reduces inflammation, used in the treatment of gastric ulcer. *Formula:*

$C_{34}H_{50}O_7$ *Synthesized from glycyrrhizic acid, a derivative of licorice root, carbenoxolone increases the ability of cells to bind protein, thus, it is believed, increasing the secretion of protective mucus.* 1974 Collier's Encyclopedia Year Book, p336 [**1965**, from *carb*on + *-ene* hydrocarbon + *ox*ygen + *-ol* alcohol or phenol + ket*one*]

car bomb, an explosive device concealed in a motor vehicle that is set off as an act of terrorism. *A full-scale resumption of the Provisional IRA's bombing campaign may have been temporarily averted by the capture on Saturday of the largest quantity of bomb-making materials ever found in the province. If it had got through, the haul would have enabled terrorists to make up to 60 car bombs.* Times (London) 1/19/76, p1 [**1972**] —**car bombing:** *After a ten-week trial at Winchester, eight young men and women were found guilty of complicity in the London car-bombings.* Annual Register of World Events in 1973, p29

carbon-copy, *v.t.* to make an exact copy of; to duplicate. *But what Ariane Mnouchkine and her collaborators have achieved can't be carbon-copied any more than what Jean Vilar was doing at Avignon and Suresnes around 1950.* Manchester Guardian Weekly 9/4/71, p14 [**1962**, verb use of *carbon copy* a copy made with carbon paper; an exact copy]

carbon date, the age of a fossil, artifact, etc., measured by the amount of radioactive carbon in it. *Weapon points were found . . . where they had lain in conjunction with the skeletons of animals, and could therefore be dated by the carbon 14 test: most of the animals were long since extinct, and the approximate carbon date was between six and seven thousand years ago.* Atlantic 7/64, p38 [**1958**]

carbon-date, *v.t.* to date the age of (a fossil, artifact, etc.) by measuring its content of radioactive carbon. *The tools are unsophisticated and generally unlike any other known New World artifacts . . . The tools themselves, being stone, could not be carbon-dated. Therefore, dates had to come from analysis of volcanic ash that overlies some of the sites, and from the shells.* Science News 5/13/67, p447 [**1967**]

carbon fiber, a synthetic fiber of great strength and lightness, made by carbonizing acrylic fiber at very high temperatures. See also HYFIL. *Development of carbon fibres, first produced in the U.K. and subsequently used for a revolutionary plastic material for aircraft and precision engineering, began to evolve on an international scale.* Britannica Book of the Year 1970, p426 [**1966**]

carborane, *n.* a compound of carbon, boron, and hydrogen having unusual thermal properties (also used attributively). *The existence of complete series of polyhedral borane anions and carboranes was not apparent at the beginning of the present decade.* Science 7/12/68, p153 *One of the most promising of recent approaches has been the inclusion of carborane clusters in polymer chains.* New Scientist 4/10/69, p64 [**1965**, blend of *carbon* and *boran*e + *-ane* (chemical suffix)]

carborne, *adj.* carried in or traveling by motor car. *The shopping public is . . . increasingly car-borne.* Times (London) 3/16/70, p13 *The car locator systems now being considered by the* [police] *department have two essential segments: a small carborne radio transmitter and a permanently based sensing device.* NY Times 11/5/67, pA129 [**1958**]

carceplex, *n.* a molecular complex consisting of a large molecule in which a smaller molecule has been chemically trapped. *A carceplex consists of a "carcerand"—a hollow "prison" molecule—and a "guest" molecule trapped inside. These guest molecules . . . exist in a state of matter different from the familiar states represented by solids, liquids, gases and electrically charged plasmas.* NY Times 3/21/89, pC1 [**1989**, from Latin *carcer* prison + English com*plex*]

carcerand, *n.* a large, hollow molecule in which a smaller molecule is chemically trapped. Compare CARCEPLEX. *A "carcerand," from the Latin word for a prison . . . allows chemists to study the differences in properties between a small molecule in solution and the same molecule imprisoned within another molecule where its movements would be restricted. Carcerands* *themselves turn out to be highly insoluble.* Science News 8/8/87, p92 [**1987**]

carcinoembryonic antigen, a protein substance causing the body to produce antibodies against it (antigen), found in the cells of certain cancer tumors as well as in the normal cells of a fetus. *Abbreviation:* CEA *Whatever progress has been made toward developing biochemical tests* [for early detection of cancer] *is based on the findings that tumors and embryonic tissues share . . . several enzymes and structural proteins not found in mature healthy tissues. The two most important of these substances are carcinoembryonic antigen, which was first found in colon tumors, and alpha-fetoprotein, which was first discovered in liver tumors.* 1976 Collier's Encyclopedia Year Book, p61 [**1967,** from *carcino-* tumor, cancer + *embryonic*]

card[1], *v.t. U.S. Slang.* to require an identification card of (someone) to prove legal age (often used as a way of excluding someone from entering a night club, etc.). *Blacks are not the only people who are particularly likely to be carded by disco doormen.* New Yorker 12/13/76, p145 [**1976,** verb use of noun *card,* short for *identification card*]

card[2], *n.* **play the** (or **one's**) _____**card.** to use a (particular) gambit or tactic so as to gain an advantage or attain a goal. *He plays the human rights card by noting that violaters such as Argentina, Chile, Haiti, Nicaragua and Ethiopia were recipients of some $600 millions in the last year.* Manchester Guardian Weekly 7/9/78, p7 *During his visit, Teng had played his "U.S. card" six different ways. He left conservatives at odds and the Soviets fretful.* Burlington Free Press (Vermont) 2/6/79, p1 [**1973**] ►This is a new version or variant of several older figurative expressions derived from cardplaying, such as *play one's cards* (*right, well,* etc.), *play one's cards close to the vest* (or *the chest*), *play one's best card,* etc.

card-carrying, *adj.* openly avowed; confirmed; inveterate. . . . *the first hint of Greene as a new man, as a card-carrying representative of the modern condition, comes when, in 1920, he is sent, astonishingly and at the age of sixteen, to an analyst in Kensington after an abortive attempt to run away from home.* New Yorker 10/2/71, p129 [**1963,** an extended sense of the term used in politics to describe a member of the Communist Party (that is, one who carries a membership card) as distinguished from Communist sympathizers, and later applied to anyone devoted or strongly attached to a particular party, doctrine, etc., as "a card-carrying capitalist" or "a card-carrying Democrat"]

cardioactive, *adj.* stimulating the heart's activity. *Wildenthal developed a method for maintaining these* [fetal mice] *hearts in organ culture in the contractile state for 3-4 weeks and found that they responded normally to a number of cardioactive drugs, such as acetylcholine and ouabain.* McGraw-Hill Yearbook of Science and Technology 1971, p53 [**1971,** from *cardio-* heart + *active*]

cardiogenic shock, shock due to an impairment in the output of blood by the heart. *Today heart muscle or pump failure is the leading cause of death in CCUs. Cardiogenic shock due to pump failure is related to the size of the myocardial infarction, or heart muscle death, and despite heroic measures, the mortality rate remains formidable.* Americana Annual 1974, p376 [**1968,** from *cardio-* heart + *-genic* originating in]

cardiomyopathy, *n.* progressive weakness, enlargement, etc., of the heart muscle. *Six to 20 or more months of complete bed rest is apparently saving people with . . . diseases of the heart muscle itself—disorders generally called cardiomyopathies.* NY Times 11/24/66, p58 [**1966,** from *cardio-* heart + *myopathy* disease of the muscles]

cardiopulmonary resuscitation, the full form of CPR. *Cardiopulmonary resuscitation . . . is "a psychomotor skill that needs practice," a New York Heart Association spokesman said. "A person can do mouth-to-mouth resuscitation without special training. It's the chest compression that can be dangerous. Done incorrectly, it can crack ribs and possibly puncture internal organs."* New York Post 1/30/79, p28 [**1973**]

cardioversion, *n.* restoration of normal heartbeat by using electric shock. *The preferred treatment for sustained ventricular tachycardia* [abnormally fast heart action] *is an intravenous injection of lidocaine* [a local anesthetic]. *If that fails, normal rhythm can usually be restored by delivering a mild and carefully timed electric shock through the chest wall, a procedure called cardioversion.* Scientific American 2/71, p47 [**1963,** from *cardio-* heart + *version* a turning]

care, *v.* **could care less,** *U.S. Informal.* not to care at all; be completely indifferent (to). *But wearing a baggy, pinstriped '40s suit, Mitchum looks as if he could care less what the film is going to do for his career.* Women's Wear Daily 4/18/75, p14 *Asked if she would vote this year,* [she] *said, "I never have and I never will. I didn't watch the debates, and I could care less."* New York Post 10/27/76, p35 [**1966,** alteration of (*I*) *couldn't care less,* an expression that became popular in the 1940's, probably by influence of the earlier (1930's) *I couldn't agree more;* see the derivations in Eric Partridge's *A Dictionary of Catch Phrases,* 1977] ►The widespread use of this expression in American English during the 1970's prompted considerable discussion both in the popular press and in scholarly journals. According to a note in *American Speech* (45, 1-2, 1973, p29), its use by the columnist Abigail ("Dear Abby") Van Buren was promptly corrected by several of her readers, and Theodore M. Bernstein, the late style editor of *The New York Times,* called it a "degenerated" expression that "makes no sense."

caregiver, *n.* a person who provides care for the very young, sick, or elderly. . . . *the link between early "attachments" to a primary caregiver and later adaptation at school.* Science News 4/27/85, p266 [**1970**]

care label, a label on a garment or fabric providing instructions for its cleaning. *The office thought the industry should consider whether . . . all clothing should have non-detachable care labels.* Times (London) 2/17/77, p3 [**1967**]

Carey Street, *British.* bankruptcy. *Boys may . . . be content with casements . . . divided into economical panes that a chap can risk putting a missile through without bringing his parents into Carey Street.* New Scientist 12/14/67, p641 [**1967,** after the name of the street in London where the Bankruptcy Court was formerly located]

Caricom or **CARICOM** (ˌkærəˈkɑm), *n.* acronym for *Caribbean Community* or *Caribbean Common Market,* a common market established in 1974 by ten countries of the eastern Caribbean which comprised the earlier Caribbean Free Trade Association from 1968 to 1973. *Haiti and Surinam applied to join Caricom, and diplomatic relations were established between Caricom countries and Cuba.* Britannica Book of the Year 1975, p230 [**1974**]

carnapper or **carnaper,** *n.* a car thief. *The seats have massage units to reduce driving fatigue (or jiggle when you sleep), the tires light up at night, and if a carnapper tries to break into all this luxury, the doors give him an electric shock.* NY Times 9/9/68, p48 *Carnapers stole here early this morning a Volkswagen car owned by former Rep. Florante C. Roque.* Manila Chronicle, Philippines 7/6/65, p1 [**1965,** from *car* + *kidnapper* or *kidnaper*]

carousel or **carrousel,** *n.* **1** a circular conveyor, as for the delivery of luggage at an airport. *Older people . . . found it hard to tug their cases off the carousels.* Which? 11/70, p352 **2** a circular tray for a slide projector, having slots from which each slide is dropped or pushed in front of the lens and then returned to its slot. *Houziaux has invented a teaching machine to remove some of the load from lecturers. His automatic tutor is based on a carousel of 35-mm slides, a magnetic tape recorder, and a small computer that handles the logic decisions on what to ask the pupil next.* New Scientist 11/29/73, p654 [**1962** for def. 1; **1971** for def 2; extended senses of the term for a merry-go-round]

carpool or **car-pool,** *v.i. U.S.* to join a car pool; take turns in driving each other to work, shop, etc. Compare VANPOOL. *In Houston, Texas, five friends and neighbors car-pool daily to their jobs at Shell Oil Company's headquarters.* Woman's Day

10/74, p4 [**1966**, verb use of *car pool* (1940's)] —**carpooling** or **car-pooling**, *n.*: *The Senate commanded Zarb to promulgate, within 90 days, precise standards of energy conservation covering everything from decorative lighting to carpooling and mass transit use.* Tuscaloosa News (Alabama) 4/24/75, p4

carry-on, *adj.* small enough to be carried aboard an airplane by a passenger. *Coats and carry-on baggage are stowed in large overhead storage compartments.* Time 1/19/70, p41 [**1955**]

cartoon, *n.* a computer printout forming a pictorial display or image (also used attributively). *A geological cartoon representation of gross geological relationships in the Eastern Alps. That part of the section above the line 1-1 is well established, that below the line is inferred.* Nature 9/22/72, p203 [**1970**]

car-top, *v.t., v.i.* U.S. to transport on top of an automobile. *Transportability (it can't be car-topped, needs a special trailer) and ease of construction were secondary.* Popular Science 5/74, p100 [**1968**]

cascade effect, a series of events in which one causes or produces the next, often intensifying each other. *In the case of the Navy, it's a mixed picture. Apparently the Navy is badly afflicted by the loss of highly trained technical men and the cascade effect—if you're short of technicians, those left have to work harder, spend more time at sea, and this creates more unhappiness, which leads to more shortage.* Forbes 5/26/80, p37 [**1976**]

case, *n.* **get off one's case**, U.S. Slang. leave one alone; stop annoying or harassing one. *Our 17-year-old daughter seems to be a puritan. She gets very angry when anyone in our family discusses sex . . . When I've tried to talk with her about the subject she will say something like "Get off my case."* New York Post 5/12/80, p22 [**1979**]

cash and carry, a store that sells goods, usually at a discount, on the basis of cash payments and no services. *The number of cash and carries has grown from 398 in 1967 to 610 at the end of last year. Retailers of all sorts have turned to the cash and carry to help them compete against the cut prices in supermarkets.* Times (London) 3/16/70, p15 [**1966**]

cash bar, U.S. a bar at a party or reception at which alcoholic drinks are sold. *The twentieth reunion of the class of '52 was to consist principally of a daylong gathering at the Myopia Hunt Club in Hamilton, Massachusetts. There were to be seminars, and lunch, followed by golf and swimming, then a cash bar and dinner.* Atlantic 7/72, p80 [**1972**]

cash cow, U.S. Finance. a regular and reliable source of income or profit. *Karin Lissakers of the Carnegie Endowment quotes a banker in . . . an unguarded moment: "That (unmentioned country) is a cash cow for us. We hope they never repay!"* Manchester Guardian Weekly (Washington Post section) 6/19/83, p17 [**1978**]

cashless society, a society in which transactions of payment or other exchange of funds are made by credit card, computer, or other electronic technology. Also called CHECKLESS SOCIETY. See DEBIT CARD and ELECTRONIC FUNDS TRANSFER (SYSTEM). *Computerized checking accounts—the electronic transfer of funds from the consumer's checking accounts to the merchants' accounts—have brought six Long Island, New York, communities closer to the "cashless society."* Encyclopedia Science Supplement (Grolier) 1979, p98 [**1972**]

cashpoint, *n.* an electronic machine, often outside a bank, from which money can be withdrawn by inserting a card and keying in an identification number. Also called AUTOMATIC TELLER. *Its cashpoints feed out notes so new and clean they rasp the hand like fine sandpaper.* Sunday Times (London) 10/12/86, p58 [**1985**]

cassette, *n.* a small cartridge of magnetic-tape reels that can be inserted into a tape player for automatic playback or recording. *In addition to more two-year community colleges, which this obviously requires, the commission urges a big expansion in off-campus education—correspondence courses, TV lectures, home teaching cassettes.* Time 12/7/70, p60 —*v.t.* to record (on tape, film, or videotape) for replay on a cassette. *The most*

recent programmes have been in the entertainment field—EVR has cassetted 150 films. New Scientist 1/13/72, p84 [**1960** for noun; **1972**, verb use of the noun]

Castle Catholic, a derogatory term in Northern Ireland for a Catholic who supports British rule of Northern Ireland. *The SDLP [Social Democratic Labour Party] can no more choose who should lead the Unionist Party than the Unionists can—as they used to pipe-dream—select Castle Catholics (Uncle Toms) for power-sharing.* Manchester Guardian Weekly 7/28/73, p10 [**1973**]

Castlerobin bomb, a complicated home-made bomb fitted with booby traps to prevent defusing. *Bomb technology has also declined in other ways. There has been a sharp fall-off in the incidence of sophisticated arming circuits and an absence for some months of the complex "Castlerobin" bombs with anti-handling devices.* New Scientist 9/21/72, p487 [**1971**, perhaps from *Castle* (Catholic) + (round) *robin*]

Castroism, *n.* another word for FIDELISMO or FIDELISM. *I am certainly not in favor of* Castroism *or Maoism making headway in Latin America.* Saturday Review 7/2/66, p22 [**1960**]

Castroist or **Castroite**, *n., adj.* other words for FIDELISTA or FIDELIST. *He* [Che Guevara] *claimed that South America would be* Castroist *within five years.* Britannica Book of the Year 1967, p249 *But the* Castroite *Venezuelan guerrillas, fighting a representative, popular, and rich government, are not about to take Caracas.* Atlantic 11/66, p36 [**1960**]

CAT[1], abbreviation of CLEAR AIR TURBULENCE. *CAT . . . the meteorologists think, develops near the crest of a standing wave* [of air]. New Scientist 3/19/70, p544 [**1963**]

CAT[2], *n.* acronym for COMPUTERIZED AXIAL TOMOGRAPHY. See also CAT SCAN, CAT SCANNER. *In CAT the patient is put on a revolving table and X-rays are shot from all angles to get information so that the computer can construct a two-dimensional picture of a slice through the patient's brain, for example.* Science News 11/18/78, p348 [**1975**]

catalytic converter, an antipollution device in automobiles which contains a chemical catalyst for oxidizing the pollutant exhaust gases (carbon monoxide, nitrogen oxides, and hydrocarbons), thereby converting them to harmless products (carbon dioxide, nitrogen, and water vapor). *The catalytic converter won't work on a diesel because the temperature of a diesel's exhaust is too low to sustain the converter's chemical reactions.* Encyclopedia Science Supplement (Grolier) 1981, p200 [**1959**]

catastrophe, *n.* any of the sharp discontinuities treated by catastrophe theory. *Dr. Zeeman suggested that many real events—a sudden change in a chemical reaction, the sudden buckling of a steel girder, the sudden decision of a dog to attack, the sudden differentiation of growing cells into an embryo—could be represented as "catastrophes" on suitable mathematical surfaces.* Encyclopedia Science Supplement (Grolier) 1979, p101 [**1973**]

catastrophe theory, a system in mathematics proposed for describing a discontinuity or phenomenon of sudden change in a continuous process, such as behavior, financial cycles, or some other state, by fitting the attributes of the change into a geometric model consisting of dimensional planes that describe the change. *Catastrophe theory has been particularly interesting in its applications to the biological and social sciences, perhaps because discontinuous and divergent phenomena abound there. For example, Thom suggests applications not only in embryology but also in the theory of evolution, in reproduction, in the process of thought and in the generation of speech.* Scientific American 3/76, p60D [**1972**, proposed by René Thom]

Catch-22 or **catch-22**, *n.* **1** a hidden difficulty involving a puzzling paradox. Compare DOUBLE-BIND. *The Catch-22 of* [movie] *sequels goes something like this: In order to sell, stress has to be laid on the original success; but the more sharply focused these earlier memories, the more pallid the successor.* Jaws 2 *is a case in point.* Maclean's 7/10/78, p59 **2** a condition whereby one fails no matter what action is taken because of a paradoxical rule or situation. *"Getting an agent is Catch-22,"* Hoffman says. *"You can't get one unless you're published and* *you need one to get published."* Newsweek 12/24/73, p83 **3** Attributive use: *There is a "Catch-22" aspect to the story. Because discrimination prevented many women and minority workers from getting jobs in the past, they have no seniority; because they have no seniority, they are the first to be laid off.* Newsweek 12/2/74, p72 [**1970**, from *Catch-22*, title of a novel (1961) by the American writer Joseph Heller, born 1923. The title refers to an absurdly paradoxical Air Force rule by which a pilot is considered insane if he keeps flying combat missions without formally asking to be relieved; if, however, he does put in such a formal request, he is adjudged sane and may not be relieved.]

Catch-23, *n. U.S.* a new or more intricate Catch-22. *The speech showed that Kissinger . . . has come to accept what Washington insiders call the "Catch-23" of the oil business. Put simply, the idea is that to escape the political clutches of the cartel, the West will have to develop vast new sources of energy . . . The catch is that the very act of producing all this new energy may lead to a glut of oil and a sharp drop in its price, thus undercutting the price of the new energy.* Newsweek 2/17/75, p25 [**1973**; see the etymology of CATCH-22]

catch-up, *n.* **play catch-up,** *U.S.* **1** *Sports.* to try to overtake an opposing team by playing unconventionally, taking risks, etc. *Leading Oakland in the American League's Western Division by 7 games, the Royals bask in the front-runner's knowledge that this year playing catch-up is for other guys.* Time 8/23/76, p63 **2** Figurative use: *There is yet time to develop the requisite technologies for a number of vulnerable materials before such situations arise, rather than playing catch-up as in the case of energy technologies alternative to oil.* Science 2/20/76, p633 [**1971**]

catecholamine, *n.* any of a class of hormones, such as adrenalin, that act upon the nerve cells. *[Lithium] may act by interfering with the metabolism of the catecholamines, which are involved in all brain activity.* Science News 4/18/70, p390 [**1955**, from the chemical substances *catechol + amine*]

catecholaminergic, *adj.* activated by or producing catecholamine. Compare DOPAMINERGIC, NORADRENERGIC, SEROTONERGIC. *The regions of catecholaminergic neurons (caudate nucleus, substantia nigra, hypothalamus, and locus coeruleus) were dissected out under a microscope from frozen sections of the brain.* Science 1/23/76, p290 [**1973**, from CATECHOLAMINE + Greek *érgon* work + English *-ic*]

catenaccio (ˌkɑːtəˈnɑːtʃiːou), *n.* a formation in soccer using four defenders on the defensive line, three players in midfield, and three on the attack. *Juventus, winner of 15 national titles . . . represents the conservative, traditional style known as catenaccio (literally, door bolt). The emphasis is on tight defense, with the opponent's attacks being used as springboards for counterthrusts and breakaway strikes, by swift forwards.* Time 6/4/73, p40 [**1964**, from Italian]

CAT scan, an X-ray picture made by a CAT SCANNER. Also called CT SCAN. *The CAT scan can detect certain abnormalities that ordinarily can be diagnosed only through surgery, including hematoma of the liver (a blood mass caused by injury) and tumors of the pancreas.* NY Times 5/8/76, p9 [**1976**]

CAT scanner, a machine which produces three-dimensional X-ray pictures by COMPUTERIZED AXIAL TOMOGRAPHY (CAT). Also called CT SCANNER. *Mrs. Hancock . . . especially praises the new machine that diagnosed the growth in the right hemisphere of her brain. The machine, known as a CAT scanner, produced in minutes an X-ray picture revealing the deadly tumor that had escaped her physician's notice and conventional diagnostic efforts . . .* Wall Street Journal 12/10/75, p1 [**1975**]

CAT scanning, the act or process of producing X-ray pictures with a CAT SCANNER. Also called CT SCANNING. *CAT scanning came of age in 1976. The abbreviation CAT stands for computerized axial tomography. This is a technique that makes possible precise diagnosis in many cases where the abnormality is unclear or undetectable by conventional X-ray or radioactive scans.* Americana Annual 1977, p322 [**1976**]

catsuit, *n. British.* a one-piece pantsuit. *His [the designer's] suits are either one-piece worsted cat-suits, or trousers and jerkin-type top.* Times (London) 5/31/68, p10 [**1963**]

cattle show, *U.S. Informal.* a public gathering of Presidential candidates running in a primary election campaign. Compare BEAUTY CONTEST. *In a cattle show, national candidates are herded into a ballroom, which then becomes a kind of stockyard-showcase. Local politicians poke them to see if their flesh is pressable; national pundits prod them to find variances in their views; the local party profits on ticket sales.* NY Times 3/10/83, pA27 [**1979**]

CATV, originally the abbreviation of *Community Antenna Television* (an early system of cable television), now used as an abbreviation for CABLE TELEVISION. *Conventional TV broadcasters do have very real grievances, for CATV could be piratical unless properly regulated. It was started to bring television to isolated or poor reception areas. CATV entrepreneurs raised hilltop antennas, plucked the signals of distant channels from the air and then relayed them, generally by coaxial cable, direct to subscribers' TV sets.* Time 6/1/70, p66 [**1964**]

Cayley (ˈkeɪli:), *n.* the material that fills large highland depressions on the moon creating a smooth undulating terrain. It is typically a breccia type of rock with light color and smooth surface. *The Cayley is the plains-forming fill unit that is scattered throughout the entire Central Highlands. It is characterized by mostly smooth to undulating terrain. "The Cayley must be volcanic, because it fills in like bathtub rings," says Muehlberger.* Science News 4/8/72, p236 [**1972**, from *Cayley Plain,* where it was first encountered, named for Sir George *Cayley,* 1773-1857, a British pioneer of aviation]

CB, abbreviation of *chemical and biological.* Compare CBW. *They [U Thant's consultant experts] called clearly for the accession of all states to the 1925 Geneva Protocol, . . . and an agreement to halt the development, production and stockpiling of CB agents.* New Scientist 7/17/69, p107 [**1964**]

CBer or **C.B.er** (ˌsi:ˈbi:ər), *n. U.S.* an owner or operator of a CB radio. *The first is the practice of many CBers to spend hours in their parked autos enthusiastically modulating with anyone who can hear them.* Daily News (New York) 6/5/77, p16 [**1963**] ►Although CB radio was introduced in the United States in 1945 with the establishment of the Citizens Radio Service, it was used mainly by sportsmen and professional people until the early 1960's, when it attracted the interest of the general public.

Though CB radios exist in other English-speaking countries, they are called by different names. The abbreviation *CB* is the popular name both in the United States and Canada. The official Canadian equivalent is General Radio Service or *GRS.*

CBW, abbreviation of: **1** chemical and biological warfare. *Several years ago the Campaign for Nuclear Disarmament claimed there was a highly secret chemical warfare establishment in Cornwall. Those who thought they knew their British CBW scene were politely sceptical.* Science Journal 12/70, p8 **2** chemical and biological weapons. *Which countries are, in the future, most likely to use CBW on an extensive scale? Would these be the smaller powers? . . . "From that point of view, interest in CBW would be centred in the Third World, in nonnuclear powers."* New Scientist and Science Journal 7/15/71, p139 [**1964**]

CCD, abbreviation of CHARGE-COUPLED DEVICE. *The CCD can also function as an image sensor. A silicon CCD is an excellent optical detector throughout the visible spectrum—potential wells can be created by shining a light on it. Thus a completely solid state version of a television camera pickup tube, or vidicon, can be made of a CCD array.* World Book Science Annual 1973, p304 [**1970**]

CCU, abbreviation of *coronary care unit.* Compare ICU. *It has been estimated that at least two-thirds of sudden deaths are due to unrecognized and untreated disorders of the cardiac rhythm. To prevent such disasters, it seemed logical to bring the trained personnel and equipment of the CCU to the patient* *outside the hospital as quickly as possible.* 1975 Britannica Yearbook of Science and the Future, p276 [**1971**]

CD, abbreviation of COMPACT DISK. *Because there is no groove in a CD, there are none of the mechanical problems involved in keeping a phonograph needle in a groove, hence no skipping, sticking or distortion.* Suburbia Today 5/1/83, p23 [**1982**]

CD-ROM (ˌsiːˌdiːˈrɑm), acronym for *compact-disk read-only memory* (an optical disk used to store computer data). *"CD-ROM" is . . . an extremely compact new form of data storage . . . The CD-ROM disks on the market for personal computers today have a storage capacity of about 550 megabytes of data.* Washington Post 5/26/86, pF15 [**1983**]

CEA, abbreviation of CARCINOEMBRYONIC ANTIGEN. *The researchers have found that if CEA is present in the blood of a person above a specified amount, he or she very likely has cancer. If the protein recedes in the blood of a person being treated for cancer, the recession is a good sign that treatment is working.* Science News 6/9/73, p367 [**1970**]

cedi (ˈseidiː), *n.* the basic unit of money in Ghana. 1.02 cedi equals $1. *Ghana's economic crisis, represented by the recent 44 per cent devaluation of the cedi, is on a scale that would threaten the existence of the government in many African countries.* Times (London) 1/10/72, p5 [**1965**]

celebutante, *n.* a young woman who becomes a celebrity on her first appearance in society or in the arts. . . . *the Hollywood celebutante Brigitte Neilson . . .* Sunday Times (London) 9/18/88, pG13 [**1986**, from *celeb*rity + deb*utante*]

celiac, *n.* a person who has celiac disease, a digestive disorder chiefly of young children, characterized by diarrhea and abdominal swelling. *Wheat, or more specifically wheat gluten, is known to be especially toxic to celiacs. Gluten is the sticky plant protein found in cereal grains. When it is removed from the diets of celiacs, their psychotic behavior diminishes.* Science News 1/31/76, p69 [**1976**, noun use of *celiac, adj.*]

cell, *n.* a small geographical area in which a group of radiotelephones can communicate through a single radio transmitter. *As a vehicle in which a telephone call is in progress on a particular channel moves from one cell to another, the call is automatically transferred to the neighboring cell.* Encyclopedia Science Supplement (Grolier) 1985, p329 [**1978**]

cell fusion, a method of producing new cells in the laboratory by placing together cells of different types or from different species until two cells fuse their nuclei. *The scientists collected some of these cells and used a process called cell fusion to join them with a type of cell that grows easily in the test tube. From the new combination cells, the scientists isolated and established a line of combination cells that constantly synthesize antibodies against the sheep red blood cell antigen.* World Book Science Annual 1978, p299 [**1975**]

cell-mediated immunity, immunity produced by T cells directly attacking viruses, foreign tissue, etc., rather than by antibodies such as those secreted by B cells. *Scientists at the Georgetown University School of Medicine have found that women's natural cell-mediated immunity against German measles is lowered during pregnancy. Cell-mediated immunity constitutes an important defense against viral infections.* Science News 10/20/73, p253 [**1972**]

cell therapy or **cellular therapy**, a method of rejuvenation or physical restoration by the injection of suspensions of cells prepared from the organs of embryonic sheep. *Abbreviation:* CT *Last week, for instance, there was this fellow I was confronting who believes that almost any sickness (except infections) can be cured by injecting suspensions of appropriate cells from foetal sheep. It's called cell therapy.* New Scientist and Science Journal 8/19/71, p424 *Cellular therapy is not generally accepted by the medical profession in Europe and it is not officially permitted in the United States.* 1972 Britannica Year Book of Science and the Future, p84 [**1960**]

cellular engineering, the scientific alteration of cell structure or substitution of cells as medical treatment for certain conditions and as basic research into biological phenomena. It is similar to and overlaps with genetic engineering. *The new techniques, as well as marrow grafts represent an attempt at "cellular engineering" to correct the life-threatening effects of birth defects.* NY Times 5/14/76, pD12 [**1972**]

cellularized, *adj.* divided into cells or small compartments. *The directors also tell shareholders that the Manchester Miller will be converted this summer into a fully cellularized container vessel which will help meet the demands for space on the company's Montreal container services.* Times (London) 4/21/70, p22 *When Richard Nixon's entourage visited the White House, one campaign aide expressed surprise at how "cellularized" Lyndon Johnson's staff is.* Time 11/22/68, p19 [**1968**]

cellular phone or **cellular telephone,** a mobile telephone unit, especially in a motor vehicle, capable of extending communication over a wide geographical area by means of low-power radio transmitters linking many smaller areas called cells. Also called MOBILE PHONE. *The dark blue Lincolns cruise the Washington streets from sunup to midnight. Inside are shadowy predators of the political jungle curled around their cellular phones, eyes alight and voices urgent, positioning themselves in the great power struggle that has now been joined.* Time 12/3/84, p24 [**1984**]

cellulite, *n.* a substance made up of fat, water, and wastes that is supposed to form unsightly lumpy pockets beneath the skin. *Cellulite cannot be burned off by conventional diets, says Ronsard: even when poundage is pared away, this "superfat" remains.* Time 3/10/75, p76 [**1971**, from French, coined by Nicole Ronsard, a French dietitian, from *cellule* cell]

cenosphere (ˈsenəˌsfir), *n.* a thin-walled, glassy ball of calcined clay in which gases have been trapped during cooling, found in fly ash. *The balls, called cenospheres, can withstand extremely high pressure. They can be used to provide buoyancy in deep-ocean operations, as a closed-pore insulation in a space shuttle design, and for making light-weight floating concrete.* World Book Science Annual 1974, p273 [**1971**, from *ceno-* empty (from Greek *kenós*) + *sphere*]

centerfold, *n.* an illustrated center spread that is extra long and has to be folded into a magazine or book, and unfolded to be seen in full. *On one such occasion, a Phantom pilot was surprised to see his Soviet counterpart hold up a centerfold from, of all things, Playboy magazine.* Time 6/28/71, p20 [**1967**]

centimillionaire, *n.* a millionaire who has a hundred million or more dollars (also used attributively). *Ordinarily, David Rockefeller, chairman of the Chase Manhattan Bank and a centimillionaire in his own right, would expect to have no trouble at all negotiating a loan from his friendly neighborhood banker.* Time 1/12/70, p47 [**1968**, from *centi-* a hundred + *millionaire*]

central casting, *U.S.* the casting department of a film studio. Often used figuratively, as in **straight from central casting**, stereotyped, typical, or conventional. . . . *almost everyone in the Italian theatre seems to be noisily auditioning for a part in a rather dated play about the Italian theatre. And most of the applicants are straight from central casting.* New Yorker 10/21/67, p92 [**1958**]

central city, *U.S.* a city that is the center of a metropolitan area. Also called CORE CITY. Compare INNER CITY. *The Times has expressly concerned itself with the problems of the central cities despite the fact that these views may not jibe with those of many of its suburban readers.* NY Times 3/17/70, p42 [**1963**]

central dogma, **1** the theory that the transmission of genetic information is an irreversible process always determined by the nucleic acid DNA (deoxyribonucleic acid, the carrier of genetic material in the cells). See the first quotation. Compare TEMINISM. *For more than a decade, most scientists have accepted the "central dogma" of molecular biology without question. Stated simply, that dogma holds that the heredity information in living cells is always passed along in the same direction: from the "double helix" DNA molecule to the single-stranded messenger RNA molecule, which in turn directs the synthesis of protein— which is essential to all life.* Time 7/20/70, p57 . . . *Dr. H. M. Temin, now at Wisconsin University, claimed to have found in* *a cell invaded by an RNA virus a stretch of DNA that matched with the viral RNA. The RNA seemed to be acting as a template for DNA synthesis—in direct contravention of the central dogma.* New Scientist 12/31/70, p607 **2** *any idea which is accepted unquestioningly. But in America for the last century, the image of the clinician-researcher has been increasingly the model, and it is now central dogma for medical educators, who accept it unquestioningly.* NY Times 10/16/70, p41 **[1967]**

centrism, *n.* a moderate or middle-of-the-road position in politics. *He [Willi Stoph, Prime Minister of East Germany] has acted as a mediator between people of differing opinions, always supporting the principle of "centrism," which would seem to explain why his position has never been challenged.* Times (London) 3/14/70, p6 **[1965]**

cents-off, *adj. U.S. and Canada.* having to do with a promotion of a product in which its price is reduced a few cents when a shopper presents a coupon with the purchase. The coupon is an obligation under which the manufacturer reimburses the retailer for the cents the latter takes off the price of the product. *"Cents off" specials . . . are in reality the regular price.* Maclean's 8/74, p64 *Cents-off coupons continued to show growth and widespread consumer acceptance.* Britannica Book of the Year 1976, p209 **[1963]**

cerebral death, another name for BRAIN DEATH. *Death of the brain, called cerebral death, is currently used by Cooley and many other heart surgeons as the yardstick for selecting [heart transplant] donors.* Americana Annual 1969, p335 **[1969]**

cesium clock, a type of atomic clock which measures time by the vibration frequency of atoms of the element cesium. *The Navy men borrowed several cesium clocks from the United States Naval Observatory. These are among the most precise clocks in existence.* NY Times 8/10/68, p27 **[1957]**

CETA ('si:tə), *n. U.S.* a revenue-sharing program in which state and local governments receive federal funds to provide job training and public-service jobs for the unemployed. *Federal funds—chiefly CETA—that once helped the libraries to pay staff are now drying up.* New York Post 12/1/78, p20 **[1976,** acronym for *Comprehensive Employment and Training Act,* an act passed in 1973 which established this program that expired in 1982]

CETI, abbreviation of *communication with extraterrestrial intelligence.* Compare SETI. *At a September CETI meeting, participants felt that the best way of determining whether thinking beings indeed lived in outer space lay in analyzing radio waves of extraterrestrial origin for possible information content.* 1972 Compton Yearbook, p430 **[1971]**

CFC, abbreviation of CHLOROFLUOROCARBON. . . . *there has been a steady search for substitutes for the CFCs. If you recall, CFCs, according to Rowland and Molina, were getting up into the ozone layer and destroying our protection against ultraviolet from the Sun.* New Scientist 10/19/78, p248 **[1977]**

CFM, abbreviation of CHLOROFLUOROMETHANE. *Chlorofluorocarbons F-11 and F-12 (otherwise known as chlorofluoromethanes or CFMs) rise into the lower stratosphere where they produce chlorine atoms that deplete the ozone thus increasing human exposure to harmful ultraviolet rays and causing extra cases of skin cancer.* New Scientist 9/23/76, p627 **[1976]**

cGMP, abbreviation for CYCLIC GMP. *Michel Simon, working at Gif sur Yvette in France, claims that cGMP is converted directly into cAMP [cyclic AMP] at each beat of a frog's heart.* New Scientist 5/27/76, p465 **[1974]**

chainbelt, *n.* a belt made with interlinked metal rings. . . . *Accessories were often called body-jewels and were chain-mail type networks of linked metals, chainbelts, . . . snake bracelets and arm bracelets, and slave footstraps.* 1970 World Book Year Book, p342 **[1970]**

chairperson, *n. U.S.* a person who presides at a meeting; a chairman or chairwoman. *And a group of women psychologists thanked the board for using the word "chairperson" rather than "chairman," but argued that too much sexual discrimina-*

tion still exists within the APA [American Psychological Association] and in the academic world. Science News 9/11/71, p166 **[1971]**

challenge grant, a sum of money given in proportion to the amount raised by public contribution; a matching grant. *Deservedly, HVP [Hudson Valley Philharmonic] is nationally recognized. The New York State Council has designated it a "primary institution": NEA has awarded it a prestigious Challenge Grant (they receive $1 for every $3 raised).* Time 8/25/80, p36 **[1980]**

Chandler wobble or **Chandler's wobble,** a variation of the earth's rotation upon its axis. *The Earth's pole undergoes a nutation [oscillation], the Chandler wobble, with a predominant 14-monthly period whose motion is somehow kept going despite the substantial effects of viscous damping forces.* New Scientist and Science Journal 1/21/71, p105 **[1967,** named after Seth Carlo *Chandler,* 1846-1913, American astronomer, noted for his determination of the laws of variations of the earth's pole]

channel, *n.* a person through whom invisible beings, spirits, or forces supposedly communicate. . . . *J.Z. Knight, the "channel" for Ramtha.* Atlanta Journal/Constitution 11/22/87, pJ10 **—v.t.** to supposedly communicate with (invisible beings, spirits, or forces). *"Not all the channeled voices are from outer space."* Atlanta Journal/Constitution 11/22/87, pJ10 **[1971]**

channeling, *n.* **1** *Physics.* the ability of accelerated nuclear particles or ions to pass through the atomic rows and planes of a crystal or similar solid. *Channeling takes place in extremely perfect crystals, which have a precisely regular array of atoms. This regular array leaves unobstructed channels between planes of atoms. Particles that enter the channels in the right way are constrained to move along them by the forces exerted on them by the atoms in the walls of the channels. And so the particles go right out the other side of the crystal.* Science News 1/5/80, p5 **2** the act or process of supposedly communicating with invisible beings, spirits, or forces. *The extraterrestrials who turn up in the course of channeling . . . appear almost unfailingly wise and benevolent.* Time 12/7/87, p66 **[1967** for def. 1; **1971** for def. 2]

chaos, *n. Mathematics, Physics.* the random behavior generated by any deterministic system. *The determinism inherent in chaos implies that many random phenomena are more predictable than has been thought . . . Chaos allows order to be found in such diverse systems as the atmosphere, dripping faucets and the heart.* Scientific American 12/86, p46 **[1983]** **—chaotic,** *adj.: Chaotic behavior has recently been observed in the output of lasers operated in unstable regimes and in the interaction of laser radiation with atoms and molecules.* McGraw-Hill Yearbook of Science and Technology 1989, p251

charbroil, *v.t.* to broil over hot charcoal. *Since nobody charbroiled steak for us or handed round copies of McCall's, our diversions were few.* Sunday Times Magazine (London) 5/16/71, p66 **[1963]**

charge-coupled device, a semiconductor chip with an array of cells in which electrical charges can be stored or shifted between cells by means of electrical pulses applied to a pair of external terminals, used chiefly to store visual or binary information. *Abbreviation:* CCD *Charge-coupled devices store data at densities perhaps ten times as great as those of conventional semiconductor arrays and are easier and cheaper to build because they require no internal connections.* Britannica Book of the Year 1973, p191 **[1972]**

charged particle beam, another name for PARTICLE BEAM (def. 2). *Dr de Geer notes that in the past two years some Americans have said that the Russians have been building a new military device, a charged particle beam. Such a beam would be directed at incoming nuclear missiles.* Times (London) 12/7/77, p20 **[1977]**

charge nurse, a nurse charged with the supervision of a ward. *Besides, strange as it may seem, I had been favorably impressed by Dr. Stevens, the chief of surgery, by Jerry Baker, the resi-*

dent, and by Sharon Avery, the charge nurse. William A. Nolen, M.D., The Making of a Surgeon, 1970, p23 [**1961**]

charisma, *n.* strong personal appeal or magnetism, especially in politics. . . . *even in a democracy, high intelligence and courage can bring leaders to the fore without the aid of charisma or demagoguery.* NY Times 6/28/71, p30 [**1960**] ►Originally a theological term for a supernatural grace or gift bestowed by God on select individuals (from Greek *chárisma*), the word began to be widely applied in the 1960's to various celebrated figures and personalities, especially political candidates. It is often roughly equated with "sex appeal" and "glamour."

charismatic, *n. U.S.* a Christian who believes in charismatic gifts (such as the gift of speaking in tongues and healing by the laying on of hands), especially a member of a church practicing the teachings and methods of American pentecostalism. Compare NEO-PENTECOSTAL. See also EXORCISM. *Among Pentecostal Christians, both Roman Catholic and Protestant, exorcism through "deliverance" prayers has become as common as speaking in tongues. Many of these "charismatics" believe that they have already been filled by an outside force—the Holy Spirit—and have received the Pentecostal "gift" for discerning other spirits, which enable them to spot any poor sinner who has let a demon get inside.* Newsweek 2/11/74, p66 [**1970,** noun use of the adjective]

Charlie or **Charley,** *n. U.S. Military Slang.* **1** a Vietcong guerrilla. . . . *as one American official has put it, "everything that moves in Zones C and D is considered Charlie."* New Yorker 2/7/70, p36 **2** the Vietcong. . . . *Colonel Braim issued a final order to his battalion commanders: "You've got 18 hours left. Go out and kill some Charley."* Time 4/13/70, p29 [**1965,** shortened from *Victor Charlie* or *Victor Charley,* the communications code name for *V.C.,* abbreviation of *Vietcong*]

charm, *n. Nuclear Physics.* a quantum unit with the value of $+1$ for any quark and -1 for its antiquark. See QUARK. *Of the several different quarks thought to exist, one was differentiated by the property known as charm, a quantum number that must be conserved during any interaction among particles. The year was notable for a series of experimental results that all tended to confirm the existence of charm.* Britannica Book of the Year 1978, p584 [**1974,** named by the American physicists Sheldon L. Glashow and James Bjorken "for we were fascinated and pleased by the symmetry it brought to the subnuclear world"]

charmed, *adj.* possessing or exhibiting the characteristics of charm. *According to the revised quark picture, the psi particle is a hadron consisting of a charmed quark and a charmed antiquark.* Scientific American 3/78, p50 [**1975,** from CHARM + -ed]

charmonium (tʃɑːˈmouniːəm), *n.* any particle, such as the psi particle, with the characteristics of charm; a charmed particle. Compare ORTHOCHARMONIUM, PARACHARMONIUM. *The discovery of the charmonium was an event of the utmost importance in elementary-particle physics. Nothing so exciting had happened in many years. For believers in quarks the new particle was the first experimental indication that a fourth quark existed.* NY Times Magazine 7/18/76, p36 [**1975,** from CHARM + -onium, as in *muonium, pionium*]

Charon (ˈkerən), *n.* a satellite of Pluto, discovered in 1978. . . . *Subsequent studies confirmed the existence of the satellite, offering estimates of 2,700 km (1,600 mi) for its diameter and a separation of about 19,000 km (12,000 mi) from Pluto. As a name for the new moon, discoverer Christy suggested Charon, the boatman who ferried souls of the dead into Pluto's underworld, although Persephone, who was Pluto's queen, might be equally appropriate.* Britannica Book of the Year 1979, p204 [**1978**]

charrette (ʃəˈret), *n.* a meeting of a group assisted by experts in various fields to discuss problems. . . . *the charrette depends on the constant interplay of ideas. Its most important aspect is the participation of people normally outside the decision-making process.* Time 5/11/70, p40 [**1970,** from French, cart (in the phrase *en charrette* in a cart), perhaps originally so called in allusion to the practice of French architecture students of work-

ing hastily on their design drawings in carts which took them to their school]

charts (tʃɑrts), *n.pl.* Usually, **the charts,** a list of the best-selling or most popular items of a kind (in a particular week, month, etc.). *Freud gives us the psycho-analytical insights without which no deserving American novel could possibly hit the charts.* Listener 1/22/76, p92 . . . *in popular music, if you're not on the charts every minute of the day, you really feel you're a failure, and it's not like that in acting.* NY Times Magazine 12/10/78, p100 [**1965,** used originally in reference to recordings of popular songs]

chatcom, *n. U.S. Informal.* an informal and usually humorous interview program on television or radio. *Late Night is different: a chatcom whose mixture of the real and the surreal keeps the viewer agreeably off-balance . . . Late Night means to prove . . . that "most people are instrinsically funny."* Time 3/22/82, p69 [**1982,** from *chat* + *comedy,* patterned after SIT-COM]

chat show, *British.* another name for TALK SHOW. *Genuinely spontaneous good talk is the rarest thing, even in real life, and almost unknown in the chat show.* Sunday Times (London) 8/29/71, p22 [**1969**]

chauvinism, *n.* exaggerated loyalty to members of one's own sex; a superior attitude toward the opposite sex. *Israeli society does not discourage a woman, once she has married and had children, from having a career and equal financial status with men—if she can manage it. The married women I met concurred in this view—or felt impelled, out of chauvinism, to pretend that they did.* NY Times Magazine 11/26/78, p114 [**1972,** abstracted from MALE CHAUVINISM and FEMALE CHAUVINISM] —**chauvinist,** *n.: Chauvinist* [Michael] *Caine prefers his wife to be at home. "She's not going to make a career out of this," he predicted confidently.* Time 3/3/75, p49 —**chauvinistic,** *adj.: Linda Wolfe's new book, Playing Around: Women and Extramarital Sex . . . may cause some chauvinistic husbands of the old school to sit bolt upright in their easy chairs and howl with rage and alarm.* NY Sunday News 6/29/75, p18

cheapo, *adj. U.S. Slang.* cheap (in its various senses). *"Raging Bull" has the air of saying something important, which is just what he loved those cheapo pictures for not having.* New Yorker 12/8/80, p222 [**1972**]

cheap shot, *U.S. and Canada.* **1** *Sports.* an intentionally rough and underhanded action against an opposing player. Compare BLINDSIDE. *In football, a cheap shot is a tackle or block delivered when the player on the receiving end is unable to defend himself—stretching to catch a pass, for example, or being wrestled down by another player.* NY Times Magazine 1/25/81, p9 **2** *Figurative.* an unfair and contemptible action or statement directed at an easy target. *Bruce Porter's article . . . about Utica's political aberration—*[Mayor] *Ed Hanna—contains one omission and two cheap shots which call for a response.* NY Times Magazine 10/10/76, p82 [**1967**]

cheap-shot artist, *U.S. and Canada.* a person who takes cheap shots at opponents. *"Who Is Attacking the Teamsters Union?" The ad supplied its own answer: "An unholy alliance of political midgets, some lying media gossip peddlers and a few self-appointed labor 'reformers' whose secret motives are destructive and un-American." It termed Fox "a cheap-shot artist."* NY Times Magazine 11/7/76, p92 [**1967**]

checkbook journalism, the payment of large sums to public figures for exclusive journalistic interviews. *In 1965, the Press Council, after investigating all aspects of chequebook journalism, condemned as immoral the practice of rewarding criminals for their disclosures for public entertainment.* Times (London) 6/6/73, p18 *The Frost-Nixon deal carries Watergate checkbook journalism to its greatest extreme to date . . . Frost argues that since Nixon is out of office, the interviews are not news but a memoir and therefore immune to the checkbook charge.* Time 8/25/75, p58 [**1963**]

checkless society, another name for CASHLESS SOCIETY. *It is projected that in the 1980s the "cashless" or, more appropriate-*

ly, "checkless" society will come into being. The means for this new financial system will be the debit card, which . . . will be used to initiate a transaction at the bank itself, at a retail outlet, or at a remote unattended location where money can be deposited or withdrawn around the clock. McGraw-Hill Yearbook of Science and Technology 1977, p173 [**1965**]

checkoff, n. U.S. the opportunity of making a contribution from a part of one's refund or dividends or of adding an additional amount to one's payment for use in a specific program, such as political campaign funding. This is a proposal to establish an "income-tax checkoff" on tax returns. A box on tax forms would enable taxpayers to add to the taxes they owe, or subtract from the amount the government owes them, by a stated amount. Harper's 8/77, p19 [**1973**, originally (since the early 1900's) applied to the system of withholding union dues from workers' wages]

Checkpoint Charlie, a crossing point between two hostile forces and territories. Compare BERLIN WALL. Governments, it appears, are watching not only world affairs and their Checkpoint Charlies but also football. Times (London) 6/5/70, p16 "We take our copy to Checkpoint Charlie" a reporter for Al Anwar explained, referring to the dividing line between Christian and Moslem quarters of the City . . . NY Times 5/3/76, p3 [**1970**, from the name of the checkpoint between East and West Berlin where foreigners could cross over]

check trading, the practice of selling bank checks to a customer, who then repays the amount of the check plus interest in installments. But so ill-defined is check trading's status that a recent court case indicated that it could possibly be a form of money lending. Times (London) 4/3/70, p25 [**1967**]

chemical laser, a laser that uses the energy of chemical reaction rather than electrical energy. Chemical lasers differ from ordinary lasers in that molecules with abnormally large amounts of energy are produced by particular chemical reactions, not by some external source of radiation. Times (London) 2/26/70, p63 [**1966**]

Chemical Mace, another name for MACE. A Chicago policeman wields a pressure can of Chemical Mace in an attempt to subdue antiwar demonstrators . . . 1969 Collier's Encyclopedia Year Book, p181 [**1966**]

chemigation, n. the irrigation of crops with chemicals, such as fertilizers and pesticides. Chemigation is usually done with so-called microsystems, which use special piping to drip small amounts of chemicals at the base of plants. World Book Science Annual 1987, p216 [**1986**]

chemoimmunotherapy (ˌkiːmouiˌmyuːnouˈθerəpiː), n. a medical treatment combining immunotherapy with chemotherapy. There were indications that immunotherapy (stimulation of the body's immune system) combined with other treatments might be of value. For example, chemoimmunotherapy with anticancer drugs and BCG (attenuated tubercle bacillus) might induce definite increases in the remission rate in malignant melanoma. Britannica Book of the Year 1976, p384 [**1976**, from chemo- chemical + immuno- immunological + therapy]

chemosensing (ˌkiːmouˈsensiŋ), n. the detection of a chemical by a living cell or cells. But the extremely important ecological and behavioral roles of chemosensing are just beginning to be appreciated and understood by science. Science News 8/7/71, p98 [**1971**] —**chemosensor**, n.: Just as bacteria detect attractants by means of chemosensors rather than indirectly through some secondary benefit, so the bacteria are equipped with other chemosensors that detect repellents directly; they do not simply sense the repellents by experiencing some harm they do. Scientific American 4/76, p43

chemosensory, adj. of or relating to the stimulation of sensory organs by chemical substances. Some fishes have been found to possess almost incredible chemosensory acuity. Harold Teichmann of the University of Giessen was able to condition eels to respond to concentrations of alcohol so dilute that he estimated the animals' olfactory receptors could not have re-

ceived more than a few molecules. Scientific American 5/71, p99 [**1971**]

chemosterilant, n. a chemical substance used in chemosterilization. The use of chemosterilants—compounds which sterilise insects and make them unable to breed—has been a promising recent development in man's war against insect pests. New Scientist 10/22/64, p210 [**1962**]

chemosterilization, n. sterilization of insects, rodents, and other pests by chemicals that effect the reproductive organs or drive, especially of males. Chemosterilization—a weapon used successfully to control insect population—is now pointed at rats. Science News 10/11/69, p329 [**1968**]

chemotaxonomy (ˌkiːmoutækˈsanəmiː), n. the classification of plant and animal organisms by their chemical constituents rather than by their appearance. Chemotaxonomy has really gotten started only in the past several years, and even less is known about the chemotaxonomy of marine organisms than about that of land animals. Marine organisms are exceedingly difficult to classify chemically, because of the plethora of organisms to be found in the vast marine environment. Encyclopedia Science Supplement (Grolier) 1972, p174 [**1963**, from chemo- chemical + taxonomy]

cheongsam (ˈtʃɔːŋˈsaːm), n. a dress with a high collar and slit skirt, worn especially by Chinese women. Tell her you've always thought she'd look beautiful in a cheongsam. And you'd like to take her to a little shop where she can buy one. The shop is in Hong Kong . . . and the cheongsam is that devastating slit-skirted dress women wear in the Orient. Advertisement in New Yorker 10/24/64, p73 [**1957**, from Cantonese cheuhng sāam long dress]

chereme (ˈkeriːm), n. a basic signal unit in AMERICAN SIGN LANGUAGE. Ameslan has fifty-five cheremes. Nineteen identify the configuration of the hand or hands making the sign; twelve, the place where the sign is made; and twenty-four, the action of the hand or hands. Eugene Linden, Apes, Men, and Language, 1974, p18 [**1974**, from Greek cheír hand + English -eme unit of language (as in phoneme basic unit of speech)]

cherry red, British Slang. another name for BOVVER BOOT. Their [the skinheads'] hair is shaved within an eighth of an inch from the scalp, and they are dressed in oversized workpants, thin red suspenders and hobnailed, steeltoed boots costing about $10 and known as "cherry reds." Time 6/8/70, p37 [**1970**]

Chicana (tʃiˈkaːnə), n. a Mexican-American woman or girl; a female American of Mexican birth or descent (often used attributively). Says Chicana Leader Cecilia Suarez: "Our issues are bread-and-butter ones; Women's Lib is trying to get equal job opportunities, but we are still trying to get our women into school." Time 3/20/72, p31 [**1972**, from Mexican Spanish, feminine of Chicano]

Chicano (tʃiˈkaːnou), n. a Mexican American; a person of Mexican birth or descent living in the United States (often used attributively). Denied to blacks, assimilation for years robbed the Chicano community of a nucleus of leadership. Today the forfeiture of this newly acquired cultural awareness seems to the young Chicano a prohibitive price to pay. Atlantic 6/71, p45 [**1969**, from Mexican Spanish Chicano, from the Chihuahua dialect pronunciation of Mexicano Mexican as (metʃiˈkaːnou)-with loss of initial unaccented syllable]

chicken, n. U.S. Slang. a young or adolescent male prostitute. Along Selma Avenue and Sunset Boulevard, male and female teen-agers, many of them runaways, line up under the guise of hitchhiking. Grandfatherly "chicken hawks," men in their 50s and 60s, haggle with "chickens," teen-age boy hustlers, through the windows of Cadillacs. Time 8/15/77, p23 [**1973**]

chicken hawk, U.S. Slang. a man who preys on boys for sexual purposes, especially one who solicits young male prostitutes. Most of his time now is devoted to tracking down molesters of young girls and "chicken hawks," street parlance for men with a sexual preference for boys. People 10/9/78, p99 [**1973**]

chicken run, a derisive term used in Rhodesia (now Zimbabwe) for the route or flight taken by whites out of the country in anticipation of black rule. *More than 1,700 white Rhodesians joined the exodus from the country last month, setting a record for any month since Rhodesia broke away from Britain in 1965. The previous record for those taking "the chicken run" as whites call it, was in May 1977 when there was a net loss of 1,339.* Manchester Guardian Weekly 11/5/78, p6 [**1977,** from *chicken* coward + *run* trip, flight (as in *milk run*)]

chicklet or **chicklette,** *n. U.S. Slang.* a young woman; a girl. *There is some show-stopping (if irrelevant) footwork by a trio of pretty chicklets billed as Extraordinary Spooks.* Time 12/27/68, p47 [**1968,** diminutive of *chick,* slang term for a girl, originally a shortening of *chicken,* also slang for a girl]

Chicom (ˈtʃaɪˌkam), *n. U.S.* a Chinese communist (also used attributively). *Also to be heard from are the ChiCom dreaders with their dire forebodings about the mighty Red Chinese nation, a dedicated monolith poised to crush all Asia at any provocation.* Time 1/27/67, p7 [**1955**]

child abuse, harmful treatment of a child by a parent or other adult, including physical, psychological, and verbal abuse. Compare BABY-BATTERING, CHILD-BATTERING. *"Child abuse occurs in all walks of life," Dr. Horowitz said. "Doctors and lawyers, too, batter their kids. Ten per cent of children under 5 years of age who come in with trauma are cases of child abuse."* NY Times 1/6/74, p36 [**1972**]

child-battering, *n.* the act or practice of inflicting harmful physical abuse on a child by an adult. Compare BABY-BATTERING. *Child-battering is an unspeakable act that can never be justified, leaving unerasable scars on the child's mind as well as body.* Psychology Today 11/78, p96 [**1972**] —**child-batterer,** *n.: Not all the cases are in deprived areas: there are child-batterers in middle-class districts, but they are not easy to detect. In a multi-storey block of flats, a child in pain will be heard screaming and someone may complain. Even so, a case of child-battering is very often difficult to prove.* Listener 11/22/73, p690

childproof, *adj.* that a child cannot open or otherwise tamper with; safe for children. Also called CHILD-RESISTANT. *It [a car] has all the usual features including childproof locks . . .* Sunday Times (London) 5/2/71, p13 *Legislation is now in preparation to . . . require producers of household poisons to render their containers "childproof" by making bottles and packages harder to open.* Time 12/12/69, p64 [**1956**]

Children of God, a sect of the Jesus Movement whose members hold the world to be near destruction. *The Children of God eschew tobacco, liquor and premarital or extramarital sex, devoting themselves within their nearly self-sustaining communes to chanted prayers, hymns sung ecstatically, an almost constant study of the Bible, meditation and conversing in languages that they say come to them through prayer on the spur of the moment.* NY Times 11/29/71, p41 [**1971**]

children's rights, the fair treatment of children; protection from abuse and exploitation sought for or extended to children. *The father of six is also a keen advocate of children's rights.* Maclean's 6/4/79, p30 [**1978**]

child-resistant, *adj.* another term for CHILDPROOF. *The introduction of child-resistant packaging for children's aspirin in 1976 has reduced the number of children accidentally poisoned to less than half the 1975 figure.* Times (London) 8/12/77, p14 [**1975**]

chilidog (ˈtʃɪliˌdɔːg), *n. U.S.* a frankfurter with chili con carne on it. Compare CORNDOG. *"What is for chow?" "Chilidogs." "He'll be back. Daumier does love his chilidog."* New Yorker 4/1/72, p31 [**1971,** from *chili* + (*hot*) *dog*]

chilling effect, *U.S.* an action or situation that dampens or discourages the exercise of free speech. *Another argument against reporters taking the stand is the so-called "chilling effect." This holds that the very act of subpoenaing a reporter to testify or to turn over his notes . . . has an inhibiting effect on potential news sources or on reporters themselves.* NY Times 12/15/76, pB10 [**1965,** apparently coined by Justice William Brennan in Supreme Court case of *Dombrowski v. Pfister* (380 U.S. 479)]

chillout, *n. U.S.* a period of uncomfortably cold indoor temperatures caused by the shortage of fuel for heating. *There is one major hitch: if refineries produce enough gasoline to meet peak demand this summer, they may have to curtail heating-oil output enough to threaten more chillouts next winter.* Time 4/16/73, p88 [**1973,** patterned after *blackout* and *brownout* in the supply of electricity]

chimurenga (ˌtʃiːmuːˈrɛŋgə), *n.* a war of liberation in Africa, especially a war to establish black rule. *The broadcasts from Mozambique, which call upon the young men to cross the border and join the guerrillas in their camps, talk of the chimurenga . . . in the chimurenga of 1976, the blacks are using Kalashnikov Ak-47 assault rifles, grenade launchers and 60-mm. mortars.* NY Times Magazine 7/11/76, p31 [**1967,** from Shona (a Bantu language), literally, strife, rebellion]

China syndrome, a catastrophic nuclear accident resulting from an uncontrollable MELTDOWN. . . . *Such a meltdown, some fear, would lead to the so-called China Syndrome—a nuclear lava flow of such intense heat that it would burn its way through its thick steel capsule, through the nine- or 10-foot thick reinforced concrete slab, and down deep into the soil beneath the plant, in a manner that would recall the childhood fantasy of digging through the earth to China.* NY Times Magazine 6/20/76, p41 [**1973**]

China watcher, an expert student or observer of Communist China and its government. Also called PEKINGOLOGIST. *The official New China News Agency spends a lot of money each day spreading the propaganda throughout the world. The great bulk of it is ignored by all but the most dedicated China Watchers.* Manchester Guardian Weekly 4/3/69, p10 [**1966**]

Chinese restaurant syndrome, a group of symptoms which appear in some people after eating Chinese food. Also called KWOK'S DISEASE. *Reports appeared in the U.S. press of a so-called Chinese restaurant syndrome (headache, dizziness, flushing), which was attributed by some authorities to the excessive use of monosodium glutamate (MSG).* Britannica Book of the Year 1970, p350 [**1968**]

chinois (ʃiːˈnwɑ:), *n.* a fine-meshed metal strainer for kitchen use. *The British housewives who attend the cookery courses . . . are all sent in search of two utensils vital to the tips they are taught—a conical metal sieve called a chinois, and a pan with a rounded copper bottom for making the perfect omelette.* Times (London) 6/1/76, p6 [**1972,** from French]

chip[1], *n.* a very small piece of silicon on which integrated circuits can be printed. Also called MICROCHIP. Compare WAFER. *Over the last decade, for example, the number of components that a designer can pack on a single silicon chip has increased a thousandfold. This means that the entire electronic system for a desk calculator is contained on three silicon chips, each no more than one eighth of an inch square.* New Scientist 12/10/70, p441 [**1967**]

chip[2], *n.* short for BARGAINING CHIP. *If Turner had been able to report the real state of affairs that the Soviet crop was poor . . . the President could have used the need for grain as a chip in the ongoing SALT negotiations.* Maclean's 3/6/78, p59 [**1973**]

chip-kick, *British.*—*n.* (in rugby, soccer, etc.) a short, often lofted, kick aimed to gain a more advantageous position by repossession after chasing the ball or by a throw-in after kicking the ball so it goes out of bounds. Compare GARRYOWEN. *Barry John, from fly-half, put in the most delicate and perfect of chip-kicks to bamboozle the defence.* Sunday Times (London) 5/23/71, p22 —*v.t., v.i.* to kick with a chip-kick. *An aberration by the lively Burton, chip-kicking good loose ball away in the Australian 25, happily led up to a five yard scrummage and try No. 2.* Times (London) 1/5/76, p5 [**1969,** probably from *chip* short, lofted shot (in golf) + *kick*]

Chiron (ˈkaɪrən), *n.* another name for OBJECT KOWAL. *Chiron travels around the Sun in an eccentric orbit which takes it from inside the orbit of Saturn out to the orbit of Uranus.* McGraw-

Hill Yearbook of Science and Technology 1979, p102 [**1978**, named by its discoverer after the centaur *Chiron* in Greek legend, who was a descendant of the gods Saturn and Uranus]

Chisanbop (ˈtʃizənˌbɑp), *n.* trademark for a system of calculating arithmetically with the fingers and thumbs, invented by Sung Jin Pai, a Korean mathematician. It is used especially to teach elementary arithmetic. *With Chisanbop, the fingers are used to count to 99, with larger numbers being carried over by memory or written down. On the right hand the thumb stands for one unit with a place value of five, while each finger represents one additional unit. On the left hand the thumb stands for 50, with each finger representing 10.* Maclean's 1/8/79, p37 [**1976**, from Korean, literally, finger counting]

chlordecone (ˈklɔrdəkoun), *n.* the generic name of KEPONE. *Chlordecone is the common chemical name of Kepone, which was originally developed by the Allied Chemical Corporation . . .* NY Times 4/8/76, p28 [**1972**, from *chlor-* chlorine + *dec-* ten + *-one* ketone]

chlorinated hydrocarbon, any of a class of synthetic pesticides, formed by a chlorine-carbon bond, that are among the most persistent of environmental poisons. *The most troublesome pollutants among pesticides are the so-called hard pesticides, principally the chlorinated hydrocarbons—DDT, dieldrin, aldrin, endrin, lindane, chlordane, heptachlor, and some of their relatives.* Science News Yearbook 1970, p306 [**1956**]

chlormadinone (klɔrˈmædəˌnoun), *n.* Also called **chlormadinone acetate.** a drug used to prevent pregnancy. *Like the other man-made hormones that constitute the pill, chlormadinone is built up from chemicals extracted from the root of the Barbasco plant, a species of wild Mexican yam.* Sunday Times (London) 7/9/67, p3 [**1963**]

chlorofluorocarbon, *n.* any of various compounds of carbon, chlorine, fluorine, and hydrogen, used especially as refrigerants and aerosol propellants but restricted in use during the 1970's because of their suspected depletion of the ozone shield of the atmosphere. *Abbreviation:* CFC Compare HALOCARBON. See also AEROSOL. *In America, where aerosols have been used to dispense everything from toothpaste to chocolate whip and chantilly cream, the suggestion that the Earth might literally be scorched to death as a result caused profound alarm. In 1975 there was a 15 per cent drop in the manufacture of chlorofluorocarbons, largely due to lost aerosol sales. In Europe there was reaction too, but the authorities have not followed the American rush to ban chlorofluorocarbons.* Times (London) 11/1/77, p10 [**1959**, from *chloro-* chlorine + *fluoro-* fluorine + *carbon*]

chlorofluoromethane, *n.* any of various chlorofluorocarbons used especially as refrigerants and aerosol propellants. *Abbreviation:* CFM Compare HALOMETHANE. See also AEROSOL. *Every day, millions of aerosol cans of cleansers, deodorants, shaving cream, and other household items release chlorofluoromethanes, propellant gases that may be reducing the atmosphere's ozone layer, which protects the earth from the sun's ultraviolet radiation.* World Book Science Annual 1976, p280 [**1970**, from *chloro-* chlorine + *fluoro-* fluorine + *methane*]

choke point or **chokepoint**, *n.* any route that cannot be easily bypassed; a geographic point for which there is no immediate alternative in travel or communication. *To quote from the Survey, "(the Soviet) access to the open seas passes through a number of choke points (such as the Bosphorus, Gibraltar, and the Greenland-Iceland-United Kingdom gap . . ."* Times (London) 5/31/76, p8 [**1966**]

cholinomimetic (ˌkoulənoumiˈmetik), *adj.* similar to or imitating acetylcholine (chemical which transmits nerve impulses), especially in its ability to affect the flow of impulses in the nervous system. *The direct effects of the cholinomimetic agents on transmission in bladder ganglia underscore the complexity of drug actions at ganglionic synapses.* Science 2/11/72, p661 —*n.* a cholinomimetic agent. *Such substances, known as cholinomimetics, work by mimicking the action of chemicals found normally in the nervous system.* Time 3/30/70,

p47 [**1968**, from acetyl*choline* + connecting *-o-* + *mimetic* mimicking]

chopper, *Slang.*—*v.i.* to fly by helicopter. *Whenever he* [General Creighton W. Abrams] *can, he choppers to the field and once a month flies to Bangkok to visit his wife.* Time 2/15/71, p19 —*v.t.* to transport by helicopter. *A four-ship British task force anchored in the bay and began choppering food, clothing, medicine and water purification pills to the remote coastal areas.* Time 12/7/70, p28 [**1965**, verb use of *chopper, n.,* helicopter (1951)] —*n.* **1** a motorcycle, especially one that is custom-built with the front suspension extended to place the front wheel farther forward than is customary. *My wheel or chopper is a light pistachio-coloured two-stroke motorino, that cost in lire the equivalent of £60.* Sunday Times (London) 8/8/71, p22 **2** Also called **chopper bike** or **bicycle,** a bicycle with high handlebars and tall back support. *"Chopper" bicycles have already been criticised on safety grounds. Now a group of researchers at the Royal Victoria Infirmary, Newcastle, has found that children riding choppers have a greater chance of ending up in hospital if they have an accident than children on other bicycles.* New Scientist 11/1/73, p338 [**1969**]

chop shop, *U.S.* a place where stolen cars are stripped and disposed of. *The most interesting part of the display was the part dealing with self-destructing labels for vehicles. A sign described this as "an experimental component identification planned to thwart 'chop-shop' operators* ["These places that just take these things and chop them up," a man in a blue suit said] *and auto thieves.* New Yorker 10/22/79, p35 [**1979**]

choreology (ˌkɔriˈɑlədʒiː), *n.* the study or writing of dance notations. *. . . a discussion of choreology, the art of writing down dances, in which the aims and merits of the two leading systems are more clearly and fairly assessed than in many longer accounts.* Times (London) 11/20/78, p15 [**1970**, from *choreog*raphy + *-logy* study of] —**choreologist**, *n.: Sitting on a chair by the piano . . . is the company's official notator, or choreologist, as he is titled—a man named Jurg Lanzrein, who is jotting down symbols on a large pad as he takes note of this or that bit of action.* New Yorker 10/22/73, p51

chozrim (kɔːzˈriːm), *n.pl.* Israelis who return to Israel after having emigrated. Compare YORDIM. *The Government also makes attractive loans to returnees, including housing loans, and permits a range of exemptions for the stiff customs levies. "From April 1976, when our budget year began, until last October,"* said Yoram Shachal, Zarankin's boss, "the chozrim numbered 3,400." NY Times Magazine 1/16/77, p24 [**1977**, from Hebrew, literally, returnees]

Christingle service (ˈkrisˌtiŋgəl), a Christmas service in the Church of England at which purses of money are brought forward by children for the Children's Society, and in return each donor receives an orange tied with a red ribbon and pierced with a candle surrounded by raisins and jellies on sticks. *A Christingle service is to be held in Canterbury Cathedral, with Dr. Ramsey receiving the purses from children, on December 28 at 3 pm.* Times (London) 12/22/72, p15 [**1972**, probably from *Christ*mas + *ingle* fire, flame (from Scottish Gaelic *aingeal* fire, light)] ►In informal usage, the decorated orange is called a *Christingle.* It symbolizes the world, while the candle is a symbol of the light of the world, the raisins and jellies represent the fruits of the earth, and the red ribbon symbolizes the life of Christ.

Christmas tree (bill), *U.S.* a legislative bill that provides benefits for various special-interest groups, especially because of numerous amendments not directly related to the main part of the proposed law. *Next came what members called the "Christmas Tree," wherein they traded amendments to help their friends and screw their enemies. Hung on the tree were guarantees of fuel to buses, truckers, the tour business, farmers, the building trades, schoolteachers.* New Times 2/22/74, p22 [**1971**] ►This term was originally applied to a tax bill affecting foreign investors that was passed in 1966 and signed "with reservations" by President Lyndon B. Johnson, who noted that it would "confer special tax windfalls and benefits upon certain groups."

Christmas tree effect, *Astronomy.* the hypothesis that the change in frequency of light emissions from some quasars is not due to their motion but to internal changes. *In order to save modern physics from such forbidden speeds some very ingenious models have been devised, such as the Christmas tree effect, which says that the apparent motions are really a series of well-timed blinks of a string of stationary components.* Science News 4/24/76, p267 [**1973**]

chromodynamics, *n.* the theory dealing with the COLOR FORCE. Also called QUANTUM CHROMODYNAMICS. See QUARK. *The differentiation by "color" refers to the fact that quarks seem to behave as if they carried three different kinds of charge—not electrical charge, but something analogous to it. The study of the "color" of both matter and antimatter suggested the name "chromodynamics," which has nothing to do with real, visible color.* NY Times 9/2/79, p28 [**1976,** from *chromo-* color + *dynamics*] —**chromodynamic,** *adj.: How the charmonium states change into one another, resemble one another and differ from one another is extremely important for an understanding of the characteristic called charm and of the chromodynamic force that holds these structures together.* Science News 2/9/80, p85

chromon, *n.* a hypothetical constituent of quarks that determines the property of COLOR. *The color of the composite system is determined by preons called chromons; there are four of them, one with the color red, one yellow, one blue, and one colorless.* Scientific American 4/83, p63 [**1983,** from Greek *chrôma* color + English *-on* elementary unit]

chronobiology, *n.* the study of rhythmical or cyclical changes in living organisms. *Many other areas of classical agricultural phenology, intensive phenological ecosystems studies, and medical phenology (chronobiology and allergies caused by seasonal discharge of pollen and spores) are under investigation in many parts of the world.* McGraw-Hill Yearbook of Science and Technology 1976, p323 [**1976,** from *chrono-* time + *biology*] —**chronobiologist,** *n.: Chronobiologists are not completely sure why humans have seasonal or "circannual" rhythms, but according to Halberg, these changes are not just psychological. Blood pressure, cholesterol levels and hormones are all implicated.* Science News 4/10/76, p233

chronon, *n. Physics.* a hypothetical quantum of time. *In 1976 Dr. [Robert] Ehrlich found that the lifetimes of all known elementary particles were consistent with being an integral number of "chronons." He put the magnitude of the chronon at 2 $\times$ $10^{.23}$s.* New Scientist 5/4/78, p291 [**1978,** from Greek *chrónos* time + English *-on* elementary unit]

chronotherapy, *n.* a treatment for insomnia by adjusting the patient's rhythm of sleeping and waking. *Here's how "chronotherapy" works: For each of six days, the person is kept up three hours longer than the previous day . . . More or less permanently, then, the patient is regularly able to fall into a normal night's slumber within minutes after retiring at his desired bedtime.* Modern Maturity 8-9/83, p92 [**1980**]

chuff, *v.t.* **chuff up,** *British Slang.* to cheer up; encourage; please. *"This other guy started ahead of me by about 20 yards," Brown said, "so I sprinted up beside him and said 'I'm clapped out.' It chuffed him up a bit and I ran along his slip stream . . ."* Sunday Times (London) 8/22/71, p17 [**1971,** back formation from *chuffed*]

chuffed, *adj. British Slang.* pleased; happy. *I gather, Nessie, that you are very shy, but if you could at least show yourself for a few minutes this summer the Colonel and lots of other people would be frightfully chuffed.* Punch 6/18/69, p897 [**1957**]

chunnel, *n.* a tunnel for railroad trains built under a channel of water. *In recent years the idea of a channel tunnel—popularly known as the "chunnel"—has been revived.* NY Times 7/17/66, pD12 [**1957,** blend of *channel* and *tunnel*]

churn, *v.t., v.i. Slang.* to increase unnecessarily the amount of business transacted in a brokerage account, the number of return visits in a professional practice, etc., in order to generate more income. *Churning: Unnecessarily requiring patients to report or to return to a health center for additional treatment.* NY Times 8/31/76, p54 *Stories abound of customers' accounts being "churned," traded recklessly to generate commissions.* Maclean's 5/16/77, p70 [**1968**]

chutzpah or **chutzpa** ('hutspə), *n. U.S. Slang.* brazen audacity; shameless impudence; nerve; gall. *Takara was so adept at copying that it set some kind of Japanese record for chutzpah. Its first models were almost exact duplicates of the chairs produced by the leading U.S. manufacturer, Chicago's Emil J. Paidar Co.* Time 8/10/70, p61 [**1958,** from Yiddish *khutspe,* from Hebrew *ḥutspāh*]

chymopapain (ˌkaimoupə'paiən), *n.* a protein-digesting enzyme of the tropical papaya plant, used as a meat tenderizer and experimentally as a drug to relieve pressure and pain on nerve roots. *The FDA [Food and Drug Administration] sometimes criticized for not allowing new drugs on the market, has allowed 15,302 persons to be injected with chymopapain, a nonsurgical treatment for damaged spinal discs.* National Review 10/24/75, p1156 [**1973,** from Greek *chȳmós* juice + English *papain* an enzyme in papaya juice]

ciao (tʃau), *interj.* **1** greetings. *Crowds of children were swimming off the rocks along the Posillipo . . . they sometimes looked up to us and waved, and she waved back or called out "Ciao," while I set out a jug and glasses on a table between us.* Shirley Hazzard, The Bay of Noon, 1970, p152 **2** good-by. *In Mexico City, for example, the Italian ciao has virtually replaced adiós among college students . . .* Atlantic 7/67, p100 [**1957,** from Italian, from dialectal *ciaou,* alteration of *schiavo* slave (originally in *sono vostro schiavo* I am your slave), from Medieval Latin *sclavus* slave]

cigar, *n.* **close, but no cigar,** *U.S. Informal.* not quite good enough to succeed or to achieve a desired result. *[Bobby] Poe, as the saying goes, came close, but no cigar, as a singer, songwriter and manager during two decades of aiming toward American Bandstand.* Washington Post, Magazine Section 2/5/78, p4 [**1952,** probably in allusion to the carnival game in which great strength is required to ring a bell and the person who succeeds is rewarded with a cigar. See Gerald Cohen's discussion of the origin of the phrase in *Comments on Etymology* 17, 13-14 (April 1988), p4-6.]

Cigarette, *n.* or **Cigarette hull,** a type of large inboard motorboat with an open cockpit, used for offshore racing. *Driving a deep-vee Cigarette hull to vie with Kudo was Betty Cook, Paul's wife, who became the first woman in the sport's history to compete in the open class . . . her boat was the 36-ft Cigarette Kaama.* 1976 Collier's Encyclopedia Year Book, p513 [**1974,** so called for its shape]

cigarlet (sə'garlit), *n.* a short, thin cigar. *Hitherto a cigar filler crop has been produced in sufficient volume for internal commercial purposes, and a variety of Rhodesian-made cigars and cigarlets has been on the market for some years.* Rhodesia Herald 2/16/73, p14 [**1968,** from *cigar* + *-let* small, short]

ciggy or **ciggie** ('sigi:), *n. Informal.* a cigarette. *Local ciggies are cheap—say 12p a packet.* Sunday Times (London) 12/28/75, p34 [**1962,** by shortening]

cilantro (sə'læntrou), *n.* coriander, especially in reference to its use in Mexican cooking. *The vegetable section burst with feathery bunches of parsley and pungent fresh cilantro, enough tropical fruits to suggest a headdress for Carmen Miranda, tiny emerald-green tomatoes, prickly cactus leaves, and at least eight kinds of chili peppers.* NY Times 6/5/76, p13 [**1965,** from Spanish, ultimately from Latin *coriandrum*]

cimetidine (sai'metəˌdi:n), *n.* a drug that inhibits the secretion of acid in the stomach, introduced into the United States and Canada from Great Britain in 1977 for use in the treatment of peptic ulcers and various gastrointestinal diseases. *Formula:* $C_{10}H_{16}N_6S$ *Cimetidine works because it blocks the action of histamine, which stimulates the secretion of gastric acid.* Maclean's 12/25/78, p39 [**1977,** from *cyano-imidazol-methyl-guanidine,* chemical constituents of the drug]

Cinderella services, medical and social services provided to the mentally and physically handicapped, the aged, and the chronically ill. *The Cinderella services of primary care include . . . services directed to people in their homes, and special programs for identified groups of medically and socially dependent people.* JAMA [Journal of the American Medical Association] 3/11/83, p1279 [**1976**, from the figurative sense of *Cinderella*, "a neglected or despised member, partner, or the like" (OEDS 1840)]

cine-, a combining form meaning "motion picture," "film," "cinema," very productive during the 1960's. Some recent examples of its use: —**cinecult**, *n.attributive: Langlois showed the films, and for a short time Van Peebles was a cinecult celebrity.* Time 8/15/71, p43 —**cine-holography**, *n.: Research workers have been talking about cine-holography ever since the laser turned Dennis Gabor's idea of holography into a useful tool rather than a curiosity.* New Scientist 8/27/70, p420 —**cineménage**, *n.: Like Polonsky's Willie Boy, Andy Warhol is here, and as I feared when I wrote about "Flesh" last week it must have been his temporary absence from his cineménage which made that film likeable.* Sunday Times (London) 1/25/70, p54 —**cine-record**, *v.t.: The child was left to 'play' in the room for 10 minutes while the experimenter cine-recorded the behaviour from an adjoining cubicle.* Science Journal 2/70, p69

cineangiogram, *n.* a motion-picture record of a fluoroscope showing the passage of a radioopaque substance through the blood vessels. *The raw material for the image analysis is a cineangiogram—an X-ray cine film taken of the heart after the injection of a radio-opaque dye. The dye absorbs X-rays, so the film follows its progress through the heart.* New Scientist 3/25/76, p680 [**1976**, from *cine-* motion picture + *angiogram*]

cinefluoroscopy, *n.* motion-picture photography of a fluoroscopic examination. *The crocodile's heart is analogous to a mammal's. Both direct measurements and cinefluoroscopy confirm that its four chambers can pump blood from the body to the lungs and from the lungs to the body without mixing.* Scientific American 4/76, p117 [**1976**, from *cine-* motion picture + *fluoroscopy*]

cinema novo or **cinema nôvo**, a movement of radical filmmakers of Brazil, noted especially for the combination of fantasy and melodrama in their work. *Brazil had released Glauber Rocha's early films* Barravento *and* Terra em Transe, *Ruy Guerra's* Os Fuzis, *and Carlos Diegues's* Ganga Zumba, *all 'guerrilla' films representing the* cinema nôvo. Annual Register of World Events in 1972, p441 [**1970**, from Portuguese *cinema nôvo* new cinema]

cinematheque (ˌsinəmə'tek), *n.* a movie theater showing experimental and unconventional films. *Spearheaded by [Andy] Warhol, the underground has begun to emerge from the cellars of the cliquish film societies that provided their original audiences. Today, almost every major American city boasts at least one "cinematheque" where these pictures, shot on 16mm film, are constantly on display.* 1969 World Book Year Book, p120 [**1965**, from French *cinémathèque* a motion-picture film library]

cinéma vérité (si:nei'maveiri:'tei), a type of documentary film or film-making that attempts to capture the sense of documentary realism by spontaneous interviews, the use of a hand-held camera, and a minimum of editing of the footage. Also shortened to CINÉVÉRITÉ. *Shot in* cinéma vérité *format over a period of four months last summer,* Carry it On *revolves around Harris' arrest in July for noncooperation with the draft.* Time 8/24/70, p61 [**1963**, from French *cinéma-vérité*, literally, cinema-truth, cinema-realism]

cinephile ('sinəˌfail), *n. British.* a lover of motion pictures; a movie fan. *August is always a lean month for cinephiles in search of new French films.* Manchester Guardian Weekly 8/21/71, p14 [**1963**]

cinévérité (ˌsi:neiveiri:'tei), *n.* short for CINÉMA VÉRITÉ. *Nevertheless in that moment a scene was rigged for the camera. Not even the most stringent piece of* cinévérité *has ever been completely free of that kind of thing.* Listener 12/19/68, p826 [**1964**]

cingulotomy (ˌsiŋgyə'latəmi:), *n.* a form of psychosurgery in which incisions are made into the cingulum (bundle of association fibers) of the brain. *Ten of the subjects had experienced more than one psychosurgical operation, including four who had three cingulotomies.* Science News 5/14/77, p315 [**1972**, from *cingulum* + connecting *-o-* + *-tomy* surgical incision] —**cingulotomist**, *n.: H. T. Ballantine of Massachusetts General Hospital is probably the most prolific cingulotomist, and he does it for alleviation of intractable pain as well as for various "neuropsychiatric illnesses" such as depression, anxiety states, and obsessional neuroses that have not proved amenable to other kinds of treatment.* Science 3/16/73, p1110

CINS (sinz), *n. U.S.* acronym for *Child(ren) In Need of Supervision. These children, who are variously labelled Persons in Need of Supervision (PINS), Children in Need of Supervision (CINS), Juveniles in Need of Supervision (JINS), or Wayward Minors, depending on the state they live in, will be guilty of nothing more serious than being a burden or a nuisance.* New Yorker 8/14/78, p55 [**1972**]

circadian (sər'keidi:ən), *adj.* functioning or recurring in 24-hour cycles. *If man does indeed possess a circannual clock and its nature becomes accessible to investigation, the implications may be as important as those of the circadian clock, to which we are all biologically bound.* Scientific American 4/71, p79 [**1959**, from Latin *circā diēm* around the day + English *-an*]

circadianly, *adv.* in 24-hour cycles. *Temperature and urine flow are but two among many physiological functions which fluctuate circadianly, and they could be influenced by the great variety of circadian fluctuations in our environment . . .* New Scientist 2/9/67, p350 [**1967**]

circadian rhythm, the 24-hour cycle of physiological activity in living organisms governed by the biological clock. See also BODY CLOCK. Compare BIORHYTHM. *Biologically, however, the scientists expressed great interest in the phenomenon called circadian rhythm—man's biological clock that regulates his normal body cycles.* Science News 10/10/70, p304 [**1963**]

circalunadian (ˌsərkəlu:'na:di:ən), *adj.* characterized by or occurring in the 24-hour, 50-minute cycles of the lunar day. *This change in periodicity when an organism is placed in constant conditions is a property of almost all clock-controlled biological rhythms. Since tidal rhythms follow the lunar day, they are called circalunadian (about a lunar day).* Scientific American 2/75, p70 [**1975**, from Latin *circā* around + *lūna* moon + *diēs* day + English *-an*]

circannian (sər'kæni:ən) or **circannual** (sər'kænyuəl), *adj.* functioning or recurring in annual cycles. *Following investigations of hibernation in five species of ground squirrel (Citellus), E. T. Pengelley and K. H. Kelly, from the University of California, Riverside, have suggested that these animals have a similar internal rhythm of approximately a year. They have named this faculty a "circannian" rhythm . . .* New Scientist 12/22/66, p688 *The discovery of a circannual clock in hibernators has of course been followed up with investigations of other animals marked by conspicuous annual changes in behavior or physiology.* Scientific American 4/71, p75 [**1966**, from Latin *circā annum* around the year + English *-ian* or *-al*]

circuit breaker, *U.S.* a rebate on property tax or income tax granted by a State to low-income homeowners or renters to help them cope with rising property taxes. *Measures already in use in about 30 states, known as circuit breakers, accomplish this: The state assumes part of the household's property tax (only for senior citizens in some states, for all ages in others) whenever the tax exceeds a specified percentage of income.* Today's Education 9-10/78, p47 [**1972**, transferred use of the term for a switch that interrupts an electric circuit when the current gets too strong]

circular file, *U.S. Slang, Humorous.* the wastepaper basket (especially of an office). *A petition to amend the tax law was sent to Governor Carey's office in April but Mr. Bourke said "it probably went into the circular file somewhere."* NY Times 9/19/76, pA20 [**1967**]

circumgalactic, *adj.* surrounding or revolving about a galaxy. *Because the permitted galactic source distributions lead to a soft X-ray flux which peaks at low galactic latitudes . . . the observed increase in flux at high latitudes must arise from an extragalactic or circumgalactic component.* Nature 6/16/72, p380 [**1970**]

circumglobal, *adj.* revolving or traveling about the earth; circumterrestrial. *These big balloons are also bearing payloads for Project Boomerang, the "poor man's satellite," on circumglobal missions.* New Scientist 1/10/74, p55 —**circumglobally**, *adv.*: *"Because they are distributed circum-globally . . . peregrines provide an ideal focus for international cooperation," said Dr. Ward, who is chief of the Ecological Research Office.* NY Times 2/15/76, pA73 [**1974**]

circumplanetary, *adj.* surrounding or revolving about a planet. *Mariner 10 will conduct a search for dwarf satellites, nevertheless, but if W. R. Ward and M. J. Reid are on the right track, the search will be more fruitful on the surface than in circumplanetary space.* New Scientist 11/1/73, p353 [**1973**]

circumstellar, *adj.* surrounding or revolving about a star. *What is this cool object? . . . Harold L. Johnson and V. C. Reddish of the University of Arizona have argued that it may be an extremely bright supergiant star that has been reddened by either interstellar dust or a circumstellar envelope of some kind.* Scientific American 8/68, p59 [**1966**, from *circum-* around + *stellar* of a star]

cislunar, *adj.* of or referring to space between earth and moon. *This indicated a low concentration of dust of interplanetary space, perhaps 1/10,000 of that found near the earth and 1/100 of that in cislunar (earth-moon) space.* Americana Annual 1964, p606 [**1956**, from *cis-* on this side + *lunar* of the moon]

city, *n.* U.S. and Canadian Slang. someone or something of a specified character; a (specified) condition, situation, person, prospect, etc. *In a CBS-TV special called* Funny Papers *. . . It turned out that Daddy Warbucks is straight city, but Carroll O'Connor is pretty sexy.* Time 1/17/72, p32 *". . . I get on a talk show, I get talking and whoa!* Trouble city!" Rolling Stone 1/11/79, p86 [**1972**, abstracted from FAT CITY]

civex ('siveks), *n.* a system for reprocessing nuclear fuel in a breeder reactor in such a way as to avoid production of pure plutonium, which can be used to make nuclear weapons. *The United States cannot prevent a nation from going nuclear—peacefully or militarily—if it wants to, he said, even with civex. Civex is only designed to prevent subnational groups and terrorists from misusing it for military aims, he said.* Science News 3/4/78, p132 [**1978**, apparently from *civ*ilian (i.e., nonmilitary) + *ex*traction]

CJD, abbreviation of CREUTZFELDT-JAKOB DISEASE. *All three natural diseases, scrapie, kuru and CJD are caused primarily by rather unusual types of viral agent, although it is recognised that genetic factors may considerably affect the length of incubation.* New Scientist 11/18/76, p381 [**1972**]

C-J disease, short for CREUTZFELDT-JAKOB DISEASE. *Scrapie, kuru, and C-J disease will all "take" if inoculated into the brain of a chimpanzee.* Harper's 1/77, p29 [**1972**]

cladistic (klə'distik), *adj.* based on hereditary factors and relationships. Compare PHENETIC. *. . . statematists . . . developed methods of classifying animals for other purposes: numerical (phenetic) classifications, based on relative degrees of similarity and ignoring evolutionary history and, at the other extreme, the cladistic classifications, based on assumed lines of descent while ignoring similarity.* Britannica Book of the Year 1970, p169 [**1960**, from *clad-* (from Greek *kládos* sprout, branch) + *-istic*, as in *statistic*] —**cladistics, cladist**, *n.*: *Cladistics is a systematic method of classifying living things on the basis of shared features, such as the mammary glands and hair of mammals. It all sounds innocent enough, but cladists do not have much time for fossils as a primary source of information. This both infuriates the traditionalists and leads the cladists to revolutionary conclusions about relationships between living things.* Sunday Times (London) 11/23/80, p4

cladogram ('klædə,græm), *n.* a diagram of sequences in an evolutionary tree. *Immunological distances are . . . apportionable along derived cladograms and thus serve as reliable indicators of phylogenetic affinities among the taxa being compared.* Nature 4/22/76, p700 [**1966**, from *clado-* (from Greek *kládos* branch) + *-gram* diagram]

clambake, *n.* a group of marine animals living in areas of the ocean floor heated by a hot spring. *Leading the observers to the hot water veins was the unusual presence—for these 2,700-meter depths—of large groups of animals clustered around them, apparently thriving in the 9C-warmer-than-usual water. Though well-known in shallow water, this is the first known occurrence of such clusters in the deep sea. The scientists have taken to calling these clusters of animal communities "clambakes."* Science News 3/19/77, p183 [**1977**, transferred sense of the earlier (1830's) meaning "a gathering at which clams are baked"]

clam diggers, U.S. trousers cut off at midcalf. *Clam diggers or pedal pushers, this midcalf length is very fashionable. This pair is styled in white cotton after sailor's pants.* NY Times Magazine 3/21/76, p75 [**1976**, so called from their original use in digging for clams] ▶The term was applied to such pants in the 1940's and revived in recent years.

clanger ('klæŋər), *n.* British Slang. a resounding blunder (especially in the phrase **drop a clanger**). *He has good reason for embarrassment for the Americans seemed to have dropped a fair sized clanger.* Sunday Times (London) 4/28/68, p34 *Nobody disputes, of course, that it was a crashing clanger but the deep breathing now going on seems a bit more than is warranted.* Manchester Guardian Weekly 5/11/67, p6 [**1958**]

clapometer, *n.* a meter for measuring the applause of an audience. *The applause and the laughter gave off warmth, like a fire. The clapometer was bursting itself, registering 98, a record. "You're bringing the house down," Hughie Green said.* Times (London) 6/12/76, p8 [**1972**, from *clap* to applaud + connecting *-o-* + *-meter*]

clapped-out, *adj.* British Slang. ruined by decay, neglect, or waste; dilapidated. *. . . he owned a huge, clapped-out Chrysler which carried eight people . . .* Punch 10/23/68, p569 *Effluent and over-fishing have also made dangerous inroads into the beds . . . "Now look at the beds. Bloody clapped out they are: It takes me a tide to pick what I used to in an hour."* Sunday Times (London) 6/6/71, p24 [**1960**]

clap track, prerecorded applause added to a sound track. *John played rhythm guitar, George the lead, and afterwards, when a "clap track" (the sound of people clapping) was dubbed over, everyone except Lennon's wife, Yoko Ono, rushed into the studio to join in the applause.* Newsweek 3/26/73, p100 [**1973**, patterned after LAUGH TRACK]

class action, a legal action brought on behalf of all to whom the case applies. *The legislative program described by [former Congressman] Ottinger would amend: Federal law to broaden the right of citizens to bring "class actions" against polluters and to provide a fund to help defray legal expenses in such actions.* New Yorker 5/9/70, p116 [**1968**]

classism, *n.* discrimination based on class distinctions. Compare AGEISM, SEXISM, SPECIESISM. *The council says in its book "Human (and Anti-Human) Values in Children's Books," that it advocates "a society which will be free of racism, sexism, ageism, classism, materialism, elitism, and other negative values." It evaluates children's books to determine the degree to which they "help achieve such a society."* NY Times 7/10/77, p9 [**1971**]

clast, *n.* Geology. a rock fragment; piece of broken rock. *In 1971 H. A. Lee pointed out that the most commonly used methods in glaciated terrain include sampling of heavy clasts, basal till, and eskers.* McGraw-Hill Yearbook of Science and Technology 1973, p205 [**1972**, back formation from *clastic, adj.*, consisting of broken pieces of older rock]

claustrophobic, *n.* a person who has an abnormal fear of enclosed spaces. *Thomas H. Budzynski, at the University of Colorado Medical Center, has been applying EEG [electro-*

encephalograph] *biofeedback procedures to anxiety problems and psychosomatic disorders. Stutterers and claustrophobics can be taught to relax without the use of tranquilizers.* Science News 11/6/71, p316 [**1965,** noun use of the adjective (1889) meaning prone to or suffering from claustrophobia]

claw, *v.i.* **claw back,** *British.* to retrieve (money spent on increased government benefits and allowances) in the form of additional taxes. *Above that level, the 15 per cent proposed surcharge evens things out, but not enough to claw back the big concessions on the first £2,000 of income.* Guardian (London) 4/22/72, p15 [**1953**]

claw-back, *n. British.* **1** retrieval by the government of money spent on increased benefits and allowances by a corresponding increase in taxes. *His* [Mr. Ian Macleod's] *alternative Budget proposals, given the money available, would have been a 10s. family allowance increase with claw-back which could cost £30m.* [million]. Times (London) 4/16/70, p2 **2** a drawback. *The pleasure* [in the Diaries of Samuel Pepys] *is various and pervasive—even with its occasional claw-backs. It is in drink and food, in drinking wine with anchovies; in travel on the river, in walking by moonlight; in his singing and music; in company, theatre-going, sights, sounds, ceaseless curiosity . . .* Manchester Guardian Weekly 12/5/70, p18 [**1969,** from CLAW BACK]

claymore mine, Also shortened to **claymore.** an electrically detonated mine that sprays small metal pellets. *. . . the constant going off of claymore mines, rockets, and other forms of ammo would get on his nerves . . .* Harper's 8/69, p63 *The homemade Claymore is a wooden box a foot long, four inches wide, six inches deep.* Sunday Times (London) 10/31/71, p10 [**1961,** probably named after the *claymore* sword of the Scottish Highlanders]

clean, *adj.* free from the use of narcotic drugs. Compare DIRTY. *. . . only one-tenth of heroin addicts are ever completely "clean again." In Washington, where the quality of drugs is poor and withdrawal less dramatic than in say, New York or Chicago, Dr. Dupont and several ex-addicts claim that 10 per cent is far too pessimistic a figure.* Times (London) 3/13/70, p11 [**1963**]

clean room, a thoroughly sterilized room used for laboratory work, the manufacture of critical spacecraft parts, etc. *Soldering iron handle for use in clean rooms helps eliminate potential dust and solder contamination while insulating fingers against high temperature.* Science News 9/18/65, p191 [**1960**]

clear air turbulence, a violent disturbance in air currents, caused by rapid changes of temperature associated with the jet stream. Clear air turbulence is characterized by severe updrafts and downdrafts that affect jet aircraft flying at high altitudes. *Abbreviation:* CAT *To the airline pilot, the wave means "clear-air turbulence." This sounds strange, since for the glider it is so smooth. But the glider stands still in the wave. The jet flies through it at 550 mph, with maybe a 70 mph tailwind added, and then the wave is like a thank-you-ma'am in the road, taken too fast: it can lift the passenger right out of his seat and put the coffee on the ceiling.* Harper's 11/71, p129 [**1959**]

Cleocin (kli:'ousən), *n.* a trademark for CLINDAMYCIN. *Cleocin . . . appears especially useful in treating infections caused by anaerobic bacteria, those that thrive without oxygen, such as Bacteroides most commonly found in patients after surgery or during drug or radiation therapy that impairs their normal defense mechanisms against infection.* World Book Science Annual 1974, p283 [**1970**]

client, *n.* **1** short for CLIENT STATE. *Washington and Moscow must bring their clients to heel in order to avoid involvement in another armed confrontation.* NY Times 11/1/70, pD15 [**1958**] **2** a person viewed euphemistically as a subject of regulation by a government agency or public authority. *In the world of prisons notable advances have also been made recently in prettying-up the nomenclature. Guards are now "correctional officers"; solitary confinement punishment cells, "adjustment centers"; prisons, "therapeutic correctional communities"; convicts, "clients of the Department of Correc-*

tions." NY Times 9/5/73, p41 [**1973,** originally (1920's) applied to a social worker's case]

client state, a dependent state or government. Also shortened to CLIENT. *. . . the peace movement had not taken Nixon's politics serious until November 3rd. Now we know that his true intention is to continue a pro-West client state in Vietnam.* New Yorker 1/3/70, p42 [**1955**]

climbout, *n.* the immediate, steep climb of an aircraft during takeoff. *Noise on takeoff will be less offensive than the 747 because the SST* [supersonic transport] *climbout will be steeper and faster.* NY Times 12/1/70, p47 [**1962**]

clindamycin (ˌklində'maisən), *n.* a semisynthetic antibiotic used against infections caused by anaerobic bacteria. *Formula:* $C_{18}H_{33}C1N_2O_5S$ *Trademark,* CLEOCIN. *The study was useful medically since it showed that one of the drugs, clindamycin, reached the fetus in sufficient amounts to control syphilis.* Newsweek 6/24/74, p74 [**1970**]

Clio, *n.* a statuette presented annually as an award for the best production, acting, etc., in commercial advertisements during the year on American television. *In honor of such memorable performances, this year, for the first time, the American TV Commercials Festival is awarding a Clio, the industry's equivalent of an Oscar, to the best actor in a commercial.* Time 4/28/67, p57 [**1966,** named after *Clio,* the Greek muse of history]

cliometric, *adj.* of or relating to CLIOMETRICS. *Genovese . . . is the first historian to combine such traditional sources as government records and slaveholder diaries with extensive use of the slaves' own narratives in a picture of slavery as a whole— and with at least a few cliometric citations as well.* Saturday Review 1/11/75, p23 [**1970,** from *Clio,* the Greek muse of history + *metric* of or involving measurement] **—cliometrically,** *adv.: Dr. Fogel of the University of Chicago has cliometrically calculated that railroads were not so crucial to industrial growth as the traditional wisdom has pictured them.* Encyclopedia Science Supplement (Grolier) 1970, p290

cliometrics, *n.* the study of history by the use of advanced methods of mathematical analysis, particularly the processing of large quantities of historical data through computers. *The book* [Time on the Cross, by Robert W. Fogel and Stanley L. Engerman] *is sure to produce new interest in the burgeoning science of cliometrics, the manner of applying computers to the reconsideration of social and economic phenomena, . . .* Manchester Guardian Weekly 4/27/74, p5 [**1970,** from CLIOMETRIC] **—cliometrician,** *n.: Together they are the leading edge of a new wing of historians known as cliometricians because their methods marry Clio, the muse of history, to the practice of quantifying the past with the help of computers.* Time 6/17/74, p98

clo (klou), *n.* a unit for measuring the amount of insulation or warmth provided by a garment. *The unit of thermal resistance used by the clothing industry is the clo. Wool fibre, several centimeters thick, down and the new 3M material have clo values of 0.9, 1 and 1.8 respectively. Therefore a thinner barrier of microfibre than down gives equal warmth.* New Scientist 8/14/80, p537 [**1956,** from *clo*thing]

clockwork orange, someone deprived of his individuality by scientific conditioning and made into an automaton. [Albert] *Bandura feels the behavior-modification process is misunderstood by the public. "They see salivating dogs, shocks, clockwork oranges. They misunderstand the process," he says.* Science News 3/16/74, p181 [**1972,** from *A Clockwork Orange,* title of a novel (1962) by the British author Anthony Burgess, born 1917, about transformation of a deviant and violent personality by exposure to a form of aversion therapy. The phrase is from the Cockney expression "queer as a clockwork orange."]

clofibrate (klou'fai,breit), *n.* a drug that lowers cholesterol levels in human beings and removes fats from tissues. *Particular attention is being focused on clofibrate, a substance that sharply reduces the levels of cholesterol and other fatty substances in the blood.* NY Times 11/24/68, pD10 [**1964**]

clomiphene (ˈklɑmə‚fiːn), *n.* Also called **clomiphene citrate.** a fertility-inducing drug. *This substance, clomiphene, makes a false biological signal to the hypothalamus and causes it to set in train the sequence of events which leads to ovulation.* Science Journal 6/70, p46 [**1963**, shortened from *chloramiphene*]

clone, *n.* **1** a person or thing that is an exact duplicate, or appears to be an exact duplicate, of another; a carbon copy; replica. *Both blond and blue-eyed, Mr. Driver and Mr. Haddow agree that they are clones, then fall to squabbling over who is the original.* NY Times 7/20/79, pC3 **2** a person who acts in a mindless, mechanical fashion; automaton; android; robot. *Elsewhere, they suggest the possibility of using clones for work involving radiation or dangerous chemicals, or for fighting wars.* Manchester Guardian Weekly (Washington Post section) 9/24/78, p17 [**1978,** figurative senses of the noun *clone,* meaning two or more individuals duplicated or propagated asexually from a single (sexually produced) ancestor, from Greek *klón* twig] —**v.t. 1** to reproduce or propagate asexually. *Cauliflowers have been cloned at the National Vegetable Research Station . . . Simply by cutting slices of cauliflowers, at their market-ready stage, and putting them in nutrient solution a single plant can be made to yield many more plants.* New Scientist 6/18/70, p581 **2** Figurative use: *Since it costs about $2 billion to design and tool up for an all-new plane and engines, most of the new generation will be cloned from present models, scaled down in size and outfitted with the latest technology.* Time 8/14/78, p57 —**v.i.:** *Cloning, or duplication of identical organisms, as has been achieved with frogs, is not genetic engineering in the real sense, he* [Dr. James Danielli] *asserts, nor are efforts to create test-tube babies, although cloning and creating life in a test tube are often canopied under the heading of genetic engineering.* Science News 9/4/71, p152 [**1959,** from *clone, n.*] —**cloning,** *n.: Added to these possibilities is the often-dreaded question of cloning. This has turned out to be the subject that catches the imagination, that titillates movie audiences and shows up so often in science fiction.* Robert Cooke, Improving on Nature, 1977, p10

clonidine (ˈklounə‚dain *or* ˈklounə‚diːn), *n.* a drug that lowers high blood pressure, found also to block and reverse the effects of withdrawal from heroin and other narcotics. *Formula:* $C_9H_9Cl_2N_3$ *The scientists suggest that clonidine and naltrexone may be used in sequence to first effect a nearly painless withdrawal from heroin and then to maintain the ex-addict in a prevention program. Neither of the substances is addictive—giving them a significant advantage over methadone maintenance, say the researchers.* Science News 8/5/78, p85 [**1972,** probably irregular from *cyclo-* cyclic + a*nilide* + *-ine* (chemical suffix)]

closed caption, a caption to aid the deaf and hard of hearing, used in a system of restricted transmission of television-program captioning. *The programs are to be encoded with what are called "closed" captions—subtitles that are invisible on all television sets except those specially equipped to make them appear.* NY Times 10/5/76, p89 [**1976,** shortened from *closed-circuit caption*] —**closed captioning:** *The closed captioning system operates through the imposition of encoded visual subtitles on Line 21 of the TV vertical blanking interval—a portion of the screen that does not ordinarily contain video information.* Deaf American 4/79, p7

closed-loop, *adj.* of or relating to an automatic control process or unit that adjusts or corrects itself by a feedback mechanism. Compare OPEN-LOOP. *Closed-loop systems, where the experiment is directly controlled by computer, are currently being developed. Their prototypes can be seen in industrial control systems, where . . . devices, ranging from elevators to oil refineries, are controlled automatically.* Scientific American 9/66, p163 [**1958**]

close-look satellite, an earth satellite used for detailed military photo reconnaissance. *With their shorter lifetime in orbit, the close-look satellites had less stringent reliability requirements than the area-surveillance models and were therefore able to reach full operational status more quickly.* Scientific American 2/73, p19 [**1972**]

closet, *adj.* hidden; covert; secret. *But for the G.I.s in the rear areas, there was another enemy to fight: hard drugs. To find out why, I invited a "closet" addict from Army headquarters in Saigon to come over and talk.* Time 2/5/73, p23 [**1968,** extended from earlier (1600's) sense of "private; secluded"]

closet homosexual, a person who hides his homosexuality; a covert homosexual. *I know men in high and low places in society, in government, at work, who would shrivel in shame if people suspected that they were even closet homosexuals.* Saturday Review 2/12/72, p28 [**1972**]

closet queen, a slang term for CLOSET HOMOSEXUAL. *The whole first part of the movie nags us with the author's exposure of his characters; the actively "normal" parents, for instance, have created a hyperaggressive daughter who wants to "mold" men, and a son who wants to be a girl and who winds up, literally, as a closet queen.* Atlantic 4/71, p99 [**1968**]

closet queer, *U.S.* derogatory slang term for CLOSET HOMOSEXUAL. *"Hell, he's one of those tough fags," would be the answer. But he's married and has three children, I would point out about someone else. "A closet-queer, obviously," the answer would shoot back.* Harper's 9/70, p39 [**1970**]

clothback, *n.* a clothbound book. *The appearance in print of the first of the Nuffield Advanced Science courses will be enthusiastically welcomed by many. First, perhaps, by those already using the trial materials, who can discard 5 lb of duplicated loose leaves for a pair of large pocket-sized clothbacks.* New Scientist 10/1/70, p44 [**1970**]

cloth-cap, *adj. British.* of or belonging to the laboring or working class, particularly in opposition to other classes. *So-called top hat pension schemes are spreading in popularity and, even if they are not yet in vogue among cloth cap workers, their use is no longer confined to the very highly paid executives for whom they were first designed.* Times (London) 6/11/66, p17 [**1959,** from the *cloth caps* commonly worn by workers in Great Britain]

cloth-eared, *adj.* having, or as if having, cloth ears. *The public world is dominated today by the cloth-eared and insensitive noisemongers.* New Scientist 4/16/70, p101 [**1965**]

cloth ears, defective or tone-deaf hearing. *"They've got cloth ears. Sometimes you get someone left behind who swears you didn't even call the flight . . ."* Sunday Times (London) 10/9/66, p5 [**1965**]

clout, *n. U.S.* power, influence, or prestige, especially in politics. . . . *in the waning months of his Administration, he* [President Johnson] *no longer had enough clout left to force through a scheme which was bound to infuriate virtually every member of Congress.* Harper's 9/68, p16 [**1963,** figurative sense of the term for a heavy blow with the hand]

cloxacillin, *n.* a synthetic form of penicillin effective against germs that have developed resistance to natural penicillin. Compare AMPICILLIN, OXACILLIN. *The antibiotic was cloxacillin, as this is effective against the staphylococcus that causes about half the infections found both at the end of lactation and at calving.* Times (London) 1/8/68, p11 [**1964,** from its chemical name *chl*orophenyl-methyliso-*ox*azolyl penic*illin*]

cloze (klouz), *adj.* of or based on the cloze procedure. [J. Wesley] *Schneyer (1965) explored the effects of the cloze procedure upon the reading comprehension of sixth grade pupils. Two types of cloze exercises were used; one built on every-tenth word deletions and the other on noun-verb deletions.* Eugene Jongsma, The Cloze Procedure as a Teaching Technique, 1971, p9 [**1960,** alteration of *close, v.,* as used originally in Gestalt psychology and later in communication theory in the sense of "to complete a pattern parts of which are missing or have been deleted"]

cloze procedure, a testing procedure for comprehension in reading which measures the ability of a reader to supply words which have been systematically deleted from a reading selection. *The "cloze procedure" has been developed to enable teachers to determine the ability of the child to handle materials; it will also indicate the ability to handle concepts as well* *as word and sentence structures.* Robert M. Wilson, Diagnostic and Remedial Reading for Classroom and Clinic, 1972, p247 [**1958**]

Club of Rome, an international group of business people, economists, and scientists who periodically issue reports and predictions about global problems of food, population, industry, environment, and other factors of survival. *In its famous doomsday treatise four years ago, the Club of Rome depicted a world consuming its resources and polluting itself at a rate that—if continued—would ensure its early destruction. The only hope for global salvation was suggested in the report's title:* The Limits to Growth. Time 4/26/76, p12 [**1972**, so called because the group was founded in Rome]

cluster bomb, a bomb consisting of a number of small fragmentation bombs or several explosive canisters. *The new US Administration has embargoed the sale of cluster bombs using fuel/air explosives (FAE) to Israel.* New Scientist 2/24/77, p443 [**1965**] —**cluster-bombed**, *adj.: A better measure of the peace process is to be found in the collapse of Israeli-Egyptian negotiations, and in the cluster-bombed villages of south Lebanon.* Harper's 8/78, p75 —**cluster bombing**: *The majority of the population actually live in the areas serviced by ERA* [Eritrean Relief Association], *where there are over 600,000 displaced persons and where daily napalm and cluster bombing causes an ever-increasing number of civilian casualties.* Manchester Guardian Weekly 11/19/78, p2

cluster college, one of a group of small autonomous liberal-arts colleges within a university, modeled on those of Oxford and Cambridge. . . . *some forty American universities already have taken steps toward the development of smaller units or "cluster colleges," each enrolling no more than 200 to 1,000 students and each with its own basic faculty which is selected on the basis of talent for teaching undergraduates.* Saturday Review 8/17/68, p53 [**1963**]

cluster headache, a type of severe, disabling headache occurring several times daily or every two or three days, usually for a period of time and then recurring later. *Cluster headache is an exquisitely painful type of migraine. Its victims are primarily middle aged men, although women and people as young as 20 years of age may be affected. The headaches come in blindingly painful bunches . . .* Encyclopedia Science Supplement (Grolier) 1979, p243 [**1953, 1972**]

CM, abbreviation of COMMAND MODULE. . . . *Meanwhile, the third Apollo 11 crew member, Michael Collins, circled the moon in the CM, one of the few Americans unable to watch Armstrong and Aldrin.* Encyclopedia Science Supplement (Grolier) 1970, p304 [**1965**]

CNC, abbreviation for *computer numerical control.* Compare DNC. *Development of the CNC systems, each of which has its own built-in minicomputer to run a machine tool, was held back because of relatively high costs.* 1973 World Book Year Book, p411 [**1972**]

co-anchor, *U.S.* —*v.t., v.i.* to anchor (a television or radio program) jointly with another or others. *Barbara Walters was brought from the "Today" show to co-anchor ABC's evening news with Harry Reasoner. Then NBC, not to be outdone in on-camera personability, brought up David Brinkley from Washington to co-anchor with John Chancellor.* New Yorker 10/31/77, p123 —*n.* a person who co-anchors. *The drop in the "Today" show ratings over the last year might perhaps be attributed to her NBC co-anchor Jim Hartz.* NY Times 4/24/76, p55 [**1969**]

Coanda effect (kou'ændə), the property or tendency of any fluid passing a curved surface to attach itself to the surface. It is also called the WALL-ATTACHMENT EFFECT, and is an important principle of fluidics. *A common demonstration of the Coanda effect is seen when a falling jet of water from a tap defies gravity and runs along a spoon or jar just brought into contact with it.* Science Journal 12/68, p53 [**1954**, named after Henri *Coanda*, a French engineer who described the effect in 1932]

coat protein, a protein that acts as a protective sheath for a virus, making it resistant to antibodies of the host organism. *The putative coat proteins prepared from different clones of one strain of* T. brucei *differed in composition. This supported the view that coat protein is the variant antigen . . .* Nature 1/1-8/76, p15 [**1976**]

coattail, *adj. U.S. Politics.* based on the ability of a strong candidate to carry weaker ones along to victory. See also COATTAILS. *On Capitol Hill, Rockefeller promoted "coattail power"— meaning that he can get more Republican Congressmen elected in November than Nixon.* Time 6/28/68, p13 [**1964**]

coattails, *n.pl. U.S. Politics.* the ability of a strong candidate to carry weaker ones along to victory. *Paul O'Dwyer, an anti-war McCarthy supporter, upset strong Kennedy and Humphrey men in the Senatorial primary, suggesting that McCarthy had coattails.* Harper's 5/69, p83 [**1954**, from the idiom *ride on someone's coattails* to get ahead by sticking closely to someone who is advancing or successful]

coat-trailing, *adj. British.* provoking; provocative. *This consensus—the conventional wisdom of parliamentary liberalism—is expressed with force and charm in Humphrey Berkeley's new book and in spite of his engagingly coat-trailing title, most of his attention is devoted to it.* Listener 4/11/68, p476 [**1959**, from the British idiom *trail one's coat* (for someone to tread on), meaning to provoke an attack or quarrel; the original idiom was *drag* (or *trail*) *one's coattails*]

COBOL or **Cobol** ('kou₁bɑl), *n.* acronym for *Common Business Oriented Language*, a computer language widely used in industry and government. Compare ALGOL, BASIC, FORTRAN. *Compiler writers learnt their trade and eventually standard languages emerged: Algol and Fortran for scientific purposes and Cobol for business applications.* Science Journal 10/70, p96 [**1960**]

cochair, *v.t.* to chair jointly; share the chairmanship of. *The occasion was a press conference to announce a forthcoming backgammon tournament in Las Vegas that was being co-chaired by Magriel and the venerable jack-of-all-games Oswald Jacoby.* New Yorker 12/5/77, p40 [**1968**]

cockamamie or **cockamamy**, *U.S. Slang.* —*adj.* foolish, absurd, or nonsensical. *If there are some confining or irritating or cockamamy rules of the house . . . these should be explained in advance.* Atlantic 9/70, p118 —*n.* something foolish, absurd, or nonsensical. *Arlen characterized the drama as "a ninety-minute uninterrupted cliché . . . the most asinine and inept piece of cockamamie that I'd seen all year."* Harper's 8/69, p100 [**1960**, probably an altered form of *decalcomania* the fad or mania for using decals]

cockapoo or **cockerpoo**, *n.* a dog that is the hybrid offspring of a cocker spaniel and a miniature poodle. *I have a cockapoo: it's a cross between a cocker and a poodle.* Atlantic 10/71, p84 [**1971**]

cockpit, *n. Geology.* an enclosed depression with no evidence of a dry valley. It is a feature of the limestone topography of Jamaica. *To the south of the fault there are well developed cockpits whilst to the north the landscape is physically disarmingly similar to the chalk downlands of southern England.* Geographical Magazine 10/72, p35 [**1972**]

cocooning, *n.* the habit or tendency to withdraw into the privacy of one's home, especially during one's leisure time. Compare COUCH POTATO. *Gandy says his clients are spending a lot more time at home, curled up with good books, good music, and VCR movies. Some refer to this as cocooning.* Christian Science Monitor 2/12/88, p24 [**1987**]

code, *v.i.* **code for,** to specify the genetic code for synthesizing (a particular protein, etc.). . . . *they contain more than enough RNA—about 3300 nucleotides—whereas only 3000 or so are needed to code for the three proteins.* New Scientist 12/18/69, p590 [**1966**]

code dating, the practice of placing coded information on perishable products to indicate date of manufacture, expiration of shelf life, or time limit for sale. See BAR CODE. *Consumerism* is not about to fade away; rather, it is begetting a spate of legislation to regulate retailers' conduct, including unit and dual pricing and code dating. 1971 Collier's Encyclopedia Year Book, p460 [**1971**]

code word or **codeword**, *n.* **1** a seemingly inoffensive word or expression which conceals an offensive meaning or message. Compare WORD. *Those who advise us that "law and order" is a codeword for racism will have a bit of difficulty pinning the racist tag on Coleman Young, first black mayor of Detroit.* National Review 2/1/74, p120 *Initially, the Arabs were stunned when Carter endorsed "defensible borders" for Israel (code word for no return to the 1967 frontiers).* Time 3/28/77, p27 **2** another name for CODON. *Information for the synthesis of protein molecules is stored as a sequence of code words in the DNA of the cell nucleus and is transcribed as a similar sequence onto RNA messenger molecules.* 1976 Britannica Yearbook of Science and the Future, p62 [**1968** for def. 1; **1964** for def. 2, probably short for *genetic code word*] ► *Code word* in the sense of definition 1 is now used to attack opponents or to question motives by ascribing a concealed ("code") meaning to a slogan or other expression. This usage developed during the 1960's in the civil-rights movement, when politicians calling for "law and order" were accused by civil-rights leaders of using the phrase as a "code word" for suppressing the struggle for civil rights.

codon ('kou,dan), *n.* a group of three chemical bases in a certain order, forming the genetic code for producing a particular amino acid. Also called CODE WORD. *A sequence of three nucleotides—known as a codon—is required to specify one amino acid . . . The codon which consists of three uracil residues, for example, specifies the amino acid phenylalanine; other codons act as punctuation marks, coding for the beginning and end of a protein.* Science Journal 11/70, p57 [**1962**, from *code* + *-on* (unit of genetic material)]

codswallop, *n. British Slang.* nonsense; rubbish. *"That what they teach you up college?" sneered Hidius Bulbus . . . "Filling your head with a lot of radical Christian codswallop about equal rights."* Punch 1/17/68, p74 [**1963**, originally a phrase *cod's wallop*]

co-edition, *n.* one of several editions of the same book published by two or more companies at the same time, usually in different countries. *Italian publishers are in unison in complaining about rising costs, but with sales depressed, they do not feel they can raise prices . . . One way out of the problem that several publishers have found is "co-editions," books with a lot of art work utilizing Italians' graphic skills. They are printed in Italy under the name of a foreign publisher with a translation of the text provided by the foreign house and sold in both countries.* NY Times 1/25/76, pC40 [**1969**]

coevolution, *n.* the simultaneous evolution of two or more unrelated, but often mutually dependent, forms or organisms. *They conclude that the prime function of these ubiquitous plant substances is as ultraviolet pigments. They have probably played an important part in the coevolution of flowers with ultraviolet-sensitive insects.* New Scientist 8/24/72, p375 [**1967**] —**coevolutionary**, *adj.: Gilbert draws attention to . . . the coevolutionary advantages of pollen feeding not only to the Heliconius butterflies but also to the plants from which they are able to collect limited but continuous amounts of pollen.* Nature 7/14/72, p76

coevolve, *v.i.* to undergo coevolution; evolve simultaneously, especially in response to one another. *They found that the eaters and the eaten progressively evolved in close response to each other—coevolved. (Some plants developed defensive alkaloid poisons. Some caterpillars acquired a taste for alkaloids. The plants diversified wildly. The caterpillars diversified with them. What evolved really was the relationship, stably dynamic, unpredictable and sure.)* Harper's 4/74, p105 [**1972**]

coffee-table, *adj.* of or relating to coffee-table books. *Presumably, therefore, its* ["The Atlas of the Universe"] *buyers will be mostly schools and libraries with a smattering of coffee-table enthusiasts.* New Scientist 11/12/70, p339 [**1966**]

coffee-table book, an oversized, expensive, and richly illustrated book, usually dealing with a specialized subject and designed for display on a coffee table or the like. *Like many coffee-table books, this one is very scholarly, and I suppose that the accuracy and intelligence of presentation is intended to make up for the book's physical unwieldiness.* Manchester Guardian Weekly 9/6/69, p19 [**1962**]

Cogas, *n.* acronym for *coal-oil-gas*, applied to the gasification of coal or oil. *A consortium of companies is developing the Cogas (coal-oil-gas) process, in which carbonization is accomplished in a fluidized bed of coal at comparatively low temperature.* Scientific American 5/76, p27 [**1973**]

co-generation, *n.* the production of heat and electricity from the same facility, especially by using the steam left over from industrial processes to generate electric power. *Many industries examined the feasibility of co-generation—simultaneously producing process steam for manufacturing and electricity. The Administration considered offering new incentives to encourage industry to try this system. Among the items being considered were a 30 per cent tax credit for co-generation investment.* 1978 World Book Year Book, p312 [**1976**, coined by the American physicist Amory B. Lovins, born 1948]

cognitive dissonance, *Psychology.* the holding of contradictory attitudes at the same time or the performing of acts that conflict with one's beliefs. Compare DOUBLE-BIND. *Cognitive Dissonance Theory . . . holds that people cannot easily entertain two ideas at once, if these ideas are basically at odds with each other. One way out of such a dilemma, should it arise circumstantially, is to come down heavily on one side. With rationalisations, counterarguments and, if possible, outside support, the other side of the dilemma is routed.* Listener 9/6/73, p298 [**1968**]

cognitive therapy, a method of treating mental and emotional problems by trying to change faulty thinking patterns. *Cognitive therapy has been used with tremendous success, and recently it has been championed as an alternative to psychiatric drugs, which presumably act directly on the mood centers of the brain.* Science News 1/28/84, p58 [**1978**]

cohabitee, cohabitant or **cohabitor**, *n.* a person who lives with another without being married to him or her. *The burden of their message is that a full and meaningful and ever-deepening relationship between cohabitants can only be achieved if each cohabitee continually strives to discover more and more about the nature of him/herself and his/her mate.* New Scientist 10/4/73, p51 *Cohabitors frequently draw up a contract for themselves outlining their respective duties and areas of ownership.* Ruth Rejnis, Her Home, 1980, p137 [**1973**, from *cohabit* to live together as husband and wife without being legally married (c1530) + *-ee* or *-ant* or *-or; cohabitant* in the general sense of one who dwells together with others has been in use since the 1500's]

Cointelpro (,kouin'telprou), *n.* acronym for *counterintelligence program*, a program of the U.S. Federal Bureau of Investigation to disrupt by secret actions the activities of individuals or groups regarded as a threat to domestic security. *Mr. Kelley has stated that Cointelpro is a thing of the past which has been "purged" from bureau operations, but . . . the F.B.I. withheld for two weeks from Denver police information about yet another Socialist Workers Party burglary carried out by one of its informants.* NY Times 8/3/76, p28 [**1975**]

cokehead, *n. U.S. Slang.* a person addicted to cocaine. Compare CRACKHEAD. *Many cokeheads take sedative pills like methaqualone, brand-named Quaaludes (tons of which are illegally imported).* Time 7/6/81, p59 [**1970**, from *coke* cocaine (OEDS 1908) + HEAD]

COLA, *n. U.S. and Canadian.* acronym for *cost of living adjustment* (or *allowance*). . . . *Johnston and his right-leaning cohorts in cabinet are convinced that bending to the clerks' demands—particularly for a COLA . . . clause—would open the floodgates.* Maclean's 10/13/80, p32 [**1976**]

cold, *n.* **1 come in from the cold,** to come out of a condition of isolation or neglect. *Taking advantage of the blizzard condi-*

tions they have spent a period of "splendid isolation" . . . at the bleakest of training waters, even in normal conditions at Ely . . . So it is with great interest that we await for an enigmatic Cambridge [boating crew] *to "come in from the cold".* Times (London) 3/10/70, p12 **2 in from the cold,** back into favor; no longer in a condition of isolation or neglect. *After the arrests were made, they at first wanted to keep their cover, but now, after a month of enjoying the real world again, they are happy to be in from the cold.* Time 1/9/78, p14 **[1967,** popularized by the title *The Spy Who Came in From the Cold,* a bestselling novel (1964) of espionage by John Le Carré (pseudonym of David Cornwell, former British diplomat); also reflecting the catch phrase *out in the cold*]

Cold Duck, *U.S.* an inexpensive mixture of sparkling burgundy and champagne. *The Nation's thirst for Cold Duck began to rise last August . . . Whether they were moved by the fad or frugality, New Year's revelers decided that Cold Duck was just the tipple with which to see out the inflationary old year and toast in the uncertain new one.* Time 1/12/70, p47 **[1970,** translation of German *Kalte Ente,* alteration of *kalte Ende* cold ends, a phrase used to describe leftover wines mixed and served at the close of a party]

cold mooner, a person who believes that there is no thermal or volcanic activity in the moon's core and that the craters on the moon were formed by the impact of meteorites rather than by volcanic activity. Compare HOT MOONER. . . . *probably most of the moon's craters were formed by meteorite impact and not by volcanic activity. The cold mooners, led by Dr. Harold Urey, are definitely in the ascendant.* Manchester Guardian Weekly 11/29/69, p3 **[1969]**

cold shutdown, a complete stoppage of the activity of a nuclear reactor. *By extinguishing the fission reaction, the control rods reduced the power output of the reactor by 93 percent, but the reactor was a long way from "cold shutdown."* Harper's 10/79, p16 **[1979]**

cold-turkey, *v.i., v.t. U.S.* to quit a habit or addiction abruptly. *If you are not cold-turkeying, try to figure out which cigarettes are most important to you. After breakfast? After dinner? Some people find they can cut down to just four or five a day this way.* Harper's Bazaar 4/74, p124B *What all this means, of course, is that taking leave of your local club for foreign destinations no longer obliges you to "cold turkey" tennis entirely . . .* Town and Country 4/75, p114 **[1974,** from the noun phrase *cold turkey* (1920's) an addict's sudden deprivation of the drug habit]

Cold Warrior, a politician or statesman who plays an active part in the power struggle between the Soviet Union and the western nations known as the Cold War. *The selection of Robert McNamara and Roswell Gilpatric for the Department of Defense (although neither was an enthusiastic Cold Warrior) affirmed further the continuing delegation of foreign policy to businessmen and the New York Establishment.* Harper's 7/70, p50 **[1959,** blend of *Cold War* and *warrior]*

collage, *v.t.* to compose in the form of a collage; assemble, combine, or paste (a collection of odd parts or pieces) on a surface to form an artistic composition. *The platform is painted and collaged in Rauschenberg's customary manner, with such random objects as a tennis ball, a rubber heel, a shirt sleeve, and numerous action photographs from magazines and newspapers.* New Yorker 2/29/64, p84 **[1964,** verb use of the noun]

collapsar (kəˈlæpˌsɑr), *n.* another name for BLACK HOLE. *These dimouts could not be due simply to a black hole passing in front of Epsilon Aurigae; the collapsar would have to be improbably large to cause that effect.* Time 4/5/71, p32 **[1971,** from *collapse* + *-ar,* as in *quasar* and *pulsar]*

collectibles or **collectables,** *n.pl.* items suitable for collecting, especially rare or outdated objects of little intrinsic value. *One finds Art Deco restaurants, shops with plants and baskets, shops with secondhand clothes (now called "antiques" and viewed as high fashion), and shops filled with the less-than-antiques that used to be called "junk" and are now called "collectibles."* New Yorker 11/22/76, p127 *The popularity of collectables from the past—such as a vogue for items of the 1930s*

and 1940s—may be a measure of the times. 1971 World Book Year Book, p125 **[1952; 1963,** noun use of the adjective (1600's)]

collectivism, *n.* the tendency to act or think as a group instead of individually. *The entrapments of collectivism are overwhelming: TV and radio, which permeate our privacy and destroy the aloneness out of which it becomes possible to learn to build a self; drugs, which smash the mirror of personal identity; . . . the debilitation of the arts; the great gray educational machine; the devaluing and disparaging of the imagination . . .* NY Times 10/13/70, p45 **[1966]** ► The usual sense of *collectivism* is that of collective economic control by the state, as in a socialist country.

collector, *n.* short for SOLAR COLLECTOR. *The temperature that can be achieved when solar radiation is absorbed in a collector—the absorbing device—depends on how intensely the collector concentrates the energy.* New Yorker 2/9/76, p63 **[1976]**

collegiality, *n.* the doctrine of the Roman Catholic Church that the bishops, as spiritual descendants of the Apostles, collectively share ruling power over the Church with the Pope. *Thus the theological concept of "collegiality," endorsed at the* [Vatican] *council means that bishops are not to be regarded as agents of the home office in Rome, but as co-governors of the church along with the Pope.* NY Times 3/9/68, p15 **[1965]**

collide, *v.t.* to strike together; bring into collision. *At Cambridge, a bypass that allows beams of electrons and positrons to be stored in the accelerator's ring so that they may be collided has recently been completed, and beams of both positrons and electrons successfully held in it for a sufficient amount of time. The next steps are to store the two kinds of particles simultaneously, collide them and increase the beam intensities . . .* Science News 3/21/70, p299 **[1961]** ► The transitive verb has been regarded as archaic or obsolete since the 1800's.

Colombian gold, a potent South American variety of marijuana. Compare ACAPULCO GOLD. See also THAI STICK. *They loiter on the sidewalk, trying to buy marijuana from the storklike black youth who can say, "Colombian gold" in a carrying whisper without moving his lips.* NY Times Magazine 1/23/77, p30 **[1976,** so called from its frequent place of origin and bright yellow color]

color, *n.* any of three hypothetical quantum states which combine to produce the strong force that binds quarks. *More complex versions of this theory have been proposed since its introduction in 1963, including the idea that the three basic quarks are subdivided still further by quantum properties called colors.* 1977 Britannica Yearbook of Science and the Future, p157 **[1975,** so called because when the colors of red, yellow, and blue light combine the result is white, suggestive of the neutralized state in which combined quarks should be] **—colored,** *adj.: Although the quark rules imply that we will never see a colored particle, the color hypothesis is not merely a formal construct without predictive value.* Scientific American 10/75 (page not known)

Color Abstraction, the style of color-field paintings. *Taken together, the Olitski retrospective at the Whitney, the Kelly at the Museum of Modern Art, and the Hamilton at the Guggenheim evoke the dominant avant-garde styles of the nineteen-sixties: Color Abstraction and Pop Art.* New Yorker 10/15/73, p113 **[1973]**

color-code, *v.t.* to code or key by the use of different colors to denote different items or categories. . . . *return envelopes have been color-coded with orange trim for Ontario, green for Quebec.* NY Times 3/19/67, p22 **[1957]**

color-field, *adj.* of or designating a form of abstract art that relies more on color than on form. *A number of exhibitions were devoted to artists who had worked in the 20th century. Works by the colour-field abstractionist Jules Olitski were shown at the Pasadena (Calif.) Museum of Modern Art . . .* Britannica Book of the Year 1975, p87 **[1967]**

color force, the strong force which binds quarks. See CHROMODYNAMICS, GLUON. . . . *The nuclear force is regarded as a mere indirect manifestation of a more basic* color force *responsible for the permanent entrapment of quarks. Color is used in this* *new technical sense with no relation to the ordinary meaning of the word.* NY Times Magazine 7/18/76, p29 **[1976]**

colorization, *n.* the act or process of colorizing. *Organizations and individuals passionately have opposed colorization on the ground that it crassly alters the creative work of others.* Americana Annual 1987, p376 **[1986]**

colorize, *v.* to add color to (black-and-white motion pictures) by means of a computer programmed to assign various colors to different values of black-and-white images. *As the process grows more widespread, dozens of famous films are being "colorized," and the trend is provoking a fierce debate on both sides of the Atlantic.* NY Times 8/5/86, pA1 **[1979]**

color-key, *v.t.* another word for COLOR-CODE. *The Forum's color theme invades the 25-acre parking lot. Season ticket holders get three color-keyed tickets, one for parking in the right colored area, the second for entry to the reserved seats (follow the coppertone or gold pathway), and the third for admission to the Forum Club.* Maclean's 12/67, p58 **[1965]**

color man, *U.S.* a radio or television announcer who adds color or variety to the broadcast of a public event by providing background information on the participants, describing or analyzing their actions, etc. *He [Wally Schirra] also signed on to be Walter Cronkite's color man on CBS's play-by-play coverage of the Apollo space shots.* Esquire 1/73, p182 **[1971,** from *color* meaning "interest, vividness"] ►The following variants of *color man* have also been recorded: —**color announcer:** *The Second Annual Unofficial Miss Las Vegas Showgirl Pageant, with host Steve Allen, color announcer Phyllis Diller and judges Louis Nye, Rip Taylor and Jane Meadows.* TV Guide 2/1/75, pA78 —**color babbler:** *There is one short scene in which Dick Button, playing a TV color babbler, describes the moves of a Japanese wrestler in terms of figure skating, the only sport his character knows anything about.* Time 8/21/78, p53

COM or **com,** abbreviation for *computer output microfilm,* a computer printout made directly on microfilm. *Microfilm may thus take some of the load off computer memories. At the same time, it may also help break the bottleneck of computer printout through a great new range of systems known as computer-output-microfilm, or COM for short.* Encyclopedia Science Supplement (Grolier) 1973, p412 **[1970]**

comanagement, *n.* another name for WORKER PARTICIPATION. Also called COSUPERVISION. *"Let each one choose quite freely the type of society he wants. . .but we must reject with the utmost vigour formulas which under diverse labels aim through comanagement at unionizing and paralysing the management of firms."* Times (London) 1/14/76, p18 **[1976]**

combi, *n. British, Informal.* combination. *When business is slack at weekends, the aircraft are turned into "combis"—with half the cabin carrying passengers and the other half cargo.* Times (London) 11/4/76, pVII **[1969,** by shortening]

combination drug, an antibacterial drug made up of two or more active ingredients. *First to go from the drugstores, and already decertified by the FDA [Food and Drug Administration] are many of the "combination drugs," so called because they contain two antibiotics, or an antibiotic and one of the sulfa drugs. . .* Time 7/25/69, p38 **[1969]**

combinatorics, *n.* a branch of mathematics that deals with the permutations and combinations of elements in finite sets. *Niven writes an informal, clear algebra of combinatorics for high school students and mathematical amateurs.* Scientific American 12/66, p145 **[1964]**

combine, *n.* an artistic work made up of a combination of painting, collage, and construction. *His [Merce Cunningham's] feeling that any movement can be part of a dance has its echo in the assemblages and combines of Robert Rauschenberg, among others.* New Yorker 5/4/68, p78 **[1963]**

combined immunodeficiency disease, a disease characterized by the absence of both T cells and B cells in the body. It is usually fatal and occurs among the young who die of such secondary conditions as pneumonia and sepsis. *Abbreviation:* CID *In 1972 Hilaire Meuwissen of the Albany (N.Y.) Medical Center and his*

colleagues identified three infants who had serious combined immunodeficiency disease and who also lacked a particular enzyme in their red blood cells. Science News 2/28/76, p138 **[1973]**

comb-out, *n.* a combining and arranging of the hair to form a hair style or keep it in place. *Vanessa [Redgrave] washed her own hair in midafternoon, then summoned Beverly Hills Coiffeur Carrie White for a comb-out and had her add a cascading fall for greater thickness.* Time 4/21/67, p58 **[1962]**

come, *v.* **1** *U.S. Slang.* **come down,** to happen; occur. *"We would be better off if this [slavery] hadn't come down—if we were left alone," a young man commented.* Time 3/7/77, pK2 **[1977] 2** *Especially U.S.* **come on,** to make a strong impression; have a strong effect (shortened from the phrase *come on strong*). In the phrase *come on like gangbusters,* the reference is to the name of an old radio program that came on the air with a crescendo of loud sounds. [Senator] *Muskie is not coming on like gangbusters. He is coming on the way Ohio State plays football, slowly and methodically, doing one thing at a time with just enough momentum to keep going forward.* Atlantic 6/71, p6 **[1968] 3 come out,** to become openly homosexual. *Today's homosexual can be open ("come out") or covert ("closet"), practicing or inhibited, voluntary or compulsive, conscious or unaware, active or passive, manly ("stud") or womanly ("fem") . . .* Saturday Review 2/12/72, p24 **[1972] 4** *U.S. Slang.* **where one is coming from,** what one feels or experiences. *The book is a record of what the natives are into, what they have going . . . whom they are getting it on with, where they're coming from, and what's coming down.* New Yorker 4/24/78, p157 **[1977]**

comex, *n.* acronym for *commodity exchange. Comex ordered that trading in the silver market be restricted to the liquidating of existing contracts and it also sharply raised the down payments on silver and gold futures contracts, which made it more difficult for speculators to finance their transactions.* Manchester Guardian Weekly 2/3/80, p3 **[1976]**

comint or **COMINT** ('kɑmint), *n.* the system or process of gathering intelligence by intercepting communications. *Comint organizations . . . endeavour to intercept as much enemy signal traffic as possible.* New Scientist 3/2/72, p466 **[1969,** acronym for *communications intelligence*]

comix ('kɑmiks), *n.pl.* comic strips of the underground press, characterized by disorganized and purposely offensive subjects and characters. *The advertisement continued: "The largest selection of your favourite comix along with searing pungent coverage of up-to-the-minute topics and dirty small ads."* Times (London) 1/18/73, p2 **[1972,** humorous alteration of *comics* (influenced by *mix*)]

command module, the unit or section of a spacecraft which contains the control center and living quarters. *Abbreviation:* CM *The crew of Apollo 13 returned safely to the earth on April 17, 1970. The astronauts remained in the lunar module until just before reentry into the earth's atmosphere; they then moved into the command module . . . and jettisoned the lunar module.* 1971 Britannica Yearbook of Science and the Future, p126 **[1962]**

commerciogenic, *adj.* having commercial appeal. *. . . the introduction of many new foods tailored for convenience, novelty, and economy. Such "commerciogenic" foods were criticized by some U.S. nutritionists.* Britannica Book of the Year 1975, p306 **[1974,** from *commercial* + connecting -*o*- + -*genic,* as in *photogenic, mediagenic*]

commodification, *n.* the turning of works of artistic or cultural value into commodities or articles of trade. *Guilbaut's cultural analysis . . . consists of routine attacks on the commodification and trivialization of art under capitalism.* New Republic 2/20/84, p41 **[1984,** from *commodity* + -*fication*]

common-area charge, *U.S.* money paid periodically to cover the costs of maintaining areas and services that everyone uses, as in a condominium. *Rents will be $8.50 a year per square foot, plus a common-area charge.* NY Times 5/26/76, p67 **[1976]**

Common Cause, an independent political organization, founded in the United States in 1970, devoted to reform of governmental practices that are not responsive to the needs or wishes of the people. *The post-Watergate reforms—many of them brought about by the zeal of Common Cause and other agitators for righteousness—have led to disclosure of political and moral as well as financial assets and liabilities.* New Yorker 5/8/78, p145 [**1971**] —**Common Causer:** *The sampling here . . . ranges from cynical wheeler-dealer to idealistic Common Causer.* Saturday Review 4/8/72, p49

Common Marketeer, one who favors joining the Common Market, especially in Great Britain. *Blackpool has as big and variegated a fringe this week as Edinburgh at festival time. Thirty-six meetings: . . . Friends of Israel, enemies of Israel, Common Marketeers and anti-Marketeers.* Manchester Guardian Weekly 10/3/70, p11 [**1962**]

common-site picketing or **common-situs picketing**, *U.S.* the picketing of a subcontractor at a construction site by members of a union. Also called SITUS PICKETING. *Ford said collective bargaining provisions of the bill have great merit, but "it is to the common situs picketing title that I address my objections."* Tuscaloosa News (Alabama) 1/3/76, p1 [**1976**]

communard, *n.* a member or inhabitant of a commune. *To live in a commune . . . undermines the property ethic . . . When a dozen people share the bills, they can afford to carry a couple of communards who want to take a week off, or who want to try to survive by selling newspapers, or selling marijuana, or pan-handling.* Manchester Guardian Weekly 3/27/71, p6 [**1970**]

commune, *n.* a place where anyone can stay for as long as he or she likes, living and usually sharing work or expenses with other inhabitants. *A major purpose of . . . communes—organized by such varied movements as hippies, political radicals, religious groups and humanistic psychologists—is to seek a sense of family warmth and intimacy . . .* Science News 7/25/70, p68 [**1967**]

Communicare, *n. British.* a community center which provides a wide range of social welfare services. *At Killingworth the people have been 'given' a lot—Communicare, for example. This is a complex of health, pastoral, youth and sports centres, and a good library. It is a fine idea, and well-used.* New Statesman 1/3/75, p8 [**1968**, from *community* care, probably patterned after *Medicare* (U.S.), *denticare* (Canada)]

communications gap, a failure of understanding, usually because of a lack of information, especially between different age groups, economic classes, political factions, or cultural groups. *. . . our modern Technological society is now so complex that its problems can only be managed by innumerable cadres of specialists. As a result there is a growing gulf—a widening "communications gap"—between the governors and the governed.* New Scientist 5/30/68, p445 [**1968**]

community home, *British.* a reform school. *One of the most controversial innovations of the 1969 Act was the care order under which the local authority can put children into community homes.* Times (London) 1/2/76, p9 [**1972**]

community medicine, general practice medicine for families and individuals. Also called FAMILY MEDICINE or FAMILY PRACTICE. *There were no general practitioner models in the teaching hospital, nor did the hospital exhibit any interest in what is now called community medicine (a new term for general practice).* Scientific American 9/73, p141 [**1971**]

commute, *n.* a trip to and from work by a commuter. . . . *a liberal-minded chap in a New York suburb put his house on the market and got ready to move to one where there was more room for his family and which was an easier commute.* Saturday Review 10/12/68, p16 [**1958**, noun use of *commute, v.i.*]

commuter belt, a suburban area typically inhabited by commuters. . . . *a marked contrast emerges between the industrial and rural counties on the one hand, and the middle-class commuter belt on the other.* Times (London) 4/27/66, p6 [**1963**]

commuterland or **commuterdom**, *n.* the suburbs where commuters live. . . . *at the gates to commuterland, in Grand Central Station . . .* Time 10/13/67, p38 . . . *the past sixty years have seen the growth of commuterdom, with all its attendant frustrations, health hazards, and crazy economics.* Manchester Guardian Weekly 9/5/68, p13 [**1959**]

commuter tax, an income tax levied by a city on people who commute to work there. *Let me state unequivocally that I will be proud to continue these same payments in the form of a commuter tax to insure such fine departments as the New York City Fire Department and Police Department.* NY Times 2/5/67, p44 [**1967**]

Comoran ('kɑmərən) or **Comorian** (kə'mɔri:ən), *adj.* of or relating to Comoros Islands, an island country in the Indian Ocean, independent (except for Mayotte) since 1975. *Only weeks after the mercenary takeover of the Comoros, black African statesmen . . . expelled the Comoran delegation from the annual Organization of African Unity conference in Khartoum, the Sudan.* High Times 1/79, p112 —*n.* a native or inhabitant of Comoros. *The Comorians have competed for some time with the Malagasy for jobs as dock workers, guards and municipal employees, reports from the area, which was calm, today said.* NY Times 12/24/76, pA7 [**1973**, from *Comoro* + *-an* or *-ian* (adjective and noun suffixes)]

comp, *U.S. Informal.* —*v.t.* to compensate. *The group was flown free from New York by Las Vegas Hilton, is . being comped for rooms, meals and beverages at that hotel; . . .* Esquire 3/74, p44 —*n.* compensation. *Willis's company-paid supplemental unemployment benefits ran out three weeks ago. "I've been coming down here for about five weeks," said the soft-spoken bachelor. "I'm still drawing* [state] *comp, but that doesn't make it."* Newsweek 3/3/75, p58 [**1974**, by shortening]

compact disk or **compact disc**, **1** a digital disk without grooves whose sounds are picked up by a laser. *Abbreviation:* CD *Still, many see the compact disk as a potentially enormous growth area for the languishing consumer audio-electronics industry.* NY Times 3/18/83, pD1 **2 Compact Disc,** a trademark for such a disk. *Philips invented the Compact Disc system, which produces an hour of digital sound from a grooveless 12-cm disc when a laser "reads" it.* New Scientist 11/5/81, p374 [**1978**]

compact object, any of a class of very dense astronomical bodies, including neutron stars, quasars, and X-ray bursters. *For over 50 years compact objects have fascinated scientists who have found in them arenas for the discovery of new effects through the application of physical principles under extreme conditions.* Science 1/27/84, p387 [**1984**]

compander or **compandor**, *n.* a device used for companding. *Unlike the Dolby B system now in use for tapes, or the DBX companders (compressor/expander), the Burwen filter can remove noise from existing program material.* Popular Science 7/74, p12 [**1967**, blend of *compressor* and *expander*]

companding, *n.* the process of compressing transmission signals over a communications channel and expanding them upon reception; use of a COMPANDER. *The terminal also performs important associated functions such as "companding." This function is a quasilogarithmic compression of the analogue signal before or concurrent with A/D* [analog-to-digital] *conversion and a corresponding expansion after or concurrent with D/A* [digital-to-analog] *conversion.* Scientific American 9/72, p138 [**1969**, from *compander* + *-ing* (noun suffix)]

company, *n.* **the Company,** *U.S. Slang.* the Central Intelligence Agency. *The congressional hearings came after Journalist Carl Bernstein's charges in the Oct. 20 issue of* Rolling Stone *magazine that at least 400 employees of American news organizations have worked directly for or informally aided the CIA over the past 25 years . . . Most of the relationships had ended, Bernstein added, but as of 1976 some 50 American journalists were still bound by secret agreements with "the Company."* Time 1/9/78, p12 [**1975**]

comparable worth, the concept that men and women whose jobs are comparable in skills, training, and responsibility should earn the same pay. *On April 11, the U.S. Commission on Civil*

Rights rejected the idea of comparable worth as "profoundly flawed" and said it was not a remedy for sex discrimination in the workplace . . . Women's rights groups denounced the decision. 1986 World Book Year Book, p258 [**1981**]

comparative advertising, advertising in which a competing product is named and compared unfavorably with the advertised product. *Others argued that comparative advertising made messages more pointed and informative by allowing them to stress specific product attributes instead of emphasizing such intangibles as the glamour or romance associated with the product.* 1978 Collier's Encyclopedia Year Book, p478 [**1975**] ►The British equivalent is *knocking copy* (1950's).

comparison-shop, *v.i., v.t.* to compare the prices, merchandise, or service of (competing establishments) to obtain the best value. *We comparison-shopped supermarkets in the Los Angeles, Chicago and New Jersey areas and found that most organ meats are still a bargain.* McCalls 7/73, p36 [**1966**, back formation from *comparison shopper* (1950)]

compatibility, *n.* the ability of computer software or hardware to be used with different models or systems without adaptation. *The TRS-80 Model 4, Radio Shack's latest desktop computer, offers compatibility with existing Model III software and a wide range of advanced features.* Popular Computing 11/83, p46 [**1983**]

compatible, *adj.* (of computer software or hardware) able to be used with different models or systems without adaptation. *The Systemcard is completely compatible with the IBM PC and requires no translation software.* Popular Computing 10/83, p28 [**1981**]

compiler, *n.* a computer program which translates instructions written in a computer language to the internal code (machine language) of a specific computer. *A computer cannot work directly with a program written in a high-level or assembly language. The instructions have to be translated into a machine language . . . Special programs called compilers and assemblers translate high-level and assembly languages into machine language.* 1981 World Book Year Book, p548 [**1962**]

compiler language, the coding system of a compiler. Also called ASSEMBLER LANGUAGE or ASSEMBLY LANGUAGE. *For our purposes, the compiler language can also be translated into a logical form in which the computer can think. The machine can then make deductions and, more important, inductions . . .* New Scientist 6/15/67, p657 [**1967**]

complementary, *adj.* (of a DNA or RNA molecule) having two strands that are specific for each other, so that each strand can serve as a template for synthesizing new molecules. *It is known that the genetic information within a cell . . . is coded into the sequence of molecules that make up the long strands of DNA (deoxyribonucleic acid). As necessary, the message is transcribed into complementary RNA (ribonucleic acids), which in turn translate the information into a sequence of amino acids (proteins) that carry out the instructions.* 1978 Collier's Encyclopedia Year Book, p89 [**1966**]

completist, *n.* one who sets completeness or completion as a goal (also used attributively). *The "completist attitude," which has governed several projects, fi .ds the company [Columbia Records] in the position of either having finished or nearing the end of the complete recorded works of Stravinsky, Varèse, Webern, Schönberg, and Copland . . .* Saturday Review 9/28/68, p59 [**1955**]

composite, *n.* a strong, lightweight, plasticlike material composed of two materials bonded together, one serving as a matrix surrounding the fibers or particles of the other. *Voyager was the first aircraft ever built entirely of composites.* World Book Science Annual 1988, p300 [**1987**]

comprehensivist, *n.* **1** a person who advocates general or broad knowledge and study; one who opposes specialization. *A self-described comprehensivist,* [R. Buckminster Fuller] *has been urging us for decades to realize that human societies, like biological species, court extinction when they become overspecialized.* Harper's 4/72, p58 **2** *British.* a supporter or advocate of COMPREHENSIVIZATION. *The NFER* [National Foundation for Educational Research] *report revives hopes that good education is a likely product of good comprehensive schools, especially those which enjoy long-term stability . . . Its use as ammunition by die-hard comprehensivists intent on shot-gun marriages between schools could result in rather less contented bedfellows.* New Scientist 6/15/72, p605 [**1970**]

comprehensivization or **comprehensivisation**, *n. British.* the process of making a school or schools comprehensive by providing a curriculum for students of all levels of ability. *So, 30 years on, we seem to have come back to the position we were in about secondary education, when our predecessors were concerned with creating some attempt at equality in secondary education. Now the same arguments are going to be brought forward about the comprehensivisation of higher education.* Listener 5/23/74, p661 [**1965**]

compressed speech, speech reproduced at a faster than the normal rate without loss of understandability by being fed into a machine which automatically clips out certain sound segments. *Some 48 Virginia children with Negro dialects have learned to speak better English through compressed speech. They learned considerably faster than with normal language instruction . . . Lessons were initially presented at 100 words per minute, a little less than normal speaking rate, and then increased to 50 percent faster than normal.* Science News 11/25/67, p516 [**1965**]

compu-, combining form for "computer," as in the following:
—**computalk**, *n.: Computalk . . . My article, "Talking to the Computer," (4 December, p. 498) was not intended as a learned paper describing and justifying all the techniques used in our recognition processes.* New Scientist 1/8/70, p76
—**Computicket**, *n.: Another, about to be introduced, is Computicket which will link every kind of entertainment from baseball to ballet to local outlets like supermarkets . . .* Time 5/31/68, p51 —**compuword**, *n.: Nevertheless, when questioned recently in fluent computalk at the House of Commons terminal by the leader of the Opposition, who asked about the implications of taking a strong policy against South Africa, the computer's only reply was the enigmatic compuword, "benn".* New Scientist 1/1/70, p19 [**1963**]

compulsory, *n.* a required demonstration of skills in figure skating, gymnastics, and the like. *All nine judges have placed Miss Linichuk and her partner in first place after the compulsories . . .* Times (London) 3/11/78, p15 [**1968**, noun use of the adjective]

computational linguistics, the use of computers to collect and correlate linguistic information. . . . *computational linguistics—studies in parsing, sentence generation, structure, semantics and statistics, and including experiments in translation . . .* NY Times 11/25/66, p29 [**1964**]

computeracy, *n.* another name for COMPUTER LITERACY. *Or he* [Robert K. Logan] *may be reaching his conclusion that the next great revolution in thought lies in computer literacy or "computeracy," as he prefers to call it, because the term computer literacy "conveys the erroneous conception that literacy—the use of the alphabet—and computeracy are basically the same."* NY Times 7/31/86, pC21 [**1979**, from *computer* literacy]

computer crime, a crime committed by obtaining illegal access to a computer and manipulating records stored in it with transactions that transfer funds in bank accounts or possession of other assets. *While some reported computer crimes involve the theft or embezzlement of only thousands of dollars, quite a few involve very large sums; a million dollars from a computer crime is considered a respectable but not an extraordinary score.* New Yorker 8/22/77, p38 [**1972**] —**computer criminal**: *He made another point which helps explain why the computer criminal does not bear the social stigma of other kinds of thief: "Computer crime, to those who engage in it, is not like stealing a purse from an old lady; it imparts to theft a nice, clean quality."* Times (London) 7/10/78, p12

computer dating, the arrangement of social engagements between single men and women by programming a computer to match their characteristics according to prescribed types; matchmaking by computer. *But the director, Brian De Palma,* and the producer, Charles Hirsch, who wrote this movie ["Greetings"] together . . . threw in another plot, about a computer dating service, that is very low-grade stuff. New Yorker 12/21/68, p91 [**1968**]

computer-enhanced, adj. (of a photograph) improved in distinctness, clarity or intensity by the use of a computer to control developing. Computer-enhanced photography is nothing new to astronomers, but its use has now expanded to bring out very faint features on photographic plates taken by earthbound telescopes. Encyclopedia Science Supplement (Grolier) 1979, p99 [**1976**]

computer enhancement, improvement in the quality of a photograph, especially one taken at great distance, by programming a computer to lighten lighter segments and darken darker segments of the original image. Images of 185-kilometre squares of ground recorded by the Landsat Earth resources satellite with computer enhancement have shown that up to 30 per cent more of the state of Maryland is involved in strip coal mining than had previously been recognised. New Scientist 8/26/76, p428 [**1976**]

computerese, n. **1** the terminology or jargon of scientists and others working with computers. Ziegler [White House press secretary], who worked in Haldeman's advertising agency, mixes computerese into his briefings: he talks of "inputs" and "outputs," of "implementing" a policy within a "time frame" . . . Time 6/8/70, p18 **2** another term for COMPUTER LANGUAGE. It can be programmed in English, instead of "computerese." This means it can be re-programmed by your own staff to fit your expanding operations. Advertisement in Saturday Review 1/13/68, p35 [**1960**]

computer game, any of various games that use electronic circuitry programmed to rules of play, often showing progressive steps of the game with flashing lights or a display screen. Compare VIDEO GAME. Simon, an electronic computer game . . . challenges any ability to remember its seemingly random flashes of colored lights and gives the raspberry to any player who forgets the sequence . . . Saturday Review 12/79, p40 [**1979**]

computer graphics, art or design produced on computers. The objective of most computer-graphics programs is easily stated: to represent objects of some kind and to provide a means for manipulating them. Scientific American 6/70, p65 Computer graphics: new tool of industrial designers. Encyclopedia Science Supplement (Grolier) 1970, p339 [**1969**]

computerist, n. a person trained or skilled in the use of computers. Also called COMPUTERMAN. Pick up any "documentation" (called "instructions" in the real and ordinary world), and you are apt to be immediately bombarded by gibberish, at best intimidating to the neophyte and portentous to the versed computerist. Much of the idiom could really be written in English. NY Times 11/16/82, pC6 [**1982**]

computerizable, adj. that can be programmed for analysis, control, etc., by a computer. The other main reason he [Dr. Kendall] gives for the Edwards committee appointment was that it needed someone who understood computer systems, and who could discern "the aspects of the organization which were computerizable." New Scientist 5/15/69, p368 [**1965**]

computerization, n. the use of computers; mechanization or automation by means of computers. Some people in the trade believe that computerization will eventually result in great master lists of all magazine readers and all gadget buyers. New Yorker 9/24/66, p158 ". . . In a world of increasing mass production, automation and computerization, values based on a sense of extraordinary quality are irrelevant." Saturday Night (Canada) 1/68, p41 [**1957**]

computerize, v.t. to analyze, control, or equip with computers. Demand was very heavy for integrated circuits, the "chips" that are being used to "computerize" products ranging from children's toys to machine tools. Americana Annual 1980, p255 —v.i. to change to the use of computers in commerce, industry, etc.; adopt computerization. It is vital if Britain is going to computerize that there should be a sufficient supply

of people with experience, ingenuity—and genius—to programme our computers. Times (London) 1/7/65, p14 [**1958**]

computerized axial tomography, X-ray photography in which images of an internal part of the body are combined by computer into a single cross-sectional picture. Abbreviation: CAT Computerized axial tomography consists of passing a fan-shaped beam of X-rays through a patient's body to radiation detectors on the opposite side as the patient or X-ray apparatus is rotated stepwise around a single axis. 1978 Britannica Yearbook of Science and the Future, p363 [**1976**]

computer language, any of various alphabetical and numerical systems for programming computers according to rules of grammar or logic. Also called PROGRAMMING LANGUAGE. To apply computers to everyday problems, the user needs to know . . .: 1. What he wants to do and the specific logical steps necessary to perform that job. 2. The grammar and syntax (subsequently described) of a particular computer language, so he can communicate his desires to the machine. Van Court Hare, Jr., Introduction to Programming: A BASIC Approach, 1970, p110 [**1958**]

computer literacy, the ability to understand and use computers. Also called COMPUTERACY. Before the computer revolution can really be effective in the schools, educators agree that "computer literacy" must be attained by more people. U.S. News and World Report 1/8/79, p39 [**1979**]

computer-literate, adj. capable of understanding and using computers. Just as a literate person can say, "That's a hollow argument" or "That's an unsupported assertion" or "That's a beautiful poem," so a computer-literate person should be able to say, "That computer output is useless (or worse) in this situation" or "That's an elegant model." Such literacy goes beyond "computer penmanship." Popular Computing 11/83, p11 [**1978**]

computerman, n. another term for COMPUTERIST. For the computerman or management theoretician it is tempting to design the ideal system, extracting the most from the computer, handling information in the most efficient way . . . Times (London) 9/25/70, p26 [**1965**]

computer model, a description constructed by a computer program that is designed to describe a system, project, etc., and is capable of showing the effects of variations applied to it. Mr. Michael Noble, Minister of State for Trade and Industry, said that "the age of the computer model is now with us and, from the heated debates about such models, as applied recently to the environment, it is evident that the institute is being born at an auspicious moment when there is as evident a need for a great deal of sound scientific research in the methodology and application of systems analysis." Nature 10/13/72, p361 [**1972**] —computer modeling: Computer modeling could save NASA considerable time and money in designing the new space shuttle, narrowing down design possibilities from perhaps a hundred at the outset to less than a dozen, which would require the precision of wind tunnel testing to choose between them. Science News 10/13/73, p236

computer science, the science of computers, including computer design, devising of computer languages, programming, data processing, and related specializations. D. L. Slotnick ("The Fastest Computer") is professor of computer science and director of the Center for Advanced Computation at the University of Illinois. Scientific American 2/71, p12 [**1965**]

computer scientist, a specialist in some aspect of computer science. Effective work by computer scientists and behavioural psychologists is going on, but it is not to be learned about here. New Scientist and Science Journal 5/20/71, p478 [**1968**]

computer virus, a subprogram or routine secretly inserted into a standard computer program or operating system, where it is able to copy itself and from which it may be spread to other programs and computers. Also shortened to VIRUS. See also INFECTION, VACCINE. Computer viruses, depending on their instructions, can destroy data, display an unexpected message, *make a disk unusable, or wreak some other form of havoc.* Philadelphia Inquirer 3/27/88 (page not known) **[1988]**

computery, *n.* **1** computer systems; computers collectively. *The problems for this Beckenham-based group, which has recently been adding computery and sophisticated mechanical filing systems to its staple lines of sales and book-keeping stationery and loose-leaf binders, were twofold.* Times (London) 3/16/70, p24 **2** the use, manufacture, or operation of computers. *The key element in the campaign, though, will be straightforward economy, rather than any high-flown appeal to rationalisation and computery.* Sunday Times (London) 1/14/68, p31 **[1965]**

computistical, *adj.* statistically computed; having to do with statistical computations. . . . *manuscript 54, a complicated collection of computistical texts, many of which are accompanied by diagrams.* Times Literary Supplement 11/3/72, p1348 **[1972,** from *compu-* (combining form for "computer") + sta*tistical*]

comsat, *n.* **1** a communications satellite; an artificial earth satellite that transmits or relays electronic signals from one point to another on earth. . . . *Europe is at last beginning to develop real skill in building sensible space technology—comsats, navigation satellites, weather satellites* . . . Science Journal 10/70, p5 **2** Also, **Comsat** or **COMSAT,** the Communications Satellite Corporation, a U.S. government-sponsored commercial system for launching communications satellites. *Transmissions between the United States and Europe accounted for four hours and 45 minutes of satellite time, the company, known informally as Comsat, said.* NY Times 4/2/68, p31 **[1962,** from com*munications* sat*ellite*]

Comsymp, *n. U.S.* one who sympathizes with the Communist party or its aims. *Ron Gostick makes a living telling people Trudeau is a Comsymp. You'd be amazed how many people believe him.* Maclean's 9/68, p56 **[1961,** from *Communist sympa*thizer**]**

COMUSMACV (ˌkɑməsmæk'viː), *n.* acronym for *C*ommander *U*nited *S*tates *M*ilitary *A*ssistance *C*ommand, *V*ietnam. *"There is no military solution to this problem of Vietnam," said General William C. Westmoreland to me. "The solution has to be one hundred per cent political." This was in August 1964 in Saigon. He had by then been COMUSMACV, the chief U.S. Military adviser, for about six months.* Harper's 11/70, p96 **[1970]**

concelebrant, *n.* a clergyman who celebrates the Mass jointly with another. *The office of the Most Rev. Terence J. Cooke, Roman Catholic Archbishop of New York, said yesterday that he would be the chief concelebrant at the requiem mass* . . . NY Times 6/7/68, p21 **[1965]**

conceptual art or **concept art,** a form of art in which the works are intended to reflect an idea or concept in the artist's mind during the process of creation. Also called PROCESS ART or IMPOSSIBLE ART. *Some U.S. museums also began to document the avant-garde "process" or "concept" art, which involved only ideas and their realization in a situation, or a series of events, that did not always produce objects or traditional works of art.* 1970 Compton Yearbook, p359 **[1968]**

conceptual artist, another name for CONCEPTUALIST. *As for the work of the conceptual artists—those who feel that the idea alone is what counts, and that the artist's idea, sketched or written down, need not necessarily be carried out—Geldzahler finds it provocative, but he doubts whether it will have much historical value.* New Yorker 11/6/71, p113 **[1971]**

conceptualist, *n.* an artist who creates works of conceptual art. Also called CONCEPTUAL ARTIST. *Such earthworkers, antiformers, processors, and conceptualists as* [Robert] *Morris, Carl Andre, Walter de Maria, Robert Smithson, Bruce Nauman, Richard Serra, Eva Hesse, Barry Flanagan, Keith Sonnier, Dennis Oppenheim, and Lawrence Weiner have been enjoying increasing prestige.* New Yorker 1/24/70, p62 **[1970]**

concerned, *adj.* involved in or troubled about current social or political problems. *And what of our idealistic, "concerned" youth? Do we see them demonstrating and protesting against the inhumanities perpetrated by the Viet Cong as they "liberate" Southeast Asia? No, Sir, they are much too busy* . . . *find-*

ing fault with America's defense of democracy. Time 7/13/70, p4 **[1958,** extended sense of the term meaning anxious or worried]

concert, *n.* a stage performance by a comedian or other entertainer (often used attributively). *His most famous works are hybridized: concert performances filmed piecemeal and then edited into one-man movies. Highly unusual in style and content, two have been enormously successful:* Richard Pryor Live in Concert *and* Richard Pryor Live on the Sunset Strip. 1983 Britannica Book of the Year, p88 **[1975,** extended use of *concert* meaning a performance by a musician or musicians]

Concorde (kɑŋ'kɔrd), *n.* the commercial supersonic aircraft produced jointly by Great Britain and France. *The British prototype of the new British-French Concorde made its debut at Bristol Airport this year. The jet transport is designed for commercial operation at 1,200 mph—twice the speed of sound.* 1970 Collier's Encyclopedia Year Book, p83 **[1963]**

concrete poem, a poem in the style of concrete poetry. See also CONCRETE POETRY. Compare CALLIGRAM. [Ian Hamilton] *Finlay's concrete poem is part of a wave of poetic experimentation that has been rising in Western Europe and South America recently.* NY Times Book Review 2/25/68, p4 **[1958]**

concrete poet, a writer of concrete poetry. Also called CONCRETIST. *Concrete poets hammer words, syllables and individual letters into every conceivable permutation or physical shape.* New York Times Book Review 2/25/68, p4 **[1966]**

concrete poetry, a form of avant-garde poetry in which words, letters, or fragments of words or letters are arranged in shapes and patterns to form a combined poem and drawing. Also called CONCRETISM. *Concrete poetry is all too often confused with the "Calligrammes" of Apollinaire and their modern equivalents in which lines of text are ingeniously manipulated in order to imitate natural appearances.* Sunday Times (London) 10/15/67, p32 **[1958]**

concretism, *n.* another name for CONCRETE POETRY. *Their main idea is to carry over the text of vanguardist poetic experimentation into popular songs; and their selection of lyrics ranges from Oswald de Andrade to Concretism.* Britannica Book of the Year 1969, p478 **[1968]**

concretist, *n.* another name for CONCRETE POET. *The dumbstruck poet may now make his mark as a "concretist," practicing a definition-defying new discipline derived in equal measure from pop art, typewriter doodles and the undeniable truth that a poem is, after all, just so many letters arranged on a page.* Time 4/12/68, p59 **[1966]**

condo ('kɑndou), *n. Especially U.S.* short for CONDOMINIUM (in both senses). *Semiretired attorney William Heiberger, for instance, was told that the myriad rec facilities at Century 21, his North Miami Beach condo, would cost him a mere $25 a month.* Newsweek 3/25/74, p78 *The going market value for these opulent condos is between $80,000 and $90,000.* Advertisement, Town & Country 11/72, p196 **[1970]**

condominium, *n. U.S.* **1** an apartment house in which each apartment is bought and owned individually as if it were a house. The land the building is on is usually held by a corporation. . . . *the lack of interesting events in the lives of the twenty-thousand-a-year technical and professional intelligentsia in the garden suburbs and the highrise condominiums, lies at the root of their* . . . *truculent rhetoric.* Atlantic 5/65, p97 **2** a unit in such an apartment house (also used attributively). *Come see the exciting condominium choices at Trump Plaza, where Palm Beach comes to life. Two and three bedroom condominium residences, penthouses and grand penthouses priced from $299,200 to $1,800,000.* NY Times Magazine 2/28/88, p60 **[1962,** from the legal sense (in Roman law) of joint ownership of the same property with individual right of disposal]

conference call, a conference over the telephone between a group of people linked by a central switching unit. *Tuesday a bunch of us neighbors found ourselves being notified to stand by to come in for a conference call initiated by the White House.* NY Times 11/19/70, p47 **[1970]**

confluence model, a theory which relates intellectual growth to family size and the years between the birth of children. It holds that as the number of young children increases the intellectual level of the family unit drops. *The confluence model also addresses the question of differences in intellectual test performance among different national, regional and ethnic groups.* Science News 4/17/76, p246 [**1976**]

conformational, *adj. Chemistry.* of or relating to the three-dimensional forms or conformations assumed by molecules in various states. *Six-member ring of cyclohexane, C_6H_{12}, (a solvent used in paint remover) can exist in various shapes known as conformational isomers, or conformers.* Scientific American 1/70, p59 [**1967**]

conformational analysis, the analysis of molecular shapes or conformations, especially to explain the chemical and physical properties of compounds. *Conformational analysis has revolutionized man's understanding of the structure of compounds. The properties of substances yet to be synthesized can be predicted with far more accuracy than previously.* Encyclopedia Science Supplement (Grolier) 1970, p298 [**1967**]

confrontationist, *adj.* **1** seeking, supporting, or advocating confrontation. . . . *the confrontationist politicians of our time . . . have learned the value not of committing violence but of provoking it.* Harper's 4/70, p52 **2** clashing with traditional values, methods, etc. *Dubuffet . . . leads Ragon to wonder whether the part played by confrontationist artists is at all different from that of conformists.* New Yorker 6/6/70, p56 [**1968**]

confrontation state, a country that is hostile to a neighbor or bordering country. *The* New York Times *conceded that the sale to the Saudis of sixty F-15s would "alter the balance of forces in the Middle East." The Israelis issued a statement suggesting that the Saudis might "transfer the planes to confrontation states engaged in active fighting with Israel, or employ mercenaries, probably Americans, to fly the planes."* Harper's 5/78, p19 [**1976**]

Confucian, *adj.* (in Communist China) of or associated with the traditional teachings of Confucius and therefore backward-looking; reactionary. *A new attack today in the official daily, Jenmin Jih Pao, equated unidentified "capitalist roaders" in the party with "Confucian disciples" who favored a restoration of the revisionist line.* NY Times 2/14/76, p6 [**1974**] —**Confucianist**, *n.: This year's campaign against Confucianists and rightists was only the latest in a long series of rectification efforts in Chinese Communist Party history.* 1975 Collier's Encyclopedia Year Book, p177

conglomeracy, *n.* the formation of commercial conglomerates. *In America the trend to diverse big business togetherness—otherwise known as conglomeracy—is sharply underscored by the announcement that the Weiss Noodle Company has been acquired by Iron Mountain Incorporated.* Listener 4/6/69, p53 [**1969**]

conglomerate, *n.* a huge business corporation formed by the acquisition and merger under unified control of many companies or industries operating in diverse and often entirely unrelated fields. . . . *many old-line publishers have surrendered their character to become part of a conglomerate empire.* Atlantic 6/70, p125 [**1964**]

conglomerator (kən'glɑːməˌreitər) or **conglomerateur** (kənˌglɑmərə'tœr), *n.* the organizer or head of a conglomerate. *So it comes as a pleasant surprise to find this Scots conglomerator bringing Scottish, English and European textiles to the market on a modest, not to say downright low, forward P/E* [price-earnings ratio] *of 11.6.* Sunday Times (London) 4/20/69, p27 *Conglomerateur Charles Bluhdorn figured that Evans was just the man to run Gulf & Western's new bauble, Paramount, and put him in charge.* Time 1/11/71, p31 [**1967**, from *conglomerate + -or* or *-eur* (as in *entrepreneur*)]

congressperson or **Congressperson**, *n. Especially U.S.* a member of the United States Congress. *By 8:30 she was attending a meeting of freshman congresspersons. This was an attempt*

on the part of new members to get to know, at least, each other, since there are 435 members of the House. Harper's Bazaar 4/73, p127 [**1972**, from *Congress + -*PERSON]

conk, *v.t. U.S.* (*Black English*) *Slang.* to straighten (kinky hair) by rinsing it with lye, using pomade, etc. *First in Boston, then as a teen-ager in the early 1940s, he* [Malcolm X] *donned a zoot suit and painfully "conked" his hair.* Time 2/23/70, p88 . . . *street youths with elaborately straightened or "conked" hair, like the ones Dr. King had talked to in pool halls in Birmingham.* NY Times 4/10/68, p33 [**1964**, from earlier *conk, n.,* slang word for a hair straightener, the hair-straightening process, and ultimately the head]

conkout, *n. U.S. Slang.* a breakdown. *"Good morning, sweeties! I'm Sherri, your new Penn Central conductor. If any little old things like delays, derailments, engine conkouts, or fires make you feel icky-poo, you just come and tell little ol' Sherri."* Cartoon legend, New Yorker 11/14/70, p55 [**1970**, from *conk out* to break down]

conmanship, *n.* the art or skill of a confidence man or trickster. *Whether he was selling snake oil to farmers in the Southwest (his three-page sales pitch is a masterpiece of W.C. Fieldsian conmanship) or living it up in those all-purpose ashrams known as "studios" in Greenwich Village,* [Kenneth] *Rexroth was on top of the left-wing game.* Time 2/25/66, p76 [**1966**, from *con man + -ship,* probably influenced by *-manship* (see the entry -MANSHIP)]

connection, *n.* **1** a place through which narcotics or other illegal goods are smuggled. *At least 15 other foreigners have been detained in the Soviet Union on narcotics charges in the last year, reflecting a growing concern of the Soviet authorities about the "Moscow connection," as some Westerners here have nicknamed the Moscow transit route.* NY Times 8/25/76, p10 **2** any secret or conspiratorial relationship. *Lyndon Johnson used to tell intimates that he blamed Cubans for Kennedy's death. Last week, the Castro connection was the chief topic of testimony before the House Select Committee on Assassinations.* Time 10/2/78, p22 [**1972**, probably extended from earlier sense (1930's) of "a narcotics drug dealer or supplier," and more lately reinforced by *The French Connection,* the movie version (1971) of a book (1969) by Robin Moore]

Conrail, *n. U.S.* acronym for *Consolidated Rail (Corporation),* a federally subsidized private operator of several northeastern railroads, formed in 1976. *Unlike Amtrak, Conrail is a private corporation, formed by congressional mandate from the ruins of half a dozen bankrupt carriers; but like Amtrak, Conrail is federally funded, the difference being that Amtrak's funds are grants, while Conrail's funds are, in effect, loans.* Americana Annual 1978, p504 [**1976**]

conscientization, *n.* a movement in Latin America to raise the consciousness of the uneducated and underprivileged. *Paolo Freire, a prominent Brazilian educator . . . has claimed that he could teach fifteen million illiterate Brazilians to read in six weeks if the government would allow all its teachers to use his method—a method based on what Freire calls the principle of "conscientization," or "awakening the political conscience of the deprived."* New Yorker 4/25/70, p68 *Returning to El Salvador, Father Grande decided to carry out a similar experiment in "conscientization" in the fertile valley of Aguilares, 20 miles north of the capital.* NY Times Magazine 5/6/79, p42 [**1970**, from Portuguese and Spanish]

consciousness, *n.* **raise one's consciousness**, to develop or increase one's political, social, or personal awareness, especially in behalf of a cause. *But we know what they're doing in the movie: they illustrate the various humiliations to which aging women are subject, and they spell things out—loss of self-esteem, problems of identity. They're in the movie to raise our consciousness.* New Yorker 3/6/78, p99 [**1970**]

consciousness-expanding, *adj.* another word for MIND-EXPANDING. *LSD has been called a "mind-expanding" or "consciousness-expanding" drug; its use has been advocated to increase human creative potential, since some people who have* *taken the substance report strong subjective feelings of creative drive.* Britannica Book of the Year 1968, p652 **[1962]**

consciousness-raiser, *n.* **1** a person involved in or devoted to consciousness-raising. *During the last federal election in the fall of 1972 left-nationalist consciousness-raisers succeeded in persuading only 5 per cent of voters to worry about American economic domination.* National Review 4/12/74, p428 **2** something designed or intended to raise one's consciousness. *Varda One, editor of* Everywoman, *says that words like manglish, as she calls the English language, and herstory are "reality-violators and consciousness-raisers."* Casey Miller and Kate Swift, Words and Women, 1976, p135 **[1974]**

consciousness-raising, *n.* a method, act, or instance of increasing or developing awareness of one's condition, needs, motives, etc., as a means of achieving one's full potential as a person (often used attributively). *Abbreviation:* CR *She* [a member of NOW (National Organization for Women)] *described consciousness-raising as "opening the door to the mind—questioning what is happening, why is it happening, does it have to happen that way?" . . . One young mother charged that marriage and motherhood had deprived her of her own identity. She feels consciousness-raising has been her salvation.* Herald Statesman (Yonkers, N.Y.) 6/26/72, p15 **[1972]**

conspecific, *n.* an animal or plant of the same species as another. *The honeypot is thus much more vulnerable than other ant species to the crushing jaws of its conspecifics, and when death is so likely to result from combat, slavery becomes preferable.* New Scientist 6/10/76, p580 **[1972,** noun use of the adjective (OED 1859) meaning "of the same species"]

constant-level balloon, the type of balloon used in the GHOST (Global Horizontal Sounding Technique) to collect atmospheric data. *Instead of rising vertically for a flight lasting only a few minutes, the constant-level balloon is designed to settle at a preselected altitude and to stay aloft for weeks or months, roving over the face of the earth.* 1970 Collier's Encyclopedia Year Book, p337 **[1955]**

construct, *n.* an object produced by a constructivist painter or sculptor. *There is no sense of precariousness in Camargo's geometry. The calculations are precise and cool, and, because of the seeming absence of all chance, his constructs are as reposeful as the interior of a church.* New Scientist 1/24/74, p218 **[1974]**

consumable, *n.* something that can be consumed. *"Marooned," a science-fiction film . . . in which a group of astronauts stranded in a spaceship waited for rescue while their supplies of power, oxygen, and water—which engineers call "consumables"—dwindled.* New Yorker 4/25/70, p28 **[1955,** noun use of *consumable, adj.*]

consumerism, *n.* public demand for greater safety and quality in consumer products; popular opposition to unsafe or defective goods. See also NADERISM. *The consumerism movement has . . . made customers more concerned about prices and less interested in change for the sake of change.* Time 5/18/70, p83 *"Consumerism" involves new approaches to judging and influencing corporate behavior; it presents new concepts of corporate responsibility, including protection of the safety and health of citizens and a meaningful choice for consumers in the products they buy.* Americana Annual 1971, p51 **[1968]**

consumerist, *n.* an advocate of consumerism. *Lately, not only the quantity but the quality of TV sales spiels for children have become targets of reform-minded parents' groups, consumerists and federal officials.* Time 4/19/71, p61 **[1971]**

consumerization, *n.* the act or practice of promoting or emphasizing mass consumption of goods, especially as the basis of a sound economy. *Mindful of the Western Pop artists who had played on the consumerization of U.S. life . . .* NY Times Magazine 5/8/77, p34 **[1976,** from *consumer + -ization*]

contact inhibition, the cessation of cell division when the surface of one cell comes into physical contact with the surface of another cell. *It has been suggested . . . that one of the factors in the control of cell division is "contact inhibition." Abercrombie noted that cells in tissue culture continue to divide*

until they establish contact, at which point they stop dividing . . . no one knows how contact inhibition works. Scientific American 6/69, p49 **[1966]** —**contact-inhibitable,** *adj.: The study of surface differences between cells that are contact-inhibitable and cells that are not is being hotly pursued because one key to the governance of the cell cycle may be found here.* Scientific American 1/74, p64 —**contact-inhibited,** *adj.: Probably the most widely studied phenomenon in cell culture is that of contact inhibition of division. This occurs when normal cells are grown until they form a layer a single cell thick over the surface of the culture vessel, at which point (the saturation density), cell division decreases dramatically and the cells are said to be contact-inhibited.* Nature 2/27/75, p689

contact visit, a prison visit during which a prisoner is permitted to have physical contact with visitors. *Following the ruling Spenkelink was allowed "contact" visits with his 67-year-old mother, Lois, and his fiancee, Carla Key of Jacksonville.* New York Post 5/25/79, p2 **[1976]** —**contact visiting:** *Currently, in city facilities where contact visiting is not yet in effect, inmates are separated from their visitors by Plexiglas windows and they must speak to each other by telephone. Contact visiting would allow them to speak with a table between them, and would enable them to kiss, hug or hold hands.* NY Times 9/28/76, p76

containerization, *n.* the shipping of cargo in large prepacked containers. Also called CONTAINERSHIPPING. *The pioneer in containerization was the Sea-Land Line, created by Malcolm McLean.* 1968 Collier's Encyclopedia Year Book, p485 *If the container revolution moves along the path predicted . . . the number of dockers (whose main job is to handle the general traffic due for containerisation) could be reduced by ninety percent over the next fifteen years.* Punch 7/12/67, p66 **[1958]**

containerize, *v.t.* to equip or design (a ship) to carry cargo in prepacked containers of a standard size. *Two factors are leading to present enthusiasm: the emergence of large, containerized vessels as the wave of the shipping future, and the development of propulsion reactors that are more efficient and smaller than those used in the Savannah.* Science News 3/29/69, p316 **[1958]**

containerport, *n.* a seaport with facilities to load and unload containerized cargo. *A containerport at Port Newark at a standstill as a result of strike.* NY Times 10/4/77, p26 **[1976,** from *container*ship + *port,* by analogy with *seaport*]

containership, *n.* a containerized ship. *Containerships, several of which are already in service and many more of which are on order, the study noted, have a big advantage over conventional freighters in that they spend much less time in port loading and unloading.* NY Times 2/4/68, p82 **[1958]**

containershipping, *n.* another name for CONTAINERIZATION. *Containershipping, which is the most likely area of application, has already experienced more drastic upheavals in its methods of operation than nuclear propulsion.* New Scientist and Science Journal 5/13/71, p380 **[1965]**

containment boom, a floating barrier used to encircle an oil spill and prevent its spread. Compare CYCLONET. *The high-seas containment booms, rated effective in 5-foot seas and 20-knot winds, and seaworthy in 20-foot seas and 40-knot winds, lose their effectiveness in rougher weather.* NY Times 12/30/76, p10 **[1976]**

content-addressable memory, a computer memory whose storage locations are made accessible by identifying any part of their contents (rather than by identifying the position of specific contents). *Content-addressable memories, in which partial knowledge of a stored word is sufficient to find the complete word, would be extremely useful in some applications. Electronic content-addressable memories have never been common because the cost per bit is far higher than it is for location-addressable memories.* Scientific American 9/77, p135 **[1970]**

contextualism, *n. Architecture.* the principle that a structure should fit naturally into its surroundings. *In the new spirit of contextualism, or blending in, the design successfully linked the Romanesque and aggressively modern buildings that* *flanked it with yet a third style that might be called 19th century industrial.* Americana Annual 1987, p108 [**1986**; earlier meanings apply to philosophy and literary criticism]

contextualize, *v.t.* to place in context, especially one that is appropriate. *Aretha's Greatest Hits, an album so well contextualized that it stands solidly on its own as a fabulous musical experience, marks off intervals in a celebrated recording career.* Saturday Review 1/29/72, p49 [**1972,** from *contextual + -ize*]

continentalization, *n.* **1** the process of assuming the character of a continent or mainland. *Another change obvious at a glance is what might be called continentalization. The town* [London] *is full of French, Italians, Spaniards, and you overhear strange accents on the streets—whiffs of exotic languages.* Harper's 7/67, p50 **2** *Geology.* the formation of a continuous land mass. *As the Black Sea plate was forced beneath its northwesterly neighbour the ocean gradually closed. Metamorphism and granitisation then produced a "continentalisation" of the rocks which is virtually complete in Hungary but still happening in the Black Sea basin.* New Scientist 12/24/70, p538 [**1965** for def. 1; **1970** for def. 2]

contingency management, a method of treatment used in behavior modification that controls events or other things that cause a reaction in order to reinforce desired behavior. *Briefly, contingency management procedures rest on the notion that behavior is controlled by its reinforcing consequences. There are positive and negative reinforcers, which refer to stimuli or events that an individual desires or avoids, respectively.* McGraw-Hill Yearbook of Science and Technology 1976, p52 [**1976**]

contra or **Contra,** *n.* a member of the right-wing rebel military forces that oppose the Sandinistas in Nicaragua. *Even those Hondurans who are ideologically at odds with the Sandinistas fear that action by contras from Honduran soil could result in the situation getting out of hand.* Manchester Guardian Weekly 8/7/83, p11 [**1983,** from American Spanish, short for *contrarevolucionario* counterrevolutionary]

contracept, *v.t.* to prevent the conception of. *The conventional excuse for contracepting and aborting babies is that catch-all cop-out, the "population explosion."* NY Times 10/14/70, p47 [**1965,** back formation from *contraception*]

contract, *n. Underworld Slang.* an assignment to kill someone for pay. Compare HIT², OPEN CONTRACT. *"There's one thing I haven't told you," Jones says, cupping his hands around a cigarette. "I don't know if it should be in the story . . . I've done some hits—you know, a contract. It was right after I got out of prison, and I needed some bread."* Harper's 11/74, p92 *Some policemen believe that a West End mobster named "Lucky" has put a contract out for Savard.* Maclean's 5/31/76, p24 [**1963**]

contract marriage, a marriage in which a man and woman agree to be married for a specified period. Compare OPEN MARRIAGE, SERIAL MARRIAGE. *Another alternative is the contract or renewable marriage, in which both partners agree to live with each other monogamously for a stated length of time, say four years.* Maclean's 4/19/76, p30 [**1976**]

contrarian, *n. U.S.* a person who is contrary to the ideas of others, especially a stock speculator who does not follow the popular trends in buying and selling stock. *Like all other investors, contrarians follow the obvious credo of buy low, sell high. But they avoid buying or selling at obvious times. They also avoid securities heavily favored by analysts, the ones that most investors buy, because contrarians believe that mob psychology has already made the stocks too expensive.* Time 10/17/83, p70 [**1966**]

controlled substance, *U.S.* any drug that has the capacity to modify behavior and whose possession and use is regulated by law. *Lasco had* [been] *convicted at 17 of aggravated assault, breaking and entering, and possession of controlled substances.* New York Post 10/10/79, p18 [**1972**] ►The term derives from the *Controlled Substances Act,* passed in 1970, which specified as potentially harmful or dangerous certain drugs ranging from amphetamines and barbiturates to heroin, marijuana, and LSD. It imposed a penalty for illegal possession of any controlled substance.

convenience food, canned, quick-frozen, dehydrated or other prepackaged food that is easy to prepare for eating. *The convenience food market continued to expand. To increase the flavour of these prepacked foods, processors used new flavour enhancers. The wider implications of the usefulness of convenience foods were shown in a cookery demonstration (by a blind woman) held in New York to celebrate the 1,000th copy of* The Braille Cookbook of Convenience Foods. Britannica Book of the Year 1968, p290 [**1955**]

convenience store, a small general store that is open long hours for the convenience of late shoppers. . . . *the string of armed robberies might have been brought on partly because the usual pressures of the holiday season had been intensified by hard times—tempting a few ordinarily respectable citizens to stop in at their local convenience store for more than just a carton of milk and some lunch meat.* New Yorker 4/30/79, p115 [**1965**]

conventional, *adj.* not using nuclear weapons. *Their* [the Soviets'] *large conventional forces have finally been matched by strategic weapons which are, roughly, a match for America's.* Robert G. Kaiser, Russia, 1976, p 464 [**1958**]

conventional wisdom, the generally accepted attitude or opinion; popular belief. *The conventional wisdom about starting newspapers in New York City is that it can't be done.* New Yorker 3/14/70, p28 *Sad to say, large chunks of these essays on contemporary America are conventional wisdom at its most conventional and least wise.* Manchester Guardian Weekly 10/18/69, p19 [**1961**]

convergence, *n.* a reduction of differences between Communist and non-Communist societies. See DÉTENTE. *Party ideologists . . . denounce Western scholars who suggest that convergence is underway. They try to persuade their people that, while great powers with differing social systems can live side by side in peace, the ideological battle must go on with undiminished fury.* 1976 World Book Year Book, p152 [**1970**]

converger, *n.* a person who excels in close logical reasoning. Compare DIVERGER. *By his work at Cambridge, Liam Hudson established in common coinage the terms converger and diverger to describe types of personality. The classical converger is a cool, analytical person with a "rational, unimaginative" approach to problems, . . . The diverger, on the other hand, has a grasshopper mind and sees connections between seemingly unrelated subjects.* New Scientist and Science Journal 5/13/71, p367 [**1966**]

cook-off, *n. U.S.* a competition of creativity in food preparation and cooking ability. *Given the apparent eagerness of notables to display their culinary prowess, celebrity cook-offs could become the biggest thing in fund raising since Girl Scout cookies.* Time 10/18/76, p112 [**1973,** patterned after *bake-off* (1952); compare FLY-OFF]

cook-up, *n.* something improvisational; something concocted. *These disputed pictures are different. They are cook-ups. And on top of the absurdity of ascribing them to Palmer, their pedigree leaves me in doubt.* Times (London) 8/7/76, p13 [**1971,** from the verb phrase *cook up*]

cool, *Slang.* —*n.* calm detachment; self-control or restraint. *A man was nothing in prison without his cool, for prison was the profoundest put-on of them all—it said, dig, man, you are here suffering for your crime.* Harper's 3/68, p115 . . . *he ambled down Main Street in big town and small, flaunting his difference and his cool.* Saturday Review 11/16/68, p36 Used especially in the phrases: —**blow one's cool,** to become emotional; get excited. *Twice a month, the troops got a newsletter from the boss* [Thomas Reddin, Chief of Police in Los Angeles] *with a one-paragraph message. One typical caveat: "Don't blow your cool and be the one who starts an incident."* Atlantic 3/69, p92 —**keep one's cool,** to stay calm; control oneself. *I managed to keep my cool, however, and told him I wouldn't sign an exclusive contract with anyone.* Times (London) 11/9/68, p19

—**lose one's cool,** to become emotional; get excited. *He* [Pierre Trudeau] *"lost his cool" in London during the January meeting of Commonwealth prime ministers when reporters dogged his steps in public and showed insatiable curiosity about his personal life.* Americana Annual 1970, p148 —**adj.** all right; satisfactory. *Geraldine insinuates herself while feigning a search for a glass in my kitchen: ". . . I know the kinda scene you look for. You want to have it all your way, don't you, Colonel? That's cool with me."* Harper's 8/70, p84 —**v.t. cool it, 1** to keep calm; calm down. *Several fights broke out, with some students shouting, "Cool it, cool it."* NY Times 5/10/68, p36 *But if Mr. Heath (and for that matter, Mr. Wilson) is really sincere about wanting "One Nation" then there surely is one obvious answer. Cool it.* Punch 2/23/72, p231 **2** to remain detached; not get involved. . . . *he* [John Gielgud], *like Dean Martin, only needs to play on his public image—to cool it.* New Yorker 1/27/68, p108 **[1964]**

coolie jacket or **coolie coat,** a jacket, usually quilted, resembling that formerly worn by laborers in China. *Quilted "coolie" jackets and vests, frog closings, mandarin collars, and other classic oriental touches found their way into sportswear fashions.* Americana Annual 1976, p247 **[1972]**

coop, *v.i. U.S. Slang.* to sleep during the night inside a parked police car while on patrol duty. *You recall reading about the policemen who like to sleep on duty? Well, it appears that while 'cooping,' as they call it, they tend to fall out of their prowl cars.* New Yorker 11/29/69, p50 **[1968,** verb use of earlier noun, meaning a policeman's regular shelter, derived from chicken *coop*]

co-op, *n.* short for COOPERATIVE. . . . *The basic difference between co-ops and condos is that the condominium owner actually owns a particular unit. The cooperative owner does not own the unit in which he or she lives.* Americana Annual 1981, p271 **[1959]**

coopérant (kouɔpei'rā), *Anglicized* **cooperant** (kou'ɑpərənt), *n.* a participant in the program of French assistance to underdeveloped countries. *Claustre was captured in the spring of 1974 while exploring pre-Islamic tombs with a young French* coopérant—*roughly the equivalent of a U.S. Peace Corpsman—and a West German doctor and his wife.* Time 2/14/77, p38 *There are more than 200 "cooperants" doing jobs roughly equivalent to Peace Corps jobs.* Manchester Guardian Weekly (Le Monde section) 6/6/76, p14 **[1973,** from French, literally, cooperator]

cooperative, *n.* Also used attributively. **1** an apartment house owned and operated by the tenants. Shortened to CO-OP. *Five cooperatives for newly-arrived immigrants have been established in the past two years, and a 30-unit co-operative for women is being organized in Toronto.* Maclean's 9/22/80, p55 **2** an apartment in such a building. *The cooperative apartment is owned by the tenants of the apartment complex. The tenants own a portion of the entire property, similar to the undivided interest that condominium owners have in their common areas.* Americana Annual 1981, p271 **[1955]**

cooperativity, *n.* the tendency of the first in a series of molecular bindings to promote the binding of the second (**positive cooperativity**) or to retard the binding of the second (**negative cooperativity**). *An interesting and important feature is that the iron sites can interact, so that when some of them have bound oxygen the others acquire it more readily. The mechanism is thought to involve strains transmitted through the intervening protein structure, and the resulting cooperativity serves to promote efficient oxygen uptake and release in the circulating blood.* McGraw-Hill Yearbook of Science and Technology 1977, p306 **[1972,** from *cooperative* + *-ity*]

cooperativize, *v.t.* to make or turn into cooperatives. *All the old trades have been "cooperativized"—tinkers, tailors, cobblers, blacksmiths, carpenters, etc.* NY Times 7/10/76, p3 **[1972]** —**cooperativization,** *n.: The outcome of the manysided development of the national economy in the conditions of industrialization and agricultural cooperativization, has been the continuous expansion of the country's resources.* Times (London) 12/29/72, pI

Cooper pair, a pair of electrons with equal and opposite momentum and spin, which attract each other and combine through an interaction involving the lattice of positive ions. *A Cooper pair can in a sense be regarded as a new particle, with twice the charge and mass of an electron, that can exist only in a metal. The effective diameter of a Cooper pair is called its coherence length and is on the order of a hundred-thousandth of a centimeter.* Scientific American 3/71, p77 **[1967,** named after Leon N. Cooper, born 1930, an American theoretical physicist who was one of the proponents of a theory of superconductivity which posited the formation of electron pairs under certain conditions]

co-opt, *v.i.* to make additional appointments. *The Government, it was suggested, should press on with the production of a unified service with the establishment of area health boards having an elected membership with powers to co-opt.* Times (London) 10/5/68, p5 —**v.t.** *U.S.* to take over; absorb. *Says Fred Kent, coordinator for New York's Environmental Action Coalition: "It is irresponsible for business to say that they* [Continental Oil Co., Scott Paper Co., Sun Oil Co.] *support us. They are just trying to co-opt us."* Time 5/4/70, p16 . . . *a Republican Party based in the "Heartland" (Midwest), West, and South can and should co-opt the Wallace vote.* Atlantic 10/69, p18 **[1963,** extended from the earlier meaning of "commandeer, appropriate, preempt"]

Coordinated Universal Time, another name for UNIVERSAL COORDINATED TIME. *In their article Cannon and Jensen compared the Coordinated Universal Time (UTC) time scales during 1972 of seven laboratories and concluded that "the scale of the Royal Greenwich Observatory (RGO) was running at an anomalous rate," even though they recognized that it was "the most stable clock of all."* Science 2/6/76, p489 **[1972]**

coordinates, *n.pl.* clothing matched in color, fabric, design, etc., to produce a harmonious effect in combination. *And there's striped and plain co-ordinates and Him and Her outfits for brothers and sisters, and some of the little girls' dresses and little boys' shorts are completely reversible—they're awfully practical.* Punch 3/24/65, p451 **[1955]**

cop, *v.i.* **cop out,** *U.S. Slang.* **1** to go back on a commitment; withdraw from involvement. *"A few Episcopal clergymen promised to go along, but at the last minute they copped out because of their big hangups on their families."* New Yorker 3/14/70, p118 **2** to give up a principle, a cause, etc.; to compromise. *"A man must be involved, engaged and committed." "And if he is not?" "He is a fink. He has copped out. He has opted for middle-class affluence."* Times 5/28/68, p46 **[1958,** from the earlier slang meaning "to plead guilty, especially to a lesser charge in order to avoid a trial," chiefly in the phrase *cop a plea*, from *cop* to take, seize, steal]

Cope's rule, the theory that among animals that do not fly, body size increases with evolutionary development. *The chances are, however, that this one too was a somewhat miniature version of the large individuals common a million years later. The pressures of evolution may have enhanced the statures of them all. A gradual increase in body size of this sort is a common, and repeated, feature of evolution in groups of species and is known as Cope's rule.* New Scientist 4/8/76, p72 **[1976,** named after Edward Drinker Cope, 1840-1897, an American paleontologist]

copilot, *n. U.S. Slang.* an amphetamine. *"Go Ask Alice," records the entry of 15-year-old Alice into the world of drugs . . . of taking "Dexie," marijuana, "copilots," LSD, heroin, everything.* NY Times Book Review 5/7/72, Part II, p1 **[1972,** from its popularity with truck drivers to ward off sleep]

cop-out, *n. U.S. Slang.* an act of copping out; retreat; compromise. . . . *this book is weakened by incomplete thoughts and bad connections, and by the presence of a small crowd of inviting characters left standing on the edges of the story . . . Davis comes close enough—close to Amis, anyway—to make his cop-out a real disappointment.* New Yorker 4/20/68, p189 *"That was no strategy," one of them observed bitterly, "that was a cop-out."* NY Times 3/24/68, pD1 **[1965]**

co-president, *n.* an executive who shares the position of president with another. *As for Richard Cooke, he was also co-president of the Hawaiian Electric Company and of the Hawaiian Agricultural Company.* New Yorker 3/11/72, p39 [**1965**]

coprological, *adj.* of or having to do with obscenity in literature and drama; scatological. *It [Arrabal's "Le Jardin des Délices," a play] has some offensive scenes, for example, at the end of the first act, when an indecent word is translated into coprological action.* Sunday Times (London) 1/11/70, p53 [**1967**, from Greek *kópros* filth, dung, but directly derived from earlier *coprology* (1856)]

co-prosperity, *n.* mutual or cooperative prosperity (also used attributively). *One guess from where the outside stimulus in the 1970s and 1980s might come: Japanese "protection" of Korea; "tutelage" for Indonesia; "co-prosperity" with the Philippines?* Atlantic 3/71, p80 *In some official quarters there is a mounting suspicion that Japan is a natural economic predator, committed to establishing its "co-prosperity sphere" by guile rather than force.* Times (London) 3/31/70, pII [**1963** ►This term, used in the 1930's and in World War II to describe Japan's economic policies toward occupied territories in China and the Pacific, has been associated in the West with Japanese economic expansion since World War II.

copulin ('kɑpyəlin), *n.* the sex attractant of female monkeys. *Monkeys produce a collection of simple volatile fatty acids—"pheromones"—called copulins . . . whose function is to lure the male. The female's sexual activity parallels the levels of copulins, being highest at midpoint and falling off towards the end of the menstrual cycle.* New Scientist 2/6/75, p302 [**1972**, from *copulate* + *-in* (chemical suffix)]

core city, *U.S.* another name for CENTRAL CITY. *The core cities were left to decay, and local governmental agencies were left to fight the problems with minimal funds and few dedicated officials.* Saturday Review 1/13/68, p36 [**1965**]

core melt, another term for MELTDOWN. *The likelihood of a core melt in any one reactor is only once every 20,000 years.* U.S. News & World Report 3/29/76, p55 [**1976**]

corequake, *n.* a violent structural disruption in a planet, star, etc., originating in its core. Compare CRUSTQUAKE. *Stimulated by the plausible suggestion that heavier neutron stars might possess a solid inner neutron core, M. Ruderman, J. Shaham and I have suggested that these giant speed-ups might arise as a result of corequakes which represent the sudden release of elastic energy stored in a solid neutron lattice deep in the stellar interior.* New Scientist 5/30/74, p546 [**1972**]

co-residence, *n. British.* residence at a university by members of both sexes. *While agreeing that more places should be made available for women undergraduates at Oxford, many dons fear that uncontrolled moves towards co-residence would mean that the women's colleges would be relegated to a second-class status.* Times (London) 3/15/77, p4 [**1972**]

core time, the part of a working day when most or all employees are present, especially when starting and quitting times are staggered. Compare FLEXTIME. *Core times in a typical U.S. plan might stretch from 9:30 a.m. to noon and from 1:30 to 4 p.m. Employees may arrive as early as 7 a.m. and stay as late as 6:30 p.m. The only requirement, aside from being present at core time, is that at week's end an employee's total hours meet the company requirement of, say, 40 hours.* Reader's Digest 10/78, p210 [**1972**]

co-riparian, *n.* one that has rights to the use of a river jointly with another. . . . *India's indifference to East Pakistan's rights as a co-riparian to a fair share of the waters of the Ganges at Farakka places in dire jeopardy the future of over twenty million people.* NY Times 10/24/70, p30 [**1967**]

corndog, *n. U.S.* a frankfurter dipped in hot cornbread batter, cooked, and eaten on a stick. Compare CHILIDOG. *Some junk food richly deserves that name, although it must be remembered that one man's meat is another man's corndog.* Time 7/4/77, p45 [**1977**, from *corn*bread + hot *dog*]

corner reflector, an arrangement of prismatic mirrors that is used to reflect laser light directly back towards its source. It is used in interplanetary measurements. *Another promising technique is measuring the round-trip travel time of ultrashort laser pulses beamed to earth satellites and particularly to the special mirrors, known as corner reflectors, placed on the moon by American astronauts and by unmanned Russian spacecraft.* Scientific American 6/76, p71 [**1965**, from its resemblance to the corner of a room where floor and walls meet]

cornichon (kɔrni:'ʃɔ̃), *n.* a gherkin or any other small sour pickle. *The food at the party was exceptionally good: pâté and tiny sour cornichons, two whole Scotch salmon with mustard-and-dill sauce, wheels of Brie, and other first-rate items.* New Yorker 10/24/77, p33 [**1966**, from French, ultimately from *corne* horn]

cornrow, *v.t., v.i. U.S.* to arrange hair into flat braids or pigtails. *"We all suffered through our mothers cornrowing our hair when we were little," Miss Taylor said, "and we couldn't wait to get out of it." But cornrowing is back, although beauticians don't like to talk about that because you don't need to go to a beauty parlor to do it.* New York Post 3/8/77, p15 **—n.** a hairstyle of flat braids or pigtails close to the scalp, often intricately patterned. *Cicely Tyson has worn cornrows for years, but not until blond, white Bo Derek wears them will anyone admit that they are beautiful.* Time 2/25/80, p5 [**1971**, originally southern Black English dialect; so called from the resemblance of a row of short pigtails projecting from the head to a row of cornstalks]

coronal hole, a dark portion in the corona of the sun characterized by low density of matter. *Each of the coronal holes measures more than three hundred thousand miles across, and is a good deal cooler and less dense than the corona. They are thought to be the major source of the solar wind—a stream of electrons and protons which radiates continuously from the sun.* New Yorker 9/6/76, p40 [**1975**]

coronavirus, *n.* any of a group of spherical viruses with many minute projections which suggest the solar corona. The coronavirus group includes those for the common cold, avian infectious bronchitis, and mouse hepatitis. Compare ON-CORONAVIRUS. *The human coronaviruses, however, were initially only capable of growth in organ culture, but after a period of adaptation by this means they could be grown on standard continuous cell cultures.* Nature 3/10/72, p81 [**1968**, from *corona* + *virus*]

corotate, *v.i.* to rotate with, or at the same time or rate as, another body. *The Jovian satellites, and probably the Saturnian satellites, offer obstacles to corotating plasma fields as the inner planets offer obstacles to the solar wind. Voyager will investigate the interactions of satellites with the planetary plasmas during the mission.* New Scientist 8/18/77, p401 [**1965**] **—corotation**, *n.: How far out do you go before corotation of the sun and corona changes; that is, before the corona starts to drag behind.* Science News 2/28/70, p227

corporate raider, a person or company that makes a tender offer or starts a proxy fight to forcibly gain control of a corporation. Also shortened to RAIDER. *Lunchtime at Le Cirque is more than socialites devouring tasty bits of gossip, and corporate raiders swallowing companies whole.* Vanity Fair 4/89, p202 [**1988**]

correctional facility or **correction facility**, *U.S.* a prison. *Having got permission to land, we started to come in low over the Green Haven Correctional Facility. The last thing we saw from the air was some of the inmates out in the yard, playing basketball.* New Yorker 11/13/78, p56 [**1972**]

correctional officer or **correction officer**, *U.S.* a prison guard. *The first fruit of the committee's report was the outbreak of renomenclaturing in 1970, under which guards became "correction officers," prisons metamorphosed into "correctional facilities," and other euphemisms banished other unpleasantnesses.* New Yorker 10/31/77, p95 [**1972**]

correspondent bank, *U.S.* a large bank that provides banking services to smaller banks, such as holding their deposits, clearing their checks, and acting as their agent or consultant in large transactions. *Few bankers thought Lance was wrong to seek personal loans from correspondent banks, which provided services for the banks he ran in exchange for interest-free accounts.* Time 9/19/77, p18 [**1963**] —**correspondent account:** *Correspondent accounts, which are non-interest-bearing pools of money that small banks deposit in larger banks in another city to expand services to their customers there, are described by bankers as a standard and very beneficial practice.* NY Times 9/25/77, pA30

corset, *n. British.* a restriction placed on banks in order to control the money supply by reducing profits from interest-bearing deposits. *The Government has chosen the so-called "corset," which holds back the growth of bank deposits, as its main weapon in bringing the growth of the money supply under control. The measure immediately hits back at the sharp growth in lending to consumers and the service industries revealed in banking figures published earlier last week and their contribution to the money supply.* Manchester Guardian Weekly 6/18/78, p5 [**1976**, so called from its constricting effect]

cortical braille, a system of stimulating the visual cortex to produce braille cells (a group of phosphenes forming a unit of perception) so that a blind person can perceive braille symbols without touching them. *The patient who has a high-school education is a very poor braille reader . . . consequently, he rarely uses tactile braille. He believes, and we concur, that he will become considerably faster at 'cortical braille' with practice, particularly when he can control the rate of presentation through a modified tablet now being interfaced with the computer.* Nature 1/15/76, p112 [**1976**]

corticopontine cell (ˌkɔrtəkouˈpɑnti:n), one of a group of cells in the cortex of the brain that transmits visual stimuli to the pons Varolii which connects the two hemispheres of the brain. *The technique calls for electrically stimulating the axons of corticopontine cells . . . at their far end, so that a spike is conducted along the fiber and invades the cell body.* Scientific American 11/76, p97 [**1976**, from *cortico-* cortex + *pontine* of the pons Varolii]

Cosa Nostra (ˈkousə ˈnoustrə), a name for the Mafia crime syndicate in the United States, originally used as a secret name by its members but made public by the informer Joseph Valachi in 1962. *We understand and sympathize with the sentiment of a spokesman for the recent Italian-American Unity Day rally that "what we resent emphatically is this myth that anybody whose name ends in a vowel is Mafia or Cosa Nostra."* NY Times 7/6/70, p30 [**1963**, from Italian *cosa nostra* our thing, our business]

cosmetic, *n.* something that decorates or embellishes, especially by covering up defects. *Attorney General John Mitchell's expressed preference for the term "quick entry" over the scorned catchword "no-knock" provides glaring evidence of the way in which Government currently uses words as cosmetics to delude the public and even itself.* NY Times 7/27/70, p26 *By the twentieth century artists were no longer performing a unique role: the creation of images which filled a deeply felt need of their culture, and which they alone could provide. Inevitably many people began to regard their work as "primarily decorative"—a cosmetic of society rather than food for its soul.* Harper's 7/70, p23 —**adj. 1** of the surface; superficial. *Environmental problems are cosmetic, not systemic. Unemployment and inflation, however unpleasant for those immediately involved, are technical faults and certainly nothing to justify any interference with the free price system.* Harper's 7/70, p58 **2** of or for effect in order to impress or influence others. *. . . there are cynical people who say Mr Nixon's tour [of Europe to discuss Middle Eastern problems with European political leaders] is done for its 'cosmetic value' to the Republican Party.* Listener 10/1/70, p450 [**1963**]

cosmeticize or **cosmetize,** *v.t.* to make more attractive or easier to accept. Compare SANITIZE. *He [Sir Val Duncan] promised that Rio Tinto would "cosmeticize" its opencast copper mine, and enthused on the miraculous abilities of modern earthmoving equipment.* New Scientist 11/12/70, p317 *"We have not*

Vietnamized the war; we have cosmetized it," the New York Republican [Senator Charles Goodell] *said in his opening statement. "Behind the façade of this Potemkin village, the facts of Vietnam remain as ugly as ever."* Times (London) 2/4/70, p6 [**1966**] ► In the literal sense of "to treat with cosmetics," *cosmeticize* was already used in the 1800's: *"1860 All Year Round* No. 47.493 The skins that were not hard red, were of a ghastly cosmeticised whiteness." (*OED*) The form *cosmetize* has no earlier record.

cosmo-, an old combining form meaning "universe" or "world," reborrowed from Russian *kosmo-* in the 1960's with the new meaning of "outer space," "space travel," and equivalent to English *astro-* (as used in *astronaut, astrospace,* etc.). Compounds with *cosmo-* were often taken whole from the Russian (with conventional adaptations of form and spelling), as the best-known one, *cosmonaut* (Russian *kosmonaut*); but the derivative COSMONETTE and compounds such as *cosmodog* are formed in English. The following are some examples. —**cosmodog,** *n.: After 22 days in orbit in their Cosmos 110 satellite— longer than any other living beings have spent in space— Cosmodogs Veterok and Ugolyok were brought down to a safe landing in Russian Central Asia.* Time 3/25/66, p43 —**cosmodrome,** *n.: The landing stage of the station; called Cosmodrome, continued to send back to earth temperature and radiation measurements.* Science News 9/26/70, p269 —**cosmograd,** *n.: Soviet officials . . . emphasize the importance of space stations and, with Salyut's initial success, talk of it as a cornerstone for clusters of vehicles forming "cosmograds"— space cities.* NY Times 6/13/71, p6 —**cosmonautics,** *n.: Consistently, Soviet scientists—in the tradition of Ziolkowsky, the founder of Soviet cosmonautics—have spoken of the importance of manned space-stations in Earth-orbit.* New Scientist 2/9/67, p325

cosmogenic, *adj.* originating from cosmic rays. *The possibilities that cosmogenic . . . He^3 [an isotope of helium] in dust can be used for identification, can enable inference of an influx rate, and can contribute to atmospheric He^3 were suggested by Mayne.* Science 3/1/68, p941 [**1967**]

cosmonette, *n.* a Soviet spacewoman. *Cosmonette Valentina herself was a textile worker, night school student and Young Communist functionary until she got interested in parachuting as a hobby (she made 126 jumps) and was picked for astronaut training.* Time 6/21/63, p26 [**1963**, from *cosmon*aut Soviet astronaut + *-ette* (feminine suffix)]

cost-benefit, *adj.* of or relating to cost-benefit analysis. *A power company contemplating a possible new plant or installation will reach its decision through the usual cost-benefit calculations.* Scientific American 9/71, p192 [**1964**]

cost-benefit analysis, an analysis or estimate of cost efficiency. *The prime difficulties of cost-benefit analysis manifest themselves as various aspects of the one central problem: how to place a monetary value on goods and services for which no market exists.* New Scientist 8/20/70, p374 [**1963**]

cost-cut, *v.t.* to cut the cost of (an operation, enterprise, etc.). *The reason is that the stockpile may be cost-cut right out of existence. "JPL has said in a letter to the NSF [which sponsors the U.S. Antarctic Research Program] that they can no longer afford to maintain the Antarctic Simulator after July 1."* Science News 5/4/74, p285 [**1971**, back formation from *cost-cutting,* adj.]

cost efficiency or **cost effectiveness,** the efficiency of an operation, system, etc., in terms of the ratio of its cost to the benefit anticipated from it. *. . . a university is so much plant that should be kept in full production all the year round, its staff made to earn their living, and its management governed by strict cost-efficiency considerations.* Times (London) 4/23/70, p12 *Today, when cost-effectiveness is all and image building for the general public is too expensive, the commercial giants are less lavish with their patronage and more careful of its destination.* New Scientist 5/14/70, p345 [**1964**]

cost-efficient or **cost-effective,** *adj.* efficient in terms of the ratio of cost to anticipated benefits. *Mr. Heath and the Shadow Cabinet agreed that a vast amount of public money was being* *poured into development areas without producing a cost-efficient return.* Times (London) 2/2/70, p1 *New category of cost-effective light-metal components with three to five times better strength and stiffness to weight ratio . . . New category of cost-effective high-temperature components with higher creep strength and oxidation resistance.* New Scientist 9/10/70, p517 **[1967]**

cost inflation, another name for COST-PUSH. *There are two quite different kinds of inflation: demand inflation, when, through credit expansion and tax reduction, money demand is allowed to rise much faster than productive capacity: and the cost inflation which follows.* Manchester Guardian Weekly 6/6/70, p23 **[1967]**

cost-push, *n.* Also called **cost-push inflation** or COST INFLATION. inflation in which rising costs of labor and production increase prices even when demand has not increased. Compare DE-MAND-PULL. *For instance, the Radcliffe committee declared there was no limit to the increase in the velocity with which money could be made to circulate, and therefore no significance in the quantity of it. There was the never-ending debate between cost-push and demand-pull.* Times (London) 4/11/70, p2 *In South Africa, the international ailment of cost-push inflation is claiming another victim. In spite of a high average annual growth rate of around 6 per cent during the past decade, South Africa's retail price index inflated by a modest 2 per cent a year.* Manchester Guardian Weekly 9/12/70, p6 **[1957]**

costumey, *adj. U.S.* consisting of or characterized by clothing that is overly elaborate or affected to attract attention. *I have grown weary by now with the costumey aspect of Las Vegas. Everywhere, someone is dressed in a bastard version of some ancient or modern national dress.* Harper's 11/69, p36 **[1968]**

cosupervision, *n.* another name for WORKER PARTICIPATION. *M Ambroise Roux, . . . president of the Compagnie Générale d'électricité, said that joint works committees had become an "organ of challenge much more than an organ of cooperation." Cosupervision presented grave dangers.* Times (London) 1/14/76, p18 **[1976]**

co-surveillance, *n.* another name for WORKER PARTICIPATION. *The committee's report, issued in February, proposed a whole series of reforms, including the idea of "co-surveillance" (cosupervision) by up to one-third representation of worker members, sitting with shareholder representatives on supervisory boards or boards of directors exercising supervisory functions.* Britannica Book of the Year 1976, p407 **[1976]**

cot death, *British.* another name for CRIB DEATH. *Breastfeeding could prevent cot death in very young babies, the report says. It criticizes the habit of propping up the baby unattended, in cot or pram, with a bottle of milk.* Times (London) 5/11/70, p3 **[1970]**

couchette (ku:'ʃet), *n.* a train compartment with a sleeping berth. *There is no reason why B.R., with some imaginative timetabling, should not allow us to travel in comfort between London and Switzerland between 7 p.m. and 7 a.m. with dinner, breakfast and couchette thrown in for the price of the cheapest (and most uncomfortable) flight.* Observer (London) 7/5/64, p12 **[1954,** from French, literally, small bed]

couch potato, *U.S. Informal.* a person who spends much time watching television or videotapes. Compare COCOONING. *Couch potatoes, as their name implies, are happiest when vegetating "all eyes" in front of Television.* Jack Mingo, et al., The Couch Potato Guide to Life, 1988, p10 **[1982]**

counter-, a very productive prefix in the three senses listed below. **1** opposing; in opposition. —**countereffect,** *n.: The movie ["The Confession"] plays it very close and stays with the particulars, and at first the semi-documentary look and the bureaucratic realism have a counter-effect—the film seems to be non-involving.* New Yorker 12/12/70, p172 —**countergovernment,** *n.: In order to provide some opposition to the one-party government, and also to pacify the Cambodian left, Sihanouk took the extraordinary step of setting up a "countergovernment," a kind of shadow cabinet with no real power ex-*

cept to criticize, but nevertheless an opposition of sorts. Atlantic 7/70, p36 —**counterstimulus,** *n.: The troubled and turbulent times that this great Republic has been experiencing during the Vietnam war have brought about an atmosphere of discontent, disquiet and confusion . . . As a counterstimulus, it would appear that we shall need a change in our national leadership that possesses those rare and essential qualities of dedication, humbleness and inspiration, . . .* NY Times 9/70, p46 **2** in return or retaliation; retaliatory. —**counteraccusation,** *n.: To accusations of "Traitor!" and counter-accusations of "Reactionaries!", the communists and other political groups clashed in an unprecedented shouting match.* Times (London) 4/29/70, p6 —**counterstrike,** *n.: Much of Rand's reputation rested on its studies for the Defense Department on such harsh possibilities as various kinds of nuclear threat, strikes and counterstrikes, including calculations of projected casualties.* Time 7/5/71, p10 **3** corresponding or equivalent. —**counterattractive,** *adj.: While it is true that there was virtually no counter-attractive facility to Hanover in a war-damaged Germany at the time it was built . . .* Times (London) 2/17/70, p19 —**counterlogic,** *n.:* [Friedrich] *Meckseper seems to demonstrate by creating a counter-logic, that the world is simply too complex and interesting to be perceived and classified in an inflexible, absolute way.* Manchester Guardian Weekly 10/17/70, p21

counteradvertising, *n. U.S.* advertising which refutes the claims of other advertisements. *The FTC also advocated that broadcasters allow "counteradvertising" by groups that oppose a product or a message that regular advertisers are trying to push. Under the proposal, for example, antipollution forces would be entitled to free time to rebut auto-company commercials.* Time 1/22/73, p70 **[1972]** ►Synonymous terms which have appeared in recent years have been *counterad, countercommercial, countermessage,* and *counterspot.*

countercultural, *adj.* relating to or characteristic of the counterculture. *We would create the options of communal living, of single women raising their children, and of women (not their doctors or the state) deciding whether to end an unwanted pregnancy. Some of our proposals are "countercultural," such as communal families or free medical care centers or abortions on demand.* Atlantic 5/70, p96 **[1970]**

counterculture, *n.* the special culture made up of those, chiefly of the younger generation, who have rejected the standards and values of established society. *With its narcotics and hallucinogens, its electrically amplified noise and stroboscopic lights and supersonic flights from nowhere to nowhere, modern technology helped to create a counter-culture whose very disorder serves admirably to stabilize the power system.* Lewis Mumford, The Pentagon of Power, 1970, plate legend [27] *According to Robert Glessing's recent book,* The Underground Press in America, *some 400 newspapers and magazines now serve the counter culture . . . The preferred name for this considerable activity is "alternative media."* Atlantic 11/70, p112 **[1969]**

counterculturist, *n.* a member of the counterculture or one who is sympathetic to its standards and goals. *Ideally, the counterculturist seeks to enter a world of real experiences, where plastics, computers, sonic booms and acquisitive instincts, do not scar the primeval beauty of the human soul . . .* New Scientist and Science Journal 1/21/71, p142 **[1971]**

counterdemonstrate, *v.i.* to demonstrate publicly in order to offset the effect of another public demonstration. *The desire for all and sundry to demonstrate and counterdemonstrate has made the police a permanent buffer at a time when recruiting to full strength has been disallowed . . .* Times (London) 2/17/70, p4 **[1970]**

counterdemonstrator, *n.* a person who counterdemonstrates. *Boston marchers filed past counterdemonstrators carrying signs saying "Hardhats for Soft Broads."* Time 9/7/70, p12 **[1958]**

counter drug, a drug sold without a doctor's prescription. *Then, at the age of 70, he [Sir Derrick Dunlop] retired . . . to become a director of the Sterling-Winthrop Group Limited, the wholly owned British subsidiary of an American pharmaceutical com-*

pany selling ethical and counter drugs. New Scientist 1/17/74, p151 [**1974**, short for *over-the-counter drug*]

counterdrug, *n.* a drug that creates a distaste for heroin, alcohol, or some other habit-forming substance. *Antabuse is a counter-drug that produces an aversion to alcohol.* Science 1/7/72, p32 [**1972**, from *counter-* opposing + *drug*]

counterinsurgency, *n.* military action against guerrillas or other insurgents (often used attributively). *The British effort in Malaya is a recent example of a counterinsurgency effort which required approximately ten years before the bulk of the rural population was brought completely under control of the government, the police were able to maintain order, and the armed forces were able to eliminate the guerrilla strongholds.* NY Times 6/13/71, pD35 *"If the federal government handled Negro aspiration as it handles the revolt in South Vietnam,"* [I.F.] *Stone writes at one point, "we would be sending counterinsurgency teams South to kill civil-rights agitators."* Maclean's 3/68, p80 [**1962**]

counterinsurgent, *n.* a person who engages in counterinsurgency. *They cannot invoke the Geneva Convention because as counterinsurgents trained to operate behind enemy lines or in hostile areas, they carry arms and use them in combat.* NY Times 6/2/67, p7 —*adj.* of or relating to counterinsurgency. *Vietnam was consciously made into a test of liberal international policy by the Kennedy and Johnson Administrations—of liberal "nation building," carried on behind a shield of Green Beret counter-insurgent warfare, against the Asian Communist "model" of radical national transformation.* New Yorker 7/3/71, p36 [**1964**]

counterintuitive, *adj.* running counter to intuition; not consistent with what one knows or perceives intuitively. *I find this hypothesis of counter-intuitive behaviour attractive, my own unaided intuitions having been inadequate to deal with more complex systems than I could enumerate.* Times (London) 3/9/70, p25 [**1967**]

counterphobic, *adj.* relating to or expressing a preference for something feared. *Just as with the alcohol drinker, his drug of choice contains the counterphobic anticipation of more total dissolution, here of psychic boundaries rather than inhibitions. It is not accidental that adverse reactions to marijuana sharply diminish when the effects of the drug are thoroughly familiar to potential users.* Norman E. Zinberg and John A. Robertson, Drugs and the Public, 1972, p76 [**1970**, from *counter-* opposing + *phobic*] —**counterphobically**, *adv.*: *"Please come right over," said the Playwright, in a fragment of forthright dialogue counterphobically opposed to his usual ambiguous and allusive circumlocutions.* Saturday Review 10/21/72, p54

counterproductive, *adj.* producing undesirable results. *[There are] a number of interrelated problems in Africa which it is dangerous and counter-productive to deal with in isolation.* Manchester Guardian Weekly 8/8/70, p8 [**1958**]

counterterror, *n.* opposing or retaliatory terror. *Gene Browning, a moderate black intellectual, decides that the wanton killing of a black boy by a New York cop must be met with counterterror.* Harper's 12/69, p135 [**1956**]

counterterrorism, *n.* opposing or retaliatory terrorism. *There is a fear that Communist terrorism will provoke rightist counterterrorism until such tension is built up that the rightists, in conjunction with the army, will try to topple the Government on the ground that it cannot maintain security.* NY Times 1/22/68, p14 [**1954**]

counterterrorist, *n.* a person who engages in counterterrorism. *Terrorists and counterterrorists trying to outwit each other in the calm setting of Geneva.* New Yorker 8/10/68, p15 [**1954**]

counterviolence, *n.* the use of violent methods to resist or put down violence. *The violence . . . exemplified by lynchings and other unlawful injuries, has provoked counterviolence in many quarters, and the time has come when the nation must restore good will and cooperation, regardless of race or color if we are to be a healthy nation.* NY Times 10/31/70, p29 [**1958**]

country, *n.* short for *country music* or COUNTRY-AND-WESTERN. *Austin's musicians . . . have made the city the fastest-growing country-music center in the U.S. Nashville, still the capital of country, may provide more regular work.* Time 9/9/74, p70 —*adj.* of or relating to such music. *Eleven straight years in which her records have been on the top of the country hit charts have allowed her to buy 2,300 acres in Tennessee—a spread that includes the entire town of Hurricane Mills.* Newsweek 12/4/72, p67 [**1967**]

country-and-western, *n.* U.S. a stylized form of country music, especially of the western United States, now usually played with electric guitars. *Abbreviation:* C & W or C-and-W Compare BLUEGRASS. *People say rock 'n' roll is a combination of rhythm and blues and country-and-western, but really it's just blues and country.* Time 1/12/70, p40 [**1959**]

country rock, a blend of country music, especially country-and-western, and rock music. Compare ROCKABILLY. *Synthesis was the password for popular music . . . In an appropriate conclusion to the most eclectic decade in American popular music, the year was flooded with such new combinations as jazz-rock, folk-rock, and country-rock.* Americana Annual 1970, p578 [**1969**]

courseware, *n.* instructional materials designed for or stored in computers. *Control Data Corporation, a Minneapolis company, reports it has tapped the skills of almost 2000 educators since 1973 to create nearly 7000 hours of courseware on 750 subjects from basic English to ancient Egyptian.* Publishers Weekly 3/20/81, p26 [**1978**, from *course* + soft*ware*]

covert action or **covert operation**, a secret and often illegal operation conducted by a police force or intelligence branch of government. *Veteran agency operatives often say that without covert action the C.I.A. would be nothing but a collection of sophisticated professors with mounds of intelligence, and the agency itself would be only a more specialized version of the State Department.* NY Times Magazine 9/12/76, p115 *Colby also said that this eight million dollars' worth of covert operations in Chile had been approved beforehand by the National Security Council's 40 Committee, which was assigned the responsibility for authorizing all such operations.* New Yorker 4/10/78, p45 [**1975**]

cowabunga (ˌkɑuəˈbəŋgə), *interj.* a surfer's cry when riding the crest of a wave. *Shouting . . . "Cowabunga!" they climb a 12-ft. wall of water and "take the drop" off its shoulder . . . till the wave carries them in to the hot white shore where gremmies, ho-dads and wahines watch in wonder.* Time 8/9/63, p49 [**1963**, from a made-up exclamation used on the *Howdy Doody* television show in the early 1950's]

cowboy, *v.i.* U.S. to work or live as a ranch hand. *Ten children survived, and seven of them were boys, and they all cowboyed—except one who roughnecked in the oil fields near Houston and one who took up pentecostalism and died from shock while caressing a prairie rattler at a revival meeting.* New Yorker 6/6/77, p47 [**1968**, verb use of the noun (1860's)]

coyote, *n.* Slang. a smuggler or exploiter of illegal immigrants to the United States, especially from Latin America. *Sometimes coyotes—smugglers of human beings—abandon their charges, as they did in July 1980 when 12 Salvadorans died in the Arizona desert from lack of food and water.* World Book Year Book 1986, p77 [**1977**]

CPA, abbreviation of CRITICAL PATH ANALYSIS. *CPA is a technique for showing all the connexions and interrelations in time of the activities that make up a project.* Times (London) 3/11/68, p26 [**1968**]

CPR, abbreviation of CARDIOPULMONARY RESUSCITATION, a combination of mouth-to-mouth breathing, or other ventilation techniques, and chest compression, used to provide emergency life support. *CPR consists of hard pressure on the lower breastbone 60 to 70 times a minute (to force blood out of the heart) alternating with mouth-to-mouth ventilation.* Time 11/26/73, p71 [**1973**]

CPU, abbreviation of *central processing unit* (of a computer). *The central processing unit (CPU) provides the computer with* *arithmetic, logical and control capabilities. The arithmetic unit of a CPU provides for the simplest of arithmetic operations; namely, nothing more than addition, subtraction, multiplication and division . . . Together the primary storage and the CPU are the heart of the computer.* Encyclopedia Science Supplement (Grolier) 1971, p138 **[1967]**

c quark, short for *charmed quark. Other studies of meson states, in which the b quark and the c quark are components, had been carried out at electron-positron colliders.* Lawrence W. Jones, 1979 Britannica Yearbook of Science and the Future, p378 **[1976]**

CR, abbreviation of CONSCIOUSNESS-RAISING. *But the makeup of what are popularly called "CR" groups has not changed perceptibly since those early days of the women's rights movement. Now, as then, the consciousnesses being raised are overwhelmingly white, middle class and college-educated.* NY Times 11/27/76, p17 **[1976]**

crack[1], *v.i., v.t.* in various phrases: —**crack on,** *British Slang.* to go on; carry on. *There she was cracking on about having colour TV so I said mmm, yes, isn't science wonderful . . .* Advertisement, Punch 9/11/68, p4 —**crack up,** *U.S. Slang.* to cause to laugh or to laugh uncontrollably; convulse with laughter. *And then Fred shouts: "I am the great pumpkin!" The whole room cracks up.* Harper's 7/71, p49 **[1968]**

crack[2], *n.* concentrated cocaine in a pellet form which can be smoked. Also called ROCK. *Cocaine can also be smoked in an extremely pure form called* crack. *The effect of crack is 10 times more intense than cocaine, and so crack is even more addicting—and dangerous. Even infrequent or first-time crack users can die from an accidental overdose, because cocaine constricts the blood vessels and causes the heart to beat too fast or—in some cases—to stop altogether.* World Book Science Annual 1988, p157 **[1986]**

crackback, *n. U.S. Football.* a block at knee level on a linebacker or defensive back by a pass receiver coming from the blind side of the field. *The crackback is a major cause of knee injuries. But it is also legal and effective, and as O.J. says happily, "J.D.'s got himself such a reputation for the crackback that guys are always looking for him out of the corner of their eye."* Newsweek 11/26/73, p68 **[1972,** from *crack, n.* a blow + *back* player behind the line of scrimmage]

crackhead, *n. U.S. Slang.* a person addicted to crack. *The drug is most popular in the inner city; a recent survey by the cocaine hotline indicates that most abusers are men between the ages of 20 and 35, and that more than half the nation's so-called crackheads are black.* Time 6/2/86, p16 **[1986,** from CRACK[2] + HEAD]

crack house, a place in which crack users congregate. *Unlike the youths who can often be seen selling crack and smoking in crack houses in the poorer areas of the city, experts say, affluent crack users are less public in their habits and are less likely to be noticed.* NY Times 6/8/86, p42 **[1986.** See CRACK[2].]

craftsperson, *n.* a person who is skilled at a craft or crafts. *About 100 craftspersons from all parts of the state will have booths to demonstrate their work and their wares, including glassblowing, batik and leather work.* NY Times 10/7/77, pC10 **[1974]**

crank, *v.i.* **crank up,** *U.S. Slang.* to get ready; prepare. *On the morning of March 10th [Senator Birch] Bayh instructed his staff to crank up for an all-out fight against the nomination. . .* New Yorker 12/5/70, p143 **[1967]**

crash, *v.t., v.i.* **1** *U.S. Slang.* to sleep or lodge free. See also CRASH PAD. *"When a transient arrives looking for a place to crash," says one communard, "We send him to a motel."* Time 3/30/70, p10 **[1969] 2 v.i.** (of a computer) to become inoperative because of a malfunction in the hardware or software. *Viruses . . . can modify a program's operation, causing computers to malfunction or crash.* Yonkers Herald Statesman 4/17/88, pH19 **[1977]**

crash barrier, *British.* a center guard rail of an express highway to prevent head-on collisions. *If international agreement can be achieved, he [Dr. J. P. Bull] believes, it will be possible to make direct comparisons between the hazards facing road users in one country with those in another. Controlled trials could then be held to test, for example, the optimum design of crash barriers, the control of pedestrian crossings.* New Scientist 4/18/68, p110 **[1963]**

crash pad, *U.S. Slang.* a place in which one may sleep or lodge free or without invitation. *Lately, the Berkeley police have taken to dawn busts [raids] on the communal "crash pads" which litter any big university town.* Manchester Guardian Weekly 10/31/70, p24 *One thing we discovered was that there were a series of hostels, or "crash pads," along our route, where it was even possible to get free meals.* NY Times 6/20/71, p10 **[1967]**

crashworthy, *adj.* able to withstand a crash. *But [Ralph] Nader contended that automakers should build "crashworthy" cars that would not cause bodily injury in a "second collision" after the accident itself.* Time 12/12/69, p65 **[1965]**

crater, *v.i. U.S. Slang.* to die (literally and figuratively). *"Don't let him crater on me!" "Crater" is Ben Taub slang. It means die.* Life 11/6/70, p29 *Thirty seconds later a young woman is apologizing for being tardy: her car has cratered; she's been detained by repairs.* Atlantic 1/72, p72 **[1970,** probably extended from the earlier (OEDS 1917) transitive sense "to destroy with crater-forming artillery shells"]

crawl, *n.* a list of credits, titles, announcements, etc., shown on television. *The crawl, or credit list, of the show, which usually appears (it is omitted when the show runs long) at the end of every program,. . .* New Yorker 5/6/72, p43 **[1962]**

crawling peg, *Economics.* a system by which a country's exchange rate can be frequently adjusted, to reflect current market conditions. *. . . the crawling peg . . . would allow each parity to be moved up or down by a small amount each year.* Punch 12/11/68, p852 *An esoterically named idea . . . is known as the "crawling peg." A nation's exchange rate would automatically change by small increments, upward or downward, if in actual daily trading on the foreign exchange markets it had persisted on the "floor" or "ceiling" established by the present rules for a specific period of time.* NY Times 12/1/68, pD3 **[1966]**

crawlway, *n.* a passageway with a very low ceiling. *When the rocket is ready, the transporter will lift it and its launch tower, and clank onto a special crawlway, as wide as the New Jersey Turnpike and almost 8 ft. thick (to support the 17.5-million-lb. combined weight of the transporter and its load).* Time 3/26/65, p49 **[1965]**

crazy, *n. Slang.* a crazy or eccentric person. *Then waiting down in the subway . . . and being jammed in the car with all those faces looking at you, and maybe somebody in there shouting out loud to themselves or laughing or maybe saying something to you because there are so many crazies around now.* New Yorker 2/21/70, p36 *Like the best of all goons, clowns or assorted crazies, he [Jerry Rubin] is deadly serious. "We are not protesting 'issues'; we are protesting Western civilization."* Manchester Guardian Weekly 11/7/70, p19 **[1966,** noun use of the adjective]

creamer, *n.* a powdery creaming agent similar to dried milk but made of corn syrup solids and other ingredients, used especially in coffee. . . . *"coffee, light," in the North, is coffee that is light-colored because of the great amount of cream, half-and-half, milk, nondairy creamer, or other, uh, creaming agent, it contains.* NY Times Magazine 1/27/80, p9 **[1969]**

creation science, another name for SCIENTIFIC CREATIONISM. *Rejecting an appeal by state officials of Louisiana, the Supreme Court upheld the judgment of two lower courts by declaring unconstitutional a "balanced treatment" Louisiana statute that forbids the teaching of evolution in public schools unless a doctrine called creation science is taught as being equally valid.* Scientific American 8/87, p14 **[1981]**

creative, *n. U.S.* a creative person. . . . *he [an adman named Jerry Della Femina] heads his own agency and is one of the more abrasive of the young "creatives" who have risen fast in* *a mercurial business.* Time 6/22/70, p78 *Maybe all this recent talk about creativity is pushing the creatives to the top.* NY Times 2/5/68, p53 [**1968**, noun use of the adjective]

credibility gap, a gap or discrepancy between a government leader's public statements and positions on public affairs and his actual deeds, leading to a weakening of the government's or leader's credibility. *Nevertheless, he* [Whitney M. Young, Jr.] *added, the Administration "faces a credibility gap of enormous proportions" with blacks. He noted that Nixon had "asked black Americans to judge him by his deeds and not his words; we have done that—and we have been greatly disappointed."* Time 8/3/70, p7 [**1966**]

CREEP or **Creep**, *n.* a derisive acronym for *Committee to Re-elect the President*, the campaign committee whose activities led to the Watergate scandal. *The officials in charge of CREEP apparently shared the illusions that lie at the heart of the Agency—that the politics of a country can be guided by tapping the phone of a Larry O'Brien or a Spencer Oliver, or by employing someone like Donald Segretti to write fake letters.* Harper's 1/74, p56 [**1972**]

creepy-crawly, *n. British. Used informally or as baby talk.* a crawling insect, or something likened to one. *And all this gentle safari in perfect safety—there are* no *poisonous snakes,* no *deadly creepy-crawlies,* no *tropical diseases.* Sunday Times (London) 9/7/69, p50 [**1959**] ►The adjective use of *creepy-crawly,* especially figuratively (as in *a creepy-crawly feeling*), is well-established in British English, attested since the 1890's.

cremains, *n.pl.* the ashes of a cremated corpse. *Any contact with the idea of dying takes place on a totally unrealistic level, buoyed up by semantic fiddling (the loved one passes into everlasting slumber, reposes in a casket, has his cremains hygienically dissolved, rests for all eternity in a memorial park) . . .* Punch 10/16/63, p577 [**1963**, blend of *cremated* and *remains*]

crescent of crisis, another term for ARC OF CRISIS. *One tragedy of Afghanistan is simply its geography: it lies along the eastern tier of the "crescent of crisis," which in an oil-short world has become strategically vital to both the West and the Soviet Union.* Time 1/14/80, p23 [**1980**]

Creutzfeldt-Jakob disease (ˈkrɔitsfeltˈyaːkɔp, *Anglicized* ˈkrɔitsfeltˈdʒeikəb), a degenerative disease of the human nervous system that causes mental deterioration and death. This disease is important in the study of viruses with a long incubation period (slow viruses) because of its similarity to certain other diseases caused by such viruses. *Abbreviation:* CJD Also called JAKOB-CREUTZFELDT DISEASE. *The first neuropathological studies of kuru brain in 1967 immediately suggested a close similarity between kuru and Creutzfeldt-Jakob disease (CJD) of man, first described in early 1920.* New Scientist 11/18/76, p381 [**1971**, named after Hans Gerard *Creutzfeldt* (1883-1964) and Alfons M. *Jakob* (1884-1931), who first described it]

crib, *n.* a trench lined on the sides and covered with concrete to dump atomic waste so that the radioactive contents can gradually seep into the soil through the dirt bottom. *One crib already rests on so intense a concentration of plutonium that the dump could conceivably explode and spew the toxic plutonium into the air.* Newsweek 8/20/73, p80 [**1973**]

crib crime or **crib job**, *U.S. Slang.* the mugging of an old person. Compare PUSH-IN CRIME. *. . . "crib" crimes—muggings in which old people are accosted at their own front doors and pushed into their apartments, where they not only lose their belongings but suffer physical abuse as well.* NY Times 12/14/76, p42 *The young hoods . . . plan what they call a "crib job," because it is as easy as taking money from a baby.* Time 11/29/76, p22 [**1976**]

crib death, the sudden death of an infant without any warning symptoms of known cause. *Crib deaths have been attributed to viral infections, immune reactions to certain foods, chronic oxygen deficiency, and other possible but so far unascertained causes. The technical name is* SUDDEN INFANT DEATH SYNDROME. *In the United States, Dr Marie Valdes-Dapena of the School of Medicine at Temple University, a leading authority*

on cot deaths, published two maps of the city of Philadelphia, with crib deaths marked on one, and areas due for demolition on the other—the maps were virtually identical. Science Journal 1/71, p72 [**1963**]

criminalization, *n.* the act of making criminal. *There is evidence, too, that criminalization of the distribution of drugs has caused much collateral crime with drug addicts, "to support their habits," as the President's Crime Commission puts it, "stealing millions of dollars worth of property every year and contributing to the public's fear of robbery and burglary."* Norval Morris and Gordon Hawkins, The Honest Politician's Guide to Crime Control, 1970, p9 [**1964**]

criminalize, *v.t.* to make criminal; to declare (a person or activity) to be criminal. . . . *A President's Judicial Advisory Council Policy Statement* (1964) *has characterized the activities of the* [Narcotics] *Bureau as exceeding legal rightfulness in "criminalizing" by executive fiat and administrative dictum those addicted to addicting drugs who for decades have been prevented from going to a doctor for treatment unless it was under the aegis of Lexington Jail, and thru police channels.* Atlantic 11/66, p108 [**1966**]

crinotoxin (ˌkrinəˈtɑksən), *n.* an animal poison produced by a specialized gland and released through pores of the skin. See ZOOTOXIN. *Little is known about the biological or chemical properties of most crinotoxins, although much recent research has concentrated on the structure and synthesis of certain frog and toad crinotoxins.* 1977 Britannica Yearbook of Science and the Future, p229 [**1976**, from *crin* in substance that stimulates secretion of certain glands (from Greek *krínein* to separate) + connecting *-o-* + *toxin*]

crisis center, a place established as a headquarters or other center of operations from which a disaster is monitored, emergency relief is controlled, psychological counseling is available, or other assistance is given during a time of difficulty. *Mrs. Washington describes Poe as a kind of crisis center where pregnant teen-agers can count on support from their classmates and teachers in an informal atmosphere.* Tuscaloosa News (Alabama) 1/8/73, p5 [**1972**]

crisis management, the expert handling of a crisis or emergency so as to reduce or eliminate danger, damage, or the like, especially in government, law enforcement, and industry. *The President's Commission also concluded that the N.R.C.* [Nuclear Regulatory Commission] *itself, when it was called upon to provide crisis management, performed with marked ineptitude.* New Yorker 11/12/79, p45 [**1978**] —**crisis manager:** *The Administration's crisis managers met in the Situation Room of the White House. The danger of spreading conflict was obvious.* NY Times Magazine 3/18/79, p104

crisis of capitalism, a fiscal crisis attributed, especially by Marxists, to structural flaws or weaknesses in the capitalist system. *Another worldwide crisis of capitalism is upon us. Why it has appeared and what consequences it portends for the economic system in which we live are the questions I wish to consider here. But first we should take note that it is another crisis of capitalism. From its earliest days, capitalism has always been as critically ill as it has been intensely alive.* New Yorker 8/28/78, p52 [**1976**]

critical mass, a sufficient number or amount to bring about a desired result efficiently. *A few thought more liberals would help (four percent) and a few thought more conservatives (five percent). But the critical mass (a plurality of over forty percent) grouped itself around a nonpartisan, nonideological solution: throw all the rascals out.* Esquire 9/75, p100 [**1972**, figurative use of the physics term meaning "the minimum amount of fissionable material needed to achieve a chain reaction"]

critical path, variant of CRITICAL PATH ANALYSIS. . . . *Discusses Critical Path Analysis and PERT scheduling technique by tracing a project from initial planning. Management attempts to maintain the project and target data by shifting of resources to critical areas as the critical path for the project shifts from one area of work to another.* Science News 5/17/69, p468 [**1959**]

critical path analysis, a method of planning and controlling a complex operation by using a computer to show all the connections and interrelations in time that constitute the operation. *Abbreviation:* CPA Compare NETWORK ANALYSIS. *The key element is the techniques that take advantage of the computer's ability to handle vast masses of data and to solve large numbers of equations very quickly. Among the techniques that have been applied most widely are critical path analysis (C.P.A.) and the closely related program evaluation and review technique (P.E.R.T.).* NY Times 1/9/67, p149 [**1960**]

cromolyn sodium ('krouməlin), a drug for preventing attacks of bronchial asthma. *Formula:* $C_{23}H_{14}Na_2O_{11}$ *Cromolyn Sodium . . . offers a fresh approach for asthma treatment. It is a powder-type medication administered through an aerosol inhalator directly into the lungs much the same way the previously mentioned nebulizers are used.* Joe Graedon, The People's Pharmacy, 1976, p180 [**1973**, from the chemical name (*disodium*) *cromo-glyc*ate + *-in* (chemical suffix)]

crossbusing, *n.* U.S. another name for BUSING. *Charlotte supports the forty-third largest school system in the United States, and is the first of such size to implement extensive crossbusing.* Atlantic 11/72, p18 [**1964**]

cross-dress, *v.i.* to dress in the clothing of the opposite sex. *Classes 1, 2, and 3 include transvestites, ranging from those who occasionally wear the clothes of the other sex in private to those who are only comfortable when "cross-dressing" in public.* Harper's 5/78, p51 [**1978**] —**cross-dresser**, *n.: By the end of the Victorian era, despite all the contrary evidence, female cross-dressers were dismissed as inconvenient myth.* Manchester Guardian Weekly 3/12/89, p29 —**cross-dressing**, *n.: . . . a scholarly analysis of women's cross-dressing from the 1700s to World War I.* Manchester Guardian Weekly 3/12/89, p29

cross-frontier, *adj.* occurring between two or more unrelated businesses, professions, or other interests and activities not generally associated with one another. *British companies have shown most interest in the activities of the European Community's "Marriage Bureau," set up two and a half years ago to foster cross-frontier cooperation between medium and small companies.* Times (London) 1/10/76, p17 [**1970**]

cross-holdings, *n.pl.* British. reciprocal holdings of shares by two or more companies. *Through a series of cross-holdings, Dunlop has, broadly speaking, a 49 per cent interest in Pirelli operations in Italy and other countries in the EEC, and 40 per cent elsewhere, while Pirelli has similar interests in Dunlop's operations.* Times (London) 12/15/72, pXII [**1966**]

cross-modal, *adj.* of or relating to the association of two different modes of perception in animals. *. . . apes can match objects by touch to photographs of identical objects. To do this the brain must compare information from two senses, an operation called cross-modal integration. For instance, learning to read requires the association of sounds with written words, and the association of written words with their meanings.* Science News 10/23/71, p281 [**1971**]

crossover, *n.* **1** (of music) the act or process of crossing over in style or appeal. *The ability of a few artists to effect a "reverse crossover"—moving from white audiences to black audiences—was reflected in the energetic and soulful singing of Leo Sayer. His singles, such as "How Much Love," enjoyed popularity on both black- and white-oriented radio stations.* 1978 World Book Year Book, p413 **2** music which crosses over in style or appeal (often used attributively). Compare FUSION. *The latest trend is crossovers—songs that make the country charts while also getting on the pop or the middle-of-the-road listings. In fact, a song stands a poor chance of reaching the top spot on one chart without at least appearing on another.* Tuscaloosa News (Alabama) 6/11/75, p8 [**1972**, from CROSS OVER]

cross over, **1** to shift from one style of music to another, as from jazz to rock. *Billy Cobham, the drummer, and George Duke, the pianist, are two jazz musicians who have "crossed over," as the saying goes, about as far as one can cross.* NY Times 6/28/76, p23 **2** (of music) to transcend limits of style or appeal. *Fusion enjoys a crucial advantage over mainstream and avant-garde jazz: it "crosses over" a wide range of radio formats, a key*

element to selling any music today. Rolling Stone 1/11/79, p43 [**1972**]

cross-ownership, *n.* U.S. ownership by a company of one or more newspapers and radio or television stations. *Today, 104 TV outlets are owned by newspaper publishers, many in the papers' hometowns. This practice, known as "cross-ownership," has been criticized by some liberals and conservatives alike, and last week the Justice Department took steps to deprive three major publishers of their hometown interests.* Newsweek 1/14/74, p43 [**1973**]

crossply tire, a tire built up from plies laid across one another. *The new Terylene tyre cord is strong, durable and has a high stretch resistance. It is more resilient to impact than rayon and does not develop flat spots like nylon. Both crossply and radial-ply tyres can be made from Terylene.* New Scientist 3/19/70, p559 [**1965**]

cross-reactive, *adj.* likely to undergo an immunological cross-reaction. *This phenomenon is also referred to as cross-reactivity between various HL-A antigens . . . if this nonreactive cell suspension has an HL-A antigen which is cross-reactive with the stimulating antigen, it may absorb out all antibody activity from the antiserum, which becomes nonreactive even against cells from the stimulating donor.* McGraw-Hill Yearbook of Science and Technology 1972, p399 [**1972**, from earlier (1959) *cross-reaction* (reaction between an antibody and nonspecific antigen)] —**cross-reactivity**, *n.: Quantitative assay of immunological cross-reactivity between antigens on foetal and tumour cells is particularly important as it was demonstrated recently that the common antigen of foetal and tumour cells is distinct from the tumour-specific transplantation antigen, at least in chemically induced rat tumours.* Nature 11/3/72, p41

cross-subsidize, *v.i., v.t.* to support an unprofitable operation out of the profits of another operation. *Another source of waste may have been the practice of cross-subsidizing, by which the federal government in effect forces transportation companies to pay for losing tracks, bus routes, and air routes by charging rates for the more frequently used lines that are higher than they would be if they were determined independently.* 1976 Collier's Encyclopedia Year Book, p549 [**1972**] —**cross-subsidization**, *n.: Cross-subsidization occurs when some users of a facility are charged less than the costs of providing for them, and the resulting losses are financed by other users, who pay more than their costs.* Times (London) 4/14/76, p24

cross-trading, *n.* the business of a shipping line in which it conveys cargo between foreign ports. *Cross-trading, as it is called, still represents probably about 40 per cent of the total earnings of British liner shipping after more than a decade of growing nationalism on world trade routes in which developing countries have demanded substantial new carrying rights in many trades.* Times (London) 1/16/76, p19 [**1976**]

Crow Jim, *U.S. Slang.* prejudice against whites by blacks. *. . . blacks bullied whites, the smell of Crow Jim was in the air; one set of values had collapsed, as yet not replaced by anything else.* Harper's 1/71, p36 [**1964**, reversed from *Jim Crow* prejudice against blacks]

crown ether, *Chemistry.* a combination of ethers shaped like crowns, with a ring made of carbon atoms and indentations made of oxygen atoms. *Many-atom ring systems (crown ethers and cryptates) containing oxygen, nitrogen, or sulfur were shown to have high affinity for inorganic cations, and an anion-complexing cryptate also was reported.* Britannica Book of the Year 1978, p245 [**1973**, from the crownlike shape of the arrangement]

CRP, abbreviation of *Committee to Reelect the President. Mitchell's admission that he had known about some of the dirty work going on in the C.R.P. while he was its director and his claim that he had kept the President in the dark about it to insure his reëlection implied that this demonstrated the President's innocence of any malfeasance.* New Yorker 8/13/73, p21 [**1973**]

cru or **c.r.u.** (kru:), *n.* acronym for *collective reserve unit,* the name of an international currency or monetary unit for use along with other currencies in the reserves of the world's central banks. *France even came up with one version of a plan to establish the "cru". . . to be issued in proportion to each country's supply of gold, only to turn away from it again.* Time 3/29/68, p55 **[1965]**

cruise, *v.i., v.t. U.S. Slang.* to go about (from place to place) in search of a sexual partner. *The film's psychosexual turmoil is heightened still further by the director's linkage of these two milieus: gays cruise in cop costumes, and off-duty cops cruise in S-M drag.* Time 2/18/80, p67 **[1972]**

cruise control, a computer-controlled mechanism that regulates the speed of an automobile after it is set by the driver. *Fears about its [an automobile's] thirst (20-25 mpg) were easily assuaged by the advantages of air-conditioned comfort in an automatic with the ultimate luxury—a "cruise control" button. Pressing it caused the car to maintain a constant speed, even up and down hills, without even a foot on the accelerator.* Sunday Times (London) 4/12/81, p21 **[1974]**

cruise missile, a guided missile directed by a computerized navigational system. *Unlike a ballistic missile, which is powered and hence usually guided for only a brief initial part of its flight, after which it follows a free-fall trajectory governed only by the local gravitational field, a cruise missile requires continuous guidance, since both the velocity and the direction of its flight can be unpredictably altered by local weather conditions or changes in the performance of the propulsion system.* Scientific American 2/77, p20 **[1968]**

cruiseway, *n. British.* a stream or canal that has been improved to accommodate pleasure boating. *It is not only uneconomic to enlarge the cruiseways, it is undesirable. Their chief attractions—human scale, as an open museum of industrial archaeology with historic canalside buildings and canal "plant," the segregated pedestrian towpath system, the fact they are hedged in by buildings to form a strange secret world in the towns and pass through unspoilt remote countryside—are precisely the factors that make them so expensive to enlarge.* New Scientist 7/19/73, p163 **[1967]**

crunch, *n.* Usually, **the crunch. 1** financial pressure; economic squeeze. *Both Drs. Hilst and Blair cautiously conceded that existing systems in Western Europe and Japan may be ahead of those in the United States—because, Dr. Hilst says, the crunch on resources came sooner in these more thickly populated areas.* Science News 10/10/70, p301 **2** the decisive or critical moment; turning point or crisis. *Similarly, take its assurance on the palmy days of early 1957 of intention to maintain "free and innocent passage" for shipping through the Strait of Tiran, only to do nothing when the crunch came 10 years later.* Times (London) 6/8/67, p11 **[1957]**

crush barrier, *British.* a steel barrier for restraining crowds. *Crush barriers were overturned and town councillors waiting to be presented were swept aside as they [15,000 people in Fiji] fought their way to meet the Queen.* Times (London) 3/5/70, p6 **[1963]**

crustquake, *n.* a violent structural disruption in a planet, star, etc., originating in its crust rather than its core. Compare CORE-QUAKE. *Two especially large speed-ups, corresponding to a relative frequency jump of a few parts in a million, separated by a period of 29 months, have been observed for the Vela pulsar. Both the magnitude and frequency of these speedups pose a severe problem for crustquake theory; interpreted as crustquakes, the fractional change in the oblateness of the star in a 'quake' of this magnitude would be almost 10 per cent.* New Scientist 5/30/74, p546 **[1972]**

cruzado (kru:ˈzeidou *or* kru:ˈza:dou), *n.* the monetary unit of Brazil, equal to 100 centavos. It replaced the cruzeiro in 1986. *Under Sarney's plan, the cruzeiro was replaced by a new currency, the cruzado, at the rate of 1,000 old cruzeiros for one cruzado, with the cruzado initially set at 13.8 to the U.S. dollar.* 1987 Collier's Encyclopedia Year Book, p163 **[1986]**

cryobank (ˈkraiouˌbæŋk), *n.* a place for storage of sperm at extremely low temperature. *There are approximately 20,000 to 30,000 artificial inseminations in the United States each year, of which between 2,000 and 4,000 result in pregnancy, according to Dr. Cappy Rothman, head of the Southern California Cryobank, a sperm bank.* Washington Post 8/3/82, pA3 **—v.t.** to preserve in a cryobank. *Since the birth, in 1954, of the first baby produced by insemination with sperm that had been frozen and thawed, the methodology for cryobanking human semen has undergone continuous refinement.* Patient Care 5/30/83, p18 **[1980,** from *cryo-* freezing (from Greek *krýos* icy cold) + *bank]*

cryobiology, *n.* the study of the effects of freezing and low temperatures on living things. *Robert Nelson, president of the [Cryonics] society, said it was a "nonprofit society formed to educate the public in the field of cryobiology, which encompasses freezing techniques on all biological matter."* NY Times 1/20/67, p44 **[1960]**

cryocable, *n.* an underground electric cable supercooled to increase its conductive quality. *By economising on materials, GE hopes to bring cryocables within commercial practicability. It envisages an underground cryocable system capable of carrying 3500 MVA or more, with three cables to a 20 in. diameter steel pipe.* New Scientist 6/15/72, p623 **[1972]**

cryoelectronics, *n.* a branch of electronics dealing with the effects of supercooling in transmitting electric power. *Concise treatment of the whole range of cryoelectronics which includes low temperature effects of conductors, insulators and semiconductors, superconduction in machines, magnets and cables, microwave effects, cryotrons and memories.* Science News 9/8/73, p146 **[1973]**

cryonic, *adj.* of or relating to cryonics. *When brothers Terry and Dennis Harris last saw their mother 10 years ago, she was . . . reclining on a cloudy bed of liquid nitrogen in "cryonic suspension"—a bizarre process once ballihooed as "man's first serious bid for immortality."* Maclean's 5/12/80, p31 **[1980]**

cryonics, *n.* the preservation of bodies from decay by a freezing process. *The widespread application of cryonics might result in a sudden loss of population in an unpleasant year, to be followed by overpopulation when times improved. There is the question of how the thawed person would adjust to a strange society. One can also imagine staggering legal headaches.* 1969 Britannica Yearbook of Science and the Future, p408 **[1967,** from *cryo-* freezing (from Greek *krýos* icy cold) + *-nics,* as in *bionics]*

cryoprecipitate, *n.* a substance obtained by cryoprecipitation, now referring specifically to a concentrate of blood-clotting protein. *In its frozen state, this cryoprecipitate kept indefinitely and could be quickly processed for intravenous infusion in a solution averaging ten to 20 times the potency of plasma.* Time 8/16/68, p36 **[1968]**

cryoprecipitation, *n.* chemical precipitation achieved by freezing, now used especially for a method of concentrating the blood-clotting protein needed in large amounts to treat hemophiliacs. *Cryoprecipitation, so-called because it is effected at low temperature, enables the antihemophilic factor from a pint of blood to be concentrated in a volume of only 10 ml.* [milliliters]. Britannica Book of the Year 1969, p498 **[1968]**

cryopreservation, *n.* the preservation of living tissues by supercooling. *Currently, doctors at Downstate Medical Center in Brooklyn, N.Y., are perfecting a technique of preserving corneas in human-tissue culture, thereby circumventing the potential hazards of cryo-preservation.* Newsweek 8/27/73, p62 **[1972]**

cryoprobe, *n.* an instrument for freezing tissues, usually with liquid nitrogen, in order to destroy, remove, or operate on them. *The central gas-cooled cryoprobe has a cap for treating wide, shallow areas, such as malignant skin lesions.* World Book Science Annual 1969, p96 **[1966]**

cryoprotectant, *adj., n.* variant of CRYOPROTECTIVE. *Offerijns has actually frozen them ["pacemaker" cells of the heart], using a cryoprotectant agent called dimethyl sulfoxide*

(*DMSO*), *and revived 80 percent of them successfully.* Science News 8/19/72, p125 [**1972**]

cryoprotective, *adj.* providing protection against supercooling. *They found that embryos exposed to dimethylsulphoxide, a cryoprotective (antifreeze) agent and cooled at 0.3 to 2.0 degrees C. per minute gave the best chances of survival.* Science News 6/30/73, p419 —*n.* a cryoprotective agent. *Of particular importance is the influence of cryoprotectives on the degree of concentration of salts, especially sodium chloride and potassium chloride, in the remaining liquid phase during initial freezing.* McGraw-Hill Yearbook of Science and Technology 1975, p151 [**1971**]

cryoresistive, *adj.* supercooled to reduce resistance. *Transmission cables insulated with compressed gas, cables cooled to the temperatures of liquid nitrogen (called cryoresistive transmission lines), and cables cooled even more so that they become superconducting are all being developed as options to the conventional underground power lines.* Science 12/1/72, p968 [**1970**]

cryosurgeon, *n.* a surgeon who specializes in cryosurgery. *Cryosurgeons use cold to kill the cells of a malignant rectal tumor. The frozen cells decay in 7 to 10 days.* World Book Science Annual 1969, p96 [**1969**]

cryosurgery, *n.* surgery in which freezing temperatures are used to destroy or remove tissues. *He [Dr. John Milton McLean] was a leader in clinical research on the use of hormone ACTH [adrenocorticotropin] to treat inflammations of the eye and in the basic work on the new cryosurgery (freezing-surgery) of the eye, especially in retinal detachment.* NY Times 5/3/68, p47 [**1962**]

cryosurgical, *adj.* of or relating to cryosurgery. *The significance of the introduction of this cryosurgical equipment was that cold could be safely and accurately applied to any part of the body to which the tip of the probe could be introduced, and the tissue surrounding the probe could be independently frozen and destroyed.* Britannica Book of the Year 1970, p517 [**1965**]

cryptand, *n. Chemistry.* any of a group of compounds having a basketlike structure with a central cavity into which an atom of a metal may easily fit. *The complexes that are formed when crown ether or cryptand molecules . . . enclose positively charged alkali ions are the structural basis of alkalides (and of electrides).* Scientific American 9/87, p68 [**1978**, from *crypt* + lig*and* ion or molecule that establishes bonds (OEDS 1952)]

cryptate, *n. Chemistry.* a compound in which atoms with unbonded electrons cluster around a metal ion in a symmetrical arrangement. *A novel type of complex has recently been prepared, in which the metal ion is quite literally surrounded by its coordinating groups: it is, in effect, trapped within a tiny organic cage. Called* cryptates, *these complex ions were first made by J.M. Lehn, J.P. Sauvage and B. Dietrich of the Institut de Chemie, Strasbourg.* New Scientist 7/16/70, p121 [**1970**, from *crypt*- hidden, latent (from Greek *kryptós*) + -*ate* (chemical suffix)]

crypto-, combining form formerly used chiefly in scientific and technical compounds with the meaning "hidden," "secret," but gradually extended to more general applications, especially in the sense of "veiled," "disguised," "not open and aboveboard." A sampling of recently formed compounds with *crypto-* includes the following: —**crypto-censorship**, *n.: What is needed is not some form of crypto-censorship by external bodies but self-censorship, or self-inspection made by a body which is largely, but not wholly, composed of representatives from the several branches of television itself.* Times (London) 3/5/70, p10 —**crypto-colonial**, *adj.: Calling the house "weirdo," the neighbors sued on the ground that Eustice's dream was "inharmonious" with their own ranch-style and crypto-colonial homes.* Time 9/26/69, p56 —**crypto-commercialism**, *n.: Let us have honesty, straight dealing, clean breasts, an end to subterfuge and shamateurism and crypto-commercialism.* Punch 2/21/68, p271

cryptobiote, *n.* an organism that survives in a state of metabolic inactivity. *Cryptobiotes could be revived after exposure to a*

temperature close to absolute zero; at this temperature metabolic processes, if they proceed at all, must be extremely slow and the destructive effects of oxygen must be minimal. Scientific American 12/71, p33 [**1971**, back formation from CRYPTOBIOTIC]

cryptobiotic, *adj.* surviving in a state of metabolic inactivity. *It is not known just how long a cryptobiotic organism can persist in a state of suspended animation. Some nematodes have been revived after being kept in the dried condition for 39 years.* Scientific American 12/71, p31 [**1965**, from *crypto-* hidden, latent (from Greek *kryptós*) + *biotic*]

cryptoexplosion structure, a crater or similar geologic feature formed by a sudden explosion, as that caused by the impact of very large meteorites, and characterized by a circular depression, uplifted bedrock in the center, shatter cones, and often rock deformations unrelated to volcanic activity. *Both Mars and the moon are dotted with surface craters, mostly created by impact. Some scientists believe the terrestrial craters that most closely resemble lunar and Martian craters are a class called cryptoexplosion structures.* Science News 4/1/72, p218 [**1967**, from *crypto-* hidden + *explosion;* so called because of the lack of precise evidence for the cause of the explosion]

cryptosystem, *n.* a system for using or deciphering a secret code; a cryptographic system. *The major powers . . . use machines to generate ciphers so strong that, even given a cryptogram and its plaintext, and all the world's computers of this and the next generation, a cryptanalyst would need centuries to reconstruct the cryptosystem and use the reconstruction to read the next message.* NY Times Magazine 5/16/76, p67 [**1968**, from *crypto*graphic + *system*]

cryptozoology, *n.* the study of and search for legendary animals. *Cryptozoology, according to Dr. George Zug—Chairman of the Department of Vertebrate Zoology at the Smithsonian's Museum of Natural History, who examined the photographs of the Loch Ness monster taken in 1975—is the study of mysterious animals of unexpected occurrence in time and space.* Smithsonian 6/83, p92 [**1983**]

CS, a symbol for a tear gas widely used in military and riot-control operations. Compare BZ, GB, VX. *The principal short-term incapacitant now in military use is CS (orthochlorobenzalmalonitrile). . . . named after its American discoverers, Ben Carson and Roger Staughton of Middlebury College.* Scientific American 5/70, p21 *CS is a lachrymator, a respiratory irritant, a sternutator, a vesicant and a lung irritant.* New Scientist 6/18/70, p579 [**1960**]

CSM, abbreviation of *corn, soya, milk,* used as the name of a powdered blend of corn meal, soybean flour, and dry milk marketed as a food supplement. *Although the U.S. Department of Agriculture has made a food made of corn, soybeans and milk, called CSM, it is a gruel, really a baby food, Prof. Brownell says.* Science News 5/11/68, p454 [**1966**]

CT, abbreviation of CELL THERAPY. *This book . . . is an exhaustive examination (with case histories) of the doctors of all stripes who deal in youth-giving formulas and operations—cell therapy (CT), facelifting . . .* Harper's 1/69, p106 [**1969**]

CTOL ('si:ˌtɑl), *n.* acronym for *conventional takeoff and landing. Also, there are the greatly improved noise pollution characteristics of VTOL compared not only with conventional aircraft (CTOL) but with short takeoff and landing craft (STOL) as illustrated in the accompanying comparison of noise 'footprints'. . .* Science Journal 3/70, p5 [**1970**]

CT scan, variant of CAT SCAN. *Sawada and his colleagues performed CT scans on the brains of 21 acute carbon monoxide poisoning patients. The scans revealed abnormalities in 11 of the patients; the outcome for all but one of them was poor.* Science News 5/17/80, p314 [**1977**]

CT scanner, variant of CAT SCANNER. *The CT scanner . . . produces television-like pictures of the inside of the body and can detect a minute cancerous growth.* Maclean's 5/14/79, p42 [**1976**, *CT*, abbreviation of *computerized tomography*]

CT scanning, variant of CAT SCANNING. *CT scanning—the X-ray technique pioneered by EMI for photographing "slices" of the body—has swept the US medical scene so rapidly that there has been no time for a proper evaluation, according to the report.* New Scientist 5/19/77, p380 **[1976]**

CTT, *British.* abbreviation of CAPITAL TRANSFER TAX. *Those who choose life in the Channel Islands or the Isle of Man as the answer to our tax evils will find this does not work at all for CTT, because they are deemed to have a United Kingdom domicile for all time.* Times (London) 1/29/77, p18 **[1977]**

C-type virus, a virus containing RNA (ribonucleic acid) that causes leukemia in animals and is thought also to cause cancer in humans. Also called TYPE C VIRUS. *Biologists have . . . known for years, in fact, that some viruses—and especially a few that cause cancer in birds and mammals—carry no DNA of their own. They carry no doublestranded genetic codebook of their own at all. Instead, these viruses, known as the C-type viruses, merely carry a simple singlestrand bit of RNA that contains all of their own virus-building instructions.* Robert Cooke, Improving on Nature, 1977, p61 **[1970,** probably from Cancer-*type*]

Cubanologist, *n.* an expert on Cuba and Cuban politics. *But like other Cubanologists, who sit in Florida and observe Havana via the microfilms in a university library, Dr. Suarez does not assess Castro's achievements by reference to the past.* Manchester Guardian Weekly 12/21/67, p11 **[1967]**

Cuban sandwich, *U.S.* See the quotations for the meaning. *What Tampa calls "Cuban sandwiches" are made of Cuban bread, sliced open and filled overpoweringly with ham, pork, sausage, cheese and dill pickles.* NY Times Magazine 10/17/76, p82 *That familiar long sandwich crammed with a meal's worth of edibles—what is it called? In New York it is a hero sandwich; in the South, it is known, unheroically, as a poor boy. Pennsylvanians call it a hoagie, New Englanders a grinder and Floridians a Cuban sandwich.* Time 12/4/78, p81 **[1976]**

cube, *n.* short for FLASHCUBE. *Flashbulbs were being partly replaced by flashcubes which were basically four bulbs in expendable reflectors, the cube turning after each shot.* Britannica Book of the Year 1970, p615 **[1969]**

cuchifrito (ˌkuːtʃiːˈfriːtou), *n.* a cube of pork dipped in batter and deep-fat fried. *One night over cold cuchifritos and a hot pinball machine, Willie had a vision of the triumph of love over induction.* Harper's 10/68, p50 **[1964,** from American Spanish, from *cuchi* hog + Spanish *frito* fried]

cued speech, a method of communication for the deaf which combines lip reading with manual signs by associating particular sounds with certain hand positions. *The Gallaudet schools also are experimenting with a method known as "cued speech," developed in 1966 by R. Orin Cornett, vice-president of Gallaudet College. Cues consist of 12 hand signals that, when used with lip reading, allow a deaf person to see clearly any word that is spoken.* 1975 World Book Year Book, p162 **[1973]**

cuisine minceur (kwiˌziːn minˈsər, *French* kwiˌziːn mæˈsœr), an earlier name for NOUVELLE CUISINE. *Les Prés is run by Michel Guérard, high priest of the cuisine minceur, the technique of low calory cooking that appeals to slimmers as well as lovers of good food.* NY Times 10/23/77, p16 **[1975,** from French, literally, slimness cooking]

cult-figure, *n.* a person or figure that is the object of a cult or popular adulation. *We have not, so far, come up with a cult-figure to equal Father Christmas. Lenny Lent, while productive interimwise, lacks the folklore attributes we are looking for.* Punch 2/23/66, p269 **[1966]**

culturalization, *n.* the process of acquiring the ways, attitudes, and habits of a culture. *To become a human being, the hominid [animal resembling man] must acquire a human nature, and this he does through the culturalization process in which he is conditioned. Human nature, then, is what Homo sapiens learns from his culture.* NY Times Book Review 2/25/68, p14 **[1968]**

cultural revolution, **1** a complete transformation of the institutions of a culture or society. *We need an alternative program, an alternative both to development and to merely political revolution. Let me call this alternative program either institutional or cultural revolution, because its aim is the transformation of both public and personal reality.* Saturday Review 10/17/70, p57 *Legally sanctioned paths toward change, as far as Kate Millett is concerned, are simply not enough. She calls for a "cultural revolution, which must necessarily involve political and economic reorganization [but] must go far beyond as well."* Time 8/31/70, p19 **2** Usually, **Cultural Revolution.** the name of a major drive led by Mao Tse-tung, begun in 1966 and lasting several years, to enforce Maoist ideology and purge China of revisionist leaders and mandarin influences. *The Communist Chinese threat was not rated as serious. The country's 2.75 million troops had their hands full stabilizing the countryside after the upheaval of the Cultural Revolution.* 1970 World Book Year Book, p217 **[1966]**

cultural revolutionary, an advocate or supporter of cultural revolution. *The cultural revolutionary risks the future on the educability of man.* Saturday Review 10/17/70, p57 *Going beyond yoga, many cultural revolutionaries are adopting—or at least sampling—an imported version of the dietary discipline of the Zen Buddhists.* Time 11/16/70, p59 **[1970]**

culturati (ˌkəltʃəˈrɑːtiː), *n.pl.* the cultured class; cultured people. *It is a measure of the isolation of the planning profession that its revolutionaries should be amiable culturati filled with nostalgia for "civilised" cities (especially Italian cities) of the past and with little grasp of the social pressures of today.* New Scientist and Science Journal 12/16/71, p180 **[1966,** formed in English from *culture* on the analogy of *literati* (the educated class)]

culture gap, a difference between cultures that creates difficulties in understanding. *Oh dear, it seems that we are faced here with what the anthropologists call a culture gap, which can be crossed only by a certain stretching of the imagination on your side, a certain amount of deliberate explication on mine.* Harper's 8/70, p60 **[1966]**

culture shock, the discomposure and disorientation a person experiences when thrust into a foreign culture or a new way of life. [Alvin] *Toffler argues: "Future shock arises from the superimposition of a new culture on an old one. It is culture shock in one's own society. But its impact is far worse. For most travelers have the comforting knowledge that the culture they left behind will be there to return to. The victim of future shock does not."* Time 8/3/70, p13 **[1963]**

cumecs (ˈkyuːmeks), *n.* acronym for *cubic meters per second. The flood flow in Woolwich Reach moving upriver during a surge tide is some 4000 cumecs, whereas a high flow over Teddington Weir following heavy rains or snow melt could be of the order of 300 cumecs.* New Scientist 1/4/73, p44 **[1970]**

curate's egg, *British.* something that is of mixed quality; something good in parts only. *Purcell's* Dido and Aeneas *seems to be extraordinarily resistant to a wholly successful recorded performance. What we have had up to and including this one is a series of six curate's eggs.* The Gramophone 4/68, p551 *With a business so diversified as Harrison & Crosfield's—which spans rubber and tea planting, tin mines, insurance broking, chemicals and general import-export—the average year tends to be something of a curate's egg.* Times (London) 10/30/68, p22 **[1958]** ▶Originally used as a simile, as in "excellent in parts, like the curate's egg." The allusion, according to the *OED Supplement,* was to a story which first appeared in *Punch* concerning "a meek curate who, having been given a stale egg by his episcopal host, stated that 'parts of it' were 'excellent' (*Punch* 9 Nov. 1895, p 222)."

curl, *n. Surfing Slang.* the curve of water formed on top of a breaking wave. *The transition from the smooth to the broken part of the wave occurs, in a good surfing wave, with water springing from the wave crest in a sheet—a "curl" in surfers' terminology—which covers a pocket of air, the "tube."* New Scientist 7/6/78, p8 **[1969]**

currency snake, another name for SNAKE. *Chancellor Schmidt and President Giscard . . . still hope that an enlarged and improved currency snake will be an important step in the direction of eventual economic and monetary union within the Community.* Manchester Guardian Weekly 10/29/78, p1 [**1976**]

current sheet, another name for MAGNETODISK. *One of the most impressive characteristics is the enormous distance to which the current sheet extends into space.* McGraw-Hill Yearbook of Science and Technology 1978, p335 [**1976**]

cursor, *n*. a flashing symbol or signal, often a small square of light, that can be moved to any position on the display screen of an electronic typesetter, computer, etc., to indicate where a change is to be made. *"Now, suppose you want to get a little color into this," Butsikares said, and he began tapping keys—marked with arrows pointing up, pointing down, pointing sideways—around the word "HOME." A tiny square of light known as the "cursor" began to move up the face of the tube. It was something like the bouncing ball that used to hop from word to word in song lyrics on movie screens.* New Yorker 2/10/75, p31 [**1972**, extended sense of the earlier term for a sliding part of any instrument (such as a slide rule or a filter placed on a radar screen) that facilitates computing or sighting, from Latin *cursor* runner]

cursus honorum ('kərsəs hɑ'nɔrəm), *Latin.* course of honors; sequence of offices (originally referring to the series of offices leading up to the Roman consulate). *Indeed, some might find it remarkable that such a* cursus honorum—*Dean of King's College London, Dean of Exeter, Dean of St. Paul's—should have fallen to so liberal a thinker.* Times (London) 3/14/70, pIV [**1959**]

curtain-up, *n. British.* the rise of the curtain at the start of a performance. *The bows before curtain-up for the conductor was a mark of honour from the Edinburgh audience for their fellow-countryman James Loughran, just appointed to the Hallé.* Times (London) 12/22/70, p11 [**1963**, from the phrase *curtain up!*, used as a warning call to the cast and crew]

curve ball, *U.S.* a trick or ruse. *. . . numbers of people will argue heatedly that Government half-truths, cover-ups, obfuscations, sophistries, euphemisms and curve balls are permissible tools of the trade so long as a "real lie" (meaning outright and provable) is not employed to gull the people.* NY Times 6/29/71, p37 [**1961**, from the baseball term for a ball that swerves just before reaching the batter]

cushioncraft, *n*. a vehicle that travels on a cushion of air; an air cushion vehicle or hovercraft. *Britten Norman, the Isle of Wight aircraft manufacturer, has decided to sell its subsidiary making the ten-seat cushioncraft.* Times (London) 2/19/70, p23 [**1959**]

cutesy or **cutesie** ('kyu:tsi:), *adj. U.S.* self-consciously or affectedly cute. *. . . a gossipy backstage operetta of fights, love affairs and campy humor. The music that interrupts the cutesy dialogue is standard Mozart.* Time 6/7/68, p4 *Start with the cutesie title* [Bashful Billionaire, The Story of Howard Hughes, by Albert B. Gerber]. *Pursue the mysteriously jumbled chronology. Endure a prose style whose principal interest is a rare, fossilized quaintness.* NY Times Book Review 2/25/68, p10 [**1961**, from *cute* + *-sy* or *-sie*, as in *artsy, gutsy*, etc.]

cutout, *n. Slang.* a person or business used to conceal contact or connection between members of a clandestine operation, as in espionage. *The firm* [U.S. Recording Company] *operated as a "cutout," or front, for the FBI's purchase of eavesdropping equipment; the idea was to prevent targets of wiretapping—such as gangsters or spies—from learning the bureau's capabilities simply by examining government purchasing records.* Time 4/5/76, p23 [**1966**]

cutting edge, the forefront or vanguard of something. *The Tatham approach represents the cutting edge of contemporary management thinking in electronics and high technology.* Maclean's 9/7/81, p39 *Ever since it outlawed public school segregation in 1954, the U.S. Supreme Court has been on the cutting edge of civil rights advances. Now, however, the Jus-*

tices may be on the verge of a historic rollback. Time 10/24/88, p78 [**1978**, in allusion to the sharp edge of a cutting instrument]

CVI, abbreviation for *common variable immunodeficiency*, a condition marked by decreased numbers of antibodies (immunoglobulins). *People with CVI have normal numbers of B lymphocytes—the cells that make antibodies—but the cells fail either to synthesize or to secrete antibodies.* World Book Science Annual 1976, p296 [**1975**]

cyanoacetylene (ˌsaiənouə'setəˌli:n), *n*. a large organic molecule discovered in cosmic gas clouds. *Cyanoacetylene is the first interstellar molecule whose complexity approaches that required for amino acids. It contains 5 atoms: a hydrogen and a nitrogen connected to either end of a 3-atom carbon chain.* Encyclopedia Science Supplement (Grolier) 1971, p56 [**1967**]

cyanobacterium (ˌsaiənoubæk'tiri:əm), *n., pl.* **-teria** (-'tiri:ə). any of a group of blue-green algae lacking a distinct nucleus. *The modern chloroplast, for example, may be derived from a cyanobacterium that was engulfed by another cell and that later established a symbiotic relationship with it.* Scientific American 9/78, p116 [**1978**, from *cyano-* blue + *bacterium*]

cybernated, *adj*. automated through computers. *Papers and panel discussions on basic assumptions, computing machines and cybernated systems, and on the evolving and the future society.* Science News 7/16/66, p44 [**1962**, from *cybern*etics + autom*ated*. See CYBERNATION.]

cybernation, *n*. automation through the use of computers. *To begin with, I believe that cybernation—the complete adaptation of computer-like equipments to industrial, economic, and social activity—will represent a quantum jump in the extension of man.* Saturday Review 7/15/67, p21 [**1962**, coined by Donald N. Michael, a U.S. communications expert, from *cybern*etics + autom*ation*]

cybernetist, *n*. an expert in cybernetics (the comparative study of complex calculating machines and the human nervous system). *Indeed, everything which a physicist does with energy, a cybernetist does with information: namely, he studies receiving, storing, transmitting, transforming and using information.* Encyclopedia Science Supplement (Grolier) 1970, p292 [**1970**] ►Earlier variant names are *cyberneticist* and *cybernetician*.

cyberphobia, *n*. an excessive fear of computers. *He estimates that nearly a third of the nation's office workers suffer from "cyberphobia"—a fear of computers that can cause vertigo, nausea, hysteria and cold sweats.* Washington Post 11/8/82, p1 [**1981**, from *cybern*etics + *phobia*] —**cyberphobe**, *n.: . . . the cyberphobes bead with cold sweat before those little green screens.* Christian Science Monitor 6/21/82, p22 —**cyberphobic**, *adj.: The next step . . . is to develop specific methods for minimizing cyberphobic reaction when a new computer is introduced.* Discover 2/81, p6

cyborg ('sai,bɔrg), *n*. a human body or other organism whose functions are taken over in part by various electronic or electro-mechanical devices. *It is also possible that whenever biological life reaches the intellectual level at which the physiological organism can understand itself (i.e., the stage which Man has just attained), then inorganic components are used for the replacement of defective or worn-out biological ones. In fact, the Cyborg (which is the name recently coined for animal-machine integrations) is possibly the ultimate form for any race.* New Scientist 9/11/69, p541 [**1962**, contraction of *cy*bernetic *org*anism]

cycleway, *n. British.* a road or lane reserved for cyclists. *A scheme to provide cycleways through Central London's parks has been suggested.* Listener 2/7/74, p179 [**1963**, from *cycle* (OED 1881, short for *bicycle* or *tricycle*) + *way*]

cyclic AMP, a chemical compound that acts as an intercellular messenger in carrying out the action of hormones, especially the hormones of the pituitary gland. *In a series of experiments she* [Dr. Jane Shaw] *is attempting to define the relationship between prostaglandins and a substance called cyclic AMP, a chemical widely recognized as a mediator of hormonal effects.* Science News 10/10/70, p306 [**1968**, *AMP*, abbreviation of adenosine monophosphate, a compound of adenosine (a constituent of nucleic acid) and one phosphate group]

cyclic GMP, a chemical compound that functions as a messenger to stimulate the action of hormones and that interacts with the related chemical CYCLIC AMP in cellular metabolism. *A second cyclic nucleotide, guanosine 3', 5' monophosphate (cyclic GMP), is also present in all living systems, but until recently few investigators have studied the relation of this compound to regulatory processes. It has now been proposed that cellular regulations may be influenced by the interaction of cyclic AMP and cyclic GMP.* Science 10/12/1973, p149 [**1970**, *GMP*, abbreviation of *guanosine monophosphate*, a compound of guanosine (a constituent of nucleic acid) and one phosphate group]

cyclo-cross, *n.* a sport which combines cycling and cross-country running. *Cyclo-cross was invented neither for the competitor nor the paying spectator but for the television viewer.* Sunday Times (London) 1/21/68, p18 [**1968**]

cyclonet, *n.* a mechanical device for separating oil and water in an oil spill, which relies on the affinity of substances of different weights for different vortices a cyclonet creates. Compare CONTAINMENT BOOM. *Now a French company, Alsthom, has developed a device for clearing oil slicks—the cyclonet which it claims meets the two fundamental requirements of speed and simplicity.* New Scientist 11/15/73, p481 [**1973**, from French, from *cyclo-* circular, rotating + *net* clean]

cyclophosphamide, *n.* a drug derived from nitrogen mustard, used especially to control leukemia. *Formula:* $C_7H_{15}Cl_2N_2O_2P$ *Modern drugs such as methotrexate and cyclophosphamide are extremely valuable in the treatment of many cancers and especially leukaemias where, in most cases, an increase in survival time has been achieved.* Science Journal 3/70, p63 [**1962**, from *cyclo-* cyclic compound + *phosph*orus + *amide*]

cyclo-pousse (ˌsiːklouˈpuːs), *n.* (Southeast Asia) a pedaled or motorized rickshaw; pedicab. *I have been pedalled uncomplainingly through a snow storm by a Hanoi cyclo-pousse boy clad in cotton shorts and singlet, and in the end he argued logically, at length, but without temper, about the fare.* Punch 5/15/68, p701 [**1965**, from French *cyclo-pousse*, from *cyclo-* bicycle or tricycle + *pousse* rickshaw, short for *pousse-pousse*, literally, push-push (though a rickshaw is pulled rather than pushed)]

cyclosporine or **cyclosporin** (ˌsaiklouˈspɔrin), *n.* an immunosuppressive drug derived from certain fungi, effective in stopping the rejection of transplanted tissue without destroying the body's immune system. *Unlike other immunosuppressive drugs, cyclosporine does not shut down parts of the immune system that enable the body to resist infection.* World Book Science Annual 1985, p242 [**1979**]

cygnet, *n.* a highly energetic and penetrating form of radiation detected underground and believed to come from the constellation Cygnus and certain other celestial sources. *These cygnets have become the ugly ducklings of underground astronomy.* Science News 1/3/87, p8 [**1986**, from *Cygnus*, a northern constellation in the Milky Way; form influenced by *cygnet* young swan]

cyproterone acetate (saiˈproutˌroun), a drug which suppresses the hormone testosterone, used to control sexual hyperactivity in males. *Formula:* $C_{24}H_{29}Cl0_4$ *. . . abnormally high libido could be dampened by an antiandrogen, cyproterone acetate.* Britannica Book of the Year 1968, p508 [**1968**, from *cyclo-* cyclic compound + *prop*yl univalent radical of propane + testos*terone*]

cytochalasin (ˌsaitoukəˈlæsən), *n.* any of a group of structurally related fungal by-products that inhibit the activity of contractile elements in cells, causing the arrest of cytoplasmic division, the migration of cell nuclei, and other effects on cellular processes. *The great value of the cytochalasins as research tools, in spite of present ignorance of their precise mode of action, is that they appear to achieve their reversible impact on cell behavior with a minimum of undesirable side effects such as inhibition of respiration or protein synthesis.* McGraw-Hill Yearbook of Science and Technology 1975, p155 [**1966**, from *cyto-* cell (from Greek *kytos*) + Greek *chálasis* loosening]

cytokinin (ˌsaitouˈkainən), *n.* a plant hormone that directs the differentiation of cells into the roots and shoots of young plants. Compare ABSCISIC ACID, BRASSIN, KINETIN. *The cytokinins are closely related to adenine, one of the bases found in nucleic acids, and compounds with strong cytokinin activity occur in transfer RNA.* New Scientist 11/20/70, p393 [**1965**, from *cyto-* cell + *kinin* a growth-promoting substance in plants (from Greek *kinein* to move)]

cytomegalovirus (ˌsaitouˌmegəlouˈvairəs), *n.* a virus which causes a disease of the central nervous system similar to infectious mononucleosis, attacking and enlarging cells, and is characterized by inclusion bodies in the cell nucleus. *Cytomegalovirus and herpes simplex virus have led to brain damage, deafness, blindness and other malformations of the central nervous system.* Science News 1/12/74, p20 [**1968**, from *cyto-* cell + *megalo-* enlarged + *virus*]

cytosol (ˈsaitəˌsɔːl), *n.* the liquid component of cytoplasm; cytoplasm without other cellular components that are associated and usually suspended in it. *Although long-chain fatty acids are at best poorly soluble in aqueous media, a mechanism to account for the apparent facility with which they traverse the cytosol (aqueous cytoplasm) has not been identified.* Science 7/7/72, p56 [**1972**, from *cytoplasm* + *sol*ution] —**cytosolic**, *adj.*: *Homogenisation of a tissue in vitro also gives dilution of the cytosolic GSP [glutathione peroxidase] . . . to concentrations that are less inhibitory than those in vivo.* Nature 4/15/76, p632

cytostatic, *n.* any drug or combination of drugs that inhibits the multiplication of cells, used especially in the treatment of cancer. *If we set aside hormones, which, as we have seen have equally wide scope but limited effectiveness, the cytostatistics are the first really general treatment of the disease of cancer, the first means of reaching—of controlling or preventing—lesions that are spread throughout the organism.* Lucien Israel, Conquering Cancer, 1978, p97 [**1976**, noun use of the adjective (1957), from *cyto-* cell + *static* (from Greek *statikós* causing to stand)]

Cytrel, *n.* British trademark for a tobacco substitute made from cellulose, used in cigarettes. Compare NEW SMOKING MATERIAL. *Supplements like Cytrel reduce tar and nicotine in cigarette smoke to very low levels, firmly anchoring synthetic/tobacco mix smokes at the foot of the tar league tables.* New Scientist 7/29/76, p228 [**1975**]

D

D/A, abbreviation of *digital-to-analog. The processing includes the analogue-to-digital (A/D) conversion before transmission and the inverse digital-to-analogue (D/A) conversion after transmission.* Scientific American 9/72, p138 **[1972]**

dab, *v.t. Slang.* to fingerprint. *Wall Street firms are required to "dab" . . . every employee from messenger boy to president.* Times (London) 2/6/70, p25 **[1970,** from the noun *dab* fingerprint (OEDS 1926)]

daisy printer or **daisy wheel,** a wheel in a typewriter or word processor that prints from letters mounted on the ends of spokes radiating from a spindle. *Daisy-wheel typewriters can't create double-sized characters or draw charts and graphs. But if you want to use a different type face—italic, for example— just change daisy wheels.* World Book Science Annual 1986, p334 **[1977]**

dalasi (dɑ:ˈlɑ:si:), *n.* a monetary unit introduced into Gambia in 1971 to replace the Gambian pound. See BUTUT. *There had also been a record peanut crop (accounting for over 90% of exports) at unprecedented world prices, averaging 747 dalasis per ton (and reaching over 1,000 dalasis) as against 491 dalasi in 1973.* Britannica Book of the Year 1975, p317 **[1971,** from the Gambian name of a coin worth originally 4 shillings]

Dalek or **dalek** (ˈdɑ:lek), *n. British.* a robot that talks with a rasping, monotonous voice. *The Brothers have returned (BBC 1, Sunday) a bit dusty from their absence. Chairman Merroney still betrays all the emotion of a Dalek.* Listener 2/12/76, p180 *So, like programmed daleks, the French military planners proceed to their "second generation." This consists of 18 intermediate range ballistic missiles . . . each in an underground silo on the ironically named Plateau d'Albion.* Times (London) 7/26/73, p16 **[1963,** said to have been coined by one of the writers of the "Dr. Who" B.B.C. science-fiction television series from an encyclopedia volume DA-LEK]

Dalkon Shield, a trademark for a metal and plastic intrauterine contraceptive device shaped somewhat like a shield. *By this time, scientists had concluded that a multifilament tail on the Dalkon Shield functioned like a wick, collecting bacteria and causing a higher-than-normal incidence of uterine infections among shield users.* NY Times 3/23/80, pD22 **[1973]**

damageability, *n.* the capacity to inflict or sustain damage. *Perhaps the first guide is to do with damageability. The child has to learn to recognize two classes of object he might unwittingly spoil.* Times (London) 10/21/70, p14 *In an effort to cut the costs of highway accidents, insurers accelerated their studies of the damageability and reparability of automobiles.* Americana Annual 1974, p296 **[1970,** from *damage* + *-ability*]

damage control, 1 any means used to minimize or reduce the damage caused by an accident, crime, financial loss, adverse publicity, or other calamity. *Their first goal is to prevent stolen goods from disappearing forever. . . although with limited resources they have essentially undertaken a damage-control mission.* NY Times Magazine 12/13/87, p46 **2** Figurative use: *It's a stunning scene where old grudges and suspicions are suddenly dredged up and flung in a fit of emotion, devoid of damage control.* Washington Times 1/23/89, pE1 **[1959]**

dammit, *n.* **as near as dammit,** *British Slang.* very nearly; almost. *I am no longer a Reuters correspondent, but clearly this affectedly casual conversation was as near as dammit an apology for what had happened to me in Peking.* Manchester Guardian Weekly 5/15/71, p6 **[1961,** in earlier formula: as _____ as clammit (1908)]

damp squib, *British Slang.* something that has no effect or that fails completely; anything ineffective. *In contrast there is a strong body of union opinion which believes the whole demonstration will be a damp squib.* Times (London) 1/9/71, p2 *But with approximately £86 million spent on information services. . ., compared with the damp squib that Dr. Mellanby reports for scientific research, a real information firework display is going on in the technological development area.* New Scientist 5/11/67, p358 **[1847, 1958,** the earlier meaning was a joke or lampoon (a squib) that falls flat, as a squib (firecracker) whose powder is damp]

dan, *n.* one of several grades or ranks of proficiency in Japanese sports and games. *Iyeda has been playing the ancient Oriental board game constantly since he was eight, now ranks as a fifth Dan professional (ninth Dan is highest) in his native Japan, where GO has been the national indoor game for as long as anybody can remember.* Time 4/22/66, p48 **[1966,** extended use of the term used in judo (OEDS 1941)]

dance language, the series of patterned movements by which honeybees communicate. *He* [Karl von Frisch] *proved conclusively for the first time that fish can hear, and bees, he deduced, can distinguish between odours and communicate with each other through a dance language.* Britannica Book of the Year 1974, p510 **[1968]**

dancercise, *n.* group dancing as a type of physical exercise. *Witnessing a performance of Les Ballets Jazz de Montréal is much like watching a "dancercise" class work itself into a quasi-religious lather of shimmying, shaking, jiving, and high-kicking.* Maclean's 2/1/82, p61 **[1967** trademark, **1981,** blend of *dance* and *exercise*]

D & D, abbreviation of *Death and Dying. Study courses for nurses, nuns, priests, and ordinary folk—all these have sprung up within the last few years. Thanatology, the "science" of D&D, is here fullblown.* National Review 11/22/74, p1356 **[1974]** ▶ The abbreviated phrase derives from the title of a pioneering book, "On Death and Dying" (1969) by Elisabeth Kübler Ross.

Dane particle, a large spheroidal virus particle found in the blood of a person infected with serum hepatitis. *When a serum containing antibody against hepatitis B was reacted with a serum containing the various antigenic particles, all three particle forms were agglutinated: the 22-nanometer spheres, the filamentous forms, and the 42-nanometer "Dane particles." If the blood samples were treated with a detergent to remove the outer shell of the Dane particle, however, the naked core was not agglutinated with the other particles.* Scientific American 7/77, p46 **[1971,** named after David M. S. *Dane,* a British medical scientist who led the research team that first detected the particle in 1970]

dangle-dolly, *n. British.* a small doll hung in a car window as a charm or decoration. *A leading fancy goods manufacturer. . . looked forward to an increasing Americanisation of British campaign methods, and saw no reason why, next time, Heath or Wilson dangle-dollies should not be hanging in the rear-windows of every car in the land.* Punch 3/30/66, p457 **[1965]**

dapsone, *n.* a drug that inhibits the growth of the bacteria that causes leprosy, used also in treating some forms of dermatitis. *Formula:* $C_{12}H_{12}N_2O_2S$ *The well-established anti-leprosy drug Dapsone. . . has been found to reduce inflammation pain and swelling without the side effects of cortisone-type drugs.* New Scientist 9/29/77, p799 **[1952,** from *di*aminodi*p*henyl *s*ulf*one*, the chemical name]

Dari ('dɑːriː), *n.* a variety of modern Persian spoken chiefly by the Tadzhik ethnic group. *The lower house of the Shura, or parliament, seldom had a quorum and spent most of its session on a linguistic issue—whether civil servants should know both Pushtu and Dari (Persian), Afghanistan's two official languages.* Americana Annual 1973, p65 **[1972]**

dark comedy, 1 another name for BLACK HUMOR. *The literary movement known as Black Humor or Dark Comedy, which achieved a certain inflated prominence in the early sixties, has lately shown signs of reaching some condition of impasse or exhaustion.* Atlantic 7/68, p89 **2** another name for BLACK COMEDY. . . . *there is scarcely any need to mention the vast terrain that has lately been opened up in the name of black comedy, sick comedy, or, more conventionally, dark comedy.* NY Times 10/16/66, pB1 **[1966]** ▶ The term *dark comedies* has long been used by dramatic critics to describe several of Shakespeare's comedies, notably *All's Well That Ends Well, Measure for Measure,* and *Troilus and Cressida,* that are characterized by a pessimistic tone, an underlying seriousness of purpose, and unconventional endings.

dark matter, *Astronomy.* a hypothetical form of matter that does not emit or absorb electromagnetic radiation. *Most astronomers agree that there must be more matter in the universe than has been observed to date. They often refer to this as the "missing mass" problem, and many now believe that this missing matter is unlike ordinary matter that gives off or absorbs light, hence the name—dark matter.* World Book Science Annual 1986, p229 **[1985]**

dark repair, the repair of a damaged or broken strand of a molecule of DNA with the help of special enzymes but without the use of light. Compare EXCISION REPAIR, RECOMBINATIONAL REPAIR. *The second system excises radiation-induced damage from one strand of DNA and resynthesizes the missing segment by using the opposite, complementary strand of DNA as the template. Since this mode of repair does not require light it is called a dark repair process.* 1973 Britannica Yearbook of Science and the Future, p303 **[1969]**

darobokka (ˌdærəˈbɑkə), *n.* a drum struck with two hands, used in Egypt and North Africa. . . . *the atmosphere was charged by groups of musicians beating a variety of drums—tablas and darobokkas—giving a pulsating beat to accompany the eerie rhythm provided by reed and bamboo pipes.* Times (London) 12/18/70, p20 **[1970,** from Arabic *darabukka* tambourine]

dartist, *n.* a person who plays the game of darts. *In the U.K. Unicorn world championships, dartists from 16 nations competed for top honours.* Britannica Book of the Year 1977, p648 **[1971,** from *dart* + -*ist;* the form perhaps influenced by *artist]*

dart tag, a small metal dart with a plastic streamer attached, inserted into the back of a fish as an identifying tag. *For small fish, small dart tags that were fired from a "pistol" also came along, as did dart tags that were inserted in an incision cavity.* NY Times 1/13/76, p27 **[1976]**

daruma (dɑːˈruːmɑː), *n.* a Japanese doll used as a good-luck symbol. See the quotation for details. *Some three weeks earlier, one member of the Lockheed staff had brought a large* daruma—*a papiermâché figure of a famous Buddhist monk of that name—to the room. Traditionally, in Japan, when a wish is made, the left eye of a daruma is painted in, and if the wish comes true the right eye is also painted in.* New Yorker 1/23/78, p74 **[1963,** from Japanese, after *Daruma,* the Japanese name of Bodhi*dharma,* the legendary founder of Zen Buddhism]

dashiki (dəˈʃiːkiː), *n.* a loose, shirtlike, pullover garment originally from Africa, usually short-sleeved and having bright colors. *At Burroughs, there were several black students, wearing Afro haircuts and dashikis.* New Yorker 5/16/70, p110 **[1968]**

DAT, abbreviation of *digital audiotape. Unlike CDs, which cannot be used to copy live music or other recorded tapes, the DAT is . . . able to rerecord and play back sounds.* Encyclopedia Science Supplement (Grolier) 1988, p319 **[1985]**

data, *v.t. U.S.* to compile or possess detailed information about (a person or group). *By the mid-Fifties the FBI not only had all "card-carrying" Communists in the U.S. identified and "dataed," but had the Soviet intelligence services, the KGB and the military GRU, so thoroughly penetrated that it could actually influence their direction.* National Review 9/14/73, p993 **[1973,** verb use of *data, n.*]

data bank, 1 a collection of records stored in a computer system so that any data may be extracted from it or organized as desired. Also called DATA BASE. *In defence of databanks, one can point to major benefits in medicine, in research, in industry and in commerce which stem directly from the centralization of information.* Times (London) 11/18/70, p12 **2** Transferred sense. any data storage system. *The nucleic acid content of many of the extranuclear organelles makes sense on this theory, as do many special mechanisms for the transmission of organelle instructions that are not recorded in the central nuclear data bank.* Scientific American 5/71, p128 **3** the place where such a collection is kept or stored. . . . *alarmed individuals fear that our rights to liberty and privacy will vanish. One target of criticism is the proposed central data bank in Washington, D.C., which is to contain important facts on all residents and citizens of the United States.* Encyclopedia Science Supplement (Grolier) 1970, p238 **[1967]**

data-bank, *v.t.* to put or store in a data bank. *As data banks proliferate, so will the indiscriminate use of the material they contain. And that raises the question whether an American citizen has a constitutional or legal right not to be data-banked, computerized, stored, exchanged and possibly damaged—materially or in reputation—by the process.* NY Times 7/7/70, p38 **[1970]**

data base, another name for DATA BANK. *The programs are written to retrieve and process information stored in a pre-arranged way in the computer's peripheral units—such as magnetic tape decks or discs. Any alterations to the way in which this store of information (the data base) is arranged . . . usually requires alterations to all the relevant programs.* New Scientist 4/16/70, p117 **[1962]**

data buoy, a buoy equipped with weather sensors and transmitters, used especially to obtain early warnings of storms and other meteorological events. *The inability to obtain regular meteorological data from a variety of fixed points in the oceans has long posed a problem to weather forecasters. A network of sophisticated data buoys was seen as a good way to solve the problem.* Science News 6/24/72, p407 **[1972]**

data capture, the simultaneous automatic recording and processing of data, as by means of equipment connecting distant locations with a central computer or processing unit. *A brief review of this type must unfortunately pay scant attention to many sectors of even the hardware market. These include . . . the development in data capture, one of the most vital areas of computing.* Times (London) 12/4/72, pII **[1969]**

dataflow, *n.* Also **data flow.** the flow or transfer of data between computers or within a network of computers. *Differing national laws governing such areas as consumer information disclosure, transborder data flow and currency exchange pose substantial challenges for software developers. How soon will there be a truly international electronic payment system?* Washington Post 6/9/85, pH2 **[1982]**

data link, a communications link for direct transmission of data from one or more distant points to a central computer or processing unit. *Digital communication systems, often called "data-links," are beginning to appear in increasing numbers. The data-link is bound to proliferate. It is the natural communication medium for the pulse trains that pass between digital electronic devices.* Times (London) 5/26/77, p18 **[1963]**

data logger, an instrument that receives data in the form of electrical signals and records them in digital form. *The output is primarily via data loggers and a computer, and consists in part of a digitised continuous body heat map from which the experimenters can study the body's heat patterns.* New Scientist 12/21/72, p703 **[1962]**

datamation (‚deitə'meiʃən), *n.* the automatic processing of data, especially as a branch of commerce and industry. *In the field of computer technology the distinction between hardware and software has lately been blurred by the introduction of the term* firmware. *At the same time, datamation has been adopted as the new term for computer processing.* Language Teaching Abstracts 1/72, p72 [**1963**, from *data* + auto*mation*]

dataphone, *n.* a telephone apparatus for transmitting data, such as information into a computer. *One of industry's main criticisms at the present time is of the weak marketing methods of the Post Office. Industry spokesmen say that if they were allowed to sell telephones, extension telephones, dataphones and other instruments direct to the public they could sell a lot more than they can now sell to the Post Office.* New Scientist and Science Journal 7/1/71, p14 *The telephone companies expected to continue . . . activities in the area of data communications, including Data-Phone and private-line facilities that served more than 100,000 teletypewriters.* 1970 Britannica Yearbook of Science and the Future, p150 [**1958**]

Dataroute, *n.* a Canadian telecommunications system for the transmission of data in digital form. *Canada's new Dataroute system is designed to provide low rates for a digital transmission service that is needed because of the increasing flow of business information and the increasing use of computers in Canada . . . The new system utilizes a type of transmission called data under voice.* Americana Annual 1974, p578 [**1974**]

data set, an analog-to-digital or digital-to-analog converter used in data communications. *"Modem" is a contraction of modulator-demodulator. Modems, also known as data sets, adapt alphanumeric information (letters and numerals) for transmission over standard voice channels. Questions and answers, or requests and acknowledgements, flow in rapid message bursts from agents' terminals to the central computer and back again.* Scientific American 9/72, p136 [**1972**]

data-undervoice, *n.* Also spelled **data under voice.** a method of digital data transmission in which the data signals and voice signals are sent simultaneously over a microwave radio relay system by using different frequency bands for the data signals and the voice signals. *Abbreviation:* DUV *The new development achieved during 1971 that would eventually link machines in most cities of the U.S. was a technological breakthrough known as data-undervoice (or DUV). What made DUV so significant and its potential impact so far-reaching was that it could be used on the existing microwave radio relay network, a transmission facility that reaches almost every corner of the U.S.* 1973 Britannica Yearbook of Science and the Future, p215 [**1972**]

Datel or **datel** (dei'tel *or* 'deitel), *n.* a service of the British postal system, providing high-speed transmission of data by computer for subscribing business firms. Compare PRESTEL. *An extension of Telex is Datel, the provision of high speed data links for computers.* Sunday Times (London) Magazine 6/20/71, p23 [**1967**, from *data* + *Telex*]

dating bar, *U.S.* a bar in which single men and women meet and date socially. *In city after city, run of the gin-mill bars have been turned into "dating bars." What converts an ordinary bar into a dating bar is a weekend admission fee (usually $1), a large welcome for single girls, and a good neighborhood.* Time 9/15/67, p37 [**1967**]

daunomycin ('dɔːnə‚maisin), *n.* an antibiotic derived from a species of streptomyces or produced synthetically, used as an anticancer drug. *Formula:* $C_{27}H_{29}NO_{10}$ *Other newly synthesized drugs include the anti-tumour agents adriamycin and daunomycin.* Britannica Book of the Year 1980, p240 [**1973**, from Italian *daunomicina,* from *Daunia,* region in southeastern Italy + -*micina* -mycin (ultimately from Greek *mýkēs* fungus)]

dawk, *n. U.S.* a person who disapproves of wars but is unwilling to oppose and propagandize actively against war; a compromiser who is neither a hawk nor a dove. . . . *the House Republican Conference last week issued a 37-page indictment of Lyndon Johnson's conduct of the war. In it, the Republicans did their agile best to sail with the doves and swoop with the hawks. The result was a dawk . . . However, the Republican dawks could* not convincingly square their criticism of U.S. war policy with their insistence that they still support the war. Time 9/30/66, p12 [**1966**, blend of *dove* and *hawk; a Time* coinage]

day-care, *U.S.* —*adj.* concerned with the care of preschool children (usually of working mothers) outside their homes. *The board unanimously endorsed a proposal to set up work incentives for welfare recipients and to expand counselling services, family planning and day-care services.* NY Times 5/22/68, p1 —*n.* Also **day care.** the care of small children or anyone needing supervision outside their homes (also used attributively). *For years, day-care centers have provided recreation for millions of children and respite for their parents, and now more and more centers are being established across the country to meet the day care needs of the elderly and their families.* NY Times 9/5/77, p18 *The worst difficulties all boil down to lack of day care . . . It's happening all over the country and it seems to me that day care should become the responsibility of central government instead of local authorities.* Sunday Times (London) Magazine 5/11/75, p34 [**1958**]

Day-Glo, *n.* the trade name of a fluorescent paint that gives off a variety of brilliant colors when exposed to light (often used attributively). *Galleries uptown and in Soho exhibit paintings of parked trucks, geometrics in plastic or marble, designs that flare up in Day-Glo or neon, . . .* New Yorker 3/6/71, p73 *The George Mitchell Choir, greasepaint and day-glo and soft-shoe, was hamming it up on the jetty.* Sunday Times (London) 4/14/68, p15 ". . . *After the drug-crazed, Day-Glo 60's, plants and healthfood stores were a natural."* NY Times Magazine 12/14/80, p29 [**1951**]

daylight, *v.i.* to work at a regular daytime job. *When [Lily] Tomlin isn't working before the cameras or a concert audience she's likely to be working on new characters. Recently she turned up without make-up and with hair piled atop her head at a Burbank supermarket, where she daylighted for four days perfecting her "Dot, the checkout lady."* Newsweek 4/21/75, p90 [**1975**, verb use of the noun, on the pattern of *moonlight, v.* (1957)] —**daylighting,** *n.: These are just two instances of the irregular employment practices—"black labour" the trade unions call it—which have always been part of the Italian way of life. They go well beyond moonlighting, which presupposes daylighting or a regular daytime job in the first place.* Times (London) 10/24/77, p27

Day 1 or **Day One,** *Informal.* the first day of any period of time; the very beginning. *From Day 1, fashion has dictated that women's tender toes be squeezed into a pointed-toe shoe that ignores the realities of human anatomy.* NY Times Magazine 9/2/79, p47 [**1976**]

day-sailer, *n. Especially British.* a small sailboat used for short pleasure trips. *In the following years he [Uffa Fox] designed dozens of boats from dinghies and day-sailers to cruisers and ocean-racers, and achieved a high place among the world's leading marine architects.* Times (London) 10/27/72, p16 [**1964**, from *day*time + *sail, v.* + -*er*]

dazibao ('da:dzi:'bau), *n., pl.* -**baos.** another name for WALL-POSTER. *Li Chun-kuang, a young teacher at the Conservatory of Music, in August 1975 posted up a dazibao criticising the leadership of the Ministry of Culture for its dead hand on China's cultural life and specifically for suppressing "The Pioneers," a film extolling China's oilfield workers.* Manchester Guardian Weekly 1/30/77, p2 [**1972**, from Chinese (Pinyin) *dazibao,* literally, big-character poster]

d.b., abbreviation of *double-breasted* (suit, jacket, coat, etc.). *. . . a squat man in a shiny d.b. sharkskin equably engages my mother in a twenty-minute discursion . . .* Atlantic 5/71, p30 [**1966**]

dBA, abbreviation of *decibel A* (a unit for measuring noise in which A represents a weighting scale for loudness). *The PNdB* [perceived noise decibel] *is somewhat different from the dBA frequently used in assessing traffic and industrial noise because it contains a weighting factor dependent on the masking effect of high frequency noises in addition to the usual ear sen-*

sitivity frequency response. New Scientist and Science Journal 3/18/71, p605 **[1968]**

DCE, *Economics.* abbreviation of *domestic credit expansion,* a British measure of changes in the money supply that excludes foreign exchange reserves and overseas government borrowing. *Statistically, the DCE approximates to the rise in the money supply plus the balance of payments deficit, although the purity of this equation is marred by such tiresome conventions as that changes in the non-deposit liabilities of the banking sector are excluded from the money supply, but included in DCE.* Times (London) 1/15/76, p19 **[1970]**

DCS or **D.C.S.,** abbreviation of *Dorsal Column Stimulator,* a small electrical device that supplies impulses to stimulate the spinal nerves and relieve pain. *During a brief operation, the D.C.S. is implanted in the skin . . . with the source of the pain determining its position; for example, if the patient suffers from leg pain, the D.C.S. is implanted just above the point at which the nerves from the leg reach the spinal column.* NY Times Magazine 1/30/77, p50 **[1973]**

DDVP, abbreviation of *dimethyl dichlorovinyl phosphate,* the full chemical name of the insecticide DICHLORVOS. *Recent work by Swedish biochemist Göran Löfroth . . . raises doubts about the wisdom of letting the organophosphorous insecticide DDVP be freely available in Britain.* New Scientist 10/23/69, p171 **[1955]**

de-, a very productive prefix, with various meanings shown below: **1 a** to do the opposite of (an action). —**debureaucratize,** *v.t.: Thus authority must be sweepingly decentralized and debureaucratized . . .* Harper's 6/70, p114 —**deconsolidate,** *v.i.: It sold control of W.S.F. [Westinghouse Saxby Farmer, a company] to the West Bengal Government for 1 rupee, and was able to deconsolidate.* Times (London) 7/1/70, p27 —**deglaciate,** *v.t.: . . . the apparent presence of microblade groups in the southern Yukon around 7000 b.c. suggests that these groups were advancing into newly deglaciated territory hard upon the retreating Cordilleran ice.* Britannica Book of the Year 1969, p102 —**deideologize,** *v.t.: But the time has come: Unflinchingly to get down to the task of demythologizing and deideologizing the teaching office in the church.* NY Times 6/3/71, p39 **b** opposite of. —**deconsolidation,** *n.: Helped by the deconsolidations, by recovery in Australia, and by exceptionally high profits in semiconductors at home, the recovery in group profits last year was spectacular.* Times (London) 7/1/70, p27 —**deculturalization,** *n.: . . . he [the French painter Jean Dubuffet] . . . proposes "institutes for deculturalization, nihilistic gymnasiums as it were, where particularly lucid instructors would give a course in deconditioning and demystification lasting several years, in such a way as to equip the nation with a thoroughly trained body of negationists who will keep confrontation alive . . ."* New Yorker 6/6/70, p56 —**de-isolation,** *n.: At stake, in the process of China's de-isolation, are questions of great significance to all nations: the control of nuclear weapons, the resolution of the Indochina war, peace in a quadripolar East Asia (U.S., U.S.S.R., Japan and China), scientific and technical cooperation, the war against poverty and hunger.* NY Times 10/28/70, p46 —**descrambler,** *n.: . . . industry is facing a serious problem in this area [guaranteeing privacy] and may be willing to pay for devices that limit access to any communications link to those with the correct "descrambler".* New Scientist 6/4/70, p470 **2** to remove or take away (something specified) from an object. —**debarb,** *v.t.:* [Senator] *Muskie smiled, gulped a glass of water, showed his ability to debarb a question.* Time 1/18/71, p9 —**deblur,** *v.t.: Any photograph which is out-of-focus or limited by an optical effect can be deblurred.* New Scientist and Science Journal 5/6/71, p304 —**de-ink,** *v.t., v.i.: Scrap paper that is used to make some form of paperboard for packaging can be used as it is, but if the recycled paper must be white, the scrap must be de-inked. De-inking is an expensive process, and causes its own form of pollution.* New Scientist and Science Journal 4/29/71, p259 —**de-oil,** *v.t.: In the lab, both seem to de-oil feathers without affecting their waterproofing properties, and field trials are soon to be undertaken with five birds.* New Scientist and Science Journal 6/10/71, p608 —**depod,** *v.t.: At the same time it* [the pea] *is the most popular green vegetable, but particularly irk-*

some to prepare fresh, involving all available members of the family in depodding operations. Times (London) 2/16/70, pIII

deaccession, *v.t., v.i.* to sell or exchange pieces of a museum's collection or any other formal collection. *A good number of paintings in the original donation, none of them fakes, did turn out to be wrongly attributed, and were deaccessioned by the university as we began to rebuild the collection.* Atlantic 5/75, p28 —**n.** the act or practice of deaccessioning a part of an art or other collection. *Richard F. Brown, director of Fort Worth's Kimbell Museum of Art, felt that . . . the "principle" of de-accession is right although he might "disagree with the particular object chosen for de-accession."* Newsweek 1/29/73, p76 **[1972,** from *de-* do the opposite of + *accession***]**

de-acquisition, *n.* **1** a piece to be deaccessioned from a collection. *When it was announced seven months ago that museum director Thomas Pearsall Field Hoving's de-acquisitions would include Picasso's "Women in White" and Manet's "Boy with a Sword," it aroused the kind of reaction that has made Hoving a controversial figure ever since he was Mayor Lindsay's parks commissioner.* Newsweek 10/16/72, p117 **2** the act or process of deaccessioning. *After much public debate and recrimination because of alleged secrecy and disregard of the public interest in handling several* de-acquisitions *(selling or exchanging works), the Metropolitan Museum of Art presented its own guideline for future transactions . . .* 1974 World Book Year Book, p527 **[1972]**

deadee (ded'i:), *n.* a portrait of a dead person painted from a photograph. *There are "deadees" (painted after their lifetimes), and portraits from life.* NY Times 1/6/68, p31 **[1968]**

Dead Hand, another name for RAYNAUD'S PHENOMENON. *Known as "Dead Hand" or "White Fingers"—and most recently as Vibration Syndrome—Raynaud's Phenomenon produces the same numbness and pain as a normal hand which is exposed to extreme cold for long periods but it occurs after only brief exposure to mild cold and takes much longer to overcome.* Sunday Times (London) 3/23/69, p5 **[1969]**

dead letter box or **dead letter drop,** a place for depositing secret messages and other material without having to come in direct contact with the recipient. *It was said that ever since coming to West Germany Guillaume had been collecting intelligence material and dispatching it to his masters—either by radio, by courier or through 'dead letter' boxes.* Annual Register of World Events in 1974, p156 *The Soviet newspaper* Izvestia *published details of a year-old case in which they had discreetly expelled an attractive young American woman, obviously a CIA operative, caught planting money, poison and cameras at what the thriller books call a "dead letter drop" for another agent to pick up.* Maclean's 7/10/78, p47 **[1971,** so called in reference to a post-office dead letter, which cannot be delivered or returned**]**

dead-on-arrival, *n.* an electronic circuit which fails to operate when first used in equipment. *Even with this high pre-delivery rate* [of rejected circuits] *circuits received are not free from defects. To quote from a report by the Rome Air Development Center in the US: "Recent experience indicates that dead-on-arrivals constitute up to five per cent or more of the received product."* New Scientist and Science Journal 7/8/71, p75 **[1971,** extended sense of the technical term (usually abbreviated as DOA) for a sick or injured person who is pronounced dead upon arrival at a hospital**]**

de-aestheticization, *n.* the removal of aesthetic qualities from art. *The movement toward de-aestheticization is both a reaction against and a continuation of the trend toward formalistic overrefinement in the art of the sixties, and particularly in the rhetoric that accompanied it.* New Yorker 1/24/70, p62 **[1970]**

de-aestheticize, *v.t.* to rid (art or a work of art) of aesthetic qualities. *Di Suvero builds sculptures out of the beams of wrecked buildings, and Oldenburg de-aestheticizes bath fixtures by sewing them together out of cloth.* New Yorker 7/1/67, p73 **[1967]**

deafferented (di:'æfərəntid), *adj.* having the afferent or sensory nerve fibers (which convey impulses to the central nervous system) severed or otherwise interrupted. *Monkeys can even learn to perform new conditioned responses with deafferented extremities with vision occluded.* Science 12/8/72, p1114 [**1972**]

deal, *v.* **deal up**, *U.S.* to promise a defendant who is a minor figure in a criminal case a degree of immunity from prosecution in return for information that will help convict someone who is more important or charged with a greater crime. *But the plea bargaining has its own controlling strategy—"dealing up" for testimony ever closer to the top—and [Charles] Colson by that measure was the biggest catch yet.* Newsweek 6/17/74, p17 [**1974**]

de-Americanize, *v.t.* to reduce American involvement in. *Under the Johnson Administration, according to [Defense] Secretary Laird, "Vietnamization" meant "de-Americanizing" the war.* NY Times 8/1/70, p22 [**1966**]

death education, a program of courses that provides information about death and the problems and needs of the dying. Compare D & D. *Many critically ill patients suffered greatly from loneliness. To help solve this problem, a number of medical schools, hospitals, colleges, and even high schools and churches began to give courses in death education.* World Book Encyclopedia (1979), Vol. 5, p53 [**1979**]

death squad, any of various unofficial vigilante groups in Latin America whose members murder petty criminals, suspected leftists, etc. *What causes alarm is the serried ranks of the Latin American diaspora—exiles spread over several continents—is that the victims of the assassination schemes are for the most part political moderates, and there seems to be no geographical limit to the operations of the death squads.* Manchester Guardian Weekly 10/3/76, p8 [**1969**]

death star, another name for NEMESIS. . . . *many stars in the galaxy are part of double star systems, in which both members orbit a common center of gravity. Perhaps, they speculated, the sun has a dim, undiscovered companion star—a death star, the press called it—with an orbit that brings it close to the solar system every 26 million years. As the star nears, its gravitational pull disturbs the inner Oort Cloud, spilling comets from it and causing an extinction.* Discover 5/84, p26 [**1984**]

death therapy, supportive therapy for patients suffering from terminal diseases; advice, reassurance, and other guidance given to help patients and their families cope with their imminent death. *John Parkins: "I've heard of death therapy, death counseling, and I think it's a good idea. Not for me, because I found out about my sickness early, and I provided my own therapy."* Maclean's 4/73, p24 [**1973**]

debit card, a card enabling a bank customer to withdraw cash at any time from any of the bank's automatic teller machines and to charge purchases of goods and services directly to funds on deposit in the bank. *It is projected that in the 1980s the "cashless" or, more appropriately, "checkless" society will come into being. The means for this new financial system will be the debit card, which is planned to replace the credit card of today.* McGraw-Hill Yearbook of Science and Technology 1977, p173 [**1975**, patterned after *credit card* (1956)]

deboost, *v.i.* to reduce the thrust of a spacecraft, missile, etc., in flight, especially in order to lower the orbiting altitude of a spacecraft or to slow down a warhead before impact. *This combination would prevent anti-ballistic missile radar . . . from ascertaining the point of impact until the rocket "deboosts"— about three minutes and 500 miles from target.* Time 11/10/67, p15 —**n.** a reversing of the thrust of an orbiting spacecraft, artificial satellite, etc. (also used attributively). *The second "de-boost" maneuver dropped Orbiter 2 from its taxiing orbit of 1,150 miles high and 130 miles low to a new orbit of 1,149 miles high and 31.3 miles low.* NY Times 11/17/66, p15 [**1966**]

decametric, *adj.* of or equivalent to a decameter (10 meters) in wavelength. Compare DEKAMETRIC, DECIMETRIC. . . . *the satellite could clear up the puzzling problem of Jupiter's 'deca-*

metric' radiation bursts by studying their spectrum in a new frequency range. Science Journal 5/68, p17 [**1962**]

decapacitate, *v.t.* to inhibit capacitation in (sperm). *There was a further theoretical difficulty in the way of the fertilization of human eggs, arising from the fact that it was necessary to use ejaculated sperm. The seminal plasma was believed to contain decapacitating factors, that is, substances that inhibit capacitation.* Scientific American 12/70, p48 [**1964**]

decapacitation, *n.* a process by which certain substances in seminal plasma inhibit capacitation. *The achievement of human fertilization in vitro . . . has enlarged the stock of information on capacitation and decapacitation revealed by the fertilization of hamster eggs in vitro.* Scientific American 12/70, p48 [**1961**]

deca-rock, *n.* another name for GLITTER ROCK. *Wedged between the regression of nostalgia and the perversity of deca-rock is the real core of the pop product—the myriad soft and hard rock bands, and the individual singer-songwriters, both black and white.* Newsweek 12/24/73, p48 [**1973**, short for *decadent rock*]

decathlete (di'kæθ,li:t), *n.* an athlete who competes in the decathlon (a ten-event track and field contest). *Gerhard Auer, No. 3 in the West German boat, was once a decathlete, accumulating over 6,500 points.* Times (London) 9/7/70, p11 [**1968**, blend of *decathlon* and *athlete*]

decet ('desət), *n.* another name for DECIMET. *Gell-Mann's quarks explain the elementary-particle families in his Eightfold Way classification system. They combine by threes to form a 10-member family, the baryon decet.* World Book Science Annual 1975, p85 [**1974**, from *dec-* ten (from Greek *déka*) + *-et*, as in *octet, sextet*, etc.]

decidophobia, *n.* a fear or avoidance of deciding something, especially something important. *Without Guilt and Justice. Walter Kaufmann. Wyden. An influential scholar of Nietzsche unsparingly attacks the American disease of "decidophobia"— an unwillingness to make fateful decisions—proposing "moral autonomy" as a cure.* 1974 Collier's Encyclopedia Year Book, p109 [**1972**, coined from *decide* + connective *-o-* + *phobia*] —**decidophobe**, *n.*: *The decidophobe often restricts himself, Kaufmann says, by making one of ten major choices that automatically eliminates the need for many future decisions.* Time 3/6/72, p52

decimet ('desəmet), *n.* a group of ten nuclear particles with approximately the same mass, hypercharge, and isotopic spin. Also called DECET. *The grouping of these families of elementary particles into superfamilies (octets, decimets and so on) was proposed independently in the early 1960's by Murray Gell-Mann and Yuval Ne'eman.* Scientific American 7/74, p55 [**1965**, from Latin *decimus* of ten + English *-et*, as in *octet, sextet*, etc.]

decimetric, *adj.* of or having to do with radio waves ranging from 0.1 to 1 meter in length, or a frequency of 300 to 3000 megahertz. Compare DECAMETRIC, DEKAMETRIC. *Trapped particle species will be the object of a University of California experiment—the Jovian trapped radiation detector, which will endeavour to relate these particles to the decimetric radio emissions.* New Scientist 3/9/72, p537 [**1966**, derivative of *decimeter* unit of length equal to a 10th of a meter]

decision table, a tabular listing of conditions to be considered in defining a problem, together with the actions to be taken under each of the conditions. *Often easier to draw than a flow chart, a decision table still shows the essential conditional features of a computation sequence. Some users prefer decision tables because of their compactness and summary qualities.* Van Court Hare, Jr., Introduction to Programming: A BASIC Approach, 1970, p109 [**1970**]

decision tree, a graphic representation of alternative courses of action, risks, and possible results, used as an aid in decision-making. Compare EVENT TREE. *The fourth channel questions facing Sir John Eden, the Minister of Posts and Telecommunications, can be laid out in the form of a relatively simple decision tree. First, he must decide whether to allocate the fourth* *channel now or postpone the decision . . . Second, he must decide who should be responsible for the fourth channel. And finally, he must decide how this responsibility, once assigned, should be discharged.* Listener 10/25/73, p543 [**1968**]

decompress, *v.i.* to pass from a state of stress and become less tense; relax. *"If you grew up in Georgia, you know how to decompress," Rusk recently told an acquaintance who wondered how he had adjusted to his comparatively tranquil postgovernment life. "My mother would decompress by sitting down in a rocking chair and taking a five-minute nap."* New Yorker 2/6/78, p62 [**1971,** figurative sense of the term meaning to reduce or relieve pressure (as of air or gas)] —**decompression,** *n.: Each morning the finance minister awoke, determined to leave public life and end the 15 years of grueling, 12-hour days to spend more time with his family. By midafternoon he would waver, recalling his nine years in cabinet as a power in national affairs and anticipating a difficult decompression to private citizen.* Maclean's 9/19/77, p63

deconstruct, *v.t.* **1** to subject (a text) to deconstruction. *Inherit the Wind still has its moments—when, for instance, Robards de-constructs "the pleasant poetry" of the Book of Genesis.* New York Magazine 3/21/88, p78 **2a** to destroy the structure of; break down. *Asked by the subcommittee chairman, Rep. Dan Mica, D-La., what it would cost to "de-construct" the top floors, Dertadian said it would be as much as the U.S. has already actually spent to build the chancery.* Manchester Guardian 5/3/87, p16 **b** to do away with; destroy. *Feminist ideology continues to deconstruct the culture of aging, and many women claim to be growing older with pride and affirmation.* Ms. magazine 6/89, p26 [**1973** for def. 1; **1987** for def. 2]

deconstruction, *n.* a method of literary criticism that reduces the language of a text to a multiplicity of possible meanings rather than any specific meaning ostensibly intended by the author. Also called DECONSTRUCTIVISM. *He makes the refreshing suggestion that his exemplary American texts will prove resistant to deconstruction, an analytic-associative technique honed on the glinting self-referentiality of the poetry of Mallarmé, because both criticism and poetry "in the American grain" affirm "the self over language."* NY Times Book Review 1/31/82, p8 [**1973**] —**deconstructionist,** *n.* **a:** *Deconstructionists maintain that language is such an unstable and slippery medium that any text can be shown, under analysis, to subvert or contradict its own claims to meaning.* NY Times Book Review 5/12/85, p32 **b** Attributive use: *Deconstructionist criticism, as practiced in this country, has tended to cast literature—indeed all language—in the uncomfortable position of being unable to refer to anything outside of its own figurative nature.* NY Times Magazine 12/6/87, p112

deconstructivism, *n.* **1** another term for DECONSTRUCTION. *Practitioners of the new literary critical movement in question are divided over its precise definition, as well as over what it should be called. "Revisionist criticism" has been suggested, and also the French-derived term "deconstructivism."* Harper's 10/79, p93 **2** a movement in modern architecture that seeks to change conventional ways of perceiving form and space by producing buildings of sharp, clashing angles, skewed shapes, and incomplete forms. *Deconstructivism is highly theoretical; . . . its proponents want to change our fundamental perceptions of buildings. They do not accept the conventions of architectural culture—floors, walls, windows, doors, and ornamentation.* NY Times 6/26/88, pH29 [**1979** for def. 1; **1988** for def. 2] —**deconstructivist,** *adj.: Then the guests arrive . . . I join them at the massive buffet and try to keep up with a rapid-fire debate about deconstructivist architecture.* Vanity Fair 11/88, p230

decontaminate, *v.t.* to remove the secret or sensitive parts of (a classified document) to make its publication harmless. *It was only when Secretary of Defense Laird refused to decontaminate and declassify the documents for the Foreign Relations Committee that men who had worked on the papers and reporters who had heard about them set out to expose the blunders and the cover-up.* NY Times 6/20/71, p13 [**1971**]

deconvolution, *n.* the unfolding or unwinding of a convoluted line or form, especially one produced by a computer; act or

process of deconvolving. *Close examination and comparison of the red absorption band of chlorophyll oligomers, $(Chl_2)_n$, and a variety of photosynthetic organisms by computer deconvolution techniques give considerable support to the thesis that antenna chlorophyll in green plants and in blue-green algae has spectral properties and a structure very similar to those of chlorophyll oligomers, $(Chl_2)_n$.* McGraw-Hill Yearbook of Science and Technology 1974, p128 [**1972**]

deconvolve, *v.t.* to unfold or unwind (a convoluted line or form, especially one produced by a computer). *Theoretically, photographs from a single moving observation site such as an aircraft can be deconvolved by a computer to obtain neutral wind speed.* Nature 11/3/72, p32 [**1972**]

decoupage or **découpage** (ˌdeikuːˈpɑːʒ), *v.t.* to decorate with decoupages (paper cutouts). *The first decision to make is what to decoupage. I have found that decoupage is best applied to wood. The most frequently used article to decoupage is a wooden plaque . . .* Lesley Linsley, Découpage: A New Look at an Old Craft, 1972, p12 [**1972,** verb use of the noun (1950's)]

decouple, *v.t.* **1** to reduce the shock waves of (a nuclear explosion) by detonating underground. *. . . scientists can keep the seismic signals from secret tests so small in size [by] testing in underground cavities which "decouple" explosive shock from surrounding earth and drastically reduce the seismic signal.* NY Times 4/19/63, p42 [**1960**] **2** to separate or split up. *Raising such issues might arouse suspicion that, with new missiles in Europe, the United States was ending its guarantee that its intercontinental strategic forces would counter aggression against the allies—that America was "decoupling" its own defense from that of NATO.* NY Times Magazine 12/9/79, p57 [**1966**] —*v.i.* **1** to become separated; split up. *Eventually the universe had cooled enough for oppositely charged particles to combine, rendering normal matter electrically neutral, and so matter decoupled from radiation.* Scientific American 12/86, p62 [**1966**] **2** to eliminate the dependence of one country upon another, especially of a developing country upon an industrialized one. *The case for "decoupling," as it is called, is an increasingly common theme in some of the developing countries and also among some sympathetic politicians in the industrialized West.* Manchester Guardian Weekly 7/27/80, p5 [**1977**]

decrement, *v.t.* to show a decrease in or on. *Apart from becoming one of the main instruments to identify us electronically to the banking system, they [bank cards] may also be used as a sort of portable bank account. In this case it will be the card itself, not the account held at the bank's computer centre, which is decremented as we make our payments.* New Scientist 7/23/70, p181 [**1966,** verb use of decrement, *n.*]

decriminalize, *v.t.* **1** to remove from the category of a crime; declare to be noncriminal. *Glasser would decriminalize heroin and make it available in pharmacies for addicts.* NY Times Magazine 7/2/72, p8 *The Alaska state bar voted Saturday to support legislation to decriminalize use of marijuana. By a vote of 54-30 at their annual convention, the state bar members urged that legislation be drafted to eliminate all criminal penalties for possession, sale and possession with intent to sell marijuana.* News (Mexico City) 6/17/73, p2 **2** to free (a person or activity) from liability to criminal prosecution or penalty. *The recommended removal of all penalties for the private possession of marihuana would do much to decriminalize a large number of those involved with this drug.* Saturday Review 4/15/72, p21 *Homosexuality was decriminalised, and homosexuals came to be treated with unprecedented tolerance.* Listener 12/18/75, p8 [**1972,** from de- + CRIMINALIZE; also 1963 as *v.i.* in the sense of "rehabilitate criminals through psychiatric treatment"]

decruit (diːˈkruːt), *v.t. U.S.* to try to place (older or unneeded employees) in another firm or in a less critical position in their present firm. *Under today's conditions, in which many industries are actively recruiting, the decruiting effort can be more effective . . . The main problem is bringing together companies releasing people and companies which may be able to employ those being let go.* (Newsletter of) Edward Gottlieb & Associates, New York City, 2/15/74 [**1974,** from de- do the opposite of + re*cruit*] —**decruitment,** *n.: Co-Op Denmark is processing the decruitment program, and a survey of 1285 Danish managers over 50 showed that 70% preferred downgrading to retirement.* Time 5/15/78, p77

dedicated, *adj.* designed or used for a particular task or purpose. *These are, however, what are known as dedicated computers: one in the washing machine to control the cycles, another in the microwave oven to allow a sequence of preparations to be programmed, and so on.* NY Times 7/2/85, pC4 [**1969**]

deek, *n. U.S. Slang.* a policeman. . . . *the two policemen are familiar to the inhabitants of this gallery. The regulars long since recognized them as "deeks"—street slang for cops—but not because they had seen the policemen's snapshots or because they were white (other whites congregate here).* New Yorker 11/16/83, p175 [**1983,** variant of *dick* detective (OEDS 1908)]

deep cover, 1 concealment of an informant's or secret agent's identity or location by use of elaborate security or protective guises. *The author . . . readily admits to having served briefly as a deep cover agent in the CIA after leaving college.* National Review 2/20/76, p169 2 Transferred use: *Student records . . . often bulge with personal information—much of it unsubstantiated—such as the political and sexual leanings not only of the student but also of his parents. Ever since the Family Educational Rights and Privacy Act went into effect in late 1974, these records have been kept under deep cover.* Time 2/2/76, p44 [**1963**]

deep pocket, *Informal.* 1 Often, **deep pockets.** a large amount of capital; strong financial resources. *By bringing in a partner with deep pockets . . . the company was in a position to offer a more attractive deal . . .* NY Times 10/30/86, pD4 *You don't sue the perpetrator; you sue the party with the money—the one with the "deep pockets."* American Banker 11/3/86, p4 2 a person or company with strong financial resources. *The requirement that deep pockets pay damages if codefendants cannot is called the "doctrine of joint and several liability."* Christian Science Monitor 3/7/86, p3 [**1975**]

deep space, space beyond the earth and the moon (as distinguished from *outer space* in the sense of the space immediately beyond the earth's atmosphere). *This will be the first time such a large, sophisticated mass has operated in the violent temperature ranges of deep space. What are the effects? To find out, the spacecraft will be positioned for some 4-½ hours with one side constantly facing the sun.* NY Times 10/8/67, pM6 [**1952**]

deep structure, (in generative-transformational grammar) the basic or underlying structure of a sentence from which its surface or phonetic expression is generated. Compare SURFACE STRUCTURE. *Transformational-generative grammar assigns to each sentence a "deep structure" in attempt to generalize about language—and reproduce, from all constituent parts, all the possible sentences of a language.* NY Times 6/8/72, p49 [**1965**]

deep-think, *n. U.S. Slang.* extreme bookishness; academic, pedantic, or esoteric thought (often used attributively). *A plague of deep-think pseudosociology has presented American Big Sports as a model, a metaphor, a paradigm and a proof for American Big Imperialism, American Big Oppression, American Big Sexism, and all the other U.S. Bigs including Infantilism.* Newsweek 12/11/72, p71 [**1963,** back formation from *deep thinker*]

deep throat, *U.S. and Canadian.* a highly placed anonymous informer on criminal activities in government. *Experience has taught, for example, that the media must be able to protect the identity of confidential sources, "deep throats," in order to maintain access to crucial information; neither General Motors nor A & P has that problem.* NY Times 5/14/78, pD18 [**1973,** from the nickname of an informer (or several informers) who, according to the American journalist Bob Woodward, provided him with "deep background" on the Watergate affair (1972-74); originally the title of a pornographic motion picture which was widely exhibited in 1972]

de-escalate, *v.t., v.i.* to reduce in scale or size. *The debate followed the adoption of a resolution charging the Administration with failing to de-escalate the war and with pursuing a*

policy of redistributing bombing targets. NY Times 6/21/68, p7 *Those who might be expecting in these excerpts some of the qualities imparted to this* [musical] *work by Elisabeth Schwarzkopf, Nicolai Gedda, and Erich Kunz in their famous Angel production are warned to de-escalate their expectations.* Saturday Review 11/25/67, p90 [**1964**]

de-escalation, *n.* a reduction in scale or size. . . . *a slow de-escalation of the warlike postures of Egypt and Syria behind a smokescreen of incidents not quite large enough to provoke a new Israeli riposte . . .* Listener 7/13/67, p37 [**1965**]

de-escalatory, *adj.* designed to de-escalate. . . . *the hope was that if Washington made the first de-escalatory move, Hanoi might match it . . .* Atlantic 10/69, p110 [**1968**]

deet, *n. U.S.* the commercial name of a widely used insect repellent. *The natural product and authentic deet showed identical repellency to* Aedes aegypti *mosquitoes. However, deet has been reported to show some attraction for pink bollworm moths in laboratory tests.* Science 1/5/68, p99 [**1961,** from the abbreviation dt of the chemical name *diethyl toluamide*]

deexcitation, *n.* a lowering or being lowered from an excited or high-energy state. *When an extremely energetic proton collided with a target nucleon, a highly excited and complex state would be generated. Most of the time this state would lose energy with the emission of such strongly interacting particles as pions and kaons. Occasionally, however, deexcitation would result in part from the emanation of virtual photons that would decay immediately into lepton pairs.* Scientific American 10/78, p73 [**1964,** from *de-* do the opposite of + *excitation* a raising to a higher energy level]

deexcite, *v.t.* to diminish the high-energy level of (an atom, electron, etc.). See EXCIMER. *The density of the corona is so low that the atoms are not deexcited by collisions before they have a chance to radiate the energy.* Scientific American 10/73, p72 —*v.i.* to be deexcited. *The excited state then de-excites down through lower excited levels until finally it reaches the ground, or stable, state of the nucleus.* 1970 Britannica Yearbook of Science and the Future, p378 [**1960,** from *de-* do the opposite of + *excite* raise to a higher energy level]

defect action level, another name for ACTION LEVEL. *CU* [Consumers Union] *urged the Food and Drug Administration to establish and enforce a sound Defect Action Level for meat and poultry pot pies. A Defect Action Level sets limits on the extraneous matter—commonly known as filth—permissible in food products before the FDA may take regulatory action without further evidence of a health hazard.* Consumer Reports 2/76, p67 [**1976**]

defective agent or **defective virus,** any of a class of viruses that contain only a small amount of genetic material and can therefore replicate only in the presence of a normal virus. *The delta agent* [is] *a defective virus that exists only in conjunction with the hepatitis B virus.* Science News 10/18/86, p244 [**1974**] Also called DI PARTICLE.

defectology, *n.* the study of the causes and remedies of defects in human development or mechanical composition. *The Research Institute of Defectology is supported by faculties in Moscow, Kiev, Leningrad and other cities where teachers have been trained to care for handicapped children since 1920.* Science News 7/2/66, p3 *Like corrosion science, welding defectology is not the most glamorous of spheres of scientific activity.* New Scientist 3/13/69, p565 [**1966**]

defensive medicine, the practice by physicians of ordering an unusual number of laboratory tests and diagnostic consultations in order to protect themselves from possible malpractice suits. *The practice of "defensive medicine" is increasing among California physicians, surgeons and hospitals in the face of a rising volume of malpractice lawsuits . . . The practice also includes the refusal to treat high-risk patients.* NY Times 1/27/74, p20 [**1970**]

defuel, *v.t.* to remove the fuel rods of a nuclear reactor. *Unfortunately, removal of the sump water, expected to be among the most difficult tasks of the clean-up operation, must be accom-*

plished before full scale decontamination and defuelling of the reactor can begin. New Scientist 9/11/80, p766 [**1980**]

defuse, v.t. **1** to remove the critical element in (an explosive situation); exert a calming or moderating influence upon. *President Nguyen Van Thieu has defused chronic student protest by releasing jailed students. He also succeeded in mollifying the raucous disabled war veterans, who roll to their riots in wheelchairs, by granting them more liberal benefits.* Time 9/7/70, p17 **2** to lessen the force or effect of; weaken. *It would be nice to say the young girl puts up, as Anne Baxter did against Bette Davis, menacing competition. The truth is that Miss Bacall defuses and obliterates every other talent on stage.* Manchester Guardian Weekly 4/11/70, p16 [**1958**, figurative senses of *defuse* to remove the fuse from a bomb, etc.]

defuser, n. one who exerts a calming or moderating influence in a critical situation. *Why should a man so meticulously outspoken have fiercely attacked last week the work of reporters in Nigeria who merely wrote what they saw. Chiefly, it is because his style and skill as a public man is as a defuser of explosive predicaments.* Sunday Times (London) 1/25/70, p11 [**1967**]

degear, v.i. British, Finance. to reduce the amount of a company's fixed-interest debt and replace it with equity capital. *Whittingham acquired a significant proportion of its land bank near the top of the market. And, while it may be of sparse comfort to shareholders who have ridden the shares from 1973's 170p to yesterday's 19p, the group has now cleared its books of unrealistically valued land and has begun the uphill struggle to degear.* Times (London) 2/18/76, p25 [**1976**, from *de-* do the opposite + *gear* (1930's) to borrow money so as to increase the amount of total capital in relation to equity capital]

degender, v.t. to remove reference to gender in. Compare DESEX. See also HE/SHE. *Among the ideas: degendering language; letting men wear modes of clothing that were equivalent to skirts (caftans, togas and such); giving children nonsex-identification names; having unisex public bathrooms and taking sex off application forms.* NY Times 6/11/74, p46 [**1974**]

degradability, n. susceptibility to chemical decomposition. . . . *in the wake of moves to ban DDT in several states and foreign countries . . . The Federal commission will study the evidence of the "degradability and persistence, and the adequacy of our knowledge of their chronic and acute effects upon human health . . ."* Science News 5/3/69, p423 [**1969**]

degradable, adj. susceptible to chemical decomposition. . . . *there has been a reduction of the residual amounts of synthetic detergent material in the board's river sources of supply after the complete substitution in packets of washing powder retailed in Britain of anionic detergents which are biologically degradable.* Nature 5/30/68, p1202 *In the past year or so, however, public indignation over litter and garbage has caused industry to ask chemists whether self-destroying, or quickly degradable, plastics might be devised to replace indestructible, unburnable and incompressible glass, aluminum and plastics, which comprise the largest segment of consumer waste.* Science News 8/7/71, p92 [**1963**]

dehire, v.t. U.S. to discharge from hired employment. Compare DESELECT. *The pinched corporation . . . fires the chairman of the board. Fires is a rude word, but the bouncing of the boss is happening now on such a scale that Wall Street is mushrooming with firms sporting the weird names of "Dehiring Consultants, Inc." and "Executive Adjustment Advisers." Their function is to find painless ways of easing company presidents into "early retirement." In a depression, the boss is sacked and jumps from a window. In the "recedence," he is "dehired".* . . . Manchester Guardian Weekly 9/5/70, p22 [**1965**]

deindex, v.t. **1** to remove or separate (income, interest rates, and the like) from cost-of-living or inflation rates. *The aim here is to encourage what the Chancellor called "hard work and initiative." The proposals to tax certain short-term benefits, deindex others and reduce and tax strike benefits will produce an outcry from the unions, the Labour Party and the poverty lobbies.* . . . Manchester Guardian Weekly 4/6/80, p5 **2** to remove

from a cost-of-living index or similar economic indicator. *If there is no possibility to deindex recipients, then it's only fair that we protect taxpayers through an indexation of taxes.* Time 7/28/81, p58 [**1979**, from *de-* + INDEX] —**deindexation**, n.: *Or will it* [an interview] *be remembered for all that dogged detail over possible changes in union immunities and de-indexation of social benefits?* Times (London) 1/13/80, p12

deinstitutionalize, v.t. **1** to divest or free (a church, hospital, or other institution) of its institutional character. *As the function of teacher becomes despecialized, so (from our perspective) the process of education becomes deinstitutionalized and is freed to be reconfigured with the "other" processes of our integral lives—perhaps in forms hard to recognize.* Saturday Review 8/19/72, p31 **2** to enable (an inmate, patient, etc.) to live away from an institution; remove from an institution. *It is a really visionary little organization, anxious to deinstitutionalize the disabled and to encourage young people especially to lead normal, independent lives.* Times (London) 1/5/72, p5 *"We're institutionalizing everybody,"* [Governor] *Brown tells a group of hospital workers to whom he is extolling the virtues of limited growth. "And I'd like to deinstitutionalize everybody. I'd like to have a community that has a more human spirit to it."* Manchester Guardian Weekly (Washington Post section) 7/2/78, p18 [**1967**] —**deinstitutionalization**, n.: *Does "deinstitutionalization" represent an enlightened revolution or an abdication of responsibility? It is probably too early for a definitive judgment, but it is not too soon to review the issues raised by this aspect of the community mental health movement and to consider how such a well-intentioned reform as deinstitutionalization could have created so many problems.* Scientific American 2/78, p46

déjà entendu (deiʒɑ: ɑ̃tɑ̃'dʏ), recognition of something already understood or something heard or seen before. *Lindsay may also have a sense of déjà entendu about the current judgment, popular in some circles, that it is hopeless for him even to consider entering the national race.* New Yorker 8/21/71, p68 *Around To the Shores of the Polar Sea (Radio 4), for instance, there hung an air of déjà entendu that stereophony could not dispel nor radiophonic cold winds blow away.* Listener 2/26/76, p246 [**1965**, from French, literally, already understood]

déjà lu (deiʒɑ: 'lʏ), recognition of something already read or encountered before in one's reading. *Her first book suffers inevitably from a sense of déjà lu. It not only draws heavily on those earlier articles, it trades on childhood experiences shared to some extent by every reader.* Time 5/21/73, p102 [**1960**, from French, literally, already read]

dekametric, adj. of or having to do with radio waves ranging from 10 to 100 meters in length, or a frequency of 3 to 30 megahertz. Compare DECIMETRIC. *This magnetosphere is believed to be the source of the decimetric (not to be confused with the dekametric) radio emanations that come from the planet.* Science News 9/30/72, p216 [**1970**, alteration of earlier DECAMETRIC, from *decameter* unit of length equal to 10 meters]

deke (di:k), n. Especially Canadian. a maneuver in ice hockey and some other sports that deceives an opponent and draws him away from a defensive position. *He gave them such a fantastic series of dekes, you know what happened? They crashed into each other and knocked each other down.* New Yorker 3/27/71, p114 [**1961** (1960 A Dictionary of Canadianisms), alteration of *decoy*. Spelled also *deek* and used both as a noun and a verb, the term became current in Canada in the early 1960's.]

Delaney amendment or **Delaney clause**, an amendment of the U.S. Food, Drug and Cosmetic Act which forbids the use of any food additive or other substance that is shown to cause cancer in animals or people, regardless of the amount. *If the suspect tumors can indeed be linked to saccharin (rather than to impurities in the drug or to other factors), the FDA* [Food and Drug Administration] *will once again invoke the Delaney amendment.* Science News 3/3/73, p134 [**1970**, named after James J. Delaney, born 1901, U.S. Congressman from Long Island City, N.Y., author of the amendment] ► Although twenty years old at the time, the Delaney amendment became the focus of intense controversy during the 1970's. The amendment became extremely controversial as scientific analysis became more sophisticated and it became possible to detect extremely minute quantities of substances. Many scientists believe there is no need to ban a useful substance if the amount used is safe, asserting the proper role of the investigator is to make an analysis of the RISK-BENEFIT RATIO, in which the hazards of using a substance are balanced against the benefits. Other scientists believe the Delaney clause is necessary for the protection of the consumer.

delawyer, *v.t. U.S.* to eliminate the need for a lawyer's services in (a legal proceeding). *Procedural reforms such as no-fault insurance offer ways to "delawyer" particular problems. In New Zealand, virtually all lawsuits for personal injuries (not just auto accidents) have been abolished; these injuries are now handled through a nationwide insurance system.* NY Times Magazine 2/8/76, p21 **[1976]** —**delawyerization,** *n.: Group legal service plans, extensive use of paralegal aides for routine functions, . . . "delawyerization" through arbitration, no-fault systems of compensation, and encouragement of less expensive lay alternatives—such reforms would improve access to services and reduce costs for the vast majority who are neither wealthy nor impoverished.* Harper's 2/76, p86

deletion, *n.* the removal or loss of a section of genetic material from a chromosome. *The first mutation was a deletion that removed a "letter" from the genetic message; the second mutation inserted an extraneous letter. Such mutations are called "frame-shift" mutations since they cause succeeding bases to be "read" in incorrect groups of three.* Scientific American 1/71, p46 **[1970]** ► A similar earlier (1920's) sense of *deletion,* used in cytology, is "the loss or breaking off of a piece of chromosome in a cell."

deli ('deli:), *n. U.S.* short for *delicatessen. And it's time for lunch. He goes out and buys a pastrami sandwich at the deli.* New Yorker 6/21/69, p37 **[1954]**

delir (di'lir), *v.i.* to be delirious; experience delirium; hallucinate. *Ten years before, in Serbia, the only woman he had ever loved—another man's wife—had become pregnant by him. She suffered a miscarriage, and died the next night, deliring and praying.* New Yorker 5/19/73, p36 **[1973,** back formation from *delirium]*

deliver, *v.i. U.S.* to carry out or fulfill an expectation; make good. *Nixon will have to deliver spectacularly to retain his present thin edge, and it now looks as if he would be doing well to hold his own.* New Yorker 10/23/71, p158 *This autumn the President has a major opportunity to deliver on his pledge.* NY Times 10/28/70, p46 **[1959,** shortening of *deliver the goods* (1940's)]

deliverance, *n.* the freeing of a person from the influence or control of evil spirits. *Seldom do all the church members accept the practice of deliverance and sometimes the church splits. But in many cases, exorcism leads to increases in church attendance and financial support.* NY Times 11/29/74, p33 **[1974]**

Delphi, *n.* a method of forecasting future developments, especially in an area of technology or science, by collating and summarizing the ideas of a group of experts. *Delphi is a class of routines for getting panels of experts to work anonymously together, perhaps by way of consoles, with feedback from a controlling group that compares and contrasts the answers and the relative expertise.* Scientific American 5/70, p146 Often used attributively. —**Delphi method:** *He intends to apply the so-called Delphi method in backing future productions—a kind of consensus forecasting technique in which panels of different experts are called in.* Times (London) 3/9/72, p19 —**Delphi process:** *Such a consensus is sought through the participation of 12 to 15 qualified experts whose judgments will be obtained, combined, and refined in a systematic way—a variant of the Delphi process that has been used extensively to apply expertise to important issues not yet open to analysis.* New Yorker 11/12/73, p171 —**Delphi technique:** *Clearly, what we need is a way of utilising the advantages of a meeting while at the same time also avoiding its many disadvantages . . . the Delphi technique, pioneered by Dr Olaf Helmer at the United*

States Airforce, RAND Corporation . . . *has been used in the development of weapons systems and some leading British firms have used the method in developing both production techniques and the products themselves.* New Scientist 10/10/74, p90 **[1963,** after *Delphi,* ancient site in Greece of the Delphic oracle]

Delphology, *n.* the study of methods for making accurate forecasts of future developments, especially in technology and science. Compare FUTURISTICS. *Today's futurologists have elaborated the procedures. They draw data from more disciplines and process them with computers. They talk of Delphology, of model-building, of scenarios.* Saturday Review 1/1/72, p15 **[1969,** from *Delphi* (the site of the Delphic oracle) + *-ology* study of]

delta agent or **delta virus,** a defective virus that can exist only in combination with the virus which causes serum hepatitis. *The delta agent . . . believed to be on the rise world-wide, can make chronic hepatitis B infection lethal.* Science News 10/18/86, p244 . . . *when the delta virus combines with another virus that causes hepatitis B infection, it produces a much more deadly infection than hepatitis B alone.* NY Times 8/4/87, pC6 **[1986]**

Delta blues, country music influenced by the blues. *Muddy Waters is the kind of dirty blues, down-home blues, funky blues or straight blues—most properly known as Delta or country blues.* Time 8/9/71, p40 **[1970,** named for the Mississippi delta region in southern Louisiana]

delta waves, large, slow brain waves marking the deepest level of sleep. *High-amplitude delta waves in sleep are almost typical of youth. With increasing age, however, the EEG* [electroencephalogram] *of the delta waves becomes smaller and flatter.* 1970 Britannica Yearbook of Science and the Future, p310 **[1966]**

demagnify, *v.t.* to reduce to microscopic size, especially for storage; miniaturize. *These systems are really transmission electron microscopes working in reverse. Instead of a specimen there is a mask, and instead of magnifying the object formed by the specimen the object formed by the mask is demagnified.* Scientific American 11/72, p41 **[1960]**

de-man, *v.i., v.t.* **1** *British.* to reduce the manpower of a plant, industry, etc.; remove from a job or employment. *One expert estimated recently that one employee in three was surplus in British airlines. But de-manning on this scale would cause great disruption to industrial relations.* New Scientist 3/22/73, p673 **2** *U.S.* to deprive of manhood or virility; emasculate. *The girl here is a prototypical Woman as seen by the Male Chauvinist Pig—brainy, too alert, de-manning; and the man in the film is women's lib prototypical Man—expecting working women to do their jobs without talking about them and to get on with the cooking in good time.* New Yorker 7/9/73, p19 **[1971]**

demand-driven, *adj.* caused by increased demand for a product or service. *Given that health care is essentially a demand-driven industry—that is, that a large part of its costs are the result of increased demand for more and better services and technology—how can we, as a society, place limits on spending without also limiting medical progress?* NY Times 2/19/84, p28 **[1980]**

demandeur (dəmãn'dœr), *n.* one who makes a request, as before a court of law; petitioner. *As things worked out, SALT did not begin in the summer, as the President suggested. Both sides wanted talks, but neither would be pushed. The Nixon Administration began by feeling pushed, and refused to be rushed. Now Moscow, having been cast in the role of demandeur by Washington, would not be hurried.* New Yorker 5/19/73, p112 **[1966,** from French]

demand inflation, another name for DEMAND-PULL. *There are two quite different kinds of inflation: demand inflation, when, through credit expansion and tax reduction, money demand is allowed to rise much faster than productive capacity; and the cost inflation which follows.* Manchester Guardian Weekly 6/6/70, p23 **[1968]**

demand-pull, *n.* Also called **demand-pull inflation**. inflation caused by excessive demand for goods and services forcing the cost of production higher and therefore raising the market price. Compare COST-PUSH. . . . *demand-pull [is] an excessive pressure of demand on productive capacity—so that cost-push, or the rising cost of the factors of production, is seen simply as a consequence of demand-pull.* Manchester Guardian Weekly 8/22/70, p22 [**1958**]

demand-side, *adj.* of or advocating an economic policy designed to stimulate demand for goods and services that will be met by increased employment. Compare SUPPLY-SIDE. *Demand-side economists, who have long held sway, emphasize Federal budgetary and monetary policies as a means of manipulating demand for goods and services and, thereby, spurring the production side of the economy.* NY Times Magazine 3/23/80, p33 [**1979**]

de-Maoification, *n.* another term for DE-MAOIZATION. *While Teng has not directly attacked the memory of the Great Helmsman, a gradual process of de-Maoification is under way in China.* Time 11/27/78, p40 [**1977**] —**de-Maoify**, *v.t.:* *The real question in Peking at the end of the year, with the Central Committee meeting in the Great Hall of the People, and purple ink on the wallposters outside, was not whether Mao should be de-Maoified two years after his death.* Manchester Guardian Weekly 1/1/79, p10

de-Maoization, *n.* the repudiation or reversal of the policies of the Chinese Communist leader Mao Tse-tung (Mao Zedong), 1893-1976. *Just as the de-Stalinisation debate in Russia was part of the struggle for power between Stalin's successors, so the de-Maoisation debate is a sign of a similar struggle now going on in Peking.* Manchester Guardian Weekly 5/7/78, p9 [**1969**, patterned after *de-Stalinization* (1957)]

de-marketing, *n.* the allocation of scarce goods to meet demand. *The word [de-marketing] popped up like a pothole with the arrival of the fuel and energy crunch. Some companies, hurt by shortages, found that they had to scurry to satisfy demand rather than increase demand, and that process became known as de-marketing, i.e., undoing, backing off, holding the line.* Advertising Age 4/8/74, p14 [**1974**]

demento, *n.* U.S. Slang. a demented person; lunatic. *All the electronic gear in Miami could not replicate the effect of 60,000 live dementos in Little Rock's War Memorial Stadium on a humid October night.* NY Times Magazine 1/1/78, p19 *Treman Cottage . . . has two small public rooms, hardly suitable for a peripheral lurker of any description, much less the brooding Heathcliff of the playing field Ms. Godwin saw. Can she have been peering through her curtains at some other lone demento?* Harper's 4/80, p4 [**1978**, from *demented* + *-o* as in *wacko, weirdo*]

demi-mini, *adj.* shorter than mini. . . . *they [five girls] all wore tiny, frothy demi-mini shifts, which barely covered their behinds and seemed designed to show even more leg than they had.* New Yorker 9/16/67, p41 —*n.* a skirt or dress shorter than mini. . . . *Designer Mary Quant, 32, grandam of Chelsea's [London] fashion hippies, decided to hike the hems still higher . . . Mary has designed demure little matching boxer shorts for the birds to wear with their demi-minis.* Time 11/18/66, p26 [**1966**]

demi-pension (dəmi:pä'syē), *n. French.* an arrangement in a boarding house, hotel, etc., to eat only some meals, usually the noon meal; (literally) half-board. . . . *a regrettable tendency on insisting that his guests take at least demi-pension (from £2 10s. per head) which wouldn't be so bad if his restaurant were not mediocre compared with some of the others.* Sunday Times (London) 9/14/69, p65 [**1951**]

demiworld, *n.* a world or sphere on the fringes of conventional, wealthy, or reputable society; demimonde. *Nor is there any need to make imaginative leaps into Crane's inner life since Crane himself reported what it was like for him to experience the demiworld of the city, the* Commodore *disaster, and the battlefields of Greece and Cuba.* Atlantic 11/68, p48 *Home in New York, his* Scrutiny *byline and his impressive set of academic credentials opened the doors of literary society, a demi-*

world about which Podhoretz writes entertainingly and knowledgeably. Time 1/19/68, p67 [**1967**] ▶ *Demiworld* is a partial translation of French *demimonde*. The only earlier evidence for *demiworld* is an 1862 quotation from the London *Times* in the *OED:* "The bye-world . . . which the French call the *demi-monde.* The demi-world or bye-world is an alluring theme." The *OED* labels the entry *nonce-word*.

demo, *n.* a sample or type of record, play, etc., used for demonstration. [Bernard] *Purdie [a guitar and drum player] finally got a job with Lonnie Youngblood's orchestra, went on the road, returned, and went out again, with Les Cooper's band . . . Then he started making demos, or demonstration records. "When they make the demo the master, that's the big break. Mine came when they made the master of 'Mercy, Mercy' from our demo."* New Yorker 11/18/67, p56 [**1966**]

Demochristian, *n.* a member of one of the Christian Democratic political parties of Europe. *Both of Italy's main parties, the Christian Democrats and the Communists, face this in somewhat flabby condition. The Demochristians are in far the worse shape. They have ruled almost since World War II, first by themselves and then in varying coalitions.* NY Times 4/23/72, p15 [**1966**, from *Democ*ratic + *Christian*]

demographics, *n.pl. Especially U.S.* statistics of populations, including size, distribution, economic status, etc.; demographic data. *Who bought the first 125,000 mopeds? The demographics are unsettled: Ed Kaufman, M.B.A. director of communications, says that more women than men are buying, but mopeder Gloria Alvarez . . . says she has yet to see another woman mopeder.* NY Times Magazine 5/15/77, p97 *To the surprise of no one, the demographics of today's jazz consumer reveal an older, more mature fan: mostly male, college-educated and between the ages of twenty and thirty.* Rolling Stone 1/11/79, p43 [**1967**, from *demographic, adj.* (OED 1882)]

demographic transition, a major change in the patterns of fertility and mortality of a population. *Three stages of the demographic transition can usually be detected in every population. The first stage is characterized by high and almost equal birth and death rates and by a low rate of growth. That pattern has existed in most populations throughout most of history. In the second stage mortality declines and is followed by a lagging decline in fertility, so that the rate of population growth is high. The third stage is characterized by low birth and death rates and therefore by a rate of growth that declines gradually.* Scientific American 3/73, p15 [**1971**]

demonetarize, *v.t.* to withdraw from use as a monetary standard. *The ban on private ownership is being lifted as one step in a longterm U.S. effort to demonetarize gold—that is, unlink it from currency values and turn it into just another commodity the price of which can go down as well as up without affecting—or afflicting—the international monetary system.* Time 1/6/75, p84 [**1973**, alteration (influenced by *monetary*) of *demonetize* (1852)] —**demonetarization**, *n.: The Italians' tactics, it is felt in Paris, have been to divert attention from their own monetary waywardness by going over to the attack, and insisting on a demonetarization of gold and the creation of a fully institutionalized monetary union, with a central intervention fund.* Times (London) 7/28/72, p7

demonology, *n.* a grouping of persons or things viewed by their opponents as evil, harmful, or disruptive influences. *Like his patron, the President, [Murray] Chotiner is one of the fixtures of liberal demonology, and one, as it happens, who can never be counted out.* Atlantic 10/70, p52 *Prof. Amitai Etzioni's Sept. 5 "Topics" column "Genetic Manipulation and Morality" is another contribution to the demonology of genetic engineering that obscures the important dilemmas of health policy requiring open-ended public discussion and participation.* NY Times 9/26/70, p28 [**1956**, figurative sense of the term for a belief in or a treatise on demons]

demotivate, *v.t.* to cause to lose motivation or incentive. *The fact was that tax today in Britain started at too low a level and increased at too fast a rate. The present tax levels demotivated people and drove them out of the country.* Times (London)

11/7/78, p4 [**1974**] —**demotivation,** *n.: A study in managerial demotivation is provided by a survey of over 500 executives published yesterday. It shows that 51 per cent of the respondents believe themselves to be less keen to obtain promotion than they were five years ago.* Times (London) 6/1/77, p21

demystification, *n.* the act or process of demystifying; enlightenment. . . . *he* [the French painter Jean Dubuffet] *proposes "institutes for deculturalization, nihilistic gymnasiums as it were, where particularly lucid instructors would give a course in deconditioning and demystification lasting several years* . . . New Yorker 6/6/70, p56 *In an age of unfolding rationality and demystification of the world, this numerical growth of scientists, technologists and technicians has been accompanied by the development of a new faith and a new priesthood.* New Scientist and Science Journal 12/16/71, p165 [**1964**]

demystify, *v.t.* to rid of mystifying elements; enlighten. . . . *what the mature William Blake fails to make clear can often be demystified with the help of the commentator and the textual exegesis.* Sunday Times (London) 2/16/69, p12 [Robert] *Morris, of course, maintains that his aim is to demystify the viewer. Says he of his sculpture: "You don't have to explore it. The information is given at once."* Time 5/17/68, p60 [**1959**]

demythify, *v.t.* to remove the myths from; strip or rid of mythical aspects. *They are equally convinced of the need for provoking rebellion through a school play. But while Franc considers the play as a chance to demythify the politico-religious system oppressing their comrades, Angelo wants to incite a trauma which will allow them to "take over."* Manchester Guardian Weekly (Le Monde section) 2/24/73, p19 [**1964**, variant of *demythicize* (1951); perhaps influenced by DEMYSTIFY] —**demythification,** *n.: Then there is that class of film that doesn't quite make it into the Top Ten, but which has given pleasure all the same: Peter Bogdanovitch's Paper Moon; The Long Goodbye, Robert Altman's demythification of Raymond Chandler.* Times (London) 12/28/73, p7

denasserization, *n.* the repudiation or reversal of the policies of Gamal Abdel Nasser, 1918-1970, the president of Egypt from 1956 until his death. *Before the October 1973 war, the great slogan of the initial cautious phase of denasserisation was the "correction" (of the arbitrary, repressive excesses of the great man's rule), and few people—Communists, Moslem brothers, or anyone else—could quarrel with that.* Manchester Guardian Weekly 6/28/75, p9 [**1971**; compare DE-MAOIZATION]

dendroclimatic, *adj.* of or relating to dendroclimatology. *The great age of these trees makes them of enormous scientific interest. They are important in dendro-climatic research—the study of climatic change as revealed by tree-ring data—and for the study of past fluctuations in the concentration of radiocarbon in the atmosphere.* Geographical Magazine 6/72, p639 [**1972**, from *dendro-* of trees (from Greek *déndron* tree) + *climatic*]

dendroclimatology, *n.* the study of past climates and climatic conditions by analysis of the annual growth rings of trees. *Dendroclimatology is a subdiscipline of dendrochronology in which the annual variations in climate are reconstructed from variations in characteristics of dated rings. Tree-ring evidence for past climatic variation is unique in that the climatic information is precisely dated to the year.* McGraw-Hill Yearbook of Science and Technology 1973, p311 [**1953**] —**dendroclimatologist,** *n.: A dendroclimatologist, seeking to reconstruct variations in past climate, tries to exclude or minimize the effects of as many nonclimatic factors as possible by choosing extreme sites where climate is almost always the limiting factor in the growth of trees.* Scientific American 5/72, p93

deniability, *n. U.S.* the ability of the President or other high government official to deny having any knowledge or connection with an illegal or improper activity. *Brzezinski is known to believe that the President should have broad flexibility, including "deniability"—that is, that it should be possible to carry out operations in a way that would enable the President to deny he knew about them. The question of accountability for such operations was one of the basic issues raised in the recent examination of our intelligence activities.* New Yorker 5/1/78, p112 [**1973**, from *deny* + *-ability*] ►This term first appeared during the Watergate affair in reference to claims that the President was unaware of the wrongdoings of his subordinates.

denimed ('denəmd), *adj.* wearing denim clothing. *By 7:30 the East and South cellblocks finish breakfast. The yard fills with denimed convicts streaming from the messhalls.* Harper's 2/72, p40 *In front of the stage the denimed crowd drew into a solid mass after darkness.* Times (London) 8/25/73, p3 [**1968**]

denticare, *n.* (in Canada) a government-sponsored program of free dental care for children. *There are no signs that denticare will stir up the militant professional opposition aroused by medicare. Dr. Campbell* [of the Manitoba Dental Association] *thinks most dentists accept denticare as inevitable but will try to gain a hand in controlling the plan.* Maclean's 1/67, p1 [**1964**, from *denti-* teeth, dental + *care*, patterned after *Medicare*]

denturist, *n.* a dental technician who sells and fits false teeth, as distinguished from a licensed dentist. *In spite of major public support for denturists, on April 24 the provincial legislature voted 21-20 against legislation that would have granted them the right, which they hold in three provinces, to fit dentures for the public.* Americana Annual 1973, p508 [**1964**, from *denture* + *-ist*] —**denturism,** *n.: Bootleg dentistry—a dental laboratory technician illegally selling low-cost dentures directly to the public—had occurred sporadically in the U.S. for decades. Although these bootleg technicians had generally been kept under close surveillance, there were indications that denturism, as this activity was often called, might be expanding.* Britannica Book of the Year 1974, p464

denuclearization, *n.* the act or process of denuclearizing. *Restoration of Japanese sovereignty and denuclearization of the island* [Okinawa] *is long overdue.* NY Times 6/18/71, p39 [**1958**]

denuclearize, *v.t.* to ban or remove nuclear arms from (a place or region). *Just this month the Soviet Government took the embarrassed step of associating itself with the Spanish Communist underground party in calling for the elimination of American bases and denuclearizing the Mediterranean.* NY Times 5/13/70, p40 . . . *they "would agree not to manufacture, receive, store, or experiment with nuclear arms or nuclear launching artefacts," and to work jointly with the other Latin American republics for the area to be declared a denuclearized zone.* Times (London) 11/25/64, p11 [**1958**]

denucleate, *v.t.* to remove the nucleus or nuclei from (an atom, molecule, animal cell, etc.). *Fusion of mammalian eggs, in this case from mice, has been reported by Dr. Christopher Graham of Oxford. Using an influenza-like virus that for some unknown reason causes membranes to fuse, he has fused mouse egg cells with cells from mouse spleen and bone marrow, getting hybrid cells with double nuclei that may have undergone one cell division. But this has not yet been accomplished with denucleated egg cells, and no timetable is yet available.* Science News 3/29/69, p304 [**1969**; earlier *denucleated* (OED 1892)]

denucleation, *n.* removal of a nucleus or nuclei from an atom, molecule, animal cell, etc. . . . *at the foot of the 17-metre suction pipe, just above the suction valve, is a pressure vessel designed to act as a denucleation chamber. The operating cycle of the pump is as follows: (1) Close the discharge valve and apply a pressure of 300 atm to the bellows, by pumping oil into the pressure vessel surrounding the bellows. Maintain this pressure for 10 seconds to ensure denucleation of the water in the denucleation chamber and suction pipe.* New Scientist 1/29/70, p199 [**1970**]

de-orbit, *v.t.* to take out of orbit. *First of all, warheads de-orbited from satellites could reach their targets so quickly that a defending nation would lose the previous minutes of warning for which the United States has purchased such costly facilities as the Ballistic Missile Early Warning System.* Atlantic 8/63, p49 —*n.* the act of taking or coming out of orbit. . . . *the astronauts will make the eighth and final firing of their main rocket. This should begin the de-orbit, thrusting the spaceship earthward, its nose pointed downward at a forward angle.* NY

Times 10/20/68, pD11 *The critical factor will be to determine the moment of de-orbit.* New Scientist 11/16/67, p424 **[1963]**

deoxyribonucleoside (diːˌaksəˌraibouˈnuːkliːəˌsaid), *n.* a compound formed by the pentose sugar deoxyribose and a purine or pyrimidine base. It results from the removal of the phosphate group from a deoxyribonucleotide. *A communication by Berger, Tarien and Eichorn . . . describes proton magnetic resonance and optical spectroscopic studies of the interaction of the copper (II) acetate dimer with various ribonucleosides and deoxyribonucleosides.* Nature 10/20/72, p429 **[1968**, from *deoxyribo*se + *nucleoside*]

deoxyribonucleotide (diːˌaksəˌraibouˈnuːkliːəˌtaid), *n.* a nucleotide (compound that is the main constituent of nucleic acid) containing the pentose sugar deoxyribose. *As lability to alkali is a characteristic of ribonucleotides as opposed to deoxyribonucleotides, the next step was to see whether ribonucleases had the same effect, and so indeed it proved.* Nature 10/20/72, p428 **[1964**, from *deoxyribo*se + *nucleotide*]

dependency-prone, *adj.* tending or likely to become psychologically dependent on a drug or drugs. *Drug users may be grouped into three categories. The first consists of dependency-prone persons who, because of psychological and personality problems, have become heavily immersed in drug use and drug subcultures . . . The ghetto dweller, suffering the shock of cultural displacement and the hopelessness of a filthy slum, is in this category.* Norman E. Zinberg and John A. Robertson, Drugs and the Public, 1972, p12 **[1969]**

depollute, *v.t.* to free from pollution. . . . *May Christmas grow more comely and muted. And the world a fraction depolluted.* New Yorker 12/26/70, p23 *There is no question that just as technology has polluted the country, it can also depollute it.* Time 5/10/68, p43 *The cheapest desalted water in the US still costs 10 times as much as depolluted fresh water in water-short areas.* Sunday Times (London) 4/9/67, p31 **[1960]**

depollution, *n.* the act or process of depolluting. *The air was cleansed, slums cleared, the desert on the wrong side of the tracks converted into the Golden Triangle, and a small beginning made in the depollution of the Allegheny and Monongahela rivers.* Atlantic 2/68, p134 **[1968]**

depressurization, *n.* the removal or release of air pressure from a pressurized interior. *The explosion was caused by depressurization. It happened when the pressure inside the aircraft, kept at equivalent to that at about 8,000 ft., forced its way through the fuselage as the machine climbed into thin air at 25,000 ft.* Times (London) 9/25/70, p2 . . . *"human error and mechanical failure between them caused creeping depressurization in the spacemen's nine-foot cabin and deprived the astronauts of life-supporting oxygen on the final phase of their journey."* Time 7/12/71, p41 **[1969]**

deprivation dwarfism, a condition of stunted physical growth in children due to the lack of affection or to other forms of emotional deprivation. *Furthermore, when these children are removed from their stressful surroundings, their growth hormone switches on again and they show typical catch-up growth. This phenomenon was first described under the name of deprivation dwarfism by Lytt I. Gardner of the Upstate Medical Center of the University of New York and by Robert M. Blizzard and his colleagues at the Johns Hopkins Hospital.* Scientific American 9/73, p42 **[1969]**

deprofessionalize, *v.t.* to make less oriented toward a profession or professions. *A Yale spokesman denied that the dismissal signalled a change in policy, but Mr. Brustein . . . saw it as part of a plan, supported by Yale's new president, A. Bartlett Giamatti, to "deprofessionalize" the school, opening it up to students not interested in theater careers and introducing academic courses in addition to dramatic skills.* NY Times 6/25/78, pD9 **[1884, 1978]** —**deprofessionalization**, *n.: For to Illich the barefoot doctors represent the brightest jewel in the crown of the "deprofessionalisation" of medicine.* New Scientist 12/12/74, p835

deprogram, *v.t.* to change the beliefs or convictions of (a person, especially a youth, who is thought to have been misled into joining a sect or cult), chiefly by forceful preaching and attempts at persuasion. *Joe Alexander Jr. had been scheduled to deprogram Mike. But he was delayed on another case and the initial task was left to a group of ex-Moonies.* Daily News (New York) 12/3/75, p54 *Vigilantes have engaged in kidnaping and "deprogramming" U.S. members of oddball religious groups for years.* Time 12/18/78, p52 **[1973**, from *de-* do the opposite of + *program, v.*] —**deprogrammer**, *n.: Ted Patrick, who calls himself a "deprogrammer" of wayward young people, was found guilty last night of falsely imprisoning two young Denver women.* NY Times 5/3/74 (page not known) —**deprogramming**, *n.: In an interview Mr Heys told me that he has trained about four deprogrammers through the use of the POWER [Peoples Organized Workgroup on Ersatz Religions] manual and said that "several" successful deprogrammings have been carried out.* Times (London) 4/4/77, p4

deradicalize, *v.t.* to cause to abandon or retreat from an extreme position in politics. *Today [David] Obst's [a literary agent] cigars are longer than his hair, and he admits that hobnobbing with publishing fat cats has tended to deradicalize him.* Newsweek 1/6/75, p60 **[1971]** —**deradicalization**, *n.:* The New York citadel of New Left politics, had gone too far for too long. Somebody somewhere had to expose this intellectually treasonous, anti-American publication and the new tough-minded Commentary was the appropriate site . . . As another chapter in Commentary's de-radicalization process, there was not a shadow of a doubt about the eventual outcome of "The Case." Esquire 4/72, p112

derecognize, *v.t.* to withdraw recognition or formal acknowledgment of (a country, etc.). *The nervousness stems primarily from the fact that the United States, the Taiwanese government's staunchest ally and protector, will probably extend full diplomatic recognition, either this year or next, to the Chinese Communist government in Peking and will simultaneously "derecognize" Taiwan.* New Yorker 6/13/77, p72 **[1961]** —**derecognition**, *n.: How many of these pacts could or should survive "derecognition"? . . . How could the U.S. continue to supply arms to a government whose legitimacy it no longer formally recognizes? Government lawyers have been preparing briefs on these and other questions, and the State Department has retained some private law firms . . . to study the legal ramifications of derecognition.* Time 11/6/78, p48

deregulate, *v.t.* to remove controls from; free from regulation or control. *Dr Whitehead suggested 'de-regulating radio'—that is, to impose no requirements at all for community service as a condition for licence-holding on a long-term basis.* Listener 3/9/72, p296 *The White House also sought to persuade Congress and the courts to deregulate the price of gas.* Britannica Book of the Year 1974, p289 **[1963]** —**deregulator**, *n.: The deregulators are not uncaring or unthinking. To them, the choice is between excessive, strangling regulation and something less.* Time 11/27/78, p87 —**deregulatory**, *adj.: They ran up against a team of American negotiators in full deregulatory flight, adamant that they were not going to be deflected from their main demand to have cheap fares at once, whatever the effect might be on the airlines.* Times (London) 3/22/78, p23

deregulation, *n.* the removal of controls from; a freeing from regulation or control. *Airlines tried to meet new competition under deregulation, mainly by slashing labor costs. The pilots union urged re-regulation of fares, contending that airline costcutting amid rampant fare discounting could threaten air safety along with their jobs and salaries.* 1984 World Book Year Book, p504 **[1963]**

derepress, *v.t.* to activate (an enzyme) or induce (a gene) to operate by disengaging the repressor. *The group . . . now hopes to find out how genes are repressed and derepressed—turned off and on—so that genes can be made to operate when required.* Americana Annual 1970, p437 **[1960]**

derepressor, *n.* another name for INDUCER. *There is evidence that molecules known as repressors and derepressors play a role in turning genes, and protein synthesis, on and off.* Science News 2/28/70, p215 **[1965]**

Dergue (dərg), *n.* Usually **the Dergue.** the socialist ruling council of Ethiopia, established as the provisional government after the overthrow of Emperor Haile Selassie in 1974. Also spelled DIRGUE. *The military administration, the Dergue, has . . . announced a jargon-heavy political programme which included the rights to form political parties and to demonstrate (provided such activities were "anti-feudal, anti-bureaucratic, anti-capitalistic and anti-imperialistic").* Manchester Guardian Weekly 5/2/76, p10 [**1975,** from Amharic, literally, committee]

dermaloptical vision (dərmə'lɑptəkəl), technical name for EYE-LESS SIGHT. *It is not clear from this paper just which parapsychological phenomena "obviously do happen"; the only ones which the authors unambiguously support as authentic, such as Kirlian photography and Rosa Kuleshova's "dermaloptical vision"—the alleged ability to "see" colours by touching them—are explicitly stated not to be parapsychological.* New Scientist 2/13/75, p398 [**1972,** from *dermal + optical*]

dermatoglyph ('dərmətə,glif *or* dər'mætə,glif), *n.* one of the surface lines, markings, or patterns of the skin. *Besides uncovering factors that contribute to the molding of individual dermatoglyphs, Green hopes studies of skin cells in culture will provide clues to greater mysteries of control of cell movement and of local influences on development.* Science News 7/8/78, p24 [**1970,** back formation from *dermatoglyphics* (OEDS 1926) the study of skin markings or patterns, from Greek *dérmatos* skin + *glyphikós* of carving]

derrière-garde (,deri'er'gɑrd), *n.* another name for ARRIÈRE-GARDE. [Alec] *Wilder has steadily applied these principles to his own work, which comprises an astonishing canon. He has, with amusement, called himself "the president of the derrière-garde," but he is a unique and adventurous composer, who has written a huge body of music, both popular and formal, most of it nearly unknown.* New Yorker 7/9/73, p37 [**1963,** from French *derrière* behind + *garde* guard (as in *avant-garde*); probably formed in English]

DES, abbreviation of *diethylstilbestrol. Several women told the panel that cancer had claimed the lives of their "DES daughters" and another woman, whose mother had taken DES during pregnancy, blamed the drug for the cancer operation last year that left her unable to bear children.* New York Post 2/28/75, p21 [**1972**]

desalivate, *adj.* having the salivary glands removed. *In a second series of experiments, the researchers applied vaseline to the lips of desalivate pups every two hours during the daytime.* New Scientist and Science Journal 1/21/71, p107 [**1971**]

deschool, *v.t.* to abolish traditional schools in (a society, etc.). *The radical deschooling of society begins, therefore, with the unmasking by cultural revolutionaries of the myth of schooling.* Saturday Review 10/17/70, p68 *To eliminate the "social addiction" to attending school, his deschooled world would replace most formal classes with networks of "learning exchanges."* Time 6/7/71, p25 [**1970**]

deschooler, *n.* a person who advocates the elimination of compulsory schools and their replacement with voluntary learning centers. *From deschoolers and free schoolers, from the radical right and the radical left, the education system is under attack, and so are the teachers who work in it.* Times (London) 10/11/72, p12 [**1970,** from *deschool + -er*]

descriptor, *n.* a symbol or group of symbols that identifies a particular subject in the storage unit of a computer. *To make the process totally computerized, the descriptors filed in the computer would also have to be obtained from the fingerprint by an automatic reading device.* Science News 5/25/68, p495 *Each flight would be assigned a descriptor for use by the computer. As the flight proceeds, the computer would simultaneously calculate the plane's position, search its data bank for other aircraft in the area, operate the display screens of air route centers, and provide data for evaluation by the controllers.* 1969 Collier's Encyclopedia Year Book, p234 [**1965**]

deselect, *v.t. U.S.* to discharge (a trainee) during training. Compare DEHIRE. *. . . . I couldn't help recalling my own experience in the Peace Corps in Malawi. Nowhere else can a person be fired by being told he has been "selected out" or "deselected."* Time 10/3/69, p7 *The road from applicant to trainee to overseas volunteer is a hard one. Many individuals do not follow through. Many are "de-selected."* NY Times 6/24/68, p7 [**1968**]

desertification (,dezərtəfə'keiʃən), *n.* the process by which land turns into a desert, especially by the encroachment of a neighboring desert or through excessive grazing or cultivation. *The creation of deserts or desert-like conditions is termed desertification. Generally thought of as the degradation of lands by natural and human means, desertification results in the diminution or destruction of the land's biological productivity. The process of desertification is at least as old as civilization but only recently has it been recognized as a serious global problem.* Science News 10/29/77, p282 [**1973,** from *desert + -ification* a making or causing to become]

desex, *v.t. U.S.* to remove sexual or sexist references from. Compare DEGENDER. *Firemen will become fire fighters and kennelmen will become kennel attendants in the latest round of official "desexing." The city Civil Service Commission Wednesday approved the "desexing" of 170 job titles in an effort to eliminate sex discrimination.* Tuscaloosa News (Alabama) 9/15/74, p5c *On a printed form not yet completely desexed, all plebes* [at West Point] *were asked: "What was the highest rank you attained in the Boy Scouts?"* Time 7/19/76, p74 [**1974,** from *de-* remove + *sex*, or extended from earlier senses: a. to castrate or spay (OEDS 1911); b. to deprive of sexual characteristics or appeal (1962)]

desi ('dezi:), *n. U.S.* short for DESIGNATED HITTER. *(No one has yet suggested an effective estoppage or cease-and-desist for the sportswriters who have begun to refer to the tenth man as the "desi.")* *This year, the American League bashed 1,552 homers, as against its 1971 total of 1,484—the designated hitters again making the difference.* New Yorker 11/19/73, p184 [**1973**]

designated hitter, *U.S. Baseball.* a tenth player who may be named in the lineup to bat for the pitcher anywhere in the batting order. *Abbreviation:* DH *In his first winning move, Robinson entered his own name in the Indians' line-up as designated hitter—then stepped up to the plate in his first turn at bat and belted one of those home runs that will live in legend and in the memories of the 56,000 roaring fans who saw it.* Newsweek 4/21/75, p57 [**1973**]

designer, *adj.* designed by and bearing the signature of a noted fashion designer. *Neither will you refer to your pants as slacks, trousers or cut-offs. But jeans are OK. Especially designer jeans.* Daily News (New York) 1/21/79, p5 *What kind of elegance? The idea of a "designer fragrance," all too familiar today, probably did not exist before Chanel.* Connoisseur 2/88, p46 [**1966,** adjective use of the noun]

designer drug, *U.S.* a narcotic made so that it does not fall under the category of a CONTROLLED SUBSTANCE. *They are "designer drugs"—designed, that is, to get around the law. The drugs are created by underground chemists who tinker with the molecular structure of illegal narcotics to produce variants that are not explicitly banned by federal law. Thus it is legal to make and use designer drugs. But it is by no means safe.* Time 4/8/85, p61 [**1983**]

desk study, *British.* a study made without extensive field and laboratory investigation. *Approval is being sought from the Government by the Water Resources Board to carry out a detailed survey for a new scheme to develop the Wash as a fresh water supply. The details are contained in a report published yesterday. Estimates made in the desk study put the cost of the first reservoir at £25m.* Times (London) 9/11/70, p2 [**1963**]

desktop, *adj.* designed to be used or placed on top of a desk. Compare LAPTOP. *Precisely because every model must compromise on some aspect or another of desktop computers, each manufacturer comes up with a different formula in hopes of striking the perfect balance.* Gannett Westchester Newspapers 4/26/87, pH2 [**1958**]

desktop publishing, publishing by means of personal computers and special programs. *Desktop publishing moved to the* *forefront of new and efficient ways to use personal computers . . . for easy and inexpensive preparation of school newspapers, corporate reports, and virtually any other publication that combines text and graphics on the same page.* Encyclopedia Science Supplement (Grolier) 1987, p101 **[1984]**

desmosine ('dezməsain), *n.* an amino acid formed in elastic tissue as the linking medium that gives the tissue its elasticity and stability. *Elastin incorporated two previously unrecognized amino acids, which they named desmosine and isodesmosine (from an original Greek root word meaning "bond"). These two amino acids were found to perform cross-linking functions in elastin.* Scientific American 6/71, p49 **[1968,** from Greek *desmós* band, bond + English *-ine* (chemical suffix)]

desmosome ('dezməsoum), *n.* a thickened part of the cell membrane by which epithelial cells are attached to each other. *The first suggestion that cells were linked by special channels came from electro-physiological experiments. Lanthanum staining and electron microscopy then demonstrated that definite structures, classified morphologically as either tight junctions, desmosomes, or gap junctions, existed between cells.* New Scientist 7/11/74, p62 **[1968,** from Greek *desmós* band, bond + English *-some* body]

desorb, *v.t.* to restore (an absorbed or adsorbed substance) to its original state. *Puraq's new process* [of desalting seawater] *uses a hydrophylic polymer solvent which can be made to desorb water by heat. The result is desalination nearly 50 per cent cheaper than by distillation.* New Scientist 1/29/70, p203 **[1964,** earlier "to remove from a surface" (OED 1924)]

despin, *v.t., v.i.* to neutralize the effect of revolving motion by revolving an attached object in the opposite direction at the same speed. *To maintain permanent radio illumination of the Earth the horn aerial mounted at one axis is mechanically despun in the opposite direction to spin stabilization.* Science Journal 1/70, p18 *It also is essential that the satellite does not spin, for that would wrap the antennas around it. The "despinning" began on Monday.* NY Times 7/11/68, p14 **[1960]**

destabilize, *v.t.* to render (a government) unstable or incapable of functioning. *There was little ideological difference between the two parties, but the BLP was reportedly somewhat more to the right . . . and less concerned about allegations of U.S. Central Intelligence Agency plots to "destabilize" Barbados and other governments in the region.* Britannica Book of the Year 1977, p163 **[1974,** specialized sense of the verb "to make (anything) unstable, deprive (something) of stability"] **—destabilization,** *n.: Between 1970 and 1973 the C.I.A. had spent five million dollars in Chile on "destabilization" (a euphemism for making it impossible for a government to govern).* New Yorker 4/10/78, p45

destress, *v.t.* to eliminate excess strain on. *Immediate measures to guarantee the track's safety and eventual destressing (a heating process) of the entire existing mileage should prevent further serious trouble on these lines, Major Rose* [Major C. F. Rose, an inspecting officer of railways] *says.* Times (London) 4/2/70, p2 **[1969]**

desublimate, *v.t.* to divest of the ability to sublimate one's instinctive or primitive impulses. *For Rico is persistently, irremediably desublimated: weakwilled, anxious to please, full of doubts and scruples, and inevitably "underneath" in relation to the assorted sublimates with whom he comes in contact.* Times (London) 5/1/72, p8 **[1969]**

desuete (di'swi:t), *adj.* outdated; outmoded. . . . *our artistic history and heritage we learn backwards, astonished to find what were once hailed as strokes of trenchant originality emerging from earlier now neglected and desuete masters.* Manchester Guardian Weekly 5/1/71, p19 **[1971,** from French *désuète,* from Latin *dēsuētus,* past participle of *dēsuēscere* to disuse. As a direct borrowing from Latin *dēsuētus,* the form *desuete* existed in English during the 1700's. It is found in Bailey's *Universal Etymological English Dictionary* (1727) and defined as "out of use." The French form *désuète* (feminine of *désuet*) has been recorded only since the 1800's]

desynchronized sleep. See the quotation for the meaning. Compare SYNCHRONIZED SLEEP. See also PARADOXICAL SLEEP. *The two distinct states of sleep that we all experience differ in so many ways that they are usually given two separate names. The state characterized by eye movements, dreams, and irregular, desynchronized brain waves is called D-sleep for dreaming or desynchronized sleep. Such sleep is also called rapid eye movement (REM) sleep, or paradoxical sleep, because it is very light in some ways and very deep in others.* 1977 World Book Year Book, p112 **[1974]**

DET, abbreviation of *diethyltryptamine,* a hallucinogenic drug. Compare DMT, STP. *The group also includes some drugs, not used in medicine, generally referred to as STP, DMT and DET; these have not been controlled before.* Times (London) 3/12/70, p1 *The use of LSD (lysergic acid diethylamide) appeared to decline during 1968, as did the use of some other hallucinogens, or psychedelics, such as STP, DMT and DET.* Americana Annual 1968, p483 **[1966]**

détente (dei'tɑnt), *n.* the improvement of relations between countries, political groups, etc., that have opposing views or interests. *Kissinger's solution was detente (he wasn't the first to come up with the idea, but he was the one to get it implemented). Detente, as the French writer Andre Fontaine neatly put it, was not the same as peace or else it would have been called peace. It was an arrangement whereby a combination of political, military, technical and commercial agreements were reached for the expressed purpose of preventing the sort of confrontation that would end in mutual annihilation. For a time, roughly between the summers of 1972 and 1975, the process was working.* Manchester Guardian Weekly (Washington Post section) 7/10/77, p17 *Working harder for détente than any other statesman, Tito this year visited Moscow, Peking and Washington. His formula for détente is a balance of forces between the Soviet Union and the United States, relative political stability within their alliances, progress toward disarmament and freedom for all nations to develop independently.* NY Times Magazine 12/3/78, p182 **[1973,** extended use from early 1900's sense of easing of tensions between nations, from French, literally, slackening]

detox ('di:ˌtɑks), *n.* short for *detoxication* or *detoxification* (used especially in reference to the part of a hospital or a clinic where alcoholics or drug addicts are treated). *"I went to detox again . . . and it's been five years since I came out and I haven't had a drink or pill since."* NY Times Magazine 8/6/78, p11 **—v.t.** short for *detoxicate* or *detoxify. "They did get me detoxed and clean. They told me I was an alcoholic. . ."* NY Times Magazine 8/6/78, p38 **[1972** for verb; **1975** for noun]

developed, *adj.* having high industrial and commercial production; economically and technologically advanced or self-sufficient. *A company which wants to make money should not invest in a developed country. It should head for the Third World.* Manchester Guardian Weekly 2/29/76, p5 *The world's so-called "developed" section—Europe, Russia, North America, temperate South America, Australia, New Zealand, and Japan—had a total population of about 1.2 billion.* 1978 World Book Year Book, p443 **[1962,** from past participle of *develop;* also used earlier of skilled workers (OED 1859)]

developing, *adj.* not yet developed; lacking in technology or in capital, resources, etc., and often dependent on economic aid. Compare EMERGING. *At stake was the critical issue of future economic cooperation between the OPEC countries, 14 developing states, and the industrial nations which included Canada, the U.S., Japan and the nine European Common Market countries.* Maclean's 2/9/76, p41 *Largely rural developing nations—like India, Brazil and Tunisia—realize that computers can speed the time it takes them to develop into industrialized powerbrokers.* Science News 9/23/78, p214 **[1962,** from present participle of *develop*]

developmental biology, the study of the development of organisms. *Specifically, the question developmental biology seeks to answer concerns the way in which a single fertilized cell can grow into an organized mass of millions of cells, of many dif-*

ferent types, all functioning together as a whole. New Scientist and Science Journal 1/28/71, p174 [**1957**]

Development Decade, a ten-year program sponsored by the United Nations to promote the economic and social development of Third World countries. The first Development Decade was from 1961-70. *On the economic and social side, by contrast, the responsible heads of the main UN programmes laboured unceasingly throughout the year to put their machinery in good shape to meet the challenge of the Second Development Decade.* Annual Register of World Events in 1970, p332 [**1970**]

Devil's Triangle, another name for BERMUDA TRIANGLE. *Ships and planes disappear, time skips a beat, and earthlings board extraterrestrial craft, all in the Atlantic region known as the Bermuda, or Devil's Triangle—or so a continuing stream of books insists.* 1976 Collier's Encyclopedia Year Book, p161 [**1975**]

Devlinite ('devlə,nait), *n.* a supporter or follower of Bernadette Devlin, born 1947, an Irish Catholic civil rights leader in Northern Ireland and member of the British House of Commons. Compare PAISLEYITE. *We must, in the next year, get together, all of us, Paisleyites, Devlinites, civil rights groups, students, Orangemen, I.R.A.* [Irish Republican Army] *men, the lot, we must prove once and for all that we cannot be left any longer in the dead hands of our Unionist masters. . .* Atlantic 9/70, p62 [**1970**]

devolatilize, *v.t., v.i.* to make or become free of volatile matter. *The CO_2 acceptor process uses lignite rather than coal. The moisture content of the lignite is removed by flash drying, and the lignite is devolatilized and transferred into the gasifier unit.* McGraw-Hill Yearbook of Science and Technology 1970, p151 [**1965**, probably re-formed as back formation from *devolatilization* (1963) but found earlier (OED 1868)] —**devolatilization**, *n.: Complete devolatilization of the coal was not achieved, the amount of volatile matter remaining being equivalent to 20 to 70% of the original volatile matter content.* Nature 4/21/72, p398

devolve, *v.t.* (in British politics) to grant under a policy of increased self-government to the elected legislative body of a political entity in the United Kingdom. *Most of those who want complete "devolution," and many of those who want more powers than Mr. Wilson is proposing to devolve, have joined the Scottish Nationalist Party.* NY Times 1/24/76, p6 [**1974**] —**devolver**, *n.: "It is hardly possible to proceed with the present proposals," Mr Mackintosh says, "when there are prominent opponents in the Cabinet and among English backbench MPs on both sides of the House, when the devolvers among Scottish Labour and Liberal MPs can scarcely bear to commend the proposals, and the Secretary of State almost breaks into tears every time he has to defend the project."* Times (London) 1/12/76, p2

dex, *n. Slang.* a tablet of dextroamphetamine, a stimulant. Also called DEXIE. *Gets drunk once a month on 3.2 beer. Pops a dex or a downie occasionally, especially during exam week. Tried marijuana at a be-in last summer and would do it again if someone had it lying around.* Harper's 9/71, p63 [**1966**, short for *Dexedrine*, a trademark for *dextroamphetamine*]

dexed, *adj. Slang.* stimulated by dextroamphetamine pills: high on dexes. *Thus, your basic Tequila Sunrise is not merely one of those chic, absurdly yin, innocuously thirst-quenching drinks (so prized by dehydrated athletes, entertainers, and heavily dexed writers working against viciously unfair deadlines), it is also Bombsville-oh-roonie.* Saturday Review 8/12/72, p25 [**1972**]

dexie or **Dexie**, *n. Slang.* another name for DEX. *"Go Ask Alice," records the entry of 15-year-old Alice into the world of drugs and sex . . . and finally death (perhaps murder, possibly self-induced) after several months of taking "Dexie," marijuana, "copilots," LSD, heroin, everything.* NY Times Book Review, Part II 5/7/72, p1 [**1967**, short for *Dexedrine;* see DEX]

dextranase ('dekstrə,neis), *n.* an enzyme manufactured by a fungus of the penicillium family, capable of preventing formation of dental plaque by streptococci. . . . *a certain enzyme,*

called dextranase, blocks the decay process by preventing the formation of dental plaque, a sticky substance deposited on the teeth by certain bacteria. Americana Annual 1969, p454 [**1968**, from *dextran* the bacterial product forming plaque + *-ase* enzyme]

DH, abbreviation of DESIGNATED HITTER. *The New York Yankees and Kansas City Royals have each tried a half-dozen men as DH (although the Yanks may have found their No. 1 in newly acquired Jim Hart).* Honolulu Star-Bulletin 4/23/73, pC1 [**1973**]

diabetologist, *n.* a specialist in diabetes or diabetic disorders. *Meeting recently in Boston, 34 of the nation's leading diabetologists joined forces to denounce the FDA warning* [against the use of tolbutamide, an antidiuretic drug] *and question the study upon which it was based.* Time 12/21/70, p41 [**1965**, from *diabetes* + *-ologist* specialist in]

diabolus ex machina (dai'æbələs eks 'mækənə), *pl.* **diaboli ex machina** (dai'æbə,lai). *Latin.* devil from a machine; an evil person or thing introduced into a story or account to provide an explanation or resolve a problem. The term means the same as its model, *deus ex machina,* except that here the subject personifies evil rather than any (impersonal or benevolent) being. *He* [Victor Alba] *seems to have swallowed quite uncritically the propaganda of Argentine nationalists. Thus, he undertakes to explain Latin-American history with a diabolus,* or rather *diaboli ex machina.* NY Times Book Review 8/11/68, p7 [**1961**]

Dial-A- or **dial-a-**, a combining form used, often as part of a trademark, to designate a service obtained by dialing a particular telephone number. —**dial-a-bus**: *Dial-a-bus, an innovation of London transport operates in Hampstead Garden Suburb. The 16-seat vehicles, which run every 15 minutes, pick up customers at their homes and at several fixed stops, and the driver will also stop when hailed if it is safe to do so.* 1976 Britannica Yearbook of Science and the Future, p408 —**Dial-A-Joke**: *The telephone company sponsors Dial-A-Joke and about a dozen other such service announcements. What is its newest?* Dial-a-Trivia. NY Post 1/5/79, p18 —**Dial-A-Meal**: *Dial-A-Meal operates from kitchens in Knightsbridge but when John Hildreth expands it will be into restaurants rather than to buy more kitchen premises.* Times (London) 4/10/72, p14 —**dial-a-park**: *When visiting the greater Washington metropolitan area, you can call for up-to-date information about activities in National Capitol Parks. The dial-a-park number is 426-6975.* Southern Living 5/73, p18 —**dial-a-programme**: *Who would pay? Commercial interests might, if they were allowed to link up a whole city, so that Rediffusion for example, installed its dial-a-programme system in Liverpool or a comparable area.* Listener 9/20/73, p365 —**dial-a-ride**: *To accommodate the new commuting patterns Altschuler foresees the need for much more flexible modes of transportation—he mentions car pools, buses, dial-a-ride.* National Review 8/15/75, p810 —**Dial-A-Shrink**: *"In San Francisco one has been able to buy conversation—more or less sensitively tuned instant friendship—as reported in Psychiatric News previously. Now New York . . . not to be outdone, has a new service for the emotionally forlorn—'Dial-A-Shrink'."* Thomas Szasz, The Myth of Psychotherapy, 1979, p209 [**1961**, apparently abstracted from earlier (1957) trademark *Dialaphone*, a machine dialing a telephone automatically]

dialogue des sourds (dya'lɔːg de 'sur), a discussion in which the participants pay no attention to each other's arguments. *Steering the discussion back to Minuteman, the Americans sought to explain that all elements of each side's strategic forces must be "survivable"; for one element—Minuteman, say—to become vulnerable would create dangerous anxieties, hence instability. The Russians replied, in effect, Why are you so worried about Minuteman when your sea-based forces will always remain intact and available for the second-strike role? It was a dialogue des sourds.* New Yorker 5/26/73, p86 [**1963**, from French, DIALOGUE OF THE DEAF]

dialogue of the deaf, translation of DIALOGUE DES SOURDS. *Better communication is no panacea for every industrial dispute . . . But English reserve does seem to lead, all too often, to a* *muted dialogue of the deaf.* Times (London) 2/15/74, p14 [**1970**]

dial-up, *adj.* of or relating to access by telephone lines to a computer terminal or other electronic equipment. *The Post Office's involvement includes the holding of the pages of information at a computer centre, and the provision of the dial-up service, which enables users to call up the information they want via their telephones.* Times (London) 7/28/78, p17 [**1972**, originally referring to the use of a dial telephone to initiate a station-to-station telephone call]

diamantane ('daɪəmən,teɪn), *n.* a hydrocarbon having the same spatial arrangement of carbon atoms as the diamond. *But a report (Tetrahedron Letters, 1971, p 1671) has now appeared . . . of the facile conversion of diamantane for the first time into functional derivatives suitable for the introduction of the diamantane nucleus into potential drugs.* New Scientist and Science Journal 8/5/71, p301 [**1970**]

diamondoid, *adj.* having the form of a diamond. *However, the large diamondoid hydrocarbon diamantane, although known, was extremely difficult to prepare and has thus remained a chemical curiosity.* New Scientist and Science Journal 8/5/71, p301 [**1970**]

diamond ring, a great ring of sunlight that appears briefly when the moon covers the solar disk during an eclipse. *There is a considerable drop in temperature, and, about half a minute before totality, things become much darker, the air seems to be very still, the famous "diamond ring" appears followed by Baily's Beads, and just at the instant of totality the light fades completely, the corona appears, and the eclipse is total. The diamond ring and Baily's Beads are caused by the Sun shining through the valleys on the limb of the Moon.* New Scientist 7/12/73, p91 [**1963**]

diazepam (daɪ'æzə,pæm), *n.* a chemical substance widely used as a tranquilizer. Trademark, VALIUM. *Finally, hostile tendencies can often be remarkably controlled by drugs, like Librium and diazepam, which are not sedatives, and which do not depress the general level of cerebral activity, but which act specifically and selectively on the aggressive circuits.* New Scientist 3/21/68, p623 [**1961**, from *di-* two + *az-* nitrogen + *ep-* besides, distinctive + *-am* ammonia]

diazotroph (daɪ'æzə,trɑf), *n.* any nitrogen-fixing bacterium that converts diazo compounds (compounds having two nitrogen atoms, N_2, united with carbon) into nitrates. *The term "diazotroph" refers to an N_2-fixing organism. Two well-known and much-studied diazotrophs are Clostridium, a strict anaerobe (grows and fixes N_2 only in the absence of O_2), and Azotobacter, an aerobe (grows and fixes N_2 only in presence of O_2); both are widely distributed in soils.* McGraw-Hill Yearbook of Science and Technology 1977, p17 [**1977**, from *diazo* + *-troph* one that nourishes (from Greek *trophē* nourishment)]

dibbler, *n.* an Australian mammal, regarded as extinct since the 1800's and rediscovered in 1967. See the quotations for details. *The animal is the rat-like marsupial, Antechinus apicalis, popularly known (to those who have even heard of it) as the Dibbler. Mouse-brown in colour with a long snout and a short tail it had apparently been dibbling away on the outskirts of a big city, undisturbed because nobody even suspected it was there.* New Scientist 6/8/67, p577 [**1967**]

dichlorvos (daɪ'klɔrvəs), *n.* an organic phosphate used as an insecticide in aerosol form or by impregnating a resin strip with it. Also called DDVP. *For example, one gallon of Dichlorvos, a chemical in common use for fly control, could, if applied with maximum efficiency, kill 100 square miles of dense locust swarm.* Times (London) 11/24/70, p18 [**1964**, contraction of the full chemical name dimethyl *dichlorovinyl* phosphate]

dichophase ('daɪkou,feɪz), *n.* Biology. a stage during the interphase following cell division when the cell may either differentiate or proceed toward another division. *After mitosis the new daughter cells have to decide whether to go through the whole cycle again producing more daughter cells, or to become specialised and perform a specific tissue function, ultimately to die as the nucleus degenerates. This time of decision is known*

as the dichophase. New Scientist 10/4/73, p28 [**1964**, from Greek *dicho-* in two, separate + English *phase*]

dictabelt, *n.* a plastic belt on which dictation is recorded in a dictating machine. *Special prosecutor Jaworski states that the dictabelts the White House finally surrendered likewise have blanks at the most important spots.* Wells News Service (Newtown, Pa.) 2/15/74 (page not known) *My secretaries in New York, Los Angeles, Washington, and San Francisco . . . get dicta-belts from me every day.* New Statesman 9/5/75, p284 [**1967**, from *dictation* + *belt*]

diddly-bop ('dɪdli:,bɑp), *Especially U.S. Slang.* **—n.** a light, rhythmic sound. *Smiling thinly, he sabotages each phrase; sometimes by putting small diddly-bops into the accompaniment, sometimes by asking her sharply not to touch the piano.* NY Times 10/5/77, p28 **—adj.** light; bland; dull. *I want to have coke up my nose, not this diddly-bop candy.* High Times 1/79, p8 [**1965**, perhaps from *diddle* to trifle away + *bop*, as in *bebop*]

diddy-bop ('dɪdi,bɑp), *v.i. U.S. Slang.* to walk with a light, rhythmic motion, as if dancing. *To top off the show, Smith's 19-year-old sister Doris diddy-bopped out in a 1972 bridal outfit: a strapless white Lurex gown worn with a white fake-fur jacket and a gauzy veil with a feather stuck in the side.* Time 8/7/72, p52 [**1968**, probably imitative]

die-in, *n.* a public demonstration in which participants lie as if dead, imitating the effects of a lethal weapon. See -IN. *About 100 members of PANG (People Against Nerve Gas) stage a "die-in" on a street in downtown Seattle, Wash., May 17, 1970, to protest the shipment of nerve gas through the area.* Britannica Book of the Year 1971, p766 [**1970**, patterned after earlier (1960's) *sit-in*, etc.]

dielectrophoresis (,daɪɪ,lɛktroufə'ri:sɪs), *n.* a process that forces uncharged particles in a liquid to move toward the charged area of a nonuniform electric field, used for separating mixtures, such as a suspension of living and dead cells. *Dipolar molecules experience a net force in a strongly inhomogeneous electric field and migrate toward the region of maximum absolute field strength. This migration, called dielectrophoresis, will continue until a concentration gradient reflecting equilibrium with diffusion is attained.* Science 6/23/72, p1335 [**1968**, probably blend of *dielectric* conducting across, nonconducting + *electrophoresis*]

diesel, *v.i. U.S.* (of an internal-combustion engine) to continue firing after the ignition has been shut off. *We also found that when hot, the engine would often diesel (run on) after the ignition was switched off.* Popular Science 1/71, p16 [**1971**, verb use of *diesel* or *Diesel, n.* (OEDS 1894), a type of internal-combustion engine in which such brief idling occurs] **—dieseling**, *n.: And my wife's car is a grade-A gasser. She comes home from the supermarket, parks in the garage, . . . remembers that she left her pocketbook in the car, walks back to the garage— and finds the engine still gasping, chugging, and slobbering like one of the bulldogs after a run at a squirrel. Around Motown, they call that phenomenon "dieseling." If we wanted a diesel, we'd buy one.* Newsweek 12/4/72, p99

diesohol ('di:zə,hɔ:l), *n.* a mixture of diesel oil and ethyl alcohol, used as fuel for diesel engines. Compare GASOHOL. *As prices for petroleum products rise the economics should become favorable for gasohol and for the diesel fuel-ethanol combination, called diesohol.* 1979 Britannica Yearbook of Science and the Future, p313 [**1978**, from *diesel* + *alcohol*]

dietary fiber, roughage in vegetables and fruits, eaten to promote health. Often shortened to FIBER. *Dietary fiber was the latest dietary component to be hailed as the one that does it all. Dietary fiber should not be confused with crude fiber; it includes structural polymers of cell walls, celluloses, hemicelluloses, pectin, lignin, and undigested polysaccharides, and may be three to seven times more plentiful in a diet than the crude fiber included in food composition tables.* 1978 Britannica Yearbook of Science and the Future, p319 [**1976**]

diet pill, *U.S.* any of various hormones, diuretics, etc., in tablet form, prescribed to reduce weight by speeding up metabolism.

Sam Fine, a Food and Drug Administration official, said today that the decision to seize large quantities of diet pills in Dallas and Abilene had been based on medical evidence that showed the pills produced insomnia, nervousness and symptoms of heart failure. NY Times 1/24/68, p33 [**1968**]

Digger, *n.* any of a group of hippies devoted to helping others, especially other hippies, as by giving them free food and clothing. . . . *the Diggers with their hazy ideas about free stores and co-operative farms—whatever their failings, these are part of the utopian anarchist tradition which has always bravely refused to knuckle under the proposition that life must be a bad, sad compromise with the Old Corruption.* Listener 12/5/68, p755 [**1966**, named after the *Diggers*, a group of English idealists in the 1600's who applied communistic principles to agriculture, digging and planting publicly held lands]

digital, *adj.* **1** displaying information electronically in the form of numerical figures. *Advances in microelectronics technology have greatly reduced the cost of solid-state digital watches.* Encyclopedia Science Supplement (Grolier) 1975, p388 *As we passed through Times Square bound for the IRT* [subway], *a digital thermometer informed us with a twinkle that it was ninety degrees.* New Yorker 8/2/76, p21 **2** of or having to do with the recording of sound by means of electrical signals coded into binary digits. *The move from analog to digital TV sets is viewed as one of the most significant changes in television since the introduction of color. In some ways it parallels the shift from analog to digital that is also starting in the phonograph industry, with the introduction of the digital audiodisk.* NY Times 3/17/83, pD2 *David Atherton's red-blooded direction with the London Sinfonietta and a high-powered cast was superbly presented in spectacular digital sound (Decca, 3 discs.)* Manchester Guardian Weekly 12/20/81, p21 —*n.* a digital device, especially a timepiece, thermometer, or gauge. *Everyone is now sobering up as to the projections for digitals. Of 50 million watches of all kinds sold in the United States this year, perhaps 1.5 million will be digitals.* NY Times 7/20/75, pC1 [**1964** for def. 1, extended from the sense of "using digits" (as in *digital computer*); **1960** for def. 2]

digital disk or **digital disc,** a sound recording whose quality is enhanced by processing with a digital computer. *The digital revolution creeps up on us. By the end of 1982 we are promised the first fully digital discs, compact and metallic, gleaming with rainbow colours, their music free from all interference. They will be tracked by a laser beam on a completely new kind of player.* Manchester Guardian Weekly 12/20/81, p21 [**1980**]

digitization, *n.* the conversion of data into numerals or numerical form. *There are two distinct processes: one involves the digitization of contours (using a D-Mac electronic digitizing table) to convert a pre-existing contour map into machine-readable form; the contours can then be re-created at a different scale or on a different projection or in conjunction with different secondary information, using computer-driven draughting devices.* Geographical Magazine 8/72, p778 [**1966**, from *digitize* (1953) to convert into digits + -*ation*]

dihydrotestosterone (dai,haidroutes'tastəroun), *n.* the biologically active form of the male sex hormone testosterone, produced by addition of two hydrogen atoms, and considered to be responsible for enlargement of the prostate gland. *In the time of "the sere, the yellow leaf," the testicles send decreasing amounts of testosterone to the prostate. But testosterone is metabolized, along the way, to another form of the male hormone, dihydrotestosterone (DHT).* NY Times Magazine 2/16/75, p65 [**1970**, from *dihydro-* combined with two atoms of hydrogen + *testosterone*]

dilatancy, *n.* the expansion of rocks under increasing groundwater pressure, believed to be a precursor of earthquakes (often used attributively). *The onset of dilatancy can . . . be detected from observations of ground surface level changes, inclination changes, density changes (through gravitational effects), and magnetic changes, all of which stem from the slight volume change of the dilatant rock mass.* New Scientist 2/12/76, p342 [**1973**, extended sense of the geological term

(OED 1885) meaning the expansion of granular material, such as sand, caused by rearrangement of the particles]

Dillon's Rule, *U.S.* the rule that if a state contests the powers of a municipal corporation, the judicial decision will always favor the state. *The rule is named after the legal commentator John F. Dillon, and it grows out of the fact that this nation's Constitution does not mention the powers of cities but only the powers of states. The states establish cities as their own creatures, granting them, as Dillon's Rule has it, no powers other than those clearly implicit in the establishing statutes.* New Yorker 3/17/73, p29 [**1973**]

dimethylnitrosamine (dai'meθəlnai'trousəmi:n), *n.* a cancer-producing chemical found in certain foods and in tobacco smoke. *Abbreviation:* DMN or DMNA *Most German beers, and perhaps American brews too, contain trace quantities of dimethyl nitrosamine—a known animal carcinogen. The German Cancer Research Center in Heidelberg announced last week that it had tested 158 beers in a two-year study.* Science News 1/20/79, p40 [**1968**, from *dimethyl* having two methyl radicals + *nitrosamine* an organic compound]

dimuon ('dai,myu:ɑn), *n. Nuclear Physics.* a pair of muons (heavy nuclear particles) that may result from the decay of particles governed by the interactions of neutrinos at high energy. Compare TRIMUON. *Several explanations that involve only conventional processes and particles might be invoked to account for the dimuon events. One of the most obvious is the hypothesis that the second muon is created by the decay of a charged pion or kaon produced in the initial neutrino interaction.* Scientific American 1/76, p53 [**1975**, from *di-* two + *muon*]

dink, *n. U.S. Army Slang.* a derogatory name for a Vietnamese. *Young GIs soon learned that there were Army names for Vietnamese too: gook, dink, and slope.* Harper's 5/70, p55 [**1968**, of unknown origin]

dinner theater, a restaurant where a theatrical production is presented during or following dinner. Compare CAFÉ THÉ-ÂTRE. *Some years ago, store owners discovered the lure of one-stop shopping. Today showmen are making the same discovery. In a converted pancake house in San Diego, a former laundry in Kansas City, a onetime illegal gambling casino in New Orleans and countless other locations, they are drawing packed houses to dinner theaters.* Time 6/3/74, p52 [**1960**]

dioxin (dai'ɑksən), *n.* a very persistent and highly poisonous impurity present in herbicides. Its full name is 2,3,7,8-tetrachlorodibenzo-*p*-dioxin. . . . *extensive teratogenic, or fetus-deforming, effects were discovered in chick embryos when the dioxin, or a distillate predominantly consisting of it, was present at concentrations of little more than a trillionth of a gram per gram of the egg.* New Yorker 3/14/70, p124 [**1970**]

dioxirane (dai'ɑksə,rein), *n. Chemistry.* any of a new class of organic compounds consisting of two hydrogen, one carbon, and two oxygen atoms, believed to be important intermediaries in reactions that produce photochemical smog. *Richard Suenram and Frank Lovas of the US National Bureau of Standards detected dioxirane, the simplest member of the new family, using low temperature microwave spectroscopy during studies of the reaction between ethylene and ozone.* New Scientist 6/22/78, p325 [**1977**, probably from *di-* two + *oxy-* oxygen + ring + -*ane* (suffix used in names of hydrogenated carbon compounds)]

DI particle, another name for DEFECTIVE AGENT. *Marcus and Sekellick studied DI particles that arise from vesicular stomatitis virus, which causes a cattle disease. The genetic material in that virus is a single strand of RNA, and most of the DI particles contain shorter pieces of that RNA. One set of DI particles, however, contains RNA consisting of two regions that can bind together into a double-stranded structure.* Science News 5/14/77, p308 [**1977**, abbreviation of *defective interfering particle*]

diplomaism, *n.* undue emphasis on the acquisition of an academic degree, especially as a qualification for hiring personnel. *The obvious question is whether a degreeless society would pro-*

duce enough skilled people to bring technology under control. It is one thing to lambaste the tyranny of diplomasim, but quite another to expect nations to function without high standards of excellence. Time 6/7/71, p26 [**1971**]

diplomatic shuttle, an act or instance of engaging in SHUTTLE DIPLOMACY. Often shortened to SHUTTLE. *It was a diplomatic shuttle, but not exactly in the Kissinger mode: no custom-fitted Air Force jet, no phalanx of aides, bodyguards and reporters. British Envoy Ivor Richard last week hopped from capital to capital in southern and eastern Africa in a modest chartered twin-engined Hawker Siddeley executive jet.* Time 1/17/77, p30 [**1975**]

directed-energy weapon, another name for BEAM WEAPON. *There are a couple of hundred (overtrained) blue-eyed boys in Los Alamos, New Mexico, working on hunter-killer satellites and directed energy weapons like satellite-launched high-energy lasers.* Rolling Stone 1/11/79, p78 [**1977**]

direttissima (ˌdirə'tisəmə), *n. Mountaineering.* direct ascent. *The first winter ascent by climbers of the North Face of the Matterhorn (14,688 ft.) was achieved today by Dougal Haston, of Eiger direttissima fame, and Mike Burke, also an experienced mountaineer.* Times (London) 2/13/67, p1 [**1965,** from Italian, literally, most direct]

Dirgue (dərg), *n.* a variant of DERGUE. *The crucial victim executed was General Aman Andom, until recently the chairman of the provisional military government or Dirgue.* Manchester Guardian Weekly (Washington Post section) 11/30/74, p15 [**1974**]

dirt bike, a lightweight motorcycle for use on dirt roads. . . . *no discussion of parks is complete without mentioning the latest and most loathsome menace of all, the off-road recreational vehicle . . . The list of this ubiquitous blight is unending and includes: dirt bikes, 4 WD's, hovercrafts and amphibious half-tracks.* Maclean's 8/13/79, p16 [**1970**]

dirty, *adj.* **1** being on drugs; using drugs. Compare CLEAN. *Two weeks ago four new men came into the group meeting and each admitted he was then "strung-out." Each was given 10 days to appear on the list as "clean." At the meeting 10 days later each was "dirty" and each swore that the agreement had been "clean after 10 days" and that therefore they should not be punished.* Times (London) 5/2/70, p9 [**1970**] **2** (of a floating rate of exchange) manipulated by a country to influence the exchange rate of its currency in its own favor on the money markets. *As it is now the present system is a "dirty," or controlled, float. The Common Market countries which have agreed to a joint float intend to hold their currencies within a 2 ¼ % band around the par values compared with a margin of 4 ½ % allowed for other world currencies.* Auckland Star (N.Z.) 3/31/73, p10 —*v.t.* to manipulate (a floating rate of exchange). *Because trading was light, central bankers rarely had to "dirty" the float by intervening in the market to maintain the float's new relationships.* Newsweek 4/2/73, p74 [**1973**]

dirty pool, *U.S. Slang.* unfair or dishonest conduct; foul play. *They charged that officials of Harrison, a sprawling town of which Purchase is a small corner, had resorted to "dirty pool" by secretly presenting the bill in Albany and getting it passed by means of an exchange of favors among state legislators.* NY Times 4/13/68, p29 [**1956**]

dirty tricks, underhanded actions or activity by government agents or political hirelings, designed to disrupt or subvert the machinery of an electoral campaign, a political convention, an established government, etc. *To my mind, the dirty tricks campaign run by the Committee to Reelect the President was far more sinister than the Watergate break-in and wiretapping. After all, those were illegal acts which, once discovered, could be dealt with; the dirty tricks campaign represented something more; it reflected an attitude, an unethical and odious attitude, toward the whole of political life.* Maclean's 12/73, p66 [**1973**] ▶ This usage attained wide currency during the Watergate hearings of 1973. However, the term's use in a political context is older. The following pre-Watergate quotation suggests that the term was established in U.S. government circles well before the date (1966) of the quotation itself: *Whether or not po-*

litical control is being exercised, the more serious question is whether the very existence of an efficient C.I.A. causes the United States Government to rely too much on clandestine and illicit activities, back-alley tactics, subversion, and what is known in official jargon as "dirty tricks." Times (London) 4/26/66, p9 The phrase *dirty trick* in the sense of a despicable or malicious act has been known since the 1600's.
—**dirty trickster:** *Is Charles Colson, famous dirty trickster and convert, a feigning Christian? I don't think so. I believe he may be the truest American Christian since Andrew Carnegie—the man Mark Twain took as the perfect specimen.* NY Times Magazine 8/1/76, p8

dirty war, the use of terrorism, death squads, or other unorthodox means of waging war. *In December 1985 a civilian court convicted and stripped of their rank five former junta members for crimes committed during their campaign against dissidents and terrorists—the so-called dirty war during which at least 9,000 Argentine citizens disappeared.* 1987 Collier's Encyclopedia Year Book, p133 [**1960**]

disadapt, *v.t.* to make unable to adapt. *There were certainly consequences for concern from the latest Soyuz 9 flight which set a new long duration space flight record for man—18 days. The two cosmonauts remained 'disadapted' to normal gravity for much longer than would have been predicted on a basis of the previous (American) longest duration flight—the 14-day Gemini 7 mission.* Science Journal 12/70, p4 [**1963;** earlier in the obsolete sense "to render unfit" (OED 1611)]

disaggregative, *adj.* **1** broken down or separated into component parts. *Some of the differences between neoclassical economics and ecology . . . may be conveyed to the economist if he is asked to envision a disaggregative economics built ab initio around the existence of market imperfections.* Science 10/27/72, p393 **2** of or involving separate or discrete units. *In demonstrating the usefulness of a "system dynamics" approach to specific problems considered at a disaggregative level—as is done effectively in the papers on "DDT Movement in the Global Environment"; on "Mercury Contamination"; and on "The Eutrophication of Lakes"—this objective may have been achieved.* New Scientist 3/22/73, p680 [**1972,** from disaggregate collective (1828)]

disambiguate, *v.t.* to rid (a sentence, statement, etc.) of ambiguity. *Given a syntactically ambiguous grammar, it is possible to use semantic information to disambiguate its syntax and construct a similar unambiguous grammar.* New York 10/17/70, p145 [**1963**]

disaster film or **disaster movie,** a motion picture whose plot revolves around a catastrophic event. *It's not every disaster film that will cause audiences to long for the realism of* The Towering Inferno. . . *or the convincing effects of* Earthquake. *This movie* [City on Fire] *makes even* The Swarm *look good.* People Weekly 10/22/79, p26 *Danger can be presented in hundreds of ways that are not objectionable, without gore or sadism. The great success of the disaster movies proves this point.* TV Guide 7/2/77, pA7 [**1975**]

disbenefit, *n.* a lack or absence of benefit. *It has not occurred to many that the argument should be about the superiority of SST* [supersonic transport], *all things considered, as a means of getting from here to there. It should be about the benefits to the thousands and the disbenefits to the millions.* Saturday Review 3/2/68, p51 [**1968**]

disbound, *adj.* having a torn, loose, or poor binding; having come unbound. *As the author's trustee, the owner of a library has the moral responsibility of preserving his books in the best possible condition and thus to hand them on to posterity in a perfect state of preservation. Disbound copies should be rebound, new leather backs should be made where they have been cracked or been lost completely, . . .* New Scientist 12/24/70, p552 [**1970**]

disc, *n.* short for DISCOTHÈQUE. Less common than DISCO. *After that, how about a night on the town at one of the local discs.* Advertisement, New Yorker 11/22/69, p115 [**1969**]

discaire (dis'ker), *n.* a person who selects the records to be played at a discothèque. *Upstairs, underneath the arches, couples shake, shuffle, or glide—depending on the whims of the discaire—from nine to three-thirty every night.* New Yorker 5/9/70, p6 [**1966,** from French]

discipling (də'saipliŋ), *n.* **1** the practice in the neo-Pentecostal movement of grouping followers into small units under the guidance of a leader whom the disciples obey and are expected to give one tenth of their income to. *Leaders of the charismatic movement who oppose the teaching about discipling say that the seeds of a new denomination have already been planted.* NY Times 9/16/75, p31 **2** Attributive use: *The two went to the nation's highest corrections officer and asked to take 12 prisoners out of confinement for two-week "discipling" sessions at Fellowship House, in Washington.* NY Times Magazine 8/1/76, p48 [**1975**] ▶ The OED records *discipling* as a verbal noun and participial adjective with several obsolete senses derived from the obsolete verb *disciple*]

disclination, *n.* (in the geometric model of a solid) displacement by rotation rather than by linear motion (translation). Compare DISPIRATION. *The study of disclinations has its origins in the physics of crystalline solids, but as it happens disclinations are seldom observed in ordinary three-dimensional crystals such as those of metals. They do appear in the arrays of oriented molecules called liquid crystals. What is more, they are important structural elements in many ordered materials other than conventional crystals, such as the protein coats of viruses. Disclinations can even be observed in the pattern of fingerprints, in the pelts of striped animals such as zebras and in basketwork.* Scientific American 12/77, p130 [**1972,** from *dis-* (as in *dislocation*) + in*clination*]

disclosing agent or **disclosing tablet,** a vegetable dye that is absorbed by plaque adhering to the teeth. *A sure-fire way to detect plaque is to use a "disclosing agent" (tablet or liquid) before or after brushing and flossing. When chewed or swished in the mouth, these agents stain the plaque, making it readily apparent . . . Dentists advise using a disclosing agent, at first, every time you clean your teeth, to detect hard-to-get areas.* Reader's Digest 2/74, p221 [**1972**]

disco ('diskou), *n.* **1** short for DISCOTHÈQUE. *There are some most luxurious and comfortable camp sites on the coasts of Europe, many with their own swimming pools, private beaches, supermarkets and even discos . . .* Times (London) 6/6/70, p26 [**1964**] ▶ *Disco* is also used as a combining form, as in the following: —**disco-pub,** *n.: Rivals Watneys have had a great success with their Birds Nest disco-pubs and Charrington may just have learnt a lesson there.* Times (London) 6/17/70, p27 —**discoset,** *n.: With an astonishing falsetto* [Tiny Tim] *rose to the top of "the charts" . . . He was on the Greenwich Village boîte circuit for a time until he improvised a gig at The Scene, a Manhattan nightery that adopted him as the darling of the discoset and launched his rise to broader public acclaim.* Britannica Book of the Year 1969, p166 **2** music played in discothèques, especially such music with a strong bass rhythm and simple melody (often used attributively). *The hustle, which is believed to have had its origins five years ago in the black and Puerto Rican bars of Queens, is danced to "disco," a black-based rhythm and blues characterized by a strong, rhythmic bass guitar, that in itself is achieving wide popularity.* NY Times 7/12/75, p27 ▶ *Disco* in this sense is also used as a combining form, as in the following: —**discophile,** *n.: Just as in adults' clothing, labels or logos have found their way to the backs of children's jeans . . . and to the collar of jersey dresses with slit skirts meant to be worn by pubescent discophiles.* NY Times Magazine 3/9/80, p62 —**discospeak,** *n.: Disco may be on its last legs and New Wave may be over the crest, but the hottest action right now is "rapping." One of the biggest-selling singles of the past two months is a funked-up, 12-incher called Rapper's Delight, which features the ribald discospeak of three New Jerseyites who call themselves the Sugarhill Gang.* Maclean's 2/11/80, p32 —*v.i.* to dance to disco music. See ROLLER DISCO. *It was a hot night the following Spring and she was at Studio 54 and she was discoing with a kid who looked*

like Bruce Jenner. New York Post 1/12/79, p18 [**1975** for noun def. 2; **1978** for verb]

disco jockey, *U.S.* an announcer or master of ceremonies at a ballroom where disco is played. Compare TALK JOCKEY. *They [the musical pieces] are cunningly selected by the all-important disco jockeys who keep a hawk's eye on the floor and choreograph the dancers by changing the pace and style of the records and tapes.* Time 6/27/77, p56 [**1977,** influenced by *disc jockey* (1940's) a radio announcer of recorded popular music]

discothèque or **discotheque** ('diskə,tek), *n.* a nightclub or other place of entertainment where customers or performers dance, sing, etc., to recorded music. *The young generation loves the noisy nightclubs and the discothèques.* NY Times 4/29/67, p16 —*v.i.* to dance to recorded music at a discothèque. *Most older men will only react by trying doubly hard to prove how young they are, sweating it out on the tennis court or discothequing it way past their bedtime.* Time 2/21/69, p35 [**1954,** from French *discothèque,* literally, record library, from *disque* disk, record + *-thèque,* as in *bibliothèque* library; originally applied to a record shop, then to a café or bar where customers chose records to be played from a selection]

discothèque dress, a short, low-necked dress, often black and with frills at the hemline, originally worn by go-go girls at a discothèque. *In a series of crepe discothèque dresses, Miss Keenan dropped a flutter of fine pleats from a round yoke or pressed them flat on lowbelted dresses.* NY Times 11/16/66, p46 [**1964**]

discouraged worker, *U.S.* an unemployed person of working age who is not actively looking for a job. *That eight million people are officially "unemployed"—looking for work and unable to find it—is only part of the problem. An additional million discouraged workers have stopped looking.* NY Times 3/7/87, p26 [**1980**]

discoverist, *adj.* favoring or advocating the DISCOVERY METHOD. *The "discoverist" school owes much to the Swiss psychologist Jean Piaget who said that a child's capacity to learn increasingly complex tasks must develop at its own speed over a period of time. He emphasized the need for exploration and organizing activities on the part of the student.* Science News 3/24/73, p187 [**1973**]

discovery method, a method of instruction in which students pursue knowledge on their own and work out their own solutions to problems under the guidance of a teacher. *Lectures by the teacher and textbooks have been a good deal replaced by "discovery methods"—groups working on joint activities that may bring aspects of traditional subjects together in various ways, with each of the children pursuing his own strongest interests.* New Yorker 10/29/73, p134 [**1961**]

discovery procedure, *Linguistics.* a theoretical procedure by which analysis of a corpus leads to discovery of basic units making up particular structural aspects of a language. *Chapters 4-7 describe the development of Chomsky's transformational grammar . . . The principal stress is on the rejection of 'discovery procedures' in favor of an evaluation procedure, and on the creativity (or 'open-endedness') of human language as setting a goal for grammatical theory that requires going beyond a corpus.* Language 6/72, p420 [**1965**]

discrete, *n.* a separate piece of equipment, often a component part of a large system, such as a high-fidelity record playing system. *This is a bleak outlook when most manufacturers of discretes are—to quote an industry marketing manager—"up to our ears in transistors", having built up heavy stocks in expectation of sales that did not materialise.* New Scientist and Science Journal 1/14/71, p52 [**1967**] ▶ The OED includes a noun use of the adjective *discrete* in the sense of "a separate part": "1890 J. H. Stirling *Gifford Lect.* xviii 353 Break it up into an endless number of points . . . an endless number of discretes."

disfluency, *n.* **1** inability to speak fluently, often in reference to a condition of stuttering. *Himself a stutterer who simply seemed to outgrow his problem, he "found the Iowa approach to 'disfluency' faintly depressing. . . As a theory it seemed too much of a patchwork—a psychological insight here, a contribution from sociology there, a little neurology, a little anthro-*

pology, a leavening of old-fashioned common sense." NY Times 9/27/77, p43 **2** an instance of this. *According to a study conducted by one of Johnson's graduate students, these normal childhood "disfluencies" occur on the average of fifty times for every thousand words spoken. For instance, a child may come running into the house shouting, "I-I-I want some ice cream."* New Yorker 11/15/76, p142 [**1976,** from *dis-* lack of + *fluency*]

disgrunt, *v.t.* to say or remark with disgust; express displeasure. *The other two jurors went on to give the prize to Stewart Brand, the collator, leading one critic to disgrunt that next year they'll give it to a Xerox machine.* NY Times Book Review 4/30/72, p47 [**1972,** back formation from *disgruntled;* form influenced by the verb *grunt*]

dishy, *adj. Slang.* desirable; comely. *Kaleidoscope: A fast-paced mod-style gambling story set in a glossy background of boutiques and casinos. Nifty plot and Susannah York as a dishy doll make up for Warren Beatty's lack of presence.* Maclean's 3/67, p80 [**1961,** from *dish,* slang word for a comely girl or woman]

disinform, *v.t.* to provide with distorted or false information. *Advocates of the change say, in justifying it, that foreign intelligence services today are increasingly using so-called influencing agents for subverting, deceiving and disinforming French public opinion, that they receive their training, instructions and remuneration from abroad.* Manchester Guardian Weekly (Le Monde section) 7/30/78, p13 [**1978,** back formation from DISINFORMATION]

disinformation, *n.* distorted or false information designed especially to mislead foreign intelligence agents (often used attributively). *I wrote a memo to New York about both rumors, Mao's illness and his alleged double. The memo questioned whether this was a piece of "disinformation" to influence the leadership struggles in Peking, or whether Mao had really been taken ill.* Leona and Jerrold Schecter, An American Family in Moscow, 1975, p297 [**1955,** translation of Russian *dezinformatsiya,* a word used as part of the title of a special branch of the Soviet secret service]

disintermediate, *v.i. U.S.* to withdraw money from intermediate institutions (as savings and commercial banks) for direct investment at higher interest rates in the securities market. *In my very next column it will be my duty to inform . . . readers how they can successfully "disintermediate"—i.e., pull their money out of the banking system and get a higher short-term yield with safety.* Newsweek 5/6/74, p75 [**1974,** back formation from DISINTERMEDIATION]

disintermediation, *n. U.S.* heavy withdrawals from savings banks for direct investment in the securities market. *In addition, the refinancing got high marks from Wall Street because of the Government's effort to lessen "disintermediation".* . . NY Times 5/2/68, p67 [**1968**]

diskette, *n.* another name for FLOPPY DISK. *Some 442 million information documents of all types . . . are filed with the I.R.S. each year by employers, corporations and banks. About 42 percent of these documents are furnished in the form of magnetic tape, disk or diskette, and the rest are provided on paper slips similar to the forms individual taxpayers receive through the mail.* NY Times 1/17/78, p51 [**1973,** from DISK + *-ette* (diminutive suffix)]

disk pack or **disc pack,** a stack of magnetic disks that can be inserted in or removed from a disk drive as a unit. *Another way to provide input data that can be read by the computer is to use machine-prepared data files in the form of magnetic tapes or removable disk packs.* Encyclopedia Science Supplement (Grolier) 1969, p361 *How many magnetic drums or disc-packs are needed to hold 10^{12} bits?* Science 1/71, p28 [**1963**]

disparlure ('dispar,lur), *n.* a synthetic sex attractant for the female gypsy moth, more persistent than the natural attractant. Compare GOSSYPLURE. *Our experiments clearly showed that disparlure is a more potent sex lure than any of the related compounds. The two compounds that elicited the next-largest responses are 20 and 100 times less effective.* Scientific Ameri-

can 7/74, p34 [**1972,** from New Latin (*Porthetria*) *dispar,* the gypsy moth + English *lure*]

dispiration, *n.* (in the geometric model of a solid) displacement by spiral or helical motion. Compare DISCLINATION. *Dispirations constitute a third class of lattice defects; they are based on screw symmetry, which combines translational and rotational components. Screw symmetry can exist in a periodic structure made up of units that are not spherical, such as the small cones here.* Scientific American 12/77, p136 [**1972,** from *dis-* (as in *dislocation*) + Latin *spira* coil, spiral + English *-tion*]

displaced homemaker, *U.S.* a married woman who has lost her means of support by divorce, separation, or the death or disability of her husband. *The term displaced homemaker was invented by another Californian, Tish Sommers, 64, who was divorced at 57 and "discovered I was part of an invisible problem, one of the women who had fallen through the cracks, too young for social security, too old to be hired, not eligible for unemployment insurance because homemaking is not considered work."* Time 1/1/79, p64 [**1978**]

disposable, *n. U.S.* an object to be thrown away after it has served its purpose, such as a bottle or container after its contents have been removed. *Using disposables of all varieties, including hypodermic syringes and needles, was saving hospitals large sums of money but had created new problems—how to dispose of some 18 lb of garbage per patient per day, and keeping the 1.2 billion stainless steel needles from being salvaged and used by drug addicts.* 1971 Britannica Yearbook of Science and the Future, p225 [**1958**]

dissolved gas, natural gas found in a dissolved state in petroleum. Compare ASSOCIATED GAS. *A third type of accumulation is also found, in which the natural gas is dissolved in the oil. This is known as "dissolved gas."* Encyclopedia Science Supplement (Grolier) 1975, p183 [**1975**]

distribution satellite, a communications satellite of relatively low power, that retransmits signals to small geographical areas. *These distribution satellites would be largely supplemental, adding to the facilities now available through land lines and microwave relays.* Saturday Review 10/24/70, p23 [**1968**]

ditsy or **ditsey** ('ditsi:), *adj. U.S. Slang.* **1** somewhat flighty or eccentric; dizzy. *He thinks women who want equality are ditsey little twitches—ruthless, no-souled monsters who take men's jobs away from them.* New Yorker 12/6/76, p182 **2** overly elaborate; busy. *His classic-cut skirts feature ditsy floral patterns.* People Weekly 5/2/88, p77 [**1976,** of uncertain origin]

diverger, *n.* a person who excels in far-ranging and imaginative thought. Compare CONVERGER. *Many people of obvious intellectual ability gain low scores on conventional intelligence tests but high scores on tests containing questions to which there is no one correct answer. Such people are defined as divergers; convergers on the other hand, gain higher marks on intelligence tests than on open-ended tests. When the two sets of tests were applied to English sixth forms, it was found that the science specialists tended to be convergers and the arts specialists divergers.* Times (London) 3/30/68, p5 [**1966**]

diving reflex, a physiological response found in human beings and other mammals, in which submersion of the head in cold water immediately slows the heartbeat and diverts oxygen-rich blood to the brain, heart, and lungs, delaying suffocation and the possibility of brain damage. *Now a number of other survivals from what might have been cold-water drownings are reported . . . by Martin J. Nemiroff, a University of Michigan physiologist. He reports that the survivals are primarily due to a mechanism that he calls the "diving reflex." . . . The diving reflex, Nemiroff continues, is especially strong in younger persons. He believes that it is a physiological vestige of the birth process from earlier times, when the transition from placental oxygen to the earth's atmosphere was a more hazardous affair than it is today.* Science News 9/24/77, p200 [**1975,** so called because it is the means by which diving mammals, like the porpoise and seal, remain submerged without breathing for long periods]

D.I.Y., *British.* abbreviation of *do-it-yourself. The fact that not only the makers of shockers, but the garages which sell them, can do well out of the spares market is stressed in SAMA's promotional material for garages: "Sell shocks on your accessory counter and catch the D.I.Y. motorist as well. It's bouncing business! A new pair of shocks can make more profit than a pair of spotlamps or a pair of tyres or a new battery."* Sunday Times Magazine (London) 5/30/71, p29 **[1955]**

dizygous (dɑɪˈzaɪɡəs), *adj.* derived from two separate zygotes and therefore genetically different; fraternal. *Abbreviation:* DZ *One of the best ways of throwing light on problems like these is by the study of pairs of monozygous and dizygous twins reared together.* Nature 11/10/72, p69 **[1970,** from *di-* two + *zyg*ote + *-ous;* synonymous with *dizygotic* (1930)]

DMBA, abbreviation of *dimethylbanzanthracene,* a cancer-producing chemical used experimentally to determine resistance to cancer, especially on the skin of rodents. *DMBA induced cancers (papillomas) in 60 per cent of the "old" grafts compared with only 25 per cent in the "young."* New Scientist 2/1/73, p230 **[1965]**

DMN or **DMNA,** abbreviation of DIMETHYLNITROSAMINE. *In two of ten samples of hot dogs obtained from a local supermarket, he discovered . . . the highest levels of DMN ever found in meat up to that time. No safe level of DMN has been established.* Atlantic 10/72, p90 **[1970]**

DMSO, abbreviation of *dimethyl sulfoxide,* a colorless liquid extracted from paper-pulp wastes, used as an industrial solvent, and in medicine chiefly to relieve pain and inflammation. *DMSO hemolyzes or breaks red cells.* Science News 5/30/70, p530 **[1963]**

DMT, abbreviation of *dimethyltryptamine,* a hallucinogenic drug. Compare DET. *. . . there are chemists in laboratories in Toronto, Montreal and Vancouver who produce amphetamines and psychedelic drugs, LSD, STP, DMT and other molecular variations.* Times (London) 2/23/70, pIV **[1964]**

DMZ, abbreviation of *demilitarized zone.. . . at an OAS-sponsored* [Organization of American States] *meeting of the Central American foreign ministers in Costa Rica on June 4, Honduras and El Salvador agreed to establish a demilitarized zone (DMZ) 1.8 mi. on either side of their common border.* Britannica Book of the Year 1971, p376 **[1960]**

DNA fingerprint, a distinctive pattern of bands formed by repeating sequences of base pairs of satellite DNA in every individual, used as a biochemical means of identification. Also called GENETIC FINGERPRINT. *Except for identical twins, even close relatives can be distinguished by these DNA fingerprints.* Science News 12/21-28/85, p391 **[1985]**

DNA fingerprinting, the technique of analyzing satellite DNA in a specimen of body tissue or fluid to reveal an individual's DNA fingerprint. Also called GENETIC FINGERPRINTING. *It is envisaged that DNA fingerprinting will revolutionize forensic biology particularly with regard to the identification of rape suspects.* Science News 12/21-28/85, p391 **[1985]**

DNA polymerase (ˈpɑlɪməˌreɪs), an enzyme that promotes the formation of new nucleotides of DNA (deoxyribonucleic acid, the carrier of genetic information in the cells) by a process of replication. Compare RNA POLYMERASE. *. . . it has more recently been shown that besides its copying abilities, DNA polymerase can repair strands of DNA damaged by ultra-violet light.* Times (London) 5/25/70, p5 **[1964]**

DNase (ˈdiːˌenˈeɪs), *n.* an enzyme that promotes the hydrolysis of DNA (the genetic material in cells). *The smallpox virus is known to make several enzymes. Two of these enzymes are known as DNases. Their function has not been known. What the New York City cytobiologists have found is that one of these DNases is released after the smallpox virus enters a host cell. The DNase then switches off the synthesis of the host cell's DNA.* Science News 7/7/73, p3 **[1967,** short for deoxyribonuclease (OEDS 1946)]

DNC, abbreviation of *direct numerical control.* Compare CNC. *In DNC, the computer with overall control passes information to the machine tools which otherwise would have to read-in their instructions from tapes. The DNC computer thus performs more of a production control and data management function rather than just simple system control.* New Scientist 1/27/72, p196 **[1971]**

D Notice, *British.* a government memorandum requesting newspapers not to publish specific items of secret information in the interests of national security. *By accident, D Notices had given a vast amount of protection to national interests which the Government could not have got in any other way.* Manchester Guardian Weekly 7/13/67, p4 **[1940, 1961,** from *D,* abbreviation of *Defense*]

dobra (ˈdoubrə), *n.* the unit of money of São Tomé and Príncipe (island country off the west coast of Africa). **[1979,** from Portuguese *dobra,* literally, a fold, from Latin *dupla,* feminine of *duplus* double]

dock, *v.i.* (of a spacecraft) to connect with another orbiting spacecraft. *The manned orbital workshop was assembled yesterday when the three-man ferry craft Soyuz 11 docked with the Salyut, a big instrumented station that was sent aloft without a crew on April 19.* NY Times 6/9/71, p20 **—v.t.** to connect (orbiting spacecraft). *The space program puts great dependence on computers . . . The machines are used to set orbiting patterns, dock vehicles and help perform many other functions—even help design spacecraft.* NY Times 1/9/67, p135 **[1951,** back formation from *docking*]

dockaminium or **dockominium** (ˌdɑːkəˈmɪniːəm), *n. U.S.* a berth for a boat or ship sold as a piece of real estate. *The two- and three-bedroom units are priced from $212,500 to $285,000. The complex includes a boating clubhouse and more than 140 boat slips or "dockaminiums" which property owners can purchase at prices beginning at $20,000.* Gannett Westchester Newspaper 9/30/84, pJ1 *The salesmen insist that these are not boat slips at all, but rather "dockominiums."* NY Times 6/24/87, pB1 **[1984,** from *dock* + cond*ominium*]

docking, *n.* the joining of orbiting spacecraft (also used attributively). *Rendezvous and docking in orbit is a difficult operation: even with men in charge. The first Gemini attempt nearly ended in disaster.* Science Journal 1/68, p10 *The simple task of clamping Agena's tether to Gemini's docking bar is an exhausting struggle.* Time 9/30/66, p54 **[1960]**

docking adapter, a tunnel-like passage formed by the joining of orbiting spacecraft. Compare AIRLOCK MODULE. *In spite of the grumbling, the clothing was quite versatile: if the astronauts planned to spend much time in the docking adapter, which was usually chilly, they could pull on golden-brown jackets.* New Yorker 8/30/76, p37 **[1973]**

docu-, a combining form meaning "documentary." **—docu-fantasia,** *n.: It'll be the second time this year that Mitchell has floored her guitar for floodlights, having just finished Shadows and Light, an original mélange of concert footage and fantasy sequences which is being described in film circles as a "docufantasia."* Maclean's 9/8/80, p38 **—docuhistory,** *n.: . . . The Lisle Letters bear a deceptive title, for the 1,677 documents themselves compose only about one-half of the 4,000 pages and 2 million words; the remainder is Miss St. Clare Byrne's voluminous editorial comments. The combination is a new kind of historical production—docuhistory—in which the voice of the past speaks in concert with the imagination of the living, producing a duet between the living editor and the records of the dead.* Manchester Guardian Weekly 5/31/81, p18 **—documusical,** *n.: Johnny Cash, who used to have a segment about railroading on his weekly series, will do an hour-length ABC special, 'Ridin' the Rails,' Nov. 22. Producer Nick Webster calls it a 'documusical,' with songs and dramatic recreations about America's railroads.* TV Guide 8/3/74, p36 **—docu-reenactment,** *n.: That's the message one gets from an almost totally 'reenacted' documentary presented by ABC News's often innovative-or-bust 'Close-up' series . . . Some basic matters are touched on too lightly in this docu-reenactment.* Christian Science Monitor 7/15/83, p20 **[1961,** abstracted from *documentary,* as in DOCUDRAMA]

docudrama ('dɑkyə‚drɑ:mə), *n.* a television dramatization based on facts, often presented in the style of a documentary to impart a sense of authenticity. *Described as "fact-based," this is the story of Caryl Chessman, who spent 12 years in San Quentin before being executed in May 1960. Like all fact-based television, whether it be labeled true story or docudrama, this dramatization is not without a point of view or, if you will, a strong bias.* NY Times 9/23/77, pC24 *There isn't a shred of new evidence in the docudrama, according to Peter Pearson who co-authored and directed* The Tar Sands. Maclean's 2/21/77, p59 *Viewers here will be able to pass judgment on these matters of opinion when the docu-drama appears on BBC 1.* Times (London) 8/31/78, p16 [**1959,** from *docu*mentary + *drama*] ▶ This term parallels the formation of other words made by shortening through blending in component words, such as *psychodrama* (1937, from *psycho*logical + *drama*) and *sociodrama* (1943). Originally, *docudrama* may have referred only to theatrical productions, since the term is listed among "Vocabulary Newcomers" in the *1961 Annual Supplement of the World Book Encyclopedia* as "Short for documentary drama," a phrase used to describe several new plays of the 1959-61 season, including *The Miracle Worker, The Rivalry* (between Lincoln and Douglas), and *The Wall.* However, as applied to television and motion pictures, *docudrama* does not seem to have come into common usage until 1976. —**docudramatist,** *n.: There ought to be a truth-in-labeling law to separate truth and fiction. But who could write it, and who would pass it? Since there won't be any such law, everybody concerned— and TV docu-dramatists most of all—should be held more accountable for fat content and fact content, properly labeled.* Time 9/19/77, p93 —**docudramatize,** *v.t.: David Susskind wanted to docudramatize the Black Sox scandal.* Esquire 1/2/79, p72

docutainment (‚dɑ:kyə'teinmənt), *n. U.S.* a television or other entertainment based on or including documentary material. *"I call it 'variety docutainment,'" says the production's executive producer . . . "We'll be using documentary inserts combined on stage with drama, song, and dance."* Washington Post 12/21/83, pC1 [**1983,** from *docu-* + enter*tainment*]

DOD, abbreviation of *Department of Defense* (of the United States). *Even allowing for growth in military-age population, DOD found that it could not expect to get more than 2,000,000 men, at least 700,000 short of pre-Viet Nam needs.* Time 1/10/69, p25 [**1960**]

DOE[1], abbreviation of *Department of Energy* (of the United States, formed in 1977). *"The existence of DOE means 17,000 hungry cunning people in this town depend on OPEC for their livelihood."* New York Post 2/3/79, p9 *Both the Senate Energy Committee and DOE predict that by 1985 greater production of natural gas will save the nation 1.4 million bbl. a day in imported oil.* Time 10/9/78, p24 [**1978**] ▶ Though Great Britain was first to create a Department of Energy, in 1974, the abbreviation DOE has been more generally applied to the Department of the Environment which was created earlier.

DOE[2], abbreviation of *Department of the Environment* (of Great Britain, formed in 1971). *The DOE—as it has come to be called—swallowed and quickly set about digesting three other independent and quite powerful ministries: Transport, Public Building and Works and Housing and Local Government, which had responsibility for town and country planning.* Times (London) 4/12/72, pV [**1972**] ▶ See the note under DOE[1].

doggy bag, *U.S.* a bag containing leftover food given to customers at a restaurant to carry home, supposedly to feed their dog. *Asher's wife couldn't finish her turkey sandwich. The elderly waitress put it in a doggy bag for her. . . .* New Yorker 11/7/70, p44 [**1964**]

do-it-yourselfer, *n.* a person who makes and repairs things at home. *To the do-it-yourselfer, shopping for lumber for a weekend carpentry project is often a confusing experience because sizes are never as stated.* NY Times 6/6/71, pB30 [**1953**]

do-it-yourselfery, *n.* the activity of a do-it-yourselfer. *Heywood's research had suggested that do-it-yourselfery allied to*

car ownership had a growth potential of its own. Sunday Times (London) 7/7/68, p36 [**1965**]

do-it-yourselfism, *n.* the practice of being a do-it-yourselfer. [Philip] *Slater . . . is perceptive and provocative when analyzing American do-it-yourselfism and even the much-prized American family as devices that ensure further loneliness and isolation.* Time 6/1/70, p87 [**1954**]

dojo ('doudʒou), *n.* a place where instruction is given in various arts of self-defense. *Special gymnasiums, called dojos, were set up to give private lessons in such martial arts as judo and karate.* 1970 Compton Yearbook, p444 [**1964,** from Japanese *dōjō*] ▶ An earlier citation of *dojo* refers specifically to judo.

dokusan (‚dou‚ku:'sæn), *n.* a formal private meeting between a Zen master and a disciple. *My teacher . . . said nothing, viewing my frustrated maneuvers at each dokusan with an amused smile.* Philip Kapleau, Zen: Dawn in the West, 1980, p191 [**1976,** from Japanese]

Dolby or **dolby** ('doulbi: *or* 'dɔ:lbi:), *adj.* of, relating to, or produced by any of various electronic devices that reduce or eliminate noise in recording sound for tapes and in radio broadcasting, especially of recorded music. *Dolby noise reduction plus a simple electronic trick could mean much better reception for people listening to stereo broadcasts. Noise reduction on cassette tape recorders to reduce "tape hiss" is now a well-known technique.* New Scientist 7/18/74, p130 [**1969,** abstracted from *Dolby System* (1966), the trademark for such devices, named after Ray *Dolby*, born 1933, their American inventor]

Dolbyized, *adj.* made or provided with a Dolby device or equipment. *Speaking of cassette recorders, with the exception of "Dolbyized" models, you can count on one finger the number of models that have a hi-fi signal-to-noise ratio of 50 db.* Popular Photography 8/71, p99 [**1971**]

dolce vita ('doultʃei 'vi:tɑ:). Often also **la dolce vita.** *Italian.* a life of sensuous pleasure and luxury; (literally) the sweet life. *. . . the Swiss mistrust any kind of* dolce vita. NY Times 5/22/67, p49 *But he is widely regarded as "an international playboy," with a penchant for fast cars and* la dolce vita. Sunday Telegraph (London) 3/1/64, p2 [**1961,** from *La Dolce Vita,* title of an Italian film (1959) directed by Federico Fellini, dealing with the life of pleasure-seeking socialites]

doll, *n. Especially U.S. Slang.* a stimulant or depressant drug in pill form. *Jacqueline Susann . . . has made the word "doll" a synonym for pill.* Harper's 10/69, p65 *Snow, junk, smack* (heroin); *cough medicine* (codeine); *sleeping pills, dolls* (barbiturates); *downers* (tranquilizers); *drink, booze* (alcohol). Encyclopedia Science Supplement (Grolier) 1974, p281 [**1966;** see VALLEY OF THE DOLLS]

dolly, *n. Slang.* a tablet of methadone (narcotic used as a substitute for heroin). *Methadone* [is] *known on the street as "dollies"* (*Dolophine is the trade name of methadone in tablet form*). Harper's 6/70, p76 [**1970**]

dolly bird, *British Slang.* a young, slim, attractive, and usually fashionably dressed girl. *"You American Jews," she* [an Englishwoman] *said, "are so romantic. You think every little dolly bird is Delilah. . ."* John Updike, Bech: A Book, 1970, p147 *There is unfairness, of course, that a man in his forties can get a dolly-bird (God help him, the one she provides him with) whereas a woman in her forties is more likely to be high and dry.* Manchester Guardian Weekly 10/23/71, p21 [**1964**]

dolorology (‚doulə'rɑlədʒi:), *n. U.S.* the scientific study of pain. *Not until the specialty of dolorology began to emerge did the study of pain itself gain a new emphasis and respectability.* NY Times Magazine 1/30/77, p13 [**1977,** from Latin *dolor* pain + *-ology* study of]

dolosse (də'lɑsə), *n., pl.* **-ses** or **-se.** a concrete casting used in large numbers that diminishes the force of waves on a beach or dike by breaking them up. *Public Service engineers estimate that 69,000 dolosse, each weighing anywhere from 6½ to 42 tons, will be needed. The dolosse will interlock with one another, providing thousands of spaces into which sea water can* *slosh, spending its energy.* NY Times Magazine 6/4/72, p80 [**1972**, probably from Afrikaans, from the Setswana word for an animal knucklebone used in witch doctors' rites]

dolphinarium, *n.* a large pool in which dolphins are kept and observed, especially for public entertainment. *Regardless of one's point of view on keeping wild animals in captivity . . . the fact remains that it is only by such close proximity that the general public can get to know, and perhaps appreciate, these animals for the beautiful creatures they are. It is with this in mind that we should perhaps welcome the establishment of the London Dolphinarium.* New Scientist and Science Journal 4/15/71, p174 [**1968**, from *dolphin* + *-arium,* after *aquarium*]

dominance hierarchy, an order of dominance among animals, in which members of a group establish rank by aggressiveness, size, etc. *Lacking language, and dependent for communication on a repertoire of about two dozen sounds and gestures, baboon troops are held together by a dominance hierarchy headed by three or four central males that cooperate to keep order in the troop, control access to females, and provide defense against predators.* Natural History 4/72, p25 [**1972**]

domino, *n.* any of a group of things so positioned that if one of them should fall, all the others would fall in turn, like a row of dominoes (often used attributively). *Most foreign policies proceed from certain perceived truths—Vietnam is a domino, Greece is the southern flank of NATO, Communism is monolithic. . .* Atlantic 6/70, p4 *East Bloc representation* [at the celebration of the UN's 25th anniversary] *suffered from a domino sequence of dropouts.* Time 10/26/70, p36 [**1954**, first recorded in the phrase *'falling domino' principle*]

domino theory, a hypothesis stating that if one thing or idea is disposed of, those allied or associated with it will be disposed of in turn, like a falling row of dominoes. *Chavez's next target was the Guimarra Vineyards, the largest table-grape growers in America, themselves controlling 10 percent of the annual crop, and a company not especially beatified by its enlightened view of the labor movement. His strategy was a San Joaquin Valley version of the domino theory: knock over Giumarra, and other growers will fall in line.* Atlantic 6/71, p40 . . . *if there is "action" on the book in the shops, the owners will order more. Which means people calling up and ordering or coming in and buying it. It's the domino theory. One book bought is another book sold.* Saturday Review 10/31/70, p6 [**1965**, from the theory, first advanced in the administration of President Eisenhower in the mid-1950's, that if one country in southeast Asia falls to the Communists, the others will fall in turn]

domsat ('dɑm,sæt), *n.* a communications satellite restricted in operation to a particular country (often used attributively). Compare LANDSAT, MARISAT, SEASAT. *The whole collection of the companies' domestic satellite systems is called Domsat. It will handle telephone, television, telegraph, and data transmission traffic within the United States.* Americana Annual 1973, p578 [**1972**, acronym for *domestic satellite,* on the model of *comsat* (communications satellite), *Intelsat* (International telecommunications satellite), etc.]

don, *n.* a leader in the Mafia. *Of the dons of the golden age who had children, only a few seem to have followed their fathers into the rackets. Most law-enforcement officials agree with Puzo: men like Colombo are hardly the equal of their predecessors.* Harper's 8/71, p56 [**1952**, from Italian *don* a form of address for noblemen, priests, and wealthy gentlemen; (literally) master, from Latin *dominus* lord]

donor card, a card indicating that certain organs or body parts may be used in transplant surgery upon the bearer's death. *"If a person carries a donor card saying he wishes his organs to be used in the event of his death, that should overrule any objection by the coroner unless there is a reason, such as damage to the body, why the organ should not be used."* Times (London) 2/29/80, p2 [**1970** from earlier sense of blood donor's card identifying blood group (1964)]

do-nothinger, *n.* one who adopts or is committed to a do-nothing policy. *Mr Ford is not a do-nothing President for lack of thrust; he is a do-nothinger from conviction.* Manchester

Guardian Weekly 12/7/74, p1 [**1970**] ▶ The older noun *do nothing* (1500's) has the general meaning of "one who does nothing; a lazy person; idler."

dontopedalogy (ˌdɑntoupeˈdælədʒiː), *n.* a natural propensity or talent for putting one's foot in one's mouth (that is, for saying something indiscreet, foolish, or embarrassing). Compare FOOT-IN-MOUTH DISEASE. *At the other extreme, and refreshingly so, is her* [Queen Elizabeth's] *husband, Prince Philip, who looks remarkably like Stan Musial and is a self-confessed expert in the art of "dontopedalogy," as he calls it: opening his mouth and putting his foot in it.* Time 6/27/69, p26 [**1960** coined by Prince Philip, born 1921, the Duke of Edinburgh from *donto-* (from Greek *odoús, odóntos* tooth) + *pedal* (from Latin *pedālis* of the foot) + *-logy* (as in *physiology, psychology,* etc.)]

doodley-squat, *n. U.S. Slang.* a minimum; nothing. *Ohio Democrat Senator Howard Metzenbaum . . . accuses consumers of doing "doodley-squat." Consumer advocates deny doing nothing and add that they have neither the money nor the power to lobby Congress like big business.* Maclean's 3/24/80, p46 [**1980**; compare earlier *doodley* (1950), carnival term meaning "nothing", and *doodle-e-squat* (1940's), carnival term meaning "broke, penniless"]

doomsdayer, *n.* one who predicts or warns of imminent catastrophe; alarmist. Also called APOCALYPTICIST or APOCALYPTICIAN. *Miller assails the conservationists and doomsdayers on "spaceship earth" who fail to see how the price mechanism and changing technology can keep us from running out of scarce resources.* National Review 11/22/74, p1369 [**1974**]

Doomsday Machine, a hypothetical machine designed to trigger automatic nuclear destruction under certain conditions without anyone being able to stop it. *But weapons technology continues to "progress," and it is possible that the "ultimate" in weaponry, the so-called Doomsday Machine that can destroy all human life, will become not only technologically feasible but inexpensive.* 1969 Britannica Yearbook of Science and the Future, p402 [**1960**] ▶ The concept of the Doomsday Machine was popularized by Herman Kahn, the author of *On Thermonuclear War* (1960).

doomster, *n.* another word for DOOMSDAYER. See ECODOOMSTER. *Mr Colin Robinson . . . begins by pooh-poohing the prophecies of doom, repeats all the facts and estimates we know only too well as though they were something new, and ends by reaching the same conclusions as the doomsters.* Times (London) 1/8/73, p16 [**1972**, either from *doom* + *-ster* or extended from the old Scottish law term (1600's) meaning "one who dooms or pronounces sentence; a judge or executioner"]

doomwatch, *n.* a watching for or warning of impending doom; alarmism (also used attributively). *Dear Bernard Levin! His maverick messianic urge is drawing him deeper and deeper into ideological difficulties. In his latest piece of political doomwatch (directed against Mr Heath, for a change), he . . . forecasts an upsurge of bloody revolt against what Harold Macmillan, no less, once castigated as the "casino society.". . .* Times (London) 7/3/73, p17 [**1970**] —**doomwatcher,** *n.: Of course the excesses of the doomwatchers need to be pinpointed, but by the same token of scientific caution it is appropriate to criticize with equal rigour the optimistic view that science can solve everything; and here Nature has been silent.* Nature 10/6/72, p353 —**doomwatching,** *n.: The road forward does not lie through the despair of doomwatching nor through the easy optimism of successive technological fixes.* New Scientist 8/28/75, p483

doorstep, *British.* —*adj.* of or having to do with door-to-door solicitation of sales, contributions, political support, etc. *Mr Pat Duffy (Attercliffe), chairman of the Motor Industry Select Committee, criticised the lack of consultation by Ministers. Mr Riccardo, chairman of the Chrysler Corporation, had behaved like a hustling doorstep salesman.* Manchester Guardian Weekly 12/28/75, p3 —*v.i.* **1** to go from door to door in order to solicit sales, canvass for political support, make an investigation, etc. *For those who lived and sweated through these Watergate summers and winters the report . . . brings back the* *familiar smell of John Sirica's courtroom, the pudgy face of that inoperative liar Ronald Ziegler, the endless door-stepping on the trail of John Ehrlichman and Archibald Cox and John Dean.* Manchester Guardian Weekly 10/26/75, p10 **2** to wait on, or as if on, a doorstep. *As our crisis stretches from weeks into months, it seemed time to learn how the other half of the journalistic world lives. There they are, nearly every day staked out in wet and windy streets waiting for endless crunch meetings to come to a crunch, or at least an end. Door-stepping, we call it in the trade.* Times (London) 1/29/74, p12 [**1962** for adj.; **1974** for verb] —**doorstepper**, *n.: It seemed to owe a lot to his* [Roy Hattersley] *own experience of workaday life in Yorkshire as the only child of a local government officer, adolescent deviller and doorstepper for the local Labour Party machine, graduate of Hull University and then a Sheffield city councillor.* Times (London) 10/23/76, p18

doorway state, *Nuclear Physics*. a theoretical intermediate state between a simple and a more complex nuclear interaction. *According to quantum theory the underlying sharp compound resonance states into which the doorway state can dissolve must all have the same spin and parity (intrinsic symmetry) as the molecular doorway state, since the total spin and parity are conserved.* Scientific American 12/78, p68 [**1968**, so called from the figurative doorway through which the initial simple reaction must pass to become a complex system]

doo-wop, *Slang*. —*adj*. characteristic of a style of rock'n'roll group harmony music popular in the 1950's and early 1960's. *The Steinettes . . . sounded like a fifties doo-wop group, or a takeoff on a fifties doo-wop group—with a lead singer belting it out and the three others snapping their fingers while singing "doo-wop" or "sha-la-la" or "doo-doo-doo" or words to that effect.* New Yorker 7/2/79, p78 —*n*. doo-wop music. *. . . their fine harmonies, which veered between the related styles of black gospel and streetcorner doo-wop were applied to refreshing effect, adding a welcome new flavour to well-known songs like "Let's Get It On."* Times (London) 6/16/80, p7 [**1972**, imitative of the background harmony]

dopamine ('doupə,mi:n), *n*. a hormone produced by the adrenal glands that is essential to the normal nerve activity of the brain. *Some of the symptoms of parkinsonism may be due to lack of the neural chemical dopamine in the brain. . . .* 1970 Collier's Encyclopedia Year Book, p214 *The use of L-Dopa is based on the belief that Parkinson's disease is the result of a deficiency of a substance called dopamine in the brain. L-Dopa is a naturally occurring substance that leads to the formation of dopamine.* NY Times 5/8/68, p49 [**1959**, contraction of dihydroxyphenylethylamine]

dopaminergic (,doupəmə'nərdʒik), *adj*. producing or activated by dopamine. *Results of recent research in the most common type of idiopathic Parkinsonism—a disorder of the central nervous system—appear to indicate that the disease is related to degenerative changes in the corpus striatum, substantia nigra, and related dopaminergic neurons.* McGraw-Hill Yearbook of Science and Technology 1972, p307 [**1971**, from dopamine + Greek érgon work + English -ic]

dopant ('doupənt), *n*. an impurity added in small quantities to a semiconductor to improve its conductive capacity. *The technique is now becoming increasingly important in making semiconductors, whose electrical properties are dominated by certain impurities ("dopants") in concentrations sometimes as low as one part in 10^8.* New Scientist 2/6/69, p282 *A typical integrated circuit crystal . . . contains an acceptor dopant such as boron. The amount of dopant may be approximately one dopant atom for every 107 silicon atoms. . .* Science Journal 10/70, p42 [**1963**, from dope, v., to treat or coat one substance with another + -ant (noun agent suffix)]

dopehead, *n. Slang*. a drug addict. *Says . . . a mechanical engineer and teaching elder at the Platte Valley Baptist Church in Columbus: "It would be horrible if the sheriff comes someday when I'm gone and gives Loralea and the children a summons, when they let the dopeheads and potheads run loose. The dedicated Christians I know are not going to stop educating their children simply because of any whimsical decree of some*

court." Time 6/8/81, p54 [**1980**, from *dope* narcotic drug (1889) + HEAD]

Doppler-shift or **Dopplershift**, *v.t.* to cause an apparent shift in (the wave frequency or spectral lines of a source). *Direct information about the constitution, location and velocity of interstellar clouds can be gained by detecting molecules and measuring their position and the amount by which their spectral features are Dopplershifted.* Scientific American 3/73, p56 [**1969**, verb use of *Doppler shift* (1951) the apparent change in wave frequency as the source or the observer moves towards or away from the other]

dork, *n. U.S. and Canadian Slang*. a dull, stupid person. *Martha's son, Stokely, spends most of his life in the office of a therapist who is trying to put the kid in touch with his childhood. "I'm only 10 years old, you dork," Stokely tells him.* Maclean's 4/7/80, p61 [**1972**, probably a figurative sense of earlier U.S. taboo slang *dork* penis (Wentworth and Flexner, *Dictionary of American Slang*, revised edition, 1967)] —**dorky**, *adj.: She asked Kate what she thought of Cle. 'He's dorky,' Kate responded. She said she didn't like his glasses.* Sunday Times (London) 9/18/88, pG13

dormin, *n*. another name for ABSCISIC ACID. *The story began several years ago when Professor P.F. Wareing, of the University College of Wales at Aberystwyth, found that the formation of dormant buds by sycamore trees in response to the shortening days of autumn was due to an increase in a growth-inhibitory substance in their leaves. He called this substance dormin.* New Scientist 9/5/68, p503 [**1965**, from *dormant* + -in (chemical suffix)]

dormobile, *n. British*. a small van equipped as a dwelling and often having a roof that raises to accommodate space for a bunk; camper. *As the horse-drawn carriage declined in use, so we lost the need and hence the ability to refer to the differences which 80 years ago were freely expressed by words like phaeton, brougham or landau. But, of course, we've balanced such losses with words which distinguish between convertibles, fastbacks, dormobiles and minibuses.* Listener 8/2/73, p151 [**1969**, from earlier (1952) *Dormobile*, trademark for a vehicle of this kind, apparently from *dormitory* + auto*mobile*]

dose-response, *adj*. showing the relationship of dosage (of a drug, gas, radiation, or other substance) to the physiological effect produced. See PHARMACOKINETICS. *A dose-response chart would have a line going from zero to maximum dose, with the rise accelerating and the time span shortening in proportion to the increasing dose.* NY Times Magazine 3/25/79, p84 *Remarkably little data have been obtained on human dose-effect and dose-response relationships for microbes and their products. We know far more about dose-response relationships in the toxicology of food additives and pesticides, than for most microbial toxins.* New Scientist 12/13/79, p861 [**1972**]

DOT, abbreviation of *Department of Transportation* (of the United States). *This means that about another $50 million . . . will become available for the controversial airliner. The total is considerably short of the $290 million DOT wanted for the current fiscal year.* Science News 1/9/71, p23 [**1967**]

dot-matrix, *adj*. of or having to do with a printing process or device using a rectangular pattern of small dots to generate characters on a printer or computer display screen. *The dot-matrix impact printers . . . use dots arranged close together to make letters.* Encyclopedia Science Supplement (Grolier) 1982, p124 [**1975**]

dotted-line, *adj*. having to do with a direct relationship; lineal; close. *And the man had replied: Yes, I understand that those rules apply in ordinary situations, but my situation is not quite ordinary. You see, I have a dotted-line reporting relationship with the vice-chairman. Government relations reports to him, but I don't report to him through them; I'm doing something directly for him.* Harper's 3/80, p62 [**1979**, from the use of dotted lines to represent relationships on an organizational chart]

double, *n. Horse Racing*. a bet on the winners of the first two races of the day (the "daily double"). *Of course I discovered* some interesting possibilities in the first race, and interest soon grew into excitement. I hustled to the track, bet my "doubles," and prepared to take my place in the sun. Atlantic 10/67, p78 [**1959**]

double-bind, *n.* Also, **double bind. 1** a situation of crisis in behavior resulting from repeated subjection to conflicting pressures. *There are times, says R.D. Laing, when people need to go mad. Reminding us that schizophrenia literally means "broken hearted," he suggests that feelings of terror and despair are often the result of "double-binds," in which, without conscious malice, one person is repeatedly subjected to simultaneous, absolutely contradictory injunctions and attributions about who he is, or how he feels or what he thinks, until he can no longer tell who he is, or what he feels or thinks.* NY Times 1/19/76, p27 **2** Transferred use. dilemma. *The act of writing autobiographical fiction contains a double-bind of which most writers, probably, are aware. To give fictitious form to a personal experience means that the writer is hiding behind his characters; and yet to come clean, to say, "this is me, and this is how I behaved," immediately removes one of the essential props of fiction: the illusion that the reader is being told all that the author knows.* Sunday Times (London) 6/22/75, p34 [**1962,** coined by the American anthropologist Gregory Bateson in 1956]

double-blind, *adj.* based upon a method of testing in which neither the identity of what is being tested nor its possible effects are disclosed to the subject or the one administering the test until its completion. *The ideal way to determine that two like products are equal in therapeutic action would be to compare them in extensive, double-blind clinical studies.* Science News 10/31/70, p350 *Dr. Lawther also uses other members of his staff for "double-blind" experiments, in which neither the subject nor the technician knows exactly what is going on.* New Yorker 4/13/68, p83 [**1950** in specialized sources; widely applied after 1963]

double-book, *v.t.* to accept two reservations for (the same hotel room) so as to help insure its occupancy in the event of a cancellation. *"Even when we double-booked the rooms once and had to turn people away, they said 'Never mind, dear, we know it's not your fault.'"* Times (London) 8/17/70, p5 [**1960**]

double-deal, *v.i.* to practice deception; cheat; deceive. . . . *it is Don Lope who is ill and she who double-deals pretending to call a doctor for him with her finger pressed firmly down on the telephone rest.* New Yorker 9/26/70, p124 *I am double-dealing once more by choosing only new recordings for the top ten.* Sunday Times (London) 12/17/67, p21 [**1967,** back formation from *double-dealing, n.* (before 1529) or *double-dealer* (1547)]

double-digit, *adj. Especially U.S.* equaling or exceeding a rate of 10 per cent (up to a possible 99 per cent). *The runaway economy, beset by 14% inflation and double-digit interest rates, continued to race beyond . . . control.* Daily News (New York) 5/27/79, p5 *Double-digit inflation and steadily rising unemployment do not admit of bromides about 'men of goodwill' and 'getting round the table' unless they are accompanied by some hard policy proposals and some intelligible discussion of priorities.* New Statesman 5/16/75, p645 [**1974**] ► Although *double-digit* in its current sense became widespread in mid-1974 (probably influenced by the earlier British *double-figure*), the compound appeared on occasion in special contexts, as in the following 1959 quotation: *The editors boasted: "Although these three books were written by Shulman at the age of eight, critics have pointed out that they show the insight and penetration of a man of nine." Now Humorist Shulman, 40, has advanced into the double-digit years.* Time 8/31/59, p68

double dipping, *U.S.* **1** the practice or policy of allowing a retired soldier or civil servant to earn a salary from a new government job while receiving a pension or other benefits from the first job. *The critics, including many Congressmen, consider "double dipping" typical of the ways in which the military pension system has become overly generous and helped to inflate military manpower costs.* NY Times 4/10/77, p3 **2** passing into verb: *Controller Harrison J. Goldin will move next week to break a deadlock that has stymied attempts to identify*

retired cops who have been "double-dipping"—earning excess amounts of money from city jobs while receiving disability pensions. Daily News (New York) 2/24/78, p5 [**1975**] —**double dipper:** *If the panel has its way, there would also be an end to double-dippers, those who draw two Federal paychecks because they have "retired" from the military and later found a place for themselves in the civilian bureaucracy.* NY Times 4/16/78, pD2

double-figure, *adj. Especially British.* variant of DOUBLE-DIGIT. *Earlier controls and tariffs on imports had proved largely ineffective in dealing with double-figure inflation which had been accelerating over the past two years reaching more than 40 per cent during September alone.* Times (London) 10/4/76, pX5 [**1966,** probably transferred from *double figures* (occasionally *double-figure*) a score of 10 or more, especially in cricket (OEDS 1860)]

double-helical, *adj.* consisting of two strands that coil around each other to form a double spiral or helix. *Until the dramatic announcement of the double-helical structure of DNA, there was complete ignorance of how a chemical substance could carry out the multifold activities needed for a genetic substance.* Atlantic 2/68, p91 [**1968**]

double helix, the double-helical structure of a molecule of DNA. Compare ALPHA HELIX. *The irony was that the physicists-turned-biologists and their immediate collaborators promptly . . . discovered the double helix, and opened up vistas of genetic engineering that were anything but "safe."* Atlantic 9/70, p98 *Chargaff's* [the biochemist, Erwin Chargaff's] *rules then suddenly stood out as a consequence of a double-helical structure for DNA. Even more exciting, this type of double helix suggested a replication scheme much more satisfactory than my briefly considered like-with-like pairing. Always pairing adenine with thymine and guanine with cytosine meant that the base sequences of the two intertwined chains were complementary to each other.* James D. Watson, The Double Helix, 1968, p196 [**1954**]

doubleknit, *n.* a fabric knitted with a double stitch to provide it with twice its usual thickness (often used attributively). . . . *Adele Martin's eloquent understatement in wool doubleknit.* New Yorker 9/23/67, p168 *Behind this huge production of Crimplene in Britain lies a modern and technically advanced doubleknit industry consisting of about 100 firms.* Sunday Times (London) 4/30/67, p27 *Save up to $2.33 on this special buy of polyester doubleknits. Scoop up anywhere from 1 to 5 yards lengths . . . all first quality fabrics.* Advertisement, Sunday News (New York) 6/25/72, p98 [**1964**]

double nickel, *U.S. Slang.* the nationwide highway speed limit of fifty-five miles per hour (established in 1973). *"Drive 55" would probably have disappeared with the gas lines had it not been for the discovery that the limit reduced fatal accidents; Washington estimates the saving at 4,500 lives a year. Hence the "double nickel" has won the support of the National Highway Traffic Safety Administration as well as consumer groups.* NY Times 2/5/79, pA18 [**1976,** originally citizens band radio slang for 55 (two fives = two nickels)]

Douglas bag, a plastic bag for collecting exhaled air or for administering respiratory mixtures. *The inspired air is fed from cylinders so that the gas mixture can be varied, and a reservoir and sampling tubes enable the gas that the athlete breathes to be sampled. Then from the expired air another sample is taken and the total expired air can be collected in a Douglas bag.* Science Journal 11/70, p37 [**1963,** named after C. G. *Douglas,* 1882-1963, an English physiologist]

dove, *n.* a person who is opposed to war or to confrontation of force; person who seeks accommodation with an enemy instead of making war. Compare HAWK. *In our opinion, the general run of Americans—whether hawks or doves, or neither—are deeply preoccupied with the war.* New Yorker 1/13/68, p19 . . . *both Hawks and Doves are unanimous that the Vietnamese war must be brought to an immediate end if the United States economy is to avoid further disruption.* Times (London) 4/11/68, p17 [**1962**]

dovish or **doveish,** *adj.* opposed to war or to the use of force in a conflict; tending to seek accommodation with an enemy instead of making war. Compare HAWKISH. *Mr. Eban is widely regarded as the most "dovish" member of the Israel Cabinet, and one who would certainly negotiate a real peace now, if he could.* Times (London) 2/18/70, p1 . . . *New Hampshire is considered hawkish and Wisconsin dovish.* . . Harper's 12/68, p53 *The President . . . wants it on a schedule best calculated to enhance his political position while undermining that of hawkish spokesmen for escalation and doveish prophets of cataclysm.* Atlantic 1/68, p6 **[1966]**

down, *Especially U.S. Slang.* —*adj.* depressing; gloomy; downbeat. *I don't like down movies. I like up movies.* New Yorker 8/5/72, p21 *Primarily, a down week with a couple of lighter spots, specifically the lunches with two of our professors.* New Yorker 3/20/78, p90 —*n.* another word for DOWNER (def. 1). *In Hollywood, a boy of eleven . . . has been pushing "ups" (amphetamine and methedrine pills) and "downs" (barbiturates, tranquilizers) since he was nine. . .* Time 2/16/70, p36 —*v.i.* to take downers (depressant drugs). *Amphetamines and barbiturates also have two faces. They are a familiar item in the doctor's armamentarium and, as such, reassuring. And yet excessive "upping" or "downing" can cause severe psychic dislocation, certainly as damaging as any of the effects of LSD.* Norman E. Zinberg and John A Robertson, Drugs and the Public, 1972, p49 **[1967** for adj.] (but compare OED 2, *adj.* 3 Obs. in which 'down spirits' appears in quote dated 1645; **1969** for noun; **1972** for verb]

downburst, *n.* a strong downdraft creating a sudden destructive air current near the ground. *Some meteorologists maintain that many so-called downbursts are actually downdrafts—common sinkings of air within a cloud that do not reach the ground. But Fujita maintains that it's a question of intensity and dimensions. He says downbursts not only originate higher in clouds than do downdrafts (13 kilometers as opposed to 6 or 7 km for downdrafts), but they come very near or actually reach the ground.* Science News 3/17/79, p170 **[1978,** patterned after *downdraft* a downward current of air (1849)]

downconvert, *v.t.* to change by means of downconverter. Compare UPCONVERT. *The signals are down-converted to i-f, passed through a filter to limit the receiver bandwidth to 100 kHz, amplified, up-converted to 135.6 MHz, and transmitted earthward.* McGraw-Hill Yearbook of Science and Technology 1969, p95 **[1968]**

downconverter, *n.* a converter that transforms radiant energy to a lower frequency. Compare UPCONVERTER. *For over 20 years, silicon point-contact diodes were used in microwave-receiver down-converters (units which translate the incoming microwave frequency to a lower intermediate frequency).* McGraw-Hill Yearbook of Science and Technology 1969, p213 **[1968]**

downcycle, *n.* a downward or declining cycle in business or the economy. *Mr Charles Baker, the IISI secretary, told a press conference that a survey among its 27 members gave reason to believe that "the downcycle is at an end and that a turnaround has come for all countries."* Times (London) 1/22/76, p20 **[1976]**

downer, *n. U.S. Slang.* **1** a sedative or depressant drug. Also called DOWN. Compare UPPER. *The premiere involved a student who refused to pop "uppers" and "downers" like the rest of the kids. The comic relief, provided mostly by the school's bicep-brained athletic director (Jerry Van Dyke), was a downer.* Time 9/28/70, p66 . . . *Janis [Joplin, a rock singer], along with her famous Southern Comfort, harbored a sometime penchant for downers and hardstuff.* NY Times 10/27/70, p45 **2** a dull, tiresome person or thing. . . . *depressing people were "downers," a bad experience was a "bummer."* Harper's 3/70, p69 **3** a lessening or decrease in force, intensity, etc. *This does not mean that America has seen the last of revolutionary violence. The movement has always been characterized by uppers and downers, and this spring may bring more uppers than anybody cares to see.* Time 2/22/71, p14 **[1966]**

downhiller, *n.* a downhill racer in a ski competition. *Miss Chaffee, a product of the same ski country that had produced the great Andrea Mead, had been the team's outstanding downhiller.* NY Times 12/14/67, p66 **[1967]**

downlink, *n.* transmission of data signals, etc., from a spacecraft or satellite to the ground (often used attributively). Compare UPLINK. *Oscar 6 contained a translator that received signals in the 145.9-146.0 MHz range (uplink) and retransmitted them at 29.45-29.55 MHz (downlink). In this manner more than 1,000 amateurs on all continents successfully conducted two-way communications via the satellite.* Britannica Book of the Year 1974, p661 **[1969]**

down-looking, *adj.* (of radar) transmitting signals downward, used to detect low-flying aircraft or missiles and to direct the guidance system of a missile. Compare SIDE-LOOKING. *Given the American decision to deploy cruise missiles aboard B-52 bombers, it was not surprising to learn that the Soviet Union was constructing towers along the Russian borders several hundred feet high to house "down-looking" radar.* Annual Register of World Events in 1977, p338 *The missile is also provided with a downlooking radar altimeter capable of resolving objects on the ground smaller than the map squares from a height of several kilometers.* Scientific American 2/77, p22 **[1972]**

down-market, *Especially British.* —*adj.* of or for the lower-income consumer; of a lower grade or quality. Compare UP-MARKET. *Not so very long ago, for instance, Harold Macmillan's staid and dynastic publishing house might have disdained anything so down-market as the biography of a sex-pot. But they have just bid £12,000 for a potential 'breast-seller'—the life story of Raquel Welch.* Sunday Times (London) 6/1/75, p28 —*adv.* in or into the down-market field. *Readers who have asked about the matter can be told that there is no reason to believe the paper will move 'down-market' in search of popularity.* Listener 12/27/73, p875 **[1970** for adj.; **1973** for adv.]

downpress, *v.t.* to oppress; keep in a state of subjugation (a word used by Rastafarians about the Jamaican government, especially in the lyrics of reggae music). *By 1970 or so the Rastas were saying . . . something quite specific about Jamaican politics: The System was downpressing the people, capitalism was the plague, and the Hugh Shearer government—as the current embodiment of Babylon—was going to burn.* Harper's 7/77, p12 **[1977]** —**downpressor,** *n.:* . . . *it is most odd that this Caribbean wild man [singer Bob Marley], with his dreadlocks, his ganja-inspired revelations, has attracted such a hysterical following. A gospel of death to the "downpressors" does not seem in keeping with these tame times.* NY Times Magazine 8/14/77, p24

down quark, a type of quark (hypothetical nuclear particle) possessing a charge of $-\frac{1}{3}$ and a spin of $+\frac{1}{2}$. Also called D QUARK. *To explain the common, well-behaved particles such as neutrons or protons requires two quarks (and their corresponding antiquarks) designated "up quark" and "down quark" or "neutron quark" and "proton quark" depending on whether one uses California or eastern American terminology.* Science News 5/8/76, p293 **[1976,** so called in reference to the downward spin it is supposed to exhibit]

downscale, *adj. U.S.* below a certain scale, especially of income or wealth; not upscale. *The Ewings' ranch house is certainly cast in the same image, but, as the advertising people say, it is definitely downscale from "Giant." Large but not huge; white, serene, and grandly suburban.* New Yorker 3/24/80, p116 *Last week the Sunday Times acquired a document from within CBS setting out "the TAPE formula for motion pictures and television movies." The computer analyses plot, social content and the ethnic makeup of the cast . . . Ideally, a screen hero should be from a "downscale" social background, the central conflict should be on a "desert island" and most of the characters should not be older than 25.* Sunday Times (London) 7/18/82, p4 **[1966, 1980,** patterned after UPSCALE]

downsize, *v.t. U.S.* to reduce the overall size and weight of (an automobile). *For the 1978 model year, GM [General Motors] downsized its four intermediate cars . . . trimming their length by about 8 inches and their weight by up to 825 pounds.*

1978 Collier's Encyclopedia Year Book, p143 [**1976**, from *down, adv. + size, v.*]

Down's syndrome, a congenital disorder characterized by mental retardation, short stature, and a flattened facial profile. Also spelled **Down syndrome**. *Down's syndrome, or mongolism* [is] *a genetic disease that results from an extra No. 21 chromosome in the child's cells.* NY Times 6/3/71, p41 [**1961**, named after John L. H. *Down*, 1828-1896, an English physician who first described the characteristics of this disorder]

downstream, *adj., adv.* **1** in, of, or toward the distribution and marketing end of any industry. Compare UPSTREAM. *A third cost is the losses when the project is delayed. The scheduled time of many "downstream" events, such as tooling and the availability of manufacturing facilities, are tightly linked to the schedule of R & D.* Scientific American 9/78, p92 *Oil countries, notably Iran, are also showing a growing interest in investing "downstream."* Auckland Star (N.Z.) 2/10/73, p18 **2** *Molecular Biology.* in or toward the end point of a genetic segment or transcription. *Pierre Chambon of the French National Center for Scientific Research in Paris in March 1981 reported that, when his group of researchers made deletions by approaching a gene from the downstream side, they began to destroy promoter activity when they reached a point some 200 molecules from the beginning of the gene.* World Book Science Annual 1982, p285 [**1963** for def. 1; **1980** for def. 2]

downwelling, *n.* the lowering or depressing of the ocean under the pressure of tectonic plates. *One of the puzzles of the gravity interpretation is that both upwellings (plumes) and downwellings (trenches) lead to gravity highs.* Nature 12/29/72, p540 [**1968**, patterned on UPWELLING]

doxycycline (‚dɑksə'saikli:n), *n.* a broad-spectrum antibiotic derived from tetracycline. *Formula:* $C_{22}H_{24}N_2O_8$ *The drug is doxycycline, a synthetic form of tetracycline that, in larger doses, is also used to treat gonorrhea.* Newsweek 12/9/74, p71 *A drug to prevent traveler's diarrhea—an antibiotic called doxycycline—was found.* Science News 12/23-30/78, p451 [**1966**, from *deoxy-* containing less oxygen than (from *de-* less, fewer + *oxy*gen) + tetra*cycline*]

dozen, *n.* **the dozens**, *U.S. Slang.* a ritualized game or contest in which two participants exchange insults directed against each other's relatives. *Playin' the dozens in inner-city schools may cause more fights and disruptions than any other activity. The dozens or playin' the dozens has many names, but most youngsters probably refer to the game as "talkin' about moms"—making derogatory allegations about mothers.* Today's Education Sept./Oct. 1975, p54 [**1972**] ▶ This phrase emerged in the 1970s as linguists and social scientists began to investigate Black English and Afro-American culture in general. Among blacks the term is known to have been used at least from the 1920's.

DP, **1** abbreviation of *data processing. As the report puts it: "Forecasting specific developments in the data processing (DP) field is far more difficult than predicting general trends."* New Scientist 10/30/69, p240 **2** abbreviation of DURABLE PRESS. *Durable press (DP) has touched off a revolution that is affecting the entire apparel industry and even such non-apparel commodities as sheets and blankets.* 1967 Collier's Encyclopedia Year Book, p535 [**1969** for def. 1; **1965** for def. 2]

D particle, an elementary particle believed to be composed of a charmed quark and an ordinary anti-quark. *Physicists from SLAC and the University of California, Berkeley, reported the discovery of the genuinely charmed particle. Large numbers of them appeared in experiments at SLAC. The new particle is called the D particle. It is electrically neutral* [and] *is about twice as heavy as the proton.* 1977 World Book Year Book, p453 [**1977**]

d quark, short for DOWN QUARK. *Strangeness is among these approximately conserved quantum numbers; as a result weak interactions can convert an s quark into a u or a d quark and strange particles can decay through weak interactions into lighter nonstrange hadrons or into leptons.* Scientific American 10/77, p59 [**1976**]

dragon, *n.* **chase the dragon,** to take or use an opiate, especially heroin. *All around me were burning candles the addicts use to light their silver papers to chase the dragon.* Sunday Post-Herald (Hongkong) 7/1/73, p1 *Out of the conflict, which has distinct political overtones, one immediate issue has emerged— what to do about White House and Congressional proposals for involuntary, random urinalysis tests for hard drugs, especially in Europe and aboard ships, where opiate use is referred to as "chasing the dragon."* NY Times 7/30/78, pD4 [**1961**]

dragsville, *n. Slang.* something that is boring. Compare DULLSVILLE. *"Anti-smoking week will not be sanctimonious," Mr. Sidey promised last week. "In fact it will be anything but dragsville."* Manchester Guardian Weekly 12/19/68, p4 . . . *University? That's just dragsville.* Sunday Times (London) 9/24/67, p35 [**1959**; see -VILLE]

dragway, *n. U.S.* a road or course used for drag races; the paved racing area of a drag strip. *Then, with a blast and crackle of its jets,* Kiss of Death *comes out of the gate, and seven seconds later we watch it spitting and sparking at the dark end of the dragway. Fumes drift over the drag strip.* Harper's 1/76, p22 [**1976**]

drained weight. See the quotation for the meaning. *And unit price based on net weight is at best misleading. A better way, CU* [Consumers Union] *believes, would be to state "drained weight" on the labels of cans. Drained weight is the actual weight of the solid food—or net weight minus liquid weight.* Consumer Reports 1/76, p6 [**1976**]

dramedy ('dræmədi:), *n. U.S.* a situation comedy containing elements of realistic drama. *The so-called dramedy . . . didn't punch the viewer with a joke every 30 seconds, used one-camera film instead of videotape, and was shot indoors and out.* NY Times 6/26/88, pH1 [**1978**, from *drama* + com*edy*]

drawdown, *n. U.S.* a reduction; cutback. *Last week, in what may be the beginning of a worldwide drawdown, the President announced that 14,900 troops will be brought home from various stations abroad.* Time 7/18/69, p14 *There has been "drawdown," as the services call it, on military supply inventories throughout the world.* NY Times 4/23/66, p30 [**1966**, from the verb phrase *draw down*]

dreadlocks, *n.pl.* hair which has formed matted clumps from lack of grooming, worn especially by Rastafarians. *The communal group's life-style soon brought objections from neighbors. Members refuse to bathe with soap, and many wear their hair in unkempt dreadlocks.* Time 8/14/78, p16 [**1960**, from *dread* fear + *locks*, so called from the supposed fear by non-Rastafarians of the *dread*ful power of faithful Rastafarians]

dream factory, **1** a motion-picture studio. *What with Hollywood and Disneyland, the Los Angeles metropolitan area is the home of American fantasy. But last week saw an event for which sheer unreality had even the dream factories beaten.* New Scientist 2/8/73, p290 **2** the motion-picture industry. *Old Nick making money for the front-office men: another potboiler about the Devil is rampant in the dream factory . . . a thing called "Exorcist II: The Heretic."* New Yorker 7/18/77, p70 [**1966**]

dream machine, the television industry. *Back in the dream machine, BBC 1's Barlow continues on whatever, at his level, a beat is called. He has been given 'smart new surroundings (a flat with two telephones), and reports to various smooth operators of the manipulative mandarin class.* Listener 1/16/75, p83 [**1971**, from *The Great American Dream Machine*, a program of topical satire on the public television network in the United States]

dreamscape, *n.* a dreamlike picture or view. *The book* [The Holy Well by Valentin Katayev] *is a dreamscape—Fellini is the unavoidable reference—as an old man in hospital, hearing his blood drip into a bottle, reviews his life.* Manchester Guardian Weekly 8/17/67, p11 [**1955**, from *dream* + *-scape* view, scene]

Dr. Feelgood, **1** a physician who regularly prescribes amphetamines or other stimulants for patients. *Was there a "Dr. Feelgood" in the White House, dispensing chemical happiness to his co-workers? . . . The doctor denied it.* Maclean's 8/21/78, p22 **2** Attributive and transferred use: *The Carter Administra-*

tion has responded with a Dr. Feelgood litany that the dollar's health is sound. . . But the world's money traders are not buying that happy talk. Time 10/9/78, p45 [**1972**]

drillship, *n.* or **drill ship**, a ship designed to drill for oil under water. *He notes that the Soviet Union has contracted with a Finnish shipyard to build a drill ship reinforced for work in polar ice. It will reportedly be able to encase its drill hole and drill apparatus so that oil and gas can be extracted—something the Glomar Challenger cannot do.* NY Times 8/10/82, pC1 [**1972**]

drin, *n.* a group of toxic chemicals made of chlorinated hydrocarbons, used chiefly as insecticides. *Mancus Fox, Under Secretary of State for the Environment, told the House that the drins should indeed be controlled, but that they are not in wide use. We are affected mostly by discharges of dieldrin from our mothproofing industry, largely based in Yorkshire.* New Scientist 3/13/80, p859 [**1980**, abstracted from al*drin* (OEDS 1949), diel*drin* (OEDS 1949), etc.]

driography (drai'agrəfi:), *n.* a printing process using a flat-surfaced plate and special inks, making unnecessary the use of water to keep nonprinting areas free of ink. *With an attractive combination of wit and clarity, Mr. [James] Moran singles out some of the more portentous exhibits, notably those which indicated improvements in photogravure and driography; and the emergence of optical character recognition devices.* Times Literary Supplement 5/12/72, p556 [**1970**, from *dry* + *lithography*] —**driographic**, *adj.*: *A necessary adjunct of the driographic system is that the printing ink be optimized for use with the Dry Plate.* McGraw-Hill Yearbook of Science and Technology 1972, p340

drip-feed, *British.* —*adj.* of or for feeding intravenously. *A baby was wheeled on a hospital trolley across a busy main road as a nurse held a drip-feed bottle because the men refused to turn out.* Times (London) 10/19/70, p2 —*n.* a course of intravenous feeding or the apparatus for it. . . . *every senior officer in the Sudanese command was stricken with a most terrible illness. The Ambassador, who is not a very young man, had to retire to bed for five days and was even on a dripfeed.* Manchester Guardian Weekly 7/17/71, p11 [**1963**; earlier (OEDS 1907) used in reference to lubricating machinery]

drip irrigation, another name for TRICKLE IRRIGATION. *Probably the principal benefit, which is not matched in other techniques, is that drip irrigation supplies plants with the precise amount of water they need.* Scientific American 11/77, p65 [**1971**]

drip painting, **1** a form of action painting executed by dripping or splattering paint instead of by using brushstrokes. *In addition, he [André Masson, an artist] squeezed color directly onto his canvases from a special tube, thereby antedating the drip paintings of Jackson Pollock by 20 years.* Time 4/5/68, p44 **2** the style or technique of making such paintings. *Pollock's modifications of painting tend toward an emulation of writing. In throwing, dribbling, and blotting his pigments, he brought paint into closer approximation of the resiliences of verbal utterance. The essential form of drip painting is calligraphy.* New Yorker 5/6/67, p168 [**1958**]

driveability or **drivability**, *n.* the quality of characteristics of design that make an automobile easy to drive. *These substantial reductions in emissions were accomplished . . . at relatively small cost, although penalties were incurred in both fuel efficiency and driveability.* Science 1/25/74, p254 *The car I used was a Volvo 144 fitted with Michelin M + S winter tyres, each studded with 120 tungsten carbide spikes. These project only a millimetre or two from the tread, but totally transform a car's drivability.* Times (London) 2/8/73, p31 [**1972**]

drive-through, *adj.* designed or arranged to be seen while riding in one's automobile. *Shuster had been impressed by the large number of people who traveled to Africa primarily to visit the game parks and believed that a drive-through zoo would appeal to the American public.* Americana Annual 1975, p52 [**1969**]

drive-up window, *U.S.* a window through which patrons can be served while seated in their cars. *Zip Food Stores in Denver adds drive-up windows at five of its seven small markets.* Wall Street Journal 4/8/65, p1 [**1963**]

droid, *n. Informal.* android (used figuratively). *So far, Nader has contacted his allies Jane Fonda and Robert Redford about possible work and the Nader droids are reading through the real-life Nader's Raiders files looking for "anything of social significance."* Maclean's 10/20/80, p41 [**1980**, shortened form of *android*]

droog, *n.* a member of a lawless gang; gangster. *Trotskyist, in Labour terminology, is virtually synonymous with hooligan, hoodlum, ruffian, droog.* Times (London) 1/27/72, p16 [**1967**, from the word for a young gangster in Nadsat, an artificial language used in the novel *A Clockwork Orange* (1962), by Anthony Burgess, British author, born 1917, from Russian *drug* friend]

droop, *n.* Often, **the droop.** another name for BIG DRESS. *On a recent sunny day on Fifth Avenue, the droops were out in droves, completely concealing even the shapeliest woman's protrusions and inversions.* NY Times 8/27/75, p29 [**1975**]

drop, *n. Slang.* a place used by spies to deposit secret messages or information. *Szolky [Gunmar Szolky, a secret agent] himself, in his forthcoming autobiography "Under Twelve Flags," maintains that he passed the entire period in Oslo managing a combination tobacconist's shop and foreign-agents' "drop," which was "blown" when a quisling agent found himself smoking a chart of harbor defenses.* New Yorker 4/6/68, p38 —*v.t. Slang.* to swallow or ingest (a drug, especially a narcotic). *For every pain or problem we take a drink, smoke a cigarette of one type or another, or drop a pill.* NY Times Book Review, Part II,2/13/72, p22 *He [Ken Kesey] was dropping tabs of acid when most others were still getting high on root beer, and the "Acid Tests" he began on the West Coast of America all but turned-on an entire generation.* Times Literary Supplement 2/25/72, p209 —*v.i.* **drop out**, to reject or withdraw from conventional society because of disillusionment with its standards and values. *Being a hippie, to them, means dropping out completely, and finding another way to live, to support oneself physically and spiritually.* Harper's 6/70, p94 [**1958** for noun; **1962** for verb]

drop-in, *n.* **1** a person who drops in to a place; a casual visitor. *The pilot was Captain Itchy Bourne. . . He despised all generals, especially drop-ins from Washington.* Harper's 3/70, p18 [**1963**] **2** a place where people drop in or visit casually. *The rubbish came from Alice's Restaurant, a drop-in for dropouts built out of a deconsecrated church in Stockbridge, Mass.* Manchester Guardian Weekly 2/21/70, p20 [**1948, 1970**] **3** a dropout who rejoins conventional society without giving up unconventional ideas and ways of living. *Howard Bannister (Ryan O'Neil). . . is pursued by a madcap young thing. Judy Maxwell, a drop-in who has majored in everything and remembered it all, and who is determined to prise Howard away from Eunice.* Listener 6/29/72, p878 [**1967**, patterned after *drop-out*]

dropout, *n.* **1** a person who withdraws from any segment or institution of established society to join groups of radicals, hippies, etc. *And by the end of the decade, there was a marked reaction among white middle-class Americans against the rebellious Negroes, the defiant university students, and the social drop-outs.* 1970 World Book Year Book, p25 **2** a Jewish emigrant from the Soviet Union who is supposedly going to Israel but emigrates to another country, especially the United States. *An early Israeli attempt to stop the dropouts involved trying to establish an air link between Moscow and Tel Aviv. In that way, Russian Jews might be flown directly to Israel, thus eliminating the Vienna stopover and the refugees' option to go elsewhere.* Time 11/22/76, p37 [**1967** for def. 1; **1976** for def. 2; earlier use of *dropout* (OEDS 1930) refers to students who have left school, especially before completing a course of study]

drownproofing, *n.* a means of protection against drowning. See the quotation for details. *A new technique of water survival called "Drownproofing" has been in official use as part of the* training program here since April. It has virtually superseded conventional swimming instructions in water survival courses. The marine is taught to relax in the water and to allow the head and upper torso to sink beneath the surface at a 45 degree angle. Then, with a slow easy arm and leg motion, the head is raised above the surface; the man takes a deep breath and then relaxes again, exhaling slowly while under water. Marines in full combat uniforms with packs and rifles have stayed afloat using this method for an hour or more. NY Times 10/15/67, pA7 [1959]

Dr. Strangelove, variant of STRANGELOVE. *The anti-nuclear lobby would have us believe that the nuclear industry is run by an army of Dr Strangeloves motivated by nothing more than a desire for personal glory and profit.* New Scientist 8/29/74, p498 [1966]

druggy, U.S. —n. a person who takes drugs. . . . *the various student types . . . joiners and doers, druggies and drunks.* NY Times 11/25/70, p37 *Presumably they meant the movie to observe, without either condemning or condoning, some of the oddities in our midst—Hell's Angels, greasers, skinheads, druggies, etc.* Manchester Guardian Weekly 12/18/71, p21 **—adj.** having to do with taking drugs. *"Can't You Hear Me Knocking" [a record], by contrast, is a stylistic meeting place for old and new. It begins with that familiar buzzing, distorted guitar sound and inimitable druggy sentiments. . .* Time 5/17/71, p34 [1968]

drugola (drə'goulə), n. U.S. Slang. illicit payments made by narcotics dealers to secure protection from police or other legal interference. . . . *Federal investigators throughout the country are looking for friendly witnesses who will be granted immunity for telling what they know about payola and drugola.* Newsweek 7/30/73, p62 [1973, patterned after *payola, gayola,* etc.]

drugpusher, n. another word for a *pusher* (of narcotics). *In a routine part, nightclub proprietress in league with drugpushers, she [Patricia Neal] showed what real acting can do with the most unpromising, thin material.* Punch 8/7/68, p204 [1955]

drummer, n. **march to** (or **hear**) **a different drummer,** U.S. to be different from others; act unconventionally. *Massachusetts voters march to a very different drummer indeed. For many of the independent-minded Yankees, the situation was a source of pride rather than puzzlement—"the other 49 states are all wrong" was the unastonished explanation of Marty Kelly who delivers beer in the Boston area.* Newsweek 11/20/72, p32 *In the new world of the tour, one man, who came to the circuit as recently as 1967, obviously hears a much different drummer. That is Trevino, a throwback not to the nineteen-fifties but practically to the nineteen-thirties. He is an anachronism: the last of the ex-caddies to become a great champion.* New Yorker 4/28/73, p120 [1972, abstracted from an epigram in Thoreau's *Walden:* "If a man does not keep pace with his companions, perhaps it is because he hears a different drummer."]

druzhinnik (dru:'ʒi:nik), n., pl. **druzhinniki** (dru:'ʒi:niki:). a civilian auxiliary policeman in the Soviet Union. *The Druzhinniki . . . assist the police in preventing crime, combating hooliganism and drunkenness, and controlling crowds. They are also to be found guarding courtrooms during political trials.* Times (London) 6/27/70, p7 [1964, from Russian *druzhinnik,* from (*Narodnaya*) *Druzhina* (People's) Patrol + -*nik* (personal suffix)]

DRV or **DRVN,** abbreviation of the *Democratic Republic of Vietnam* (official name of North Vietnam). *Most of the DRV delegation are no strangers to Paris. They count French scholars and journalists who follow Vietnamese affairs among their friends, and with a sure touch they can direct a foreigner to good Parisian restaurants.* Atlantic 12/68, p6 *As far as Hanoi is concerned, the D.R.V.N. comprises all of Vietnam.* NY Times 10/6/68, pD11 [1967]

dry, v. **dry out,** to receive treatment for alcoholism or drug addiction; be free of dependence on alcohol or drugs. See DETOX.

Elizabeth dried out for a while and then had a relapse, drinking more heavily than before. Time 4/22/74, p80 [1963]

D sleep, short for DESYNCHRONIZED SLEEP. Compare S SLEEP. *Though there is no assurance that cats dream in D Sleep, the psychiatrists acknowledge, the very fact that the animal brains undergo human-like electrical patterns during sleep justifies the cat as "a reasonable subject for our study of the brain as a dream process generator."* Science News 12/17/77, p405 [1974]

DSRV, abbreviation for *Deep Submergence Rescue Vehicle. DSRV-1 was launched on January 24 and is undergoing trials in shallow water. Ultimately the craft will be able to rescue 24 men at a time from a disabled submarine at depths of 5,000 feet (1,500 meters).* Americana Annual 1971, p515 [1966]

dual pricing, pricing of packaged goods to show both the actual price and the price per pound or other unit. *Consumerism is not about to fade away; rather, it is begetting a spate of legislation to regulate retailers' conduct, including unit and dual pricing and code dating.* 1971 Collier's Encyclopedia Year Book, p460 [1970]

dual slalom, another name for PARALLEL SLALOM. *The final race was the first dual slalom in World Cup history. In a format borrowed from the professional tour, the skiers raced side by side down parallel courses in direct eliminations.* 1976 World Book Year Book, p459 [1976]

Duchenne dystrophy (du:'ʃen), a form of muscular dystrophy. *Muscular dystrophy is in fact a group of diseases. In the best known, Duchenne dystrophy, which is inherited and affects only boys, the muscles start to waste away from an early age.* Times (London) 6/30/70, p16 [1964, named after Guillaume Armand *Duchenne,* 1806-1875, a French neurologist who described various forms of the disease]

duck hook, a deviation of a golf ball from its intended course, usually in the path of an erratic curve. *Too many of the tee shots, at least half, developed a bend about 150 yards down the fairway and disappeared to the left in a sudden, ugly, discouraging curve. Duck hooks, as the professional golfers call them, miserable duck hooks.* Maclean's 7/73, p35 [1967]

dude, n. U.S. Slang. any male; a man or boy; fellow. *"Compared to the Tombs, you know, it was okay. . . Every time I went there dudes in the receiving line would be sick. . . There was so many dudes in the 'A' pen once that I couldn't sit down. Some of them getting sick on the floor; the dude next to me was moaning about his bust."* Harper's 11/74, p89 *Each time I suggest a program of self-development, they respond with overwhelming enthusiasm. Black teen-agers—some of the roughest, most street-wise dudes you will ever meet—respond to that appeal.* NY Times Magazine 4/18/76, p71 [1970, extended from the original sense of a city slicker, a dandy (1880's)]

duende ('dwendei), n. Spanish. (literally) elf; demon. But see the quotations for other meanings. . . . *the quality of the Spanish character—which Michener sums up in one evocative word, duende, meaning "mysterious and ineffable charm."* Time 5/17/68, p84 . . . *he has that essential flamenco ingredient which America's own great ethnic dance expert, La Meri, describes as duende (a "demon"), which means that "the dancer must be possessed."* Saturday Review 1/6/68, p36 *As a Latin, Busoni approaches the idea of death through a feeling for what Lorca called duende—that Spanish apprehension of the dark magic of death which lurks behind life and behind all great works of art.* Listener 4/14/66, p556 [1924, 1954]

dukawallah ('du:kə,wɑlə), n. a shopkeeper in Kenya and some other parts of eastern Africa. *The first Asians went to East Africa well ahead of the British. . . They became the colony's 'dukawallahs' (or shopkeepers), running every kind of establishment from the smart shops in the capital to tiny stores in dusty African villages.* Listener 3/7/68, p294 [1959, from *duka* shop (1924, from Swahili) + -*wallah* (Anglo-Indian suffix for one connected with)]

duke, v.i., v.t. Especially U.S. Slang. **1** to fight or hit with the fists. *While the book is most certainly addressed to educators, we are not mistreated with stuff about "pattern of errors" or* *"interference of home tongue"* or *"mainstream demands,"* terms which hallmark the language-arts battles when folks be duking in the faculty lounge about the speech of black students. NY Times Book Review 9/3/72, p3 *"If the cat didn't have a gun available when he got into an argument, he'd probably just duke (punch) the other person," says ghetto-bred Sgt. Fred Williams. "The other guy might end up with a busted lip, but he'd still be alive."* Newsweek 1/1/73, p21 **2 duke it out,** to fight, especially until someone wins. *There is nobody in our organization that takes second place when it comes to getting up and duking it out. Just because we wear suits and ties doesn't mean we're afraid to get into that kind of thing.* Maclean's 1/8/79, p8 [**1972,** verb use of the slang noun *dukes* the fists (1874), especially in the phrase *put up one's dukes*]

duke-out, *n. Especially U.S. Slang.* a fistfight. *Take the last all-House duke-out. It was, distressingly enough, over ten years ago. Although there have been a fair number of fistfights in the capitol since, none has qualified as total Fist City.* Atlantic 3/75, p48 [**1975,** probably from *duke*, verb, on the pattern of *shoot-out* and *breakout*]

dukes-up, *adj. Especially U.S. Slang.* ready to fight; pugnacious. *Aside from a dukes-up debut as official opposition, for two months the party had stood as still as the slate-gray autumn that hung on here almost supernaturally long.* Maclean's 3/74, p10 *Did the blame for that lie with the Communists, who bickered endlessly with their Socialist allies during the campaign? Not to hear Marchais tell it. "We bear no responsibility," he said in a dukes-up, three-hour speech. The cause, he asserted, was purely the Socialists' "obstinacy."* Time 5/8/78, p37 [**1974,** abstracted from *put one's dukes up*]

Dullsville or **dullsville,** *U.S. Slang.* **—n.** a condition of utter dullness; something very dull. Compare DRAGSVILLE. *. . . the thirty-seventh President tips ketchup on his cottage cheese. "Stylewise," a lady columnist impaled the new regime, "it looks like backward to Dullsville for the next four years in the nation's capital."* Manchester Guardian Weekly 1/23/69, p4 **—adj.** very dull. [President Lyndon] *Johnson is square, folksy and dullsville, sounding just like dozens of boring politicians from the past.* Time 10/7/66, p17 [**1960**]

dumb, *adj., v.* **dumb down,** *U.S. Informal.* to make less intelligent; lower the intellectual level of. *They are generally blamed . . . as having been a major force in dumbing down textbooks nationwide.* Atlanta Constitution 10/22/87, pA17 *There are jobs that will be dumbed down . . . simply because of the retraining costs.* Harrisburg (PA) Sunday Patriot-News 2/21/88, pF4 [**1933, 1983**]

dumdum, *n. Chiefly U.S. Slang.* a stupid person; a dumbbell (also used attributively). *The police commissioner can expose himself in the middle of 42nd Street and no one'll pay attention to him. Yet all you need is one dumdum in the mayor's office pointing to a cop and saying, 'I like that boy,' and the next day he's got a promotion.* Harper's 9/71, p87 [**1968,** from the reduplication *dum(b)-dum(b)*]

dummy head, a device resembling a human head with a microphone in each ear, used to receive sound for binaural and quadraphonic sound reproduction and transmission. *The new QB-phonic system makes a recording using two conventional dummy heads, one in front of and one behind a baffle, to capture front and rear sounds and transmit them in four channels via a conventional CD-4 quadraphonic disc. The four channels are processed by introducing delays and frequency filtering, to compensate for the path in air which the sound must take when reproduced by loudspeakers instead of headphones.* New Scientist 3/24/77, p701 [**1976**]

dump, *n.* Computers: *When computers hit a snag they often print out dense reams of digits, which represent all the data that's been given to them. This is called a "dump." Searching out the error in a dump is referred to as "debugging," and it occupies much of any programmer's time.* Atlantic 3/70, p67 **—v.t.** U.S. Football: *A team is not "defended against" but "defensed," and he who would describe a quarterback caught behind the line of scrimmage as having been "dumped" rather than "sacked" reveals his status as a postulant before the mys-*

teries. Time 11/19/70, p37 **—v.i. dump on,** *U.S. Slang.* to attack verbally; criticize severely. *They [homosexuals] have also made it a practice to "trash" (wreck) restaurants, publishing houses, and other businesses that discriminate against the third world of sex; "dump on" (heckle) religious leaders, such as Billy Graham, who don't like them; and "zap" (confront) politicians until they express themselves one way or the other on equal housing and employment rights for homosexuals.* Saturday Review 2/12/72, p24 [**1956** for noun; **1963** for verb]

dune buggy, a small, lightweight car designed especially for driving on sand dunes and beaches. *A new and popular outdoor hobby was the building and driving of "dune buggies," cars modified especially for daring drives on sand dunes.* 1969 Compton Yearbook, p269 [**1966**]

dunemobile, *n.* a vehicle for riding on sand dunes. *A popular sport in the area of the mammoth Sleeping Bear Dune, west of Traverse City, Michigan, is to ride the dunemobiles at high speed over the shifting sands.* Encyclopedia Science Supplement (Grolier) 1972, p181 [**1972,** from *dune* + auto*mobile*]

duoplasmatron, *n.* an apparatus that produces a stream of ions, as of argon or oxygen. *The ions used for sample bombardment are generated in a hollow-cathode duoplasmatron ion source that is capable of producing ions of a wide variety of gases, including those of a highly electronegative character.* Science 2/25/72, p853 [**1964,** from *duo-* double + *plasma* highly ionized gas + *-tron* an accelerating device, as a *cyclotron*]

duorail, *n.* the conventional railroad consisting of two rails, as distinguished from the monorail. *Because the duorail is for the present favored, the new rapid-transit systems being built in the metropolitan areas of the Americas and Europe are underground railways powered by electric traction.* 1969 Compton Yearbook, p450 [**1967**]

duplex, *n.* a double-stranded DNA or RNA molecule. *Another method of repair occurs in the dark and in cells containing certain repair enzymes. In this process, known as excision repair, a damaged strand of the DNA duplex is removed and replaced by undamaged DNA replicated from the other strand of the duplex.* Britannica Book of the Year 1975, p444 [**1963,** from the adjective, meaning "twofold" (OED 1817)]

durable press, a textile-manufacturing process in which creases, pleats, etc., are set more or less permanently into fabric by the use of chemicals. *Abbreviation:* DP Also called PERMANENT PRESS. *In furnishings, the great growth of durable press and soil-resistant shirts made much of the older stock obsolete.* New Yorker 1/8/68, p124 *The first limited success was an all-cotton durable-press shirt marketed this year.* Time 10/10/69, p61 [**1965**]

dustbinman, *n. British.* a garbage collector. *The first major confrontation over inflationary wage demands came when local authority workers employed in what were called 'the dirty jobs'—dustbinmen, sewage workers, and street sweepers—began a series of selective strikes.* Annual Register of World Events in 1970, p40 [**1970**] ▶ This term seems to be competing with the earlier Briticism, *dustman* (1700's).

dust cloud, a mass of interstellar matter made up of gases, molecules, and other particles; cloud of cosmic dust. *A typical dust cloud with a diameter of one light-year and a density of 1,000 molecules of hydrogen per cubic centimeter will attenuate light by about four magnitudes and ultraviolet radiation by a factor perhaps as large as 10^{24}.* Scientific American 3/73, p62 [**1965**] ▶ The nebular hypothesis in astronomy holds that stars arise from the condensation of dust clouds.

dust head, *U.S. Slang.* a habitual user of ANGEL DUST. *"Dust heads," as users are called, say that $3 for a marijuana cigaret laced with the hallucinogenic-like drug is a pretty cheap high.* Daily News (New York) 2/24/78, p29 [**1978,** from angel *dust* + HEAD]

dustoff, *n. U.S. Military Slang.* another name for MEDEVAC. Often used attributively. *. . . . virtually all battlefield casualties are picked up by aerial ambulances, the so-called "dustoff"* *medical helicopters.* NY Times 5/21/67, pA22 [**1967**, so called from the dust they raise during their rapid descent and takeoff]

dust tail, the part of a comet's tail consisting of dust particles blown away from the coma by pressure of the sun's radiation. Compare GAS TAIL. See also ANTITAIL. *The observations from Skylab just after Comet Kohoutek swung past the Sun suggest that particles up to 1 mm in diameter were ejected from the nucleus. This is 100 times larger than particles that usually form the dust tails of comets.* McGraw-Hill Yearbook of Science and Technology 1975, p51 [**1975**]

duty solicitor, a government-appointed solicitor in Great Britain, charged with representing indigents. *The duty solicitor, apart from giving advice to a defendant, would have the advantage of being able to talk to court officials on an informal basis where he finds this desirable.* Times (London) 5/1/72, p2 [**1972**]

DUV, abbreviation of DATA-UNDERVOICE. *DUV, part of the Bell System's Dataphone Digital Service, allows 1.5 million bits of information to be transmitted per second.* 1975 World Book Year Book, p269 [**1975**]

D.W.I., abbreviation of *driving while intoxicated. The D.W.I. offender is generally an individual under pressure, anxious about financial or domestic troubles.* Time 1/5/70, p28 [**1968**]

dye laser, a chemical laser using the fluorescence of certain organic dyes, such as rhodamine and fluorescein, to produce intense coherent light over a wide range of possible frequencies. *The tunability of the dye laser is its most striking characteristic; therefore much work has been done in this area. The gross selection of wavelength can be achieved by properly choosing the dye.* McGraw-Hill Yearbook of Science and Technology 1970, p234 [**1967**]

dykey, *adj. Slang.* lesbian. *One interlude, however, is entirely free of stylistic ties. On the road, Robert and Rayette pick up two dykey hitchhikers. One is sullen. The other (Helena Kalliniotes) delivers a ten-minute broadside at "man."* Time 9/14/70, pK11 [**1968**, from *dyke* a female homosexual, lesbian (1942) + -*y* (adj. suffix)]

dynamic, *adj.* (of a computer memory) requiring electrical recharging to retain data; not static. *The memory sold in highest volume in 1979 was the 16-K dynamic random access memory (RAM; K = 1,024 bits). In 1979 a new type of 16-K dynamic RAM was successfully manufactured in high volume. (In a dynamic RAM, data must be refreshed periodically or it will be lost.)* Britannica Book of the Year 1980, p449 [**1967**]

dynamic positioning, a system to automatically control the positioning of a ship by computer. *The ship maintains its position by a process called "dynamic positioning."* . . . *If the ship begins to drift, the computer automatically activates the appropriate screws (propellers) to hold the ship in position.* World Book Science Annual 1972, p122 [**1967**]

dynamic scattering, a process in which transparent liquid crystals become opaque and scatter light by application of a charge of electricity, used especially in producing display screens for computers. *In 1968, the RCA laboratories discovered the so-called "dynamic scattering" effect by enclosing a thin film (a few microns thick) of nematic material between transparent conducting plates and applying several tens of volts.* New Scientist 12/14/72, p652 [**1968**]

dynamite or *sometimes* **dynomite**, *adj.* (restricted to an attributive position before nouns) *U.S. and Canadian Slang.* superlative; extraordinarily good. *Conceded an Arledge aide last week: "CBS ought to be congratulated. It was dynamite TV."* Time 11/28/77, p47 *She is no longer a dynomite mom. They used to talk these things over, share enthusiasms.* New Yorker 1/23/78, p25 *After a dynamite opening . . . at the Palladium last night, Elton John went up to 54th Street's Studio 54 and ran into—of all people—Goldie Hawn.* New York Post 10/19/79, p7 [**1976**, popularized by the character "J.J." in the television situation comedy series *Good Times*]

dynamite charge, another name for ALLEN CHARGE. *Because hung juries are becoming common in political and complicat-*

ed criminal cases, prosecutors argue that the dynamite charge is necessary to push juries along—that it is difficult to get 12 people to agree on anything and that the criminal process would get stalled if jurors were not told they must decide cases.* NY Times 10/8/72, pD6 [**1972**]

dynein ('dɑinin), *n.* a form of the enzyme ATPase whose action provides the energy for the movement of cilia. *The microtubules of cilia are associated with a protein of high molecular weight. This protein, which Gibbons named "dynein," is an adenosine triphosphatase. Dynein forms arms or projections that are attached to one tubule (the A tubule) of the outer doublets.* Science 9/28/73, p1237 [**1965**, coined by Ian Gibbons, an American molecular biologist, from *dyne* the unit of force (from Greek *dýnamis* power) + -*in* (chemical suffix)]

dysautonomia (disˌɔ:təˈnoumi:ə), *n.* an inherited disorder of the nervous system, found chiefly among Jews of European descent, in which sensory perception and many automatic functions are impaired. *Dysautonomia, transmitted through a recessive gene, affects the autonomic, or automatic, nervous system, which regulates such basic processes as respiration, digestion, blood circulation, and responses to pain, heat and cold.* New York Post 6/25/72, p58 [**1954**, from *dys-* abnormal, defective + *autonomic* (nervous system) + -*ia* disease, as in *pneumonia, diphtheria,* etc.]

dysautonomic, *adj.* of, relating to, or affected with dysautonomia. *Mercifully, not every dysautonomic child has all the symptoms, but some of them have so many that they cannot attend regular school and require constant care.* Newsweek 3/19/73, p56 —*n.* a person affected with dysautonomia. *When NGF [nerve-growth factor] levels were determined . . . the results showed a striking discrepancy: dysautonomics, compared with normal subjects, had a threefold increase in blood-serum levels of a substance immunologically equivalent to NGF.* Scientific American 12/76, p53 [**1973**, from *dysautonomia* + -*ic*]

dysbarism ('disbəˌrizəm), *n.* paralyzing cramps caused by a sudden reduction of air pressure. . . . *farther up* [than three miles], *man becomes subject to "the bends," or dysbarism. Nitrogen in his tissues is released because of the low atmospheric pressure.* 1970 Compton Yearbook, p564 [**1967**, from Greek *dys-* bad + *báros* weight, pressure + English -*ism*]

dysfunction, *v.i.* to cease to function properly or normally; to break down. *Looking at "the dysfunctioning of Arab society," Beirut Social Psychologist Halim Barakat says, "Men alienated from established orders have alternatives."* Time 8/9/71, p23 *"I'm convinced that the next ruling generation is going to be all pillheads. I'm convinced of it. If they haven't dysfunctioned completely to the point where they can't stand for office."* Atlantic 8/66, p40 [**1966**, verb use of *dysfunction, n.* (1916)]

dyslexic, *n.* a person affected with dyslexia (impairment in reading ability). *The conventional figure of the incidence of dyslexics in this country* [Great Britain] *is 4 per cent of backward readers.* Sunday Times (London) 7/11/71, p21 *To the parents of a dyslexic, the child's behavior may be profoundly perplexing. Often the child exhibits exceptional ingenuity and creativity, yet fails totally at school.* NY Times 2/5/68, p41 [**1961**, from *dyslexia* (1888) + -*ic*]

dysmelia (disˈmi:li:ə *or* disˈmeli:ə), *n.* a deformed condition or development of the limbs. *The deformities are usually severe, and the upper limbs are more severely affected than the lower limbs. This variation in the degree of the defect is also observed in human cases of thalidomide dysmelia.* Nature 10/20/72, p461 [**1972**, from New Latin, from *dys-* bad + Greek *mélos* limb]

dystopia, *n.* the opposite of a utopia; a place where all is bad or a condition in which all is evil. . . . *some of the best-known SF* [science fiction] *is pure jeremiad. . . The generic type is what Heinlein once called the "If This Goes On" story: take a current trend, carry it to extremes, and show a society—usually a dystopia, i.e., a perverted and malevolent utopia—built from the results.* 1981 Britannica Yearbook of Science and the Future, p39 *It may be that only a vision of Utopia can combat the dystopia of contemporary life.* Time 1/18/71, p15 [**1868, 1952,**

---

from *dys-* bad + u*topia*] ► The coinage of *dystopia* (where all is bad) as the opposite of *utopia* (where all is good) suggests that the initial *u-* (from Greek *oú* not) has become associated with the prefix *eu-* (from Greek *eu-* good) and that Sir Thomas More was surely punning on this phonetic connection in his coinage of *utopia*.

dystopian, *adj.* of or relating to a dystopia; the opposite of utopian. . . . *the deformed, the insane and the defective become the new elite. Madness and destruction ensue . . . Despite such familiar dystopian details,* Intensive Care *has little in common with the average science-fiction novel, far more with social-* commentary-as-critique such as Orwell's 1984 and Butler's Erewhon. Time 5/18/70, p88 [**1962**]

dystrophication (ˌdistrəfəˈkeiʃən), *n.* the pollution of streams, lakes, etc., by domestic and industrial wastes and runoff from fertilized agricultural areas. See also EUTROPHICATION. *The sea can probably tolerate the runoff indefinitely but along the way the nitrogen creates algal "blooms" that are hastening the dystrophication of lakes and estuaries.* Scientific American 11/70, p115 [**1970**, from *dystrophic* depleted in nutrients (said of a lake) + *-ation*]

E

Eames chair (i:mz *or* eimz), a plywood or molded plastic chair shaped to fit the contours of the body. *The Eames chair is hardly a pure work of art; it is a utilitarian object, produced by impulses both sacred and profane. Considered even as a practical chair, it has flaws. But as an object of contemplation, as an instant replay of social change during the past twenty years, the Eames chair is invaluable.* Newsweek 5/14/73, p81 [**1946, 1964,** named after Charles *Eames,* 1907-1978, an American designer, who introduced it in the 1940's]

ear candy, *U.S. Slang.* music, especially popular music, that is pleasing to the ear; a smoothly arranged and softly played musical composition. *Synthesizers are enjoying a particular vogue . . . because, in the words of one composer-arranger, "they fulfill pop music's never-ending quest for fresh ear candy."* Time 2/27/84, p96 *While not in Dolby's class, Wang Chung produces some fairly highbrow synthesized ear candy.* Stereo Review 5/84, p83 [**1984**]

ear-catcher, *n.* something that attracts attention by its sound; a catchy tune, lyric, etc. *Demonstration records in my collection tend to sort themselves out into two changing piles: one predictably of ear-catchers designed to send listeners through the roof; the other, equally important, of "guess-whats."* Manchester Guardian Weekly 5/1/69, p21 [**1958,** patterned after *eye-catcher* (OEDS 1923)]

early warning system, anything that detects danger early. *Sixth, the UN would be asked to set up an international early warning system for the ill-effects of man-made pollutants.* New Scientist 6/1/72, p489 *Essentially the committee has two roles in respect of drugs: it licenses the release of new products and it maintains an early warning system for the detection of unexpected adverse effects from drugs.* Times (London) 1/24/73, p11 [**1966,** transferred sense of the term originally (1946) used for a system of early warning of aerial attack]

ears, *n.pl. U.S. Slang.* a citizens band radio set. *Ears—The C.B. radio. As, "Got your ears on, good buddy."* NY Times 12/17/75, p47 *Because of overcrowding, many a CB enthusiast (called an "apple") is strapping an illegal linear amplifier ("boots") on to his transceiver ("ears") which is limited by the Federal Communications Commission ("Big Daddy" in the US) to an output power of no more than five watts.* New Scientist 6/30/77, p764 [**1975**]

earth art, a form of art that changes some natural object or scenery to fit a concept of the artist. Also called LAND ART. *"When I get discouraged," says* [Michael] *Heizer, "I go back to painting," but the core of his work—by now the most extensive accomplishment in what has come to be called "earth art"—is out-of-doors, dug, blasted and chiseled into sections in the land in Nevada and California.* Newsweek 11/18/74, p113 *—earth artist: Peter Hutchinson, a British earth artist, has cultivated bread molds on the lip of an active volcano in Mexico.* New Yorker 2/5/72, p42

Earth Day, a day in April set aside by environmentalists to dramatize the need for pollution control. See also EARTH WEEK. *By the time Earth Day dawned on April 22, ecoactivists of all ages were suffused with quasi-religious fervor.* Time 1/4/71, p34 [**1970**]

earthday, *n.* the 24-hour day of the earth applied to measuring time on other celestial bodies, artificial satellites, etc. *For just over 14 earthdays the sun will not shine on the barren surface of the Sea of Rains, where the Lunokhod began its historic mission last Tuesday.* Times (London) 11/24/70, p6 [**1963**]

earthlubber, *n.* a person who stays on earth and has not traveled in outer space; one who is not a space traveler. *The applied ver-*

sion, probably no sooner than the 1900s, could provide direct power in space to space stations, spacecraft and other recipients using its own, self-generated laser beam. But efficient, high-powered lasers have also been a long-sought goal of weapons developers, so earthlubbers will be watching too. Science News 5/15/76, p309 [**1973,** from *earth* + *lubber,* patterned after *landlubber*]

earthquake lights or **earthquake lightning,** flashes of bright light occurring during an earthquake, believed to be caused by electric discharges from the earth's crust. *The subject of earthquake lights is fascinating. Few scientists have worked on the question . . . Nevertheless, observations have been made for many years, and the existence of earthquake lights is well established. One hypothesized explanation is linked to the piezoelectric effect in quartz-bearing rock.* Science News 1/7/78, p3 *A puzzling but rare phenomenon known as earthquake lightning—flashes of lightning caused by an earthquake.* Times (London) 11/23/70, p10 [**1970**]

earth resources satellite, an artificial satellite that gathers data on the earth's natural resources. *Somewhat of a dark horse in space has been the earth resources satellite. Such vehicles were not even included in early planning. But when astronauts returned with stories of how well they could see the earth below, geologists conceived the idea of the Landsat series of multi-spectral scanning satellites.* NY Times Magazine 1/29/78, p22 [**1968**]

earthrise, *n.* a view of the earth from the moon or from a spacecraft orbiting about the moon, in which the earth seems to be rising above the moon's horizon. *The earthrise is seen over the lunar horizon from the Apollo 12 spacecraft . . .* 1970 Compton Yearbook, p436 [**1969,** patterned after *sunrise*]

Earth Shoes, a trademark for square-toed shoes with thicker soles in front than in back, designed to lower the heel below the rest of the foot for greater comfort. Also spelled **earth shoes.** *She got rid of the demure blue patent pumps she had been wearing and substituted earth shoes, supremely comfortable but odd-looking with their lowered heel. "I hadn't worn them before because I thought people would think them ugly," she explained.* Maclean's 8/74, p7 *The people are your usual mixture of ages, etc. Some are wearing Earth Shoes, some are wearing Gucci loafers.* New Yorker 2/3/75, p22 [**1973,** so called because they were introduced into the United States from Denmark (where they originated) on Earth Day (April 22) of 1970]

earth station, a station on earth equipped with electronic apparatus to receive and rebroadcast signals transmitted from outer space. Compare SATCOM. *Every single piece of equipment in the satellite must operate flat-out* [at top capacity] *in order to provide today's services, and their signals can be picked up only by giant 90- or 100-foot diameter Earth stations costing several million pounds.* New Scientist 7/2/70, p13 [**1963**]

earth time, time measured by the 24-hour rotation of the earth, especially as a measure of time on other celestial bodies. *The General Conference's 1967 redefinition of the second did not resolve a conflict that had long been going on between proponents of atomic time and proponents of earth time. Astronomers had, naturally, been partial to earth time, and, indeed, all time had for centuries been considered their province. But even the astronomers had their differences.* New Yorker 8/27/73, p55 [**1968**]

Earthwatch or **earthwatch,** *n.* a proposed network of stations to monitor world-wide environmental pollution. *We will have an "earthwatch" to monitor and measure the growing sickness of* *the planet, and perhaps not too late, to have its warnings respected.* Natural History 10/72, p103 *The difference between the Center and Earthwatch is fundamental: the Center's mission is to observe and report; Earthwatch's will be not only to act as an early-alert system but to take that information and use it to assess the world environment in all facets and make suggestions for changes.* Harper's 3/73, p51 [**1972**]

Earth Week, a week in April set aside for expression of public concern over the pollution of the earth's atmosphere. Compare EARTH DAY. *To celebrate Earth Week (this year's version of Earth Day, spread over April 18-24), New York's Bronx Zoo set up this ominous "Animal Graveyard." Each of the 225 tombstones commemorates a species that has become extinct since 1600 . . .* Time 4/26/71, p59 [**1970**]

earthwork, *n.* a work of art which uses as a medium some natural material, such as earth, mud, rocks, sand, and ice, and is usually exhibited in photographs. See also ECOLOGICAL ART. *Earthworks protest aga·· the constricting museum-gallery system organized around u ...ndful of aesthetic platitudes by asserting the nostalgia of artists for invention, craftsmanship, and expressive behavior.* New Yorker 1/24/70, p62 [**1969**]

earthworker, *n.* an artist who makes earthworks. *The earthworkers may bring their massive mounds . . . into the galleries, or they may leave their sculptures far away, in the form of imprints inscribed in a desert, a dry lake, mud, and ice.* 1970 Collier's Encyclopedia Year Book, p117 [**1969**]

Earth-year or **earth-year**, *n.* time measured by the 365-day year of the earth, especially as a measure of time on other celestial bodies. *As Pluto moves in its orbit, the pole points farther away from the Earth each year. The effect of having the pole in the orbital plane is to make a season at one of the poles last for about half the time that Pluto takes to revolve around the Sun. Thus, there would be roughly 124-Earth-years of summer with constant sunlight, followed by 124-Earth-years of winter with constant darkness.* 1974 World Book Year Book, p203 [**1967**]

easy meat, *British Slang.* an easy thing to do, obtain, etc. *. . . he himself says modestly,"It's easy meat,playing for England."* Sunday Times (London) 6/1/69, p22 [**1958**] ▶This is a secondary sense. The earlier meaning implies a passive or impotent victim, e.g. "Unarmed citizens are easy meat for gunmen," to coin an example. Partridge (*Dictionary of Slang,* 1950, p1040) gives " 'She's easy meat'—of a not invincible chastity," which is doubtless the origin.

eating disorder, any of various psychological conditions involving abnormal eating habits, such as anorexia nervosa and bulimia. *Researchers estimate that 5 to 10 per cent of the adolescent girls and young women in the United States suffer from eating disorders.* World Book Science Annual 1987, p60 [**1986**]

Eaton agent, an organism resembling the virus of pleuropneumonia (pleurisy with pneumonia), believed to cause various mild forms of pneumonia. *Mycoplasma pneumoniae, or Eaton agent, a microorganism intermediate in several respects between viruses and bacteria, is probably responsible for most cases of what used to be called primary atypical pneumonia or, loosely, virus pneumonia.* Britannica Book of the Year 1968, p529 [**1962**, named for Monroe D. *Eaton,* born 1904, an American bacteriologist]

Eblaite ('eblə‚ɑit *or* 'i:blə‚ɑit), *n.* an ancient Semitic language discovered in cuneiform inscriptions on several thousand clay tablets excavated in northern Syria between 1975 and 1979. *Scholars have been electrified by the parallels between the language of the tablets and the language of ancient Hebrews. Eblaite, as the language is referred to, seems to be a West Semitic form unlike Sumerian, Akkadian or any of the other ancient languages known to modern science.* New York Post 6/9/76, p60 —**adj.** of or relating to Eblaite or to the kingdom of Ebla. Also, EBLAN. *The language of the tablets, unknown until now, has been named Eblaite by the researchers. It is related to the Biblical Hebrew that was used about one thousand years later. One of the most important tablets is one containing a vocabulary of Eblaite and Sumeric words.* Science News 8/21/76,

p118 [**1976**, from *Ebla,* an ancient city at Tel Mardikh, near Aleppo, Syria + *-ite*]

Eblan ('eblən *or* 'i:blən), *adj.* variant of EBLAITE. *The existence of the Eblan kingdom was not unknown; ancient Sumerian, Akkadian and Egyptian texts refer to it. However, Paolo Matthiae, 36, and Giovanni Pettinato, 41 . . . were the first to explore Ebla's ruins, which they located some 30 miles south of modern Aleppo.* Time 10/18/76, p63 [**1976**]

Ebola virus (i'boulə), a virus that causes very high fever and internal hemorrhaging. It was first identified in Zaire and Sudan in 1976. *Another hitherto unknown tropical virus, named Ebola virus . . . joins a growing list of fatal haemorrhagic fever viruses found in Africa, of which Lassa fever and Marburg disease (the so-called green monkey disease) are the most notorious.* Times (London) 3/21/77, p17 [**1976**, named after a river in northern Zaire]

ebullism ('ebyə‚lizəm), *n.* the bubbling of body fluids resulting from a sudden reduction of air pressure. *The absence of an atmosphere on the Moon brings hazards of suffocation with a time of useful consciousness limited to a few seconds due to lack of oxygen and the ebullism—boiling of body fluids—due to lack of atmospheric pressure.* Science Journal 5/69, p104 [**1956**, from Latin *ēbullīre* to bubble or boil up + English *-ism*]

EC, 1 European Community. *On April 3, China signed its first trade agreement with the European Community (EC), not only to bring itself closer to the industrial strength of western Europe, but also, in the words of Peking, "to support its struggle against hegemony (Soviet domination)."* Americana Annual 1979, p157 **2** Eastern Caribbean. *The member countries of the Eastern Caribbean Currency Authority (ECCA) refused, initially, to hand over EC$3 million to Grenada . . .* 1979 Annual Register of World Events, p93 [**1969** for def. 1; **1977** for def. 2]

ECCM, abbreviation of *electroniccounter-countermeasure.* Compare ECM. *Electronic Counter Measures against such missiles might include sending out scrambling radio signals to distort the beam . . . Needless to say, most of this equipment is highly classified. It also becomes obsolete very quickly as opponents learn their own ECCM.* Harper's 10/72, p74 [**1968**]

ecdysone ('ekdə‚soun), *n.* a hormone that regulates growth and molting in insects. Compare ECDYSTERONE. *The insect hormone ecdysone, which controls the metamorphosis of insects, achieves its effect by acting directly on DNA.* Britannica Book of the Year 1967, p511 [**1956**, from *ecdysis* the shedding of skin, molting + *-one,* as in *hormone*]

ecdysterone (‚ekdə'steroun), *n.* a hormone, related to the molting hormone ecdysone, isolated from crustacea and insects and also from some plants. *One technical problem that has hindered research related to ecdysterone is the lack of a precise physicochemical technique for quantifying tissue and circulating titers of this hormone.* David W. Borst and John D. O'Connor, "Arthropod Molting Hormone: Radioimmune Assay," Science 10/27/72, p418 [**1967**, from *ecdysis* molting + *sterol* + *-one,* as in *hormone*]

echocardiogram, *n.* a record or tracing made by echocardiography. *The ultrasound technique involves bouncing sound waves off the heart. The sound waves are of such high frequency that they cannot be detected by human ears. Using equipment that costs $20,000, cardiologists can view the anatomical features of the heart in a form called an echocardiogram.* Encyclopedia Science Supplement (Grolier) 1975, p234 [**1975**]

echocardiography, *n.* the use of ultrasonic apparatus for diagnosing cardiac tumors, diseased valves, etc. See also ULTRASONOGRAPHY. *Sound waves reflected from cardiac tissues (echocardiography) disclose heart chamber size, the status of myocardial contraction, and heart valve and tissue configuration.* 1981 Britannica Yearbook of Science and the Future, p357 [**1965**]

echo effect, a delayed consequence or repetition of an event. Compare RIPPLE EFFECT. *It is possible, indeed, that births will temporarily continue to rise slightly in an "echo effect" of the postwar baby boom, now that women born after World War II,* many of whom apparently delayed the birth of their first child, are bearing children. 1978 Collier's Encyclopedia Year Book, p453 [**1971**]

echo encephalography, the use of ultrasonic apparatus for diagnosing tumors and lesions in the brain. See also ULTRASONOGRAPHY. *Echo-encephalography got its start in 1954 when Lars Leksell, a Swedish neurosurgeon, reported the use of pulsed ultrasound to reveal lateral shifts in certain structures which normally lie in the medial plane of the brain.* Science News 2/3/68, p118 [**1960**]

echovirus, *n.* or **ECHO virus**, a type of picornavirus associated with various kinds of meningitis, intestinal disturbances, and respiratory illnesses in human beings. *Polioviruses, reoviruses, echoviruses and infectious hepatitis virus still circulate widely.* New Scientist 9/10/70, p530 [**1955**, formed from its full name, enteric cytopathogenic *h*uman *o*rphan virus; called "orphan virus" because it is not known to cause any of the diseases it is associated with. Compare REOVIRUS.]

ECM, abbreviation of ELECTRONIC COUNTERMEASURE. Compare ECCM. *All the Nato programmes on which the successes and failures in the recent Middle East fighting obviously have a bearing—ECMs, SAMs, anti-tank guided weapons, tank gunnery and armour—will now be critically reviewed.* Manchester Guardian Weekly 11/24/73, p5 [**1958**]

eco-. The prefix *eco-* (with the meaning "of or dealing with ecology," "ecological and _____") has gained wide use growing out of the concern over pollution of the environment. Some of the new terms formed with *eco-* are listed here. —**ecoalimental, ecometabolic, ecopathogenic**, *adj.*: *Ecological death manifests itself when animals die from starvation, dietary deficiencies or ingestion of "wrong" foods (ecoalimental), from infection by pathogens however transmitted (ecopathogenic), from the effects of foreign matter deposited in or on tissues (ecometabolic) or by lethal physical forces operating mechanically from outside the animal (ecophysical).* New Scientist 3/21/68, p625 —**eco-atmosphere**, *n.*: *The scientists under Dr John Kirmiz have determined this mixture the "eco-atmosphere", in line with their previous studies of the jerboa's ecoclimate.* Science Journal 9/68, p5 —**ecocrisis**, *n.*: *The ecocrisis is as good an opportunity as any to start building a Brave New World, but for God's sake let's be careful how we go about it.* New Scientist and Science Journal 5/27/71, p535 —**ecopolitical**, *adj.*: *The Council on Environmental Quality has been in operation for only nine months; but it has already totally changed the eco-political situation in the United States.* New Scientist 10/8/70, p59 —**eco-theologian**, *n.*: *The eco-theologians argue that man's despoliation of nature has drawn encouragement in part from mistaken or misapplied Christian concepts.* Time 6/8/70, p49 See also the entries below.

eco-activist, *n.* a person who is very active in matters pertaining to the protection of the environment from pollution. *Why the new vegetarian trend? It is inexpensive, for one thing. Moreover, the eco-activists are concerned by the amount of DDT and other chemicals in meat.* Time 11/16/70, p59 [**1969**]

eco-activity, *n.* any project or undertaking to combat pollution or improve the quality of the environment. *There are numerous "eco-activities" that can be performed by individuals or local school and community groups . . . Right: old car tires are used in an experiment to stop soil erosion along Minnesota's Rum River. Local students furnished the labor and later planted trees inside the tires.* Encyclopedia Science Supplement (Grolier) 1970, p172 [**1970**]

ecocatastrophe, *n.* a large-scale or world-wide disaster resulting from uncontrolled use of pollutants. *Gordon Rattray Taylor . . . suggests that overcrowding in the mushrooming cities of South America and Asia will eventually bring about social disruption followed swiftly by political and technological collapse. In his view, this is the form Doomsday will take, beating . . . ecocatastrophe by a short head.* New Scientist 9/10/70, p542 [**1969**]

ecocidal, *adj.* relating to or causing ecocide. . . . *beyond that lie the use of ecocidal weapons—herbicides in Vietnam—and*

"humane incapacitants." Manchester Guardian Weekly 8/15/70, p18 [**1970**]

ecocide, *n.* the destruction of the earth's ecology through the uncontrolled use of pollutants. Compare BIOCIDE. . . . *And presumably nothing has caused such joy in Vietnam as the prospect of peace after two decades of war, strife, death and ecocide.* Tehran Journal 3/1/73, p4 *The irony of development is that to the extent that it succeeds, the world situation worsens and the dangers of ecocide are increased.* New Scientist and Science Journal 7/15/71, p158 [**1970**, from *eco-* + *-cide* killing, as in *suicide, genocide*, etc.]

ecodevelopment, *n.* development which balances economic and ecological factors. *Rich nations should atone for years of economic exploitation by paying appropriate reparations to the developing countries. For the Third World itself the policy for the future should be one of ecodevelopment, this representing a synthesis of the conflicting needs of the environment and economic growth.* New Statesman 12/26/75, p808 [**1975**, from *eco*nomic and *eco*logical + *development*]

ecodoom, *n.* large-scale ecological destruction; obliteration of a balanced natural environment. Compare DOOMWATCH. . . . *the prophets of ecodoom, whom predict early disaster unless men achieve a radical revision of their collective goals and behaviour.* Times (London) 8/21/73, p13 [**1972**, from *eco-* ecological + *doom*]

ecodoomster, *n.* one who predicts or warns of ecodoom. See DOOMSTER. *Men of goodwill can defend humanity from technological doom, granted an extension of scientific training . . . and of British-style social democracy. A soothing conclusion for those who attended the lectures at Stanford, on which this book is based, but words which are scarcely likely to carry much conviction with the ecodoomsters committed to a cataclysmic view of the world's fate.* Manchester Guardian Weekly 10/8/78, p20 [**1973**]

ecofact, *n.* a natural object, such as a bone or a seed, found together with artifacts at an archaeological site. *The evaluation of ecofacts reveals such information as what food people ate and whether they grew crops or gathered wild plants.* World Book Encyclopedia 1988, pA-599 [**1988**, from *eco-* + arti*fact*]

ecofallow, *n.* a method of farming that combines reduced tillage and crop rotation to control weeds and conserve soil moisture. *Ecofallow markedly increased the grain yields of wheat and sorghum. In this connection, wheat yields increased 6% and 8% and grain sorghum yields 31% and 47% with minimum and no tillage, respectively, above the 10-year average yields of these two crops obtained with conventional tillage.* McGraw-Hill Yearbook of Science and Technology 1977, p341 [**1977**, from *eco-* ecological + *fallow*]

ecofreak, *n. Slang (often disparaging).* a fervent conservationist or environmentalist. Also called ECONUT. *Sierra Club members, taunted as "ecofreaks," report that they are being subjected to the most severe criticism they have ever encountered.* Atlantic 11/73, p24 *The presenter, Malcolm MacEwen, said that 'some people tend to dismiss Friends of the Earth as doomsters or ecofreaks, but I have found that responsible scientists don't share this view.'* Listener 3/14/74, p339 [**1972**, from *eco-* ecological + *freak*]

E. coli (i: 'koulɑi), partial abbreviation of *Escherichia coli*, a common rod-shaped bacillus of the intestinal tract, strains of which have been grown in large amounts and used extensively in experiments dealing with protein synthesis, genetic transmission, immunity, enzymology, etc. *The discovery of sigma factors in E. coli bacteria early last year caused considerable excitement in molecular biological circles, for the factors constituted the first control elements found in living cells that could act directly to turn on genes.* New Scientist 12/3/70, p363 [**1955**]

ecological art, the art of making or sculpturing earthworks. *If ecological art . . . sounds eccentric, it is. But it is also demanding. Its practitioners sweat and swim, dig trenches, hack through ice, suffer desert winds or the muscle ache of long* climbs—all for the sake of a few photographs and a memory. Time 6/29/70, p62 **[1970]**

ecology, n. any balanced or harmonious system. *The introduction of a comprehensive computerized data base into a large company could well upset the 'ecology' of the firm to such an extent that it could take ages to re-establish a stable balance . . .* Science Journal 10/70, p36 **[1970,** extended sense of the technical term for the balanced relationship between organisms and their environment]

ecomone ('ekoumoun), n. a hormone associated with or affecting the balance of nature; ecological hormone. *A consideration of the role of ecomones in the establishment of relations between organisms in the networks of the biochemical continuum is also lacking.* Nature 9/15/72, p177 **[1972,** from *eco-* ecological + hor*mone*]

econiche, n. protected habitat in which an organism or species can survive. *But if these unnatural recombinants escaped from the laboratory, particularly during the experimental stages, they might tuck into some econiche where naturally evolved control mechanisms couldn't touch them.* Science News 3/20/76, p188 **[1976,** from *eco-* ecological + *niche*]

economic crime, a crime involving the illegal use of money or acquisition of wealth, especially in Communist and Third World countries. *A March 25 decree increased penalties for a number of "economic crimes" and imposed the death penalty for embezzlement, smuggling, corruption, and unauthorized disposal of foreign currency.* 1976 Collier's Encyclopedia Year Book, p553 *Two Soviet officials were executed for economic crimes. Mikhail Y. Leviyev, the manager of a Moscow state store and a Jew, had embezzled $2.7 million worth of goods, while Yuri S. Sosnovski, the director of a division of the Timber and Wood Processing Ministry, had accepted bribes of $140,000 from a Swiss businessman.* Americana Annual 1976, p564 **[1975]**

economic zone, short for EXCLUSIVE ECONOMIC ZONE. *But they point to a middle level of threats and problems that include . . . friction with neighbouring States over fishing grounds, oil, or other ocean resources, and illegal immigration, as well as the general role of maintaining sovereignty over Australian territories including coastal waters and the adjacent "economic zone," if this becomes international law.* Manchester Guardian Weekly 1/11/76, p8 **[1973]**

econut, n. Slang (usually disparaging). an enthusiast about ecology; an ECOFREAK. *Current delays must now be laid at the door of the "econuts" who are opposing the . . . plans to drill into the granite rocks, for example, even when the authority makes it clear that this would be a purely scientific exercise that does not imply later use of the site as a waste disposal facility.* New Scientist 10/20/77, p132 **[1972,** from *eco-* ecological + *nut* enthusiast]

ecopolitics, n. **1** the study of politics in terms of economic factors. *Though Americans tend to think of West Germany and Japan as the economic giants now, and suppose their own strength is poised on the tip of missile launchers, that perception itself is a reflection of the new dominance of ecopolitics. Neither Germany nor Japan owns a warhead, and both rely on the United States for defense. Yet they are powers of recognized importance in the modern world.* NY Times 12/31/78, pD3 **2** the study of politics as affected by ecological issues. *A bimonthly New Ecologist (no relation) will concentrate on more topical material, including "ecopolitics" and the more practical aspects of living in a "post-industrial" society.* New Scientist 12/8/77, p623 **[1973** def. 1, from *economic* + *politics;* **1971** def. 2, from *ecological* + *politics*]

eco-pornography, n. advertising or publicity that exploits and profits from public interest in ecology and pollution control. *Environmentalist groups still abound, the advertising industry is still cashing in on the bandwagon by presenting companies and products as ecology-conscious (eco-pornography is the word that has been coined for such practices) and politicians still pay plenty of lip service to the issue.* Nature 4/28/72, p422 **[1971]** —**eco-pornographer,** n.: *Drag the favorite whipping boy, DDT, around the stage for an exemplary flogging.*

A tip of the hat to Silent Spring, *and a pox of the throat to the eco-pornographers of Madison Avenue.* National Review 7/20/73, p799

ecotage ('ekə,ta:3), n. sabotage of polluters of the environment, especially to dramatize the need for pollution control and conservation programs. *Ecotage, or sabotage for ecological reasons, was used increasingly by some conservation activists in 1971. Ecotage activities ranged from dumping dye into sewage-treatment tanks to show how pollution travels down waterways, to sawing down roadside billboards.* 1972 World Book Year Book, p298 **[1972,** from *eco-* ecological + sabo*tage*]

ecotecture ('ekə,tektʃər), n. architectural design that subordinates immediate and practical needs to environmental factors. *Architect Sim Van der Ryn . . . has already coined a phrase for the new style of building: "ecotecture." At a Berkeley conference he once termed the practitioners "outlaw builders." Whatever . the label, the craftsmen were individualists who apparently do their best work alone.* Time 11/5/73, p75 **[1972,** from *eco-* ecological + archi*tecture*]

ecotelemetry, n. another name for BIOTELEMETRY. *Biotelemetry, or ecotelemetry, is an important new tool which enables the biologist to acquire information at a distance from an unrestrained living organism and its environment.* McGraw-Hill Yearbook of Science and Technology 1969, p115 **[1969]**

ecotopian or **Ecotopian,** Informal. —**adj.** of or having to do with an ecologically ideal society. *The desire to preserve the landscape was popularized in a 1975 novel, Ecotopia, in which a new nation is shut off from the U.S. because of its radical environmental laws. "The long-term trend, especially in the Northwest, is still toward Ecotopian ways," says author Ernest Callenbach. Mr. Callenbach may be right. In a November referendum election, voters decided to keep stringent, statewide land-use planning laws that tightly rein in new development.* Christian Science Monitor 2/23/83, p3 —**n.** a person who adopts an ecotopian way of life. *"If there is such a thing as the 'solar lifestyle,' or 'the solar experience,' the activist is living it . . . Whether we call them dropouts or ecotopians, it is clear that they are already trying to live in the future, like a new generation of pioneers creating their own environment beyond the physical frontier."* Graduate Woman (American Association of University Women) July/August 1981, p30 **[1981,** patterned after *utopian* (1551)]

ECR, abbreviation of *electronic cash register. The long predicted ECR invasion . . . hit Europe five weeks earlier when the giant German Kaufhof chain installed three different ECR systems in three different stores.* New Scientist 11/2/72, p273 **[1972]**

Ecstasy, n. Also **ecstasy.** U.S. Slang. another name for MDMA. *The drug's advocates—including a number of psychologists and psychiatrists who use Ecstasy in treating their patients—claim that the drug breaks down emotional barriers between people while causing no harmful side effects.* 1986 World Book Year Book, p295 **[1985]**

ecu or **ECU** (ei'ku:, *sometimes* 'i:'si:'yu:), n. acronym for *European Currency Unit,* a money of account in the European Common Market, created to settle debts among members and to act as a standard in floating currencies within a narrow range. See SNAKE. *In the longer term, however, members of a united Europe might increase trade more with themselves than with the U.S., and a strong, viable ecu ultimately might rival the dollar as a real reserve currency.* Time 12/18/78, p69 *The annexe suggested that ECUs would be used to support the system and implied that they would have a hybrid character.* Times (London) 9/6/78, p21 **[1972,** influenced by French *écu,* a coin]

ecumaniac, n. a fanatical or extremely enthusiastic promoter of ecumenism or the union of all Christian churches. *The 'ecumaniacs'—as hostile religious separatists like to call them—have come to believe that it is their religious duty to break down the barriers between denominations.* Maclean's 7/6/63, p26 **[1954]**

ecumenopolis (,ekyume'napəlis), n. the world viewed as one continuous city. *To emphasize its scholarly austerity, Constan-*

tinos Doxiadis concludes with an article (as unreadable as it is unbelievable) not on megalopolis, but on ecumenopolis—the world itself as a city—the ultimate end of man as a social animal. Saturday Review 11/25/67, p35 [**1964**, coined by Constantinos A. Doxiadis, 1913-1975, a Greek architect and engineer, from Greek *oikouménē* the world + *pólis* city. See also EKISTICS.]

ED, abbreviation of *Education Department* (the U.S. Department of Education). *I worked hard through much of my time at ED on the Carter Administration's major domestic initiative for the year, the Youth Act of 1980.* NY Times Magazine 1/11/81, p46 [**1981**]

EDB, abbreviation of *ethylene dibromide*, a pesticide and antiknock agent in gasoline, linked with sterility and suspected of causing cancer in humans. *There are questions about how much EDB is actually used; the effectiveness of vapor recovery devices and the extent to which they are used; how much people actually use self-service pumps; and on and on.* Science 2/9/79, p527 [**1963**]

Eddington limit, *Astronomy.* the maximum brightness attainable by a celestial object of a given mass. Also spelled **Eddington's limit.** *If A0620-00 were indeed this far away, the implied x-ray luminosity would be . . . much larger than the Eddington limit for a star.* McGraw-Hill Yearbook of Science and Technology 1977, p427 [**1972**, named after Sir Arthur Stanley Eddington, 1882-1944, who discovered the relationship between the mass and luminosity of stars]

edifice complex, *U.S.* infatuation with large and costly building projects. *Continued the Ambassador: "If we could turn it* [an apartment-dining complex in India] *over to the Smithsonian it would make a marvelous memorial to a certain kind of mentality. But that isn't really practical, is it? . . . Let this sad ending be a lesson to the next U.S. Administration tempted by an edifice complex."* Time 8/6/73, p8 [**1973**, a pun on *Oedipus complex;* perhaps first applied to Gov. Nelson Rockefeller's enthusiasm for building the New York State Mall in Albany, N.Y.]

edit, *n.* short for *editing* or *editorial,* used especially in journalism and film-making. [Joseph] *Strick tosses in so many starts of parades and tourist views that at times the movie* ["Tropic of Cancer"] *feels like a travelogue . . . luckily, the fast edit keeps the action from sagging.* New Yorker 3/7/70, p96 *As I read your edit in your issue of May 8, I felt like jumping up onto a soapbox and replying, "I'm glad you asked that question."* Punch 6/19/68, p893 **—v.t.** *Molecular Biology.* to alter (a gene) by genetic engineering. *Although a gene of any size can in principle be made by chemical DNA synthesis, for large genes it is probably more practical to isolate the natural gene and then, when necessary, merely "edit" the gene with chemically synthesized DNA.* Science 9/19/80, p1403 [**1960** for noun; **1979** for verb]

Edsel ('edsəl), *n.* a product that does not correspond to the wishes or requirements of the time; a failure. *Some retailers, indeed, were heard to predict that the midi would prove to be "the Edsel of the fashion industry."* 1971 Compton Yearbook, p412 . . . *it is compatible with the IBM PC. Still, one can't help wondering if the Macintosh will turn out to be Apple's Edsel.* Creative Computing 3/84, p246 [**1971**, originally the name of an unpopular automobile manufactured by the Ford Company between 1957 and 1962, named after *Edsel* Ford, 1893-1943, an American automaker]

educational park or **education park,** *U.S.* a group of elementary and secondary schools built on a large tract of land, with many facilities used in common. *The most promising answer, said the Commission, is a new concept called education parks . . . The parks replace several racially segregated schools with one wholly new establishment.* Science News 2/25/67, p185 *The commission called educational parks, or clusters of schools, a "revolutionary" technique that might provide common experiences for children of different backgrounds.* NY Times 2/14/66, p27 [**1963**]

educationese, *n.* the jargon used by people associated with the field of education. *What kind of person is it who enjoys the aes-*

thetics of a bell shaped curve, the rhetoric of educationese, or the poetry of the primer? Saturday Review 1/21/67, p74 [**1958**, from *education* + *-ese* language or jargon]

educrat, *n. U.S.* a representative or official of an educational system, agency, or institution. . . . *he* [Governor Claude R. Kirk, Jr., of Florida] *early exhibited a flamboyant affinity for newspaper headlines . . . and a remarkable talent for colorful invective (education leaders are referred to as "educrats" or wielders of "blackboard power").* Saturday Review 4/20/68, p64 [**1968**, from *education* + *-crat,* as in *bureaucrat*]

-ee, a very productive suffix meaning "one who is _____ed"; freely added to verb stems to form nouns paralleling agent nouns in *-er;* but also added to intransitive verbs and meaning "one who _____s" (as in *escapee*); and sometimes also added to adjectives (as in *deadee*). **—adaptee,** *n.: The adaptee then cannot tell the difference between yellow and white, ie is yellow-blind.* New Scientist 5/6/71, p353 **—blackmailee,** *n.: That you can't ever protect a man's reputation by invading his privacy; . . . that the underlying relationship of the FBI to passing Administrations—at least in the internal security area—is in part the relationship of the blackmailer to blackmailee . . .* Atlantic 11/70, p52 **—deferee,** *n.: In any case, affluent college deferees do not compare in number with those who, often by the accident of poverty, unfortunately have physical or mental-defects that cause deferment or rejection.* Harper's 8/66, p27 **—meetee,** *n.: Some meetings should be . . . mercifully brief. A good way to handle the latter is to hold the meetings with everybody standing up. The meetees won't believe you at first. Then they get very uncomfortable and can hardly wait to get the meeting over with.* Times (London) 5/5/70, p27 See also DEADEE, FRANCHISEE, MERGEE.

EER, abbreviation of *energy efficiency ratio* (the cooling power of an air conditioner in relation to electric power used). *Many brands of air conditioners now come with a number called the energy efficiency ratio (EER). The EER is derived by dividing the number of BTUs of cooling capacity by the unit's wattage.* Encyclopedia Science Supplement (Grolier) 1975, p196 [**1975**]

EEZ, abbreviation of EXCLUSIVE ECONOMIC ZONE. *There was an almost universal extension of fishery limits to 200 mi (as a partial EEZ) or claims of a full EEZ over 200 mi.* Britannica Book of the Year 1978, p488 [**1978**]

Effie, *n. U.S.* an award presented annually by the advertising industry for effective advertising. *Coke, coincidentally, won an Effie (for marketing moxie) and Alka-Seltzer a Clio (for performance) from the admen themselves.* Time 6/19/72, p52 [**1970**, from the feminine name *Effie,* chosen for its resemblance to the word *effective*]

EFTS or **EFT,** abbreviation of ELECTRONIC FUNDS TRANSFER SYSTEM. *E.F.T.S. (also referred to in some circles as the "checkless society") is a plan to eliminate paper by moving money among major financial institutions via computer.* NY Times 10/5/76, p65 *Most publicized EFT activities involve consumer funds transfer services, for example . . . the use of automated teller machines (ATMs) . . .* McGraw-Hill Yearbook of Science and Technology 1977, p143 [**1973**]

egg, *n.* (with) **egg on one's face.** embarrassed and humiliated. *Bob Strauss, for the first time during exemplary service for an Administration conditioned to ineptitude, "got egg on his face" (in the words of one long-time political associate).* New York Post 8/24/79, p23 [**1964**]

egg transfer, the surgical transfer of an ovum from the uterus of one female to that of another. Compare EMBRYO TRANSFER. *Another reason for an egg transfer (from a donor) might be that patient's serious genetic defects. Or if she is unable to interrupt her career outside the home in order to complete a pregnancy, as may become the case more often in these days of women's liberation, she could have her baby by surrogation.* Joseph Fletcher, The Ethics of Genetic Control, 1974, p67 [**1974**]

ego-state, *n.* any of three states of consciousness, identified as Parent, Adult, and Child according to transactional analysis that typifies how one will interact with people in different situations. See P-A-C. *The three ego-states of T.A. do, of course, par-*

allel the Freudian description of the psychic apparatus, but whereas the emphasis in classical psychoanalysis is on the sexual experience of the growing child, the emphasis in T.A. is on the growing child's sense of his or her own worth or lack of worth. NY Times Magazine 11/19/72, p43 [**1967**, coined by Eric Berne, 1910-1970, Canadian-born psychiatrist who founded the transactional analysis method of psychotherapy]

ego trip, something done to boost one's ego, often characterized by self-indulgent behavior. *The speeches, generally addressed directly to the camera, become uncomfortably hortatory, or somewhat smug and self-righteous ego trips.* Saturday Review 7/1/72, p63 [**1969**] —**ego-tripper**, n.: *"Public access could become the first electronic soapbox," says Global Village co-director John Reilly, "if it can only survive its ego-trippers."* Newsweek 4/9/73, p86 —**ego-tripping**, n., adj.: *What is overlooked in the inevitable discussion of the alleged ego-tripping in Mailer's writing is that these more "modest" selves are often at work in the sounds and turns of his sentences—questioning the assertive, the heroic, the outrageous self.* Atlantic 10/72, p80

eightfold way, *Nuclear Physics.* a theoretical classification of strongly interacting elementary particles into groups called multiplets and supermultiplets, whose relationship is established by their having nearly the same mass, hypercharge, and isotopic spin. Also called SU(3) SYMMETRY. *In the Eightfold Way, each combination of 3 fictitious objects, called quarks, makes a different baryon* [heavy elementary particle]. World Book Science Annual 1968, p170 [**1961**, from the Buddhist term for the eight steps to be followed to attain enlightenment; so called from the original suggestion that this classification would explain the relationship among a group of *eight* different elementary particles]

eighty-six or **86**, v.t. *U.S. Slang.* to refuse to serve (a customer). *On the evening of July 22, Mr. Mailer was filming a dream sequence at the house of Alfonso Ossorio in East Hampton, when Mr. Smith came into the house. "He told me, 'You're 86'd.' " Mr. Smith recalled yesterday. This is a barroom phrase that means "you're banned in here."* NY Times 7/31/68, p29 [**1959**, originally rhyming slang noun for *nix*, used in the jargon of cooks, waiters, etc., to indicate that there is nothing left of an item ordered from the menu; later applied to a person who is refused service for being disorderly, unable to pay, etc.]

ejaculatorium, n. a room in a sperm bank set aside for donors to discharge semen. *Some bank. The bankbook is called* The Semen Depositor's Handbook . . . *Home collection, the booklet notes, is preferred, but the bank also maintains its own ejaculatorium in Manhattan.* Time 1/3/72, p52 [**1972**, from *ejaculate* + *-orium*, as in *sanatorium*]

ekahafnium (ˌekəˈhæfniːəm), n. a provisional name given to ELEMENT 104. *Using Mendeleev's naming scheme, some researchers have called the new element ekahafnium. The Russians gave it the name kurchatovium. The right to name new elements is given to the discoverers and the name is later approved by the International Union of Pure and Applied Chemistry. By year-end neither name has been adopted by IUPAC.* Science News Yearbook 1970, p265 [**1970**, from *eka-* beyond (in the periodic table) + *hafnium*]

ekalead (ˌekəˈled), n. a hypothetical chemical element beyond the transactinide series; element 114. . . . *element 114, which we have mentioned so often, proves to be homologous with that very stable element lead; it can therefore be called "eka-lead," using the terminology of Dmitri Mendeleev, the originator of the periodic table.* Scientific American 4/69, p66 [**1968**, from *eka-* beyond (in the periodic table) + *lead*]

ekistical, adj. of or relating to ekistics. *The profound thing about the transition [from farm to town] is, and put this down in your ekistical notebook, it's rural-suburban.* Harper's 12/70, p103 [**1970**]

ekistics (iˈkistiks), n. the study of communities and settlements of people, especially with a view to improving them by extensive planning. . . . *since we do not know what kind of life the future rural dwellers employed in agriculture would like to have, we should use the term "cities" as meaning all sorts of*

human settlements in the sense that ekistics, the science of human settlements, studies them. Britannica Book of the Year 1968, p17 [**1959**, coined by Constantinos A. Doxiadis, 1913-1975, a Greek architect and engineer, from Greek *oikistikós* of settlements or dwellings. See also ECUMENOPOLIS.]

Ekman layer, a layer of ocean water whose flow is at right angles to the wind's direction. *Thus the wind in the southern half of our square basin representing the North Atlantic transports water to the north in the thin Ekman layer.* Scientific American 1/70, p117 [**1969**, named after the Swedish oceanographer V. Walfrid *Ekman*, who first described it in the early 1900's]

ekpwele (ekˈpweilei), n. *sing. and pl.* the monetary unit of Equatorial Guinea (a country in western Africa) since 1973. *African place names were also substituted for Spanish ones in other areas, and the name of the currency unit was changed from the peseta to the ekpwele.* 1974 Collier's Encyclopedia Year Book, p253 [**1973**, from the local name in Equatorial Guinea]

elastohydrodynamic, adj. dealing with the elasticity of fluids under force. *Sometimes the film of lubricant is so thin, and the fluid pressures acting on the bearing surfaces are so high, that the elastic deformation of these surfaces cannot be ignored; the regime is then called elastohydrodynamic.* Science Journal 2/69, p74 [**1967**]

elastohydrodynamics, n. the study of elastohydrodynamic effects. *The sound introduction to elastohydrodynamics could readily have been extended to deal with realistic machine components to the advantage of the student.* New Scientist and Science Journal 4/15/71, p174 [**1966**]

el cheapo, *U.S. Slang.* variant of CHEAPO. *Some of those old el cheapo pictures were, in the last analysis, more entertaining than this rather too impeccable film.* Time 7/23/79, p80 [**1979**]

eldercare, n. *U.S.* any program of low-cost medical care for elderly people, especially one providing regular preventive care to supplement Medicare. *In addition, many members of Prosser's eldercare program look forward to the monthly hospital outings as social occasions that give them a chance to see friends.* Time 2/11/74, p60 [**1965**, from *elderly* + *care*] ►This term first appeared for the American Medical Association's plan proposed as an alternative to Medicare which was adopted by Congress in the same year. Since then, *eldercare* has been applied to other private medical-care plans for the aged.

electric, adj. played with electrically amplified instruments. *Joe Boyd, a brilliant young American record producer . . . had come here originally to run a British subsidiary for the creative Elektra company of America, at that time making the difficult transition from folk to electric rock.* Times (London) 4/18/70, pIII *Gerde's Folk City is pondering a move to the West Village while two former centers of electric pop, the Night Owl and Generation, remain closed.* NY Times 7/5/68, p21 [**1968**]

electride, n. any of a class of chemical compounds formed with atoms of metallic elements joined by unpaired electrons and analogous to sodium chloride. *Electrides . . . provide a fascinating opportunity to study the interactions among electrons in solids. By synthesizing electrides from a variety of materials, one can vary the geometry of the anionic cavities and their relation to the surrounding cations. The resulting properties may make it possible for electrides to become a basis for economically useful new materials and devices.* Scientific American 9/87, p66 [**1977**, from *electron* + *-ide* chemical compound]

electro-, a combining form with several meanings listed below, used with great frequency in technical terms. **1** electric (of, charged with, or run by electricity) or electrical (accompanied by, involved in, or relating to electricity). —**electroconductivity**, n.: *Compared with some other instruments, such as the electro-conductivity recorder for measuring SO₂, it* [the instrument] *offers the advantage of being insensitive to ammonia. On the other hand, its sensitivity to all sulphur compounds is a mixed blessing.* New Scientist 10/15/70, p118 —**electrodermal**, adj.: *The main significance of this finding, Dr. Mednick says, lies in its correlation with another group of data showing that the disturbed children were markedly ab-*

normal in tests of their galvanic skin responses (GSR). The GSR is a measure of electrodermal conductivity regulated by the autonomic nervous system, which is largely in charge of regulating the body's internal stress reactions. Science News 7/4/70, p15 —**electroduct,** *n.: The Milan company was to have supplied and mounted high-tension wires in the tract of the electroduct between Caboara Bassa and the South African border.* Times (London) 12/19/70, p4 —**electromechanization,** *n.: The innovations will include large-scale, dual-purpose desalting plants; electromechanization of farms and of means of transportation; electrification of the metal and chemical industries, and more effective means for utilizing wastes.* Scientific American 11/70, p21 —**electrosensory,** *adj.: . . . influence of electric organ control system on electrosensory afferent pathways in mormyrids* [African freshwater fishes] *. . .* Advertisement in Scientific American 3/70, p18
2 by or with electrolytic decomposition. —**electroslag,** *adj.: The purist would probably query the description of electroslag remelting as an arc process . . .* New Scientist 5/21/70, p395
3 a electronic. —**electromusic,** *n.: The first part* [of "Stages," a ballet] *has electromusic by Arne Nordheim.* Sunday Times (London) 5/2/71, p35 **b** electron. —**electrophile,** *n.: Then by dividing heterolytic* [cell-destroying] *reagents into nucleophiles and electrophiles, he* [Sir Christopher Ingold, F.R.S.] *saw the basis of a scheme interrelating a great range of chemical reactions.* Times (London) 12/10/70, p10 See also the entries below.

electroacupuncture, *n.* a form of acupuncture using electrically vibrating needles. Compare STAPLEPUNCTURE. *Much more spectacular and immediately verifiable was our observation of four simultaneous major operations performed at the Affiliated Hospital. The only anesthetic was electroacupuncture—a new application of the ancient technique.* Science 1/7/72, p21 **[1972]**

electrogasdynamic, *adj.* producing electric power by electrogasdynamics. *The U.S. Department of the Interior granted $680,500 to Gourdine Systems, Inc. . . . to demonstrate the feasibility of transforming coal directly into cheaply transmittable electricity at the mine by using electrogasdynamic (EGD) generators.* 1967 World Book Year Book, p330 **[1966]**

electrogasdynamics, *n.* the conversion of heat energy directly into electricity by sweeping charged particles through an electric field in a stream of gas. *Electrogasdynamics (egd for short) is a novel means of generating electricity. The principles involved are, however, quite simple. Small particles of dust (or smoke, fog, etc.) are charged in a low-voltage region and transported by a gas stream to a high-voltage region, where the charges are removed. Work is done on the particles in moving them against the electric field and electricity generated.* New Scientist 3/5/70, p457 **[1967]**

electroglow, *n.* a strong emission of ultraviolet light occurring on the sunlit side of various planets, especially Uranus. *Voyager 2 found that the glow was of yet another variety, which requires both UV sunlight and electrons, and Voyager scientists dubbed it "electroglow."* Science News 2/1/86, p72 **[1986]**

electrohydraulic, *adj.* producing mechanical or chemical energy by electrohydraulics. *In a rock fragmentation study, scientists found that an electric spark jumped between two electrodes submerged in water could produce a shattering pressure pulse much like the blast wave generated by conventional explosives. This "electrohydraulic effect" could one day offer a safer, more effective rock-breaking method.* 1971 Americana Annual, p470 **[1966]**

electrohydraulics, *n.* the conversion of electrical energy directly into mechanical or chemical energy by the controlled discharge of high-voltage electric arcs submerged in water or another liquid. *For example, in the hard rock mining of copper an electrical energy system could replace explosives and thereby avoid the production of noxious fumes in the mine. We have built a system based on electrohydraulics and tested it both in the laboratory on three tonne boulders and in a copper mine.* Science Journal 3/68, p64 **[1966]**

electronhole drop or **electronhole droplet,** a liquid form of electrical energy produced by a laser beam in a semiconductor crystal. *The object of the photograph is called an "electronhole drop." It contains an equal number of negatively charged electrons and positively charged "holes" from which electrons have been dislodged by a beam of laser light.* NY Times 5/19/75, p18 **[1975]**

electronic art, a form of art that uses electronic materials, such as moving and flashing light displays, as the artistic medium. Compare LUMINAL ART. *Electronic music inspired him* [Nam June Paik, a Korean] *to make electronic art, just as the Russian composer Scriabin made a motorized light display to accompany his* Prometheus *half a century ago.* Time 1/28/66, p49 **[1966]**

electronic church, *U.S.* religious television and radio programs aimed at mass audiences, often presented in the style of regular shows and conducted by preachers of great personal appeal. Compare TELEVANGELIST. *The 200 participants heard the growth statistics of the "electronic church": Over the past 15 years, membership in the National Religious Broadcasters, an umbrella organization for television and radio evangelical groups, has risen from 104 to 900; . . . religious radio stations are being founded at a rate of one a week, television one a month.* NY Times 2/10/80, pD10 **[1979]**

electronic countermeasure, an electronic device that misdirects the guidance system of an enemy missile. *Abbreviation:* ECM. *By an electronic summer,* [Israeli defense minister] *Dayan meant clashes between Soviet-built, radar-controlled Egyptian surface-to-air missiles and Israeli jets equipped with electronic countermeasure (ECM) devices.* Time 7/20/70, p18 **[1958]**

electronic funds transfer system, a system for transferring money from one account or location to another by computer. *Abbreviation:* EFTS or EFT Also called **Electronic Funds Transfer.** *"The elimination of what is now known as money could be achieved with the implementation of an electronic funds-transfer system . . ."* Times (London) 2/10/73, p22 **[1973]**

electronic game, another term for VIDEO GAME. *The largest electronic games are designed for commercial establishments, and many are played in . . . arcades.* World Book Encyclopedia 1988, Vol. 6, p203 **[1980]**

electronic intelligence, variant of ELINT. *Completing the electronic intelligence are details of the frequencies and operating patterns of Soviet radar gathered by RC-135 four-engine jets, which are based at secret locations in Britain and are supposed to stay over international air space.* Manchester Guardian Weekly 1/13/85, p18 **[1961]**

electronic journalism, *Especially U.S.* coverage of news by television. Compare BROADCAST JOURNALISM, PRINT JOURNALISM. *All three networks emphasized citizenship and the tireless high-mindedness of electronic journalism. None mentioned the high-pricedness. This year the combined coverage cost some $10 million, roughly what the presidential candidates together spent on TV commercials—with about the same results.* Time 11/20/72, p61 **[1971]** —**electronic journalist:** *Television journalists are probably more subtly manipulated by the people in the street than by corporate public relations directors. This is a terrible dilemma for the electronic journalist. How can he decide when an event is real or merely the concoction of a radical public relations expert?* 1971 Compton Yearbook, p454

electronic mail, 1 a system for sending messages by computer, telex, facsimile telegraph, or other electronic means instead of by post. *For instance, the Integrated Electronic Office (IEO) sold by Datapoint . . . offers electronic mail and computerized information retrieval: on both fronts it is a rival to the Prestel viewdata system that Aregon, a subsidiary of the UK's National Enterprise Board, is attempting to export.* New Scientist 2/28/80, p658 **2** the messages sent by such means. *For instance, with "wait" set at 7 A.M., you can insert the disk before leaving the office, and the computer will call up at the appointed hour and have all your electronic mail waiting for you in the morning.* NY Times 8/19/86, pC4 **[1977]**

electronic smog, nonionizing radiation (such as radio and television waves or radar) emitted into the environment in such quantities as to constitute a potential health danger. *In the United States alone, radio waves are emitted not merely by the 10,000 or so commercial radio and television stations but also by some 250,000 relay towers for telephone, teletype, and TV hookups; 15 million Citizen's Band radios; millions of microwave ovens; communications satellites and the immensely powerful transmitters that link us to them; radar at airports and in planes; diathermy machines; burglar alarms; and automatic garage door openers. . . . The result is a pervasive "electronic smog" whose biologic effects we are just beginning to understand.* Saturday Review 1/7/78, p35 **[1978]**

electronic warfare, the use of electronic devices for military purposes, such as the interruption of enemy communications by electronic interference. *Electronic warfare, or EW as it is referred to by military-industrial insiders, is a rapidly expanding field of pushbutton defense technology that has already revolutionized modern air warfare. It has also spawned a subculture of EW buffs in the military and electronics industries.* Harper's 10/72, p74 **[1972]**

electronograph, *n.* **1** a device using an electron tube to produce images on a fine-grain photographic emulsion exposed to an accelerated beam of electrons. *It is remarkable that the ultimate in sensitivity, the standard of comparison for a dozen ingenious up-to-date developments, remains the electronograph.* Scientific American 5/70, p139 **2** an image produced by an electronograph. *Because the electron beam is focused, an 'electron picture' (electronograph) results.* Science Journal 3/70, p14 **[1970]**

electronography, *n.* the use of electronographs. *The cost of electronography to the user is high. Every time an exposed photographic plate is removed, the air destroys the highly reactive photosurface.* Scientific American 5/70, p139 **[1955]**

electron spin resonance, reversal of the spin of unpaired electrons by an electromagnetic field, used especially in spectroscopic analysis. *Electron spin resonance (ESR) spectroscopy of free radicals can detect the order and structure of biological membranes, the binding of drugs and other small molecules to proteins, the presence of drugs in biological specimens, translational diffusion within biological membranes, and the properties of the enclosed volume of cells and spheroidal model membranes.* McGraw-Hill Yearbook of Science and Technology 1976, p191 **[1952]**

electropaint, *v.t., v.i.* to deposit paint on (a metal surface) by an electrolytic process. *Ford's tests consisted of driving sets of cars (some with galvanised bodyworks, others electropainted) through salt water fast enough for spray to penetrate every crevice in the bodywork.* New Scientist 11/9/72, p334 —*n.* the paint used in electropainting. *Pollution consciousness stimulated interest in water-based and powder coatings, and water-based electropaints were being used throughout the world to prime automobile bodies.* 1973 Collier's Encyclopedia Year Book, p366 **[1966, from** *electro*lytic + *paint*]

electrophorese (i̥lektrəfə'ri:z), *v.t.* to subject to electrophoresis (a method of separating molecules of a substance, such as blood plasma). *A second method has been used by Gitlin . . . in which blood cells are gently lysed and their contents electrophoresed in the presence of antihaemoglobin antisera.* Nature 10/27/72, p488 **[1968, back formation from** *electrophoresis*]

electrophotograph, *n.* an image produced on film by Kirlian photography. Also called KIRLIAN PHOTOGRAPH. *The Kirlians report that their electrophotographs show certain points on the human body radiating light flares more forcibly than the areas around them and that these points correspond exactly to the 741 acupuncture points mapped out by the ancient Chinese. It is also reported that they have produced photographs showing that a plant is diseased before the physical symptoms of the disease appear.* Science News 9/29/73, p202 **[1973]**

electrosensitivity, *n.* the ability of an animal to sense or detect some object from naturally occurring electric signals; biological sensitivity or responsiveness to electricity. *Aspects of electrosensitivity in which the fish senses its own electric organ dis-*

charge will not be treated here except to say that weakly electric fish can locate prey and other objects, can maneuver in the environment, and can even control their posture by utilizing their own electric organ discharge. McGraw-Hill Yearbook of Science and Technology 1977, p205 **[1972]**

electrosleep, *n.* a state of deep sleep induced by passing a mild electric current through the brain. *In a dark, quiet room electrodes are attached to the relaxing patient's eyes and mastoids (the protruding bone behind the ear). A very low-amplitude, pulsating direct current is then passed through the patient's head for up to two hours. The procedure is repeated daily for at least 10 days. The technique, known as cerebral electrotherapy (CET or electro-sleep), is supposed to induce and enhance a state of natural sleep.* Science News 1/12/74, p29 **[1967]**

electroweak, *adj. Physics.* uniting the weak and the electromagnetic forces. *Any theory that unifies weak and electromagnetic forces requires there to be corresponding particles exchanged so as to generate the weak nuclear force. It turns out that there must be at least three such particles; two electrically charged, $W \pm$, and one neutral, $Z°$. Salam and Weinberg have formed a rather detailed model of the resulting "electroweak" interaction, which predicts that the masses of $W \pm$ and $Z°$ are each nearly 100 times the mass of a proton. This is too large for such particles to be produced in experiments with existing accelerators, so higher energies are needed.* New Scientist 4/10/80, p78 **[1978, from** *electro*magnetic + *weak*]

element 104, a radioactive chemical element with atomic number 104 in the periodic table and the first of the transactinide series. Also called KURCHATOVIUM, RUTHERFORDIUM, EKAHAFNIUM, and UNNILQUADIUM. . . . *Ghiorso and four associates announced in April 1969 their discovery of element 104—which the effervescent Ghiorso describes as the "hippie" element, because of what he called its somewhat hairy characteristics.* Encyclopedia Science Supplement (Grolier) 1970, p277 **[1965]**

element 105, another name for HAHNIUM. Also called UNNILPENTIUM. *The high stability of element 105 surprised the team of scientists. It contradicted present nuclear theories predicting a half-life of only milliseconds for element 105. This will probably lead to a revision of existing nuclear theories.* 1971 World Book Year Book, p251 **[1969]**

element 106, a radioactive chemical element with atomic number 106 in the periodic table and the 14th of the synthetic transuranium elements. It was synthesized independently by American and Soviet scientists in 1974. Also called UNNILHEXIUM. *On the basis of its projected position in the periodic table, element 106 is expected to have chemical properties similar to those of tungsten (atomic number 74).* McGraw-Hill Yearbook of Science and Technology 1976, p175 **[1974]**

element 107, a radioactive chemical element with atomic number 107 in the periodic table. Soviet physicists claimed to have synthesized it in 1977 by bombarding bismuth with nuclei of chromium. Also called UNNILSEPTIUM. *Scientists have predicted the positions of element 107 through 168 in the periodic table. From these positions, the scientists figure that there are several "islands of stability" at the unstable high end of the table.* Encyclopedia Science Supplement (Grolier) 1977/1978, p302 *For element 107, the "eka-rhenium" which was searched for in the prefission era, seven events have been found . . .* McGraw-Hill Yearbook of Science and Technology 1985, p446 **[1976]**

element 108, a radioactive chemical element with atomic number 108 in the periodic table. It was synthesized in 1984 by West German physicists and had one isotope, with mass number 265. Also called UNNILOCTIUM. *In 1984, another isotope of element 106 was identified by a West German group . . . The group first detected it in their discovery of element 108.* World Book Encyclopedia 1988, Vol. 6, p222 **[1984]**

element 109, a radioactive chemical element with atomic number 109 in the periodic table. It was synthesized in 1982 by West German physicists and had one isotope, with mass number 266. Also called UNNILONIUM. . . . *all elements from element 102 through element 109 were produced by* *bombardment with ions heavier than helium.* 1984 Britannica Yearbook of Science and the Future, p370 [**1983**]

element 126, a superheavy chemical element believed to exist in nature and the subject of intense research especially during the late 1970's. *Great excitement was caused by the announcement last June that a group of physicists had found evidence for the existence of element 126 and some other ultraheavy elements in samples of monazite, an ancient mineral from Africa. Skepticism and controversy were generated when various experiments could find no such evidence in other pieces of monazite.* Science News 2/5/77, p85 [**1976**]

eleventh commandment, any rule observed, or to be observed, as strictly as if it were an addition to the Biblical Ten Commandments (often used humorously). *A reporter asked Reagan if he were violating his promise to abide by the G.O.P.'s Eleventh Commandment—thou shalt not smite thy fellow Republican.* Time 3/15/76, p16 . . . *a blasphemous breaking of his own eleventh commandment: Thou shalt prune all trees.* Book Digest 5/80, p127 *I grew up believing in an Eleventh Commandment: Thou Shalt Always Eat a Good Breakfast.* Cuisine 6/84, p50 [**1975**]

ELF or **elf**, abbreviation of *extremely low frequency*, a frequency range between 30 and 300 hertz in the radio spectrum. *Research projects should take advantage of the opportunity to learn of the effects of weak ELF fields, knowledge also relevant to life under ordinary power lines and among electrical appliances.* Science News 8/13/77, p102 [**1962**]

elint ('elint), *n.* **1** Also **Elint** or **ELINT.** the act or process of gathering intelligence by electronic monitoring, especially from ships, aircraft, or other listening posts. Compare COMINT, HUMINT, IMINT, SIGINT. *The first requirement of electronic intelligence, or Elint, is to be able to recognise what is hostile (or potentially hostile) and what is not. The only way to do this is to intercept every possible transmission and identify as much as is practicable, thus building up a library of known transmissions.* New Scientist 3/2/72, p467 **2** a ship, aircraft, or other listening post that uses electronic equipment to gather intelligence (often used attributively). *"How would we feel if a Russian 'elint' suddenly showed up four miles off our Polaris base of Charleston, S.C., in company with three Soviet destroyers?" one official asked.* NY Times 6/12/68, p6 [**1961**, acronym for *el*ectronic *int*elligence]

ELISA or **Elisa** (i'li:sə *or* i'laisə), *n.* a test used chiefly to safeguard blood supplies from contamination by the virus that causes AIDS. Compare WESTERN BLOT. *In an ELISA, broken-up pieces of the AIDS-related virus are stuck on a solid surface and washed with blood. If AIDS antibodies are in the blood, they'll stick to the virus.* Science News 3/9/85, p148 [**1985**, from *e*nzyme-*l*inked *i*mmuno*s*orbent *a*ssay]

elliptical, *n.* a galaxy of elliptical shape and without spiral arms. *Ellipticals, by contrast, seem to possess little gas or dust, usually contain late-type dwarf stars and exhibit scant rotation.* Scientific American 6/70, p26 [**1963**, short for *elliptical galaxy*]

El Tor (el 'tɔr), a strain of the bacillus that causes cholera, widely prevalent in Asia, Africa, and Europe since the early 1960's. It causes a mild form of the disease and so spreads undetected in areas where hygiene is poor. *Exactly ten years after its appearance in Indonesia the El Tor variety of cholera reached Western Europe and was reported in the Saragossa area of Spain in July.* Britannica Book of the Year 1972, p449 [**1963**, from the name of the Egyptian quarantine station on the Sinai Peninsula where it was first isolated in 1905]

Élysée (eili'zei), *n.* the government of France. *The Elysee's creed is that the line laid down by M Harmel must be followed to the bitter end.* Manchester Guardian Weekly 7/11/70, p22 [**1967**] ►Literally the *Élysée* is the name of the official residence of the presidents of France, but like the *White House, Whitehall,* and the *Kremlin* the name is also used to designate the national government.

EM, abbreviation of *electron microscope* or *electron microscopy. The EM tissue samples after therapy showed the formation of the collagen and new bone in the former defect.* Science

News 3/18/72, p184 *Most EM studies show a very restricted extracellular system of 150-200 angstrom gaps* . . . New Scientist 11/28/68, p513 [**1968**]

emalangeni (,eima:la:ŋ'geini:), *n.* the plural of LILANGENI. *The Umbuluzi dam scheme, which would irrigate 8,000 ha, was allotted a further 3 million emalangeni.* Britannica Book of the Year 1977, p638 [**1977**, from siSwati (a Bantu language) *ema*-plural prefix + *-langeni* root form for "money"]

embourgeoisification (em,burʒwa:səfə'keiʃən), *n.* the adoption of bourgeois or middle-class practices and values. Compare GENTRIFICATION. *I heard a great deal about the Circle 333 Trust: and no one spoke of it as the philanthropic institution which Miss Pickering describes. Many people I spoke to did fear being evicted by the Trust; they were frightened, too, that they would not be able to afford the 'fair rents' which would be charged after conversion, and saw the Trust as yet another agent of creeping, expensive embourgeoisification.* Listener 3/8/73, p311 [**1973**, blend of earlier *embourgeoisement* and *bourgeoisification* (1937)]

embryoid, *n.* a plant or animal form having the structure or function of an embryo. *These cells are then cultured, and from them are grown embryoids and eventually whole "pomatoes"* [a hybrid plant produced from a potato and a tomato]. New Scientist and Science Journal 4/29/71, p263 [**1963**]

embryo transfer, surgical transfer of an embryo to another female, a technique used especially to increase the birth rate of a specific strain of animal. Compare EGG TRANSFER. *"Embryo transfer" . . . involves (1) injecting a cow with a "follicle stimulating hormone" (a serum, for instance, from pregnant mares) which causes her reproductive system to release five, six or even as many as a dozen ova instead of a single egg; (2) inseminating her artificially; (3) removing the resultant embryos by surgery; and (4) implanting each in an ordinary cow, which then assumes the task of bringing it to term and delivering it to the expectant world of cattle buyers.* Atlantic 9/73, p51 *Last March, the government's Ethics Advisory Board concluded that research on in-vitro fertilization and embryo transfer was "acceptable" in hospitals that receive Federal money.* Reader's Digest 6/79, p112 [**1973**]

emergicenter, *n. U.S.* a walk-in clinic for treating minor medical emergencies. . . . *part of a trend of taking certain specialized medical services out of the hospital to less expensive settings . . . is the rise of the "emergicenter"—a cross between a hospital emergency room and a family doctor's office.* U.S. News & World Report 8/17/81, p50 [**1981**, from *emergency* + connecting *-i-* + *center*]

emerging, *adj.* recently created; newly independent. Compare DEVELOPING. *The white racist attitudes that are part of the problem at home have also been an often unconscious element in the policy failures of the white political leadership vis-à-vis the emerging nations, most recently in Africa.* NY Times Magazine 4/18/76, p13 [**1975**, from present participle of *emerge*]

EMG, abbreviation of *electromyograph* (instrument for recording differences in the electric potential of muscles). *Surface EMG recordings were made from both arms during sleep.* Science 7/14/72, p159 [**1967**]

emiocytosis (,emi:ousai'tousis), *n. Biology.* a process of cellular excretion by which the membrane of a granule fuses with the cell membrane and the granule is discharged through an opening in the fused membranes. *The newly formed insulin, proinsulin, and C-peptide are subsequently transferred from the Golgi apparatus to storage granules which discharge by fusing with the plasma membrane in a process known as emiocytosis.* McGraw-Hill Yearbook of Science and Technology 1973, p233 [**1973**, from New Latin, from Greek *emeîn* to vomit + New Latin *cyt-* cell + *-osis* process or condition] —**emiocytotic**, *adj.: In summary, the present findings suggest that the emiocytotic release of insulin is coupled with an endocytotic process, leading to the relocation of membranous material from the cell membrane into an intracellular vacuolar system.* Science 8/10/73, p562

emission control, regulation of the amount of pollutants released into the air, as from the exhaust of a motor vehicle or the smoke from a factory. *Before the advent of emission controls, the principal criteria used in developing an engine calibration were smooth operation, fuel economy, performance, and absence of knock. With the enactment of the Clean Air Act of 1970 (and amendments), a limitation on the amount of hydrocarbons, carbon monoxide, and oxides of nitrogen also became part of the criteria. To some degree these criteria are incompatible.* McGraw-Hill Yearbook of Science and Technology 1981, p113 **[1973]**

EMP, abbreviation of *electromagnetic pulse* (pulse of radiation produced by a nuclear explosion). *It is known that EMPs can erase the memory tapes in computers which form vital parts of present and future aircraft subsystems. Without these tapes such aircraft as the presidential airborne command post (a converted Boeing 747) and the North American Rockwell B-1 strategic bomber would be rendered ineffective.* New Science 3/16/72, p601 **[1963]**

empaquetage (āpak'taʒ), *n.* a work of conceptual art consisting of an object wrapped tightly in canvas or other material and tied to form a distinctive bundle or package. *Chicago's newest monumental "art work" was, for a few days, the entire Museum of Contemporary Art, which was "wrapped" by the master of* empaquetage, *Christo* [a Bulgarian-born New York artist]. Americana Annual 1970, p102 **[1966,** from French, packaging, package]

empty nester, a person whose children have grown up and left home. *"Empty nesters," ready to sell their homes after their children have left, have a strong incentive through capital gains tax laws to reinvest quickly in home ownership.* NY Times 2/1/76, pH8 *Like their grown children, the empty-nesters are intent on living well.* Maclean's 7/76, p52 **[1962]**

empty nest syndrome, a form of depression supposedly common among women whose children have grown up and left home. *We knew, of course, about the empty-nest syndrome but were not perceptive enough to recognize it in ourselves. It did not occur to us that to grow gracefully into a new kind of life required an affectionate search for the neglected, unused parts of ourselves.* McCall's 1/73, p138 **[1972;** see EMPTY NESTER]

empty set, another name for NULL SET. *Every finite set of n elements has 2^n subsets if one includes the original set and the null, or empty, set. For example, a set of three elements, ABC, has $2^3 = 8$ subsets: ABC, AB, BC, AC, A, B, C, and the null set.* Scientific American 3/71, p106 **[1960]**

EMR, abbreviation of *educable mentally retarded. Children diagnosed as educationally mentally retarded (EMR) . . . were assigned to special small classes offering a different instructional program from that in the regular classes. To qualify for this special treatment, children had to have IQs below 75 as well as lagging far behind their age-mates in scholastic performance.* Arthur R. Jensen, Genetics and Education, 1972, p5 *Likewise, there is little dispute that the education offered in EMR classes is academically far inferior to that in regular classes. Among other things, witnesses testified that EMR students aren't expected to progress beyond the third to fifth grade level (while peers continue on to the twelfth grade).* New Scientist 8/3/78, p337 **[1970]**

emulate, *v.t.* to do the work of (another computer) without requiring extensive modification of the program or routine worked on. *The 1400 series was so popular that many newer computers were emulating them—that is, running 1400-series programs unmodified. The 9700 incorporated the capability of emulating the 1400-series machines much more flexibly than before, taking another step toward what might eventually become basically incompatible lines of computers from various manufacturers that can nevertheless run one another's programs through emulation.* Britannica Book of the Year 1973, p192 **[1965]** —**emulation,** *n.: Counterfeiting became possible because an IBM 370/145, for example, could be made to look like an ICL 1904A by replacing the IBM microprogramming with a new set that makes the machine language look like an ICL machine. Quite basic conventions vary between IBM and ICL; during a sorting operation whether the numbers are listed before or after the letters must be accounted for in the microprogramming. This form of mimicry is sometimes known as emulation.* New Scientist 6/22/72, p690 —**emulator,** *n.: In general, an emulator consists of special logic . . . which simulates the most frequently used instructions of the emulated computer.* McGraw-Hill Yearbook of Science and Technology 1967, p155

enarchist ('en,arkist) or **enarch** ('en,ark), *n.* a high-ranking French civil service administrator selected from the top graduates of the École Nationale d'Administration (National School of Administration). *The first generation of "enarchists" now dominate at the policy level of government in the same way that "polytechniciens" [graduates of the École Polytechnique] for generations have held sway over top posts in industry and finance.* Science 7/19/68, p249 *There have been constant complaints from outside that the "Enarchs" are arid technocrats and often precious with it.* Manchester Guardian Weekly 8/14/69, p15 **[1968,** from French *énarque,* formed from *ÉNA,* initials of École Nationale d'Administration + *-arque* -arch (ruler or leader)]

encapsidate (en'kæpsə,deit), *v.t.* to enclose (a virus particle) in a protein coat, which makes the particle stable and transmissible. *Conventional viruses are made up of nucleic acid encapsidated in protein, whereas viroids are characterized by the absence of encapsidated proteins. In spite of their small size, viroid ribonucleic acids (RNAs) can replicate and produce the characteristic disease syndromes when introduced into cells.* McGraw-Hill Yearbook of Science and Technology 1977, p417 **[1972,** from *en-* to put in + *capsid* + *-ate* verb suffix] —**encapsidation,** *n.: Only when enough coat protein has accumulated to permit the formation of "disk" aggregates can the assembly of virus particles begin. This would delay the encapsidation of virion RNA thereby allowing time for synthesis of early proteins and (−) strands.* Nature 4/29/76, p763

encephalitogen (en,sefə'laitədʒən), *n.* a virus or other substance that causes encephalitis. *This basic polymer is both encephalitogenic and is not a general non-specific immunosuppressive agent (our unpublished results). Whereas it efficiently suppresses the disease when administered after the basic encephalitogen, it cannot prevent the disease when injected intravenously in saline before the basic brain protein.* Nature 12/29/72, p565 **[1964,** back formation from earlier *encephalitogenic* (OEDS 1923) causing or able to cause encephalitis]

encephalization quotient, index to a ratio of body weight to brain weight, used to describe animal development. It is computed as a comparison of actual brain weight of any given specimen to average brain weight for animals of the same class and size. *Until the Isthmus of Panama rose just a couple of million years ago, South America was an isolated island continent . . . Here the herbivores display no increase in brain size through time. Their average encephalization quotient remained below 0.5 throughout the Tertiary, and they were quickly eliminated when advanced carnivores crossed the isthmus from North America.* Natural History 1/75, p26 **[1970]**

encephalomyocarditis (en,sefəlou,maiəkar'daitis), *n.* a virus disease, especially of children, characterized by inflammation of the brain and the heart muscle. *Although the ribosomes readily translated globin mRNA and poly U at normal rates, they were unable to translate encephalomyocarditis virus RNA.* New Scientist 8/31/72, p422 **[1964,** from *encephalitis* inflammation of the brain + *myocarditis* inflammation of the heart muscle]

enchilada, *n.* **the whole enchilada,** U.S. Slang. the complete or entire affair; the whole matter or thing. Compare BIG ENCHILADA. *Villa readjusted his sunglasses against the blazing Mexican noon and stared out across the vast expanse. "So this is it," he murmured. "The whole enchilada."* New Yorker 6/6/77, p39 **[1977]**

encounter, *n.* U.S. an encounter group session. *As encounters multiplied and perspective deepened, Jane (Howard) found herself kicking pillows and hurling finger paint with the worst* *of them—and feeling, as a result, relieved of some fossil fears.* Time 7/27/70, p74 [**1967**]

encounter group, a group of people taking part in sensitivity training. Also called SENSITIVITY GROUP and T-GROUP. *Sensitivity training sessions . . . also known as encounter groups . . . share several common attributes. The programs are designed to place people in a group situation. Through a mixture of physical contact games and no-holds-barred discussions about each other's strengths and failures, each group member hopefully will feel less constricted.* Encyclopedia Science Supplement (Grolier) 1970, p78 [**1967**]

encounter grouper or **encounter groupie**, a member of an encounter group. [John] *le Carré's set-painting and weather reports are, as ever, top of the line. He reveals himself as a talented parodist, especially receptive to the counterfeit yelps of lovers and the cheapjack philosophy of encounter groupers wasting away with their terminal cases of Kahlil Gibran.* NY Times Book Review 1/9/72, p7 *It is powerful stuff . . . ending with the same character in the throes of what encounter groupies call a 'primal'.* Listener 11/6/75, p622 [**1972**]

encryption (en'krɪpʃən), *n.* the act or process of putting information into a cipher or code. *"Encryption" is in and "encoding" is out . . . Mr. Carter used both the old word and the new in explaining SALT verification: he claimed that the treaty "forbids the encryption or the encoding of crucial missile-test information."* NY Times Magazine 11/18/79, p18 [**1964**, from *encrypt* (1958) to encipher (from *en-* put into + *crypt*ogram) + *-ion*] —**encryptor**, *n.: The . . . encryptor will have two applications in this new financial network. The first application will be for authentication. Each cardholder will have some form of personal identification number as a requirement for access to the network. To provide added security, this number may be encrypted.* McGraw-Hill Yearbook of Science and Technology 1977, p174

endangered, *adj.* threatened with extinction. *A notable example: The signing by President Nixon of the Endangered Species Act "to prevent the importation of endangered species of fish and wildlife into the United States . . ."* Encyclopedia Science Supplement (Grolier) 1970, p188 *The black rhino, of which there are about 300 in the reserve, is recognized as an endangered mammal and has been placed on the official list of threatened species compiled by the International Union for the Conservation of Nature.* Science Journal 4/70, p12 [**1964**]

end-consumer, *n.* the ultimate consumer of a manufactured product. Also called END-USER. *The result is that foreign business is faced with a global market, including the end-consumer, the complex distribution system, the powerful domestic competitors, and last but not least the Government.* Times (London) 6/17/70, pIV [**1970**]

endgame, *n.* a contest in its final stage. . . . *the Viet Cong struck at Tet. It hit every provincial capital in South Vietnam, more than half the district capitals, seized the American Embassy for twelve hours, and held the city of Hué for twenty-two days. The American public never recovered, and from that point on, the Vietnam War was an endgame.* Atlantic 11/70, p86 [**1965**, transferred sense of the term for the final stage of a game, especially chess]

endocast, *n.* an internal cast of a primitive cranium or other hollow bodily structure. *A plaster endocast . . . was made by Mr R.J. Clarke and its volume was determined by water displacement by Mrs Margaret Leakey and Dr A. Walker.* Nature 10/20/72, p468 [**1972**, from *endo-* within, internal + *cast*]

endocytose (,endousai'touz), *v.t.* to absorb or incorporate by endocytosis. *One particularly important role is in endocytosis. In this process, damaged portions of the cell surface and even potentially damaging substances that bind to it are sucked, or endocytosed, into the cell.* World Book Science Annual 1975, p119 [**1975**, back formation from ENDOCYTOSIS]

endocytosis (,endousai'tousis), *n. Biology.* a process of cellular ingestion by which the cell membrane folds inward to enclose and incorporate foreign substances. Compare EMIOCYTOSIS. *Macrophages' role in life is to roam the body and scavenge for-*

eign material they come across. By a process known as endocytosis, macrophages can engulf particles of substantial size. New Scientist 1/11/73, p64 [**1963**, from New Latin, from *endo-* within, internal + *cyt-* cell + *-osis* process or condition] —**endocytotic**, *adj.: The uptake is thought to occur by engulfment of bacteria into vesicles formed by invagination of the plasmalemma during plasmolysis and concomitant degradation of the cell wall, rather than by a strictly endocytotic process.* Nature 10/20/72, p455

endonuclease (,endou'nu:kli:,eis), *n.* an enzyme that breaks up strands of DNA (deoxyribonucleic acid, the carrier of genetic information in the cells) into discontinuous segments. Compare EXONUCLEASE. *The enzyme is an endonuclease, able to clip—in the test tube at least—the newly formed DNA helix into fragments shorter than the original RNA template.* New Scientist 11/5/70, p257 [**1962**, from *endo-* inner + *nuclease* an enzyme that hydrolyzes nucleic acid]

endoperoxide (,endoupə'rɑksaid), *n.* any of a group of highly oxygenated compounds that are precursors of prostaglandins (modified fatty acids with hormonelike functions) and convert naturally to THROMBOXANE and PROSTACYCLIN. *Endoperoxides can be changed by enzyme action into various prostaglandins, including those that produce fever, pain and inflammation.* NY Times 10/30/79, pC1 [**1974**, from *endo-* internal (as in a ring rather than a side chain) + *peroxide*]

endorphin (en'dɔrfin), *n.* one of a group of polypeptides present in the brain that control various physiological responses. Each endorphin has certain properties of morphine and acts as a natural pain suppressant or opiate of the body. Compare ENKEPHALIN. *This past October, Dr. Roger Guillemin of the Salk Institute reported on several other endorphins, all produced by the brain, that seem to play important roles in a host of bodily activities. "Alpha-endorphin" seems to be a natural tranquilizer; "gamma-endorphin" makes even timid rats angry and aggressive; other endorphins appear to turn the nightly switch of sleep on and off.* NY Times Magazine 1/30/77, p52 *Injected into animals, in laboratory tests, the endorphins (a chain of up to 31 amino acids) acted as pain-killers.* Maclean's 12/13/76, p76 [**1975**, from *endogenous* within + *m*orphine]

endorse, *v.t.* **endorse out**, (in South Africa) to send away from an urban to a rural area as part of a system of controlling the influx of black Africans into the cities. *If an African is caught without his reference book, or violates one of a host of other restrictive regulations, he can be put in jail or fined or "endorsed out"—sent, that is, to a "homeland" that he may never have seen and to which he has no ties.* New Yorker 2/10/68, p37 [**1963**]

endosulfan (,endou'səl,fæn), *n.* a powerful insecticide containing chlorinated sulfate. *Endosulfan is extremely toxic to fish: concentrations in the water as low as 0 00002 parts per million cause death.* New Scientist 4/16/70, p114 [**1965**] ▶German and Dutch spellings (*endosulvan* and *endosolvan*) have also appeared in English language publications (*Time, Manchester Guardian Weekly,* and *World Book Year Book*).

end-stopped, *adj.* marked by stops or pauses at the end of a movement. *Ballet has accustomed us to phrases that congeal into moments our eye can seize on; modern dance has accustomed us to big, emphatic changes of the whole body's shape. But Tharp-dancing is rarely end-stopped: The dancers seem almost constantly on the move—sliding and twisting and jabbing their feet through the music, executing small, fluid shrugs and circles with God knows how many parts of their bodies simultaneously.* NY Times Magazine 1/4/76, p12 [**1976**, extended sense of the term applied in poetry to lines that end with a stop or pause (OED 1877)]

Endsville, *adj. U.S. Slang.* the largest, greatest, or most wonderful. *At the windup of his two-week tour, Soviet Cosmonaut Georgy Beregovoy announced that New York was strictly Endsville . . .* Time 11/21/69, p46 [**1957**, from *end* (in the U.S. slang phrase *the end* the best or most exciting, often *the living end*) + *-ville* (see the entry -VILLE)]

end-user, *n.* another name for END-CONSUMER. *Independent peripheral men in the US aren't happy with IBM's contention* *that the new price structure is in the end-user's best interests. The Computer Peripherals Manufacturers Association has announced that it will file with the US Department of Justice a request that it consider peripherals very seriously in its current anti-trust lawsuit against IBM.* New Scientist and Science Journal 2/4/71, p244 [**1963**]

enemies list, a list of people regarded as one's enemies and therefore liable to reprisal. Compare HIT LIST. *Whatever the propriety of putting a distinguished man of science on an enemies list, it must be acknowledged that the list makers followed the custom of treating the learned with some decorum.* New Scientist 7/19/73, p152 [**1973**] ▶This term became current in 1973 with the disclosure growing out of the Watergate investigations that the White House kept such a list during the Nixon administration.

energy, *n.* Often used attributively in such phrases as **energy accounting** and **energy gap** in referring to the supply or sources of energy or of energy-producing substances such as petroleum, coal, and natural gas. See also ENERGY AUDIT, ENERGY CRISIS. —**energy accounting:** *By now, most people working on energy questions have heard of energy accounting. This extension of the accountant's art adds up all the energy required for components of a system in order to determine the overall energy requirement.* New Scientist 5/18/78, p444 —**energy company:** *The legislation might also break up "energy companies," requiring a firm to participate in only one energy source, such as coal or oil, but not both. Supporters of this legislation believed lower energy prices could result.* Americana Annual 1977, p196 —**energy gap:** *Energy conservation seems much too modest a method to take seriously for a problem like the energy gap. People scoff. "America," they say, "did not become great by conserving."* NY Times Magazine 6/4/78, p110 —**energy industry:** *Specialist banks have been established to serve the energy industry.* Times (London) 4/1/76, p25 —**energy plantation:** *The Energy Research and Development Administration (ERDA) has recently written several large contracts for the study of biomass energy systems, which would have trees, grasses or other crops grown on "energy plantations" as a source of either electric power or synthetic fuels.* Scientific American 3/76, p60B [**1970**]

energy audit, a systematic check of the use of energy within an establishment to determine where savings in the output of energy can be achieved. *His mission: to convince them that outside experts should do "energy audits" of schools and hospitals to see what forms of insulation and heating devices would make them more energy efficient.* Time 6/20/77, p75 [**1977**] —**energy auditor:** *Healthy savings can be achieved by some of the big things energy auditors look for, such as attic insulation.* Christian Science Monitor 1/8/80, p24

energy budget, an estimate of the amount of energy obtained and expended by an organism or ecosystem. *Small creatures generally have a high metabolism because they require more energy to keep warm than do larger mammals. Therefore, the two researchers say small animals' "energy budget" . . . may account for these animals' greater need for sleep.* Encyclopedia Science Supplement (Grolier) 1987, p81 [**1950, 1980**]

energy crisis, an acute shortage in the supply of energy-producing fuels, especially oil and natural gas. *In one sense, the term energy crisis means simply that the supplies of fuels and power are less than we want, or that they might cost much more in the future. In another sense, an enlargement of the first, it refers to a tangled web of problems concerning the quality of the environment and the availability, marketing, and growing demand for energy resources.* Science 11/17/72, p703 *The energy crisis hasn't yet hit Boise with anything like an instructive impact. Gas is not only plentiful but a good deal cheaper than it is in the East, even though the nearest refinery is on the coast, 400 miles away.* Harper's 11/74, p40 [**1970**]

energy-intensive, *adj.* requiring great expenditure of energy for production. *In the case of copper, feasible new sources may indeed be found: high-copper-content manganese nodules on the ocean floor, for instance (energy-intensive aluminum being*

a bad example). Science News 2/12/72, p101 [**1967**, patterned after *capital-intensive, labor-intensive,* etc.]

energy paper, a dry sheet of paper fiber impregnated with potassium persulfate and powdered carbon, that serves as the active material of a dry-cell battery and is easily replaceable when the battery runs out of power. *To the world of dry cells and storage batteries Dutch scientists have added a new concept: "energy paper."* Science Journal 1/68, p13 *A potential use for this "energy paper" is to power cordless appliances such as electric shavers.* NY Times 8/2/68, p45 [**1968**]

energy structure, a type of kinetic art structure having motorized, mechanical, or electronic parts. *Sculptors' work took many forms, from figurative to nonobjective, from funk to energy structures.* Americana Annual 1970, p99 [**1970**]

enfant chéri (ā'fä ʃei'ri:), *French.* a cherished or pampered child (used chiefly figuratively in English). *Aix has entertained hope in recent years of purchasing a painting or two by the city's enfant chéri, Paul Cézanne, but the going rate is out of reach.* Saturday Review 10/17/70, p44 . . . *Ivory Coast had a trade balance of thirty-two million Central African francs in 1969. She is the enfant chéri of France, showered with loans and French capital that have helped her diversify her economy . . .* Atlantic 11/71, p88 [**1955**]/

enforcer, *n. Ice Hockey.* a very strong and aggressive player used by a team to intimidate or fight opposing players. *Every team employs swashbuckling . . . "enforcers." Chicago Black Hawk defenseman Keith Magnuson has taken boxing lessons from a former world bantamweight champion and knocks out many an opponent with one blow. Philadelphia Flyers' Dave "Hammer" Schultz . . . excels at another job: ferocious attacks on opposing teams' stars.* Reader's Digest 3/76, p34 [**1976**, extended from the underworld sense of one employed to enforce discipline by violence]

engineered food, food treated or prepared scientifically to increase its nutritional value and storage life or to replace or supplement other conventional food. Compare FABRICATED FOOD. *Nutritional research has added two new terms to the food vocabulary: fabricated food and engineered food. Fabricated food covers all kinds of imitation foods, chiefly meat (beef, pork, and poultry), milk, and egg products. The meat substitutes are chiefly made from soybean fibers and most dairy analogs from different types of soybean protein. Engineered food, although now used interchangeably for fabricated food, is a term which indicates that food has been fortified or supplemented and shows evidence of improved nutrition.* 1972 Collier's Encyclopedia Year Book, p247 [**1971**]

English disease, a term often used to describe various problems of labor management, first given widespread notice in Great Britain, such as excessive attention to work rules, apparent control of management policy by shop stewards, absenteeism, etc. Also called ENGLISH SICKNESS. *At the same time, rapidly rising costs of factory production—first noticeable in Britain and nicknamed "the English disease"—have become manifest in other countries of west Europe and in North America.* Times (London) 5/25/66, p18 [**1966**] ▶*English disease* and *English sickness* appear to be translations of French *la maladie anglaise* or German *die englische Krankheit.* Formerly, *English disease* was sometimes applied to various ailments once associated with Great Britain, such as rickets and bronchitis. According to the *OED, English disease* or *English Malady* was used in the 1700's to mean low spirits or melancholy.

Englishment, *n.* an English rendering or version of a foreign work. *Aristophanes, with an easy Greek candor about bodily functions, . . . used a number of words unknown to Queen Victoria even in translation, and when Arrowsmith did translate them (in a larruping fine Englishment, an early draft of which Arrowsmith read to me and I read back to him one great evening years back in Rome) they turned out to be too colorful for the American stage . . .* Saturday Review 8/13/66, p22 [**1966**, from *English, v.,* to translate into English + -*ment*]

English sickness, another name for ENGLISH DISEASE. *In fact, "the English sickness" is a term widely used in Europe to de-*

scribe high levels of absenteeism, restrictive practices and wild-cat strikes . . . Science Journal 4/4/70, p26 [**1969**]

enhance, v.t. to improve the quality of (a photograph) by computer. See COMPUTER-ENHANCED. *Once more, in a complex, time-consuming process, the computer is used to enhance the images by altering the contrast and adding "cosmetics" and by filling gaps caused by the loss of data bits on the trail between the camera in the spacecraft and the computer on earth.* 1975 Collier's Encyclopedia Year Book, p45 [**1974**, extended from the general sense of add to, heighten]

enhanced radiation, **1** a large amount of radiation in the form of high-energy neutrons and gamma rays, capable of contaminating almost instantly all living things exposed to it when released in a nuclear explosion that produces relatively little heat and blast. *The neutron warhead is a refinement of nuclear technology that could, according to its proponents, devastate by "enhanced radiation" (what an adjective to modify a noun synonymous with death) invading columns of infantry and artillery but cause little damage to the territory being invaded.* New Yorker 8/1/77, p58 **2** Attributive use: *It might also be said in favor of enhanced-radiation devices that, as the systems of this new generation of tactical nuclear weapons are currently planned, they incorporate features other than enhanced radiation.* Scientific American 5/78, p50 [**1976**]

enhanced radiation weapon, a nuclear device designed to release enhanced radiation. *Abbreviation:* ERW Compare BEAM WEAPON, MININUKE. *The neutron bomb releases most of its energy in the form of instant radiation, particularly neutrons, instead of doing so in the form of blast and heat like the fission weapons which Nato already has. This is why scientists like to call it the enhanced radiation weapon . . . and journalists opt for the neutron bomb—which fits more easily into the single column headline in a newspaper.* Times (London) 4/8/78, p4 [**1976**]

enhanced recovery, another name for TERTIARY RECOVERY. *For the long-term, new sources for gas must be found, but development of them will also depend on the price people are willing to pay for this clean, convenient fuel. So-called "enhanced recovery" techniques can squeeze new gas out of old fields at a cost of $1.50 to $2.50 per Mcf* [thousand cubic feet]. Science News 2/26/77, p135 [**1976**]

enkephalin (en'kefəlin), n. either of two polypeptides that are natural pain suppressants or opiates of the body. Enkephalins are produced in the pituitary gland and are related to the endorphins. Compare ENDORPHIN. See also LEU-ENKEPHALIN, MET-ENKEPHALIN. *A variety of evidence suggests that the enkephalins are neurotransmitters for specific neuronal systems in the brain which mediate the integration of sensory information pertaining to pain and emotional behavior.* McGraw-Hill Yearbook of Science and Technology 1978, p271 [**1975**, coined by John Hughes and Hans Kosterlitz, University of Aberdeen, from Greek *enképhalos* brain + English *-in* (chemical suffix)]

enriched, adj. containing many stimuli, especially more than usual in a standard laboratory environment. *The number of dendrites and dendritic spines . . . increased under enriched conditions, which included more sensory stimuli, and decreased under impoverished conditions, where such stimuli were reduced.* NY Times 5/22/76, p11 *. . . one rat is placed in an enriched environment and the third is put in an impoverished environment.* Scientific American 2/72, p22 [**1972**]

enterobacteria, n.pl. intestinal bacteria, especially those belonging to a large family of rod-shaped bacteria that includes E. coli. *A permanent, vigilant body to monitor the epidemiology of enterobacteria would save time, money, anguish, and probably lives too, the next time danger arises.* New Scientist 11/27/69, p444 [**1966**, from *entero-* intestines + *bacteria*]

enterobactin, n. a substance produced by enterobacteria that has an inhibiting effect on other bacteria. *Pacifarin, found in certain batches of whole wheat and dried egg and produced by bacteria, protects mice infected with mouse typhoid. It was identified as enterobactin (a compound of known structure), recently discovered by biochemists at the University of Califor-*

nia, Berkeley. 1972 Britannica Yearbook of Science and the Future, p251 [**1971**, from *enterobac*teria + *-in* (chemical suffix)]

enteropathogenic, adj. producing intestinal disease. *In particular, studies at the research station in Stock, Essex, on enteropathogenic strains of Escherichia coli . . . and on bacterial drug resistance . . . are unique, and unlikely to be taken over elsewhere.* New Scientist and Science Journal 4/8/71, p68 [**1968**, from *entero-* intestines + *pathogenic*]

enterprise zone, an area of high unemployment and poverty in which the government encourages business enterprise by various economic incentives, such as reduction of taxes and suspension of zoning laws. *New York and West Virginia joined 28 other states in authorizing enterprise zones to encourage companies to bring new growth to declining areas.* 1987 World Book Year Book, p481 *Steven's most interesting ideas concern the establishment of tax-free "enterprise zones" in such areas as Cape Breton and Vancouver Island.* Maclean's 4/22/85, p46 [**1979**] —**enterprise zoning**: *"Enterprise zoning is an effective method of improving chronically depressed neighborhoods."* NY Times 7/28/85, pA24

enthalpimetry (en,θælpə'metri: or en,θæl'pimətri:), n. the measurement of total heat content generated or absorbed by a substance, used especially to follow the progress of a chemical reaction. *Enthalpimetry depends on the fact that almost all reactions are associated with the evolution or absorption of heat.* New Scientist 2/8/68, p300 *Peak enthalpimetry is a novel approach that is applicable to biochemical and clinical analysis. The salient feature is rapid mixing of a reagent stream with an isothermal solvent stream into which discrete samples are intermittently injected. The temperature versus time of the resulting product stream is recorded with the aid of a thermistor circuit that has a sensitivity of 0.00001°.* McGraw-Hill Yearbook of Science and Technology 1975, p397 [**1968**, from *enthalpy* total heat content + *-metry* measurement] —**enthalpimetric**, adj.: *Another reason may well be that many of the analytical problems to which the enthalpimetric method has been applied had earlier been solved in other ways, and the particular virtues of this technique were not made apparent.* New Scientist 2/8/68, p300

Entisol ('entai,sɔːl), n. (in U.S. soil taxonomy) any of a group of soils lacking distinct soil horizons, found in all parts of the world and under a wide variety of vegetation. *Soil taxonomy identifies taxa called soil orders that require greatly different amounts of time for development. Entisols, for example, are found on recent deposits, whereas Oxisols may require millions of years to form from unweathered material.* McGraw-Hill Yearbook of Science and Technology 1976, p367 [**1972**, probably from *entire* + *-sol* (from Latin *solum* soil)]

entrain, v.t., v.i. *Biology.* to alter (the circadian rhythm of an organism) so that it adjusts to or synchronizes with a different 24-hour cycle. *Circadian rhythms are so widespread among animals that we were not surprised to find them in the house sparrow. Its locomotor rhythm is readily entrained by artificial light cycles. If the phase of the entraining cycle is shifted, there are three to six transient, or intermediate, cycles before the bird reorients its activity to the new regime.* Scientific American 3/72, p24 [**1972**, specialized sense of the term meaning "to draw away; bring on as a consequence" (OED 1568)] —**entrainment**, n.: *Through their entrainment feature, circadian clocks would adjust daily to the natural 24-hour cycle of earth rotation, regardless of the rhythm's natural frequency.* 1972 Compton Yearbook, p547

entry-level, adj. of or being at the beginning, first, or lowest level. *This demographic reality poses a big problem for employers like hotels and restaurants and fast-food chains who hire most of their workers at the entry-level wages of the federal minimum.* Manchester Guardian Weekly 3/22/81, p18 *The Tandy 102 ($499) is the latest version of a very popular entry-level laptop.* Connoisseur 9/88, p160 [**1981**]

envenomate, v.t. to inject with a venom. *Envenomated rabbits do not show any significant prolongation of clotting time; there are, however, still unconfirmed claims concerning the decrease of oxidative phosphorylation in mitochondria of mice*

intoxicated with cobra venom. Science 7/28/72, p321 **[1972]**
►Coined to distinguish from verb *envenom* (1200's) meaning "to put poison on" or "fill with bitterness."

environment, *n.* a work of environmental art. *Dada has contributed to every new technique employed in this century that it did not actually invent—collage, which is everywhere; its extension, assemblage, which includes junk sculpture, "found" objects and a hundred cousins; the "environment" as well as the Happening; kinetic sculpture, whether motorized or not, and on and on.* NY Times Magazine 3/24/68, p30 **[1962]**

environmental, *adj.* of or relating to environmental art. *From the desire to be totally encompassed by the work came the wall-size dimensions of the drip canvases, so suggestive to later "environmental" painters and sculptors.* New Yorker 5/6/67, p167 **[1964]**

environmental art, a form of art that encompasses the spectator with a fixed image or object. *Luminal, minimal, and three-dimensional pop art have contributed to the development of environmental art in rejecting fixed walls and standard spaces and in becoming concerned with the commercial and urban world beyond the galleries.* 1969 Collier's Encyclopedia Year Book, p115 **[1967]**

environmental biology, the branch of biology dealing with the interrelationships of organisms and their environment; ecology. *According to Dr Rene Dubos, professor Emeritus of environmental biology at Rockefeller Institute in New York . . . "All over the globe and at all times in the past, men have pillaged nature and disturbed the ecological equilibrium, usually out of ignorance, but also because they have always been more concerned with immediate advantages than with long range goals."* Buenos Aires Herald 3/3/73, pIII **[1972]**

environmental engineer, a specialist in the reduction of pollution and contamination of the environment. *The environmental engineer, a direct descendant of the civil (sanitary) engineer, now uses the scientific and technological advances contributed by applied chemists, chemical engineers, industrial engineers, hydrologists, hydraulic engineers, biologists, statisticians, and aerospace engineers, to achieve a balance . . .* Engineering Special (University of Alabama), 4/11/72, p9 **[1972]**

environmental impact statement, a review of the possible consequences that a proposed idea or project may have on the environment. See IMPACT STATEMENT. *A group of middle-class whites in Newark had been able to block a highly controversial low-income housing project by bringing a long series of challenges to the project's environmental impact statements.* Harper's 12/77, p50 **[1973]**

environmentalism, *n.* the interests and activities of environmentalists; concern with the quality of the environment, especially with the effects of uncontrolled pollution of the atmosphere. *The arguments in the United States over environmental problems have not yet reached these basic levels, even though environmentalism got its first major impetus here.* Science News 2/12/72, p101 **[1972, derivative of ENVIRONMENTALIST]**

environmentalist, *n.* **1** a person concerned with problems of the environment and especially with the effects of uncontrolled pollution on the earth's atmosphere. Compare ANTIPOLLUTIONIST. *Some environmentalists reject all of modern technology and call for a return to a simple, pastoral life free of fumes, artificial chemicals and any noise but the chirping of birds and the croaking of frogs.* Science News 6/19/71, p413 *The concern of environmentalists for ecological hazards is justified.* NY Times 9/25/70, p42 **2** an artist who creates environmental art. *Other environmentalists see their works as means to engage the viewer in a new kind of emotional release . . . "People become part of the art object," [Tony] Martin explains. "They score it. They compose it. I supply the format."* Time 5/3/68, p42 **[1969 for def. 1; 1968 for def. 2]** ►The term *environmentalist* was originally used around 1920 in the sense of "one who advocates or supports the theory that the environ-

ment is the dominating force in effecting change or development, rather than a person's heredity or initiative."

environmental science, the group of sciences dealing with the environment and now especially with the effects of pollution. *As a group of marine biologists, we are actively involved in various facets of environmental science—a less emotive and more encompassing term than pollution studies.* Times (London) 3/31/70, p9 **[1967]**

environmentology, *n.* the study of environmental problems; science concerned with the quality of the environment. *In creating an executive committee on environmentology with past president E. W. Tucker as chairman, the American Veterinary Medical Association (AVMA) recognized the interrelationship of environment with most activities engaged in by practitioners.* 1974 Britannica Yearbook of Science and the Future, p336 **[1973]**

enzyme engineering, the use of enzymes in technology; application of enzymes or enzymatic processes to agriculture, industry, etc. *Chromosomal material that controls the enzymatic synthesis of fruit-fly protein or silkworm protein can be transferred to bacteria in such a way that the progeny synthesize these proteins. Likewise, the genes that are responsible for skin proteins in frogs can be transferred to bacteria in such a way that the progeny synthesize the proteins. Such methods have led to the expansion of a field called "enzyme engineering," which has great scientific and technical potentials.* Americana Annual 1975, p382 **[1972]**

EPA, abbreviation of *Environmental Protection Agency* (of the United States, established in 1970). *. . . a major "redirection" of the EPA's research program . . . tends to shift the agency away from development of pollution control technology and toward a narrower mission of supporting the agency's regulatory functions.* Science 2/9/73, p550 **[1970]**

ephemeralization, *n.* the practice or process of producing goods that are for temporary use or that are to last for only a short time. *"Ephemeralization" is the key word in Buckminster Fuller's bulging lexicon. To him it means increasing the obsolescence rate of all goods in order to speed up the recycling of elements. The corollary is "regenerative" or inflamed consumerism.* NY Times Book Review 1/16/72, p4 **[1960, coined by R. Buckminster Fuller from ephemeral + -ization]**

epidermin, *n.* a fibrous protein that is the main constituent of the epidermis. *Considerable uncertainty exists about the structure of the fibrinogen molecule. It was classified by Astbury with a-keratin, epidermin, and myosin because it gave an X-ray diffraction pattern which indicated a molecular structure similar to these α-proteins.* Nature 5/5/72, p9 **[1966, from epidermis + -in]**

episome, *n.* a genetic particle in the cells of bacteria that may exist autonomously in the cytoplasm or may be a part of the chromosomes. *Infectious particles of this kind, called episomes, are known to carry factors determining fertility, the ability to produce particular bacterial antibiotics called bacteriocins, and drug resistance.* Britannica Book of the Year 1967, p505 **[1960, from epi- outer + -some body]**

epitope, *n.* the part of an antigen that determines or influences the specific antibody which will react with the antigen. Compare IDIOTOPE. *The specific patterns that are recognized by antibody molecules are epitopes: patches on the surface of large molecules such as proteins, polysaccharides and nucleic acids. Molecules that display epitopes are called antigens.* Scientific American 7/73, p52 **[1973, from epi- on, upon + -tope place (from Greek tópos)]**

EPNdB, abbreviation of *effective perceived noise decibels*, a unit of measure of the effects of noise on the hearing, based on the type of sound and its intensity and duration. *Anyone familiar with EPNdB figures will appreciate that these values are literally fantastic. It means that the QTOL's [quiet takeoff and landing (airplane)] "90 EPNdB footprint," the plot of noise forming a contour at 90 effective perceived noise decibels, lies almost wholly within the boundary of most airports. In practice, it would mean that people living even near the airport would sel-*

dom hear the aircraft above the general background of urban noise, whether indoors or out. New Scientist 7/19/73, p138 **[1971]**

Epstein-Barr virus, a herpesvirus that causes infectious mononucleosis and is found associated with various types of human cancers. It was first isolated by the British virologists M. A. Epstein and Y. M. Barr in 1964. *Added to the evidence linking the Epstein-Barr virus with Burkitt's lymphoma, and the burgeoning knowledge about animal cancer viruses, this result will strengthen the growing conviction that viruses are an essential causal determinant for human cancer.* New Scientist 11/22/70, p162 **[1969]**

ept, *adj.* able; clever; effective. See EPTITUDE. *It is different because it is inept, and those other businesses are very ept indeed. They are eptest at getting what they want from the Administration and fighting for what they want until they get it.* Atlantic 9/73, p114   *The obvious answer is summed up by a White House official's sardonic crack: "Politically, we're not very ept."* NY Times Magazine 6/6/76, p15 **[1938, 1966,** back formation from *inept*]

▶Since a number of words with the prefixes *in-, un-, dis-,* etc., have no counterparts of opposite meaning with the same base form, there has been a tendency, especially since the 19th century, to create such equivalents, usually for humorous effect. An example of this from the 1600's is *scrutable,* derived from the then 150-year-old *inscrutable.* Although the words *ept* and *eptitude* seem to have become fairly current in recent years (perhaps in part by influence of *apt* and *aptitude*), similar words are sometimes created by writers for the nonce, occasionally by the whimsical dropping of what is not a negative prefix or not even a real prefix, without expecting them to catch on. For example: *armingly* (from *disarmingly*), *delible* (from *indelible*), *gainly* (from *ungainly*), *pensable* (from *indispensable*), *trepid* (from *intrepid*), *ertia* (from *inertia*).

eptitude, *n.* fitness; ability; effectiveness. *What makes Huntford's Anglo-Saxon hackles rise is less the cleverness and thoroughgoing eptitude of the Social Democratic persuasion-cum-administration machine . . . than the supine attitude of the Swede-in-the-street.* NY Times Book Review 2/27/72, p6 **[1967,** back formation from *ineptitude*]

E.Q., abbreviation of ENCEPHALIZATION QUOTIENT. *In order to analyze the progressive evolution of encephalization in the mammals, I have computed average E.Q.'s and standard deviations for samples of fossil and living ungulates and carnivores and plotted them as a set of normal curves.* Scientific American 1/76, p95 **[1973]**

equal opportunity, 1 equality in employment regardless of color, race, religion, sex, etc.; nondiscriminatory practices in hiring employees. Compare AFFIRMATIVE ACTION. *The last revenue-sharing funds impounded by the federal courts in a legal dispute over equal opportunity in Chicago's police department were released to the city on June 21.* 1978 World Book Year Book, p249 **2** Attributive use: *From now on, Zumwalt declared, Navy commanders will be graded on their own performance in handling racial problems under their command. "The Navy has made unacceptable progress in the equal opportunity area," the CNO warned sternly. "Response which lacks commitment from the heart is obstructionist."* Newsweek 11/20/72, p35 **[1925, 1963]**

Equal Rights Amendment, a proposed amendment to the United States Constitution providing for equal rights of both sexes. *Abbreviation:* ERA *The Equal Rights Amendment . . ., which provides that "equality of rights under the law shall not be denied or abridged by the United States or by any State on account of sex," cannot go into effect until 38 states have ratified it.* 1976 Collier's Encyclopedia Year Book, p198 *The polls . . . showed that 60 to 70 percent of the people favored an Equal Rights Amendment. People always favor rights.* NY Times Magazine 4/11/76, p31 **[1972]**

▶In the United States the Equal Rights Amendment, popularly known as *ERA* (pronounced ˈiːˈɑrˈeɪ), was first introduced in Congress in 1923. For 48 years women's-rights groups continued to propose the amendment without success, until Octo-

ber 12, 1971, when the House of Representatives approved the amendment followed by the Senate on March 22, 1972.

The campaign for state ratifications touched off a bitter national debate, and though Congress extended the deadline for ratification to June 30, 1982, the ERA was defeated.

equal time, *U.S.* **1** an equal amount of free air time given, usually at the same hour of another day, to an opposing political candidate, party, group, or citizen, to broadcast their views over radio or television. Compare FAIRNESS DOCTRINE. *Blair Clark, the Senator's campaign manager, announced his intention of requesting the three national television networks for equal time for the Senator before Tuesday's primary election in Wisconsin.* NY Times 3/31/68, p57 **2** Transferred sense. an equal opportunity to reply to any charge or opposing view. *The request for equal time comes from Emma Wallop, a small-town Midwestern widow and retired nurse who wakes one day to discover that her former boarder, Randy Rivers, has published a bestselling novel entitled* Don't Look Now, Medusa. *A tinplated* Spoon River Anthology, *it has as its main character a small-town Midwestern landlady, like Emma herself . . .* Time 10/19/70, p90 **[1959]**

equipe (eiˈkiːp), *n.* a sports or racing crew and its equipment; team. . . . *Rothmans revealed yesterday that they are forming a full-time* equipe, *complete with four aircraft and pilots, which will tour round the air shows this summer.* Times (London) 5/20/70, p29 **[1937, 1956,** from French *équipe* gang, crew]

ER, abbreviation of *emergency room. By late afternoon, the ER starts filling up. Half the patients are brought in by the police.* U.S. News and World Report 11/19/79, p52 **[1965]**

ERA or **E.R.A.,** abbreviation of EQUAL RIGHTS AMENDMENT. *Yet the problems of the ERA could not be entirely interpreted as a rebuke to women's rights. The sweeping simplicity of the amendment—"Equality of rights under law shall not be denied or abridged on account of sex"—made many voters, especially women, nervous. The anti-ERA lobby, led by Phyllis Schlafly . . . conjured up the prospect of unisex public toilets, and end to alimony, women forced into duty as combat soldiers.* Time 1/5/76, p7 **[1972]**

ERDA (ˈərdə), *n.* acronym for *Energy Research and Development Administration* (of the United States, 1974-1977). *By bringing together the energy research activities of several different departments and agencies, ERDA is designed to encourage development of many diverse energy sources without the nuclear bias of AEC's* [Atomic Energy Commission] *programs.* Science News 10/19/74, p248 **[1974]**

ergosphere, *n. Astronomy.* a hypothetical enclosed region that may surround a black hole. . . . *a body that enters this ergosphere can be influenced by the black hole without being completely captured by it.* Science News 12/26/70, p480 **[1970,** from Greek *érgon* work, energy + English *sphere*]

eroduction, *n.* another name for SEXPLOITER. *Crowded into insanitary homes or the dormitories run by their company, the Japanese seek escape through alcohol, television or* eroductions, *the sex films specialising in torture and disembowelment.* Sunday Times (London) 10/31/71, p77 **[1965,** from *erotic production*]

eroticist, *n. Especially British.* **1** a person who exhibits or is subject to strong sexual desire. *The fully aware eroticist, by the same token, must always subscribe to the code which he transgresses, otherwise his pleasure will lose its edge.* Times Literary Supplement 3/3/72, p234 **2** a person who produces or distributes erotic material; pornographer. *The most popular adult film, he* [Charles Roarty, the hotel's director of marketing] *says, is* Vixen, *directed by Russ Meyer, the master eroticist.* Times (London) 9/25/72, p12 **[1972,** derived from *eroticism* (1885) erotic character, quality, or condition]

erotologist, *n.* a specialist in erotology. The Devil Drives: A Life of Sir Richard Burton *by Fawn Brodie. The author maps the life of the flamboyant Victorian explorer, linguist and erotologist . . .* Time 8/11/67, p3 **[1967]**

erotology, *n.* erotic literature and art. *Crammed down and spilling over with assorted entertaining gobbets of history, bibacity and erotology.* Times (London) 8/1/70, p7 [**1966**]

erotophobic, *adj.* fearing or hating sexual expression or activity. *. . . 'we live in what some of the sociologists call an erotophobic environment', in which the mention of sex is 'detested' and 'taboo'.* Listener 4/13/72, p485 [**1972**, from *erotic* + connecting *-o-* + *phobic*]

error box, *Astronomy.* a quadrilateral representation of an area in the sky delimiting the approximate location of a celestial object or event. *X-ray observing equipment characteristically locates a source within a certain "error box" that may contain several candidates for visual identification, and the task is to make the error box smaller or pick the likeliest candidate.* Science News 8/5/78, p88 [**1971**]

error catastrophe, a theory of aging in which an increase in defective protein causes cell functioning to break down. *These results provide evidence for Orgel's theory of ageing, which suggests that one cause of ageing could be the accumulation of errors in protein synthesis, leading to a gradual but irreversible breakdown in the accuracy of the protein synthesizing machinery and finally to a lethal "error catastrophe."* Nature 7/7/72, p26 [**1972**, perhaps coined by Leslie Orgel in the early 1960's]

ERTS (ərts), *n.* **1** acronym for *Earth Resources Technology Satellites*, a U.S. space program for studying earth resources by means of satellites. *. . . by the time the ERTS becomes a practical proposition it may be found that it has been pre-empted in many of the fields in which it was to have found use.* Science Journal 12/69, p9 **2** any of the series of artificial satellites scheduled to be launched under this program. *The observations made aboard ERTS will be applied to agriculture, cartography, geology, geography, hydrology, hydrography and oceanography.* Science News 7/25/70, p64 [**1968**]

ERW, abbreviation of ENHANCED RADIATION WEAPON. *The point, cheering to the military, is that with ERW you get proportionately less heat and blast and more radiation . . . than from conventional nukes, knocking out the enemy in his tanks without unnecessarily devastating several square kilometers of territory.* Manchester Guardian Weekly 2/19/78, p9 [**1976**]

ESB, abbreviation of *electrical stimulation of the brain* (the stimulation of specific areas of the brain by the insertion of electrodes). Compare PACEMAKER, STIMOCEIVER. *Delgado and his co-workers at the Yale School of Medicine worked with cats and monkeys and learned to produce definite changes in eating, sleeping, fighting, playing and sex behavior. When applied to humans, ESB was able to evoke such feelings as fear and friendliness, pain and pleasure.* Science News 4/13/74, p245 [**1963**]

esbat, *n.* a meeting of witches. *Alex Sanders, 44, likes to call himself the King of the Witches . . . Esbats at the Sanderses' include dancing, chanting, feasting and the fondling of various ritual objects.* Time 4/27/70, p96 [**1952**, probably from Old French *esbat* a frolic, gambol (French *ébats*), from *esbatre* to frolic, ultimately from Latin *ex-* out + *battere* to beat]

escalate, *v.t., v.i.* to increase or expand in scale or size. *We have escalated war and moral numbness; we cannot de-escalate in a day.* Saturday Review 9/24/66, p64 [**1959**, extended from the earlier sense of raise prices, wages, etc. (1952) and originally to climb by an escalator (1922)]

escalation, *n.* an increase or expansion in scale or size, especially in the scale of a war. *The North Koreans want the Communist Powers to play the game of escalation, but only Russia has the military resources needed for this.* Manchester Guardian Weekly 8/25/66, p7 [**1959**]

escalatory, *adj.* leading to or involving increase in scale or size, especially of a war. *Simply to carry on as things stood was bound to lead to defeat; the U S had to make some sort of escalatory move.* Sunday Times (London) 4/13/69, p50 [**1965**]

escape mechanism, a means of escaping a danger. *Perhaps the most surprising and best-studied escape mechanism is antigen-*ic modulation: the ability of cancer cells to mask or lose antigen in the face of immunological attack.* Scientific American 5/77, p22 *Adds New York Bullion Trader James Sinclair, long a fervent backer of gold and silver: "Under the present circumstances, gold has become an outright escape mechanism."* Time 1/28/80, p63 [**1977**, figurative sense of the psychology term for an unconscious reaction or process of avoiding something unpleasant]

escapologist, *n.* a person who is adept at extricating from difficult situations. *. . . I can't help saluting the work put in by Alberto Lionello, a slippery* maestro *of comic embarrassment—not so much a born escapologist as a born escapologist—who reminds me of Peter Sellers without the narcissism.* New Yorker 10/21/67, p108 [**1967**, figurative use of earlier (OEDS 1926) meaning of a performer who escapes from handcuffs, chains, confinement in a box, etc.]

►Other earlier meanings of escapologist are one who escapes from daily concerns and duties (figurative, 1936) and one who escapes as from prison (literal, 1946).

escapology, *n.* the skill or methods of an escapologist. See ESCAPOLOGIST. *Even by the high standards of Mr. Wilson* [Harold Wilson, then British Prime Minister], *who is no beginner when it comes to shooting himself out of a tight corner, this was one of his finest moments in the art of parliamentary escapology.* Times (London) 12/19/67, p1 [**1967**]

Esky, *n. Australian.* a trademark for a portable container for keeping drinks cold. Popularly spelled **esky**. *"I knew there was an Esky full of lemonade for the pilot when he got thirsty and I thought I might get it."* Australian Women's Weekly 2/7/79, p14 *No less popular is Rugby League football, where raucous fans with well-stocked "eskies"—beer coolers—scream and swill and brawl with Sydneyesque abandon.* National Geographic Magazine 2/79, p228 [**1962**, probably shortened and altered form of *Eskimo*]

ESL, abbreviation of *English as a second language.* Compare TEFL. *This text . . . is intended for beginning and intermediate students of English as a second language and is designed to teach the student skills essential to success in an English speaking community, but which are not normally presented in the ESL classroom.* Advertisement by UCIS Publications, Pittsburgh, Pa., 1976, p4 [**1967**]

ESOL ('i:sɔl), *n. Especially U.S. and Canadian.* acronym for *English for Speakers of Other Languages. Learning to omit a distinction is just as hard, often even harder, than learning to make one; Spanish-speaking learners of ESOL have that kind of problem when they have to learn to say* they *in English where Spanish would have* ellos *or* ellas. J.L. Dillard, Black English, 1972, p272 [**1969**]

ESOP ('i:sap), *n.* acronym for *Employee Stock Ownership Plan* (any of various plans that promote stock ownership among company employees). *ESOP's have become increasingly popular . . . as a combination of an employee bonus plan and as a source of inexpensive capital for the company.* NY Times 9/3/76, pD1 [**1976**]

-esque, **1** an adjective suffix, meaning "resembling or suggesting the style, ideas, etc., of _____," commonly attached to the names of famous or prominent people. —**Disneyesque**, *adj.* [Walt Disney, 1901-1966, American film producer]: *Frommer is very proud of the hotel, but something in the way he speaks of it reveals a sort of show-business notion of place that is almost Disneyesque. He seems to believe, that is, in atmosphere, foreignness as theater, Europe as stage set.* Harper's 7/72, p45 —**McLuhanesque**, *adj.* [Marshall McLuhan, 1911-1980, Canadian communications specialist]: *The words seem slightly grandiloquent in a McLuhanesque age when all is known at once, the future long discounted, and uniformed options line up by the numbers.* Time 7/26/71, p7 —**Reaganesque**, *adj.*: *His* [Jimmy Carter's] *foreign policy reflexes are uncertain and briefly Reaganesque.* Manchester Guardian Weekly 3/9/80, p1
2 In the sense of "like a _____," "resembling that of a _____," the suffix appears in such words as the following: —**goblinesque**, *adj.*: *An element of the goblinesque: the porcupine*

dome of the Parliament House . . .; the ubiquitous, unendearing cupids . . . New Yorker 6/4/66, p90 **—robotesque,** *adj.: Hanus Thein's production may once have had some point; here in Holland it was blunted and paralysed, as witness the stagnant grouping and robotesque movement of the company in the Hussite scenes.* Times (London) 7/4/70, p21

ESR, abbreviation of ELECTRON SPIN RESONANCE. *In . . . ESR, a strong magnetic field is applied to the sample and the energy absorption is measured when the odd electrons flip their spins from being aligned in the same direction as the field to being aligned in the opposite direction.* Scientific American 8/70, p72 **[1955]**

essentic (e'sentik), *adj.* showing emotion by outward expression. *Anger, for instance, has an "essentic form" characterized by a short duration and a strong outward thrust . . . The essentic form of joy is a representation of a mental leap outward: there is a downward pressure followed by a rebound that exceeds the initial thrust.* New Scientist 12/31/70, p580 **[1970,** from Latin *essent-* (stem of *essens* being) + English *-ic*]

est, *n.* a system of consciousness-raising and self-realization. *With a dollop of almost every Eastern and Western discipline from Zen Buddhism to Dale Carnegie, "est" promises self-realization in a shiny new package—a 60-hour feel-it-don't-think-it training session developed by Erhard.* Newsweek 2/17/75, p49 *Est's route to increased potential is a Zen-like one: you are perfect as you are; since you cannot be other than what you are, it's okay not to be okay.* Psychology Today 11/78, p136 **[1974,** from acronym of *Erhard Seminars Training,* founded in 1971 by Werner Erhard, American entrepreneur] **—estian,** *adj.: If somebody tells me he will phone me at 3:00 with, say, some information I need, I know he will phone. If he calls instead at 3:20, we will have an estian conversation "acknowledging" that "he broke an agreement," "getting clear about it," "cleaning it up" and "taking responsibility" for it.* New Times 10/18/74, p49 **—estie,** *n.: It was the concluding session of the training, and the factorylike positioning of the tables and chairs, the beaming, interchangeable "esties," the steady handclapping, made me feel as if I were being processed on an assembly line.* NY Times Magazine 5/2/76, p56

establishment or **Establishment,** *n.* **1** Usually, **the Establishment.** the ruling groups or institutions of a country; a nation's power structure. Compare POWER STRUCTURE (definition 1). *If the Establishment means anything, it means big government and big business, and between them they pay most of the bills for big science.* Atlantic 9/70, p97 *It is the Establishment—the elders, the politicians, the military-industrial complex, the Administration, the press, the university trustees, the landlords, the system—that represses the black, exploits the poor, stultifies the students, vulgarizes American life. And it is the Establishment, of course, that wages the war in Vietnam—in the widespread protest against which the underlying class and generational clashes were dramatized and sharpened.* NY Times 8/9/68, pD1 **[1955] 2** the ruling circle of any institution (usually preceded by a modifier). *A sizable minority of senators tried unsuccessfully to reduce the size and influence of the military establishment by cutting the weapons procurement requests of the Department of Defense.* Americana Annual 1970, p239 *In the years covered by Dos Passos' informal memoir, The Best Times, the underdog was anybody who did not belong to various Establishments such as Big Business or the various governments that had made World War I.* Harper's 1/67, p97 **[1945, 1961] 3** conventional society. *Now this has got to go both ways, not just from me—the middle-class, balding, middle-aged Establishment-type person—but from you young folks here who feel strongly on the other side. It's all right for some of you to tell us we've got to listen. But it's got to go both ways.* Harper's 12/70, p80 *The revival of pearls, downgraded in past years for representing the tired chic of the establishment, was one of the big accessory events . . .* Americana Annual 1970, p290 **[1923, 1957]** ►In *The Changing English Language* (1968), Professor Brian Foster points out that *Establishment,* in the sense of "some well-entrenched group manipulating society from behind the scenes," had been used at various times in Great Britain long before the wide currency it attained during the 1960's. As a notable early instance

of its use he cites a letter written in 1770 in which *establishment* was used to designate the religious ruling circles of the day.

establishmentarian or **Establishmentarian,** *adj.* of, belonging to, or favoring the Establishment. *In Pine Bluff, Ark., she* [Martha Mitchell] *was an average, Middle American high school girl. In wartime Washington, or postwar Forest Hills, or more recently in establishmentarian, suburban Rye, N. Y., she was little more than part of the background . . .* Time 11/30/70, p31 **—n.** a person who belongs to or favors the Establishment. *Galbraith himself has defined the true Establishmentarians as the pivotal Republicans who are given top posts in Democratic Administrations.* Harper's 11/67, p54 **[1960** for adj.; **1964** for noun]

eta meson, an elementary particle of zero spin and neutral electric charge, with a mass of 1072 times that of an electron. *The particular experiment involves the decay of the eta meson into 3 pi mesons (one with positive charge, one with negative charge and the other neutral).* New Scientist 7/9/70, p64 **[1962,** from *eta* the 7th letter of the Greek alphabet; patterned after *pi meson,* etc.]

etch pit, any one of numerous depressions found on the planet Mars, similar to the depressions found on earth where melting and evaporating permafrost has caused the surface to cave in. *In the region of Novus Mons a smooth finely striated area covers a rough terrain to a uniform depth like a thick layer of syrup. The layer has etch pits and could be water ice—a martian glacier—since it and others similar surround a high land area.* New Scientist 2/24/72, p423 **[1963,** extended sense of the technical term used for tiny pits in the surface of metal or crystal]

ethacrynic acid (,eθə'krinik), a powerful synthetic diuretic substance, used to treat acute pulmonary edema, congestive heart failure, and other conditions. *Formula:* $C_{13}H_{12}Cl_2O_4$ *Before they undertook their research, they knew that a chemical inhibitor of sodium ion reabsorption into the kidney cell, ethacrynic acid, also inhibits calcium ion reabsorption into the kidney cell.* Science News 4/22/72, p263 **[1965,** from *ethyl*ene + *ac*etic + butyr*yl* + phe*nol*ic *acid*]

ethambutol (e'θæmbyu,tə:l), *n.* Often, **ethambutol hydrochloride.** a synthetic drug that inhibits the growth of tuberculosis bacilli. *Two new antituberculosis drugs became available: ethambutol hydrochloride, a synthetic; and rifamycin, an antibiotic. These agents, when used in conjunction with the older, established drugs . . . delayed development of bacterial resistance to those compounds.* 1971 Britannica Yearbook of Science and the Future, p224 **[1963]**

ethephon ('eθəfɑn), *n.* a synthetic chemical used to regulate growth of various plants. *Ethephon . . . was used by growers to regulate the maturity of walnuts so that they would all be ready for harvesting at the same time. The chemical was also used to induce flowering in pineapples, and to regulate the harvesting of sour and sweet cherries.* World Book Science Annual 1973, p255 **[1972,** from chloro*ethane* phos*phon*ic acid]

ethidium (i'θidi:əm or e'θidi:əm), *n.* Often, **ethidium bromide.** a chemical substance that binds differentially to adjacent bases of DNA, used in biochemical research. *Several properties of plasmids support the idea that they are ancestral to the mitochondrial genome. They are similar in size to mitochondrial DNA's, and share the property of being supercoiled circles and of being subject to elimination by acridines and ethidium.* Science 8/18/72, p580 **[1967,** from *ethyl* + *-id* + *-ium* (chemical suffixes)]

ethnic, *Especially U.S.* **—n. 1** a member of a racial, cultural, or national minority group. *All sports are now saturated with ethnics.* Harper's 4/70, p89 *Just who are you anyway? Catholics, Protestants, Jews? Are you all from central and southern Europe? Then are Poles ethnics? Would Scandinavians consider themselves ethnics?* NY Times 10/16/70, p41 **2 ethnics,** *pl.* racial, cultural, or national background. *. . . I think anyone whose parents were not intellectuals will have the same complete gap between his adult and highschool selves, even though class and ethnics don't seem to be involved.* Harper's 2/68, p6 **[1945, 1961** for def. 1; **1968** for def. 2]

ethnicism, *n.* emphasis on ethnic identity; separation into ethnic groups. *In a fever of ethnicism, Italians, Jews, Orientals, Blacks, Hispanics and others have withdrawn into themselves, causing all unmeasured social damage.* NY Times Magazine 9/24/72, p68 **[1972]** ►The now archaic meaning of this term was paganism (1600's). The related term *ethnicity* (1950's) means ethnic quality and ethnic separatism.

ethnic purity, *U.S.* racial, cultural, or national homogeneity within a neighborhood or community. *White liberals appeared to be more put off by Carter's remarks than the blacks. Says one Midwestern liberal leader: "The question is whether or not 'ethnic purity' is a code word, and if so, is it calculated to lose 5% of the black vote and pick up 12% of Wallace's support? Or was it just a blunder?"* Time 4/26/76, p16 **[1976]** ►The phrase, used by Jimmy Carter in the 1976 Presidential campaign, was probably an attempt to show sympathy for ethnic feeling, but it was widely interpreted as a veiled reference to the support of segregation in housing.

ethno-, a combining form meaning "of or relating to ethnic groups; ethnic; cultural." *Ethno-* is used to form technical terms, chiefly in anthropology. **—ethno-law,** *n.: Biennial Review of Anthropology . . . appraises recent research papers in the areas of ethno-law.* Science News 5/30/70, p541 **—ethnomycologist,** *n.: A Mexican hallucinogenic-mushroom cult . . . was discovered several years ago by the Yankee ethnomycologist R. Gordon Wasson.* New Yorker 4/25/70, p130 **—ethnopsychiatry,** *n.: As for the mission stations, Mr. Kerr read the commission a paper on ethnopsychiatry by Dr. Cawte, who had studied the Kalumburu mission station in the remote Kimberleys of Western Australia.* Times (London) 9/30/65, p11 **—ethnoscience,** *n.* and **ethnosemantics,** *n.: . . . the following topics . . . surely ought to figure in an introductory text in anthropological linguistics, if only for historical reasons: . . . paralinguistics, kinesics* [communication by gestures and facial expressions], *ethnoscience, semiotics, ethnosemantics . . .* Language 3/70, p234 See also the main entries below.

ethnoarcheology, *n.* a branch of archeology that studies the culture of a particular group. See GARBAGEOLOGY. *Ethnoarcheology . . . is another new endeavor based largely on the new paradigm, one in which archeologists in increasing numbers are doing fieldwork in living societies . . . Here the guiding question is not only how does technology reflect other subsystems but "how does it reinforce, enforce, and even determine the tasks and functions that it is involved with?" It is in pursuit of this problem that ethnoarcheology has developed.* Science 5/11/73, p617 **[1969,** from *ethno-* of cultural groups + *archeology*]

ethnocide, *n.* the willful destruction of the culture of an ethnic group, especially as a government policy of acculturation or assimilation. *I do not believe that Mr. Stolz would be particularly concerned to defend himself from inclusion in the category of those missionaries who, by the verdict of Bishop Alejo Ovelar, "are implicated in the grave crime of ethnocide," because he would see nothing wrong in the destruction of the racial identity of Indians for which he feels little but contempt.* Sunday Times Magazine (London) 1/26/75, p47 **[1972,** from *ethno-* cultural group + *-cide* a killing, patterned after *genocide* (1944)]

ethnogenesis, *n.* the formation or evolution of an ethnic group. *It is but natural that such a long-standing ethnogenesis, comprising a great variety of components, bequeathed to us an extremely rich spiritual dowry in Neolithic, Thraco-Dacian and Latin traditions.* Times (London) 12/29/72, pVIII **[1962]** **—ethnogenetic,** *adj.: One would have to study, in some quantitative way, the effects of anesthetic drugs on native-born Chinese living in China, on first- or second-generation Orientals living in Hawaii or California, on transplanted third-generation subjects in whom the ethnogenetic lines have remained unmixed, and finally on hybrids in order to determine the possible effect of intermarriage between races.* 1974 Britannica Yearbook of Science and the Future, p57

ethnopharmacology, *n.* use of traditional medicinal substances by a particular culture; folk medicine. *The recent creation of the Journal of Ethnopharmacology attests to a growing interest*

in exploring medical use of plants among primitive peoples. Science News 8/2/85, p75 **[1968]**

ethogram, *n.* a detailed description of the behavior of an animal. *This book is an expression of an emerging trend to look at human behaviour in much the same way as ethologists of the early 'thirties began to look at animal behaviour. In particular, it is a step in the process of constructing an "ethogram" of our own species; the step characterized by pinpointing, in the seemingly bewildering variety of movements that constitute "behaviour," a core of relatively simple "elements" which can be seen with fair regularity and constancy in all individuals of a species or population.* Nature 8/25/72, p471 **[1936, 1968,** from *etho-* behavior (from Greek *éthos* character) + *-gram* tracing, record]

etorphine (i:'tɔr,fi:n), *n.* a synthetic drug related to morphine. *Etorphine was first synthesised in 1963 and has been widely employed to immobilise game animals in Africa.* New Scientist and Science Journal 9/23/71, p664 **[1968,** from *et-* (perhaps from *ether*) + m*orphine*]

Etrog, *n.* an award presented annually since 1967 by the Canadian Film Awards Committee (incorporated in 1979 into the Academy of Canadian Cinema) for filmmaking achievements in Canada. The Etrog is a 12-inch gold-finished statuette mounted on a marble base. *The Etrogs will be awarded on the last evening of the festival and most Canadians can assess the judges' decisions after-the-fact when the films are generally released. Among the unseen nominees are George Kaczender's In Praise of Older Women starring Karen Black and Etrog nominees Helen Shaver (best actress), Marilyn Lightstone and Alberta Watson.* Maclean's 9/4/78, p13 **[1977,** named for Sorel *Etrog,* a Canadian sculptor who designed the statuette]

ETS (ˌiːˌtiː'es), *v.i. U.S. Military Slang.* to be discharged from service, especially on completion of one's tour of duty. *He summarized life since his discharge: "Remember you guys gave me a giant banana split the day I ETSed* [got out on schedule]? *Well, it's been downhill since then. I came back to Cleveland; stayed with my dad, who was unemployed. Man, was that ever a downer. But I figured things would pick up if I got wheels, so I got a car."* Harper's 6/72, p69 **[1970,** from abbreviation of *Estimated Time of Separation,* patterned after *ETA,* estimated time of arrival]

eucaryote or **eukaryote** (yu:'kæri:out), *n.* a cell with a visible nucleus. Compare PROCARYOTE or PROKARYOTE. *The bacteria and their close relatives the blue-green algae comprise the so-called prokaryotic group; they are all micro-organisms. The second group, the eukaryotes, includes all other types of cell, whether animal, plant, protozoal or fungal.* New Scientist 9/24/70, p624 **[1961,** from *eu-* good, true + *caryote* or *karyote* cell nucleus (from Greek *káryon* nut, kernel)]

euglenid (yu:'gli:nid), *n.* any one-celled flagellate organism related to or resembling the euglena. *Mitotic cell division was the crucial genetic step toward further evolutionary advance. There must have been numerous dead ends, variations and byways. Evidence of just such uncertain gradualism is found today among the lower eukaryotes, for example the slime molds, the yellow-green and golden-yellow algae, the euglenids, the slime-net amoebas and others.* Scientific American 8/71, p56 **[1968,** from New Latin *Euglenida* the order of organisms including the euglena and related forms]

euphenics (yu:'fi:niks), *n.* a science dealing with ways of improving the human race by technological means, such as organ transplantation, prosthetics, and genetic engineering. *We now encourage certain measures for correcting the symptoms of genetic disease (euphenics) and for reducing their frequencies (eugenics). Both measures can be extended and should be with a generous measure of discretion and good judgment, especially in the case of eugenics.* Science News Letter 1/1/66, p5 **[1963,** coined by the American geneticist Joshua Lederberg, born 1925, from *eu-* good + *phen-* appearance + *-ics,* on the analogy of *eugenics* (race improvement by hereditary control) and *euthenics* (race improvement by social and environmental control)]

euphobia (yu:'foubi:ə), *n. Humorous.* fear of good news (thought of as a prelude to bad news). See GOOD NEWS. *Euphobia—the fear of good news—was the useful word coined to describe this kind of reaction. We could hardly have got through the year without it. Never did silver linings adorn so many dark clouds. Mr. Callaghan, announcing a "booming Britain" early in the year, was worrying about slump in the very same speech.* Manchester Guardian Weekly 1/1/79, p3 [**1977**, from *eu-* good + *phobia* fear]

euphorigenic, *adj.* inducing euphoria. *R.S. Cahn . . . cast doubt on the euphorigenic activity of cannabinol.* McGraw-Hill Yearbook of Science and Technology 1971, p260 [**1971**]

Eurailpass, *n.* a tourist pass for traveling at a discount on European railroads. *All together, 104,000 Eurailpasses were sold in 1970, and travel agents expect sales to rise by 45% this year.* Time 7/19/71, p56 [**1961**, blend of *European* and *railroad pass*]

Euro-, a combining form which has gained wide currency in several specialized meanings since the 1970's, most often used in the three senses listed below. **1** of Europe, especially western Europe. —**Eurodump**, *n.: Due to national sensibilities, no one is publicly advocating a European repository or series of "Eurodumps." Individual countries will develop their own disposal strategies.* New Scientist 2/14/80, p463 —**Eurofreeze**, *n.: The Eurofreeze created wartime-like refugee conditions for those caught on impassable highways, in crowded train stations and in befogged airports.* Time 1/18/71, p20 —**Euroman**, *n.: The growing similarities between Europeans have enabled investigators for the first time to draw a sketch of the composite Euroman . . . Euroman is roughly 34, married and has 1.5 children.* Time 5/31/71, p22 —**Euro-politics**, *n.: . . . Mr. Heath himself has said virtually not a word about political Europe since he became Conservative leader: when he did talk Euro-politics he was speaking for the Macmillan administration.* Manchester Guardian Weekly 10/24/70, p10 —**Euroworld**, *n.: No other European financial centre has been able to provide that special combination of tradition, highly-developed markets and institutions, ease and speed of dealing, and predilection for international affairs which has established the City of London as the hub of the Euroworld.* Times (London) 4/13/70, pII **2** of or relating to the European money market. —**Eurocapital**, *adj.: Of all the activities of the merchant banks today, possibly the most important internationally are the Eurocurrency markets and the Eurocapital markets which the London merchant banks created.* Times (London) 4/13/70, pV2 —**Eurofranc, Euromark, Euroyen**, *n.: Even when . . . the various Euroyen, Eurofrancs, Euromarks and so forth are subtracted, there exists no reasonable external source for these funds . . .* Harper's 2/80, p48 —**Eurofund**, *n.: . . . various developments, not least the build-up of a vast, $30,000 million pool of hot, mobile and virtually-uncontrolled international Euro-funds, have strained the whole structure to its limits; and that the thing is only held together by string, tape and central bankers will-power.* Sunday Times (London) 10/5/69, p36 See also the main entries EUROBOND, EUROCURRENCY, EURODOLLAR. **3** of or relating to the European Economic Community or Common Market. —**Euro-executive**, *n.: So much for the Euro-executive's remuneration; but what of the way he has to work in order to gain it?* Times (London) 8/18/70, p21 —**Euro-farmer**, *n.: Euro-farmers sink into the currency quagmire.* Sunday Times (London) 10/5/69, p30 —**Euromerger**, *n.: Dunlop and Pirelli plan to amalgamate operating interest in the first substantial "Euromerger" since Royal Dutch Shell and Unilever were established before the war.* Manchester Guardian Weekly 3/7/70, p24 —**Eurospeech**, *n.: Naturally, a form of Euro-speech has grown up. "Convergence" means "reducing Britain's share of the Budget." "Concertation" means doing things together. "Sheepmeat" is Euro for lamb and mutton. "A common transport infrastructure process" means building the Channel tunnel.* Manchester Guardian Weekly 3/23/80, p19 See also the main entries EUROCRACY, EUROPE.

Euro, *adj.* European. *Another suggestion is that the elections could be held on the same day as the general elections, and some of the MPs elected in Westminster could also be Euro MPs with seats in Westminster, as well as being directly elected to Strasbourg.* Times (London) 3/11/77, p18 —**n.** a proposed European monetary unit. *The day of a truly unified Eurocurrency—or "Euro" as moneymen call it—is still far away.* Time 4/17/72, p82 [**1972**, abstracted from the combining form *Euro-*]

Eurobank, *n.* a European bank, especially one holding deposits from various European and other countries. *It is not only American companies which obtain finance from Eurobanks: many European concerns in the high-interest countries also have recourse to this "fountain of short-term money."* Times (London) 5/24/72, pXII *As the recycling goes forward, Eurobanks may face liquidity problems, given the current lightness of most money markets.* Forbes 9/1/74, p23 [**1966**, from *Euro-* European + *bank*]

Eurobanker, *n.* **1** a banker in a Eurobank. *A prominent newcomer is Stanislas Yassukovich, an American with French and Russian parents who in a couple of years has made the European Banking company, one of the consortium banks, one of the market's strongest newcomers. The press calls such men Eurobankers.* NY Times 12/25/76, p21 **2** a bank which is part of the Eurobank system. *You would think the currency settlement and the queues of borrowers would be good for number one Eurobanker, Germany's Deutsche Bank. Deutsche Bank will be a gainer from multinational companies extending their German business in a bigger EEC.* Sunday Times (London) 12/19/71, p42 [**1971**]

Eurobond, *n.* a bond issued by an American or other non-European corporation for sale in European countries. *Issued abroad by both U.S. and foreign companies and usually payable in dollars, Eurobonds are used to tap the $60 billion in American money that is sloshing around Europe.* Time 8/9/71, p54 [**1967**]

Eurocentric, *adj.* having the European Economic Community as its center; principally concerned with the Common Market. Compare EUROPOCENTRIC. . . . *the Federal German Chancellor, Helmut Schmidt, and the French President, Valery Giscard d'Estaing, were preparing their own Eurocentric response to what they also had begun to fear might turn into the complete collapse of the dollar as the world's reserve currency.* Manchester Guardian Weekly 11/26/78, p6 [**1963**]

Eurocheque, *n. British.* a check drawn on a bank that is a member of a group of European banks allowing their customers to write checks that will be accepted by other member banks. *Under the Eurocheque system the Briton travelling abroad can get up to the equivalent of £30 in cash from a Continental bank.* Daily Telegraph (London) 11/13/76, p21 [**1968**]

Euroclear, *n.* the clearing house for transactions of Eurobanks. *Euroclear is based in Brussels and already has some 164 members.* Times (London) 6/1/70, p22 [**1970**]

Eurocommunism, *n.* a form of Communism adopted by some Western European Communist parties that emphasizes working within the existing democratic political systems to achieve social change. *The word "Eurocommunism" . . . was coined by a Yugoslav named Franj Barberi, who invented the phrase in one of his articles in Milan's Il Giornale.* NY Times 10/10/77, p27 *Eurocommunism is a mouthful of a word which both the Soviet Union and the United States are finding difficult to swallow. It is an in-word, invented to describe a new version of Marxism which preaches obedience to the Western law of the ballot box and independence from Moscow.* Maclean's 7/25/77, p37 [**1976**, from *Euro-* European + *communism*] —**Eurocommunist**, *n., adj.: Santiago Carrillo's 218-page Eurocommunism and the State is the strongest written argument for Eurocommunism yet made by one of its leading proponents. The book sounds all the familiar Eurocommunist themes: independence from Moscow, democratic plurality, universal suffrage, respect for human rights.* Time 7/11/77, p32

Eurocracy, *n.* the officials or administrators of the European Economic Community or Common Market. *The average Briton is still afraid of the EEC's [European Economic Community's] high food prices and fearful of losing British sovereignty to the Brussels-based Eurocracy.* Time 7/5/71, p19 [**1971**, derived from the earlier (1961) term *Eurocrat* (a Common Market official), formed on the analogy of *bureaucrat, bureaucracy*]

Eurocratic, *adj.* of or relating to the administration of the European Economic Community or Common Market. *Britain could accelerate this process, to the security of all. But if under Eurocratic fostering it goes ahead with Britain outside instead of inside, Britain's prospects and position will be prejudiced by 1980, and probably even by 1975.* Times (London) 6/19/70, p11 **[1970]**

Eurocredit, *n.* financial credit in the Eurobank system. *Until now the Eurocredit market has been completely uncontrolled, and recently some leading German banks have been urging cautious lending policies on market participants to keep it this way.* Times (London) 3/4/76, p18 **[1976]**

Eurocurrency, *n.* currency of various countries deposited in European banks and used in the European money market. Also called EUROMONEY. *Last week a committee headed by Luxembourg's Prime Minister, Pierre Werner, handed in a report suggesting how the Common Market countries can create a new "Eurocurrency" that would acquire some of the privileges and powers of the dollar.* Time 10/26/70, p108 **[1963]**

Eurodollar, *n.* Eurocurrency in dollars. . . . *the Eurodollar* [is] *a U.S. currency that never goes home, because it is barred from the United States.* NY Times 7/29/70, p38 **[1960]**

Euromoney, *n.* another name for EUROCURRENCY. *Today the defence possibilities in line with the market are much more favourable owing to the attraction of the Euromoney market which has since grown enormously.* Times (London) 6/24/70, p29 **[1970]**

Euronet, *n.* a scientific and technical data communications network linked by computers, operated by the European Economic Community. *The international aspect is important because data networks will ultimately transcend all national boundaries. Euronet, the EEC packet-switched network, is due to start early next year and several similar systems are already operating in the US to which it and existing European systems will be connected.* New Scientist 6/29/78, p918 **[1976,** from *Euro-* European + *network*]

Europarliament, *n.* variant of EUROPEAN PARLIAMENT. *Although Sir Peter did not actually introduce question time to the Euro-parliament, as is sometimes claimed, he and his fellow delegates from Britain injected it with a liveliness and vigour it had not known before. A competent linguist, he impressed his fellow Europeans with his energy and enthusiasm for the European cause.* Economist 4/23/77, p62 **[1962]**

Europarliamentarian, *n.* a member of the European Parliament. *Then in Strasbourg, where Reagan is to address the European Parliament, Deaver skipped an appointment with Europarliamentarians so that he could stroll about town.* Newsweek 3/11/85, p19 **[1978]**

Europarliamentary, *adj.* of or having to do with the European Parliament. *The terrorist told interrogators that he had first wanted to kill the "king of England" as well as the President of the European Parliament. He said he changed his mind after discovering that Britain was ruled by Queen Elizabeth II and the Europarliamentary President was a woman, Simone Veil. Agca told police that "as a Turk and a Muslim," he would not kill a woman.* Time 6/1/81, p34 **[1979]**

Europatent, *n.* a patent for inventions, valid in all or most European countries. *The first convention provides for a so-called Europatent. The Europatent scheme will be open to all European countries and a single granted Europatent will in many respects function effectively as a national patent in each of the separate European countries belonging to the convention (around 20 so far). Thus any one Europatent will for most practical purposes serve as some 20 separate national patents.* Times (London) 6/2/72, p21 **[1962]**

Europe, European, Europeanism, Europeanist. This group of terms gained currency (especially in Great Britain) in specific reference to the European Economic Community, better known as the Common Market. To join *Europe* means to gain

entry into the Common Market; a *European* is one who favors such a move; *Europeanism* is either the advocacy of or the movement supporting such a move; and *Europeanist* means tending toward or supporting Europeanism. *Mr Shore has long been sceptical about the advantages of joining Europe, and Mr Hattersley is a passionate and long-standing European.* Manchester Guardian Weekly 4/4/70, p8 *The highly uncertain future if Britain does not go into Europe has not yet been adequately explained or understood, according to some anxious pro-Europeans.* New Yorker 7/3/71, p64 *We have insisted for too long on maintaining the status quo in NATO, ignoring the powerful trend toward Europeanism and the towering strength of the European Common Market.* Saturday Review 7/30/66, p22 *Men under the age of 50 are more likely to be Europeanist than men over 50.* Times (London) 6/30/70, p6 *The Europeanists note that the nations of Western Europe contain 320 million people with a spending power of $385 billion, exports of $96 billion and imports of $102 billion.* Time 5/31/71, p22 **[1957]**

European Monetary System, a monetary system to stabilize exchange rates of the currencies of member countries in the European Economic Community. *European Community governments are close to agreement on a package of measures to strengthen the European Monetary System, and today the European Commission intends to finalise formal proposals to implement them. The measures, which won the approval of nine member states at a meeting of the Community's monetary committee last week, fall short of the significant step towards monetary union.* Financial Times 11/28/84, p1 **[1978]**

European Parliament, the popular name of the Assembly of the European Community, the legislative and advisory branch of the European Economic Community. Since 1979 it has consisted of 410 deputies elected by the voters of member nations. See MEP. *British Ministers are becoming concerned at the increasing demands of the European Parliament to have more influence over Common Market decisions. Leaders of the European Parliament have been applying more pressure recently on the EEC Council of Ministers to consult them over a wide range of policy questions.* Manchester Guardian Weekly 11/5/78, p4 *The European parliament . . . will advise the European Commission and Council of Ministers, the two administrative bodies of the Common Market, formally known as the European Economic Community.* Sunday News (New York) 6/10/79, p8 **[1961]**

Europlug, *n.* an electric plug with prongs designed to fit any of the different types of sockets used in European countries. *From the outset of discussions, the Dutch wanted to keep . . . the Euro-plug, which the British bitterly opposed on safety grounds. It is possible to insert the Euro-plug into both round and square pin UK sockets between the Earth and live holes, reversing polarity and making the body of any connected appliance live.* New Scientist 7/8/76, p77 **[1965]**

europocentric or **Europocentric**, *adj.* having Europe as its center; principally concerned with Europe or Europeans. Compare EUROCENTRIC. *How far Marx's nineteenth century europocentric vision is totally applicable to the second half of the twentieth century is debatable.* New Scientist 2/27/69, p473 *He* [a historian] *knows that for half a millennium the nations of Western Europe were destined to predominate. Thus, it is natural for him to have a Europocentric view of the modern world, to believe that non-Western cultures are below par if not permanently inferior.* Saturday Review 9/3/66, p11 **[1934, 1958]**

Europort, *n.* a European port serving as a major import and export harbor, especially for the Common-Market countries. *Rotterdam Europort is prepared to deepen its channel to 80 ft. to take 500,000-ton tankers, Franz Posthuma, managing director of the port, said in a paper read in London last night.* Times (London) 1/9/68, p18 **[1968,** translation of Dutch *Europoort*]

eusocial (yu:'souʃəl), *adj.* completely or perfectly social. *It is both intrinsically interesting and particularly well written, although lovers of the old, romantic, anthropomorphic style will be both shocked and disappointed to find that for Wilson the honeybee is "just one more eusocial apoid."* Natural History

2/72, p87 [**1972**, from *eu-* good, true, truly + *social*] —**eusociality**, *n.: There are three levels of increasingly complex behavior on the way to eusociality. The lowest level, communal behavior, is characterized by an aggregation of female insects, all belonging to the same generation; once the females have aggregated they build a communal nest for their young.* Scientific American 3/76, p101

euthanasia, *n.* ▶The development of artificial means to keep dying patients alive by drugs, organ transplants, and respirators has led to a renewed interest in euthanasia, a term traditionally defined as painlessly putting to death the incurably and painfully diseased. This definition has been criticized by those who hold that euthanasia no longer means "putting to death painlessly" but rather "letting die with dignity."

The new definition is based on the distinction between AC-TIVE (or POSITIVE) EUTHANASIA, where treatment is *administered* to hasten death, and PASSIVE (or NEGATIVE) EUTHANASIA, in which treatment is *withheld* to hasten death. Both forms are illegal in most countries, but while RIGHT-TO-DIE groups may condemn active euthanasia or "mercy killing" (a popular term since the 1930's), most support or advocate passive euthanasia on the grounds that prolonging life in the terminal stage of incurable illness disregards the rights or will of the patient (see LIVING WILL, INFORMED CONSENT), causes needless deterioration, dependence, and pain, and amounts to a prolongation of dying rather than of life.

euthanize (ˈyu:θəˌnaiz), *v.t.* to put to death painlessly; perform euthanasia on. *At its five New York shelters—one in each of the five boroughs—the A.S.P.C.A. will be able only to find adoptive homes for 10 per cent of the animals that will be brought in next year. The rest will be "euthanized."* NY Times 12/29/78, pB5 [**1969**, from *euthanasia* + *-ize*]

eutrophicate (yu:ˈtrɑfəˌkeit), *v.i.* (of streams, lakes, etc.) to be or become polluted by the introduction of phosphates, nitrates, and other substances that promote growth of algae. *Even in the short run eutrophicating influences can greatly damage aquatic ecosystems.* Science News Yearbook 1970, p297 . . . *the increased growth of vegetation in the water and the proliferation of algae in huge blotches of green slime . . . causes lakes to eutrophicate, or age, before their time.* NY Times 11/15/70, pD12 [**1966**, back formation from EUTROPHICATION]

eutrophication (ˌyu:trəfəˈkeiʃən), *n.* the pollution of streams, lakes, and other bodies of water by phosphates, nitrates, and other substances that cause rapid growth of algae, which deplete the water of oxygen. See also DYSTROPHICATION. *Eutrophication literally means "nourishing well," but in current usage it refers to the inadvertent nourishing of algae in lakes to the detriment of other living things.* Scientific American 11/70, p46 *Scientists agree, however, that detergent phosphates are not the only cause of the accelerated eutrophication. Also implicated are the phosphates from human wastes and from agricultural fertilizer run-off, as well as nitrates and organic compounds that end up in the water.* World Book Science Annual 1972, p285 [**1964**, originally (1940's) used to describe a natural chemical enrichment process in lakes; from Greek *eútrophos* enriched, thriving]

eutrophied (ˈyu:trəfi:d), *adj.* eutrophicated; polluted. *A group of University of Wisconsin scientists tried using alum applied directly to the surface of the eutrophied Horseshoe Lake in eastern Wisconsin.* Science News 5/29/71, p370 [**1971**, from *eutrophy*, *n.*, well-nourished condition (in English in this sense since the 1700's) + *-ed* (adjective suffix), apparently with influence of *atrophied*]

EVA, abbreviation of *extravehicular activity* (activity outside a space vehicle). *The crew expected therefore to find a lot of fine-grained material but after the first seven hours stay (EVA) outside the lunar module, Schmitt could only report seeing coarse grained material similar to mare basalts but with a high percentage of plagioclase.* Science News 12/16/72, p388 [**1965**]

evapotranspire *v.t.* to cause the loss of (water) from soil by both evaporation and transpiration. *Water-use efficiency can be expressed in a variety of ways, such as tons of hay or bushels of potatoes per acre-inch of water evapotranspired, crates of marketable lettuce per acre-foot of water, or as a weight ratio, kilogram per kilogram.* McGraw-Hill Yearbook of Science and Technology 1967, p165 [**1967**, back formation from *evapotranspiration* (OEDS 1948) the loss of water from soil by evaporation and transpiration]

événement (eivenˈmã), *n. French.* event; incident (in the sense of a major social and political development). *Clouds of acrid tear gas hung over the chestnut trees of Left Bank boulevards, just as they had during the shattering* événements *of May 1968 that tore France apart and led directly to the fall of Charles de Gaulle.* Time 6/8/70, p37 *During the evenements of May and June, 1968, the red flag of communism and the black flag of anarchism fluttered side by side on the occupied Theatre de l'Odeon. Inside, of course, the whole intelligentsia of Paris listened in on the discussions by day and by night.* Manchester Guardian Weekly 8/7/71, p18 [**1968**] ▶This word, first recorded in 1660, became obsolete after the 1670's and was reborrowed as a result of the events of 1968 in France referred to in the quotations, since this is the term used by the French for this and other happenings of a violent and controversial character. The attraction of the word is that in a partisan situation it is neutral, like the Irish "troubles."

event, *n.* **1** *Nuclear Physics.* the production of a nuclear particle by causing other particles to collide. *After analyzing thousands of collisions researchers came up with about 200 "events" in which charmed particles seem to have been produced.* Maclean's 1/10/77, p48 **2** an accidental failure or breakdown, especially in a nuclear reactor or power plant. See BLOWDOWN, EXCURSION, MELTDOWN. *That same month, there was another nuclear event. It happened at the Hanford reactor, in Richland, Washington. This nuclear plant spewed 60,000 gallons of radioactive water into the Columbia River, forcing the reactor to shut down. It happened accidentally—although the nuclear industry would probably prefer to say it happened eventfully.* Esquire 5/22/79, p80 [**1962** for def. 1; **1968** for def. 2]

event horizon, *Astronomy.* the boundary of a black hole. *If we drop things radially into a black hole we shall never quite see them penetrate the event horizon; they will endlessly spiral around it at a rate given by the angular velocity of the black hole. Someone falling in however would pass through the event horizon in what to him would be a perfectly finite time.* New Scientist 1/8/76, p54 [**1969**]

eventing, *n. Especially British.* **1** equestrian competition including dressage, cross-country riding, and show jumping, usually lasting three days. *Eventing is a comparatively new sport, but in 1976 it is estimated that 250,000 people went to the Badminton Horse Trials, and the number of people watching show jumping on television is second only to soccer.* Times (London) 11/19/76, p14 **2** Passing into verb: *Interviewer: Would you like to cook Captain Phillips's breakfast before he goes off to work, for example?*

Anne: I can manage that. It's easy. Especially when he's eventing, because he's not going to get more than a cup of coffee. Listener 11/15/73, p661 [**1965**, from *event* + *-ing* action or process connected with] —**eventer**, *n.: The only rider to be hurt was Sarah Glyn, a three-day eventer and the owner and rider of The-Wheeler-Dealer. She broke her collarbone in a fall from another horse during the dressage.* Times (London) 4/9/77, p5

event tree, a diagram with labeled branches designed to show all the possible consequences of a particular event, especially an accident or failure in a system. Compare FAULT TREE. *Event tree for pipe failure. An event tree can be constructed showing the initial failure of a pipe break and showing all possible choices of success (up) and failure (down) of the functions shown.* McGraw-Hill Yearbook of Science and Technology 1976, p61 *An "event tree" defines an initial failure somewhere within a system. It then traces, like a genealogy—hence the name "tree"—the consequences of that failure down through related equipments and procedures.* Encyclopedia Science Supplement (Grolier) 1977-1978, p181 [**1976**]

Everywoman, *n.* a typical woman; the prototype of womanhood. *A political wife, in a sense, is a contradiction in terms . . . She must be the model of purity and probity at home, but she must be Everywoman outside, with a ready smile and a cheerful word for all the importuning bores on the campaign trail.* Time 10/7/74, p15 [**1968**, patterned after *Everyman* interpreted as the typical man, after the name of the hero of an English morality play of the early 1500's]

evoked potential, the electrical response arising from the cortex of the brain upon stimulation of a sense organ. *With human subjects it is possible to measure these signals by recording evoked potentials: small changes in the electrical properties of the scalp produced as a result of activity of the brain. Because they are objective indicators of certain brain functions evoked potentials have clinical applications.* Scientific American 10/73, p99 [**1968**]

EW, abbreviation of ELECTRONIC WARFARE. *A whole range of EW equipment has been developed to gather and coordinate as much data as possible about the adversary's radar (land, sea, air, surveillance, weapon control, navigation, etc.), command and control, and communication systems, a form of EW known as Elint (electronic intelligence).* New Scientist 5/10/73, p351 [**1972**]

exa-, a prefix meaning one quintillion (10^{18}) of any standard unit in the international meter-kilogram-second system of measurements. Compare PETA-. *One discovery was the development of an analytical technique to identify the presence or absence of a single atom among 10 exa—that is, 10 quintillion (10,000,000,000,000,000,000)—other atoms . . .* Encyclopedia Science Supplement (Grolier) 1977-1978, p299 [**1976**, perhaps alteration of *exo-* outer, from Greek *exō-* out of, outside]

exacta, *n. U.S.* (in horse racing) a method of betting in which the bettor picks the horses to win and to place in the exact order of the finish. Also called PERFECTA. *Since exacta wagering calls for the bettor to pick the precise 1, 2 finish (unlike a quiniela gambling, in which 1, 2 or 2, 1 do not matter) two payoffs were in order to the holders of winning ninth-race exacta tickets.* NY Times 1/31/68, p34 [**1964**, from American Spanish, short for *quiniela exacta* exact quiniela (*quiniela*, a bet on the first two finishers of a race in any order)]

excess, *v.t. U.S.* to suspend the assignment of (a public school teacher or other civil servant) because a particular kind of job has been eliminated or declared overstaffed. Excessed employees usually continue on the payroll until they are dismissed. *According to a spokesman for the Board of Education, 243 supervisors were "excessed" last November and transferred out of their districts, although subsidized funds enabled some of them to return. The spokesman said that 165 of the 243 were due to be laid off next month unless additional funds were found.* NY Times 1/20/76, p28 [**1976**, verb use (OED 1888) of noun and adjective (OED) *a*1400]

excimer ('eksəmər), *n.* a substance (dimer) formed by the union of atoms in an excited state. *A new form of laser that uses two gases has been developed at the Lawrence Livermore Laboratory in California. It is called a two-excimer laser. The term excimer means that atoms that are energetically excited come together and form molecules, and the molecules then emit the laser light. "Two excimer" means that molecules of two different elements are involved.* Science News 6/16/73, p391 [**1961**, from *excit*ed "raised to a higher level of energy" + di*mer*; stress and articulation modeled on *polymer*]

exciplex ('eksə,pleks), *n.* a complex or aggregate of excited states produced in a dye laser. *The key to such laser tunability lies in a reversible chemical reaction that forms the 'exciplex', or excited state complex . . . an exciplex reaction—unlike a normal chemical reaction—takes place only when the molecules of the dye are in an electronically excited state, just before the emission of light. The molecules are excited by directing light pulses into the dye solution (pumping). Once excited, the molecules of the dye react with a chemical present in the solution, and another form of the dye is created. This is the excited state complex, or exciplex.* Science Journal 11/70, p17 [**1966**]

excisionase (ek'si:zə,neis), *n.* a viral enzyme that promotes the excision of the DNA of the virus from the genetic material of the bacterial host cell. Compare RESTRICTION ENZYME. *Similar studies of the reverse process—the excision of viral DNA from the bacterial chromosome . . . have shown that excision requires in addition to integrase the product of a second viral gene (called excisionase). The virus thus introduces into the host cell enzymatic machinery for cutting and joining the viral and host DNA at specific sites to bring about the insertion and excision of the provirus.* Scientific American 12/76, p111 [**1976**, from *excision* + *-ase*, a suffix meaning enzyme]

excision repair, the removal of damaged or mutant base sequences in a molecule of DNA and their replacement by correct ones. Compare DARK REPAIR, RECOMBINATIONAL REPAIR. *Another method of repair occurs in the dark and in cells containing certain repair enzymes. In this process, known as excision repair, a damaged strand on the DNA duplex is removed and replaced by undamaged DNA replicated from the other strand of the duplex.* Britannica Book of the Year 1975, p444 [**1971**]

excitonic, *adj.* of or involving excitons (excited electrons in a crystal structure). *There is a variety of excitonic processes, however, that give rise to electrical conductivity.* McGraw-Hill Yearbook of Science and Technology 1968, p161 *In most cases excitonic fluorescence is quite efficient: In the substance anthracene, for example, 95 percent of the impinging light is reradiated as fluorescent light.* Science News 4/19/69, p378 [**1958**, from *exciton* (OEDS 1936) + *-ic*]

excitonics, *n.* the study of excitons (excited electrons in a crystal structure). *The recent developments in excitonics could have an important bearing on the study of energy-transfer mechanisms such as those involved in photosynthesis by living plants.* Scientific American 5/69, p56 [**1969**]

exclusionary rule, a rule established by the U.S. Supreme Court that evidence obtained by methods which violate the constitutional rights of the accused cannot be introduced in the trial of a criminal case. *Especially galling are those who escape because of legal rules: drug pushers caught dirty but without proper search warrant, Mafiosi discovered through an illegal wiretap, thugs whose car was stopped by cops acting without probable cause. In such cases, the catchall—or lose-all—complication is the exclusionary rule, which provides that evidence seized illegally may not be used in court.* Time 3/8/76, p44 *The primary purpose of the exclusionary rule is to deter police misbehavior. Without the rule, the U.S. Supreme Court has held, lawmen could violate—with impunity—citizens' Fourth Amendment rights to be free of unreasonable searches and seizures. The rule against illegally obtained evidence has applied in Federal courts since 1914, and in 1961, the Court extended it to the states. The decision outraged law-enforcement officials, but it did force them to train policemen in the niceties of constitutional rights.* Newsweek 6/4/79, p86 [**1959**] ► Also known in legal circles as the *Weeks Doctrine* (after the case of *Weeks v. the U.S.*, 1914) or the *Suppression Doctrine*.

exclusive economic zone, the area of coastal waters and their undersea beds whose fishing and mineral resources a country claims exclusive rights to exploit or license others to make use of. *Abbreviation:* EEZ. Also shortened to ECONOMIC ZONE. *Another unresolved issue is an exclusive economic zone stretching from the new 12-mile limit of the territorial sea, an area where each coastal nation has full jurisdiction, to a limit of 200 or more miles if the continental shelf is particularly broad. Coastal countries would enjoy sovereign rights to prospect and exploit such natural resources as fisheries and off-shore oil and gas fields in their exclusive economic zones.* NY Times 8/1/76, p19 [**1975**]

excursion, *n.* an uncontrolled chain reaction in a nuclear reactor that uses high-energy neutrons to produce fissionable material (fast-breeder reactor). Compare MELTDOWN. *If the temperature of the core rose and gas bubbles of sodium were to form in the coolant, less neutrons would be captured by the sodium than before, thus the reaction would tend to increase. This can lead to the hypothetical "excursion."* New Scientist

12/9/76, p574 [**1963**, extended sense of the original meaning "escape from confinement" (OED 1579)]

executive clemency, reduction in the penalty of a convicted criminal by the chief executive of a government, such as the President of the United States or the governor of a State. *Executive clemency is not a pardon. Mr. Nixon also denied . . . that he had offered executive clemency to McCord in exchange for his silence.* Manchester Guardian Weekly 5/26/73, p3 *There is no practical difference between commutation of sentence and Executive clemency.* Time 6/17/74, p3 [**1973**]

executive privilege, *U.S.* the privilege claimed for the executive branch of the U.S. government by the President of withholding information from the legislative and judicial branches. *Obviously executive privilege is essential to protect the inner working of Government. Obviously also it is liable to grave abuse. A decade ago President Kennedy tried to end the practice by which lesser officials in the executive branch assumed this authority on their own cognizance. "Executive privilege," he wrote Representative Moss in 1962, "can be invoked only by the President and will not be used without specific Presidential approval." NY Times Magazine 2/6/72, p50 Sparked by the Pentagon Papers affair, charged of excessive secrecy, of improperly concealing information, were leveled at the executive branch. In response, administration spokesmen argued that withholding information deemed by the President or his delegates not in the public interest was a proper exercise of executive privilege, a right intrinsic in the doctrine of separation of powers.* Americana Annual 1972, p185 *Attorney General Richard G. Kleindienst had asserted unlimited executive privilege for all two and a half million employees of the executive branch, and had just told the senators that if they had any objections they could impeach the President.* New Yorker 4/28/73, p30

▶Although the concept of executive privilege goes back to the very beginnings of American Constitutional history, the term itself first appeared in the 1940's and did not attain widespread currency until the 1970's. According to the American Constitutional expert, Raoul Berger, "The very words 'executive privilege' were conjoined only yesterday, in 1958" (Raoul Berger, *Executive Privilege: A Constitutional Myth*, 1974, p 1). However, Fred R. Shapiro, of the New York School of Law (in "A Computer Search for the Origin of *Executive Privilege*," *American Speech* 59, 1, 1984, p 60), traced the term back to August, 1940, when it occurred once in a U.S. Court of Appeals opinion in *Glass v. Ickes*. In this case, Glass contended that Cabinet Secretary Harold Ickes was liable for defamation and that his presumed immunity by virtue of his office did not apply to communications to the general public. The Court's opinion differed: *No such limitation is justified by the language of the Supreme Court in the Vilas case nor has this court recognized such a distinction. On the contrary, we have previously held a communication, released generally to the press, within this executive privilege.* (*Federal Reporter, Second Series*, vol. 117, p 277).

The words "executive" and "privilege" first appeared together in a relevant context (though not in combination) in a speech made in the Senate by Charles Pinckney (1757-1824), the South Carolina delegate to the Constitutional Convention of 1787: *"No privilege of this kind was intended for your executive, nor any except that which I have mentioned for your legislature."* See also FREEDOM OF INFORMATION.

Exercycle, *n.* a trademark for a stationary bicycle used for exercising indoors. Also popularly spelled **exercycle**. *Fischer passed part of every day swimming, playing tennis, lifting weights, skipping rope, riding an Exercycle, doing sit-ups and pummeling a 300-lb. bag. "You gotta stay in shape," he says, "or it's all over."* Time 7/31/72, p34 *She [Isabel Perón] eats sparingly, pedals an exercycle, watches TV, . . . and plays canasta with a maid.* Daily News (New York) 4/16/79, p7 [**1967**, blend of *exercise* and *cycle* bicycle]

exfiltrate, *v.i., v.t. U.S. Military Slang.* to get out of a hostile area stealthily or unnoticeably; slip out through the enemy lines. *During the night, the Vietcong remnants tried to "exfiltrate" (American jargon for to slip out), but ran up against the blocking force and were turned back after an exchange of fire.*

Times (London) 6/19/68, p4 *. . . Corporal Courcey stays with the doomed native garrison instead of being exfiltrated (Army jargon for decamping) with the other Americans.* Sunday Times (London) 1/7/68, p39 [**1968**, from *ex-* out + in*filtrate*]

exfiltration, *n. U.S. Military Slang.* a slipping out of a hostile area. *"Why don't you pick the best area for exfiltration?" the ground commander suggested. "I really like that little knoll over to the west where you can see the exfiltration trails in the woods there," Captain Reese said.* New Yorker 3/16/68, p83 [**1968**]

exit poll, a poll taken of voters as they leave the voting place. *Some of the networks' "exit-polls" on primary days showed that Democrats favored Kennedy on the questions of who would handle the economy better and who was a better leader, but that when it came to the question of "honesty" or "trust," they favored Carter.* New Yorker 6/23/80, p56 [**1976**]

exit tax, a tax paid by citizens with state-subsidized academic training who wish to emigrate from certain Communist countries of eastern Europe. *. . . before she could leave [Czechoslovakia] she still had to pay an "exit tax" of three hundred crowns at the state bank.* New Yorker 7/23/79, p80 [**1972**]

Exner's center. See the quotation for the meaning. *Exner's center is a motor association area for the part of the primary motor cortex which controls the hand and thus it is part of the structures underlying writing.* McGraw-Hill Yearbook of Science and Technology 1972, p391 [**1970**, named after Siegmund Exner, 1846-1926, an Austrian physiologist, who first described Exner's plexus, the layer of nerve fibers in this area of the brain]

exoatmosphere, *n.* the outermost region of the earth's atmosphere. *The larger Spartan's [an antiballistic missile] job would be to provide an "area defense" by engaging enemy warheads in the exo-atmosphere—roughly 300,000 ft. up.* New Scientist 6/29/67, p772 [**1967**, possibly a back formation from *exoatmospheric*]

exoatmospheric, *adj.* of the exoatmosphere; designed for the exoatmosphere. *. . . some experts say the Moscow part of the Soviet missile defense system is based upon what is called an "exoatmospheric" rocket, or a defensive missile designed to intercept incoming missiles above the atmosphere.* NY Times 2/5/67, p67 [**1966**]

exobiologist, *n.* a specialist in exobiology. *Even Ponnamperuma, a highly respected exobiologist (extraterrestrial biology) at NASA's Ames Research Center in California, admits that only a thumbprint on a beaker could introduce amino acids into a meteorite sample.* Time 12/14/70, p67 [**1962**]

exobiology, *n.* the study of life outside the earth. *As man enters the second decade of the Space Age, exobiology—that branch of planetary science concerned with the search for extraterrestrial life—will prove itself or be forgotten. It will not always be a science in search of a subject.* 1970 Britannica Yearbook of Science and the Future, p193 [**1960**]

Exocet ('eksə,set), *n.* a French-built missile with a heat-seeking radar guidance system, used as an air-to-surface or surface-to-surface weapon, chiefly against ships. *The Exocet . . ., with a range of about 30 to 40 miles, is designed to skim close to the water's surface after being launched far from its target.* NY Times 6/5/84, pA4 [**1970**, from French, from *exocet* flying fish]

exocytosis, *n.* a process by which cellular substances active in the transmission of impulses are released outside the nerve cells. *From ultrastructural and biochemical studies, it now seems certain that the tiny bag-like structures, or vesicles, seen in nerve endings, act as storage sites for transmitter substances. At the moment, interest centres around the mechanisms by which their contents are released into the extracellular space. The most plausible model is that of "exocytosis", in which the membrane of the storage granule fuses with the membrane of the cell, and the secretory products are lost through an opening in the fused membranes.* New Scientist 6/4/70, p464 [**1963**, from *exo-* outside + *cyto-* cell + *-osis* process or condition]

exoelectron, *n.* an electron emitted from a surface atom of a metal, especially under conditions associated with stress. *Since such processes are exothermal, or heat-emitting, Kramer called the electrons exoelectrons. Although his explanation for the mechanism of electron emission is not accepted today (for example, the exoelectron emission in solidification is believed to be associated with changes in volume and the accompanying breakup of surface layers), the term exoelectron has survived.* Scientific American 1/77, p76 [**1963**, from *exo-* outer + *electron;* but see quotation for origin of term]

exohormone, *n.* a hormonal secretion by an organism which affects the olfactory organ of another organism so as to alter its behavior in a certain way. Compare PHEROMONE. *If a goat's kid is taken away for only two hours from birth, the mother will reject it when it is returned. They probably become conditioned to its smell, or exohormones, at this time.* Science Journal 1/68, p31 [**1968**]

exon, *n.* a segment of DNA that specifies the genetic code for a protein, as distinguished from an intervening sequence (INTRON). *In 1979, NIH* [National Institutes of Health] *molecular biologists Dean H. Hamer and Philip Leder chemically removed the introns from the DNA of a tumor virus called SV40, which infects both monkey and human cells. They cut the DNA into introns and exons with restriction enzymes, then used a linking enzyme to join the exon pieces in the right order.* World Book Science Annual 1981, p207 [**1979**, from *ex-* outer, outside + *-on,* unit of genetic material]

exonuclease (ˌeksou'nu:kliːˌeis), *n.* an enzyme that breaks up the strands of DNA which had been segmented by the enzyme endonuclease. *A circular structure for DNA was first described in 1962 . . . This conclusion was based on experiments showing the resistance of this viral DNA to digestion by exonuclease, enzymes which degrade DNA starting only at free ends of DNA molecules.* Science Journal 8/69, p46 [**1969**, from *exo-* outer + *nuclease* an enzyme that hydrolyzes nucleic acid]

exonumia, *n.* the study and collection of items other than coins and paper currency, such as tokens, medals, and coupons. *It is possible, but not likely, that rare pieces will turn up in junk boxes. It is more likely that the rare ones, such as the illustrated token from North Jellico, Tenn., will have to be purchased from one of a handful of dealers who specialize in exonumia.* NY Times 11/27/66, pB26 [**1966**, from *exo-* + *-numia,* extracted from *numismatics*]

exonym ('eksəˌnim), *n.* any of the names given in different countries or languages to the same geographical feature or area (for example, the river *Vistula* in English, a transfer from Latin, has the exonyms *Wisła* in Polish, *Visla* in Russian, and *Weichsel* in German). *The crusade against exonyms will continue in New York until the next conference in five years time of the United Nations group of experts on geographical names.* Times (London) 6/1/72, p4 [**1972**, from *exo-* outside + *topo*nym place name]

exorcism, *n.* ►The ancient practice of expelling evil spirits by conjurations and religious or magical ceremonies has been revived in recent years, especially among CHARISMATICS of the NEO-PENTECOSTAL movement. Many of the churches, disliking the term exorcism, prefer to use the word DELIVERANCE in its place. The popularity of exorcism has grown in proportion to the increasing interest in the occult and the appearance of many books and films dealing with the existence of demons. Probably the most widely read of these books was *The Exorcist* (1971), a novel by William Peter Blatty about a teen-age girl possessed by a demon; an extremely successful motion picture based on it was released in 1973.

exotic, *adj. Nuclear Physics.* highly unstable and hard to capture. *The newer exotic particles—K's* [K mesons], *sigmas and antiprotons—also belong to both* [electromagnetic and strong nuclear] *forces, and they will be especially useful in investigating the outer layers of the nucleus.* Science News 11/14/70, p385 [**1970**]

expanded cinema, another name for INTERMEDIA. *Expanded cinema, sometimes called intermedia, the recent experiments in combining film with live actors and musicians, will be the* subject of five of the 27 events, including two forums and a demonstration. NY Times 9/7/66, p51 [**1966**]

expansion, *n. U.S. and Canadian.* Often used attributively in such phrases as **expansion club** and **expansion pool** in referring to a sports team formed by buying a franchise from a professional league that expands and allows the new team to draft players from established teams in the league. **—expansion city:** *Even ice hockey has been absorbed. Seven of the eight expansion cities are American. Canadians cannot buy a franchise. Consequently, many Canadian hockey players are living rather ingrown expatriate lives in Oakland and L.A.* Harper's 7/71, p30 **—expansion club:** *The Philadelphia Flyers, 1974 Stanley Cup winners, believe in the violent approach to the game. Although a relatively young team, they became the first of the expansion clubs to win the championship last year.* NY Times Book Review 3/23/75, p36 **—expansion draft:** *Each NBA team froze seven players on its roster and Klein was then allowed to select two of the remaining men from each team in a special expansion draft.* Britannica Book of the Year 1967, p140 **—expansion pool:** *The new look in the league came when six additional franchises were created in an expansion pool. The six clubs were lumped together in the newly formed Western Division, and the six existing clubs played in the Eastern Division.* 1969 Collier's Encyclopedia Year Book, p523 **—expansion team:** *Expansion teams, such as the Caps and the Kansas City Scouts (who also changed coaches last month after more than a dozen straight losses), are typically launched with fourth-class flotsam—arthritic veterans and immature, unskilled rookies.* Maclean's 2/9/76, p45 [**1966**]

expert system, a computer program that incorporates the knowledge and reasoning of an expert in a specialized field, such as an area of medicine or finance. *Among the best-known expert systems are programs that contain medical information that can help doctors diagnose illnesses.* World Book Science Annual 1987, p351 [**1972**]

expletive deleted, *U.S.* an expression indicating the omission from print of a vulgar or obscene word or phrase. *3-foot 10-inch Hervé Villechaize plays a manservant in "The Man with the Golden Gun." On his professional résumé, Villechaize notes firmly: "I am not available for Santa's helper, baby New Year, elves or other (expletive deleted) like that."* Newsweek 9/2/74, p44 *To an outsider to the field of astronomy, the range of reactions to the term "Janus," listed in many references as the 10th moon of Saturn, is often a bit of shock. Responses range from acceptance to tolerant smiles to expletive deleted.* Science News 1/29/77, p69 [**1974**]

Expo, *n.* **1** a large national or international exposition. *There was some talk at first that Fairmount Park, the site of the Philadelphia Centennial Exposition of 1876, be used for the Bicentennial Expo, but park lovers and environmentalists quickly killed that idea.* Saturday Review 7/1/72, p30 **2** Also, **expo.** any large exhibition. *There are now hundreds of stores specializing in personal computers. This thing has taken off like a skyrocket. This expo* [a three-day exhibition of personal computers] *had five thousand people in here yesterday.* New Yorker 11/14/77, p40 **3** Used in combination: *At the Oceanexpo meeting at Bordeaux, France was revealing a potential second generation mining system.* New Scientist 10/13/77, p20 [**1963**, short for *Exposition*]

exposure age, the length of time a meteorite is exposed to cosmic radiation before falling into the earth's atmosphere. *Measured exposure ages range from some tens of thousands of years up to two billion years. The most obvious way to arrive at an exposure age is simply to measure the concentration of some stable spallation product and then to divide this value by any rate at which the nucleus is produced.* Scientific American 7/73, p67 [**1973**]

express, *v.t.* Usually *(passive)* **be expressed** or *(reflexive)* **express oneself.** to cause (a gene) to synthesize the specific protein it codes for by the processes of transcription (producing messenger RNA) and translation (making the protein from the information encoded in messenger RNA). See RECOMBINANT DNA RESEARCH. *Whether the gene would express itself (start making insulin) is not known. But bacterial genes have already* been introduced into human cell cultures and have expressed themselves in those cells. Science News 1/6/73, p13 *A cell makes mRNA when a gene, which is a section of a DNA strand, is to be expressed. In most cases, genes express themselves by causing specific proteins to be made.* World Book Science Annual 1977, p248 [**1968**, extended from an older sense used in genetics, "(of a gene or genetic character or effect) to be manifested in the observable character or phenotype of an organism"]

expression, *n.* the process by which a gene synthesizes a specific protein; manner in which a particular gene expresses itself. See SENTENCE, SYNONYM, WORD. *The expression of certain genes can be experimentally controlled in bacteria.* World Book Science Annual 1972, p338 *The recent advances in understanding gene function and expression stem largely from the new and sometimes controversial scientific technology called recombinant DNA research.* NY Times 5/22/79, pC1 [**1968**]

extencisor (ek'sten,saizər), *n.* a mechanical device for exercising and strengthening the fingers and wrist. *Dr. Robert P. Nirschl of Arlington, Va., recommends squeezing a rubber ball and doing forearm curls with a five-pound weight; he also advises the use of an extencisor.* NY Times Magazine 11/12/72, p32 [**1972**, apparently irregular blend of *extensor* and *exerciser*]

external fertilization, the fertilization of an egg, especially a human ovum, outside the body by introduction of sperm into an egg cell surgically removed from an ovary. Also called IN VITRO FERTILIZATION. *Another, potentially more vexing, argument is that external fertilization constitutes "interference with nature." . . . Some observers fear that external fertilization experiments will lead to a science fiction nightmare—a "brave new world" in which procreation will be moved from the bedroom to the laboratory . . . Counterbalancing the possible problems of external fertilization are substantial potential benefits.* 1979 Collier's Encyclopedia Year Book, p341 [**1974**, extended from an earlier zoological usage (c1943) describing normal fertilization in certain invertebrates, fish, and amphibians that takes place after eggs have left the female body]

externalization, *n.* U.S. the method of transacting sales of stock by transmitting orders to buy and sell to the floor of a stock exchange. *Internalization refers to two separate types of securities transactions that now are prevented by the regulations of the New York Stock Exchange but may be permitted if the S.E.C. issues specific rules. As opposed to externalization, where orders to buy and sell stock are transmitted to the floor of an exchange, internalized orders would be handled completely within the confines of a broker's office.* NY Times 1/17/77, p37 [**1977**]

extra-, a very productive prefix, added chiefly to adjectives and meaning "outside (the area or province of)," "beyond (the scope of)," as in the examples below. —**extrachromosomal,** *adj.: It appears . . . that enterobacteriaceae* [pathogenic bacteria that affect the intestinal tract] *can transfer multiple resistance from one organism to another and even from one species to another by means of extrachromosomal hereditary factors.* 1967 Collier's Encyclopedia Year Book, p124 —**extramaternal,** *adj.: Our abiding image of Flaubert is of a mother's boy bachelor, working through the night, calling "Maman!" on waking, growing stout on huge Norman meals, finding his only extramaternal devotion in the self-imposed martyrdom of his art.* Manchester Guardian Weekly 9/7/67, p10 —**extraneural,** *adj.: Rabies virus is . . . generalized throughout the organism in every extraneural organ and tissue.* Science Journal 4/70, p37 —**extra-political,** *adj.: No doubt the lessening of a certain kind of partisan zeal can be attributed in part to a spreading disenchantment with the whole political order and a growing absorption with extra-political forms of expression.* New Yorker 6/8/68, p120 —**extrareligious,** *adj.: The father, on the other hand, lives in northern New Jersey, where "temples, Hebrew schools and extrareligious facilities abound."* Time 8/16/68, p57 —**extra-subjective,** *adj.: . . . philosophers who profess not to believe in the reality of the extra-subjective world admit the*

existence of other men and that they have the same subjective experience as themselves. Harper's 5/68, p74

extracurricular, *n.* an extracurricular activity. *Besides attending nightly cheerleader practices, she's* [Judy Bell] *Tracy's representative to Girls State, one of eight girls who represent the school at a statewide leadership conference, on the yearbook staff, and in enough extracurriculars that she'll be listed in the high school* Who's Who. Saturday Review 11/11/72, p64 [**1965**, noun use of the adjective (OEDS 1925)]

extralunar, *adj.* found or existing outside the moon. *A small fraction* [of lunar breccias and fines] *(1 or 2 percent) is an extralunar component of meteoritic or cometary origin, most readily identified by a relatively high content of nickel and platinum-group elements, which are found only in low concentrations in the crystalline rocks.* Scientific American 10/71, p53 [**1958**]

extrapolability, *n.* the ability to extrapolate or make projections from available data. *We explored many traditional processes and sites, and from our observations are now trying to extrapolate what we can about ancient methodology. Obviously the degree of extrapolability from evidence or* [from] *crafts extant today must vary enormously from case to case.* Science 3/1/68, p935 [**1968**]

extraterrestrial, *n.* a creature from another planet. *"Much commotion was made over the discovery of the image of a 'Martian god' complete with space suit, found in cliffs overlooking the Sahara . . . Such publicity is due, of course, to widespread popular interest in the possibility of contact with intelligent extraterrestrials. But for this very reason, we must examine critically any purported artifacts uncovered."* Saturday Review 8/6/66, p42 [**1957**, noun use of adjective *extraterrestrial* outside the earth]

extravehicular, *adj.* **1** outside an orbiting space vehicle. *Major Edwin Aldrin, the co-pilot of the Gemini 12 spacecraft, successfully completed his last extravehicular activity today when he stood up in the hatch to photograph two star clusters and experiment with a sextant.* Times (London) 11/15/66, p6 **2** of or for activity outside a space vehicle. *In the extravehicular configuration, the constant-wear garment is replaced by the liquid-cooling garment and four items are added to the intravehicular suit: extravehicular visor, extravehicular glove, lunar overshoe, and a cover over umbilical connections on the front of the suit.* Encyclopedia Science Supplement (Grolier) 1969, p329 [**1964**]

ex-works, *adv. British.* directly from the factory. *It may be that some clerk has developed the habit of putting down the value ex-works and not the price at which it is being sold.* Times (London) 2/21/70, p16 [**1955**]

eye, *n.* the angle from which a graphic image is viewed on a computer screen. *In addition to three-dimensional manipulation of an object, the program offers separate but simultaneous manipulation of the "eye," the viewing point. A motion programmer lets you step your drawing through a series of manipulations and then play back the sequence under automatic computer control.* Popular Computing 11/83, p117 [**1983**]

eyeball, *n.* **eyeball to eyeball,** face to face. *. . . you had to get right in there with Williams, stand eyeball to eyeball, and plant the zinger on him, bang . . .* Harper's 6/69, p74 *The manager must always decide, or manage, in the selection of objectives and goals and the formation of basic policy. Personnel handling and 'eyeball to eyeball' negotiation are also not fit subjects for stimulation or modelling.* Science Journal 11/68, p87 [**1962**]

eye contact, a meeting of eyes; direct look at the eyes, exchanged with another. *Bruce Kramer, Harry Reem's lawyer, recalls: "For seven weeks I saw a jury that was friendly and receptive. We maintained eye contact. After the film was shown they wouldn't look us in the eye."* NY Times Magazine 3/6/77, p36 *The eyes of the wolf also communicate a great deal (as in the domesticated dog, but perhaps more so). Subordinates are constantly attentive to the leader, and as soon as eye* *contact is made, they submissively avert their eyes.* New Yorker 4/24/78, p57 [**1965**]

eye-in-the-sky, *n., pl.* **eyes-in-the-sky.** electronic ground surveillance apparatus used in aircraft or artificial satellites. Compare SPY SATELLITE. *Police are also deploying night vision equipment on their helicopters. Lockheed's Airborne Night Observation Device and similar equipment manufactured by RCA and International Telephone and Telegraph give the police a nocturnal eye-in-the-sky, peeking in on unsuspecting persons.* New Scientist 6/15/72, p620 *The CIA . . . has been trying to keep tabs on Soviet agriculture with eye-in-the-sky photo satellites, and its findings have been reasonably accurate in the past.* Time 11/28/77, p88 [**1966,** patterned after earlier *spy-in-the-sky* (1960); perhaps influenced by *pie in the sky,* a pleasant prospect (c1918), from the IWW song of Joe Hill *Pie in the Sky* (c1912), which contained the refrain, "You will eat, bye and bye, In that glorious land above the sky, Work and pray, live on hay, You'll get pie in the sky when you die."]

eyeless sight, the ability to sense the colors of objects, and sometimes further developed to sense printed matter, through sensitivity of the skin, especially in the fingertips. Also called SKIN VISION. Technical name, DERMALOPTICAL VISION. *Certain investigators believe that another manifestation of radiesthesia may be involved in such psychic phenomena as reading print or identifying colors with the hands (eyeless sight), a medium's communication with someone by other than the five senses while utilizing some object associated with that person (object reading, or psychometry), and dowsing.* 1973 Britannica Yearbook of Science and the Future, p80 [**1972**] ▶ The term was first used in a more general sense in 1924 in a book entitled *Eyeless Sight; a Study of Extra-Retinal Vision and the Paroptic Sense,* translated from the French by C.K. Ogden. In the original work, *Vision Extra-Retinienne* (1920) by the French Nobel Prize-winning novelist Jules Romains, there was an account of his research concerning the faculty of seeing without the use of the eyes. When the book was ridiculed by many scientists Romains abandoned his research, but it was taken up again in the 1960's in connection with the field of parapsychology. However, there are much earlier accounts of eyeless sight by Robert Boyle, the English chemist, followed by occasional accounts in the 1800's. In the 1930's there was research in this field in Brazil. See the article "Eyeless Sight" in the *Encyclopedia of Occultism and Parapsychology* by Leslie Shepard, Gale Research Company.

eyelift, *n.* popular name for BLEPHAROPLASTY. *There has also been news of hair transplants for Frank Sinatra, Roy Clark and Strom Thurmond, . . . face and breast architectural work for Cher, and eyelift, facelift, and breast reduction for Phyllis Diller . . .* Time 10/23/78, p97 [**1978,** patterned after *facelift*]

eyes-only, *adj. U.S.* (of confidential information) intended to be read only by the recipient and not passed along to others; top-secret. *[J. Edgar] Hoover sent the Rowley letter to six senior bureau officials on an "eyes-only" basis. There is no record of FBI meetings or discussions of those allegations.* Manchester Guardian Weekly (Washington Post section) 10/10/76, p15 *In February, Walker received an "eyes only" message from an old friend, Army Chief of Staff General Bernard W. Rogers. The communication assured him that Rogers was working to line up another "four-star slot" for him and implied that there would be no problem in finding one.* Time 10/9/78, p37 [**1972,** abstracted from the phrase *for your eyes only,* a heading put on intelligence reports: *For Your Eyes Only* is a collection of espionage stories (1960) by British author Ian Fleming]

eyewall, *n.* a layer of turbulent funnel-shaped clouds around the eye (calm center) of a storm. Also called WALL CLOUD. . . . *Hurricane Debbie . . . was some 800 miles east of Puerto Rico. Planes flew there to dump their crystals, in hopes of causing supercooled water droplets in the hurricane's eyewall to condense.* Science News 8/23/69, p153 [**1966**]

F

fabricated food, food mixed with cheaper substitutes, such as vegetable fiber, as part of the ingredients to replace traditional varieties of meat, milk, eggs, etc. Compare ENGINEERED FOOD. *Scientists and industry analysts predict a surge in the use of so-called fabricated foods—items that are not in the form or shape we're used to or contain ingredients not usually associated with the products.* Tuscaloosa News (Alabama) 8/21/75, p11 [**1970**]

fabric sculpture, a sculptured work made of pieces of cloth. Compare FIBER ART. *And perhaps some nostalgia for literalism is expressed in the newly fashionable mode of fabric sculpture, which painstakingly scissors, pieces, and pokes into being illustrations as rich and nappy as Pyle's and as broadly luminous as Maxfield Parrish's.* New Yorker 8/14/78, p96 [**1971**]

Fabry's disease, an inherited metabolic disorder caused by the deficiency of a galactoside enzyme, allowing accumulation of a fatty acid in body tissue. See ALPHAGALACTOSIDASE. *Fabry's disease . . . can give rise to a characteristic skin lesion, angiokeratoma, and the patients may die in middle age of a cerebral artery hemorrhage or renal failure.* Science 8/11/72, p527 [**1967**, named after Johannes *Fabry*, 1860-1930, a German dermatologist who first described (in 1898) the skin rash caused by the disease]

FAC, abbreviation of *forward air controller. The FACs—forward air controllers who spot targets from tiny two-engine Cessnas for the fighter-bombers—were also forced to fly dangerously lower. During one four-hour mission, FAC Captain Conrad Pekkola, 32, dodged 15 SAMs as he circled the area between Khe Sanh and the DMZ.* Time 4/17/72, p39 [**1965**]

face, *v.i., v.t.* **face off**, *U.S.* to confront (an opponent) in a test of strength, will, endurance, etc. *They don't write fan mags the way they used to when . . . Hedy Lamarr and Joan Bennett faced off in one of Hollywood's "dangerous feuds."* Saturday Review 1/22/72, p71 [**1955**]

facedown, *n. U.S.* a confrontation between opponents. *The eleven-man Czechoslovak Presidium has vowed to fight down the line for liberal reform and independence in the facedown with the eleven-member Politburo.* Time 8/2/68, p18 *The other cowboy in the electoral facedown, Barry Goldwater, will no doubt make the political counterblow of flicking the new coins into the air and putting six shots through them before they hit the ground.* Punch 8/12/64, p227 [**1964**, from *face down*, probably patterned after *showdown*]

face fly, a fly closely related to the common housefly, found throughout the United States and Canada. *A serious problem in the United States is the face fly, which breeds on cattle dung, then attacks the eyes of cattle.* Science News 5/30/70, p532 [**1960**]

face-off, *n. U.S.* a confrontation between opponents. *How elemental the face-off* [between generations] *can become was demonstrated last week in Monterey, Calif., when the state unemployment-insurance office ruled that jobless men with long hair can no longer collect unemployment benefits.* Time 6/8/70, p12 *Mr. Soll tells us that the draft was the secret of American success in various cold war face-offs.* NY Times 6/30/71, p40 [**1959**, from FACE OFF]

facility trip, *British.* a trip taken at the expense of a government, business, etc., often to promote its interests; junket. *But what about those shadowy areas where perks are part of the public relations world in which a journalist cannot avoid existing: the facility trip, the publisher's party, the Christmas drinks, the lunch at the Savoy?* Listener 5/31/73, p713 [**1973**, so called from the hotel, car, and other facilities usually provided on such trips]

faction, *n.* a book based on or consisting of facts but written in the form of a novel and published as fiction. *He promises his publisher a "faction"—one of the mixtures of fact and fiction craved by the present age.* New Yorker 9/2/72, p71 *Alex Haley called* Roots *a work of "faction," blending fact and fiction, but the distinction wasn't made all that clear on TV, embarrassing Haley deeply.* Time 9/19/77, p93 [**1966**, blend of *fact* and *fiction*]

factionalize, *v.t. U.S.* to divide into opposing groups; separate into factions; make factional. *The Republicans plan to push hard for more than a year to put it over. And with the Democrats certain to be factionalized in at least some areas, the GOP'ers feel they'll have a good chance.* Honolulu Star-Bulletin 4/2/73, pA4 [**1971**, from *factional* involving factions, partisan (OED 1650) + -*ize*]

factoid, *n.* **1** a published statement taken to be a fact by virtue of its appearance in print; some account or event that is unsubstantiated but widely accepted. *He* [Norman Mailer] *speculates at length on fictionalizing biography, treating the actual person much as a novelist treats an imagined one. What this amounts to in* Marilyn *is . . . juggling facts, guesses, and factoids as suits his fancy, with the result that he loses authority as both biographer and novelist.* Harper's 10/73, p108 **2** a book consisting of factoids. *At any rate factoids were booming. The previous year had given us* The Amityville Horror: A True Story, *about which author Jay Anson later said: "I have no idea whether the book is true or not."* Richard de Mille, the Don Juan Papers, 1980, p104-105 [**1973**, coined by the American novelist Norman Mailer from *fact* + -*oid* resembling] —**factoidal**, *adj.: Also from Farrar, Straus: Tom Wolfe's "The Right Stuff," probably factoidal, too, about . . . the early astronauts.* NY Times 6/25/79, pC13

FAE, abbreviation of FUEL AIR EXPLOSIVE. *FAE bombs were first used in combat in 1967, by the US Marines in Vietnam. One-hundred-pound BLU-73 FAEs—containing the highly volatile ethylene oxide, which burns spontaneously without oxygen—were used to detonate mines and defoliate trees across areas of over 700 sq.m.* New Scientist 1/19/78, p151 [**1973**]

faggotry, *n. Slang (derogatory use).* homosexuality. *I remember what I used to hear about—the computer dating, the hectic beach resorts, the girls who complained that a wave of faggotry was upsetting the balance.* Harper's 2/70, p64 [**1966**, from *faggot*, slang word for homosexual, of unknown origin]

faggy, *adj. Slang (derogatory use).* effeminate; homosexual. *Coco* [a musical] *is more of a bore than a bomb . . . The production seems to squelch almost everyone connected with it. Only René Auberjonois as a faggy designer manages to filch an occasional moment of amusing exuberance.* Time 12/26/69, p31 [**1963**, from *fag* (OEDS 1923), slang word for homosexual, shortened from *faggot* (1914), of unknown origin]

fag hag, *U.S. Slang.* a woman who consorts habitually or exclusively with male homosexuals. *Homosexuals who felt socially isolated would sit together at mealtime, as much to escape the careless insults of faggot jokes as to ward off the loneliness. Girls who stop to talk to them still risk being called "fag-hags."* NY Times Magazine 3/12/78, p16 [**1972**, from *fag* homosexual + *hag* ugly old woman or witch]

fail, *n. U.S.* the failure of a broker or brokerage firm to deliver securities by a given time. *The main measuring device for the seriousness of back-office trouble was the amount of what Wall*

Street calls "fails." Fails, which might more bluntly be called defaults, occur when on the normal settlement date for any stock trade—five business days after the transaction itself—the seller's broker for some reason does not physically deliver the actual sold stock certificates to the buyer's broker, or the buyer's broker for some reason doesn't receive them. New Yorker 7/3/73, p50 [**1968**, noun use of the verb]

fail-safe, *adj.* **1** designed to stop or alter an operation automatically in the event of a malfunction. *A fail-safe reel brake prevents accidental spilling of tape in case of power failure.* Science News 1/27/68, p102 **2** guaranteed not to fail; safe from failure; foolproof. *A master plan was worked out, beautifully turned and fail-safe on paper—and the team went bankrupt before lunch.* Manchester Guardian Weekly 9/26/68, p6 —*v.i.* to stop or alter an operation automatically in case of some malfunction. *Those with gas central heating will have cursed the irony of a system which fails-safe when the electrical power supply is severed.* Manchester Guardian Weekly 12/19/70, p13 —*v.t.* to make or cause to be fail-safe. *One problem with Venera 4, says Dr. Drake, was that its equipment "was not failsafed. If it failed and gave erroneous readings, there was no way to know." He hopes this one is fail-safed.* Science News 5/31/69, p525 [**1948, 1958,** popularized by the *Fail-Safe* system developed by the U.S. Strategic Air Command, in which bombers sent into enemy territory on the basis of an unconfirmed order can be prevented from completing their mission by withholding its confirmation or by other automatic safeguards]

fairness doctrine, *U.S.* a principle in licensed radio and television broadcasting of providing reasonable opportunity for different points of view in a controversial issue of public importance to be broadcast. Compare EQUAL TIME. . . . *the Federal Communications Commission ruled that under the so-called "fairness doctrine," all broadcasters who carry cigarette advertising must also carry announcements and programs telling of possible perils of smoking.* NY Times 9/13/68, p55 [**1964**]

fake book, *U.S.* a book reproducing the melodies or similar shorthand versions of copyrighted popular songs without permission of the copyright owners. . . . *Burton Lane, a major Broadway composer . . . sat at an upright in the well of the courtroom and played 15 popular songs from the original sheet music and from a "fake book" published by Rose and sold to musicians.* NY Times 4/20/66, p39 [**1958**]

fall, *v.* **fall about**, *British, Informal.* to be overwhelmed with laughter; to break up laughing. *"The thought of producing a book in that time is enough to make us fall about,"* chortled Bodley. *Yes, but hold on a minute, the book is only 16 pages long and we here on* The Times *produce similar miracles nightly, except Saturdays.* Times (London) 1/19/73, p14 [**1967**]

fallout, *n.* a by-product or residue of something, usually unexpected. Compare SPINOFF. *A sublime piece of technological fall-out from space technology is a means of purifying foul-smelling sewage and converting it into sterile drinking water.* New Scientist 7/2/70, p20 *From the research that produced the rocket motors, liquid propellants, space suits and other necessities of space flight emerged . . . unexpected applications—in medicine, industry, and the home—for materials, equipment, and services that had been created for use in space. Such by-products are called "spin-off" or "fallout."* 1970 Compton Yearbook, p574 [**1957**, extended from the earlier (OEDS 1950) sense of the radioactive dust or particles that fall to earth after a nuclear explosion]

FALN or **F.A.L.N.**, abbreviation of *Fuerzas Armadas de Liberación Nacional,* Spanish for Armed Forces of National Liberation, the name of a Puerto Rican terrorist group demanding independence for Puerto Rico. Compare INDEPENDENTISTA. *"WE DON'T DESERVE THIS" was the headline over an editorial in the* News *on August 4th, the day after the F.A.L.N., a fanatical group advocating Puerto Rican independence, had planted several bombs in Manhattan office buildings, killing one person.* New Yorker 9/5/77, p74 [**1975**] ►The same name

and abbreviation were earlier (1963) used by a Venezuelan terrorist organization.

false color, a photographic process using infrared film, on which images of highly contrasting colors differentiate temperatures of sources of heat by variations of infrared radiation to detect camouflage and environmental pollution, to survey crops, forests, and other natural features of the earth's surface, and to aid in the study of other planets. *Earth crater in Saskatchewan was photographed in false color by Skylab astronauts. It is Deep Bay Crater at south end of Reindeer Lake. It is nine kilometers across and 100 million years old.* Scientific American 1/77, p85 [**1968**] —**false-color**, *adj.*: *Global color variations on Mars are shown in this "false-color" composite assembled from photographs taken by Viking I shortly before it entered its circum-Martian orbit.* Science News 11/12/77, p327

family, *n.* **1** *U.S.* one of the operational units of the Cosa Nostra or Mafia. *A Mafia family is a group of individuals who are not necessarily blood relatives.* NY Times 5/9/67, p38 *The boss of one Cosa Nostra "family" is said to have given a half-million dollars in cash, divided five ways, to five of his lieutenants for Christmas.* Harper's 2/69, p86 *The Luchese family . . . was suspected of being in the narcotics traffic* NY Times 12/23/67, p11 **2** a group of hippies living together, as in a commune. *He [Elia Katz] also repeatedly encountered hypocrisy: e.g., among the health food faddists in Pennsylvania and, most notably, in the bosom of the "Family" in Taos, New Mexico.* Saturday Review 1/22/72, p78 *The term "snuff film" itself dates to the days of Charles Manson and his family.* New York Post 10/1/75, p28 [**1954** for def. 1; **1972** for def. 2]

family ganging, *U.S.* the practice of giving medical treatment to several members of a family covered by medical insurance when only one member has requested or needs care. *Abuses such as "ping-ponging," in which patients who come to the clinic with a single complaint are referred to a string of different specialists, and "family ganging," in which a physician treats all accompanying family members whether or not they are sick, were documented earlier this year by Senator Frank Moss, a Utah Democrat who posed as a Medicaid patient during his own investigation of the facilities.* NY Times 10/6/76, p1 [**1975**]

familygram, *n. U.S.* a brief radio message transmitted by relatives to a sailor at sea. *Crewmen also begin to worry inordinately about friends and relatives on shore. The Navy tries to soothe their fears with "familygrams"—radioed messages received when the sub surfaces.* Time 9/17/73, p65 [**1962**, from *family* + *-gram,* as in *telegram*]

family hour, *U.S.* a television viewing period, usually from 7 to 9 p.m., when programs containing excessive violence or sexual material are barred and only programs regarded as suitable for viewing by parents and children together are shown. Compare FRINGE TIME, PRIME TIME. *The family hour is still in effect at three networks, spokesmen there say, though the term "family hour" is not officially used anymore. "There is," as one network put it, "a greater sensitivity exercised during the 8-9 p.m. hour."* New York Post 3/28/79, p45 [**1975**]

family jewels, *U.S. Slang.* shameful secrets; skeletons in the closet (applied to various underhanded activities or operations engaged in especially by members of the U.S. Central Intelligence Agency). See DIRTY TRICKS. *A turncoat . . . gave up to congressional investigating committees delicious CIA secrets, among them the notorious 693-page list of the "family jewels"—such tricks as the surveillance of journalists, interception of mail, drugging of unknowing CIA employees, assassination attempts against Fidel Castro, Patrice Lumumba, Rafael Trujillo. This, he says, is where the mole business probably got started.* Manchester Guardian Weekly (Washington Post section) 6/11/78, p17 [**1978**] ►The term is also recorded in various slang dictionaries as an old taboo phrase meaning "testicles." The term *jewels* was already used in this sense before 1500 (see the *Middle English Dictionary*).

family medicine, another name for COMMUNITY MEDICINE. *My 14 years at the Steiner School . . . provided a solid, deeply hu-*

manistic basis for the pursuit of my M.D.-Ph.D. program and a career in family medicine—a "newly emerging" medical discipline devoted to the holistic approach to the patient. NY Times Magazine 10/30/77, p78 [1966]

family practice, another name for COMMUNITY MEDICINE. *A new specialty, known variously as community medicine or family practice and stressing a general and person-oriented approach to medicine, was gaining in popularity.* Britannica Book of the Year 1973, p456 [1973]

family therapy, a form of psychotherapy in which the therapist involves a family group (especially parents and children) in treating one member of the family. [Mel] *Roman, a professor of psychiatry at Albert Einstein College of Medicine, sees family therapy as the wave of the future. "Family therapy says we're all in this together. No one's at fault. Everybody is responsible."* Daily News (New York) 4/17/79, p43 [1977] —**family therapist:** *For an hour a week over a period of eight weeks, I had sat behind a one-way mirror in an observation room in a psychiatric clinic and watched and listened to their sessions with a new breed of healer called a family therapist.* New Yorker 5/15/78, p39

Fanconi's anemia, a constitutional anemia of children, resembling pernicious anemia. *They have discovered that cells from patients with Down's syndrome (mongolism) and Fanconi's anaemia—two diseases which Miller had proved to predispose toward leukaemia—are more susceptible to SV40 transformation.* New Scientist and Science Journal 3/18/71, p596 [1967, named after Guido *Fanconi*, 1882-1940?, a Swiss pediatrician who first described the disease]

Fanonesque or **Fanonist** or **Fanonian,** *adj.* characteristic of the radical political ideas of Frantz Fanon, 1925-1961, a revolutionary leader in Algeria, who believed in a world-wide peasants' revolution against colonial oppression. *A young West Indian named Errol improbably arrives to rent a room, and Mr. Didcot eventually takes him into his confidence. The plot unfolds in a sort of Fanonesque parable.* Saturday Review 4/22/72, p87 *His simple answer to this very large and difficult question is given in what have become familiar Fanonist terms, though stated in his own peculiar language.* Manchester Guardian Weekly 7/10/71, p18 [1970]

fantasmo, *adj. Informal.* supremely fantastic; **a** most strange or fanciful. *The figures that populate his [Richard Condon's] books are, instead, fantasmo embodiments of various sorts of foaming mania.* Time 10/23/72, p106 **b** that is so good, quick, high, just, etc., as to be unbelievable. *Antioch College, Yellow Springs, Ohio, the absolute fantasmo super-pinnacle of academic liberalism, has been completely wiped out for the last six weeks by a student strike and the occupation of key buildings.* National Review 6/22/73, p671 [1972, from *fantastic* + *-mo,* as in *supremo* (from Spanish, supreme)]

fantasy, *n.* a coin of questionable origin or purpose, especially one issued by a country for sale to coin collectors rather than for use as legal tender (also used attributively). *Growing concern over increasing activities in the manufacture and distribution of counterfeits, fantasies, and copies brought about the formation of an international committee to publicize these coins wherever found.* Britannica Book of the Year 1967, p618 [1966]

Faraday cup, a device that captures charged particles and determines their type, charge, and direction. *Large numbers of projectiles are required in nuclear-reaction studies. The projectiles that do not strike a nucleus simply joggle their way through the electron clouds of the atoms in the target and continue on in a well-defined beam. They are caught in a Faraday cup, where their accumulated charge is used as a measure of the beam's intensity.* Scientific American 10/72, p105 [1967, named after Michael *Faraday*, 1791-1867, English physicist and chemist]

farm, *n.* **buy the farm,** *U.S. Military Slang.* to be killed in action; die while in service. *Schwarzkopf needed to know what was going on. "Are you sure you need a jungle penetrator?" he said. "You know they're risky even in the daylight."*

"Sir," Cameron answered, "the only thing I can tell you is that two of my people have bought the farm, and if I don't get it two more will." New Yorker 3/15/76, p95 [1967, alteration of earlier Air Force slang *to buy a farm,* meaning to crash, recorded in *The United States Air Force Dictionary* (by W.A. Heflin, 1956)]

far-out, *adj.* **1** (literally) far removed in space; very distant in space. *Although Pluto, the solar system's most far-out planet, has appeared to be growing slightly dimmer for the past ten years, this is not a permanent change.* Science News 3/22/69, p285 **2** (figuratively) far removed from the ordinary; very unconventional. Compare WAY-OUT. *I got away from writing vaguely autobiographical snips for the New Yorker market to writing some far-out, inventive pieces.* NY Times Magazine 1/14/68, p41 *I'll put it this way. He was a brainy individual. He was smart. That impressed me. But he was a little far out for a small community like this.* Harper's 12/70, p75 [1954]

far-outer, *n.* one who is very unconventional; a non-conformist. *For one thing, there's the question of warmth—after all, what are coats for—so only the most hardy far-outers wear them as short or shorter than their skirts.* Sunday Times (London) 1/8/67, p40 [1967]

fastback, *n. U.S.* **1** an automobile with lines that slope down from the midsection to the rear in an unbroken curve. Compare NOTCHBACK. *Ever-changing tastes of American car owners slowed the trend toward fastbacks. Motorists reiterated a preference for. . . rear fenders with pronounced bustles in the trunks.* Americana Annual 1967, p109 **2** a racing boat with a stern that slopes down in an unbroken curve. *When preliminary Cup races began in Newport,* Mariner *continued to lose embarrassingly to* Courageous *and* Intrepid. *Working 20 hours a day back at the drawing board and test tank, Chance designed a modified fastback.* Time 7/29/74, p63 [1962 for def. 1; 1974 for def. 2]

Fastback, *n.* a breed of pigs that are more economical and leaner than other breeds, first produced in 1970 in Great Britain. *Main customers for the Fast Back are the bacon curers and pork butchers, who sell whole sides of bacon, or joints of meat with the crackling and fat still intact.* Sunday Times (London) 5/16/71, p52 [1970]

fast breeder or **fast-breeder reactor,** a breeder reactor (atomic power plant able to produce its own fuel as well as generate power with almost no loss of fissionable material) that uses fast or high-energy neutrons to produce fissionable material. Compare THERMAL BREEDER. *In a fast breeder reactor, atoms of nonfissionable plutonium are converted into fissionable atoms of plutonium-239.* 1969 Collier's Encyclopedia Year Book, p403 [1954]

fast food, *U.S.* food prepared in a standardized form and served quickly, such as hamburgers, frankfurters, fried chicken, and pizza. *Fast food failed to supply adequate vitamin A, biotin, folacin, pantothenic acid, iron, or copper.* 1982 Britannica Yearbook of Science and the Future, p322 *American racetracks . . . have become as indistinguishable as their fast food.* Maclean's 6/18/79, p31 [1954]

fast-food, *adj. U.S.* that specializes in serving fast food. . . . *frozen foods, packaged foods, TV dinners, fast-food franchises, preservatives and additives all stem from a culture that made pragmatism, step saving and time saving virtues in themselves.* Time 11/16/70, p63 [1951]

fast-forward, *v.t., v.i.* to wind a cassette tape rapidly forward. *. . . she shifted her focus from within to without, suggesting the mechanism of a hypersensitive tape-recorder that could fast-forward or rewind with the flick of an invisible switch.* NY Times Magazine 1/19/75, p50 —*n.* the process of fast-forwarding. *A characteristic of all Beta machines is that the video tape remains laced round the rapidly rotating video head drum during "fast-forward" and "rewind."* New Scientist 5/10/79, p441 —**adv.** by fast-forwarding. *Thanks to remote control units for TV sets, viewers can instantly turn off the sound during a commercial break, dial-hop from one station to another, or run fast-forward through commercials on pro-*

grams that have been taped on videocassettes. Fortune 1/21/85, p68 [**1972,** from earlier adjective (OED 1948)]

fast lane, *U.S. Informal.* a style of living that is filled with activity and excitement, often to an unrestrained or reckless extent. *"Times have changed," Mr. LeFrak says. "We're living in an instant society. People want to have it all; they want more time to enjoy life." "You might call it life in the fast lane," he adds. "I call it progress."* NY Times Magazine 6/28/87, p64 [**1978,** figurative use of *fast lane* (OEDS 1966) lane of a highway used by drivers to pass slower cars]

fast track, rapid advancement or acceleration, especially in education and business. . . . *there arose in business the phenomenon of the "fast track," as Dr. Robert H. Hayes of the Harvard Business School and others have called it. Companies took relatively young and inexperienced employees, compressed 15 years of training and experience into five, transferred them all over the country and very quickly gave them positions of real responsibility.* NY Times Magazine 3/8/81, p24 [**1965,** figurative use of the racing term (1934) for a dry track that is easy to run on]

fast-track, *adj.* rapid; advanced; accelerated. *Meanwhile, the Government has approved the use of fast-track planning procedures, which minimise the scope for public scrutiny and debate and enable the Minister of Energy to override the decisions of any tribunals.* Manchester Guardian Weekly 7/12/81, p2 —*v.t.* to put on a fast track; advance rapidly; accelerate. *The National Development Bill . . . was designed to facilitate (or 'fast-track') such projects as major energy developments beyond the reach of what the Government clearly regarded as onerous and time-consuming land-use . . .* 1979 Annual Register of World Events, p321 *In many Japanese companies, promotions may come as infrequently as once every ten years, a glacial pace that would drive fast-tracking U.S. managers crazy.* Time 3/2/81, p74 [**1967** for adj.; **1979** for verb]

Fatah (fɑːˈtɑː), *n.* variant of AL FATAH. *"Fatah therefore decided to send guerrilla cadres into Israel," he reported. It was the border from which the Israelis least expected any trouble.* Egyptian Mail 2/17/73, p4 [**1968**]

fat city, *U.S. Slang.* **1** an excellent condition, situation, or prospect. *"Mr. Huston, just what does the expression 'fat city' mean?" "It's a jazz musician's term," Huston said. "It's a dreamer's term, meaning no boundaries to the possibilities. It's the pot of gold at the end of the rainbow.* New Yorker 8/5/72, p21 **2** (*ironical use*) a poor or undesirable condition, situation, or prospect. . . . *the novel [Leonard Gardner's "Fat City"] fails to show how or why its principal characters wind up in "fat city" (argot for "out of condition" as well as for a loser's vain dreams) . . .* American Scholar Winter 1972, p148 [**1965;** the sense of def. 2 derives from such slang phrases as *a fat lot* (OEDS 1892) and *a fat chance* (1906), both ironical uses implying "very little, hardly any"; the use of *city* probably influenced by the slang suffix *-ville* (as in *dullsville*), literally, town, village]

fat farm, *U.S. Slang.* a health resort or spa for overweight people. *As waistlines keep expanding, so too do beauty resorts—the places that thin people like to call fat farms.* Time 3/2/70, p64 *Last week the First Tuesday segments dealt with a weight-reduction "fat farm" and a Christian anti-Communist crusade.* Time 4/11/69, p42 [**1969**]

fat-mouth, *v.i. U.S. Slang.* to talk excessively, especially without taking action. *They have to do something, have to move, where they can no longer sit back and fat-mouth about it, because the country will be on fire.* Atlantic 5/70, p61 [**1970**]

fault tree, a diagram with labeled branches that show all the possible consequences of accident or failure in a system. Compare EVENT TREE. *One group of nuclear critics is . . . especially critical of the particular analytical methods used for risk projections (called fault tree analysis). The method concentrates on minor design comparisons and does not reveal gross design errors.* Science News 8/24-31/74, p117 [**1974**]

faux naif (fou nɑːˈiːf), *French.* falsely naïve; apparently but not actually simple or artless. *Dossena never admitted to being a forger, and no one ever managed to prove that he was deliber-*

ately trying to deceive . . . It was others who claimed that his pieces were by Donatello or Simone Martini or an unknown Greek of the fifth century. He made a statement to a reporter . . . which may or may not have been faux naïf. Harper's 2/68, p26 *Wood's work is very* faux naif *and Nicholson painted better when he was under the influence of Mondrian.* Listener 6/20/68, p818 [**1958**]

fave rave, *Slang.* an infatuation with a popular performer, especially a singer. *He* [David Cassidy] *was hired, therefore, as an actor, but as soon as he was seen on screen he was snatched by the American fan magazine market, always at the ready to replace a current fave rave.* Times (London) 7/30/73, p15 [**1967,** from *fave* (short for *favorite*) and *rave* infatuation, craze]

fax, *n.* **1** short for FAX MACHINE. *Today's faxes are as user-friendly as a toaster.* Money 7/88, p87 **2** a copy of graphic material sent or received by a fax machine. *Even more aggravating, unsolicited faxes use your electricity and your facsimile paper.* NY Times 10/2/88, p52 —*v.t.* to send by a fax machine. *Restaurant owners fax menus to nearby offices . . . Radio stations encourage listeners to fax their song requests.* NY Times 10/2/88, p52 [**1948, 1976**]

fax machine, an electronic device that transmits and receives facsimiles of graphic material over telephone lines. *Corporate high-rollers fire off memos from the rear of limousines, using portable fax machines.* NY Times 10/2/88, p52 [**1976,** short for *facsimile machine*]

FBS, abbreviation of *forward-based system. Primary components of the FBS are aircraft carriers and shorter-range aircraft and missiles, which are based in several countries of Western Europe as well as in South Korea.* Americana Annual 1977, p336 [**1971**]

FEA, abbreviation of *Federal Energy Administration* (of the United States, 1974-1977). *The FEA figures that a 25% tax credit for such purchases as storm windows and doors, and insulation for unfinished attics could lead to a reduction of 50,000 to 100,000 bbl. a day.* Time 10/14/74, p34 [**1974**]

feasibility study, a study to determine the desirability and practicability of adopting a plan or system. *An essential ingredient of the sensible feasibility study on which Mintech has embarked, therefore, is an assessment of the value which the main categories of intercity traveller put on different aspects of the journey.* Science Journal 3/70, p5 *A feasibility study must consider many factors, one of the most important being the assurance that the industrial plant can at all times utilize all, or practically all, of the steam generated from processes such as the fuel gas processes for the contracted quantities of solid waste to be accepted.* McGraw-Hill Yearbook of Science and Technology 1978, p126 [**1971**]

Federales (ˌfeideiˈrɑːleis; *Anglicized,* ˌfedəˈræleiz), *n.pl.* Mexican federal troops (sometimes used in the singular). *Died. Lucio Cabañas, 37, Mexican guerrilla and folk hero; of wounds suffered in a gun battle with Federales; in the Sierra Madre del Sur above Acapulco.* Time 12/16/74, p69 *At the Palace, she said she was strapped to a table while a Federal interrogated her with applications of an electric cattle prod . . . until she passed out.* NY Times Magazine 5/1/77, p50 [**1967,** from Mexican Spanish, short for Spanish *Fuerzas Federales* Federal Forces]

Feebie, *n. U.S. Slang.* a member of the U.S. Federal Bureau of Investigation. . . . *on their left stands a man in a very dark suit, with very dark tie, very dark glasses, very white shirt, and very bald head; a cop, FeeBie, CIA, something like that.* Atlantic 1/68, p36 . . . *Secret Service agents derisively call the FBI men "Feebies."* Time 2/28/69, p14 [**1968,** from an irregular pronunciation of the abbreviation *FBI*]

feedback, *n.* a reciprocal effect of one person or thing upon another; a reaction or response that modifies, corrects, etc., the behavior of that which produced the reaction or response. *Primitives treat things and animals as people, and experience feedback from them.* Manchester Guardian Weekly 3/21/70, p18 *Outsiders are unable to penetrate the continuing feedback between the* [Army Engineers] *Corps and the congressional committees.* Atlantic 4/70, p55 *Twelfth in a monthly series of* *'open ended' problems featuring feedback from readers.* Science Journal 12/69, p30 [**1943, 1959,** extended use of earlier (OEDS 1920) *feedback* a process in electric machinery]

feedback inhibition, a form of cellular control by which an enzyme catalyzing the production of a substance in a cell is inhibited at a certain level of accumulation of that substance, thereby balancing the amount produced with the amount needed. *In biosynthetic pathways biochemists have often observed that the enzyme catalysing the first reaction unique to a particular pathway is inhibited by the end-product of the pathway—the so-called "feedback inhibition." This inhibition is of the "allosteric" or shape-changing type—the inhibiting molecule binds to a site on the enzyme distinct from the catalytic site, and the inhibition is mediated by a conformational change in the enzyme.* New Scientist 1/8/70, p47 [**1964**]

feedforward, *n.* the control of a feedback process by anticipating any defects in the process before it is carried out. *This more "intelligent" type of control is known as "feedforward" as opposed to feedback, and essentially it involves locating the sensor at the input end.* Times (London) 5/7/70, p33 *Consider another and a peculiarly interesting example of feedforward: what you have it in mind to say before you have begun to put it into any sort of words. This feedforward can be very definite. It can unhesitatingly reject any and all of your efforts to say it. "No," you note, "that isn't it at all."* Saturday Review 2/3/68, p16 [**1961**]

feed-in, *n.* a gathering of people to receive free food. *Even food, modest but nourishing, was provided for penniless but hungry travelers at two or three daily "feed-ins."* NY Times 6/20/71, p10 [**1967,** see -IN]

fee-for-service, *n.* separate payment for each medical service received by a patient (often attributive). *Prepaid groups . . . had earned good reputations for giving high quality care more cheaply than did the traditional fee-for-service system. The groups worked on a fixed budget and had an incentive to keep people well and out of the hospital where care is very expensive.* NY Times 5/17/76, p16 [**1973**]

feelgood, *n.* **1** Usually spelled **Feelgood.** variant of DR. FEELGOOD. *The best way to guard against Feelgoods and charlatans is for the medical profession to keep its own house in order. We ought not to ask doctors to make the ethical decisions that are the responsibility of all society. But conversely, only physicians can protect us from quacks.* Newsweek 12/25/72, p29 **2** (*used disparagingly*) **a** a carefree, blissful state; perfect contentment. Compare BLISSOUT. *The chief exponents of psychic feelgood tend to come from Asia, California and the psychological sciences, no one of which has an impressive record at making people feel good.* NY Times Magazine 5/15/77, p12 **b** Attributive use: *Some critics, especially those who dislike Neil Simon (with whom Ross has collaborated closely), dismiss him as a "feel-good" director whose style reeks of old fashioned 1950's-style seamless sleekness.* NY Times Magazine 11/12/78, p17 [**1972**]

feelie, *n.* an art object or medium which the spectator can feel as well as see, smell, and sometimes hear (also used attributively). *Some of the confections are merely art-student capers, the "feelies" for example, where the visitor has to push himself through a narrow gangway of rotating sausages of soft foam.* Sunday Times (London) 4/14/68, p11 *"You see, we asked a hundred and thirty-seven art consumers what they wanted in a work of art," Mr. Laing said . . . "Women tended toward feelie things and free forms,"* Mr. Phillips called from across the room. New Yorker 4/30/66, p35 [**1966**] ►The term *feelies* was first used in Aldous Huxley's *Brave New World* (1932) for a kind of escapist cinema of the future in which spectators could experience the sensations displayed on film with the aid of knobs attached to their chairs. The following quotation alludes to this in the context of a present-day "happening": *. . . with strobe lights* [special lights for fast action photography], *sounds, movies, and dancing all going on at once, we approach the "feelies" of* Brave New World. Saturday Night (Canada) 3/67, p11

feet, *n.pl.* in various idioms: **1 die on one's feet,** to collapse, fail, or break down. *Now this most promising of African economies* [Nigeria] *is liable to die on its feet, even if it does not disintegrate into chaos.* Manchester Guardian Weekly 8/17/67, p1 [**1963**] **2 find one's feet,** *British.* to become firmly established or settled. *We look in satisfied bemusement at the rise of the working classes since 1970. We have not yet proved more responsible than the middle-class supremacy of a hundred years but we have only had four years to find our feet in.* New Statesman 6/27/75, p824 [**1961**] **3 vote with one's feet,** to show one's disapproval of a condition by leaving or escaping from it. *. . . the 40,000 draft dodgers now in Canada have voted in the ultimate way—with their feet.* Manchester Guardian Weekly 3/27/71, p6 [**1966**]

fellate (fə'leit), *v.i., v.t.* to perform fellatio (on). *The blow she had struck was with an ice pick and . . . it was fatal. On August 15, 1975, she was acquitted in a North Carolina courthouse; her defense of self-defense—Alligood had forced her to fellate him, so she killed him—stood up.* Maclean's 5/16/77, p64 [**1968,** back formation from *fellatio*]

felt-tip pen or **felt-tipped pen,** a pen with a felt point, used for labeling, drawing, etc. . . . *underlined the most compelling passages with a yellow felt-tip pen for future reference.* Time 9/2/66, p36 *. . . felt-tipped pens, filled with waterproof ink, obtainable in black and various colours.* Times (London) 4/8/67, p21 [**1957**]

FeLV, abbreviation of *feline leukemia virus* (a retrovirus causing lymphosarcoma, a kind of cancer, in cats and shown to be spread by contagion). *Hardy and Old find that overt infection with FeLV and incidence of leukaemia is highest in cats living in communities. Blood relationships between the animals has no influence.* New Scientist 8/9/73, p308 [**1973**]

fem, *adj. U.S. Slang.* effeminate. *Today's homosexual can be open ("come out") or covert ("closet"), practicing or inhibited, voluntary or compulsive, conscious or unaware, active or passive, manly ("stud") or womanly ("fem").* Saturday Review 2/12/72, p24 [1972, probably an extended use of *fem, femme,* slang for female or feminine, from French *femme* woman]

female chauvinism, exaggerated pride in, or loyalty to, the female sex. *Now for a notorious example of female chauvinism:* Notable American Women, 1607-1850 . . . *edited by Edward T. James (traitor!) and sponsored by (naturally) Radcliffe College. Just what are the qualifications of these 1,359 women? Judge for yourself: There are actresses like Laurette Taylor and Alma Gluck, artists like Helen Hokinson and Mary Cassatt, heroines like Pocahontas.* Saturday Review 5/6/72, p70 [**1972,** patterned after MALE CHAUVINISM] —**female chauvinist:** *You know, there are a lot of women I know in the music business that like to say, "Oh, well I just couldn't make it because, you know, the men held me back," and all this sort of female chauvinist bull. And it just seems to me that the better I got at what I did, the less trouble I had from that kind of attitude.* Maclean's 10/2/78, p4

Fem Lib or **Femlib,** *n.* another name for WOMEN'S LIB. *Jenkins loves the hooting and hollering and bashings and splatters of college football, Fem Libs be damned.* Harper's 1/71, p95 *Should the conditions of Femlib take over, the cultural fallout will be stupendous.* NY Times 11/11/70, p45 [**1970**]

femme (fem), *n. Slang.* a lesbian who adopts a feminine role. *Among lesbians, a butch, dyke or bull dyke is a mannish woman who seeks a femme—a passive, dependent partner.* Time 9/8/75, p43 [**1961,** from French *femme* woman]

femto-, a prefix meaning one quadrillionth (10^{-15}) of any standard unit in the international meter-kilogram-second system of measurements (SI UNIT). *There are international agreements about names and prefixes to be used, and it does not help understanding if in one line the authors adhere to the adopted usage (pg for picogram) and then in another call a femtogram (fg) an Emich.* Science 5/24/68, p872 [**1961,** from Danish *femten* fifteen]

femtometer, *n.* one quadrillionth of a meter. *Although the* [gold atom] *nucleus is 10^{15} times denser than the remainder of the* *atom, even in it there is a great deal of "empty space." Each nucleon has a diameter of approximately one femtometer (10^{-15} meter); the center-to-center distance between neighboring nucleons is some two femtometers.* Scientific American 10/72, p101 [**1972**]

fender-bender, *n. U.S. and Canadian Slang.* **1** a collision between automobiles. *An automobile accident is unpleasant anywhere, but it would be hard to top the hassle of a Moscow fender-bender as I discovered recently when my little Russian-made Zhiguli (modeled after the Italian Fiat 124) slid into a bread truck at an intersection.* Manchester Guardian Weekly (Washington Post section) 11/16/75, p20 **2** a driver involved in such a collision. *This system of compensating those who have suffered injuries in car accidents—by trying to figure out which fender-bender was at fault—is about the most chaotic one that could have been devised.* NY Times 2/18/68, pD4E [**1966**]

fenfluramine (fen'flurə,mi:n), *n.* a drug used as an appetite depressant in the treatment of obesity. *Formula:* $C_{12}H_{16}F_3N$ *Our Medical Correspondent writes: Ponderax (fenfluramine) is widely used to reduce appetite in overweight patients and is generally regarded as very safe. In contrast with other slimming pills, such as amphetamines, it has no stimulant effect and is not addictive.* Times (London) 3/15/73, p3 [**1970**, from *fen-* (variant of *phen-* phenyl) + *fluor-* fluorine + *amine*]

fenitrothion (fə,nitrou'θaiən), *n.* a highly toxic yellow oil that contains phosphorus and inhibits the enzyme cholinesterase, used to kill insects and other pests. *Formula:* $C_9H_{12}NO_5PS$ *The codling moth that is responsible among other pests for maggoty apples is on the wing, and if you can reach your apple trees a spraying with a good insecticide such as fenitrothion (Fentro) would be worth while, especially if you have only a light crop.* Times (London) 7/9/77, p11 [**1965**, from *fen-* (variant of *phen-* phenyl) + *nitro-* nitric (acid) + *-thion* containing sulfur (from Greek *theîon* sulfur)]

fenthion (fen'θaiən), *n.* a highly toxic brown liquid that contains phosphorus and inhibits the enzyme cholinesterase, used to kill insects and other pests. *Formula:* $C_{10}H_{15}O_3PS_2$ *At a park 40 miles south of Nashville, a contact poison called Fenthion, mixed with diesel fuel, was sprayed on roosting birds. Fenthion kills by attacking the birds' nervous system.* NY Times 2/29/76, p33 [**1968**, from *fen-* (variant of *phen-* phenyl) + *-thion* containing sulfur (from Greek *theîon* sulfur)]

Fermiology, *n.* the quantum-mechanical concepts and theories of Enrico Fermi. *While the "Fermiology" of matter is extensively explained in textbooks, the understanding of non-Fermi electrons is another matter entirely.* Science 7/14/72, p156 *The gradient from momentum space representations ("Fermiology") to real space representations (clustering, localization) crosses the frontier between physics and chemistry.* Nature 7/21/72, p130 [**1972**, from Enrico *Fermi*, 1901-1954, Italian-born American physicist + *-ology* study of]

ferredoxin (,ferə'daksən), *n.* a plant and bacterial protein containing iron and sulfur, whose function is to transfer electrons from one enzyme or group of enzymes to another. *Ferredoxins . . . have no enzymic activity themselves, but nevertheless have a wide variety of applications . . . Because of the simplicity and efficiency of ferredoxin, advocates of the chemical evolution theory of the origin of life have proposed that it was among the first proteins to be synthesized on earth.* McGraw-Hill Yearbook of Science and Technology 1977, p354 [**1962**, coined by the American biochemists Leonard E. Mortenson, Raymond C. Valentine, and James E. Carnahan, from Latin *ferrum* iron + English *redox* oxidation-reduction + *-in* (chemical suffix)]

fertility drug, a drug that combats infertility in women by stimulating ovulation. See, for example, CLOMIPHENE. *Fertility drugs are useful when infertility is caused by failure of the woman's body to produce an egg each month that is capable of being fertilized. Failure to ovulate accounts for 20 per cent of infertility cases.* NY Times 6/20/71, p7 [**1965**]

festival seating, *U.S.* unreserved seating, especially at a rock music concert. *How many lives before the punitive and inhu-*

man policy of festival seating at rock concerts is outlawed? Time 1/7/80, p6 [**1980**]

fetal alcohol syndrome, a group of defects in a newborn, including mental retardation and abnormally small head size, resulting from an excessive consumption of alcohol by the mother during pregnancy. *A group of French researchers first recognised what has come to be called the "fetal alcohol syndrome" (malformations and behavioural damage) after a study of 9000 mothers in 1963.* New Scientist 1/11/79, p76 [**1977**]

fetologist, *n.* a specialist in fetology. *By being able to monitor growth and development continuously, fetologists would be able to catch, and perhaps treat, sickness that occurs in the natural womb but does not show up until after birth.* Atlantic 5/71, p48 [**1966**]

fetology, *n.* the medical study of the growth, development, and diseases of fetuses. *In what amounts to a quiet medical revolution, a new specialty called fetology is being created, and with it a new breed of doctor whose main concern is caring for unborn patients.* McCall's 1/67 (page not known) . . . *researchers . . . have been devising ways to save babies when a women's natural machinery fails and the fetus is born too soon. This new branch of medicine is called "fetology."* Atlantic 5/71, p45 [**1965**, from *feto-* fetus + *-logy* study of]

fetoprotein, *n.* a protein found normally in significant amount in the blood serum of a fetus, especially ALPHAFETOPROTEIN. *Other cancers are associated with the reappearance of fetoproteins, for example, carcinoembryonic antigens, found in colonic cancer.* McGraw-Hill Yearbook of Science and Technology 1974, p263 [**1973**, from *feto-* fetus + *protein*]

fetoscope, *n.* an optical instrument for direct observation of the fetus in the womb. *Another instrument that is becoming useful in diagnosing genetic and birth defect problems afflicting the unborn child is the fetoscope, a device which actually allows the doctor to look inside the womb. The fetoscope uses thin optical fibers—which themselves are still being developed and improved—to pipe light into the uterus and then carry the image of the fetus out.* Robert Cooke, Improving on Nature, 1977, p93 [**1971**, from *feto-* fetus + *-scope* instrument for viewing] —**fetoscopy,** *n.: The fetus can also be examined by ultrasound waves or, still as an experimental procedure, by fetoscopy (direct visual inspection) or by sampling the fetal blood. The optimum time for such prenatal tests is about the 16th week of gestation, and additional time may be required for tissue culture, bringing the fetus close to the period of viability.* Scientific American 1/77, p24

fettucine Alfredo, a dish made with fettucine (Italian noodles), butter, Parmesan cheese, black pepper, and often heavy cream. *Kelly was addressing an audience over a luncheon of fettuccine Alfredo at Toronto's crusty La Scala restaurant.* Maclean's 12/11/78, p41 [**1966**, from Italian *fettucine all' Alfredo*, named after *Alfredo*, the owner of a restaurant in Rome noted for this dish]

Feynman diagram ('feinmən), a graphic representation of various interactions of elementary particles, such as electrons, positrons, and photons. *Electromagnetic and weak processes exhibit striking similarities when depicted in the form of Feynman diagrams. Such diagrams symbolize the interactions that underlie subnuclear phenomena, for example the collision between two particles, which physicists refer to as a scattering event.* Scientific American 7/74, p53 [**1968**, named after Richard P. *Feynman*, 1918-1988, an American nuclear physicist who devised it]

F factor, a genetic factor that enables bacteria either to donate genetic material to other bacteria or to become the recipient of such material. *The F factor, which determines sexuality and conjugation in E. coli . . . is infectious, can transmit itself sequentially by conjugation and is an intact duplex DNA loop (of about 62 megadaltons), and there is about one of these F plasmids for every chromosome.* Scientific American 4/73, p22, [**1972**, from Fertility *factor*]

fiber, *n.* short for DIETARY FIBER. *Read the modern literature on nutrition written for the public to see how little space is de-*

voted to the need for fiber or, as grandmother used to call it, roughage. Washington Post 4/27/75, p6C [**1975**]

fiber art, the art of producing three-dimensional structures by weaving, winding, or otherwise shaping fibers on special frames to form artistic designs. Compare FABRIC SCULPTURE. *Most fiber art exploits the expressive potential of the fiber itself, playing up the hairiness of rope, emphasizing the sleekness of plastic yarns, or revealing unexpected qualities in wool.* Saturday Review 5/20/72, p58 [**1972**]

fiberfill, *n.* synthetic fiber or filament used as filling in clothing, pillows, quilts, etc. *The arms alone have burlap, fiberfill, muslin and batting back to back beneath the velvet.* New Yorker 11/18/67, p249 [**1955**]

fiberoptic or **fiberoptical**, *adj.* of, relating to, or using fiber optics. *Hemorrhage from the upper gastrointestinal tract remained a serious problem. Early diagnosis as to site and source, essential to successful treatment, was facilitated by prompt fiberoptic endoscopy.* Britannica Book of the Year 1971, p482 *The American Telephone and Telegraph Company announced last week that it plans to build a fiberoptical transmission system to carry telephone and other signals . . . using laser pulses rather than electric voltages to carry the information.* NY Times 1/27/80, pD20E [**1961**]

fiber optics, **1** a bundle of flexible glass or plastic filaments which can transmit light around curves and into inaccessible locations. *Fiber optics have been fabricated from materials that transmit light in the ultraviolet to the infrared region; the frequent dependence of scientific instrumentation on responses in this spectral region should give impetus to using such fibers in the design of this equipment.* McGraw-Hill Yearbook of Science and Technology 1971, p308 **2** the branch of optics using fibers or filaments to transmit light. *Technological progress in fiber optics, especially during the past ten years, has given the engineer an important additional tool for transferring information by means of light. The medical investigator can use a bundle of flexible fibers both to illuminate internal parts of a living body and to return an image or other analytical information.* Science 1/12/68, p183 [**1956**]

fibre-tip pen, *British.* a pen with a tip made of fibers pressed together; a kind of felt-tip pen. *The directors wear short grey overall jackets, their breast pockets charged with fibre-tip pens.* Sunday Times Magazine (London) 5/18/75, p17 [**1969**]

fibrinbioplast (ˌfaibrɪnˈbaiəˌplæst), *n.* a synthetic fibrous material used to replace human tissue. *Known as the Euroamerican Technocorporation, it will produce and market the Hungarian biochemical invention "fibrinbioplast," a human tissue substitute, usable in 30 different kinds of surgical operations.* Americana Annual 1973, p340 [**1973**, from *fibrin* fibrous protein + *bio-* living + *-plast* formed matter]

fibrinopeptide (ˌfaibrənouˈpepˌtaid), *n.* a protein substance formed in the process of blood clotting. *The fibrinopeptides of man and chimpanzee have been found to be identical in all 30 of their individual chemical sub-units . . . The fact that the genes of man and of the chimpanzee specify identical fibrinopeptides implies that the two species shared a common ancestor comparatively recently* [five million years ago]. Times (London) 2/18/70, p13 [**1969**]

fibrogenesis (ˌfaibrəˈdʒenəsis), *n.* the production or proliferation of fibrous tissue. *Inhalation of the various fibre types results in pulmonary fibrogenesis and an increased incidence of bronchogenic tumours in animals.* Nature 12/1/72, p256 [**1969**, from *fibro-* fiber + *genesis*]

fiche (fiːʃ), *n.* a card, strip of film, etc., used in indexing or cataloguing data. *Although the PVC* [polyvinyl chloride] *paper used is only about a third of the thickness of a microfilm fiche (0.002 in against 0.006 in) it is sufficiently opaque to take printing on both sides . . .* New Scientist 12/31/70, p601 *There is a strong possibility that a uniform, computer-supported fiche system will be developed over the next few years to prevent gaps from appearing in the records—not to*

"lose" people, as it were. New Scientist and Science Journal 3/11/71, p529 [**1959**, from French]

Fidelism (fəˈdelˌizəm), *n.* Anglicized form of FIDELISMO. . . . *that generation* [the young people] *is now trying out various kinds of anarchism, Trotskyism, Maoism, and Fidelism.* Manchester Guardian Weekly 10/10/68, p6 [**1960**]

Fidelismo or **fidelismo** (ˌfiːdeˈliːzmou), *n.* Communist revolutionary activity in Latin America based on the theories and practices of Fidel Castro, born 1927, Communist premier of Cuba. Also called CASTROISM. *It is too easy to dismiss* fidelismo *with the undoubtedly true judgments that the image of Fidel Castro in Latin America is not remotely as effective as it was in the first year or two of the revolution . . .* NY Times 1/2/67, p18 *. . . the incident served to underline the widening differences between the traditional Latin-American Moscow-based Communism and the Cuban variety, often referred to as Fidelismo.* Britannica Book of the Year 1968, p436 [**1958**, from Spanish *Fidelismo*, from *Fidel* Castro + *-ismo* -ism]

Fidelist (fəˈdelist), *n., adj.* Anglicized form of FIDELISTA. *"All of these countries have been inspired by the success of the Cuban revolution,"* claims Desnoes, an introspective revolutionary who calls himself a Fidelist. Times (London) 7/28/67, p8 *The apparent solution of his difficulties with the Kremlin has removed the danger of a potentially ruinous split between "Fidelist" and the old-line Communist groups.* NY Times 4/28/63, p11 [**1961**]

Fidelista or **fidelista** (ˌfiːdeˈliːstə), *n.* a supporter or advocate of Fidelismo. Also called CASTROIST or CASTROITE. . . . *if the fidelistas now accept the less revolutionary Soviet approach, Communism, as they have always said, becomes a relatively pallid force in contemporary Latin America.* Atlantic 1/70, p84 —*adj.* favoring or supporting Fidelismo. *The colony is British . . . At the same time, British Guiana is a part of South America. If it should go openly Fidelista, the whole of Latin America will feel the consequences.* Wall Street Journal 4/16/63, p34 [**1959** for noun; **1962** for adj., from Spanish *Fidelista*, from *Fidel* Castro + *-ista* -ist]

fido, *n.* a coin minted with an error or defect. *Edward Wallace, author of "A Numismatography of the Lincoln Cent". . . is an authority on minting errors and "coined" the word, Fido, to indicate mistakes in coinage. He derived the word—now popular in numismatic circles—by taking the first letters of freaks, irregulars, defects and oddities that occur in the production of monies.* NY Times 10/20/68 (page not known) [**1966**; see the quotation for the word's origin]

FIDO or **Fido**, *n. U.S. Aerospace.* an engineer concerned with the dynamics of a space flight, such as velocity, elevation, and changes in altitude and direction. *In the front row . . . sat three Flight Dynamics Engineers, the men responsible for the ship's trajectory: from right to left, the Guidance Officer, or GUIDO, who was the chief navigation officer, the Flight Dynamics Officer, or FIDO, who plotted the trajectory and made sure the spacecraft followed it; and the Retrofire Officer, or RETRO, who was in charge of the spacecraft's reëntry into the earth's atmosphere.* New Yorker 11/11/72, p49 [**1969**, from Flight Dynamics Officer]

field-effect, *adj.* relating to or using the effect produced by a varying electric field. *Field-Effect Electronics . . . covers the theory and applications of field effect transistors. Both junction and insulated gate transistors are given intensive coverage.* Science News 3/11/72, p176 *The alternative is the liquid crystal display (LCD), which takes only a fraction of the power of an LED display and therefore can be left on all the time. But despite improvements made lately with so-called field-effect liquid crystals, which use polarising filters over the display and background reflecting surface, these are still difficult to read in dim light or in the dark.* New Scientist 10/30/75, p285 [**1953**]

field-ion microscope, an extremely powerful microscope in which the emission of electrons of positive ions is used to produce a magnified image of the emitting surface on a fluorescent screen. *In the field-ion microscope, it it possible not only to observe the positions of individual atoms on a metal surface* *at low temperatures, but also to follow the movement of the atoms when the specimen is heated.* New Scientist 7/30/70, p224 **[1952]**

fifth force, *Physics.* a hypothetical force in nature intermediate in range between the gravitational and electromagnetic forces, which are infinite in range, and the strong and weak nuclear forces, which do not extend beyond the radius of an atomic nucleus. *Unlike gravity, the theoretical fifth force would be a repelling force. But it would influence objects only within a limited range; estimates are from a few feet to thousands of feet.* NY Times 3/4/86, pC11 **[1976]**

filamentous virus, a virus consisting of clusters of fine filaments. *Viruses can be readily observed in experimentally infected sensitive (indicator) strains that are lysed by viral infection. The filamentous virus . . . (about 10 nm in diameter) is first observed in the nucleus and, later, after lysis of the nuclear membrane, in the cytoplasm.* McGraw-Hill Yearbook of Science and Technology 1975, p411 **[1971]**

filiale (fil'yal), *n.* a subsidiary company in France. *This could mean that such outstanding problems as the present Westinghouse-EDF imbroglio may go on for some time yet, although it is unlikely that the new government will veto the Creusot-Loiret-Westinghouse nuclear filiale.* New Scientist 7/27/72, p204 **[1971, from French]**

film noir ('film 'nwar), a type of relentlessly gloomy motion picture photographed in dark tones and suggestive of evil. *The movie [The Big Heat] is . . . designed in light and shadows, and its underworld atmosphere glistens with the possibilities of sadism—this is a definitive film noir, with a few stunningly choreographed nasty scenes.* New Yorker 4/27/81, p28 **[1958, from French, literally, black film]**

filmography, *n.* **1** writings dealing with motion pictures. *This important book [The Haunted Screen, by Lotte H. Fisner] . . . is essential for any real follower of the cinema to add to their bookcase of filmography.* Manchester Guardian Weekly 1/3/70, p18 **2** a list of the films of a particular actor, director, etc. *Citadel Press, for example, has been publishing for several years now its* The Films of . . . *series, which includes complete filmographies of such performers as Bogart, Chaplin, Bette Davis, W.C. Fields, and, perhaps best of the lot, William K. Everson's perceptive annotations on the careers of Laurel and Hardy.* Saturday Review 11/4/67, p51 **3** a book or article dealing with the films of a particular actor, director, etc. *Books about the movies are tumbling from the presses with the frequency of cookbooks: star autobiographies, illustrated filmographies of their careers . . .* Harper's 11/70, p130 **[1962, from film + bibliography]**

fine-tune, *v.t.* to make fine adjustments in; regulate. *No single, central planning agency can fine-tune a diversified modern economy.* Time 3/29/71, p24 **[1970]**

fingerprint, *n.* short for DNA FINGERPRINT. *Fingerprints obtained from different tissues or body fluids of a particular individual are identical.* McGraw-Hill Yearbook of Science and Technology 1988, p153 **—v.t.** to identify (something) through a distinctive mark, trace, or impression. *"We're now trying to purify the atypical cholinesterase, to fingerprint it, then perform amino acid sequencing to see if we're right."* Science News 6/26/71, p438 *. . . a convenient, foolproof method was devised for "fingerprinting" missiles and other metal objects. In this method of photomicrograph or a replica of the metallic microstructure is used as a positive and unique means of identification.* Americana Annual 1968, p473 **[1970 for noun; 1955 for verb]**

fink, *v.i.* **fink out**, *U.S. Slang.* to back out; retreat. *Naturally, ARENA [a Brazilian political party] dominated Congress and so when Castella Branco decreed that the next President would be elected by Congress, the opposition finked out.* Time 10/7/66, p38 **[1963, from fink, v.i., slang for "to act as an informer," from fink, n., slang for "informer," originally, "strikebreaker," of unknown origin]**

fink-out, *n. U.S. Slang.* an act or instance of backing out; retreat. *The cop-out is like a fink-out, only more graceful. It is getting away with a renege.* New Yorker 6/24/67, p43 **[1967]**

Finlandization, *n.* the adoption by a non-Communist country or political area of a foreign policy like that of Finland, which aims to maintain friendly relations with the Soviet Union. *It would be idiotic to yield to political pressures and start weakening Nato's defense by pulling out U.S. troops just as the Russians have strengthened their forces. The psychological effect might produce the "Finlandization" of a free Europe that had come to doubt both itself and its greatest external friend.* NY Times 4/3/70, p36 *. . . there is a foreign policy called Finlandisation, which allows more independence than Rumania has.* Manchester Guardian Weekly 5/22/69, p7 **[1969]**

Finlandize, *v.t.* to cause (a country or political area) to adopt a policy of neutrality or accommodation in its relations with the Soviet Union. *Direct confrontations are unnecessary. The Russians can succeed better by indirection. They hope to Finlandize Western Europe.* New Yorker 7/19/76, p43 *Urho Kekkonen said that "Generally speaking, Finlandization should also be taken to refer to political conciliation with the Soviet Union, and I have noticed with satisfaction that there are many others who want to be Finlandized in this sense. In this sense it seems that only China and Albania do not want to be Finlandized."* Americana Annual 1976, p250 **[1972, back formation from FINLANDIZATION]**

firebase, *n.* a military base established especially to deliver heavy gunfire against an enemy. *The South Vietnamese came out of Sophia, one of their firebases near Tchepone, in a reasonably orderly fashion.* Manchester Guardian Weekly 3/27/71, p5 *Along the way, the raiders would set up permanent firebases to make sure that the trail was permanently closed.* Time 2/8/71, p19 **[1968]**

firebomb, *v.t.* to attack with incendiary bombs. *Since 1968 dozens of abandoned slum tenements in the East Village have been firebombed.* NY Times 6/19/71, p27 *In the meantime, attempts to firebomb the floating oil and burn it up were proving as unsuccessful as local efforts to dissolve it with detergents.* Science News 4/8/67, p328 **[1959, verb use of fire bomb an incendiary bomb]**

firebreak, *n.* a check in the escalation from conventional wars or weapons to all-out nuclear wars or weapons. *NATO says it needs neutron bombs to counter large concentrations of Warsaw Pact tanks. But conventional anti-tank missiles would probably do the job better at much less cost. They would also be less risky. Neutron warheads are likely to erode the gap between conventional and nuclear weapons—the so-called "firebreak"—and thus increase the probability of nuclear war.* New Scientist 10/26/78, p250 **[1962, transferred sense of the term (DAE 1884) for a strip of cleared land used to check the spread of a forest or prairie fire]**

fire brigade, *U.S. Military Slang.* a highly mobile military unit organized to handle emergency outbreaks or attacks. *The U.S. is likely to keep two airmobile divisions . . . on hand after the other fighting units have been withdrawn. These units will serve as "fire brigades," taking advantage of their mobility to rush to any location where it appears that the ARVN . . . is in trouble.* Time 1/26/70, p10 **[1955, extended meaning of the term for a group of fire fighters]**

firestorm, *n. U.S.* a violent, devastating outburst; explosion; storm. *Following the "Saturday Night Massacre" of Cox, Richardson, and Ruckelshaus, the White House was inundated by a "firestorm" of indignation (the figure employed by General Alexander Haig). The subsequent fortnight brought demands from a variety of sources that the President resign.* National Review 11/23/73, p1281 *The announcement that Sergeant Major Lymo Hascarni . . . had tied up the coveted big game (against, it is rumored, keen bidding from Liechtenstein and Bolivia) created an initial firestorm of protest from American basketball fans.* New Yorker 10/21/74, p36 **[1967, figurative sense of the term (1940's) meaning the windstorm accompanying the explosion of incendiary or atomic bombs]**

firmware, *n.* programs or data stored permanently in a computer's read-only memory (ROM) and not changeable by the operator with normal keyboard operations. Compare HARDWARE, SOFTWARE. *Efforts also were made to transfer some of the functions of software—the programs of instructions to computers—to small, high-speed memories which could operate as "assistants" to computer processing circuitry. Both magnetic and LSI [Large-Scale Integration] memories were investigated for this function, which was given the new label "firmware."* 1968 World Book Year Book, p274 *A modular construction, in which the basic computer consists of a standard box with wiring and power supplies capable of coping with the maximum memory capacity, to which is added the right hardware and firmware for the particular job . . .* New Scientist 1/7/71, p27 **[1968]**

first cousin, something or someone closely connected with another; a close relation. *On November 6, on the island of Amchitka in the Aleutians, a seismic event occurred that, though not an earthquake, was a first cousin to one.* Americana Annual 1972, p247 *Herr Alfred Tetzlaff is the hero of West Germany's hottest new situation comedy. He is a first cousin to both* All in the Family's *Archie Bunker and his relative, Alf Garnett of the BBC comedy series* Till Death Us Do Part. Time 5/13/74, p96 **[1968,** figurative use of the term for a child of one's uncle or aunt, parallel to earlier use of *cousin*]

first-strike, *adj.* (of a nuclear weapon or deterrent) openly deployed and vulnerable to destruction, and therefore designed only for an initial attack that would reduce or eliminate the enemy's power to retaliate. Compare SECOND-STRIKE. . . . *the Poseidon* [is] *effective against hardened targets; it can, therefore, be regarded as a first-strike weapon.* New Scientist 9/24/70, p619 **—n.** an attack by first-strike weapons. . . . *the Soviet ICBMs are certain to be vulnerable to a US first-strike. This may account for the continued deployment of the SS-11 and SS-13 missiles on the philosophy that they are intended to provide a residual second-strike capacity should a US first blow be made.* New Republic 3/28/70, p14 **[1962]**

first-strike capability, the ability of a nuclear power to attack another power's missile silos with first-strike weapons, thereby reducing or eliminating its ability to retaliate. *The Americans argued that the U.S. is not seeking a first-strike capability that could knock out the Soviet nuclear force in a surprise attack.* Time 11/28/69, p36 *The effect might be a period of dangerous nuclear nervousness, with each side tempted to shoot first if it thought the other was approaching a first-strike capability.* NY Times 2/6/68, p42 **[1962]**

First World, the chief industrialized countries within the political power bloc of the world, including many of the countries of Western Europe, the United States, Japan, and the Soviet Union (often used attributively). *At times he* [Dom Helder] *has used his foreign platforms for stinging denunciations of terror and torture in Brazil; more often he tries to prick the conscience of the First World for its complicity in the Third World's troubles.* Time 6/24/74, p61 *I was dismayed to read Dr. Hanlon's column, which is libellous and has obviously been printed because of the knowledge that it is difficult for Third World Scientists to take legal action against a "First World" journal.* New Scientist 2/6/75, p339 **[1974,** patterned after THIRD WORLD]

FIS, *British.* abbreviation of *Family Income Supplement. Even FIS families, who receive a supplement because of their low wages, sometimes have to pay income tax.* Times (London) 1/27/72, p16 **[1972]**

fiscal drag, *Economics.* the depressing effect on economic growth of an excess of tax collections over government expenditures. *Even in places where taxes seem most onerous, among them Scandinavia and Britain, there is an increasing drive towards adjustments intended to eliminate fiscal drag and taxation of the purely paper capital gains that inflation brings.* NY Times 7/30/78, pD3 **[1972]**

fish-eye, *adj. Photography.* **1** covering an extremely wide angle of view, usually such that a distorted image is created. *Several of the photographs, all of which are big enlargements,*

impressively displayed, are visually strong. A few, taken with the so-called "fish-eye" lens, are attempts at interpretation to give an impression of the complete environment . . . NY Times 2/19/67, pB30 **2** using or made with an extremely wide-angle lens. *The 160° "fish-eye" cameras were synchronized to less than a tenth of a second for each pair of eight-second exposures.* New Scientist 3/68, p540 **[1961]**

fish-in, *n.* a protest demonstration in which a group engages in illegal fishing at a particular body of water to force a confrontation with authorities who had banned fishing there. *Marlon Brando came here one or two winters ago to the Nisqually River to fish with the Nisqually Indians in their "fish-in" protest against unfair treatment by the state of Washington.* Atlantic 5/66, p36 **[1964,** see -IN]

fishkill, *n.* a large-scale destruction of fish by water pollution. *He was at Escambia Bay talking about "fishkills"—that's three or four acres of pollution-poisoned fish piled 15-feet high, and the kills happen 300 times a year.* NY Times Magazine 3/12/72, p112 **[1962]**

fish protein concentrate, a tasteless, odorless, and durable fish flour made by pulverizing dried whole hake and similar species, used as food or as a dietary supplement. *Fish protein concentrate (FPC) is a second approach to feeding on the world's hungry populations. FPC is on the verge of worldwide mass production except in the U.S.* 1970 Britannica Yearbook of Science and the Future, p170 **[1962]**

fission-track dating, a method of determining the age of rocks and other geological formations by counting the number of characteristic tracks left by the spontaneous fission or uranium 238 during the lifetime of each sample. The number of tracks is proportional to the age of the sample. *Fission-track dating is direct and visual and has proved to be applicable to many materials and over an enormous range of ages. The critical factor is the uranium content of the material to be dated. A concentration of one part per million—which is common in rocks—provides enough tracks to date an object older than some 100,000 years easily.* Scientific American 6/69, p34 **[1965]**

fitness center, a gymnasium. *Metropolitan Tower was graced by a "24 hour concierge," a "state of the art security system," a "24 hour catering kitchen," a "private fitness center."* Spy (The New York Monthly) 3/88, p102 **[1988]**

five, *n.* **take five,** *Slang.* to take a rest; relax. *Being a peripatetic President is tiring, so Cuba's Fidel Castro decided to take five—on a reviewing stand in Ethiopia's Revolution Square. As Colonel Mengistu Haile Mariam, Ethiopia's head of state, chatted away, Castro slumped in his chair and watched a parade.* Time 10/2/78, p89 **[1965,** extended sense of the phrase meaning "take a five-minute break," used (since the 1920's) especially during rehearsals for a play, concert, etc.]

fix, *n Informal.* something whose supply becomes continually necessary or greatly desired. *Some viewers, of course, outraged at the loss of their favorite soap operas and talk shows, would have preferred it canceled before it had even started. "Is this* [televising of House of Commons session] *going to happen every day?" was a repeated bleat from those deprived of their Monday soap fix.* Maclean's 10/31/77, p20 *I wondered, too, why he, a serious writer, even did these shows year in and year out, and whether or not he was gearing up for another round of publicity not to promote the book, because the book still wasn't finished, but to convince himself, meanwhile that he was alive, to get a fix.* NY Times Magazine 7/9/78, p23 **[1976,** figurative use of the slang term for a shot of a narcotic]

fizzbo, *n. U.S.* the sale of a house without the services of a real-estate broker. *'Fizzbo' is the pejorative term that realty brokers give to "for sale by owner" home transactions. It's a dirty word in most agents' books—it means no commissions.* Newsday 4/5/86, p5 **[1986,** from pronunciation of the abbreviation *fsbo,* from *for sale by owner*]

flack, *v.i. U.S. Slang.* to act as someone's press agent. *Bill Woestendiek, the newsman fired by Washington's WETA-TV because his wife was hired to flack for Martha Mitchell* [wife of the then attorney general], *has a new job* . . . Time 6/15/70, p40 [**1966,** verb use of *flack* (1946), slang term for a press agent]

flackery, *n. Slang.* publicity; promotion. *There were also slogans minted by a Manhattan advertising agency and mimeographed press releases that smacked of big-city flackery.* Time 5/23/69, p21 . . . *Belly-Button . . . happens to be a very funny book. Funny enough, perhaps, to sell well even without flim-flam or flackery.* Maclean's 4/67, p110 [**1962,** from *flack,* slang term for a press agent + *-ery,* noun suffix denoting occupation or profession]

fladge (flædʒ), *n. Especially British Slang.* flagellation as a form of sexual perversion; flogging. *The two big bookstalls in Trastevere go in for porn and fladge, modulating through books of Nazi atrocities to the anthropozoology of Desmond Morris.* Times (London) Literary Supplement 8/4/72, p916 [**1972,** altered and shortened form of *flagellation*]

flag, *v.t. U.S. Military use.* to put a flag of special color on a file folder or card to stop it from being altered or processed in any way. . . . *Wilson was able to order Colonel James D. Kiersey, chief of staff at Fort Benning, to "flag" Calley's records, an Army procedure freezing any promotion or transfer for a soldier.* Harper's 5/70, p81 [**1968,** extended from the earlier verb sense (OEDS 1934) "to mark with a flag or tag in order to find easily"]

flagellin (fləˈdʒelin), *n.* the fibrous protein from which the flagella of bacteria is made up. *There are two genes, called* H1 *and* H2, *that encode the protein flagellin, which is the main component of the flagellar filament.* Science 9/19/80, p1370 [**1955, 1969,** from *flagell*um + *-in* (as in *protein*)]

flag of necessity, *U.S.* a foreign flag under which a ship is registered and sailed to avoid strict regulation, paying certain taxes, etc. *In the United States the flag of convenience is bluntly called the flag of necessity, for without it owners would not be able to operate in what is a very competitive market.* Times (London) 3/19/70, pV [**1967**]

flagship, *n.* **1** the chief or leading item of a group or collection. *Located in the city's plush southeastern section, Myers Park High School has long been the flagship of Charlotte's educational system, known for its legions of National Merit Scholars and All-State quarterbacks.* Atlantic 11/72, p20 *The patents, Bunker Ramo claimed, cover crucial components used in IBM's 360 and 370 computer series—the "flagships" of its computer line.* Newsweek 3/11/74, p74 **2** Attributive use: *Although the Beacon was the first Copley newspaper . . . the editorial tone of the fiercely conservative chain is set by the flagship paper, the* San Diego Union. Harper's 4/70, p77 [**1955,** figurative use of the naval term]

flak, *n. U.S.* **1** criticism; censure. *". . . we now have a tough anti-pollution law, and the city is taking a lot of flak because its own incinerators won't be upgraded in time for the deadline set by that law."* New Yorker 5/10/69, p60 **2** exchange of criticism; a heated quarrel or argument. *In spite of the current flak between Mayor Lindsay and Edward Logue, the tough, intelligent, battlehardened former [urban] renewal administrator of Boston and New Haven who was picked to head the state corporation, the potential for the city is unlimited.* NY Times 5/20/68, p46 [**1963,** figurative senses of *flak* antiaircraft gunfire (1940), from the German acronym formed from Fliegerabwehrkanone antiaircraft cannon]

flake[1], *n. U.S. Slang.* a very unconventional or eccentric person. *For kicks, [skier Jean-Claude] Killy races fast cars and jumps from airplanes; he has tried his hand at bullfighting, and he has a well-deserved reputation as something of a flake.* Time 2/9/68, p34 *He [Dizzy Dean] was a "flake" a full generation before that word came into use, and none of his fun-production exists today.* NY Times 8/2/68, p36 [**1962,** perhaps back-formation from FLAKY]

flake[2], *n. U.S. Slang.* an arrest to meet a quota or to satisfy pressure for police action. See the quotation for details. *"An accommodation collar,"* he [Patrolman William R. Phillips] *said, is an arrest, to satisfy superior officers, that is presented in court*

with such weak evidence that acquittal is assured. "A flake," *however, is the arrest, on known false evidence, of a person for something he did not do.* NY Times 10/20/71, p36 [**1971,** probably so called from the flimsiness of the evidence submitted]

flake[3], *v.i.* flake out, *Slang.* **1** to lose consciousness. . . . *what is the Greek national drink anyway?—oh, yeah, ouzo, and everybody eventually flakes out.* Maclean's 6/67, p56 *Mr. Michael Nyman, a psychiatric worker at the unit, said that people taking the mixture "flaked out" after having hallucinations.* Times (London) 4/29/68, p2 **2** to get out; leave; disappear. *By the way, both of us agree that* Norwegian Wood *and* Day Tripper *are not undecent. Where did you get that idea? Take our advice: state the right facts or flake out!* Time 7/15/66, p9 [**1960** for def. 1; **1963** for def. 2; the original meaning, still current, is to fall asleep or collapse from fatigue (OEDS 1942)]

flakey, *adj.* variant spelling of FLAKY. *An officer might handle vast sums of money, the temptations were enormous, and there was some flakey behaviour.* Manchester Guardian Weekly 10/13/73, p19 [**1972**]

flak jacket, a padded jacket with small steel plates sewn in place to protect the trunk of the body from bullets or shrapnel, originally used by air force pilots. *On the corner of Tu Do and Le Loi, in the heart of Saigon, a military policeman in a flak jacket stood with a transistor radio pressed against his ear.* NY Times 6/6/68, p33 [**1953**]

flako, *adj. U.S. Slang.* drunk. *Yet they greeted Harry with a fireside grudging gruffness that said, flako or otherwise, he was another daddy and welcome.* Atlantic 2/71, p81 [**1971,** from the phrase *flaked out* worn out (from drunkenness) + *-o,* as in *blotto, wino*]

flaky, *adj. Slang.* very unconventional; eccentric or crazy. Also spelled FLAKEY. *"Andy is a great guy to room with. He's flaky of course, but not quite as crazy as I am.* NY Times 3/31/67, p42 *If a kid can't take being in a class, it's pointless to force him to stay. He can get more out of figuring out why he wanted to leave—just as we can now talk to the kid who was punching me and ask why he acts so flaky.* Atlantic 3/69, p67 [**1957,** probably so called from the idea of being flighty or lightheaded]

flame-out, *n. U.S.* **1** the act or fact of being destroyed or crushed; destruction or extinction. *But now the great surge that carried racial justice briefly to the top of the nation's domestic agenda in the 1960s has been stalemated—by war, economics, the flame-out of the old civil-rights coalition.* Newsweek 2/19/73, p29 **2** some person crushed by a sense of defeat or something destroyed by the loss of an exciting or fascinating quality. *A man often faces the jolting realization that he cannot accomplish all his early dreams, and, more important, begins to think seriously for the first time about the inevitability of death. Some flameouts simply sink into depression, others start to drink heavily.* Time 4/13/70, p90 [**1970,** figurative use of an earlier meaning (1950) the extinction of flame in the combustion chamber of a jet engine]

flame stitch, another name for BARGELLO. *You will look for bargello or "flame stitch" in vain in the "Dictionary." I could find nothing in any of the illustrations under that or any other name that looked like it. Bargello means, literally, police headquarters in Italian. Bargello (also called "Florentine stitch" today) obviously takes its name from the great museum of sculpture in Florence.* NY Times Magazine 6/11/72, p57 [**1965**]

flanken, *n.pl. U.S.* cooked ribs of beef cut from the flank. *I picked out flanken in horseradish with boiled potatoes and lima beans, a cup of noodle soup, a large roll, a cup of coffee, and a piece of cake—all for sixty cents.* New Yorker 7/31/71, p35 [**1966,** from Yiddish, from German *Flanken* sides, flanks (of beef, etc.)]

flap, *n.* a concentration of sightings of unidentified flying objects in a small area within a short period. *A sharp increase in the total number of the U.F.O.s sighted during the past year has, of course, caused considerable excitement in local flying-saucer circles . . . As for 1966, it got off to a very promising start with the U.F.O. flap in Michigan. We talked the Michigan* *flap over with three local ufologists and found them both elat-ed and alarmed.* New Yorker 4/9/66, p32 [**1966**]

flappable, *adj.* tending to be excited or confused in a crisis. *As he demonstrated for a nationwide audience while he was being questioned by newsmen after the assassination attempt, Chief Reddin is not easily flappable. A round-faced man with dark eyes, he breaks into a wide, thin smile every few minutes, under normal circumstances.* NY Times 6/6/68, p21 [**1962,** back for-mation from UNFLAPPABLE]

flare, *n.* short for FLARE PASS. *No self-respecting football fan would dare to offer advice without couching it in jargon: red dogs, crack-back blitz . . . flares, and loops.* Harper's 1/72, p22 [**1972**]

flare pass, a quick pass in U.S. football to a back heading toward the sideline. *We will miss watching men like Humm throw flare passes with such a low trajectory that only defense men six inches high could intercept.* New Yorker 9/30/72, p106 [**1965**]

flash, *U.S. Slang.* —*v.i.* **1** to experience the effects of a psyche-delic drug. . . . *if they [drug addicts] are not stoned out of their skulls or have not flipped or flashed or freaked out, they rap about the people over thirty who have ruined their lives . . .* New Yorker 12/5/70, p218 [**1970**] **2** Usually, **flash on.** to ap-preciate immediately; understand quickly. *"I really flashed on that song."* Time 8/17/70, p32 *If you "dig" something, you "flash on it," "turn on," "get into it."* Harper's 7/69, p60 [**1969**] —*n.* the initial effect of a narcotic. Compare RUSH. *Many speed freaks still prefer to inject speed with particular impurities be-cause amphetamine laced with other substances, such as ether, is thought to produce a heavier flash or more intense rush than pure methamphetamine does.* Saturday Review 7/8/72, p38 [**1967**]

flashback, *n.* the recurrence of a hallucination originally expe-rienced under the influence of a hallucinogenic drug. *This de-cline [in the use of LSD] has been due, in part, to the bad "trips" that terrified many users, the frequency of disturbing "flashbacks," and the prolonged anxiety states and psychotic reactions that were experienced.* Americana Annual 1970, p486 [**1968,** extended sense of the literary and motion-picture term (OEDS 1916) for a return to an earlier occurrence in the midst of a chronological sequence of events]

flash-cook, *v.t.* to cook, or sometimes to sterilize, by a very short exposure to intense heat, such as infrared radiation. *Dairy Custard is the first test of a new technology called aseptic can-ning, which gives a fresher tasting product because cans are flash-cooked for six seconds rather than sterilised for 60 min-utes.* Sunday Times (London) 7/4/71, p38 [**1966**]

flashcube, *n.* a small disposable plastic cube containing a flash-bulb on each of four sides that revolve into place as a photo-graph is taken. *Flashbulbs were being partly replaced by flashcubes, which were basically four bulbs in expendable re-flectors, the cube turning after each shot.* Britannica Book of the Year 1970, p615 [**1965**]

flasher, *n. Slang.* a person who exposes his genitals in public, usually suddenly and briefly. Compare STREAKER. *Sara never rides the subway. She fears—not necessarily in the following order—murderers, rapists, purse-snatchers, flashers and all of the seamy types who take advantage of rush-hour crowds to rub up against women.* NY Times 1/12/78, p18 [**1974,** from *flash* to display + *-er*]

flash-forward, *n.* a motion-picture or literary technique, in which a scene of a future event is given ahead of its occurrence in a chronological sequence. *The hero . . . is killed in a flash-forward at the start of the story, and the movie that follows is a sort of drowning man's vision of everything that was ever dear to him.* New Yorker 9/5/70, p64 *Using flash-back and flash-forward from these prison reflections, Dennis Potter slowly built a believable picture of a complex personality.* New Scientist and Science Journal 12/23/71, p229 [**1955,** patterned after *flashback*]

flashlight fish, any of a family of fishes, especially *Photo-blepharon palpebratus,* that emit light from special lumines-cent organs. *The Atlantic flashlight fish lives in more than 500 feet of water and only enters lesser depths to feed during dark-ness. Its light organs, which may be seen by divers as far as 50 feet away, contain glowing bacteria and can be covered with a lid. Nealson plans to study the relationship between the fish and its bacteria.* Science News 3/4/78, p135 [**1975**]

flash pack, *British.* a product displaying a reduced price on the package. *"Flash-packs," as they are called in the trade, are largely responsible for housewives' confusion over grocery prices. It is hard to remember the "real" price of an article if you hardly ever pay it. There can be 40 or 50 flash-packs on show in a big supermarket at any one time.* Times (London) 9/8/72, p12 [**1970**]

flat pack, a thin, sealed package of semiconductors with leads connecting the unit to microelectronic circuits. *The Chinese diode-transistor logic element uses a method of packaging (de-veloped in the U.S.) called the TO-5 package; the transistor-transistor element uses what is called flat pack.* Scientific American 12/72, p14 [**1968**]

flat-plate collector, a group of flat metal-and-glass plates to ab-sorb solar radiation, mounted over air ducts or tubes carrying liquid that are heated by the energy absorbed from the plates. *Flat-plate collectors sloped toward the south in Madison, with a slope equal to the latitude, will have incident on them an av-erage daily radiation of 3.4 kw-h/m² in January and 5.6 kw-h/m² in July. These data illustrate the gains to be obtained by orienting a collector in a favorable manner.* Science 1/16/76, p144 [**1976**]

flat time sentence, *U.S.* a prison sentence that is specified by law and cannot be reduced by judiciary discretion or parole. *The legislatures in Maine, California and Indiana have al-ready adopted "flat time" sentences, which have a specified number of years. These sentences are usually shorter than "in-determinate" terms, where the maximum is high and a judge has broad discretion to sentence a defendant to, say, five to 15 years.* NY Times 12/19/76, pD8 [**1961**]

flat water, a lake or other similar body of water without turbu-lence and current. *They [canoeist] read the journal of the American Whitewater Affiliation. To them, a lake is not a lake but "flat water."* New Yorker 3/21/70, p128 [**1970**]

flavodoxin, *n.* an electron-carrying protein containing ribofla-vin and associated with oxidation-reduction reactions in bacte-rial cells. Compare RUBREDOXIN. *Consistent with their reductive character, ferredoxins, and flavodoxins, proteins oth-erwise typical of anaerobes, have been implicated in nitrogen fixation by Azotobacter and also by the aerobic root nodule system.* McGraw-Hill Yearbook of Science and Technology 1974, p308 [**1971,** from *flavo-* flavin, flavoprotein (literally, yel-low) + *redox* oxidation-reduction + *-in* (chemical suffix)]

flavomycin, *n.* an antibiotic derived from soil bacteria and re-lated to streptomycin. *Regulations will also be made so that from 1 March, 1971, flavomycin and virginiamycin can be used as feed antibiotics available without prescription though subject to some conditions, including the extent and method of use.* New Scientist and Science Journal 2/25/71, p433 [**1970,** from *flavo-* yellow + *-mycin* fungal substance (ultimately from Greek *mýkēs* fungus)]

flavon, *n. Nuclear Physics.* a hypothetical constituent of quarks that determines electric charge. *In the allocation of electric charge, however, a complication arises. If there are only two flavons and if they are the sole carriers of electric charge, not all of the charge values observed in nature can be reproduced.* Scientific American 4/83, p63 [**1981,** from FLAVOR + *-on* ele-mentary particle]

flavor, *n. Nuclear Physics.* a specific type or variety of quark, such as the down quark or the strange quark. *The different kinds of quarks . . . are known technically as flavors. They fol-low the universal rule that each particle of matter is matched by a companion antiparticle that is equal in mass but opposite in electrical charge.* World Book Science Annual 1978, p324 *Experiments of recent years led to the grouping of differ-ent quarks in terms of at least five "flavors" and three "colors."*

Such names are merely conveniences, and have no more meaning than numbers. NY Times 9/2/79, p28 **[1975]**

flea collar, a collar for dogs and cats, containing a substance to kill fleas and ticks. *The message, complete with merry jingle, was a commercial for flea collars for dogs and cats.* Times (London) 11/4/78, p11 **[1953]**

flesh, *n.* **press (the) flesh,** *Especially U.S.* to shake hands. [Pete V.] *Domenici is a breathless, ebullient crowd pleaser, while strong, low-key Jack Daniels, in contrast, is a diffident public speaker who prefers to press the flesh with individual voters in a kind of Western one-on-one campaign.* Time 11/6/72, p58 *The state assemblymen . . . stayed at the rear of the crowd for a while to clap shoulders, press flesh, show off their memory for names, and often mention, incidentally, next week's fund-raiser.* New Yorker 9/4/78, p86 **[1972]** ►According to William Safire (*Safire's Political Dictionary,* 1978), the phrase was first used by Lyndon B. Johnson in 1960. The expression may have originated in black jazz slang.

fleshette, *n.* one of a spray of darts exploded as an antipersonnel weapon. *In Vietnam there was added yet a third shell, the canister round, a blunt-nosed bullet which exploded on impact and distributed 9800 "fleshettes," which look like little roofing nails with barbs on the end; the canister round was for use against people, or personnel.* Atlantic 11/70, p63 **[1969,** alteration (influenced by *flesh*) of *fléchette* a small dart-shaped projectile, from French]

flesh-printing, *n.* an electronic tracing or recording of the protein patterns found in the flesh of fish to help identify and study them. *Scientists and wildlife officials in Ohio are developing a method of electronic "flesh-printing" to help trace the migration patterns of fish. By making pictures of the protein patterns in walleye pike fillets, they hope to match the fish with their birth waters and thereby make it easier to chart, control and increase the walleye population.* NY Times 7/16/68, p36 **[1968]**

flexi-, a combining form meaning "flexible," used originally (1960's) in various trademarks (*Flexi-Van, Flexiprene*) but now freely used to form compounds such as the following: **—flexibacteria,** *n.pl.: Some researchers studying the growth of filamentous bacteria, called flexibacteria, in Yellowstone National Park geyser pools, believed that the formation of stromatolites by flexibacteria may have taken place in the Precambrian.* 1974 Britannica Yearbook of Science and the Future, p202 **—flexi-cover,** *n.: One is left wondering whether, for it to survive and quench the thirst of the further education of students rather than just the academics, Copley's Camden may not have to become more workaday: go into flexi-covers and on to less beautiful paper.* Times (London) 5/27/77, pIII **—flexinomics,** *n.* [*flexi* + economics]: *Vice President Spiro Agnew sounded off in Las Vegas about "the strange, new 'flexinomics' being tested and scrapped by a desperate candidate" whom he did not have to name.* Newsweek 9/25/72, p33 **—flexi-roof,** *n.: On television, meanwhile, they showed a lovely flexi-roof, called a Gridshell, which inscrutably reverses the effect of a draped fisherman's net, and by imitating that sort of lattice-work, becomes convex rather than concave. Clever stuff.* Listener 3/27/75, p415 **[1972]** See FLEXITIME.

flexible time, another name for FLEXITIME. *The company working day is lengthened, normally in Germany from seven in the morning till seven in the evening. And two quite different types of working time are introduced—"flexible" time, during which employees have the choice of being in or not, and "core" time, when everybody should be present at desk or workbench.* New Scientist 3/16/72, p602 **[1972]**

flexiplace, *n.* a workplace at home connected by a computer to an office. *Now that idealized world to come is undergoing heated revision as more and more people use their homes as places for computerized work. In experimental projects across the U.S. several hundred clerical and professional workers have agreed to abandon the office and work at home on computer terminals electronically linked to their firms' office computers.*

In management jargon they are "telecommuting" and work at "flexiplaces." Time 1/30/84, p63 **[1984]**

flexitime, *n.* variant of FLEXTIME. *In the search for improving the work environment, flexitime has become a legitimate option. What began as an experiment is no longer a novelty, and most of its users are convinced that its benefits far outweigh any shortcomings.* Reader's Digest 10/78, p210 **[1973]**

flextime, *n.* the staggering of working hours to enable each employee to work the full quota of time but at periods most convenient for the individual. Also called FLEXITIME, FLEXIBLE TIME, GLIDING TIME. *Flextime is especially appreciated by working parents, who can choose either to see their children off to school in the morning or to pick them up after classes, and sports enthusiasts, who can play golf or tennis in the early morning or late afternoon. Supervisors report that productivity generally improves under Flextime—since employees can work at the hours when they feel most alert—and that absenteeism drops.* Time 1/10/77, p52 **[1972,** from *flexible* + *time*]

flight attendant, a person who attends passengers in an airplane. *A few of the new words will give the flavour of their enervating bowdlerisation. Salesmen becomes sales persons. Maids becomes house workers. Airline stewardesses becomes airplane flight attendants. Foremen becomes supervisors, jury foremen becomes jury forepersons.* Sunday Times 5/4/75, p18 *American Airlines agreed today to rehire 300 flight attendants who were dismissed between 1965 and 1970 because they became pregnant and to pay them a total of $2.7 million.* NY Times 10/4/77, p40 **[1947, 1974]**

flight capital, funds transferred from one country to another, usually to avoid impounding or losses resulting from taxation, inflation, devaluation, etc. *Swiss officials are considering a variety of measures aimed at toughening the regulation of the country's 553 banks . . . Many of the possible reforms affect the way the banks handle funds from abroad—including stolen funds, flight capital, tax-dodge money and other unsavory negotiables that have found their way into the Swiss system, no questions asked.* Time 7/18/77, p74 **[1962,** from the phrase *flight of capital,* long used in economics to designate the movement of capital out of a country] **—flight capitalist:** *Judging from the financial statistics of Swiss banks, it is more the exception than the rule for the flight capitalists to be caught.* NY Times 5/11/76, p52

flightworthy, *adj.* capable of flight or of being used in flight. *. . . Shepard underwent surgery, and examination by National Aeronautics and Space Administration physicians found his condition flightworthy.* Science News 5/31/69, p527 *But "a considerable amount of development is still necessary before these sensors become production, flightworthy hardware."* Times (London) 3/20/70, p33 **[1969]**

flip, *v.i.* Often, **flip out.** *Slang.* to lose one's mind; go crazy. *"He goes to Notre Dame and that's all right, but he mustn't even hear about Chartres. Sheila, you've flipped."* Harper's 4/68, p71 *Kingsley Hall* [is] *an anti-hospital in London where "people who flipped out, or near to it, could stay and go through whatever they had to go through without drugs, electric shocks, or other psychiatric hocus pocus."* Manchester Guardian Weekly 4/18/70, p15 **[1950, 1961,** shortened from the slang expression *flip one's lid* (1949)]

flip chart, a chart to display information in sequence, consisting of large sheets attached at the top that can be turned over one after the other. *The apparently dreaded flip-charts that were mentioned are quite simply one of the many methods used to help experts in highly technical areas communicate graphically in the course of lectures, etc.* Times (London) 11/10/74, p20 **[1956]**

flip-flops, *n.pl.* or **flip-flop sandals,** flat sandals, made of composition rubber, held on the foot by a thong that goes between the toes and over the instep. *A woman in Tampa said that her daughter had left home on October 28th—wearing a white blouse, pink pants, and green "flip-flops"—and had not been in touch since.* New Yorker 4/15/72, p132 *We have passed whole families climbing up in wellington boots and flip flops, and people climbing Striding Edge at Hellvelyn without maps* or compasses. Times (London) 8/23/77, p11 [**1969,** so called from the flip-flopping motion of the sole hitting against the foot]

flipping, *Slang.* —*adj.* (used as a mild intensive) confounded; blooming. *"You seem to think you're in a flipping hotel, not in a hospital."* Times (London) 9/21/70, p7 *If private business is so much more efficient than any Government agency why don't we farm out the whole flipping government operation to some private business?* Wall Street Journal 3/4/65, p12 —*n.* U.S. See the quotation for the meaning. *The bill contained other provisions which Wallace contends never would have passed on their own merits: abolition of garnishments on the first $80 of a worker's pay; outlawing "flipping," or charging interest on interest, a common loan-sharking practice.* NY Times Magazine 1/2/72, p33 [**1911, 1948** for adj.; **1969** for noun]

flip side, the reverse; the other or opposite side. *The manoeuvring . . . and the hustling which is the flip-side of showbiz.* Sunday Times (London) 3/28, p7 *Barbra's marked resemblance to Fanny* [Brice] *is more than nasal. She is the flip side of Cinderella—the homely girl who made it.* Time 10/4/68, p63 [**1962,** extended use of *flip side* (OEDS 1949) the back or second side of a phonograph record]

FLIR, *n.* acronym for *forward-looking infrared,* an electronic device to detect objects in the dark, used by the military in night fighting. *The FLIR . . . heat-sensitive system is like a television camera that can see at night. Objects show up on a screen, defined by the heat they are giving off, which is picked up by the camera. FLIR was initially developed for use in aircraft but now can be used by ground troops as well.* Manchester Guardian Weekly (Washington Post section) 10/24/76, p15 [**1976,** so called because it was originally intended for use in the nose of an airplane]

float, *v.i.* to fluctuate in value on the international monetary market in response to supply and demand rather than by government support or regulation. *Overseas, the currency fluctuations caused by the high price of oil forced France to stop supporting the price of the franc—allowing it to float against other currencies.* Newsweek 1/28/74, p56 [**1965**] —*v.t.* to allow (a currency) to float. *The Germans are angry with the French for floating the franc and thus trying to underprice German exports.* Time 2/11/74, p38 [**1970**] —*n.* **1** *British.* a sum of small change with which a shopkeeper, tradesman, etc., begins the day's work. *"What's that, then?" I asked, pointing at the drawer. "That's my float," she grunted. "I'm not parting with that".* Sunday Times Magazine (London) 3/26/72, p63 [**1955**] **2** the act or process of floating a currency or currencies. *According to West German officials, the collective float against the dollar by six of the nine Common Market countries would be a "dirty" one.* Cape Times 3/17/73, p4 [**1970**]

floatfishing, *n.* fishing while floating down a river in a boat. *After an unsuccessful effort to find a school of small bluefish that we hoped to catch for bait we anchored off the mouth of Lookout Bight and Barden Inlet . . . The latter named species* [pinfish] *are most commonly used in the area when floatfishing for kings, but Earnhardt believes the young blues are much better.* NY Times 10/24/76, pE8 [**1963**]

floating decimal point, a decimal point that is automatically moved into place as each operation is performed on an electronic calculator. *On top of that, the machine has a minus sign indicator. A floating decimal point. True underflow for calculations beyond 8 digits.* Advertisement, New Scientist 5/3/73, p285 [**1973**] ▶The concept of the *floating decimal point* (OEDS 1948) was introduced with the early calculating machines.

flokati (flou'kɑ:ti:), *n. sing.* or *pl.* an inexpensive shaggy rug made in Greece. *Personally, I would still choose wood which does not show signs of wear on the main traffic routes, is not ruined if somebody drops a bottle of ink over it, and improves rather than deteriorates with age. It helps even cheap rugs such as goatskin, Greek flokati, and Italian . . . druggets look ex-*

pensive. Times (London) 6/26/76, p22 [**1966,** from Modern Greek *phlokátē*]

flooding, *n. Psychology.* a method of treating a phobia by controlled exposure of the patient to the cause. Compare IMPLOSION. See also AGORAPHOBIA. *Flooding consists of directly confronting the patient with the situation or object that is feared. Instead of simply imagining the stimulus (as in desensitization), the phobic is safely exposed to it. As with desensitization, the stimuli are carefully graded and presented in a systematic way, with the patient relaxing between encounters.* Encyclopedia Science Supplement (Grolier) 1979, p62 [**1969,** from gerund of *flood, v.,* to deluge, overwhelm]

floor-crossing, *n.* the act or practice of voting with members of the opposing party in a legislative body, especially in a parliament modeled after the British parliament. Maclean's: *Is the two-party system here to stay? Will Congress MPs now defect to Janata?*

Desae: *We will stop defections by law. We certainly do not approve of floor crossing. We will probably have three parties rather than two, but the plethora of parties will disappear.* Maclean's 4/4/77, p59 [**1967**] —**floor-crosser,** *n.*: *That well-known floor-crosser Reg Prentice . . . made his debut on the Conservative back benches last week.* Times (London) 11/11/77, p14

floor-through, *n. U.S.* an apartment that takes up an entire story of a building. *The trust she came into at twenty-one allowed her to live in a large floor-through, to decorate it, and to give dinner parties.* Harper's 2/70, p48 [**1964**]

floppy, *n.* short for FLOPPY DISK. *Just as CDs are replacing records and tapes in home sound systems, they are beginning to replace certain kinds of books, microfilms, even floppies (the most commonly used type of computer disks) . . .* Encyclopedia Science Supplement (Grolier) 1987, p107 [**1979**]

floppy disk or **floppy disc,** a transportable magnetic disk on which to store data in a digital computer memory. Also called DISKETTE. *A one-ounce "floppy" disk can contain as much information as 3,000 punch cards. It can also be reused and is read much faster than cards by a computer.* 1976 Britannica Yearbook of Science and the Future, p322 *The BBC is now working towards the storage of word data on floppy discs to control the electronic generation of characters in synchronisation with the transmission of a feature film. This provides ideal source of English language sub-titles for foreign movies.* New Scientist 9/30/76, p696 [**1972**]

flops, *n.* a unit of speed in the operation of a computer, often used in combination, as in *megaflops* (one million flops) and *gigaflops* (one billion flops). *Much more powerful than mainframes, supercomputers are the tools of sophisticated researchers. These machines typically perform up to 35 million floating-point operations per second (flops), computations in which the location of the decimal point may vary from number to number. Because of their multimillion-dollar price tags, fewer than 100 supercomputers are in use in the United States. The iPSC, selling for $200,000 to $500,000, can perform up to 10 million flops.* World Book Science Annual 1986, p241 [**1985,** from *f*loating-point *op*erations per *s*econd]

Flory temperature ('flɔri:), a temperature at which a particular polymer dissolved in a suitable solvent exhibits properties that differentiate it from other polymers. *Dr. Flory called this the "theta temperature." He found that when any polymer was studied at its "theta temperature," the measurements of its properties could be compared to those of different polymers. Polymer chemists now know it as the Flory temperature.* NY Times 10/16/74, p31 *The Flory temperature . . . became the basis for the development of hundreds of different plastics and synthetics.* Time 10/28/74, p52 [**1974,** named after the American chemist Paul J. *Flory,* born 1910, who discovered it]

floss, *v.i.* to clean the teeth with dental floss. *Effective brushing, flossing, and irrigation of the teeth pry loose the colonies referred to as dental plaque.* Americana Annual 1978, p174 [**1973,** verb use of the noun]

flower bond, a United States Treasury bond purchased below face value and, until 1976, redeemable at face value if used to pay Federal estate taxes. Now return on the bond is partly taxable as a capital gain. *"Flower bonds," Federal Government issues that can be purchased at discounts and later cashed in at face value to pay a deceased owner's Federal estate taxes, are not subject to capital gains taxes.* NY Times 5/22/76, p32 [**1975**, thought to be so called from the association of *flowers* with the deceased bond holder]

flower child, a young hippie who proclaims peace and benevolence, especially by carrying around or handing out flowers as a symbol of love. . . . The Joshua Tree, *by Robert Cabot. It is about a meeting in the Mojave Desert of a rich old desert rat from the lost frontier, and a sort of psychedelic flower-child from California.* Harper's 9/70, p96 [**1967**]

flower people, flower children. *This is the London of our day, Carnaby Street costumes, flower people, pot, pop art and promiscuity.* Listener 12/19/68, p833 *"You see, I think the hippie type of dropping out is wrong," Father Kirk was saying. "I don't think you should stress the value of that type of dropping out. The flower people's dropout was always narcissistic, sensation-centered, passive."* New Yorker 1/25/68, p66 [**1967**]

flower power, a slogan used by flower children, modeled on the term BLACK POWER. . . . *it soon became obvious that few hippies cared at all for the difference between political left and right, much less between the New Left and the Old Left. "Flower Power" (their term for power of love), they said, was nonpolitical.* 1968 Collier's Encyclopedia Year Book, p79 *As they walked to pick up their diplomas, many of the girls handed Mr. Lindsay a daisy or carnation and whispered: "Flower power."* NY Times 6/3/68, p33 [**1967**]

flueric ('flu:ərik), *adj.* another word for FLUIDIC. *So far this "flueric" system has been tested only on a small scale, but Carl J. Campagnuolo and Allen B. Holmes seem to foresee no insurmountable difficulties.* New Scientist 5/16/68, p351 [**1968**, from Latin *fluere* to flow + English *-ic* (adj. suffix)]

fluid fuel, liquid, gas, and chemical fuels collectively. *Throughout the world fluid fuels are replacing solid fuels because their technical advantages in transport, handling, storage, processing and use have a large monetary value.* Times (London) 4/22/70, p26 [**1970**]

fluidic, *adj.* using the interaction of fluid streams of gas, air, or liquid to perform functions of instrumentation, control, etc., which would otherwise be performed by purely mechanical or electrical mechanisms. Also, FLUERIC. *The signal in fluidic devices is carried by the flow of a liquid, just as the signal in electronic circuits is carried by the flow of the electrons . . . a fluidic device is not disturbed, as is an electrical device, by cold, heat, radiation, or minor vibrations. Fluid circuits can thus work in places where electronic circuits cannot, such as inside nuclear reactors and in the heart of a jet.* World Book Science Annual 1968, p311 [**1960**]

fluidics, *n.* the science or technology of using fluid streams or fluidic devices instead of purely mechanical or electrical mechanisms to perform functions of instrumentation, the control of machinery, the processing of information, etc. (also used attributively). . . . *fluidics engineers are now thinking more in terms of integrating their devices into the whole system of operating a process or machine, rather than just mimicking electronic logic with fluids.* New Scientist 3/26/70, p612 [**1960**]

fluidized-bed combustion, the burning of fuel, especially coal, in a hot, fluidized bed of fine particles to reduce nitrous-oxide fumes and increase heating efficiency. *The Energy Research and Development Administration (ERDA) worked to improve the technology of coal utilization. The ERDA program concentrated on coal liquefaction and gasification and fluidized-bed combustion (FBC).* 1978 World Book Year Book, p259 [**1977**]
—**fluidized-bed combustor:** *A fluidized-bed combustor is a furnace chamber whose floor is slotted, perforated, or fitted with nozzles. Air is forced through the floor and upward through the chamber. When the chamber is partially filled with particles of either reactive or inert material, this material will "fluidize" at an appropriate air flow rate. At fluidization, the bed*

of material expands (bulk density decreases) and exhibits the properties of a liquid. McGraw-Hill Yearbook of Science and Technology 1978, p123

flukicide, *n.* a chemical substance that kills parasitic flatworms or flukes. *There has also been improvement in flukicides, while diethylcarbamazine has controlled parasitic bronchitis in cattle and sheep. . .* Times (London) 11/9/70, pVIII [**1970**, from *fluke* + *-icide* killer, as in *germicide, herbicide*]

fluorescent, *adj.* of bright or glowing appearance. *Presently, a woman entered, a brown gamine with a certain look of money about her, like a faint shimmer along her limbs. She was already a trifle awash, on the arm of a pretty, perfumed, fluorescent youth whom she introduced to Fawzi by his first name and sang, "Isn't he beautiful?"* Harper's 10/70, p72 —**n.** a fluorescent light. *There* [on Wall Street], *mid the canyons of cold steel and glass. . .the plucky Californian* [Nixon] *worked hard and long under flickering fluorescents until he had achieved those legal and financial victories that were to prepare him for the presidency.* Atlantic 2/71, p86 [**1963** for adj., figurative use of the term meaning "having fluorescence"; **1971** for noun]

fluorescer (,flu:ə'resər), *n.* **1** a fluorescent substance. . . . *what further inducement could be offered to the housewife to buy one brand rather than another? It had to be more than mere cleanliness, and so fluorescers. . .were incorporated in detergents to "add brightness to whiteness".* New Scientist 10/16/69, p122 **2** See the quotation for the meaning in chemistry. *Fluorescers are molecules which absorb ultraviolet radiation, passing to an unstable high-energy level in the process, and emit visible light when they return to the stable state.* New Scientist and Science Journal 6/3/71, p593 [**1904, 1959**]

fluoroplastic or **fluorplastic**, *n.* any of a group of plastics made from fluoropolymers. *The real problem comes from burning: some plastics (eg, polystyrene and ABS) give off dense, sooty smoke; others (eg, PVC and chlorinated polythene) give off hydrochloric acid gas; the fluorplastics (eg, Teflon) give off fluorine; and all the thermoplastics melt and clog up grates and burners.* New Scientist 5/18/72, p390 [**1971**, from *fluoro-* polymer + *plastic*]

fluoropolymer, *n.* any of various polymers made by replacing the hydrogen atoms in hydrocarbon molecules with fluorine. *Substitution of fluorine on a carbon will induce a chemical shift of approximately 0.3 eV on the adjacent carbon. This information allows chemical characterization of fluoropolymer systems that formerly could not be analyzed by conventional techniques.* McGraw-Hill Yearbook of Science and Technology 1974, p168 [**1964**, from *fluoro-* fluorine + *polymer*]

fluxoid, *n.* a form or quantum of magnetic flux associated with the passage of a current in high magnetic fields. *Fluxoids participate in two types of interaction of special importance. First, they interact with the current and are driven in a direction mutually perpendicular to the direction of current flow and to the direction of the magnetic field. Therefore fluxoids created by the self-magnetic field of a current are driven from the surface to the interior of the conductor.* Scientific American 4/72, p89 [**1965**, from *flux* + *-oid*]

flux tube, a flow of charged particles producing large bursts of radio energy, occurring at a point along the magnetic field between the planet Jupiter and its satellite. *The flux tube is simply the ensemble of the lines of magnetic force from Jupiter's magnetosphere that pass through Io.* Scientific American 8/79, p72 *A "flux tube," within which there is an electrical current of several million amperes, connects Jupiter to its satellite Io. It would take more than 20 times the power-generating capacity available on the Earth to equal the power expended by this current.* 1981 Britannica Yearbook of Science and the Future, p256 [**1980**]

fly-cruise, *n.* a pleasure cruise in which air travel is used to reach the cruise ship's port of embarkation and to return from the port of landing. *How much baggage am I allowed to take on a fly-cruise? Usually a little more than the regular airline allowance. But as every cruise differs on this point it is essential to check at the time of booking. There is, of course, no limit on traditional port-to-port cruises.* Sunday Times (London)

10/19/69, p63 —v.i. to go on a fly-cruise. *The concept of fly cruising is, and was then, a familiar one, and some might say that Lord Mancroft was merely extending the idea to its logical conclusion, opening the cruise to a wider market.* Times (London) 12/19/70, p18 [**1967** for noun; **1970** for verb]

fly-drive, *n.* travel in which a tour provides air transportation and car rental (often used attributively). *Canvas Holidays. . . has 35 camps, with fly-drive holidays tied in, and with choices of fishing, tennis, boules, water-skiing, or just exploring.* Times (London) 1/4/77, p7 —v.i. to travel in this way. *I have read Roland Gelatt's "Ups and Downs of a Fly-Drive". . . and would like to add some pointers based on my own experiences "fly-driving" in England, Holland and Belgium.* NY Times 1/9/77, pH31 [**1976**] —**fly-driver**, *n.: I shudder at the thought, suggested by Mr. Gelatt's itinerary, of a novice "fly-driver," weary with jet lag, jumping from his airplane into a strange car and attempting the treacherous and unfamiliar climb to Ronda.* NY Times 1/9/77, pH31

flying squad, any highly mobile group organized for special tasks. *One approach is to equip and staff special ambulances as mobile coronary care units expressly for heart attack patients. . . Such ambulance teams, called "flying squads," have now been introduced in many major Russian cities.* Scientific American 7/68, p26 . . . *Alderman Frederick Hall, chairman of the education committee, said that one of the points brought up was a suggestion that a "flying squad" of teachers be set up to help schools where the staff problems were greatest.* Times (London) 1/12/67, p3 [**1961**, extended use of the earlier term (OEDS 1927) for a police squad trained and equipped for rapid pursuit]

fly-off, *n. U.S.* **1** a competitive demonstration of flight capability between two or more aircraft. *The contract is the first under the Pentagon's new "fly-before-you-buy" policy—and was won by Fairchild after its prototype competed in a "fly-off" with one made by Northrop Corp.* Newsweek 1/29/73, p55 **2** Attributive use: *A flyoff competition between the two prototypes is tentatively scheduled for 1976; the winner will become the army's new attack helicopter.* 1974 Collier's Encyclopedia Year Book, p121 [**1967**, probably patterned after *bake-off* (1952); compare COOK-OFF]

flypost, *v.t. British.* to post with bills or notices in haste, especially to avoid detection. . . . *someone has flyposted the area with yellow stickers reading "Jesus commands, Love one another."* Sunday Times (London) 8/24/69, p4 [**1961**, probably from the phrase "to post on the fly"]

FOBS (fɑbz), *n.* acronym for *Fractional Orbital Bombardment System,* a nuclear-weapon system in which warheads are delivered to targets on earth from an orbiting space vehicle in order to escape detection by conventional radar. Compare MOBS. *German substitutes often tend to be tongue-twisters, such as "atombombensatellitensystem" for fractional orbital bombardment system. Like their American colleagues, defense experts here simply call it "fobs."* NY Times 12/3/67, p21 *In midsummer and late September the Soviet Union launched and recovered two FOBS, marking new tests of this vital system, which is capable of delivering nuclear bombs from outer space.* 1971 Collier's Encyclopedia Year Book, p465 [**1967**]

foco, *n.* a small guerrilla center radiating revolutionary activity throughout a country. *By going over to the counter-attack on the other hand, it [the guerrilla unit] catalyzes the people's energy and transforms the foco into a pole of attraction for the whole country.* Saturday Review 8/24/68, p18 . . . *the foco theory has never been disproved. The most serious criticism is that it does not necessarily bring warring revolutionary factions to coalesce around it. This was undoubtedly achieved by Castro's foco in the Sierra Maestra, but the experience has not been paralleled since.* Manchester Guardian Weekly 5/23/70, p19 [**1967**, from Spanish, focus]

fogbroom, *n.* a device to thin or disperse fog. *He [Wesley Bellis, of the New Jersey Department of Transportation] set up a research group, which finally evolved a "fogbroom," in 30-in. by 48-in. aluminum frame strung with a half mile of nylon* thread and rotated at 86 r.p.m. by a base-mounted motor. Time 7/14/67, p38 [**1966**]

Foggy Bottom, an informal name for the U.S. State Department, often used with humorous or mocking intent in allusion to the supposed fogginess of its official statements or policies. *And so, while I may sound critical, my purpose is to shed some light on what goes on in the labyrinths of Foggy Bottom, and try to stimulate some concern about how to induce qualified and talented people to go to work for their government and help formulate and carry out an intelligent foreign policy.* Atlantic 2/67, p45 [**1959**; *Foggy Bottom* was originally a regional name applied to Hamburgh, a town which became part of Washington, D.C., and especially to its swampy southern portion with noxious nighttime fog]

FOI, abbreviation of FREEDOM OF INFORMATION. *Last month Convicted Felon Gary Bowdach told a Senate subcommittee that he had filed "scores" of FOI requests with the FBI for himself and fellow inmates at the federal penitentiary in Atlanta "to try to identify informants." Why? "To eradicate them," Bowdach replied.* Time 9/25/78, p27 [**1976**]

folate, *adj.* of or relating to folic acid, a constituent of the vitamin B complex. . . . *folate deficiency constitutes a considerable problem both in the U.S. and in the United Kingdom, It is particularly serious among alcoholics, . . . and the poor, especially those who are elderly and tend to neglect their meals.* 1970 Britannica Yearbook of Science and the Future, p252 [**1969**, from *folic* acid + *-ate* (adj. suffix)]

folivore, *n.* an animal, especially a primate, that feeds on leaves. Compare FRUGIVORE. *The three-toed sloth is a primitive mammal that . . . hangs in the forest canopy, and reaches out occasionally to pluck leaves from three favorite tree species, and is thus classified an "arboreal folivore" (a tree-dwelling leaf eater).* Science News 7/24/76, p58 [**1972**, from Latin *folium* leaf + English *-vore,* as in *carnivore*] —**folivorous**, *adj.*: *Presbytis entellus and Gorilla gorilla are the only folivorous primates that do forage extensively on the ground.* Science 5/26/72, p871

folkie, *n. Slang.* a folk singer. *"Pop" singers, disc jockeys, rock 'n rollers, bands, folkies, balladists and others will give free concerts in the open air.* Times (London) 1/12/66, p13 . . . *the bill included Kris Kristofferson, the first out-front early-sixties-type folkie to become a star in five years or so . . .* New Yorker 9/25/71, p120 [**1966**]

folk mass, a mass using folk music, often with audience participation in the singing. *When his wife-to-be, Joan Bruder, the daughter of an apartment-house superintendent, had come down from Mount Holyoke to visit him on weekends . . . she had worshipped at St. Thomas More Church, the Roman Catholic chapel where Richard Herrin now played guitar at folk masses.* NY Times Magazine 5/7/78, p82 [**1965**]

folknik, *n. Slang.* a devotee of folk songs or folk singers. *She [Mary Martin, a manager of singers] spent nights and Sundays in the company of various Toronto folkniks, including Ian Tyson, who was then designing labels for Resdan bottles.* Maclean's 4/2/66, p21 [**1958**; see -NIK]

folk-pop, *n.* popular music with elements of folk-song melody and lyrics (often used attributively). *Not content with hyphenated forms, such as folk-pop or jazz-rock, the group attempts an ambitious fusion of folk, pop, or jazz and with classical and contemporary music and various ethnic strains.* NY Times 4/13/76, p28 *In the past two months, East Germany has arrested dozens of intellectuals, harassed citizens seeking to emigrate to the West, and exiled its leading folk-pop hero, Balladeer Wolf Biermann.* Time 1/24/77, p38 [**1965**]

folk rock, a type of rock 'n' roll music with elements of folk-song melody and lyrics. . . . *the Byrds popularized folk rock, infusing a steady, driving rhythm into four-part harmonies overdubbed several times, electrified folk guitar picks and strums, and a steady, straight time bass line.* Saturday Review 10/26/68, p82 [**1965**]

folk-rocker, *n.* a folk-rock musician. *At first glance, [Peter] Serkin looks more like a folk-rocker than he does like a concert* *pianist. His hair is modishly shaggy, his dress casually disheveled, his talk typically teen.* Time 2/24/67, p50 [**1966**]

folkster, *n. U.S.* a folk singer. *An outfit known as Orphan will share the stage with a group called Travis Shook and the Club Wow through Monday, Jan. 15. In addition, some folksters named Patchwork will be here Wednesday and Thursday, Jan. 10-11.* New Yorker 1/13/73, p5 [**1963,** from *folk* (*singer*) + *-ster,* as in *hipster, mobster,* etc.]

foodaholic, *n.* a person having a strong desire for food; person obsessed with eating. See -AHOLIC. *Lynn* [*Redgrave*] *admits that she once had a weight problem. "At 23, when I made 'Georgy Girl,' I was a foodaholic," she said. She dieted and trimmed her 5-foot-10 frame to a slim 135 pounds soon afterward and successfully maintains that weight.* Sunday News (New York) 3/23/75, p11 [**1975,** alteration of earlier (1965) *foodoholic,* from *food* + alc*oholic*] ►The earlier spelling *foodoholic* was recorded by Margaret M. Bryant in "Blends are Increasing," *American Speech,* Fall-Winter 1974: Are you a foodoholic suffering from creeping overweight? *New York World Telegram and Sun 3/30/65, p19*

food processor, an electric appliance that cuts, slices, chops, shreds, minces, and otherwise processes food at high speed. *A food processor may be less expensive to manufacture than a blender, but the Cuisinart food processor does not come cheap.* Daily News (New York) 8/19/79 "You" section, p10 [**1974**]

food science, the technical study of the preparation and processing of foods (sometimes including the science of nutrition and dietetics). *Professor Alastair Frazer, who holds numerous posts in food-science and sits on the Health Ministry's own committee on drug-safety, declared that "chronic vitamin deficiency has never before been investigated or recognised as a disease."* Sunday Times (London) 5/5/68, p4 [**1963**]

food stamp, a stamp issued by the U.S. government to recipients of welfare and unemployment benefits to purchase food. *My fellow Jerseyan, Melvin James Suplee (letter Oct. 18) has taken an angry pen in hand to protest the issuance of food stamps to General Motors strikers who desire to feed their families. "Outrageous," he says, for taxpayers to subsidize men on strike.* NY Times 11/7/70, p28 [**1956**]

food stylist, one who prepares food to be photographed for advertisements, cook books, and the like. *Frequently these companies require Maggie's assistance for photography. She is a veteran food stylist, and never 'doctors' or otherwise tampers with the food.* Cook's Magazine Mar/Apr 1983, p12 [**1977**]

foot-in-mouth, *adj.* characterized by "putting one's foot into one's mouth." See FOOT-IN-MOUTH DISEASE. *Treasury Secretary David Kennedy is becoming an increasing source of embarrassment to the Nixon Administration. His chronic foot-in-mouth habits, which are costly in terms of both dollars and prestige, began to be revealed the moment that he was appointed.* Time 10/17/69, p62 [**1963**]

foot-in-mouth disease, the habit or condition of saying something awkward or embarrassing, that is, "putting one's foot in one's mouth." Compare DONTOPEDALOGY. *President Nixon's latest onset of foot-in-mouth disease unfortunately came just as the American Trial Lawyers' (barristers) Association was about to hold its annual meeting in Miami . . . [The lawyers] unanimously agreed that calling any man guilty who is still sitting in the prisoner's box was "a very serious error."* Manchester Guardian Weekly 8/15/70, p5 [**1968,** formed as a pun on the technical term *foot-and-mouth disease*]

footpad, *n.* one of the cushioned or padded feet of a soft-landing spacecraft. *Extension is activated by a switch in the LM* [lunar module] *. . . The footpads, about 37 inches in diameter, are made of 2 layers of spun aluminum bonded on aluminum-honeycomb core.* Encyclopedia Science Supplement (Grolier) 1969, p327 [**1967**]

footprint, *n.* **1** the area within which debris from a spacecraft, satellite, etc., is predicted to land. *The so-called "footprint" of debris could be as large as 4,000 miles long and 100 miles wide, but its size will be affected by a variety of factors, including whether the spacecraft "skips" slightly when it first encounters*

the earth's atmosphere. NY Times 7/11/79, pA18 **2** any area marked or affected by a force. *Engine manufacturers have been working for the past four years to develop hush kits and claim to have had a large degree of technical success. Fitted to new BAC 1-11 airliners, the Rolls kits have reduced the 90-decibel noise "footprint" produced on the ground by the two Spey engines from 25 to 12½ square miles.* Times (London) 3/19/76, p5 [**1965,** transferred from the original sense (1500's) of "a mark made by a foot"]

footwell, *n.* the hollow space containing the accelerator, foot brake, etc., at the driver's feet in a motor vehicle. *Since I tested the car, additional cool-air vents have been provided in the footwells—I certainly found it too stuffy in warm weather unless a window was opened.* Daily Telegraph (London) 5/17/72, p13 [**1959**]

force de dissuasion ('fɔrs də di:swa'zyɔ̃), *French.* another term for FORCE DE FRAPPE; (literally) force of dissuasion. *France continued to concentrate on development of its force de dissuasion, or independent nuclear deterrent force.* Britannica Book of the Year 1968, p268 *Even the famous little nuclear force de dissuasion must now advance more slowly.* NY Times 7/3/68, p34 [**1963**]

force de frappe ('fɔrs də' frap), *French.* striking force, especially a nuclear striking force. Also called FORCE DE DISSUASION. *The French government, not pleased by the aggressive sound of force de frappe, prefers to call its creation a force de dissuasion. The theory behind the force is that not even a nuclear power would want to destroy France at the possible cost of the retaliatory death of even a few million of its own people.* Time 11/17/67, p34 [**1960**]

format, *v.t.* to lay out the format or arrangement of (computer data). *The signal processor formats the position data for readout in a manner similar to the technique used in the automatic position-determination system for Omega* [a satellite navigation system]. McGraw-Hill Yearbook of Science and Technology 1969, p95 [**1964,** verb use of the noun]

Formula 5000, a racing car powered by an engine of up to 5000 cubic centimeters displacement. *In the seven-race Formula 5000 series, the Lola-Chevrolets driven by Brian Redman of England and Mario Andretti of Nazareth, Pa., won three races each, and Redman won the series. These cars looked like Indianapolis cars, but their stock-block engines were much cheaper.* 1975 World Book Year Book, p215 [**1973**] ►*Formula refers to the engine and design specifications to which the car is built for a particular race.*

Formula One or **Formula I,** a racing car powered by an engine of from 1500 up to 3000 cubic centimeters displacement. *The drivers' championship was raced in Formula One cars with single seat, open cockpit, and open wheels.* 1974 Collier's Encyclopedia Year Book, p485 *These are the élite, and they are no more a conspiracy than are the Continental circus of Formula 1 drivers—they are simply self-selecting.* Times Literary Supplement 6/2/72, p630 [**1965**] ►See the note under FORMULA 5000.

for-profit, *adj. U.S.* organized or existing to make profit; profit-making. *By . . . direct competition the for-profit chains have driven many nonprofit hospitals also to combine into chains.* Scientific American 12/86, p38 [**1980**]

FORTH or **Forth,** *n.* a computer language that uses common English words, used especially for computer games and real-time applications involving control of machinery. *Whereas most high-level languages are somewhat abstract—dealing with variables, relations, formulas—FORTH feels very direct.* Whole Earth Software Catalog 1985, p166 [**1973**]

FORTRAN or **Fortran** ('fɔr,træn), *n.* acronym for *Formula Translator,* a computer language used for writing programs involving scientific and algebraic computation. Compare ALGOL, BASIC, COBOL. *A computer is no better than the software that controls its operation. The BESM-6 can be programmed in Fortran and Algol, the two universal languages for scientific computer work.* Scientific American 10/70, p107 [**1956**]

forward-based, *adj.* (of missiles or other weapons) based or situated close to the target; short-range. *Abbreviation:* FB, as in FBS (forward-based system). *The chief purpose of the forward-based aircraft is to counter the seven hundred-odd Soviet medium- and intermediate-range ballistic missiles (MR/IRBMs) targeted on the cities of America's European allies.* New Yorker 5/26/73, p86 [**1971**]

Fosbury flop ('fazbəri:). Also shortened to **Fosbury.** a style of high jumping in which the jumper goes over the bar headfirst and stretched out faceup to land on the back. *Eighteen months ago he had the experience every Fosbury Flop jumper dreads when he jumped in training, missed the pit, and landed on his head.* Sunday Times (London) 8/10/75, p19 —*v.i.* to use the Fosbury flop. *He watches the high-jumper carefully as he hurls himself into space* backward—*what must it feel like to that Fosbury-flopping guy?* NY Times Book Review 9/24/72, p4 [**1968**, named after Dick *Fosbury,* an American athlete who, as an Oregon State University student, originated it at the Olympic Games of 1968]

found, *adj.* (of artistic works or materials) appropriated from nature or the environment; not fashioned by the artist but taken as found and adapted for their aesthetic value or effect. *Basically, Pop Art is "found" art; its most potent effect is the hallucination of mistaking the street for a museum or the astonishment of Molière's character at learning that he has been speaking prose.* New Yorker 11/8/69, p168 [**1968**, abstracted from the term *found object,* translation of French *objet trouvé*]

found poem, a piece of prose rearranged to the form of a poem by breaking down a paragraph into rhythmical units, etc. *"Found poems" aren't a new idea: William Butler Yeats produced one thirty years ago from the prose of essayist Walter Pater. And the opposite process—presenting poetry as if it were prose—is as old as the Bible.* Maclean's 5/2/66, p22 [**1966**]

four-channel, *adj.* another name for QUADRAPHONIC. *Last November RCA dropped one shoe in the path of Columbia's advancing four-channel record band wagon.* Saturday Review 4/22/72, p41 [**1970**]

four-color conjecture, the hypothesis that only four colors are needed to color any map on a plane surface so that no adjacent regions will be the same color. *The normally restrained world of higher mathematics was jolted in the summer of 1976 when news from the University of Illinois indicated that a team of mathematicians had resolved the century-old four-colour conjecture.* Britannica Book of the Year 1977, p505 [**1963**, variant of earlier *four-color problem* (OEDS 1879)]

four modernizations, a program to modernize China's agriculture, industry, national defense, and science and technology. Compare GREAT LEAP FORWARD. *"What do you think of our Four Modernizations?" the young factory technician looked at me expectantly over his cup of tea, and then answered his own question. "They are fine in theory," he said; "The problem is implementation."* Time 4/28/80, p33 [**1978**, announced in January 1975 by Premier Zhou Enlai (Chou En-lai)]

fourplex, *n. U.S.* a house or building containing four separately owned apartments; a four-family condominium. Also called QUADROMINIUM. *At their best, fourplexes combine the economics of scale (common walls, roofs and plumbing) with the land-use advantages of cluster housing.* Newsweek 11/20/72, p106 [**1972**, from *four* + *-plex,* as in *duplex, triplex*]

fourth market, *U.S.* the trading of unlisted securities directly between investors. Compare THIRD MARKET. *Often talking simultaneously over two telephones—one connected to a buyer, the other to a seller—[Donald] Tomaso arranges direct trades between large institutional investors. He is one of the handful of entrepreneurs who run the "fourth market," so named because it bypasses the more conventional methods of trading securities: the stock exchanges, the over-the-counter market, and the market for listed stocks created by brokers who are not members of the exchanges.* Time 10/26/70, p110 [**1965**]

Fourth Revolution, the introduction of electronic and computerized instruction in schools. *The first of [Sir Eric] Ashby's revolutions was the shift from home instruction to the school; the*

second, the adoption of the written word as a tool of education; the third, the invention of printing and the use of the book. The Fourth Revolution lies in the future with the electronic media. New Scientist 6/22/72, p705 [**1972**, coined by British biologist and educator Eric Ashby in a 1967 report for the Carnegie Commission on Higher Education]

Fourth World, the world's poorest and most underdeveloped countries in Africa, Asia, and Latin America. Compare FIRST WORLD, SECOND WORLD, THIRD WORLD. . . . *the ruler of Abu Dhabi will create a development fund of $3 billion, and other Arab producers may be pressed to "invest" in a development bank—where they probably will practice "neocolonialism" on their poorer brothers, who are now called the Fourth World.* Harper's 6/74, p68 [**1974**, patterned after THIRD WORLD; coined by Robert McNamara, president of the World Bank, to distinguish such countries from the oil-rich nations of Asia, often grouped with the Third World]

four-wall, *v.t. U.S.* to rent a theater for the entire run of (a motion picture) and collect all the ticket receipts. *I bypassed the distributors, and that got me into hot water. So now I'm four-walling the movie—leasing the theater for $240,000, paying for everything, including advertising, and taking whatever receipts I can get.* NY Times 9/23/77, pC6 [**1974**, from the earlier (1954) adjective *four-wall,* referring to indoor theaters in contrast to drive-ins, and later (1967) applied to the kind of arrangement described above]

foxy, *adj. U.S. Slang.* very attractive to the opposite sex. *If a woman is "sexy" she is over 30 and not to be trusted. The replacement is* foxy, *a "counter word" with plenty of connotation but no denotation.* NY Times Magazine 3/21/76, p111 [**1971**, apparently derived from Black English *fox,* meaning an attractive young girl, popularized by the boxer Muhammad Ali in the 1960's]

FPC, abbreviation of FISH PROTEIN CONCENTRATE. *FPC could be manufactured to meet a child's minimum daily protein requirement of ten grams for about one cent.* 1970 Britannica Yearbook of Science and the Future, p334 [**1962**]

fractal, *n.* any of a class of highly irregular and fragmented shapes or surfaces that are not represented in classical geometry (often used attributively). *Fractals arise in many parts of the scientific and mathematical world. Sets and curves with the discordant dimensional behavior of fractals were introduced at the end of the 19th century by Georg Cantor and Karl Weierstrass. Until now their use has been limited primarily to theoretical investigations in advanced mathematical analysis. Like the Koch curve, they were considered too bizarre for application to the real world.* Science News 8/20/77, p123 *Some fractal sets are curves, others are surfaces, still others are clouds of disconnected points, and yet others are so oddly shaped that there are no good terms for them in either the sciences or the arts.* Advertisement leaflet for FRACTALS, a book by Benoit B. Mandelbrot, 1979, p2 [**1975**, from Latin *frāctus* (past participle of *frangere* to break) + English *-al*]

fractal geometry, the branch of geometry that deals with fractals. *As pointed out in "Ants in Labyrinths" (SN: 1/21/84, p42), the increasing popularity of fractal geometry . . . stems from the vast diversity of physical problems that can be viewed as variations on a similar theme.* Science News 2/18/84, p99 [**1980**]

fracturation, *n.* the breaking or fracturing within a mass of rock. *There are several systems for describing the degree of fracturation of a rock. A widely used specification is known as RQD (rock quality designation). This is defined as the percentage of a rock core, usually in total lengths of about 3m (10 ft), naturally intact over lengths of 100mm (4 ins) or more.* New Scientist 1/15/70, p100 [**1970**]

frag, *v.t. U.S. Military Slang.* to kill or injure (a fellow soldier or superior officer), especially by means of a fragmentation grenade. *The lieutenant proceeded to make life miserable for the GI. Finally, the GI approached Karabaic and said, "I'm going to frag the bastard."* Saturday Review 1/8/72, p12 [**1970**, from *frag*, short for *fragmentation grenade*, a type of hand grenade often employed in fraggings]

frameshift, *adj. Molecular Biology.* present because of the deletion or insertion of one or two bases in the DNA chain, so that the sequence of bases is read in incorrect groups of three during translation. Compare MISSENSE. *These mutagens are called frameshift mutagens because the reading frame of the messenger RNA (mRNA) is shifted by the addition or deletion of a base, and this effect distinguishes them from the usual mutagens that cause base pair substitutions.* Science 4/7/72, p47 [**1971**]

franchise, *n.* right to exercise control; jurisdiction. *So they— Robert Lovett, Paul Hoffman, John J. McCloy, the Dulles brothers (who began under the Democrats), William Burden, William Foster, Paul Nitze, and many others—were recruited . . . In time it came to be supposed, not the least by those involved, that such men had an exclusive franchise on foreign policy.* Harper's 7/70, p49 [**1970**, extended sense of the term for the exclusive right of marketing a product or service in a particular territory]

franchisee, *n.* one who is franchised by a company to operate a retail store, branch, etc. *Some may require considerable capital on the part of the franchisee, as in setting up a hotel in the Holiday Inns chain, or none at all beyond one's time in becoming a franchisee of a hearing aid company.* Times (London) 10/16/67, p22 [**1963**]

francicize or **francisize**, *v.t. Canadian.* to cause to adopt or change to the French language. *Whether Quebec separates or not, there is a feeling among Anglos that things will never be the same for them as the province moves to "francicize" business and restrict the right to English-language education for newcomers.* Maclean's 4/4/77, p18 [**1977**, from Canadian French *franciser* (literally) to make French]

francization or **Francization**, *n. Canadian.* the process of adopting or changing to the French language (often used attributively). *Now, business firms that wish to be eligible for government premiums, subsidies, concessions, contracts, etc. must hold "francization" certificates. Individuals who wish to join professional corporations—a prerequisite to many types of employment—must demonstrate their proficiency in French.* Linguistic Reporter 12/75, p3 [**1974**, from Canadian French *francisation*, from *franciser* to FRANCICIZE] ►In the sense of "the act of making French in nationality, customs, manners, etc.," *Francization* was borrowed from French *francisation* in the late 1800's (OED 1888), and revived during 1959-1962 to designate President DeGaulle's plan for Algeria's complete integration with France. The Canadian use of the term appeared in July, 1974 with the passage of Quebec's Official Language Act.

Franco, *n., pl.* **-cos.** *Canadian.* —*n.* a Canadian of French descent; French-speaking Canadian. *Liberal Pierre de Bane . . . thinks that discussion will speed a settlement—but while agreeing with him that everybody should have their say, I doubt that the question can ever be settled to everyone's satisfaction, or that true affection can be induced as between Francos and Anglos in Canada.* Province (Vancouver) 6/9/73, p4 —*adj.* of or relating to French Canadians. *Heady with the new sense of Franco preeminence after more than a century of Anglo power, the radicals feel the time has come to be decisive. It may well be, experts say, that Levesque has chosen caution.* Manchester Guardian Weekly (Washington Post section) 11/12/78, p16 [**1973**, abstracted from *Francophone*, perhaps by influence of ANGLO]

Francophone or **francophone**, *n.* a French-speaking native or inhabitant of a country in which French is only one of two or more official languages (often used attributively). Compare ANGLOPHONE. *. . . the Francophones are worried about the patois spoken by some Canadians and cruelly call it joual, to represent the pronunciation in some places of cheval.* Manchester Guardian Weekly 8/7/69, p15 [**1900, 1962**, from French *Francophone*, from *Franco-* French + Greek *phōné* voice, speech]

Francophonic or **francophonic**, *adj.* French-speaking. Compare ANGLOPHONIC. *It should, after all, be remembered that the French not only continue to cherish their cultural, legal and social community of francophonic states, but are actively wooing new recruits such as Quebec.* Times (London) 8/14/70, p7 [**1962**]

Francophonie or **francophonie**, *n.* **1** the French-speaking countries and communities of the world collectively. *When Gabon's conferring of sovereign attributes on Quebec at a Francophonie conference caused Ottawa to break relations, the Gabonese begged the Canadians to relent on the ground that they were sorry . . .* Times (London) 8/5/70, p8 **2** the unification of French-speaking countries and communities into a commonwealth. *Francophonie, a term that emphasizes the common cultural elements in the French-speaking world, has largely replaced the stillborn "French Community" as the ruling concept, but important military and economic links remain in addition to the common culture.* Americana Annual 1969, p43 [**1967**, from French *Francophonie*]

franglais or **Franglais** (frɑːn'glei), *n., adj.* French containing many English words and expressions. Compare FRENGLISH. *Franglais permits a Frenchman to do* le planning *et research on* le manpowerisation *of a* complexe industrielle *before taking off for* le weekend *in* le country. Time 7/22/66, p30 [**1963**, from French *franglais*, blend of *français* French and *anglais* English] ►The term *Franglais* was popularized in the mid-1960's by René Etiemble, a professor of comparative languages at the Sorbonne, especially in his book *Parlez-Vous Franglais?* in which he proposed French equivalents for Anglicisms to stop what he considered a misuse of the French language.

franglification, *n.* the introduction of English words and expressions into French. *Hugely enjoyable and informative survey of the French temper, from* le bébé boom *(which started it all) . . . to the monster-development of Languedoc and the franglification of language and social life . . .* Times (London) 5/30/70, p22 [**1970**, from French *franglification*, formed irregularly from FRANGLAIS + the suffix *-fication*]

Franquista (fræn'kistə), *n.* a follower of the policies of Francisco Franco (1892-1975), dictator of Spain from 1936 to 1975, especially one of the ultraconservative members of the BUNKER (often used attributively). *Waiting for the ceremonies to begin, the crowd began to chant. "You notice it! You feel it! Franco is here!" Then the Spanish national anthem boomed over the loudspeakers, and the Franquistas snapped to attention and put their palms forward in the straight-arm Fascist salute.* Time 12/4/78, p58 [**1972**, from Spanish, from *Franco* + *-ista* -ist]

fratricide, *n.* the destruction of nuclear missiles launched in a second wave by the explosion of the warheads of the missiles fired in the initial attack. *An additional factor in a massive attack involving many warheads arriving at about the same time in the same area is "fratricide" among the incoming missiles. In a concentrated attack the atmospheric disturbances created by the first warheads to arrive must necessarily destroy, disable or deflect many of the warheads that arrive later.* Scientific American 11/76, p35 [**1974**]

freak, *Slang.* —*n.* **1** a drug addict. *. . . the Skippy heiress is twenty-two and some kind of pill freak who busts up cocktail parties in New York.* Atlantic 5/70, p76 [**1967**] **2** *U.S.* an addict of anything; a devotee or enthusiast. Compare HEAD. *. . . this is a solid book. Something from which the casual moviegoer as well as the dedicated film freak can learn.* Harper's 4/70, p107 [**1908, 1946**] **3** a person who has broken away from conventional society, especially a hippie. *. . . the use of marijuana is extensive, and the number of freaks—people given to long hair, beads, and joss sticks—grows every year.* Harper's 3/70, p66 [**1970**] —*v.i., v.t.* **1** to get or make extremely excited, as if under the influence of a hallucinogenic drug. *None of their writing has the force of the classic texts . . . None matches, say, those extraordinary paeans to self-disorientation found in Jerry's* [Jerry Rubin's] *touchstone parable of the Yippies freaking the college newspaper editors . . .* Atlantic 3/71, p63 **2 freak out**, *Slang.* **a** to come or put under the influence of hallucinogenic drugs. *The undergraduates attracted there* [the University of California at Santa Barbara] *might not be strong on scholarship but they would be . . . more given to surfing than* *freaking out on drugs.* Manchester Guardian Weekly 3/14/70, p13 **b** to experience or produce sensations or reactions similar to those induced by hallucinogenic drugs; make or become extremely excited. . . . *Abbie Hoffman gleefully showered dollar bills onto the floor of the New York Stock Exchange . . . to freak out the straights.* Time 2/2/70, p13 **c** to break away from the mores of conventional society, politics, etc.; to change radically. *Kudlow . . . switched to the Kennedy campaign, and, after the assassination, "freaked out" and joined the S.D.S.* [Students for a Democratic Society], *because it seemed to be "the only ballgame in town."* New Yorker 1/3/70, p37 **[1965]**

freak-out, *n. Slang.* **1** a person who is under the influence of a hallucinogenic drug. *Have the vast quantities of decibels hammered into their bones by disc-jockeys, pop groups, and hippy-hippy freak-outs violently fertilized their growth buds and sent them shooting early for the ceiling?* New Scientist 5/16/68, p329 **2** the action or conduct of a freak-out. *In my favorite bar in New York people theorized endlessly. The one-killer theory, the two-killer theory, the witchcraft theory, the LSD freak-out theory, etc.* Harper's 11/70, p55 **[1966]**

freaky, *Slang.* —*adj.* of or relating to freaks or freak-outs. *The crowd chanted with Ginsberg. They were of a generation which would try every idea, every drug, every action—it was even possible a few of them had made out with freaky kicks on tear gas these last few days* . . . Harper's 11/68, p108 Performance *casts Mick as a freaky rock singer who has given it all up* . . . Time 8/24/70, p61 —*n.* a person who has freaked out; a freak. . . . *most of the dwellings in the street had been painted in . . . odd shades like cream and eau-de-nil, fraught, no doubt, with some underground significance in the secret codes of these peripheral freakies.* Punch 10/22/69, p660 **[1966 for adj.; 1969 for noun]**

Freddie Mac, *U.S.* nickname for the Federal Home Loan Mortgage Corporation. Compare GINNIE MAE. *On a smaller scale, "Freddie Mac" operates to purchase existing loans from savings and loans, and 1974 was expected to establish a record high purchase total.* Americana Annual 1975, p285 **[1974,** patterned after earlier (1953) *Fannie Mae,* nickname for the Federal National Mortgage Association (from its abbreviation, *FNMA*)]

free agent, *U.S. and Canadian Sports.* a player who is not under contract to any professional team or club. *Under the Rozelle Rule . . . if a player becomes a free agent by playing out the option of his contract and then signs with another team, the new team must compensate the old club with players or draft choices.* NY Times 10/19/76, p47 **[1963]** ▶In sports this term was originally applied to nonprofessional players who attained fame for some skill or performance. The term gained wide currency in 1976, when a U.S. Court of Appeals ruled against the "reserve clause" which bound a professional baseball player to a particular team or to any team he was traded to. Soon football, baketball, and hockey made many players free agents. In turn the ROZELLE RULE (see the quotation above) was attacked because it effectively stopped teams from hiring free agents by failing to set a limit on the compensation a team would have to pay to the player's old team. —**free agency:** *Earlier in the day, before the game, I had asked a couple of the Phillies veterans what they thought about free-agency and the enormous new sums of money that some players have begun to earn.* New Yorker 4/25/77, p110

freebase, *v.t.* **1** to purify (cocaine) by removing the salts and other additives with ether and heating it, often to inhale the fumes. *The Los Angeles police say* [Richard] *Pryor told them that the accident occurred while he was "free-basing" cocaine.* Time 6/23/80, p10 **2** to use (freebased cocaine). *He was currently treating . . . a cocaine dealer who free-based and smoked an astounding 15 grams a day.* NY Times 6/27/81, pA10 —*v.i.* to freebase cocaine. *He and several other players experimented with "freebasing".* . . . Tuscaloosa News 6/9/82, p27 —*n.* **1** cocaine that has been freebased. *These doses are taken either by injecting the substance, like heroin, or by smoking a highly concentrated and chemically altered form called "freebase," made by treating the white powder with ether.* NY Times 6/27/81, pA1 **2** Attributive use: *Perhaps the most im-*

portant new public health problem in the United States in 1986 was the rapidly increasing abuse of the smokable, or "freebase," form of cocaine called crack. 1987 Collier's Encyclopedia Year Book, p421 **[1980]**

freebie or **freebee,** *n. Slang, Chiefly U.S.* **1** something obtained free of charge; something gratis. *I settled for a pair of freebees to an evening of Off Broadway theatrics.* New Yorker 5/28/66, p40 **2** one who gets or gives something free of charge. *Third, there are the "freebees," the blue-chip gamblers who are transported and accommodated solely on their reputations as gamblers* . . . Sunday Times (London) 10/27/68, p4 **[1954,** originally (1942) an adjective, *freebee* or *freeby,* meaning free of charge, with the endings *-bee* or *-by* unexplained]

freedom of information, freedom from governmental interference with the flow of information, especially unrestricted public access to government records and documents that do not violate an individual's privacy or endanger national security. *Abbreviation:* FOI *"Ninety per cent of the civil servants would like freedom of information. It's as they reach the top echelons and surround the ministers that they oppose it. There is an element of corruption and blatant incompetence."* New Scientist 10/13/77, p92 **[1967]** ▶The U.S. *Freedom of Information* Act (1967) was designed to prevent the executive branch from withholding information from Congress and the public. It was revised in 1974 to allow for judicial review of a complaint against the executive branch for withholding information. See EXECUTIVE PRIVILEGE.

free-fire zone, *Military use.* an area in which any moving thing may be fired upon or bombed. *To avoid hitting innocent civilians, most missions are carried out in "free-fire zones".* . . . *kept under strict dusk-to-dawn curfew.* Time 7/21/67, p25 **[1967]**

free-for-aller, *n. British Slang.* one that ignores rules and restrictions to gain advantage. *"In the absence of a statutory incomes policy the trade union movement recognises the obvious. The unions are not free-for-allers."* Manchester Guardian Weekly 4/18/70, p8 **[1966]**

free-free, *adj. Astrophysics.* unrestricted as a result of the movement of free electrons in highly ionized gas. *For the immediate neighbourhood of the Sun it is possible to use a combination of observations such as the difference in arrival times of pulsar signals at different frequencies or the relative intensities of the spectral lines of neutral and ionized calcium, combined with data on free-free absorption and emission.* Nature 8/11/72, p311 **[1965,** from the phrase "free-free absorption" used in one of the Ossian poems by the Scottish poet James Macpherson, 1736-1796, to describe a dream of heaven]

free lunch, *U.S. and Canadian.* something that seems to be free but is not. *Many Republicans campaigned on the Kemp-Roth plan to cut federal income taxes by 33% over three years . . . Even though voters want tax reductions, they were skeptical of a scheme that sounded so much like a free lunch.* Time 11/20/78, p18 **[1978,** abstracted from the expression "there ain't no such thing as a free lunch," perhaps used originally in allusion to the practice common in the mid-1800's of giving saloon customers a free lunch with the purchase of drinks]

free-return trajectory, the trajectory of a spacecraft toward a lunar or planetary orbit which provides for an automatic return to earth if the spacecraft is unable to enter the proper orbit. *. . . reestablishment of a free-return trajectory was within the capability of both the service and the lunar modules' propulsion system.* Americana Annual 1970, p27 **[1968]**

free school, a school in which pupils are free to choose and pursue their own subjects of interest without formal classroom instruction. Compare ALTERNATIVE SCHOOL. *In hundreds of tiny private "free" schools and in public classrooms in nearly every state, the fixed rows of desks and the fixed weekly lessons have been abandoned.* Time 1/3/72, p44 **[1926, 1968]** —**free schooler:** *From deschoolers and free schoolers, from the radical right and the radical left, the education system is under attack, and so are the teachers who work in it.* Times (London) 10/11/72, p12

free speecher, *U.S.* a student radical who agitates against the academic and political establishment. *There are some, of course, who'd like to make flag-raising compulsory, which would negate the very philosophy and spirit which gives the symbol meaning. Amongst them might be some "free speechers" who hiss and shout down the expression of opposing views.* NY Times 7/4/70, p20 [**1966**, originally applied to members of the 1964 *Free Speech* Movement on the Berkeley (University of California) campus]

free university, an independent college or university organized chiefly by students to study subjects of interest to them without the usual academic restrictions of grades or credits. . . . *the so-called "free university," which eliminates the traditional boundaries between students and faculty, one academic discipline and another, the cognitive (knowing) process and the affective (feeling) process.* Time 11/9/70, p55 [**1968**]

freeze-etching, *n.* a method of preparing specimens for study under an electron microscope by freezing and then fracturing them to show internal structure in three dimensions. *Branton used a new technique, called freeze-etching, to investigate the lamellas. He first quick-froze isolated chloroplasts and pieces of leaf in liquefied freon and then fractured them. The frozen specimens broke along natural planes of weakness, such as the interface between the surfaces of internal structures. This exposed a three-dimensional face with contours that revealed the surfaces of the structures.* World Book Science Annual 1969, p273 [**1965**]

freeze-fracture, *v.t., v.i.* to prepare a specimen for observation under an electron microscope by FREEZE-ETCHING. *Freeze-fracturing calls for freezing a sample of tissue at minus 150 degrees Celsius in liquid Freon and transferring the sample to a chamber that is then pumped down to a high vacuum. The tissue is fractured by passing a microtome knife through it.* Scientific American 5/78, p141 [**1970**]

freeze frame, a single frame of a film, videotape, or videodisk that is held motionless like a still photograph. *Already second-generation video recorders are here, with slow motion, freeze frame, high speed search, remote control and so on.* Sunday Times (London) 4/6/80, p92 [**1960**, a frozen shot on television]

freezenik, *n. U.S. Slang.* a person who supports the freeze on the production of nuclear weapons. *Having failed in a shabby effort to brand the freezeniks as dupes of the Kremlin, Mr. Reagan now approaches arms control through the Gospel.* NY Times 3/11/83, pA30 [**1983**; see -NIK]

freightliner, *n. British.* a train that carries a large quantity of freight packaged in containers. *The Eastern Region of British Railways said they felt they would be able to maintain all freightliner and company trains, but the London Midland Region had to cancel one freightliner, running from Manchester, Liverpool and Birmingham to Harwich.* Times (London) 6/25/68, p21 [**1965**]

Frelimo or **FRELIMO** (frei'li:mou), *n.* a leftist guerrilla organization of Mozambique that fought against Portuguese control from 1964 to 1974. In 1975 it became established as the ruling political party of the newly independent country. *Frelimo's crucial support comes, however, from the Soviet Union and China. The Soviet Union supplies most of Frelimo's weapons. Many Frelimo members have been trained in the Soviet Union or in China for guerrilla, terror, and propaganda activities.* National Review 8/17/73, p885 [**1967**, from Portuguese, acronym for *Fre*nte de *Li*beraçao de *Mo*çambique, Front of Liberation of Mozambique]

French fact, *Canadian.* the dominance of the French language and culture in Quebec, recognized especially after the emergence of the separatist movement in the 1960's; Quebec's French heritage and nationalism. *For many, the election crystallised the need to make a decision—to stay or leave; to accept the French fact and integrate, or pull up roots and start fresh elsewhere.* Maclean's 4/4/77, p18 [**1974**]

Frenglish, *n, adj.* English containing many French words and expressions. Also spelled FRINGLISH. Compare FRANGLAIS. *It may be that one man's misfortune is another's good luck, and*

that "Frenglish" is none of a Frenchman's business. But at least it ought to be understood that language-borrowing isn't a one-way street. Manchester Guardian Weekly (Le Monde section) 1/29/72, p14 [**1963**, blend of *French* and *English*]

freshperson, *n.* a freshman (used to eliminate supposed reference to sex in *freshman*). See -PERSON. *Your poem "To His Coy Mistress" is under attack again, this time from a girl who wrote a paper on it for her college course in freshperson English. Here's the crux of her argument.* Intelligence Digest 2/74, p63 [**1972**]

Friedmanite, *n.* a monetarist, especially one who supports the theories of the American economist Milton Friedman, born 1912, who advocates direct regulation of money supply by the government instead of manipulation of taxes, federal programs, etc., to regulate the economy. Compare NEO-KEYNESIAN. *For, although debate has raged passionately in the United States for years between the Friedmanites and the Keynesians, the British Keynesians have been markedly slow to take the Friedman challenge seriously or to respond to it in terms.* Times (London) 3/13/70, p10 [**1968**]

Friedmann universe, a model of the universe based on Einstein's general theory of relativity, in which the universe does not expand indefinitely but reaches a state of maximum distention after which it begins to contract, both the expansion and contraction being of identical duration. *Numerous observations have shown that the universe appears to be pervaded by a background flux of electromagnetic waves that represent a blackbody at a temperature of 2.7 degrees K. Most cosmologists take this background as a relic of the original "big bang" that started the universe. On the whole this radiation is isotropic, the same in all directions, but some theories predict a minute anisotropy . . . This leads to some cosmological conclusions: We live in a highly closed Friedman universe.* Science News 8/18-25/73, p108 [**1973**, named for Alexander *Friedmann*, a Russian mathematician who constructed the model in the 1920's]

Friends of the Earth, an organization of conservationists and environmentalists. Compare GREENPEACE. *In less than two years the Friends of the Earth has precipitated action on issues ranging from wildlife protection and combating pollution from plastic packaging to exposing the risks to national parks and designated areas from oil drilling and types of mining development new to Britain.* Times (London) 6/29/72, p4 [**1972**]

Friend virus, a virus that causes enlargement of the spleen in mice and replacement of normal spleen cells with cancerous ones. *A virus called the Friend virus is known to cause leukemia of the spleen in experimental animals.* Science News 1/11/75, p21 [**1967**, named after Charlotte *Friend*, born 1921, an American microbiologist]

fringe theatre, *British.* **1** a theater that stages low-cost and usually experimental plays. . . . *unfortunately the unreliable standards at fringe theatres reflect the pressure of productions staged under economic pressure. The Bush, Shepherd's Bush is the latest fringe theatre to make a desperate appeal for subsidy, and their current evening show, Dracula, provides a case for official support.* Listener 2/15/73, p223 **2** experimental drama such as that staged in fringe theatres. *The Great Ban, which opened in London's Soho district last week, stars York as a former actress who lapses into confused reveries, childhood recollections, and a brief impression of Marilyn Monroe. "An unintentional parody of all the worst excesses of fringe theater," blasted* Time Out *magazine.* Time 1/26/76, p42 [**1970**]

fringe time, the period of television broadcasting before or after prime time. Fringe time in the United States is usually considered as from 5 to 7 p.m. and 11 p.m. to 1 a.m. Compare PRIME TIME. See also FAMILY HOUR. *Most TV stations refuse to sell time to politicians in the middle of their news programs, and that wipes out most of the valuable evening "fringe time."* NY Times 1/13/76, p17 *"We feel that original programming works best in fringe time,"* said Dick Ebersol, the head of NBC's late-night operations. TV Guide 7/10/76, pA1 [**1976**]

Fringlish or **fringlish**, *n., adj.* variant spellings of FRENGLISH. *If they did not watch out, they thought gloomily, they would soon descend to using* fringlish *words like cul-de-sac instead of* *the proper French term* impasse. Manchester Guardian Weekly 4/24/69, p16 [**1969**]

Frisbee, *n.* Also popularly spelled **frisbee** or **frisby**. a trade name for a small plastic disk sailed in the air as a toy or in games. *My gaze passes beyond this student and through the dirty, mullioned windows to the lawn outside where a group of three seniors spin a frisbee in the spring air.* Harper's 9/68, p50 *In streets all over the town students were gaily throwing frisbies . . . which travel such a satisfactory distance with so little effort.* Times (London) 5/4/70, p8 [**1957**, from the name (altered by the inventor, Fred Morrison) of the *Frisbie* bakery in Bridgeport, Connecticut, whose pie tins presumably inspired the invention of this flying disk]

Frisbee golf, a game similar to golf but played with a Frisbee instead of a golf ball and clubs. *Frisbee golf rules are much the same as ordinary golf's, with each throw counting as one "stroke."* NY Times Magazine 6/12/77, p24 [**1977**]

fritz, *v.i.* **fritz out**, *U.S. Slang.* to go out of order; break down. *. . . when the television camera fritzed out on the lunar surface, Astronaut Alan Bean had a moment of atavism. Like any other 20th century man confronted by the perversity of nonfunctioning machines, he whacked it with his hammer.* Time 11/28/69, p18 [**1969**, from the slang phrase *on the fritz* in disrepair (OEDS 1903)]

'Fro, *n. U.S.* short for AFRO. *One G.I. summed it up: ". . . The regs [Army Regulations] say you can grow your hair this long, but the first sergeant says he don't care what the regs say, because he don't like no black man with a 'Fro."* Time 12/14/70, p40 [**1970**]

frog hair, *U.S. Slang.* money for use in political campaigns. *Disturbingly, many of the plaque owners were contractors or architects who stood to benefit from making political contributions—"frog hair," as such funds are known locally.* Time 2/4/74, p29 [**1972**, paralleled on *hen's teeth*, as in the phrase *scarce as hen's teeth* (1858)]

front, *n.* **1** the dividing surface between two different elements, similar to a weather front. *The pumping station was completed in May 1951, in response to a water shortage . . . It delivered 100 million gallons a day during the drought of 1985, its last use . . . In 1985 "New York City was mercilessly criticized for starting [pumping] in July, when the river flow is lower and the salt front is farther north, threatening the city of Poughkeepsie," which takes its water entirely from the river.* NY Times 5/7/89, pL9 [**1989**] **2 up front**, *U.S. Informal.* **a** in advance. *The book then went to thirty other publishers. Change this, change that, they said. Mostly change the title. One offered $40,000 up front if all the proper changes were made.* Harper's 5/74, p44 **b** in an open or straightforward manner. See UP-FRONT, *adj. He* [John G. Heimann] *. . . held that it would be better to finance such projects "up front"— that is, with Government appropriations or other means that permitted full and clear public knowledge of the total costs.* NY Times 11/13/76, p21 **c** in the open or foreground. *Vanocur is at ABC as an executive, Newman is a media star in his own right, and Chancellor works up front, using his face muscles more than his leg muscles.* New Yorker 10/31/77, p124 [**1974**]

front burner, on the (or **one's**) **front burner**, taking precedence or priority over others; of immediate and major concern. Compare BACK BURNER. *In the U.S., most China analysts interpreted last week's pronunciamento as indicating that détente with Washington was still on Peking's front burner.* Newsweek 9/10/73, p43 [**1970**]

front-end, *adj. U.S.* provided or paid in advance to start a project. See FRONT MONEY. *The report advocates "front end" support which would involve large payments for R & D at the start of a programme that could reap commercial rewards later on.* New Scientist 6/29/78, p893 [**1970**, probably abstracted from FRONT-END LOAD]

front-end load, sales commissions and other expenses that make up part of the early payments of an investor under a long-term contract for the purchase of mutual-funds shares. *The holders were paying for the privilege of having their money managed by portfolio wizards. Half of their first year's investment often went for the original sales commission, and late in 1966 the Securities and Exchange Commission indignantly declared these charges—the "front-end load"—to be excessive.* New Yorker 7/3/73, p38 [**1963**, so called because the "load" (commission and other charges) is paid at the beginning or "front end"]

front-end processor, a unit in a data-processing system which forwards data from terminals to the computer and back again. *The role of the communication-control unit varies with the system. It can act essentially as a computer and perform several functions, including routing commands and messages, checking errors and converting one data format to another. The unit is often called a front-end processor.* Scientific American 9/72, p126 [**1972**]

frontenis (fran'tenis), *n.* a Latin-American ball game resembling handball and consisting essentially of jai alai or pelota played with tennis rackets. *Mexico has been the world's leading frontenis power for seventeen years, and in Mexico City alone there are three thousand frontenis courts.* New Yorker 11/2/68, p191 [**1968**, from American Spanish *frontenis,* blend of Spanish *frontón* a jai alai court and *tenis* tennis]

front four, *U.S. Football.* the four-man defensive line (two tackles and two ends) in a professional team. *So that is the jolly mood of the Cowboys one game into the season . . . There is that excellent front four of Larry Cole, Jethro Pugh, Bob Lilly and George Andrie.* NY Times 9/27/70, Sports Sec., p4 [**1966**]

frontlash, *n. U.S.* a reaction which offsets or neutralizes a backlash. *In 1964, a widely predicted "white backlash" against the Negro movement failed to materialize. It apparently was swallowed in what President Johnson called the "frontlash" against Barry Goldwater and the fear that he would drop nuclear weapons.* NY Times 9/7/66, p42 *Frontlash from the second Vatican Council, to borrow one of President Johnson's remarkable neologisms, is now being strongly felt among English Roman Catholics.* Saturday Night (Canada) 4/67, p42 [**1964**, from *front* + back*lash*]

front-line, *adj.* of or having to do with a country that is close to or borders on a hostile nation or area of potential conflict. *As more of the Rhodesian countryside falls to the rebels, squabbling over territory could easily flare into fighting. Efforts by Nyerere and other front-line leaders to heal the breach have been to no avail.* Time 10/9/78, p56 *One thing making such "front-line" states as Malaysia and Thailand more hostile to the boat people is the fear that the developed nations will cream off the most highly qualified and leave them with the rest.* Economist 7/14/79, p13 [**1976**]

front money, *U.S.* money paid, given, or shown in advance to initiate or support an undertaking; front-end money. *I've written six novels; if each had required $70,000 in front money, I'd still be making cement full-time.* National Review 12/19/75, p1480 [**1931, 1964**]

Frostbelt, *n.* another name for SNOWBELT. *Like most conventional wisdoms, the arbitrary antithesis between "Sunbelt" and "Frostbelt" is a crutch that has crippled understanding of cities and their problems, and should be eschewed. In some of the frostiest of the "Frostbelt cities—notably St. Paul, Minneapolis, Milwaukee, and Chicago—urban problems have been far less severe than in cities like St. Louis, Baltimore, and Oakland, where the snow falls less often or not at all.* Harper's 12/78, p46 [**1978**]

frostbite boating, *U.S.* another name for FROSTBITING. *For frost-bite boating enthusiasts a mouton vest or parka would be heart-warming.* NY Times 2/9/68, p31 [**1968**]

frostbiter, *n. U.S.* a sailboat used in frostbiting. *We've got everything here from ten-foot frostbiters, for winter racing, to fifty-foot yawls . . .* New Yorker 8/22/64, p69 [**1964**]

frostbiting, *n. U.S.* the sport of sailing or racing a sailboat in the winter months. Also called FROSTBITE BOATING. *Everett B. Morris, who died Tuesday at age 67, had fun writing about boats—from frostbiting in Port Washington, L.I., where his funeral service will be held this morning, to America's Cup* *drama off Newport, R.I., and ocean racing to Bermuda.* NY Times 2/17/67, p31 **[1967]**

frostbound, *adj.* lacking in warmth; frozen. *Relations with France seemed as frostbound as ever, despite the thaw in Guinea's relations with some French-speaking West African countries . . .* Annual Register of World Events in 1968, p329 **[1960]**

froth, *v.t.* to cover or invest with something light and trifling. *The Church of Santa Maria della Salute, whose facade is frothed with baroque winged statues, has been closed . . .* Atlantic 1/71, p23 *It seemed wrong to show Komarov's black bordered portrait laced with the teleprinty call sign and frothed up with the newsreel music.* Listener 5/4/67, p599 **[1967,** verb use of *froth, n.,* something unsubstantial or of little worth]

frozen frame, a single image held momentarily still in the midst of a motion-picture sequence. . . . *the jump cut in which you see, for instance, a pickle shrinking bite by bite because the intervening film has been cut out; or the frozen frame, when the camera makes its point by stopping and holding a motionless shot of Sophia Western laughing, or a model wearing Supphose.* Maclean's 1/1/66, p38 **[1966]**

frug, *n.* a rock 'n' roll dance performed with little or no movement of the feet but with rhythmic motions of the hips, arms, head, and shoulders. . . . *but the internal movements she had been detecting recently seemed a bit more like those of "a small, enthusiastic elephant dancing the frug."* Punch 8/18/65, p232 —*v.i.* to dance the frug. . . . *people grasped the sense of the youth movement by watching Mademoiselle's College Board members and other young things frugging in minidresses at Cheetah.* NY Times 7/25/66, p18 **[1964,** of unknown origin]

frugivore (ˈfruːdʒəvɔr), *n.* an animal, especially a primate, that feeds on fruits. Compare FOLIVORE. *Those primate species that can utilize cellulose in leaves are referred to as folivores and are distinguished from frugivores, which cannot utilize cellulose. Of course, these basic categories do intergrade, since folivores may supplement their leaf diet with fruit.* Science 5/26/72, p869 **[1972,** from Latin *frūgis* fruit + English -*vore,* as in *carnivore*]

Frye boot, a trademark for a heavy leather boot that reaches the calf and is adapted from traditional western boots. *The Frye boot is the obligatory accompaniment to the down jacket . . . Frye boots—and they are everywhere around you—bag at the ankles so the wearer looks like a basset hound with old legs, wrinkled from the hard life it's known. Some of the Frye boots are decorated in Western designs; some are plain; all are heavy, thick-toed, good for stomping, or kicking a mugger.* NY Times Magazine 1/25/76, p46 **[1976]**

fry-up, *n. British Informal.* **1** a dish of fried food, usually leftovers quickly prepared in a frying pan. *With a deft flick Fred flung half a dozen bangers into his vintage frying pan, reached for the cracked cup containing the drippings from a month's fry-ups . . .* Sunday Times (London) 4/11/71, p11 **2** the making of such a dish or dishes. *You and Roy must come back for lunch. We'll have a good old fry-up.* New Yorker 9/18/71, p37 **[1966]**

FSO, abbreviation of *foreign service officer.* *"You were in Bonn?" "Three years." "Well, they probably thought that a change of scene. . ." "But I am an FSO." "You'll come to like it here,"* the chief of section said. Atlantic 8/72, p68 **[1965]**

fuel air explosive, a cluster bomb that sprays vaporized fuel producing an explosion over a large area when ignited. *Abbreviation: FAE The bomb . . . is called a "fuel-air explosive." At a preset height, a film of kerosene-like inflammable liquid is squirted out to form a circle as much as 30 feet in diameter.* Manchester Guardian Weekly (Washington Post section) 10/24/76, p15 **[1973]**

fuel cycle, the process which nuclear fuel undergoes in a reactor or in recycling for renewed use. *The alternative being favored is the "once through," or "throwaway" fuel cycle, in which the depleted, highly radioactive fuel rods from nuclear power plants, containing about 1 percent of unspent uranium 235 and an equal amount of plutonium, would simply be*

stored indefinitely. Scientific American 5/78, p81 **[1976,** short for *nuclear fuel cycle*]

fuelish, *adj. Especially U.S. and Canadian.* using excessive fuel. A word to the fuelish: *Beginning Labor Day weekend, Canadians will again be bombarded by an advertising campaign urging energy conservation. The federal government will spend $820,000 in newspapers, magazines and on television encouraging homeowners to save fuel by reinsulating.* Maclean's 8/76, p13 **[1975,** from *fuel* + -*ish,* coined as a pun on *foolish*] —**fuelishly,** *adv.: The world's collecting temper, already burning on a short fuse, was further aggravated by an international fuel shortage. Admonitions that people not be "fuelishly" wasteful did nothing to dampen the fires.* 1975 World Book Year Book, p173

full-court press, *U.S.* a vigorous, full-scale attack or offensive. *At the beginning of the year, and especially in his State of the Union address, he* [President Carter] *seemed to be pulling back from some of his most controversial proposals. But now he has gone to a full-court press.* Times (London) 4/6/78, p5 **[1977,** figurative sense of the basketball term (1951) for a defensive tactic in which strong pressure is applied on the offensive players all over the court in order to upset and disorganize them]

full-service, *adj.* that provides complete service in a particular line of business. *He likes to describe his business as "the only full-service walk-in retail store for trial lawyers" and "Toys R Us for attorneys." He sells and rents not only detailed plastic models of herniated disks (his most popular items) but also models of pelvises, legs, jaws, hearts, knees, eyes (two sizes), spines, wrists, shoulders (from five different manufacturers), hands, brains, and other body parts. Lawyers use the models to create compelling courtroom exhibits in personal-injury lawsuits.* Atlantic 4/88, p62 **[1972]**

fulsome, *adj.* **1** very flattering or complimentary; profuse in praise. *I believe quite firmly that dictionary users have a real right to know what language attitudes are. If, in giving a formal talk, I say /núwkyələr/ and get blackballed for it, I have a perfect right to know what I did wrong. And I also have a right to know that when I use 'fulsome praise' to mean great and sincere praise, many will construe it as an insult.* Language 6/70, p248 *It is more or less commonly accepted . . . that "fulsome" (that is, "grossly excessive") means something like "extremely good or favorable" ("The chairman gave a fulsome eulogy of the speaker").* American Scholar Spring 1972, p241 **2** full; rounded; complete. *The announcement that Prime Minister Begin is to come to Canada in the near future underlines my conviction that Sadat should be invited so that Canadians may have a fulsome view of the Middle East situation.* Maclean's 10/2/78, p17 **[1968,** altered senses of the term meaning (since the 1300's) "offensive to normal tastes or sensibilities"] —**fulsomely,** *adv.: We have been hearing so much, so fulsomely, about new-wave rock in the past year, that it was a distinct occasion to . . . listen to one of pop's greatest old-wave masters.* Times (London) 4/15/78, p11 ►As the quotations under definition 1 show, this usage is viewed with disfavor in some quarters. Yet it has been gaining currency, probably because the first syllable is taken to mean "full" or "abundant" and therefore connoting approbation. The following quotation illustrates the usage in a neutral context: *In a serenade that made strong men quiver, fulsome colleagues rose to pay tribute to his decision to tolerate a compromise on the pending civil rights bill.* NY Times 2/27/68, p42 Historically the original meaning of *fulsome* was not pejorative, but rather the opposite. Derived from *full* + -*some,* the word meant "characterized by abundance, possessing or affording copious supply; abundant, plentiful, full" (OED *c*1250). Applied to the body, it meant "full and plump, fat, well-grown" (1340-70). Imperceptibly, however, these meanings shifted by extension to "overgrown" and then to "coarse, gross, offensive to the senses," and finally, "offensive to good taste, especially from excess." The new senses represent a revival of the original approbative use of the word, as in the following quotation, in which *fulsome* means "very full": *Just heard someone on the radio say something like "Once you've known the rich, fulsome taste of organically grown fruits and vegetables and natural whole grains. . ." I'd never heard* fulsome, *which is usually used or* misused in the term "fulsome praise," misused in quite that way before. But I like "the rich, fulsome taste." Fulsome is perhaps the most contra-onomatopoeic word in English. It sounds like full and wholesome, but in fact it means "disgusting, offensive." Saturday Review 7/21/79, p10

Fu Manchu mustache, a mustache that comes down vertically at the sides of the mouth; a thin, drooping mustache. Compare ZAPATA MUSTACHE. *He was a tall boy with a lot of curly hair and a Fu Manchu moustache.* Harper's 7/76, p29 **[1964,** named after *Fu Manchu,* a sinister Chinese doctor in the novels (1932-1948) of the English mystery writer Sax Rohmer]

funabout, *n.* any of various small motor vehicles used to drive about for pleasure or sport. *Beach buggies, those curious bathtub-shaped funabouts based on Volkswagon Beetle components, are all the rage in the United States.* Times (London) 9/10/70, p15 **[1970,** from *fun* + run*about*]

Fun City, a nickname for New York City. *Shortly after 10 p.m., in what tourists call the Big Apple and Fun City, Monty was in bed watching a western on black and white TV.* Maclean's 3/74, p69 **[1966]**

fundi (ˈfundi:), *n.* (in eastern and southern Africa) a skilled person; expert. *I get sick after the sack—ulcers and headaches, and the young medical fundi tells me it's my alcohol consumption . . .* Rhodesia Herald 4/20/73, p10 *The stress on cooperative production and on village involvement—through the survey team, training of local* fundis, *village meetings, etc.—provides a basis by which the village can control both the production and use of these technologies . . .* New Scientist 9/14/78, p758 **[1972,** from Swahili, from Bantu *fund-* instruct, teach]

fund-raiser, *n. U.S.* a formal dinner or other social gathering to raise funds; a fund-raising function or event. *White House aide Jerry Jones says Ford's trip to Georgia, a week before Reagan was to announce, was Ford's "last speech to a Republican fundraiser for a long time and maybe forever."* National Review 12/5/75, p1326 *He* [Woodie Guthrie] *was perhaps an even bigger hit with the upper-middle-class liberals and leftists at fund-raisers than he was among the poor.* New Yorker 12/13/76, p149 **[1970,** apparently extended from earlier meaning (1957) "a person who raises funds"]

fun fur, a garment made of an inexpensive or imitation fur or assembled furs, usually for casual wear. *The inexpensive items, commonly referred to as fun furs . . . included rabbit, various types of lamb, raccoon, fox, calfskin, bobcat, bassarisk* [a kind of civet cat], *and muskrat.* Britannica Book of the Year 1970, p369 **[1959]**

funk, *v.i. U.S. Slang.* to swing pleasurably (to agreeable music). *There were organic peanut-butter-and-honey sandwiches to eat, free liquor and carrot juice to drink, live rock from a group called the Stoneground to funk to . . .* Newsweek 11/26/73, p116 **[1973,** back formation from FUNKY]

funk art or **funk,** *n.* a type of pop art created from strange or bizarre objects, usually of a recognizable form, such as a huge toothbrush or a typewriter with finger-shaped keys. . . . *San Francisco's William Wiley is, at 31, an elder statement-maker of the West Coast's cheerfully crude funk art movement.* Time 2/28/69, p41 **[1966]**

funk artist, a person who produces funk art. *What they discovered . . . was regional groups with a common outlook, like the West Coast's "funk artists," whose gamy, gutsy assemblages have been shown in many national exhibits.* Time 12/22/67, p32 **[1967]**

funkiness, *n. U.S. Slang.* funky quality. *The Fillmore* [a rock theater in New York City], *patronized by the children of the bourgeoisie, strives for (and achieves) a certain level of funkiness.* New Yorker 1/23/71, p25 **[1968]**

funky, *adj. U.S. Slang.* fine; excellent. *"That's a funky jacket, Kit Carson."* Time 8/17/70, p32 *Kathy* [Kathy Buday, an American girl] *scattered a handful of pants round the room—pants in different painted fabrics. "Persian, Indian, Tunisian, and this one's funky Marseilles." Everybody laughed.* Sunday Times (London) 5/21/72, p41 **[1968,** originally (about 1950) a

black jazz term meaning earthy, emotional, rooted in the blues]

funny car, a type of drag-racing car with the body of a conventional automobile, a supercharged engine in the middle, and the driver's seat in the back. *The weirdest vehicle we have ever laid eyes on moves through the crowds toward the starting line aboard a large pickup truck. Its hood yawns. We have, emblazoned in gold and black flowing letters,* Kiss of Death . . . *This may be a Funny Car, but there's nothing much funny about it.* Harper's 1/76, p20 **[1976]**

fun run, a running race that encourages participation rather than performance. *The children will be supervised in a warm-up session and accompanied on a fun run in the village of Rhinebeck, followed by a cool-down period.* Putnam County News and Recorder 8/3/83, p4 **[1976]**

funsome, *adj.* having or loving fun; given to amusement. *Back to Charlie* [a perfume]*—a name that POW! set it apart from all the others, no matter how beautiful, evocative, descriptive, Frenchy they were. The others were selling luxury and haute couture and mystique and sophistication and elegance and status and all those yummy things we're so good at. Charlie was absolutely SOMETHING ELSE: flip and forthright and free of funsome.* Drug & Cosmetic Industry 3/83, p22 **[1983,** from *fun* + *-some,* as in *winsome, frolicsome,* etc.]

fuoro (fyuːˈbrou), *adj.* of or having to do with any of a group of very young, distant, variable stars (T Tauri stars) that exhibit eruptive activity which changes their brightness, spectrum, and apparent shape. *Although two of the fuoro stars have remained close to peak brightness for years, V 1057 appears to be sliding back to its previous condition. It has declined by a magnitude and a half in five years. So perhaps the fuoro phenomenon is not permanent, and after* n *number of years, the star goes back to the T Tauri class again.* Science News 1/10/76, p27 **[1976,** coined by Viktor Ambartsumian, an Armenian astronomer, from *FU Ori*onis, a nebula in which the first star of this type was observed]

Furbish lousewort, a rare, endangered species of lousewort (genus *Pedicularis*) discovered in Maine in 1880 and thought to be extinct until rediscovered in 1976. See SNAIL DARTER. *The Furbish lousewort, despite its unprepossessing name, is not without certain modest charm when it first emerges in the springtime along the steeply sloping banks of the St. John River. Its leaves are delicate and fernlike. Its stem is slender and, in due season, it diffidently puts forth two or three pale yellow blossoms.* NY Times Magazine 6/4/78, p39 **[1976,** named after Kate *Furbish,* its discoverer]

furor colligendi (ˈfyuːrɔr ˌkɑlɔˈdʒendɑi), *Latin.* a rage for collecting. See COLLECTIBLES. *Both brothers* [Albert and Henry Berg] *were collectors; when they were boys—they were the sons of a tailor—both worked as pages in the Cooper Union Library, where early browsing led to the* furor colligendi. New Yorker 3/25/72, p30 **[1971,** patterned after the older Latin phrases *furor loquendi* (a rage for speaking), *furor scribendi* (a rage for writing), etc.]

fuse, *n.* **have a short fuse,** *U.S.* to get excited or angry easily; to "blow up" easily or quickly. See also SHORT FUSE. *The press is also now on to the fact that* [Senator Edmund] *Muskie can have a short fuse, and they poke and prod to see if he will explode.* Atlantic 4/71, p25 *"He's* [Hartzog is] *very hard on his people. He cracks the whip. And he has a short fuse."* New Yorker 9/11/71, p60 **[1968]**

fusion, *n.* a blend of jazz and rock or other popular musical styles (often used attributively). Compare CROSSOVER. *Fusion enjoys a crucial advantage over mainstream and avant-garde jazz: it "crosses over" a wide range of radio formats, a key element to selling any music today. Top Forty, Album Oriented Radio (AOR) and progressive FM radio regularly include fusion artists like Stanley Clarke, Weather Report and Chick Corea on their playlists.* Rolling Stone 1/11/79, p43 **[1976]**

future shock, a state of stress and disorientation brought on by a quick succession of changes, especially in new standards of behavior and values, in society. Compare CULTURE SHOCK.

What brings on future shock . . . is a rate of social change that has become so fast as to be impossible for most human beings to assimilate. . . "Future shock arises from the superimposition of a new culture on an old one. It is culture shock in one's own society." Time 8/3/70, p13 *Future shock, he* [Alvin Toffler] *says, can make us ill, physically and mentally; it robs us of the power to decide, deprives our children of the roots we took for granted, and it has ruptured marriage.* Atlantic 8/70, p112 [**1965**, coined by the American author Alvin Toffler]

futuristics, *n.* the art or practice of making forecasts about future developments, especially in science and technology, and future trends, as in art, fashion, etc., and their effect upon society. Compare DELPHOLOGY. *Some writers, such as Bertrand de Jouvenel, have objected to the term 'futurology', because an 'ology' is a science which deals with things that exist, and the future* per definitionem *never exists, so let us call it 'futuristics'.* Innovations, 1970, p102 [**1970**]

futurological, *adj.* of or relating to the forecasting of future developments in science and technology. *The conference he* [Arthur Bronwell, dean of engineering at the University of Connecticut] *organised in 1959 with the US National Science Foundation, the Engineers' Joint Council and many other learned bodies, sparked off a great deal of the systematic "futurological" thinking that was much a characteristic of the 'sixties.* New Scientist 12/24/70, p562 [**1970**]

futurologist, *n.* a person who studies or makes forecasts about the future developments in science and technology and their effect upon society. *The coming superpower is not China but Japan which, by late this century or early next one, will possess the largest gross national product in the world. Such is the considered opinion of Herman Kahn, futurologist . . .* NY Times 8/5/70, p34 [**1967**, derived from earlier *futurology* (OEDS 1946)]

fuzzball, *n. U.S. Slang.* a derogatory term for a police officer. *"Ten years ago, police were pigs," said Moell, who works at criminal hearings. "Now they are fuzzballs and slimes."* Fort Wayne Journal-Gazette 9/21/86, p10A [**1986**, from *fuzz* slang term for police (1920's)]

fuzzbox, *n.* an attachment on an electric guitar that gives a fuzzy quality to the sound (often used attributively). See FUZZ TONE. *There's a passage in one old song, "I Could Write a Book," when her voice turns sweetly gruff, an almost exact vocal gloss on modern fuzzbox guitar.* Sunday Times (London) 5/9/71, p31 [**1968**]

fuzzbuster, *n. U.S. Slang.* an electronic device for detecting radar. High Times: *What's been the greatest technical advance in the marijuana smuggling business?* Eby: *The fuzzbuster. Modify that box just a little bit and you can tell whenever radar is coming at you.* High Times 1/79, p53 [**1977**, from *fuzz* slang term for the police (1920's) + *buster* one that busts; so called because it destroys the effectiveness of police radar]

fuzzbuzz, *n. U.S. Slang.* fuss or inconvenience; bustle; commotion. *Descending from ship or train or plane, with a minimum*

of immigration fuzzbuss, the F.F. [Foreign Friend] *sees the world's most intensively cultivated fields, wheat and rice and sorghum and countless vegetables, pressing to the edge of every road, rail and airport runway.* Time 10/23/78, p62 [**1960**, probably from *fuzz* a blur + *buzz* humming sound, formed to suggest confusion and noise]

fuzzify, *v.t. Informal.* to muddle or confuse. *Fuzzifying . . . is the presentation of data, concepts, programs or goals in what appear to be precise terms while permitting a flexibility of future interpretation.* Washington Post Magazine 1/23/83, p14 *Gee, Dr. Fotheringham, you've certainly managed to fuzzify the muddification.* Maclean's 3/8/82, p68 [**1976**] —**fuzzification**, *n.: We've come a long way since Texan Maury Maverick used the term gobbledygook to describe the language of the Potomac. We have witnessed a refinement of that inelegant communicative art, and have experienced the development of professional fuzzification as a means of assuring tranquility to the ship of state.* Washington Post Magazine 1/23/84, p14

fuzz tone, a fuzzy quality given to the sound of an electric guitar by distorting certain amplified sound waves. *Either vibrato or tremolo can be added to tones electronically, and a variety of novelty effects, such as "fuzz tone," can be produced.* McGraw-Hill Yearbook of Science and Technology 1971, p276 [**1968**]

fuzzy logic, a form of logic which tries to take into account ill-defined or vague terms such as "very," "somewhat," and "mostly". *Computers give blunt answers. Yes or no, black or white. Researchers in artificial intelligence are trying to teach their machines a little subtlety: to encode the shades of grey characteristic of human thought. One approach that is producing good results is "fuzzy logic," an idea thought up by Dr. Lotfi Zadeh, at the University of California at Berkeley . . . This is how it works. When a conventional expert system is given the task of deciding whether a man is tall it will reply yes to anybody above say, six foot and no to everybody else. This is doing an injustice to an English word. Tall has a less precise (and more useful) meaning in conversation—taller than the local average, tall for your age, taller than broad, etc.* Economist 3/30/85, p89 [**1969**] —**fuzzy logician**: *"Fuzzy logic provides just the principles needed to deal with large-scale models of the vagueness of the real world," says computer scientist and fuzzy logician Constantin Virgil Negoita of New York's Hunter College.* Encyclopedia Science Supplement (Grolier) 1987, p117

fuzzy set, a mathematical set whose elements converge or overlap with those of other sets. *In many fields of science, problems having an element of uncertainty and imprecision are conventionally treated according to the concepts and methods of probability theory. However, there are also situations in which the imprecision stems not from randomness but from the presence of a class or classes (that is, fuzzy sets) that do not possess sharply defined boundaries.* Science 12/8/72, p1069 [**1964**]

G

G, a symbol used in the United States to designate motion pictures recommended for general audiences. *The Motion Picture Association of America's Production Code and Rating Administration . . . has been classifying movies (G, PG, R or X) for the stated purpose of providing the public with information that would forestall the impulse toward local censorship.* NY Times 7/3/73, pB1 [**1968**] ►Symbols for a voluntary system of rating films were introduced in the United States in November, 1968 by the Motion Picture Association of America.

While the rating system adopted in the U.S. is relatively new and controlled by the film industry, the British have been rating films since 1914. In Canada, each province has its own film censorship board.

GABA ('gæbə), *n.* acronym for *gamma-aminobutyric acid,* an amino acid occurring in the central nervous system of mammals. *In mammals, GABA is a compound almost exclusively confined to the brain, where it is present in high concentrations.* New Scientist 7/23/70, p174 [**1958**]

gab line, *U.S.* a telephone service that for a charge per minute allows a caller to engage in conversation with someone. Also called TALK LINE. *He might have . . . the opportunity to listen in on 976-MEET, "Philadelphia's Wild Party line," or almost any of the other so-called gab lines now operating in the Philadelphia area.* Philadelphia Inquirer 2/14/88, p1-A [**1988**]

gag order, *U.S.* a court order prohibiting members of the news media from reporting or publicly commenting on an issue that is before a court of law. Compare PRIOR RESTRAINT. *When the Supreme Court last year virtually banned direct "gag orders" on the press, reporters thought they had won a decisive victory. But the victory has since been diluted by the emerging possibility that indirect curbs may be legal, a trend for which the Supreme Court last week provided support.* NY Times 1/15/78, pD7 [**1976**, perhaps from a combination of *gag rule* limiting debate in a legislature and *restraining order*]

Gaia hypothesis or **Gaia theory** ('geiə or 'gaiə), the theory that the planet earth is the core of a unified living system which regulates itself much like an organism does. *It is the Gaia theory's insistence that the earth is a self-controlling, whole system, not a conglomeration of disconnected parts and discontinuous functions, that has drawn the interests of scientists.* NY Times Magazine 11/23/86, p67 [**1981**, from *Gaia,* Greek name for (mother) earth in mythology]

gal operon, a group of genes which control the metabolism of galactose sugar in bacteria, important in genetic research. *In the middle of the duplex there was an unpaired region where the picked-up segment of bacterial DNA (including the gal operon) was not complementary to the viral DNA.* Scientific American 12/76, p111 [**1972**, *gal,* short for *galactose*]

galvanic skin response, a measure of the resistance of the skin to the flow of electricity between two electrodes attached to a person's hand, used to indicate the degree of stress or anxiety of the subject. *Prior to meditation, volunteer meditators and control subjects took the Minnesota Multiphasic Personality Inventory (MMPI) and were measured for spontaneous galvanic skin response (GSR). GSR is a measure of the degree of stability of the autonomic nervous system which is correlated to such things as resistance to stress and reduced physical impulsivity.* Science News 9/8/73, p152 [**1962**]

game-breaker, *n. U.S. Football.* a play or player that determines the outcome of a game. *With the new 3-4 defense choking off the long run and seamless zone defenses in the secondary denying all but the perfectly thrown pass, the big play is often the game-breaker in the N.F.L.* [National Football League] *this sea-*son. *Often that play comes from the little men, especially on kickoff and punt returns.* Time 12/5/77, p75 [**1969**]

game park, a large tract of land, especially in Africa, set aside as a game preserve. Compare SAFARI PARK. *Because the game parks offer so much that is unique, they are regarded as Kenya's number one tourist attraction; and this is as it should be, for nothing can compare with the experience of viewing in such surroundings.* Times (London) 8/26/78, p11 [**1963, 1970**]

game plan, *U.S.* a carefully planned course of action; strategy. *Now that there are signs of a change in the trend of the economy, it is timely to make a preliminary judgment on how the so-called "game plan"—the Administration's strategy for overcoming inflation without recession—has been going.* NY Times 10/20/70, p45 [**1941, 1970**, originally a sports term for the strategy to be used in a game]

game show, *U.S.* a television program built around a game or contest in which the players or contestants are scored and the winners are given prizes. *Game shows are one of the embarrassing little secrets in American Pop culture. Even confessed TV addicts do not readily admit that they watch the games . . . But the games survive. . . Currently there are 30 hours of game shows on networks' weekly daytime schedules.* Time 2/18/80, p85 [**1961**]

gamma-ray astronomy, the study and detection of sources of celestial gamma radiation, including the study of GAMMA-RAY BURSTS. *Gamma-ray astronomy finally achieved a measure of sophistication with the launch of the American SAS-2 satellite in 1972 and the European COS-B satellite in 1975. In addition to the detection of a flux of gamma rays whose intensity varies with the 33-millisecond period of the pulsars in the Crab Nebula, a dozen other sources were revealed in data analyzed as of mid-1977.* Britannica Book of the Year 1978, p207 [**1966**]

gamma-ray burst, a sudden, short, powerful emission of gamma rays detected by orbiting astronomical satellites about five times a year. *Abbreviation:* GRB Compare X-RAY BURST. *Gamma-ray bursts are stirring the kind of excitement among astronomers and astrophysicists that the discovery of pulsars, quasars and X-ray stars did in the 1960's. Gamma-ray bursts are short in duration, sometimes less than one second, and staggering in their power.* Encyclopedia Science Supplement (Grolier) 1974, p24 [**1974**]

gamma-ray laser, another name for GRASER. *Packing the wallop of a miniature A-bomb and able to penetrate a wall several feet thick, the gamma-ray laser . . . could create a revolution in scientific research and weapon development.* Science News 1/5/74, p8 [**1974**]

gamma surgery, a surgical operation in which gamma rays from pellets of radioactive cobalt are used to destroy cancerous cells, to relieve Parkinson's disease, etc. *Gamma surgery also opens up a new perspective in the surgery of pain. With only a bloodless procedure involved, a patient with advanced cancer can be spared the extra stress of a conventional operation, and could possibly be treated at a much earlier stage.* New Scientist 12/3/70, p377 [**1970**]

gangbang, *n. U.S. Slang.* sexual relations by a group of males with one female. *There were of course those other girls, demented atrocities who lay impassively in boiler rooms, behind schoolyard handball walls, or in the sand traps of the nearby golf course while a group of us would swagger our way through a gangbang. .* Harper's 8/70, p83 [**1967**] —*v.t. U.S. Slang.* **1** to subject to a gangbang. *"Even male politicians don't get the kind of viciousness that women get as routine. It is like being* *gang-banged in public.*" Time 3/20/72, p31 **2** to hang around or belong to a gang. "*Lotta people say just because I'm 16, 'You need to quit gangbangin' cause you still got a life in front of you.' But I feel I better do it while I'm young. . . If you ask me, gangbangin' ain't gone never die,*" says De Bam. "*They's just too many people that want to be a gang member.*" People Weekly 5/2/88, p44 [**1972**]

gangle, *v.i.* to move awkwardly or loosely. *Men who go in for mime belong to a special physical type. . . Their limbs can't be called gangling because they are controlled so efficiently but they would gangle if they could.* Punch 2/12/69, p247 [**1957**, back formation from *gangling*, *adj.*, awkwardly or loosely built (OED 1808)]

Gang of Four, a group of high officials of the Chinese Communist party that opposed westernizing influences in Chinese culture and modernization of industry. Its members were arrested and purged in the power struggle following the death of Mao Tse-tung (Mao Zedong) in 1976. See CONFUCIAN, ANTI-CONFUCIAN, CAPITALIST ROADER. *We heard* [in China] *denunciations of the Gang of Four for past abuses from almost everyone. Their removal from power is said to be the most significant political event since the 1949 revolution. The Gang of Four and Lin Piao are clearly the current domestic villains, and they are blamed for the excesses of the Cultural Revolution and the suppression of modern development. It has been said that radical movements thrive when some devil has been identified for condemnation. The Gang of Four certainly fills that role admirably.* Science 2/9/79, p514 [**1976**, so called in reference to Mao's wife, Chiang Ching, and three of her allies, who led the radical faction in the Shanghai Communist Party organization]

gang shag, another name for GANGBANG. *The novel* [The Story of O], *it was earnestly proposed, explored the paradox that only in slavery can one find perfect freedom. A flogging here, a gang shag there, these are a small price to pay for release from the endless naggings of free will.* Time 1/5/76, p63 [**1927, 1976**]

Ganzfeld ('ga:nts,felt), *n. Psychology.* **1** a blank surface, such as a screen, used to prevent interference with internally produced visual imagery, especially in testing for extrasensory perception. *Sargent is one of many to have used Ganzfeld in telepathy and is probably the most successful in obtaining "good" results; a parallel series of experiments at Edinburgh have failed to show any significant effect.* New Scientist 10/18/79, p199 **2** Attributive use. Also, Anglicized **ganzfeld.** *Sitting alone with Ping-Pong ball halves over my eyes, a red light shining in my face and earphones piping the sounds of the sea into my head, I must have looked as foolish as I felt. But I had asked for it. This was the ganzfeld setup in the parapsychology lab at Maimonides. My task was to think out loud for 30 minutes while someone on the outside listened but did not answer.* Science News 11/10/73, p300 [**1973**, from German, from *ganz* whole, all + *Feld* field]

garage sale, a sale of old or used household belongings, held in a garage or other part of a house. Compare TAG SALE, YARD SALE. *Garage sales, especially those in old neighborhoods, are a sometime source of interesting old things, although the truly worthwhile old stuff may not be out for sale simply because the householder thinks of it as junk.* American Home 3/76, p82 [**1967**]

garbageology, *n.* the study of a culture or society by examining and recording the contents of its refuse. See ETHNOARCHEOLOGY. *The unarguable theory behind this garbageology is that if we can learn about ancient peoples by studying their garbage, we can learn even more about present society the same way: "It's all there in the trash," the professor says.* National Review 2/6/76, p70 [**1971**, from *garbage* + *-ology* scientific study]

garbologist, *n.* a garbage collector. Compare SANITATIONMAN. *Sanitation worker, Ronald Whatley, has suggested a new title for workers in his profession—"Garbologists."* NY Times 9/16/68, p47 *One dustman in court last week called himself a garbologist.* New Scientist 1/13/66, p97 [**1966**, from *garb*age

+ *-ologist*, as in *biologist, zoologist,* etc.; perhaps influenced by Australian English *garbo* garbage collector]

garbology (gɑrˈbɑlədʒiː), *n.* variant of GARBAGEOLOGY. *Among aficionados and practitioners of the new pop science of garbology . . . there's a saying: Garbage doesn't lie.* Suburbia Today 5/1/83, p8 [**1983**] ▶Perhaps this is becoming the preferred term.

GARP, *n.* acronym for *Global Atmospheric Research Program. One of the tasks of GARP is to collect data describing the complete atmosphere, i.e., from the surface to about 30 km (19 mi). Since the inception of GARP there has been significant progress in the development of satellites equipped with radiometric instruments that can measure surface temperatures as well as the distributions of temperature and humidity with altitude.* 1978 Britannica Yearbook of Science and the Future, p283 [**1974**]

garri ('gɑriː), *n.* a staple food of Nigeria, made of ground cassava. *. . . garri is regarded by relief doctors* [in Biafra] *as a mere "filler" without real nutrient value.* Sunday Times (London) 1/11/70, p13 *. . . Biafra's farmers have actually produced a surplus of yams and garri.* NY Times 3/31/68, p44 [**1926, 1964**]

garryowen, *n. Rugby.* a high, hanging kick used to advance the ball down the field. Compare CHIP-KICK. *The provincial XV includes five men on national duty at Lansdowne Road on Saturday. One of these is the stand-off, Ward, and it may safely be assumed that all Munster rugby men are praying not only that he will be on target as a goal kicker but also as a hoister of garryowens, under which his forwards will advance like the hounds of hell.* Times (London) 10/31/78, p8 [**1965**, from *Garryowen*, the name of an Irish rugby club noted for its use of such kicks]

gas, *n.* Usually, **a gas.** *U.S. Slang.* a great pleasure; a delight; joy. *. . . as black Percussion Man Warren Duncan says, "It's a gas to ride the buses, see all the mountains and the jack rabbits and road runners. And the concerts are wild."* Time 11/2/70, p66 [**1957**]

gas chromatograph, the apparatus used in gas chromatography. *. . . the gas chromatograph . . . separates hydrocarbon molecules of different kinds according to their volatility.* 1969 Collier's Encyclopedia Year Book, p406 [**1952**]

gas chromatography, another name for GAS-LIQUID CHROMATOGRAPHY. *Gas chromatography is a procedure whereby a volatile mixture is separated into its components by a moving inert gas passing over a sorbent. . . As a method of separating the individual components of a complex mixture gas chromatography has no equal.* Scientific American 6/69, p115 [**1958**]

gasdynamic laser, a gas laser in which the mixture of gases is energized by burning fuel instead of by means of electrical discharges. Compare GAS LASER. *A gasdynamic laser theoretically able to produce thousands of kilowatts of infrared light has been developed by Avco Corp.* Science News 5/30/70, p529 [**1970**]

gas-guzzling, *adj.* Especially *U.S. and Canadian.* consuming excessive quantities of fuel. *Chevys sold in 1985 will be compacts or subcompacts. Engines will be smaller and more fuel-efficient, using fuel injection and turbocharging (which force feeds air into the engine and improves combustion) to maintain at least some of the peppiness of a gas-guzzling V8.* Time 10/9/78, p93 *The smart folks in the sportfishing industry decided a while back that the days of heavy tackle, expensive boats, and gas-guzzling outboards might be headed for trouble, so they bet on fly-fishing.* NY Times 6/6/79, pA26 [**1968**, coined by George Romney, former head of American Motors Company] **—gas guzzler:** *Ever since North Americans faced the fact that fuel reserves are finite, some drivers of the big cars with huge V-8 engines have felt guilty. While they reveled in powerful six-seaters, environmentalists kept telling them their gas-guzzlers were sinful.* Maclean's 11/28/77, p69

gas laser, a laser that produces its intense beam of light by exciting a tube filled with a mixture of gases such as neon and helium or carbon dioxide and nitrogen. Compare GASDYNAMIC LASER. *Gas lasers are usually excited by electrical discharges.*

But this method has limitations, particularly when large volumes of gas are involved. In general, the energy generated by a gas laser increases as the volume increases. New Scientist 10/22/70, p164 **[1970]**

gas-liquid chromatography, a method of analyzing the chemical substances of a mixture by combining it with a gas such as nitrogen and passing it through a liquid solvent. Also called GAS CHROMATOGRAPHY. Compare THIN-LAYER CHROMATOGRAPHY. *Clarks Ltd, the shoe manufacturers, will not accept leather from tanners who use whale oil. Its chemist, Michael Fletcher, employs a refined analysis, based on gas-liquid chromatography, to detect sperm oil.* New Scientist 11/15/79, p499 **[1952]**

gasohol ('gæsə,hɔːl), n. **1** a blend of gasoline and ethyl (grain) alcohol, used as fuel in internal-combustion engines. Compare DIESOHOL. *In half a dozen major cities, Brazilians now fill the tanks of their car with "gasohol," a mixture of 80 percent gasoline and 20 percent ethyl Alcohol.* Manchester Guardian Weekly (Washington Post section) 9/10/78, p15 *Supporters of gasohol say that its use will conserve scarce petroleum supplies and also reduce surplus farm crops, which can be used to produce alcohol.* NY Times 1/14/79, p40 **2 Gasohol**, a trademark for such a product. *Nebraskans just completed two million miles of on-road testing of Gasohol—a trademarked blend of 10 percent ethyl (or grain) alcohol and 90 percent unleaded gasoline.* Science News 10/29/77, p280 **[1974**, from *gas*oline + alc*ohol*] ►The gasoline-alcohol mixture was first developed in the U.S. in the 1930's and sold in the Midwest under the trade name Agrol (from *ag*ricultural alc*ohol*). The term *gasohol* became current after the energy crisis of 1973-74 led to a search for alternate sources of fuel.

GASP, n. U.S. acronym adopted by various antismoking and antipollution groups. *Kessiloff is an advocate of GASP (Group Against Smoker's Pollution) who feels that cabdrivers have a right to clean air in their taxis. A Winnipeg ordinance prohibits drivers from smoking while carrying passengers but no such law extends to cab patrons.* Maclean's 3/22/76, p24 **[1969]** ►This acronym has been used as the name for *Group Against Smoke and Pollution, Gals Against Smoke and Pollution, Greater Washington Alliance to Stop Pollution,* etc.

gas-ripened, adj. ripened by treatment with ethylene gas. *The regulation stated that the vine-ripened tomatoes had to be larger than gas-ripened tomatoes produced in the U.S.* Consumer Reports 1/76, p5 **[1976]**

gas tail, the part of a comet's tail that consists of ionized molecules blown away from the coma by the solar wind. Compare DUST TAIL. See also ANTITAIL. *A color photograph of Comet Bennett showed the dust tail to be yellowish. . . The gas tail, on the other hand, was blue, because of characteristic emissions of the ionized molecules present.* Encyclopedia Science Supplement (Grolier) 1974, p12 **[1974]**

Gastarbeiter ('gɑːst,ɑrbaitər), n. sing. or pl. a worker in West Germany who has come from another country (mainly Italy, Yugoslavia, Turkey, or Spain) to supplement the labor shortage. *In social terms, the gap between what the Germans call* Gastarbeiter *(guest worker) and his host has remained wide.* Time 6/8/70, p39 **[1964**, from German, literally, guest worker]

gastrinoma (,gæstrə'noumə), n. a disease characterized by multiple ulcers in the stomach, caused by excess secretion of gastrin, resulting from a pancreatic tumor. Compare ZOLLINGER-ELLISON SYNDROME. *While some specialists remain skeptical of the value of cimetidine in the treatment of other ulcer diseases, they are virtually unanimous in acclaiming it for gastrinoma.* NY Times Magazine 11/6/77, p76 **[1977**, from *gastrin* + -*oma* diseased condition]

gastroplasty, n. a surgical method of treating gross obesity by sectioning off a small, upper portion of the stomach with a row of stainless steel staples so that the patient is left with a much smaller stomach. *The gastroplasty technique was pioneered in the 60's by Dr. Edward Mason at the University of Iowa, then abandoned until last year when modifications made the operation more effective.* Maclean's 5/7/79, p13 **[1979**; earlier

(1940's) broadly defined in medicine as plastic or reconstructive surgery on the stomach]

gat (gɑːt) or **gath** (gɑːθ), n. a complex rhythmic passage that usually marks the final movement or section of a raga, the traditional Hindu musical form. *An element of lively humour marked the* gat *when the percussionist, Manik Rao Popatkar, engaged the sitar in some brisk rhythmic dialogues with the tabla.* Times (London) 3/29/68, p13 *Mr.* [Ravi] *Shankar himself is, of course, a prodigious virtuoso on the sitar, and to me the most memorable event of the evening was a gath performed by him, with tabla (drum) accompaniment by Alla Rakha. . .* New Yorker 9/21/68, p138 **[1966**, from Sanskrit]

gate, n. one of the locations in the nervous system, especially along the spinal cord, at which pain signals are controlled according to the GATE-CONTROL THEORY. *Twirling the acupuncture needles these researchers hold creates a flood of sensations—but none that contain pain—racing to the gates. These sensations, in effect, overwhelm the capacity of these "gates" so that the pain sensations of a surgical procedure are not transmitted to the areas of the brain where pain is registered and felt by the patient.* NY Times 6/4/72, pD7 **[1968]**

-gate, a combining form added to nouns and meaning any scandal resembling Watergate; a scandal involving charges of corruption and usually of cover-up. The following are examples of its use: **—Cattlegate:** *B. Dale Ball, director of the state Agriculture Department, was accused by several state legislators of masterminding a "Cattlegate" coverup to minimize the problem. . .* Americana Annual 1978, p330 **—Hollywoodgate:** *Judy Garland's ex-husband Sid Luft has accused David Begelman, president of Columbia Pictures and a central figure in the unfolding "Hollywoodgate" drama, of embezzling up to $100,000 from the late singer while managing her career.* New York Post 1/30/78, p1 **—Irangate:** *The recent White House scandal has been a windfall for wordsmiths. . . First come the five -gates: Reagan's Watergate, Reagangate, Irangate, Contragate, and Armsgate.* American Speech, Summer 1987, p187 **—Koreagate:** *The continually expanding scandal over the Park regime's influence peddling on Capitol Hill has already been called a "Koreagate."* Manchester Guardian Weekly 12/5/76, p6 **—Lancegate** [Bert *Lance*, former director of Office of Management and Budget]: *Although Lancegate has encouraged the British press to expose the financial shenanigans of Tory Reginald Maudling, the question is asked: Why are the Americans doing this to themselves?* NY Times 9/29/77, p35 **—Muldergate:** *The South African government seems to have given little thought to former information minister Connie Mulder, who was forced to drop from the government parliament and party positions because of the "Muldergate" scandal.* Weekly Review (Nairobi, Kenya) 3/30/79, p19 **—Nannygate:** *Canada's "Nannygate" furor—touched off by Transport Minister Otto Lang's attempt to arrange a free armed forces flight for his family's Scottish nanny. . .* Maclean's 1/24/77, p46 **—Oilgate:** *Had the government proclaimed a stern law and then winked at its offenders? Who knew about the misdeeds? How much did they know? The affair that Britons were dubbing "Oilgate" threatened to reach into the highest places.* Time 10/2/78, p43 **—Pearlygate:** *Having decreed as recently as December that it was time for journalism to abandon the tired old -gate suffix in the naming of scandals, I am now given a humbling lesson in the error of dogmatism. Its source is the scandal of the warring television preachers, for which there is only one possible name: Pearlygate.* NY Times 3/28/87, p27 **—Quakergate:** *Quakergate is the new scandal brewing, and two Pennsylvania congressmen are accused.* People Weekly 2/13/78, p32 **[1973**, abstracted from WATERGATE] ►Most words formed with -*gate* last only for the newsworthiness of the event: *Dallasgate, Floodgate, laborgate, Muldergate,* or as a nonce word to relieve some writer's style: *headachegate* or *sewergate.* However, the combining form persists in spite of the short life of most of the creations that make use of it. A discussion of -*gate* words by I. Willis Russell and Mary Gray Porter appeared in the "Among the New Words" column of *American Speech,* 53, 3 (*Fall* 1978).

gate-control theory or **gate theory**, a theory that assumes the existence of specific locations in the body at which sensation of pain can be blocked off from awareness. See ACUPUNCTURE. *An increase in the sensory input at the site of needling* [in acupuncture] *and application of electricity might send impulses up the spinal cord to the brain and jam the circuits—in line with* [Pat] *Wall's pain gate-control theory.* Science News 8/5/72, p84 *One theory of pain that has been widely cited as a possible explanation of acupuncture is the so-called gate theory, developed by Wall and Ronald Melzack. This theory rejects the long-held idea that sensations of pain are transmitted directly from the receptors to the brain via nerve structures.* 1974 Britannica Yearbook of Science and the Future, p60 **[1968]**

gateway drug, a soft drug, such as alcohol, that often leads the user to turn to hard drugs. *Marijuana is often the gateway drug for other illicit drug use, specifically cocaine and heroin. For example, studies show that among those who reported using marijuana only 3 to 10 times, more than 20 percent have gone on to try cocaine.* NY Times 4/13/86, pD24 **[1985]**

Gatorade ('geitər,eid), *n.* a trade name for a soft drink containing glucose, citric acid, sodium bicarbonate, potassium chloride, etc., used by athletes instead of water to replenish rapidly lost body fluids and salts. . . . *Winnie Palmer, Arnold's* [the golfer Arnold Palmer's] *wife . . . was carrying a container and explained that she had been dispatched at the ninth green to find some Gatorade.* New Yorker 7/5/69, p70 **[1967**, named by James Free, a colleague of J. Robert Cade, the inventor of this drink, because it was an "aid to the Gators", University of Florida football team; the suffix *-ade* is from *lemonade, orangeade*]

gauchesco (gau'tʃeskou), *adj.* of or having to do with a type of Spanish poetry whose character, language, and setting derive from the life of the gauchos of South America. *I travelled up and down Argentina and Uruguay, lecturing on Swedenborg, Blake, the Persian and Chinese mystics, Buddhism, gauchesco poetry.* . . New Yorker 9/19/70, p86 **[1970**, from American Spanish, from *gaucho* + Spanish *-esco -esque*]

gauchist ('gouʃist), *n.* Anglicized form of GAUCHISTE. *He* [Eugene Ionesco] *believes that the "gauchist" movement contains a fundamental Fascist element.* Manchester Guardian Weekly 6/12/69, p17 **[1969]**

gauchiste (gou'ʃi:st), *n. French.* a political radical; a leftist (also used attributively). *It was a mass demonstration ordered by La Gauche Proletarienne* [The Proletarian Left], *a militant Maoist group made up of amalgamated gauchistes.* . . New Yorker 6/13/70, p97 *Long-haired gauchiste (leftist) students in blue jeans and suede jackets stopped motorists in the Latin Quarter and flipped their cars over to form makeshift barricades.* Time 6/8/70, p37 **[1970]**

gauchos, *n.pl.* baggy trousers usually reaching, and often gathered at, the ankles, similar to those worn by South American gauchos. *Knickers and gauchos, hip-huggers, bellbottoms and jeans—all-are currently outselling dresses of any length.* Time 1/11/71, p38 **[1971]**

gauge particle, *Nuclear Physics.* any of a group of elementary particles whose function is to transmit forces between other particles. *When the Sun lights the Earth, the energy is transmitted from the one celestial body to the other by photons, the gauge particles of electromagnetism. And when the Earth attracts the Moon, the two exchange gravitons, the gauge particles for gravity.* Encyclopedia Science Supplement (Grolier) 1987, p307 **[1986]**

gauge theory, *Physics.* any theory that attempts to establish relationships between fundamental physical forces such as electromagnetism, the weak force, the strong force, etc. Compare HIGGS BOSON. *Nearly 11 years ago Abdus Salam and Steven Weinberg independently proposed a simple "gauge theory" which would unify two of the fundamental forces of nature: the weak interaction, which is responsible for the "beta decay" of atomic nuclei and allows the Sun to burn, and the electromagnetic interaction which creates light and chemical forces. To everyone's delight the . . . theory fitted beautifully with two great discoveries in the 1970s: neutral currents (discovered,*

incidentally, in Gargamelle) and the charmed quark. New Scientist 4/20/78, p151 **[1977]**

Gault, *adj. U.S.* of, relating to, or providing legal protection and rights to minors. Compare MIRANDA. *The Gault decision established, nationwide, children's right to counsel, though only in the adjudication stage. The Court, however, has yet to address itself to the question of the rights of so-called status offenders, or PINS.* New Yorker 8/14/78, p56 **[1973**, from the Supreme Court ruling (1967) that Gerald *Gault* was denied due process under the Fourteenth Amendment when committed to reform school without being informed of his rights]

gavel-to-gavel, *adj. U.S.* from beginning to end of a conference, meeting, etc. *The U.S. Senate voted to allow gavel-to-gavel coverage of congressional proceedings on the C-SPAN channel; some critics felt the move would improve public accountability; others said it would encourage showboating.* Americana Annual 1987, p511 **[1974]**

gay, *n. U.S. Slang.* a homosexual. *The City Council has twice failed to report out a bill forbidding discrimination against gays.* . . . Newsweek 2/26/73, p32 **[1971**, noun use of *gay, adj.*, homosexual (OEDS 1935)]

Gay Lib, 1 a militant movement of homosexuals demanding greater civil rights and protesting discrimination in business, etc. *Why, ultimately, would I not subscribe to Gay Lib—or to Women's Lib, or Black Power, or Welsh Nationalism? It is because, though it may be that I am 'gay' or a woman or black or Welsh, I don't want to make it the business of my life.* Listener 8/16/73, p220 **2** a member or supporter of this movement. *Being a politician, Mr Jenkins may calculate that the Gay Libs can muster more votes than the Christian community can.* Times (London) 9/3/76, p13 **[1972**, shortened from GAY LIBERATION on the pattern of WOMEN'S LIB]

Gay Liberation, *U.S.* another name for GAY LIB. . . . *a skinny, semi-hysterical young man lunged at him* [Senator Edward Kennedy] *with a placard, stumbling and shrieking, "What is your position on Gay Liberation?"* New Yorker 12/4/71, p49 *Increasingly, homosexuals are creating their own parainstitutions, including churches. And with the proliferation of such radical groups as the Gay Liberation Front, . . . they are taking to the streets.* Time 7/13/70, p6 **[1970]**

gayola (gei'oulə), *n. U.S. Slang.* undercover payments made by homosexual establishments for permission to operate without interference. . . . *it is generally acknowledged that homosexual bars, steam baths, restaurants, and moviehouses everywhere in this country pay "gayola" to crime syndicates and to law enforcement agencies.* Saturday Review 2/12/72, p23 *There is also a constant opportunity for blackmail and for shakedowns by real or phony cops, a practice known as "gayola."* Time 1/21/66, p41 **[1966**, from *gay, adj.*, homosexual + *-ola* (as in *payola*, U.S. Slang word for graft, blackmail, or any similar payment)]

gazar (gə'zɑr), *n.* a gauzy silk fabric, often sequined with shiny metal. *Givenchy's turquoise gazar dress has white beading and bare midriff.* NY Times 3/16/68, p18 . . . *prettiest in purple gazar, ruffled at the high neck and sleeves, at Patou.* . . Sunday Times (London) 8/25/68, p39 **[1967**, from French, from *gaze* gauze]

gazump (gə'zəmp), *British.* —*v.t.* to subject (the buyer of a house) to demands for a higher price after the purchase has been arranged. *The rapid increase in prices, the growing number of people with mortgages in their pockets, has meant that there is little time to be choosy before you are gazumped.* Guardian (London) 5/12/72, p21 —*n.* an act or instance of gazumping. *The brass-faced gazump is bad enough, but now the gazumpers are finding sneakier ways to dun the househungry.* News of the World (London) 5/14/72, p8 **[1971**, alteration of earlier British slang *gazoomph* to swindle (OEDS 1928), of unknown origin]

GB, a symbol for a lethal nerve gas (fluoroisopropoxy methyl phosphine oxide), usually combined with an explosive for use as a bomb. The gas was formerly known by its German name, Sarin. *The U.S. Army planned to bury at sea some 27,000 tons* of surplus chemicals including GB, an organic phosphorus nerve gas. . . Americana Annual 1970, p162 According to a U.N. report, less than one drop of GB can paralyze and kill a victim within minutes of contact. NY Times 8/6/70, p32 [**1954**]

GDP, abbreviation of GROSS DOMESTIC PRODUCT. The need [in Trinidad] is to build up agriculture, which only accounts for 9 per cent of the gross domestic product, and manufacturing (16 per cent of GDP) as against petrol and asphalt which accounts for 25 per cent of the GDP and 80 per cent of the island's exports. Manchester Guardian Weekly 5/2/70, p4 . . . GNP [gross national product] equals GDP plus net factor payments on foreign investments. . . Britannica Book of the Year 1971, p273 [**1962**]

gear, n. British Slang. high quality; style; class. In the first cafe he went into someone sold him six librium [a tranquilizer] pills. "It was my sort of cafe, my sort of people—of course they had gear."Times (London) 9/22/70, p10 [**1964**, from earlier British slang gear, adj., smart or fashionable (OEDS 1951), probably from the phrase in top gear in style]

geep (gi:p), n. the offspring of a goat and a sheep. Also called SHOAT. Hundreds of people have claimed success in breeding shoats or geep (hybrids between sheep and goats). . . A male goat cannot fertilise a sheep but a ram can easily fertilise a female goat; in fact the fertilisation rate is as high as normal. But after six weeks of normal development the foetus dies showing the classical signs of rejection. New Scientist and Science Journal 7/8/71, p66 [**1970**, blend of goat and sheep]

gelato (dʒeˈlaːtou), n., pl. **-ti** (-tiː). a rich, creamy Italian ice cream, often made with fruit. Why, sitting in the Piazza Navona, eating a gelato, was I suddenly reminded of the Trinity? Because a fountain is an archetype of a self-giving self-renewing God. NY Times Magazine 3/16/86, p69 [**1953**, from Italian]

GEM (dʒem), n. acronym for GROUND EFFECT MACHINE. For mass transportation there are air cushion vehicles or ground effects machines (GEM) that use huge fans to draw air downward and up underneath the machine and create a cushion of air several feet high. GEM can travel over land, water, ice, marsh, mud or desert. . . Science News Letter 5/9/64, p298 [**1959**]

gemellologist (ˌdʒeməˈlalədʒist), n. a scientist who specializes in the study of twins. Sixteen pairs of twins may not sound like a large number of people on whom to base any generalisations, but as twin studies go it is not a bad sample. Roughly speaking, there are 100 million twins in the world, about a third of them identical.

Set beside this, however, gemellologists, as students of twins call themselves, say that only 80 pairs of identical twins who have been separated at birth have ever been studied. Sunday Times (London) 5/25/80, p34 [**1979**, from Latin gemellus, geminus twin + English -ologist]

gender bender, a person or thing that minimizes sexual differentiation or emphasizes bisexuality. . . . The cult hallows ambiguous sexuality: Mr. David Bowie, the rock star "gender bender", is a key hero. Economist 12/27/80, p48 [**1980**]

gender gap, U.S. the apparent differences in values or attitudes between the sexes. Differences between the sexes may seem out of fashion, but one new distinction is enjoying a vogue: Women are voting more often for Democrats than men, pollsters say. Surveys probing the touted "gender gap" have suggested that . . . Republicans ought to beware, for women are especially sensitive on the subjects of war and social justice. NY Times 12/10/82, pA35 [**1982**]

gene bank, a place in which specific genetic materials are stored alive for study and research. The idea behind creation of such "gene banks," of course, isn't really anything new. Plant breeders have been collecting, sorting, and storing plant materials gathered from all over the world for years, especially for use in plant-breeding experiments. Robert Cooke, Improving on Nature, 1977, p117 [**1972**]

gene deletion. See the quotation for the meaning. Researchers are studying a number of possible techniques that might be

used to remove unwanted genes (gene deletion), supply missing genes (gene insertion), or alter whole blocks of characteristics simultaneously (genetic surgery). 1971 Collier's Encyclopedia Year Book, p6 [**1971**]

gene insertion, the insertion of missing genes in the genetic inventory of a cell or animal. Compare GENE DELETION. For gene insertion, Professor Edward L. Tatum of Rockefeller University, a Nobel Prize winner, envisions the use of nuclear grafts from other cells; the feasibility of such additions has already been proven in experiments with microorganisms. More recently, other scientists have experimented with the use of viruses for gene insertion. 1971 Collier's Encyclopedia Year Book p6 [**1971**]

gene mapping, the process of determining where a particular gene is located on a chromosome. Gene mapping may go beyond determining whether an unborn child will inherit a certain disease; it actually promises to correct many genetic disorders. If, for example, a defective gene could be removed and another normal gene inserted in its place on the map of human chromosomes, many genetic disorders could be prevented. 1980 Britannica Yearbook of Science and the Future p355 [**1978**]

general adaptation syndrome, physical and mental changes by which the body responds to prolonged stress. See the quotation for the details. [Selye] concluded that the body responds to continued stress in three stages, which together he called the general adaptation syndrome: the alarm reaction, in which the person or animal becomes aware of the stressor; the stage of resistance, in which the body adapts to the stressor; and the stage of exhaustion, in which the body loses its ability to adapt World Book Science Annual 1977, p31 [**1972**, coined by Hans Selye, Canadian physician born in Austria in 1907, an authority on stress]

Generalitat (ˌʒenəraːliˈtaːt), n. the autonomous government of Catalonia reestablished in 1977. The Generalitat's executive council has been installed in the old Gothic palace which was its headquarters before and during the Civil War. Manchester Guardian Weekly (Le Monde section) 3/19/78, p11 [**1976**, from Catalan, from (Diputació del) General (de Catalunya) Deputation of the General of Catalonia, the body's original name + -itat -ity]

generate, v.t. to derive or predict (a grammatical sentence) by a set of rules of operation or transformation. Surface structures—the sentences we actually speak and hear—are not "like" the kernels from which they are generated by transformational rules. New Yorker 11/15/69, p225 [**1956**]

generation gap, **1** the differences in social values, behavioral attitudes, and personal aspirations of one generation and that of the next generation, expecially the generation of adolescents and young adults and that of their parents. "What generation gap?" asks University of Michigan Psychologist Joseph Adelson, who argues that "an overwhelming majority of the young—as many as 80%—tend to be traditionalist in values." Time 8/17/70, p35 Do you want to bridge the generation gap? Have a look at some of the books now being written for today's teenagers. Guardian (London) 5/18/72, p13 **2** Transferred sense: Meanwhile ICL [International Computers Limited] is finishing designs on a new series of machines that will make the 1900 series obsolete within 18 months or two years. Thus the generation gap between computers inside and outside eastern Europe seems likely to be perpetuated. Scientific American 10/70, p106 [**1967**]

generative, adj. of or based on the derivation or prediction of grammatical sentences by operational or transformational rules. He [Noam Chomsky] adds . . . that there will "definitely someday be a physiological explanation for the mental processes that we are now discovering." Does this confident assertion signify that generative linguistics is committed to materialism to a view of consciousness as being purely or simply neurochemical? Some of its adherents seem to think so. . . New Yorker 11/15/69, p227 [**1959**]

generative-transformational grammar, a system of rules of operation and transformation for deriving all the grammatical sen tences of a language for more basic underlying strings. Compare TRANSFORMATIONAL GRAMMAR, PHRASE-STRUCTURE GRAMMAR. *The dominant linguistic influence at present is the theory of generative-transformational grammar developed by Noam Chomsky. This theoretical position taken by Chomsky has led to a great deal of psychological research in addition to reviving some traditional philosophical problems, particularly nativism versus empiricism, or competence versus performance.* McGraw-Hill Yearbook of Science and Technology 1968, p317 [**1965**]

generativist, *n.* a follower or advocate of generative linguistics. Compare TRANSFORMATIONALIST. . . . *theories come and go, and the linguists of the future may be better prepared by exposure to a broad range of issues, rather than to the hang-ups of tagmemicists, stratificationalists, generativists, or whatever.* Language 9/70, p667 [**1965**]

genesis rock, a rock or rock formation thought to be contemporary with the formation of the planet, moon, or other celestial body where it is found. *In addition the Apollo 15 astronauts returned a piece of anorthosite, a plagioclase-rich rock formed at depth. It had been hoped that the sample would prove to be a "Genesis rock" as old as the moon itself—about 4.6 billion years—but this hope was not realized: the rock was dated as 4.15 billion years old.* Americana Annual 1972, p303 *Important clues to the origin of the solar system lie in "genesis rocks." These are rocks that have retained their character from nearly 4.6 billion years ago.* Scientific American 1/75, p24 [**1972**]

gene splicing, another name for RECOMBINANT DNA RESEARCH. See SPLICE. *Gene splicing, the much-heralded technique generally known as recombinant DNA research, became more of a reality during the year. Gene splicing involves newly developed techniques by which scientists can incorporate genetic material from one organism into the DNA of another.* 1978 World Book Year Book, p473 [**1977**]

gene therapy, the treatment of a genetic disorder by replacing defective genes in the cells with normal ones that can synthesize a missing substance, such as an enzyme. *Other strategies of gene therapy . . . would be to implant normal cells (cells with the right genes and chromosomes) in developing embryos, or to synthesize viruses to carry the needed enzymes.* Joseph Fletcher, The Ethics of Genetic Control, 1974, p55 *The success obtained by Berg and colleagues Richard Mulligan and Bruce Howard is the first glimmer of a different and still distant vision, that of "gene therapy"—replacing defective genes with their normal counterparts.* Science News 10/28/78, p292 [**1972**]

genetic alphabet, the set of symbols for the four chemical bases of DNA (deoxyribonucleic acid, the carrier of genetic information in the cells) that combine in various ways to form the genetic code. *Most DNA consists of sequences of only four nitrogenous bases: adenine (A), thymine (T), guanine (G) and cytosine (C). Together these bases form the genetic alphabet, and long ordered sequences of them contain in coded form much, if not all, of the information present in the genes.* Scientific American 4/70, p24 [**1970**]

genetic code, the biochemical code by which the four bases in the DNA molecule combine, usually in units of three, to store genetic information and specify the synthesis of particular amino acids and proteins. See also CODON. *The last of the 64 triplet "words" of the genetic code was deciphered by geneticists at the University of Cambridge. . . It was found that the triplet UGA (the bases uracil, guanine, and adenine) . . . signals the end of a protein chain during protein synthesis in the cell.* Encyclopedia Science Supplement (Grolier) 1969, p72 [**1961**]

genetic copying, the duplication of a genetic inventory. *Terms such as "genetic surgery," "genetic copying," "gene insertion," and "gene deletion" are beginning to appear in the scientific journals, and references to genetic manipulation and genetic engineering are common. The potential control of genetic material stems directly from the molecular biologists' fairly recently acquired ability to manipulate and experiment with the*

living cell rather than merely observe it. 1971 Collier's Encyclopedia Year Book, p6 [**1952**]

genetic counseling, the counseling of prospective parents on possible inheritable defects, based chiefly on examination of the parental chromosomes or of the fetal cells in the amniotic fluid of a pregnant woman. Compare GENETIC SCREENING. *People who know or suspect the possibility of an inherited disorder in their family often want to know if they are likely to have a child with the disorder. Genetic counseling is available to these people and their physicians.* Encyclopedia Science Supplement (Grolier) 1977/1978, p61 [**1974**] **—genetic counselor:** *As a dividend, the test also ascertains the sex of the child. "But do you want to know?" my friends asked. Of course. I was dying to know. "We'll be glad not to tell you," said Lynn Godmilow, my genetic counselor at Mount Sinai Hospital.* NY Times Magazine 11/26/78, p28

genetic engineer, a specialist in GENETIC ENGINEERING. *He* [Dr. Edward Tatum, a pioneer of molecular biology] *. . . hinted, at least, at the culture of embryos in the laboratory, destined to develop into adults whose physical and, possibly, intellectual characteristics had been chosen in advance by the genetic engineers.* New Scientist 6/23/66, p762 [**1966**]

genetic engineering, 1 the scientific alteration of genes or genetic material to produce desirable new traits in organisms or to eliminate undesirable ones. Compare EUPHENICS. *The development of techniques for isolating pure genes brings us one step closer to practical genetic engineering. . . Once the biological break-through arrives, genetic engineering, like nuclear engineering, can be used to attain both good and bad ends.* 1970 World Book Year Book, p35 *"Genetic engineering" implies that an alteration in the genetic complement of the fertilized egg is being effected.* Times (London) 2/28/70, p7 **2** any form of human intervention in hereditary processes to alter the character or nature of an organism. . . . *customs, like monogamy, primogeniture, prohibitions against incest, nationalism, war, and commerce have played their part in the de facto policy of genetic engineering of the human species.* 1970 Britannica Yearbook of Science and the Future, p82 [**1966**]

genetic fingerprint, another name for DNA FINGERPRINT. *No two people have the same genetic fingerprint, unless they are identical twins.* McGraw-Hill Yearbook of Science and Technology 1988, p153 [**1987**]

genetic fingerprinting, another name for DNA FINGERPRINTING. *The method is reliable enough for genetic fingerprinting to have been accepted . . . as evidence in criminal cases; it has also been used to determine paternity in zoo primates.* Scientific American 6/88, p33 [**1988**]

genetic load, the accumulated mutations contained in all the genes of a species. *We are learning more about the gene pool and genetic load, but many questions remain unanswered. We know very little about . . . the relative proportions of balanced and mutational load produced by the common mutagenic agents.* Scientific American 3/70, p106 [**1955**]

genetic marker, a gene or genetic characteristic that can be identified and followed from generation to generation. *In 1973 it was discovered that the great majority of patients suffering from ankylosing spondylitis have a characteristic "genetic marker," HA W-27. This marker could be used to identify persons at risk of developing ankylosing spondylitis.* Encyclopedia Science Supplement (Grolier) 1975, p271 [**1967**]

genetic screening, study of the genetic composition of an individual to find and correct inherited defects or to detect defects that may be passed on to offspring. Compare GENETIC COUNSELING. *The best known and most widely used type of genetic screening is the testing in early infancy for the condition known as PKU (phenylketonuria), a disorder that may doom its victims to incurable mental retardation. The ill effects are preventable by adherence to a strict diet, if the dieting begins early enough in infancy.* NY Times 6/24/75, p55 [**1972**]

genetic surgery. See the quotation for the meaning. *Researchers are studying a number of possible techniques that might be used to remove unwanted genes (gene deletion), supply missing* ones (*gene insertion*), *or alter whole blocks of characteristics simultaneously* (*genetic surgery*). 1971 Collier's Encyclopedia Year Book, p6 [**1964**]

gene transplantation, another name for RECOMBINANT DNA RESEARCH. *In a letter to two major scientific publications in July 1974, a group of leading biologists proposed a six-month ban on most research in this area so that scientists could have an opportunity to better evaluate the hazards of gene transplantation.* Americana Annual 1975, p265 [**1974**]

genital herpes, a viral disease in which vesicles occur in the genitals. *These two viral forms are responsible for the common cold sore, herpes keratitis (a severe eye infection) and genital herpes, a venereal disease more common than syphilis.* Science News 6/5-12/76, p361 [**1976**]

genitality, *n.* the focus of attention on genital organs. *At one point we find [Norman] Mailer cheering Germaine Greer for saying in her book,* The Female Eunuch . . . *that clitoral stimulation is "the index of the desexualization of the whole body, the substitution of genitality for sexuality."* Atlantic 7/71, p42 [**1968,** from extension of meaning "normal sexual response in the genital organs" (1950's)]

genogram ('dʒenə‚græm), *n.* a graph that traces the connections in the behavior of several generations of the same family; psychological family tree. *One of the new tools in this effort is called the genogram, in which the interplay of generations within a family is carefully graphed so that repetitive patterns of behavior can be clearly identified.* NY Times 1/21/86, pC1 [**1986**]

Gentle People, a term applied to any of various groups of people noted for their nonviolent creed, such as the flower children and certain American Indians. *It is the manners of the Gentle People that give their jamborees an air of prelapsarian innocence.* Times (London) 8/31/70, p7 . . . *the Gentle People refused a police order to stop playing bongo drums and reciting a Buddhist love chant on the grass of a small park.* NY Times 6/4/67, pD3 [**1967**]

gentleperson, *n.* U.S. a replacement of *gentleman* and *gentlewoman* to avoid reference to the individual's gender. See -PERSON. *The ideological egalitarianism of these gentlepersons is uninhibited by thought, by analytical rigor, or by moral refinement. One gets the creepy feeling that, really, the lot of them make no distinction between the way of life of a free or relatively free society, and the way of life of a totalitarian society.* National Review 6/20/75, p685 [**1975**] ►The capitalized, plural form *Gentlepersons* is occasionally used as a neutral salutation in letters.

gentrify ('dʒentrə‚fai), *v.t.* **1** to convert (a poor or working-class property or area) to one that is more expensive or exclusive, especially in order to raise property value. *He and others in the community are complaining that the new people, almost all of them white, are prosperous, civic-minded and far too eager to buy and renovate rundown houses. These newcomers are "gentrifying" working-class Islington and should be resisted, not welcomed, Mr. Pitt, a 31-year-old community worker, says.* NY Times 9/22/77, pA2 **2** Figurative use: *Labour's class of '71 was a younger and more radical group than the previous Labour administration. It had recovered from the Sporle corruption case in the late 1960s and was—in its own words—a gentrified council, dominated by professional people from Putney rather than people from the working-class areas.* Times (London) 12/17/76, p30 [**1973**] —**gentrification,** *n.: a From Boerum Hill in Brooklyn to Capitol Hill in Washington the fastest growing social problem was not the departure of the white middle class; it was the displacement of the poor and nonwhite, as affluent, taxpaying professionals bid up the prices on brownstone houses and cooperative apartments in what once were dismissed as unsightly slums. Urban specialists now refer to this process as inner-city "gentrification."* Harper's 12/78, p42 **b** Transferred use: *Such pretentions are compounded by the usual inverted snobbery of the middle classes who have "gone slumming" to save a bob or two and then, to their amazement, enjoyed it. To that extent Skytrain is to cheap travel what early Islington was*

to the property market. It's "gentrification" of the air. Manchester Guardian Weekly 1/29/78, p19

geo-. The prefix *geo-* (meaning "of the earth" or "encompassing the whole earth") has generally been attached in the past only to technical terms, such as *geobotany, geomagnetism, geomorphology,* etc. Newer usage, as shown in the examples below, has extended it to less scientific and more socially oriented applications. See BIO- and ECO- for similar use of these prefixes. —**geocide,** *n.: . . . Money has moved on, out of rails, into madness and real estate on the moon, futures in black air and dead waters, a corner on cobalt, a bull market in geocide.* New Yorker 4/18/70, p44 —**geohygiene,** *n.: The problem of geohygiene (earth hygiene) is highly complex and closely tied to economic and social problems. This problem can therefore not be solved on a national and especially not on a local basis.* NY Times 7/22/68, p15 —**geopoetry,** *n.: The theory* [that the sea floor moves the land masses above it] *was so unorthodox and tenuous that Hess* [the American geologist Harry Hess] *cautiously called it "geopoetry." It was soon to become geofact.* Time 1/5/70, p36 —**geo-warfare,** *n.: The final chapter* [of Physics of the Earth by T. F. Gaskell] *. . . introduces an entirely new viewpoint—geo-warfare—with melting ice-caps flooding major cities, artificially induced earthquakes and associated tidal waves (tsunamis) wreaking havoc and weather control bringing a new meaning to cold war.* Science Journal 4/70, p83

geocorona, *n.* a region of ionized hydrogen surrounding the earth at a distance of forty to eighty thousand miles from its surface. *The geocorona, which is produced by the solar wind—a varying flow of protons and electrons from the sun—streams away from the earth on the side opposite the sun, and the moon will be at right angles to that stream, so Dr. Page expects a spectacular shot of the earth looking like a comet with a bright front and a tail thousands of miles long.* New Yorker 4/8/72, p108 [**1960,** from *geo-* earth + *corona* a ring or halo]

geographical medicine, a branch of medicine dealing with the influence of geographical and climatological factors on general health, longevity, disease, etc. *Among the great advances in medical science since World War II has been the growth of a new discipline: geographical medicine. This field of investigation involves intensive study of populations, particularly of populations that have migrated from one environment to another.* Scientific American 7/70, p42 [**1970**]

geomagnetic storm. See the quotation for the meaning. *The term geomagnetic storm is used for worldwide fluctuations in the Earth's field with a scale of about 100 over a period of several hours, caused by the impact of a solar plasma front on the magnetosphere. A number of Russian scientists have claimed that there is a real association between geomagnetic storms and the incidence of various human diseases.* Nature 1/29/76, p302 [**1972**]

geometrodynamics, *n.* the use of multiple connected geometrical structures to study electric, magnetic, and gravitational phenomena as parts of a single process. *"There is nothing in the world except empty curved space. Matter, charge, electromagnetism and other fields are only manifestations of the curvature of space." John Wheeler, prophet of geometrodynamics wrote these words in 1957 and remains as passionately committed to this philosophy as he was then.* New Scientist 9/26/74, p828 *Even modern approaches such as geometrodynamics get a mention.* Nature 2/6/75, p485 [**1972,** from *geometric* + connecting *-o-* + *dynamics*]

geophysical warfare, the modification of environmental conditions, such as weather and cosmic radiation, as a weapon of war. *Perhaps the most exotic form of geophysical warfare concerns tampering with the electrical behaviour of the ionosphere, that ionised region of the atmosphere which extends from 50 km or so up to hundreds of kilometres above the surface of the Earth. Techniques for disturbing radio communication by "punching holes" in the ionosphere with nuclear explosions have long been discussed.* New Scientist 6/17/76, p629 [**1972**]

geopressured, *adj.* under great pressure from geologic forces. *The most speculative, but perhaps also the largest, potential* source of natural gas is the geopressured zone of the Gulf Coast. This zone. . . consists of large aquifers at depths of 2500 to 8000 meters. These aquifers are characterized by high temperatures (above 150°C) and pressures that are as much as twice those of conventional water at comparable depths. At such temperatures and pressures . . . nearly all organic matter is eventually converted to methane. Science 2/13/76, p550 [1968, from geo- earth, of the earth + pressured]

geoscientist, n. an expert or specialist in any of the earth sciences, such as geophysics, geology, oceanography, or seismology. . . . in Iceland, an excited conference of more than fifty local historians, geoscientists and applied scientists recently discussed the problems posed by the return of a most unwelcome visitor accompanying the cooling climate—the Arctic drift ice. New Scientist 3/6/69, p508 [1968]

geostationary, adj. orbiting over a fixed position above the earth and therefore at the same rate as the earth moves. The geo-stationary, or synchronous, satellite's speed is not 680 miles per hour as Shayon indicates but approximately 6,850 miles per hour. Saturday Review 8/10/68, p63 [1961]

geostationary orbit, the orbit of a synchronous satellite; an orbit in which a communications satellite moves at the same rate as the earth does, at an altitude of about 22,000 miles above the equator, so that it can act as a fixed relay station. Also called GEOSYNCHRONOUS ORBIT. . . . the next generation of Intelsat IV satellites, the first of which is due to be placed in geostationary orbit over the Atlantic next year. Science Journal 11/70, p23 [1966]

geosynchronous orbit, another name for GEOSTATIONARY ORBIT. This project should be seen as a possible first move towards a longer-term target which might be a European capacity equivalent to a two-ton-information-transfer satellite in geosynchronous orbit in the 1980s, providing this proves viable. Times (London) 11/22/68, p23 [1968]

geotextile, n. a very strong, impermeable synthetic fabric, used in the construction of highways, bridges, railroad tracks, and the like. Polypropylene fibers are finding a hot new market in what is called geotextiles. Business Week 5/18/81, p140D Companies . . . in America and . . . in Britain are weaving geotextiles into strong and water-impermeable materials whose internal structure, like a mattress, is full of pockets . . . such materials can take a lot of weight—up to 40 tonnes per metre width. And their pockets can be filled (even underwater) with quick-set cement to make them still stronger. Economist 2/18/84, p85 [1979]

ger, n. a round tent stretched over a collapsible wooden framework, used in Mongolia. They [Mongols] see nothing shameful in living in a Ger (a felt, canvas and wood tent, which is called a yurt in other parts of central Asia). Times (London) 10/27/70, p8 [1964]

geriatric, n. a geriatric patient; one suffering from a disease of old age. Writing to the local newspaper last week, a £14-a-week nurse suggested a solution to the miner's dispute: ban all hospital treatment for miners, and send geriatrics and mental defectives back to their pit villages. New Statesman 1/25/74, p105 [1974, noun use of the adjective (1920's)]

gerontophobia (dʒə,rɒntə'foubi:ə), n. fear, dislike, or hatred of old age or old people. See AGEIST, GRAY POWER. A few years ago the great intellectual enemy of the movement was called gerontophobia—fear of aging, loathing of the aged. . . The target has shifted from gerontophobia to ageism. . . Gerontophobia could be inflicted only upon the old. Ageism, on the other hand, is a social prejudice against people of any age. Just as whites might be victims of black racism, and men may sometimes be the objects of female chauvinism, so young people can be (in early America actually were) targets of ageism too. New Republic 12/2/78, p35 [1978, from Greek gérōn, -ontos old man + English phobia]

Gestalt therapy (gə'ʃtɑːlt), psychotherapy based on Gestalt psychology. There are also numerous workshops in Gestalt therapy, an approach devised by the late German Psychiatrist Frederick S. Perls. One of the newest and most rebellious branches of psychology, Gestalt theory seeks to celebrate man's freedom, uniqueness and potential. Time 11/9/70, p55 [1970]

get, v. **get off on,** U.S. Slang. to get a thrill from; be pleased by; enjoy greatly. "A lot of people get off on getting into a loft," says Mrs. Walz, whose guest lists are sprinkled with Upper East Side names. "Some uptown people have never seen a loft before, so it's fun for them to stand in the street and yell and release themselves." NY Times 9/15/77, The Home Section, p25 [1973] ►An earlier meaning of this phrase is "to get high on," perhaps from to get off "to feel the effects of a drug," and to get on "to smoke marijuana."

gherao (ge'rɑːou), n. (in India and Pakistan) a form of protest demonstration in which the demonstrators surround a building, as of an office or plant, and prevent anyone from entering or leaving. Compare BANDH. In West Pakistan, a wave of wildcat strikes continued to sweep the cities. . . Some invoked gherao, a tactic borrowed from India in which workers barricade employers in their offices until wage demands are met. Time 3/28/69, p29 —v.t. to subject to a gherao. The directors of one steel concern were "gheraoed" next to the blast furnace. . . NY Times 5/25/67, p8 [1967, from Hindi, literally, encirclement]

ghetto blaster, U.S. Slang. a large portable radio, often combined with a cassette tape player; a box². For fogies who carry briefcases through the streets instead of huge "ghetto-blaster" radios, this is rap music. Wall Street Journal 12/12/84, p1 [1982; so called because of their popularity in inner-city ghettos, where they are often played at full blast]

GHOST (goust), n. **1** acronym for Global Horizontal Sounding Technique, a method of collecting data about the atmosphere by means of radio-equipped balloons launched to float at fixed altitudes. In the Global Horizontal Sounding Technique (GHOST), balloons containing three-ounce (about 85-g) radio transmitters are launched to float at specified levels in the Southern Hemisphere. Tracked by the radio signals emitted, they provide data on winds at various levels in the atmosphere. 1969 Britannica Yearbook of Science and the Future, p152 **2** any of the balloons used to collect atmospheric data. Two GHOST flights of limited duration will be carried out over the United States in July and August to prove the balloons' ability to carry a heavy payload. Science News 4/18/70, p394 [1965]

ghost, U.S. **—n.** an absentee who is counted as present at school or at work. "High schools were being allocated funds according to the total register, although many pupils attended class sporadically. So the high school division created the category of long-term absentee, defined as any youngster absent from school for 20 consecutive school days. This was the first official acknowledgment of the existence of this part of the school population. These are your ghosts." NY Times 11/14/76, pL7 **—v.i.** (of an absentee) to be counted as present. The waterfront investigation began in response to reports of widespread "ghosting" by many longshoremen, who were listed on payrolls by their foremen even though they were not present. NY Times 4/19/76, p14 [1976]

ghost station, British. an unused or unstaffed railroad station. . . . a three-dimensional "map" or model of the London beneath our feet, with its 550 miles of sewers, its railways, ghost stations, pipes, cables and hidden passages, and rivers such as the Fleet and the Walbrook. Times (London) 11/30/70, p3 [1963]

gi or **gie** (giː), n. the costume worn for judo or karate (often used in combination, as judo-gi, karate-gi). To make the point, an attendant karate expert, properly dressed in his gi, emphatically chopped a couple of boards into splinters . . . New Yorker 11/17/80, p47 All karate students start out as white belts wearing a uniform called a "gie." Observer (Eastchester, N.Y.) 7/20/72, p4 [1963, from Japanese -gi, combining form of ki clothing]

giant otter, a rare, endangered species of otter (Pteronura brasiliensis), up to seven feet in length, found in South America. In September last year the International Fur Trade Federation announced a voluntary ban on trading in skins of the tiger, snow *leopard, clouded leopard, La Plata otter and giant otter.* Times (London) 1/26/72, p16 [**1971**]

gigabit ('dʒigəˌbit), *n.* a unit of information equivalent to one billion bits of binary digits. Compare KILOBIT, MEGABIT, TERABIT. *The four-minute-mile for electronics engineers has been the gigabit computer, a computer that can process a billion bits of information per second.* Science News 4/4/70, p345 [**1970,** from *giga-* one billion (from Greek *gígas* giant) + *bit*]

giggle-smoke, *n. U.S. Slang.* marijuana. . . . *the young soldier was saying that here in Vietnam cannabis, pot, the weed, giggle-smoke, grass, Mary Jane, call it what you will, is readily available and freely used.* Manchester Guardian Weekly 6/20/70, p6 [**1970**]

GIGO ('gaiˌgou *or* 'giːˌgou), *n.* acronym for *garbage in, garbage out* (in reference to unreliable data fed into a computer that produces worthless output). *Most of us are familiar with GIGO—garbage in, garbage out—and we try in our systems to eliminate the vast printouts from the computer.* New Scientist and Science Journal 3/11/71, p575 *New technology and curriculum changes, he says, can be beneficial, but "it's a matter of GIGO—Garbage In, Garbage Out. You put garbage into a computer, you get garbage out." Simply investing money into new ideas isn't enough.* Science News 3/24/73, p186 [**1966**]

gimme cap ('gimiː), *U.S.* a visored cap with a clasp for adjusting it to any head size. . . . *Jay Dusard has photographed many modern cowboys with seeming realism . . . you will not see his cowboys fixing a baler or wearing the increasingly common "gimme" caps. They wear broadrimmed hats, chaps and kerchiefs. They ride horses, not pickups. They look just like cowboys should look.* Newsweek 12/12/83, p98 [**1978,** from *gimme* representing an informal pronunciation of *give me;* apparently so called from their being given out freely upon request ("gimme one") as a promotion item by various companies whose names often appear on the caps]

Ginnie Mae, *U.S.* **1** nickname for the Government National Mortgage Association. Compare FREDDIE MAC. *"Ginnie Mae" has been more active than ever before, particularly in the area of "pass-through" securities where "Ginnie" guarantees securities issued by lenders that represent loans in which the net principal and interest on the mortgage loan are passed through to investors each month.* Americana Annual 1975, p285 **2** a stock certificate issued by this agency. *Ginnie Maes—which normally come in minimum amounts of $25,000—provide both high interest yields and also return part of your investment to you each month. Any brokerage firm can provide you with complete details.* New York Post 12/1/78, p65 [**1975,** from pronunciation of the abbreviation *GNMA,* patterned after earlier (1953) *Fannie Mae,* nickname for the Federal National Mortgage Association (from its abbreviation, *FNMA*)]

girlcott, *v.t.* (said of women, in humorous analogy to *boycott*) to join in a boycott against someone or something prejudicial to women. *The Y.W.C.A., Feminists in the Arts, Radicalesbians, National Organization for Women—and anyone of taste—will find much to girlcott in* Quiet Days in Clichy [a motion picture]. Time 10/12/70, pJ9 [**1959**]

giveback, *n. U.S.* the surrendering of fringe benefits or other advantages gained previously by a labor union, usually in return for an increase in wages or other concessions by management. *New York City and its Transit Authority are both demanding givebacks to compensate for pay increases sought by their unions.* NY Times 3/26/78, p1 *Murdoch got most of the rest of the staff cut he was looking for by laying off eighteen people at the bottom of the seniority roll. That left an imposing list of givebacks still on Murdoch's "must" list.* New Yorker 1/22/79, p61 [**1978,** from the verb phrase *give back*]

given, *n.* something taken for granted; a fact. *Loneliness is a human given, and commitment and the public aspects of a relationship are probably things we'll always want.* New Yorker 11/28/70, p76 *The access of moneys to power is simply one of the givens in Washington.* Atlantic 3/71, p22 [**1965,** noun use of the adjective] ▶The noun has been formerly restricted in use to technical contexts in logic and mathematics.

give-up, *n. U.S. Stock Market.* a practice in which financial institutions, such as mutual funds, instruct brokers executing transactions for them to yield part of their commissions to other brokers, usually ones who have been performing services for the institution. *At issue was Fidelity's use of what are known as "give-ups." This is the cushion of the sales commissions on stock transactions that the broker actually handling the trade frequently gives to another broker on the instructions of his customer, generally a mutual fund.* NY Times 7/24/68, p53 [**1968**]

glam, *n. Informal.* short for *glamour. A champagne reception before the awards had the glitz and glam the Genies need, and the stars turned out in relative force—Jack Lemmon, Donald Sutherland, Helen Shaver, Margot Kidder, Lee Majors, Céline Lomez.* Maclean's 3/31/80, p49 [**1961**]

glasnost, *n.* an official policy of open and public discussion of problems and issues in the Soviet Union. *Furthermore, in this period of glasnost and uneasy détente, there are people in both governments who perceive the joint exploration of Mars as contributing to world peace.* New Yorker 6/8/87, p81 [**1985,** from Russian *glasnost'* a being public, public knowledge; also found in earlier references in English from 1972]

glasphalt, *n.* a material made from glass for paving roads. . . . *an experimental product called "glasphalt" . . . uses finely ground glass granules to replace the rock aggregates now used as a construction material for highways.* Time 3/16/70, p62 [**1970,** blend of *glass* and *asphalt*]

glass arm, an injured or sore arm resulting from tendons weakened or damaged by throwing or pitching balls. *Countless more suffered chronic maladies ranging from the annoying, like athlete's foot and jock itch, to the exotic and painful, like glass arm (loss of throwing ability from damaged tendons, common in baseball players), hollow foot (a strained instep found in ballet dancers) and web split (splitting of skin between the fingers).* Newsweek 4/2/73, p65 [**1966,** patterned after *glass jaw* (of a boxer)]

glass cord, cord made of fiberglass. *Another material that may make possible cheaper radials in glass cord. Glass cord can save tiremakers as much as $1 per tire, and some companies have already started to make glass-belted radials.* Encyclopedia Science Supplement (Grolier) 1972, p397 [**1968**]

glasshouse effect, British name for GREENHOUSE EFFECT. *According to Dr Sawyer the direct effect of carbon dioxide on mankind is negligible, with atmospheric content now being 319 parts per million to be compared with about 290 parts per million at the end of the nineteenth century. The indirect effect—the trapping of heat within the atmosphere, the so-called glasshouse effect—is however not so easily evaluated.* Nature 5/5/72, p5 [**1972**]

glassteel, *adj.* made of glass and steel. *The only trouble is that the Sondheim score does not have any integrity. It flirts with various styles, and is as neutral and eclectic as the glassteel skyscraper projections used as a backdrop.* Harper's 7/70, p108 [**1970**]

glass tissue, *British.* a fabric made of fiberglass. *Glass tissue, of which the initial annual production will be about 60 square metres, can be used as a base for roofing materials, wall covering, and other building purposes.* Times (London) 4/2/76, p20 [**1976**]

GLCM, abbreviation or acronym of *ground-launched cruise missile.* See CRUISE MISSILE. *The GLCM (or "glickum," in Pentagon jargon), to be deployed in Britain, West Germany and Italy, and later, perhaps, in Belgium and The Netherlands, is a dry-land version of the U.S. Navy's Tomahawk sea-launched cruise missile. It is designed to be a subsonic weapon with a range of about 1,500 miles and a lot of maneuverability. . . .* Time 12/24/79, p30 [**1979**]

gleamer, *n.* a cosmetic for making the skin of the face gleam. *Some* [candidates for Miss Teenage America Pageant in Texas] *wore pancake or foundation and blotches spread, islands of* *makeup holding up smaller islands of blusher or gleamer.* Harper's 3/70, p98 **[1970]**

Gleitzeit ('glait,tsait), *n.* German word for FLEXTIME. *"Flextime," the term which the jargon-ridden world of management has inevitably given the concept, has its origins in West Germany. Gleitzeit, or gliding time, has already been applied there on a substantial scale.* Times (London) 4/19/72, p23 **[1971,** contraction of German *gleitende Arbeitszeit* gliding worktime]

gliding shift, a work shift that functions on flextime. *In 1970, Lufthansa German Airlines tried out the system in one of its offices. It then extended it to many other units and now is considering putting its technical workshops on a comparable program, with "gliding shifts."* U.S. News and World Report 6/19/72, p102 **[1972]**

gliding time, *Especially British.* another name for FLEXTIME. Compare SLIDING TIME. *In West Germany some 3500 firms have adopted "gliding time." In one form of the plan, company doors are open from 7 am to 7 pm and factory or office workers can come in any time they like provided they are around for "core time" from 10 am to 3 pm.* New Scientist 1/4/73, p27 **[1972,** translation of German *Gleitzeit*]

glitch, *n.* **1** *U.S. Slang.* a sudden mishap or malfunction. *Goofs and glitches always creep into the early blueprints for any new aircraft. . .* Time 3/1/68, p52 **2** an unexpected deviation; hitch; snag. . . . *the discovery rate of new oil precedes its economic exploitation by a decade or so. Since discovery in the U.S. peaked in about 1956, U.S. production would itself peak in the 1970's. The Alaskan find put a notable glitch in the curve but cannot edit the handwriting on the wall.* Scientific American 9/79, p42 **3** *Astronomy.* a sudden change in rotation of a celestial body, especially a pulsar. *From the Earth one sees, first, a long slow decrease in the pulsar frequency as radiation saps the spin energy of the pulsar; strains build up in the crust, causing the glitch, and instantaneously the frequency increases. . . Based on those ideas a mathematical model of the glitch has been developed.* Times (London) 1/13/76, p14 **—v.i.** to undergo a glitch. *Several times, however, the Crab and Vela pulsars were observed to begin suddenly to pulse faster, or "glitch." This was attributed to "starquakes," in which the star suddenly readjusted its shape for its slower rotation period.* Britannica Book of the Year 1977, p152 **[1962** for def. 1; **1970** for def. 2; perhaps from Yiddish *glitsh* a slipping, *glitshen* to slip] ▶Originally a *glitch,* as defined by astronaut John Glenn, was a momentary change in voltage in an electrical circuit.

glitterati (,glitə'ra:ti:), *n.pl.* fashionable people, especially those who conspicuously attend to cultural endeavors and social events. *The Soviet embassy threw its annual celebration of the Revolution of 1917 a few days ago, and the glitterati of Washington swarmed in as usual to the stone box of a building that hunkers down on 16th Street.* Time 11/24/80, p27 **[1956,** blend of *glitter* and *literati* the learned or literate class (OED 1621)]

glitter rock, a form of rock music in which performers wear glittering makeup and costumes. Also called DECA-ROCK. *Going solo, he* [Lou Reed] *anticipated and helped launch both the underground and the glitter rock extravagances of the early 70s.* Time 4/24/78, p79 *"Glitter" rock appeared to be fading fast, although the antics of such as David Bowie and Alice Cooper continued to sell to live and television audiences.* Americana Annual 1975, p478 **[1973]** **—glitter rocker:** *Outfitted in an orange and white soccer uniform—and mink warm-up coat— Glitter Rocker* **Elton John** *came to the Los Angeles Coliseum last week to greet his newest employee.* Time 3/15/76, p46

glitz, *n. U.S. and Canadian.* glitzy condition or appearance; dazzle. *Helping Creley and Negin recreate the glitz and glitter of Paris gone-by are Richard Adams as Chevalier, Taborah Johnson and Josephine, Liliane Stilwell as Piaf and Barbara Law as Mistinguett.* Maclean's 11/27/78, p4 **[1978,** back formation from GLITZY]

glitzy ('glitsi:), *adj. U.S. and Canadian.* glittering; dazzling; showy; flashy. *This son of Glasgow. . .dreamed of crowning Toronto's new boom-town status with a genuinely glitzy film festival.* Maclean's 10/3/77, p70 *Individuals like Rachel and*

Geri Wagner are bright, educated. . . They can be seen in Bloomingdale's, Marshall Field, Neiman-Marcus; in glitzy restaurants, health clubs, tennis courts, theaters and bookstores. NY Times Magazine 12/3/78, p35 **[1966,** probably from German *glitz(ern)* to glitter + English *-y*]

GLM, abbreviation of GRADUATED LENGTH METHOD. *In GLM, beginners start without poles and are first taught how to walk up the hill herringbone style. This is accomplished by Chaplinesque manoeuvres of the feet.* Maclean's 1/74, p25 **[1972]**

global tectonics, another name for PLATE TECTONICS. *"Analysis of the sedimentary, volcanic, structural and metamorphic chronology in mountain belts," they* [Dr. John F. Dewey of Cambridge University and Dr. John M. Bird of the State University of New York] *write, "and consideration of the implications of the new global tectonics (plate tectonics) strongly indicate that mountain belts are a consequence of plate evolution."* Science News 8/15/70, p143 **[1970]**

global village, a term coined by Marshall McLuhan (see MCLU-HANISM) to designate the world of the late 20th century, in which the electronic communications media have radically reduced the distance and isolation of people from each other, restoring to humans some of their original sense of being part of a village or tribe. *There are no boundaries in a global village. All problems will become so intimate as to be one's own. No problem can arise at one point without affecting all points immediately and emotionally, and world government will become a fact even if no one, due to past prejudices, particularly wants it. . .* Saturday Review 10/24/70, p19 *With its steadily growing membership, the U.N. promises to become an ever more faithful mirror of Marshall McLuhan's "global village."* Time 10/26/70, p39 **[1960]**

glosser, *n.* any shiny or glossy cosmetic, especially one for the lips. *Miss Japan curled her eyelashes with a pair of tiny tongs. Miss Lebanon creamed off her shoulder with a cotton wool ball and Miss Bahamas smacked her lips over a raspberry flavoured glosser.* Sunday Times (London) 11/16/75, p43 **[1974,** from *gloss, v.* to make glossy + *-er*]

glucan ('glu:kən), *n.* a large carbohydrate isolated from the cell wall of bakers' yeast and other fungi, shown experimentally to be effective in the treatment of microbial diseases. *These polysaccharides are glucans which are commonly referred to in the literature as dextran, they form a major component of the bacterial plaque matrix, and may be responsible for adhesion of the bacterial plaque to tooth enamel.* Nature 7/28/72, p219 **[1967,** from *gluc*ose + *-an* suffix indicating an anhydride of a carbohydrate]

glucoreceptor, *n.* a cell in the brain, sensitive to the presence of glucose. *Experiments . . . had demonstrated that the satiety centers contain cells that are particularly sensitive to glucose and hormones, such as insulin, to which the rest of the brain does not respond. We suggested that the rate at which these cells, called glucoreceptors, take up glucose from the blood determines whether the satiety centers are active and the feeding centers quiet or, conversely, whether the satiety centers are quiet and the feeding centers active.* World Book Science Annual 1973, p121 **[1972,** from *gluc*ose + *receptor*]

glue-sniffing, *n.* the habit or practice of inhaling the fumes of certain kinds of glue, often for the intoxicating effect of the toluene present. *Dock C. Reeves Jr., 19 years old, a drugstore delivery-man with a medical history of glue-sniffing, died yesterday not long after his family found him lying beside a paper bag and an empty glue tube in their home.* NY Times 5/24/68, p23 **[1963]**

gluino, *n.* a hypothetical nuclear particle that is a weakly interacting form of the gluon. *A scenario with supersymmetry: gluinos from within a proton and an antiproton collide, and make supersymmetric gluinos, each of which decays into two quarks and one photino.* Discovery 4/85, p52 **[1985]**

gluon, *n. Nuclear Physics.* a component of subatomic particles that has neither mass nor charge and that holds together quarks to form strongly interacting elementary particles; the carrier of the strong force. See COLOR FORCE. *If a fundamental theory* *of matter called quantum chromodynamics, or QCD, is correct, the gluon must exist, and if the scientists had failed to find it in their new experiment, much of the theoretical work in physics in the past decade would have been in serious doubt.* NY Times 9/2/79, p1 [**1972**, from *glue* + *-on* elementary particle]

glycosylate ('glaɪkəsə,leit), *v.t. Biochemistry.* to add a carbohydrate chain to (a protein) to form a glycoprotein. *One of the general facts that seems to have emerged is that proteins with carbohydrate chains attached to their outer end always span the membrane. The histocompatibility antigens have such chains (or in technical terms, are glycosylated).* New Scientist 10/20/77, p152 [**1971**, back formation from *glycosylation*]

glycosylation (,glaɪkəsə'leiʃən), *n. Biochemistry.* the addition of a carbohydrate chain to a protein to form a glycoprotein. *In vitro synthesis of interferon should permit one to approach the question of the role of carbohydrate substitutions in interferon activity. Interferon has long been known to be a glycoprotein but whether the glycosylation is essential for activity remains unclear.* Nature 2/5/76, p363 [**1963**, from *glycosyl* carbohydrate radical derived from a glycose (simple sugar) + *-ation*]

gnome, *n. Especially British.* a banker or financier, especially one doing business in the international money market. . . . *export prices rise, the balance of payments runs into trouble, the gnomes gather, the pound trembles, and the Government of the day deflates the economy.* Manchester Guardian Weekly 8/22/70, p12 [**1965**, abstracted from the phrase *gnomes of Zurich,* coined in 1964 by the former British Foreign Secretary George Brown to describe the international currency speculators located in Zurich, who he thought were determined to profit from their speculations on the value of the British pound]

gnotobiology (,noutoubaɪ'alədʒi:), *n.* the branch of biology dealing with organisms or conditions that are either free of germs or associated only with a few known germs. *A highly specialized segment of the ultraclean technology is gnotobiology, the raising of germ free animals, largely for research purposes.* Science Journal 4/70, p46 [**1963**, from *gnoto*biotic free of germs or associated only with known germs (OEDS 1949) + *biology*]

go, *adj. Slang.* **1** *Aerospace.* ready for launching; ready to start or use. *After conferring with launching crews, flight controllers, the far-flung tracking teams and the weatherman, William C. Schneider, the mission director, said: "Everything is at this time 'go.' "* NY Times 4/4/68, p10 **2** ready for or favorable to a project or activity. Compare NO-GO. *"We're getting married next year." She was suddenly in a go condition with all the assurance of a woman on familiar ground.* Punch 8/14/63, p224 *But all systems are not "go" for the Nassau-Suffolk economy despite boosts of contracts. . .* NY Times 4/15/63, p109 [**1961**]

go-aheadism, *n.* enterprise; initiative. *Part of the income from the antiquities of Herculaneum . . . is going into the pockets of a few who show a kind of Neapolitan go-aheadism.* Manchester Guardian Weekly 7/18/70, p13 [**1970**] ▶The use of this word in the 1800's is recorded in the *OED* with one citation: "1846 C. Kingsley in *Life* (1877) I. 143 It is the new commercial aristocracy, it is the scientific go-a-head-ism of the day, which must save us." The *OEDS* (1933 edition) antedates the use with an 1838 citation from James Fenimore Cooper, using the form *goaheadism.* The word has probably been in continuous, though unrecorded, use since then.

gob pile, *U.S.* a large accumulation of refuse from a mine, especially slime and silt from washing coal. *Sixty miles to the east, near the village of Nokomis, a second gob pile will soon be coming down, ending the runoff of sulfuric acid water into a tributary of the Kaskaskia River.* NY Times 11/26/76, pB14 [**1972**, from earlier attributive use as in gob-stuff (OED2 1839)]

Godardian, *adj.* characterized by a free and daring use of the camera, improvised scripts, and unconventional staging. Partner *is a Godardian exercise of repetitions, monologues, slogans, alienation effects, cheeky political symbolism.* Listener 10/8/70, p497 *Of the directors who emerged in the 1960s, the most strikingly successful in 1970 was Bernardo Bertolucci, who seemed entirely to have overcome his phase of Godardian imitation (Partner).* Britannica Book of the Year 1971,

p195 [**1966**, from Jean-Luc *Godard,* born 1930, a French motion-picture director noted for his cinematic innovations + *-ian*]

godfather, *n. Slang.* **1** the head of a Mafia family or other group involved in organized crime. Compare DON. *We meet a Puerto Rican Godfather who radiates pride of family and neighborhood connections and has incorporated tape cassettes into his numbers operation to avoid incriminating policy slips.* Newsweek 6/17/74, p98 **2** Transferred sense: *Through direct-mail bombardment, the right alerts its friends to a particular cause and adds to its converts. In this letter-box war for American minds, the top general is Viguerie, who is considered by friend and foe alike the "godfather" of the New Right.* Time 10/3/77, p24 *Some critics say the I.R.A. has become a children's army. . . The youngsters, they say, are manipulated by a little band of experienced "godfathers" who make the plans but never risk their own lives.* NY Times 2/13/78, pA12 [**1972**, popularized by *The Godfather,* title of a motion picture (1972), based on a novel (1969) by Mario Puzo but known earlier from US Government hearings on organized crime (OED2 1963)]

God's Eye, a small cross made of twigs, branches, etc., around which colored yarn or thread is wound in geometric patterns, popular in Mexico and the southwestern United States as a decoration or as a symbol of good fortune. *An ancient and comparatively little known craft that is presently undergoing a revival in this country is the making of* ojos de dios (*God's Eye*) *hangings and talismans.* NY Times 7/11/76, pB29 [**1966**, translation of Mexican Spanish *ojo de dios,* literally, eye of god; so called because it originally represented the eye of a deity (and was used in worship) among some Indians]

God slot, *British Slang.* a religious program on radio or television. *Just as we have to be given God-slots at chosen times, so, it seems, we must have our* [comedy programs] *carefully allocated. Let us pray. Let us laugh.* Times (London) 7/25/77, p9 [**1972**]

God squad or **God committee**, *U.S. Slang.* **1** a group of advisors to a hospital staff on ethical procedure in cases of terminal illness, severe birth defects, elective surgery, etc. *The whole concept of an ethics committee to determine the fate of any patient is one that is being discussed with increasing frequency in medical and legal circles not just in the United States but also throughout the world. Such committees go by different names and sometimes are irreverently called "God Squads" and "God Committees."* NY Times 6/27/76, pA1 **2** any group of religious leaders. *As he prepared for his July 15 speech on energy policy, Carter invited a variety of national leaders to the presidential retreat at Camp David, Md. They included, on one occasion, a cluster of leading religious officials who came to be called the "God Squad." After the session, the God Squad issued a statement supporting the intent of Carter's program. . .* Britannica Book of the Year 1980, p598 [**1973**]

gofer ('goufər), *n. U.S. Slang.* an office assistant whose duties include running errands for the staff. *She plays an inadvertent career girl, jilted by the rounder she put through medical school, and working as a "gofer" at a Minneapolis TV station.* Time 9/28/70, p66 [**1968**, alteration of *go-for,* so called from being told to *go for* coffee, newspapers, etc.]

goggle, *n.* Usually, **the goggle.** *British Slang.* television. . . . *there is no proof that watching the inflammatory material which appears on the goggle drives kids to rape, or arson, or flagellation. . .* New Scientist 5/28/70, p432 [**1970**, shortened from GOGGLEBOX]

gogglebox, *n. British Slang.* television. Compare IDIOT BOX. *The very speed of television's development might have led to some initial resistance to it, even resentment of it. " 'Gogglebox' and 'idiot's lantern' are hardly terms of affection and respect."* Manchester Guardian Weekly 1/9/69, p8 [**1958**]

go-go, *Chiefly U.S.* —*adj.* **1** of or relating to the lively dancing and music performed at discothèques or similar nightclubs. *Following the people will come supermarkets, golf courses, yacht clubs, and go-go girls.* Saturday Review 9/23/67, p72 **2** lively; energetic; enterprising. *There is a go-go spirit in Ford Motor offices that is unmatched in the auto industry.* Time

7/20/70, p66 **3** very fashionable; stylish; chic. . . . *he was dressed for action, in a white polo shirt, red cardigan sweater (very go-go, being double-breasted) and tan slacks.* Maclean's 3/67, p52 **4** of or relating to go-go funds. *Stocks of franchising companies. . . have been among the Street's latest go-go favorites.* Time 3/9/70, p62 —**n. 1** discothèque dancing. *It's golf and go-go, saunas and sunsets; paisleyed walls and chairs of patent leather.* Advertisement in New Yorker 4/20/68, p149 **2** short for GO-GO-FUND. . . . *the go-gos constantly outperform everyone else.* Time 9/22/67, p17 [**1962**, shortened from earlier *a-go-go, adj.*, of or relating to discothèque dancing, from French *à-gogo* aplenty (used in the names of discothèques). The English meanings were influenced by the verb *go*, the French form *gogo* being often taken as a reduplication of the English verb.]

go-go fund, a type of investment fund that tries to accumulate large earnings in a short time and therefore may engage in risky, speculative stock-market operations. Also shortened to GO-GO. *It has been this area of the market that has been patronised most heavily by the so-called "go-go" funds—the performance funds that show no hesitation to play the market like professional day-traders.* Sunday Times (London) 10/15/67, p46 [**1966**]

go-kart, *n.* a small, open, four-wheeled racing car for one person. Also shortened to KART. *A school that has its own land yacht, wind tunnel, go-kart and canoeing clubs . . . may sound like a well-endowed foundation or an expensive way to go about education.* Times (London) 1/23/67, p9 [**1959**, from *Go-Kart*, a trademark for such a racing car]

gold, *adj. U.S.* of or designating a phonograph record that has sold a million copies or an album with sales of a million dollars. Compare PLATINUM. *His records sell extremely well—since 1964 he has had three gold albums . . . and three gold singles.* New Yorker 3/1/69, p38 [**1969**, so called from the award, a gold phonograph record, given to the performers] ►In Canada *gold* is applied to records that have sold between 50,000 and 100,000 copies: . . . *the first album she recorded for RCA. . . went "gold" (it sold more than 50,000 copies in Canada).* Maclean's 9/5/77, p31

goldbug, *n. Informal.* a person who hoards gold, especially as a hedge against inflation. *Among gold investors there is a fringe coterie that treats gold as a religion, as a way of life, as being valuable above all else. They are the "gold bugs," and part and parcel of their monomaniacal acquisitiveness is the dogma that the world's economic system is destined to collapse into anarchy—but soon.* Maclean's 9/24/79, p14 [**1968**] ►Earlier meanings were (1) a kind of beetle with a golden shine (1843), and (2) an advocate of the gold standard (1878), both American English.

golden age club, *U.S.* any of various social or recreational organizations for elderly people. *Mrs. Mills continued to serve the A.W.V.S.* [American Women's Voluntary Services] *until recently. In 1962, as its national chairman, she directed the activities of its members, who work in nurseries and playrooms in children's hospitals, in golden age clubs and in veterans' and community hospitals.* NY Times 5/2/68, p48 [**1956**]

golden-ager, *n. U.S.* an old or elderly person. *There are no euphemisms in Dutch for being old—no "senior citizen," no "golden-ager".* . . New Yorker 8/15/70, p57 [**1961**]

golden handshake, *Especially British.* **1** a large sum of money given as severance pay to induce an employee to retire early. *O'Farrell, with 3 ½ years of a five years' contract to go, was assured of a golden handshake of about £40,000, while the other two, not under contract, were "compensated."* Manchester Guardian Weekly 1/6/73, p28 **2** the payment of such a sum of money. *You make the proposal that the golden handshake is the solution to the job stagnation problem in British universities.* Nature 2/13/75, p496 [**1960**]

golden oldie or **golden oldy,** something old or long-established that is very popular or is being revived to become popular. *Their latest album (Grateful Dead, Warner Bros K66009, stereo, £3.99), which is made up of live excerpts from such shows, contains . . . such golden oldies as 'Johnny B. Goode'*

and *'Not Fade Away'.* Listener 1/27/72, p123 *But football, truly a Golden Oldie, remains as it is—a sport in which not all the participants can be picked up simultaneously by a single camera.* New Yorker 11/27/78, p126 [**1966**]

golden palm, a motion-picture award presented annually at the Cannes Film Festival in France. *The golden palm for the best short film went to Marcell Jankovics, a Hungarian director, for Kuzdok ("The Fight").* Times (London) 5/28/77, p3 [**1967**, translation of French *palme d'or*]

golden parachute, an employment contract guaranteeing continued salary and benefits when control of a company is transferred to new owners. Compare TIN PARACHUTE. *Legally, though, it is not yet clear that golden parachutes will float. Although takeover lawyers such as Martin Lipton say they strongly recommend that clients faced with a hostile tender offer give their top executives such contracts, many corporate lawyers believe golden parachutes are illegal when they are adopted during a tender offer fight to create a financial obligation that will scare off potential acquirers.* NY Times 11/30/82, pD2 [**1982**; patterned after GOLDEN HANDSHAKE]

Golden Triangle 1 an area of southeastern Asia growing a large portion of the world's raw opium. It consists of the Yunnan province in China, northeastern Burma, northern Thailand, and northern Laos. See BROWN SUGAR. *Both the opium and the morphine base almost certainly originated in the so-called "golden triangle" where the opium poppy grows in abundance.* Bangkok Post 4/22/73, p1 . . . *Thai coöperation in stemming traffic in narcotics in the so-called Golden Triangle—the area where Burma, Laos, and Thailand come together.* New Yorker 7/14/75, p79 **2** any geographic area characterized by high yield or productivity. *In the area of greatest population concentration, the birth rate was found to be more than double that of the outlying regions. The result of this trend could be to entrench the so-called Golden Triangle, the industrial area that extends from the Midlands of England to the Gulf of Genoa.* Nature 1/1-8/76, p2 [**1972**]

goldie, *n. U.S.* a gold record or album. *In the three years since he emerged from the ashes of the legendary Jeff Beck group to record "The Rod Stewart Album," the wiry singer who almost became a soccer pro has had two gold solo albums and another goldie with his group, Faces.* Newsweek 9/11/72, p75 [**1969**, from GOLD + *-ie* (diminutive suffix)]

gold rush, a rush to buy gold, especially as a hedge against inflation. *The gold rush is on. At Barclays Bank they had sold well over a thousand new-minted sovereigns with a week of issuing them. At Barclays at Marble Arch they cost £61.50 plus commission just before Christmas.* Manchester Guardian Weekly 1/6/80, p5 [**1963**, extended sense of the term for a sudden rush to goldfields in search of gold (1876 DAE)]

golf ball, a ball-shaped, movable metal device on which the characters are located in certain electric typewriters. *Quaternary Geology has passed straight from golf-ball typewriter to printed page, missing the editorial proofreading that could have corrected a number of grammatical incoherences and spelling errors.* New Scientist 9/6/79, p741 [**1966**]

GOM, abbreviation of *Grand Old Man*, used in describing an old and venerable person or thing. *Second comes to the GOM of English racing, Lord Rosebergy, born in 1882, the year after St Simon, and happily still going strong.* Sunday Times (London) 11/2/69, p21 *The Pennsylvania has been the G.O.M. of railroads, often a key to their mergers, gobbles, and grabs. . .* Atlantic 7/68, p87 [**1964**, originally referring to Gladstone (OEDS 1884)]

gomer ('goumər), *n. U.S. Slang.* an obnoxious or otherwise undesirable person. *In hospital parlance, a "gomer" is a disgusting, filthy old man.* St. Louis Post-Dispatch 9/14/80, p3 *In the inside lingo of the medical profession, . . . a gomer is a patient (often called a player) who is whining and otherwise undesirable. The term is said to be an acronym for "Get Out of My Emergency Room," but may originate in "gomerel," Scottish dialect for simpleton, influenced by the television hillbilly Gomer Pyle.* NY Times Magazine 11/9/80, p16 [**1966**]

Gondwana (gɑndˈwɑːnə), *n.* a hypothetical supercontinent comprising Australia, Antarctica, Africa, and sometimes including India and South America, believed to have existed for millions of years before splitting up during the Cenozoic era (about 60 million years ago). *Advocates of* [continental] *drift are challenged to say exactly how the present continents fitted together to form Pangaea, or alternatively to reconstruct the two later supercontinents Laurasia and Gondwana, which some theorists prefer to a single all-embracing land mass.* Scientific American 10/70, p30 [**1965**, named after *Gondwana*, a region of central India inhabited by the Dravidian *Gond* people. The region is noted for its unusual geological formations.]

gonzo (ˈgɑnzou), *adj. U.S. Slang.* crazy or wild; extremely eccentric; bizarre. *Gonzo Journalism supplements the techniques of the novelist with the techniques of the lunatic.* Atlantic 7/73, p100 *Politics, in any case, has nothing to do with this gonzo record, which transcends mundane concerns and speaks, as rock henceforth* must *speak, to universal themes alone.* National Review 6/21/74, p707 *Rock's gonzo guitarist Ted Nugent . . . began grandstanding. . .* People Weekly 10/2/78, p95 [**1972**, from Italian *gonzo* simpleton, blockhead, perhaps shortened from *Borgonzone* Burgundian] ►The phrase *gonzo journalism* first appeared in the book *Fear and Loathing in Las Vegas* (1971) by Hunter S. Thompson, a correspondent for the magazine *Rolling Stone*, in reference to his reporting.

good buddy, *U.S. Informal.* **1** form of address used especially by CB radio operators. *"Hey, there, eastbounders. You've got a Smokey in the grass at the 93-mile marker . . . he's takin' pictures." "Aaay, we definitely thank you for that info, good buddy. We'll back 'em down a hair."* NY Times Magazine 4/25/76, p64 **2** a CB radio operator. *Perhaps the biggest problem is overcrowding, which can turn "good buddies" into nasty rivals. CBers are supposed to limit calls to five minutes, and those who do not are called "ratchet jaws."* 1977 World Book Year Book, p267 [**1976**]

good news, *U.S. and Canadian.* a pleasant person or a desirable or satisfying condition. *A two-year-old says* bastek *for* basket *until she reaches a state of readiness to make the change. When that happens. . . her memory bank rings up* basket *for all time. The child experiences a flash of delight: getting it right is good news.* Maclean's 1/73, p32 *Bradley is good news on many levels. Ten years' service as a city councilman have made him a professional specialist in urban problems.* Newsweek 7/23/73, p27 [**1972**, patterned after BAD NEWS an undesirable or troublesome person or condition] ►In the early 1970's *good news, bad news* jokes became a fad in the United States. According to *Time* magazine (June 5, 1972, p 75), "The gags probably originated a few years ago as spoofs of the in-flight announcements made by airline pilots. For example: 'This is your captain speaking. I have some good news and some bad news. The good news is that we're ahead of schedule. The bad news is that our navigational equipment has failed and we have no idea where we are.' "

Others have dated jokes back to high school and college use in the 1950's, to parlor games of the 1940's, and even to comic vaudeville routines of World War I vintage.

Good News Bible, a modern-English translation of the Bible, published by the American Bible Society in 1976. *The accuracy of the latest and much-heralded translation of Holy Scripture, the Good News Bible, the millionth copy of which has just been presented to the Queen, has been challenged by Dr Eric Kemp, Bishop of Chichester. He says he finds it incredulous that those famous words of St Paul about "flesh" and "lower nature" have, in his episcopal view, been altogether mistranslated.* Manchester Guardian Weekly 2/6/77, p4 [**1976**, *Good News*, from *gospel*, in Old English *gōdspell* or *gōdspel*, *gōd* good + *spel* news, story, tidings]

good ole boy 1 *U.S.* a Southerner who is typically easy-going, unpretentious and gregarious. *The core of the good ole boy's world is with his buddies, the comfortable, hyperhearty, all-male camaraderie, joshing and drinking and regaling one another with tales of assorted, exaggerated prowess.* Time 9/27/76, p47 *This is the world of the Good Ole Boy, the country hick from down in the hollow, his innocent, God-fearing*

eyes scanning the world of corruption laid out before him at every crossroad grocery store, supermarket, and shopping center. Harper's 9/76, p18 **2** Transferred sense: *If I could take a transsexual and make her seem like everybody's best friend—just a good ole boy—then I succeeded.* Maclean's 6/11/79, p6 [**1976**, *ole* alteration of old (as in *Grand Ole Opry*) to represent Southern pronunciation]

goose, *v.t. Slang.* **goose up**, to push or prod; raise; lift. *The book needs goosing up.* Times (London) 7/10/72, p7 *But what's the use of goosing up wages if the cities' workers live in dreary, faceless prisons.* Maclean's 6/28/76, p52 [**1972**, figurative use of earlier (1880's) slang sense of "to poke in the buttocks so as to startle"]

gork, *n. Slang (disparaging use).* a person who has lost brain function as a result of senility, stroke, disease, etc. *Like many other physicians, I have cared for hopelessly brain-dead people (referred to by the less genteel as "vegetables" or "gorks") who, due to the tragedy of our technological times, have been maintained by machines and nutritious solutions.* Harper's 11/74, p127 [**1972**, of unknown origin]

gorp, *n. U.S.* a mixture of dried fruit and nuts, seeds, etc., used for snacks. *We carried water, lunch, and gorp. Gorp is a secret strengthening mixture favored by climbers and other desperate types, consisting of peanuts, raisins, dried apricots (optional), and bittersweet chocolate bits.* Atlantic 6/74, p49 [**1972**, probably related to earlier U.S. slang verb *gorp* to eat greedily, of unknown origin]

gospel, *n.* a form of religious music developed by American blacks, combining elements of the spiritual, the blues, and jazz (often used attributively). Compare SOUL MUSIC. *His* [Neil Diamond's, a composer of pop and rock songs] *song delve ingeniously into hard and soft rock, blues, gospel, even country rock. . .* Time 1/11/71, p40 *By turning a small dial they can experience classical Indian music, jazz, folk songs of Appalachia, hard rock, blues bands, the Nashville and Detroit sounds, gospel music. . .anything.* NY Times 9/1/68, pB12 [**1955**]

gossyplure (ˈgɑsəpˌlur), *n.* the sex attractant of the pink bollworm, a larva which feeds on cotton bolls. Compare DISPARLURE, MUSCALURE. *Gossyplure proves the old adage that nothing exceeds like excess. When it is sprayed on a cotton field, it so saturates the air with female pink bollworm moth pheromone that. . . they soon become so accustomed to the scent that they no longer respond to it. The result: a sharp drop in the population of caterpillar young.* Time 5/22/78, p95 [**1976**, from New Latin (*Pectiniphora*) *gossypiella* the pink bollworm + English *lure*]

go-stop, *n. British.* another name for STOP-GO. *"If we are to consolidate our improved position and avoid a return to all the evils of stop-go, or go-stop as I prefer to call it, I am sure that any substantial or indiscriminate relaxation would be wrong."* Manchester Guardian Weekly 2/7/70, p8 [**1965**]

Gothic or **gothic**, *n.* a novel, motion picture, or play characterized by a lurid or gruesome atmosphere; a work in the Gothic style. *This little gothic in a high-school setting has a script by Lawrence D. Cohen taken from Stephen King's unassuming potboiler about a miserable, repressed high-school senior . . . who has never been accepted by other kids.* New Yorker 11/22/76, p177 [**1972**, noun use of the adjective; see GOTHICKRY]

Gothick, *adj. Especially British.* characteristic of a lurid or gruesome medieval atmosphere; grotesque; macabre. *The point of* Dance Macabre *seems to be Gothick horror—a bit outmoded in the theatre, I thought, although in literature there is still a strong demand.* Times (London) 3/7/68, p7 [**1959**, deliberate archaic spelling of *Gothic, adj.*, in the sense of "medieval suggestive of romance, the supernatural, etc." The Gothic novel, such as *Wuthering Heights*, was a genre of the 1800's that was revived in the 1970's.]

gothickry, *n. British.* a Gothic theme, mood, or style. *But it is an earlier genre of gothickry that predominates, a world (or other world) in which the hero can write about the "miasma of hatred which, even to this day, seems to rise through the soil* *of his grave."* Times (London) Literary Supplement 3/10/72, p272 [**1971**, from GOTHICK + -*ry*, noun suffix]

GPM, abbreviation of GRADUATED PAYMENT MORTGAGE. *GPM's, insured by the Federal Housing Administration (FHA), enabled many more families to buy their first homes. Under this plan, introduced in 1976, payments increase gradually for a specific number of years and then level off.* 1979 Compton Yearbook, p166 [**1978**]

grab, *v.t. Slang.* to cause (a person) to react; make an impression on. . . .*the Women's Liberation Front. . .is charging the Cormorants with discrimination in hiring practices. How does that grab you?* New Yorker 2/21/70, p37 [**1963**]

grade creep, *U.S.* the automatic promotion of people in the civil service by regularly raising the level of their jobs in the job classification system (GS-1, GS-2, etc.). *Agriculture Secretary John A. Knebel, conceding that the Ford Administration failed to prevent a "grade creep" in jobs in his department over the past eight years, has appealed to agency officials to tighten safeguards against over-grading Government posts.* NY Times 1/9/77, p36 [**1976**]

graduated length method, a method of ski instruction in which beginners start on short, maneuverable skis and advance through progressively longer skis as their ability improves. *The Graduated Length Method makes it possible to develop skills in a week that take several seasons on long skis. I later discovered that GLM is a source of great annoyance to skiers who have had to learn the long, hard way.* Maclean's 1/74, p25 [**1972**]

graduated payment mortgage, *U.S.* a mortgage on which monthly payments are low in the early years after purchase of a house, rising gradually thereafter. Compare VARIABLE RATE MORTGAGE. *Graduated payment mortgages (GPMs) are new, too, and were also created for the young house hunter. Here payments rise as the homeowner gets older, on the theory that his or her income will be rising as well. Graduated payment mortgages come in government-insured, privately-insured, and uninsured programs.* Ruth Rejnis, Her Home, 1980, p25 [**1976**]

graft-versus-host, *adj.* of or denoting a condition in which transplanted cells of a donor attack the cells of the recipient's body, instead of the more common reaction in which the recipient's body rejects the transplanted cells. *In bone marrow and thymus transplants, one runs the added risk of the transplanted tissue rejecting the patient to whom it is given. Thus, donor marrow cells produce lymphocytes that recognize the patient's tissue as being foreign to themselves. The result, known as graft-versus-host (GVH) disease, is usually deadly unless the reaction is very mild.* Science 4/13/73, p170 [**1963**]

grammaticality, *n. Linguistics.* the degree of grammatical acceptability of a sentence. *"He didn't deny that 'Floyd broke the glass' could be made more explicit in, say, 'Floyd caused the glass to become broken,' but he said that the meaning was derived semantically. The argument is still raging, and other young linguists have joined in. Very often the debate turns not on any evidence—for there really isn't any evidence yet—but on intuitions of grammaticality. . .* New Yorker 5/8/71, p85 *Lakoff makes a very important point here regarding a non-native speaker's ability to make the sort of grammaticality judgements required for transformational research.* Language 3/70, p150 [**1961**]

Grammy, *n., pl.* **Grammys** or **Grammies**. *U.S.* a gold-plated replica of an old-fashioned phonograph awarded annually by the National Academy of Recording Arts and Sciences. *Another album, "Goin' Out of My Head," won a Grammy award as the best instrumental jazz performance of 1966.* NY Times 6/16/68, p68 [**1959**, shortened from Gramophone, trade name for an early phonograph + -*y* (diminutive suffix)]

granadero (ˌɡrɑːnaˈðeirou), *n.* a member of a special military or police force in Mexico, used especially to quell riots. *The crack regiment of* Granaderos *marched in and the college was put*

under military rule. Times (London) 4/18/70, pI [**1968**, from Spanish, grenadier]

grandfather, *U.S.* —*adj.* relating to or based upon rights or privileges possessed prior to the passage of a new law or regulation. *Some lawyers opposed to the Concorde insisted that it would be perfectly legal to lay down noise rules that would bar the Concorde and, under a "grandfather" exemption, still allow other planes now using the airport and exceeding those new noise limits to keep operating at Kennedy.* NY Times 10/10/77, p12 —*v.t.* to exempt (a person or company) from the restrictions of a new law or regulation. *Cablecasting. . .systems in the top 100 markets operating on March 31, 1972, are "grandfathered"—not required to conform to new regulations—until March 31, 1977.* Britannica Book of the Year 1973, p656 *As a subdivision that had been filed before the new laws went into effect, Chambers Point was exempt from their requirements— what real-estate people call "grandfathered."* New Yorker 10/30/78, p152 [**1965** for adj., from *grandfather clause* (1900), a clause in the constitution of some Southern states formerly used to restrict voting rights to those whose fathers or grandfathers voted before the Civil War; **1968** for verb, verb use of the adjective]

grand unified theory, *Physics.* any theory which unifies the four forces of nature: gravity, electromagnetism, the strong force, and the weak force. *These so-called grand unified theories (known somewhat unfortunately, by the acronym GUTs) are still not at the stage where they can be experimentally verified. However, in some formulations the effect of the other forces mixed in with the strong force is to induce a breaking of the hitherto infallible law of baryon conservation.* 1982 Encyclopedia Science Supplement (Grolier), p304 [**1979**]

granny, *adj.* of or in the style of granny dresses. *Bluejeans, granny gowns, polka-dot clamdiggers, slouch hats, dashikis, and ponchos are not uncommon. . .* New Yorker 10/30/71, p106 *Girls in hot pants with granny shawls over bare breasts.* Sunday Times (London) 5/23/71, p12 [**1965**]

granny annexe, *British.* a part of a house set aside as an apartment for an old relative. Also called GRANNY FLAT. *A ground floor "granny annexe,"—with no stairs and easy access to the garden—is a sensible way of helping elderly relatives who want to retain their independence, yet need to know that someone is close at hand.* Times (London) 9/9/78, p10 [**1978**]

granny dress, a loose dress reaching from the neck to the ankles, similar to those formerly worn by elderly women or "grandmothers." Some granny dresses have long sleeves and ruffles at the neck and wrist; others have low scoop necks and high waistlines like the Empire style. *Some of the many teenage girls in the audience wore long granny dresses. . .* NY Times 1/22/68, p24 [**1965**]

granny flat, *British.* another name for GRANNY ANNEXE. *Each house has its own minor idiosyncrasies. They come in either left- or right-handed versions; you can choose brick, timber or stone for the walls, put in a games room under the stairs, create a granny flat.* Sunday Times Magazine (London) 10/17/82, p70 [**1979**]

granny glasses, gold- or steel-rimmed eyeglasses, similar to those often worn formerly by elderly women. *She* [a young woman] *was wearing gold granny glasses on her little heart-shaped face. He didn't know if her cheeks were flushed or rouged.* John Updike, Bech: A Book, 1970, p148 [**1965**]

granola, *n.* a mixture of dry oats, brown sugar, nuts, raisins, etc., used especially as a health food. *One nice thing about a working-class commune: bacon and eggs and potatoes for breakfast—no granola.* Harper's 6/72, p72 *Other health foods— crunchy granola, for example—and all the up-to-the-minute superheroes have also been recreated with paint and glitter; $7, in sizes ranging up to 12.* New Yorker 11/26/73, p107 [**1970**, originally a trademark, ultimately from Italian *grano* grain, wheat, corn + -*ola* a diminutive suffix]

grantsman, *n.* an expert or specialist in obtaining grants of money, as for research. *To help communities, school boards, and others obtain federal funds for projects, a new kind of spe-*

cialist has appeared—the "grantsman"—who is familiar with the technical forms and formal language. Saturday Review 12/17/66, p82 *The institutional grant, money provided to colleges and universities for their own purposes, rather than to individual researchers. . .would provide institutional stability as well as support for younger scientists now at a competitive disadvantage when pitted against experienced grantsmen.* Science News 7/27/68, p77 [**1966**, back formation from *grantsmanship*]

grantsmanship, *n.* the art of obtaining grants of money, as for research, from various foundations or other donors. *On most U.S. campuses these days, grantsmanship—the fine art of picking off research funds—is almost as important to professorial prestige as the ability to teach or carry out the research once a grant is landed.* Time 3/17/67, p34 [**1964**; see -MANSHIP]

Gran Turismo (ˌgrɑːntuːˈriːzmou), a type of automobile built to the high standards required of racing automobiles. *Abbreviation:* GT *Roughly, a Gran Turismo: Must be very fast but still carry passengers in great comfort. Must handle well—partly because of tighter suspension, which gives a bumpier ride than most Detroit models, partly as a result of superior brakes, steering, shock absorbers, and tires. Should have distinctive styling.* Business Week 1/21/67, p56 [**1959**, from Italian, literally, grand touring]

graphicacy, *n.* skill in the graphic arts. Compare ORACY. *It seems that the individual who excels in literacy, numeracy and graphicacy (all needed in good measure by the first-class geographer) is indeed rare.* Times (London) 4/19/77, p12 [**1972**, from *graphic* + -*acy* (noun suffix), patterned on *literacy*]

graphicate, *adj.* skilled in the graphic arts; able to draw, map, engrave, etc. *The new BA studies start this coming October and are much more broadly construed aiming to nurture numerate, literate and graphicate geographers experienced in the applications of their subject to real problems.* Geographical Magazine 7/72, p673 [**1972**, from *graphic* + -*ate* (adj. suffix), patterned on *literate*]

graphite fiber, a fibrous material made of graphite, similar to fiberglass. *Thornel is a remarkable graphite fiber, produced by Union Carbide, which when used to reinforce high performance plastics, creates a material that can have five times the strength and stiffness, for equal weight of metals.* Scientific American 1/77, p69 [**1970**]

graphoscope, *n.* a computer display unit on which the data displayed can be modified by the use of a light pen or similar device. *An exciting and recent development of the alphascope principle is the graphoscope. In this system, communication is by drawing and there are many clever devices to enable the user to draw on the scope as well as to obtain output from it.* New Scientist 6/4/70, p7 [**1970**, probably as a new coinage from *grapho-* writing or drawing + -*scope* instrument for viewing, though known in the sense of "a viewer" as early as 1879]

graphotherapy, *n.* the diagnosis and treatment of mental or emotional problems through handwriting; the manipulation or alteration of handwriting as a form of therapy. *Like its parent, graphology, graphotherapy has many critics who equate it with such pseudo-sciences as phrenology and astrology. Both also have their advocates.* Time 9/21/70, p51 [**1956**, from *grapho-* writing + *therapy*]

graph theory, *Mathematics.* the study of sets of points joined by lines. *While the solution to this problem is of no practical use to cartographers, the century-long endeavor to solve it generated a whole new branch of mathematics called graph theory that has been of crucial importance to the development of such fields as operations research and computer science.* 1978 Britannica Yearbook of Science and the Future, p353 [**1953**]

GRAS (græs), *n.* acronym for *Generally Recognized as Safe,* used by the U.S. Food and Drug Administration as a label for food ingredients not considered to be harmful or dangerous. *Ralph Nader and his eager followers are now turning their angry attention to the list of food ingredients listed as GRAS—generally recognized as safe.* New Scientist 7/30/70, p232 *Heretofore saccharin has been on the agency's so-called*

GRAS list—a list of several hundred food substances "generally recognized as safe." NY Times 6/23/71, p28 [**1969**]

graser, *n.* a device similar in function to a laser, which uses gamma rays to produce a beam of great energy and penetrating power. Also called GAMMA-RAY LASER. *Grasers. . .are hypothetical devices which would generate coherent radiation in the range of 0.05-5A (0.0005-0.5 nm) by inducing radiative transitions between isomeric nuclear states. They are not to be confused with so-called nuclear lasers, in which the radiation generated is of optical frequency although the laser is pumped by nuclear radiation.* McGraw-Hill Yearbook of Science and Technology 1976, p228 [**1974**, acronym for gamma-ray amplification by stimulated emission of radiation; patterned after *laser*]

grass, *n. Slang.* marijuana. *One youth held his grass out to me, and said, "Ain't it the weirdest. Get caught with this, and they can give you five years; drop napalm bombs good, and they give you a medal."* Atlantic 1/68, p39 *Where have all the hippies gone?. . .Today Haight-Ashbury ("Hashberry") resembles a ramshackle holiday town when the season is over. . .Nobody offers flowers now, or issues invitations to a pad for a free meal and a share of "grass."* Manchester Guardian Weekly 10/17/68, p19 [**1943, 1965**]

grasshopper, *n. U.S. Slang.* a marijuana smoker. *I could not see how they were more justified in drinking than I was in blowing the gage. I was a grasshopper, and it was natural that I felt myself unjustly imprisoned.* E. Zinberg and John A. Robertson, Drugs and the Public, 1972, p206 [**1968**]

grass mask, a breathing mask attached to a marijuana pipe to conserve the smoke. *Contemporary pipes are also made of metal, glass and acrylic plastic. The grass mask is a pipe fitted with a plastic nose shield to ensure that you lose nothing you want to inhale; the water pipe filters the smoke through water, wine or whatever flavored cooling agent you like.* NY Times Magazine 3/21/76, p21 [**1976**]

grass skiing, the sport of racing down grassy or straw-covered slopes on specially designed skates. *Beachy Head is one of several sites being examined by a committee set up by the ski club to promote grass skiing.* Times (London) 7/27/70, p2 *A new form of skiing called grass skiing used what looks like a cross between a roller skate and a tractor belt.* Britannica Book of the Year 1971, p724 [**1970**]

Grasstex, *n.* a trademark for a type of tennis court surface. See the quotation for details. Compare ASTROTURF, HAR-TRU. *The new courts, known as Grasstex, are composition courts with grit-free surfaces. It was felt that this surface, with its top layer of natural fibres reinforced by emulsified asphalt, provided a cushioning effect that, in Cumberland's view, made Grasstex preferable to its sister product, Laykold.* Times (London) 9/24/76, p11 [**1976**, from *grass* + texture]

gravitational lens, *Astronomy.* a lenslike effect produced by the strong gravitational field of a massive object, such as a galaxy, causing light reflected from a quasar or other very distant object to bend or intensify as it passes through the field. *What had not been observed was the more extreme case—deflection of light by a gravitational field so strong that it acts as a lens if on the line of sight. But now astronomers believe they have found the first evidence for just such a gravitational lens.* Science News 6/16/79, p389 [**1979**]

gravitational radiation, radiation of GRAVITATIONAL WAVES. *Our own galaxy is a spiral type with most of the matter in a plane. Gravitational radiation may be emitted by objects in orbits lying in this plane.* Popular Science 5/72, p192 *Gravitational radiation is supposed to be detected by vibrations that it causes as it passes through large aluminum cylinders.* Science News 8/18-25/73, p108 [**1970**]

gravitational waves, energy-carrying waves involving gravitational forces. The existence of such waves was considered hypothetical until 1969, when their discovery in laboratory experiments was announced. Also called GRAVITY WAVES. *When Einstein postulated his general relativity theory in 1916, he realized that it predicted the existence of gravitational* *waves. Similar to electromagnetic waves, which are generated by accelerating electric charges, gravitational waves would be radiated by accelerating masses, such as binary stars, and would travel through space at the speed of light.* New Scientist 10/15/70, p122 [**1937, 1959**]

gravitino, *n.* a hypothetical elementary particle with a spin of 3/2, postulated in the theory of SUPERGRAVITY. *Others are worried by the growing complexity of the theories and the proliferation of the supposedly "basic" building blocks of matter. There is talk of hundreds of them: quarks of different "colors" and "flavors," gluons that bind them inseparably, leptons, bosons and, in one formulation that includes gravity, "gravitinos."* NY Times 8/6/79, pA9 [**1977**, from *gravit*on the unit particle of gravitational force (1942) + *-ino,* as in *neutrino*]

gravity waves, another name for GRAVITATIONAL WAVES. *Gravity waves are thought to be a form of energy similar to electromagnetic radiation and travel at about the speed of light.* 1970 Britannica Yearbook of Science and the Future, p382 [**1930, 1959**]

gravlax ('grɑːvˌlɑːx), *n.* salmon marinated with fresh drill sprig, spices, and cognac. *Among the appetizers, the Cognac-cured gravlax and daily pasta specials are standouts.* Connoisseur 9/88, p65d [**1975**, from Swedish, short for *gravad lax,* literally, buried salmon; so called from its being tightly packed when cured]

gray, *n.* an international unit for measuring absorbed doses of ionizing radiation, equal to 1 joule per kilogram. It is intended to replace the older name *rad. Among the SI's* [Système International] *derived units with special names are those for. . .radioactivity (the becquerel, or spontaneous nuclear transitions per second) and absorbed dose of radiation (the gray, or joules per kilogram).* Scientific American 3/76, p60A [**1975**, named after Louis Harold *Gray,* a 20th-century British radiobiologist]

gray-collar, *adj. U.S.* of or relating to workers who perform technical services of repair or maintenance. Compare PINK-COLLAR, STEEL-COLLAR. *Two decades ago, in 1948, the ratio of production to service jobs was just the reverse—55 to 45. By 1975, only one out of three jobs is expected to be in production. . .Blue-collar, gray-collar, and farm employment combined will just barely exceed the white-collar total, a balance that economists would have pronounced ludicrously improbable half a century ago.* 1968 World Book Year Book, p105 [**1968**]

graymail, *n. U.S.* a threat of possible public exposure of government secrets during prosecution in a trial. *The graymail problem extends beyond espionage—to bribing foreign officials, lying to Congress about intelligence activities abroad, and investigating and harassing innocent dissidents. . .Secret proceedings would not eliminate graymail. But the procedure would let all parties know where they stand and reduce the number of cases that cannot be prosecuted.* NY Times 7/25/79, pA22 [**1973**, originally a term used in the Central Intelligence Agency as a euphemism for *blackmail.* Compare GREENMAIL.]

Gray Panther, a member of an organization promoting the interests of the elderly in America. Compare GREEN PANTHER. *Gray Panthers have been on the prowl nationwide for over six years. As they prey on the various existing forms of ageism, they deftly uncover issues of trenchant public interest: health care, housing, income security, utilities, crime.* The New Old: Struggling for Decent Aging, 1978, p310 *Associations are being spawned in great profusion by the age movement which. . . They range from cultural and political and economic organizations of high sophistication to basement centers where "senior citizens" in rocking chairs listen to Lawrence Welk and make macaroni jewelry. The Grey Panthers rage against those places as "geriatric playpens." Others rail against the Grey Panthers too.* New Republic 12/2/78, p34 [**1974**, from *gray*-haired or hair + *panther;* patterned on BLACK PANTHER]

gray power, *U.S.* the power of the elderly to assert their rights. See AGEISM, GERONTOPHOBIA. *Consider the Gray Power reflected in the congressional bill banning mandatory retirement at sixty-five.* New Yorker 12/12/77, p122 *Age is yet another denominator. The group awareness of senior citizens—*

"Gray Power"—is a considerable phenomenon in Florida, Arizona, and California. At the other end of the age chart, more and more legal rights are being defined for children. Harper's 5/78, p41 [**1977**, from *gray*-haired or hair + *power;* patterned on BLACK POWER]

graywater, *n.* waste water which can be recycled, as from a sink or washing machine, and does not drain from toilets and other sources of heavy contamination. *His pamphlet on graywater (recycled water from sink and shower) had been adopted by the local water utility as the western drought tightened.* Atlantic 1/78, p61 [**1978**]

GRB, abbreviation of GAMMA-RAY BURST. *We compared notes and gained confidence that these quite unexpected GRBs were real. They occur at an unpredictable time, in unpredictable parts of the sky and last no more than a few seconds. During 4½ years of nearly constant alert, we found 41 GRBs that had activated two or more distant satellites.* World Book Science Annual 1976, p201 [**1975**]

Great Leap Forward, the name of a large-scale economic program of rural collectivization and rapid industrialization instituted in China by Mao Tse-tung (Mao Zedong) between 1958 and 1961. Compare FOUR MODERNIZATIONS. *The economic ideas with which Mao Tse-tung instituted the Great Leap Forward included the economic fallacy that as a man could produce more in a day than he could consume—by value—more manpower in China would be no handicap so long as everyone was a full-time producer—and this was one aim of the Great Leap.* Times (London) 4/17/68, p8 [**1958**]

great room, *U.S.* a living area in a house that serves as a living room, dining room, family room, and sitting room. *Contractors across the country are trying to build smaller houses that will still look attractive. Instead of a living room and a separate family room, more builders this year will offer a single "great room." Others are eliminating garages and extra baths, or leaving part of the home for the buyer to finish.* U.S. News and World Report 2/9/81, p76 [**1978**]

Great Society, **1** the name given to former President Lyndon B. Johnson's program of social welfare. *The New York Republican* [Governor Rockefeller] *said that recent inflationary pressures cutting into purchasing power might have done more to harm low-income persons than "the so-called Great Society" has helped.* NY Times 5/23/68, p23 **2** Transferred sense (to society as a whole): *Wheeler Ranch* [a hippie commune] *is a microcosm of Society. . .Just about everything that happens in Society happens here. After all, take away the long hair and we look like everyone else, with the same needs and basic desires. But the important thing to remember is that, like the Great Society, we are diverse.* Harper's 8/70, p8 [**1964**]

green ban, (in Australia) the refusal of trade union members to work on environmentally and socially objectionable projects. *As leader of the 40,000-member Australian Builders' Laborers Federation, he* [Jack Mundey] *was the bloke who invented the green ban—labor's veto over projects that threaten the environment. Shop steward, spare that tree.* Maclean's 6/28/76, p52 [**1974**]

green belt, a strip of land adjacent to a desert which has been irrigated and planted in order to stop desertification. *One of the most tangible products of the UN conference will probably be six "transnational" or cooperative intergovernmental experimental projects, involving 29 countries, that have been developed to halt desertification and to demonstrate how countries can work together to solve common problems. These projects include establishment of "green belts" in the northern and southern fringes of the Sahara, to extend from the Atlantic Ocean to the Red Sea, to limit grazing and allow regeneration of some of the region's lost farming land.* Science News 10/29/77, p285 [**1977**] ▶The earlier (1930's) meaning of this term is an area of parkland set aside around a city or town to restrict further urban growth or development.

Green Berets, 1 the nickname of a unit of the U.S. Army, officially called Special Forces. *The halcyon years were 1964 and 1965. "Back then," one Special Forces sergeant major growled recently, "the Green Berets were Vietnam, baby."* NY Times

8/31/68, p4 **2 Green Beret,** a member of the Green Berets. *One stroboscopic sequence. . .starts out slyly as a somewhat tasteless spoof of suicidal Buddhists in Vietnam, then suddenly brings on miniskirted nuns, pursued by coolie-hatted VCs, who in turn are being hunted—and destroyed—by Green Berets.* Harper's 9/68, p108 **3 green beret,** the beret worn by Green Berets as part of their uniform. *These are just a few items of a diversified trade that includes everything from aircraft to the famous green berets (which are made in Toronto).* Maclean's 2/68, p13 [**1955,** from the name of the commando unit 1949]

green card, 1 *U.S.* a permit, originally green-colored, which allows foreigners to live and work as resident aliens in the United States. See also GREEN-CARDER. *The man had just come in from Mexico on a "green card," or visa, which is a symbol of the most serious obstacle that Chavez's organizing effort faces: the century-old effort of California farmers to depress wages and undercut resistance by pitting one group of poor people against another.* New Yorker 6/21/69, p50 **2** *British.* a green-colored insurance document covering motorists against accidents in foreign countries. *Insurance companies have been known, however, to refuse to extend cover even for countries which recognise the green card as well as for those where it is not valid.* Guardian (London) 5/13/72, p17 [**1963** for def. 1; **1959** for def. 2]

green-carder, *n.* *U.S.* a foreigner who holds a green card. *Workers pulled out on strike were readily replaced by scabs and green-carders—foreign nationals (in this case Mexicans) with U.S. work permits.* Atlantic 6/71, p40 *"Green-carders" can become citizens after five years of residence—and pay taxes, be drafted, and qualify for Social Security while they wait.* New Yorker 6/21/69, p55 [**1966**]

green currency, any of the artificial units of account, such as the green pound, created in 1969 to protect the European Economic Community's common farm prices from the fluctuations of the currencies of its member nations. *The present debate about German farming, whether held in France, Italy or Britain, centres on money. It is claimed that the green currency system is used by the West German Government to keep up the incomes of part-time smallholders.* Times (London) 11/13/78, p1 [**1977**]

greenfield, *adj.* *British.* of, relating to, or built in a rural or undeveloped area. *In this study we have considered plants of the kind which may be decided upon for "greenfield" construction in the UK some years ahead.* New Scientist 5/4/72, p253 *It is becoming apparent that greenfield sites close to urban areas are in short supply and it is probable that future development will be concentrated on the refurbishment of existing premises.* Times (London) 6/12/78, p12 [**1963**]

green gold, vegetation as a valuable natural resource, as in producing alcohol from cellulose or fodder for animals. *"Green gold" is the object of the most meticulous concern on the part of agricultural researchers: "We have two natural resources here, water and the sun. They give us grass."* Manchester Guardian Weekly (Le Monde section) 5/6/79, p14 [**1953**] ►An earlier meaning of *green gold* (OEDS 1935) is an alloy of gold and silver.

greenhouse gas, a gas that warms the atmosphere by trapping heat of the long-wave solar radiation reflected from the earth's surface. *Carbon dioxide and other radiatively active gases such as methane, ozone, fluorocarbons and oxides of nitrogen. . . are the greenhouse gases.* Scientific American 6/87, p37 [**1982;** patterned after *greenhouse effect* (OEDS 1937)]

greenlining, *n.* *U.S.* any of various methods used to combat the practice of REDLINING. *Now a spirited fight against redlining is mounting across the U.S. by the residents of declining neighborhoods. Their tactic: to make investments in the inner city financially attractive to lenders once again, a process that community groups call "greenlining."* Time 5/27/74, p72 *One pressure tactic, called "greenlining" by a Chicago community group, the Citizens Action Program, which has employed it, is to threaten to withdraw residents' savings deposits en masse from institutions that decline to make mortgage and home improvement loans in the depositors' neighborhoods.* NY Times 1/26/76, p46 [**1974,** patterned after REDLINING]

green lung, *British.* a park or other area of planting in a city. *The English with their gift for enjoying their country have managed to preserve fragments of the ancient past. The parks, "the green lungs," once the hunting preserves of the early monarchs, which give London such refreshment today, are a prime example.* Atlantic 5/70, p131 [**1962,** in reference to production of oxygen in plants]

greenmail, *U.S.* —n. **1** the practice of buying a large block of a company's shares of stocks as if to threaten a takeover so that the company will be forced to repurchase its stocks at a higher price. *Mr. Steinberg's good fortune added momentum to a drive underway in Congress to outlaw greenmail. Many legislators, and the Securities and Exchange Commission, argue that such arrangements protect management and enrich speculators, but leave stockholders out in the cold.* NY Times 8/26/84, pE8 **2** the money paid by a company to repurchase its stocks from investors attempting greenmail. . . .*some analysts say stockholders will not allow the company to pay "greenmail" to escape.* . . NY Times 7/19/84, pD1 —v.t. to subject to greenmail. *St. Regis has been greenmailed twice. . . Last week Disney and St. Regis faced the fact that greenmail is like blackmail: a company that pays once merely invites new demands.* Time 7/30/84, p89 [**1984,** from *green* money + -*mail,* as in *blackmail.* Compare GRAYMAIL.] —greenmailer, n.: *When a company pays a premium price to buy back stock from someone who is trying to take it over, all the shareholders get shortchanged. The only beneficiaries are the managers of the company, who get to keep their jobs, and the greenmailers, who are encouraged to use the tactic again and again.* Washington Post 5/14/84 (page not known)

green monkey disease, another name for MARBURG DISEASE. *The mystery fever from which scores of people are reported to have died in the southern Sudan and across the border in Zaire is caused by the Marburg virus—the "green monkey disease"—the World Health Organization said today.* Times (London) 10/15/76, p9 [**1967**]

Green Panther, *U.S.* (*used disparagingly*) a militant or vocal protector of the natural environment. Compare GRAY PANTHER. *There is another problem. To minority groups, sensitivity about the landscape goes hand in hand with indifference to human needs. In the ghetto, environmentalists are known as "Green Panthers."* Atlantic 11/73, p26 [**1973,** from *green,* color associated with environmentalists + *panther;* patterned on BLACK PANTHER]

Green Paper, *British.* a government document in which a proposal or idea is put up for discussion, usually printed on green paper to distinguish it from a White Paper, which presents fixed policy. Compare BLACK PAPER. *The Government's Green Paper on economic strategy, "The Task Ahead," presents a decidedly cautious assessment of Britain's economic prospects.* Manchester Guardian Weekly 3/6/69, p9 *Last week, the British government published a green paper (green for discussion) called "A Framework for Government Research and Development" (Cmnd 4814).* New Scientist and Science Journal 12/2/71, p14 [**1967**]

Greenpeace, *n.* a militant environmentalist movement involved especially in protecting animals from whalers, trappers, and other hunters. Compare FRIENDS OF THE EARTH. *The shambling New Brunswick Liberal. . .is about to be subjected to the piranha-like peckings of Greenpeace, the scruffy band of ecofreaks who take on nations—and usually win.* Maclean's 2/21/77, p64 *The seal hunt is indeed a sickening and unnecessary event. . .Greenpeace seeks a ban on the commercial hunting of harp and hood seals. We believe that only the aboriginal hunt can be justified, provided that this limited hunting can be proven to be within safe environmental boundaries.* New Scientist 4/13/78, p83 [**1972**]

green pound, the unit of account by which farm prices are expressed in sterling within the European Economic Community. See GREEN CURRENCY. *He [Agriculture Minister Peter Walker] persuaded his European colleagues, moreover, to ac-*

cept a devaluation of 5 per cent in the "green pound," the national unit of exchange for farm produce. Manchester Guardian Weekly 7/1/79, p3 [**1974**]

green power, the power of money. "*We give the public what it wants,*" *the theatre producers still cry, meaning of course they cater to the side of the public that has the most green power (that is, money).* Manchester Guardian Weekly 4/11/68, p12 "*'Green Power' is important for the Negro now. Pride and dignity come when you reach in your pocket and find money, not a hole.*" Time 8/11/67, p14 [**1967**]

green revolution, the large-scale development of inexpensive and high-yield varieties of wheat, rice, and other grains, especially to improve the economy of underdeveloped countries. *. . .the "green revolution" in the third world is at last showing results. . .There is a real chance that over the next ten years agricultural productivity will increase dramatically in the rice growing countries of South-East Asia.* Manchester Guardian Weekly 1/3/70, p12 *. . .the Green Revolution [is] the development through "genetic engineering" of new cereal varieties whose introduction into developing countries has enormously increased crop yields and helped exorcise threats of famine.* NY Times 10/25/70, p12 *Nonetheless, many U.S. environmentalists remain skeptical about the Green Revolution precisely because it depends so heavily on agricultural chemicals.* Time 11/22/71, p52 [**1969**]

green time, the length of time during which traffic is able to move uninterruptedly through a series of traffic lights showing a green light. *The basic idea is to make more efficient use of the precious "green time" that keeps traffic moving on the roadways. Ideally, the computer program coordinates traffic signals so that platoons of vehicles can run smoothly from one green light to another, with a minimum number of stops for red lights or congestion.* Popular Science 1/71, p53 [**1968**]

greenway, n. *Especially U.S.* a strip of parkland, usually connecting larger parks, designed for pedestrians and bicyclists (often used attributively). "*Our next proposal, by the way, is for an eight-block Ruppert Greenway, running from Central Park, through the Green here, to Carl Schurz Park, on the East River.*" New Yorker 6/24/72, p28 *Governor McCall and others favor a program of public acquisition of "greenway" land along both banks, but the program has lagged.* Encyclopedia Science Supplement (Grolier) 1973, p215 [**1966**]

gremmie, n. *U.S. Slang.* a surfer who is new or poor at the sport. "*A lot of gremmies come out just to impress girls, and all they do is sit on their popouts.*" "*What's a popout?*" we asked. "*A crummy board,*" the boy said. "*Machine-made. And you can see the fibres going in all different directions in the resin.*" New Yorker 6/17/67, p24 [**1962**, a diminutive of *gremlin*, a U.S. slang word for anyone annoying or troublesome]

grey area, *British.* a geographical area showing low employment but not poor enough to qualify for special government assistance. *The future of grey areas—places which have fallen between the two stools of prosperity and real depression—is of great importance in this corner of Britain.* Times (London) 6/1/70, p7 [**1963**]

gridlock, n. **1** a complete stoppage of all vehicular traffic due to the blocking of major intersections by long lines of vehicles. *It could be serious. . .the Beltway jammed to gridlock with Volvos.* Manchester Guardian Weekly 11/30/80, p17 *Gridlock quickly replaced such tired terminology as logjam, bumper-to-bumper, glut of cars, wall-to-wall parking lot.* (New York) Daily News 4/13/80, pD **2** Transferred sense. any complete stoppage of activity due to overcrowding. *Sometimes, the entire city seemed to be jammed in telephone gridlock with everyone on the phone and no one getting through.* New Yorker 11/19/84, p99 *The legislature of California is in legislative gridlock.* Roger Mudd, NBC News 7/18/83 [**1980**]

grief therapy, supportive therapy for the bereaved; psychological help for those who have sustained the death of a spouse, a child, etc. Compare DEATH THERAPY. *So successful was the first attempt that five grief therapy groups are now operating. Each is composed of both men and women in similar stages of grief and need. As the need for a highly-trained counselor ebbs, a counselor of less expertise is gradually worked into the group.* The New Old: Struggling for Decent Aging, 1978, p429 [**1973**]

Grinch or **grinch** (grintʃ), n. *U.S. Informal.* a person or thing that spoils the enjoyment or plans of others; spoilsport; killjoy. *No print-medium Grinch is arguing that humor aimed at the young doesn't have a place in the video spectrum.* Newsweek 5/7/79, p72 *The grinches noted that. . .the 80386's are simply faster versions of the I.B.M. PC-AT.* . . NY Times 1/6/87, pC7 [**1969**, from the name of the character in *How the Grinch Stole Christmas* (1957), a children's story by Dr. Seuss (Theodor Seuss Geisel), an American writer and illustrator, perhaps inspired by earlier use in Kipling's works (1872)]

griot (griːˈou or ˈgriːɑt), n. a traditional poet, musician, and storyteller of western Africa. *Ouologuem writes a griot—"a troubadour, member of a hereditary caste whose function it is to celebrate the great events of history and to uphold the God-given traditions.*" New Yorker 11/13/71, p187 *By working backward through slave records, talking to linguists and finally interviewing African griots, native oral historians, he* [Alex Haley] *succeeded in tracing his slave ancestor, Kunta Kinte, back to a particular village, Juffure, in an interior section of Gambia.* Newsweek 8/5/74, p74 [**1820, 1959**, from French, probably of African origin (compare Wolof *gewel* oral historian)]

grody (ˈgroudiː), adj. *U.S. Slang (chiefly teenage use).* disgusting; gross. *It's Saturday, and she would rather be shopping or out with friends. But you don't expect to hear her displeasure in a different language. "Omigod, Mom, like that's totally beige. . .I mean grody to the max, just gruesome. Gimmie a royal break." If you're wondering if your daughter is suffering from some new disease, you should know that a bubbling rapid-fire speech pattern is only one of the symptoms.* NY Times (Connecticut Weekly) 12/12/82, p4 "*Val*" *is really a sort of satire of slang, a goof on language and on the dreamily dumb and self-regarding suburban kids who may actually talk like that. It would come out all wrong if a minister were to compose his sermon in Val. "The Lord is awesome," he would have to begin. "He knows that life can sometimes be, like, grody—grody to the max! Fer shirr!*" Time 11/8/82, p91 [**1982**, probably alteration of GROTTY, with pronunciation influenced by GROSS]

grok (grɑk), v.i. *U.S. Slang.* to communicate meaningfully or sympathetically. "*I was thinking we ought to get together somewhere, Mr. Zzyzybyzynsky, and grok about our problems.*" New Yorker 3/15/69, p35 *Esalen* [a growth center] *T-groups frequently use the term grokking in their touch therapy.* . . Time 3/29/71, p61 [**1967**, from a "Martian" term for the power of perception and communication possessed by the hero of the science-fiction novel *Stranger in a Strange Land* (1961) by the American writer Robert Anson Heinlein, born 1907]

groove, *Slang.* **—n.** something very enjoyable, wonderful, or outstanding. *It's* [a discothèque] *in the vaults—below a crêpe-and-shish-kebab establishment of the same name—and it's generally considered to be a groove.* New Yorker 4/27/68, p7 *Asked how he felt about his release in exchange for the Krogers, Mr. Lorraine beamed: "It's a groove."* Sunday Times (London) 10/26/69, p2 **—v.i. 1** to enjoy oneself; have fun. "*Moovin' and groovin' with Big Daddy Madman Mathews on sooooo-oulful 1600 WXKW 76 degrees in the big bag outside and time for: Muuuuu-sic!*" Atlantic 3/70, p67 *But as a black American, who is probably Black Beach Boy Fan No. 1, I close my eyes to their shoddy politics and simply groove on the music.* Time 9/27/71, p2 **2** to be enjoyable; be fun. "*Life as it is. . .really grooves.*" New Yorker 12/20/69, p35 **3** to associate (with), especially because an emotional bond has been formed. *. . .it is Radical Chic that prompts the Carter Burdens "to groove, as they say, with the Young Lords and other pet primitives from Harlem and Spanish Harlem. . ."* Time 6/15/70, p87 **—v.t.** to cause to groove. "*What better way to groove my contemporaries on earth than to decorate their material life with mind-expanding design?*" New Yorker 11/28/70, p157 [**1959**, from the slang phrase *in the groove* in perfect form

(OEDS 1933), from which *groovy,* meaning excellent, very good (OEDS 1937) also derives]

gross, *U.S. Slang.* —*adj.* unpleasant, dirty, nasty, disgusting, etc. (a general term of disapproval applied to anything objectionable). *True enough, "gross" has always meant something coarse and vulgar. But as used by the teens, it runs the gamut of awfulness from homework to something the cat contributed to the ecology.* Saturday Review 7/29/72, p71 —*v.t.* Usually, **gross out.** to affect with disgust, horror, shock, etc. *Instead of subtle plot twists, they* [horror films] *offer dangling limbs, effusing guts and gruesome decapitations—and audiences are lining up in droves to be "grossed out."* New York Post 6/7/79, p35 [**1968** for verb; **1972** for adj., extended from the original meaning (OED 1532) "extremely coarse in behavior or morals"]

gross domestic product, the gross national product of a country minus the net payments on foreign investments. *Abbreviation:* GDP *One of the most important agents of change was the tourist, whose spending generated an increase in local consumption, in imports, and in the gross domestic product.* Annual Register of World Events in 1969, p112 *In terms of one key indicator, per capita gross domestic product, the developed economies registered an increase of 43 percent in the course of the decade, compared with only 27 percent for the underdeveloped economies.* Scientific American 9/72, p64 [**1964,** patterned after *gross national product* (1940's) the total monetary value of all goods and services produced in a country during a year]

gross-out, *U.S. Slang.* —*n.* someone or something disgusting, boring, or otherwise objectionable. *Well, it's just toooo much* (late '40s). *A real drag* ('50s), *a bad trip* ('60s), *and naturally, a gross-out* ('70s). *As the new decade approaches, so does a new lingo of youth.* San Francisco Examiner & Chronicle 4/1/79, pA12 —*adj.* variant of GROSS. *Disgusting; wild or orgiastic, as in "That was a real gross-out party."* American Speech Spring-Summer 1973, p157 [**1973,** from GROSS OUT, *v.*]

gross social product, *Economics.* the total monetary value of all goods produced in a nation during a certain period of time; gross national product minus the value of services. *Abbreviation:* GSP *At the beginning of the current decade investments in fixed and working assets in Yugoslavia amounted to some 43 per cent of the gross social product (GSP) of the country, perhaps a world record. That could not be sustained, and the aim is to reduce investments to almost half that proportion of national income. Only modest success has been achieved. Investments have gone down to some 36 per cent of the GSP last year.* Financial Times 9/7/83, p15 [**1979**]

grotty ('grɑti: *or* 'grɑdi:), *adj. Slang.* **1** unpleasant, dirty, disgusting, etc.; gross. . . . *a rather grotty individual, manifestly a hippie, accosted the clerk in charge.* New Yorker 12/26/70, p21 **2** *Especially British.* run-down; shabby; dreary; mean. . . . *a grotty suburb where the shops and the public services have not caught up with modern affluence.* Times (London) 6/1/70, p7 [**1964,** shortened from *grotesque* + *-y* (adjective suffix), with the form perhaps influenced by *grotto* (a cavern or crypt]

ground effect machine, another name for, AIR CUSHION VEHICLE. Compare SURFACE-EFFECT SHIP. *Among the various novel craft that ride on a cushion of air is the class known in the United States as. . .ground-effect machines—GEM is the usual acronym—and in the United Kingdom as hovercraft, because they are free of the Earth's surface.* McGraw-Hill Yearbook of Science and Technology 1966, p366 [**1959,** so called because of the effect of the ground in trapping the air to form a cushion]

ground pollution, environmental pollution caused by the seepage of toxic chemical wastes buried in the ground, especially in dumpsites and landfills. *Ground pollution's greatest threat is to the national drinking supply. More than 100 million Americans depend upon ground water as the major source of life's most vital fluid.* NY Times Magazine 1/21/79, p41 [**1979**]

groundprox, *n.* a navigational device in an aircraft which alerts a pilot to change the craft's altitude to avoid crashing into the ground. *Groundprox* (New Scientist, *vol. 68, p 280) is a system for warning a pilot that he is flying into the ground. At the heart of the Plessey system is the Plessey MIPROC, which processes inputs such as the altimeter reading and emits an electronically synthesised command—"pull up" or "climb"—if the plane is in danger.* New Scientist 3/4/76, p508 [**1975,** short for *ground pro*ximity warning system]

ground-to-ground, *n.* a land-to-land rocket or missile. *"Tomorrow, we'll get three divisions in here, four, we'll get two hundred B-52s, we'll get ground-to-grounds, and whole batteries of Lazy Dogs, we'll get nuclear. . ."* Punch 2/21/68, p258 [**1968**]

ground truth, information about the earth obtained by direct examination of features on the ground in order to verify information gathered by satellite or other airborne means. *The atmosphere may prove to be so dense that it will throw the instruments off; indeed, scientists involved in these experiments, some of whom are skeptical about the accuracy of data from an orbiting spacecraft, will be scattered around the world to get what they call "ground truth."* New Yorker 5/5/73, p128 [**1971**]

grouper, *n. U.S.* **1** a member of an encounter group. *When, for instance, the spirits of some grouper noticeably sag, he may be rocked tenderly in the air on the hands of the others. Tears are a summons to "cradle": the moist-eyed one is warmly and multiply embraced.* Time 11/9/70, p55 **2** one who takes part in group sex. *Many columns of ads for wife-swappers, lesbians, homosexuals, groupers, sadists, masochists. . .* Harper's 2/70, p54 **3** one of a group of young people who have pooled their resources to rent a vacation cottage. *The three young women decided to become "groupers" and take part shares in "Snug Cozy," which means that for $375 each they will be allowed to spend every other summer weekend there, with a group of 13 other hopefully amiable "groupers," no more than 8 of whom will be allowed per weekend.* NY Times 3/26/76, p41 [**1970** for defs. 1 and 2; **1966** for def. 3]

group grope, *U.S. Slang.* **1** petting or similar sexual play by a group of people. *Nevertheless she'd gone along with group-grope, gang-bang. . .and other perversions for her plump pal's sake, deferring her preferences to his.* Harper's 10/72, p82 **2** a form of encounter-group therapy which stresses close physical, and especially tactile, contact between members of a group. *It's a group grope at Esalen. . .an orgy of touching, palpating, feeling, stroking.* NY Review of Books 1/26/78, p22 [**1969**]

groupie, *n. Informal.* **1** a teen-age girl who is a fan of rock 'n' roll singing groups and follows them where they perform. *It seems that rock bands prefer San Francisco groupies to New York groupies; the latter, being coldhearted Easterners, are only out for conquests; Bay Area chicks really dig the musicians as people, not just bodies, and stay afterward to do their housework.* New Yorker 10/23/71, p170 **2** a follower or admirer of a celebrity; fan. *Steve Doyle. . .is a groupie. No, not the kind of groupie that chases after rock singers. Steve's serious. He works for his idol, and his idol happens to be a presidential primary contender.* Saturday Review 6/10/72, p22 *Groupies have been around a long time—camp followers of the rich or famous, this heavyweight champion or that president. John F. Kennedy took several groupies into the White House with him.* New York Post 10/13/78, p59 **3** a devotee or enthusiast; aficionado. Compare JUNKIE. *Court groupies and Hearst case buffs arrived from all over the country; some had taken leaves from their jobs to see as much of the six- to eight-week trial as possible.* Time 2/16/76, p46 . . .*a radical-chic restaurant where Toronto artists, entrepreneurs and culture groupies hang out.* Maclean's 12/11/78, p6 [**1967**] **4** *Especially U.S. Informal.* a consortium or group of associated companies designated by the term *Group. Last year's groupies included the Medallion Group, the American Recreation Group, the Wellington Fund reorganized as Vanguard Group of Investment Companies and Clinton Oil, to the Energy Reserves Group.* NY Times 5/23/76, pC17 [**1971**]

Group of 77, a group of United Nations diplomats representing the underdeveloped countries of the world. *The 114 third-world nations, represented by the so-called "Group of 77," would have the "common heritage of mankind" husbanded by an international body generally referred to as the Authority.*

NY Times Magazine 7/17/77, p32 *The Group of 77 (the term used to describe developing countries in the North/South negotiations) formulated a tough draft of the code.* New Scientist 11/2/78, p354 [**1967**, so called because originally it represented 77 nonaligned nations at the United Nations Conference on Trade and Development]

Group of Ten, a group of leading financiers representing the United States, the United Kingdom, Canada, France, West Germany, Belgium, the Netherlands, Italy, Sweden, and Japan, organized in 1962 to support with loans the International Monetary Fund whenever required and to consider various reforms of the international financial system. *It became known today that the next such discussion will take place over the weekend at Basel, Switzerland, where representatives of the world's leading central banks, the so-called "Group of Ten," will meet for a new round of talks on the international monetary situation.* NY Times 6/8/68, p47 [**1964**]

group-think, n. the handling of any problem by a group, such as a commission, a board of directors, or a research team (also used attributively). Compare THINK TANK. *The trend to group-think began earlier in this century when governments, along with universities and big businesses, decided that more progress could be made if assorted experts were brought together in one place to discuss a multidimensional question.* Time 1/19/70, p18 *Philanthropy, Ford-style, moreover, is a group-think affair. Decisions are shaped by over a hundred men.* Harper's 1/66, p85 [**1959**]

groupuscule ('gru:pə,skyu:l), n. a very small or minor group. *He [Raymond Marcellin, the French Minister of the Interior] banned the "Gauche Proletarienne" [a leftist group], ostensibly because he considered it the most dangerous of the groupuscules.* Manchester Guardian Weekly 7/11/70, p6 [**1968**, from French, from *groupe* group + min*uscule* very small]

growth center, a center or institute providing sensitivity training, Gestalt therapy, or other means for the development of people's potentials. *One index of the rapid expansion of encounter groups has been the proliferation of "growth centers" that use various group methods designed to help individuals enhance their creativity, self-knowledge, and ability to work with others.* 1972 Britannica Yearbook of Science and the Future, p410 *A similar event last year drew 850; last April, 6,000. Since January 1969, when Donald Clark counted 37 "growth centers"—established sites for the development of human or group potentials—the census has risen past 100.* Time 11/9/70, p54 [**1970**]

growth fund, a mutual-fund investment company whose stated goal is growth or appreciation in capital value. *Some giant growth funds have run into trouble over their asset valuations.* Sunday Times (London) 2/9/69, p32 [**1963**]

grunge, n. U.S. Slang. something that is bad, inferior, ugly, or boring. *Your average American rock-and-roll fan can stand the Dolls' brand of high-strung urban grunge only if it comes from somewhere besides New York—preferably England.* New Yorker 11/19/73, p234 [**1965**, corresponding to the adjective GRUNGY]

grungy, adj. U.S. Slang. bad, inferior, ugly, or boring. *". . .real people are pretty grungy actors when you come right down to it. Like all those schlockmeisters on 'Candid Camera.'"* New Yorker 7/19/69, p20 *The film* ["McCabe and Mrs. Miller"] *develops a striking ambience, thanks mostly to the talents of Production Designer Leon Ericksen, who constructed a Western town that is simultaneously grungy and beautiful.* Time 7/26/71, p43 [**1965**, of unknown origin]

grunt, n. U.S. Military Slang. an infantry soldier or marine. *But it is his [Nixon's] support of the troops which is even more extraordinary. Were his motive genuinely that of wanting to praise the poor grunts in Vietnam, even according to the prevailing mythology of heroism (a mythology to which the grunts themselves no longer subscribe), it would be a motive worthy and deserving of worthy language.* Harper's 7/70, p31 *The sergeant grabbed the sleeping grunt by the throat and*

told him: *"If I were a V.C., you would be dead."* Time 1/25/71, p31 [**1965**]

gruntwork, n. U.S. and Canadian Informal. low, menial work. *Humble Baluchi and Pakistani workers. . .do the gruntwork of the* [Gulf] *states' lavish modernization programs.* Maclean's 3/31/80, p27 . . .*the dirty, tedious gruntwork needed to make a campaign successful.* NY Times 1/25/81, pE21 [**1972**, from GRUNT + *work*]

GSP, abbreviation of GROSS SOCIAL PRODUCT. *Although the West German economy is showing its customary resilience to the worldwide economic recession, it could not remain immune to it. After a 1.8 percent rise in the Gross Social Product (GSP) last year, a decline of between 1 and 2 percent is predicted for this year coupled with yet another massive balance of payments deficit.* Scientific American 7/81, p61 [**1979**]

GSR, abbreviation of GALVANIC SKIN RESPONSE. *GSR is a measure of the degree of stability of the autonomic nervous system which is correlated to such things as resistance to stress and reduced physical impulsivity.* Science News 9/8/73, p152 *The GSR showed that he was under no unusual stress. His heart rate remained essentially the same.* World Book Science Annual 1974, p144 [**1964**]

GT, abbreviation of GRAN TURISMO. *The Austin 1300 GT is neither high geared, quiet nor relaxing, but a quick and entertaining version of British Leyland's front-driven family car.* Times (London) 9/10/70, p15 [**1964**]

guaranteed annual income or **guaranteed income**, another name for NEGATIVE INCOME TAX. *For many years proposals have come from various positions in the political spectrum recommending a "negative income tax" or a guaranteed annual income.* Americana Annual 1970, p562 [**1968**]

guerrilla theater, a type of dramatic presentation of short antiwar or antiestablishment plays, usually in pantomime and in any public place where an audience will gather. Also called STREET THEATER. *The defendant, Daniel Jay Schacht, was a member of a "guerrilla theater" group which presented skits protesting the Vietnam war. In one skit he wore an army uniform as a costume.* 1971 Collier's Encyclopedia Year Book, p583 [**1968**]

guest worker, another name for GASTARBEITER. *Like the Swiss, the Germans have turned to foreign labour (here they are called guest workers) to help out.* Times (London) 9/22/70, p22 [**1970**]

Guevarist, n. a follower of the Argentine-born Latin American revolutionary Ernesto (Ché) Guevara, 1928-1967, or of his ideas of implementing revolution through guerrilla tactics to pave the way to social reform (also used attributively). *In Ceylon, Government forces claimed they had crushed the revolt by Guevarist rebels in many parts of the island, but admitted the fighting was still going on in some provinces.* Manchester Guardian Weekly 4/24/71, p3 [**1968**]

GUIDO or **Guido** ('gaidou), n. U.S. Aerospace. an engineer in charge of a space flight; the chief navigation officer in a mission-control center. Compare RETRO, FIDO. *The men in the* [front row] *never feel more like pilots than during a rocket burn. As soon as the GUIDO got the trajectory information from the FIDO, he punched the numbers into a white keyboard in front of him, preparatory to loading (or, as GUIDOs say, "uplinking") the data into the computer aboard the spacecraft.* New Yorker 11/11/72, p107 [**1969**, probably from *Guidance* Officer]

gulag or **Gulag** ('gu:,la:g), n. **1** a shortened name for GULAG ARCHIPELAGO. *Perhaps the most profound influence of all. . . was the moral impact in the West of Alexander Solzhenitsyn whose revelations of the character and scale of the Gulag made it electorally imperative as well as morally necessary for the Western Communist parties to come to full terms with Stalinism.* Manchester Guardian Weekly 11/20/77, p5 *Dissent was punished long before there was a gulag. It was in recognition of this simple but basic fact that the Founders took such pains to disperse power and safeguard individual freedoms.* NY Times 6/13/78, pA18 **2** a forced labor camp, especially for political prisoners. See ZEK. *To tell these workers that they are foreigners, living in black gulags, and can express their political voice only in distant homelands is sheer fantasy.* Time 6/27/77, p37 [**1974**, from Russian *GULag*, acronym for *Glavnoye Upravleniye Lagerei* Chief Administration of (Corrective Labor) Camps; popularized in *The Gulag Archipelago*]

Gulag Archipelago, the network of prisons and forced labor camps in the Soviet Union established by Stalin for criminals and political prisoners. Also shortened to ARCHIPELAGO. *All the aggressive elements, all the influential elements in society—this was especially the case in Britain—admired what they called the 'unprecedented progressive experiment taking place in the USSR', while we were being strangled by the cancerous tentacles of the Gulag Archipelago, while millions of hard-working peasants were being sent to die in Siberia in midwinter.* Listener 3/25/76, p358 . . .*a horror that can be thought of only in the images conjured up by the words "Auschwitz" or "Gulag Archipelago."* NY Times Magazine 11/19/78, p42 [**1974**, from *The Gulag Archipelago*, a series of books by Aleksandr Solzhenitsyn, Russian author, born 1918]

gullwing door, a car door that opens upwards from the body so that it resembles the extended wings of a gull. *The De Lorean team believe their product is a good one with its stainless steel covered body and gullwing doors.* Sunday Times (London) 8/10/80, p47 [**1966**]

gundown, *n.* the act of shooting or killing with a gun. *This aborted son of a godfather seems a compendium of every gangster classic since "Little Caesar"—complete with the obligatory gundowns in barbershop and restaurant, initiation blood ritual, tribal meetings and formalized Sicilian mating dances.* Newsweek 11/27/72, p100 [**1969**, from the verb phrase *gun down*]

gunge, *n. British Slang.* a soft, sticky mass; goo; gunk. *Carl Sagan and B.N. Khare have obtained a rough match between the interstellar infrared bands and those they have obtained from solid residues produced by discharge or ultraviolet irradiation of various gaseous mixtures of chemically abundant compounds. . .They call this solid material tholin (after the Greek word for muddy), but it seems likely that chemists will continue to call this rather familiar material "gunge."* New Scientist 1/11/79, p93 [**1969**, probably alteration of *gunk* (1940's), originally *Gunk*, a U.S. trademark for a liquid soap]

Gunn, *adj.* of or based upon the Gunn effect. *A Gunn device generates oscillations as a result of the curious manner in which the conduction electrons behave in n-type gallium arsenide.* New Scientist 3/20/69, p643 *At top right is a cylindrical copper mounting for a Gunn oscillator, a tiny crystal of gallium arsenide that can be made to emit microwaves simply by applying a steady voltage across it.* Scientific American 8/66, p23 [**1965**]

Gunn effect, the emission of microwaves and the simultaneous decrease of direct current flow in a semiconductor when it is subjected at a certain critical level to electrical voltage. *In the past year the emphasis in solid-state microwave devices has been on making practical Gunn effect microwave devices to replace the much larger and more clumsy microwave tubes used in radar and other applications. In addition, due to the interest inspired by the Gunn effect, different types of solid-state devices based on it are being developed and show considerable promise.* 1970 Britannica Yearbook of Science and the Future, p380 [**1964**, named after Ian *Gunn*, of International Business Machines, who discovered the effect in 1963]

guns and butter, *U.S. Politics.* a policy of putting equal emphasis on both military and economic programs (often used attributively). . . . *while it may be true technically and from a monetary point of view that you can have guns and butter, it is a fact of life that where your heart is there your money will go, and the heart of the Administration is in that war in Vietnam.* NY Times 4/2/67, p76 *President Johnson's guns-and-butter policy has produced an estimated $25,000 million to $35,000 million budget deficit, which must be covered by higher revenues.* Sunday Times (London) 3/24/68, p32 [**1966**, originally the term

was *guns before butter* (1930's), giving the highest priority to military expenditures]

gunship, *n.* a helicopter equipped with armament to support ground troops and protect transport helicopters from ground fire. *The man in the rear flies the helicopter and fires the rockets and Gatling-type six-barreled machine guns fixed on stubby wings on each side. The forward man fires a six-barreled minigun in a movable chin turret under the nose. "This is what we call a professional gunship," said Col. J. Elmore Swenson of Columbus, Ga.* NY Times 1/7/68, p5 *This time a hail of fire from a battalion of U.S. defenders and the miniguns of circling American gunships stopped the assault short of the fort's outer fences.* Time 12/8/67, p30 [**1965**]

guru, *n.* **1** a leading figure in some field. *The object of all this praise from one of the gurus of the current fashion scene is an intense, red-headed, strong-willed high-school dropout who owns two shops in Toronto. . .* Maclean's 11/19/66, p14 **2** an expert or authority. *The prime-time football and other changes lead some TV ratings gurus to predict that ABC, which reduced the Nielsen numbers gap about 4% last year, will make equal headway this season and approach parity with CBS and NBC, now in a virtual tie for first place.* Time 10/5/70, p79 **3** a long, loose outer garment similar to the ones worn by Indian holy men (also used attributively). *It seems like a wonderful idea for a play: a handsome young man with long blonde hair and beard, wearing a silver lamé guru, arrives in a Mediterranean city in the company of 12 lovely girls.* Times (London) 4/25/68, p15 *While certain exhibitors focused on such items as Nehru jackets and the toga-like Guru shirts, others brought traffic through their doors with more conventional clothing and furnishings.* NY Times 4/3/68, p69 [**1963**, extended from the earlier meaning of a religious guide or teacher, especially in Hinduism (OEDS 1826)]

Gush Emunim ('gu:ʃ emu:'ni:m), a militant, religious, and ultranationalistic movement in Israel. *Government officials spoke of a plan to establish 20 more Jewish settlements in the West Bank over the next four years, but when members of Gush Emunim, the fanatical religious organization, tried to found two illegal settlements on the hills above Jerusalem last week, soldiers quickly evicted them.* Time 1/8/79, p34 [**1976**, from Hebrew, literally, bloc of the faithful]

gut, *adj. U.S. Slang.* **1** felt deeply or instinctively; visceral. *The welfare changes. . .reflect the gut feeling of many Congressmen that large numbers of welfare recipients are either too lazy or too unmotivated to work.* Time 8/25/67, p17 *There is, as they would phrase it, little "gut reaction" in favour of trade unionism among American workers.* Manchester Guardian Weekly 4/27/67, p1 **2** basic; vital. *The trick is to go where the people are, he went on, and "tackle the gut issues—jobs, substandard housing, education."* NY Times 1/21/68, p84 [**1956**]

GUT, *n.* acronym for GRAND UNIFIED THEORY. *But for physicists, the saltmine experiment is of immediate importance. If those tell-tale flashes are detected it will confirm that scientists are on the way towards achieving one of the chief goals of physics—a Grand Unified Theory (known to the initiated as a GUT).* Sunday Times (London) 1/13/80, p12 *One obvious difficulty lies in the difference in strengths of the forces, but GUTs suppose that this arises from a symmetry-breaking effect.* New Scientist 4/23/81, p220 . . .*thus came the marriage of GUTs and creation: It was just when the once-joined forces began to differentiate. . .that space launched into rapid inflation.* NY Times Book Review 9/25/83, p9 [**1980**]

gutfighter, *n. U.S.* a hard-hitting, tough adversary. *President Nixon came to office convinced that he could govern only if he overcame his old reputation as a gut fighter and followed the politics of reconciliation. . .* NY Times 10/28/70, p47 *To his detractors, he is a "Facile" Frank Fasi, an arrogant gutfighter who shoots from the lip and to hell with the consequences.* Time 2/23/70, p44 [**1961**]

Guts Frisbee. Also, **Guts.** a game in which competing teams throw and try to catch a lightweight plastic disk. Compare ULTIMATE FRISBEE. *There are well-developed games like Guts, where teams of five, 15 yards apart, engage in an all-out, 100* m.p.h., *flying disk war.* NY Times Magazine 7/18/76, p47 [**1971**]

GVH, abbreviation of GRAFT-VERSUS-HOST. *Recent experience suggests that if donor and recipient have identically matched tissues, GVH disease will be mild and will subside of its own accord, but proof of this has yet to be established.* Science News Yearbook 1970, p81 [**1963**]

gyplure, *n.* a synthetic form of the sex attractant of the female gypsy moth. *Pheromones* [olfactory hormones] *control ant behavior and much insect mating. An artificial pheromone (gyplure) can be synthesised to attract gypsy moth males into an insecticidal trap.* New Scientist and Science Journal 2/25/71, p412 [**1960**, from *gyp*sy moth + *lure*]

gypsy cab, *U.S.* a taxicab that is licensed only to pick up passengers who call for a cab, but that often cruises illegally for fares. *The law requires that the gypsy cabs be painted so that they do not resemble taxis operated with police medallions or that they carry letters six inches high saying that they are not licensed to pick up passengers while cruising.* NY Times 7/15/68, p21 [**1966**]

gyrase, *n.* an enzyme which changes double-helix DNA into superhelical DNA. *Gyrase uses energy from ATP molecules to* "super coil" *the DNA double helix in the direction opposite the twist of the helix. The stored mechanical energy from such super coiling makes a local region of the helix easier to open. . .Gyrase so far has been best studied as an aid to replication of DNA, but recently scientists have begun investigating its potential role in RNA production.* Science News 6/10/78, p372 [**1977**, from *gyr*ate + *-ase* enzyme]

gyro ('yɪrou; *Anglicized* 'dʒɑɪrou, 'gɪrou), *n.* a type of Greek sandwich. See the quotation. *Soyer circled the area, took his time, and settled for a Greek gyro—mounds of thinly sliced, garlicky pressed beef and lamb on pita bread.* New Yorker 10/23/78, p101 [**1972**, from Modern Greek, from Greek *gŷros* turn, rotation; so called from the meat being roasted on a spit]

gyrodynamics, *n.* the study of the dynamics of rotational motion. *Although he has spent most of his life in an academic environment, starting at Edinburgh University where he was awarded a PhD for his study of gyroscopes,* [Leonard] *Maunder's work has kept him in close touch with industry. He has also carried out research on engineering dynamics and gyrodynamics and the stress analysis of structures.* Times (London) 7/23/76, p19 [**1976**, from *gyro-* circle, spiral + *dynamics*]

H

habitat, *n.* a vessel to house researchers or scientists under water over an extended period of time while they are conducting their work. See also AQUANAUT, SEALAB. *Four scientists from the U.S. Department of the Interior spent two months in a four-room habitat, Tektite I, nearly 50 feet below the surface of the sea. . . Because internal and external pressures were identical, a floor hatch in the habitat's wet lab could be kept open permanently for ready access to the water.* Americana Annual 1970, p517 *Diving from the barge Hugh Gordon, they were using a "habitat"—a watertight vessel that attaches to the pipe—to cut out the damaged section.* Sunday Times (London) 12/15/68, p41 **[1968,** transferred sense of the term for a place where an animal or plant lives (OED 1796), from Latin]

hack, *v.i. U.S. Slang.* to manipulate computer programs expertly; engage in the practices of a hacker. *One of the most arcane [games] is played on U.S. campuses by subcultures of bright computer-science undergraduates who call themselves hackers. For solitary entertainment, these young adults spend long hours hacking—inconsequentially toying with complex programs—at the terminals of university campuses.* Britannica Book of the Year 1981, p399 **[1981,** back formation from HACKER]

hacker, *n. U.S. Slang.* an expert computer enthusiast, especially one highly skilled in the manipulation of computer programs. *Computer hackers may mean no harm, but amusements that can result in the destruction of, say, irreplaceable medical records ought to be firmly discouraged.* Washington Post 12/2/83, pA14 *Hackers . . . almost whimsically probe the defenses of a computer system, searching out the limits and the possibilities of the machine. Despite their seemingly subversive role, hackers are a recognised asset in the computer industry, often highly prized.* NY Times 7/26/81, pF4 **[1975,** probably from the slang verb *hack (around)* to fool around, play around (1950's) + *-er*]

hadal ('heidəl), *adj.* of or relating to the very deep part of the ocean, ranging from depths of 6500 to 11,000 meters. *Later the reader is taken from the intertidal with its diverse wealth of life progressively lower over the floor of the continental shelf and slope eventually to the profound depths of the ultra-abyssal or hadal zone.* Nature 5/19/72, p180 **[1964,** from *Hades* the nether world + *-al*]

hadron, *n.* any of a class of strongly interacting elementary particles that include the baryons, antibaryons, and mesons. *Now more than 200 kinds of particles have been observed, mostly of the strong interacting kinds called hadrons. . .* 1970 Collier's Encyclopedia Year Book, p431 **[1962,** from Greek *hadrós* stout + *-on*, as in *meson, proton,* etc.]

hadronic, *adj.* of or relating to a hadron or hadrons. *It has been found that a photon with a billion times as much energy as a photon of visible light behaves as hadrons do when it is allowed to interact with hadrons. The discovery that the photon has this hadronic character at very high energies, although it was unexpected, has now been incorporated into a new group of theories that make the hadronic photon respectable.* Scientific American 7/71, p94 **[1962]**

Hageman factor ('hægəmən *or* 'heigmən), a substance in blood plasma necessary for rapid coagulation of blood. *In addition to promoting clotting, activated Hageman factor can initiate the function of other enzymes in the blood plasma which ultimately increase vascular permeability, contract isolated smooth muscles, induce pain and dilatation of the blood vessels (thus increasing blood flow to the area), and even cause the white blood cells to stick to injured areas of blood vessels and subsequently traverse this barrier into surrounding tissues.*

McGraw-Hill Yearbook of Science and Technology 1971, p133 **[1963,** named after a patient in whom a deficiency of this substance was first noticed]

hahnium, *n.* an artificial radioactive chemical element with the atomic number 105, atomic weight of 260, and half-life of 1.6 seconds. It is produced by bombarding californium with nuclei of nitrogen. Also called ELEMENT 105. *A new element, number 105 in the periodic table, has been synthesized by workers at the Lawrence Radiation Laboratory of the University of California. The element has been named hahnium, after the late German physicist Otto Hahn.* Scientific American 6/70, p48 **[1970]**

haircurling, *adj.* causing or spreading terror; frightening; hair-raising. *Passengers have hair-curling stories about many of the little lines, including engine failures, landings with the landing gear retracted, and even running out of gas.* Time 7/18/69, p69 **[1954]**

hair implant, a graft or grafting of strands of artificial hair (usually made of an acrylic fiber) stitched into a bald area of the scalp or attached to small metal barbs forced into the scalp under pressure. Compare HAIR TRANSPLANT. *Hair implants have been advertised by a number of clinics across the country. . . Unlike the transplantation of actual hair from one part of the scalp to another, synthetic implants trigger the body's natural defense mechanisms, usually causing the rejection of the artificial hairs.* Newsweek 2/19/79, p54 **[1974]**

hairologist, *n. U.S.* a specialist in the care and treatment of hair. *Fancier shops now boast resident "hairologists" whose only mission is to prescribe the proper natural treatment and conditioning for feeble follicles.* Time 7/16/73, p59 **[1973,** from *hair* + *-ologist,* as in *cosmetologist* (1920's) a specialist in cosmetics]

hair shirt, 1 an imposing of penance, austerity, or self-sacrifice. *If low real interest rates and falling inflation are so important . . . then the hair shirt is the only answer.* Financial Times 10/3/85, p6 **2** a person who advocates austere and self-sacrificing remedies. *Although Orwell was certainly a bit of a hair shirt himself, he seemed to have a hair shirt's impatience with other hair shirts.* Christian Science Monitor 2/8/85, p27 **[1956,** extended senses of the term for a rough shirt made of horsehairs worn as a penance (OED 1737) and figurative use (OED 1889)]

hair transplant, a graft or grafting of one's own hair by removing follicles and inserting them in a bald area of the scalp. Compare HAIR IMPLANT. *He's a no-sell advertisement for hair transplants; his hasn't taken, and he combs the few remaining blond strands from left to right over the crown of his head.* Maclean's 3/73, p29 **[1973]**

hair-weaving, *n.* the weaving or sewing of a hairpiece or wig into a balding person's remaining hair. *The process is called "hair-weaving," and it was developed in Harlem several years ago to provide long straight hair for Negro women whose own hair had been damaged by frequent straightening treatments and who didn't want to wear wigs.* NY Times 4/15/68, p38 **[1968]**

Haldane principle, the principle that government research agencies be completely insulated from government departments that benefit from the research. *The National Research Council has evolved into the embodiment of the so-called Haldane principle that government research and development should be the responsibility not of mission-oriented departments but of an independent agency.* Nature 8/11/72, p305 **[1966,** named after J.B.S. *Haldane,* 1892-1964, British geeticist who headed the committee which enunciated this principle]

half-board, *n. British*. the provision of a bed, breakfast, and one other meal each day, as by a hotel or boarding house (often used attributively). *We were grateful we had only half-board so that we could justify eating outside the hotel at least once a day.* Times (London) 4/1/77, pIV [**1975**, patterned after *full board* (1910) the provision of a bed and all meals]

half-life, *n*. a period of flowering or prosperity preceding decay or decline. *Alas, in the mercurial cosmetics business, almost all products have short half-lives, and Charlie sales have started to decline. But before they did, Bergerac and Revlon were ready with both an explanation and a new product.* Time 12/11/78, p90 [**1963**, figurative of "the time it takes half of a particular substance to break down or decay" (OEDS 1907)]

half-marathon, *n*. a foot race of 13.2 miles, approximately one half the length of a marathon. *The Kenyan was running his first 15-km race, but he had splendid credentials on either side of the distance, owning the world's fastest road performance at 10,000 meters (27:55) and one of the fastest at the half-marathon (1:02:07).* Sports Illustrated 2/15/82, p20 [**1978**]

hallucinant, *n*. something that produces hallucinations. *This is the core of last week's excitement in which . . . the sudden disclosure of a full military alert, official scare treatment given to threats at the borders, and the trumpeted arrest of a Communist Party leader served as somewhat unnerving hallucinants.* Times (London) 7/13/70, p5 [**1932, 1964**]

hallucinogenic, *n*. a drug that produces hallucinations. *Known medically as hallucinogenics or psychotogenics, these drugs [LSD, mescaline, and psilocybin] are still subject to intense research.* Time 9/26/69, p46 *One is struck by student boldness in searching for pot and other hallucinogenics, and the comparative ease with which they secure them.* Saturday Review 8/17/68, p55 [**1967**, noun use of *hallucinogenic, adj*. (OEDS 1952)]

halobacteria, *n.pl.; sing.* **-ium.** rod-shaped bacteria of a group that thrives in areas with very high salt concentrations. *Halobacteria are salt-loving cells that inhabit stagnant puddles and salt flats at the edge of tropical seas. . . They turn water orange and red herrings red and turn sunlight into chemical energy on their "purple membranes." These bacteria are, all in all, very strange organisms.* Science News 3/6/76, p149 [**1976**, from *halo-* salt (from Greek *háls, halós*) + *bacteria*]

halocarbon, *n*. a compound of carbon and one or more halogens (fluorine, chlorine, etc.). Compare CHLOROFLUOROCARBON. *Concern over the tenuous, but vital, ozone layer which surrounds the Earth has centered around the possible effects of exhaust gases from supersonic transport and the space shuttle, and latterly those which may result from the halocarbons used in packaged aerosol canisters.* New Scientist 5/29/75, p492 [**1964**, from *halogen* + *carbon*]

halocline, *n*. a sharp discontinuity in the salinity of sea water, usually at a depth of about 180 feet. *There has been a marked decrease in the oxygen content of deeper waters, the report* [on water pollution] *states, and "if this development continues, the whole water mass below the halocline will probably turn into a lifeless 'oceanic desert' such as found in the Black Sea."* Times (London) 3/6/70, p7 [**1969**, from *halo-* salt (from Greek *háls, halós*) + English *-cline* a layer (from Greek *klínein* to slope)]

halomethane, *n*. a compound of methane and one or more halogens (chlorine, fluorine, etc.). Compare CHLOROFLUOROMETHANE. *Halomethanes . . . used as refrigerants or as propellants for aerosol spray cans, are another hazard to the earth's ozone shield.* Americana Annual 1975, p175 *Among other nasty organic and man-made intruders, every sample contained chemicals called halomethanes, which some scientists believe can cause cancer in humans.* Maclean's 3/20/78, p16 [**1975**, from *halogen* + *methane*]

haloperidol, *n*. a tranquilizing drug used in the treatment of acute and chronic psychosis. *Formula:* $C_{21}H_{23}ClFNO_2$ *Doctors know that two groups of drugs, which include chlorpromazine*

and haloperidol, are remarkably effective in relieving the thought disorders, hallucinations and extreme withdrawal of schizophrenia, a chronic psychosis that affects one person out of every 100. Time 1/14/74, p57 [**1967**, from *halogen* + *piperidine* + *-ol*]

halothane, *n*. a nonflammable general anesthetic administered by inhalation. *One theory, supported by some evidence, is that halothane may undergo a chemical change in the body and produce a substance toxic to the liver in susceptible individuals.* Britannica Book of the Year 1970, p495 [**1957**, from *halogens* (group of elements) + *ethane* (a gas)]

hammer, *n. U.S. Slang*. **1** an accelerator. *"Yeah, good buddy, you got a county mounty there at marker three-oh. He's eastbound and he's got the hammer down."* Family Circle 8/76, p20 **2 drop the hammer**, to accelerate. *And "modulating," (talking) while "dropping the hammer" (accelerating) is more dangerous to the driver than to his speech.* Time 1/2/78, p36 [**1975**]

hanamichi (hɑːnɑːˈmiːtʃiː), *n*. a raised runway leading to the stage in the Japanese Kabuki theater. Compare HASHIGAKIRI. *Hanamichi is the ramp extending from stage to rear of theatre which allows the actor to show off at close quarters . . . hanamichi will be on view at Sadler's Wells from August 15 when a Japanese Kabuki season opens.* Times (London) 8/3/77, p14 [**1952, 1971**, from Japanese, from *hana* flower + *michi* way]

hand, *v.* **hand up**, *U.S.* to deliver (an indictment) to a higher judicial authority. *Both men pleaded not guilty to the charges, which were handed up by a special grand jury.* NY Times 5/14/76, p1 ►The verb phrase *hand down* means "to announce (a legal decision or opinion)." A judge hands down a decision, whereas a grand jury hands up an indictment.

handle, *n. U.S.* Usually, **have** or **get a handle on**, to have a means of directing or guiding; control. *It follows that if we could only get a better handle on the arms-building phenomenon, we could do something about it; turn it around.* Manchester Guardian Weekly (Washington Post section) 5/29/77, p15 *Carter's State of the Union speech failed to convince foreign moneymen that the Administration has a handle on the economy's problems.* Time 1/30/78, p20 [**1972**]

handoff, *n*. the condition or period in which control of an aircraft is transferred from one airport's control tower to another. *On handoff from Los Angeles' FAA air-route traffic center to San Diego's FAA Approach Control Facility, he* [the pilot] *reported Lindbergh Field in sight.* Encyclopedia Science Supplement (Grolier) 1982, p337 [**1963**]

hands-on, *adj*. designed for or encouraging personal participation or involvement. *Skyline is a "magnet" school, attracting students from all over the city to its special offerings; it also is a new concept in "career education" (not to be confused with "vocational education") that combines fast-paced academic work with hands-on training for real jobs.* Saturday Review 11/11/72, p37 *"Kids are sick to death of being told in science classes to keep their hands off equipment. This* [Ontario Science Centre] *is a strictly 'hands-on' concept."* New Scientist 5/21/81, p480 [**1969, 1971**, patterned after *hands-off, adj.* (OED 1902)]

handtector (ˈhænd,tektər), *n*. a hand-held electronic metal detector, used especially in airports to screen for the presence of weapons. *Held close to a person's body the handtector detects any inordinate amount of metal . . . hidden beneath the clothing.* New Scientist 4/6/72, p17 [**1972**, from *hand* de*tector*]

hang, *v. U.S. and Canadian Informal*. in various phrases: **1 hang in there**, to hold on or hang on. *He* [Richard M. Nixon] *has a long history of coming from behind, they say, and of confronting adversities, and it would be in his nature to hang in there and fight.* Atlantic 5/71, p6 **2 hang loose**, to stay calm; relax; take it easy. *In the meantime, my survival plan is to hang loose, trust my own perceptions, and wear out my Rod Stewart and Joy of Cooking records.* New Yorker 2/26/72, p81 *"In Marin Countyese, people talk of being laid back, mellow, hanging loose and getting their thing together."* NY Times

Book Review 10/16/77, p54 **3 hang tough,** to remain firm in resolve; persevere. *Washington has adhered to a policy of "no concessions" to the terrorists. It will not accede to demands put forward as a condition for the hostages' release, it will not negotiate such terms, and it will not put pressure on other Governments to yield. In the interests of deterring future terrorism, America hangs tough.* NY Times Magazine 7/18/76, p7 *Chrétien decided to hang tough rather than give in to opposition demands for sweeping cuts in personal income taxes.* Maclean's 11/27/78, p22 **4 let it all hang out,** to be carefree or uninhibited; let one's hair down. *Most whites can probably translate, even if they can't use, such terms as "rap" (talk), "rip off" (steal), "hang-up" (pre-occupation) and "let it all hang out" (what J. Edgar Hoover did in that interview this week).* NY Times 11/22/70, pD11 **[1968]**

hang five or **hang ten,** *Surfing Slang.* to curl the toes of one (*hang five*) or both (*hang ten*) feet over the edge of a surfboard. *Hanging Five, or Ten occurs when a surfer hooks his toes over the end of the board.* 1968 World Book Year Book, p590 **[1962]**

hang-glide, *v.i.* to ride a hang glider. *More often she* [Lily Tomlin] *plunges at random into her seemingly inexhaustible repertory of impersonations: a crazy woman of the streets, a quadriplegic whose goal is to hang-glide off Big Sur.* New Yorker 4/4/77, p81 *In May Frenchman Jean-Marc Boivin, 29, intends to climb* [the Matterhorn], *ski down its 60-degree east face, climb the north face, then hang glide down—all within 24 hours.* Times (London) 2/6/80, p11 **[1974,** back formation from HANG GLIDER or HANG GLIDING]

hang glider, 1 a device somewhat like a kite. The rider controls the gliding and soaring while holding onto a bar suspended from the kite. It is usually launched by running off a hill or cliff. Also called ROGALLO. *My first hang glider has a sail consisting of .004-inch polyethylene. The machine weighed 40 pounds empty. It served me well for many ground-skimming flights until the sail began stretching, which degraded the glide ratio.* Scientific American 12/74, p139 **2** the rider of such a device. Also called ROGALLIST, SKY SURFER. *"It is the most beautiful, the quietest, the cleanest sport," says one hang glider. "It is as close to the elements as you can get," says another. "It is the ultimate natural high."* Sunday News (New York) 9/16/73, p28 **[1930, 1972]** —**hang gliding:** *It's called hang gliding, sky surfing or self-soaring—one of man's fantasies since the mythical days of Daedalus and Icarus. But in the past three years, self-propelled flying has become a reality—and one of the fastest-growing sports in the country.* Newsweek 9/17/73, p82

hangout, *n. U.S.* disclosure, exposure, or openness. *As Alan, Peter Firth is equally astonishing; he and Roberta Maxwell as the stable girl play the most blazingly effective nude scene in our age of Total Hangout.* Newsweek 11/4/74, p60 *For Congress to agree to less than full cooperation from Korea would be to acquiesce in a kind of cover-up, in what not so long ago was dubbed a modified limited hangout.* NY Times 1/8/78, pD18 **[1974,** from the phrase *let it all hang out*] ►This term was in part popularized by use in the White House tapes transcribed during the Watergate affair.

hangtime, *n. U.S. Football.* the amount of time a punt stays in the air. The longer the hangtime, the greater the opportunity for the defensive team to tackle the receiver. *A whistle sent the Mariners into a punting drill and a football soared into the sky above the treetops of this affluent North Shore community. It wasn't a particularly long kick, but Rush liked the hangtime.* NY Times 8/26/76, p41 **[1971]**

hangup, *n. Slang.* **1** a psychological or emotional problem. *Aldous is the most interesting Huxley for moderns. That's because he touched modernity's hangups at so many points.* NY Times 6/27/68, p41 . . . *man's racial hangups and his misconceptions about his evolution have led to aggression, violence, and war.* New Yorker 11/2/68, p192 **2** any problem or difficulty, especially one that causes annoyance or irritation. *That big hangup for drivers caught in traffic lineups—the overheated engine—could soon become a thing of the past.* Maclean's 3/68, p4 *My hangup with Dr. Menninger and others who pontificate on violence is that they seem to be saying that they have*

answers. Saturday Review 10/5/68, p21 **[1959,** from the slang phrase *hung up.* See HUNG-UP.]

happening, *n.* a spontaneous or improvised public performance, display, spectacle, or the like, often involving the audience or spectators. *The student protest movement continued in West Berlin and in many university towns in the Federal Republic, 'happenings' often being staged by the Socialist Students' Federation under the direction of the Federation's chief ideologist, Herr Rudi Dutschke.* Annual Register of World Events in 1967, p251 *The show is self-styled as a Happening, and, considered on its own terms—as an attempt to simulate spontaneity, that is—it is a failure. . .* New Yorker 1/6/68, p68 *What was happening was a Happening—a combination of artists' ball, carnival, charade, and a Dadaesque version of the games some people play.* Time 8/19/66, p36 **[1959,** specialized use of the term meaning an event or something that happens]

happenstantial, *adj. U.S.* accidental; happening by chance. *We are not "others," say women, we are human beings like you in whom there exists merely a happenstantial sex difference.* Atlantic 12/73, p96 **[1958,** patterned after *circumstantial* (adjective form of *circumstance*); from *happenstance* (blend of *happen* and *circumstance*)]

happy hour, a time in the early evening when alcoholic drinks are served, especially at a club bar or cocktail lounge, sometimes at reduced prices. *So, this being the content of your happy hour, you decide to break your iron-clad rule, that rule of rules, and have eleven drinks instead of the modest nine.* New Yorker 7/17/71, p26 *A recruit needs neither height (five-feet two-inches will do) nor education (grade 8) to begin making $536 a month and having the privilege of buying beer for 40 cents a bottle during Happy Hour.* Maclean's 11/6/78, p23 **[1961]**

happy talk, a form of news broadcasting in which reports are tailored to an informal style with emphasis on light subjects. *What Happy Talk means in fact is that the consumer-listener-viewer gets an inverted perspective of the world in which he lives. Even for domestic news, he is fed reaction rather than analysis.* Listener 8/30/73, p295 *I think broadcast journalism has done much to expand news definitions . . . something which I think is long overdue. Yes, there have been excesses . . . the happy talk, the newscasters in clown suits.* Columbia Journalism Review, March/April 1976, p83 **[1973]**

haptic lens, a contact lens which covers the white of the eye. Compare MICRO-CORNEAL LENS. *The haptic lens is a part sphere designed to align with the sclera—the visible white part of the eye—and stabilised by evenly fitting the lens over the sclera so that it moves as the eye moves.* New Scientist and Science Journal 9/23/71, p688 **[1971,** *haptic* from Greek *háptein* to fasten + English *-ic*]

hardball, *n. U.S. and Canadian Slang.* Often, **play hardball,** (to use) tough, aggressive methods and tactics (often used attributively). *The inducements ranged from the withholding of campaign appearances by the First Family to the granting of photographs with the President. . . It was hardball of the rawest kind, an insider's game that one would not previously have associated with the softspoken Washington outsider.* NY Times Magazine 12/17/78, p34 *The sense of discouragement left by the breakdown of the private meetings caused the publishers to issue an ultimatum to Moffett. . . At a meeting with the publisher's negotiators, Moffett said, "Evidently, you guys have decided that you are going to play hardball."* New Yorker 1/29/79, p62 *B.C. Health Minister Jim Nielsen's hardball legislation, which reflects the increasingly inflexible stances adopted by both sides, was stalled in the B.C. house late last week, but is almost certain to be passed.* Maclean's 4/13/81, p35 **[1973,** figurative use alluding to "serious" or "professional" baseball (as opposed to *softball*); a usage popularized by Patrick J. Buchanan, a White House speechwriter during the administration of President Nixon]

hard bubble, an aberrant magnetic bubble that causes disruption of the memory in a computer, usually formed spontaneously in the operation of a circuit. Also called QUANTIZED

BUBBLE. *The hard bubbles are more stable than the previously known "normal" bubbles and have different dynamic properties. Instead of moving only parallel to the drive field, the hard bubbles have a velocity component perpendicular to the field and would in general move at some angle to it.* Science News 10/21/72, p264 **[1972]**

hard copy, printed copy of the output of a computer or data-processing system. *Some keyboards used for perforating tape are converted typewriters and therefore generate hard copy; others are designed solely for tape perforation and therefore operate "blind," that is, without preparing any record of keystrokes other than the punched paper tape. Hard copy seems to be advantageous for relatively untrained or part-time operators but less advantageous for the professional.* McGraw-Hill Yearbook of Science and Technology 1970, p159 **[1964]**

hard-core, *adj.* **1** completely uninhibited, graphic, or explicit in presenting or describing sexual acts. Compare SOFT-CORE. *The exploration of unacknowledged desires is the process that is the most compelling structural requirement in hard-core pornography.* Harper's 2/75, p47 *That breakthrough film which uses hard-core sex as a dramatic expression of meaningful human relationships has yet to be made.* New York Post 11/29/75, p14 **2** hard to cure of addiction; resisting treatment. *Mostly, the users, even the heroin users, weren't strung-out hard-core junkies. I'd say many of them came from middle-class families.* New Yorker 7/3/73, p61 **—n.** Also, **hard core.** hard-core pornography. *California is busy withdrawing the liquor licences of strip-joints and bars putting on sex-shows. Hard-core may fetch the customers, but hard liquor brings in the profits: and hundreds of such saloon-keepers have suddenly developed a passionate concern for the Constitution in general and the First Amendment in particular.* Listener 7/27/73, p120 *He had seen it during World War II, when he served as a Navy lieutenant. In Casablanca, as watch officer for his ship, he had seen his men bring back locally produced pornography. He knew the difference between that hardest of hard core and much of what came to the Court. He called it his "Casablanca Test."* Bob Woodward and Scott Armstrong, The Brethren, 1979, p194 **[1963** for adj. def. 1, **1972** for def. 2; **1973** for noun]

hard disk, a rigid disk to store data in a computer, larger in capacity than a floppy disk. *Unlike cassette tape and floppy disks, the standard Winchester hard disk is permanently attached to its recording unit, so you need a separate recording device for creating backups. Perhaps the least expensive solution is to copy the hard-disk data onto floppy disks, especially if you already have a floppy-disk drive for reading in purchased software.* Popular Computing 9/83, p168 **[1976]**

hard dock, a joining of orbiting spacecraft by mechanical coupling. *Finally, they depressurized the command module, went to an open-cockpit condition to carry out a dramatic series of maneuvers—and achieved a hard dock.* Newsweek 6/4/73, p60 **[1971]** **—hard-dock,** *v.i.*: *Their frustrations were far from over. At least five attempts to redock with the space station after the futile repair work failed. The crew finally hard-docked late the first night by hot wiring the retract mechanism of the docking probe with a cable.* Science News 6/2/73, p353

hard drug, any drug that is considered physically as well as psychologically addictive, such as heroin and morphine. Compare SOFT DRUG. *. . . the maximum penalties are to be reduced for the use not only of cannabis but of heroin and other hard drugs as well.* Times (London) 3/13/70, p11 *The money spent on gambling increased fourfold. Hard-drug usage—heroin, cocaine—multiplied ten times over. Gradually the plot of history and the quirks of society grew nastier—Suez, Profumo, the 1966 Moors murder trial.* Time 7/6/70, p71 **[1966]**

hard-edge, *n.* a form of abstract painting characterized by the use of austere, sharply defined, geometric forms, often set off by strong colors. *Pink and mauve are the dominant colors in the recent works of a second-generation Abstract Expressionist, who has stuck to his guns through Pop, hard-edge and minimal.* Time 5/11/70, p2 *Post-painterly or "hard-edge" abstraction cleaned up the gooey mess and substituted neatly defined geometrical shapes in chaste combinations. Optical art, also, is*

neatly defined and geometrical in its pattern. NY Times Magazine 2/21/65, p12 **[1961]**

hard-edger, *n.* a painter of hard-edges. *Peter Hutchinson. . . Another hard-edger with genes from shaped canvases and minimal sculpture. . .* NY Times 11/25/67, p35 **[1967]**

hardened, *adj. Military use.* underground and especially protected against missiles or bombs by heavy concrete construction. *. . . . the Poseidon* [is] *effective against hardened targets; it can, therefore, be regarded as a first-strike weapon.* New Scientist 9/24/70, p619 *Hardened silos require a huge weight of explosives for their destruction.* Time 8/3/70, p11 **[1960]**

hardhat, *n. U.S.* **1** a construction worker. *When construction workers, some of them with crowbars, wade into a group of students, laying about them indiscriminately, not everyone joins in denouncing the hardhats.* Saturday Review 10/10/70, p20 **2** an outspoken conservative or reactionary, especially one who believes in suppressing opposing opinions. *. . . the hard-hats who commit violence and spread a disregard for personal rights are as fanatical as any bomb-thrower.* NY Times 7/7/70, p38 *Gradually, Gandhi's white-capped protégé became a hardhat on the Tibetan border question. . .* Time 6/14/71, p41 **[1970,** extended senses of *hardhat*, the protective metal hat or helmet worn by mining and construction workers (1953)]

hard line, rigid adherence to an attitude or policy, especially in politics. Compare I SOFT LINE. *French propaganda and French diplomacy encouraged the Biafrans to adopt a hard line and refuse a compromise.* NY Times 1/23/70, p46 **[1957]**

hard-line, *adj.* following a hard line; rigid and inflexible; uncompromising. *Albania also continued to express its opposition to the Soviet hard-line policy toward Czechoslovakia.* Americana Annual 1970, p72 *On the crucial issue of Vietnam, Clifford carries with him to the Pentagon an exceedingly hard-line philosophy.* NY Times Magazine 1/28/68, p20 **[1957]**

hard-liner, *n.* one who adopts or follows a hard line. Compare SOFT-LINER. *This campaign, and, even more, the present efforts of Dr. Husak to get rid . . . of some of the more clumsy "hard-liners" only confirms what was stated in my article: that the economic paralysis caused by the purges is depriving the Soviet Union of important supplies.* New Scientist 12/10/70, p470 **[1960]**

hard-lining, *adj.* taking a hard line. *The government of Premier Lon Nol* [of Cambodia], *under increasing pressure from the harder-lining elements in the National Assembly to strengthen the war effort, declared national mobilization.* Time 7/6/70, p24 **[1958]**

hard porn, hard-core pornography. Compare SOFT PORN. *Ain't Misbehavin' (Focus) is an extraordinary compilation film which relies heavily on naughty footage from private (sic) collections from 1907 to the Forties. Not hard porn, it nevertheless contains some surprisingly rude bits from the earliest days that have earned it, some 70 years later, an X certificate.* Listener 3/6/75, p314 **[1975]**

hard rock, the original hard-driving rock 'n' roll, played with a regular beat, often on electronically amplified instruments. Compare SOFT ROCK. *Miss* [Roberta] *Flack's success with "The First Time Ever I Saw Your Face" symbolized the competition offered hard rock by a softer, gentler sound.* 1973 World Book Year Book, p429 **[1967]**

hardscape, *n.* the manufactured or constructed objects in a designed landscape, such as paving stones, benches, and fountains. *Joseph O'Connor, head of New England Life's development operations, is treasurer for the design and rebuilding of Copley Square. The winning design has been selected, and funds to carry out the project are now being raised. "The hardscape budget alone," says O'Connor, "is $3 million."* Boston Globe 12/5/85 (page not known) **[1985,** from *hard* + land*scape*]

hard science, any of the natural or physical sciences, such as physics, chemistry, biology, geology, and astronomy. Compare SOFT SCIENCE. *On the campuses, the people in the 'soft sci-*

ences' are arguing with the people in the 'hard sciences.' The physical sciences and engineering bring in more research money. NY Times 6/2/68, p61 [**1966**]

hard scientist, a specialist in a hard science. *The numbers here differ from those previously published due to the increased number of total responses from "hard scientists" (569) now available due to questionnaires that came in late.* New Scientist 7/31/69, p235 [**1966**]

hardstuff, *n. U.S. Slang.* hard drugs collectively. . . *Janis* [Joplin], *along with her famous Southern Comfort, harbored a sometime penchant for downers and hardstuff.* NY Times 10/27/70, p45 *"They go to one of these hard-stuff parties. They get hooked—and they're done for. Done for! Done for!"* New Yorker 12/7/68, p62 [**1955**]

hardware, *n.* **1** the electronics, circuitry, and other physical components of a computer, often including equipment such as terminals, printers, disk drives, processing units, etc. Compare FIRMWARE, SOFTWARE. *The designer of a total computing system (i.e., one that includes hardware and the associated software, or programs) can choose either hardware or software implementation of the desired instructions. For example, it is possible to build . . . a piece of hardware with a wide instruction repertoire. . .* Van Court Hare, Jr., Introduction to Programming: A BASIC Approach, 1970, p153 [**1947**] **2** the physical equipment of a rocket, missile, or other space vehicle, as distinguished from its design plans, its fuel, etc. *The AAP* [Apollo Applications Program] *was a much-desired plum for space industries, since NASA's most likely choices for the future would be ones making use of existing Apollo hardware.* Science News 6/18/66, p490 [**1960**] **3** the physical equipment or facilities of any complex system. *While the Federal government, under the plan, would provide 90 per cent of the money for planning grants, research and pilot projects, . . . it will provide only 50 per cent of the costs of "hardware"—that is, new correctional centers, crime laboratories and police academies.* NY Times 2/12/67, pD7 [**1968**]

hard-wired, *adj.* **1** (of a computer circuit or component) wired directly to a computer. *The decoding of the instruction can be done in several ways. One method employs a "hard-wired" decoder, in which an array of gates selects a unique combination of active output lines for each possible combination of bits in the operation code.* Scientific American 9/77, p89 *The coordinates, speed, course and other data of other nearby vessels can also be entered, either via the keyboard or directly from another source via a hard-wired link.* New Scientist 11/2/78, p360 **2** Figurative use: *It appears to me that there are a long list of such human traits and that a large percentage of them are shared with primates. For example the facial expressions of human beings really appear to be hard-wired and in many instances comparable to those found in the chimpanzee.* NY Times 2/26/78, pD18 [**1969, 1971**] —**hard-wiring**, *n.: It is preeminently a clandestine device, hidden away, and so the first constraint the bug-maker meets is size. The next is the means of passing on the signal—radio transmission, carrier wave system, or directly by cable. In the trade, the use of an ordinary cable is known as "hard wiring."* New Scientist 11/23/78, p600

Hare Krishna ('hɑːre 'krɪʃnə), **1** the title of a Hindu chant or mantra dedicated to the god Krishna, adopted as the informal name of a sect (def. 2). *Paroled at 20, he* [David Hoyt] *drifted to the flowering world of San Francisco's Haight-Ashbury, where he became a member of the Hare Krishna cult and custodian of the Radha Krishna temple.* Time 8/3/70, p31 . . . *Senator Burdick introduced Ginsberg to his colleagues as the Pied Piper of the drug movement—from newspaper pictures of the poet chanting "Hare Krishna" at one of Leary's sellout psychedelic celebrations or marching across Sheridan Square with a big grin on his face and with a homemade sign saying "POT IS FUN!" pinned to his overcoat.* New Yorker 8/17/68, p36 **2** a member of the International Society for Krishna Consciousness, a sect devoted to the Hindu god Krishna; a follower or adherent of KRISHNA CONSCIOUSNESS. *The tangible outcome of the arranged marriage among the Hare Krishnas can be seen in certain temples in the Western U.S. In Los Angeles, seventy*

married devotees are raising fifty infants under five years old in Dallas, about two hundred Hare Krishna offspring aged five to fourteen from all over the world attend a special Sanskrit school. Harper's 5/74, p9 [**1967**, from Hindi, literally Lord Krishna]

harmolodic, *adj.* combining harmonies, melodies, and rhythms in new, unconventional ways. *Through the 1960's, Mr. Coleman formulated what he called the "harmolodic" system which broke down traditional harmonies and rhythms; he wrote chamber music, jazz tunes and a symphony, "Skies of America," which was recorded in 1972.* NY Times 6/30/85 pA44 —*n.* a harmolodic style or composition. *That word "harmolodic" gets hurled around a great deal these days, but Mr Coleman has never offered a really succinct definition. Basically, it is music that concentrates on counterpoint, with horns, guitars, and even electric basses all playing independent melody lines, often in different keys.* NY Times 9/9/81, pC7 [**1972** blend of *harmony* and *melodic*; invented by Ornette Coleman (1950's)] —**harmolodics**, *n.: On "Consume" and "Ska'd to Move," he's polyrhythmic, approximating the "harmolodics" of James "Blood" Ulmer and Ornette Coleman.* Washington Post 6/4/82, p27 KNITTING FACTORY, 47 E. Houston St., near Mulberry St. (219-3055)—A second-floor music and performing space, where people come to ponder the meaning of harmolodics. . .* New Yorker 10/12/87, p6

hartree ('hɑːˌtriː), *n.* a unit of energy in nuclear physics, approximately equal to 27.21 electron volts. *Orbital energy is given below each diagram in hartrees, and charge density is plotted in electrons per cubic bohr.* Scientific American 4/70, p58 [**1970**, named for Douglas R. *Hartree*, born 1897, English theoretical physicist]

Har-Tru ('hɑːˌtruː), *n. U.S.* a trademark for an artificial surface for tennis courts, made from crushed greenstone. Compare ASTROTURF, GRASSTEX. *Many American tennis enthusiasts, I am sure, have wondered if we were not too hasty in ripping up the grass courts used for the championships at Forest Hills and replacing them with Har-Tru.* New Yorker 10/9/78, p148 [**1976**, from *Hard* + *True*, a reference to the physical quality of such courts]

harvest index, the percent of total plant weight represented by the harvested product. *With many crops, particularly cereals, the trend is to increase the harvest index, that is, weight of harvested product/total plant weight of the crop, and this is of special significance for multicropping in that an overabundance of vegetative parts tends to delay maturity.* Nature 9/1/72, p9 [**1970**]

Harvey Smith, *British Slang.* a V-sign made with the palm of the hand inwards, regarded as a gesture of contempt. *One of the best things in this book by Desmond Morris and others is a photograph of Mrs. Thatcher on the occasion of some earlier election grinning all over her face and presenting a cheery Harvey Smith, presumably under the impression that she was giving a victory sign.* Manchester Guardian Weekly 5/20/79, p21 [**1972**, from the name of a show jumper who popularized it]

hash, *n. Slang.* hashish. *Should marijuana and hash (the leaf and resin of the cannabis plant) be subjected to severe penalties, while addictive drugs like alcohol and tobacco are passed by society?* Sunday Times (London) 4/4/71, p11 *Heroin was present in both envelopes. Or it might be a bag of marihuana or "hash," or even barbiturates.* Harper's 4/67, p36 [**1959**]

hashhead, *n. Slang.* a person who is addicted to hashish or marijuana. *"The hippies come here for the pot, of course," says a young visitor from New York—and indeed Morocco is a hashhead's delight.* Time 1/31/69, p42 [**1967**; see HEAD]

hashigakari (ˌhɑːʃiˌɡɑːˈkɑːriː), *n.* a bridgelike passageway over which performers enter or leave the stage in the Japanese No theater. Compare HANAMICHI. *By now one is used to the formalised stage, the raised rosewood platform, the pine-tree background, the hashigakari (or bridgeway) leading to a curtained doorway.* Manchester Guardian Weekly 6/16/73, p22 [**1967**, from Japanese, from *hashi* bridge + *-gakari* between two]

hash marks, *U.S. and Canadian.* the broken inbounds lines or markers on a football field. *The hash marks are used to position the ball on the playing field after it has been downed either out of bounds or too close to the boundaries to permit reasonable play. Moving the hash marks closer to the center of the field has given offensive players—particularly wide receivers and running backs—more room to maneuver, while the defenses have more ground to cover. Also, field-goal kickers now enjoy a better angle.* Time 10/16/72, p47 [**1967**, so called from their supposed resemblance to *hash marks* or military service stripes]

hash oil or **hashish oil,** tetrahydrocannabinol (THC), the active ingredient of marijuana and hashish. *Hash oil is hard to detect; it can be mixed with coffee or wine, and because it has no distinctive odor, it is often dabbed onto ordinary cigarettes and smoked in public with impunity.* Newsweek 9/11/72, p63 *Mr Salman said today that about 4,000 kilograms of the drug and 34 kilograms of hashish oil had been confiscated by the police in recent months and added that "the authorities have stepped up efforts to crack down on the hashish trade."* Times (London) 9/7/77, p6 [**1972**, so called because of its resemblance to motor oil]

hassle, *v.t. U.S. Informal.* to abuse or harass. *I'd like to be able to . . . wear my hair long without getting hassled.* NY Times 10/15/70, p47 *Jesus Christ loved, he took abuses and he would love some more. He wore long hair and a beard, and when they hassled him, he taught more love.* Time 4/6/70, p79 [**1966**, from earlier *hassle, v.i.,* to fight or quarrel (1951), from *hassle, n.,* a fight or struggle (1945), originally a U.S. dialectal word]

hat, *n. Especially U.S. Slang.* any bribe or illicit bonus, such as that offered as graft for protection against prosecution, or the extra money collected by the recipient rather than through a bagman. *The discussion about enlarging the staff turned on the question of whether the plainclothesmen should hire a civilian to make the monthly pickups from the gamblers. This finally was rejected because the policemen involved did not want to lose the $200 monthly bonus or "hat" for the dangerous job of making the pickups themselves.* NY Times 5/7/72, pD11 *The black market prices—what Greeks refer to as "the hat"—are the difference between what the government says the local butcher can charge for a piece of veal, and what the shopper actually has to pay for it. Some Athenians say that the hat is driving their household expenses up by 15% a year.* Time 2/19/73, p82 [**1971**, from the expression "buy yourself a hat" used in offering an initial bribe]

hatchback, *adj. U.S.* (of an automobile) having a hatch in the back on the sloping roof. *The basic list price of the Vega 2300 is $1,950, which (with federal excise tax and dealer preparation) comes out to $2,091 for a two-door sedan, $2,197 for a "hatchback" coupe, and $2,329 for a station wagon.* Time 9/21/70, p92 [**1970**]

hatter's shakes, a trembling of the muscles and limbs formerly found among workers in hatmaking and now attributed to mercury poisoning. See also MINAMATA DISEASE. *The features in chronic mercurialism are an inflammation of the mouth, muscular tremors—the famous hatter's shakes—and a characteristic personality change.* New Yorker 8/22/70, p68 [**1955**] ►Only the *OED* enters this term, in the form *hatters' shakes,* with a supporting quotation of 1902 from the British Medical Journal: "Muscular tremors ('hatters' shakes) are most often observed in those engaged in dusty post-carotting processes." Recent interest in the widespread occurrence of mercury poisoning, resulting from eating fish contaminated with mercury from industrial chemicals, has provided an explanation of the old idiom *mad as a hatter,* which, so far as we know, has never been satisfactorily explained before. The following quotations suggest the source of the idiom: *The bizarre mental symptoms of mercury poisoning gave rise to the phrase, "mad as a hatter," in the 19th century, when mercury compounds were used to treat felt in hatmaking.* Science News 4/18/70, p388

haut (ou), *adj.* having a high tone or style; high-class. *We who suffered the pangs of stretching out now hang loose, line up at the cinema, down an egg cream at the haut café, and, after hours, in copious time, enjoy a mellow joint with friends.* Harper's 10/71, p32 *In fact, I was green with envy under my gray cheeks. Here was a man of the* hautest *of haut-mondes. A fabulous winter vacationer on the slopes of Mount Sybaris.* NY Times Magazine 12/26/76, p4 [**1970**, abstracted from such phrases as *haut monde* and *haut ton,* ultimately from French *haut* high; compare obsolete *haut* high, haughty (OED 1430)]

havurah (xɑ:ˈvuːrɑ:), *n., pl.* **havurot** (xɑ:vuːˈrout), any of various informal Jewish fellowship groups formed, especially in colleges and universities in the United States, as an alternative to traditional, synagogue-centered activities and practices (often used attributively). *Each such group—there are now hundreds all over the U.S.—is a close-knit community that meets for prayer sessions, meals, classes and discussions on Judaism. While* havurah *members do not necessarily live together or pool their finances, they share an intense commitment to making religion part of everyday living.* Time 1/10/77, p57 [**1972**, from Hebrew *hābhurāh* fellowship]

hawk, *n.* a person who favors war or advocates military solutions in a conflict. Compare DOVE. *In our opinion, the general run of Americans—whether hawks or doves, or neither—are deeply preoccupied with the war.* New Yorker 1/13/68, p19 *Politicians in Washington have often cited the emotive words "Munich" and "Czechoslovakia" in recent years, but only to draw an analogy useful to the hawks on Vietnam.* NY Times 7/28/68, pD3 —*v.i.* to be or act as a hawk; be hawkish. *So in the early Seventies, with [Ronald] Reagan suddenly charging out of the West, hawking on the war, he may be able to play some of Nixon's older roles, talking about Victory, attacking No-win policies. . .* Harper's 2/70, p76 [**1962**, shortened from *warhawk,* a term originally applied in the United States to one who favored war with France during the diplomatic crisis of 1798 and later to one advocating war against England in 1811; the current term *hawk* first appeared in 1962 in connection with the Cuban missile crisis, to characterize those who advocated demanding from the U.S.S.R. that it remove its missiles from Cuba, in contrast to the DOVES, who favored a peaceable approach]

Hawking effect, *Astrophysics.* the simultaneous creation and absorption of particle-antiparticle pairs by a black hole or mini-black-hole. *Thus we have outlines of atomic physics, elementary particle physics, quarks, gauge theories, relativity, black holes, the wave-particle nature of light, gluons, gravitons, the Hawking effect, and a host of other weird and difficult concepts.* New Scientist 1/3/80, p30 [**1977**, named after Stephen W. *Hawking,* born 1942, British physicist who proposed the existence of mini-black-holes]

hawkish, *adj.* warlike; favoring war or advocating military solutions in a conflict. Compare DOVISH. *An article about W.W. Rostow, the most "hawkish" of the President's advisers on Vietnam, quoted Rostow as saying, "The duty of men is to prevent war and buy time."* New Yorker 2/24/68, p43 *His [President Kennedy's] second year was climaxed by the Cuban missile crisis, which he handled with firmness, but without the bluster of some of his hawkish advisers who pressed him to bomb and invade the island.* Harper's 12/66, p110 [**1965**]

Hawthorne effect, an improvement in the performance of workers, students, etc., resulting from the attention of researchers seeking means to achieve such an improvement. Compare HEISENBERG EFFECT. *In the Oak School experiment the fact that university researchers, supported by Federal funds, were interested in the school may have led to a general improvement of morale and effort on the part of the teachers. In any case, the possibility of a Hawthorne effect cannot be ruled out either in this experiment or in other studies of educational practices.* Scientific American 4/68, p23 [**1968**, named after the Western Electric Company's *Hawthorne* Works in Chicago, where experiments during the 1920's to improve working performance yielded this effect]

Hayflick limit, a natural limit to the lifetime of cells in a culture. *If the fibroblasts come from old tissue their potential for divid-*

ing in culture is much reduced: the average number of divisions declines by 0.20 for each year of the donor's life in human tissue. Leonard Hayflick of Stanford University, the man whose name has been given to this limited division potential (the Hayflick limit), believes the laboratory observations do have some relevance to the normal ageing phenomenon. New Scientist 11/29/73, p615 [**1971**, named after Leonard Hayflick, born 1928, an American microbiologist who discovered it]

haylage ('heilidʒ), n. partly dried hay stored in a silo; silage containing from 40 to 60 percent dry matter. However they function structurally, they always delight and instruct, and the book abounds in them. For example: —Adolph Oien's invention of the "free stall barn"; —how to make hay, haylage, and silage. Harper's 7/80, p81 [**1960**, from hay + silage]

hazardous waste, any waste material perilous to health, especially one having permanent damaging effects on the human body. The rules, about 2,000 pages long, set standards for landfill sites for hazardous wastes. In addition, a detailed "cradle-to-grave" manifest system to monitor hazardous wastes from the time they are generated, through shipping, to ultimate disposal is required by the regulations, which define "hazardous wastes" as those which are corrosive, explosive, ignitable, reactive, or toxic. 1981 Collier's Encyclopedia Year Book, p238 [**1978**]

Hazchem ('hæz,kem), n. British. a system of labeling containers of potentially dangerous chemicals by a special code to facilitate their safe handling or disposal in an accident. The immediate appeal of Hazchem is due to its simplicity and directness—it tells the fireman exactly what he wants to know. However, hopes that it would gain acceptance widespread enough to forgo legislation have been dashed. "The absence of specific and obligatory rules for all operators and hauliers is seriously weakening" the development of Hazchem, Bill Aston (Deputy Chief Constable of Cleveland Constabulary) told a conference. New Scientist 5/5/77, p262 [**1976**, from hazardous + chemical]

H-bomb, v.t. to bomb with a hydrogen bomb. . . . can we really believe that the GPO [General Post Office] tower in Tottenham Court Road would continue to function if London is H-bombed? New Scientist 12/31/70, p610 [**1964**, from H-bomb, n. (1950), patterned after A-bomb, n., v.]

HCS, abbreviation of human chorionic somatomammotrophin, a hormone that originates in the outermost membrane of the amniotic sac enclosing the fetus (chorion) and promotes growth, mammary development, and milk secretion. Later, the developing placenta produces a polypeptide hormone called human chorionic somatomammotrophin, or HCS. By and by the placenta produces this hormone in enormous quantities—about a gramme a day. This alone suggests the hormone is functional. But till now there has been no convincing explanation of its function. New Scientist 7/5/73, p4 [**1971**]

HDL, abbreviation of high density lipoprotein, a lipoprotein containing more protein than lipids and carrying excess cholesterol out of body tissues to the liver for excretion. Compare LDL and VLDL. Any cholesterol program should be directed, at least in part, toward raising the supply of these "good" cholesterol-disposing HDLs in the bloodstream, as opposed to the "bad" cholesterol-depositing LDLs. Time 11/21/77, p119 [**1974**]

head, n. **1** a drug addict. "Why don't she and I, Mr. Bech, smoke some marijuana together as a dry run? That way she can satisfy her female curiosity and I can see if we could stand a trip together. As I size her up, she's much too practical-minded to be a head; she just wants to make the sixties scene, and maybe to bug you." John Updike, Bech: A Book, 1970, p83 **2** a devotee; fan. . . . just how interested are people in film? It is assumed that the young think of nothing else, yet when Derek Hill organised an excellent collection of foreign films from the Counter Festival . . . in July, the cinema was nearly empty most of the time. . . What was it that kept these young film-heads away? Listener 10/22/70, p560 [**1936, 1955**, ab-

stracted from compounds such as hophead (an opium smoker 1911)]

head count, Informal. a census or poll. Some members of Congress did assume that the White House must have made a head count and found enough backing, at least in the Republican dominated Senate, to avoid rejection of the Saudi deal. Time 9/7/81, p10 It's bound to be a generalized figure, because it's impossible to take a detailed head count. NY Times 4/4/63, p10 [**1958**]

head counter, Informal. **1** a census taker. Official head counters now put the white-collar multitude around 30 million. Wall Street Journal 5/7/63, p1 **2** one who takes polls; a pollster. ". . . am afraid," said a Democratic head-counter recently, "that we have enough votes to override." NY Times 1/27/70, p42 [**1960**, from HEAD COUNT]

head end, a location in a cable television system where a central antenna receives, amplifies, filters, and sometimes changes the frequency of a signal before it is passed into the cable leading to local subscribers (often used attributively). Whatever the source, the signals go into the "head end," which is the master control station and nerve center of a cable system. . . . If the signals are exceptionally weak, they are usually boosted by a pre-amplifier so that the head-end equipment can process them satisfactorily. Scientific American 10/71, p22 [**1969**]

headhunt, Slang. —v.i., v.t. to recruit executives for a corporation. . . . the board felt that a good consulting firm, with a strong track record for executive "headhunting," could assist in the normally chaotic selection process. Atlantic 4/71, p42 . . . the new ex-Slater managing director Allan Baxter (head-hunted by K I M) wanted to carry out his own programme before coming back for consultation. Sunday Times (London) 11/2/69, p30 —n. an instance of headhunting. There must be a dozen or so institutions out there seeking the strength and the imagination Bennis offers. They should be grateful for getting a headhunt for free. Atlantic 6/71, p34 [**1966**]

headhunter, n. Slang. one who engages in headhunting, as a personnel agent or management consultant. . . . you're how and everything you do works and they're calling you for a job and the headhunters are crying for you. . . Time 6/22/70, p78 Julius Sakala is, temporarily at least, a municipal head-hunter. Times (London) 12/30/70, p13 [**1960**]

head restraint, a support for the head attached to the back of an automobile seat to prevent injury to the neck by a sudden jolt in a crash. The devices may have been made in Detroit, but they were mandated in Washington, and they join a formidable list of items forced on Detroit in the past few years: head restraints, shoulder belts, engine blow-by devices, side marker lights, locking steering columns, fire-resistant fabrics, impact-resistant fuel tanks. Newsweek 9/18/72, p76 [**1972**]

head shop, a shop selling psychedelic artifacts, such as glowing posters, sticks for burning incense, and paraphernalia used in drug taking. Also called PSYCHEDELICATESSEN. Local, state, and federal authorities are increasingly concerned about the growth of head shops that propagandize and glamorize the illegal drug industry among vulnerable youth. Christian Science Monitor 11/21/79, pB1 Before long, we were double-parked on St. Marks Place in a colorful swirl of head shops and ice cream stores, advertising such flavors as Acapulco Gold and Panama Red. Harper's 9/71, p92 [**1967**; see HEAD]

headteacher, n. British. a person in charge of a school. Hundreds of headteachers have been told that they could go on writing confidential reports on potential university entrants. Times (London) 3/5/70, p2 [**1958**] ▶Headteacher is the generic term for all heads of state schools, used often by officialdom and unions. Headmaster is considered a more prestigious term for the same job.

head-to-head, U.S. —adj. fought very closely. In the offensive line, Southern Cal's huge tackle Ron Yary earned at least a draw in a head-to-head battle with Green Bay's All-Pro defensive end, Willie Davis. Time 8/9/68, p56 The Democratic primary in Nebraska May 14 was to have been a head-to-head match between the two anti-Administration candidates, per-

haps driving the loser out. NY Times 5/3/68, p30 **—n.** a con-test or fight at very close quarters. *It* [the Sheridan tank] *cannot stand against any of the Russian tanks in a head-to-head, and its highly sophisticated mechanisms make it difficult to use in places like jungles or deserts, where, on the one hand, the engine exhausts become clogged and overheated and, on the other, the combination of sand and heat makes it intolerable to operate.* Atlantic 11/70, p65 [**1962,** patterned after *hand-to-hand, adj.* (OED 1836)]

head trip, *Slang.* **1** an informal psychological or exploratory excursion into the mind. *"Folie En Tête" is her own title for this book, and exactly right. A head-trip, lasting 180,000 words.* Sunday Times (London) 7/18/71, p26 *"*[Robert] *Crumb is creating a whole new way of thinking, a whole new head trip," says Gary Arlington. "People really relate to his stuff. It's like opening up your mind and seeing it in a mirror."* NY Times Magazine 10/1/72, p68 **2** to engage in a head trip. *Dr John Lilly did much of his celebrated dolphin research with US military money. When, however, he shifted from studying the dolphin mind to exploring the inner recesses of his own—head tripping to Americans—military interest in the man ought properly to have ceased.* New Scientist 7/19/73, p176 [**1971**]

head-up display, a secondary visual display of data relayed from instrument readings, projected on a windshield enabling a driver or pilot to keep the eyes on the course or path ahead. *Twelve Yorkshire police cars are currently testing head-up displays—projections of the car's speed onto the windscreen.* New Scientist 11/22/73, p546 *The other development, the head-up display, also enhances automatic-landing safety by helping the human pilot, having been brought down to the runway by electronics, to make the transition from instruments to the outside world by optically putting all essential instrument data in the windscreen.* Times (London) 9/4/78, pVII [**1960**]

headwork, *n.* the use of the head to propel the ball in soccer. *Oxford generally looked the more dangerous, partly because the clearances of their defenders went to their own forwards with greater regularity and partly because their headwork was also better directed.* Times (London) 12/10/70, p5 [**1965**]

health maintenance organization, an organization that provides subscribers with comprehensive health care for a fixed fee. *Abbreviation:* HMO *Health maintenance organizations can be a third option for the Medicare recipient. An HMO is a one-stop shopping center that offers a broad range of health services—including hospitalization, preventive care, diagnosis, and nursing—for a fixed monthly or yearly premium. We believe that the kind of care a good HMO provides can be ideal for older people.* Consumer Reports 1/76, p27 *Five years ago, President Nixon coined the term Health Maintenance Organization to describe prepaid health groups—those organized medical services that allow a family to pay one set fee for almost all medical care.* NY Times 5/17/76, p16 [**1971**]

health spa, a commercial gymnasium specializing in weight reduction. Also shortened to SPA. *Those who are not able to go to Belgium, to Wiesbaden, or to Bath, can nevertheless go to their local health spa. . . It may offer a pool, steam room, sauna, exercise equipment, massage room, and the like.* American Speech, Spring-Summer 1975, p29 [**1975**]

HEAO, abbreviation of *high-energy astronomy observatory,* any of a series of unmanned earth satellites that gather data on X-ray stars, gamma-ray bursts, and other astronomical phenomena, the first of which was launched in August, 1977. *HEAO-1, at 7,000 pounds (3,175 kg) the heaviest unmanned earth orbiting satellite ever launched, carried a new generation of experiments that dwarfed earlier rocket and satellite experiments.* Americana Annual 1978, p443 [**1971**]

hear, *v.t. U.S. Slang.* to understand or agree with. *Some slang improves an adjective . . . and some varies with inflection:* I *hear ya can mean "I understand," or "I agree". . . depending on the tone of voice.* NY Times Magazine 1/18/81, p8 *The down-filled women still wear cowl-necked sweaters and carry Louis Vuitton handbags. The down-filled people . . . regard "Saturday Night Live" and Steve Martin as funny. They say "I*

hear you," meaning "I understand what you're saying." Harper's 3/80, p65 [**1970**]

hearing-ear dog or **hearing dog,** a dog trained to alert a person who is deaf or hard of hearing to such significant sounds as a doorbell, smoke alarm, crying infant, or alarm clock. *Guide dogs for the blind are already a familiar sight, and in recent years a few deaf Americans have become owners of "hearing-ear dogs", which alert them to noises that they would not hear.* New Scientist 4/2/81, p12 *Representative Frederick W. Richmond, Democrat of Brooklyn, on Monday urged the adoption of a Federal program to train "hearing dogs" for the deaf and hard-of-hearing, patterned after Seeing-Eye dogs for the blind.* NY Times 2/22/78, pA5 [**1978,** patterned after *Seeing Eye dog* a guide dog trained to lead the blind]

heat, *n. U.S. Slang.* the police. . . . *out the door comes this great big porcine member of the heat, all belts and bullets and pistols and keys and flashlights and clubs and helmets.* New Yorker 7/19/69, p20 [**1966,** extended from the U.S. slang term for intense police activity, especially in the phrase *the heat is on*]

heat island, an industrial area or populated region in which the heat radiated is measurably greater than in the surrounding area. *The first report of the Royal Commission on Environmental Pollution mentions that temperatures are usually higher in urban areas than in nearby rural areas and that the warmth of the city helps to reduce space heating costs. These urban 'heat islands', as they have been termed, affect the distribution of atmospheric pollution, and geographers have pioneered their study.* Geographical 8/72, p787 [**1964**]

heat pipe, a pipe containing fluid to transfer heat from one end to the other by a difference in pressures without external pumping or supporting mechanisms. *Heat pipes—first developed for space applications . . . may soon be used by electronics engineers. These devices can transfer heat from a component such as a high power transistor or valve to an external heat sink* [device that absorbs heat] *with fantastic efficiency.* New Scientist 3/5/70, p461 [**1964**]

heat-seeking missile, a guided missile with an infrared device to home in on objects that radiate heat, such as aircraft engines and factory facilities. *In Guinea over the last eight weeks "Estrela" heat-seeking missiles have been used with some effect against the Portuguese air force.* Manchester Guardian Weekly 6/9/73, p7 [**1966**]

heave-ho, *v.i., v.t.* to heave or lift with force. . . . *the* [Congolese] *women who, apparently 12 months* [sic] *pregnant, nonetheless are constantly hauling and heave-hoing on this packing case of merchandise or that basket full of provisions.* Manchester Guardian Weekly 8/7/71, p17 *The distance from our court to the top of the hill was a full hundred yards of fairly steep incline and slippery footing, but the tires were chopped loose from the ground, and a groaning mass of men heave-ho'd the snow car up the ramp and onto the runway.* New Yorker 1/18/64, p84 [**1964,** from *heave ho!* the cry used by sailors when raising the anchor, etc.]

heavy, *adj. Slang.* important or serious. *"Marcuse is heavy stuff."* Time 8/17/70, p32 *Something serious is "heavy," something relaxed is "laid back."* Harper's 7/69, p60 **—n.** *Surfing Slang.* a very large wave. *We see them* [surfers] *in every size of wave, from the regular 4-ft. rollers off S. Africa to the house-size "heavies" off Hawaii, and their skill (and occasional accidents) are fascinating to watch.* Punch 3/6/68, pv [**1968**]

heavy-metal, *adj. Especially U.S.* of or relating to a type of rock music with a heavy beat and sometimes harsh amplified instrumental effects. *The next kings of that musical thunder known as heavy-metal rock might very well be an English rock quartet called Queen.* NY Times 1/18/76, pB17 *This is heavy-metal music with easy-listening inflections, rock fierce enough for the FM stations, flighty enough to fit right into TOP 40 AM radio.* Time 9/25/78, p76 [**1974,** partly from the association with the names of rock groups that popularized it (1964): *Led Zeppelin* and *Iron Butterfly;* partly from the amplified "metallic" guitar effects in the music]

heavy rail, of or belonging to a system of trains running as part of a conventional railroad system. Compare LIGHT RAIL. *Transit specialists generally consider heavy rail transit, such as the subways, surface and elevated trains of the New York City system, to be the best and most efficient way to move large numbers of people through heavily traveled corridors.* NY Times 9/13/77, p22 [**1976**]

heavy rock, another name for PROGRESSIVE ROCK. *Heavy rock remained a vital force. One of the most broadly accepted groups was Aerosmith, whose lead singer, Steve Tyler, was compared with Mick Jagger of the Rolling Stones.* 1977 World Book Year Book, p417 [**1973,** from HEAVY + ROCK]

hedge fund, *U.S.* an investment fund set up as a limited partnership for investing private capital speculatively. *A small hedge fund called, friends of mine who manage $2 million. They differ from mutual funds in the sense that they are very unregulated; operate with relatively little money; can go long, sell short, or write options. The managers of a hedge fund take 20 percent of the profits if there are profits.* Atlantic 6/71, p47 *The hedge funds, so-called, have been operating on borrowed money in order to concentrate the capital gains of their customers.* Harper's 11/69, p56 [**1968**]

hegemony or **hegemonism,** *n.* a Chinese Communist term for an expansionist foreign policy. *This became a central theme of Chinese pronouncements. The conflict in Vietnam could be seen as "resistance to hegemony." In 1972 Mao decreed: "Dig deep, store rice, never seek hegemony." He was surely referring to a presumed military threat from the United States, even as he was referring to the Soviets.* Daily News (New York) 2/4/79, p42 *He* [Vice-Premier Teng Hsiao-ping] *then flew to Thailand, Malaysia and Singapore, signing scientific exchange agreements and preaching endlessly against Soviet "hegemonism."* Time 1/1/79, p13 [**1970,** special use of *hegemony* "leadership or dominance of a state" as translation of Chinese (Pinyin) *baquanzhuyi,* literally, doctrine of domination; **1965** *hegemonism,* patterned after *imperialism*] ▸This use began to appear in American and Chinese joint communiqués after the establishment of trade and other relations between the two countries in 1971 (see CODE WORD and PING-PONG DIPLOMACY).

heightism, *n.* an attitude of contempt for or discrimination against short people. *Worst of all, we usually end up marrying a short man, thereby having to share the life of one of those less successful victims of heightism.* Time 10/25/71, pBI-1 [**1971,** patterned after *ageism, sexism, racism*]

heimish ('heimiʃ), *adj. Especially U.S. Slang.* cozy; friendly; informal. *The restaurant attracts this crowd not only because of its* heimish *cuisine but because of its five-man team of countermen, a couple of whom mainly provide countertalk entertainment and a couple of whom mainly provide food.* New Yorker 5/15/78, p28 [N.Y. Mayor] *Koch served as a street speaker then, and again four years later, developing a style that is more* haimish—homey—*than sophisticated or rousing.* Time 10/3/77, p23 [**1964,** from Yiddish, literally, homelike]

Heimlich maneuver ('haimlik), a first-aid procedure to dislodge food or some object from a person's windpipe. The rescuer embraces the choking victim from behind, beneath the rib cage, and presses a closed fist under the breastbone with a quick upward thrust. Compare HEIMLICH'S SIGN. See also CAFE CORONARY. *Frank Field's report on the Heimlich maneuver to help someone who is choking on food resulted in 300 similar letters citing life-saving instances. You see, on News Center 4 Frank does a lot more than just give weather reports.* NY Times 11/19/76, pC26 [**1975,** named after Henry J. *Heimlich,* born 1920, an American surgeon who devised the procedure]

Heimlich's sign, a proposed hand signal to indicate that one is choking on food. Compare HEIMLICH MANEUVER. *"Heimlich's sign" is a universal signal that the victim can use and that a rescuer can recognize to indicate that this accident has occurred. The victim grasps his neck between thumb and index finger of one hand to signal "I'm choking!"* Encyclopedia Science Supplement (Grolier) 1976, p229 [**1976**]

Heinz bodies, aggregates of hemoglobin visible in red blood cells in certain conditions. *The unstable haemoglobins are a group of well-defined haemoglobin variants associated clinically with haemolytic anaemia of varying severity. The nature of the amino-acid substitutions reduces the stability of the haemoglobin molecule, and this results in precipitation within the red cell and formation of characteristic inclusions called Heinz bodies.* Nature 11/17/72, p180 [**1970,** named after Robert *Heinz,* 1865-1924, German physician who first described them]

Heisenberg effect, a change in a subject under investigation due to the effect of the investigative process. Compare HAWTHORNE EFFECT. *No one does or can do the same things on stage that he does unobserved. It's the popularized Heisenberg effect: The act of observing inevitably changes the process under observation.* NY Times Magazine 5/15/77, p18 *Second, there is the possibility of a Heisenberg effect; the act of trying to outguess market psychology itself becomes a factor in the psychology and may invalidate the conclusion.* Times (London) 9/21/70, p20 [**1968,** named after Werner K. *Heisenberg,* 1901-1976, German physicist, in allusion to the *uncertainty* (or *indeterminacy*) *principle* of quantum mechanics developed by him in 1927]

heliborne, *adj.* carried or done by helicopter. *Man for man, the U.S. troops may lack some of their enemies' jungle skill, but the rapid availability of firepower and heliborne mobility have tipped the scales decisively in their favor.* Atlantic 10/66, p14 [**1963,** from *heli-* helicopter + *borne,* as in *airborne*]

helicity, *n. Nuclear Physics.* the direction of the spin of an elementary particle. *Depending on which way the spin turns, the particle* [neutrino] *can be compared to a left-handed or right-handed screw, and this combination of spin and forward motion is called helicity.* Science News 3/28/70, p318 *Helicity can only be defined for particles with non-zero spin angular momentum; and stated very simply, a particle has helicity + 1 if it is seen as spinning counter-clockwise while approaching an observer, while if the observer sees the particle as spinning clockwise, it has helicity* −1. New Scientist 3/19/70, p545 [**1958,** from *helic-* (for *helik-,* stem of Greek *hélix* spiral) + *-ity* quality or state]

helihop, *v.i.* to go short distances from place to place by helicopter. *At 3:35 p.m., the shuffling exercise routine in Mountjoy Prison was noisily disturbed when a helicopter suddenly settled in the yard, scattering prisoners in all directions. One Mountjoy warder thought it was a surprise visit from Defense Minister Patrick Donegan, who is fond of helihopping round the country.* Time 11/12/73, p74 [**1966,** from *heli-* helicopter + *hop*]

helilift, *v.t.* to transport by helicopter, especially in an emergency. *Almost immediately, 1,000 reinforcements were helilifted to the heights commanding the battered town.* . . Time 3/15/71, p24 [**1965,** from *heli-* helicopter + *lift,* as in *airlift*]

helipad, *n.* a landing and take-off area for helicopters. *Minutes later, two paratroop platoons from the 101st Airborne Division at nearby Bien Hoa landed on the embassy's rooftop helipad.* Time 2/9/68, p17 [**1961,** from *heli-* helicopter + *pad*]

heliskiing, *n.* skiing on high mountains reached by helicopter. *For the dedicated disciples of winter who follow the snow from continent to continent, heli-skiing is the ultimate experience and the top of the mountain is the last frontier.* Maclean's 1/9/78, p52 [**1976,** from *heli*copter *skiing*]

helium shakes or **helium tremors,** another name for HIGH-PRESSURE NERVOUS SYNDROME. *The high-pressure neurologic syndrome is indeed called "helium shakes" in diver's vernacular, but in truth has nothing to do with helium. The high pressure neurologic syndrome has been clearly shown to result from increased hydrostatic pressure. Indeed, helium tends to offset it, but inadequately.* Science News 5/29/76, p339 [**1970**]

helium speech, an unnatural, squeaky quality in the voice of undersea explorers, divers, etc., when communicating by telephone with the surface, due to interference by the helium gas contained in the pressurized mixture of gases breathed undersea to prevent nitrogen narcosis or "the bends." *There is an urgent requirement for speech converters to unscramble the extraordinary 'Donald Duck' noises of helium speech, and although these have been developed, they mostly at present require bulky equipment which has to be placed onboard the surface support vessel.* Science Journal 6/68, p25 [**1968**]

helper T cell, a T cell that bolsters the activity of B cells. *Studies of AIDS victims' blood revealed a harmful imbalance in the amounts of two varieties of T lymphocytes, a type of white blood cell. The two types of T cells perform opposite functions. Helper T cells, which normally make up 40 to 60 per cent of all T cells in the blood, boost immune activity. Another 15 to 30 per cent are suppressor T cells, which dampen immune activity. In AIDS patients, the situation is reversed, with suppressor T cells predominating.* World Book Science Annual 1984, p275 [**1978**]

helping profession, *U.S.* any profession, such as vocational guidance or occupational therapy, whose purpose is to help people improve their lives and cope with everyday problems. *If you are a social worker or a counsellor of some sort, you are a member of the* helping professions *and you say things like, "We want to study how government impacts on families." Forty percent of the delegates at these conferences are* helping professionals. *The other 60% are just plain folks, or grass roots delegates.* Daily News (New York) 6/12/80, p79 [**1980**]

hembar, *n.* a hybrid variety of barley developed in 1969 by the U.S. Department of Agriculture. *Hembar yields 15 to 35 per cent more grain than other varieties with similar climate and soil requirements.* World Book Science Annual 1969, p250 [**1968**, coined by Dr. Robert T. Ramage, research scientist of the U.S. Department of Agriculture in Arizona from arbitrary prefix *hem-* + *bar*ley]

hemiretina, *n.* half of the retina of the eye. *The Polaroid filters are arranged so that each eye receives a different image. Using a technique developed by Bela Julesz of the Bell Telephone Laboratories, the author presented one random-dot pattern to the right hemiretina of the right eye and a slightly different random-dot pattern to the right hemiretina of the left eye. In other trials the pattern was presented to the left hemiretinas.* Scientific American 3/73, p75 [**1970**, from *hemi-* half + *retina*]

He-Ne laser ('hi:'ni:), a laser that is activated by exciting a mixture of helium and neon gases. *The visible output of these He-Ne lasers is a coherent beam of monochromatic light at a frequency of 6328 angstroms.* Atlantic 6/71, p93 *The experiment raises anew the serious question of how to define the metre. The error of the NBS* [National Bureau of Standards] *result arises mainly from comparing the miserable standard of length, based on incoherent krypton radiation, with the He-Ne laser.* New Scientist 11/16/72, p376 [**1971**, *He-Ne* from *He,* symbol for helium + *Ne,* symbol for neon]

hepatitis A, the form of viral hepatitis occurring naturally through infection and often epidemic, formerly called *infectious hepatitis. The hope for a vaccine to hepatitis A may require isolation of the virus or, in the far distant futⁱ re, the use of recombinant techniques to clone the viral antigens in large quantities. Purcell says.* Science News 12/2/78, p392 [**1978**]

hepatitis B, the form of viral hepatitis transmitted by injection of contaminated blood or blood products, formerly called *serum hepatitis. At least two separate teams of investigators reported using recombinant DNA techniques to produce viral antigens (surface proteins recognized by antibodies) from the hepatitis B virus, which can then be used to manufacture a vaccine against the disease; these antigens cannot be harvested in sufficient quantities by other techniques.* 1981 Collier's Encyclopedia Year Book, p160 [**1978**]

hepatocarcinogen, *n.* a substance that causes cancer of the liver. *It is interesting that in the two most sophisticated parts of the world, Europe and North America, liver tumours are the least common, and so far no known experimental hepatocarcinogen has been unequivocally implicated in human liver cancer.*

New Scientist 8/30/73, p494 [**1972**, from *hepato-* liver + *carcinogen*]

hepatocyte, *n.* a cell of the liver. *Specific fluorescence was also found in the cytoplasm of spindle-shaped cells growing out from the original liver tissue and it was considered that these fibroblast-like cells phagocytosed the antigen produced by the hepatocytes.* Nature 1/25/74, p177 [**1972**, from *hepato-* liver + *-cyte* cell]

heptathlon (hep'tæθlɔn), *n.* a two-day competition for women in the Olympic Games, consisting of seven events that include the 100-meter hurdles, high jump, shot-put, and 200-meter run on the first day, and the long jump, javelin throw, and 800-meter run on the second day. *In the heptathlon (the most grueling event for a female athlete) she* [Jackie Joyner-Kersee] *set a world record with 7,291 points.* 1989 Collier's Encyclopedia Year Book, p87 [**1988**, from Greek *heptá* seven + *áthlon* exercise of skill; patterned after *pentathlon*]

herb, *n. U.S. Slang.* marijuana. *"My parents didn't make enough money. I used to burglarize places that had the stuff I wanted. I didn't like people feeling sorry for me." "Selling herb is the easiest life there is . . . until you get busted."* NY Times Magazine 10/23/77, p40 [**1977**, perhaps patterned after *weed* and *grass,* earlier (1930's) slang terms for marijuana]

Herbig-Haro object ('hərbig'ha:rou), any of a number of small bright nebulas believed to be associated with the early stages of stellar formation. Compare YSO. *Herbig-Haro objects are another of the many curious classes of objects in the sky. Small, nebular and reddish, they have spectra consisting of emission lines of various elements with a very weak continuous spectrum in the background. Efforts to explain what they are have not adequately fit the data, but some astronomers have suggested that Herbig-Haro objects may be very early phases of stellar evolution.* Science News 10/28/78, p296 [**1972**, named after George *Herbig,* an American astronomer, and Guillermo *Haro,* a Mexican astronomer, who first discovered such objects]

hereditarian, *adj.* maintaining that individual traits are determined chiefly by heredity. *Eysenck shows his bias and wastes time by calling the second type of theory hereditarian and the third type environmentalist.* Manchester Guardian Weekly 6/26/71, p11 *. . . current studies do not support either an "environmentalist" or a "hereditarian" interpretation of differences in intelligence. . .* Saturday Review 11/16/68, p96 [**1966**, adjective use of the noun *hereditarian,* in use since the mid-1800's]

hermatype, *n.* a coral that forms reefs. *It should be noted that there are two kinds of stony corals: those that build true reefs and those that do not. The reef-building corals—called hermatypes from the Greek* hermatos, *"mound"—contain within the inner tissue layer a symbiotic alga that speeds the calcification process.* 1977 Britannica Yearbook of Science and the Future, p205 [**1976**, back formation from HERMATYPIC]

hermatypic, *adj.* reef-building. *He* [Thomas F. Goreau] *experimentally demonstrated the supreme significance of the endozoic algae (zooxanthellae) present within all hermatypic corals in the necessarily high rate of calcification possessed by these reef builders.* Times (London) 5/7/70, p15 [**1963**, from Greek *hérma* reef + English *-typic* of the type]

heroin baby, the infant of a woman addicted to heroin, usually born prematurely and with a craving for the drug. Compare BOARDER BABY. *At Kings County Hospital in Brooklyn, one in every 50 births is reported as a heroin baby. No one knows how many others are not diagnosed or reported. In 1971, the births of more than 550 heroin babies were recorded by the Department of Health in New York City.* NY Times Magazine 1/9/72, p18 [**1972**]

he/she, he or she (used as a pronoun of common gender when the antecedent may be either male or female). *The author rejects volunteer work as merely a way "to fill in the time" and claims that he/she needs "real work."* NY Times 9/5/77, p17 *Parents are wise not to make flat statements telling the teen what he/she should or should not do and letting it go at that.* New York Post 3/9/79, p24 [**1976**, patterned after combinations such as *and/or*] ▶ Recent concern over sexism in language causes many writers to avoid using *he* as a genderless antecedent (e.g. "If a person wishes to succeed, *he* must work hard"). The most common replacement is "he or she."

According to some writers, the search for a genderless pronoun to replace *he* where "he or she" is meant is unnecessary and wasteful, since we already have such a pronoun. The word is the plural form, *they*. In the following passages, two authors, separated by a span of 20 years, argue for its acceptance: *The English language most needs . . . one word to mean "he or she." Nobody is likely to go as long as an hour without encountering this need. We have the plural "they" to apply to the genders indiscriminately; why must we be deprived of an equivalent singular word? "Everybody," says the average person defiantly, "should speak as they please." "Wrong!" thunder the grammarians. "The antecedent 'everybody' being singular, you must say '. . . as he or she pleases.'" So again . . . we have a Hobson's choice.* NY Times Magazine 9/11/55, p27 *In the stubborn case of the masculine generic pronoun, the candidate that seems most likely to succeed is a word already in wide use,* they. *Despite grammarians' efforts to restrict it to plural antecedents, they is already commonly used both in speech and writing as an alternative to the awkward "he or she." What critics of this usage seem not to know, or decline to acknowledge, is that* they *and its inflected forms have been used for centuries by reputable writers from Shakespeare ("Everyone to rest themselves") to Shaw ("It's enough to drive anyone out of their senses") to Scott Fitzgerald ("Nobody likes a mind quicker than their own").* Casey Miller and Kate Swift, Words and Women, 1976, p135

hesiflation (ˌhezəˈfleiʃən), *n. Economics.* a condition of halting, spasmodic growth accompanied by high inflation. Compare BOTTLENECK INFLATION, SLUMPFLATION. *During 1977 the world economy suffered through sporadic periods of four different types of economic conditions: stagflation (slowing "real" growth and accelerating inflation), hesiflation (a stuttering economic growth pattern combined with strong inflationary pressures), disinflation (a selective slowing down but not elimination of inflation), and deflation (sharp price declines in certain economic sectors).* Britannica Book of the Year 1978, p644 [**1978,** from *hesi*tation + in*flation*]

hetero, *adj.* attracted to members of the opposite sex; not homosexual. *The German boy is formal, rather earnest and inclined to homosexuality. The Englishman is a cocky landowner, romantic at heart and hetero.* Punch 12/31/69, p1101 **—***n.* a person who is hetero. *Now perhaps it is psychologically or even medically true that homosexual persons, in the nature of their persuasion, are somehow less trustworthy and stable than heteros.* Harper's 11/69, p108 [**1933, 1957,** shortened from *heterosexual, adj., n.*]

heterofil ('hetərəfil), *adj. British.* (of a synthetic fiber or fabric, especially nylon) composed of more than one type of filament to reduce static electricity, improve resistance, etc. *A British fibre producer announced plans to make textiles by the spun-bonded process, using heterofil fibres of his own invention.* Britannica Book of the Year 1974, p377 [**1968,** from *hetero-* other, different + *fil*ament]

heterojunction, *n.* another name for HETEROSTRUCTURE. *A heterojunction comprises a layer of gallium-aluminum-arsenide over gallium-arsenide leads. It serves to reduce the size of the region in which electronic interactions take place, thus reducing the operating current and, hence, the heat generation.* 1971 Britannica Yearbook of Science and the Future, p185 *Heterojunctions can be made between different semiconducting materials with the same or different conductivity types.* Scientific American 7/71, p36 [**1960**]

heteronuclear RNA, a form of ribonucleic acid (RNA) found in the nucleus of mammalian cells. *In recent years, it has become apparent that in mammalian cells the appearance of messenger RNA is preceded by the synthesis of a "giant" species of RNA, called heteronuclear RNA (or HnRNA), which is confined to the nucleus. The role of HnRNA is still unclear; it may be concerned with events taking place strictly within the nucleus, or it may be the precursor of messenger RNA (or it may be*

both). New Scientist 6/8/72, p560 [**1971,** special application in biology from earlier use in chemistry (1900)]

heterophobia, *n.* fear or dislike of members of the opposite sex. Compare HOMOPHOBIA. *. . . there is strong evidence that many homosexuals suffer from a condition referred to as heterophobia—or fear of the opposite sex.* Sunday Times (London) 5/9/71, p8 [**1971,** from *hetero-* other + *phobia*]

heterosex, *n.* the condition of being heterosexual (attracted to members of the opposite sex); heterosexuality. Compare HOMOSEX. *Although this alliance too has its ideological implications—it is presumably what heterosex would be like if all the pressures of role-playing were removed from men and women—it fails, and its failure comprises the central dramatic development of the story.* NY Times 1/19/78, p26 [**1972**]

heterosexist, *adj.* discriminating against homosexuals. *At least one heterosexist assumption expressed in Signe Hammer's article should not pass unquestioned. There are some of us who as daughters competed with Daddy to possess Mommy, and who later in life competed with other men in the search for lovers or wives.* Ms. magazine 1/79, p4 [**1979,** blend of *heterosexual* and *sexist*]

heterostructure, *n.* a semiconducting device made up of several different types of semiconductors, used in lasers (often used attributively). Also called HETEROJUNCTION. *Minute sandwich-like "heterostructures" composed of two or more different semiconducting materials show great promise as cheap, efficient carrier-wave generators for use in mass communications.* Scientific American 7/71, p32 *The new laser, a double heterostructure diode, employs four thin alternating layers of gallium aluminum arsenide and gallium arsenide.* Science News 9/12/70, p219 [**1970**]

hexadecimal, *adj.* using the decimal number 16 or its equivalent as a base, especially in computer arithmetic systems. *The hexadecimal numeral system uses the base 16, as contrasted with the base 10 of the decimal system and base 2 of the binary system.* Encyclopedia Science Supplement (Grolier) 1971, p143 [**1954,** from *hexa-* six + *decimal*]

hexosaminidase (ˌheksəsəˈminəˌdeis), *n.* either one of a pair of enzymes, a deficiency of which causes various degenerative diseases of the central nervous system. *The Baltimore program owes its origin to several recent scientific discoveries in the field of molecular biology. One was the identification of the enzyme hexosaminidase-A, the lack of which causes Tay-Sachs disease.* Time 9/13/71, p40 [**1969,** from *hexosamine* an amine derivative of a hexose + *-id* related to + *-ase* enzyme]

HGH, abbreviation of HUMAN GROWTH HORMONE. *HGH could be a boon to nursing mothers. Twenty-two Mexican women who complained of insufficient milk secretion were given daily injections of HGH for a week. All of their babies recorded significant weight gains during the period. . .* Time 1/18/71, p23 *. . . HGH is used to treat dwarfism, which occurs in about 20,000 individuals in the United States.* Science News 12/20/69, p570 [**1959**]

HHS, abbreviation of *Health and Human Services,* a department of the U.S. Government. *In May U.S. President Jimmy Carter formally inaugurated the Department of Health and Human Services (HHS), a successor to the Department of Health, Education, and Welfare. Subsequently the HHS announced a two-year program to assess new medical technologies on the basis of their "social consequences" to determine if they should be funded under Medicare and Medicaid. The first assessment would cover heart transplants.* Britannica Book of the Year 1981, p420 [**1980**]

Higgs boson or **Higgs particle,** *Physics.* a hypothetical particle with a spin of 0, whose existence is assumed by the Weinberg-Salam theory. *Subatomic particles theoretically acquire mass by interacting with particles called Higgs bosons. No such particle has ever been observed, however.* World Book Science Annual 1987, p301 *One still unverified prediction of the standard model is the existence of a particle more massive than the W or Z, the so-called Higgs particle, which is responsible for the breaking of the simple underlying symmetries of the* *model*. 1986 Britannica Yearbook of Science and the Future, p367 [**1974**, named after Peter W. *Higgs*, a British physicist who first proposed it in 1964]

Higgs meson, another name for the HIGGS BOSON. *Higgs mesons, an exotic class of new particles as massive as atomic nuclei, will be the physics of the next decade . . . The role of the Higgs mesons has been played down—except at a highly abstract level. For although in theory they orchestrate the symmetry break-up Higgs mesons are not easily seen. They are likely to be very heavy (7 to 100 GeV) and will interact only weakly with ordinary matter.* New Scientist 2/17/77, p381 [**1974**]

high, *adj*. **be high on**, to be excited about; be especially fond of. *. . . Almond goes for obsessions and fatalities and an elliptical style—he's very high on portents.* New Yorker 12/12/70, p177 *'Well, the word is going round,' he* [a press agent] *says, 'that Zanuck is very high on you just now.'* Manchester Guardian Weekly 5/23/70, p15 [from the phrase *be high on* be under the influence of a narcotic drug (OEDS 1932)]

high camp, sophisticated use of the artistically banal or mediocre. Compare LOW CAMP. [Michael] *Sahl may have actually used a piece by Ernst, de Bériot, or one of the early nineteenth-century boys. That would make his score very high camp indeed.* Harper's 9/69, p34 *What we don't learn here is that Joan Crawford movies are now a symbol of High Camp . . .* Atlantic 11/68, p142 *We'll pay even more for 'Peyton Place'. And in return they* [our American friends] *will buy that appalling spy thriller Bernard Goldblatt describes as the epitome of high camp.* Listener 6/13/68, p770 [**1954**, from *high* great or extreme + CAMP]

high five, *U.S.* an informal gesture of greeting or congratulation in which two people slap the raised palms and fingers of their hands together. *One does not ask for a high five . . . the participants must know intuitively when an event worthy of a high five has occurred.* NY Times Magazine 12/18/88, p18 [**1980**]

high-level, *adj*. intensely radioactive. Compare LOW-LEVEL. *The AEC has 80 million gallons of liquid waste at their defence establishments in Hanford, Washington; Idaho Falls, Idaho; and Savannah River, Georgia. The waste is temporarily in ground-level tanks but the AEC hopes to store the high-level waste in geological formations, other than salt, which are located directly beneath the establishments.* New Scientist 3/16/72, p589 [**1971**]

high-level language, a computer programming language which employs terms and grammar often found in the vocabulary of the user. *A variety of computer languages enable the computer and the user to "communicate" with each other. The most popular high-level language for home-computer use is BASIC (an acronym for Beginners All-purpose Symbolic Instruction Code). Although not the most powerful language, its English instructions are relatively simple to master.* 1978 Collier's Encyclopedia Year Book, p205 [**1964** *high-level programming language*]

highlighter, *n*. a cosmetic used to highlight or emphasize facial features. *The natural look became the big thing, but it was not natural to produce—you had to learn how and where to put all the new subtly coloured highlighters, shadows, blushers and how to handle the battery of brushes that went with them.* Times (London) 10/22/70, p16 [**1970**]

high-pressure nervous syndrome, a condition of nausea, dizziness, and tremors often experienced by deep-sea divers, thought to be caused by the effects of respiration of a helium-oxygen mixture under high pressure. Also called HELIUM SHAKES. *Commercial divers can now descend to 1,000 feet by breathing a helium-oxygen mixture, but using this mixture also exposes them to the high-pressure nervous syndrome, characterized by mental deficits and trembling hands. Adding nitrogen to this breathing mixture can reduce the dangers of the syndrome.* Science News 11/6/76, p296 [**1973**]

high profile, an attitude or position that is direct, open, and emphatic; a conspicuously clear-cut stance. Compare LOW PROFILE. *Following his inauguration, the President adopted what*

in current terminology might be called a fairly "high profile" on Biafran relief. Atlantic 6/70, p6 [**1970**, patterned after LOW PROFILE]

high-rise, *adj*. **1** very tall; multistory. *Corbusier proposed to stack people vertically in high-rise towers so that the surrounding land could be freed for parks and playgrounds.* Time 10/23/64, p55 **2** raised up; elevated. *High-rise shoes run the gamut of style, color and height.* Time 8/21/72, p46 *"High-rise" handlebars, which force a small child to steer with elbows at chinlevel, and the long, narrow "banana" seats, which invite additional passengers, are major contributors to instability—and may cause additional accidents.* Reader's Digest 8/74, p38 —*n*. a high-rise building (often used attributively). Also spelled HI-RISE. Compare LOW-RISE. *"We're abating taxes on the land, we're not going so heavy for high-rises. Nobody will be ashamed to live in the houses we're building."* Harper's 8/68, p39 *The typical high-rise terrace does not seem like much of a blessing at first glance. But no matter how mingy, charmless, wind-torn and useless these shelves-in-the-sky might appear, they are potential sources of year-round luxury and additional living space.* NY Times Magazine 2/17/80, p68 [**1953** for adj.; **1963** for noun]

high-riser, *n*. *U.S.* See the quotation for the meaning. *Demand rose to new heights in the mid-1960s with the introduction of high-risers—those small-wheeled children's bikes with elongated "banana" seats, tall "ape-hanger" handlebars, and moderate $30-$50 price tags.* Time 6/14/71, p60 [**1971**]

high-tech, *n*. **1** a style of design or interior decoration that uses objects and articles normally found in factories, warehouses, restaurant kitchens, etc., or that imitates the stark functionalism of such equipment. Also spelled HI-TECH. *High-tech, in case you haven't heard, is the tag line for a home furnishings trend that's catching on fast. It's an interior design style that uses utilitarian industrial equipment and materials, out of context, as home furnishings.* Daily News (New York) 2/11/79, p8 **2** Attributive use: *A cultural and administration center in construction now by Vasconi and Pencreac's is a far more sophisticated building, but its version of the current "high-tech" vogue of mechanical effects, with its brightly colored metal panels, has little to do with anything else around it.* NY Times Magazine 11/19/78, p168 [**1978**, coined by Joan Kron and Suzanne Slesin, American interior decorators, from *high*-style *tech*nology]

high-technology, *adj*. of or relating to advanced, highly specialized, and sophisticated technology. Compare LOW-TECHNOLOGY. *High-technology goods such as computers, aircraft and electronics comprise the most vital part of the U.S. export mix.* Newsweek 2/19/73, p61 *A five-year study by the Commerce Department of six "mature" corporations (such as General Motors and Bethlehem Steel), five "innovative" companies (including Polaroid and IBM) and five "young high-technology" firms (among them, Marion Labs and Digital Equipment) turned up some telling figures.* Time 10/2/78, p63 —*n*. Usually, **high technology.** advanced, highly specialized, and sophisticated technology, involving extensive research and development. *Professor Jewkes went on to argue that the only thing that is "high" about high technology is the level of risk involved. High technology is technology that private companies will not finance because they cannot see a reasonable return on their investment.* Nature 11/10/72, p66 [**1967**]

high-temperature superconductor, any of a class of nonmetallic mineral compounds that can conduct electric current with no resistance at temperatures above 77 Kelvin (the boiling point of liquid nitrogen) or higher. *The new high-temperature superconductors . . . may revolutionize various technologies by allowing electricity to flow without losses and without much cooling—making magnetically levitated trains feasible, for example.* Science News 12/19-26/87, p390 [**1986**]

high-voltage, *adj*. high-powered; dynamic. *Her* [Nadine Gordimer's] *principal problem, never really overcome, is how to join a low-key character to high-voltage politics without diminishing interest in either. Bray is too often a laboriously illustrated abstraction of honor and decency whom Miss*

Gordimer attempts to quicken with some peculiarly imprecise and subjective imagery. Time 11/16/70, p103 [**1954**]

hijack, *n.* the act or crime of stealing or taking over by force a vehicle in transit, especially an airplane. Compare SKYJACK. *Michael said they were well looked after during the hijack but is was a frightening experience because the guerrillas filled the cockpit with explosives.* Times (London) 9/14/70, p4 [**1968,** noun use of *hijack, v.* (OEDS 1923)]

HILAC ('haɪˌlæk), *n.* acronym for *Heavy Ion Linear Accelerator,* a machine for accelerating ions of heavy particles, such as those of carbon and helium, to velocities capable of initiating nuclear reactions. *The rebuilt HILAC . . . at Berkeley* [California] *is also due for operation in 1972. It is expected to produce viable beams of particles as heavy as uranium.* New Scientist 7/2/70, p8 [**1956**] ►*HILAC* has the appearance of having the ending *-ac* (or *-AC*) that is used in the names of computers (*ENIAC, SEAC, UNIVAC*), in which it stands for Automatic Computer. Actually, the ending in *HILAC* is *-LAC,* for Linear *Ac*celerator, its linearity being what distinguishes it from the *-tron* type of circular accelerators, such as *cyclotron, bevatron, synchrotron.*

Hilbert space, *Mathematics.* a space with an infinite number of dimensions generalized from ordinary or Euclidean space. *A special kind of Banach space called Hilbert space had the property that numerous splittings of a desirable kind existed.* Britannica Book of the Year 1972, p447 [**1964,** named for David Hilbert, 1862-1943, a German mathematician]

him/her, *Especially U.S.* him or her (used as the objective case of HE/SHE to indicate common gender). *I could not help children if I did not believe that every child is as positive as his/her unique life situation allows him/her to be.* NY Times 10/17/77, p28 [**1977**]

hindcast, *v.i.* to provide weather information based on the record of past atmospheric conditions. Compare BACKCAST. . . . *Mayer is gearing up to provide weather information to offshore drillers. By "hindcasting" from historical data, he says the company can tell a potential offshore bidder, for example, how fierce the worst storms will be at projected drilling sites.* Forbes 12/15/75, p66 [**1959,** patterned after *forecast*]

Hinglish, *n.* a blend of Hindi and English spoken in India. . . . *now that the British-born teachers have gone home, English is on its way to becoming a native language—or, rather, native languages. (One native language has already been given the name Hinglish. It uses English parts of speech for more complicated functions, as in this Hinglish sentence: "Dekho great democratic institutions kaise India main develop ho rahi hain," which in English is "See how the great democratic institutions are developing here in India.")* New Yorker 9/9/67, p96 [**1967**]

hip, *n. U.S. Slang.* the condition of being alert or wise to what is new, smart, stylish, etc. *Grooviness* [at the discothèque "Yellowfinger's"] *merges with aplomb, and hip attains a state akin to quiet well-being.* New Yorker 9/19/70, p7 [**1965,** noun use of *hip, adj.,* alert, informed, up-to-date (OEDS 1904)]

hip-hugger, *adj.* clinging to the hips. See also HIP-HUGGERS. *There are separates, too, such as long jackets, stovepipe hip-hugger trousers, very full shorts, and box-pleated skirts that hook up with bridle bits of silver metal.* New Yorker 8/26/67, p82 [**1962**]

hip-huggers, *n.pl.* trousers that start about an inch and a half below the waistline and cling closely to the hips. *Knickers and gauchos, hip-huggers, bellbottoms and jeans—all are currently outselling dresses of any length.* Time 1/11/71, p38 [**1965**]

hippie or **hippy,** *n.* a person who breaks away from conventional society, espousing complete freedom of expression, typically by wearing unconventional clothes and letting the hair go ungroomed, and maintaining a philosophy of love and fellowship. Hippies often live in communes and engage in free love and the free use of drugs. Compare FLOWER CHILD, YIPPIE. *A few wear the garb of hippies—beards, beads, jeans, long gowns— but most are simply young men and women dressed for midsummer comfort.* NY Times 8/6/68, p25 *Robert Morley, playing a retired General, reacts to his children's strange behaviour*

by becoming a hippy himself and finally living up a walnut tree. Punch 3/6/68, pvi —*adj.* of, relating to, or characteristic of hippies. *Almost every newspaper account emphasized the hippie dress and hair, yet I don't think more than a small fraction of the population there affected that style.* Atlantic 1/68, p39 [**1966,** originally (1950's) "a person who is very or overly hip" (i.e., excessively eager to be ahead in the latest styles, extremely unconventional), from *hip, adj.,* alert, informed, up-to-date, + *-ie* or *-y,* diminutive suffix]

hippiedom, *n.* the realm or world of hippies; hippies as a group. *All in all* Hair [a musical] . . . *seems to be a truer and fairer representation of hippiedom than anything the theater has offered so far.* Saturday Review 1/13/68, p95 [**1967**]

hippiness or **hippieness,** *n.* the quality or condition of being a hippie. *You can make sense out of a* [rock] *group like Exodus— with their veneer of Dutch hippieness they bring to mind the Indonesians who waltzed around the Rembrandtsplein* . . . Manchester Guardian Weekly 7/24/71, p15 [**1967**]

hippyism or **hippieism,** *n.* adherence to hippie values, practices, and style. *Oppressed by a hippyism which seemed, in its elected rags, to mock the peasants in their enforced rags, I put on a collar and tie (the first ever seen in Deya) and spoke on Shakespeare, the ambitious, the money-getter, the ultimate bourgeois.* NY Times 12/11/70, p47 [**1967**]

hip-shooting, *adj. U.S.* haphazard, reckless, or impulsive. *"Structuralism" is an umbrella-word if ever there was one, and Dr. Martin makes it cover a number of dim definitions. Under the umbrella he delivers a great many hip-shooting generalizations about American culture, America today, the incompatibility between American and Christian directions, etc.* Saturday Review 4/8/72, p61 [**1968,** from the phrase *shoot from the hip* (figurative use) act or speak recklessly or impulsively]

hire, *n. Informal.* a person who is hired; wage earner; employee. *To cut labor costs, Crandall introduced a two-tier wage system under which younger hires were paid less than veteran workers.* Time 10/16/89, p52 [**1978,** extended from the sense of act of hiring (OED 1615)]

hi-rise, *n.* another spelling of HIGH-RISE. . . . *atop the hi-rise treble-glazed flats that fringe Regent's Park, company directors nudge their mistresses on to the balconies of £50,000 penthouses to admire the view* . . . Punch 5/7/69, pviii [**1968**] ►*Hi-rise* is an example of the use of the phonetic spelling *hi* instead of *high.* This spelling has wide currency in such words as *hi-fi* (for high-fidelity), *hifalutin,* and (chiefly in the U.S.) *hijinks.*

his/her, *Especially U.S.* his or her (used as the possessive form of HE/SHE to indicate common gender). . . . *the author's suggestions regarding what needs to be researched about est, for example, effects on the trainee's sense of responsibility, his/her freedom from resentment, "righteousness" and domination, and his/her flexibility in points of view.* Psychology Today 11/78, p147 [**1977**]

Hispanic, *n. U.S.* a Spanish-speaking person of Latin-American origin or descent, living in the United States. *The 68-person unit includes twelve blacks, twelve Hispanics, and two women; all of them . . . can be called instantly when a hostage action develops.* Newsweek 6/25/74, p90 [**1972,** noun use of the adjective (1897)]

Hispano, *adj., n.* another name for HISPANIC. *About 15 per cent of Denver's students are black and another 20 per cent are Hispano* (the local term for those with Latin-American roots). *Most of the blacks live in central or northwestern Denver. The Hispanos are also concentrated in a few areas.* NY Times Magazine 11/19/72, p41 [**1972,** short for *Hispano-American* (1900), originally applied to the descendants of Spaniards living in the southwestern U.S.; later (1960's) extended to include Mexican-Americans of the same area]

histidinemia (ˌhɪstədɪ'niːmiːə), *n.* a hereditary disorder associated with a high level of the amino acid histidine in the blood and characterized by lowered growth rate and increased susceptibility to infection. *In humans, physicians disagree as to the ef-*

fect of the biochemical abnormality. At first it appeared to be associated with mental retardation and speech defects, but now many human geneticists believe histidinemia produces no demonstrable effect on the nervous system. Science News 2/5/77, p86 [**1967,** from *histidine* (coined as German *Histidin* in 1896, from Greek *histion* tissue, web) + *-emia* blood condition (from Greek *haima* blood)]

histocompatibility antigen, any of various proteins in the blood that stimulate rejection of foreign tissue, used as markers to determine genetic compatibility between different tissues for a successful graft or transplant. Compare HLA. See also H-Y ANTIGEN. *At the root of the rejection problem in transplantation surgery are the histocompatibility antigens, the cellular markers which label the grafted tissue as foreign and lead to its attack by the host's immunological defence mechanism.* New Scientist and Science Journal 6/24/71, p733 [**1969,** from *histocompatibility* (OEDS 1948), from *histo-* tissue (from Greek *histós* web) + *compatibility*]

histocompatible, *adj.* exhibiting compatibility of graft tissue. *Adoptive transfer of autoimmune encephalomyelitis between histocompatible guinea pigs has been regularly used recently to elucidate the mechanisms of autoimmune diseases.* Science 3/1/68, p995 [**1964**]

histoincompatibility, *n.* incompatibility of graft tissue; graft rejection. . . . *these animals have virtually no immunological reactivity, so we felt confident that our test would not be complicated in any important way by histoincompatibility reactions between cells and hosts.* New Scientist and Science Journal 7/8/71, p90 [**1948, 1971**]

Histosol ('histə,sɔːl), *n.* (in U.S. soil taxonomy) any of a group of wet soils consisting mainly of organic matter such as forest litter and plant residues. *Most of the soils formerly called Intrazonal are included in the orders of Vertisols, Inceptisols, and Histosols.* McGraw-Hill Encyclopedia of Science and Technology 1971, p489 [**1971,** from *histo-* tissue (from Greek *histós* web) + *-sol* (from latin *solum* soil)]

hit¹, *v.i., v.t. Slang.* to give oneself or another person an injection of narcotics; to shoot up. *I* [Jeffrey, a nineteen year old boy] *started hitting up once a day, and a couple of months later I started shooting two and three times a day.* Time 3/16/70, p18 *How did he become an addict? "You mean, who hit me first? My friend, Johnny."* NY Times 2/23/70, p26 [**1953,** verb use of *hit, n.,* injection of a narcotic drug (1951)]

hit², *n. Underworld Slang.* a planned murder, especially one carried out by a mobster. *Indeed, mob sources have been saying that Nunziata's death was a "hit," ordered by the Gambinos because they feared the detective might talk about the heroin thefts.* Time 1/1/73, p92 *"I've done some hits—you know, a contract. It was right after I got out of prison, and I needed some bread."* Harper's 11/74, p92 [**1963,** from the slang verb meaning to kill (1950's)]

hit³, *n.* a successful comparison or matching of two items of data in a computer. *The computer responds with a postings count (a tally of the number of items in the data-base "hits" which match the search statement) and a list of these is held in a temporary store and assigned a number by which it can be identified for printing or for incorporation in a subsequent search statement.* New Scientist 1/12/78, p77 [**1970,** extended from the sense of "a successful stroke" (OED 1815)]

hi-tech, *n.* **1** another spelling of HIGH-TECH. *Laid out in hi-tech and Romper Room, Sesame Place has no passive amusement-park rides, no static display enclosed in glass.* Discover 10/80, p108 **2** shortened form of HIGH-TECHNOLOGY. *The result is the Canada-France-Hawaii Telescope, latest hi-tech toy for Canada's scientists.* Maclean's 3/24/80, p21 [**1979**]

hit list, *Slang.* **1** a list of persons to be killed. *At the end of June, the Red Brigades issued a "hit list" of thirty prominent anti-Communist journalists and editors.* Harper's 9/77, p99 **2** a list of persons or projects to be removed or eliminated. Compare ENEMIES LIST. *A particular sore point was Carter's original "hit list" of 32 water projects. The President compromised and re-*

stored 14 of the originally doomed projects. Time 6/6/77, p11 [**1976;** see HIT²]

hit man, 1 *Underworld Slang.* a man paid to murder; a hired killer. *A mobster hit man named Joseph Rodriguez was spilling detail after gory detail about the 1972 slaying of Mafia Boss Emmanuel ("Nello") Cammarate.* Time 5/31/76, p46 *In his confession to the FBI, Townley has named six Cubans he recruited as hitmen against Letelier. Three of them have been arrested in the past two months. Two more are on the run from the FBI.* Listener 6/22/78, p791 **2** Transferred sense: *Every* [ice hockey] *team employs swashbuckling "hit men" and "enforcers." Chicago Black Hawk defenseman Keith Magnuson has taken boxing lessons from a former world bantamweight champion.* Reader's Digest 3/76, p34 [**1970;** see HIT²]

hit squad or **hit team, 1** a group of hit men. *Dellacroce dispatched hit teams of his own toward Danbury . . . Belatedly, Morris Kuznesof, chief federal probation officer in Manhattan, wrote Danbury Warden Raymond Nelson that he had received information "from a highly reliable source that an attempt to murder Mr. Galante will be made at your institution.* Time 11/13/78, p37 **2** a group or unit of terrorists. *They* [the German Baader-Meinhof gang] *are a self-appointed hit squad for a revolution none of them have yet been able to articulate. Whatever the jargon of their ransom notes, they . . . horrify most older people on the left here, who blame them, reasonably, for the backlash the entire left endures after each gloating act of third-generation violence.* New Yorker 3/20/78, p44 [**1976;** see HIT²]

hit woman, *Underworld Slang.* a woman paid to murder. *Blanche Wright, accused 'hit' woman.* Dispatch (White Plains, N.Y.) 2/14/80, pA14 [**1980**]

HIV, abbreviation of *Human Immunodeficiency Virus,* the retrovirus that causes AIDS by invading and destroying the helper T cells of the body. *Researchers hope that their experimental vaccine will stimulate the body to produce vast numbers of . . . killer T cells that would be able to recognize and destroy any of the variant forms of HIV.* World Book Science Annual 1988, p274 [**1986**]

hive-off, *n. British.* the formation of a new or subsidiary company by distribution of stocks. The equivalent U.S. term is *spin-off. To involve governments in the collaboration between companies or changes in industrial structure (mergers, take-overs, "hive-offs," etc.), adding the complexities of diplomacy and international financing to the normal burdens of running the affairs of large companies.* New Scientist 9/6/73, p566 [**1965,** from the verb phrase *hive off* to separate or remove from a larger unit]

HLA or **HL-A,** abbreviation of *human leucocyte antigen* or *histocompatibility locus antigen,* histocompatibility antigens in white blood cells of humans. *Compatibility between donor and recipient, generally highest among relatives, is gauged according to similarities in two individuals' immune systems as measured in the H-LA . . . system.* Science News 3/21/70, p297 *The individuality of tissue from different human beings is asserted primarily by the protein products of genes at four loci on the short arm of chromosome No. 6; the major histocompatibility complex, designated HLA. Genes A, B and C code for antigens inserted in the cell membrane, and gene D is apparently involved in the manufacture of antibodies.* Scientific American 1/78, p64 [**1967**]

HMO, abbreviation of HEALTH MAINTENANCE ORGANIZATION. *The best (and biggest) of the HMOs take care of their members with 65 percent less hospitalization than the national average (even excluding the chronically ill): HMO subscribers and their families don't go into the hospital as often and don't stay there as long when they do. Yet, by and large, they are satisfied: HMOs have grown steadily and now service over six million people, a number equal to the entire population of Sweden.* Saturday Review 1/7/78, p11 [**1973**]

HnRNA, abbreviation of HETERONUCLEAR RNA. *Investigators of this critical process have identified markers for following the parts of the HnRNA that are degraded, as well as markers for following the parts converted to m-RNA. This work has* *helped clarify the role of the strange polyadenylic acid (poly-A) sequences, 200 units long, that are added at the end of the HnRNA molecules before m-RNA is produced.* Americana Annual 1975, p126 [**1971**]

ho (hou), *n. U.S. Slang.* a prostitute. *Much of the Milners' evidence runs counter to prevalent beliefs, like the one that pimps are sinister Svengalis who entice innocents into prostitution by stringing them out on heroin or other hard drugs. "The truth is," say the Milners, "that only a few of the hos are masochists or junkies."* Newsweek 1/15/73, p70 [**1971**, alteration (influenced by Black English pronunciation) of *whore*]

hobbit, *n.* one of a fictitious race of genial, lovable, elflike creatures with furry feet created by the British writer John Ronald Reuel Tolkien, 1882-1973. *Few Nepalese or Tibetans have heard of it* [the kingdom of Mustang] *either: the Tibetans who have called it 'the land of Lo'—which makes it sound as if it were inhabited by Hobbits.* Listener 12/26/68, p864 *He is intensely vivid about Melbourne . . . its complex social structure, its railways and tramways, its hobos, hobbits and habits.* Sunday Times (London) 5/19/68, p58 [**1962**] ► *The Hobbit* was published in 1937, followed by *The Lord of the Rings*, a trilogy, of which *The Fellowship of the Ring* was published in 1954. Hobbits are the main characters in the books.

hoc tap, the Vietnamese term for RE-EDUCATION. *But "rehabilitation" does not involve only those who served under the former regime. Everyone is subjected to "hoc tap," a kind of retraining course (without surveillance or travel away from home) that comprises talks and discussions on revolutionary policies and on Vietnam's recent history.* Manchester Guardian Weekly (Le Monde section) 2/8/76, p13 [**1976**, from Vietnamese]

ho-dad, *n. Surfing Slang.* a person who doesn't surf or who surfs poorly or amateurishly. *This book* [Surf 's Up! An Anthology of Surfing] *assembles a couple of dozen pieces on this dazzling sport . . . Cartoon columns from California papers make argot such as* ho-dad *and* cowabunga *clear to the uninitiate.* Scientific American 12/66, p148 [**1962**, of uncertain origin]

hog, *n. U.S. Slang.* **1** a motorcycle, especially a large one. *A hog, of course, is a motorcycle, and the Angels have long been first among riders of the open road.* Time 3/22/71, p10 **2** a large automobile. *His name was Teddy Johnson but they called him 'Eldorado' because that was the kind of hog he drove. He was involved in numbers and other hustles and used the Post Office job for a front.* Atlantic 12/73, p80 [**1967**, probably so called from its *hogging* the road]

hoisin sauce, a thick dark-red sauce made with soy beans, garlic, and various spices, used in Chinese cooking. *Most large towns will have one Chinese grocery store (those restaurants have to get their stuff somewhere) and you can find hoisin sauce, oyster sauce, dried mushrooms, and suddenly you can cook just about any dish you've ever eaten in your local Chinese restaurant, and a good many others besides.* Maclean's 9/73, p54 [**1965**, from Chinese (Canton)]

hold, *n.* **on hold**, *U.S.* **1** on a telephone connection held open automatically until someone is available to take the call. *Phone calls sometimes come in from Florida, Nova Scotia, and Missouri; the callers may be put on hold for an hour or more. They do not seem to mind.* New Yorker 8/14/78, p39 [**1965**] **2** Figurative sense. in a suspended state; put off; delayed. *"A massive reorganization of our elevator operation, based on a two-year engineering study, has been 'on hold' for over a year pending the results of the Department of Investigation-Housing Authority probe," Mr. Christian said.* NY Times 8/25/76, p33 [**1973**]

hold-harmless, *adj. U.S.* relating to or designating a part of a government aid program that spares the recipient group or locality from further harm or deterioration, usually by providing aid equal to or above that of a specified year. *Pending disputes involve a so-called "hold-harmless" provision, under which the Federal Government is to absorb program costs above the amount paid by state and local governments during 1972 in the former welfare grants for the aged, blind and disabled poor.* NY Times 4/11/76, p38 [**1976**, from the legal phrase *hold*

harmless to make free from loss of liability, originally (OED 1418) *save harmless*]

holding pattern, **1** a circular pattern flown by an aircraft above or near an airport while it waits to be cleared for landing. *Actually I was not over New York at all; I was in a "holding pattern" over Allentown, Pennsylvania.* Harper's 10/68, p38 **2** Figurative use. a condition in which no progress is made; a static or stationary situation. *Analysts noted that prices in recent sessions have been in a "holding pattern" pending fresh news developments.* NY Times 3/23/76, p48 *While most nonprofit arts organizations manage to stay in business, recent studies for the National Endowment for the Arts (NEA) suggest that the spiral of labor and other costs has forced them into a "holding pattern."* 1978 World Book Year Book, p132 [**1954**]

holding tank, *U.S.* a tank on a boat for holding sewage to be pumped out at a dockside station. *Whatever the size of a holding tank, however, critics point out that its contents end up in municipal sewage plants—which in turn dump their often undertreated effluent into waterways.* Time 5/3/71, p45 [**1971**]

hold time, a delay in the countdown or launching operations of a rocket or missile. *Fortunately, the countdown schedule had been padded with enough precautionary hold time to enable technicians to replace the oxygen without delaying the launch.* Time 12/27/68, p13 [**1968**]

-holic, a variant of -AHOLIC, as in: **—carboholic** [from *carbo*hydrate + *-holic*]: *To remedy the problem, I have devised a special diet for carboholics (detailed in my book. Dr. Solomon's Easy No-Risk Diet), which balances the proportion of carbohydrates, protein and fats.* New York Post 12/29/76, p30 **—chocoholic** [from *choco*late + *-holic*]: *Mrs. Marcus, a self-professed chocoholic, has left no mint patty unturned in her search for the ultimate chocolate experience.* NY Times 5/16/79, pC1 **—colaholic** [from *cola* + *-holic*]: *The "cola-holics" reported a strong craving for their favorite drink and complained that without it, they could not perform as well when studying and taking exams.* Prevention 7/74, p87 **—computerholic:** *There are clearly more "computerholics" in Britain than many in the business ever imagined.* New Scientist 5/19/77, p405 **—crediholic** [from *credit* + *-holic*]: *Only a handful are true "crediholics"—people who get some kind of excitement about always being in debt and in a bind about paying bills. Most simply yield to the temptation to overspend.* Time 2/28/77, p39 **—mariholic** [from *marijuana* + *-holic*]: *So—just like the speed freaks, alcoholics, mariholics and junkies—people using liquid diets against a virus or diarrhea, others undergoing diuretic therapy, and those who just prefer drinking to eating,* all *are raising their own B vitamin requirements.* Rich Wentzler, The Vitamin Book, 1978, p28 **—petroholic:** *It is, of course, the craving for crude that keeps the game going. Petroholic economies everywhere remain excessively hooked on Demon Oil.* Time 5/7/79, p70 [**1972**]

hollow foot, a foot with an abnormally high longitudinal arch. *Countless more suffered chronic maladies ranging from the annoying, like athlete's foot and jock itch, to the exotic and painful, like glass arm (loss of throwing ability from damaged tendons, common in baseball players), hollow foot (a strained instep found in ballet dancers) and a web split (splitting of skin between the fingers).* Newsweek 4/2/73, p65 [**1973**]

Holocaust, *n.* **the Holocaust**, the Nazi destruction of European Jewry in World War II. *Before the Holocaust and the foundation of the state of Israel . . . the Zionist settlers in Palestine, the "Yishuv," already thought of their return to the land . . . as having a quality of idealism so dedicated that it would symbolically purify Jewish existence . . .* Harper's 11/67, p77 [**1967**, specialized use of *holocaust* recorded in phrases such as *Nazi holocaust* as early as 1942]

hologram, *n.* a record or reproduction of an image produced on a photographic plate or film by holography. . . . *lasers alone can produce coherent beams strong enough to make holograms.* Science News 5/10/69, p460 *Included in the exhibits displayed by International Business Machines at Edinburgh is a computer-generated hologram.* Times (London) 8/9/68, p17 [**1952**, from Greek *hólos* whole + English *-gram* record, but first recorded description in 1949]

holograph, *v.t.* to make a hologram of; produce by holography. *The main purpose of the meeting, however, was to show the extent to which holography can be used to make accurate engineering measurement. This stems from the fact that a hologram stores a faithful three dimensional record of the object being 'holographed', and the reconstructed image can be matched against the object itself.* Science Journal 3/68, p86 [**1967**]

holographic, *adj.* of, relating to, or done by holography. *The original problem with holography was that whereas it was easy to record the square of the amplitude of the diffraction pattern, the phase is usually lost, and without a record of the phase the holographic reconstruction is poor except for very special objects.* Scientific American 9/68, p154 [**1964**]

holography, *n.* a lensless method of photography in which a three-dimensional image is recorded on a photographic plate or film by means of laser light. The laser light is split into two beams that interfere with each other to form a pattern which depends on the shape of the photographed object. When the pattern on the plate or film is then exposed to visible light, a three-dimensional image of the object is formed. *But still more spectacular is use of the laser as the basis for a new type of photography called holography. Laser light projected through a photographic film with holographic techniques, gives a real three-dimensional image with a wealth of detail and a remarkable depth of focus.* Science 2/16/68, p702 *Holography differs from photography in that it uses the coherent properties of laser light to record all the information in an arrangement of light rays on a piece of photographic film.* New Scientist 2/26/70, p394 [**1964**]

holon ('hɔlɒn), *n. Philosophy.* any whole which is a part of a larger whole; a distinct entity. *By remembering the dynamic status of these "holons"—at one moment the nodes from which other branches spring, at another the boughs that lead to the main trunk—the scientist will overcome the atomistic fallacy: the erroneous image of complex units as mere composites of small, divisible parts.* New Yorker 3/6/71, p107 *Things of all kinds are made of holons—things like hearts and livers, where people are concerned—which have a natural tendency towards autonomy but also a tendency towards integration. But people are also holons, and they are in part impelled by the 'integrative tendency', which accounts for ESP, clairvoyance, psychokinesis and the other phenomena by which Arthur Koestler is fascinated.* Listener 2/10/72, p187 [**1970**, coined by the Hungarian-born British author Arthur Koestler, 1905-1983, from Greek *hólos, hólon* whole]

holophone, *n.* a device for recording an acoustical hologram. *A holophone records patterns in time in a manner analogous to the way an optical hologram records patterns in space.* New Scientist and Science Journal 1/21/71, p105 [**1968**]

holoscope, *n.* an optical instrument for producing holographic images. *A suggestion to combine the optical non-linear effects with holography has led to a proposal that can in principle yield a "holoscope", a true three-dimensional microscope that could be used in much the same way as a normal two-dimensional one.* New Scientist 7/13/67, p97 [**1967**]

holoscopic, *adj.* of or based upon complete or overall observation; comprising everything in sight. *Daiches found himself "licensed Platonist", i.e. ready to relate judgments on novels, literature, to the rest of creation—history, nature of man, etc.; "holoscopic" view.* Sunday Times (London) 5/21/72, p40 [**1972**]

home-beat, *n. British.* a policeman's beat in or near the area in which he lives. *PC Prendergast's home-beat is at the more commercial end of Notting Hill, with boarding houses and small and large hotels.* Times (London) 7/31/72, p3 [**1971**]

homeboy, *n. U.S. (especially Black English) Slang.* a boy or man from one's own hometown, region, or community. *"I didn't*

know how to read or write 'cause I was always out with the homeboys." People Weekly 5/2/88, p47 [**1967**]

home computer, a microcomputer for home use. Compare PERSONAL COMPUTER. *A new generation of home computers is beginning to emerge. With these, you take them home, plug them in, and begin using them. Costs vary widely and there is a lot of market maneuvering.* Encyclopedia Science Supplement (Grolier) 1979, p113 *Since 1975, when home computers made their debut, some 200,000 have been sold, despite a serious dearth of programs.* Daily News (New York) 2/4/79, p3 [**1977**]

home confinement, *U.S.* a term of imprisonment served in one's home and carried out by monitoring signals from an electronic transmitter attached to the prisoner to determine his or her whereabouts. *A growing number of states have introduced . . . home confinement as a punishment, generally for nonviolent crime.* 1987 Collier's Encyclopedia Year Book, p207 [**1986**]

homeland, *n.* any of various regions of southern Africa set aside by the Republic of South Africa as separate tribal states. *The second of South Africa's nine tribal homelands to be granted "independence," Bophutha Tswana (literally meaning "that which binds the Tswana) is not recognized by any country in the world except South Africa and another homeland, Transkei, which became independent last year.* Time 12/19/77, p40 [**1963**, extended from the original sense (OED 1670) "one's native land"] ▶The usual name for such regions or states during the 1950's and 1960's was *Bantustan* (from *Bantu* + *-stan*, as in *Baluchistan, Pakistan, Afghanistan*). During the 1970's *homeland* replaced Bantustan, which seemed to convey a racial tone.

home-port, *v.t.* to establish a port for (part of a naval fleet) in a location near its theater of operations. *Junta leaders, who have given up their American limousines in favor of Mercedes-Benzes, have blocked the U.S. Navy's plans to home-port a Sixth Fleet aircraft carrier in Greece.* Time 4/19/74, p41 *Both vessels will be home-ported at Lahaina and according to Drew, will operate in waters south of Hawaii with their catches slated for export and the local market.* Honolulu Star-Bulletin 2/5/73, pC20 [**1972**, from the noun phrase *home port*] —**home-porting**, *n.: The rationale of what is called "home-porting" here* [in Athens] *is that this affords the Sixth Fleet essential facilities, strengthening its position as a key force on NATO's flank and also as a guardian of U.S. commitments to Israel. But Athenian comfort and culture for the wives and kiddies are not required for that.* NY Times 10/15/72, pD15

homeschool, *v.* to teach one's own children at home. —*v.i.* THE COMPLETE HOME EDUCATOR, *Mario Pagnoni . . . Explains how computers work and how families can use them at home; how and why the Pagnonis homeschool.* John Holt's Book and Music Store brochure, HOMESCHOOLING, 1986, p1 —*v.t. For Peter Bergson and Susan Shilcock, who are home-schooling their four children in Bryn Mawr, Pennsylvania, learning is a function of neither construction projects nor prescribed texts. "Our children's lives involve massive amounts of what the outside world would call play," says Bergson, who makes his living as an educational consultant.* Atlantic 4/88, p22 [**1986**] —**homeschooler**, *n.: The parents who are homeschoolers can be found anywhere along a continuum of educational philosophies, stretching from a free-form, non-directive approach to a regimented, almost institutional style of teaching.* Atlantic 4/88, p22

home shopping, shopping by telephone from a commercial television program devoted to selling goods and services at a discount to viewers who call in their order when an item is offered or displayed. *"Home shopping is quick, clean,* [and] *painless," says the Roper study.* Wall Street Journal 11/4/87, p39 [**1985**]

homesteading, *n. U.S.* short for URBAN HOMESTEADING. *The "homesteading" scheme, whereby citizens could gain title to dilapidated houses by repairing them and living in them for a minimum period, was gaining in popularity.* Britannica Book of the Year 1975, p363 [**1975**]

hominization, *n.* the act or process of making human in character or nature. *. . . . dehumanization of the living worker was* *complemented, paradoxically, by the progressive hominiza-tion of the machine—hominization in the sense of giving the automation some of the mechanical equivalents of lifelike motion and purpose . . .* New Yorker 10/17/70, p131 **[1953,** from *homin-* (stem of Latin *homō* human being) + *-ization;* formed on the pattern of *humanization*]

homme (ɔːm), *n.* the French word for "man," used in English in various French compounds, as the following: **—homme d'affaires** (ˈɔːm daˈfer), a businessman; (literally) man of affairs. *Henri Micmacher is an homme d'affaires in the strict French sense. He is the founder-president of Pronuptia, the Paris-based marriage-gear multiple that in 1971 reckons to sell upwards of 46,000 wedding dresses.* Sunday Times (London) 6/27/71, p49 **—homme de confiance** (ˈɔːm də kɔ̃ˈfyɑs), a man of trust; a right-hand man. *Around the death-bed of General Franco, an anxious crowd of would-be successors clusters: Admiral Carrero Blanco, the sometime submarine commander who has been the Caudillo's* homme de confiance *for 30 years . . .* Times (London) 10/30/70, p10 **—homme du monde** (ˈɔːm dY ˈmɔ̃d), a man of the world. . . . *Michel Piccoli [is a] good actor: one of those Frenchmen who excel at playing strong, not quite handsome, amused, interestingly jaded, middle-aged* hommes du monde, *a category nonexistent in contemporary American and English acting.* New Yorker 9/5/70, p64 **—homme du sys-tème** (ɔːm dY siˈstem), a man of the system. *In turn unreconstructed Tory . . . Whig, and Liberal, he adapted to most major shifts in political ideas and practices. Party affiliation is in one sense irrelevant, for Palmerston was a great placeman on the eighteenth-century model, and* homme du système *who happily worked it without questioning its basic assumptions.* Manchester Guardian Weekly 12/12/70, p18

homo, *n.* the Latin word for "man," used in various Latin compounds to describe some essential characteristic or quality, on the analogy of established scientific terms such as *homo sapiens* ("rational man") and *homo faber* ("worker man"), including: **—homo americanus,** American man. *What Perosa finds in* [F. Scott] *Fitzgerald's fiction is a comedy of manners "with all its tragic implications," a way of writing through which he was able to define that unique creature,* homo americanus. Saturday Review 10/26/68, p42 **—homo aquaticus,** aquatic man. *. . . the name of Commandant Jacques-Yves Cousteau is so familiar, with his celebrated conception of* homo aquaticus, *which he predicted at the Congress of Underwater Activities in London in 1962.* New Scientist 2/20/69, p390 **—homo insip-iens,** foolish man; the opposite of *homo sapiens. Thus, in dread of the fate of* homo insipiens, *more people, it would seem, are inclined to take time off to look again at the question: why?* Times (London) 10/17/70, p14 **—homo ludens,** playful or sportive man. *The Cyprus problem is anyway absorbingly complex. It embraces almost every aspect of the diplomatic game and* homo ludens *cannot fail to have an entertaining time delving into its subtleties on the spot.* Listener 1/12/67, p53 **—homo maniacus,** mad man. *Witnessing this worldwide obduracy, writers as disparate as Naturalist Konrad Lorenz and Novelist Arthur Koestler have redefined Homo sapiens as* Homo maniacus . . . Time 6/7/68, p30 **—homo mathematicus,** mathematical man. *This nearly perfect insulation of the national security managers leads them into the trap of collecting isolated facts and figures. McNamara was of course the leading specimen in the national security bureaucracy of* homo mathematicus, *i.e., men who behave, and believe that other men behave, primarily in response to "hard data," usually numbers (infiltration rates, "kill ratios," bomb tonnage).* Harper's 11/71, p57 **—homo neuroticus,** neurotic man. *"Homo neuroticus," says Mrs. Szasz, "de-animalizes his pets in exactly the same way he de-humanizes himself."* Time 2/14/69, p50

Homo habilis, an extinct species of man believed to have been the earliest toolmaker, about 1,700,000 years ago, whose fossil fragments were discovered in the early 1960's at the Olduvai Gorge in northern Tanzania. *Today one of the great questions is whether the earliest known manlike creature,* Homo habilis, *was actually a maker of tools.* 1969 Britannica Yearbook of Science and the Future, p232 **[1964,** from Latin *homō habilis* skillful man]

homophile, *n.* a person attracted to members of his or her own sex; a homosexual. *But to Dr. Ullerstam this* [a Swedish law prohibiting homosexual contacts until the age of eighteen] *seems unfair because "it causes the homophiles the greater suffering than would appear at first sight* [since] *youths between fifteen and eighteen are often the most attractive and most available objects for the homosexual urge."* Saturday Review 7/9/66, p30 **—adj.** concerned with the rights or the welfare of homophiles. *Homophile activists contend that there would be more happy homosexuals if society were more compassionate . . .* Time 10/31/69, p42 *There are, nowadays, increasing exchanges between the medical profession and the nonpatient—what Larry Littlejohn of San Francisco's homophile Society for Individual Rights (SIR) calls "impatient"—homosexuals. These exchanges are not always pleasant occasions . . .* Saturday Review 2/12/72, p28 **[1960,** from *homo-* the same, of the same species + *-phile* (one) attracted to]

homophobe, *n.* a person who fears, dislikes, or hates homosexuals. *I went to see Michael England, the pastor of the Metropolitan Community Church, in the Castro, to ask about the impact of AIDS on the gay community. I had no idea what his position on the baths might be. When the subject came up, England, a robust, energetic man of thirty-eight, told me that he had been working closely with Dr. Silverman on the issue. "I trust Silverman," he said. "The man is not in any way a homophobe—his sole agenda is to save lives."* New Yorker 7/28/86, p56 **[1979,** back formation from HOMOPHOBIA or formed from *homo*sexual + *-phobe* (as in *Anglophobe*), from Greek *-phóbos* fearing]

homophobia, *n.* fear, dislike, or hatred of homosexuals. *The task force reached an agreement that secular society should forbid job discrimination against homosexuals and repeal laws that regulate the private sexual behavior of consenting adults. It urges the church to work against "homophobia," the fear and loathing of homosexuals.* Time 1/30/78, p85 **[1969,** from *homo*sexual + *phobia*] **—homophobic,** *adj.: Herbert Gold is a heterosexual. Although it is possible for straights to write positive articles about gays, Gold's treatment leaves something to be desired. While obviously not rabidly homophobic, his consciousness, sensitivity and awareness are not what they could be.* NY Times Magazine 12/4/77, p34

homopolynucleotide (ˌhoumᵊˌpɑliːˈnuːkliːᵊˌtaid), *n.* a substance composed of nucleotides of the same kind. *At Merck, Sharpe and Dohme a process for the preparation of homopolynucleotides has been scaled up to commercial level using immobilized polynucleotide phosphorylase covalently coupled to cellulose.* McGraw-Hill Yearbook of Science and Technology 1974, p176 **[1968,** from *homo-* same + *polynucleotide*]

homopolypeptide (ˌhoumᵊˌpɑliːˈpeptaid), *n.* a substance composed of peptides of the same kind. *Homopolypeptides provide good model systems for various aspects of proteins. Recent advances in high polymer and solid state physics have enabled the vibrational aspects of the simpler homopolypeptides to be treated as normal—but complicated—polymers.* Nature 7/7/72, p38 **[1966,** from *homo-* same + *polypeptide*]

homo sap, short for *homo sapiens,* used humorously with allusion to *sap* (a fool). *Meanwhile, the solar system has been visited by aliens who seem to want to eliminate homo sap.* Sunday Times (London) 5/2/71, p37 *The earliest fact, and the latest, is differences increasing and multiplying, with Homo sap struggling to lasso and harness their circumambience for the varying uses of his struggle to keep on struggling.* Saturday Review 10/1/66, p29 **[1966]**

homosex, *n.* the condition of being homosexual; homosexuality. Compare HETEROSEX. *Yet other doctors propose that the physical basis of homosex stems from a "first," or primal, pleasurable, satisfactory "touch response." But as far as we got is where that covey of blind men was in describing the elephant.* Saturday Review 2/12/72, p27 **—adj.** homosexual. *Paul Guilbert . . . an avowed homosexual, wanted to take a male escort to his high school junior prom, whereupon, predictably, an eruption of publicity. Homosex rights and parents' rights collided when Guilbert's parents refused permission, thus letting* *the school off the hook, whew, and forestalling an ACLU suit on Guilbert's behalf.* National Review 5/11/79, p597 [**1972**]

honcho, *n. U.S. Slang.* chief; headman; boss. *Mr. Komer expects to be able to name these 45 key provincial honchos, and he hopes to place civilians in at least a quarter of the posts.* NY Times 6/4/67, pD1 *Nicholas Johnson, the [Federal Communications] commission's most outspoken liberal (who has also called for more public involvement in TV), recently criticized Nixon for clearing [Dean] Burch's appointment with broadcasting honchos before announcing it.* Time 11/21/69, p24 [**1953**, originally U.S. Army use in Asia, from Japanese *hanchō* group leader]

honky or **honkie,** *n. U.S. Slang (used disparagingly).* a white person. *Mr. Lehman Brightman, a militant South Dakota Sioux who is now president of the United Native Americans in Berkeley, California, comments angrily: "Even the name Indian is not ours—it was given us by some dumb honky who got lost and thought he'd landed in India."* Times (London) 3/10/70, p10 [**1967**, originally used among blacks in the U.S. at least as early as 1946, of unknown origin]

honor box, *U.S.* a type of newspaper vending machine. See the quotation. *The blue-and-white newspaper-vending machines that have been multiplying on city streets as newsstands approach extinction . . . are called "honor boxes," because they open when the price of a paper is deposited, the customer being trusted to take just one.* New Yorker 1/22/79, p56 [**1978**]

hook, *n.* **1** variant of HOOKER (def. 2). *The author of several how-to-do-it books (among them* Writing Articles that Sell, *which she uses as the text for her course), she [Louise Boggess] points her students straight toward the mass writing market. In her streamlined, practical lessons the emphasis is unabashedly on formula writing that will sell. Her very first assignment is how to write a "hook," meaning an arresting opening sentence. What does she think of the word "The" for an opener? It doesn't exactly grab her, she admitted.* Atlantic 7/70, p53 **2** *Surfing Slang.* the crest of a breaker. *To the surfer each breaker has a "hook," or crest, a "shoulder," the calm portion behind the hook, and a "shore break," the final surge ending in the inevitable "soup," or foam.* NY Times 8/10/65, p31 [**1970** for def. 1; **1964** for def. 2]

hooker, *n. Slang.* **1** a hidden difficulty; catch. *With neither a colonizing past to overcome, nor an imperialistic present to dissemble, with tireless diplomats and an abundant store of selfless common sense, Canada can be trusted by nearly everyone. But—and this is the hooker—Canadian statesmen will only be effective if they speak softly while they carry their slim dispatch cases from capital to capital, from crisis to crisis.* Maclean's 10/74, p57 **2** an intriguing or catchy opening, as of a show or a story. Also called HOOK. *Her [Barbara Walters'] values are conventional, whether they pertain to the structure of a television program ("It should have a hooker, a teaser and a conclusion"), social intercourse . . . or society in general.* NY Times Magazine 9/10/72, p46 [**1967** for def. 1; **1968** for def. 2]

hoot, *n. Slang.* something hilariously amusing or funny. . . . *'The Projector' [a play] was a marvellous hoot, it was a very elaborate parody but everybody thought it was the real thing.* Manchester Guardian Weekly 6/5/71, p16 *After dinner, all the chaps chuck their clubs in a heap, and the wives have to pick a club and go off with the owner; it's going to be an absolute hoot!* Punch 12/17/69, p990 [**1942, 1963**, noun use of *hoot, v.,* to laugh (OEDS 1925)]

hootch, *n. Slang, chiefly U.S. Military use in Asia.* **1** a thatched hut in which natives live. *They found in the village "undefended and unarmed women, children and old men in their hootches"—American soldiers' slang for grass-thatched huts.* Times (London) 11/18/70, p6 *At Phuoc Vinh, a black 1st Cavalry trooper recently dragged a wounded white from a rocketed hootch when no other black or white dared to venture in.* Time 9/19/69, p19 **2** (by extension) any house or dwelling. *It is a minor point, but if Mr. Dareff would have us believe that the term "hootches" is used to make fun of or belittle the Vietnamese for the way they live, I would like to point out that this term is used universally here in Vietnam to describe any dwelling,*

including our own, and that there is nothing "jocular" or malicious or belittling about the word at all. Saturday Review 8/24/68, p35 [**1960**, from Japanese *uchi* house; the form was probably influenced by *hutch*]

hooter, *n. British Slang.* a nose. *. . . there are estimated to be over 500,000 people in this country [Great Britain] hooked on the ludicrous custom of impelling fermented tobacco-powder up their hooters.* New Scientist and Science Journal 2/4/71, p229 [**1958**]

hoot owl, *U.S.* the midnight shift in a mine, factory, or the like (often used attributively). *The newer men, the trainees, can be shuttled around at will. On the hoot owl they usually end up as laborers.* Harper's 12/71, p102 [**1968**, in allusion to the owl's nocturnal habits]

horizontal divestiture, the disposal of a company's holdings in operations or businesses producing products similar to its own. *Mr. Carter favors horizontal divestiture—prohibiting energy companies from owning competing forms of fuel—and the issue seems sure to be discussed early in the year.* NY Times 1/9/77, pC35 [**1975**]

horizontal proliferation, increase in the number of nations that possess nuclear weapons. *"Horizontal proliferation" or sideways spread . . . is the danger that seventh, eighth, and nth countries will acquire the means to make bombs.* Manchester Guardian Weekly 1/29/78, p10 *It is clearly recognized by both sides that vertical proliferation and horizontal proliferation need to be attacked as mutually inseparable problems.* NY Times 1/15/78, pD20 [**1976**]

hors d'oeuvre, 1 (adverbial use) outside the major concern; apart from the main undertaking. *Adolfo . . . was an important boutiquier when other custom milliners ventured no farther hors d'oeuvre than an occasional scarf or handbag.* New Yorker 10/18/69, p158 **2** (noun use) something beyond the main concern; something peripheral. *Restraints on free speech are usually hors d'oeuvres for the Supreme Court, but when Congress outlawed draft card burning to squelch antiwar dissent, the Justices backed the law, 7 to 1.* NY Times 6/20/68, p32 *. . . dictionaries . . . of space and medical terms, and a number of other little compendia that look substantial in a table of contents but are essentially mere hors d'oeuvres.* Saturday Review 11/19/66, p49 [**1956**] ▶The common meaning of *hors d'oeuvre* in both French and English is "appetizer," "side dish." In French the form is usually hyphenated and does not take a plural *-s.*

horsenapping, *n.* **1** the theft of a horse, especially a racehorse. *The horsenapping at Claiborne happened in late June. Somebody cut a wire fence and made off with Fanfreluche, a mare that had been Canada's horse of the year in 1970 and had produced a colt that won the same distinction twice.* 1978 World Book Year Book, p56 **2** Attributive use: *This lady has unwisely taken her eye off her $3,700 thoroughbred gelding "Prince," evidently unaware that horsenapping gangsters could get up to $5,000 for him on the Belgium-Luxembourg underground meat market.* High Times 1/79, p105 [**1978**, from *horse* + kidnapping]

hospice, *n.* an institution for the care of the terminally ill. *From Britain has come the idea of the "hospice," an in-patient facility specially designed for the dying: cheerful, homelike, full of plants and families (including young children). There are about thirty such places in Britain now, but the idea has been slower to take root in the United States. The hospice in New Haven, for instance, has been in operation with a home-care program for more than two years.* The New Old: Struggling for Decent Aging, edited by Ronald Gross, Beatrice Gross, and Sylvia Seidman, 1978, p159 [**1976**, extended from the older meaning (1890's) of a home for the destitute or the sick]

hospitality suite, a room or set of rooms in which guests of a company or organization are received and served refreshments. *NBC, with great aplomb, secured for itself two aged but air-conditioned railroad parlor cars, parked them on a spur across from the convention hall and went into business with* *the most elegant hospitality suite in town.* TV Guide 8/28/76, pA2 [**1963**]

host, *n.* a computer used simultaneously by various operators at different terminals; multiple-access computer. *An example is the situation where a central computer—a "host" in the current jargon—wishes to communicate with a variety of different types of terminal. At present this entails not only having a separate access port for each terminal active at a given moment, but also providing special support software for each terminal type.* New Scientist 5/13/76, p352 [**1970**, specialized sense of the term meaning one who provides lodging for guests (OED 1303)]

host-specific, *adj.* living on or in a particular species of host. *The plague bacterium is transferred from rat to rat by a particular flea which like all other fleas is host-specific; ordinarily it will feed on the blood of rats and rats alone.* Times (London) 2/21/70, pIV [**1964**]

hot dog, *U.S. Slang.* a very skillful athlete, especially one able to perform stunts. *We had this one* [basketball] *player, Alston Mackintosh, from Oleander College in Nebraska, who could hit nine out of ten from the foul line with his back to the basket. He was a real hot dog, but when we had him move up to the pros he couldn't take the pressure.* Atlantic 3/66, p131 [**1958**, probably from *hot dog!* exclamation used to show pleasure, admiration, etc.]

hot-dog, *U.S. Slang. —adj.* very skillful; able to perform stunts. *I think I told you about Roscoe in one of my other letters. He's a hot-dog surfer and he used to be real wigged on Zen.* New Yorker 12/31/66, p28 **—v.i.** (of a skier, skateboarder, etc.) to perform acrobatics or stunts. *"And when I ski, I hotdog. I wouldn't recommend it for everyone, but racing no longer gives me the expression I need; I had to progress from there. Hotdogging lets me be free; I enjoy self-realization in sport."* Town and Country 1/75, p57 [**1963**] **—hot-dogger,** *n.: For advanced practitioners, a whole new style of baroque skiing has developed. Known as "free-style," "exhibition" or "hot-dog" skiing, the form emphasizes acrobatic stunts rather than downhill speed. Hot-doggers build up repertoires of twists, turns, spins and somersaults.* Time 12/25/72, p60

hothouse, *v.t. Education.* to begin teaching (children) at a very early age in order to stimulate or advance their mental development. *All this commotion has caused concern among childhood specialists, who now talk about such topics as "hothousing"—forced intellectual growth. Naturally, they say, there is nothing wrong with early education that is "developmentally appropriate"; but too often, what these specialists are seeing goes far beyond that.* Christian Science Monitor 3/28/86, pB1 [**1966**, verb use of noun; originally used of plants grown in a hothouse in order to speed ripening]

hot line, 1 a direct teletype line open for instant communication between leaders of different governments in case of an emergency. *Walt. W. Rostow, the President's national security adviser, was calling to report that the "hot line" was being activated from Moscow. Since the hot-line link between Washington and Moscow was first put into operation on Aug. 30, 1963, it had conveyed nothing more dramatic than New Year's greetings and hourly testing messages.* Time 6/16/67, p15 **2** a telephone line constantly open for communication in an emergency. . . . *drug abuse is a serious problem that can be dealt with only by a coordinated community effort. In such efforts a variety of orthodox and innovative services are interlocked to provide treatment and preventive services. Hot lines, storefront clinics, and rap sessions are backed up by emergency medical clinics and hospital facilities.* Americana Annual 1971, p255 **3** *U.S. and Canada.* a radio or television program which broadcasts conversations with people who telephone the studio with questions, problems, etc. *About 20 orators arose, one after another, to espouse everything from (predictably enough) free university tuition to local night shopping and radio hot lines.* Maclean's 9/17/66, p3 [**1963**, originally (early 1950's) a U.S. Air Force term for a direct telephone line between distant bases]

hotliner, *n. Canadian.* the host of a radio or television program which broadcasts conversations with people who telephone the studio. *Al, our muckraking, scabpicking, intrepid, Icelandic but otherwise clean-living reporter, was interviewed on the spot by A.C. Grudge, the well known hotliner.* Province (Vancouver) 4/28/73, p53 *The unlikely events lurched to a start last November when Vancouver radio hot-liner Ed Murphy offered to send his listeners a list of Murphy-collected government boondoggles and examples of waste.* Maclean's 10/23/78, p66 [**1973**, from HOT LINE a radio or television call-in program + *-er*]

hot mooner, a scientist who believes that there is thermal or volcanic activity in the moon's core and that this activity, rather than the impact of meteorites, produced the lunar craters. Also called VULCANIST. *Hot mooners who believe that the moon has or once had a molten core like the earth's are still hot mooners.* Sunday Times (London) 1/11/70, p7 *The meetings of GLEP* [Group for Lunar Exploration Planning] *are a little like auctions, with scientists . . . dickering with geologists who want rocks from the highlands—and even hot-mooners bargaining with cold-mooners to go to sites they think may be volcanic.* New Yorker 1/9/71, p69 [**1970**]

hot pants, close-fitting short pants, cut high on the leg, worn by women in place of a skirt or in combination with a split skirt. *The accepted generic term, hot pants, lends the style the leering inference of an adolescent joke. But short shorts are no joke, they are serious business . . .* Time 2/1/71, p48 [**1970**, probably suggested by the slang expression "to have *hot pants,*" meaning to be sexually aroused]

hot rock, an underground heat reservoir without the water needed to bring its geothermal energy to the surface. *The US Department of Energy (DOE) expects to make LASI the lead agency for the country's "hot rock" geothermal programme. While the US has so far exploited only conventional hydrogeothermal resources where there is underground water available to bring the energy to the surface, the DOE estimates that there is something like a hundred times as much energy in hot dry rocks.* New Scientist 3/23/78, p784 [**1975**]

hot spot, 1 *Geology.* any of various regions of the earth where molten material in the earth's mantle is carried upwards, heating the crust above. See PLUME. *The oceanic "hot spots" which may be the source of mid-Pacific volcanic islands may be several hundred km wide and may well up from mantle depths.* New Scientist 11/29/73, p607 *Scattered around the globe are more than 100 small regions of isolated volcanic activity known to geologists as hot spots. Unlike most of the world's volcanoes, they are not always found at the boundaries of the great drifting plates that make up the earth's surface; on the contrary, many of them lie deep in the interior of a plate. Most of the hot spots move only slowly, and in some cases the movement of the plates past them has left trails of extinct volcanoes. The hot spots and their volcanic trails are milestones that mark the passage of the plates.* Scientific American 8/76, p46 **2** *Medicine.* a cell or other part of the body that is susceptible or predisposed to a disease, infection, or the like. *The scientists cited other studies that have failed to show relationships between cancer and air pollution, and Dr. Demopoulos said that misattribution of cancer "hot spots" to air pollution or other factors can be dangerous because it inhibits the search for the real causes.* NY Times 3/4/79, pD7 [**1971** for def. 1; **1977** for def. 2]

hot tray, a tray with an electric heating element built in underneath its surface to keep food hot. *The magazine had gotten a surprisingly negative response to an ad for hot trays that ran in the sample issue (The slogan was: "Women: stand up for your right to sit down at dinner time").* Saturday Review 7/15/72, p10 [**1970**]

hot tub, a large tub or vat that is electrically heated or filled with hot water, used for bathing, often in a group, as a form of relaxation or physical therapy. Also called SPA. *He could clearly hear the burbling sounds of water in the fiber-glass and redwood hot tub that had been installed in the backyard.* Time 6/18/79, p62 *How does the young modern executive unwind after work? By dipping into a swimming pool? No, the pool is yesterday's status symbol. The hot tub is the wave of the future,* *according to spa manufacturers and dealers across the country.* Today (New York) 9/20/79, pB2 [**1973**] **—hot tubbing:** *Santa Barbara has become the center of a new fad called "hot tubbing"—outdoor communal soaking at temperatures of 104 to 120 degrees.* Newsweek 8/20/73, p50

hot-wire, *v.t. Slang.* to start the engine of (an automobile, airplane, etc.) by short-circuiting the ignition switch. *Her David-and-Jonathan 16-year-olds hustle pool-players for money, hot-wire cars, get shot at, flunk chemistry exams.* Sunday Times (London) 12/5/71, p43 *Well, on Columbo, the millionaire would plot the perfect murder. He would attend a business convention in another city, secretly fly back by hot-wiring an associate's private plane, drown the girl.* Time 11/26/73, p118 [**1966**]

house, *n. U.S. Education.* a subdivision of a large elementary or secondary school, consisting of 200 to 300 students under the instruction and guidance of a particular team of teachers, counselors, and other educational professionals. *"It's a lot more work, but it's very stimulating," says Elizabeth Ophals, a social-studies teacher . . . in New York City, where houses and team teaching were adopted last year.* Time 6/26/89, p51 [**1989**]

housebroken, *adj. U.S.* socially acceptable; tame. *She* [Marian Anderson] *used dreadful arrangements, sentimental and bathetic, and the housebroken, white-washed tunes she sang were designed to tweak the white conscience ever so slightly while perpetrating the stereotype of the black man as a shiftless creature but amiable, stupid, endowed with a natural lyric gift and a conviction that he is "Gwine to Hebbn."* Atlantic 9/70, p120 [**1959**, figurative sense of the U.S. term applied to domestic animals trained to be clean indoors. The British equivalent is *housetrained.*]

househusband, *n.* a married man who manages a household (the correlative of *housewife*). *In his final album, househusband* [John] *Lennon sings to his son Sean: "Life is what happens to you while you're busy making other plans."* Maclean's 12/22/80, p3 *A trivial household chat between this column and the good husband? Maybe, but the President would err gravely if he took a cavalier attitude when millions of American househusbands* [are] *gathering in the barbershop and supermarket . . .* NY Times 9/3/70, p32 [**1955**]

houseperson, *n.* a person who manages a household. See -PERSON. *That evening on TV, she* [Margaret Thatcher] *looked a winner: her sang froid, hairdo, and clarity of diction perfect, but her well-known persona of a chilly suburban houseperson infused with a new warmth, real or assumed.* New Statesman 2/7/75, p172 *One may empathize with the plight of the Mesa Verde houseperson by getting down on hands and knees to try the back-straining job of grinding a few dried red, blue and yellow corn kernels in a stone mortar.* NY Times 2/22/76, pJ7 [**1975**, used to replace *housewife* or HOUSEHUSBAND]

house-sit, *v.i. Especially U.S.* to live in and take care of a house while the regular occupants are away. *If you want to house-sit in a remote vacation home for a year or so, pick the area where you want to go, contact local real estate agents who may know of these homes, and write letters of inquiry to resort directors.* NY Times 12/10/78, p14 [**1977**, back formation from *housesitter* (1973), patterned on *baby-sitter*] **—house-sitter,** *n.:* House-sitters, NY Suburbs, Summer. *Suburban home with nice garden and cat looking for reliable "au pair" caretakers during owner's absence from July through mid-September.* NY Review of Books 3/4/76, p39

houtie (ˈhoutiː), *n.* a derogatory term used in Zimbabwe to refer to a black African. Compare AF. See also TERR. *Then, with perhaps an unfortunate turn of phrase, he added: "The catchword of the battalion is 'We just want to slay houties.' "* *Afterwards Colonel Rich explained to foreign correspondents that the term "houtie" meant Africans. It is in fact an Afrikaans word meaning "wooden head" and has tended to replace "kaffir" and "munt" as a derogatory term for blacks.* Times (London) 5/15/76, p4 [**1976**, shortened from Afrikaans *houtkop,* literally, wooden head]

hoverbed, *n.* a device for supporting a person with burnt or ulcerated skin on a cushion of air. *The block will provide all inpatient services needed to complete the accident and emergency centre next door. It will have a regional burns unit, including two revolutionary "hoverbeds" for badly burned patients.* Belfast Telegraph 2/2/73, p3 [**1967**, from *hover-* (as in HOVERCRAFT) + *bed*]

hovercraft, *n. sing.* or *pl. Chiefly British.* a vehicle that travels above ground or water on a cushion of air produced by fans. Also called in the United States AIR CUSHION VEHICLE and GROUND EFFECT MACHINE. . . . *4,000 tons was unlikely to be the limit of size in hovercraft. They could travel faster than ships and carry cargoes more cheaply than aircraft, and so fall neatly between the two in operating costs. There might be a vast market for cargo hovercraft as large bulk carriers on the Atlantic and other trans-oceanic routes.* Annual Register of World Events in 1967, p408 [**1959**]

hoverferry, *n. British.* a hovercraft to ferry passengers across water. *The world's first semi-amphibious hoverferry . . . showed its paces yesterday in special trials and sped along the Solent at 38 knots.* Times (London) 5/7/70, p24 [**1961**]

hoverpad, *n. British.* a metal plate forming the base of a hovercraft or hovertrain. *The full scale test vehicle will be 24 metres long and will employ both the prototype hoverpads and linear motor envisaged for a 100-passenger commercial version . . .* Science Journal 5/70, p17 [**1964**]

hoverport, *n.* a port or terminal for hovercraft. *The new car ferry and hoverport at Dover will further enhance what is already, though few are aware of it, the world's leading port for international passenger traffic by sea.* Times (London) 5/1/70, p15 [**1964**]

hovertrailer, *n. British.* a hovercraft for carrying heavy loads over a marsh, bog, mudflats, plowland, and the like. *Two hovertrailers linked side by side have been used to transport a 27-ton tracked piledriver over marshy ground along the line of an electricity transmission line in Holland.* New Scientist 6/21/73, p756 [**1967**]

hovertrain, *n.* a high-speed train that rides on a cushion of air over a concrete track. *The promoters of hovertrains see their vehicles as providing a coarse, high-speed network, which, by allowing the ordinary trains to run at less diverse speeds, will vastly increase the capacity for goods and intermediate distance passengers, as well as enable the service to be improved.* New Scientist 1/1/70, p25 [**1961**]

HPV, abbreviation of HUMAN PAPILLOMAVIRUS. *Human papillomavirus (HPV) has been known as the causative agent of warts of the human skin and condylomata of the genitalia for over half a century.* McGraw-Hill Yearbook of Science and Technology 1988, p376 [**1984**]

H-ras (ˌeitʃˈræs) *n.* a human gene of the ras group. *Scientists learned in 1983 that yeast cells contain two genes that are similar to a human cancer gene known as H-ras. Because they are so like the human gene, the two yeast genes are also called ras. Mutant yeast strains that lack both ras genes cannot grow, indicating that the genes serve some important function in the normal growth of a yeast cell.* World Book Science Annual 1986, p288 [**1985**, from *H*uman + RAS]

HTGR, abbreviation of *high temperature gas-cooled reactor* (a nuclear power reactor using uranium and thorium as fuel, graphite as moderator, and helium as coolant). Compare HTR. *With a total absence of combustion products the HTGR is certainly the most environmentally attractive source of energy available today.* Science News 11/17/73, p307 [**1968**]

HTLV, *n.* any of several retroviruses linked to various forms of leukemia and formerly thought to include the virus that causes AIDS. Compare HIV. . . . *a retrovirus called HTLV-1, which was put forward as the leading candidate for the cause of AIDS. HTLV-1, initially reported in 1981, had been found to cause a rare type of leukemia in southern Japan and the Caribbean islands. HTLV originally stood for human T-cell leukemia virus but now the initials are used for human T-*

lymphotropic retroviruses to broaden the name. NY Times 4/24/84, pC3 [**1983**]

HTR, abbreviation of *high temperature reactor* (a nuclear reactor in which the temperature is high enough to generate mechanical power). *Both in Germany and the United States, there is great interest in the HTR system as the medium term for generation.* Times (London) 8/9/72, p6 [**1967**]

huayco ('waikou), *n.* a large landslide common in Peru. *Although a mud–and earthslide (called* huayco) *covered Yungay, and a nearby village beneath tons of debris and took thousands of lives, the principal cause of the high death toll was strong earth vibration that led to the collapse of innumerable poorly designed structures.* Britannica Book of the Year 1971, p661 [**1970**, from American Spanish, from Quechua]

hub-and-spoke, *adj.* of or having to do with a system of transportation, especially of small airlines, by which passengers or freight are carried on branch routes to a central city to make connections for transportation to a large metropolitan area. *Another post-deregulation trend . . . was hub-and-spoke operations* [that] *depend largely on feeder traffic.* Americana Annual 1987, p526 *Hub-and-spoke systems make for many shorter, better-filled and hence more profitable flights than nonstops.* NY Times Magazine 11/1/87, p44 [**1981**]

Hubble constant or **Hubble's constant,** an astronomical measure used in calculating the velocity at which galaxies recede according to the HUBBLE LAW. *Most astronomers agree that the universe is expanding, but they have never been able to get an accurate measure of the rate of that expansion, the so-called Hubble constant . . .* Science News 11/29/69, p505 *Drs. Marc Aaronson, Jeremy Mould and John Huchra turned the clock back by recomputing the number known as Hubble's Constant, or H, used to figure time and distance in the universe. They found that H, the ratio of an object's speed (relative to our galaxy) to its distance from our galaxy, is 95, not 50.* NY Times 11/18/79, pD7 [**1952**, named after the American astronomer Edwin P. *Hubble*, 1889-1953]

Hubble law, the astronomical observation that the velocity of the recession of galaxies is proportional to their distance from our own galaxy, as shown by the systematic shift of lines in the spectra of the galaxies toward the red in linear proportion to their distance from us. *For some time Arp has argued that the extremely large red shifts of quasars—which according to the Hubble law indicates that they are the most distant known objects in the universe—did not arise entirely from their distance and recessional velocity but from some other cause.* Science Journal 10/68, p9 [**1933, 1962**, named after Edwin P. *Hubble* (see HUBBLE CONSTANT) who formulated the law in 1929]

HUD (həd), *n.* acronym for *Housing and Urban Development* (full name, Department of Housing and Urban Development), a department of the U.S. government created in 1965. *When George Romney visited Warren, Mich., in July, he learned how sensitive community feelings are. Romney was cursed and hissed, as he explained HUD's aspirations to let more of the blacks who work in Warren's auto plants live in the town.* Time 9/7/70, p51 [**1965**]

huelga ('welgɑ:), *n. Spanish.* a labor strike, often in the phrase *la huelga* (the strike). . . . *if* [Cesar] *Chavez is able to continue* [the boycott against grape growers] *despite his precarious health, there seems little doubt that, in the end,* la huelga *will prevail.* 1970 Collier's Encyclopedia Year Book, p405 *Here and there is the emblem of U.F.W.O.C.* [United Farm Workers Organizing Committee, in Delano, California], *a square-edged black eagle in a white circle on a red background, over the word "HUELGA," which in Spanish means "strike."* New Yorker 6/28/69, p43 [**1965**]

huevos rancheros ('hweivous rɑ:n'tʃerɔs), a Mexican dish of fried or poached eggs with tomato sauce. *The most widely known dish in the Southwest breakfast repertory, huevos rancheros, derives its name from the region's ranching heritage.* NY Times Magazine 1/24/88, p42 [**1986**, from Spanish, literally, ranch eggs]

Hugo, *n.* an award given annually for the best work in science fiction. *The yearly awards for excellence in science fiction are called Hugos . . . With greater justice, they might be called Herberts, in recognition of Herbert George Wells.* Saturday Review 1/1/72, p14 [**1967**, named for *Hugo* Gernsback, 1884-1967, American editor, publisher and inventor, who founded the first science-fiction magazine, *Amazing Stories*, in 1926]

humalin, *n.* insulin made for humans through genetic engineering. *New biological technologies, including gene-splicing, have . . . led to such new products as spray bandages, artificial organs and microelectronic limbs. Just weeks ago, the Food and Drug Administration approved the marketing of "humalin"— human insulin made artificially from gene-splicing techniques.* NY Times 11/27/82, p23 [**1982,** from *huma*n + insu*lin*]

human growth hormone, a synthetic form of the pituitary hormone somatotropin, which regulates growth of the human body. *Abbreviation:* HGH *The creation of the synthetic "human growth hormone" (H.G.H.) was the work of Dr. Choh Hao Li and Dr. Donald Yamashiro, of the hormonal research laboratory of the University of California.* Times (London) 1/7/71, p7 [**1959**]

humanistic psychology, a branch of psychology dealing with the emotions, needs, and potential development of the normal individual. *Although* [Abraham H.] *Maslow later became president of the American Psychological Association, he saw his own humanistic psychology as a "third-force" alternative to strict Freudianism and its off-shoots, which rules the psychoanalytic profession, and to the behavioristic psychology that had become dominant in most university psychology departments.* New Yorker 1/5/76, p42 [**1971**] —**humanistic psychologist:** *No one could have mistaken the Squaw Valley meeting of the humanistic psychologists for an academic conference.* NY Times Magazine 12/17/72, p19

human papillomavirus, a virus that causes warts or wartlike growths on the human skin and genitalia. *Abbreviation:* HPV. See PAPOVAVIRUS. *Before the carcinogenesis of human papillomavirus drew the attention of investigators, type II herpes simplex virus . . . was suspected as the causative agent of uterine cervical cancer.* McGraw-Hill Yearbook of Science and Technology 1988, p376 [**1983**]

human potentials movement, a social movement to improve the self-respect of individuals and their relationships with others chiefly in group sessions that make people aware of their own feelings and sensitive to the feelings of others. See also SENSITIVITY TRAINING, ENCOUNTER GROUP. *The leaders of the human potentials movement should see this movement in a larger social context, and concentrate on the re-establishment of smaller social units and natural groups in society at large. Otherwise the movement becomes just another empty institution void of significance and meaning outside the four walls of the joy seminars . . .* Time 11/30/70, pNY4 [**1970**]

human-powered, *adj.* powered by a person or persons, not by an engine or other machine; powered by human energy. *Both solar craft were designed by aeronautical engineer Paul MacCready of Aerovironment Incorporated in Pasadena, Calif. He had earlier won fame, plus prize money, with his human-powered* Gossamer Condor, *which made aviation history in 1977, and the* Gossamer Albatross, *a human-powered plane that flew across the English Channel in 1979.* World Book Science Annual 1982, p251 [**1961**]

human rights. ▶This 200-year-old phrase rose to new prominence in 1976 as the expression of a major political policy of the U.S. government. As a theme of his inaugural address and in addressing the United Nations in 1977, President Jimmy Carter emphasized that body's responsibility to promote human rights throughout the world: All the signatories of the UN Charter have pledged themselves to observe and to respect basic human rights. Thus, no member of the United Nations can claim that mistreatment of its citizens is solely its own business. The term *human rights* has been in the English language since the French Revolution, perhaps first used by Thomas Paine, in his *Rights of Man* (1791), where he translated the French *droits de l'homme* as "human rights." Considered self-evident in meaning, it was not defined in dictionaries until the late 1970's.

human sciences, the formalized studies or sciences that deal with the activities of human beings, such as anthropology, language, literature, psychology, religion, and sociology. *The magisterium's role is to express "what is true," [Yves] Congar emphasized, while today's theologian is expected to chart new modes of defining those truths. "The theologian must be in constant contact with human sciences, with latest developments in all kinds of thought . . ."* Time 11/13/72, pNY13 *Acquisition of language by humans is among the most recalcitrant problems in human sciences.* New Scientist 11/22/73, p526 [**1943, 1971** loan translation of German *Geisteswissenschaften* (1883)]

human services, *U.S.* aid provided to improve social conditions, such as that given by child welfare bureaus and public health clinics or free medical care for the elderly. *Somehow "human services" strikes me as vague, but it distinguishes the activity of that department from, say, canine services . . . Most important, it will relieve congressmen of the onus of having voted for "more welfare."* NY Times Magazine 10/28/79, p9 [**1967**]

humint or **HUMINT**, *n.* the gathering of secret intelligence by the use of spies (as opposed to electronic surveillance, etc.). *Among the more practiced perpetrators of mayhem on the English language are members of the US intelligence community. Already they have flattened the phrase communications intelligence (the fruits of electronic surveillance or code breaking) into "comint" and reshaped human intelligence (information from spies) into "humint."* Time 7/25/77, p30 [**1977**, blend of *human intelligence*]

humongous (hyu:'maŋgəs), *adj. U.S. Slang.* extremely large or great; colossal; tremendous. *Her normal speaking voice has a light Southern accent. She uses expressions like "the whole megillah" (meaning the whole long story) and "humongous" (meaning huger than huge and more tremendous than tremendous).* New Yorker 8/16/76, p26 *The surge of slang is, in a word, humongous. Go for it!* San Francisco Sunday Examiner & Chronicle 4/1/79, p12 [**1976**, apparently a fanciful coinage from *huge* and *monstrous*]

180-degree or **hundred-and-eighty-degree**, *adj.* complete; hundred-percent. *Still, as one diplomat in Paris noted, "The Chinese now are open and forthcoming; the slogans, polemics and jargon have disappeared from their conversation. It's a 180-degree change from the old days."* Newsweek 1/22/73, p31 *Taft, as you'll recall, was a stick-in-the-mud on most economic and social issues, but . . . midway in his senatorial career he did a hundred-and-eighty-degree turnabout on this issue, and became a forceful advocate of federal aid to education.* New Yorker 2/3/75, p21 [**1972**, figurative use of the measurement of a straight angle, one equal to a complete turnabout or the opposite side of a circle or arc] ►As an adverb in the sense of "completely" the form *180 degrees* is also sometimes used, as in the following quotation: *I mean, those glancing insights, those adolescent knight-errantries, aren't they old news? Haven't our tastes altered 180 degrees?* Time 2/7/72, p50

hung-up, *adj.* Also, **hung up.** *Slang.* **1** having psychological or emotional problems. *The men who become prisoners are the most obvious criminals: clumsy, stupid, impulsive, hung-up. Some have gotten what they deserve, some are oversentenced, some belong in mental institutions, some shouldn't be in any institution.* Atlantic 1/66, p52 *But she admits her songs are not yet very commercial. "I usually write them when I am very emotionally disturbed, really hung-up," she explains.* Times (London) 3/1/68, p13 **2 hung up on, a** obsessed or preoccupied with. *Each is hung up on his syndrome (which often takes the form of atavistic racial fears), unable to live without it.* NY Times Magazine 1/14/68, p31 **b** emotionally attached to; infatuated with. *"Solid citizen Albert," Harper says sardonically, "hung up on a chick—at your age"* . . . Punch 6/8/66, p853 [**1957**, originally used in the sense of being delayed or stymied by a difficulty and unable to proceed]

hunter-killer satellite, an artificial satellite designed to search out and destroy enemy satellites. Also called KILLER SATELLITE, SATELLITE KILLER. See ASAT. *Last year's resumption of Soviet tests of a hunter-killer satellite in earth orbit has moved the United States to draw up its own plans to wage war in space.* Manchester Guardian Weekly (Washington Post section) 1/23/77, p16 *There are a couple of hundred (overtrained) blue-eyed boys in Los Alamos, New Mexico, working on hunter-killer satellites and directed energy weapons like satellite-launched high-energy lasers.* Rolling Stone 1/11/79, p78 [**1976**, extended from the older (1948) meaning of *hunter-killer* designed for finding and destroying enemy submarines]

hush kit, *British.* a combination of sound-absorbent linings and modified jet pipe nozzles fitted to jet engines to reduce noise. *Engine manufacturers have been working for the past four years to develop hush kits and claim to have had a large degree of technical success. Fitted to new BAC 1-11 airliners, the Rolls kits have reduced the 90-decibel noise "footprint" produced on the ground by the two Spey engines from 25 to 12½ square miles.* Times (London) 3/19/76, p5 [**1973**]

hustle or **Hustle**, *n.* a lively dance for couples done to disco music, characterized by intricate footwork, dips, and spins. *Each week an extra kick or a fancy turn sets off a new variation and a new challenge. There is the advanced hustle, which resembles a jitterbug, the beginner's hustle, which is the dance reduced to its simplest steps, and the Latin hustle, which has the most complicated footwork and spins. There is also a Bronx hustle, Queens hustle, Brooklyn hustle and scores more that do not have names.* NY Times 7/12/75, p27 —*v.i.* to dance a hustle. *Again, as in times long past, "Would you like to dance?" means "Can you dance?" There's no more ad libbing, no way to fake it. Either you Hustle—or you sit. If the question can be answered affirmatively, there is then the moment while you figure out which Hustle your partner is dancing.* Sunday News (New York) 1/11/76, p41 [**1975**]

hyaline membrane disease ('haiələn), a respiratory disease of newborn babies, especially when born prematurely, due to the formation of a hyaline or glassy film over the interlining of the lungs. Also called RESPIRATORY DISTRESS SYNDROME. *Each year, 50,000 U.S. infants die soon after birth—at least 25,000 of them from respiratory distress syndrome (RDS). Also called hyaline membrane disease, RDS is caused by the inability of an infant's lungs to extract oxygen from the air and pass carbon dioxide out of the body.* Time 12/7/70, p94 [**1953**, *hyaline* from Greek *hyálinos* of glass, from *hýalos* glass]

H-Y antigen ('eitʃ'wai), a protein that determines the action of the male chromosome (Y chromosome) in mammals, found on the surface of cells in males. *Mary Lyon, at Harwell, and her colleagues in America, showed that only the Y chromosome carried the genetic blueprint for production of a surface protein, the so-called HY antigen, which acted as the stimulus for developing testes.* Annual Register of World Events in 1975, p360 *The Y chromosome sex determinant gene was identified in all seven of them [hermaphrodites]. Specifically, the protein that is encoded by this gene, the so-called H-Y antigen, was present in cells from all the subjects.* Science News 10/16/76, p246 [**1976**, from *h*istocompatibility + *Y* chromosome + *anti*gen; so called because it was originally thought to be a HISTO-COMPATIBILITY ANTIGEN, since it caused skin grafts in genetically identical mice to be rejected when male skin was grafted on females]

hybridoma, *n.* a hybrid cell formed by CELL FUSION. *Tissue typing . . . is the labour to which immunologists foresaw the end when they made the first antibody-secreting hybridoma: a hybrid between an ordinary mouse antibody-secreting cell, which has only a limited lifespan, and an immortal tumour cell from a mouse myeloma.* New Scientist 7/27/78, p271 *Hybridoma technology is . . . nearly ready for application in research, diagnosis and possibly treatment. This is the result of fusing two different kinds of cells—lymphocytes fused to myeloma cells provide information for producing just that one pure antibody.* New York Post 12/24/79, p13 [**1978,**

from *hybrid* + *-oma* mass, tumor, as in *myeloma* a malignant tumor of the bone marrow]

hybrimycin (ˌhaibrəˈmaisən), *n.* any of various antibiotic drugs made by combining the components of other antibiotics. . . . *the new antibiotics were given the name hybrimycins, since they can be considered hybrid antibiotics, with the streptamine or 2-epistreptamine ring coming from streptomycin or spectinomycin, respectively, and the remaining rings coming from the neomycins.* McGraw-Hill Yearbook of Science and Technology 1971, p121 [**1969,** from *hybri*d + *-mycin,* suffix in the names of antibiotics derived from soil bacteria (from Greek *mýkēs* fungus)]

hycanthone, *n.* a chemical substance that causes mutations in bacterial and mammalian cells, used as a drug in the treatment of schistosomiasis. *Formula:* $C_{20}H_{24}N_2O_2S$ *Sterling-Winthrop Research Institute has produced hycanthone, a one-shot treatment for schistosomiasis, a worm disease almost as widespread and devastating as malaria, and has reported 80 percent cure rates.* 1971 Collier's Encyclopedia Year Book, p336 [**1970,** from *hy*droxymethyl thio*xanthen*one, part of the chemical constituents]

hydrilla, *n.* a soft aquatic weed that was introduced from Asia into Florida in the 1960's as an aquarium plant and that has since spread throughout the southeastern United States. *This year, the almost indestructible hydrilla has blanketed the 1,600-acre lake* [Trafford], *choking fish and destroying navigation.* Newsweek 1/13/75, p74 *Hydrilla . . . appears to have the potential of becoming the most serious submersed weed problem in the United States. It is a major problem in the Panama Canal Zone and in several other countries.* McGraw-Hill Yearbook of Science and Technology 1978, p96 [**1970,** from New Latin *Hydrilla* (*verticillata*), the species name, probably diminutive of Latin *hȳdra* hydra]

hydrofracturing, *n.* **1** a method of opening a passageway for oil by pumping water under high pressure down an oil well that has gone dry to crack the rock and allow more oil to seep into the well, used also to pump water to and from hot rock reservoirs for use as a power source (also used attributively). *The challenge is to sink wells and shatter this rock so that water from the surface can penetrate it and become heated. The hot water or steam would then be piped up and used to drive a power plant. Holes must be drilled into such rock and some process, such as underground nuclear explosions or "hydrofracturing," must be used to shatter the rock so that water can penetrate it.* NY Times 11/5/72, pD8 **2** Passing into verb: *At the deepest level attempted, 5,320 meters, the tests reached the 1,000-bar safety threshold of the well pipe without hydrofracturing the local gabbro zone.* Science News 4/24/76, p267 [**1970,** from *hydro-* water + *fracturing* cracking]

hydrogasification, *n.* the conversion of coal into gas by reacting it with hydrogen at high pressures to yield methane. *A $5.7-million pilot plan for hydrogasification of coal will be built by Procon, Inc., a subsidiary of Universal Oil Products, for the Institute of Gas Technology at a Chicago site, the magazine Chemical Week reports.* NY Times 8/15/68, p62 [**1954,** from *hydro*gen + *gasification*]

hydrogasifier, *n.* an apparatus used in hydrogasification. *As an example, if Bituminous Coal Research is successful in developing a low-cost gas producer, it might be used with a steam-iron variation of the Institute's hydrogasifier to produce methane at an economically attractive price. Again, the Kellogg molten salt process might produce hydrogen for a hydrogasifier.* New Scientist 4/27/67, p214 [**1966**]

hydrolab, *n.* a vessel designed for research under water for an extended period. *Meanwhile, after years of having the hydrolab underwater laboratory-residence used primarily for testing man's survival in a strange environment, scientists have begun to use the facility for extensive research at 50-foot depths near the Bahamas. From March 13 to 20, ichthyologist C. Lavett Smith of the American Museum of Natural History, and two companions, lived in the 16- by 8-foot habitat to study*

the microcosm around a coral reef. Science News 4/7/73, p221 [**1969,** from *hydro-* water + *lab*]

hydronaut, *n.* (in the U.S. Navy) a person trained to work in undersea vessels engaged in search and rescue missions and in research projects. Compare AQUANAUT. *Hydronauts—the men who will operate the U.S. Navy's deep submergence vehicles—are being trained in a unique dry-land device that simulates operation of the bathyscaphe Trieste II.* Science News 3/25/67, p286 [**1961,** from *hydro-* water + *-naut,* as in *astronaut*]

hydrophilic, *n.* a contact lens made of plastic material that absorbs water to become soft and flexible. Usually called SOFT LENS. *It is estimated that within a couple of years between 30 and 40 per cent of the contact lens market will be taken by the hydrophilics.* Sunday Times (London) 10/24/71, p10 [**1971,** noun use of the adjective meaning "readily absorbing water"]

hydroplaning, *n.* the skidding of a motor vehicle on a wet road which results from the building up of a wedge of fluid between the moving tires and the pavement to a point where the tires lose contact with the road. Also called AQUAPLANING. *Film* ["Grooving for Safety"] *illustrates a new technique currently being employed to prevent tire hydroplaning, by putting narrow grooves in highways to provide an escape route for the water and improving tire traction.* Science News 2/22/69, p180 [**1969,** from the earlier term (1909) for traveling in a hydroplane]

hydroskimmer, *n. U.S.* an air cushion vehicle designed to travel over water. *Several ACVs called Hydroskimmers, have already been built for the U.S. Navy by Bell Aerosystems Company, Buffalo, N.Y.* Science News 6/4/66, p445 [**1961**]

hydrospace, *n.* the space beneath the surface of the sea. Also called INNER SPACE. *Other categories of plot include a growing preoccupation with "inner space" or "hydrospace" (the word used, incidentally, in a recent advertisement in New Scientist)—the opening up of the watery four-fifths of our own planet.* New Scientist 12/22/66, p691 *. . . the boom . . . is coming in the exploration and exploitation of what the hard men in the shipping world are learning to call hydrospace.* Sunday Times (London) 10/13/68, p33 [**1960**]

Hyfil, *n.* a trade name for a plastic or resin strengthened with carbon fiber. *Rolls-Royce has had Hyfil fan blades fitted to some engines in Standard VC10s . . .* Times (London) 5/7/70, p2 *In the UK, 'Hyfil' compressor blades are an excellent example of such a carbon fibre/resin application.* New Scientist 7/10/69, p68 [**1966**]

hylology (haiˈlɑlədʒi:), *n.* the study of the properties of materials used in science and technology; materials science. *The problem in arriving at these priorities, of course, is the very diversity of what constitutes "materials research." As a separate discipline, the field has existed for only about two decades, and only now has the Academy suggested that the term "hylology" (the study of matter) be applied to this amorphous realm.* Science News 1/26/74, p53 [**1974,** from Greek *hȳle* substance, matter + English *-ology* study of]

hype, *Slang.* **—n. 1** something that artificially stimulates sales, interest, etc., such as advertising or promotion. *Detached from hype and trend, almost entirely dependent upon their fine heads and solid musicianship, there are a few groups and a few individual performers in the new music who endure . . .* Time 2/2/70, p3 **2** any trick or stunt to attract attention. *The original plan* [of the yippies] *was to hold a vast free rock-folk festival and bring together in a Community of Consciousness 'technologists, poets, artists, community organisers and visionaries' . . . despite talks of plans the yippies were basically interested in improvising scenarios as they went along—using the Convention as a blank canvas for their revolutionary artistry. The talk, the publicity, the putting on, the 'hype' worked.* Listener 10/31/68, p566 **3** a person or thing publicized or promoted through hype. . . . *the performer who is written off as a hype becomes no longer the darling of the underground in-crowd, whatever his sincerity or intrinsic merit.* Times (London) 8/13/70, p10 **—v.t.** Usually, **hype up. 1** to stimulate artificially; promote, especially with tricks or stunts. *They're* [producers of sports programs on television] *so lacking in confidence in the* *attraction of the games they televise that they feel they have to hype them up with some hysterical commentator in order to get anyone to watch them.* Saturday Night (Canada) 8/65, p31 **2** to stir up in feeling; excite. *But Sandy . . . is so hyped up about the Boston opening Sept. 4 that some fear she may blow all the fuses.* Time 9/1/67, p47 [**1962**, from *hype*, U.S. slang term for hypodermic injection of a narcotic drug (OEDS 1933) and possibly influenced by the meaning "morphine user" (OED2, 1924)]

hyped-up, *adj. U.S. Slang.* exuberant; excited. *Tom Wolfe is known for his frenetic, grammar-released, hyped-up tonal style.* NY Times 8/12/68, p37 [**1968**, from the verb phrase *hype up*]

hyper-, a very productive prefix, meaning over; excessively; super-. Words formed with *hyper-* typically include: —**hyperaggressive**, *adj.: The whole first part of the movie nags us with the author's exposure of his characters; the actively "normal" parents, for instance, have created a hyperaggressive daughter who wants to "mold" men . . .* Atlantic 4/71, p99 —**hypercautious**, *adj.: . . . the hypercautious instincts of the politically insecure youths who now occupy the upper reaches of the Administration . . .* Manchester Guardian Weekly 3/6/71, p4 —**hyperfine**, *adj.: Apparent small shifts in the velocity may be attributed to hyperfine atomic structure because the 1.35-cm H_2O line is in fact a blend of six hyperfine energy transitions.* New Scientist and Science Journal 7/29/71, p243 —**hyperinflation**, *n.: What a magnificent drain on our resources with the complex consequences of stock market boom and bust, uncontrolled inflation with its inherent danger of hyperinflation . . .* NY Times 11/7/70, p29 —**hyperslow**, *adj.: Duvalier affected the staring gaze, whispered speech and hyperslow movements recognized by Haitians as signs that a person is close to the voodoo spirits.* Time 5/3/71, p26 —**hyperspecialization**, *n.: ". . . The remarkable thing is that at a time of overwhelming technical sophistication, expertise and hyperspecialization, professionals are discovering a common purpose—the well-being of people."* Time 5/24/71, p45 —**hyperverbal**, *adj.: He* [Paul Newman as Rheinhardt in "WUSA"] *is hyperverbal and is given to self-lacerating bitter tirades . . .* New Yorker 11/7/70, p165

hyper, *adj. U.S. and Canadian Slang.* overly excited or stimulated; emotionally charged. *The quiz kids are about as sensitive as meat grinders. They scratch and claw for every point, lips smacking and eyes glittering . . . One boy was so hyper he fell off the set minutes before the game was to begin; he climbed back up and did the show with a broken wrist.* Maclean's 2/73, p85 *One of Culver's characteristics, noted by his friends, is objectivity about himself. As he talks now about the staff, this comes out, "I know I can be hyper and intimidating and aggressive, and I have to be careful not to expect too much of them."* New Yorker 9/11/78, p65 [**1942, 1971**, adjective use of the prefix HYPER-, or perhaps shortened from *hyper*active]

hyperalimentation, *n.* intravenous feeding that provides the necessary foods and nutritive substances to patients who cannot ingest them through the alimentary canal. *Thousands of people across the country who cannot digest or absorb their food are benefiting, though less conveniently, from . . . intravenous hyperalimentation. By using this technique, which involves pumping nutrients directly into the bloodstream, doctors are able to keep alive patients with shortened guts, inflamed bowels, and immunological defects that prevent proper digestion of food.* Time 10/9/78, p104 [**1970**]

hyperbaric, *adj.* of or relating to the use of oxygen under high pressure, especially in medical operation and experimentation. *Still another way to increase the amount of oxygen available to human tissues is . . . to supply oxygen to him in a hyperbaric chamber, in which the total gas pressure is increased to two or three atmospheres.* Scientific American 2/66, p63 *The revival of hyperbaric medicine in the mid-fifties contributed greatly to awaken interest in pressure physiology.* McGraw-Hill Yearbook of Science and Technology 1967, p2 [**1963**, from *hyper-* + *-baric* (from Greek *báros* weight, pressure + English *-ic*)]

hypercharge, *v.t.* to charge to excess; supercharge. *Harold Wilson said in October 1965 that the atmosphere in Rhodesia was hypercharged with fear. If it was true then, it is even more true today. The events of the past few months seem to have paralysed us.* Manchester Guardian Weekly 1/26/67, p6 —**n.** *Nuclear Physics.* a quantum number which is equal to twice the average electric charge in a group of strongly interacting particles. *Each eight-fold way multiplet consists of several subgroups of particles having the same mass, hypercharge and isotopic spin.* Science News Letter 2/6/65, p85 [**1965** for verb; **1956** for noun]

hypercomplex, *adj.* **1** of or designating the most structurally complex cells of the visual cortex. *A typical complex cortical cell responds only to a slit, a bar or an edge. Cortical cells also have stringent requirements for the width and orientation of the stimulus. Hypercomplex cortical cells require that the stimulus also have a specific length.* Scientific American 12/72, p78 **2** of or designating any algebraic number or system involving quaternions. *Buff studied hypercomplex analysis, which deals with a calculus for functions of quaternions, variables in complex mathematics analogous to numbers.* Science News 3/7/70, p244 [**1969** for def. 1; **1970** for def. 2]

hyperlipidemia (ˌhaipərˌlipəˈdiːmiːə), *n.* an abnormally large amount of fatty or oily substances (lipids) in the blood. *It is currently recommended that children with one of the known genetic forms of hyperlipidemia (elevated blood levels of certain fats) be placed on an appropriate diet.* Americana Annual 1973, p452 *A national register of people suffering from hyperlipidaemia, a rare form of heart disease, is being compiled in Oxford . . . Hyperlipidaemia is a severe biochemical abnormality characterized by a greatly increased level of fats in the blood—not cholesterol but triglycerids.* Times (London) 10/24/78, p2 [**1969**, from *hyper-* excessive + *lipid* + *-emia* blood]

hyperlipoproteinemia (ˌhaipərˌlipəproutiˈniːmiːə), *n.* an abnormally large amount of lipids and proteins combined (lipoproteins) in the blood. *Dr M.C. Stone (Leigh Infirmary, Lancashire) discussed the role of diet in the management of hyperlipoproteinaemias. He and his collaborators have developed a simple method for studying the serum lipoprotein pattern by a combination of membrane filtration and nephelometry.* Nature 7/28/72, p194 [**1969**, from *hyper-* excessive + *lipoprotein* + *-emia* blood]

hypermarket, *n. British.* a very large ground-floor store, usually built in the suburbs. *Hypermarkets—monster out-of-town shops, perhaps up to 10 times bigger than a big supermarket—are the latest challenge to traditional shopping.* Sunday Times (London) 6/6/71, p46 *. . . they commissioned an independent survey of the probable effects of the proposed hypermarket.* Listener 12/30/71, p919 [**1970**, translation of French *hypermarché* very large market, after *supermarché* supermarket]

hyperrealism, *n.* a style of painting and sculpture characterized by extremely lifelike representation of persons and objects. *Hyperrealism, as predicted, is popping up in the galleries, represented here by Michael Leonard, who has actually been practising it for some time. His style is immaculate, his subjects intimate, the tone as green and shady as a day in the park.* Manchester Guardian Weekly 8/26/72, p21 [**1970**] —**hyperrealist**, *adj., n.: Robert Bechtle/Alan Kessler—Hyperrealist paintings of California back yards by a painter who has a deadly eye for the banal. / What looks like well-worn tools offered up at a lawn sale—handsaws, files, hatchets, crossbars—are really hand-carved-and-painted wooden sculptures.* New Yorker 1/2/78, p7 *The proof of a really good exhibition is whether it makes you see things differently afterwards, and the exhibition of American Hyper-realists and European Realists at the National Centre of Contemporary Art (CNAC) in Paris did just that.* Manchester Guardian Weekly 5/11/74, p21

hypervariable minisatellite, any of a class of short segments of satellite DNA, containing repeating sequences of base pairs whose number varies from individual to individual. *Since hypervariable minisatellites are completely specific to an individual, they provide a powerful tool for paternity testing.*

McGraw-Hill Yearbook of Science and Technology 1988, p153 [**1987**]

hypervelocity, *n.* extremely high velocity, as that of spacecraft or of nuclear particles. *I had independently and in advance of Harrison developed the idea of achieving controlled fusion by the impact of macroparticles accelerated to hypervelocities.* New Scientist 10/5/67, p47 *The surfaces of the* [lunar] *glass spheres and rocks show minute craters, which are the result of hypervelocity impacts of tiny particles . . .* McGraw-Hill Yearbook of Science and Technology 1971, p274 [**1955**]

hypnodrama, *n.* the acting out of a situation under hypnosis; psychodrama performed by a hypnotized person or persons. *We were to be hypnotized, and were then to participate in hypnodrama. We encircled the fieldstone fireplace in the center of the large dining hall as Ira Greenberg of the Camarillo, Calif., State Hospital led the session. He described hypnosis as a "control of our controls." It was a technique, he said, that enabled us to concentrate deeply and regress to forgotten states; once these states were recalled, hypnodrama could be used to act them out, enabling us finally to gratify the unsatisfied nurture needs of infancy.* NY Times Magazine 12/17/72, p22 [**1966,** from *hypnosis* + *drama*]

I

iaido (iːˈɑidou), *n.* a Japanese form of fencing using a single-edged sword slightly curved toward the point. *In martial arts activities closely related to kendo, the 17th All-Japan Iaido (Quick-Sword-Draw) Championships were held on October 31 in Fukushima Prefecture.* Britannica Book of the Year 1977, p201 [**1976**, from Japanese, from *iai* drawing a sword + *-dō* way]

-ian, a suffix now used chiefly to form adjectives of proper names in the sense of "relating to or characteristic of," and attached mainly to the names of well-known or famous persons. Primarily adjectival, *-ian* may be used also as a noun suffix; the variants *-an* and *-ean* are much less common. The following is a selection of currently common forms with *-ian:* —**Beckettian**, *adj.* [Samuel *Beckett*, born 1906, Irish playwright and novelist]: *The painful story of a writer balancing his "obligation to express" against his conviction that there is, in the end, "nothing to express" is Beckettian drama of a high order.* Saturday Review 10/3/70, p43 —**Borgesian**, *adj.* [Jorge Luis *Borges*, 1899-1986, Argentinian writer]: *Here are no visions and, in the Borgesian sense at least, no nightmares.* Times (London) 12/24/70, p5 —**Brechtian**, *adj.* [Bertolt *Brecht*, 1898-1955, German playwright]: *Edward II, translated by Eric Bentley, has been called Brecht's only tragedy; a reworking of Marlowe's play, it has been transmuted through the Brechtian intelligence into a grimly poetic drama about a beleaguered king railing against an unanswering universe.* Saturday Review 11/26/66, p41 —**Chomskian**, *adj.* [Noam *Chomsky*, born 1928, American linguist]: *. . . Chomskian generative and transformational grammar is one of those specialized conjectures which, by sheer intellectual fascination and range of implication, reach out to the world of the layman.* New Yorker 11/15/69, p217 —**Hitchcockian**, *adj.* [Alfred *Hitchcock*, 1899-1980, British film director]: *Particularly risky is the idea of filming an old-fashioned Hitchcockian murder mystery in all its creaking intricacy.* Time 6/22/70, p89 —**Ivesian**, *adj.* [Charles Edward *Ives*, 1874-1954, American composer]: *. . ."The Yale-Princeton Football Game," a little musical joke, with typically Ivesian quotations from popular marches . . .* New Yorker 12/12/70, p178 —**Nabokovian**, *adj.* [Vladimir *Nabokov*, 1899-1977, Russian-born novelist and poet]: *Equally Nabokovian are the extremes of opinion about the master's Russian translation of "Lolita."* Manchester Guardian Weekly 2/27/71, p18 —**Wodehousian**, *adj.* [P. G. *Wodehouse*, 1881-1975, British writer of humorous novels]: *A Wodehousian phrase leaps to mind as the perfect description for Marin's educational philosophy: the most frightful bilge!* Saturday Review 10/17/70, p55 —**Woolfian**, *adj.* [Virginia *Woolf*, 1882-1941, British novelist]: *Thus a lifelong love of technical language for its own sake pays off. The material isn't, as it were, orchestrated in a Woolfian way, nor is there anything like the immemorial moaning that Tennyson combines with geology.* Atlantic 5/70, p69

iatrogenesis (aiˌætrouˈdʒenəsis), *n.* the inducing of a disease, disorder, symptom, etc., by a physician through treatment, diagnosis, or other medical activity. *I include in clinical iatrogenesis the inevitable unwanted side effects of most powerful treatments or interventions which are foreseen and accepted by the doctor; those which are not foreseen, either because of his negligence, or because of his ignorance, or because of lack of scientific evidence on such treatments—this is a second category. Third, I include there all that damage that results from wrong judgment systems breakdown; lack of communication between patient and doctor; mix-up of information in the treatment establishment.* Maclean's 12/13/76,

p4 [**1976**, from Greek *iātrós* physician + English *genesis* origin]

IBA, abbreviation for *Independent Broadcasting Authority* (of Great Britain). *In the meantime he pursued his case against the ITV [Independent Television] documentary on Andy Warhol before the Appeal Court. Counsel for the Independent Broadcasting Authority said the IBA's board had now seen the film and fully concurred with its executive's decision that it be broadcast.* Listener 2/1/73, p137 [**1971**, replacing earlier (1954) *ITA*, abbreviation of Independent Television Authority]

ibuprofen (ˌaibyuːˈproufen), *n.* a drug which reduces the inflammation of arthritis and rheumatism without the gastrointestinal upset associated with aspirin. *Formula:* $C_{13}H_{18}O_2$ *In 1974 Boots won the Queen's award for export achievement. One of its drugs, ibuprofen, contributed significantly to that success.* Times (London) 2/2/77, p20 [**1970**, from *iso*butylphenyl*pro*pionic acid + *-fen* (probably alteration of *phenyl*)]

IC, abbreviation of INTEGRATED CIRCUIT. *An IC is a circuit consisting of up to 20 transistors and diodes on a microscopic chip of silicon . . .* 1970 Britannica Yearbook of Science and the Future, p167 *New integrated-circuit technology, and large-scale integration (LSI) in particular, should also have an impact on memory design—the report predicts that by 1975 superfast IC memories will be competitive with ferrite-core memories on the basis of cost considerations alone.* New Scientist 1/7/71, p20 [**1966**]

ice, *v.t.* U.S. Slang. **1** to kill. *When a white student broke a ban on drugs by giving LSD to an unprepared Ethiopian student, blacks threatened to "ice" him if he ever returned to Old Westbury.* Harper's 9/71, p61 **2 ice out**, to ignore or exclude socially. *It [Washington] is not a big city, and when a lady is down and out and getting herself dumped from someone's guest list there, it is not the same as getting herself iced out in New York or Chicago. There are not that many guest lists that everyone wants to get on, and Washington is poorer for that.* Harper's 7/70, p66 [**1965**, figurative senses of the verb meaning to cool with ice or become ice, freeze]

iceberg, *n.* **the tip of the iceberg**, a small or superficial part of something; that which appears only on the surface. *. . . the news article reported only the tip of the iceberg. Hidden is a serious situation for engineers in the United States and Great Britain.* Manchester Guardian Weekly 5/9/70, p2 *. . . subclinical infection by the cholera vibrio, in which the host shows no sign of illness, is common. This situation is similar to that of poliomyelitis or viral hepatitis, where the manifest cases of illness represent only the tip of the iceberg, with a much larger number of persons carrying the infection and spreading it unknowingly.* Scientific American 8/71, p16 [**1963**]

ice-minus, *adj.* of or designating a strain of bacteria developed by genetic engineering to resist the effect of ice formation on plants. *The researchers believe that spraying this ice-minus bacteria on plants . . . will prevent the growth of the normal bacteria which do catalyze frost formation, and thereby minimize frost damage to crops.* 1987 Collier's Encyclopedia Year Book, p156 [**1984**, from *ice* + *minus* lacking, non-existent]

icescape, *n.* a landscape consisting of ice, especially the polar landscape. *The whole icescape was awash with light—a cold, weird winter light which has transformed the pressure ice into foaming white breakers and ice floes into tranquil lagoons.* Sunday Times (London) 2/9/69, p6 [**1965**, from *ice* + *-scape* view, scene] ►Earlier sense of *icescape* (OEDS 1904) is a painting or picture showing an ice scene, on the pattern of *land-scape* and *seascape*.

ice station, a scientific research station in the Arctic, serving especially to monitor ice movement, weather, sea, and other environmental conditions. *Charles Knight . . . has had several periods of residence and work on drifting ice stations in the Arctic; he notes that one of them, ARLIS I (Arctic Research Laboratory Ice Station I) "was the first attempt at an austere station, and it did succeed in being austere."* Scientific American 1/73, p11 [**1968**]

icon, *n.* a picture or drawing representing a command to a computer, such as the picture of a garbage can representing the command to erase a file. *Icons, little pictures that represent such functions as "openfile" or "trash," can be clicked on or off with a mouse pointing device.* NY Times 9/23/86, pC7 *The corner icons are, clockwise from upper left, the move-window, help, grow-window, and close-window icons. The help icon, when clicked on, always gives a window—sometimes several—of explanatory information.* Byte 5/85, p101 [**1982**, transferred sense of *icon* picture, image]

ICU, abbreviation of INTENSIVE CARE UNIT. *Nearly every patient in the ICU is attached to a respirator, with a tube running from his nose to a white accordion-pleated cylinder, encased in glass, that expands and then flattens with a rhythmic sighing sound.* NY Times Magazine 5/23/76, p80 [**1972**]

IDDM, INSULIN DEPENDENT DIABETES MELLITUS, *Renal failure is seen in 50% of IDDM patients after 20 or 30 yr of diabetes.* Merck Manual, 15 ed., p1071 [**1987**]

identikit (ai'denti,kit), *n. British.* **1** a device used in police work to reconstruct faces from memory by using line-drawn variations of facial features to make a composite picture that approximates the description supplied by witnesses (often used attributively). Compare PHOTO-FIT. *Parts of the picture—for instance, of a face—can be lifted with a light pen and deposited on another face across the screen. This makes the construction of identikit-style pictures easier than before. The computer can even be programmed to divide the picture in two and replace the left with the right half and then the right with the left.* New Scientist 9/29/77, p798 **2** Figurative use: *Twenty-five years as a policeman had taught him that no character was without its complications, its inconsistencies. Only the young or the very arrogant imagined that there was an identikit to the human mind.* P.D. James, Shroud for a Nightingale, 1971, p154 [**1962**, from *identity + kit*; originally from the trademark spelled *Identi-Kit*]

identity crisis, a time of disturbance and anxiety when a person is in a self-conscious stage of personality development or adjustment, occurring especially during adolescence. *In the course of analyzing [George Bernard] Shaw's essay, [Erik] Erikson refers to Shaw's "identity crisis," and calls the long period of lonely, introspective writing a "moratorium"—an "interval between youth and adulthood" when one tries to achieve an inner and outer coherence.* New Yorker 11/14/70, p75 *For Mrs. Frank Schiff, the former Gloria O'Connor, being an identical twin was never a problem in any sense. She and her sister, Consuelo, now the Countess Rodolfo Crespi of Rome, never went through an identity crisis.* NY Times 6/21/71, p34 [**1954**]

idiot box, *Slang.* television. Compare GOGGLEBOX. *Anyone still wondering how the idiot box got its name hasn't been watching the TV commercials directed at housewives lately. Most are like messages from beyond Lewis Carroll's looking-glass . . .* Maclean's 5/68, p34 [**1959**]

idiot light, *Informal.* a warning light, usually red or yellow, that turns on when something goes wrong in an automobile or other machine. *Auto makers to date have provided the driver with only the most minimal information—gas level, coolant temperature, oil pressure, and battery charge—via dashboard gauges and idiot lights.* Saturday Review 6/10/72, p49 [**1968**]

idiotope ('idi:ou,toup), *n.* the part of an idiotype that behaves as an antigenic epitope when reacting with another antibody. *When antibodies produced by animal A are injected into animal B, animal B will produce antibodies against the idiotypic*

epitopes ("idiotopes") of the injected antibody molecules. Scientific American 7/73, p58 *Idiotopes . . . are self-antigens or autoantigens that play an important role in the regulation of the immune response.* McGraw-Hill Yearbook of Science and Technology 1988, p472 [**1973**, from *idio*type + epi*tope*]

idiot's lantern, *British Slang.* television. *It is still fashionable in some circles to dismiss television as the idiot's lantern or the goggle-box and to condemn it as a purveyor of poor shadowy substitutes for the "real thing" . . .* Punch 2/19/69, p284 [**1969**]

idiotype ('idi:ou,taip), *n.* the structure of an antibody that determines the specific antigen with which the antibody will react. *There are probably over a million different idiotypes in the body. Each B-lymphocyte and all of its offspring manufacture just one variety.* World Book Science Annual 1982, p168 *On each cell these two classes of receptor share the same antigenic specificity and idiotype, which probably means that they have the same variable region.* New Scientist 9/19/80, p1353 [**1972**, from Greek *ídios* one's own, distinct + English *type*, but also perhaps special application in biology from earlier use in chemistry (1865)] —**idiotypic**, *adj.: By recognizing idiotypic determinants on other antibodies and cellular antigen receptors, the immune system is able to balance responses to individual challenges . . .* McGraw-Hill Yearbook of Science and Technology 1988, p472 —**idiotypically**, *adv.: But the current report is the first to demonstrate that idiotypically identical antibodies . . . have identical light and heavy variable regions.* New Scientist 3/14/74, p669

IF, abbreviation of INTERFERON. *On being invaded by a virus, cells begin to make IF. The IF molecules do not take on viruses directly; instead, the interferon goes to surrounding cells and stimulates them to manufacture other substances.* Reader's Digest 11/79, p130 *If all goes well, they will make possible ample supplies of what is now a rare, extremely expensive, but promising new cancer drug: interferon, or, as scientists abbreviate it, IF.* Time 3/31/80, p60 [**1979**]

Ig, abbreviation of IMMUNOGLOBULIN, used especially in combination with a letter to designate any of various types. —**IgA**, a protein antibody acting against bacteria. *Our skin acts as a formidable barrier against infection, but our other coverings are not so impervious: the mucous membranes that line our lips, the soft covering of our eyes, the inside of our nose and cheeks, the linings of our mouth, throat and stomach. To keep organisms from entering through these moist, open surfaces, our body in its evolutionary wisdom coats them with IgA antibodies, which will attack any microbe, stopping it from getting into the bloodstream or down into the deeper layers of our bodies.* Reader's Digest 10/76, p263 *A protective immunological substance called secretory IgA is abundant in mother's milk. Studies have found that secretory IgA appears to prevent viruses from locking themselves to the membranes of living cells, the first step in infection.* Sunday News (New York) 9/23/79, p42 —**IgD:** *In man, there are two minor or less abundant classes, IgD and IgE, which have delta and epsilon heavy chains, respectively. Although the function of IgD is unknown, IgE antibodies are responsible for reaginic hypersensitivity reactions.* McGraw-Hill Yearbook of Science and Technology 1975, p238 —**IgE**, a protein antibody acting against allergic substances. *Further experiments indicated that this substance, called reagin, is produced in allergic people in response to such allergens as molecules from pollens and foods. It is similar to the way immunoglobulins, or antibodies, are produced . . . Then, in 1967, immunologists Kimishige and Teruko Ishizaka, a husband-and-wife team at the National Jewish Hospital and Research Center in Denver, proved that reagin was a new type of immunoglobulin, now called immunoglobulin E, or IgE.* World Book Science Annual 1977, p154 —**IgG**, a protein antibody causing agglutination of bacterial cells. *Some antibodies called IgG and IgM, may pass from the blood into the mouth in the minute amounts of fluid that normally seep out of the crevices where the gingivae meet the teeth. These crevicular antibodies adhere to bacteria and enhance the action of certain white blood cells, which engulf and destroy S. mutans.* Americana Annual 1978, p174 —**IgM**, a protein antibody acting against gram-negative bacteria. *However, IgM, the phylogenet-*

ically and ontogenetically earliest immune globulin, can be produced in large amounts despite the most severe malnutrition. McGraw-Hill Yearbook of Science and Technology 1978, p21 **[1965]**

igloo, *n.* a portable plastic structure having a dome shape, used as a protective covering. *The tariff applies to point-to-point consignments using the full 125 in. by 88 in. and 108 in. by 88 in. pallets with nets or igloos.* Times (London) 12/3/70, pV **[1963,** earlier in the sense of a rounded permanent structure (OED2, 1956)]

illegitimate, *adj. Genetics.* not occurring through the regular mechanisms of transmission; irregular. *Homologous crossing-over shuffles alleles, or variants, of the same gene and thereby promotes genetic diversity. In unequal crossing-over, a somewhat rarer event, the chromosomes are not perfectly aligned; nonhomologous segments cross over and recombine by means of some still uncertain process of "illegitimate" recombination, giving rise to more radical rearrangements of the DNA, including the duplication of genes.* Scientific American 5/81, p69 **[1978]**

imageable ('imidʒəbəl), *adj. Psychology.* (of a word, phrase, etc.) able to evoke a mental image. *This attribute [imagery-concreteness] is highly correlated with performance in memory tasks, such that imageable, concrete words are remembered better than nonimageable, abstract words.* New Scientist 10/5/72, p32 **[1967,** from *image, v.,* to represent, portray + *-able,* earlier in the sense of concepts of the mind (OED2, 1864)] —**imageability,** *n.: Most work in imagery and memory has concerned attributes of verbal items. The two chief properties which have been investigated are imageability (usually abbreviated to "I") and concreteness (C).* New Scientist 10/5/72, p32

image-builder, *n.* one engaged in image-building. *He [Robert T. Bartley, Commissioner of the U.S. Federal Communications Commission] warned of "the inherent danger of the broadcast operations' becoming a tool and image-builder for the corporate conglomerate. . . ."* Saturday Review 2/4/67, p56 **[1964]**

image-building, *n.* the use of publicity and advertising to create or maintain a favorable impression before the public. *The program also gave a sympathetic hearing to policemen and showed the difficulties they labor under in a city the size of New York and some of the new techniques of image-building being employed to reach the communities they serve.* NY Times 5/28/68, p95 *It was only recently that a prominent firm of chartered accountants in London took the bold step of using film for image-building.* Times (London) 3/23/70, p23 **[1963]**

IMINT ('imint), *n.* intelligence obtained through aerial photography. *The most solid evidence the U.S. has about events in Central America comes from IMINT (image intelligence). The photographs of airfields and military encampments in Nicaragua were taken by SR-71 Lockheed reconnaissance planes, so-called Blackbirds, that are capable of flying higher than 80,000 ft. and at speeds of more than 2,000 m.p.h., as well as by U.S. satellites orbiting more than 100 miles above the earth.* Time 3/22/82, p22 **[1982,** acronym for *image intelligence*]

immersion, *n.* an intensive course of oral instruction in a second language, especially in a bilingual area. . . . *four Ottawa-area school boards have spent the past three years experimenting with new ways of teaching French, including "immersion," a program in which at least 50% of the curriculum is taught in French.* Maclean's 5/17/76, p54 Attributive use.—**immersion course:** *Discussing his public speaking style, he once told me: 'I've been taking immersion courses in French, you know. Some of my friends say what I really need is an immersion course in English.'* Time 11/13/72, p35 —**immersion method:** *Papers by David Reibel and Leonard Newmark explore the strategies of the immersion method [in] language learning.* Times Literary Supplement 4/14/72, p425 —**immersion school:** *In Winnipeg, a total of 1,123 students were enrolled in immersion courses this fall, and Ecole Sacre-Coeur, the city's largest immersion school, recorded a jump in enrollment from 334 to 560 students between 1974 and 1975.* Maclean's 11/1/76, p21 **[1965]**

immune complex, *Medicine.* an aggregate formed by an antigen and its antibody. Immune complexes may cause agglutination, precipitation, and other immunological reactions. *Anti-DNA antibodies are the hallmark of this disease, and such antibodies are demonstrable in virtually all cases. Circulating immune complexes of DNA—anti-DNA undoubtedly cause some of the lesions of acute nephritis and vasculitis.* 1975 Britannica Yearbook of Science and the Future, p280 **[1973]** —**immune complex disease:** *In the light of the evidence that the kidney disease was caused by an antigen-antibody complex, it was called "immune complex" disease.* Scientific American 1/73, p26

immune surveillance, another name for IMMUNOLOGICAL SURVEILLANCE. *Cellular immunity evolved specifically to hunt down and destroy cancer cells that are constantly emerging in all of us. This concept of "immune surveillance" was taken up and championed by Sir Macfarlane Burnet and is now accepted, in some form, by most immunologists.* New Scientist 9/26/74, p807 **[1973]**

immunity bath, *U.S. Law.* a grant of immunity allowing a witness to confess to any crime without risking future prosecution. Compare USE IMMUNITY. *The traditional reluctance of Congress, the courts, and the executive branch to wield such a potent weapon [immunity] carelessly grew out of several factors—among them the fear that corrupt prosecutors would give "immunity baths" to those guilty of serious crimes.* New Yorker 4/12/76, p99 **[1969]**

immuno-, a combining form now widely used in the physical sciences to denote any study, process, technique, etc., involving immunological or antibody-producing properties and reactions. See the examples below and the main entries which follow. —**immunochemical,** *n.: Miles-Yeda, Ltd. . . . a subsidiary of Miles Laboratories, Inc. in the U.S., makes isotopes and immunochemicals.* 1971 Britannica Yearbook of Science and the Future, p385 —**immunodiffusion,** *n.: He [Orjan Ouchterlony, a Swedish biologist] put a few drops of solution containing antigen in one well and a like amount of antibody solution in the other. The fluids diffused toward each other through the gelatinous agar and reacted at an intermediate zone. There a thin white crescent was precipitated in the otherwise clear gel. The crescent indicated the chemical neutralization of the antigen by the antibody. The technique is known as immunodiffusion . . .* Scientific American 9/69, p248 —**immunoparalysis,** *n.: . . . experience with protracted immunoparalysis maintained with the aid of immunosuppressant chemicals over periods of years to prevent destruction of transplanted organs was observed to be associated with a definitive increase in the frequency of cancer in these patients.* 1972 Britannica Yearbook of Science and the Future, p291 —**immunopharmacology,** *n.: The word immunopharmacology does not appear, between immunochemistry and immunotherapy, in any of the medical dictionaries that I have consulted but its use as the title of this book will probably cause it to be defined in their next editions. In the meantime, I take immunopharmacology to be the study of how and why applied chemical substances induce or modify immune processes.* New Scientist 8/1/68, p253 —**immunoradioactive,** *adj.: . . . they [a team of researchers] are optimistic enough about their results, in experiments with . . . induced tumors in mice, to be talking about an immunoradioactive anti-cancer serum in the foreseeable future.* Science News 7/6/68, p22 —**immunoradiotherapy,** *n.: According to [Professor R.C.] Nairn, the results so far achieved with phosphorus-32 are "a very promising beginning to the exploration of possible immunoradiotherapy of cancer in human patients".* Science Journal 8/68, p11

immunoadsorbent or **immunoadsorbant,** *n.* a chemical substance that adsorbs antigens or antibodies. *EBV-infected cells are homogenized and the immunoadsorbent is immersed in the mixture. The antigens cling to the antibodies and when the immunoadsorbent is removed, the antigens come with it. The antigens are then freed from the immunoadsorbent and concentrated.* Science News 7/14/73, p32 *Gluteraldehyde fixation of the cells . . . has been widely used in immunology to make fixed preparations of antigens (immunoadsorbants) which allow the adsorption and isolation of antibody and cells* *bearing antibodylike receptors.* McGraw-Hill Yearbook of Science and Technology 1976, p400 [**1973,** from *immuno-* immunological + *adsorbent* or *adsorbant*]

immunoassay, *n.* analysis of the characteristics of a bodily substance by testing its immunological or antibody-producing reactions. Compare RADIOIMMUNOASSAY. *Gonadotrophins from chorionic tissue are produced mostly in early pregnancy and can be assayed either biologically or by immuno-assay . . .* New Scientist 4/9/70, p66 [**1959**]

immunocompetence, *n.* the ability to produce or maintain immunity. *The best picture that could be assembled at this stage of the story was that the bursa and thymus, as "central" lymphoid tissues, secreted some hormone-like factor needed for the immunocompetence of lymphocytes in "peripheral" lymphoid tissues like the spleen.* New Scientist and Science Journal 12/9/71, p81 [**1971**]

immunocompetent, *adj.* capable of producing or maintaining immunity. *The antibody-forming cells are frequently designated as immuno-competent cells.* McGraw-Hill Yearbook of Science and Technology 1969, p104 [**1963**]

immunocyte, *n.* an immunity-producing cell that attacks other cells of the body. *Those pathogenic immunocytes that cause autoimmune disease are also curbed by the system of surveillance: in this instance the autoimmune process and the surveillance mechanism are both attributed to the same system of thymus-dependent immunocytes.* New Scientist 12/10/70, p466 [**1963,** from *immuno-* + *-cyte* cell]

immunodeficiency, *n.* inability of the immune system to produce antibodies in sufficient number or strength to fight infection. *The granulocytes and macrophages in our bloodstream are only part of our immune system. Indeed, if they were all we had, we would not survive long. Those children born with immunodeficiency have all the granulocytes they need, yet they die within months from infections.* Reader's Digest 10/76, p262 [**1971,** from *immuno-* immunological + *deficiency*] —**immunodeficient,** *adj.: One experimental approach to treating immunodeficient individuals, who are likely to die of overwhelming infection if their immune systems cannot be restored, is transplantation of bone marrow or thymus tissue.* Science 4/13/73, p169

immunodeficiency disease, any disease caused by a deficiency in the immunity mechanism of the body. *The ability to transplant bone marrow material successfully . . . will mean a lot more than the treatment of relatively rare immunodeficiency diseases. Solving the graft-versus-host reaction will mean that virtually any congenital blood disorder . . . will be curable by simply replacing the patient's own blood-forming tissue with that from a donor.* New Scientist and Science Journal 5/13/71, p397 [**1969**]

immunoelectrophoresis (‚imyənoui‚lektroufə'ri:sis), *n.* a method of identifying complex proteins through their immunological reactions after electrically induced separation from a substance such as blood plasma. *"Antigen and antibody preparations from many species, as well as from various individuals of a given species, have become available commercially in recent years. Hence numerous experiments involving . . . immunoelectrophoresis are within the reach of the enterprising amateur."* Scientific American 9/69, p258 [**1958,** from *immuno-* + *electrophoresis* electrically induced separation of substances]

immunoelectrophoretic, *adj.* of or relating to immunoelectrophoresis. *He [Dr. Tristram Freeman] was best known for his studies of a rare hereditary complaint . . . and of the dynamic exchanges of several plasma proteins and more recently for his modifications and application of the Laurell technique, an immuno-electrophoretic method for analyzing blood plasma proteins in terms of a dozen or more well-defined circulating proteins.* Times (London) 11/23/70, p10 [**1955**]

immunofluorescence, *n.* the labeling of antibodies with a fluorescent dye to reveal antigens, viruses, etc., when viewed under ultraviolet light. *Utilizing a technique of immunofluorescence, these investigators demonstrated gamma E [a type of immunoglobulin] antibody-forming cells in lymphoid*

organs of the tracheal mucosa, pharynx, and intestinal tract, although they were essentially absent in the spleen and lymph nodes . . . 1970 Britannica Yearbook of Science and the Future, p267 [**1960**]

immunofluorescent, *adj.* of or relating to immunofluorescence. *Indirect immunofluorescent techniques show cross immunity reactions.* Science News 5/11/68, p462 [**1959**]

immunoglobulin, *n.* a globulin or protein in the blood that acts like an antibody and produces immunity. *Abbreviation:* IG *Gamma globulin or immunoglobulin is one of the key antibody proteins which lymphocytes produce in response to microbial invasion.* Science News Yearbook 1970, p88 *A newborn pig has very little gamma globulin (the principal antibody protein) in its serum. Apparently it acquires gamma globulin and other immunoglobulins from its mother's colostrum when it begins to suckle.* Scientific American 6/66, p98 [**1959**]

immunohematologic, *adj.* of or relating to immunohematology. *Pathology of Sickle Cell Disease—Joseph Song-Thomas, C.C., 1971, 460 p., photographs, $26. A reference book to the multiphasic manifestations of sickle cell anemia, discusses the hemoglobin molecule, genetic mutation, biochemical aspects, immunohematologic manifestations, incidence, complications and therapy.* Science News 7/10/71, p31 [**1954**]

immunohematology, *n.* the study of the immunological or antibody-producing properties of the blood. *Professor Jean Dausset is a member of the Faculty of Medicine at the University of Paris and is Director of Immunohaematology at the Georges Hayem Centre in Paris.* Science Journal 7/68, p51 [**1954**]

immunological surveillance, a monitoring process by which the body's immune system detects foreign cells. Also called IMMUNE SURVEILLANCE, IMMUNOSURVEILLANCE. *Immunological surveillance, first proposed by Macfarlane Burnett, is now widely accepted in principle, even though it begins to look in need of some modification. The theory says that T cells roam the body looking for foreign cells, including incipient cancers, which are summarily destroyed.* New Scientist 9/13/73, p606 [**1973**]

immunomodulator, *n.* a drug used to stimulate activity of the body's immune system. Also called IMMUNOSTIMULANT. *The virus hides itself well in the cell, and because infection appears to persist for life, Hirsch and several others predicted that lifelong treatment will be needed. And, as has happened with cancer therapy, a combination—probably an antiviral drug in concert with an immunomodulator—may be necessary.* Science News 4/27/85, p261 [**1984**]

immunoprecipitation, *n.* the process of separating a substance in an insoluble form by combining specific antibodies and antigens. *As a rule immunoprecipitation procedures are necessary to visualise the small amount of virus-specific polypeptides. The specificity of the immunoprecipitation was checked as follows. Immunoprecipitation of control injections . . . by addition of anti-AMV [Avian Myeloblastosis Virus] serum, gives rise predominantly to two polypeptides with molecular weights of 190,000 and 50,000, respectively.* Nature 2/26/76, p698 [**1972**]

immunoregulation, *n.* the process by which the immune system of the body is regulated. *Understanding T-cell suppression is potentially important to understanding immunoregulation. For example, it is possible that allergic individuals have congenital or acquired deficiencies in this suppressive activity that permit uncontrolled production of allergy-causing antibody. It may be that desensitization works in the treatment of some allergies by boosting the number of suppressor cells.* World Book Science Annual 1975, p306 [**1974**]

immunorepressive, *adj.* another word for IMMUNOSUPPRESSIVE. *The doctors in charge increased the dosage of immunorepressive drugs as soon as it was discovered that the period of rejection was being experienced . . .* Times (London) 2/10/68, p4 [**1968**]

immunosorbent, *n.* another name for IMMUNOADSORBENT. *The role of animal rotaviruses in human disease and the exchange of rotaviruses is not known . . . This report describes the use* *of an enzyme-linked immunosorbent assay to distinguish members of the rotavirus group.* Science 7/21/78, p259 [**1974**]

immunostimulant, *n.* another word for IMMUNOMODULATOR. *Besides the special diet, he [Steve McQueen] now takes a variety of "immunostimulants," including live cells from fetal pigs and cattle, the controversial cancer drug laetrile and a lot of vitamins and dietary supplements. . . Clinic physicians say his tumors have shrunk.* Newsweek 10/20/80, p65 [**1978**]

immunosuppress, *v.t., v.i.* to suppress the immune response of (an organism) against a foreign substance. *Further studies are under way to confirm that the technique selectively immunosuppresses at the cellular and subcellular levels.* Science News 5/6/72, p295 *There is evidence that those individuals in whom the capacity to respond to an immunological challenge is decreased, i.e., those who are immunosuppressed, have a high incidence of cancer.* 1976 Britannica Yearbook of Science and the Future, p364 [**1967**, back formation from IMMUNOSUPPRESSION]

immunosuppressant, *n.* an immunosuppressive drug. It is used especially to suppress rejection of grafted or transplanted tissue. Also called IMMUNOSUPPRESSOR. *. . . it is the lack of an effective immuno-suppressant, free of any deleterious effect on the bone marrow, which is a major difficulty in human organ transplantation.* Science Journal 3/70, p66 —*adj.* another word for IMMUNOSUPPRESSIVE. *. . . Hundreds of projects, ranging from cancer research, antibiotics and immunosuppressant drug research to cosmic radiation studies, are feeling the pinch.* Science News 11/23/68, p530 [**1965**]

immunosuppression, *n.* the suppression by the use of drugs, radiation, etc., of the immunological reaction of the body to foreign substances, especially to prevent the rejection of grafts or transplants by the recipient's body. *In order to coerce the body into accepting a donor's organ, full immunosuppression has been necessary . . . often leading, unfortunately, to fatal secondary infection.* New Scientist 11/6/69, p281 [**1965**]

immunosuppressive, *adj.* causing immunosuppression. Also, IMMUNOREPRESSIVE, IMMUNOSUPPRESSANT. *Reports from transplant surgeons that immunosuppressive drugs given to their patients to suppress organ rejection foster the rise of cancer are additional evidence of the relationship between cancer and immunity and the need for moderation in drug therapy.* Science News Yearbook 1970, p76 —*n.* an immunosuppressive agent or drug; an immunosuppressant. The Development of Modern Surgery by Frederick F. Cartwright. *A brief topically arranged history of surgery from the era before antisepsis and anesthesia to the present era of antibiotics and immunosuppressives.* World Book Science Annual 1968, p283 [**1963**]

immunosuppressor, *n.* another word for IMMUNOSUPPRESSANT. *In a study of 400 patients who received kidney transplants, it was found that 15 of them developed lymphomas, cancer of the lymphatic system . . . most of the patients who developed lymphomas had received antilymphatic serum in addition to chemical immunosuppressors.* Americana Annual 1970, p157 [**1970**]

immunosurveillance, *n.* another name for IMMUNOLOGICAL SURVEILLANCE. *This new work has now established that it is the antibodies in myasthenics which are behind the diseases' symptoms. For some reason the immuno-surveillance of these patients has broken down, and they are interpreting their own acetylcholine receptors as "foreign," and coating them with antibody. There is no hint just yet as to the reason why this should be happening.* New Scientist 9/14/78, p769 [**1974**]

IMP or **imp**[1], abbreviation of *International Match Point,* a unit of scoring used in European contract bridge tournaments. *The Italians staged an incredible rally. They won by 26 IMP's, 215-189, with the entire margin swinging on the 92nd deal.* 1976 Collier's Encyclopedia Year Book, p209 *With eight boards to be played Scotland were trailing by 24 imps, but in a great rally they scored 28-4 imps to make the match an exact tie.* Times (London) 1/20/76, p14 [**1963**]

Imp or **imp**[2], *n.* acronym for *indeterminate mass particle,* a hypothetical nuclear particle with no well-defined rest mass. *One of the first things to come up is an explanation of why all searches for free quarks have failed to find them. Imps have the property that their size increases rapidly with age. This means that very soon after quarks are produced they get too large to interact effectively with electrons and ionize atoms.* Science News 1/14/78, p23 [**1977**]

impact aid, *U.S.* Federal financial assistance to a school district where children of government employees attend school. *"Impact aid," as it is called, goes to four hundred and fifteen of the four hundred and thirty-five congressional districts. This year, the Administration proposed to reduce funds for children whose parents are federal employees but do not live in federal installations, on the theory that these people do pay property taxes.* New Yorker 2/27/78, p64 [**1970**]

impacted, *adj. U.S.* **1** financially burdened by the demand on public services, especially schools, caused by the sudden influx of many new residents into an area. *Nixon . . . proposed that $1.5 billion in federal funds be made available to "racially impacted areas" over the next two fiscal years to help desegregating school districts meet their special needs . . .* Time 4/6/70, p12 *Funds were also earmarked for the following: federally "impacted" areas, that is, areas where the families of federal workers had swollen school enrollments ($1.026 billion) . . .* 1967 Compton Yearbook, p232 **2** designed to relieve an impacted area. *This is the $600 million included in the Democratic bill for the program ungrammatically called "impacted aid"—that is, Federal assistance to certain school districts to help them bear the impact of the children of Federal employees on their education costs.* NY Times 1/27/70, p42 [**1963**]

impact statement, a review of the possible consequences of a proposed idea or project, especially one affecting the environment. *In the first draft of an impact statement on the transportation of radioactive materials near and through large, densely populated areas, the agency counted in 1975 in New York City approximately 280,000 radioactive shipments including twelve shipments of the Brookhaven spent elements or thirteen per cent of the national total.* New Yorker 11/13/78, p146 [**1973**]

imperial presidency, the Presidency of the United States viewed as exceeding in power and authority the executive role provided by the Constitution. *One area in which the imperial presidency is as regal as ever is the matter of international airline routes: by law the President can bestow on any airline of his choice the right to fly between any American city and any foreign one and he need not bother to state a reason.* Time 1/16/78, p46 [**1973**, from *The Imperial Presidency* (1973), by Arthur M. Schlesinger, Jr., born 1917, American historian] —**imperial president:** *The "imperial" Presidents in global affairs—from Roosevelt to Nixon—did not so much usurp their great powers as find them conferred because public fears and ambitions were then so widely shared.* NY Times 2/19/78, pD16

implied consent, *U.S. Law.* consent to forfeit certain rights or to assume certain responsibilities when one applies for some privilege, such as a driver's license. *The governor also paid tribute to the "implied consent" law which allows testing of drivers suspected of drunkenness.* Tuscaloosa News (Alabama) 6/19/74, p6 [**1969**] ►This term should not be confused with INFORMED CONSENT.

implosion, *n. Psychology.* a method of treating a phobia by dramatically confronting the patient with the situation or object feared. Compare FLOODING. See also AGORAPHOBIA. *A more drastic technique, similar to throwing a baby into a pool to teach it how to swim, is known as "implosion"—a patient might be driven to a large empty field and left there for hours to cope with his fears. The theory is that terror drains away once it is faced directly.* Time 11/7/77, p58 [**1969**, specialized sense of the word meaning "a bursting inward"]

impossible art, another name for CONCEPTUAL ART. *Happenings, "impossible art," auto-destruction art, multi-media events are alternative pursuits that can engage an artist's in-*

ventive powers . . . Manchester Guardian Weekly 1/10/70, p20 **[1970]**

impoverished, *adj.* containing fewer stimuli than those provided in a standard laboratory environment. *The team found that rats placed in "enriched" environments—cages holding toys, mazes and other rats—developed, among other things, thicker cerebral cortices than those isolated in bare, or "impoverished," cages.* NY Times 5/22/76, p11 **[1972]**

impressionist, *n.* a performer who does imitations or impersonations, especially of famous people. [Rich] *Little was once described as the "most accurate, original, daring and dependable impressionist this side of Xerox."* Current Biography 1975, p249 **[1964,** from *impression* an imitation or impersonation (OEDS 1953) + *-ist*]

impulse buyer, a person who often buys on whim without much or any consideration of cost, quality, or utility. *While the Colts might be described as impulse buyers, they seem downright cautious compared to the Monacos, who bought their house without ever having seen the inside.* NY Times 6/30/71, p46 *A new range of McVitie and Price cake packages, designed by Richard Lonsdale-Hands Associates, will be on display in supermarkets this week, designed to attract the "impulse" buyer.* Times (London) 3/11/70, p25 **[1959]**

impulse purchase or **impulse buy,** something purchased impulsively, especially without consideration of cost, quality, or utility. *Write out a list and stick to it. Impulse purchases will be thrust at you; most of them you don't* really *need.* Maclean's 8/74, p16 *Our games are cheap enough to be impulse buys.* Times (London) 9/26/71, p61 **[1962]**

in-¹, a combining form of the preposition *in,* meaning "within," "during," etc., frequently used in combination with a noun to form adjective modifiers. Such compounds are derived from corresponding prepositional phrases, as e.g., *in-college activities* derived from *activities in college, in-depth interview* from *interview in depth.* The compounds are ordinarily pronounced with a main stress on *in-* as well as on the normally accented syllable of the other member ('in-ca'reer, 'in-'city); but there may be a main stress only on *in-* when it is in contrast with *out-* ('in-,state 'students). See the following examples as well as the main entries IN-COMPANY, IN-COUNTRY, IN-HOUSE. **—in-car,** *adj.: Systems for improved highway safety, for instance, will include automatic guidance and control, in-car visual and audible hazard warnings* . . . Science News 8/3/68, p107 **—in-career,** *adj.: Whether in-career re-education will be best inside or outside universities is a matter for debate* . . . New Scientist 10/3/68, p31 **—in-city,** *adj.: It* [a commuter railroad line] *is not designed to stop every half-mile, nor to service in-city passengers.* Harper's 1/66, p68 **—in-home,** *adj.: Last year the three syndicated weeklies. . . countered the research studies of regular magazines purporting to show an impressive pass-along readership with studies of their own, demonstrating a greater in-home readership and superior retention value.* Saturday Review 1/8/66, p111 **—in-prison,** *adj.: With few exceptions, in-prison schooling had previously been limited to the high school level.* 1967 Compton Yearbook, p397 **—in-process,** *adj.: The primary purpose of in-process measurement is to ensure that a workpiece is manufactured to the desired size.* New Scientist 4/20/67, p140 **—in-state,** *adj.: The land-grant colleges and state universities were founded as publicly supported institutions where in-state students would be able to obtain a college education for minimum rates.* NY Times 11/5/67, pA85 **—in-station,** *adj.: Demanding that their in-station hours be cut from 56 to 50 a week, 278 of Kansas City's firemen last month got around state laws by playing sick for four days* . . . Time 8/5/66, p47

in-², a combining form of the adjective *in,* used in the sense of "favored by connoisseurs as the latest, most up-to-date, or exclusive (item of its kind)" to form noun compounds. In compounds with *in-²* the main stress falls on the first syllable ('in, as 'in-,jargon, etc.). See the following examples and also the entry IN-CROWD. **—in-jargon,** *n.: . . . instead of teaching, the two speakers conducted a precious duologue of in-jargon.* Sunday Times (London) 12/3/67, p28 **—in-language,** *n.: Of course this 'in-language' invariably provokes misunderstanding, or*

feigned misunderstanding, on the part of the sensible persons in the play. University of Leeds Review 10/71, p223 **—in-thing,** *n.: . . . if widows are the in-thing now, can unwed mothers be far behind?* Saturday Review 10/19/68, p8 **—in-word,** *n.: . . . It is not, of course, beyond the realms of possibility that the disclosure of these seats as the Prime Minister's top 13 is no more than an exercise to galvanize the party workers to new levels of achievement and to send yet another "frisson"(Mr. Wilson's latest in-word) through the Tory machine.* Times (London) 6/8/70, p7

-in, a combining form of the adverb *in,* introduced in the 1960's by the black civil-rights movement in a number of nouns formed from verb + *-in* on the analogy of *sit-in,* such as *kneel-in* (in segregated churches), *ride-in* (in segregated buses), *swim-in* and *wade-in* (in segregated swimming pools and beaches), and so on.

The original meaning was soon extended to the staging of any kind of public demonstration, as in LIE-IN (blocking traffic), SMOKE-IN (for legalization of marijuana), and TEACH-IN (by college professors criticizing government policies).

A third development was the weakening of the earlier meanings to cover any kind of gathering by a group, as for socializing. This meaning is exemplified by BE-IN (originally a social gathering of hippies or flower children), LOVE-IN, SING-IN, and LAUGH-IN. Other main entries with *-in* are FISH-IN, PAINT-IN, PRAY-IN, SIGN-IN, SLEEP-IN, WORK-IN. The following is a sampling of compounds not separately entered in the book: **—bike-in,** *n.: Alternate modes of nonpolluting transportation called for "bike-ins," balloon ascensions and pedestrian parades.* Time 4/27/70, p46 **—camp-in,** *n.: As illustrated by the extra squads of policemen patrolling the Capitol, there is a latent fear in Congress that the camp-in will set off violence.* NY Times 5/26/68, p71 **—eat-in,** *n.: Knives, forks and plates, not notepads and pencils, are set on the highly polished boardroom table at the weekly directors' meeting of W. Purdy Ltd. The weekly eat-ins are a vital part of quality control* . . . Sunday Times (London) 4/18/71, p53 **—gay-in,** *n.: Last June's much-publicized "Gay-In" gathering in Manhattan's Central Park with smaller assemblages in other cities, had nationwide reverberations . . . thousands of marchers paraded placards and chanted slogans—"Better Blatant than Latent," "An Army of Lovers Cannot Lose," pre-empting Plato's defense of love between Spartan soldiers* . . . Saturday Review 2/12/72, p24 **—mail-in,** *n.: The Ministers of Finance and Economy and of Agriculture were all victims of the chicken mail-in, which was organized in protest against a recent influx of imported eggs from Belgium.* Times (London) 7/29/70, p4 **—prance-in,** *n.: The quality of this Israeli prance-in often verges on the amateur* . . . New Yorker 4/13/68, p7 **—study-in,** *n.: The Youth Culture may be using big words to hide some facts—as in the battle against parietal rules which stand for boys' rights to have girls in dormitory rooms for individual study-ins and not, as the Yale Daily News stressed, for sleep-ins.* NY Times 1/7/68, pD11

incap, *n. Military Slang.* an incapacitating chemical agent or drug; an incapacitant. *. . . the employment of "incaps" (i.e., incapacitating chemicals) which, if used against whole populations, will be bound to cause widespread deaths as well as general degradation.* New Scientist 4/4/68, p42 *Considerable interest had focused on psychic or hallucinatory chemicals. Dubbed "incaps" (for incapacitating agents), they are designed to disorient temporarily rather than kill* . . . Time 9/6/68, p40 **[1968]**

incapacitant, *n.* a chemical agent or drug designed to incapacitate a person or animal temporarily by inducing sleepiness, dizziness, disorientation, etc. See also INCAP. *How are we to ensure that the new wave of military morality is not simply due to obsolescence and still more pathological projects? It may take the death of a few military sheep around Dugway Proving Ground to make CBW a property too hot for any administration to harbour, and beyond that lie the use of ecocidal weapons—herbicides in Vietnam—and "humane incapacitants."* Manchester Guardian Weekly 8/15/70, p18 **[1961]**

incendive, *adj.* capable of setting fire; incendiary. *A spark struck from such a surface* [rusty steel smeared with aluminum] *has a miniature thermite reaction which is exothermic [heat-releasing] and can prove more incencive to inflammable vapours than a spark struck from the impact of steel on steel.* New Scientist 5/14/70, p349 [**1959**, from Latin *incendere* to set on fire + English *-ive*]

Inceptisol, *n.* (in U.S. soil taxonomy) any of a group of widely distributed soils of recent origin, characterized by a slight development of soil horizons. *The remaining broad groups of soils, the Alfisols, Entisols, Spodosols, and many Inceptisols, fall between the two extremes, both in nutrient losses during formation and in fertility levels. Mountainous regions, with their great variety of soils, also belong to this intermediate group. Collectively these occupy about 35% of the land surface.* McGraw-Hill Yearbook of Science and Technology 1972, p374 [**1971**, from *inception* + *-sol* (from Latin *solum* soil)]

incinderjell, *n.* jellied gasoline combined with napalm and used in flamethrowers and fire bombs. *The issues and living horror of the war disappear in a deadened, bureaucratic language—'incinderjell', 'the other side', 'body counts' of dead 'communists' reported with dream-like exactness.* Listener 2/22/68, p244 [**1967**, alteration of *incendiary gel*]

incognoscenti (in,kounyou'ʃenti:), *n.pl.* uninformed persons; uninitiates. *The religious affairs department of the BBC does its very best to be ecumenical . . . Thus, the other day it broadcast as its Sunday morning service an act of worship by a chapter of the Society of Friends (Quakers, I had perhaps better say, for the benefit of any incognoscenti, who might, by chance, read this column).* New Scientist 2/14/80, p506 [**1970**, from *in*- not + *cognoscenti* (1778) well-informed persons (from Italian)]

income maintenance, *U.S.* money paid by a government to provide the poor with a regular income. *They have shown, for example, that it is possible to provide the poor with a secure income without killing their motivation to work, suggesting that a "negative income tax" or "income maintenance" system could be a viable policy.* Psychology Today 11/78, p24 [**1972**]

incomes policy, any government policy to check inflation resulting from wage and cost increases. *Galbraith urged the cause of a militant incomes policy in the form of direct wage-price controls—a message that President Nixon put into effect in August 1971, to the great advantage of the country and the President's re-election prospects.* Newsweek 11/13/72, p88 *What is needed, therefore, is some kind of government participation in the wage bargaining process—an incomes policy, in short—which will directly secure a reduction in the size of pay claims. This is not a piece of straightforward economics, like controlling the money supply, but more in the nature of continuous or repeated exercises in internal diplomacy.* Listener 3/8/73, p313 [**1963**] ►The term was originally used by British economists and referred chiefly to a policy of the Labour government during the 1960's. It began to be used in the United States about 1970.

incommutation, *n. U.S.* another name for REVERSE COMMUTING. *In regard to Westchester, the report explained the growth of incommutation as a result of the movement of major companies and industries into the suburbs, combined with the decision of employees to remain in the central cities.* Herald Statesman (Yonkers, N.Y.) 1/22/74 (page not known) [**1974**, from *in* + *commutation*]

in-company, *adj.* carried on within a company or business. *In-company supervisor training sessions should be arranged in order to improve the supervisor's understanding of his role in the management team and the functions of other departments.* Times (London) 2/9/70, p19 [**1966**; see IN-¹]

in-country, *adj.* carried on within a country, as distinguished from its borders or neighbors. *The Defence Department, he said, was not responsible for "in-country" activities in Laos.* Times (London) 3/4/70, p5 [**1954**; see IN-¹]

incrementalism, *n.* a policy of improving or enlarging current social programs by making small, gradual changes in them. *Richard Nathan of the Brookings Institution, the spokesman for "incrementalism", notes the rapid expansion of most social welfare programs since the late 1960s and concludes that sup-*

port for the poor has increased so much that nothing radically different needs to be done. Manchester Guardian Weekly (Washington Post section) 6/5/77, p18 [**1974**] —**incrementalist,** *n.: "A crypto-deviationist antipeople incrementalist, I have been guilty of optimism about the use of social-science knowledge in the management of public affairs,"* New York's Senator Daniel P. Moynihan wrote a decade ago. NY Times 1/20/80, pD20

in-crowd, *n.* an exclusive set or circle of acquaintances; a group of insiders; clique. *. . . the magazine's [New York magazine] critics still point to its smug, In-crowd perspective.* Time 4/11/69, p55 *. . . the performer who is written off as a hype becomes no longer the darling of the underground in-crowd, whatever his sincerity or instrinsic merit.* Times (London) 8/13/70, p10 [**1967**; see IN-²]

IND, abbreviation of *investigational new drug*, (the status of) a drug approved by a regulatory agency for experimentation and research. *The Committee for Freedom of Choice in Cancer Therapy . . . point to the plot of the U.S. Food and Drug Authority granting Andrew McNaughton an IND—permission to test a new drug on humans—then 10 days later taking it away when he didn't come up with the required information on the drug's safety.* Maclean's 1/76, p26 [**1970**]

indépendantiste (ǣdeipādǎ,ti:st), *n.* a supporter or advocate of political independence for the Province of Quebec. Compare PÉQUISTE. [Camille] *Laurin explains that he became an indépendantiste partly through his experience with Canadian medical groups and associations, in which, over the years, he felt less and less as though he belonged. "I wasn't part of the club,"* he says. Maclean's 1/10/77, p29 [**1968**, from Canadian French, from French *indépendant* independent + *-iste* -ist]

independentista (,inde,penden'ti:sta:), *n.* a supporter or advocate of political independence for Puerto Rico. Compare FALN. *Statehooders and independentistas agree on only one thing—that commonwealth status is colonial status, and degrading. By and large statehooders are conservatives, the commonwealth leaders are left-centrists, and the independentistas are leftists.* Harper's 12/77, p18 [**1967**, from Spanish, irregularly formed from *independencia* independence + *-ista* -ist]

in-depth, *adj.* going deeply into a subject; very thorough; comprehensive. *. . . he has spent hours reading Government cables, memoranda and classified files to brief himself for in-depth discussions.* NY Times Magazine 1/28/68, p70 *This time-lag is a serious handicap to Mr Nencini's book because he offers an in-depth report of the whole event in much the same way as he would cover it for his own Florentine paper.* Sunday Times (London) 10/22/67, p55 [**1957**, from the phrase *in depth.* See IN-¹.]

index, *v.t.* to adjust (income, rates of interest, etc.) to price changes in goods and services as reflected by the cost-of-living index. *As a social objective, it would seem that more and more people feel that something better should be done for pensioners. That to index their pensions so that cost of living rises are compensated for at least once a year is a minimum.* Guardian (London) 3/25/72, p18 [**1972**, verb use of *index*, *n.* (for *cost-of-living index*), probably patterned after French *indexer*, *v.*]

indexation, *n.* variant of INDEXING (def. 1). *Basically, indexation simply means attaching escalator clauses based on some relevant yardstick of inflation to various long-term contracts. Wages and rents, for example, would be raised periodically to keep step with the cost of living. Interest payments on bonds and bank deposits would be adjusted upward or downward in line with the inflation rate (chart). And the tax system would be readjusted so that corporate and individual income gains that merely reflect inflation are not taxed away, resulting in a loss of real income.* Business Week 5/25/74, p147 [**1960**, from *index* + *-ation*]

index crime, *U.S.* any of the most serious types of crimes on which statistical reports are published annually in the Uniform Crime Reports of the Federal Bureau of Investigation. *Of the seven index crimes in the Uniform Crime Reports, four are crimes of personal violence—murder, aggravated assault, rape, and robbery. They account for about 13 percent of all the index* *crimes in the country. The remaining three index crimes are burglary, larceny of $50 or more, and auto theft; these crimes against property make up the remaining 87 percent of serious crime.* Norval Morris and Gordon Hawkins, The Honest Politician's Guide to Crime Control, 1970, p56 [**1970**]

indexed, *adj. Economics.* adjusted to changes in a cost-of-living index (or a similar indicator of changes in the value of money). *It is the indexed National Savings Bond recommended by the Page Committee. For ordinary savers—and a few still survive— it would be a rock of assurance in the flood of inflation.* Manchester Guardian Weekly 7/26/74, p15 *Brazil has now developed into what could be termed an "indexed economy," where practically every area of the economy has some sort of adjustment mechanism for inflation.* NY Times 4/7/74, pF14 [**1972**]

index fund, *U.S. Finance.* an investment fund made up of stocks selected for their relative values to match the performance of the market over a period of time. *Index funds, though popular, are few. Their clients include other institutions, some of which buy shares because their managements believe that they must put at least some of the money they control into the index to avoid accusations of investing imprudently.* NY Times 1/14/77, pD2 [**1976**, so called from its being based on Standard & Poor's index of 500 stocks]

indexing, *n. Economics.* **1** adjustment of income, prices, interest rates, etc., to a cost-of-living index or similar indicator of change in the value of money. *A band of conservative economists . . . are vigorously touting "indexing," a system that in theory preserves the buying power of money by tying all paper values to a price indicator.* Time 5/13/74, p110 *The new handy pain reliever we're being offered instead of a miracle cure, is called "indexing"—a way to adjust nearly everybody to the realities of rising prices; a system that hitches incomes, various other payments and taxes to changes in the cost-of-living.* Maclean's 11/74, p118 **2** a correlating of the prices of basic commodities to the prices paid by underdeveloped countries for industrial imports. *Mr. Kissinger is opposed to the concept of "indexing," a system of linking the price of oil and other raw materials to the cost of industrial goods that poor nations must import.* NY Times 5/3/76, p3 [**1972**]

index-link, *v.t. Especially British, Economics.* to adjust according to a cost-of-living index or similar indicator. *Of all the factors which have contributed to the drop in consumption the most important has been tax increases . . . A commitment by the Government to index-link cigarette tax would be a major reform. A move to make the tax progressively steeper would be an even better deterrent.* Manchester Guardian Weekly 6/12/77, p10 [**1970**] **—index-linked,** *adj.: There are more than one would think, in the private sector, who also have index-linked pensions.* Listener 1/15/76, p41 **—index-linking,** *n.: "Index-linking is not the panacea some people make it out to be—indeed it can create a false sense of security," says another company.* Sunday Times (London) 6/1/75, p49

Indianness, *n.* **1** the condition of being an American Indian. *. . . after mastering the meaning of Negritude and machismo they would have to grapple with the meaning of Indianness.* New Yorker 4/18/70, p103 **2** a quality suggestive of India and its culture. *Gandhi always thought that a common thread of Indianness would somehow hold the two together.* Time 12/6/71, p13 [**1934, 1964**]

indomethacin, *n.* an analgesic drug used in the treatment of arthritic disorders to reduce inflammation and fever. *Formula:* $C_{19}H_{16}C1NO_4$ *This manoeuvre might well eliminate the gastrointestinal side-effects of drugs such as indomethacin used to treat rheumatoid diseases.* New Scientist and Science Journal 6/24/71, p745 [**1963**, from the chemical constituents *indo*le + *methy*l + *ac*etic acid + *-in* (chemical suffix)]

inducer, *n.* a theoretical component of the operon that helps to activate genes. Also called DEREPRESSOR. *The French scientists advanced the theory, now substantially verified, that genes are controlled by a negative mechanism. That is, they are kept turned off by a "repressor" until another substance, an "inducer," comes along and disengages the repressor, thus allowing the gene to express itself.* Encyclopedia Science Supplement

(Grolier) 1970, p108 [**1967**, earlier in biochemistry in the sense of an agent causing production of an enzyme (1953)]

industrio-, a combining form meaning "industrial" or "industrial and _____." **—industrio-economic:** *We may expect to see before very long something resembling an industrio-economic "inner cabinet" consisting of the Chancellor of the Exchequer, the President of the Board of Trade, the Minister of Labour, the Minister of Technology and the Prime Minister.* Manchester Guardian Weekly 9/7/67, p4 **—industrio-nuclear:** *Having heard that football was a vital metaphor for understanding industrio-nuclear America, we drove to Washington to discover what could be learned about the country.* NY Times Magazine 10/3/76, p6 **—industrio-scientific:** *Basically, the qualifying concept is "plant used in manufacture" (with special dispensations for ship-repairing, mining, quarrying, construction and industrio-scientific research, and for computers, ships and hovercraft).* Sunday Times (London) 12/4/66, p54 [**1966**]

inertia-reel belt, a seat belt with a take-up reel which adjusts automatically the length of the belt to fit people of different sizes. Compare PASSIVE RESTRAINT. *Early belts were often poorly designed, being difficult both to adjust and to release. Furthermore, static belts can hold the driver in so effectively that he is unable to reach essential controls. Finally, they tend to drag on the floor and get dirty. Most of those points have been met by the inertia-reel or automatic belt, which has become increasingly popular in the past two years or so.* Times (London) 7/15/76, p31 [**1964**]

inertia selling, *British.* See the first quotation for the meaning. *"Inertia selling"—that is, sending unsolicited goods to potential customers and charging for them if not returned—has been under attack in the press.* Punch 3/27/68, p460 *Mr. Weitzman, Labour member for Stoke Newington and Hackney, North, said inertia selling might not be carried out on a wide scale but something had to be done to stop it.* Times (London) 3/12/70, p4 [**1968**]

I.N.F. or **INF,** abbreviation of *Intermediate-range Nuclear Forces,* the European-based nuclear weapons of the United States and the Soviet Union (often used attributively). *The withdrawal of the U.S.S.R. from the INF talks of course worries us. The Soviet position on this seems to me to overlook the fact that their deployment of SS-20s threatened the balance of power in the first place.* Time 1/2/84, p39 *The polls show that the public supports the I.N.F. treaty.* NY Times 12/22/87, pA27 [**1984**]

infect, *v.t.* (of a computer virus) to penetrate and pass into (a computer program or operating system). *The virus infects the operating system and program disks of any computer it comes in contact with, and these pass the virus on to still other computers.* World Book Science Annual 1989, p246 **—infection,** *n.: Infections by viruses, programs that can secretly spread between computers and alter and destroy data, have increased dramatically. For example, the software trade association Adapso reported in March that there were 30,000 virus infections in the last two months of 1988.* NY Times 5/30/89, pC1 [**1988**]

infill, *adj.* designed to fill in a vacant space or area. *On aircraft noise, however, the report is considerably "softer." It proposes that new and infill housing should be allowed in areas that government policy would not allow.* New Scientist 2/12/76, p338 [**1964**]

infinity microphone, an extremely sensitive and far-ranging listening device concealed in a telephone. Also called **infinity transmitter** or **infinity bug.** *And the CIA is believed to be making extensive use of the "infinity microphone"—a device billed as the world's most effective bug. Hitched to the victim's telephone, it can transmit either phone conversations or voices in the room; it uses telephone current for power, and can't be found with a radio detector.* Newsweek 7/30/73, p17 *The "infinity" bug . . . can be used from any corner of the world's telephone system . . . The phone never rings, and instead the caller is able to eavesdrop through the infinity bug's microphone.* New Scientist 11/23/78, p601 [**1973**]

infirmatory, *adj.* tending to invalidate or weaken; making infirm or insubstantial. . . . *a large number of papers have been published in the journals critical of Dr. Eysenck's* [Hans J.

Eysenck, a psychologist] *thinking or infirmatory of his demon-strations in the field of introversion-extraversion studies.* New Scientist 7/30/70, p254 [**1970**] ►This word is labeled obsolete in the OED on the evidence of its only quotation from John Ayliffe's *Parergon* (1726). The current use may be a revival of the old word or a new independent formation patterned after *affirmatory, confirmatory,* etc.

inflatable, *n.* any of various functional structures or units made of strong plastic that can be inflated. *The most popular toys are the inflatables: an 8-foot-long sausage and a 10-foot-square air mattress that looks like an upside-down wading pool.* Time 4/26/71, p56 . . . *Boat Shows at Earl's Court have given a boost to the inflatables . . . These lightweight, easily transport-ed and amazingly robust small boats are exactly what a certain type of British family has been wanting for years.* Sunday Times (London) 12/29/68, p39 [**1954**, noun use of adjective]

inflationary, *adj. Astronomy.* of or having to do with a model of the Big Bang theory which postulates that in the first fraction of a second following the cosmic explosion in which it originat-ed, the universe underwent an extremely rapid expansion. *Even more "dark matter" is implied in the inflationary con-cept of the universe, put forward a few years ago by Alan H. Guth of the Massachusetts Institute of Technology.* NY Times 4/28/87, pC3 [**1983**]

inflation-proof, *v.t.* to protect (investments, savings, etc.) from inflation, especially by indexing. *So far as the Civil Service is concerned, the cost of inflation-proofing the pensions of 260,000 retired civil servants was 1.5 per cent of the wages bill for the Civil Service, at a time when, on the basis of outside pay movements, the salaries of serving civil servants were being in-creased by 32 per cent.* Listener 1/15/76, p41 [**1973**]

influenza A, B, and **C,** three types of influenza viruses having different degrees of virulence. *Part of the problem of distinc-tions among the strains of influenza viruses may have been re-solved in 1972 when the World Health Organization adopted new nomenclature for influenza viruses. The gist of the seman-tic change was that different strains of the viruses—such as A_1, A_2, and so forth—should henceforth all be classified simply as influenza A.* Science 4/9/76, p131 *Influenza C is an insignifi-cant cause of human illness. Influenza B is a perennial prob-lem but does not change dramatically and rarely causes widespread epidemics or severe illness. Influenza A is another story . . . The A flu virus has been the cause of all the deadly pandemics of influenza for which a cause has been estab-lished—that is, all the global outbreaks since the flu virus was discovered in 1933.* NY Times 7/23/76, pA22 *Both kinds of variation are observed in influenza A viruses, but only anti-genic drift has been detected in influenza B viruses. Influenza C is rarely isolated.* Scientific American 12/77, p91 [**1972**]

inflump, *n.* another name for SLUMPFLATION. *Albert Sommers, economist for the business-oriented Conference Board and the man who coined the term "inflump" to describe the current mess, argues that renewed stimulus would become politically inevitable—and since it would be mistimed, the effect would inevitably be more inflation.* Newsweek 2/24/75, p65 [**1975**, blend of *inflation* and *slump*]

infobit, *n.* an item of information in a data bank. *Rights will be threatened in this new world of the 21st Century, property rights and copyrights in particular. Will the data base owners track down and pay the originators of every "infobit" ac-cessed? When new material is assembled from original works will recognition be given the true authors?* Library Journal 10/1/82, p814 [**1982**, from in*fo*rmation + *bit*]

in-form, *adj. British.* in good form; well conditioned and coached for competition. *One in-form player Revie did not pick was Birmingham's Trevor Francis. "He is definitely a player for the future. I was tempted to put him in this time, but I have been happy with the players up front," Revie said.* Times (London) 11/3/76, p10 [**1964**]

informatics, *n.* another name for INFORMATION SCIENCE. Com-pare TELEMATICS. *It was agreed in Amsterdam that an intro-*

duction to Informatics should form an integral part of general education in schools. Times (London) 9/2/70, p9 [**1967**]

informational picketing, *U.S.* picketing by workers to publicize demands or grievances. *Under an executive order, unionized Government workers are prohibited from picketing. But union lawyers said the picketing ban should exempt so-called "infor-mational picketing," such as is conducted in Kentucky and New York.* NY Times 10/3/76, p45 [**1976**]

information art, art concerned with the communication or rep-resentation of information. . . . *to arrive at found objects, ready-mades, conceptual art, information art, anti-form heaps, earth art it is necessary only to discard Picasso's compositional objectives in "Man with a Hat" and to elaborate upon his past-ed-in news items and aging paper (processed art).* New Yorker 3/11/72, p118 *Harold Rosenberg moans on . . . about the seri-al follies of Pop Art, Sharp-focus Realism, Conceptualist Art, Information Art, Earth Art.* Listener 2/5/76, p156 [**1972**]

information pollution, a profusion of information, especially un-necessary or redundant information produced by researchers, journalists, broadcasters, etc. *One of the subjects which he hinted strongly that he would like the panel . . . to consider is "information pollution." If there is too much information, he said, there is a danger that people will ignore all of it and return to idiosyncratic politics, based on gut reaction.* New Sci-entist 6/12/75, p594 [**1973**]

information science, the study of the means by which informa-tion is processed or transmitted through computers and similar automatic equipment. Also called INFORMATICS. *The new chairs will bring the total to 47. Their professors will teach in-formation science (a new field of study connected with com-puters), music, English, economics, pure mathematics, applied mathematics, and accounting.* Times (London) 8/11/64, p9 [**1960**]

information system, any method of processing information, es-pecially by a data-processing system. *Information science and technology is concerned with devising means for providing more efficient access to documents and improving the dissemi-nation of information. To accomplish these tasks it is necessary to gather together large quantities of raw information and to process them into a form that is more easily transferable and usable. When these processing procedures are integrated into an efficiently functioning unit, the result is called an informa-tion system.* 1973 Britannica Yearbook of Science and the Fu-ture, p258 [**1971**]

information technology, the application of computers and tech-niques of using computers to the handling of masses of data. *In any case, the revolutionary impact of information technology has been greatly exaggerated by students of "megatrends." Like all technologies, the computer solves problems that are de-fined not by technology itself but by the prevailing social pri-orities.* New Republic 8/13-20/84, p28 *Contemporary information technology embodies a convergence of interest be-tween electronics, computing and communications, which is being promoted by the rapid development of microelectronics.* New Scientist 4/26/79, p254 [**1975**]

informed consent, consent to surgery or medical experiment conditional upon the patient's or subject's understanding of what is involved. *A California law giving mental patients the right to refuse convulsive therapy and psychosurgery . . . re-quires informed consent by the patient or, with court permis-sion, a guardian.* New Scientist 9/1/77, p535 *Some skeptics doubt that enough embryo transplants have been done on pri-mates and other mammals to justify trials on man and also wonder if the patients know enough about the risks to give "in-formed consent."* Time 7/31/78, p69 [**1974**]

informercial or **infomercial,** *n. U.S.* a television commercial in the form of a program featuring demonstrations or discussions of various products or services. *Leading advertisers, though, are testing a totally new type of commercial, or "informercial" as they call them, that will soon be used widely on cable televi-sion. These will range in length from 30 minutes to four hours. Sears, for example, could buy half an hour of air time to ex-plain how to redecorate a porch.* Time 5/18/81, p69 *There are* *even new (and rather clumsy) coinages ". . . infomercials," . . . to convey the subtle melding of program material and advertising appeals.* TV Guide 5/8/82, p38 [**1981,** blend of *information* and *commercial*]

infotainment, *n.* *U.S.* television or other entertainment based on or including factual information. *The airwaves are now flooded with syndicated "infotainment" shows that give TV viewers. . . peeks at the public and private lives of their favorite celebrities . . .* Newsweek 8/26/85, p42 [**1985,** from *information* + enter*tainment*]

infradian, *adj.* of or relating to biological rhythms or cycles that recur less than once per day. *Neurobiologic rhythms are organized according to the complexity of the space in which they operate and the frequency at which they recur. Figure 1a defines rhythms in three frequency ranges: less than one per day (infradian), about one per day (circadian) and more than one per day (ultradian).* McGraw-Hill Yearbook of Science and Technology 1977, p147 [**1977,** from *infra-* below + Latin *diēs* day + *-an*]

infrared astronomy, a branch of astronomy dealing with the nature and sources of infrared radiation in space. *Infrared astronomy is beginning to study such things as intensity variations and polarizations in infrared sources, to chart their positions more accurately and to obtain better resolution of their spectra.* Science News 9/7/74, p150 [**1965**]

infrasonics, *n.* sound waves below the frequency of those audible to the human ear, especially as produced during severe storms. *At the other end of the sound spectrum are frequencies below those which can be heard. This is the world of infrasonics. The noise here ranges from about 20 cycles per second down to one cycle per second.* Sunday Times Magazine (London) 1/26/75, p20 [**1969,** from *infrasonic, adj.* (1920's)]

infrasound, *n.* a very low-frequency sound wave produced in the atmosphere by phenomena such as thunderstorms, hailstorms, and tornadoes. . . . *the deflection of infrasounds at high altitude may well supply us with additional information about winds at these heights—heights which tend to be inaccessible to both balloon and satellite experiments.* New Scientist 6/18/70, p568 [**1930, 1965,** from *infra-* below + *sound*]

inhalation therapy, the treatment of respiratory disorders by the use of oxygen, aerosols, gas mixtures, and the like. *A chief of service at the hospital . . . was treated during a recent illness by high school dropouts who had completed a course in inhalation therapy.* NY Times 8/16/68, p29 [**1968**] —**inhalation therapist:** *There are 500 registered inhalation therapists in the United States, and only six in New York City.* NY Times 8/16/68, p29

in-house, *adj.* being within or done within a business firm, organization, etc. *It [Bell System] employs, for example, as many PhDs as Britain produces annually and has an inhouse technical education programme equivalent in size and sophistication to a fair-sized university.* New Scientist 6/24/71, p770 *While a few companies—Ford is one—employ their own in-house anthropometric specialists, most rely on outside consultants.* Time 11/15/68, p62 [**1954;** see IN-¹]

initialism, *n.* an abbreviation formed from the initial letters of a phrase (such as *NATO* for *North Atlantic Treaty Organization* and *MRV* for *multiple reentry vehicle*), as distinguished from abbreviations formed by contraction (*doz.* for *dozen*) or by substitution (*lb.* for *pound* and *xtal.* for *crystal*). *By 1960, when the Gale Research Company of Detroit published the first edition of what is now called Acronyms and Initialisms Dictionary (lumping wordlike acronyms with unpronounceable abbreviations) 12,000 of both were already on the loose.* Time 7/20/70, p61 [**1965**]

injectable, *n.* a drug or medicine that may be injected directly into the bloodstream. . . . *Dr. Kramer said the injectables are most often used by persons who formerly took amphetamines orally, as pep-pills. They graduated to main-lining to enhance the drugs' stimulating effects.* NY Times 8/1/67, p27 *Implantable time capsules, once-a-month pills and long-*

term injectables are also on the horizon, he says. Science News 12/23/67, p615 [**1956,** noun use of *injectable, adj.*]

injection, *n.* the process of putting a satellite or spacecraft into a calculated orbit. Also called INSERTION. *"We were flying blind during lift-off and injection," says Bill Collier, . . . Mariner II was safely delivered, apparently thriving in its adult environment, and on its way to Venus.* Time 3/8/63, p79 [**1959**]

ink-jet, *adj.* of or designating a high-speed printing or typing process in which jets of ink are broken up into magnetized droplets and deflected under computer control to form letters and numbers on paper. *Ink-jet printing. A wide variety of methods exist involving continuous flow and stop/start jets of ink aimed at plain paper. The Mead Dijit system uses 512 continuous jets of ink which are acoustically broken up into tiny equal sized drops in precise follow-my-leader columns.* New Scientist 6/10/76, p575 [**1973**]

inner cabinet, *British.* a committee or other small group within an organization that performs unofficially the advisory function of a cabinet. *The one hope of avoiding an all-out interunion dispute now lies with the Trades Union Congress. Its "inner cabinet," the finance and general purposes committee, hopes to call in all the parties next week to discuss the long drawn out row.* Manchester Guardian Weekly 1/16/69, p22 *The meeting was also told that Hebdomadal council, the university's "inner cabinet", had appointed a committee to listen to the views of the students' elected representatives.* Times (London) 3/3/70, p2 [**1969** extended from earlier use of a group in government (OEDS 1900)]

inner city, *U.S.* the part of a city usually inhabited by large numbers of poor or disadvantaged people, viewed apart from other sections and suburbs where the middle-class groups live. Compare CENTRAL CITY. . . . *most outer-city integration has been restricted to areas contiguous to black sections of the inner city, leaving heavier concentrations of poorer blacks at inner-city lines, and a few in middle-income and upper-income suburbs farther away from the city.* NY Times 6/1/71, p28 *It is clear that the twin concepts of decentralization and community control of the schools developed in response to the failure of the schools in the inner city and have little or nothing to do with the sometimes excellent schools serving the city's middle-class, predominantly white students.* Saturday Review 11/16/68, p95 [**1963**]

inner-city, *adj.* of or relating to an inner city. *In inner-city schools, 60% of the pupils who made the 10th grade dropped out before completing the 12th.* Britannica Book of the Year 1969, p39 *Projects range from national parks and seashores to historic sites and inner-city playgrounds.* 1979 World Book Year Book, p272 [**1965**]

inner space, 1 another name for HYDROSPACE. . . . *In the House of Commons last week the Prime Minister told a questioner that the case for international control had still to be made out. Perhaps the British report on marine science and technology which is expected shortly will shed light on this and other problems arising from the new interest in what the Americans called "inner space".* New Scientist 10/24/68, p174 **2** the subconscious part of the mind. *Three letters, on a drawing of three cubes, appeared not long ago on a fence at the University of Wisconsin with the slogan: Your Campus Travel Agent—One Trip Is Worth A Thousand Words. Just about everyone at Wisconsin knew what kind of "trip" that was: the voyage into "inner space," the flight into or out of the self, provided by LSD.* Time 6/17/66, p46 **3** the quality or suggestion of depth in an abstract painting. *Kandinsky and Malevich were 'diagonal invaders' of horizontal or vertical Renaissance space. They used diagonals to create 'inner space' by breaking down interiorising outer space.* Listener 3/7/68, p318 [**1958** for defs. 1 and 2; **1968** for def. 3]

Innigkeit ('inix,kait), *n.* *German.* whole-hearted sincerity and warmth (applied in English only to musical works). *Blumine has in fact a very characteristic innigkeit—a Mahlerian simple poignancy—which might well benefit a work whose progress from a child's heaven to a satanic hell has often seemed abrupt and unreal.* Listener 6/29/67, p865 *In Beethoven's F minor* quartet (the early C minor had been promised—one of those high-handed last-moment changes so regrettably popular with Russian visitors) their playing was smooth and thoughtful, portentous of the innigkeit rather than the urgency of the later Beethoven. Times (London) 11/21/66, p14 A quarter of a century ago it was generally accepted that Bruno Walter was pre-eminent as a Mozart conductor. Nobody, it was believed, so achieved the Innigkeit of the Mozart symphonies and operas. Harper's 8/64, p106 [1964]

inoperative, adj. deprived of force or effect; nullified; invalidated. Whenever necessity required him to swear loyal reconciliation and fealty to the King of France, his mortal enemy, he promptly engaged in treacherous intrigues with the King of England, leaving his knightly oaths to become, in the White House word, inoperative. Atlantic 9/73, p44 Suddenly the "official spokesman" of a great national leader is telling us things which, a day or so later, turn out to be "inoperative." New York Post 2/3/79, p9 [1973] ►The usage was popularized by President Nixon's press secretary, Ronald Ziegler, who referred to contradictory statements as being "inoperative." The word has existed in English in the sense "not working or operating" at least since 1631 (OED).

insertion, n. another name for INJECTION. Insertion: the process of boosting a spacecraft into an orbit round the Earth or moon. Sunday Times (London) 7/13/69, p13 [1962]

insider trading, the buying and selling of stocks based on information obtained from persons with secret knowledge of likely stock price changes on the stock market. Insider trading is now illegal in the United States. The SEC regards insider trading as grossly unfair to the investing public because someone with privileged access to important knowledge exploits that advantage. Americana Annual 1987, p198 [1963] —insider trader: The definition of an insider trader under the terms of the Bill is drawn as wide as possible to include anyone who deals in the shares of a company if he has information which "is not generally available" and which, if it were, "would be likely to materially affect the price" of the shares. Times (London) 7/21/78, p17

inside skinny, U.S. Slang. secret or confidential information. Compare SKINNY. It was clear to everyone that he had inside information, "inside skinny," as Nora called it. Atlantic 5/73, p45 On balance, the book is well worth reading (with appropriate grains of salt), but to get the real inside skinny we shall have to wait until you-know-who's memoirs tell us what the butler really saw. National Review 9/14/73, p1007 [1972, probably from the idea of getting inside the skin of a subject]

insonify, v.t. to charge (an object) with high-frequency sound waves, especially to form an acoustical hologram (that becomes a three-dimensional picture when reconstructed with laser light). Compare SONICATE. A variety of interesting scanning schemes is possible by choosing various combinations of scanning motion involving four basic elements. These elements are (1) the source of sound used to insonify the object, (2) the object, (3) the receiver, and (4) the pointlike light source. McGraw-Hill Yearbook of Science and Technology 1973, p218 [1965, from in- into + Latin soni- (combining form of sonus sound) + English -fy to make]

Instamatic, n. a trademark for a lightweight, fixed-focus camera with a nonadjustable lens, made by the Eastman-Kodak company. "Hey, there's Sonny Bono," said Carol Troy. "Where's my Instamatic?" New Yorker 11/29/76, p33 "It would be difficult to catch from so frail a craft," I laughingly said. "Catch? Dew, there's a simpleton you are. Instamatics we use, not harpoons. We make pictures." Punch 1/21/77, p107 [1964, from instant + automatic]

instance, n. give a for instance, U.S. Informal. to give an example or illustration. "Give me a for-instance, Rabbi," Dr. Muntz suggested. "All right. Since we're talking about wills, I'll give you an example from the laws of inheritance." Harry Kemelman, Wednesday the Rabbi Got Wet, 1976, p205 "I'll give you a for instance," a man named Irving Goltz told us while he chewed on a fried chicken wing. "My real name was Irving. For a while there, they called me Sidney, and then, all of a sudden,

they were calling me Sussy. Don't ask me why." New Yorker 6/26/78, p26 [1959, 1971, blend of the phrases give an instance to give an example, and for instance for example]

instant, adj. 1 produced or occurring in what seems to be an instant; involving little or no preparation, planning, thought, etc. For present tastes, honed to instant violence, it is by no means obvious that Shakespeare outwrote Marlowe. [Ian] McKellen's Richard [II] is Shakespeare's, full strength and without eccentricity, a prince refined down to holy innocence . . . Time 9/19/69, p51 The reorganization of the Army (the Socialists favour the creation of "instant soldiers" with basic training limited to six months). Times (London) 4/10/70, p6 Mr. [Keith] Jenkinson pointed to a 1928 double-deck bus which has taken him eight years to renovate and is the third oldest in existence. "That's one bit of instant history the Americans are not going to get." Manchester Guardian Weekly 4/17/71, p9 2 characterized as being very quick, especially too quick to be of much value. In this instant world of today people, sadly, have short memories . . . Times (London) 4/21/70, p12 [1962, originally applied to premixed or precooked foods (OEDS 1912)]

instant book, a book, such as an anthology or a reprint of a government report, that requires little editing or rewriting to prepare for printing. Yale University Press has simply reprinted this surprisingly readable document (The Double-Cross System in the War of 1939 to 1945) on the coded doings of Garbo, Tricycle and the rest, and bargain-priced the instant book at $6.95. Time 3/13/72, p83 [1968]

instant camera, a camera which takes individual photographs and develops each picture soon after it is taken. See INSTANT PHOTOGRAPHY. The resultant small size of the negative means that it must be enlarged for printing and viewing. This both adds a process which is missing from the instant cameras, such as the Polaroid, and can introduce defects that are absent on the original negative. New Scientist 12/23-30/76, p720 [1964]

instantize, v.t. to make available in instant (premixed, precooked, etc.) form. . . . . the department contracted . . . for the purchase of "instantized" nonfat dry milk for distribution in welfare programs. Americana Annual 1970, p58 . . . when foods become unrecognisable, what shall we do? The formulated, instantised, convenience foods will no longer look like meat, milk, cereal or vegetable. New Scientist 12/24/70, p560 [1962]

instant lottery, U.S. a lottery in which the players can immediately determine from the markings on the ticket whether they have won a prize, without having to wait for a drawing. The game will be a variation of the state's most recent instant lottery in which players rubbed off a wax covering to reveal a set of numbers. In the new lottery, each ticket will cost $1 and will contain 16 numbers. There are six ways to win, depending on which numbers are shown to be circled when the wax is rubbed off. NY Times 8/31/77, p33 [1976]

instanton, n. Physics. a hypothetical quantum unit for the interaction occurring between states of the lowest energy. Compare AXION. It now seems likely that the key to understanding QCD [quantum chromodynamics] relies on a detailed knowledge of the vacuum state—that is, a state of zero energy. Previously believed empty, it appears to contain "pseudoparticles" otherwise called instantons, which can affect the interactions between the quarks. New Scientist 3/30/78, p858 Instantons are mathematical, but they have a physical effect: In their presence the gluons feel forces. So nothing can affect something. Science News 4/15/78, p228 [1978, from instant + -on elementary unit or particle, first proposed by Gerard't Hooft, University of Utrecht]

instant photography, a photographic process that develops each picture soon after it is taken. The manufacturing of film and cameras for instant photography, with the photographic darkroom incorporated into the film itself, has been dominated by the Polaroid Corporation. NY Times 4/13/76, p47 [1976]

instant replay, U.S. and Canadian. a videotaped replay of an event, especially a play in sports, which can be shown as soon as the event is completed. The corresponding British term is

ACTION REPLAY. *TV instant replay multiplies analysis and assigns error: in the press boxes, after a goal has been scored, sportswriters and sportcasters rush to the TV screen for the instant replay, usually shown in slow motion. When a goalie looks bad on a goal now, he looks bad over and over again. Instant replay might pick up the forward who missed his check, or the defenseman out of position: what it never fails to pick up is an awkward miss or a faked-out drop to the ice.* Maclean's 2/73, p80 **[1973]**

instructional television, *U.S.* closed-circuit television programs designed as courses for instruction within the classroom. *Abbreviation:* ITV *After more than a decade of intensive effort and the expenditure of hundreds of millions of dollars, instructional television seems to have arrived at a limbo of promise and partial success.* Saturday Review 11/19/66, p88 **[1966]**
▶British English seems to have no direct equivalent. *CCTV* (for *Closed-Circuit Television*) is often used to mean instructional television.

instrumental learning, *Psychology.* a form of conditioning in which the subject learns to respond according to the result of the effects (good or bad) of his or her previous responses. *Two types of learning are classical conditioning and instrumental learning. Classical conditioning begins with an unconditioned stimulus. The conditioned stimulus that is paired with it comes to substitute for it in producing the unconditioned response. In instrumental learning a conditioned stimulus is presented along with an opportunity to respond in various ways. The correct response is reinforced, or rewarded.* Scientific American 1/70, p31 *In a typical experiment, if a rat showed a slight increase in its heart rate, it would be rewarded by electrical stimulation of certain areas of the brain known to produce pleasure to the animal. This was then followed by a further increase in heart rate, which was called instrumental learning.* Britannica Book of the Year 1970, p168 **[1956]**

insulin-dependent diabetes mellitus. See quotation for meaning. *Insulin-dependent diabetes mellitus (IDDM or Type I) defines a group of patients who are literally dependent on exogenous insulin to prevent . . . death.* Merch Manual, ed. 15, p1069 **[1987, from earlier medical use in the phrase** *insulin-dependent* **(1977)]**

insulinoma, *n.* a benign tumor of the islets of the pancreas (islets of Langerhans) that secretes insulin. *The best-known example of this is the insulinoma of the pancreas, which causes the plasma to contain an unusually high amount of insulin much of which can be in the form of "pro" insulin.* McGraw-Hill Yearbook of Science and Technology 1977, p415 **[1962, from** *insulin* + *-oma* **tumor (from Greek** *-ōma,* **noun suffix)]**

Intal, *n.* a trademark for CROMOLYN SODIUM. *It took Fisons, a British company, seven years to get its Intal, an anti-bronchial medication, approved by American authorities, even after registration was granted in Britain.* NY Times 3/21/76, pC6 **[1969, from** *interference with al*lergy**]**

integrase, *n.* a viral enzyme that promotes the insertion of the virus's DNA into the genetic material of a bacterial cell. Compare EXCISIONASE. *The enzyme product of a specific viral gene (dubbed integrase) is required for the insertion of viral DNA; mutant viruses lacking this enzyme are unable to enter the lysogenic state.* Scientific American 12/76, p109 **[1974, from** *integra*tion + *-ase* **(suffix meaning enzyme)]**

integrated circuit, an electronic circuit hundreds of times smaller than a wired circuit, produced on a single chip of silicon in such a way that the components are completely integrated and cannot be grouped or redistributed in another way and still perform the same electronic function. *Abbreviation:* IC Also called MICROCIRCUIT. Compare MONOLITHIC CIRCUIT. *Integrated circuits have been used chiefly in computers and low-frequency instrumentation, but now they can be applied in VHF, UHF and microwave apparatus.* New Scientist 10/15/70, p13 *Integrated circuits have just reached the colour television business and are already vital components in the computer industry: electronics for mass-produced cars, desk calculators, and further ahead, the household computer, are on a long list*

of areas the industry would like to penetrate. Manchester Guardian Weekly 4/11/70, p22 **[1959]**

integrated circuitry, components or equipment consisting of integrated circuits. Also called MICROCIRCUITRY. *The effects of the rapidly falling price of integrated circuits can still surprise even those in close touch with this field. The W. German subsidiary of Texas Instruments exhibited integrated circuitry to replace the traditional string and pulley drive of radio receivers.* New Scientist 11/12/70, p329 **[1970]**

integrated injection logic, a type of integrated circuit used in microprocessors and semiconductor memories. *The circuit is an example of the semiconductor technology called integrated-injection logic, or I²L. A distinguishing feature of I²L circuits is that some regions of the chip function as elements of more than one transistor.* Scientific American 9/77, p70 **[1976]**

integrated optics, the use of highly compact units of optical fibers to control and guide the flow of light in optical instruments and devices activated by or using light, such as in communication systems. *The need for transmission, repeating, and receiving terminals for the fiber links has given rise to yet a new field, "integrated optics." In this area the effort is aimed at duplicating for light the feat that integrated electronics has already achieved for electricity, the ability to manipulate the flow of light in miniature, monolithic optical circuits.* 1975 Britannica Yearbook of Science and the Future, p47 **[1974]**

intelligent, *adj.* **1** capable of processing data by a built-in microprocessor. *The second method is to cut telecommunications costs. An intelligent terminal can run its own software without a telephone line being kept open all the time to the remote "central computer".* New Scientist 5/3/79, p355 **2** (of a machine) able to solve problems, make fine distinctions, and perform other logical operations. Compare SMART. See also ARTIFICIAL INTELLIGENCE. *A new electronic camera from Japan represents a step towards the concept of the "intelligent" camera—one which can decide for itself how to produce the best possible photograph from any given set of circumstances.* New Scientist 5/18/78, p452 *The eye of the gadget "memorizes" the underside of the object it is guarding, and of course the alarm "hits" if that object is removed. In addition, it is so "intelligent" that it knows immediately if a piece of paper or even a sliver of the same material it is guarding is slid under the object in an attempt to remove it without detection.* NY Times Magazine 12/17/78, p108 **[1969]**

Intelsat, *n.* **1** acronym for *International Telecommunications Satellite (Consortium)*, an organization of over 70 member nations formed to control and promote work in global communications by means of satellites. *. . .America is prepared to supply rockets to Europe even for communications satellites which would bring competition to US-comsats. The question of how this could be achieved without violating the Intelsat rules, however, has yet to be solved.* New Scientist 10/1/70, p16 **2** any of several communications satellites launched under the auspices of Intelsat. Compare COMSAT. *The Intelsats launched by the Communications Satellite Corporation provide commercial service over vast areas by being stationed in synchronous orbits above the Atlantic and the Pacific oceans.* Encyclopedia Science Supplement (Grolier) 1968, p298 **[1966]**

intensive care unit, a medical unit equipped with life-saving and monitoring devices for providing 24-hour in-hospital care for severely ill patients, or immediate out-of-hospital care in emergencies, especially heart attacks. *Twenty years ago hospitals employed 1.5 persons to care for each patient. Today the ratio is almost 3 to 1 nationally and much higher in specialized intensive care units.* NY Times 2/25/68, p51 *Doctors at the Royal Victoria Hospital, Belfast, are operating a new crash-call system which is saving the lives of people having coronary attacks at home, by sending a mobile intensive-care unit to the patient's own door.* Sunday Times (London) 8/6/67, p2 **[1963]**

intensivism, *n.* the breeding and raising of animals herded together in a small area. *Wherever intensivism has taken control, severe problems of disease and environmental damage have* *arisen.* Times (London) 11/15/72, p24 [**1968**, from *intensive (husbandry)* + *-ism*]

inter-, a prefix meaning "between" or "among," now used chiefly to form adjectives, as in the following recent formations: —**interauthority,** *adj.: In the second case inter-authority arrangements could be made for recruiting pupils from outside the immediate area.* Times (London) 3/25/70, p10 —**intercentre,** *adj.: . . . saturation signalling involves a large volume of inter-centre communication and with conventional techniques it can only be employed in networks of limited size and with limited traffic capacity.* New Scientist 12/31/70, p596 —**interdealer,** *adj.: It appears to be technically feasible to use a central computer to record and report interdealer quotations for some or all over-the-counter securities on a continuing basis.* NY Times 2/19/68, p60 —**interfirm,** *adj.: The Stock Exchange yesterday announced details of price fractions for which inter-firm accounting computers will be programmed after decimalization.* Times (London) 3/11/70, p28 —**intersyllabic,** *adj.: Rhythmically, the production follows a metrical pattern as fixed as that of the metronome with which it opens. Lines are broken up with blows of a strap, or even split up with intersyllabic pauses.* Times (London) 5/22/70, p6

interabang (in'terə,bæn), *n.* another spelling of INTERROBANG. *Thanks to the American Type Founders Co., Inc., an easy solution is at hand: the interabang* (‽) *a punctuation mark . . . for such rhetorical questions of daily life as "Who forgot to put gas in the car" or "What the hell."* Time 7/21/67, p38 [**1967**]

interactive fiction, a computer game or video game in which an adventure, mystery, or other story is developed through the player's interaction with the story's characters. *Interactive fiction allows players to become heroes as they engage in . . . feats of derring-do simply by typing in commands on the computer's keyboard.* Encyclopedia Science Supplement (Grolier) 1987, p113 [**1980**]

interconnect, *adj. U.S.* of or having to do with the interconnection of private telephone facilities with the general telephone network. *Virtually overnight, an "interconnect" industry sprang up offering Bell customers the chance to buy a variety of new terminal equipment—and interconnect it to A.T.&T.'s lines.* NY Times Magazine 11/28/76, p114 [**1973**, adjective use of the verb]

interdate, *v.i. U.S.* to go out on dates with members of a different religion or denomination. *Among the Catholic students 74 per cent interdated frequently and 66 per cent thought it likely they would marry non-Catholics.* NY Times 11/8/65, p33 [**1965**]

interdit (æter'di:), *adj. French.* prohibited. *Karisimbi [a high peak in NW Rwanda, in central Africa] was strictly interdit. Provided, however, that I undertook to go straight up and down, he would in my case waive the rules.* Times (London) 9/17/66, p9 *There are hamburgers and hot dogs—and quiche Lorraine and bifsteck tartare as well: Moët et Chandon champagne and Coca-Cola are both on the menu. Empty seats are interdit.* Time 11/2/70, p56 [**1966**] ►In French there is a noun *interdit* as well as the adjective. The feminine of the adjective is *interdite,* a form recorded in the OED as an obsolete variant of *interdict, n.* and *v.* But *interdit, adj.* is an independent loan from modern French.

interface, *n.* something that serves to connect or coordinate different systems; the boundary joining any two parts, persons, or things. *"Interface" refers to anything that mediates between disparate items: machinery, people, thought. The equipment that makes the computer's work visible to the user is often called an "interface," and the word is used highly metaphorically, as in "the interface between man and the computer, between the scientist and society,"* Atlantic 3/70, p66 *Last week, the Biological Engineering Society celebrated the tenth anniversary of this broad interface between medicine and technology with a conference in Oxford.* New Scientist 4/16/70, p117 *And it is exactly at the "interface" between that Darwinian-Mendelian theory of random mutation and natural selection and the recent discoveries in genetics and biochemistry that one finds some of the most characteristic speculative argu-

ments in current science. New Yorker 3/6/71, p108 —*v.i., v.t.* to match, harmonize, or work together smoothly. *This was to be a full-dress affair, including inflated space suits, which have to "interface"—a space-age verb meaning, roughly, to coordinate—with equipment in the cabin.* New Yorker 1/11/69, p42 *Putting the computer to work meant complex programming, interfacing of instrument and computer, of man and machine.* Scientific American 5/70, p114 *I like big companies. They're very important. They have money. I'm offering them a chance to interface with new products right from the start.* New Yorker 2/27/71, p34 [**1963**, extended senses of *interface, n.,* the touching surface of two objects that are joined (OED 1882)]

interferon (,intər'fir,an), *n.* a protein produced in the cells of many vertebrates that prevents the replication of viruses by its sensitivity to foreign nucleic acid. *Abbreviation:* IF . . . *acute virus infection can be cured by stimulating the body's production of interferon.* World Book Science Annual 1969, p317 *Interferon, once hailed as a potential panacea for virus diseases, has fallen from grace in some scientists' eyes, as is a focus of controversy among those who continue to believe in its future.* Science News Yearbook 1970, p112 [**1957**, from *interfere* + *-on* (chemical suffix)]

intergenerational, *adj.* occurring or existing between two or more generations. *Mothers in Poverty: A study of Fatherless Families . . . An assessment of alternative explanations of the intergenerational transmission of poverty.* Science News 5/16/70, p493 *They [most parents] may give a child the name of a relative to strengthen feelings of kinship, to keep alive an intergenerational awareness, or possibly to make a legacy more likely.* Science Journal 9/70, p39 [**1964**]

interleave, *n.* the correlation, by means of successive numbers, of physically separate locations of storage units in a computer. *One reason why Sigma 5 gets more efficient as it grows larger is that when memory modules are added interleave and overlap occur. This not only increases the effective speed of the central processor but raises input/output capability too.* Scientific American 2/67, p11 [**1967**]

interleukin-1, *n.* a protein secreted by various cells that functions especially in stimulating the production of T cells. *Interleukin-1 . . . is a protein with a molecular weight of 17,000 daltons that is synthesized primarily by the phagocytic white blood cells called macrophages.* Scientific American 7/87, p83 [**1980**, from *inter-* + *leuk*ocyte + *-in* (protein suffix)]

interleukin-2, *n.* **1** a protein secreted by T cells activated by certain antigens, important as mediators of cellular immunity. *Helper T cells may also react to an encounter with antigens by releasing lymphokines, substances including interleukin-1 (IL-1), interleukin-2 (IL-2), interferon, and chemotactic factors (chemical attractors of cells) that activate lymphocytes, macrophages, and a variety of other cells.* 1986 Britannica Yearbook of Science and the Future, p164 **2** this protein produced by genetic engineering, used experimentally in the treatment of cancer. *The experimental therapy involves treating white blood cells removed from the patient with a genetically engineered substance called* interleukin-2. *The white cells, which are then reinjected into the patient, attack the cancerous cells.* 1986 World Book Year Book, p395 [**1983**, from *inter-* + *leuk*ocyte + *-in* (protein suffix)]

intermedia, *n.* the use of many different devices and techniques from any artistic form to produce a show, exhibition, or other entertainment. This may include such a potpourri as exotic theatrical lighting combined with motion pictures and sound from tapes on a backdrop behind a full ballet (often used attributively). Compare MIXED MEDIA, MULTIMEDIA. *That a great many Western artists for a great many years have quarreled with received definitions of artistic media, genres, and forms goes without saying: pop art, dramatic and musical "happenings," the whole range of "intermedia" or "mixed-means" art, bear recentest witness to the tradition of rebelling against Tradition.* Atlantic 8/67, p29 *Lyla Hay, Gerald Hoke, Arthur Wagner, and Bronislav Radakovich perform well and strenuously amid the taxing conditions posed by this sort of experimentation. And there is no gainsaying the uniqueness of the event. Yet it* does make the play much more difficult to follow, as well as compelling the theatergoer to sit on the floor for two hours. Since this form of environmental "intermedia" theater is in its early stages, one is inclined to forgive its imperfections and distractions. Saturday Review 5/20/67, p64 [**1966**] ►This word should not be confused with *intermedia* in the sense of musical or dance interludes, which is the plural of *intermedium* (a term with several technical senses, originally from Latin, in which it is the neuter of *intermedius*, from *inter-* between + *medius* middle). The word herein is a new English formation of *inter-* + *media* means of communication, expression, or entertainment (plural of *medium*).

intermediate, *n. U.S.* an automobile between the standard and the compact models in size. Compare SUBCOMPACT. *The intermediates, the Chevrolet's Chevelle and the Pontiac, Oldsmobile and Buick models received major changes for 1968 and get minor grille and trim facelifts for 1969.* NY Times 3/26/68, p32 *General Motors and Ford restyled their standard-sized cars for 1971, adopting the trend toward ventless front windows and concealed wipers that became paramount on the redesigned 1970 intermediates.* Americana Annual 1971, p130 [**1968,** noun use of adjective]

intermediate boson or **intermediate vector boson**, another name for W PARTICLE. *The disagreement between the Utah result and present theory suggests that additional sources of cosmic-ray muons exist. One possibility is the intermediate boson—a hypothetical particle never seen by experimenters.* New Scientist 9/25/69, p633 *The present theory of the weak interaction predicts that its quantum should be a so-called intermediate vector boson, which can come in two varieties, positively or negatively charged, designated W-plus or W-minus.* Science News 10/9/71, p253 [**1958**]

intermediate technology, a form of technology that combines small scale, simplicity, and self-sufficiency with present-day tools and methods. Compare ALTERNATIVE TECHNOLOGY, APPROPRIATE TECHNOLOGY. *Providing practical edge to the theory, a number of intermediate or "appropriate" technology groups, inspired by Schumacher's philosophy, now exist in several Western nations, including Germany, Switzerland, Canada, and the United States.* East West Journal 9/77, p30 *What the poor need most of all is simple things—building materials, clothing, household goods, agricultural implements—and a better return for their agricultural products . . . All these are idea fields for intermediate technology.* E.F. Schumacher, Small Is Beautiful, 1973, p186 [**1973**]

intermodal, *adj.* **1** combining different ways of transportation into one system. *Both vessels are part of an intermodal system in which United States Freight uses railroads to "piggyback" trailers and container vans to ports for delivery.* NY Times 5/4/68, p78 **2** used in an integrated system of transportation. *Unit trains are high-speed trains made up of about 100 permanently coupled flatcars, each able to carry two intermodal containers.* Sunday Times (London) 4/6/69, p56 [**1963**]

internalization, *n. U.S.* a method of transacting sales of stock securities within brokerage offices instead of transmitting trading orders to the floor of an exchange. Compare EXTERNALIZATION. *For the public . . . internalization could lead to drastic changes in the way that securities are bought and sold. Although there is no question that it would result in more sites where Big Board stocks are traded, in addition to the exchange itself, there is a raging controversy among those with and without axes to grind as to whether it would lead to better prices and greater access to the marketplace by the individual investor.* NY Times 1/17/77, p37 [**1977**]

internal pollution, the excessive and often harmful ingestion of a variety of synthetic substances in drugs and foods. *Dr. Beaconsfield, an American, is a specialist in the long-term effects of drugs upon various body tissues and cells. He earlier coined the term internal pollution and was instigator of this proposal for independent action by the scientific community.* NY Times 6/20/71, p50 [**1971**]

interoperability, *n.* **1** the ability to operate together or jointly; cooperation. *Defenders of the existing regime—although*

many concede there is scope for greater "inter-operability" between the home and foreign services—contend that . . . the Foreign Office has developed a sharp commercial edge while remaining a political instrument which is still the envy of others, including the Americans and the French. If it were to be integrated with the home departments what would happen to its superb communications?* Manchester Guardian Weekly 5/1/77, p4 **2** coordination of communication systems, equipment, etc., used by member countries in an alliance. *While nationalistic pride will probably continue to prevent full standardization, there have been gains in what NATO jargon terms interoperability. Two years ago, for example, few of the airbases in NATO countries could service any but their own warplanes. By next year, most bases will be able to accommodate all NATO aircraft.* Time 12/11/78, p43 [**1965,** from *inter-* one with the other, between + *operability* condition of being operable]

interoperable, *adj.* capable of operating together or reciprocally. *In other respects the two nations' forces are working in parallel and Skynet* [The Royal Navy's military satellite communications system] *is compatible and interoperable with the US Defence Communication Satellite system . . .* Science Journal 3/70, p13 [**1966**]

interpandemic, *adj.* occurring between pandemic outbreaks of a disease. *Our present vaccine policy . . . recommends the preferential immunization of the estimated 45 million Americans unusually susceptible to influenza complications (pneumonia and death) even in interpandemic years.* NY Times 2/13/76, p33 [**1970,** from *inter-* between + *pandemic*]

interpopulational, *adj.* occurring or existing between populations or between different groups, especially groups considered as separate species, cultures, etc. *I wonder whether he would agree that there are no known IQ tests which are capable of overcoming the interpopulational cross-cultural barrier?* Listener 12/30/71, p907 *Interpopulational developmental comparisons . . . helped to clarify what in the past seemed to be an aberrant course of leaf development.* McGraw-Hill Yearbook of Science and Technology 1971, p253 [**1971**]

interpulse, *n.* a secondary or intermediate pulse occurring in a pulsar. *There may be two pulses in the pulsar, a main pulse strong in radio but weak in X-ray and an interpulse strong in X-ray but weak in radio.* Science News 1/27/73, p58 [**1969,** from *inter-* between + *pulse*]

interrobang (in'terə‚bæŋ), *n.* a punctuation mark (‽) intended to express simultaneously a question and an exclamation, as in certain rhetorical questions (How about that?! Who needs him?!). Also spelled INTERABANG. [Martin K.] *Speckter's device, which he prefers to call the interrobang ("bang" is printer's slang for an exclamation point), remained just an idea until Detroit Graphic Artist Richard Ishbell casually included it in the Americana face he was designing.* Time 7/21/67, p38 [**1962,** from *interro*gation point + *bang*]

interrupt, *n.* **1** a temporary stop; interruption. *Sigma 5 can deal with foreground real-time interrupts in 6 microseconds without losing control of any of its other jobs, yet every background user will get his answers faster than he needs them.* Scientific American 2/67, p11 **2** any breach, separation, or gap. *Wide though the interrupt be that divides us, runers* [makers of runes] *and counters, from the Old World of the Plants . . . we nod them as neighbors . . .* New Yorker 11/21/70, p58 [**1957,** noun use of verb]

intersensory, *adj.* involving the use of all or several senses at the same time. . . . *such is the power of intersensory whatever-it-is that any one of four golfers, sizing up to a simple chip shot of, say, 40 yards, knows suddenly that nothing can prevent him socketing it.* Sunday Times (London) 11/26/67, p20 [**1964**]

interstate, *n. U.S.* a highway extending between States; an interstate highway. *Since the restaurant adjoined a motel, most of the breakfast crowd were regular denizens of the Interstate: traveling salesmen; irritable young matrons of hair curlers with inert infants in tow; members of some obscure rock combo, all surly and haired-over.* Saturday Review 9/2/72, p13 *The wildcat blockades, which began early in the week on* *interstates in the East and quickly spread to other parts of the country, led to angry confrontations with police.* Newsweek 12/17/73, p74 [**1965,** noun use of adjective (1844)]

intervening sequence, the full name of INTRON. *They recognized these unattached segments as introns, or intervening sequences—sections of DNA that do not code for proteins. Introns are found only in cells with nuclei and thus are not in viruses.* World Book Science Annual 1984, p161 [**1983**]

intervention, *n. U.S. Education.* instruction or tutoring of children by their parents. Compare HOMESCHOOL. *I, for one, am tired of the past decade's scramble to discover some magic period during which interventions will have particularly great payoffs. Some experts emphasize the nine months in utero; Pines and White, the period between 8 and 18 months; others, the entire preschool period; and yet others emphasize adolescence.* NY Times Magazine 1/18/76, p42 [**1976**]

intifada or **intifadeh** (ˌintəˈfɑːdə), *n.* a popular uprising of Palestinian Arabs against Israeli occupation of the West Bank and Gaza Strip, begun in 1988. *The intifada became a focal point of political and social change among the Palestinian Arab community in the territories.* Americana Annual 1989, p294 *And in a poorer quarter, Sabha Mubarak . . . said, "The intifadeh has held our heads high."* NY Times Magazine 12/18/88, p34 [**1988,** from Arabic *intifāda* uprising]

into, *prep.* **be into, 1** *Slang.* to be deeply involved or interested in. *"Yes, I am into a new thing, dear child. It's called embroidery."* New Yorker 8/1/70, p21 . . . *he doesn't want to be President. He isn't into that. You know. Into power.* New Yorker 4/11/70, p161 *Career Plans* [of 1971 Teen-ager]. *Digs working in leather, wood, metal, and the cane fields of Cuba (for a month). Is also into making music, films, and videotapes.* Harper's 9/71, p65 [**1969**] **2** to be in debt to. . . . *he* [a Japanese truck driver] *was a hi-fi nut who made his own equipment, which he could have got from Philco for $200 cheaper, and he was into us for several hundred dollars for some acoustical components.* Maclean's 10/67, p80 [**1967**] ▶Definition 2 is an old slang usage just emerging into general use. Partridge (*Dictionary of Slang*, 1950) calls it a Canadian colloquialism, citing a 1932 source. It also occurs in Saul Bellow's *Adventures of Augie March,* 1949: "I said I'd stop Frazier's credit at twenty-five dollars. It was a lie; . . . he was already into me for nearer to forty."

intra-, 1 a prefix used chiefly to form adjectives (both technical and nontechnical) with the sense of "situated, occurring, carried on, etc., within or inside," as in the following formations: —**intracloud,** *adj.: Zeroing in on intracloud lightning . . . lightning strokes between and within clouds are difficult to study and document because weather conditions usually prevent visual and photographic observations.* Science News 3/28/70, p320 —**intragovernmental,** *adj.: In what is fast becoming an ugly intragovernmental feud over the creation of an electronics and broadcasting giant, the Justice Department insisted that the FCC had violated the law by not holding more complete hearings.* Time 2/10/67, p58 —**intraoffice,** *adj.: They were impatient with committees that took months to study proposals and with intra-office and interagency reports that delayed action.* NY Times 4/14/68, pD13 —**intraregional,** *adj.: . . . the remarkable rate of increase in intraregional trade cannot go on forever, and eventually there will be a need for wider markets.* Time 2/3/67, p29 —**intraunion,** *adj.: The intra-union controversy, regarded as a bid by Negroes to gain more power within their union made idle half the fleet of 2,800 buses and drastically reduced service on elevated and subway rapid transit trains.* NY Times 7/4/68, p8 —**intrazonal,** *adj.: The Chilean delegate—Pedro Daza—told startled delegates . . . that the only beneficiaries of tariff reductions to date had been foreign multinational companies. Intrazonal trade had increased, but so had the region's dependence on foreign capital.* Manchester Guardian Weekly 12/19/70, p22 **2** in the following occurrence *intra-* has become an adjective modifying the noun with which it is combined, and meaning "inside, internal": —**intra-trading,** *n.: The increase* [in exports] *of nearly 16 per cent was close to the average of 17 per cent for all countries covered, and virtual-*

ly at the estimated average, if Common Market intra-trading is excluded. Times (London) 5/6/70, p26

intractable, *adj. Mathematics.* a problem for which a polynomial algorithm cannot be given. Compare NP-COMPLETE. *The inclusion of guessing in the definition of these problems suggests strongly to many mathematicians that* P *and* NP *are not the same set and hence that efficient algorithms can never be found for the intractable problems in the class* NP. Scientific American 1/78, p105 [**1977**]

intrapreneur (ˌintrəprəˈnur), *n.* a corporation executive empowered to act as an entrepreneur in undertaking new ventures. *Pinchot argues that entrepreneurs and intrapreneurs have similar motivations. Both are pushed primarily by the desire to accomplish something . . . Pinchot says that companies should try to tap employees' interest by giving them the freedom and the financial backing to chase their ideas. If they succeed, they may get a bonus or a promotion. But for intrapreneurs, the real payoff is the feeling of success—"I did it, and it worked."* Time 2/4/85, p36 [**1980,** from *intra-* within + entre*preneur*]

intrauterine device, a contraceptive loop, coil, ring, etc., placed within the uterus as a physical barrier to implantation of a fertilized ovum. *Abbreviation:* IUD See also LIPPES LOOP. *At the 14 municipal hospitals the free birth-control services will include provision of pills, intrauterine devices, and contraceptives as well as advice on the spacing of children.* NY Times 6/17/68, p41 . . . *the Pill and intra-uterine devices are not permitted.* Times (London) 6/2/67, p9 [**1965,** earlier *intrauterine appliance* (1931)]

intravehicular, *adj.* of, relating to, or used inside a space vehicle. Compare EXTRAVEHICULAR. *The intravehicular space suit consists of: fecal containment subsystem, constant wear garment, biomedical belt, urine collection transfer assembly, torso limb suit, integrated thermal micrometeoroid garment, pressure helmet, pressure glove, and communications carrier.* Encyclopedia Science Supplement (Grolier) 1969, p329 [**1969**]

intravenous, *n.* an injection or transfusion into a vein or an intravenous feeding or series of such feedings. *"Do you want me to rub your arm?" Ellie asked. "I don't think I dare. You have intravenouses going in both your hands."* New Yorker 11/21/70, p66 [**1960,** noun use of *intravenous, adj.,* going into a vein]

introgressant, *n.* a gene of one species which is acquired by another species through hybridization. *The problem is to find a good scale to measure the proportions in which the parental species are represented in a sample of introgressants.* McGraw-Hill Yearbook of Science and Technology 1968, p121 [**1968,** from *intro-* into + *-gress* go (as in *progress, regress*) + *-ant* (noun agent suffix)]

intron, *n.* a segment of DNA that has no specific genetic code. Full name, INTERVENING SEQUENCE. Compare EXON. *The split gene is first transcribed into a large RNA copy. The noncoding regions, the introns, are then cut out and the gene fragments, exons, are joined together in a process known as splicing. The resulting messenger RNA travels out of the nucleus and into the cytoplasm where its genetic code is translated into protein.* New Scientist 5/10/79, p453 [**1979,** from *intro-* inward, inside + *-on,* unit of genetic material]

Intropin (ˈintrəpin), *n.* the trademark for a drug that stimulates the action of the heart. *Intropin (dopamine hydrochloride), a compound that increases the heart's ability to contract and may restore blood pressure when it is dangerously low during shock, such as after a heart attack or open-heart surgery. Although chemically related to adrenalin and other stimulant drugs, Intropin exhibits differences in activity, especially in increased blood flow to the kidneys and less abnormal heart rhythm.* World Book Science Annual 1977, p268 [**1976**]

invandrare (ˈinˌvandrɑːrə), *n. sing.* or *pl.* a worker who has immigrated to Sweden to take advantage of the labor shortage and high wages. *Most* invandrare *in Sweden work in clean, progressive factories, and they work by law, for Swedish wages. Predrag takes home eighteen hundred kronor a month after taxes—about four hundred and ten dollars—which is more* *than five times what he used to make in Yugoslavia.* New Yorker 3/22/76, p48 **[1976,** from Swedish, literally, immigrant] ►This is the Swedish equivalent of the German GASTARBEITER.

investigative reporting or **investigative journalism,** news gathering by investigation, as of crime or corruption when official investigation is lagging. *Two prominent Japanese journalists, at a luncheon meeting with their foreign colleagues here the other day, talked for two hours in Japanese about the problem and used "investigative reporting" in English throughout.* NY Times 4/11/76, p4 *Autopsy reports on* New Times *magazine—the Jan. 8 issue now on the stand is the last—cite a new and supposedly rampant virus as the cause of death: reader apathy about investigative journalism.* Arizona Republic (Phoenix, AZ) 1/1/79, pA7 **[1951, 1964]**

invitational, *n.* a sports event restricted to invited guests or participants. *As Decker prepared for this week's Sunkist Invitational in Los Angeles. . . .* Newsweek 1/21/85, p16 **[1968,** noun use of the adjective]

in vitro fertilization, another name for EXTERNAL FERTILIZATION. *In-vitro fertilization, the method by which Louise Brown was conceived . . . was developed in England by Dr. Patrick Steptoe and physiologist Robert Edwards to help women who cannot conceive because their Fallopian tubes are blocked.* Reader's Digest 6/79, p110 **[1974]**

inworks, *adj. British.* carried on or taking place within a factory or works. *He added: "In hindsight, it might have been sensible to announce it, but there was no major hazard involved. It was a purely internal, local, inworks business."* Times (London) 12/11/76, p2 **[1976]**

I/O, abbreviation of *input-output* (operations or parts of a computer). *The disparity in the speed of electromechanical I/O and electronic components resulted in ineffective use of the more expensive resources (processor and memory), since these were often idle pending completion of the slower I/O operations.* McGraw-Hill Yearbook of Science and Technology 1977, p42 **[1971]**

iodine-xenon dating, a method of determining the age of a geological specimen by calculating the time it has taken radioactive xenon to decay into the iodine present in the specimen. *Iodine-xenon dating has established that iron sulphide in the Orgueil carbonaceous meteorite is one of the oldest known meteoritic mineral phases, and probably dates from the condensation stage of the early Solar System.* Nature 1/22/76, p189 **[1967]**

iodochlorhydroxyquin (͵aiədou͵klɔrhai'draksəkwin), *n.* a drug used to treat amebic dysentery and infections caused by certain protozoans and bacteria. *Formula:* C_9H_5ClINO *Another potentially harmful drug that the vacationer may encounter in many countries is an anti-diarrheal preparation called Entero-Vioform (iodochlorhydroxyquin). When taken for long periods, says the Medical Letter, this remedy can sometimes produce eye and nerve damage.* Newsweek 6/11/73, p116 **[1972,** from *iodo-* iodine + *chlor-* chlorine + *hydroxyl* + *quino*line]

Ioffe bar (yɑf 'i:), one of a set of current-carrying bars used to increase the strength of a magnetic field in a nuclear fusion reaction. *. . . by adding several current-carrying bars, called Ioffe bars, around the plasma and parallel to the axis, a true magnetic well can be created.* World Book Science Annual 1969, p345 *In addition extra current-carrying structures are often used to improve the stability of the plasma. These structures were originally proposed on theoretical grounds in 1955 by Harold Grad of New York University. They were first used successfully in an experimental test in 1962 by the Russian physicist M.S. Ioffe. The straight rods used by Ioffe in his experiment have come to be called Ioffe bars, but such stabilizing structures can assume various other shapes.* Scientific American 2/71, p52 **[1964]**

ion etching, the technique of eroding materials such as metals, glass, polymers, body tissue, etc., atom by atom, by bombarding them with high-energy ions, in order to reveal their smallest structural features. *The technique of ion etching has now been applied to a wide variety of specimens. Typical examples are metallurgical specimens usually polycrystalline and showing characteristic grain boundary formation.* New Scientist 2/5/70, p256 **[1965]**

ion implantation, a process of making semiconductor devices by implanting electronically the necessary impurities into silicon chips instead of diffusing them. *This month has seen the marketing of the first transistor device produced using the new technology of ion implantation.* New Scientist 2/19/70, p358 *Ion implantation in metal oxide semi-conductors would allow higher switching speeds, reduction in size, and will allow easier fabrication of three-dimensional devices.* World Book Science Annual 1972, p357 **[1965]**

ionophore, *n.* any of various substances capable of transporting ions across lipid barriers in a cell. *The class of compounds known as ionophores has attracted increasing attention during the past decade because of the remarkable cation selectivities shown by these substances. Their ability to carry ions across lipid barriers caused the term "ionophores" to be suggested in 1967 for all compounds having this property. These compounds are generally cyclic, although several are known in which cyclization occurs only upon complexation with a cation. Those studied initially were of natural origin, namely valinomycin, nonactin, and monesin.* McGraw-Hill Yearbook of Science and Technology 1974, p245 **[1967,** from *ion* + connecting *-o-* + *-phore* combining form meaning thing that carries (from Greek *phóros* carrying)]

ippon, *n.* a full-point score in judo, equivalent to a knockout in boxing. *Last night the first judo gold medal was won by the strong and skillful heavyweight from the Soviet Union, Serge Novikov. He threw his opponent, Gunther Neureuther, forcibly on to his back to score an* ippon *to which there is no reply, ending a scheduled 10-minute bout in 79 seconds.* Times (London) 7/28/76, p11 **[1967,** from Japanese, point]

I.R.A. or **IRA** ('ai'ar'ei *or* 'airə), *U.S.* abbreviation of *individual retirement account.* Compare KEOGH PLAN. *I.R.A.'s were established by the Employee Retirement Income Security Act of 1974 to allow individuals not covered by an employer pension plan to set up a plan of his or her own. With an I.R.A., a person can put 15 percent of his earnings each year up to a maximum of $1,500 in a special account and build up an untaxed nest egg until normal retirement age.* NY Times 3/18/76, p61 **[1974]** ►The Tax Reform Act of 1986 restricted I.R.A.'s for many taxpayers.

irenology, *n.* the study of peace, especially as part of international relations. *Peace-making is at last becoming a subject of serious study, engaging some of our most talented scholars. Variously called "Peace Studies," or "Irenology," this is rapidly developing as an independent field.* Pamphlet published by The Christophers, New York, 2/74 *Irenology has received new impetus with an infusion of fresh ideas about human conflict from the fields of psychology, anthropology, sociology, economics, politics and history.* Murdoch University (Australia) Handbook and Calendar 1975, p66 **[1974,** from *iren*ic, ultimately from Greek *eirēnē* peace, + English *-ology;* compare *polemology* (1938) the study of war]

Ir gene, a gene that determines immunological response to various antigens, such as viruses. *The discovery of the existence of Ir genes was only the first of several surprises. The next came when attempts were made to man them—that is, pinpoint the location of the genes among the chromosomes. It turned out that not only were they nowhere near the genes controlling antibody structure, but that they appeared to be tucked away right in the middle of the genes determining graft rejection, those coding for the so-called histocompatibility antigens.* New Scientist 5/25/72, p431 *The interaction between T cells and B cells that leads to antibody production . . . requires that both types of cell have identical IR genes.* World Book Science Annual 1975, p306 **[1972;** *Ir* abbreviation of *immune response*]

irghizite ('irgə͵zait), *n. Geology.* a tektite rich in silica, discovered in Kazakhstan, U.S.S.R. *The irghizites are small black objects averaging about half a gram in weight. (Most tektites weigh a few grams.) They are warty, twisted objects . . . Their* *chemical composition according to Kurt Fredrikson of the Smithsonian Institution, is remarkably uniform from specimen to specimen; it is unlike that of any local rocks and is very similar to that of the tektites found in Java.* Scientific American 8/78, p116 [**1977,** from *Irghiz,* a town near which it was discovered in a shallow crater + *-ite* rock, mineral]

iridology, *n.* a method of inspecting the iris of the eye which is supposed to aid in medical diagnosis. Compare SANPAKU. *Iridology can identify an organ that has degenerated enough to become cancerous. The basis for iridology is the neuro-optic reflex, an intimate marriage of the estimated half million nerve filaments of the iris with the cervical ganglia of the sympathetic nervous system.* Esquire 1/78, p56 *Hoax or not, iridology has only an organ that has degenerated enough to been practised and studied in Europe since the first iridology chart was developed in the early 1800s. There are now an estimated 10,000 European practitioners, though North America has only about 1,000, most of them in the United States.* Maclean's 2/6/78, p58 [**1971,** from *irid-* of the iris (from Greek *íris, íridos* iris) + *-ology* study of] —**iridologist,** *n.: The eye has been called the window to the soul. Less poetically, iridologists call it the map to the body's trouble spots.* Maclean's 2/6/78, p56

Iris, *n.* acronym for *infrared intruder system,* an alarm system which is set off when a beam of infrared light is interrupted. *Iris (infrared intruder system) is . . . effective over distances of up to 200 metres between its two component parts, a beam transmitter and sensor. The infrared beam is very narrow—a 40 mm cylindrical "pipe" links the two components, which work off a 12 volt dc supply.* New Scientist 8/24/72, p386 [**1972,** influenced by the proper name *Iris*]

iron, *n. Slang.* **pump iron,** to lift weights; be a weight lifter. *When Lisa Lyon, 26, met muscleman-actor Arnold Schwarzenegger two years ago . . . she began to pump iron, and—voila—today the 5-3 cutie can heft 265 lbs. like straw.* New York Post 10/19/79, p7 [**1976,** popularized by the motion picture "Pumping Iron" (1977)]

iron-pumper, *n. Slang.* a weight lifter. *The generation now turning 40 is the one that never trusted anyone over 30. Its members . . . are among the most fanatical cyclists, joggers, iron-pumpers, lap-swimmers, rope-jumpers and cross-country skiers.* Time 6/6/77, p83 [**1977,** from *pump iron* (see IRON)]

irrelevance, *n.* absence of contemporaneity; failure to address oneself to issues that are current. Compare RELEVANCE. . . . *writers like Mark Twain and Stephen Crane, despite their "irrelevance," were more important than Eldridge Cleaver and Rap Brown.* 1970 Collier's Encyclopedia Year Book, p105 [**1970**]

irrelevant, *adj.* having no bearing on issues that are current. Compare RELEVANT. *Ronnie, now 24, later chose not to join his father's "irrelevant" business, won a conscientious-objector status after a harrowing legal battle, and started writing a novel.* Time 8/17/70, p38 [**1969**]

irtron, *n.* a galactic source of strong infrared radiation. *To satisfy theoretical and observational constraints imposed by the shape of the spectrum shown in the figure, the size of the emitting region in the galactic center must be made much smaller than the observed diameter. Thus it is necessary to break up the source into many smaller sources. These sources must be nearly identical in all their physical properties, and have been named irtrons because of their characteristic infrared spectrum.* McGraw-Hill Yearbook of Science and Technology 1971, p209 *Irtrons radiate fantastic amounts of energy, in some cases many times more than the total power emitted by all the stars in the largest galaxies.* Science News 5/9/70, p464 [**1970,** from infrared spectrum + *-on,* as in *electron, neutron,* etc.]

ISBN, abbreviation of *International Standard Book Number,* a number assigned to new books, especially to facilitate ordering. *The International Standard Book Number (ISBN) for numbering of books by publishers was widely adopted . . . , in September further progress was made with the introduction of the International Standard Serials Number for the identification*

of periodical publications . . . Britannica Book of the Year 1973, p413 [**1972**]

ISD, abbreviation of *international subscriber dialing,* a system of direct dialing of telephones between participating countries. *Users of Britain's 15 million telephones with international subscriber dialling are now able to dial Moscow direct. ISD has also started to Bombay.* Times (London) 11/16/76, p4 [**1972**]

island of stability, a group of superheavy chemical elements with highly stable nuclei. Compare SEA OF INSTABILITY. *For a number of years efforts have been under way at the University of California, Berkeley, and at Dubna in the Soviet Union to create elements in the so-called "island of stability" centered on 114 by smashing heavy atoms together. Likewise, various researchers have reported evidence that such elements exist—or that they have left behind their decay products.* NY Times 6/18/76, pB6 [**1970**]

isobutyl nitrite, a colorless liquid chemical prepared from isobutyl alcohol, inhaled by drug users for its stimulant effects. *Formula:* $C_4H_9NO_2$ Also, BUTYL NITRITE. *A kind of poor man's cocaine, isobutyl nitrite is known to users as a "popper" because its effects are similar to those of its restricted chemical cousin, amyl nitrite. Poppers have become the newest cheap kick for increasing numbers of people: manufacturers estimate that 5 million Americans regularly inhale the chemical, both on the dance floor and later in bed. Some people use it as a quick upper during the day.* Time 7/17/78, p16 [**1978**]

isoenzyme, *n.* one of two or more chemically different forms of the same enzyme. Also called ISOZYME. *Chymotrypsin-A and chymotrypsin-B* [a pair of digestive enzymes] *are the most closely related, their sequences differing only in about 20 per cent of the positions, and as their catalytic activities and specifications are practically identical they can correctly be considered as isoenzymes—"twins" in the family.* New Scientist 3/19/70, p547 [**1960,** from *iso-* equal + *enzyme*]

isoglucose, *n.* a sugar substitute extracted from starchy crops such as maize and wheat flour. *Taxation of competing products should not be used as a means of disposing of food surpluses by compelling consumers to eat the dearer product. This principle is breached by the present proposal by the European Commission to tax isoglucose—a cheap sugar substitute made from cereals—to make it less competitive with sugar.* Times (London) 2/16/78, p12 [**1977,** from *iso-* alike (from Greek *ísos* equal) + *glucose*]

isolated camera, a television videotape camera that is focused on a single player or a single area of play during a game in order to permit immediate replay of any segment involving the player or area of play. *In the spring and summer it is baseball, and winter and fall it is football, beginning shortly after lunch on Saturday . . . and then the whole thing again on Sunday, a vast swirl of bats, swings, passes, kicks, touchdowns, stolen bases, shown again on instant replay, slow-motion, split-screen, and isolated camera . . . The ball game is on.* Atlantic 3/68, p77 [**1965**]

isometrics, *n. pl.* or *sing.* exercises for strengthening muscles by tensing one set of muscles, especially against an immovable object. *Taking issue with those who dismiss high blood pressure as a hazard,* [Dr. William S.] *Breall draws attention to the danger of "weight lifter's hypertension." A man performing "severe isometrics," he explains, markedly increases his blood pressure because he tenses his arm or leg muscles and cuts down the flow of blood through them.* Time 7/20/70, p46 [**1962,** from *isometric, adj.,* denoting muscular contraction occurring against resistance + *n.pl.* suffix *-s*]

Isoprinosine (ˌɑisouˈprinəsiːn), *n.* a trademark for an experimental drug used to fight viral infection by stimulating the B cells and T cells of the immune system. *Formula:* $C_{52}H_{78}N_{10}O_{17}$ *Thirty-nine volunteers were randomly chosen to receive either Isoprinosine or a placebo tablet. They were then challenged with a cold virus. Of the 19 volunteers receiving Isoprinosine, 5 became ill, whereas 14 out of 20 in the placebo group did.* Science News 3/20/76, p187 [**1971**]

isospin, *n. Nuclear Physics.* a quantum number based on the theory that the neutron and proton are different states of the same particle. *Drs. Berman, Fultz and Kelly suggest that the discrepancy is due either to a complicated and unexpected mixing together of isospin states (isospin is a number, with no simple physical meaning, that represents mathematically the difference between neutrons and protons) or to a component of the strong nuclear force whose action does depend on electric charge.* Science News 10/17/70, p320 [**1963**, contraction of *isotopic spin*]

isozyme, *n.* another name for ISOENZYME. *Another enzyme being studied in assessing possible carriers is lactic dehydrogenase (LDH) which exists in five configurations—or isozymes—in normal muscle. In analyses of muscle samples, Dr. Emery found an apparent shortage of one of these isozymes in six known carriers* [of Duchenne dystrophy]. New Scientist 8/27/64, p480 [**1959**]

isozymic, *adj.* of or relating to isozymes. *Population geneticists are presently having a field day describing isozymic variation in natural populations, however, and are finding a wide array of allelic diversity at many if not most loci of the genome.* Science 1/5/68, p72 [**1959**]

i.t.a. or **ITA**, abbreviation of *Initial Teaching Alphabet*, a system designed to teach the early stages of reading, consisting of 44 letters and code symbols, supposedly to give a closer phonetic regularity than traditional spelling. *Another difference was that, with the middle-class children, Bereiter tried out a phonetic alphabet called ITA. Harper's 1/67, p60 She is one of those with the longest experience of i.t.a.—and as an employee of a school system at a high level.* Science News 3/25/67, p274 [**1964**]

ITV, 1 abbreviation of INSTRUCTIONAL TELEVISION. *With certain honorable exceptions, ITV has merely transferred conventional teaching techniques to the screen or served as a conduit for other media: films, slides, etc.* Saturday Review 11/19/66, p89 **2** *British.* abbreviation of *Independent Television* (the British commercial television network). *The real danger of a council . . . is that it would interrupt the direct dialogue between the BBC and its audience, and I should think that what I have said probably would be just as true of ITV.* Listener 4/7/66, p498 [**1966** for def. 1; **1958** for def. 2]

I²L ('aɪ'tuːˌel *or* 'dəbəlˌaɪ'el), abbreviation of INTEGRATED INJECTION LOGIC. *I²L is already faster than all the MOSFET technologies. On the other hand, the compact architecture of integrated-injection logic makes it a natural candidate for large-scale integration.* Scientific American 9/77, p81 [**1976**]

IUCD, abbreviation of *intrauterine contraceptive device.* See INTRAUTERINE DEVICE. *". . . Just today, I* [a woman doctor in charge of a Family Planning Center in Delhi] *have had a total of five patients, and I have had to remove the I.U.C.D.s from three of them, because of the bleeding."* New Yorker 9/9/67, p86 *It is claimed in official circles that the IUCD or the Loop has come to stay in India.* New Scientist 2/16/67, p408 [**1963**] ►*IUD* is the current preferred abbreviation. *IUCD* is the older form.

IUD, abbreviation of INTRAUTERINE DEVICE. See also IUCD. *Vasectomies and IUDs can make the future a bit brighter. It's the present that bothers me.* New Scientist 5/1/69, p262 *Although oral contraceptives, when well used, are the most effective method and require only the taking of a tablet for three weeks out of four, in practice in many communities the use-effectiveness (i.e. method and patient failures) is no better than that of the intra-uterine device (I.U.D.).* Practitioner 4/72, p486 [**1965**]

Ivorian, *adj.* of or relating to the Ivory Coast (a republic in western Africa, independent since 1960). *The black Ivorian élite, who can be seen enjoying an "elevenses" of caviar and champagne, support the President's free enterprise system.* Sunday Times Magazine (London) 10/10/71, p43 —*n.* a native or inhabitant of the Ivory Coast. *It is hardly surprising that Mr Houphouet-Boigny has sounded the call for "Ivorisation." He has his Finance Minister, Konan Bedie, and Minister of the Plan Mohamed Teikoura Diawara, working actively to increase the role of Ivorians in national life.* Manchester Guardian Weekly (Le Monde section) 3/24/73, p15 [**1966**, from French *Ivoirien*, from Côte d'*Ivoire* Ivory Coast + *-ien* -ian]

-ization, noun suffix now often used in the sense of "the transferring of establishments, institutions, or positions of authority or power (to a specified ethnic or national group)." The suffix is added to proper-name adjectives and nouns usually ending in *-an.* —**Ivorianization:** *One explanation is that Mr. Yacé has been pressing behind the scenes for more vigorous application of a program of "Ivorianization," in which foreigners in high corporate and governmental positions are replaced by Ivorians.* NY Times 7/14/76, p2 —**Libyanisation:** *In the first of two articles from Tripoli, David Hirst reports on how Libyanisation is going awry.* Manchester Guardian Weekly 3/6/71, p4 —**Malaysianization:** *But some misunderstandings still prevail over the policy of Malaysianization.* Times (London) 11/27/70, pIV —**Moroccanization:** *King Hassan . . . continued his direct control of political life and sought to extend the 'Moroccanization' of agriculture, industry and commerce.* Annual Register of World Events in 1973, p234 —**Zairianization:** *Marred by corruption, mismanagement, and political favoritism, the "Zairianization" of small- and medium-sized foreign firms had seriously disrupted some sectors of the economy.* Americana Annual 1977, p557 [**1958**] ►The new meaning of this suffix developed from the practice of replacing foreign managers with native citizens, especially non-Europeans, as part of the process of decolonization and the emergence of independent African and Asian nations during the 1960's and 1970's.

-ize, suffix now often used to form transitive verbs in the sense of "to transfer (establishments, institutions, or authority) to members of a specified ethnic or national group." Such verbs often derive by back formation from nouns in -IZATION. —**Algerianize:** *"By 1980, the El Hadjar metal works will be 100 per cent Algerianized." There are 5,000 workers at El Hadjar now; within eight years there will be 15,000.* NY Times Magazine 4/23/72, p22 —**Ivorianize:** *The decision-making posts in the Civil Service are now totally Ivorianized and private firms have had to report and say what their plans are in this direction between now and 1980.* Times (London) 3/25/77, pII —**Jordanize:** *Moves were also made to "Jordanize" the armed forces after the hijacking of a Jordanian airliner on November 6, 1974, by members of a group calling itself the "free officers."* 1976 Collier's Encyclopedia Year Book, p311 [**1958**]

J

j, *n. U.S. Slang.* a marijuana cigarette. Also spelled JAY. *If they have never heard the terms in Vietnam, the POW's will quickly learn about "bummers" ("unpleasant experiences, especially with drugs"), "joints" ("marijuana cigarettes, jays, j's, reefers") and "munchies" ("to be hungry, usually after ingesting marijuana").* Newsweek 2/12/73, p68 [**1973,** from abbreviation of joint (OEDS 1952), slang for marijuana cigarette]

J, *n.* variant of J PARTICLE. *The discovery two years ago of the heavy particles called psi or J continued to reverberate through all of particle physics, extending this year to the discovery and later to the photographing of particles that openly show the property called charm.* Science News 12/18-25/76, p387 [**1974**]

jackboot, *n.* **1** rough, bullying measures to achieve compliance or submission; jackboot tactics. *Communist Eastern Europe (there's a handy cliché) has suffered particularly from this kind of reporting. At the crudest level, the area is regarded as a grey, monolithic bloc of Slavic peoples suffering under the Soviet jackboot . . .* Maclean's 8/11/80, p4 **2** a person who uses rough, bullying measures. *Makarios, now President of Cyprus, considers Grivas a trigger-happy jackboot bent on grabbing full power on the island.* Time 4/1/66, p24 —*v.t.* to make by using rough, bullying measures to achieve compliance or submission. *German (Communist) troops were jackbooting their way around the northwestern section of Czechoslovakia for the first time in 23 years . . .* NY Times 9/1/68, pD3 [**1955** for noun, def. 1, earlier isolated instances 1768 and attributive use, (OED2, 1910); **1966** for def. 2; **1968** for verb; figurative senses of the term meaning a type of heavy military boot]

jackboot tactics, rough, bullying measures to achieve compliance or submission. *"With this first attempt by the Government to bludgeon this Bill through with jackboot tactics in the face of a one-day strike called solely over the issue we are discussing, it would be quite improper for this committee to continue its sitting,"* he [Edward Taylor, leader of the Opposition] said. Times (London) 3/18/70, p26 [**1970;** compare attributive use jack-minority (OED2, 1910)]

jack-up, *n.* **1** *U.S.* an increase. *Summing it all up, Eliot Janeway, the economist, gave this assessment in his weekly newsletter: "We see very little practical hope of avoiding another jack-up in short-term rates at the very time when foreign pressure on the dollar comes back on hard."* NY Times 5/17/68, p73 **2** a type of rig for off-shore oil drilling, on which legs are lowered to the sea bed from the operating platform. *There are three main methods for drilling and maintaining wells: from a platform (fixed, jack-up, or floating) or a ship; from remote-controlled equipment on the sea floor; or from manned equipment on the sea floor . . .* New Scientist 12/3/70, p366 [**1965,** from the verb phrase jack up to increase, raise]

Jacob-Monod (ˈdʒeikəbməˈnɑd; *French* ʒaˈkɔːbmɔːˈnou), *adj.* of or relating to the theory that genes are controlled by the mechanism called the operon, first advanced by the French scientists François Jacob and Jacques Monod. *The achievement [isolation of the lac operon] clears the path for a detailed study of the workings of the Jacob-Monod mechanism in the test tube under controlled conditions.* Encyclopedia Science Supplement (Grolier) 1970, p109 *While the phage DNA is integrated it betrays its presence only by a small number of proteins which function as typical Jacob-Monod repressors keeping its infective genes shut off and dormant.* New Scientist 1/22/70, p145 [**1969**]

Jacuzzi (dʒəˈkuːziː), *n.* **1** a trademark for a device which swirls water in a bath. *West Coast home furnishing shows this fall feature . . . Waterford wood stoves from Ireland, as often and as prominently as Jacuzzis and hot tubs last year.* Maclean's 11/27/78, p14 **2** a bath equipped with such a device. *I don't blame them for saying they'll move the team to Jidda if the city here won't build them a new upper deck and an executive Jacuzzi.* New Yorker 12/11/78, p37 [**1966**]

Jag, *n. Slang.* a Jaguar sports car, especially the classic two-seater coupe. *The police streak past: important ones in Mercedes, middle ones in Jags, plain coppers in Volkswagen beetles with blue lights on top.* Sunday Times (London) 10/17/71, p62 [**1959**]

Jakob-Creutzfeldt disease (ˈyaːkɔpˈkrɔitsfelt; *Anglicized* ˈdʒeikəbˈkrɔitsfelt), variant of CREUTZFELDT-JAKOB DISEASE. *It was diagnosed as Jakob-Creutzfeldt disease, and there are few recorded cases of it. Something about a galloping degeneration of the nerve cells. The prognosis for him: up to six months. Cause? Nobody knows.* Reader's Digest 9/76, p31 [**1973**]

jamais vu (ˌʒɑːmeˈvuː; *French* ʒameˈvy), *Psychology.* the illusion that one has never experienced the situation one is in, although it is in fact a familiar situation. *The experience of having been somewhere before—déjà vu—is said to be a purely physical experience which affects the frontal lobe of the brain which provides the impression that one has dreamt the identical situation previously. The same explanation is applied to the opposite feeling—jamais vu—when one momentarily fails to recognize a familiar situation.* Auckland Star (New Zealand), (Weekender section), 3/31/73, p3 [**1968,** from French, literally, never seen, patterned on déjà vu (OEDS 1903)]

jams, *n.pl.* **1** a clipped and contracted form of *pajamas. He went among the people and took on the people's ways . . . he bought six-packs and electric back-yard rotisseries, he wore His-'n-Hers flowered at-home jams, he joined the Thursday Evening Swingin' Couples League at the Nutley Bowlmor Lanes.* New Yorker 3/14/70, p34 **2** swim trunks with a pajama-like drawstring around the waist, used by male surfers. Compare BAGGYS. *There will also be ascots (which can double as belts), walking shorts, swim trunks and surfers' "jams," kneelength trunks with drawstring waists.* NY Times 1/22/68, p36 [**1966**]

Jane Crow, *U.S. Slang.* discrimination against women. *Men hate an "uppity" woman; they also hate an "aggressive" woman. Ours has been a Jane Crow society for several thousands of years.* Time 1/18/71, p2 [**1971,** patterned after *Jim Crow* (discrimination against blacks), with *Jane* as in *Jane Doe* (fictitious name for any female)]

J.A.P. or **JAP** (dʒæp), *n. U.S. Slang.* acronym for *Jewish American Princess* (used disparagingly to refer to a rich or spoiled Jewish girl or woman). Compare JEWISH PRINCESS. *Q. What do J.A.P.s most often make for dinner? A. Reservations.* Leo Rosten, Hooray for Yiddish, 1982, p168 [**1980**]

Japlish, *n.* a blend of Japanese and English spoken in Japan. *A great many Japanese speak English nowadays (or at least "Japlish," as the American colony calls it), and their words are usually understandable.* Harper's 1/63, p54 *Perhaps one of the most indicative—and amusing—effects of American influence has been the infiltration of American English into other languages. Japanese sometimes sounds like Japlish: masukomi for mass communications, terebi for TV, demo for demonstration and the inevitable baseballism pray bollu, storiku and hitto.* Time 7/22/66, p30 —*adj.* of or in Japlish. *A word of warning to tourists and others: the Japlish veneer can be deceptive. The Japanese may use more English words, but they still think like*

Japanese. Times (London) 11/26/70, p12 [**1960**, blend of *Japanese* and *English*]

japonaiserie (ʒapɔːnɛ'zriː), *n.* a style or work of art characteristically or distinctively Japanese. *Mr. Helpmann's most recent ballet, "Yugen," is a piece of japonaiserie based on a Noh play* . . . NY Times 5/29/67, p28 [**1965**, from French, from *Japonais* Japanese + *-erie* -ery] ▶Introduced by French writers in the late 1800's, *japonaiserie* was used in English at the turn of the century, but only in the plural form *japonaiseries* and with the specific sense of "Japanese ornaments." The preferred English form for the latter sense has been *Japanesery* (since the 1880's), formed from *Japanese* + *-ery* but probably on the model of the French word.

jargonaut ('dʒɑrgə,nɔːt), *n. Humorous.* a person who uses jargon excessively. *So* Clinical *is inexorably coming to mean something like its opposite; and the doctors will have to invent a new word for their purpose. There is poetic justice of a sort if this happens. Members of the medical profession have often been unscrupulous and piratical Jargonauts with other men's jargon themselves.* Times (London) 4/1/76, p16 [**1963**, blend of *jargon* and *argonaut*, probably influenced by *argot*]

jawbone, *U.S. Slang.* —*v.t.* to use jawboning on; influence by jawboning. . . . *every price increase that happens to catch the public's eye must be "jawboned" to death by the Government.* NY Times 1/2/66, pD2 *Since June, Feather has been jawboning his union chiefs on the virtues of labor discipline on the shop floor.* Time 9/19/69, p32 —**adj.** using or characterized by jawboning. *So many workers in so many industries have already got such big increases that those still on the waiting list won't pay any heed to jawbone appeals.* NY Times 6/16/70, p46 [**1965**, back formation from JAWBONING]

jawboning, *n. U.S. Slang.* **1** strong urging or warning by an influential person to leaders in industry, labor, etc., to comply with certain regulations and restraints. *Lloyd Bentsen, in his victorious Texas senatorial campaign, frequently advocated "jaw-boning" or Presidential persuasion, and voluntary wage-price guidelines, as anti-inflation weapons.* NY Times 12/20/70, pD11 *Lecturing business and labor on their responsibilities to hold down prices and wages—jawboning as it was called in the Johnson Administration—has been foregone.* Harper's 3/70, p48 **2** another word for JAW-JAW. *"Please, can I have the thirty cents this week without the jawboning?"* Cartoon legend, New Yorker 3/13/71, p34 [**1965**, from *jawbone, n.,* the bone of the jaws + *-ing*]

jaw-jaw, *Slang.* —*v.i.* to talk at great length; to engage in a long discussion. *So the novelty of the reaction to the latest call for a European Summit is not in any changed assessment of the super-Powers' intentions, but in the feeling that it is time at last to start jaw-jawing.* Manchester Guardian Weekly 12/13/69, p12 —*n.* drawn-out or lengthy talk; long discussion. *Despite considerable jaw-jaw, the Soviet combat brigade in Cuba is not going anywhere for the moment. For that and other reasons, neither is the Strategic Arms Limitation Treaty.* NY Times 10/7/79, pD1 [**1954**, reduplication (in isolated instance 1831) of the slang verb *jaw* to talk (OED 1748)]

Jaws of Life, a hydraulic device shaped like a pair of scissors in which the jaws are used to force apart or lift things, especially in rescue work. *Dale Greene doesn't remember the crash, the way his car wrapped around the tree trunk* . . . *All he knows is that he is alive, and he gives credit to a machine called "the Jaws of Life," which freed him from the wreckage in around five minutes.* NY Times 9/6/76, p17 [**1976**, probably patterned after KISS OF LIFE]

jay, *n. U.S. Slang.* a marijuana cigarette. Also spelled J. *Several enterprising youths mingled with the crowds selling buttons saying "Have a Nice Jay" for $1 (jay is another word for marijuana cigarette) and bags of what they said were "legal smoking herbs" for $4.* NY Times 5/16/76, p28 [**1973**, from pronunciation of *j*, abbreviation of *joint*]

jazz loft, *U.S.* an upper floor in a building used as a club or concert hall where jazz, especially experimental jazz, is played. Compare LOFT JAZZ. *Various and assorted jazz players—some of them are competent unknowns, some are established veter-*

ans, and others are downright famous—turn up to jam in thi (for the most part) mainstream jazz loft. New Yorker 2/12/79 p8 [**1976**]

jazzothèque ('dʒæzə,tek), *n.* a night club where both jazz musi and recorded music for dancing are played. *The success of th dancing policies at the Rainbow Grill and the Riverboat ha led the Half Note, which has been a nondancing jazz club fo 10 years, to clear some space for dancers. The club is now call ing itself a "jazzothèque".* NY Times 1/6/68, p24 [**1968**, from *jazz* + disco*thèque*]

jazz-rock, *n.* a blend of jazz and rock 'n' roll rhythms. *Synthesi was the password for popular music in 1969. In an appropriat conclusion to the most eclectic decade in American popula music, the year was flooded with such new combinations a jazz-rock, folk-rock, and country-rock.* Americana Annua 1970, p578 *Neither jazz-rock nor soul-jazz is the pure, uncu stuff of mainline jazz; both belong to what an earlier, mor idealistic age would have called "commercial" music.* Atlanti 2/71, p105 [**1968**]

jazz tap, tap-dancing to jazz music or rhythms. *Lynn Dally, ar tistic director, and Keith Terry, company percussionist, sper two weeks as part of the faculty at the Colorado Dance Festiva in Boulder earlier this month. Their teaching, Miss Dally indi cates, "focuses on the rhythm patterns" of jazz tap, which sh values as "both musical and physical expression."* NY Time 6/26/83, pB11 [**1979**]

J curve, *Economics.* a curve showing that after devaluation o a country's currency, its trade deficit normally worsens before it improves, reflecting the higher import prices resulting from the devaluation. *In the case of the United States, the "J" curv appeared to be immobilized at the bottom of the "J," and ex perts searched for the reasons.* 1988 Collier's Encyclopedi Year Book, p261 [**1973**]

jeaned (dʒiːnd), *adj.* wearing jeans. Compare DENIMED. *They'r 22,* . . . *jeaned and meticulously casual; perfectly young* Maclean's 9/73, p36 *There was a festive atmosphere in th square as jeaned supporters settled down with their blankets t pass the night there and to see how their party would do.* Time (London) 6/22/76, p7 [**1968**]

jeanswear, *n.* jeans of various styles for chiefly casual wear *Jeans departments are readying themselves for a flood of relat ed jeanswear which designers are beginning to produce.* NY Times Magazine 4/29/79, p116 [**1979**]

jellies, *n.pl.* another word for JELLY SHOES. . . . *the exhibit in cludes everything from "jellies" (transparent, rubbery shoes) t petroleum products, linens to electronics, antiquities to cannec samples of roasted moose snout.* Newsweek 9/22/80 p65 [**1980**]

jelly bomb, an incendiary bomb made with jellied gasoline; a fire bomb. *"Stones is nothing. You've got to wait till the jell bombs come over. Half the time you've got time to throw then back."* Sunday Times Magazine (London) 4/11/71, p17 [**1952**

jelly shoes or **jelly sandals**, shoes or sandals made of rubber o flexible plastic in bright colors. *They're called "jelly shoes," anc if they'd been around when Charlie Chaplin made a meal o his boot in "The Gold Rush," the little tramp would probabl have selected them for dessert.* NY Times 6/1/80, p2 *There ar also jeans, dresses, shirts, jelly sandals and red-and-white striped swim suits.* NY Times Magazine 3/15/81, p64 [**1980**]

je-m'en-foutisme (ʒəmɑ̃fuˈtiːzmə), *n. French.* lack of concern o interest; literally, "I-don't-care-ism." . . . *here is the terrible harvest of those years of mutual mistrust, disunity and despai at the losses of 1914-18,* je-m'en-foutisme *and defeatism i France.* Punch 4/9/69, p545 *Jenny McDade, who wrote it caught very accurately the mixture of indifference and para lysing rigidity in adults and its opposition to the high aim. and plain contrary* je-m'en-foutisme *of Kathy her heroine, th school-leaver in question.* Listener 5/18/67, p666 [**1954**]

Jensenism, *n.* the theory that intelligence, as measured by IQ tests, is largely determined by heredity. *I think part of the rea son I paid as much attention to it [the heredibility of intelli* ence] *as I did when I wrote the* Harvard Review *article was hat I felt that it had been totally neglected in American psy-hology, and especially in American educational psychology. Part of 'Jensenism' could probably be seen as a reaction against xtreme and, to me, unreasonable environmentalism.* Arthur ensen, Listener 1/4/73, p14 [**1970**, from Arthur R. *Jensen,* an American educational psychologist, born 1923, who suggested he theory + *-ism*] **—Jensenist,** *n., adj.: Critics of the Jensenist ine say that his conclusions are illogical and based on inade-uate evidence.* Science Journal 9/70, p9 **—Jensenite,** *n., adj.: More chilling is the call by some jensenites for the exercise of 'eugenic foresight" or that of the physicist William Shockley or voluntary sterilization programs for people with lower han normal IQs.* Harper's 10/73, p25 *He firmly believes in he Jensenite figure of 80 per cent as the proportion of an indi-idual's IQ that is inherited in advanced countries, and indeed hinks that the figure for real intelligence (whatever that is) is till greater.* New Scientist and Science Journal 9/30/71, p722

esus freak, *U.S. Slang.* a person who is enthusiastic about or nfatuated with the person and message of Jesus Christ; espe-ially, one of the Jesus People. *Todd Henning, 20 . . . turned rom "freaked-out motorcycle addict" to "Jesus freak" when he isited the Love Inn . . .* NY Times 6/15/71, p45 [**1970**, from esus + FREAK (def. 2)]

esus Movement or **Jesus revolution,** a Protestant Christian novement in the United States, consisting chiefly of young eople who worship and spread the teachings of Jesus Christ ndependently of any of the established churches of denomina-ions. Compare CHILDREN OF GOD. *The sect* [Children of God] ad its origins among a small group of conservatives within he Jesus Movement, a nationwide Fundamentalist movement mong youth, and served only as a reactionary facet of that roup until early 1970, when it mushroomed into a full-ledged sect.* NY Times 11/29/71, p41 *The Jesus revolution, ike the others, has a flavor peculiarly American. Its strong Pentecostalism emphasizes such esoteric spiritual gifts as peaking in tongues and healing by faith.* Time 6/21/71, p39 [**1971**]

esus People, the people who make up the Jesus Movement; he body of chiefly young people who emphasize an intense personal relationship with Jesus Christ. *The Jesus People, also nown as Street Christians or Jesus Freaks, are the most visible; t is they who have blended the counterculture and conserva-ive religion . . . Some, but by no means all, affect the hippie tyle; others have forsworn it as part of their new lives.* Time /21/71, p39 *Mr. Ross and fellow occupants of Love Inn are Jesus People," part of a nationwide movement of youths who re "turning on to Jesus" and dressing up the old-time religion n hippie garb.* NY Times 6/15/71, p45 [**1971**]

esus shop, *U.S.* a store specializing in popular religious articles used by members of the Jesus Movement, such as posters, but-ons, and shirts inscribed with Biblical verses and religious mes-ages. *It* [Telegraph Avenue] *now looks little different from nany another street in the San Francisco Bay area (except for ts Jesus shops, symbols of the brand of freaked-out Christiani-y that has replaced Flower Power as a culture) . . .* New Scien-ist and Science Journal 6/3/71, p588 [**1971**]

etabout, *n.* a person who travels by jet aircraft. *Kuala Lumpur, s well as other cities, is taking on the look of Bangkok or Sin-apore: luxury hotels; . . . loads of "jetabouts," mostly Aus-ralians crammed into Boeings for two days here, two there, vith a glimpse of the country between hotel rooms.* Manchester Guardian Weekly (Le Monde section) 7/13/74, p13 [**1974**, pat-erned after *gadabout, layabout,* etc.]

et belt or **jet flying belt,** a special belt equipped with flying gear nd attached to a small jet-powered engine, designed to enable person to take off in flight to a height of about 25 feet and fly hort distances. *Under development since 1965, the . . . Jet Belt ogged its first manned free flight on April 7, 1969, when Rob-rt F. Courter, Jr., lifted off a runway apron at Niagara Falls nternational Airport and piloted the system over a 300-foot el-iptical course.* Encyclopedia Science Supplement (Grolier) 970, p373 *A Buck Rogers-style Army "jet-flying belt" that is*

expected to transport a soldier over the treetops at 60 m.p.h. for as far as ten miles. Time 7/15/66, p21 [**1966**]

jetboat, *n.* a boat propelled by a jet engine. *Thus Sir* [Edmund Hillary] *was feted as a pilgrim on his voyage from the mouth of the Ganges for more than 1,500 miles upstream to the point where the expedition's jet boats could no longer struggle with the Himalayan torrent . . .* Manchester Guardian Weekly 3/11/79, p22 [**1963**]

jetborne, *adj.* carried or transported by jet aircraft. *It* [The Hil-ton's "Day-Hour Plan" ($12 for the first three hours, $3 an hour thereafter)] *is intended to make life easier and less expensive for today's jet-borne businessman, who often zips in and out of two or three cities in a single day.* Time 8/9/68, p55 [**1966**]

jeté (ʒəˈtei), *v.i. Ballet.* to leap from one foot to the other. *Since the show's emphasis is on the ability of dancers to act, as well as to glissade, jeté and pirouette, the show has also become an actor's workshop.* NY Times Magazine 5/2/76, p19 *And you'll gasp as a tightrope walker jetés across the wire while playing a haunting theme on the oboe.* People Weekly 5/2/88, p106 [**1968**, verb use of the noun, ultimately from French]

jet fatigue, another name for JET SYNDROME. *The popular name for this disruption of rhythmic biological function on flights spanning many time zones is jet fatigue, a temporary affliction known not only to tourists but also to wide-ranging businessmen and government officials.* NY Times 9/15/68, pD11 [**1968**]

jetfoil, *n. Especially British.* a jet-powered hydrofoil. *In Sep-tember P&O is making a brave financial commitment to the Thames and, three times a day, its jetfoil will 'fly' down the river from the heart of London to Belgium and back for less than it costs to go by plane.* Listener 5/10/79, p638 [**1974**, from *jet* + hydro*foil*]

jet-hop, *v.i.* to travel from place to place by jet aircraft. . . . *he announced a series of surprise summit meetings that will have him jet-hopping from island to island and coast to coast over the next two months.* Time 12/6/71, p22 [**1952**]

jet-lag, *n.* Also **jet lag.** an upset of the body clock resulting from travel by jet through several time zones in twelve hours or less. . . . *jet-lag remains a medically unsolved problem with doctors urging that the best thing that any business man can do with his few hours saved by flying supersonically is to have a few more Martinis in his New York hotel when he arrives.* New Sci-entist and Science Journal 4/15/71, p133 *"I don't generally do this sort of thing, actually I have as low an opinion of inter-views as you do—" "How do you know I have a low opinion?" Jet-lag was getting to Bech; irritability was droning in his ears.* John Updike, Bech: A Book, 1970, p139 [**1966**] **—jet-lagged,** *adj.: Five jet-lagged unicorns, having recovered from their 40-hour flight from San Diego Zoo, are now settling down happily in the deserts of Oman.* Sunday Times (London) 3/16/80, p51 **—jet-lagging,** *adj.: Right from the jet-lagging start, I was knocked out by the place. The morning light when we got off the plane at Sydney had a delicate silvery quality.* Life 4/82, p8

jet set, the wealthy social set that gathers in fashionable places in many parts of the world, often traveling by jet plane. *While it's true that the jet set may have felt vulnerable for the first time, the rest of the country, and certainly the urban dweller, has been in the grip of that fear for at least ten years.* Harper's 1/71, p6 **—adj.** Usually spelled **jet-set.** of or relating to the jet set. . . . *his campaign managers created a new image of him* [Pierre Trudeau] *as the youthful, debonaire, "with-it" man of the jet-set age.* Americana Annual 1970, p694 *That* [lead poi-soning] *is not a jet-set or beautiful-people concern—but a sim-ple matter of life and death for the children of poverty.* Harper's 1/71, p6 [**1960**] ►This term became popular in the early 1960's and quickly replaced such older terms of similar meaning as *café society* and *smart set.* Though it may have been a felicitous coinage by a society news reporter, there is ev-idence indicating that the term was used during the 1950's in a special sense that may have foreshadowed the current mean-ing. The sense in which *jet set* was used between 1956 and 1958 was that of a group of youngsters in the Soviet Union, especially in Moscow, who had adopted a "fast" Western style of life. The following two 1956 quotations use the term in this sense; the second quotation suggests the possible origin of the term. *Orders for the crackdown of the Soviet "jet set" of juvenile delinquents came straight from Communist boss Khrushchev . . .* Newsweek 9/3/56, p12 *This is the Soviet "Jet Set," an element of the younger generation that is causing great concern to the country's leaders and to the Communist party. The term was originated by a young member of a foreign embassy staff in Moscow and refers to the Soviet youth who are attracted by things foreign—specifically Western things and especially clothing, hair styles, jazz, movies, automobiles—and who go in for restaurants, hard drinking, wild parties and the gay life generally.* NY Times 11/4/56, p14

jet-setter, n. a member of the jet set. *We can condone photographic safaris as a means through which the jet-setters can escape their intolerable boredom.* NY Times 5/5/68, pD15 [**1963**]

jet syndrome, the symptoms of JET-LAG. Also called JET FATIGUE. *Symptoms of biorhythm upset, known popularly as the jet syndrome, are experienced by jet airplane travelers who fly through several time zones in 12 hours or less. The local time between their place of departure and their destination may differ by 5, 6, or even as much as 10 hours.* World Book Science Annual 1968, p115 [**1968**]

Jetway, n. a trademark for the movable covered corridor that telescopes out from an airport terminal to an airplane to load or unload passengers. Commonly spelled *jetway. Mobile lounges need a larger labour force to run them than jetways and therefore open the airport to greater risk of shutdown through labour disputes.* Times (London) 9/23/72, pIX [**1960**]

Jew for Jesus, a member of a missionary group evangelizing among Jews and maintaining they are Jews who accept Jesus as the Messiah. *Some of the recent returnees, however, are hardly what Israeli legislators had in mind: zealous young Jews for Jesus whose purpose in coming to the Promised Land is to engage in aggressive Christian evangelism.* Time 3/26/73, p111 [**1972**]

Jewish Christian, 1 a person claiming to be both a Jew and a Christian, especially a JEW FOR JESUS. *Though Jewish Christians come from all ages and backgrounds, they are predominantly young spiritual refugees from secularized Jewish homes, liberal synagogues, the drug culture or radical politics.* Time 6/12/72, p67 **2** of or pertaining to Jewish Christians; claiming to be both Jewish and Christian. *The aggressiveness of some groups toward the conversion of Jews and the appearance of "Jewish Christian" sects aroused some apprehension among Jewish leaders.* Britannica Book of the Year 1973, p584 [**1972**]

Jewish Princess, U.S. and Canadian Slang. a rich or spoiled Jewish girl or woman. Compare J.A.P. *She is a kind of reverse Jewish princess: she goes through life gratefully accepting the pleasures and amenities that come her way, and if they are not the particular pleasures and amenities she ordered—well, so much the better.* New Yorker 10/20/86, p79 *To add the necessary dramatic tension, he's lower class and a bit of a slob while she's rich and Jewish-princess chic.* Maclean's 3/16/81, p63 [**1980**]

jhala ('dʒɑːlə), n. a heavily cadenced passage ending the second movement of a typical raga, the traditional Hindu musical form. [Ravi] *Shankar delighted his audience with an exquisite alap, jor and jhala in raga Darbari Kanad: music great enough to send even the initiates into ecstasies.* Times (London) 11/19/68, p14 [**1966**, from Sanskrit]

jiggle, n. U.S. and Canadian Slang. the display, especially on television, of women engaged in actions that show sexually suggestive bodily movements. *As the women, dressed in sports hotpants, crashed into each other in the playing arena, the opportunities for jiggle were obviously endless.* 1979 Collier's Encyclopedia Year Book, p542 *Pierre Berton's real value is . . . in refusing to move to Los Angeles, like his old CBC inferiors, so as to write scripts at $200,000 for sitcoms that glorify jiggle.* Maclean's 2/11/80, p56 [**1978**]

jiggly, adj. U.S. Slang. sexually suggestive; titillating. *NBC has catapulted itself out of last place in the Nielsen ratings with "jiggly" shows and promotional ads.* New York Post 10/24/79, p15 [**1978**]

jingo, v.i. to sound of jingoism; express loud or aggressive patriotism. *The flags waved and the speeches jingoed when the United States embarked on its first armed adventure in Asia.* NY Times 5/25/70, p32 *. . . he never descends into the loathsome smocks-and-ale jingoing that infected the essays of his contemporaries, such as Hilaire Belloc.* Sunday Times (London) 3/9/69, p58 [**1969**, verb use of *jingo, n.*, a chauvinist]

JINS (dʒinz), n. U.S. acronym for *Juvenile(s) In Need of Supervision.* Compare MINS. *These children, who are variously labelled Persons in Need of Supervision (PINS), Children in Need of Supervision (CINS), Juveniles in Need of Supervision (JINS) or Wayward Minors, depending on the state they live in, will be guilty of nothing more serious than being a burden or a nuisance.* New Yorker 8/14/78, p55 [**1972**]

job action, U.S. a protest by workers without undertaking a general strike, such as a slow-down or work-to-rules action. *The Uniformed Fire Officers Association yesterday voted a "job action"—the refusal to perform nonfirefighting duties—to back up demands for more manpower.* NY Times 7/26/68, p16 *During the afternoon, the city had applied for and been granted an injunction against the firemen's job action.* New Yorker 1/16/71, p83 [**1968**]

job bank, a computerized job-placement service run by a government department. *The computer is an ideal tool for compiling and cleaning lists, so both DoE [Department of Employment] and DL [Department of Labour] developed computer job banks which produce periodic print-out lists of available jobs.* New Scientist 8/31/72, p437 [**1971**]

job centre, British. a variant of JOB BANK. *The cost of each job centre placing, based on the job centre's running costs, including premises, salaries and other expenses, is £22. How many private employment agencies do the job so cheaply? Job centres place 30 per cent to 40 per cent more people in jobs than the older-type offices they replace.* Times (London) 11/25/76, p17 [**1971**]

job-hop, v.i. to go from job to job; change jobs frequently. *After leaving Washington in the mid-1950s, he [Najeeb Halaby, President of Pan-Am] job-hopped, serving briefly as operating vice president of Servo-mechanisms Inc. and later organizing his own law firm in Los Angeles.* Time 1/19/70, p43 [**1970**, patterned after *table-hop, island-hop*, etc.]

job-hopper, n. a person who job-hops. *Boyden's prospects are rarely aware that Boyden is aware of them as potential job hoppers.* Time 10/13/67, p63 *Employers don't like early job hoppers.* Sunday Times (London) 7/25/71, p45 [**1955**]

jock, n. U.S. Slang. an athlete, especially at a college (often used attributively). *Not every college jock gets a campus building named after him. But not every college jock becomes President of the United States. Gerald R. Ford, a football All-American at the University of Michigan in the 1930's did, and last night he was at his alma mater for the dedication of his Presidential Library.* NY Times 5/3/81, pD13 *The only funny performance is by Michael Meyer as Brenda's jock brother, a big gregarious, simple-minded, good-hearted lug who has exactly the right moves of the athlete—shoulder-rolling, ass-slapping, gum-chewing—all down pat.* Atlantic 7/69, p108 [**1963**, extended sense of *jock* an athletic supporter or jockstrap (OED 1952)]

jockette, n. U.S. a female jockey. *They had to fight their way into the racetrack a few years ago, but now lady jockeys are becoming a common sight. What hasn't been resolved is what to call them. Sometimes people around the track call women jockeys "guys"—or girl jockeys, women jockeys, lady jockeys, even jockettes.* Family Circle 3/73 (page not known) [**1969**, from *jockey* + *-ette* (feminine suffix)]

Joe Sixpack, U.S. Slang. an average blue-collar male. *To bring all these new people into its ranks, however, the G.O.P. is going to have to modify its country club image: Joe Sixpack does not* *belong to a country club.* Time 7/21/80, p10 [**1973**; so called from the popularity of sixpacks of beer among working males]

jog, *v.i.* to run at a measured or regular trot or pace as a form of physical exercise. *While jogging one after another, they suddenly stopped, did a series of strenuous push-ups—or energetic deep knee bends or vigorous hops into the air—and then resumed jogging.* Time 2/28/72, p60 [**1967**; known orally in the late 1940's] **—jogger,** *n.: To the astonishment of foreigners, forest paths and parks seem to be crowded with joggers.* Times (London) 10/23/74, pvi **—jogging,** *n.: Jogging does call for a tremendous effort—merely to get going—and for the kind of mental resolve a man must have to get out of bed and do push-ups.* Saturday Review 4/22/72, p6

jogger's nipple or **joggers' nipple,** an irritation of the nipples caused by the rubbing of a jogger's shirt against the skin. *The current crop of sports injuries goes beyond the routine pulled muscle and the torn ligament to a wide range of problems, from heart attacks to jogger's nipple (an irritation to the point of bleeding suffered by runners of both sexes who neglect to protect the upper body with an undershirt or proper running bra).* NY Times Magazine 10/5/80, p42 [**1978**]

jogging pants, ankle-length pants similar to sweat pants, worn especially in cold weather for jogging. *Hunting, fishing, and hiking clothes were extremely popular. Among these items were . . . jogging pants tied at the ankle, and billowing sweat shirts.* 1977 Collier's Encyclopedia Year Book, p260 [**1974**]

jogging shoe, a soft sneaker or sneakerlike shoe with a cushioned sole, designed for jogging. *The piece begins as Gordon and Setterfield circle the space slowly in a jog-walk. They wear satin gym pants, white shirts, jogging shoes. An atmosphere of trial, of self-tempering, begins to gather.* New Yorker 5/15/78, p126 [**1976**]

John, *n. U.S. Slang.* See the quotations for the meaning. *Despite the fact that a recent New York law makes the "John," or customer, guilty as well as the prostitute, the New York District Attorney's office sees fit not to prosecute the male customer but only the woman he exploits.* Atlantic 3/70, p104 . . . *a prostitute is arrested after having committed a sex act with her customer, known in the trade as a "John," after "John Doe."* NY Times 8/15/67, p27 [**1953**]

John Bircher, another name for BIRCHER. . . . *the bitterness with which they [Negroes] are pursued produces its own reaction. The ultra-conservative Governor, Mr Ronald Reagan, is part of this. So are the John Birchers, who are at their strongest in the red-neck South of this enormous State [California].* Manchester Guardian Weekly 10/3/68, p10 [**1961**]

joint, *n. Racing Slang.* a small battery-operated device for applying an electric shock, used illegally to stimulate a racing horse. *For years, dishonest jockeys have experimented with tiny hand-carried shock-makers that can be applied to the horse's neck in the homestretch. But the "joint" is usually an unreliable accomplice, because many horses become angry and contrary when the men on their backs give them electric shocks.* Newsweek 7/9/73, p59 [**1972**]

joint custody, a legal agreement between divorced or separated parents to share the custody of their children. *Six-year-old Tommy Mastin, the central figure in a controversial child-rearing arrangement known as joint custody, leads something of a double life in Gainesville, Fla. On Mondays, Wednesdays and Sundays, Tommy lives with his father at Oak Forest, a luxury apartment complex on the city's south side.* NY Times 5/24/76, p24 [**1976**]

joint float, a controlled float of the currencies of several countries, established to prevent large fluctuation in any one of the currencies, especially the controlled float established in 1972 by France, West Germany, Belgium, the Netherlands, Luxembourg, Norway, Sweden, and Denmark. Compare SNAKE. *Mounting speculation about impending adjustments to currency parities within the European joint float . . . caused much uncertainty and much confusion in European financial centres.* Times (London) 1/31/76, p15 [**1973**]

Jonah word, any word which a chronic stutterer has difficulty uttering in ordinary conversation. *A person trained in the Van Riper method may attack a Jonah word like "mother" by prolonging the first syllable into a long mooing sound. The result may not be exactly like normal speech, but it is better than trying to talk through sealed lips. For some reason, prolonging the vowel sound often gets the stutterer through the block and into the next word.* New Yorker 11/15/76, p146 [**1976**, from *Jonah*, the name of the Biblical character, in allusion to one who brings bad luck, a jinx]

Jones or **jones,** *n. U.S. Slang.* **1** Often, **the Jones.** drug addiction. *A gang member named Sly, 22, a tall black who lost a college basketball scholarship because of his habit, put it this way: "I was arrested three times for robbery and larceny. Drugs were ruining my life. But then the Brothers got hold of me and wouldn't let me out of their sight. You get a guy on the Jones and that's what you have to do."* Time 4/3/72, p18 **2** a narcotic, especially heroin. *"Jones" is slang both for heroin and its craving (as in "his jones came on him so bad"). The top ghetto jones-man, as pragmatic as a dumdum bullet, hunts his upstart challengers with stunning, careless cruelty.* Newsweek 10/14/74, p120 [**1968**, apparently from the common proper name *Jones*, but the connection is obscure]

jor, *n.* the rhythmic second movement of a typical raga, the traditional Hindu musical form. Compare ALAP, GAT. *In the second movement,* jor, *a pulse or beat is introduced against which the musician constructs his phrases.* Listener 4/11/68, p480 *Jazz and rock 'n' roll periodicals have run involved disquisitions on the technicalities of the tabla, the tamboura, the alap and the jor.* NY Times 12/20/66, p58 [**1966**, from Sanskrit]

Josephson effect, the effect produced by a Josephson junction. *. . . the Josephson effect (a quantum phenomenon whereby, near absolute zero, current can flow without resistance across an insulating gap).* New Scientist 5/23/68, p407 *The Josephson effect, one of the most important in solid state physics, can be used for detecting microwave radiation and low voltages, among many other purposes.* Times (London) 4/15/70, p13 [**1963**, named for Brian D. *Josephson*, an English physicist who predicted this effect in 1962]

Josephson junction, the junction formed by two superconductors separated by a thin insulating layer, across which current will flow without resistance and generate radio waves when subjected to a certain voltage. *A Josephson junction is a unit in which two superconductors are joined by an electrically bad connection. That is, there may be some insulator between them, or a narrow air gap, or their surfaces may be rough so that there is only contact at certain points and not over the whole surface. If a driving voltage is applied to such a junction, an oscillating current will flow across it, and it will emit microwave radiation.* Science News 9/6/69, p172 [**1965**]

jostle, *v.i. U.S. Slang.* to pickpocket. *Robert Baldwin, charged with "jostling," . . . was convicted by a single judge and sentenced to one year in prison.* Time 7/6/70, p42 [**1965**]

jostler, *n. U.S. Slang.* a person who pickpockets. *A woman detective picked a prosecutor's pocket in Queens Criminal Court Monday to demonstrate how "jostlers"—the police terminology for pickpockets—work.* NY Times 6/2/65, p33 [**1965**]

joual (ʒuːˈal), *n.* a dialect or patois of Canadian French, used chiefly by uneducated French Canadians. *Nor is it a question of slang. French-Canadian slang [as spoken in Quebec] is called* joual—*a corruption of the word* cheval—*and is as different from the correct French Canadian as Cockney is from English.* Maclean's 3/5/66, p44 *He [Jean Drapeau, Q.C., Mayor of Montreal] speaks fluent English and a French that bears no trace of* joual—*an archaic and affectedly rustic way of speaking French that is common to many citizens of the province [Quebec], of all classes, and that purists are currently trying to discourage.* New Yorker 4/29/67, p33 **—adj.** of or like joual. *Because the language [used in a popular radio and TV show, "Seraphin"] is very* joual, *it's a very popular language, and the situations are so true to the myth . . .* Saturday Night

(Canada) 2/68, p30 [**1962**, from Canadian French *joual*, a rendition of the joual pronunciation of French *cheval* horse]

Joviologist (͵dӡouvi:'alədӡist), *n.* astronomer who specializes in the study of the planet Jupiter. *It's been scarcely four months since Pioneer 10 gave earthlings their first good look at Jupiter, and the Joviologists are still finding new causes for excitement every time they reexamine their data.* Science News 4/13/74, p236 [**1974**, from Latin *Jovis* genitive of *Jupiter* + English *-ologist* student of]

joy stick, a control lever, as for controlling a cursor on a computer display screen, that can be moved in any direction. *The same computer linkage makes it possible for space ships to seem, for the first time, to make curvilinear movements. It also offers the special-effects person a joy stick with which he or she can make the little model spacecraft pitch and roll in a newly convincing way.* Encyclopedia Science Supplement (Grolier) 1982, p329 [**1963**, extended sense of earlier (OEDS 1910) control lever of an airplane]

J particle, another name for PSI PARTICLE. *The most striking feature of the J particle is its very long lifetime. The J particle lives from a hundred to a thousand times longer than all known mesons of heavy mass. Whenever objects in nature are found much more stable than expected, there is reason to be curious. There must be some hidden cause, some yet unknown effects of new principles that change the anticipated course of events.* McGraw-Hill Yearbook of Science and Technology 1976, p226 [**1975**, named by Samuel C. C. Ting of the Massachusetts Institute of Technology, who led in its discovery at the Brookhaven National Laboratory in Long Island, New York, partly from the initial letter of *jump* and partly because the letter *J* resembles the Chinese character for *Ting*]

J-psi particle, another name for PSI PARTICLE. *What the two scientists had to tell each other was precisely the same thing: using different techniques, both had discovered a new subatomic particle—now known as the J/psi particle—a finding that turned the field of elementary particle physics on its collective ear.* Maclean's 1/10/77, p48 [**1977**]

juco ('dӡu:kou), *n. U.S. Informal.* a junior college. *Robinson joins Garrett and Smart as a "juco" product, an increasingly popular breed* [of basketball player] *at four-year universities.* Christian Science Monitor 12/2/87, p18 [**1987**, acronym for *junior college*]

judicare, *n. U.S.* a government-sponsored program providing free legal services to the poor. *For all the argument over the pros and cons of judicare, there is agreement that too many of the nation's poor still go without legal help.* Time 4/21/80, p98 [**1966**, from *judi*care + *care*, patterned after MEDICARE]

judoman, *n.* a person who participates in judo wrestling matches or competitions. *The* Black Belt Yearbook *listed 102,569 judo players in the United States and named Seino, Graham, and Coage among the top 10 judomen in the nation.* 1969 Collier's Encyclopedia Year Book, p527 [**1969**] ►This term seems to be interchangeable with the older term *judoka* (from Japanese *jūdōka*, recorded in English since 1952. *Judoka*, however, is used both in the sense of a judo wrestler and an expert in judo. Another term for the latter meaning is *judoist* (OEDS 1950).

jugate, *n. U.S.* a button showing two heads, especially one which pairs the pictures of a Presidential candidate and his running mate. *Pollack's own collectibles run heavily toward buttons. He owns more than 50,000. He keeps them in file drawers in his bedroom. If he could find the button of his dreams, it would be the Cox-Roosevelt 1920 campaign button. "I guess everybody owns things about owning a Cox-Roosevelt jugate," he said. "It goes for $2500 on up. I've seen one; I've touched it."* New York Post 9/13/75, p9 [**1974**, noun use of the adjective (OED 1887) meaning joined or overlapping, as two busts on a coin]

jugular, *n.* the most vulnerable point of an opponent (especially in the phrase **have an instinct for the jugular**). *His detractors often accuse Vice President Spiro Agnew of having an instinct for the jugular.* Time 6/1/70, p6 *The chief virtues in a political machine are plodding patience, an utter lack of imagina-*

tion, unsqueamishness in the face of greed and brutality, and a feel for the jugular. New Yorker 5/8/71, p138 **—adj.** aiming for the jugular; cutthroat; murderous. . . . *Mr. Scranton will not get far in the jugular combat of national politics without a more lionlike approach.* . . NY Times 7/28/65, p30 [**1960**, from the *jugular (vein)*, in which a puncture or break may prove fatal]

juice, *n. U.S. Slang.* **1** money made from illegal activities, such as kickbacks from sales, protection money, bribes, or usurious interest rates on loans. . . . *the service known as 'juice,' which is the California gambling profession's euphemism (in Florida the term is 'ice') for 'protection' money.* Estes Kefauver, Crime in America, 1951, p17 *At least two murders and perhaps more have been connected to the loan shark, or "juice" racket, as it is called here, as well as beatings and threats.* NY Times 6/9/68, pA29 [**1927**, **1960**] **2** favorable standing; position, power, or influence. *This Las Vegas is a jet-age Sodom, a venal demimonde in which the greatest compliment that can be paid a man is to say that he has "juice" (influence in the right places).* Time 7/11/69, p24 *"The important thing now is I got juice as an actor,"* [Steve] *McQueen went on. "That means you choose your material, you pick your situations."* NY Times 12/4/66, pB13 [**1935**, **1951**] **3** narcotic drugs. [Glady] *Smith hammered home the point that this was Jones' fault, not the system's, and launched into a discussion of do's and don'ts of going for an interview. Don't . . . resort to street slang. . . "I've got to pick up my juice".* . . New Yorker 11/23/81, p159 [**1957**, **1972**]

juicehead, *n. U.S. Slang.* a habitual drinker of alcoholic liquor; tippler. *If anybody wanted to get stoned the guy who owned the pad made them go up on the roof. Juice-heads drank Red Mountain.* . . New Yorker 9/9/67, p41 [**1955**, from *juice* liquor + HEAD]

juice man, *U.S. Slang.* a person who lends money at exorbitant interest rates; a loan shark. . . . *a professional criminal . . often must make a loan from a "juice man," a loan which may involve an interest rate of 20 per cent a week.* NY Times 8/20/67, pA35 [**1961**, from JUICE (def. 1) and *man*]

juicer, *n. U.S. Slang.* a heavy drinker of alcoholic liquor. . . . *"A lot of people are worn out from last night, especially the juicers. The difference between the juicers and the heads is that the juicers sometimes get a little obstreperous but the heads go sit quietly in a corner someplace."* New Yorker 5/13/67, p40 [**1967**]

juke, *U.S.* **—v.t.** to pretend to make a movement or play in American football to mislead (an opponent); fake. *"My game is to juke the tough guys,"* he [O.J. Simpson] *says. "I put the okey doke on them, just bounce around and look for daylight. No one is going to get me to put my head in Dick Butkus' lap."* Time 12/24/73, p57 **—n.** an act of juking in American football; a fake. *Pruitt puts on "a lot of jukes and lateral movement" so that he does not get hit head on.* Time 12/5/77, p76 [**1973**, originally (1958) verb intransitive, probably from earlier verb (OEDS 1937) *juke* to dance, ultimately of West African origin]

jumbo, *n.* short for JUMBO JET. *When the Concordes are delivered to BOAC in 1975 the airline will have a fleet of five super sonic and 60 subsonic jets, which will include at least a dozen Jumbos.* Daily Telegraph (London) 5/26/72, p1 *At the new Kansas City, Mo., jetport, one of the few in operation to have been specifically designed for the jumbos, passengers walk only 175 ft (or a minimum of 85 ft) from bus or car door to aircraft.* 1971 Britannica Yearbook of Science and the Future p278 [**1966**]

jumbo jet, a jet aircraft with a passenger capacity of about 500 people and a freight capacity of about 200 tons. Also shortened to JUMBO. Compare MEGAJET. See also SUPERJET. *Discussing high-capacity airliners ("jumbo jets") the director-general said a matter of prime concern was the problems on the ground these would bring with them.* Times (London) 5/24/66, p8 *The design of the terminal buildings, runways, and other facilities of civil aerodromes, to meet the problems created by the introduction of jumbojets, is one of the most complex puzzles of modern life.* New Scientist 7/11/68, p72 [**1964**]

jump cut, an abrupt transition from one filmed shot or scene to another due to the excision of intervening film. . . . *French director Jean-Luc Godard . . . cut directly from scene to scene without fades or dissolves, and even introduced jump cuts— unmatching actions—within a scene.* 1969 World Book Year Book, p115 **[1953]**

jump-cut, *v.i.* to make jump cuts. *He* [William Conrad, producer-director of the motion picture "Brainstorm"] *recklessly jump-cuts from scene to scene, using gimmicky transitions or linking one sequence to another with trick dialogue.* Time 6/18/65, p80 **[1965]**

jumping gene, *Informal.* another term for TRANSPOSON. *Dr. Hugh Bollinger of N.P.I. said amaranth seemed to share with corn the characteristic of "jumping genes" or the ability to transpose pieces of genetic material from one part of a chromosome to another. Jumping genes may help to speed the laboratory "evolution" of new improved plant types.* NY Times 10/16/84, pC1 **[1981]**

jump jet or **jump-jet**, *n. British.* a jet aircraft designed for short vertical take-off and landing. Compare V/STOL. *A Hawker Siddeley . . . "jump jet" aircraft, piloted by Flight-Lieutenant John Farley, coming in to land in a forest clearing during a demonstration yesterday at Royal Aircraft Establishment, Bedford.* Times (London) 9/27/66, p20 *Can't think why King Hussein wants to buy Harrier jump-jets. Isn't the Jordanian Air Force nervous enough as it is?* Punch 6/26/68, p907 **[1964]**

jump jockey, *British.* a rider in a steeplechase. *Graham Thorner, that most determined of jump jockeys, rode his heart out three times over fences in stamina sapping conditions at Worcester yesterday for a double on When Lad and Breakwater and a neck second on Toy Flag.* Times (London) 1/25/77, p12 **[1970]**

jump-start, *v.t. U.S.* to bring to life; revive. *The New York Times has recently described efforts to jump-start: the region's stalled economy, a draft-Trump movement, a discussion about curriculum, the once-stalled Gephardt campaign. The New Yorker's chairman told The Washington Post that new advertising sections were necessary to jump-start the magazine.* NY Times 3/3/88, pA3 **[1988,** figurative sense of the term meaning to give an automobile engine a *jump-start* (a start by means of jumper cables)]

jump suit or **jumpsuit**, *n.* a one-piece garment resembling a parachutist's uniform, used especially for casual wear. *She's lithe, but you wouldn't mistake her for a man, and the sky-blue driver's jump suit matches her eyes.* Maclean's 9/17/66, p19 *The fashions include jumpsuits for both men and women. . .* NY Times 7/11/68, p40 **[1964]**

jump-up, *n.* (in the British West Indies and Guyana) an informal dance. *". . . You go for a swim with the local leader. You have some rum and a bloody good lunch, then you have a jump-up, and the proper shindig."* Sunday Times (London) 6/13/71, p9 *Georgetown, Guyana, Dec. 10—The pale leaves in the American Ambassador's garden shone moistly last night in the colored lights set up for his pre-Christmas jump-up.* NY Times 12/12/66, p24 **[1955]**

junction grammar, a method for converting the grammatical rules of a language into an alphanumeric code to facilitate machine translation. It was developed by Eldon G. Lythe, an American linguist at Brigham Young University. *The science of machine translation is an extension of linguistics research; once the language analysis has been refined, the computing tasks become relatively trivial. The Utah system is based on a model of language structure developed in the 1960s and known as junction grammar (JG). The essence of JG is the "J-tree" representation, which breaks down a sentence into a kind of "family tree" in which the language equivalent of a "mother" (or father) in the tree is known as a "node".* New Scientist 3/13/80, p836 **[1976]**

junk bond, *U.S.* a high-risk, noncorporate bond that is bought at less than face value. *What they will also get is a piece of a fund that specializes in deep-discount bonds—sometimes known as "junk bonds"—that have enabled FIFI over the last several years to run up one of the most enviable performance records in the industry. Junk bonds, because they carry a much higher risk quotient than corporate bonds, typically offer a much higher return.* NY Times 1/29/77, p28 **[1976]**

junk food, food that is high in calories and low in nutrition, such as candy, soft drinks, and potato chips. *One thing most camps try to do is cut down on junk food children are accustomed to.* NY Times Magazine 3/20/77, p91 *"There is a huge junk food industry providing empty calories . . . the trouble is that these junk foods will not fill the nutritional gap, though big profits could be made."* Times (London) 2/25/77, p5 **[1973]**

junk gun, another name for SATURDAY NIGHT SPECIAL. *The 1968 Federal Gun Control Act banned the import of many of these so-called "junk guns." But under pressure from various gun lobbyists, the landing of gun parts was not stopped. This led naturally to the profitable gun-assembly business.* Time 11/26/73, p131 **[1973]**

junkie, *n. Informal.* one who is addicted to some (specified) thing; enthusiast; devotee. Compare GROUPIE (def. 3). *For all I know, people may exist who like to see their names in print. John Lennon and Yoko Ono were said to be print junkies.* Listener 11/15/73, p671 *The campaign of antisepsis began soon after he* [Solzhenitsyn] *was expelled from the Soviet Union in 1974. ("He suffered too much—he's crazy." "He's a Christian zealot with a Christ complex." "He's an agrarian reactionary." "He's an egotist and a publicity junkie.")* Harper's 7/76, p34 *Barbara Mikulski, a Democratic member of Congress from Baltimore . . . told me why she was here: "I'm a new-idea junkie. In 1968 and 1972, the Party wasn't in touch with what was going on out there with the people."* New Yorker 1/15/79, p60 **[1972,** transferred and figurative use of the slang word for a drug addict (1920's)]

junk sculptor, an artist who makes junk sculptures. *Long before the tachiste painter* [action painter] *or the junk sculptor, the American Indian shaped art from sand, bone, feathers— whatever he had at hand.* Time 1/14/66, pE1 **[1966]**

junk sculpture, the art of making three-dimensional figures from material usually found in junkyards, such as scrap metal, broken glass, pieces of wood and rubber, and other discarded items. *Students interested in musicology, junk sculpture, the Theater of the Absurd, and the literary dicta of Leslie Fiedler can go somewhere else.* Harper's 9/69, p14 **[1963]**

Juno, *n.* an award presented annually in Canada for outstanding achievements in music. The corresponding U.S. award is the GRAMMY. *It's no surprise that he* [Murray McLauchlan] *has assumed the mantle for a generation. Yet his appeal goes far beyond these confines. The Junos he has accumulated tell part of the story—three in country categories, two for folk-singer and one for composer of the year.* Maclean's 4/23/79, p56 **[1973,** probably named after *Juno,* queen of the gods in Roman mythology, used as the code name of the beach in Normandy on which Canadian forces landed on D-day, June 6, 1944]

jurimetricist or **jurimetrician**, *n.* an expert in jurimetrics. *Being, in this enterprise, jurimetricists and not legal historians, they* [the authors] *chose the molds of analytic rather than historical jurisprudence for the ordering of their materials.* Scientific American 9/66, p296 *. . . econometricians, polimetricians, psychometricians, jurimetricians are all rapidly proliferating species of a genus of mathematically minded scholars who are infiltrating the academic world armed with computers and many of the analytical tools of higher mathematics.* Encyclopedia Science Supplement (Grolier) 1970, p287 **[1966]**

jurimetrics, *n.* a branch of law using scientific tools and research in dealing with legal matters. *This ambitious project* [a nationwide study of the jury system] *brings lawyers and social scientists together in the search for truth and understanding. . . The two worlds of discourse have become one. This fruit of the union of jurisprudence and social science has inevitably been christened "jurimetrics."* Scientific American 9/66, p295 **[1949, 1964,** from *juris*prudence + *-metrics,* as in biometrics, psychometrics, etc.]

Juso ('yu:ˌsou), *n.* any of a group of young leftist members of the Social Democratic Party of West Germany. *One problem is that one can't talk about the Social Democrats at the moment without discussing their left-wingers, especially the powerful young socialist movement known as Jusos for short. The Jusos, roughly speaking, are moderate Marxists educated during the student upheavals four or five years ago: their aim is gradually to phase out capitalism by reforms,rather than revolution.* Listener 1/31/74, p139 *His* [Chancellor Schmidt's] *first order of business was to lay down the law to the young Marxists, known as Jusos, whose demands for nationalization, more welfare programs and more state controls were angering the conservative workers who were the party's backbone.* NY Times Magazine 5/2/76, p82 [**1971**, from German, short for *Jungsozialisten*, literally, young socialists]

juvabione, (ˌdʒu:vəˈbɑioun), *n.* a terpene of the balsam fir which is a naturally occurring hormone similar to the juvenile hormone that prevents insects from reaching sexual maturity. *William Bowers and his colleagues at the Insect Physiology Laboratory, Agricultural Research Service (ARS), Beltsville, Maryland, isolated and determined the structure of this "paper factor," now called juvabione. Juvabione, which is found in the wood of the balsam fir, only affects members of one family of "bugs."* Science 8/31/73, p834 [**1968**, from *juv*enile (hormone) + *Abies* (balsamea), New Latin name of the balsam fir + hor*m*one]

juvenile hormone, 1 a hormone, secreted by the corpus allatum (a gland behind the brain of insects), that controls the metamorphosis from the larval to the adult stage. *Juvenile hormones play a regulatory role in the molting process of insects. They are of much interest because of the possibility of their application to the selective control of insect populations.* 1972 Britannica Yearbook of Science and the Future, p216 *A chemical analogue of the juvenile hormone has now been produced at Mysore, and large scale treatment of pests with this chemical would reduce their numbers, while avoiding problems of residual toxicity, or the development of resistant strains.* New Scientist 12/5/68, p560 **2** a synthesized form of this hormone, used to prevent development of maturation of insect pests. *Juvenile*

hormone is a possible DDT substitute in killing insects. Science Journal 2/70, p20 [**1940, 1964**]

juvenile-onset diabetes or **juvenile diabetes,** the former name of a type of diabetes that develops early in life (usually before the age of 20) and is much more severe, although less widespread, than MATURITY-ONSET DIABETES. *Juvenile-onset diabetes is treated with injections of insulin derived from the pancreases of cows and pigs. The patient's diet must also be controlled so that the minimum amount of insulin is required and so that concentrations of sugar in the blood do not fluctuate too widely.* World Book Science Annual 1978, p54 [**1976**] —**juvenile-onset diabetic** or **juvenile diabetic:** *There are an estimated 10 million diabetics in this country; one million juvenile diabetics, most of whom suffer from absolute insulin deficiency.* NY Times Magazine 4/9/78, p98 ▶The terminology has shifted to a distinction between TYPE I INSULIN-DEPENDENT DIABETES MELLITUS or (IDDM) and TYPE II or NON-INSULIN-DEPENDENT DIABETES MELLITUS (NIDDM).

juvenilization, *n.* an arrest in the development or maturation of an insect, especially by action of juvenile hormones. *72% of the treated* Pyrrhocoris *larvae formed adultoids which showed effects ranging from a marked juvenilization of the wings to the formation of supernumerary sixth instar larvae. By contrast, untreated larvae in similar conditions consistently formed normal adults.* Nature 6/23/72, p458 [**1972**]

juvenocracy, *n.* rule or government by young people. *A young McGovernite woman, 24-years-old, demanded to be made vice chairman of the Platform Committee to represent youth, "an oppressed minority." The Committee rushed to oblige. Then, on television, she spoke about "child molesting," and, according to the* Village Voice, *gave "the most rotten, bigoted speech of the whole Convention." The perils of juvenocracy.* National Review 10/27/72, p1180 [**1972**, from *juven*ile + connecting -*o*- + -*cracy,* as in *aristocracy*]

juvie or **juvey,** *n. U.S. Slang.* a detention home for juvenile delinquents. *Dot and Meg . . . had sculpted a large eye together in an art class, and they had asked for permission to take it with them when they left. "But the teacher at juvey said, 'You have to finish it,' " Meg said.* New Yorker 2/25/67, p128 [**1967**]

K

K or **k**, *n.* a unit of computer memory capacity equal to 1000 (or 1024 in the binary system) characters, bytes, or words. See KILOBYTE. *Does the idea of a 10 million K RAM stretch credulity too far? It shouldn't because this device is already here. Dutch electrotechnical giant Philips recently demonstrated a random access memory (RAM) that can hold up to 10^{10} bits of information, that can be written on by a user and on which any bit, or character, can be located within a quarter of a second.* New Scientist 11/23/78, p611 [**1966**, from *k*, symbol for *kilo-*, prefix for 1000]

kabele (kɑːˈbeilei), *n.* variant of KEBELE. *In addition, there are mass organizations with great power, such as the peasants' associations, the trade unions and the kabeles, or urban dwellers' associations. Originally created by the Dergue and the ideologues, they now have millions of members and their own imperatives. Their tribunals sit on criminal and civil cases. Kabele leaders collect rents and can evict tenants.* NY Times Magazine 1/8/78, p26 [**1977**]

kabouter (kəˈbɑutər), *n.* any of a group of Dutch political activists promoting pacifism and anarchism. *The Dutch protesters passed on all they had learnt about . . . pollution to an Antwerp offshoot of the* kabouters *(literally dwarfs or pixies), Holland's newest antisociety movement. But protest was in vain.* Times (London) 5/31/72, pIII [**1970**, from Dutch]

kainic acid (keiˈinik), a chemical substance derived from a species of red alga, used especially to kill intestinal worms. *Formula:* $C_{10}H_{15}NO_4$ *Kainic acid, a potent substance that is now the standard treatment for intestinal parasites, comes from a red seaweed, Digenia simplex, eaten by the Japanese from time immemorial for the same purpose.* New Scientist 11/2/78, p367 [**1962**, probably from Greek *kainós* new + English *-ic* (adj. suffix)]

kalashnikov (kəˈlɑːʃniˌkɔːf), *n.* a Soviet submachine gun, used especially by Arab guerrillas. *A ragtag group of fedayeen bearing kalashnikovs, hand grenades and often Pepsi-Cola bottles, swarms around the headquarters area.* NY Times 10/30/70, p41 *They consist of forays across the border by from 40 to 100 men armed with Russian mortars, rockets, recoilless guns and kalashnikov automatics. . .* Times (London) 1/12/72, p10 [**1970**, from Russian, from the surname *Kalashnikov*, probably name of the inventor]

kalimba, *n.* a small, hollow piece of wood, usually about eight inches long, with metal strips inserted along it lengthwise that vibrate when played with the thumbs. *This modern version of the tribal instrument is tuned to play Western music and is held in both hands with the palms upward.* Compare MBIRA. *Buckley blends unusual "noises" into the music: clinks, kalimba, calliope, gunfire, and an odd assortment of rhythm instruments.* Saturday Review 10/26/68, p89 [**1966**, from a Bantu word]

kamagraph, *n.* **1** a type of printing press that can reproduce exactly an original painting specially made for it. *Max Ernst, the well-known dada and surrealist painter; Edouard Pignon, a French abstractionist; and the late René Magritte, the extraordinary Belgian surrealist who died this year, have all executed special work for the kamagraph.* 1968 Collier's Encyclopedia Year Book, p131 **2** a reproduction of a painting made by the kamagraph. *Kamagraphy faithfully produces 250 perfect copies of a painting on a special press, destroying the original in the process. . . Each kamagraph looks as though the artist had painted it by hand.* Time 6/23/67, p49 [**1967**, back formation from KAMAGRAPHY]

kamagraphy, *n.* a method of reproducing an original painting so that both the color and raised brush stroke on canvas are duplicated. The canvas has to be specially made for the type of press used in kamagraphy. *A French process called kamagraphy has been developed by engineer André Cocard, with the backing of art collector and vintner Alexis Lichine. It is capable of reproducing 250 copies of a painting, each of which looks as if it had been painted by hand.* 1968 Collier's Encyclopedia Year Book, p131 [**1967**, from French *kamagraphie*, probably from Sanskrit *kāma* + French *-graphie* representation or record of something]

Kampuchea (ˈkɑːmpuˈtʃiːə), *n.* the official name of Cambodia since 1975. See KHMER ROUGE. *A vitriolic attack on Canada's record in Indochina and its treatment of the underprivileged at home has been made by the government of Cambodia, now known as Democratic Kampuchea. Canada's hands are said to be "stained with the blood of the people of Kampuchea" . . . say the Cambodians.* Maclean's 9/25/78, p25 [**1976**, from Khmer (language of Cambodia)] —**Kampuchean**, *adj., n.: Speaking two days after Vietnam and the Soviet Union signed a friendship and cooperation treaty in Moscow, Mr Wang said at a banquet last night: "The Chinese Government and people resolutely support the Kampuchean people's just struggle in defence of their independence."* Times (London) 11/7/78, p9 *Peking's technicians have been providing expertise in telecommunications and irrigation, while 49 North Koreans attempted (unsuccessfully, as it turned out) to teach the Kampucheans to fly MiG aircraft.* Time 1/22/79, p33

kaon (ˈkeiˌɑn), *n.* any of a group of mesons having masses from 966 to 974 times that of an electron. Also called K-MESON. Compare MUON. *The neutral kaon and antikaon always appear in the experiments as particular combinations of the two, denoted $K^\circ 1$ and $K^\circ 2$.* New Scientist 8/1/63, p255 [**1958**, from *ka* the letter K (in *K-meson*) + *-on* elementary particle]

kaonic (keiˈanik), *adj.* containing or producing kaons. Also called K-MESIC. Compare MUONIC. *To date Wiegand has been able to put kaons in orbit around 24 different elements ranging in mass from lithium to uranium. The X rays emitted by the "kaonic" atoms are analyzed by a nuclear X-ray spectrometer. . .* Scientific American 7/69, p52 [**1965**]

Kaposi's sarcoma (kəˈpousiːz), a cancer of the skin and mucous membranes characterized by multiple purplish lesions on the extremities, formerly rare and benign but now an often fatal disease associated with AIDS. *Mwebe tells me he thinks the disease had appeared by 1980. One of his uncles died of Kaposi's sarcoma that year. Last year his uncle's wife and one of his girlfriends died of "classic AIDS immunosuppression."* Vanity Fair 7/88, p115 [**1961**, named after Moritz *Kaposi*, 1837-1902, a Hungarian dermatologist who first described it]

karate, *v.t.* to strike or beat with blows used in karate (a Japanese method of fighting with the hands and feet). See also KARATE-CHOP. *Wow, dearie, did you miss the action! A wolf was bugging me, so I gave him a shot of Mace, karated him, and called the fuzz.* New Yorker 9/14/68, p129 [**1966**, verb use of the noun (OEDS 1955), from Japanese]

karate-chop, *n.* a sharp slanting stroke with the hand used in karate. *"I'm Larry Taylor," a breathless, sharp-featured young man said, offering a karate-chop handshake to Jay Steffy. "I'm Jay Steffy," Jay Steffy said, karate-chopping back.* New Yorker 12/5/70, p49 —*v.t., v.i.* to strike with a karate-chop. *. . . the wife . . . can karate-chop hell out of her husband.* Time 5/11/70, p62 [**1963**]

karateka, *n.* a karate expert. *Karatekas, those fearsome exponents of the Japanese technique of self-defence called Karate—a sort of tougher version of Judo—often display their prowess by breaking plates, blocks of wood and even bricks with their bare hands.* New Scientist 7/7/66, p8 [**1966,** from Japanese]

kareeba or **kareba,** *n.* a short-sleeved shirt worn with matching trousers by Jamaican men. *The guests sauntered from booth to booth viewing . . . the latest kareebas.* Week-End Star (Kingstown, Jamaica) 9/28/73, p6 *He* [Michael Manley] *was wearing a blue* Kareba *suit, the open-necked, loose-fitting African garb he popularized in Jamaica in line with third-world fashion.* NY Times Magazine 7/25/76, p32 [**1972,** probably of African origin]

karma, *n.* an aura or quality (good or bad) felt to be emanating from a person, place, or thing. *Disney World alone attracts 1,000,000 visitors a month to its 27,000 acres of fun and games—and school is not even out yet. "It's great karma, man," noted one long-haired California youth as he emerged from the Mickey Mouse Review.* Time 5/15/72, p77 *Laid back though they are, Los Angelenos can be as touchy as anyone else when the karma feels wrong.* Maclean's 12/27/76, p28 [**1970,** extended sense of the Hindu and Buddhist term (OED 1828, from Sanskrit) meaning the acts and thoughts that determine a person's fate; hence, fate or destiny]

Karman cannula or **Karman catheter,** a device for performing an abortion by vacuum aspiration. See the quotation for details. *The Karman cannula is a narrow, blunt, flexible plastic tube, closed at the end and notched. Attached to any vacuum-creating apparatus it effects suction abortion in about two minutes. Since the cannula is blunt and soft, the risk of uterine perforation is virtually nil.* Harper's 4/74, p107 [**1972,** named after Harvey *Karman,* an American designer of surgical instruments, who invented it]

kart, *n.* short for GO-KART. *A second hand Class One kart can be picked up for £20 or £30.* Sunday Times (London) 10/16/66, p17 [**1959**]

karting, *n.* the sport of driving or racing a go-kart. *Followers of a fairly new pursuit are also being wooed, and on July 12 a karting week is being held. From what I am told, karting is becoming skilled and highly competitive and can also be a fine spectator sport.* Times (London) 3/30/68, p26 *Kart racing is for the young, and for the not so young—a happy way to taste the thrills of speed, even at 25 m.p.h. Now a competition sport, karting attains sensational speeds of 60, 70 and even 100 m.p.h.* Time 5/21/65, p5 [**1959**]

Kawasaki disease (ˌkɑːwɑːˈsɑːkiː), a disease of young children, characterized by acute fever, congested blood vessels, skin rashes, red feet and hands, and swollen arms and legs. *Kawasaki disease, another puzzling illness, hit 46 children in Massachusetts between April and June. More than 600 cases of the disease have been reported in the United States between 1976 and 1980. The disease, first diagnosed in Japan in 1967, most often affects children under 5.* 1981 World Book Year Book, p336 [**1980,** named after Tomisaku *Kawasaki,* a Japanese pediatrician who first described the disease]

KCIA or **K.C.I.A.,** abbreviation of *Korean Central Intelligence Agency. For all of its zeal, the KCIA is regarded in Washington as a ham-handed offspring of the U.S. CIA—which has helped finance the KCIA in the past. The KCIA does not bother to gather intelligence from South Korea's closest enemy, North Korea.* Time 11/29/76, p14 [**1976**]

kebele (kəˈbeilei), *n.* any of the self-governing neighborhood associations formed in the towns and cities of Ethiopia by the military government which deposed Emperor Haile Selassie in 1974. Also spelled KABELE. *To manage the confiscated urban property and to act as agents of administration, the government established a series of kebeles. The kebele is thus the basic urban unit of the Ethiopian revolution—what the soviet was to the Russian Revolution and the commune was to the Chinese revolution.* New Yorker 7/31/78, p40 [**1976,** from Amharic]

Keller plan or **Keller method,** a method of college instruction in which the subject matter of a course is divided into study units students are allowed to master at their own pace. Also called PSI. *The Keller Plan as applied to science instruction in college was the subject of a comprehensive survey during the year. Evaluation of the results of a large number of experimental and questionnaire-type investigations revealed a surprisingly consistent advantage of PSI over the orthodox lecture-discussion procedure.* 1975 Britannica Yearbook of Science and the Future, p195 [**1973,** named after Fred S. *Keller,* an American psychologist who proposed it in 1968]

Kenyapithecus (ˌkiːnnyəˈpiθəkəs), *n.* either of a pair of humanoid apes believed to have lived from 14 to 20 million years ago, identified by the British paleontologist Louis S. B. Leakey from several skeletal fragments he discovered in the vicinity of Lake Victoria in Kenya between 1962 and 1967. *Moreover, a stratum at Fort Ternan, Kenya, containing the bones of* Kenyapithecus, *an ape-like creature probably in the line of human development, has been dated at 14 million years old.* 1971 Britannica Yearbook of Science and the Future, p397 *Though Leakey still insists that* Kenyapithecus *is a hominid, most other scientists now believe that he is an ape.* Time 8/29/69, p38 [**1962,** from *Kenya* + New Latin *pithecus* ape]

Keogh plan (ˈkiːou), *U.S.* any of various plans by which self-employed individuals set aside part of their yearly income as a tax-deferred annuity or retirement fund. Compare I.R.A. *Keogh plans permit self-employed people . . . to deduct each year as much as 15 percent of what they earn (up to a maximum of $7,500 annually), tuck the money into an insurance annuity, mutual fund or savings bank, and pay no taxes on the interest or dividends credited to the account until they retire.* NY Times 12/27/76, pC14 [**1976,** named after Eugene J. *Keogh,* born 1907, a Congressman from Brooklyn, N.Y., who sponsored a legislative bill for such a plan]

Kepone (ˈkiːˌpoun), *n.* a trademark for a highly toxic chlorinated hydrocarbon formerly widely used as a pesticide. Formula: $C_{10}Cl_{10}O$ Also spelled **kepone.** Generic name, CHLORDECONE. *Kepone . . . is shown to cause brain and liver damage, sterility and possibly cancer in exposed workers. Allied Chemical Corporation, the manufacturer, was fined $13 million for dumping Kepone-laden wastes into Virginia's James River, destroying the fishing industry downstream.* NY Times 1/9/77, pC39 *Industrial waste from the plant, laced with the pesticide kepone, flowed through the city's sewer system.* New Yorker 1/3/77, p65 [**1972**]

Kevlar, *n.* a trademark for a strong, lightweight, synthetic fiber developed to substitute for steel in automobile tires, cables, and many other products. Generic name, **aramid.** *Lined with Kevlar, a synthetic fiber that is lighter than nylon and five times as strong as steel, these contemporary garments are virtually bulletproof and knife-resistant. Already worn by police in seven U.S. cities, the "soft body armor" also has considerable appeal within the bulletprone private sector as well.* Newsweek 2/24/75, p56 [**1973**]

key, *n. Slang.* a kilo of a drug, especially hashish. *There are profits aplenty. A $10 or $20 "key" of Lebanese hash can fetch $1,500 or more in the U.S. . . .* Time 4/13/70, p36 [**1968,** a respelling of *ki* in *kilo* based on the pronunciation]

keyboard, *v.t.* **1** to enter (information) into a computer by the use of a keyboard. *After the encyclopedia, consisting of many volumes, has been keyboarded into the computer, the computer under instruction withdraws the material on a specified subject from its memory storage and sets it up for publication as a separate book or pamphlet. . .* Scientific American 5/69, p68 **2** to typeset (copy) on a machine operated by a keyboard. *Corrections are made by keyboarding the complete line in which the error occurs.* New Scientist 6/22/67, p716 [**1961,** verb use of the noun]

keyboardist, *n.* a person who plays a musical instrument with a keyboard, such as a piano or organ; a pianist, organist, accordionist, etc. *Edmunds assembled the musicians for the LP, including keyboardist Chuck Leavell, bassist Phil Chen and ex-*

Rockpile drummer Terry Williams. Rolling Stone 12/88, p11 [**1955, 1976**]

keypad, *n.* a small panel or console with a set of buttons for operating an electronic calculator or other machine. *Telephones equipped with a 12-button keypad can be used for data communication or retrieval—for example, in a shop to check a customer's credit balance or in a factory to record job progress or staff attendance.* Times (London) 6/8/76, p10 [**1967,** patterned after *keyboard*]

keyphone, *n.* British. a push-button telephone. *Looking exactly like a conventional instrument, except for its 10-button keypad in place of the rotary dial, the Keyphone is being sold to the public as "the phone with the modern touch."* New Scientist 4/11/74, p65 [**1967,** from *key*board + *phone*]

keystroke, *v.t.* another term for KEYBOARD. *All publications . . . have to be keystroked at some new state of their life cycle.* Library Journal 3/1/67, p975 [**1966**]

khanga or **kanga** (ˈkɑːŋgə), *n.* a colorful cotton fabric or garment of East Africa, with traditional patterns printed on the borders. Also called KITENGE. *One-of-a-kind khangas from Kenya are used as body wraps and head wraps, or the ends may be tied to form a carryall. Made of hand-printed cotton, they've been prewashed until they're as soft as oversize hankies.* NY Times Magazine 4/11/76, p100 [**1963,** from Swahili]

Khmer Rouge (kəˈmer ˈruːʒ), the Communist guerrilla force (and from 1975 to January 1979 the Communist government) of Cambodia (Kampuchea). *In "The Politics of Food," an apologia for the evacuation of Phnom Penh, the Indochina Resource Center criticizes the use of the term "Khmer Rouge" as pejorative and/or illiterate. But it is used by Sihanouk and it will be employed in this article in the same sense as he employs it—as a shorthand for that section of the FUNK [National United Front of Kampuchea] which took control of Cambodia after April 17, 1975.* New York Review of Books 3/4/76, p24 *In order to counterbalance a neutrality hitherto tilted towards the Khmer Rouge, Thailand sent the 50,000 refugees into a sector held by the Vietnamese and their allies in Phnom Penh.* Manchester Guardian Weekly (Le Monde section) 7/1/79, p11 [**1970,** from French, literally, Red Khmer]

khoum (kuːm), *n.* a monetary unit in Mauritania introduced in 1973, equal to 1/20 of a ougiya. *At the end of June, on the same day as a total eclipse of the sun brought hundreds of visitors to Mauritania, the new currency was launched. The denominations were the ougiya (worth 5 CFA francs) and the khoum (worth one CFA franc).* Annual Register of World Events 1973, p274 [**1973,** from Arabic]

kickboxing, *n.* a form of boxing, especially popular in Oriental countries, in which kicking with bare feet is permitted. *From karate, Mr. Rothman and his friends have graduated to the more dangerous kickboxing, an Americanized karate. Wearing boxing gloves and sneakers, the kickboxers fight full force and Mr. Rothman admits "you can get hurt." He described it as the "ultimate" in fighting and self-defense.* Observer (Eastchester, N.Y.) 7/20/72, p4 [**1971**] —**kickboxer,** *n.: In the featherweight contest Cambridge's Griffin understandably came out somewhat perplexed against Oxford's former Thai kickboxer, Weeraworawit.* Times (London) 3/4/78, p17

kickturn, *n.* the lifting of the front of a skateboard and moving it left or right by pressing down and pivoting on the back wheels. *Children preferred boards with "kicktail" curves, helpful in performing such stunts as kick-turns.* Times (London) 12/1/77, p2 [**1965**]

kicky, *adj. U.S. Slang.* lively; spirited; racy. . . . *Bergdorf was taking no chances. As a postscript, it brought out some kicky styles to preview its new fur boutique.* NY Times 8/15/68, p42 . . . *we've added kicky new nightlife to all the land/water sports, unstinted luxury and loving Personal Service.* New Yorker 4/20/68, p139 [**1965,** from *kick, n.,* slang word for energy, excitement, stimulation, etc., + *-y* (adj. suffix)]

kidology (kiˈdɒlədʒi:), *n. British, Informal.* a subject of humor or ridicule; something comic or laughable. *It is hard to see their [French wines] making much headway here in Britain where*

the indiscriminate use of the word Château is a popular piece of kidology. Times (London) 11/22/76, p17 [**1964,** from *kid* to joke with, fool, tease + *-ology* study of]

kidvid, *n. U.S.* children's television programs (often used attributively). *Yet, beyond those business-as-usual cartoons, a greening has been transforming the kid-vid wasteland, and the catalyst is yesteryear's bore—educational (now public) television.* Saturday Review 9/16/72, p54 *It's a new world for Anne, an innocent abroad now in that special region of televisionland known as kidvid, an industry within an industry where, says one broadcaster, "We don't think of them as little people, but as little customers."* NY Times Magazine 1/5/75, p15 [**1971,** from *kid* child + *video*]

killer bee, 1 an African honeybee (*Apis mellifera adansonii*), usually black with yellow abdominal bands, noted for its extreme aggressiveness when disturbed. *Such behavior has earned the insect names like the "killer bee" or the "Mau Mau bee." The bee is also a hard worker and an excellent producer of honey, especially in tropical and semi-tropical environments. It was for these reasons that Brazilian authorities decided, in 1956, to import the African bee.* Encyclopedia Science Supplement (Grolier) 1976, p93 **2** any of various hybrids of this African bee and native Brazilian bees that have been spreading from Brazil since the late 1950's, attacking in swarms anything that disturbs their hives. Also called AFRICANIZED BEE. *The northward and southward expansion of the bees' range from the original point of release [has] . . . led to predictions that the "killer bees" might eventually spread a reign of terror throughout the U.S.* Scientific American 1/76, p63 [**1976**]

killer cell, a type of lymphocyte that fights off viral infections and tumors without activation by other cells of the immune system. Also called NATURAL KILLER CELL. *T lympocytes may be turned into "killer cells" that destroy any foreign cells they encounter just as they do when they reject grafted tissue.* Scientific American 6/77, p116 [**1976**]

killer satellite, another name for HUNTER-KILLER SATELLITE. *Killer satellites are small spacecraft. They carry an explosive charge which destroys itself and any nearby satellite on detonation.* Times (London) 12/16/77, p16 [**1972**]

killer T cell, a type of T cell that destroys viral, bacterial, and other foreign matter in the body, especially with helper T cells. *Now in the great war waged by the immune system against foreign invaders, the suppressor T-cell is no fifth column. If the killer T-cells were left unrestrained, they might start knocking off innocent body bystanders. The suppressor T-cells are thought to keep in check the incidence of autoimmune disease by hindering the killer T-cells.* Science News 4/29/78, p278 [**1978**]

killer weed, another name for ANGEL DUST. *Angel dust . . . is called killer weed because it causes numbness in the arms and legs and because it makes some users feel "dead."* Daily News (New York) 2/23/78, p5 [**1978**]

kill ratio or **kill rate,** the proportion of combat casualties on either side, used as a yardstick for estimating military effectiveness or success, especially in antiguerrilla warfare. Compare BODY COUNT. . . . *those Nigerians who had escaped the crossfire had fled northward into the forest, leaving behind 41 dead, the Biafrans said. They put their losses at three killed and a dozen wounded. The lieutenant was pleased with the kill ratio.* NY Times 8/11/68, pA3 *Israeli reconnaissance watched them [Soviet-made SA-2s within eleven miles of the west bank of the Suez Canal] but no effort was made to bomb them for fear Russian MIGs would respond. In North Viet Nam the same type of SA-2s had a "kill" rate of less than one success per 1,000 firings.* Time 7/20/70, p18 [**1953**]

kill shot, a shot in racquet games that is very difficult or practically impossible to return. *Third, the squash ball is smaller and not as lively as the racquetball. Combined with the smaller court and the telltale, this leads to longer rallies and puts the emphasis on skillful placement of shots rather than power. Very few points are ended by an irretrievable "kill" shot—a* *bread-and-butter play in racquetball or tennis.* Money 12/77, p93 [**1976**]

kilobit, *n.* a unit of information equal to one thousand bits or binary digits. Compare GIGABIT, MEGABIT, TERABIT. *Pulse code modulation (PCM) gives very high quality speech reproduction but is an expensive and highly complex system requiring a digit rate of about 64 kilobits/second.* Science Journal 3/70, p12 [**1961,** from *kilo-* 1000 + *bit* binary digit]

kilobyte, *n.* a unit of computer information equal to one thousand bytes. Compare MEGABYTE. *The data are recorded on the magnetic tape inside the cartridge in a diagonal fashion. Each stripe contains 4 KB (kilobytes) of data. A total of 67 diagonal stripes represents one cylinder on disk.* McGraw-Hill Yearbook of Science and Technology 1976, p148 [**1970,** from *kilo-* 1000 + *byte* unit of computer information usually equal to 8 bits]

kilometrage (kə'lɑmətridʒ), *n.* the number of kilometers covered or traveled. *He* [the lorry driver] *is paid according to milage (or rather kilometrage).* Times (London) 6/23/76, p14 *The difference between a united and divided Jerusalem is nothing in terms of kilometrage, but everything in terms of having a unified capital.* NY Times 4/9/76, p2 [**1976,** from French *kilométrage*]

kina ('ki:nə), *n.* the monetary unit of Papua New Guinea (an independent country since 1975). *In line with a decision made in the spring of 1974, Papua New Guinea adopted a new currency as of April 19, 1975. The kina, which is divided into 100 toeas, will circulate with the Australian dollar, to which it is equivalent, until the end of the year.* 1976 Collier's Encyclopedia Year Book, p398 [**1975,** from the native name]

kindling, *n.* a physiological process in which a series of small events, actions, or reactions lead up to, and perhaps stimulate a larger event, such as a seizure or permanent pattern of behavior. *Some scientists believe true kindling represents a kind of learning process and speculate that it may hold clues to the way permanent memories are formed in the brain.* NY Times 2/2/88, pC3 [**1988,** transferred sense of *kindling* fire-starting materials]

kinetic, *adj.* of or relating to kinetic art; involving motion or the suggestion of motion produced by mechanical parts, colors, lights, etc. *The University of Iowa dedicated its new museum and commissioned for it a large kinetic fountain by the Belgian surrealist Pol Bury.* Americana Annual 1970, p101 *Dada has contributed to every new technique employed in this century that it did not actually invent—collage, which is everywhere; its extension, assemblage, which includes junk sculpture, "found" objects and a hundred cousins; the "environment" as well as the Happening; kinetic sculpture, whether motorized or not, and on and on.* NY Times Magazine 3/24/68, p30 [**1957**]

kinetic art, a form of art involving any sort of movement or motion, whether through the use of mobile parts, motor-driven mechanisms, and the like, or through the use of light effects, optical illusions, etc. Also called KINETICISM. Compare LUMINAL ART. *Of particular interest was the use of light and motion in sculpture, especially in constructions designed for spectator participation. . . "Options," a large group show that originated at the Milwaukee Art Center . . . featured kinetic art that reacted to touch, weight, and body heat.* Americana Annual 1969, p95 [**1964**]

kinetic-energy weapon, a missile that relies on laser beams to find its target and on kinetic energy for its destructive effect. *Kinetic-energy weapons move at more or less ordinary rocket speeds and deliver explosive charges to their targets.* Science News 5/2/87, p276 [**1987**]

kineticism, *n.* another name for KINETIC ART. *Manhattan's avant-garde Jewish Museum is currently showing 102 works by kineticism's established practitioners, Jean Tinguely and Nicolas Schöffer.* Time 1/28/66, p44 [**1966**]

kinetic kill vehicle, a weapon designed to destroy a nuclear warhead by force of impact. *This system would not employ directed-energy weapons at the outset; instead it would rely on kinetic kill vehicles.* Scientific American 6/87, p18 *Such data* *is critical for a "kinetic kill vehicle," a vital weapon of the Star Wars system.* Philadelphia Inquirer 2/14/88, p21A [**1987**]

kinetin ('kainətən), *n.* a plant hormone, a type of cytokinin, originally derived from yeast. Compare ABSCISIC ACID, BRASSIN. *Cultured plant cells normally need the hormone kinetin in order to divide and grow.* World Book Science Annual 1967, p268 . . . *kinetin, the first growth factor isolated, promotes growth by a "stop-and-go" signal and by affecting a plant's growth habits.* . . Americana Annual 1969, p130 [**1955,** from *kinet-* motion + *-in* (chemical suffix)]

kininogen (kai'ninədʒən), *n. Biochemistry.* an inactive precursor in the blood of any various kinins (polypeptides forming in tissues in response to injury). *A recent report described the immunoglobulin E (IgE) mediated release of a new mediator . . . which is an arginine esterase and generates kinin from kininogen.* McGraw-Hill Yearbook of Science and Technology 1977, p126 [**1963,** from *kinin* (abstracted from BRADYKININ) + connecting *-o-* + *-gen* thing that produces (from Greek *-genēs* born)]

kinky, *adj. Slang.* **1** involving or appealing to sexually unconventional or perverted tastes. . . . *the current "The Right Honourable Gentleman," on which Littler collaborated, contains references to a man sleeping with two women at once and other kinky behaviour.* Observer (London) 8/30/64, p4 **2** sexually deviant. *Obscenities, it was complained, had been introduced by "kinky" authors into television plays.* Times (London) 4/12/66, p6 **3** unconventional in a sophisticated way; offbeat. *". . . there's the danger of making everything the same in an effort to be way out,"* she [the actress Susannah York] *added thoughtfully. "I loathe really kinky clothes."* NY Times 10/4/66, p44 *But today they report huge sales of bed jackets for bedtime television, kinky underwear and the . . . leg-o'-mutton blouse.* Times (London) 3/21/66, p13 [**1959,** extended senses of *kinky* full of kinks or curls, twisted; also figuratively, queer, eccentric (1860's)] ►*Kinky* in reference to clothing (see definition 3 and also the entry *kinky boot*) is used especially to suggest the type of feminine attire or accessory that is associated with fetishism and sexual stimulation.

kinky boot, *British.* a knee-length or thigh-length boot, especially of black leather, worn by women. *It was the year that satire became an industry; that the Derby winner, Relko, was tested for dope; that women adopted the fashionable long 'kinky' boot.* Annual Register of World Events in 1963, p1 [**1964**]

Kirlian, *adj.* of or relating to Kirlian photography. *Those who are interested in the details of how to make Kirlian motion pictures may feel free to write to me.* Science News 12/1/73, p339 *Among the factors that obviously influence a person's Kirlian signature, explains physicist William Tiller of Stanford University, are chemical changes on the skin surface brought about by such unmysterious substances as sweat and body oils, the topology of a person's fingerprints, the electrical energy in the outer cells of the skin and physical buckling of the film when the electric spark passes through it.* Newsweek 3/4/74, p55 [**1970,** from the name of Semyon D. and Valentina K. *Kirlian*, Russian researchers in electricity who invented KIRLIAN PHOTOGRAPHY]

Kirlian photograph, an image obtained on film by Kirlian photography. Also called ELECTROPHOTOGRAPH. *The body's aura, he continued, is more intense inside a pyramid. He took from his desk two Kirlian photographs of a living butterfly. The one made outside the pyramid showed only a faint white aura. The one made inside showed a bright blue aura that extended several inches beyond the butterfly's wings.* Scientific American 6/74, p118 [**1972**]

Kirlian photography, a process that records on photographic film the field radiation of electricity supposed to surround living things. By passing an electric charge through an object a bright glow is detected emanating from the object. Also called RADIATION-FIELD PHOTOGRAPHY. See BIOPLASMA. *Work in Russia recently has photographed, by Kirlian photography, the energy emissions from the acupuncture points.* New Scientist 8/10/72, p309 *Kirlian photography . . . produces star-*

tling photographs of pulsating, multicolored lights streaming from the human body and from plants. Science News 9/29/73, p202 *Many psychics and their followers believe that paranormal powers may be dependent on mysterious auras or "energy flows," phenomena that they say can be recorded by Kirlian photography.* Time 3/4/74, p70 [**1972**]

KISS, n. U.S. Informal. acronym for *Keep It Simple, Stupid.* *Even some of the military planners concede that the complex mission violated an old Army rule called KISS, meaning "keep it simple, stupid."* Time 5/12/80, p33 [**1980**]

kiss-and-tell, adj. revealing private or confidential matters known through personal intimacy. *TV sports executives and announcers are a notoriously thin-skinned lot. It's no wonder, then, that the talk of the business right now is former ABC exec Jim Spences' kiss-and-tell memoir* [Close and Personal: The Inside Story of Network Television Sports]. Sports Illustrated 5/30/88, p83 [**1970**, from the verb phrase *kiss and tell* "to recount one's sexual exploits" (OEDS 1695)] ►The adjective *kiss-and-tell* became especially prominent in 1988 in news stories about books by former White House members and intimates of President Reagan, such as David Stockman, Michael Deaver, Donald Regan, and Larry Speakes. The verb phrase is of long standing in English, perhaps best known from the line "Oh fie Miss, you must not kiss and tell," in Congreve's *Love for Love* (1695). The expression is older, however, having appeared in Charles Cotton's *Burlesque upon Burlesque* (1675): "And if he needs must kiss, and tell,/I'll kick him headlong into Hell." The phrase is also found in the works of other English and American writers, such as Rudyard Kipling and A.B. Lindsley. As pointed out by John Algeo in *American Speech* 64, 1 (1989), p 66, "All of the early uses of the expression [*kiss and tell*] are in predicate function and have an explicitly sexual meaning. The current voguish use, however, is attributive, refers to books, and has the more general sense of 'revealing private or confidential matters that are embarrassing to the person written about.' "

kiss of life, British. **1** another term for MOUTH-TO-MOUTH RESUSCITATION. *Simon pulled himself out of the water. He folded his dressing gown under Munter's head, forced back his neck, and felt in the gaping mouth for dentures. There were none. Then he fastened his mouth over the thick lips and began the kiss of life.* P.D. James, The Skull Beneath the Skin, 1982, p317 **2** an act that gives back life; something that revitalizes. *The Government's kiss of life for Rolls* [-Royce] *could be very misleading if it is seen as a sign of a volte face by the Government over propping up ailing companies.* Manchester Guardian Weekly 11/21/70, p22 *The question of Britain's possible entry into the Common Market, for long declared to be a dead issue in the House of Commons, was given the kiss of life today by Sir Alec Douglas-Home.* Times (London) 6/2/65, p12 [**1961**, probably patterned after the earlier phrase *kiss of death* (OEDS 1948) though the meanings are wholly unrelated]

kitemark, n. the registered certification mark of the British Standards Institution, indicating compliance of a manufactured product with the Institution's standards of performance. *But the new regulation comes at a time when the BSI "kitemark" standard—set with the aid of belt manufacturers—is coming under expert criticism.* Sunday Times (London) 1/15/67, p8 [**1952**]

kitenge (ki'teŋgi:), n. another name for KHANGA. *Women and girls were so committed to minis that when those dresses were banned they immediately saw an alternative in the kitenge . . . and began tying them around their legs.* Voice of Uganda 3/14/73, p6 [**1964**, from Swahili]

kitschy, adj. artistically shallow or vulgar, but slickly professional; gaudy or ostentatious. *Flamboyant orange hat, half-blouse breaking into white tassels below full breasts lent a kitschy, high-school-queen quality.* Harper's 9/69, p84 *I am jealous of the scenery here for the Gibichung Palace, but the trees by the Rhine are Kitschy. . .* Times (London) 3/25/70, p17 *. . . those of us who are writers, teachers, community leaders, makers of opinion can bury our outmoded, liberal, laissez-faire ideas about freedom of expression at any cost—and help to cramp and cripple the mass appeal of pornography by making it démodé, by pointing out its kitschy insipidity, by expos-*

ing its infantilism, by laughing it to scorn. Atlantic 8/71, p26 [**1964**, from *kitsch* inferior works of art or literature (OEDS 1941, earlier *Kitsch*, 1926), from German *Kitsch*]

kiwi fruit, an edible fruit resembling a large gooseberry, produced by a New Zealand vine and sold in the United States as a delicacy. *Chinese gooseberries, also known as kiwi fruit, are in metropolitan markets for the third season in increased quantities.* NY Times 8/13/66, p12 [**1966**, from *kiwi*, a nickname for a New Zealander, originally the Maori name of the apteryx, a New Zealand bird]

Kleinian, adj. of or relating to the theories of Melanie Klein, 1882-1960, a German pioneer in child psychology who emphasized infant sexuality and argued that the psychoanalytic technique could be applied to very young children. *This is something that psychoanalytic thought itself has often failed to grasp; wherever psychoanalytic theory stops short at tracing back human ills to an aboriginal calamity, whether in the tribal life of our remote ancestors, as in Freud's own early work, or in the early life of the individual child, as in much Kleinian theory, then at this point the psychoanalytic movement does less than justice to its own insights, and takes over the outlook of the fatalistic religions whose neurotic character it has been instrumental in exposing.* Listener 5/18/67, p650 —n. a follower or supporter of Melanie Klein's theories. *. . . "Kleinians" maintain that paranoia is full-blown in the first year of life.* Harper's 8/68, p57 *Freudians believe the Kleinians overemphasize the early months of life and neglect adult experience and environmental factors.* Encyclopedia Science Supplement (Grolier) 1969, p276 [**1955**]

kleptocracy, n. government by thieves. *In the course of a quite long digression about the Federal Republic of Cameroon, which he seems to regard as one of the less wicked kleptocracies, Mr. Barnes makes no reference to the part played in its history by the Union des Populations Camerounaises. . .* Manchester Guardian Weekly 7/10/71, p18 [**1968**, from *klepto-* theft + *-cracy* government]

klick or **klik**, n. U.S. Military Slang. a kilometer. *Sipping lemonade or good Russian vodka, they trade experiences. Nothing to the north for 20 klicks (kilometers). All quiet at Kompong Speu, but the city* [Phnom Penh] *is deserted and still smoldering from a Communist mortar attack that morning.* Time 7/6/70, p24 *"O.K., well, there's one hootch down there about a klik south of us that we want you to get," the ground commander said.* New Yorker 3/16/68, p86 [**1966**]

kludge, Slang. —n. any clumsily improvised system, design, or the like. *A Kludge is that familiar product of design endeavour—"an ill-assorted collection of poorly-matching parts forming a distressing whole."* New Scientist 12/22/66, p699 *A kludge (rhymes with "sludge") is an improvised lashup often involving adhesive tape and string. It works fine, but only as long as it's pampered, and no one trips over a wire.* John Prenis, Computer Terms, 1977, p45 —v.t. to produce (any system, design or the like) by clumsy improvisation. *The kiosks that it has been testing in supermarkets since December have yielded disheartening results. "The concept is intellectually perfect," says Chairman Walter A. Forbes, "but it's just not that easy. You can't just 'kludge' together a system, sell at a discount, and get rich."* Business Week 3/25/85, p78 [**1962** for noun; **1983** for verb; origin unknown]

klutz, n. U.S. Slang. a clumsy, awkward person. *Candice* [Bergen] *is generally hailed as heiress apparent to Grace Kelly, but the princess role does not quite fit. Says she: "Basically I'm the klutz who makes a terrific entrance to the party and then trips and falls and walks around with food in her hair."* Time 11/2/70, p83 [**1967**, from Yiddish *klots*, literally, a block or lump, corresponding to German *Klotz*]

klutzy, adj. U.S. Slang. awkward and clumsy. *. . . the sad, klutzy ballerinas of the Music Hall pollute children's first live experience of dance.* New Yorker 1/17/70, p72 [**1965**]

K-mesic, adj. another word for KAONIC. *. . . in 1952 physicists at Rochester and Pittsburgh identified X-rays originating from pi-mesic atoms. Since then muonic atoms (mu mesons in atomic* *orbit) and K-mesic atoms were discovered.* New Scientist 9/17/70, p566 [**1958**]

K-meson, *n.* another word for KAON. *Usually the beams consist of . . . K-mesons with about 1,000 electron masses. K-meson beams have been particularly valuable recently in the production of further new particles.* Listener 4/30/64, p711 [**1954,** from earlier *k particle* (OEDS 1949)]

kneecapping, *n.* the act of shooting or drilling through the kneecaps of a person as a punishment. . . . *I.R.A. "hit men" punish detractors and defectors, by subjecting them to "kneecapping." "It used to be done with guns," Clutterbuck will tell a class matter-of-factly, "but lately they've been running an electric drill through the knee in such a way that even after medical treatment there's a peculiar, easily identifiable walk."* New Yorker 6/12/78, p60 *The Red Brigades . . . last week took responsibility for the "knee-capping" of three more Italian industrial figures.* NY Times 7/9/78, pD2 *Passing into verb. Terrorists 'Kneecap' 10 At School In Italy.* New York Post 12/12/79, p43 [**1975**]

knee-jerk, *adj.* reacting without much thought or in a predictable or automatic way (like the reflex of the foreleg produced when a light blow is delivered to the knee). *Rauh was instantly denounced by some for responding in the usual knee-jerk liberal fashion. . .* New Yorker 12/5/70, p83 *The board seems to encourage the local state of political apathy, depending on entrenched hacks and knee-jerk Republicans to turn out the winning vote.* Harper's 10/71, p74 **—n.** a person whose reactions are predictable or automatic, especially in politics. *The most notorious Congressman from Iowa is cranky old H.R. Gross, a seventy-year-old knee-jerk best remembered for castigating the Reverend Bill Moyers for dancing the frug in the White House. . .* Harper's 3/69, p52 [**1963**]

kneeling bus, *U.S.* a bus with a pneumatic suspension system that will lower its body to the level of a curb so that passengers do not have to negotiate a step. *Pledging that his own administration would be "sensitive to the special needs of the aging," Mr. Koch promised, among other things, . . . the deployment of "kneeling" buses "on routes where they will serve the greatest number of people who need them."* NY Times 8/29/77, p21 [**1977**]

kneeroom, *n.* enough room in front of a seat of an automobile, airplane, etc., to keep one's knees in a natural, comfortable position when seated. *More people are buying Rolls-Royces today than ever before. . . More front headroom and rear kneeroom could be devised by reducing the bulk of their cushions and backrests, without detracting from comfort.* Times (London) 4/16/70, p18 [**1970**]

knee-slapper, *n. U.S.* a hilarious joke. *If T.R. [Theodore Roosevelt] is President when he is fully dressed, went one knee-slapper, what is he with his clothes off? Answer: Teddy bare.* Time 12/5/69, p56 *"How's the World Treating You," an English comedy at the Music Box, is full of knee-slappers like that one, but it does have the benefit of a couple of rowdy music-hall performances by Patricia Routledge and Peter Bayliss.* New Yorker 11/5/66, p128 [**1958**]

knees-up, *n. British.* a lively party or celebration. *I'm sure the Ferryboat at Whitchurch won't mind my saying that they're good for a knees-up any night of the week.* Manchester Guardian Weekly (Le Monde section) 5/30/70, p14 *The street party . . . wasn't exactly a Cockney "knees-up," but everyone was having a ball.* Maclean's 6/27/77, p40 [**1963,** from a popular song beginning *"Knees up,* Mother Brown!" and a dance associated with it]

knocker-up, *n., pl.* **knockers-up.** *British.* a person who brings the resident of a house to the door in order to prepare the ground for someone else to solicit, canvass, etc. *Three hundred yards away, Michael Whincup, the candidate, is canvassing with six knockers-up.* Times (London) 3/11/66, p8 [**1965**] ►In old industrial areas, especially mining, houses used to have a slate outside on which was written a time. A "knocker-up" would then tour the streets rousing workers for a shift of work, acting as an alarm clock. A *knocker-up* as used in the quotation would rouse the residents and ask if they would like to meet the

candidate. The candidate would be called across to those who said yes.

knockoff, *n. U.S.* a copy or reproduction of the design of a textile or apparel product. [Coco] *Chanel had long since refused to join the cabal of Paris designers who tried to prevent style piracy. . . Private customers paid $700 for the original; buyers, intent on knockoffs, paid close to $1,500.* Time 1/25/71, p38 *Copying designs to sell for less has a name in the industry. It is called the "knockoff."* NY Times 1/25/66, p44 [**1963**]

known quantity, a well-known or familiar person or thing. *411 dailies with 30 million circulation back Ford. They tend to emphasize that he is a known quantity.* Time 11/8/76, p13 *Have people become so accustomed to the series idea from television viewing that they go to another Dirty Harry movie because it's a known quantity?* New Yorker 1/24/77, p86 [**1976,** patterned after *unknown quantity,* an algebraic term]

knuckle-walk, *v.i.* to walk as chimpanzees and gorillas do, with the knuckles of the hands touching the ground. *Orangutans adjust to walking on a cage floor with a variety of hand postures, but they cannot knuckle walk.* McGraw-Hill Yearbook of Science and Technology 1967, p132 *Russell Tuttle, also of the University of Chicago, suggested that the initial divergence between man and ape may have occurred in the arboreal habitats through differential use of forelimbs and hind limbs and before the evolution of knuckle-walking.* 1971 Britannica Yearbook of Science and the Future, p291 [**1967**] **—knuckle-walker**, *n. The first component separates quadrupedal cercopithecoids from both knuckle-walkers.* Nature 8/10/73, p373

koban, *n.* a police substation in Japan. *Foot patrols are characteristic of police work in Tokyo, and every few city blocks has a koban, or police booth, manned by one to a dozen men who patrol the neighborhood constantly. Each koban policeman is responsible for about 150 households, and is required to visit each of these households at least twice a year.* Americana Annual 1975, p197 [**1967,** from Japanese *kōban*]

kobo, *n.* a unit of money in Nigeria. See the quotation for details. *The naira will be made up of 100 kobo . . . the name is a corruption of the word "copper" and the popular term here* [in Nigeria] *for the penny, a copper coin. . . The kobo, symbolized by a lower-case k, will be produced in coins of one-half kobo, 1, 5, 10 and 25 kobo. A 50-kobo paper bill will be produced.* NY Times 8/9/72, p14 [**1972**]

Kohoutek (kə'houtek), *n.* a comet discovered on March 7, 1973 beyond the orbit of Mars by Lubos Kohoutek, a Czech astronomer working at the Hamburg Observatory. See OORT'S CLOUD. *What set Kohoutek apart from other comets is that this passage was subjected to more scientific observation than ever before. The attention resulted because Kohoutek was discovered while still distant from the Sun.* McGraw-Hill Yearbook of Science and Technology 1975, p51 [**1973**]

Kojah ('koudʒɑ:), *n.* a mutant variety of mink. See the quotations for details. *Last year, too, there appeared Kojah mink (rare and expensive), a mink so long-haired that it resembles sable. Nobody I have asked knows whence it sprang, and the thing is a real mystery, because I hear that neither minks nor sables believe in miscegenation.* New Yorker 11/8/69, p179 *Called "Kojah" for reasons best understood by the trade (although the name does have a bit more class than "mable" or "sink"), the fur is much thicker and softer than conventional mink and less bulky than sable.* Time 1/31/69, p47 [**1969,** of uncertain origin]

komiteh (kou'mi:tei), *n.* any of the revolutionary committees with wide police powers formed in Iran after the deposition of the Shah in 1979. *Ayatollah Mahdavi Khani, supreme commander of the komitehs, announced they would be phased out and their militiamen incorporated into the now-moribund national police force. Prime Minister Mehdi Bazargan again attacked the komitehs, calling for an end to their "rule of revenge."* NY Times 4/29/79, p2E [**1979,** from Persian, probably from English *committee*]

Kondo effect, *Metallurgy.* an increase in the resistance of dilute alloys of magnetic materials in a nonmagnetic environment as the temperature is lowered. *Disappearing superconductivity has been observed once before in certain alloys which exhibit the "Kondo effect" (a minimum in electrical resistance at low temperatures). The new compound ErRh4B4 shows no sign of a Kondo effect.* New Scientist 6/30/77, p778 [**1969,** named after J. *Kondo,* a physicist who predicted it in 1964]

kook, *n. Slang.* an odd, crazy, or eccentric person. *"Don't think that just because he talked about those way-out rockets he's a kook,"* cautioned a fellow officer. Time 10/4/63, p37 —**adj.** silly or crazy; KOOKY. *Premier Bill Bennett, master of all that is kook and strange in British California, is an apple in a grove of oranges, a misfit who cannot understand why everyone will not play by his own rules.* Maclean's 1/14/80, p56 [**1959** for noun, **1980** for adj.; probably shortened from KOOKY]

kooky, *adj. Slang.* odd; crazy; eccentric. . . . *this study of a kooky girl* [Petulia] *is also, from the orthodox point of view, kookily narrated. . . Seldom has the kooky girl character been seen in anything but a comedy; almost for the first time here we are made to realise the havoc she can cause.* Punch 6/19/68, p899 *The first group includes* Vogue, Harper's Bazaar *and* Queen, *and shows expensive clothes mainly for thirties and upward age-group, although pressure of the so-called swinging image has resulted in space for young 'kooky' clothes.* Gillian Freeman, The Undergrowth of Literature, 1967, p16 [**1959,** probably alteration of *cuckoo, adj.,* U.S. slang word meaning crazy (OEDS 1918)]

Koreagate, *n.* See the quotation for the meaning. *The scandal, which is sometimes called "Koreagate" here, gained public attention last fall through American newspaper reports that Park Tong Sun, a Korean businessman in Washington, had made payments in cash to American legislators to obtain favorable consideration of American military and economic support of South Korea.* NY Times 1/9/77, pA12 [**1976,** from *Korea* + -GATE]

koza, *n.* a staff unit in Japanese universities for teaching and research, consisting of a professor, an associate professor, several assistants, and technical personnel. *Each koza is funded separately and functions almost independently, with each worker making a virtual lifetime commitment to this particular group.* Science News 8/19/78, p125 [**1972,** from Japanese, literally, academic chair, professorship]

K-point, *n.* the point in the landing area in ski jumping beyond which there is insufficient space for a safe landing. *Last week in St. Moritz, Switzerland, Horst Bulau was poised on the inrun atop the 75-m ski jump. After a first and second at Sapporo, Japan, and a historic double win at Thunder Bay, Ont., Bulau was atop the ski jumping world. He had just jumped 94m. landing at the "K-point," the critical landing distance.* Maclean's 2/8/82, p41 [**1982,** partial translation of German *K-Punkt,* shortened from *kritischer Punkt* critical point]

KREEP, *n.* a yellow-brown glassy mineral obtained on the moon, noted for its unusual chemical composition. *Another Apollo 12 find of general agreement was that of an exotic component called KREEP by some—for high content of potassium, rare earth elements and phosphorus—found in rock 13 and in other material dated about 4.5 billion years old.* Science News 1/23/71, p62 *The lunar regolith has been found to contain particles of unusual chemical composition, high in potassium, phosphorus and certain metals known as rare-earth elements. These mineral fragments have been dubbed* kreep *(from K, the chemical symbol for potassium, rare-earth elements and P, the chemical symbol for phosphorus).* Encyclopedia Science Supplement (Grolier) 1971, p43 [**1971**]

Kremlinologist, *n.* an expert in Kremlinology. Also called SOVIETOLOGIST. *"Will they be content to stop at that point, or will they continue to grind out more ICBM's? We simply don't know,"* one top Kremlinologist in Washington conceded. NY Times 2/25/68, pD2 [**1960**]

Kremlinology, *n.* the study by Western political scientists of the policies, practices, etc., of the Soviet government. Also called SOVIETOLOGY. Compare PEKINGOLOGY. *If the West had*

grasped at that time [the post-Stalin thaw of 1953-1957] *the opportunity provided by the division among the Soviet leaders on the problem of Germany, the two halves of Germany might by now have been unified. There were many other equally promising avenues to explore, as the diplomatic cliché has it, but the diplomatists were not interested, because this was "Kremlinology"—an inexact science if ever there was one.* Manchester Guardian Weekly 11/3/66, p10 [**1958**]

Krishna, *n.* short for HARE KRISHNA. *Forrest Nichols, a security guard at O'Hare in charge of regulating solicitors, said that each Krishna averaged $125 to $150 a day in solicitations and that the airport got about five complaints a week about them.* NY Times 12/22/76, p31 [**1973**]

Krishna Consciousness, a form of Hinduism devoted to the god Krishna, founded in the United States in 1966 by Swami Prabhupada (A.C. Bhaktivedanta), an Indian guru born in 1896 in Calcutta. See HARE KRISHNA. *Some meditation practices are avowedly religious and integral to the beliefs of the group itself such as with Hinduism, Buddhism, the Vedanta Society, Sivananda Yoga, Krishna Consciousness, and the Self-Realization Fellowship.* New York Post 2/26/77, p23 [**1970**]

Krugerrand, *n.* a one-ounce gold coin of South Africa, with the obverse showing a bust of President Paul Kruger, first struck in 1967. *Gold is the country's major export and the advertising campaign behind the Krugerrand is designed to help South Africa sell more of the precious metal. The coin is being promoted not for its numismatic value—as a collector's item—but as a convenient way to own gold.* NY Times 10/9/76, p28 [**1967,** from Afrikaans, from Paul *Kruger* (1825-1904) + *rand* South African monetary unit]

Kugelblitz or **kugelblitz,** *n.* a very rare type of lightning that appears in the form of blazing spheres which move slowly and disappear without an accompanying sound. Its common name is the English equivalent *ball lightning. Writing in Nature (vol 245, p 95) R.C. Jennison of the University of Kent at Canterbury, proposes that the mysterious spheres of Kugelblitz (the more dramatic-sounding Teutonic name) may be some sort of stable standing waves of electromagnetism; the balls, usually about 20 cm in diameter, are "a phase-locked loop of electromagnetic radiation in the intense field associated with lightning activity."* New Scientist 9/27/73, p792 [**1968,** from German *Kugelblitz,* literally, ball lightning]

kumite (ku'mi:ti:), *n.* a sparring event or exhibition in karate, similar to sparring in boxing except that attacks are stopped just short of contact with the target. *Japanese also won the men's team kumite final as well as the individual and team titles in the kata (prescribed forms), for both men and women.* Britannica Book of the Year 1978, p255 [**1965,** from Japanese, literally, set hand]

kundalini (ˌkundəˈliːniː), *n.* (in Hindu yogic tradition) the mystic life force or spiritual energy which lies dormant at the base of the spine until it is awakened by the practice of yoga. *The mystics want "a lofty class of men," of scientists with elevated kundalinis who will keep watch over the race.* Harper's 11/72, p125 *Kundalini, often referred to as the "serpent power" because it is symbolized by a coiled snake, can be concentrated and channeled through the spine into the brain—a process . . . not yet identified by modern science. The systematized process for accomplishing this upward flowing of energy is known as kundalini yoga.* John White, Kundalini, Evolution and Enlightenment, 1979, p21 [**1971,** from Sanskrit *kuṇḍalinī,* literally, coiled up]

kung fu, a Chinese method of fighting without weapons in which the hands and feet are used to strike blows at vulnerable parts of the body. See WU SHU. *Unlike the hard, powerful style of karate, kung fu involves softer, fluid movements, all of which have philosophical meanings. "Kung fu is a way of life,"* says Ronald Dong, an instructor in the White Crane Kung Fu School in San Francisco. Newsweek 5/7/73, p76 *A Chinese Buddhist monk, expert in the deadly art of kung fu, who uses his skill only in self-defense. . .* Maclean's 1/74, p78 [**1966,** from Chinese (Canton) *kung fu,* literally, boxing art]

kurchatovium (ˌkɑrtʃə'touviːəm), *n.* the name given by Soviet scientists to ELEMENT 104. See the quotation for details. *Russian physicists had reported . . . that they had succeeded in synthesizing element 104, which they named kurchatovium in honor of the Russian physicist I. V. Kurchatov. The Berkeley group then synthesized element 104 by a different method and challenged the Russian finding, naming their discovery rutherfordium in honor of the British physicist Lord Rutherford.* Scientific American 6/70, p49 [**1966**]

kuromaku ('kuːrə'mɑːkuː), *n. sing.* or *pl.* a Japanese of great power and influence, especially one who acts behind the scenes. *The system also involves the behind-the-scenes machinations of the kuromaku, or "black curtain" wirepullers—influential power brokers whose connections with violent rightwing nationalist groups and gangsters enable them to use coercion and intimidation to accomplish what money and influence alone cannot.* NY Times Magazine 11/21/76, p105 *A few days later he introduced Kotchian to another of Japan's top power brokers, Ryoichi Sasakawa. Like Kodama, Sasakawa was a kuromaku; in fact, now that Kodama is in trouble as a result of the Lockheed scandal, and is sick besides, Sasakawa is regarded as the last of Japan's great old-time fixers.* New Yorker 1/23/78, p69 [**1974**, from Japanese, literally, black curtain, a term taken from the Kabuki theater and extended to mean "wirepuller, manipulator"]

kuru, *n.* a fatal disease of the human nervous system similar to scrapie in sheep. Kuru, occurring in natives of the New Guinea highlands, is characterized by tremors and fits of giggling followed by loss of muscular coordination and speech, inability to swallow, and other degenerative symptoms. *Kuru . . . was found to be caused by a virus that persists in the tissues for long periods of time before symptoms appear.* 1970 Britannica Yearbook of Science and the Future, p271 *Kuru, one of the strangest and most insidious diseases known, is fading away in its New Guinea habitat, apparently because of a ban on ritualistic cannibalism.* NY Times 6/12/71, p33 [**1957**, from the native name of the disease, roughly meaning "shivers"]

kvell, *v.i. U.S. Slang.* to enjoy oneself thoroughly. The New York Spy *is a useful and terribly bright guide to New York, conscientiously kvelling through 'the city's pleasures', charmed alike by brutal manners, as chronicled by Tom Wolfe, and the Jewish takeover (London swings but Jewish New York kvells).* Listener 12/28/67, p849 [**1967**, from Yiddish *kveln*]

kvetch, *U.S. Slang.* —*n.* a habitual complainer or faultfinder. *The subway graffiti had begun to include phrases like "Medea Is a Yenta" and "Kafka is a Kvetch."* Atlantic 1/68, p43 —*v.i.* to whine, complain, or find fault. . . . *what is a Jewish mother for, except to* kvetch *a little?* Harper's 9/69, p92 *"Stuyvie is a reactionary," said one of the classmates. But he is an amiable one, not given to angry kvetching, a twinkly-eyed bachelor who'd rather talk about pot-smoking escapades in Mexico, his efforts at preserving the California backland from suburban tractation. . .* Atlantic 10/68, p70 [**1963**, from Yiddish *kvetsh, n.* or *kvetshn, v.,* literally, squeeze]

kwacha ('kwɑːtʃə), *n.* the new monetary unit of Zambia (since 1969) and of Malawi. *Malawi's decimal currency was to be introduced in March 1971; the new unit, the kwacha, is divided into 100 tambolas.* 1970 Compton Yearbook, p188 . . . *Zambia changed to a decimal currency and replaced the pound, shilling, and pence with the kwacha (meaning "dawn"), which equals US $1.40, and the ngwee (meaning "bright"), which is one-hundredth of a kwacha.* 1969 Collier's Encyclopedia Year Book, p624 [**1966**]

Kwanza, *n.* an Afro-American cultural festival celebrated during the seven days preceding New Year's Day. *Although Africans themselves don't celebrate Kwanza, it has been growing in popularity in black communities here since the early 60s, when it was developed by Los Angeles black leader Maulana Ron Karenga, founder of the organization US.* New York Post 12/31/73, p7 [**1971**, from Swahili *kwanza* beginning; so called probably in reference to a festival of first fruits]

kwanza, *n.* the unit of money of Angola, equal to 100 lweis. *On January 8 the Finance Ministry announced the introduction of a new currency, the kwanza (named after the nation's main river), to replace the Portuguese escudo.* 1978 Collier's Encyclopedia Year Book, p123 [**1977**]

KWIC (kwik), *n.* acronym for *key-word-in-context* (designating an index in which key words are listed alphabetically but within a fixed amount of context). *A second type of bibliographic information retrieval device is the key-word-in-context (KWIC) index, which has become widely used, particularly as a device for retrieving information from current materials.* McGraw-Hill Yearbook of Science and Technology 1967, p16 [**1959**]

Kwok's disease, another name for CHINESE RESTAURANT SYNDROME. *Several years ago, Chinese restaurants became a centre of scientific attention as a result of what was later called "Kwok's disease"—numbness in the back, followed by general weakness, and palpitations—a syndrome caused by too lavish addition of the flavouring agent monosodium glutamate to the chop suey.* New Scientist 3/28/74, p796 [**1972**, named after Robert *Kwok,* an American physician, who first described it]

kyudo ('kyuː;dou), *n.* a Japanese method of archery used to develop concentration and coordination. *Those who prefer a less physically demanding exercise may use their weekly practice time for kyudo. . .* NY Times 6/25/67, p7 [**1967**, from Japanese *kyūdō* archery]

K-Z syndrome, a group of symptoms in liberated prisoners of war, including anxiety, insomnia, memory lapse, and guilt for surviving. Compare STOCKHOLM SYNDROME. *K-Z syndrome has been identified, but causal connections between captivity and clinical observations remain tenuous due to lack of information. It may be that all or part of the K-Z syndrome will show up in returned Vietnam POW's, but the evidence is inconclusive so far.* Science News 3/21/81, p188 [**1979**, from *K-Z,* irregular abbreviation of German *Konzentrationslager* concentration camp + English *syndrome*]

L

laboratory disease, a disease induced, especially in laboratory animals, for experimental purposes. *This graft-v.-host syndrome is a "laboratory disease" procurable at will by a variety of methods, most simply by inoculating newborn mice or rats with a few million lymphocytes from adult donors of another strain.* Scientific American 4/74, p43 [**1974**]

labor-intensive, *adj.* requiring great expenditure of labor to increase productivity or earnings. . . . *a labor-intensive textile mill in Arusha, or an agricultural project, would in theory be preferred to a modern, highly mechanized factory in Dar es Salaam.* NY Times 1/5/70, p36 *The service sectors have in common the fact that they are disproportionately labor-intensive rather than capital-intensive, even though some sectors (particularly transportation and communication) have extremely high ratios of capital to output.* Scientific American 11/71, p20 [**1957**]

lac, *adj.* of or relating to the lac operon. . . . *the lac repressor binds to DNA that contains the lac genes* . . . Scientific American 6/70, p43 [**1961**]

lac operon, the operon which controls the metabolism of lactose (milk sugar). *Boston: The isolation in pure form of a set of six bacterial genes known as the lac operon has been accomplished by a group led by Dr. Jon Beckwith of the Harvard Medical School* . . . Science Journal 1/70, p14 [**1969**]

lactoferrin (ˌlæktəˈferin), *n.* an iron-binding protein found especially in mammalian milk, important in providing resistance to certain infections. *Lactoferrin . . . deprives certain bacteria, most often staphylococcus and E. coli, of the iron they need to survive.* NY Times Magazine 7/8/79, p42 [**1973**, from lacto- milk + Latin *ferrum* iron + English *-in* (chemical suffix)]

lacto-ovo-vegetarian, *n.* another name for OVO-LACTARIAN. *Technically, I'm a lacto-ovo-vegetarian, which means that I eat milk products and eggs as well as vegetables. A stricter vegetarian is called a vegan.* New Yorker 3/17/75, p32 [**1952, 1975**, from lacto- milk + ovo- egg + *vegetarian*]

ladder polymer, a high-temperature polymer consisting of two molecular chains which are intermittently linked like the two sides of a ladder. *The use of conventional straight-chain polymers seems to be restricted by an upper temperature limit of about 550°C, but the ladder polymers (so-called because of their integral cross-linked structure) offer more exciting possibilities.* New Scientist and Science Journal 6/24/71, p761 [**1971**]

laddertron, *n.* an electrostatic generator (for accelerating charged particles) consisting of a ladderlike series of metal rungs separated by plastic insulating material to form a current-carrying belt. *The laddertron . . . has a much greater current carrying capacity than either the conventional belt or the pelletron and has the advantage of greater mechanical rigidity.* Nature 5/26/72, p192 [**1972**, from ladder + -tron (accelerating) device, as in *cyclotron, bevatron*]

Laetrile (ˈleiəˌtril), *n.* the trademark for an anticancer drug obtained by hydrolyzing amygdalin (a compound derived from almonds, apricot pits, and other seeds) and oxidizing the resulting glycoside. It is supposed to release cyanide into the body to kill cancer cells. *Formula:* $C_{14}H_{15}NO_7$ Often spelled **laetrile**. Also called VITAMIN B₁₇. *We drive up a dusty sidestreet to a makeshift former warehouse which houses the Cytopharmaca factory, where primitive equipment and a handful of lethargic Mexicans in lab coats grind the small brown apricot kernels imported from U.S. canning factories into a fine white, cyanide-rich powder that emerges, several steps later, as the yellow tablets and pale serum known as Laetrile.* Maclean's

1/76, p23 *The notion of using Laetrile as a cancer drug got its first major impetus in the United States in 1920 when Ernst T. Krebs Sr., a California physician, tried apricot pits as a cancer treatment. Laetrile received another big shove in 1952 when Ernst T. Krebs Jr., a biochemist, developed a purified form of Laetrile for injection.* Science News 8/6/77, p92 *Doctors at the Massachusetts General Hospital . . . testified that a child named Chad Green showed signs of cyanide poisoning as a result of oral Laetrile treatments given him by his parents.* Science 2/9/79, p528 [**1949, 1968**, from *l*-mandelonitrile, the chemical name of the compound, from levorotatory + German *Mandel* almond + connecting -o- + English nitrile] —**Laetrilist**, *n.*: *If, say the Laetrilists, the pancreas fails in its mission, these cells scatter throughout the body . . . and this, they say, is the basis of cancer.* NY Times Magazine 11/27/77, p48 ▶Although patented by a British firm in 1958 and banned by the U.S. Food and Drug Administration from importation and interstate shipment and sale since 1963, Laetrile's sudden popularity in the 1970's stirred controversy over whether patients' rights to select their own treatment should override the government's efforts to protect its citizens from treatment whose claims of medical effectiveness, either as a cure or a preventive, remain unproved. The U.S. Surgeon General has also warned that the drug's high concentration of cyanide may be lethal.

Laffer curve, *Economics.* a curve showing a correlation between tax rates and economic activity. See the quotation for details. *The "Laffer curve" . . . is a simple parabola, drawn to demonstrate that if the tax rate were 100 per cent, revenues would be zero. If the tax rate were zero, revenues would be zero. As tax rate rises, so does revenue—up to a point where tax evasion builds up, people prefer leisure and unemployment to work, and the growth of output slows down.* Manchester Guardian Weekly 7/30/78, p4 [**1978**, named after Arthur Laffer, born 1940, an American economist who devised this curve]

Lagrangian point (ləˈgreindʒiːən), *Astronomy.* a location between heavenly bodies where centrifugal force neutralizes gravitational force so that an object in that location remains stationary. Also called LIBRATION POINT. See SPACE COLONY. *Back in 1772 the astronomer Joseph Louis Lagrange showed that in those places any object remained stationary with respect to the moon. As the moon moved about the earth, any object in either of those places would also move about the earth in such a way as to keep perfect step with the moon. The connecting gravities of earth and the moon would keep it where it was . . . The two places ideally are regions in space and are called "Lagrangian points."* Saturday Review 6/28/75, p12 [**1962**, named after Joseph Louis Lagrange, 1736-1813, the French mathematician and astronomer who postulated the existence of such points]

laid-back or **laidback**, *adj. Slang.* calm, cool, and relaxed; nonchalant. See LAY. *Yates' tenacity in a fight might come as a surprise to those whose judgment is based on his apparent laidback manner.* Chicago Sun Times 10/3/76 (page not known) *Of all the clichés about west coast living . . . the most offensive is that life out here is "laid back," as if even the most aspiring members of the artistic community are sitting around waiting for someone to peel them a grape while the real hustlers are back east getting things done.* Maclean's 1/9/78, p62 *Sharks, the ad tells us, are "built for destruction," but then so is the barnacle in a laid-back sort of way.* New Scientist 11/2/78, p377 [**1969**, perhaps originally in allusion to the posture of riders on motorcycles fitted with a long seat and a backrest]

Laingian ('læŋiːən), *adj.* of or having to do with the theory that mental illnesses are understandable as natural and often therapeutic responses to stress in family and other social situations. See ANTIPSYCHIATRY. *She* [Doris Lessing] *began in that novel to explore the theme of non-verbal consciousness: the now-familiar Laingian argument that language is the first and strongest of the prison-houses with which our civilisation enslaves the free self.* Listener 5/10/73, p623 —*n.* an adherent or follower of Laing's theories and therapeutic methods. . . . *although I find Dr. Redler's reluctance to bare "innermost feelings" both admirable and utterly unique among Laing's followers, I remain in my "arrogance" (suspicion would have been a better word, but Laingians are wretchedly imprecise in their use of the language), more than a little dubious.* Harper's 7/71, p10 [**1967** for adj.; **1971** for noun, from R.D. *Laing,* born 1927, Scottish psychiatrist, who formulated the theory]

Lakoda (lə'koudə), *n.* a shorn fur-seal skin resembling glossy suede. *A midicoat of Lakoda in its natural caramel uses black beaver for the collar and cuffs, the hem, and the edging of the deep slits that go up the sides to the hips* . . . New Yorker 11/8/69, p179 [**1961,** from the name of an area on the Pribilof Islands in the Bering Sea, where the skin is obtained]

Lamaze (lə'mɑːz), *adj.* of or relating to a form of painless childbirth obtained through psychoprophylaxis. Compare LEBOYER. *The method is known as . . . the Lamaze Method of "natural" childbirth . . . The mother is given little or no anesthetic and relies on her knowledge of the psychology of childbirth and of specially developed breathing rhythms and relaxing techniques to make the delivery easier.* Encyclopedia Science Supplement (Grolier) 1971, p265 [**1965,** named after Fernand *Lamaze,* a French obstetrician who developed this form of childbirth in the 1950's from Pavlov's studies of the conditioned reflex]

lambda, *n.* a virus which infects the bacterium Escherichia coli, important for its ability to incorporate the E. coli genes into its own system and transfer them to the cells of other organisms (often used attributively). See LAMBDOLOGY. *In particular, lambda has played a crucial role in our understanding of how genes are controlled at the molecular level, and of the events that lead up to copying out of these genes (in the form of messenger RNA) in the process of transcription.* New Scientist 6/29/72, p727 [**1965,** from the Greek letter λ, perhaps because of a resemblance in shape]

lambdology, *n.* the study of the virus lambda. *"Lambdology" has long remained an esoteric science. The book attempts to make it accessible to all biologists. This is a very welcome effort, since the results and concepts emanating from the study of phage lambda will undoubtedly find applications in a variety of other fields; they already inspire the thoughts of those who study genetic recombination, DNA replication, cell differentiation, morphogenesis, and the transformation of animal cells by oncogenic viruses.* Science 2/11/72, p617 [**1972,** from LAMBDA + -*ology* study of] —**lambdologist,** *n.: Lambdologists . . . have laid bare in extraordinary and fascinating detail the complicated biology of bacteriophage lambda.* Nature 1/14/72, p82

lame, *adj. U.S. Slang.* not up to date; unsophisticated; naive. *Anyone who does not know that he* [Mark Lindsay] *is the positively super-fab lead singer of Paul Revere and the Raiders is obviously lame . . . or perhaps just over 25 and into the twilight of life.* Time 6/2/67, p26 [**1959**]

LAN, abbreviation for LOCAL AREA NETWORK. *By the middle of the 90s, today's local area networks (LANs) will have become much faster, far more flexible, considerably easier to use, and much more central to the way we work.* MicroAge 4/2/89, p4 [**1988**]

land art, another name for EARTH ART. *Richard Long . . . is part of a movement called Land Art, in which artists have returned to wildernesses and ancient places. He may simply rearrange natural elements in situ.* Sunday Times Magazine (London) 5/30/82, p45 [**1970**]

lander, *n.* a space satellite or vehicle designed for landing instead of orbiting. Also called LANDING VEHICLE. Compare

SOFT-LANDER. *The Mars 3 lander also took to the surface instruments for measuring atmospheric temperature and pressure, for mass-spectrometric determination of the chemical composition of the atmosphere, for measuring wind velocities and for determining the chemical composition and physical and mechanical properties of the surface layer.* Science News 12/25/71, p422 [**1961**]

landing vehicle, another name for LANDER. *The most impressive signal was produced by the impact of the spent upper stage of the Apollo 12 landing vehicle.* Science Journal 3/70, p83 [**1969**]

Landsat ('lænd,sæt), *n.* a United States artificial satellite designed to gather data about the earth's natural resources; an EARTH RESOURCES SATELLITE. *Landsats . . . make fast, accurate and cheap surveys of forests and crops . . . Landsats have located deposits of copper, chromium and manganese as well as new sites for tuna and shrimp fishing.* NY Times 2/5/78, pD18 [**1975,** from *Land* sa*tellite*] ▶Formerly called ERTS, this type of satellite was renamed *Landsat* in 1975.

land-to-land, *adj.* launched from the ground at a target on the ground. Compare GROUND-TO-GROUND. *The Jordanian Ambassador alleged that in the attack on the town and neighbouring villages Israel used land-to-land rockets for the first time.* Manchester Guardian Weekly 6/6/68, p3 [**1965**]▶The term is used in contrast to *air-to-air, air-to-ground, surface-to-surface,* and similar collocations.

Langmuir probe, a device to measure plasma density by calculating the potential of electric discharge along a probe in a plasma-filled tube. *The oscilloscope traces represent the signals picked up by a Langmuir probe, a small wire used to detect the local value of the plasma density or the electric potential.* Scientific American 7/67, p81 [**1963,** named after Irving *Langmuir,* 1881-1957, an American chemist]

language, *n.* short for COMPUTER LANGUAGE. *NEAT/3, a language with built-in simplicity, incorporates simple English instructions with powerful tools that enable the computer to generate its own program.* Scientific American 4/68, p149 [**1956**]

language laboratory, typically, a room or rooms equipped with interconnected tape recorders having one permanent master track and one erasable student track for receiving language instruction. *Recent developments in the use of the language laboratory for programmed learning and practice drills have made possible the more efficient use of the teaching resources of the school* . . . Times (London) 1/16/67, pII [**1931, 1963**]

language planning, the formulation and implementation of a program to standardize a language, as by choosing between alternative forms, dropping archaisms, etc., or to control language development, as by recommending new usage and meanings, or to promote use of a language or dialect, as by selecting among dialects for different purposes (such as in religion, education, law courts, etc.) or selecting a standard dialect. *Language planning . . . has its own built-in dialectic between goals such as modernization, unification, and tradition; every decision involves a compromise.* Times Literary Supplement 7/7/72, p773 *There is an unwritten and unspoken assumption that with the advent of cultural pluralism, many of the abuses against minorities would vanish . . . Unfortunately, studies of language planning in other countries clearly demonstrate that the issue is not merely one of a policy of language change, but also a conscious shift in the power structure.* Word 4/78, p50 [**1968;** see *Introduction to a Theory of Language Planning* (1968), by V. Tauli]

language universal, any linguistic feature that is found in all natural languages. Also called LINGUISTIC UNIVERSAL. *The child is limited by his innate linguistic endowment, the inborn sense of abilities which are reflected in language universals and which are common to all children speaking all languages in all cultures.* Listener 12/2/71, p760 [**1966;** see *Language Universals with Special Reference to Feature Hierarchies* (1966), by J.H. Greenberg]

Lantian Man ('læn'tyæn). See the quotation for the meaning. *The Lantian Man from Shensi Province, discovered in 1964 in south central China, is earlier* [than Peking Man], *possibly dating from 500,000-600,000 years ago, and also more like Java Man in form.* 1968 Collier's Encyclopedia Year Book, p48 [**1964**, revised spelling of earlier *Lantien Man*, named for the county of *Lantien*, in Shensi province, China, where its fossil remains were discovered]

lapidescent (ˌlæpəˈdesənt), *adj.* resembling a stone, especially a stone monument; stonelike. *He* [Thomas Hudson, a character in Hemingway's book] *is curiously apart, a lapidescent presence, half man, half monument, adored but unapproachable, given to periods of almost hieratic muteness and immobility.* Times (London) 10/12/70, p6 [**1970**, from Latin *lapidēscentem*, present participle of *lapidēscere* to become stony. Compare *lapidescent, adj.* in the OED, meaning "having a tendency to solidify into stone," with citations from 1644 through 1811.]

laptop, *n.* **1** a portable computer. *Often weighing in at less than 15 pounds, the new laptops . . . often come equipped with the same memory as desktop machines.* NY Times 4/12/87, p6 **2** Attributive use: *Laptop computers continue to offer shoppers the most diverse hardware choices.* Gannett Westchester Newspapers 4/26/87, p2 [**1985**, patterned after *desktop*]

large-scale integration, a miniaturization technique for fabricating a hundred or more integrated circuits as a unit on a chip of silicon. *Abbreviation:* LSI *An extension of the integrated circuit is seen in the developing technology of large-scale integration—LSI. Instead of components being tied together, as in an integrated circuit, complete circuits will be wired together on a chip into a piece of equipment such as a communications subsystem or a computer.* Encyclopedia Science Supplement (Grolier) 1967, p331 [**1966**]

large-statured, *adj.* consisting of relatively tall trees and shrubs. *Large-statured forests (moist forests of the Temperate Zone, where nutrients are abundant, and certain tropical rain forest) have a net productivity* [of solar energy fixed by green plants] *ranging up to several thousand grams per square meter per year.* Scientific American 9/70, p70 [**1970**]

lasable, *adj.* capable of being lased. *His scheme is to introduce into the room traces of a "lasable" gas chosen so that its excitation-frequency lies in the invisible ultraviolet, and its emission frequency in the visible.* New Scientist 11/17/66, p369 [**1966**]

lase (leiz), *v.i.* to emit the intense light beam of a laser. *Many lasers, as I have described, are excited (or "pumped," as we say in the laboratory) by light. Others may be made to lase by radio waves, or by an electric current, or by chemical reactions.* National Geographic Magazine 12/66, p864 —*v.t.* to subject to laser light beams. Compare MASE. . . . *bean sprouts appeared at the soil surface seven days after planting in the lased samples and nine days in the control sample.* New Scientist 2/5/70, p261 [**1962**] ▶ Derived by back formation from LASER. The following early quotation describes this development. *Everybody is his own etymologist, and almost overnight the acronym LASER becomes the noun laser and, finally, the verb to lase.* Bulletin of the Atomic Scientists 11/63, p16

laser ('leizər), *n.* any device that emits a very narrow and intense beam of coherent light or other radiation of a single wavelength either continuously or in pulses. A laser uses light to stimulate the emission of more light by excited atoms, molecules, or other physical systems. Its light may be used to cut or melt hard materials, remove diseased tissue, transmit signals, etc. (often used attributively). *Lasers provide extremely intense sources of energy at virtually any desired wavelength in the ultraviolet, visible, infrared, or microwave regions of the spectrum.* Scientific American 5/79, p114 [**1960**, acronym formed from *l*ight *a*mplification by *s*timulated *e*mission of *r*adiation; patterned after earlier *maser* (1955)]

laser bomb, **1** a bomb with nonnuclear explosives, released by an aircraft and guided to its target by laser beams. *Those laser bombs, according to the protesters, have since caused havoc to the dike systems of North Vietnam, thus endangering the lives of thousands of peasants when the monsoon season brings* flooding. New Scientist 9/28/72, p590 **2** a hydrogen bomb detonated by a laser beam. *A "laser bomb" would be an H-bomb in which the intense heat of a laser beam—perhaps the most powerful and concentrated form of light in the universe—would be used to trigger the hydrogen explosives, instead of the A-bomb trigger now required.* Sunday Post-Herald (Hongkong) 6/24/73, p7 [**1970**; earlier (1967) *laser-guided bomb*]

laser cane, a walking stick that emits infrared laser light which is reflected by surrounding objects and received as tones in a light-sensitive device to help blind people detect obstacles. *Laser canes provide an optical echo at three vertical angles, warning the blind user of objects overhead and at his feet, as well as straight ahead. The laser cane communicates its information by both tones and touch.* World Book Science Annual 1976, p73 [**1975**]

laser card, **1** a small plastic card that has information stored on it to be read by a laser. *Subscribers will receive a laser card on which several hundred pages of . . . text are recorded, in place of the conventional printed paper. The card will be slotted into a personal reader and the pages will appear on a television screen.* Financial Times 12/24/84, p4 **2** LaserCard. a trademark for such a card. *Matsushita, one of Japan's largest manufacturers, has licensed Drexler's LaserCard. The LaserCard stores 2 megabytes of information on a credit-card-size optical strip.* Byte 12/84, p10 [**1981**]

laser disc, another name for OPTICAL DISK. *Todays videodiscs differ radically . . . from one another. The most sophisticated is the optical disc, or laser disc. The player for optical discs is the first home product to incorporate a laser.* World Book Science Annual 1983, p131 [**1980**]

laser fusion, nuclear fusion induced by high-energy pulses of radiation from a laser. See LAWSON CRITERION. *The laser fusion concept, on the other hand, eliminates the whole problem of magnetic containment. A pellet of frozen hydrogen is dropped into a relatively simple round vessel made of metal alloys. This vessel, as first designed, is filled with molten lithium to absorb heat. Midway in its descent the pellet is hit by a short, powerful pulse of laser light through a porthole in the sphere. The burst of energy instantly sets off a small thermonuclear reaction.* Fortune 5/74 (page not known) [**1972**]

laser gyro, a gyroscope having a ring of laser light instead of a wheel to indicate change in direction, used especially in guidance systems for space flight. *Britain claims world-class skills in laser gyros and logic array chips.* U.S. News & World Report 5/27/85, p45 [**1975**]

laser memory, a computer memory that retrieves information by a scanning laser beam. *The first laser memories were of the block-oriented variety; thus they were quite slow (requiring many milliseconds) in locating a block but then could read a block of 150,000 bits extremely quickly, about three bits every microsecond.* 1976 Britannica Yearbook of Science and the Future, p321 [**1975**]

laser printer, a device that prints words, diagrams, and other material from a computer by projecting an image of electronic impulses generated by a laser and reproduces copies similar to those made by a photocopying machine, used especially in desktop publishing. *The laser printer places a nearly professional-quality printing plant in the hands of an individual.* NY Times 9/3/85, pC4 [**1979**] —**laser-printed**, *adj.: Once the page is finished, it is printed on a laser printer. In quality, the laser-printed page rivals the output of expensive typesetting machines, and it can be used as "camera-ready" copy for an offset printing press.* Encyclopedia Science Supplement (Grolier) 1987, p101

laser ranging, a method for determining precise distances by measuring the time it takes a pulse of laser light to return from an object. *Lageos* [Laser Geodynamic Satellite] *has its* raison d'être *the experimental assessment of the possibilities of laser ranging in studies of movements of the Earth's crust and its poles. It may also serve for measuring solid Earth tides and, as a necessary adjunct of accurate plate movement determinations, the more precise fixing of reference points on the world's* *land-masses.* New Scientist 6/3/76, p525 **[1968]** —**laser ranger:** *The "laser ranger," a very precise surveying instrument, is another application. It is really laser radar and is sometimes called lidar.* World Book Science Annual 1974, p204

laser surgery, the destruction of living cells by the beam of a laser. . . . *a multi-disciplined team of surgeons, physicists, engineers and technicians is required if laser surgery is to be conducted effectively and safely.* New Scientist 7/27/67, p190 **[1967]**

LASH or **lash,** *n.* a system of shipping in which barges loaded with cargo are placed on board the ship directly instead of being unloaded (often used attributively). *With the inauguration of a new route, a special containerization method called LASH has crossed from Europe to America. LASH stands for Lighter Aboard Ship; lighter refers to a 380-ton, 61-foot-long barge, which carries the cargo.* Science News 5/2/70, p424 *Shipowners also hastened the introduction of combined oil-bulk carriers, . . . liquid gas carriers, and lash vessels in which laden barges are floated directly into a large hull.* Times (London) 8/12/70, p18 **[1965]**

L-asparaginase (ˌelæspəˈrædʒəˌneis), *n.* a bacterial enzyme used in inhibiting the growth of certain forms of cancer. *A new drug was added to the list of agents deterrent to, but not curative of, acute leukemia. An enzyme, L-asparaginase, seems to starve leukemic cells of certain nutrients and thereby kill them.* 1968 Collier's Encyclopedia Year Book, p354 **[1963,** from *L-asparagine* (the *L-* or levorotatory form of the amino acid asparagine) + *-ase* enzyme]

Lassa fever, a highly contagious and usually fatal virus disease believed to be transmitted by mice, first identified in 1970 in Lassa, a village in western Nigeria. *Lassa fever had already proved so deadly that one of the world's most expert virologists had fallen ill of the disease, a lab assistant and two nurses had died of it, and research with the virus had been abandoned until more exacting safety precautions could be devised.* Time 2/23/70, p42 **[1970]**

last hurrah, *U.S. and Canadian.* a final act or effort at the end of a career. *It isn't enough to dismiss Richard Daley's victory as the truly last hurrah: that phrase has been applied to him every four years, and each time he has been born again out of the phoenix flame of his presumably dead self.* NY Post 2/28/75, p37 **[1972,** originally applied to the final campaign of a veteran politician, from *The Last Hurrah,* the title of a novel (1956) about an Irish-American political boss (believed to be modeled on Mayor James M. Curley of Boston), by Edwin O'Connor, 1918-1968]

Las Vegas Night, *U.S.* a legal gambling event conducted by a nonprofit organization to raise money. *Under the regulations set up by the* [New York State] *Legislature last year, religious and charitable organizations can hold Las Vegas Nights once a month to raise money for themselves. Games are limited to blackjack, roulette, craps and other competition where players are pitted against the house. Prizes are limited to $1,000 a game a night, with top prizes of $100 for each players.* NY Times 1/30/77, p35 **[1973,** from *Las Vegas,* Nevada, famous for its gambling casinos]

lateral thinking, thinking which seeks to avoid being caught up in details in order to range as widely as possible to include all aspects of a problem or topic. . . . *there is another way. This involves 'lateral thinking' and the assumption that no existing way of doing anything is likely to be the best. This means that adequate is not the end of the search but the beginning. It is a matter of trying to do things in a different way and then seeing whether that different way offers any advantages. If not, then the exercise in flexibility is its own reward.* Science Journal 7/69, p31 **[1966]**

latifundism (ˌlætəˈfənˌdizəm), *n.* the practice or condition of holding land in large estates. *The great landholdings—the latifundia—were broken up at the time, but a new latifundism has arisen.* NY Times 7/10/67, p28 **[1967,** from American Spanish *latifundismo.* See the etymology of LATIFUNDIST.]

latifundist (ˌlætəˈfəndist), *n.* the owner of a latifundium or large estate. *It is necessary for every urban guerrilla to keep in mind always that he can only maintain his existence if he is disposed to kill the police and those dedicated to repression, and if he is determined to expropriate the wealth of the big capitalists, the latifundists and the imperialists.* Time 11/2/70, p20 **[1970,** from American Spanish *latifundista,* from Spanish *latifundio* a latifundium (large landed estate) + *-ista* -ist]

Latin Americanist, an expert in the history, institutions, and other cultural elements of Latin America. *Professor Hale . . . shows an acquaintance with European political thought rare among United States Latin Americanists.* Times Literary Supplement 12/8/72, p1503 **[1972]**

Latin rock. See the quotation for the meaning. *This quintet, spearheaded by two sharp-voiced girls . . . from Ipanema could begin a rush to what's been called Latin rock—a striking compound of bossa nova, rock and jazz.* Sunday Times (London) 1/19/69, p58 **[1969]**

laugher, *n. U.S. and Canadian Slang.* a game so absurdly one-sided as to be laughably easy to win. *The game was a laugher, 8-0 jets. The level of play was often closer to senior amateur than to NHL* [National Hockey League] *professional.* Maclean's 3/73, p56 **[1963]►**Originally restricted to baseball games.

laugh-in, *n.* a situation or event marked by hilarity, often one staged for this purpose. . . . *students at Cambridge proposed to organise a "laugh-in." The idea, apparently, was that the participants in the demonstration should disperse themselves in various parts of the hall, and then, in the course of Mr Healey's speech, first one and then another would burst into peals of laughter.* Manchester Guardian Weekly 3/21/68, p6 **[1968;** see -IN]

laugh line, a wrinkle at the outer corner of the eye supposedly formed from habitual smiling or laughing. *We sat next to Ralph Brasco, a rangy man with plenty of laugh lines around his eyes, who has been with the Department of Sanitation for ten years.* New Yorker 8/15/70, p20 **[1968]**

laugh track, a recording of audience laughter added to a sound track, especially of a previously filmed television show. *"That 'laugh track' was the most deplorable thing I ever heard in my life," says Mr. Quine. "It was even laughing on the straight lines!"* NY Times 11/20/66, pB19 **[1955]**

launching pad, a place from which something starts; springboard. *Then came the Kennedys, John burst onto the political scene using vast sums of money, clever-exploitation of television, cadres of advance men, personality-projection techniques, and the launching pad of Presidential primaries.* Saturday Review 11/2/68, p20 **[1959,** figurative sense of the term for a rocket- or missile-launching platform (1951)]

launch vehicle, a rocket used to propel a spacecraft, artificial satellite, etc., into an orbit or trajectory. *The earliest launch vehicles were derived from the ballistic missiles developed by the United States and Russia after World War II.* 1970 Compton Yearbook, p556 **[1964]**

launch window, the time when astronomical conditions permit the launching of a spacecraft under the most favorable conditions. . . . *the 20-day period centered around the launch date allowing travel between planets on an orbit requiring the least amount of energy. This is the so-called "launch window" used to hurl space vehicles from earth to the moon, or to Venus or Mars.* Science News 9/3/66, p165 **[1964;** see WINDOW]

launder, *v.t.* **1** to give (money obtained illegally) the appearance of being lawfully gained, usually by channeling it through a respectable enterprise. See MONEY-WASHING. *It was Lansky who developed the worldwide network of couriers, middlemen, bankers, and frontmen that allows the underworld to take profits from illegal enterprises, to send them halfway around the world and then have the money come back laundered clean to be invested in legitimate businesses.* Atlantic 7/70, p65 **2** to make (any illegal commodity, etc.) seem lawfully obtained; give (something) the appearance of being acceptable. *Some authorities suspect that much of the food Havana is now importing* *from other countries actually is U.S.-grown and has been "laundered" by international traders before being shipped to Cuba.* Parade 9/26/76, p9 **3** to remove any blemish from; clear of faults; whitewash; sanitize. *But now, after a year in Nowheresville, Bourne has been laundered—and born again.* Maclean's 5/7/79, p39 [**1970,** from the idea of "cleansing" "dirty" money] ►**Launder,** def. 1 became current during the 1972-74 investigations into the Watergate scandal, in connection with funds contributed to the Nixon campaign that were deposited in a Mexican bank and then used to finance various illegal campaign activities.

laundry, *n.* a place, usually in a foreign country, where money from an illegal source is laundered. *For no flourishing power block will tamely submit to a sudden and arbitrary exclusion from influence. It will resort to the Mexican laundries and to other roundabout routes, preferably within the law but, well, if it can't be done legally . . .* National Review 1/18/74, p77 [**1974**] ►*Laundermat* was used in this sense in 1969: *On a more complex level, Wall Street crime involves the use of secret foreign bank accounts and other financial gimmicks to defraud the U.S. Government and to provide a convenient "laundermat" for organized crime in "bleaching" illegal profits from narcotics and gambling. Thus cleansed the money can be reinvested in legitimate businesses.* Newsweek 12/15/69, p90

laundry list, *Chiefly U.S.* a detailed and usually long list of a variety of items. *Four brief paragraphs . . . describe the President's proposed welfare reforms and revenue-sharing program, as well as a laundry list of social concerns (health, education, housing, transportation, equal voting rights, etc.).* NY Times 2/3/70, p42 [**1958,** so called from the practice of keeping an itemized list of the items sent to a commercial laundry]

lavalier or **lavaliere** (ˌlævəˈlir), *n.* a very small microphone hung around the neck or clipped to the clothing of the user (also used attributively). *Another kind of microphone, the* lavalier, *. . . may be in camera view, or hidden in the clothing.* 1974 World Book Year Book, p570 *A series of group sessions was held in which the speech of each member (picked up from a lavaliere microphone) was recorded on a separate track.* William Labov, Sociolinguistic Patterns 1972, p210 [**1960,** extended sense of the term (1950's) for a pendant hung from a chain worn around the neck, ultimately from the name of the Duchess of *La Vallière,* mistress of Louis XIV]

Lawson criterion, *Physics.* **1** the requirement that for a nuclear fusion reaction to yield a gain in energy the product of the confinement time of plasma (highly ionized gas), measured in seconds, and the density of the plasma, measured in ions per cubic centimeter, must exceed a certain number, usually 10^{14}. *The fundamental criterion for a successful fusion reactor is that it should confine the hot fuel long enough so that a sufficiently large fraction will react and thereby release appreciably more energy than was invested in fuel heating. This is known as Lawson's criterion.* 1973 Brittanica Yearbook of Science and the Future, p112 **2** Also called **Lawson number.** a number which indicates the gain in energy obtained in a fusion reaction. *The Lawson number, expressed in seconds per cubic centimeter, specifies the break-even condition on the assumptions that no more than a third of the energy released must be fed back to sustain the reaction.* Scientific American 6/74, p24 [**1969,** named after the British physicist J.D. *Lawson,* born 1923, who formulated it in the 1950's]

lay, *v.i.* **lay back,** *Slang.* to relax; take it easy. *A society that has no heroes will soon grow enfeebled . . . Its individual members will also be enfeebled. They will "hang loose" and "lay back" and, so mellowed out, the last thing of which they wish to hear is heroism.* Harper's 11/78, p33 *After a three-year hiatus from composing, Valdy has decreed "there'll be no more laying back."* Maclean's 1/22/79, p4 [**1978,** derived from LAID-BACK]

layered look, a fashion in clothes in which garments of various types and lengths are worn one over the other; the fashion of LAYERING. *The best season classics for women are pre-washed jeans topped by a printed T-shirt, a front-tied work shirt, wrapped head, espadrilles, wooden bangle bracelets and a pouchy canvas shoulder bag. This layered look offers the*

added option of taupe-tinted aviator sunglasses and a perfect tan. Herald Statesman (Yonkers, N.Y.) 8/21/75, p13 [**1972**]

layering, *n.* the wearing of garments of various types and lengths one over the other. *Layering, the art of piling garment upon garment, also aided a rich look. Layering savvy consisted of double blouses, multiple sweaters of varying lengths, pants under tunic dresses, jumpers over dresses, double coats (a paper-thin rain shell over a warm wool, knit, or fur version), hoods under hats, and shawls over everything.* 1976 World Book Year Book, p309 [**1971,** coined in 1950 by Bonnie Cashin, born 1915, an American fashion designer]

layperson, *n.* a person who does not belong to the clergy or to a profession or, sometimes, to any specified group; a layman or laywoman. *Hospital ethics or review committees . . . have been looked to by some laypersons as possible arbitrators of the decisions to begin or discontinue extreme efforts to maintain life.* Harper's 8/78, p29 *In a field where the layperson is typically either ignorant or misinformed, "The Tenant Survival Book" will be a serviceable handbook for the curious and the convinced alike.* NY Times Book Review 11/19/72, p48 [**1972;** see -PERSON]

Lazy Dog, *U.S. Military Slang.* a type of bomb that explodes in midair and scatters steel pellets at high speed on the target area. *". . . Tomorrow, we'll get three divisions in here, four, we'll get two hundred B-52s, we'll get ground-to-grounds, and whole batteries of Lazy Dogs, we'll get nuclear . . ."* Punch 2/21/68, p258 *The Lazy Dog is an advanced antipersonnel weapon introduced last spring.* New York Times 1/13/67, p8 [**1965**]

LBO, abbreviation of LEVERAGED BUYOUT. *Though LBOs represent only 4 percent of Milken's high-yield financing, they inevitably make the newspaper headlines.* Insight 6/12/89, p10 [**1989**]

LCD, abbreviation of *liquid crystal diode* or *display,* a device in which a transparent liquid turns opaque when an electric current is passed through it, used to obtain dark numbers on a light field in digital watches, calculators, etc. Compare LED. *The second advice I would give, despite arguments to the contrary from many experts, is that you should buy LCD models. The letters stand for Liquid Crystal Display and that means that you have a continuous display of hours and minutes or, where relevant, date, month and seconds.* Times (London) 5/14/77, p23 [**1973**]

LD, abbreviation of LEARNING-DISABLED. *The LD youngsters, although of average or better than average intellectual level, had either failed a grade or were near failure and were about two years behind controls in oral reading achievement.* Science News 12/10/77, p389 [**1977**]

L.D.C., abbreviation of *less developed country. But if OPEC has made life uncomfortable for Americans, its effect on the world's poor countries has been much more painful. For some of these nations—known in the accepted jargon as less-developed countries, or LDCs—the price increase for fuel has been a severe problem. For others it has been a catastrophe.* New Republic 6/16/79, p5 [**1967**]

LDL, abbreviation for *low-density lipoprotein,* a lipoprotein containing more lipids than protein, thought to carry cholesterol from the liver to various tissues. Compare HDL and VLDL. *Cholesterol destined for delivery to the body tissues circulates in a package termed LDL, or low-density lipoprotein (high levels of which are correlated with heart disease).* New Scientist 3/16/78, p730 [**1976**]

lead-free, *adj.* another word for NONLEADED. *True or false: lead-free gasoline is the best thing to come down the freeway since the V-8 engine. True, according to the oil companies that recently switched to unleaded or low-lead fuels and are promoting them as an antipollution measure. False, from the viewpoint of the Ethyl Corp., the nation's largest producer of lead additives for gasoline.* Time 9/14/70, p51 *Two British oil companies and the American Gulf yesterday said they were* *ready to market a lead-free petrol in the United Kingdom.* Times (London) 3/9/70, p1 **[1970]**

leading indicators, *U.S.* a list of selected stock prices or other indicators of business activity that usually show trends in the national economy. *As Miller told* TIME *Washington Economic Correspondent George Taber: "The economy is slowing. The leading indicators are down. I see housing starts down in the first quarter compared with the first quarter of last year."* Time 4/30/79, p70 **[1963]**

leadless, *adj.* another word for NONLEADED. . . . *oil companies have begun to market leadless gas.* Encyclopedia Science Supplement (Grolier) 1970, p159 **[1970]**

leaflet, *v.i.* to distribute leaflets. *Leafletting on New York's Lower East Side for ten years would not reach the housewife in Escanaba, Mich. but thirty seconds on the six o'clock news would.* NY Times 12/22/70, p33 **[1962,** verb use of the noun]

leafleteer, *n.* a person who hands out leaflets. *When I left the plant there were leafleteers at the gate distributing* Workers' Power. Harper's 6/72, p69 **[1970,** from *leaflet, v.i.,* to distribute leaflets (1962) + *-eer* one connected with] ►*Leafleteer* in the sense of "a writer of leaflets" is found in the late 1800's.

league table, *British.* a tabulated comparison of performance in any field. *It is possible to make a league table of top jobs now and see whether specializations contribute directly to incomes, using the quarterly salary survey tables of the* Cornmarket Careers Register. Times (London) 6/24/68, p26 **[1959,** so called from the tables of performance records of athletic or sports associations]

leakproof, *adj. U.S.* protected or secure against the disclosure of secret or confidential information. *The President . . . continues to urge that the six leaky congressional committees dealing with intelligence be consolidated into one leakproof joint committee.* Time 3/1/76, p11 **[1976,** figurative extension of *leakproof* (OEDS 1926); influenced by *leak* disclosure of secret information]

leaky, *adj.* not secure against disclosure of secret or confidential information. *IBM's Operating System for Multiprogramming with a Variable number of Tasks (OS/MVT) does not prevent unauthorised reading of files when used on certain computers. The system is used widely, but is commonly known to be leaky and is being replaced increasingly by other IBM operating systems which provide better security.* New Scientist 6/16/77, p626 **[1976,** figurative extension of *leaky* (OED 1606); influenced by *leak* disclosure of secret information]

lean, *v.* **lean on**, *Informal.* to put pressure or coercion on (someone). *Disappointed when he did not earn a higher position in the Nixon Administration, he said: . . . "When things are going great they ignore me, but when things get screwed up, they lean on me."* Time 3/11/74, p13 *"Otherwise, building societies must equally be free to enter the money market for credit and offer and charge competitive interest rates without being leaned on by the Government as we have in the past," he* [Leonard Boyle] *said.* Manchester Guardian Weekly 9/1/73, p8 **[1965]**

leap second, a second of time as measured by an atomic clock, that is added or omitted each year by international agreement to compensate for changes in the earth's rotation. See UNIVERSAL COORDINATED TIME. *In the new regime, the adjustment will be made by inserting a whole second called a leap second when this becomes necessary.* Times (London) 1/4/72, p11 **[1971,** patterned on *leap year*].

learning curve, a representation of the progress shown in acquiring adeptness or practical experience in a field. *The airline that will be first with the most 747s, and thus must cope with every one of the bumps in what airmen call a new plane's "learning curve," is Pan American.* Time 1/19/70, p40 **[1967]**►Originally a term in psychology (1922), *learning curve* was broadened in application in the 1960's.

learning disability, a condition associated with the nervous system which interferes with mastery of a skill such as reading and calculation with numbers. *With widespread confusion and un-* *certainty surrounding both the causes and effects of various types of learning disabilities, it is not surprising that a wide variety of terms has been applied to the condition. A recent Government report found 38 different names in common use, including minimal brain damage or dysfunction, psychoneurological inefficiency, cerebral dysfunction, neurological handicap, perceptual handicaps, communication disorder and association deficit pathology. A number of more specific terms are also in common use: dyslexia (inability to read), dysgraphia (inability to write), dyscalculia (inability to manipulate numbers) and developmental aphasia (inability to receive or express spoken words).* NY Times Magazine 3/2/75, p15 **[1960,** patterned after *reading disability* (1930's)]

learning-disabled, *adj.* having a learning disability. *Abbreviation:* LD *Only the special-education teachers know which children have been designated as moderately retarded, emotionally impaired or learning disabled.* Psychology Today 4/75, p36 **[1974]**

leash law, a law or ordinance requiring that dogs be kept on a leash in public places. *Angry residents have been demanding tougher leash laws. Some people have taken to shooting any dog, even a neighbor's innocent pet, that wanders onto their property.* Time 5/4/81, p56 **[1978]**►The term *leash-laws* is recorded in Bailey's Dictionary (1721) in the sense of laws to be observed in hunting or coursing; the sense is labeled obsolete in the OED.

leather[1], *n.* **hell-bent for leather**, as fast as possible; very fast. *General Tolson said that he had expected initial resistance to be light but that he had told his commanders to advance cautiously. "The worst trap we could get into here would be to go hell-bent for leather, thinking we've got it easy," he said.* NY Times 4/4/68, p19 **[1959]** ► Reference is made to this phrase in Harold Wentworth's *American Dialect Dictionary* (1944) as a variant for *hell for leather,* for which it supplies citations from several sources. The *ADD* gives for *hell-bent for leather* the date 1919 and locates it in western Massachusetts. However, the earliest quotation in our files is from a British source ("Perhaps it is no wonder that so many of us are hell-bent for leather." Sunday Times (London) 4/12/59, p19) and we have confirmed its current use among both American and British speakers.

leather[2], *adj.* of, having to do with, or frequented by homosexuals who project a tough masculine image. *David Scott endorsed her candidacy . . . after that, he took her to gay leather bars and campaigned vigorously with her.* New Yorker 7/28/86, p47 **[1972;** so called from their customary leather outfits]

leatherjacket, *n.* a person wearing a leather jacket, especially such a person belonging to a gang of toughs, delinquents, etc. *. . . the leatherjackets stare listlessly ahead dreaming of their Utopian England taken over by strip-cartoon sadists.* Times (London) 5/5/72, p9 **[1959]**

Leavisite ('li:vǝ,sait), *n.* a follower or supporter of the English literary critic Frank Raymond Leavis, 1895-1978, noted for his controversial attacks on contemporary literary values. *. . . in his memoirs, he* [a Cambridge ex-professor] *makes his historical reference to the notorious nuisance the "Leavisites" were in his time.* Times (London) 4/28/70, p11 **[1962]** —*adj.* of Leavis or the Leavisites. *They* [followers of Leavis] *argue that in the era of the breakdown of values, and in the absence of religion, our only connection with the past of the "organic community" is through the English books of the Great Tradition, as chosen by the Leavisite priesthood.* Saturday Review 3/12/66, p21 **[1958]**

Leboyer (lǝbɔ:'yei; *Anglicized* lǝ'bɔiǝr), *adj.* of or relating to a method of childbirth that is as painless as possible for the newborn by avoiding the use of forceps, using a quiet, dimly lit room for delivery, and placing the infant in a warm bath upon birth. Compare LAMAZE. See also ALTERNATIVE BIRTHING. *If additional follow-up studies continue to show beneficial effects for children born the Leboyer way, it seems likely that nonviolent delivery may become an accepted way of birth.* Science News 1/22/77, p59 *She hopes to avoid birth trauma for William by using the Leboyer method—low lights, soft music* nd a bath of water at 101 degrees. Sunday Times (London) /4/82, p14 [**1976**, named for Frederick *Leboyer*, a French obstetrician who presented his ideas to *Birth Without Violence* ᴸ975)]

ᴇch, *adj.* lecherous. *The question can be taken or left for what* ᵗ *is as long as Friedman sticks to the mimicry of detective-story* ᵗ*ialogue, journalism clichés, police-blotter prose, and the series* ᶠ *burlesque lech-skits that give* The Dick *its basic shape.* Time /7/70, p62 [**1964**, adjective use of the noun meaning lechery ᴸ830) and a lecher (1943)]

ᴇching, *adj.* given to lechery; dissolute. *He* [Whittaker Chambers] *felt guilty for his painful birth, guilty for his "hatred"* ᵗ*f his parents, and guilty for his love of his brother Richard,* ᵗ *wild, leching lad who committed suicide at 22.* Time /10/67, p66 [**1963**, from present participle of *lech* to be a ᵉcher, behave lustfully (OEDS 1911), verb use of the noun]

ᴸED, abbreviation of ʟɪɢʜᴛ-ᴇᴍɪᴛᴛɪɴɢ ᴅɪᴏᴅᴇ. Compare ʟᴄᴅ. ᴸED's are most often used in small sizes, which mates them ᵂell to small portable devices such as pocket calculators. Scienᵗific American 6/73, p72 [**1968**]

ᴇft-brain, *n.* the left hemisphere of the brain (often used attribᴸtively). *The brain's two large cerebral hemispheres . . . are* ᴺow commonly known as left-brain and right-brain. The reaᵗᵒn is that, once the corpus callosum has been cut, the two sides ᵗf the brain appear to possess such independent capacities and ᴺental properties that each merits a separate name.* Encycloᵖedia Science Supplement (Grolier) 1976, p50 *They conclude ᴸhat while alcohol can affect left-brain functions, such as ᵖeech and language, such disruptions did not show up using ᴸhe amount of alcohol employed in their study.* Science News ᴸ/30/77, p281 [**1976**, perhaps abstracted from *left-brained* ᴼEDS 1890)]

ᴇftfield, *n. U.S.* a position outside the center of action; the sideᴸines. *Ambitious sons of famous fathers are hardly unique in ᵖolitics. With personality continuing to outweigh party loyalty ᴸs a political asset, an increasing number of candidates are ᵉmerging from leftfield to give voters surprising options.* Time ᴸ/9/70, p14 [**1959**, figurative sense of the baseball term (usualᴸy spelled *left field*); from the fact that the left field is far off ʳom the home base]

ᴇghemoglobin (ˈlegˌhiːməˈgloubən), *n.* the oxygen-carrying pigᴹent in legumes, essential for symbiosis with nitrogen-fixing ᵇacteria. *There is now evidence that the enigmatic leghemogloᵇin in Azotobacter of root nodules, which is not essential for ᴺitrogenase activity, serves to provide oxygen to the system at ᵃ very low concentration.* McGraw-Hill Yearbook of Science ᵃnd Technology 1974, p308 [**1968**, from *leg*ume + *hemoglobin* ᴸhe oxygen-carrying substance in the blood]

ᴇgionellosis (ˌliːdʒənəˈlousis), *n.* another name for ʟᴇɢɪᴏɴ-ᴺᴀɪʀᴇꜱ' ᴅɪꜱᴇᴀꜱᴇ. *Although legionellosis (also known as Leᵍionnaires' disease) affects 125,000 persons in the United States ᵃnnually, early diagnosis of this life-threatening pneumonia ᵗs not possible unless physicians take biopsy samples . . .* Sciᵉnce News 6/6/81, p358 [**1979**, from New Latin *Legionella pneumophila*), the bacterium causing the disease + *-osis*]

ᴇgionnaires' disease or **legionnaire's disease,** a serious and ꜱometimes fatal form of pneumonia characterized by high ᶠever, chills, abdominal pain, and lung congestion. It is caused ᵇy *Legionella pneumophila*, a previously unclassified species ᵗf small, rod-shaped, gram-negative bacteria. *From such ꜱtudies it appears that Legionnaires' disease is caused by a comᴹon bacterium present in soil or water. In four instances the ᵗrganism was discovered in air-cooling or air-conditioning ᵉquipment. The organism may be trapped in these devices, ꜱprayed as an aerosol to the surroundings, and then inhaled by ᵃ susceptible individual.* New Scientist 11/30/78, p670 [**1976**, ꜱo called because the disease was first identified in an outbreak ᵃt an American Legion convention in Philadelphia in July ᴸ976]

ᴇg warmers, knitted coverings for the legs extending from the ᵃnkles to the upper thighs. *Practicality is never far from realᴸife fashion, so last chilly winter found all the trendy girls . . .*

well preserved against chilblain on the nether half. Legwarmers, accessory of every freezing dance rehearsal room, emerged as a stylish cover-up for girls who had never heard of an entrechat. Times (London) 3/30/76, p10 [**1976**]

Leidenfrost phenomenon (ˈlaidənˌfrɔːst), *Physics.* **1** a phenomenon in which a hot surface repels a liquid by generating a thin layer of insulating vapor. *You may use many common household liquids in place of water in investigating the Leidenfrost phenomenon, but first you should eliminate any that are flammable or likely to explode near an open fire or on a hot surface.* Scientific American 8/77, p129 **2** an analogous hypothetical phenomenon applied to the relationship of matter to antimatter in the boundaries where particles and antiparticles meet. *If matter and antimatter are separated, there must be boundary regions, and in these regions annihilations should occur. The annihilations should produce gamma rays that would go a long distance from their source. Neither of these effects are observed. Some astronomers invoke the so-called Leidenfrost phenomenon: A few annihilations at the border maintain a pressure that keeps large amounts of matter and antimatter apart.* Science News 3/31/73, p212 [**1967**, translation of German *Leidenfrostsche Phänomen*, named after Johann G. Leidenfrost, 1715-1794, a German physician who discovered the insulating phenomenon]

leisure suit, a suit for informal wear, consisting of an open-collar, shirtlike jacket and matching trousers. See ꜱʜɪʀᴛ-ᴊᴀᴄᴋᴇᴛ. *They posed for photographs, Mr. Badillo sober in a navy-blue suit, Mr. Hirschfeld resplendent in an open-collared leisure suit.* NY Times 8/29/77, p21 [**1972**]

LEM (lem), *n.* acronym for *lunar excursion module* (the earlier name of the ʟᴜɴᴀʀ ᴍᴏᴅᴜʟᴇ). Compare ʟᴍ. *Sitting on its four stilted and saucer-footed legs, the all-white LEM resembles a weird, buglike denizen from outer space.* World Book Science Annual 1965, p52 [**1962**]

lemon law, *U.S. Informal.* a law that requires a manufacturer or dealer to repair a defective product provided the buyer reports the defects within a specified period. *Governor Kean today signed a "lemon law" to protect buyers of defective new automobiles . . .* NY Times 6/21/83, pB1 [**1981**, from *lemon*, slang word for something (now especially a manufactured product) that turns out to be defective or worthless (originally U.S., 1909)]

lentivirus, *n.* any of a group of slow viruses that undergo frequent structural changes and cause various infectious diseases in sheep, horses, and other animals. *The AIDS virus may be closely related to animal lentiviruses.* Encyclopedia Science Supplement (Grolier) 1988, p230 [**1986**, from New Latin *Lentivirus*, the genus name, from Latin *lenticulāris* lenticular + New Latin *virus* virus]

leone (liːˈoun), *n.* the basic unit of money in Sierra Leone. *An agreement for a ten-million leone Japanese loan to Sierra Leone will be signed in two weeks time, it was exclusively confirmed in Freetown yesterday.* Daily Mail (Freetown) 11/23/79, p1 [**1964**, from Sierra *Leone*]

leopard-skin cease-fire, a cease-fire in which each side remains in control of the areas it occupies. See ʟᴇᴏᴘᴀʀᴅ ꜱᴘᴏᴛ. *Elsewhere in the country, the Communists have been maneuvering to put themselves in as advantageous a position as possible when the projected leopard-skin cease-fire occurs.* New Yorker 1/13/73, p78 [**1972**, so called from the spotty or irregular arrangement of the areas occupied, suggesting a leopard's skin]

leopard spot, any of a number of separate areas held by a military force, especially at the time of a cease-fire. *The exact number of these isolated strongpoints or clandestinely administered villages will only be known when the communist leadership emerges after the ceasefire. The Americans insist that the leopard spots are relatively few, but anticipate many claims and much flag competition in the Mekong Delta.* Times (London) 11/23/72, p8 *The war itself . . . has exacerbated the divisions between the nation's Christian and Moslem communities and the Palestinians, who, in Lebanon as refugees, became embroiled in its civil fighting. The war also has left the nation in a state of "leopard spots," de facto partition, with dif-*

ferent factions in control of noncontiguous areas. NY Times 11/14/76, pD1 [**1969**; see LEOPARD-SKIN CEASE-FIRE]

leopon ('li:ə,pɒn), *n.* the offspring of a leopard and a lioness. *The zoo is trying to mate its leopon . . . with a tiger.* Times (London) 12/16/67, p6 [**1967**, blend of *leopard* and *lion*; compare *tigon* (OEDS 1927) the offspring of a tiger and a lioness]

leptonic, *adj.* of, relating to, or belonging to the class of elementary particles (leptons) that partake of the weak interaction. *. . . the number of known leptons has remained constant at four for the last decade, while the number of known strongly interacting particles, or hadrons, has been increasing rapidly. The basic leptonic quartet consists of the muon, the electron, and the neutrinos associated with these two particles. Many experimental searches have attempted to add to this list, but without success.* Science Journal 12/70, p12 [**1957**, from *lepton* (OEDS 1948) + *-ic*]

Lesch-Nyhan syndrome ('leʃ'naihən), a genetic disorder of male children. See the quotations for details. *Lesch-Nyhan syndrome, a rare form of cerebral palsy, is such a ruinous disease. Victims of the most severe cases are mentally retarded, spastic and aggressive, and they compulsively mutilate themselves by biting their lips and fingers.* Science News 8/6/83, p90 *The lack of the IAP* [inosinic acid pyrophosphorylase] *gene in humans causes the Lesch-Nyhan syndrome, a distressing disease in children resulting in early death.* New Scientist and Science Journal 3/11/71, p532 [**1964**, named after Michael *Lesch* and William L. *Nyhan*, American physicians who first described the syndrome]

lesion, *v.t.* to cause a lesion in. *Jouvet also has a critical experiment he wants to perform. If dreams are the replay of the genetic code, they should not be affected by the environment. Earlier, he recalled that he had lesioned in cats the "brake" that prevents them from moving while they dream.* New Scientist 3/15/73, p604 [**1972**, verb use of the noun]

less developed, economically underdeveloped, especially in technology and industry. *Less-Developed Nations experienced even more severe inflation than the industrial countries.* 1977 World Book Year Book, p307 *There are hundreds of millions of poor people in the less developed countries, and very few trained experts.* Britannica Book of the Year 1978, p338 [**1963**] ▶ See L.D.C. and the note under DEVELOPING.

lethal injection, injection of a lethal drug into the body of a person condemned to death. *The death total included the first woman executed since 1962, convicted murderer Margie Velma Barfield, 52, who died on Nov. 2, 1984, of a lethal injection in a Raleigh, N.C., prison.* 1985 World Book Year Book, p455 [**1977**]

lethal yellowing, a disease of palm trees first discovered in Jamaica and becoming widespread in the United States, caused by a viruslike microorganism. *The primary cause of the epidemic called "lethal yellowing" seems to be a virulent mycoplasma—a microorganism without cell walls. The organism is so low in the order of things that it cannot be classified as either plant or animal.* Encyclopedia Science Supplement (Grolier) 1977/1978, p196 [**1973**]

letterform, *n.* a sheet of stationery for writing letters. *A sturdy lined letterform for children will surely induce the most recalcitrant to get down to the "thank-you" letters which they have to be bullied into writing after birthdays and parties.* Times (London) 9/11/70, p8 [**1970**; an earlier sense is that of the design of a letter in printing type (1908)]

leu-enkephalin (,lu:en'kefəlin), *n.* a chemical that overcomes or reduces pain, produced normally in the brain and consisting of a peptide chain having the amino acid leucine at its end. . . . *a large research group from Sandoz Ltd in Basle report the analgesic effects of met- and leu-enkephalin when injected directly into mouse brains. Met-enkephalin is more potent than the leu- variety, but both bind less strongly to brain receptors than does morphine.* New Scientist 6/10/76, p578 [**1976**, from *leucine* + ENKEPHALIN]

levamisole (lə'væmə,soul), *n.* a drug originally used as a deworming agent, found to stimulate cellular immunity and used experimentally in the treatment of cancer and other diseases *Formula:* $C_{11}H_{12}N_2S$ *Many researchers believe that one of the body's two immune mechanisms, . . . cell-mediated immunity apparently retards cancerous growth. By a yet-undefined mechanism, levamisole increases cellular immunity when it is below normal.* World Book Science Annual 1977, p264 [**1976** from *levorotatory* + *ami*de + alteration of *a*zole]

level-peg, *v.i.* British. to maintain a balanced condition or position, as between rivals; remain on equal terms. *Conversions have been level-pegging with repurchases, while the trust is about 40 per cent, liquid to meet further possible encashments* Sunday Times (London) 5/26/68, p26 [**1959**]▶Originally a term from cribbage, this word occurs invariably in the form *level-pegging* and appears to be used largely among journalists and radio and television commentators.

level playing field, a condition of equality or evenhandedness; equal terms. *Even if the guests* [on the television program *Nightline*] *are in a studio 50 feet away, they talk to him* [Ted Koppel] *through the camera as if they were on the other side of the world. The physical arrangement provides a level playing field when other guests are somewhere else.* Newsweek 6/15/87, p53 [**1981**]

leverage, *v.i., v.t. U.S. Finance.* to speculate or cause to speculate on borrowed money in the expectation that large profits will be made on the money through investment. . . . *as the prospectus warns: ". . . short-term trading investing in put and call options written by others, the purchase and sale of warrants, selling short and leveraging through borrowing are all speculative techniques which carry with them greater risk of loss and which will result in greater turnover of the fund's portfolio. . . ."* NY Times 2/20/68, p64 [**1957**, verb use of *leverage, n.,* the property which a security has of showing a relatively large increase in profits in relation to a small change in its price]

leveraged buyout, *U.S. Finance.* the purchase of a company with borrowed money to be paid back largely from the profits obtained from the purchase. *Abbreviation:* LBO *Maxwell Communications acquired Macmillan Publishing in a $2.62 billion leveraged buyout.* Americana Annual 1989, p157 *Leveraged buyouts annoy and puzzle Congress, and many members feel they must do something about them.* Insight 6/12/89, p10 [**1976**]

levodopa (,levou'doupə), *n.* a drug that raises the level of dopamine in the brain. Antiparkinsonism drugs, *Levodopa (L-dopa, levodihydroxyphenylalanine) has been found effective in relieving the distressing rigidity, tremors, and mental depression of Parkinson's disease.* 1970 Collier's Encyclopedia Year Book, p214 [**1969**]

lexigram, *n.* any figure or symbol used to represent a word. *So far the scientists have created 125. To avoid ambiguity, explains* [Ernst] *von Glaserfeld, each lexigram has only one meaning, unlike English in which most words have more than one definition.* Science News 6/2/73, p360 [**1973**, from Greek *léxis* word + English *-gram* something written; compare earlier (OED 1836) *lexigraphy* a system of writing in which each character represents a word]

lexis, *n.* vocabulary; lexicon. *Its* [the Oxford English Dictionary's] *twelve volumes provided the most thorough and lively account of a language ever attempted, a definite canon of the English léxis.* Sunday Times (London) 3/24/68, p10 [**1960**, from Greek *léxis* word, speech]

lez, *n., pl.* **-zes.** *U.S. Slang (often used disparagingly).* a lesbian. *In an editorial expressing approval of the Supreme Court's refusal to consider the case of a man who was denied a job by a state government because of his homosexuality, the* News *broadened its views on the subject only to the extent of offering its readers a larger selection of sobriquets: "Fairies, nances, swishes, fags, lezzes—call 'em what you please."* New Yorker 7/15/72, p64 [**1972**, alteration (influenced by the pronunciation) of earlier (1956) *les,* short for *lesbian*]

LGM, abbreviation of *little green man* (a whimsical reference to intelligent extraterrestrial life). See SETI. *Looking for*

GM's: Intelligent aliens may be neither little, green, nor men, but if any are there, NASA wants to look for them. Science News 11/20/76, p332 **[1968**, originally applied to pulsars by their discoverer, the English astronomer Antony Hewish (born 1924); so called from the popularized characterizations of exterrestrial beings found in early science fiction and fantasy writings]

H-RH, abbreviation of *luteinizing hormone-releasing hormone,* a hormone secreted by the hypothalamus (now also produced synthetically) that causes the pituitary gland to release luteinizing hormone, which in females stimulates ovulation and estrogen production and in males stimulates release of testosterone. *LH-RH plays a key role in the onset of puberty, is the mediator responsible for the release of the ovulatory quota of LH* [luteinizing hormone], *and is necessary for normal implantation and maintenance of pregnancy.* McGraw-Hill Yearbook of Science and Technology 1978, p164 **[1971]**

Lib or **Lib,** *adj.* of or relating to WOMEN'S LIB. *The Lib Movement was rich in documentation of the conditioning processes. Writer after writer rummaged in her past, hunted out childhood details with a bearing on the making of modern femininity.* Atlantic 3/70, p116 *There are now 24 girls in the lib lobby, but the deal is still the same as was worked out at that famous dormitory feast in Houston. They won't play unless the tournament guarantees minimum prize money . . .* Sunday Times (London) 6/27/71, p20 **[1970]—n.** *Informal.* freedom from discrimination. *Susan Struck won a near three-year "maternity lib" battle. The Air Force, reversing its stand on automatic dismissal for giving birth, has reinstated her to active duty.* NY Times 12/3/72, p2 *The authors reject any suggestion that the study is a call for children's suffrage or other simplistic notions associated with kids' lib, but at the same time they talk about the "dimensions of the struggle ahead . . ."* Maclean's 1/20/78, p41 **[1970,** short for *liberation,* as in *Women's Lib, Men's Lib,* etc.]

libber, *n. Informal.* **1** a member or follower of Women's Lib; Women's Liberationist. *The doctor sees through Kate and sees Sheila's worth. Achievement has made her more lovable. It's a pop conversion of women's liberation into: The libbers get the princes.* New Yorker 2/3/75, p86 **2** a member or follower of any liberation group. *'Gosh, I never expected the happy ending', exclaims the narrator at the end of yet another of Ms Kavan's bleak forays among ghastly freakers-out and assorted libbers: nor did the reader.* New Statesman 3/28/75, p424 **[1971,** abstracted from *Women's Libber*]

libbie, *n. U.S. Informal* (*used disparagingly*). a member or follower of Women's Lib; LIBBER. *Decter's major charge against the libbies is that, basically, they seek not equal responsibility with men but flight from responsibility, that, faced with those choices before them regarding their individual modes of existence, women, having made their choices, are now unwilling to bear the consequences.* National Review 12/22/72, p1416 **[1971,** from *lib* + *-ie* (diminutive suffix)]

liberate, *v.t.* to free from social biases or restrictions, now especially those based on sexual differences. *In nearly half a dozen cities, women swept past headwaiters to "liberate" all-male bars and restaurants.* Time 9/7/70, p12 **[1970]**

liberated, *adj.* freed from a rejecting traditional sexual and social roles, especially the passive or secondary role traditionally assigned to women in society. *From her* [Linda Wolfe's] *feminist point of view, she contends that liberated women now enjoy the sexual freedom that men have always enjoyed, and that they are, therefore, behaving as shabbily as men have always behaved sexually.* Sunday News (New York) 6/29/75, p18 *Though a successful working woman, and "liberated" in many respects, she will marry no man who is on a social or intellectual level lower than her own.* NY Times Magazine 8/29/76, p18 **[1970,** from past participle of *liberate, v.,* influenced by Women's *Liberation, liberationist,* etc.]

liberationist, *n.* a member or follower of any liberation group, especially of Women's Liberation. *While certain liberationists might applaud the idea of freeing women from the nine-month pregnancy period, they might be appalled at the exploi-*

tation of another woman. NY Times Magazine 3/5/72, p48 *Emma Lou Thornbrough's* T. Thomas Fortune: Militant Journalist *recovers the life and times of a black liberationist who lived from 1855 to 1928 and became one of the country's leading journalists.* Americana Annual 1973, p416 **—adj.** advocating or supporting liberation, especially Women's Liberation. *In June a group of young women . . . launch a monthly news magazine to be called Spare Rib. As its clever, acid title suggests, its tone will be liberationist.* Times (London) 4/24/72, p7 **[1970,** abstracted from *Women's Liberationist*]► The 19th-century use of this term (OEDS 1869) was restricted to the members of the "Liberation Society" of England which advocated disestablishment. The current form is an independent derivation.

liberation theology, a Christian theological movement which views God as acting through historical processes to free mankind from social and political oppression. Also called THEOLOGY OF LIBERATION. *Some advocates of "liberation theology" have indeed embraced violence, joining guerrilla movements. But more have expressed their convictions peacefully. In Honduras, priests helped to found the National Peasant Union, a force for land reform; in Ecuador, priests organized Indian cooperatives; in Brazil, Chile and El Salvador they have spoken out forcefully against violations of civil rights by the ruling regimes.* NY Times 1/30/79, pA18 **[1972]—liberation theologian:** *For liberation theologians like Brazil's Boff* [a Franciscan friar in Brazil, author of *Church: Charisma and Power*], *the base communities are also the true pillars of the church to be—as he puts it, the "church being born from the faith of the poor."* Time 2/4/85, p56 **—liberation theologist:** *A group of liberation theologists . . . worked round the clock preparing documents on the desperate state of Latin America's masses.* NY Times Magazine 5/6/79, p44

Libermanism, *n.* the economic ideas and theories of the 20th-century Russian economist Yevsei Grigorevich Liberman, especially his advocacy of less bureaucratic planning and control of marketing and his stress on profit sharing for workers and management. *The revisions, grouped together in Russia under the term Libermanism, permit everything from market pricing of some consumer goods to incentive bonuses in factory piecework and decentralized planning—all untouchable in Marxist dogma.* Time 5/10/68, p38 **[1965]**

Lib-Labbery, *n. British.* alliance between the Liberals and Labour supporters. *First, the absence of an unequivocal declaration by Liberal leaders that in the event of a close finish there would be no Lib-Labbery in the new parliament and second, Mr. Thorpe's echo of the Labour gibe at Mr. Heath's reference to a possible devaluation of the pound if Labour came to power.* Manchester Guardian Weekly 6/27/70, p2 **[1965,** from *Lib-Lab* (the name given in the early 1900's to a member of the British Liberal Party who favored the policies of the Labour Party, and more recently used to describe anything involving both Liberals and Labour supporters) + *-ery* actions or activity, here also having a connotation of shady dealings, as in *skulduggery*]

libration point, another name for LAGRANGIAN POINT. *All libration points, however, are not alike . . . Points L-1, L-2, and L-3 are fairly unstable. The other two points—L-4 and L-5—seem to be fairly stable. Space scientists are now very interested in those "stable" points.* Encyclopedia Science Supplement (Grolier) 1975, p358 **[1973,** so called because an object at a Lagrangian point is likely to *librate* or sway at times under the influence of the competing gravities of the bodies between which it is located]

Librium, *n.* Also popularly spelled **librium.** the trade name of a drug (generic name, *chlordiazepoxide*), used especially as a tranquilizer. *I called the psychiatrist, but his answering service told me he was away on a month's vacation. I dined forlornly on hot milk and Librium and was asleep before ten . . . and awake before three.* New Yorker 5/31/69, p34 *In the first cafe he went into someone sold him six librium pills.* Times (London) 9/22/70, p10 **[1960]**

lichenometric (ˌlaɪkənəˈmetrɪk), *adj.* of, relating to, or based on lichenometry. *. . . a growing number of carbon-14 and li-*

chenometric dates for moraines from southern Alaska and the western U.S. leaves open the possibility that one or more episodes of glacier expansion, as yet unrecognized in most areas, may have occurred during this interval. Scientific American 6/70, p109 [**1958**]

lichenometry (ˌlaikə'nɒmətri:), n. the measurement of the diameter of lichens to establish their age or the age of the area in which they grow. Although not as precise or reliable as other methods of dating neoglacial moraines, lichenometry has proved to be particularly useful in certain nonforested arctic and alpine regions and, under ideal circumstances, is applicable over intervals as great as 4,000 years. Scientific American 6/70, p109 [**1957**]

lid, n. U.S. Slang. a small package containing from 22 grams to one ounce of marijuana. Day or night, it is crowded with hippies, feeding the hunger that follows a smoke of marijuana, coming down off an LSD trip, or looking for a lid of "pot" or a tab of "acid." NY Times 1/8/68, p1 [**1966**]

lidar ('lai,dar), n. a radarlike device that uses light beams to detect objects or changes invisible to the eye. Essentially, lidar is an instrument analoguous to radar in that it is composed of a transmitter which emits energy to space and a receiver which detects that portion back-scattered by obstacles in its path. Recent applications in the lower atmosphere include cloud height measurements, haze layer and visibility determinations, dimensions of plumes and clouds of particulates, water vapor profiles, accurate distance measurements, clear-air turbulence, and other aeronautical problems. McGraw-Hill Yearbook of Science and Technology 1971, p109 [**1963**, from light + radar]

lie-in, n. a lying down of a group of people in a public place to disrupt traffic, etc., as a form of protest or demonstration. Last week pollution protesters staged a lie-in at government offices in Tokyo. Time 12/27/71, p40 [**1963**; see -IN]

lifeboat ethic or **lifeboat ethics,** a set of values which in a crisis assigns priorities according to urgency or expediency rather than on the basis of humanitarian or other moral principles. Dr. [Garrett] Hardin, an ecologist at the University of California, Santa Barbara, is well known as an advocate of triage or "the lifeboat ethic," in world food matters. He has argued that as global food shortages become more intense, the United States should not grant food aid but instead should permit famines to reduce the number of people in developing countries. NY Times 12/5/76, p67 Is there a basis for hope that the circular dilemma of runaway population growth, poverty, and hunger can be solved? The neo-Malthusians despair that the gap between population and food can ever be overcome and fear that governments may be forced to practice triage and lifeboat ethics. Manchester Guardian Weekly (Washington Post section) 11/26/78, p18 [**1974**, by analogy with an overcrowded lifeboat from which a number of passengers must be cast for the rest to survive]

life care, a type of housing in which apartments and medical services are purchased for life. As you have probably guessed, life care does not come cheap. Costs of the apartments range from $20,000 for an efficiency unit to $50,000 and more for a two-bedroom unit for two apartment occupants. After paying the initial buying fee, a resident pays a monthly service charge, like rent or a condominium maintenance fee, which varies but generally starts at from $400 to $500. Ruth Rejnis, Her Home, 1980, p117 [**1963**]

life president, Also, as a title, **Life President.** the president of a republic, especially in Africa, who is elected to or assumes the presidency for life. Also called PRESIDENT-FOR-LIFE. President Banda is not only life-president of the country, but life-president of the ruling Malawi Congress Party as well. He is also his own Minister of Agriculture, Foreign Affairs, Public Works and Justice. Times (London) 7/4/78, p16 [**1972**]

lifer, n. U.S. Military Slang. a career officer or soldier. The old ones, the lifers, know everyone in the Army, from four-star generals on down, and an extraordinary bond grows between them. Atlantic 10/70, p82 [**1964**, extended from the original

meaning of a person sentenced to prison for life (attested sinc the early 1800's)]

life scientist, a scientist who specializes in one or more of th sciences dealing with living organisms. Many groups tried t build machines for scanning real images or photographs wit a view to automating tedious laboratory processes such as ce counting . . . Unfortunately the life scientists, who first dre attention to the possibilities, were unable to make very wide u of the limited systems available. New Scientist and Scienc Journal 9/23/71, p676 [**1968**, derived from life science (1949]

life-support, adj. **1** containing or providing the necessar equipment, material, or treatment to keep a person alive, espe cially in adverse circumstances. Also to be deferred was the de velopment of improved space suits, life-support backpacks and astronaut maneuvering units for use with the shuttle. Bri tannica Book of the Year 1976, p627 The fetus reaches viabil ty (the capability of surviving, given the appropriate life support facilities) . . . ordinarily at about 24 weeks. Scientifi American 1/77, p22 **2** of or involving the capacity to suppor life, especially wild life. The final category was life suppor value, including a marsh's ability to absorb carbon dioxide produce oxygen, support waterfowl and other animals an protect cities and beaches from the damaging effects of storm NY Times 1/8/76, p24 —n. Also, **life support.** the equipment material, or treatment necessary to keep a person alive. Basi life support is an emergency first-aid procedure that include . . . the proper application of cardiopulmonary resuscitatio (CPR). Americana Annual 1975, p372 New legislation was u gently required, some doctors urged, to make it easier to decid when life-support should be discontinued. Annual Register o World Events in 1975, p358 [**1970**, abstracted from LIFE SUPPORT SYSTEM]

life-support system, any system designed to support the physio logical processes essential to life. The earth supports man be cause of its biological richness; any diminution in this richnes endangers the "life-support systems" that sustain man. Boyc Rensberger, The Cult of the Wild, 1977, p227 Each astronau has a life-support system to supply him with breathing an suit-pressurizing oxygen and water for the liquid-cooled gar ment. For added safety, the secondary system has been im proved for the Apollo 14 mission. Science News 1/2/71 p2 [**1959**]

liftback, n. an automobile with a slanted back that opens up ward. The Celica models comprise a 1600 two-door coupé an a range of two-litre liftbacks with tailgate and folding rea seat. Times (London) 1/12/78, p70 [**1973**, patterned afte HATCHBACK]

lifting body, a gliderlike wingless spacecraft with sufficien aerodynamic lift and maneuverability to reenter the earth's at mosphere in the manner of a conventional airplane. An experi mental lifting body also hangs in Space Hall. It was one of th test craft that resulted finally in the development of the spac shuttle. This one, the M2-F3, is simply a flattened, delta shaped fuselage designed to maneuver in space and then re enter the atmosphere and glide to a landing. 1979 Britannic Yearbook of Science and the Future, p21 [**1963**]

ligase ('lig,eis), n. an enzyme with joining properties, importan in the synthesis and repair of deoxyribonucleic acid (DNA). . all newly made DNA is synthesized in a discontinuous man ner. These discontinuous segments are then joined by an en zyme, ligase, to produce a continuous strand. 1970 Britannic Yearbook of Science and the Future, p299 [**1961**, from Latin ligāre to bind + English -ase (suffix meaning enzyme)]

light, n. (see the) **light at the end of the tunnel,** (to glimpse) the prospect of success during a long and perilous venture. The Sec retary of State has repeatedly said that he will not help compa nies where there is no light at the end of the tunnel . . . Even now there are serious doubts whether the group is capable o eking a profit four years hence. Manchester Guardian Weekly 3/11/72, p10 A proposal for a federal Ireland . . . could be the light at the end of the tunnel—in contrast to further well meaning British suggestions, which only add fuel to the fire National Review 8/30/74, p979 [**1967**]►The expression wa opularized during the Vietnam War by U.S. government pokesmen predicting the imminent victory of South Vietnam nd an end to the American involvement in the war. Oppoents of the war frequently ridiculed the expression, and some f them attributed the light to an onrushing train coming from he other direction.

ight-day, *n.* the equivalent of a day in a light-year. See also uotation under LIGHT-MONTH. *If a quasar's radiation varies vith a period of, say, four days, then the radius of the quasar an be no greater than four light-days.* Science News 11/8/69, 437 [**1964**]

ght-emitting diode, a semiconductor that emits light whenevr a suitable electric current is applied across it, used widely to roduce the glowing digits in electronic calculators, digital vatches, etc. *The most popular type of display on present and-held calculators is the light emitting diode (LED). This ives small, red digits which can switch rapidly.* New Scientist /31/73, p549 [**1970**]

ght guide, an optical fiber or bundle of fibers used in a commuication system in which messages are coded into pulses of ght transmitted through the fibers. *Light guides offer a number of advantages over transmission by metallic conductors. Since the light in a light-guide transmission system is tightly onfined to the inner core of each fiber, signals cannot leak between adjacent fibers and give rise to "cross talk."* Scientific American 8/77, p47 [**1971**]

ight-minute, *n.* the equivalent of a minute in a light-year (the distance light travels in a year). Compare LIGHT-SECOND. *Suppose that the Sun is suddenly switched off. We on Earth, about ight light-minutes away, will see a dark spot appear in the entre of the Sun some eight minutes after switch off.* New Scientist 2/6/75, p313 [**1925, 1975**]

ight-month, *n.* the equivalent of a month in a light-year. See he quotation for details. *We pointed out in a previous footnote hat a light-year is the distance traveled by light in a year. The units light-month, light-week and light-day have been derived n the same way. A light-month is about 500,000,000,000 miles; a light-week, about 115,000,000,000 miles; a light-day, about 16,000,000,000 miles.* Encyclopedia Science Supplement (Grolier) 1968, p62 [**1963**]

ight pen, a small photoelectric cell in the form of a pen, used o put new information into a computer by sensing light from he screen of a cathode-ray tube and transmitting the light impulses to the computer. *The engineer in charge can then correct he diagram with a single light-pen, and the machine will retranslate the diagram into numbers.* Times (London) 7/18/68, p24 *The most common graphic input is the light pen. This does not emit light but is a hand held light detector, effectively just a photocell with a limited field of view. When it detects light from the screen it sends a signal to the computer.* Science Journal 10/70, p71 [**1962**]

ight pipe, a fine glass fiber or transparent plastic rod that conducts light. *Light pipes . . . have, until now, absorbed and lost too much light. While high losses are acceptable for many applications—over short lengths in scientific instruments, for example—low loss fibres are essential for long distances.* New Scientist 9/21/72, p488 *The Vivitar VI keeps the negative cool by carrying the light from lamp to negative by means of a Lucite "light pipe" illumination system.* NY Times 10/3/76, p34 [**1961**]

ight piping, *Botany.* the transmission of minute quantities of ight down the stem of a plant to its parts underground. *Botanists at Stanford University in California announced in August 1984 that young seedlings—and perhaps mature plants as well—transmit small amounts of light through their stems and roots down to depths of at least 4 or 5 centimeters (1.6 to 2 inches). The natural phenomenon, known as light piping, affects the way a seed grows into a plant. Light acts as a trigger that starts or otherwise controls the various life processes of plants when special pigments in a plant absorb light.* World Book Science Annual 1986, p235 [**1985**]

light pollution, the excessive glare of street lights, advertising signs, and the like, in a city and its environs. Compare SOUND POLLUTION. *Looking for possible new sites Walker prepared maps of California and Arizona on which he drew exclusionary circles around regions where urban light pollution was too strong for good observatory siting.* Science News 12/15/73, p382 [**1971,** patterned after earlier *air pollution, thermal pollution,* etc.]

light rail, of or belonging to a railroad system built with light rails and using lightweight rolling stock, such as streetcars. Compare HEAVY RAIL. *Brookline passengers board a "light rail" vehicle, one of 175 modern trolley cars for the Massachusetts Bay Transportation Authority system.* 1978 World Book Year Book, p509 [**1976,** shortening of *light railway* (OED 1868)]

light-sculpture, *n.* a sculptured work made of transparent material and electric wiring that causes it to light up. Compare SOUND SCULPTURE. *The show looks great. A blue neon light-sculpture, designed by artists Val Strazoveck and Cork Marchesky, dominates the stage.* Maclean's 9/74, p82 [**1968**]

light-second, *n.* the equivalent of a second in a light-year (the distance light travels in a year). Compare LIGHT-MINUTE. *The sun is 500 light-seconds away, the nearest star 100 million light-seconds distant, the "edge" of the universe 400 million billion (4 × 10[17]) light-seconds away, and ever receding.* 1974 Britannica Yearbook of Science and the Future, p409 [**1973,** patterned after earlier *light-month, light-week, light-day*]

light show, a display of colored lights in kaleidoscopic patterns usually accompanied by music. *Arthur, 154 E. 54th St. . . . Tiny tables, a minimal light show, and rampant recorded rock that shifts to the rampant live sounds of the Bubble Gum Machine.* New Yorker 7/6/68, p4 [**1966**]

light-water, *adj.* of, using, or relating to ordinary water, H_2O, as distinguished from *heavy water* (deuterium oxide, D_2O). *While American technology of light-water reactors becomes progressively adopted in western Europe—Britain remaining for the time being faithful to the technology that she herself developed—future generations of reactors are being investigated.* New Scientist 12/10/70, p434 [**1956**]

light-week, *n.* the equivalent of a week in a light-year. See also the quotation under LIGHT-MONTH. *So there is now evidence for the existence of a continuous sequence of objects which generate energy by means as yet unknown . . . These objects appear to produce up to 100 times the luminosity of a normal galaxy in a volume which does not exceed light-weeks in diameter.* Science Journal 2/70, p61 [**1967**]

like, *conj.* U.S. Slang. as if to say; so to speak. *"Afterward, a girl came up to me and said, 'You look kinda interested in this; did you know there are civil rights for women?' And I thought like wow, this is for me."* Time 8/31/70, p19 *"Man, when I'm high (snapping his fingers). . . like, I'm inside myself. I'm outside myself (snap, snap)."* NY Times 1/11/68, p18 *". . . you're one of those who will never like cop out on the true scene and split for the Establishment bread."* New Yorker 10/25/69, p61 [**1959**]

Likud (liːˈkuːd), *n.* a right-wing coalition party in Israel that was formed in 1973 and became the ruling party in May 1977. *To the surprise of Washington, if not to that of his countrymen, Begin became Premier after his Likud coalition won a narrow victory in last May's national election, thereby ending 29 years of Labor-led coalition governments.* Time 1/2/78, p13 [**1973,** from Hebrew, literally, alliance, union]

likuta (liˈkuːtə), *n., pl.* **makuta.** a monetary unit of Zaire, equal to 1/100 of a zaire. *Currency: The monetary unit is the Zaire (Z.) divided into 100 makuta (K.) each worth two American cents. "Makuta" is the plural form of the word "likuta." One Z. equals two U.S. dollars.* NY Times 6/27/71, pK5 [**1967**]

lilangeni (ˌliːlɑːŋˈgeiniː), *n., pl.* **emalangeni.** the monetary unit of Swaziland introduced in 1974. *As Swaziland is part of the Rand Monetary Area, visitors do not even have to change money. South African rand and the local currency, the lilangeni (plural emalangeni) which is pegged to the rand, are used* *interchangeably.* Times (London) 9/6/78, pI [**1976**, from siSwati (a Bantu language) *li-*, singular prefix + *-langeni*, the root of the word for money]

L.I.M., abbreviation of LINEAR-INDUCTION MOTOR. *The TACRV* [tracked air cushion research vehicle] *propelled by the L.I.M. will ride on thin cushions of air on a fixed U-shaped guideway which contains a central vertical aluminum reaction rail.* Times (London) 5/29/70, p29 [**1970**]

limiting nutrient, a chemical which retards eutrophication. *Some researchers have claimed that internal sources of carbon may sometimes be the limiting nutrient in lake eutrophication and that phosphates and nitrogen may be less important than earlier thought.* Science News 10/7/72, p238 [**1971**]

limo, *n.* short for *limousine. One night . . . a black limousine rolled up to the front portico* [White House] *at the appointed hour . . . Out of the limo stepped Spiro Agnew.* Time 3/30/70, p20 *Weyman hopped out, shook hands with Siegel, and introduced the young lady as his wife. "You ride in the limo, dear," he said to her breezily, helping her out of the Daimler. . .* New Yorker 11/23/68, p96 [**1965**] ►An isolated early use in print has been found by David Shulman (*American Speech*, Summer 1988, p 116): *"It was the fastest ride the old Grayne limo had made."* NY Evening Journal Magazine 3/12/32, p4

Limousin (li:mu:ˈzɑ̃; *Anglicized* ˌliməˈzi:n), *n.* any of a breed of hardy beef cattle from France. *Further, the new breed had to be evaluated competitively against native breeds. It was under these regulations that Limousin cattle were subsequently imported from France and Simmental cattle from Germany and Switzerland.* New Scientist 2/15/73, p357 [**1970**, named for a region in central France]

limousine liberal, *U.S.* a wealthy liberal. *Canada is most fortunate to have a Premier who is willing to tell the bleeding hearts and limousine liberals what he thinks of them and who will also take whatever strong measures are necessary to rid his country of Communist murderers.* NY Times 10/26/70, p36 [**1969**]

linar, *n.* See the quotation for the meaning. *Radio astronomy, having coined the words quasar and pulsar, has now added linars to the growing list of strange objects inhabiting the visually dark areas of space. Linars—based on the words line and star—are point sources which emit with extraordinary energy, at wavelengths characteristic of the spectral line of particular chemical compounds.* Manchester Guardian Weekly 8/15/70, p15 [**1970**]

lincomycin, *n.* an antibiotic derived from a kind of streptomyces (soil microbe), found effective against certain bacteria that are resistant to penicillin. *Although not a broad-spectrum antibiotic, Lincomycin is effective against the most important gram-positive organisims, including resistant staphylococcus.* 1966 Collier's Encyclopedia Year Book, p195 [**1963**, from *linco(lnensis)*, name of the variety of streptomyces from which the drug is derived + *-mycin*, as in *streptomycin, actinomycin,* and other names of antibiotics]

line, *n.* Usually, **the line.** *U.S. and Canadian.* the betting odds set by bookmakers for a number of non-racing sports contests, especially in football. *For years, the "line"—which is what the point spread for a number of games is called—came from a group of experts, in Minneapolis.* NY Times Magazine 1/2/77, p15 *The line, published in many daily newspapers, establishes for bookmakers and bettors across the continent the team favored to win each game and by how many points.* Maclean's 1/22/79, p35 [**1964**]

linear-induction motor, an electric motor that produces thrust directly without torque by the movement of the magnetic field which creates a linear impelling force rather than a rotating force. *Abbreviation:* L.I.M. Also called LINEAR MOTOR. *A linear induction motor is like a regular rotary motor that has been sliced open and laid out flat. Both rotary and linear motors produce force by the interaction of a magnetic field and a current induced by the field. The movement of the rotor inside the stator of a rotary motor produces torque (a twisting force) which then must be transformed to thrust, usually through the*

form of gears connected to a wheel. The interaction of the ma▨ netic field in a linear-induction motor, however, produce▨ thrust directly. 1970 Britannica Yearbook of Science and th▨ Future, p390 *Vehicles with linear induction motors flo▨ above the rail or rails, and may achieve speeds of 300 miles p▨ hour or even more. In Britain, Professor Eric Laithwaite's pr▨ totype vehicle is expected to run in Cambridgeshire in 197▨* Dennis Gabor, Innovations: Scientific, Technological, and S▨ cial, 1970, p29 [**1964**]

linear motor, short for LINEAR-INDUCTION MOTOR. *Laithwai▨ pioneered the renewed development of linear motors, whic▨ are like normal induction motors, cut across the circumferen▨ and rolled out flat, with the rotor laid down as a metal rail, an▨ the stator clamped beneath the moving field which impels ▨ along . . .* New Scientist 7/9/70, p69 [**1957**]

line item, an item in a fiscal budget to which a separate line ▨ assigned to emphasize its importance. *Conspicuously absen▨ from that budget . . . was a budgetary line item for develop▨ ment of the Observer* [a spacecraft] *itself.* Science New▨ 10/19/85, p250 [**1981**] **—line-item,** *adj.: One thing the legisla▨ tors wanted was the governor's agreement not to use his line▨ item veto to delete $300 million in local projects that the mem▨ bers in each house would select for their districts.* NY Time▨ 6/21/81, pD4

line judge, a person who watches for violations in the line i▨ various sports, such as football and tennis. *He finally lost th▨ third set, 7-5, on what seemed a really bad call by a lin▨ judge—. . .* New Yorker 9/30/67, p108 [**1964**]

liner pool, a swimming pool made with a heavy vinyl lining in▨ side an excavated hole. *He finally decided, rightly, that for th▨ do-it-yourself enthusiast the "liner" pool is the best bet. . . . No▨ surprisingly, these liner pools evidently take up about 80 per▨ cent of the American home pools market.* Times (London▨ 4/15/72, p8 [**1971**]

lingua franca, any standard language that is widely used as ▨ general medium of communication. *This is exactly the sam▨ thing as happens in certain countries where register switchin▨ may involve different languages: the mother-tongue may b▨ used in the home, a lingua franca such as English, French▨ or Russian in the schools, the lawcourts, and government of▨ fices.* Listener 1/13/66, p53 *Back when Erasmus and Grotiu▨ wrote in Latin, they had readers throughout the Continen▨ With the disappearance of that lingua franca, writers in th▨ emerging major languages lost little; but Holland's writer▨ were left with a parochial vernacular.* Saturday Review▨ 7/2/66, p23 [**1955**, extended sense of the term for a hybrid lan▨ guage used as a common trading jargon (OED 1678)]

linguistic universal, another name for LANGUAGE UNIVERSAL▨ *In relation to the total number of spoken languages, our studie▨ remain statistically almost insignificant. 'It is still prematur▨ to expect,' says one linguist, 'that we can make any except th▨ most elementary observations concerning linguistic universal▨ and expect them to be permanently valid. Our knowledge o▨ two-thirds or more of the world's languages is still too scant▨ (or in many instances non-existent).'* George Steiner, On Diffi▨ culty, 1974, p152 [**1971**]

linkage, *n.* a principle or policy of bargaining, especially in in▨ ternational relations, in which diverse or unrelated issues ar▨ linked in an attempt to force an agreement on at least one issu▨ which by itself would be less likely to be resolved. *He* [Henry Kissinger] *also reaffirmed his commitment to the concept o▨ "linkage" which he defined as an understanding of the interre▨ lationship of foreign policy issues, and called President Car▨ ter's decision to cancel the B-1 bomber "a unilatera▨ unreciprocated concession" that violated the linkage principle▨* NY Times 9/20/77, p6 *The issue of linkage—that is, relatin▨ Israeli withdrawal from the Sinai Peninsula to politica▨ changes for the occupied West Bank and Gaza Strip—remain▨ a major stumbling block.* Time 12/11/78, p52 [**1973**] ►The▨ term was popularized by Henry Kissinger as assistant to the▨ President for national security affairs (1969-75). Its first use i▨

political context was by James N. Rosenau in *Linkage Politics* 1969).

inkman, *n. British.* **1** (in soccer, rugby, and field hockey) a player who acts as a link between the center forwards and backs. *Using Brindley as a deep-lying linkman, Staffordshire set up the openings, only for Goh and Flood to turn them back time after time.* Times (London) 11/9/70, p12 **2** a moderator or coordinator, especially of a radio or television discussion program. *Tommy Steel will appear as linkman and commentator.* Sunday Times (London) 5/5/68, p51 **3** an intermediary; a go-between. *The new setup at Broadcasting House [appointment of Charles Curran as Director-General of BBC] looks a little as though the Director-General is in risk of being downgraded to the role of link man between the Governors (more specifically the chairman) and the staff.* Manchester Guardian Weekly 3/15/68, p8 **[1960]**

inksland, *n.* See the first quotation for the meaning. *A links-and—a links, for short—is a stretch of sandy soil deposited by the ocean and whipped into dunes and fancifully shaped sand hills by the winds off the sea.* New Yorker 8/1/70, p60 *Carnoustie, however, like so many seaside links . . . is nothing much to the eye, being on a comparatively flat expanse of reclaimed linksland.* Sunday Times (London) 7/7/68, p24 **[1964]**

Link trainer, a trade name for a set of audio-visual aids for training people to drive a motor vehicle. *In the Link trainer, the pupil finds that it is like being in the cinema, with a wide screen. The film shows a driver's view of real traffic. The pupils respond to the conditions shown in the film, and to instructions . . .* New Scientist 6/11/70, p527 **[1970]** ▸The original *Link trainer* (OEDS 1937) was a flight simulator for giving flying instruction on the ground.

iposome ('lipə,soum), *n.* a microscopic membranous capsule made by the action of ultrasonic vibrations on a suspension of fats in water. Liposomes are used especially to enclose a drug or other substance to be released in a specific part of the body. *During the year, liposomes were successfully tested as an experimental form of cancer treatment, used to carry drugs selectively to the site of a tumour. They were also used for the first time to treat diseases caused by lack of essential enzymes.* Annual Register of World Events in 1974, p397 **[1968,** from *lipo-*fat (from Greek *lípos*) + -*some* body; an earlier (1940's) meaning of this term is a droplet of fat in the cytoplasm of a cell] —**liposomal,** *adj.: The researchers are now tagging the liposomes with antibodies that should help direct the liposomal-packaged enzymes to the appropriate target cells. Weissmann remains optimistic that liposomal-enzyme packets will eventually benefit persons with various defective or deficient enzymes.* Science News 7/22/78, p60

iposuction (,lipə'sək ʃən), *n.* cosmetic surgery in which excess fat is removed from the body by suction. Also called SUCTION LIPECTOMY. *Liposuction, a procedure that vacuums fat from problem areas, surpassed breast augmentation as the most popular cosmetic procedure.* 1988 Collier's Encyclopedia Year Book, p311 **[1987]**

ipotropin, *n.* a hormone of the pituitary gland that promotes the breakdown of fat in the body and that is a chemical precursor of the natural opiates of the brain called endorphins. *The C-terminal region of lipotropin, named C fragment, has been found as an intact polypeptide in the pituitary gland and the C fragment is also released from lipotropin by mild digestion with trypsin in vitro.* Nature 4/29/76, p793 *In schizophrenics an enzyme defect might lead to an imbalance in the endorphins produced from the original large pituitary chemical (known as beta lipotropin). Different enzyme deficiencies might lead to the variety of symptoms seen in different kinds of schizophrenia.* Times (London) 11/4/76, p14 **[1964,** from *lipotropic* preventing the accumulation of fat (from Greek *lípos* fat + *tropé* a turning) + -*in* (chemical suffix)]

Lippes loop ('lipis), a loop-shaped plastic intrauterine device, named after its inventor, the American physician Jack Lippes. Also called THE LOOP. *The Lippes loop, for example, has shown infection rates of only 0.4 and 0.7 per 100 woman-years, and*

the few pelvic infections that have occurred cleared up quickly. Science News 2/1/69, p117 **[1964]**

LIPS or **lips,** acronym for *logical inferences per second* (a measure of the speed with which a computer solves a problem). Compare MIPS. *They will be so much more powerful that where today's machines can handle 10,000 to 100,000 logical inferences per second, or LIPS, the next-generation computer will be capable of 100 million to 1,000 million LIPS.* NY Times 8/2/83, pC14 **[1982]**

lipspeaker, *n.* a person who is skilled in using lip movements to communicate with the deaf. *"Lip Speakers" are used. These are people who are easy to lip-read and they repeat what is being said without "voice." It is not strictly simultaneous translation because the lipspeakers try to use the main speakers's actual words, and run two or three words behind.* New Scientist 10/12/78, p125 **[1977,** patterned after *lip reader* (OEDS 1912)]

lip-synch ('lip,siŋk), *v.i., v.t.* to move the lips in synchronization with recorded sound, words, voices, etc., often silently. *"Please bear with me tonight, Licia. The old persona's on the fritz, and I'm just lip-synching."* New Yorker 10/21/72, p31 *Unlike a true NHL [National Hockey League] player, Dryden didn't . . . mark off an entire section by lip-synching his way through* The Godfather. Maclean's 2/73, p27 **[1970,** verb use of noun phrase *lip synch, lip sync* short for *lip synchronization*]

liquid chromatography, chromatography renamed to distinguish it from *paper chromatography, gas chromatography,* and other methods. *Another technique, this one for separation of complicated mixtures, became prominent this year. The technique is liquid chromatography, and although the principles involved have been well known for a long time, there was an explosion of interest this year because of the newly discovered power of the method for separating nucleotides, the sugar-base compounds that are the building blocks of DNA and RNA.* 1973 Collier's Encyclopedia Year Book, p219 **[1972]**

liquid membrane, a thin film of oil encapsulating a water globule or water surrounding a globule of oil, stabilized by an agent that reduces surface tension. Liquid membranes are able to isolate a substance from its surroundings or to separate it from other substances. *The team tested both aspirin and phenobarbital and found that liquid membrane solutions will remove 95 percent of each drug within five minutes from acidic solutions (such as those found in the stomach).* Science News 4/17/76, p246 **[1976]**

liquid protein, a preparation of concentrated protein, once widely used as a food substitute to reduce weight but later considered unsafe as a diet. *Liquid protein consists, essentially, of protein processed from the gelatin in cowhide or from some other source of connective tissue. It supposedly provides patients with just enough low-calorie nutrition to help them survive the rigors of near-starvation diets.* Science News 7/29/78, p70 **[1967]**

lisente (li'senti:), *n.* plural of *sente,* a monetary unit of Lesotho equal to 1/100 of a loti. *The currency is the Loti (plural* Maloti) *divided into 100* Lisente *which is at a par with the South African* Rand. Statesman's Year-Book 1984-85, p786 **[1980,** from Sesotho]

lit crit ('lit 'krit), *Especially British, Informal.* **1** literary criticism. *Alas, the title is a publisher's trick, concealing a fairly orthodox work of literary criticism: criticism, it is true, dressed up a little and fitted into a thesis, but lit crit nonetheless.* Listener 9/27/73, p416 **2** a literary critic. *Unfairly, the novel that is an "easy read"—accomplished, well-paced, absorbing, rather than knotted up in sensitivity—seems to be a disadvantage with lit crits.* Times Literary Supplement 8/25/72, p985 **[1963,** from *lit. crit.,* abbreviation of *literary criticism*]

Litek ('laitek), *n.* the trademark for a fluorescent light bulb designed to last up to ten years and consume 70 percent less energy than ordinary bulbs. *Unlike a conventional light bulb, the Litek bulb has a magnetic coil that is energised by electronic circuitry in its base. The coil produces a magnetic field that excites mercury gas in the bulb. The gas emits ultraviolet light,* which produces visible light as it strikes a phosphor layer on the inside surface of the bulb. New Scientist 3/18/76, p626 [**1976**, probably irregular acronym for *Light Technology Corp.*, the company established by its inventor, Donald D. Hollister, an American physicist, to develop the device]

literarism, *n.* emphasis on literary or humanistic values. *Dr.* [Frank R.] *Leavis's lecture at Bristol on "'Literarism' versus 'Scientism'", printed in the Times Literary Supplement this week, is a heartening sign.* Times (London) 4/25/70, p9 [**1963**]

lithium, *n.* a salt of the element lithium, used as a psychotherapeutic drug. Also called **lithium carbonate**. *Dr Michael Pare of St Bartholomew's Hospital spoke of the use of lithium to hold back the recurrence of attacks of depression.* Listener 10/18/73, p515 [**1967**]

lithoprint, *n.* a print reproduced by lithography. *His enchanting drawings (transformed into big, clear-coloured lithoprints in limited editions of 100 each) are in a gallery run by his mother in the purlieus of his architect father's office.* Sunday Times (London) 4/6/69, p30 —*v.t.* to print by lithography. *The several hundred local natural history publications, often duplicated or lithoprinted, offer an easy outlet for young artists.* New Scientist and Science Journal 1/28/71, p206 [**1969**]

lithospheric, *adj.* of or belonging to the solid rock part of Earth. *According to the theory of plate tectonics, lithospheric slabs spread apart at mid-ocean ridges and thrust under other slabs at ocean trenches.* Science News Yearbook 1970, p154 [**1969**, from *lithosphere* the part of the Earth's crust consisting chiefly of solid rock + -*ic* (adj. suffix)]

lithotripter ('liθou,triptər), *n.* a device that disintegrates stones in the kidney or gall bladder by means of ultrasonic waves directed against the stones from outside the body. *The lithotripter, a machine that crushes kidney stones without any kind of incision, is being used in a growing number of Americans.* Encyclopedia Science Supplement (Grolier) 1987, p226 [**1986**, alteration or replacement of earlier *lithotriptor* (1847) a surgical instrument for rubbing down or crushing stones in the bladder, ultimately from Greek *líthos* stone + *thrýptein* to crush, with spelling influenced by Greek *tríbein* to rub]

litmus test, a decisive test. . . . *Israel wants the planes now, while it can still get them. At the same time, the sale, which has the support of sizable groups in both the House and Senate, is regarded in Israel as a kind of litmus test of U.S. intentions.* Time 6/22/70, p28 *But the litmus-test of a liberal regime must surely be the freedom of the individual from arbitrary arrest and punishment, and in this respect France has become not more liberal but less.* Times (London) 5/4/70, p4 [**1957**, so called from the use of *litmus* paper to test a solution for acidity or alkalinity. An older term with the same meaning is *acid test.*]

litter bag, *U.S.* a plastic or paper bag, often sealable, in which litter can be put. *Continental Can, whose products—often used, can often be spotted in America's lush countryside, is this month launching "a massive anti-litter program" throughout its plants and district sales offices. They've handed out over 100,000 litter bags as well as a lot of print and promotional material.* NY Times 6/6/68, p78 [**1968**]

litterbug, *v.i. U.S.* . . . to litter a public place with wastepaper, refuse, etc. . . . *Arlo Guthrie launches into 18 minutes and 20 seconds of wildly seriocomic semitrue narrative-plus-song about how he helped a friend named Alice clean out her place in Stockbridge, Mass., dumped the refuse over a cliff, was arrested for litterbugging and fined $50* . . . Time 1/15/68, p45 [**1968**, verb use of *litterbug, n.* (OEDS 1947)]

Little Neddy, *British.* one of a number of industry-wide committees under the National Economic Development Council (popularly called *Neddy*); any one of the Economic Development Committees. *The Little Neddy for the hotel and catering industry has just published the result of a survey it commissioned among foreign travel agents.* Punch 5/24/67, p766 [**1963**]

live-in, *adj.* **1 a** living in the place where one is employed. Compare LIVE-OUT. . . . *the Hetheringtons have no live-in maid. A woman comes three days a week to clean. Alec uses the*

maid's room as a study. New Yorker 7/29/67, p37 **b** requiring one's living in the place where one is employed. *The nine member faculty-student committee proposed that Miss LeCla be denied several campus privileges because she had lied to th college when she said she had an off-campus live-in job, an violated the housing regulations.* NY Times 4/19/68, p53 **c** living with another, especially as a cohabitee. *Steve McQueen live-in girl friend in Bullitt will probably need some fanc footwork to escape agony in her new film.* . . . Time 2/7/69 p33 **2** relating to or involving living in a particular place as a inhabitant, resident, etc. Also, LIVING-IN. . . . *Dr. Jastrow wen on from a discussion of the moon to a discussion of the live-i prospects on Mars (quite promising; colonies likely)* . . . Ne Yorker 1/10/70, p17 —**n. 1** See the quotation and the entr -IN. *Twenty-two social workers who have been staging a protes live-in at the office of the City Department of Labor were a rested last night after seven days of sleeping, washing clothe and cooking in the halls of the building.* NY Times 10/18/66 p47 **2** a live-in person. Compare COHABITEE, ROOMMATE. Se also MARRIAGE. *Now she devotes her time to writing, pottery Ben, her live-in (American for permanent boy friend . . . friends, cats and plants.* Manchester Guardian Weekly 3/6/77 p19 [**1955** for adj.; **1966** for noun]

live-out, *adj.* not living in the place where one is employed Compare LIVE-IN (def. 1 a). *He [Arthur Ochs Sulzberger] ha a live-out cook, but he likes to bend over the stove himself, an sometimes prepares family meals.* New Yorker 1/18/69 p41 [**1969**]

liveware, *n.* the personnel involved in computer work, such a operators, programmers, and systems analysts. Compare MID DLEWARE. *Computing people, programs and machines—in th jargon, liveware, software and hardware—will be busy inter acting next week at the British Computer Society's Datafair '7 conference and exhibition at Nottingham University.* Time (London) 4/6/73, p32 [**1966**, patterned after *hardware, soft ware*]

living-in, *adj.* another word for LIVE-IN (def. 2). *Apart from car ing for its five living-in patients and the 15 to 20 who visit ι from home, Dr Kelleher believes that the unit still has a vita role to play.* Sunday Times (London) 6/11/67, p2 [**1955**]

living will, a document expressing a person's wish to be allowec to die in case of an incurable illness or injury rather than be kept alive by artificial means. *It also would have provided fo litigation to enforce a so-called living will, stipulating that lif sustaining treatment be abandoned should the signer "by rea son of brain damage or degeneration" become "permanentl incapable of giving directions."* 1977 Collier's Encyclopedi Year Book, p336 [**1972**]

LM (lem; so pronounced from the former spelling LEM, fo *lunar excursion module*), abbreviation of LUNAR MODULE *After more than two hours on lunar ground, Armstrong anc Aldrin returned to the LM, lifted off the moon, and reentered lunar orbit.* 1970 Collier's Encyclopedia Year Book p492 [**1967**]

LNG, abbreviation of *liquefied natural gas. Technology is cur rently being developed for the use of liquefied natural gas LNG, as a motor fuel.* NY Times 1/13/67, p22 [**1964**]

loadmaster, *n.* a crew member of a heavy transport aircraf who is responsible for the cargo. *The aircraft [Douglas C-47s carry a crew of eight—pilot, co-pilot, navigator, flight mechan ic, load master (who also drops the flares), two gun loaders, anc a Vietnamese Air Force liaison officer.* New Scientist 8/17/67 p328 [**1961**]

lobby-fodder, *n. Chiefly British*, a politician regarded as on primarily serving the needs of lobbyists. *It is the first porten in this Parliament that Conservative backbenchers will nc more be lobby-fodder on some issues than 30 or 40 Labou backbenchers were in the last Parliament* . . . Times (London 11/2/70, p9 [**1959**]

lobotomized, *adj.* dulled or sluggish, suggesting the aftereffect of a lobotomy. *It was the life and times of a tightly clustered and rather faceless group, which ended with a robotlike square* *dance. Mr. Sheppard's lobotomized shuffle was a joy to watch.* NY Times 2/5/68, p29 . . . *Acting President* [Peter Regan of The State University of New York at Buffalo] *was explaining his reasons for calling the police onto the campus, a speech greeted for the most part with a lobotomized silence.* Atlantic 4/71, p50 **[1968]**

local area network, a system in which a series of computers, printers, and other devices are linked by telephone lines, as in an office or building. *Abbreviation:* LAN *Other trends, like local area networks linking users in a particular building, say, are reborn each year.* NY Times 3/10/87, pC4 **[1985]**

-lock, *noun combining form.* complete stoppage of movement; (vehicular or pedestrian) traffic jam. —**aqualock** [*aquatic* + *-lock*]: . . . *"aqualock" among the ships and boats in the harbor produced gridlock in lower Manhattan, the first deputy commissioner of the City Transportation Department, Samuel I. Schwartz, said. The "aqualock" slowed the ferries' crossings, creating long lines of waiting of cars and passengers, he added.* NY Times 7/4/86, p6 —**boatlock:** *While Coast Guard officials feared "boat-lock," the mood of the harbor was one of jubilant if sun-burnt revelry* . . . Washington Post 7/5/86, pA1 —**cablock:** *Crowds brimmed the streets conquering gridlock, boatlock, a taxi strike cablock* . . . NY Times 7/6/86, p12 —**limolock:** *The largest gathering ever of world leaders paralyzed* . . . *the city with the weeklong flutter of parties, protests and police overtime. "Limo-lock entered the vernacular.* Newsweek 11/4/85, p21 —**pedlock** [*pedestrian* + *-lock*]: . . . *another new form, "pedlock," had come along to describe a pileup and immobilization of pedestrians.* NY Times 4/1/82, pC19 **[1982,** abstracted from GRIDLOCK]

lock-away, *n. British.* a long-term security. *At this level and in view of the prospects the shares should be regarded as a widows' and orphans' lock-away rather than a performance stock.* Times (London) 4/9/70, p28 **[1964]**

lockdown, *n. U.S.* a condition or period in which the inmates of a prison are kept in their cells all day under maximum security. *The shooting occurred nine days after the officials lifted a month-long "lockdown," prompted by gang-related racial battles in July in which three prisoners were killed.* NY Times 8/29/77, p18 **[1974,** from the verb phrase *lock down*]

locked, *adj.* **locked in,** not open or susceptible to changes; committed. . . . *most of the senators who were finally to vote for Carswell* [as a Supreme Court justice] *had already announced their intention, and they were, as the Washington saying goes, "locked in."* New Yorker 12/12/70, p58 **[1953]**

lock-in, *n. U.S.* a protest demonstration in which a group locks itself within a building, office, etc. *In their maneuvering over the bill, the Democrats staged a lock-in in the House, and the Republicans held a sit-out in the Senate.* Time 10/18/68, p27 *They have organized petitions, demonstrations, sit-ins, lock-ins and progressively more violent means to protest causes.* NY Times Magazine 3/3/68, p16 **[1965,** from earlier use in labor demonstrations (1920)]

lock-on, *n.* **1** the automatic tracking of an object by radar. *When an air-to-air training missile "sees" its target, a new microminiaturized signal amplifier developed by Hughes tells the pilot that lock-on has been achieved.* Scientific American 5/67, p83 **2** the forming of an airtight connection for underwater passage between submarines, rescue and exploration craft, etc. *Back at the surface, a lock-on device enables divers to transfer to a larger chamber on board, releasing the sub to return to work with a fresh diving team.* Sunday Times (London) 4/23/67, p8 **[1958** for def. 1; **1967** for def. 2; from the verb phrase *lock on*]

lock-out, *n.* an underwater compartment in which the air pressure is sufficient to prevent water from entering through the compartment's open port. *Some of the modifications which are being considered, are as follows: a lock-out which will allow entry and exit of divers at work sites down to 1000 feet* . . . New Scientist 11/17/66, p341 **[1966]**

lockstep, *n.* a rigid pattern or arrangement. *When Manning came to Stanford in 1964, he was determined to break the tra-*

ditional lockstep of three-year law school curriculums. Time 10/5/70, p69 —*adj.* rigid; unbending. *Mrs. Handy's lockstep methods (copy the great novelists, read the "Masters of the Far East," stay away from girls) produced a handful of published novels* . . . New Yorker 10/30/71, p155 **[1954,** from *lock step* a mode of marching in close order]

lockwasher, *n.* or **lock washer,** *Cell Biology.* a helical form occurring in the structure of protein as a result of some dislocation. *Making the solution abruptly more acidic (down to pH5) converts the disks directly into short helical "lock washers" of just over two turns, in length; the lock washers then stack in imperfect register and eventually anneal to yield helixes of indefinite length that are structurally very similar to the virus particle except that they are devoid of viral RNA.* Scientific American 11/78, p64 **[1971,** transferred sense (from their similarity of shape) of the term for a kind of washer designed to prevent the loosening of a nut]

locomotive, *adj.* having the capacity to stimulate or accelerate economic growth. *What can be done? The OECD* [Organization for Economic Cooperation and Development] *recommends prompt efforts by West Germany and Japan, two "locomotive" economies, to speed up growth. Since Japan is already trying to stimulate its economy, the obvious target of the OECD appeal is West Germany, which has consistently rejected expansionist economic policies.* Time 1/9/78, p45 **[1977,** transferred sense of adjective "having the power of locomotion . . ." (OED 1657)]

locust years, years of deprivation and hardship. *Yet before these locust years of Labour, we had the Conservative years of rising prosperity.* Times (London) 5/27/70, p8 *Those were terrible years—'the locust years,' Churchill has called them.* Harper's 7/65, p90 **[1962]** ▶ The phrase used by Winston Churchill (see the second quotation) was in reference to the depression years preceding World War II. Its origin is the biblical verse (Joel 2:25) "And I will restore to you the years that the locust hath eaten . . ."

lo-fi, *adj.* of a standard or inferior quality of sound reproduction; not hi-fi. . . . *most of the hi-fi sound that Cole created for next week's Andy Williams special will be wasted when it is fed through the nation's strictly lo-fi TV sets.* Time 4/26/68, p38 —*n.* lo-fi sound, reproduction, or equipment. *Finally, despite Mr. Kolodin's warning of the "lo-fi," we would "urge" the purchase of this set* [Allan Berg's *Lulu*] *as a significant item in Toscanini's recorded legacy, and as a definite contribution to any collection in which these selections are of interest.* Saturday Review 7/29/67, p53 **[1958]**

loft, *v.t.* to launch into space. *The more I hear about the McGeorge Bundy Foundation's plan for lofting communications satellites into space in order to extend the scope of Educational TV broadcasting, the more I wish it (and him) well* . . . New Yorker 1/7/67, p80 **[1961]**

LOFT (lɔːft), *n.* acronym for *low frequency radio telescope*. *LOFT would be designed for observation at frequencies between 0.5 and 10 megahertz, a range that is reflected by the ionosphere and cannot be observed from the ground.* Science News 9/5/70, p202 **[1970]**

loft jazz, *U.S.* an innovative form of jazz, often performed in an informal setting, such as a loft. Compare JAZZ LOFT. *There are other signs that New York's loft jazz, one of the few authentic underground musical activities left in the city, is about to go overground on a national scale.* NY Times 6/4/76, pC17 **[1976]**

log, *v.i., v.t.* **1 log in** or **log on,** to register, especially with a computer as an authorized operator. *Anything you can do off line should be done before you log on. If you get stuck on something, don't be reluctant to log off, figure out what you're doing, and log back on.* Popular Computing 10/83, p71 **2 log off,** to terminate one's use of a computer. *She also makes efficient use of* . . . *other services that allow her to save her place in the session, log off, and come back to where she left off.* Popular Computing 10/83, p72 **[1963]**

lognormal, *adj.* having a normal or symmetrical logarithmic distribution. *Distributions that are not normal come in for gen-*

uine attention (although not enough time is spent on the log-normal case), and tests of significance and regression methods are given brief but quite usable explanations. Scientific American 8/67, p126 [**1945, 1958,** from *log*arithm + *normal*]

loid (lɔid), *Slang.*—*n.* a strip of celluloid used by a burglar to push back the bolt of a spring lock (also used attributively). *A "loid" expert wiggles a celluloid or piece of Venetian blind strip in a door crack to open a spring lock.* Harper's 2/67, p51 —*v.t.* to unlock (a door) with a loid. *It takes an experienced thief to "loid" (open with a strip of celluloid) a door if it is fitted with a spring lock that is not double-locked.* Times (London) 11/4/68, p8 [**1958,** from cellu*loid*]

loliginid (lɒlə'dʒinid), *adj.* of or belonging to a family of long-bodied cylindrical squids. *In addition, LaRoe's work has proved that tropical loliginid squid grow much faster than previously believed. His squid reached maturity within five months after hatching, contrary to the belief that it would take three years.* Science Journal 2/70, p14 [**1963,** from Latin *lōligo, lōliginis* cuttlefish + English -*id* (adj. suffix)]

lollipop, *n. British.* a pole bearing a large disk, used as a sign to stop the traffic by a person assigned to help children cross the streets at schooltime (often used attributively). *Top-hatted they stream from the school, one boy picks up the lollipop sign—which is hidden in a bush—and traffic is brought to a halt.* Sunday Times (London) 3/9/69, p5 [**1959**]

Lomotil (lə'moutəl), *n.* a trademark for a drug that temporarily paralyzes the peristaltic contractions of the alimentary canal, used especially to treat traveler's diarrhea. *Formula:* $C_{30}H_{32}N_2O_2 \cdot HCl$ *Lomotil is an "anti-diarrhoeal" creeping into common usage in the rich world. Salesmen on missions abroad take it in their emergency medication packs, lest they succumb to "Delhi belly."* New Scientist 3/31/77, p786 [**1969**]

longueur (lɔːŋ'gər), *n.* a variant spelling of *longueur,* meaning a long or tedious passage in a book, play, etc. The original spelling was taken directly from French, and was apparently first used by Lord Byron in his epic poem *Don Juan* (1821). However, evidence showing the use of the simplified English spelling has been accumulating since the late 1950's, as the following quotations indicate: *All of the Irish critics welcomed the play as a fine piece of historical drama . . .* Sean White wrote *The Irish Press* that *"it has strength despite its central longueurs."* NY Times 5/24/63, p16 *The piece* [Grande pièce symphonique by César Franck] *is loose in construction and, as so often with Franck, one feels that its* longueurs *could do with a little pruning.* Gramophone 4/68, p540 [**1957**]

longhair, *n. Slang.* a person wearing long hair, especially a male hippie. . . . *rampaging hardhats . . . have been hunting down longhairs in the canyons of downtown Manhattan.* NY Times 5/18/70, p28 [**1969**]

longstop, *n. British.* a person or thing that serves to check, hold back, or prevent something undesirable, especially as a last resort. *In fact, session after session major Bills are sent to the Lords so late that the peers cannot be expected to act as efficient longstops.* Times (London) 3/30/70, p6 [**1957,** from the *long stop* in cricket, who stops the balls that pass the wicket-keeper]

long-term memory, the part of the memory which consists of a permanent store of information. *Long-term memory has no obvious limits on the amount which we can store in it, but . . . forgetting in long-term memory arises largely because the material is inaccessible—the information is still stored in the system but we can't get it out.* New Scientist 2/24/72, p428 [**1970**]

longuette (lɔːŋ'get), *n.* another name for MIDI. . . . *strangers busied themselves with . . . the bulging dossier of* Women's Wear Daily *evidence of the arrival of its "longuette."* New Yorker 10/10/70, p167 [**1970,** from French *longuette, adj.,* somewhat long; longish]

look-ahead, *n.* the ability of a computer to perceive or calculate in advance different possibilities, steps, etc. *Look-ahead . . . is defined in Hayes and Levy's excellent book on the first world computer chess championship. Stockholm, 1974 as "the search for a solution to a problem by examining the branches of a tree of possibilities."* Times (London) 4/15/78, p9 —*adj.* characterized by or involving this ability. See INTELLIGENT. *When the scheme was actually implemented in the late 1950's with an IBM 704 computer, a look-ahead search of two full moves took eight minutes.* Scientific American 6/73, p93 [**1972**]

look-down, *adj.* variant of DOWN-LOOKING. *Low-flying aircraft can only be tracked by a look-down radar since the ground masks land-based radars. Neither the MiG-25 nor any other Soviet aircraft has a look-down radar that works over land.* Science News 3/5/77, p147 [**1972**]

looking-glass, *adj.* completely inverted or reversed; topsy-turvy. *How long do we think the looking-glass politics and Marie Antoinette economics that Faisal practises can serve in Saudi Arabia? The cracks in the façade are still tiny but they are clearly to be seen.* Manchester Guardian Weekly 5/11/67, p5 [**1963,** in allusion to Lewis Carroll's *Through the Looking Glass*]

loon, *v.i. British Slang.* to spend time foolishly; frolic or clown *'Looning about on our bikes' means riding far beyond the speed limit, chasing along the pavement, riding straight over roundabouts; it also means buzzing oncoming motorists and playing chicken with trucks.* Listener 7/12/73, p37 [**1966** probably back formation from *loony* foolish, crazy (1872)]

loon pants, Also **loon trousers** or **loons,** *n.pl. British.* tight-fitting pants that flare from the knees down, designed for informal wear. *Dress manufacturers who are in despair at the number of young customers in loon pants and T-shirts might now consider hiring not a designer but another Johann Strauss to restore a desire for expensive extravagant dress.* Times (London) 12/5/72, p15 [**1971,** from LOON or panta*loon*]

loop[1], *n.* a circular condition in which something reacting to a stimulus produces a stimulus of its own that acts upon the source of the original stimulus. *There is no escape from the conclusion that the press is now part of the political process. We are in a loop without exit signs. We influence politicians. We are influenced by polls. The American people are polled. They provide answers based upon what they have read or seen or heard. Politicians set their agendas on the basis of what tracking polls tell them. It's conceivable that this loop is destructive to the continuation of a vibrant and free democracy.* NY Times 11/13/88, pD3 [**1976**]

loop[2], *n.* **the loop,** another name for LIPPES LOOP. *Three years ago, family-planning experts here thought the intrauterine device, the loop, would be the answer to a population increasing at the rate of more than a million a month.* NY Times 8/16/68, p8 [**1962**]

loose cannon, *U.S. Informal.* a dangerous person or thing that has gone out of control. *After all, Young had been something of a loose cannon . . . as ambassador to the United Nations, a black who seemed quick to find racism all around him.* The News and Observer, Raleigh, N.C. 5/28/82, p5A [**1977,** in allusion to the state of a cannon improperly secured on a warship]

loosey-goosey, *adj. U.S. Slang.* uncoordinated because of excessively loose or supple movement of the body. *He is long off the tee, and he uses an unorthodox, cross-handed style for putts because "I'm too loosey-goosey doing it the regular way."* Time 6/27/69, p56 [**1967,** from the rhyming slang phrase *loose as a goose*]

lophophorate (ˌloufə'fɔrit), *n.* an invertebrate animal having a fan of ciliated tentacles (lophophores) about its mouth, especially an extinct species (*Odontogriphus omalus*) discovered in 1976 and believed to have been the source of the toothlike, conical fossils called conodonts. *The discovery of a new Cambrian lophophorate . . . with conodont-like teeth from the Burgess Shale of British Columbia was described as highly significant. It represented still another type of possible "conodont animal" found in the fossil record in the past few years and suggested that some conodonts were lophophorates.* 1978 Britannica Yearbook of Science and the Future, p288 [**1977,** from *lophophore* (from Greek *lóphos* crest, comb + -*phóros* bearing) + -*ate* (noun suffix)]

lordotic, *adj.* of or relating to the characteristic arching posture of certain female mammals during mating. *In contrast, even when given high doses of estrogens, the capacity for showing normal female behavior—such as the "lordotic" response, typical in female rats and guinea pigs, in which the back is deeply arched and the genitals raised and presented to the male—was dramatically diminished. It was as if, during the period of prenatal life, some inner behavioral dial had been set at "male."* NY Times Magazine 5/7/72, p103 [**1971,** derivative of *lordosis* arching posture (1941). The original meaning of *lordotic* (1856) was pertaining to or affected with an anterior curvature of the spine.]

Lordstown syndrome (lɔrdz͵taun), *U.S.* a condition of restlessness and discontent among workers resulting from the sameness of automated assembly-line work. *Union leaders . . . contended that what passed for job dissatisfaction—the so-called Lordstown syndrome—was not new, could be resolved by increasing job security and pay through traditional collective bargaining procedures, and was at most limited to special work situations and special circumstances.* Americana Annual 1974, p331 [**1973,** named after the fully automated assembly plant of General Motors in *Lordstown,* Ohio, where workers first went on strike over the job dissatisfaction issue]

Lorentz force, a force acting on an electrically charged particle moving through a magnetic field. *Lorentz force, named for the Dutch physicist H.A. Lorentz, tends to make a charged particle entering a magnetic field travel at right angles to both the direction of its original motion and the lines of force.* Scientific American 5/63, p88 [**1961,** named after the Dutch physicist Hendrik Antoon *Lorentz,* 1853-1928]

lossmaker, *n. British.* a business or industry that shows consistent losses or deficits. *What happens when two companies, both lossmakers, merge into one? The answer, as often as not, is one big lossmaker.* Manchester Guardian Weekly 1/23/71, p22 [**1963**]

lossmaking, *adj. British.* showing consistent losses or deficits. *He started by picking up a 40% stake in the lossmaking Carson's chocolate business in March 1964.* Sunday Times (London) 8/15/71, p41 [**1964**]

loti (ˈlouti:), *n., pl.* **maloti.** the monetary unit of Lesotho, equal to 100 lisente. *This January, for example, Lesotho announced that it would mint its own currency, the loti (plural, maloti), equal to one South African rand. The loti, however, will supplement, rather than replace the South African rand.* 1981 Collier's Encyclopedia Year Book, p464 [**1980,** from *Sesotho*]

lotus position, a sitting position with the legs folded and intertwined and the hands resting on the knees, used in yoga. *His thing, once he discovered the lotus position can work up an appetite, included four scrambled eggs, ham, the half chicken, bread and butter, and a quart of milk.* Saturday Review 10/24/70, p10 [**1962,** a loan translation of Sanalern't *padmāsana (padma* lotus + *āsana* posture), so called in allusion to the lotus leaf which, though it rests on water, does not become wet, and thus symbolizes detachment]

Lou Gehrig's disease, a disease of the central nervous system accompanied by degeneration of the muscles. *In Boca Raton, Fla., physician Murray Sanders of the Sanders Research Institute is experimenting with a combination of venoms from the cobra and African snake, the krait, to treat victims of a central nervous system disease called amyotrophic lateral sclerosis, also known as Lou Gehrig's disease because it killed the great baseball player.* World Book Science Annual 1977, p351 [**1965,** named after Henry *Lou*is *Gehrig,* 1903-1941]

lovastatin (͵ləvəˈsteitin), *n.* a drug that decreases cholesterol by blocking the enzyme which regulates cholesterol production in the liver. *The FDA approved lovastatin, a drug shown to reduce total cholesterol levels by 32% and levels of low-density lipoproteins (LDLs), the so-called "bad" cholesterol, by up to 39%.* Americana Annual 1988 p348 [**1987,** of uncertain origin in]

love beads, colored beads worn about the neck as an ornament and symbol of brotherly love. . . . *a group of bright, radical in-*

terns . . . sported the abundant hair, bell bottom trousers, love beads, and other symbols of the disaffected young . . . NY Times 11/29/70, pD8 [**1968**]

love-bombing, *n. U.S.* the outpouring of contrived affection by members of a cult towards a potential convert. *Love-bombing, a term coined to describe the typical pattern of early encounters with cults, overwhelms the visitor with a barrage of apparent fellowship, concern and affection, purveyed by solicitous and ever-smiling devotees.* NY Times 11/28/78, pA22 [**1975**]

love bug, a small black fly of the southeastern United States, related to the March fly. The love bug flies only during daylight, feeds on dead vegetation, and appears at springtime in very large numbers, often covering windshields and clogging radiators of automobiles. *An exotic new driving hazard faces motorists in the American resort of Miami this summer—the love bug. The love bug population, report scientists, is on the increase and is spreading down the Florida peninsula at the rate of 20 miles every year. The love bug is a flying insect rather like an elongated housefly.* Sunday Times (London) 7/13/75, p8 [**1966,** so called because these flies are often seen in pairs during their mating season]

love-in, *n.* a public gathering of people for the purpose of celebrating love or demonstrating against war, etc. *Only once in a while did he have time to remember that there was a . . . world of junkies, hippies, freaks, and freaks who made open love at love-ins, be-ins, concerts, happenings, and on the stage of tiny theaters with invited guests.* Harper's 3/71, p44 [**1967,** see **-IN**]

lovestruck, *adj.* affected strongly with love. *But the production keeps it [Ugo Benelli's performance in Giovedì Grasso] in the perspective of a coherent ensemble where all characterizations are balanced, even to the scatty, lovestruck housemaid (Janet Hughes) and the dimwitted reluctant elderly seductress (Johanna Peters in best form).* Times (London) 10/27/70, p11 [**1964,** patterned after *moonstruck, thunderstruck,* etc.]

lowball, *v.t. U.S. Informal.* to give a deliberately low appraisal or estimate of, especially so as to deceive. *Bankers sometimes lowball your net worth by 20% to 30% for an unsecured loan . . . Some will also lowball the value of the car or home you want by 20% to 30%.* Money Magazine 6/89, p96 [**1981,** from automobile dealers' slang *lowball, n.,* a low price given verbally to a customer and later repudiated (1956)]

low camp, (used as both a noun and adjective phrase) unconscious or unsophisticated use of the artistically banal or mediocre. Compare **HIGH CAMP.** *In his novel* A World in the Evening *Christopher Isherwood gave the first literary definition. He divided camp into two schools, 'high' and 'low'. Low camp he defined very accurately as a female impersonator 'imitating Marlene [Dietrich] in a seedy nightclub', but by inventing high camp he liberated the word from its purely homosexual connexions . . .* George Melly, Revolt Into Style, 1970, p177 [**1967**] ►See the note under **CAMP.**

Lower Forty-eight or **Lower 48,** *U.S.* the forty-eight states of the continental United States excluding Alaska. *People arrive steadily. And people go. They go from Anchorage and Fairbanks—let alone the more exacting wild. Some, of course, are interested only in a year or two's work, then to return with saved high wages to the Lower Forty-eight.* New Yorker 6/20/77, p49 [**1976**]

low jinks, *Informal.* irreverent or coarse behavior; vulgar jokes or pranks. *The Acting Company brought an intriguing production of "Twelfth Night" to the Kennedy Center's Terrace Theater last night—intriguing because it dares to go against the grain. Shakespeare's comedy about the befuddlement of lovers and the low-jinks of carousers on the island of Illyria is customarily viewed as one of his merrier efforts.* Washington Post 3/24/82, pB3 [**1957,** from *low* coarse, vulgar + *(high) jinks* unrestrained merrymaking (OED 1842)]

low-level, *adj.* not intensely radioactive. *Solidified high-level wastes are generated by commercial reprocessing plants that remove waste fission products from fuel that has been used in nuclear power stations; low-level wastes are contaminants in* solid materials, principally in the transuranium elements (such as plutonium) generated at AEC installations. 1971 Collier's Encyclopedia Year Book, p385 [**1970**]

lowlight, n. Informal. the least prominent or interesting part of an event, subject, or the like. He spent the rest of his article discussing 10 "lowlights of the 1978-79 Supreme Court term" that he said demonstrated the Court's great insensitivity to important civil liberties principles. NY Times 1/13/80, pD7 [**1966**, patterned after highlight (OED 1658)]

low profile, **1** a deliberately low-keyed or understated attitude or position; a restrained, inconspicuous stance. Also called LOW SILHOUETTE. Ultimately, a far more vexatious issue than any of Japan's economic problems is the nation's future role in Asia and the world. Japan today simply stands too tall and too rich to maintain a low profile . . . Time 3/2/70, p37 **2** a person who shows or cultivates a low profile. We now have a government of "low profiles," gray men who represent no identifiable place, no region, no program. Harper's 4/70, p87 [**1964**, translation of Japanese teishisei, from tei low + shisei posture, the motto of the Hayato Ikeda cabinet (1960-1964)]

low-rent, adj. U.S. Slang. shoddy; sleazy. Penn and Teller play two low-rent types living off the land of show business. NY Times Magazine 12/4/88, p84 The Italian publisher Longanesi brought out a low-rent docunovel . . . about sex, drugs, models, the Mafia and death. Spy (The New York Monthly) 3/88, p58 [**1988**]

lowriding, n. U.S. a style of cruising in an automobile practiced especially in California and New Mexico. See the quotation for details. Farther east, on Whittier Boulevard, young Hispanics express themselves with a unique form of Saturday night fever known as "low riding"—cruising in ornately decorated autos equipped with hydraulic pumps that lower the chassis to within inches of the roadway so as to produce showers of sparks as the car bounces along the street. Time 10/16/78, p52 [**1978**] —**lowrider**, n.: The custom is called lowriding. The car a lowrider drives—almost always a sedan produced by the General Motors Corporation—is also called a lowrider. New Yorker 7/10/78, p70

low-rise, adj. (of a building) having few stories and no elevator. In a layout of predominantly "low-rise" (not tall) new buildings there would be a larger element of private housing than had been usual in new towns. Times (London) 6/24/67, p3 [**1957**]

low silhouette, another term for LOW PROFILE (def. 1). The Soviet military men, as well as the civilians, generally try to maintain an extremely low silhouette. Time 6/22/70, p33 [**1968**]

low-tech, adj. of or having to do with LOW-TECHNOLOGY. Fantasy, on the other hand, usually has a low-tech, medieval setting that is clearly no simple variation on the earth we know . . . Names, Vol. 30, no. 2, 1982, p60 —n. a style of design or interior decoration typical or imitative of early technology. Late-50's low tech, the décor in her public rooms was harsh, metallic and fluorescent. NY Times Magazine 5/11/80, p66 [**1979**]

low-technology, adj. of or relating to old, unsophisticated technology limited to the production of basic commodities. Because the U.S. no longer commands such a high share of the world's high-technology market, it no longer can offset its large imports of low-technology items such as shoes and clothing. Time 10/2/78, p59 [**1973**]

L-PAM ('el'pæm), n. a nitrogen mustard used as an anticancer drug. Formula: $C_{13}H_{18}Cl_2N_2O_2$ Fisher and his colleagues at the 34 centers have found a 36 percent reduction in death two years after giving patients the drug L-PAM as an adjunct to a radical mastectomy. Science News 2/5/77, p91 [**1974**, from l-phenylalanine mustard]

LRF, abbreviation of luteinizing (hormone) releasing factor, a hormone secreted by the hypothalamus that causes the release of luteinizing hormone (which stimulates cells in the ovary and the testes). Also called LH-RH. Compare TRF. The results of the experiments may prove to be even more important if further ex-perimentation shows LRF can affect copulation in humans. LRF may be helpful in the treatment of impotence in males where no organic defect can be found. It may also become useful as a cure for frigidity and infertility in women. Science News 7/14/73, p21 [**1970**]

LRV, abbreviation of lunar roving vehicle. See also LUNAR ROVER. Certainly the lunar Rover was a high-cost vehicle, but it was a pilot-research vehicle. The LRV made possible one of the most prolific scientific explorations ever attempted. Science News 9/18/71, p184 [**1969**]

LSI, **1** abbreviation of LARGE-SCALE INTEGRATION. Compare MSI. LSI . . . involves building up very complex electronic networks on tiny chips. A major step beyond current solid-state technology, it would permit packaging the entire circuit for a high-performance radio in a space one-thousandth the size of today's typical transistor. 1969 Collier's Encyclopedia Year Book, p80 **2** a unit or array of integrated circuits. . . . the central processor for a high-capacity computer could be built from perhaps 100 LSI chips, making such a computer readily portable. Scientific American 2/70, p29 [**1967**]

lucid dream, a dream during which the sleeper is aware of dreaming and therefore has some control over it. The lucid dream is an altered state of consciousness (ASC), a drastic change in the pattern of your mind's functioning. Harper's 12/74, p111 [**1974**]

luddite, n. one who is strongly opposed to increased mechanization or automation in any field (often used attributively). Also spelled **Luddite**. In American estimates, however, port capacity can be greatly increased by quick installation of modern equipment—if the Indian Government is really determined to override the Luddite resistance of the wharf labour. Times (London) 12/29/65, p5 [**1962**, from the proper name Luddite, applied in the early 1800's to any group of English workers who went about destroying manufacturing machinery for fear that the use of the machines would put them out of work; ultimately from Ned Ludd, a Leicestershire "village idiot" who in the 1790's broke some stocking frames]

ludditish, adj. characteristic of a luddite; showing Ludditism. Not many years ago it was considered regressive and ludditish even to suggest the need for control of technology. Saturday Review 3/2/68, p53 [**1968**]

Ludditism or **Luddism**, n. strong opposition to increased mechanization or automation in any field. In an uprising against ignorance and psychopathology Ludditism has no place . . . Manchester Guardian Weekly 6/19/71, p20 There is the Data flow project, aimed at increasing their productivity: "Through systems men are just as susceptible to Luddism as anyone else," McQuaker comments. Sunday Times (London) 4/16/67, p24 [**1964**, originally used in the sense of "the beliefs and practices of the 19th-century Luddites"]

lude, n. a slang name for QUAALUDE. Compare QUAD². Because "ludes," as the students call them, are so abused as a "fun" drug, pharmacists are constantly on the watch for phoney prescriptions. Maclean's 8/21/78, p22 [**1978**, short for Quaalude]

Luing ('lu:iŋ), n. a breed of beef cattle produced by crossing the offspring of Shorthorn bulls and purebred Highland cows. Welsh Black cattle have spread far beyond the borders of the principality to produce beef on all but the highest hills, while the newest on the scene is the Luing. Times (London) 8/14/72, p14 [**1970**, named for the island of Luing off the west coast of Scotland, where the breed was produced]

luminal art, a form of art that uses the arrangement or projection of colored electric lights to create images, moving patterns, flashing designs, etc. Also called LUMINIST ART. Along with everything else, art has gone electric . . . The new luminal art has suddenly emerged as both international and popular. A record 42,000 visitors showed up when Kansas City's Nelson Gallery staged a month-long "Sound Light Silence" show last November. Time 4/28/67, p36 [**1967**]

luminist art, another name for LUMINAL ART. Although interest in kinetic and luminist art remained high in 1969, there was a reaction against the technologically elaborate and sensation-rich work of recent years. Many artists turned to projects designed to give subtle aesthetic experiences devoid of sophisticated engineering or aggressive electronics. Americana Annual 1970, p99 [**1970**]

luminosity, n. Nuclear Physics. the number and density of accelerated particles in a beam. The higher-energy, higher-luminosity storage rings would also be very useful for the study of the weak interaction. The weak interaction tends to get overwhelmed by strong-interaction effects at low energies. At higher energies it should come into its own. Science News 5/19/73, p329 [**1973**]

lumisome ('lu:mə,soum), n. a light-emitting particle in the cells of animals that emit light; a unit particle of bioluminescence. "Lumisomes" contain all the various molecules which have previously been identified as part of the bioluminescent system. So the list of sub-cellular organelles increases, and lumisomes take their place with lysosomes, peroxisomes and the rest. New Scientist 7/12/73, p66 [**1973**, from Latin lūmen, -inis light + English -some body]

lumpectomy (,ləm'pektəmi:), n. the surgical removal of a tumor in the breast. Also called TYLECTOMY. In the "simple" mastectomy, the breast is removed but the lymph nodes are not touched, and in the "partial" mastectomy or "lumpectomy," only the tumor and a surrounding section of normal breast tissue are excised. Newsweek 10/7/74, p34 [**1972**, from lump + -ectomy surgical removal from Greek ektomé a cutting out] ►The name is new; the surgical procedure has been practiced since before World War II.

lumpenprole or **lumpenprol** ('ləmpən,proul), n. one of the lumpenproletariat; an unintellectual, unenlightened worker. Once we were one-dimensional, then (in an appendix) we were revolutionary students, a little later flower-people, hippies, counter-culture cadres (a blend presumably of Marx's Bohemia and lumpenproles?). Manchester Guardian Weekly 2/17/73, p26 The Autograph Hound, by John Lahr (Knopf). An interesting, if somewhat shallow, first novel . . . that takes us through one frenetic week in the life of Benny Walsh: lumpenprol, loser, busboy, autograph collector. New Yorker 3/17/73, p129 [**1971**, short for lumpenproletarian (1930's) influenced by prole (1930's) a proletarian]

lunanaut, n. another name for LUNARNAUT. A member of the White House space council gives firm assurance that "neither side" had, until recent accidents, killed an astronaut or cosmonaut (but why, at the present stage, not lunanaut?). Times (London) 10/5/67, p8 [**1965**, from Latin lūna moon + English astronaut]

lunar mass, the mass of the moon (7.35 x 10^{25} g.), used as an astronomical unit of mass. As measured from radio signals received at Earth, the motion of the spacecraft provided a new estimate of the mass of Jupiter—heavier than previously thought by 1 lunar mass. Also, it showed the lunar masses of the Galilean satellites as being: Io, 1.22; Europa, 0.67; Ganymede, 2.02; and Callisto, 1.44. McGraw-Hill Yearbook of Science and Technology 1975, p383 [**1974**]

lunar module, a lightweight manned spacecraft carried by a larger spacecraft and detached while in lunar orbit so that it may land on the surface of the moon. Abbreviation: LM Compare COMMAND MODULE, SERVICE MODULE. The lunar module 's the first of its kind, a new generation of spacecraft too weak to lift itself from the earth, too vulnerable to fly through the atmosphere without burning up. So specialized is the strange vehicle that it even is designed in two sections—one to land on the moon and the other to take off again. Science News 3/1/69, p218 [**1967**]

lunarnaut, n. an astronaut who travels to the moon; a lunar astronaut. Also called LUNANAUT. . . . deprivation of nasal satisfaction may prove irksome and nerve-ragging to future long-stay lunarnauts and the provision of an interesting aromatic background may be as necessary to their well-being as the maintenance of an artificial atmosphere. New Scientist 3/14/69, p316 [**1965**, from lunar + astronaut]

lunar rover or **lunar roving vehicle,** a vehicle for exploratory travel on the lunar surface. Also called MOON CAR, MOON CRAWLER, MOON ROVER. The Lunar Roving Vehicle looks like a two-tone buckboard; the chassis is silvery, and the four plastic fenders (which will prevent the astronauts from being sprayed with dust) are brown. New Yorker 7/17/71, p42 [**1964**]

lunarscape, n. a view of the lunar surface. The moon began to show out over the North Sea. It was huge, and through my powerful binoculars I was able to study its face. The lunarscape looked like some great contoured globe. Manchester Guardian Weekly 8/15/70, p12 [**1965**, from lunar + -scape view, scene]

lunchtime abortion, Informal. an abortion performed by vacuum aspiration. May we remind our correspondent that legal abortion is not nearly as safe as she would like to think? . . . Even the Karman catheter (lunchtime abortion) carried at least a 13 per cent complication rate. New Statesman 5/16/75, p661 [**1972**, so called because of the short time it usually takes to complete it]

lungs, n.pl. Chiefly British. breathing spaces, such as small parks that might be placed in overpopulated or traffic-congested areas. Designs for urban living provide for "Landscaped areas," created either as "lungs" or to resolve an architectural dissonance. Manchester Guardian Weekly 4/18/70, p11 [**1970**, from a use popular in the 1800's, as in the phrase lungs of London (1808)]

lunilogical, adj. of or relating to study of the moon, especially its geology. The winning lunar roving vehicle concept consists of a collapsible four-wheel vehicle to provide surface transportation on the Moon for two astronauts, their hand tools, other equipment, lunilogical samples and experiments. Science Journal 1/70, p16 [**1970**]

Lunokhod (,lu:nə'xɔ:t), n. a vehicle designed by Soviet scientists for scientific exploration on the lunar surface, powered by solar cells and directed by radio signals from earth. The news agency called the Lunokhod "a self-propelled scientific laboratory", and said that it "fundamentally extends" the area of exploration. Times (London) 11/18/70, p1 [**1970**, from Russian Lunokhod, literally, moonwalker]

luteinizing hormone-releasing factor, the full name of LRF. Still another hormone, luteinizing hormone-releasing factor (LH-RH or LRF), is secreted by the hypothalamic region of the brain. LH-RH serves as a master switch over luteinizing hormone, the sex hormones and ovulation. Science News 2/10/73, p93 [**1970**]

luteolysin (,lu:ti:ou'laisən), n. a chemical substance which destroys the corpus luteum even if an egg has been fertilized, studied to develop an effective contraceptive pill. A further method—impossible at the moment—would be to use synthetic analogues of the gonadotrophins as specific antagonists to them. Luteolysins, as yet unknown in man, could be used to prevent the formation or growth of the corpora lutea. Science Journal 3/68, p87 [**1968**, from (corpus) luteum a ductless gland important in maintaining pregnancy in animals + lysin a substance causing dissolution]

luxon, n. any elementary particle with zero mass that moves at the speed of light. Compare TARDYON. Other particles with proper mass of zero, such as neutrinos and gravitons, also travel at the speed of light. Bilaniuk suggested that all such zero mass particles be termed "luxons" from a Latin word for "light." Saturday Review 7/8/72, p54 [**1971**, from Latin lūx light + -on elementary particle]

lwei (l'wei or əl'wei), n. a monetary unit of Angola, equal to 1/100 of a KWANZA. The currency is the kwanza divided into 100 lwei. Coins are of 50 lwei, 1, 2, 5 and 10 kwanza; notes are of 20, 50, 100, 500 and 1,000 kwanza. Statesman's Yearbook 1984-85, p82 [**1978**]

Lyme arthritis (laim), earlier name of LYME DISEASE. Alerted by the Connecticut data, doctors in Massachusetts, Rhode Island and New York have since discovered instances of Lyme arthritis in their own areas. These cases suggest that the disease may have been misdiagnosed or overlooked in the past and may actually be widespread. Time 6/13/77, p56 [**1976**, named after *Lyme*, a town in southern Connecticut where the disease was first observed in 1975]

Lyme disease, an infectious disease marked by large reddened areas of the skin, chills and fever, fatigue, and often arthritic, neuralgic, and cardiac symptoms, caused by bacteria carried by a species of tick. *Lyme disease is an affliction of summer. It is a tickborne bacterial disease that is most likely to be contracted during the months of June through September, when youngsters and adults are outdoors, walking barelegged in woods and long grass.* Scientific American 7/87, p78 [**1980;** see LYME ARTHRITIS]

lymphokine, *n.* any of various chemical agents secreted by T cells which have been activated by suitable antigens. Lymphokines are involved in cell-mediated immunity and other processes affecting cells. *The T-lymphocytes receive the antigen in an appropriate form through the intermediary of the macrophages. Some of them kill the foreign microbe cells directly. Others secrete various lymphokines, substances that take part in the defense through various mechanisms.* Lucien Israel, Conquering Cancer, 1978, p20 [**1971,** from *lympho*cyte lymph cell + Greek *kīneîn* to move]

lymphotoxin, *n.* a lymphokine having a toxic effect on cells derived from a tumor. *One of these mediators is known to attract inflammatory (white) cells and another can keep the inflammatory cells at the site of the infection. A third mediator, lymphotoxin, can destroy uninfected as well as infected cells, and a fourth is the now well-known substance interferon, which can inhibit the replication of viruses.* Scientific American 1/73, p25 [**1972,** from *lympho*cyte lymph cell + *toxin*]

lysocline, *n.* a layer of water in the sea where certain chemical substances undergo dissolution. *When marine organisms die and sink to about 4,000 meters, they cross the "lysocline," below which calcium carbonate redissolves because of the high pressure.* Scientific American 11/70, p106 [**1970,** from *lyso*-dissolution + *-cline* layer (as in *thermocline* and *syncline*]

lysosomal, *adj.* of or relating to lysosomes. *The membrane serves to protect the rest of the cell from the contents of lysosomes, because uninhibited action of lysosomal enzymes cause cell death.* Times (London) 9/23/68, p6 [**1957**]

lysosome, *n.* a cellular granule containing enzymes which cause the chemical decomposition of substances entering the cell. . . . *in arthritis the damage to the joints might be caused by some agent rupturing the lysosomes and allowing enzymes to leak out* . . . Annual Register of World Events in 1968 p377 [**1955,** from *lyso*- dissolution + *-some* body]

lysostaphin (ˌlaisəˈstæfən), *n.* an enzyme that destroys staphylococcal bacteria by disintegrating the bacterial cell wall. *Enzymes may offer an alternative to antibiotic therapy in treating staph infections that cannot be blocked by known antibiotics. Preliminary research on dogs with acute staph infections of heart valves suggests an enzyme called lysostaphin is a potential cure for such infections in human beings.* Science News 11/11/67, p469 [**1967,** from *lyso*- dissolution + *staphylo*cocci + *-in* (chemical suffix)]

M

M₁, M₂, M₃. See these entries in their alphabetical places (**M-one, M-two, M-three**).

ma and pa, variant of MOM AND POP. *Says Roger Kennedy, terminal manager for a grocery wholesaler: "We've been reluctant to hire women because the job involves unloading heavy cases at Ma and Pa grocers."* Time 4/26/76, p100 *Ali's Alley, 77 Greene St., between Spring and Broome Sts . . . Sort of a ma-and-pa jazz loft, owned and managed by drummer Kashied Ali.* New Yorker 1/15/79, p6 **[1963]**

Mace (meis), *n.* Also spelled **mace.** the trade name of a nerve irritant with a tear gas base, which produces a burning sensation in the eyes, throat, etc., used in the form of an aerosol spray as a temporary incapacitant. Also called CHEMICAL MACE. *Mace temporarily incapacitates, but it contains no toxic ingredient other than tear gas and the risk with Mace is negligible when compared with conventional weapons, the team reported.* NY Times 6/8/68, p18 **—v.t.** Also spelled **mace.** to attack or disable with Mace. *I've been maced in the face and tear-gassed and hit on the head.* Atlantic 3/70, p62 **[1967]**

machine art, a form of art that uses mechanical, electronic, magnetic, or similar devices as objects of art. **—Machine Art: E.A.T. (Experiments in Art and Technology)** *became an international organization. Its more than 35 chapters encouraged the development of machine art all over the world.* Americana Annual 1969, p95 **[1969; an earlier meaning (OEDS 1945) is artworks, produced by a machine]**

machine intelligence, another term for ARTIFICIAL INTELLIGENCE. *IBM describes the assembler as a programmable, adaptable machine tool, not a robot. Though it is similar to work carried out by machine-intelligence researchers at Edinburgh University, its designers insist they are not in the artificial intelligence business.* Times (London) 3/26/76, p19 **[1966]**

machine language, the coding system that a computer uses to process information. Compare COMPILER LANGUAGE, COMPUTER LANGUAGE. *Programming in machine language is a dying art because it is too intimately involved with the machine design and with numeral systems that are not easy to handle.* Encyclopedia Science Supplement (Grolier) 1971, p159 **[1956]**

machine-readable, *adj.* able to be processed directly by a computer. *These [information-handling] functions all involve the manipulation of digital information. Therefore they can be handled by machines, with great savings in time and labor over manual techniques, provided that the basic records are available in a machine-readable medium such as punched cards.* Scientific American 9/66, p228 **[1961]**

machine sculpture, a sculpture in the form of a mechanical, electronic, or similar device. Compare MACHINE ART. *But the ultimate comment on technology came from the American artist Tinguely who built machine-sculptures that could be exhibited only once—because they destroy themselves.* New Scientist 3/12/70, p513 **[1970]**

machine time, the amount of time a computer or other machine is in operation on a specific job. *In my environment the majority of user time, not machine time but user time, is spent in writing and running short programs.* New Scientist 9/12/68, p548 **[1968]**

machine translation, translation from one language into another by an electronic computer. *Information stored in microfilm, microdots, magnetic tape, computers, and in other machine-manipulatable form, can be retrieved from any distance. Access will be speeded up by the use of advanced techniques in classifying and indexing, machine translation, and electronic scanning.* McGraw-Hill Yearbook of Science and Technology 1970, p82 **[1949, 1956]**

macro-, combining form meaning "large" or "large-scale," formerly used to form scientific terms but since the 1960's introduced into the common or general vocabulary, as in the following examples: **—macrochange,** *n.: Revolutions, including the Russian one, made the mistake of insisting that the macro-change, of the whole system, should come before micro-change, of the life style.* Manchester Guardian Weekly 4/18/70, p15 **—macrocontract,** *n.: With a macro-contract worth some £30 million, neither side can afford to make mistakes.* Sunday Times (London) 10/19/69, p37 **—macro-energy,** *n.: . . . few scientists would aver that either quantum theory or relativity is wrong. It is thought instead that both must be incomplete, missing some essential facts about nature. The incompleteness must lie somewhere in the interface between the macro-world and macro-energy and the micro-world and micro-energy.* Encyclopedia Science Supplement (Grolier) 1970, p64 **—macrophallic,** *adj.: Freedom from constraint has not resulted in any great efflorescence of erotic art, but merely a dreary duplication of commercial porn, meaty, masturbatory, with its inevitable distortions, brutalised women and macrophallic faceless men.* Sunday Times (London) 4/23/72, p43 **—macroplan,** *n.: Whatever the macro-plan, every graduate has a right to be considered in terms of what he needs to get out of his job and how he will be utilized by it.* New Scientist 5/28/70, p418 **—macroscale,** *n.: Meteorology is one of the few sciences which continually and consistently acquires a mass of reliable data on a macroscale.* Encyclopedia Science Supplement (Grolier) 1968, p113 **—macrosociology,** *n.: At a session devoted to macrosociology, papers were presented on "The Comparative and Evolutionary Study of Macro-Institutions" . . .* Americana Annual 1968, p603 **—macrostrategy,** *n.: But it is impossible for a government nowadays to have no macro-strategy; and Mr. Heath's Carshalton speech in 1967 gave a glimpse of one.* Times (London) 11/1/68, p27 **—macroworld,** *n.: The illustrations—and it is hard to leave them alone—cover both the micro- and macroworld of nature.* NY Times 8/3/68, p27

macro, *n.* an instruction in a programming or computer language that is automatically translated into several instructions in a machine language. *Once your macro is given a name, the program will automatically execute all the keystrokes recorded whenever the macro is called up. You no longer have to learn a computer language and become a programmer to use macros.* NY Times 9/16/86, pC4 **[1963,** short for *macroinstruction* (1959)**]**

macrobiotic, *adj.* of or relating to macrobiotics. *Macrobiotics, like many panaceas, can be many things to many people. Some think it confers superhuman strength . . . For many, yoga and macrobiotic diets have become a substitute for drugs.* Time 11/16/70, p60 **—n.** a follower or adherent of macrobiotics. *Most macrobiotics, as Ohsawa's devotees call themselves, try to follow his other nine diets, which are graduated from six to minus three to include increasing amounts of fish and vegetables—organically grown—along with brown rice.* Time 11/16/70, p59 **[1962,** from Greek *makrobiotos* long-lived, prolonging life; so called from the belief that a macrobiotic diet confers longevity**]** ▶The term was originally used in the sense of "relating to the prolongation of life" (OED 1797).

macrobiotics, *n.* a dietary system based on the Zen Buddhist division of the world into the opposite and complementary principles of *yin* and *yang,* in which a balanced diet consists of a 5 to 1 proportion of yin (organically grown sugar, fruits, vegetables) to yang (meat, eggs, etc.). *"Rice, unpolished rice, is the basis of macrobiotics . . . It is a cleansing diet. Physically, mentally, and spiritually."* New Yorker 5/16/70, p46 [**1965,** originally used in the sense of the art or science of prolonging life (OED 1862)]

macroengineering, *n.* engineering dealing with extremely large and complex projects (also used attributively). *For the first time a one-day discussion was held on "macroengineering" projects—the construction of things so big size alone makes them different from all other things. Past examples include the pyramids and the Panama Canal (successful) and Charlemagne's Rhine-Danube canal (a flop).* NY Times 2/19/78, pD7 [**1964**]

macrolide, *n.* any of a class of antibiotics made by species of streptomyces, characterized by a ring structure of large size. *There exists a class of antibiotics known as the polyene macrolides, which have been known for some 15 years as potent and effective therapeutic agents against a wide variety of fungal infections of Man.* New Scientist 10/17/68, p120 [**1960,** from Polish *makrolid,* apparently from *makro-* macro- + *lakt*id lactide (substance formed from lactic acid)]

MACV (mæk'vi:), *n.* acronym for *Military Assistance Command, Vietnam,* the official name of the U.S. military command in South Vietnam. *We have also recently told MACV that we have a high priority requirement for night photorecce of key motorable routes in Laos.* NY Times 6/13/71, pD37 [**1965**]

MAD (mæd), *n.* acronym for MUTUAL ASSURED DESTRUCTION (a concept of nuclear deterrence based on the ability of each side in a conflict to cause intolerable damage to the other in retaliation for a nuclear attack). *In the acronymically MAD era of mutually assured destruction, atomic warfare is clearly absurd.* New Scientist 9/14/78, p785 [**1973,** coined by Donald G. Brennan, born 1926, an American military strategist and mathematician]

MADD, *n.* acronym for *Mothers Against Drunk Driving. Laws in 23 states . . . have established that alcohol servers can be held responsible for injuries caused by drunk drivers. MADD supports this concept of third-person liability and wants to expand it to each state.* Christian Science Monitor 5/28/86, p5 [**1986**]

Mad Hatter's disease, another name for MINAMATA DISEASE. Compare HATTER'S SHAKES. *Two American physicists, however, have sifted the evidence and offer the explanation that Newton had a classic case of Mad Hatter's disease—mercury poisoning.* New Scientist and Science Journal 12/30/71, p274 [**1971**]

Maffei galaxy (mɑ:f'fei:), either of two galaxies which are part of the local group (of relatively close galactic systems). *The Maffei galaxies, obscured by the Milky Way dust, appear as small, faint, diffuse patches.* World Book Science Annual 1972, p266 *According to preliminary estimates, Maffei 1 and Maffei 2 appear to be about three million light-years away, or not quite twice as distant as the Andromeda galaxy. The identification of the new galaxies began in 1968 when Paolo Maffei, a young Italian astronomer working in the Laboratory of Astrophysics in Frascati, reported finding two strange objects quite close together in infrared photographs of one of the dustiest regions of the Milky Way, between the constellations Perseus and Cassiopeia.* Scientific American 3/71, p45 [**1971**]

mafia or **Mafia,** *n.* any secret or exclusive society; a closed circle or clique. *Back in Paris she drew support from Andre Gide, Andre Maurois, Francois Mauriac, and others from the Twenties literary mafia.* Manchester Guardian Weekly 8/22/70, p11 *The composers' Mafia, with its dedication to atonality and the production of new noises, holds no terrors for him* [Gian Carlo Menotti]. New Yorker 1/3/70, p44 [**1964,** extended use of the name of the secret criminal society (OED 1875)]

Mafiology, *n.* the study of the Mafia crime syndicate. *These key events in current Mafiology are skilfully described from young Bonanno's viewpoint.* Times (London) 3/16/72, p11 [**1971,** from *Mafia* + *-ology* study of]

magainin (mə'geinin), *n.* any of a group of broad-spectrum antibiotics obtained from secretions in the skin of certain species of frogs. *The magainins . . . kill bacteria, funguses, the yeas that often infects AIDS patients, and protozoans like those tha cause malaria.* NY Times 8/10/87, pA20 [**1987,** from Hebrew *māgēn* shield + English *-in*]

magazine, *n.* a television program comprised of various new and entertainment features linked together as a series (ofte used attributively). *Later this year ABC and NBC will intro duce their own versions of the magazine format, which is basi cally an hour-long collection of documentary-type reports . . At this rate television may soon offer more "magazines" tha the corner newsstand.* Time 3/27/78, p83 [**1975,** earlier (OED: 1936) used only of radio programs]

magcon, *n.* a concentration of magnetic material on the surface of a moon or planet. *Magnetic concentrations ("magcons") i the lunar surface could, if of sufficient extent and fiel strength, interact locally with the solar wind when the mag cons are on the daytime lunar side.* Nature 4/21/72 p381 [**1972,** from *mag*netic *con*centration, patterned afte MASCON]

magic bullet, a drug or other medicinal agent that is able to de stroy specific disease-causing bacteria, viruses, cancer cells, o the like without harming the host. *. . . we are forced to con clude that zinc is no magic bullet. That is to say, it is a dru, like other drugs. Magic bullets are rarer than people like t think. There are, for example, insulin-resistant diabetics. An the famous antibiotics are far from being comprehensively ef fective.* New Yorker 9/12/77, p116 *Another important facto in the development of an effective cancer therapy is that should act like a "magic bullet," killing cancer cells whil doing a minimum of damage to normal ones.* Scientific Amer can 5/78, p92 [**1967,** originally used in reference to the pio neering efforts of the German biochemist Paul Ehrlich (1854 1915) to discover a chemical that would kill bacteria withou harming human beings, which led to his discovery of the an tisyphilitic drug arsphenamine]

Magic Marker, *U.S.* the trade name of an instrument for mark ing and drawing, consisting of a metal tube which holds quick drying, waterproof ink and a thick felt tip which transmits th ink onto a surface. *Poring all day over legal tomes, scrawlin, notes with a Magic Marker on a clip board, using Lati phrases, he* [Lenny Bruce] *experienced a heady pleasure.* N Times Magazine 6/27/71, p22 [**1956**]

magic mushroom, 1 a mushroom of western North Americ containing psilocybin, an alkaloid which produces hallucinato ry effects when eaten. *The autumn rains and fertile pasture propagate thousands of little mushrooms of the psilocybe spe cies, commonly known as magic mushrooms. Renowned fo their ability to produce a vividly colored "high" when a fe are ingested, the mushrooms annually attract hundreds o "psilocybarites" . . . to the river valleys of the Pacific North west.* Maclean's 10/16/78, p16 **2** Transferred use. any hallu cinogenic mushroom. *In the ancient Near East, there was a other "magic mushroom" cult, which probably influenced th religious concepts of the Greeks, Jews, and early Christian and which still lingers in Siberia.* Norman E. Zinberg and Joh A. Robertson, Drugs and the Public, 1972, p68 [**1966**]

magic realism or **magical realism,** a style in literature in whic magical and fantastic events are interwoven with a seemingl realistic narrative. *The original boom novelists were Carlos Fu entes of Mexico, Julio Cortázar of Argentina, Mario Varga Llosa of Peru, and Gabriel García Márquez of Colombia. A four . . . experimented with language and structure, often in jecting fantasy and fragmenting time and space. The boon produced a style known as "magical realism," which blende dreams and magic with everyday reality.* World Book Encyclo pedia (1988), Vol. 12, p113 [**1986**]

magic spot, a compound of guanosine and four or five phos phate groups, whose appearance in cells is believed to inhib the synthesis of ribosomal RNA. *A further twist to the story o ribosomal RNA synthesis was . . . an unusual substance guanosine tetraphosphate (ppGpp), otherwise christene* *"magic spot." This has the interesting property that its amount in bacterial cells is inversely correlated with the rate of riboso- mal RNA synthesis; the more magic spot a cell contains, the less ribosomal RNA it makes.* New Scientist 2/10/72, p326 **[1970,** so called from the unexpected spots this compound causes to appear on chromatograms used to analyze the nucleotide com- ponent of bacterial cells]

mag-lev or **maglev,** *n.* a high-speed railway train riding on su- perconducting magnets over a magnetic field that is around the rails that guide the train (often used attributively). *But the most interesting possibility is to try to use magnetic levitation to lift trains. The German mag-lev system uses attractive mag- nets pulling up towards a steel plate. A railway rail is T- shaped, which means there are two surfaces that magnets could pull up against on each rail.'* New Scientist 9/20/73, p685 **[1968,** from *mag*netic *lev*itation]

magnesium pemoline, a combination of the stimulant pemoline and magnesium hydroxide, used as a drug to stimulate the nervous system. *Tests on student volunteers in America have shown that a drug, Magnesium Pemoline, increases the speed and accuracy of their work when they are tired.* Sunday Times (London) 10/27/68, p3 **[1965]**

magnetic anomaly, a pattern of alternating bands of rock hav- ing normal and reversed magnetization. *The age of the rocks lying 40 miles west of the ridge implies that they have travelled at an average rate of 0.8 centimetres a year since the time they were extruded from the ridge. This agrees well with the figure estimated from the magnetic anomalies of the ocean floor.* Times (London) 10/3/68, p13 **[1967]**

magnetic bottle, a magnetic field or fields to confine plasma (highly ionized gas) in a controlled thermonuclear reaction. *A magnetic bottle is the only known container that will hold a plasma for the time it takes to undergo fusion.* Discover 12/80, p18 **[1956]**

magnetic bubble, a tiny, circular magnetic domain that can be moved at extremely high speed through an integrated circuit on a wafer of crystalline material. Each bubble represents a unit of binary information, so that its movement from one cir- cuit to another can form a single calculation in a computer. Also called BUBBLE and BUBBLE DOMAIN. *Magnetic bubbles are small cylindrical domains within a piece of magnetized matter in which the magnetization is opposite to that of the bulk of the material. The domains can be made to move by application of a driving field.* Science News 10/21/72, p264 **[1970]**

magnetic domain, a zone of uniform magnetization in a thin film of ferromagnetic material. *A magnetic domain is that por- tion of a substance in which the electron orbits of all the atoms are lined up in the same direction. A magnetic domain is in ef- fect a small magnet within the substance. A substance will act as a large magnet when all or most of its magnetic domains (lit- tle magnets) line up in the same direction.* Encyclopedia Sci- ence Supplement (Grolier) 1972, p390 **[1970]**

magnetocardiogram, *n.* the record or tracing made by a magne- tocardiograph. *Using careful shielding that excluded magnetic disturbances from outside sources, [Dr. Cohen] . . . produced what he called magnetocardiograms, which are symmetrical with electrocardiograms taken from the same subjects.* NY Times 5/30/67, p18 **[1963]**

magnetocardiograph, *n.* a cardiograph that records heart action in the magnetic field around the heart. . . . *it is . . . too early to assess the long-range potential of the magnetocardiograph.* NY Times 5/6/67, p33 **[1963]**

magnetodisk, *n.* a cylindrical region of strong magnetic lines on the boundary of a magnetosphere. *According to one model of this magnetodisk or "current sheet," it resembles the wide, floppy brim of a fedora hat, with one side cocked up and the other cocked down. Close to Jupiter, the sheet lies in the plane of the magnetic equator.* 1976 Britannica Yearbook of Science and the Future, p31 **[1974]**

magnetogasdynamics, *n.* the study of the interaction of mag- netic fields and plasma (highly ionized gas). *Elements of Magnetogasdynamics—[by] L.E. Kalikham . . . Deals with the*

theory of magnetogasdynamics, various problems involved in the motion of plasma, the investigating methods employed and selected applications. Science News 1/7/67, p22 **[1960]**

magnetopause, *n.* See the first quotation for the meaning. *The outer boundary of the magnetosphere, where there is a transi- tion from the terrestrial to the interplanetary magnetic field, is called the magnetopause.* McGraw-Hill Yearbook of Science and Technology 1968, p239 *The space probes show that at about ten earth radii, the earth's geo-magnetic field ends its conflict with the interplanetary environment. The magnetic field goes through a series of rapid fluctuations at that distance from earth. This is known as the magnetopause.* Listener 6/27/68, p829 **[1963]**

magnetoplasmadynamic, *adj.* using plasma (highly ionized gas) in magnetic fields to generate power. *NASA's engine, being tested at Lewis Research Center in Cleveland, is called a magnetoplasmadynamic (MPD) arc thruster. An electric arc heats the argon or xenon propellant until it is ionized into a plasma, which is then forced through a "nozzle"—is actually a cone-shaped magnetic field—to produce thrust.* Science News 4/1/67, p298 **[1963]**

magnetosheath, *n.* a thin region surrounding the magne- tosphere of a planet that acts like an elastic medium transmit- ting the kinetic pressure of the solar wind onto the planet's magnetic field. *Yet far stranger discoveries remain. Some half a million miles later—twice the distance from the earth to the moon, a surprisingly small distance on Jupiter's vast scale—the spacecraft left the tumultuous magnetosheath and entered the magnetosphere proper, the main body of the planet's magnetic field.* Science News 12/8/73, p356 **[1968]**

magnetosphere, *n.* **1** an area of radiation formed by the earth's magnetic field which extends up to 40,000 miles from the earth and protects it from dangerous particles. *The moon, unlike the earth, is not protected from the solar wind—it has no magnetic field and, therefore, no shielding magnetosphere.* Science News 12/23/67, p611 **2** any similar area around a heavenly body. *This low-frequency electromagnetic radiation, which was suggested first by Pacini and later by James E. Gunn and myself at Princeton, is inevitable if the pulsars are magnetic neutron stars spinning in a vacuum. Peter Goldreich and Wil- liam Julian at the California Institute of Technology have shown, however, that such a star must have a magnetosphere, a plasma-filled region surrounding the star.* Scientific Ameri- can 1/71, p56 **[1959** for def. 1; **1967** for def. 2]

magnetospheric, *adj.* of the magnetosphere. *The length of the magnetospheric tail is uncertain. It has been observed by Nor- man Ness and John Wolfe to extend at least 10^3 R$_e$ in the anti- solar direction.* McGraw-Hill Yearbook of Science and Technology 1968, p239 **[1961]**

magnetotactic, *adj.* exhibiting magnetotaxis. *Richard Blake- more of the Woods Hole Oceanographic Institution reported finding bacteria that respond to magnetic forces by swimming toward the earth's north magnetic pole. Blakemore called these organisms "magnetotactic."* Encyclopedia Science Supple- ment (Grolier) 1976, p67 **[1976]**

magnetotail, *n.* the elongated part of the earth's magne- tosphere that extends away from the sun in a form resembling the tail of a comet. See SUBSTORM. *The continuum seems to consist of two components, one which fills the whole magne- tosphere and magnetotail and which is permanently trapped between the plasmasphere and magnetosheath, and another component which can penetrate the magnetosheath to propa- gate freely into the solar wind.* Nature 4/22/76, p686 **[1971]**

magnetotaxis, *n.* movement of an organism in response to a magnetic field. *Iron-rich beads probably play a role in magne- totaxis in bacteria. The bacteria crowd to one edge of a water- drop under the influence of the earth's magnetic field, then migrate in opposite direction when a magnet is placed there.* World Book Science Annual 1977, p309 **[1963,** from *magneto*- magnetic + *taxis* movement (in a particular direction) in reac- tion to an external stimulus]

magnetotelluric, *adj.* of or relating to the magnetic areas of the earth. *There were also two outstanding sessions on paleo- and archeomagnetism, which included some interesting new results. New studies are underway on . . . magnetotelluric phenomena.* Science 3/1/68, p1002 [**1953**, from *magneto-* magnetic + *telluric* of the earth]

magnet school, *U.S.* a school with superior facilities or curricula, designed to attract enrollment by pupils, especially of different races. *The concept of magnet schools with the educational excellence to draw enough white students to accomplish voluntary integration has shown such promise that it is being viewed as a way to help Boston out of its school busing brouhaha.* Wall Street Journal 5/19/75, p1 [**1972**]

magnon, *n. Nuclear Physics.* a quantized wave propagated by the deviation of a nuclear spin in a magnetic field. *. . . nuclear spins relax by interacting with the electronic spin system— through the emission or absorption of spin waves (magnons).* Scientific American 7/69, p65 [**1964**, from *magnetic* + *-on*, as in *electron, neutron,* etc., a term suggested as early as 1941 by the Soviet mathematician and physicist Lev D. Landau (1908-1968)]

magnox, *n.* a British type of nuclear reactor fueled by rods of natural uranium encased in magnesium alloy cans. *At the end of its program of magnox-type reactors, the U.K. abandoned this system in favour of the AGR (advanced gas cooled, graphite-moderated reactor) type . . .* Britannica Book of the Year 1970, p365 [**1953**, from *Magnox*, trade name of the magnesium alloy]

mag wheel, *U.S.* a shiny metal rim or wheel of a sports car. Mag wheels have no hubcaps. *It is Del Rio Customs, a garage that equips cars with elaborate racing stripes and mag wheels.* Time 6/3/74, p65 [**1972**, *mag* short for *magnesium,* the metal used to give it a silvery appearance]

Maharishi (ˌmɑːhəˈriːʃiː), *n.* Often spelled **maharishi.** any guru or sage. *Like our maharishi-seeking hippies of today, St. Francis of Assisi considered dirtiness as among the insignias of holiness . . .* New Scientist 9/18/69, p565 [**1966**, extended use of the title of a Hindu guru or spiritual guide, from Sanskrit *mahā* great + *rishi* sage, seer; the form of the compound in Sanskrit is *mahārshi*]

mail bomb, an explosive device hidden in a letter or parcel so that it may explode when opened by the recipient. *Last October, Taiwan's governor, Shieh Tung-min, had his left hand amputated after he was injured by a bomb mailed inside a dictionary, and two other officials had close escapes from other mail bombs.* New Yorker 6/13/77, p86 [**1972**, perhaps replacing the earlier (1948) *letter bomb*]

mail center, *U.S.* a business establishment that provides mailboxes for patrons. *Storefront businesses that rent postal boxes— sometimes called "mail centers"—began springing up in California about five years ago, according to Mr. Baer. This was a response to the shortage of boxes at United States Post Offices, he said. Although there are now more than 1,000 such centers nationwide, few of them are on the East Coast, Mr. Baer said.* NY Times 11/11/82, pC3 [**1982**]

mail cover, *U.S.* the screening and holding up of certain types of mail by postal officials, especially at the request of the recipient of such mail. *When a person is subjected to a mail cover, the Post Office records the name and address of anyone sending mail to him, as well as the postmarking and the class of mail. First-class mail is not delayed or opened, the department says.* NY Times 2/24/65, p26 [**1965**]

mailgram, *n. U.S.* a letter transmitted electronically between post offices for regular mail delivery. *Mailgrams, a combination of letter-telegram, which are cheaper than telegrams and faster than a letter, now exceed U.S. telegram volume. On Sept. 6, 1974, mailgrams were first transmitted by satellite.* Americana Annual 1975, p466 [**1970**, from *Mailgram*, trademark of the service developed jointly by the U.S. Postal Service and the Western Union Telegraph Co.]

main, *v.t. Slang.* to inject (heroin or a similar drug) into a vein; mainline. *. . . all my friends were on heroin. I snorted a couple of times, skinned a lot, and after that I mained it.* Time 3/16/70, p17 [**1970**]

mainframe, *n.* the central processor and immediate access store of a computer. *The emphasis during the year was on small computers and calculators and on peripheral equipment; the latter grew at twice the pace of the "mainframe" business.* Britannica Book of the Year 1970, p321 [**1964**]

mainstream, *v.t., v.i. U.S.* to place (handicapped or exceptional children) in regular classes with normal students whenever possible; integrate into the academic mainstream. *The Philadelphia School District is committed to mainstreaming, or enrolling mildly-handicapped students in regular classes . . . They are also mainstreaming the gifted. Since the mathematics curriculum is non-graded, the student can easily move from a special class to a regular class.* Report from Association of American Publishers, Inc., New York, 3/2/76, p4 [**1974**, verb use of the noun] —**mainstreaming**, *n.: In the U.S. advocates of "mainstreaming" became more insistent that handicapped students could get effective education in regular classrooms . . . Advocates of mainstreaming recognized the necessity of having some separate special education facilities and programs.* Britannica Book of the Year 1976, p306

mainstream smoke, the smoke that passes through the length of a cigarette or cigar. See PASSIVE SMOKING. *First, a distinction must be drawn between two types of cigarette smoke. The gases which a smoker draws into his mouth are called mainstream smoke, while the smoke which drifts off the tip of a cigarette is called sidestream.* New Scientist 8/9/73, p313 [**1973**]

mainstreet, *v.i. U.S. and Canada.* to campaign for election along the main streets of towns and districts. *From the Irish and black community of Dorchester to the Italian North End, Boston has witnessed a merry binge of mainstreeting, leafletting and parties with some of the excitement of a mayoral election.* Time 6/14/71, p20 [**1965**, verb use of *main street*]

maintenance drug, a narcotic given legally to an addict in doses large enough to maintain the drug's effect and prevent withdrawal symptoms. See METHADONE MAINTENANCE. *At present, [Herbert Jay] Sturz concedes the advantages of oral methadone over heroin as a maintenance drug. Both are addictive, but oral methadone lasts 24 to 36 hours while heroin, which must be injected, lasts only four to six hours, requiring repeated injections.* NY Times Magazine 7/2/72, p7 [**1972**]

mai tai (ˈmaɪ ˈtaɪ), a drink made from assorted rums, lime, sugar, and pineapple. *[Richard Nixon] spent an effervescent night on the town with David and Julie Eisenhower, dining on mai-tais, crab Rangoon, sweet-and-sour pork and almond duck at Trader Vic's.* Newsweek 10/15/73, p22 [**1963**, from Hawaiian]

major, *n.* Usually, **majors**, *pl.* a large oil-producing company. Compare SEVEN SISTERS. *Together these eighteen or twenty "majors" control an astonishing 94 per cent of America's crude-oil reserves, 70 per cent of its crude-oil production, 86 per cent of its gasoline sales. Even the phrase "oil company" has become a misnomer, for the majors are much more than that.* Newsweek 3/4/74, p12 [**1963**]

major-medical, *n. U.S.* a broad form of health insurance, providing coverage for large surgical, hospital, and other medical expenses. *But a man who had almost died could need a haven, and surely the room was that. His own and yet not his own. Enclosed, privileged, paid for by major-medical, suspended below the roof and above the street.* New Yorker 6/5/65, p36 [**1965**]

makuta (məˈkuːtə), *n.* the plural of **likuta.** *The Congo devalued its currency about two-thirds yesterday and introduced a new currency system of zaires, makuta and senghi.* Times (London) 6/26/67, p17 [**1967**]

maladapt (ˌmæləˈdæpt), *v.t.* to adapt poorly or improperly. *Speaking of criminals, some governments have engaged in some evil practices, using the tools of your trade, science. Suppose neurology makes great strides in the future in terms of things it's possible to do with the mind, and some government maladapts your discoveries.* Maclean's 4/19/76, p4 [**1976**, back formation from *maladapted* (1956) or *maladaptation* (1877)]

maladept (ˌmæləˈdept), *adj.* not adept or skilled; inexpert. *Within the Conservative and Labour parties, the most likely candidates for these seats are Westminster MPs ready to retire from the back benches, candidates who have unsuccessfully fought a British election, and those too youthful or maladept to have been nominated.* Times (London) 2/11/76, p14 [**1976**, from *mal-* badly, poorly + *adept*]

mal de siècle, (ˌmal də ˈsyeklə), a term denoting weariness of life or pessimism of a melancholy sort, roughly equivalent to *Weltschmerz* and *taedium vitae. All the belief systems that have served society for hundreds of years have gone, resulting in the modern mal de siècle—a frustration which has "led to the rejection of science as a pursuit and objectivity as a moral attitude."* New Scientist 12/10/70, p431 [**1959**, Anglicization of French *mal du siècle*, literally, sickness of the age. The French form is attested in English since 1926 (OEDS).]

male bonding, fellowship or camaraderie among males. *Buried within . . . the Gilgamesh epic is an adolescent-male myth of the wonderful world without women which still surfaces in male writings. It is the earliest extant tale of male bonding and the diabolic influence of women.* Elizabeth Fisher, Woman's Creation, 1979, p323 [**1970**]

male chauvinism, excessive male pride or exaggerated loyalty to members of the male sex. Compare SEXISM. See also CHAUVINISM. *Historically hampered by archaic laws and antique moral codes, European women have accepted their lot much more readily than their American counterparts. Recently, however, growing numbers, taking a cue from their more combative sisters across the Atlantic, have launched their attack on male chauvinism.* Time 8/17/70, p23 [**1970**]

male chauvinist, a person who exhibits male chauvinism; a man who regards himself as superior to women. Compare SEXIST. *During the past several years higher education has experienced a series of crises. The newest, and in the long term perhaps the most significant, development is the issue of discrimination against women . . . Male chauvinists would like to think that the current uproar is the work of a few militant troublemakers . . .* Science 1/14/72, p127 [**1970**]

male chauvinist pig, a derogatory or humorous term for a man who regards himself or all men as superior to women. *Abbreviation:* MCP *Now somebody . . . hit on the idea of having him proclaim himself the world's ranking male chauvinist pig. Grinning from ear to ear, he put out the most outrageous possible statements about the pathetic inferiority of women, except in the boudoir and the nursery. He actually succeeded in baiting into fury the brave but totally humourless vanguard of Women's Lib.* Listener 9/27/73, p398 [**1972**, from MALE CHAUVINIST and *pig*, a derogatory slang term for an obnoxious person] —**male chauvinist piggery:** *In its single-minded, five-year assault on male chauvinist piggery, the women's liberation movement has spawned hundreds of practical guides to help sisters infiltrate everything from karate to carpentry.* Newsweek 2/4/74, p78

malibu board (ˈmæləˌbuː), a streamlined plastic surfboard, usually about 9 feet long. *Then, when the swell brought in good surf, it was malibu boards, skegs, and washouts as the surfers took over the place.* Times (London) 9/21/70, p3 [**1964**, named after *Malibu* Beach, on the Pacific, in southern California, much frequented by surfers]

malolactic (ˌmælouˈlæktik), *adj.* of or relating to the conversion of malic acid to lactic acid and carbon dioxide in wine by the bacterium *B. gracile. A Nicolas buyer told me that some cooperatives and private growers in the Midi had to be taught how to vinify correctly: "Some of them didn't know that wine undergoes two fermentations—one alcoholic, the other malolactic."* Manchester Guardian Weekly (Le Monde section) 9/8/73, p13 [**1967**, from *malic* + connecting *-o-* + *lactic*]

maloti (məˈloutiː), *n.* the plural of LOTI. *On Jan. 19, 1980, Lesotho issued its new currency, the loti (plural, maloti), backed by South Africa's rand, and launched the Lesotho Monetary Authority.* Britannica Book of the Year 1981, p490 [**1980**]

mammograph, *n.* an X-ray picture of the breast. *This image Dr. Wolfe and many other radiologists agree is far clearer and more detailed than film mammographs because there are sharp lines between areas of differing tissue density, such as between cancerous and normal tissues.* NY Times 3/25/68, p25 —*v.t.* to take an X-ray picture of the breast. *Mammography has been controversial since at least the 1960s, when large studies, such as one by the Health Insurance Plan of Greater New York, gave breast cancer screening in under-50s a bad name. The focus then turned to mammographing only those women with clearly defined risk patterns, leaving the rest to feel their own breasts for lumps or let their doctors do it.* Maclean's 3/3/80, p45 [**1968** for noun; **1980** for verb]

man[1], *n.* **the Man,** *U.S. Slang.* **1** the white man; white society personified. *The Man systematically killed your language, killed your culture, tried to kill your soul, tried to blot you out . . .* Time 4/6/70, p71 *"Nobody in the North believes now in integration because they've never had it, but here, in an economic and social way, they've had integration all along, though of course entirely on the Man's terms . . ."* John Updike, Bech: A Book, 1970, p122 **2** the police. *". . . I catches up with one fella in an alley after he put my TV in a truck. He keeps denyin' what I seen him do with my own eyes, so I blasts him and takes him bleedin' down to the Man."* Maclean's 12/67, p27 *To the bombers and kidnappers the Man is Authority. He is every policeman.* Manchester Guardian Weekly 11/7/70, p1 **3** the Establishment in general; the system. *Kent and Cambodia were made to order for radicals. Something like Dowdell's death was made for them: 'The pigs got Tiger. You can't trust the Man. Come on with us.' I can hear them now.* Harper's 12/70, p59 [**1962** for defs. 1 and 2; **1970** for def. 3; originally used by Southern blacks to counteract the whites' use of "boy" in addressing or referring to black men]

man[2], *n.* ►Concern during the 1970's with eliminating sexism in the English language focused especially on the word *man.* In an attempt to DEGENDER the language, the extensive use of the occupational suffix *-man,* as in *fireman, policeman,* etc., was criticized as implicitly favoring the male sex. Likewise critics contended that the use of *man* in the generic sense (*working man, early man, man as toolmaker*) obscures the role of women in society. Some efforts to restrict the use of *man* have met with a degree of success. *The National Conference of Catholic Bishops will vote next month on a . . . second proposal [that] would authorise the priests to "substitute an inclusive word or phrase" in the church's prayers wherever "the generic term 'man' or its equivalent is found."* Manchester Guardian 10/25/79, p5 In Old English, *man* had two of the primary senses, meaning "human being" (as opposed to animals) and "adult male" (as opposed to women). While this twofold sense of *man* existed originally in other Germanic languages, the generic sense of "human being" was subsequently taken over by a derivative, as in German and Dutch *Mensch,* Swedish *människa,* Danish *menneske,* etc. English, however, did not develop such a derivative and *man* retained the built-in ambiguity. Accordingly many large publishing houses established guidelines to avoid sexist language, and they have succeeded in popularizing such nongender terms as *camera operator, firefighter, police officer,* and *mail carrier.* Even less male-oriented terms such as *chessman* and *man-made* are replaced by "chess piece" and "of human origin." At the same time many words with feminine endings are avoided in favor of neutral substitutes, such as *flight attendant* and *homemaker* in place of *stewardess* and *housewife.* However, it seems doubtful that certain time-honored feminine and masculine designations, such as the distinguishing pairs *master/mistress, hero/heroine, duke/duchess* will disappear.

managerialist, *n.* one who believes in managerial planning or control in business, government, etc. (also used attributively). *"No doubt some cynics and managerialists will deride them [local city councils] as 'mere talking-shops.' It is perhaps more likely . . . that they will make local government a reality to many people who now ignore or stand aside from it."* Manchester Guardian Weekly 2/14/70, p8 [**1965**]

man amplifier, a mechanical or robotic device attached to a person, who maneuvers it to perform activities that are beyond the normal human capacity or strength. Compare WALKING MACHINE. *General Electric has a family of other augmentor robots, including . . . Hardiman, which is worn by its human operator as a sort of outside skeleton enabling him to lift a 1,400-pound load exerting 30 pounds of force. The Hardiman exoskeleton is typical of a whole class of augmentors, called man amplifiers.* Science News 3/9/68, p238 [**1965**]

Manchurian candidate, a person who has been brainwashed by some organization or foreign power and programmed to carry out its orders automatically. *Embarrassing pop-psychology aside, the Schlafly-Ward thesis seems to be that Kissinger is a sort of Manchurian Candidate, planted in government by . . . members of the Council on Foreign Relations. He totally subscribes, say the authors, to the CFR one-world, better-Red-than-dead philosophy.* National Review 6/6/75, p624 [**1972**, from *The Manchurian Candidate*, title, of a novel about a brainwashed assassin (1959) by Richard Condon, born 1915, American novelist, and of a motion picture (1962) based on the novel]

mandate, *v.t.* to order or require officially; make mandatory. *By mandating Canadian content in radio and television programming, government has effectively subsidized the communicating class, . . .* Harper's 6/79, p31 [**1967**, verb use of the noun]

Manhattanize, *v.t.* to build up (a city) with high-rise office and apartment buildings and other large-scale projects. *The net result of this has been to "Manhattanize" Paris (Maine-Montparnasse and the Defense areas are among the less glorious examples of this trend).* Manchester Guardian Weekly (Le Monde section) 8/31/74, p11 [**1972**, from *Manhattan,* borough of New York City noted for its skyscrapers + *-ize*] —**Manhattanization**, *n.: The expansion of the financial-district high rises is part of a process now known in San Francisco as Manhattanization . . . The business leaders of the Bay Area have for some years been transforming San Francisco into a center of financial institutions and corporate headquarters which they see as Wall Street West.* Newsweek 12/19/77, p116

manifold, *n. Mathematics.* a topological space or surface. See the quotations for details. *Manifolds are objects of primary interest in present-day topology. They are spaces built by pasting together pieces that look like ordinary Euclidean space. If the dimension of the Euclidean space is* n, *the manifold is called* n-*dimensional. One way to study a manifold is to try to break it into simple pieces resembling triangles; if the procedure is successful, it is said that the manifold has been triangulated.* Britannica Book of the Year 1970, p491 *In a pure mathematical sense, we can have manifolds with any number,* n, *of dimensions.* Edna E. Kramer, The Nature and Growth of Modern Mathematics, 1970, p460 [**1957**]

man-month, *n.* one month of an individual's work taken as a unit of time in business and industry. *In-depth studies will involve . . . "up to 60 man-months of professional effort over a period of 18 months." Preliminary studies will involve "up to 18 man-months of professional effort over 12 months."* New Scientist 5/24/73, p473 [**1971**, patterned after earlier *man-hour, man-week,* etc.]

man-on-man, *adv., adj. U.S. and Canada.* (in team sports) of or in a defensive position in which one defenseman is assigned to one offensive player. *. . . they were "gambling," trying to cover Green Bay's wide receivers too tightly—mostly because they were forced into single man-on-man coverage by the blitzing tactics of the Kansas City linebackers.* Time 1/27/67, p52 [**1963**]

man-portable, *adj.* capable of being carried or moved by a man (as distinguished from several men or a vehicle). *"The tactical world," he said, "will be dominated by systems that are cheap and widely distributed: man-portable antitank and antiaircraft weapons, unmanned remotely piloted vehicles . . ."* NY Times Magazine 2/23/75, p36 *Deferred—a helicopter borne antitank missile and the Milan man-portable missile.* Manchester Guardian Weekly 3/27/77, p5 [**1973**]

man-rad, *n.* a dose of one rad (100 ergs per gram) per individual, used as a unit of absorbed radiation. Compare MAN-REM. *The annual cost in the United Kingdom of health physics services in the hospitals together with the costs of structural shielding*

amounted to some £580,000 per year. This resulted in a consequential saving of 140,000 man-rads, that is about £4 per man-rad saved. Nature 1/4/74, p6 [**1972**]

man-rate, *v.t.* to certify (a rocket or spacecraft) as safe for manned flight. *After it* [a new Soviet booster] *has been man-rated, however, and used in orbital rendezvous and docking missions, the USSR will have achieved a major platform for further advance . . .* New Scientist 3/21/68, p631 *The general question of the reliability of unmanned spacecraft has always been a thorny problem for NASA. Manned spacecraft have redundant systems—back-up systems in case one fails. This method, called "man-rating a spacecraft," is costly.* Science News 6/19/71, p416 [**1963**]

man-rem, *n.* a dose of one rem (1 roentgen of high-voltage X-rays) per individual, used as a unit of absorbed radiation. Compare MAN-RAD. *"The total future cost of one man-rem in terms of health costs paid in present dollars, is between $12 and $120."* Science 2/14/75, p509 [**1973**]

-manship, combining form meaning the art or tactic of using (something specified) to gain an advantage. The form was abstracted from *gamesmanship, lifemanship,* and *one-upmanship,* terms coined by the English humorist Stephen Potter, born 1900, on the model of *sportsmanship.* Some recent examples of its use are: —**growthmanship**, *n.: Like President Nixon, who used to poke fun at growthmanship, Lekachman seems to hold that the New Economists exaggerate the importance of growth and GNP* [gross national product]. Harper's 10/70, p9 —**Housemanship**, *n.: It was by a stroke of sheer Housemanship—not normally his best asset—that the Secretary for Trade and Industry managed to sail through the debate with such surprisingly little personal damage.* Manchester Guardian Weekly 8/7/71, p7 —**Marxmanship**, *n.: Like ten others whose Marxmanship was slightly off target, he was able, unlike Ali, to cite a passage about the mole from Marx, but not the right one.* Times (London) 3/13/70, p10 —**quotemanship**, *n.: Mr. Boller . . . has identified no less than 22 distinct varieties of quotes currently used in the art of quotemanship, not counting the nonquote or out-of-context or spurious quotes.* NY Times 5/31/67, p45 —**ringmanship**, *n.:* [Boxer Henry] *Cooper's finest bit of ringmanship seems to have gone unnoticed by the British press.* Times (London) 11/13/70, p17 —**stockmanship**, *n.: Some farmers are working far too hard themselves and haven't been able to pay attention to details, like concentrating on stockmanship and keeping down wastage . . .* Sunday Times (London) 1/25/70, p13 —**winemanship**, *n.: Winemanship has long held the status of an art in Europe, and when fine French and German wines began flowing across the Atlantic, the expertise came too. Vines, vineyards and vintages were soberly debated. Wine-tasting sessions became social events and the sniffy phrases of oenology became part of the language.* Time 10/19/70, p51

mantle plume, a large upwelling of molten material from the earth's mantle. Also called PLUME. See HOT SPOT. *Mantle plumes are . . . hypothesized by some scientists to account for, among other things, the creation of volcanic island chains in the Pacific.* Science News 8/17/74, p105 [**1972**]

Maoist ('mauist), *n.* a follower or supporter of the Chinese Communist leader Mao Zedong (Mao Tse-tung) or his doctrines. *The young Maoists, more influenced by the idea of Götterdämmerung than perhaps they know, are for burning down and starting over.* NY Times 4/4/68, p58 [**1964**, noun use of the adjective (1951)]

Maoize ('mau,aiz), *v.t.* to bring under the influence of Mao Zedong (Mao Tse-tung) or his doctrines. *Mao demolished . . . others who did not share his own mystical concept of the revolution. He hoped to replace them with freshly radicalized, totally Maoized youth who would be prepared to spend their lives in permanent struggle.* Time 7/12/71, p22 [**1968**]

Mao jacket, another name for NEHRU JACKET. *Mr. Lanvin expressed his disapproval of "extravagances" such as the Mao jacket, the evening turtle neck, and pendant and chain jewelry.* NY Times 5/22/68, p50 [**1967**]

mao-tai ('mau'tai), *n.* Also, **mao tai**. a potent Chinese liquor distilled from millet. *Speeches of welcome accompanied by toasts in the fiery colourless* mao-tai *begin early and may go on sporadically to the soup (the last course).* Listener 10/4/73, p443 [**1965**, from Chinese *mao tai* (*Maotai,* town in China where it is made)] ►This term was popularized in the West after President Nixon's visit to China. It should not be confused with MAI TAI.

maraging steel ('mar,eidʒiŋ), a very strong iron alloy containing little or no carbon and consisting chiefly of nickel with lesser amounts of other metals. *A relatively new steel, known as maraging steel, has been used in extremely fine gauge in the making of the case of the third stage of the Black Arrow rocket for putting British research satellites into orbit. This is an age-hardened steel which avoids the risk of distortion and scaling associated with high-temperature heat treatment and quenching.* New Scientist 7/25/68, p185 [**1962**, *maraging,* from *mar*tensite (the hard component of quenched steel) + -*aging*]

Marburg disease ('mar,bərg), a contagious, often fatal virus disease characterized by high fever and hemorrhaging, transmitted to humans by West African green monkeys of the species *Cercopithecus aethiops.* Also called GREEN MONKEY DISEASE. *Three laboratories . . . have now confirmed that specimens from the Sudan/Zaire fever contain a virus similar to that of Marburg disease. Several hundred people have already died in the current outbreak, and as a result control measures have been tightened up at ports and airports throughout the world.* New Scientist 10/28/76, p199 [**1969**, named after *Marburg,* West Germany, where several laboratory technicians died from the disease in 1967 after handling green monkeys]

Marburg virus, 1 the virus causing MARBURG DISEASE. Compare EBOLA VIRUS. *The World Health Organization said today that studies with electron microscopes of specimens received from Zaire and the Sudan revealed a virus that appeared to be similar in form to the Marburg virus.* NY Times 10/15/76, pA5 **2** another name for MARBURG DISEASE. *If we did not study viruses in the laboratory, we would be helpless against outbreaks of new diseases, such as the Marburg virus or Lassa fever of recent years.* 1974 Britannica Yearbook of Science and the Future, p301 [**1971**]

margarita (,margə'ri:tə), *n.* a cocktail made with tequila, lime or lemon juice, and an orange-flavored liqueur. *With regard to beverages, the question restaurateurs ask is, what about a mixed drink? Do you have to specify the precise amount of gin and the precise amount of vermouth that go into a martini or the minutely measured quantities of tequila and Cointreau in a margarita?* NY Times Magazine 11/25/79, p31 [**1963**, from American Spanish, probably from the name *Margarita* Margaret]

marginalize, *v.t.* to omit, exclude, or ignore, especially by leaving on the fringes of society or isolating from the course of progress. *In three countries the challenge to an emerging Latin American type of socialism . . . to solve towering economic and social problems which effectively leave half the populations marginalized has already begun.* Times (London) 10/31/70, p12 [**1968**]

mariculturist, *n.* one who engages or specializes in sea farming. *The man who studies agriculture stands in a different place from the man who studies mariculture. There are other differences between the two fields but not so basic as the need for the mariculturist to swim.* Science Journal 12/69, p30 [**1969**, from *maricultur*e (CD 1909) + -*ist*]

marine science, all the sciences dealing with the sea and its environment, including marine biology, oceanography, and similar specializations. *However, for any MP interested in marine science, a study of what the Canadians are attempting would be well worth while. For example, there is the project for control of the ice-cover on the Gulf of St Lawrence.* New Scientist and Science Journal 1/28/71, p195 [**1968**]

Marisat ('mærə,sæt), *n.* a satellite for maritime communications of the U.S. Navy, commercial shipping, and offshore industries. Compare LANDSAT. *The first launch of a communications payload during the reporting period was that of Marisat 3, on Oct.*

14, 1976. This geostationary maritime communications satellite was stationed above the Indian Ocean. Marisat 1 and 2 cover the Atlantic and Pacific oceans, and thus Marisat 3 completes the Marisat system's global coverage of shipping lanes. McGraw-Hill Yearbook of Science and Technology 1978, p342 [**1976**, from *Mari*time *sa*tellite]

Markarian galaxy (mar'ka:ri:ən), any of a class of galaxies characterized by unusual shapes and a strong emission in the ultraviolet part of the spectrum. *The Markarian galaxies, under their broad umbrella of excess ultraviolet, contain many different types: Seyferts, Zwicky objects, Haro blue galaxies, many giant galaxies, many dwarf galaxies, distant galaxies and close galaxies; even quasars might be numbered among them. One of them, Markarian 132, is the brightest object in the universe with an absolute magnitude of about minus 27.* Science News 8/18-25/73, p117 [**1969**, named after B.E. *Markarian,* an Armenian astronomer who discovered the first such galaxies in 1968]

markup, *n. U.S.* the process of putting a legislative bill into final form (often used attributively). *Almost all congressional committees do their most important work—deciding the final details of legislation—in secret; these are called "mark-up" sessions.* Atlantic 9/72, p17 *The Judiciary Subcommittee is now beginning its markup of the bill, and the best estimate is that the measure will reach the House floor for consideration in April.* Association of American Publishers, Inc., 2/20/76, p2 [**1967**, from the *mark up* of a bill with various proposals, compromises, etc., by members of the committee in charge]

MARMAP ('mar,mæp), *n.* acronym for *Marine Resources Monitoring Assessment and Prediction,* a survey of the kinds and amounts of living marine resources available to the United States. *The U.S. National Marine Fisheries Service is, for example, conducting a research program (MARMAP) designed to reveal the distribution of larvae and breeding areas over the continental shelf of North America.* Americana Annual 1974, p367 [**1971**]

Marmes man ('marmis), a prehistoric human being whose fossil bone fragments were discovered in 1965 in the state of Washington and dated as being over 11,000 years old, making it the oldest human remains in the Western Hemisphere. *Preliminary study of the skull bones, finger and wrist bones, teeth, and fragments of rib and long bones indicates that Marmes man was a Mongoloid, having a broad-cheeked, flat face. Most of the human bones are charred and split like those of the animals with which they were found, which suggests that human beings were eaten by occupants of the site.* 1969 Collier's Encyclopedia Year Book, p107 [**1968**, named for R.J. *Marmes,* a rancher on whose property the bones were discovered]

marriage encounter, a method of renewing and enhancing marital relationships in which a small group of married couples meet, usually on a weekend, and engage in frank discussions and exploration of feelings between husbands and wives. *Abbreviation:* ME *Dialoguing is what Marriage Encounter is all about. It is a technique you will not learn . . . except during an encounter weekend, a form of communication that cannot be taught properly by one couple or through the printed word. It is also a very sensitive undertaking.* Daily News (New York) 7/31/79, p29 *The* marriage encounter, *a movement Catholic in origin but nondenominational in outlook and participation . . . There is nothing typically Catholic about either the marriage encounter or the charismatic renewal, or indeed about much that is new in the Catholic Church.* American Speech, Summer 1979, p88 [**1975**]

Marsokhod (,marsə'xɔ:t), *n.* a vehicle designed by Soviet scientists for scientific exploration on Mars. See also LUNOKHOD, PLANETOKHOD. *In addition to discussing future Lunokhod explorations of the moon, the Soviets also described similar automated stations and robots for Venus, Mats and Mercury. These they call "planetokhods" or "marsokhods."* Science News 11/21/70, p397 [**1970**, patterned after Russian *Lunokkhod,* literally, moonwalker]

Marsquake, *n.* a major seismic disturbance on the planet Mars. *Even though the Viking 1 lander successfully touched down,* *it suffered a few malfunctions. Its seismometer refused to uncage upon command and remained out of order permanently. Thus, no data on Marsquakes could be recovered.* 1977 Britannica Yearbook of Science and the Future, p396 [**1974**]

martial artist, a practitioner of the martial arts, such as karate and kung fu. See WU SHU. *Martial artists who dispatch their enemies by puncturing their jugulars bare-fingered are on a level of combat which is either too high or too low for this scenario.* Listener 9/5/74, p310 [**1970**, derived from *martial arts* (1930's) the Oriental arts of self-defense]

Martianologist, *n.* a person who engages in scientific study of the planet Mars. *Notably absent in all the Mariner pictures are the networks of "canals" that some Martianologists began putting into their drawings a hundred years ago.* Scientific American 5/70, p26 [**1970**]

MARV, *n.* acronym for *Maneuverable Reentry Vehicle*, a rocket-launched offensive missile with several nuclear warheads that can be maneuvered to change course or vary speed to avoid interception by defensive missiles during reentry into the earth's atmosphere. *Also included under this heading are $248 million for advanced research on MARV's, a "follow on" generation of highly accurate maneuverable reentry vehicles.* Scientific American 3/74, p44 —*v.i.* to equip with a MARV warhead. *They invented MIRV's (multiple independently targetable re-entry vehicles) and are now busy MARVing (MARV's are maneuverable re-entry vehicles) the MIRV's, so that they can be maneuvered right onto their targets.* NY Times 2/18/76, p37 [**1972**, patterned after MIRV]

marvie or **marvy**, *interj. U.S. Slang.* a shortened and altered form of *marvelous.* *"O sad Arthur, how marvie!" cried the entranced Lambie.* New Yorker 3/14/70, p34 *When Donna heard the news, she clapped her hands. "Marvy—now we can go on the trip together!"* New Yorker 10/17/70, p39 [**1965**]

mascon ('mæs,kan), *n.* **1** a massive concentration of dense material lying about 30 miles below the lunar surface, and characterized by a higher-than-average gravity. *The most remarkable property of the mascons is that the five most pronounced examples coincide with circular lunar seas, such as Mare Imbrium; none lies under the large, irregular maria.* 1970 Britannica Yearbook of Science and the Future, p120 **2** a similar feature on the planets or their moons. *We have already noted the detection on the Martian surface of mascons, analogous to the lunar areas of especially high gravity.* New Scientist and Science Journal 12/30/71, p247 [**1968**, from *mass concentration*]

masculinist, *n.* a person in favor of male rights or privilege. *Economic discrimination against women has a direct parallel in the unfair treatment accorded the Negro. Lest old-fashioned masculinists panic, all that the new-style feminists really demand is the opportunity for a mediocre woman to get as far as a mediocre man.* NY Times 7/18/68, p31 *No militant masculinists stooped to conquer; indeed almost the only men to be seen on the premises, apart from the staff, were male journalists invited to help celebrate the occasion.* Times (London) 10/13/67, p8 [**1918, 1964**, patterned after *feminist*]

mase (meiz), *v.i.* to generate and amplify microwaves. Compare LASE. *Many substances have been made to "mase" and "lase"—that is, to behave like masers or lasers.* Encyclopedia Science Supplement (Grolier) 1964, p308 *No significant overestimation of the mass of the coronal clouds would result from this small degree of masing and no significant selections of incoming clouds would occur.* Nature 3/30/68, p1238 [**1962**, back formation from *maser* (OEDS 1952), a device that generates and amplifies microwaves]

mask, *n. Electronics.* a kind of photographically produced stencil used in the fabrication of integrated circuits to cover up selected areas on the semiconductor chip for metal deposition or etching. *The end product from an integrated-circuit design service is the mask itself. Even now most IC masks are produced by a draughtsman who first lays out the masks hundreds of times full size on a board about four feet square. The final mask is made by a process of successive photo-reductions. This mask, which might be about one eighth of an inch across, is repeated several hundred times across a two-inch silicon slice.*

New Scientist 12/10/70, p441 . . . *if one is designing the mask for an integrated electronic circuit, the objects to be represented are the transistors, resistors, gates, wiring and other elementary components from which the circuit is to be built.* Scientific American 6/70, p65 [**1967**]

masscult, *adj.* of or relating to drama, art, music, and other forms of culture spread by the mass communications media, especially television. *Their* [literary magazines'] *golden age lasted from World War I to the communications, or "masscult," revolution of the mid-1950's* . . . NY Times 9/11/67, p47 [**1963**, contraction of *mass* and *cult*ure]

mass driver, a device for propelling or launching materials from the moon or other body in space to a space colony under construction. *Getting off the earth itself may always be difficult and rather expensive. But, once you are in space, some old but still untried ideas for propulsion become feasible. We have heard about the mass driver, for instance, which hurls rocks and might be used for fetching asteroids.* Listener 7/6/78, p13 [**1975**]

master class, an advanced class in music, art, etc., taught by a distinguished musician, artist, and the like. *Old singers* . . . *teach. And the best of them conduct master classes.* Times (London) 2/26/70, p16 [R.B. Kitaj] *says of the two Venetian Agonies in the Garden (painted by brothers-in-law, Mantegna and Bellini): "Their spectacular compositions are like the stuff of master-classes I wish I could have attended."* Sunday Times (London) 5/25/80, p62 [**1963**]

matching fund, **1** a sum of money given by some individual or institution, usually in proportion to that raised by public contribution. The matching fund is an inducement to obtain enough money in total to pay for some project. *Along with such institutional changes, the European science ministers endorsed an international matching fund for support of four-or-five-year, pilot interdisciplinary research programs, as well as establishment of reserve funds in each participating nation for projects approved by international committees.* Science News 3/30/68, p303 **2 matching funds**, *pl.* the sums of money contributed to match the individual contributions. *The New York Philharmonic was still without a permanent music director for the 1970s, while in many cities, efforts were underway to raise matching funds to meet the 1971 deadline set by the monumental Ford Foundation program to increase orchestral endowments.* 1969 World Book Year Book, p420 [**1957** for def. 1; **1969** for def. 2]

matching grant, another name for MATCHING FUND. *I've received a matching grant from the NEA* [National Educational Association] *for the production of a number of chapbooks. It's good to have that money as I've been unable to purchase materials for the next chapbook.* Saturday Review 1/6/79, p59 [**1962**]

materials-intensive, *adj.* requiring great use of or expenditure on materials. *The relatively less materials-intensive switching technology is substituting for transmission technology, a trend that has been given enormous impetus by the integrated circuit which is doing for switching what it is doing for calculators.* Science 2/20/76, p731 [**1972**, patterned after CAPITAL-INTENSIVE, LABOR-INTENSIVE]

materials science, the study of the properties and uses of materials, such as glass, metals, polymers, etc. *Materials science is a very wide subject since it includes metals, ceramics, glasses and polymers, together with a great deal of solid state physics, and it is a difficult task to write about these related topics with equal ease, as Fishlock has done.* Science Journal 1/68, p85 *Efforts are now being made to see the subject in the broader background of materials science and there are signs that this name* [soil mechanics] *is slowly passing out of use in favour of soil engineering or some similar appellation.* Science 1/71, p81 [**1961**]

matière (ma'tyer), *n.* artistic matter or material. *In a series called "Los Espejos" (The Mirrors), he* [Manuel Rivera] *once again uses his unusual matière to trap light as if in a mammoth spider web and spin all manner of bewitching effects.* Time 11/25/66, pE1 *Lecture Four. The matiere of verse dem-*

onstrated further in Wallace Stevens; who isn't my poet. Manchester Guardian Weekly 8/7/71, p19 [**1963**, from French, matter, material]

matrix, n. **1** an ordered table or two-dimensional array of variables, especially for use in computer programming. *Dr. Warner's group has been working for two-and-a-half years on computer diagnosis. They have set up a "matrix"—a device for statistical analysis—that comprises some thirty-five different disease entities and fifty-seven symptoms known to be associated with congenital defects.* NY Times 5/28/63, p19 **2** an array of circuit elements designed to perform a particular function, especially in a computer. *The diodes on each character unit are connected to a matrix of seven horizontal wires . . . The other side of each diode is connected to one of five vertical wires. In this way, any one diode can be switched on individually by applying a voltage across selected horizontal wires and vertical wires in the matrix.* Science Journal 11/70, p16 [**1963** for def. 1; **1952** for def. 2]

matrix isolation, *Chemistry.* the trapping of molecules in an inert solid (the matrix or background material) to observe them in isolation. *Illinois researchers went back more than 100 years . . . to trace the steps leading to the video tape recorder, oral contraceptive pills, the electron microscope, magnetic ferrites . . . the matrix isolation—a technique for 'freezing' chemical reactions to study intermediate products.* Science Journal 4/69, p9 [**1968**]

maturity-onset diabetes, the former name of a type of diabetes that is more widespread, occurs later in life, and is usually less severe than JUVENILE-ONSET DIABETES. *Maturity-onset diabetes (because it usually shows up after the age of 40) definitely "appears to have a strong hereditary tendency," the editorial continues. "It has been calculated that 60% of the children of two maturity-onset diabetics will themselves develop mild diabetes by the age of 60."* Scientific American 2/76, p56 [**1976**] —**maturity-onset diabetic:** *All maturity-onset diabetics are found concordant as opposed to only 50% of juvenile-onset diabetics. This suggests that in maturity-onset diabetics inheritance is the primary factor, while in some juvenile-onset diabetics environmental factors are consequential.* McGraw-Hill Yearbook of Science and Technology 1978, p139 ►The terminology has shifted to a distinction between TYPE I or INSULIN-DEPENDENT DIABETES MELLITUS (IDDM) and TYPE II or NONINSULIN-DEPENDENT DIABETES MELLITUS (NIDDM).

mau-mau, v.t. U.S. Slang. to terrorize. . . . *his* [Norman Mailer's] *demonstration of the inadequacies and distortions of Kate Millett's Sexual Politics is convincing and indicates that the English Department of Columbia University had been mau-maued by that termagant of Women's Lib.* Harper's 6/71, p9 [**1970**, popularized by the American journalist Tom Wolfe, author of *Radical Chic and Mau-mauing the Flak Catchers*, from *Mau Mau* a secret society of Kikuyu terrorists in Kenya, also used in Afro-American slang as a name for a militant member of the Black Muslims or Black Panthers]

Maunder minimum, a period of irregular solar activity between about 1645 and 1715, characterized especially by the virtual absence of sunspots. *During a 70-year period in the late 17th and 18th centuries, sunspots and other signs of activity all but vanished from the sun. Historical evidence for this period, called the "Maunder minimum," coincided with a very clear picture of the minimum shown as a radiocarbon anomaly in tree rings formed at the time.* Science News 3/5/77, p152 *Auroral displays occur during periods of high solar activity but, during the Maunder minimum, far fewer aurorae were recorded than in either of the 70-year periods preceding or following.* New Scientist 8/25/77, p467 [**1976**, named after E. Walter *Maunder*, a 19th-century British solar astronomer who first described it in 1890; so called because of the minimal solar activity recorded]

maven or **mavin**, n. U.S. Slang. an expert or connoisseur. *Much of the credit for the Cinderella publishing story goes to Robert Gottlieb, then the editorial genie in residence at Simon & Schuster, now the mavin at Alfred Knopf.* Time 9/12/69, p78 *Participants at a conference put together by microcomputer maven Ben Rosen last summer were asked to rank the*

companies they believed would dominate the personal computer market by 1985. Datamation 12/82, p89 [**1968**, from Yiddish *meyvn*, from Hebrew *mēvīn*]

max, n. U.S. Informal. the greatest possible amount; maximum. *A . . . new single from southern California has been riding the airways to the max this summer providing parody-rocker Frank Zappa with his first mainstream hit.* Newsweek 8/2/82, p61 —v.i. Usually, **max out.** to reach a maximum. *The average late-night restaurant does about three turns. Amsterdam's "is doing very well," he said. "They're just about maxing out on the covers"—industry jargon meaning that the restaurant is feeding people as fast as it can.* NY Times 4/18/85, pD1 —v.t. to perform or execute to one's maximum capacity. *Scott has just finished maxing the push-up test at 68, where he was ordered to stop (with one more just for the drill sergeant's satisfaction).* Washington Post 10/3/82, pF1 [**1979**, originally teenage slang, shortened from *maximum*]

maxi, n. **1** a skirt, dress, coat, etc., reaching to the ankle or just above it; a maxiskirt, maxidress, maxicoat, etc. Compare MICRO, MIDI, MINI. *When you have seen one maxi, you have seen them all, though Saint Laurent makes his droopier than ever with mufflers and downdragged crochet berets, but pantsuits have infinite variations.* Sunday Times (London) 2/2/69, p58 **2** the ankle-length style of fashion. *In their desperation to whet consumer demand by the good, old American economic device of forced obsolescence, the industry's merchants, manufacturers and editors have been touting the midi, the maxi and other varieties of lowered hemlines.* NY Times 7/5/68, p50 **3** something very large. *The worst outbreak so far this year occurred on April 3 and 4, when a fusillade of 100 tornadoes, more than half of them maxis, struck in a 14-state area over a 12-hour period. More than 300 people died.* Science News 9/7/74, p152 —adj. **1** reaching to the ankle or just above it; ankle-length. *Teen-agers and college girls rushed for maxi coats and shops reported good sales in the style.* Americana Annual 1970, p287 **2** larger or longer than usual. *As fashions grow minier, accessories are waxing maxier. Witness the popularity of superwatches—huge, outsize timekeepers that measure 3 in. across and come with round, square and octagonal faces.* Time 11/10/67, p47 *In the Dublin suburbs there is a mini-car in nearly every garage, and downtown the traffic jams are becoming very maxi.* Saturday Review 9/23/67, p4 [**1967**, from *maxi-*]

maxi-, a new prefix derived from *maximum* (on the analogy of *mini-*), used with the two meanings given below: **1** reaching down to the ankle; long. —**maxicoat**, n.: *Along Belgrade's Terazije, maxicoats and Longuettes, velvet knickers and leather gaucho pants abound, as do swinging discothèques, modish butiks and the most daring skin magazines.* Time 3/29/71, p29 —**maxidress**, n.: *To relieve the sterile monotony of nurses' uniforms, Fashion Designer Pierre Cardin recently unveiled three new creations at a London showing. Two of his designs— nunlike wimples with white maxidresses—were harmless affairs that might make ward nurses look functional if not fashionable.* Time 11/16/70, p67 —**maxilength**, n.: *Both in Paris and in the United States, couturiers showed maxilengths (almost floor-sweeping) but were commercially cautious and kept enough of their styles short.* 1970 World Book Year Book, p342 —**maxi-shorts**, n.pl.: *The middle-aged American who waddled down the steps of the expensive Spinzar Hotel in his rainbow maxi-shorts would hardly have glanced at the woman who came towards him from out of the shadows, her hands cupped, her face haggard and vacant.* Listener 2/29/68, p270 **2** very large. —**maxi-order**, n.: *After announcing his latest orders last week in New York, Pao hopped a plane for Tokyo to look for shipyards interested in another maxi-order.* Time 7/5/71, p53 —**maxi-taxi**, n.: *Those most favoured by your correspondents seem to be the post-bus and the mini-bus (or maxi-taxi).* Times (London) 10/8/70, p11

maxsaver, n. U.S. the lowest airfare, usually requiring advance purchase of nonrefundable round-trip tickets for weekday flights. *The range of ticket prices widened . . . when major airlines in competitive markets reduced their lowest fares, known* *throughout the industry as maxsavers.* NY Times 1/23/88, p52 [**1988,** from *maximum + saver*]

mayo, *n.* short for *mayonnaise. Dottie . . . said gently, "So sorry. Then run down to the corner and get me a ham and cheese on rye and tell them to hold the mayo."* Atlantic 1969, p118 *We were sitting at a luncheonette counter the other day, just about to bite into a b.l.t. down, with mayo, when a familiar voice addressed us from an adjacent stool.* New Yorker 7/10/71, p20 [**1960**]

MBD, abbreviation of MINIMAL BRAIN DYSFUNCTION. *The hyperkinetic child is being recognized as a true behavioral aberration or diagnostic entity. Also called MBD, for "minimal brain dysfunction," this handicap causes children to be extremely overactive, distractible, of short attention span, impulsive, aggressive, and fluctuant in mood. Great trials to their parents and teachers, these children can apparently be calmed down by antidepressive drugs.* 1973 Collier's Encyclopedia Year Book, p377 [**1971**]

MBFR, abbreviation of *mutual and balanced force reduction,* designating the proposal that the armed forces in both western Europe under NATO and eastern Europe under the Warsaw Pact be simultaneously and proportionately reduced. *One prime aim of NATO diplomacy now ought to be to rescue the talks on MBFR from a state of relaxed and (apparently) amiable deadlock and to introduce a needed note of stridency.* Manchester Guardian Weekly 11/6/77, p10 [**1971**]

mbira (əmˈbiːrə), *n.* a hollow piece of wood, usually about eight inches long, with metal strips, inserted lengthwise, that vibrate when played with the thumb. The instrument is tuned to play tribal music while held in both hands with the palms upward. *. . . he was making music with a mbira, a kind of African hand-piano. His brother, who is three years his junior, was accompanying him on a kalimba, he said, which is a modern version of the mbira and was designed by his father, Dr. Hugh Tracey, a well-known South African musicologist.* NY Times 6/4/66, p27 [**1966,** from a Bantu word]

McLuhanism, *n.* **1** the ideas and theories of the Canadian writer and communications specialist Marshall McLuhan, 1911-1980, especially his emphasis on the influence of electronic communications and the mass communications media in radically reshaping society. *On a superficial level Joel Lieber's provocative novel bears out the basic precept of elementary McLuhanism: the medium is the message.* Saturday Review 5/6/67, p36 **2** a word or expression peculiar to Marshall McLuhan. *These movies are all "non-linear," to use a favorite McLuhanism; they refuse to follow A-to-Z patterns . . .* Saturday Night (Canada) 10/68, p56 [**1965**]

McLuhanite, *n.* a follower or supporter of Marshall McLuhan and his ideas. *As the McLuhanites are so fond of pointing out, television—and particularly the commercials—had accustomed them* [audiences at movie houses] *to seeing more, and faster.* Saturday Review 12/28/68, p18 **—adj.** of or relating to McLuhan or McLuhanism. *Also, there is some kind of joke on McLuhanite coolness; Chance* [the central character of *Bad News,* by Paul Spike] *is a walking television screen . . .* New Yorker 9/25/71, p133 [**1967**]

McLuhanize, *v.t.* to put under or subject to the control or influence of television, computers, and other forms of electronic communications media. *Among the nonelectronic press, a gnawing feeling grows that their efforts are becoming obsolete. This is hardly so, as the sales of Theodore White's books can attest. But the fear of being McLuhanized into irrelevance has forced the pen-and-pencil men to fight back.* Atlantic 10/68, p124 *The thesis of Australia in the seventies as a model McLuhanized society is fervently denied by publishers.* Times (London) 3/31/70, pVI [**1968**]

MCP, abbreviation of MALE CHAUVINIST PIG. *A senator who voted against her* [Anne Armstrong] *might once have been thought unchivalrous, but in the liberated air of today, he would be branded by every woman in his state as an MCP— male chauvinist pig.* Listener 1/15/76, p38 *Some MCPs still regarded woman as a sex object . . . sexist and racist attitudes*

had to be rubbished once and for all. Manchester Guardian (London) 12/28/79, p10 [**1972**]

MDA, abbreviation of *methylenedioxy-amphetamine,* a hallucinogenic drug derived from amphetamine. Compare DPT, MDMA, PMA, PCP. *MDA . . . has a high abuse potential, is without currently accepted medical use in treatment in the United States and lacks accepted safety for use under medical supervision.* Science News 8/18-25/73, p110 [**1972**]

MDC, abbreviation of *more developed country. Of particular relevance is the development of insight and assessment of policy alternatives that could lead to narrowing of the gap between the less developed (LDC) and more developed (MDC) countries.* New Scientist 11/21/74, p565 [**1973,** patterned after LDC]

MDMA, abbreviation of *methylenedioxy-methamphetamine,* a stimulant drug that relaxes inhibitions, used in the treatment of phobias. Also called ECSTASY. *But there were some protests in May when the DEA* [Drug Enforcement Administration] *announced that, effective July 1, 1985, it was placing a one-year prohibition on the drug MDMA—commonly known as Ecstasy—while research continued into the drug's possible harmful effects.* 1986 World Book Year Book, p295 [**1985**]

ME, abbreviation of MARRIAGE ENCOUNTER. *ME was born in Spain in the 1950s, the brainchild of Gabriel Calvo, a young priest working with couples in Barcelona. It was discovered in 1968 by an American Jesuit, Chuck Gallagher, who saw in it the antidote for the "overemphasis on personal fulfilment in today's life," as he explains.* Maclean's 5/2/79, p6 [**1979**]

meal pack, *U.S.* a frozen meal prepackaged in a tray to be heated before serving. *Meal packs constitute 30 percent of all lunches served in New York City public schools.* NY Times 9/29/77, p39 [**1976**]

meals on wheels, a service that brings a hot meal daily to the home of an elderly or disabled person. It is usually a private service subsidized by government. *Islington council said: "We have heard that from tomorrow our refuse collectors, sewermen, baths plant operators and drivers, except those on meals on wheels and health and welfare vehicles, are on strike."* Times (London) 9/29/70, p4 [**1961**]

means-test, *v.t. British.* to make (Welfare benefits) dependent upon the outcome of an examination of the financial means of an unemployed or disabled person. *The state retirement pension is below what is commonly regarded as the poverty line and many old people do not claim the means-tested benefits to which they are entitled, either because they are not aware of them or because they find the process of claiming too cumbersome or too humiliating.* Times (London) 4/20/70, p9 *The means-tested state which we are now entering may have a profoundly disturbing long-term effect on incentives and attitudes to work.* Daily Telegraph (London) 5/5/72, p9 [**1963**]

meat and potatoes, *Slang.* **1** the most important or basic part. *Other trade books do better but only sensational best-sellers can recover production costs on the Canadian market alone. Textbooks remain the meat and potatoes of publishing in Canada.* Maclean's 7/67, p65 **2** Often, **meat-and-potatoes.** basic; fundamental. *Chapter six discusses very briefly equipment and methods of observation. It is a pity these subjects are so perfunctorily covered, for this is the kind of "meat and potatoes" information amateur astronomers . . . are eager to glean from an experienced observer.* New Scientist 8/15/68, p351 [**1955**]

mechanical, *n.* **1 mechanicals,** *pl.* the operational or functional parts; mechanics. *Many regulations, particularly in relation to TV, prevented advertisers from using international campaigns if the basic mechanicals—artwork, films, and so on—were not produced in Italy by Italians.* Britannica Book of the Year 1967, p66 **2** any nonessential participant. *Frivolity seems to me the only, precarious excuse for this novel—a let-out, for instance, for treating the income-earning group as characters and the rest as 'mechanicals'.* Listener 2/1/68, p148 [**1967** for def. 1, noun use of adjective; **1968** for def. 2, extended from earlier meaning (1590, OED) a handicraftsman]

mechatronics (ˌmekəˈtraniks), *n.* the design, manufacture, and use of miniaturized components in electronic circuits. *"The big buzzword in Japanese electronic circles now," Mr. Strom said, "is mechatronics—a recognition that miniaturizing the mechanisms has become even more important than miniaturizing circuitry."* NY Times 11/25/82, pC8 [**1982**, blend of *mechanism* and *electronics*]

MECO (ˈmiːkou), *n.* the point in a space flight when the main engine of a spacecraft is shut down. *Houston: Columbia, Houston, if you have a couple of seconds, we'd like another run through or description of that pogo-ing effect that you noticed near MECO. Columbia: O.K. This was after MECO. It was during the dump. Houston: Columbia, Houston, we're not copying you right now. We did copy that it was after MECO and not before MECO.* NY Times 4/13/81, pA13 [**1981**, acronym for Main Engine Cut Off]

medallion, *n. U.S.* **1** a license or permit to operate a taxicab, issued in the form of a medallion which is purchased by the licensee. *. . . a government contract is awarded to the bidder who will best serve the government's interest or to the one who submits the lowest bid. The theory is extended to taxicab medallions and turnpike concessions . . .* New Yorker 9/26/70, p56 **2** a taxicab driver with such a license. *"If medallions want to start a fight, all right, but don't go looking for trouble," he said.* NY Times 7/10/68, p36 [**1963**]

me decade, a name applied to the 1970's to characterize the seemingly obsessive preoccupation individuals had with their personal happiness or self-gratification during that decade. Compare ME GENERATION. *Broadly, the premise of the "me decade". . . is that great numbers of people are disdaining society to pursue existence as narcissistic massage buffs, omsayers, encounter groupies and peacocks.* Time 12/25/78, p84 *The conservative 1970s were called the "Me Decade," especially by people clinging to the myth that the 1960s were years of selflessness. Odd, isn't it, that the slogan of the "selfless" '60s was "Do your own thing."* Newsweek 11/19/79, p59 [**1977**, coined by the American journalist Tom Wolfe, born 1931]

medevac (ˈmedəˌvæk), *U.S.* —*n.* military helicopter used to carry the wounded from combat areas to hospitals. *The two wounded Aid Men continued to crawl about and administer care. There would be no medevac; there was no landing zone for it . . .* Harper's 1/67, p77 —*v.t.*, **medevacked, medevacking.** to transport by a medevac. *At My Lai, Ridenhour reported, one soldier shot himself in the foot so that he would be Medevacked out of the area.* Time 11/28/69, p23 [**1965** for noun; **1969** for verb; from *medical evacuation*]

media event, 1 an event deliberately staged or promoted for extensive coverage by the communications media; a pseudo-event. *The reason that some phenomenon or other is declared to exist as a trend is that powerful interests have invested in that existence. (The "media event," which is no event at all until the network camera crews tramp in to make it so, is one example of the attempt to shape the world to subjective corporate fiat.)* New Yorker 3/13/78, p93 **2** a minor event made to seem important by excessive or exaggerated publicity. *The vogue phrase for coverage that overwhelms an occasion and by magnification distorts it is "media event."* Time 3/8/76, p62 **3** a special or outstanding event, especially in broadcasting or communications. *Among the top "media events" of 1977 were David Frost's historic televised interviews with former President Richard Nixon, presented in four 90-minute segments at weekly intervals.* Americana Annual 1978, p119 [**1972**]

mediagenic (ˌmiːdiːəˈdʒɛnik), *adj. Especially U.S.* suitable for or appealing to the broadcasting or communications media. [Gerald] *Ford hopes to find someone youngish and mediagenic, politically moderate enough to balance his own brand of Midwest conservatism.* Newsweek 8/19/74, p32 [**1972**, from *media* + *-genic*, as in *photogenic, telegenic, radiogenic*]

mediaman, *n.* another name for MEDIAPERSON. *Not everyone has been bored. I have found people to be more polite and philosophical than is usual at election time, as if they wanted to identify themselves with the impartial experts and media-*

men, *rather than the partisans: there has been a tendency to look down on politicians, who actually hold* beliefs *and make* decisions. Listener 2/28/74, p260 [**1974**]

mediamorphosis, *n.* the transformation or distortion of facts by the media. *Thus, where the Vice President is concerned after this reinauguration, the question is not what* [he] *is really like. Mediamorphosis notwithstanding, a great many people seem to know, and from all electoral accounts, he seems to be doing just fine.* Newsweek 1/29/73, p9 [**1971**, from *media* + *metamorphosis*]

mediaperson, *n.* a reporter or correspondent of one of the media. *The Braves' attendance so far strongly suggests that if Hank should waft the record-breaker during a home game the deed will be witnessed by more mediapersons than Atlantans.* Newsweek 7/16/73, p52 [**1973**; see -PERSON]

media-shy, *adj.* fearful of the media; nervous about being interviewed or reported on by journalists. *A man who was involved with the Monkees from their conception to demise, but who is media-shy and insists on remaining anonymous, tells me he has seen it happen to every person he's known who becomes the object of mass worship.* Atlantic 10/73, p64 [**1973**, patterned after *camera-shy* (1920's)]

Medibank, *n.* the national health insurance program of Australia. *More than two million Australians have begun a 24-hour strike in protest against proposed changes to Medibank, the national health scheme introduced by the former Labour Government.* Times (London) 7/12/76, p1 [**1975**, from *medical* + *bank*]

Medicaid, *n. U.S.* a joint state and federal program that provides financial benefits for medical service to the poor or disabled (often used attributively). *Generally, a family of four with one wage earner is now eligible for Medicaid if it has an income of $6,000 or less.* NY Times 1/9/68, p31 [**1966**, from *Medical aid*]

Medicaid mill, *U.S.* a private clinic where several doctors offer medical services under the Medicaid program, engaging in excessive or illegal billing for services that are unnecessary or never performed. See PING-PONG, FAMILY GANGING. *The investigation of Medicaid mills is unusually difficult because, unlike nursing homes and day-care centers, they usually do not exist as corporate entities. Rather, groups of doctors share an office, with each billing Medicaid separately under his own name.* NY Times 10/6/76, p1 [**1975**, patterned after *diploma mill, propaganda mill,* etc.]

Medicare, *n. U.S. and Canada.* a government health-insurance program providing low-cost hospital and medical care, especially for people over sixty-five (often used attributively). *Medicare, which became effective on July 1, 1966, offered inexpensive health care for most of the nation's elderly citizens.* 1967 Compton Yearbook, p289 *In Florida, a general practitioner was paid $191,000 from the Medicare treasury in a single year.* Science News 5/24/69, p497 [**1962**, from *Medical care*]

medichair, *n.* a chair with electronic sensors to monitor the physiological activity of a person. *. . . scientists have developed an instrumented chair that gives a person a quick basic medical check-up in one sitting . . . This medichair was demonstrated for the first time yesterday at the opening session of the annual meeting of the Aerospace Medical Association in Las Vegas.* NY Times 4/19/66, p37 [**1966**, from *medical chair*]

medigap, *n.* a policy of supplemental health insurance that provides coverage of some or all medical, hospital, and other costs of health care not provided by Medicare and Medicaid. *Revised medigap policies were required this year . . . About 22 million of 33 million Medicare beneficiaries have supplemental insurance.* NY Times 5/13/89, p50 [**1976**]

mediocritize (ˌmiːdiːˈakrətaiz), *v.t.* to make mediocre; reduce to the ordinary or banal. *Leticia Kent, a journalist and a critic, describes Barbara* [Walters] *as "chameleonlike. At first she was anti-student and antifeminist. She was even against women wearing slacks . . . 'Today' is one of the most mind-controlling programs, and the banal patter on the show is appalling. She* exercises a mock-critical role. Everything is mediocritized, I don't know if it's her, or the medium." NY Times Magazine 9/10/72, p50 [**1972,** back formation from *mediocritization* (1968), from *mediocrity* + *-ization*] —**mediocritization,** *n.: I subscribe more to my own theory of our general mediocritization (or would if the word itself were less unwieldy). People who are led to feel that it is basically desirable to let mass-produced precooked frozen foods nourish their families are perhaps the general run, or will be in a few years.* Esquire 8/70, p124

MEDLARS ('med,larz), *n. U.S.* a computerized system for obtaining bibliographical data compiled from medical literature. Compare MEDLINE. *The National Library of Medicine, in Bethesda, Maryland, has an information-retrieval service (MEDLARS) designed to index the medical literature in twenty-three hundred periodicals.* New Yorker 10/24/70, p63 [**1964,** from *Med*ical *L*iterature *A*nalysis *a*nd *R*etrieval *S*ystem]

MEDLINE ('med,lain), *n. U.S.* a direct-line computerized system for obtaining bibliographical data compiled from medical literature, introduced in 1972. *In using MEDLARS, a physician or researcher would generally write or telephone a request for a search on a given topic to the National Library of Medicine in Washington. A week or longer would lapse before he would receive the results. Now, through MEDLINE, each user installation would have its own computer terminal connected to a centralized data processing system and would be able to search a large body of the more frequently used medical literature and receive listings of relevant citations in minutes.* 1973 Britannica Yearbook of Science and the Future, p259 [**1972,** from *MED*LARS + *line* telephone or communications line]

medullin (mə'dələn), *n.* a prostaglandin isolated from the medulla of the kidney, used in the treatment of high blood pressure. *A kidney substance called medullin, which at St. Vincent Hospital, Worcester, Mass., was first tried on a patient with high blood pressure and reduced it to a normal level, was found to be a member of the prostaglandin family.* Science News Letter 6/18/66, p481 [**1966,** from *medull*a + *-in* (chemical suffix)]

mega-, *combining form.* **1** very large; bigger than most of its kind. —**mega-association,** *n.: The closer links which are already developing within the personal finance industry, could be logically developed into a mega-association for all parties.* Times (London) 6/27/70, p13 —**megacity,** *n.: And among the new moralists analogous doubts exist concerning . . . the noisy, ugly, chaotic, increasingly dangerous and ever-spreading mega-cities . . .* Harper's 2/68, p61 —**megagame,** *n.: However, there are plenty of people who like tennis the way Ashe and Graebner play it. It is the megagame.* New Yorker 6/7/69, p56 —**megamillionaire,** *n.: Nelson Aldrich Rockefeller, 59, a megamillionaire via the Rockefellers, a political patrician through the Aldriches . . .* Time 3/8/68, p21 **2** one million (in units of measurement). —**megabar,** *n.: The pressure needed to produce metallic hydrogen may well be less than a megabar; laboratory equipment will just about stretch to 600 kilobars at the moment.* New Scientist 1/9/69, p81 —**megadecibel,** *n.: The controversy over Viet Nam was raised several megadecibels by widespread speculation that the Johnson Administration was considering use of tactical nuclear weapons in the war.* Time 2/23/68, p10 —**megarad,** *n.: With simple calibration the radiation dosage can be read off directly in megarads.* New Scientist 3/21/68, p638 [from Greek *mégas* large, great]

megabit, *n.* a unit of information equivalent to one million bits or binary digits. Compare GIGABIT, KILOBIT, TERABIT. *In the lower band the system will provide 16 high speed digital broadband channels, each capable of supporting a data rate of 500 Megabits/sec.* Science Journal 10/70, p19 [**1957,** from *mega-* one million + *bit*]

megabyte, *n.* unit of computer information approximately equal to one million bytes. Compare KILOBYTE. *Edinburgh University, according to Computing magazine, has requested permission from the Universities Computer Board to install 1,600 megabytes of Telex disc memory.* Times (London)

11/12/76, p16 [**1973,** from *mega-* one million + *byte* unit of computer information usually equal to 8 bits]

megadose, *n.* a very large dose of a drug, medicine, vitamin, etc. *Studies with college students in Canada have shown that megadoses of vitamin C can protect against the common cold.* Science News 7/28/73, p60 —**v.t.** to provide with a megadose. *In the scramble for a cure in the past half-century, patients have been lobotomized, tranquilized, psychoanalyzed, starved, chilled, shocked with electricity and mega-dosed with vitamins.* Maclean's 12/26/77, p42 [**1972,** from *mega-* very large + *dose*]

megajet, *n.* a jet aircraft larger and faster than a jumbo jet. Compare JUMBO JET. *Compared with today's Boeing 747, for instance, these new 'megajets' would cruise 40 per cent faster with some 250 per cent more payload.* Science Journal 9/70, p47 [**1970**]

megamachine, *n.* a term coined by Lewis Mumford to describe a social system so dominated by technology that it resembles a gigantic machine which functions without any regard for human needs and objectives. See also MEGATECHNICS. *What is needed to save mankind from the megamachine—or whatever controls the megamachine—is to displace the mechanical world picture with an organic world picture, in the center of which stands man himself.* Lewis Mumford, New Yorker 10/31/70, p85 *The megamachine was "invisible" because its tens of thousands of intricately interacting parts were human.* Harper's 10/67, p110 [**1967**]

megastructure, *n.* a very large building. *Arcology is architect Paolo Soleri's master city of the future. Integrating architecture with ecology, it is a total planned environment—dwellings, factories, utilities, cultural centers—within a single megastructure 1-2 miles wide and up to 300 stories high.* Encyclopedia Science Supplement (Grolier) 1971, p287 [**1965**]

megatanker, *n.* a very large tanker, especially one exceeding 200,000 tons. Compare SUPERSHIP. *Japan, which has concentrated on the construction of these megatankers, in 1972 launched 13 million tons of merchant ships representing nearly 50 percent of the total world tonnage and nearly double the total output of Sweden, West Germany, Great Britain, Spain, and France.* 1974 Collier's Encyclopedia Year Book, p540 [**1970**]

megatechnics, *n.* a term coined by Lewis Mumford to describe the large-scale mechanization of a highly technological society. See also MEGAMACHINE. *Under the impulsion of unprecedented "megatechnics"—"nuclear energy, supersonic transportation, cybernetic intelligence, and instantaneous distant communication"—the far-flung settlement patterns of Megalopolis are resistlessly expanding in many parts of the world, transforming man and the earth.* Harper's 10/67, p108 [**1967**]

megatonnage ('megə,tənidʒ), *n.* the total destructive force in megatons (one megaton = one million tons of TNT). *In a queer display of morbid mathematics Defense Secretary Melvin Laird has summed the megatonnages of strategic nuclear explosives possessed by the United States and the Soviet Union, and he has concluded quite absurdly, that Russian infinity is a greater quantity than American infinity.* NY Times 11/19/70, p46 [**1954**]

megaversity, *n.* a very large university, with an enrollment of many thousands of students. Compare MULTIVERSITY. *Under [John A.] Hannah, M.S.U. [Michigan State University] has grown from a sleepy agricultural college of 6,390 students into a 5,000-acre "megaversity" with an enrollment of 42,541 and an annual budget of more than $100 million.* Time 3/21/69, p34 [**1968,** from *mega-* very large + uni*versity*]

megavitamin, *adj.* of or based upon the ingestion of very large dosages of vitamins. *The use of very large amounts of vitamins in the control of disease has been called megavitamin therapy. Megavitamin therapy is one aspect of orthomolecular medicine. It is my opinion that in the course of time it will be found possible to control hundreds of diseases by megavitamin thera-*

py. Linus Pauling, Vitamin C and the Common Cold, 1970, p70 **[1968]**

me generation, the adult generation of the ME DECADE. *It may have taken them a little longer, but right now . . . middle-class blacks have been seized by the "Me Generation." They are looking at themselves, their bodies, their minds, their golf swings, wardrobes and investment portfolios.* NY Times Magazine 12/3/78, p140 *The quest for identity also accounted for the self-improvement programs associated with the human-potential movement—a farrago that included such quick-fix therapies as "primal scream" and "rolfing." Much of it, observers complained, typified the "me" generation's insistence on magical solutions and gratification.* Newsweek 11/19/79, p96 **[1977**, coined by the American journalist Tom Wolfe, born 1931; term influenced by NOW GENERATION**]**

megillah (məˈgilə), *n.* **a whole megillah,** *Slang.* a long, complicated story or affair. *"There's a whole megillah about being a straight man. It's supposed to be so difficult . . ."* Manchester Guardian Weekly 8/30/75, p18 **[1957**, translation of Yiddish *a gantse megile*, in allusion to the *Megillah* (Hebrew *megillah* roll, scroll) of Esther in the Old Testament, read out loud during the holiday of Purim**]**

mellotron (ˈmeləˌtran), *n.* an electronic musical instrument programmed by computer. . . . *the cold, windswept string tone of the Mellotron, a keyboard instrument which simulates—but not quite—the sound of an orchestra.* Times (London) 12/22/70, p11 **[1968**, apparently formed from *mello*w + *elec*tron*ic***]**

melodica, *n.* a small wind instrument resembling a harmonica but having a pianolike keyboard. *There was a service on Sunday conducted by the captain, with music provided by the senior technical officer on the flute, and an engineer officer with his melodica.* Times (London) 4/26/67, p3 **[1961**, from *melodic*, on the analogy of *harmonic, harmonica***]**

meltdown, *n.* the melting of the fuel core of a nuclear reactor. Compare BLOWDOWN, EXCURSION. See also CHINA SYNDROME. *What concerns these nuclear engineers . . . is a "meltdown," which can occur if a reactor loses the water used to control the temperature of its uranium core.* Time 3/8/76, p69 *Even if there were to be a meltdown, the release of radioactivity would be retarded by the very strong reactor vessel, which typically has walls six to 12 inches thick.* Scientific American 1/76, p25 **[1965**, from the verb phrase *melt down***]**

memcon (ˈmemˌkan), *n. Especially U.S., Informal.* a memorandum of a conversation. *The U.S. negotiators prepare memorandums known as "memcons" on any "unofficial" point—or hint—of substance a Russian offers, and the Soviet side presumably does the same.* Time 8/14/78, p11 **[1973**, from *mem*o + *con*versation**]**

memory bank, the storage unit or data bank of a computer. *Participating entertainment enterprises like theaters and sports arenas are linked by sales outlets in such spots as railroad stations, travel agencies, department stores and even supermarkets. At most of those locations, buyers tell a sales clerk what event they want to see and when. By pushing buttons on a console, the clerk queries a regional computer's "memory bank" and gets an instant reading on what seats are available. Customers then can have their tickets printed electronically on the spot.* Time 8/29/69, p57 **[1952]**

memory drum, a reel of magnetic tape or a cylinder on which data are recorded in the memory unit of a computer. *The memory drum of a computer at a medical college holds millions of pieces of evidence regarding the results of certain types of treatment based on particular symptoms.* Americana Annual 1967, p104 **[1958]**

memory trace, a chemical change occurring in the brain when new information is absorbed and remembered. *The two most popular chemical contenders for this elusive "memory trace" . . . have been ribonucleic acid (RNA) and protein. The learning process is assumed to produce changes in these molecules which then, on recall, alter in some way the properties of the*

neural synapses and allow the memory to be expressed. New Scientist 7/27/67, p206 **[1924, 1951]**

ménage à quatre (meiˌnɑːʒ ɑ ˈkatrə), a household of four people whose relationship involves sexual intimacy between all or several of the members. *Trevor, in hospital with broken limbs (having slipped on a frog!), is visited by a liberated Irene with Shirley and Eric, all ready for a* ménage à quatre. Listener 1/29/76, p121 **[1963**, from French, literally, household of four, patterned after *ménage à trois***]**

menazon (ˈmenəˌzan), *n.* a systemic insecticide used widely because of its low toxicity to mammals. *Dr. A. Calderbank, already a veteran of insecticide and herbicide research . . . was jointly responsible for the discovery of the powerful aphicide menazon . . .* New Scientist 9/25/69, p665 **[1961**, irregularly formed from the names of some of its chemical components: di*me*thyl, tria*z*in, thi*on*ate**]**

mengovirus (ˈmeŋgouˌvairəs), *n.* a virus that causes inflammation of the brain and heart muscle (encephalomyocarditis). It belongs to the picornavirus group. *There are shifts in allegiance to various hypotheses as new findings occur; for example, early studies with vaccinia* [and] *mengovirus . . . all indicated that interferon acts at a translation level.* Nature 8/18/72, p369 **[1970**, from *Mengo*, apparently the name of its discoverer + *virus***]**

mensch (mentʃ), *n. U.S. Slang.* a respected person; a decent human being. *The Warren Commission unleashed an army of investigators to dredge up the facts about* [Jack] *Ruby (né Jacob Rubenstein, alias J. Leon Rubenstein), the seedy Dallas stripjoint owner who yearned to be a* mensch, *a pillar of the community . . .* Time 1/13/67, p16 **[1953**, from Yiddish *mentsh*, literally, a person, human being, from German *Mensch***]**

Men's Lib or **Men's Liberation**, *U.S.* an organization of males whose aim is to free men from their traditional image and role in society. *The members of Men's Lib say they are tired of "having to prove our masculinity twenty-four hours a day" and believe that if their cause should prevail, "outmoded concepts would disappear in the face of reality."* New Yorker 12/19/70, p101 **[1970**, patterned after *Women's Lib, Women's Liberation***]**

menstrual extraction, a method of terminating possible pregnancy by evacuating the uterus. *In several gynecological offices and clinics the technically legal process of "menstrual extraction" is now being employed as a means of terminating suspected pregnancy at its earliest stage. The procedure involves . . . drawing out most of the uterine lining . . .* 1974 Collier's Encyclopedia Year Book, p348 **[1972]**

menu, *n.* **1** *Figurative use.* any list or program of items. *German theatre . . . directors face diminishing audiences, bored with over-familiar theatrical menus . . .* Manchester Guardian Weekly 9/19/70, p7 *Students . . . are so bright that they are bored with the standard academic menu.* NY Times 7/20/70, p26 **2** a computer program that presents choices, especially of tasks for the computer to do or categories of information for it to work with. *To select a particular brush the artist calls up a list of what is available—a menu—on the screen (some systems have the menu displayed on a separate screen.* New Scientist 12/10/81, p754 **—v.t.** *Informal.* to arrange; program. *Menu, meaning a computer's directory of functions, is turning up now as noun and verb, as in "Let me menu my schedule and I'll get back to you about lunch."* NY Times 11/8/82, p92 **[1953** for noun def. 1; **1971** for noun def. 2; **1982** for verb**]**

MEP, abbreviation of *Member of the European Parliament.* See EUROPEAN PARLIAMENT. *It has already been laid down in Strasbourg that MEPs "shall vote on an individual and personal basis" and "they shall not be bound by anyone's instructions and shall not receive a binding mandate." Moreover, "it is not desirable that chairmen or members of committees should enter into direct contact, as MEPs, with governmental or other national authority." The Community interest is meant to override the national interest.* Time (London) 8/8/77, p15 **[1976]**

merc (mərk), *n. Informal.* a mercenary. *A squad of Dutch and West German mercenaries invaded the platform and took pos-*

session—on behalf of the foreign minister himself. In a daring predawn raid six days later, Bates and four other armed men retook Sealand and ousted the mercs. High Times 1/79, p108 [**1967,** by shortening]

mercenarism, n. the act or practice of being a mercenary soldier. Derek Roebuck, professor of law at Tasmania University, another member of the commission, said it was not improper for the court to establish a crime of mercenarism as international and national law. Times (London) 7/1/76, p7 [**1976**]

merchants of death, a term of opprobrium for manufacturers or sellers of arms, who presumably profit more than others from war. The military-industrial complex is at once more and less than the name implies. As a catch phrase, it may be on its way to surpassing in notoriety "merchants of death," the term that grew out of Senator Gerald Nye's investigation of the arms industry in 1934. Time 4/11/69, p21 [**1963,** a revitalized term popular in the 1930's]

mergee, n. one party to a merger. Elsewhere in the motel—we learn later—the rival corporation, Penta, has chosen a more ingenious method: they tell their mergees that it seems important only that the change be comfortable for everyone; why not just divide into pairs of compatible people, and Penta will choose among these two-man teams. Atlantic 10/71, p85 [**1964**]

meritocracy (,merə'tɑkrəsi:), n. **1** a ruling class in society consisting of those who are most talented or have the highest intellect. [Michael] Young is most widely known as the author of The Rise of the Meritocracy [first published in 1958]. The book portrays a 21st-century Britain in which the social revolution has thrown up a ruling elite selected, not by birth or wealth, but by intellectual ability as demonstrated in examinations. Science 4/26/68, p403 **2** a system of education which stresses advancement of those who are most talented or have the highest intellect. Selection of pupils by ability is not so much a device of meritocracy as an accepted method of increasing teaching productivity. Times (London) 2/17/65, p13 [**1958,** from merit + -ocracy, as in aristocracy]

meritocrat ('merətə,kræt), n. a member of a meritocracy. It urges a programme of action for the children—the potential drop-outs who are too often ignored in an education system which often seems devoted only to the able and the clever—the meritocrats. Times (London) 5/8/68, p10 [**1960**]

meritocratic (,merətə'krætik), adj. of or belonging to a meritocracy. The managerial revolution has been much more thorough in America and on the Continent than in Britain, where nepotism and the old boy network still hamper progress towards meritocratic rule in the Civil Service, industry, commerce and finance. Punch 10/19/66, p572 [**1958**]

Mertensian mimicry (mər'tenzi:ən), Zoology. close resemblance of a noxious animal to one that is less noxious. Three major forms of mimicry have been observed, or at least are thought to exist, in nature—Batesian mimicry, in which a defenseless organism bears a close resemblance to a noxious one; Mullerian mimicry, in which noxious species tend to resemble each other, and Mertensian mimicry, in which a mimic is more strongly protected than its model. Science News 2/26/77, p139 [**1977,** named after R. Mertens, a herpetologist who first described this type of protective mimicry]

mesc, n. Especially U.S., Slang. mescaline. [Relevant Teenager 1971] is off everything at the moment—pot, hash, speed, acid, STP, mesc, psyl, coke, scag—because "It's all a bummer, man; I got my head together." Harper's 9/71, p63 [**1970,** by shortening]

mesclun (mes'klœ or 'mesklən), n. a French salad consisting of a mixture of tender young lettuces, spicy wild green herbs, and sometimes edible flowers. Clearly mesclun gives a whole new sparkle to the green salad. NY Times Magazine 12/6/87, p134 [**1987,** from French (originally dialectal), from Old French mescler to mix, from Medieval Latin misculare to mix thoroughly, from Latin miscēre to mix]

mesocyclone, n. a cyclone of up to ten miles in diameter that develops in the vicinity of a large thunderstorm. The Norman instrument, operated by the National Severe Storms Laborato-

ry and the National Weather Service, sweeps oncoming storms with a radar beam and monitors echoes of the beam returned by water droplets and ice crystals. The echoes are translated into a display which can indicate to meteorologists the characteristic signatures of mesocyclones, from which tornadoes are born, and the tornadoes themselves. New Scientist 4/6/78, p7 [**1975,** from meso- midway, intermediate + cyclone]

meson factory, a particle accelerator designed to produce intense beams of mesons with which to probe atomic nuclei. A new generation of machines, called meson factories, should yield a sharper dimension in the study of what goes on in atomic nuclei . . . The Los Alamos facility is the most energetic of the meson factories now under construction. It will be a linear accelerator, 1,800 feet long, that will accelerate protons or negative hydrogen ions to energies between 100 million and 800 million electron volts. The protons, striking various targets, will produce pi and mu meson beams. Science News 10/11/69, p332 [**1966**]

mesoscale ('mesou,skeil), adj. intermediate between large-scale and small-scale. Dr. H.A. Panofsky, a Pennsylvania State University meteorologist, pointed to weaknesses in the knowledge of mesoscale meteorology, the meteorology of areas 10 to 20 miles in diameter, or about the size of many urban areas. Such knowledge, in the form of sophisticated mathematical models, is badly needed, he says, so that meteorologists can help air pollution control officials. Science News 1/30/71, p81 [**1957,** from meso- middle + scale]

mesoscaph or **mesoscaphe** ('mesou,skæf), n. an undersea vessel designed for medium depth exploration of the seas. The mesoscaphe can drift along with the Gulf Stream at depths ranging from 500 to 2,000 feet, as the scientists aboard study their environment with cameras, hydrophones, water samplers, and plankton nets. Encyclopedia Science Supplement (Grolier) 1969, p144 [**1964,** from French mésoscaphe, coined by its inventor, the French deep-sea explorer Jacques Piccard, born 1922, from Greek mésos middle + skáphē vessel]

mesosome, n. a structure on cell membranes that is concerned with the formation of the cross wall when a cell divides. The key to their theory [as to how DNA enters bacteria] is the mesosome, a structure which can be observed in electron micrographs of bacteria . . . It is the point at which DNA is attached to the cell membrane. New Scientist 10/16/69, p113 [**1960,** from meso- middle + -some body]

message, n. a unit of the genetic code which specifies the order or sequence in which amino acids synthesize a particular protein. The genetic message is carried from the nucleus to the cytoplasm in the form of messenger ribonucleic acid (messenger RNA). Science Journal 11/70, p57 [**1963**]

message unit, U.S. a unit used by a telephone company to charge for calls that are timed, such as long-distance calls. But then Joe Smith got tough: "Come off it, bo'. You wanna meet Mr. Howard Hughes or not? Time is money and you have just cost me 10 message units, though life is cheap here in Mexico." NY Times Book Review 2/27/72, p55 [**1963**]

messenger, n. a chemical substance which carries or transmits genetic information. A theory of messenger-RNA (mRNA) was offered, designating one type of RNA as a messenger between the DNA templates in the nucleus and the protein-manufacturing RNA in the cytoplasm. Encyclopedia Science Supplement (Grolier) 1965, p40 [**1961**]

messenger particle, Physics. any pointlike subatomic particle that transmits a fundamental force of nature. The graviton, the photon, the gluon, and the weakon are messenger particles. The particle relationship to the weak force is more complicated. In one weak reaction, a neutron changes into a proton by emitting a messenger particle called a weakon or W particle, which in turn is quickly transformed into an electron and an electrically neutral counterpart of the electron called a neutrino. World Book Science Annual 1987, p189 [**1986**]

messenger RNA, a ribonucleic acid which carries genetic messages from the DNA (deoxyribonucleic acid) in the nucleus of a cell to the ribosomes in the cytoplasm, specifying the particular protein or enzyme to be synthesized. *Abbreviation:* mRNA Compare RIBOSOMAL RNA, TRANSFER RNA. *Because coding experiments are done with RNA, genetic codes are usually given in terms of messenger-RNA rather than DNA.* World Book Science Annual 1967, p300 **[1961]**

meta-, combining form meaning "going beyond or transcending the usual kind of (a specified person or thing)," used chiefly in technical terms such as the following: —**metaculture,** *n.: Activities such as reading, writing, private communication, learning, previously framed with silence, now take place in a field of strident vibrato. This means that the essentially linguistic nature of these pursuits is adulterated; they are vestigial modes of the old "logic." Yet we are unquestionably dealing with a literacy, with codes of recognition so widespread and dynamic that they constitute a "meta-culture."* Atlantic 8/71, p41 —**metahistorian,** *n.: A historian writes the history of a period, a metahistorian compares different periods in order to derive common rules.* New Scientist 3/12/70, p525 —**metaprogram,** *n.: When you take hold of ecology, it will help if you have a firm understanding of the order of nature and if you have a good metaprogram.* New Yorker 5/2/70, p30 —**metavolcanic,** *adj.: Westmoreland [Westmoreland Minerals (mining)] and its partners have said the banded iron formation adjoins 2,000 ft. to 3,000 ft. wide metavolcanic zones . . .* Times (London) 2/2/70, p23

metallide ('metə‚laid), *v.t.* to subject (a metal) to metalliding. *Molybdenum, for example, is a relatively soft metal; when boron is metallided into it, the resulting surface alloy is apparently second in hardness only to diamond.* Science News 7/15/67, p66 **[1967,** from metall-, combining form for metal (as in *metalloid* a non-metal used in alloys) + -ide (suffix of chemical compounds)]

metalliding ('metə‚laidiŋ), *n.* a process of strengthening the surface of metals by diffusing the atoms of one metal through high-temperature electrolysis into the surface of another. The resulting surface alloy is harder than any mechanically applied coating or plating. *Metalliding, a process patented by General Electric Company, created alloys at the outer layer of a wide variety of metal substances. The process places both the alloying and base metals in a bath of molten fluoride salts and applies direct current electricity between them. Ions of the anode (alloying metal) flow to the cathode (base metal) and diffuse into it, forming the alloyed surface.* World Book Science Annual 1968, p290 **[1967,** gerund of *metallide, v.*]

metalloenzyme, *n.* an enzyme containing metal ions that are essential for its activity. *Enzymes in which transition metals are tightly incorporated are called metalloenzymes, since the metal is usually embedded deep inside the structure of the protein. If the metal atom is removed, the protein usually loses its capacity to function as an enzyme.* Scientific American 7/72, p57 **[1955,** from *metallic* + connecting -o- + *enzyme*]

metaphor, *n.* something concrete thought of as resembling and hence representing an idea, quality, or condition; a symbol. *His metaphor for the insincerity of the governmental approach is the moratorium on whale hunting taken at the Stockholm conference.* Maclean's 6/73, p76 *One of Mr. Nixon's tax dodges provides a metaphor for his relation to the places where he spends his time.* Harper's 7/74, p4 **[1971,** extended sense of the term meaning an implied comparison in language, e.g. "the sea of life," "Life's but a walking shadow," etc.]

met-enkephalin (‚meten'kefəlin), *n.* a painkilling chemical produced in the brain and consisting of a peptide chain having the amino acid methionine at its end. Compare LEU-ENKEPHALIN. *Met-enkephalin is more potent than the leu- variety, but both bind less strongly to brain receptors than does morphine.* New Scientist 6/10/76, p578 **[1976,** from *methionine* + *enkephalin*]

meter maid, *U.S.* a female member of a traffic bureau or police department who patrols metered parking areas and gives traffic summonses for parking violations. *The city [New York] itself is hazardous for me now. I started on a walk one afternoon during my last visit, but the wind was so strong I had to lean against walls and hold on to No Parking signs. A Meter Maid*

was soon watching me censoriously, no doubt thinking I was drunk. Harper's 2/68, p41 **[1956]**

meth, *n. U.S. Slang.* methamphetamine (a stimulant drug). Also called SPEED. *"It sounds like I'm knocking her. I'm not. She was a good kid, if she hadn't been so freaked out on meth."* NY Times 10/16/67, p53 **[1967]**

methadone maintenance, the use of methadone as a maintenance drug in treating heroin or morphine addiction. *Addicts attempting to withdraw from heroin, morphine, or the like . . . go to treatment centers for methadone maintenance. The largest program is in New York City and is headed by Dr. Vincent Dole and Dr. Marie Nyswander, who began the push for methadone maintenance and have done most of the original clinical research.* Norman E. Zinberg and John A. Robertson, Drugs and the Public, 1972, p112 **[1972]**

methanogen (mə'θænə‚dʒən), *n.* any of a group of methane-producing microorganisms genetically distinct both from bacteria and from plant and animal cells. Also called (as a group) ARCHAEBACTERIA. *The most striking thing about the methanogens is that they survive only in warm environments entirely free of oxygen—on the sea floor, in sewage, in the stomachs of cattle or in the hot springs of Yellowstone National Park. They thrive by converting carbon dioxide and hydrogen into methane, the principal component of natural gas.* Newsweek 11/14/77, p53 **[1977,** coined by Ralph S. Wolfe, an American microbiologist, from *methane* + connecting -o- + -gen (suffix meaning something that produces)] —**methanogenic,** *adj.: They were all conspicuously remote from the other bacteria. This cuts right across any classification on the basis of form; but then it is quite reasonable to suppose that form in bacteria is not the important evolutionary pointer that it is in higher, many-celled animals. Is there any other indication in the methanogenic biochemistry that these organisms are distinct from other bacteria?* New Scientist 12/1/77, p565

methaqualone (‚meθə'kweiloun), *n.* a nonbarbiturate drug that reduces anxiety and induces sleep, widely used as a narcotic. *Formula:* $C_{16}H_{14}N_2O$ *Trademark,* QUAALUDE. See SOPOR. *Because methaqualone was believed to be non-addictive when it first went on the U.S. market in 1965, it was not placed under the special Federal restrictions that govern substances whose harmful potential has been proved, including morphine, barbiturates, LSD and amphetamines.* Newsweek 2/12/73, p65 **[1961,** from *methyl* + connecting -a- + *quinazolinone*, chemical components of the drug]

methicillin (‚meθə'silən), *n.* a synthetic penicillin that has proved effective against penicillin-resistant staphylococci. *Another six days later there were signs of bacterial infection in the lungs, and the doctors prescribed methicillin.* New Scientist 1/18/68, p118 **[1961,** contraction of the full name di*meth*oxy-*ph*enylpen*icillin*]

methotrexate (‚meθou'trek‚seit), *n.* a drug that is an antagonist of folic acid and is used in the treatment of leukemia. *If a doctor has at hand a drug he believes to be beneficial, it is hard to dissuade him from using it. A case in point is a drug called Methotrexate, a highly toxic anticancer drug. Physicians have been prescribing it in the treatment of psoriasis, even though the Food and Drug Administration has not approved it for such use. Some 20 years ago physicians stumbled onto the fact that, though Methotrexate does not cure psoriasis, the drug suppresses the scaly, itchy symptoms of the skin disease . . .* Science News 6/6/70, p549 **[1955,** probably irregularly formed from the full chemical name *meth*ylamino p*t*eroylglutamic *ac*id + *-ate* (chemical suffix)]

methyl atropine, a chemical compound that inhibits the transmission of nerve impulses. *. . . Smith and his colleagues applied methyl atropine to the lateral hypothalami of killer rats. This chemical, which blocks the action of acetylcholine, turned the formerly deadly rats into harmless pacifists . . .* New Scientist 2/70, p342 **[1970]**

methylmercury, *n.* a highly toxic compound of mercury widely used in technology and as a pesticide. *Ultimately, scientists fear, its [mercury's as a fungicide] hazard to human beings may prove equally great. The Swedes solved their problem by* banning the use of one extremely pervasive compound, methylmercury, and shipping it to the United States, where it is now used to treat wheat seed. Atlantic 9/70, p25 [**1968**]

methylphenidate (ˌmeθəlˈfenəˌdeit), n. a drug used as a stimulant, especially in the treatment of mental disorders. *The idea that hyperactivity has a biological basis is further strengthened by the dramatic change in behavior produced in many of these children by a stimulating drug (such as amphetamine or methylphenidate).* Scientific American 4/70, p98 [**1962,** from *methyl* + *phenyl* + *-id* + *-ate* (chemical suffixes)]

methysergide (ˌmeθəˈsərˌgaid), n. a drug derived from the fungal nerve poison ergot. *A newer drug, methysergide, also derived from the nerve poison, is effective in reducing the number and severity of migraine headaches in about 70 per cent of patients.* Encyclopedia Science Supplement (Grolier) 1969, p167 [**1962,** apparently from *methyl* + blend of *serotonin* and *ergot* + *-ide* (chemical suffix)]

metical (ˌmetiˈkɑːl; *Anglicized* ˈmetiˌkæl), n. the monetary unit of Mozambique, introduced in 1980. Finance and Trade. *monetary unit: metical (new currency, introduced in June 1980 to replace the former escudo at par), with (Sept. 22, 1980) a free rate of 28 meticals to U.S.$1 (68 meticals = £1 sterling).* Britannica Book of the Year 1981, p550 [**1981,** from Portuguese, from Arabic *mithqāl* a unit of weight or money in various Moslem countries]

metric, *adj.* **1 go metric,** to adopt the metric system of measurement. *Going metric will not deprive us of the use of fractions where they are convenient: we can continue to count in halves and quarters as well as in twos, tens, and dozens.* Manchester Guardian Weekly 8/29/70, p15 **2** (of a country or person) using or accustomed to a metric system of measurement. *In a metric Britain, Manchester will be 296 km from London, not 184 miles. The motorist will have to drive within speed limits of 50 and 120 km per hour.* New Scientist 4/30/70, p247 [**1960**]

metricate (ˈmetrəˌkeit), v.t., v.i. to convert to the metric system; change to metric units. Also, METRIFY. *The cost of metricating road signs, which the Government were examining, would eventually have to be considered by local authorities.* Times (London) 10/28/70, p7 [**1965**]

metrication, n. conversion to the metric system. Also, METRIFICATION. *Mr Benn said he no more approved or disapproved of metrication as such, than he approved or disapproved of having ten fingers. But three quarters of our exports (he said 75 per cent) were to metric countries. It was good to share the same calendar, to agree on Greenwich Mean Time, and to have common units of measurement.* Manchester Guardian Weekly 3/7/70, p14 [**1965**]

metrification, n. British. another word for METRICATION. *The crowning glory of all was decimal coinage, but there was still time to retract. He [Lord Somers] had not heard a good word for it. Now there was a threat of metrification of weights and measures. That was the last straw. Before long there would be a move to drive on the right.* Times (London) 4/17/70, p6 [**1965**]

metrify (ˈmetrəˌfai), v.t., v.i. British. another word for METRICATE. *Although the Confederation of British Industry hopes that 75 per cent of Britain's industries will have metrified by 1975, there is as yet no official equivalent of the Decimal Currency Board, charged with supervising the change.* Sunday Times (London) 3/31/68, p10 [**1965**]

metro or **Metro,** U.S. and Canadian. —*adj.* of, relating to, or extending over a region including a large city and its suburbs. *The Valley of the Sun—Metro Phoenix—includes the satellite cities of Scottsdale, Paradise Valley, Tempe, Mesa (founded by Mormons), Glendale, and the retirement communities of Youngstown and Del Webb's Sun City.* Town And Country 1/76, p99 —*n.* a municipal government extending over a metropolitan area. *Metro handles public transit, police, welfare, ambulance services, and housing for the elderly. Local governments take care of many services, from firefighting to parking lots.* Harper's 12/74, p15 [**1962,** short for *metropolitan (area)*]

Metroliner, n. U.S. a high-speed train of the Amtrak railroad network. *The metroliner, electrically propelled with aluminium coaches, has neither quite the panache nor the speed of the Japanese Tokkaido Line, but it has cut the travelling time from Washington to New York, a distance of 226 miles, by nearly ninety minutes to two and a half hours.* Manchester Guardian Weekly 1/31/70, p6 [**1969**]

metronidazole (ˌmetrəˈnaidəˌzoul), n. a drug used to treat trichomoniasis (a disease infecting the vagina and causing abortion and sterility in cattle), used experimentally in cancer chemotherapy. *Formula:* $C_6H_9N_3O_3$ *A kind of shock wave ran through the community of chemotherapists not long ago when Sutherland of Great Britain showed that metronidazole, which I have already mentioned in connection with radiotherapy, not only sensitized cells to radiation but, independently of radiation, could also kill cells in phase G—a result that is yet to be confirmed but the possible significance of which can be readily imagined.* Lucien Israel, Conquering Cancer, 1978, p106 [**1963,** from *metro-* (from Greek *mḗtrā* uterus, cervix) + *ni*troimi*dazole,* chemical constituent of the drug]

Mexicali revenge (ˌmeksəˈkæliː), Slang. traveler's diarrhea acquired in Mexico. *He brought his own food, water, and liquor to Acapulco to avoid the embarrassment of his 1970 trip when nearly all of his guests developed classic cases of "Mexicali revenge" after being fed local produce.* Atlantic 7/73, p38 [**1973,** from *Mexicali,* city in northwestern Mexico]

Mexican brown, a type of dark-colored heroin produced in Mexico. Compare BROWN SUGAR. *William Smitherman, the U.S. attorney in Arizona, says his state has become perhaps the most important conduit for heroin entering the country. So-called "Mexican brown" cascades across the Nogales frontier, often in light aircraft that skim the desert to avoid radar surveillance.* Maclean's 11/15/76, p34 [**1975**]

MIA or **M.I.A.** (ˌemaiˈei), n. Especially U.S. a member of the armed forces reported as missing in action. *"We shall under no circumstances abandon our POWs or MIAs (missing in action) wherever they are,"* he [President Nixon] *said.* Times (London) 10/17/72, p6 [**1968,** from the abbreviation of *missing in action*]

Michaelis constant (maiˈkeilis), Biochemistry. a measure of the affinity of an enzyme for the substance it acts upon, equal to the concentration at which the reaction occurs at 50% of the maximal rate. *Symbol:* km *In the oyster adductor muscle, as in other organisms, malic enzyme is fully reversible; however, the Michaelis constants for pyruvate and carbon dioxide are so high that in vivo the oyster enzyme probably functions only in the direction of pyruvate production.* Science 12/8/72, p1057 [**1970,** named after Leonor *Michaelis,* 1875-1949, an American chemist]

mickey, n. take the mickey out of, British Slang. to act in a teasing or mocking manner towards (someone); mock; ridicule. . . . *there [on television] were Bird, Wells, Fortune, and Barry Humphries taking the mickey out of Kenneth Harris, Lord Devlin, Mark Lane, etc., and the next thing I knew I was laughing.* Manchester Guardian Weekly 2/16/67, p14 [**1952,** alteration of earlier *take the mike out of* (OEDS 1935)]

Mickey Mouse, U.S. **1** Military Slang. **a** anything that is unnecessary or unimportant. *A central concern now is the steady leak of talented officers, most of them young captains, majors, and lieutenant colonels. A study is under way to find the causes, but the most sensitive army officers already know them. They are four: the repeated Vietnam tours, the antimilitary atmosphere in the country, the low pay, and (for the younger men) the anachronistic spit-and-polish, the Mickey Mouse.* Atlantic 11/70, p81 **b** a muddled situation; a mix-up; foul-up. *Logistically so far, the only big Mickey Mouse, in G.I. parlance, was a brief shortage of canvas-and-rubber jungle boots (leather footgear rots in Viet Nam's steamy climate); they were flown in directly from Stateside manufacturers.* Time 12/10/65, p15 **2** Student Slang. an easy or simple college course. *Some popular opinion persists, of course, that college courses in "the movies" are a kind of trade-school apprenticeship or something easy to relax with ("Mickey Mouse" in today's campus par-*

lance). Harper's 10/65, p68 **3** simple; easy; unimportant. *"This is no Mickey Mouse business," said E. James Strates . . . "In the old days you put together a funhouse for $3,000, now it can cost $40,000."* NY Times 9/25/67, p41 [**1965** for def. 1; **1958** for def. 2; **1967** for def. 3; named for the Walt Disney animated cartoon character, in allusion to its childish appeal, its simplicity, triviality, etc.]

mickey-mouse, *v.i.* to synchronize the background music with the action, as in an animated cartoon. *The choreography, by Norman Maen, is the feeblest element in the film, with too much unimaginative "Mickey-mousing", matching each note in the score with some movement rather than creating an overall style of dance.* Times (London) 7/6/67, p8 [**1967**]

micro, *adj.* shorter than mini; mid-thigh or higher. *The hem was the same place it was last year—everywhere. Couturiers pegged it all the way from micro to floor level.* 1970 Collier's Encyclopedia Year Book, p232 **—n. 1** a skirt, dress, or other garment that is shorter than mini. *Hemlines go to all lengths. In extremes, there are micros, which barely cover the buttocks; minis, maxis and the nineteen-thirties length, which is well below the knee but still shows some shin.* NY Times 1/22/68, p36 **2** short for MICROCOMPUTER. *The real importance of micros, he notes, rests upon the fact that both processor and memory circuits have become units of mass production. Some peripheral machines are also moving in the same direction.* Times (London) 9/12/77, p7 [**1970** for adj.; **1968** for noun def. 1, **1972** for noun def. 2]

micro-, *combining form.* **1** very small; miniature. **—microdevice**, *n.: . . . automation is increasingly used in the production of the micro-devices and circuits which in turn are assembled into further automation systems.* Times (London) 5/7/70, p33 **—microfile**, *n.: Having selected the appropriate microfile from his folder, by means of one of 65 keywords (eg "filter"), the engineer inserts it into a reader and selects the page he wants by scanning down the first column.* New Scientist 7/10/69, p71 **—microinstability**, *n.: More than a hundred kinds of microinstabilities have been identified, and fusion researchers have been trying to find magnetic-bottle configurations that will be able to reduce the microinstabilities to acceptable proportions.* World Book Science Annual 1972, p222 **—microzone**, *n.: No one regional center can be pinpointed as the place from which agriculture emerged. Rather, there were a series of agricultural developments stemming from a number of environmental niches or microzones.* World Book Science Annual 1968, p267 **2** microscopic. **—microcrater**, *n.: . . . Mr. Gold* [Thomas Gold, an astrophysicist at Cornell University] *. . . had found microscopic craters—three or four craters, sometimes, to a speck of dust—and he was certain these microcraters proved that much of the dust on the moon came from space . . .* New Yorker 4/4/70, p92 **—microparticle**, *n.: . . . the search continues for facts about the similarities and differences between "organized elements," microfossils, and microparticles formed from amino acid polymers.* Encyclopedia Science Supplement (Grolier) 1969, p78 **—microworld**, *n.: Chemists and molecular biologists have unraveled many of the intricate processes needed to create the microworld of the living cell.* Scientific American 9/70, p125 [from Greek *mikrós* small]

microblade, *n. Archaeology.* a thin sliver chipped delicately from a prepared flint core, usually with parallel edges. *Late in the Upper Paleolithic and during the ensuing Mesolithic, it became the fashion to make smaller and smaller bladelettes. Commonly inserted as "side blades" into lateral grooves in antler and bone projectile points, such "microblades" lacerated the flesh of wounded game animals and thus promoted free bleeding and rapid death.* Britannica Book of the Year 1969, p101 [**1954**]

microbody, *n.* See the quotation for the meaning. *Ever since the electron microscope became available, microscopists have noted little particles within cells which they were unable to identify with any particular function. In a fit of divine inspiration, they named these particles "microbodies." Over the past few years,* [Professor Christian] *de Duve has discovered that these microbodies contain an enzyme system which could con-*

ceivably constitute the primitive respiratory system of the cell. The particles always contain an oxidase enzyme of some type, capable of indirectly converting oxygen to hydrogen peroxide. They also contain a catalase enzyme, which can convert hydrogen peroxide to water. New Scientist 6/27/68, p675 [**1954**]

micro book, a very small book which requires the use of a magnifying glass for reading. *The micro book is already much more than an idea. A company called Micro & Cine Books Ltd has been set up in Jersey and has taken premises to make the hardware—the readers and covers. Davies and his co-worker are intending to form their own publishing company in Alderney, which they have recently adopted as their base.* New Scientist 12/31/70, p601 [**1970**]

microburst, *n. Meteorology.* an intense downward surge of cool air sometimes occurring during a thunderstorm. *Since microbursts are often accompanied by rapid changes of wind speed and direction, they pose a threat to aircraft during take-off and landing. A microburst may have caused a fatal crash that killed 153 people when a Pan American Boeing 727 crashed near New Orleans in 1982.* World Book Science Annual 1986, p254 [**1983**]

microcalorie, *n.* one millionth of a calorie. *Heat flow through the ocean crust is on average 1.2 microcalories/cm²/s except in active regions such as mid-ocean ridges.* Science Journal 8/69, p42 *The heat flux of the moon is about two-tenths to three-tenths of a microcalorie per square centimeter per second, or about a sixth to a third that of the earth.* Science News 11/28/70, p414 [**1969**, from *micro-* one millionth (as in *microgram, microfarad*) + *calorie*]

microcapsule, *n.* a very small or microscopic capsule of a chemical substance, drug, etc. *Chang showed that his microcapsules of asparaginase broke down asparagine* [an amino acid] *when suspended in an asparaginase solution, and so he tested the technique in animals.* New Scientist and Science Journal 1/28/71, p171 [**1961**]

microcassette, *n.* a very small audiotape cassette. *Personal portables now have built-in AM, FM and even TV audio. They may have Dolby B or DBX noise reduction and take metal tape or microcassettes. They can record in stereo and become part of your home system.* Washington Post 1/7/83, p24 [**1979**]

microchip, *n.* another name for CHIP¹. *Electronic engineers have seen the future, and it is incredibly small. It is also cheap, easy to produce, stupefyingly fast, infinitely versatile, and magnificently convenient. It is, in a word, the microchip, a ladybug-sized bit of electronic scrimshaw that may change our lives as profoundly as the industrial revolution.* NY Times 2/14/78, p68 *Microchips are highly reliable, but should one fail, mechanical back-ups will keep the car running.* Discover 10/80, p44 [**1975**]

microcircuit, *n.* another name for INTEGRATED CIRCUIT. *Ferranti have introduced a new and advanced airborne computer known as the Argus 400—the first machine incorporating fully integrated silicon microcircuits to be developed and built in Europe.* Times (London) 8/10/65, p10 [**1959**]

microcircuitry, *n.* **1** another name for INTEGRATED CIRCUITRY. *If they can get a transmitter into that fabled olive in the vodkatini, then they could pack a fine old array of microcircuitry into a mouse's saddle-bags.* New Scientist 6/10/65, p702 **2** microscopic circuits. *Ganglion cells, however, fall into certain classes, indicating considerable order in the microcircuitry between them and the receptor cells.* McGraw-Hill Yearbook of Science and Technology 1969, p344 [**1959** for def. 1; **1965** for def. 2]

microcirculation, *n.* circulation of the blood through the capillary vessels. *But in the microcirculation, other factors—chemical messengers—seem to be at work. The red of a sunburn, for example, doesn't come from reaction of the brain or nerves. Ultraviolet light striking the skin causes it to release a compound called histamine. That body drug causes tiny arteries and capillaries to dilate so that blood suffuses the skin—sunburn.* Science News 12/2/67, p547 [**1959**]

microcomputer, *n.* a very small, low-cost electronic computer containing one or more microprocessors. *The heart of the microcomputer is a tiny chip of silicon packed with thousands of transistors. This chip, called a microprocessor, functions in the same way as the central processing unit in a standard computer. Thus small-scale memory systems and other units can be linked with the chip to produce a complete microcomputing device.* Encyclopedia Science Supplement (Grolier) 1975, p90 [**1972**]

microcontinent, *n.* a slab of continental rock thought to have been isolated and separated from a larger parent continent during the process of continental drift. *Rockall Bank is supposed to be one such isolated fault block—a microcontinent left behind in the splitting apart of Greenland and northern Europe. Its east and west boundaries represent the torn edges of the splitting; its southwestern one, a transform fault dislocating the ocean floor in a shearing movement.* New Scientist 6/24/76, p701 [**1965**]

micro-corneal lens, a contact lens covering only part of the cornea of the eye. Compare HAPTIC LENS. *Micro-corneal lenses cover only two thirds of the surface area of the cornea—the transparent bulge in front of the pupil—and must be aligned with its curvature.* New Scientist and Science Journal 9/23/71, p688 [**1971**]

microcrack, *n.* a microscopic crack in a material such as glass or chrome. *The low strength of glass is attributed to the presence of microcracks in the glass surface which drastically reduce the overall stress needed to cause fracture.* New Scientist 2/27/69, p457 —*v.i., v.t.* to produce microcracks (in a material). *At low thicknesses the deposits of chrome thrown by the new method are microporous, while thicker coatings are microcracked, which according to concentrated testing, gives a far greater resistance to corrosion.* Times (London) 5/22/70, p27 [**1950** for noun; **1955** for verb]

microculture, *n.* **1** a small, narrowly confined geographical area, whose inhabitants are considered to have their own ways and fashions that form a cultural unit within a nation, state, or other larger area. *That part of Texas where I first lived was some microculture. Puritanism in theory. Tobacco Road in practice.* New Yorker 4/6/68, p58 **2** a culture of microscopic organisms, tissue, etc. *"To clean the specimens I used a microculture slide in the form of a glass plate containing 12 depressions, each approximately one centimeter wide and four millimeters deep . . ."* Scientific American 5/67, p144 [**1964**]

microdot, *n. Slang.* a small pill containing the hallucinogenic drug LSD in highly concentrated form. *. . . one senior officer said last night: "I am deeply concerned about the use of this completely new form of LSD. Normally the drug produces hallucinations, but these microdots create fear, terror and suicidal tendencies."* New York Post 1/3/72, p5 [**1971**] ▶An earlier sense of *microdot* is that of a photograph reduced to the size of a dot for purposes of secrecy, etc.

microearthquake, *n.* a small earthquake, especially of a magnitude of less than 2.5 on the Richter scale. Also called MICRO-QUAKE. *. . . improved electronic equipment and modern developments in seismometer design should enable the new instrument to sort out artificial vibrations from those caused by local microearthquakes . . .* Science News 3/28/70, p320 [**1965**]

microecology, *n.* a branch of ecology concerned with environmental conditions in very small areas. *Too little is still known about microecology to allow for meaningful generalizations about the significance of impenetrable microsites for the protection of polluting chemicals against attack.* New Scientist 8/31/67, p440 [**1960**]

microelectronic, *adj.* of or relating to microelectronics. *And without the voracious demand of the computer industry we would not have seen such a rapid advance in electronic, and especially microelectronic, technology.* Science Journal 10/70, p42 [**1960**]

microelectronics, *n.* the branch of electronics dealing with integrated circuits. *Microelectronics, the use of extremely small circuits to replace larger and more costly tubes and transistors, will make such throw-away devices "economically useful . . ."* Science News Letter 4/3/65, p213 [**1952**]

microencapsulate, *v.t.* to enclose (something small) in a microcapsule. *Numerous metabolic diseases, many of them fatal in early infancy, have their roots in a lack of an appropriate enzyme in the liver, and all are presumably targets for liposome therapy. The technique has the advantage over other attempts that are being made to microencapsulate enzymes for therapy in that liposomes are constructed of "natural" materials.* New Scientist and Science Journal 7/15/71, p122 [**1965**]

microencapsulation, *n.* encapsulation in microcapsules. *But today striped paint is no more ridiculous than . . . copying paper that needs no carbon, or drugs that taste pleasant yet later (according to a precisely designed time schedule) release unpalatable medicants into the body, or packaged perfume painted invisibly on to paper for release months or years later, or petrol in the form of an apparently solid brick that can be sliced with a knife. These and many other equally startling but useful products all owe their existence to microencapsulation.* Science Journal 2/70, p62 [**1961**]

microfilament, *n.* an extremely fine and very long fiber in the cytoplasm of cells, associated with protoplasmic movement and cytoplasmic division. *Cytological and biochemical studies have demonstrated that microfilaments are virtually identical to actin, one of the major contractile proteins found in all skeletal, cardiac, and smooth muscle cells. The cytological evidence centers on the observation that microfilaments in a wide variety of animal and plant cells interact with a portion of the other major muscle protein, myosin.* McGraw-Hill Yearbook of Science and Technology 1977, p155 [**1970**] —**microfilamentous**, *adj.*: *The actin and myosin of the microfilamentous system interacted with each other while floating just under the membrane.* New Scientist 6/5/75, p553

microform, *n.* any material on which something can be reproduced in greatly reduced form. *The master files of the more than 3.2 million patents issued since 1790 will be put on microfilm, videotape or another microform for quick retrieval and public sale.* NY Times 1/25/66, p55 *Paper would be impracticable but microform might be the answer.* Sunday Times (London) 9/24/67, p2 —*v.t.* to reproduce on microfilm or other material; make copies of on microform. *The Massachusetts Institute of Technology . . . is planning to "microform" its entire engineering library.* NY Times 1/9/67, p139 [**1960** for noun; **1967** for verb]

microgravity, *n.* a condition of very low gravity, especially one approaching weightlessness. *Another, more subtle, effect you'll experience is the way your posture alters in microgravity. If you relax and allow yourself to just float, you'll naturally assume a neutral body position. In this posture, your arms float away from and just in front of your body. You're bent slightly at the waist, your knees are flexed, and your toes point a bit. The toe pointing makes it hard for you to stand erect with your feet flat on the floor. To correct this, special attachments for your boots have been developed.* Space Shuttle Operator's Manual 1982, p2.6 [**1981**]

microlens, *n.* a lens for photography on a microscopic scale. *Walon Green, who directed the picture and shot a good portion of the photography as well, used microlenses and extreme slow motion to get awesome footage of mayflies living out their brief lives . . .* Time 7/19/71, p48 [**1971**]

micromachining, *n.* the machining of very small parts, such as the components of microcircuits. *Micromachining has received much publicity in the past, and forms the mainstay of Laser Associates' range of systems . . . An example of this would be the drilling of a very fine hole in a hard material to a depth many times the diameter.* New Scientist 4/16/70, p101 [**1960**]

micrometastasis (ˌmaɪkroʊmə'tæstəsɪs), *n., pl.* **-tases** (-təsiːz). the spread of small, residual cancerous growths from one organ to another. *Studies of breast tissue removed during surgery have revealed that even when there was only one small identifiable lump in the breast, there were, in a majority of cases, micrometastases elsewhere in the breast, the lymph nodes of* *the armpit and the nodes beneath the* pectoralis major, *or major chest muscle.* Time 11/4/74, p109 [**1974,** from *micro-* ery small + *metastasis* spread of cancerous cells (from Greek *metástasis* removal)]

micrometeoroid, *n.* a tiny meteoroid; a meteoroid so small that it will not disintegrate upon entering the earth's atmosphere. *A satellite is being developed to reach 172,000 miles into space and gather data on micrometeoroids, tiny bits of matter no larger than grains of sand.* Science News Letter 8/29/64, p133 [**1954**]

microminiaturization, *n.* the production of microminiaturized objects or parts. *Now, microminiaturization has entered the field; large-scale integrated (LSI) circuits are smaller and more complex than their predecessors.* Encyclopedia Science Supplement (Grolier) 1971, p27 [**1955**]

microminiaturize, *v.t.* to reduce (electronic circuits, etc.) to a size smaller than miniature. Also, SUBMINIATURIZE. *The transistorized lock . . . could be microminiaturized and adapted to any number of combinations.* NY Times 5/20/67, p49 [**1959**]

micropolis (mai'krapəlis), *n.* a miniature or compact city; a small area containing many of the facilities of a city. *Colony Square, a hundred-and-one-million-dollar project that is described by its builders as a "micropolis," will have two office towers, a hotel, a shopping center, luxury apartments, town houses, condominiums, and a two-thousand-car underground garage, all on eleven acres of land about a mile from the center of the city.* New Yorker 12/31/73, p33 [**1972,** from *micro-* very small + Greek *pólis* city; patterned after *metropolis*]

micropopulation, *n.* the population of microorganisms living in a particular habitat. *Bdellovibrio bacteriovorus, discovered in 1962 by H. Stolp of Berlin-Dahlem, is the only bacterium so far known which lives as a parasite on other bacteria. It is not a virus bacteriophage but a true bacterium. First discovered in Berlin, it was found later by Dr. Stolp in soil samples from Mexico, Venezuela, Greece, Malta, Australia, Ceylon, Japan and from other countries. It can be considered therefore as a common member of the micropopulation of soil and water.* New Scientist 2/2/67, p282 [**1967**]

microprism, *n.* any of the minute prisms in the focusing screen of a camera that produce a blur when the subject is not in proper focus. *The viewfinder in the Contax RTS has some unique features. In addition to the interchangeable viewing screen with a central micro-prism, an illuminated scale across the top of the finder area indicates the maximum aperture of the lens in use and the actual aperture setting.* NY Times 9/26/76, p36 [**1965**]

microprobe, *n.* an instrument using a very fine-focused electron beam, usually in combination with optical apparatus, to analyze the chemical composition of rocks, minerals, glasses, alloys, etc. *In the laboratory, I have seen a laser instrument called a microprobe that permits quick and easy analysis of any object without damaging it.* National Geographic Magazine 12/66, p868 [**1958**]

microprocessor, *n.* a small silicon chip containing the circuitry for a central processing unit of a computer. See MICROCOMPUTER. *Microprocessors, the small-scale computing units on silicon chips that serve as the processing units of microcomputers, are being used to control fuel and emissions and gasoline mileage on some 1977 and 1978 automobiles. And cars may soon come equipped with microprocessor-controlled safety devices.* Encyclopedia Science Supplement (Grolier) 1979, p98 [**1970**]

microprogram, *n.* special data in the memory of a computer, used as part of a more complex program or to control the operations of a subordinate computer. *We can also expect to see new devices, possibly based on the use of amorphous materials, employed in very fast semi-fixed stores used for microprogrammes.* Times (London) 3/6/70, p29 —*v.t.* to provide (a computer) with a microprogram. *. . . a given microprogrammed machine may be easily adjusted to duplicate the characteristics of another machine, so that programs written in machine language for other computers can be handled without*

reprogramming. Van Court Hare, Jr., Introduction to Programming: A BASIC Approach, 1970, p413 [**1953**]

micropublication, *n.* a book, periodical, or the like, published in greatly reduced form, especially on microfilm or microfiche. *Most micropublications have been produced not for their qualities of space saving and archival permanence, but because they can provide cheap good quality reproductions for a very small market . . . Micropublications can be economically viable even if as few as five copies are sold, and are able, therefore, to provide on the most specialised subjects information that would otherwise be inaccessible.* New Scientist 4/27/72, p230 [**1971**]

micropublish, *v.i., v.t.* to publish in greatly reduced form, especially on microfilm or microfiche. *An important development in micropublishing, the production of newspapers on microfilm is announced today. From January 1 The Washington Post will be micropublished by Newspaper Archive Developments Ltd., a subsidiary of Times Newspapers Ltd.* Times (London) 10/12/78, p21 [**1970**]

microquake, *n.* another word for MICROEARTHQUAKE. Compare SILENT QUAKE. *McNally and her six co-workers would also help design the experiment, based on their work with monitoring swarms of "microquakes" in Southern California.* Science News 12/16/78, p422 [**1973**]

microsample, *n.* a minute or microscopic sample of a substance. *Protons are also being used in many laboratories to analyze microsamples, such as air- and water-pollution filtrates.* McGraw-Hill Yearbook of Science and Technology 1974, p435 [**1973**]

microskirt, *n.* a skirt that is shorter than a miniskirt. *The trouble is that with maxicoats, culottes, microskirts and trousersuits all in vogue, even the Hemline dictate is just a matter of personal predilection.* Sunday Times (London) 10/12/69, p27 [**1966**]

microstate, *n.* another name for MINISTATE. *Other events included . . . proposals that a special UN membership category be created for "microstates."* Britannica Book of the Year 1970, p463 [**1962**]

microstudy, *n.* a study of a very small, specific, or minor part of a subject or field. *One of the important conclusions emerging from the discussion was the view that anthropology needs to expand its horizons beyond microstudies to deal with the national and international considerations that can impinge upon even the most apparently isolated village.* 1975 Britannica Yearbook of Science and the Future, p192 [**1972**]

microteaching, *n.* a method of training teachers. See the quotation for details. *After sixteen years both as a student at Stanford University and a teacher in the university's Graduate School of Education, Allen claimed much of the credit for "microteaching," an intensive teacher-preparation program involving skill development through the use of videotape, differentiated staffing, and flexible scheduling in secondary schools, among other achievements.* Saturday Review 3/4/72, p48 [**1971;** so called from the analysis of very small segments of practice teaching employed in this method]

microtektite, *n.* a microscopic variety of tektite found deep in ocean sediments. *But ocean sediments in some regions, notably near Australia and the Ivory Coast, contain small glassy objects called microtektites which are reckoned to be the fine-grained components of the so-called "strewn fields" of larger tektites.* New Scientist and Science Journal 8/5/71, p299 [**1967**]

microtexture, *n.* the small structural characteristics or composition of a rock, stone, etc. *The basic facts about designing road surfaces giving good wet grip have been known for a decade or more. The first such fact is that if a surface is to provide good wetted friction at any speed, it must have a coarse microtexture or adequate fine-scale roughness at the 0.01-0.10 mm size level.* New Scientist 1/13/77, p67 [**1965**] —**microtextural,** *adj.: The aim of the conference was an assessment of the role of . . . microtextural and microtectonic information in the interpretation of geological processes.* Nature 4/8/76, p483 microtransmitter, *n.* a very small electronic transmitting device, used in surveillance, tracking, and the like. *Other devices spray the thief with incapacitating chemicals or phosphorescent dyes or even tag the poor devil with a microtransmitter so that he can be pursued, if need be, to the four corners of the earth.* NY Times Magazine 12/17/78, p108 [**1973**]

microtubule, *n. Biology.* a minute tubular filament in cells, consisting of the protein tubulin and functioning especially in forming and maintaining cellular shapes. *The microtubules are very fine tubes averaging 250 angstroms in diameter. They are found in cilia, in the tail of sperm cells, in the mitotic spindle of a dividing cell and in the cytoplasm of many types of cell.* Scientific American 10/71, p77 [**1963**]

microvascular, *adj.* of or relating to the very small vessels of the circulatory system, such as the capillaries. *Precise formations of the microvascular system and other spaces in organs of dead animals are revealed in detail when this liquid silicone compound is injected.* Science News 9/9/67, p262 [**1959**]

microvilli, *n.pl.* microscopic hairlike parts growing on the surface of a cell. *The photographs from the scanning electron microscope show that on day 4 of the reproductive cycle the epithelium is covered by a regular carpet of thread-like microvilli . . .* New Scientist and Science Journal 8/12/71, p356 [**1953**]

microwave, *n.* short for MICROWAVE OVEN. *Although microwave ovens take 50 per cent more power than conventional ovens, the microwaves are nevertheless the cheaper servants.* Saturday Review 1/1/72, p59 [**1972**] —*v.t., v.i.* to bake, cook, or heat in a microwave oven. *Never microwave eggs in the shell and never microwave a whole egg without pricking the yolk with a toothpick to break the outer membrane . . . When a recipe calls for sautéing . . . microwave, stirring occasionally, until cooked as desired.* Weight Watchers Quick and Easy Menu Cookbook, 1987, p15 [**1978**]

microwaveable or microwavable, *adj.* capable of being prepared in a microwave oven. *Frozen food comes on plastic plates now, not in tin pans, and it's microwavable.* New Yorker 4/29/85, p30 [**1982**]

microwave oven, a usually portable oven in which food can be cooked rapidly and uniformly with heat produced by microwaves. Also MICROWAVE. *Microwave ovens are being used in more and more homes because they cook food quickly, but they raise the question of the effects of prolonged exposure to their low-level radiation.* Encyclopedia Science Supplement (Grolier) 1977, p190 [**1961**]

microwave sickness, an illness described in Russian medical literature as caused by low-intensity microwave radiation that affects the circulatory, cardiovascular, and central nervous system. *The Soviets recognize a distinct "microwave sickness" among radar workers and others exposed to microwaves on their jobs. This "sickness" is characterized, they say, by headaches, irritability, anxiety, disturbed sleep, fatigue, forgetfulness, decreased efficiency, and inability to concentrate.* Encyclopedia Science Supplement (Grolier) 1977/1978, p193 [**1976**]

midcourse, *adj.* for or during the middle part of the course of a spacecraft, aircraft, etc. *During the uneventful, 73-hour coast [of Apollo 11 toward the moon], only one of the four planned midcourse corrections was necessary. After breakfast Thursday, Collins prepared for the minor course-correction maneuver.* 1970 World Book Year Book, p66 —*n.* the middle part of the course of a spacecraft, aircraft, etc. . . . *the small rocket engine which can manoeuvre the space craft slightly in midcourse was needed only to direct Ranger to the sunny rather than the dark side of the moon.* Times (London) 8/1/64, p6 [**1959** for adj.; **1964** for noun]

midcult, *n.* cultural characteristics associated with the middle class, typified by conventional and moderately intellectual values and ideas. *If there is any clerical rival to Dr Billy Graham in President Nixon's affections, Fr Hesburgh is the man. In their different ways, all three men exercise a ministry to Mid-*

cult. Manchester Guardian Weekly 4/17/69, p5 [**1960,** contraction of *mid*dle-class *cult*ure]

Middle America, a broad cross section of the American population conceived as politically middle-of-the-road or moderate, belonging to the middle-income class, and geographically situated chiefly in the midwestern states. *To call Salina Middle America, however, would not be entirely accurate. "We have some pockets of intolerance," says Whitley Austin, editor of the Salina Journal, "but most of the people simply try to be fair." Salina is an accumulation of American eras. Ladies wait for men to open doors for them.* Time 7/13/70, p14 [**1968**] ►The term *Middle America* has long been used by geographers in an entirely different sense, to denote the region between the United States and South America which includes Mexico, Central America, and the West Indies.

Middle American, **1** a person belonging to Middle America. *Who precisely are the Middle Americans? . . . They make up the core of the group that Richard Nixon now invokes as the "forgotten Americans" or the "Great Silent Majority," though Middle Americans themselves may not be a majority of the U.S.* Time 1/5/70, p9 **2** of or belonging to Middle America. . . . Newsweek *wrote on December 1, 1968: "Her [Mrs. Richard Nixon's] looks and taste are classic Middle American, even as her husband's are."* 1969 Collier's Encyclopedia Year Book, p3 [**1968**]

middle distillate, a petroleum product that is volatilized at medium temperatures in oil refineries. *The allocation program for the so-called "middle distillates"—including heating oil and diesel fuel—gives priority to all fuel-producing firms, farmers, mail transportation, cargo freight and vital community services such as hospitals and mass transit.* Newsweek 12/10/73, p92 [**1952, 1973**]

middle manager, a person occupying an intermediate position in management, such as an executive who is responsible for day-to-day operations but not for overall policymaking. *The workers are currently finalising a structure which will create a government council, which appoints a general manager. The existing middle-managers and foremen are expected to retain their present jobs. All the unskilled men and women will continue to have full interchangeability between jobs.* Sunday Times (London) 1/12/75, p50 [**1966,** from earlier (1940's) *middle management*]

middle-of-the-road, *adj.* of or relating to the type of popular and standard music that appeals to a broad audience. *No matter what critics and prophets looked for, sales of records showed that the public was reacting against the amateurism that characterized much rock music, preferring the greater craft and professionalism of such middle-of-the-road singers as the Carpenters.* 1975 Collier's Encyclopedia Year Book, p448 [**1973,** so called because such music avoids extremes of fashion or innovation, employing familiar, established themes and styles]

middlescence, (ˌmidəˈlesəns), *n.* the period or condition of life between about 40 and 65; the middle age of a person's life. *The Spouse Gap* [by] *Robert Lee and Marjorie Casebier. Middlescence—the new crisis years of marriage—is the subject of this unique book. The authors examine problems that face middle-aged married couples and offer some exciting possibilities for bridging "the spouse gap" and recreating a full life together.* Atlantic 11/71, p142 *A humorist has called our condition "middlescence." . . . But we will stick with the original putdown: middleaged.* New York Post 2/10/79, p15 [**1965,** from *middle* (*age*) + -*escence*, as in *adolescence* and *senescence*] —middlescent, *adj.: Most of us, however, in middlescent years—say about 30 to 65 years old—just want to get and stay in shape, manage our stressful lifestyle, live a little longer.* Jewish Week-American Examiner 8/26/79, p28

middleware, *n.* a computer software designed for tasks that are intermediate between control programs and application programs. Middleware includes any program needed for the chosen tasks of a particular installation. *According to Mr. Barney Gibbens of Computer Analysts and Programmers, middleware is a collection of techniques . . . based on a design approach in which the controls—for example, the checking and recovery of large files—are divorced from the application programs. Each can then move independently of the other.* Times (London) 4/6/73, p32 [**1970,** from *middle + ware,* as in *software, hardware,* LIVEWARE]

midi ('midi:), *n.* **1** a skirt, dress, or other garment reaching to the calf, usually the mid-calf. Also called LONGUETTE. Compare MAXI, MICRO, MINI. *If I died, what would they bury me in? A mini? A midi? Pants? I know, this isn't important.* Atlantic 5/71, p66 **2** the style or length characterized by hemlines at the calf. *What you seemed to miss is that for the individual, fashion should be FUN! In variety and change there is that fun. As for the midi, let's hope it helps to bring back those qualities so sadly lacking from the recent sartorial scene: grace, elegance and good taste.* Time 10/5/70, p4 **—adj.** reaching to the calf. *The mid-calf-length midi had, according to one fashion expert, "become merely an extra, whether as coat, cape, pants, or late-day dress.* **2** U.S. designer Anne Klein had shown midi coats in her fall collection but cut them shorter "after getting the message from the stores' buyers."* Britannica Book of the Year 1969, p337 *In this case, it is a series of sandwich-board capes in midi and maxi lengths.* NY Times 7/11/68, p40 [**1967,** from *mid + -i,* as in *mini* and *maxi*]

midi-, combining form meaning of medium or intermediate size; mid-sized. It is added to nouns, as in the following examples: **—midibus,** *n.: The National Bus Company's experimental rural "midibus" has been running around the Fenland villages for a month and most people seem to think it a good idea.* Times (London) 6/23/76, p3 **—midicarrier,** *n.: The whole concept of switching from Nimitz class carriers, which cost $2,000 million each, to midi-carriers costing half that much, will have to be reevaluated.* Manchester Guardian Weekly (Washington Post section) 6/19/77, p17 **—midicomputer,** *n.: Midicomputer for laboratory automation. Charles Sederholm of IBM Corp., Palo Alto, Calif., has pioneered the effort for the laboratory automation concept.* McGraw-Hill Yearbook of Science and Technology 1971, p62 [**1970,** generalized from MIDI]

midlife crisis, a crisis or turning point experienced on becoming middle-aged, caused especially by the realization that one's youth is over. See MIDDLESCENCE. *The Center for Applied Behavioral Sciences in Topeka, Kan., gives seminars in which executives are taught how to solve personal problems, how to relax and how to cope with "midlife crisis."* NY Times Magazine 11/20/77, p50 *Mid-life crisis; should you take a lover or redo your house?* Vogue 9/78, p506 [**1965**]

mid-rise, *adj.* midway between low-rise and high-rise; not excessively tall. *The biggest newsmakers in architecture . . . were arguably not these high-profile urban public buildings but their lowly suburban counterpart—the mid-rise office building.* 1988 Collier's Encyclopedia Year Book, p121 [**1987**]

migraineur (mi:grə'nœr), *n.* a person who suffers from migraine headaches. *Migraineurs also speak of small white skunks with erect tails, the rippling pattern of windblown water, mice and rats, Turkish carpets and Brobdingnagian or Lilliputian vision. Migraineur Lewis Carroll is thought to have conceived his scenes for "Alice's Adventures in Wonderland" during his auras.* NY Times Magazine 5/8/77, p52 [**1971,** from French *migraine* migraine + *-eur* agent suffix]

migronaut ('maigrə,nɔ:t), *n.* a person who is forced to travel as a migrant for lack of a country that will admit him or her; displaced person. Compare BOAT PEOPLE. *Called "shuttlecocks" or "migronauts" in the press, these Asians have traveled from airport to airport throughout the world until the British, faced with Amin's decree, have finally relented and agreed to take in every British citizen.* Atlantic 12/72, p34 [**1970,** from *migrate + connecting -o- + -naut* traveler (as in *astronaut*)]

Milankovitch (mə'læŋkə'vitʃ), *adj.* of or relating to the theory that slow cyclic changes in direction and tilt of the earth's axis and eccentricity of its orbit are linked to major climactic changes. *On the face of things, the Milankovitch process seems to explain very satisfactorily the climatic fluctuations of the past two million years, the so-called Quaternary Ice Age. But sceptics have doubted whether quite small changes in insolation could account for such major features as the advance of*

an ice sheet. Times (London) 5/7/76, p19 [**1975,** named for Milutin *Milankovitch,* a Yugoslav geologist who published this theory in 1941] **—Milankovitcher,** *n.: Looking outside the Earth itself, the solid basis of present work is seen both in the latest developments of the "Milankovitchers," and in the recurring (but now at last established) idea of a link between solar activity and climate.* New Scientist 8/28/75, p470

militaria, *n.pl.* a collection of objects having to do with the military, such as firearms, decorations, uniforms, etc. *During his last years he spent much of his time in trying to gather together writings, militaria and other possessions left by the Field-Marshal.* Times (London) 12/23/70, p10 [**1959,** from Latin *mīlitāria,* neuter plural of *mīlitāris* military]

military-industrial complex, the combination of a strongly entrenched military establishment and a large war matériel industry, viewed as a powerful interest group controlling American economic and foreign policy. *This basic issue [the neglect of domestic problems] aroused intense emotion and led to vigorous denunciations of the "military-industrial complex," which presumably had a stake in a high level of international tension to justify more arms for soldiers, greater profits for businessmen, and reelection of congressmen who brought jobs and money to their constituents.* Americana Annual 1970, p729 [**1961**] ▶The term was probably first used by President Dwight D. Eisenhower in his Farewell Address, delivered on January 17, 1961. It appears in the following passage: "In the councils of government, we must guard against the acquisition of unwarranted influence, whether sought or unsought, by the military-industrial complex. The potential for the disastrous rise of misplaced power exists and will persist."

Minamata disease (,minə'ma:tə), poisoning by ingestion of methylmercury. Also called MAD HATTER'S DISEASE. *In the early 1950's fishermen and their families around Minamata Bay in Japan were stricken with a mysterious neurological illness. The Minamata disease, as it came to be called, produced progressive weakening of the muscles, loss of vision, impairment of other cerebral functions, eventual paralysis and in some cases coma and death. The victims had suffered structural injury to the brain.* Scientific American 5/71, p15 [**1957,** from *Minamata,* a town in western Kyushu, Japan]

mind, *n.* **blow one's mind,** *Slang.* **1** to experience or cause to have drug-induced hallucinations. *. . . he regularly turned on with marijuana or blew his mind with LSD.* NY Times 3/21/66, p1 *In one episode, some hippies offer him coffee and "blow his mind" with the new mind-expanding drug.* Maclean's 9/67, p89 **2** to cause to lose control over one's mind; to excite, stir, shock, etc., to an extreme degree. *Then [at the annual conference of U.S. Student Press Association held in Washington], on screens on three walls, flashed gory Viet Nam scenes from Communist propaganda movies. . . The film was meant to blow the minds of the viewers, but they blew their cool instead. Some raced around trying to pull the plugs of the projectors; other tried to get their hands on the organizers.* Time 2/16/68, p47 [**1967**]

mind-bender, *n. Slang.* **1 a** a hallucinogenic drug. *STP is a new, untested drug, resembling both amphetamine pep pills and the active ingredient in mescaline, the cactus-derived mind-bender.* Science News 7/22/67, p80 **b** a user of drugs, especially hallucinogenic drugs. *In recent years, youthful mind-benders have tripped (or thought they did) on everything from airplane glue to morning-glory seeds, from nutmeg to black tea.* Time 4/7/67, p60 [**1967**] **2** a person who uses subtle means to influence, persuade, or pressure others. *What the Republican mind-benders are thinking about is individualized communication—computerized mail and telephone on a scale new to politics—and subtle use of television, all designed to touch basic attitudes, the voter's "value profile,". . .* Harper's 12/71, p97 [**1963**]

mind-bending, *adj. Slang.* **1** causing hallucinations; hallucinogenic. *In dealing with student dissidents, perhaps a more effective coolant might be the joint (marijuana cigarette), which has sealed many a youthful alliance. Indeed there is a precedent for such get-togethers in the American Indian ceremony of the peace pipe, which was often filled with "kinnikinnick"—a* *mind-bending admixture of hemp and the inner bark of dogwood.* Time 6/7/68, p31 **2** distorting the perception; causing mental stupor or derangement. *Already "mind-bending" gases for military purposes are said to be at an advanced stage of development, if not actually on the active lists; their proponents suggest that they are more humane than bullets.* New Scientist 4/21/66, p151 **3** mind-boggling. *The theoretical mathematics of the situation* [mining metals] *are positively mind-bending. Howarth and Chambers claim that 300,000 tons of ore has already been stockpiled at El Sobrante.* Sunday Times (London) 1/25/70, p29 [**1965**]

mind-blow, *v.t. Slang.* to blow the mind of; excite, stir, shock, etc. *It can mind-blow a long-haired GI to know he'll have to live straighter to survive in Sweden than in the Army or in America.* Listener 10/22/70, p540 [**1970,** back formation from *mind-blowing;* see MIND, def. 2]

mind blower, *Slang.* **1** a hallucinogenic drug. *There are at least three different classes of psychedelic drugs, each with very different molecular structures. To complicate matters further, two chemicals with almost identical structures can have very different psychedelic properties: one might be a real mind-blower and the other as ineffective as a sugar lump.* New Scientist 6/27/68, p703 **2** a user of drugs, especially hallucinogenic drugs. *For most of the 19th century's mind blowers, opium meant laudanum, an alcoholic solution of the drug used as a common painkiller.* Time 5/30/69, p55 **3** a mindblowing experience. *There is the hysteria of The Who and the pure rhythmic orgasm of Ten Years After. They all help to make* Woodstock *as unique on film as it was in fact, "the mind blower," as John Sebastian puts it, "of all time."* Time 4/13/70, p103 [**1968**]

mindblowing, *Slang. —adj.* **1** hallucinogenic. . . . *the poet celebrates the mindblowing effects of LSD and laments at the same time his lost childhood.* Times (London) 5/4/68, p21 **2** exciting, stirring, shocking, etc., to an extreme degree. *My doctor and I agreed that while I was in the hospital I would not hang around with my friends outside anymore. I only saw them for an hour or so in the evenings on the way home, and they thought it was very mystical and mind-blowing to be in the hospital.* Atlantic 3/69, p43 **—n.** the act of blowing one's mind. . . . *the editors* [of Krazy Kat, a selection of George Herriman's comic strips] *. . . try to acclimatize the work into the world of "mind-blowing" and "psychedelia;" as usual, the strip evades all such Kategories.* New Yorker 3/14/70, p156 [**1967**]

mind-boggling, *adj.* causing the mind to boggle; overwhelming. *The permutations of play-offs are mind-boggling.* Times (London) 8/1/71, p17 [**1964**] **—mind-bogglingly,** *adv.: The filmtown reporting of the day was mind-bogglingly dull.* National Review 1/23/76, p46

mind-expander, *n.* a mind-expanding or hallucinogenic drug. *Dr. Laverne said that the effects of Vietnamese marijuana were sometimes surprisingly similar to those induced by hallucinogenic and psychotogenic agents such as L.S.D., mescaline and other so-called mind-expanders that have been used experimentally, illicitly, and proved harmful to the body and central nervous system of humans.* Times (London) 3/26/70, p7 [**1970**]

mind-expanding, *adj.* intensifying and distorting perception; psychedelic. *LSD has been called a "mind-expanding" or "consciousness-expanding" drug; its use has been advocated to increase human creative potential, since some people who have taken the substance report strong subjective feelings of creative drive.* Britannica Book of the Year 1968, p652 [**1963**]

mindon ('main,dan), *n.* a hypothetical particle of matter that carries mental or telepathic messages. *Columbia University's Gerald Feinberg . . . thinks that psychic transmissions may one day be linked to as yet undiscovered elementary particles, so-called mindons or psychons.* Time 4/23/73, p86 [**1972,** coined by the Hungarian-born British writer Arthur Koestler, 1905-1983, from *mind* + *-on* elementary particle or unit]

mini, *n.* **1** a short skirt, dress, etc., especially one ending 2 to 4 inches above the knee; a miniskirt, minidress, etc. *The passing girls, dressed in their gray, tan, and dark-blue conservatively cut suits, look as if they were afraid to wear minis.*

Atlantic 2/68, p34 **2** the style or length of fashions characteristic of the miniskirt. *"The midi will get time, but not equal time with the mini,"* predicts Henri Bendel [a fashionable women's clothing store in New York] *President Geraldine Stutz.* Time 5/12/67, p68 **3** anything miniature in size. *The Micro 16 does not pretend to be a pale imitation of a large machine: it is intended to be, and indeed is, a highly effective mini. It is no accident that the machine should be "highly thought of" by active users in the small machine field, myself included.* New Scientist and Science Journal 5/20/71, p484 **4** *British.* short for *minicar* (a small automobile). See MINI-. *A mini and a Cadillac belong to different species which may require different rules. When it comes to exhaust gases, anyway, the exhalations of a mini are negligible compared with a Cadillac's.* Manchester Guardian Weekly 11/3/66, p9 **—adj.** **1** reaching well above the knee; very short. *Minis, which ruled city streets all summer, were still applauded in fashion shows. . . The maxi coat, worn over the mini dress, was symbolic of the times.* Americana Annual 1970, p287 **2** very small; miniature. *Increasing interest in equipment for camping was evidenced by the great variety of improved camping stoves and the number of "mini" refrigerators and stoves suitable for outdoor and trailer use.* Britannica Book of the Year 1967, p289 *This little girl played a sort of mini Eliza Doolittle and she alone breached the wall around Blandings Castle.* Manchester Guardian Weekly 3/2/67, p13 [**1961,** from MINI-]

mini-, *prefix.* currently used with the two meanings given below. **1** of very small size, duration, or importance; miniature or minor. **—miniboom,** *n.: After enjoying a miniboom for nearly a decade, the* [Yugoslavian] *economy, which manages to combine capitalistic profit incentives within a Communist framework, has run into a severe inflationary problem.* Time 8/9/71, p21 **—minicomputer,** *n.: The Apollo Systems Division of General Electric has designed the security system, which consists of a vast array of sensors on-line to a minicomputer, to watch everything.* New Scientist and Science Journal 6/3/71, p597 **—minidose,** *n.: . . . the contraceptives of the next generation may include a minidose pill taken once a day every day.* NY Times 11/12/67, pD7 **—minipark,** *n.: A plan to create "100 vest-pocket or miniparks" in the city's slum areas was reported last night by the New York Urban Coalition.* NY Times 6/24/68, p32 **—minisurvey,** *n.: A thousand and one eccentric facts, odd anecdotes, shaggy dog stories, and mini-surveys about the Bolton pubs are here poured lovingly forth.* Manchester Guardian Weekly 1/2/71, p19 **—miniwar,** *n.: Three times since 1968, disagreements between sides have resulted in actual miniwars.* Time 9/28/70, p16 **2** reaching well above the knee; very short. **—minidress,** *n.: Marbel Junior, who showed up in a periwinkle blue and white flowered dinner jacket, had the last word in the show—a bridal minidress with a veil twice as long as the dress.* NY Times 5/13/68, p50 **—minishorts,** *n.pl.: In Paris, minishorts are an every-night, run-of-the-disco affair.* Time 2/1/71, p32 [from *miniature,* reinforced by *minimum.* The form first became popular in Great Britain through the appearance of the *Mini Minor,* a small car produced in 1960 by the British Motor Corporation. The consequent appearance of other *minicars* and of the *minicab,* a small taxicab, furthered the use of *mini-* as a prefix.]

minibike, *n. U.S.* a small motorcycle. See the quotation for details. *That the minibike owners cut a funny figure is due not only to their physique but also to the new bike's low frame, small wheels and elevated handle bar, which are designed to drastically reduce the amount of necessary agility.* NY Times 5/30/68, p35 [**1968**]

mini-black-hole, *n. Astronomy.* a hypothetical black hole of extremely small size, with a mass as low as 1/100,000 of a gram. Compare HAWKING EFFECT. *Most papers on black holes (those warped regions of space from which light cannot escape) deal with entities of stellar or galactic mass. Stephen Hawking injected some variety with his idea that mini-black-holes in the mass range 10^{-5} to 10^{-15} g might also exist. These have the astonishing property that quantum fluctuations cause them to evaporate. . .* New Scientist 6/2/77, p527 [**1973**]

minibudget, *n.* a supplemental budget introduced to adjust the economy of a country, especially during fiscal emergencies.

Chrétien and his officials . . . produced one budget and two minibudgets in the year, to turn the economy around. Concedes a battered Chrétien: "The job is tougher than I expected." Maclean's 9/25/78, p15 [1966]

minibus, *n.* a small vehicle with the seats arranged as in a bus, designed to take more passengers than an automobile. *There were two charter flights full of United supporters, to say nothing of 16 intrepid voyagers through the snows on a 4,000-mile round trip from Manchester in a minibus.* Times (London) 3/23/68, p8 [1958]

minicalculator, *n.* a pocket-size electronic calculator, consisting of a numerical keyboard and a lighting panel on which the digital readout appears. Also called POCKET CALCULATOR. *A typical minicalculator will add, subtract, multiply, or divide, giving an eight-digit answer with a floating decimal point.* Americana Annual 1973, p265 [1972]

minicell, *n.* a small bacterial cell produced by an abnormal division process and able to transfer episomes (extra-chromosomal particles) from or into normal cells. *The scientific palm of the week must undoubtedly go to that bizarre little object the minicell. For no fewer than three papers have appeared in different journals of the past few days, describing how these tiny cells, formed by a pinching off of one end of* Escherichia coli *bacteria, have been used to package up specific portions of the microbes' DNA.* New Scientist 8/13/70, p325 [1967]

minicourse, *n.* a brief course of study. *The idea of a short January term, sandwiched between the regular semesters, has become institutionalized in recent years, and students on hundreds of campuses will be staying around next month for so-called minicourses.* NY Times 12/15/76, pD21 [1972]

minifestival, *n. Especially U.S.* a small-scale festival; a festival in miniature. *Churches will serve as sites for afternoon concerts and social suppers, and local groups will also be involved in "minifestivals," a group of outdoor activities taking place in various parks and gardens that will feature South Carolina storytellers, gospel and blues singers, puppets, mimes, crafts and instant theater.* NY Times Magazine 5/22/77, p37 [1976]

minimal, *adj.* of or relating to minimal art. *Minimal forms still massively demand their unrewarding space, but they are countered by weirdly eccentric shapes that are frankly frivolous, at least unpredictable.* Time 6/3/69, p42 *The inherent detachment of Pop's aestheticized banalities prefigures the "pure" objects of Minimal sculpture. . .* New Yorker 11/8/69, p169 **—n. 1** minimal art. *Ironically, though current trends in United States art are unrepresented at the American Pavilion, they are in evidence at "foreign" pavilions, where the echoes of pop, op, and minimal resound.* NY Times 6/22/68, p29 **2** a work of minimal art. *On the ground floor [of the Guggenheim Museum], Robert Morris' I-beam minimals; on the first tier, Fukushima's arched* Blue Dots. Time 10/27/67, p43 [1965]

minimal art, a form of art that reduces shape, color, etc., to its simplest or most basic elements, avoiding embellishment or dramatization. Also called MINIMALISM, REDUCTIVISM. *But the whole category of Minimal art seems to have been created around the least important aspect of the work: its use of simple "primary" shapes. . . The best Minimal art, like some of Donald Judd's, for example, is in a sense explosive, carrying a charge of compressed energy behind its blank surfaces.* Times (London) 3/18/70, p15 [1965]

minimal artist, a painter, sculptor, or other artist who works in minimal art. Also called MINIMALIST. *Minimal artists whose works were seen in one-man shows in New York included Sol Lewitt, Robert Smithson, Charles Ross. . .* Americana Annual 1969, p95 [1968]

minimal brain dysfunction, a disorder of undetermined mechanism exhibited in the behavior and/or learning capacities of some children, but generally overcome to a degree with maturity. It is often characterized by poor muscular coordination, brief span of attention, difficulty in perception and verbalization, hyperactivity, eye imbalance, etc. *Abbreviation:* MBD. *Some scientists use the term minimal brain dysfunction to describe a collection of behavioral symptoms that are presumed*

to represent a disturbance of brain activities. World Book Science Annual 1974, p348 *What is the cause of hyperactivity? . . . It is possible that these children sustained some brain damage during pregnancy or birth; however, the data in support of this are not compelling and certainly do not justify the alternative description of the condition as "minimal brain dysfunction."* New Scientist 11/2/78, p351 [1962]

minimalism, *n.* **1** another name for MINIMAL ART. *But he [Andy Warhol] gives dramatic clarification to Minimalism by minimalizing the artist, too, and the world he inhabits.* New Yorker 6/12/71, p105 **2** musical style or form that uses the most basic elements and avoids embellishment or dramatization. *Paradoxically, "minimalism". . . took as its foundation precisely those aspects of music that seemed to be fundamental—the scale, the sequence, the tonal I-V-I progression. . .* NY Times 11/23/82, pC11 **3** a narrative style in fiction that avoids lengthy description or elucidation, is often restricted to bare dialogue, and uses few or simple dramatic devices. *The art of pantomime . . . lent her [Colette's] literary art something of its silence, its effective minimalism.* New Yorker 12/29/80, p69 *A kind of minimalism has always characterized Vonnegut's prose. . .* Atlantic 5/73, p106 [1969]

minimalist, *n.* an artist, composer, or writer who practices or uses minimalism. *Nonetheless it [representational and figural sculpture] is outclassed numerically and formally by the minimalists, a useful term but essentially as misleading as nonobjective once was for the positive statements of geometrically abstract art.* Saturday Review 11/25/67, p42 *The moral would seem to be that minimalists should stay minimal; it is safer for them that way.* Manchester Guardian Weekly 12/18/71, p20 **—adj.** of or relating to minimalism or minimalists. *Tony Smith, usually taken as the original minimalist sculptor (after the pyramids and Goethe's sphere on a cube) is well represented by large sculptures and ill served by some barely adequate paintings.* Manchester Guardian Weekly 5/1/69, p20 [1967]

minimill, *n.* a small-scale steel mill utilizing locally collected scrap metal. *The increasing. . . construction of minimills near large cities with ample scrap supplies will further open markets for steel scrap.* Science 2/20/76, p672 [1972]

miniminded, *adj.* mindless; stupid. *In recent months, producers have become shrewdly sensitive to the public's insatiable appetite for escapist epics, for jumbo-budgeted, miniminded movies that rock no boats and make no statements bulkier than "Beware of the Shark!"* NY Times Magazine 2/8/76, p34 [1965]

minimine ('mini,mi:n), *n.* a poisonous substance obtained from the venom of bees. *At the California Institute of Technology, an injection of minimine—a toxic polypeptide isolated from the bee venom—into fruit fly larvae was found to result in one-quarter-size adults that were normal in every way except that their individual cells were miniature.* 1973 Britannica Yearbook of Science and the Future, p338 [1971, from *minim* very small (amount or size) + *-ine* (chemical suffix)]

minimum purchase, *U.S.* a minimum amount that can be purchased at one time, especially a minimum amount of gasoline that must be sold to each purchaser in order to prevent drivers from topping off their gas tanks. See ODD-EVEN. *Several states including New Jersey are intensifying efforts to make sure that gasoline stations comply with "minimum purchase" rules. Motorists with four- and six-cylinder cars are restricted to buying no less than $4 worth of gasoline; motorists with eight cylinder autos must buy at least $8 worth.* Christian Science Monitor 11/20/79, p10 [1979]

minimum tillage, another name for NO-TILLAGE. *For millennia, farmers have turned over the land with plows before tilling it, cultivating it and putting in seed. Now, machines are available that combine several operations in a process called minimum tillage. One machine, on which Garst and a partner hold the patent, cuts a V-shaped furrow in unplowed land and simultaneously drops in seed. Says Garst: "In a sense, we have gone back to the pointed stick."* Time 11/6/78, p101 [1977]

mininuke, *n. Especially U.S. Slang.* a small nuclear weapon designed for use in combat. Compare ENHANCED RADIATION WEAPON. See also WARFIGHTING. *A better way to describe the* *present device would be to consider it as only one type of a new generation of what have been called "mininukes." By being able to control the amount of radiation, fallout and blast from these tiny H-bombs, the Pentagon can now deploy nuclear weapons capable of performing a whole new range of tactical functions.* Science News 7/23/77, p61 [**1975,** from *mini-* small, little + *nuke* nuclear weapon]

minipill, *n.* a pill containing a very low dose of a drug, especially an oral contraceptive having only one-tenth of the progesterone and none of the estrogen present in larger pills. *The minipill was developed for one reason alone: because it was believed to provide safe contraception.* New Scientist 1/29/70, p187 *Researchers are working upon minipills, injections or implants that might be good for a year, pills that would induce abortion if a woman had conceived but didn't yet realize it, and pills for men.* New York Post 8/4/71, p70 [**1970**]

miniplanet, *n.* a small or minor planet. See OBJECT KOWAL. *The solar system yielded yet another of its secrets in November when Charles Kowal of the Hale Observatories, Pasadena, Calif., announced discovery of a "miniplanet" circling the Sun between the orbits of Saturn and Uranus.* Britannica Book of the Year 1978, p205 [**1977**]

miniseries, *n.* a short series of dramatizations, performances, or the like. *There has been friction behind the scenes over a low-budget miniseries called* Royal Suite, *whose installments are linked, like those of Neil Simon's* Plaza Suite, *by the fact that they all take place in the same hotel room.* Maclean's 9/20/76, p62 *Twenty-eight concerts are scheduled between now and next June; you can buy subscriptions to the entire program or one of seven mini-series.* NY Times 9/23/77, pC22 [**1973**]

mini-ski, *n.* a short ski worn by beginners or in ski bobbing. *Mini-skis, they* [a group of West German physicians] *claimed, would help the beginner learn faster; reduce the skier's fear of falling; in case of falling, result in fewer sprains and fractures.* Maclean's 12/68, p80 [**1967**]

miniskirt, *n.* a skirt that reaches well above the knee; a mini. *Miniskirts are more than just provocative, according to British revenue authorities—they are tax evaders as well. . . A tax official explained that a 12½ per cent purchase tax is charged only on skirts longer than 24 inches from waist to hem. Anything shorter is classified as children's clothing and hence is not taxable.* NY Times 7/16/68, p28 [**1965**] —**miniskirted,** *adj.: Miniskirted office girls with paper cups of yogurt lolling prettily on a greensward. . .* Saturday Review 8/12/72, p40

ministate, *n.* a very small country, especially one of the recently established independent small states of Africa or Asia. Also called MICROSTATE. *South Africa's economic predominance radiates from here to three ministates of Botswana, Lesotho and Swaziland.* NY Times 1/26/68, p70 *A U.S. resolution on ministates was shelved when smaller countries indignantly opposed the idea that very small states should take associate rather than full membership, thus relinquishing the right to vote, and the obligation to pay dues.* 1970 World Book Year Book, p537 [**1966**]

minisub, *n.* a very small submarine, especially one equipped to explore and monitor the underwater environment. *The minisub* Alvin *. . . was used for recovering the H-bomb lost off the Spanish coast.* New Scientist 9/22/66, p655 *Two scientists cruising by in a Mini-Sub, an underwater observatory, watched wide-eyed as the sharks swam through the repellent to devour the tuna chunks.* Maclean's 4/2/66, p15 [**1959**]

minitank, *n.* a highly mobile lightweight tank. *Pentagon researchers have designed a vehicle with rapid acceleration so it could scoot for cover before an antitank missile could hit it. The 20-ton minitank would carry an armor-piercing 75mm gun for destroying heavy tanks while racing around the battlefield.* Manchester Guardian Weekly (Washington Post section) 11/27/77, p16 [**1973**]

minitanker, *n. British.* a small ship or truck carrying some liquid; a small tanker. *Whisky is to be exported from Scotland by pipeline and "minitanker", the shipping firm of Christian Salvesen and Co., of Leith, announced yesterday.* Times (London) 5/18/67, p23 *Petrol is supplied free, either by the client filling up at the company's garage or from a mini-tanker which regularly visits the special parking places.* New Scientist and Science Journal 9/2/71, p520 [**1967**]

minor tranquilizer, any of a group of mild tranquilizers used to treat anxiety or tension, that are usually ineffective in serious neurotic or psychotic disorders. *In a country where 100 million people are regular consumers of alcohol (of them, 10 million are alcoholics), where doctors write an estimated 100 million prescriptions each year for the so-called "minor tranquilizers," such as Valium and Librium, the age-old practice of mixing alcohol and drugs has reached unprecedented and staggering proportions.* NY Times Magazine 8/6/78, p10 [**1969**]

minoxidil (mɪˈnɑksəˌdɪl), *n.* a drug used in the treatment of high blood pressure, found also to have the property of stimulating hair growth when applied as a lotion to bald spots in certain individuals. *Says Dr. Anthony Zappacosta of Bryn Mawr, Pa who prescribed the drug for several patients, some of whom were bald: "In most cases hair grows on the scalp for about eight weeks, attaining normal thickness and a length of around three-quarters of an inch. Then it falls out, and the growing process begins again." Such hair today, gone tomorrow results do not bother some medical students, they reportedly have been rubbing a crude minoxidil lotion on their thinning peaks.* Time 1/26/81, p57 [**1967,** from *amino-* + *oxy*gen + *piperidinyl*]

MINS (mɪnz), *n. U.S.* acronym for *Minor(s) In Need of Supervision.* Compare JINS. *Legislatures rewrote juvenile codes to include Gault rights, but deep-seated public apathy and the resistance of the "child savers" had not extended reform beyond label changing. To deny Gault-type hearings to children not accused of specific crimes, new categories were devised with amusing acronyms: PINS, CINS, or MINS (persons, children, or minors in need of supervision).* Britannica Book of the Year 1973, p409 [**1972**]

MIPS (mɪps), *n.* acronym for *million instructions per second.* Compare LIPS. *The Army's plans for a network of 288 processing elements, each with a processor—for input, arithmetical operations and output—were hit by lack of money after only 11 were built. Nevertheless, those 11 can handle a total throughput of 100 MIPS. Simulation of the full array suggested it could handle 800 MIPS.* New Scientist 4/21/77 p140 [**1974**]

miracle fruit, the fruit of a West African tree (*Synsepalum dulcificum*) of the sapodilla family, containing a substance that makes sour food taste sweet. Compare SERENDIPITY BERRY. See also MIRACULIN. *Miracle fruit comes from a wild shrub, in tropical West Africa, whose red berries have long been used by natives to make their sour palm wine and acid maize bread more palatable. Its secret is a taste-modifying protein.* New Scientist 1/1/70, p21 [**1964**]

miracle rice, a hybrid rice seed that yields twice or three times the amount per harvest as traditional varieties. *The new strains of "miracle rice" that have brought self-sufficiency in food supply to many other Asian nations have failed to take hold in North Viet Nam, partly because workers assigned to collective farms are unwilling to give the new strains the intensive care they require.* Time 8/24/70, p24 [**1969**]

miraculin (məˈrækyəlɪn), *n.* a protein derived from MIRACLE FRUIT. Compare MONELLIN, THAUMATIN. *Miraculin is a glycoprotein from the miracle berry which modifies the taste of food so that even sour foods taste sweet. Miraculin was marketed at one time by the Miralin Corporation as a sweetener in dietetic foods.* McGraw-Hill Yearbook of Science and Technology 1976, p181 [**1973,** from *miraculo*us + *-in* (chemical suffix), named after the MIRACLE FRUIT]

Miranda (məˈrændə), *adj. U.S.* of, relating to, or upholding the legal rights of a person suspected of a crime to remain silent and to be represented by a lawyer, especially during questioning by police. Compare GAULT. —**Miranda card:** *Police used a "Miranda card" to read a Mexican immigrant his rights before arresting him in connection with the barroom slaying of Ernesto Miranda—the man whose name was given to a landmark Su-*

preme Court decision on defendants' rights. New York Post 2/2/76, p15 —**Miranda rule:** *The report acknowledges that factors in the poor conviction record may include . . . such restrictions on police power as the still controversial Miranda rule, which requires the arresting officer to inform the suspect of his rights to counsel and to remain silent.* Time 9/26/77, p60 —**Miranda warning:** *The United States Supreme Court . . . has once again limited the application of the so-called Miranda warnings, further narrowing the conditions under which a suspect must be advised of his legal rights.* NY Times 1/30/77, pD2 [1977, from the Supreme Court ruling (*Miranda* vs. Arizona, 1966) in the case of Ernesto *Miranda*, a Mexican immigrant convicted of a crime in 1963 in Phoenix, Arizona]

mirex or **Mirex,** *n.* a highly toxic and persistent chlorinated hydrocarbon compound, used widely as an insecticide, especially to control fire ants. *Mirex may again be used against the fire ant in the southern states despite the program's recent cutback.* Natural History 1/76, p16 [1962, origin uncertain; perhaps alteration of Greek *mýrmēx* ant] ▶Despite its frequent appearance in print with an initial capital, *mirex* is not registered as a proprietary name or trademark.

MIRV (mərv), *n.* acronym for *Multiple Independently-targeted Reentry Vehicle,* an offensive missile having multiple warheads that can be guided within a pattern to different targets so as to penetrate an enemy's antiballistic missile shield. Compare MRV. *MIRV's threaten the viability of the fixed land-based missile component of the strategic force and provide pressures for the development and deployment of new systems.* Scientific American 1/71, p24 —*v.t.* to equip with a MIRV. *MIRVing the Polaris system allows a dozen warheads to be fitted to a single Poseidon missile.* NY Times 11/3/68, pD17 [1967]

miscode, *v.t.* to provide with a wrong or faulty code; code incorrectly. *Experiments with a mutant of a microorganism,* Neurospora, *show, for example, that the mutant DNA miscoded a single amino acid in the sequence of structural protein in the membrane. As a result of this seemingly minor alteration, the entire membrane was defective.* Science News 5/23/70, p510 [1965]

misevolution, *n.* abnormal evolution of a cell, viral particle, etc. *According to Dr. Temin, human cancer is probably brought about by a "misevolution of a normal cellular information transference process"—a mistake that can be caused in several ways, viruses perhaps being one of the ways.* Encyclopedia Science Supplement (Grolier) 1976, p91 [1972, from *mis-* bad, wrong + *evolution*]

misfuel, *v.i., v.t.* to supply (a motor vehicle) with the wrong type of fuel, especially leaded gas in a vehicle designed for unleaded gas. *As long as gas—and especially unleaded gas—remains in short supply, many motorists will undoubtedly keep right on misfueling their cars whatever the consequences.* Newsweek 7/16/79, p78 [1979]

missense, *adj. Molecular Biology.* involving or resulting from the insertion of a different amino acid from that which is usual in a polypeptide or protein molecule. Compare NONSENSE. See also FRAMESHIFT. *The additional material consists of amino acids added on to the N-terminal, or start of the molecule. Although this could be an artefact of the cell-free system, investigation shows that there are no major "mis-sense" errors . . . , no termination or initiation errors, and essentially no breakdown of the product during the incubation.* New Scientist 8/8/74, p309 [1961]

missionary position, the face-to-face position in sexual intercourse with the male on top of the female. *In the South and Midwest . . . said one lawyer, "the law proscribes even married people from using anything but the missionary position" in their sexual relations.* New York Post 6/21/75, p23 [1969, apparently so called because of the belief that it was not practiced in primitive societies until its introduction by missionaries]

mission control, a command center that controls space flights from the ground. *Instead of launching the cosmonaut team, Soviet mission control had to raise the orbit of Salyut 2 by engine thrust on 4 April.* New Scientist 4/19/73, p157 [1964] —**mission controller:** *By the following day, mission controllers had*

devised a kind of Rube Goldberg extension of the damaged fender, using four plastic terrain maps and two clamps. This seemed to work well enough. Newsweek 12/25/72, p46

mission specialist, a scientist responsible for coordinating scientific experiments aboard a spacecraft or during space exploration. Compare PAYLOAD SPECIALIST. See also PI. *"Mission specialists," . . . with a variety of scientific and engineering backgrounds, may become involved with spacewalks, payload handling and maintenance, and actual experimental operations. All six of the selected women are in the mission-specialist category.* Science News 1/21/78, p36 [1977]

Mister Charley or **Mister Charlie,** *U.S. Slang, chiefly Black English.* the white man. Also spelled MR. CHARLEY or MR. CHARLIE. *"What Congress did to Adam* [Clayton Powell] *was a direct insult to the entire black community. It was 'Mister Charley' saying, 'Out you go, niggah!' It's a very emotional issue around here."* NY Times 3/3/68, p109 *And if his* [the black student's] *education does open the world to him, he may find himself cut off from his old community. He is an "Uncle Tom," the most dread and spirit-shattering of epithets, not because he laughs at Mister Charlie's jokes but because he is interested in mathematics.* Atlantic 7/67, p39 [1960]

Mitbestimmung ('mitbə‚ʃtimuŋ), *n.* (in West Germany and some other European countries) the right of workers to participate in corporate management; codetermination. Also called WORKER PARTICIPATION. *West German unions are normally famous for their self-restraint, and one source of moderation has been* Mitbestimmung: *that means the election of workers onto boards of management as opposed to boards of directors.* Listener 1/31/74, p139 [1970, from German, from *mit* with, together with (co-) + *Bestimmung* decision, determination]

mitose, *v.i.* to undergo cell division. *The small DNA tumour viruses—polyoma virus and simian virus 40—share the property of inducing nondividing cells which they infect to initiate a round of DNA synthesis; if the cells are non-permissive and survive, they subsequently mitose.* Nature 6/16/72, p371 [1972, back formation from *mitosis*]

mixed media, a combination of various media, such as the use of water colors and oil in painting or tapes, films, phonograph records, photographs, and slides, used in an artistic or educational presentation. Also called MULTIMEDIA, with the exception of painting. *Mr. Rubin was propelled into mixed media, he said, by seeing so many bad but interesting examples, including some of Andy Warhol's work in Greenwich Village.* NY Times 8/19/67, p17 [1962]

mixed-media, *adj.* using mixed media. Also called MULTIMEDIA, with the exception of painting. *More galleries experimented with mixed-media exhibitions making use of the wonders of modern technology.* Britannica Book of the Year 1971, p105 [1967]

MLR, abbreviation of *minimum lending rate,* the official interest rate of the Bank of England, which corresponds to the U.S. Federal Reserve discount rate. *There was considerable political pressure on the Government, not least from its supporters, to intervene either by making funds available at a low rate of interest, as was done by the previous government, or by lowering MLR.* Manchester Guardian Weekly 7/15/79, p3 [1973]

MMT, abbreviation of *Multiple Mirror Telescope. The MMT is the first of a new class of large telescopes: it has a number of small mirrors, rather than a single large one, collecting the light from stellar objects. The six 72-inch mirrors have the light gathering power of a single 176-inch mirror, making MMT the world's third largest telescope.* New Scientist 6/8/78, p647 [1973]

mnemon ('ni‚mɑn), *n.* a minimal unit of information stored in the brain or nervous system; a theoretical unit of memory encoded in a nerve-cell pathway. *If a mnemon in an octopus brain is thought of as a single word on a signpost—a simple "Stop" or "Go"—then the mnemons in a human brain must be equivalent to whole sentences, paragraphs, even books, containing elaborate "programs" for guiding our future thoughts,* *feelings, and actions.* New Yorker 8/16/76, p23 [**1965**, from Greek *mnémē* memory + English *-on* elementary unit]

mobile genetic element, another term for TRANSPOSON. *Barbara McClintock, a Long Island geneticist whose PhD is in botany from Cornell, received this award for her discovery of mobile genetic elements in plants, which she theorized more than 30 years ago. The elements became apparent only within the last 10 years.* Christian Science Monitor 12/8/83, p35 [**1981**]

mobile missile, a missile that can be moved through underground tunnels to any one of several launch sites. *In reaction to the threat, the West European powers agreed to the installation of American Pershing II mobile missiles and the ground-launched Cruise Missile.* Americana Annual 1980, p229 [**1960, 1976**]

mobile phone, another name for CELLULAR PHONE. *A new mobile phone that we are now developing may become as easy to use as a home telephone.* U.S. News & World Report 2/12/79, p63 [**1979**]

MOBS (mɑbz), *n.* acronym for *Multiple Orbit Bombardment System,* a nuclear-weapon system in which earth satellites carry warheads that may be released from space upon earth targets, thus escaping detection by conventional radar. *Some observers here fear that the recent Russian shots may represent a step upward from this FOBS system to the so-called MOBS—multiple-orbit bombardment system—that Soviet officials have discussed publicly since 1961.* NY Times 4/3/68, p1 [**1967**]

mocamp ('mou͵kæmp), *n.* a tourist camp providing various facilities for campers. *If you're touring Turkey, stay at BP Mocamps. Here's a welcome for campers and caravanners. And more. Like hot and cold water, toilets, showers, kitchen, laundry and ironing facilities.* Times (London) 11/1/67, pII [**1967**, from *mo-* (as in *motor, motel,* and *mobile*) + *camp*]

mod, *adj.* extremely up-to-date and fashionable in style of clothes, makeup, music, art, etc.; avant-garde. *More often than not, the music that enhances these mod liturgies comes from an electric guitar pulsating to a rock beat.* Time 10/12/70, p43 *Carnaby Street, in the West End in London . . . is the Mecca of the "mod" fashions which became so popular that nearly every department store in America which caters to the young opened special shops for them.* Harper's 5/67, p28 **—n. 1** a mod person. *These are the mods—short for moderns—who care more about looking "smart" than any other segment of the population, male or female. The British public became aware of them when the Beatles were first popular.* NY Times 2/24/65, p43 *Starting out as an adjective to describe clothing, "mod" has continued on to become a noun denoting an extremely up-to-date person or group, as well.* Springfield [Mass.] Republican 7/15/67 (page not known) **2** mod style or fashion. *The look of "chic mod" she says she is trying to achieve starts with a pointed doll's face engulfed in brass gold hair, and with caramel colored eyes rimmed with the thinnest line of black pencil.* NY Times 2/7/68, p50 [**1965**, originally *mod, adj.,* "of or relating to the *Mods*," a group of young British working-class boys in the late 1950's who acted like dandies and wore ultrafashionable clothes, *Mods* being a shortened form of *moderns*]

mode-locked, *adj.* (of a laser) having its light phases modulated so as to produce pulses of extremely short duration. *The development of the "mode-locked" pulsed laser perhaps offered the single most important technological advance in chemical dynamics of excited states.* 1972 Britannica Yearbook of Science and the Future, p211 *The extremely high peak power that can be got in pico-second pulses from such "mode-locked" lasers promise fresh insights into interactions of light and matter.* Scientific American 9/68, p121 [**1966**]

modem ('mou͵dem), *n.* an electronic device for converting signals from one form to another to facilitate transmission. *Handling data on conventional speech circuits requires the conversion of digital information into analog form, by modulators and demodulators (modems) which also protect the tele-*

phone circuits from damage. Science Journal 10/70, p62 [**1961**, from *mo*dulator + *dem*odulator]

moderacy, *n.* the holding of moderate opinions, especially in politics; moderateness. *So who did he pick as sacrificial victims? Why those very models of leftish moderacy [who] were sacked from the front bench for the heinous offence of voting against the government. . .* Manchester Guardian Weekly 3/11/84, p4 *. . . if Saudi Arabia were to make any such overtures in the field, America, as a proponent of Saudi moderacy and as the godfather of the Israeli-Egyptian Peace Treaty in all its documents and appendages, might be placed in a rather delicate position.* Summary of World Broadcasts (BBC) 11/23/81 [**1978**] ▶*Moderacy* is found in the OED with the label *Obsolete* and one citation dated 1601. The word has been revived on the model of *supremacy, diplomacy, literacy,* etc. See also GRAPHICACY, ORACY.

modularize, *v.t.* to make modular or break into units; build (something) into modules or units. *We are an anxious people. Our cosmetic media and modularized lifestyles attempt to hide this fact but it haunts every feature of existence.* NY Times 10/8/70, p47 [**1959**]

modulate, *v.i. U.S. Slang.* to talk over a CB radio. *The person who installs a CB set and adopts a "handle" (nickname) and starts "modulating" on the air, is creating a character and reaching out to others while still maintaining anonymity.* Time 5/10/76, p79 [**1976**]

module, *n.* **1** a self-contained, standardized, and interchangeable unit or component, as in a computer or other machine. *One reason why Sigma 5 gets more efficient as it grows larger is that when memory modules are added interleave and overlap occur.* Scientific American 2/67, p11 **2** a unit in an aircraft or spacecraft, that has a specific function and is often designed to function apart from the main craft as a self-contained, self-supporting unit. *An operational crew module which could be used in an emergency for escape and survival is to be fitted to the American F111 fighter-bomber. . .* Times (London) 3/29/66, p5 [**1955** for def. 1; **1961** for def. 2]

mogul, *n.* a moundlike elevation on a ski slope. *Becky's eyes and face hesitated, but she obeyed. Easily, solid on her skis, she swung down among the moguls and wind-bared ice, and became small, and again waited.* New Yorker 3/9/68, p35 [**1961**, probably from Norwegian *muge, mugje* (feminine *muga*) a heap or mound; form influenced by English *mogul* a prominent person]

moldy fig, *U.S. Slang.* an old-fashioned or outmoded person or thing. *Holden Caulfield [hero of J.D. Salinger's The Catcher in the Rye] is a moldy fig; the Lord of the Flies has been swatted. This year, the unquestioned literary god on college campuses is a three-foot high creature with . . . the improbable name of Frodo Baggins [hero of J.R.R. Tolkien's The Lord of the Rings].* Time 7/15/66, p54 [**1966**, originally (1940's) applied by progressive jazz fans to lovers of traditional jazz]

mole, *n.* **1** a machine that bores holes through soil and rock, used especially to make tunnels. *The tunnel borer, or mole, has 36 cutters, weighs 200 tons, and is designed to cut through sandstone and siltstone at the rate of 20 feet (6 meters) per hour. A laser beam guides the machine through the rock formation.* Americana Annual 1972, p689 **2** a secret intelligence agent who builds a legitimate cover over a period of years but not engaging in spying activities until he or she is tapped for an important mission. Also called SLEEPER. *A 'mole' is, I think, a genuine KGB term for somebody who burrows into the fabric of a bourgeois society and undermines it from within—somebody of the Philby sort who is recruited at a very tender age.* Listener 1/22/76, p90 *A leak is detected in Castle's department. Counter-intelligence suspects a "mole"—the word used to designate a traitor in one's secret midst, a burrower from within who is working under the mandate of a foreign espionage organization.* New Yorker 5/8/78, p151 [**1965** for def. 1; **1974** for def. 2; both transferred senses of *mole* burrowing mammal]

molechism or **molecism** ('mɑlə͵kizəm), *n.* any virus, viewed as an infective agent possessing the characteristics of both a living microorganism and a nonliving molecule. Also called OR-GANULE. *Outside the cell, the virus may lie inert like a crystal or bit of dust. It comes alive only when it invades an intact living cell in order to reproduce. Yet while in the cell, it is no longer a virus since it has become part of the genetic material of the cell. For most virologists, viruses fall between the smallest living organism and the largest inert chemical molecules. According to the late Dr. Thomas Rivers of Rockefeller University, a virus could be appropriately described as a "molechism" or an "organule."* Newsweek 1/20/69, p63 [**1968;** *molechism,* from *mole*cule + *chemical* + organ*ism; molecism,* from *mole*cule + organ*ism*]

molecular astronomy, a branch of astronomy concerned with the molecules found in interstellar space, especially as they relate to galactic and stellar evolution. *That was more or less the picture of the interstellar medium in 1968, the year marking the birth of molecular astronomy as we now know it.* Scientific American 4/73, p52 [**1970**]

molecular fossil, a molecule of organic material extracted from rocks older than the oldest known fossils, used to study the early evolution of life on earth. *The exciting studies of Calvin, who has attempted to prove the existence of what he calls "molecular fossils," have not, however, firmly established the biogenic nature of these substances.* Science Journal 4/69, p36 [**1965**]

molecular genetics. See the quotation for the meaning. . . . *molecular genetics, which accounts for heredity in terms of nucleotide base sequences, had become established as a separate discipline. . .* Encyclopedia Science Supplement (Grolier) 1970, p123 [**1963**]

Mollisol ('malə,sɔːl), *n.* (in U.S. soil taxonomy) any of a group of soils with well-defined horizons, formed under vegetation and usually yielding rich cereal crops. *Mollisols. These soils of cool-temperate grasslands have been formed in weakly weathered regoliths on young land surfaces. Major areas are in the north-central United States and adjacent Canada, the Ukraine and Siberia, and the pampas of Argentina.* McGraw-Hill Yearbook of Science and Technology 1972, p372 [**1960,** from Latin *mollis* soft + *-sol* (from Latin *solum* soil)]

mom and pop, *U.S.* **1** of or relating to a small, family-run retail business. Also called MA AND PA. *Shortages of natural gas have forced industries and utilities in some areas to switch to oil. . . Something had to give. What gave were the "mom and pop" independent filling stations.* Science News 5/26/73, p342 *"It's a Mom and Pop deli. That's Pop."* Cartoon legend, New Yorker 11/29/76, p45 **2** Transferred use: *What started out as a "Mom and Pop" television shop, with two reporters and six line producers, has grown into a factory, employing more than 70 people, including 21 producers and 16 film editors.* NY Times Magazine 5/6/79, p29 [**1962** for def. 1; **1966** for def. 2; so called because many such businesses are operated by a husband and wife]

moment of truth, the decisive or critical moment at which one must confront a challenge or ordeal without evasion. *As the excruciatingly painful moment of truth nears on voting a half-billion dollars of new taxes, a rash of substitute proposals can be expected from lawmakers. . .* NY Times 3/1/66, p34 *Owen's* [movie director Don Owen's] *moment of truth came after the screening of his first rough version of the film* ["The Ernie Game"]. Maclean's 10/67, p111 [**1956,** originally meaning the moment in a bullfight when the matador confronts the bull with the final sword thrust, probably first used in this sense by Ernest Hemingway in his book *Death in the Afternoon* (1932) as a translation of Spanish *momento* (or *hora) de la verdad*]

mommy track, *U.S.* the career path of women who are willing to trade advancement and high pay for the opportunity to devote more time to their families. *Felice Schwartz in an article in the January-February issue of the* Harvard Business Review. *. . suggests relegating most working mothers to a gentler path, which wags have dubbed the Mommy Track.* Time 3/27/89, p72 *Real estate already has the two-tier system* [in which] *the "mommy track" is residential property—men sell commercial real estate.* Ms. magazine 6/89, p22 [**1989**]

Monday clubber, *British.* a right-wing Tory. Compare TRIBUNITE. *The 11 contenders for John Boyd-Carpenter's safe seat include a strong contingent of Monday Clubbers, headed by Dr Rhodes Boyson, headmaster of Highbury Grove Comprehensive School.* Times (London) 2/4/72, p12 [**1970,** from *Monday Club* (1962), a British right-wing Conservative social and political organization]

M₁ or **M-1** ('em'wən), *n. Economics.* money supply consisting of currency and demand deposits. Compare M₂, M₃. *The Fed reported that the basic money supply, known as M-1 and referring to currency in circulation plus checking account balances, had climbed from $304.3 billion in the statement week ended Sept. 8 to $308.8 billion in the week ended Sept. 15.* NY Times 9/24/76, pD1 [**1974;** *M,* abbreviation of *money*] ►M₁ represents the generally accepted idea of money. According to economists who favor this basic definition, there is a well-established relationship between the growth of M₁ and the overall course of the economy. Other economists dispute this and propose the broader concepts of M₂ and M₃ which incorporate money that can be readily converted into M₁. Some go further and include large certificates of deposit (M₂ or M₂ prime), and savings bonds and credit union shares (M₄), and so on. Only M₁, M₂ and M₃, however, are generally in use among economists.

monellin ('manəlin *or* mou'nelin), *n.* a protein derived from an African berry, having a taste about 30,000 times sweeter than sugar. Compare MIRACULIN. *Many other sweeteners, both naturally occurring and synthetic, are in various states of research and development. These include monellin (from the serendipity berry) and thaumatin, both protein sweeteners.* McGraw-Hill Yearbook of Science and Technology 1976, p182 [**1972,** from *Monell* Chemical Senses Center at the University of Pennsylvania (where the protein was isolated) + -*in* (chemical suffix)]

monensin (mou'nensən), *n.* a fermentation product of a species of streptomyces, widely used as an additive to beef cattle feed. Monensin is also noted for its ability to carry ions across lipid barriers. See IONOPHORE. *Monensin is less soluble in acid and base than in octanol, so it remains within the membrane. It picks sodium ions from the basic solution, carries them across the membrane and releases them into the acid solution.* Science News 11/30/74, p348 [**1974,** from (*Streptomyces cinna) monensis,* the name of the organism from which it derives + -*in* (chemical suffix)]

monetarism ('manətə,rizəm), *n.* the economic doctrine or theory of the monetarists. *The lecture was a full-blooded onslaught on "the new monetarism", the doctrines of the Chicago school of economists led by the celebrated Professor Milton Friedman.* Times (London) 3/13/70, p10 *Monetarism, the belief that the state of the economy can be decisively manipulated through regulating the flow of money, became an accepted cult in the White House after Dr Burns had left it to assume the chairmanship of the Federal Reserve Board.* Sunday Times (London) 8/8/71, p4 [**1969**]

monetarist ('manətərist), *n.* an advocate or supporter of the theory that a balanced economy depends on the money supply. Compare NEO-KEYNESIAN. *Alaric Shepherd there reveals himself as an uncompromising monetarist . . . , insisting that "as John Stuart Mill once said, nothing is more important than money." He is, he confessed to our man, well advanced with his own magnum opus, a definitive 1,000-page* Monetary History of the United Kingdom and Europe. Times (London) 4/21/70, p25 —*adj.* of monetarists or monetarism. *Broadly, the monetarist school remains confident that a recovery cannot be far off, since the monetary policy of the Federal Reserve Board remains expansionary.* Manchester Guardian Weekly 11/28/70, p22 [**1963**]

money, *n.* **on the money,** *U.S. and Canadian Slang.* on target; precisely to the point. *Peter Klappert's article "Let Them Eat Wonderbread" on a political double talk from a poet's vantage point was right on the money.* Saturday Review 11/4/72, p28 [**1971,** patterned after similar older phrases such as *on the button, on the nose*]

money market fund, a mutual fund that specializes in investments in short-term instruments of credit. *People can often get the money at 8.5% interest and then put it into money market funds yielding at present about 14%.* Time 4/14/80, p78 *When managers of money-market funds believe interest rates will continue rising, they shorten the average time to maturity of the securities in their portfolios. And when they believe rates will fall, they begin to lengthen the maturities.* Money *magazine* 12/81, p82 [**1977**]

money-washing, *n.* the act or practice of channeling illegally obtained funds to make them seem legitimate; laundering of money (often used attributively). See LAUNDER. *The undercover activities reportedly ranged from disrupting the Democratic primaries to secret fundraising, questionable "money-washing" operations and the preparation of dossiers on various prominent Democrats.* Newsweek 2/12/73, p26 [**1972**]

mongo, *n. U.S. Slang.* objects of salvage, especially as considered of use or value by scavengers. *Arson is a common means of covering up other crimes, such as robbery. "Mongo" hunters, usually drug addicts, will set fires and then come back to the scene after the excitement has died down to steal any valuable items that they can find; the term "mongo" is a slang expression for the lead piping, copper fixtures, and other such material that is stripped from the building and then sold to junk dealers. Tenants have even burned their run-down buildings in order to be relocated to better housing.* 1980 Collier's Encyclopedia Year Book, p238 [**1979,** perhaps alteration of *mungo* inferior wool made from felted rags and wastes (OED 1857), of unknown origin]

monobuoy, *n.* a large floating structure anchored several miles offshore to serve as a mooring place for megatankers or other large vessels that cannot be accommodated at a conventional port. See SUPERPORT. *The journey from Thistle's tanker loading buoy, 130 miles north-east of the Shetlands, to the Humber monobuoy took the tanker two days, and discharge of the cargo about 24 hours.* Times (London) 4/17/78, p19 [**1972**]

monoclonal antibody, an antibody produced in the laboratory by fusing cells that are genetically distinct and cloning the resulting hybrids so that each hybrid cell produces the same antibody. *Biologists are trying to obtain a monoclonal antibody that will bind interferon, a natural substance that fights viral infections. . . Other active areas of research already underway include development of monoclonal antibodies that enhance organ transplants, that diagnose and monitor leukemia and that detect subtle changes in the nervous system.* Science News 12/23-30/78, p447 *The technique for making monoclonal antibodies was developed only five years ago. . . A whole new industry is developing to exploit the potential of these highly precise antibodies. Their first use is likely to be in medical diagnosis such as the important task of identifying hepatitis infections in a person or blood sample.* NY Times 1/27/80, p31 [**1972**]

monohull, *n.* a sailing vessel with a single hull. *Well, the design of the monohull can be improved—there is constant experiment with materials—and the multihull, with everything in its favour, could do the voyage extremely quickly.* Sunday Times (London) 2/2/69, p50 *Slowly multihull boats are gaining ground against the traditional monohulls.* Sunday Times Magazine (London) 4/11/71, p20 [**1967**]

monokini, *n.* **1** a one-piece bikini. *The one-piece got briefer and briefer until it reached the limit with the topless swimsuit, or as the French called it, the "monokini."* Sunday Times (London) 5/5/68, p60 **2** a man's bikini. . . . *Young and amazingly inventive Spanish "coiffeur-architect" Truderro, whose recently launched black-and-yellow salon (he works wearing only a jet monokini, a trained canary perched on his shoulder) has attracted EVERYONE.* New Yorker 4/10/65, p92 [**1964**]

monolithic, *n.* short for MONOLITHIC CIRCUIT. *Monolithic integrated circuits are used for arithmetic and logic functions in the new computers. The central processors use what is called monolithic systems technology (M.S.T.) . . . Monolithics are*

also used as storage devices in the high-speed buffer memories. Times (London) 7/3/70, p27 [**1970**]

monolithic circuit, an integrated circuit fabricated entirely on a single crystalline silicon chip. *In the next five or ten years we may well expect to see the development of automated methods for the manufacture of monolithic circuits and very large-scale integrated circuits which will further increase the reliability and speed of tomorrow's computers as well as cut their cost.* Van Court Hare, Jr., Introduction to Programming: A BASIC Approach, 1970, p19 [**1963**]

mononucleate, *adj.* having only one nucleus in a cell. *Here shall be concerned with the mononucleate hybrid cells that are produced when the nuclei of two cells (and occasionally three) fuse together as the heterokaryon* [cell in a fungus] *divides.* New Scientist and Science Journal 7/8/71, p90 [**1957**]

monosexual, *adj.* of, relating to, or for one sex only. Compare UNISEXUAL. *Or, when uninhibited, do the younger women of all tribes perform ritual monosexual dances to satisfy some urge of which we yet know little?* Times (London) 1/21/71 p11 [**1964**]

monotechnic, *n.* a school specializing in a single technical subject. *We could learn much from the American system of higher education, . . . and also from the Russian model where* mono-technics *of high educational as well as vocational standing greatly outnumber the traditional universities.* Listener 9/1/66, p297 [**1967,** noun use of the earlier adjective (1904), from *mono-* single + *-technic,* as in *polytechnic*]

monounsaturate, *n.* a monounsaturated oil or fat, often used in diets. *The Federally funded Intersociety Commission for Heart Disease Resources also called for an over-all national policy to prevent premature heart disease. . . The commission's diet calls for . . . keeping polyunsaturated fats (corn oil, safflower oil, soybean oil and cottonseed) at less than 10 per cent of calories with the rest of dietary fats consisting of monounsaturates (peanut and olive oil).* NY Times 12/20/70, pD7 [**1970**]

monster, *n. Especially U.S. Slang.* a singer or musician of very broad public appeal; a musical superstar. *Behind the headlines the Average White Band is an exciting group with the potential to be what the music business calls "monsters," musically and commercially.* Newsweek 3/24/75, p81 [**1974**]

monstre sacré (mɔ̃strə sa'krei), *pl.* **monstres sacrés.** a celebrity whose eccentric or unconventional behavior is excused or admired by the public. Jean Cocteau: The Man and the Mirror *is most vivid in recounting the great friendships that linked the writer-artist to such fascinating figures as . . . Picasso, and Colette, as much of an individualist and a* monstre sacré *as Cocteau himself.* Saturday Review 5/25/68, p22 [**1959,** from French, literally, sacred monster]

Montagnard (ˌmɑntə'nyɑrd), *n.* Also spelled **montagnard.** one of an aboriginal people living in the highlands of South Vietnam (often used attributively). Also called YARD. *But there are still great numbers of Vietnamese for whom French is a second language, particularly the mountain tribesmen (the so-called Montagnards)—and the Vietcong.* New York Review of Books 3/17/66, p8 *When 600 montagnard tribesmen graduated recently from the Pleiku Montagnard Training Center, they each took back to their mountain villages some new concepts in farming, a saw, a knife—forged from the leaf of an old truck spring—and a gun.* NY Times 1/2/68, p2 [**1962,** from French, literally, mountaineer]

Montezuma's revenge (ˌmɑntə'zu:məz), *Slang.* traveler's diarrhea acquired in Mexico or from eating Mexican food. Also called AZTEC TWO-STEP, MEXICALI REVENGE. *"I do hope this doesn't last too long. I had a Mexican meal last night and I've got Montezuma's revenge,"* said one of the dozen or so photographers shuffling about in the cold and wet.* Times (London) 1/6/77, p17 [**1962,** named after *Montezuma* II, 1480?-1520, an Aztec ruler of Mexico during the Spanish conquest]

Montonero (ˌmɑntou'nerou; *Anglicized* ˌmɑntə'nirou), *n.* a member of a left-wing Peronist organization in Argentina, engaged in urban guerrilla activities. *In recent months, the Montoneros, a political and guerrilla organization of Marxists and* *leftist followers of the late President Juan Domingo Perón, have repeatedly denounced the activities of the Argentine military intelligence in Mexico and other countries where there are Argentine exiles.* NY Times 1/29/78, p13 [**1970**, from Spanish, literally, bushwhacker, guerrilla]

mood drug, a drug, such as a stimulant or tranquilizer, that affects or alters one's state of mind. *There is some opposition to the use of mood drugs for children. Traditionalist Freudian psychiatrists believe that behavior and learning problems are psychological, not physical or chemical in origin.* Time 8/10/70, p44 *"Overuse of mood drugs is becoming increasingly acute," he said recently.* Sunday Times (London) 10/24/71, p6 [**1970**]

Moog synthesizer (moug), an electronic keyboard instrument for generating a large variety of sounds. *Baroque composers did not write for these great outsized modern harpsichords, anymore than they did for the piano, or the Moog Synthesizer.* Atlantic 5/70, p124 [**1969**, named after the American engineer Robert A. *Moog*, born 1934, who invented it]

moon car, another name for LUNAR ROVER. *Its hollow, wiremesh wheels snapped into place, and the moon car was lowered to the ground.* Time 8/9/71, p6 [**1965**]

moonchild, *n.* a person born under the sign of Cancer, June 21-July 21. *She was a Cancerian, a Moon child with no light of her own but the reflected light of the Sun.* New Yorker 4/3/71, p40 *Into his life and villa moves the external present in the form of Jill, a rich moonchild on the run from a mother in Connecticut and a pusher in New York.* Times (London) 4/6/72, p7 [**1969**, so called because of the influence of the moon on the house of Cancer; used instead of *Cancer* because of association with the disease]

mooncraft, *n.* a spacecraft for traveling to the moon. Also called MOONSHIP. *When the Russians are ready they may launch a fully-fuelled propulsion module and join the two components of a mooncraft in Earth-orbit.* New Scientist 3/21/68, p631 [**1962**]

moon crawler, another name for LUNAR ROVER. *Lunokhod-1, Russia's moon crawler, this week became the first vehicle to travel across the lunar surface.* Manchester Guardian Weekly 11/21/70, p3 *"Moon mobiles" and an unmanned "moon crawler" that looked very much like the current Russian Lunokhod were being considered until the manned Apollo outran the unmanned Surveyor.* Science News 6/12/71, p404 [**1970**]

Moonie, *n.* a follower of the Reverend Sun Myung Moon and member of his Unification Church; an adherent of Moonism. *The Greens have a personal motive for their campaign. Last year, two of their children left home to cast their lot in with "the Moonies"—7000 hardcore converts who live in guarded "training centres" across the US.* Fiji Times 1/10/76, p12 *The Federal Government, however, has some ways of coping with the cults. At the moment an interagency task force . . . is being organized to investigate the financial transactions of the Moonies.* Time 12/11/78, p38 [**1975**, from Sun Myung *Moon*, born 1920, Korean industrialist and religious leader + -*ie*]

mooning, *n. U.S. Slang.* the act or practice of displaying one's buttocks. Compare STREAKING. *And one boy rhapsodizes about his success at "mooning," a boyish trick of sticking one's bare behind out the window at passing girls. All these things are essentially ugly and debasing. Yet Grease treats them unevasively and with good comic effect.* Saturday Review 7/15/72, p64 [**1972**, from *moon* or *moons*, old slang noun (1700's) meaning buttocks]

Moonism, *n.* the beliefs, teachings, and practices of the Reverend Sun Myung Moon and his Unification Church, combining elements of fundamentalist Christianity and Buddhist philosophy. *Six days later I was to get a new insight into Moonism—this time by observing an intense process of withdrawal which has become known in the language of religious cultism as "deprogramming."* Daily News (New York) 12/3/75, p54 [**1975**, from Sun Myung *Moon* (see MOONIE) + -*ism*]

moon pool, a shaft in the center of a deep-sea mining ship, through which equipment is lowered and raised. *There was also a giant "moon pool" in the ship's bottom, with doors that could swing open to take aboard bulky "mining machinery" from below.* Newsweek 3/31/75, p31 [**1971**]

moonport, *n.* a launch complex for preparing spacecraft to travel to the moon. *The board of inquiry was expected to order the entire spacecraft removed from its booster and taken to the Merritt Island, Fla., moonport for step-by-step disassembly.* Science News 2/18/67, p161 [**1963**, from *moon* + *port*, patterned after *airport*]

moonrock, *n.* a rock sample from the moon. See KREEP for example. *There is something bizarre about the exchange in Moscow recently of a minute quantity of Apollo moonrock for an even more minute quantity of Luna 16 moonrock.* New Scientist and Science Journal 6/24/71, p766 [**1963**]

moon rover, another name for LUNAR ROVER. *As an example of sheer technological innovation, however, nothing aboard Apollo 15 quite beats NASA's new LRV (for Lunar Roving Vehicle), more commonly known as the "moon rover."* Time 7/26/71, p38 [**1970**]

moonship, *n.* another name for MOONCRAFT. *Dropping into the calm seas 300 miles north of Hawaii several feet per second faster than planned, the moonship created a mighty splash.* Time 8/16/71, p28 [**1963**]

moonwalk, *n.* an exploratory walk on the moon's surface. *During their 66 hours on the moon—twice the duration of Apollo 14's lunar stay—they plan to venture out of their LM on three moonwalks for periods of up to seven hours and distances as far as five miles.* Time 2/22/71, p37 [**1966**]

moonwalker, *n.* a person who takes a moonwalk; a moon explorer. *The board, chaired by Edgar Cortright, Director of NASA's Langley Research Center and including Earth's first moonwalker Neil Armstrong, spent seven weeks studying photographs of the crippled service module taken by the Apollo 13 astronauts. . . .* Science Journal 9/70, p4 [**1966**]

MOR (ˌemˌouˈɑr), *U.S.* abbreviation of MIDDLE-OF-THE-ROAD (used especially in radio programming). *"Now a copyright like 'I Write the Songs' is worth something; a Sinatra will work it into his act, for instance. Or—and this is certainly something you didn't see a few years ago—a song will break MOR [middle of the road, easy listening] and then cross over to top-40."* NY Times Magazine 4/24/77, p86 [**1973**]

Moral Majority, an American movement of evangelical Christians, seeking to effect moral changes in politics and society. *As described by the Rev. Jerry Falwell, spokesman for the Moral Majority, the agenda includes constitutional amendments to ban abortion and reinstitute school prayers, legislation to restrict pornography and drug use—and opposition to the Equal Rights Amendment.* Manchester Guardian Weekly 12/14/80, p17 *Mr. Wildman, chairman of the Coalition for Better Television, had threatened to boycott products of companies sponsoring "offensive" programs. Since his coalition claims membership of 400 mostly conservative groups, led by Moral Majority, and has at least $2 million for its campaign, the boycott threat gave pause to advertisers.* NY Times 6/28/81, pD7 [**1980**]

morning-after pill, an oral contraceptive that could prevent pregnancy even if taken one or several days after intercourse. Compare ABORTION PILL. *Dr. Chang and Dr. Pincus had been working recently on a new pill, known popularly as the "morning-after" pill. It affects the egg after ovulation.* NY Times 8/24/67, p35 [**1967**]

morph, *n.* a variant form of an animal species. *There were also differences between the various "Morphs", i.e., winged or wingless, viviparous or oviparous; between the sexes; and between aphids of the same type collected on different dates.* New Scientist 7/29/65, p283 [**1955**, from Greek *morphé* form]

morphactin (mɔrˈfæktən), *n.* any one of a group of chemical compounds, derived from fluorene and carboxylic acid, which affect plant growth when applied at various stages and in varying strengths. *Morphactin . . . need merely be applied to the leaves of young cucumber plants that are beginning to flower. The chemical causes the flowers' ovaries to develop into fruit without first being pollinated, as is normal.* World Book Science Annual 1972, p282 [**1966**, from *morph*ogenesis + *act*ive + *-in* (chemical suffix)]

MOS, abbreviation of *metal oxide semiconductor*, used in integrated circuits, especially of the large-scale integration or LSI type. *. . . . more circuits are being fabricated on a single silicon slice, with the trend from MOS devices to MSI (medium scale integration), applied to devices with up to 100 circuits or so on one chip) and then to LSI (large scale integration), with more than 100 circuits on one chip.* New Scientist and Science Journal 7/8/71, p78 [**1964**]

MOSFET ('mɑs,fɛt), *n.* acronym for *metal oxide semiconductor field effect transistor,* a type of transistor widely used in microprocessors, computer memories, and other electronic circuits. *In a typical MOSFET two islands of n-type silicon are created in a substrate of p-type material. Connections are made directly to the islands, one of which is called the source and the other the drain. On the surface of the silicon over the channel between the source and the drain a thin layer of silicon dioxide (SiO_2) is formed, and on top of the oxide a layer of metal is deposited, forming a third electrode called the gate.* Scientific American 9/77, p74 [**1967**]

Mossad (,mou'sɑ:d), *n.* the secret intelligence service of Israel. *Mr Shamir is a former leader of the Stern Gang, the most ruthless of the underground movements that harried the British out of Palestine, and a former senior official of the Mossad, Israel's secret service.* Manchester Guardian Weekly 3/16/80, p8 [**1976**, from Modern Hebrew *Mosad* agency, short for *Mosad Elyon Lemodiim Ubitahon* Supreme Agency for Intelligence and Security, the full name of the organization]

Mössbauer spectroscopy ('mœs,bauər), spectroscopic study using the Mössbauer effect for analysis and measurement. *With very few exceptions the application of Mössbauer spectroscopy to biology has involved measurement and interpretation of the resonant gamma-ray absorption of ^{57}Fe, the stable isotope which makes up 2% of the iron in nature.* McGraw-Hill Yearbook of Science and Technology 1977, p305 [**1962**, named after Rudolf *Mössbauer*, born 1929, a German physicist who discovered the *Mössbauer* effect, enabling changes in gamma radiation to be measured with great precision]

moto ('moutou), *n.* one of the heats that make up a cross-country motorcycle race. *A Grand Prix motocross race actually consists of two heats, or "motos," each lasting for about 45 grueling minutes.* Newsweek 7/9/73, p58 [**1973**, back formation from *moto-cross* (OEDS 1951) a cross-country motorcycle race]

motor home, a motor vehicle with a long body designed and furnished to serve as living quarters for recreational travel or for camping. *Steve Ford . . . is touring scenic backwaters of the Far West with his boyhood friend Kevin Kennedy in a 27-ft. motor home.* Time 10/11/76, p24 [**1966**] ▶Not to be confused with a *mobile home* (1950's), which is a trailer designed to be used as a permanent, year-round home and which ranges from 29 to 70 feet in length and 8 to 14 feet in width.

motor hotel, a motel, especially one situated in a city and built like a hotel but providing parking and other facilities for motorists. *It is Trust Houses' first "purpose-built" motor hotel, with 28 double bedrooms, good parking space, and service and petrol filling stations.* Times (London) 2/9/65, p16 [**1965**]

motor inn, another term for MOTOR HOTEL. *Though outwardly in strong shape, with 46 restaurants and six motor inns as well as its food-processing, the company has recently been having trouble keeping earnings up to snuff.* Time 4/21/67, p25 [**1967**]

Motown ('mou,taun), *n.* a style of rhythm and blues with a strong beat, which originated in Detroit, Michigan (often used attributively). *Think of Michael Walden: he plays funky, Detroit low-down, Motown. But he plays better than most of the famous names, and he's only 22.* Manchester Guardian Weekly (Le Monde section) 3/8/75, p14 *Would* you *want to hear*

French hits from the past 30 years done with a Motown bea New York Post 4/20/79, p45 [**1970**, from the trademark of record company based in Detroit, a blend of *Motor Town*, nick name for Detroit]

mouse, *n.* a device to control a cursor or other image on a com puter display screen. *True, there is a whole new generation o software that manipulates cursors on screens by using mic those palm-sized, button-eared plastic rodents only recentl ushered onto the computer stage. Move the mouse on your des and the mouse sends a signal up its tail, causing the cursor t make a matching move on the video monitor. Press an ear bu ton, and you can "pick up" a block of text and position it else where on the screen.* NY Times 10/25/83, pC3 [**1965**]

mouth-to-mouth resuscitation, a method of artificial respiratio in which a person's mouth is placed tightly over the victim and air is blown every few seconds into the victim's mouth t inflate the lungs. Also called (*British*) KISS OF LIFE. Compar CPR. *One of them . . . appeared lifeless, but firemen restore his breathing by mouth-to-mouth resuscitation and oxygen* NY Times 4/26/63, p18 [**1961**]

movement, *n.* Usually, **the Movement**, the Women's Liberatio movement. Also called WOMEN'S MOVEMENT. *My editor i New York, Lisa Drew, began writing "Ms." on her letters to me The feminist Kate Millett had just written a grumpy Double day book,* Sexual Politics, *and the office was full of The Move ment.* Maclean's 1/73, p32 [**1970**]

mover and shaker, *U.S.* a person of power and influence. *Fou years after the death of his legendary father, Illinois state Sen ator* [Richard M.] *Daley has begun to emerge as a mover an shaker in his own right.* Newsweek 8/18/80, p26 *For Wash ington's movers and shakers, being an "outsider" in the city social life is worse than living in Baltimore. There is a bris trade in bits of advice on how to "make it" and how to tel what's "in" and what's "out."* NY Times Magazine 1/4/81 p68 [**1974**]

MRCA, abbreviation of *multi-role combat aircraft,* a swing wing type of combat aircraft jointly developed by Great Brit ain, Italy, and West Germany. *The third partner in the MRC project is Italy, and each of the three countries will have it own assembly line for this advanced fighter-bomber with it variable-geometry wing and top speed well over twice that o sound.* Times (London) 6/22/77, Special Report: West Germa ny, pV [**1970**]

Mr. Charlie or **Mr. Charley**, variant spellings of MISTER CHAR LEY and MISTER CHARLIE. *Tipped off that some other farmer were confused and might vote for white-sponsored candidates he* [Mr. Ickes] *asks them: "You going to vote for Mr. Charle (the white man)? What's Mr. Charley ever done for you?"* Wal Street Journal 8/10/65, p1 *"Adam Clayton Powell is the vica for the man who always wants to spit in Mr. Charlie's face, says John Morsell, assistant executive director of the N.A.A.C.* Time 4/4/69, p19 [**1960**]

Mr. Clean, *Informal.* a person of impeccable morals or reputa tion, especially a politician or other public figure regarded a incorruptible. *The board . . . handed the top job to Jerr MacAfee, a tough, outspoken Texan who was dubbed "Mr Clean" by the* Toronto Star *during his term as president of Gul Oil Canada Ltd.* Maclean's 2/9/76, p47 *The Lockheed payoff are clearly an example of what the Japanese poetically refer t as* kuroi kiri (*black mist*), *or corruption. Ironically, Premie Miki could profit from the public anger; he has earned a repu tation as his party's Mr. Clean.* Time 2/23/76, p36 *There wer serious fears that Mr Callaghan might have damaged his repu tation as "Mr Clean" by confirming his son-in-law's appoint ment.* Manchester Guardian Weekly 5/22/77, p1 [**1971**, from the trademark of a liquid cleanser]

mRNA, abbreviation of MESSENGER RNA. *. . . mRNA in DNA may also be the basis for the timing cycle that regulates cell ac tivity. They isolated unique classes of protozoan mRNA whos concentrations varied periodically.* Britannica Book of the Yea 1970, p543 [**1961**]

MRV (ˌemˌɑrˈviː), abbreviation of *multiple reentry vehicle.* Compare MIRV. . . . *MRVs (for multiple re-entry vehicles) . . . and in a pre-planned pattern, but they cannot be steered to widely separated targets.* Time 5/4/70, p40 *Just recently* [Defense] *Secretary Laird announced that the Russians were testing an SS-11 system with three multiple reentry vehicles (MRV's), which lack the capability for being independently targeted.* Scientific American 1/71, p16 [**1969**]

Ms. (miz), abbreviated title used instead of *Miss* or *Mrs. The proliferation of Women's Lib-oriented journals has served to standardize the movement's special jargon . . . Unliberated honorifics like "Mrs." and "Miss" are replaced by the noncommittal "Ms."* Time 8/31/70, p18 *As an old-fashioned man, the President prefers the old conventions, such as addressing a woman as "Miss" or "Mrs." rather than the new, liberated, status-less "Ms."* New York Post 1/3/72, p26 *The elections committee of the California Senate has passed a Bill allowing women to sign the electoral roll as Ms.* Daily Telegraph (London) 2/12/72, p6 [**1949, 1970**] ►Although apparently coined in the 1940's, *Ms.* did not come into general use until the 1970's. Our single 1949 quotation is from Mario Pei's *The Story of Language,* p. 79: ". . . *feminists, who object to the distinction between Mrs. and Miss and its concomitant revelatory features, have often proposed that the two present-day titles be merged into a single one, 'Miss' (to be written 'Ms.'), with the plural Misses' (written 'Mss.'), even at the cost of confusion with the abbreviation for 'manuscripts.' "*

MSI, abbreviation of *medium-scale integration,* a method of producing a number of integrated circuits on a single chip of silicon. Compare LSI. . . . *more circuits are being fabricated on a single silicon slice, with the trend from MOS* [metal-oxide-semiconductor] *devices to MSI (medium scale integration, applied to devices with up to 100 circuits or so on one chip) and then to LSI (large scale integration), with more than 100 circuits on one chip.* New Scientist and Science Journal 7/8/71, p78 [**1968**]

MSR, abbreviation of *missile site radar,* an electronic radar used at antiballistic missile sites. Compare PAR. *Missile-site radars, or MSR's, were to be deployed at every ABM* [antiballistic missile] *site.* Scientific American 8/69, p24 [**1965**]

MSY, abbreviation of *maximum sustainable yield,* the largest amount of a natural resource that can be taken every year without impairing the ability of the resource to renew itself. *From a strictly biological point of view, the optimal harvest strategy is to remove no more and no less than the MSY each year. . . . In the case of the whales, by adding economic to biological considerations, one finds that the optimal harvest strategy may be to harvest at a rate either above or below the MSY.* 1978 Britannica Yearbook of Science and the Future, p310 [**1972**]

M₃ or **M-3** (ˈemˈθriː), *n. Economics.* the overall money supply of a country, including M_2 and deposits in savings and loan associations and the like and certificates of deposit. *According to figures for October, M₃ (a money supply measurement which includes cash as well as current and deposit bank accounts) was rising at an annual rate of 14 and a half per cent—compared to the target range of 9 to 13.* Manchester Guardian Weekly 12/4/77, p1 [**1974;** *M,* abbreviation of *money*] ►See the note under M₁.

M₂ or **M-2** (ˈemˈtuː), *n. Economics.* the money supply of a country, including M_1 and commercial-bank time deposits except certificates of deposit. *M₂, the broader category of money supply, climbed $1,700m in the latest week, averaging $711,900m against a revised $710,200m a week earlier.* Times (London) 9/21/76, p15 [**1974;** *M,* abbreviation of *money*] ►See the note under M₁.

mucopeptide, *n.* a polymeric substance consisting of chains of mucopolysaccharides and peptides, found especially in the cell walls of many bacteria. Also called MUREIN, PEPTIDOGLYCAN. *The cell envelope, the outer portion of the bacterial cell, is a complex structure consisting of an inner plasma membrane and a rigid mucopeptide layer, the cell wall proper, that confers strength and shape.* Scientific American 11/69,

p121 [**1959,** from *muco-* mucous + *peptide* a combination of amino acids]

Mud Man or **mudman,** *n.* one of a native people of Papua New Guinea who daub themselves with mud and wear grotesque clay masks to frighten their enemies. *In this anthropologist's dream world, many people—like the Mud Men of Goroka—still live in something akin to the* Stone Age. Newsweek 11/19/73, p69 [**1971**]

muggee (ˌməˈgiː), *n.* a person who is attacked or robbed violently; the victim of a mugger. *It is no use saying a mugger is a symptom of social problems. For someone in a dark street who is about to become a muggee, the 'symptom' is the problem.* Newsweek 9/16/74, p53 *Old Sam is full of ideas: in a press release . . . he suggests that, when attacked, the muggee should "try not to make any ethnic slurs . . . soft whistling or humming are okay while you are being stripped of your valuables."* Maclean's 3/22/76, p14 [**1972,** from *mug, v.* + *-ee*]

Mujahedin (muːˌdʒɑːhəˈdiːn), *n.pl.* Moslem guerrillas active especially in Iran and Afghanistan (often used attributively). . . . *the Mujahedin, a fanatical group of Muslim activists with a mixed set of political beliefs, who played a prominent part in the overthrow of the Shah.* New Yorker 6/9/80, p72 *The Mujahedin strategy is to keep whittling away at Khomeini's increasingly disjointed government.* Time 9/14/81, p41 [**1979,** from Arabic *mujāhidīn,* plural of *mujāhid,* fighter, guerrilla, from *jihād* fight, jihad (holy war)]

multi-, a productive combining form with the sense of "many" in adjective compounds (*multichannel, multicultural,* etc.) and "multiple" in noun compounds (*multiprocessing*). Some newly formed compounds follow: —**multibillion,** *adj.: What would be the practical and scientific benefits of a multibillion dollar space station?* New Scientist and Science Journal 1/28/71, p184 —**multichannel,** *adj.: This new technique, which can carry multi-channel telephony, telegraphy and all forms of data information, was proved feasible by the experimental Telstar satellite in 1962.* Times (London) 12/13/67, pV —**multicultural,** *adj.: After years of bi-bi* [bilingual, bicultural, etc.] *talk, I am delighted to understand from your Editorial that Canadians are encouraged to preserve our society as a multilingual and multicultural one.* Maclean's 3/68, p72 —**multiscreen,** *adj.: Taking his cue from the multiscreen effects exhibited at the 1964 New York World's Fair, John Frankenheimer shot many of the sequences for Grand Prix, his auto racing extravaganza, to make the vast, curving Cinerama screen contain three or more separate images working in counterpoint.* 1968 Collier's Encyclopedia Year Book, p372 —**multitrack,** *adj.: Recording studios also offer new technical means of composing, through such devices as the echo chamber, multi-track recording and tape superimposition.* Time 8/29/69, p47

multi-access, *adj.* of or relating to the sharing of one computer by two or more users simultaneously. Also, MULTIPLE-ACCESS. *. . . the chance to gain experience in using multi-access techniques, which allow a number of designers to use the computer together, each communicating with it from a separate terminal.* New Scientist 7/13/67, p78 [**1966**]

multiband, *adj.* combining two or more wavelength exposures. *Vertical aerial view of part of the Carrizo Plains, California, at near right was taken using ordinary Ektachrome film and reveals little trace of the phenomena rendered starkly visible in the enhanced multiband photograph at far right. Such pictures are produced by combining two or more narrow band exposures.* Picture legend, Science Journal 6/69, p64 [**1969**]

multicompany, *adj.* controlling or operating diverse companies or a variety of companies. *Litton, which prefers to be known as a multicompany company rather than a conglomerate, says the new unit will not only give counseling in the marketing of products and services but also will prepare the graphics.* NY Times 7/9/68, p61 [**1968**]

multiflex, *adj.* of or relating to a complex offensive system of formations in American football in which the backs and ends may assume a number of different positions to confuse the opposing team. *Because it takes a great deal of experience, poise* *and ability to run Harvard's multiflex offense, the loss of Davenport is even more crippling.* NY Times 9/23/77, pD14 [**1977**, from *multi-* many + *flex*ible]

multihull, *n.* a sailing vessel having two or more hulls joined by a common deck, as a catamaran. Compare MONOHULL. *Slowly multihull boats are gaining ground against the traditional monohulls. . . What is the point of multihulls? They are an alternative to the basic boat problem of stability.* Sunday Times Magazine (London) 4/11/71, p20 [**1960**]

multi-industry, *adj.* involved or operating in widely different industries. *The men who are challenging established firms with exuberance and even effrontery are the builders of conglomerates—those multipurpose, multi-industry companies that specialize in hodgepodge acquisitions.* Time 3/7/69, p55 [**1969**]

multimarket, *adj.* involved or operating in various widely different markets. [Assistant Attorney General Richard Wellington] *McLaren is becoming the most active—and visible—trustbuster since the days of Teddy Roosevelt; his broadsides have helped chill investor enthusiasm for multimarket companies.* Time 5/23/69, p61 [**1968**]

multimedia, *adj.* **1** using a combination of various media, such as tapes, film, phonograph records, photographs, and slides, to entertain, communicate, teach, etc. Also called MIXED-MEDIA. *The twenty-fourth Edinburgh International Festival opens this year on August 23 when Sir John Barbirolli conducts Beethoven's ninth symphony, and ends on September 12 with the last late-night performances of the Military Tattoo and of the multimedia rock musical* Stomp. Times (London) 4/28/70, p7 **2** involving the use of different communications media in the same place. *These standards apply both to multimedia information centers with print and audiovisual materials and to schools with separate libraries and audiovisual centers.* Americana Annual 1970, p420 —*n.* the use of more than one medium of communication or entertainment at one time. Also called MIXED MEDIA. *Concerts and demonstrations of multimedia were given in schools, colleges, theatres, museums, warehouses, and barns, in a variety of musical, nonmusical, unmusical, and antimusical presentations.* Britannica Book of the Year 1969, p549 [**1962** for adj.; **1971** for noun]

multimeric, *adj.* Chemistry. (of a group of molecules) held together by weak bonds. *There are two possible ways in which such multimeric DNA molecules might be generated—by recombination or by some failure to terminate replication—and evidence for one or other mechanism has been obtained by workers investigating the replication of various phages and viruses.* Nature 5/26/72, p196 [**1968**, from *multimer* group of molecules held together by weak bonds (from *multi-* many + *-mer* part, as in *polymer*) + *-ic*]

multinational, *adj.* having branches, subsidiaries, plants, and the like in many countries. *The multinational company has been a key factor in increasing skills, creating jobs and promoting economic growth in the developing world, and in trebling the international flow of investment capital in the past ten years.* Listener 11/22/73, p696 —*n.* a multinational company. Also called TRANSNATIONAL. *Some multinationals have been described as "sovereign states." The metaphor is more than apt, and one consequence of its currency is that the federal intelligence community no longer automatically equates the national interest with the multinationals' investments.* Harper's 12/74, p52 [**1968** for adj.; **1971** for noun; earliest adj. meaning (OEDS) 1926), "consisting of many races or nationalities"] —**multinationalism,** *n.*: *As chairman and chief executive officer of the Singer Co., Kircher, 57, runs a worldwide enterprise that could serve as a model of U.S.-based corporate multinationalism.* Newsweek 11/20/72, p98 —**multinationality,** *n.*: *In engine production in particular, opportunities for moving towards multinationality and market expansion are real and attainable: it is substantially this path that the whole European Motor industry is taking.* Times (London) 2/23/72, pVI

multipack, *n.* a package containing two or more individually packaged products, sold as a unit (often used attributively). *Despite the increasing number of "multipack" foods, such as Chef*

Boy-ar-Dee's lasagna with canned meat sauce, canned grate cheese, and packeted pasta, frozen foods continued to be eate in the U.S. at the rate of 68 lb. per person per year. Britannic Book of the Year 1969, p289 [**1967**]

multiphoton, *adj.* involving a number of photons. *As ionisatio cannot take place with the absorption of a single photon, mo laser physicists believe that multiphoton processes are in ope ation.* New Scientist 1/20/72, p130 [**1970**]

multiple, *n.* a mass-produced painting, sculpture, or other arti tic work. . . . *present-day American artists have tried to proje themselves directly into the surroundings of the majorit through products midway between art and supermarket orn ments and spectacles, such as light displays and Happening posters, color prints, banners, and multiples.* New Yorke 2/21/70, p87 *The artist who becomes interested in multiple takes the first step towards involving himself with the d mands of technology.* Times (London) 3/26/68, p7 [**1968**, nou use of the adjective]

multiple-access, *adj.* another word for MULTI-ACCESS. *Th "multiple-access time-sharing" arrangement does much mo than place additional computational ability at the comman of the engineer.* Sunday Times (London) 5/14/67, p33 [**1966**

multiple aim point system, a system for reducing the vulner bility of stationary missile silos to nuclear attack by shuttlin missiles within underground tunnels in a series of empty silo See MX. *One solution to the theoretical problem has been th proposed "multiple aim point" system (MAP) for deployin ICBMs—a shell game in which the US Minuteman force woul be deployed in only a small proportion (say 10 percent) o greatly increased numbers of missile sites.* Manchester Guard ian Weekly 10/29/78, p7 [**1978**]

multiplet, *n.* a group of two or more nuclear particles that ar similar in properties such as mass and spin but have differen charges. Compare SUPERMULTIPLET. *Early in 1964 order we brought to the nuclear "jungle" by the SU-3 theory unde which the 100 or so known nuclear particles are grouped int families, or multiplets, of eight or ten members.* Science New Letter 2/6/65, p85 [**1929, 1952**, from *multiple* + *-et*, after *do blet, triplet*]

multiprobe, *n.* a spacecraft carrying several other craft de signed to be released as planetary probes. *Weighing nearly ton, the multiprobe resembled a tall hatbox, about 2.5 mete across and 2.9 meters high, with four large, conical mushroon growing on its lid. "Resembled"—past tense—because th mushrooms are no longer there. The radio signal was the fir step in setting them free, to become individual, instrumen laden probes.* Science News 11/25/78, p356 [**1978**]

multiprocessing, *n.* the use of two or more computer processo which have access to a common memory and can execute se eral programs simultaneously. *Multiprocessing, like multipr gramming, got off to a slow start because of the associate complexities in coordination and control, but a number o multiprocessing systems are now in operation and many mo are planned.* McGraw-Hill Yearbook of Science and Technolo gy 1967, p151 [**1961**]

multiprocessor, *n.* a computer unit consisting of several proce sors, used in multiprocessing. *In construction, ours will be memory-oriented multiprocessor system—that is, it will be ab to carry out a number of operations, simultaneously, aroun the same memory. . .* New Scientist 11/16/67, p20 [**1961**]

multiprogramming, *n.* the handling of several programs concu rently by a single computer. *System 370 Models 155 and 16 the company states, have been developed to meet emergin needs such as large data bases, remote-access computing an high-throughout multiprogramming.* Times (London) 7/3/7 p27 *At its cleverest, it uses a Univac operating system to d more multiprogramming than seems decent.* New Scientist an Science Journal 12/2/71, p30 [**1959**]

multiracialism, *n.* a political or social system in which all raci groups are accorded equal rights and opportunities. *Whe progress there was toward multiracialism during the 1953-6 period when Southern Rhodesia was federated with what a* *now Zambia and Malawi is now being reversed.* NY Times 3/24/68, pD9 [**1958**]

multiresistant, *adj.* resistant to various antibiotics. *In the right environment such as the intestinal tracts of cattle being fed a number of different antibiotics, multiresistant strains develop rapidly.* Manchester Guardian Weekly 1/18/68, p7 [**1964**]

multispectral, *adj.* capable of sensing emissions from several spectra, especially from parts of the visible, infrared, and microwave spectra. *The possibility of aerial survey lies in multispectral photography, especially with infrared or "false" colour photography using a line scanner.* New Scientist and Science Journal 7/15/71, p122 [**1966**]

multitasking, *n.* the performance of two or more tasks concurrently by a computer. Compare SINGLE-TASKING. *Multitasking refers to a computer doing several things at once; for example, printing, copying and computing. Networking is the interaction of one computer with several others in an office, in a sort of electronic kaffeeklatsch. Both functions are pretty much limited to 16-bit machines.* NY Times 10/18/83, pC6 [**1966**, from *multi-* + *tasking*, gerund of *task, v.*]

multi-track, *v.t.* to record, especially on tape, on several sound tracks. *On Heart Food she is helped a lot by engineering, which has enabled her to multi-track her vocal lines.* Rolling Stone 5/24/73, p56 [**1972**, verb use of earlier (1950's) adjective, as in *multi-track recording*]

multiversity, *n. U.S.* a very large university made up of various divisions, extensions, campuses, etc. Also called POLYVERSITY. *The rebellion at Berkeley centered on the indifference of multiversity's mechanism to the personal needs of the students.* Saturday Review 3/2/68, p53 [**1963**, coined by Clark Kerr, born 1911, former president of the University of California, from *multi-* + *university*]

munchable, *Informal.* —*adj.* suitable for eating as a snack. *"Empty" calories? True. That's what makes things like . . . Planter's Cheese Curls so munchable and yet so steadfastly unsatisfying.* Washington Post 10/14/81, pB1 —*n.* Usually, **munchables,** *pl.* munchable food; snack. *They called it the Great Cookie War when two giant companies promoted their newest munchables in Kansas City in 1983.* Economist 8/3/85, p26 [**1980**]

munchies, *n.pl. U.S. Slang.* a desire for food, especially after smoking marijuana (often in the phrase *to have the munchies*). *If they have never heard the terms in Vietnam, the POW's will quickly learn about "bummers" ("unpleasant experiences, especially with drugs"), "joints" ("marijuana cigarettes, jays, j's, reefers") and "munchies" ("to be hungry, usually after ingesting marijuana").* Newsweek 2/12/73, p68 [**1971**, from earlier slang *munchie* (OEDS 1917) something to munch on, a snack]

muni ('myu:ni:), *n. U.S. Informal.* a municipal bond or other security issued by a city. *Paragon . . . mounted an expensive advertising campaign aimed at peddling "munis" to the masses and last year sold $750 million worth of securities.* Newsweek 1/13/73, p82 [**1973**, short for *municipal*]

muon ('myu:,ɑn), *n.* an unstable elementary particle that partakes of the weak reaction and has a mass about 207 times that of an electron. Compare KAON. *Except for the mass difference the muon does not appear to be any different from the electron.* Nature 7/14/72, p86 [**1953**, from *mu-*meson (former name of the *muon*) + *-on* elementary particle]

muonic (myu:'ɑnik), *adj.* of, containing, or producing muons. Compare KAONIC. *Extensive studies of the sizes and shapes of nuclei have been made using muonic atoms.* New Scientist 1/11/68, p92 [**1955**]

muonium (myu:'ouni:əm), *n.* an isotope of hydrogen consisting of a positively charged muon and an electron. *In many respects the muonium atom resembles the simplest ordinary atom, the atom of hydrogen which consists of a proton (p^+) and an electron. In fact muonium can be considered a lighter isotope of hydrogen. In both atoms the nucleus is a comparatively heavy positively charged particle (either a proton or a muon) that is*

surrounded by a much lighter negatively charged particle (an electron). Scientific American 4/66, p93 [**1957**]

Muppet, *n.* any of a group of puppets manipulated by the hands of one or more persons representing animal characters and people, which became popular in 1970 on the American television show for children *Sesame Street. In its simplest form a Muppet is a sleeve, one end of which is so stitched as to allow a human hand to operate as the thing's mouth; above that are sewn two glass eyes. How these lengths of felt are then transmuted into live, endearing individuated and, above all, hilariously funny characters I dare not begin to analyse. It cannot depend wholly on the skill of the hidden forearms responsible for the manipulation; maybe it is a magic inherent in the felt.* Times (London) 10/25/76, p10 [**1970**, alteration of *puppet;* coined by Jim Henson, who created this group of puppets]

murein ('myur,i:n), *n.* another word for MUCOPEPTIDE. *Murein contains an amino sugar, muramic acid, which is not found in higher organisms. . .* New Scientist 7/10/69, p64 [**1964**, from Latin *mūrus* wall + *-ein,* after *protein*]

Murphy game or **Murphy,** *n. U.S. Underworld Slang.* See the first quotation for the meaning. *"The Murphy game" is underworld argot for a slick maneuver in which a victim puts his cash in an envelope and gives it to the con man, who makes a fast sleight-of-hand switch and hands back an identical envelope stuffed with newspaper strips. It was named after an Irishman who was arrested many times for perpetrating such tricks.* Time 4/16/65, p16 *Everybody should have a car. . . How are you going to get it? You can get it selling drugs. You know, you can get it playing the Murphy.* NY Times 9/4/66, pD5 [**1959**]

Murphy's Law, any of various humorous rules of thumb. See the quotations for examples. *Your reference to Murphy's Law touches on only part of that ancient Irish potentate's laws. . . His set of the laws of life refer with circularity to nothing, everything and anything. They are: 1) nothing is as easy as it looks; 2) everything takes longer than you think it will; and 3) if anything can go wrong, it will.* Letter to the Editor, Time 4/13/70, p6 *Murphy's Law states that if it is possible to connect two things together the wrong way round, then someone will do it that way.* New Scientist 9/21/67, p601 *"Recently,"* [Roger] *Baker writes, "I learned of a governing principle known as Murphy's first law of biology. It states: 'Under any given set of environmental conditions an experimental animal behaves as it damn well pleases.' "* Scientific American 6/70, p143 [**1958**]

muscalure ('məskə,lur), *n.* the sex´ attractant of the female housefly, first isolated and identified in 1971. *Initial field tests of muscalure, a newly identified sex attractant for houseflies, showed that the attractant more than tripled the response of flies to several traps and baits.* 1974 Britannica Yearbook of Science and the Future, p159 [**1973**, from Latin *musca* fly + English *lure*]

muscle car, *Chiefly U.S.* a medium-sized automobile with a large engine and heavy-duty suspension system, designed for high power and speed. *. . . . a thunderous avalanche of Barracudas, G.T.O.s, Javelins, Challengers, Hondas, Harleys, Cougars, Vettes, pickups, Furys, Darts, choppers, and various aging muscle cars as the players and spectators come dragging out of the parking lot.* New Yorker 8/30/76, p28 [**1968**]

muscle pill, an informal name for ANABOLIC STEROID. *A group of West German sports doctors is challenging the Olympic ban on anabolic steroids, contending the "muscle pills" are harmless to physically mature athletes if dosages are carefully controlled.* NY Times 10/27/76, p48 [**1976**]

museque (mu:'seikei), *n.* a slum area in Angola. *Luanda has two faces. One is of a town of fine old colonial buildings and modern blocks of flats, built by the Portuguese for their own use. The other is of the museques, the sprawling shanty towns that encircle the city and which are rarely seen by whites except from the window of a passing car.* Times (London) 2/6/76, p14 [**1972**, from Portuguese]

musicassette ('myu:zəkæˌset), *n.* a small cassette of musical tape recordings. *As yet, of course, musicassettes are more for the uncritical listener to popular music (as the preponderance of pop in the cassette repertoire would indicate), the background-music listener, and those who want compact recordings they can play on battery portable machines.* Saturday Review 5/25/68, p50 [**1966**, from *music + cassette*]

Muslim, *n. U.S.* another name for BLACK MUSLIM. *He knows the alternatives: the Muslims and the black nationalists or, on the other hand, the ageless kind of self-abasement and self-delusion which he and others associate with the effort to beg and pray for a pittance here and there from the white man.* NY Times Magazine 4/21/68, p135 [**1961**, transferred use of the name for any follower of Islam]

mutagenicity (ˌmyu:tədʒəˈnisəti:), *n.* the inducement of mutations; the use of agents (mutagens) that cause genetic aberrations. . . . *chemical mutagenicity promises to become a boiling issue in the 1970's with controversies already having erupted over cyclamates, pesticides . . . and many other substances.* Science News 3/28/70, p314 [**1956**]

mutagenize ('myu:tədʒəˌnaiz), *v.t.* to induce mutation in. *Their approach was systematically to make individual tests on each of several hundreds of colonies from a heavily mutagenized stock of E. coli. This technique had already been successfully used to locate a mutant of E. coli lacking a ribonuclease activity.* Science Journal 3/70, p14 [**1966**]

mutual assured destruction, the full name of MAD. *Referring to reports and warnings issued by the more vigorous critics of SALT, Culver says, "One of their major pegs is that the Soviets do not share our strategic-nuclear-doctrine concepts of deterrence and mutual assured destruction. . ."* New Yorker 9/11/78, p51 [**1973**]

MX, *n.* an experimental intercontinental ballistic missile with multiple warheads, designed to be moved within underground tunnels. *Most ominous is the plan to develop the huge mobile ICBM, the MX, that would be equipped with as many as ten nuclear warheads. This deadly counterforce weapon would threaten Soviet ICBM forces and invite a similar response.* New York Review of Books 3/22/79, p38 [**1976**, from the abbreviation of *missile, experimental*]

my ('em'wai), abbreviation of *million years. Previously, evi-*

dence for rocks older than about 3400-3500 my, has been sketchy, with an age for a Minnesota gneiss of 3550 my. . .* New Scientist and Science Journal 12/2/71, p11 [**1969**]

mycotoxin, *n.* a poison produced by a fungus. *At the second* [symposium of the Third International Congress of Food Science and Technology] *participants discussed . . . the significance of aflatoxin and other mycotoxins.* New Scientist 9/17/70, p578 [**1962**, from *myco-* (from Greek *mýkēs* fungus) + *toxin*]

myoelectric, *adj.* using electric currents produced by muscular contraction to actuate movement of an artificial limb, such as an arm or a hand. *Most other myoelectric controlled prostheses require two sets of electrodes, one for opening and another for closing.* Science 1/71, p13 [**1955**, from *myo-* (from Greek *mŷs* muscle) + *electric*]

myotherapy, *n.* the application of pressure to relieve muscular pain. *Myotherapy was described as a refinement, an enlargement and a jelling of Dr. Hans Kraus' trigger point injection theory, acupressure, biofeedback and other pain relief methods.* Medical Tribune 1/14/81, p1 [**1980**, coined by Bonnie Prudden, an American physical therapist, from *myo-* muscle (from Greek *myós*) + *therapy*]

mysterium, *n.* a hydroxyl radical identified as emitter of a distinctive pattern of radio frequencies in several regions of the Milky Way. *In fact, one of the first groups to discover the hydroxyl line named it "mysterium" because they did not believe it could be hydroxyl emission.* Scientific American 10/67, p50 [**1965**]

myth, *v.t.* to make mythical; turn into or contrive a myth. *Edward Plowman also observes that "in the drug scene many kids develop a spiritual awareness. . . They believe in a spiritual reality. They've seen visions and demons. Thus a conservative Christianity, which hasn't mythed away God and angels, appeals to them."* Time 8/3/70, p31 [**1970**, verb use of the noun]

mythogenic, *adj.* of or having to do with the forming of myths. *Religious institutions are now disintegrating, the two researchers believe, because religion has cut itself off from its "principal sources of nourishment—the soul, the symbolic and mythogenic process, the psychic energy resources."* Time 10/5/70, p73 [**1964**, formed as an adjective to *mythogenesis* (1887)]

N

NAA, abbreviation of NEUTRON ACTIVATION ANALYSIS. *NAA has already been used in the crime laboratory to detect counterfeit ancient Roman and Greek coins, which are a lucrative field for forgers. The procedure can also detect coins that are genuinely ancient but were forgeries when they were first made. In addition, NAA can detect forged stamps.* 1969 Collier's Encyclopedia Year Book, p164 [**1964**]

NAAQS, abbreviation of *National Ambient Air Quality Standards. NAAQS were established for such pollutants as sulfur dioxide, nitrogen dioxide, hydrocarbons, carbon monoxide, photochemical oxidants (smog formers), and particulate matter. These standards will probably be tightened.* 1979 Collier's Encyclopedia Year Book, p245 [**1978**]

nacho ('natʃou), *n., pl.* **nachos.** a taco tortilla or chip baked with cheese and Mexican pepper. *A recent meal began with nachos, the appetizer made with cheese and beans and chilies baked on tortillas; fried Spanish sausage; and guacamole.* NY Times 4/30/71, p22 [**1967**, from Mexican Spanish]

NAD, abbreviation of *nicotinamide adenine dinucleotide*, an electron-carrying coenzyme necessary for the conversion of glucose to alcohol and for the removal of hydrogen from compounds. *During alcohol metabolism, the ratio of $NADH_2$ to NAD increases. Since the availability of the hydrogen acceptor NAD is important for the dehydrogenation of alcohol to acetaldehyde, the resulting $NADH_2$ must be continually reoxidized back to NAD by other oxidation-reduction reactions.* New Scientist 11/30/67, p540 [**1961**]

Naderism ('neidər,izəm), *n.* another name for CONSUMERISM. *The phenomenon [consumerism] was also called "Naderism," because of the successful crusades of a young lawyer, Ralph Nader, against unsafe automobiles, industrial hazards, and environmental pollution.* Americana Annual 1970, p725 . . . *it will be interesting to see whether the thinking behind the Sherman and Clayton Acts (to say nothing of militant Naderism) eventually penetrates the Brussels bureaucracy.* New Scientist and Science Journal 8/19/71, p431 *Naderism was not for Britain.* Times (London) 3/2/72, p10 [**1969**, from Ralph *Nader*, born 1934, U.S. lawyer engaged in consumer protection + *-ism*]

Naderite ('neidə,rait), *n.* an advocate of consumerism, especially one who follows methods used and advocated by Ralph Nader. *Lowell F. Jones, a businessman in Minnesota who ran afoul of the consumerists a couple of years back, has a horrifying tale to tell. The Naderites play plenty rough.* . . National Review 5/10/74, p507 **—adj.** of or relating to the form of consumer protection practiced and advocated by Ralph Nader and his group. *Although British consumerists like to feel they can tub-thump with the best of them, it's noticeable that our brand of consumerism is generally very much more respectable than the American Naderite sort.* Listener 7/12/73, p67 *Of dispute there is plenty, with strong contributions and interjections from such inexorable critics as . . . James Turner, Naderite author of The Chemical Feast, and founder and co-director of Consumer Action for Improved Food and Drugs.* New Scientist 8/8/74, p345 [**1972**, from Ralph *Nader* + *-ite;* see NADERISM]

naff, *v.i.* **naff off**, British Slang. go away; beat it; disappear. . . . *the Queen via her press staff, gave editors a short, sharp and public "request" to tell the scribes and telephoto lens artists who had been plaguing the royals at Sandringham to naff off.* Economist 1/7/84, p44 [**1983**]

Nahal (na:'ha:l), *n.* **1** a branch of the Israeli army. See the quotation for details. *The casualties were soldiers belonging to Nahal, an élite corps which combines military training with the establishment of agricultural settlements in exposed or remote areas.* Times (London) 12/31/70, p6 **2** Also spelled **nahal.** a settlement established by Nahal. *In practice, Israel has already founded six "Nahals"—agricultural settlements manned by soldiers—at points in or near the Jordan Valley. . .* Manchester Guardian Weekly 3/28/70, p13 *For that reason, the government has established there a necklace of nahals, fortified camps manned by young Israelis who are equally able to farm or to fight.* Time 1/4/71, p28 [**1961** for def. 1; **1968** for def. 2; from Modern Hebrew acronym for "youth pioneers and fighters"]

nail bomb, a homemade explosive consisting of nails tied around sticks of dynamite. *A nail bomb looks very much like half a brick and often the only means of distinguishing between a stone-thrower and a nail-bomber is that a light enough stone may be thrown with a flexed elbow whereas a nail bomb is usually thrown with a straight arm as in a bowling action.* Times (London) 4/20/72, p5 [**1970**] **—nail bomber:** *The lives of the soldiers were at risk from attendant snipers and nail bombers.* Manchester Guardian Weekly 4/29/72, p6

naira ('nairə), *n.* a unit of money in Nigeria. See the quotation for details. *On Jan. 1, 1973, Nigeria will scrap her system of Nigerian pounds, shillings and pence, borrowed from her colonial ruler, Britain, and begin a decimal currency system with units of money called the naira and the kobo. . . The naira—the name is adapted from the word Nigeria—will be the major unit of exchange and will have a value about half that of the current Nigerian pound, or $1.53.* NY Times 8/9/72, p14 [**1972**]

naive, *adj.* **1** not having or showing formal training, techniques, etc., in art; lacking artistic sophistication. *"Curious paradox: the youngest among the world's great powers . . . the United States possesses the oldest, the most original, and just about the most authentic naive painters," admitted Paris' Figaro Littéraire with an air of astonishment. The show consisted of 111 naive American paintings from the collection of Edgar William and Bernice Chrysler Garbisch. . .* Time 2/9/70, p54 **2** not previously subjected to a test, experiment, etc.; unconditioned. *The experiments just described have shown that fear of the dark, acquired by training, can be transferred to naïve animals by material extracted from the brain of trained donors.* Nature 3/30/68, p1261 [**1957** for def. 1; **1961** for def. 2]

naked ape, a human being. *Honest adults who can still remember themselves when young will probably have difficulty recalling anyone more revolting whom they met in later life. The transient ambition of the adolescent naked ape is to live a life of high tragedy. Parents, therefore, should never try to understand their offspring.* New Scientist 10/22/70, p161 [**1967**, a term popularized by the British anthropologist Desmond Morris in his book *The Naked Ape* (1967)]

naked call, U.S. an option to buy a stock or other security not actually owned by the seller. *So far this month there have been more than enough buyers to snap up the shares. Some were speculators who had sold "naked calls"—that is, speculators had sold to other investors options to buy at pre-fixed prices that the sellers of the options did not own. As the deadline approached two weeks ago for the options to be exercised, the option sellers had to rush into the market.* Time 2/2/76, p52 [**1976**]

naloxone (næl'aksoun), *n.* a chemical substance that acts as an antagonist to narcotics by blocking the nerve receptor sites that absorb the narcotics. *Formula:* $C_{19}H_{21}NO_4$ Compare

NALTREXONE. *An antagonist, such as naloxone, is chemically similar to a specific drug—in this case, morphine. When given to an addict, it blocks the euphoria usually produced by heroin, or the analgesic effect of morphine.* Newsweek 3/19/73, p55 *The experimenters found they could reverse the effects of the beta-endorphin, which has some of the characteristics of morphine, by injecting naloxone, a chemical used as an antidote for morphine overdose.* NY Times 11/7/76, pD7 [**1964,** from *N-al* lyl*nor*oxymorph*o*ne, the chemical name]

naltrexone (næl'treksoun), *n.* a nontoxic chemical substance used experimentally as an antagonist of narcotics. *Formula:* $C_{20}H_{23}NO_4$ Compare NALOXONE. See also CLONIDINE. *Multiple emulsions (oil in water in oil) containing the narcotic antagonist Naltrexone are being developed as "timed-release" drug systems for addicts. Naltrexone blocks the opiate "high," but must be injected too frequently for successful use in outpatient treatment centers.* Science News 4/17/76, p246 [**1973,** from the chemical components *N-al* lyl + *-trex-* (as in *methotrexate*) + *-one* (chemical suffix)]

name, *n.* **the name of the game,** the essential thing; the thing that really counts. *Well, all right, I said. The name of the game is trust; you've got to trust things.* James Dickey, Deliverance, 1970, p206 *"Some of them [refugees] have slipped back to the Pathet Lao," said an American official at the time, "but we have rounded up most of the population, and the name of the game is control of the population."* Atlantic 7/71, p10 [**1966,** from the fact that in certain games, especially card games, the game's object is expressed by its name, as in the expressions *to have gin, to get twenty-one, to call rummy,* etc.]

Namibian, *adj.* of or belonging to Namibia, the name by which African nationalists call the territory of South-West Africa (after *Namib,* the coastal desert area) in the Republic of South Africa. *Proponents of Namibian independence accuse South Africa of genocide and racial extermination, claiming that blacks are herded into "concentration camps" to be killed off as a result of inadequate medical attention.* Time 7/5/71, p27 —*n.* a native of Namibia. *We as sponsors of the Friends of Namibia Committee, on the third anniversary of the Namibians' imprisonment, appeal for their release and repatriation.* Manchester Guardian Weekly 2/20/71, p2 [**1968**]

nannofossil ('nænou,fasəl), *n.* a small or microscopic fossil. *Up to 60 percent of the rock consists of nannofossils, relics of the smallest kinds of plankton, according to a report by Robert E. Garrison of the University's geology department.* Science News 10/7/67, p348 [**1963,** from *nanno-* very small (variant of NANO-) + *fossil*]

nano-, combining form meaning "one billionth," used in units of measurement involving submicroscopic objects, velocities, etc., as in the following examples. —**nanoequivalent,** *adj.: Coulometric analysis is the quantitative determination of materials by measuring the amount of electricity necessary for their complete reaction. . . Accuracy and precision compare favorably with other methods and range from a few hundredths of a per cent at the hundred microequivalent level under ideal conditions to approximately 10% at the five nanoequivalent level.* McGraw-Hill Yearbook of Science and Technology 1967, p146 —**nanometer,** *n.: . . . A typical clay particle could be shaped like a flat plate 100nm × 1000nm × 10nm covered by a water layer 200nm thick (1 nanometer is $10^{-9}m$).* Science 1/71, p79 —**nanomole,** *n.: Most, if not all, effects result from block of conduction in nerve axons. Conduction is blocked in isolated, desheathed frog sciatic nerves by a solution [of tetrodotoxin, a poisonous compound] containing about 3 nanomoles per liter.* McGraw-Hill Yearbook of Science and Technology 1968, p387 —**nanowatt,** *n.: The new COS/MOS units, on the other hand, operate on nanowatts of power in the quiescent state and use greater power only during the instant of switching information.* Scientific American 3/68, p17 [from Greek *nânos* (and Latin *nānus* dwarf)]

nanoamp ('nænou,æmp), *n.* one billionth (10^{-9}) of an ampere. *Rats with induced currents of between 5 and 15 nanoamps in amputated limbs quite definitely achieve a striking degree of organised recovery and partial regeneration compared with*

controls. New Scientist 1/20/72, p127 [**1972,** from NANO- + *amp,* short for *ampere*]

nanoatom ('nænou,ætəm), *n.* one billionth (10^{-9}) of an atom of any element. *The initial rate of respiration was 216 nanoatoms of oxygen per minute. The addition of 0.1 mM glucose induced an increased rate of oxidation (270 nanoatoms per minute) which lasted approximately 50 seconds.* Science 10/13/72, p127 [**1972,** from NANO- + *atom*]

nanosurgery, *n.* surgery performed on microscopic parts of cells, tissues, etc., under an electron microscope. *Informed researchers believe that as equipment grows more sophisticated, tomorrow's surgeons will use such mind-defying techniques as nanosurgery, 10,000 times finer than the microsurgery now employed in pediatrics, and dependent on improvements in electron-microscopy and laser instrumentation now under study in the United States and France.* Encyclopedia Science Supplement (Grolier) 1967, p181 [**1967**]

Napoleonism, *n.* the policy of a ruler or a country of assuming unlimited control over subject peoples or nations. . . . *the traditional Latin American leader's custom of renouncing ultimate power as soon as he had won it (for fear of accusations of "Napoleonism"), were less significant than the internal political and social divisions.* Sunday Times (London) 4/6/69, p27 *Without our nation standing up against Russia's modern day mad dog Napoleonism Europe itself would not remain independent through the 1970s.* Manchester Guardian Weekly 6/6/70, p2 [**1966,** originally (1800's) applied to Napoleon I and his dynasty]

narc or **nark,** *n. U.S. Slang.* a federal narcotics agent. *I guess you know this town is on a bum trip—narcs everywhere and no good weed going unpunished.* New Yorker 2/21/70, p34 *Most speed freaks get to a point where they're seeing narks in the trees with cameras. . .* NY Times 10/17/67, p44 [**1967,** shortened from *narcotic agent* or *detective*] ▶By coincidence the British slang term for a police informer is also *nark.* The latter, however, came from Romany (the Gypsy language) *nāk,* meaning nose, and has been used since the 1800's.

narco-terrorism, *n.* terrorist practices used by narcotics smugglers and dealers against government interdiction. *Narco-terrorism . . . originated in the "Golden Triangle," the opium-producing areas of Burma, Thailand, and Laos, but reached a new high in the 1980's in certain Latin-American countries.* 1987 Collier's Encyclopedia Year Book, p95 [**1987,** from *narcotics* + *terrorism*]

narrative art, another name for STORY ART. Jean Le Gac— *Photographs and printed commentary (the genre has been labelled "narrative art") by a French practitioner who works in the touching belief that the time and effort required of the viewer to digest his lengthy captions and relate them to the pictures is well spent.* New Yorker 2/2/76, p11 [**1975**]

narrowcasting, *n. U.S.* transmission of television programs by cable; CABLECASTING. *Arnie Rosenthal's "The Big Giveaway," New York cable television's first game show, began live narrowcasting on public-leased Channel J from a Manhattan Cable TV studio on East Twenty-third Street to eighty thousand apartments and houses and eight thousand hotel rooms and a couple hundred bars on the southern half of Manhattan Island.* New Yorker 3/15/76, p26 [**1972,** from *narrow* + *-casting,* as in *broadcasting,* because of the limited range of cable transmission] ▶This term has been in existence for over thirty years, although not in the sense recorded here. In the Fall 1978 issue of *American Speech* ("Among the New Words," p. 217), I. Willis Russell and Mary Gray Porter traced the word back to 1948 as "a term used by its opponents to describe subscription radio."

NASDAQ ('næz,dæk), *n. U.S.* acronym for *National Association of Securities Dealers Automated Quotations,* a computerized information system providing price quotations on securities traded over the counter. *At least 30,000 publicly traded over-the-counter issues remain outside the NASDAQ system, an association spokesman estimated. For these securities, the primary source of data is the National Quotation Bureau, which* compiles quotations from about 750 securities dealers. NY Times 12/29/76, p37 [**1968**]

nasty, n. a nasty person or thing. *Starring Jean-Paul Belmondo and Alain Delon as two lovable crooks in prewar Marseilles, the film has had enormous success in Paris and elsewhere and hits London while the iron is hot. Nice nasties are de rigueur these days.* Manchester Guardian Weekly 8/8/70, p21 . . . *Nasties—they're the newest social force, waiting in the wings to displace the last 1960s social force, the Flower People. They've always been around, the Nasties—disguised as merely unpleasant people, as persons with hateful, mean, offensive characters.* Saturday Night (Canada) 2/68, p27 [**1935, 1959**, noun use of the adjective]

national lakeshore, *U.S.* a recreational area adjoining a lakeshore, preserved and administered by the Federal government. *The nation's first National Lakeshore, Indiana Dunes on the shores of Lake Michigan, was established on September 8.* 1973 World Book Year Book, p282 [**1972**]

Native American, *U.S.* an American Indian. *The Indians . . . have suffered a great deal from the white man, though of course they suffered a great deal from fellow Native Americans before whitey arrived. And not all the statistics are exactly genocidal in their implications.* National Review 4/27/73, p487 *There were disappointed minorities—black, Spanish-speakers, Native Americans—who had felt that the partisanship the privileged, young upper middle class had shown during the civil rights movement in the 1950s and 1960s had been insincere, self-indulgent and fleeting.* Margaret Mead, Culture and Commitment, 1978, p110 ►This name was popularized in the early 1970's by civil-rights activists and perhaps derives from *Native American Church* (known since the early 1950's), referring to a religious denomination of American Indians which combines traditional Indian beliefs and rituals with Christianity.

Ironically, the name *Native American* was used in the 1840's to refer to a member of the Know-Nothing political party (the Native American Party) whose aim was to keep control of the U.S. government in the hands of native-born citizens.

In the southwestern United States, *Native American* (DA 1811) has been used to refer to Spanish-speaking residents of European ancestry.

natural killer cell, another term for KILLER CELL. *Natural-killer cells have long been thought to be part of the body's immune system. Scientists theorize that the appearance of a malignant cell in the body normally arouses the killer cells, which . . . destroy the cancerous cell. Interferon not only helps recruit these defensive cells but also magnifies their destructive power.* World Book Science Annual 1981, p298 [**1979**]

nautical archaeology, the branch of archaeology that deals with the recovery and study of historic or ancient objects (as those found in shipwrecks) from beneath the sea. *The first move in making nautical archaeology in Britain a true academic discipline and establishing an appropriate university qualification is the inauguration of an Institute of Maritime Archaeology at the University of St. Andrews.* New Scientist 6/28/73, p825 [**1972**]

NC, abbreviation of NUMERICAL CONTROL. Compare APT (def. 3). *Milling and drilling operations were the most common NC applications, followed by turning operations. Many other NC systems were used in wire manufacturing, flame cutting, gas and arc welding . . . plating, metal grinding, glass cutting . . . and complex metal contouring.* Britannica Book of the Year 1970, p421 [**1966**]

nebbish, n. a person who is pitifully unfortunate. . . . *the center of the play is Mr. Gammell's black-comedy Hitler. He starts as a bandy-legged nebbish: jumpy, up tight, the least-likely-to-succeed mobster you have ever seen.* NY Times 8/8/68, p28 —adj. pitifully unfortunate. *The central character is so nebbish he has not even a name.* Times (London) 4/6/68, p21 . . . *a perversion, a monstrous contained exultation . . . is manifested in certain daredevils, paranoid psychopaths who, after nebbish lives, suddenly feel themselves invulnerable in the certain wooing of sweet death.* . . Atlantic 9/69, p57 [**1959**, from

the Yiddish interjection *nebekh* pitiful, a pity, probably from a Slavic word related to Czech *nebohy* poor, Polish *niebożę* poor devil]

necklace, *v.t.* (in South Africa) to kill by setting fire to a gasoline-soaked tire placed around the victim's neck. *"The comrades executed many of those suspected collaborators, often by 'necklacing' them. . ."* World Book Year Book 1987, p470 [**1987**]

Neddy, n. *British.* nickname for the National Economic Development Council of Great Britain. Compare LITTLE NEDDY. *A Neddy-sponsored questionnaire sent out to 2,000 firms in the wool trade, is the first phase of a £80,000 survey designed to establish the competitiveness of the British wool textile industry and how it can increase profitability.* Times (London) 4/18/68, p21 [**1962**, alteration of the abbreviation *NEDC* for National Economic Development Council]

needle, n. **1** a spur, goad, or stimulus. . . . *there is plenty of time for the newer helmsmen to come to the fore. One hopes they do, for without the constant needle of improving competition the men at the top will find it difficult to improve any further.* Times (London) 3/16/70, p8 **2** a barbed or sarcastic remark. *More than* [Will] *Rogers,* [Bob] *Hope has become the friend of politicians and statesmen, tycoons and sportsmen. . . He kids the starch out of them, and they feel better for it; a needle from Hope becomes an emblem instead of a scar.* Time 12/22/67, p48 **3** the needle, *Especially U.S. Slang.* narcotic drugs. *James Baldwin also told him* [Daniel Snowman]: *'When I was growing up in the streets of Harlem, most of my generation—for reasons I had no difficulty to discover—perished on the needle . . . by and by, white kids—sons and daughters of Pan Am, sons and daughters of General Electric—. . . they hit the needle, too.'* Listener 10/17/68, p505 *"She is inscrutable. How she managed to protect her children is a mystery. None of us has been in prison. None has been on the needle."* NY Times 6/3/63, p19 **4** thread the needle, to accomplish a difficult task. . . . *Mr. Udall . . . expressed hope that the committee "can succeed in making the compromises and threading the needle" to get authorization for the central Arizona plan, which conservation groups have fought successfully so far.* NY Times 1/27/67, p13 [**1955**]

needle therapy, another name for ACUPUNCTURE. *In the intervening days, I found acupuncture to be almost a part of the dove-gray Paris air. Every day I met someone who was either going or had gone for needle therapy.* Saturday Review 2/19/72, p47 [**1972**]

needle time, *British.* (in radio broadcasting) the programmed air time devoted to recorded music. *The pirate radio broadcasters, who escaped the restrictions of "needle time" (limitation on the broadcasting of records imposed under British copyright legislation), claimed large audiences among young listeners for their round-the-clock output of "pop" music interspersed with advertising.* Britannica Book of the Year 1967, p723 [**1962**]

negabinary (ˈnegəˌbainəri:), *adj., n.* (expressing) a negative binary number. *The answer to the question about negabinary palindromes is that the smallest composite number that is palindromic in negabinary is 21. Its plus form is 10101, its minus form is 111111.* Scientific American 5/73, p105 [**1973**, from *nega*tive + *binary*]

negative euthanasia, another name for PASSIVE EUTHANASIA. *Negative euthanasia refers to withdrawal of treatment from a patient who as a result is likely to die somewhat earlier than he otherwise would. . . Many of those who favor negative euthanasia also recognize that appropriate care of the terminally ill may include "positive" procedures, such as giving morphine, (which, among other effects, may advance the moment of death).* Scientific American 9/73, p60 [**1972**]

negative income tax or **negative tax,** direct payments by the government to any family or individual whose income falls below a specified level, often proposed as a replacement for present welfare programs in the United States. *Abbreviation:* NIT Also called GUARANTEED ANNUAL INCOME or GUARANTEED INCOME. . . . *the unemployed in the United States have* begun to demand not just the right to work but a guaranteed annual income whether they work or not. Far from being considered a shocking proposal, the idea has been advanced independently by middle-class reformers under the somewhat specious label of the "negative income tax." New Yorker 10/31/70, p54 *This coupled with his* [the Chancellor of the Exchequer's] *proposal to investigate and discuss publicly the tax-credit system, more commonly known as negative income tax.* Times (London) 5/5/72, p17 **[1967]**

negative interest, *Finance.* money deducted from or paid on interest. *Treasury bills are now 7.5% to 8.5% on an annual basis, CDs slightly higher. But inflation is at 12% to 13%. So you have a negative interest rate that swells the demand for credit.* Forbes 8/15/74, p27 *Switzerland, traditional safe citadel for flight capital from all over the world, two weeks ago in effect slammed shut its bank vaults to foreigners. Among other things, it ordered banks to charge foreigners 40% a year "negative interest" for the privilege of keeping deposits in Swiss francs.* Time 3/20/78, p61 **[1973]**

negative option, the choice one has of keeping and paying for or accepting the obligations of an unsolicited product received in the mail or of returning it to the sender. The practice is also called INERTIA SELLING in Great Britain. *Unsolicited credit cards may be new to Great Britain, but they are notorious—and illegal—in the US. The chaos that followed the launches of the US versions of Access several years ago brought such a public outcry that two years ago today a law took effect banning unsolicited cards. Even the negative option or inertia selling technique used by Lloyds Bank, where the consumer has 10 days to refuse the card, is banned in the U.S.* New Scientist 10/26/72, p206 **[1972]**

négociant (neigɔ:'syã), *n. French.* dealer; merchant. *It used to be practicable for French negociants to hold wines in their cellars until they had matured and could be sold for almost immediate drinking.* Manchester Guardian Weekly 5/16/70, p17 **[1955]** ►As used in English, the meaning of the word is close to being "a wine dealer," equivalent to French *négociant en vins.*

negritude ('negrə,tu:d), *n.* **1** the distinctive qualities or characteristics of Negroes, especially African Negroes. Also called NEGRONESS or BLACKNESS. . . . *the whole-hearted attempt by other Negroes to emphasize their Negroid features and hair texture shows their pride in their "negritude"—a word currently in fashion in Negro communities.* Time 8/27/65, p19 **2** pride in the cultural and artistic heritage of Negroes, especially African Negroes. *One is forced to conclude that the noble doctrine of negritude, the poetizing of what is best in the Black African tradition to achieve a world-wide communion among Negroes meanders all too frequently into this area of racial hatred.* Saturday Review 6/11/66, p69 **[1950,** from French *négritude,* literally, the condition of being a Negro**]**

Negroness, *n.* the condition or quality of being Negro. Also called BLACKNESS or NEGRITUDE. *"The Negroness that we are is there. There's no way to get out of it."* NY Times 4/24/66, p17 **[1946, 1958]**

Nehru, *n.* a Nehru jacket or coat. *Mr. Goring will sell the men's bags, but he will "emphatically not" wear them. "On the other hand, I wouldn't wear Nehrus or those damn beads either, so you can't go by me," he said.* NY Times 6/6/68, p50 **[1968]**

Nehru jacket or **Nehru coat,** a long, narrow jacket or coat with a high collar. Also called MAO JACKET. *Variations on the narrow "Nehru" jacket with the stand-up collar continue. . .* NY Times 5/24/67, p46 *Those who feel that tuxedos are old-fashioned are trying out the long mandarin-collared Mao or Nehru coats.* Time 3/1/68, p43 **[1967,** named after Jawaharlal Nehru 1889-1964, prime minister of India, who wore this type of jacket or coat**]**

Nehru suit, a suit consisting of a Nehru jacket and tight pants. *Mr. Tillotson, a tall, mustached man, appeared unperturbed in black Nehru suit with gold neck chain and white ruffles at cuffs and neck. . .* NY Times 6/24/68, p42 **[1963]**

nellie, *adj. Slang.* feminine; effeminate. . . . *it* ["The Boys in the Band"] *was also full of lachrymose seriousness about the miseries and heartbreaks of homosexuality. It was like "The Women," but with a forties-movie bomber-crew cast: a Catholic, a Jew, a Negro, a butch faggot, a nellie fagot, a hustler, and so on. . .* New Yorker 3/21/70, p166 **[1971,** from the feminine name *Nellie,* nickname of *Helen*]

Nelly, *n.* **not on your Nelly,** *British Slang.* certainly not; not likely; not on your life. . . . *Home said "that would mean me investing in another man's career. Not on your Nelly!"* Sunday Times (London) 5/15/66, p9 **[1941, 1961,** shortened from *not on your Nelly Duff,* rhyming slang for *not on your puff,* "puff" being a little-known slang word for "(breath of) life." There is a vulgar tinge to *not on your Nelly,* probably left over from *Nelly Duff, duff* being a slang word for the buttocks.**]**

Nemesis, *n. Astronomy.* a hypothetical companion star to the sun that may create disturbances in the earth's atmosphere; DEATH STAR. *They suggested that this star, which became known as Nemesis, follows an elongated orbit around the sun that takes it through the Oort cloud every 26 million to 30 million years. . . According to this theory, the gravitational pull of Nemesis disturbs the orbits of the comets, sending some of them hurtling down to Earth.* 1986 World Book Year Book, p108 **[1984,** named after *Nemesis,* Greek goddess of retribution and vengeance**]**

neo-, combining form meaning "new" or "new version of," attached chiefly to names or designations of doctrines, beliefs, theories, systems, etc. New compounds formed with *neo-* include: **—neoconservative,** *adj.: Judaism and Christianity have always placed primacy in man. Now this primacy is being attacked by what I call the neoconservative ecological approach to life.* Time 8/23/71, p31 **—neofeminist,** *n.:* "Are you still against abortion?" [Ellen] *Willis* [a rock critic] *asks, alluding to a position I had once taken which gave me, for a time, some small notoriety among the rest of the neo-feminists.* Harper's 11/69, p28 **—neo-Maoist,** *adj.: If a neo-Maoist China is to take shape after the cultural revolution and the ninth congress one can say that it is still very murky and that its institutional life is not in sight yet.* Times (London) 2/21/70, p7 **—neonationalism,** *n.: . . . that signs that "middle-class radicalism and neo-nationalism" were growing in West Germany could no longer be denied.* NY Times 5/11/68, p13 **—neopopulism,** *n.: Once dismissed as a racist demagogue, Alabama Gov. George Wallace brings a quirky but potent neopopulism to 1972 Presidential politics—as witnessed by his triumph in the Florida Democratic primary.* Newsweek 3/27/72, p3 **—neorevisionist,** *adj.: One of the Maoists' main targets is the Marxist Communist Party, branded by Peking as neorevisionist to distinguish it from the pro-Moscow Communist Party.* Times (London) 2/26/70, p6 **—neorevisionist,** *n.: . . . the Indian Marxists have often been denounced by Radio Peking as "neo-revisionists."* Manchester Guardian Weekly 7/18/70, p5 See also the main entries below.

neoantigen, *n.* an immunity-stimulating protein formed in a cell infected by a slow virus. *Immune complexes of antibody and circulating neoantigens are deposited and lead to inflammation, as in lupus nephritis. Antibody may also combine with neoantigens on tissue cells . . . so that inflammation results in various tissues.* McGraw-Hill Yearbook of Science and Technology 1975, p240 **[1971,** from *neo-* new + *antigen*]

neocolonial, *adj.* supporting or practicing neocolonialism. *At one session with the press—before the discovery of the Vietcong camp—he* [Prince Sihanouk] *passionately denounced the United States for ever coming to Vietnam as "a military and neocolonial power". . .* New Yorker 1/13/68, p86 **—n.** a neocolonial power. *For many Africans, he* [Moise Tshombe, then premier of Katanga, Republic of the Congo] *became a symbol of the "neocolonials" (the Belgians) and the "imperialists" (the Americans).* NY Times 7/5/67, p12 **[1961** for adj.; **1965** for noun**]**

neoconservatism, *n.* a moderate form of conservatism that favors many liberal reforms while opposing big government and that often sides with business interests on political and economic issues. *What is not often realized, however, is how much of* *the currently fashionable "neoconservatism" is made possible by the rapid exertions of government in the recent past to meet the real problems of this society.* Manchester Guardian Weekly (Washington Post section) 2/5/78, p15 *A cluster of mandarins, including the Harvard triumvirate of Nathan Glazer, Daniel Bell and James Q. Wilson, and New York's tart-tongued Sen. Daniel Patrick Moynihan modulated their New Deal progressivism into a cautious new social critique, dubbed "neoconservatism" by socialist Michael Harrington.* Newsweek 11/19/79, p95 **[1960]**

neoconservative, *U.S. —adj.* of or characterized by neoconservatism. *To be sure, there are signs of change in the intellectual community. A few neoconservative intellectuals like Irving Kristol, Edward Banfield, and Pat Moynihan are leaning in the New Majority direction.* Harper's 6/73, p70 **—n.** an adherent or advocate of neoconservatism. *The neoconservatives' claim that big government tends to become unpopular and eventually illegitimate deserves more attention than liberals or radicals have given it. Unfortunately, it also deserves more attention than neoconservatives have given it.* NY Times Book Review 7/1/79, p17 **[1964]**

neo-Dada, *n.* a movement which rejects traditional art forms or theories in contemporary art. Also called NEO-DADAISM. *Abstraction, neo-Dada and other up-to-date tendencies can be seen flourishing among "unofficial" works of the younger generation.* NY Times 10/13/67, p24 . . . *the appeal of "anti-art" was irresistible to many young art students, and critics now gravely talk about neo-Dada . . . however, it is not the label that matters but the wit and talent that may go into these assemblages of discarded objects.* Atlantic 2/66, p94 **[1962,** from NEO- + *Dada* movement in art and literature (OEDS 1916) which rejected conventional standards and values, ultimately from French meaning hobbyhorse]

neo-Dadaism, *n.* another name for NEO-DADA. *Perhaps a change in the air encouraged . . . the recent revival of surrealism and neo-Dadaism.* Times (London) 7/16/66, p7 **[1960]**

neoexpressionism, *n.* a style of painting characterized by bold forms, strong color and a crude and heavy technique. It is a reaction to minimalism and began to appear in the late 1970's. *While the imagery of neoexpressionism is always in some degree representational, it otherwise has nothing in common with contemporary Realism.* NY Times 7/12/81, pD23 **—neoexpressionist,** *n.: Meanwhile, the art establishment embraced the Neoexpressionists, with major shows of Eric Fischl at the Whitney . . ., Enzo Cucchi at the Guggenheim, and David Salle at the Philadelphia Institute of Contemporary Art.* 1987 Collier's Encyclopedia Year Book, p138 **—neoexpressionist,** *adj.: Neo-expressionist painters Eric Fischl and David Salle, both in their 30's, had museum surveys of their bold, representational work.* 1987 World Book Year Book, p197 **[1961]**

neoglacial, *adj.* of or relating to the formation of new glaciers, or readvance of older glaciers, particularly during the so-called Little Ice Age in the northern hemisphere between 1600 and 1850. *Carbon-14 dates of vegetation, peat or soil overrun by glacier ice provide direct ages for neoglacial advances, and dating of organic matter in recessional or advance deposits associated with neoglacial moraines may provide important limiting ages.* Scientific American 6/70, p105 **[1960]**

neoimperial, *adj.* of or characterized by neoimperialism. Also, NEOIMPERIALIST. *This analysis could embrace not just neoimperial China and neoimperial Russia.* NY Times 3/17/68, pD12 **[1968]**

neoimperialism, *n.* a revival or recurrence of imperialism. *Their* [the Moorish kings'] *rule was broken by the French conquest in the 19th century, but Morocco still claims its former lands, including much of the Algerian Sahara, the northern parts of Senegal and Mali and all of Mauritania. Morocco's territorial claims are plainly unacceptable to its neighbors, who brand them "neo-imperialism," and embarrassing to its friends.* Time 2/17/67, p24 **[1957]**

neoimperialist, *n.* one who supports neoimperialism. *I believe that, in fact, we are in danger of seeing the isolationists of the*

1920s and 1930s replaced by the neoimperialists, who somehow imagine that the United States has a mandate to impose an American solution the world around. Atlantic 1/67, p55 **[1956]**

neoism (ˈniːoʊˌizəm), *n.* newness as a value in politics, art, and the like. *Now, too, the troubled consciences are evident in the electoral campaigns, where new and old philosophies are competing against each other, within the Republican Party and on the school board. In these two areas, political ideals nowadays are sold as "pragmatism" and "neo-ism" (which means that as long as what a candidate says sounds new and practical, it should not matter to voters that he or she doesn't have a coherent set of values).* Washington Post 8/29/82, pC8 **[1982]**

neoisolationism, *n.* a revival or recurrence of isolationism. *More than one high official has expressed concern that disillusionment about the Indochina War and preoccupation with domestic ills will bring on neoisolationism in the United States.* Atlantic 1/71, p4 *He* [Richard M. Nixon] *is still very much the internationalist . . . at a time when neo-isolationism is spreading through the country.* Harper's 1/68, p23 **[1952]**

neoisolationist, *adj.* of or characterized by neoisolationism. *This month's magazine offers a considerable dose of anti-neoisolationist nourishment: two articles on Egypt and the Middle East situation, reports on Berlin, Canada, and China policy; as well as a lighthearted exercise in the ways of England . . .* Atlantic 1/71, p4 **—n.** one who supports neoisolationism. *Isolationism, it would seem, is once again on the rise. President Nixon has used the term neo-isolationist to describe certain of his senatorial critics who would alter U.S. foreign policy or who seek a greater role for the Congress in shaping it.* Time 5/31/71, p18 **[1950]**

neo-Keynesian, *adj.* of, characterized by, or based upon government spending and tax adjustment as the major influential factors in economic growth. [Senator Hubert H.] *Humphrey pledges to continue the neo-Keynesian policies that have helped stimulate the nation to 7-½ years of unprecedented growth in jobs, wages and production.* Time 10/25/68, p31 **—n.** a supporter of a neo-Keynesian fiscal policy. Compare MONETARIST, FRIEDMANITE. *It was also recognized that monetary policy could be effectively exploited for purposes of stabilization policy, and this position is accepted by Neo-Keynesians and monetarists alike.* Times (London) 9/7/70, p19 **[1959]**

neomort (ˈniːoʊˌmɔrt), *n.* a body whose brain is dead but with some other organs kept functioning by a respirator and other artificial means. . . . *the neomort by definition has no functioning central nervous system.* Harper's 9/74, p26 *"Should neomorts arise. . ." Toward the programme's end I gathered that . . . even with most advanced techniques, the management of these semicadavers is exceptionally difficult beyond 24 hours: they need, so it appears, much of the same amount of nursing as anyone with a totally incapacitating stroke—and that is quite a lot.* Times (London) 6/19/76, p10 **[1974,** coined by Willard Gaylin, an American psychiatrist, from *neo-* new + Latin *mortuus* dead]

neo-Pentecostal, *adj.* of or relating to a movement in Protestant and Catholic churches of the United States which emphasizes Pentecostal beliefs and practices such as faith healing, speaking in tongues, and the exorcism of demons. See DISCIPLING, EXORCISM. *She had a session with a pioneer in the Neo-Pentecostal movement that was just then beginning to introduce healing and other "gifts of the Holy Spirit" into mainstream churches.* Time 4/26/76, p42 **—n.** a member of a neo-Pentecostal church or sect; a CHARISMATIC. *The most radical innovation among neo-Pentecostals is the creation of charismatic "households" in which married couples, singles, clergy and nuns come together for shared prayer and mutual support.* Newsweek 6/25/73, p85A **[1971] —neo-Pentecostalism,** *n.: Roman Catholic "neo-Pentecostalism," a movement that stressed prayers and speaking in tongues, attracted thousands.* 1973 World Book Year Book, p177 **—neo-Pentecostalist,** *n.: Like other Neo-Pentecostalists, Stapleton believes in miraculous physical heal-*

ings, but has played down her own involvement in them. Time 4/26/76, p42

neophilia (ˌniːəˈfiːliːə), *n.* a love of novelty; a great interest in anything new. *What was best in the dream—the idealism of the Ban the Bomb movement, a general exuberant impulse toward freedom—finally went mad. . . Booker mainly blames the communicators—the fad-conscious journalists, the telly talkers, the trendy film makers—who turned Neophilia into an industry.* Time 7/6/70, p71 *Indeed, the opportunity to explore a complex area can be used instead of food or water as a reward to induce a rat to choose one passage rather than another. This well-developed neophilia has led some writers to use the term "curiosity drive" to refer to it. . .* Scientific American 1/67, p85 **[1966]**

neophiliac, *n.* a person characterized or affected by neophilia. *What on earth do the Beatles, Harold Wilson, Twiggy, and Kenneth Tynan have in common? . . . They are Neophiliacs— lovers of "the new"—and they are doomed to live out the damnation of all ultramodern men: "Keeping pace with pace."* Time 7/6/70, p71 **[1969]**

Neorican (ˌniːouˈriːkən), *U.S. —n.* a New Yorker of Puerto Rican origin or descent. *Manny Santel is doubtless the luckiest man in Mosquitos. A skilled worker and union leader at the Aguirre mill, he won a $17,000 lottery. . . But he is an exception, a relatively sophisticated returnee from New York (those who come back are called* Neoricans, *a term touched with envy and resentment).* Time 2/16/76, p15 **—adj.** of or being a New Yorker of Puerto Rican origin or descent. *His ragged Spanish also has caused problems, although it is now improving. Terry and her Neorican friends at school are severely rebuked by classmates if they are overheard speaking in English.* NY Times Magazine 11/12/78, p90 **[1972,** influenced by *neo-* new, from NUYORICAN]

neovascularization, *n.* the growth or spread of new capillaries in the body, especially in a tumor. *Neovascularization also seems to be important in some diseases other than cancer. For example, one would like to know why capillaries invade the vitreous humor of the eye in diabetes and overrun the cornea in trachoma, leading in both cases to blindness.* Scientific American 5/76, p73 **[1976]**

nepheloid layer (ˈnefəˌlɔid). See the quotation for the meaning. *Several years ago Drs. Maurice Ewing and Edward M. Thorndike detected turbid layers in the deep waters several kilometers off the East Coast of the United States. They called these areas nepheloid layers and found them to be a suspension of clay-sized mineral particles.* Science News 10/4/69, p304 **[1965,** from Greek *nephélē* cloud + English *-oid*]

nerd (nərd), *n.* **1** *U.S. and Canadian Slang.* a foolish or ineffectual person; jerk. Also spelled NURD. *As the novel begins, the hero, another loser named Walter Starbuck, is serving time for a contemptible minor role he played in the Watergate scandal. . . He's 67 years old and a nerd, but he still has lots of energy.* Sunday News (New York), Leisure section 8/26/79, p7 **2** *U.S. Slang.* an enthusiast; fan. *"In a way, you could say we're more film nerds than film critics," said a member of the group named Mason Wiley, who told us that he graduated from Columbia Journalism School in 1978 and now works as Judith Crist's factotum. "We're the sort of people who go to see a film at the Museum of Modern Art and rush to get a seat in the front row."* New Yorker 2/18/80, p29 **[1957** for def. 1; **1980** for def. 2; possibly an alteration of earlier slang (1940's) *nert* stupid or crazy person, itself an alteration of *nut*] **—nerdy,** *adj.: Playing with numbers is no longer a nerdy accountant's game.* Manchester Guardian Weekly 1/31/88, p19

nerve agent, a gas or other substance used in chemical warfare that attacks the nervous system. *Work on toxins is "too expensive", studies of the operational feasibility of incapacitating agents (such as LSD) have stopped, and there is no further interest in carbamates. Stocks of five nerve agents (T-2715, GB, GD, GF and VX) are kept at Nancekuke and, at present, a total of about 100 lb is in the store.* New Scientist 11/5/70, p281 **[1963]**

nerve growth factor, a protein that stimulates the growth of sympathetic and sensory nerve cells. *Abbreviation:* NGF *Nerve growth factor is a protein found in special abundance in mouse salivary glands and in certain snake venoms. It has a unique biological activity as a potent and specific stimulant of the growth of postganglionic sympathetic neurons and sensory neurons. These effects are seen most prominently in the sympathetic or sensory ganglia of young animals when the neurons are not fully developed.* Science 1/12/73, p171 **[1966]**

net economic welfare, *U.S. Economics.* a measure of a country's economy, consisting of the gross national product corrected to account for certain non-material factors, such as the cost of industrial pollution and the value of expanded leisure. *The new indicator, which M.I.T.'s Samuelson calls "net economic welfare," or N.E.W., is based on a pioneering study of Yale Professors William Nordhaus and James Tobin. Basically, N.E.W. tries to measure some of the more slippery realities not included in G.N.P.* Time 4/9/73, p98 **[1973]**

nettle, *n.* **1** something vexing or nettlesome; irritation; vexation. *The Minister* [Dr. Hillery, the Irish Republic's Minister of External Affairs] *said that someone had to deal with the nettle of the Orange Order.* Times (London) 7/9/70, p1 *. . . I made a lot of money but spent every cent, and the commuting was an endless nettle.* New Yorker 10/18/69, p188 **2 grasp the nettle,** to attack a difficulty boldly; deal promptly and firmly with a problem. *Still, with the audacity that has made the Warren Court the most fascinating institution in this usually predictable Capitol city, the Justices grasped the nettle on Monday and announced that they will rule on Mr. Powell's case.* NY Times 11/24/68, pD11 *And with John Davies about to grasp the Ministry of Technology end of the nettle with characteristic brusqueness, the laboratories of the Atomic Energy Authority, especially Harwell, are suffering renewed and damaging queasiness.* Manchester Guardian Weekly 8/8/70, p10 **[1963]** ▶ *Nettle* in the sense of "something vexing" represents a new meaning, most likely derived from the verb *to nettle,* "to vex or irritate," rather than by extension from the noun's literal meaning ("a plant with stinging leaf hairs").

The idiom *grasp the nettle* (attested in the *OED* since 1884) may be a distant echo of Shakespeare's "Out of this nettle, danger, we pluck this flower, safety" (King Henry IV, II.iii.10). The idiom must have originated among country dwellers, who were aware that the nettle is harmless if grasped tightly and quickly.

nettle-grasper, *n.* a person who attacks a difficulty boldly. *The problem for the Foreign Office is what you do about such regimes. The nettle-graspers are all for firm decisions and quick recognition, the slitherers for "playing it long." The technique is to let the coup cool and tactfully look the other way till you can be sure who has won and what you think of him.* Manchester Guardian Weekly 11/1/69, p11 **[1963,** from the idiom *grasp the nettle*]

network, *v.* **1** *British.* to broadcast or telecast over a network. **—v.t.:** *More than ever this year's American elections are being fought over the airwaves—especially on television. . . First there's the great set-piece networked from coast to coast and paid for by the candidate, an operation not to be embarked on very often.* Listener 10/10/68, p461 **—v.i.:** *It became one of Scottish Television's most popular programmes and was the first originating in Scotland to be networked.* Times (London) 4/26/68, p9 **[1952,** from the noun meaning a broadcasting system (OEDS 1914)] **2** to meet informally with groups of people who share interests or causes. **—v.i.:** *Many* [films] *are rented to schools, churches, interested organizations, grassroots activists. New Day maintains a mailing list of more than 4,000 people who have subscribed to past films. "Also, if you've networked with people when you were doing a film, you have a natural interest in seeing their reaction to the film," says Durrin.* Washington Post 4/20/83, pB7 **[1980]** **—n. 1** a system that links together a number of computers. *Networks enable computer users to share files and expensive peripheral equipment.* 1986 World Book Year Book, p265 *The real market for over-30-megabyte hard disks is in network situations where two or more microcomputers share a hard disk to ease the exchange and updating of information.* NY Times 9/9/86, pC4 **[1973]** **2** a group of people who work together informally to promote ommon goals. *Written by an author experienced in the field,* *Networking features practical information on how women can* *help each other find better jobs, become more effective in their* *present jobs, and offer moral support, plus useful tips on start-* *ng a network, finding contacts, more. Network directory in-* *luded.* Book Chat, Winter 1980, p32 [**1980**]

network analysis, the mathematical or statistical study of net- works and their connecting lines, points, branches, etc. Com- pare CRITICAL PATH ANALYSIS. *A modern society is to a large* *extent a system of networks for communication, transportation* *and the distribution of energy and goods. The complexity and* *cost of these networks demand that existing networks be effec-* *ively used and that new networks be rationally designed. To* *meet this demand there has evolved a new discipline called* *network analysis.* Scientific American 7/70, p94 . . . *the ap-* *plication of scientific techniques in government as in business* *management is very useful. It is enough to mention operational* *research, network (critical path) analysis, etc.* New Scientist */9/70, p96 [**1962**]

network analyst, a specialist in network analysis. *Network ana-* *ysts rely heavily on graph theory, a branch of mathematics* *hat was founded with Leonhard Euler's formulation and so-* *ution of the first graph-theory problem in 1736.* Scientific American 7/70, p94 [**1970**]

networking, *n.* **1** a computer system in which several comput- ers and data banks are linked together (also used attributively). *Time-sharing and networking are "multi-access" systems. Sev-* *ral individuals or companies have access to and can use a sin-* *gle computer system. In all such systems, each user has the* *impression that the entire computer is at his disposal. Actually,* *he machine may be serving many users at once.* Encyclopedia Science Supplement (Grolier) 1975, p98 *Networking is the in-* *eraction of one computer with several others in an office, in* *a sort of electronic kaffeeklatsch.* NY Times 10/18/83, p18 **2** the promotion of political goals or the exchange of ideas and in- formation among people who share interests or causes. *"Recre-* *ational activities offer time to network with colleagues,"* *counsels* Working Woman *magazine in an article on conven-* *ions. (The article also recommends "networking at breakfast.')* Harper's 9/83, p13 [**1973** for def. 1; **1972** for def. 2] —**net-** **worked,** *adj.: Mainframes, as large computers are called, will* *be needed only for work requiring special facilities—large pro-* *grams, graphics display and so on—so it would be sensible to* *build networked systems enabling expensive machines to serve* *a large number of users. Networking also means that particular* *jobs can be run on special machines rather than many ma-* *chines handling all types of jobs which is inefficient.* New Sci- entist 9/7/78, p669

neural net, short for NEURAL NETWORK. *It's becoming evident* *that neural nets . . . are well suited to many signal processing* *and biotechnology problems.* Science News 8/1/87, p76 [**1987**]

neural network, 1 a network of units in a computer that are thought of as resembling the interconnections among nerve cells. *Improvements in neural networks . . . have sharpened* *computers' ability to discern and absorb information.* NY Times 9/15/87, pC12 **2** a computer having such a network. *The new computers are called neural networks because they* *contain units that function roughly like the intricate network* *of neurons in the brain.* NY Times 9/15/87, pC1 [**1987**]

neuraminidase (ˌnurəˈminəˌdeis), *n.* an enzyme that hydrolizes neuraminic acid (a fatty acid in the spinal cord) and attacks mu- cous cells and substances. *The enzyme neuraminidase, injected* *into mice as a post-coital contraceptive, seemed to be the most* *effective base for a "morning-after pill" of any yet tried.* New Scientist 12/31/70, p608 *The enzyme, known as neuramini-* *dase, can attack the mucus of saliva, nasal secretion, sputum* *or egg white and so on.* Science Journal 1/70, p40 [**1957**]

neurobiological, *adj.* of or relating to neurobiology. *As work in* *this field frequently forms part of a wider programme of* *neurobiological research, it is not possible to isolate a figure for* *expenditure on research into epilepsy alone.* New Scientist and Science Journal 1/28/71, p195 [**1954**]

neurobiologist, *n.* a specialist in neurobiology. . . . *neuro-* *biologists . . . uncovered a link between calcium and the estab-* *lishment of the classic Pavlovian conditioned response. Drs.* *Robert Grenell and Eduardo Romero . . . elicited responses at* *will by manipulating the cellular chemical in a living brain.* Science News 3/7/70, p246 [**1957**]

neurobiology, *n.* the branch of biology that deals with the nervous system. . . . *much basic research is being carried out* *by the council and the universities, particularly in the field of* *neurobiology, and may well throw light on the problems of ep-* *ilepsy.* New Scientist and Science Journal 1/28/71, p195 [**1959**]

neurochemical, *n.* a chemical substance that affects the nervous system or some part of it. *Several neurochemicals, when ap-* *plied to a specific area of the brain, appear to control killing* *behavior in laboratory rats. . .* Science News 2/21/70, p197 —*adj.* of or relating to neurochemistry. *The most logical* *direction for neurochemical research is perhaps to carry for-* *ward the work of neurophysiologists by elucidating the chemi-* *cal changes that accompany action potentials and synaptic* *transmission.* New Scientist and Science Journal 8/26/71, p462 [**1967** for noun; **1963** for adj.]

neurochemist, *n.* a specialist in neurochemistry. *Probably one* *of the most baffling aspects of brain research concerns the na-* *ture of consciousness. Neurophysiologists and neurochemists* *have yet to find the exact seat of consciousness or to explain* *how it functions.* Encyclopedia Science Supplement (Grolier) 1968, p105 *Chemical transmitters are attracting a good deal* *of attention from neurochemists at the moment.* New Scientist and Science Journal 12/16/71, p145 [**1958**]

neurochemistry, *n.* the chemistry of the nervous system. *As a* *basic science, neurochemistry has continued to advance, and* *many of its observations have been of great clinical impor-* *tance. It has been found that disturbances of vitamin B6 (pyri-* *doxine) may cause seizures. This vitamin is an essential* *nutritional cofactor, without which the brain enzyme which* *produces gamma-aminobutyric acid (GABA) fails to function.* Americana Annual 1962, p528 [**1955**]

neurodepressive, *adj.* acting as a nerve depressant. *When preg-* *nant rats are treated with atropine, a neurodepressive drug, no* *later than the third day of pregnancy, implantation of a ferti-* *lized egg is delayed. . .* Science News 1/17/70, p63 [**1970**]

neuroendocrinologist, *n.* a specialist in neuroendocrinology. *These organic compounds [amines], which were thought to act* *as chemical mediators (neurohumors) at synaptic junctions* *(where the endings of nerve cells come into contact) in the cen-* *tral nervous system, were of interest to neuroendocrinologists.* *Most of these compounds are found in high concentration in* *the hypothalamus.* 1969 Britannica Yearbook of Science and the Future, p389 [**1960**]

neuroendocrinology, *n.* the endocrinology of the nervous sys- tem. *Neuroendocrinology research was expected to establish* *the pathways in the brain that regulate the hypothalamic hor-* *mones and the role of the amines in the control of these path-* *ways.* 1969 Britannica Yearbook of Science and the Future, p389 [**1958**]

neuroethology, *n.* the branch of ethology dealing with the nervous system; study of the neural basis of animal behavior. *Jörg-Peter Ewert ("The Neural Basis of Visually Guided Behav-* *ior") is professor of zoology and head of the department of* *neuroethology at the newly founded Gesamthochschule Kassel* *(Integrated University of Kassel) in West Germany.* Scientific American 3/74, p16 [**1972**]

neurogenetics, *n.* the branch of genetics dealing with the nervous system; study of the genetic development, features, etc., of the nervous system of animals. *Current neurogenetics* *is based primarily on research with animals such as mice, Dro-* *sophila, Paramecium, Daphnia, and nematodes, in which it is* *difficult or impossible to study the physiology of particular* *neurons.* Science 2/28/75, p760 [**1972**] —**neurogeneticist,** *n.:* *The team, coordinated by . . . neurogeneticist Dr. Eva Ander-* *mann, is trying to stop the death toll from Tay-Sachs—six fam-* *ilies have now lost sons and daughters to the disease—by*

identifying couples who both carry the Tay-Sachs gene muta-
tion and thus run a 25% chance of having a Tay-Sachs child.
Maclean's 4/19/76, p57

neurohemal organ (ˌnurouˈhi:məl), an organ of the circulatory
system having neurological importance. *According to Bruce*
Johnson, in the cockroach Periplaneta *secretory material is re-*
leased from the granules in the axons along the whole length
of the cardiac nerves; that is, the nerves themselves act as
neurohemal organs where the hormone is released into the cir-
culating blood. . . Britannica Book of the Year 1967,
p173 [**1953,** from *neuro-* nerve or nervous system + *hemal* of
or relating to the circulatory system]

neurokinin (ˌnurouˈkainən), *n.* a protein substance that causes
dilation of blood vessels and has an undetermined effect on
nerves. *In 1960 a polypeptide, neurokinin, was isolated by*
Wolff and his colleagues in the USA, from the subcutaneous
tissues near the temporal blood vessels in patients during an
attack of migraine. New Scientist 1/27/66, p208 . . . *sub-*
stances around the headache site, referred to as "headache
fluid," . . . among which are two miniature proteins called
bradykinin and neurokinin, are believed to make nerves sensi-
tive to pain. Encyclopedia Science Supplement (Grolier) 1969,
p166 [**1960,** from *neuro-* nerve or nervous system + *kinin* any
of various proteins involved in dilation and contraction of tissue, from Greek *kīneîn* to move]

neuroleptic, *n.* a tranquilizing drug, especially one used to treat
schizophrenics. *Schizophrenics treated over long periods with*
neuroleptics have sometimes shown symptoms typical of en-
dogenous depression and have attempted suicide. New Scientist 11/21/68, p417 [**1958,** from French *neuroleptique,* from
neuro- nerve or nervous system + *-leptique* -leptic (as in *epi-*
leptic)]

neurolinguistics, *n.* the study of the relationship between the
human nervous system and language. *The field of neuro-*
linguistics is concerned with elucidating the relationships be-
tween language and the central nervous system; it draws upon
the research, analytical tools, and hypotheses of linguistics,
psychology, neurology and neuroscience. Since the 19th centu-
ry the principal source of data has been the patient with brain
damage; hence, for ethical as well as practical reasons, the ac-
cumulation of knowledge in this field has been slow and diffi-
cult. McGraw-Hill Yearbook of Science and Technology 1976,
p287 [**1961,** coined by the American linguist Edith C. Trager,
born 1924]

neurometrics, *n.* the measurement and analysis of the electrical
activity of the brain and nervous system by means of computers. *Recent work in "neurometrics," . . . revealed consistent*
variations in populations of learning-disabled children. To
date, this approach has allowed discrimination of disabled
children from normal children with 93% accuracy. 1980 Britannica Yearbook of Science and the Future, p220 [**1972**]

neuropharmacological, *adj.* of or relating to neuropharmacology. *Apart from their clinical effects these various poisons*
have proved novel tools in neuropharmacological research, es-
pecially in elucidating the mechanism of nervous conduction.
New Scientist and Science Journal 12/9/71, p119 [**1959**]

neuropharmacologist, *n.* a specialist in neuropharmacology.
The effects of the new drug [magnesium pemoline] *on rats are*
impressive. Those given the compound learned from four to
five times faster than untreated rats. They also retained what
they had learned longer, Dr. N.P. Plotnikoff, an Abbott neuro-
pharmacologist, reported. Science News Letter 1/1/66,
p6 [**1966**]

neuropharmacology, *n.* the study of the effects of drugs on the
nervous system. . . . *brain-control chemistry (neuropharma-*
cology) is making very rapid progress. I see no reason for as-
suming that the human brain will lose its individuality after
losing contact with its body. . . Even when the body is very
weak and ailing, the brain continued its active life if it is not
exhausted by physical pain. Encyclopedia Science Supplement (Grolier) 1969, p233 *Chronicles the development of*
neuropharmacology during the past 10 years. Of particular
importance are the chapters on central nervous pharmacology

with the microiontophoretic technique of drug application.
Science News 1/16/71, p38 [**1955**]

neuroregulator, *n.* any of a group of chemical substances that
function specifically in communication between nerve cells, including substances that transmit impulses between nerve cells
(neurotransmitters) and those that amplify or dampen neuronal activity. *A seemingly diverse group of substances, neu-*
roregulators have in common a role in communication process-
es among neurons. In that respect, they differ from substances
such as glucose and oxygen, which are involved primarily in
the metabolic maintenance of the cell. They also differ from
second messengers, such as cyclic AMP and cyclic guanosine
monophosphate (GMP), which help to translate neurotransmit-
ter or neuromodulator signals into metabolic events. It only re-
cently has become clear that many neuroregulators in the
brain do not satisfy the criteria for neurotransmitters. Science
5/26/78, p965 [**1978**]

neuroscience, *n.* any of the sciences dealing with the nervous
system, such as neurology, neurochemistry, etc., or these sciences collectively. *Although the prospects of, for example,*
greater self-knowledge through neuroscience, are exciting, we
know that self-knowledge does not necessarily give rise to wis-
dom and that there is fear that neuroscience will be misapplied
in mind-control. Times (London) 11/26/70, p12 [**1963**]

neuroscientist, *n.* a specialist in any of the neurosciences. *Amer-*
ican neuroscientists at the meeting hailed his [Levon A. Matini-
an's] *findings as a monumental achievement which might*
make it possible to treat victims of spinal cord injury, brain in-
jury, stroke, and multiple sclerosis successfully. Until recently,
neuroscientists thought that repairing damaged nerves in the
brain and spinal cord was impossible. 1977 Collier's Encyclopedia Year Book, p353 [**1965,** from NEUROSCIENCE + *-ist*]

neurotransmitter, *n.* a chemical substance that transmits impulses between nerve cells. *Norepinephrine is a neuro-*
transmitter, a substance responsible for carrying a signal
across the gap between two neurons. Neurons that use norepi-
nephrine as a neurotransmitter have a role in the control of
mood, learning, blood pressure, heart rate, blood sugar and
glandular function. Science News 4/17/71, p266 *In the brain,*
as elsewhere in the body, the transmission of nervous impulses
from one cell to another is due to the release at nerve endings
of chemicals called neuro-transmitters; these include acetyl-
choline and noradrenalin. Times (London) 1/6/71, p4 [**1961**]

neutercane, *n.* a storm with high winds, which originates to the
north of the normal Atlantic hurricane area. *A neutercane*
comes into being when pretropical storm conditions and an in-
vading cold air mass coincide. Winds are driven both by the
heat of condensing water vapor and the push of the cold air
mass. NY Times 9/10/72, pD13 [**1972,** from *neuter* + hurri-
cane]

neutral current, a weak interaction between nuclear particles
in which no charge is exchanged. *Towards the end of 1973,*
physicists had taken a big step towards unifying the laws of
the universe into a single, cohesive system, with their discovery
of so-called 'neutral currents'. These had unified the mathe-
matics describing radioactivity and electro-magnetism. Annual Register of World Events in 1975, p395 *A neutral-current*
process is one in which two particles interact without exchang-
ing a unit of electric charge. If a neutrino strikes a proton and
bounces off, and the neutrino remains a neutrino and the pro-
ton remains a proton, that's a neutral-current interaction. . .
A search for neutral-current processes was undertaken, and
they were discovered in 1973. Science News 7/8/78, p20 [**1974**]

neutralist, *n.* a geneticist who attributes genetic variation to
random disappearance of different forms or stages of organisms. *Neutralists and selectionists have also diametrically op-*
posed explanations for the mechanisms by which genetic
variability is maintained within a species, particularly in the
form of protein polymorphism: the coexistence in a species of
two or more different forms of a protein. Scientific American
11/79, p117 [**1975,** *neutralist* originally (OED 1623) meant one
who maintains a neutral political attitude]

eutron activation analysis, a method of analyzing the composition of a substance by radioactive bombardment with neurons to identify the elements present by their characteristic adiation. *Abbreviation:* NAA Compare ACTIVATION ANALYSIS. *. . . neutron activation analysis, [is] a technique which detects race elements by bombarding them with neutrons so they give ff characteristic gamma rays. . .* Science News 3/7/70, 245 *. . . neutron activation analysis offers a sensitive method for comparing bearing wear. The method can detect wear 'ue to a few minutes' running, as well as abnormal wear.* New cientist 7/30/70, p241 **[1951]**

eutron bomb, another name for ENHANCED RADIATION WEAPON. *The Pentagon proposal to introduce a new generation of actical nuclear weapons into Europe is truly alarming. Included are the so-called "neutron bombs," a term used to describe new 8-inch nuclear artillery shells and new warheads or Lance surface-to-surface missiles. These weapons, under development since 1972, are designed to produce a prompt burst f neutrons and gamma-rays capable of delivering sufficiently arge radiation doses at ranges of several hundred metres to inapacitate exposed persons in a matter of minutes and kill almost all of them in a day or two.* New Scientist 7/14/77, 68 **[1961]** ►Although references to this weapon appeared in rint sporadically during the 1960's, they became frequent and videspread after President Carter's announcement in 1977 hat he supported military requests for its development.

eutron poison, an element that readily absorbs large numbers f neutrons. The rods used in a nuclear reactor to control a hain reaction are made of these elements. *The operation of he reactor might also have been modified by a decrease in the quantity of neutron poisons present. . . In this way neutron poisons may have been "burned out" of the ore soon after the eactor began operating. If the initial amounts of elements uch as lithium and boron were large enough, this effect could ave been a major factor controlling the reactor.* Scientific American 7/76, p40 **[1963]**

'EW, U.S. abbreviation of NET ECONOMIC WELFARE. *NEW is he corrected version of GNP—corrected (1) to subtract from he conventional calculation those* non-material disamenities *hat have been accruing as costs to our economy whether or not hey have been recognized and charged against the industries and activities that cause them and corrected (2) to add in items rrationally excluded from GNP (such as housewives' services n the home, value of expanded leisure and so forth).* Newsweek 4/9/73, p102 **[1973]**

New Age or **new age, 1** a popular cultural movement concerned with mysticism, metaphysics, astrology, spiritualism, nolism, and occultism. *Many elements of the New Age, like 'aith healing, fortune-telling, and transmigration of souls, go back for centuries.* Time 12/7/87, p62 **[1971] 2** the contemporary era especially as manifested by offbeat trends and movements. *It was impossible not to marvel at the eclectic riot of privileged consumerism that heralded itself as the New Age; and we could live lightly and opulently not only on the earth but under it as well: one entrepreneur was showing off his range of pine coffins.* Harper's 4/81, p25 **[1979] 3** Also **new age music.** a form of popular music influenced by jazz and characterized by soft, restrained playing, slow rhythms, and improvisation on such instruments as the piano, flute, harp, and synthesizer. *George Winton's pastoral piano is the essence of New Age music—serene, introspective and quietly inventive.* Washington Post 12/1/85, pG7 *The popularity of the new age radio program, "Music From the Hearts of Space" and the quiet but steady sales of new age albums are reason enough for record sellers to compound the confusion between new age music and postminimalist classical music. There's no clear division. . .* NY Times 9/29/85, pC25 **[1985**, a revival of a long-popular term for describing occultism and religious interests as n *The New Age: A Democratic Review of Politics, Religion, and Literature* (1894 ff), *New Age* (a publication of freemasonry, 1904 ff), and possibly in part stimulated by earlier use (1944) in Alice Bailey's *Discipleship in the New Age*]

New Ager ('eidʒər), **1** a person who plays or enjoys listening to New Age music. *Other New Agers, however, are less strident than Halpern; Jonathan Goldman, the founder of NESH* [New England Sound Healers], *played guitar in the Boston rock band The Silencers only four years ago.* Daily News 6/16/85, p20 **2** an adherent of the New Age cultural movement. *Some New Agers, says Alev, are children of the sixties who still haven't found the answers they've been looking for.* Ladies Home Journal 8/87, p48 **[1985]**

New Alchemist, a member of a group advocating methods of agriculture that utilize renewable resources, avoid the use of pesticides, and protect the environment from the destructive aspects of modern technology. *The New Alchemists built a greenhouse that is heated by solar energy, grows most of the community's food supply, and recycles its own wastes.* NY Times Magazine 2/29/76, p65 **[1975**, from *New Alchemy* Institute, organized in 1972 by John Todd, an American oceanographer and biologist, to study and explore alternative methods of agriculture]

new archaeology, an approach to archaeology that makes extensive use of technological and statistical apparatus and seeks to establish scientific procedures to explain and test theories about the past. *The innovative methodological developments of the so-called new archaeology became part of standard operating procedure, and schisms between proponents of alternative approaches were less pronounced.* Britannica Book of the Year 1976, p129 **[1972]** —**new archaeologist**: *The new archaeologists define culture differently from traditional archaeologists. They recover more data as they dig, and they ask different questions of their data.* 1980 Britannica Yearbook of Science and the Future, p235

new economics, the policy, based on Keynesian theory, of a flexible adjustment of taxes and government spending to influence or improve the economy; the policy of the neo-Keynesians. *In the thirty-odd years since Roosevelt and the peacetime New Deal, the national Democratic Party has won elections on five major policies. . . The policies were:*

(1) Implementation of the New (or Keynesian) economics. This insured, as all liberal Democrats believed, that the economic system worked. Harper's 7/70, p44 **[1965]**

New Federalism, a policy of shifting responsibilities such as social welfare programs from the Federal government to the States, advocated by Presidents Richard Nixon and Ronald Reagan. *Two years of liberal encomiums to decentralization have intellectually legitimized the concept, if not the name, of states' rights and have set the stage for the widespread acceptance of Nixon's "New Federalism."* Harper's 1/70, p32 *President Reagan wants to reduce the flow of funds and has proposed giving state governments control of much of what is left. He talks of a "New Federalism," in which Washington would be less dominant and would turn back many responsibilities to state governments.* NY Times 6/21/81, pD5 **[1968]**

New Federalist, a supporter or advocate of New Federalism. *To the New Federalists, morality in a nation is determined not by government policy, church decree, or social leadership—what is moral is what most people who think about morality at all think is moral at a given time.* Atlantic 5/70, p22 **[1970]**

New Journalism, journalism characterized by personal involvement of the reporter, deeply probing interviews, psychological speculation, and use of dramatized chronology, detailed description, etc. *According to Tom Wolfe, the New Journalism has taken on the sacred trust abandoned by the novel, social realism. There is something to this idea, but the reader quails when Wolfe energetically compares the decade of such figures as Rex Reed, Dick Schaap, Jimmy Breslin, Gay Talese, and Tom Wolfe to the age of Balzac and Dickens.* Atlantic 7/73, p99 **[1972]** —**New Journalist**: *I worry about the health of Dr. Hunter Thompson. . . He is the most creatively crazy and vulnerable of the New Journalists, seemingly, and scattered throughout his dispatches are alarming reports on his health.* Harper's 7/73, p92

New Left, a movement of political radicals opposed to the traditional liberals of the left and calling for revolutionary changes in government, civil rights, foreign policy, education, and other areas affecting society. Also called RADICAL LEFT. *The "New Left," represented by groups such as the National Mobilization Committee to End the War in Vietnam and the Students for a Democratic Society, had no doubt that the nation had become a sick society, characterized by poverty, racism, violence, and war.* Americana Annual 1969, p714 **[1960]**

New Leftist, a member of the New Left. *The New Left thinks of the poor as victims and believes that the conservatives think of them only as failures. . . The New Leftists have a mystical faith in the purity and wisdom of the poor, "uncorrupted" by the Establishment—an idea that the New Right rejects as nonsense.* Time 4/28/67, p15 **[1960]**

new math, a method of teaching mathematics, especially in elementary and secondary schools, by emphasizing concepts instead of rules and drills and by using such tools as set theory, nondecimal numeration systems, and symbolic logic. *The old math lasted for centuries, the new math for something more than a decade. . . A growing number of educators are awakening to the realization that while students trained under the new math that has dominated math education in the United States since the early 1960's may know why two and two equal four, they don't necessarily know that they do equal four.* NY Times 4/10/77, p18 **[1967**, short for *new mathematics* (1958)**]**

new penny, *pl.* **new pence**. the British penny in the newly established decimal system (effective February 15, 1971), equal to one 100th of a pound and corresponding to 2.4 pence in the old system. A new penny is worth 2.4 American cents. *Abbreviation:* p *The economic crux of the matter . . . is to be found in that shoppers' table, which turns both nine and ten old pence into four new pence—an anomaly brought about by the necessity of "rounding up" or "rounding down" the old sums to convert them to the nearest equivalent in new coins.* New Yorker 11/21/70, p192 *The minimum cost of a call would go down from 6d.—the equivalent of 2½ new pence—to 2 new pence with a compensating adjustment in the length of the call.* Times (London) 2/20/70, p13 **[1966]** ►Since the appearance of this term it has been noticed that many people in Great Britain, some of them highly literate, have been using the plural form *new pence* in the singular, as "one new pence." This is an interesting development, since few would ever have said "one pence" under the old system. Thus in a circular letter sent out in February 1972 by the managing director of a London unit trust (mutual fund), the following appears: "After careful consideration of all the relevant facts and costings we have come to the conclusion that we can offer our existing unit holders the opportunity of increasing their investment at a discount of 1 new pence per unit."

New Politics, a development in American politics, associated especially with the figures of Senators Eugene J. McCarthy, the late Robert F. Kennedy, and George S. McGovern, in which emphasis is placed upon intense participation of voters in the political processes rather than on party machinery. *The young radicals are probably not nearly so important as they sometimes seem, and what is called the New Politics may matter even less than they do.* Harper's 3/70, p58 **[1967]**

New Right, a political movement standing for conservatism and nationalism in response to both the New Left and the traditional or established conservatives. *"I belong to the New Right in Japan . . . and I agree with the New Left on one thing—that what the Japanese were taught after the war about American peace and democracy was not true."* Manchester Guardian Weekly 12/12/70, p7 *True to its ideal of detachment, the Voice avoids the excesses of partisan politics. . . And the paper that claims to have discovered the New Left has recently discovered a New Right, rebelling against the upper-class gentility of Bill Buckley.* Time 11/11/66, p52 **[1966]**

news hole, *U.S.* the space devoted to news and features in a newspaper or magazine; nonadvertising space. *Newspapers have much more room, and it is easier for them to expand the news hole.* Newsweek 5/27/74, p87 **[1962]**

newsmaker, *n. U.S.* a newsworthy person or event. *Scatterbrained, overstimulated, and insecure in her role as a newsmaker, Martha [Mitchell] likes to tell herself and others about* her "projects" and "accomplishments." Time 11/30/70 p33 *Such pictures as these made in the frontline of combat reveal field photojournalism itself as one of the real newsmakers of the year.* Saturday Review 3/11/67, p134 **[1954]**

New Smoking Material, British trademark for a tobacco substitute with a cellulose base, used in cigarettes. *Abbreviation:* NSM Compare CYTREL. *In the Hammersmith tests, 200 men smoked cigarettes containing 30 per cent New Smoking Material (a cellulose synthetic) and ordinary cigarettes for 20 months, without knowing which they were smoking.* New Scientist 6/17/76 p619 **[1973]**

newsperson, *n.* a person who reports the news; a reporter, correspondent, or newscaster. *Some of "Today's" critics charge that it is unseemly for a newsperson to do commercials.* Newsweek 5/6/74, p58 *We are used to chairpersons, of either sex, camerapersons, newspersons (they usually work for "media"), and congresspersons.* Times (London) 11/24/77, p1 **[1972; see -PERSON]**

newsreader, *n. British.* a news announcer. *Robert Dougall, the B.B.C. newsreader, has been nominated as president-designate of the Royal Society for the Protection of Birds, an organization in whose affairs he has taken an active interest for the past 20 years.* Times (London) 9/14/70, p8 **[1959]**

new wave, a more restrained and sophisticated form of punk rock developed in the late 1970's. *Unlike the Stranglers and other bands who wish to dissociate themselves from the punk by calling themselves "new wave," the Clash still play the driving, relentless songs that forced the invention of the pogo dance.* Times (London) 12/14/79, p11 *Punk soon turned to new wave, which especially in the United States meant a more deliberately clever, even arty approach to rock minimalism.* NY Times 8/13/79, pC16 **[1977]**

Nextel ('nekstel), *n.* the trademark for a synthetic substance that resembles blood, used in plays, motion pictures, etc. *Besides looking realistic when applied, Nextel coagulates and cakes as it dries, just like real blood. But here the similarity ends: Nextel dries to a soft powder that can be simply brushed off costumes, thus reducing cleaning costs.* Saturday Review 6/10/72, p51 **[1972]**

N galaxy, a galaxy distinguished by a starlike central nucleus Compare SEYFERT. *A program of photographic monitoring of quasars, N galaxies and Seyfert galaxies has been carried out over the last two years at the University of Florida. . .* Science News 12/5/70, p424 **[1968**, *N* for *nuclear*]

NGF, abbreviation of NERVE GROWTH FACTOR. *When a minute amount of NGF is added to an isolated sympathetic ganglion in a laboratory tissue culture, projections sprout in large numbers from the cell cluster, forming a halo of nerve fibers around it in six to 10 hours.* Scientific American 12/76, p52 **[1966]**

ngultrum (əŋ'gultrəm), *n.* the monetary unit of Bhutan, introduced in 1974. *Bhutan's first currency notes were released in Thimphu in April. Called ngultrums, they were at par with the Indian rupee, which would remain legal tender.* Britannica Book of the Year 1975, p109 **[1974**, from Bhutanese (a Tibetan language)]

ngwee (əŋ'gwi:), *n.* a new monetary unit of Zambia (since 1969). See the quotation for details. *Zambia changed to a decimal currency on January 16, replacing pounds, shillings, and pence with kwacha (1 kwacha = $1.40) and ngwee (100 ngwee = 1 kwacha).* Americana Annual 1969, p756 **[1966]**

Nibmar or **NIBMAR** ('nib,mar), *n.* acronym for *no independence before majority African rule,* a statement by Great Britain and members of the British Commonwealth demanding proportional representation for the black population in white-ruled dependencies before granting independence. *Afraid that [Prime Minister Harold] Wilson might come to terms with the Rhodesian regime, they [the Commonwealth leaders] demanded that he agree to something called NIBMAR—an acronym standing for "No Independence Before Majority African Rule."* Time 9/23/66, p31 *Britain, he [Sir Colin Crowe, Britain's chief representative to the United Nations] said, had* never accepted a commitment to Nibmar from the United Nations. Times (London) 11/12/70, p6 [1966]

NIC, acronym for *newly industrialized country,* a country that has begun to show rapid industrial development. *None of the hemisphere's "NIC's" has been redefining its foreign policy in terms of national priorities more vigorously than Mexico. . .* NY Times 7/6/80, pD3 [1978]

nickel-and-dime, *v.t.* or **nickel and dime,** *U.S. Informal.* **1a** to pay close attention to minor expenditures. *Joe DePrimo, 25, returned from Vietnam with a Bronze Star and worked his way through New York's Richmond College with the help of G.I. benefits and part-time jobs. . . "I nickeled-and-dimed it all through college," says DePrimo, the first in his family to get a degree.* Newsweek 3/5/73, p24 **b** to get or achieve by paying close attention to minor expenditures. *But this is not the first time Mr. Carter has tried to wriggle out of a tough political problem by compromising with special economic interests. And what passed for good tactics last fall has become bad strategy. The economy is rapidly being nickled and dimed into double digit inflation.* NY Times 2/2/78, pD18 **2** to treat cheaply or stingily, especially by paying too close attention to minor expenditures. *J. Paul Getty once kept a pay phone at his English mansion, but he wasn't the sort to nickel and dime his women—except possibly his wives.* Time 6/28/76, p38 [1963]

nidate ('nai,deit), *v.i. Embryology.* to become implanted in the uterus. *In 1971, Shettles was the first investigator to actually implant an artificial or laboratory conceptus in a woman's womb, doing it at the implantable or "blastocyst" stage of sixty-five or more cell divisions (about five days' growth). . . The egg transfer was done only to see if it would nidate, which it did; it was not done to bring it to birth.* Joseph Fletcher, The Ethics of Genetic Control, 1974, p66 [1962, back formation from nidation (1892), from Latin *nīdus* nest + English *-ation*]

Nielsen rating, *U.S.* the percentage of households tuned in to a specified radio or television program, based upon an automatic sampling of households by the A.C. Nielsen marketing research organization. *Nielsen ratings were based on mechanisms—"audimeters"—inserted in a sampling of television sets, keeping a record of stations tuned. Their use in radio had dated from 1935, but they became especially prestigious in television.* Erik Barnouw, Tube of Plenty, 1975, p133 *This was the decade in which culture was quantified as never before in our mass society, where numbers tell the story from political polls to Nielsen ratings to box-office grosses.* Newsweek 11/19/79, p112 [1951]

nif gene, a gene involved in nitrogen fixation. *One of the earliest goals of such work—as should be obvious with the emphasis on soybeans—is to try to make the nif gene settle into a type of plant where it's not normally found.* Robert Cooke, Improving on Nature, 1977, p135 *Even if nif genes could be incorporated into the cells of a plant such as corn, that would probably not be enough to create a self-fertilizing crop. One problem that would remain to be solved, for example, is the protection of the nitrogenase from oxygen.* Scientific American 3/77, p81 [1974; nif, from nitrogen-fixing]

niggle, *n. British.* a petty or trifling complaint. *The chapter on media gives some useful analytical data but does not describe how different constituents should be sterilized. I would like personally to have seen more on the turbidostat and other types of culture vessel. . . However, these are just niggles.* New Scientist 3/19/70, p575 [1956, recorded as dialect (1886)]

nightside, *n.* **1** the side of a planet, moon, etc., that faces away from the sun and is thus in darkness. *Temperatures on the nightside of the planet [Mars] were very low, dropping down to −85F.* Encyclopedia Science Supplement (Grolier) 1970, p322 **2** the dark or unilluminated side of anything. [Elias] *Lönnrot awoke the nightside of the nineteenth-century professional and middle-class mind, represented by himself, and connected it with the prehistoric culture of subarctic medicine men.* Saturday Review 8/19/67, p73 [1951 for def. 1; 1967 for def. 2]

night-sight, *n.* a gun sight for use under adverse lighting conditions, especially at night. *Our marksman, who saw him clearly*

through his night-sight, asked the platoon commander for permission to fire at him. Manchester Guardian Weekly 11/6/71, p12 [1969]

nightwatchman, *n. Cricket.* a usually second-rate batsman sent in to defend the wicket until the close of play, late in the day. *In the fifth over Holder trimmed Aftab's bails with his second ball and the fifth was caught by Turner off the nightwatchman Wasim Bari's glove and shoulder.* Sunday Times (London) 5/2/71, p24 [1963]

-nik, a slang suffix used to form nouns. *Sputnik,* whose successful launch in 1957 heralded the birth of the Space Age, was the model for *beatnik,* which became widely current in the late 1950's. *Beatnik* inspired the coinage of a number of nouns ending with the Russian personal suffix *-nik,* meaning "one who does or is connected with something." Most of the new *-nik* words closely followed the meaning of *beatnik* in denoting a person who rejects standard social values and becomes a devotee of some fad or idea or takes part in some mode of life. This class of words included *folknik* (folk-song devotee), *peacenik, protestnik, jazznik, filmnik* or *cinenik* (movie fan), and *Vietnik* (one who opposes U.S. involvement in Vietnam). Many words in *-nik* are in some degree derogatory. **—cinenik:** *Secter chose the 1965 Commonwealth Film Festival in Wales for the movie's* ["Winter Kept Us Warm"] *world premiere and it enchanted the ciné-niks there.* Maclean's 11/19/66, p23 **—citynik:** *A kibbutz is a collective settlement, where all are equal, each giving according to his abilities and receiving according to his needs . . . The day starts at dawn—in mid-summer this means four o'clock. It is surprising how quickly a reasonably healthy citynik adjusts to the hours and graft.* Sunday Times (London) 1/4/70, p67 **—computernik:** *Despite the alarums of the computerniks and the current promulgation of the notion (from over the Canadian border) that bound volumes are doomed to obsolescence, the book would appear to be here to stay.* Saturday Review 10/22/66, p59 **—filmnik:** *Another favorite is urbane, eccentric Woody Allen, who is currently flipping the filmniks by writing a Japanese movie in which the dubbed-in sound track is totally different from what is occurring on-screen.* Time 3/4/66, p27 **—goodwillnik:** *This editor didn't once ask me if I knew anything about music or had any right to write about it. Or, for that matter, whether I could write about anything. He wanted a goodwillnik, and whatever my feelings about this man's regulations, I think it was most admirable of him to spell them out.* Atlantic 9/70, p117 **—nogoodnik:** *Lew Archer's job is to find a 17-year-old girl who has run off with a 19-year-old nogoodnik.* NY Times 3/3/68, p37 See also the main entries FREEZENIK, PEACENIK, VIETNIK.

nil norm, *British.* a standard of minimum wage and price increases set by the government, limiting increases of a specified maximum to underpaid workers or where the increase results in productivity. Also called ZERO NORM. *But for all the traditional wage demands some principle does need to be hammered out to establish who will be permitted to breach the nil norm.* Sunday Times (London) 8/14/66, p8 *There can be little doubt that the £1 a week rise would not qualify as an exception to the nil norm laid down in the summer.* Manchester Guardian Weekly 2/1/68, p8 [1966]

Nimby, *n. Slang.* opposition by a community or a group within a community to the establishment in its midst of a public facility which it regards as undesirable, such as a prison, a waste dump, a shelter for the homeless, or a drug rehabilitation center. *Because of the Nimby syndrome, the garbage chain is becoming so tortuous that the solid-waste industry is considering shipping our household garbage to third world countries.* NY Times 9/23/88, pA34 [1980, from acronym for *Not in my back yard*] **—Nimbyism,** *n.: Leading Tory opponents of the Channel Tunnel link were . . . still threatening a rough ride for the scheme through Parliament, despite winning a partial victory for Nimbyism.* The Independent (London) 3/8/89, p3

Nine, *n.* **the Nine,** the nine nations of the European Economic Community from 1973 to 1981. *The Nine are due to agree then on a new round of farm price increases, which would go hand in hand with Britain's second alignment to Community price levels under the timetable set out in the Treaty of Accession.*

Manchester Guardian Weekly 3/9/74, p7 *Said one French diplomat: "Kissinger is attempting to bring the Nine into an Atlantic system whereby they will be able to take only decisions that are approved in Washington."* Time 4/1/74, p26 **[1973]** ►The European Economic Community, popularly known as the Common Market, or between 1957 and 1973, *the Six*, comprised Belgium, France, Italy, Luxembourg, The Netherlands, and West Germany. On January 1, 1973, Denmark, Ireland, and Great Britain joined the group, known thereafter as *the Nine*. Then, in May 1979 Greece was accepted as the tenth member, effective as of January 1, 1981, and the Common Market *Nine* came to be known as *the Ten*.

nine-ball, *n. U.S. Slang.* a variety of pocket billiards. See the quotation for details. *For the hustler, nine ball is the best game. The first nine balls—eight solid-colored balls and the nine ball with a yellow stripe—are racked in a diamond with the one ball in front and the nine ball in the middle. The rules are simple: the lowest numbered ball on the table must be hit first, and whoever makes the nine ball wins.* Atlantic 4/70, p67 **[1966]**

1984, *n.* a date symbolizing a totalitarian society in which all truth and freedom is suppressed and people live in a totally regimented and dehumanized state. *Throughout the campaign, the political uses of television advertising and packaging of candidates were heralded by proponents as the inescapable wave of the future and by doomsayers as the ominous forerunner of 1984.* Time 11/16/70, p14 **[1959**, from the novel *1984* by George Orwell, 1903-1950, which is set in such a society]

nine-to-fiver or **nine-to-five**, *n. Slang.* a person who holds an office job with regular hours, usually nine in the morning to five in the evening. *At Grand Central you can't tell the action crowd from the nine-to-fivers. Singapore Sammy stopped there to put a saw on Carry-Me-Back in the fifth at Roosevelt and wound up on the 5:14 to Greenwich.* Time 4/19/71, p12 *In the course of their rejection, [the hippies] have created a new way of looking at things and a new context in which to live. Dedication to the work ethic has produced the alienation that the hippies see all around them in the "nine-to-fives."* Britannica Book of the Year 1968, p790 **[1959]**

ninja (ˈnindʒə), *n.* a practitioner of the martial art of making oneself elusive or invisible through disguises and other artifices. *So obsessed was Japan with the secret negotiations surrounding Mr. Nixon's trip to China that for months the Japanese spoke of national-security adviser Henry Kissinger as a* ninja—*the magician of Japanese legends who performs supernatural acts and practices sorcery.* International Newsweek 9/11/72, p28-29 *Today, ninja practice their art not as espionage, but as a traditional martial art with a nonviolent philosophy.* World Book Encyclopedia (1988), Vol.13, p234 **[1972**, from Japanese]

nit, *n.* a unit of brightness in the meter-kilogram-second system. See the quotation for details. . . . *let's look at some of the units you get on to when you have sorted out mass and weight . . . I noticed wild things like the* Nit *"a unit of luminance in the MKS system which is the equivalent to one candela per square metre"; and the* Slug *"a unit of mass in the foot pound system . . . The slug is also called a gee pound."* Punch 9/11/68, p364 **[1953**, from Latin *nitēre* to shine]

NIT, abbreviation of NEGATIVE INCOME TAX. *Under the NIT, the tax scales would be continued downward past the zero-tax line . . .* Time 2/8/71, p15 **[1967]**

Nitinol (ˈnitə,nɔːl), *n.* a nonmagnetic alloy of titanium and nickel. See the quotations for details. *In 1968 a nickel-titanium alloy, 55-Nitinol, was discovered to have the ability to regain its original shape after being heated and then cooled below a certain temperature, crushed, and subsequently reheated. This "memory" property is expected to make Nitinol a valuable component of fire-extinguisher activators.* 1969 Compton Yearbook, p324 *One of the fascinations of the behavior of plastics is that when certain kinds of plastic are molded in a distinct form, then melted so that the form is lost and then allowed to cool, they resume much the same form. Called "plastic memory," the phenomenon has an analogue in a little-known metallic alloy. The metal is named Nitinol from its constitu-*

ents (*nickel and titanium*) and the place where it was discovered 10 years ago (*the Naval Ordnance Laboratory*). Scientific American 3/71, p47 **[1968]**

nitty-gritty, *n.* **1** the practicalities or details. *But they got bogged down in the nitty-gritties of negotiation . . .* Manchester Guardian Weekly 4/10/71, p1 *How many meetings, finally at the nitty-gritty, are interrupted by your secretary asking if you want to take a call . . .* Harper's 3/70, p87 **2 get down to the nitty-gritty**, to get down to the fundamentals or details. *. . . Dr. Swanson . . . can really understand people in a gutsy way. And he's not afraid to get down to the nitty-gritty of unpleasant problems . . .* NY Times 6/27/67, p20 **[1961**, of uncertain origin]

Nixon Doctrine. See the first quotation for the meaning. . . . *the Nixon Doctrine [was] enunciated by the President on Guam last July, that the U.S. from then on would avoid military commitments that might lead to ground-combat interventions similar to Viet Nam.* Time 4/13/70, p17 *The Nixon Doctrine, although not officially applicable to Europe, has some worrying implications for Europe. It implies that America is ready to expend money and technology on behalf of her allies but no longer ready to shed her own blood. It also implies that American help is conditional on self-help.* Manchester Guardian Weekly 8/12/72, p15 **[1970]**

NLP, *U.S.* abbreviation of *neighborhood loan program*, a state-sponsored plan that provides low mortgage and down-payment requirements, designed especially for redlined sections of a city. *The neighborhoods eligible for the NLP are chosen in consultation with municipal officials. They have to be basically stable and primarily residential, areas where decay and blight have not reached too advanced a stage and where financing has been difficult.* Ruth Rejnis, Her Home, 1980, p24 **[1979]**

NOAA (ˈnouə), *n.* acronym for *National Oceanic and Atmospheric Administration* (of the United States). *Specifically, NOAA will be concerned with determining atmospheric conditions that make for pollution, the effects of pollution on weather, and contaminants in fish.* Science News 3/27/71, p212 *Formed in 1970, NOAA absorbed the activities of the Environmental Science Services Administration, which was abolished.* 1972 Britannica Yearbook of Science and the Future, p174 **[1969]**

no-cut contract, *U.S. and Canada.* a contract in professional sports guaranteeing that the signer will not be eliminated from a team's roster. *Joe Thomas reportedly is demanding a five-year, no-cut contract at more than $350,000 a year with the Baltimore Colts. Thomas, who has been credited with rebuilding the franchise, is the pro football club's general manager.* NY Times 1/5/77, pA18 **[1976]**

nod, *n.* **on the nod**, *British.* without formality; by tacit agreement or acknowledgment. *The agenda, usually the cause of great friction, was accepted "on the nod".* Sunday Times (London) 1/12/69, p4 *With the Royal Exchange will die more than two centuries of tradition of trading mostly done "on the nod," with scarcely a written contract to be seen.* Manchester Guardian Weekly 7/11/68, p10 **[1959]**

no-fault or **no fault**, *Especially U.S.—adj.* **1** of or relating to a form of automobile insurance by which accident victims are compensated for damages or expenses by their own insurance company, whether the accident was their fault or not. *Specifically, the hearings were to focus on a modified no-fault bill introduced by Senator Bernard G. Gordon, a Peekskill Republican. The bill is designed to end much of the current reliance on litigation-oriented settlements for auto accidents.* NY Times 3/5/72, pD4 **2** of or denoting a form of divorce which is granted without either party having to prove the other guilty of causing the dissolution of the marriage. *Already accepted by 25 of the United States, the no-fault concept eliminates the adversary role; the courts accept an acknowledgment of irretrievable marriage breakdown by both spouses as sufficient grounds for divorce.* Maclean's 4/19/76, p30 **3** of or involving any method of reaching a settlement or awarding damages without having to resort to legal action. *A related "no fault" plan was recently endorsed by the American Medical Associa-*

tion. *"When a patient is aggrieved, he should be paid appropri-ate compensation, and he should not have to take his chances in court to get it,"* [Gerald J.] *Lustic says.* Scientific American 3/75, p49 —**n.** any system in which the fault, guilt, or responsi-bility of a party is eliminated as the basis for compensation or settlement. *There remains, for instance, the right to sue in court for damages sustained in an auto accident. And as long as this right remains, there's no pure no fault.* Honolulu Star-Bulletin 4/2/73, pA10 [**1967**]

no-frills, *adj.* stripped to or providing the bare essentials; with-out extras or embellishments. Also, **no-frill.** *In 1974 the CAB flatly rejected a proposal by London-based Laker Airways to fly regular "no-frills" flights between New York and London for $125 each way.* Harper's 9/75, p28 [**1960,** from the phrase *(with) no frills*]

no-go, *adj.* **1** *Slang.* no in a favorable condition for proceeding. Compare GO. *. . . in space jargon this was potentially a "no-go" situation; with no alternative open except to abort the mis-sion.* Manchester Guardian Weekly 6/19/69, p13 **2** *British.* not to be entered without special allowance; barred to designated persons, groups, etc. *Is it a form of UDI* [Unilateral Declaration of Independence] *at Liverpool, or is Liverpool to be a no-go area?* Daily Telegraph (London) 5/5/72, p9 [**1958** for def. 1; **1971** for def. 2]

no-growth, *adj.* designed to prevent, decrease, or restrict growth (as of an area, a population, or an economy). *Califor-nia's legal system is already clogged with lawsuits provoked by local zoning restrictions or "no growth" rulings.* Atlantic 11/73, p31 [**1972**]

no-hair theorem, *Astronomy.* the axiom that black holes of the same mass, charge, and spin are indistinguishable regardless of what they are made from. *Apart from these three properties* [mass, angular momentum and electric charge] *the black hole preserves no other details of the object that collapsed. This con-clusion, known as the theorem "A black hole has no hair," was proved by the combined work of Carter, Werner Israel of the University of Alberta, David C. Robinson of King's College, London, and me. The no-hair theorem implies that a large amount of information is lost in a gravitational collapse.* Sci-entific American 1/77, p36 [**1976**]

NoHo (ˌnouˌhou), *n.* an area of New York City, in lower Manhat-tan, noted as a growing center of avant-garde art, music, film, and fashion. *The Newport-New York Jazz Festival may be los-ing some of its stars to mass culture and failing to tap the loyal audience that listens to the avant-garde in the lofts of SoHo and NoHo, but one suspects that it will continue to survive and prosper.* NY Times Magazine 6/12/77, p87 [**1976,** from its being situated North of Houston Street]

noise pollution, 1 the production of noise by motor vehicles, jet planes, machinery, etc., viewed as harmful to people and the environment. *Man is an adaptable animal. Without realizing it, he has become accustomed to excessive noise pollution in his environment. But Dr. Alexander Cohen of the U.S. Public Health Service's National Noise Study says, "This sonic boom is not something you adapt to easily."* 1970 World Book Year Book, p132 **2** the loud sound or noise itself. *Also, there are the greatly improved noise pollution characteristics of VTOL com-pared not only with conventional aircraft (CTOL) but with short take off and landing craft (STOL) as illustrated in the ac-companying comparison of noise 'footprints'. . .* Science Jour-nal 3/70, p5 [**1967**]

no-knock, *adj.* *U.S.* of or deriving from legislation granting po-lice the authority to enter upon premises without announcing or identifying themselves. *The "no-knock" and "preventive-detention" provisions of the District of Columbia Crime Con-trol Act have violated, respectively, the public's right to be se-cure against unreasonable searches and seizures and the traditional presumption of innocence.* New Yorker 4/10/71, p30 [**1969**]

no-load, *adj., n.* See the quotations for the meaning. *The mutu-al savings bank industry is preparing a pilot test of its long-discussed plan to offer mutual fund shares to the public. As things now stand, the savings bank plan calls for a "no-load"* fund, in which shares would be sold without sales commis-sions, and investment management fees would be closely relat-ed to the actual cost of managing the fund. NY Times 12/16/66, p73 *A handful or so Canadian funds are "no-loads"—are offered without any sales charge and are generally available through investment dealers.* Maclean's 10/68, p22 [**1963**]

-nomics, a combining form for "economics," usually attached to the name of a public figure espousing a particular economic theory or policy. See also REAGANOMICS. —**Nixonomics,** *n.:* *Some economists, of course, were disposed to give Nixonomics little or no credit for this rosy outlook.* Newsweek 10/18/71, p29 —**Trudeaunomics,** *n.:* *In this special issue,* **Maclean's** *ex-amines the Trudeau Era, beginning with . . . Ian Urquhart's discussion of Trudeaunomics . . .* Maclean's 4/3/78, p1 —**Volckernomics,** *n.* [after Paul *Volcker,* director of the U.S. Federal Reserve System]: *Though widely considered as long overdue medicine, Volckernomics caught everyone from corpo-rate treasurers to Zurich goldbugs off guard and pushed Wall Street into a brief but panicky tailspin.* Time 1/7/80, p35 [**1969**]

non-. 1 *Non-* in its original sense of "not," "lacking," or "oppo-site of" continues to be freely used to form noun and adjective compounds. A sampling of such formations includes: —**non-black,** *n.: At the University of Natal, non-white students . . . refer to whites as "non-blacks."* Manchester Guardian Weekly 8/22/70, p7 —**noncolor,** *n.: In interior decoration, the most popular hue is a noncolor, beige. Names too are sexually equiv-ocal; one child out of five has a name like Robin or Leslie or Dana.* Time 10/12/70, p57 —**noncommitted,** *adj.: . . . what the KGB* [secret service agency of the Soviet Union] *conscious-ly fears is bad publicity in the West and among non-committed nations.* Sunday Times (London) 1/12/69, p50 —**non-degradable,** *adj.: For centuries man's nondegradable waste ma-terials have generally been hauled, along with the degradable wastes, for disposal in open gulleys or abandoned pits.* En-cyclopedia Science Supplement (Grolier) 1971, p233 —**nonestablishment,** *adj.: However, it is widely held that Mr. Trudeau became the darling of the Liberals, and now their champion, because he was a lone outsider, a nonestablishment man who spoke coolly and directly on fresh ideas.* NY Times 4/14/68, pD10 —**nonpolluting,** *adj.: The Fishmans believe that biking is a healthy, friendly, quiet, inexpensive, non-polluting, fast, and practical means of transportation, and ap-parently a lot of New Yorkers agree with them.* New Yorker 9/26/70, p28 —**nonstick,** *adj.: The Hotpoint 6150 free-standing cooker, for example, is equipped with four high-speed rings set in a lift-up hot top; two auto-timed ovens—one fitted with non-stick coated panels, and a Pan-guard device to pre-vent liquids boiling over.* Times (London) 3/12/70, p8 **2** An ex-tension of *non-* appearing with increasing frequency indicates not so much the opposite or reversal of something as rather that that "something" is not true, real, or worthy of the name. In this use, *non-* is prefixed to a noun and often carries such con-notations as "sham; pretended; pseudo-; mock; fraudulent." In the older use *non-* is part of a yes-or-no classification: a state-ment is either *sense* or *nonsense;* but here *non-* makes a com-ment or a criticism: a *non-book* pretends to be a book; a *nonpolicy* is a vacuum where a policy should be. Apparently the first popular term in which *non-* bore this meaning was *non-book,* as the following early quotation suggests: *. . . we owe to Professor Daniel J. Boorstin of Chicago the concept of the pseudo-event, which is an event taking place only in order to be reported in the newspapers, just as we owe to* Time *maga-zine the notion of the non-book, which is a book published in order to be purchased rather than to be read.* Harper's 4/64, p117 —**nonactor,** *n.: Mitchum is simply and gloriously him-self in spite of everything—one of the most powerful and ex-pressive non-actors in the business.* Manchester Guardian Weekly 12/19/70, p17 —**nonevent,** *n.: The most stupendissi-mo non-event of the Fall Publicity Season so far was the big, big Sophia Loren press conference at Radio City Music Hall.* New Yorker 10/3/70, p30 —**noninformation,** *n.: There is an-other view of question time . . . as it was once cleverly, if un-fairly, described "the ritual exchange of non-information."* Times (London) 4/16/70, p5 —**nonissue,** *n.: The "voting ma-*

chines" fiasco [in Trinidad] *has always been a major non-issue which has said more about the sterility of official opposition than the corruption of the Government.* Manchester Guardian Weekly 5/23/70, p3 —**nonplay**, *n.: Jimmy Shine—Dustin Hoffman does his brave best to make us believe that this nonplay by Murray Schisgal is a touching comedy about the ignominy of young manhood; for all his bravery and talent, it is not enough.* New Yorker 12/28/68, p2

nonachiever, *n. U.S.* **1** a student who fails to achieve passing grades. *The most recent serious disturbance at our high school was set off not by blacks, but by a gang of white "nonachievers" from relatively low-income families, who started a fight with long-haired middle-class white seniors.* NY Times Magazine 4/9/72, p104 **2** any person, especially a youngster, who lacks accomplishment. *With scoreboard lights flashing and father shouting, a boy has much more than his self-evaluation at stake. The rewards after the game are sweet for the achiever, but bitter for the nonachiever. There is no overt punishment, just the punishment of being left out.* 1974 World Book Year Book, p101 **[1972,** patterned after *underachiever* (1953), *overachiever* (1953)]

nonactin (nə'næktin), *n.* an antibiotic derived from a species of streptomyces, noted for its ability to carry ions across lipid barriers. *Formula:* $C_{40}H_{64}O_{12}$ *The class of compounds known as ionophores has attracted increasing attention during the past decade because of the remarkable cation selectivities shown by these substances . . . These compounds are generally cyclic, although several are known in which cyclization occurs only upon complexation with a cation. Those studied initially were of natural origin, namely, valinomycin, nonactin, and monensin.* McGraw-Hill Yearbook of Science and Technology 1974, p245 **[1968,** probably from *non-* not + *act*ive + *-in* (chemical suffix), because of its unusual inertness to chemical compounds]

nonaddicting or **nonaddictive,** *adj.* not causing addiction. *The U.S. Food and Drug Administration was ready to approve release of a new analgesic that New York's Winthrop Laboratories say is "in the morphine range of potency" but is nonnarcotic—and, they hope, nonaddicting.* Time 7/7/67, p45 *We would prefer to use a heroin antagonist (a nonaddictive drug which makes the addict ill if he takes heroin), but the best one available . . . just can't be had in this country yet.* Sunday Times (London) 10/29/67, p9 **[1957]**

nonaerosol, *adj.* not using a propellant, especially a fluorocarbon, under pressure. See AEROSOL. *The Bristol-Myers Company has introduced an antiperspirant deodorant pump spray . . . It is the first nonaerosol deodorant spray to be marketed in South Africa.* NY Times 9/23/77, pD9 **[1977]**

nonaligned, *n.* one that opposes political alignment with a larger power; a neutralist. *The two groups in Indonesia opposing each other are the "nonaligneds" and the "interventionists."* Manchester Guardian Weekly 5/30/70, p6 **[1966,** noun use of the adjective]

noncampus, *adj.* not having a campus; providing instruction from other than a specific location or headquarters. *A somewhat similar development, begun in the 1971-72 academic year, was the Vermont Regional Community College, a noncampus, community-based instructional system that covered much of the state.* Britannica Book of the Year 1973, p265 **[1972]**

noncandidacy, *n.* the status of a noncandidate. *In addition to repeatedly asserting his non-candidacy,* [Senator Edward M.] *Kennedy had made some forceful speeches in recent months.* New Yorker 12/4/71, p47 **[1963]**

noncandidate, *n.* a person who has not announced or is unwilling to announce his or her candidacy for an office. *One of the most maddening candidates in a political race is the noncandidate. He is the fellow who is being talked for a race but who will just never admit his candidacy until the last minute.* Tuscaloosa News (Alabama) 3/25/69, p4 **[1964]**

nonconsumptive, *adj.* not consuming, destroying, or exploiting natural objects or resources. *He* [Edward Hoagland] *is a "nonconsumptive" user of the forest, a man with exceptional powers*

of observation, reflection and appreciation. He neither hunts nor fishes but takes long solitary hikes and prefers conversing with old farmers, trappers and woodsmen. Time 4/2/73, p88 **[1970]**

noncontact, *adj.* of or involving a game or contest in which no physical contact occurs or is required between the players or competitors. *In Michigan, New Jersey, New York, and Indiana, girls won the right to play on noncontact boys' teams.* Americana Annual 1974, p535 **[1972]**

noncooperativity, *n.* the lack or absence of COOPERATIVITY. *The three different enzymes shown exhibit respectively noncooperativity (top row), positive cooperativity (middle row) and negative cooperativity (bottom row).* Scientific American 10/73, p63 **[1973]**

noncountry, *n.* a country that lacks the characteristics of most countries, such as a homogeneous population, natural borders, and a history as a nation. *The reason Cyprus is unable to handle its own affairs is not that it is a nonaligned country but a noncountry. Its Greek-speaking and Turkish-speaking population don't think of themselves as Cypriots the way French-speaking Swiss and German-speaking Swiss consider themselves Swiss.* NY Times 8/27/72, p15 **[1970,** patterned after *non-book, nonplay;* see NON- def. 2]

nonearthly, *adj.* originating or existing outside the earth. *Man has long regarded the stars, sun, moon and planets as the homes of gods and demons. In countless myths, man is helped and civilized by them. In some tales, the extraterrestrial (nonearthly) beings are fully human, at least physically. These themes have survived in present-day science fiction and fantastic stories, including many flying-saucer reports.* Encyclopedia Science Supplement (Grolier) 1972, p9 **[1970]** ►This term is preferred in an outer-space context to *unearthly,* which is suggestive of the supernatural or unnatural.

nonet (nou'net), *n.* a group of nine nuclear or subatomic particles. *There are other resonances with quantum numbers similar to the A2 meson. Under the SU(3) scheme they form a nine-particle configuration: three A2 mesons, four K* (pronounced K-star) mesons, and two f⁰ mesons. To reconcile the A2 meson with current theory, it is necessary to show that the other members of its SU(3) nonet display similar double structure.* New Scientist 10/29/70, p211 **[1963]** ►The only previously recorded sense of this word is "a group of nine musical instruments or voices." As used in nuclear physics, the term was probably adopted on the analogy of *quartet, sextet, octet,* etc., where the meaning "any group of _____" is well established.

nongraded, *adj.* **1** without a proficiency rating. [Robin] *Widdows, as the second highest non-graded driver, gains six points.* Times (London) 3/31/70, p13 **2** *U.S. Education.* not divided into grades. *Nongraded classes, for example, permit a precocious five-year-old to take some classes with six-, seven-, and eight-year-olds, and the rest with youngsters his own age.* Saturday Review 11/16/68, p104 **[1968** for def. 1; **1963** for def. 2]

noninvasive, *adj. Medicine.* **1** not invading healthy cells or tissues. *It is being given to patients who had noninvasive cancer of the bladder and who are at high risk of getting new bladder cancers.* Science News 6/23/79, p414 **2** not involving the introduction of instruments into the interior of the body. *A long-time avocational interest in the field of particle physics has led Rubenstein to a current research project on the use of a synchrotron radiation for noninvasive angiography.* Scientific American 3/80, p21 **[1979]**

nonleaded or **nonlead,** *adj.* containing no tetraethyl lead (an antiknock additive which is a contributor to air pollution). Also, UNLEADED, LEAD-FREE, LEADLESS. *The two most desired types of gasoline components for nonleaded gasolines are highly branched paraffins and the common aromatic components such as benzene, toluene, and xylene.* McGraw-Hill Yearbook of Science and Technology 1971, p212 *News that British Petroleum and Shell are to produce non-lead petrol for cars in Britain will revolutionize the engineering side of car manufacture in the next year or two.* Times (London) 3/10/70, p5 **[1955]**

nonmarket, *adj.* not included in the labor market. *Economists . . . have traditionally chosen not to measure a housewife's productivity because it falls in the so-called nonmarket sector, along with such activities as charity work and unpaid political canvassing.* NY Times 1/13/76, p39 **[1976]**

non-nuclear, *n.* a non-nuclear power; a nation with an arsenal of only conventional weapons. Compare NUCLEAR. *So far, negotiation under the heading 'nonproliferation' has virtually been between the Americans and the Russians and it has been about Germany. This is indeed something, but negotiation between nuclears and non-nuclears has scarcely begun.* Listener 2/9/67, p186 **[1956, noun use of the adjective]**

nonorgasmic, *adj.* unable to have orgasm. Compare ANORGASTIC. *Higher levels of glucose and insulin, as well as lower levels of nitrogen, phosphorus, cholesterol, and calcium, were found in the blood of "nonorgasmic women."* 1977 Britannica Yearbook of Science and the Future, p364 **—n.** a nonorgasmic person. *Deprived of a stable father-figure, a non-orgasmic in this study seemed to be unable to face the blurring of personal boundaries which goes with full physiological orgasm.* Listener 4/26/73, p549 **[1973]**

nonoxynol-9 (nə'nɑksə,nɔːl), *n.* a spermatocide widely used in contraceptive creams, foams, and lubricants. *Similar experiments in the United States have shown that another spermicide, nonoxynol-9, can also kill the AIDS virus in test tubes.* **[1967,** formed from a recombination of *nonylphenol* and *ethylene oxide]*

nonpermissive, *adj.* Biology. not permitting replication (of genetic material, viruses, etc.). Compare PERMISSIVE. *Temperature-sensitive mutants of bacteria had been obtained that are defective in initiating DNA replication at a high or nonpermissive temperature, where the mutation is phenotypically expressed.* Britannica Book of the Year 1973, p420 **[1972]**

nonprint, *adj.* that does not include printed matter, such as books, magazines, and newspapers, but is recorded on tapes, films, and the like. *In its celebration of reading, this annual event (the 16th), sponsored by the American Library Association and the National Book Committee, again failed to recognize the presence of nonprint media in libraries.* Americana Annual 1974, p346 *In general, nonprint materials reflect the worst kind of tokenism. An example we viewed of this was a film on women narrated by a man with the only women speaker in the film being one who spoke against the equal rights amendment.* "Women: A Recommended List of Print and Non-Print Materials . . .," Mediacenter (New York), 5/75, p6 **[1968]**

nonproliferation, *n.* the halting of the spread of nuclear weapons among nonnuclear powers by common consent (often used attributively). *The Soviet Union would like the solution of nonproliferation to add dimensions and a sense of realism to the problems of outlawing nuclear weapons.* NY Times 6/28/68, p1 **[1963]**

nonproliferation treaty, a treaty signed by 93 nations as of December 1969 and ratified by more than 43 nations on its effective date, March 5, 1970, whereby countries not possessing nuclear weapons agreed never to produce or acquire them in order to halt their proliferation. *Abbreviation:* NPT See also SALT. *For more than a year the United States delayed testing a peaceful nuclear device called Cabriolet in order not to complicate negotiations on the nuclear nonproliferation treaty.* Science News 5/11/68, p449 **[1964]**

nonself, *n.* any material that produces an immune response in the body. *It is therefore a matter of great biological and modical significance that the system sometimes goes awry in such a way as to give rise to the diverse group of disorders known as autoimmune diseases. Such disorders result when the immune system, which ordinarily distinguishes self from nonself with great precision, begins to attack certain of the body's own cells.* Scientific American 2/81, p80 **[1965]**

nonsense, *adj. Molecular Biology.* **1** that does not specify a particular amino acid in the genetic code. *The experiment was undertaken on the hypothesis that there would be no complementary stretches in the two heavy strands of the two*

phages except those provided by the sense and nonsense bases of the lac operon. The hypothesis was confirmed.* Scientific American 1/70, p50 **2** that results from the presence of nonsense sequences in the genetic code. Compare MISSENSE. *They [Drs. J. and M. Gross] also demonstrate that the mutation is recessive to the wild type gene in partial diploids, that it is the result of an amber nonsense mutation and that the polymerase lesion has little or no effect on the ability to carry out genetic recombination.* Science Journal 3/70, p14 **[1961]**

nonstandard analysis, *Mathematics.* a method of studying the properties of infinitely large and infinitely small numbers, and of systems that incorporate such numbers. *Nonstandard analysis, a revolutionary new approach to classical calculus, is deeply rooted in mathematical logic and perhaps in the very reasoning processes of mathematics itself.* 1977 Britannica Yearbook of Science and the Future, p355 **[1961, 1971,** invented in 1960 by the German-born American logician Abraham Robinson, 1918-1974]**

nontarget, *adj.* not being the object under attack, study, experimentation, etc. *They pointed out that while such substances would be of potential use against a broad spectrum of pests, they might, by the same token, affect nontarget species.* Britannica Book of the Year 1974, p424 **[1971]**

non-thing, *n.* **1** something nonexistent; nothing. *She [Germaine Greer] cannot blame female weakness because she has convinced all of us that this is a non-thing.* Time 8/14/72, p8 **2** something insignificant; meaningless thing; trifle. *. . . a large and deadening apparatus which explains among other non-things that William Dean Howells spelt 'millionaire' with two n's, or that in Tom Sawyer on a specified number of occasions 'ssst!' is printed as 'sssst!'* Listener 11/29/73, p751 **[1972]**

nontuplet, *n.* one of nine offspring born at one birth. *Geraldine Brodrick gave birth last week to nontuplets (nine babies) in Australia, the first such recorded birth.* NY Times 6/20/71, p7 **[1971,** from Latin *nōnus* ninth + English *-tuplet* as in *quintuplet, sextuplet,* etc.]**

noodge (nudʒ), *n.* variant of NUDZH. . . . *Rabbi Ben Kaddish, the holiest of all ninth-century rabbis and perhaps the greatest noodge of the medieval era.* New Yorker 6/20/70, p31 **[1968]**

No. 1 ('nəmbər 'wən), *Informal.* **1** one's own welfare; number one. *Robert Ringer's* Looking Out for No. 1 *was part of an entire I'm-terrific library of aggressive narcissism.* Time 1/7/80, p38 **2** chief; principal; number one. *And Dr. Henry Palacios, of St. Elizabeth's Hospital in Washington, D.C., says his statistical research has convinced him that fine-particulate air pollution is now the No. 1 cause of a whole range of respiratory diseases—chronic sore throats, repeated colds, hay fever, asthma, bronchitis, pulmonary emphysema—and some skin diseases.* NY Times Magazine 11/4/79, p130 **[1977,** new spelling of *number one,* recorded since 1704 (OED2)]**

noradrenergic (,nɔrədrə'nərdʒik), *adj.* producing or activated by the adrenal hormone noradrenaline (norepinephrine). Compare CATECHOLAMINERGIC, DOPAMINERGIC, SEROTONERGIC. *Injections of amphetamines such as Dexedrine or amphetaminelike drugs such as Ritalin stimulate the noradrenergic systems and usually make a normal person more active and enhance his pleasurable experiences.* World Book Science Annual 1974, p350 **[1963,** from *noradrenaline* + Greek *érgon* work + English *-ic]*

Nordic, *adj.* of or relating to ski competition involving cross-country racing and ski jumping. Compare ALPINE. *A series of errors and mishaps added interest to the Olympic men's 4 × 10 kilometres cross-country relay race . . . in which Finland took their second Nordic gold medal of the games.* Times (London) 2/12/76, p10 *Nordic disciplines gained more active following outside their traditional north European strongholds, especially in Switzerland and the U.S.* Britannica Book of the Year 1977, p732 **[1954,** so called from such competition having originated in the Nordic or Scandinavian countries]**

North, *n.* the industrialized, technically and economically advanced countries of the world. *During a four-day Conference on International Economic Cooperation held in Paris last week* *by 16 industrialized nations and 19 "poor" ones (which included some* nouveau riche *oil-producing countries), the North made what it considered a generous offer, especially given its painfully slow economic recovery. The South grudgingly accepted the package, but termed it quite inadequate and refused to give anything in exchange.* Time 6/13/77, p30 **[1975,** so called because most of the industrialized countries lie in the northern latitudes] ▶ *North* and *South* are economic designations into which the countries of the world can be roughly divided. The *North/South* distinction first appeared in the expression *North-South dialogue,* referring to a protracted debate concerning the obligations and expectations of each group of countries in a redistribution of the world's wealth.

Norwalk agent, a cube-shaped viral particle identified in 1972 as the causative agent of intestinal flu. *They decided to examine stool specimens from hepatitis A patients using immune electron microscopy. Kapikian had previously used this method for detecting, in a stool filtrate, the Norwalk agent, which is similar to the hepatitis A virus. The Norwalk agent was found to be associated with a form of acute infectious nonbacterial gastroenteritis—intestinal flu—in humans.* Science News 12/8/73, p359 **[1972,** named after *Norwalk,* Ohio, where it was first isolated]

nose, *n.* **rub one's nose in,** to cause one to experience closely (something unpleasant, especially as a punishment). *In the view of one leading Republican who finally cast a crucial vote against* [appointment to the Supreme Court of George H.] *Carswell, the choice was also an attempt to rub the Senate's nose in the mess it had made of the* [Judge Clement F.] *Haynsworth nomination.* New Yorker 12/5/70, p61 *Robert Carr, in an attempt to show that he is not rubbing deregistered noses in the dirt, has indicated that they can set up separate friendly societies to get these tax advantages.* Sunday Times (London) 11/14/71, p60 **[1963]**

noseguard, *n.* the defensive player in American football directly opposite the offensive center; a middle guard. *The Princeton coach also expressed pleasure with the play of his defensive line, especially Pete Funke, the noseguard, and two tackles, Matt McGrath and Joe Luncie, both sophomores.* NY Times 9/28/77, p32 **[1976,** probably so called from his central position on the defensive line]

nose job, *Informal.* cosmetic surgery to reshape the nose; rhinoplasty. *He attacked O'Hare as a cosmetic surgery junkie. She has had nine nose jobs, an eyelid lift, and hair transplant.* Time 5/14/79, p106 **[1963]**

nose wheelie, *U.S.* the raising of a skateboard's back wheels off the ground by putting one's weight on the front. *So many children perform "nose wheelies" and "tail wheelies" (tipping back or front) that some skateboards are now being manufactured with snubbed noses and flipped-up tails.* Encyclopedia Science Supplement (Grolier) 1977, p260 **[1976]**

nosh, *Slang.* —*v.t., v.i.* to nibble or snack. *The politician, equipped with a trowel and the Fixed Smile, gobs mortar on a cornerstone, or noshes his way along the campaign trail.* Time 10/12/70, p42 *Nor could any of it have been described as dainty noshing.* Sunday Times (London) 12/7/69, p49 —*n.* **1** *U.S.* a snack. *Advertising copy will stress that the company makes everything from "soup to nosh." (A nosh is a snack.)* NY Times 4/9/65, p40 **2** *British.* food. *While on the subject, couldn't one of the dining-rooms be turned into a Chinese restaurant, sort of? I've always found Chinese nosh both cheap and filling—tasty, too.* Punch 2/14/68, p220 **[1957** for verb; **1963** for noun; from Yiddish *nashn, v.,* to nibble, *nash, n.,* a nibble, snack]

nosher, *n. Slang.* a person given to eating snacks. . . . *hot meal vending machines in the lobby for late night noshers, help yourself breakfasts and make-your-own-beds.* Sunday Times (London) 3/23/69, p28 **[1957]**

noshery ('nɑʃəri:), *n. Slang.* a restaurant. *Richard Newport's Space-1999-with-touches-of-Conran restaurant is more than an expense account, sturgeon-egg noshery.* Times (London) 7/14/77, p14 *Pronto, a trendy East Side Italian restaurant, is offering a Sunday brunch for the first time, and similar affairs*

at other nosheries are S.R.O. Time 10/2/78, p88 **[1963,** from NOSH, *v.* + *-ery,* as in *eatery, bakery]*

no-show, *n.* **1** a person who fails to show up, as for an appointment. *The Levitt audit said there was no requirement to determine when . . . the "no-shows" had become ineligible, and hence no chance to recover any fraudulent payments. The "no-shows," the report said, might involve deaths, moving away from the city or changes in income.* NY Times 6/2/76, p23 **2** an act or instance of not showing up; nonappearance. *In many instances, say prosecutors around the country, the loss of one key witness means no case. Though statistics of witness no-shows are spotty and hard to come by, a recent study in high-crime Brooklyn, N.Y., by the Vera Institute of Justice found that as many as half the witnesses required to come to court for trial just did not show up.* Time 9/11/78, p41 **[1966,** transferred senses of the term (1940's) meaning "a person who reserves a seat on an airplane, etc., and neither cancels nor claims it"]

no-strings, *adj.* free of conditions or obligations. *Following the February £13m no-strings pay deal, which gave manual employees rises of £4 to £5 15s. a week, union officials have been conducting a wages and conditions survey of motor plants in Britain.* Times (London) 8/18/70, p15 **[1953,** from the phrase *with no strings attached]*

notaphily (nou'tæfəli:), *n.* the collecting of banknotes as a hobby. *Notaphily is the name of the hobby, and, as Mr. Narbeth points out in "Collect British Banknotes," it has one great advantage over other hobbies—"You are actually saving money and getting real pleasure from it . . . "* Manchester Guardian Weekly 12/12/70, p17 **[1970,** from Latin *nota* note (for banknote) + English *-phily* love of (from New Latin *-philia,* from Greek *philía* love)] —**notaphilic,** *adj.: Biafran £1 notes were printed, but it appears the war with the Nigerian Government ended before they were used. However, the notes found their way on to the notaphilic market.* Times (London) 1/27/76, p17 —**notaphilist,** *n.: Another kind of note which is highly prized was produced by the Chinese of the Ming dynasty—the Ming vases, you might say, of the notaphilists.* Manchester Guardian Weekly 6/12/71, p17

not-for-profit, *adj. U.S.* not formed to make profit; nonprofit. *Ever since the United States Customs Service moved out of the building, several years ago, the New York Landmarks Conservancy (a not-for-profit organization that preserves and reuses buildings of architectural and or historical significance) and the Custom House Institute . . . have been putting on a variety of shows.* New Yorker 9/11/78, p29 **[1966]** ▶ During the 1970's this term became almost as common in the United States as *nonprofit.*

no-tillage or **no-till,** *n.* a method of farming in which a seedbed is prepared without tillage by spraying a covering of mulch with herbicide and applying fertilizer (often used attributively). Also called MINIMUM TILLAGE, ZERO TILLAGE. *Differences in response of crops to tillage do exist on different soils, and tillage system selection should be tailored to specific soil characteristics. No-tillage is the most desirable system under some conditions, while moldboard plowing may be the most desirable system under others.* McGraw-Hill Yearbook of Science and Technology 1978, p79 *We experimented with no-till corn and soybeans last year. No-till worked especially well on land that had a good mulch.* Progressive Farmer 6/74, p29 **[1971]**

nouveau pauvre (nu:'vou 'pouvrə), *pl.* **nouveaux pauvres.** *French.* one who has become poor recently. *One of every four Americans 65 or over lives at or below "the poverty line." Some of these 5,000,000 old people were poor to begin with, but most are bewildered and bitter nouveaux pauvres, their savings and fixed incomes devoured by spiraling property taxes and other forms of inflation.* Time 8/3/70, p49 **[1958,** patterned after *nouveau riche]*

nouveau roman (nu:'vou rɔ:'mɑ̃), *pl.* **nouveaux romans.** a type of novel developed chiefly in France in the 1960's by such writers as Alain Robbe-Grillet, Michel Butor, Marguerite Duras, and Claude Mauriac, characterized by lack of moral, social, or psychological comment and by precise descriptions that suggest the mental state of the person experiencing or seeing them. Also called ANTI-ROMAN. *The detailed objectivity of the narration, giving every event movement by movement, the device of addressing the reader by the vocative . . . and the drifting plotlessness of the book, are hallmarks of the* nouveau roman. Times (London) 5/19/66, p18 *The characters are many and the story jumps from one to another, often (in the manner of the* nouveau roman) *with no names other than "he" or "the boy" to tell you whose episode it is.* Harper's 7/65, p112 [**1961,** from French, literally, new novel]

nouvelle cuisine (nu:'vel kwi'zi:n), a light, simplified form of French cooking introduced in the late 1970's. Also called CUISINE MINCEUR. *That is how it all began. Gault and Millau just had to lick their formula into shape (Millau's training as a journalist helped), and they were away. Among their shrewder coups was the invention of the term* nouvelle cuisine, *to describe the new school of lighter, more inventive, and less complicated cooking, which often combines unexpected ingredients.* Manchester Guardian Weekly (Le Monde section) 3/23/80, p13 *They moved on to La Recolte, the hotel's four-star and spectacularly decorated* nouvelle cuisine *restaurant, where people lingered over late lunches in Mozartean splendor.* Margaret Truman, Murder At The FBI, 1985, p135 [**1977,** from French, literally, new cookery]

now, *adj. Slang.* very fashionable or up-to-date; belonging to the Now Generation. *. . . sure as God made little green banknotes, you're bound to find that someone's been doing something you didn't, something more In, something more Now.* Punch 12/17/69, p990 *Bullitt, I find, is completely typical of the "now" look in American movies—a swift-moving, constantly shifting surface that suggests rather than reveals depths.* Saturday Review 12/28/68, p18 [**1963,** revival of adjective use recorded from 1444-1875]

NOW or **N.O.W.** (nau), *n.* acronym for *National Organization for Women. Women's Liberation formally began with the founding in 1966 of the National Organization for Women, which remains the largest and most influential movement group, the original umbrella under which other groups pressed their individual programs. N.O.W. has led assaults in Congress and the courts on issues ranging from child care to abortion reform.* Time 3/20/72, p29 *The Women's Campaign Fund and NOW both contributed to Miss Holtzman's primary . . .* NY Times Magazine 10/19/80, p31 [**1966,** influenced by *now* immediate]

NOW account, *U.S.* a savings account which may be used by the depositor to write checks against, much as if it were a checking account, and which usually bears interest. *The NOW accounts were clearly popular, and were a particular boon to pensioners who were recently authorized to have their Social Security checks deposited directly in a savings bank.* NY Times 5/12/76, p31 [**1973,** from *NOW,* abbreviation of *negotiated order of withdrawal,* the checklike instrument used in such accounts]

nowcast, *v.i.* to provide a description of atmospheric conditions as they occur or develop. *The capability of meteorologists to analyze current weather conditions and to provide very short-range forecasts continued to improve in 1984. This scale of weather description and short-period forecasting is referred to as* nowcasting. 1986 Britannica Yearbook of Science and the Future, p287 [**1983,** patterned after *forecast,* BACKCAST]

Now Generation, a name applied to the generation of young people of the late 1960's to characterize their concern with current trends, fashions, issues, etc. *The more mature of the unmarried in the Now Generation say that, far from promoting promiscuity, the pills impose a sense of responsibility.* Time 4/7/67, p20 *"The police don't understand the now generation and the now generation doesn't dig the fuzz."* NY Times 9/22/68, pB32 [**1967**]

no-win, *adj.* **1** not likely to be won; not leading to victory. *For a long time, these officials looked the other way. Why? Well, they said, they were afraid that active efforts to find out which children were in the extortion ring and to punish them would expose them to charges of "police tactics." The principal's main* concern was that it was a "no-win" situation. NY Times Magazine 9/26/76, p65 **2** not played or engaged in to win; noncompetitive. *An offshoot of a 1973 New Games Tournament, staged by* Whole Earth Catalog *Creator Steward Brand, the foundation is now a growing national enterprise. Its goal is nothing less than to change the way Americans play, mainly by replacing competitive games with cooperative "no win" pastimes.* Time 9/11/78, p54 [**1962,** from *no, adj. + win, v.*]

NO$_X$ (nɑks), *n.* acronym for *nitrogen oxide* or *nitrogen oxides.* [Robert] *Fri also announced a one-year delay of implementation of the 1976 standards for emissions of nitrogen oxides (NO$_x$). EPA will recommend a modified NOx standard to Congress this fall, and Fri says some sort of special electronic feedback catalyst system will be required to meet that new standard.* Science News 8/4/73, p71 [**1972**]

NP-complete, *adj. Mathematics.* of or belonging to a class of problems that are impractical to solve because no polynomial algorithm can be given. *Several typical examples can be used to illustrate the wide variety of problems currently known to be NP-complete. One example is known as the Traveling Salesman's Problem. In this problem a salesman is given a list of cities and a road map telling him the shortest route between each pair of cities. The salesman would like to begin at his home city, visit all the other cities, and return to his home city, traveling the least total distance in the process. The problem of finding this shortest route has recently been shown to be an NP-complete problem.* 1978 Britannica Yearbook of Science and the Future, p184 *Since NP-complete problems capture the difficulty of all other problems in NP, it is widely thought today that all NP-complete problems are computationally intractable. A proof that a problem is NP-complete is usually considered a strong argument for abandoning further efforts to devise an efficient algorithm for its solution.* Scientific American 1/78, p107 [**1976,** from *nondeterministic polynomial + complete*]

NPT, abbreviation of NONPROLIFERATION TREATY. *As of Dec. 9, 1969, the NPT had been signed by 93 governments, 22 of which had ratified it.* Americana Annual 1970, p248 [**1967**]

NRC, abbreviation of *Nuclear Regulatory Commission,* a U.S. government agency established in 1975 to regulate the operation of nonmilitary nuclear facilities, especially nuclear power plants. *At a press conference at which the NRC was sharply criticized for complacency and being too close to the nuclear industry, Rep. James Weaver, D-Ore., also raised the possibility of blocking licenses for new plants until the dangers of nuclear facilities are brought into focus.* Today (New York) 4/3/79, pA2 [**1976**]

NREM sleep ('en,rem), another name for SYNCHRONIZED SLEEP. *These two phases are already present in the infant from birth on. Compared with the adult there are a number of differences: in the nature of some of the brain wave criteria; in the fact that infants invariably begin sleep with an REM phase whereas adults start NREM sleep; and so on.* New Scientist 4/4/74, p16 [**1965;** *NREM,* acronym for *nonrapid eye movement*]

NSM, abbreviation of NEW SMOKING MATERIAL. *The controversial NSM advertisements were approved by the authority and the Department of Health before they appeared . . . Unlike those for cigarettes, these advertisements can make health claims and do not have to carry a health warning. Critics argue that they could mislead smokers.* Times (London) 7/6/77, p19 [**1973**]

nu body, another name for NUCLEOSOME. *About half of the DNA in chromatin was found to be associated with nu bodies and the remainder with the threads connecting them; recent data, however, suggests that more, perhaps over 70%, of the chromosome DNA is associated with nu bodies.* 1977 Britannica Yearbook of Science and the Future, p344 [**1976;** *nu,* said to be derived from the Greek letter *nu* but probably short for *nucleus*]

nuclear, *n.* **1** a nuclear weapon, especially a missile armed with an atomic warhead. *The highest common interest on either side of the Iron Curtain is in survival. A strategic nuclear exchange* would have a catastrophic effect on both. The West, moreover, is unlikely to initiate the use of nuclears. The Russians have a superiority in conventional forces at their disposal which is unlikely to diminish. Times (London) 2/27/70, p9 **2** a nuclear power; a nation with an arsenal of atomic weapons. Compare NON-NUCLEAR. So far negotiation under the heading "non-proliferation" has virtually been between the Americans and the Russians and it has been about Germany. This is indeed something, but negotiation between nuclears and non-nuclears has scarcely begun. Listener 2/9/67, p186 [**1962** for def. 1; **1967** for def. 2; noun uses of the adjective]

nuclearism, n. emphasis on nuclear weapons as a deterrent to war or as a means of attaining political and social goals. The most extreme state of contemporary deformation is a pattern which may best be called "nuclearism." By this term I mean to suggest the passionate embrace of nuclear weapons as a solution to our anxieties (especially our anxieties concerning the weapons themselves), and as a means of restoring a lost sense of immortality. That is, one turns to the weapons, and to their power, as a means of restoring boundaries. Nuclearism, then, is a secular religion, a total ideology in which grace, the mastery of death, is achieved by means of a new technological deity. Atlantic 10/70, p106 [**1969**]

nuclearist, n. a person who supports nuclearism. An instant myth seems to be emerging that nuclear threats are highly effective. Recently ex-President Eisenhower referred to some he had made at a time of stalemate in negotiations to end the Korean War, and which he is quoted as believing conjured an immediate settlement . . . President Eisenhower's threats must have been a godsend to China's nuclearists . . . Manchester Guardian Weekly 10/20/66, p15 This deity is seen as an all-powerful force, capable of both apocalyptic destruction and unlimited creation, and the nuclear believer, or nuclearist, allies himself to that force and feels thereby compelled to expound the virtues of his god. Atlantic 10/70, p106 [**1952**]

nuclear medicine, the use of radioactive materials and of instruments detecting nuclear radiation in the diagnosis and treatment of diseases. . . . nuclear medicine [is] a new medical specialty which has developed largely under the support of the Division of Biology and Medicine of the AEC [Atomic Energy Commission]. The main accomplishment of this discipline is a vast improvement in the diagnosis of cancer and many other diseases. Atlantic 4/71, p32 [**1952**]

nuclear winter, a condition of subfreezing temperatures lasting up to a year or more, predicted by scientists as one of the consequences of a limited nuclear war. A bold new theory states that with the explosion of even a fraction of the stored up arsenal of nuclear power presently on Earth, there will be a so-called "nuclear winter," caused by a devastating dust storm of soot and smoke, like that observed temporarily on Mars. Christian Science Monitor 12/14/83, p10 [**1983**]

nucleocapsid (ˌnuːkliːouˈkæpsid), n. the nucleic acid of a virus together with the shell enclosing it. The RNA of the influenza virus is found in five to seven discrete pieces, each in its own nucleocapsid, and its total mass is about 4 million daltons. Each of the pieces . . . is an intact gene that controls at least one characteristic of the virus. Science 6/8/73, p1044 [**1972,** from nucleo- nucleic acid + CAPSID outer shell of a virus]

nucleochronology, n. the chronology or sequence of time in which chemical elements are formed from the nuclei of hydrogen, especially in the evolution of stars and planets. These nucleochronologies, coupled with the observed abundances of heavy elements in the stars and theories of star formation, have been used by various investigators in proposing detailed theories of the entire history of the galaxy. Further work on the correlation of nucleochronology with other astronomical information should yield important results in the near future. Scientific American 1/74, p77 [**1972,** from nucleo- nucleus + chronology]

nucleochronometer, n. a chemical element or isotope that serves as a standard for measuring or determining nucleochronology. We have estimated the relative p-process production of ^{146}Sm and propose a measurement which would

enable it to become a nucleochronometer. Nature 1/23/72, p447 [**1972,** from nucleochronology + -meter measuring device]

nucleocosmochronology, n. the chronology or time sequence of the formation of the universe or any part of it, such as the solar system, determined especially by nucleochronology. The history of these countless nuclear events is written in the chemical elements out of which the earth and the rest of the universe are made. By properly interpreting this history we can assign a date to the formation of those elements. From this date we can infer the age of the universe itself. The scientific discipline that is concerned with these techniques is called nucleocosmochronology. Scientific American 1/74, p69 [**1972,** from nucleo- + cosmo- universe + chronology]

nucleonium (ˌnuːkliːˈouniːəm), n. an elementary particle consisting of a nucleus and an antinucleus in a bound state, formed when matter and antimatter come into contact. To understand the process by which nucleonium is formed in a matter-antimatter encounter, one may consider a specific, hypothetical example of a collision between a neutral atom X and a singly ionized antiatom Y, which is lacking one positron. McGraw-Hill Yearbook of Science and Technology 1974, p102 [**1974,** from nucleon nuclear particle + -ium (suffix for chemical elements)]

nucleophile, n. a substance that is strongly attracted to atomic nuclei. Then by dividing heterolytic reagents into nucleophiles and electrophiles, he saw the basis of a scheme interrelating a great range of chemical reactions. Times (London) 12/10/70, p10 [**1953**]

nucleosome, n. the basic structural unit of chromatin, the constituent of chromosomes, consisting of a roughly spherical body made up of 200 base pairs of DNA and eight basic protein molecules called histones. Also called NU BODY. Chromatin is the DNA and protein package that makes up the chromosomes of higher organisms, and it is generally believed to consist of a series of gobs of DNA-plus-protein, arranged like pearls on a string. The gobs are known as nucleosomes, and the holy grail of chromatin research has been the nucleosome crystal. Once he has a crystal, the molecular biologist can use the most powerful tool in his possession—X-ray crystallography—to solve its structure. New Scientist 9/22/77, p727 Each nucleosome contains two molecules each of the four histone types H2A, H2B, H3, and H4. Closely associated with the histones to form the nucleosome "core" are 140 base pairs of the DNA; the remaining DNA is less closely associated with histone and forms a bridge or linker between adjacent cores. McGraw-Hill Yearbook of Science and Technology 1978, p278 [**1976,** from nucleo- + -some body] —**nucleosomal,** adj.: They suggest that H1 is bound to a short (30 base pair) terminal stretch of nucleosomal DNA which can be removed by nuclease treatment . . . without significantly disturbing the basic nucleosome structure. Nature 4/15/76, p577

nucleosynthesis, n. the process by which chemical elements are created from the nuclei of hydrogen. Further points in favour of lunar water, free or combined, are that the universe consists practically entirely of hydrogen and helium—hydrogen being the starting material for nucleosynthesis in stars—and that oxygen is now known to be abundant in the Moon's crust . . . Science Journal 5/69, p92 For more than a decade astronomers have agreed that the heavy elements which are built up in stars by nucleosynthesis are dispersed throughout galaxies by supernova explosions. New Scientist and Science Journal 3/25/71, p663 [**1960**]

nude mouse, any one of a laboratory-bred strain of mice that have no thymus glands and therefore lack the immune defenses provided by T cells. There is also the case of the "nude mouse." The nude mouse is . . . very prone to disease. But it is not more prone than any other mouse to cancer. So it seems that T cells cannot be playing a very large part in the natural defence of the body against cancer. More recent research has shown clearly that there are tumour-killing cells, both in the blood of cancer patients and in that of normal people. But they are not (or apparently are not) T lymphocytes. Nude mice, for instance, have them. What they are remains, for the time being, *mystery.* New Scientist 2/2/78, p291 [**1974,** so called from its being hairless]

nudzh or **nudge** (nudʒ), *n. U.S. Slang.* a nuisance; bore; pest. Also spelled NOODGE. *"He's not a writer, he's a nudge. On the phone twice a day asking how's it going!"* NY Times Book Review 12/7/72, p56 *Discharged from prison, Lou Jean Poplin—sometime beautician, full-time nudzh—must first spring her husband . . . from the minimum-security prison.* Time 4/15/74, p92 [**1968,** from Yiddish *nudyen* to bore, pester, from Russian *nudnyi* tedious, boring; related to *nudnik* a bore, pest 1920's)] ▶The spelling *nudge* was influenced by the English word *nudge* push, poke (pronounced nədʒ).

nuke (nuːk), *U.S. Slang.* —*n.* **1** a nuclear weapon. *The guessing game of "enoughness" goes on unabated, its premise being "We must not have too many nukes or the enemy will feel threatened, but we must not have too few or he will attack."* New Yorker 1/9/71, p60 *"I worked with the people, so I knew what they were doing," Walkley* [James Walkley, a former Air Force sergeant, who used to work on target planning at Hickam Field in Hawaii] *said. "With a nuke, you'd have to drop a certain type on a certain type of target."* Cleveland Press 4/7/72, p2 [**1959**] **2** a nuclear-powered electrical generating station. *According to the Hudson River Fishermen's Association, the nuke was directly responsible for the death of between 310,000 and 475,000 fish in a six-week period last year alone.* Time 9/13/71, p49 [**1969**] —*v.t.* **1** to attack with nuclear weapons. *There is another minority among Vietnam veterans: hawks, whose feelings are quite the opposite of these men's, who proclaim that the difficulty in Vietnam was not that we have done too much but that we have done too little, that we should 'nuke Hanoi', as they put it in that grotesque idiom.* Listener 8/31/72, p270 [**1967**] **2** *Figurative.* to destroy. *That play, too, was quickly nuked by poor ticket sales.* Americana Annual 1987, p522 [**1976**] **3** to microwave. *Nothing that can't be set to rights by nuking a little frozen za.* Fairfax Journal (Virginia) 9/7/88, pA10 [**1988**]

null set, *Mathematics.* a set with no members. Also called EMPTY SET. *Mathematics has available for this purpose* [an impossible event] *the null or empty set, symbolized by ∅. The null set is a subset of every aggregate and hence is useful in connection with many other issues.* Edna E. Kramer, The Nature and Growth of Modern Mathematics, 1970, p261 *Every finite set of n elements has 2^n subsets if one includes the original set and the null, or empty set. For example, a set of three elements, ABC, has 2^3 = 8 subsets: ABC, AB, BC, AC, A, B, C, and the null set.* Scientific American 3/71, p106 [**1966**]

number, *n.* **do a number on,** *Chiefly U.S. and Canadian Slang.* **1** to hurt or harm, especially by deception or trickery. *I was on my own among male relatives, male bosses, male lovers who were all, at one time or another doing numbers on me.* Maclean's 11/74, p19 *The wife was shaken. "If I'm doing a number on the kid, I want to know about it,"* Mrs. Bryan said. New Yorker 5/15/78, p40 **2** to make fun of in a sly or mocking way; subject to derision or ridicule. *Fearless Johnny Carson stepped out before the camera last night on his "Tonight" show and did a number on his new boss, NBC president Fred Silverman . . . with this line: "Freddy Silverman has just canceled his mother."* NY Post 12/1/78, p10 *In fact, there is a real social disadvantage for those of us who are limited to one standard language, and others sometimes do a number on us because of it. Black Americans who successfully navigate in the white offices of standard English, for instance, still employ the mother tongue, sometimes to remind the white folks around them that black is beautiful or proud or indomitable.* Manchester Guardian Weekly (Washington Post section) 1/6/80, p17 **3** to flirt with, especially in a subtle or devious manner. *I coolly flicked the ashes of my Lucky Strike—into my half-finished brandy and soda. I don't think she noticed—her big baby blues were too busy doing a number on my bloodshot brown ones.* Spectator, Winter 1979, p15 **4 do a number,** to do a (specified) act, performance, or routine. *"I did a bag-lady number on one of the platforms here in the bus station last year, and I almost got arrested. They thought I was the real thing."* New Yorker 10/17/77, p40 [**1974,** patterned after *do a job on* with apparent

extension from the phrase *do one's number* to perform one's act or routine in a show, etc.]

number cruncher, *Informal.* a computer designed to perform complicated and lengthy numerical calculations. *Figures of 40-50 MIPS have been claimed for . . . the Texas Instruments Advanced Scientific Computer (ASC) in contrast to a conventional giant number-cruncher like the CDC 7600 at 10 MIPS.* New Scientist 6/17/76, p626 *Aiming to develop their own "number crunchers," as the fast new U.S. machines are called, Moscow is designing a large computer, specified the BESM-10. Supposedly, it will be capable of 15 million operations per second.* Time 8/1/77, p45 [**1966,** so called for its ability to break down large computational tasks] —**number crunching,** *Informal: A new HP 1000 F-Series computer system—the Model 45—provides number-crunching power previously obtainable only with much larger and more expensive systems.* Scientific American 9/78, p104

numbered account, a bank account identified only by a number and not by the holder's name. *Most* [Swiss] *banks try to dissuade depositors from opening a numbered account on the grounds that Swiss banking secrecy covers all accounts. The vetting of credentials is much stricter, the deposit higher (as much as $50,000 for some banks) and one pays for the service. In return, the identity of a holder of a numbered account is known only to two or three high bank officials.* Manchester Guardian Weekly 6/9/73, p27 *Along with a more or less stable currency, Panama now has, under Torrijos, banking laws of alluring flexibility: numbered accounts like Switzerland's, no local taxes on offshore earnings, no restrictions on taking money out of the country.* New Yorker 8/16/76, p72 [**1965**]

number runner or **numbers runner,** *U.S. Slang.* a person who collects bets in the form of an illegal lottery known as a numbers game. *Mother played the numbers like everyone else in Harlem but she was scared about Daddy being a number runner. Daddy started working for Jocko on commission about six months ago when he lost his house-painting job, which hadn't been none too steady to begin with.* Louise Meriwether, Daddy was a Number Runner, 1970, p21 [**1958**]

number two, *Slang.* second; not in the most important or powerful position. *As long as Russia feels the understandable necessity to catch up in the arms race, the language of economic priorities is distorted for her in a way that it need not be for the US as number one super-Power. It just does not pay to be number two.* Manchester Guardian Weekly 4/25/70, p17 [**1965**]

numéraire (nʏmeiˈrer), *n. French.* standard for currency exchange rates. *The Bretton Woods agreement, hammered out by an international panel of experts, headed by Harry Dexter White, of the United States, and John Maynard Keynes, of Britain, established the dollar as the numéraire, or measuring rod, against which the value of other currencies was set, and also as the principal currency in which the reserves, or national savings accounts, of other nations would be held.* New Yorker 10/23/71, p118 *Not only can they* [SDRs] *be used as the numéraire for currency values, they can also be modified to form the basis for further increases in national reserves in the future.* Times (London) 3/3/72, p17 [**1964**]

numerical control, a method of machine-tool automation using perforated tape carrying coded instructions. *Abbreviation:* NC *Numerical control means a fully automatic control system which works from numerical information, of the kind found on an engineering drawing . . . A digital computer is used to prepare punched or magnetic tape containing full machining instructions.* New Scientist 5/12/66, p362 [**1952**]

numerically-controlled, *adj.* automated through numerical control. *Now, numerically-controlled machine tools have been developed which offer a 5-axis capability and could do everything that Molins* [Machine Company] *required, without any movement of the workpieces from one machine to another.* New Scientist 9/14/67, p563 [**1952**]

numerical taxonomy, the classification of plant and animal species based on a quantitative analysis by means of computers. *In the second edition of their work on numerical taxonomy, Peter*

Sneath and Robert Sokal stated: "Numerical taxonomy is a revolutionary approach to biological classification . . . Instead of qualitatively appraising the resemblance of organisms on the basis of certain favored characters, a taxonomist using this new methodology will attempt to amass as many distinguishing characters as possible, giving equal weight to each." 1975 Britannica Yearbook of Science and the Future, p338 [**1974**]

numero uno ('nu:mə,rou 'u:nou), *U.S. and Canada.* the first, best, or most important of a kind; number one. *All the Bicentennial rhetoric and campaign jingoism can't cover up the fact that we're not Numero Uno.* Time 6/21/76, pE6 *Now along comes the 22-year-old Miss Evert, numero uno, a two-time defending champion, with a winning streak on clay that spans four years and 112 matches.* NY Times 9/10/77, p19 *Margaret Laurence's* The Stone Angel *was adjudged numero uno, a popular choice.* Maclean's 3/20/78, p67 [**1963**, from Spanish *número uno* or Italian *numero uno*]

nunchakus (nu:n'tʃɑ:ku:z), *n.pl.* See the quotation for the meaning. *The radical taste tends . . . to nunchakus, which go back more than 500 years. They were . . . invented by Japanese peasants for self-defence when metal weapons were forbidden to all but the Samurai, and have been revived by Tokyo students for their frenzied battles with the police. Nunchakus are two hardwood sticks, about 14 inches long and 1¼ inches in diameter, connected by a rawhide or nylon cord. Eight stickmen abreast, it is claimed, can clear a street in no time. The sticks have 30 inches of reach, making frontal assaults impossible.* Manchester Guardian Weekly 5/2/70, p11 [**1970**, from Japanese]

nuplex, *n.* a nuclear-powered complex of industrial manufacturers. *The obvious answer is to initiate, or promote, energy-consuming industries in the vicinity of these stations, creating at each point a nuclear powered agro-industrial complex—or "nuplex".* New Scientist 7/10/69, p60 *Dr Finniston mentioned the building of large industrial complexes in arid coastal regions; of "nuplexes" centred on large nuclear reactors using seawater.* Manchester Guardian Weekly 9/13/69, p9 [**1967**]

nurd (nərd), *n. U.S. and Canadian Slang.* variant of NERD. *When Collins condescends to the help of a greenhorn (John Lazarus)—a nurd in heavy, black-rimmed glasses and an early-morning bouffant—he does it because it amuses him, temporarily. The kid's a klutz, but he's also a link with the outside world.* Maclean's 12/18/78, p49 [**1965**] **—nurdy,** *adj.: The nurdier clients want foil. They don't want golden-brown Brillo pads. "They want potatoes cooked in an oven in foil," Otto says. "If the potatoes are in foil, that's gourmet."* New Yorker 2/19/79, p92

nurse practitioner, a registered nurse with preparation in primary health care. *In the interests of efficiency and economy, the New Medicine will make greater use of ancillary medical personnel. Nurse-practitioners (i.e. registered nurses with extra training) can competently perform many of the physician's traditional tasks. They can take medical histories, conduct a physical examination, deliver babies and provide 75 per cent of all care required by children.* Maclean's 1/7/80, p40 [**1966**]

nurturance, *n.* the action or process of nurturing; the providing of sustenance and care. *Reverence for such neglected "feminine" values as gentleness and nurturance becomes an excuse to bad-mouth women who display "masculine" characteristics like self-assertion or who don't want to preside as goddess of the organic kitchen.* New Yorker 10/23/71, p170 [**1938, 1953**]

nurturant, *adj.* providing sustenance and care. *Social scientists apply the term "nurturant" to typical female professions such as child care, teaching, nursing or social work.* Encyclopedia Science Supplement (Grolier) 1971, p81 [**1938, 1951**]

nut, *n.* **1** core; basic part. *The nut of [Jeremy] Bray's argument . . . is that the government's role in managing the economy would be more effective if the blanket approach were replaced by a new structure providing two kinds of centres of analysis and demand management: management agencies for each industry and also for each locality.* New Scientist 10/2/69 p4 *. . . you go and do your thing and we'll go and do ours— just the way it's always been, but without tackling the nut of the problem, effective politics.* NY Times 10/16/70, p41 [**1969**] **2 do one's nut** or **do one's nuts**, *British Slang.* to act or work like one who is crazy. . . . *Macdonald has been doing some extra-mural lobbying of the Home Office to spread the word of his famine warnings. In his own words: "I've been doing my nut about saying why do we have to wait for the house to be on fire . . . "* Sunday Times (London) 4/18/71, p9 *Don't tell us, after the rich crop of British Rail announcements about increased seat reservation fees, and another five shillings on sleepers, that they aren't doing their nuts to get themselves out of the red.* Punch 8/20/69, p286 [**1960**]—**v.t.** *British Slang.* to strike with the head. *While they [skinheads] favor the boot as a primary weapon, they also use their heads to "nut" or butt a victim, and whatever other weapons come to hand: bricks, rocks, bottles, knives and razors.* Time 6/8/70, p37 *I jumped up and nutted him, and this other kid jumped on his back.* Sunday Times (London) 9/21/69, p22 [**1963**]

nuts and bolts, the basic features or components. *While Laird has immersed himself in day-to-day Pentagon business in order to learn the nuts and bolts of the Defense Department, Packard has taken on the long-range, tasks.* Time 3/28/69, p15 *With that philosophic fundamental out of the way, what of the nuts and bolts of printed news in the years ahead? . . . Here those two columns of* What's News *on the front page of* The Wall Street Journal, *and the news-magazines, point the way.* Saturday Review 10/10/70, p64 [**1967**, noun use from earlier (1952) adjectival phrase meaning basic or practical]

nutter, *n. British Slang.* a crazy or eccentric person. *Much of this is born of solitariness, a detached curiosity, and affection for the shabby and odd, the nutters of the species.* Manchester Guardian Weekly 2/20/71, p20 [**1958**]

Nuyorican or **Newyorican** (,nu:yɔr'ri:kən), *adj., n. U.S.* variant of NEORICAN. *A book of poems by more than a dozen of these Nuyorican writers, "Nuyorican Poetry, an Anthology of Puerto Rican Words and Feelings," has just been published by William Morrow & Company, in English and Spanish or both—a "Nuyorican dialect" that the writers see as just being born.* NY Times 5/14/76, pD17 *Puerto Ricans on the island have a name for these reverse migrants: Neoricans (sometimes spelled Newyoricans). As Neoricans, the family of Manuel Oritz-Peña is typical, a microcosm of the returning islanders.* NY Times Magazine 11/12/78, p20 [**1972**, from Spanish *Nueva York* or English *New York* + Puerto *Rican*]

NVA, abbreviation of *North Vietnamese Army. . . . millions of people in Vietnam . . . have risked their lives, their fortunes, and their sacred honor to fight off the NLF, the VC, the DRV, the NVA, and all the others with alphabetical tags that simply spell "the enemy."* Atlantic 3/69, p28 [**1966**]

O

OAO, abbreviation of *Orbiting Astronomical Observatory*, an unmanned scientific satellite of NASA, designed for astronomical research from a circular orbit around the earth. Compare OGO, OSO. *The OAO satellite was planned as a general observing facility as well as for the specific experiments mentioned. Three months before the satellite was launched, NASA placed notices in general astronomical publications announcing that the satellite, like earth-based observatories, would be made available to guest observers for their own research.* Science News Yearbook 1969, p148 *Although the first OAO malfunctioned, the second one (launched on Dec. 7, 1968) has been an outstanding success and has produced a wealth of important new astronomical data.* McGraw-Hill Yearbook of Science and Technology 1971, p300 [**1962**]

OAPEC (ou'eipek), *n.* acronym for *Organization of Arab Petroleum Exporting Countries*, a subgroup of OPEC. *By way of explanation, OAPEC spokesmen argued that a sizable increase was warranted because "persistent erosion" of the dollar and inflation in the developed countries had cut the real price of a liquid barrel of oil almost by half since 1973.* Time 10/9/78, p94 [**1969**]

OAU, abbreviation of *Organization of African Unity*, an association of African countries formed in 1963. *Nigeria and Tanzania carry special weight within the OAU, the first because it is black Africa's most populous and militarily most powerful state, the second because it is the spokesman of the front-line states (in the Rhodesian conflict).* Manchester Guardian Weekly (Le Monde section) 7/9/78, p11 [**1963**]

obduct, *v.t. Geology.* to push (one crustal plate of the earth) on top of another. Compare SUBDUCT. *In Newfoundland, however, they recognize examples of their first category of ultramafic rocks—sheet-like masses analogous to ophiolite complexes of oceanic lithosphere obducted later than the Permian.* Nature 12/15/72, p383 *Many recent reports on the nature of ophiolites from various parts of the world have clearly pointed up the problem of comparing oceanic lithosphere with preserved slabs of supposed older oceanic crust obducted onto the margins of continents.* McGraw-Hill Yearbook of Science and Technology 1974, p393 [**1971**, from Latin *obductus*, past participle of *obdūcere* to cover over, from *ob-* over + *dūcere* to lead; formed on the analogy of SUBDUCT]► *Obduct* in the general sense of "to cover over" is recorded in the OED as obsolete since 1646. Compare SUFFOSION. **—obduction,** *n.: Alpine orogeny . . . was probably preceded by subduction or obduction of the Tethyan plate along the European continental margin.* Nature 3/31/72, p222

Obie ('oubi:), *n.* an annual award given by a newspaper for the best off-Broadway plays and performances presented in the American theater. *Meanwhile, he [James Coco] was acting (six Broadway shows, 25 off-Broadway), collecting two Obies for off-Broadway performances . . . and being entirely forgotten by audiences and casting directors when his shows were over.* Time 1/12/70, p37 [**1966**, from the pronunciation of the letters *OB*, abbreviation of OFF-BROADWAY.]

Object Kowal ('kouəl), *n.* a planet about 100 miles (160 kilometers) in diameter, discovered between Saturn and Uranus in 1977. See MINIPLANET. *The new planet's . . . motion is locked in resonance with the movement of Saturn. The time for five revolutions of Saturn in its orbit is almost exactly equal to that for three revolutions of object Kowal. There are also possible resonances with Jupiter and Uranus, a situation which would make the orbit of the new planet particularly stable.* New Scientist 2/2/78, p300 [**1977**, named after Charles *Kowal*, the as-

tronomer who discovered it at the Hale Observatories in Pasadena, California]

obsidian dating, a method of determining the age of a geological or archaeological specimen containing volcanic glass (obsidian) by measuring the amount of water absorbed. *In contrast one can agree that the wealth of detail in the section on obsidian dating is fully justified because this is a technique which by virtue of its low cost and relative simplicity should be within the technical competence of a small archaeological unit to set up and operate, and the chapter provides enough practical detail to make this possible.* Nature 8/11/72, p360 [**1968**]

obviosity, *n.* something obvious; a plainly evident remark, inference, detail, etc. *The recent* Preliminary Report on Soccer Hooliganism, *prepared by a Birmingham research group under Dr J.A. Harrington for the Minister of Sport, contains so many obviosities, and betrays so little knowledge of the game (not to speak of group psychology), that it has irritated people inside it (not to speak of psychologists).* Listener 2/29/68, p286 *Who says there's nothing charming about obviosities, clichés and an 1890 style? . . . In this book Smith is openly sentimental, seldom hesitates to use a cliché, and isn't afraid of being obvious. As a result "Shelter Bay" . . . has the kind of touching charm that a less unsophisticated author couldn't have given it.* Maclean's 3/6/65, p46 [**1959**, from *obvious*, on the pattern of pairs such as *porous, porosity*]

occupational medicine, a branch of medicine dealing with the treatment and prevention of disorders related to one's occupation or work. *Murray has admiration for some of the French legislation which insists that the employer of 3000 people must have a full-time doctor trained in occupational medicine.* New Scientist 6/14/73, p697 [**1970**]

oceanaut, *n.* another name for AQUANAUT. *Food, clothing and shelter used to be enough to get explorers to their goals. In the deep oceans, however, as in space, the most important consideration is air. Oceanauts can only begin their quests encumbered by the huge air tanks to which they are presently bound.* Science News 8/5/67, p138 [**1962**, from *ocean* + *-naut*, as in *astronaut*]

ocean engineering, a branch of engineering dealing with the design and development of equipment for use in the ocean, such as underwater sensing devices. *Dr Ken Ridler of NRDC was . . . roaming up and down the country trying to whip up enthusiasm for ocean engineering and broadcasting the fact that this was one area where the corporation would be pleased to invest its money.* New Scientist 7/13/72, p75 [**1965**]

ocean-floor spreading, another name for SEA-FLOOR SPREADING. *Ocean-floor spreading processes, Talbot contends, swept the "scum" together, piling it up in a skimming action to form "micro-continents."* New Scientist 4/6/72, p6 [**1972**]

oceanics, *n.* the scientific exploration and study of the ocean. *A science of the seas is rapidly emerging. It's called oceanics. Through research in this vital and promising field, Bendix has already made a number of interesting and significant contributions . . . We have developed techniques for operating electronic systems at depths of 18,000 feet, and transmitting data from these systems to the surface.* Time 5/8/64, p80 [**1964**]

oceanization, *n.* the gradual conversion of crustal material characteristic of continents to the type of material found beneath the oceans. *The Soviet tectonician Belousov has gone so far as to invoke extensive 'oceanisation' of continental crust to account for the ocean basins; he has in consequence totally rejected plate tectonics and explains first order structures exclu-*

sively by vertical motions. Nature 2/6/75, p396 [**1960**, from *ocean* + *-ization*]

ocean-thermal, *adj.* relating to or making use of the temperature differences between the (warm) surface water and (cold) deep water of the ocean. *William E. Heronemus, a University of Massachusetts professor who has done extensive research in both wind-power and ocean-thermal technology, believes that if we wanted to, we could have the first commercial-sized ocean-thermal-differences power plant in place and making electricity in the Gulf Stream off Florida within six to eight years.* NY Times Magazine 3/16/75, p46 [**1974**]

ochratoxin (ˌoukrəˈtaksən), *n.* any of various highly poisonous substances secreted by some strains of a mold found in grain. Grain feed containing ochratoxin may find its way into eggs and meat. *Some of the history of ochratoxin A demonstrates the point. First encountered in South Africa in the early 1960s, this toxin is produced by the mould* Aspergillus ochraceus *isolated from grain.* New Scientist 4/22/76, p170 [**1972**, from (*Aspergillus*) *ochra*ceus, the species of mold + *toxin*]

Ocker (ˈakər), *n. Australian Slang.* a type of uneducated and boorish Australian. Compare ALF GARNETT, ARCHIE BUNKER. *A legacy of colonial brutality and puritanical inhibition still sends the Ocker in search of sporadic release through "rorts" of formidable rowdiness and binds him to a veritable cult of intolerance and ethnocentricity.* New Yorker 1/3/77, p58 [**1971**, from the name of a character played in a television series by the Australian actor Ron Frazer; *Ocker* is a common Australian variant of the name *Oscar*] —**Ockerism**, *n.: The new Australian boorishness is known as Ockerism, from a slob-like character called Ocker in a television series—the embodiment of oafish, blinkered self-satisfaction.* Listener 9/12/74, p334

OCR, abbreviation of *optical character recognition*, the ability of a computer unit to optically "read" printed material and convert it into computer code without manual keyboard operation. *Optical character recognition (OCR), as practiced by the new generation of machines that read, is one of filtering, selecting and reducing from the detail present in each character on the paper just sufficient information to allow the correct identity to be decided with certainty.* Science Journal 10/68, p67 [**1966**]

octaphonic, *adj.* of or having to do with high-fidelity sound transmission or reproduction over eight different channels. *In addition, Philips hints, the CD can theoretically accommodate a video track, for opera fans, or quadraphonic and even octaphonic sound, for audio buffs. All one has to do is buy a new player, which will probably be priced at about $500, and replace what may be an extensive, expensive record library.* NY Times Magazine (Home Design section) 4/13/80, p87 [**1978**]

octopush, *n.* a form of hockey invented in Great Britain, played in a swimming pool. See the quotation for details. *Octopush, for the benefit of unaquatic land-lubbers and ignoramuses, is a new form of underwater hockey . . . The game is played by teams of six . . . The object of the game is to propel or shovel the puck . . . along the bottom of the pool and into the opponents' gull* [goal]. Times (London) 2/18/70, p11 [**1970**, blend of *octopus* and *push*]

OD or **o/d**, abbreviation of *overdose* (applied to narcotics taken in excess or to drug users sick or dead from an overdose). *"When I was shooting up . . . I liked to hear about the ODs* [overdose cases], *and I'd think I was brave for taking it."* Time 3/16/70, p25 *The doctor released them as not o/d . . . and I said they could sit in the waiting room, but one took some more pills in there and the doctor got mad and said we should put them out.* Times (London) 8/17/70, p6 —*v.i. Slang.* to become sick or die from an overdose of a narcotic. *. . . they were just about to start shooting a film called* Zaccariah, *a rock, shlock, cowboy musical turn-of-the-century thing starring Ginger Baker, when the drummer OD'd and had to be replaced.* Atlantic 2/71, p104 [**1960** for noun; **1970** for verb]

odd-even, *adj. U.S.* of or having to do with a system of odd and even numbering, especially in relation to a method of restricting the sale of gasoline in a period of shortage, the sales being contingent upon a matching of odd and even numbered days

on the calendar with odd and even license plate numbers. See MINIMUM PURCHASE, TOP OFF. *Panicky motorists bluffed an bribed to beat the odd-even system, and station operators too most of the heat.* Newsweek 7/2/79, p24 *Maryland would r impose odd-even rationing if the state projected that gasolin supplies would fall substantially below expected deman Odd-even plans have proved to be a comparatively simpl method of cutting long lines at gas stations when supplies b come tight.* Christian Science Monitor 11/20/79, p10 [**1979**]

OEM, abbreviation of *original equipment manufacturer* (manufacturer of computer, agricultural, earthmoving, or othe equipment, that purchases semifinished machines or parts c machines to add to its products before distributing them in var ious markets). *There are only 200 employees with Dietz work ing on the design and production of its new Mincal 62 machine. Many of these computers are sold on the so-calle original equipment market, or OEM, to other manufacturer for incorporation in systems tailored to particular applica tions.* Times (London) 12/4/72, pII [**1971**]

off, *n.* **from the off**, *British.* from the beginning; from the star *My employer, Mrs. Heyley, was a woman of seventy . . . Sh had spent forty formative years in India, and after twenty-fou hours I had new insight into why the natives were so keen t see the sun set on the Empire. Heredity had thrust our roles o us from the off: behind her lay generations of sahibs and a d rect link with Clive of India.* Punch 1/4/67, p32 —*v.t. U.S Slang.* to kill. *Then he described how* [Alex] *Rackley was take from the bed to a car and then to the river. "At the swamp, Ale was offed," said Sams. "Warren* [Kimbo] *shot him first. Lonni* [McLucas] *hit him a second time. We were told not to com back unless he was dead."* Time 5/11/70, p29 [**1966** for noun **1968** for verb]

off-air, *adj., adv.* **1** directly from a radio or television broadcas with a sound or videotape recorder. *Indeed all domestic ma chines have in common the provision of sockets which enabl them to record programs "off-air" with the minimum of fus and so breach copyright with the maximum of ease.* New Scien tist 4/6/78, p9 [**1971**] **2** broadcasting by cable instead of ove the airways. Compare ON-AIR. *Essentially, these rules requir that systems in the top 100 markets must have at least 2 broadcast channels . . . for each off-air channel and nonvoic return communication capacity.* Britannica Book of the Yea 1973, p656 [**1961**]

off-book fund, a secret fund used for improper or illegal dis bursements of money. *The company disclosed it had funnele $65,000 to $90,000 in corporate funds through an "off-book fund between 1968 and 1973. The money was used for commis tic political contributions.* NY Times 5/29/76, p1 *BP says tha the four off-book funds in four counties have been closed Funds in those accounts totalled £126,000, of which abou £56,000 was paid to minor government officials, custom offi cials, "in order to get them to perform duties which they wer not otherwise obligated to perform."* Times (London) 6/4/77 p1 [**1976**, so called from its being *off the books*, i.e., not on an official bookkeeping record]

off-Broadway, *n.* the segment of the New York professiona theater outside of Broadway (the traditional theatrical center noted for its introduction of experimental plays, often by un known playwrights. Compare OFF-OFF-BROADWAY. *The hope of the American theater has sometimes been placed in off Broadway: in terms of sustained achievement this amounts t wistful thinking. Of the several playwrights who got their star off-Broadway, only Edward Albee has remotely fulfilled hi promise.* Time 5/17/68, p63 *Theatre began to happen. Broad way was sick and timid, unwilling and unable to put on darin new works or revive the classics. Off-Broadway, basing itsel in and around the* [Greenwich] *Village area, began to rock the American theatre with* [Edward] *Albee's plays and the lates works from Europe.* Saturday Night (Canada) 10/66, p25 —*adj.* of or relating to off-Broadway. *Vinie Burrows, who play Bobo in "The Blacks," the long-running Off Broadway play b Jean Genet, has been invited to appear on June 26 at Antioch College.* NY Times 6/18/63, p33 [**1957** for noun; **1953** for adj.

offenseful, *adj.* full of offense. *Self-control, silence. But with each year, to the murmur of trees and the clamor of birds, that separation seems more offenseful and the offense more absurd.* New Yorker 5/23/70, p44 [**1970**] ►The last recorded use of this word was by Shakespeare in *Measure for Measure* (II.iii.26): "So then it seems your most offenceful act was mutually committed?"

off-island, *n.* an off-shore island. *The off-islands may seem to be just across the nautical street but the journey can still be an experience on a rough day.* Sunday Times (London) 2/23/69, p63 —*adj.* U.S. visiting or temporarily residing on an island; being an off-islander. *. . . the rival Territorial Party—more conservative than its opposition but by no means a political outpost of the Republican Party—administered something of a drubbing to the Democrats. This upset afforded small comfort to off-island Republicans here, though, because while the Guamanians are American citizens, they cannot vote in our Presidential elections.* New Yorker 2/13/65, p42 —*adv.* See the quotation for the meaning. . . . *one islander was heard to remark recently that he never carried more than 30 cents in his pocket unless he planned to go off-island.* NY Times 6/27/71, p3 [**1965** for noun; **1961** for adj.; **1971** for adv.] ►Early use of *off-island* (OEDS 1917) referred only to Nantucket Island, off Massachusetts, as did *off-islander* (OEDS 1882).

off-islander, *n.* U.S. a temporary or seasonal resident of an island. Compare ON-ISLANDER. *. . . local businessmen gladly pocket the $20 million a year spent annually on bus trips, post cards and clam chowder. In fact, the tourist trade is growing so rapidly that many "off-islanders," the regular summer residents, are concerned lest their historic hideaway lose its charm.* Time 7/26/68, p67 [**1961**; see the note at OFF-ISLAND]

off-off-Broadway, *n.* the segment of the New York professional theater producing low-budget and often highly experimental plays that would not be presented in Broadway and off-Broadway theaters. Compare OFF-BROADWAY. *Actually the distinction between the two is quite real. Off Broadway still comes under the jurisdiction of the actors union (although at reduced rates). Off-off Broadway is completely outside the union because it never takes place in a "real" theatre; instead, Off-off Broadway uses cafés, rooms, lofts, churches, and in the case of two plays I saw recently the back room of a saloon in the East Village* [Greenwich Village] *. . .* Manchester Guardian Weekly 10/17/68, p21 —*adj.* of or relating to off-off-Broadway. *It would seem that these off-off Broadway playwrights are emerging in a period when no producer can expect to present their unconventional works except at a financial loss.* Saturday Review 6/10/67, p20 [**1967**]

off-price, U.S. —*adj.* offering merchandise below the retail price suggested by manufacturers. *Yet among the off-price practitioners are some that have struck the fancy of professional investors and market watchers. Two such companies . . . have particularly intrigued a number of analysts because of their growth rate and the appreciation of their stock.* NY Times 3/13/83, pC15 —*adv.* at a price lower than that suggested by manufacturers. *Mr. Syms, whose business is buying and selling merchandise off-price ("we are not discounters"), said that his personal exposure has helped the business.* NY Times 8/30/77, p25 [**1955** for adj.; **1977** for adv.]

offput, *v.t.* British. to disconcert; embarrass. . . . *the peculiarity of a faith that can revel in medieval plumbing in the 1970s and be so offput by the female of any species that not even a cow is allowed to pasteurise here.* Manchester Guardian Weekly 11/7/70, p15 [**1970**, back formation from *off-putting* disconcerting (1828), formed from the phrase *putting off*]

off-road, *adj.* made or used for traveling off public roads and highways, such as dune buggies, snowmobiles, and heavy trucks are. *The American deserts are among the last wild areas remaining in the United States. These beautiful, fragile environments are now being laid waste by the mindless operation of off-road vehicles.* Time 1/12/76, p7 *The complaints, which came from about five British manufacturers, concerned the prices of 30-tonne and 15-tonne Russian trucks of the type of off-road operations such as earthmoving and quarrying.* Times (London) 2/10/77, p19 [**1968**] —**off-roader**, *n.: To the rest of us,*

an abundance of specialized life forms provides opportunity for study and quiet reflection—re-creation of mind and body that often conflicts with the tumultuous pursuits of off-roaders. Time 1/12/76, p7

offshore fund, an investment company operating from abroad, usually as an investment trust or mutual fund. *The SEC* [Securities and Exchange Commission] *proposed that previously unregulated hedge funds (private funds) as well as offshore funds (outside the United States) be subjected to controls.* 1972 World Book Year Book, p522 [**1970**]

off-the-job, *adj.* **1** not on the job; done or happening while away from one's work. *Douglas* [a training officer] *says the off-the-job study is essential because it removes the pressures and distractions of the shop-floor.* Times (London) 2/9/70, p19 **2** being off one's job; laid off or unemployed. *In addition to the usual demands . . . he* [Walter Reuther] *is insisting on a "guaranteed annual income." . . . for union members with seniority, it would involve some sort of new company-financed plan enabling an off-the-job worker to maintain "his normal living standard" for up to a year.* Time 7/21/67, p51 [**1956** for def. 1; **1967** for def. 2]

off-the-rack, *adj.* **1** ready-made; available for immediate purchase or use. *Rome's off-the-rack clothes are represented by Fabiani's culotte suit with reversible shell.* NY Times 9/8/65, p54 **2** *Figurative.* having little individuality, as if made for mass production. *The off-the-rack excitement of a doomed or disabled athlete's last hurrah, in a competitive arena is glib enough to turn us into snickerers.* Maclean's 10/8/79, p58 [**1963**]

off-the-shelf, *adj.* **1** ready-made; available for immediate purchase or use. *Both of these systems are built with "off-the-shelf" items from parts available to any heating and plumbing contractor.* Progressive Farmer 3/77, p7 **2** Transferred use: *. . . an off-the-shelf covert team running the war in Costa Rica with arms and drugs and terrorist trafficking.* Vanity Fair 5/88, p66 [**1966**]

off-the-wall, U.S. Slang. —*adj.* unconventional; unusual. [Denis] *Brian knows how to startle the over-interviewed with off-the-wall questions that get surprising answers: Ever see a ghost? What makes you cry?* National Review 1/4/74, p47 Goin' South *has a consistent personality that reflects the off-the-wall sensibility of its hero. Nicholson's straight-faced use of unappetizing extras makes us see the whole film through Moon's somewhat stoned eyes.* Time 10/9/78, p100 —*adv.* Also, **off the wall.** unconventionally. *"I just thought it was off-the-wall funny," says Lear. "When I told my wife Frances about the idea, she said, 'Norman, this time you've gone too far—even for you.' But it worked. It was funny."* Time 4/5/76, p74 [**1974**, probably from handball or squash court usage, meaning "not expected, startling"]

ofuro (ou'fu:rou), *n.* a large tub or vat filled with hot water, used in Japan for bathing. *The concept of the hot tub, essentially a wooden tub filled with hot water (102 degrees Fahrenheit to 105 degrees Fahrenheit as a rule), is hardly new—the Japanese have been bathing communally in their ofuros for centuries.* NY Times 10/13/77, p48 *The Japanese custom of the communal bath, ofuro, with one large tub of hot water shared by all members of a family, presented a perfect opportunity for the early application of solar energy on a commercial scale.* Science News 4/22/78, p263 [**1964**, from Japanese]

OGO, abbreviation of *Orbiting Geophysical Observatory*, an unmanned scientific satellite of NASA, designed for gathering physical data about the earth. Compare OAO, OSO. *The satellite, OGO-IV (Orbiting Geophysical Observatory), was put into a polar orbit for a study of the relationship between particle activity, aurora and airglow, the geomagnetic field, and the effects of sources of electromagnetic energy in the atmosphere.* Times (London) 1/19/68, p13 [**1961**]

-oholic, a variant of -AHOLIC, as in: —**bloodoholic**, *n.:* [Yury] *Mamleev writes about such Soviet bizarreries as a psychopathic vampire, a kind of bloodoholic, who is trying to stay on the wagon, or at least on the Moscow bloodmobile (he manages to refrain from killing people when he gets a job in a bloodbank).*

NY Review of Books 2/19/76, p12 —**Cokeoholic,** *n.: Does it help your election choice to know that Trudeau's office contains a regular box of chocolates to appease his sweet tooth? And that Clark is a Coke-oholic, who relishes junk food?* Maclean's 5/1/78, p88 [**1973**]

oilberg, *n.* **1** an oil tanker with a capacity of 200,000 tons or more; a very large oil-carrying ship. *But the oilbergs have made at least as big an impact on shipbuilding as they have on the oil industry.* Sunday Times (London) 5/4/69, p37 **2** a large mass of oil floating in the sea. *No scientists are willing to forecast the effects of the oil now spreading seaward from the* Argo Merchant. *Most believe that if the globs of oil, called oilbergs because most of their mass is below the surface, continue to move east, the damage will be held to a minimum.* Time 1/10/77, p45 [**1966,** from *oil* + ice*berg*]

oil diplomacy, diplomacy involving relations between oil-importing and oil-exporting countries. *A prime goal of U.S. oil diplomacy over the past two years has been to break up the Organization of Petroleum Exporting Countries.* Time 1/19/76, p54 [**1975**]

oil minister, a government official in charge of or representing the interests of an oil-producing country. *At the June meeting of OPEC in Quito, Ecuador, the Shah's oil minister, Jamshid Amuzegar, blocked a move by Saudi Arabia to lower the price of oil by $2 on the posted price of $11.65 per barrel.* Atlantic 9/74, p20 [**1974**]

oil patch, *U.S.* **1** an oil-producing area. *Out in the Texas oil patch they tell the story of a young man, fresh from engineering school, who reported to one of the leases of a large oil company.* Birmingham News 3/23/80, pF3 **2** the petroleum industry in general. *Instead of being an aggressive explorer, Gulf is known in the oil patch for being cautious. It drills wells around already established basins . . .* Christian Science Monitor 5/21/82, p11 [**1976,** from *oil* + *patch* piece of ground]

oil spill, the accidental escape of oil into a body of water, often resulting in the destruction of water plants and birds and the pollution of shoreline. See CYCLONET, SKIMMER. *If we can't stop all the oil spills, can we at least clean up the messes they cause? That takes technology and trained people, and cleaning up oil spills is a new and primitive art. Equipment and techniques do exist—floating booms and chemicals to corral the oil, pumps and skimmers to pick it up, straw and "sorbents" to mop it, chemicals to disperse it, materials to sink it, microorganisms to eat it.* NY Times Magazine 4/9/78, p33 *Specifically, we have been warned:—that the pollution of the seas by oil spills and chemical runoff may be annihilating the phytoplankton that renews much of the oxygen in the atmosphere . . .* Theodore Roszak, Person/Planet, 1978, p35 [**1970**]

oil weapon, the threat of withholding oil or raising its price, used as a means of pressuring or controlling countries that depend upon oil imports for their energy needs. See PETRO- *The new President . . . was a keen opponent of President Nixon of the United States and an advocate of the so-called 'oil weapon'. It came as no surprise, therefore, when on 16 April he announced the nationalization with compensation of the 22 oil companies operating within Venezuela, to be completed in 24 to 36 months.* Annual Register of World Events in 1974, p105 [**1974**]

Okazaki fragment, piece, or **segment** (ˌoukə'zɑːki:), a fragmentary form of bacterial DNA, occurring during replication and later linked with other fragments to form the long double-helical strand of the typical DNA molecule. *Some enzyme other than the usual RNA polymerase may be . . . involved in starting off the Okazaki fragments of bacterial DNA.* Nature 11/3/72, p14 [**1968,** named after Refii *Okazaki,* a Japanese geneticist who first identified the fragments]

Oklo phenomenon ('ouˌklou), the occurrence of a series of natural nuclear chain reactions during the accretion of a rich deposit of uranium over a billion years ago in what is now a uranium mine in southeastern Gabon. *It is not generally appreciated that a natural example of geological containment of high-level wastes for many millions of years exists at the site of a uranium mine in Gabon. The "Oklo phenomenon" as this has come to be termed, is an occurrence of natural chain fission reaction which took place in a uranium deposit in Precambrian times and which were moderated by groundwaters. Many of the resultant actinides and fission-products are still fixed in the host rocks in the reactor zones despite 1800 million years of subsequent exposure to geological processes.* New Scientist 4/27/78, p226 [**1976,** named after *Oklo,* the uranium mine where the phenomenon was discovered in 1972]

Okun's law, a formula in economics by which an increase in unemployment is correlated with a decline in the gross national product. *Okun's Law, that is, asserts that growth in production must exceed some minimum value in order to keep unemployment from rising as labor productivity increases and the need for labor declines, relative to output.* New Yorker 2/16/76, p90 [**1970,** named after Arthur M. *Okun,* 1928-1980, an American economist who devised the formula]

Old Left, the leftist movement, predominantly Marxist in ideology, that represented the radical element in politics before the emergence of the New Left (often used attributively). *The Old Left had a program for the future; the New Left's program is mostly a cry of rage. The Old Left organized and proselyted playing its part in bringing about the American welfare state. But it is precisely big government, the benevolent Big Brother that the New Left is rebelling against.* Time 4/28/67, p14 *And just as Establishment becomes a devil-image, so do other terms such as (in different ways) "confrontation" and "youth" become god-images. It is true that these god- and devil-images can illuminate many situations, as did such analogous Old Left expressions as "the proletarian standpoint," "the exploiting classes," and "bourgeois remnants" . . .* Atlantic 10/69, p86 [**1960**]

Old Leftist, a member of the Old Left. *En route to the United Nations, a handful of anti-antiwar demonstrators managed to pelt the peace parade with eggs. New York police on horseback—in contrast with the "Cossack" image so many Old Leftists apply to them—kept the countermarchers from breaking up the parade.* Time 4/21/67, p15 [**1967**]

oleophilic, *adj.* attracting oil to itself. *The French authorities used . . . chalk treated with a film of stearate to make it "oleophilic" or oil-attracting.* New Scientist 6/11/70, p529 *Sawdust treated with appropriate silicones is water repellent but strongly oleophilic and will soak up many times its weight of oil.* Science Journal 2/70, p21 [**1957,** from *oleo-* oil + *-philic* attracting]

olfactronic, *adj.* of or relating to olfactronics. *Another aspect of the olfactronic approach to detecting sources through their airborne signatures is the variety of possible ways in which this can be done. Any set of measurement, together with the numerical values, that adequately characterizes an airborne effluent in the presence of irrelevant impurities in air, can be used as an olfactronic signature.* New Scientist 9/15/66, p623 [**1966**]

olfactronics, *n.* the analysis and detection of odors by sensitive instruments and techniques. *Eventually olfactronics may be used to guard bank vaults against burglars . . . as well as to stand guard as fire alarms and sentries against the Vietcong.* NY Times 7/16/67, pD8 [**1964,** from *olfac*tory + *-tronics,* as in *electronics*]

oligomeric (ouˌligə'merik), *adj.* of or characteristic of a chemical compound with a few recurring subunits, in contrast to a polymeric or monomeric compound. *The best understood enzymes contain only one protein chain; but most enzymes are in fact composed of a small number of protein sub-units associated together. This oligomeric structure is useful in allowing certain control functions to operate . . .* New Scientist 5/14/70, p320 [**1957,** from *oligomer* (OEDS 1952, from *oligo-* few + *-mer* as in *polymer*) + *-ic*]

olim (ou'li:m), *n.pl.* Jewish immigrants to Israel. Compare CHOZRIM and YORDIM. *The founders of modern Israel called themselves olim: pilgrims, "those who ascend."* Time 6/7/71, p52 *Positively, the nation feels refreshed by olim, the homecoming immigrants, justified in its deepest purpose, and strengthened to build a new life on its corner of the earth.*

Times (London) 9/16/67, p10 [**1967**, from Hebrew, literally, those who ascend]

Olympiad, *n.* a variant of OLYMPICS. *After Varna, Fischer did play from time to time in international chess—notably at the Havana Olympiad in 1966.* New Yorker 10/28/72, p76 *Preeminent in women's bridge was the British pair, Mrs. Rixi Markus and Mrs. Fritzi Gordon. They were runaway victors in the women's Pairs Olympiad.* Britannica Book of the Year 1975, p193 [**1961**, extended sense of *Olympiad* the Olympic Games (OEDS 1907)]

Olympics, *n.* a series of contests patterned on the Olympic Games by including a variety of events, having an international representation, etc. *Keith Brown of Baltimore took individual honors at the National Junior Olympics that ended today by becoming the first athlete in the 10-year history of the event to win three gold medals.* NY Times 8/24/76, p26 *It may be inspiring to watch tiny Nadia Comaneci arch into a flawless parallel-bar handstand . . . but for sheer spine-tingling, heartrending drama and a basic tug deep in the stomach, nothing can compare with the World Culinary Olympics.* Maclean's 12/13/76, p31 [**1976**, extended sense of *Olympics* the Olympic Games (OED2, 1928)]

OMA ('oumə), *n.* U.S. acronym for *orderly marketing agreement,* a negotiated agreement between governments to restrict imports of a specific product when they jeopardize the employment, production, and sales of the importing country's industry. *The Administration has negotiated an OMA limiting imports of Japanese color-TV sets to 41% of their 1976 level (a restriction that obviously has not stopped Zenith from concluding that it will benefit by becoming a foreign manufacturer. Another OMA limits imports of shoes from Korea and Taiwan to 25% and 20% respectively.* Time 10/17/77, p53 [**1977**]

Omah ('oumɑː), *n.* another name for SASQUATCH. *At the same time, a more modest effort is under way to track down the Western Hemisphere's own Abominable Snowman—a large, shaggy, ape-like creature variously called Sasquatch or Bigfoot or Omah that is said to roam the mountains and forests of the Pacific Northwest.* New Yorker 10/9/72, p40 [**1972**, of uncertain origin; perhaps related to *Omaha*]

OMB, abbreviation of *Office of Management and Budget,* a U.S. government agency established in 1970 to replace the Bureau of the Budget. *Those whose pet projects have been cut out of Federal budgets allege that the OMB is the real power in the Government, a kind of bureaucratic Cardinal Mazarin.* Science News 5/22/71, p349 [**1970**]

ombudsman, *n.* **1** a government official appointed to investigate the grievances and protect the rights of private citizens. *Now, at last, we have the Ombudsman, whose business it is to investigate charges of bad administration, and lay reports which the Commons can accept as thorough market research among the consumers of politics.* Times (London) 3/4/68, p8 *New Zealand has installed an ombudsman; several American states are talking about doing the same thing; and now four Canadian provinces as well as the federal government are either looking at bills, or being urged to look at bills, that would make federal and regional* ombudsmen *part of our own parliamentary system.* Maclean's 4/18/64, p6 **2** someone to complain to or report a grievance to. *Harvey Schmedemann, a local liquor dealer, . . . had come to protest to the newspaper, his only ombudsman that day, a mimeographed newsletter thrust by a hippie into the hand of his eleven-year-old son as the boy walked across the University of Kansas campus.* Harper's 12/70, p59 **3** any person who champions or defends individual rights. *Like many of my generation, I knew her [Eleanor Roosevelt] somewhat, not well. How could one not know her, since she was everywhere, doing everything—columnist, lecturer, traveler constantly crisscrossing the country, ombudsman for every injustice, agitator for every cause that needed help, one-woman lobby?* NY Post 11/15/71, p46 [**1959**, from Swedish, literally, commissioner]

ombudsmanship, *n.* the position or authority of an ombudsman. *The series of programmes under the heading. The Scientists,*

now being shown on commercial television are the best of their kind so far to emerge from the perennial funfair. Late on Saturday night is scarcely the ideal time for such viewing but one must be thankful for small mercies especially since the opposition at that hour is devoted to football and the loquacious ombudsmanship of Bernard Braden. New Scientist and Science Journal 6/3/71, p597 [**1966**]

ombudswoman, *n.* a female ombudsman. . . . *Of course, if people felt closer to their councillors they might be able to wrest more expansive replies from the town hall. Perhaps the only answer is for more councillors to see themselves as Ombudsmen and Ombudswomen, and to leave less discretion to the routine decisions taken by officials.* Manchester Guardian Weekly 10/21/65, p6 [**1961**]

omega, *n.* or **omega meson**, a highly unstable and short-lived elementary particle with a mass 1540 times that of an electron. Compare PHI, RHO. *Physicists had supposed that the photon, or light particle, was the sole intermediary of electromagnetic forces. But experimental evidence has shown that photons approaching hadrons tend to turn themselves into one of the mesons called phi, rho or omega. Thus, it appears that electromagnetic forces are mediated to leptons directly by photons and to hadrons by phi, rho or omega.* Science News 4/10/71, p250 [**1961**]

omnicide, *n.* the destruction of all life. *The subject of nuclear omnicide has proliferated in the pages of the Guardian to such an extent and such marked lack of conclusion, I think the perspective of the debate should be changed.* Manchester Guardian Weekly 8/10/80, p2 [**1959**, from *omni-* all + *-cide,* on the pattern of *homicide, suicide*]

omnifaceted, *adj.* covering all facets. *The Great Depression! In these troubled times, how could more words about those troubled times become a national bestseller? The answer is that Studs Terkel's omnifaceted study of the latest major societal breakdown in the U.S. seems remarkably relevant to 1970.* Time 7/20/70, p76 [**1970**]

omnifocal, *adj.* (of a lens) having a focal length that varies imperceptibly from one part to another. *Now an optical company in Ohio offers to solve this problem with an "omnifocal" lens which has power that's gradually increased from top to bottom with no blurred area or transition zone.* Maclean's 2/20/65, p1 [**1962**]

omnisex or **omnisexual**, *adj.* of or involving individuals or activities of all sexual types. *Chief attraction was the New York Dolls, a gaudy "omnisex" rock group.* Newsweek 11/12/73, p69 *The Dice Man is a blackly comic amusement park of a book, replete with vertiginous roller coaster rides of the spirit, feverish omnisexual trips through the tunnel of love.* Time 11/1/71, p60 [**1971**, from *omni-* all + *sex(ual)*] —**omnisexuality**, *n.: Nothing much for anyone, actually, in this film about the omnisexuality of a footman hero (Michael York) who sidles up to an Austrian countess (Angela Lansbury) and also to her son and to everyone else in sight.* New Yorker 1/15/72, p16

OMS, abbreviation of *Orbital Maneuvering System. The nominal flight plan begins, understandably, with getting into orbit, by means of successive firings of yet two more rocket engines, together called the Orbital Maneuvering System, or OMS.* Science News 3/21/81, p187 [**1981**]

on, *adj.* British Slang. **1** having a favorable potential; easily possible. . . . *the candidate . . . recovered sufficiently to win a storm of applause with "So you see, old boy, that while I agree with you denationalisation just isn't on: Labour's made such a howling mess of these industries that no one in his senses would ever buy them back!"* Punch 9/25/68, p421 **2** all right; seemly. [Brett] *Whiteley* [a London painter] *himself is now in the U.S., at the start of a $500-a-month Harkness Foundation scholarship . . . and is already hard at work on an American series, including a collage portrait of Folk-Rock Singer Bob Dylan. Says Whiteley: "Dylan is the outsider. He's the most on person in America."* Time 11/10/67, p42 [**1963**]

on-air, *adj.* broadcast or broadcasting over the airways, instead of transmission by cable. Also, OVER-THE-AIR. Compare OFF-

AIR. *A WNET spokesman noted that both the total amount raised by the station and the size of the average donation exceeded the levels of all previous on-air campaigns for funds.* NY Times 3/23/76, p62 *Cable-TV's greatest objection to the bill is that it establishes the principle that cable owes fees for all the on-air television programs it carries.* Americana Annual 1975, p546 [**1973**]

on-board, *adj.* installed or carried aboard a craft or vehicle. *In the satellite, they* [special frequency-control devices] *would decrease the frequency of incoming signals to a frequency band in which they could be efficiently amplified by on-board equipment before being increased again and radiated back to Earth.* New Scientist 10/22/70, p178 *Lufthansa, the West German airline, is considering the abolition of on-board food service on short domestic flights . . .* NY Times 5/20/68, p93 [**1961**]

on-camera, *adj., adv.* within range of a television or film camera; being televised or filmed. *"We're going to make you a star," she quotes him as saying, as he volunteered to choose her on-camera clothes and eyeglasses.* Atlantic 8/75, p86 *The Strategy was to keep her on-camera but away from confrontation.* Time 5/14/79, p32 [**1962**]

oncogene ('aŋkə,dʒi:n), *n.* a tumor-producing gene. *The* [Robert Heubner] *theory itself states that human cancer is viral in origin and is caused by a more or less hypothetical entity called the oncogene. This, according to Heubner, is an extra piece of genetic material (presumably DNA) passed on from generation to generation. Originally the oncogene was part of an RNA virus but at some unspecified time it incorporated itself into someone's DNA and has been passed on ever since; a tiny time bomb implanted in the nucleus of each cell.* Harper's 11/71, p101 [**1969**, from Greek *ónkos* tumor + English *gene;* influenced by *oncogenic* tumor-producing]

oncornavirus (aŋ,kɔrnə'vairəs), *n.* any of a group of tumor-producing viruses that contain RNA. Compare CORONAVIRUS, PAPOVAVIRUS, RETROVIRUS. *We now report that six oncornaviruses, including the human "candidate" virus RD-114, can be distinguished from each other. Even immunologically similar viruses from the same species can be identified as to type. This technique permits rapid identification of a new virus isolates by comparison with known strains.* Science 6/1/73, p972 [**1970**, from *onco-* tumor + *RNA* + *virus*]

one-liner, *n. U.S.* a very brief joke or witty remark. *. . . your mass audience doesn't laugh at that kind of stuff. . . . See if you can think up some one-liners.* NY Times 10/11/70, pD13 [Senator Eugene] *McCarthy had a one-liner for everyone in Washington, and the reporters who found favor were those who learned to leer and feed straight lines.* Harper's 5/69, p84 [**1964**] ▶An earlier use of *one-liner* was a headline consisting of one line of type (OEDS 1904).

one-night stand, *Slang.* an act of sexual intercourse engaged in casually, as with a stranger. *Most men, Hite found, are repelled by machismo, oppose casual encounters (even a one-night stand should have some emotional connection) and value the closeness of sex.* [**1963**, extended sense of the term for a single performance of a play, show, etc., in a town by a touring company (DA 1880)]

one-on-one or **one-to-one,** *adj., adv. U.S. and Canada.* with one competitor, candidate, etc., directly confronting another; on a person-to-person basis. *They acknowledge that she now has a sizable, varied political base but suspect that it is unexpandable and that, one-on-one after a contentious primary, she will lose.* NY Times Magazine 6/26/77, p38 *Ellis Rabb was alarmingly persuasive as the older actor. Once again Mamet had demonstrated his particular talent for one-to-one conversations.* Americana Annual 1978, p493 [**1967** for *one-on-one,* originally a sports term (especially basketball and football); **1965** for *one-to-one,* extended from the sense (used in mathematics, statistics, etc.) of "matching exactly one element with another," as in *one-to-one correspondence* (OED2, 1873)]

onetime, *adj.* on only one instance; occurring only once. *. . . unlike police who deal with homicide or other major crimes, who have onetime or rare contact with their customers, the po-* lice *who handle problems of morality rather than injury, crimes like prostitution and drug addiction, tend to develop a peculiar rapport with the people with whom they war.* Atlantic 1/67, p44 [**1959**] ▶The older meaning of *onetime, adj.* (since the 1880's) is "of some earlier time; former," as in *a onetime history teacher.*

one-time pad, a cryptographic method in which a secret message is coded in a cipher system devised especially and only for use on a single occasion. *. . . the main cipher-using Powers began to shift over to the one system that even Friedmann's methods cannot readily break: one-time pad. The German diplomatic service was using this in the early 1920s; the Russians took it up from 1930; even the British were using it by 1943. Mr Kahn shows, indeed, that it is theoretically unbreakable. Messages in it are prepared from a page of random figures, of which only the sender and the receiver have copies; no page is ever used twice.* Manchester Guardian Weekly 2/22/68, p10 [**1953**]

one-up, *v.t.* to score an advantage over; go one better. *The Liberals have had a variety of plans. John Wintermeyer, the party's 46 year old leader, first one-upped the socialists by endorsing the Saskatchewan plan, dithered, finally about-faced and produced a Tory-like scheme at the Liberal convention a month ago.* Canada Month 3/63, p10 *Trying to be funny, he said to the salesgirl: "That horse is a fake." She one-upped him: "Yet, so was the original."* Saturday Review 12/21/68, p6 [**1963**, partly from the sports phrase *be one up on* (an opponent), meaning to lead in a game by one point, but chiefly a back formation from *one-upmanship* (the art or practice of being one up on one's friends), a term coined by the English humorist Stephen Potter, and the title of one of his books, published in 1952. See also -MANSHIP.]

on-islander, *n. U.S.* a permanent resident of an island. Compare OFF-ISLANDER. *Traditionally, the Vineyard . . . has been a haven of tranquillity, offering respite from the cares of the metropolis—a place where . . . tourists, especially day-trippers, were tolerated rather than sought. This is how the "on-islanders" want to keep it. On the other hand, there is much to attract "off-islanders."* NY Times 6/27/71, pJ3 [**1971**]

onlend, *v.t., v.i. British.* to lend (borrowed funds) to others. *The aim of the "corset," reintroduced as part of the June economic package, is to restrict the capacity of the banks to bid in funds which they then on-lend, creating new bank deposits and increasing the money supply.* Times (London) 8/18/78, p15 [**1972**]

Oort's Cloud (urts *or* ɔrts) or **Oort Cloud** (urt *or* ɔrt), a great swarm of comets traveling in elliptical orbits around the solar system at distances of up to 13 trillion miles from the sun. *Comets exist by the billions in . . . Oort's Cloud, coalesced from the swirling dust and gases in the original solar nebula, from which the sun, earth and other planets and moons were formed.* Time 12/17/73, p91 *The Oort cloud itself, and the comets that compose it, . . . may have been formed along with the rest of the solar system, some 5,000,000,000 years ago.* Encyclopedia Science Supplement (Grolier) 1981, p7 [**1965**, named after the Dutch astronomer Jan H. *Oort,* born 1900, who first proposed its existence]

op or **Op,** *n.* short for OP ART. *'Op' was a form of abstract design depending largely on optical illusion to create its effects. This could at times be combined with movement and thus become a type of kinetic art.* Annual Register of World Events in 1965, p427 —*adj.* of or characterized by op art. *In the new Op paintings and textile designs, discussed here in July, squares, circles, rectangles and ellipses jangle against one another as violently as they do in daily life.* Scientific American 9/65, p222 [**1964**]

op art or **Op art,** a form of abstract art that relies heavily on optical illusion. Also called OPTICAL ART. *There is an obvious but superficial sense in which Op art (discussed in this department last July) can be called mathematical art. This aspect of Op is certainly not new. Hard-edged, rhythmic, decorative patterns are as ancient as art itself, and even the modern movement toward abstraction in painting began with the geometric forms* *of the cubists.* Scientific American 4/66, p110 [**1964**, shortened from *optical art*, on the analogy of *pop art*]

op artist, a person who produces op art. Also called OPTICAL ARTIST. *Now, hard on the heels of op artists, who address their work to the retina, has come a widespread number of "kinetic" artists, who try to combine mechanics and art.* Time 1/28/66, p44 [**1965**]

op-con or **ops-con,** *n.* U.S. operations control. *"Burns, we want control of this operation. If there is an operation. We've got men on the ground, we've got very good op-con. American interests are involved, and don't forget that. This is what the Deputy Director wants, and that is what we will have."* Atlantic 8/72, p71 *He led me up a narrow flight of stairs to a gallery overlooking a control room at Goddard, very much like the Mission Control Room in Houston, which is called Operations Control, or OpsCon, and from which engineers sitting at four rows of consoles were supervising the communications and tracking network.* New Yorker 4/17/71, p129 [**1971**, by shortening]

OPEC ('oupek), *n.* acronym for *Organization of Petroleum Exporting Countries,* formed in 1960. Compare OAPEC. *The economists, with their trained inability to understand the real world, had an even simpler solution. Paper money (dollars, marks, etcetera) would flow to OPEC, whose members would have to spend it, lend it, or bury it in the sand. If they spent it, we would get the oil, and pay for it with our exports, a workable exchange even if at unfair prices.* Harper's 3/75, p45 [**1960**] ▶The abbreviation appeared occasionally (mostly with periods, as *O.P.E.C.*) during the 1960's. With the advent of the energy crisis of the early 1970's the organization and its abbreviated name gained world-wide prominence.

Op-Ed page, U.S. a newspaper page featuring articles by columnists and other writers. *The Op-Ed page—so named because it runs opposite a newspaper's editorial page—became a journalistic tradition with the rise of the personal column. Pioneered by the Pulitzers in the old New York morning* World, *the Op-Ed provides a variety of viewpoints in dozens of major metropolitan dailies.* Time 8/10/70, p32 [**1970,** shortened from *Opposite Editorial page*]

open admissions, U.S. another name for OPEN ENROLLMENT. *With surprising fervor, the City University of New York (CUNY) has set out to help break the poverty cycle of young people—both white and black—who graduate with serious educational deficiencies from the city's high schools each year. Under its new "open admissions" policy, CUNY was taking such students despite their academic shortcomings, even admitting some of them directly into its four-year colleges.* Time 9/28/70, p36 [**1969**]

open classroom, U.S. a classroom, especially at the elementary-school level, in which the activities are informal, individualized, and centered on open-ended investigation and discussion of subjects instead of formal instruction. *An open classroom means nothing to me unless it means that a child learns in that classroom that learning is not dependent at every level on the presence of a teacher.* NY Times 6/8/71, p39 *Critics . . . claim that the open classroom fails to equip children with basic skills and facts, and that it will result in placing students at a disadvantage in selective examinations for jobs and college entrance.* World Book Science Annual 1972, p307 [**1971**]

open contract, *Underworld Slang.* a murder assignment open to any mobster. See CONTRACT. *According to some reports, there had been an "open contract" on Joe for months—that is, virtually ever since the Colombo shooting . . . Some detectives insist, however, that they never heard of any such thing as an "open contract" until the phrase began to appear in the press; mob bosses, they insist, don't leave such matters to chance.* NY Times Magazine 6/4/72, p96 [**1972**]

open corridor, another term for OPEN CLASSROOM. . . . *children wander through their classrooms like free souls—sprawling on the floor to read library books that they themselves have chosen, studying mathematics by learning how to cope with family food bills, chattering and painting and writing, writing, writing. Their teachers glide purposefully from*

group to group and from child to child, guiding, correcting, encouraging. All this adds up to a new style of elementary instruction that has been called "informal education" or "open classrooms" or "open corridors." Newsweek 5/3/71, p60 [**1971**]

open-date, *n.* a date stamped on packaged food to show when the food was packaged or when it is no longer fresh (often used attributively). Compare PULL-DATE. *New labeling regulations came into force in Britain, and comprehensive proposals were made for a system of open-date marking of prepacked foods.* Britannica Book of the Year 1973, p306 —*v.t.* to put an open-date on (packaged food). *I congratulate those manufacturers who have been willing to open-date their products.* NY Times 9/1/77, p30 [**1971**] —**open-dating,** *n.: Mr. Leonard Reeves-Smith, chief executive officer of the National Grocers' Federation, said: "We have always maintained that agitation for open-dating did not represent the view of the majority of consumers. The average housewife has few complaints about freshness."* Times (London) 3/16/73, p14

open education, a system of instruction, especially at the elementary-school level, emphasizing individualized activities and free discussions, as an alternative to traditional methods of instruction. See ALTERNATIVE SCHOOL. *[John]* Bremer, 45, is, after all, a noted advocate of "open education," the creator of Philadelphia's innovative Parkway School (the "school without walls," where students use the community as their place of learning).* Maclean's 3/74, p77 [**1973**]

open-ended, *adj.* having no fixed time limit. . . . *the Government was proposing to introduce "open ended" drinking hours, so that we can behave like real members of the Common Market.* Manchester Guardian Weekly 11/21/70, p11 *The months before L.B.J.'s [President Lyndon B. Johnson's] decision not to run again were the worst; to her [Mrs. Johnson], the thought of another campaign seemed like "an open-ended stay in a concentration camp."* Time 11/9/70, p18 [**1953, 1970**]

open enrollment, U.S. a policy of unrestricted admission to a college or university that permits poor or unprepared students to matriculate. Also called OPEN ADMISSIONS. *The open enrollment policy for the city universities will be a mistake. In order to maintain the high academic standards of this city, it is imperative that the existing standards of CUNY be maintained.* NY Times 1/7/70, p42 [**1962**]

openers, *n.pl.* Usually, **for openers.** *Informal* to begin with; as a starter. *For openers, just after he got back to New York, he won world-wide attention when his report . . . became an issue in the 1960 presidential campaign.* Time 9/14/70, p79 [**1967**]

open-heart, *adj. Surgery.* performed on the interior of the heart while maintaining circulation by means of a heart-lung machine. . . . *in the 1950s, with the development of the heart-lung machine—a mechanical device which substitutes temporarily for the heart and lungs—the procedure known as open-heart surgery became feasible.* Saturday Review 7/1/67, p50 *Since last March at the National Heart Hospital alone he has performed 219 "open heart" operations.* Sunday Times (London) 3/30/69, p6 [**1957**]

open housing, U.S. prohibition of racial or religious discrimination in the sale or rental of a house, apartment, or other dwelling (often used attributively). *"You have to earn at least $10,000 or $12,000 a year to move to the Cleveland suburbs," remarked Gerta Friedheim, young, petite Cleveland Heights housewife who heads the Suburban Citizens for Open Housing, an organization pushing for integration of the outer city.* NY Times 6/1/71, p28 *Nova Scotia's open-housing laws prohibit racial segregation only in overcrowded tenements and in apartments too expensive for Negroes.* Maclean's 11/67, p1 [**1953**]

open-loop, *adj.* of or relating to an automatic control process which has no feedback or self-corrective mechanism. Compare CLOSED-LOOP. . . . *almost all skilled muscular activities seem to exhibit many "open-loop," pre-programmed characteristics. An open-loop system (one that draws little or no information from the thing it governs) can always be operated more effectively than a closed-loop one, provided that its task is well de-*

fined and not subject to major disturbances. New Scientist 6/30/66, p830 [**1954**]

open marriage, a form of marriage in which the spouses agree to remain socially and sexually as independent as if they were single. Compare CONTRACT MARRIAGE, SERIAL MARRIAGE. *Others are trying to meld the two modes through "open marriage" covenants that permit each party to form a variety of relationships—by no means just physical—with members of the opposite sex.* Newsweek 7/16/73, p58 *Advocates of "open marriage" have argued that the partners in a monogamous relationship need the freedom to develop as individuals outside the bonds of the relationship while retaining primary emotional ties with the wife or husband.* Estelle Fuchs, The Second Season, 1977, p221 [**1973**, coined by George and Nena O'Neill, U.S. anthropologists and authors of the book *Open Marriage* (1973)]

open sentence, *Mathematics.* an equation containing one or more unknown quantities. *Decision procedures—sometimes called algorithms—are familiar in everyday mathematics. For example, the technique of long division represents a decision procedure for the predicate "x is divisible by y," where x and y can be any natural number. (A predicate is an open sentence: one that can be completed by assigning names to its variables.)* Scientific American 3/71, p55 [**1965**]

open-space, *adj.* of or characterized by the use of movable partitions and furniture as space dividers instead of rigid partitions and walls. *Although traditional concepts of architectural design still appealed to some, a contemporary concept, the open-space plan, gained increasing popularity in the early 1970's . . .* Americana Annual 1972, p351 *A return to basics, if it is projected as a cure, is bound to prove as disappointing as open-space architecture.* Manchester Guardian Weekly (Washington Post section) 12/18/77, p12 [**1972**]

open university, a college or university without regular classroom instruction. *Under the auspices of the State University, New York opened its first "open university." It teaches its students largely by remote control—mailed assignments, television, tape recordings, and independent study. These are augmented by periodic guidance, discussion, and testing sessions with faculty members at specially designated learning centers.* 1972 World Book Year Book, p331 [**1971**, probably influenced by the *Open University* (1966), a British educational institution providing courses for adult students based on correspondence and television and radio broadcasts]

operand, *n.* any of the items of information involved in a computer operation. *By means of a fine-grained separation of the computer's functional units a high degree of overlapping has been attained. Current efforts in "pipelining" the processing of "operands" will allow a further significant increase in speed.* Scientific American 2/71, p76 [**1956**, extended from earlier (OED 1886) meaning of a quantity to be operated on]

operator, *n.* the part of the operon that activates and regulates the structural genes. Also called REGULATOR GENE. *According to a now classic hypothesis in genetics, there are two classes of genes. The first consists of structural genes that, through RNA, determine the sequence of the amino acids and thus the structure of protein. The second class of genes, called operators, control the first, turning them on and off to regulate gene expression. Working as a unit, a package of structural and operator genes is called an operon.* Science News 11/29/69, p494 [**1961**]

opera window, a small ventless window on either side of the back seat of an automobile, usually behind a rear side window. Imperial *Le Baron by Chrysler makes its 1975 appearance with only minor styling changes, the most conspicuous of which is a new narrow opera window for rear seat passengers.* Ebony 1/75, p74 [**1972**, patterned after *opera light* either of two outside lights by the passenger doors of an automobile]

operon, *n.* a cluster of linked genes functioning as a unit in controlling the production of proteins. Compare LAC OPERON. *An operon is a chromosomal unit consisting of a group of adjacent structural genes, which are regulated together, and the operator, which coordinates their activities.* 1968 Collier's Encyclo-

pedia Year Book, p149 *The group . . . now hopes to find ou how genes are repressed and derepressed—turned off and on—so that genes can be made to operate when required. This concept, known as the operon concept, was first formulated by the French scientists François Jacob, André Lwoff, and Jacques Monod, who won the 1965 Nobel Prize.* Americana Annual 1970, p437 [**1961**, from OPERATOR + -*on* (unit of genetic material)]

opioid, *n.* a synthetic drug that resembles morphine, heroin etc., in its effects. Often used attributively. *The I.G. Farbenindustrie laboratory at Höchst am Main created methadone in the search for a morphine substitute late in the Second World War, when Germany was cut off from opium supplies Yet it is a narcotic—an "opioid"—for in action it is fundamentally similar to morphine or heroin, and it is fully as addictive* New Yorker 10/1/73, p97 [**1957**, from *opium* + -*oid*, suffix meaning "(one) like"] ►An *opiate* (OED 1603) is a preparation or natural derivative of opium (e.g. morphine, codeine). An *opioid* is a synthetic substitute for an opiate that differs from it chemically but resembles the action or effect of an opiate. But *opiate* has also been used since the early 1950's in the sense of a synthetic substitute for the natural opiate.

opportunistic infection, an infection which develops in people with a deficiency of the immune system, especially with such conditions as AIDS. *AIDS is characterized by a disorder of the immune system that makes victims susceptible to a wide variety of so-called opportunistic infections. Such infections result from organisms that rarely cause disease in people whose immune systems are working normally. Pneumocystis carinii, for example, causes a type of pneumonia in some patients whose immune systems have been compromised by chemotherapy for cancer and it occurs commonly among AIDS victims.* NY Times 5/24/83, pC3 [**1962**]

opster, *n.* U.S. Slang. an op artist. Compare POPSTER. *"Sculpture: New York Scene," a bright, concentrated little group show . . . ranging from the intricate light-and-shadow wall reliefs of the opster Ben Cunningham to the ingenious carved wood mechanical devices of Robert Zakarian . . .* NY Times 3/18/67, p25 [**1965**]

Optacon ('aptə,kan), *n.* a trademark for an electronic device that enables a blind person to read ordinary printed matter by touch. The device consists of a small camera connected to light detectors and vibrating tactile pins that convert printed characters of a text into a vibrating pattern of the shape of the characters which can be felt by the blind person's fingertip. *The Optacon is primarily a reading aid: a letter beneath the camera excites a corresponding pattern of vibration in the tactile array, which the user can feel with the index finger. Nearly 2,000 blind people use the Optacon, and after a year or two of experience they can read 40 to 60 words per minute.* New Scientist 5/19/77, p394 [**1970**, from *optical-to-tactile* converter]

optical, *adj.* of or relating to op art. *Leaving aside the question of the contemporary fashion for "optical" painting, Vasarely's work shows—indeed it largely created—two important trends in abstract art today.* New Scientist 5/20/65, p491 [**1965**]

optical art, another name for OP ART. *There is the Klee of the early 1930s, the precursor of optical art, in whose canvases flickering and apparently changing patterns of iridescent colours dance around firm linear designs whose strength creates a high degree of tension between colour and form.* Times (London) 7/22/65, p15 [**1964**]

optical artist, another name for OP ARTIST. *The Manhattan optical artist [Josef Levi] has devised several new dizzying exercises with illuminated shadow boxes superimposed on black and white perforated metal screens.* Time 2/7/69, p4 [**1964**]

optical astronomer, a specialist in optical astronomy. *Now, the optical astronomers turned to one of their most powerful tools: the spectrograph which separates light into its component wave lengths by passing it through a prism or a series of fine lines etched on a glass plate.* Time 3/11/66, p51 *Before 1960 radio astronomers had identified and catalogued hundreds of radio sources: invisible objects in the universe that emit radiation at radio frequencies. From time to time optical astrono-*

mers would succeed in identifying an object—usually a galaxy—whose position coincided with that of the radio source. Thereafter the object was called a radio galaxy. Scientific American 5/71, p56 [**1965**]

optical astronomy, the branch of astronomy that uses telescopes for direct observation of the heavens (as distinguished from *radio astronomy, X-ray astronomy,* etc.). *The first machine to automate completely one of the important processes of optical astronomy has been commissioned at the Royal Observatory, Edinburgh. The machine, called GALAXY, is used to locate and measure the star images on photographic plates from the Observatory's 400 mm Schmidt telescope. A single plate taken by the Schmidt may contain tens of thousands of star images, all in perfect focus.* Science Journal 3/70, p14 [**1960**]

optical disk or **optical disc**, a videodisk using laser beams to record and transmit sounds and images. Also called LASER DISC. *Perhaps, for example, a large optical disk memory will serve as an archive. It could store a year's accumulation of documents and replace filing cabinets throughout a large organization.* Scientific American 8/80, p138 *But the optical disc, which uses lasers to read and write information onto a transparent surface, promises to replace its magnetic cousin eventually. One optical disc can store up to 200 million bytes of information.* New Scientist 10/29/81, p310 [**1977**]

optical fiber, one strand of fiber optics. *Optical fibers are a means of manipulating light that is rapidly finding use in many fields. Some recent developments are their use in chromatography, automatic titrations, and control of chemical reactions.* McGraw-Hill Yearbook of Science and Technology 1971, p308 *Equally, nobody has yet produced glass which meets all the challenging requirements of optical fibres . . .* Science Journal 12/70, p68 [**1970**]

optoacoustic, *adj.* of or having to do with the modulation of light energy by means of sound waves. See ACOUSTOOPTICS. *Some of the recent studies in the field of measuring atmospheric contaminants have been concerned with the use of the optoacoustic method in determining the level of concentration of trace gases in the lower atmosphere.* McGraw-Hill Yearbook of Science and Technology 1977, p140 [**1971**, from *opto-* of vision or light, optical + *acoustic* of sound]

optoelectronic, *adj.* using a combination of optical and electronic systems or devices. *. . . the underlying reason for the lack of production hardware seems to be that, as soon as a function has been performed by an opto-electronic device, another research team has found a way to do the same thing without using light at all.* Science Journal 5/70, p43 [**1955**]

optoelectronics, *n.* the combined use of optical and electronic systems or devices. *A shaft of light is a neat way of coupling electronic circuits together in such a manner as to suppress "noise" passing from one to another. Here, then, is an application for opto-electronics in computers, data transmission and communication systems, where the trend towards miniaturization is meeting problems with the bulkiness of the transformers normally used to isolate bits of the system.* New Scientist 8/12/65, p387 *Optoelectronics, albeit using incoherent light, has also found its way into the video cassette field via a new video disc system being developed by Philips.* New Scientist and Science Journal 4/29/71, p266 [**1959**]

optronic, *adj.* another word for OPTOELECTRONIC. *France's Thomson-CSF is developing an optronic surveillance system called Scorpion, which is sized to be used on a Brevel-type RPV or light air-craft . . . The optronic section housing the camera has provisions for a laser designator, and stabilization of the Scorpion system offers a steady image regardless of carrier aircraft vibrations, according to the officials.* Aviation Week & Space Technology 4/28/86, p113 [**1985**]

optronics, *n.* another name for OPTOELECTRONICS. *Germany's fundamental role and the absence of a combined defence structure rule out any military programme, while planning is not currently popular in a Europe where the winds of liberalism are blowing. Whence the idea of a civilian European cooperation programme in six advanced technology sectors—*

optronics, . . . new materials, supercomputers, high-powered lasers, artificial intelligence and ultra high-speed microelectronics. Manchester Guardian Weekly (Le Monde section) 7/7/85, p11 [**1967**, blend of *optical* + *electronics*]

oracy ('ɔrəsi:), *n.* the ability to express oneself orally and to understand the speech of others. Compare GRAPHICACY. *Why is there such great interest in dyslexia and no interest in disfunctional oracy? In all but the deaf, effective oracy precedes any effective literacy: in learning literacy a functional ability to communicate in the mother tongue is thus a condition of being communicated with thereafter in literacy from the printed page.* Times (London) 12/6/73, p9 [**1965**, from *oral* + *-acy* (noun suffix), patterned after *literacy* (1883), *numeracy* (1959)]

oral, *n. U.S. Informal.* a secretly recorded conversation, not filmed or videotaped. *That was recorded in what the F.B.I. called an "oral," a group conversation taped in stereophonic sound through a pair of microphones concealed at opposite ends of Mr. Dorfman's office near Chicago's O'Hare International Airport. The bugs were so sensitive that the jury could hear a clock ticking and jet aircraft taking off in the distance.* NY Times 12/16/82, pP20 [**1982**, noun use of the adjective]

oral biography, a biography based on and containing interviews with relatives and acquaintances of the subject. *Like Jean Stein and George Plimpton's "Edie: An American Biography," an oral biography of Edie Sedgwick, and Peter Manso's more recent "Mailer: His Life and Times," Mr. Potter's book is less a biography than an exercise in gossip, an excuse for people to talk about themselves and settle old scores under the guise of reminiscing about the celebrated figure they have known.* NY Times Book Review 2/2/86, p15 [**1974**]

oral history, **1** the tape-recording of interviews with persons who witnessed or participated in historical events. *Since 1970 . . . oral history has evolved into a full-blown movement, feeding the mills of scholarship and gossip alike with thousands of miles of taped reminiscences, justifications (both candid and self-serving), secrets and trivia.* Newsweek 8/5/74, p74 **2** a historical account based on tape recordings or typescripts of such interviews. *A $100,000 grant from the Ford Foundation is supporting an oral history of the civil-rights movement during Dr. [Martin Luther]* King's *lifetime.* NY Times Magazine 11/26/72, p68 **3** any account based on verbal recollections or information, as distinguished from written records. *She never spoke of him with anything but affection . . . Yet at one time, according to the oral history of the town, she and Jake had decided on divorce.* Harper's 2/73, p25 **—oral historian:** *The historian must be prepared to see and define the problems and to remind and even spur as well as to check and supplement the forgetful subject. In short, a tape recorder does not of itself make an "oral historian."* Science 3/7/75, p827 [**1971**] ►Although the term *oral history* was used occasionally in the 1960's by historians, chiefly in connection with the John F. Kennedy Library, it became very current about 1972, as the method attained popularity both among social historians and writers on contemporary affairs.

orange paper, a document published by a British or Commonwealth ministry in which a program of reform or modification of existing policy is proposed. *The first step toward that goal followed in the same year with publication of a government "orange paper" that proposed, as a key element of reform, the provision of "an acceptable basic annual income for all Canadians"—in effect, a guaranteed annual income aimed especially at the "working poor."* Maclean's 6/14/76, p23 [**1976**, patterned after GREEN PAPER]

orature, *n.* the oral poems and narratives of a preliterate people or nation. *The Greeks had vast and complex oral heritages that might more accurately be called their orature.* Tom McArthur, Foundation Course for Language Teachers 1983, p41 [**1981**, from *oral* literature]

orbital, *n. British.* a highway going around the suburbs of a city. *First priority for roads, after the orbitals outside Greater London, is Ringway 2 (North and South Circular Roads).* Times (London) 2/3/70, p2 [**1970**, noun use of the adjective (1933)]

orbital steering. See the first quotation for the meaning. . . . *orbital steering* [is] *a process in which atoms within enzymes are held at precise angles to permit them to join and form new molecular compounds in biochemical reactions.* Science News 6/27/70, p618 *A new concept that enzymes facilitate chemical reactions by precisely guiding the angles of approach of atoms in the reacting compounds has been proposed by Daniel E. Koshland, Jr., of the University of California at Berkeley. Koshland presented evidence for this concept, which he calls orbital steering* . . . Scientific American 8/70, p46 [**1970**]

Oreo, *n. U.S. Slang.* a derogatory name for a black man who is part of the white establishment or is in favor of working within the white establishment. *Trouble is Negroes been programmed by white folks to believe their products are inferior. We've developed into a generation of Oreos—black on the outside, white on the inside.* Harper's 3/69, p61 [**1968**, from the trade name for a chocolate cookie with a vanilla cream filling]

org, *n. Informal.* organization. *Inside the Toronto org, I saw one ceremony that might be construed as worship. It was an hourlong "Sunday service" opening with a recitation of the Scientology creed, which is reminiscent of the United States Declaration of Independence.* Maclean's 6/74, p77 [**1936, 1962**, by shortening]

organic metal, *Chemistry.* a polymer with high electrical conductivity. *"Organic metals" are tantalizing chemists and physicists both with the challenge of understanding unusual properties and the potential for novel technological applications* . . . *But the new materials are surprisingly good conductors, and their conductivity is strictly temperature dependent. Although they conduct electricity, these solids retain organic characteristics (such as solubility in organic solvents) that may offer a number of new industrial possibilities.* Science News 9/10/77, p171 [**1977**]

organo-, combining form for "organic," now used especially in forming adjective compounds designating organic insecticides, fungicides, bacteriocides, etc., as in the following examples: —**organochlorine**, *adj.: In one of the most competent surveys ever of the organochlorine scene, the report points out that by 1963 Britain used only 1 per cent of the 60,000 tons of organochlorine insecticide used in the United States, a position which has probably improved since then.* New Scientist 11/5/70, p255 —**organomercuric**, *adj.: This disease* [smut disease of barley] *cannot be treated by organo-mercuric compounds, probably because it is so deep seated in the seed.* New Scientist 11/20/69, p403 —**organophosphate**, *adj.: Organophosphate pesticides, although highly toxic, are being used in increasing amounts because they are far more biodegradable than chlorinated hydrocarbons such as DDT.* Science News 2/20/71, p130 —**organophosphorous**, *adj.: The organophosphorous insecticides inhibit the enzyme cholinesterase, which normally breaks down acetycholine following the transmission of the nerve impulse across the synapse.* McGraw-Hill Yearbook of Science and Technology 1971, p319

organohalogen (ɔr,gænou'hælədʒən), *adj.* of, relating to, or denoting any of a group of highly toxic organic compounds containing one or more halogens. *Three categories of waste disposal were included in the proposed regulations. The first was for agents totally banned. These were the organohalogen compounds, such as the organochlorine pesticides and polychlorinated biphenyls.* Times (London) 2/16/72, p7 *The Convention prohibits the dumping at sea of certain dangerous substances, including . . . organohalogen compounds and highly radioactive materials.* Nature 1/1-8/76, p5 [**1972**]

organologist, *n.* a specialist in the study of musical instruments. *The Met's organologist is a professional devoted to studying the history, use, and construction of musical instruments—of which the museum owns some 4,000, including the world's oldest piano.* NY Times Magazine 7/8/79, p17 [**1976**, derived from *organology* the study of musical instruments (OEDS 1959), from *organ* musical instrument (from Latin *organum*, from Greek *órganon*) + *-ology* study of]

organule ('ɔrgənyu:l), *n.* another name for MOLECHISM or MOLECISM. *Organule or molecism? . . . Whether viruses are*

molecules or organisms depends on how you look at them, and it is always important to have more than one point of view. Science Journal 3/68, p90 [**1968**, from *organism* + *molecule*]

org-man, *n. U.S.* short for *organization man*, one who gives himself up wholly to the business or to the institution with which he is associated. *They* [white Anglo-Saxon Protestants] *grew great as initiators and entrepreneurs. They invented the country, its culture and its values; they shaped the institutions and organizations. Then they drew the institutions around themselves, moved to the suburbs, and became org-men.* Harper's 4/70, p86 [**1970**]

Oriental, *n.* a Jew of Middle Eastern or North African origin or descent. *The Orientals hold down the majority of the service and production jobs in Israel. Some twenty-five to fifty per cent of the Europeans (depending on date of arrival) are in professional and managerial posts, as against only ten to fifteen per cent of the Orientals.* New Yorker 4/7/73, p74 [**1972**, short for *Oriental Jew* (OEDS 1938)]

Oriental Shorthair, any of a breed of green-eyed cats with a long body of uniform color, developed in Europe by crossing Siamese with other oriental cats. *Newly recognized by the Cat Fanciers Association, the Oriental Shorthair cat is one of this country's newest breeds, combining the stylized body type of the Siamese with the richest colors of the other shorthair felines.* NY Times 1/28/79, pL7 [**1979**]

-oriented, a combining form added to nouns to form adjectives meaning "geared to, directed toward," now increasingly used as in: —**action-oriented**, *adj.: Magic Mountain: No Disneyland imitator, this park is an action-oriented playground featuring thrills and excitement.* National Observer 6/9/73, p16 —**change-oriented**, *adj.: "Then again, these hillmen are implacably tradition-bound, or 'not change-oriented,' to use the expression of an unusually disheartened visiting sociologist.* Atlantic 10/76, p283 —**cops-and-robbers-oriented**, *adj.: . . . a welcome relief from the strident, cops-and-robbers-oriented dramas of commercial television.* New Yorker 3/24/75, p79 —**golf-oriented**, *adj.: "It was," says the Rangers' golf-oriented center, Peter Stemkowski, "like getting a two on a par-five hole."* Boys' Life 12/72, p10 —**identity-oriented**, *adj.: . . . The American Indian is a classic example. He was identity oriented, occasionally warlike and hostile, but seldom motivated by aggression or fear. The American frontiersmen were survival-oriented, and all but eliminated the Indian in the acquisition of power and land.* Saturday Review 2/19/72, p27 —**land-oriented**, *adj.: It's estimated that Southern city dwellers spent $1.4 billion on land-oriented recreation last year.* Progressive Farmer 1/73, p20 —**outdoor-oriented**, *adj.: As pleasant and hospitable as their surroundings, they take obvious pride in their outdoor-oriented life-style.* Reader's Digest 12/71, p148 —**sports-oriented**, *adj.: Ironwood, Palm Desert. Exclusive sports-oriented community on 900 acres.* Town and Country 6/74, p43 [**1950**, from the past participle of *orient, v.* "to adjust, correct, or put into the right relationship" (OED 1850)]

orienteer, *n.* a person who engages in orienteering, the sport of competing with others to get first through an unknown area with the use of a compass and topographical map. *Furthermore, Swedish orienteers bled their way into medical history a few years ago following an epidemic of the disease.* Sunday Times (London) 10/10/71, p30 [**1965**, back formation from *orienteering* (OEDS 1948)]

orogenics, *n.* the process of mountain formation. *Because the book is primarily concerned with the effects of the Caledonian, Hercynian, and Alpine orogenics in Europe, no detailed stratigraphy is given. Caledonian movements are seen only on the Scandinavian Peninsula, but without any comparison or correlation with the British Isles the account is rather brief.* Science Journal 12/70, p82 [**1970**, from *orogenic, adj.*, relating to mountain formation (OED 1886)]

orphan drug, a drug not manufactured because only a small number of patients might purchase it. *The Senate Dec. 1 cleared legislation designed to encourage drug companies to develop drugs for rare disabling diseases. The bill—the "Or* *phan Drug Act"—had received final House approval Dec. 14.* Facts on File 1982, p99 [**1982**, figurative use of *orphan*, because the diseases for which the drugs are needed do not receive attention and funding for research, + *drug*]

orphan virus, a virus not known to be the cause of a disease. *A considerable number of viruses recently isolated from the feces of healthy as well as ill individuals are not known to produce disease. . . . These viruses . . . are called orphan viruses, and those isolated from humans are known as ECHO viruses.* P.L. Carpenter, *Microbiology*, 1955. [**1954**]

orthocharmonium (ˌɔrθoutʃarˈmouniˌəm), *n.* a name for the PSI PARTICLE according to the charm theory. See QUARK. *They designate the charmed-quark-charmed-antiquark bound state as "charmonium" and say that what has been found is specifically orthocharmonium.* Science News 1/25/75, p60 [**1975**, from *ortho-* straight + CHARMONIUM]

orthodonture, *n.* the straightening or adjusting of irregular teeth; orthodontics. *More and more adults are wearing braces on their teeth, and smiling, because orthodonture today can be done with braces that are removable for special occasions.* NY Times Magazine 11/26/78, p130 [**1969**, from *orthodontics* the branch of dentistry dealing with the straightening of teeth (OEDS 1909) + *-ure* (noun suffix), as in *denture;* perhaps influenced by an alteration in the pronunciation of *orthodontia* (OEDS 1849)]

orthodox sleep, the dreamless part of sleep, during which the body undergoes no marked changes. *There are two basic kinds of sleep: 'orthodox' sleep and 'paradoxical' sleep. During orthodox sleep there are no dreams and measurements of brain waves show a slow 'alpha' rhythm.* Science Journal 12/69, p78 *After about an hour of this orthodox sleep phase, a change occurs and paradoxical sleep begins and lasts about 10 minutes before orthodox sleep is resumed . . . I believe that orthodox sleep (non-rapid eye movement, non-dreaming, or slow wave sleep) serves a function for the growth and renewal of general bodily tissues, and that paradoxical sleep (rapid eye movement or dreaming sleep) is important for brain growth and renewal.* New Scientist 4/23/70, p170 [**1967**]

orthoferrite, *n.* any of a class of crystalline materials in which specific areas of magnetism can be induced by the application of electric current, used especially in computers to store and transmit data. *For several years, Bell scientists have been experimenting with thin wafers of crystalline materials known as orthoferrites, which are compounds of iron oxides and such rare-earth minerals as ytterbium, thulium and samariumterbium.* Time 9/5/69, p37 *Bubble domains were first found in a class of materials called orthoferrites, compounds of rare earths, iron and oxygen. They have the general chemical formula $RFeO_3$, where R is any of the rare earths or the element yttrium.* Science News 5/8/71, p318 [**1956**, from *ortho-* straight + *ferrite* an iron compound]

orthomolecular, *adj.* of or based upon a theory formulated by the American chemist Linus Pauling, born 1901, according to which disease may be caused by deficient molecular concentrations of essential substances in the body, so that cures may be effected by combining medical treatment with dietary and vitamin therapy to overcome the molecular deficiency. *Another way in which the disease* [diabetes] *can be kept under control, if it is not serious, is by adjusting the diet, regulating the intake of sugar, in such a way as to keep the glucose concentration in the blood within the normal limits. This procedure also represents an example of orthomolecular medicine.* Linus Pauling, Vitamin C and the Common Cold, 1970, p66 *His* [Linus Pauling's] *approach, which he calls orthomolecular psychiatry, involves giving the brain "the right molecules in the right amounts," and he is currently trying to discover the optimum concentrations for specific individuals. This is a radical approach to mental health, one not endorsed by most medical researchers.* World Book Science Annual 1969, p382 [**1968**, coined by Linus Pauling from *ortho-* straight, correct, exact + *molecular*]

orthophoto or **orthophotograph,** *n.* a composite photograph of terrain, made by joining narrow strips of other photographs so

that the finished picture is fully correct in scale, position, etc. *The orthophoto produced in this manner, although similar in appearance to an aerial photograph, is in fact quite different. Whereas an aerial photograph of rolling or mountainous terrain will have inherent scale and angular distortions, the orthophoto is true to scale; shapes, angles, and distances are correct.* McGraw-Hill Yearbook of Science and Technology 1972, p245 *Despite developments in air survey techniques, leading to the introduction of orthophotographs . . . conventional cartographic resources are now unable to keep pace with the accelerating rate of information collection.* Times (London) 5/21/76, p15 [**1964**, from *ortho-* straight + *photo(graph)*]

orthotic, *adj.* of or relating to orthotics. *The list of practical factors that prevail against myoelectric systems is long and specialized. It led me to the conclusion that the short-term control of remote manipulators is easier to achieve than the long-term control of orthotic arms by a paralyzed patient in a wheelchair.* New Scientist 3/26/70, p629 [**1955**]

orthotics, *n.* the rehabilitation of injured or impaired joints or muscles through artificial support. . . . *shortages existed in all of the other rehabilitation disciplines: occupational therapy, prosthetics and orthotics, social work, speech pathology and audiology, rehabilitation counseling . . .* Britannica Book of the Year 1969, p510 [**1957**, from *ortho-* straight, correct + *-tics,* as in *prosthetics*]

orthovoltage, *n.* X-ray radiation therapy using voltages of 200,000 to 500,000 volts (often used attributively). *It is unlikely that further sophistication of either radiation dosage or localization will result in an increased rate of cure (witness the rather disappointing gains in progressing from orthovoltage to the accelerator* [the use of proton beams in radiotherapy]). Science 6/9/72, p1071 [**1967**, from *ortho-* straight, normal + *voltage*]

ORV, abbreviation of *off-road vehicle.* . . . *the continued heavy use of ORVs may greatly erode these coastal islands.* 1982 World Book Science Annual, p242 *He's a businessman who drives dune buggies and a member of the Eugene Sandbugs, one of the dozens of off-road-vehicle (ORV) clubs in Oregon.* Encyclopedia Science Supplement (Grolier) 1987, p197 [**1974**; see OFF-ROAD]

ORVer (ˈɔrvər), *n.* U.S. Informal. the owner or driver of an off-road vehicle. *Recently the road was ordered closed by the state, denying ORVs access to the beach and its shorebird areas. ORVers have protested . . .* Encyclopedia Science Supplement 1987, p200 [**1986**]

Orwellism, *n.* the manipulation or distortion of facts for propaganda purposes. See also 1984. *President Nixon may have been wounded in the mid-term elections but his election night insistence that the blood on his face was nothing less than the blush of victory can now be seen as a triumph of public relations. At least, an interesting example of the progress of Orwellism in national politics.* Manchester Guardian Weekly 12/5/70, p5 [**1970**, earlier *Orwellianism* (1967); so called in allusion to a society completely controlled by propaganda in the novel *1984* by George Orwell. The adjective *Orwellian* (OEDS 1950) has been much used to describe such a totalitarian society.]

OSHA (ˈouʃə), *n.* U.S. acronym for *Occupational Safety and Health Administration,* created by Congress in 1971. *OSHA was empowered to set national standards to replace a welter of conflicting health and safety guidelines, send inspectors to factories, stores and offices to check on compliance, levy stiff fines on violators and even order unsafe businesses to close down.* Time 7/8/74, p48 [**1971**]

osmolality, *n.* degree of the pressure operative in osmosis. . . . *X-ray diffraction studies of hemoglobin spacing in human red cells showed that . . . when the cells shrank, the spacing changed much more slowly with external osmolality, presumably because the molecules were so close together that they could not easily become more tightly packed.* Scientific American 2/71, p95 [**1959**, from *osmolal* of or relating to the *osmol,* a unit of osmotic pressure (from *osmosis* + *mol* molecular weight in grams) + *-ity* (suffix denoting quality, condition, or degree)]

osmolarity, *n.* the quality or tendency characteristic of osmosis. *The most important functions of the kidney are to keep constant the volume, osmolarity and composition of the fluid which surrounds the cells of the body.* New Scientist 6/24/65, p868 [**1953,** from *osmolar* of or relating to osmosis (from *osmol*, a unit of osmotic pressure + *-ar*, adj. suffix) + *-ity*. See the etymology of OSMOLALITY.]

OSO, abbreviation of *Orbiting Solar Observatory,* an unmanned scientific satellite of NASA, designed for solar research from a circular orbit around the earth. Compare OAO, OGO. *The OSO weighs about 500 lb, of which 200 lb are scientific experiments. They are launched at the rate of about one per day by a Delta rocket from Cape Kennedy into a 300-nautical-mile circular orbit at an inclination of 33°.* McGraw-Hill Yearbook of Science and Technology 1968, p363 *In addition to picture-taking experiments, each OSO contains instruments that monitor the UV and x-ray radiation emitted by the entire solar disk.* McGraw-Hill Yearbook of Science and Technology 1971, p301 [**1962**]

ossobuco (ˌɑsouˈbuːkou), *n.* an Italian dish of braised veal shanks, made with olive oil, white wine, anchovies, etc. Also spelled *osso bucco. There are five pastas costing $3.75 and $4.00, and three entrées at $6.25, including osso buco.* National Review 7/18/75, p780 [**1961,** from Italian, (literally) bone marrow]

ostomate, *n.* a person who has undergone a colostomy, ileostomy, or similar operation. *Assuming no further complications— for example, a recurrence of cancer—an ostomate's life expectancy is no different from that of anyone in the general population. Once recovery is complete, an ostomate can lead a normal life.* NY Post 12/1/79, p25 [**1966,** from *ostomy* + *-ate* noun suffix]

ostomy, *n.* any operation in which a part of the intestine or urinary tract is removed and an artificial opening (stoma) is made for the passage of waste products; a colostomy, ileostomy, ureterostomy, etc. *An ostomy may become necessary because part of the intestine or urinary system is affected with cancer or an inflammatory disease . . . Although the ostomy operation involves major surgery, it is a relatively safe procedure.* NY Post 12/1/79, p25 [**1961,** abstracted from *colostomy, ileostomy,* etc.]

Ostpolitik (ˈɔːstpouliˌtiːk), *n.* **1** a policy of the West German government to establish normal diplomatic and trade relations with the Communist countries of eastern Europe. Compare WESTPOLITIK. *In the West, the big change was Willy Brandt's narrow victory in the West German elections last October, and the formation of a new Bonn coalition government dominated by the Social Democrats, prepared to abandon the rigidities of the Adenauer foreign policy of the last twenty years and embark on an entirely new and dynamic course of Ostpolitik.* Atlantic 7/70, p26 **2** a similar policy of any western nation. *Nixon as a risk-taker is something of a surprise . . . But his Ostpolitik is daring. It is a repudiation of his entire past.* New Yorker 10/23/71, p156 [**1961** for def. 1; **1971** for def. 2; from German, Eastern policy]

OTB, abbreviation of *off-track betting,* a state-licensed system in the United States for placing bets away from the track where the horses are racing. *Seems that the OTB computers that are linked with those at the race track developed a colic or something, and wagers at the fourteen shops around town had to be recorded manually.* New Yorker 7/31/71, p65 [**1964**]

OTC or **O.T.C.**, abbreviation of: **1** *one-stop inclusive tour charter,* an airline tour package that combines low-cost air fares with discount arrangements at a single destination. *To their credit, travel agents have devised ingenious plans to make the tourist's dollar work more efficiently. This year's prime example: the one-stop-inclusive tour charter, or OTC. Approved last fall by the Civil Aeronautics Board, OTC plans to allow travelers to choose among dozens of destinations at prices that include air fare, hotel room, ground transportation, taxis and tips.* Time 8/23/76, p53 [**1976**] **2** *over-the-counter.* See the

quotation for the meaning. *The market is for "over-the-counter" stocks—those not generally listed on an exchange but bought and sold largely over the telephone by brokers.* Wall St. Jnl 4/2/63, p1 [**1957**]

OTH, abbreviation of OVER-THE-HORIZON. *Unlike conventional radar, over-the-horizon, or OTH, radar is not restricted in its range by the curvature of the earth. By reflection from the ionosphere OTH radar can penetrate to great distances, making possible the detection of missiles soon after they are launched.* Scientific American 2/73, p22 [**1967**]

ougiya or **ouguiya** (wɑːˈgiːyə), *n.* the monetary unit of Mauritania introduced in 1973. See KHOUM. *In a second slap at France, the republic of Mauritania replaced the French franc with a new currency unit called the ougiya.* Newsweek 8/27/73, p36 [**1973,** from Arabic]

outachieve, *v.t.* to surpass in achievements; do better than. *In fact, getting along with parents has never been easy in the U.S. America has almost begged for trouble by expecting children to out-achieve their parents, yet wanting them still to look up to them.* Time 8/17/70, p39 [**1960**]

outasite or **outasight** (ˌɑutəˈsait), *adj. U.S. Slang.* **1** very advanced or unconventional; far-out. *The new film surrealists (the outasite ones) can make you suddenly think of a very large, strong, cheery wrestler, with thumbs the size of most people's wrists, trying with all his might to thread a needle.* New Yorker 8/29/70, p51 **2** out of this world; incomparable; wonderful. *Chances are that parents will never like Janis Joplin or Country Joe and the Fish, no matter how many times you insist they're outasight. So save your confrontations for topics that you consider important.* Time 8/17/70, p38 [**1968,** contraction of *out of sight;* also found earlier as *outa sight* (1893)]

outer city, *U.S.* the outskirts of a city; the suburbs. *A small, growing number of black families is increasingly able to penetrate the new Outer Cities of America, the swelling bands of suburbs that ring the stagnating inner cities.* NY Times 6/1/71, p1 [**1971**]

outgun, *v.t.* to surpass; outdo; be better than. . . . *I should now go on . . . with a "ten best" list full of incontrovertible masterpieces. I can't do it; but I can and do suggest that my 10, whittled down despairingly from an initial list of 30, comfortably outguns Philip Hope-Wallace's for the theatre in sheer talent and the proper use of the medium's widening possibilities.* Manchester Guardian Weekly 12/26/70, p18 [**1952,** extended use of *outgun* meaning to have more weapons than or to outshoot]

outlaw country, another name for PROGRESSIVE COUNTRY. *B.W. Stevenson, also on the bill, is a country-music performer who spills over into rock; probably he could fit into the currently popular "outlaw country" genre. He filters his country sounds through present day rock-and-roll.* NY Times 2/15/76, p65 [**1976**]

out-of-body, *adj.* characterized by or involving dissociation from one's own body; having to do with parapsychological phenomena in which one sees the body and its surroundings from an external position in space. *Noyes speculates that out-of-body experiences may be projections the brain makes to negate death, to pretend we are only witnessing it as a spectator.* Maclean's 6/14/76, p50 [**1971,** alteration of earlier (1946) *out-of-the-body*]

outplace (autˈpleis), *v.t. U.S.* to place in a new job before actual discharge from a company; help secure new employment. *Instead of simply bouncing a subordinate, the boss can send him to a firm that specializes in helping unwanted executives to find new jobs. The practitioners have even coined a euphemistic description for the process: "outplacing" executives who have been "dehired."* Time 9/14/70, p83 [**1970**]

outplacement, *n.* the act or process of outplacing (also used attributively). *The boom in outplacement was triggered by the 1974-1975 recession, which prompted a wave of severe personnel cutbacks in dozens of major corporations.* NY Times 3/18/79, pC3 *The outplacement firms have their critics. Some industrial psychologists feel that an executive who has been* *ired* needs the determination to reassess his abilities and find *a* job on his own. Time 9/14/70, p83 **[1970]**

outrageous, adj. U.S. Slang. used admiringly, especially by *t*eenagers, of something shocking, daring, etc. Compare AWE-*S*OME. But that is not at all what's wanted by the fans of Kiss (*a*t least according to the kids I talked to). What they want is *o*utrageousness. ("Outrageous," spoken with heavy emphasis *o*n the "rage" and overweening approval in the voice, is today's *s*lang for defiant of flamboyant behavior, going against the *r*ules: 50's-style rebellion with a twist. Think of James Dean in *d*rag.) NY Times Magazine 6/19/77, p66 R. Couri Hay, celebri*t*y columnist for the National Enquirer and star and producer *o*f his own celebrity-interview show on Channel C, local cable-*T*V station: "The invitation was first-class. All the important *m*edia people were there. The narrated slide show of Elvis was *o*utrageous. I just couldn't believe the dialogue." New Yorker 1/27/78, p34 **[1977]**

outreach, n. U.S. any deliberate and systematic effort to pro-*v*ide health care, jobs, and other social services to needy groups *o*r communities (often used attributively). A joint committee *s*tudy . . . showed that 1890 colleges had significant capabili-*t*ies in areas involving nutrition, environmental quality, psy-*c*hology, consumer education, rural development, community *h*ealth, and outreach to the rural poor. Saturday Review *5*/23/72, p48 His was also the first black gospel group to play *a*t Nashville's Grand Ole Opry. His Soledad concert was ar-*r*anged at the request of an independent ex-con outreach group *c*alled The Way Inn. As for his own motivations in singing the *L*ord's praises to such a group of desperate men, Crouch ex-*p*lains: "I'll hook them any way I can." Time 1/9/78, *p*14 **[1967**, extended sense of the term meaning "act of reach-*i*ng out" (OED 1870)]

outseg, v.t. U.S. Slang. to be more segregationist than; to sur-*p*ass in degree of segregationist policy. Governors Spiro Agnew *o*f Maryland and Winthrop Rockefeller of Arkansas won office *e*ven though their Democratic opponents "outsegged" them . . Time 10/13/67, p19 [Albert] Brewer . . . acquired a repu-*t*ation as an effective administrator, and, most important, he *h*as no intention of being "Out-segged" by [George C.] Wal-*l*ace. Manchester Guardian Weekly 4/4/70, p14 **[1963**, from *o*ut- better than + seg, shortened from segregationist]

outsource, v.t. in manufacturing, to acquire (parts) from non-*u*nion or foreign suppliers, especially to cut costs. Compare *S*OURCE. Without an agreement that limits wage demands in *r*eturn for job security, the prospect is that an increasing num-*b*er of union jobs will be transferred abroad—where labor and *p*roduction costs are lower. Indeed, one crucial element of the *a*greement Fraser is seeking would commit GM and Ford to *s*top "out-sourcing the work." Maclean's 2/1/82, p37 Harry *E*llis said in effect that companies had left themselves free to *o*utsource spare parts . . . Washington Week in Review, PBS, *9*/21/84 **[1982]**

Oval Office or **Oval Room**, Especially U.S. the office of the *P*residency of the United States. And if Congress should decide *t*hat a President is no longer to be held broadly accountable for *t*he conduct of his most personal appointees, it would obviously *e*ncourage future Presidents to wink at every sort of skuldug-*g*ery so long as nothing could be traced to a specific directive *f*rom the Oval Office. Harper's 5/74, p15 Neither corruption *o*f language nor corruption extending from the Oval Room can *m*uch longer mask the perilous need for the new energy re-*s*ources so long suppressed. Nation 1/5/74, p16 [Oval Office 1969; Oval Room 1974; transferred from the literal sense of the *p*rivate office of the President, a large oval room in the White *H*ouse]▶In the current sense this term became popular in the *c*ontext of the Watergate affair. In its literal sense it appeared *i*n the 1930's, when the office was built.

Oval Officer, an appointee to the staff of the President of the *U*nited States. John J. Wilson, attorney for former Oval Offi-*c*ers Haldeman and Ehrlichman, said that, realistically, he ex-*p*ected them both to be indicted. National Review 3/15/74, *p*290 **[1974]**

overachieve, v.t., v.i. to do or perform better than expected. . . . this succinct yet passionate ballet overachieves its immedi-ate purpose by choreographically summing up the Dumas story with a series of brilliantly visualized cinematic-style vi-gnettes. NY Times 5/2/68, p58 What do you do after you've climbed to the pinnacle of rock stardom, over-achieving your wildest childhood dreams? Maclean's 10/2/78, p1 **[1967**, figu-rative sense of the educational term meaning to achieve higher grades than predicted by intelligence tests (OEDS 1953)]

overbook, v.t., v.i. to make more reservations for accommoda-tions than are actually available in an airplane, ship, hotel, etc. When Mr. Humphries continued to protest a senior official told them the aircraft was overbooked and that they had been taken off the flight on his orders. Times (London) 8/14/67, p2 And let the CAB [Civil Aeronautics Board] look closely at the custom of making passengers wait on stand-by only to be put aboard half-empty planes at the last minute—yes, I know people over-book and then fail to show up, but that knowledge does noth-ing for my personal convenience when some clerk has snarled my reservation . . . Saturday Review 8/31/68, p7 **[1903, 1959]**

overdose, v.i. **1** to become sick or die from an overdose of a nar-cotic. He overdosed in Miles's bathroom and cut himself in a fall. Newsweek 3/26/73, p22 Dr Gisela Oppenheim, con-sultant psychiatrist at the drug dependence unit at Charing Cross Hospital, said she wrote to Dr Vignoles asking him not to prescribe for one of her patients. "This boy's life is in danger as he is overdosing," she wrote. Times (London) 3/14/73, p3 **2** Figurative use: Though Wenders overdoses on mood, he creates the right apprehensiveness for a Highsmith story. But he's try-ing to do eighteen other things, too; he "enriches" the plot with incidental speculative themes. New Yorker 10/17/77, p176 By day's end, the children will be pale and testy, overdosed on an-ticipation and excitement. NY Times 12/24/78, pD1 **[1972**, verb use of the noun, probably influenced by the earlier (OED 1758) transitive verb meaning "to give too large a dose to"]

overdub, v.t. to add (one or more vocal or instrumental parts) to a recording. Apparently Crosby, Stills and Nash went back to the studios to overdub their vocals on "Suite: Judy Blue Eyes", but the rest are left as originally played. Times (London) 7/18/70, p7 . . . the album comes complete with a disclaimer from Heart and an admission that Mushroom had remixed and overdubbed the material without the band's cooperation. NY Times 9/2/77, pC15 **[1962** —n. the addition of recorded vocal or instrumental parts to a recording; the blending of several or multiple layers of sound in one record. In 1971 Mike Oldfield began work on a composition entitled 'Tubular Bells' and now, after 2,300 overdubs, 'Tubular Bells' is available on record as the first release from Virgin Records of Notting Hill Gate. Lis-tener 6/7/73, p775 **[1965 for verb; 1973 for noun]**

overexploitation, n. the exploiting of a natural resource beyond the level of natural replenishment. Improved technology of fishing existing stocks ought to be accompanied by increased knowledge of the biology of commercially important fish so that natural fluctuations in stocks may be understood. More-over, improved international cooperation should limit overex-ploitation of important stocks. New Scientist 12/3/70, p374 **[1961]**

overground, adv., adj. **1** in the open; public or publicly. The new force [an officer corps] saw little serious combat. But it be-came of pivotal importance in both the overground and under-ground politics of Burma under the Japanese and it saw itself very much in the Japanese mould. Manchester Guardian Weekly 5/11/74, p6 **[1943, 1961] 2** belonging to or recognized as acceptable to, established society or culture. Next, I got a part in what you might call an "overground" movie—huge budget and lots of stars. New Yorker 9/9/67, p40 When the American activist Abbie Hoffman published his "handbook of survival and warfare," . . . the book clearly bore a price and, beneath the spoof imprint "Pirate Editions," that of an "over-ground" publisher, Grove Press. Times Literary Supplement 1/21/72, p66 **[1961]**

overinterpretation, n. interpretation beyond a necessary or jus-tified point. Like most cosmogonic conjectures, Gamow's model is not strictly "scientific". There are traces of metaphysical *speculation, of over-interpretation, of pictorialized facile concepts, and perhaps, even of suppressed religious memories. Yet no original thinker can resist the temptation to make gigantic extrapolations.* New Scientist 10/1/70, p39 [**1959**]

overkill, *n.* **1** the ability to annihilate an enemy or objective several times over. *What does being ahead mean when possessing more or less overkill cannot be translated into anything that is militarily or humanly meaningful?* NY Times 11/2/70, p47 **2** something that causes harm by exceeding the required or safe limits. *This prospect of recession raised fears in certain quarters that the nation's fiscal and monetary authorities, in their desire to correct inflation, might pursue restrictive policies too long, leading to economic overkill.* Americana Annual 1970, p125 [Theodore] *Kheel feels that the crunch is demanded by the very nature of representative bargaining. He readily concedes that bargaining under deadline pressure can lead to miscalculations, contract inequities, and in what he calls "overkill," meaning long and bitter strikes* . . . New Yorker 8/1/70, p44 **—v.i.** to kill or destroy several times over. *We maintained armed forces to defend a non-existent Empire and spent uselessly and prodigally in a vain attempt to keep abreast of the titans in capacity to kill and overkill, and in doing so we saddled ourselves with expensive commitments that hindered industrial re-equipment and social spending on housing and education.* Punch 11/27/68, p751 [**1958**]

overmike, *v.t. U.S.* to amplify too much with a microphone. *Because the show, like all Broadway shows, is damnably overmiked, it is hard to tell what the quality of her voice may be.* New Yorker 5/2/77, p90 [**1972**, from *over-* too much + *mike, v.* (1957) to transmit on or use a microphone]

overprescribe, *v.i., v.t.* to prescribe medicine unnecessarily or in excess of what is required. *There are rogues in any profession, and in this situation there are three possible culprits apart from the farmer himself. There is the agricultural merchant who bends the regulations, there is the veterinary surgeon who overprescribes, and finally there is the unscrupulous retail pharmacist* . . . New Scientist 3/28/68, p679 *I cannot tolerate the overprescribing of unnecessary and expensive drugs which in my opinion is largely due to this pressure.* Times (London) 10/12/67, p9 [**1953**]

overprescription, *n.* the act or practice of overprescribing; unnecessary or excessive prescription of medicines. *Dr.* [Ian] *Hindmarch blames overprescription by doctors as the main source of illicit amphetamines. He added: "Some doctors to me are pushers. They give out up to 100 at a time to avoid being pestered weekly."* Times (London) 11/4/70, p6 [**1967**]

overqualified, *adj.* exceeding the minimum requirements for eligibility; being overly qualified. . . . *applications are flooding colleges across the country. The problem is how to cull the lucky few from the overqualified many. Forced to refine their criteria, admissions directors now seek "high-energy" students (basal metabolism readings may be next) and especially "interesting people."* Time 3/28/69, p41 . . . *it is often hard to get the message across to personnel men "who make points hiring overqualified people for less than they're worth" and plant managers who get promoted by cutting costs.* NY Times 2/3/68, p30 [**1963**]

override, *n. U.S.* the act of overriding or nullifying. *A few days before the scheduled Assembly vote, Tony Daugherty,* [Governor Jerry] *Brown's legislative liaison chief, told me, "In all candor, we have not worked it the way we would a normal override." With the backing of strong Democratic majorities* . . . *Brown had never been overridden; in fact there had been only two successful overrides of a governor's veto in all the years since Earl Warren.* Atlantic 1/78, p36 [**1974**, noun use of the verb] ►*Override* as a noun has been in use (OEDS 1946) to mean a device for taking over operation of an automatic control.

overshoot, *n.* a miss of an intended objective resulting from aiming too high or trying for too much. *He* [the Soviet cybernetist Vadim Alexandrovich Trapeznikov] *sees the market economy as a system with high gain and strong feedback, possessing self-regulation, but troubled by overshoots; in contrast,*

in the Soviet system there is low gain and very weak feedback "depriving it of automatic functioning and correction fo minimum losses." New Scientist 12/17/70, p515 [**1962**, noun use of the verb]

oversing, *v.i.* to sing more loudly or with more interpretatio that is justified. . . . *Marenka and Jenik, though, both tende to over-sing in what is, after all, London's smallest regula opera house.* Times (London) 7/27/70, p5 [**1962**]

overspend, *n. British.* **1** the act of overspending; excessiv spending. . . . *in the words of the report, that "the larger th proposed technological step, the larger the probability of ove spend."* Manchester Guardian Weekly 8/11/73, p15 **2** a amount overspent; overexpenditure. *An overspend c £100,000 is a probability, therefore.* Sunday Times (London 5/30/71, p22 [**1971**, noun use of the verb]

overstayer, *n. British and Australian.* a visitor to a country wh remains longer than permitted by the terms of the entry visa *"I do not think an unconditional amnesty is right, but I thin the Home Office could adopt a much more liberal attitude t overstayers, particularly to people from Cyprus or Rhodesia.* Times (London) 9/17/76, p4 *Auckland Police Associatio chairman P. Ngata says the methods used to track down over stayers were "quite abhorrent."* . . . *He had a departmen memo which said that police were to round up illegal imm grants and overstayers of all races.* National Business Review (Auckland, N.Z.) 11/10/76, p5 [**1976**]

overstretch, *n.* overextension of military forces. *By concentrat ing Britain's role in the European defence theatres the Nav was increasingly able to match commitments and meet th problem of overstretch.* Times (London) 3/10/70, p9 [**196**(noun use of the verb]

overswing, *v.i.* to swing too hard and with too much follow through. *When he is up against a long course like the August National,* [Gary] *Player, who is not a big man, has a tendenc to overswing in search of added yardage, and as a result, he i far off balance more than occasionally at the finish of a ful shot.* New Yorker 5/2/70, p100 [**1970**, verb use of the nou (OEDS 1926)]

over-the-air, *adj.* variant of ON-AIR. *Although studies have bee prepared proposing or assuming the end of over-the-air broad casting in favour of cable, such efforts seem hardly more tha academic exercises.* Britannica Book of the Year 1973 p657 [**1972**]

over-the-horizon, *adj.* of or denoting a type of radar that use reflections from the ionosphere to detect objects beyond th horizon. *Abbreviation:* OTH *The department is spendin $50,000 to explore over-the-horizon radar as a spotting tool Used now to give distant early warning against missiles, sub marines and warships, a single radar installation of this typ located at, say, Denver could cover the entire 1,500-mile borde from the Gulf of Mexico to the Pacific.* Newsweek 9/17/73 p19 [**1967**]

over-the-transom, *adj.* unsolicited. *Anderson works chiefl with his established sources in government, turning over mos of the over-the-transom tips to the younger men for investiga tion.* Time 4/3/72, p43 [**1972**]

over-tonnaged, *adj.* having too great a tonnage; oversized for its kind. *Russian expansion has not been in the bulk trades— which are free and open to all and in which she is under tonnaged—but in the liner trades, which are largely closed anc in which she is already over-tonnaged.* Times (London 6/13/77, p19 [**1968**] **—over-tonnaging,** *n.: The report statec that this would produce over-tonnaging which in turn woula reduce the efficiency of vessel utilization and result in in creased shipping costs.* Times (London) 1/12/76, p17

overwithhold, *v.t. U.S.* to withhold too large an amount of (per sonal tax) from a taxpayer. *Some developments, such as the fed eral refund of overwithheld income taxes in 1972, were expected to stimulate the economy further in the first half, par ticularly if, as some estimates have it, more than $5 billion i* *handed back to consumers who were overwithheld.* Americana Annual 1973, p243 [**1972**]

OVIR (ou'vir), *n.* the Soviet government bureau that issues exit visas for foreign travel. *I could enumerate for you a few of the innumerable bureaucratic atrocities of OVIR, not that anyone knows them all. But I could give you a list of the names of all those criminals, down to the women clerks.* New Yorker 5/9/77, p38 [**1972,** from Russian, acronym for (the Russian equivalent to) *Office of Visas and Registrations*]

ovoid, *n.* Geology. a region or body having a rectangular shape with rounded corners. *Each of these ovoids* [on one of the moons of Uranus] *is 200 to 300 kilometers (120 to 180 miles) across, and they are unlike anything ever seen in the solar system.* World Book Science Annual 1988, p114 [**1987,** transferred sense of the noun meaning egg-shaped object]

ovolactarian, *n.* a vegetarian whose diet includes dairy products and eggs. Also called LACTO-OVO-VEGETARIAN. *"Ovolactarians" supplement their plant food with eggs and milk; "granivores" eat only seeds and grains; "fruitarians" consume only fruits; "vegans" refrain from utilizing any animal product whatever.* Time 3/10/75, pK5 [**1975,** from *ovo-* egg + Latin *lactārius* of milk + English *-an*]

Ovonic, *adj.* of or relating to the Ovshinsky effect; using glassy material for a semiconductor. *Commercial switches, known as Ovonic devices, have been developed, which will drop their resistance rapidly by several orders of magnitude when suitably biassed. They will either stay "on" when the voltage is removed, or snap "off" again—although not quite so rapidly—when the current falls below some holding value.* New Scientist 7/16/70, p128 *The Ovonic switch is an inherently symmetrical semiconductor which can be changed instantaneously from a high-impedance blocking state simply by increasing the voltage or current above a given threshold level.* Times (London) 2/13/70, p27 [**1968,** from *Ov*shinsky effect + *-onic,* as in *electronic*]

Ovonics, *n.* the use or application of Ovonic devices or of the Ovshinsky effect in electronics. *Other fields of application for Ovonics lie in a.c. control where the bidirectionality of Ovonic switches will be of prime importance.* Science Journal 8/69, p78 [**1968**]

Ovshinsky effect, the property exhibited by certain amorphous glass-based compositions of switching from a state of high electrical resistance to one of low resistance depending on the level of the voltage applied with reference to chemical composition of glass or a glasslike substance. *By experiment with glass, he* [Ovshinksy] *discovered that if a particular voltage of electricity were introduced, the electrons in the glass would race out of their individual sequestrations collectively, like tribesmen hidden in the hills awaiting a chieftain's signal to attack. The signal to the electrons is now known as "the Ovshinsky effect." To achieve "the Ovshinsky effect" the voltage must be matched precisely to fit each combination of chemicals in the glass; the voltage must also be varied with the thickness of the glass.* Saturday Review 12/14/68, p68 *. . . the so-called Ovshinsky effect . . . is exhibited by amorphous glass films containing certain amounts of arsenic, germanium, silicon, and tellurium . . . This mechanism has applications ranging from simple alternating or direct current switching to logic and memory functions in computers.* World Book Science Annual 1969, p298 [**1966,** named after the American inventor Stanford R. Ovshinsky, who discovered it]

own-brand, *adj. Chiefly British* another term for OWN-LABEL. *The principles of own-brand groceries date back to the turn of the century when stores such as Lipton and Home & Colonial did much of their own packaging.* Times (London) 2/16/70, pIX [**1967**]

owner-occupation, *n. British.* occupation of a house by its owner; homeownership. *The truth is that less homes have been built for owner-occupation in the last six months than in the same period a year ago.* Listener 3/24/66, p431 *"Freedom to choose between tenancy and owner-occupation over a wide range of rents and prices is . . . (an) essential ingredient in the*

satisfaction of housing needs", the plan says. Times (London) 9/25/70, p3 [**1958**]

own-label, *adj. Chiefly British.* bearing a retail store's label as brand name instead of the manufacturer's label. Also called OWN-BRAND. *Denis Defforey, director-general of Carrefour hypermarket group, has stirred up rival distributors and many manufacturers by introducing 50 own-label items costing up to a third less than equivalent branded goods.* Times (London) 6/15/76, p21 [**1961**]

oxacillin, *n.* a semisynthetic form of penicillin that is resistant to neutralizing by penicillinase (the enzyme which destroys natural penicillin). *He was also given heavy doses of antibiotics, including a gram of chloramphenicol, a gram of oxacillin, two million units of penicillin . . .* Atlantic 3/70, p50 [**1962,** from *ox*ygen + *azole* + penic*illin*]

Oxbridgean or **Oxbridgian,** *n.* a student or graduate of Oxford or Cambridge University. *His* [John Ney's] *evidence is personal observation, engagingly wicked gossip, and literary quotation, with which he is as apt as an eighteenth-century Oxbridgean with the Latin tag.* Atlantic 5/70, p132 —**adj.** of or relating to Oxford or Cambridge Universities. *Hard on the heels of the US ping pong team were Arthur Galston and Ethan Signer, respectively professors of biology at Yale and MIT, and the first American scientists to visit China for two decades . . . Galston I encountered during and after a mini press conference in the ivy-covered, Oxbridgian atmosphere of Yale.* New Scientist and Science Journal 6/17/71, p706 [**1959,** from *Oxbridge,* a blend of *Ox*ford and Cam*bridge,* used as a collective name to distinguish this type of traditional institution from the newer British universities. *Oxbridge* was apparently first used by Thackeray in *The History of PendennisThe boom in outplacement was triggered by the 1974-1975 Arthur Pendennis, the novel's hero, attends. In 1928 Virginia Woolf revived the name in a series of lectures published in 1929 as A Room of One's Own.*]

Oxisol, *n.* (in U.S. soil taxonomy) any of a group of highly weathered and leached soils of tropical regions. *Oxisols may require millions of years to form from unweathered material.* McGraw-Hill Yearbook of Science and Technology 1976, p367 [**1960, 1972,** from *ox*ide + *-sol* (from Latin *solum* soil)]

oxygen walker, a small portable oxygen tank for persons suffering from emphysema or other lung diseases, and heart disease. *My father used a newly developed Union Carbide "oxygen walker" for over a year prior to his death from emphysema in 1970. The "walker" was filled from a liquid oxygen tank and its use enabled him to retain mental alertness and a certain degree of physical mobility in spite of the emphysema and the tranquilizing medications that he was receiving.* Science News 11/6/76, p291 [**1976**]

ozeki (ou'zeiki:), *n.* a champion sumo wrestler ranking immediately below the grand champion. Compare YOKOZUNA. *Me, I'm a belt man. It is a thing of joy to witness my favorite, a trim but powerful ozeki, or champion, named Takanohana, come out of the . . . initial charge, with his legs crouched and his head up and his arms slashing away at his opponent.* NY Times 1/6/74, pJ11 [**1966,** from Japanese *ōzeki*]

ozone shield, the layer of ozone about 20 to 40 miles above the earth's surface that shields the earth from excessive ultraviolet radiation. *Man's assaults on the ozone shield, in the form of SST flights, aerosol sprays and other chemicals, are continuous and could permanently deplete the layer.* Time 2/23/76, p46 *Atmospheric chemists have predicted that man-made chemicals will thin the earth's ozone shield, the sun's harsh rays will then increase skin cancer prevalence and alter global climate. Now by jet, laboratory experiments and computer, the chemists are challenging and substantiating that gloomy prediction.* Science News 9/23/78, p212 [**1976**] ►Earlier terms for this part of the atmosphere were the still current *ozone layer* (1951) and *ozonosphere* (1952).

ozone sickness, a condition caused by inhalation of ozone seeping into jet aircraft at altitudes over 40,000 feet. It is characterized by itchy eyes, headaches, chest pains, and drowsiness. *Because ozone sickness is such a recent peril to air safety, many vexing questions remain unanswered. Why does the sickness* *hit frequently during the early months of the year? Why does it occur more often over the Pacific Ocean? What's the best remedy? Pan Am has already installed charcoal filters in its six 747SP jets, and the company reports the problem solved.* Maclean's 4/17/78, p30 [**1978**]

ozonesonde ('ou‚zoun‚sɑnd), *n.* a radiosonde (a radio-transmitting instrument package carried aloft by a balloon) designed to measure the distribution of ozone above the earth and transmit the data back to earth. *In the past two years there has been an increased emphasis on several aspects of antarctic meteorology, . . . albedo programs, meteorological studies aboard the Eltanin, and the inclusion of vertical coverage through radiometersondes, ozonesondes, and gammasondes.* Bulletin of Atomic Scientists 1/64, p29 [**1960**]

Ozymandian (ɑzə'mændiːən), *adj.* of or alluding to the huge size of a statue of Ozymandias, the Greek name of the Egyptian king, Ramses II. . . . *he has already taken amateur tennis out of the lingering Ozymandian shadow left by Rod Laver . . . who won the grand slam of tennis last year by capturing the Australian, French, English, and American championships.* New Yorker 7/27/63, p91 . . . *the Shah's Ozymandian megalomania, symbolized by a $100 million fete he staged at Persepolis in 1971 to celebrate the 2,500 years of the Persian Empire.* Time 1/7/80, p12 *Volcker charges that by letting the deficit run toward $100 billion, the White House has all but abandoned its fight against inflation. It is these Ozymandian budget deficits that are soaking up private capital . . .* Time 2/8/82, p52 [**1963**, from *Ozymandias* (1817), title of a sonnet by Shelley in which the poet describes the huge, but broken and abandoned statue of the king]

P

p, abbreviation of *penny* or *pence* in the British decimal system (introduced in February, 1971) in which a pound equals 100 new pence, as in *4p, 53p,* etc. See also NEW PENNY. *The unfamiliarity of the new coinage, with pence abbreviated to "p" rather than "d", at 100 to the pound, will be the least distressing aspect of the change.* Times (London) 4/17/68, p11 **[1968]**

pa'anga (paː'ɑːŋgə), *n.* the monetary unit of the kingdom of Tonga, at par with the Australian dollar. *Tonga has decided against calling its new decimal currency unit the dollar because the native word, "tola", also means a pig's snout, the soft end of a coconut, or, in vulgar language, a mouth. The new unit, to be introduced next year, will be called "pa'anga", which has only two alternative meanings—a coin-shaped seed and, not surprisingly, money.* Times (London) 5/21/66, p8 **[1966, from Tongan]**

pablum, *n.* **1** a source of nourishment; fuel. *In one week Spiro Agnew ascribed moral decay to the universities, Dr Spock, and the Presidential Commission on Campus Unrest, which, he said, had produced a report which 'was sure to be taken as more pablum for the permissivists'.* Listener 10/22/70, p538 **2** something intellectually watered down or insipid; pap. *"You can go to Hollywood as a second assistant unit manager for ten years, make the long, stultifying climb, and finally turn out predigested pablum."* New Yorker 7/23/66, p24 **[1960, from Pablum, trade name for a bland but very nourishing cereal for infants, with meaning (especially for def. 1) influenced by pabulum food, nourishment (from Latin pābulum fodder)]**

PAC (pæk), *n.* a political committee organized by a special-interest group to promote legislation or political candidates that favor their interests. *The fact is PACs and corporate financing of elections are part of the new political reality in the United States.* Tuscaloosa News 10/20/82, p4 *Subsidized by millions of right-wing PAC dollars and riding the coattails of the Reagan landslide, 16 brand-new Republicans were elected to the Senate in 1980.* Spy (The New York Monthly) 2/89, p82 **[1982, acronym for political action committee]**

P-A-C, abbreviation of *Parent, Adult, Child,* used in transactional analysis to designate the three ego-states within every individual. *The analysis of transactions in terms of P-A-C is what the theory of T.A. is all about. There is no doubt in the minds of its advocates that T.A. works better than other methods. As Dr. Harris once wrote: "If only one hour were available to help someone, the method of choice would be a concise teaching of the meaning of P-A-C and the phenomenon of the transaction."* NY Times Magazine 11/19/72, p43 **[1972]**

pacemaker, *n.* an electronic device for relieving certain symptoms of neurological disorders by sending signals to electrodes implanted under the scalp. *In the last year, three dozen* [epileptic] *patients have had the pacemaker implanted. . .Even if the pacemaker's results turn out to be short lasting, experts believe that the fact that it works at all could lead to a new understanding of how the brain controls movement and perhaps to simpler nonsurgical methods of treating abnormal movement disorders.* NY Times 9/22/73, p15 **[1973, transferred from the earlier (1951) sense of an artificial pacemaker for the heart, a device implanted near the heart to control its beat]**

pachycephalosaur (ˌpækəsə'fælə,sɔr), *n.* a plant-eating dinosaur of the Cretaceous period, characterized by a thickened, dome-shaped skull covered with knobs and spines. *Pachycephalosaurs probably used their reinforced skulls as battering rams during competitive courtship display—rather like living goats and sheep.* McGraw-Hill Yearbook of Science and Technology 1973, p163 **[1973, from New Latin Pachycephalosaurus, the genus name, from pachy- thick (from Greek pachýs) +** cephalo- head (from Greek kephalḗ) + saurus lizard (from Greek saûros)] **—pachycephalosaurian,** *adj.: Galton. . .has suggested that the greatly thickened skull roof of the pachycephalosaurian dinosaurs was correlated with the use of the head in pushing and ramming during intraspecific combat, like that seen today in mountain sheep.* Nature 4/29/76, p748

pachyosteomorph (ˌpæki:'asti:ə,mɔrf), *n.* an evolutionary level characterized by heavy bone structure (also used attributively). *As a number of separate lineages approached and attained the pachyosteomorph level of organization in the late Middle and early Upper Devonian, arthrodires underwent a remarkable burst of secondary adaptive radiation, to become the dominant fishes of the time.* McGraw-Hill Yearbook of Science and Technology 1971, p313 **[1970, from Greek pachýs thick + ostéon bone + morphḗ form]**

pacifarin (pə'sifərən), *n.* a bacterial substance that prevents certain germs from causing disease while permitting them to survive within the organism they have invaded. *Pacifarin, found in certain batches of whole wheat and dried egg and produced by bacteria, protects mice infected with mouse typhoid. It was identified as enterobactin (a compound of known structure), recently discovered by biochemists at the University of California, Berkeley.* 1972 Britannica Yearbook of Science and the Future, p251 **[1963, from pacifier + -arin, as in heparin]**

Pacific Rim, the nations of Asia that border on the Pacific Ocean, and those island nations located in it. . . .*an invitation to become a founding father to the stripling Australian National University, in Canberra, now one of the great institutions of the Pacific Rim.* Connoisseur 4/88, p151 **[1969]**

packet, *n.* a segment of data or information processed as a unit in a computerized communications system. *A customer's message was treated as one or more packets, about 1,000 or so bits in length, with its destination address and other relevant information included among the bits. The packet could route itself through a special communications network, which generally utilized minicomputers at the junction or branch points.* 1975 Britannica Yearbook of Science and the Future, p216 **—v.t.** to segment data or information into units for processing in a computerized communications system. *Most terminals do not have the capability to "packet" their data, so a "terminal processor" at the local exchange is interposed to accept the characters sent by the terminal, packet them, and convert them if necessary into a standard format.* New Scientist 5/13/76, p352 **[1973 for noun; 1976 for verb]**

packet-switched, *adj.* using a packet-switching communications system. *New data transmission services—in particular packet switched links now being introduced, in which blocks of data from different users are interleaved along main communication links—raise new problems of data security.* New Scientist 3/2/78, p593 **[1972]**

packet-switching, *n.* the transmission of data or information in segments over a computer network, each unit of transmission restricted to a maximum size and bearing a specific address (often used attributively). *The technique. . .is known as "store and forward" or packet-switching. Messages are temporarily stored as they arrive at a centre; only when the message has been completely and accurately received is it forwarded to the next centre; and so on in succession through the various centres en route.* Times (London) 5/17/72, pIII **[1971]**

Pac-Man defense, *U.S. Finance.* a defense tactic in which a company threatened by a hostile takeover bid launches its own takeover bid for the company that threatens it. *There was a vague feeling of distaste for. . .the Pac-Man defense in* which. . .the target company bids to acquire the would-be acquirer. NY Times 10/6/82, pD1 [**1982**, from *Pac-Man*, trademark of a video game in which attackers are sometimes swallowed up by their intended victims]

pad, *n. U.S. Slang.* **1 the pad**, graft which is received by and shared among various members of a police precinct or department for ignoring illegal activities. *When a cop was transferred to a new post, the pad from his old station kept up for another two months.* Time 11/1/71, p23 *Mr. Armstrong said the testimony would show how the gamblers of the city paid off the policemen on a regular monthly basis after they had been placed on what is called "the pad." Narcotic bribes, the counsel said, usually "are made on an individual score basis."* NY Times 10/19/71, p47 **2 on the pad**, sharing in the graft collected by policemen of a precinct or department for ignoring illegal activities. *"I never knew a plainclothesman," said Phillips, "who wasn't on the pad." And yet for years it went further than that: it was as if the whole town was on the pad, as if a sidewalk couldn't be cleaned without grease, as if the garbage could not be carted without paying grease. . .* NY Post 10/20/71, p47 [**1971**, so called from the secret pad on which the names of policemen accepting graft were listed]

page, *v.t.* **1** to contact someone by sending a radio signal to a small portable receiver that has a warning sound activated by the radio signal. *An executive moving from country to country will be accessible to paging in any of the company's establishments by carrying a pager in his pocket, as he would a pen.* Times (London) 4/27/73, p15 *A thief was caught in Sydney, Australia, when police "paged" him in the pocket paging device he had stolen.* Reader's Digest 1/80, p82 **2** to contact and regulate (an electrical appliance) by means of an electronic remote-control device operated by a keyboard. *The digital signal pages only those wall modules set to the number you keyed. If you page a light, for example, you can also page it to turn on, off, or you can even dim it. . .You can page an appliance such as your coffee maker or toaster to turn on or off.* Science News 5/5/79, p304 [**1960**, specialized use of the verb meaning to find or contact someone by means of a page boy (OEDS 1904) or a public-address system (1920's)]

page-turner, *n.* a very interesting book, especially a fast-moving novel that is an adventure story, science-fiction or detective story. *As they say in the story departments out at The Burbank Studios, this one is a real page turner.* New Yorker 10/30/78, p155 *If it is possible to ignore the moral issues that West himself raises and then drops,* Proteus *can be clear sailing. Connoisseurs of page-turners will feel right at home in a world where a woman can still be described as a "leggy redhead," where grins are "crooked," where a Jewish character says "oy vay" and a Scotsman says "aye."* Time 1/22/79, pK6 [**1969**]

paint-in, *n.* an undertaking by a group of people to paint or decorate the exterior of buildings or other structures to improve, or show the need to improve, the appearance of a run-down area. *Depressed by the sight, Jane Shay, a staffer at the nearby National Trust for Historic Preservation, organized a one-day paint-in by a group of Washington high school art students. The result was a half-mile mural in which [were] green trees, pink pigs. . .Tricia [Nixon] even walked down on the day of the paint-in and added a few dabs herself.* Time 6/20/69, p64 [**1965**; see **-in**]

pair, *v.t. U.S.* to combine the white and black pupils of (schools that are close to each other). *The administration of Pres. Jimmy Carter seemed to be leaning toward busing and pairing (or clustering) schools to mix students from predominantly white or black schools. Under the pairing plan, an elementary school is formed from two or more different schools so that students will attend a racially mixed class even though they may reside in segregated neighborhoods.* Britannica Book of the Year 1978, p343 [**1964**]

pair bonding, the act or condition of forming a monogamous bond or union. *Similarly pair-bonding, which is the ornithologists' in-phrase for procreative conjunction between sexually ardent cocks and hens, can be welded by the formal presentation of food (courtship feeding) or duetted songs which, in certain African bush-shrikes, reach a state of harmonic perfection rarely matched by human vocalists.* New Scientist 6/17/65, p768 [**1965**, from *pair-bond, n.* (1940)]

paired-associate learning, *Education, Psychology.* a form of learning in which words, numerals, pictures, etc., learned in pairs become associated so that one of the pair can serve as a stimulus to recall the other. *Paired-associate (PA) learning apparently differs from serial learning mainly in benefiting to a larger degree from past verbal experience. PA learning can be more influenced by verbal mediational processes than serial learning.* Arthur R. Jensen, Genetics and Education, 1972, p264 [**1963**, from *paired associates* (1937)]

Paisleyism, *n.* a movement in Northern Ireland founded by Ian Paisley, born 1926, head of the Free Presbyterian Church of Ulster, directed against ecumenical and other efforts to draw together Catholics and Protestants. *Whether or not one agrees with all aspects of Brian Moore's analysis of the unhappy Ulster situation, he is correct in perceiving that its solution lies in bringing this festering evil to a head and performing the necessary surgery. . .Once this is done and the evil spirits of Paisleyism exorcized, I think that the "Wearers of the Green" and their largely Scot protagonists of the Six Counties will rediscover their common humanity and basic Celtic heritage.* Atlantic 12/70, p34 [**1966**]

Paisleyite, *n.* a follower of Ian Paisley; a supporter of Paisleyism. Compare DEVLINITE. *Two Irish independents already have broken through and taken their seats in the Commons, and on June 18 there are to be Paisleyites and Devlinites in the field. . .* Times (London) 5/19/70, p1 **—adj.** of or relating to Paisleyites or Paisleyism. *Martin Waddell's whimsical portrait of an Ur-Protestant Ulster bigot is a bad case of bandwaggonry. . .Augustus Harland, the Paisleyite monster whose diary this purports to be, is a grotesque parody of a human being.* Listener 10/22/70, p555 [**1966**]

Paki, *n. British Slang.* a Pakistani. *"Cruising" by Gerald Walker is a sharp, terse piece of work, half novel and half thriller. . .Whether the hated object is queers, blacks or Pakis, the inadequacies breeding the hatred are faithfully put down here.* Sunday Times (London) 6/6/71, p32 [**1964**, by shortening]

palazzo pajamas (pə'lɑ:tsou), a woman's garment for lounging or semiformal wear, consisting of loose, wide-legged trousers and a matching jacket or blouse. *All these varieties continued into the nineteen-sixties, when they were joined by such other forms as palazzo pajamas (wide enough to sweep around a palace in), culottes, pants dresses and pants suits.* NY Times 4/30/68, p52 [**1965**]

palazzos (pə'lɑ:tsouz), *n.pl.* or **palazzo pants**, women's loose, wide-legged trousers. *Unlike jeans, which tend to reveal everything, palazzos conceal everything, even fat hips, skinny thighs and thick calves.* Time 9/11/72, p49 *She* [M. McPartland] *is wearing an ensemble that has clearly been thought out to the last fold: a close-fitting cranberry turtleneck, a gold belt, brocaded cranberry-and-gold palazzo pants, and a gold pocketbook.* New Yorker 1/20/73, p56 [**1968**, from PALAZZO PAJAMAS, ultimately from Italian *palazzo* palace, large mansion]

paleo- or (*British*) **palaeo-**, combining form meaning "ancient," "prehistoric," or "of geological times," usually attached to names of established branches of science or to words describing some measurable physical phenomenon or activity. Compounds include: **—palaeochronology**, *n.*: *All dating methods based on counting the ridges of fossil shells and corals are necessarily hazardous because the animals may miss out growth ridges in a systematic fashion and many species of fossil "clock" have no exact living counterpart against which to be regulated. In spite of these and other pitfalls, which further research may be expected at least to make more evident, the subject of palaeochronology is one of the most promising and least well trodden fields of science.* Times (London) 6/4/70, p13 **—palaeoengineering**, *n.*: *We have been examining the palaeoengineering of Pteranodon ingens, the largest pterodactyl and also the largest flying creature ever to exist. . .* New Scientist and Science Journal 12/23/71, p202 **—paleozoogeography**, *n.*: *. . .hope has been entertained that major* *gaps in knowledge of the fossil record will be filled. . .by new finds in Antarctica, China, and Australia. But the presence of North American and European genera in these faunas poses new problems of paleozoogeography.* McGraw-Hill Yearbook of Science and Technology 1971, p312 See also the entries below.

paleoenvironment, *n.* the oceanic or terrestrial environment in the time before the ages of human history. *As it enters its second decade, the Deep Sea Drilling Project is shifting its objectives. The Challenger's most recent voyage, Leg 63, completed the transition. . .from hard rock geophysics and tectonics to paleoenvironment—studies of changes in ocean ecology with time as reflected in the sediments.* Science News 1/6/79, p6 **[1957]** —**paleoenvironmental,** *adj.: After a basic introduction from the geologist's viewpoint, the book discusses the occurrence of organic residues in freshwater sediments and sedimentary rocks, and evaluates both the importance of these residues in paleoenvironmental and related problems, and their role as biochemical fossils.* Science News 2/6/71, p101

paleogenetics, *n.* the study of the genetics of fossil animals and plants. *Cytochrome c is a key molecule in the final stages of the "burning" of foodstuffs for the provision of energy in living cells, forming part of a chain along which electrons are passed—eventually—to water. It has also become the star of the young science of chemical palaeogenetics, enabling evolution to be studied at the molecular level.* New Scientist 7/16/70, p119 **[1965,** from *paleogenetic* (1886)]

paleohabitat, *n.* the habitat of an animal that lived in the time before the ages of human history. *Further, systems of biostratigraphy based on different organisms have been conceived in isolation, not integrated, and these systems can individually apply no further than the principal paleohabitat (represented by facies—rock sequences reflecting major Earth environments) of the studied organism.* McGraw-Hill Yearbook of Science and Technology 1974, p118 **[1972]**

paleoichthyologist, *n.* an ichthyologist who specializes in fossil fish. *The Gogo fish fauna thus offers excellent opportunities for studies in sedimentary petrology and paleoecology, fields which are usually ignored by paleoichthyologists.* McGraw-Hill Yearbook of Science and Technology 1971, p312 **[1964,** earlier *palaeichthyologist* (1897)]

paleoprimatology, *n.* the study of prehistoric primates. *Palaeoprimatology is a subject the very existence of which depends on the fact that teeth, unlike other parts of the body, are immutable, being "fossils" from the start; and it is hardly surprising that most of our knowledge of evolutionary lineages has been formulated under the "tyranny of the teeth."* New Scientist 9/13/73, p642 **[1972]**

Palestinian, *n.* any Arab who lived in Palestine until its division in 1948 between Israel, Egypt, and Jordan, and who supports the establishment of a state or homeland in any part of the region. *That also struck me—how similar the Palestinians are to the Israelis. I was surprised to find the Israelis are closer to the Palestinians in temperament and character and even appearance than the Palestinians are to the Egyptians.* NY Times 7/9/78, pE2 **[1968,** extended sense of the name for any native or inhabitant (Arab, Christian, or Jew) of Palestine since Biblical or Roman times]

palimony ('pælə,mouni:), *n. U.S. Slang.* alimony or its equivalent demanded by a person for having lived with someone without being married. *The latest case of "palimony" involves a Los Angeles court demand. . .by Kayatana Harrison for $4 million of the fortune amassed by comic Flip Wilson, who, she says, was a longtime, live-in boyfriend.* Newsweek 2/19/79, p59 *The Lee Marvin palimony case. . .shows that—married or not—people who live together cannot avoid a shared responsibility.* Daily News (New York) 4/20/79, p35 **[1979,** blend of *pal* and *alimony*]

palindrome, *n. Molecular Biology.* a segment of double-stranded DNA (the genetic material in cells) having identical but inverted sequences of nucleotides on both strands. *A 24-nucleotide stretch reads identically (with one flaw) in opposite directions beginning at its center. The researchers suggest that this segment could bind a protein important for messenger RNA function. Mirror-image sequences, called palindromes, of a different type are known in bacteria, but such an arrangement of nucleotides has not been described in globin or other mammalian genes.* Science News 5/7/77, p295 **[1974,** transferred sense of the term (c1629) meaning a word, number, etc., that reads the same backward and forward] —**palindromic,** *adj.: Restriction enzymes. . .recognize a single palindromic nucleotide sequence on the DNA helix and make staggered cuts in both chains of the helix whenever this sequence appears.* Scientific American 1/77, p48

palliative care unit, *Especially Canadian.* a hospital facility for the care of the terminally ill. *Abbreviation:* PCU Compare HOSPICE. *Charette is one of the stars in a film just released by the National Film Board of Canada called* The Last Days of Living. *His co-stars are a dozen patients, at the Royal Victoria Hospital (RVH) who are dying of cancer, their families, and the staff of the palliative care unit at the RVH.* Saturday Gazette (Montreal) 2/2/80, p45 **[1975]**

palytoxin (,pælə'taksən), *n.* a highly poisonous substance discharged by polyps, especially as protection against octopuses. *The scientists collected some of the polyps* [limumake-o-Hana], *ground them up, and extracted some of the poison, which is called palytoxin. They learned several things about the palytoxin, but its incredible potency was the most interesting.* World Book Science Annual 1972, p376 **[1971,** probably from Greek *palýnein* to strew, sprinkle + English *toxin*]

PAN [pæn], *n.* acronym for: **1** peroxyacetyl nitrate. . . .*the principal constituents of smog. . .include ozone, an unstable toxic form of oxygen; nitrogen dioxide, an irritating reddish brown gas; peroxyacetyl nitrate (PAN), an explosive liquid; aldehydes; and acrolein, a poisonous, colorless or yellowish liquid.* Encyclopedia Science Supplement (Grolier) 1971, p244 **2** polyacrylonitrile (a polymer of acrylonitrile, used for making synthetic fibers). *While in principle a number of precursor fibres could give rise to carbon fibres with very good mechanical properties, this has yet to be established. PAN (polyacrylonitrile) may have special advantage, in that the nitrogen atoms may play a part in stabilizing the structure.* New Scientist 2/5/70, p254 **[1966** for def. 1; **1969** for def. 2]

Pan-Africanist, *n.* an advocate or supporter of the political union of all African nations. *Since its independence in September 1966, Botswana has sought to steer a balanced course between the political pressures of Pan-Africanists and the pressures resulting from strong economic ties with the Republic of South Africa.* 1968 Collier's Encyclopedia Year Book, p157 —**adj.** of or relating to Pan-Africanists or their policies. *He did not refer to the split between the A.N.C.* [African National Congress] *and another organization in South Africa, the Pan-Africanist Congress, but said that the A.N.C. intended to wage war from within, not invade from outside.* Times (London) 3/11/68, p2 **[1959]**

Pan-Asianist, *n.* an advocate or supporter of the political union of all Asian nations. *"To my father it was completely different—he was a pan-Asianist who believed in a unified Asia free of colonialist rule", says Miss Maw.* Times (London) 4/13/68, p10 **[1968]**

panchreston (pæn'kres,tan), *n.* an explanation designed to cover or to fit all possible cases equally well; a catch-all explanation or proposition. *Finally I would like to suggest that there has been a tendency in psychoanalysis for the concept of infantile psychosexuality to have lost the original freshness and vigor with which it was presented, and to have become a dogma, and even a panchreston, a kind of vacuum cleaner gobbling up many varieties of behavior and reducing them all to the same tired explanations. . .* Science News 2/25/67, p178 **[1967,** an extended sense of obsolete English *panchreston* universal medicine, panacea (recorded in the OED with citations from 1632 through 1706), from Greek *pánchrēston,* neuter adj., good for everything, from *pan-* all, everything + *chrēstós* useful, good]

pancuronium (,pænkyu'rouni:əm), *n.* or **pancuronium bromide,** a synthetic drug similar to curare, used as a muscle relaxant.

Formula: $C_{35}H_{60}Br_2N_2O_4$ *Pancuronium. . . .acts on muscle fibers as it does on motor nerve terminals.* Science 11/17/72, p754 *An investigation indicated that at least 18 of the victims—including nine of those who died—had been given Pavulon, or pancuronium bromide, a synthetic variant of curare, the lethal plant toxin used by South American Indians to tip poison darts. Anaesthesiologists sometimes administer Pavulon to surgical patients to relax their muscles.* Time 3/22/76, p47 [**1967**, probably from *pan-* all, general + *cu*rare + *-on* + *-ium* (chemical suffixes)]

panda car, *British.* a police prowl car. *Five children, who formed a "secret five club" and helped catch two thieves, are to be given a ride in a police panda car as a reward.* Times (London) 3/17/70, p2 *The Panda car got on to us.* Times (London) 2/3/72, p5 [**1967**, from the color configuration of the cars]

Pangaea (pæn'dʒi:ə), *n.* a hypothetical continent that included all the land masses of the earth before the Triassic period (about 200 million years ago) when continental drift began with the breaking away of the northern group (Laurasia) from the southern group (Gondwana). *According to our reconstruction, Pangaea was a land mass of irregular outline surrounded by the universal ocean of Panthalassa: the ancestral Pacific.* Scientific American 10/70, p35 [**1924, 1958**, possibly coined in the 1920's by Alfred L. Wegener, a German geologist, from Greek *pan-* all + *gaîa* land]

pangram, *n.* a sentence made up to include all the letters of the alphabet. *The pangram, an ancient form of word play, is an attempt to get the maximum number of different letters into a sentence of minimum length.* Scientific American 9/64, p222 [**1964**, from *pan-* all + *-gram* letter, as in *anagram*]

pangrammatic, *adj.* of or relating to a pangram. *Also represented: Sotadic* [palindromic] *verses, pangrammatic rubaiyat and problems in alphametics (alphabet arithmetic).* Time 9/17/65, p72 [**1953**]

pantdress, *n.* a dress with a skirt divided and sewed like trousers; a dress with culottes. *At far left, a Persian pantdress in pure wool (with a matching mini-nightie, about $60).* Maclean's 12/67, p35 *This time, it is a more coordinated trend—pant-skirts, pant-dresses, pant-suits, tops and pants, and so on, as contrasted with the single item it used to be, he said in a recent interview here.* NY Times 7/15/68, p43 [**1964**]

Panther, *n.* short for BLACK PANTHER. *His* [Bobby Seale's] *trial in New Haven for complicity in the murder of a fellow Panther kept the campus in a state of near-hysteria throughout the last term.* Harper's 8/70, p18 *. . .the alleged bias for "activists," typically meant that delegates were presidents of youth organizations or youth members of town councils, not Weathermen or Panthers as the word suggests.* Harper's 8/71, p26 [**1968**]

panti-, Also spelled **panty-**. a combining form designating panties worn with some other garment as one piece. **—panti-slip**, *n.: She has introduced a. . ."panti-slip," a bit of nylon tricot edged with lace and worn with a matching camisole.* NY Times 1/8/66, p16 **—panti-tights**, *n.pl.: "Sorry," the man in overalls said, "We're right out of them. What about a pair of panti-tights?"* Manchester Guardian Weekly 4/11/70, p14 **—pantyleg stocking**: *Gold and silver pantyleg stockings (at $4 each) are selling so fast stores can't keep them in stock.* Time 12/2/66, p53

pantskirt, *n.* a divided skirt resembling trousers; culottes. *The pants and pantskirt as shown by Marc Bohan at Dior are for the country and around the house.* Times (London) 8/3/64, p11 [**1964**]

pantsuit, *n.* Also spelled **pants suit**. a woman's suit with matching jacket and trousers. *The people strolling down Kasr el Nil, Cairo's most fashionable shopping district, look better dressed than in past years. There is only an occasional miniskirt or pantsuit, but the clothes generally seem more stylish and the shop windows brighter and better stocked with locally made shoes, purses, textiles.* Atlantic 1/71, p40 *Partisans of the pants suit argued that women were wearing pants anyway and the*

suit was neater than haphazard tops and slacks. 1967 Collier' Encyclopedia Year Book, p210 [**1964**]

pantyhose, *n. pl.* or *sing.* Also spelled **pantihose**. a woman's gar ment worn from the waist down to replace both panties an stockings, originally made for wear with miniskirts. *There are now not only government dollar stores* [in Cairo, Egypt] *but string of busy boutiques on Sharwabi Pasha Street as well openly offering Parisian perfumes, German pantyhose, Britis woolens, Italian slacks and bras, American Techmatic razors fancy French cravats, all at outrageous markups.* Atlantic 1/71 p40 *"The stretchiest stockings and panti-hose yet, resultin from a new concept of hosiery manufacture," were announced by the British firm Pretty Polly.* Britannica Book of the Yea 1969, p339 [**1963**]

paparazzo (ˌpɑ:pə'rɑ:tsou), *n., pl.* **paparazzi** (ˌpɑ:pə'rɑ:tsi:). a aggressive free-lance photographer who pursues celebrities t take their pictures wherever they go. *Off for a month's vaca tion from the attentions of Rome's paparazzi went Sophic Loren, 35, with her husband, Italian Film Producer Carle Ponti, and their 18-month-old son Cheepy (C.P. Jr.).* Time 7/20/70, p32 *United States District Court Judge Irving Ber Cooper ruled yesterday that the activities of Ronald E. Galella the self-styled "paparazzo" photographer, had "relentlessl invaded" the right to privacy of Mrs. Aristotle Onassis and had interfered with the protective duties of the Secret Service.* NY Times 7/6/72, p1 [**1961**, from Italian, from *Paparazzo*, sur name of a free-lance photographer in the motion picture *L Dolce Vita* (1959)]

paper add, *U.S.* a recording that is listed on a radio station': playlist although it has been played infrequently or not at all *Although paper adds aren't illegal, they are dishonest, and Radio & Records has on occasion stopped publishing playlists of stations that engage in the practice.* Rolling Stone 3/88, p181 [**1988**]

paperback, *v.t. Chiefly British.* to publish as a paperback. *The suspect they may have a best-seller on their hands but the think it's too bulky to paperback.* Sunday Times (London) 2/16/75, p56 [**1960**, verb use of the noun]

paper factor, a terpene of the balsam fir which is a naturally oc curring insect juvenile hormone. *Paper factor is highly effec tive in killing the cotton stainer bug, which destroys up to hal the cotton crop in Asia, Africa and South America each year.* NY Times 11/29/66 (page not known) *The tree synthesizes what we named the "paper factor," and this substance accom panies the pulp all the way to the printed page.* Scientific American 7/67, p17 [**1966**, so called for the fact that it was first discovered in newsprint]

paper gold, another name for SPECIAL DRAWING RIGHTS. *When it was first proposed that the world's reserves be supplemented by new drawing rights in the IMF* [International Monetary Fund]—*a matter of giving the fund the right to print "paper gold" in carefully controlled quantities—the Americans launched the idea that the rights should be awarded in the first place to the poor countries.* Manchester Guardian Weekly 9/27/69, p22 *. . .the far from reassuring phrase "paper gold" became the common nickname for S.D.R.s.* New Yorker 10/23/71, p130 [**1966**]

paperless, *adj.* transferring information or data without the use of paper. *An experimental paperless service in San Francisco already provides computer transfer of funds from the accounts of industrial corporations to those of their employees. . .* New Scientist and Science Journal 5/13/71, p386 [**1965**]

paper trail, a record compiled from letters, notes, and other written sources. *Under this law the Government can not "monitor the paper trail" to track down bribers.* NY Times 8/16/81, pD19 *"Whatever the accident" that might strike a nuclear plant, there would always be a paper trail in the agency's files showing that somebody had previously worried about that kind of thing.* New Yorker 4/13/81, p74 [[**1976**]]

papovavirus (pə'pouvəˌvairəs), *n.* any of a group of viruses containing DNA which are associated with or known to cause various types of tumors and growths in mammals. See HUMAN

PAPILLOMAVIRUS. *The virus. . .found in 8 out of 18 kidney-transplant patients, belongs to a group known as the papovaviruses, the human version of which has only recently come to light.* New Scientist 2/8/73, p285 *The human papovavirus belongs to the same group of viruses as the monkey virus SV40, which is known to cause tumours on rodents.* Times (London) 2/6/73, p14 [**1962**, from *p*apilloma-*po*lyoma-*vac*uolation + *virus*]

Papua New Guinean (ˈpæpyuːə), a native or inhabitant of Papua New Guinea, an independent country (since Sept. 16, 1975) consisting of the eastern half of New Guinea and a chain of islands including the Bismarck Archipelago, Bougainville and Buka in the Solomon Islands, and the Trobriand Islands; Papuan. *In 1976, in an attempt to establish a sense of national identity, Papua New Guineans were encouraged by the prime minister to wear national dress to work every Friday.* Britannica Book of the Year 1977, p550 [**1972**]

PAR (pɑr), *n.* acronym for *perimeter acquisition radar*, a radar forming the outermost part of an antiballistic missile system. See also MSR. *Theoretically, enemy missiles would be picked up soon after launch by PAR (perimeter acquisition radar), which would inform the central control system.* Britannica Book of the Year 1970, p253 [**1967**]

para (ˈpærə), *n.* **1** short for *parachutist, paratrooper, paracommando,* etc. *But these days the image of Saint-Cyr* [French military academy] *is that of an electronic scientist rather than that of a future cavalry officer, or even "para."* Manchester Guardian Weekly 3/21/70, p7 *The Belgian paras sustained only seven casualties in rescuing the hostages.* Time 12/4/64, p28 **2** *U.S. Informal.* a paraprofessional. *It was also agreed that para-professionals would receive annualized salaries, that they would be paid for 52 weeks instead of 44, as in previous years, and that paras would be included in a pension system.* NY Times 2/18/79, pE9 [**1958** for def. 1, from French; **1979** for def. 2, by shortening]

para-, a combining form abstracted from *paramilitary, paramedical,* etc., and meaning "related to but not quite," "supplementary to," "subordinate to." In this sense, extended from *para-,* meaning "beside" or "near," the form has become very productive in various professional circles, appearing in such compounds as the following: —**para-academic,** *adj.:* [Paul] *Goodman has, in great measure, become the spokesman of the alienated and the rebellious, and he has become a sort of roving prophet for the independent students who are establishing free universities and similar para-academic organizations.* Saturday Review 2/18/67, p82 —**parabiospheric,** *adj.: . . .as a terrestrial envelope the biosphere obviously has a somewhat irregular shape, inasmuch as it is surrounded by an indefinite "parabiospheric" region in which some dormant forms of life are present.* Scientific American 9/70, p45 —**para-church,** *n.: . . .groups that don't attract or seek publicity, that meet in upper rooms. . .This is sometimes called the para-church, the church of the future which is beginning to take shape. . .* Manchester Guardian Weekly 12/12/70, p14 —**para-governmental,** *adj.: It seems that the Viet Cong set up a much more efficient political and para-governmental structure in certain areas than was previously realised.* Sunday Times (London) 2/25/68, p8 —**parapolitical,** *adj.: To elucidate the parapolitical function of modern spying. . .* Time 4/4/62, p62 —**parareligious,** *adj.: For instance, the religious or para-religious sects of the West Coast may seem as mysterious to an East Coast observer as primitive societies.* NY Times Magazine 1/28/68, p37

paracetamol (ˌpærəˈsiːtəˌmɔːl), *n.* a drug used to relieve headaches and reduce fever. *And a terribly natural-looking box of Healthcraft Pain Relief Tablets which in fact are powerfully laced with Paracetamol—which is the modern form of headache drug, the aspirin de nos jours.* Sunday Times (London) 7/4/71, p17 [**1963**, from *para-* near, related to + the chemical name *acetam*idophen*ol*]

paracharmonium (ˌpærətʃɑrˈmouniːəm), *n.* a hypothetical form of the PSI PARTICLE according to the charm theory. Compare ORTHOCHARMONIUM. *Paracharmonium (a version with slightly different quantum numbers, but still charmed) should also* *exist at a slightly different mass, and they think it ought to be looked for.* Science News 1/25/75, p60 [**1975**, from *para-* beside, supplementary + *charmonium*]

paradoxical sleep, any of about five periods in a night's sleep, each period lasting about ten minutes, during which dreams occur and the body undergoes marked changes, including rapid eye movement, loss of reflexes, and increased brain activity. Also called REM SLEEP. Compare ORTHODOX SLEEP. *After about an hour of this orthodox sleep phase, a change occurs and paradoxical sleep begins and lasts about 10 minutes before orthodox sleep is resumed. . .in paradoxical sleep, unlike orthodox sleep, the blood flow through the brain is increased far above waking levels.* New Scientist 4/23/70, p171 [**1962**]

parafoil, *n.* a combination of parachute and airfoil. *The U.S. Navy's "parafoil" performs like an airfoil in providing a gliding descent permitting the parachutist to guide it—quite different from the vertical descent of conventional parachutes.* 1969 Compton Yearbook, p345 *. . .a revolutionary parachute invention. . .known as the para-foil, would enable pilots bailing out over enemy territory to glide like birds until they reached safety. . .* NY Times 8/13/67, pA15 [**1967**]

paragraph loop, a loop in figure skating in which a series of turns are introduced at various points of the circles. *He kept his head, and laid down a final paragraph loop which, while not faultless, was better than anything either Curry or the third skater Michael Fish produced.* Times (London) 12/3/70, p16 [**1964**, from earlier *paragraph* in figure skating (1930)]

parajournalism, *n.* unconventional journalism. See also UNDERGROUND PRESS. *. . .perhaps the current fad for first person parajournalism, where the reporter—me, say—looks into his own heart for information about politics, war, or suffering, and tells what he finds there in long loping sentences all stuffed with literary allusion and neighborhood bar slang—I'm a scholar and good fellow, too—may have gone too far.* Atlantic 8/71, p85 [**1965**]

parajournalist, *n.* a practitioner of parajournalism. *It is difficult to pinpoint exact and usable definitions of this parajournalism. But let us try, following MacDonald as he castigates a Wolfe review of Mailer's latest novel and berates the reviewer as again playing parajournalist because his technique was "to jeer at the author's private life and personality—or rather his persona. . ."* Atlantic 6/66, p89 [**1966**]

parajournalistic, *adj.* of or relating to parajournalism or parajournalists. *A wave of parajournalistic publications, the so-called underground press, was mounting a serious challenge to established dailies.* Americana Annual 1970, p503 [**1970**]

parakiting (ˈpærəˌkaitiŋ), *n.* the act or sport of soaring in a parachute while being towed by a motorboat, car, or other fast vehicle. *In parakiting, the water skier becomes airborne when his trailing parachute pops open.* Time 3/30/70, p42 [**1970**, from *para*chute + *kite* + *-ing*]

paralanguage, *n.* the qualities of voice not usually analyzed phonemically that nevertheless assist in communication, such as tone of voice, sighing, drawling, etc. *That particular methodology called generative-transformational did not include paralanguage, kinesics, or cultural influences.* Verbatim 5/15/78, p2 [**1958**, from *para-* alongside + *language*]

paralegal (ˈpærəˌliːgəl), *adj.* of, relating to, or associated with the law in an auxiliary capacity. *It was epitomized in a letter from a young paralegal worker, Adam Bennion, to Charles R. Nesson, a Harvard Law School professor who was one of the defense attorneys.* Atlantic 8/73, p12 —*n.* a paralegal aide. *Operating with local foundation financing out of a refurbished downtown factory building, the clinic's three attorneys and three paralegals can devote personal attention to individual problems that overburdened legal-aid attorneys and probation officers do not have time for.* Time 4/18/77, p46 [**1968**, from *para-* near, subordinate + *legal*]

paralinguistic, *adj.* of or relating to paralanguage. *Wolfram. . . rejects the possibility of 'careful' and 'casual' speech, as Labov had done, on the grounds that interpretation of paralinguistic cues is open to subjective bias.* Language 9/70, p772 [**1958**]

—**paralinguistics,** *n.: And there seems to be no references to. . . paralanguage, kinesics, ethnoscience, semiotics.* Language 3/70, p234

parallel computer, a computer having several processors that enable it to handle a large number of operations at the same time instead of serially. See PARALLELISM, PARALLEL PROCESSING. *The computer is the ILLIAC IV, and it is the first truly parallel computer—that is, a computer capable of working on a problem in parallel, simultaneous operations. The ILLIAC IV can do 64 identical operations in parallel.* Encyclopedia Science Supplement (Grolier) 1972, p122 [**1970,** from *parallel,* adj. "concurrent," in reference to computer operation (1948)]

parallelism, *n.* or **parallel computation,** the simultaneous handling of a large number of computations for a problem by a parallel computer. *The advantages to be gained by parallel computation are still largely unknown. In some important applications parallelism can increase the computation speed almost indefinitely. It is important to note that in some situations there is no substitute for speed. That is, one hour of computation at 100 MIPS cannot be replaced by 100 hours at 1 MIPS. Examples of this include weather prediction (it does no good to take 48 hours to compute a 24-hour weather forecast).* 1975 Britannica Yearbook of Science and the Future, p219 [**1974**]

parallel processing, performance of many operations simultaneously on a parallel computer. *Another way to handle the series of small steps is to assign each to a different microprocessor so that they can be computed simultaneously; this is called parallel processing.* Science News 8/24/85, p118 [**1960**]

parallel slalom, a slalom skiing race in which two competitors race at the same time over courses roughly equivalent in length and difficulty. Also called DUAL SLALOM. *The Nations' World Series, a new event, was notable in that it provided that amateur circuit with its first taste of head-to-head "parallel slalom" skiing, with two skiers racing down parallel courses against each other, rather than against the clock.* 1975 Collier's Encyclopedia Year Book, p504 [**1974**]

Paralympics (ˌpærəˈlimpiks), *n.* an international sports competition patterned on the Olympics, in which the participants are paraplegics or others confined to wheelchairs. *These four, and 380 other handicapped athletes from 31 states, are competing in the 20th national Wheelchair Games. . .The top finishers in the various classes—determined by the severity of the handicap—will represent the United States in the upcoming "Paralympics" in Toronto, Aug. 3 through 11, against teams from 51 other countries.* NY Times 6/12/76, p15 [**1965,** from *para*plegic + *O*lympics]

paramedic, *n. U.S.* a medical technician or other auxiliary worker in medicine (also used attributively). *In a fresh and growing trend, more than 40 training programs for doctors' assistants are under way across the country. The graduates, already numbering in the hundreds, are tagged with clumsy names—paramedic, clinical associate, health practitioner. . .Started by Duke University in 1965, paramedic studies are wideranging—from community health to bacteriology and psychosomatic medicine, plus techniques such as regulating intravenous infusions and operating respirators.* Time 11/9/70, p38 [**1970**] ►This term should not be confused with the military term *paramedic* (OEDS 1951), meaning a parachuting medical corpsman in the armed forces and deriving from *para*chute + *medic.* The word entered here is a back formation of *paramedical,* which means related to medicine in an auxiliary capacity.

paramenstrual, *adj.* of or relating to the paramenstruum. . . . *the para-menstrual failure rate in "O" level candidates was 17 per cent for girls whose menstrual loss lasted up to four days. . .* Sunday Times (London) 12/29/68, p3 [**1968**]

paramenstruum (ˌpærəˈmenstruəm), *n.* a period of eight days comprising the four days preceding menstruation and the first four days of menstruation. *Recent studies have shown that in women half of all medical and surgical admissions to hospital occur during the paramenstruum. . .At this time women appear to have a lowered pain threshold, lowered resistance to in-*

fection, and an increased tendency to fever and allergy. Times (London) 9/30/70, p14 [**1966,** from New Latin *para-* beside, near + *menstruum* menstruation]

parameter, *n.* any defining or characteristic factor. . . .*the President at least understands "the parameters of the problem."* Time 8/3/70, p9 *The mind with all its parameters and limits ingrained through years of constant failure to aim beyond the "feasible" and "allowable," the "probable."* Atlantic 11/70, p65 [**1964,** extended use of the sense "a measurable factor" which helps with other such factors to define a system" (1927)]

paramilitarism, *n.* the ideals and spirit of militarism among paramilitary groups (i.e. civilian groups organized on a military basis). *Parties for the Panthers have become fashionable in New York in the last three weeks—ever since the Leonard Bernsteins gave one and were denounced for doing so in an editorial in the Times. . .[which] talked about the Panthers' "Mao-Marxist ideology and Fascist paramilitarism". . .* New Yorker 2/14/70, p33 [**1961**]

paramilitarist or **paramilitary,** a member of a paramilitary force. *It was feared that the failure of the warring Catholic and Protestant factions* [in Northern Ireland] *to reach any kind of agreement on power-sharing would inspire paramilitarists on both sides to try to fill the political vacuum.* Manchester Guardian Weekly 3/7/76, p1 *Senator Wilson was firmly opposed to violence and, unlike most Ulster politicians, did not carry a gun; his body had thirty knife wounds. Responsibility for this deed was claimed by a group of Protestant "paramilitaries" calling themselves the Ulster Freedom Fighters.* New Yorker 5/8/78, p61 [**1973,** from *paramilitary,* adj.] ►These terms have been applied chiefly to the paramilitary units in Northern Ireland.

paramyxovirus (ˌpærəˌmiksəˈvairəs), *n.* any of a group of viruses that includes the viruses causing mumps and various respiratory diseases. *The presence of intranuclear inclusions distinguishes measles virus (and the closely related distemper and rinderpest viruses) from paramyxoviruses such as mumps, parainfluenza, and Newcastle disease virus, which are morphologically very similar but produce only cytoplasmic inclusions in infected cells.* McGraw-Hill Yearbook of Science and Technology 1971, p263 *The two workers point out that cases of diabetes have been reported in man after an attack of mumps, a disease which is caused by one of the paramyxoviruses.* Times (London) 11/27/68, p9 [**1962,** from *para-* + *myxovirus* the virus causing influenza]

paraphernalia, *n.pl. Slang.* See the quotation for the meaning. *In the argot of the drug world, it is "paraphernalia": the necessary accouterments to merchandising heroin. The small glassine enveloped or "bags," used to package heroin are paraphernalia. So, too, are the legal, harmless powders used to dilute the drug, usually quinine, dextrose, lactose or mannite.* Time 7/20/70, p15 [**1970,** transferred sense of the term meaning personal belongings or equipment]

paraphysics, *n.* the study of physical phenomena attributed to psychic forces; the physical aspects of parapsychology. *Professor Werner Schiebeler of Ravensburg Polytechnic has lectured on "An Introduction to Parapsychology and Paraphysics," in addition to his normal lectures, since 1970.* New Scientist 3/6/75, p566 [**1973,** from earlier (1950's) *paraphysical* relating to such phenomena as telekinesis, levitation, etc., from *para-* beside + *physical*] ►In recent years *paraphysics* has been suggested by some students of extrasensory phenomena as a replacement of *parapsychology,* on the grounds that these phenomena cannot be adequately accounted for by psychology and their proper area of study might be physics.

paraprofessional, *n.* a person engaged to assist the work of professionals, as in teaching, nursing, social work, etc.; an aide or assistant in a professional field who does not have full professional training. . . .*classes were proceeding, with regular teachers and "para-professionals," mostly mothers, to help out with classes in reading and in English, which is taught by modern adult methods of language instruction.* New Yorker 10/5/68, p44 —*adj.* acting as a paraprofessional; being an aide or assistant to professionals. *There is some talk now of using para-*

professional help, trained on the job like interns. In some schools, mothers already are supervising lunch hours and study periods. Eventually they may be accepted into classrooms, with other assistants such as qualified volunteers or unemployed artists, peace workers, the retired, almost anyone with a BA and common sense. Maclean's 5/67, p64 [**1967**]

parasailing ('pærə,seilıŋ), n. the act or sport of soaring in a parachute while being towed by a motorboat, car, or other fast vehicle. The ultimate panoramic view is probably best gained by parasailing, where the intrepid traveller is attached to a parachute and pulled along behind a motorboat to rise in the air like a kite over the water. Times (London) 2/18/78, p13 [**1969**, from parachute + sailing]

parastatal (,pærə'steitəl), adj. serving the state or government indirectly or in an auxiliary capacity; working with the state though not officially a part of it. The [Uganda] Government monopoly of importing is to be exercised through parastatal bodies, such as the National Trading Corporation, and the Uganda Development Corporation. Times (London) 5/19/70, p22 —n. a parastatal group. . . .the parastatals were still almost wholly outside central control; and little had been done to curb the penchant of the STC [State Trading Corporation] for importing luxury goods. Manchester Guardian Weekly 10/23/71, p6 [**1967**]

para-transit, n. a system of transportation, often without fixed schedules or routes, that uses automobiles, vans, and buses to carry passengers and usually supplements an urban transit system. Para-transit was the rather sinister name given to another range of cheap solutions aimed at bridging the gap between private cars and conventional public transport. Para-transit covered a multitude of services, including shared taxis, jitney buses, dial-a-ride, and car pools. Britannica Book of the Year 1976, p673 [**1973**]

parawing, n. a glider which incorporates a sail-shaped, parachute-like device that unfurls to act like a wing during descent. The National Aeronautics and Space Administration said. . . that it would negotiate a contract. . .for research flight testing on an all-flexible combination of parachute and wing called a parawing. NY Times 5/30/67, p23 [**1960**]

parenting, n. **1** the process of caring for and raising a child. Our study of adopted children, Growing Up Adopted, published recently, indicated that. . ."it is the single-minded, unconditional desire, together with the emotional maturity to provide a loving, caring home, which is the hallmark of good parenting."Times (London) 10/30/72, p8 "When we ask whether sex determines parenting, we can say that neither males or females are innately programmed to parenthood nor do they inherit distinct styles of parenting. . .Parenting is mostly learned from identification with models." New Republic 1/5-12/74, p31 **2** the act or process of producing offspring; reproduction; procreation. The eight modes or methods of parenting can be listed very simply. (1) The coital-gestational way. (2) Artificial insemination of a wife with her husband's sperm, without any assistance or input from a third party. (3) Artificial insemination of a woman with a donor's sperm. (4) Egg transfer from a wife, inseminated by her husband and then transferred to another woman's womb for substitute gestation. . . Joseph Fletcher, The Ethics of Genetic Control, 1974, p40 [**1959**]

parietals (pə'raiətəlz), n.pl. U.S. visitation rules in a dormitory for members of the opposite sex. . . . Yale students. . .have rejoined the nationwide battle for liberalized "parietals"—campus term for women's visiting hours in male dormitories, or vice-versa. NY Times 12/17/67, pD9 [**1967**, noun use of parietal, adj., of or relating to visiting hours within college walls, ultimately from Latin pariēs wall]

park-and-ride or **park-ride**, adj. U.S. designed to enable suburban commuters to park their cars at railroad stations, bus terminals, etc., and complete their trip into the city by public transportation. From park-and-ride facilities to bus—rapid transit transfer terminals, Chicago's commuters are increasingly able to step from one mode of transportation to another quickly and conveniently. Science News 9/15/73, p170 Metro. . .took over and revived the countywide trans-

portation network, creating a park-ride system to bring in suburbanites. Time 12/77, p36 [**1966**]

parking orbit. See the first quotation for the meaning. The United States has used "parking" orbits on its Ranger shots to the Moon. Under this technique, the probe and a booster rocket are "parked" in orbit around the earth. At the appropriate point in the orbit, the booster is re-ignited, sending the vehicle toward its goal. NY Times 4/3/63, p14 After getting away satisfactorily from its "parking orbit" round the Earth, Lunik IV was slated to be functioning quite as planned and the 250 ft. radio telescope at Jodrell Bank picked up its signals when the vehicle was above the horizon. New Scientist 4/11/63, p73 [**1960**]

Parkinson's Law, any of various satirical observations made by the English writer, Cyril Northcote Parkinson, born 1909, especially concerning time and work. As Parkinson's Law observes, work expands to fill the time available for doing it. With twice as much time at its disposal, Congress created twice as much work, which meant twice as much governing. NY Times Magazine 7/9/78, p6 [**1955**]

parochiaid, n. U.S. governmental aid to parochial schools. Litigation on parochiaid is likely to go on for several years. But lawyers are fairly sure that Lemon's broad principles, plus the anti-aid line-up reflected by the court's near unanimity, will eventually require a drastic rearrangement of the Catholic education. Time 7/12/71, p53 [**1971**, patterned after Medicaid]

parole, n. **1** the discretionary authority, granted to the Attorney General by the U.S. Immigration and Nationality Act, to admit refugees into the country on an emergency basis. The bills differ. . .substantially in how they allot policymaking power. Mr. Eilberg would end the discretionary "parole" authority extensively used by attorneys general and replace it with congressionally written guidelines. Mr. Kennedy would retain parole and give the executive branch flexible new authority to cope with unexpected refugee flows. Manchester Guardian Weekly (Washington Post section) 4/9/78, p16 **2** Attributive use. In 1973. . .Attorney General John Mitchell granted Soviets "parole" immigration status—reserved for persons being given refuge from persecution in their homeland. NY Times Magazine 9/26/76, p27 —v.t. to admit into the country under parole. A section of that act [Immigration and Nationality Act] states that the Attorney General "may in his discretion parole into the United States temporarily. . .any alien applying for admission," and this section was invoked by the Ford Administration shortly before the fall of Vietnam to allow up to a hundred and fifty thousand refugees from Vietnam and Cambodia to enter the country. New Yorker 9/5/77, p35 [**1967**, transferred sense of the term (a1616) meaning the discretionary release of a prisoner] ►Although parole in this unrecorded sense has existed since the passage of the 1952 Immigration and Nationality Act, the term appeared infrequently in print and only when a new influx of refugees raised questions about their admission and status. The wave of refugees from southeastern Asia (see BOAT PEOPLE) during the 1970's brought the word into currency.

parrot's perch, a device or method of torture. Describing one regular torture, the parrot's perch, the document says victims are suspended from a horizontal pole, with their knees doubled over the bar and their hands tied to their ankles behind their backs. Manchester Guardian Weekly 2/1/76, p6 [**1972**, translation of Portuguese pau de arara (literally) perch of ara (a kind of macaw)]

Parsons table, a square or rectangular table of simple design, with the legs extending from the four corners of the underside of the tabletop. The eclectic approach, combining traditional French and English styles with such contemporary designs as the Parsons table, steel-and-glass or steel-and-leather pieces, the wall system, and sectional upholstered pieces became fairly widespread. 1972 Collier's Encyclopedia Year Book, p286 [**1967**, named after Parsons School of Design in New York City]

participational, adj. (of a show or exhibit) involving the participation of the spectators or the audience. In spite of its premature closing, the participational section of the Morris exhibition was valuable because of the discussion and thought it provoked among artists and public alike. Manchester Guardian Weekly 6/19/71, p12 *The $30 million Ontario Science Center opened in September in Toronto. The Center features hundreds of "participational" exhibits that are operated by push buttons.* Americana Annual 1970, p687 [**1970,** earlier in the general sense of requiring participation (1959)]

participatory democracy or **participant democracy.** See the quotations for the meaning. *Both the Negroes and the antiwar groups have made use of the politics of marches, sit-ins and mass demonstrations. But those who practice this "participatory democracy" can ultimately achieve their objectives only if they work through electoral processes and win control of Congress and the Presidency.* NY Times 5/6/68, p46 *These "alternate institutions" frequently emphasize values similar to those of a therapeutic community: group cohesion and commitment; open communication, particularly about personal problems; helping and being helped by peers, and "participant democracy," meaning involvement of the entire group in decision-making.* Scientific American 3/71, p42 [**1966**]

participatory theater, a form of theater in which the plays include participation or physical involvement by the audience. [The contemporary theater] *is trying to rediscover its preverbal origins, and it is trying to isolate what it is that theater can uniquely do that films and television cannot do. . .These ventures in dramatic exploration are also intimately related to an attempt to bridge the we-they gap in the actor-audience relationship—what is popularly called "participatory" theater.* Time 2/23/70, p68 [**1970**]

particle beam, 1 a stream of charged nuclear particles produced in a particle accelerator. *Particle beams. . .are the source for much of what is known about the structure of the atom and its constituent particles. To create such a beam, negatively charged electrons, positively charged protons or the charged nuclei of atoms may be swung past successive rows of magnets in devices called accelerators, speeding up each time a magnet is passed and acquiring more energy.* NY Times 12/4/78, pD11 **2** a stream of charged nuclear particles directed through the atmosphere by a beam weapon. Also called CHARGED PARTICLE BEAM. *Particle beams fired from the ground or space at close to the speed of light—186,000 miles a second—have been suggested as a means of stopping enemy nuclear missiles before they reach the U.S.* New York Post 1/22/79, p12 [**1977**]

particle-beam weapon, a beam weapon that fires particle beams. *The idea of a particle-beam weapon is to produce a copious burst of energetic particles, be they electrons, protons, ions (or, as the Soviets now seem to be suggesting, neutral [?] particles), send them X kilometers through the atmosphere and zap! there goes your capital city ("biological target") or, more likely, zap! there goes your incoming cruise missile.* Science News 8/19/78, p117 [**1977**]

particle physicist, a specialist in particle physics. *Even particle physicists and molecular biologists would be hard put to point to new discoveries, insights and ideas rivalling those in the field of astronomy in the near-miraculous 10 years since 1961.* New Scientist and Science Journal 8/5/71, p334 [**1966**]

Parti Québécois (par'ti: keibe'kwa:), a political party in Quebec advocating political independence and separation from the rest of Canada. Formed in 1968, it gained control of the provincial government of Quebec in 1976. See PÉQUISTE. *The victory of the Parti Québécois in the November 15 election implied on the part of the voters a willingness to put. . .the question of independence to a referendum. If it does not pass, and if the PQ is elected once more, the question will be put again.* Maclean's 12/13/76, p12 *Surely—this book was published three years after the Parti Quebecois came to power, remember—there will be in the final chapters a revaluation, a reconsideration of the dogmas of a decade ago.* Globe and Mail (Toronto) 1/7/80, p10 [**1968,** from French]

parton ('par,tan), *n.* any of certain concentrated charges into which a proton or neutron may break up under nuclear bom-

bardment. *Richard P. Feynman of Cal Tech has been developing a theoretical model of the nucleon that may explain the inelastic-scattering results. He has given the name "parton" to the unknown constituents of the proton and the neutron that inelastically scatter high-energy electrons. Feynman assumes that partons are point particles. He and others have examined the possibility that partons may be one or another of the great array of previously identified subnuclear particles.* Scientific American 6/71, p73 *The partons may rapidly recombine to make another proton, in which case the scattering will be elastic. Alternatively, they may recombine to make one or more other particles, in which case the scattering will be inelastic.* 1970 Britannica Yearbook of Science and the Future, p375 [**1969,** from *part*icle + prot*on* or neutr*on*]

partwork, *n.* a book or set of books published one part or fascicle at a time. *Purnell's three most successful part-works* [were] *The History of the Second World War (launched in October 1966 and extended from 96 to 120 parts), The History of the Twentieth Century (launched in 1968), and The History of the First World War (launched in 1969). . . Britannica Book of the Year 1970, p644 An architect who started doing illustrations for the IPC partwork Birds of the World has since abandoned the set-square and become a full-time artist. . .* New Scientist and Science Journal 1/28/71, p206 [**1969**]

parvo, *n.* short for PARVOVIRUS. *The "scare story" of the year with regard to animal disease was the widespread outbreak of a highly contagious and fatal parvovirus infection, commonly dubbed "parvo." The disease had been recognized in Australia in 1978 and may have been present in Texas about that time.* 1982 Britannica Yearbook of Science and the Future, p360 [**1980**]

parvovirus, *n.* any one of a group of small viruses found in various animals, especially a virus transmitted by dog feces and causing a serious and often fatal disease of dogs. *In less than two years parvovirus has raced across the U.S. and overseas, killing thousands of dogs. . .Many scientists believe that it is a recent mutant of the bug that causes feline panleukopenia, or cat distemper.* Discover 10/80, p11 [**1965,** from Latin *parvus* little + English *virus*]

parylene ('pær,əli:n), *n.* a plastic derived from an isomer of xylene (paraxylene) by polymerization. *The product, named parylene, has been successfully used as a dielectric, or insulation, on capacitors. . .* NY Times 2/18/65, p43 *It's a skintight plastic coat so thin you would never know it's there. Yet it covers the bee completely, right down to the individual hairs on the bee's knees. It was done to protect specimens in a natural history museum. But we didn't spend 12 years on a new plastic just to protect bees. We developed parylene to protect things like bees—fragile, complex things so intricate in shape they are next to impossible to coat.* Scientific American 11/66, p33 [**1965,** from *paraxylene*]

PASCAL (pæs'kæl), *n.* a computer programming language used especially in education and scientific research. *Thus, while ALGOL was mostly limited in its uses to calculations involving the numbers and arrays that appear in mathematical computation, PASCAL provides a convenient tool for writing well structured programs that manipulate much more general types of data such as alphabetic strings and records and lists.* 1980 Britannica Yearbook of Science and the Future, p297 [**1971,** named for Blaise *Pascal,* the 17th century philosopher and physicist, by its developer, Niklaus Wirth, a Swiss computer scientist who published it in 1971; the capitalized form is patterned after such acronyms as *ALGOL, COBOL, FORTRAN,* and *BASIC*]

passalong, *n. U.S.* an increase in the costs of a producer or someone who provides a service, that is passed along in the form of increased prices, rent, etc. *This meant that production costs could no longer be offset to the same degree, and, in industry after industry, the consequent cost increase was passed along to the consumer in the form of higher prices. As this "pass-along" accelerated, prices began rising at an inflationary rate.* NY Times Magazine 11/19/78, p48 [**1977,** from the verb phrase *pass along*]

passenger cell, a white blood cell that is accidentally implanted with an organ from a donor. *Earlier, people had tried to explain Summerlin's reports by saying that organ culture must work by clearing away "passenger cells" that for some reason provoked rejection. Lafferty's rationale was more intricate.* New Scientist 2/26/81, p528 **[1979]**

pass-fail, *adj.* of or relating to a system of crediting academic work in which a student passes or fails but otherwise is not graded. *There has been much discussion of grading reforms; but the only major change, if it can be called that, has been the introduction of some options to take a certain number of courses on a pass-fail basis, without any indication of the actual quality of the work performed.* NY Times 8/9/70, p7 *"I believe we have gained a great deal in suggesting grading instead of somewhat more rigid pass-fail standards," he said.* Times (London) 4/20/70, p2 **[1959]** —*n.* the system in which a student either passes or fails a course instead of receiving a grade in numbers or letters, such as A, B, C, etc. *As with many other colleges of late, Hobart and William Smith also offer such options as. . .pass-fail instead of grades, study off-campus or abroad or at another school, and independent study in a major field.* NY Times 6/25/72, pD9 —*v.t.* to pass or fail (a student) instead of giving a grade in letters or numbers. *I would much have preferred to pass-fail my students. They could have relaxed more and learned more if we'd all concentrated on education instead of grades.* National Observer 7/1/72, p10 **[1972]**

passive belt, an automobile safety belt that automatically holds an occupant in a seat, especially by laying across a shoulder upon the closing of a door. *In model year 1982, all standard-size cars will get an automatic protective system; in 1983, mid-size cars* [will] *get a passive belt or air bag.* Christian Science Monitor 5/8/79, pB7 **[1977]**

passive euthanasia, the causing or hastening of the death of an incurably ill or injured person by withholding life-sustaining treatment. Also called NEGATIVE EUTHANASIA. Compare ACTIVE EUTHANASIA. *In the United States, most right-to-die measures introduced in 15 states from 1969 through 1974 would have permitted only the withholding or termination of treatment (so-called passive euthanasia) or, occasionally, the administration of pain-killing drugs in dosages that risk death.* 1977 Collier's Encyclopedia Year Book, p336 **[1975]**

passive restraint, a safety device in an automobile that automatically protects a passenger from serious injury in an accident. *Passive restraints are devices designed to protect occupants in collisions, without the need for occupants to take any active step, such as buckling belts. The air-bag, which automatically inflates in a crash, or passive belts, which are attached to the front door and automatically fold across front-seat occupants when the door closes, have been tested and can meet the Government's requirement.* Times (London) 7/4/77, p20 **[1970]**

passive smoking, the inhalation by nonsmokers of smoke from other people's cigarettes, cigars, and pipes. *Although the amount was small relative to that measured in smokers, the doctors said, "the fact that some nicotine is present in the urine of almost all nonsmokers suggests that episodes of passive smoking are common in urban life."* International Herald Tribune 2/4/75, p3 *In a study at the Long Beach Veterans Administration Hospital, Aronow tested the effects of passive smoking (breathing smoke-contaminated air) on ten men with severe-coronary-artery disease.* Time 7/17/78, p73 **[1971]** —**passive smoker**: *Throughout the country, "passive smokers" are beginning to speak out. Growing numbers of nonsmokers are trying to rid their environment of a pervasive pollutant that is a general nuisance to most and a genuine health hazard to some.* NY Times 11/22/78, pC1

pastiche, *v.t., v.i.* to combine (various works, styles, etc.) into a mixture or hodgepodge. . . . *the unfortunate Victorian habit of "reviving", that is, pastiching, the Renaissance, the Baroque and just about every other style of the past.* Times (London) 10/17/70, p20 **[1957, verb use of the noun]**

pasties ('peisti:z), *n.pl.* a pair of small adhesive coverings on the nipples of female performers, worn chiefly to comply with laws against indecent exposure. *Orgiastic rock music, go-go girls (some of them topless, which in Toronto means with pasties), surly waiters, raw prole* [proletarian] *vitality.* Maclean's 11/68, p76 *Typical of the elaborate revues being offered by the hotels is "Toujours Paris". . .Among the performers are. . .a long line of tall, beautiful, plastic-looking showgirls who wear rhinestone pasties instead of brassieres.* NY Times 8/5/68, p20 **[1961]**

pataphysical, *adj.* of or relating to pataphysics, an imaginary science satirizing scientific and scholarly thought and writing, invented by the French surrealist writer Alfred Jarry, 1873-1907. *"They* [the Czech producers of Alfred Jarry's play "Ubu Roi"] *had a perfectly good program printed up, a ten-page job including a detailed description, in the best 'pataphysical' jargon, of that crazy machine you saw giving off sparks as the curtain went up. The idea being to get the spectator into the proper 'pataphysical' spirit Jarry believed in—you know, anarchist, antiscientific, irreverent."* Atlantic 2/65, p114 **[1964, from *pataphysics* (OEDS 1945) + *-al*]**

pat-down search, *U.S.* a search, especially for concealed weapons, conducted by running the hands over a person's outer clothing; a frisking. *Everyone trying to enter the courtroom is scanned by electronic devices; there is a pat-down search by guards who also rummage through purses and briefcases; photographs are taken of each new visitor.* Time 7/19/76, p43 **[1974]**

pathotype, *n.* a pathogenic or disease-producing type of organism. *The organism* [Pseudomonas solanacearum], *earlier considered to be a soil inhabitant and an omnivorous root invader, primarily of solanaceous species such as tobacco, tomato, and potato, has revealed itself as a "species" comprising different races and pathotypes, each with its own specific disease-causing characteristics.* McGraw-Hill Yearbook of Science and Technology 1971, p331 **[1971]**

patient-day, *n.* a unit for calculating the cost of running a hospital, clinic, etc., based on the expense of providing care and facilities to one patient for one day. *More specifically, planners must decide such things as the average hospital cost per patient-day, the number of patient-days per capita and ultimately the share of national income that is devoted to health care.* Scientific American 9/73, p159 **[1967, patterned after *man-day* (OEDS 1925)]**

patienthood, *n.* the quality or condition of being a patient. *Miss MacKenzie obviously cannot report, except by hearsay, on the operation itself, but about the painful explorations prior to it and about the trip back, complete with a couple of frightening detours, she is brilliantly precise. Hers is the best account of the psychology of patienthood in a modern hospital I've ever read.* Harper's 5/71, p111 **[1970]**

patrial ('peitri:əl), *n.* a native or natural-born citizen of a country, and in Great Britain, one who has such status by adoption or naturalization or whose parent or grandparent had such status. *Commonwealth citizens with a grandparent born here would not need a work permit or be subject to supervision. But they would not share the privilege of "patrials" or immunity from deportation and they would have to apply initially for entry.* Manchester Guardian Weekly 2/3/73, p11 **[1971, noun use of the adjective meaning "of one's native country" (OED 1629)]**

patriality, *n.* the condition of being a native or natural-born subject or citizen of a country. *Patrials are defined as "all people who are citizens of Britain by being born here, or become citizens by adoption, registration, or naturalisation in the UK, or who have a parent or grandparent who was born here or acquired citizenship by adoption, registration, or naturalisation.". . .In some cases, where patriality depends on ancestral connection, a certificate issued through the British High Commissioner in his own country will be needed as proof of that right.* Manchester Guardian Weekly 3/6/71, p8 **[1971, from *patrial* of one's native country + *-ity*]**

patriate, *v.t. Canada.* to transfer the authority to amend (Canada's constitution, embodied in the British North America Act of 1867) from the British government to Canada's federal government. *For most Canadians,. . .the failure to agree on a simple thing like patriating the constitution must seem puzzling. But it is not patriation that has proven so contentious. Rather, it is the division of powers between Ottawa and the provinces.* Maclean's 11/13/78, p26 [**1966**, from Latin *patria* native country + *-ate*, (verb suffix), influenced by *repatriate*] —**patriation,** *n.: "The maintenance of the legitimate and historical powers of the provinces may be at stake if patriation is carried forward unilaterally," Premier Peter Lougheed of Alberta declared this week.* NY Times 4/10/76, p2

patrimonial sea or **patrimonial waters,** the waters within which a coastal state may exercise sovereignty over natural resources. Compare EXCLUSIVE ECONOMIC ZONE. *In principle, Australia is ready to accept new laws which would provide a territorial sea of 12 miles, a patrimonial sea of 200 miles, and retain existing rights to explore the continental shelf even if it extends beyond 200 miles.* Manchester Guardian Weekly 6/30/73, p6 [**1972**]

Patriotic Front, a black nationalist organization formed in Zimbabwe-Rhodesia in 1976 as an alliance of ZANU and ZAPU to represent a united front against the white Rhodesian government. *The Patriotic Front has the full backing of the black African states most closely involved in the Rhodesian conflict and claims to be the political voice of the guerrillas fighting against white minority rule.* NY Times 1/16/77, p7 [**1976**]

patterning, *n.* a form of physical therapy guiding brain-damaged or brain-deficient children through the individual movements of creeping, crawling, walking, etc., on the theory that following the pattern of those functions that the brain has failed to develop will help to develop them through therapy (also used attributively). *"Patterning" is a rigid physical treatment for children handicapped by brain damage, mental retardation or reading disabilities.* Time 5/31/68, p42 *The "patterning" treatment for retarded and brain-damaged children, the efficacy of which was questioned by a group of medical and health organizations recently, has been vigorously defended by its developers.* NY Times 5/26/68, p55 [**1968**]

Pave Paws, acronym for *Precision Acquisition of Vehicle Entry, Phased Array Warning System,* a radar system that detects ballistic missiles launched at sea at a range of over 3,000 miles. *Pave Paws has no moving parts. Its thin 2° beam is electronically focused and steered at high search rates by 10,000 antenna elements fixed to two faces of the radar building. Quick to note that the military operates facilities today which are 20 times more powerful than Pave Paws, Lt. Col. Paul T. McEachern who presented the case for the Air Force, repeatedly assured residents that "the power densities will be well below the values at which any health impact will occur."* New Scientist 2/2/78, p30 [**1976**]

Pavulon ('pævyə,lɑn), *n.* a trademark for PANCURONIUM. *To suppress the shivers, the infant was dosed with Pavulon, a derivative of curare; a poison used by South American Indians to paralyze game.* NY Times Magazine 6/11/78, p32 [**1970**]

Pax Americana, peace enforced by American power. The term was modeled on *Pax Romana,* the peace imposed by Roman might under the Caesars, and *Pax Britannica,* a later term with the same connotation applied to the British Empire. *Mr. Steel's final advice to America should warm British hearts—at any rate nostalgically. It is that Pax Americana should model itself on Pax Britannica which although often "insufferably smug and hypocritical" reserved its power "for situations it could hope to control and which were directly related to the national interest."* Punch 2/28/68, p321 *In the opinion of many European experts, the Kremlin has a more ambitious objective: to alter the status quo by exchanging the Pax Americana for a Pax Sovietica.* Newsweek 10/18/71, p17 [**1963**]

Pay Board or **pay board,** a government board in charge of establishing general standards for wage increases. Compare PRICE COMMISSION. *U.S. Pay Board announced guidelines on the granting of fringe benefits to workers.* Britannica Book of the Year 1973, p43 *Phase Two of the Government's anti-inflation programme officially began, and the new Pay Board formally came into being to hear unions' complaints that the*

present freeze was dealing unfairly with their members. Listener 4/5/73, p437 [**1972**]

pay cable, *U.S.* a system for transmitting a fixed number of special television programs by coaxial cable for a monthly charge. *For the first time in its long, flickering career, pay television—now known as "pay cable"—is making a highly visible challenge to the networks' oligarchic hegemony over video entertainment.* Newsweek 3/31/75, p73 [**1974**]

payload specialist, a specialist on scientific experiments aboard a spacecraft. Compare MISSION SPECIALIST. See also PI. *Two British and six American scientists are on the short list from which two candidates will be chosen for a new breed of astronaut, called payload specialists, to carry out 13 experiments on the second flight of Spacelab 2 in 1981.* Times (London) 4/29/78, p5 [**1977**]

pazazz (pə'zæz), *n.* another spelling of PIZZAZZ. *His* [John Turner's] *campaign manager, John Claxton, son of Brook Claxton, the Liberal Minister who held the seat from 1940 to 1953, mounted a campaign that has had few equals anywhere for sheer pazazz.* Saturday Night (Canada) 5/66, p34 *"I don't see what's wrong with the floor we have," said the King. "Square," said the Queen. "Square, square, square. Montina Corlon's different. It's got pazazz."* New Yorker 1/16/65, inside cover [**1965**]

PBB, abbreviation of POLYBROMINATED BIPHENYL. *PBBs, which are no longer manufactured for use in this country, had been used as a flame retardant. In 1974 that chemical was accidently mixed with animal feed in Michigan and contaminated livestock and food. Recent studies have identified adverse health effects on some farm residents.* Science News 11/5/77, p297 [**1976**]

PBS, abbreviation of *Public Broadcasting Service,* the network of noncommercial television stations in the United States. *In what it called an "experiment," PBS abandoned floor reporting and trained its cameras only on speakers at the rostrum. This technique, the network said, would give viewers a delegate's-eye view of the proceedings.* Newsweek 9/4/72, p89 [**1971**]

P.C., *U.S.* abbreviation of *Professional Corporation. A doctor whose medical practice has been incorporated for tax purposes must use the initials "P.C.," for professional corporation, after his name.* NY Times 1/30/76, p10 *Mr. Goodfriend, whose firm has helped half a dozen other law firms make the switch from partnership to PC in the last nine months, said that most PCs are small firms with one or two lawyers.* National Law Journal 6/4/79, p10 [**1976**]

PCB, abbreviation of *polychlorinated biphenyl,* any one of a group of highly toxic and persistent chemical substances used in industry especially as electrical insulators and in plastics manufacture. Since 1976 the manufacture of PCBs has been discontinued in the United States. *In Ontario alone, more than 220 tons of deadly polychlorinated biphenyls or PCBs are currently being stored as liquid waste under varying conditions at sites throughout the province—many of them in urban areas—because there is no incinerator anywhere in Canada capable of destroying them.* Maclean's 10/2/78, p50 [**1966**]

PCM, abbreviation of PROTEIN-CALORIE MALNUTRITION. *The biochemical lesions in PCM are still incompletely understood but are of obvious importance. The syndrome has been called the greatest killer of infants and young children and the major cause of retarded child growth and development in today's world.* McGraw-Hill Yearbook of Science and Technology 1971, p298 [**1971**]

PCP, a trademark for the depressant drug phencyclidine, used illegally in powder form as the narcotic popularly called ANGEL DUST. *The San Francisco office of the United States Department of Justice's Bureau of Narcotics and Dangerous Drugs was feverishly trying to locate what is believed to be the largest manufacturing plant of PCP in California. Phencyclidine hydrochloride is a hallucinogen, an animal tranquilizer which provides an acid-like high and, doctors say, gradually damages the brain.* Rolling Stone 5/24/73, p30 [**1970**, from the abbrevition of *phenylcyclohexylpiperidine*, also (by contraction) the rug's generic name *phencyclidine*]

CPA, abbreviation of *para-chlorophenylalanine*, a drug which reduces the level of serotonin and is widely used in clinical research to treat a variety of conditions, including intestinal tumors and schizophrenia. *The drug, known as PCPA or para-chlorophenylalanine, is commonly used to interfere with the synthesis in the brain of another chemical which affects mood and sleep.* Times (London) 5/4/70, p11 **[1968]**

PDL, British. abbreviation of POVERTY DATUM LINE. *The PDL is, in fact, so low a standard that most social researchers use the concept of the Minimum Effective Level to express the minimum income needed for an African family to lead a decent life.* Manchester Guardian Weekly 3/17/73, p4 **[1973]**

peacenik, n. U.S. Slang. a person who engages in peace demonstrations; an active opponent of war. Compare VIETNIK. *What is the real offense of a long-haired peacenik who holds his fingers in a V as the hardhats come marching by?* Harper's 8/70, p45 *When Barbara Howar was asked on the CBS special how somebody with her peacenik views could keep going out with Kissinger, she said, in a reply cut from the show, "Politics make strange bedfellows."* Harper's 1/71, p61 **[1963; see -NIK]**

Peace People, a movement of Catholics and Protestants organized to promote peace in Northern Ireland. *There were the Peace People, for instance, who over the past two years and despite their failings, have at least proved to Protestants, that Catholics truly want an end to violence and to Catholics that the Protestants desire likewise.* Times (London) 8/24/78, p12 **[1976]**

peace sign, 1 a V-shaped sign made with the fingers as an expression of peace. . . .*an admiring article by Tom Cawley, a reporter for the Binghamton Press, which was flanked by a large, smiling picture of* [Mayor John] *Lindsay giving the peace sign.* . . New Yorker 12/25/71, p54 **2** another name for PEACE SYMBOL. *Peter Stowe, an economics professor at Southern Illinois University, was haled into court under the law. In their car's rear window, his wife had stuck a* [U.S.] *flag decal with a peace sign where the stars should have been.* Time 7/6/70, p14 **[1969]** ►The V-shaped sign with the fingers was formerly (especially in World War II) called the *victory sign* and represented the *V* in Victory. The current use of the sign to indicate peace represents an adaptation of the upside-down *V* in the peace symbol.

peace studies, a course or program of studies dealing with the subject of peace among nations and the means of achieving it. Compare IRENOLOGY. *Some £75,000 was raised during 1972 toward the establishment of a chair of peace studies at the University of Bradford, Yorkshire.* Britannica Book of the Year 1973, p591 **[1952]**

peace symbol, the sign ☮ used as a symbol of peace. Also called PEACE SIGN. *American Opinion magazine, published by John Birch Society Founder Robert Welch, compared the familiar peace symbol to an anti-Christian "broken cross" carried by the Moors when they invaded Spain in the 8th century.* . .*Any resemblance, however, is probably coincidental. The peace design was devised in Britain for the first Ban-the-Bomb Aldermaston march in 1958. The lines inside the circle stand for "nuclear disarmament." They are a stylized combination of the semaphore signal for N (flags in an upsidedown V) and D flags held vertically, one above the signaler's head and the other at his feet).* Time 11/2/70, p6 **[1970]**

peak experience, a profoundly affecting spiritual or mystical experience. *In place of the behaviorists' mechanistic concept of human nature as a network of conditional responses,* [Abraham] *Maslow posited a human nature that is partly species-wide and partly unique. Most of us, according to Maslow, are capable, moreover, of what he termed "peak experiences"—breakthrough moments of deep emotional understanding or intensity, the most dramatic examples of which are the spiritual revelations of saints and mystics.* New Yorker 1/5/76, p42 **[1962]**

peak shaving, the pumping out of liquefied natural gas from storage tanks during periods of peak demand. *Cryogenic storage of natural gas is a rapidly growing technique; at 76 locations in the U.S. "peak shaving" operations involving liquefied natural gas are in use or under construction. There is no technical reason why a similar peak shaving technique cannot be employed with liquid hydrogen.* Scientific American 1/73, p16 **[1960**, so called because the natural gas is "shaved off" during periods of great demand]

PEC, abbreviation of PHOTOELECTROCHEMICAL CELL. *In effect, a PEC cell splits H_2O just as may be done in electrolysis by electrical current from a battery or other energy source. But in this case, the energy comes from sunlight.* World Book Science Annual 1977, p261 **[1976]**

pecs, n. U.S. Informal. pectoral muscles. *The great Las Vegas pose-off: Checking out the pecs.* . .*of a new wave of female athletes.* Newsweek 5/14/85, p54 **[1966**, short for *pectorals* pectoral muscles (OED 1828)]

pedal-steel guitar, an electronic guitar with usually ten strings that is mounted on a stand and connected to pedals which are used to modulate the sound and produce gliding effects. *In Canada, even the sweet attraction of a pedal-steel guitar is given added juice by the cockiness, vitality and winner's aura of the Canadian West.* Maclean's 10/13/80, p51 **[1969]**

pedestrianization, n. the act or process of pedestrianizing. *The scheme to ban cars from Bond Street is essentially to make it a parade, although pedestrianization can have a commercial appeal.* Times (London) 3/18/68, p7 **[1964]**

pedestrianize, v.t. to convert (a street, etc.) to use by pedestrians; make free of vehicular traffic. *Eventually it intends to pedestrianise Low Street and turn the whole centre into a traffic-free area.* Sunday Times (London) 11/19/67, p30 **[1962]**

-pedia or **-paedia**, a combining form used in names of sections of an encyclopedia. See the quotations for examples of words using this combining form. *The first volume, propaedia, will be introductory.* . .*Next comes micropaedia, a 10-volume ready-reference dictionary of 10,300 pages, lavishly illustrated in colour. Finally, there is macropaedia, 19 volumes of substantive essays ranging the world of learning.* Times (London) 1/12/74, p12 *The Alphapedia was conceived as a finding device for the Colorpedia.* Harper's 12/77, p105 **[1974**, abstracted from *(en)cyclopedia* or *(en)cyclopaedia*]

pedochemical (ˌpiːdouˈkeməkəl), adj. of or having to do with the chemical composition of, or changes in, soil. *The sources of trace metals in soils include those derived from geochemical and pedochemical weathering of rocks which make up the parent materials of soils.* McGraw-Hill Yearbook of Science and Technology 1974, p381 **[1974**, from Greek *pédon* soil + English *chemical*]

peel, v.i. **peel out**, U.S. Slang. to accelerate sharply in an automobile so that the tires leave rubber marks on the pavement. *As an adolescent man is freer to drive a car carefully rather than "peel out" and display the "horsepower" of his car—a vicarious display of his own power.* NY Times 6/17/71, p41 **[1963]**

peer review, review before publication of a scientific or scholarly work by referees or experts in the appropriate field or fields of knowledge, who must approve the work before it is published. *In particular, the spotlight is on a part of the process known as peer review, which scientific journals rely upon to weed out inaccurate claims and research findings. Editors, if favorably disposed to manuscripts submitted for publication, send them to scientists, or "peers," considered experts on the topic of the manuscript.* NY Times 6/6/89, pC3 **[1971]**

Pekingologist or **Pekinologist**, n. other names for CHINA WATCHER. . . .*professional China watchers—often referred to as Pekingologists, or, more flippantly, as dragonologists—are constantly sifting through the raw material that Hong Kong provides them with.* New Yorker 2/12/66, p44 . . .*Fleet Street is said to be desperate for reliable Pekinologists who can churn* out a thousand weekly words on the Chinese enigma. Punch 4/2/69, p478 [**1962**]

Pekingology or **Pekinology**, *n.* the study of the policies, practices, etc., of the Chinese Communist government in Peking. Compare KREMLINOLOGY. *. . .practitioners of the recondite art of Pekinology say that if Chairman Mao died tomorrow the party leadership probably would fall. . .* NY Times 4/3/66, pD6 [**1962**]

pelican crossing or **pelican,** *n. British.* a crosswalk with traffic lights that can be activated by a pedestrian. *One particular concern is the pelican crossing: old people tend to distrust them, fearing that the lights will change before they can reach the other side of the road, and will deliberately choose other (and more dangerous) places to cross.* Times (London) 2/19/76, p27 *The GLC* [Greater London Council] *survey. . .studied 40 pelicans which had been converted from zebras; 31 pelicans where there had been no previous controlled crossing, and 32 pelicans with vehicle-actuated equipment.* New Scientist 6/24/76, p702 [**1966**, formed irregularly from pedestrian light controlled, and patterned on zebra crossing (1952) a crosswalk painted with black and white stripes]

pelletron, *n.* an electrostatic generator of metal beads or pellets separated by insulating material to form a current-carrying belt for accelerating charged particles. Compare LADDERTRON. *Charge flows off smoothly after contact, so there is no spark abrasion. In most Pelletrons the returning pellets are charged opposite to the ingoing ones to give current doubling.* McGraw-Hill Yearbook of Science and Technology 1976, p316 [**1972**, blend of *pellet* and *-tron*]

pelvic inflammatory disease, a general inflammation of the female pelvic cavity that can lead to infertility by damaging the Fallopian tubes. *Abbreviation:* PID *"Pelvic inflammatory disease," said Dr. Nancy Lee of the Centers for Disease Control, "can be caused by a multitude of organisms, some that are sexually transmitted and others from a woman's own body."* NY Times Magazine 12/6/87, p120 [**1980**]

pemoline, *n.* **1** a drug used to relieve depression; a stimulant. *Pemoline has been known sometime to be a mild brain stimulant, midway in strength between Amphetamine and coffee.* Sunday Times (London) 10/27/68, p3 **2** a shortened form of MAGNESIUM PEMOLINE. *Widely hailed as a memory-improving drug, pemoline—tradenamed Cylert by Abbott Laboratories—has been the focus of several independent studies since it was first publicized two years ago.* Science News 1/6/68, p14 [**1961**, perhaps from its chemical components *pher-ylimino-oxazolidinone*]

pence, *n. sing.* or *pl.* See the footnote under NEW PENNY.

pend, *v.t.* to leave undecided; postpone a decision on. *. . .the United States Atomic Energy Commission has spread a security blanket over what may be a basic innovation in controlled fusion technology. It has done this by "pending" the settlement of nine patent applications filed by KMS Industries Inc. . .* New Scientist 7/16/70, p134 [**1970**, verb use of *pending, adj.,* as in *with cases still pending, patent pending,* etc. (1797)]

penny, *n.* **two a penny,** *British.* very plentiful or common and therefore not valued. The equivalent U.S. phrase is *a dime a dozen. It is, of course, an isolated church in many ways, and foreign theologians, two a penny in Oxford or in Boston, are curiosities in Sofia.* Times (London) 4/4/70, p10 *Winston Churchill had little money of his own, hardly enough to keep him living in the style demanded in the 4th Hussars. He found in India that subalterns were two a penny and invited nowhere. Life in cantonment offered less than no opportunity.* Listener 10/27/66, p612 [**1960**] ► *Ten a penny* is also used in England in the same sense.

pen register, an electronic device connected to a subscriber's telephone line at an exchange that prints the numbers called and the date, time, and duration of telephone calls. *Because a pen register automatically keeps a record of whom someone calls, when, and how often, and because the phone company, some businesses, law enforcement, and the intelligence community use them, pen registers are becoming the focus of a new*

kind of debate over a citizen's right to privacy as guarantee by the Fourth Amendment. Science 2/17/77, p749 [**1966**, pa terned after earlier *pen recorder*]

pentadecapeptide (͵pentə͵dekə'peptaid), *n.* a proteinlike mole cule consisting of 15 amino acids. *In the report, published i July, 1972, the investigators describe how they isolated an a tive substance they named "scotophobin". . .In view of the uncertainty as to the precise structure, they synthesized thre pentadecapeptides. They reported that one had biological an chemical properties identical to those of the naturally occu ring material.* 1974 World Book Year Book, p226 [**1972**, fron *pentadeca-* fifteen (from Late Greek *pentadeka-*) + *peptide*]

pentatonism, *n.* the use of a pentatonic or five-tone musica scale. *Pentatonism exists only on the frontier with Bolivia, bu an archaic tritonic* [three-tone] *song, the* Baguala, *sung to th* caja, *can still be heard in the high mountains of the north-wes* Times (London) 7/4/70, p30 [**1970**]

penton, *n.* a group of five interdependent units in the oute protein shell of a virion (virus particle). *After a further days. . .during which time there is a loss of pentons from th virion and a consequent greater susceptibility to disruption DNA was extracted from purified virions.* Nature 4/14/7² p347 [**1966**, from *pent-* five + *-on* elementary unit]

penturbia (pen'tərbi:ə), *n. U.S.* small cities or towns that attrac new residents because of their simple way of life, cheap lan and housing, and often job or business opportunities. *Long-ru growth will be greater in penturbia than anywhere else in th nation.* Atlantic 9/87, p108 [**1987**, from *pent-* five + sub*urbi* (because it supposedly represents the fifth major social migra tion in American history)]

people journalism, a form of journalism, chiefly pictorial, de voted to the activities of celebrities. *"People journalism". . . had its origins in Time magazine, in a department called "Peo ple," which was eventually allowed to swing as a single be tween its own covers on supermarket counters. Even we, at th Times company, have spawned an "Us." In "people journal ism," the media become as important as the personages the cover.* NY Times 12/6/79, pA30 [**1979**]

people meter, a remote-control device that measures televisio ratings by requiring participating viewers to punch a series o buttons each time they watch television. *People meters. . .hav logged prime-time network viewership at nearly 10 percen below previous ratings, which were based on the diary system* Atlantic 8/88, p12 [**1987**]

people mover, any of various means for transporting peopl quickly between two fixed points. *. . .a "people mover," a vehi cle smaller than a streetcar, for West Virginia University i Morgantown. . .will provide continuous service between th old campus in town and the new campus in the suburbs of thi small mountain city.* World Book Science Annual 1972 p375 *. . .rail-oriented, change-of-mode centers will be strate gically located throughout the region. They will enable com muters to change from car to rail transportation and, possibly in the New York City center, to change from subway to a noise less pedestrian conveyor called a "people mover."* NY Times 6/20/71, p22 [**1970**]

people sniffer, the nickname of a portable chemical and elec tronic apparatus that can detect the presence of hidden per sons. *United States troops refer to the gadget as the "people sniffer." It leads American officers here in the Mekong delta to enemy hide-outs by "sniffing out" the kind of ammonia odors given off by the human body.* NY Times 8/18/68 pA3 [**1965**]

Pepper Fog, a trade name for a PEPPER GAS. *After a decade o assorted riots, the nation's 400,000 policemen are armed with more lethal weapons than some of history's major wars re quired plus Mace and Pepper Fog, undercover agents, comput ers and helicopters.* Time 7/13/70, p34 [**1969**]

pepper gas, a riot-control gas that forms a thick haze and causes irritation of the throat and nasal passages. Also called by the trade name PEPPER FOG. *About 225 state and city policemen, armed with pepper gas, submachine guns, rifles and shotguns,* *repelled the mob, at first with truncheon blows.* Times (London) 7/9/70, p5 [**1970**]

pepstatin (pep'stætin), *n.* a chemical compound that inhibits the action of certain enzymes, which break down proteins. Pepstatin has been isolated from various species of streptomyces. *Pepstatin could become a valuable tool for investigating the role of renin in various forms of experimental hypertension.* Science 2/11/72, p656 [**1972**, from pepsin + *-stat* inhibiting substance + *-in* (chemical suffix)]

peptidoglycan (ˌpeptədou'glɑiˌkæn), *n.* another name for MUCO-PROTEIN. *The walls of all penicillin-sensitive organisms contain a structural component called peptidoglycan. . .* Nature 4/10/75, p482 [**1966**, from *peptide* + connecting *-o-* + *glycan* chemical name for a polysaccharide]

péquiste or **Péquiste** (pei'ki:st), *n.* a member of the PARTI QUÉBÉCOIS. Compare INDÉPENDANTISTE. *The Péquistes are off and running. A referendum is promised (its timing is uncertain but the general expectation is that it will come in about two years) and ministers speak confidently of their future as an independent nation.* Times (London) 6/3/77, p1 —**adj.** of or relating to the Parti Québécois. *Let's suppose that the péquiste government succeeds in its first 18 months in office in delivering the goods on the rather modest pledges it made during the campaign.* Maclean's 12/27/76, p8 [**1973**, from Canadian French *péquiste*, from (the French pronunciation of) *P.Q.*, abbreviation of Parti Québécois + *-iste* -ist]

perbromate (pər'brouˌmeit), *n.* a salt of perbromic acid. *Preliminary studies showed that the perbromate ion has physical and chemical properties between those of the perchlorate and periodate ions.* 1970 Britannica Yearbook of Science and the Future, p141 [**1968**; the term was originally used in 1866 for a different preparation]

perbromic acid, a compound of bromine in its highest oxidation state (HBrO₄), first synthesized in 1968. It lies between the analogous perchloric and periodic acids. *An inconsistency in the reactions of members of the halogen family that has plagued inorganic chemists since the middle of the nineteenth century was cleared up this year at Argonne National Laboratory, Argonne, Ill., by Dr. Evan H. Appleman. He synthesized perbromic acid in which bromide has a valence equal to that of seven hydrogen atoms.* Science News Yearbook 1969, p181 [**1968**; the term was originally used in 1864 for a different preparation]

perceived noise decibel. See the quotation for the meaning. *Abbreviation:* PNdB or PNdb *Flight tests of 707 and DC-8 aircraft have shown that fan noise can be decreased 10-15 perceived noise decibels by the use of such [sound-absorbing] linings. The perceived noise decibel is a unit of measurement of the human annoyance caused by noise exposure.* McGraw-Hill Yearbook of Science and Technology 1971, p425 [**1965**]

perennity, *n.* continuance for a long time; permanence; perpetuity. *M Chirac told party officers yesterday that his objectives were to insure the perennity of Gaullism and to win the next general election.* Times (London) 12/20/76, p4 [**1972**, from French *pérennité*, from Latin *perennitās*, from *perennis* perennial] ►This is a reborrowing or revival of a 17th-century word. The OED records it as obsolete, citing three instances of its use in 1597, 1641, and 1713. The related word *perenniality* (derived from *perennial*) has been in use since the mid-1800's though not nearly as frequently as the synonyms *permanence* and *perpetuity.*

perestroika (ˌperə'strɔikə), *n.* a restructuring of Soviet society, especially in economic policy. *Bukharin's greatest importance today, by far, is as the intellectual forerunner of perestroika.* Manchester Guardian Weekly 12/6/87, p1 [**1986**, from Russian, literally, rebuilding but found earlier in official translations (1981)]

perfecta, *n. U.S.* another name for EXACTA. *For horseplayers who hopefully bet on exactas, perfectas, quinellas, doubles, and such, I can report that one afternoon last week at the Fair Grounds in New Orleans, an exacta paid $25,257.* New Yorker 2/20/71, p107 [**1968**, from American Spanish, short for *quiniela perfecta* perfect quiniela]

perfluorochemical (pərˌflu:ərə'keməkəl), *n.* any of a group of chemical compounds in which hydrogen has been replaced by fluorine. Emulsions of such chemicals have been used in experiments as short-term substitutes for blood. *The perfluorochemicals, like blood itself, can carry oxygen and carbon dioxide, since both of these gases are very soluble in these compounds.* 1974 Collier's Encyclopedia Year Book, p172 —**adj.** of or relating to such chemicals. *Research toward breathable liquids has progressed from pressurized saline to the use of perfluorochemical liquids.* Science News 9/28/74, p202 [**1973**, from *per-* of the highest valence + *fluoro-* fluorine + *chemical*]

performance art, a form of theatrical performance or presentation which combines dancing and acting with music, photography, films, and other art forms. Compare INFORMATION ART. *Related to the "happenings" of the '60s was the Performance Art of the '70s, theatrical in presentation or form and sculptural in concept. The artist or performers present an internalized commentary between their bodies and the environment . . . Performance Art was centered in the U.S., England, and West Germany.* Britannica Book of the Year 1977, p144 *Performance art. Distinctions between painting, sculpture, theater, and choreography were merged and blurred. Diaghilev's teams of composer, dancer, and painter, were reconstituted often in one person.* New York Post 12/29/79, p15 [**1971**] —**performance artist:** *One of the most controlled and happens to like words, although he classifies himself as a dancer, not a writer. (I don't know of many writers who have been attracted to the form; those who have been have generally seen it as no occasion to lay their verbal gifts aside).* New Yorker 5/15/78, p126

performance contract, *U.S.* a contract by a private educational business firm to improve the educational performance of public-school students to a specified level for an agreed-on fee. *Roger R. Sullivan, president of Behavioral Research Laboratories, which has performance contracts operating in seven cities but was not one of the companies used in the test, said: "We feel that a performance contract, done properly, can be a great asset to American education."* U.S. News and World Report 2/14/72, p52 [**1971**] —**performance contracting:** *More than 30 cities have experimented with "performance contracting," and one poll showed that two-thirds of the nation's school board members were interested in trying it.* Time 2/14/72, p42 —**performance contractor:** *The program was further marred by a number of complaints that employees of the performance contractor were using corporal punishment to control and discipline students.* NY Times 1/2/72, pD7

performance theater, a form of theater in which productions are developed cooperatively by the actors. *Some of the brightest moments in U.S. theater in 1970 were to be found on the avant-garde front, in particular, with what was sometimes referred to as "performance theater." In this new kind of work . . . actors . . . either improvised without a written text, or freely adapted an old (dramatic or nondramatic) text, or had a text written to suit their needs by a playwright who worked with them as a member of the company.* 1971 Compton Yearbook, p458 [**1970**]

periapsis (ˌperi:'æpsis), *n.* the point in the orbit of a satellite body closest to the center of the celestial body around which it is orbiting. . . . *its [faster-orbiting vehicle's] companion, in a 50° orbit with apoapsis 20500 miles and periapsis 530 miles, undertakes the scrutiny of selected areas of Mars to gain a better idea of surface and atmospheric changes, seasonal variations, and the still enigmatic dust storms and Martian clouds.* New Scientist and Science Journal 5/6/71, p305 [**1964**, from *peri-* near + *apsis* orbit]

pericynthion (ˌperi:'sinθi:ən), *n.* another name for PERILUNE. Compare APOCYNTHION. . . . *as the moon travelers neared pericynthion—their closest approach to the lunar surface—Mission Control radioed a "go" for lunar orbit.* 1969 World

Book Year Book, p48 [**1959,** from *peri-* near + *Cynthia* goddess of the moon]

perilune, *n.* the point in a lunar orbit nearest to the center of the moon. Also called PERICYNTHION. Compare APOLUNE. *After being tracked for several days the spacecraft would be further slowed so that its perilune, or closest approach, would be reduced to about 28 miles above the lunar surface, which would be the primary altitude for photography.* Scientific American 5/68, p60 [**1960,** from *peri-* near + French *lune* moon (from Latin *lūna*)]

perinatology (‚perənei'taləd3i:), *n.* the medical study of the period around childbirth, especially the period including five months preceding birth and the first month after. [The] *chief of the Maternal and Child Health Center's division of perinatology described to the press and a large number of hospital personnel today the problems that were posed in caring for and then separating the twins.* NY Times 9/29/77, p39 [**1976,** from *perinatal* (1950's) of or relating to the period around childbirth (from *peri-* around + *natal*) + *-ology* study of] —**perinatologist,** *n.*: *At the same time that perinatologists have been concerning themselves with what goes on in the life of the fetus during its nine months of development, the birth process itself has become safer for the newborn, most dramatically through the use of fetal-heart monitors.* NY Times Magazine 7/11/76, p21

peripheral, *n.* any part of the electromechanical equipment of a computer, such as magnetic tape, high-speed printers, keyboards, and displays. *The first peripherals were highly mechanical and not well matched to the demands of the electronic computer. There has been a gradual conversion from these all mechanical peripherals to the electro-mechanical and onwards to the electro-mechanical-optical.* Science Journal 10/70, p75 *Peripherals include a card reader operating at three cards per minute, a line printer operating at 300 lines per minute and a paper tape reader.* New Scientist and Science Journal 6/3/71, p572 [**1964,** noun use of the adjective in this sense (1956)]

periphonic, *adj.* of or relating to an omnidirectional or multispeaker sound system. *A little of Third Ear Band's nursery doodling goes a very long way indeed, with or without electronic backing . . . But the French pieces were almost as uneventful, even with benefit of this excellent multi-channel, so-called periphonic, sound.* Times (London) 6/25/70, p7 [**1970,** from *peri-* all around + *phonic* producing sound]

peritus (pe'ri:tus), *n., pl.* **periti** (pe'ri:ti:). one of the theological experts serving as consultants at the Second Vatican Council (1962). *Father Baum, a peritus (adviser) at the Second Vatican Council, believes that condemnation of contraception is a matter of discipline that involves neither the church's infallibility nor divine revelation, and thus is subject to change.* Time 4/22/66, p43 . . . *Charles Davis, Britain's leading Roman Catholic theologian, . . . was . . . one of the "periti," the experts who gave bishops advice on theological and intellectual issues during the Vatican Council.* NY Times 1/12/67, p10 [**1963,** from New Latin *peritus,* from Latin *perītus, adj.,* skilled, expert]

permanent press, another name for DURABLE PRESS. *Recently a completely new process emerged, and is rapidly gaining ground in the USA, Europe and Japan. It is known by a variety of names, but possibly the most general is "permanent press".* New Scientist 7/20/67, p151 *Foreign competition is most severe in man-made-fiber textiles, the most rapidly rowing segment of the industry since advancing technology gave the world wash-'n'-wear shirts and permanent-press pants.* Time 4/18/69, p61 [**1964**]

permissive, *n.* another word for PERMISSIVIST. *It* [a proposal for a world-wide cricket tour] *also irritates the extreme cricket-establishment people, some of whom seem to relish the thought of the tour, barbed wire and truncheons and all, to show that they are not going to be dictated to by the long-haired permissives.* Times (London) 2/5/70, p9 —**adj.** *Biology.* permitting replication (of genetic material, viruses, etc.). Compare NON-PERMISSIVE. *In non-permissive primary mouse embryo cells*

some 24 h after infection with SV40 [a virus] *the extent and pattern of transcription are almost identical to that in permissive cells late in infection.* Nature 10/13/72, p368 [**1967** for noun; **1972** for adj.]

permissivism, *n.* the beliefs and attitudes of permissivists. *But the most impressive tributes to "the high priest of permissivism," as he* [Dr Spock] *once described himself, were casual. Not a single baby cried during the 90 minutes of protest.* Manchester Guardian Weekly 10/17/68, p3 [**1968**]

permissivist, *n.* a person considered excessively indulgent toward unacceptable behavior or attitudes. Also called PERMISSIVE. *In one week Spiro Agnew ascribed moral decay to the universities, Dr. Spock, and the Presidential Commission on Campus Unrest, which, he said, had produced a report which 'was sure to be taken as more pablum for the permissivists'.* Listener 10/22/70, p538 *So theatrical permissivists should ask themselves whether, if there must be censorship, it is not better from their point of view that it should remain with a rationally indefensible institution, which is in no position to enforce for long unpopular or unjustifiable standards.* Times (London) 2/16/66, p13 [**1966**]

peroxisome (pə'raksə‚soum), *n.* See the quotations for the meaning. *Recently the cells of higher organisms have been found to contain organelles called peroxisomes, whose major function is thought to be the protection of cells from oxygen. The peroxisomes contain enzymes that catalyze the direct reduction of oxygen molecules through the oxidation of metabolites such as amino acids and other organic acids.* Scientific American 9/70, p113 *Peroxisomes, tiny enzyme packages that may be a key to control of plant and animal growth, have been discovered in plants. They were previously known to exist in human cells; . . . peroxisomes appear to break down glycolic acid molecules that would otherwise play a role in growth. Slow-growing crops, including spinach, wheat and tobacco, are abundant in peroxisomes, while fast-growing crops such as corn have few.* Science News 2/8/69, p141 [**1965,** from *peroxide* + *-some* body]

peroxyacetyl nitrate, a highly toxic element in smog. *Activated by sunlight, nitrogen oxides combine with waste hydrocarbons from automobile exhaust to produce the noxious final product of photochemical smog, peroxyacetyl nitrate, often referred to as PAN.* New Yorker 10/2/71, p78 *Volume I . . . describes the web of photochemical reactions that desert sunlight spins daily in the warm pool of Los Angeles air out of the hydrocarbons and nitric oxide from a million manifolds. It is a remarkable story: the reducing agents turn into fierce oxidants that crack rubber, irritate the eyes and yellow the citrus groves. The products are many, the reagents not few. Ozone and peroxyacetyl nitrate are two recognizable and voracious oxidants.* Scientific American 9/70, p240 [**1966**]

perp, *n. U.S. Slang.* a person who has committed a crime. *Police are notorious for creating new words by shortening existing ones, such as "perp" . . ., "ped" for pedestrian and "wit" for witness.* Fort Wayne Journal-Gazette 9/21/86, p10A [**1986,** short for *perpetrator*]

persistent, *adj.* (of toxic chemicals, especially insecticides) hard to decompose; chemically stable and therefore degradable only over a long period of time. *As 1969 came to a close, the bureaucratic infighting had begun, with makers of DDT carrying on a delaying action on Hardin's* [Secretary of Agriculture Clifford Hardin's] *first ban. Action against other persistent pesticides, such as aldrin, dieldrin, and endrin, and those containing lead and mercury, is also in prospect.* Science News Yearbook 1970, p310 [**1963**]

person, *n.* ► **1.** *Redefinition of "person" to exclude unborn child.* One far-reaching refinement of the meaning of *person* occurred in January, 1973, when the U.S. Supreme Court ruled (in *Roe v. Wade*) that "the word person, as used in the 14th Amendment, does not include the unborn." As this meant that a fetus is not entitled to constitutional protection until it becomes "viable" (defined as at approximately seven months), the ruling invalidated the antiabortion laws of many states, in effect legalizing abortion in the United States. **2.** *Use of "per-*

ons" to replace "people." *Person* in the plural has for some me been invading the domain of *people;* it is the universal plu-al in notices, for example: "Capacity 13 persons." This plural ow produces sentences such as "How many persons attended he lecture?" and "Their best friends are usually persons in-olved in the arts." **3.** *Use of "person" as a genderless designa-ion.* More generally, person is increasingly used as a eplacement for both *man* and *woman.* For example, a classi-ed advertisement may seek a "person Friday" instead of a girl Friday." To a lesser extent, *person* replaces *boy* and *girl,* specially for teenagers; for younger boys and girls *child* re-ains acceptable, though it tends to be displaced by *person* in stitutional surroundings, such as schools and hospitals. The ost obvious new use of *person* is to replace *-man* or *-woman* a many established compounds. See -PERSON below. The fol-owing quotation illustrates the use of *person* to eliminate refer-nce to gender: *Chairman briefly became chairperson, but any now settle simply for chair, as in "she was the chair of he committee.". . . The Naval Academy wisely insists that its omen will be called midshipmen. Person is still acceptable hen used independently to designate either a man or a oman. When White House Press Secretary Ron Nessen men-ons future Government appointees, he is very careful these ays to speak of person instead of man.* Time 1/5/76, p13

erson-, a combining form sometimes used in place of *man* and oman in compounds to avoid reference to the individual's ender. **—person-ness,** n.: *Thomas Savage's* Daddy's Girl *(Bal-ntine, 95c) is . . . a "lost lady" story about cheeky, bright arty Linehan . . . seeking some assurance of her own person-ess.* Saturday Review 4/29/72, p74 **—person-trip,** n.: *The umber of "person-trips" (one person taking one trip) exceeded 60 million* NY Times 6/27/76, pJ25 **[1970]**

erson, a combining form used in place of *man* and *woman* in ompounds to avoid reference to the individual's gender. Often, however, compounds in *-person* are applied specifically o women, as when a prime minister who is a woman is referred o as a *statesperson,* and such usage defeats the purpose of the eplacement. The plural of compounds ending in *-person* may e *-persons* or *-people.* Some of the commonly used compounds re main entries in this book, e.g., ANCHORPERSON, LAYPER-ON, SPOKESPERSON. Some compounds in *-person* (e.g. *hench-erson*) are fabricated facetiously or for comic effect. The ollowing are recent examples of the use of this combining orm. **—businessperson,** n.: *If there is a budding business-erson in your vicinity, check the local Farmers Home Admin-stration office listed under the U.S. Department of Agriculture n the telephone book.* Woman's Day 3/74, p24 **—coun-ilperson,** n.: *No caption-writer in his normal senses would sol-mnly employ such ludicrous words as "councilpersons" and chairpersons" and "salespersons."* National Review 2/6/76, 92 **—fisherperson,** n.: *Check your impulse to indulge in salty ernacular, especially when among veteran fisherpersons.* New Yorker 9/6/76, p24 ►The U.S. Department of Labor ses *fisher* instead of *fisherperson* or *fisherman. Fisherperson* as tautologous as *fisherman;* in both terms the *-er* performs he same function as *man* or *person.* **—henchperson,** n.: *This eek Chairperson Mitchell and her henchpersons looked at the ay education brainwashes girls into accepting a submissive omestic role.* Listener 3/1/73, p286 **—houseperson,** n.: *The astry Bureau is supposed to (and probably does) busy itself in eaching the British housepersons to take more interest in bet-er pastry.* Manchester Guardian Weekly 10/19/75, p21 **—marksperson,** n.: *The Army has decided that all women sol-iers donning their new uniform after June 30 must become ualified "markspersons" with the M16 rifle.* Tuscaloosa News Alabama) 3/26/75, p8 **—repairperson,** n.: *Need a Fix? . . . Making home repairpersons from finger smashers.* National Observer 5/25/74, p6 **—spaceperson,** n.: *Applications are in-ited from suitably qualified candidates for the post of the irst British spaceperson.* Times (London) 6/3/77, p1 **—work-erson,** n.: *The actual manufacture and distribution of the fix-ures themselves is . . . rather a matter for the engineers than or workpersons.* Esquire 12/72, p226 **—yachtsperson,** n.: *If ou are a yachtsperson and have never visited Edgartown, go. own and Country 8/74, p37 **[1972,** generalized chiefly from

chairperson (1971), though influenced by earlier *salesperson* (OEDS 1928) and perhaps *tradesperson* (OED 1886)]

personal computer, a microcomputer that fits in a small area, such as a desk top, and can be programmed and operated by one person. Compare HOME COMPUTER. *We started a little per-sonal-computer manufacturing company in a garage in Los Altos in 1976. Now we're the largest personal-computer compa-ny in the world. We make what we think of as the Rolls-Royce of personal computers. It's a domesticated computer. People ex-pect blinking lights, but what they find is that it looks like a portable typewriter, which, connected to a suitable readout screen, is able to display in color.* New Yorker 11/14/77, p41 *We visualized the personal computer in the 1980s as a notebook-sized package whose front side was a flat-screen re-flective display, like a liquid-crystal watch face . . .* World Book Science Annual 1979, p185 **[1976]**

personal flotation device, U.S. and Canada. any device de-signed to keep a person afloat. *Abbreviation:* PFD *Personal flo-tation devices, (as the Coast Guard calls life jackets, life vests and other kinds of life preservers), must be bought in the prop-er size—and not necessarily "the bigger the better."* Popular Mechanics 6/73, p30 **[1972]**

personal rescue enclosure, U.S. another name for BEACHBALL. *Hard-pressed for elbow room in the shuttle's crew-carrying or-biter section, engineers at the National Aeronautics and Space Administration's Johnson Space Center in Houston have devel-oped the beachball, called the "personal rescue enclosure," as a compact escape system to replace bulky spacesuits in case the orbiter becomes disabled or a crew member is injured.* Science News 5/22/76, p327 **[1976]**

person-day, n. Statistics. a unit of time designating one average day of one person's normal activities. *In that year* [1960] *people in California spent some 235 million person-days in specified outdoor recreational activities, primarily swimming, picnick-ing, fishing and boating.* Scientific American 2/70, p91 **[1970]**

personkind, n. the human race; humanity (used in place of *mankind* to eliminate the reference to *man). Readers and writ-ers of both sexes must resist onefully any meaningless neolo-gisms. To do less is to encourage another manifestation of prejudice—against reason, meaning and eventually per-sonkind itself.* Time 10/23/72, p79 *There really are people who think it is very funny to refer to "personkind". . . and one clown even wrote a letter to the* Daily Another Newspaper *be-ginning "Person," instead of "Sir."* Times (London) 1/13/76, p14 **[1972]** ►*Humankind* is an alternate term that has been re-corded in the language since about 1645.

person-year, n. a unit of work equivalent to the work done by one person in one year, usually calculated without absence, or a unit of life lived in one year, used to calculate medical or pop-ulation statistics (used in place of *man-year* to eliminate the ref-erence to *man). The results of a massive study—"based on a total of 29,217 person-years of experience"—into the effect of a cholesterol-lowering diet on deaths from coronary heart dis-ease have just been published in Lancet.* New Scientist 10/26/72, p190 **[1972]**

PERT (pərt), n. acronym for *Program Evaluation and Review Technique,* a method of network analysis for planning a com-plex operation by using a computer. See the quotations for de-tails. *Using PERT, Raborn set precise timetables for each phase of the enormously complicated program, thus assured that everything would mesh without time-wasting gaps or overlaps in the schedule.* Time 4/23/65, p20 **[1959]**

pesewa (pə'sewə), n. a unit of money in Ghana. See the quota-tion for details. *The pesewa means a penny in the Ghanaian Fante language, and the cedi, which is worth 100 pesewas, is derived from a word meaning a small shell.* Times (London) 7/14/65, p11 **[1965]**

PET, abbreviation of *positron-emission tomograph* (or *tomog-raphy),* a diagnostic machine (or method) similar to the CAT scanner (or scanning) but using radioactive tracers to detect ab-normal biochemical activity. *First generation PETs (such as the whole-body scanner installed in London's Hammersmith Hos-*

pital last year) incorporate detectors made of sodium iodide crystals. The Canadian team uses a different material, bismuth germinate, which is more sensitive to positrons. It permits higher counting rates, more rapid scanning and lower radiation doses. New Scientist 2/28/80, p656 **[1980]**

peta-, a prefix meaning one quadrillion of any standard unit in the international meter-kilogram-second system of measurements. *In deriving units the SI* [Système International] *emphasizes that they should be formed from the base and supplementary units in a coherent manner. One result of this principle is a series of 16 prefixes that should be applied to the basic units to indicate large or small quantities. For large quantities they are deka (10¹), hecto (10²), kilo (10³), mega (10⁶), giga (10⁹), tera (10¹²), peta (10¹⁵) and exa (10¹⁸).* Scientific American 3/76, p60A **[1975,** possibly from the Greek root *peta-* spread out]

Peter Principle. See the first quotation for the meaning. *Everybody has heard of Educator Laurence Peter's "Peter Principle," which holds that employees advance until they are promoted to their level of incompetence.* Time 4/13/70, p13 . . . *much blame must attach to the* [U.N.] *administrative system, which has not only set out to prove Parkinson's Law, but which religiously follows the Peter Principle of promoting mediocrities.* Manchester Guardian Weekly 7/25/70, p6 **[1968]**

petnapper, n. U.S. one who practices petnapping. *With the increasing number of animal care bills before Congress, medical researchers are worried that they might get hog-tied along with the petnappers.* Science News 4/30/66, p317 **[1966]**

petnapping, n. U.S. the kidnaping of pet animals. *The United States acted in 1966 to curb "petnapping." Under a federal law signed by President Lyndon B. Johnson in August, animal dealers who steal pets and sell them to research laboratories may be fined up to $1,000 and sentenced to a maximum of one year in jail.* 1967 Compton Yearbook, p111 **[1966]** ►Though *petnapping* and *petnapper* are formed on analogy with *kidnaping* and *kidnaper* the traditional American forms *-naping* and *-naper* have been supplanted by the spellings *-napping* and *-napper*, which are more usual in Britain.

petro-. Originally *petro-* was used as the combining form of Greek *pétra* meaning "rock" or *pétros* meaning "stone," as in *petrography.* Later, *petro-* became a combining form for "petroleum" (= rock oil) and was used chiefly to form technical or scientific terms such as *petrochemical* and *petrolization.* A new meaning arose during the mid-1970's that of "based on or having to do with the wealth and power of the oil-exporting countries, especially those of OPEC." The following are some examples. See also PETRODOLLARS and PETROPOWER. —**petrocrat,** n. [petro- + bureaucrat]: *A new order is the ultimate goal of the petrocrats. Their aim is to lead many of the Third World nations in an economic revolution.* Time 1/6/75, p12 —**petrocurrency,** n.: *Part of sterling's strength may be its position as the "petro-currency" . . .* Manchester Guardian Weekly 7/15/79, p3 —**petromoney,** n.: *The boom in Arab property purchases in London has attracted its fair share of Saudi money. Hotels and apartment buildings have fallen to the tidal wave of petro-money.* Times (London), Special Report: Saudi Arabia 9/24/76, pII —**petropolitics,** n.: *The energy crisis . . . may have been artificially imposed, but its implications stretch far beyond petropolitics.* Time 12/3/73, p44

petrodollars, n.pl. surplus dollars accumulated by oil-exporting countries, especially when used for loans and investments in oil-importing countries. *Iran, seeking investment outlets for its petrodollars, said it had tentatively agreed to infuse $300 million into the ailing carrier, enough to ease Pan Am's current financial strain.* Newsweek 3/3/75, p60 —**petrodollar,** singular noun and attributive use: *There are many other kinds of help we could give the Arabs . . . but all they seem to want from us is arms. Since 1973, we have sold them more than $12 billion worth. Not that we mind. It is an effective way to recycle the petrodollar.* Harper's 5/78, p21 . . . *the unpredictable financial consequences of the massive petrodollar surpluses being acquired by the oil states.* Manchester Guardian Weekly 11/16/74, p3 **[1973]**

petropower, n. **1** the financial or political power of oil-rich countries. *It was a devastatingly ironic example of petropower. The Libyan Arab Foreign Bank will lend Fiat $104 million and spend an additional $311 million to buy newly issued Fiat stock and bonds.* Time 12/13/76, p65 **2** a country having power based primarily on possession of abundant supplies of petroleum. *Iran has thus blossomed into a formidable petropower—a regional political force that must be reckoned with and even, perhaps, one of the world's potentially great nations.* Britannica Book of the Year 1975, p37 **[1975]**

PFD, *U.S. and Canada.* abbreviation of PERSONAL FLOTATION DEVICE. *The big "must" of course is that the PFD's must be designed to float a person in a safe position, and pass a stiff leak test.* Consumer Contact (Ottawa, Canada) 6/72, p1 *Coast Guard approved PFD's may include life rings, buoyant cushions, buoyant vests, or buoyant jackets . . . You are legally required to carry at least one PFD for every person in the boat.* Field and Stream 4/73, p83 **[1972]**

PG, 1 a symbol used in the United States to designate motion pictures not restricted to any age group but requiring parental discretion and guidance. The approximate British equivalent is A. *The picture meticulously avoids nudity, and gets its reward: a PG rating from the M.P.A.A.* New Yorker 12/23/72, p55 *In Whatever Happened to Randolph Scott, the Statler Brothers examine the plight of the movie-oriented family man who must plow through G, PG, R and, especially X ratings.* Time 5/6/74, p53 **[1968,** abbreviation of Parental Guidance] **2** abbreviation of PROSTAGLANDIN. *Their* [doctors'] *experience is too limited, the researchers concede, for them to recommend routine use of prostaglandins for abortion, and they urge a more extensive trial . . . when the technique of PG abortion is simplified and improved, it is likely to be more acceptable than surgery—both emotionally and aesthetically—to many women.* Time 2/9/70, p40 **[1969]**

PGM, abbreviation of *precision-guided munition. The development of PGMs was greatly stimulated by the very effective use made of laser-guided bombs in Vietnam . . . A PGM may be an air-to-air, air-to-surface, surface-to-air, or surface-to-surface weapon and may be fired from an artillery piece, aircraft, ship, or vehicle, or be launched by an individual soldier.* New Scientist 5/8/75, p305 **[1975]**

PG-13, a symbol used in the United States for motion pictures rated PG but suggesting guidance for children under 13. *Your July 9 Current "Movie Violence Gets New Label" listed the new movie labels as announced by the industry. They list P for general audiences, PG for parental guidance suggested, PG-13 suggesting special guidance for children under 13, R for restricted and X to mean no one under 17 admitted.* U.S. News & World Report 8/13/84, p4 **[1984]**

phallocrat ('fælə,kræt), n. one who believes in the superiority or rule of the male sex; a male chauvinist. *Granted, not every art historian has been as nobly certain of the natural order as that unruffled Italian phallocrat; yet the fact remains that until quite recently, the work of women artists did not have a history.* Time 1/10/77, p60 **[1977,** from French *phallocrate,* from Greek *phallós* penis, phallus + *krátos* rule] —**phallocratic,** adj.: *A young heart trapped in an aging body, the private energy crisis of nature, is a suitable case for fictional treatment. But the phallocratic and medical detail meant to be portentous becomes absurd.* Times (London) 6/30/77, p14

pharmacogenetic, adj. of or relating to pharmacogenetics. *A major advance pharmacologists are now serving up to physicians has to do with "pharmacogenetics," the study of genetically triggered individual responses to drugs. More and more clinicians are tuning in to pharmacogenetics. It should help them prescribe more rationally . . . Known pharmacogenetic conditions appear to adhere to the general principles established for inborn errors of metabolism.* Science News 6/26/71, p438 **[1962]**

pharmacogeneticist, n. a specialist in pharmacogenetics. *Some pharmacogeneticists advocate screening individuals who are to receive succinylcholine* [a muscle relaxant] *before surgery for* *heir pseudocholinesterase activity.* Science News 6/26/71, 439 **[1967]**

harmacogenetics, *n.* the study of the interaction of genetics nd drugs. *A body of knowledge, called pharmacogenetics, was ccumulating that showed that the fate of a drug in the body, r even the nature and extent of its therapeutic effect, depends n certain cases upon a discrete genetic trait.* 1970 Britannica earbook of Science and the Future, p278 **[1960,** from *pharaco-* drug (from Greek *phármakon*) + *genetics*]

harmacokinetics, *n.* **1** the reaction of the body to particular rugs; the way a drug is absorbed, distributed, metabolized, tc., in the body. Compare BIOAVAILABILITY. *The magnitude f the antitumour effect depends on a complex interaction beween cell kinetics and pharmacokinetics.* New Scientist /27/73, p748 **2** the study of the absorption, distribution, metabolism, etc., of drugs. *From pharmacokinetics . . . has come he concept of minimal alveolar concentration (MAC), which s defined as the concentration of an anesthetic that must be resent in the lungs before anesthesia can be achieved.* Britanica Book of the Year 1969, p491 **[1960,** from *pharmaco-* drug rom Greek *phármakon*) + *kinetics*]

hase, *v.t.* **phase down,** to reduce gradually; reduce by phases. *he secretary said that the programme to phase down Amerian air operations in Indo-China and turn over more of the air ffort to the South Vietnamese "is solidly based and progressng, if anything, ahead of schedule."* Times (London) 11/6/70, 8 **[1967,** from PHASEDOWN, *n.,* probably patterned after *hase out* to end or discontinue by phases]

hased-array, *adj.* having or based on a complex of electronially steerable radiating elements in place of a mechanically roated antenna. *These phased-array radars, with computer omplexes, could sight incoming missiles more than 1,000 iiles away . . .* Americana Annual 1970, p464 *"Phasedrray" aerials scan by means of a pattern of controlled delays etween the signals passing through the different elements of he aerial.* New Scientist 9/23/65, p738 **[1965,** from *phased rray* "an array of antennas" (1938)]

hasedown, *n.* the gradual reduction of a program or operaon. *. . . I believe we should proceed with our phasedown orthwith and carry it through expeditiously to completion— hat is, until all U.S. Army, Navy, Marine Corps and Air Force ersonnel, except Embassy guards, are out of Vietnam.* NY imes 6/27/71, pD15 *The best scope for achieving economies n clerical staff will probably come on the female side, where he turnover is rapid and any required phasedown can thus be cquired easily in a relatively short time.* Times (London) /12/68, p17 **[1963,** probably patterned after *breakdown, omedown,* etc.]

hencyclidine (fen'siklə,di:n), *n.* a depressant drug used to imnobilize animals, and illegally as a narcotic popularly known s ANGEL DUST. *Formula:* $C_{17}H_{25}N$ *Abbreviation:* PCP *And if ou want to see a Siberian tiger, Panthera tigris altaica, "immoilized with phencyclidine and promazine . . ." turn to the hotographs.* New Scientist 5/14/70, p345 *By any name, hencyclidine (PCP) is the most dangerous drug to hit the treets since LSD became widely available a decade ago.* Time 2/19/77, p53 **[1959,** short for *phenylcyclo*hexyl piper*idine*]

henetic (fi:'netik), *adj.* of or relating to a method of classificaion of organisms based on overall or relative degrees of simiarity among the organisms to be classified. Compare CLADISTIC. *A good example of new phenetic data was provided y C.G. Sibley who summarized his thousands of pieces of data n proteins in bird muscle and eggs. The protein data were reated in the same way as the more classical morphological ata; a classification was derived based on degree of similarity.* cience 2/9/68, p659 **[1960,** from *phen-* (from Greek *phainein* o show forth) + *-etic,* as in the term *phyletic* (based on phylum r line of descent), with which *phenetic* is contrasted]

henetics, *n.* the phenetic system of classification. *This is a ladistic (or branching) approach toward forming a classificaion and markedly differs from the methodology of phenetics vhich emphasizes the degree of similarity independent of the*

way in which similarity was achieved. Science 2/9/68, p659 **[1968]**

pheromone ('ferə,moun), *n.* any of a class of complex chemical substances secreted especially by insects to produce a specialized response in other insects of the same species. *These chemical messages have been termed pheromones, and in insects they have a wide range of functions, from sex attractants and trail markers to alarm pheromones and those which participate in maintaining the social structure of a colony.* McGraw-Hill Yearbook of Science and Technology 1971, p323 **[1959,** from *phero-* (from Greek *phérein* to carry) + *hormone*]

phi, *n.* or **phi meson,** a highly unstable and short-lived elementary particle with a large mass and zero charge. *Physicists had supposed that the photon, or light particle, was the sole intermediary of electromagnetic forces. But experimental evidence has shown that photons approaching hadrons tend to turn themselves into one of the mesons called phi, rho or omega. Thus, it appears that electromagnetic forces are mediated to leptons directly by photons and to hadrons by phi, rho or omega.* Science News 4/10/71, p250 **[1962]**

Philadelphia chromosome, an abnormally small chromosome found in the blood-forming cells of many patients with chronic myelocytic leukemia. *In each chapter appropriate and informative tables and figures are included: the lack of a picture of a metaphase with the Ph¹-chromosome (Philadelphia chromosome) is regrettable since the chromosomal anomaly is the only consistent and characteristic one established to date for any mammalian malignancy.* Science 4/27/73, p401 **[1963,** so called because it was discovered by Peter C. Nowell of the University of Pennsylvania School of Medicine in *Philadelphia*]

Phillips curve, a curve showing a correlation between rates of unemployment and rates of inflation. See the quotation for details. *The Phillips curve . . . lays it down that the rate at which wages rise is inversely proportional to the level of unemployment—that is, that the greater the pressure on the labour market (and hence the lower the level of unemployment), the faster the price of labour will rise.* Manchester Guardian Weekly 3/14/70, p22 **[1966,** named after A.W.H. *Phillips,* born 1914, a British economist]

phone-in, *n.* another name for CALL-IN. *One of the most exciting potentials this year has been the phone-in—not so much for anything it's yet achieved, but for the developable importance and excitement of acquiring presently-participating listeners.* Listener 12/30/71, p915 **[1963]**

phone phreak, Also spelled **phone freak.** a person who uses electronic equipment illegally to make free telephone calls. Also shortened to PHREAK. *Placing the signals related to a call on separate circuits . . . will also increase greatly the difficulty that so-called "phone phreaks" have in placing long-distance calls without paying toll charges by using devices that imitate the phone system's internal tone signals.* NY Times 1/18/76, p37 **[1972,** *phreak,* alteration of *freak* by influence of *phone*] **—phone phreakdom:** *The pharaoh of phone phreakdom, a loose-knit organization of tech heads who try to rip off the phone company with sophisticated home-concocted electronic devices, got busted in nearby Stroudsburg last year by Ma Bell's security squad for operating a computer "capable of theft of telecommunications service."* High Times 1/79, p40 **—phone phreaking:** *A new offensive against "phone phreaking" may have claimed its first victim last month. An alleged phone phreak had dialled a motoring organisation . . . But, in mid-call, his line was abruptly crossed by the Post Office's special phone phreak detectives.* New Scientist 4/3/75, p29

phonoangiography (,founou,ændʒi:'ɑgrəfi:), *n.* examination of blood vessels by monitoring the sound made by the bloodstream. *Phonoangiography, which picks up sound just as a stethoscope does, is being used to detect hardening of the arteries. A normal artery is silent.* Science News 11/7/70, p368 *The sound of blood flowing through the vessels is picked up by a sensitive microphone, recorded on magnetic tape, and analyzed by phonoangiography—a new method of locating and estimating size of arterial obstructions.* World Book Science

Annual 1972, p326 [**1970,** from *phono-* sound + *angiography* examination of the blood vessels]

photic driver, a weapon combining strobe lights and ultrasound, for use in riot control. *The Army has stopped short of introducing the strobe lights of the projected "photic driver" with their ability to induce epileptic fits, but its use could still be guaranteed to produce another anti-Army and communally divisive outcry.* New Scientist 9/20/73, p668 [**1973,** *photic* of or using light, from Greek *phōs, phōtós* light]

photino (fou'ti:nou), *n. Nuclear Physics.* a hypothetical particle which, according to the theory of supersymmetry, is a weakly interacting form of the photon. *The same experiments at CERN prompted Joseph Silk of the University of California at Berkeley, Keith Olive of the Fermi National Accelerator Laboratory in Batavia, Ill., and Mark Srednicki of the University of California at Santa Barbara to consider photinos as candidates for the unseen or dark matter that astrophysicists believe is plentiful in the universe; which would account for the cohesion of clusters of galaxies and also ensure that the universe has a closed geometry.* Science News 7/13/85, p23 [**1983,** from *photon* + *neutrino*]

photobotany, *n.* the branch of botany that studies the effects of light on plants. *The author starts with the basic physics of radiation . . . then moves on to techniques, to radiotoxic effects, shuns photobotany (chlorophyll doesn't appear even in the index), and then speeds to photo-reception and its underlying mechanisms.* New Scientist 7/2/70, p39 [**1970**]

photochemical, *n.* a chemical produced by the action of light on a substance. . . . *the Environmental Protection Agency, created in December, 1970, set air-quality standards in 1971 for six principal pollutants of urban areas. These were sulfur oxides, carbon monoxide, particulates (soot and smoke), hydrocarbons, nitrogen oxides, and photochemicals.* World Book Science Annual 1972, p34 [**1971,** noun use of the adjective (OED 1859)]

photocube, *n.* a transparent plastic cube usually filled with a piece of spongy material to hold a photograph up against the inside of each surface so that it may be displayed. *Perspex photocube—an ingenious way of displaying six different photos, price £2, postage 1s.6d. extra, from Presents of Sloane Street, London, S.W.1.* Times (London) 11/13/70, p15 [**1970**]

photodegrade, *v.t., v.i.* to decompose by the action of light, especially sunlight. *Kenneth W.L. Moilanen and Donald G. Crosby of the University of California at Davis have demonstrated two routes by which DDT may have photodegraded into PCBs, using wavelengths which occur in sunlight.* New Scientist 5/24/73, p462 [**1973,** back formation from *photodegradation* (1950's)] —**photodegradable,** *adj.: One pound of active ingredient is 900 times as effective as a pound of pesticide and must be applied only half as often, the developers claim. The fibers, made of an acetal resin, are photodegradable and the EPA found the system had no ill effects on wildlife, soil and water.* Science News 6/3/78, p360

photodissociate, *v.t.* to dissociate chemically by the absorption of light. *A meteorite impact, Veverka suggests, could crack the fragile crust, producing a huge fountain of dilute ammonia that is quickly photodissociated by ultraviolet light onto hydrogen and nitrogen.* Science News 1/1/77, p12 [**1962,** back formation from *photodissociation* (1925)]

photoelectrochemical cell, an electrochemical cell that produces current when exposed to light, used experimentally to convert solar power to chemical energy. *Abbreviation:* PEC *As might be suspected, the central element of the photoelectrochemical cell is the photoelectrode. Virtually any electrode material will give photoeffects, and it has been known for over 100 years that irradiation of an electrode can result in the nonspontaneous flow of electric current in the external circuit.* McGraw-Hill Yearbook of Science and Technology 1978, p14 [**1972**]

photoelectrode, *n.* an electrode that is stimulated to action by light. *Another idea that the team came up with was to etch the photoelectrode to improve light pick-up. Whereas previously*

they had at best achieved power conversion efficiencies around 1.2 per cent, after etching efficiencies improved around 9 per cent. New Scientist 6/10/76, p579 [**1973**]

photoenvironment, *n.* an environment marked by the presence of light. *The layer [of plankton], which had migrated down ward at dawn, rose again by 50m. at eclipse totality, some thr hours after sunrise, lagging slightly because the rate of swi ming was too slow to permit the animals to maintain the selves exactly in the optimal photoenvironment.* Britanni Book of the Year 1976, p469 [**1965**]

photo essay, an article or book presenting a subject chie through photographs. *What is the future of the self-publishe photo essay? It may not replace the coffee-table spectacula the scholarly monograph, or the book pegged to current even but the new photography book is finding a growing audien of its own.* Saturday Review 12/2/72, p67 *"The Other Ham, ton," a photo-essay on the black community of Bridgeham ton, Long Island, has been published by Grossman.* Ne Yorker 2/11/74, p128 [**1971**] —**photo essayist:** *When Life ma azine ceased publication on December 29, some observers sa the era of the black-and-white photo essay in print was ove What had in fact happened, however, was that the photo essa ist had moved on to other media—even as reader interest w moving—while* Life *(and* Look, *which had died a year earlie stuck stubbornly to their old patterns.* 1973 World Book Ye Book, p462

photofabrication, *n.* the use of photography in the manufactu of integrated circuits by photoengraving semiconductor su faces on a small silicon wafer or chip. *Photofabrication star with drawings and by chemistry and optics transforms the into the objects, usually with a reduction in linear scale.* Scie tific American 4/67, p47 [**1966**]

Photo-Fit, *n. British.* the trademark for a system of reconstruc ing faces by using photographic alternatives of five basic faci features (forehead, eyes, nose, mouth, and chin) to make a com posite photograph that approximates the description supplie by witnesses. *Also commonly spelled photofit. The police ha distributed photofit likenesses of the three men who murdere Signor Occorsio in his car as he was leaving his home to go t the law courts.* Times (London) 7/12/76, p4 [**1970**]

photographica, *n.pl.* items of interest or of value to devotees photography, such as antique cameras and related equipmer once owned by famous photographers. *At many of the world leading auction houses the traditional emphasis on the fi arts and expensive jewelry has had to make room, in recen years, for a new phenomenon: the burgeoning sales of phot graphica, the images and equipment identified with the fir years of photography.* 1978 Collier's Encyclopedia Year Boo p46 [**1972,** from *photograph* + *-ica* by analogy with such word as *erotica* and *esoterica* or from plural of (assumed) New Lati *photographicum*]

photoisomerize, *v.t.* to change the isomeric form of (a sub stance) by the action of light. *Exposure to light photoisomerize the retinal* [visual pigment of retina] *and initiates a series o changes in the configuration of opsin as its deep red color is re placed by light yellow.* 1973 Britannica Yearbook of Scienc and the Future, p301 [**1963,** back formation from *photoisomer ization* (1926)]

photonovel, *n.* a novel in the form of photographs, usually wit dialogue inserted in the style of comicstrip balloons. *Mr. Steu art, as head of Fotonovel Publications, presides over a staff c 15, turning out two 168-page photonovels a month.* NY Time Book Review 7/22/79, p27 [**1978,** from Spanish *fotonovel* from *foto* photo + *novela* novel]

photo op, *U.S. Informal.* short for PHOTO OPPORTUNITY. *The operate in the slick new tradition of political handlers, whos job is to reduce a campaign to photo ops and sound bites.* Tim 11/21/88, p144 [**1988**]

photo opportunity, *U.S. and Canada.* a session in which publici ty pictures are taken of celebrities or government officials. Th British equivalent is *photocall. A husky, bearded veteran o Vietnam War coverage who now watches the White House fo*

CBS, ruminated glumly on the morning's events: "This is the sort of thing that eats up our time. Photo opportunities, briefings, releases, more photo opportunities. Most of it doesn't mean a damn thing. But the White House grinds it out and we eat it up." NY Times Magazine 5/15/77, p22 **[1976]**

photopolarimeter, *n.* an instrument combining telescopic, photographic, and polarimetric (measuring polarized light) apparatus for producing detailed images of planetary features. *Most intriguing of all, light measurements by Pioneer's imaging photo-polarimeter will enable computers on earth to construct about ten pictures of the planet* [Jupiter] *that will show features as small as 250 miles across.* Time 3/15/71, p46 **[1971]**

photorealism, *n.* a style of painting and sculpture having the realism of a photograph. Compare HYPERREALISM. *Photorealism's sudden emergence in the Whitney's "New Realism" show of 1970 caught most critics unprepared: Those who had cut their eyeteeth on various kinds of abstraction . . . were at a loss when confronted with these huge, photographically meticulous canvases that looked like oversized picture postcards.* National Review 5/11/73, p530 **[1961]** —**photorealist**, *n., adj.: To the photorealists of the turn of the sixties, nudity, reproduced to the last pore and hair curl, ranks with automobiles and storefronts as preferred data of painting and sculpture.* New Yorker 11/4/72, p121

photosensor, *n.* a device that is sensitive to light. *In a study of commonly used type fonts, for instance, it has been found that 24 rows of photosensors are necessary to recognise unambiguously a typical character. In contrast, the number of vertical columns in the photosensor array is determined primarily by psychological considerations: many columns lead to a higher reading rate.* New Scientist 12/24/70, p554 **[1962]**

photovoltaics, *n.* the use of photovoltaic cells, especially solar cells, for the direct conversion of sunlight into electricity. *But even in California the science of photovoltaics is in its infancy, and the cells remain expensive and not very efficient.* Time 4/30/79, p75 **[1973]**

phrase marker, an abstract representation of the grammatical structures in a sentence. *"Now, the fundamental idea of transformational grammar is that the bracketed and labelled representation of a sentence is its surface structure, and associated with each sentence is a long sequence of more and more abstract representations of the sentence—we transformationalists call them phrase markers—of which surface structure is only the first . . ."* New Yorker 5/8/71, p53 **[1963]**

phrase-structure grammar, a grammar consisting of phrase-structure rules. Compare GENERATIVE-TRANSFORMATIONAL GRAMMAR. *Considerable progress has been made . . . in using computers to manipulate languages, both vernaculars and programming languages. Grammars called phrase-structure grammars and transformational grammars supply the theoretical backdrop for this activity.* Scientific American 9/66, p166 **[1966,** from *phrase structure* (1957)]

phrase-structure rule, one of the rules governing the construction of the phrasal constituents of a sentence. *The problem is this: phrase structure rules and transformations are local; they define well-formedness conditions on individual phrase-markers and on pairs of successive phrase-markers . . . Phrase structure rules and transformations turn out to be special cases of derivational constraints.* Language 9/70, p627 **[1970]**

phreak, *n.* short for PHONE PHREAK. *So far, British phreaks have tended to avoid the sophisticated electronic devices used by many US phreaks.* New Scientist 4/5/73, p23 **[1972]** ▶*Phreak is also an easy variant of freak for any whimsical purpose. For example, name phreak is Herb Caen's term for a person who contributes a note on an oddity in a personal name to his column in the San Francisco Chronicle.*

phytochrome, *n.* a protein pigment in plants. See the quotation for details. *Phytochrome molecules regulate such processes as germination, growth, and flowering, turning these functions on and off in response to the length of days and nights.* 1967 World Book Year Book, p247 **[1960]**

PI or **P.I.**, *U.S.* abbreviation of *principal investigator,* a scientist or scholar in charge of a particular experiment or study. *One source quotes a high official in the NASA Pioneer office: "If Pioneer survives, it'll be the first time in this mission that I've been right and all the PI's (principal scientific investigators—the experimenters) have been wrong."* Science News 11/24/73, p325 **[1969]**

Piagetian (ˌpiːəˈʒeiən), *adj.* of or relating to the Swiss psychologist Jean Piaget, 1896-1980, or his theories of child development. *Collection of articles representative of the theoretical and empirical research derived from Piagetian theory, focus is on intellectual development of the young elementary school child . . .* Science News 8/17/68, p171 —*n.* an advocate or supporter of Jean Piaget and his theories. *Quite possibly, Piagetians sometimes speculate, adolescents' fascination with their ability to visualize alternatives is what makes them so eager to test new life-styles and utopian ideals.* Time 12/12/69, p42 **[1960]**

picadillo (pikəˈdilou; *Spanish* piːkɑːˈdiːyou), *n.* a Spanish and Latin American dish of ground meat mixed with tomatoes, garlic, onion, olives, and capers. *Who would have ever guessed, for instance, that the old Mexican street near downtown Los Angeles that looks as if it was restored by the MGM set department . . . would have one place that served delicious hand-patted soft tacos packed with picadillo . . .* Atlantic 4/74, p68 **[1965,** from Spanish, literally, ground meat, hash]

picloram (ˈpaiˌklɔrəm), *n.* a highly active and persistent herbicide, used extensively for defoliation in Vietnam. *The recently introduced chemical, picloram, is one of the longest-lived pesticides and would contaminate the ground for years.* Manchester Guardian Weekly 2/21/70, p6 **[1964,** formed backwards from the chemical name *aminotrichloropicolinic* acid]

picornavirus (piˌkɔrnəˈvairəs), *n.* any of a group of viruses containing ribonucleic acid, including the poliovirus, rhinovirus, and similar viruses. *The picornaviruses are a third category. "Pico" stands for very small, and "rna" is added because they contain ribonucleic acid, which is conventionally abbreviated to rna.* Times (London) 9/3/65, p14 *FMD* [foot-and-mouth disease] *is caused and transmitted by a picorna virus (one of the smallest known disease-producing organisms) of which there are seven major types and at least 50 subtypes.* 1969 Britannica Yearbook of Science and the Future, p339 **[1962;** see the first quotation for the etymology]

picosecond, *n.* one thousand billionth (10^{-12}) of a second; a trillionth part of a second. *Laser pulses lasting about a trillionth of a second, or one picosecond, can now be measured accurately for the first time, making it possible to measure picosecond events in atoms and molecules.* Science News 12/2/67, p537 *Closely spaced picosecond pulses have been observed in Q-switched ruby and neodymium/glass lasers.* New Scientist 12/28/67, p767 **[1962,** from *pico-* trillionth (from Spanish *pico* peak) + *second*]

picture telephone, another name for the VIDEOPHONE. . . . *the life of existing television cameras may now be extended by forming the tube at higher temperatures. The manufacture should be cheaper, involving only silicon and silicon compounds. The development of picture telephones . . . is brought a step nearer with this advance.* Times (London) 3/30/70, p8 **[1962]**

PID, abbreviation of PELVIC INFLAMMATORY DISEASE. *Several surveys in different countries have now found that women using IUDs are at increased risk of getting these infections, which are known as pelvic inflammatory disease, or PID. In Oxfordshire, for example, older upper-income women using the coil had two to three times the risk of PID compared with non-users.* Times (London) 7/6/80, p6 **[1980]**

pierced earring, *U.S.* an earring made for insertion in a pierced ear. *Employed by a costume jewelry company, Miss Robbe travels all over the country promoting the company's earrings. The package deal includes the purchase of a $6 pair of pierced earrings. With this purchase, the customer may sign a permis-*

sion slip and have her (or his) ears pierced free of charge. Tuscaloosa News (Alabama) 12/31/71, p8 [**1965**]

pig, *n. Slang.* a policeman. *The news that in only 19 per cent of the riots were the police called in also makes nonsense of the New Left's equally mulish contention that the "pigs" are the Establishment's unfailing resort.* Manchester Guardian Weekly 1/24/70, p5 . . . *Jake was murdered in a shoot-out in Chicago where three pigs were killed and seven were wounded.* New Yorker 2/13/71, p72 [**1967**] ►*Pig* is a hostile or insulting epithet used to describe policemen and sometimes other law-enforcement officers. The use of *pig* in this sense was part of British underworld slang throughout the 1800's. The current use may be a re-emergence of a very old expression. —**v.i. pig out,** *U.S. Informal.* to stuff oneself with food; gorge. *Johnson reports some colleges have informal groups of women who "pig out" regularly in frantic feasting.* Time 11/17/80, p94 [**1980**]

piggyback, *v.t., v.i. U.S. and Canada.* to add or join up to something else as an extra load (in various transferred and figurative uses). *The Senate is engaged in its old game of trying to piggyback a tax-cut rider onto important legislation—this time a bill raising the debt ceiling.* Business Week 6/22/74, p108 *A Mackenzie Valley pipeline transporting this U.S. gas provides us as Canadians with access to our frontier gas which can "piggyback" on the U.S. gas.* Maclean's 5/30/77, p22 [**1968**, extended from the verb sense "to carry loaded truck trailers on railroad flatcars" (1953)]

piledriver, *n.* **1** a person who hits or strikes with great power or impact. *Hill, a 6-ft. 3-in. 212-lb. pile driver, rewarded them by leading the league in rushing* . . . Time 4/6/70, p79 *Her [Jeanne-Marie Darré's] piano playing has immense vitality, propelled by a phenomenal technique. But she is made of blood, bone and brain* . . . *and she is not a piledriver.* NY Times 8/22/66, p41 **2** (in wrestling) a slamming downward of an opponent's head so that it hits the canvas. *I was coerced into becoming wrestling correspondent* . . . *Friday night became Majestic night, a night immersed in grapevine, arm and head lock, body slam and press, piledriver, full and half nelson, Boston crab, head scissors, flying mare, leg snatch and folding press, bear hug, knockout and submission.* Manchester Guardian Weekly 12/26/70, p23 [**1962**]

Pilipino (ˌpiləˈpiːnou), *n.* one of the two official languages of the Philippines (the other being English). *Pilipino is a variation of Tagalog, the language of the people of the Manila area. More than half the people of the Philippines speak Pilipino* . . . World Book Encyclopedia (1989), Vol. 15, p374 [**1936, 1961,** from Tagalog *pilipino,* from Spanish *Filipino* Philippine]

pill, *n.* **the pill,** an oral contraceptive in pill form. *The pill is an extremely effective means of birth control, but it can only work if the patient remembers to take it.* Science Journal 11/70, p14 *Newspapers, magazines, television and even newsreels have carried on a noisy debate over the last year on whether the Pill, by far the most popular contraceptive, is safe.* Saturday Night (Canada) 3/67, p17 [**1957**]

pillhead, *n. Slang.* a person addicted to taking pills, such as tranquilizers, barbiturates, and amphetamines, to combat depression, insomnia, anxiety, etc. *There were five other patients "in residence" when I arrived and during my six-month stay, the population totalled only nineteen—fourteen narcotic addicts, two marijuana smokers and two "pillheads," including me.* Maclean's 9/4/65, p31 *Mr. Leech told the children, in group discussions, using the slang of the "pillheads" and "junkies", that on Tuesday he buried an addict of 23* . . . Times (London) 3/28/68, p3 [**1965;** see HEAD]

pimp, *v.t., v.i. U.S. Slang.* to profit from or live off another, as a pimp does. *"I think it unfortunate that black personalities, or leaders (those who actually command people), allow themselves to be used, pimped, in this way."* New Republic 4/4/70, p29 *"That child been pimpin' off his mother since he was three years old."* Time 1/11/71, p43 [**1942** *pimp on,* **1970,** verb use of the noun; cf. *pimp, v.i.* (OED 1636) to work as a pimp; pander]

piña colada (ˈpiːnyə kouˈlaːdə), an alcoholic drink made with pineapple juice, coconut (syrup, milk, or meat), and rum.

Norma inspected his work. "These are wild," she said. "There's only one thing to do: get some piña coladas and stay up all night. I'm game." New Yorker 8/21/78, p32 [**1967,** from Spanish, literally, strained pineapple]

pin-fire, *v.t.* to treat (a horse) for splints and other leg ailments by anesthetizing and applying electric needles to the affected part. *Woodlawn was pin-fired below the knee last spring after injuring himself just before Cheltenham. The Hennessy Gold Cup is his next objective, and all being well he will be trained in the new year for the Grand National.* Times (London) 11/4/67, p7 [**1962**]

ping-pong, *v.t., v.i. U.S.* to refer (a patient) needlessly to various specialists, especially in a clinic. See FAMILY GANGING. *The Senate investigators, all of whom had been pronounced in excellent health by Congressional doctors at the beginning of the inquiry,* . . . *were "ping-ponged" to neurologists, gynecologists, internists, psychiatrists, podiatrists, dentists, ophthalmologists, pediatricians.* NY Times 9/5/76, pD1 *The sending of a patient to eight or ten doctors for needless, Medicaid-reimbursed tests and treatments is known to the trade as "ping-ponging."* New Yorker 12/13/76, p121 [**1975,** earlier *ping-ponging, n.* (1972); extended from the figurative verb sense "to bounce or toss back and forth" (1952), from *Ping-Pong,* trademark for table tennis equipment]

ping-pong diplomacy, the establishment of trade and other relations between the United States and the People's Republic of China, begun when an American table tennis team went to China in 1971. *The extraordinary transformations of the past two years, commencing almost ludicrously with "ping-pong diplomacy," but going on to* . . . *the de facto exchange of diplomatic recognition between Washington and Peking, did not result from some wishful brain-wave of Nixon or Kissinger.* National Review 3/30/73, p352 [**1971**]

pink-collar, *adj. U.S.* of or relating to occupations in which women predominate. *Working women are still disproportionately herded into so-called pink-collar jobs—teaching, clerical and retail sales work. The median salary for American women last year was only 60% that of American men.* Time 11/28/77, p14 *The "silent 80%" is what they're often called—the women who do the low-paid, dead-end, unglamorous pink- and blue-collar jobs.* Sunday News (New York) 12/9/79, p3 [**1977,** patterned after *white-collar* (1928), *blue-collar* (1950); compare GRAY-COLLAR]

pink spot, a chemical substance (DMPEA or dimethoxyphenylethylamine) that is closely related to the hallucinogenic drug mescaline, discovered in the urine of non-paranoid schizophrenics, where its presence may be a biochemical indication of schizophrenia. *Dr. Arnold J. Friedhoff of the New York University School of Medicine, one of the first to identify DMPEA, or the pink spot, in the urine of schizophrenics, presents further evidence on its metabolic pathways.* Science News 5/25/68, p503 [**1965,** so called because the presence of the substance is indicated by the appearance of a pink spot on the porous chromatographic paper used in the analysis of urine]

PINS (pinz), *n.pl. and sing. U.S.* acronym for *Person(s) In Need of Supervision,* a legal term for a child or adolescent with behavioral problems. *The Family Court Act defines PINS as any youngster under 16 "who is a habitual truant or who is incorrigible, ungovernable or habitually disobedient and beyond the lawful control of parent or other lawful authority."* NY Times 12/14/76, p42 *There are, for many reasons, still far more girls than boys who are PINS, and girls are usually confined in institutions for far longer periods than boys.* New Yorker 8/14/78, p58 [**1968**]

pinstriper, *n. U.S. Informal.* a business executive. *[The airline] has to attract more business travelers if it hopes to survive. "Pinstripers are not buying our product, for very good reasons," Burr acknowledges. "We've got to change."* Business Week 5/12/86, p31 [**1986,** from *pinstripe* suit, as typical of a business executive + *er*]

Pinyin (ˈpinˈyin), *n.* a system for transliterating Chinese into Roman characters. *The new system, known as Pinyin, for the Chinese word meaning "transcription," has been adopted in* he United Nations and by the United States Board on Geographic Names, which determines the spelling of place names or Government use . . . In switching to the Pinyin style, The Times will retain a handful of well-known conventional names, such as Peking and Canton, because they are deeply rooted in English usage. For some names the previous spelling systems coincide, as in Shanghai. NY Times 2/4/79, p10 [1963]

The Pinyin system was introduced in China in 1958 as a teaching aid, but it was not utilized to communicate with foreigners until 1979. Until then the most widespread Romanized system was the Wade system, devised in the mid-1800's by Sir Thomas Wade, a British diplomat and Chinese scholar and revised by H.A. Giles for his Chinese-English Dictionary (1892). In the Pinyin system, the late Chairman Mao Tse-tung's name is rendered Mao Zedong, and the late Premier Chou En-lai's name is spelled Zhou Enlai. Some examples of place names are:

Conventional Spelling	Pinyin
Canton	Guangzhou
Fukien	Fujian
Kiangsu	Jiangsu
Nanking	Nanjing
Peking	Beijing
Szechwan	Sichuan
Tientsin	Tianjin

ionium (pai'ouni:əm), *n.* a short-lived quasiatom consisting of a pion (pi-meson) and a muon, unstable nuclear particles. *Pionium is produced in the decay of the K meson to a muon, a pion, and a neutrino. In about one in ten million decays the muon and pion remain bound together by their electrostatic attraction. The resulting neutral pionium atom moves undetected away from the line of the K beam.* New Scientist 6/10/76, p578 [1976, from *pion* (OEDS 1951) + -*ium* (suffix for chemical elements)]

ion therapy, a method of destroying cancer tumors by concentrating an intense beam of pions on the cancerous tissue and causing a miniature atomic explosion that damages the atoms and molecules of the target cells. *"It will take years to say whether pion therapy is superior to other treatments," says Malcolm Bagshaw, a radiation oncologist from Stanford University, who is visiting Los Alamos. "We are looking for local control where cancer has started. We probably can't do much about a cancer that has spread through the body." Nevertheless, pion therapy will have to show significant improvements over alternates, to be worth the expense and effort.* Science News 12/9/78, p414 [1970]

piquada (pi'ka:də), *n.* a small electric needle used as an instrument of torture. *Technology also has a place. One instrument widely used in some Latin American torture centres is an electrical refinement of the straight pin called the piquada, which is inserted under the victim's fingernails.* New Scientist 7/19/73, p141 [1972, alteration of Spanish *picada* puncture]

piscicide ('pisə,said), *n.* the extermination of fish, especially all fish in a given area. *Yet I was unable to detect any evidence of mass piscicide in the Sonic's track. The only dead fish I saw was a 6 in. specimen pointed out by Mr. Tolar himself.* Times (London) 8/21/63, p5 [1960, from *pisci-* fish + -*cide* killing, as in *genocide*]

pit, *n.* **the pits,** *U.S. Slang.* the worst; the most undesirable or unpleasant place, condition, circumstance, etc. Compare ARMPIT. *"Get me back into the novel or marry me," Emma told Kugelmass. "Meanwhile, I want to get a job or go to class, because watching TV all day is the pits."* New Yorker 5/2/77, p38 *They take a special delight in bad-mouthing the old hometown and state. First of all, this state was good enough for them for about 55 years. Suddenly, it's the pits!* New York Post 10/10/78, p91 [1953, probably from plural of *pit* a deep place; abyss; hell]

pit lizard, *U.S. Slang.* a female fan or follower of automobile racing drivers. *Some of the women stand out because you see them there every day . . . "Pit lizards," camp followers, or dedicated racing fans, whatever you choose to call them, they are part of the scene and their presence is pleasing to racing men.* Atlantic 6/73, p77 [1972, patterned on *lounge lizard* (1920's)]

pit road, the road off an automobile racing course where the pits are located to service the competing cars. *The race stewards had declared that no replacement cars would be allowed to start the race and neither would any driver who had failed to complete the first lap, which meant that all those who finished the lap in the pit road would also be excluded.* Times (London) 7/19/76, p8 [1976]

pixel ('piksəl), *n.* one of the photographic elements of a television image or picture. *The Vidicon converted each picture into an image consisting of 200 lines with 200 picture elements ("pixels") per line, making a total of 40,000 pixels per picture.* Scientific American 5/70, p28 [1969, from *pix* (picture) element]

pizzazz or **pizazz** (pə'zæz), *n. U.S. Slang.* showy quality; flashiness. Also spelled PAZZAZZ. *In a high-rolling state [Florida] that likes politics with pizazz, [Governor Reubin] Askew is a nonsmoking teetotaler who devotes most of his spare time to Presbyterian Church activities.* Time 5/31/71, p15 [1962, of unknown origin, from earlier (OEDS 1937) meaning of liveliness, vitality, pep]

PKU, abbreviation of *phenylketonuria* (an inherited condition in which the body cannot metabolize the amino acid phenylalanine, resulting in brain damage and mental retardation in infancy). *Dr. David Y. Hsia, a professor of pediatrics at Northwestern University, reported yesterday findings that confirm that a special diet permits normal brain development in children born with the defect called phenylketonuria, or PKU.* NY Times 5/3/68, p18 [1957]

PL, abbreviation of PRODUCT LIABILITY. *Many PL problems relate directly to product quality control and reliability.* McGraw-Hill Yearbook of Science and Technology 1974, p361 [1974]

planeside, *n.* the area beside an airplane. *I arrive back at Kennedy Airport a veritable Adonis of virility and hedonistic masculinity. But by the time I walk from planeside to a taxi, a cold wind sweeps across the airport and wipes away the whole four weeks' work.* Saturday Review 8/31/68, p6 —*adj.* at the planeside; beside an airplane. *In a planeside interview, General Abrams said that, although the Communists had the ability to launch new offensives, "I don't know about" the magnitude of such ability.* NY Times 3/28/68, p3 [1968]

Planetokhod (plə'netə,xɔ:t), *n.* a vehicle designed by Soviet scientists for scientific exploration of the planets. See also LUNOKHOD, MARSOKHOD. *The vehicle is called Lunokhod-1. The hybrid Russian word means "moon vehicle" or "moon walker", and Soviet scientists are predicting that other such vehicles, named Planetokhod or Marsokhod, will eventually move over the surface of the Planets.* Times (London) 11/18/70, p1 [1970, patterned on Russian *Lunokkhod*, literally, moon walker]

Planet X, *Astronomy.* a hypothetical planet orbiting the sun in a region beyond Pluto and within the Oort Cloud. *Astronomers . . . have revived interest in finding Planet X, the putative (assumed to exist) body that has long been sought beyond Neptune and Pluto.* Encyclopedia Science Supplement (Grolier) 1986, p15 [1985]

planholder, *n.* a shareholder in a pension plan. *When the planholder reaches retirement, he draws a pension expressed in units—helping to offset subsequent rises in the cost of living.* Sunday Times (London) 8/20/67, p18 [1965]

planification (,plænəfə'keiʃən), *n. Especially U.S. and Canada.* the act or process of planifying; systematic planning. *He also expects the increase in business concentration to erode the functioning of markets, necessitating ever more "planification of capitalism".* . . Harper's 6/76, p102 *As for his government of technocrats and bureaucrats, nearly all of us, French and English, businessmen and workingmen, have been frustrated to the screaming point by their planifications, financial chaos and the obvious fact that most of their programs create more problems than they solve.* Maclean's 11/1/76, p14 [1967, from French, from *planifier* PLANIFY]

planify ('plænə,fai), *v.t. Especially U.S. and Canada.* to plan systematically; subject to thorough planning. *"We have estab-*

lished in recent years the most planified market that ever existed," said Louis Camu, chairman of the Banque de Bruxelles. "Every day the price for eggs, for example, is fixed by a computer in Brussels and then transmitted to the people who buy, sell and transport them." Time 4/23/73, p79 [**1973**, from French *planifier*]

planned obsolescence, the manufacture of products designed to deteriorate or become outdated after a shorter period of time than might normally be expected. Compare WASTE-MAKER. *After about two years, the makers wisely claim, the bracelets lose their power and must be replaced—a sort of magical planned obsolescence.* Time 7/6/70, p56 [**1956**]

plantimal ('plæntəməl), *n.* a living cell formed by fusing the protoplast of an animal cell with that of a plant cell. *Already, in some instances, cells as different, as distantly related as a mouse and man, as tobacco plant and man, have been induced to fuse and form new cells which were neither man nor mouse, neither plant nor animal. Indeed, those plant-animal hybrids are already being called "plantimals." Such strange new hybrid cells haven't yet been grown up successfully into strange new creatures.* Robert Cooke, Improving on Nature, 1977, p130 [**1976**, from *plant* + an*imal*]

plasma panel, a panel displaying information from an electronic computer or the like, consisting of an array of gas-filled cells which can be selectively ignited to display any letter, number, diagram, etc. [Jurg] *Nievergelt programmed Race Track for the University of Illinois's Plato IV computer-assisted instruction system, which uses a new type of graphic display called a plasma panel.* Scientific American 1/73, p108 [**1972**]

plasmapause, *n.* the upper limits of the region above the atmosphere that contain layers of plasma or highly ionized gas. Compare PLASMASPHERE. *But the spacecraft will be far beyond the plasmapause, the outer boundary of the ionosphere, and beyond the magnetosphere for most of the time.* Science Journal 3/70, p73 [**1966**]

plasma physicist, a specialist in plasma physics. *Typically, plasma with a density of 10^{14} nuclei per cu.cm must be held together for about one second. To bring this about is the dream of plasma physicists.* New Scientist 10/24/68, p186 [**1968**]

plasma physics, a branch of physics dealing with plasma or highly ionized gas, especially as it appears in a wide range of cosmic phenomena and as it is used in controlled thermonuclear reactions. *Hydrogen bombs achieve fusion from the extraordinary temperatures and enormous pressures generated by atomic explosions, which are clearly untenable for peaceful thermonuclear power: controlled fusion must meet the stringent demands of plasma physics nonviolently.* Encyclopedia Science Supplement (Grolier) 1971, p367 . . . *plasma physics* [is] *the study of balanced mixtures of free ions and electrons.* 1970 Britannica Yearbook of Science and the Future, p421 [**1958**]

plasmasphere, *n.* an envelope of highly ionized gas about a planet. Compare PLASMAPAUSE. *Since none of Jupiter's outer satellites seems to affect the planet's radiation, the plasmasphere evidently does not have a long tail extending to satellite orbits beyond Io.* New Scientist and Science Journal 7/1/71, p8 [**1966**]

plasma torch, a device that produces plasma or ionized gas for vaporizing, melting, or reducing any substance, such as metal or waste products. *In addition to vaporizing solids, plasma torches could also be used to heat liquids.* Science News 3/7/70, p250 [**1959**]

plasmid, *n.* a small, circular segment of DNA that replicates in bacteria independently of the bacterial chromosome. *To clone a fragment of DNA one "recombines" it with a vector that can be introduced into a host bacterium and multiply in it. The vector can be a plasmid (a circular bit of nonchromosomal bacterial DNA) or a bacteriophage (a virus that infects a bacterium). The vector DNA is cleaved at a unique site by an enzyme called a restriction endonuclease.* Scientific American 5/81,

p61 [**1964**, originally (1952) meaning any extrachromosom hereditary determinant]

plasmon ('plæz,mən), *n.* Physics. a quantum of longitudinal e citation of an electron gas. *Graphite is known to have a shar plasmon at about 7eV* [electron volts]. McGraw-Hill Yearboc of Science and Technology 1976, p174 [**1956**, from *plasm* (highly ionized gas) + *-on* elementary particle or unit]

plastic, *adj.* not natural or real; synthetic; artificial. *In mic interview with Yippie Jeer-leader Jerry Rubin, some 30 Yipp yahoos stormed the studio stage, screeching obscenities, knoc ing over equipment, squirting Frost with water and insul ("You are a plastic man. You have been dead for years").* Tim 11/23/70, p36 *Now that so many of the young seem to wea their hearts on their sleeves, it is hard to tell which ones are re and which ones are plastic.* Harper's 8/67, p19 —*n.* short fc PLASTIC MONEY. *With plastic, the overall financial picture ge blurred in the psychological distance the consumer imposes be tween the use of his card and his own money supply—as if th two weren't quite connected. Maclean's 8/27/79, p46 The came the . . . credit squeeze in March. Many people simp stopped using their cards, and some people even sent them t the White House as a symbol of swearing off demon plasti* Time 9/29/80, p67 [**1963** for adj., figurative use of *plastic*, a synthetic material; **1979** for noun, abstracted from PLASTI MONEY]

plasticated, *adj.* plastic, synthetic, or artificial (chiefly figura tive use). *Marco Ferreri's* The Last Woman [a film] *is set in a immediately recognizable context—a modern industrial wast land of high-rise apartment blocks and plasticated entertair ments.* Times (London) 10/15/76, p13 [**1972**, from pas participle of *plasticate*, *v.* (1929) to knead rubber by means c a plasticator or (1962) to make plastic by adding a plasticizer]

plastic bullet, a bullet made of polyvinyl chloride plastic an discharged from a specially designed gun, used in riot contro Compare RUBBER BULLET. *The grim news from Belfast f cused attention for the first time on the plastic bullet, the slee er among the new generation of British anti-riot weapon. Basically it is rather shorter than a rubber bullet and made o PVC. A cylinder 1½ inches in diameter and rather over fou inches long, it looks like a thick white lump of candle.* New Sc entist 12/16/76, p672 [**1972**]

plastic credit, the use of credit cards in place of cash or check Compare PLASTIC MONEY. *We were told then and now that th advantage of plastic credit is that it reduces paperwork, consol idates all bills down into one (to be paid by a single check a the end of the month), and moves us rapidly, inexorably to ward the "checkless society."* Newsweek 6/30/75, p11 [**1971**]

plastic memory. See the quotation for the meaning. *One of th fascinations of the behavior of plastics is that when certai kinds of plastic are molded in a distinct form, then melted s that the form is lost and then allowed to cool, they resum much the same form. Called "plastic memory," the phenome non has an analogue in a little-known metallic alloy. Th metal is named Nitinol . . .* Scientific American 3/71 p47 [**1967**]

plastic money, credit cards. *One advantage of using "plasti money"—bank credit cards in place of cash—was the interes free ride if monthly bills were paid on time. But now the fre ride is rapidly disappearing, and users of Master Charge card and Bank-Americards should take notice.* NY Times 9/11/76 p27 *Plastic money is taking on a new form that seems sure t make it even more widespread on the British banking scene* New Scientist 2/17/77, p398 [**1974**]

plate, *n.* one of a number of vast crustal blocks that comprise according to the theory of plate tectonics, the land masses o the earth and that are believed to produce the drift and frag mentation of continents. Also called TECTONIC PLATE. *Earth quakes occur because each plate is rigid and moves agains another plate with great resistance.* Encyclopedia Science Sup plement (Grolier) 1971, p13 *Both of these plates* [the Caribbe an and Atlantic] *are moving westward, but the Atlantic plat is moving faster and is being forced under the Caribbean . .* Science News 3/6/71, p170 *According to the sea-floor* spreading hypothesis, large plates of the Earth's crust are slow-*ly moving relative to one another, like giant slabs of floating* *ice.* McGraw-Hill Yearbook of Science and Technology 1971, p430 [**1965**, earlier theoretical use (1904)]

plateglass ('pleit,glæs), *adj.* of, relating to, or designating the newer British universities founded especially since the 1950's. *The collective academic phenomenon now known as the Plateglass universities coincides with a break in the great grad-uate bull market of the 1950s and 1960s.* Manchester Guardian Weekly 5/22/71, p13 *The new universities, particularly the new foundations, which are familiarly called "the plateglass universities" because of their architecture, were expected to be innovative institutions, breaking away from conventional models of organization, course structure, and degrees.* Science 6/1/73, p938 [**1968**, so called because of the *plate glass* often used in the building of these universities, in contrast to the *red-brick* universities built in the 1800's]

plate-tectonic, *adj.* of or relating to PLATE TECTONICS. *During Permian and Triassic time, between about 200 and 250 million years ago, the quiet of the western coast of South America grad-ually gave way to rumblings brought on by the incipient breakup of the supercontinent Pangaea and the onset of the plate-tectonic cycle that is still under way.* Scientific American 3/73, p65 [**1969**]

plate tectonics, a theory of the structure of the earth's surface, according to which the land masses of the earth consist of vast crustal blocks called plates, which are bounded by seismically active trench systems, mountain chains, etc., and which are slowly driven sideways by convection currents or other forces kept in motion by the earth's internal heat. *In accordance with plate tectonics, the Pacific Ocean is spreading apart along the East Pacific Rise, much like the sea-floor spreading that is oc-curring along the Mid-Atlantic Ridge.* 1972 Britannica Year-book of Science and the Future, p232 *It would therefore be well to lay out the rules of plate tectonics—the set of conditions which are believed to govern the behaviour of features on the Earth's surface. . . Plate tectonics has been adequately tested in other parts of the world and has shown its ability to predict, amongst other things, the direction of the movement accompa-nying earthquakes.* Science Journal 8/69, p39 [**1969**]

platinum, *adj.* of or designating a record album that has sold a million copies. Compare GOLD. *The Austin sound—redneck rock or progressive country—began crossing over from country to pop charts and racking up sales once scarcely dreamed of in the country field. In the past two years, three such albums have gone platinum, in trade parlance (i.e., sold 1 million copies).* Time 9/18/78, p81 [**1971**, so called from the award, a platinum album, given to the performers]

PLATO or **Plato** ('plei,tou), *n.* a computer-based individualized system of instruction. *Plato operates through visual display ter-minals that connect directly to the large-scale computer and interact through lesson materials in the computer's memory. Users see their instructional materials in the form of text, num-bers, animated drawings, and other graphics. The student in-teracts with the computer-stored lesson materials in somewhat the same manner as with a teacher.* NY Times 4/15/76, p57 [**1963**, acronym for *Programmed Logic for Automatic Teaching Operations*]

platoon, *v.t., v.i. U.S. Sports Slang.* to substitute (a player) for another, usually putting in one specializing in a particular play or position. *Later,* [Gil] *Hodges* [manager of the New York Mets] *decided to "platoon" him* [Cleon Jones] *by playing him only against lefthanded pitchers.* Time 9/5/69, p52 [**1967**, verb use of the noun *platoon* a group of football players special-izing in either offensive or defensive plays]

playbook, *n.* a book containing diagrams of a football team's plays. *They spend most of their time watching films of their next opponents or studying the 'play-book' which sets out the dozens of moves they have to learn before the next match.* Sun-day Times (London) 9/28/69, p22 [**1963**]

player, *n. U.S.* a person or group that plays an important part in any activity involving several parties. *A major player in the*

year's merger activity was Texas Air Corporation. 1987 Col-lier's Encyclopedia Year Book, p115 [**1986**]

playgroup, *n.* a type of improvised nursery school for preschool children, privately formed and supervised usually in some neighborhood facility. *Mothers find difficulty in getting baby-sitters, but the playgroups in church premises and the adven-ture playgrounds are welcomed.* Times (London) 3/20/70, pII [**1942, 1962**]

playlist, *n.* a list of musical recordings broadcast by a radio sta-tion in a given period. *Out of the blue, DJ Gene Baxter and music director Todd Fisher dug up "Red Red Wine"—which had risen to only Number Thirty-four when first issued in 1984—and added it to the station's playlist last June.* Rolling Stone 12/88, p20 [**1975**]

playmaking, *n.* **1** the action or practice of an offensive player, as in basketball. *In the zone-defense game the team with the sharpshooters will probably win. The playmaking team will suffer. And because playmaking is more exciting than stand-ing around potshotting the basket, the elimination of the zone defense has improved the pro game.* NY Times Magazine 1/25/76, p27 [**1960**] **2** another name for *playwriting.* Chau-vinism aside, the piece is recognizable anywhere as a tour de force *which creates its own form of dramatic life while dis-pensing entirely with plot, character, illusion, and every other element normally used in play-making.* Times (London) 1/26/72, p10 [**1963**]

playpit, *n. British.* a small pit, sometimes filled with sand, for children to play in. *Columbia* [Maryland] *. . . is America's showpiece city of the future. . . This private enterprise venture into community creation is a regular weekend draw . . . The village shopping centres have good stores as well as sculpture and playpits for the children.* Manchester Guardian Weekly 5/8/71, p15 [**1971**]

plea-bargain, *Especially U.S.* —*n.* Often spelled **plea bargain.** an agreement between a prosecutor and a defendant in a crim-inal case, in which the defendant is allowed to plead guilty to a less serious offense in order to avoid going through a long and costly trial on the original, more serious charge. *Encouraging plea-bargains as a means of expediting the criminal process is a mere palliative, and ultimately self-defeating.* NY Times 12/13/76, p35 *Twenty-two of them said that they had pleaded guilty because of a plea-bargain—an offer made through counsel to the effect that if they pleaded guilty, they would re-ceive lesser sentences than if they fought their cases and were convicted.* Times (London) 9/24/77, p13 —*v.i.* to make a plea-bargain. Compare DEAL UP. *Miller plea-bargained with Jawor-ski to get Kleindienst off with a misdemeanor charge.* Time 9/9/74, p14 *The effect of the 1972 decision was to change North Carolina's discretionary into a mandatory death penalty law. There can still be discretion, opponents of the penalty claim, even where the penalty is mandatory under the law. The prosecution can plea-bargain and bring a lesser charge, and the governor can exercise executive clemency.* National Review 5/9/75, p494 [**1968**, for noun; **1973** for verb; a shortening of *plea-bargaining* (1963)] —**plea-bargaining,** *n.: Some eighty per cent of the convictions obtained in New York State are the re-sult of plea-bargaining—pleading guilty to a lesser offense than the original charge in the hope of obtaining leniency.* New Yorker 10/24/77, p66

pleiotypic (,plaiə'tipik), *adj.* characteristic of cellular multiplica-tion or growth. *Important parameters determining rate of growth include membrane transport, protein and RNA synthe-sis, and protein degradation. These characteristics fluctuate in a coordinated way with fluctuations in growth rate; together they are known as the pleiotypic programme.* New Scientist 7/12/73, p64 [**1971**, from *pleio-* more, multiple (from Greek *pleíōn*) + *typic*]

PLO (,pi:,el'ou), abbreviation of *Palestine Liberation Organiza-tion,* a military and political organization representing the Pal-estinian Arabs, founded in 1964 and dedicated to the reunification of pre-1948 Palestine as a secular Arab state. Compare AL FATAH. *It is not malicious or propagandist to offer the view that Israel is not at present helping to expand the* *peace process begun at Camp David. Neither, for that matter, is the PLO, whose charter explicitly calls for the destruction of the State of Israel and whose occasional utterances do little to dilute that unacceptable commitment.* Manchester Guardian Weekly 7/8/79, p10 **[1965]**

PL/1, abbreviation of *Programming Language One*, a very simple computer language for general programming needs. *Although there is a proliferation of languages already—such as Cobol, devised by the United States Department of Defence for commercial work, and I.B.M.'s Fortran (scientific) and PL-1 (general purpose)—they are costly investments and are beginning to look clumsy.* Times (London) 4/26/68, p25 *Contrasted with machine language, the PL/1 program is almost self-explanatory. (PL/1 is an abbreviation for Programming Language One.)* Encyclopedia Science Supplement (Grolier) 1971, p158 **[1965]**

plotter, *n.* a peripheral output component of a computer system for analysis of data. *Another output device is the plotter, which can make plots from computer-generated data.* Encyclopedia Science Supplement (Grolier) 1971, p146 **[1956]**

PLR, *British.* abbreviation of PUBLIC LENDING RIGHT. *I would be opposed to PLR if it infringed on public libraries, but librarians are not expected to work for nothing.* New Statesman 12/19/75, p796 **[1969]**

PLSS (plis), *n.* acronym for *Portable Life-Support System. A backpack portable life-support system (PLSS) provides moonwalking astronauts with oxygen and temperature control for up to four hours of activity outside the spacecraft.* 1970 Compton Yearbook, p567 **[1968]**

plug, *v.t.* **plug into**, to use electronic equipment, especially to listen to something or be in communication with someone. *A third-grade classroom in Minot, North Dakota's third largest city, population 33,477. Five children were plugged into a tape recorder, listening to a story and following it in the books in front of them.* Atlantic 7/70, p88 *The place is completely wired for closed-circuit television, so anybody in any of the rooms can be plugged into what's going on in any other room. We'll also be able to do live telecasts from here over national hookups.* New Yorker 3/14/70, p30 **—n. pull the plug, 1** to remove life-support equipment, such as a respirator, from a person who is permanently comatose, irreversibly brain-damaged, or terminally ill. *He also foresees—perhaps thinking wishfully—that "Community Ethics Boards" will be empowered to "pull the plug" in cases where meaningful life has ended.* NY Times 1/25/76, pC56 *The Euthanasia Society claims 50 to 60 per cent of medical men pull the plug when life chances are nil and the prognosis is negative.* New York Post 5/14/79, p24 **2** Figurative use: *Cowles, pointing out that* Harper's *is, in effect, being kept afloat by the parent Minneapolis Star and Tribune Co., even hinted he might pull the plug in preference to "indefinitely" subsidizing the magazine.* Time 3/22/71, p48 **[1968** for verb; **1966** for noun but earlier figurative sense, in British use in reference to a mechanism for flushing a toilet (1961)]

plug compatible, capable of being connected in auxiliary or peripheral functions to various computers. *The 1970 IBM took in more than $1.1 billion in revenues from peripheral products that were plug compatible with its mainframe units. All other manufacturers of plug compatible equipment combined took in a little more than $100 million on products designed for IBM computers.* Harper's 5/74, p82 **[1974]**

plugola (plə'goulə), *n.* indirect or incidental promotion of a product or person on radio or television. *Aside from two skill-testing parlor games,* Family Feud *and* The $20,000 Pyramid, *all the current shows celebrate the theater of cruelty and the entertainment values of Las Vegas. Masochistic contestants meet fourth-rate Hollywood celebrities in a neon-lit orgy of product plugola group hysteria and psychological mayhem.* Time 2/18/80, p85 **[1972,** originally (1959) meaning an undercover payment for casually mentioning or displaying a product on another sponsor's program, from *plug* to promote or publicize + *-ola,* as in *payola* (1938)]

plumber, *n. U.S.* a person whose job is to investigate and stop leaks of government secrets. *Ford is not averse to that important, although unofficial, branch of government called cronyism. Cronies, if they are well placed and well chosen, can tell even a President what he needs to know, and perform a few tasks without the aid of "plumbers."* Harper's 8/74, p22 **[1972]** ▶The term became current during the Watergate affair. The White House plumbers were assigned in 1971 to investigate security leaks, but soon thereafter turned to various illegal activities which included the Watergate burglary.

plum book, *U.S. Informal.* an official government publication that lists the available government positions which the President may fill by appointment. *While the number of positions in the plum book is about 5,000, the turnover would be only about half that number since many apolitical persons would be retained.* NY Times 11/21/76, pA28 *There are about 350,000 federal civilian employees in and around Washington, but when Mr. Carter arrived in town he could make only 2,200 appointments from what is known as the "Plum Book." This document, which is in fact yellow and entitled Policy and Supporting Positions, presents the Administration with the list of available patronage.* Harper's 6/77, p34 **[1965,** from *plum* a choice position or appointment (OED 1891)]

plume, *n.* short for MANTLE PLUME (often used attributively). *The mechanism that generates hot spots must be sought in the mantle. They may be surface manifestations of "plumes": rising, columnar currents of hot but solid material. The plumes might well up from below the asthenosphere, at a phase-change boundary a few hundred miles inside the mantle.* Scientific American 8/76, p49 **[1971]**

plus, *adv.* in addition; furthermore. *The DMG-12's manually operated gull-wing doors are regarded as safer than conventional ones because they are not jarred open as easily. Plus, says DeLorean, "they add sex appeal."* NY Times Magazine 10/28/79, p45 **[1963]** ▶Sometimes analyzed as a conjunction, *plus* in this use always means "in addition" and usually introduces a clause or sentence rather than connecting two simple nouns.

PMA, abbreviation of *paramethoxyamphetamine,* a potent hallucinogenic drug derived from amphetamine. Compare DPT, PCP. *Other than the hallucinogens presently controlled by the Act though, only two others have found their way to the illicit market in any quantity. These drugs, called PMA and MDA, are derivatives of amphetamine.* New Scientist 12/9/76, p572 **[1967]**

PMS, abbreviation of PREMENSTRUAL SYNDROME. *Dr. Norris of Tufts says that the syndrome may in fact be several diseases. "If progesterone works," he says, "it may be because some cases of P.M.S. are due to progesterone deficiency, and others relate to some abnormality in the hypothalamus-pituitary axis on which progesterone has some effect."* NY Times 3/7/82, p75 **[1969]**

PNdB or **PNdb**, abbreviation of PERCEIVED NOISE DECIBEL (a standard unit for measuring noise, based on the type of sound and its intensity). *Although both the Douglas company and the airlines contend that the new aircraft [jumbo jets] will be within the noise standard of 112 PNdb (Perceived Noise decibels), the authority has maintained that its information shows the craft will be noisier on take-off and landing than the present jets.* NY Times 12/28/66, p66 *For instance the monitored noise limits for jet take-offs which are designed to ensure that the first major built up area does not receive noise above 110 PNdB (perceived noise decibels) by day or 102 PNdB by night, often mean that the aircraft's engine power must be reduced as soon as a safe height is reached . . .* Times (London) 8/28/70, p7 **[1959]**

pneumocystis, *n.* a virulent form of pneumonia caused by a parasitic organism. *Almost 60 percent of the pneumocystis patients died. In some cases, pneumocystis preceded the cancer. The disease center has no statistics on the incidence of pneumocystis in the general population, but said that its occurrence was extremely unusual . . .* NY Times 8/29/81, p9 **[1981,** from

Pneumocystis (carinii), the species of parasitic protozoan causing this disease]

poblacion (ˌpoublɑːsiˈoun), n., pl **-ones** (-ˈounes). a shanty-town or slum in Chile. *During the three turbulent years of Salvador Allende's administration, the poor of the poblaciones never wavered in their support of his government.* Newsweek 10/8/73, p54 [**1971**, earlier, a community, district, or other administrative unit (1926), from Spanish *población* village, settlement]

poblador (ˌpoublaˈdɔr), n., pl. **-dores** (-ˈdɔːres). an inhabitant of a poblacion in Chile. Compare ROTO. *Yes, tracts such as this one do continue to be circulated in Chile. This particular one covers everything—infant mortality, malnutrition, school dropouts, prostitution by young children, and evictions of the pobladores.* Manchester Guardian Weekly (Le Monde section) 8/8/76, p12 [**1966**, from Spanish, villager, settler]

pocket, n. U.S. Football. a small, heavily protected area in the backfield for the passer, usually the quarterback. . . . *Myers seldom runs a roll-out; he is a drop-back "pocket" passer, throws what the pros call a "soft ball"—a pass that reaches the receiver slightly nose up, is therefore easier to catch.* Time 10/18/63, p94 [**1963**]

pocket calculator, another name for MINICALCULATOR. *I also have my own pocket calculator, which goes up to a million dollars and you could leave the housekeeping to me, leaving yourself free to fly around to Washington, Paris, etc.* Punch 3/26/75, p518 *The promise lies in the continuing advance in military technology based on microelectronics, symbolized by the ubiquitous pocket calculator.* Scientific American 10/78, p55 [**1973**]

point, n. U.S. a charge or fee discounted by a lender from a loan, usually one percent of the loan's face amount, by which the effective interest rate is substantially increased. *"Points" are a means by which a lender, operating under a legally fixed ceiling, can get a mortgage interest rate equivalent to other market rates on invested money such as on safe corporate bonds, which now yield better than 6.5 per cent.* NY Times 5/8/68, p17 [**1967**]

point in time, U.S. and Canada. a particular time. Used especially in the phrases: —**at that point in time**, then. *Saying "at that point in time," when you mean "then," requires a lot of time and wears down the audience.* NY Times 8/11/74 (page not known) —**at this point in time**, now. *"At this point in time, dinner is served."* Cartoon legend, New Yorker 6/23/73, p41 [**1973**] ►This phrase became a cliché during the Watergate hearings (1973-74), although evidence of its earlier use in scholarly and literary sources has been cited (see *American Speech*, Spring-Summer 1973, pp 159-60). For example: *Daringly, in section 5* [of "The Bear"], *he takes us back to a point in time three years before Isaac's act of renunciation.* Cleanth Brooks, William Faulkner: The Yoknapatawpha Country, 1963, p269. Also found in similar uses, such as *point of time* (1737).

point man, U.S. and Canada. a representative in dealings with others, especially with others who are considered opponents. *As the head of the 10-member "interest section" in Havana, Mr. Lane will be serving as a direct channel of communications with the Cubans and as the point man for American policy.* NY Times 9/2/77, pA3 [**1972**, extended use of the sense of a soldier in front of a military patrol (1944)]

point-of-sale, adj. of, relating to, or placed in the location where sales are made or recorded in a store, etc. *Abbreviation:* POS *A kit with a slew of point-of-sale material had to be prepared and sent to agents by Aug. 23, and an ad to recruit new agents had to be made and placed.* NY Times 9/21/76, p60 *Electronic cash registers linked to computers—point-of-sale systems, in the jargon—are continuing their move into the main department stores. A £2m commitment to 500 point-of-sale terminals for 12 regional stores was announced yesterday by Lewis's, one of the department store companies.* Times (London) 8/3/77, p17 [**1953**]

pointy-head, n. U.S. Informal (often derogatory). an intellectual; egghead; highbrow. *He shouted some and lied some, but he*

told those people they were being screwed by pointy-heads in Washington and New York—and they clapped hands. NY Times Magazine 3/12/72, p106 [**1972**, back formation from POINTY-HEADED]

pointy-headed, adj. U.S. Informal (often derogatory). intellectual; eggheaded; highbrow. *Groups widely believed to have been at the center of the shifting conspiracy against the common weal have at various times included . . . the pointy-headed bureaucrats, the Establishment, the system, the straights, the New Left nihilists, the Mafia, the oil companies, the media, and the CIA.* Harper's 6/74, p52 *Before Frank Mankiewicz arrived on the scene, the few people talking about NPR* [National Public Radio] *at all were saying the wrong things: "Pointy headed" . . . "elitist" . . . "inaccessible" . . . were some of the comments.* Christian Science Monitor 11/20/79, p816 [**1968**, coined by George C. Wallace, born 1919, former governor of Alabama]

poison pill, U.S. any means of finance used by a company to make it too costly for a hostile company to acquire it through a tender offer. *The tin parachutes, of course, are also a form of a poison pill, which are conditions established by a corporate board to make a takeover prohibitively expensive. Poison pills thus far have had mixed results in courtroom tests of their legality.* NY Times 3/19/87, pD1 [**1987**]

Polavision (ˈpoulaˌviʒən), n. a trademark for motion picture equipment that develops its film in the cartridge automatically after the film is exposed, introduced by the Polaroid Corporation in 1977. See the quotation for details. *The system, christened Polavision, uses three minutes of special Super 8 film sealed in a non-standard cassette which fits only a Polaroid camera. After exposure the cassette is loaded into a Polavision player. A small sachet containing just 12 drops of developer is automatically ruptured and the film is rewound and processed. Ninety seconds later it is ready for projection by the player onto a back projection screen the size of a small TV set.* New Scientist 4/13/78, p88 [**1977**, from Polaroid + vision]

polemological, adj. of or relating to polemology (the study of war). *There is a French Institute of Polemology in Paris and a Polemological Institute at Groningen in the Netherlands.* NY Times 8/26/68, p35 [**1968**, from polemology (1938) + -ical]

polemologist, n. an expert in polemology (the study of war). *Polemologists say two things helped Israel's victory, at the material level, over the Arab armies: they were the Startron* [an aid for improving night vision] *and the American-made 155 cannon.* Manchester Guardian Weekly (Le Monde section) 1/9/77, p11 [**1970**, from polemology (1938) + -ist]

pole position, an advantageous position. *Berlin-based Schering is one of those companies with a US twin of the same name formed by confiscation of its American interests in the war. The German company retained a pole position in hormone research which led to the Pill.* Sunday Times (London) 9/12/71, p50 [**1960**, figurative sense of the racing term for the advantageous position of a contestant on the inside (near the infield) of a track]

police lock, a metal bar that sets against a door and extends diagonally out to the floor. *The first thing I saw was the apartment door. It was closed and the police lock was on. Its bar was in place, braced between the door and the floor. There was no way the woman could have entered the apartment.* New Yorker 3/1/76, p34 [**1972**, perhaps because these locks are recommended by police for their effectiveness]

police procedural, a detective story in which police procedures used to detect crime are of central interest. *Laidlaw is also the first police procedural by Scottish Author William McIlvanney.* Time 6/27/77, p56 [**1967**]

policier (ˌpouliˈsyei), n. a detective story; whodunit. *The film climaxes, as all policiers apparently must, with a car chase, but it is nowhere near as interesting as the successful off-casting of nice Hal Holbrook as a heavy.* Time 2/11/74, p64 [**1969**, short for French roman policier, literally, police novel]

polimetrician, n. a political scientist who specializes in mathematical and statistical methods of study and research. . . .

econometricians, polimetricians, psychometricians, jurimetricians are all rapidly proliferating species of a genus of mathematically minded scholars who are infiltrating the academic world armed with computers and many of the analytical tools of higher mathematics. Encyclopedia Science Supplement (Grolier) 1970, p287 [**1970,** from *poli*tical + -*metrician* one who measures]

Polisario (ˌpouliˈsɑːriːou), n. **1** Also, **Polisario Front.** a guerrilla organization fighting for independence of the former Spanish Sahara (Western Sahara) ceded by Spain to Mauritania and Morocco in 1976 (often used attributively). *France is supporting Mauritania and Morocco against the Polisario in what is in practice a latter-day colonial war between Arabs.* Manchester Guardian Weekly 1/1/78, p1 *Algeria and the Polisario Front, a Saharan nationalist movement, want independence for the area's nomad population. They have armed guerrillas who say they will fight to the death for the area, now occupied by more than 20,000 Moroccan troops.* NY Times 5/16/76, pA15 **2** a member of this organization. *The Moroccan army launched a search-and-destroy campaign against the Polisarios. Apparently in response, Algerian units crossed into the Sahara.* Time 2/9/76, p42 [**1975,** from Spanish (*Frente*) *Polisario,* acronym for (Frente) *Po*pular para la *Li*beración de *Sa*guia el Hamra y *Rio* de Oro (Popular Front for the Liberation of Saguia el Hamra and Rio de Oro, the two zones of Western Sahara]

political animal, a person who is gifted or knowledgeable as a politician. *He* [the Rev. Wilfred Wood] *has the command of language and certainly the understanding. But he lacks the wish of the true political animal to act for effect.* Times (London) 4/20/70, p4 [**1966**] ► The phrase was originally applied by Aristotle to humans in the sense of their being social creatures.

Pollutant Standards Index, U.S. a standard index for measuring the amount of air pollution. *The Pollutant Standards Index will gauge air quality on a scale from 0 to 500. Intervals will be geared to the measured levels of five major pollutants: carbon monoxide, oxidants, particulates, sulfur dioxide and nitrogen dioxide.* NY Times 8/24/76, p31 [**1976**]

pollution tax, a proposed tax on companies or their products that create environmental pollution. *Mr. Miller said that if special financing was needed to help meet the new noise rules, he preferred a so-called "pollution tax" in the form of a tax imposed on planes in inverse proportion to the amount of noise suppression achieved. Revenues would be allocated for further noise-reduction efforts.* NY Times 12/2/76, p51 [**1972**]

pollutive, adj. causing pollution. *The diesel engine has a similar amount of development work behind it and is a naturally less pollutive engine than the spark ignition one.* New Scientist 7/2/70, p12 [**1970**]

poly (ˈpɑliː), n. **1** British, Informal. a polytechnical school. *Those people who feel that polys should be "upgraded to university status" are implicitly and unfairly judging them as second-rate institutions.* New Scientist and Science Journal 5/27/71, p514 *Is the growth in student members to be stopped in universities and slowed down in polys, in spite of bigger age groups, higher proportions reaching A-levels, and more demand for women's places?* Manchester Guardian Weekly 11/2/74, p10 **2** polyester fiber. *Brushed Nylon Gown with matching trim, back placket and elasticized sleeve cuffs. Comfortable 100% brushed nylon with poly trim.* Carroll Reed, Winter Holiday 1979-1980 Catalog, Item B, p20 [**1967** for def. 1, short for *polytechnic, n.* (OEDS 1836); **1974** for def. 2, short for *polyester* (1929)]

polybrominated biphenyl (ˌpɑliːˈbrouməneitid baiˈfenəl), any of a group of highly toxic and persistent chemicals related to the polychlorinated biphenyls, used as a fire retardant and additive in plastics, and regarded as a dangerous contaminant. *Abbreviation:* PBB *600 pounds of a closely related chemical, polybrominated biphenyl, were shipped to a Michigan cattle feed plant in 1973. The contaminated feed nearly wiped out the state's dairy industry.* Maclean's 2/9/76, p55 *The chemical, polybrominated biphenyls, or PBB's, is a close relative of PCB's, an industrial pollutant that has become widespread through the environment and has been shown in heavily ex-*

posed people in Japan and upstate New York to cause liver and thyroid abnormalities, nerve damage, skin lesions, pregnancy problems and, in laboratory animals, cancer and growth retardation. NY Times 8/12/76, p20 [**1976**]

polycentric, adj. characterized by polycentrism. *After the success of Tito's revolt against Moscow* [Palmiri] *Togliatti conceived of "polycentric" Communism. This means adjusting party methods in each country to national traditions and requirements.* NY Times 1/18/65, p34 [**1956**]

polycentrism, n. the existence or establishment of a number of independent political centers within the framework of a single political movement or ideology. *No longer was Moscow the undisputed centre of all Communist thought and policy. Polycentrism, as the new trend was called, corroded the once strictly unified command position and ideological faith.* Britannica Book of the Year 1968, p230 [**1956**]

polycentrist, n. an advocate or supporter of polycentrism. *Many more responsible non-communists were becoming polycentrists, including General de Gaulle.* Times (London) 7/7/66, p7 [**1963**]

polychlorinated biphenyl (ˌpɑliːˈklɔrəˌneitid baiˈfenəl). Also shortened to **polychlorobiphenyl,** n. one of a group of chemicals widely used in industry as electrical insulators and in plastics manufacture, recently detected in wildlife at levels approaching the concentration of DDT and similar insecticides. *Polychlorinated biphenyls, another group of chlorinated hydrocarbons that are industrial pollutants, have become similarly dispersed throughout the global ecosystem.* McGraw-Hill Yearbook of Science and Technology 1971, p320 *Scientists have recently become concerned over contamination of the environment by polychlorinated biphenyls (PCB's), industrial compounds which have much in common with chlorinated pesticides. The PCB's are persistent poisons, they are attracted to fatty tissues of organisms and they are concentrated up the food chain.* Science News 7/25/70, p69 [**1962**]

polydrug, adj. of or relating to the use of many kinds of narcotics. *What most concerns the military are "polydrug abusers," servicemen taking a mixture of drugs that become addictive. Abuse seems to be greater in units outside the United States, and the drugs vary. In Korea, the problem is barbiturates. In Germany, it is heroin, methaqualone and amphetamines. In the United States, it is LSD, cocaine, heroine, and PCP, or phencyclidine, commonly known as "angel dust."* NY Times 7/30/78, pD4 [**1972**]

polyether, n. See the first quotation for the meaning. *A polyether is a thermoplastic material that contains ether-oxygen linkages, —C—O—C—, in the polymer chain.* 1972 Britannica Yearbook of Science and the Future, p216 *All three versions* [of furniture] *are available in either Burma teak, or prime beech and are fitted with specially composed polyether foam cushions.* Times (London) 3/28/68, p9 [**1957**]

polyglass tire or **polyglas tire,** an automobile tire with polyester fiber cord and a double fiberglass ply belt molded around the outside, designed for better traction and longer tread wear. *A new "polyglass" tire of bias-belted construction became widely used on U.S. 1970-season models.* Britannica Book of the Year 1970, p417 [**1968,** from *poly*ester + fiber*glass* or fiber*glas*]

polygraph, v.t. to give a lie-detector test to. *"Polygraph them all. I don't know anything about polygraphs and I don't know how accurate they are," the President said, "but I know they'll scare the hell out of people."* Time 7/29/74, p20 [**1971,** verb use of *polygraph* lie detector (1923)]

poly I:C (ˈpɑliː ˈaiˈsiː), a synthetic chemical compound that stimulates the production of the antivirus protein interferon by its resemblance to the RNA (ribonucleic acid) core of infectious viruses. . . . *several groups reported that poly I:C, a synthetic double-stranded RNA, that induces the production of interferon, an antiviral protein produced by animals, was effective as a protective agent against some viral diseases.* 1971 Britannica Yearbook of Science and the Future, p239 *Perhaps the most exciting prospect is that a recently-recognised compound, known for short as polyI:C, induces the body's own cells to* *create the natural anti-viral agent called interferon . . .* Sunday Times (London) 1/4/70, p8 [**1969,** shortened from the chemical name *poly*inosinic: poly*c*ytidylic acid]

polylogue ('pɒliˌlɔːg), *n.* **1** a conversation involving a number of characters in a play, etc. *Radio writers are sometimes advised to eschew monologue in favour of the less artificial polylogue; Mr Curram's excellence in soliloquy suggests one reason for this recommendation: the majority of actors cannot carry it off as he can.* Times (London) 3/18/72, p8 **2** discussion involving a number of participants. *It is much too soon to speculate what will come of the parleys that began in December 1975. They would be useful even if the "polylogue" among the more than two dozen countries, deemed to be representative of developed and developing countries, merely begins to reveal the priorities among the numerous aims of the participants.* Science 2/20/76, p640 [**1961** for def. 1; **1941, 1961** for def. 2; from *poly-* many + dia*logue*]

polyoma virus, a virus containing DNA and associated with various tumors formed in mammalian animals. *A number of viral agents of cancer in lower animals, such as the polyoma virus in mice, Rous sarcoma virus in chickens, and certain leukemia viruses in mice and hamsters, provide models for the study of related human diseases.* Britannica Book of the Year 1968, p515 [**1958,** from *poly-* many + *-oma* tumor]

polyribosomal, *adj.* of or relating to polyribosomes. *In the unaltered cytoplasm surrounding these areas ribosomes were gathered into polyribosomal aggregates, indicating very active synthesis of protein.* Science Journal 4/70, p36 [**1962**]

polyribosome, *n.* a cluster of ribosomes linked by messenger RNA functioning as a unit in synthesizing proteins. Also called POLYSOME. *The ribosomes on the surface of the endoplasmic reticulum are arranged as polyribosomes with a spiral configuration.* McGraw-Hill Yearbook of Science and Technology 1967, p426 *A cluster of ribosomes translating a given strand of mRNA forms a polyribosome.* New Scientist and Science Journal 6/24/71, p735 [**1962**]

polysome, *n.* another name for POLYRIBOSOME. *What probably happens is that there is a regular cycle of association and dissociation of subunits, so that the 30S and 50S subunits meet upon the mRNA molecule and progress along the message as 70S ribosomes among a whole string of them, called a polysome.* New Scientist and Science Journal 2/25/71, p410 [**1962**]

polyversity, *n.* another name for MULTIVERSITY. *Once an idea supported only by a few, notably Mr. Eric Robinson and Professor Robin Pedley, the development of the comprehensive university of "poly-versity" has been supported this year both by the National Union of Students and the National Union of Teachers.* Times (London) 4/6/70, p2 [**1970,** from *poly-* extensive + uni*versity*]

Pomeranchuk theorem (ˌpɒməˈræntʃək), *Physics.* a theorem which states that in a high energy region a particle and its antiparticle should have approximately the same total cross section when interacting with a target. See POMERON. *The Pomeranchuk theorem is based on the symmetry of matter and antimatter. It says that although the proton-antiproton cross section can at low energies be a little larger than the proton-proton cross section, at high energies the two cross sections should tend to the same value.* Science News 3/17/73, p165 [**1970,** named after Isaak Y. *Pomeranchuk,* 1913-1966, a Soviet theoretical physicist, who postulated it]

pomeron ('pɒməˌrɒn), *n. Physics.* a theoretical "pole" formed in a high energy region where total cross sections of interacting particles have become constants (also used attributively). *For "elastic" two-body scattering, where only momentum and angular momentum are exchanged (the particles remain themselves), the appropriate "Regge pole" is called the "Pomeron" after the Russian physicist Pomeranchuk. The Pomeron differs markedly from all other Regge families. If the Pomeron were simple, then the total cross sections (or interaction rates) for hadron-hadron scattering would remain constant (or decrease) as the energy is increased.* New Scientist 3/27/75, p797 [**1967,** from *Pomer*anchuk theorem + *-on* elementary unit or particle]

Pompe's disease ('pɒmpəz), a metabolic disorder that prevents the normal storage of glycogen in the body. *In Pompe's disease glycogen builds up in the liver, heart and muscle and the average age at death is five to six months.* New Scientist 12/27/73, p890 [**1970,** named after J. C. *Pompe,* a Dutch physician of the 1900's]

Pong, *n.* Often popularly spelled **pong.** a trademark for any of various video games simulating such sports as hockey and tennis. *Clutching a handful of quarters, the college student settled in at a video console. Twiddling a set of dials, he sliced an electronic table-tennis "ball" back and forth across the screen. As the game wore on, he muttered intently: "I'm a prisoner of pong."* Newsweek 12/17/73, p91 *My dream is to be an airline stewardess, but I'm not old enough. In the meantime, I operate a pneumatic tie-wrap gun and make harnesses for electronic pong games.* NY Times Magazine 9/4/77, p9 [**1973**]

pony car, *U.S.* a medium-sized automobile. *NASCAR* [National Association for Stock Car Auto Racing] *is very seriously considering switching from full-size models to so-called "pony" cars, the Dodge Aspens, Chevrolet Novas, Ford Granadas and such, beginning with the 1978 season.* NY Times 10/28/76, p55 [**1976,** originally (1968) applied specifically to certain small, sporty cars modeled after the Ford Motor Company's Mustang, suggesting the name *pony*]

Ponzi scheme, a type of investment fraud in which initial investors are paid off with funds taken from subsequent investors lured by the promise of large profits. *To be successful, a Ponzi scheme relies on a single prime condition: the mobility of money as expressed by the concentration of capital and the dispersal of debt. An individual persuades a great many people to give him a good deal of money. A few are repaid handsomely to inspire confidence; the rest are paid in dribs and drabs to hint of future earnings. As practiced by a bank, it consists of accepting deposits, lending them to qualified borrowers, and then relending the same money to other qualified borrowers, increasing the principal and interest payments while decreasing the amount of real money in the system.* Harper's 2/80, p57 [**1973,** named after Charles *Ponzi,* a swindler who devised such a scheme in 1919-1920 and within six months defrauded investors of more than 10 million dollars]

pooper-scooper, *n. Especially U.S.* a scooplike device for picking up the droppings of a dog, horse, etc. *Though most New Yorkers' initial reaction was that the law is probably unenforceable, retailers reported brisk sales of sanitary devices ranging from 15c disposable cardboard shovels to $11, long-handled pooper scoopers equipped with a flashlight for nocturnal emitters.* Time 8/14/78, p73 [**1972,** *pooper,* from *poop,* U.S. slang (chiefly a children's) term for feces + *-er,* suffix added to rhyme with *scooper* device used to scoop up]

poor-mouth, *v.i., v.t. U.S.* to claim or complain of poverty. [Eugene] *McCarthy's advertising campaign, despite the McCarthy camp's constant poor-mouthing on the subject, wasn't exactly modest . . .* New Yorker 9/21/68, p169 *"I sell a few hides to pay the taxes," he poor-mouthed, suggesting an improbable picture of himself in a dinner jacket leading a tallowy cow down a dusty arroyo to keep the sheriff from foreclosing on his splendid Palo Corona Ranch at Carmel, California.* Atlantic 10/68, p70 [**1967**]

poove, *n. British Slang.* an effeminate male; a male homosexual. *After shaves are for pooves.* Sunday Times (London) 10/10/71, p42 [**1962,** alteration of earlier *poof* (OEDS c1850-60), probably ultimately from French *pouffe* puff]

poovey or **poovy,** *adj. British Slang.* of or like a poove; homosexual. *Ralph fell in love with Carrington and Lytton fell in love with Ralph, so they all joined in a ménage à trois . . . Volume one ended with Lytton severed from his protracted idyll of intellectual and poovey bliss at Cambridge . . .* Punch 2/21/68, p282 *You could not possibly prefer the poovy drips on the moon, or the thick skinheads of Hussite Prague in this production.* Times (London) 7/4/70, p21 [**1967**]

pop[1], *adj.* of or relating to the popular arts and fashions, especially those reflecting the values and mores of the younger generation. *. . . . I just don't believe that many young persons in* *this swinging pop society are left ignorant of the facts of life because of inertia or reticence on the part of our official guardians.* New Scientist 10/29/70, p232 *The attraction was the assembly of American pop groups and singers whose names may not be well known to a wide public, but who have great drawing power in the pop world.* Times (London) 6/29/70, p2 *He believes in little except himself. Unfortunately, that self is mainly composed of pop-culture fragments, miscellaneous emotions and loose social ties.* Time 7/6/70, p74 [**1958**, shortened from *popular,* originally in such terms as *pop music, pop singer, pop song* and later especially in the phrase *pop culture*]

pop² or **Pop,** *n.* short for POP ART. *There were about a hundred and fifty paintings on view in the huge Main Hall, reduced in size and otherwise modified by draperies, and they ranged from Op and Pop to Picasso.* New Yorker 2/24/68, p100 —*adj.* of or characterized by pop art. *The works of pop painter Roy Lichtenstein were among those chosen to represent the United States at the Venice Biennial, one of the world's most prestigious exhibitions.* 1967 Compton Yearbook, p250 [**1962**]

pop³, *v.t.* **1** *Slang.* to swallow (a drug in pill form), especially habitually. *The word from Wall Street is that executives of finance and insurance companies are popping pills these days to tranquilize their nerves as they watch the news for the latest take-over attempts in their industries.* NY Times 8/2/68, p46 . . . [Members of the crew] *described the two hijackers as anti-Vietnam war hippies who signed on in the United States. For the whole of the voyage they were "popping pills and blowing marijuana".* Times (London) 3/17/70, p1 **2** *British.* to fasten with poppers. *The invaders don midi leather skirts popped up the side with three-quarters of the poppers undone . . .* Times (London) 7/21/70, p7 [**1968**, extended sense of *pop* to inject a drug (1935)]

pop art or **Pop art,** an art form that uses everyday objects, especially popular mass-produced articles such as comic strips, soup cans, and posters, as its subject matter and sometimes also as the artistic material or medium itself. Also shortened to POP or POP. *Pop art is thought to be the art of everyday things and banal images—bathroom fixtures, Dick Tracy—but its essential character consists in redoing works of art. Its scope extends from Warhol's rows of Coca-Cola bottles to supplying the "Mona Lisa" with a mustache.* New Yorker 11/8/69, p167 [**1957**]

pop artist, an artist who produces works of pop art. *Discarding all subtleties, the pop artists commented on life today by bombarding us with its most familiar images. Cans of Campbell's soup, neon signs, billboard blowups all combine to reproduce the face of the contemporary United States.* 1969 Compton Yearbook, p53 [**1962**]

popout, *n. Surfing Slang.* a mass-produced, and often poorly made, surfboard. *"A lot of gremmies come out just to impress girls, and all they do is sit on their popouts." "What's a popout?" we asked. "A crummy board," the boy said. "Machine-made. And you can see the fibres going in all different directions in the resin."* New Yorker 6/17/67, p24 [**1963**]

popper, *n.* **1** *British.* a snap fastener or gripper. The traditional term in Britain is *press-stud. It fastens with poppers sewn under the buttons so that you do not have the bother of making tiny buttonholes.* Times (London) 2/18/70, p12 *If your body is a tall one, these body shirts simply don't work, especially if, like the one I tried last week, the only fastening is at the crotch, with poppers. Take one breath, the poppers unpop, the garment slides upwards relentlessly.* Daily Telegraph (London) 5/15/72, p12 **2** *Slang.* an ampule of amyl nitrite, inhaled by drug users for its stimulant effect. *Later Roman tells me that just before the crucial take he gave her a popper—i.e. crushed an amyl nitrite capsule under her nose.* Sunday Times (London) 11/7/71, p43 **3** *Slang.* another name for ISOBUTYL NITRITE. *As a result of aggressive marketing, poppers quickly spread to avant-garde heterosexuals. Marketed under such trade names as Bullet, Crypt and Locker Room, isobutyl nitrite is sold openly in some record stores, boutiques and pornographic bookstores. Poppers sell for $4 to $6 for about half an ounce, enough for up to 15 sniffs.* Time 7/17/78, p16 [**1959** for

def. 1; **1969** for defs. 2 and 3, so called from the popping sound made when it is broken open]

pop-rock, *n.* popular music in the style of rock with a strong beat, repetitive phrasing, electronic instruments, etc. (often used attributively). *The millionaire pop-rock star Mick Jagger, leader of the Rolling Stones . . .* NY Times 11/9/76, p28 [**1966**, from *pop* (short for *popular*) + *rock*] —**pop-rocker,** *n.: Vancouver's pop-rocker Nick Gilder has the look of a Vienna Boys Choir refugee and the sweet high sound of a castrato, so no wonder he's trying to change his image.* Maclean's 11/13/78, p45

popster, *n. U.S. Slang.* a pop artist. . . . *a "Floating Biennale" yacht, anchored in the Grand Canal at the '64 Venice Biennale . . . was raided by the police. They made off with a giant anatomical detail, rendered on canvas by popster Harold Stevenson.* NY Times 10/16/66, pB3 [**1963**]

pop-top, *adj.* having a ring attached to a metal tab in the top, that can be pulled to open the can. *Insert finger, tug and quaff: in those few seconds, the aluminum ring atop a pop-top can of beer or soda fulfills its function and becomes instant junk. Garbage men hate the rings because the sharp edges can cut.* Time 9/21/70, p84 [**1963**]

popularist, *adj.* seeking popular interest or participation; appealing to or involving the general public. *What emerged was a popularist outlook (Hightower called it "human") and the determination to dissolve painting and sculpture into broader aesthetic streams.* New Yorker 10/10/70, p150 *There is no doubt that, after two years of passive and effacingly popularist administration, the President of All the People [Mr. Nixon] tried to become President of Most of the People; a President who saw an opening to the bilious, ulcerated right.* Manchester Guardian Weekly 11/14/70, p3 [**1970**]

population genetics, a branch of genetics dealing with the frequency and distribution of genes, mutants, genotypes, etc., among animal and plant populations. Also called QUANTITATIVE GENETICS. *The study of population genetics has in general become a powerful tool for unraveling human history and prehistory and particularly for solving problems of the origin and dispersal of plants and animals. Each individual study, however, brings out limitations in both the organism being investigated and the approach made to the study. To obtain greater precision in the interpretation of complex events it is therefore desirable to study a number of species.* Scientific American 11/77, p100 [**1949, 1972**] —**population geneticist:** *The book, in fact, represents a useful contribution in an area of enquiry shared by population geneticists, taxonomists and natural historians.* Nature 5/5/72, p55

population inversion. See the first quotation for the meaning. *. . . population inversion . . . is a situation in which enough gas molecules are brought down to a lower energy level to prevent the loss of energy all at once.* Science News 5/30/70, p529 *. . . the thermally excited gas molecules undergo a temporary "population inversion," which is the essential prerequisite for laser action.* Scientific American 7/70, p52 [**1961**]

pop wine, *U.S.* a sweet, fruit-flavored wine. Also called SODA-POP WINE. *The alcoholic tide has been pushed higher by the fast-selling, inexpensive pop wines, which disguise their alcoholic content with sweet fruit flavors.* Time 4/22/74, p76 [**1971**, probably from *pop,* as in *soda pop* carbonated soft drink]

porn or **porno,** *n. Slang.* **1** pornography (also used attributively). *Printed matter is still the most common form of porn, much of it supplied by such relatively new publishing houses as Los Angeles' Oxford Bindery and Manhattan's Olympia.* Time 11/16/70, p92 *Foreigners now provide 60 per cent of the customers in Denmark's porno business and one difficulty is getting the country's sexport through the customs barriers of less liberal countries.* Sunday Times (London) 10/19/69, p24 **2** a pornographic movie. *People who wouldn't ordinarily go to pornos go to porno-spoofs, which always have an adolescent anti-establishment air about them.* New Yorker 11/6/71, p189 **3** a writer of pornography. *The right-wing National Democratic Party derides [Gunther] Grass as a "porno," be-*

cause his works are peppered with four-letter words. Time 9/5/69, p27 [**1962** for def. 1; **1968** for def. 2; **1958** for def. 3]

porn- or **porno-**, variant combining forms meaning "pornographic" or "pornography," freely attached to many words, sometimes to form puns such as *pornfield* and *pornucopia.* The following are some examples of use: **—pornbook,** *n.: the author is content to employ his demonic imagination on an almost routine device for writing a pornbook: the step-by-step story of filming the most elaborate stag flick in history.* Time 8/24/70, p64 **—pornfield,** *n.: Browsers are not noticeably furtive. A young actor cheerfully leafs his way through the pornfield, whistling Mozart.* Times Literary Supplement 2/11/72, p159 **—porno-chic,** *n.: Undoubtedly one of the major trends of the year was not towards the art film, but towards porno-chic.* Times (London) 1/10/76, p5 **—pornoflick,** *n.: An occupational hazard of film criticking is coming to hate movies, to sit grim-faced through laff-riots, yawn during thrillers, peek at a newspaper by the light of a 10-watt aisle bulb during porno-flicks . . .* National Review 11/9/73, p1251 **—pornoland,** *n.: Another nice quiet restaurant, this one in a contradictory location, is the Ceylon India Inn at 148 West 49th, deep in the heart of pornoland.* NY Times 4/9/76, p33 **—porno-violent,** *adj.: "A Clockwork Orange" might be the work of a strict and exacting German professor who set out to make a porno-violent sci-fi comedy.* New Yorker 1/1/72, p50 **—pornshop,** *n.: Their researchers have caused them to travel hundreds of yards, from one Soho pornshop to another and one saloon bar to several more.* Times (London) 2/8/72, p12 [**1963,** abstracted from PORN and PORNO]

pornobiography, *n.* a pornographic biography. *The mildly lascivious may be grateful that he gives the longest plot summary of* Genarvon *I know of, and prints the entire text of* Don Leon, *a not very titillating piece of pornobiography.* Saturday Review 10/17/70, p32 *The Music Lovers—Ken Russell seems to have invented a new genre of pornobiography. In this film, Tchaikovsky is the chief victim of Russell's baroque vulgarity.* New Yorker 12/11/71, p24 [**1970**]

pornography, *n.* a description or portrayal of any activity regarded as obscene. *In recent years the movies and television have developed a pornography of violence far more demoralizing than the pornography of sex, which still seizes the primary attention of the guardians of civic virtue.* Saturday Review 10/19/68, p23 [**1963**]

pornotopia, *n.* an ideal place or setting for the activities envisioned in pornographic literature. *Both kinds of writing tend to regard the world as a pornotopia. Reality is conceived as the scene of exclusively sexual activities and human and social institutions are understood to exist only insofar as they are conducive to further sexual play.* Steven Marcus, The Other Victorians, 1966 (British edition), p194 [**1966,** from porno–graphic + utopia]

porny, *adj. Slang.* pornographic. *Partly because of the visual quality and the use of pastels, you don't get that depressed, crummy feeling that usually settles in with the first shots of porny pictures.* New Yorker 11/6/71, p188 [**1961**]

poromeric (ˌpɔrəˈmerik), *n.* an extremely porous polymeric plastic material, used for shoe uppers instead of leather. *Nevertheless, the poromerics—because they "breathe" and thus simulate the properties of leather—are still the only suitable alternative to natural leather in men's footwear.* New Scientist and Science Journal 4/1/71, p37 **—adj.** made of poromeric; very porous. *The leading entry is Du Pont's leather-like poromeric material, Corfam, introduced in shoe uppers in 1964.* Sunday Times (London) 1/15/67, p53 [**1963,** from porosity + polymer + -ic]

portability, *n. U.S.* the condition of permitting workers to transfer pension contributions and entitlements to another pension fund when they change their place of employment. *But one feature of the proposed Senate legislation rankles business. Both bills provide for "portability"—which allows employees to change jobs and carry accumulated pension benefits with them without having to start from scratch at the new job.* Newsweek 9/24/73, p98 [**1969,** specialized sense of the word

meaning the quality or state of being portable, fitness to be moved from one place to another (OED 1667)]

POS, abbreviation of POINT-OF-SALE. *Point-of-sale (POS) equipment emerged with unexpected strength as a giant in the retail industry. POS systems were basically real-time, data-collection computer terminal systems. They replaced traditional electromechanical cash registers and checkout devices.* Britannica Book of the Year 1977, p208 [**1972**]

posigrade, *adj.* **1** producing thrust in the direction in which the vehicle is moving. *It was also necessary to take into account time delays in the spacecraft and booster for relays, valves, and mechanical equipment to operate, a figure for the last boost of thrust from the engines as they "tail-off" after shutdown, and another figure for the thrust of the small, posigrade rockets that give the spacecraft a gentle separation push away from the booster.* 1965 World Book Year Book, p48 **2** of or from a posi-grade rocket. *Command Pilot Schirra made a number of ground-computed corrective maneuvers. To change his elliptical orbit into a circle that reached up closer to Gemini 7, he made several "posigrade" burns—bursts from his forward thrusting rockets.* Time 12/24/65, p35 [**1961** for def. 1, **1965** for def. 2; from positive + retrograde]

position, *v.t. U.S.* to market (a product or service) by appealing to a particular segment of the market in order to emphasize uniqueness and difference from the competition. *Sports Illustrated positioned itself as a third newsweekly instead of just another sports magazine, and its circulation rose.* NY Times Magazine 1/25/76, p56 *How much slick advertising can a college undertake before compromising the tone of the specific institution and higher education in general? Admissions directors now attend professional workshops in marketing, and they seek Madison Avenue advice on "positioning" their product among rivals.* Harper's 3/78, p27 [**1973**]

position paper, a document which presents the position of a political group, government, trade union, etc., on an important issue. *They got out an eleven-page policy statement, called a "position paper," which after performing the vulgar necessity of attacking President Johnson and the Administration for "laxity" in enforcing the fair (i.e. equal) employment laws, went on to say something on their own account.* Manchester Guardian Weekly 9/9/65, p2 [**1960**]

positive euthanasia, another name for ACTIVE EUTHANASIA. *The situational ethicist, who derives much of his philosophical base from classical utilitarian, or consequential ethics, sees relatively little difference between negative and positive euthanasia, that is, between allowing to die and causing to die.* Scientific American 9/73, p60 [**1972**]

posslq or **POSSLQ** (ˈpɑsəlˌkyuː), *n.* acronym for a *person of the opposite sex sharing living quarters. It is, in any case, a term guaranteed to cool all ardor: if there is a motive and a cue for passion, there is equally a posslq for its deflation.* Vogue 8/81, p90 *The Feds, as usual, screwed it up by creating POSSLQ, . . . which could refer to married couples as well as unmarried or newborn twins, or just about anybody.* National Review 5/25/79, p658 [**1979,** coined by the U.S. Census Bureau]

Possum, *n. British.* a nickname for an electronic device or equipment by means of which a paralyzed person may telephone, type, or operate certain types of machines. *Basically Possum is an electronic aid which enables very severely disabled persons to exercise control over electric and electromechanical equipment.* Sunday Times (London) 6/13/71, p11 [**1961,** from Latin *possum* I am able, used because of its resemblance to the initials of the technical name of this device, *P*atient *O*perated *S*elector *M*echanisms]

postcode, *British.* **—n.** a combination of letters and numbers identifying a postal area in Great Britain, used for accelerating mail deliveries. The corresponding system in the U.S. is called ZIP CODE. . . . *a postman at the letter-coding desk has each envelope put in front of him and types out its postcode on a keyboard at his fingertips.* Sunday Times Magazine (London) 6/20/71, p17 **—v.t.** to provide with a postcode. *On the letters side, 13 offices were equipped with code-sorting machinery, although not all were fully operational. Almost every address in* *the U.K. was expected to be postcoded by early 1973.* Britannica Book of the Year 1973, p558 [**1967** for noun; **1972** for verb]

postconciliar, *adj.* existing or occurring after the Vatican ecumenical council of 1962-1965. *The post-conciliar attitude seems to draw attention above all to the value of personal and social relationships as the expression of the pattern of God's love on earth.* Times (London) 2/24/68, p9 . . . *the doctrinaire course being steered by church authorities in the postconciliar period* [is] *a course which in many issues (birth control, mixed marriages, celibacy, episcopal election, the Dutch church, the creed of Paul VI) has been paid for by serious burdens to individuals and to the church.* NY Times 6/3/71, p39 [**1965**]

posted price, a price for crude petroleum used as a reference for calculating the taxes and royalties paid by oil companies to the oil-producing countries. *Posted prices are not the prices at which the companies sell the oil but are a yardstick against which the revenues and royalties which make up the producer countries' revenue are calculated.* Egyptian Mail 6/2/73, p4 *The central concept was "the posted price," a figure that in principle—though not in fact—represented the price at which crude-oil extracting divisions of the companies sold oil to their refining divisions.* New Yorker 1/20/75, p64 [**1963**]

post-fade, *n.* a mechanism for turning on and off the erasing head of a tape recorder to erase unwanted passages from a recording. *Post-fade on an open reel machine is an answer to the prayer of anyone taping music off-air and seeking to eliminate dull tracks and much of the excruciating disc-jockey chat.* New Scientist 12/23-30/76, p719 [**1976**]

post-modern, *adj.* **1** of or relating to POST-MODERNISM; characterized by a departure from or rejection of twentieth-century modernism in the arts. *"Post-modern". . . denotes a period in which the radical aberrations of modern thought and modern art have at last been shaken off . . . If some outstanding modernist artists can be admired as masters, the post-modern critic argues, they are illuminated craftsmen, like artists of other times, and owe nothing to vanguardist dogmas.* New Yorker 2/20/78, p99 *In his latest book,* The Language of Post-Modern Architecture *(1977),* Jencks [the English architecture critic Charles Jencks] *complains that "any building with funny kinks in it, or sensuous imagery" has come to be labeled Post-Modern, and suggests that the term should be restricted to hybrid, "impure" buildings that are designed around historical memory, local context, metaphor, spatial ambiguity and an intense concern with architectural linguistics.* Time 1/8/79, p52 **2** following or going beyond the modern in ideas, values, technical advances, etc. *Europeans since the Second World War mostly have been content to accept America at the evaluation we ourselves are inclined to set—as the "postmodern" society, model for the world, or social laboratory for mankind . . .* New Yorker 1/24/77, p69 [**1965** for def. 1, **1956** for def. 2; from *post-* coming or developing after + *modern*]

post-modernism, *n.* a movement or style in art, architecture, literature, etc., characterized by a departure from or rejection of twentieth-century modernism (including modern and abstract art, avant-garde writing, functional architecture, etc.) and represented typically by works incorporating a variety of classical or historical styles and techniques. *My ambition has been to write splendidly engaging stories without turning my back on the history of what's happened in our medium and in our culture since the decline of realism at the turn of the century. Some critics have called this postmodernism, and that seems to me a useful term to describe it, so long as it's not a mindless atavism or regression which denies that the first half of the century has happened.* NY Times Book Review 9/24/72, p36 *Postmodernism has no use for vanguards. In fact, the essential connotation of "post-modern" may be "a period without vanguards."* New Yorker 2/20/78, p100 *In architecture, postmodernism meant the reaction against the long-running supremacy of the International Style, which froze architectural form into ice cubes of space, by a growing number of architects including an apostate International stylist, Philip Johnson.* Newsweek 11/19/79, p118 [**1971**, from *post-* coming or developing after + *modernism*, patterned on *post-impressionism* (*c* 1910), etc.] —**post-modernist**, *adj., n.: The controversy over*

modern art was never merely between the artists and their public . . . a generation of artists has arisen which considers itself "post-modernist." NY Times Book Review 12/31/72, p6 *In this war of words,* [Reyner] *Banham accused* [Charles] *Jencks and the post-modernists of not being able to reject modernism totally.* NY Times 12/31/78, p21

postneonatal, *adj.* of, relating to, or occurring during the first year of infancy. *Deaths in the postneonatal period appear to be roughly in step with the increased number of births . . . The authors call for more research into the phenomenon, which caused two deaths a thousand live births in the areas concerned.* Times (London) 5/11/70, p3 [**1958**, from *post-* after + *neonatal* newborn]

post-object art, a form of art that attempts to eliminate or minimize the art object itself by stressing the theories, ideas, or personality of the artist. Also called ANTI-OBJECT ART. *Although there were at least two large exhibitions of post-object art—the "ungainly genres" as they are called—interest in such production may have waned as its sensationalism has given way to difficult searches for quality. The Walker Art Center offered "Projected Images," an exhibition by six artists who use film and video to create light environments.* 1975 World Book Year Book, p529 [**1971**]

post-painterly, *adj.* of or characterized by a style of painting that uses traditional painterly qualities of color, form, and texture in producing nonobjective works, such as hard-edges. *At the Metropolitan, the largest displays are by so-called object-makers—"post-painterly" canvases: that is to say, smooth-surfaced, cool, and tending to blend with their setting.* New Yorker 12/6/69, p184 [**1965**]

post-synch, *v.t., v.i.* to synchronize sound with motion-picture action after a scene or film has been photographed. *Tati always dubs and post-synchs his sound tracks after shooting—every word of the script, and also every buzzer and every clicking high heel on overpolished tiles, which are noises that he often raises above words, following the reality of people's attention and throwing film convention out of the window.* New Yorker 1/27/73, p46 [**1960**, short for *post-synchronize* (1950's)]

pothead, *n. Slang.* a person who habitually smokes marijuana. *. . . the implied assumption that the pothead, through the influence of marijuana alone, stands a 10 per cent chance of being drawn ineluctably on to the "hard" drugs is an example of tendentious reasoning masquerading as hard fact . . .* New Scientist 10/31/68, p267 [**1959**, from *pot* marijuana + HEAD]

pothole, *v.i.* to explore caves as a sport or hobby. *Four potholers were found suffering from exposure yesterday after being missing for more than 12 hours. They were with 10 others potholing on the Pennines at Casterton, near Kirkby Lonsdale, Westmoreland.* Times (London) 10/26/70, p4 [**1959**, verb use of *pothole* a cave entered from the surface; known orally in the early 1950's]

povertician (ˌpɑvərˈtiʃən), *n. U.S. (derogatory use).* a person in the administration of a government antipoverty program, especially one who profits privately from such a program. *Despite some successes, Lyndon Johnson's War on Poverty is too well remembered as one in which benefits often trickled up to the so-called poverticians—the programmers, social workers and suppliers to the needy.* Time 8/29/77, p18 *The Koch administration's distaste for what the Mayor has called "poverty pimps" and what Deputy Mayor Herman Badillo describes as "poverticians" has been a hallmark of its opening days in office.* NY Times 1/24/78, p24 [**1977**, from *poverty* + *-ician*, as in *politician*]

poverty datum line, *British.* another name for POVERTY LEVEL. *Seven companies were paying some employees below the poverty datum line (PDL) which is defined as the lowest possible amount on which a family can live under humanly decent conditions in the short run.* Times (London) 12/15/77, p1 [**1973**]

poverty level, a minimum level of income set as the standard of adequate subsistence, below which a person or family is classified as living in poverty. *It is said that 24.3 million Americans—more than 10 percent of the population—were classified* *as poor in 1974, up from 23 million in 1973 . . . The poverty level is defined as an annual income of $5,038 for a nonfarm family of four.* NY Times 2/2/76, p13 *Widespread complacency in West Germany about unemployment may cause have shaken by the disclosure that at least a million people are living below the poverty level because they or their breadwinners are out of work.* Times (London) 2/2/78, p5 [**1966**] ►The earlier variant *poverty line* (OEDS 1901) continues to be used.

poverty trap, *British.* a condition in which people receiving government benefits cannot increase their income without losing some of those benefits. *The poverty trap (he said) is a scandal; it is becoming virtually impossible for the family below the national wage to improve its position.* Times (London) 1/30/76, p6 [**1972**]

Powellism, *n.* a movement in British politics led by (John) Enoch Powell, born 1913, Conservative Member of Parliament, characterized especially by advocacy of laissez-faire economics and exclusion of black immigrants from Great Britain. *Powellism is a combination of racism, archconservative economics, and a touch of prickly isolationism.* Time 6/29/70, p21 *What the press calls Powellism, as though it were already a rightist political pressure group for discontented small people, as Poujadism was in France in the fifties, is having the immediate effect of filling the mailbags of M.P.s and the newspaper correspondence columns with letters of violent approval or condemnation.* New Yorker 5/11/68, p98 [**1965**]

Powellist, *adj.* another word for POWELLITE. . . . *the Conservatives, refreshed in Opposition from their ideological wellsprings, are likely for a year or two to be more Powellist in economics and more disposed to fasten legislative chains on the unions.* Manchester Guardian Weekly 9/5/68, p12 [**1968**]

Powellite, *n.* a follower or supporter of Enoch Powell; an adherent of Powellism. *He* [Mr. Maudling] *has long been at odds with the extreme free-market views of the Powellites, and now his friends at Westminster and the City are hearing his scornful dismissal of the doctrine of the "high-wage, low-cost economy" that Mr. Heath uses to justify Tory opposition to incomes legislation and all the parliamentary Orders that flow from it.* Times (London) 3/18/68, p8 —*adj.* of or relating to Powellites or Powellism. Also, POWELLIST. . . . *a massive Conservative majority would bring back to Westminster a lot of members who, if not overtly Powellite, would sympathise with the kind of conservatism for which Mr Enoch Powell stands.* Manchester Guardian Weekly 9/27/69, p12 [**1965**]

power, *v.* **1 power down,** to reduce the power consumption (of a spacecraft). *"I would like to make sure that the LM* [lunar module] *is okay before we power down the CSM* [command and service modules]*."* Times (London) 4/18/70, p6 **2 power up,** to increase the power consumption (of a spacecraft). *Because of the cold which had restricted the astronauts' sleep to only two or three hours and caused them considerable discomfort, the lunar module was powered up three hours earlier than planned—nine hours before entry into the earth's atmosphere.* Times (London) 4/18/70, p1 —*adj. U.S. Informal.* **1** involving powerful individuals. *I wasn't there to hear my son's valedictorian address because I was at a power lunch with network executives.* Valerie Harper, on Larry King Live, CNN-TV, 12/3/87 **2** expressive of power; dynamic. *Yellow ties are on their way out . . . with pink and red the new power colors.* Wall Street Journal 1/28/87, p1 [**1965** for noun def. 1; **1970** for noun def. 2; **1986** for adj.]

power base, *U.S.* a foundation of political support for a campaign, a policy, etc. *These progressives are young and ambitious, confident of their ability to build an effective power base in Georgia without the rural white supremacists.* NY Times 5/19/68, p49 . . . *his* [Mr. Faulkner's] *power-base in the Unionist right might have been used to make successful reform where O'Neill was bound to fail.* Sunday Times (London) 11/14/71, p16 [**1959**]

power broker, *U.S.* a person who manipulates power by influencing people in positions of power. *Politicians, on the other hand, know exactly where he stands, and another of the contradictions of* [Senator Henry] *Jackson's candidacy is that it*

disturbs a number of Democratic and Republican power brokers alike. Time 11/22/71, p28 . . . *it is difficult to think of such faculty persons as anything but cynics or fanatics to whom the ends of power justify the means. The means, alas, include the students, black and white, who serve as cannon fodder for the "cause.". . . the power brokers among the faculty will be busy at the same old stands, ready as ever to seduce the innocent.* NY Times 4/17/70, p36 [**1961**]

power game, *Especially British.* any scheme or maneuver to increase one's power over others. *Presentation of a journalists' union card can tighten up slack service in a restaurant in no time at all. While I was there, one other sort of power game was taking place: the elections for a new head of the painters' union. Grants, bursaries and priceless travel awards are in the gift of the person who holds this post and it necessarily carries a fair degree of pull.* Listener 6/8/78, p724 [**1958**]

power-sharing, *n.* a proposed coalition between the Protestant and Catholic factions in the government of Northern Ireland. *Privately, Government officials as well as Catholics and Protestants in Northern Ireland held out scant hope that the Government's plan for resumption of a convention of Catholics and Protestants could achieve a breakthrough on the issue of power-sharing.* NY Times 1/13/76, p1 [**1970**]

power structure, 1 the structure of established groups or institutions that hold power in a country. Compare ESTABLISHMENT (def. 1). *But the Congress cannot be expected to submit passively to the processes of decay, however far advanced these may seem to be. It still represents what in America would be called "the power structure."* Atlantic 2/68, p20 *"You struggle to make it as a person—not a white or a Negro—in the white world, inside the white power structure, and then you go back to the ghetto when you're in a position to do something."* Maclean's 3/68, p39 **2** the ruling circle of any institution. [Sam] *Massell* [candidate for mayor of Atlanta] *countered with charges of anti-semitism and claimed that his opponents were members of a business "power structure" trying to keep control of Atlanta.* Americana Annual 1970, p316 [**1960**]

power tower, a power station which generates electricity with solar energy. The tower, which is surrounded by mirrors, is equipped with a device that absorbs their reflections and converts the solar energy to heat, which produces steam used to drive turbine generators. *Despite a solar research budget that has soared from less than $1 million to $290 million, the cost of making electricity from photovoltaic cells or from a power tower on which a field of mirrors is focused remains out of sight.* NY Times 12/5/76, pC7 [**1972**]

PPB or **PPBS,** abbreviation of *Planning-Programming-Budgeting (System),* a system of planning in business, government, research, etc., in which benefits are measured in relation to final costs and alternative ways of reaching goals are examined to select the least costly method. *The basic idea is Planning, Programming and Budgeting, or PPB. Rand worked on the system for the Defense Department and the initials PPB are firmly lodged in the Rand vocabulary. PPB means that the initial research and analysis is tied firmly and logically to the final budget in terms of benefit received, not just output.* NY Times 4/29/68, p32 *The PPBS, which began in the Defense Department and now is the rule throughout the Government, has these aims, as set forth by President Johnson . . .* New Scientist 7/14/66, p81 [**1966**]

PQ, abbreviation of PARTI QUÉBÉCOIS. *The PQ, whose platform calls for Quebec to break away from the Canadian confederation but to establish a customs union with Canada after independence, took over the government of the province by winning 70 of the 110 seats in the provincial legislature.* 1978 Collier's Encyclopedia Year Book, p466 [**1970**]

P.R. or **p.r.,** *v.t. U.S. Informal.* to influence, persuade, or manipulate by means of public relations. [Joe] *McGinniss expressed doubts that any conceivable advertising campaign could resell the President. "It's a lost cause," the writer said. "They seem to have finally p.r.'d themselves into a corner that they can't p.r.*

themselves out of." Time 7/9/73, p20 [**1966**, from the abbreviation of *public relations*]

practolol ('præktǝ,lɔːl), *n.* a beta-blocking drug used to control irregular heart rhythms. *Formula:* $C_{14}H_{22}N_2O_3$ Compare PROPRANOLOL. *At a conference prompted by concern about adverse reactions to practolol, a useful drug which produces adverse reactions in a small number of patients, Sir Eric said: "Modern medicines have become so powerful that there must be some doubt about the ability of one person to comprehend fully every new production."* Times (London) 4/1/77, p4 [**1969**, from *propoxyace*tanilide (chemical constituent of the drug) + *-olol,* as in *propranolol*]

prasadam (prǝ'sɑːdǝm), *n.* (in Hinduism) food, usually fruit, offered first to God or to a saintly person who thereby confers a blessing and purification upon the person eating it. *There's a big feast of "prasadam"—the Hindu-style veggies which they claim bestow spiritual rewards in the very tasting.* NY Times Magazine 5/1/77, p40 [**1972**, from Sanskrit]

prayer breakfast, *U.S.* a Christian prayer meeting combined with a breakfast. *The prayer-breakfast movement, evangelical in origin, has been taken up enthusiastically by mainline Protestant churches and by Mormons and Christian Scientists. It is nondenominational in emphasis, like the great revivals and crusades.* NY Times Magazine 8/1/76, p9 *Nowadays, no politician in the vicinity of Atlanta at the appropriate time would dream of skipping the Governor's Annual Prayer Breakfast.* New Yorker 2/6/78, p46 [**1966**]

pray-in, *n.* the gathering of a group of people to listen to sermons, improvise prayers, etc., as a form of protest or demonstration, especially in a church, synagogue, or other house of worship. *More than 3,000 Roman Catholics went to Westminster Cathedral yesterday for a "pray-in" called by an ad hoc group of laity, opposed to the Pope's ruling.* Sunday Times (London) 8/18/68, p1 *They relied on persuasion, oral and written, and experimented with such non-violent techniques as preach-ins and pray-ins . . .* New Yorker 5/2/70, p127 [**1963**; see -IN]

preaddict, *n. U.S.* a person who has tried or experimented with a narcotic and is therefore considered a potential addict. *But under American conditions—with heroin, so to speak, widely available except to investigators—research into occasional users would be difficult and its meaning debatable, for many American specialists automatically consign all such users to the ranks of what they call pre-addicts.* New Yorker 10/1/73, p81 [**1967**]

pre-AIDS, *n.* another name for AIDS-RELATED COMPLEX. *Q. What is the so-called pre-AIDS syndrome? A. There are many names for signs and symptoms that have been associated with infection by the AIDS virus: AIDS-related complex, AIDS-related conditions, . . . or pre-AIDS. These symptoms include fatigue, weight loss, swollen lymph nodes and fever.* U.S. News and World Report 8/5/85, p66 [**1983**]

preatmospheric, *adj.* coming or occurring before the formation of the atmosphere. *The shallow craters could be the result of preatmospheric bombardment of the planet* [Venus]. Science News 8/4/73, p72 [**1972**]

prebiotic or **prebiological**, *adj.* before the appearance of living things. *. . . James P. Ferris of the Salk Institute for Biological Studies . . . assumes that the earth's atmosphere in prebiotic times contained methane, nitrogen, and water.* World Book Science Annual 1967, p263 *The interface from prebiological to biological evolution is more likely to be recognized in terms of molecular structural changes rather than morphological remains.* McGraw-Hill Yearbook of Science and Technology 1971, p5 *. . . these two simple chemicals* [formaldehyde and ammonia] *have recently been detected in space; and a reaction between them to yield amino acids is assumed to be an essential step in the chemical evolution that preceded the emergence of life. Ergo: such pre-biotic evolution could have occurred elsewhere in the Galaxy.* New Scientist 12/10/70, p425 [**1958**]

prebiotic soup, another name for PRIMORDIAL SOUP. *There is a big gap between any of the postulated "prebiotic soups" and*

the simplest organism subject to natural selection. To narrow the gap a little, many people have suggested that the first organisms did not use all the current amino acids. New Scientist 12/29/66, p740 [**1966**]

precarcinogen, *n.* a chemical precursor of a cancer-producing substance. *The concept that the chemical to which the animal is exposed is often not the molecular species which induces the tumour has given rise to a new group of terms: precarcinogen, for the parent compound; proximate carcinogen for more carcinogenically active decomposition products; and ultimate carcinogen for the product which reacts with some critical cellular component and thus induces cancer.* New Scientist 8/23/73, p433 [**1973**]

precensorship, *n.* censorship imposed, especially by the government, on secret or classified information prior to its being printed or published by a newspaper, magazine, etc. *The Times knew about the U-2 overflights of Russia before Powers was shot down, and The Times knew of the plans for the Bay of Pigs invasion. Bowing to implicit precensorship and to the argument of "national security," The Times did not publish its knowledge.* NY Times 6/27/71, p14 [**1960**]

preclear, *v.t.* to clear in advance; certify as safe beforehand. *At the present time, FDA* [Food and Drug Administration] *approval is somewhat academic because the agency does not regulate IUDs before they appear on the market, though if legislation giving FDA broad authority to preclear all types of medical devices materializes, the situation may change . . .* Science News 8/8/70, p121 [**1970**]

preconciliar, *adj.* existing or occurring prior to the Vatican ecumenical council of 1962-1965. Compare POSTCONCILIAR. *I am theologically a profound conservative. I could teach with deep relish a course in preconciliar theology. I would like to have lived in the Middle Ages, one of the high points of man's spirit.* New Yorker 4/25/70, p68 *Everyone tends to exaggerate the mutual isolation of pre-conciliar days and to forget what two world wars accomplished in bringing Christians together.* Sunday Times (London) 1/22/67, p10 [**1967**]

pre-emptive, *adj.* launched to prevent the enemy from attacking first; initiated on the basis of evidence that an enemy attack is imminent. *But our offensive ICBM's (the Minutemen) will scarcely avail us if Soviet strategy calls for a Soviet pre-emptive (surprise) attack.* NY Times 7/14/70, p36 *No less ominous than an American or Israeli intervention in Jordan is the threat . . . of a preemptive strike against the missiles installed by the Russians and Egyptians in breach of the military standstill agreement.* Manchester Guardian Weekly 9/26/70, p3 [**1959**]

prefade, *v.t.* to cause (a new fabric or garment) to look faded. *With the rise of George McGovern, the Democrats have donned the love-beads, prefaded denims and purple sunglasses of affluent liberalism.* NY Times Magazine 8/6/72, p9 [**1972**]

pregalactic, *adj.* existing before the formation of a galaxy or galaxies. *If the technique of comparing brightness and color distribution works throughout as well as hoped, it may provide a thread on which to hang details of a theory of galactic evolution from the gassy chaos of the pregalactic universe through ellipticals and spirals to disks.* Science News 11/6/76, p300 [**1976**]

prehormone, *n.* a rudimentary or incipient hormone. *A description of the nature of the skin hormone naturally released by irradiated skin was finally provided in 1936 by Adolf Windaus of the University of Göttingen. He demonstrated that 7-dehydrocholesterol is the natural prehormone that is found in the skin and showed how it becomes calciferol on ultraviolet irradiation.* Scientific American 12/70, p82 [**1970**]

premenstrual syndrome, a group of physical and emotional changes that may precede the onset of menstruation. *Abbreviation:* PMS *Megadoses of B-6, a vitamin that is water-soluble and therefore promoted as "safe at any dose," are used by so-called orthomolecular psychiatrists to treat schizophrenics. B-6 also has been touted as a cure for premenstrual syndrome.* Washington Post 11/4/83, pD5 [**1983**]

pre-metro, *n.* an underground railway system for streetcars. *Interest continued in light rail systems, ranging from the "pre-metros" of such cities as Bonn and Brussels to revived streetcar (tram) systems and very light systems, such as those at airports.* Britannica Book of the Year 1978, p680 [**1968,** from *pre-* before + *metro* underground railway, subway]

prenuclear, *adj.* **1** before the age of nuclear weapons. *In earlier, prenuclear times, American Presidents responded to such depredations with fleets, Marines and righteous cannon fire— as when Thomas Jefferson dispatched U.S. frigates under Stephen Decatur to clean out the Barbary pirates who menaced American trade in the Mediterranean.* Time 9/21/70, p12 **2** lacking a visible nucleus. *These other organisms have cells with nuclei and specialized organelles or specialized intracellular structures; they are called eukaryotic (truly nucleated), whereas bacteria and blue-green algae are prokaryotic (prenuclear). It would be surprising if the autotrophs on the lowest rungs of the evolutionary ladder were anything but prokaryotic.* Scientific American 5/71, p30 [**1958** for def. 1; **1971** for def. 2]

preon, *n. Nuclear Physics.* any of various hypothetical constituents of a quark or a lepton that determines its particular character. *The rationale for the preon model begins with the observation that every quark and lepton can be identified unambiguously by listing just three of its properties: electric charge, color and generation number. These properties, then, suggest a straightforward way of organizing a set of constituent particles. Three families of preons are needed.* Scientific American 4/83, p63 [**1981,** probably from *prequark* + *-on,* as in *proton, neutron,* etc.]

preppie or **preppy,** *U.S. Informal.* —*n.* a student or graduate of a preparatory school. *No longer believe that Harvard students are all rich preppies tracing their Harvard histories back almost as far as the Saltonstalls . . .* Harper's 10/70, p103 —*adj.* relating to or characteristic of preppies, especially in dress and behavior. *The audiences get preppier and preppier every week.* New Yorker 6/4/79, p6 *In New York, trendy folk are "preppy" in cashmere sweaters draped casually about the shoulders, collegiate style polo shirts, straight cut slacks . . . and soft leather moccasins.* Sunday Times (London) 5/18/80, p35 [**1962** for noun; **1971** for adj.] ▶In most use the term carries a pejorative connotation.

preprocessor, *n.* a computer program for performing preliminary operations on data before further processing. *PM3 is a translator that allows programs to be written in a shorthand, thus saving programming time. Known as a Cobol preprocessor, PM3 takes shorthand statements and converts them to proper Cobol statements that will be accepted by the computer.* New Scientist 11/30/72, p510 [**1967**]

preprogram, *v.t.* to program beforehand for automatic control. *Many behavioral scientists and neuroscientists now believe that much of the brain's activity is preprogramed and that some unknown portion of it is genetically determined.* Science News 11/25/78, p362 [**1958**]

preprohormone, *n.* a large molecule that is the precursor of a prohormone. *Preprohormones seem to exist only at stages before the final protein gets off the production line. And Günter Blobel and his associates believe that its function is as a production directive.* New Scientist 8/4/77, p291 [**1977,** from *pre-* before + PROHORMONE]

preproinsulin, *n.* the preprohormone of proinsulin. *The researchers concluded that insulin is made on the ribosome as part of the much larger preproinsulin. Evidence suggests that the extra amino acid sequence is needed to guide the newly synthesized hormone from the ribosomal surface . . . to the Golgi apparatus in which the hormone is stored as proinsulin.* 1978 World Book Year Book, p221 [**1975,** from *pre-* before + PROINSULIN]

prepsychotic, *n.* a person with a predisposition to psychosis. *LSD has inspired a number of horror statistics, and it is certainly true that there is danger of long-term damage or difficult reentry into society for prepsychotics and teenagers who use the drug casually and without proper supervision.* Norman

E. Zinberg and John A. Robertson, Drugs and the Public, 1972, p49 [**1972,** noun use of the adjective (1950's)]

prequark, *n. Nuclear Physics.* a hypothetical particle from which all quarks and leptons are made. *A fully successful composite model [of quarks] might resolve all the questions left unsettled in the standard model. Such a hypothetical theory would begin by introducing a new set of elementary particles, which I shall refer to generically as prequarks. Ideally there would not be too many of them. Each quark and lepton in the standard model would be accounted for as a combination of prequarks, just as each hadron can be explained as a combination of quarks.* Scientific American 4/83, p62 [**1981**]

prequel ('pri:kwəl), *n.* **1** a sequel dealing with earlier events than those shown or described in the previous work. *It is a pleasure to report that the execution of the "prequel" (the coining of such words should be punishable by a slow and ugly death) to* Butch Cassidy and the Sundance Kid *is as bad as the idea itself.* Maclean's 7/2/79, p58 **2** the work preceding a sequel. *Mr. Baker . . . has produced in "The Good Times" a memoir of such excellence that just like last time, when its prequel, "Growing Up," was published, critics all over the country are going to be . . . sweating blood trying to come up with appropriate superlatives.* NY Times 5/23/89, pC18 [**1973,** from *pre-* + *sequel*]

presence, *n.* troops of one country stationed in another by mutual agreement. *"Liberal" intellectuals and "conservative" politicians both shared the unthinking assumption behind Johnson's words to the AFL/CIO that the American "presence" abroad is by definition always good.* Manchester Guardian Weekly 11/14/70, p18 [**1958,** probably translation of French *présence,* as in *la présence française*]

presenter, *n. British.* a newscaster who introduces or coordinates a television or radio broadcast. The approximate U.S. equivalent is ANCHOR. *American television presenter Barbara Walters hit the headlines when she agreed to switch networks—from NBC to ABC—on the strength of a $5 millions contract.* Manchester Guardian Weekly 1/9/77, p19 [**1966,** from *present* to introduce (the various parts of a broadcast) + *-er*]

preservator, *n. U.S.* a person responsible for the preservation of a park, scenic or historic site, etc. *A Columbia University professor of architectural history will be named the first Preservator of Central Park, according to Edwin L. Weisl Jr., the Parks, Recreation and Cultural Affairs Administrator.* NY Times 9/29/74, p25 [**1974**]

president-for-life, *n.* variant of LIFE PRESIDENT. *As the young [Jean-Claude] Duvalier settled into his role of president-for-life, the battle for the real power in Haiti came to the fore.* Americana Annual 1973, p331 [**1972**]

presidential, *adj.* of or characteristic of a president; considered to have qualities, such as decisiveness and dignity, appropriate of a president. *The President fared better with Cathy Marceau, 23, a Los Angeles computer programmer. "Ford was very presidential," she said. "Carter seemed hesitant. Too many 'wells' and 'uhs'."* Time 10/4/76, p21 [**1963**] —**presidentiality,** *n.:* *Local political satirists and cartoonists . . . were preoccupied with variations on jokes about teeth, stumbling, grits, and calculated Presidentiality.* New Yorker 9/27/76, p60

presoak, *n.* a stain-removing substance put into water to soak laundry before washing. *The difference between a pre-soak and a detergent is mainly a difference in the concentration of active ingredients. However, both products contain essentially the same ingredients—enzymes, phosphates and surfactant, a cleaning agent.* Time 2/16/70, p86 . . . *the annual production of enzyme detergents and presoaks amounts to some two and a half billion pounds, resulting in retail sales of half a billion dollars.* New Yorker 1/16/71, p42 [**1968,** noun use of the verb]

presort, *v.t.* to sort mail before delivery to the Post Office. *Bulk posting and direct mail firms which pre-sort their letters for the Post Office are protesting against the new proposed postal charges . . .* Times (London) 7/25/70, p18 . . . *he would relent and extend the deadline for the mandatory zip-coding of* *mail and mandatory pre-sorting of business mail . . .* NY Times 2/9/66, p59 [**1963**]

press baron, a powerful newspaper publisher. *Two newspapers, Der Kurier in West Berlin and the Hamburg Abendecho, recently ceased publication, and Axel Springer, the German press baron, recently forecast that the day is not far off when German cities as large as half a million will be unable to support more than one newspaper.* Saturday Review 3/11/67, p123 *Is it not remarkable that sterling should be affected far more by the speeches or articles of a press baron than by the announcement of a multi-million pound order gained in America by Rolls-Royce?* Times (London) 5/14/68, p14 [**1958,** paralleling earlier *press lord* (1930)]

press kit, memorandums, sample newspaper articles, or other information handed out in a package to reporters and writers, especially at a press conference. *Mr Sean O Bradaigh, the Provisionals' publicity officer, who dispenses elaborate press kits in neat plastic folders to legions of journalists from Europe and America, says that Yugoslavia comes nearest to their ideal.* Times (London) 2/16/72, p14 [**1963**]

press opportunity, *U.S.* a brief news conference. *A "press opportunity" is on the schedule when the plane sets down in Omaha (whose media reach into Iowa) and now Kennedy is preparing an answer to the inevitable question about Mondale's remark.* New Yorker 2/4/80, p63 [**1980**]

press-show, *v.t.* to show to the press before public presentation; to preview. *"So far I have press-shown 18 films, to the first four of which only one critic turned up. It seems they are only interested in festivals when they are flown south with all expenses paid. The whole thing is an example of English conservatism and French curiosity."* Times (London) 7/16/70, p10 [**1958**]

Prestel, *n.* a service of the British postal system that connects subscribers to a computer by telephone and displays information from it on a television screen. Compare DATEL. *Prestel . . . is now looking increasingly less like a straightforward system that provides information by linking TV sets to a computer, and more like a fully-fledged computerised data network. Prestel's change in emphasis will undoubtedly hasten, at a rate not foreseeable a year ago, the acceptance of the "personal" computer in the home or in the office.* New Scientist 11/9/78, p418 [**1978,** probably blend of *prest*o quick + *t*elephone and *tele*vision]

prêt-à-porter (pretapɔr'tei), *n., adj. French.* ready-to-wear. *If a lady of style has gobs of money, she can still find all the exclusive, just-for-you creations her heart desires, in Paris' high-fashion houses. But the designers these days trend more to mass-market ready-to-wears, known as prêt à porter . . .* Time 8/9/68, p30 *And more ironically still, French prêt-à-porter designers are being invited ever more frequently to design for our famous ready-to-wear . . .* Punch 5/14/69, p715 [**1957**]

pretax, *adj.* another name for BEFORE TAX. *They forecast a sales gain of 8 to 10 per cent but see an almost dramatic improvement in margins as pretax earnings rise 15 to 20 per cent above those of 1967.* NY Times 1/12/68, p38 [**1955**]

pre-teen, *n. Especially U.S.* a person under the age of thirteen; a boy or girl between ten and twelve. *. . . the texts of many popular songs are so obviously coital that one wonders how they get on the radio and are sold openly to pre-teens.* Atlantic 1/67, p77 [**1959,** noun use of the adjective (1952)]

preteen-ager or **preteenager,** *n.* another name for PRE-TEEN. *In her first tournament, as a preteen-ager in Southern California, she [Billie Jean King] was ordered out of a group picture because she was wearing shorts instead of a tennis dress.* Time 3/20/72, p103 *Crime among teenagers—and even preteen-agers—has skyrocketed in recent years.* 1976 Collier's Encyclopedia Year Book, p212 [**1965**]

prewire, *v.t.* **1** to install electrical wiring during construction of a building or room, especially for equipment or services normally installed after completion. *They planned to rehabilitate conventionally the properties and create about 60 apartments . . . The apartments have fireplaces, double-glazed windows, video intercom units and pre-wiring for alarm systems under*

every window. NY Times 1/25/81, p1 **2** Figurative use: *All newborns smile, for instance, even if they are blind, and all babies tightly clutch objects placed in their palms. Both habits have apparently been prewired into the brain as firmly as the optic nerve. Such prewiring, however, resembles less a finished circuit board than a few rudimentary connections.* Newsweek 1/12/81, p71 [**1957** for def. 1; **1971** for def. 2]

Price Commission or (*especially British*) **Prices Commission,** a government commission established to regulate price increases. *Meanwhile, the Price Commission permitted only a few food processors to increase prices, and it urged the food industry to hold its requests for increases to a minimum.* 1973 World Book Year Book, p341 *'We believe it is necessary,' the Prime Minister informed one of his questioners, 'to have this as a feature'—he was referring to the Pay Board and Prices Commission—'certainly for the next three years . . . to show the world that we are going to continue to deal with inflation . . .'* Listener 1/25/73, p105 [**1972**]

primal, *n.* the release of repressed childhood emotions, as by emitting primal screams or through other techniques of PRIMAL THERAPY. *One of the major aims of the therapy is to help a person fully relive an early personality-shaping experience. When this occurs, he is said to have a primal. After a primal the patient often realizes truths about himself and gains new insights which will help him achieve significant personality changes.* Maclean's 2/74, p8 [**1972,** probably shortened from PRIMAL SCREAM]

primal scream or **primal screaming,** a scream or fit of screaming uttered by a patient in PRIMAL THERAPY. *Some of the more volatile schools of analysis (Fritz Perls' gestalt therapy, Alexander Lowen's bioenergetic approach, Janov's primal scream) teach the desirability of giving vent to one's feelings through verbal or physical acts of aggression.* Science News 10/14/72, p254 *. . . the impulse that's lately sent so many people into transcendental meditation and primal screaming and astrology and est and all the other byways of the human-potential movement.* NY Times Magazine 9/25/77, p102 [**1970**]

primal therapy or **primal scream therapy,** a method of psychotherapy developed by the American psychologist Arthur Janov. See the first quotation for details. Also called SCREAM THERAPY. *They are all patients in the pre-intensive stage of primal therapy, a new form of intensive psychotherapy which attempts to rid people of their neuroses by having them relive those early experiences that stunted the healthy development of their personalities.* Maclean's 2/74, p8 *She is an educated, upper-middle-class New York woman of 34 who . . . paid seven psychiatrists and six psychologists more than $75,000 for treatment ranging from Freudian analysis to primal-scream therapy.* NY Times Magazine 12/4/77, p46 [**1972**] —**primal therapist:** *Primal therapists believe that patients can only free themselves of these neuroses by reaching back into their childhood and fully reliving the original traumatic experiences.* Maclean's 2/74, p8

primary care, medical care basic to diagnosis and treatment of an illness or condition of the body, usually the first step in seeking specialized treatment. *The AMA, in turn, called for half of the new M.D.s to go into "primary care" specialties—general practice, internal medicine, pediatrics, and obstetrics-gynecology.* 1975 Britannica Yearbook of Science and the Future, p272 *Primary-care physicians include general practitioners, internists and pediatricians, most of whom do not perform surgery and were not hard hit by new insurance rates on the first of the year.* NY Times 1/21/76, p30 [**1974**]

primary health worker, a formal or official name for a BAREFOOT DOCTOR. *Primary health workers might be described as "first aiders," trained to recognize common symptoms that require simple treatment.* Britannica Book of the Year 1978, p339 [**1978**]

primary production, the first link in an ecological food chain, usually consisting of green plants but in some systems of analyzing the food chain it includes bacteria. *The lower forms of life have now taken over the abundant food supply once consumed by the whales. There are not a lot of different species there, but* what is there is abundant. "The abundance of life at the level of primary production of vegetation is enormous," he [Jacques Cousteau] says. Science News 2/17/73, p103 [**1970**] —**primary producer:** Several species of bacteria use reduced inorganic compounds, such as ammonia, nitrite, and hydrogen sulfide, as energy sources and fix carbon dioxide. These may also be considered primary producers. McGraw-Hill Yearbook of Science and Technology 1978, p144

primary structure, a minimal sculpture. Terms such as "primary structures" and "minimal art" are used rather loosely and interchangeably. In relation to current work, they imply a concern with basic structures and with constructions unelaborated in the traditional sense of sculpture. 1968 Collier's Encyclopedia Year Book, p129 [**1967**]

primary structurist, a minimal sculptor. Compare STRUCTURIST. In his recent works (at the Waddington Galleries) he has moved away from the elemental forms of the Situation period to elementary geometric forms, similar to those used by the Primary Structurists in America. Listener 4/20/67, p528 [**1967**]

prime, n. short for prime rate, the lowest rate of interest charged on bank loans. Said Irwin Kellner, chief economist of Manufacturers Hanover Trust: "the decline in the prime is a hope, rather than an actuality." Lawrence Kudlow, chief economist of the Bear, Stearns investment banking firm, still believes that the prime interest rate will rise to 25% by February. Time 1/5/81, p77 [**1973**]

prime time, the period of television broadcasting that attracts the largest number of viewers. Prime time in the United States is usually considered as from 7 to 11 p.m. The number of minutes that can be used for commercial messages on television is limited in industry practice to six per hour during "prime time"—which is the four hours of evening programming when most of the potential television audience has its sets on—and up to twelve per hour at other times. New Yorker 3/3/73, p60 [**1961**]

primordial soup or **primordial broth,** the mixture of chemicals which gave rise to life on earth. Also called PREBIOTIC SOUP; PROTOBIOTIC SOUP. Polymers of amino acids forming primitive proteins are formed much more readily in those dramatic laboratory reconstructions of the primordial "soup" than are crude nucleic acids constructed from nucleotides. New Scientist 1/23/69, p174 Threadlike filament of organic matter resembling decomposed plant tissue is another kind of fossil that appears in electron micrographs of the Fig Tree cherts. Some specimens are nine microns long. Not identifiable with any known organism, the filaments might conceivably be polymerized abiotic molecules from the "primordial broth." Scientific American 5/71, p32 [**1969**]

Princeton Plan, U.S. a plan to give college students a recess (usually of two weeks) in an election year so that they may work for the election of candidates of their choice. An idea widely heralded on college campuses emerged in 1970 from the student uprisings that followed the American invasion of Cambodia. Instead of seeking change through violent rebellion, why should not students work within the electoral system for reform? This was the basis for the so-called Princeton Plan . . . The plan was copied at many schools. NY Times 2/6/72, pD9 [**1970**] ►During the 1960's the term Princeton Plan was the name of a plan to achieve racial balance in public schools by pairing a school of predominantly white students with one of black students so that all students in certain grades attend the same school. Both Princeton Plans originated at Princeton University.

print journalism, Especially U.S. the gathering of news or the writing for newspapers and magazines, as distinguished from newsgathering and reporting for television and radio. Federal statute and administrative rulings impose restrictions on broadcasting that do not exist for print journalism. Time 2/4/74, p59 "Media" suggests that there is no difference in purpose and function between print journalism and television journalism; that within print journalism there is no difference in function and purpose between Time and the New York Times. Atlantic 1/75, p29 [**1972**] —**print journalist:** Earlier this

week, we of the Broadcasting Press Guild held a lunch to hand out scrolls to the winners of our 1974 television awards. I should explain that the Guild is composed of print journalists who write about broadcasting. Listener 4/10/75, p466

print press or **printed press,** Especially U.S. the editors and journalists of newspapers and magazines, or newspapers and magazines themselves, as distinguished from radio and television. Although the print press was in there plugging, the week clearly belonged to television. Newsweek 2/26/73, p55 Nixon, who by then had developed equivocal feelings, to say the least, about the printed press, could still manage a kind word on behalf of the electronic media. New Yorker 3/17/75, p41 [**1973**]

prion, n. a protein particle about 100 times smaller than a normal virus, first isolated from the brain of sheep infected with scrapie, and thought to be the cause of scrapie and other degenerative diseases of the nervous system. However, the most highly purified sample of protein is not itself infectious. They call the evasive infectious agent a prion. Science News 5/4/85, p279 [**1985,** coined by Stanley Prusiner, U.S. neurologist, from proteinaceous infectious particle, with the o and i transposed]

prioritize, v.t. **1** to arrange in order of importance; establish priorities for. I do have a special interest, based on what I hope is a creative self-perception. It is to upgrade my potential. When I prioritize my goal/objectives, that comes first. NY Times Magazine 1/16/77, p29 **2** to give preference or priority to. New York's financial problems don't come from "bloated" social services. This crisis was caused by a system that prioritizes money for the Pentagon and the banks' debt service over our needs. NY Times 10/8/77, p23 The thousand-odd delegates to the . . . conference sat dutifully in the Winter Gardens from 9 am until midnight adding composite resolutions, referring back amendments, and "prioritizing" motions as only they know how. Times (London) 4/8/78, p3 —v.i. to establish priorities. Next, you need to sift the essentials from the nonessentials. You need to establish priorities—or, as Mrs. Habeeb says, the second step is to Prioritize. In other words, just who are you and what are you? Are you a Perfectionist, a Compulsive Doer, a Lick-and-a-Promise Type, or an Out-and-Out Slob? New Yorker 10/16/78, p35 [**1972**] ►In the first quotation above, prioritize is used in a context intended to parody the jargon of social scientists. Though this and other words in -ize (e.g. finalize, widely used since the 1940's but established in Australian English since the 1920's) have had difficulty finding initial acceptance among conservative users of the language, derivatives using -ize and borrowings ending in -ize have long been a part of English. Some examples: sympathize (1591), Christianize (1593), philosophize (1594), idolize (1598), satirize (1610), monopolize (1611), realize (1611), legalize (a1716), eulogize (a1810), radicalize (1823).

prior restraint, U.S. a court order prohibiting publication of material or disclosure of proceedings deemed by the court to interfere with due process, threaten national security, and the like. Judges concerned that their trials remain valid began to issue gag orders and prior restraints on the press. They have done so 45 times since the Sheppard case, and 12 times in the past year. NY Times Magazine 3/21/76, p18 If prior restraint (prevention of publication) has a chilling effect on free speech, then obligatory disclosure of notes (enforcement of publication) has a chilling effect on free thought. New Yorker 8/14/78, p23 [**1972,** so called from its being imposed before the actual appearance of the material in print]

prisoner of conscience, a political prisoner. A great many prisoners of conscience, it claims, are sent with or without trial "to the so-called special psychiatric hospitals, where they are given forcible treatment for their supposed mental ailments". Times (London) 4/20/70, p6 [**1961**]

privatistic, adj. **1** given to or fond of privacy; seclusive. At Harvard he [Banfield] is known for his privatistic ways. Though he lunches regularly at the faculty club, he scrupulously avoids faculty committees and politics. Atlantic 9/70, p55 **2** favoring or based upon the use of private enterprise, as distinguished from collectivism. I cannot say in blanket fashion whether this Mao Myth is "good or bad." For the ordinary Chinese it seems to give meaning to things . . . The "privatistic" alternative, *anyway, in a country with per capita income perhaps one twentieth of America's, is not a glittering one.* Atlantic 11/71, p119 [**1968** for def. 1; **1972** for def. 2]

proabortion, *adj.* favoring or permitting induced abortions, especially abortion-on-demand. *"I got into the abortion issue when I started teaching criminal law in 1963." Professor* [Robert] *Bryn said recently. "I decided to study it because at first everything I came across seemed to be proabortion. So, I found some other people who were also disturbed . . . and we sort of formed our own group, Metropolitan Right to Life."* NY Times Magazine 8/20/72, p34 [**1972**, from *pro-* favoring + *abortion*] **—proabortionism,** *n.: My impression is that it is the upper middle class . . . who are the social "headquarters" of proabortionism, as of liberal attitudes in general, in this country.* National Review 1/23/76, p28 **—proabortionist,** *n.: The anti-abortionists came across as narrow and vengeful, their arguments a primitive reaction against what threatened their sexual hang-ups . . . The proabortionists came across as equally fanatical upholders of women's right to abortion.* Listener 4/26/73, p537

proactive, *adj.* active in advance; anticipating trends and working to promote their development. *A senior Administration official asserted last week that Mr. Reagan's bid . . . was a byproduct of strictly domestic political concerns. "What else is new?", he asked. "This Administration is pro-active on domestic issues. We really know how to set the domestic agenda. But we're strictly reactive when it comes to foreign policy."* NY Times 6/24/84, pD1 [**1971**, from *pro-* forward + *active*, patterned after *reactive*] ►This usage is independent of *proactive* as a term in psychology, used since the 1930's in the sense of "characterized by the dominance of first-learned material over that learned subsequently," as in *proactive inhibition of learning.*

problematics, *n.pl.* a complex of problems and uncertain conditions. *Mr. Schrag is, admirably, for pluralism, and he suggests at the end that the way out of our present predicament is to* institutionalize *(his word) pluralism in all possible ways. The assertion itself and some of the examples he then offers (decentralizing schools, police forces, health services) show that he has devoted little thought to the inherent problematics of institutionalization.* NY Times Book Review 3/5/72, p40 [**1957**, from *problematic, adj.* (OED 1609)]

problematique (prɔbləma'tiːk), *n.* the complex of interrelated problems, especially of pollution, urban decay, shortage of resources, inflation, etc., affecting technologically advanced and industrial countries. *MIT nuclear engineering professor David J. Rose proposes one partial solution: the establishment of new, interdisciplinary institutions dedicated to* problematique, *the current European term for such issues as energy, environmental quality, transportation and public health.* Science News 8/10/74, p92 *Peter Roberts . . . says that the Meadows' team model that provided the basis for* The Limits to Growth *and the earlier model developed by Professor Jay Forrester "suffered from such substantial shortcomings that they cannot be considered useful tools for enhancing understanding of the 'problematique'."* New Scientist 10/6/77, p7 [**1972**, from French, from the adjective *problematique* problematic; originally a usage of the CLUB OF ROME]

problem bank, *U.S.* a bank listed by a government regulatory agency as having financial problems. *Combining bank supervision in one agency was an idea that developed from the well-publicized "problem bank" situation. Many institutions had gotten into difficulty during the recession from bad loans, particularly those involving real estate.* Americana Annual 1977, p114 [**1976**]

procaryote (prou'kæri:ˌout), *n.* a cell without a visible nucleus. Also spelled PROKARYOTE. *Procaryotes were found in the Beck Spring Dolomite in association with the primitive eucaryotes . . . A mat of threadlike procaryotic blue-green algae, each thread of which is about 3.5 microns in diameter . . . Cells of this kind, among others, presumably produced photosynthetic oxygen before eucaryotes appeared.* Scientific American 9/70,

p112 [**1969**, from *pro-* before + *caryote* cell nucleus (from Greek *káryon* nut, kernel)]

procaryotic (prouˌkæri:'ɑtik), *adj.* not having a visible nucleus. Also spelled PROKARYOTIC. *Procaryotic cells, which lack a nucleus and divide by simple fission, were a more primitive form of life than the eucaryotes and persist today in the bacteria and blue-green algae.* Scientific American 9/70, p112 *Cells that contain a membrane-bound nucleus are termed eucaryotic (plants and animals), while those without nuclei are known as procaryotic (bacteria and blue-green algae).* New Scientist and Science Journal 8/5/71, p313 [**1968**]

process art, another name for CONCEPTUAL ART. *Some U.S. museums also began to document the avant-garde "process" or "concept" art, which involved only ideas and their realization in a situation, or series of events, that did not always produce objects or traditional works of art.* 1970 Compton Yearbook, p359 *Process art is primarily concerned with acts and effects. Richard Serra, for example, has dripped hot lead along wall intersections and leaned objects against each other in precarious positions. Bill Bollinger has spread floors with graphite and a sawdust-like compound to be disturbed by the viewer's feet and has stretched rope between various points in a room.* 1970 Collier's Encyclopedia Year Book, p117 [**1968**]

processor, *n.* an artist who creates works of process art. *Such earthworkers, anti-formers, processors, and conceptualists as Morris, Carl Andre, Walter de Maria, Robert Smithson, Bruce Nauman, Richard Serra, Eva Hesse, Barry Flanagan, Keither Sonnier, Dennis Oppenheim, and Lawrence Weiner have been enjoying increasing prestige.* New Yorker 1/24/70, p62 [**1970**]

pro-choice, *adj.* supporting the right to choose abortion. *People who believe abortion should be legal and available call themselves* pro-choice. *They like this phrase because it means they do not believe in telling anyone she should have an abortion, but that everyone should have the choice to have one if necessary. Thus, they believe in reproductive freedom. This includes access to birth control.* Daily News (New York) 6/12/80, p79 [**1978**, coined to distinguish from PROABORTION and to contrast with PRO-LIFE] **—pro-choicer,** *n.: This polarization cannot do any good. All sides of inflammatory issues of this campaign—pro-lifers and pro-choicers, proponents and opponents of the nuclear freeze, school-prayer advocates and adversaries—should heed the words of Oliver Cromwell, himself no great moderate in religious controversy; "I beseech you in the bowels of Christ, think it possible you may be mistaken."* Newsweek 10/21/84, p6

product liability, *U.S.* responsibility of manufacturers for any damage, loss, or injury caused by their products. *Abbreviation:* PL *"The whole area of product liability is getting expensive and litigious," says Dr. Alan R. Hinman, director of the Center for Disease Control's immunization division, "and the companies are self-insuring—for several million dollars' worth, even, of claims . . ."* NY Times Magazine 5/7/78, p154 [**1972**]

proette (prou'et), *n.* a female professional in sports, especially golf. *For obvious reasons, the LPGA* [Ladies Professional Golf Association] *objects to its members being called "pro" golfers, and is trying to popularize the description "proettes" . . .* Maclean's 9/68, p39 *And while no proette has ever topped $50,000 for a season, Jack Nicklaus for one has picked up that much in a single tournament.* Time 6/28/71, p41 [**1968**, from *pro* a professional + *-ette* (feminine suffix)]

pro-European, *adj.* **1** supporting or advocating the social, cultural, or economic unification of western European countries. *Maurice Schumann, 58, Minister of Foreign Affairs, combines impeccable Gaullist credentials with a pro-European outlook.* Time 7/4/69, p23 **2** favoring Great Britain's entry into the European Common Market. *The well-known differences of attitude between members of the Government over Britain's application to join the Common Market received yet another airing at the weekend with a strongly pro-European speech from Mr Roy Hattersley, the Minister of Defence for Administration.* Manchester Guardian Weekly 4/4/70, p8 **—n.** one who is pro-European. *Even Mr. Heath, the dedicated pro-European, did not often introduce the great controversial sub-*

ject of Britain's approach to membership in the European Economic Community . . . New Yorker 7/4/70, p61 [**1962**]

pro-family, *adj. U.S.* favoring large families instead of the use of abortion or other methods to curtail them; PRO-LIFE. *Many of the pro-family supporters are religious fundamentalists whose views derive from a literal reading of the Bible. Others are not so dogmatic, yet they are honestly concerned that . . . if more women continue to join the work force, if more day care centers are set up for their children, then what happens to a family structure already weakened by the pressures of American life?* Time 12/5/77, p22 *It is possible that pressure from the Republican right could force the White House to undertake a major effort to push across "pro-family" legislation on abortion and prayer in the schools . . .* NY Times Magazine 8/16/81, p30 [**1977**]

prog[1], *n. British Slang.* **1** a progressive; a person who favors progress or reform. *'Chaps like us,' observes Frank's PR cousin Adam, 'who don't believe in change, do far more for the Church than a thousand bloody progs like Pope John.'* Listener 8/29/68, p280 *The "progs" or progressives believe Tewkesbury lives too much in the past . . .* NY Times 6/1/65, p33 **2** a member of a progressive group, especially one in a political party. *By European standards the "progs," as they are known, are a moderate party which might feel most at home in the British Liberal Party, or perhaps among the west German Free Democrats.* Times (London) 3/26/70, p6 [**1965**, from earlier attributive use (1958); by shortening of *progressive*]

prog[2], *n. British, Informal.* program. *A new series of BBC-2 commences at 8 pm: . . . In tonight's prog, Anthony Smith has a look at the world's newest national park, created two years ago on the eastern border of Bavaria in West Germany.* New Scientist 6/15/72, p644 [**1972**, by shortening of *programme*]

prograde, *adj.* moving in the same direction of rotation as the celestial body being orbited. See COROTATE. *All known prograde satellites (those going the same way as the majority of rotary motions in the solar system), except Phobos, . . . are gradually increasing their distance from their planets. Retrograde satellites have the opposite condition. They come closer and ultimately crash into the planet. Thus retrograde satellites gradually disappear.* Science News 3/24/73, p180 [**1968**, from *pro-* forward + *retrograde*]

program or (*British*) **programme,** *v.t.* to cause to follow a planned sequence of steps or operations; to direct, control, or channel in accordance with a plan, schedule, or code. *To what extent can astronauts, environmentally besuited, rigidly programmed, and electronically guided to their destination, be said to resemble the courageous explorers of the past—Marco Polo, Magellan, or Amundsen, say—who travelled, in all things, hopefully?* New Scientist 12/19/68, p653 *There could hardly be a more convincing demonstration of the existence of an internal clock operating independently of the environmental conditions. Quite evidently an annual cycle of feeding and fasting is also programmed in the animal.* Scientific American 4/71, p75 *This thing is so instinctively, plus manipulatively, engineered to leave 'em crying that it could hardly fail commercially even if the actors were programmed . . . to make obscene gestures at the audience at ten-second intervals.* New Yorker 12/26/70, p53 —*v.i.* to follow a prearranged plan, schedule, scheme, etc. *Also, it is broadly hinted by the casework staff* [in the inmate "programs," *that if the inmate "programs," the U.S. Board of Parole will look more favorably at his case.* Atlantic 5/71, p34 [**1963** for verb transitive; **1957** for verb intransitive] ►While *program* is the preferred spelling of the uninflected verb form, the inflected uses usually conform to what was once considered British spelling by doubling the final consonant (*m*).

programmable, *adj.* capable of being programmed. . . . *at the moment, a highly simplified programmable logic system is more economic than stored programme control.* New Scientist 7/16/70, p20 *The mathematician's abstract world does not contain such realities—which leads mathematicians, such as Minsky, dogmatically to assert that everything which cannot be programmed cannot exist (and the corollary that everything*

that does exist must be programmable). New Scientist and Science Journal 9/2/71, p528 [**1959**]

programmetry, *n.* See the quotation for the meaning. *There are measurements as to errors found per shift of operators and per programmer, the size of files, and the use of other parts of the configuration. Yet perhaps the most exciting is in the area known as programmetry—the measurement of program performance.* Science Journal 10/70, p98 [**1970**]

programming language, another name for COMPUTER LANGUAGE. *The next development was to devise "programming languages", in which programmers could represent their directives to the computer in a form convenient for scientific or commercial work. A program in such a language is processed by another program called a "compiler", which translates it to the instruction code of the specific machine for execution.* New Scientist 4/28/66, p226 [**1959**]

program trading, the trading of stocks in a stock market by computer programs set at various levels to buy and sell. . . . *program trading is adding a new unpredictable element of volatility to an already uncertain stock market, and unsuspecting investors may be buying or selling shares at just the wrong time . . .* Arizona Republic 9/9/85, pC1 [**1985**]

progressive country, *U.S.* a form of country music that stresses social themes in the lyrics and innovative techniques in instrumentation. Also called OUTLAW COUNTRY. *The "progressive country" artists include such Nashville rebels as Waylon Jennings, Willie Nelson, songwriter Billy Joe Shaver, Tompall Glaser, and Bobby Bare. These artists share a dislike for the more facile sentimentality of mainstream country music, as well as for its tried-and-true chord changes, instrumental setups, and formulaic production.* 1975 Collier's Encyclopedia Year Book, p364 [**1974**]

progressive lens, a bifocal or multifocal lens with no outwardly visible lines and with a gradual change of focus that provides clear vision at all distances. *American Optical Corp., the largest American maker of lenses, recently introduced Ultravue, a progressive lens made of plastic.* Consumer Reports 11/77, p649 [**1976**]

progressive rock, a technically elaborate and often experimental form of rock music. Also called HEAVY ROCK. *Two progressive-rock bands—one led by former Door* [Doors, a rock group] *Ray Manzarek and another, a German specimen called Passport—share the stage . . .* New Yorker 3/24/75, p6 [**1968**] —**progressive rocker:** *Concerts grew even bigger and more depersonalized . . . It was, in the words of Robert Fripp, one of the most interesting of the British progressive rockers turned reductionist, a time for "dinosaurs."* NY Times 8/13/79, pC16

progressive soul, *U.S.* a form of soul music incorporating elements of jazz and disco music. *Rufus, the progressive soul band that features Chaka Khan as vocalist, faced high expectations at the Felt Forum on Saturday night.* NY Times 4/12/76, p37 [**1974**]

prohormone, *n.* a chemical substance that is the inactive precursor of a hormone. *The natural* [parathyroid] *hormone is initially produced as a prohormone, which is a linear chain of 106 amino acids. The prohormone is rapidly converted into its storage, or glandular, form, which is a chain of only 84 amino acids.* World Book Science Annual 1974, p263 [**1935, 1970**, from *pro-* anterior, before + *hormone*]

proinsulin, *n.* the prohormone of insulin. *It turned out that proinsulin (the inactive precursor of insulin) had a fairly low affinity for the receptor.* New Scientist and Science Journal 9/23/71, p669 *Proinsulin consists of a single polypeptide chain containing the A and B chains and the C peptide, all linked covalently.* Science 5/5/72, p482 [**1916, 1967**, from *pro-* anterior, before + *insulin*]

prokaryote, *n.* another spelling of PROCARYOTE. *Bacteria and blue-green algae are known as prokaryotes, meaning they lack the membrane-limiting nucleus possessed by nucleate organisms, or eukaryotes. (Karyon is Greek for nucleus.)* Scientific American 11/70, p24 [**1963**]

prokaryotic, *adj.* another spelling of PROCARYOTIC. *The bacteria and their close relatives the blue-green algae comprise the so-called prokaryotic group; they are all micro-organisms. The second group, the eukaryotes, includes all other types of cell, whether animal, plant, protozoal or fungal.* New Scientist 9/24/70, p624 *Only the prokaryotic blue-green algae can employ chlorophyll that is not packaged into the layered plastids of the green leaf; some bacteria, also prokaryotes, photosynthesize even without the green stuff.* Scientific American 5/71, p128 [**1968**]

pro-life, *adj.* opposed to legalized abortion, especially in advocating or supporting antiabortion laws; RIGHT-TO-LIFE. See ABORTION. *Catholics do constitute the backbone of the pro-life movement, and the action performed in defense of the sanctity of life . . . reflect a new militancy whose object will eventually be to correct other of recent years' mistaken developments besides the legalization of abortion.* NY Times 1/29/78, pD16 [**1972**, from *pro-* in favor of + *life*] **—pro-lifer**, *n.: Besides the big corporations and the unions, virtually every interest group has a representative in Washington, from the Grey Panthers, the senior citizens' campaign, to the "pro-lifers," who oppose abortion.* Manchester Guardian Weekly 9/3/78, p5 ►Like *right-to-life*, the term *pro-life* is used and promoted chiefly by antiabortionists, since it implies that those who favor unrestricted abortions are against "life."

promo, *U.S. Informal.* **—n.** an advertisement, promotional announcement, or other presentation. *The misadventures of Roger and his gifted cat are not as "marvelously funny" as the promos for the book explain on the jacket.* NY Times Book Review 4/16/72, p8 **—adj.** used for promoting some person or thing; promotional. *The boss controls the newspaper and assorted promo material, which is likely to feature pictures of himself peering knowingly into a mine face or welding machine.* Atlantic 7/73, p62 [**1962** for noun, short for *promotion* publicity and advertising; **1970** for adj.]

promoter, *n.* a functional genetic element in the Jacob-Monod model of the operon. . . . *a gene consists of 3 elements, together called an operon. The elements are a "promoter" that produces the repressor; an "operator" that starts the gene operating but is normally dampened by the repressor; and a "structural" portion, which is placed into action by the operator and does the main work of the gene.* Encyclopedia Science Supplement (Grolier) 1970, p108 *The promoter and operator sites are adjacent parts of the same DNA duplex. The promoter is the site to which the transcribing enzyme (RNA polymerase) binds in order to start transcription, and the operator is the site to which the specific repressor protein binds to stop gene expression (possibly by preventing transcription).* McGraw-Hill Yearbook of Science and Technology 1971, p213 [**1967**]

pronase ('prou,neis), *n.* an enzyme that breaks down proteins into simple compounds, derived from a species of soil bacteria and used in biomedical research. *Previously, Beatrice Mintz and Carl Illmensee of the Cancer Institute in Philadelphia had used a particular enzyme called pronase to remove the zona pellucida (protective covering) surrounding embryos. After the coverings were removed, the embryonic cells were sticky, and two embryos could be pushed together to form a single embryo.* Science News 10/22/77, p263 [**1960**, probably from *protei*nase enzyme that breaks down proteins to peptides]

pronatalism, *n.* support or advocacy of childbearing and, generally, an expanding rate of birth. *"Pronatalism" as editors Ellen Peck (author of "The Baby Trap") and Judith Senderowitz (a vice president of Zero Population Growth) explain is "any attitude or policy that is 'pro birth,' that encourages reproduction, that exalts the role of parenthood."* NY Times Book Review 2/23/75, p36 [**1972**, from earlier (1950's) *pronatalist, adj.*, from *pro-* favoring + *natal*ity birth rate + *-ist*]

pronethalol (prou'neθə,lɔːl), *n.* a beta-blocking drug that controls irregular heartbeat. *Formula: $C_{15}H_{19}NO$ . . . the selective blockade of epinephrine by the beta adrenergic blocking agent pronethalol.* Science 8/4/72, p404 [**1964**, from *pro*pyl + *amine* + *me*thyl + *naphtha*lene + *menthanol*]

pronuclear, *adj.* supporting or advocating the use of nuclear energy or nuclear weapons. *Sweden's pro-nuclear power parties won—by 58 per cent to 38 per cent—the referendum held last Sunday. The result implied that the Government should switch on two nuclear reactors as they are completed shortly. But Prime Minister Falldin, who led the anti-nuclear side, left his personal position ambiguous over future action.* Manchester Guardian Weekly 3/30/80, p7 [**1963**]

propfan, *n.* **a** an eight-bladed propeller driven by a jet engine for subsonic aircraft. *On flights of up to 1,500 miles, the prop fan would be 40% more fuel economical, since a propeller is more efficient than jet thrust during climb-outs and letdowns.* Time 8/14/78, p65 **b** Attributive use: *Lockheed, under contract from NASA, also delved into fuel-economic aircraft with . . . a four-engined, 200-passenger transport employing "propfan" engines—essentially advanced turboprop engines with smaller-diameter, eight-bladed propellers.* Americana Annual 1977, p512 [**1970**, from *prop*eller + *fan*]

Proposition 13, *U.S. and Canada.* a law or measure for reducing authority to impose taxes, especially on property, etc. (used in reference to the measure passed by voters in California in June, 1978 to reduce property taxes by more than 50 percent; often used attributively). *Appreciative of what the city [New York] had endured during the last three years of retrenchment . . . Felix Rohatyn, chairman of the Municipal Assistance Corporation said recently—"We have gone through our own Proposition 13."* New Yorker 9/4/78, p85 *The post office is caught in a vise between the union and treasury board, Ottawa's watchdog over spending. Buoyed by the Proposition 13 mood in the country, treasury board is cracking down on civil service wages as part of its program of restraint.* Maclean's 10/2/78, p23 *Sen. William Proxmire of Wisconsin . . . points out that to give American cities today what Europe got under the Marshall Plan would be to inflict mass cutbacks in urban spending that not even the lunatic fringe of the Proposition 13 crowd would espouse.* Harper's 12/78, p48 [**1978**, from the name of the California initiative, also known as the Jarvis-Gann initiative or amendment, after its authors and main sponsors, Howard Jarvis and Paul Gann]

propranolol (prou'prænə,lɔːl), *n.* a beta-blocking drug that controls irregular heartbeat, high blood pressure, and angina pectoris. *Formula: $C_{16}H_{21}NO_2$ Propranolol was found by chance to be effective in relieving mental symptoms in patients given the drug for physical disease. Propranolol is not a tranquilizer (it slows and steadies the heartbeat) but it can relieve some of the symptoms of anxiety such as palpitations and a racing pulse.* Times (London) 12/28/74, p12 [**1964**, from iso*pro*pylamino-*propan*ol (chemical constituents of the drug) + *-ol* (chemical suffix)]

proprietary, *n. U.S.* a business secretly owned by the Central Intelligence Agency. *Most of the agency's existing proprietaries, the report said, are shell corporations with paper assets that are used to provide agents with working cover or to hide the agency's operations. But the report found that the operating proprietaries had been used heavily in the past to extend the C.I.A.'s presence abroad, to provide support for paramilitary operations, to disseminate propaganda and to manage the agency's private investments.* NY Times 4/27/76, p25 [**1975**, noun use of the adjective]

prostacyclin (,prostə'saiklin), *n.* a hormonelike substance that inhibits the aggregation of blood platelets and dilates blood vessels, produced naturally by enzymes in arterial cells. *Chemists have succeeded in synthesizing a natural substance which it is hoped may lead to the prevention of heart attacks and strokes in people with atherosclerosis. The compound, prostacyclin, synthesized in America by the group headed by Dr U.F. Axen, of the Upjohn Company, is thought to protect human beings from the formation of blood clots inside healthy blood vessels.* Times (London) 4/2/77, p16 [**1976**, from *prosta*glandin + *cycle* + *-in* (chemical suffix)]

prostaglandin (,prostə'glændən), *n.* any one of 16 or more hormonelike substances produced in the tissues of mammals by the action of enzymes on certain fatty acids, found in high concentrations in seminal fluid of the prostate gland, and thought to have a variety of important functions in reproduction, nerve-impulse transmission, muscle contraction, regulation of blood pressure, and metabolism. *Abbreviation:* PG *In a 1968 report, E. J. Corey and his associates at Harvard University announced that they had developed methods for the total synthesis of five biologically potent prostaglandins . . .* 1970 Britannica Yearbook of Science and the Future, p293 *In Sweden, Britain and Uganda 200 women are using prostaglandins (instead of contraceptives) to induce abortion as soon as they miss a period.* Science News 4/3/71, p230 [**1957,** coined in German by the Swedish physiologist Ulf S. von Euler (1935) from *prosta*te *gland* + *-in* (chemical suffix)]

protectionist, *n.* one who seeks to protect wildlife; a wildlife conservationist. *Jack Berryman, who directs Wildlife Services . . . deeply resents the attacks of what he calls "the wild-eyed protectionists," who, he says, portray him and his field men as "bloodthirsty killers."* New Yorker 6/13/70, p57 [**1964**]

protective reaction, *U.S.* **1** a bombing raid on an enemy target conducted in self-defense or retaliation (often used attributively). *A secret Air Force investigation concluded that the Commander of the Seventh Air Force, Gen. John D. Lavelle, had ordered at least 28 unauthorized raids into North Vietnam and later reported them as "protective reaction"—a defensive action.* NY Times 6/18/72, pD1 *An aggressive attack by an armada of airplanes, which most speakers of English call simply an air raid, was instead spoken of as a momentary defensive strategy, a routine limited duration protective reaction.* Peter Farb, Word Play, 1974, p136 **2** Transferred use: *The same is true of people who believe themselves persecuted and harassed by "enemies" who are out to "get" them—and who, as a sort of "protective-reaction strike," persecute and harass these same "enemies."* Harper's 6/74, p52 [**1970**] ►During the early 1970's the phrase *protective reaction strike* was appropriated by protesters against the Vietnam War as a mocking euphemism. This use of the term is exemplified in the following quotation: *And, of course, Vietnam was the great source of that kind of thing. 'Bombing, bombing, why do you always say bombing?' one of the military spokesmen was quoted as saying. 'These are protective reaction strikes.'* Listener 1/15/76, p45

protein-calorie malnutrition, a form of malnutrition common in economically depressed areas, and characterized by deficiencies in protein and overall caloric intake that lead to depletion of magnesium and potassium in the body. *The spectrum of protein-calorie malnutrition (PCM as it is known to workers in the field) varies from a diet that is relatively high in calories and deficient in protein (manifested in the syndrome known as kwashiorkor) to one that is low in both calories and protein (manifested in marasmus).* Scientific American 9/76, p40 [**1971**]

protein clock, a hypothetical biological mechanism regulating the rate of evolutionary changes in the protein of a species. *By plotting the genetic differences between the flies against time, measured by the known evolution of the islands, Carson was able to predict the points at which each species evolved and the speed of the protein clock. This speed, he suggests, is a rate of 1 percent genetic difference per 20,000 years.* Science News 2/21/76, p118 [**1976,** patterned after BIOLOGICAL CLOCK]

proteinoid, *n.* a peptide-chain molecule resembling a protein molecule. . . . *the relatively small amino acid molecules combined to form protein-like macromolecules, which we called proteinoids because their building blocks were amino acids and their size was comparable to that of small protein molecules.* Encyclopedia Science Supplement (Grolier) 1969, p75 *In the past, Fox and others have demonstrated that these proteinoid microspheres can have catalytic activity, so that they take up small molecules and perform chemical reactions, that they can grow and divide . . .* New Scientist and Science Journal 6/10/71, p613 [**1956**]

Protestant ethic, a set of values held by some social scientists to be the ideological basis of the capitalistic system, including the ideas of strict personal compliance with the law, the necessity and desirability of work and thrift, and encouragement of competition and the profit motive in everyday life. *To some the Protestant Ethic—hard work is a virtue for its own sake—*

appears to have been replaced by an almost Mediterranean spirit, a spreading belief that men should work no more than they must to enjoy the good life and worldly pleasures. Time 3/23/70, p77 *The Protestant ethic and tradition of capitalism have made most middle-class Americans cherish their privacy and independence, and the dread of relinquishing them dies hard.* Encyclopedia Science Supplement (Grolier) 1971, p310 [**1956;** coined in German by the German sociologist Max Weber (1904)]

protobiont, *n.* an elementary or primordial organism. *As a preliminary stage in the total process of organic evolution, chemical evolution of course reaches its climax when lifeless organic molecules are assembled by chance into a living organism. This first form of life is what the Russian biochemist A. I. Oparin calls a "protobiont."* Scientific American 5/71, p30 [**1964**]

protobiotic soup, another name for PRIMORDIAL SOUP. . . . *the constituents of Haldane's soup (a "protobiotic soup of aminoacids, ribose, four purine and pyrimidine bases, and a source of high-energy phosphate").* Sunday Times (London) 10/3/71, p40 [**1971**]

protocontinent, *n.* another name for SUPERCONTINENT. *The Hegira Of The Indian Subcontinent About 60,000,000 Years Ago is suggested on the above map of earth's protocontinent, as Professor J. Tuzo Wilson has pictured it.* Saturday Review 3/2/68, p48 *The abundance of these [igneous] rocks in the equatorial mid-Atlantic Ridge, says Dr. Enrico Bonatti of the University of Miami, indicates that there is either a continuous layer or large blocks of continental type mantle imbedded in the mantle under the ridge. Dr. Bonatti proposes, in the June 10 Journal of Geophysical Research, that this mantle material was originally part of a layer of continental-type mantle below the protocontinent Pangaea.* Science News 7/10/71, p26 [**1958**]

proton decay, the radioactive transmutation of one chemical element into another by the emission of a proton from an unstable nucleus. *Called proton decay, it is a process in which a nucleus emits a proton and decreases both atomic number and atomic weight by one.* Science News 10/31/70, p349 *A consortium of nuclear physicists from America, England and Canada have discovered a new mode of nuclear disintegration—proton decay. The three modes already known are: emission of a beta particle (electron or positron), emission of an alpha particle (helium nucleus), and spontaneous fission (occurring only in very heavy nuclei).* New Scientist 11/5/70, p259 [**1970**]

protoporcelain, *n.* early pottery that resembles porcelain, especially ancient reddish pottery of China made white with kaolin and given a thick glaze. *Finely textured, hard-glazed "protoporcelains" of the Shang gave way to more hastily created pottery, designed for utilitarian purposes.* Science News 12/21-28/74, p395 [**1973**]

protostellar, *adj.* of or relating to the protostars (star-forming gaseous matter); giving rise to stars. *Computer simulations of spherical, protostellar clouds of stellar masses, collapsing under self-gravity, have been developed by Richard Larson and by C. C. Hayashi and his collaborators.* 1977 Britannica Yearbook of Science and the Future, p76 [**1971**]

protovirus, *n.* a primary or prototypical virus that serves as a model for others of the same kind. *According to his hypothesis, normal cells manufacture RNA, which moves to neighboring cells in the form of a protovirus, or template, and stimulates the production of a new form of DNA.* Time 4/19/71, p28 *RNA tumor viruses may have evolved when RNA coded for by one cell was transferred to a second cell, where it produced new DNA that the host DNA incorporated. In time, a DNA "protovirus" region might be established and might code for a complete RNA tumor virus particle.* 1972 Britannica Yearbook of Science and the Future, p301 [**1971**]

proved reserves or **proven reserves,** the amount of oil or natural gas that can be removed profitably from available sources. *In considering resources of oil and gas one encounters a category that has no exact counterpart in world coal statistics: the concept of "proved reserves." The term refers to discovered and well-delineated reserves that can be extracted by available* *techniques at current costs and sold at current prices.* Scientific American 9/63, p116 *The Israelis have also found major natural gas fields in the northern Sinai. Proven reserves amount to over 35 billion cubic feet.* New York Post 12/29/78, p5 [**1960**]

Provisional or **provisional,** *n.* a member of the so-called Provisional wing of the Irish Republican Army, consisting of militant extremists. Also nicknamed PROVO. *The Provisionals are more aptly defined by the things they are against.* Newsweek 10/18/71, p18 *What is known is that the arms were destined for the breakaway I.R.A. group in the North—the so called provisionals.* Times (London) 5/15/70, p5 [**1970**]

provo or **Provo**[1], *n.* any of a group of Dutch or German political activists engaging in agitation, rioting, and disruptive activities. *The youthful protesters, who used to be known as Provos (for provocateurs), rioted over almost everything from Crown Princess Beatrix's lavish wedding in 1966, when they tossed smoke bombs at the royal carriage, to the country's critical housing shortage.* Time 6/15/70, p37 . . . *Frankfurt's notorious Provos,* [are] *members of a group of youths who, as their name indicates, like to provoke the public.* NY Times 8/8/67, p35 [**1966**, ultimately a short form of French *provocateur* agitator]

Provo[2], *n.* a nickname for a PROVISIONAL. *Nevertheless, he believes, like any good Provo, that the fight must go on until Stormont is abolished not just suspended, British soldiers have left the streets of Ulster,* all *internees have been released but there are significant moves towards a United Ireland.* Sunday Times (London) 5/14/72, p15 [**1971**]

proxemic, *adj.* of or relating to proxemics. . . . *'proxemic' behaviour ranges from the distance two people maintain while engaged in conversation or the way a group of people arrange themselves, to architecture and city planning.* Times Literary Supplement 6/4/71, p653 [**1963**]

proxemics, *n.* the study of the physical degree of distance or of the arrangement of human beings or social groups as they interact. *Though territoriality . . . has been studied for many years now in connection with animal life, Dr.* [Edward T.] *Hall . . . is the first person to link the concept directly with human beings and . . . has coined a purely human word for it: proxemics.* Manchester Guardian Weekly 9/29/69, p7 [**1963**, from *prox*imity + *-emics,* as in *phonemics, morphemics,* etc.]

proximity talks, diplomatic discussions in which disputing parties occupy separate but proximate locations while a mediator moves back and forth between them. *Carter began conducting what is known in diplomacy as "proximity talks." Because Sadat and Begin were in lodges less than 100 yds. apart, Carter was able to move easily from a bilateral conversation with one to a chat with the other.* Time 9/25/78, p12 [**1973**]

PRT, abbreviation of *personal rapid transit* (an automated system of small passenger cars that stop at individual destinations by pushing a button). *For the passenger, a PRT would seem like a cross between an automatic lift and a monorail. Units will run outside on elevated beams, but they will have no driver and when they stop—often inside building lobbies—the doors will open and close automatically.* New Scientist 5/25/72, p429 [**1972**]

pseudo-event, *n.* a staged or contrived event; something arranged so that it may be publicized or reported in the news media. *I sometimes wonder what memories today's children will retain of the big pseudo-event (defined by sociologist Daniel Boorstin as a news event planned in advance) of Canada's electronic age.* Maclean's 3/67, p78 [**1962**]

pseudovirion, *n.* a virion (infectious viral particle) that contains nucleic acid from the host cell. *In another experimental approach, virus-like particles which contain pieces of cellular DNA (pseudovirions) instead of viral DNA are being used as the vector for DNA-mediated genetic modification.* Science 3/3/72, p952 [**1970**]

psi, *n.* short for PSI PARTICLE. *The first candidates were the particles discovered in 1974 at the Brookhaven National Laboratory and at SLAC* [Stanford Linear Acceleration Center], *which were named* J *or psi. It was immediately proposed that*

the psi consists of a charmed quark and a charmed antiquark, a combination called charmonium. Scientific American 4/76, p55 [**1974**]

PSI, abbreviation of *Personalized System of Instruction,* another name for the KELLER PLAN. *The most attractive feature of PSI for students was self-pacing; the students take a short examination on a unit of instruction whenever they feel they are ready and are allowed to repeat the examination without penalty or prejudice if they do not pass.* 1975 Britannica Yearbook of Science and the Future, p195 [**1973**]

psilocin ('sailəsən), *n.* a hallucinogenic drug related to DMT, derived from the mushroom *Psilocybe mexicana. Included by name as "drugs having a potential for abuse because of their hallucinatory effect," were . . . two other agents called psilocybin and psilocin . . .* NY Times 7/2/67, pD8 . . . Conocybe, Panaeolus, *and* Stropharia *. . . contain the extraordinarily biodynamic compound psilocybin, a hydroxy indole alkylamine with a phosphorylated side chain (the only indole compound with a phosphoric acid radical known from the plant kingdom) and sometimes the unstable derivative psilocin.* McGraw-Hill Yearbook of Science and Technology 1971, p357 [**1958**]

psilocybin (,sailə'saibən), *n.* a hallucinogenic drug derived from the mushroom *Psilocybe mexicana. Psilocybin, which is found in certain mushrooms, was in use by Indians when the Spanish conquerors first came to Mexico.* Encyclopedia Science Supplement (Grolier) 1969, p188 . . . *modern work with the hallucinogenic drugs such as mescalin, LSD-125, psilocybin and others which induce dreamlike states in waking subjects has also attracted research interest to the chemistry of fantasy.* Listener 5/12/66, p680 [**1958**]

psion ('sai,an), *n.* another name for the PSI PARTICLE. *Various particles, known as "psions," have been discovered in the last year and a half that are thought to possess charm as a hidden property.* NY Times 6/9/76, p17 [**1976**, from *psi* (*particle*) + *-on* elementary particle] —**psionic,** *adj.: By now, something like nine members and cousins of the psionic family have been catalogued, and there may be more to come.* Science News 6/5-12/76, p356

psi particle, any of a group of subatomic particles of large mass and exceptionally long lifetime. Psi particles are classed as hadrons composed of a charmed quark and a charmed antiquark. Also called J PARTICLE and PSION. *The main significance of the discovery of the psi particle was that it provided compelling evidence for the existence of a fourth kind of quark, which had earlier been named the "charmed" quark.* Scientific American 3/78, p50 [**1974**, so called by its discoverers (at the Stanford Linear Accelerator Center in Palo Alto, Calif.) from the resemblance of the paths made by daughter particles to the Greek letter psi (Ψ)]

PSRO or **P.S.R.O.,** abbreviation of *professional standards review organization,* a regional medical review board. *The PSRO's would be empowered to review patients' records and track down instances of unnecessary treatment and overlong hospital stays.* Newsweek 12/17/73, p94 *P.S.R.O.'s . . . were established in the hope of providing health care economically through the evaluation of the quality of care being provided in hospitals.* NY Times 1/14/78, p20 [**1973**]

psych (saik), *v.i., v.t. Slang.* **1** to lose or cause to lose resolve; break down psychologically (especially in the phrase **psych out**). *"I got a shot." "You did?" Lewis said, straightening. "I did. A spectacular miss at fifteen yards." "What happened? we could'a had meat." "I boosted my bow hand, I think. I psyched out. I'll be damned if I know how . . ."* James Dickey, Deliverance, 1970, p98 *Having discovered psychology, the cops induce "truth" by psyching the subject.* Time 4/29/66, p35 **2** to stimulate or excite (especially in the phrase **psych up**). *We were all psyched up, and as a result when we got there the shooting started, almost as a chain reaction.* Harper's 5/70, p65 *Ficker said yesterday: "I don't believe in getting the crew all psyched up."* Times (London) 9/15/70, p6 *"He's* [Harry Parker, a Harvard crew coach, is] *deadly honest," said Canning. "He's never tried to psych us, or insult us with a pep talk. Before a race, we* *et a briefing, an appraisal. Only that."* New Yorker 8/10/68, p78 [**1957** for def. 1; **1960** for def. 2]

psychedelia, *n.* **1** the realm or world of psychedelic drugs. *Dr. Timothy Leary, 49, the guru of psychedelia, heard a Laredo, Texas, jury convict him for the second time of smuggling marijuana from Mexico.* Time 2/2/70, p28 **2** artifacts associated with the effects induced by psychedelic drugs. *The kit costs $6.50 and contains a roller applicator, paint pan and three three-ounce bottles of pastel psychedelia.* Maclean's 9/67, p91 [**1966**, from *psychedelic* + *-ia,* as in *schizophrenia*]

psychedelic, *adj.* **1** mind-expanding; hallucinogenic; chemically altering the psyche so as to intensify perception. *. . . even a single dose of such psychedelic drugs as LSD may result in recurring episodes of psychosis, often resulting in depression and suicidal or homicidal impulses.* NY Times 10/9/66, pD9 **2** of or relating to psychedelic drugs or their use. *To quote from Masters' and Houston's admirable study "The Varieties of Psychedelic Experience": It is frequent and funny, if also unfortunate, to encounter young members of the Drug Movement who claim to have achieved a personal apotheosis when, in fact, their experience appears to have consisted mainly of depersonalization, dissociation, and similar phenomena.* New Yorker 10/1/66, p41 **3** suggesting or resembling the effect of psychedelic drugs; loud, bright, kaleidoscopic, etc. *Robert Wyatt, the drummer, Michael Ratledge, organist, and Kevin Ayers, bassist, are explorers of the ultimate fringe of psychedelic music, jazz, conscious distortion, electronic dadaism and shock-rock.* NY Times 7/12/68, p16 *. . . Jon Eby took the opposite approach—and put Stanfield in the middle of what we fondly believe to be the first psychedelic political poster in the history of the Tory party.* Maclean's 3/68, p23 **—n. 1** a psychedelic drug. *When I wrote these lines LSD and its chemical relative, mescaline, were the only hallucinogenic agents known. Today the number has proliferated to include psilocybin, DMT, . . . and many more now being synthesized or tested. They have a new name, the "psychedelics," meaning mind-revealing, mind-expanding or consciousness-expanding drugs.* Maclean's 6/20/64, p9 *Perhaps I am being overly solemn about Dr. Leary, psychedelics, and, by extension, Murray the K's world.* Harper's 7/66, p99 **2** a person who is addicted to psychedelic drugs. *Such dangers do not deter the acid heads or "psychedelics"—even though some users are willing to admit that they found no great "show," or had a "freak trip" (a bad one), or "tripped out" (the worst kind).* Time 3/11/66, p43 [**1956,** from Greek *psychē* soul, mind + *deloûn* to reveal, manifest + English *-ic*]

psychedelically, *adv.* in a psychedelic manner; with psychedelic effects of color, sound, etc. *Long before Expo '70 was more than an idea, Canadians began promoting it by means of a psychedelically painted school bus that travelled around both Canada and Japan.* New Yorker 6/6/70, p101 [**1966**]

psychedelicatessen, *n. U.S.* another name for HEAD SHOP. *The paraphernalia of the mind drugs was everywhere—all the sorts of things that crowd the "head shops" and "psychedelicatessens" of the Lower East Side and, of course, certain areas of the U.S. west coast.* Saturday Night (Canada) 6/67, p24 *In Los Angeles, the leading psychedelicatessen is the Headquarters, not far from the gates of the U.C.L.A. campus.* Time 2/24/67, p55 [**1966,** blend of *psychedelic* and *delicatessen*]

psychic energizer, a drug that relieves mental depression. *Monoamine oxidase (MAO) inhibitors, currently used largely as "pepper-uppers" or "psychic energizers", also tend to reduce blood pressure, but the doses needed are generally considered too dangerous for clinical purposes.* Britannica Book of the Year 1964, p653 [**1957**]

psychic healer, a person who cures the sick by means of psychic power or energy transmitted through touch, meditation, prayer, etc. *Psychic healers have achieved many cures that cannot be denied—or even explained in conventional scientific terms.* Newsweek 4/29/74, p67 *Only after he has done his persuasive best do I admit to Dr. Kirklin that I have hedged my bets. A psychic healer in New York, mobilized by a friend, will be devoting the next day to transmitting restorative waves down the Eastern seaboard specifically in my direction.* NY Times Magazine 5/14/78, p60 [**1974**] **—psychic healing:** *Psychic healing may or may not involve religious faith. Often it requires no faith at all. Some believe that anyone can heal. Others believe that only certain people can heal.* Sunday News (New York) 8/12/79, p55

psychic numbing, a denial of reality induced as a protection against overwhelming and unacceptable stimuli. *How did so many doctors manage to preside over killings while viewing themselves as idealists? . . .* [Robert Jay] *Lifton concludes that they invoked two standard psychological forms of self-delusion: the first is "psychic numbing"; at Auschwitz, for example, doctors talked compulsively about technical matters to avoid confronting the reality of all the horrors around them.* Time 6/25/79, p68 [**1970**]

psychic surgeon, a psychic healer who claims to be able to remove diseased tissues from the body. *Still farther from the pale of reason are claims of the so-called "psychic surgeons" of the Philippines and Brazil. These spiritual healers not only "cure" tennis elbow and the like, but supposedly "operate" on the critically and terminally ill without benefit of scalpel or anesthesia, removing "cancerous tissue" and other "tumours" from the credulous sufferers for substantial fees.* Britannica Book of the Year 1976, p271 [**1975**] **—psychic surgery:** *One programme was about psychic surgery, practised mainly in the Philippines. Surgeons grope into a patient's stomach and produce blood and entrails, leaving no scar. Sometimes patients say they feel better, although in some cases the blood and entrails have been shown to belong to chickens.* Times (London) 12/19/77, p12

psychoactive, *adj.* acting on the mind; affecting or altering the mental state. *Lebanese hashish contains only one important psychoactive chemical according to a report in Science (169, 3945, p 611) from an Israeli team . . .* Science Journal 11/70, p27 *. . . marijuana is a psychoactive drug and can certainly cause problems if the basic personality structure of the user is weak . . .* NY Times 6/4/71, p31 [**1961**]

psychoactivity, *n.* potency as a psychoactive agent. *These tribesmen* [in western and northeastern Siberia], *having discovered that the narcotic constituent of the mushroom is excreted with almost undiminished psychoactivity, incorporated in a ritual urine-drinking ceremony in order to take full advantage of the biodynamic principle in a region where the mushroom is rare.* McGraw-Hill Yearbook of Science and Technology 1971, p357 [**1971**]

psychobabble, *n.* psychological jargon, especially the jargon of psychotherapy groups. *It dawned on Rosen that her words were nothing more than "psychobabble" hippie argot laced with psychiatric terms to give the impression of weight and meaning.* Maclean's 4/17/78, p74 *According to the practitioners of currently fashionable psycho-babble, we live in the best of times because more and more people are "being upfront" about their feelings and "doing their own thing."* NY Times 7/18/79, pA23 *Another key verb in psychobabble is* hang, *meaning to act, behave, comport oneself. The injunction to "hang loose" is familiar and expressive, conveying a quintessentially Californian state of relaxed readiness for new experience . . .* The State of the Language, ed. L. Michaels and C. Ricks, 1980, p509 [**1976,** coined by the American author Richard D. Rosen in his Book *Psychobabble: Fast Talk and Quick Cure in the Era of Feeling* (1977), from *psycho*logical + *babble*] **—psychobabbler**, *n.: Meanwhile I stand on the roof of my Mill Valley house, watching the flood of psychobabble rising, ever rising, and wishing I knew how to turn the situation around. It won't be easy. The psychobabblers not only outnumber the rest of us, but, what is worse, they have The Force on their side.* NY Times Magazine 11/20/77, p124

psychobiography, *n.* the story of a person's life from the point of view of psychoanalysis; a psychoanalytical biography. *There are various objections to psychobiography. First, few biographers have any formal training in psychoanalysis. Secondly, which school of psycho-analytic theory is to be followed: Freud, Jung or another?* Times (London) 10/5/72, p11 *It is the paradox of psychobiography that it resolutely ignores the feasts of available information to pounce, with the trumpets at* *full blast, on a mere crumb.* National Review 8/16/74, p936 [**1931, 1965**, from *psycho*analysis + *biography*] —**psychobiographer**, *n.: Melville kept his secrets to himself, though he left behind the sort of clue that makes as cheery a sight for the psychobiographer as the first fire of fall.* Atlantic 12/75, p114 —**psychobiographical**, *adj.: Its* [the book's] *aims are simpler and less ambitious; it makes no large historiographical, mythological or psychobiographical assumptions, offering instead an inquiry into the transformations of Greek and Roman concepts of heroic virtue.* NY Times Book Review 12/10/72, p36

psychochemical, *n.* a psychoactive chemical agent. *The national and international pattern of drug abuse during 1969 reflected a continuing increase in the use of most psychochemicals.* Americana Annual 1970, p486 [**1958**]

psychoenergetic, *adj.* of or involving the use of psychic energy, as in psychokinesis (mentally influencing the movement of objects) and radiesthesia (being sensitive to energy radiations). *To move forward and reliably identify psychoenergetic effects via high-voltage photography, we must carefully monitor those physiological parameters that can directly influence the streamer process and which can be altered by mental or emotional changes in the living organism.* New Scientist 4/25/74, p163 [**1972**] —**psychoenergetics,** *n.: While the experimental conditions were not perfect, the events at Birkbeck do represent a major step forward in the new field of experimental psychoenergetics.* Science News 7/20/74, p46

psychogeriatric, *adj.* of or relating to mental illness among the elderly. *A better measure of a man's age than the state of his arteries may be the degree of his solitude, Dr. J.P. Junod, of the Geneva psycho-geriatric centre, said at an international conference on community psychiatry.* Times (London) 12/1/66, p8 [**1961**]

psychogeriatrics, *n.* the study and treatment of psychological disorders affecting the elderly. *The eastern opium dens of the past will be replaced by state controlled hallucinogenic centres which will provide a supervised escape from the technological horrors of the 21st century. In the expanding field of psychogeriatrics these drugs will become the mainstay in the management of such patients.* New Scientist 6/15/72, p637 [**1967**]

psychographics, *n.pl.* statistics of attitudes, trends, tastes, etc., of a population, used chiefly to determine marketing and advertising objectives. *They are delving into our minds and our personalities. The New Testament of Madison Avenue is psychographics. . . The shift from demographics to psychographics is changing the way America does business, giving us new products and new ways to sell them.* Daily News (New York) 8/13/85, p6 [**1968**, patterned after *demographics* (1967)]

psychohistorical, *adj.* of or relating to the psychological aspects of history. *And further efforts at deepening our psychohistorical insight could in turn help us to create new kinds of political, institutional, and legal structures appropriate to our unprecedented situation.* Atlantic 10/70, p110 [**1964**]

psychohistory, *n.* a historical account or analysis using methods of psychology and especially those of psychoanalysis. *Yes, he would attempt what no one else had even thought of daring to venture—a multi-angular psychohistory of the man whose very name suggested deep affinity with Capricorn's own verbal compulsions.* New Yorker 10/1/73, p34 [**1969**] —**psychohistorian,** *n.: When the same techniques are applied to history by psychohistorians, it is always the "psycho-" that wins over the "history." Psychohistory is just another example of the "growing habit of psychologizing," says Jacques Barzun in* Clio and the Doctors. Harper's 11/78, p98

psychological pricing, the pricing of a product to enhance its value or increase its sales appeal. *Psychological pricing is the old gimmick of taking a price to the nearest figure of nine; if normal markup methods would produce a price of, say, 25 cents for a can of peaches, the store will boost it to 29 cents and the customer will think he is getting a bargain cut down from 30 cents.* Maclean's 8/74, p63 [**1972**]

psychon, *n.* a hypothetical particle of matter bearing a psychic message. Compare MINDON. *He* [Arthur Koestler] *writes with precise lyricism about other observed or putative sub-atomic entities: quarks, mindons, psychons, the ghostly neutrinos which have no physical properties and fall in billions through space and matter . . .* Times (London) 2/10/72, p12 [**1972**, extended sense of an earlier term (OEDS 1920) meaning "a hypothetical unit of nerve impulse"]

psychopharmaceutical, *n.* a psychoactive drug. *One advantage of doxepin* [an antidepressant drug] *is its apparently low toxicity compared to other psychopharmaceuticals.* Science News 12/20/69, p581 [**1964**]

psychoprophylaxis, *n.* a method of preparing women for natural childbirth by psychological conditioning. *A gynaecologist once pointed out to me that a fundamental difference in approach to tasks—any tasks—may be one reason among many others why "psycho-prophylaxis" works so well for some women in childbirth and so badly for others . . .* Manchester Guardian Weekly 1/9/69, p17 *The Childbirth Education Association of Toronto is presently sponsoring classes in psychoprophylaxis.* Maclean's 12/67, p86 [**1959**, from *psycho*psychological + *prophylaxis* treatment to preserve health]

psychosynthesis, *n.* a method of psychotherapy combining psychoanalysis with various exercises and meditation techniques adopted from oriental philosophy and religion by Roberto Assagioli, an Italian psychiatrist. *Psychosynthesis—This multidimensional growth therapy developed in Italy now is attracting increasing attention in the U.S. It uses various forms of group and individual therapy, including meditation, written self-analysis, guided daydreams (fantasies) and music.* New York Post 2/26/77, p23 *These have included growth groups, encounter groups, T-groups, sensory-awareness training, Arica training, the Gurdjieff method, psychosynthesis, Zen, etc.* Psychology Today 11/78, p136 [**1973**, extended sense or new application of an earlier term (OEDS 1919) meaning "the integration of dissimilar or opposing elements of the psyche by means of psychoanalysis"]

psychotogen (saiˈkɑtədʒən), *n.* a drug that produces a psychotic state; a psychotogenic drug. *Herbert Weingartner, assistant professor of medical psychiatry and behavioral science at the School of Medicine, and a psychologist at Phipps Clinic, foresees a future in which some hallucinogens, more precisely those described as psychotogens, will be used in ways that will benefit the functioning of the human brain.* Johns Hopkins Journal 3/70, p1 [**1959**]

psychotogenic or **psychotogenetic,** *adj.* producing a psychotic state; causing psychosis or mental derangement. *. . . . the effects of Vietnamese marijuana were sometimes surprisingly similar to those induced by hallucinogenic and psychotogenic agents such as L.S.D., mescaline and other so-called mind-expanders that have . . . proved harmful to the body and central nervous system of humans.* Times (London) 3/26/70, p7 *Dr. Weingartner bases his conclusions on extensive research with several members of the psychotogenetic family, primarily with what has been labeled DOET (2.5-dimethoxy 4-ethylamphetamine) and DOM (2.5-dimethoxy 4-methylamphetamine), commonly called "speed."* Johns Hopkins Journal 3/70, p1 [**1956**]

psychotomimetic, *adj.* imitating or reproducing a psychotic state; affecting the mind psychotically. *A psychotomimetic snuff,* rapé dos indios, *is said to be prepared from fruits of the central Amazonian moraceous tree* Olmedioperebea sclerophylla, *but nothing is known of its chemistry.* McGraw-Hill Yearbook of Science and Technology 1971, p357 —**n.** *a* psychotomimetic drug. *Though much more has been found out about the psychotomimetic effects of the older drugs, and new ones have been discovered (e.g., psilocybin, the active ingredient of Mexico's "magic mushrooms"), LSD remains preeminent—partly because it was the first of the "modern" psychotomimetics but chiefly because it produces the most powerful psychological effects from the smallest doses.* Britannica Book of the Year 1968, p521 [**1957**]

sychotomimetically, *adv.* in a psychotomimetic manner. *The ¹-isomer is the major constituent. It appears to be quite active nd is currently being advertised as "the psychotomimetically ctive constituent of hashish", although the evidence for this laim is far from substantial.* Science Journal 9/69, p38 **[1963]**

sychotoxic, *adj.* regarded as harmful to the mind or personali-y. *Late last year the Senate whisked through a bill directing he FDA* [Food and Drug Administration] *to police the sales ecords of all firms distributing any drugs that may induce "psychotoxic effects or anti-social behavior" if taken in exces-ive quantities.* Wall Street Journal 1/27/65, p8 **[1964]**

sychrotolerant (ˌsɑɪkrouˈtɑlərənt), *adj.* able to endure cold. *lime is caused by cold resistant, or psychrotolerant, bacteria vhich are not a health hazard but which produce an objection-ble smell and change the colour of the meat.* Science Journal /70, p19 **[1959,** from *psychro-* cold (from Greek *psȳchrós*) + *olerant*]

syop (ˈsaɪˌɑp), *n. U.S. Military Use.* an action or operation in *sychological warfare. "With national elections over and the ew Government in operation, U.S. Psyop personnel should de-ote priority attention to assisting the GVN* [Government of Vietnam] *in projecting a positive image to the RVN* [Republic f Vietnam] *public," a United States Mission directive states.* NY Times 1/21/68, p9 *At Bragg, the psywar department is opeless, a grab-bag of highly sophisticated instruments to, as hey say, "use communications to influence the behavior of the arget area." To that end, psyops operatives at Bragg are study-ng the world's religions, "group dynamics," and "the social ystem." It is sociology gone berserk.* Atlantic 11/70, p79 **[1966,** rom *psychological operations]*

PTV, abbreviation of *public television* (noncommercial TV). Compare PBS. *After 20 years of rather dry, highbrow fare, PTV ame up with some creative, audience-attracting productions hat are helping to alter its old image.* 1972 Collier's Encyclo-edia Year Book, p542 **[1971]**

oublic, *adj.* **go public, a** to make for the first time a public offer-ng of stock. *"The Launching" tells the story of a small family irm of boat builders who decide to raise more capital by 'going public."* Times (London) 1/11/65, p11 **b** Figurative sense. to come before the public with confidential information; oresent private information in public. *Quickly there came more igures and helpful explanations from Mobil, Shell, Gulf, Standard of Indiana and Exxon. The decision to go public with company data, even on a small scale, represents a new era.* New Republic 1/26/74, p7 *The dispute went public at the weekend, when one of the National Weather Service forecasters, in giv-ng his bulletin, remarked: ". . . We attempt to give an honest nd scientific appraisal of weather situations and are not in-ent on scooping anybody on a news story."* Times (London) 2/15/78, p5 **[1962** for def. a; **1968** for def. b]

public access, *Especially U.S.* television broadcasting on a channel or channels set aside by law for the exclusive use of community groups and other segments of the public (often used attributively). *Some half-dozen cities have experimented sporadically with public access, and New York City's two cable operators . . . are now beaming 150 hours of do-it-yourself TV each week over their public-access channels.* Newsweek 4/9/73, p83 **[1972]**

public-interest law, *U.S.* a branch of law dealing with class ac-tion suits and other legal means of protecting the general inter-ests and welfare of the public. *Meites chose public-interest law, he says, because he "couldn't bother with the conventional lawyer's willingness to take either side."* Time 5/24/71, p44 *In the United States . . . there has developed over the last five years a new department of jurisprudence: public interest law, in which the courts are used as an integral part of the cam-paign for clean air, unpolluted rivers, quieter cities, and un-bulldozed landscapes.* New Scientist 9/28/72, p547 **[1970]** —**public-interest lawyer:** *Three public-interest lawyers in San Francisco, acting on their own, filed a class-action lawsuit against "Henry Kissinger et al." on behalf of parents in Viet-*

nam to reunite them with these non-orphans as quickly as pos-sible. NY Times Magazine 5/9/76, p14

public key, a cryptographic key used without risk of decoding by others because the letter values assigned to a second key are needed for decoding (often used attributively). *The authorised recipient of these messages has publicised his "public key," the numbers R and S. But only he knows the prime factors of R. With this knowledge, the encrypted message can be quickly rendered into plain text by a similar function C^T (modulo R). But calculation of the vital decrypting factor, T, is only possi-ble if you know the prime factors of R. And only the person who published the key will thus be able to understand such messages.* New Scientist 3/2/78, p594 **[1978]**

Public Lending Right, *British.* a royalty paid to authors based on the number of times their books are borrowed from public li-braries. *Abbreviation:* PLR *The comparatively new notion known as Public Lending Right has already placed authors on a collision course with librarians, who regard the proposed law as an intrusion and a nuisance, and with some government of-ficials, who look upon professional writing as a pleasant risk instead of as a property right.* NY Times 10/14/76, p34 **[1961]**

puka (ˈpuːkə), *n.* a small, perforated white shell common on Ha-waiian beaches, used for stringing on a wire to form a necklace or bracelet (often used attributively). *Necklaces of puka shells, liquid silver, coral birds, turquoise cylinders and African trad-ing beads are giving diamonds a run for their money these days.* NY Times Magazine 1/4/76, p38 *In a show of solidarity, Vancouver's blue-jean literati, led by aging poetry guru and University of British Columbia Professor Warren Tallman, dusted off their puka beads and held a series of parties last month.* Maclean's 10/23/78, p66 **[1974,** from Hawaiian, literal-ly, hole, perhaps short for *pukaihu* hole in a pearl shell]

pula (ˈpuːlə), *n., pl.* **-la** or **-las.** the monetary unit of Botswana, equal to 100 thebe. *The pula was introduced in 1976 replacing the South African rand which had been used as Botswana cur-rency since independence. The pula is valued at par with the rand.* Encyclopedia of the Third World 1978, p176 **[1976,** from the Setswana word for rain]

pull-date, *n.* a date, stamped on packaged food, after which the food is no longer fresh and may not be sold in its regular shelf space at full price. *The council strongly urged that labeling for processed foods include serving size, a list of ingredients, nutri-tional information, and the pull-date.* 1973 Collier's Encyclo-pedia Year Book, p248 **[1972]**

pull tab, a metal tab that is pulled to open a can or container. *They guzzle all day and night; they garland themselves with the pull tabs from beer cans.* New Yorker 3/4/72, p89 *A quick-release pull tab is provided so that when the container has served its useful purpose the protective film can be stripped away and the main body of the container disolved in water.* Times (London) 2/18/76, p24 **[1963]**

pulsar, *n.* an astronomical source of powerful radio and light waves emitted in short, intense bursts or pulses at very precise intervals. *In current theory a pulsar is the core of a star that had exploded into a supernova. It is condensed, magnetic, and spins rapidly. It is surrounded by a plasma of charged particles which gives off the optical and radio waves and also serves as a drag to slow rotation.* Science News Yearbook 1970, p218 *Pulsars have been found in all parts of the sky, but lie primarily in the Milky Way near the symmetry plane of the galaxy.* McGraw-Hill Yearbook of Science and Technology 1971, p362 **[1968,** from *pulse* + quas*ar]*

pump, *v.t.* to provide (a laser) with the energy to raise atoms in its active medium (ruby, helium, etc.) to an excited state. *Many lasers, as I have described, are excited (or "pumped," as we say in the laboratory) by light. Others may be made to lase by radio waves, or by an electric current, or by chemical reactions.* Na-tional Geographic Magazine 12/66, p864 **[1965]**

punch, *v.* **punch out,** *Informal.* to hit with a punch or punches, especially so that a person is knocked out. *Her parents split up* *when she was a baby and she has fantasies of meeting her father and punching him out.* Time 8/13/79, p70 [**1966**]

punctuated equilibrium, a modification of the Darwinian theory of evolution which maintains that natural selection acts on a species to keep it stable rather than to alter it, and that the emergence of a new species is a separate event that points up the general equilibrium in nature. *To explain this absence of gradualism, Eldredge and Gould have proposed a new idea. They call it the theory of punctuated equilibrium, which is an ungraceful way of saying that evolutionary change is concentrated in short, quick bursts when new species emerge. . . (For example, birds blown to a new volcanic island might develop into a new species.)* Discover 10/80, p89 [**1978**]

punctuational, *adj.* of or relating to punctuated equilibrium; characterized by the emergence of new species as separate or episodic occurrences over long periods of little or no change in nature. *Punctuated equilibrium provides a model for the "small" level of speciation and its consequences. But a preference for punctuational over gradual tempos may be asserted at more encompassing levels of the history of life itself. This history is not, as many people assume, a tale of slow progress, leading to greater complexity of form and greater diversity of kinds and numbers. It is, in important respects, a series of plateaus punctuated by rare and seminal events that shift systems from one level to another.* NY Times 1/22/78, pD6 [**1978**] —**punctuationalism**, *n.: The alternative theory is called . . . "punctuationalism." According to this, the diversity of life has come about as a result of sporadic adaptations by small, well-defined groups confronted by a new environment, interspersed with long periods of little or no change.* Manchester Guardian Weekly 11/26/78, p1 —**punctuationalist**, *n.: A convinced punctuationalist, he contrasts bivalves and mammals to support (unconvincingly, I believe) the hypothesis that rate of evolution is determined by rate of speciation.* Science 1/6/78, p58

punji stick or **punji stake,** a sharp bamboo spike, often dipped in excrement, which is set in camouflaged holes in the ground to pierce the legs of enemy soldiers. *A Green Beret points out to the journalist some American-made punji sticks (the movie is obsessed with punji sticks).* NY Times 6/20/68, p49 *The instructors' wives wove grass rugs and made clay cooking pots, while children helped to fashion the village's huts and whittled vicious punji stakes of bamboo.* Time 2/4/66, p18 [**1965**, *punji,* from Vietnamese, perhaps from a Tibeto-Burman language]

punk, *n.* **1** short for PUNK ROCK or PUNK ROCKER. *No matter, he survived punk, and Talking Heads are going to survive us all. Now I know why they didn't like it when I used to compare them to the Beatles, even before they had a disk to their name.* High Times 1/79, p123 *The critics heap abuse and the punks gather up each salvo like evil-smelling flowers. The game is to shock. To goad. To enrage. To move. There is no ideology. Only a vague desire for power and potency. The implements are guitar, bass and drums, amplified to an ear-bleeding volume. The music is corporate (no solos), two and three chord pedantry; endings are ragged and the words are generally unintelligible.* Maclean's 6/13/77, p42 **2** a style of clothing worn and popularized by performers of punk rock. *Classic punk is on sale at Boy, a unisex shop offering Gary Gilmore memorial T-shirts, multi-zippered jackets and shirts whose cuffs are attached to the shoulders by chains.* NY Times 9/26/77, p38 **3** a person who follows punk fashions in clothing, makeup, etc. *"The Punks are also rebelling against a very repressive atmosphere. Kids have even been arrested for wearing T-shirts some people consider offensive," adds Pamela, showing off a Punk sporting naked cowboys, another the Queen's head with an obscene connotation.* New York Post 6/9/77, p42 —*adj.* of or characteristic of punk rock, punk rockers, and the style of ragged clothes and garish makeup and decorations worn and popularized by punk-rock groups. *The British punk bands are a community linked by anger and frustration. They are, within the music world, a rebuke to the bourgeois excesses.* Time 7/11/77, p47 *Kent . . . wears yellow jeans and a t-shirt whose shoved-up sleeves are held in place with pink safety-pins. He's got a punk crew-cut, but not Paris punk. Kent is provincial punk, lead singer with a group from the Lyon suburbs called the Starshooters.* Man-

chester Guardian Weekly (Le Monde section) 1/29/78 p13 [**1972**]

punk rock, a form of rock music developed from early rock 'r roll, played and sung in a loud, aggressive, rowdy style and wit outrageous lyrics by performers usually made up in ragged c garish clothes. *Punk rock has been stealing up on us for som time now, with the original tales of torn clothes cobbled toget er with safety pins being superseded by more bizarre ones con cerning punk fans transpiercing their cheeks, Afghan zealc style, with those same safety pins.* Times (London) 11/29/7€ p11 *Actually, "punk rock," as it is called, has brought abou some useful changes in popular music, as many respected roc critics have pointed out, and its roots can be traced back to th very origins of rock itself and perhaps even a little bit farthe* New Yorker 5/30/77, p38 [**1971**, from *punk* young hoodlum —**punk rocker:** *In between cutting up their bodies with broke glass and switchblades, spitting up on stage, and thinking u new names to "shock," Punk rockers sing and play—execrably* Maclean's 6/13/77, p1

punt (punt or pənt), *n., pl.* **punt** or **punts.** the monetary unit c Ireland, known as the Irish pound until 1979, when it was sepa rated from the pound sterling. *The government detached th punt (Irish pound) from the stronger pound sterling in Marc and, for the first time in 150 years, the country had its own cur rency. Together with other European currencies, the punt fluc tuated downward against sterling.* Britannica Book of the Yea 1980, p461 *But Dublin recognises the considerable risks par ticularly if Britain stays outside. Will the Irish punt ris against the pound . . .?* Manchester Guardian Weekl 11/19/78, p5 [**1975**, from Irish Gaelic *punt* pound]

Purex or **purex,** *adj.* of or designating a system for reprocessing nuclear fuel by which both pure uranium and pure plutonium are produced. *Similar efforts would be needed in any demon stration of the existing Purex recycling process on breeder fuel That process is used in several countries, including the Unitec States, for both weapons and power programs.* NY Time 2/28/78, p49 [**1956**, from *pl*utonium *r*eduction by solvent *ex* traction, probably influenced by *pure*]

purple heart, a popular name for a tablet of drinamyl, a drug combining an amphetamine and a barbiturate. *Control ove the sale of amphetamines was first tightened up in the UK witl the passing of the Drugs (Prevention of Misuse) Act 1964. Thi act was a result of public concern over the growing use of 'pej pills' such as purple hearts, which are a mixture of amphet amine and barbiturate.* Science Journal 2/70, p7 [**1961**, sc called from the original color and shape of the tablet, in allusion to the American military award]

purple membrane, a membrane under the cell wall of halobac teria, capable of changing sunlight into chemical energy in a process resembling photosynthesis. *When light shines on the gloriously purple membrane the pigment molecules change shape slightly and shoot out a proton. This proton pumping sets up a mini-electrical potential which can be harnessed tc generate important biochemicals (particularly ATP) for the bacterium, and to transport nutrients from the outside to the inside.* New Scientist 3/11/76, p547 [**1975**]

purserette, *n.* a female purser on a ship or aircraft. *The amoun of labour involved in manufacturing clothes could be cut by a new technique that British Rail is using to make uniforms for hovercraft purserettes—the low-flying equivalent of the air hostess . . . Moulded uniforms have so far been made in small batches—about a dozen purserettes are trying them out to see how they wear . . .* New Scientist 5/28/70, p431 [**1959**]

push-in crime or **push-in job,** *U.S. Slang.* a mugging at the door of a person's home. *The Senior Citizens Robbery Unit is as signed all cases involving indoor robberies of Bronx victims over the age of 60. Many of these crimes are the so-callec "push-in" jobs that occur when a robber or group of robbers waits in a hallway for a victim to come home, and then pushes him or her into the apartment.* NY Times 11/13/76, p11 [**1976**]

put, *v.* **put down,** *Slang.* **1** to reduce in size or importance; belittle; deflate. . . . *one 19-year-old had started putting Harvey down in front of the others. "You know, Harvey," the kid had* said, "sometimes I think you're a real phony." Maclean's 8/67, p26 *The zingers that do get through* [the NBC consor's scissors] *may bruise tender sensibilities, but as* [comedian Dan] *Rowan says: "We put everybody on but we never put anybody down."* Time 3/8/68, p47 **2** to criticize. *The history of the motion-picture industry might be summed up as the development from the serials with the blade in the sawmill moving closer and closer to the heroine's neck, to modern movies with the laser beam zeroing in on James Bond's crotch. At this level, the history of movies is a triumph of technology. I'm not putting down this kind of movie: I don't know anybody who doesn't enjoy it more or less at some time or other.* Atlantic 3/66, p72 [**1958** for def. 1; **1963** for def. 2]

put-down, *n. Slang.* an act, statement, etc., meant to put down someone or something. *This growing power has made Fairchild the most feared and disliked man in the fashion-publishing field. Despite his wide blue eyes and guileless countenance, he and his No. 1 hatchet man,* WWD [Woman's Wear Daily] *Publisher James Brady, have chalked up—and delighted in—a long string of personality assassinations, cutting insults and crushing putdowns.* Time 9/14/70, p77 . . . *the rebellion has broken out. Predictably, the response to it is a gradual escalation involving a more naked use of the tactics that were supposed to prevent, but which also helped to provoke, the crisis in the first place: patronizations, put-downs, and tongue-lashings* . . . Atlantic 10/68, p55 [**1962**]

put-on artist, an expert in the put-on (prank, hoax, or spoof). *Also, though he* [Henry Ford II] *is usually forthright, he occasionally stirs suspicions that he is a bit of a put-on artist. Asked about his favorites in his art collection, he replies: "I've got a Toulouse-Lautrec; then I've got a Degas and a Manet and a Gauguin"—all the names uttered in the tones of a bored auto dealer listing the cars he cannot sell.* Time 7/20/70, p66 *We remember the kidder as a good-natured, teasing sort—that moment when he rendered his victim absurd was quickly dissipated in the general laughter that followed* . . . *Occasionally, a*

victim will try to explain away his confusion by assuming that the put-on artist is "just being ironical"—that he really means precisely the reverse of everything he says. New Yorker 6/24/67, p35 [**1967**]

PUVA ('pu:və), *n.* acronym for *P*soralen *U*ltra*v*iolet *A*, a method of treating psoriasis by the use of a particular drug (psoralen) combined with exposure to ultraviolet light. *Nearly 75 per cent of patients undergoing PUVA treatment get rid of almost all their psoriasis. However, the therapy is recommended only when other psoriasis treatments fail, because it causes a greater risk of skin cancer among psoriasis patients who have already had skin cancer or whose skin was exposed to radiation therapy before beginning PUVA treatments.* World Book Science Annual 1985, p81 [**1984**]

P.V.S. or **PVS,** abbreviation of *Post-Vietnam Syndrome* (a complex of emotional problems experienced by veterans of the Vietnam War). *"We find a lot of the guys have turned on society and turned off the VA," concedes VA Administrator Max Cleland, who lost two legs and an arm in Viet Nam. He recalls his own struggle with P.V.S. all too well: "It was like a series of secondary explosions going off in my head. I was on an emotional rollercoaster and I didn't know where I was going."* Time, 1/28/80, p30 [**1972**]

pyramid selling, *Especially British.* a method of extending the number of franchises held by a chain of stores in which a company pays its franchise holders to recruit new franchise holders, instead of restricting them to the sale of the company's products. *The new orders, issued under powers of the Fair Trading Act* . . . *"will crack down on objectionable features of pyramid selling." Significantly the new regulations will put an end to the payment of substantial sums to join a pyramid-selling organisation.* Manchester Guardian Weekly 11/3/73, p11 [**1971** RO]

Q

QC, abbreviation of QUICKCHANGE. *QC jets can expand air cargo service to small cities . . . citing new technology such as the QC jets. CAB* [Civil Aeronautics Board] *Chairman Charles S. Murphy predicted that air cargo might surpass passenger volume by 1980.* 1967 World Book Year Book, p527 *Another useful cargo carrier is the so-called QC or quickchange aircraft or convertible passenger-freighter.* Times (London) 12/3/70, pIV [**1967**]

QCD, abbreviation of QUANTUM CHROMODYNAMICS. *In the QCD theory quarks interact by exchanging a gluon, a quantum of the electromagnetic force. Naively applied, this picture is insufficient. To improve on the simple model theorists suggested that quarks have a side-to-side motion within the proton, for example a transverse momentum of their own.* New Scientist 11/9/78, p435 [**1976**]

Qiana (ki:ˈɑ:nə), *n.* the trade name of a washable and wrinkle-resistant synthetic fabric chemically related to nylon. *Qiana is said to have color, clarity, and luster equal to or better than most luxurious silks.* World Book Science Annual 1969, p274 *In the lingerie sector of Lord & Taylor, those of us known to the profession as mature women (and not in the psychiatrists' sense) will come upon the commendable and reasonably sedate bathing suits produced by Edith Lances of sea-blue Qiana, which is a man-made silk . . .* New Yorker 7/10/71, p69 [**1968**]

qiviut (ˈkivi:ˌu:t), *n.* the underwool of the arctic musk ox. *Many woolen manufacturers are enthusiastic about the principal product of the musk ox, its underwool, which the Eskimos call "qiviut." The fiber is similar to that of cashmere but about twice as long and half as thick. It can be prepared with the same machines as those used for cashmere.* Science News Letter 6/12/65, p370 [**1958**, from the Eskimo name]

Q scale. See the quotation for the meaning. *On earth, such rubble would be a very poor conductor of tremors; on the geologist's "Q" scale, a measure of how long vibrations in the earth take to die down, it would rate about 10. By contrast, the moon rubble scored at least 2,000. The difference is that the earth rubble would be filled with gases and liquids that would let the vibrations travel at high speeds, enabling them to penetrate far down into the planet.* Science News Yearbook 1970, p45 [**1970**, *Q*, abbreviation of German *Querwellen* transverse waves]

QSE, *British.* abbreviation of *qualified scientist and engineer. An average Q.S.E. in the Atomic Energy Authority is assumed to earn about £2,300, £3,350, £3,700, or £4,000 at ages 30, 40, 50, or 55 respectively.* Times (London) 7/21/70, p21 *But the number of qualified scientists and engineers (QSEs) in the world is between five and eight million.* New Scientist and Science Journal 8/5/71, p342 [**1966**]

QSO, abbreviation of QUASI-STELLAR OBJECT. *Some well-reproduced spectra of QSOs show clearly the difficulties involved in observing these objects.* New Scientist 4/18/68, p140 *The first quasars that were discovered were identified by their combination of radio and optical properties. After these first discoveries, astronomers found numerous other starlike objects that had the same unusual optical properties as quasars—that is, very large red shifts, and unusual emission spectra—but were not strong radio sources. These objects received the separate name of "Quasi-Stellar Objects, or QSO's."* Robert Jastrow and Malcolm H. Thompson, Astronomy: Fundamentals and Frontiers, 1972, p229 [**1963**]

QSTOL (ˈkyu:ˌstoul), *n.* acronym for *quiet short takeoff and landing.* Compare CTOL, STOL. *Now companies which have*

promoted the vertical takeoff and landing (VTOL) airliners for years are studying other projects. Instead of talking about "technological breakthroughs" they stress quietness. The word even gets into the title of the latest British Aircraft Corporation project, which is known as QSTOL . . . Sunday Times (London) 6/13/71, p11 [**1971**]

Q-switch, *n.* any of various devices for causing a crystal laser to produce a high-energy pulse of extremely short duration. *Q-switches are employed to obtain a very powerful pulsed output from a laser by allowing the laser to store up energy; when it reaches a maximum the blockage is quickly removed, and an intense pulse of laser radiation is emitted.* New Scientist 10/20/66, p93 —*v.t.* to cause (a crystal laser) to emit a high-energy pulse by means of a Q-switch. *Saturable absorbers have recently been used very successfully to Q-switch ruby and neodymium-doped lasers . . .* McGraw-Hill Yearbook of Science and Technology 1968, p223 [**1963**, from *Q*, abbreviation of *quantum*]

Q-switched, *adj.* capable of emitting an extremely short, high-energy pulse by means of a Q-switch. *. . . they used the 104-inch telescope to transmit and detect pulses of 50-nanosecond duration produced by a "Q-switched" (short-pulse) ruby laser.* Scientific American 3/70, p41 [**1963**]

Q-switching, *n.* the use of a Q-switch to obtain extremely short, high-energy laser pulses. *Q-switching is a technique for producing giant laser pulses by preventing lasing action until a large amount of energy has been pumped into the atoms responsible.* New Scientist 10/24/68, p205 [**1963**]

Quaalude (ˈkweiˌlu:d), *n.* a trademark for a sedative and hypnotic drug having addictive properties. Generic name, METHAQUALONE. Also called LUDE, QUAD², and SOPOR. *There's a new entry: Quaalude, the brand name of a white pill that acts as a depressant. Vassar used twenty thousand of them in three weeks, and they tell of one Brooklyn college that uses five thousand a day.* National Review 12/8/72, p1332 *It is four months since Dr. Bourne, one of President Carter's key advisers, wrote his disastrous prescription for Quaalude—time, that is, for a less hysterical view of official Washington's drug scene.* Psychology Today 11/78, p129 [**1966**]

quackupuncture, *n.* the misleading or fraudulent use of acupuncture by dishonest practitioners. *FDA is concerned that acupuncture does not fall into the category of "quackupuncture."* FDA Consumer 5/73, p23 *Acupuncture anesthesia does indeed work . . . Unfortunately, acupuncture has become an American fad instead of the subject of serious experimental research. Acupuncture in America has become transformed into "quackupuncture."* NY Times 5/28/74, p39 [**1973**, blend of *quack* and *acupuncture*]

quad¹, *adj., n.* short for QUADRAPHONIC or QUADRAPHONY. *Domestic quad listening needs two additional loudspeakers over stereo, and two more amplifiers, plus the black box which allocates some of the sound to the rear left/right and others to the front left/right.* Listener 10/23/75 (page not known) *Quad is a new medium in which the musical experience is heightened.* Newsweek 2/5/73, p65 [**1970**]

quad², *n.* a slang name for QUAALUDE. *On the street and on campus, methaqualone is known by various corruptions of its trade names: "quads" (from Quaalude, made by William H. Rorer, Inc.) . . . It was so popular among the young people who camped out at last year's political conventions that Miami Beach's Flamingo Park was dubbed "Quaalude Alley."* Time 3/5/73, p73 [**1973**, by shortening and alteration of *Quaalude*] uad[3], *n. U.S.* a unit of energy equal to a quadrillion British ›ermal units. One quad is equivalent to 24 million metric tons ̣ petroleum. *Without any new initiatives the need for import-̣ oil will rise steadily from about 12 quads at present to more ̣an 60 in the year 2000.* Scientific American 1/76, 21 *Although it is by far the most abundant indigenous ener-̣ source, coal ranks only third in consumption. Last year, it ›rovided Americans with an estimated 14.1 quads of energy, ̣ the equivalent of roughly seven million barrels of oil a day. ̣hat satisfied barely 18 percent of total energy needs. In 1973, ̣al provided 13.3 quads.* NY Times 7/16/79, pA12 [**1974**, ̣ort for *quadrillion*]

uadraphonic, quadriphonic, or quadrophonic, *adj.* of, having ̣ do with, or using quadraphony. Also called FOUR-CHANNEL, ̣UADRASONIC. *Quadraphonic music has stereo buffs drooling ̣ese days and last week was something of a milestone for the ̣ew technique: the first American recording session of sym-̣honic music in the round. The work: Bela Bartok's tumultuous Concerto for Orchestra," tailor-made for the four-speaker ̣uad play-back system.* Newsweek 1/1/73, p40 . . . *the inter-̣sting quadriphonic disc system . . . puts the sums of the two ̣ft and the two right channels into the frequency range from '0 Hz to 15 kHz, and multiplexes in the band from 20 to 45 Hz the difference signals needed to decode them.* Saturday Re-̣iew 10/31/70, p57 *This year may well mark the end of the ̣tereophonic age and the beginning of the new, all-exciting ̣nd even more complex quadrophonic age.* New Scientist and ̣cience Journal 4/8/71, p88 [**1969**, from *quadra-*, alteration ̣ *quadri-* (or *quadro-*) four + *phonic* of sound] **–quadraphonically,** *adv.: The sound track, reproduced qua-̣raphonically, makes the floor hum and the seats vibrate, and ̣he songs come out in bounteous cascades.* Time 5/6/74, p90

uadraphonics or quadriphonics, *n.* variants of QUADRAPHONY. ̣he system requires, for the best reproduction, one channel ̣ewer than the number of speakers. So a commercial model ̣ith three channels and four speakers (quadraphonics requires ̣our channels) looks the most likely development.* Times (Lon-̣on) 12/23/74, p12 [**1970**]

uadraphony (ˌkwɑdˈræfəni:), *n.* any system of high-fidelity ̣ound reproduction involving signals transmitted through four ̣ifferent channels. *The big question for me was whether, in the ̣rocess of attempting to wrap the listener of the future in ̣uadraphony, music-making would slip out by the back door.* ̣anchester Guardian Weekly 4/28/73, p23 [**1969**, from ̣UADRAPHONIC]

uadrasonic or quadrisonic, *adj.* another name for QUAD-̣APHONIC. *One of the most popular Sibelius symphonies, re-̣orded once more, this time in what is called compatible qua-̣rasonic sound; i.e., the sides can be played on a standard ̣tereo machine as well as on four-channel equipment.* New ̣orker 4/28/73, p142 *Now Davis is looking forward to Co-̣umbia's further development of quadrisonic sound, a kind of ̣ouble-stereo system that was introduced last year by Van-̣uard.* Time 9/28/70, p73 [**1970**, from *quadra-*, alteration of ̣uadri-* four + *sonic* of sound]

uadrasonics or quadrisonics, *n.* another name for QUAD-̣APHONY. *Two competing approaches to quadrasonics ̣merged: the "purist" approach, in which four separate sound ̣racks were recorded from four microphones and then played ̣ack separately to four speakers, and the "matrix" approach, ̣n which two specially encoded channels were fed into a decod-̣r where they were electronically adjusted and then split up ̣nd fed to the four speakers.* 1972 Compton Yearbook, ̣230 [**1971**]

uadro, *n.* a square section of a planned city or urban develop-̣ent, functioning as a residential unit with at least one apart-̣ent house and shopping center. *Within the one city he Arnold J. Toynbee) envisages quadros (single units of settle-̣ent) as in Brazilia, which will be of a small enough scale to ̣ngender community spirit.* New Scientist 10/15/70, ̣141 [**1970**, probably from Portuguese, literally, a square, but ̣nown earlier in English with the meaning of a square of tapes-̣ry (a1711)]

quadrominium or **quadraminium**, *n.* another name for FOUR-PLEX. *In Chicago, Dayton and some West Coast areas, four-dwelling condominiums—or "quadrominiums"—have become the fastest selling form of housing.* Time 3/29/71, p51 *The same economies are present in various other forms of new hous-ing, such as quadraminiums and townhouses.* Business Week 7/13/74, p58 [**1971**, from *quadro-* or *quadra-* four + *condo-minium*]

Qualitätswein (ˌkwɑːliːˈteitsˌvain), *n.* any German wine officially guaranteed as originating from grapes grown in several speci-fied regions. *Qualitätswein, the next rung on the ladder, is real-ly just a better grade of table wine, but it must come from a specified region, must be made from certain grape varieties and must have enough sugar in the must—the name given to the crushed grapes just before fermentation—to produce 7.5 percent of natural alcohol during the fermentation process.* NY Times Magazine 12/10/78, p178 [**1972**, from German, literal-ly, quality wine] ►The corresponding official designation for French wines is *appellation contrôlée.*

quality, *n.* a newspaper or magazine often of limited circula-tion because of its appeal to a specialized or specialized group of readers. *Not all the problems, however, are the same for all papers. The "qualities," for example, need to earn a greater per-centage of their income from advertising than the "populars," which rely more heavily on mass sales.* Manchester Guardian Weekly 7/25/70, p11 [**1970**]

quality circle, *U.S.* See the first quotation for the meaning. *On the premise that the workers often know best, the firms are forming "quality circles." These are groups of five to thirteen employees who volunteer to gather for perhaps an hour each week, on company time, in brainstorming sessions that focus on what can be done to improve output per hour worked. Su-pervisors lead the discussions and help put the recommenda-tions into practice. The result: bonuses and more job satisfaction for workers plus higher profits and productivity for firms.* Time 1/28/80, p65 *"Quality circle" groups are blos-soming at dozens of companies . . .* Newsweek 9/8/80, p58 [**1980**]

quality of life, a phrase frequently used since the 1970's to sug-gest the fundamental conditions of everyday living which make life satisfactory and rewarding, but which increased ma-terial production and improved technology have either failed to provide or actually helped to erode. *From all accounts the visitor was not amused nor, like President Pompidou, delighted with the fair's evidence of growing concern for "the quality of life" in France.* Daily Telegraph (London) 5/15/72, p9 *Nonmarket indicators of the quality of life should be sought so that we can gauge the effects of government inter-vention on our sense of well-being.* Science 5/4/79, p478 [**1969**]—**quality-of-life**, *adj.: "This is not an open city," he* [Mayor Edward Koch] *said, promising that the stern measures, including arrests for such "quality-of-life" offenses as prosti-tution, gambling, and . . . drug trafficking, would continue.* NY Times 8/30/81, pD6

quango, *n. British.* a government body or organization with in-dependent powers. See ACAS. *Quangos cover a large field. The National Enterprise Board (chairman £31,850, deputy £26,000, seven members £1,000 a year each) is a quango. So is the Water Services Staff Commission (one unpaid chairman, four members receiving £125 a year). They descend from the familiar (the Post Office) to the arcane (Committee for Tero-technology), take in the enormous (90 area health authorities), and . . . include the local (King's Lynn Conservancy Board) and the specialist (Ship's Wireless Working Party).* Times (Lon-don) 10/5/76, p4 *I notice the Right-wing Tories who attack quangos never mention the House of Lords, the biggest quango of them all.* Manchester Guardian Weekly 7/15/79, p2 *The machinery of the Dartmoor National Park Authority is an ob-ject lesson in Britain's complex bureaucracy. It operates auton-omously under its national park officer, Ian Mercer. But Mr Mercer is responsible both to this committee, which is part of Devon Council, and to the Countryside Commission, a "quan-go" financed from central government.* Manchester Guardian Weekly 1/20/80, p20 [**1973**, acronym for *quasi non-*

governmental *o*rganization; later (1976) the full name was expanded to *quasi-autonomous national governmental organization*]

quantasome, *n.* one of the granules containing chlorophyll found inside the chloroplast of plant cells. *Through the electron microscope, small leaf particles, quantasomes, resemble the stipples on the rubber surface of a table-tennis paddle.* World Book Science Annual 1969, p273 *Studies of shadowed, isolated grana have revealed a 200-A subunit in these membranes . . . The 200-A units have been termed quantasomes and are possibly related to a basic photosynthetic unit, that is, the smallest physiological unit capable of photosynthesis.* McGraw-Hill Yearbook of Science and Technology 1968, p131 [**1962,** from *quanta* (plural of *quantum* smallest unit of energy) + *-some* body; so called from its being regarded as the smallest unit or elementary particle of the cell]

quantifier, *n.* **1** a person who is skilled in quantifying or counting. *Deutsch and his colleagues agree that "both types of scientific personalities, the quantifiers and the pattern-recognizers—the 'counters' and the 'poets'—will continue to be needed."* Time 3/29/71, p32 **2** a person whose primary concern is with the quantification of data or an activity. *Near the end of his tour he had gone to Harvard, where in another and gentler time he might have been revered but now was first almost captured by the radical students and later, speaking to a group of professors, [was] asked to explain about the two Mc-Namaras, McNamara the quantifier, who had given us the body count in Vietnam, and McNamara the warm philosopher, who had delivered a speech at Montreal that had seemed to contradict his and Johnson's actual policies.* Harper's 2/71, p38 [**1963** for def. 1; **1970** for def. 2]

quantitative genetics, another name for POPULATION GENETICS. *The study of the genetic basis of individual differences in intelligence in humans has evolved in the traditions and methods of that branch of genetics called quantitative genetics or population genetics, the foundations of which were laid down by British geneticists and statisticians such as Galton, Pearson, Fisher, Haldane, and Mather and, in the United States, by J.L. Lush and Sewall Wright.* Arthur R. Jensen, Genetics and Education, 1972, p104 [**1972**]

quantized bubble, another name for HARD BUBBLE. *A stumbling block was, however, identified by workers at Bell Telephone Laboratories . . . who reported the existence of a new form of magnetic bubble, namely the "hard" or "quantized" bubble.* Nature 11/24/72, p184 [**1972**]

quantum, *adj.* of sudden, spectacular significance or effect; representing a major breakthrough. *A major lesson of the energy crisis is that we must retreat from some of our quantum technological advances.* New Times 3/22/74, p68 *Xerox . . . refers to the dry, electrostatic copying process (a quantum improvement over earlier wet photographic methods) finally developed in 1938 in a one-room laboratory behind a beauty parlor in Astoria, Queens, by a penurious patent attorney named Chester F. Carlson.* Time 3/1/76, p69 [**1971,** abstracted from QUANTUM JUMP]

quantum chromodynamics, the theory that quarks possess a quantum property called color, of which there are three that combine in each quark to produce the force that binds quarks together. Also called CHROMODYNAMICS. *For fifty years physicists have searched for a theory of strong interactions, yet it is only in the last year or so that a possible solution has emerged. This is the theory of quantum chromodynamics, which has now made the surprising prediction that a remarkable new kind of elementary particle should exist. Such a claim allows the theory to be put to experimental test.* Times (London) 2/16/78, p14 *If a fundamental theory of matter called quantum chromodynamics, or QCD, is correct, the gluon must exist, and if the scientists had failed to find it in their new experiment, much of the theoretical work in physics in the past decade would have been in serious doubt.* NY Times 9/2/79, p1 *All this is pulled together in a theory called quantum chromodynamics (QCD) analogous to the thoroughly-proved quantum electrodynamics which describes the interaction of*

particles through electromagnetic forces. Technology Revie* Dec./Jan. 1980, p11 [**1976**]

quantum electronics, the application of the laws of quantum mechanics to electronic systems and interactions. *Dr. Sil mentioned the following distinguished scientists as havin taken part in the process of re-examining the institute's polit cal work: . . . Professor Alexander Prokhorov, a pioneer o quantum electronics and a 1964 Nobel Prize winner.* Time (London) 12/3/70, p6 [**1959**]

quantum jump or **quantum leap,** a sudden spectacular advance a major breakthrough. *At this point commercial pressures le to one of those quantum jumps . . . which have been so charac teristic of the history of computing. The argument was ver persuasive. It had been realized that it should be possible to de sign complete languages, with a syntax and semantic defin tion, for the writing of programs.* Science Journal 10/7(p95 . . . *the ability of marine technology to take "quantum leaps in innovation means that a laissez-faire approach to th ocean mineral resources can no longer be tolerated.* New Scien tist 12/3/70, p372 [**1955** for *quantum jump;* **1970** for *quantu leap;* figurative sense of the term in physics denoting the sud den jump of an electron, etc., from one energy level to another

quark (kwark), *n.* a hypothetical electrically charged subnu clear particle proposed as the basic component of all strongl interacting nuclear particles (hadrons). *A quark, if it exist would have a fractional electrical charge, something previous ly unheard of in physics. Scientists around the world have bee hunting for proof that these particles exist. In 1969, four scien tists from Australia's Sydney University claimed that they de tected quarks. If this discovery is substantiated, the field o atomic physics will be revolutionized.* Encyclopedia Scienc Supplement (Grolier) 1970, p297 *Quarks are supposed to com in three configurations, each with an antiquark: one with two thirds the charge of an electron and two with one-third th charge each, one a plus and one a minus. Dr. McCusker's fiv tracks are described as being of the two-thirds variety.* Scienc News Yearbook 1970, p242 *It may be, however, that quarks d not exist as separate physical entities. They may be only mathematically convenient parameter in the model, or the may be disallowed by some law of nature yet unknown* McGraw-Hill Yearbook of Science and Technology 1971 p215 [**1964,** coined by the American physicist Murray Gell Mann, born 1929, originally as *quork,* but replaced by influenc of the phrase "three quarks" in James Joyce's *Finnegans Wake*

quark matter, *Nuclear Physics.* a hypothetical form of matte consisting entirely of free quarks. *The time when the formles particles turned into quark matter . . . was an amazingly shor time—less than one-billionth of one-trillionth of one-trillionth of one second—after the big bang.* World Book Science Annua 1988, p193 [**1985**]

quarkonium, *n. Nuclear Physics.* a hypothetical particle consist ing of a quark and its antiparticle. *This quarkonium structure (a particular kind of quark bound to its antiquark) is also repre sented in the psi particles, which are held to be a charm quark plus its antiquark. Another kind of quark that should form it flavor of quarkonium is the top quark, for which there is ye no experimental evidence. Using some relevant theory the group calculated the probable mass level at which top quarkonium might be found and conclude that is is likely t be higher than 14 billion electron-volts.* Science News 3/3/79 p136 [**1979,** from QUARK + *-onium,* as in BOTTOMONIUM CHARMONIUM]

quarter, *adj.* less than half; far from complete; very imperfect (used with a hyphen in combinations). *Some quarter-liberals i South Africa feel that oppression against the black man i white-ruled South Africa would be less intolerable if eac black man did have a black-ruled homeland nearby to which he could return if he grew too miserable under white oppres sion.* Harper's 3/70, p36 *But to take effective steps to discour age the purveying of such quarter-truths, such as the India Government has taken, is described in your editorial column as "censorship", a threat to "the freedom and the integrity of documentary producers".* Times (London) 8/29/70, p11 [**1968**

y analogy to and extended from *half-* as in *half-baked, half-witted*]

uartz watch, a watch in which high accuracy is achieved by using a vibrating quartz crystal in an oscillatory electric circuit o regulate the movement of the timepiece. *The Swiss . . . developed the first quartz watch, the heart of which was the discovery that the electric stimulation of a bar of quartz-produced ibrations were peculiarly stable.* Times (London) 11/25/76, I [**1974**]

uasar ('kwei,zɑr), *n.* another name for QUASI-STELLAR OBJECT. *'he third group of abnormal galaxies or galaxylike objects are he quasars. These objects release enormous amounts of energy hat dwarf the energy released by the Seyfert galaxies. Unlike he Seyfert galaxy, the typical quasar is also a radio galaxy. In sense, the quasars combine the properties of radio galaxies nd Seyfert galaxies, but they carry the unusual properties of hese two objects to an extreme. They are the most difficult objects of all to explain in terms of the properties of stars.* Robert astrow and Malcolm H. Thompson, Astronomy: Fundamentals nd Frontiers, 1972, p227 *The puzzling quasars are believed o be less than 10 light-years in diameter—compared with the '00,000-light-year diameter of a typical galaxy—yet they are ouring out 100 times more light than a typical galaxy of 100 illion stars.* 1969 Collier's Encyclopedia Year Book, 74 *"Quasar" is now commonly applied to starlike objects ith large red shifts regardless of their radio emissivity.* Scienific American 5/71, p55 [**1964**, from *quasi*-stell*ar*]

uasiatom ('kweizɑi'ætəm), *n.* a short-lived nuclear particle resembling an atom. *Quasi-atoms are systems in which particles ot normally found in atoms become bound together in a way nalogous to the proton and electron in a hydrogen atom and xhibit an atom-like hierarchy of discrete energy levels. Examples are positronium (electron and positron) and muonium electron and muon). Quasi-atoms are generally unstable structures either because they are subject to matter-antimatter annilation (positronium) or because one or more of their onstituents is radioactively unstable (muonium).* Science lews 6/5-12/76, p356 [**1975**]

uasicrystal, *n. Physics.* a form of solid matter having unit cells ike crystals but lacking the regular repeating pattern of crysalline ions. *"Theoretically, we've opened up a whole realm of ondensed-matter physics," says Paul J. Steinhardt of the University of Pennsylvania in Philadelphia. Steinhardt and graduate student Dov Levine introduced the idea of a 'quasiperiodic' lattice to describe these new crystals. Their oncept is based on a three-dimensional version of Penrose's tilng patterns. "We have to ask all of the same questions that one sks for crystals all over again for these quasicrystals," says teinhardt.* Science News 3/23/85, p189 [**1985**]

uasifission, *n.* a type of nuclear fission in which the target and rojectile nuclei do not fuse before splitting but retain their riginal forms. *When nuclear physicists began to strike heavy nuclei against each other in heavy-ion accelerators, they expected that projectile and target would fuse into a new compound nucleus, and the compound nucleus would then fission according to its own internal dynamics, producing two new ragments. What the physicists found instead was mostly what s called quasifission: Target and projectile form a momentariy bound system, but it seems to remember what the original nuclei were. When it splits, its fragments tend to reproduce the rojectile and target.* Science News 1/17/76, p41 [**1974**]

uasimolecule, *n.* a structure formed by a combination of quasiatoms. *Basically, electron ejection from an atom or a quasinolecule is due to the time-varying electric field acting on the lectron as the collision partners pass each other. If the collision partners have comparable atomic numbers, it must usualy be assumed that the electrons in both adjust their orbits so s to form quasimolecular states from which an electron will be removed.* McGraw-Hill Yearbook of Science and Technology 975, p115 [**1959**] —**quasimolecular,** *adj.: The large class of 'quasimolecular" transitions offers some hope to those who eek an energy storage system. These are transitions in which he upper level is a bound complex of atoms, molecules, or mixures of the two, while the lower level is a transitory state exist-*

ing only very briefly while the components of the complex fly apart. New Scientist 7/24/75, p207

quasiparticle, *n.* a unit particle or quantum of sound, light, heat, etc. (a term used especially in solid-state physics). *Soviet scientists had the honor of introducing the first quasi particles, the phonons (sound quanta in a crystal lattice), and the concepts of two others: the exciton, a specially excited state of electrons in a crystal lattice; and the polaron, a conducting electron in an ionic lattice.* 1970 Britannica Yearbook of Science and the Future, p423 [**1957**]

quasiperiodic, *adj.* occurring at irregular intervals; having varying periods. *GX5-1, an X-ray source in the constellation Sagittarius . . . is the first known example of a celestial object with quasiperiodic emissions.* Encyclopedia Science Supplement (Grolier) 1987, p6 [**1959**]

quasi-stellar object, any of a large group of astronomical bodies that are powerful sources of energy but whose exact nature has not been determined. *Abbreviation:* QSO Also called QUASAR. *The extraordinary properties of quasi-stellar objects, or quasars, were not recognized until 1963, when Maarten Schmidt discovered the red shift of 3C 273. Much excitement was generated by the discovery of objects of stellar appearance which not only were strong radio sources but had large red shifts and which might therefore be the most distant observable objects in the universe.* Science 1/19/68, p291 *The discovery of quasistellar objects, of radio galaxies and of other peculiar galactic phenomena has upset the old view that galaxies are evolving on such a long time scale that to observers on the earth they are all but unchanging. Astronomers now speak of a "violent universe" as they seek to understand the extreme physical conditions that must be present in the quasi-stellar objects and in the nuclei of radio galaxies to explain the vast fluxes of energy they emit.* Scientific American 12/70, p22 [**1964**]

Qube, *n.* the trademark for a two-way cable television system that allows subscribers to participate in some programs. *From the demonstrations I saw, Qube seem very coy about flashing up the actual size of the sample behind all its impressive percentages, and the total imponderable is, of course, over whose finger is on the button.* Listener 5/10/79, p650 [**1977**]

queen-size, *adj.* very large; extra-large. *An appealing and handsomely produced queen-size book . . .* Publishers Weekly 7/23/73, p66 [**1973**, figurative use of the term applied to a bed and meaning wider and longer than the standard size (OEDS 1959), patterned after *king-size* (1942)]

quick-and-dirty, *n. U.S. Slang.* a snack bar or lunch counter. *It was after one when he finished, and we stopped for lunch at a quick-and-dirty on East Ninety-sixth and talked shop, which he said was not unusual for him.* New Yorker 1/17/70, p23 *The office of the Massachusetts Electric Company was temporarily converted into a mock-up of a quick-and-dirty and its sign replaced with one that read AL'S BEAN POT.* Harper's 1/68, p14 —**adj.** Usually, **quick and dirty.** *U.S. Slang.* easily and cheaply made or done; of inferior quality. *President Carter announced an indefinite deferral of the reprocessing of commercial spent fuel, and Congress passed the Nuclear Antiproliferation Act, but a study by Oak Ridge National Laboratory concluded that any country with access to spent fuel could build a "quick and dirty" reprocessing plant to produce bomb-grade plutonium.* Science News 12/24/77, p438 [**1968** for noun, alteration of *quick and filthy* (1940's); **1977** for adj., probably extended from the noun]

quickchange, *adj.* capable of being converted quickly from passenger to cargo service. *Another useful cargo carrier is the so-called QC or quick-change aircraft or convertible passengerfreighter.* Times (London) 12/3/70, pIV *The first "quick change" (QC) jets, passenger planes that can be converted for cargo in a matter of minutes, went into service in 1966.* 1967 World Book Year Book, p527 [**1967**]

quick fix, *Informal.* **1** a hasty, superficial remedy or solution to a problem. *At first, Schreiber called Dreyfus' proposal a gimmicky, vote-getting "quick fix." Replied Dreyfus: "It is a quick fix, I agree. But what do they want—a slow fix?"* Time 10/16/78, p43 *Then, Gerald Rafshoon, the smooth Atlanta ad* man who helped get Mr. Carter elected, was on his way to Washington, bringing along a bag of media gimmicks and public-relations quick fixes that he is still employing today, as the President approaches another campaign. NY Times 6/3/79, p39 **2** Attributive use: The quest for identity also accounted for the self-improvement program associated with the human-potential movement—a farrago that included such quick-fix therapies as "primal scream" and "rolfing." Newsweek 11/19/79, p96 [**1966**; influenced by fix slang term for a shot of a narcotic. See FIX.]

quiet room, a locked, cell-like room used in some psychiatric hospitals to seclude intractable patients. The researchers found that persons diagnosed as schizophrenic and manic-depressive were placed in the quiet room more often than were those with personality disorders and depressive neuroses. Schizophrenics were the most frequently secluded group. Science News 6/4/76, p360 At the South Florida State Hospital, a 72-year-old woman lies . . . Dehydrated and suffering from a compound fracture of the hip, she had been left unattended in the "quiet room." U.S. News & World Report 11/19/79, p49 [**1976**]

quinacrine mustard ('kwinəkrin), a bright-yellow fluorescent compound that stains chromosomes selectively, used especially to determine the sex of fetuses during pregnancy. T. Caspersson and his colleagues at the Karolinska Institute, Stockholm, . . . showed that when hamster and bean chromosomes were stained with a compound called quinacrine mustard, and viewed with long wavelength ultraviolet light, the chromosomes fluoresced differentially along their length. New Scientist and Science Journal 3/18/71, p606 The male Y chromosome could be made to fluoresce brightly in human cells when stained with quinacrine mustard. Britannica Book of the Year 1974, p419 [**1957**] ►As an antimalarial drug, quinacrine in hydrochloride form has been known since the 1930's.

quinestrol (kwi'nestrəl), n. a long-acting, synthetic estrogenic hormone. Formula: $C_{25}H_{32}O_2$ In cases of primary sterility in women in which the drug clomiphene was unsuccessful, the addition of quinestrol (an estrogen) to the treatment regime

produced a much higher yield of successful pregnancies. 197 Collier's Encyclopedia Year Book, p345 [**1970**, from quin acid + estrogen + -ol (chemical suffix)]

quorate ('kwɔrit), adj. British. containing or consisting of a qu rum. Even if the union general meeting was quorate, the cou cil has a right to reject same by a two-thirds majority. Tim (London) 2/23/72, p13 The chairman noticed that more tha a dozen of the 18 members of the Committee had drifted fro the room and he was forced to suspend the proceedings as u quorate. New Scientist 9/4/75, p541 [**1969**, from quorum -ate (adj. suffix)]

quota system, U.S. a system in which a number or percentag of blacks, women, etc. must be admitted or hired in order t achieve equality or redress past discrimination in educatio and employment. The President ordered all government age cies to expunge any trace of a strict quota system from feder programs. Americana Annual 1973, p283 A quota system is th other side of the coin of the federal government's interventio requiring racial and economic integration. Oscar Newma Community of Interest, 1980, p25 [**1963**] ►Before its applic tion to civil rights, this term was used chiefly in reference t the system of quotas limiting the number of immigrants into country.

qwerty or **QWERTY** ('kwər,ti:), n. an informal name for th standard keyboard on typewriters in English-speaking cour tries. Typewriters have become so refined mechanically tha they almost operate themselves; the keyboard designed i 1872, however, remains basically the same. Today you and and about fifty million other people in the English-speakin world still use qwerty. Saturday Review (Science) 9/30/7 p37 The Dvorak keyboard differs from the QWERTY in seve al ways. The most important difference being the placement o the vowels, a, e, i, o, u, on the home row, off the left hand. Wor Processing World May-June 1975, p46 [**1972**, from q, w, e, r, y, the first six keys in the upper row of letters of an English alphabet typewriter's keyboard; found once (OEDS 1929) as a attributive or adjectival designation of the keyboard]

R

R, a symbol used in the United States to designate motion pictures to which persons under 16 or 17 are not admitted unless accompanied by an adult. The approximate British equivalent symbol is *AA*. *"Goin' Down the Road," which is perhaps the most uncorrupt movie in town, and a movie that will probably suffer at the box office because of its gentleness, has been rated R (or restricted) by the Motion Picture Association of America.* New Yorker 10/31/70, p131 *What was once R is now GP, and what was X only a year ago is now R.* Time 4/5/71, p40 [**1968**, from *Restricted*]

rabbit ears, a small, portable television receiving antenna with two adjustable diagonal rods. *Mr. Chapman's alternatives to public television are naive: . . . satellite-to-home transmission 'rabbit ears won't do, and the cheapest dish antenna I know of goes for $1,000—in kit form*). Harper's 11/79, p8 [**1969**, abstracted from earlier *rabbit-ear* (1955)]

racemization, n. a method of determining the age of a fossil specimen by measuring the amount of right- or left-handed rotation of polarized light passed through crystals of amino acid contained in the specimen. *The newly dated remains include a skull found in a sea cliff near Del Mar, Calif., dated at 48,000 years old, and a 44,000-year-old skull fragment found near La Jolla, Calif. The new dating technique, called racemization, measures amino acids in human bones. . . . The dating method is considered a major breakthrough in fossil dating because the carbon-14 method is reliable only to about 40,000 years into the past.* 1975 World Book Year Book, p196 [**1971**, extended sense of the chemical term for conversion of an optically active compound to one without polarized rotation that is optically inactive)]

racewalk, n. a race in walking for speed or against time. *Carl Schuler of Silver Springs, who took sixth in the 1984 Olympic 50-kilometer racewalk, was runner-up in the racewalk category at 3:30.* Washington Post 10/29/84, pC12 —v.i. to compete in a racewalk. *As Mr. Jacobson sees it, even if one doesn't racewalk, adopting the form of a racewalker can produce more benefits than other walking styles. Racewalking is moving at a very brisk pace with a long stride, while the arms are pumped up and down in the fashion of a sprinter.* NY Times Magazine 11/27/83, p112 [**1973**, back formation from *race walking* (OEDS 1954)]

rack car, U.S. a railroad freight car with racks for carrying automobiles. *With the development of three-tiered rack cars, which carry up to 18 autos, railroads were able to promise auto companies savings of up to 18% over trucks on long hauls.* Wall Street Journal 1/25/63, p1 [**1963**]

racontage (rakɔ'taʒ), n. a storytelling; anecdotage. *The foreign correspondent shares honours with the diplomat when it comes to racontage. Anyone with a taste for humour . . . will relish this pot-pourri of oriental anecdotes, exposures, scandals and adventures from the doyen of Far East reporters.* Times Literary Supplement 10/20/72, p1244 [**1971**, from French, from *raconter* to relate; cf. *raconteur* (1829) one skilled in telling stories or anecdotes]

racquetball, n. U.S. and Canada. a game similar to handball, in which two or four players strike a ball with short-handled, stringed racquets. *Racquetball is played on a regulation handball court (20 by 40 feet) with the ceiling in play and a 20-foot-high front wall as your basic target. You swing what resembles a sawed-off tennis racquet at a lively, hollow rubber ball.* Money 12/77, p91 [**1972**]

radar astronomy, a branch of astronomy that studies planets and other heavenly bodies by analyzing the echoes or reflections of radar signals sent from the earth at specific targets. *Although radar astronomy is still a very young science, it has already produced results whose scientific importance has far exceeded the most enthusiastic predictions.* Scientific American 7/68, p28 *The board report also recommended learning as much as possible about the planets from the ground up and noted that radar astronomy had done particularly well with its studies of nearer planets, especially Venus.* Science News Yearbook 1969, p83 [**1959**]

radar trap, a section of road in which the speed of vehicles is monitored by police using radar. *For the first time patrol cars will be able to measure accurately the average speed of cars without having to follow them at a constant distance or use radar traps.* New Scientist 8/23/73, p446 [**1962**, probably short for *radar speed trap* (1958) and patterned after *speed trap*]

radial, n. short for RADIAL TIRE. *Advocates of radials say that they have much more stability and wear longer than bias-belted tires.* Time 4/26/71, p49 *It is also pointed out that the majority of Michelin's tyres are steel-braced radials, unlike the other companies' textile radials.* Times (London) 3/11/70, p23 [**1971**]

radial tire or **radial-ply tire**, an automobile tire with parallel casing cords running at right angles to the wheel rim. Also shortened to RADIAL. *Radial-ply tires, long known to be safer and longer wearing, will be introduced as standard equipment on one Ford Motor Company model and will be optional on other lines for 1967 . . .* NY Times 8/19/66, p29 *But Dunlop's investment in this field is only a drop in the ocean to that which will be required of it, or for that matter any other manufacturer, if there is a call to supply radial tyres as original equipment for a mass selling car.* Times (London) 10/12/67, p20 [**1964**]

radiation-field photography, another name for KIRLIAN PHOTOGRAPHY. *Psychologists, psychiatrists, biologists and physicists, as well as investigators of psychic phenomena, are looking into Kirlian photography (also known as radiation-field photography) as a new way of observing energy fields associated with living organisms.* Science News 9/29/73, p202 *It deals with Kirlian photography, here somewhat more properly called radiation field photography.* Analog 7/76, p163 [**1973**]

radical chic, a vogue among fashionable people of socializing with radicals. *Evenings, he [John B. Fairchild, publisher of Women's Wear Daily] shuns discotheques, parties and radical chic; instead, he takes the subway and bus home to his eight-room East Side apartment, dines with Jill and their four children, and listens to Shostakovich on the stereo.* Time 9/14/70, p80 *The fashionable despair, a variation on Leonard Bernstein's radical chic, seems to me nothing more than the necessary antithesis to an earlier illusion. We were brought up on the movies of the 1940s, and most of us believed in a cardboard image of the world as false as the Wyoming afternoons painted on a studio wall.* Harper's 11/71, p115 [**1970**, coined by the American journalist Tom Wolfe in his book *Radical Chic & Mau-mauing the Flak Catchers*, 1970]

radical left, another name for the NEW LEFT. *In the half of the electorate that does not care to choose between major parties and in the somewhat larger fraction that passes up the opportunity to cast primary votes are . . . the Wallace voters and the radical right—often ideologically distinct, though not always—and the radical left.* New Yorker 9/26/70, p136 [**1969**, patterned after *radical right*]

radical right, a collective name for the extreme right-wing or conservative movement in the United States, whose ideology includes militant anti-communism and anti-liberalism. *Ten* years ago the liberal Establishment crashed down on the Radical Right with accusations of anti-Semitism, racism, and general kookiness. Birchers were nuts . . . More often than not, they were the beneficiaries of welfare-state programs, of subsidies and social security, but none of that made them suspect government any less. Harper's 8/70, p46 One solution that is more logical—to abolish the income tax—is proposed chiefly by some members of the radical right, who consider any income tax Socialistic or Communistic, and who would have the federal government simply stop spending money. New Yorker 4/10/65, p76 [1954]

radical rightism, the ideology of the radical right. One of the understandable themes in radical rightism is a social paranoia, a feeling that we are being manipulated by unseen inaccessible forces. Sunday Times (London) 3/20/66, p26 [1966]

radical rightist, a member or supporter of the radical right. Depending on the political sympathies of the accuser, blame it on the Mafia, the I.R.A., the Zionists, the Negroes, the Liberals, the Radical Rightists, or J. Edgar Hoover. Harper's 1/65, p127 [1966]

radicidation (ˌreidəsə'deiʃən), n. the irradiation of food to destroy disease germs. Radicidation, or the destruction of organisms significant to public health, such as Salmonella species, in foods and feedstuffs, would appear to offer early promise for commercialization. McGraw-Hill Yearbook of Science and Technology 1968, p182 [1964, from radiation + -cide killer (as in insecticide) + -ation (noun suffix)]

radic-lib, n. U.S. an epithet applied to liberals with leftist leanings; a radical liberal. Radic-Libs resist anticrime bills, undercut the President abroad, excuse violence while they denounce the police, support fast withdrawal from Asia, pooh-pooh pornography and keep religion out of the schools. Time 9/28/70, p8 The assault on the "radic-libs" has failed to divert the voters from their money worries, and the claim that the new Senate would contain a reliable "ideological majority" seemed to be wishful thinking. Harper's 8/71, p29 [1970]

radio astrometry, the branch of radio astronomy dealing with the magnitudes and positions of radio sources. In addition to this ability to map radio sources with fine resolution, the instrument is expected to prove valuable in radio astrometry, that is, the study of the precise positions of radio sources on the celestial sphere. New Scientist 10/19/72, p139 [1972]

radio echo sounding, a method of determining the depth of a body of water, an ice mass, etc., by measuring the echoes of very high frequency radio waves transmitted through it from the surface or the air. Contributions to the International Antarctic Glaciological Project . . . included 40 hours of aerial radio-echo sounding of the Lambert Glacier . . . Britannica Book of the Year 1975, p74 [1972]

radio galaxy, a galaxy that emits or is a source of extensive radiation. The first of the abnormal objects to be discovered were the radio galaxies. These are objects which emit intense radio signals, but look like galaxies, although sometimes their appearance is strange in comparison to that of a normal galaxy. The radio emission from the most powerful radio galaxies is equal to, and in some cases greater than, the entire output of energy from our Galaxy at all wavelengths. Robert Jastrow and Malcolm H. Thompson, Astronomy: Fundamentals and Frontiers, 1972, p220 [1960]

radioimmunoassay, n. a method of assaying the amount or other characteristics of a substance by labeling it with a radioactive chemical and combining it with an antibody to induce an immunological reaction. The availability of pure hormone has made possible the development of a very sensitive radioimmunoassay for the hormone. McGraw-Hill Yearbook of Science and Technology 1969, p121 [1962]

radioimmunological, adj. involving the use of radiolabeling in immunology. Estimation of the concentration of peptide hormones in plasma can be made by radioimmunological techniques. Britannica Book of the Year 1968, p528 [1965]

radioisotopic, adj. of or relating to radioactive isotopes, as used in power-generating nuclear reactors, as tracers in medicine,

etc. In the case of quintuple payloads Cosmos 80-84 and Cosmos 86-90 it was stated that one satellite of each group had a radioisotopic nuclear generator. New Scientist 12/30/65, p918 [1956]

radioisotopically, adv. with or by means of a radioactive isotope. Dr. Cohen notes that more than a year ago one group of workers attempted to trace a radioisotopically labeled extract through the recipient's body and found that the material had a great deal of difficulty reaching the brain. Science News 4/20/68, p376 [1970]

radiolabel, v.t. to label or tag (a substance) by adding a radioactive isotope to the substance and tracing it through one or more chemical reactions. Variations in the composition of the antisera would make each antiserum a unique target for radiolabelling with consequent variations in results. Nature 3/6/75, p67 —n. a radioactive isotope used to radiolabel a substance. The use of a radiolabel makes the technique expensive, Purcell concedes, but the expense is justified by the increased sensitivity. Science 6/16/72, p1226 [1962 for verb; 1972 for noun]

radiopharmaceutical, n. a radioactive drug used in medical diagnosis, therapy, and research. In some newer systems, a physician looked at the picture of the distribution of the radiopharmaceutical within the patient's body and then, with the aid of general-purpose computers, obtained quantitative answers to questions suggested to him by the image. 1971 Britannica Yearbook of Science and the Future, p231 In this case, doctors used one of Union Carbide's radiopharmaceuticals, which readily concentrates in brain tumors. Scientific American 7/67/, p47 [1960]

radio pulsar, a pulsar that emits radio pulses, as distinguished from optical or X-ray pulses. Russell A. Hulse and Joseph H. Taylor of the University of Massachusetts found the first radio pulsar in a binary system in July, 1974. Their discovery establishes that a neutron star can form as one of a relatively low-mass binary pair without disrupting the system. World Book Science Annual 1976, p240 [1972]

radiosterilization, n. sterilization by means of radioactive rays. The agency's programme in this field is largely a result of Hungarian initiative and Dr. B. Toth, the Hungarian Deputy Minister of Health, when opening the conference, went so far as to describe radiosterilization as one of the most useful ways of using atomic energy for peaceful purposes. New Scientist 6/22/67, p694 [1964]

radiosterilize, v.t. to sterilize by subjecting to radioactive rays. In Europe and the U.S. several new plants for radiosterilizing medical supplies were built or ordered. Britannica Book of the Year 1967, p588 [1966]

radiotoxin, n. a radioactive poison. Kuzin and Kryukova believe that the radiotoxins in the [irradiated] extracts penetrate the cell nucleus and combine with certain proteins such as histones and desoxyribonucleoproteins thus affecting the mechanism controlling the synthesis of nucleic acid. Science Journal 9/68, p9 [1968]

radiotoxologic, adj. of or relating to the study of radiotoxins. Below, scientist working in the new radiotoxologic institute in Prague, Czech. Laboratory has developed safeguards for workers experimenting with radioactive substances on laboratory animals. Picture legend, Britannica Book of the Year 1968, p528 [1968]

raga-rock (ˌrɑːgə'rɑk), n. a form of rock 'n' roll using an Indian melodic form, such as the raga, and usually including a sitar or three-stringed Indian guitar among the instruments. And Gabor Szabo, the Hungarian guitarist, has similarly attracted young audiences with his own mixture of Indian music and jazz dubbed "raga rock." 1968 World Book Year Book, p159 Such attention as he [George Harrison] got came in oddball ways. In 1965 he created a vogue for raga-rock, by introducing the sitar in Norwegian Wood. It was he who interested the rest of the Beatles in transcendental meditation. Time 11/30/70, p57 [1960]

ragtop, n. Slang. a convertible with a folding cloth top. There was perhaps a subtle message in the way Pierre Trudeau tooled *is classic 1959 Mercedes ragtop past the glinting camera lens-s on the way to joining his cabinet.* Maclean's 6/29/81, 17 [**1955,** 1967]

ag trader, *Slang.* a clothes merchant; a retailer of clothing. *What his and Davidson's King's Road Developments propose instead is an "environmentally controlled" shopping mall, predominantly of high class rag traders with restaurants and pub behind the preserved Pheasantry façade, courtyard and entrance arch.* Times (London) 8/21/70, p21 [**1970,** from earlier *rag trade* the garment industry (OEDS 1938)]

aider, *n.* short for CORPORATE RAIDER. *To deter raiders, every major American corporation is busily "restructuring" itself, to use the Wall Street euphemism.* Atlantic 5/88, p77 [**1988**]

ainbow coalition, *U.S.* a coalition of disadvantaged groups for political action. *His candidacy, he [Reverend Jesse Jackson] said, is not just one man running for office but an attempt to inspire others of what he calls a rainbow coalition—black, white and Hispanic citizens, women, American Indians and the voiceless and downtrodden"—to run for office as well.* NY Times 11/4/83, pB5 [**1983**] ▶According to the journalist Mike Kenney of the *Boston Globe,* the term was not coined by the Reverend Jackson but by Texas Agriculture Commissioner Jim Hightower, a liberal who during the 1982 campaign spoke of his support from "a rainbow coalition of blacks, browns, Anglos, blue-collar workers and yellow-dog Democrats," the latter referring to a description of a Democratic Party regular during the 1928 presidential campaign as one "who would vote for a yellow dog if the dog were a democrat."

ain date, an alternative date for an outdoor activity or performance called off because of rain. *Wednesday, July 2, at 8:30 rain date, July 3), "La Traviata."* New Yorker 7/7/75, p11 [**1972**]

ainmaker, *n. U.S. Slang.* a business executive, especially a partner in a law firm, who has high political connections and promises to use them to bring in business. *Rainmakers can come up dry: ex-Attorney General Ramsey Clark did so much free pro bono work that he lost money for his former New York firm.* Time 4/10/78, p65 *But the firm's reputation as a political one comes primarily from Mr. Shea's activities. In legal parlance, a "rainmaker" is a business-getter, and in the Shea Gould firm, Mr. Shea rattles the sky and produces thunderstorms.* NY Times 12/6/78, pB1 [**1968,** in allusion to the American Indian rainmaker (OED 1775), who promised to produce rain by supernatural means] **—rainmaking,** *n.: "Rainmaking" . . . has come to mean at the trial the promise a lawyer makes to his client to keep him happy, a promise a lawyer has no intention of keeping.* NY Times 4/28/74, p51

allycross, *n.* an automobile competition in which drivers in small groups race to achieve the fastest time around a short course. *With the reduction in rally events the other branches of the sport have blossomed—sprints, hillclimbs, rallycross, . . . and drag racing.* Times (London) 7/13/73, pVII [**1967,** from *rally + cross* (as in *moto-cross* an automobile race)]

allyman, *n.* a person who participates in an automobile rally, especially one who races cars in a rally. *But down in the forests something stirs. It is the sound of innumerable club rallymen taking part in overnight events. More drivers than ever apparently want to go rallying—but on a more reasonable scale.* Sunday Times (London) 2/2/75, p13 [**1967**]

RAM, *n.* **1** acronym for RANDOM-ACCESS MEMORY. Compare ROM. *Appropriately programmed RAM's—up to 16 kbit [kilobits] per circuit—can store any program in the machine in a 'standby" mode. Coupled with this "plug-in" programming, a user-programmable file containing two metal nitride-oxide semiconductor RAM's—each with 1 kbit per circuit—can retain information indefinitely without power.* New Scientist 5/24/76, p704 [**1957**] **2** acronym for REVERSE ANNUITY MORTGAGE. *A RAM cannot help you buy a house. It is meant for people 65 years old and over who own their homes free and clear of any mortgages. People who qualify for a RAM are able to borrow up to 80 percent of the appraised value of their house. Instead of getting a lump sum from the lender, the homeowner*

receives equal monthly payments for a specified period, such as 10 to 20 years. Christian Science Monitor 2/2/83, p11 [**1983**]

rand, *n.* the basic unit of money in the Republic of South Africa since 1961. *But, inasmuch as the blacks started off far behind the whites, their actual annual pay increase, adjusted for inflation, was two hundred and ninety-eight rands—the rand is worth a dollar and eighteen cents—as apposed to a fourteen-hundred-rand increase for the whites.* New Yorker 5/14/79, p118 [**1961,** named after The *Rand* a gold-mining area of the Transvaal, shortened from the Afrikaans name *Witwatersrand,* literally, white waters edge]

r & b or **R & B,** abbreviation of *rhythm and blues,* blues music with a strong, repetitious rhythm. *To keep track of and evaluate the enormous number of r.-&-b. singles on the market is a full-time job in itself. Yet reviewing black albums too often means being depressingly and misleadingly negative.* New Yorker 11/23/68, p135 [**1958**]

random-access memory, a computer memory in which all the data is readily accessible and each item is independent of the location or storage sequence. Compare READ-ONLY MEMORY. *What, for instance, is a 64K RAM, a product which many electronics firms are now racing to develop? Random Access Memory is the normal sort of data store used by a computer, and 64 kilobits is a measure of how much information this particular device can hold.* Sunday Times (London) 6/22/80, p19 [**1967**]

randomicity, *n.* random quality or condition; randomness. *Environmental randomicity of various kinds may have important implications in triggering evolutionary sequences that would be impossible or unlikely in nonstochastic environments.* Science 10/27/72, p392 *Most of these phenomena are characterized by a great deal of randomicity associated with the chaotic nature of turbulence.* McGraw-Hill Yearbook of Science and Technology 1977, p390 [**1936,** 1972, from *random + -icity,* as in *elasticity, electricity,* and other words formed from adjectives in *-ic*]

RANN, *n. U.S.* acronym for *Research Applied to National Needs,* a program of the National Science Foundation, created to explore ways of solving social, environmental, and health problems. *Faced with a host of federal agencies sponsoring research on fossil fuels and nuclear sources, RANN should concentrate on unconventional sources, such as solar energy.* Science 12/22/72, p1272 [**1971**]

rap, *U.S. Slang. —v.i.* **1** to have a talk; converse, especially openly and sincerely. *I went with Officers Juan Morales and Pete DiBono to the juvenile guidance center where they rap once every week with the kids in jail.* Harper's 12/70, p93 *Am I going to stay at home and get high and have a good time tonight or am I going to go out to try and rap (talk seriously) with the people, to try to organize?* Times (London) 1/7/71, p12 **2** to get along; be on good speaking terms. *[James] Buckley the candidate softly rakes "the voices of doubt and despair," claims to rap with the Silent Majority, curries the hardhat vote . . .* Time 10/26/70, p22 **—n. 1** a talk; conversation. *"Look. Around Jane Fonda you may call it a rap, but here it's still called a powwow."* Cartoon legend, New Yorker 8/8/70, p36 *Delighted and amazed that these nice, all-American kids had produced and approved so "right on" a document with such overwhelming enthusiasm, I . . . got into a rap with a tenth grader in a bikini.* Harper's 8/71, p26 **2** short for RAP MUSIC. *Rap, the streetwise, intensely rhythmic pop sound that has come roaring out of Harlem, Brooklyn and the South Bronx to influence dance music the world over, is entering a second critical phase in its evolution.* NY Times 5/18/83, pC19 [**1965,** originally black slang, probably developed from the earlier standard sense "to utter sharply or vigorously" (OED 1541)]

rap group, *U.S. Slang.* a group that meets to discuss and work out problems together. See also RAP SESSION. *. . . the New York chapter of the Vietnam Veterans Against the War instituted weekly "rap groups" where men meet and talk about their experiences and feelings.* NY Times 6/12/71, p28 *For all the visibility of . . . WITCHES [WITCH, for Women's International Terrorist Conspiracy from Hell], the heart of the [Women's*

Lib] *movement is made up of hundreds of "rap groups," usually formed on an* ad hoc *basis.* Time 8/31/70, p18 **[1970]**

rapid deployment force, a military force trained for ready or immediate deployment in distant parts of the world. *Abbreviation:* RDF *With its new "rapid deployment force," the Administration would be able, in the mid-1980's, to send 110,000 troops to the Gulf in three weeks or less.* NY Times 1/20/80, pE3 **[1980]**

rapid water, *U.S.* a nontoxic polymer slurry that is mixed with water in fire-fighting pumping apparatus to decrease friction and accelerate the rate of flow. It is manufactured under the trademark *Ucar. Engine 60, on East 143d Street, is one of the busiest fire companies in the city, and has been without rapid water since last May. When queried yesterday, a spokesman for the Fire Department acknowledged that supplies of the additive were low and that many other companies in the city equipped to use rapid water were out of it.* NY Times 8/21/76, p22 **[1976]**

rap music, a style of rock music with a very pronounced rhythmical beat and vocal accompaniment in a recitative rather than melodic style, especially used in break dancing.... *Mr. Weller began embracing American black music, and "My Ever Changing Moods" shows that he has assimilated Motown and Philadelphia soul styles, but not rap and funk music. "A Gospel," a rabid anti-patriarchal diatribe written in a Biblical jargon completely misses the improvisatory sass, humor and rhythmic vitality of the best New York rap music.* NY Times 4/29/84, pE27 **[1981]**

rap parlor, *U.S.* a euphemism for a place of prostitution. *"In 1970 we didn't have a dial-a-anything that advertised, no porno movie houses, no rap parlors and only four adult bookstores all of which were within one block of each other," he* [James M. O'Meara] *said. "Now there are adult movie houses all over the city, about 15 rap parlors, for which there's no control whatsoever, and porno bookstores everywhere."* NY Times 2/7/70, p6 **[1975,** from *rap* as in *rap session*, because such establishments disguise their illegal activities by claiming to conduct rap sessions]

rapper, *n. U.S. Slang.* a person who raps; talker. *Boulez clearly hopes there will be as many rappers as listeners.* Time 2/22/71, p38 **[1971]**

rap session, *U.S. Slang.* a discussion by a group of people, usually about a specific problem. *In every major city, women, most of them young, gather for "consciousness-raising" rap sessions, the awareness rituals of The Sisterhood.* Time 8/24/70, p12 ... *a church rap session at which a few hundred women came to talk about their abortions* ... New Yorker 11/28/70, p130 **[1970]**

rap sheet, *U.S. Slang.* a police record. *Except for so-called crimes of passion, or an occasional armed robbery, or a marijuana bust, the "Rap Sheet" of most first-timers will show from one to three pages of brushes with the law, fines, county-jail time, and probation before these men got into a California prison, or for that matter, most American prisons.* Atlantic 5/71, p34 **[1960,** from the slang term *rap* criminal charge (1903), as in *a bum rap*]

ras, *n.* any of a group of genes that are normally present in human, animal, and yeast cells, but can cause cancer under certain conditions. *Scientists learned in 1983 that yeast cells contain two genes that are similar to a human cancer gene known as H-ras. Because they are so like the human gene, the two yeast genes are also called ras. Mutant yeast strains that lack both ras genes cannot grow, indicating that the genes serve some important function in the normal growth of a yeast cell.* World Book Science Annual 1986, p288 **[1985,** from *rat* virus; so called because the original gene was found in association with a rat virus]

Rasta, *n.* short for RASTAFARIAN. *What the Rastas really believe . . . is a little hard to grasp, partly because it takes days just to understand the patois and mainly because they spend most of their waking time on the verge of vanishing into delicious, weed-induced delirium.* Maclean's 12/13/76, p52 *The*

overwhelming majority of reggae's exponents are devo Rastas. Rolling Stone 1/11/79, p97 **[1962]**

Rastafarian, *n.* a member of a cult of the West Indies, original in Jamaica, which regards Africa as heaven and the forme ruler of Ethiopia, Haile Selassie, as a god. *The government failure to cope with economic problems has led to bizarre ph nomena, such as the Rastafarians, a cult which deifies Hai Selassie, the Ethiopian ruler.* 1967 Collier's Encyclopedia Ye Book, p287 **—adj.** of or designating this sect. *In Jamaica, for e. ample, the Ras Tafarian sect believes . . . that Ethiopia's Hai Selassie is God and Ethiopia the Promised Land* ... Tim 3/23/70, p33 **[1955,** from *Ras Tafari*, the title and surname Emperor Haile Selassie]

Rastafarianism, *n.* the practices and beliefs of the Rastafarian *A significant minority of young West Indian males in Englan are rejecting the values of white, English society and expres. ing pride through Rastafarianism in being black, according a report published today by the Social Science Research Cou cil research unit on ethnic relations.* Times (London) 11/23/7 p30 **[1962,** from *Rastafarian* (see RASTA) + *-ism*] ►Accordin to Tracy Nicholas, *Rastafari, A Way of Life* (1979), Rastafarian refer to their practices and beliefs as *Rastafari.*

ratchet effect, intermittent advance, increase, growth, et *During the last decade and a half the SNP* [Scottish Nationa Party] *has advanced by a ratchet effect. If they are stuck f a moment at their latest peak that does not mean they will sta stuck forever.* Manchester Guardian Weekly 5/22/7 p4 *Because they want to be reelected, Congressmen are gene ally on the lookout for ways in which to increase governmer programs. This is because enlarged federal programs enlar the number of constituents that a Congressman can "service, thus adding to the number of voters who will be suitably grat ful on election day. The result is a powerful ratchet effect, wit federal programs and expenditures getting larger, but almo never smaller.* Harper's 6/78, p57 **[1970]**

ratchet jaw, *U.S. Slang.* a person who talks too much or too lon over citizens band radio; chatterbox. *Perhaps the biggest prob lem is overcrowding, which can turn "good buddies" into nast rivals. CBers are supposed to limit calls to five minutes, an those who do not are called "ratchet jaws." But even withou the ratchet jaws, some CBers on crowded highways or in urba and suburban areas never get a chance to talk.* 1977 World Book Year Book, p267 **[1976,** from the comparison of the mov ing jaw to the jerky motion and clattering noise of a ratche mechanism]

ratfink, *n. Slang.* a mean, worthless individual; an obnoxiou person.... *"in fitting American youth for its destiny in th free world of tomorrow, our schools may be virtually compel ling them to become a bunch of ratfinks."* Saturday Review 4/23/66, p36 ... *I should refrain from saying any more ex cept that he seems to be one of the few writers who really enjo words and use them properly, and that anyone who doesn buy a copy of this book is a rat fink.* Punch 11/24/65 p777 **[1964,** from *rat* + *fink, n.,* slang for obnoxious person; in former; (originally) strikebreaker, of unknown origin]

ratomorphic, *adj.* modeled on the behavior of experimenta rats. *You say I overestimate the dangers of the Robotomorphi or Ratomorphic view, on everyday life, but with Pavlov's dog Lorenz's grey-legged geese, Morris's naked ape, each time a analogy of behavior was taken as a homology.* Times (Londo 12/17/70, p15 *He identified the stimulus-response model i psychology with the "robot model" of man, for which Arthu Koestler has coined the epithet the "ratomorphic view of man.* Science 4/5/68, p58 **[1964]**

ratracer, *n. U.S.* **1** an aggressive, ruthless competitor.... *th students of the twenties flouted rather than protested, sa their fathers as Babbitts and stick-in-the-muds, not as capital ists and ratracers, and shook their heads over the situation, no their fists.* Atlantic 10/70, p135 ... *in the magazine literatu of the youth rebellion the father is the "rat-racer," the symbo of everything that really significant kids hate about their soci ety.* NY Times 6/18/67, pD14 **2** a person caught up in the con fusion, rush, etc., of daily commuting or travel. *Among the* easons advanced for this two-wheeled renaissance are disillu- ion with the internal combustion engine, the belief among at-racers that the physical exercise delays thrombosis, and the repeatedly proven fact that in traffic-choked cities the slender ike is the fastest means of getting from A to B. New Scientist nd Science Journal 7/1/71, p5 [**1962,** from *rat race* aggressive activity or competition (OEDS 1939) + *-er*]

raunch, *n.* **1** untidiness; sloppiness; shabbiness. *Calvin Coodge High is an actual Manhattan school building, its rust and raunch unretouched for the camera.* Time 8/18/67, p63 **2** rudeness, vulgarity, or tastelessness. *Bette Midler is . . . no treisand, her material is blue and her songs are old. Yet she's een camped out at one of Broadway's biggest theatres for sevral months now, making raunch respectable in a sellout revue alled Clams on the Half Shell.* Manchester Guardian Weekly /2/75, p20 *There are bars that are all elegance, and bars that re all raunch, and bars that breathe both elegance and raunch nd therefore are considered chic.* NY Times 7/9/76, C19 [**1964,** back formation from *raunchy* (1939)]

rave-up, *n. British Slang.* a wild party. . . . *John Bates, whose lothes with the Jean Varon label, are stocked all over the counry and who dresses debutantes for their coming out parties nd dolly girls for their all-night rave-ups.* Times (London) /20/68, p7 *Off the field the atmosphere was that of a transatantic rave-up.* Times (London) 2/23/70, p6 [**1967,** from the lang verb phrase *rave up* to express in a wild, frantic manner]

raw bar, *U.S.* a seafood restaurant, or counter at a restaurant, here raw shellfish are served. *There are numerous seafood resaurants ranging from hamburger stands, which also serve hrimpburgers and clamburgers, and raw bars, such as Frog's anding, . . .* NY Times 2/5/89, pE14 [**1943, 1986**]

azor cut or **razor haircut,** a haircut given with a razor instead f scissors. *Hair as dark as this ideally goes into a sleek and sohisticated styling of the very short tapered razor cut.* Family Circle 10/65, p60 *Now, ours is an age where life tries to imitate rt, and indeed there are a great many young guys hustling bout with earnest expressions and $35 razor haircuts . . .* Harer's 12/70, p42 [**1965**]

azor job, *British Informal.* a ruthless attack; hatchet job. *This ey passage occurs early in . . . the section which is the book's eal beginning. It sets the tone for a spectacular razor-job on american pedagogy: PhD-mills, symbol-mongering, the lot.* imes Literary Supplement 2/4/72, p127 [**1971**]

DA, abbreviation of *recommended dietary allowance. RDAs ave been published by the National Research Council's Food nd Nutrition Board for only a handful of trace elements.* Since News 8/14/71, p113 . . . *between 2 and 12% of the subects studied had intakes lower than one-half the daily ecommended dietary allowance (RDA) set by the National Reearch Council for the various vitamins and minerals.* 1971 Britannica Yearbook of Science and the Future, p194 [**1970**]

DF or **R.D.F.,** abbreviation of RAPID DEPLOYMENT FORCE. . . *the ability of the Rapid Deployment Force to deal with sitations where ground forces may be needed quickly, as in the ersian Gulf, must be made credible. But doing so will require hat we finally clarify whether the R.D.F. will be run by the Marines or by the Army.* NY Times Magazine 1/18/81, 51 [**1981**]

eaction shot, a motion-picture or television camera shot of a erformer's face to show an emotional reaction or response. *Mis [Michael Jackson's] lack of experience as a screen actor vorks partly to his advantage; his ingenuousness is touching, hough there are too many reaction shots of him being selfonsciously dear, and you want to yell "Cut!" to the editor.* New Yorker 10/30/78, p141 [**1953**]

eactor zone, an area showing the remains or evidence of the OKLO PHENOMENON. *Nature, not man, had constructed the orld's first nuclear-fission reactor. Eventually six reactor ones were identified in the Oklo pit, four of them in strata hat had not yet been mined.* Scientific American 7/76, 36 [**1976**]

read, *v.t.* to decode (a genetic message). *Each transfer RNA is succeeded by another one, carrying its own amino acid, until the complete message in the messenger RNA has been "read."* Scientific American 2/66, p30 *The first mutation was a deletion that removed a "letter" from the genetic message; the second mutation inserted an extraneous letter. Such mutations are called "frame-shift" mutations since they cause succeeding bases to be "read" in incorrect groups of three.* Scientific American 7/71, p46 [**1962**]

reading wand, *British.* an electronic device that reads and records the coded information on the labels of retail goods. *Much more information about the transaction can be entered and recorded, particularly on those ECR's [electronic cash registers] fitted with a so-called automatic reading wand.* New Scientist 4/20/72, p130 [**1972**]

read-only memory, a computer memory in which the data cannot be altered by program instructions. Also called ROM. *The decoding, timing and control circuitry . . . is principally governed by one or another of 320 instruction words (each consisting of 11 bits) delivered to the instruction register (and thence to the controller) from the read-only memory, so named because it contains a programmed set of operational instructions that cannot be changed after the manufacture of the calculator. Each instruction word, obtained from the read-only memory by nine-bit address words, establishes the operating rules that apply during one instruction cycle of 13 state times (39 clock cycles).* Scientific American 3/76, p92 [**1961**]

ready-faded, *adj.* made or designed to look faded; prefaded. *There's something rather precious about the washed-out look of, for instance, No. 50, I take it to represent fine art's answer to the ready-faded denim jean.* Listener 12/27/73, p898 [**1973**]

Reaganomics, *n.* the economic policies of President Ronald Reagan. *He [Representative Jack Kemp] is closely identified with Reaganomics and is an architect of the tax-cutting measure Mr. Reagan embraced as the centerpiece of his firstterm economic program.* NY Times 6/6/86, pA14 [**1981,** blend of *Reagan* and -NOMICS]

reaggregate (ri:ˈægrəˌgeit *for verb;* ri:ˈægrəgit *for noun*), *v.i., v.t.* to form (cells or tissue) into a new mass or aggregate. *The idea that a piece of developing tissue from an embryo can be gently teased apart into its component cells, and that these will then reaggregate to form an apparently normal test-tube version of the tissue when gently shaken in solution, stems from Aaron Moscona of Chicago.* New Scientist 1/6/72, p6 —n. tissue that has reaggregated. *Spontaneous and evoked activities in the neuronal reaggregates were often synchronized, even between clusters that were 2 to 3 mm apart.* Science 4/14/72, p183 [**1966**]—**reaggregation,** *n.: As Gierer* et al. *show that even dissociated cells show some memory of their original position, it should be possible to find what kinds of biochemical treatment before reaggregation can disrupt this memory.* Nature 10/13/72, p366

reality therapy, a method of psychotherapy to help a person accept and adjust to reality. *This step-by-step handbook is designed not to judge therapies but to explain them. Among the guide's offerings are handy capsule descriptions of the kinds of treatment available (e.g., "reality therapy": an approach emphasizing how to cope with a hostile environment).* Time 1/5/76, p64 [**1971**]

rear-end, *v.t.* to collide with the back of (an automobile or other vehicle). *It's raining, and I have to be careful driving. Very careful. There's been an accident, too. Someone has rear-ended someone else at a traffic light . . .* New Yorker 4/28/86, p40 [**1976**]

recall, *n.* a request for the return of a product by its manufacturer for some necessary repair, especially to eliminate a possible hazard to the user. *When recalls are instituted, the auto companies estimate that only between 50 and 85 per cent of recalled vehicles are actually brought in for safety checks.* NY Times 4/23/72, pD4 [**1964**]

receptorology, *n.* See the quotation for the meaning. *One of the exciting advances in cell biology in the 1970s has of course* *been the birth of receptorology, the inelegant name given to the molecular study of receptor units.* New Scientist 1/10/74, p64 **[1972]**

receptor site, an area or structure in a cell where the action of a drug or other substance takes effect. *The ways in which these proteins formed 'receptor sites', at which, and only at which, chemical messengers such as hormones could stimulate the cell to whatever action was required, was beginning to become an exact science.* Annual Register of World Events in 1975, p360 **[1972]**

recertification, *n.* renewal of certification, especially by a certification board established in some field, such as nursing and aviation. *F. Bradley MacKimm, former publisher of Medical World News and of MD Medical Newsmagazine, two of the more popular magazines for physicians, is . . . this time taking advantage of a recent development in the medical profession, recertification. From his office . . . he'll begin publishing Family Practice Recertification in April and delivering it to more than 70,000 family physicians.* NY Times 1/26/79, pD11 **[1973]**

recessionary, *adj.* of or relating to an economic recession; characterized by a setback in sales, employment, production, etc., usually following a protracted period of inflation. *He admits himself baffled by the combination of high inflationary symptoms in prices and interest rates with recessionary symptoms in output.* Times (London) 5/22/70, p8 **[1958]**

reclama (ri'klɑ:mə), *n.* a request or appeal to reconsider a decision, proposed action, or policy. *Margaret Thatcher, wrote James R. Schlesinger in Foreign Affairs magazine in 1986, "appeared at Camp David to deliver a reclama on Reykjavik."* NY Times Magazine 6/11/89, p18 **[1975,** military use, probably shortened from *reclamation* act of protesting, a protest (OED 1533)]

recombinant (ri:'kɑmbənənt), *n.* a gene or genetic substance made from recombinant DNA. *The widespread use of* E. coli *bacteria in this new genetic research increases its dangers . . . Thus every laboratory working with E. coli recombinants is staffed by potential carriers who could spread a dangerous recombinant to the rest of the world.* NY Times Magazine 8/22/76, p59 *Meanwhile, many scientists are eager to proceed with recombinant research, because DNA recombinants offer a promising lead in the search for possible links between viruses and cancer.* 1977 Collier's Encyclopedia Year Book, p164 —*adj.* of or. having to do with recombinant DNA or recombinant DNA research. *By the way: The tragic results from recombinant gene experimentation can be hypothesized also from chance mutation, and that without interference of man. No safety rules possible can prevent that from happening.* Science News 4/9/77, p227 **[1975,** so called beçause it is produced by *recombining* fragments of DNA molecules obtained from different organisms]

recombinant DNA, a form of DNA produced in the laboratory by recombining fragments of DNA molecules obtained from different organisms. The recombined molecules are introduced into a host cell and become a part of its permanent genetic complement. *Research in recombinant DNA may create viral and bacterial mutants that, should they ever escape from the laboratory, could rapidly kill off whole species of plants and animals, including the human species, and so create ecological chaos.* Theodore Roszak, Person/Planet, 1978, p35 *Human insulin has been produced at last by genetically engineered bacteria in a California laboratory—an achievement that catapults recombinant DNA technology into the major leagues of the drug industry.* Science News 9/16/78, p195 **[1975]**

recombinant DNA research, the methods and procedures by which DNA fragments from different organisms are recombined in the laboratory to produce new or altered genes which are then inserted into host cells to assume specific genetic functions. Also called GENE-SPLICING and GENE TRANSPLANTATION. *The work is called recombinant DNA research because it involves breaking apart chains of deoxyribonucleic acid (DNA), the chemical that carries genetic data, and recombining*

them in various ways. World Book Science Annual 1978, p28 *am not opposed to recombinant DNA research as such. I ha₁ said, and I still believe, there are some wonderful results to ₁ derived from genetic engineering—and some that may litera ly be essential for the survival of our civilisation. But I see al₁ a darker potential for biological and social chaos and I wou₁ hope to maximise the former and minimise the latter.* New S₁ entist 1/20/77, p150 **[1976]** ▶Recombinant DNA research generally regarded as the first major step in the developmen of genetic engineering, the process of altering, adding, or r₁ moving genes to produce new living forms and characters.

recombinational repair, self-repair of a strand of the DNA mol₁ cule. *The third mechanism is under the control of the genes i₁ volved in genetic recombination and is called recombinationa or Rec, repair. It appears to repair single-strand breaks in th sugar-phosphate backbone that are induced primarily by su₁ ionizing radiation as X rays, and by certain chemicals.* 197 Britannica Yearbook of Science and the Future, p303 **[1971]**

reconciliation room, another name for ROOM OF RECONCILI₁ TION. *Another Catholic editor, Commonweal's John Deedy, b₁ lieves the church is already "well down the road" towar elimination of individual confession. Whether those low-₁ "reconciliation rooms" will prove him wrong remains to ₁ seen.* Time 3/15/76, p44 **[1976]**

reconfigure, *v.t.* to change the form or parts of (an aircraft, com puter, etc.). *The air traffic control and navigation comple which exists today is essentially a hodgepodge of war surplu systems which have been reconfigured using modern compo nents.* Science News 6/15/68, p570 *The software must be d₁ signed so that the system is self re-configuring in the event c any hardware failure.* Times (London) 4/3/70, p27 *One of th 11 will now have to be reconfigured to accommodate the fe₁ tures that were lost on the first plane.* Science News 1/9/7₁ p24 **[1964]**

recreational vehicle, a vehicle for leisure or recreational activ ties, such as a camper or trailer. *Abbreviation:* RV Also call₁ RECVEE. *The desert becomes dotted with oases of recreationa vehicles clustered into base camps for target shooters, hunter₁ bird watchers, wild-flower enthusiasts, backpackers, bicyclist₁ fossil collectors, gem prospectors and even, improbably, fishe₁ men.* Newsweek 4/30/73, p73 *In glinting procession, ofte oblivious of the 55-m.p.h. limit, gas guzzlers and recreationa vehicles are already rolling down the interstates.* Time 7/4/77 p31 **[1966]**

rectenna, *n.* an antenna which receives microwave beams an₁ converts them into direct-current electricity. *The microwave would be beamed to the earth by a transmitting antenna, on₁ kilometre in diameter, on each satellite. The power would be r₁ ceived at antennas on the ground called rectennas, each a₁ oval about ten kilometres wide and thirteen kilometres long where the microwave energy would be rectified, or converte₁ back into electricity, and then fed into a local power grid.* Nev Yorker 2/16/81, p94 **[1975,** from *rect*ifying + antenna]

recursive, *adj.* capable of being returned to or used repeatedly *One function Professor Miller considered was the ability t₁ deal with "recursive" programmes, that is, to interrupt a cours₁ of action to undertake another—a "subroutine"—and then t₁ interrupt this in turn with the same subroutine, and so on.* New Scientist 10/15/64, p147 **[1959]**

recusal (ri'kyu:zəl), *n.* a declaring unfit as a judge; disqualifica tion of a judge. *During the hearings, a South African applica tion for the recusal of three judges—the President of the Court Sir Muhammad Zafrullah Khan, Judge Luis Padilla Nervo o, Mexico, and Judge Platon Morozov of Russia—was rejected a₁ was an offer of an all-race plebiscite in Namibia to let the peo ple themselves indicate whether they would prefer a South Af rican or UN administration.* Annual Register of World Event₁ in 1971, p224 **[1958,** from *recus*e (1600's) to reject or disqualify as a judge + *-al*]

recvee or **rec-v** (ˌrek'vi:), *n. Informal.* acronym for RECRE₁ ATIONAL VEHICLE. *In 1961, 83,500 "rec vees" were sold; las₁ year the number was 740,000. There are now some 6.5 million rec-vee families in the U.S.* Time 7/2/73, p60 *You can learn ₁* *lot about people from the vehicles they drive. Silicon Valley folk appear to favour classy pick-ups and an incredible variety of so-called recreational vehicles, Rec-Vs or RVs. These range from modest vans (though embellished with exuberant paint-schemes, bulging portholes and, so help me, bay windows) to huge monsters, in appearance part furniture pantechnicon, part meat truck.* Times (London) 11/22/78, p18 [**1972**, from re*creational + vee or v (for vehicle)]*

recyclable, *adj.* capable of being recycled. *Considering the remarkable cost of children's books and their remarkably brief life span, publishers might do well to encase their pages and bindings in some sort of ersatz (but recyclable) horn.* New Yorker 12/4/71, p177 [**1971**] —**recyclability**, *n.: In terms of its . . . utility and recyclability, glass is a natural.* Scientific American 7/73 (page not known)

recycle, *v.t.* **1** to put (wastes, garbage, etc.) through a cycle of purification and conversion to useful products. *As we look toward the long-range future—to 1980, 2000 and beyond—recycling of materials will become increasingly necessary not only for waste disposal but also to conserve resources. Richard M. Nixon, in President's Message to Congress of 2/10/70 Officials agreed that recycling would have a chance to succeed only if separation of garbage were mandatory, scavengers were controlled by penalties, convenient collections were scheduled and there were a market for the recycled materials.* NY Times 6/13/71, pA98 [**1960**] **2** *Figurative.* to put to a new or different use. *Just about every [pop music] hit or near-hit has been recycled and a fair number of them has been reactivated in single form and have reappeared in the charts.* Listener 10/4/73, p463 *Most housewives bent on recycling their talents discover that they must in fact recycle is their spirit—their initiative, perseverance, and aggressiveness.* Harper's 9/74, p93 *Recycled American series are becoming Arabian national pastimes.* I Dream of Jeannie has even hit Saudi Arabia. Esquire 8/75, p78 [**1970**] **3** to renovate (an old building), especially for another function. *The sessions . . . will include visual presentations, discussions and on-site tours and will be augmented by an exhibit of recycled old buildings done by New England architects.* Preservation News 9/74, p9 *Boston has recycled its majestic old market buildings and made them the exciting new hub of innercity life.* Time 9/4/78, p2 [**1975**] **4** to rechannel (surplus oil revenues) to oil-importing countries in the form of loans and investments. *So far, the recycling function has been fulfilled by commercial banks through the Eurodollar markets. The Arabs have been depositing dollars and (in smaller amounts) pounds sterling with banks in London and in New York. The banks, in turn, have been lending money to Britain, France, Peru, etc.* Forbes 8/15/74, p25 *Specifically, if the recycling of OPEC funds is to work at all, the Arabs must be brought into the Western financial tent—not kept out of it.* NY Times 3/30/75, p10 [**1974**. The four senses above are extensions of the original meaning (OEDS 1926) "to put again through a cycle of treatment."] —**recycler**, *n.: In the realm of ideas, Hannah [Arendt] was a conservationist; she did not believe in throwing away what had once been thought. A use might be found for it: in her own way, she was an enthusiastic recycler.* New York Review of Books 1/22/76, p8

red, *n. Slang.* a barbiturate capsule, especially Seconal (secobarbital). *Another is the case of a heroin addict who first "shot some reds" (that is, barbiturates) and then "fixed" with heroin following the barbiturates.* NY Times Magazine 11/19/72, p116 [**1966**, so called from its color]

red alert, an emergency state of readiness in the face of imminent danger. *Admissions to London hospitals [due to a flu epidemic] in the week ending at midnight on Monday totalled slightly over 2,000, above the figure for a similar period during the last hospital "red alert" two years ago . . .* Manchester Guardian Weekly 1/3/70, p24 *He [Frank C. Erwin, Jr.] has no patience with anyone or anything he considers damaging to his beloved alma mater University of Texas—and since Erwin s chairman of the university's board of regents, his antagonists re automatically on red alert.* Time 8/10/70, p54 [**1961**, extended sense of the term for an air-raid alert]

Red Army, **1** a terrorist group of Japan. The Japanese Red Army. *A fanatic, radical leftist movement whose cloudy ideology is part Mao, part Trotskyite permanent revolution, part Che Guevarism. Merged from a number of loosely knit radical groups, the Red Army . . . has been involved in terrorist exploits in Europe and the Middle East as well as Asia. The best known: the 1972 massacre at Lod Airport in which three Red Army terrorists, acting for the Palestinians, gunned down 26 people.* Time 10/31/77, p45 **2** Usually, **Red Army Faction.** a terrorist group of West Germany. *Clutterbuck goes on to say that although today's terrorists have comparable anti-authority aims, their motivations are by no means uniform. "Some, like the Palestinians and the members of the I.R.A., are nationalistic," he says. "Some, like the Red Army of Japan, the Red Brigades of Italy, and perhaps the Red Army faction of West Germany—the Baader-Meinhof Gang, in popular parlance—have broader and more widespread revolutionary goals.* New Yorker 6/12/78, p38 [**1972**, from the name of the army of various communist countries, originally the Russian Bolshevik (later Soviet Union) army]

Red Brigades, an organization of Italian terrorists of the extreme left. *The Red Brigades . . . have also been blamed for a spate of attacks, including bank raids, assassinations and bombings.* NY Times 12/16/76, p3 *Between the kidnapping and the murder of Aldo Moro in Italy, a document was issued by the Red Brigades describing the doctrine and strategy of the Italian movement. It defined the ultimate objective of the Red Brigades as "to liberate man finally from bestial exploitation, from necessary labor, from misery, from fatigue, from social degradation."* New Yorker 9/18/78, p135 *Outside, in the headlines, the Red Brigades are blowing people's knees off.* Rolling Stone 1/11/79, p79 [**1972**, translation of Italian *Brigate Rosse*]

red chicken, *Slang.* a crude form of heroin. *Most of those uncovered are turning out the crude No 3 heroin (known as . . . Red Chicken) for local consumption, but Government chemists see enough factories with the high quality No 4 heroin to suggest a sizable onward traffic, probably to America.* Listener 11/11/71, p644 [**1970**]

Red Guard, **1** a member of a movement of young Maoists of China, especially those active in the Cultural Revolution. *Such developments as . . . the rampages of the Red Guards represent momentous changes for China.* Atlantic 12/66, p26 *The Red Guards damaged a number of temples and old buildings, destroyed old books. Ancient statues were covered with red posters. The Red Guards called for the closing of churches and mosques, and for streets to be given more revolutionary names such as The East Is Red. Anything western was attacked—western dress styles, haircuts.* Listener 1/19/67, p80 **2** a member of any of various other groups of political radicals. *Japan's Red Guards are members of the Socialist opposition—aided by Communists and the Komeito (Clean Government Party)—who for the past three months have charged Sato's Cabinet with everything from fraud and embezzlement to improper installation of a toilet.* Time 11/4/66, p35 *As in all such movements there is an extremist group, called "Red Guards" in Turin, that seeks to eliminate virtually all traditional authority, to elect professors and to confer marks based on the findings of student committees.* NY Times 2/10/68, p2 [**1966**]

Red Guard doctor, a paramedic in China. *Analogous groups have also been trained in cities, such as "work doctors" in factories and "Red Guard doctors," who are housewives serving as physicians' assistants in neighborhood health clinics.* 1973 Collier's Encyclopedia Year Book, p477 [**1972**, named after the RED GUARD]

Red Guardism, the movement of the Chinese Red Guards. *By November last year Red Guardism was in full cry, and zealous youths were swarming across China on foot and by trains, buses and boats, holding aloft little red books containing quotations from Mr. Mao . . .* NY Times 3/5/67, p2 [**1967**]

redline, *v.t. U.S.* to subject (an old or blighted area of a city) to REDLINING; discriminate against by denying loans, mortgages, or insurance, especially to prospective property owners. *Banks, savings and loan associations, and other mortgage and broker-*

age houses in Detroit often "redlined" neighborhoods in the city, meaning blacks could not get mortgages in these areas. Saturday Review 8/26/72, p14 *For the community that is redlined, that has conventional mortgage and loan money withdrawn, panic sets in. Through their economic discrimination, the lending institutions ensure a community's deterioration.* Student Lawyer, 4/75, p36 *Once a collective decision is made by a group of banks to redline a community, that decision itself can become the critical factor in determining the community's future.* Oscar Newman, Community of Interest, 1980, p88 [**1967**, from *red line* supposedly drawn on a map to exclude certain areas]

redlining, *n. U.S.* the practice by certain banks, insurers, and other institutions of refusing to grant loans, mortgages, or insurance in old or blighted parts of a city because of the presumed risks involved. *Stopping banks and FHA firms from systematically denying applications for home-improvement loans in low-income neighborhoods, thus ensuring the further collapse of the neighborhood (the battle against this practice, called "redlining," has not yet been won)* . . . Harper's 12/74, p114 *Redlining involves a self-fulfilling prophecy, because an area shunned by lenders will, in fact, soon deteriorate for lack of the funds necessary for upkeep.* NY Times 9/14/75, pD2 [**1968**; see REDLINE]

Red No. 40, an artificial coloring agent used in the United States in foods, drugs, and cosmetics as a substitute for the banned RED NO. 2. *The ruling may push up the price of many consumer products. Red No. 40 costs $8.50 per lb., v. $5.50 for No. 2, and manufacturers have to use 30% to 50% more of it to get the same color intensity as with Red No. 2. Even then, the colors do not come out quite the same, so chocolate pudding may look a bit greener.* Time 2/2/76, p53 *Early in 1977 the FDA indicated that Red No. 40 may also be banned because it causes cancer in mice.* Britannica Book of the Year 1978, p393 [**1976**]

Red No. 2, an artificial coloring agent derived from naphthalene, formerly used in many foods, drugs, and cosmetics. It was banned in the United States in 1976 as a suspected carcinogen. Also called RED 2. *Red No. 2 has many advantages as a coloring agent—persistence, stability, intensity, solubility, economy—and was often chosen over other red dyes such as Red No. 40.* Science News 1/24/76, p55 *Red No. 2 gives the red colour to a wide range of foods, including jams, jellies, soft drinks, frankfurters, bottled red cabbage, salami, and blackcurrant drinks.* New Scientist 3/25/76, p659 [**1976**]

Red Power, a slogan used by American Indians, modeled on the term BLACK POWER. *As with Black Power the burgeoning Red Power movement has two components, one cultural, the other political. The Indians want some recognition, not just that they exist but that their culture has, or at least had, worthwhile values of its own.* Manchester Guardian Weekly 5/23/70, p24 *The [Mescalero Apache] tribe's demonstration of "red power" began in 1961 when leaders drew up comprehensive development plans based on tribal priorities and consultants' reports. One concern recommended the tourist complex, another, stock raising.* NY Times 6/10/71, p26 [**1968**]

red-shift, *v.t.* to shift (lines of light in stars, quasars, etc.) toward the red end or longest wave-lengths of the spectrum, indicating movement of the light source away from the observer. *In the spectra of quasi-stellar objects, however, these ultraviolet lines (both emission and absorption) are red-shifted into the visible region of the spectrum* . . . Scientific American 12/70, p24 [**1964**, verb use of *red shift* the shift of stellar light toward the red end of the spectrum (OEDS 1923)]

redshirt, *n. U.S.* a college student of athletic ability whose normal four-year course is deliberately extended by one year, usually the sophomore year, in order that he or she may develop further athletic skills. *He worked even harder in his sophomore year as a "redshirt," practicing with the varsity but not playing in any games—so that he would have an additional year of eligibility.* Time 12/7/70, p78 [**1955**, so called because of the red shirts often worn by such players during practice to distinguish them from members of the varsity]

Red 2, variant of RED NO. 2 *Red 2 has been the most widely used food color in this country, and it has always been touted as the "most thoroughly tested" of all the food colors.* Science 2/6/76, p450 [**1973**]

reductive, *adj.* of or relating to minimal art; minimal. *To judge by art magazines and museum programs, nothing new has been done in the past few years but Happenings, optical displays, and so-called primary structures and reductive paintings.* New Yorker 2/25/67, p99 [**1967**]

reductivism, *n.* another name for MINIMAL ART. *Bernard Cohen's White Plant dates from the period when his earlier 'linguistic' style had degenerated into a hothouse aestheticism the rather self-conscious reductivism of his recent exhibition was far less cloying. The odd-man-out, in that his work is figurative, is David Hockney.* Listener 8/17/67, p220 [**1967**]

reductivist, *n.* another name for MINIMALIST. *New York, architecturally closed and varied in climate, is dominated by large numbers of artists who swim in one or two schools producing closely related work—lately, the reductivists and the remainders of the Pop people.* Saturday Review 9/23/67, p55 [**1967**]

redundancy, *n. Aerospace.* the ability to provide duplication or replacement of some function in case of a failure in equipment *The Goldstone station was equipped with two completely separate systems to provide 100 percent redundancy in the reception and recording of the Ranger photographs.* Scientific American 1/66, p61 [**1962**]

reed relay, a device used as a switching unit in electronic telephone exchange systems. *One development has been a semielectronic exchange based on a device called a reed relay, in which two hairlike metal reeds are sealed in nitrogen in a glass ampoule. Because the reeds are so tiny, the time required to draw them together and to make the electrical contact is infinitesimal, and the telephone at the receiving end rings as soon as the caller has fed in the last digit.* Saturday Review 10/28/72, p41 *Reed-relay . . . switches are likely to be superseded at some time in the future by microelectronic digital switches.* Times (London) 1/5/73, p17 [**1966**]

reeducate, *v.t.* to train or drill in a program of political indoctrination, especially in a communist country. *In Vietnam, Laos and Cambodia . . . major efforts were made to revive the rural economy and to "reeducate" former opponents, but the Cambodians were clearly the most draconian in their approach.* Britannica Book of the Year 1977, p204 [**1955**, extended from earlier meaning "to educate anew, especially in order to rehabilitate or reform"] —**reeducation,** *n.: The P.R.G.* [Provisional Revolutionary Government] *has resorted to the time-honored Communist technique of "re-education" for its enemies, including some political prisoners arrested since August. Camps have been set up throughout the country for indoctrination sessions that usually last about three months.* Time 2/16/76, p30 *"Re-education" is not a punishment in the ordinary penal sense. At best it is an administrative measure of unlimited duration imposed by the victor on the vanquished.* Manchester Guardian Weekly (Le Monde section) 10/15/78, p11

reel-to-reel, *adj.* consisting of or using an open supply reel and a take-up reel for winding and rewinding magnetic tape. *Tape cartridges have their appeal, too, particularly for the in-car user, but the software repertoire for them is limited. Then there is the open reel-to-reel tape system, for which pre-recorded tapes have dropped to a mere trickle from specialist suppliers when available at all.* Listener 10/23/75, pii [**1961**]

reference beam, the beam of laser light that is aimed at the photographic plate or film in holography. *Holography is a method of recording images on film without a lens. It requires a coherent illuminating beam, divided so that one part lights the object, while the other, called the reference beam, goes directly to the film.* World Book Science Annual 1968, p221 *A low-power continuous laser, bore-sighted through the high-intensity pulsed laser, provides a continuous internal reference beam for aiming the telescope in conjunction with the television camera and reticle system . . .* Scientific American 3/70, p41 [**1966**]

reflag, *v.t.* to register under another flag. . . . *the confusion and controversy that surround the unexceptional White House plan to reflag 11 Kuwaiti oil tankers with the Stars and Stripes.* Manchester Guardian (Washington Post section) 7/19/87, p15 [**1987**]

reflexology, *n.* a method of massaging certain areas of the foot or hand to relieve nervous tension. *Once he pinpoints the cause (or causes) of the patient's symptoms, the New Doctor will be eclectic in his approach to treatment. Depending on his previous experience, he may use one or several of the following forms of therapy: meditation, psychotherapy, acupuncture, special diets and exercises, hypnotherapy, group therapy, reflexology, and manipulative techniques akin to chiropractic.* Maclean's 1/7/80, p40 [**1976**]

refusenik or **refusnik**, *n.* a Soviet citizen, especially a Jew, whose application for emigration is rejected. *I met Vladimir Sverdlin and Ilya Shostakovsky there who seemed to be close friends and who worked at organizing the "refuseniks" into some sort of cohesive body.* Times (London) 6/6/77, p8 *Anatoly Scharansky, the celebrated 29-year-old refusnik was arrested last March at the Slepak apartment, where he had stayed for six months.* New York Post 12/6/77, p45 *Orlov, who is a high energy physicist, was convicted of anti-Soviet agitation, a vague, catch-all charge often leveled at Soviet dissidents and refuseniks (persons who are refused a visa to Israel).* Science News 9/2/78, p165 [**1975**, from *refuse* + *-nik* Russian suffix meaning one who is connected with something]

reggae ('regˌei), *n.* a form of rock music of West Indian origin; also, a dance or song set to this music. See the quotation for details. *One type of music that kept within the bounds of the single [record] was "reggae," which swept Britain in the autumn of 1969. Imported by West Indian immigrants, reggae was simple, catchy, and very rhythmic; being easy to dance to, it became very popular with younger teenagers. It was also a style to which many tunes could be adapted . . .* Britannica Book of the Year 1971, p545 [**1968**, originally named in the British West Indies, but of unknown origin]

Regge ('redˌʒei), *adj.* of or having to do with a theory in particle physics that explains the behavior of strongly interacting subatomic particles in terms of mathematical poles and trajectories rather than as fundamental physical particles such as quarks. —**Regge hypothesis:** *The members of each of these families are said to lie on a hypothetical curve called a Regge trajectory . . . The idea that all hadrons lie on such trajectories, sometimes called the Regge hypothesis (even though Regge's original work did not involve hadrons), is now widely accepted.* Scientific American 2/75, p62 —**Regge pole:** *The Regge pole is an abstract mathematical way of representing an entire class of physical situations. For example, all our Type 8 spikes can be described as originating from one Regge pole, so that instead of needing an infinite number of mathematical terms to describe the behavior of Type 8 resonances, one can make do with the Regge pole alone.* Scientific American 7/74, p71 —**Regge theory:** *The development of theoretical elementary particle physics has continued in two principal areas: current algebra and the quark model, and Regge theory.* McGraw-Hill Yearbook of Science and Technology 1970, p179 —**Regge trajectory:** *Another classification scheme, known as "Regge theory," groups particles with differing masses and "spins" (internal angular momenta) into families (called "Regge trajectories"). It is found that there is a correlation between the spin and mass of each resonance within a family such that the spin is proportional to the square of the mass.* New Scientist 4/10/75, p76 [**1962**, named after Tullio *Regge*, born 1931, an Italian theoretical physicist]

Reggeism ('redˌʒeiˌizəm), *n.* another name for REGGE THEORY. *There is now good evidence that Reggeism works in the following sense. The scattering region (where virtual particle exchanges give rise to exchange forces) and the resonance region (where the real particles exist after the fashion of molecular spectra) are described by a common entity called the trajectory function.* McGraw-Hill Yearbook of Science and Technology 1970, p183 [**1970**]

regional, *n. U.S.* any of a number of small stock exchanges located in various regions of the country and serving chiefly as a secondary market for shares traded on the larger exchanges. *Wall Street brokers say that a considerable amount of United States securities business is being diverted by Canadian brokers to the regionals.* NY Times 1/8/68, p101 *Because of this growth—and the prospect of more to come—the cost of seats on the regionals has been rising steadily.* Time 9/3/65, p58 [**1965**, shortened from *regional exchange*. The British equivalent is *country exchange.*]

registered player, a tennis player of a category newly created by the International Lawn Tennis Federation, consisting of independent professionals who are eligible to play for prize money in open tournaments. *The amateurs receive only expense money; the registered players, who must be over 19 years of age, may receive cash prizes as well as expense money, as do the pros.* Americana Annual 1970, p650 *It seemed illogical, for instance, that a so-called Contract Professional, a professional who was under contract to a tennis promoter, was not eligible to represent his country in Davis Cup competition, whereas a so-called Registered Player, a professional who was affiliated with his national lawn-tennis association, was eligible.* New Yorker 10/2/71, p98 [**1968**]

regulator gene or **regulatory gene**, another name for OPERATOR. *Repressors, like the protein whose formation they repress, are coded for by genetic DNA; the genes that code for them are regulator genes.* New Scientist 2/9/67, p322 *The first known class consists of structural genes, which determine the amino acid sequence and three-dimensional shape of proteins; the second is regulatory genes, which specify whether structural genes will function and therefore control the rate of enzyme synthesis.* Science News Yearbook 1970, p103 [**1961, 1970**]

rehab, *n. U.S.* short for *rehabilitation. The vocational rehabilitation program—or "rehab" as it is often called—is jointly funded by the Alabama Department of Mental Health and the Vocational Rehabilitation Service of the state Department of Education.* Tuscaloosa News (Alabama) 9/28/75, pD1 *A runaway from a therapy group stands with his nose pressed against a steel door and shrieks periodically. "He wants to go to rehab," a recreational aide explains.* NY Times Magazine 5/21/78, p46 —*v.t.* to rehabilitate. *These were people who wanted to do good; who . . . saw slums and dreamed of humane dwelling spaces (solid 1890s structures built practically with slave labor, now rehabbed to perfection, filled with greenery and occupied by urban planning consultants).* Harper's 6/78, p43 [**1961** for noun, **1978** for verb; by shortening]

reinforce, *v.t., v.i.* **1** to encourage or strengthen (a response to a stimulus), usually by rewarding a correct response and withholding reward for an incorrect one. *If they happen to be particularly upset by their son's stomach pains (perhaps because of their own "visceral" personalities) and tend to play down the other effects, they will "reward" or reinforce the specific symptoms whenever they occur.* Encyclopedia Science Supplement (Grolier) 1970, p93 *With the red light on, push the manual feed switch to reward the bird every time it hits the switch. Continue to reinforce only as the bird pecks closer to the red light . . . A pigeon can be trained in this way in as little as 15 minutes.* Scientific American 10/70, p128 **2** to reward (a person or animal) for responding to a stimulus. . . . *we decided that this man who had been mute for 30 years had learned to be mute—or more technically had been reinforced (rewarded) by his environment for being mute.* Listener 8/29/68, p266 [**1968**]

reinforcement therapist, a practitioner of reinforcement therapy. *This principle, the reinforcement therapists insist, applies also to mental patients previously thought to be beyond psychiatric help.* Time 7/11/69, p44 [**1969**]

reinforcement therapy, psychiatric therapy designed to restore normal behavior by rewarding a patient whenever he responds normally to a stimulus, especially a stimulus in commonplace circumstances. The rewards are supposed to reinforce normal response until such response eventually becomes permanent. *For example, a withdrawn patient who makes an effort to talk with others receives certain rewards, such as extra food, candy,*

*or spending money; if he withdraws into silence, these ameni-
ties are withheld. Approximately fifty institutions in the United States are using reinforcement therapy.* Encyclopedia
Science Supplement (Grolier) 1970, p71 **[1969]**

REIT (riːt), *n. U.S.* acronym for *real estate investment trust,* a
type of lending organization that invests in real estate holdings,
such as developed property or construction projects. *Many
banks, including Chase, organized their own REITs—a move
that now seems to have been most unwise. As demand for commercial construction collapsed, many builders and property
owners were forced into bankruptcy, and the REITs and the
banks that they borrowed from were left holding the bag.* Time
1/26/76, p50 *The Value Line Investment Survey calculated recently that a group of four REITs had run up an aggregate gain
of 30% in the past three months . . . Such gains have been a
long time in coming for many REITs.* Daily News (New York)
6/4/79, p36 *The trend is now back to syndicates, which were
favored before REITs. REITs are still chancy for the first-time
investor whose every dollar must count.* Ruth Rejnis, Her
Home, 1980, p163 **[1973]**

rejaser, *n. U.S. Slang.* one who engages in or practices rejasing.
*These days, rejasers even dump junked cars neatly offshore: the
hulks act like coral reefs, attracting fish—and fishermen.* Time
4/19/71, p52 **[1971]**

rejasing, *n. U.S. Slang.* the act or practice of putting rubbish or
discarded items to useful purpose. *The biggest benefit of rejasing is that virtually indestructible objects never reach the garbage heap.* Time 4/19/71, p52 *"Rejasing'—Reusing Junk As
Something Else"—is gaining in popularity and application
throughout America . . . try it sometime.* Congressional Record, Washington, D.C. 4/21/71 **[1971,** formed as an acronym
for "*reusing junk as something else"]**

rejection front, the Arab groups or countries that oppose any
form of negotiation or settlement with Israel; rejectionists as a
united front. *The Palestinian National Congress (parliament)
has so far not been called upon to ratify the six-point agreement concluded by various Fedayeen organisations at the recent Tripoli conference. So this new platform, put together
under pressure from the Rejection Front which deliberately
rules out any compromise worked out with Israel, is still only
a paper project and could be dropped at any time for a more
conciliatory stance.* Manchester Guardian Weekly (Le Monde
section) 1/1/78, p11 **[1975]**

rejectionist, *n.* an Arab leader, group, or country that rejects
any form of negotiation or accommodation with Israel. *The so-
called rejectionists like Iraq and Libya, which oppose a permanent settlement with Israel, emerged largely discredited.* Time
12/6/76, p32 **—adj.** of or having to do with rejectionists; opposing any form of negotiation or accommodation with Israel.
*There was no comment from the rejectionist states today about
President Sadat's decision to return the latest draft Israeli-
Egyptian peace treaty for further study.* Times (London)
10/24/78, p8 **[1974]** —**rejectionism,** *n.: West Bank residents
have always tended toward the moderate end of the Palestinian political spectrum. Rejectionism, the political current that
dismisses the idea of negotiating with Israel, exists, particularly among the young; it gains and loses strength as the situation
changes but it is clearly a minority view.* NY Times 2/20/78,
p10

relationship, *n.* a euphemism for a romantic attachment or affair. *A woman banker who came to the club only once told me
she had a "relationship" but was looking for something better.
"This fellow I'm seeing," she said, "would like to move in with
me. He'd like all the conveniences of being married without the
responsibilities. But I wouldn't live with him and I wouldn't
marry him."* NY Times Magazine 8/29/76, p18 *"I told you
about Carl. He's the person with whom I'm having a relationship."* Cartoon legend, New Yorker 9/26/77, p123 **[1967]**

relativities, *n.pl. British.* the relative differences in wages within and between groups of workers. *The Government had recognised that unfairness might have arisen. It was also to take a
broad look at pay relativities, a word of which we were destined*

to hear much more. Manchester Guardian Weekly 3/16/74,
p6 **[1962]**

relet (ˈriːˌlet), *n. British.* a dwelling unit that is let or leased
anew. *Even allowing for the substantial numbers of relets from
the existing stock, the magnitude of the loss of this source of
housing in the new communities is evident.* Times (London)
1/7/76, p13 **[1969,** noun use of the verb (OED 1812), pronounced (riːˈlet)]

relevance, *n.* concern with important current issues. Compare
IRRELEVANCE. *The impetus came largely from student demands for "relevance," especially for the overdue admission of
more minority-group students. Activism has also done much to
curb the old absurdities of trivial research and needless Ph.D.s.*
Time 11/30/70, p40 *New programs offered to viewers in the
fall of 1970 put a heavy premium on the word "relevance,"
which to the networks meant dealing with social problems that
supposedly concern young people.* Americana Annual 1971,
p663 **[1970]**

relevant, *adj.* concerned with important current issues. *Either
we can commit ourselves to changing the institutions of our society that need to be changed, to make them—to use a term
which I hate—"relevant," to make them responsive or we can
sit back and try to defend them . . .* Harper's 11/69,
p86 [Adam] *Walinsky is running hard against New York State
Attorney General Louis Lefkowitz . . . The Walinsky campaign is energetic, relevant and heavily financed.* Time
10/19/70, p20 **[1969]**

REM (rem), *n.* acronym for *rapid eye movement,* the frequent
and jerky movements of the eyes which occur during the
dreaming period or state known as PARADOXICAL SLEEP. *But
rapid, almost flickering eye movements, now abbreviated in
the trade jargon to REMs, occurred in varying stretches of five
minutes to an hour, several times during a night's sleep.* Time
2/14/64, p46 **[1957]**

remote, *v.t.* to extend to great distances. *At present, Beacon
handles about 12 million passenger bookings a year. The system, which is based on Univac computer equipment, first came
into operation in 1965. By 1967, the system had been "re-
moted" to principal cities throughout the United Kingdom and
in 1968 to Paris, Amsterdam and Dublin.* New Scientist
3/9/72, p544 **[1970,** verb use of the adjective]

remote sensing, the gathering of data, usually about features of
the earth or other bodies in space, from an artificial satellite or
space probe by means of radar, aerial infrared photography,
seismography, and similar techniques (often used attributively). *Remote sensing involves the use of special cameras and
other sophisticated instruments in orbiting earth satellites.
These instruments see and record invisible as well as visible
light waves given off by objects on earth. The result is a picture
that is far more revealing than one obtained by regular photography.* 1972 Britannica Yearbook of Science and the Future,
p162 *A remote-sensing satellite could provide information on
vegetation, soil, and water infinitely faster and often more accurately than ground observation.* Americana Annual 1970,
p56 **[1972]**

remote sensor, a camera, radar unit, seismograph, or other instrument used for remote sensing. *Instruments called remote
sensors are well on the way to providing information vital to
the solution of some of the worst problems of our environment—many of them being problems that technology itself
has caused.* Encyclopedia Science Supplement (Grolier) 1972,
p392 **[1972]**

REM sleep, another name for PARADOXICAL SLEEP. *All mammals show REM sleep, but frogs and birds do not.* Scientific
American 8/70, p126 *Reserpine, which induces dysphoria
rather than euphoria, enhances REM sleep, as does LSD.*
McGraw-Hill Yearbook of Science and Technology 1971,
p171 **[1970]**

renminbi (ˈrenˈminˈbiː), *n.* the currency or legal tender of the
People's Republic of China. *The outside world was still largely
unfamiliar with the Chinese currency—the renminbi or people's currency. The basic unit of renminbi—which is abbreviat-*

ed to *RMB*—is the *yuan*, represented by the symbol *Y*, and the subsidiary units are *jiao* (*10 jiao = 1 yuan*) and *fen* (*10 fen = 1 jiao*). Times (London) 3/21/73, pIII [**1970**, from Chinese (Pinyin) *rén-mín-bi*, literally, people's currency]

rent-a-crowd or **rentacrowd**, *n. Especially British Slang.* a group of people paid or induced to form a crowd at a rally, demonstration, or the like. *In the end, the Ford campaign turned into a television extravaganza, with the President shuttling from city to city to make pre-programmed appearances before rent-a-crowds, replete with "photo opportunities" but no "question opportunities" for the press.* Maclean's 11/15/76, p61 *I wish your paper would avoid the loaded term rent-a-crowd when reporting confrontations such as the recent one in Lewisham. The implication is absurd: journalese may be cheap, but to buy the services of 4,000 demonstrators would hardly be a cost-effective exercise in such a labour-intensive field.* Manchester Guardian Weekly 9/18/77, p2 [**1961**, patterned after *rent-a-car* (1935) a car rental firm]

rent-a-mob or **rentamob**, *n. British Slang.* a group of people paid or induced to act as a mob and especially to cause a riot. *Students are the prime targets of the anti-elitists because they can be so easily organised into Rentamobs by Labour's syndicalists and their allies (and future masters) even further to the Left.* New Statesman 9/26/75, p356 *Trade unionists therefore all feel attacked and have rallied round to help our colleagues who have had 44 weeks of picketing. Charges of rent-a-mob are totally untrue and as a steward each morning, I can confirm all people I have spoken to are card carrying members of a trade union.* Times (London) 6/21/77, p15 [**1970**]

rent strike, *U.S.* refusal by the tenants of a building to pay their rent as a protest against rent increases, poor service, etc. *The tenants of the apartments at West Madison and Albany were conducting a rent strike.* New Yorker 3/13/71, p92 *The student organization also is lending moral and organizational support to the Berkeley Tenants' Union (many of whose members are students) in a widespread local rent strike.* NY Times 2/5/70, p36 [**1970**]

reovirus, *n.* an echovirus associated with respiratory and intestinal infections and found also in certain animal and human tumors. *One, called reovirus, was previously known as a common virus widely distributed in animals, but it is now being found in patients with African lymphoma.* Times (London) 9/19/67, p8 *Reoviruses, of which there are three types, have been isolated from secretions of the respiratory tract as well as of intestines, but are relatively unimportant.* Science News Letter 2/12/66, p103 [**1959**, from *r*espiratory *e*nteric *o*rphan *virus*; called "orphan virus" because it is not known to cause any of the diseases it is associated with]

repeg, *v.t.* to give a fixed value to (a floating currency). *By the year's end, the Canadian dollar, which had been floating for over two and a half years, was regarded as very unlikely to be repegged before both the international situation and Canadian-U.S. relationships achieved a higher degree of stability.* Britannica Book of the Year 1973, p529 [**1972**]

repetitive DNA, a form of DNA that contains multiple copies of a particular gene in each cell. *In all cases the repetitive DNA was located next to the single-copy DNA. The repetitive DNA was also shown to be in a sequence about 300 base pairs long, while the single-copy DNA adjacent to it was about 1,500 base pairs long.* Americana Annual 1976, p263 [**1975**]

replacement level, the birth rate needed for a population to maintain itself. *The "total fertility rate"—a figure calibrated to the average completed family size at current fertility rates— was also up about 5 percent above the first third of last year. However, the current rate of 1.84 children per woman is still below the "replacement level" of 2.1 children for American society.* Science News 8/13/77, p101 [**1974**]

replamineform (ˌrepləˈmiːnˌfɔrm), *n.* a process for duplicating organic skeletal structures in ceramic, metal, or polymer materials (usually used attributively). *Biomaterials. Further development of synthetic membranes holds the promise of creating a totally implantable artificial kidney . . . and a new "replamineform process" can help replicate living structures in*

some suitable material. Science News 1/26/74, p53 [**1972**, probably from *repl*icated + *amine* + *form*]

replant, *v.t.* to reattach surgically (a severed hand, finger, toe, etc.); implant anew. *From 1966 to 1971, the surgeons replanted 151 fingers. Eighty-five percent of the operations were successful.* Science News 6/16/73, p388 [**1973**] —**replantation**, *n.: Replantation, members of the research group stress, must be based on a patient's general condition, on the nature of the trauma, and on the time limit for survival of the replanted limb.* Science News 6/16/73, p388

replicar, *n.* a full-sized replica of a classic or antique automobile, usually sold in the form of a kit and containing an engine and other mechanical parts of modern design. *Most of the replicar companies are small, the result of individuals' efforts to meet a very present demand for the past.* NY Times 1/28/79, pL14 [**1979**, blend of *replica* and *car*]

replicase, *n.* an enzyme that promotes synthesis of RNA (ribonucleic acid) on an RNA template. *In the research, new viral RNA was produced in the test tube with the help of an enzyme, called a replicase, and strands of natural virus RNA.* NY Times 4/25/68, p20 [**1963**, from *replic*ation + *-ase* enzyme]

replicate, *v.i.* to duplicate or reproduce exactly by genetic processes. *When the cell reproduces by the process of division known as mitosis, these homologous chromosomes replicate and separate, so that each of the two daughter cells has a full complement of 46 chromosomes.* Scientific American 12/70, p46 [**1957**, back formation from *replication* (1948)]

replicon, *n.* any genetic element containing the structural gene to control its own replication. *This group . . . constitutes a replicon, of which there is just one in the E. coli chromosome and many on mammalian chromosomes. The bigger the chromosome the more replicons it has.* New Scientist 9/13/73, p607 *The replication of eukaryotic DNA has been extensively analyzed in the last few years, and significant problems that remain to be solved have been defined (for example, how are replicons turned on or off when the length of the S phase varies?).* Science 3/21/75, p1070 [**1963**, from French *réplicon*, from *réplication* replication + *-on* elementary unit]

repo, *n. U.S. Finance.* an agreement in which a seller of securities, especially government bonds, agrees to buy them back after a specified period. *Mr. Hunt believes that repurchase agreements, or "repos," are the missing link. Repos make it possible for corporations to earn interest on funds with maturities of less than 30 days.* NY Times 2/5/79, pD5 [**1963**, shortened from *repossess*, in allusion to the repurchase agreement.]

repressor, *n.* a theoretical component of the operon whose function is to repress the action of the operator. *The repressor determines when the gene turns on and off by functioning as an intermediate between the gene and an appropriate signal. Such a signal is often a small molecule that sticks to the repressor and alters or slightly distorts its shape.* Scientific American 6/70, p36 [**1957**]

reprographic, *adj.* of or relating to reprography. *The central reprographic unit is equivalent to the computer room where the main processor and general backing store are situated, while the various input devices, such as typewriters and copiers, are equivalent to the computer accessories.* Times (London) 9/27/68, p34 [**1961**]

reprography, *n.* the reproduction of graphic material, especially by electronic means. *Finally, there is reprography—which runs from simple ink and spirit duplicators through photocopying equipment to off-set lithography.* Times (London) 10/6/67, pIV [**1961**, from French *reprographie*, from *repro*duction + *-graphie* -graphy (recording process)]

repunit (ˈrepˌyuːnit), *n.* a number having one or more identical integers, such as 11, 111, 1111, etc. *"Repunits," numbers consisting entirely of 1's, produce palindromic squares when the number of units is one through nine, but 10 or more units give squares that are not palindromic.* Scientific American 8/70, p110 [**1970**, contraction of *repeating unit*]

reradiative, *adj.* capable of throwing off or reflecting radiation. *Thermal shielding to protect the* [space] *shuttle during the critical re-entry periods will probably be in the form of reradiative sheathing of such metals as columbium, rather than ablative shielding, which would have to be replaced for each flight.* New Scientist 12/11/69, p548 **[1969]**

reservation, *n.* **on the reservation**, *U.S. Informal.* remaining within a particular political party, faction, or group. *The appointment of Dean Burch . . . is another White House attempt to keep conservatives (as they say in White House lingo) "on the reservation."* National Review 3/15/74, p300 **[1971,** patterned after earlier phrase (DA 1949) *off the reservation* going outside a political party, faction, etc., as by supporting another group's candidate; originally used in allusion to Indians who left their reservations]

residency, *n. U.S.* advanced training or education in some field, analogous to medical or academic residencies. *Last winter the company instituted a series of "residencies" across the country—one- to three-week stands in Los Angeles, San Francisco, Chicago and at the University of Illinois—that combined performances with seminars and lecture-demonstrations.* Time 7/20/70, p51 **[1970]**

residual, *n. U.S.* a royalty received by a performer, writer, etc., for every repetition of a commercial or show in whose production he or she originally participated. *The network hopes to gross $1,000,000 from commercials for each rerun. The cut for Judy Garland and Oz's other 1939 stars: nothing. It was not until 1960 that film contracts began to provide residuals for actors.* Time 8/25/67, p60 **[1966]**

resistojet, *n.* a jet engine that uses electric resistance to heat liquid ammonia propellant, used chiefly to produce enough thrust to keep an artificial satellite steady during orbit. *Only one U.S. satellite, ATS-4* [Applications Technology Satellite-4], *has ever used electric propulsion as a primary system (in ATS's case, resistojets for altitude control).* Science News 11/2/68, p446 **[1968]**

resit, *v.t. British.* to take (a written examination) a second time. *So many students resit the engineering examination each year that an eventual pass rate of 80 per cent., as suggested by Mr. Alan Sim, may occur.* Sunday Times (London) 6/30/68, p15 *It is not likely that many students will, in fact, resit the examinations.* Times (London) 6/25/70, p4 **[1959]** ▶This verb has also a corresponding noun, (as in "the September *resit*," a feature of many British universities), in which the stress is on the first syllable: 'riː₁sit. Usage varies with the verb, which is pronounced either the same way as the noun or with the stress on the second syllable: riː'sit.

resmethrin, *n.* a quick-acting synthetic insecticide similar to the natural insecticide pyrethrin. *Formula:* $C_{22}H_{26}O_3$ Also called BIORESMETHRIN. *We keep them* [plastic sprayers] *about a quarter full of "Sprayday," the spray based on resmethrin which has a wonderful knock-down effect on most insects. Resmethrin is about the least harmful spray you can use as an insecticide.* Times (London) 7/10/76, p10 **[1971,** probably from *res*in + blend of *methyl* and *pyrethrin*]

resonance, *n.* an unstable elementary particle or group of particles of extremely short life. *. . . the rho meson is a particle in its own right although it is also frequently referred to as a resonance.* 1969 Britannica Yearbook of Science and the Future, p357 *A distinctive distortion, or peak, in the spectrum was found, indicating that for a brief time (of the order of 10^{-21} second) the three neutrons were bound together as one particle by the nuclear force. Such a complex body is known as resonance.* Science Journal 10/70, p23 **[1964]**

resonate, *v.i. Astronomy.* to be in synchronous motion (with oneself or another celestial body). *Amor* [an asteroid] *resonates with the earth (three orbits to eight of the earth's) in such a way that, as seen from the earth, its orbit rotates until it has a close approach to the earth.* Science News 2/17/73, p105 **[1973]**

respiratory distress syndrome, another name for HYALINE MEMBRANE DISEASE. *An artificial placenta which makes it possible to supply life saving oxygen to unborn babies suffer-*

ing from a dangerous disease known as respiratory distress syndrome has been developed by obstetricians at the Woolwich Hospital, London. Science Journal 8/68, p16 *Each year, 50,000 U.S. infants die soon after birth—at least 25,000 of them from respiratory distress syndrome (RDS). Also called hyaline membrane disease, RDS is caused by the inability of an infant's lungs to extract oxygen from the air and pass carbon dioxide out of the body.* Time 12/7/70, p94 **[1968]**

restorer gene, a plant gene that prevents sterility, isolated for use as a fertility agent. *Called the restorer gene, it restores fertility to male-sterile plants and makes possible the breeding of hybrid sunflowers of consistent high quality with good yield.* 1973 Britannica Yearbook of Science and the Future, p162 **[1969]**

restriction enzyme or **restriction endonuclease**, an enzyme that cleaves DNA strands (as of a bacterium or virus) at a specific site which matches the DNA fragment of another organism cut by the same enzyme, enabling segments of DNA from different sources to be joined in new genetic combinations. *The restriction enzyme EcoRI is an enzyme which conveniently chops DNA in such a way that the pieces have adhesive ends which can be used to stick the required gene, excised from the chromosome by the enzyme, into the replicating vehicle in which the same enzyme has hewn a suitable gap. The gap, however, must be in a part of the chromosome that the bacteriophage doesn't need in order to replicate, and that means that the particular sites on to which EcoRI likes to latch, must be on so-called nonessential parts of the genome.* New Scientist 12/12/74, p799 *Today at least 80 enzymes, called restriction endonucleases, are known to cut DNA in different specific parts of the molecule.* NY Times 11/12/78, pE9 **[1965, 1977]**

restriction site, the site at which a restriction enzyme cleaves DNA strands to be joined to the identically cut DNA of another organism. *The team synthesized an operator sequence of nucleic acid base pairs, then "glued on" two short DNA regions called restriction sites—the chemical equivalents to dotted lines where restriction enzymes can attack. They then snipped "holes" in small, circular chromosomes called plasmids and spliced in the operator region with restriction enzymes, one region per plasmid.* Science News 6/19/76, p389 **[1976]**

retard ('riː₁tɑrd), *n. U.S. Slang.* a mentally retarded person. *There are . . . heroin addicts, Air Force and CIA mental retards and Broadway Indians doing a Broadway Snake Dance.* Time 3/23/70, p49 *The younger son, self-described as "a hard-core retard," dreams of escaping to the wilds of Oregon to gambol with the bears and squirrels . . .* New Yorker 1/16/71, p76 **[1970]**

retardee (riː'tɑr₁diː), *n. U.S.* a mentally retarded person. *All but 5% of the hospital's 4,800 patients are confined there involuntarily through civil court orders; almost half are geriatrics cases or mental retardees who receive only custodial care.* Time 4/5/71, p38 **[1971]**

retarget, *v.t.* to direct to a new target. *The major outstanding question was whether Pioneer II, following along a year behind its predecessor, could safely be retargeted toward Saturn, a maneuver which would require a much closer pass to Jupiter—about 25,000 miles—for a gravity-assisted swingaround.* Science News 12/8/73, p357 *One response that Bergerac has made is to retarget Revlon's lowest-priced line, Natural Wonder, once aimed specifically at teen-agers, to reach women aged 18 to 34—not by changing the products, but by picturing slightly older females in the ads.* Time 12/11/78, p88 **[1970]**

rethink, *n. Chiefly British.* the act of rethinking; reconsideration; reappraisal. [Walter] *McNerney* [President of the Blue Cross Association of America], *in a word, seems to be in the van of the rethink of social policy now going on in the U.S.* Manchester Guardian Weekly 8/22/70, p13 *Using the metal* [titanium] *to its best advantage calls for a thorough rethink of metal-working methods and of the different avenues open to the aircraft engineer, to use different types of material . . . in an effective combination.* New Scientist 3/12/70, p503 **[1958,** noun use of the verb]

Retin-A ('retə,nei), *n.* a trademark for a substance used as a skin cream in the treatment of severe acne and found also to be effective in reducing wrinkles caused by exposure to the sun. *Formula:* $C_{20}H_{28}O_2$ *Analysis revealed that the skin treated with Retin-A grew new cell tissue to replace dead or damaged cells.* 1989 Collier's Encyclopedia Year Book, p325 [**1979**]

retinal, *n.* a yellow pigment in the retina. *The process* [by which the visual cell converts light into an electrical signal] *begins with the absorption of the incident light by the visual pigments in the disks. These pigments consist of a combination of vitamin A aldehyde, known as retinal (formerly called retinene), with a protein of the class called opsins.* Scientific American 10/70, p81 [**1960**]

retinotectal (,retənou'tektəl), *adj.* of or involving the network of nerve fibers connecting the retina with the dorsal part of the midbrain (tectum). *The mechanisms responsible for the formation of specific nerve connections have been analysed, most extensively in the retinotectal system of lower vertebrates: the axons of retinal ganglion cells connect selectively at local tectal sites to produce a map of the retina across the surface of the optic tectum.* Nature 1/18/74, p128 [**1962**, from *retino-* retina + *tectal* of the tectum]

retirement community, *Especially U.S.* a residential community chiefly or exclusively for elderly people. *The well-to-do, who constitute less than 5 per cent of the over-65 population, often live in "retirement communities" which are actually old-age ghettoes in Florida or California. Old people don't like being segregated with other old people, but it's better than being isolated in a city apartment.* Manchester Guardian Weekly 2/22/75, p16 *Youngstown is, in many ways, the prototype of the modern, self-contained American retirement community that has begun to spring up throughout the Southwest and Florida. And the generational clash here could be a preview of things to come elsewhere as the average age of Americans increases, and more of the elderly flock together to live out their days.* NY Times 1/29/76, p35 [**1963**]

retornado (,retɔr'na:dou), *n.* **1** a Spaniard who has returned to Spain after working in another country. *There is no welfare system, though—which means that young men and women who have never had a job do not get any income from the government, and neither do the* retornados, *who are coming home from West Germany and France and Switzerland at the rate of forty or fifty thousand a year.* New Yorker 3/21/77, p108 **2** a Portuguese citizen who has returned to Portugal from one of its former colonies. *He is a retornado—he came back from "over there." A colonist? Come, he hadn't been 20 years in Angola when the dream came to an abrupt end outside the mob-besieged gates of Luanda's airport.* Manchester Guardian Weekly (Le Monde section) 5/7/78, p13 [**1976**, from Spanish and Portuguese, literally, returnee]

retread, *n. Slang.* a person who rehashes old material. *Last August, I suggested in these pages that Duke Ellington be given a grant of, say, a hundred thousand dollars . . . The foundations, busy handing money out to retreads and the moribund, have been silent . . .* New Yorker 6/27/70, p52 [**1965**, from *retread, n.,* an old tire with a new tread (OEDS 1914)]

retribalization, *n.* the act or process of retribalizing; return to tribal status or to tribal practices. . . . *Hausa traders from Nigeria's north had migrated to a particular quarter of Ibadan (a Nigerian city not in Hausa territory), thus reinforcing their tribal ties for purposes of maintaining an elaborate trade network. This "retribalization" is an adaptation, in a new urban setting, to the demands of their economic and political life.* 1971 Britannica Yearbook of Science and the Future, p146 *Provided that the Bomb or the behavioral scientists do not get us first, this last phase will see reunification and integration, a sort of global retribalization.* Time 4/26/71, p64 [**1964**]

retribalize, *v.t.* to return to tribal status or to tribal ways and practices. *One of* [Marshal] *McLuhan's basic propositions is that we are crossing a technological frontier dividing the age of the collectivist from that of the individualist: We are being retribalized.* Saturday Review 4/15/67, p46 [**1963**]

retributivism, *n.* belief in dispensing punishment to criminals as an act of retribution for the injury they have caused. *Both are influential today: "retributivism" has become at least as damaging a charge on the one side as "sentimentalism" on the other: and there is an increasing readiness to listen to experts who explain away the criminal's responsibility in psychiatric terms.* Times (London) 2/24/70, p9 [**1970**]

retributivist, *adj.* characterized by retributivism. *Judicial fondness for expressionist and retributivist theories of punishment is at least partially founded on an idea that only the suffering of the criminal will appease the injured feelings of the victim.* Listener 12/30/71, p894 [**1968**]

retro[1], *n.* short for *retrorocket* (rocket producing reverse thrust). . . . *the thrust of the retro would keep it lodged in place under the craft until it had finished burning, when it would drop away.* New Scientist 9/21/67, p595 [**1961**]

retro[2], *n.* a revival of the fashions, music, plays, etc., of an earlier time (often used attributively). *The icy charms of the Group TSE's productions, beginning as far back as 1969's "Eva Peron," have been in the vanguard of the French vogue for "retro" (though the TSE is an Argentinian group, and a good deal of "retro" has been imported from the US).* Manchester Guardian Weekly (Le Monde section) 5/18/74, p14 *We thought that if we closed our eyes, retro fashion would go away. No such luck. Everything from bustiers (read the Merry Widow bra of the 1950's) to chippie shoes has been copied and is now flooding the stores. If you loved the recent Paris fashions and think that the 40's and 50's were cute, then retro is your thing.* NY Times 1/24/79, pC8 [**1974**, from French *rétro, n.* and *adj.,* probably short for *rétrospectif* retrospective]

RETRO or **Retro**, *n. U.S.* an engineer specializing in the firing and action of the retrorockets of a spacecraft. *In the front row . . . sat three Flight Dynamics Engineers, the men responsible for the ship's trajectory: from right to left, the Guidance Officer, or GUIDO, who was the chief navigation officer; the Flight Dynamics Officer, or FIDO, who plotted the trajectory and made sure the spacecraft followed it; and the Retrofire Officer, or RETRO, who was in charge of the spacecraft's reëntry into the earth's atmosphere.* New Yorker 11/11/72, p49 [**1969**, short for *retrofire officer*]

retro-engine, *n.* a rocket engine that produces thrust opposed to forward motion. *In orbit each Mariner will weigh 1200 lbs, but each carries to Mars, as well, about 1000 lbs of fuel for the 14-minute retroengine burn needed to slow it to the requisite orbital speed.* New Scientist and Science Journal 5/6/71, p305 [**1967**]

retrofire, *n.* the ignition of a retrorocket (rocket that produces reverse thrust). *After retro-fire, a marked decrease in spacecraft velocity was noted until retro-burnout occurred at 20 feet and the verniers burned alone.* NY Times 5/25/67, p43 [**1962**]

retrofit, *v.t.* **1** to modify (older equipment) to include changes made in later production of the same model or type. *To help make up for the extra pollution generated by pre-1979 engines, the agency is proposing a program of retrofitting such engines with emission-control devices as these become technologically feasible.* Science News 7/14/73, p23 **2** to provide (an older vehicle, building, etc.) with equipment modified to include changes made in later models or other improvements. *Cars in Group III cities must be retrofitted with exhaust catalysts to remove pollutants and must impose some restrictions on downtown driving.* Science News 8/4/73, p71 *The federal government has . . . shaped legislation to provide grants to cities and states for "retrofitting" public buildings with solar energy systems.* Americana Annual 1977, p95 *Conservation is often very expensive, especially when large plants must be converted to different fuels or "retrofitted" with more efficient equipment.* Time 4/25/77, p31 —*n.* the process of modifying equipment, etc., to include changes made in later models or other equipment. *We estimate that such technological improvements could cut present energy consumption by roughly one-third. These changes, however, require the production of* *new goods and services rather than a retrofit of existing systems.* Saturday Review 10/28/72, p66 *Ford is phasing in new locks and "there is a possibility of retrofit," meaning putting better locks on older cars, says Herbert Misch, a Ford vice president.* NY Times 1/11/76, pC27 [**1969**, from earlier (1956) verb and noun sense of modifying an aircraft or part of an aircraft to incorporate changes made in later productions, ultimately from *retro*active re*fit*]—**retrofittable,** adj.: *For instance, one proposed strategy is for retrofittable emission-control devices to enable older cars to meet 1975 or 1976 emission goals.* Science News 6/10/72, p372

retrograde, adj. producing thrust opposed to forward motion. *To bring a satellite to earth, scientists use devices called retrograde rockets, or, in space jargon, retro rockets.* Encyclopedia Science Supplement (Grolier) 1965, p307 [**1965**]

retroreflective, adj. reflecting light back to its source. *In the case of light three reflecting surfaces, all at right angles to one another, form a corner with the same retroreflective property.* Scientific American 3/70, p41 [**1960**]

retroreflector, n. a prismlike device that reflects a laser beam and is designed for placement on a distant object, such as a heavenly body, to calculate its distance from the earth by measuring the time elapsed to reflect a beam of light. *The* Apollo 11 *crew left retroreflectors at their landing site on the Moon for a lunar ranging experiment which is being undertaken at the present time by scientists* . . . McGraw-Hill Yearbook of Science and Technology 1971, p112 *They will also set up an improved laser-ranging retroreflector; and another solar-wind composition collecting foil.* New Scientist and Science Journal 7/29/71, p243 [**1961**]

retrospective, n. a survey or review of one's past works. . . . *Sy Oliver, the principal arranger for Jimmy Lunceford and Tommy Dorsey between 1933 and the late forties, is holding a retrospective of his work at the Downbeat with the help of a nine-piece group that includes two trumpets, two trombones, two reeds, and three rhythm.* New Yorker 5/23/70, p80 [**1964**] ▶ This term has been formerly applied only to an exhibition of the works of painters and sculptors.

retrovirus, n. any of a group of tumor-producing viruses that use RNA instead of DNA to encode genetic information. *The RNA tumor viruses, which produce animal cancers, use RNA instead of DNA to encode their genetic information. They are often called "retroviruses" because they reverse a step in one central dogma of biology: DNA makes RNA makes protein. Viral RNA, once in a cell, must create double-stranded DNA molecules. Then the viral genes can slip into an animal chromosome.* Science News 7/1/78, p6 [**1977**, from *retro*- backward + *virus*]

returnable, n. U.S. a bottle or container that one may return to a store after its use and collect a deposit included in its purchase price. *You toss away an average of 5.5 pounds of garbage per day. Use returnables. Not disposables. An incinerator just converts plastic and wax and aluminium containers into poisonous smoke.* New Yorker 4/18/70, p127 [**1970**, noun use of the adjective]

Reuben sandwich. See the quotation for the meaning. . . . *the Reuben sandwich . . . has become wildly popular in most areas of the United States . . . It is a combination of corned beef, Swiss cheese and sauerkraut served hot.* NY Times 10/10/67, p50 [**1956**, said to be named after Arnold *Reuben,* 1883-1970, an American restaurant owner]

reuptake, n. the reabsorption of a chemical substance by a nerve cell after it has relayed an impulse. *Most of the norepinephrine active at the brain synapses is "recycled," literally sucked back into the cell and conserved for future use, after relaying the nerve impulse. This sucking-back process, called "re-uptake," is the major means by which norepinephrine is "turned off."* NY Times Magazine 4/24/77, p33 [**1976**, from *re*-again + *uptake*]

rev, v.t. **rev up,** U.S. 1 to stir up. *"About the time I got out of college—I worked two and a half years between high school and college—there were a bunch of idealistic youths who had*

been revved up by a bunch of articulate and persuasive politicians in Germany." Harper's 12/70, p85 **2** to increase in tempo; accelerate. *The New London Faust (stereo)* . . . *offers lofty heights and deep lows* . . . *And the symphonic postludes have been revved up rather than intensified* . . . Saturday Review 6/24/67, p61 [**1931, 1965**, extended sense of *rev, v.,* to accelerate an engine (OEDS 1920), from *rev, n.,* revolution of an engine (1901)]

revascularization, n. the act or process of revascularizing. *The results of clinical tests were disappointing, and the medical profession dismissed the concept of surgical revascularization of the heart as being too exotic.* Scientific American 10/68, p36 *Only four years ago this and other operations to improve the circulation of blood to overtaxed hearts were either unknown or experimental. Now revascularization, or "replumbing," has become the most popular item in the thoracic surgeon's repertory of heart repairs—and with good reason.* Time 5/10/71, p40 [**1966**]

revascularize, v.t. to substitute new blood vessels to increase the blood supply to (the heart, etc.). *Specialists at the meeting today estimated that as many as 60 medical centers in the world might be doing operations to revascularize the hearts of gravely ill patients.* NY Times 2/18/67, p27 [**1965**]

revenue sharing, U.S. the distribution among local governments, especially the state governments, of a part of the revenue from Federal taxes. *At every stop except the schools, Brock's dominant theme was much the same as what President Nixon would later call "revenue sharing"—that government had to be returned to local control by way of sending the taxpayers' money back to the states, counties, cities, and towns.* New Yorker 7/10/71, p43 . . . *the opponents of revenue sharing include Mr. Nixon's two most illustrious Republican predecessors in this century: Dwight Eisenhower and Theodore Roosevelt.* NY Times 6/11/71, p35 [**1971**]

reverse annuity mortgage or **reverse mortgage,** U.S. and Canada. the transfer of a homeowner's mortgage to a bank, lending company, or the like, in return for a regular annuity. *Abbreviation:* RAM *The new equity-conversion concept is really an outgrowth of the "reverse annuity" mortgage plan.* Christian Science Monitor 4/9/82, p16 *Financial institutions have been able to offer reverse mortgage loans in Connecticut since 1978, but they have been reluctant to do so. Bankers have expressed fears about evicting elderly people who might not meet the conditions of the loans, and they have questioned the abilities of the programs to be money making, because of their long times for paying.* NY Times 12/23/84, p1 [**1983**]

reverse commuting, commutation from a city to the suburbs for work. Also called INCOMMUTATION. *Mrs. Littlefield was among several private school officials who said they had begun to notice the phenomenon of "reverse commuting" by families who had become disillusioned with what they called the "barren" and expensive life of the suburbs.* NY Times 9/15/76, p88 [**1967**]—**reverse commuter:** *But "reverse commuters," to whom the story refers, cannot afford the high housing cost of the inner-ring suburbs and therefore must live in the city while commuting to suburban jobs.* NY Times 9/4/70, p26

reverse discrimination, discrimination against individuals who are members of a dominant group by giving preferential treatment in education, employment, etc., to members of a minority group. *What has made these cases potentially explosive is the charge by those who fall outside the definition of minority groups, notably whites and Orientals, that the effect of these programs is "reverse discrimination.".* . . *Marco DeFunis had sued the University of Washington law school charging that it had practiced "reverse discrimination" against him by denying him admission in favor of less-qualified minority students.* Newsweek 5/6/74, p50 *Only a nation of saints might reasonably anticipate that a long-sustained policy of reverse discrimination will have effects other than those associated with plain discrimination; that is, perpetuation of the antagonism and other barriers that separate black from white.* Atlantic 1/78, p77 [**1969**]

reverse osmosis, the pressuring of a liquid through a semipermeable membrane against the usual osmotic flow. *Reverse osmosis . . . has been considered for some time as a way of reclaiming water from industrial effluents.* New Scientist 12/24/70, p557 *A process called "reverse osmosis" may help small-volume cheese plants solve the crucial problems of how to dispose of whey. The method removes 75%-80% of whey water, and the concentrate is shipped to larger plants for drying, thus preventing the dumping of waste whey into streams, which are polluted by the waste.* Americana Annual 1969, p50 [**1955**]

reverse transcriptase, an enzyme that causes the formation of DNA from a template of RNA, found in retroviruses. Also called REVERTASE, TRANSCRIPTASE, and (originally) TEMIN ENZYME. *. . . a sensitive assay for reverse transcriptase may prove to be, at the very least, a useful tool for the diagnosis of leukemia and perhaps other forms of cancer.* 1972 Britannica Yearbook of Science and the Future, p292 *Of the 13 milks tested only four had reverse-transcriptase activity . . . But, it should be remembered that reverse transcriptase is as yet only on trial for its cancer-forming activity; it has yet to be proven guilty in that role.* New Scientist and Science Journal 5/20/71, p436 [**1970**, from *reverse transcript* (a phrase alluding to the transcription RNA→DNA, which is the reverse of usual transcription DNA→RNA) + *-ase* enzyme]

reverse vending machine, a machine that dispenses money or credit coupons in exchange for items, such as empty bottles or other used containers, deposited in it. *Rockware Reclamation supplies a reverse vending machine that buys used aluminium cans and packs them off to the smelters.* New Scientist 9/25/86, p58 [**1986**]

revertant, *Genetics.* —*n.* a cell, organism, or strain that has reverted to an earlier type of mutation. *Examination of the chromosomes of such cells, according to Sachs, has shown that certain specific groups of chromosomes are always associated with malignancy and tend to be dropped in revertants, which conversely have more of another specific group of chromosomes, associated with nonmalignancy.* New Scientist 6/28/73, p799 —*adj.* that has reverted to an earlier type by mutation. *The first step is the isolation of revertant strains having a normal phosphatase phenotype. Genetic mapping shows that the revertants can occur in either of two ways.* Science 4/12/68, p154 [**1955**, from *revert, v.* + *-ant* (noun and adj. suffix)]

revertase (ri'vər,teis), *n.* another name for REVERSE TRANSCRIPTASE. *Recently, another important activity has been what Engelhardt calls their "Project Revertase"—revertase being the newly discovered enzyme. . . which can reproduce DNA using RNA as the template, thus reversing the central dogma of Crick about the unidirectional flow of genetic information from genes (DNA) to RNA to proteins.* New Scientist 5/9/74, p329 [**1974**, from *reverse* transcrip*tase*, the original name]

revolving door, a constantly recurring or repetitive round of activity; an automatic cycle or circular process. *The new airlift is designed to close or at least slow down the "revolving door" that allows apprehended aliens, after they have been taken back into Mexico at Tijuana, Juarez, Nuevo Laredo and other border cities, to repeat their attempts to reach the United States.* NY Times 7/25/76, p20 *The revolving door of the court system is expensive and fruitless. Prostitutes plead guilty; the judge slaps down a fine and lets them go. To pay the fine, they have to turn more tricks and soon wind up back in court.* Time 10/2/76, p48 [**1966**, figurative sense of the term (1907) for a door with sections that revolve on a central axis]—**revolving-door**, *adj.: The courts dispense a revolving-door type of trial-less justice, where 95 percent of cases are disposed of by negotiated guilty pleas and where trials in the lower courts sometimes last five minutes.* Norman E. Zinberg and John A. Robertson, Drugs and the Public, 1972, p216 *The woes of the wealthy Argonauts have become a national joke, thanks in part to the team's revolving-door policy with players, coaches and even owners. But how, oh how, do the Saskatchewan Roughriders manage to come up with a contender every year?* Maclean's 10/4/76, p65

Reye's syndrome (rɑiz *or* reiz), a rare but often fatal disease of the brain occurring among very young children, usually after a common viral infection such as influenza and associated with the administration of aspirin to treat the infection. *First, repeated changing of blood is not the only known treatment for Reye's Syndrome. Along with the blood transfusions, the child undergoes dialysis, is given a powerful drug, L-dopa, to maintain nerve impulses, and holes are drilled into the patient's skull to relieve the pressure created by swelling of the brain.* Maclean's 6/28/76, p9 [**1965**, *Reye syndrome*, named after Ralph D.K. *Reye*, 1912-1978, an Australian physician, who first identified the condition in 1963]

R factor, a genetic factor in some bacteria that codes for resistance to antibiotics and other antibacterial drugs, and that can be transmitted from one bacterium to another by conjugation. *Typhoid bacilli are among the bacteria that can acquire transferable resistance. This phenomenon occurs when bacteria that have survived exposure to an antibiotic by developing resistance to it pass on this resistance in the form of genetic material—the R factor—to other species or strains.* Times (London) 8/4/72, p14 *As in resistance to other drugs, trimethoprim-resistance is a characteristic inherited not through the main bacterial chromosome, but through the existence of an autonomous, non-chromosomal carrier of genetic information known as an R-factor. R-factor-linked resistance is particularly disturbing because of the ease with which R-factors can be transferred from one bacterium to another.* New Scientist 7/18/74, p118 [**1962**, from *Resistance factor*]

RFLP ('rif,lip), *n.* an acronym for *restriction fragment length polymorphism* (any of a group of abnormally long fragments of DNA cut by restriction enzymes, used as genetic markers in identifying defective genes). Also spelled RIFLIP. *A recently developed technique for genetic analysis has been proving to be a master key for unlocking the secrets of genetic illness. Called RLFP mapping, the method has already played a role in identifying genes that, when they are inherited in three rather than the usual two copies, are thought to cause the pathologies of Down syndrome.* Scientific American 8/87, p30 [**1985**]

rhabdovirus ('ræbdou,vɑirəs), *n.* a virus associated with various diseases transmitted by animal or insect bites. *One of the things which is known about rabies virus is that its genetic material is ribonucleic acid (RNA). Because of this property and its morphology it has been classified with the rhabdovirus group (from the Greek* rhabdos *meaning a rod). Other members of the group are four viruses spread by the bites of arthropods . . .* Science Journal 4/70, p36 [**1965**]

rhinovirus, *n.* a virus of the respiratory tract associated with the common cold. *Further, we are testing specimens from other patients with respiratory disease in order to find out how frequently hitherto unrecognized viruses can be isolated . . . It seems likely that some of these may be fastidious rhinoviruses.* Times (London) 9/3/65, p14 [**1961**, from *rhino-* nose (from Greek *rhīnos*) + *virus*]

rho, *n.* short for RHO MESON. *In the heavier nuclei more and more rhos are being produced but they are also being increasingly absorbed.* Scientific American 7/71, p94 [**1968**]

rhombochasm, *n. Geology.* a rhomboid gap formed by tension between parallel and offsetting pairs of faults. *Figure 3b, approximately middle Triassic, shows two significant changes: a second rhombochasm begins to separate the arc segment from the Palaeozoic marginal basin fragment.* Nature 4/15/76, p590 [**1958**, from *rhombo-* shaped like a rhombus (from Greek *rhómbos* rhombus) + *chasm*]

rho meson, a highly unstable and short-lived elementary particle with a mass about 1400 times that of an electron, produced in high-energy collisions between particles. Also shortened to RHO. *The electron does not strike the proton directly but interacts with it by means of a third particle, a rho meson, which bounces back and forth between them.* Science News 10/24/70, p333 *There is a class of unstable particles, the neutral vector mesons, whose members resemble photons in many ways, with two important exceptions: they have mass and they exhibit the strong force. The most prominent is the rho meson,* *which has a mass equivalent to about 750 MeV. (The mass of the proton is equivalent to 939 MeV.) Rho mesons can be created as real particles in the laboratory, and their decay products can be detected.* Scientific American 6/71, p72 [**1968**]

rhytidectomy (‚ritə'dektəmi:), *n.* cosmetic surgery that tightens the skin about the face and neck by removing fatty deposits, stretching loose muscle tissue, etc.; face-lift operation. *The face lift (rhytidectomy) corrects pendulous neck skin, wrinkled cheeks and jowls, and softens grooves from mouth to nose. Incisions are made along the frontal contour of the ear, under and behind the ear, and up the temple.* NY Times Magazine 9/25/77, p124 [**1971,** from Greek *rhytid-, rhytís* wrinkle + *ektomḗ* excision] ►Although this term has been earlier used in medicine in the sense of "surgical removal of wrinkles" (OEDS 1931), it has become in recent years generally synonymous with a face lift.

ribavirin, *n.* a synthetic ribonucleoside that inhibits the replication of both DNA and RNA in viruses by interfering with the synthesis of nucleic acids. *Formula:* $C_8H_{12}N_4O_5$ *At the present time only ara-A (Vira-A) and to a lesser extent ribavirin (Virazole) have shown promise in widespread clinical trials. Both drugs have antiviral activity at dose levels sufficiently below toxic levels to permit their systemic use.* Science News 4/10/76, p227 [**1975,** probably from *rib*onucleic *a*cid + *vir*us + *-in* (chemical suffix)]

ribosomal, *adj.* of or relating to ribosomes. *Another Nobel Prize winner, Dr. James D. Watson, of Harvard University, will report on the role of ribosomal nucleic acids in protein synthesis.* Times (London) 7/25/64, p5 [**1960**]

ribosomal RNA, a ribonucleic acid that forms part of the structure of the ribosome. *Abbreviation:* rRNA . . . *when the transplant embryos are reared through the blastula and gastrula stages, they synthesize heterogeneous RNA, transfer RNA and ribosomal RNA in turn and in the same sequence as do embryos reared from fertilized eggs.* Scientific American 12/68, p33 [**1961**]

ribosome, *n.* any of the complex particles in a cell that carry out the synthesis of protein and enzymes. *Protein synthesis is carried out by small particles, called ribosomes, located in the cytoplasm of the cell. Instructions for the construction of a particular protein are recorded on deoxyribonucleic acid (DNA) molecules located in the nucleus of the cell.* Encyclopedia Science Supplement (Grolier) 1967, p69 . . . *ribosomes consist of two subunits, each made up of RNA and many different proteins.* Americana Annual 1969, p124 [**1958,** from *rib*onucleic acid + *-some* body]

ridership, *n.* U.S. the number of passengers served by any transit system. *In many cities, bus ridership had been declining over the years until the energy crisis and Federal subsidies—which pay about three-fourths of the cost of a new bus—made buses more attractive than cars to many commuters.* Newsweek 2/25/74, p80 *Amtrak has not been failing; in fact, it has been extending its passenger train network, improving its equipment and schedules, and attracting increased ridership (up from 16.6 to 18.6 million annually).* NY Times 9/2/77, pA21 [**1969,** patterned after *readership* (1923), *listenership* (1943), VIEWERSHIP]

rifampicin (‚rifæm'paisən) or **rifampin** (rif'æmpin), *n.* an antibiotic drug, derived synthetically from a rifamycin, which inhibits the growth of bacterial cells and the replication of viruses by interfering with the action of RNA polymerases in the synthesis of RNA. *Rifampicin, an antibiotic developed for use against tuberculosis, was found to operate by inhibiting an enzyme.* Science News 4/17/71, p266 *Rifampin (rifampicin), introduced as an antituberculosis remedy . . . also demonstrated exciting possibilities as an antiviral agent . . . Most drugs that block viral growth also damage cells. Rifampin apparently does not.* World Book Science Annual 1972, p299 [**1966,** from *rifamycin* + inserted *-pi-,* from *piperazine* (a chemical constituent)]

rifamycin (‚rifə'maisən), *n.* any of a group of substances which are the fermentation products of a fungus, *Streptomyces mediterranei,* isolated from the soil in the pine forests of southern

France. Several rifamycins and their derivatives have shown antimicrobial and antiviral properties. *Another line of investigation is to take the purified enzyme and use it as a screen for agents that will inhibit the RNA-dependent DNA polymerase, but leave the normal DNA-dependent DNA polymerase alone. Already, the antibiotic rifamycin and its analogues are looking promising in this connection, and such drugs may form the basis of a possible therapy for leukemia.* New Scientist 11/12/70, p313 [**1963,** alteration of earlier (1959) *rifomycin,* from Italian *riformare* to reform + *-mycin* a fungus product (from Greek *mýkēs* fungus)]

riflip, *n.* variant of RFLP. *Each variation is unique to a certain spot on a certain one of the chromosomes in an individual's cells. Scientists have dubbed these mysterious variations "riflips," an acronym for "restriction-fragment-length-polymorphisms."* Wall St Jnl 2/3/86, p15 [**1986**]

rift zone, a large area of the earth in which a rift or fracture occurs when plates of the earth's crust move away from one another. *The location of the world's 529 known active volcanoes, relative to this model of mountain-building, is instructive because . . . 72 occur along rift zones between separating plates. Because much of the rift zone is in deep ocean water, many active, yet hidden, volcanoes await discovery.* 1971 Britannica Yearbook of Science and the Future, p44 *The discovery that metal deposits were forming in a rift zone in the Red Sea had led them to examine other rift zones, such as the East Pacific Rise, for further evidence of the nature and distribution of ore bodies.* Science News 4/24/71, p279 [**1970**]

right-brain, *n.* the right hemisphere of the brain (often used attributively). *Human beings are the only mammals whose left and right brains are specialized for quite different functions . . . Because of the distinctly human differences in left-brain and right-brain, and the variations that genetic inheritance makes possible in brain physiology—and therefore in temperament and talents—each individual brain is truly unique.* Encyclopedia Science Supplement (Grolier) 1976, p50 [**1976**]

right on, *interj., adv., adj.* U.S. Slang. a phrase or exclamation signifying agreement or approval, trust or correctness. *The phrase "Right on," which originated with the Black Panther Party, is (or was) an expression of affirmation on the revolutionary left, as in this colloquy: Speaker: Imperialism must be smashed! Audience: Right on!* New Yorker 2/7/70, p21 *Sir: Your "Catholic Exodus" article was right on. We especially concur with the comments you published concerning secular employment.* Time 3/16/70, p4 *The "mass man" of sociological terminology is the "right-on man" of black slang, gliding smoothly and simplistically, and perhaps more comfortably, over questionable assumptions, and reducing himself to a cliché in the process.* Atlantic 12/70, p47 [**1968**]

right-to-die, *adj.* permitting or advocating the withdrawal of extreme or artificial life-sustaining measures taken to prolong the life of an incurably ill or injured person. *A revolutionary "right-to-die" bill . . . will allow physicians to remove life support systems from patients who have authorized such action in advance. The act applies only in cases of irreversible injury or illness certified to be terminal by two physicians.* 1977 Collier's Encyclopedia Year Book, p177 [**1976**] ►The case of a young woman who lapsed into coma on April 1975 first brought this term and the issue to widespread public attention.

right-to-life, *adj.* advocating or supporting laws that prohibit induced abortion, especially abortion-on-demand; PRO-LIFE; PRO-FAMILY. *Right-to-life propagandists take pains to refer to male and female fetuses as "unborn boy and girl babies" and during a 1972 referendum vote on a more liberal abortion law in a midwest state they had school children call voters on the telephone, saying in a piping youngster's treble, "This is the voice of a little unborn baby."* Joseph Fletcher, The Ethics of Genetic Control, 1974, p109 *A vigorous "right to life" movement has successfully exerted pressure on some state legislatures to enact new restrictive laws and on many hospital administrators to prevent the delivery of abortion services in defiance of the decisions.* Scientific American 1/77, p22 [**1972**] ►This term and its variant, *pro-life,* emphasize the "right of the unborn to life." To avoid the implied bias, some writers prefer *antiabortion* as an objective designation and *proabortion* as its antonym.

right-to-lifer, *n.* a person who advocates or supports antiabortion laws; ANTIABORTIONIST. *A woman is a responsible individual and should be permitted to decide for herself whether or not she wants an abortion. This seems rather obvious, but the "Right-to-Lifers" apparently belong to that stifling, archaic school of thought that holds that a woman is basically irresponsible and must be told what to do with her life.* Maclean's 11/15/76, p16b *Buoyed by last week's victory, the right-to-lifers immediately began planning their congressional strategy for next year. They will press for a ban on all Medicaid abortions, without exception, and ask that these procedures be outlawed at military hospitals. They will also lobby against including abortions in any national health insurance program that Congress may consider in the future.* Time 12/19/77, p12 **[1972]**

right-to-work, *adj. U.S.* of or relating to the right of a worker to get or keep a job whether he or she belongs or does not belong to a labor union. *You might have then seen the virtue of the right-to-work policy . . . What would have been gained . . . if you sanctioned a system by which this honest and qualified ex-con were compelled to join a union against his will as the price of holding his new-found job?* Harper's 3/67, p8 *The Indiana legislature repealed its "right to work" law, reducing the number of states with such legislation to 19.* Britannica Book of the Year 1966, p8 **[1958;** known orally in the 1930's]

righty, *n. British.* a conservative or reactionary; right-winger (also used attributively). *This sounds a bit like his Righty chum, Bernard Levin, but not like any Lefty I know . . . Lefties don't demonstrate against the Soviet Union . . .* Manchester Guardian Weekly 11/28/70, p19 *England's thin red line of intellectual royalists is being overrun by "progressive" reformers who deliberately sabotage old-fashioned academic virtues . . . The Manchester Guardian called them a "tightly knit bunch of righties."* Time 10/31/69, p53 **[1967]**

ringgit ('riŋgit), *n., pl.* **-git** or **-gits.** the monetary unit of Malaysia, also known as the Malaysian dollar. *The Malaysian High Court today also fined him 15,000 ringgit (£3.750) with the alternative of another six months' imprisonment, for abetment of a criminal breach of trust.* Times (London) 1/25/77, p9 **[1967,** from Malay]

ring of fire, a belt of volcanoes surrounding the Pacific Ocean and causing violent seismic activity. *More than 80% of known active volcanoes occur on the rim of the Pacific Ocean, "the ring of fire," and in the belt from the Mediterranean Sea to Indonesia.* McGraw-Hill Yearbook of Science and Technology 1971, p430 **[1965]**

ring-pull, *adj.* having a scored metal top that comes off in one piece by pulling at a small ring attached to it. *Easy opening devices are undergoing considerable development—and ring-pull and zip-top cans are already available.* Times (London) 2/16/70, pIII **[1970]**

ringway, *n. British.* a circular road or highway; a beltway. *We tend to regard the fume-laden canyons of New York . . . and the engulfing concrete of flyovers and ringways as things that will inevitably come to this country.* New Scientist 6/18/70, p591 **[1969]**

riot shield, a shield used by members of a police or military force during a riot. *Later the Queen had a preview of some of what she will see during her jubilee visit to Northern Ireland next week. A review of the Royal Marines on Plymouth Ho included an officer and 30 men of 42 Commando, dressed for operations in Ulster and equipped with riot shields.* Times (London) 8/6/77, p2 **[1966]**

rip, *v.t., v.i.* Usually, **rip off,** *U.S. Slang.* to steal (from someone); rob, loot, or exploit. *A girl who was recording the proceedings with a portable television camera stood up and shouted, "We're sitting here, and Chemical Bank is gloating about how they're going to rip us off! Well, we're going to go into the streets and rip you off!"* New Yorker 7/18/70, p21 *For extra, unanticipated personal needs, he "rips off"—or steals. Some of those who*

take jobs in department stores or markets steal what they can . . . Some who work in restaurants or drugstores let their friends in to eat or rip what they need.* Time 6/22/70, p52 **[1967]**

ripoff, *n. U.S. Slang.* **1** an act or result of ripping off; a theft, robbery, or exploitation. *The rate of street crime is very low—because, some artists maintain, the district overlaps into Little Italy, and the Mafia does not like petty rip-offs in its own backyard.* Time 7/5/71, p33 *We asked him why he had chosen to work in this area instead of, say, in Greenwich Village. "The Village is a rip-off," he said. "Nothing but junkies, perverts—it's a bad scene."* New Yorker 6/12/71, p28 **2** one that rips off. *"Who do you have on Haight Street today?" he* [a San Francisco dope peddler] *said disgustedly . . . "You have burn artists (fraudulent dope peddlers), rip-offs (thieves), and snitchers (police spies)."* Manchester Guardian Weekly 5/2/70, p16 **[1970]**

ripography, *n. Informal.* the unauthorized photocopying of books, often in violation of copyright laws. *Canadian authors and publishers . . . rail against losses caused by photocopying, or "ripography" as it's indignantly called in the book trade. Their targets are academic institutions that copy texts and professional journals in vast quantities for classroom use but pay no royalties because the 1924 act doesn't say they must.* Maclean's 10/12/81, p51 **[1981,** from *rip*off + connective *-o-* + *-graphy,* as in *xerography*]

ripple control, a method by which a utility company helps its customers save on the cost of electric power by automatically turning off water heaters during periods of peak consumer demand, when electricity is most expensive to produce. *So far, ripple control has worked: according to test results, the system has saved roughly $60 a year per heater in electricity costs, a saving that Green Mountain Power (G.M.P.) has returned to participants in the experiment in the form of monthly $5 rebates.* Time 9/6/76, p33 *The ripple control scheme allows signals to be transmitted over the supply network so that the storage radiators can be switched on and off by the LEB* [London Electricity Board] *engineers to ensure that they only take power at the times when it is cheapest.* New Scientist 6/30/77, p784 **[1974,** from the earlier sense (1938) of a method of controlling simple switching operations from a central transmitter]

ripple effect, a gradually spreading effect. *While adding to the nation's general economic woes, the ripple effects of the housing slump seem certain to add to the pressure on government policymakers to come up with help for home building.* Wall Street Journal 12/12/74, p1 *It appears that when problems do occur, those of the wife were "least well tolerated" and produced a "ripple effect on all sexual relations" involving the couple.* Science News 7/29/78, p70 **[1966]**

ripstop, *adj.* (of a lightweight fabric, especially a synthetic fabric) designed with a series of small ridged squares to contain tearing and prevent long rips. *Most popular of all* [kites] *are the dual control stunters, capable of exciting aerobatic performances, and thanks to ripstop nylon, comparatively indestructible.* Times (London) 12/14/76, p16 **[1970]**

risk, *n.* **at risk, 1** in danger; imperiled. *The dismissal of two senior ministers and the resignation of a third in the small hours of yesterday morning shows that the policy is now at risk.* Times (London) 5/7/70, p13 **2** running the risk of becoming pregnant, especially despite the use of contraceptive measures. *There must be at least 10 million married women "at risk" in this country, and from this, I infer that however they try not to conceive, they will produce an average of two million babies a year.* New Scientist 5/25/67, p492 **[1965]**

risk-benefit ratio, the relation between the risks taken and the possible benefits derived from any undertaking (such as the administration of a powerful drug in chemotherapy). *Whereas the majority of the investigators were what we called "strict" with regard to balancing risks against benefits, a significant minority were "permissive," that is, they were much more willing to accept an unsatisfactory risk-benefit ratio.* Scientific American 2/76, p27 *Dr. Maurice B. Visscher . . . said in a review of the study in The New England Journal of Medicine that the results* had found "no consensus among physicians about what risk-benefit ratios to the individual or to society will justify either therapeutic or pure-science studies." NY Times 2/1/76, p28 [**1975**]

rite of reconciliation, (in the Roman Catholic Church) a new name for the sacrament of penance. *New procedures in the Sacrament of Penance give rise to the term* Sacrament (*or* Rite) *of* Reconciliation. *The clergymen questioned believe that the new name will eventually replace the old entirely . . .* Sacrament of Reconciliation *is milder in tone than either* Penance *or* Confession. American Speech, Summer 1979, p84 [**1976**]

RNAase (ˌɑrˌɛnˈeiˌeis) or **RNase** (ˌɑrˌɛnˈeis), *n.* an enzyme that breaks down ribonucleic acid in cells. *The RNA-ase synthesized in 1968 is found naturally in cattle, not human beings, but knowing about it may point the way to a better understanding of human cell growth and cancer.* 1970 Britannica Yearbook of Science and the Future, p294 *In bacterial extracts these enzymes of course readily mimic the activity of an RNA replicase and as a further hazard to this type of investigation the same extracts contain degradative enzymes (RNases) which will attack the newly synthesized RNA.* New Scientist 10/7/65, p14 [**1957,** from *RNA* (ribonucleic acid) + *-ase* enzyme]

RNA polymerase, an enzyme that acts upon DNA to synthesize ribonucleic acid. *. . . only one enzyme capable of catalyzing the synthesis of RNA has been isolated. Scientists have wondered how this one enzyme, RNA polymerase, could catalyze the synthesis of such differing RNA molecules.* World Book Science Annual 1969, p269 [**1962**]

roach clip or **roach holder,** *Slang.* any device used to hold the end of a marijuana cigarette when it is too small to hold in the fingers while smoking. *. . . . lists of things: lanterns, mirrors, keys "with hollow ends," . . . candles, leather handbags, bejeweled roach clips.* Harper's 4/72, p90 *An hour later, Petersen was sitting on the floor of his cabin, passing a joint on a bobbypin roach holder to his live-in girlfriend.* NY Times Magazine 7/4/76, p20 [**1967,** from *roach* (c1938) slang term for the butt of a marijuana cigarette]

roadie, *n. Slang.* a person hired to assist singers or other performers on tour. *Queen's retinue includes technicians, roadies, sound and lighting engineers—needed to manage tons of equipment, including a dry-ice smoke generator and a bubble-blowing machine. Heavy rock, indeed.* Time 2/9/76, p71 *The Rolling Stones and their roadies load up one of Al's Convairs in L.A. during the group's seven-week tour this summer.* People Weekly 10/9/78, p82 [**1969,** from *road* manager + *-ie*; probably patterned after GROUPIE]

roadman, *n.* a contestant in a race over public roads, especially a bicycle race. *The huge field of 146 riders seemed hell-bent on keeping the fast-finishing Burton well to the rear and with four laps to go and two roadmen 200 metres out in front, it seemed this has been achieved.* Times (London) 5/25/76, p9 [**1971,** from *road* race + *man*]

road rash, *U.S. Slang.* a severe scrape or bruise suffered in a fall from a fast-moving skateboard. *"You get down low on the board to cut wind resistance, and you pray that the board slows enough so you can get off," said Fred Araujo. "If you get off prematurely, you get a road rash."* NY Times 4/2/76, p38 [**1976**]

robotomorphic, *adj.* modeled on the behavior of robots. *You say I overestimate the dangers of the Robotomorphic or Ratomorphic view, on everyday life, but with Pavlov's dogs, Lorenz's grey-legged geese, Morris' naked ape, each time an analogy of behaviour was taken as a homology.* Times (London) 12/17/70, p15 *The targets of discontent were to be Neo-Darwinist orthodoxy in evolution and robotomorphic views of Man.* New Scientist 10/2/69, p22 [**1969**]

Roche lobe, a gaseous bulge formed in companion stars by each star's gravitational pull on the other. *The most widely held theory for the nova phenomenon is that the prenova is a close binary system consisting of a red dwarf, which is filling its Roche Lobe, spilling matter over towards a white dwarf companion . . .* Nature 1/22/76, p172 [**1969,** named after Edouard

Roche, 1820-1883, a French mathematician who in 1848 formulated the *Roche limit,* an area surrounding a planet within which any moon or satellite would be disrupted by the planet's gravitational force]

rock¹, *n.* a style of popular music with a rocking or heavy beat and simple melody. *Now rock has its own problems, which may well prove to be more basic than those of straight music.* Listener 12/9/71, p781 *The film's soundtrack, brief, even denies him the support of the best argument for his generation: the distinction of its music. There is hardly any rock in it at all.* NY Times 1/11/68, p42 **—adj.** of or relating to rock music. *All over Poland, Communist Party youth clubs reverberate to the latest rock sounds.* Time 11/16/70, p35 *The words by Gerome Ragni and James Rado and the music by Galt MacDermot demonstrate that a rock score can have both variety and vitality . . .* Atlantic 2/68, p133 [**1952,** short for *rock 'n' roll* (1951)]

rock², *n. U.S. Slang.* **1** another word for CRACK². *A witness testifying recently in a murder case . . . admitted he and friends had "boola'd" about three or four grams of "rock" the day he said he saw the three defendants beating up their victim.* Fort Wayne Journal-Gazette 9/21/86, p10A **2** a piece or lump of crack. *Every knowledgeable medical source . . . says that crack is instantly addictive from the first or second "rock" that is smoked.* NY Times 5/14/89, p22 [**1986**]

rockabilly, *n.* rock music with hillbilly music themes (also used attributively). *But [Charlie] Gillett is at his frequent best talking about five basic styles that finally merged into rock: Northern Bank, New Orleans dance blues, rockabilly from Memphis, Chicago rhythm and blues and vocal group rock.* Time 9/28/70, p47 *Rockabilly artists such as Elvis Presley (who combined country and R & B) inspired digressions in pop.* Saturday Review 10/26/69, p91 *Bob Dylan, seemingly unable to avoid dramatic excitement, did three songs in electric rockabilly arrangements of disarming originality with his five-man band.* NY Times 1/22/68, p31 [**1956,** from *rock* + *-a-* (as in *rock-a-bye* or *rockaway*) + hill*billy*]

rock ballet, a ballet set to rock music. *Resident choreographer Gerald Arpino, with such works as "Kettentanz" and the solemn rock ballet "Trinity," has established himself as a major artist.* Newsweek 12/24/73, p62 [**1972**]

rocker, *n. Slang.* **1** a rock song or musical. *The lyrics to "Humpty Dumpty," a rocker about the futility of waiting for the king's men to put you together, are especially good.* New Yorker 10/23/71, p175 **2** a fan of rock music, singers, etc. *Though no rock czar has yet successfully crossed over to direct films, United Artists figured he'd pull millions of rockers to see his movie.* Newsweek 9/10/73, p85 **3** a rock singer or musician. *Even in so broad a musical spectrum—part nostalgia, part status quo, part innovation—the jazz rockers are a stylish group apart.* Time 7/8/74, p37 [**1954** for def. 1, from *rock'n'roll* + *-er*; **1964** for def. 2, probably influenced by earlier (1963) *Rocker,* a type of British teen-ager given to wearing leather jackets, riding in gangs on motorcycles, and dancing to *rock'n'roll* music; **1972** for def. 3]

rocket astronomy, the collection of astronomical data from photographs, etc., taken at high altitude through instruments carried in a rocket. *. . . . the emphasis is on the more modern approach which has grown up over the past 10 years as balloon and rocket astronomy have aided observations . . .* New Scientist and Science Journal 3/18/71, p636 [**1960**]

rockfest, *n. U.S.* a rock music festival. *N.Y. Public Health Department says Watkins Glen rockfest's 600,000 attendance made it "largest public gathering ever recorded in the history of the U.S."* National Review 8/31/73, p922 [**1973,** from *rock*'n'roll + *fest* festival (from German *Fest*)]

rock-jock, *n. Slang.* a mountain climber. *. . . . if the relationship between scruffy "rock-jocks" and corporate angels is a happy one, then Canadian mountaineers—already masters of peaks in the Rockies, Alaska and the Yukon—could mount challenges to the best British, Polish and American climbers in the high peaks of Asia.* Maclean's (date not known) 82, p48 [**1980,** from *rock* + JOCK]

rock opera, a drama set to rock music. *There has been word of a black rock opera, the* first *black rock opera, and some days ago a lot of music-business people gathered in the Corinthian Room of the New York Sheraton Hotel to celebrate the news.* New Yorker 1/13/73, p22 *This book's appearance is certainly timely, just before the opening in London of the rock opera* Evita—*and, it might be remembered, a couple of years after the fall of the second Peronista régime in March 1976.* Listener 6/15/78, p771 **[1969]**

rock steady, an earlier form of reggae, a kind of rock music developed in the West Indies. *In the early and mid-60's, ska was followed by rock steady, a laid-back form of ska with less improvisation and more calypso.* NY Times Magazine 8/14/77, p28 *Mindful that ska, rock steady and reggae were once emulations of American R & B, soul and rock&roll, I can accept Marley's fascination with Seventies funk and rock idioms.* Rolling Stone 1/11/79, p98 **[1967]**

Rogallist (rou'gælist), *n.* another name for HANG GLIDER (def. 2). *Rogallists have soared off Pikes Peak (14,110 feet). In California, flights have been made from Dantes View down into Death Valley, a 5800-foot drop.* Reader's Digest 2/74, p90 **[1974,** from *Rogallo* + *-ist]*

Rogallo (rou'gælou), *n.* another name for HANG GLIDER (def. 1). *A Rogallo is basically a triangular kite. It's launched with a running jump off a hill, and the pilot controls the flight with body english.* Popular Science 5/74, p99 **[1973,** short for *Rogallo* wing or kite, a kitelike device to slow down reentry of a space probe, invented about 1962 by Francis M. *Rogallo*, an American engineer working for NASA, from which hang gliders were developed]

rolamite ('roulə,mait), *n.* a mechanical device consisting of a thin, flexible S-shaped band looped around two or more rollers so that the rollers turn without any sliding friction. *The device, christened "Rolamite," is a product of the search for suspension systems to be used in subminiature components of nuclear weapons. Because the roller-and-spring assembly does not require precision finishing, it can be produced in miniature sizes at relatively low cost.* Scientific American 12/67, p58 *Wide publicity was accorded a new mechanical device announced in October by the Atomic Energy Commission's (AEC) Sandia Corporation at Albuquerque, N. Mex. Called rolamite, this device virtually abolishes friction when used as a bearing in applications not involving large loading, pressures of less than 3,000 pounds per square inch.* 1968 World Book Year Book, p377 **[1967,** coined by its inventor, Donald F. Wilkes, an American engineer, from *roller* + *-amite* (arbitrary ending, perhaps as in *dynamite)]*

role model, a person whose behavior in a particular role serves as a model or standard for another person to follow. *Indeed, the Air Force Academy tried to encourage this process of change artificially, by bringing in 15 female officers in January 1976, six months before the arrival of the first women cadets. The young officers went through an abbreviated version of basic training, then began acting as "decoy" upperclassmen. In that way, the first real female cadets had role models of their own sex from the very beginning.* San Francisco Chronicle 12/29/79, p11 *It is suggested that black professionals are needed to provide "role models" for black children.* New York Review of Books 1/26/78, p42 *We still need a clearer picture of a role model—one that does not include excessive nurturing, competition, submission, or seduction.* Ms. 1/4/79, p4 **[1957, 1969]**

role-play, *v.t.* to play the part of or represent (someone or something) in an improvised acting out of a real-life situation. *But the command to role-play a homosexual means venturing into an unknown area of experience.* Time 11/1/71, p60 —*v.i.* to play a role or roles; enact what one conceives as an appropriate role in a particular situation. *The protean president can role-play, presenting himself as a* communal-tribal leader *on some matters, a* bureaucratic-entrepreneur *on other matters, and on still others a* problem-solver/manager. Atlantic 4/71, p52 *Do children truly lack the capacity to role-play (to temporarily assume another person's perspective), which seems to be required for effective performance in any but the most routine and* stereotyped communication situations? Or is it rather that children—even four-year-olds—have the ability to role-play but for one reason or another do not deploy the ability in certain experimental contexts? Scientific American 2/77, p104 **[1961]**

Rolfing or **rolfing**, *n.* a method of deep massage of the tissue around the muscles to make the body more supple and more efficiently oriented to the force of gravity. *Papa John has had a bad back for years, but last time he came to New York he had an hour of Rolfing, the deep-massage postural therapy, and he said the Rolfing had set him up.* New Yorker 4/7/73, p32 *The quest for identity also accounted for the self-improvement programs associated with the human-potential movement—a farrago that included such quick-fix therapies as "primal scream" and "rolfing."* Newsweek 11/19/79, p96 **[1972,** from *Rolf* massage + *-ing;* named after Ida *Rolf,* 1897-1979, an American physiotherapist who developed this system]—**rolfee, rolfer,** *n.:* *The rolfer claims that, following the rolfing program, energy flow is restored to areas of the body that have been enervated. Afterwards, the "rolfee" may breathe properly for the first time since childhood. In the course of these sessions, we are told, the rolfee is often liberated from the crippling psychic attitudes his body had preserved.* NY Times Magazine 12/17/72, p30

roll, *n.* **on a roll,** U.S. *Informal.* on a streak of success, progress, or intense activity. *"The administration has regained confidence in dealing with the Soviets," the upbeat analysis continues. "The paranoia of seeing the Soviets on a roll, the sense of the U.S. in decline, has about evaporated."* Christian Science Monitor 12/5/83, p43 **[1979]**

rollbar, *n.* a steel bar built into the roof of a car to protect the heads of passengers if the car should overturn. *If the designs work out, construction of a prototype car, incorporating such safety features as a rear-view periscope to eliminate "blind spots" and built-in roll bars, could start within a year, Mr. Rockefeller said.* NY Times 9/20/66, p41 *As vehicles become safer they become closer in construction to the vehicles which this system* [new transportation system with a car that can be slung from a monorail] *would require. Roll-bar construction will be needed to allow the vehicle to be supported from its roof.* New Scientist 1/2/69, p21 **[1954]**

rollcage, *n.* a reinforcing structure of metal bars, and sometimes wire screen, built into a car or truck or over an open seat of a tractor to protect the driver. *It would be good to see the designer Robin Herd's special rollcage adopted by all constructors, and while they are at it, could they not agree to reverse the trend for ever wider tyres?* Times (London) 3/23/72, p33 **[1972,** from *rollover* or *roll*bar + *cage]*

roller, *n.* U.S. *Slang.* a policeman. *In the black community, the police, who are sometimes called "rollers," have not been particularly popular. There are still complaints, for instance, that in fights inside the schools the police are more likely to grab a black youth and send a white one on his way.* NY Times Magazine 9/12/76, p112 **[1964]**

roller disco, *Especially U.S.* **1** a dancing to disco music while on roller skates. *It's like stereo for the feet, and from the boardwalks of Venice, California, roller-skating has spread to New York, where roller-disco is raging, and now it's beginning to shake its well behaved booty in Canadian rinks too.* Maclean's 1/8/79, p38 **2** a ballroom with a roller-skating rink for disco dancing on roller skates. *Manhattan has several roller discos, such as the Metropolis on West 55th Street, but the true mecca is in Brooklyn, where the Empire Roller Disco has become the showcase for dancers.* NY Times Magazine 7/8/79, p30 **[1978]**

rollerdrome, *n.* U.S. a roller-skating rink. *Many rollerdromes are equipped with game rooms, dance floors, and pro shops that sell skates and carrying cases on easy-payment "rollaway" plans.* Time 4/8/74, pJ13 *In New York, roller-disco moved uptown from its origins in Brooklyn rinks like the Empire Roller-drome, where skaters, mostly black, have taken disco to the third power: dancing on wheels at 20 mph.* Maclean's 1/8/79, p39 **[1974,** from *roller* skate + *-drome* race course]

roller hockey, hockey played on roller skates. *Mr Edward Heath, the former Prime Minister, is reported to have nearly* *fallen off his seat with excitement while watching a game at the new roller hockey rink at Herne Bay, Kent, which he officially opened last month. He could not understand why roller hockey was not more popular in Britain today.* Times (London) 10/20/76, p12 **[1926, 1975]**

roll-on, *adj.* **1** applied on the skin by a bottle or container fitted with a plastic roller that conveys the application without letting it spill or pour out. The principle is the same as that used to feed ink in a ball-point pen. *Among Bristol-Myers' contributions to American civilization: the first non-peroxide hair coloring (Born Blonde), the first roll-on deodorant (Ban).* Time 2/12/65, p60 *There is a roll-on night cream for breaking eyelashes, a regular problem for women who frequently add an extra flutter to what nature grew them.* Times (London) 3/10/70, p15 **2** that is equipped to carry cargo or freight loaded in trucks or truck trailers that are driven aboard. . . . *at the same time owners are branching out into new ship types: giant tankers and bulk carriers, chemical and liquid gas carriers, container and roll-on ships.* Times (London) 4/13/70, p5 **[1960]**

rollout, *n.* **1** *U.S. Football.* play in which a quarterback runs out of the area formed by blockers before passing (often used attributively). *The Cornellian had the wrong style as back-up man to Y.A. Tittle when he last was with the Giants. Old Yat was a pocket passer. Wood's preference was the roll-out.* NY Times 8/20/68, p45 *Duhon . . . was a left-handed quarterback at Tulane where he set records as a scrambling roll-out runner-passer for three years.* NY Times 9/6/68, p51 **2** the part of a landing after touchdown when an airplane slows down on the runway before it taxis to the unloading ramp. *If landings in Category III are adopted, however, the approach, flare, decrab, touchdown and possibly rollout will be performed automatically, perhaps with the pilot monitoring the events visually on electronic devices.* Scientific American 3/64, p33 *But then, two weeks following the first multiple flameout, that same plane was loaded with 128 passengers headed for Mexico City. It landed safely. But no sooner was it on the ground—still on rollout—than all four engines quit again!* Graphic 11/12/70, p3 **[1959, from the verb phrase *roll out*]**

ROM, *n.* acronym for READ-ONLY MEMORY. *The Singer Company of New York City began selling a sewing machine that used an ROM to control stitch width, length, and density.* 1976 World Book Year Book, p298 **[1966]**

roommate, *n.* a euphemism for COHABITEE. *If you are planning to acquire a roommate or have one already, be warned that you are leaving yourself wide open to more legal entanglements than even a married couple faces . . . First of all, you want to avoid getting socked with your roommate's debts. When you live with someone without being married, you assume absolutely no responsibility for his or her debts.* Esquire 9/79, p12 **[1974, transferred sense of the term for a person who shares a room with another (OED 1838)]**

room of reconciliation, (in the Roman Catholic Church) a room for confession in which the penitent and the priest can meet either face to face or separated by a screen. Also called RECONCILIATION ROOM. *Major changes are evident in all three forms* [of the rite of penance] *in the inclusion of Bible readings and prayers in which the penitent is expected to take part and the choice of speaking to a priest through a screen or openly in a special "room of reconciliation."* NY Times 3/6/76, p27 *The older* confessional, *or* confessional box, *is now joined by a* Room of Reconciliation. American Speech, Summer 1979, p84 **[1974]**

ro-ro ship, a freight ship that can carry loaded trucks, trailers, or other vehicles which drive on it at one port and drive off of it at another. . . . *ro-ro ships have made possible enormous savings in distribution costs for those willing and able to profit from them.* Times (London) 5/5/70, p1 *"Since the Channel Tunnel Study Group reported in 1964 ro-ro ships and containerization have caused sea freight rates to fall by about 40 per cent".* Science Journal 3/69, p8 **[1969, from *roll-on roll-off* (1955) + *ship*]**

rose, *n.* **come up roses,** to come out perfect. *Circa 1964-65, those* anni mirabiles *of the Great Society, everything came up roses.* Harper's 8/70, p32 . . . *if some real disaster hit us (elop-*

ing spouse, impotence, frigidity, bankruptcy, heart attack) we would have to soldier on, pretending that everything in the column was coming up roses. Times (London) 12/12/69, p24 **[1969, from the song "Everything's Coming Up Roses" in the musical *Gypsy* (1958)]**

rotator cuff, a set of muscles and tendons that secure the arm to the shoulder joint and permit rotation of the arm. Technical name, *musculo-tendinous cuff. The Brewers lost their chance at a pennant last year when their leader and prime slugger, Larry Hisle, tore a shoulder muscle—the "rotator cuff," which currently holds the No. 1 spot on the baseball Hurt Parade—while making a peg in late April, and was out for most of the rest of the campaign.* New Yorker 4/28/80, p49 **[1972]**

rotavirus, *n.* any of a group of circular viruses with spoke-like projections that are related to the reoviruses and cause acute gastroenteritis in infants and newborn animals. *Rotaviruses . . . have a similar appearance by electron microscopy, making differentiation among them difficult. Rotaviruses derived from different host species were distinguished by postinfection serum blocking virus activity in an enzyme-linked immunosorbent assay.* Science 7/21/78, p259 **[1974, from Latin *rota* wheel + English *virus*] —rotaviral,** *adj.*: *Children with rotaviral disease excrete large amounts of the virus a few days after infection.* New Scientist 3/27/80, p1009

roto, *n.* a person of the poorest class in Spanish-speaking areas of Latin America, especially Chile; a slum dweller. Compare POBLADOR. *The visiting journalist, whatever his prejudices, inevitably falls among the middle class, and that class has no more contact with the life of the Chilean "roto" than the white burghers of Johannesburg have with the black inhabitants of the township of Soweto.* Manchester Guardian Weekly 10/6/73, p17 **[1970, from American Spanish, literally broken or ragged (one)]**

rotovate, *v.t. British.* to break up or till (the soil) with a rotovator. *Not until the light soil was really dry in late April was the area rotovated twice, and set with sprouted seed.* Times (London) 12/7/70, p6 **[1962, alteration of earlier *rotavate* (1959), back formation from *Rotavator*]**

rotovator, *n. British.* a power-driven tool with rotating blades for breaking up or tilling the soil. *Mechanical rotovators and tillers will turn over the soil and applications of balanced fertilisers or composts will ensure fertility.* Sunday Times (London) 3/17/68, p16 *This meant that if I worked all this into the top four inches with a rotovator I should get good results, and I did.* Listener 12/2/71, p750 **[1970, alteration of earlier trademark *Rotavator* (1936), from *rotary cultivator*]**

round, *v.* **round down** (or **up**), to convert (currency) to the lower (or higher) value of the nearest round number. *The Decimal Currency Board have made some clear recommendations by which the new halfpenny conversion table will enable prices sometimes to be rounded down, although some may be rounded up.* Times (London) 2/18/70, p4 . . . *the confusions and ambiguities of the situation would give shopkeepers an irresistible chance to arrange things so that the rounding would usually be up, not down.* New Yorker 11/21/70, p192 **[1956]**

routinier (ˌru:ti:ˈnyei), *n.* a rigidly orthodox, conventional orchestra conductor, usually considered unoriginal and, therefore, dull. *Everything was first-rate with the exception of . . . the conductor Boris Khaikin, a tired routinier.* Manchester Guardian Weekly 1/10/70, p21 *Heger, an experienced man, conducts with a firm grip on the music but in the fashion of a* routinier, *making little effort to achieve the dynamic scheme of the opera, letting the orchestra (a good one) play in a competent rather than inspired manner.* Harper's 4/70, p117 **[1970, from French, a very conservative person, a stick-in-the-mud]**

rover, *n.* short for LUNAR ROVER. *The first rover is scheduled to take four trips of up to 32 km each with travel limited to 4.8 km radius from the landing site.* Science Journal 1/70, p16 **[1970]**

row, *n.* a line of letters or symbols displayed on a computer screen. *Displays, whether on a TV screen or a monitor, typically show 23-25 rows (a row is the equivalent of a line of type on* *a paper page). The* TRS-80 Color Computer *displays on 16 rows.* Consumer Report 9/83, p472 [**1977**]

Rozelle rule (rou'zel), *U.S. Sports.* the provision in a contract between a free agent and a professional team which requires the team to give the free agent's former team either an agreed-upon compensation or a compensation set by the league commissioner. *The superstars will be the principal beneficiaries of Judge Larson's decision that the Rozelle rule violates the anti-trust laws . . . Even with the Rozelle rule, Joe Namath was able to negotiate a two-year contract for $900,000.* NY Times 1/22/76, p34 *Through the season of 1979-1980, a Rozelle Rule applies in basketball. That is, a team hiring a free agent must compensate his old team.* 1977 World Book Year Book, p58 [**1974**, named after Alvin Ray ("Pete") *Rozelle,* born 1927, commissioner of the National Football League since 1960, who established the rule]

RPV, abbreviation of *remotely piloted vehicle,* a small, unmanned aircraft controlled by radio from the ground for use in target practice, bomb delivery, electronic reconnaissance, etc. *RPVs are, according to NASA, a safe and economic way of flight testing experimental aircraft . . . Aviation Week (22 October) reports that the USAF has set up a new organisation to manage RPV programmes, and is considering the use of RPVs fitted with warheads as "kamikaze" planes.* New Scientist 11/1/73, p339 *One of these years, we'll be getting RPVs— remotely piloted vehicles (don't you like all the initials?) That will make being a pilot a cushy job: he sits at a TV console 200 miles away and gets the RPV to provide surveillance or relay radio messages or pinpoint targets for precision bombing.* Time 5/23/77, p26 [**1970**]

rRNA, abbreviation of RIBOSOMAL RNA. *Different portions of DNA also must signal the starting and stopping points of transcriptions that produce RNA's of different types—messenger RNA (mRNA), transfer RNA (tRNA), and ribosomal RNA (rRNA)—which are used in the translation process.* Americana Annual 1967, p300 *Then virtually everyone still believed that the templates were the RNA molecules (rRNA) found in the small cellular particles called ribosomes.* New Scientist 11/24/66, p425 [**1966**]

RSVP or **R.S.V.P.** (ˌɑr,es,viːˈpiː), *v.i.* to reply to an invitation. *I have not been very good about RSVPing; I'd need a full-time secretary bringing her own stationery and stamps.* Manchester Guardian Weekly 7/4/70, p20 *Also, the party had been cleverly promoted, with each guest who had R.S.V.P.ed being sent a white beach towel and a green tank-top T-shirt that said "The Ritz" on them.* NY Times 8/13/76, pB3 [**1970**, verb use of the abbreviation (OED *a*1845) meaning "please respond" (French *répondez s'il vous plaît* reply, if you please)]

RTOL ('ɑr,toul), *n.* acronym for *reduced take-off and landing* (referring to an aircraft that uses less than half the standard runway). *Interest continues, however, in RTOL (reduced TOL—indeed, the acronymology has become so bad that at the airport conference they referred to ordinary planes as CTOL— conventional TOL) which would take off in about 1200 m.* New Scientist 4/12/73, p69 [**1972**, patterned after *VTOL* vertical take-off and landing (1950's)]

r-t-w, abbreviation of *ready-to-wear* (clothes). . . . *disasters like the midi which can happen if the r-t-w must anticipate couture by three months, should be avoided.* Sunday Times (London) 10/24/71, p37 *The r-t-w suits will be around 40 gns.* Times (London) 5/29/70, p8 [**1970**]

rubber bullet, bullet made of hard rubber and discharged from a specially designed gun, used in riot control. *Police fired rubber bullets and smoke bombs and charged with batons to disperse a crown of 10,000 on Sunday in one of the biggest anti-Government demonstrations seen here for many years.* Manchester Guardian Weekly 2/8/76, p8 [**1971**]

rubber-chicken, *adj. U.S. and Canadian.* of or having to do with the monotonous round of chicken dinners which a political figure, especially a candidate, is obliged to attend. *The listener is tempted to conclude that this therefore is merely another highly forgettable political speech, something redolent of the rubber-chicken circuit.* National Review 2/16/73, p192 *Departing*

from standard political fund-raising affairs, there wasn't a passed hat, a long-winded speaker or a rubber chicken dinner in sight last week when Consumer and Corporate Affairs Minister Warren Allmand tried to raise money for his riding association of Notre-Dame-de-Grâce. Maclean's 12/25/78, p31 [**1959**, applied to professional lecturers; **1968**, applied to political candidates; according to *Safire's Political Dictionary* (William Safire, 1978) "rubber-chicken circuit" was originally a vaudeville term referring to bookings in a number of theaters]

rubbish, *v.t.* **1** to treat with contempt; scorn; disparage. *History has dealt badly with the horse soldiers. Colonel Chivington is condemned because he won too big at Sand Creek; General Custer is rubbished because he lost too big at the Little Big Horn.* National Review 5/11/73, p536 **2** to wipe out; destroy. *With the half-a-dozen cries that could rubbish this Government and lay the United Kingdom politically waste in temporary suspension, the new year seems a fittingly brief, mellow moment . . . to praise Mr Harold Wilson.* Manchester Guardian Weekly 1/4/76, p6 *Sexist and racist attitudes had to be rubbished once and for all.* Guardian (London) 12/28/79, p10 [**1971**, from Australian English (first recorded use, 1953, in G. A. Wilkes' *A Dictionary of Australian Colloquialisms*), figurative verb use of the noun]

rubeosis (ˌruːbiːˈousis), *n. Medicine.* an abnormally reddish condition, especially of the iris. *The same procedure is used in the treatment of rubeosis, a common complication of diabetes in which the iris develops extra blood vessels. Thus enlarged, the iris cuts off circulation of aqueous humor. Previous techniques in treating rubeosis have not been satisfactory and Beckman reports his procedure is far safer to the eye.* Newsweek 9/23/74, p65 [**1974**, from New Latin, from Latin *rubeus* red + -*osis* abnormal condition]

rubidium-strontium dating, a method of determining the age of a geological specimen by measuring the radioactive decay of rubidium to strontium in the specimen. Also called STRONTIUM-RUBIDIUM DATING. *Rubidium-strontium dating has shown that the chondrites are the oldest objects scientists have sampled in the solar system. They are as old as the solar system itself, having crystallized* 4.6×10^9 *years ago.* McGraw-Hill Yearbook of Science and Technology 1974, p36 [**1970**, earlier in the phrase *rubidium/strontium method* (1950)]

Rubik's Cube ('ruːbiks), *Trademark.* a puzzle consisting of a cube formed of 26 small blocks that can be rotated on a spindle inside. Each of the cube's sides has a different color and once they are moved about it becomes a puzzle to restore the sides to their original colors. Also spelled *Rubik's cube. Büvös Kocka—the Magic Cube* [in Hungarian], *also known as Rubik's Cube—has simultaneously taken the puzzle world, the mathematics world and the computing world by storm.* Scientific American 3/81, p20 [**1980**, named after Ernö *Rubik,* a Hungarian teacher, who invented the puzzle about 1975]

rubredoxin, *n.* an electron-carrying protein found in anaerobic bacteria and associated with oxidation-reduction reactions in cells. *Also included in the iron-sulfur protein class are the rubredoxins, in which single iron atoms are attached to cysteine sulfurs. So far the rubredoxins have been found only in bacteria. The ferredoxin-type iron-sulfur clusters, on the other hand, are widespread in nature.* McGraw-Hill Yearbook of Science and Technology 1977, p353 [**1965**, from Latin *rubr-, ruber* red + English *redox* oxidation-reduction + -*in* (chemical suffix)]

ruck, *v.i. British.* to press aggressively for possession of the ball in rugby, especially as a group of forwards on a team. *The forwards, as against England, took a long time to work up to anything like effective scrummaging and rucking.* Times (London) 2/24/64, p3 *Yet he rucks with the best, and one's memory will long cherish the sight of him defying three Harlequin forwards who were trying to wrest the ball from him.* Sunday Times (London) 2/25/68, p23 [**1958**, verb use of the noun]

ruffling, *n.* cellular motion by means of thin folds that extend outward along the cells' forward edge, pulling the cell forward so that it flows over the fold as it extends new folds. *A hamster's kidney cell, magnified 16.200 times . . . travels by a process* *that is called "ruffling."* World Book Science Annual 1975, p360 [**1973,** from gerund of *ruffle, v.*]

rule, *v.* **rule in,** to decide in favor of; include (among a number of possibilities). *The odd expression "to rule in" is now current in political usage: Senator Richard Stone, Democrat of Florida, reported that an Administration witness before a Foreign Relations subcommittee "ruled out substantial military bases, but ruled in lightly manned, local facilities."* NY Times Magazine 3/30/80, p11 [**1904, 1973,** patterned after *rule out* to decide against, exclude (OEDS 1869)]

rumble strip, a strip of highway pavement built with ridges which cause a vehicle to vibrate, alerting drivers to hazardous conditions ahead. *Driving aids, both on the road and in the vehicle, are being developed. On the road, they include ribbed "rumble strips" and painted striped markings which indicate to drivers that they should slow down when approaching hazards.* Times (London) 6/18/76, p19 *Most . . . have been heading west toward Birmingham when the accidents happened. Rumble strips and other warnings have been installed to remind drivers to slow down through the interchange.* Birmingham News (Alabama) 9/26/76, p24-A [**1962**]

rumdum, *U.S. Slang.—adj.* ordinary; average. *Ponicsan finds surprising depth and touching delicacy in the rumdum lives he weaves together—dime-store and dinner women, odd-job truckers and coal-mine cripples, a mom-smothered "reader" at the cigar factory who keeps the ladies amused, and even a foraging bunch of derelicts living communistically in the town dump.* Newsweek 3/12/73, p96 **—n.** a person who is ordinary or average (as at a game or skill). *I have recently begun to play a game called racquet ball, and I find I would still rather look good than win, which is what I usually do: look good and lose. I beat the rumdums but go down before quality players.* Harper's 7/76, p72 [**1973,** probably extended sense of the U.S. slang term (1891) meaning stupefied from drink, unconscious; slang term influenced by *humdrum*]

runaway star, a member of a binary star that flies off in a straight line at high velocity when the other member of the pair explodes as a supernova. *The exploding star has to lose a lot of mass in order to release the gravitational hold on the companion, and it is interesting that there are several runaway stars in the sky, whose high speeds have always been something of a mystery. Dr Sofia suggests that they are expelled by a slingshot effect when one member of a binary sheds mass catastrophically.* New Scientist 3/30/72, p680 [**1970**]

run-of-the-, a combining form, meaning ordinary, commonplace, as in the following quotations: **—run-of-the-alley:** *The vulnerability of corporations to this kind of attack by revolutionaries or run-of-the-alley hoodlums even in the U.S. has been starkly dramatized recently by the abductions of Publishing Heiress Patricia Hearst in California and Newspaper Editor John ("Reg") Murphy in Atlanta.* Time 3/18/74, p79 **—run-of-the-house:** *Though he also treats run-of-the-house animals, like dogs and cats, Stone is best known for his work with wild species.* Newsweek 10/22/73, p122 **—run-of-the-scale:** *Rossini and Puccini could get by, Lord Drogheda thinks, with run-of-the-scale performers, but for Verdi, Wagner, Strauss, and the bel canto operas of Donizetti and Bellini, nothing but the best.* Manchester Guardian Weekly 7/26/74, p16 **—run-of-the-universe:** *Tayler's book stands back from the whizz-bang of tomorrow's funny quasar. Instead the author shows, in general terms, what is known about the physics of run-of-the-universe galaxies.* New Scientist 10/12/78, pxii [**1965,** abstracted from *run-of-the-mill* (OEDS 1930)]

run-up, *n. British.* a period leading up to some event; prelude. *In the run-up to the Greater London Council elections, the capital may show few signs of urban malaise to the visitor, in town to concentrate on the tourist or business merry-go-round.* Manchester Guardian Weekly 4/4/70, p9 *The Petit Palais show offers, also, invaluable evidence in its drawing section of the ways in which Picasso manoeuvred during the crucial run-up to the "Demoiselles d'Avignon."* Sunday Times (London) 11/20/66, p48 [**1966,** transferred sense from the term meaning

the run taken before bowling the ball in cricket or making a jump in field sports]

rurp, *n.* a type of piton shaped somewhat like a picture hook. See the quotations for details. *Scott uses a number of American rurps—their full name is "Realised Ultimate Reality Pitons"—whose blades are only 9 ¾ inches long.* Sunday Times (London) 6/15/69, p22 *Bur rurps and power drills and expansion bolts are pretty much out of fashion in Llanberis these days.* Manchester Guardian Weekly 7/31/71, p14 [**1968**]

rush, *n.* **1** the intense sensation of pleasure produced immediately after taking a narcotic. *It is clear now that science can tell us nothing about why a morphine addict says he gets a "rush" from his shot when he takes it in a deserted pad in the South End but, when given the same shot in the antiseptic ward of a modern general hospital, feels little or no pleasure.* Norman E. Zinberg and John A. Robertson, Drugs and the Public, 1972, p99 *Some people use it* [isobutyl nitrite] *as a quick upper during the day. "I carry a bottle of it with me all the time," says Ron Braun, 28, a California carpenter. "If I'm bored and want a rush, I take a sniff. It's a short break during the day."* Time 7/17/78, p16 **2** Figurative use: *It was amazing. Three layers of image . . . Pictures can be laid down layer upon layer, the way sound is edited. I got a rush, standing there, contemplating the possibilities.* NY Times Magazine 8/5/79, p42 [**1969**]

Russell rectifier, a hydraulic device for generating power from sea waves. See the quotation for details. *Russell rectifier. This device is a "wave rectifier." A large structure is divided into reservoirs, with valves designed so that waves drive seawater into a high level reservoir and empty a low level reservoir. This creates a "head" between the two reservoirs, and this can drive a water turbine.* New Scientist 5/6/76, p310 [**1976,** named after its inventor, Robert *Russell*, a British engineer]

Russian bear, a cocktail made with vodka, crème de cacao, and cream. *Americans spent an estimated $1.5-billion last year on this bland product* [vodka], *mostly to drink it mixed with fruit juices, as in Bloody Marys or screwdrivers, or even mixed with milk or cream, as in vodka milk punch or the Russian bear.* NY Times Magazine 6/8/75, p74 [**1975**]

Rust Belt or **rust belt,** *U.S.* the steel-producing and other industrial areas of the United States, especially in the northeastern region, that have been set back economically by recession and foreign competition. *In sum, the label "Rust Belt" may have had merit five years ago, but our seven-state service area that we call America's Heartland is primed and ready for the future.* AEP (American Electric Power) Report to Shareowners 1989, p12 [**1985**]

rutherfordium, *n.* one of the proposed names for ELEMENT 104. *Russian physicists had reported . . . that they had succeeded in synthesizing element 104, which they named kurchatovium in honor of the physicist I. V. Kurchatov. The Berkeley group then synthesized element 104 by a different method and challenged the Russian finding, naming their discovery rutherfordium in honor of the British physicist Lord Rutherford.* Scientific American 6/70, p49 [**1969**]

RV, 1 abbreviation of RECREATIONAL VEHICLE. *As I drive back from a weekend in another valley—the incomparable Yosemite, in the Sierra Nevada mountains—the rear-view mirror seems to show a herd of stampeding RVs chasing me down the freeway. Latter-day covered wagons, but uglier.* Times (London) 11/22/78, p18 [**1967**] **2** abbreviation of *reentry vehicle* (a spacecraft, missile, or any part of either that reenters the earth's atmosphere after completing its trajectory). *. . . defensive missiles with thermonuclear warheads can attack incoming reentry vehicles (RV's) in three general ways: with neutrons, X rays and blast, all products of a thermonuclear explosion.* Scientific American 2/68, p50 [**1968**]

R-value, *n. U.S.* a measure of the resistance to heat flow provided by insulating material. A high R-value corresponds to a high level of insulation effectiveness. Compare U-VALUE. *The insulating value of any of the materials used in walls or ceiling is determined by its R-value . . . Thickness is only an approximate indication of insulating value since 5 inches of one material may have just as much insulating value (just as high an R-*

value) as 6 inches of another. NY Times 10/10/76, pB46 [**1976,** from *Resistance*]

rya ('ri:ə), *n.* **1** a colorful handwoven rug with a deep pile, originally made by Scandinavian peasants for use chiefly as bed covers and wraps. *Mrs. Puotila's background in rug weaving is apparent in the linens she creates, for the colors she uses are as rich as those in a Finnish rya rug.* NY Times 6/4/63, p42 **2** the pattern or weave characteristic of rya rugs. *One simple stitch makes our pre-started rya hangings, rugs or cushions. Kits im-*

ported from Sweden . . . House Beautiful 3/72, p141 [**1957,** from Swedish, rug]

ryokan (ri:'oukɑ:n), *n.* a Japanese hotel or inn, especially one operated in a traditional style. *The Osaka area is heavily booked and even the tiny* ryokan, *or country inns, are doing good business.* Time 3/23/70, p32 *The most charming hotel I ever stayed at was a Japanese ryokan in the mountain spa of Kinugawa north of Tokyo.* Maclean's 3/9/63, p37 [**1963,** from Japanese]

S

Sabahan (səˈbɑːhən), *adj.* of or relating to Sabah, the former British North Borneo. *Some observers in west Malaysia believe that if the Sabah missions were to become fully Sabahan organizations the present campaign would come to and end.* Times (London) 12/30/70, p5 **—n.** a native of Sabah. *Largely overlooked in the imbroglio are the 600,000 Sabahans themselves, who, including the Moslem minority which has considerable cultural and economic influence in Sabah, would clearly prefer to stay in Malaysia.* Time 11/15/68, p45 **[1967]**

sabermetrics, *n.* measurement and analysis of baseball statistics by computer. *What sabermetrics offers is a means of recording and making available more knowledge* [to answer] *the questions that have always stirred baseball lovers.* 1984 World Book Year Book, p583 **[1984,** from *saber-*, alteration of *SABR*, acronym for *Society for American Baseball Research* + *-metrics*]

saccade (səˈkɑːd), *n.* the rapid jump made by the eye as it shifts from one fixed position to another. *What Ditchburn is mainly concerned with is not, however, a general physiology of vision, but how involuntary eye-movements, the so-called saccades and drift, affect visual performance.* New Scientist 12/13/73, p794 *First, a fast eye movement (called a saccade) carries the most sensitive part of the retina, the fovea, to the image of the target.* Scientific American 10/74, p100 **[1953,** 1966, transferred from earlier applications in ménage, music, etc. (OED 1727-41, 1876) in the sense of a jerk or jerky movement, from French]

saccharinize, *v.t.* **1** to put saccharin in; sweeten with saccharin. *The Senate version requires all products that contain the artificial sweetener to be labelled with a warning that saccharin causes cancer in animals and "may increase your risk of contracting cancer." The House, by contrast, would require such a notice to be displayed only at the shop or other retail outlet where "saccharinised" products are actually bought.* New Scientist 10/27/77, p208 **2** Figurative use: *Even his praiseworthy intention to bring great genius before large numbers of readers comes to seem suspect in the light of the corrupt and corrupting means he employs in censoring, simplifying, and saccharinizing it.* Atlantic 4/71, p95 **[1971]**

sack, *U.S. Football.* **—v.t.** to tackle (a quarterback) with the ball behind the line of scrimmage. *Namath played a half against the San Francisco 49ers, who have an outstanding pass rush—and he was sacked five times and intercepted onoe.* NY Times 9/9/77, pB12 **—n.** an act or instance of sacking. *The young defensive line he* [Joe Thomas] *drafted in 1973 and 1974 led the NFL in 1975 quarterback* sacks (*tackles behind the line of scrimmage*) *with 59.* 1976 World Book Year Book, p316 **[1969]**

SAD, abbreviation of SEASONAL AFFECTIVE DISORDER. *SAD symptoms often went away when the afflicted went south for the winter.* Encyclopedia Science Supplement (Grolier) 1987, p93 **[1985]**

sado-, a combining form meaning "sadistic" or "involving sadism." **—sado-erotic,** *adj.: We certainly get plenty for our money: a kind of all-senses collage assembled from bits of girlie photos, tropical stills, and mock-ups of sado-erotic temple carvings . . .* Manchester Guardian Weekly 4/11/70, p19 **—sado-Fascist,** *adj.: On trial at Chester last April were Ian Brady . . . and Esther Myra Hindley . . . They were charged with slowly killing a ten-year-old girl and two boys . . . "Their interests," she says of Brady and Hindley, "were sado-masochistic, titillatory, and sado-Fascist, and in the bookshops they found practically all the pabulum they needed."* Time 4/7/67, pE3 **—sado-sexuality,** *n.: It was the* One Million Years B.C. *poster of a barely wolf-skinned Raquel Welch . . . that led to her wider exposure. What is Hammer* [Films] *really promot-*ing: Sado-sexuality? Occultism? "Pure entertainment," insists Sir James* [Carreras]. Time 12/6/71, p33 **—sado-snobbism,** *n.: Client prints paperbacks for all tastes from (I think) the nasty vicarious sado-snobbism of poor FLEMING to TOLSTOY, IBSEN and old FYODOR DOSTOYEVSKY now, thank God, seeping into the Supermarkets.* Observer 8/30/64, p28 **[1954,** abstracted from *sadomasochism* (OEDS 1935), a term used in psychoanalysis for a combination of sadism and masochism]

sadomaso, *adj.* of or relating to sadomasochism. *Dodeca, however, is fated to dramatize her author's sado-maso scene.* NY Times Book Review 12/31/72, p18 **—n.** a sadomasochist. *At present, the sado-masos are in the ascendant: their crowds are bigger, their uniforms shinier, more explicit.* Listener 2/22/73, p237 **[1970,** short for *sadomasochist(ic)*]

safari, *n. attrib.* in or resembling a style of apparel originally worn by Europeans on African safaris: **—safari boot:** *Footwear often consisted of sandals and "safari" boots and some of the men were shoeless.* NY Times 8/29/77, p3 **—safari hat:** *White felt version of safari hat by Madcaps is $7 at Bergdorf's Bigi. Gray suede clutch bag by Morris Moskowitz is $55 at Bonwit's.* NY Times Magazine 9/17/72, p53 **—safari shirt:** *At Paraphernalia, the Basic Betsey at about £8 sold and sold and sold. Another seller was a bush shirt, "long before Yves Saint Laurent's safari shirt,"* explains Mrs. Young. Sunday Times (London) 11/21/71, p41 **—safari suit:** *He* [Yves Saint Laurent] *endorsed fringes, nailhead studs, vinyl raincoats and chain belts, put women in pants with his three-piece trouser suits and his "smoking" tuxedo and popularized the safari suit, the long scarf and American-style sportswear.* Newsweek 11/18/74, p74 **[1967]**

safari park, *Especially British.* another name for ANIMAL PARK. *"You are approaching lion country," a notice promises, warning you to close doors and windows against predators. The point is taken. Shopping around the safari parks certainly confirms one thought—that the low-income family on an outing these days can consider itself lucky if it gets back with its fleece.* Manchester Guardian Weekly 8/25/73, p16 *I didn't like the idea of getting animals from the wild and putting them in restricted conditions. What we needed were much more extensive spaces. The emphasis in England now is on safari parks where the animals roam in large spaces.* Maclean's 1/23/78, p8 **[1969]**

safe house, a house or other building used by intelligence agents or secret police as a place safe from surveillance. *Of the 107 prisoners interviewed by Amnesty, 71 said they had been tortured, often in "safe houses" where the methods of interrogation allegedly included prolonged beatings.* Manchester Guardian Weekly 9/26/76, p8 *Agents developing informants had no access to special "safe houses" for meetings or special untapped phones or cars with licenses that couldn't be traced to the bureau, thus making meetings with prospective informants dangerous to everyone involved.* NY Times Magazine 10/2/77, p16 **[1963]**

safekeep, *v.t.* to keep safe; safeguard. *So, banking on Dictys to safekeep her, I'd set out for Samos on a tip from half-sister Athene, to learn about life from "art."* Harper's 10/72, p80 **[1966,** back formation from *safekeeping, n.* (OED 1432)]

safe sex, sexual intercourse in which precautions are taken to avoid acquiring or spreading diseases. *The report focused on prevention of AIDS through . . . safe sex.* World Book Science Annual 1988, p308 *If he* [a doctor] *isn't practicing safe sex, then who is?* People Weekly 5/2/88, p84 **[1987]**

safety net, a guarantee of security or protection from financial or other losses; insurance. *The major London auction houses take great pains over attributions, checking with scholars and doing their own research. Nevertheless they work with a safety net in the form of their conditions of sale, which elaborately disclaim responsibility for the accuracy of attributions.* Times (London) 8/11/76, p12 *Today's move follows . . . a $3.9 billion International Monetary Fund loan and agreement by Western bankers for a $3 billion "safety net" credit to stabilize Britain's official sterling reserves.* NY Times 1/25/77, p45 [**1958**, figurative use of the term for the net to catch circus high-wire or trapeze artists or someone leaping from a building on fire]

safing, *adj. Astronautics.* designed to restore a condition of safety following a malfunction, such as a power failure. *Then came Launch Control again, reporting that the cut-off was initiated automatically by the terminal sequencer, and that "safing" procedures were now being carried out by the astronauts while Launch Control itself tried to identify the cause of the cut-off.* New Scientist 12/14/72, p645 [**1972**, probably short for *fail-safing*, participial form of *fail-safe, v.* (1949)]

Sagebrush Rebellion, *U.S.* a movement to gain state control of federally owned lands in western States. *By integrating these forces, a new conservative coalition emerged that overcame historic regional differences, linking Washington-haters in the Southern Bible Belt with the Middle Western Farm Belt and the Sagebrush Rebellion of the West.* NY Times Magazine 2/8/81, p25 [**1979**, from *sagebrush*, the state flower of Nevada, a plant associated with the Western United States]

Sahel (sə'heil *or* sə'hi:l), *n.* **1** Usually, **the Sahel.** a broad belt of semidesert on the southern edge of the Sahara, coextensive with Chad, Mali, Mauritania, Niger, Senegal, and Upper Volta (often used attributively). *Today it should be possible to put increased scientific knowledge of the Sahel and modern techniques to use, not only to help the victims of drought but also to bring drought itself under control. Unfortunately, however, the Sahel is a very marginal region as far as international economics is concerned.* Encyclopedia Science Supplement (Grolier) 1974, p157 **2** any part of the Sahel. *Finally, the existing parks are not an adequate sample of typical African ecosystems. They are heavily biased towards savannahs with their spectacular animals; sahel (arid savannah) and desert areas with their specialised plants and animals are seriously underrepresented, as are tropical forests.* New Scientist 7/27/72, p193 [**1972**, from Arabic *sāhel* shore, border] **—Sahelian,** *adj., n.: The Sahelian countries are among the poorest in the world. A new expenditure of $1 million a year would be beyond the means of most.* NY Times 9/7/77, pA12 *Even if climatologists were sure of this theory, and they aren't, it would simply add to rather than explain the Sahelians' troubles. Desertification was pinching their lives long before the rains failed here in 1968. The Sahelians have brought it upon themselves: and we—the rich, industrialized, superbly skilled, and technically superior we—have in effect been egging them on.* Atlantic 5/74, p99

Sahrawi (sɑ:'rɑ:wi:), *n., pl.* **-wi** *or* **-wis.** an inhabitant of Western Sahara (the former Spanish Sahara) ceded by Spain to Mauritania and Morocco in 1976 (often used attributively). *The Sahrawi spend a quarter of their day attacking, a quarter switching position, a quarter repairing their vehicles, and a quarter drinking tea and sleeping.* Manchester Guardian Weekly (Le Monde section) 8/29/76, p12 [**1975**, from Arabic, from *sahrā* desert, sahara]

sailboard, *n.* a kind of surfboard equipped with a hand-held mast and sail for propelling it as if it were a sailboat. . . . *the unsinkable fibre-glass sailboards that swarm like butterflies on any lake . . .* Maclean's 7/24/65, p31 *Athletically inclined men who hang around the water might welcome the challenge of a sailboard . . . skimming over the water on what is basically a surfboard with a sail.* New Yorker 12/8/80, p130 [**1962**, probably from *sail*boat + surf*board*]

sailboarder, *n.* another name for WINDSURFER. *Britain's inland water authorities have proved officiously uninterested in allowing sailboarders to use reservoirs.* Sunday Times (London) 1/11/81, p59 [**1974**]

sailboarding, *n.* another name for WINDSURFING. *Enthusiasts use it* [a beach] *for sail-boarding, water-skiing, paragliding, diving . . .* Times (London) 8/5/78, p8 [**1974**]

sailoff, *n. U.S.* a race between two or more sailing vessels. *Dennis Connor of San Diego, a former Star Class world champion, bested an international field in a sailoff in capturing the Congressional Cup in the annual match-racing series off Long Beach, Calif., in March.* 1974 Collier's Encyclopedia Year Book, p517 [**1970**, from the verb phrase *sail off*, probably patterned after FLY-OFF, *bake-off*, etc.]

salbutamol (sæl'byu:təmɔ:l), *n.* a beta-blocking drug used as a bronchodilator in the treatment of asthma and other allergies. *Formula:* $C_{13}H_{21}NO_3$ *Clearly the order of potency of the catecholamines was isoprenaline > adrenaline > noradrenaline. Salbutamol was about fourfold more potent than noradrenaline and dopamine was inactive at concentrations up to 100 μM.* Nature 2/12/76, p488 [**1969**, from *sal* salt + *but*yric acid + *am*ine + *-ol* (chemical suffix)]

saline, *n.* the injection of a highly concentrated salt solution into the amniotic sac to induce an abortion; SALTING OUT. *St. Luke's Medical Center, with 137 beds available, does six D and Cs daily, 18 salines a week.* Time 9/7/70, p48 **—adj.** of or involving saline. *The Court also held, 6 to 3, that it was unconstitutional for a state to bar the use, in abortions performed after the 12th week of pregnancy, of "saline amniocentesis," the most commonly used procedure.* NY Times 7/2/76, p1 [**1970**, extended from the earlier sense of a salt solution used in physiology]

Sally Mae, *U.S.* nickname for the Student Loan Marketing Association. *The new law also continues government guarantees for private loans to students and provides for greatly expanding that program through creating a national Student Loan Marketing Association. "Sally Mae"—as the new association is called—is designed to increase the private funds available to students by buying loan paper from banks and other private lenders.* Saturday Review 7/22/72, p38 [**1972**, from pronunciation of the abbreviation *SLMA*, patterned after *Fannie Mae* (1953), nickname for the Federal National Mortgage Association (from its abbreviation, *FNMA*)]

salonist (sə'lɑnist), *n.* another name for SALONNARD. *George Plimpton, the son of Francis T. P. and probably the best-known WASP dealer in living culture, operates like a Paris salonist among Interesting People . . .* Harper's 4/70, p89 [**1970**]

salonnard (sə'lɑnard), *n.* a person who frequents salons or circles of fashionable people (also used attributively). Also called SALONIST. *The author feels the need to enliven his salonnard gossip column with awful attempts at jocularity and whimsicality.* Manchester Guardian Weekly 2/14/70, p18 [**1970**, from French]

salsa, *n.* Caribbean dance music similar to the mambo but with elements of jazz and rock music. *At Barney Googles . . . you can hear both disco and highly spiced Latin music, called* salsa. *This blistering rhythm, Afro-Cuban in origin, is served up hottest at the Corso.* Time 7/19/76, p21 *Meanwhile the music of the Spanish-speaking dance halls deepened with a new synthesis of black Cuban and black North American genres—Salsa—of which one monument can be arbitrarily selected, a composition called* Wampo, *played by the Larry Harlow orchestra.* Times (London) 1/16/77, pI [**1975**, from American Spanish, literally, sauce]

SALT (sɔ:lt), *n.* acronym for *Strategic Arms Limitation Talks,* a round of talks between representatives of the Soviet Union and the United States on the subject of limiting the production of strategic nuclear weapons in both countries, begun in Helsinki, Finland, on November 17, 1969 (often used attributively). See SALT I, SALT II. *He* [Melvin Laird, U.S. Secretary of Defense] *is now pinning his hopes for a breakthrough on an agreement at the SALT talks.* New Scientist 7/2/70, p4 *With a new session of SALT negotiations scheduled to open this month in Vienna, the committee evidently thinks there is a* *chance to prevent a major new escalation of the arms race.* Scientific American 3/71, p44 [**1968**]

salt-and-pepper, *adj. U.S.* involving or made up of a mixture of blacks and whites. *In the upper-income areas of the outer city, there is salt-and-pepper integration, a sprinkling of Negroes here and there, but it is insignificant.* NY Times 6/1/71, p28 *Detroit is a salt-and-pepper situation. A great mix of black and white.* New Yorker 12/23/72, p38 [**1959**]

Salter duck, a mechanical device for generating power from sea waves, consisting of a line of vanes linked to form a break-water and shaped to rock in maximum response to waves. *It is called the "Salter duck"—perhaps because the device looks like a string of toy ducks bound side by side. As each individual "duck" rocks back and forth, the motion is transformed into electricity or hydraulic pressure.* Science News 5/29/76, p344 *Sea Energy Associates at Lanchester Polytechnic have also been testing Salter duck systems and have gained information on wave conditions . . . and power output.* Times (London) 4/21/78, p27 [**1976,** named after the inventor, Stephen H. Salter, a British engineer]

salting out, another name for SALINE. *The usual procedure for second-trimester abortions is saline injection, or "salting out." A heavy-gauge needle is inserted through the mother's abdomen and uterus and into the fluid-filled amniotic sac that surrounds the fetus. A half pint of amniotic fluid is withdrawn and replaced by an induction of highly concentrated salt solution. The solution usually terminates the life of the fetus within an hour.* Newsweek 3/3/75, p24 [**1970**]

SALT I, Also **SALT 1**. **1** the meetings for the first SALT agreement on nuclear weapons (1969-72) (often used attributively). *Retired Adm. Elmo Zumwalt and others have complained that one-man diplomacy put Kissinger alone at the table with Soviet experts at critical moments in SALT I when the U.S. side needed its own technical specialists to judge the give and take.* NY Times Magazine 5/30/76, p36 **2** the agreement resulting from these meetings. *Within the numerical limits of SALT 1, the Soviet Union has deployed much larger missiles than has the United States, achieving a throw-weight advantage of about three to one.* Americana Annual 1976, p210 [**1972**]

SALT II, Also **SALT 2**. **1** the meetings for the second SALT agreement on nuclear weapons (1979) (often used attributively). *SALT II is back on, says* Los Angeles Times *correspondent Robert Troth. The Soviets, says Troth, will agree to restrictions on their Backfire bomber and the United States will agree to restrictions on the range of its cruise missile.* National Review 2/6/76, p69 **2** the agreements resulting from these meetings. *SALT II will require congressional approval, and critics in Congress were quick to point out that the agreement will actually allow increases in the nuclear arsenals of both countries, thus hiking defense spending for some years to come.* 1975 World Book Year Book, p421 [**1972**]

salvage archaeology, the hasty excavation of sites about to be destroyed by construction projects, flooding, etc., in order to salvage archaeological remains. *These dams, and the lakes that form behind them, are spurring the archaeologists in a continuing race with the rising waters. "Salvage archaeology" became a way of life for anthropologists in Washington after Grand Coulee Dam created Roosevelt Lake more than 20 years ago.* Encyclopedia Science Supplement (Grolier) 1967, p30 *This is an area where the Danube narrows to run through a steep-walled canyon on its way to the Iron Gates; the site was discovered in the course of salvage archaeology in an area that will soon be flooded by a hydroelectric project.* Scientific American 4/68, p50 [**1960**]

sambo, *n.* a form of judo wrestling that originated in the Soviet Union and is now featured in international competitions. *The first-ever world championship for Sambo wrestling wound up here tonight with the Russians making an almost unchallenged sweep of the gold medal tally, giving them an insurmountable lead for the overall honors at the World Wrestling Championships.* Tehran Journal 9/15/73, p8 *The only thing that tarnishes Edinburgh's Maurice Allan's performance at Minsk last week in becoming the first Briton to win a world*

wrestling title since the 1908 Olympics is that the style in which he was successful, sambo, will not be contested at next year's Olympics. Sunday Times (London) 9/28/75, p30 [**1964,** from Russian, acronym for *samooborona bez oruzhiya* self-defense without weapons]

samink ('sei,miŋk), *n.* a mutation mink fur resembling Russian sable. *With sable pelts bringing many times the price of mink, this had long been an aim of mink geneticists. Only about 1,500 "Samink" were raised in 1972, but an expansion program was launched on the basis of the pelt's initial reception.* Britannica Book of the Year 1973, p321 [**1972,** from *sable* + *mink*]

samizdat (,sɑ:miz'dɑ:t), *n.* **1a** the practice of certain writers in the Soviet Union of secretly publishing and distributing writings banned by the government; the Soviet underground press. *By samizdat, Russians endlessly retype and clandestinely circulate the work of such banned writers as Alexander Solzhenitsyn.* Time 9/7/70, p25 *Samizdat is the hand-to-hand distribution of manuscripts, typed or photographed, of works rejected by Soviet printing houses.* NY Times 6/12/71, p1 **b** the literature or writings produced by this underground press. . . . *the authorities may be trying to break up the system of* samizdat—*of literature published in typescript which circulates privately and gives news of the proceedings of the secret police.* Listener 10/15/70, p506 *In an "Epilogue to the Russian Edition Abroad," Mr. Solzhenitsyn writes: "This book cannot be published now in our country except in samizdat because of censorship."* NY Times 6/12/71, p1 **2a** any underground press, especially in a communist country. *The book in question is Jiri Hrusa's novel "The Questionnaire," which was printed by the Prague Samizdat and is going to be published in Paris and Lucerne this autumn.* Manchester Guardian Weekly 8/27/78, p7 *New forms of* samizdat *also appeared in Poland, most significantly in the magazine* Zapis, *which specialized in good work turned down by the official magazines and publishing houses.* Britannica Book of the Year 1978, p526 **b** Attributive use: *To help coordinate nationwide* samizdat, . . . Chojecki's *printing establishment in a Warsaw apartment includes 20 typewriters, six crude presses and a skilled team of 30 people who help print, bind and distribute samizdat books.* Time 12/12/77, p55 . . . *the group has continued to work. It has produced a regular* samizdat *bulletin which chronicles cases of abuse.* New Scientist 5/25/78, p493 **3** Transferred use: *There is much to be said for innovative publishing practices whereby the major mathematical assumptions and conclusions are published, with the full proofs supplied in manuscript form to the referees and available as* samizdat *to those who care to write to the author.* Nature 2/12/76, p446 *It may be that Gedin undervalues signs of resistance to these trends: the growth of cottage industry publishing by the radical Left, the women's movement and other far from insignificant interest groups. Is this our grander, capitalist form of soul-saving* samizdat *or is it—as he might put it—just a further sign that mainstream publishing is giving up the struggle to combine righteousness with readability?* Manchester Guardian Weekly 7/10/77, p22 [**1967** from Russian *samizdat,* from *sam* self + *izdat-* (el'stvo) publishing, probably coined as a pun on *Gosizdat* the State Publishing House]

samizdatchik (,sɑ:miz'dɑ:tʃik), *n., pl.* **-chiki** (-tʃiki:). a citizen of the Soviet Union who secretly publishes and distributes writings or literature banned by the government. *"To fill their reserves," the Saratov Kommunist reported, "the* samizdatchiki *seek ties with other cities . . . They arrive with copies of the originals, which have been given abroad. Immediately, blank sheets of paper go into the typewriters. They don't sleep nights . . . (copying) literary manuscripts . . . one copy for oneself, the rest for distribution.* NY Times Magazine 9/10/72, p92 [**1972,** from Russian, from SAMIZDAT + *-chik* (agent suffix)]

sandburg ('zɑ:nt,burk; *Anglicized* 'sænd,bərg), *n.* a circular wall of wet sand, customarily built in Germany by seaside bathers to encircle themselves. It is often decorated with seashells, small sand sculptures, etc. *When the Germans take up position on the beach at the start of their holiday, they literally dig themselves in. They build what's known as a* sandburg. *The German word* burg *can mean castle, citadel, stronghold or fort.*

Certainly the German sandburg *has little in common with the sandcastles you see on the beaches of Skegness or Teignmouth . . . It serves as a family's beach headquarters and, for the period of their stay, is just as inviolable as any permanent dwelling place.* Listener 9/6/73, p302 [**1970**, from German *Sandburg* (literally) sand castle]

andinista (ˌsɑːndiˈniːstɑː) or **Sandinist** (ˈsændəˌniːst), *n.* **1** a member of a leftist military and political organization founded in 1963 in Nicaragua which overthrew the regime of President Anastasio Somoza Debayle and established a coalition government in 1979. *As any observer of Nicaraguan political life knows, there is at present no political force with any national standing except the Sandinistas.* Manchester Guardian Weekly 7/8/79, p5 **2** Attributive use: *Perhaps more than any guerrilla group in Latin America, Nicaragua's Sandinist National Liberation Front, or "El Frente," as the movement is known locally, has won the support or sympathy of broad sectors of the population, not just disenchanted youths, but non-Marxist intellectuals, conservative politicians, progressive priests and some wealthy businessmen.* NY Times 1/29/78, pIV [**1974**, revival of earlier *Sandinista* (1928), from Spanish *sandinista*, from Augusto César *Sandino*, a Nicaraguan general and rebel nationalist leader murdered in 1934 + *-ista* -ist]

S and M or **S & M**, **1** abbreviation of *Sadist and Masochist*. . . . *We just happened to be in—um, one of those bookstores on Polk Street in San Francisco that also sell 8-mm art movies, feelthy love beads, a few leather items, and posters "as you like them," and that shelve their books according to such classifications as "Homosexual," "Lesbian," "Hetero," "S & M," etc.* Saturday Review 10/31/70, p25 **2** abbreviation of *sadism and masochism. Says Zox, a Los Angeles photographer who has shot photos of women mutilating themselves: "S and M has been a trend in the arts for a while. It is just becoming a commercial trend."* Time 2/7/77, p58 [**1965**]

sand sink, a method of removing oil spilled at sea by spraying the oil with a mixture of chemically treated sand and water which sticks to the oil and causes it to sink to the bottom. *According to all the authorities concerned with the test, the Shell 'sand sink" method is eminently suitable for coping with very large oil pollution at sea.* New Scientist 6/11/70, p529 [**1970**]

sand wave, one of the moving ridges of sand on the surface of a desert or of the sea floor. *The sand waves and their movements are being studied by the Hydrographer of the Navy . . . and many other groups. A typical example is the Anglo-Dutch investigation of the Sandettie sandwave field which lies directly across one of the shipping routes into the North Sea from the English Channel.* New Scientist 10/25/73, p252 [**1972**]

sandwich bar, a restaurant specializing in sandwiches, usually served at a counter. *With him in the dock was . . . John Leonard Knight, aged 33, sandwich bar proprietor, of Peaketon Avenue, Redbridge, Essex, and William John Hickson, aged 27, company director, of Petersfield Close, Upper Edmonton . . .* Times (London) 11/25/70, p4 [**1955**]

sandwicheria, *n.* another name for SANDWICH BAR. *Restaurants, snack bars, cafés, cake shops and 'sandwicherias' are crowded.* Listener 4/11/68, p460 [**1968**, from *sandwich* + *eria*, as in *cafeteria*]

sanitation engineer, *U.S.* euphemism for a garbage and trash collector. *While the rubbish piled up last week—and newscasts reported that many of those "sanitation engineers" make more money than a lot of school teachers do—the bitterness against public servants who strike was unprecedented.* New York Post 7/9/75, p36 [**1974**] ►Not to be confused with *sanitary engineer*, who plans and manages water-supply systems, air pollution standards, etc.

sanitationman, *n. U.S.* an employee of a municipal department in charge of collecting and disposing of household refuse; a garbage and trash collector. *The lunch was provided by the Seventh Avenue Neighbors Association as its way of thanking men who do a notoriously thankless job . . . The sanitationmen left, emptying three garbage cans on their way out.* New Yorker 8/15/70, p21 [**1968**]

sanitize, *v.t.* to give a wholesome appearance to; make more palatable by removing offensive aspects or elements. *Like an aging roué looking back on halcyon days, the House Un-American Activities Committee has tried to sanitize its image. It changed its name to the House Internal Security Committee in 1969 and made abortive attempts to revive its lost vigor . . .* Time 10/26/70, p28 [**1954**, figurative sense of the verb meaning to make sanitary by disinfecting, sterilizing, etc.]

sanman, *n. U.S. Informal.* a municipal garbage and trash collector. *The garbage collectors have one of the toughest jobs in the city: such a Sanman walks as much as fourteen miles a day behind a sanitation truck, and lifts as much as six tons of garbage a day, in all kinds of weather. Sanmen get more on-the-job injuries than either policemen or firemen.* New Yorker 5/22/78, p28 [**1977**, short for SANITATIONMAN]

sanpaku (sɑːmˈpɑːkuː; *Anglicized* sænˈpɑːkuː), *adj.* characterized by an unhealthy condition that supposedly results from failure to follow a macrobiotic diet, which prescribes organically grown sugar, fruits, and vegetables in preference to meat, eggs, etc. *Ten minutes to lunch break, the publicist introduces a girl of about twenty who is very sanpaku—in fact, an inordinate amount of veinless white shows beneath the lampblack pupils—and almost intimidatingly beautiful.* Esquire 1/72, p118 SICKNESS: *If your vegetable is feeling* sanpaku (*droopiness, caused by a more than five-to-one yin-yang ratio), brew the little greenie a hot cup of Mu tea and settle down for a nice long chat.* New Yorker 8/13/73, p27 [**1963**, from Japanese, literally, three-white, from the belief that the condition is manifested by three white areas around the iris of the eye instead of the normal two on either side of the iris]

Santa Marta gold, a strong variety of Colombian marijuana. *From them* [dirt airstrips in Colombia] *fly the night planes, their holds full of bales of Santa Marta Gold. The smokers say it is better than Mexican marijuana. U.S. authorities say it is three to ten times more potent than the Mexican.* Maclean's 4/2/79, p26 [**1979**, named after its place of origin, the Sierra Nevada de *Santa Marta* (in Guajira province, Colombia), and for its golden color]

sapient (ˈseipiːənt), *n.* an early member of the species *Homo sapiens;* a prehistoric man. *New finds from the Omo region, and East Rudolf, North Kenya, have put the age of both large and small australopithecines back to the 2-3 million year mark, while African sapients from the Upper Middle Pleistocene are now known from the same region.* Science Journal 12/70, p80 —*adj.* relating to or characteristic of *Homo sapiens. . . . the mastoid of Steinheim* [man] *is sapient in form.* Nature 8/5/76, p487 [**1970**, from New Latin (*Homo*) *sapiens* (stem *sapient-*) wise or rational (man)]

SASE or **sase**, abbreviation of *self addressed stamped envelope. Marzipan! Create colorful epicurean miniatures for less. SASE $3. Box 1588, Evergreen Colo. 80439.* Harper's 2/81, p94 [**1974**]

Sasquatch (ˈsæsˌkwɒtʃ), *n.* a large, shaggy creature of legend that walks on two legs and lives in the mountains and forests of the Pacific Northwest. Also called BIGFOOT and OMAH. *Supposed sightings of Yeti and Sasquatch are disappearing evidence in favor of large manlike creatures living in the mountains of Asia and the Pacific Northwest or anywhere else. The eyewitness always turns out to be a victim of a hoax, commercially implicated, inept at keeping live specimens from getting away.* Science 10/26/73, p376 *This month's* Smithsonian *takes an engaging look at one man's determined search for the Sasquatch, an American cousin of the Abominable Snowman.* Time 1/14/74, p29 [**1972**, apparently from a Salish Indian word meaning "wild men"; (1929 Canadian use attested in *A Dictionary of Canadianisms*)]

satcom, *n.* a satellite communications center. *The difficulty of having large and small stations working through the same transponder has been circumvented by a novel technique, now adopted for the planned NATO satcom . . .* Science Journal 1/70, p16 [**1969**, from *sat*ellite *com*munications]

satellite, *v.t.* to transmit via communications satellite. *At 2 a.m. the telephone woke me. It was Peter Lynch, our contact in Tel*

Aviv (from where our film was being satellited). Listener 12/19/74, p826 *Somehow between ricocheting from Jerusalem to Damascus to Beirut to Zurich to Aswan, "satelliting" back his TV spots and getting his laundry attended to, Darius finds time to . . . unravel the dark, multilayered conspiracies of Israelis, Palestinians, the CIA and Vandenberg.* Time 12/19/77, p99 **[1974,** verb use of the noun]

satellite dish, a large dish-shaped microwave antenna that tracks and receives signals from earth satellites. *With the advent of pay TV, satellite dishes, video cassettes and increased cable services, the technology of television has already reached what viewers only a decade ago thought of as the distant future.* Maclean's 10/10/83, p69 **[1978]**

satellite DNA, a variant form of DNA (deoxyribonucleic acid, the carrier of genetic material in the cells). See the quotations for details. *Curiouser and curiouser becomes the tale of "satellite" DNA. Discovered originally in the mouse, where it constitutes some 10 per cent of the total DNA in each cell of the animal, satellite DNA can be distinguished from the rest by its different density, and by the fact that it apparently consists of repeating base sequences—i.e., multiple copies of a given sequence repeated again and again.* New Scientist 8/27/70, p406 *As much as 30 per cent of the DNA in the cells of many plants and animals has satellite properties, such as density differences, that indicate it is different from the remainder of the organisms' DNA. This strange DNA, called satellite DNA, is found in species as different from one another as mice and men.* World Book Science Annual 1972, p273 **[1970]**

satellite killer, another name for HUNTER-KILLER SATELLITE. *A "satellite killer,". . . could be ready in a year or so. The basic idea is for rockets to carry the killers into space where they will be launched to hunt their prey. Military sources have described the "killer" as a highly manoeuvrable heat-sensing cylinder, about a foot long and eight inches in diameter, that will carry no explosives. Rather, it will ram the target satellite as both vehicles fly at thousands of miles an hour.* Maclean's 2/6/78, p24 **[1977]**

satellization, *n.* the act or process of becoming a satellite or subservient to another. *Not only has Fidel [Castro] resisted satellization, but he has twisted the Cuban communist party to his own purposes—using it in 1961 to set up a new Castroite political party . . .* Harper's 5/67, p86 *They have no choice other than to align themselves with the decisions taken by others. Association is tantamount to satellization.* Times (London) 10/27/67, p8 **[1955]**

satsang ('sɑːt'sɑːŋ), *n.* a Hindu sermon or discourse. *Maharaj Ji decided to take his message of inner peace outside of India in 1970. He made his first appearance in the West in 1971 at a pop music festival in Glastonbury, Eng., arriving in a white Rolls Royce and taking the stage to deliver a* satsang *("truthgiving") for five minutes before the microphone was shut off.* Britannica Book of the Year 1974, p145 —*v.i.* to deliver a satsang. *"The Perfect Master never comes or talks exactly as prophesied," a fat mahatma in a gray business suit is* satsanging *in front of the white satin throne.* New York Review of Books 12/13/73, p38 **[1971,** from Sanskrit]

saturation dive, a dive made by saturation diving. *It is clear, however, that the "partial pressure" of oxygen should be kept between about 150 and 400 millimeters of mercury during the at-depth phase of a long saturation dive.* Scientific American 3/66, p27 **[1966]**

saturation diver, a diver who uses saturation diving. . . . *the Argyronète, a self-propelled submersible combining a house in which saturation divers can live (under sea bottom pressure) and a conventional submarine with a crew at normal atmospheric pressure.* Science Journal 2/70, p15 **[1970]**

saturation diving or **saturated diving,** a method of diving used by aquanauts to shorten the time of decompression by remaining at a given depth until the body becomes saturated with the synthetic gas mixture used for breathing. *Probably the greatest single hazard of deep dives, and especially of saturation diving, is the "bends," precipitation of bubbles of dissolved gases in the blood and tissues.* Science News 9/4/71, p139 *Captain*

[George] *Bond sought to overcome this unfavourable ratio o bottom time to decompression time with a new concept know as "saturated diving". . . The important element in saturate diving is that after six days or six months of exposure to a give depth or pressure, the diver requires a single, fixed decompres sion period.* New Scientist 10/17/68, p125 **[1966]**

Saturday night special, *U.S.* **1** a small handgun with a short bar rel, usually made from imported parts. *The company is the onl major producer of cheap pistols—"Saturday night specials"— in the city, and it continued assembling them in high volum even after Mayor Lindsay announced his determination t drive the concern out of the business or out of the city.* N' Times 3/13/73, p35 *National statistics indicated that abou half of all gun-related crimes involved "Saturday night spe cials," which . . . sell for less than $50 and are of .32 calibe or less. Although the Gun Control Act of 1958 banned importa tion of these weapons, its passage encouraged a thriving do mestic production that now turns out about 200,000 "Saturda night specials" annually.* Americana Annual 1976, p199 **2** *Fi nance.* a public offer to buy shares of a company's stocks, made without warning to prevent the company from challenging the takeover bid. *After a recent federal district court ruling, the Saturday night special (the tactic in which a predator make a lightning move to acquire a major line of stock before show ing his hand) may never be the same again.* Economis 7/14/79, p97 **[1968** for def. 1, so called because of its frequen use in barroom and street fights on weekends; **1978** for def. 2 so called from such a bid by Colt Industries, a pistol manufac turer, to acquire a small firm, in the early 1970's]

saucerman, *n.* a man from outer space; someone who travels by flying saucer. . . . *Barney and Betty Hill, a Portsmouth, N.H. couple whose "abduction" by saucermen during an auto tri was described in the fast-selling book,* The Interrupted Jour ney *by John Fuller.* Time 8/4/67, p32 *Visiting saucermen from Mars might well report back to base that all our God must be hard of hearing.* New Scientist and Science Journal 9/30/71, p722 **[1957]**

SAVAK or **Savak** (sæ'væk *or* sɑː'vɑːk), *n.* the former secret in telligence organization of Iran, abolished in 1979. . . . *Savak' primary role is domestic but it has also taken on a significan role abroad, monitoring the activities of the thousands of Irani an students in foreign colleges and universities.* Manchester Guardian Weekly (Washington Post section) 9/12/76, p17 **[1967,** from the Iranian acronym for National Security and Intelligence Organization]

saxitoxin, *n.* any of various nerve poisons obtained from shell fish that feed on toxin-forming dinoflagellates of the genus *Gonyaulax.* Mussels, clams and other filter-feeding animals *ingest the microorganisms, often concentrating the toxin in special organs. About half a milligram of the poison, called saxitoxin, is deadly to man.* Scientific American 1/73, p125 **[1962,** from New Latin *Saxi(domus giganteus)* the Alas kan butter clam, from which the poison has been isolated + English *toxin*]

scag, *n. U.S. Slang.* heroin. Also spelled SKAG. *"I started getting high on scag at 14 or 15."* Time 4/6/70, p46 *In the film* [Scag], *two young people—a black girl from the ghetto and a white boy from a middle-class suburb—have one thing in common, scag.* Science News 8/21/71, p120 **[1967,** of unknown origin]

scaling, *n. Nuclear Physics.* a property or effect of the collision of high-energy electrons with protons, in which the electrons bounce off pointlike particles that are thought to be quarks, the constituents of protons. *Recent experiments at the Stanford Linear Accelerator Center (SLAC) involving the high-energy scattering of electrons from protons show the property known as scaling. Scaling is usually interpreted as direct evidence that the electric charge inside a proton at a given instant is localized at one point or a few points, that is, at the positions of the quarks.* Scientific American 2/75, p66 **[1970,** from *scale,* proba bly in the sense of "to come off in scales, to peel"]

scam, *U.S. Slang.*—*n.* a dishonest scheme; a swindle. *A gam bling house is a sitting duck to every con man or outlaw who comes through; he is invariably convinced that he has a scam* *hat you have never seen before. Once in a very great while he 's right.* Harper's 2/71, p89 **—v.i., v.t.** to swindle, trick, or *cheat. Local citizens . . . try to avoid being scammed by . . . *ity politicians.* New Yorker 5/30/77, p96 [**1963**, of unknown *origin*]

scam, a combining form used to form nouns and meaning a *dishonest, fraudulent scheme. Abscam* (see the etymology *below*) popularized the new form which has since spawned the *following* words among many others of a nonce character: **—cabscam**, *n.: Of the New York City hacks tested during last week's "cabscam," 31 had broken the law.* Maclean's 8/18/80, *p25* **—Iranscam**, *n.: Rather more original are . . . Iranscam, and Payatollah, leading a field whose stragglers include Iran-ics, the Old Iranaround, Iranamok, and Contra-deceptive.* American Speech, Summer 1987, p187 **—petroscam**, *n.: The many petroscam comedy features Donald Sutherland as a disc jockey in a helicopter, along with Sterling Hayden . . .* Maclean's 8/4/80, p28 **—Quackscam**, *n.: Quackscam was the largest raid against game-law violators in the history of Illi-nois. The previous record-setter was in 1958, when a number of people were arrested for systematically killing ducks for sale . . .* New Yorker 3/9/81, p82 [**1980**, abstracted from *Abscam*, the code name of an undercover investigation (1978-80) of U.S. public officials, especially Congressmen, in which FBI agents posing as wealthy Arabs attempted to bribe them at secretly videotaped meetings. The name *Abscam* was formed from A*b*dul Enterprises Ltd., a bogus export-import firm that the agents used as a front + SCAM]

scan, *n.* a picture of the distribution of radioactivity in the body. See also SCANNING. *A side-view brain scan, the most common of the medical diagnostic techniques that make use of ra-dioactive tracers, reveals a brain tumor, the large dark region in the middle of the clear area.* 1971 Britannica Yearbook of Science and the Future, p231 *An improved way of scanning the brain for tumors has been reported by two California scien-tists. Their technique is claimed to give a clearer image of tu-mors deep within the brain than has heretofore been possible and also allows multiple scans in place of one or two.* Science News 9/3/66, p166 [**1953**]

scanning, *n.* a diagnostic method for detecting abnormalities in the body by the use of special photographic instruments that record the movement of an administered radioactive sub-stance as it passes through the organs, body fluids, etc. *In scan-ning, a radioactivity compound is administered to the patient, after which the compound's distribution is mapped out by a scintillation camera that detects gamma rays coming from the child.* Science News 4/6/68, p333 *. . . common studies that involved tracers were diagnoses of focal abnormalities of the brain, lung, liver, kidney, and other organs. These tests were based on a technique called "scanning," which mapped the distribution of radio-activity within the body and then dis-played the data in the form of a picture of the organ or region of interest.* 1971 Britannica Yearbook of Science and the Fu-ture, p230 [**1956**]

scanning electron micrograph, a photographic reproduction of an image formed by scanning electron microscopy. *These beau-tiful scanning electron micrographs impressively illustrate a new replication technique which enables the finer details of ice-crystal growth to be studied.* New Scientist 5/17/73, p400 [**1962**]

scanning electron microscope, an electron microscope that uses a very fine moving beam of electrons to scan a specimen so that the image obtained, though not as sharp as that provided by the standard electron microscope, contains much more detail. *Ab-breviation:* SEM *Since its introduction five years ago, the scan-ning electron microscope has established itself rapidly in a variety of fields, from microbiology to metallurgy, where the observation and understanding of surface detail is necessary.* New Scientist 2/5/70, p256 *Two different types of electron microscope are currently in use. The transmission electron mi-croscope is analogous to a conventional light microscope. The scanning electron microscope employs a flying spot of elec-*

trons to scan the object, producing a television-like image. Sci-entific American 4/71, p26 [**1953**]

scanning electron microscopy, the use of a SCANNING ELEC-TRON MICROSCOPE. *Scanning electron microscopy shows a tu-bule extending from a spore and attached to a host cell.* Science 1/25/74, p269 *The recent application of scanning electron mi-croscopy to the field of immunology has sparked interest in the surface architecture of the immune cells called lymphocytes.* McGraw-Hill Yearbook of Science and Technology 1976, p270 [**1966**]

scatterometer, *n.* a radarlike instrument equipped with several aerials for directing a radar beam, microwaves, etc., over a wide area and recording the returned signal at all angles. *The microwave radiometer and scatterometer will use radar tech-niques to penetrate cloud cover.* Science News 10/10/70, p305 [**1966**, from *scatter* + *-ometer*, as in *barometer, speedome-ter,* etc.]

scattersite housing, U.S. government-sponsored public housing designed to disperse low-income groups outside the ghetto or inner city; housing provided in scattered sites throughout a city. *The issues surrounding the battle of Forest Hills in partic-ular and the scattersite housing concept in general, are now being thrashed out in the courts rather than the streets—at least for the time being. While both sides await the decision of an appeals court on whether or not to halt construction, work continues on the project . . .* New York Post 4/24/72, p27 [**1972**]

scenario, *n.* any projected course or plan of action, especially one of several possible plans. *If either the Albanian resolution or the U.S. dual representation resolution is adopted, the scene will shift, in time, to the Security Council chamber. There, the Council will, through a complex but securely-plotted scenario, offer Peking the China seat.* New York Post 10/25/71, p5 *Unfortunately there are almost no data available on frac-ture modes for various scenarios of mission failure. An engi-neering examination of this subject is urgently needed.* Science 3/15/68, p1192 *Mr Lever* [Labour's Paymaster-General] *makes out a splendid case for "gradual but continuous" growth as the least hopeless of our alternatives, but he spoils it by fudging the wages issue . . . An alternative scenario* (to use the jargon) *might appeal to at least those Ministers who in private are sniffing eagerly for growth.* Manchester Guardian Weekly 12/12/70, p13 [**1957**, extended sense of the theatrical term for an outline or synopsis of a play]

scentometer, *n.* an instrument that analyzes the content of breath and records the extent of dust, pollutants, etc., in it. *To enforce the* [air-pollution] *code, alas, the city acquired a Scen-tometer. The device is a plastic box that contains a sensitive me-chanical sniffer through which an inspector breathes. This is a scientific means, supposedly, for calibrating stink.* Time 10/19/70, p14 [**1968**, from *scent* + *-ometer*, as in *barometer, speedometer,* etc.]

Schedule 1, a U.S. government classification of drugs that are considered to have potential high abuse and no redeeming medical value, and whose possession and use is regulated by law. *Although marijuana is still classified, with heroin, as a Schedule 1 narcotic, it has become, for many, as American as blue jeans.* NY Times Magazine 11/19/78, p60 [**1973**]

schiz (skits *or* skiz), *n. U.S. and Canadian Informal.* **1** a schizo-phrenic. *Mother Rose is drinking vodka and muscatel in the laundry and conversing with the Virgin Mary; 300-pound Le-land, an intermittently brilliant schiz, is going berserk in the basement.* NY Times Book Review 7/16/72, p30 **2** schizophre-nia. *Schiz is all tied up with religion, art, psychology, politics, and countless other things. Studying these things from the angle of schiz and schiz from these fields is doubtlessly impor-tant, fascinating, and profound . . .* Harper's 4/74, p92 [**1955**, from *schizo*, shortening of *schizophrenia*]

schizzy or **schizy** ('skitsi: *or* 'skizi:), *adj. U.S. Informal.* schizo-phrenic. *This friend of mine—a bit of a schizzy dude, to be sure, but also a B.S. from Rensselaer Poly—has been telling me that if we go on muddying up the ecosphere, all the monarch butterflies will turn against us and eat up the entire world sup-*

ply of sweet sorghum, rock salt, and anthracite coal, without which human life as we know it et cetera et cetera. New Yorker 1/20/75, p31 [**1974**, from *schizo* or *schiz* + *-y* (adj. suffix)]

schlep (ʃlep), *Informal.* —*v.i.* to move wearily or awkwardly; drag or haul oneself; toil. *"You look awful; What's the matter? That's what comes of all this* schleping *around the track? Give it up! Listen, come!"* William Peter Blatty, The Exorcist, 1971, p380 —**n.** Also spelled **schlepp. 1** a slow, dull or awkward person. *Benjamin—evidently head of the debating club, campus editor, captain of the cross-country team, social chairman of his house—transformed into a somnambulistic, clowny* schlepp . . . New Yorker 7/27/68, p52 **2** a long haul or drag. *As Mr. Moskowitz explained it, the general philosophy of the returnees was: "Why live in Wantagh and do the 'schlepp' if you don't have the kids?"* NY Times 4/8/68, p55 [**1963**, from Yiddish *shlepn* to drag] ►*Schlep(p)* as a transitive verb is recorded in the OEDS with a citation from James Joyce's *Ulysses* (1922) and another from Lincoln Steffens' *Autobiography* (1931). Its third citation is dated 1966.

schlockmeister (ˈʃlɑkˌmaistər), *n. U.S. Slang.* a purveyor of anything shoddy, mediocre, or second-rate. *The schlockmeisters seeking to capitalize on American outrage at the Iranian crisis make no apologies for their avarice. "It started out as a capitalist move, I'll admit that," says Bumper Sticker King Rachelson, "but now it's a way for me to wave the flag."* Time 12/17/79, p9 [**1965**, from *schlock* cheap, shoddy goods (see the etymology of SCHLOCKY) + German *Meister* master]

schlocky (ˈʃlɑkiː), *adj. U.S. Slang.* cheap; inferior; junky. Also spelled SHLOCKY. *Just what the marketplace doesn't need, one more schlocky Gothic series.* Publishers Weekly 12/1/75, p67 [**1968**, derived from *schlock* cheap, shoddy goods (OEDS 1915), from Yiddish *shlak* a curse]

schmear (ʃmir), *n.* **the whole schmear,** *Slang.* the whole matter, affair, or business; the works. *If there is an illiberality among us Jews, I tell Russek, it is because we never learned to sit a horse; we missed out on the whole chivalry* schmear. New Yorker 12/18/71, p33 *Seymour Krim . . . took off from the American realistic novel. His own quest took him through the whole* schmear *and he lived to see the Holy Grail turn into a booby-trapped jerry.* Times (London) 2/21/70, p1 [**1968**, from Yiddish *shmir* spread]

schmegegge or **schmegeggy** (ʃməˈgegiː), *n. U.S. Slang.* a silly or foolish person; jerk. *Richard Merkin, soon to become* GQ*'s leading source of Hemingway references, debuts a new column, Merkin on style: "Not long ago, I met a* schmegegge *who dressed like a man with a never ending gift certificate at Barneys . . . I didn't need Hemingway . . . to sense that this was a horse's ass from the old country."* Spy (The New York Monthly) 2/89, p40 [**1964**, from Yiddish *shmegege*]

schmotta (ˈʃmɑːtə), *n. U.S. Slang.* a piece of clothing; garment. *A young woman, pale, in a Victorian* schmotta. New Yorker 10/24/77, p39 [**1970**, from Yiddish *shmate* a rag, from Polish *szmata*]

schoolbook, *adj. Especially U.S.* characteristic of school textbooks; oversimplified. *Today, because of the problems peculiar to writing the history of modern mass-art forms, . . . film enthusiasts find it simpler to explain movies in terms of the genius-artist-director, the* schoolbook *hero—the man who did it all.* New Yorker 2/20/71, p89 [**1970**]

Schottky diode (ˈʃɑtkiː), *Electronics.* a rectifier with a metal semiconductor. *Tiny Schottky diodes developed at General Electric are about the size of a match. In the foreground is the silicon wafer that when sectioned will form the heart of the device.* Britannica Book of the Year 1977, p416 *"Schottky diodes" (using a metal semi-conductor junction) are simpler alternatives, and the most can be made of the structure's properties when it is applied to polycrystalline or amorphous thin-film cells.* New Scientist 12/7/78, p761 [**1968**, named after Walter Hans *Schottky,* 1886-1976, Swiss-born German physicist, whose research led to its development]

schtick (ʃtik), *n.* variant of SHTICK. *The acting's fine. The directing's clean. The writing (by Allen and Marshall Brickman)*

isn't littered with all *that much schtik.* Maclean's 5/14/79, p54 [**1959**]

schtup (ʃtup), *v.i., v.t. Slang (usually considered vulgar).* to engage in sexual intercourse. *Not bad for a couple of guys whose biggest claim to fame, for the longest time, was that you could snort and schtup in the balcony of their disco.* Vanity Fair 11/88, p170 [**1969**, from Yiddish *shtupn* to push]

schussboom (ˈʃusˌbuːm), *v.i. Slang.* to ski at high speed. *He is Bucky Scudder the skier, who flashes across moguls with such control and precision . . . as he schussbooms over a fifteen-foot dip, he hears them yell "Buuuckyyy!" as though they were yelling "Track!" in admiration of his exuberance and daring.* New Yorker 2/2/63, p37 [**1962**, from *schuss* a fast run down a straight course (OEDS 1937) + *boom, v.,* to sail very fast]

schussboomer (ˈʃusˌbuːmər), *n. Slang.* a high-speed skier. *. . . Cervenia continues to be the schussboomer's paradise. There is enough terrain hereabouts—as in most of the Alps—to make even reconstruction-minded Yankees start yodelling Dixie.* NY Times 1/20/67, p33 [**1959**]

Schwarzschild radius (ˈʃvɑrtsˌʃilt), the size at which the gravitational forces of a collapsing body in space become so strong that they prevent the escape of any matter or radiation. *A black hole is the result of uninhibited gravitational collapse . . . Eventually an object whose collapse continues reaches a limiting size that depends on its mass. The size is called the Schwarzschild radius. For the sun, it is about three kilometers. When the object shrinks to less than its Schwarzschild radius, it becomes a black hole.* Science News 12/26/70, p480 [**1965**, named after Karl *Schwarzschild,* 1873-1916, a German astronomer]

SCID, abbreviation of SEVERE COMBINED IMMUNODEFICIENCY (DISEASE). *According to current medical reports, these new techniques represent alternative therapies for children born with severe combined immune deficiency, or SCID, who without treatment rarely live more than a year.* NY Times 5/14/76, pD12 [**1976**]

science court, a proposed panel or board of scientists that would evaluate conflicting scientific claims in matters of public concern and present its findings to policymakers and the public. *The man behind the idea is Arthur Kantrowitz, chairman of the Avco Everett Research Laboratory near Boston, who sees the science court as a forum that would allow experts on both sides of technological issues to present their cases before a panel of scientist judges . . . in adversary proceedings that would be open to the general public.* New Scientist 9/30/76, p677 *The Science Court, by whatever name it might ultimately be known, offers a potential mechanism through which the status of knowledge or lack of knowledge on a controversial issue could be clarified in open forum as an input to the policymaking process.* NY Times 1/2/77, p28 [**1976**]

scientific creationism, the belief that scientific evidence supports the Biblical account of creation as an alternative explanation to evolutionary theory. Also called CREATION SCIENCE. *He [Kelly Segraves] and his lawyers insisted that they were not advocating the teaching of religion in public schools, but wanted the presentation of another scientific version, what they called "scientific creationism."* Science News 3/14/81, p165 [**1980**]

sci-fi (ˈsaiˌfai), *adj. Especially U.S.* of or relating to science fiction. *In this unpersuasive sci-fi thriller directed by John Sturges . . . it is only a matter of time until someone gravely inquires: "How worried are they in Washington?"* Time 4/30/65, p61 *Industry is still experimenting with it* [an amorphous semiconductor switch] *but is seems to make feasible the sci-fi world of TV sets hung like mirrors on the wall . . .* Maclean's 5/68, p1 [**1955**, from *science fiction,* patterned after *hi-fi* (high-fidelity)]

scintillation camera, a photographic camera that detects and records the scintillations of radioactive substances, used especially to map out the distribution of radioactive substances in the body. *The scintillation camera is capable of picturing on Polaroid film two-dimensional distribution of radioisotopes and then following the rate at which these isotopes may move* *nto and out of such organs as the liver, thyroid and kidney.* Science News Letter 5/16/64, p317 [**1964**]

cintiscanning, *n.* a method of detecting abnormalities in the body by recording with a scintillation counter the radiation of an injected radioactive isotope. *A new accelerator-produced radioactive nuclide, gallium-67, with a conveniently short half-life of 78 hours, is in many ways an ideal agent for localization of tumors by scintiscanning.* 1971 Collier's Encyclopedia Year Book, p336 [**1954**, from *scinti*llation counter + *scanning*]

cotophilic (͵skatə'filik), *adj.* having an affinity for or requiring darkness. *The measurement of the length of the day or the night was accomplished by an endogenous, or built-in, daily rhythm that consisted of two half-cycles, one photophilic ("light-loving") and the other scotophilic ("dark-loving").* Scientific American 2/76, p115 [**1960**, from *scoto-* darkness (from Greek *skótos*) + *-philic* attracted to, loving]

cotophobic (͵skatə'foubik), *adj.* of or relating to scotophobin. *Just how so small a molecule [of scotophobin] can have so dramatic a behavioural affect is baffling. The scotophobic effect seems to be very specific for this structure . . . Very probably some rigorous stereospecificity is involved in the scotophobic mechanism.* New Scientist and Science Journal 6/3/71, p559 [**1971**]

cotophobin (͵skatə'foubən), *n.* a chemical compound that is believed to be the basis of a specific conditioned response, fear of the dark, isolated from the brain tissue of rodents conditioned to fear darkness. *His [the neurochemist Georges Ungar's] theory: the memory message (that darkness should be avoided) is encoded by the rats' DNA-RNA mechanism into an amino-acid chain called a peptide, a small protein that Ungar managed to isolate and then synthesize. His name for it: scotophobin, from the Greek words for "darkness" and "fear."* Time 4/19/71, p30 [**1970**, from *scoto-* darkness (from Greek *skótos*) + *phob*ia *-ea* + *-in* (chemical suffix)]

scouse or **scouse** (skous), *British Slang.* —*n.* the dialect of Liverpool, England. *The Governors and Staff couldn't have done more to make the little blighters feel at home; . . . introducing anoraks, jeans and bobble-caps for school wear; substituting scouse for Etonian slang.* Punch 9/18/68, p420 —*adj.* of Liverpool. Also, SCOUSIAN. *. . . a man who talks in a scintillating mixture of Scouse, Irish and Welsh accents and, what with his fluent Welsh and current address in Dublin, has become a sort of Celtic scrambled egg.* Sunday Times (London) 8/22/71, p9 [**1960**, shortened from earlier *Scouse*land, slang name for Liverpool, because of the popularity of the sailor's stew called *lobscouse* or *scouse* in Liverpool]

scouser or **scouser**, *n. British Slang.* a native of Liverpool, England. *The scousers have long been renowned for their cheeky good humour.* Sunday Times (London) 12/10/67, p23 [**1959**]

scousian, *adj. British Slang.* another word for SCOUSE. *In their [the Beatles'] usual flat, Scousian manner, the boys sign on with old Fred, and the yellow submarine takes off. John thinks their journey is 'reminiscent in its way of the late Mr Ulysses', but you may think rather of Miss Alice when you see the wonders they are faced with: teapot fish, kinky-boot beasts, and the curious tricks that time can play.* Listener 7/25/68, p125 [**1968**]

SCP, abbreviation of SINGLE-CELL PROTEIN. *A promising source of protein that was expected to become available in the near future is SCP (single cell protein), consisting of an edible mass of microorganisms devoid of odor or taste.* 1971 Britannica Yearbook of Science and the Future, p197 [**1967**]

scram, *v.i.* to perform an emergency shutdown of a nuclear reactor. *The latter operation is known as SCRAM, and failure to "scram" in an emergency could lead to extremely serious consequences. Such a failure has never happened.* Scientific American 3/80, p54 [**1950**, probably from *scram*, slang verb meaning to leave or get out at once; but perhaps originally the acronym of an undetermined name, as the frequent all-capitals form suggests]

scramble, *v.i. U.S. Football.* to run with the ball without the protection of blockers. *It was Tarkenton who engineered this monumental upheaval, mainly because he bewildered the Packers with his scrambling.* NY Times 8/13/68, p31 [**1964**]

scrambler, *n. U.S. Football.* a quarterback who scrambles. *He [Quarterback Francis Tarkenton, New York Giants] is known in the trade as a "scrambler," who would just as soon run as throw, who can turn a potential 10-yd. loss into a 50-yd. gain.* Time 3/17/67, p55 [**1967**]

scramjet, *n.* **1** a ramjet (jet engine in which the fuel is mixed with air compressed by the effect of high speed) which produces thrust by burning fuel in an airstream moving at supersonic speeds. *Supersonic combustion ramjets ("scramjets") theoretically could extend flight speeds to at least Mach 14.* New Scientist 5/19/66, p429 **2** an aircraft powered by a scramjet. *A vehicle described by scientists as a forerunner of aircraft that will carry passengers at speeds of about 8,000 miles an hour at very high altitudes has made its first test flight. Called a Scramjet, the vehicle was launched Wednesday by a Scout rocket, an Air Force spokesman said.* NY Times 1/14/67, p4 [**1964**, from *supersonic combustion ramjet*]

scrapnel, *n.* fragments of metal scattered by the explosion of a homemade bomb filled with scrap metal. *In other respects the new mines bear the usual hallmarks of the IRA's crude ordnance . . . Like the electrically detonated mines before them, they are often ineptly placed so that their explosive power and scrap-metal "scrapnel" have not issued in the direction intended.* New Scientist 4/6/72, p16 [**1972**, blend of *scrap* and *shrapnel*]

scream therapy, another name for PRIMAL THERAPY. *One of the ways the psychiatrist has developed to release repressed emotion is scream therapy, described at length in his new book, "A Scream Away From Happiness."* Korea Times 3/4/73, p4 [**1973**, shortened from *primal scream therapy*] —**scream therapist**: *That is what largely accounted for the initial appeal of the psychoanalysts, and for the subsequent appeal of transactional analysts, scream therapists, antipsychiatrists, and radical therapists of all sorts. None has any truly effective methods for treating mental illness, but each spares the patient the tortures that regular psychiatrists call "treatment."* Thomas Szasz, The Myth of Psychotherapy, 1979, p45

screenwash, *n. British.* the washing done by a screenwasher. *Another new feature is the "cyclic" wipers, which give not only slow and fast speeds but, if required, one wipe every 7-½ seconds and eight wipes in conjunction with the screenwash . . .* Times (London) 3/5/70, p16 [**1970**]

screenwasher, *n. British.* an automatic windshield washer. *Screenwashers are the only way of keeping the windscreen clean on the move and are slowly being standardised.* Observer 7/12/64, p34 [**1956**]

screwup, *n. U.S. Slang.* something botched up; a bad blunder. *. . . the two men are back talking about Vietnam, about the son-of-a-bitch brigade commander who didn't give a damn about lives, only his own reputation, and some of the stupidities and screwups of the war.* Atlantic 11/70, p88 [**1960**, from the slang verb phrase *screw up* to botch up]

scrip, *n. U.S. Informal.* a prescription for a drug, especially a narcotic (also used attributively). [Leroy] *Street and his fellow addicts had for some time been able to purchase heroin through venal "scrip"(prescription) doctors in Greenwich Village, who employed bouncers to keep order in their congested waiting rooms.* NY Times Magazine 7/2/72, p9 [**1966**, short for *prescription*]

scroll, *v.i., v.t.* to move the display on a computer screen vertically or horizontally, usually one line at a time, in order to locate specific information. *The TRS-80 Color Computer displays only 16 rows. So shallow a screen is inconvenient in applications such as word-processing or in writing programs, since it forces you to "scroll" a lot. (You can scroll a computer screen to display information that has been entered but is no* *longer visible on the screen).* Consumer Report 1983, p472 [**1981**]

scuzz, *n. U.S. Slang.* a dirty, shabby person or thing. *The CC, Eighth Avenue local, was described to me as "scuzz"— disreputable—but this train, running from Bedford Park Boulevard, the Bronx, via Manhattan and Brooklyn, to Rockaway Park, Queens, covers a distance of 32.39 miles. For some of these miles, it is pleasant and for others it is not.* NY Times Magazine 1/31/82, p23 [**1968**]

scuzzy, *adj. U.S. Slang.* dirty; grimy. *Some early fumblings with girls, a lesson in how to get bluejeans properly scuzzy, and Ward's over-unsuccessful attempts to write a novel are especially memorable.* New Yorker 1/1/72, p64 [**1969**, origin uncertain; perhaps a blend of *scummy* and *fuzzy*]

SDI (ˌesˌdiːˈaɪ), abbreviation of *Strategic Defense Initiative,* a system of computer-controlled defense using lasers and nuclear ballistic missiles in outer space to intercept and destroy enemy missiles before they reach their targets. *The Strategic Defense Initiative (SDI)—also known as the "Star Wars" program—costs as much annually as the total research and development budget for all the U.S. armed services combined and stands to become the largest military research program ever undertaken, according to a newly released report.* Science News 4/5/86, p215 [**1985**]

S.D.R. or **S.D.R.s**, abbreviation of SPECIAL DRAWING RIGHTS. *. . . many economists believe that the S.D.R. represents a basic solution to the problem of providing an adequate volume of international monetary reserve to facilitate steady expansion in the volume of world trade.* NY Times 3/19/68, p68 *Over the month, the S.D.R. holdings of the developed countries rose by $66.4m. and of the I.M.F. by $12.3m.* Times (London) 3/3/70, p24 [**1967**]

S.D.S. or **SDS**, abbreviation of *Students for a Democratic Society,* any of several political organizations of radical college students, especially an American national organization formed in 1962 and split since then into various factions representing leftist, New Leftist, and anarchist views. *Chicago's Police Superintendent James Conlisk, 51, has learned a lot . . . But Conlisk's handling of the "Days of Rage" organized last fall by the Weatherman faction of the S.D.S. was restrained enough to be cited by the National Commission on Violence as a polar opposite to the "police riot" that scarred the city during the 1968 Democratic Convention.* Time 7/13/70, p41 *Neither the American nor the German group has a clearly defined program; both are primarily protest movements against the existing order. The German student movement, the SDS, is more organized; it has headquarters and leaders.* Saturday Review 9/9/67, p10 [**1961**]

Seabee, *n.* a large ship on which barges filled with cargo are loaded and transported. *Almost three football fields long, the seabee can carry up to 38 huge barges, which are lifted aboard by a 2,000-ton-capacity elevator built into the stern. When unloaded, the barges are towed into shore and can then be towed along inland waterways to their ultimate destination, thus minimizing cargo handling.* 1972 Collier's Encyclopedia Year Book, p554 *BACAT is one of a number of systems for the sea transport of barges. It is distinguished from other services, like LASH (lighter aboard ship) and Seabee, because it uses narrower barges more useful in English canals.* New Scientist 11/8/73, p412 [**1971**, perhaps influenced by *seabee* a member of the construction battalion of the U.S. Navy]

sea farming, the cultivation of marine plants and animals for food and raw materials. *Sea farming has been going on in several countries in Europe and Asia for many years. However, although the yields of food have been increased, the conclusion must be drawn that farming the sea as practiced in these countries is not fundamentally comparable with the traditional systems of agriculture, horticulture, and animal husbandry.* McGraw-Hill Yearbook of Science and Technology 1971, p17 [**1960**]

sea-floor spreading, *Geology.* the continuous formation of oceanic crust, caused by upwellings of magma from the earth's mantle at the mid-oceanic ridges when crustal plates are forced apart by the circulation of material within the earth. Also calle OCEAN-FLOOR SPREADING. *So many apparently "cataclysmic events—the giant rift that circles the earth and such hig mountains as the Himalayas, for example—have been ex plained as results of the slow and steady operation of sea-floo spreading that continues today.* Natural History 2/7? p16 *Arabia and Africa have been drifting apart for the pas four million years by a process known as seafloor spreading Molten rock from the Earth's mantle wells up through a rift i the floor of the Red Sea and spreads out evenly on either side That creation of oceanic crust is pushing Arabia and Afric apart at the rate of about 2cm a year and is responsible for th narrow trough in the centre of the Red Sea.* Times (London 3/1/77, p16 [**1961**]

sea grant college, *U.S.* a college or university receiving financia support from the government to conduct oceanographic re search. *Massachusetts Institute for Technology has bee named the "sea grant" college for Massachusetts . . . A spokes man said that the action followed seven years of M.I.T. activit in research, advisory services and education on ocean engineer ing, offshore oil, coastal management and new sea foods.* N Times 1/1/77, p18 [**1975**, patterned after *land grant colleg* (1889)]

Sealab (ˈsiːˌlæb), *n.* any of several U.S. Navy underwater vessel designed to serve as habitats for aquanauts. *The goal of th Sealabs is to develop techniques whereby men can operate o the ocean floor, venturing in and out of their compartment a will with special breathing apparatus.* NY Times 12/24/67 pD10 *Astronaut-aquanaut Scott Carpenter, leader of the un derwater teams, lived and worked in Sealab for thirty consecu tive days.* Maclean's 4/2/66, p28 [**1965**, from *Sea + laboratory*

sea of instability, a group of superheavy chemical element with highly unstable nuclei. *The element Z = 105 and A = 26. with the largest proton number is so unstable that it can onl be produced in extremely small amounts, and it disappears i a few minutes by radioactive decay. These known element form a peninsula in a plane of proton and neutron numbers surrounded on three sides by a "sea of instability."* Science 12/8/72, p1047 [**1971**]

search-and-destroy, *adj.* (in antiguerrilla warfare) involving th strategy of seeking out the enemy in a particular area in orde to neutralize or destroy his fighting forces in that area. *Afte the Lunar New Year offensive, and especially in April, the al lies began a number of search-and-destroy operations aimed a preventing a second enemy assault.* NY Times 5/6/68 p14 *South Vietnamese troops now handle almost all search and-destroy sweeps. One result has been a sharp curtailmen in U.S. casualties . . .* Time 9/14/70, p16 [**1965**]

Seasat (ˈsiːˌsæt), *n.* a United States artificial satellite designed t gather data about the ocean surface; an EARTH RESOURCE SATELLITE. *The experimental ocean-monitoring satellit known as Seasat was successfully launched on the evening o June 26, receiving its final kick into orbit from the modifie Agena rocket that is also the body of the satellite itself . . . Par of Seasat's contribution may be the ability to map the sea surface winds every 24 hours at uniform, 1,400-km intervals* Science News 7/1/78, p4 [**1974**, from *sea satellite*]

seasonal affective disorder, a mild form of depression occur ring at certain seasons of the year, especially in winter, charac terized by loss of energy and sexual drive. *Abbreviation:* SAD *Research shows that among some patients suffering from sea sonal affective disorder . . . melatonin levels rise and fall a odd hours.* Newsweek 11/25/85, p93 [**1985**]

secondhand smoke, smoke inhaled unintentionally by non smokers. *Many individuals are sensitive to what they call "sec ondhand smoke." The prohibitionists set much stock by a 197? pronouncement of a former Surgeon General, who reporte that tobacco fumes "can contribute to the discomfort of man individuals"—who, presumably, also suffer from inhaling what passes for air in city streets.* Time 1/12/76, p36 [**1976**]

Second Lady or **second lady**, *U.S.* the wife or official hostess o a country's Vice-President or second-in-command. *Going t lunch with artists is sometimes risky, but we can report (for we* *were there, and mindful of the honor) that the Second Lady carried it off with élan. The seating arrangements were a triumph of tact. Mrs. Mondale sat at the midpoint of a long, narrow table . . .* New Yorker 5/30/77, p30 [**1970**, patterned after *first Lady* wife or official hostess of the President (1940's)]

second language, 1 a language that is widely used or officially recognized in a country in addition to the national language. *English was declared the country's second language and teachers and teaching equipment were sent to make it so.* Annual Register of World Events in 1971, p211 **2** a non-native language used especially as the language of instruction in schools. *As more and more persons received specialized preparation to teach English as a second language, the stronger grew a feeling of identification with a special discipline.* Current Trends in Linguistics, Vol. 10, 1973, p308 [**1960**] ► In the sense of definition 2, the word *second* is not intended to be taken literally, since the language of school instruction referred to as a "second language" may be the third or even fourth language for many students.

second-strike, *adj.* (of a nuclear weapon) hidden or protected so that it cannot be easily destroyed, and therefore available for retaliation after an enemy attack. *Altogether, the U.S. "second-strike" deterrent force numbered about 4,000 warheads (1,700 missiles) against about 1,000 Soviet warheads.* Britannica Book of the Year 1968, p266 [**1963**]

second-strike capability, the capability of a nuclear power to retaliate with second-strike weapons after a surprise enemy attack, especially on its missile silos. *A non-aggressor nation, on the other hand, merely wants to forestall attack. This it does by aiming its missiles at a potential aggressor's cities as a retaliatory threat; then it protects these retaliatory missiles with ABMs [antiballistic missiles]. This is described as a second-strike capability.* Time 11/28/69, p36 [**1960**]

Second World, 1 the industrialized countries of the world not including the United States and the Soviet Union (often used attributively). *As far as "Second World" countries are concerned (in Chinese terminology, this refers to nations half-way between the Superpowers and the Third World), the Chinese no longer give priority to relations "between peoples," but are concentrating on links "between states." The most obvious example of that new policy is their rapprochement with the Japanese.* Manchester Guardian Weekly (Le Monde section) 11/19/78, p12 **2** the socialist or Communist countries of the world. *The Smithsonian official called for involvement in global conservation efforts of the "second world—the socialist states, whose influence can be equal to our money, and whose active participation would go a long way to rationalize the apparent disparity in motivation between the 'have' and 'have not' nations.* NY Times 12/1/76, pA18 [**1974**, patterned after THIRD WORLD] ► The two meanings of the term correspond to two methods of classification. *Definition 1* resulted from the division of countries according to their economic power. Under this classification the most developed countries (especially the U.S. and the U.S.S.R.) constitute the FIRST WORLD and the least developed countries constitute the FOURTH WORLD. *Definition 2* corresponds to the original quasi-political scheme of Communist, non-Communist, and Third World countries.

security blanket, *U.S.* **1** a blanket, toy, or other familiar object carried around by a child for a feeling of security. *A worn, torn, one-eyed teddy bear about a foot long was my "security blanket."* Ladies' Home Journal 12/73, p102 *Hutt clutches his mangy fur robe about him like a security blanket.* Time 6/17/74, p72 **2** Figurative use: *Tenure, the "security blanket" of the teaching profession, is in jeopardy at U.S. colleges. Reformers demand limits on the system's job guarantees.* U.S. News and World Report 12/11/72, p55 *The hijacker, alternating between his seat and the galley in the rear of the aircraft, apparently was holding the rear rest room as his security blanket.* Saturday Review 6/10/72, p73 [**1967**, popularized by the American cartoonist Charles Schulz (born 1922) in the comic strip "Peanuts," in which a boy named Linus is depicted as inseparable from his blanket]

security guard, a guard privately hired, especially to protect a building or maintain order. *The image of the security guard*

projected in some bitingly funny television sketches by Mr Benny Hill as a baggy-trousered recidivist with cap askew and no idea of the whereabouts of the main gate, contains just enough truth to bolster public prejudice and misgivings. Times (London) 7/7/78, p6 *At Manual Arts High School in Los Angeles, an intruder robbed a female teacher . . . "The school has a security guard," says the U.T.L.A.'s Roger Segure, "but he was on vacation and no one had replaced him."* NY Times Magazine 12/10/78, p84 [**1955**]

seed bank, a place for the storage and preservation of endangered plant species or varieties. *The United Nations Food and Agriculture Organization regards seed banks as vital to the prevention of world-wide famine . . . Left with relatively few kinds of high-yield plants that are vulnerable to pests and disease, future generations face widespread famine unless the resistant primitive varieties are preserved for crossbreeding purposes.* World Book Science Annual 1973, p13 [**1958**]

seed money, a grant of money to initiate an undertaking and provide the basis for seeking fuller funding. *This seed money covers the legal and architectural work that must be done in order for a local group (often a church) to make application for Government-subsidized financing. Once the permanent financing is obtained, the seed money is repaid and the funds can then be reemployed in a new project.* NY Times 5/4/68, p63 [**1960**]

see-through, *adj.* transparent; permitting inspection of the inside or contents of something. *The housewife, sitting with 11 other housewives, was talking about prepackaged meat wrapped with see-through tops but with cardboard on the bottom.* NY Times 5/25/68, p24 *Fascinating new see-through model computer actually solves problems, teaches computer fundamentals.* Science News 7/2/66, p11 *It remained for a myriad of advanced synthetics and plastics to make see-through sculpture a burgeoning art form in the 1960s . . .* Time 2/9/68, p52 [**1950**] **—n. 1** a see-through dress, blouse, or other garment. *Women's Wear Daily, which is more authoritative about see-throughs than breakthroughs, came up with the farthest-out rumor of all.* Time 11/19/65, p21 [**1951**] **2** the fashion of wearing see-through garments. *In fashion, as in every other important field, great mistakes are made. Nudity and see-through is one of them.* Daily Telegraph Magazine (London) 1/23/70, p32 [**1960**]

seg or **seggie,** *n. U.S. Slang.* a person who favors racial segregation; a segregationist. *When people wore the American flag then it was to show that they were not segs, because the segs of course wore the Confederate flag. Now on behalf of a stupid and futile war the segs wear the American flag, and whether we have converted them or they have converted us is a moot point.* Harper's 1/71, p35 [Senator] *Fulbright for the first time openly appealed for black votes, because he believed that he couldn't win without them and that the "seggies," who hated him for his stand on the war in Vietnam, would vote against him no matter what he did.* New Yorker 12/12/70, p107 [**1963**, by shortening]

seismic tomography, the use of seismic waves to form images of the earth's interior which are then synthesized into a single cross-sectional view. *The three-dimensional maps of the interior produced by seismic tomography have created a revolution in earth sciences by giving geologists a much clearer picture of the inner Earth.* World Book Science Annual 1987, p201 [**1985**]

selectron, *n. Nuclear Physics.* the hypothetical counterpart of an electron in supersymmetry, differing from an electron by a one-half unit. *. . . the superpartner of the spin ½ electron is the spin 0 selection.* Americana Annual 1987, p425 [**1987**, from supersymmetric + *electron*]

selenodesist (ˌseləˈnadəsist), *n.* a specialist in selenodesy. *. . . the Lunar Orbiter also carried a micrometeorite detector and enabled selenodesists to obtain more accurate data on the Moon's shape and gravitational field from precise tracking of the artificial satellite's orbit.* McGraw-Hill Yearbook of Science and Technology 1969, p218 [**1969**]

selenodesy (ˌseləˈnadəsi:), *n.* the study of the shape, dimensions, gravity, and other physical characteristics of the moon. *A rap-*

idly developing field appears to be lunar geodesy, a specialty the geodesists call "selenodesy." Science 3/1/68, p1002 [**1962**, from *seleno-* moon + *-desy,* as in *geodesy*]

self-antigen, *n.* an antibody formed in an organism in response to its own antigen. *The prediction has been made that the normal process of development of nonresponsiveness (tolerance) to self-antigens might be associated with an early maturation of lymphocytic cells and a late maturation of PAH* [primary antigen-handling] *cells.* McGraw-Hill Yearbook of Science and Technology 1971, p105 [**1971**]

self-destruct, *v.i.* **1** to cause one's own or its own destruction; destroy oneself. *An international team of scientists . . . has designed a plastic that Guillet claims will self-destruct when exposed to sunlight, but will remain intact if it is kept indoors.* Time 5/11/70, p86 **2** to disappear; evaporate. *. . . earning what seems to a writer easy money (i.e., money not acquired through the painful process of hunching over a recalcitrant typewriter); flinging words into the air where they instantly self-destruct and cannot hover around to haunt you as printed lines are wont to do. In short, lecturing.* Harper's 12/71, p30 *. . . the women had a definition of "ego" that they all agreed was appropriate to a feminist document. Then they tackled "history." . . . "our definition of 'history' is going to change as we raise our consciousness. Our definition's going to—it's going to self-destruct."* New Yorker 11/28/70, p58 [**1968**]

self-gravity or **self-gravitation,** *n.* the force of gravity which a body or system possesses or exerts upon itself or its constituent parts. *Computer simulations of spherical, protostellar clouds of stellar masses, collapsing under self-gravity, have been developed by Richard Larson and by C.C. Hayashi and his collaborators.* 1977 Britannica Yearbook of Science and the Future, p76 *Because eddies must occasionally collide with each other, turbulence within a* [interstellar] *cloud will provide an additional pressure capable of resisting self-gravitation and if the turbulence is intense enough, it may disrupt the cloud entirely.* Scientific American 6/77, p78 [**1962**]—**self-gravitating,** *adj.: The most significant difference arises from the fact that the angle between gravity and the vector* Ω *of angular velocity varies in self-gravitating bodies, while the two vectors must be parallel in the laboratory experiment.* Science 1/9/76, p81

self-noise, *n.* noise produced by a ship itself as it passes through water, as distinguished from the noise caused by the water's turbulence. *To reduce the quiet sub's self-noise (it roars its way through the water even when gliding on momentum alone), researchers are studying coatings to make the hull slip more easily along.* Science News 7/27/68, p80 *New mountings and refitting have greatly reduced self noise in Navy ships.* New Scientist 8/1/68, p225 [**1960**]

self-steering, *adj.* designed to keep a boat, etc., on a fixed course. *There was still no sign of Sir Francis* [Chichester], *by 8 a.m., Gipsy Moth continuing to sail on the self-steering gear which has made the single-handed voyage possible.* Times (London) 5/29/67, p8 [**1950**]

SEM, abbreviation of SCANNING ELECTRON MICROSCOPE. *SEM's advantage over other microscopic techniques is the ability to present a three-dimensional image more realistically.* 1972 Britannica Yearbook of Science and the Future, p311 [**1968**]

semantic net, arrangement of data in the memory of a computer, designed to parallel the characteristics of human memory. *Past experience would be no longer "stacked," as it were, in mere formal sequence but interwoven in what are called "semantic nets." Such nets seem to account for the speed and accuracy with which verbal-visual associations between past and present intervene in our cognition of a new object or situation.* New Yorker 10/28/72, p105 *A number of laboratories are exploring the use of relational structures—sometimes called "semantic nets"—for storing facts about storybook worlds extracted from English language input.* Encyclopedia Science Supplement (Grolier) 1973, p139 [**1972**]

semiamateur, *adj.* **1** not playing a sport for money but supported in part by a sponsor. *He returned to play for the Maccabi*

Tel Aviv team, a semiamateur team sponsored by a chocola company. Washington Post 9/7/78, pG1 **2** partly amateu *This Chelsea Opera Group performance . . . is a substanti undertaking for a semi-amateur group of this kind.* Financi Times 3/30/87, p17 **—n.** a semiamateur athlete. *People are r alizing that these yachtsmen are athletes . . . They're eve semiamateurs.* NY Times 2/1/87, p1 [**1978** for adj.; **1987** f noun]

semi-antique, *n.* **1** a rug or carpet approximately fifty years ol as distinguished from a genuine antique (at least 100 years old *Although the real antiques were all woven or hand-knotted b fore 1873 (a date agreeable to United States Customs), there a also valuable semi-antiques (rugs made between 1870 an 1920) and a vast quantity of modern rugs, many of them usin the same designs, the same dyes, and the same types of wool their more distinguished ancestors.* New Yorker 3/24/7 p31 **2** any rug having an antique appearance. *Sem antiques—a term used by dealers meaning the carpets a "old" or "used," from five years to 100 years old.* NY Time 6/5/76, pH8 [**1945, 1970**]

semiconservative, *adj. Genetics.* designating a form of replica tion in which the original molecular strands are conserved ind vidually rather than together. *This mode of replication termed semiconservative because the parental strands separa in the course of DNA synthesis; each daughter cell receives "hybrid" DNA molecule that consists of one parental stran and one newly synthesized complementary strand.* Scientifi American 2/67, p37 [**1957**]

semidwarf, *n.* a plant that is taller than a dwarf plant but sti below the normal size of related species or varieties. *Nonlodg ing Rice was developed at the International Rice Institute. Th varieties are semidwarfs with long stems, which hold the plan upright when the grain heads mature. Narrow leaves also ai photosynthesis by letting more sunlight penetrate.* Scientifi American 9/74, p176 [**1974**, noun use of earlier (1959) adjec tive] **—semi-dwarfism,** *n.: Further development will depend o thorough understanding of the physiological and genetic base of semi-dwarfism; the days when plant breeders simply cros the best with the best and hoped for the best are long sinc passed.* New Scientist 2/8/73, p286

semifarming, *n.* unselective or uncontrolled farming of live stock or crops. *Because natural phenomena are controlled, th modern chicken farm is true farming, while the keeping o chickens in the farmyard is semifarming. In a similar way, se farming is a case of semifarming.* McGraw-Hill Yearbook o Science and Technology 1971, p17 [**1971**]

seminarian or **seminarist,** *n.* a participant in a seminar (cours of study, conference, workshop, or the like). *Several of the firs group of seminarians (as Esalen quaintly calls its payin guests) witnessed a nearly fatal attack on Dennis Murphy.* New Yorker 1/5/76, p42 *Isaac Asimov, author of more than 10 books and one of the science-fiction seminarists, suggested tha the long-distant eventual result of space exploration might b bonds with new outer-space life-forms very different from th human.* NY Times 12/17/72, p2 [**1970**, from *seminar* + *-ian* o *-ist;* compare *seminarian* or *seminarist* a seminary student]

semistrong force or **semistrong interaction,** *Physics.* a hypothet ical force or interaction that is weaker than the strong force bu more powerful than the electromagnetic force. *If the semi strong interaction could somehow be turned off, all the spin-½ baryons would have the same mass; they would degenerate int a single state. The semistrong force splits the degenerate stat into particles of different mass, and the splitting is accompa nied by the introduction of two new quantum numbers, iso topic spin and strangeness.* Scientific American 1/76 p46 [**1976**]

Sendai virus ('sen,dɑi), a paramyxovirus that induces rapid fu sion of different types of cells. *Facilitation of this hybridizatio process by the Sendai virus permits fusion of the cells of ma and mouse and of even more disparate species.* Britannica Book of the Year 1970, p500 *The group, led by R.J. Ericsson, decide to exploit the membrane-fusing properties of Sendai virus* New Scientist and Science Journal 7/15/71, p122 [**1958**

named after *Sendai,* a city in Japan where the virus was first de-
tected]

send-up, *n.* British. a parody. *There too we are owlishly invited
to puzzle about the death of Lermontov's hero: "His digestion
was poor and his bile excessive, but otherwise he had a remarkably strong constitution." Is this a send-up of the whole business of literary scholarship and exegesis? Is Nabokov really an
irascible pedant, or is this an ingenious comic persona?* Manchester Guardian Weekly 12/17/64, p11 [**1958,** from the British slang phrase *send up* to scoff at, mock, originally public-
school slang meaning to send a boy to the headmaster to be
punished]

sene ('seni:), *n.* a monetary unit of Western Samoa equal to
1/100 of a tala. *Western Samoa, a former territory of New Zealand, which recently became independent, will change its
money system from the pound, shilling and pence to the tala
(dollar) and sene (cent) July 10.* NY Times 2/3/67, p7 [**1963,**
from Samoan, from English *cent*]

senghi or **sengi** ('seŋi:), *n.* a monetary unit of Zaire, equal to
1/100 of a likuta. *Each likuta—singular for makuta—is further
divided into 100 sengi(s). There is a raging black market for
hard currency, but penalties are stiff.* Susan Blumenthal,
Bright Continent, 1974, p335 [**1967,** from a native word, perhaps alteration of Swahili *senti* cent, from English *cent*]

senior citizenship, *U.S.* the condition of being an old or elderly
person; old age. *Educators have begun to sense that this break
in generational continuity . . . has deprived many old folks of
a desired organic contact with the future and a feeling of usefulness that is often lacking in the status of "senior citizenship."* NY Times 10/29/72, pD11 *A friend of mine in his 70s,
a very lively fellow and extraordinarily cheerful, likes to while
away his senior citizenship—what we used to call old age—by
collecting droll statistics from government sources that confute
the assumptions on which most Presidents and Congress appear to run the government.* 1978 World Book Year Book,
p49 [**1972,** from *senior citizen* (1938) + *-ship*]

sensitivity group, another name for ENCOUNTER GROUP. *A recent development has been the spread of techniques designed
to foster intensive group experience. Known by such names as
T-group, encounter group, group marathon, sensitivity group,
or synanon group, this rapidly spreading method has been
termed by Carl Rogers "the most significant social invention
of this century."* Americana Annual 1971, p562 [**1969**]

sensitivity training, training in a group, usually guided by a
leader or therapist, in which the members are supposed to gain
deeper understanding of their own feelings and those of others
in the group. *Paralleling the vogue for "sensitivity training"
and other forms of group psychotherapy is the current enthusiasm for programs which apply similar strategy to addiction.
Known as "therapeutic communities," they are modeled after
Synanon, which was launched in Santa Monica, California,
twelve years ago.* Harper's 6/70, p71 [**1954**]

Sensurround ('sensə,round), *n.* the trademark of a motion-
picture sound effect consisting of low-frequency sound signals
felt by the audience as vibrations and intended to make their
experience of the film more realistic. *Universal is constructing
several mechanical* [King] *Kongs ranging from 18 in. to 6 ft.
tall. The movie will be in color and Sensurround, the vibration
that made* Earthquake *so unpleasant.* Time 1/5/76, p71 *We
could logically have expected "Rollercoaster," the latest movie
accompanied by seat-shaking Sensurround, to have plunged us
into the boring depths of its predecessors, "Earthquake" and
"Midway."* Commercial Appeal (Memphis) 6/26/77,
p15 [**1974,** blend of *sense* and *surround*]

sentence, *n.* any sequence of nucleotide triplets or codons that
constitute a gene. Compare WORD. *The sentences describing
the amino-acid sequences of the different proteins of a cell are
arranged end-to-end in the long DNA molecules of the nucleus.
These sentences, the genes of an organism, when taken together
give directions for making all of the proteins of the cell, including all of the enzymes that the cell is capable of making.* 1976
Britannica Yearbook of Science and the Future, p62 [**1975**]

septage ('septidʒ), *n.* the waste content of a septic tank. *Peekskill Mayor George Pataki, Republican—Conservative candidate for the 91st Assembly District, has announced his support
for "regional cooperation, involving government and private
industry, to deal with the growing problem of septage and
sludge disposal," at a meeting on waste disposal at the Dept.
of Environmental Conservation offices in New Paltz last week.*
Putnam County News and Recorder 8/29/84, p1 [**1980,** from
septic tank + *-age,* as in *leafage, tonnage*]

sequenator, *n.* a machine that separates a protein into its constituent amino acids in their proper sequence. *The researchers
are using a new "protein sequenator" that requires less than 1
percent the quantity of material needed in previous protein
analyses. They predict that once the complete sequences of in-
terferons are known, they can be chemically synthesized . . .
Hunkapiller and Hood see their highly sensitive sequenator as
a biological equivalent of the physicist's high energy accelerator.* Science News 1/26/80, p52 [**1967**]

sequencer, *n.* a woman who combines a career and motherhood through sequencing. *Some experts are already warning
that the sequencer is just another doomed variation of women
trying to do it all.* NY Times 9/23/88, pA21 [**1988**]

sequencing, *n.* the practice by a professional woman of leaving
her career to bring up children and resuming professional
work several years later. Compare MOMMY TRACK. *Sequencing,
she argues, "combines the best of modern feminism with the
best of traditional mothering."* NY Times 9/23/88,
pA21 [**1988**]

sequential, *adj.* (of contraceptive pills) taken in a particular sequence to eliminate side effects. . . . *Dr. Gregory Pincus commented on the medical advertising for some newer-type
sequential and low-dosage pills: "These ads are creating a false
emphasis. There may be a minute lessening in side effects, but
since all present side effects are insignificant, I see absolutely
no advantage in sequentials."* Saturday Review 11/2/68,
p68 —*n.* **sequentials,** *pl.* sequential pills. *Some are combinations in which both the estrogen and the progestin are taken
for 21 days a month; others are "sequentials," in which the estrogen alone is taken for 14 to 16 days, and estrogen with progestin for five or six.* Time 5/2/69, p36 [**1965** for adj.; **1968** for
noun]

serendipity berry, the fruit of an African plant (*Dioscorephyl-
lum cuminsii*), containing a substance that makes sour food
taste sweet. *Mr. Ottinger said that the Library of Congress had
conducted research on artificial sweeteners and had found
eight in various stages of development, including monellin, an
extract of the West African serendipity berry.* NY Times
10/5/77, p16 [**1971,** so called from the accidental discovery of
its unusual property]

serial-access memory, a computer memory in which the time
it takes to retrieve data depends upon their location in storage.
One of the latest designs of a CCD [charge-coupled device] *serial-access memory has storage for 65,536 bits on a chip
measuring about 3.5 by five millimeters. The other principal
form of microelectronic serial-access memory exploits the mobility of magnetic bubbles.* Scientific American 9/77,
p140 [**1977**]

serial killer, a homicidal psychopath who kills repeatedly and
usually in the same predictable manner. *He'd worked in field
offices for most of his career, but a year ago had been brought
into headquarters to establish a new tactical division known as
SPOVAC—Special Office of Violent Activities (Criminal). Its
focus was on "serial killers" and mass murderers.* Margaret
Truman, Murder at the FBI, 1985, p13 [**1985**]

serial marriage, an arrangement of successive temporary marriages. . . . *the author had predicted people will gravitate towards serial marriage. In serial marriage partners remain
married for 8-10 years, then without bitterness dissolve the
marriage and start another. This way most could expect to be
married four or five times in their life.* Royal Gazette (Bermuda) 4/16/73, p20 *One English practitioner proposed that we
borrow from Latin the linguistic distinction between* pater, *the
father of fact—a distinction that might be useful in today's*

"serial marriage" society as well as in the A.I.D. [artificial insemination by donor] situation. NY Times Magazine 4/16/76, p52 [1970]

serial monogamy, the form of monogamy practiced in a SERIAL MARRIAGE. *"During the thirties and forties, we want someone who is charming, witty, intellectually stimulating and capable of keeping up with fresh demands and opportunities. In old age we seek a person who is sympathetic, understanding, and who also offers new insight into life."* Kiviloo predicts that serial monogamy may become the most popular form of union in the next century. Maclean's 4/19/76, p30 [**1972**]

serotonergic (ˌsiroutəˈnərdʒik) or **serotoninergic** (ˌsiroutə-nəˈnərdʒik), *adj.* producing or activated by serotonin, a substance that constricts blood vessels. *Fernstrom and Wurtman propose that the serotonergic nerve cells could function as "sensors" or transductors that convert information about peripheral metabolism into nerve signals.* Scientific American 7/73, p51 *Here much has been considerable controversy over whether opiate action is associated with some particular neurotransmitter. From the evidence various proponents have presented, one may conclude that the target of opiates is serotoninergic, or noradrenergic, or perhaps cholinergic.* Nature 1/11/74, p83 [**1957,** from *serotonin* + Greek *érgon* + English *-ic*]

serotype, *v.t., v.i.* to assign (a microorganism) to a particular strain on the basis of the immune response it induces in blood serum; classify according to serotype. *Dr Payne . . . said that in recent years Portsmouth has seen 331 human cases of a particular Salmonella infection: of these 271 have been traced by serotyping through the abattoir and back to the farm.* Manchester Guardian Weekly 8/29/68, p9 *The different salmonella species are distinguished by a serotyping technique perfected by the Danish bacteriologist Fritz Kauffmann in 1941 . . .* New Yorker 9/4/71, p66 [**1968,** verb use of the noun]

service module, the unit or section of a spacecraft which contains the propulsion system and supplies most of the spacecraft's consumable elements, such as oxygen, water, and propellants. *Abbreviation:* SM *The service module contains the main propulsion system that maneuvers the modules so that they can rendezvous and dock with the space station.* Encyclopedia Science Supplement (Grolier) 1971, p331 [**1961**]

servo, *v.t.* to control or assist with a servo-mechanism. *Another fundamental problem was to find a way of relieving and restoring the pressure in a conventional hydrostatic braking system without recourse to the alternative of fully powered braking . . . As already mentioned, Ferguson solved this problem with their ingenious double-sided vacuum servo, which servos the brakes on and servos them (and the driver's foot) off.* New Scientist and Science Journal 8/12/71, p359 [**1971,** verb use of *servo, n.* (OEDS 1924), short for *servomechanism*]

SES, abbreviation of *socioeconomic status,* a combination of social factors, such as education, and economic factors, such as income, used as a measure of rank in sociological studies. *The low SES child, like the average-intelligence child, is comfortable with his peers, thinks he is easy to like and perceives himself as popular.* Science News 8/21/71, p131 [**1971**]

sesshin (ˈseʃin), *n.* a long period of seclusion and meditation in Zen Buddhism, usually lasting from four to seven days. *The intensive period of Zen practice known as* sesshin *is "sustained self-effort," he* [Philip Kapleau] *explains in his book,* The Three Pillars of Zen. Time 4/9/73, p92 *With no deity to cling to,* seven days of sesshin *are a plunge into the inner self.* NY Times Magazine 6/3/79, p93 [**1972,** from Japanese, from Chinese *ch'e hsin*]

SETI, abbreviation of *search for extraterrestrial intelligence,* a program to find ways of communicating with intelligent beings elsewhere in the universe. Compare CETI. *Dubbed SETI, . . . the project is to be carried out over a period of six years by two teams of researchers. One team, at the Jet Propulsion Laboratory in Pasadena, Calif., will map the sky visible from that site using antennas at JPL's Goldstone tracking station in the Mojave Desert. The other team, at the NASA/Ames Research Center in northern California, will concentrate on our sun's cosmic neighbors, listening closely with large radiotelescopes to stars*

that lie within 100 light years of us. NY Times Magazine 10/23/77, p31 [**1976**]

Seven Sisters or **the Sisters,** a nickname for the world's seven largest oil companies. *The question asked of the international petroleum companies, the "Seven Sisters," can be asked of the grain companies as well: do they serve the interests of the United States or of themselves?* Manchester Guardian Weekly (Washington Post section) 1/25/76, p17 *In the consuming countries, meanwhile, the Sisters faced painful marketing operations.* Time 9/11/78, p42 [**1962,** transferred from the name of the Pleiades and probably influenced by the nickname for the seven Ivy League colleges originally for women]

severe combined immunodeficiency (disease), a usually fatal congenital disorder of the immune system in which the body is unable to produce the normal amount of B cells and T cells to resist infection or disease. *Abbreviation:* SCID *Severe combined immunodeficiency disease (SCID)* [is] *sometimes known as the "bubble boy" disease, named for the Texas boy who lived most of his life in a sterile bubble. He died at age 12 after a bone marrow transplant.* Science News 5/3/86, p277 [**1976**]

Sevin, *n.* a trade name for an insecticide of the carbamate group, that acts by inhibiting the enzyme cholinesterase. *Sevin a synthetic organic pesticide, has a low toxicity to animals and man and degrades rapidly, but it is highly toxic to bees.* Encyclopedia Science Supplement (Grolier) 1971, p9 [**1958**]

sex-blind, *adj.* not discriminating between the sexes; unbiased as to a person's sex. *Spokesmen for several liberal groups, including the ACLU, declared yesterday that totally sex-blind job assignments are a violation of prisoners' rights.* New York Post 3/30/77, p3 [**1974,** patterned after *color-blind* (1952) unbiased as to a person's color]

sex clinic, a clinic for the diagnosis and treatment of sexual problems. *The sex clinic is fast becoming as vital a part of the modern hospital as the emergency room and the intensive-care unit . . . But even though low-income patients can get treatment, most people who come to sex clinics are white and upper-middle class.* Newsweek 11/27/72, p65 [**1972**]

sexism, *n.* discrimination based on a person's sex; sexual prejudice; specifically, discriminatory attitudes and practices against women in business, politics, art, etc. Compare MALE CHAUVINISM. *We have heard of the extremists—ten thousand strong—called Women's Liberation, how they crop their hair short, wear baggy trousers and loose sweaters to conceal the more notable evidences of sex. "Abolish sexism!" is their slogan.* Atlantic 3/70, p82 [**1968,** patterned after *racism*]

sexist, *n.* a person who practices sexism. *Just as the New York construction workers became the arch-symbols of the brutal reaction to the long-haired antiwar movement, so the Playboy sexist has become the target of Women's Liberation.* Listener 10/22/70, p538 . . . *the women's liberationists had decided that the Tournament of Roses parade would provide a fine opportunity for letting him know that they considered him* [Billy Graham] *a sexist and a false prophet.* New Yorker 1/16/71, p85 **—adj.** practicing or characterized by sexism. *Mr. Grossman would be amazed if anyone accused him of domineering or sexist behavior. Yet tacitly condoning such behavior and finding it natural are also oppressive acts.* Harper's 5/70, p8 *Black businesswomen often contend that the toughest prejudice that they face is not racist but sexist.* Time 11/8/71, p58 [**1965,** patterned after *racist*]

sexo-, a combining form meaning "sex" or "sexual." **—sexocultural,** *adj.: Magic and Myth of the Movies has enjoyed a large underground reputation, which was blown to the world a couple of years ago as a result of the role it is made to play in the sexo-cultural pilgrimage of Myron/Myra Breckinridge in Gore Vidal's novel.* Times Literary Supplement 2/4/72, p125 **—sexographics,** *n.pl.: The Canadian hero, Adrian Dumas, tries to shake off his brutal iceman inheritance for a moral, ecological principle . . . Although set in the 1980s, it has the staleness of the '60s. Bradley's sexographics are Neanderthal, and, while there's only one murder, there are several character assassinations.* Maclean's 1/22/79, p44 **—sexoscope,** *n.: The rival Zeitung fights back with such circulation builders as sex*

crossword puzzles, a dirty-poem page and lurid sexoscopes.
Time 1/19/70, p24 —**sexotheological**, *adj.: Her delight, nostalgia, recollection, and state of total stimulation caused her to
experience that process which in theological reference works
. . . might be termed 'absolute self-fulfillment'; which, when
embarrassingly reduced, is termed by clumsy erotologists and
sexotheological dogmaticians an 'orgasm.'* Saturday Review
11/11/72, p67 [**1966**, formed on the model of *historico-*, *re-
ligio-*, and similar combining forms]

sex object, **1** someone used or serving exclusively to satisfy sexual needs. *Altogether, the Male Establishment never lets
women forget that they are all but valueless to society except
as sex objects (submissive vaginas and fruitful wombs) and as
devoted domestic servants (at home or at work) of their superior
menfolks.* Britannica Book of the Year 1973, p26 *She has an
affair with a young man named Werner whom she uses as a sex
object, but it is as unsatisfactory as it is brief.* NY Times
4/24/79, pC9 **2** an object of sexual interest, especially a sexually attractive woman. *Black actresses are beginning to be introduced as sex objects. Sheila Scott-Wilkinson is installed as
resident girlfriend to the unpleasant Detective Chief Inspector
Craven* in Special Branch (*Thames*) *and Cleo Sylvestre appeared in a supporting role in* Armchair 30 (*Thames*). Listener
4/26/73, p563 *The woman-as-sex-object, under wraps for the
past few years mainly because of the influence of the women's
movement, has returned this fall with a vengeance. You can see
her on television, in the new . . . shows such as "Flying High"
and "The American Girls," clones of "Charlie's Angels," where
she wears a lot of make-up and bares a lot of skin and is, in general, a mental midget.* New York Sunday Metro 9/17/78,
p35 [**1963**]▶ *Sexual object* is an established term in psychoanalysis meaning any person or thing, such as a fetish, toward which
sexual activity is directed, while *sex object* is a general term of
somewhat disparaging meaning in current usage, often reflecting biased male attitudes toward women.

sexploitation, *n.* the exploitation of sex in the arts, especially in
motion pictures. *But there can be no doubt that the immediate—and perhaps continuing—effects of repealing the English
obscenity laws would be to admit a flood of plays, films and
books whose only object was what is now called sexploitation.*
Times (London) 4/30/70, p11 *Russ Meyer, the Barnum of the
skinflicks, has recently been grinding out his sexploitation
films under the imprimatur of major studios.* Time 8/30/71,
p50 [**1941, 1966**, blend of *sex* and *exploitation*]

sexploiter, *n.* a motion picture produced for sexploitation. Also
called ERODUCTION. *The line between the sexploiters and the
ordinary Hollywood film was beginning to disappear . . . The
process was hastened by the Hollywood studios themselves. In
1969, Warners released* Sweet Body of Deborah *and* The Big
Bounce, *each containing more nudity than any previous film
from a major studio.* 1970 World Book Year Book, p426 [**1970**]

sex role, activity or behavior regarded as suitable to one sex but
not to the other. *. . . the amendment's backers want the law
to operate according to what a person chooses to do and is able
to do, rather than according to sex roles.* Time 3/20/72,
p68 *Her Majesty's inspectors ask all secondary schools to review their curricula from top to bottom to ensure that subject
choices are in future made on a basis of "a real equality of access" instead of traditional assumptions about sex roles.* Manchester Guardian Weekly 5/3/75, p7 [**1927, 1968**] ▶This term
of the social sciences that describes the social role of sex, such
as childrearing versus hunting, has acquired a pejorative sense
in current usage, implying that the roles assumed by the sexes
are culturally conditioned and often discriminatory towards
women.

sex shop, a shop selling pornographic books, erotic pictures,
aphrodisiacs, and other paraphernalia related to sex. *The court
. . . fully understood and had sympathy with the idea that the
area had been degraded by an invasion of the sex industry. But
the court was not concerned with sex shops: only with cinemas
showing X certificate films.* Times (London) 11/17/77,
p4 [**1970**]

sex therapy, the treatment of sexual problems, such as impotence and frigidity, by techniques involving counseling, psy-

chotherapy, and behavior modification. See SEX CLINIC. *Dr.
Helen Singer Kaplan, director of sex therapy at New York Hospital, said that "pseudo sex researchers" and untrained therapists using experimental procedures were "taking advantage of
people's vulnerability."* NY Times 1/25/76, p29 *Of the several
major areas in which behavioral improvements were being promoted, none was so fast-growing or so controversial as sex therapy. Between 4,000 and 5,000 clinics and treatment centers
were operating in the United States in 1977.* 1978 Britannica
Yearbook of Science and the Future, p392 [**1961**]—**sex therapist**: *"The scream therapist says, 'We are better than the transactional analyst,' who says, 'We are better than the group
therapist,' who says, 'We are better than the sex therapist,' and
so on."* New Yorker 5/15/78, p78

sex-typing, *n.* the assigning of sex roles; casting one into a role
deemed appropriate to the person's sex. *Anyone who has had
a girl-child and a boy-child knows that they are different.
Even in families where there is no so-called 'sex-typing', a little
girl will make a doll of anything, and a boy will put one on
top of another as soon as he can hold an object in each hand.*
Listener 1/8/76, p24 [**1941, 1972**] —**sex-typed**, *adj.: Although
women 20 and over now account for one-third of the labour
force, the vast majority are working in menial, sex-typed, or
dead-end jobs.* Britannica Book of the Year 1973, p24

sexual harassment, harassment of a person because of her or his
sex, as by making unwelcome sexual advances or otherwise engaging in sexist practices that cause the victim loss of income,
mental anguish, and the like. *The federal Equal Employment
Opportunity Commission (EEOC) issued regulations on April
11 prohibiting sexual harassment of workers by their supervisors . . . Employers are charged with the "affirmative duty" to
prevent physical or verbal sexual harassment. The EEOC's
criteria for sexual harassment included unwelcome sexual advances as a condition of employment, as a basis for any employment decision, or as creating an offensive environment
which hindered a worker's performance.* 1981 Collier's Encyclopedia Year Book, p199 [**1975**]

sexually transmitted disease, a new name for *venereal disease*
(a disease spread mainly through sexual relations with an infected individual). *STDs—Sexually Transmitted Diseases:
What You Should Know and How to Protect Yourself—Stephen
H. Zinner. Discusses the means by which these diseases are
transmitted, the expectations for treatment and cure and ways
to prevent infection.* Science News 9/21/85, p179 *Studies of
prostitutes in Nairobi have shown that a history of sexually
transmitted disease (S.T.D.) and genital ulcers caused by such
S.T.D.'s facilitate infection.* Vanity Fair 7/88, p113 [**1981**]

sexual politics, any arrangement or social order in which members of one sex seek to dominate or exploit the other. *We have
a choice between a covert sexual politics (what we've had for
centuries) and an open examination of sexual politics (what
feminism asks for). Keeping sexual politics under wraps requires, like all repression, tremendous energy.* Harper's 1/77,
p6 [**1970**, popularized by the American feminist leader Kate
Millet, born 1934, in her book *Sexual Politics* (1970)]

sexual revolution, the liberalization of traditional social and
moral attitudes toward sex, especially those that discriminate
against women. *Only briefly does* [Kate] *Millet speculate on
precisely what sort of society might be produced by the successful sexual revolution for which she calls.* Time 8/31/70,
p20 *The Sexual Revolution Conquest of the last frontier, involving the efficient management and manipulation of reproductive organs for the purpose of establishing the New
Puritanism.* Harper's 11/70, p95 [**1970**]

sexy, *adj. Informal.* having popular appeal; attracting general
interest. *Maddock, who retired as Chief Scientist at the Department of Industry last March, has applied much of his energy
in recent years to publicising his belief that "the real red meat
of the economy" is in humdrum engineering—electrical machinery, for example—rather than "sexy technology" such as
tracked hovercraft.* New Scientist 7/7/77, p5 *British Admiral
of the Fleet Sir Peter Hill-Norton dismisses the neutron bomb
as "sexy for the media* [but] *a new dimension of warfare that
we do not want to go into."* Time 4/17/78, p10 *"The farmers*

are not a sexy protest group," added his press aide. "They just can't drum up the kind of sympathy here that, say, the blacks and the feminists can." Harper's 5/78, p34 [**1965**, extended from the meaning (1920's) "concerned with sex; sexually stimulating," probably by influence of *sex appeal* in the sense of "popular appeal; general attractiveness"]

Seyfert ('saifərt), *n.* Also called **Seyfert galaxy.** any one of a group of galaxies having very small, starlike centers which exhibit broad emission lines indicative of a high state of atomic excitation. *Seyfert galaxies are a class of spiral galaxies with very bright, compact nuclei . . . Interest in Seyferts was fairly marginal until the discovery of quasars in the last decade.* Science News 6/6/70, p552 *A possible link between normal galaxies and quasars may be provided by the Seyfert galaxies, which have unusually bright nuclei similar in many ways to the sharply defined quasars.* Science Journal 4/70, p12 [**1959**, named for Carl K. *Seyfert*, 1911-1960, an American astronomer who listed and described ten of these galaxies in the 1940's]

shades, *n.pl. Especially U.S. Slang.* sunglasses. *Kay* [John Kay, a singer], *who is handsome and lean and wears shades all the time because there is something wrong with his eyes, has great stage presence.* New Yorker 8/10/68, p88 *In the street a burly figure in dark glasses stops and stares threateningly. He comes in. Eddie snatches off the man's shades. "I haven't had them off since Buddy Holly died," giggles the stranger.* Listener 12/16/71, p852 [**1958**, shortened from *sunshades*]

shadow matter, *Astronomy.* a hypothetical form of matter that interacts with ordinary matter only through gravity and not through electromagnetism or the strong or weak interactions. *Shadow matter . . . interacts with us extremely feebly and is virtually undetectable.* Science News 9/13/86, p169 [**1985**]

shambolic, *adj. British.* disorderly; in a shambles. *His office* [Mr. K. Kobayashi's, a Japanese newspaper correspondent] *in Printing House Square is so impeccably tidy that it is a contradiction and a standing reproach to the standard image of shambolic newspaper offices strewn with waste paper and inflated egos.* Times (London) 6/18/70, p9 [**1969**, irregular derivative of *shambles*, probably after such pairs as *symbol*, *symbolic*]

shape, *v.i.* **shape up. 1** to get into proper shape or condition. *Gina Hawthorn, fourth in the 1968 Olympic slalom,* [is] *shaping up for one more attempt on a British medal at the 1972 Olympic Games in Sapporo, Japan.* Manchester Guardian Weekly 10/3/70, p23 *. . . leaders punctuated demands for measures helpful to their communities with threats, often emphasized by the raised fist of revolution, that "the big fat Establishment," as one of them put it, had better shape up, because "New York's got a long, hot summer ahead."* New Yorker 9/19/70, p125 **2** *U.S.* to fall into line; behave properly; conform. *"The apparent presidential-vice-presidential view* [is] *that the economy can be saved or the casualty rate in Indochina lowered or civil peace restored if only Harriet Van Horne* [a daily columnist] *will shape up."* Time 6/8/70, p41 [**1951** for def. 1; (known orally 1952) **1963** for def. 2]

sharav, (ʃɑːˈrɑːv), *n.* a hot, dry easterly wind occurring in the Middle East in April and May. *One of the most dramatic results has been to provide a scientific basis for the tradition that ill winds such as the Föhn in Germany and the Sharav in the Near East can produce a malaise in humans. The malaise may occur because air ion imbalance affects the production of 5-HT in some individuals.* New Scientist 6/14/73, p670 *Jane goes off to visit an earlier love, Toby, now living in the uncomfortably warm climate of Israel, where the sharav is blowing and the Six-Day War is about to flare up.* Listener 4/11/74, p411 [**1968**, probably from Arabic]

shark repellent, *U.S. Finance.* any means used by a company to prevent a corporate raider from acquiring it. *There are other strategies as well—those designed as "shark repellent" ploys to ward off other unwelcome suitors.* Maclean's 4/20/81, p45 [**1981**]

s/he, *pronoun. U.S.* she or he. Compare HE/SHE. *A child's sexual orientation is determined before /s/he enters school.* American Educator, Winter 1978, p65 *An older person is called*

"cranky" when s/he is expressing a legitimate distaste with life as so many young do. The New Old: Struggling for Decent Aging (ed. Ronald Gross, Beatrice Gross, and Sylvia Seidman), 1978, p89 *A good deal of harmless fun has been poked at certain neologisms coined by the Women's Movement in its sexually egalitarian and sometimes even female supremacist zeal . . . S/he to replace the offensively sectarian yet ubiquitous use of he as an impersonal pronoun? What? Have the girls no sense of proportion?* State of the Language (ed. L. Michaels and C. Ricks), 1980, p226 [**1973**]

sheep-dip, *v.t. U.S. Slang.* to disguise (a military officer) as a civilian in order to use him as a spy in a civilian group. *American military officers engaged in C.I.A.-sponsored paramilitary operations are "sheep-dipped" for paramilitary duty—that is, they appear to resign from the military yet preserve their place for reactivation once their tour as civilians in paramilitary operations has ended.* NY Times 4/27/76, p23 [**1972**, figurative verb use of the noun meaning a disinfecting mixture into which sheep are dipped]

shekel, *n.* a monetary unit in Israel introduced in 1980, equal to 100 agorot. *When the banks reopen on Friday after a three-day holiday, a bank balance of 1,000 Israeli pounds will have become 100 shekels. The new notes bear the images of key figures in Zionism; on the 10-shekel note, for example, is a likeness of Theodor Herzl.* NY Times 9/30/80, pD7 [**1980**, from Modern Hebrew *sheqel*, revived use of the ancient Hebrew word for a silver coin that weighed about half an ounce, from Hebrew *shaqal* to weigh]

shell, *n.* a usually sleeveless and collarless overblouse. *"But my favorite dress is one that I bought for $60 in Arizona. It has a multi-colored chiffon shell over culottes, and I haven't the faintest idea who designed it."* NY Times 3/25/68, p48 [**1962**]

shepherd moon, *Astronomy.* a moon that orbits near the inner and outer edges of the rings of a planet with rings, probably holding the ring material together with the moon's gravity. *Among the first discoveries of Voyager 2 were two shepherd moons . . . that orbit the outermost Epsilon ring* [of Uranus]. World Book Science Annual 1988, p108 [**1987**]

sherpa, *n.* **1** *British Slang.* a porter. *The next most prominent rôle* [of the average husband], *sherpa, involving less and lower pay, was valued at £5 a week* (Euston portering rate). Guardian (London) 5/20/72, p12 *Herrligkoffer, like Dyrenfurth before him, was obliged to go international to raise the cash for basics like food and the sherpas' wages.* Sunday Times (London) 5/28/72, p14 **2** Also, **Sherpa.** a representative of a head of state who is charged with the preparations for a summit meeting. *"There should be a summit where there would be no proclamation of the leader in advance," said Canadian Prime Minister Pierre Trudeau. "Unstructured, without a precise agenda, and, most important, without a lengthy communique which had been written over the period of weeks and months by our 'Sherpas'—that we would be meeting at summit level to, kind of, justify that we covered all these subjects."* Christian Science Monitor 6/1/83, p3 [**1959**, from *Sherpa* a member of a tribe used for portering in the Himalayas (OEDS 1847)]

shiatsu or **shiatzu** (ʃiːˈɑːtsuː), *n.* a method of massaging or treating parts of the body by finger pressure to relieve pain, fatigue, etc. (often used attributively). Also called ACUPRESSURE. *Due to a printer's error in the article on shiatsu finger-pressure massage, page 135 of the December issue of Mademoiselle, the amount of pressure to apply was grossly overstated. The suggested pressure is not 120 pounds, but 20 pounds.* New Yorker 4/3/78, p118 *Japanese shiatsu massage is available at several locations in addition to the Salon de Tokyo . . . The undisputed Sorbonne of shiatsu is the Shiatsu Education Center of America, . . . presided over by Wataru Ohashi, generally regarded as the foremost master of the art in America.* Sunday News (New York) 6/3/79, p43 [**1967**, from Japanese *shiatsu*]

shield, *adj. U.S.* intended to protect a journalist from having to disclose confidential sources of information, as a SHIELD LAW does. *Sen. Sam Erwin (D., N.C.) says he is all for so-called shield legislation to protect the rights of newsmen, but he says it's the toughest piece of legislation he's ever tried to write.* National Review 4/13/73, p398 *Will there be a federal "shield" statute to protect the confidentiality of newsmen's sources?. . . In the House generally, he said, "proshield forces are definitely stronger than antishield forces at this time."* Time 3/19/73, p63 **[1972]**

shield law, *U.S.* **1** a law which protects journalists from having to disclose confidential sources of information. *About twenty states have "shield laws"—some of them recently enacted or expanded—to protect reporters who claim confidentiality, and the trend has drawn support from conservatives as well as liberals.* Newsweek 1/15/73, p47 *Citing the First Amendment and a New Jersey "shield law" giving a reporter the privilege of refusing to disclose confidential sources, Farber and the Times refused to turn over anything. The result: a head-on collision between the First and Sixth Amendments, between the constitutional claims of free press and fair trial.* Time 8/7/78, p74 **2** a law protecting a plaintiff's or witness's right to withhold private or confidential information. *There are now "shield laws" in 38 states to protect rape victims from inquiry during rape trials into their past sexual behavior.* 1978 World Book Year Book, p487 **[1972]**

shinkansen ('ʃiːnˈkɑːnsen), *n.* Japanese name of BULLET TRAIN. *The noted shinkansen, or bullet trains, and other trains, are to move throughout, bringing the northern frontier much more into the mainstream of Japanese life.* NY Times 5/9/76, p9 **[1973,** from Japanese, literally, new railroad]

ship, *n.* an orbiting or navigating spacecraft. . . . *"no decision has been made whether the crew will engage in extravehicular activity"—the official term for movement outside the ship.* NY Times 5/26/65, p1 **[1965,** probably shortened from *spaceship*]

shirt-jac, *n.* another word for SHIRT-JACKET, used especially in the West Indies. *In another country Mr Shah might have been summarily executed; today he is Deputy Leader of the Opposition, bedecked in a smart, beige "shirt-jac."* Manchester Guardian Weekly 7/10/77, p9 **[1964]**

shirt-jacket, *n.* a lightweight, shirtlike jacket with an open collar and either long or short sleeves. Also spelled **shirt jacket.** *True, many leisure suits have shirt-jackets rather than the traditional jacket. It's possible, but more difficult, to dress up the shirt or Western style jacket, but then the man who buys one usually intends it only for casual wear.* Daily News (New York) 7/26/75, p12 **[1879, 1973]**

shirt-suit, *n.* another name for LEISURE SUIT. *From Gordon Deighton's spring collection at Trend in Simpsons, Picadilly, W.1., this is a shirt-suit.* Times (London) 4/17/70, p18 *Polyester doubleknit leisure shirt-suits $29.99. Your ticket to a comfortable, fashion-right summer!* Daily News (New York) 7/2/75, p31 **[1970]**

shlocky ('ʃlɑkiː), *adj.* another spelling of SCHLOCKY. *If one examines books on modern movies, the stills generally look terrible—shlocky, dated, cluttered, and artificially lighted.* New Yorker 4/6/68, p162 **[1968]**

shoat (ʃout), *n.* another name for GEEP. *Their only persistent vice is letting their shoats (a cross between a sheep and a goat) wander off onto their neighbour's land.* Sunday Times (London) 6/13/71, p9 **[1971,** blend of *sheep* and *goat*] ▶The term *shoat* is also the name for a young weaned pig, in which sense it has been in English since the 1400's.

shock front, the region in which the solar wind meets a planet's magnetic field, resulting in a BOW SHOCK. *None of the spacecraft crossed the shock front at a point directly between Venus and the sun, but a profile of the front can be constructed by plotting each crossing's distance from the sun and from the sun-Venus line.* Science News 3/19/77, p185 **[1970,** extended sense of the term (1950) meaning the outer region of an atmospheric disturbance caused by a rocket, an explosion, etc.]

shock wave, Usually in the phrase **send shock waves through.** a violent, upsetting jolt caused by an explosive event, situation, etc. . . . *the last writer who send shock waves through Western literature died when Louis-Ferdinand Céline completed his life's* Voyage au bout de la nuit. Harper's 12/69, p125 *Because such securities [commercial paper] are usually bought by other*

companies that have spare cash to invest, a series of defaults could have spread financial shock waves throughout the U.S. business community. Time 12/28/70, p54 . . . *the shock waves could be felt long before the opening* [of the exhibition "New York Painting and Sculpture: 1940-1970" at the Metropolitan Museum of Art]. *Indignation and outrage resounded in the New York reviews.* New Yorker 11/6/71, p58 **[1956,** figurative sense of the technical term for the violent effect of a blast, earthquake, atmospheric disturbance, etc.]

shootout, *n.* *U.S. Soccer.* a tie-breaker introduced in 1977 by the North American Soccer League. Five players from both teams are given five seconds each to score one-on-one against the goalie; the team with the most goals receives one point to break the tie. *After a scoreless overtime, the two teams resorted to the shootout, the league's method to determine a winner when games end in a tie. Seninho converted the decisive kick in the shootout. It was the second time this season that Seninho had made the winning kick in a shootout against Washington.* NY Times 8/13/79, pC1 **[1977,** figurative sense of the term meaning a gunfight, perhaps influenced by *shoot-off* a supplementary contest to decide a tie in a shooting match]

shoot-up, *n. Slang.* the act of injecting a drug by means of a hypodermic syringe. *But the most dramatic technique is the "shoot-up" where the more serious addicts inject themselves or each other with a nausea-producing liquid. The shooting-up takes place in a crash pad of pulsating lights, acid-rock stereo, Day-Glo and even antiwar posters.* Time 12/21/70, p20 **[1970,** from the slang verb phrase *shoot up* inject a drug (OEDS 1926)]

shopping bag lady, *U.S.* a vagrant, homeless, and often elderly woman who roams a city carrying her possessions in a shopping bag or bags. Also shortened to **BAG LADY.** *On a nearby bench, apparently keeping an intermittent vigil on the vigil, were two shopping-bag ladies. They spent most of their time endeavoring to fix the mechanism of a rusty, skeletal umbrella someone must have discarded many rains ago.* Harper's 3/78, p104 *If you are not accosted by a drunk or degenerate, you might get lucky with a deranged shopping bag lady who will walk up to you, poke you in your upraised Daily News and shout something like, "Don't try to sweet-talk me, you freaking smuthound!"* Daily News (New York) 12/29/78, p26 **[1976]**

shopping mall, an outdoors or indoors shopping area in the form of a pedestrian mall. *Not all shopping malls rose in the suburbs. Although the suburban centers at least in part represented retailers' efforts to cope with downtown sales erosion by "going where the people were," the return in the 1970's of middle- and upper-income consumers to the city gradually brought about the establishment of several major urban shopping malls.* Americana Annual 1979, p430 **[1967]**

short eyes, *U.S. Prison Slang.* a child molester. *For the cons the supreme sin is to be a "short eyes"—a sexual molester of children. On this one point everyone—black, white, Puerto Rican, Muslim fanatic and tough Irish Catholic—all come together, and the short eyes gets the book thrown at him, from ostracism to the indignity of being dunked in the toilet to a final act of terrible "justice."* Newsweek 4/8/74, p81 **[1974]**

short fuse, *U.S.* a quick temper. See also FUSE. *Tully, a fellow notorious around Sausalito for his short fuse, nearly destroyed everything when, the morning after his defeat, he held Nixon's "last press conference" and told the reporters they wouldn't "have Nixon to kick around any more."* NY Times 10/13/68, pD10 *He* [Senator Muskie] *has a temper and is known to the Washington press corps variously as "testy," "peevish," and "living on the edge of resentment." But aides say he carries the short fuse in his pocket, and he can joke about it afterwards.* Atlantic 6/71, p12 **[1963]**

short-life, *adj. British.* **1** lasting only a short time; short-lived. *More than 200 delegates were turned away from a London conference on disposable and short-life garments yesterday.* Times (London) 4/9/70, p29 **2** having a short shelf life; perishable. *Short-life foods, with a recommended shelf life of three months or less, corresponding to a total life of up to as much as five months, "should be marked conspicuously with the sell by date in a prescribed form," such as* sell by 02 SEP 72 *or* sell by *02 09 72*. Times (London) 7/6/72, p2 **3** intended for transient occupancy; temporary. *The Greater London Council said in a letter pushed through her letterbox on Monday night, that it was taking possession of all the 26 short-life properties the charity was renting from it on April 1. One hundred people are housed in the 26 properties.* Times (London) 4/1/76, p7 [**1966**]

short-term memory, the part of the memory which consists of information retained for only a short time. *This type of memory is referred to as short-term, because the number of events we can hold in this fashion is strictly limited, and forgetting is extremely rapid once our attention is diverted.* New Scientist 2/24/72, p428 *The necessary conclusion is that the initial storage of information, short-term memory, involves ongoing patterns of nerve impulses in circuits of nerve cells connected together by their fibers, while long-term memory is a lasting structural change in the pathway of cells.* NY Times Magazine 2/6/77, p46 [**1970**]

shotgun, *n.* an offensive formation in American football in which the quarterback lines up several yards behind the center to receive a direct snap. *Staubach's talent is throwing from the shotgun—the old football stand-by that Coach Tom Landry had adapted for third-down passing plays. Staubach sets up 5 yds. behind scrimmage, back-pedals seven more after the snap and looks to hit any one of five receivers downfield. He says that the tactic allows him "to save a crucial couple tenths of a second"—time enough to read the defense, then choose one from a confusing mixture of possible passes in front of or behind opposing linebackers.* Time 1/19/76, p43 [**1963**]

shotmaking, *n.* the making of shots, especially successful ones, in sports such as golf, tennis, and basketball. *However, like any well-designed course, Memorial will yield to inspired shotmaking. In the first annual tournament, there were thirty rounds under par—72—and on the second round Rod Funseth birdied five of the first six holes on the second nine.* New Yorker 5/16/77, p116 [**1969**]

shoulder, *n. Surfing Slang.* the calm portion of a wave breaking on the beach. *"You want a green wave with a good shoulder," says a stripling to me. He meant the kind of surf set up, not by a strong local wind, but by a ground sea running in from the Atlantic, big, regular, green rollers that, ideally, are prevented from collapsing for as long as possible by an offshore breeze.* Sunday Times (London) 5/22/66, p21 **—adj. 1** of or denoting an intermediate season of the year during which air travel is marginal, or the periods of time each day when heavy, rush-hour traffic begins to diminish. *Under the three-season concept, fares are at a peak in the June-August summer season, come down for the September-October and April-May "shoulder" periods, and normally are at their lowest in the relatively slack winter season.* NY Times 10/27/76, p18 **2** Elliptical use: *Air fare from New York included in above prices: $312 winter, $352 shoulder, $402 peak. Day flight information from New York available on request.* National Geographic Magazine 2/79, p4 [**1962**]

shoulder harness or **shoulder belt**, an anchored strap inside an automobile, designed to be worn across the shoulder and chest together with a lapbelt to prevent a passenger from striking his or her head against the instrument panel, window, etc., especially in the event of a collision. *Padded roll bars and shoulder harnesses are standard on the Shelby Cobra, as well they might be: the $4,200 car winds up to 150 m.p.h.* Time 4/5/68, p38 *A new safety seat, with built-in shoulder belts, is being developed by the General Motors Corporation and is expected to be on the company's cars in 1971.* NY Times 9/15/68, pA46 [**1967**]

showboat, *U.S. Slang. —n.* a person who seeks or attracts public attention. *National chairmen rarely serve as showboats, and when a party controls the White House, its public image lives there.* Time 2/28/69, p22 **—v.i.** to show off; make a public display (of). *The 98-year-old ballet is traditionally noted for the gaiety of its music by Léo Delibes and the opportunity it affords a ballerina to showboat her versatility as both Coppélia and Swanilda.* Time 1/31/69, p59 *"I shall not adopt a policy of showboating on this issue," he said in announcing he would not resign.* NY Times 7/10/68, p20 [**1963** for noun, **1960** for

verb; extended uses of the term for a steamboat on which theatrical performances are given (OEDS 1869)]

shrimp boat, one of the small plastic chips which air traffic controllers place adjacent to the blips on a radarscope to keep track of the movement of individual aircraft. *What does it take to control an estimated 9,000 aircraft taxiing, taking off, flying, and landing within the U.S. at any given moment? For the FAA [Federal Aviation Agency]—overseer of all flights operating under instrument flight rules (IFR) in the U.S.—it takes 14,000 highly trained men, extremely sophisticated electronic equipment, and . . . a large supply of small plastic markers called "shrimp boats".* Scientific American 9/67, p28 [**1963**]

shrink, *n. U.S. Slang.* a psychiatrist. *"What will your shrink do with you? He's dependent on you for the payments on his car."* New Yorker 7/11/70, p20 . . . *the shrink reports only to the patient, and suitable precautions have been taken to make sure the personnel department can't tap into the data.* Harper's 3/70, p83 [**1966**, shortened from *headshrinker*, an earlier slang term for a psychiatrist (OEDS 1950)]

shrink-wrap, *n.* a protective plastic cover made by shrink wrapping. *"We can also detect pirated recordings from the shrink-wrap used to seal the record-sleeve for shop display and from the type of plastic used in the record pressing itself."* Times (London) 1/12/72, p15 [**1961**]

shrink wrapping, the wrapping of goods in a plastic film that shrinks over the package to conform to its shape when the package is subjected to heat. *The market for plastic packaging is seen to be saturated in some areas . . . In other areas the prospects are seen to glitter. They are the areas where newer kinds of packaging, like shrink wrapping, are being exploited, and the areas where the film is not used for packaging but for other purposes well served by the peculiarities of the material.* New Scientist 5/14/70, p345 [**1959**]

shtick or **shtik**, *n. U.S. Slang.* a gimmick, act, or routine, especially in a show or performance. Also spelled SCHTICK. *[Gene] Wilder has a fantastic shtick. He builds up a hysterical rage about nothing at all, upon an imaginary provocation, and it's terribly funny.* New Yorker 3/7/70, p94 *They were taping the Andy Williams Show for March 27, and Joan Kennedy was doing her piano* shtik, *like a trouper.* Time 3/22/71, p14 [**1959**, from Yiddish *shtik*, literally, piece, bit]

shuck, *n. U.S. Slang.* fake; bluff. *He* [Bob Rafelson, a film director] *and his partner, Bert Schneider, put together the Monkees and their television program. "It was a shuck, but beautiful at its own level," he said.* New Yorker 10/24/70, p41 *It took them no time at all to see that the poverty program's big projects, like manpower training, in which you would get some job counseling and some training so you would be able to apply for a job in the bank or on the assembly line—everybody with a brain in his head knew that this was the usual bureaucratic shuck.* Harper's 2/71, p108 [**1959**]

shucking and jiving or **shuckin' and jivin'**, *U.S. Slang.* a fooling or tricking of someone by creating a false impression or conveying false information; assuming a deceptive guise, posture, or facade. *"Shucking and jiving," "S-ing and J-ing"*. . . *are terms that refer to one form of language behavior practiced by the black when interacting with the Man (the white man, the Establishment, or any authority figure), and to another form of language behavior practiced by blacks when interacting with each other on the peer-group level.* Rappin' and Stylin' Out, edited by Thomas Kochman, 1972, p246 *Harry Belafonte's shucking and jiving preacher in "Buck and the Preacher" was a particularly telling portrayal. When in trouble with the white folks, he grinned and preached, for that was his protective shield, but when he was with Buck he became a sly, crafty gunslinger.* Newsweek 10/23/72, p82 *Shuckin' and jivin' is a verbal and physical technique some Blacks use to avoid difficulty, to accommodate some authority figure, and, in extreme cases, to save a life or to save oneself from being beaten physically or psychologically.* Today's Education, Sept./Oct. 1975, p52 [**1969**, originally Southern Black English phrase, from the verbs *shuck* and *jive*, both meaning to deceive, mislead (recorded since the 1920's)]

shunpike, *v.i.* U.S. to travel by automobile on side roads instead of expressways, especially to enjoy the countryside. *Besides making long trips at high speed, motorists could take part in sports car rallies, chug about in antiques, "shunpike" on quiet back roads, or watch daredevil drivers skim the Utah salt flats in jet machines.* 1964 Collier's Encyclopedia Year Book, p70 [**1963**, verb use of the noun, a U.S. term for a side road used to avoid paying a toll on a turnpike (OEDS 1853)]

shunpiker, *n.* U.S. a person who shunpikes. *Smooth roads, signposts, beautiful scenery—what more could a shunpiker want?* Saturday Review 4/22/67, p55 [**1956**]

shunt, *n.* Slang. an automobile crash or collision. *A crash—what is it like to crash at speed? During a shunt (racing slang for a crash) things appear to slow down. You watch the object that you are about to hit with a certainty that it is happening so abruptly that the wait before impact is unbearable. Already the mind is questioning what went wrong—error or mechanical failure?* Maclean's 10/31/77, p58 *The equipment is designed to reduce the high incidence of rear-end shunts on motorways and other roads carrying dense, fast traffic.* New Scientist 1/12/78, p90 [**1959**, probably noun use of the verb, to push or shove aside (OED 1706)]

shuttle, *n.* **1** short for SPACE SHUTTLE. *This shuttle is nominally a two-stage vehicle consisting of a booster (first stage) and an orbiter (second stage).* McGraw-Hill Yearbook of Science and Technology 1971, p396 **2** short for DIPLOMATIC SHUTTLE. *Thus [Ivor] Richard's shuttle has been dubbed by some officials and journalists in southern Africa a safari of salvation.* Time 1/17/77, p30 *A week of furious diplomacy for the ever-smiling Mr Cyrus Vance left observers wondering whether his new-style shuttle (was it really very different from the kind practised by Dr Kissinger?) would obtain results.* Manchester Guardian Weekly 8/21/77, p5 [**1969** for def. 1 (earlier meaning "any spacecraft used to go back and forth between earth and other points in space," 1960); **1975** for def. 2]

shuttlecock, *n.* British name for MIGRONAUT. *"My impression is that the Government will view such cases sympathetically. Nor could they return families without papers as shuttlecocks to Uganda, even if they wished."* Times (London) 9/6/72, p2 [**1970**]

shuttle diplomacy, diplomatic negotiations between hostile countries conducted by a mediator who travels between the belligerents. *The American Secretary of State hoped his latest exercise in shuttle diplomacy would lead to a formula for disentangling the warring armies and set the stage for an overall peace settlement in Geneva.* Newsweek 4/29/74, p39 *With the rise of instant communication and shuttle diplomacy, foreign ministers and heads of state rely less and less on ambassadors as intermediaries.* NY Times Magazine 7/2/78, p10 *This can best be done by . . . sending U.S. Secretary of State Vance on yet another round of shuttle diplomacy between Jerusalem and Cairo.* New York Post 2/1/79, p22 [**1974**, applied originally to U.S. Secretary of State Henry Kissinger's personalized diplomatic efforts in the Middle East] **—shuttle diplomat:** *Or consider Henry Kissinger. Understandably, Citizen K's style has changed perceptibly from that of the shuttle diplomat. To be sure, he jets by choice these days to Mexico rather than the Middle East.* Time 6/13/77, p80

siabon ('si:əbən *or* 'syɑ:bən), *n.* the offspring of a siamang (genus *Symphalangus*) and a gibbon (genus *Hylobates*). *The siabon combines the physical features of both parents and has 47 chromosomes—22 from the gibbon father and 25 from the siamang mother. A gibbon ordinarily has 44 chromosomes and a siamang has 50. Therefore, there is a greater difference in chromosomes between these two animals than there is between humans, with 46, and apes, with 48.* World Book Science Annual 1981, p231 [**1979**, from *sia*mang + gib*bon*]

Sicilian, *adj.* U.S. of or denoting a type of thick, bready, rectangular pizza (often used in the absolute form as a noun). *In addition to plain whole pizzas at $4 each, onion-laden Sicilian squares at 60 cents and Neapolitan wedges for 55 cents, Fa-*

mous Ray's offers the usual assortment of toppings. NY Times 8/17/76, p44 [**1976**]

sick building syndrome, a condition of ill health caused by absorbing toxic fumes or other pollutants found in some modern airtight buildings. Also called BUILDING SICKNESS. *A source of new concern is indoor pollution—brought on in many cases by greater energy consciousness. Some office workers in new buildings with sealed windows are coming down with what doctors call "sick-building syndrome"—eye, nose and throat irritation, headaches, dizziness, nausea, diarrhea and rashes. Officials suspect toxic fumes may be originating in insulation and paneling.* U.S. News and World Report 5/21/84, p64 [**1983**]

sickie, *n.* U.S. and Canadian Slang. a mentally ill or unstable person; psycho. *Joan Davidson's face is, I think, one of her major assets. I think maybe the defacer just wanted to get her face out of there. On the other hand, maybe he's a sickie.* New Yorker 11/4/74, p42 [**1973**]

sick-out, *n.* an organized absence of employees from their jobs on the pretext of being sick, to avoid the legal penalties that may result from a formal strike. *About 20 of Hartford's 57 black cops took part in a sick-out last year over assignment and promotion grievances.* Time 11/23/70, p13 *But the two most important ones in the legal context are the recent strikes involving the nation's postal workers and the "sick-out" by American air controllers.* Times (London) 4/6/70, p23 *The postal strike had barely ended when a sick-out by air traffic controllers continued the communications snarl. The controllers began a campaign of organized absence from their jobs, reporting illness, on March 25.* 1971 Collier's Encyclopedia Year Book, p311 [**1970**]

side, *n.* **come down on the side of**, U.S. Informal. to opt in favor of; plump for; support. *We can't come down on this side or that side of each disputed public issue because we're trying to explain far more than advocate and because some issues don't have two sides; some have three, four or half a dozen.* Times 10/24/70, p31 *"Dearly beloved, this morning I am going to come down on one side of two very large possibilities."* Cartoon legend, New Yorker 1/4/80, p65 [**1970**]

side-looking, *adj.* (of radar or sonar) transmitting signals at a slanting or acute angle to reflect a profile image. *Side-looking airborne radar, although costly, is valuable for mapping and other work in areas where constant cloud makes aerial photography almost impossible, such as in tropical rain forests.* Times (London) 4/8/76, pVI *Surface ships would use electromagnetic devices and side-looking sonar, which gives a profile of objects on the bottom.* NY Times 9/18/76, p3 [**1961**]

siderochrome ('sidərə,kroum), *n.* a chemical compound that transports iron across a cellular membrane into the cell, where the iron is metabolized. *In many cases the growth or activity of a microbial species depends upon the availability of iron. Microorganisms excrete siderochromes, which are trihydroxamates (or catechols) of low molecular weight that selectively chelate, or bind, iron.* 1978 Britannica Yearbook of Science and the Future, p338 [**1961**, from *sidero-* iron (from Greek *sídēros*) + *chrome* chromium]

side-scan, *adj.* variant of SIDE-LOOKING. *Side-scan asdic (submarine detection device) with a slant range of one kilometre has been used most successfully for geological reconnaissance of the surface of the continental shelf and upper continental slope around western Europe. The technique is equivalent to the use of side-scan radar or oblique aerial photography for examination of the surface of the land.* Science Journal 12/70, p56 *From a mooring on the loch, they [two zoologists] will lower a side-scan sonar instrument into the water and watch for any patterns of returned sound signals that suggest large moving objects below.* NY Times 6/6/76, p1 [**1967**]

sidestream smoke, the smoke that drifts off the burning end of a cigarette or cigar. Compare SECONDHAND SMOKE. *According to the Lung Association sidestream and mainstream smoke emanating from the exhalations of cigarette smokers contain high concentrations of hazardous compounds, such as carbon mon-*

oxide, tar, nicotine and 3-4 benzpyrene, which is a suspected cancer-causing agent. NY Times 9/21/77, pC21 [**1973**]

SIDS, abbreviation of SUDDEN INFANT DEATH SYNDROME. *The higher the total infant mortality, the higher the number of SIDS cases; thus everywhere (except perhaps in Ontario) the poorer children are the more frequent target.* Scientific American 3/71, p120 [**1970**]

sigint or **SIGINT** ('sigint), *n.* the gathering of secret intelligence by monitoring radio and other transmissions (ELINT) and intercepting the signals and messages transmitted (COMINT). Compare HUMINT, IMINT. *Generally speaking the larger part of the staff of all Sigint headquarters consists of scientists and engineers. Apart from actual cryptanalysis, there is a continuing need to improve intercept equipment.* New Scientist 3/2/72, p467 *Questioned by Mr John Leonard, QC, for the Crown, he said Sigint was intelligence derived from the reception and analysis of foreign communications and other electronic emissions . . . Sigint was the key component in the overall intelligence effort.* Times (London) 10/14/78, p2 [**1969**, acronym for *signal intelligence*]

sigma, *n.* **1** short for SIGMA FACTOR. *Richard Burgess and Andrew Travers of Harvard discovered a protein, known as sigma, whose sole function is to stimulate the synthesis of RNA chains. In other words, sigma is the silent partner of the enzyme RNA polymerase that catalyzes RNA synthesis.* Britannica Book of the Year 1970, p543 *Another factor which was once thought to be like sigma now appears to be quite different, because it attaches directly to DNA, not to RNA polymerase, to turn genes on.* New Scientist and Science Journal 7/22/71, p182 **2** short for SIGMA PARTICLE. *The substitute particles are all heavier than the electron. The lightest, the mu meson, is 200 times as heavy as the electron; the heaviest, the sigma, 2,400 times as heavy.* Science News 11/14/70, p385 [**1970** for def. 1; **1963** for def. 2]

sigma factor, a protein that stimulates the synthesis of chains of RNA (ribonucleic acid) by regulating the action of the enzyme RNA polymerase. . . . *the function of the sigma factor is to give the core enzyme its specificity to transcribing from a fixed point on a strand of DNA and producing RNA of defined length.* Science Journal 4/70, p17 *A team of biochemists . . . told of identifying a substance they called sigma factor, which is responsible for starting mRNA synthesis.* World Book Science Annual 1972, p338 [**1969**]

sigma particle, an unstable elementary particle having a mass approximately 2400 times that of the electron. *The heavy sigma particle and the antiproton are produced by allowing beams from the CERN [European Organization for Nuclear Research] 28-GeV proton accelerator to strike metal targets.* New Scientist 9/17/70, p566 [**1957**]

sigmic, *adj.* of or containing sigma particles. *Kaonic and sigmic atoms tend to go together, since experiments aimed at making kaonic atoms make sigmic ones too.* Science News 11/14/70, p386 [**1970**]

sign, *v.* **sign off on**, *U.S. Slang.* to approve or allow (a plan, agreement, etc.). *The military bureaucracy, most notably the Joint Chiefs of Staff, would have to "sign off" on (Washington jargon for "approve") the American proposal.* New Yorker 5/19/73, p90 *For example, people here don't really "agree" to a bill. They "sign off" on it—a subtle expression of much greater finality in a place where such things are prized—at which point they join their colleagues "on board" for the duration.* NY Times 6/7/76, p31 [**1971**, originally used in the sense of "acknowledge as received," to show by affixing a signature that the person in charge at a given level has received and will implement a particular directive]

significant other, **1** *Sociology.* any person who directly influences an individual's self-evaluation and behavior. Compare ROLE MODEL. *A significant other is usually a family member, spouse, child, employer, co-worker, or friend . . . whose acceptance and approval is sought.* The Dictionary of Cultural Literacy 1988, p409 **2** *Informal.* a person to whom one is married, engaged, or otherwise romantically or sexually attached; a spouse, fiancé(e), lover, etc. *As for [Ken] Gross's lament, I'm*

not buying his noticing (out loud, in the presence of his Significant Other, in the form of a question) "a no-fault absence of milk". . . I read that as implying that stocking the refrigerator is her responsibility. Ms. magazine 6/89, p8 [**1959** for def. 1, originally used by the American psychiatrist Harry Stack Sullivan, 1892-1949; **1979** for def. 2]

signifying or **signifyin'**, *n. U.S. Slang.* a verbal game or contest in which the participants direct playful, teasing, or clever insults against each other. Also called SOUNDING or THE DOZENS. *Mary's indignation registers quite accurately the spirit in which some signifying is taken. This brings us to another feature of signifying: the message often carries some negative import for the addressee.* Rappin' and Stylin' Out, edited by Thomas Kochman, 1972, p320 *Although many of the retorts are stereotyped insults, some players achieve real proficiency . . . Such skill in words is greatly admired in the black community, among both men and women, and "signifying" has taken on the wider meaning of "to top any preceding remark."* Peter Farb, Word Play, 1974, p123 [**1959**, from gerund of *signify*]

sign-in, *n.* the collecting of people's signatures in support of a petition, demand, etc., addressed to the government or any authoritative body. . . . *churches organized a "sign-in" urging the Government to allocate 0.75 per cent of the gross national product as international aid.* Times (London) 5/12/70, p2 [**1968**; see -IN]

Silent Majoritarian, a member of the Silent Majority. *As Mr. Goulden's article points out, Silent Majoritarians do read, although their reading patterns are different from those of intellectuals. If Eddie Rickenbacker can write a book that the Silent Majority will read, someone can do the same with the war, because the stupidity of this war transcends the boundaries between liberal and conservative.* Harper's 7/70, p12 [**1970**]

Silent Majority, *Especially U.S.* **1** the politically nonvocal section of the population that is believed to constitute the majority of Americans. Compare MIDDLE AMERICA. *It must be said that after hearing what the Silent Majority has to say, one can appreciate the turn to violence in America . . . They say they are informed yet have never heard of, let alone read, a book on the [Vietnam] war. "I don't feel we have enough information to know whether policies are right or not. Leave it to the leader."* Harper's 7/70, p12 *One political columnist saw the typical member of this silent majority as a suburbanite or small-town dweller who was deeply disturbed by high prices and taxes, crime in the streets, political demonstrations and violence, welfare "handouts," integration and black militancy, and the changing attitudes of the young toward sex, drugs, established institutions, and authority figures.* 1971 Collier's Encyclopedia Year Book, p560 **2** the general American public. *To be topped in the [TV] ratings race by Hawaii Five-O was painful enough; but to be quantitatively inferior to another fraternal combination, The Everly Brothers (darlings of the Silent Majority), was pushing Job's fate.* Saturday Review 10/3/70, p48 [**1970**, from a phrase used by President Nixon in an address to the nation on November 3, 1969: "And so—to you, the great silent majority of my fellow Americans—I ask for your support."]

silent quake or **silent earthquake,** a slippage or movement of a tectonic plate or plates, occurring without the ground-shaking or strong seismic waves that accompany observable earthquakes. Compare MICROQUAKE. *In some areas the descent of an oceanic plate generates little earthquake activity or produces "silent" quakes whose ground motions are so slow they are rarely observed.* NY Times 4/4/76, p59 *He [Hiroo Kanamori] found that the Richter scale didn't rate many significant movements of the Pacific crustal plate, and he proposed "silent earthquakes" to account for the discrepancy in the slippage and the plate's movements.* Science News 2/26/77, p139 [**1976**]

silent spring, the death of the spring season resulting from the wanton destruction of nature by toxic chemicals. *The Caspian Sea is probably the most dramatic battleground of Soviet Russia's looming silent spring and to date this battle is being lost to oil, petroleum products, industrial and city sewage, ballast and waste from ships.* NY Times 6/12/70, p38 *If we don't de-*

velop suitable pesticides—and use them—we will really have Silent Spring because there won't be any trees left for the birds to sing in. NY Times 6/27/70, p28 [**1970**, from *The Silent Spring*, a book (1962) by the American writer Rachel Carson, 1907-1964, which called public attention to the danger to ecological balance involved in the widespread use of toxic pesticides and herbicides, and which opened with a description of a spring morning with no birds left to sing]

silo buster, *U.S. Military Slang.* a nuclear missile designed to destroy enemy silos to prevent a retaliatory attack. *If MX [an experimental missile] does go into full-scale development by virtue of that argument, the gap in America's second-strike submarine force will have helped tilt the American nuclear offense toward first strike. This is because the MX would be so accurate and powerful that it would fall into the first-strike category of "silo busters," especially in the eyes of the Soviets.* Manchester Guardian Weekly (Washington Post section) 4/2/78, p15 [**1977**] —**silo-busting,** *adj.: This* [the MX] *would give Washington the means to match Moscow in what defense analysts like to call "silo-busting" capability—the ability to launch pinpoint attacks against the opposing side's missile forces.* NY Times Magazine 5/27/79, p34

silvichemical, *n.* any chemical substance derived from trees. *. . . but the research did point out two important avenues of development. One lay in the manufacture of charcoal, and the other in the development of silvichemicals. Either approach appeared to offer the possibility of a very high extraction rate for the timber . . .* New Scientist 11/3/66, p224 [**1962**, from *silvi-* (from Latin *silva* forest) + *chemical*]

simazin ('saiməzən) or **simazine** ('saimə,zi:n), *n.* a moderately toxic chemical widely used as a weed killer. *Some species might even become resistant to sprays, although the only example so far appears to be a United States groundsel reported to be undeterred by simazin and atrazin.* Times (London) 11/23/70, p13 *Simazine is only very slightly soluble in water and it breaks down quite slowly in the soil. When applied to bare soil it stays on the topmost layer, where it prevents weed germination for several months, while remaining safely out of contact with the roots of most woody plants.* New Scientist 12/24/64, p847 [**1956**, from *sim-* (perhaps for *simple*) + tr*iazine* (chemical compound with a ring of three carbon atoms)]

simulation, *n.* **1** the representation or imitation of a physical or social system or its activity by computers for the purpose of predicting the behavior of that system under certain conditions. *Political simulation may be regarded as an experimental technique through which complex political phenomena such as a political campaign or an international relations crisis involving a series of events and a number of nation-state "actors" may be recreated or forecast under quasi-experimental conditions controlled by the simulation director.* McGraw-Hill Yearbook of Science and Technology 1971, p383 **2** one such representation or model. *These methods, known collectively as simulations, involve the making of numerical models of large scale systems and solving them on high-speed computers for all imaginable configurations.* NY Times 11/15/65, p36 [**1947, 1958**]

Sindolor ('sində,lɔr), *n.* an instrument which stops the pain of the dental drill with an electric current, eliminating the need for local anesthesia. *There is even a device for that most common of all miseries, dental pain. Developed three years ago by scientists at the University of Leningrad and called Sindolor, it is attached to a dentist's drill and sends a weak current through the patient's jaw.* NY Times Magazine 1/30/77, p50 [**1973**, apparently a trademark, probably from Spanish *sin* without + *dolor* pain]

sindonology (,sində'nalədʒi:), *n.* the scientific study of the shroud of Turin, a cloth bearing the image of a life-size figure of a man thought to be Jesus Christ, kept in a chapel in Turin, Italy, since the 1500's. *Secondo Pia's photos, and better ones by Giuseppe Enrie, started the last phase in the long and vexed history of the shroud and opened up a new scientific discipline—sindonology. From the Greek sindon, via the Italian, sindone, which means shroud, sindonology is the study of the shroud—a lifelong romance with the paradox—and in particu-*

lar two questions: what is the image composed of, and by what mysterious if not miraculous process was it formed? Sindonology is the physics of miracles. Rolling Stone 1/11/79, p79 [**1964**, from (archaic or obsolete) *sindon* a shroud (from Latin, from Greek *sindōn*) + *-ology* study of] —**sindonologist,** *n.: What most fascinates sindonologists . . . is how the image got there. Historians have traced the shroud of Turin back to fourteenth-century France, a period in which many shrouds were venerated as the one from Jesus' tomb.* Newsweek 12/10/73, p83

sing-in, *n. U.S.* a musical act or event in which the audience serves as a chorus or joins in the singing. *Sing-in at Philharmonic Hall—Handel's "Messiah," directed (seriatim, fortunately) by nineteen directors . . .* New Yorker 12/19/70, p16 [**1965**; see -IN]

single, *n.* Usually, **singles,** *pl. Especially U.S. and Canada.* an unmarried man or woman. *The problem with single parents is that they don't fit in with either the married couples or the singles.* Maclean's 5/16/77, p42 *Soviet singles also complain that it is difficult to meet prospective mates, especially after they leave university life and enter the working world.* Today (Westchester, N.Y.) 1/24/79, pB8 [**1964**, noun use of the adjective]

single-blind, *adj.* of or based upon a test or experiment whose exact makeup is known to the researcher but not to the subject. *In a single-blind study, the physician knows whether he is giving a patient a drug or placebo but the patient does not know which he is receiving.* Science 1/17/75, p148 [**1963**, patterned after DOUBLE-BLIND]

single-cell protein, a protein produced from liquid or gaseous petroleum fractions that are fermented by specially treated yeast cells or other microorganisms. *Abbreviation:* SCP *Single-cell protein is designed to be used as a food supplement in those areas of the world where protein is lacking in the diet. It can be added to bread or soft drinks or introduced into the diet in other ways.* Science News Yearbook 1970, p278 [**1970**]

single-copy DNA, a form of DNA that incorporates only one gene of a particular kind in each cell. *Much effort went into understanding the relationship between two kinds of genes: those known to exist in general hundreds, or even thousands, of copies in the DNA of each cell (repetitive DNA) and those present only once (single-copy DNA). The relationship is critical, because models for gene regulation proposed that the single-copy DNA represents the active functional (structural) genes.* Americana Annual 1976, p262 [**1970**]

single-entendre, *n.* a word, expression, or statement with an unmistakable and often indelicate meaning (also used attributively). *And along New York City's Avenue of the Americas, where phalanxes of hard hats line the sidewalks at noon, passing office girls find themselves caught in a cross fire of single entendres.* Newsweek 9/3/73, p90 *Jimmy Connors is the master of the single-entendre. He says what he wants, when he wants, to whom he wants. He is a Star.* NY Times Magazine 4/10/77, p20 [**1973**, from *single* + *entendre*; patterned after *double-entendre* (OED 1673)]

singlehood, *n.* the condition of being unmarried. *It is probable that singlehood with multiple sexual and love relationships, open marriage and traditional monogamy are already the major life-style choices.* Time 12/9/74, p86 [**1973** revival or reforming of earlier use (1840)]

singles bar, *Especially U.S. and Canada.* a bar frequented by unmarried men and women. *Here is a grown, experienced, loving woman—one you do not have to go to a party or a singles bar to meet, one you do not have to go to great lengths to get to know.* New Yorker 7/3/78, p25 [**1969**]

single-tasking, *n.* the sequential performance of two or more tasks by a computer. Compare MULTI-TASKING. *But unlike Lisa, which can process several applications concurrently, Macintosh is only a single-tasking product. So although it can move data among different windows of the same application, the micro is unable to cut and paste among different applica-*

tions without forcing users to swap diskettes, the spokesman said. Computerworld 1/23/84, p8 **[1983]**

singularity, *n. Astronomy.* a hypothetical point in space at which an object becomes compressed to infinite density and infinitesimal volume. See EVENT HORIZON, WHITE HOLE, WORMHOLE. *A singularity is a mathematical point at which an object such as a burnt-out star that has collapsed under its own gravity is . . . effectively crushed out of existence, although its gravity continues to exert an influence on the surrounding space. In practice, a singularity is surrounded by a region of space so distorted by gravity that nothing can escape; it is this region that constitutes the black hole.* New Scientist 5/4/78, p307 *We do not know whether black holes, as such, exist, and whether within them singularities provide links to other realms of space and time.* Walter Sullivan, Black Holes, 1979, p267 **[1965]**

sink, *n.* natural disposal of particles in the atmosphere. *Small particles spend about 30 days in the troposphere before being washed out by rain. Gases spend varying periods there depending on the "sinks" by which each is removed from the atmosphere: incorporation into cloud droplets, reactions with other gases, loss to finely divided liquid or solid particles or the earth's surface and so on.* Scientific American 1/71, p33 **[1961]**

Sinophobia, *n.* distrust or fear of China or something having to do with China. *A stunning glimpse of . . . Sinophobia was provided; on learning of plans for some "provocative" action or attack, the two sides—the United States and the Soviet Union—would take joint steps to prevent it, or, if it was too late for that, joint retaliatory action to punish the guilty party.* New Yorker 5/26/73, p94 **[1966,** from *Sino-* of China (from Late Latin *Sīnae* the Chinese) + *phobia*]

sinsemilla (ˌsinsəˈmilyə), *n.* a highly cultivated strain of seedless marijuana. *Last March they planted some high-class seed which had produced a splendid crop. It's called sinsemilla. "That's Spanish for without seed, see. The trick is to weed out all the male plants and leave just the females. They're the ones with the high THC content."* Maclean's 12/12/77, p58 *Studies show that* sinsemillas *weed contains five times more tetrahydrocannabinol (pot's narcotic ingredient) than the common Mexican variety.* Time 6/12/78, p22 **[1975,** from Mexican Spanish, literally, without seed]

sin tax, *U.S. Informal.* a tax on tobacco, alcoholic liquor, gambling, etc. *Though federal taxes have been reduced since 1960, the cuts have been offset by severe increases in state and city income taxes, sales taxes, property taxes, Social Security taxes and "sin" taxes on liquor and cigarettes.* Time 3/13/72, p66 **[1971,** used originally (1963) in New Hampshire by opponents of state revenues which were obtained from activities regarded as of questionable value, if not sinful]

sirtaki (sirˈtɑːkiː), *n.* a Greek folk dance performed in a circle with locked arms and with sidewise, alternately crossing steps, often with improvisations by individual dancers. *He will very gently . . . lead you through a sirtaki and finish the dance solo with that chair held on high in his mouth.* Manchester Guardian Weekly 11/7/70, p15 **[1965,** from Greek]

sissy bar, *U.S. and Canada.* a curved metal support at the back of a motorcycle or bicycle seat. *Sissy bars will be lower this year.* Esquire 2/71, p60 *Personals in this publication [Easyriders,* a magazine for motorcyclists] *have a forthright stormtrooper machismo about them. The woman's place is against the sissy bar.* Atlantic 6/72, p42 **[1969,** so called disparagingly as suitable for sissies]

sister, *n.* a woman who supports or belongs to the Women's Liberation movement; a member of the SISTERHOOD. *Perhaps the most defiant of today's liberated young—the sort who are wed after seven months of pregnancy, then deliver at home with the husband superintending and a friend photographing—are making a profound statement about women, nature, and childbirth. I don't pretend to understand all of my "sisters."* Harper's 6/74, p84 *At this initial meeting seven other "sisters" and I agreed we were there not to judge, but to listen, share and support.* NY Times Magazine 5/30/76, p15 **[1972]**

sisterhood or **Sisterhood,** *n.* **1** Usually, **the sisterhood.** the group of women who support or belong to the Women's Liberation movement. Compare the MOVEMENT. *That book's* ["The Liberated Woman and Other Americans"] *stinging attack on the women's lib movement achieved for its author* [Midge Decter] *a place in the sisterhood's demonology right next to Hugh Hefner.* Newsweek 10/9/72, p104 *For the first time in history, there is a real rallying of the Sisterhood that is being led by working women and their organisations.* Britannica Book of the Year 1973, p29 **2** the bond or community formed by such women. *Does this mean that only women left in the kitchen can make it into true sisterhood? Still locked into their "sexually oppressed" state, do they find sisterhood more attractive and easier to maintain? The rejection of sisterhood in favor of ambition doesn't sit well with many feminists.* NY Times Magazine 5/30/76, p16 **[1972]**

sitcom, *n. U.S.* a type of radio or television comedy series based on contrived situations built around a character or group of characters. . . . *Nancy* [is] *a sappy-sounding sitcom with Celeste Holm set in the White House.* Time 3/2/70, p77 *The* [porno-spoofs] *genre is based on the idea of inviting you to laugh at sex—as if you were watching a dirty sit-com on TV.* New Yorker 11/6/71, p190 **[1964,** from *sit*uation *com*edy]

sitology (saiˈtɒlədʒiː), *n. Architecture.* the study of sites or locations for new buildings, especially ones that harmonize with natural surroundings. *They call on the resources of a new science called "sitology" in their proposal to call a halt to the massacre of nature and to start building without destroying our natural sites.* Manchester Guardian Weekly (Le Monde section) 1/18/75, p14 **[1975]**

situation ethics, a form of ethics based on the theory that absolute moral rules cannot be applied to specific situations or circumstances, each of which must be judged within the particular context of its occurrence. *Fletcher* [the American theologian Joseph Fletcher] *argues that situation ethics avoids the pitfalls of other approaches to morality.* Time 1/21/66, p53 **[1955,** translation of German *Situationsethik*]

situation room, a room, usually at a military headquarters, where reports are given on the current status of any action, operation, etc. *The intelligence "situation room" will keep the 15 permanent ambassadors of the NATO countries and their key military commands more fully up-to-date on Russia's political and military build-up than they have ever been before.* Sunday Times (London) 5/21/67, p7 *The President canceled minor appointments, put the White House Situation Room on special alert, and went before television cameras with a somber, seven-minute statement.* Time 6/2/67, p11 **[1967]**

situs picketing, *U.S.* another name for COMMON-SITE PICKETING. *After assuring Secretary of Labor Dunlop and the labor movement that he* [Gerald Ford] *would not veto a bill authorizing situs picketing, he reversed himself and led Dunlop to resign.* NY Times 9/6/76, p4 **[1963,** from Latin *situs* location (used in law)]

SI unit, any of the units of measurement in the international meter-kilogram-second system of measurements. *In practice it has been found that one conspicuous advantage of SI units is the simplification of calculations.* Times (London) 1/4/72, p14 **[1970,** *SI,* abbreviation of French *Système International (d'Unités)* International System (of Units)]

ska (skɑː), *n.* a kind of popular music of Jamaica, a forerunner of reggae. *The "Wailers" formed over ten years ago, in the days when 'Ska' was the popular music form in Jamaica.* Weekend Star (Kingston) 6/29/73, p15 *There was a speaker outside on the step blasting the current ska, which was a kind blend of syncopated Caribbean music, bebop and American soul, into the crowded streets.* NY Times Magazine 8/14/77, p28 **[1964,** origin unknown, perhaps imitative of a sound]

skag (skæg), *n.* variant of SCAG. *Lockhart Road, the central promenade, still throbs with pimps and barkers . . . and heroin hustlers still push "skag" at 89 cents a fix in the alleys outside.* Newsweek 2/19/73, p44 **[1972]**

skateboard, *n.* See the quotation for the meaning. . . . *the latest candidate is skateboarding. A skateboard is a surfboard scarcely larger than a steak plate, mounted on roller-skate wheels, and a skateboarder is anyone daring enough to careen over the concrete while aboard one.* Time 6/5/64, p65 [**1964**]

skateboarder, *n.* person who rides a skateboard. *On the morning of what was probably the last truly warm, gentle Saturday of 1966, we wandered off Fifth Avenue at Seventy-second Street and into the Park, strolling among the skate-boarders, bicyclists, and English baby carriages down the slope toward Conservatory Pond.* New Yorker 11/26/66, p52 [**1964**]

skateboarding, *n.* the act or sport of riding a skateboard. Also called SKURFING. *The rebirth of skateboarding has been attributed to the invention of urethane wheels by Frank Natsworthy in 1973. With a firm grip on asphalt or concrete, the new-model skateboards skim the ground like miniature surfboards* . . . New York Post 6/12/76, p25 [**1964**]

skatepark, *n.* a smooth, paved area constructed for skateboarding, frequently featuring steeply slanted hills and sharply curved banks. *Frank Nasworthy . . . is breaking ground for a $60,000, 15 thousand-square-feet-of-concrete skatepark in Ft. Lauderdale which will feature a pro shop, a game room and "amenities for the parents."* NY Times Magazine 9/12/76, p85 *It would, of course, be far better if the boards were confined to sumptuous municipal skate parks. But for the rest, and while it lasts, what would the skateboarding millions be doing if their sport were banned?* Manchester Guardian Weekly 1/15/78, p10 [**1976**, from skateboard + park]

skell, *n.* U.S. Slang. a derelict or homeless person living in a city's streets or subways. *"Wolfman Jack" is a skell, living underground at the Hoyt-Schermerhorn station in Brooklyn, on the GG line. The police there give him food and clothes, and if you ask him how he is, he says, "I'm getting some calls." Call them colorful characters and they don't look so dangerous or pathetic. These "skells" are not merely down and out. Many are insane, chucked out of New York hospitals in the early 1970's when it was decided that long-term institutionalization was doing them little good.* NY Times Magazine 1/31/82, p21 [**1982**, probably a shortened and altered form of skeleton]

ski bob, a vehicle for sliding downhill on snow, consisting of a metal frame with handlebars connected to a short pivoting ski in front, and a seat attached to a longer fixed ski in the back. The rider usually wears mini-skis for balance. *The ski-bob is rather like a converted bicycle, and the rider uses small skis on each foot for steering and stopping.* Times (London) 10/21/67, p28 *Although the first ski bob was apparently patented in the U.S. in 1892, the sport only recently started flourishing in the resort center of Crans-Montana in the Swiss Alps.* Time 3/17/67, p36 [**1968**]

ski bobber, a person who engages in ski bobbing. *In addition the ski bobber wears 18-inch-long skis. Because the weight is not taken by the legs unpleasant accidents are far rarer.* Times (London) 1/16/68, p8 [**1967**]

ski bobbing, the sport of riding a ski bob. *Ehrwald is not a centre for the relatively new sport of ski bobbing, but facilities are available in a number of resorts.* Times (London) 10/3/70, p20 [**1966**]

skidoo (ski'du:), *n.* a motorized sledge moving on endless tracks in the back and movable skis in front, used for travel on snow or ice. Also called (British) SKI-SCOOTER. *In the American and Canadian Arctic zones, the Eskimos are being "civilised" with central heating, drink, juke boxes, skidoos and hamburgers.* Sunday Times (London) 8/1/71, p6 [**1961**, from Ski-Doo, trade name of such a vehicle]

skim, U.S. Slang. —*v.t., v.i.* to conceal part of (an income, such as the winnings of a gambling casino) to avoid paying taxes. *There was evidence of skimming . . . out of the casinos in order to dodge taxes.* Time 12/21/70, p63 *He . . . denied the Assemblyman's countercharge that Mr. Rosen had been "skimming" funds contributed by the residents for the strike.* NY Times 3/1/76, p27 —*n.* an act or instance of skimming. *One of the men most responsible for exposing, or popularizing, the con-*

cept of a national criminal conspiracy called La Cosa Nostra, Pelequin has this to say about the Paradise Island transactions: *"The atmosphere seems ripe for a Lansky skim."* Harper's 12/74, p58 [**1966**, from the idea of skimming (removing) the cream off the top of milk]

skimboard, *n.* a thin, often round, surfboard about three feet in diameter, used for riding shallow water or receding waves on a beach. *Riding a skimboard, a youth glides over a comberlaved beach. Cold, treacherous currents make swimming risky.* National Geographic Magazine 11/72, p688 [**1965**, from skim act of moving lightly (over water, ice, etc.) + board]

skimmer, *n.* **1** any of various devices for collecting oil from the surface of water in an oil spill. *A fleet of skimmers is steaming from Stavanger to suck up the oil and transfer it to waiting tankers.* Times (London) 4/25/77, p1 *The French have developed skimmer gear that simply scoops up oily water and separates it into oil and water (it's said they had difficulty with this gear during the Amoco Cadiz spill). The French skimmer has one important advantage: It can be easily and quickly attached to most boats.* NY Times Magazine 4/9/78, p70 **2** U.S. a simply cut dress with straight lines, often sleeveless and with a round neck (also used attributively). *The shirt is represented in every shape and form, sometimes stopping where a shirt traditionally stops and sometimes going down a few (still a very few) inches to make a skimmer dress.* NY Times 1/5/68, p39 *A stylish clean-cut skimmer . . . neat, narrow, nubby. Deftly fashioned by The Sporting Tailors.* Advertisement in New Yorker 3/18/67, p194 [**1971** for def. 1; **1964** for def. 2]

skimming, *n.* the practice of concealing a part of the winnings of a gambling casino to avoid paying taxes. *The Mob's technique there [Las Vegas] known as "skimming," was as simple as larceny and as easy as shaking the money tree: a part of the cash profits from six . . . casinos was simply diverted before the figures were placed in the ledger books.* Time 8/22/69, p18 [**1966**]

ski mountaineering, the sport of skiing on mountains or mountainous areas. *Ski mountaineering is gaining in popularity in the Albertan Rockies, and though the sport seems like cross-country skiing, it could be lethal to confuse the two. The backgrounds for most cross-country activity are groomed trails, open fields and even golf courses; the equivalent for ski mountaineering are glacier fields, narrow passes and avalanches. In ski mountaineering all the equipment is sturdier, particularly the skis.* Maclean's 10/74, p103 [**1972**]

skin, *adj. Especially U.S. Slang.* **1** showing people in the nude; nudie. *His boss, Bruno Glober, spends working hours slathering over skin magazines . . .* Time 9/7/70, pNY6 **2** of or relating to movies, burlesque theaters, etc., showing nudes. *The skin houses were mostly playing short subjects—a girl taking a bath in a sylvan stream, a volleyball game in a nudist camp.* Harper's 7/70, p34 —*v.i. U.S. Slang.* short for SKIN-POP. . . . *all my friends were on heroin. I snorted a couple of times, skinned a lot, and after that I mained it.* Time 3/16/70, p17 [**1968**]

skin flick, *Slang.* a motion picture showing people in the nude, usually engaging in some sexual act; a nudie. *It started with sex educational films, and documentaries on pornography from Denmark and Sweden, and has continued with a profitable avalanche of skin flicks and stag movies, all totally explicit, and some of them, I understand, very well made.* Times (London) 11/28/70, p20 [**1968**]

skinhead, *n.* a type of young bigoted working-class tough wearing closely cropped hair, work pants and suspenders, and hobnailed boots, who engages in street fighting. The skinheads first emerged in Britain in the 1970's. American imitators, also called skinheads, appeared in the 1980's. Also called AGROBOY. *The skinheads . . . specialize in terrorizing such menacing types as hippies and homosexuals, Pakistani immigrants and little old ladies. "Hairies," those with long hair or hippiestyle clothing, are their particular enemies, but they are quite happy to break up a synagogue, a Chinese café or an Indian restaurant.* Time 6/8/70, p37 *A group of "skinheads" gather . . . at the main entrance to the East Village's Tompkins Square*

Park—scene of a weekend battle between demonstrators and club-swinging cops. New York Post 8/9/88, p4 **[1969]**

skinheadism, *n.* the practices of skinheads, especially the use of violent tactics or brutality against members of minority groups. *We are all conscious of the fact that many M.P.s on the Opposition side . . . are showing great courage against a different and more menacing type of skinheadism in Northern Ireland.* Times (London) 2/6/70, p8 **[1970]**

Skinnerism, *n.* the ideas and theories of the American behavioral psychologist B. F. Skinner, born 1904, especially his concept of controlling behavior through a system of rewards and reinforcements. See BEHAVIOR MODIFICATION. *The second topic (behaviour control) might, for example, be an attack on Skinnerism and end with a code of practice for psychiatrists. Such a code would contain a patient's rights section and would . . . be presented in such a way that psychiatrists, anxious for a good public image, would adopt it.* New Scientist 12/13/73, p789 **[1969]**

skinny, *n.* information or, sometimes, gossip, rumor, etc. *Wouldn't it be interesting if TV stations put critics on newcasts to probe into the efficiency of local newspapers? . . . Will we ever hear, "Hi, this is Pam Martin and I've got the revealing skinny tonight on Lewis Grizzard . . . "?* Atlanta Constitution 11/13/86, p5 **[1959]**

skinny-dip, *U.S. Slang. —v.i.* to swim in the nude. . . . *one pious Mayo farmer, coming upon his Dutch summer tenants skinny-dipping in his pond, threw them off his property . . .* New Yorker 7/25/70, p61 **—n.** a swim in the nude. *". . . I don't want to take my clothes off and march down the beach like some drunk going for a skinny-dip before an admiring throng, do you understand?"* Atlantic 9/71, p95 **[1966;** known orally in the 1940's]

skinny-dipper, *n. U.S. Slang.* a person who swims in the nude. *According to an undercover source, the skinny-dippers are a nocturnal breed and come out only at night. Of course, this is for an obvious reason: under the sun they might get well done all over. Moonlight is softer and also doesn't emphasize disfiguring (appendectomy) scars like bright sunlight.* Tuscaloosa News (Alabama) 9/5/71, p7A **[1971]**

skin-pop, *v.t., v.i. U.S. Slang.* to inject (a liquefied narcotic drug) just beneath the skin. Also shortened to SKIN. . . . *adolescents . . . inject subcutaneously (skin-pop) or into their veins (mainline) barbiturates, amphetamines, and almost anything else they can lay their hands on.* Harper's 6/70, p79 . . . *he had been using it* [dope] *for about six months, "skin-popping," or shooting it into his shoulder about two or three times a week.* NY Times 2/23/70, p26 **[1953]**

skin search, *Slang.* a search for illegal possessions by having a suspect undress. Compare PAT-DOWN SEARCH, TOSS. *So far, none of the three new guards in California's state prison system for men have been assigned to conduct "skin searches" of nude prisoners for contraband.* Time 3/26/73, p64 **[1935, 1970]** **—skin-search,** *v.t.: Prisoners . . . had been skin-searched for weapons.* Manchester Guardian Weekly 11/7/70, p7

ski-scooter, *n. British.* another name for SKIDOO. *Motorized ski-scooters used by the army on manoeuvres in Lapland.* Picture legend, Times (London) 5/13/70, pIII **[1967]**

ski touring, cross-country skiing, especially over large expanses of open country; hiking on skis as opposed to cross-country racing or downhill skiing. Also called X-C SKIING. *Ski touring represents a return to the way people skied before skiing got fancy. Scandinavians have been wild about cross-country for centuries . . .* Time 1/17/72, p68 *"Ski touring would be spoiled if too much emphasis is placed on the merchandising of fancy equipment, changing fashions, or organized area skiing, and on the promotion of the name resort."* NY Times Magazine 12/18/77, p19 **[1960]** **—ski tourer:** *Somehow the noise seems more intrusive in the otherwise peaceful countryside, particularly to snowshoers, ski-tourers and others who enjoy the stillness of winter woods.* NY Times Magazine 2/13/72, p30

skiwear, *n.* clothes appropriate for skiing. *Mr. Winter rid himself of some difficult lines, in a sales decline of from $30-*

million. "We gave up skiwear, men's wear, and teen-wear—all splinter divisions that were diluting our management effort and talent," he said. NY Times 7/15/68, p43 **[1961]**

skosh (skouʃ), *n. U.S. Slang.* a small amount; little. *A new line of Levi's for men is constructed with "a skosh more room where I need it."* Detroit Free Press 12/19/77, p6 **[1960,** from Japanese *sukoshi* a little; originally used by American soldiers in Japan and Korea in the 1950's]

skurfing, *n.* another name for SKATEBOARDING. *Skateboarding—or skurfing, as it's also called—was started four years ago in California by a group of surfing enthusiasts who were looking for something to do while the Pacific tides were out.* Maclean's 7/24/65, p26 **[1965,** blend of *skating* and *surfing*]

skybridge, *n.* another name for SKYWALK. *The scene—two of three concrete "skybridges" arching a hotel atrium, crashing down onto a jammed dance floor—is the stuff of summertime disaster movies.* NY Times 7/19/81, pD4 **[1981]**

skyclad, *adj.* without clothes; unclothed. *The main ritual is conducted every month when the moon is full. If the ceremony is indoors, it is conducted "sky-clad"—in the nude.* Time 6/19/72, p66 *Covens are encouraged, but not required, to worship outdoors, preferably "skyclad" or nude.* Sunday Post-Herald (Hongkong) 7/22/73, p22 **[1970,** from Sanskrit *digambara*] ▶The term was used occasionally in the early 1900's as an informal euphemism for "nude." Current interest in witchcraft and the occult has revived it.

skydive, *v.i.* to dive from an airplane in a long free fall as a sport, often performing various soaring maneuvers before opening the parachute. *Jim Marshall* [a football quarterback] *is a man of considerable enterprise. He skydives and sells portable telephones; he used to peddle wigs and manage a rock group . . .* Time 10/17/69, p46 *Mary Cushing . . . snorkles, surfs, skis and sky-dives . . .* NY Times 4/24/65, p21 **[1965,** back formation from *skydiver*]

skydiver, *n.* a person who skydives. Aug. 27 *Huron, O. Sky divers, leaping through an overcast from an off-course B-25, hit Lake Erie instead of their scheduled drop target at Ortners Field, Birmingham, O . . .* Britannica Book of the Year 1968, p287 **[1961]**

skyjack, *v.t.* to hijack (an aircraft) and fly it to a place other than its original destination. . . . *the guerrillas skyjacked three jet airliners and held as hostages 430 crewmen and passengers.* Time 9/28/70, p17 **—n. 1** a skyjacking. Compare HIJACK. *. . . world attention focused on the drama of a quadruple skyjack last week . . .* Time 9/21/70, p14 **2** a skyjacker. *Skyjack Minichiello becomes the hero of his homeland.* Sunday Times (London) 11/9/69, p7 **[1961,** blend of *sky* and *hijack, v.*]

skyjacker, *n.* a person who hijacks an aircraft. Also called AIR PIRATE. *The skyjacker, armed with a pistol and container of nitroglycerine, was greeted in Havana by Fidel Castro while the other 370 passengers were allowed to continue their journey.* Manchester Guardian Weekly 8/8/70, p3 **[1961]**

skyjacking, *n.* the hijacking of an aircraft. Also called AIR PIRACY. *The more than 50 skyjackings that occurred this year were taken a lot more seriously by the passengers and crews involved, however.* 1970 Collier's Encyclopedia Year Book, p84 **[1961]**

Skylab, *n.* a United States scientific space station or laboratory launched into earth orbit in 1973. Compare SPACELAB. *The programme includes the plans for Skylab, the orbiting scientific laboratory due for launching in 1972.* Times (London) 4/8/70, p6 *Skylab will, for the first time, provide our astronauts with ample room to move about when in orbit—far different from the cramped confines of the Mercury, Gemini and Apollo capsules.* Encyclopedia Science Supplement (Grolier) 1971, p329 **[1966,** from *Sky* + *lab*oratory]

sky marshal, *U.S.* a federal law-enforcement officer assigned to protect aircraft and passengers from skyjacking. *An ex-Navy man was awaiting appointment by the Federal Aviation Administration as a sky marshal—a job that he characterized as* *"a symptom of our paranoid society."* New Yorker 9/4/71, p51 **[1968]**

sky surfer, another name for HANG GLIDER (def. 2). *Most sky surfers first learn to fly on a Rogallo kite, which is often called simply a "wing."* Scientific American 12/74, p138 **[1972]**

sky surfing, another name for HANG GLIDING. *Not all new words are serious or come from the striking events of the time. From sports, for instance, there is "sky surfing," in which participants tied to delta-wing kites glide down from cliffs.* Bridgeport Sunday Post 4/14/74, pE4 **[1972]**

Skytrain, *n.* the trademark for a system of low-cost, no-frills, transatlantic flights with scheduled but unreserved one-class service, introduced in Great Britain in the 1970's by Laker Airways. *Britain's Freddy Laker has hired a Washington lawyer to protect Laker Airways' registered "Skytrain." Airlines, including Braniff, which applied for a no-reservation Dallas-London "Texas Skytrain" route, have already been warned politely but firmly to buzz off.* Time 10/10/77, p91 *"You know what I like most about Skytrain?" our friend asked. "Once and for all, it scotches the notion that flying the Atlantic . . . has anything to do with glamour . . . It's all one class on Skytrain."* New Yorker 3/8/78, p27 **[1971]**

skywalk, *n.* an overhead suspended walkway inside a building. Also called SKYBRIDGE. *On July 17, two "skywalks" collapsed onto a crowded dance floor in the new Hyatt Regency Hotel in Kansas City, Mo., killing 113 persons and injuring over 180.* 1982 Collier's Encyclopedia Year Book, p288 **[1972]**

slalom canoe, a canoe, usually with a deck, used in a canoe slalom. *As many as five modern canoes will fit on top of a car, even a bug Volkswagen—single canoes, double canoes, slalom canoes.* New Yorker 3/21/70, p129 **[1970]**

slam, *n. U.S. Slang.* Usually, **the slam.** short for SLAMMER. *This is the same Harvey Matusow who . . . ended up doing time in the federal slams for what amounted to perjury any way you slice it.* Saturday Review 11/4/72, p65 **[1960]**

slamdunk, *n. U.S.* a basketball shot made by jumping and slamming the ball forcefully down into the basket. See also STUFF. *The only one-eyed candidate who would know how to put in a slamdunk on a New York playground has new financial life, a new strategy and a better record than he has been given credit for.* NY Times 5/25/76, p35 **[1976, from slam a forceful push + dunk (shot) a high jump and throw down into the basket]**

slammer, *n. U.S. Slang.* Usually, **the slammer.** prison; jail. *No President has ever suffered the infamy and disgrace that this one did. It was even more ignominious than sitting in the slammer.* Newsweek 1/13/75, p19 *She sought to provoke Desai's Janata Party into rashly locking her up . . . Then she could argue that her stay in the slammer had purged her of guilt for abuses during her term as India's one-woman ruler.* Time 1/1/79, p68 **[1952, from the slamming of the prison cell door (analogous to lockup meaning jail)]**

SLBM, abbreviation of *submarine-launched ballistic missile.* Compare SLCM. *The sea is the most secure strategic environment, and the SLBM, as everyone agrees, is the one weapon likely to survive an uncertain future.* New Yorker 5/19/73, p97 *. . . many of the American SLBMs carried from ten to 14 warheads each.* Time 2/11/74, p18 **[1967]**

SLCM, abbreviation of *submarine-launched cruise missile.* Compare ALCM. *The Navy contemplates placing both the strategic SLCM's and the tactical SLCM's aboard the present force of several hundred attack submarines . . .* Science 2/7/75, p418 **[1970]**

sleaze (sli:z), *n. Informal.* sleazy condition or quality; sleaziness; shoddiness. *The floodgates opened in 1966 when the Supreme Court, ruling on "Fanny Hill," declared that a work is pornographic only if it is "utterly without redeeming social value"—a definition that led directly to "Deep Throat" and the sleaze of today's Times Square.* Newsweek 7/2/73, p18 **[1961, back formation from sleazy (OED c1645)]**

sleazebag or **sleazeball**, *n. Slang.* a slovenly, disreputable, or coarse person. *At various times he has called them harlots,*

sleazebags, frauds,. . . blackguards, pigs and mugs. Daily Mirror (Sidney, Australia) 9/25/86, p8 *"We're trying to reach upscale people," said Farrell. "No dodos, no porn, no sleazeballs."* Philadelphia Inquirer 2/14/88, p16A **[1986]**

sleazo, *adj. Slang.* sleazy. *Her [Bette Midler's] sleazo routines seem half-rehearsed. Her dirty jokes sound almost like last-gasp fill-ins for the cleaner lines she was supposed to deliver but forgot.* Manchester Guardian Weekly 8/2/75, p20 **[1972, from sleaze or sleazy + -o, as in dumbo, socko, weirdo, etc.]**

sleep apnea, a temporary suspension of breathing that occurs during sleep, caused by a physical obstruction in the breathing tract or by a neurological or genetic disorder. *One key question, of course, is—as with all crib-death theories—how many of the 7,500 to 10,000 deaths a year might be caused by this mechanism. Does sleep apnea cause a substantial fraction of the deaths? Or only a handful?* NY Times Magazine 5/16/76, p42 *Treatments are now available for narcolepsy and another recently discovered illness, sleep apnea. The apnea patient complains either of feeling sleepy all day, of his sleep not doing much good, or of difficulty in remaining asleep. All-night sleep recordings show that his breathing often stops for periods of 15 seconds or more during sleep.* 1977 World Book Year Book, p121 **[1976]**

sleeper, *n.* another name for MOLE (def. 2). *The CIA call them 'sleepers', I think. They're people about whom, at a certain time, you guess the pattern of their ideological development, if you're a talent spotter working for the Russian Secret service, and you winkle them into a corner, and say: 'We appreciate your feelings about this, but just keep very quiet—sooner or later we will need you and when we do we will tell you.'* Listener 1/22/76, p90 **[1955, so called from its being inactive for a time, as one who sleeps or hibernates]**

sleep-in, *n.* the occupying of a public place by a group of people to spend the night or to sleep there as a form of protest, demonstration, or indication of ownership rights. *Earlier this week, the group announced a "sleep-in" at the High Commission, but later postponed it to allow more time for the British Government to reply to their petition submitted last month.* Times (London) 3/7/70, p4 **—v.i.** to take part in a sleep-in. *She [Candice Bergen] has taken up the signal causes of her generation—sleeping-in with the Indians at Alcatraz, demonstrating against the ABM.* Time 11/2/70, p84 **[1965; see -IN]**

sleeping policeman, *British.* another name for SPEED BUMP. *The problem of designing barriers which allow cyclists to pass but deter motorists is typical. "Sleeping policemen" type humps are allowed—but only for a year at a time.* New Scientist 11/2/78, p349 **[1973]**

sleep-learning, *n.* instruction obtained by one who is asleep, usually by means of recordings, on the theory that the sleeper's unconscious is capable of absorbing the information. *"Sleep-learning" is big business in the Soviet Union, where an increasing number of civil and military establishments are setting up dormitory facilities for pumping into trainees dull but necessary information—such as foreign language vocabularies—during the time "wasted" asleep.* New Scientist 3/5/70, p446 **[1953]**

sleeve-note, *n. British.* a descriptive or explanatory note on the jacket of a phonograph record or album. *On this third [recording] . . . E. Power Briggs uses an American instrument by John Challis, and the sleeve-note gives the specification.* Gramophone 4/70, p538 **[1956]**

sleight-of-mouth, *n. Informal.* skillful use of words to deceive; verbal legerdemain. *The ambitious [William H.] Sullivan has sometimes been accused of "sleight-of-mouth" tricks—of changing his views to suit the policy of the moment.* Time 2/19/73, p21 *There are, perhaps, three-quarters of a million people in camps and prisons across the sub-continent who would win freedom from an agreement. They are not, frankly, to be sacrificed any longer to political sleight of mouth.* Manchester Guardian Weekly 4/21/73, p1 **[1973, patterned after sleight-of-hand]**

slepton, *n. Nuclear Physics.* the hypothetical counterpart of a lepton in supersymmetry, differing from a lepton by a one-half unit. *According to supersymmetry, each boson and fermion should have a partner among the opposite class of subatomic particles . . . The hypothetical fermionic partners of quarks and leptons are generically called squarks and sleptons. The partner of the electron is called the selectron.* Encyclopedia Science Supplement (Grolier) 1987, p310 **[1987,** from *s*upersymmetric + *lepton*]

slide, *n.* another name for BOTTLENECK. *It is called "slide" or "bottleneck," a style of guitar playing in which something like a piece of broken glass is used to fret the strings to produce a strong, lowdown sound. A few decades ago it was the sound of a whole genus of American music that might be called backroads blues.* Time 10/21/74, p99 **[1972]**

sliding time, *U.S.* another name for FLEXTIME. Compare GLIDING TIME. *In West Germany, some 3,500 firms have adopted "sliding time." In one form of the plan, company doors are open from 7 a.m. until 7 p.m., and factory or office workers can come in any time they like, provided that they are around for "core time," from 10 a.m. to 3 p.m., and they put in a 40-hour week.* Time 10/30/72, p97 **[1972,** translation of German GLEITZEIT]

Slim, *n.,* or **Slim disease,** a form of AIDS prevalent in Africa, characterized by uncontrolled weight loss, chronic diarrhea, and prolonged fever. *The trader says, "There are ten with Slim now, and those who have died are 120."* Vanity Fair 7/88, p116 *In Uganda, scientists suggest the Slim disease . . . came from Tanzania.* NY Times 11/21/85, pA1 **[1985]**

slimnastics, *n.pl.* exercises to help a person lose weight. *Mrs. Mason sets a no-nonsense athletic schedule. At Stanley, "every single girl, every single day, has one hour of tennis, one hour in the pool, one hour of slimnastics."* Saturday Review 8/19/72, p74 *"Straight exercise is dull," said one woman in green leotard and tights at the Yonkers Y. "I've taken slimnastics and interpretive dancing, but this seemed exciting and fun.* NY Times 11/24/74, p39 **[1967,** blend of *slim* and *gymnastics*]

slingshot, *n.* a space-flight using the gravitational pull of a celestial body to accelerate sharply, usually in order to change course. Compare SWINGAROUND. *The next flight now scheduled is . . . a "slingshot" that will pass close to Venus on its way to Mercury.* Encyclopedia Science Supplement (Grolier) 1971, p350 *Meanwhile, the long trip from Jupiter to Saturn has been productive in its own right. The "slingshot" trajectory between the worlds has carried Pioneer 11 about 16° above the plane of the ecliptic, making it the first spacecraft ever to provide earthlings with a look "down" on the solar system.* Science News 6/18/76, p391 **[1970]**

slope, *n.* **1** an economic recession. *Recession, recedence, slope, shake-out, or what have you, to the chairman of the board and the factory worker at the bench, it is something a little better than a slump and much worse than a pinch.* Manchester Guardian Weekly 9/5/70, p22 **2** *U.S. Army Slang.* a derogatory name for an Oriental, especially in Korea and Vietnam. *Young GIs soon learned that there were Army names for Vietnamese too: gook, dink, and slope.* Harper's 5/70, p55 **[1970** for def. 1; **1966** for def. 2]

slot car or **slot racer,** *U.S. and Canada.* a toy car that is powered electrically to run on a slotted track while manipulated by remote control, used in slot racing. *The track on which slot cars race is a tabletop affair, somewhat similar to the familiar model-railway layout.* Maclean's 1/22/66, p9A *Slot car lubricator increases the speed of slot racers when applied to commutator, gears, bearings and other moving parts of the car.* Science News 3/26/66, p208 **[1966]**

slot racing, *U.S. and Canada.* the sport or hobby of racing slot cars. . . . *a rapidly growing number of Americans—adults as well as youngsters—. . . have caught the slot-racing bug.* Wall Street Journal 8/27/65, p22 **[1966]**

slow infection, an infection that is often fatal, caused by a virus that is present in the body, usually for a long time (slow virus) before it becomes active. *The Fore, a primitive tribe in New*

Guinea, were the main victims of kuru, the first known slow infection of man. World Book Science Annual 1976, p57 **[1954]**

slow virus, a virus that reproduces slowly in a host cell or organism and may not cause disease for many months or years. *Evidence recently came to light that implicated slow viruses in such neurological disorders of humans as multiple sclerosis and polyneuritis as well as in rheumatoid arthritis.* 1972 Britannica Yearbook of Science and the Future, p296 **[1954]**

sluggish schizophrenia, a form of schizophrenia ascribed in the Soviet Union to political or religious dissidents. *"Even if one should accept the diagnosis of sluggish schizophrenia in these and similar cases," Chodoff said, "one must wonder why a disease without delusions, hallucinations or agitated behavior should require injections of chlorpromazine (an antischizophrenic drug) for its treatment."* Science News 9/10/77, p165 *There are no clinical symptoms for 'sluggish schizophrenia', as it is known, but one of its symptoms is described as a paranoid delusion about reforming society.* Listener 7/20/78, p70 **[1977,** translation of Russian *stértaya shizofreníya*]

slumism, *n. U.S.* the existence or proliferation of city slums. *We must show the same unhesitating commitment to fighting slumism, poverty, ignorance, prejudice, and unemployment that we show to fighting Communism.* Harper's 2/67, p83 **[1967]**

slumlord, *n. U.S.* the landlord of a neglected or abandoned building in the slums of a city. *There are rent strikes against slumlords who refuse to repair Negro tenements.* Time 8/30/63, p12 *Prosecution of slumlords is ineffective.* NY Times 1/27/65, p31 **[1953]**

slumlordship, *n. U.S.* the condition of being a slumlord. *Within the chivalric order of slumlordship he is a very minor vassal. He owns two buildings on the Lower East Side, both nearly a hundred years old; they are separated by many blocks of slums . . .* Atlantic 11/66, p128 **[1966]**

slumpflation, *n. Economics.* a condition of unemployment and business decline accompanied by increasing inflation. Also called INFLUMP. Compare HESIFLATION. *The downturn was aptly described by such words as "inflationary recession," "stagflation," or even "slumpflation"—words coined to recognize not just that inflation coexisted with recession, stagnation, or slump, but that inflation brought about such conditions.* Britannica Book of the Year 1975, p251 *The $16 billion in rebates and tax credits might be too weak to jolt the economy out of its alarming slumpflation.* Time 1/27/75, p13 **[1975,** from *slump* + *inflation*]

slurb, *n. Especially U.S.* an unsightly area on the outskirts of a large city, that has been developed with cheap housing, often indiscriminately built among gas stations, used-car lots, diners, etc. . . . *the term "slurb" was coined in California to describe sleazy, sprawling subdivisions.* Time 2/2/70, p59 . . . *cities so choked and "slurbs" so ugly that by comparison the New York-Washington corridor looks almost like a planned development.* NY Times 11/30/70, p41 **[1962,** formed from *sl-* (as in *sleazy, slovenly,* etc.) + *urb*an, but now reinterpreted as if from *slum* + sub*urb* or URB]

SM, abbreviation of SERVICE MODULE. *The service module (SM) contains the main spacecraft propulsion system and supplies most of the spacecraft's consumables (oxygen, water, propellant, hydrogen). It is not manned.* Encyclopedia Science Supplement (Grolier) 1969, p321 **[1965]**

S-M or **s-m,** abbreviation of: **1** sadomasochism. *The taboo currently under the heaviest assault is sado-masochism—sexual pleasure derived from dominating and inflicting pain on a partner or from being hurt. Porn-film makers long avoided "S-M," as it is known in the trade, because they were convinced that it would drive away customers.* Time 4/5/76, p61 **2** sadomasochist. *"The Story of O" is even more self-defeating: It's a softcore film that reduces the S-M sex of Pauline Reage's novel to a series of anguished facial close-ups.* New York Post 11/29/75, p40 **[1966]** Compare S AND M.

smack, *n. U.S. Slang.* heroin. *"I started taking smack and barbiturates."* Harper's 6/70, p79 *Countered a bearded pusher:*

"Buy one tab of acid and get a free tab of smack!" Time 8/10/70, p11 [**1960,** earlier "a small packet of drugs" (1942)]

smackhead, *n. U.S. Slang.* a user or addict of heroin. *It includes an imbecilic meeting of narcotic agents . . . and a macabre, incredibly funny conversation with a Georgia cop, who is warned of a smackhead migration to his state because they like warm weather.* NY Times Book Review 7/23/72, p17 [**1972,** from SMACK + HEAD]

smart, *adj.* **1** *U.S. Military Slang.* guided to a target by sophisticated sensor devices. *Such projectiles—the Army has named them "smart rounds," after the "smart bombs" used in the air war against North Vietnam—would carry a sensor device (infrared or electromagnetic) which could "lock on" to a target by "reading" its "signature," and correct the trajectory of a shell so that it lands on target.* Nation 1/26/74, p108 *Thousands of so-called "smart" weapons, guided bombs and antitank missiles, have been added to U.S. stockpiles overseas.* Manchester Guardian Weekly (Washington Post section) 3/13/77, p15 **2** capable of seemingly independent and rational action. Compare INTELLIGENT. *When smart traffic signals become ubiquitous . . . the cop at the intersection will become obsolete.* Scientific American 9/77, p188 [**1972**]

smart bomb, *U.S. Military Slang.* a bomb released from an aircraft and guided to a specific target by laser and television beams. *U.S. warplanes dropped laser-guided 2,000 pound "smart" bombs onto North Vietnam's only modern steel-producing facility, destroying that country's capacity to produce steel, U.S. headquarters announced today.* Daily News (New York) 6/26/72, p2 [**1972**]

smart card, a small identity card incorporating a microchip that can store extensive information about the bearer. *Experts agree that smart card technology combined with biometric measurements—finger prints, voice prints, retinal prints, something completely personal to the user of the card and impossible to alter—would provide a virtually fail-safe system. According to Smart Card Reports: "The primary advantage of these bioaccess systems is that they provide a positive user identification."* Financial Times 7/15/85, p21 [**1980**]

smarts, *n.pl.* Sometimes also *smart. U.S. and Canadian Slang.* good sense; intelligence; brains. Compare STREET-SMARTS. *Some failed simply because they just didn't have the smarts it takes to get into a U.S. medical school and stay in.* Tuscaloosa News (Alabama) 5/19/74, p4D *Mrs. Maynard said that Mr. Miller, a former West Virginia miner whom she has never met, lacks "backbone" and "doesn't have enough smart to run a union as big as the United Mine Workers."* NY Times 10/9/77, p26 *She also had the smarts, as did Shaver, to get a U.S. agency behind her.* Maclean's 11/13/78, p54 [**1968,** from *smart, adj.*]

smashball, *n.* a racquet game in which two or more players hit a ball back and forth with smashing force. *Smashball, a new racquet type game popular in Israel and Greece, comes to Central Park . . . The game resembles tennis without the bounce, court or net—or ping pong without the table.* New York Post 4/28/75 (page not known) [**1975**]

smog, *v.t.* to envelop in smog. *When we hear that Tokyo citizens are confined to their homes, that Los Angeles residents are smogged in, then we get worried.* Saturday Review 10/31/70, p32 *Furthermore, conventional geodesy depends on clear lines of sight, and in the Los Angeles basin these are often smogged out.* Science News 8/24-31/74, p136 [**1966,** verb use of the noun]

smogbound, *adj.* enveloped or surrounded by smog; covered with smog. *Smogbound, noise-deafened, misanthropic Londoners, who move out of the city to get more out of life, might be taking their high blood pressure with them.* New Scientist 1/1/70, p8 [**1970,** patterned after *fogbound*]

smogout, *n.* a condition of being completely enveloped by smog. *As these blackouts and smogouts and breakdowns continue to occur, with disastrous consequences to both the habitat and the human population, such a change may take place as*

was noted in London during the blitz . . . New Yorker 10/31/70, p96 [**1970,** patterned after *blackout*]

smoke and mirrors, manipulation or an obscuring of facts to achieve some desired result; deception. *He promised decisive action. But when he unveiled his "plan," it was all smoke and mirrors.* NY Times 2/23/89, pA23 [**1988**]

smoke detector, a device sensitive to smoke, used to warn people of a fire by making a loud sound when smoke enters its vents. It is usually encased in plastic and attached to a wall or ceiling. *Smoke detectors work either through photoelectric cells or an ionization device, but fire officials generally agree that there is minimal difference in effectiveness between the two.* Time 1/10/77, p36 [**1957,** 1977]

smoke-in, *n.* a gathering to smoke marijuana or hashish, sometimes as a demonstration for legalizing their use. *At rock festivals like Woodstock, at demonstrations like the November moratorium or July smoke-in, you make friends . . .* Manchester Guardian Weekly 10/31/70, p24 *Gone are the big smoke-ins punctuated by acid rock and strobe lights.* Time 2/22/71, p17 [**1968;** see -IN]

smoke pollution, tobacco smoke regarded as a pollutant. *To determine how much nicotine nonsmokers absorb from smoke pollution, the investigators did two series of experiments on 39 urban nonsmokers.* International Herald-Tribune 2/4/75, p3 [**1975**]

smokeshade, *n.* **1** the measure of the relative amounts of black, gray, and white particle pollutants in the atmosphere. . . . *an air pollution alert is called for when carbon monoxide readings of 10 parts per million last for four hours, coupled with high four-hour readings for either sulphur dioxide or smokeshade, a measurement of particulates in the air.* NY Times 2/9/67, p29 **2** the pollutant particles themselves. . . . *a heavy layer of dead air—a coagulated cloud of carbon monoxide from automobile exhausts, sulphur dioxide, and smokeshade (the scientists' word for visible atmospheric dirt)—spread out over the city and hovered there for days.* New Yorker 5/15/71, p117 [**1967**]

smokestack, *adj.* of or relating to heavy industry associated with the burning of coal, as in making steel or machinery. *If the stock market is any indicator, the prospects for Kennecott, as with most "smokestack" companies, are dim.* Time 4/10/78, p83 [**1976**]

Smokey or **smokey,** *n.* Also spelled **Smokey Bear.** *U.S. Slang.* a policeman or a state trooper, especially one who patrols a highway. *C.B.-ers with their colorful pseudonyms and jargon may warn of Smokey's presence—but in hundreds of instances they have helped the police catch drunken and hit and run drivers and have sped ambulances to accident scenes.* NY Times 3/7/76, pC5 *Once limited to truckers and their Smokey Bear antagonists on highway patrols, Citizens Band radio has grown to the point where about 20 million American "good buddies" have CB rigs in their cars or homes.* Time 1/23/78, p66 [**1974,** so called from the resemblance of some state troopers' wide-brimmed hats to the forest-ranger hat worn by *Smokey (the) bear,* an animal character warning against forest fires in signs of the U.S. Forest Service]

smoking gun or **smoking pistol,** a piece of definitive, indisputable evidence, especially of a crime. *It was not clear, however, whether these new allegations were what had persuaded Ribicoff and Percy to call for Lance's resignation. In fact, there may well be no "smoking gun"—no incontrovertible, black-and-white evidence of wrongdoing by Lance.* Time 11/19/77, p8 [**1974,** in allusion to the crime-fiction stereotype of a person found at the scene of a crime holding a recently fired, still smoking gun] ▶This usage arose during the Watergate affair, when evidence among the White House tapes and papers was sought to show conclusively that the President was involved in the Watergate cover-up.

SMSA, abbreviation of *Standard Metropolitan Statistical Area* (official designation of a metropolitan area in the United States). *An SMSA consists of a city of 50,000 or more and the county in which it is located, plus adjoining counties that meet* certain criteria of metropolitan character and are closely integrated with the central city, as through commuting, for example. (In New England, the basic units are towns rather than counties.) Science 5/19/72, p777 *Changes in the definition of "standard metropolitan statistical area" (SMSA), by which U.S. urban areas are outlined, were ordered on April 27 by the Office of Management and Budget. The changes added to, subtracted from, or merged various densely populated areas. As a result, 26 new areas were designated as SMSA's, 12 existing SMSA's were merged into 6 new ones, and several other SMSA's were expanded.* 1974 World Book Year Book, p259 [**1966**]

snail darter, a species of small perch that feeds on snails, discovered in the Tennessee River in 1973 and unknown elsewhere. *The 3-in-long snail darter is exerting an influence far out of proportion to its size. In June the U.S. Supreme Court stopped construction of the $116 million Tellico Dam because it would wipe out the diminutive fish, thereby violating the 1973 Endangered Species Act. Now the snail darter is endangering the very law that protected it.* Time 10/16/78, p84 [**1975**]

snake, *n.* Usually, **the snake.** a system of jointly floated currencies whose exchange rates are allowed to fluctuate within narrow limits against each other but within a wider margin against other currencies, established in 1972 by France, West Germany, Belgium, the Netherlands, Luxembourg, Norway, Sweden, and Denmark. Compare JOINT FLOAT. *The country [Sweden] also pulled out of the European monetary "snake," the collection of currencies tied to the West German mark, because Stockholm wanted to devalue the krona much more than snake rules allow. Because their economies are closely tied to Sweden's, Denmark and Norway felt obliged to devalue their own currencies by 5%, but neither followed Sweden out of the snake.* Time 9/12/77, p49 *The latest intention is that the snake (which is an arrangement by which all the member currencies are linked to each other) should be equipped with a warning system capable of identifying which currencies are responsible for undue fluctuations within the system.* Manchester Guardian Weekly 10/29/78, p10 [**1972**, shortened from *snake in the tunnel,* a name for this system derived from the graphic representation of the narrow fluctuations allowed between the jointly floated currencies that supposedly resembled a wriggling *snake,* as compared to the wider band of fluctuations permitted against other currencies of the world that supposedly resembled a *tunnel*]

snarl-up, *n.* a confusion; mix-up. *Freight business is healthier, but still recovering from nightmare snarl-ups that followed the merger three years ago.* Times (London) 2/12/70, p25 *"Beverly, was that an F and G in your part?" Conductor Aldo Ceccato once asked during a snarl-up in a recording session.* Time 11/22/71, p58 [**1960**]

snatch squad, *British.* a special detachment of soldiers assigned to help quell a riot or disturbance by seizing the most conspicuous offenders. *After two hours the Army sent snatch squads into the area to bring out trouble makers and a platoon with riot shields and clubs moved in to dismantle a temporary barricade.* Times (London) 8/5/70, p1 [**1970**]

SNG, abbreviation of *synthetic* (or *substitute*) *natural gas. Shortage of natural gas in the US now makes it necessary for that country to rely on SNG in future as a valuable energy source.* New Scientist 9/20/73, p680 [**1972**]

snob zoning, *U.S.* the use of zoning requirements (such as "one acre per house") to keep poor or less affluent people from purchasing property, especially in the suburbs. Compare REDLINING. *Also, court actions were initiated in some suburban communities to prevent the use of "snob zoning" to exclude "low-income families."* Americana Annual 1973, p337 [**1956,** 1973]

snofari (snou'fɑri:), *n.* an expedition into a polar or other snow- or ice-covered area, usually in skidoos. . . . *the short period we have been here has brought us the experience of a new kind of mountain recreation, the snofari. Tricked out like spacemen . . . we were each equipped with a kind of bobsleigh fitted with skis fore and caterpillar tracks aft and dispatched into the*

mountains. Times (London) 12/12/70, p5 [**1970,** from *snow* + sa*fari*]

snopes (snoups), *n. U.S.* an unscrupulous type of businessman or politician, especially of the southern United States. *In the heated circumstances of the present* [opposition to the nomination of Judge Harrold Carswell to the Supreme Court] *Mr. Nixon would be joining the yahoos and the snopeses.* Times (London) 4/10/70, p10 [**1962,** named after the *Snopes* family of vicious characters in the novels of William Faulkner]

snort, *n. Slang.* **1** an act of inhaling a narcotic through the nostrils. Compare TOOT. *"Everyone assumed it was coke." In fact, it was "China White" heroin. Those who sniffed became ill . . . Cher, who didn't take a snort, is credited with saving Bassist Alan Gorrie's life by walking him around all night, preventing him from lapsing into a coma.* Time 3/3/75, p49 **2** the narcotic inhaled. *At night, the whores and pimps and pushers take over . . . Want a fix? A snort (cocaine)? A smoke?* Listener 9/6/73, p304 [**1973**]

Snowbelt, *n.* the northern region of the continental United States extending east to west. Also called FROSTBELT. *Snowbelt representatives contended time after time that their region was being shortchanged. They said that the formulas were originally drawn when the Sunbelt was poor and the Snowbelt was rich.* NY Times 9/28/77, p75 [**1977,** patterned after *Sunbelt;* compare earlier *snowbelt* a region of heavy snowfalls (OEDS 1874)]

snowboard, *n.* a long, narrow board somewhat like a ski, used for riding or racing over snow. *"Once people get onto the snowboard they just fall in love with it," said Thomas J. Hsieh, Jr., editor of the International Snowboard Association magazine.* Yonkers Herald-Statesman 1/24/88, p2 [**1987**]

snowmobiler, *n. U.S.* a person who rides a snowmobile (a vehicle for traveling on snow), especially as a sport. *Snowmobilers have been accused of everything from terrorizing wildlife to vandalizing hunters' cabins.* Time 3/15/71, p62 [**1968,** from *snowmobile* (OEDS 1931) + *-er*]

snowmobiling, *n. U.S.* the act or sport of riding a snowmobile. *. . . unless you simply can't stand snow in any form, you really ought to try snowmobiling. It's a lot more thrilling than skating and less hazardous than skiing.* Maclean's 12/68, p37 [**1964**]

snuff film, a pornographic motion picture that culminates in the actual murder of a woman. *FBI agents are now zeroing in on two specific "snuff" films they believe may portray the grisly death of pretty Philadelphia English teacher Susan Reinert . . . The names of these two movies are "After Satan" and "The Satan Cult." The supposed snuff films may show people involved in her killing and perhaps the killing itself, officials believe.* New York Post 9/17/79, p15 [**1975,** from "*snuff* out" to extinguish, kill]

snurfing ('snərfiŋ), *n.* the act or sport of riding on a special board over snow. See the quotation for details. *Snow surfing (or "snurfing") through deep powder is all the rage in Utah, where two snurfers have invented the "Winterstick," a 5-foot-long, 14-inch-wide foam-cored plastic board with three small "skegs," or fins, on the underside like a surfboard. To prevent the board from running amok when the rider falls off, a safety rope is attached to the back. The snurfer hooks his feet under a strap on top, stands sideways on the board, grasps the safety line and banks off down the hill, blanketed in a powdery cloud of snow.* Newsweek 2/3/75, p69 [**1970,** blend of *snow* and *surfing*]

soaper, *n. U.S. Slang.* variant of SOPOR. *Many students here have been frantically doing soapers for more than a year, knowing little about the dangers and caring only that the pills are a great way to get loose. I appreciate TIME's report of the frightening results of methaqualone abuse.* Time 3/26/73, pK2 [**1972**]

soca ('soukə), *n.* a combination of soul and calypso music. *When he was a teen-ager, all his friends danced to the same records of Caribbean music, American soul and funk, and British rock, no matter what their ethnic backgrounds were, and Mr. Grant* *absorbed all these influences. His own music has always been cosmopolitan, and his sharp ear for rhythm has enabled him to fuse funk, reggae, West African rhythms, and the soca (soul-calypso) beat of the British West Indies into a rhythmic dialect of his own.* NY Times 3/30/83, pC27 [**1978,** from *soul* + *calypso*]

social contract, an agreement between labor unions and government in which the unions limit their demands for wage increases in exchange for economic and social policies favorable to workers. *The relative labor peace has been achieved only because the* [British] *Labor government's "social contract" with the all-powerful unions is still holding. The unions continue to accept, albeit grudgingly, the government's ceiling of a maximum 6-pound pay increase.* Wall Street Journal 11/12/76, p12 [**1974**] ►The term was introduced in Great Britain in 1974 by Prime Minister Harold Wilson, apparently echoing the 18th-century phrase for the agreement forming the basis of human society according to Rousseau's *Contrat Social* (1762).

sociobiology, *n.* the study of the biological basis of social behavior, especially as such behavior is transmitted genetically. *These models ascribe social behavior to a kind of genetic imperative—that is, behavior of individuals evolves so as to maximize their genetic contribution to the next generation. This far-reaching notion is the basis of an emerging field of inquiry known as sociobiology, which seems to be having an impact on the design of field studies of animal behavior and is also attracting the attention of social scientists as well as stirring up controversy among them.* Science 1/10/75, p50 *Sociobiology purports to offer explanations of animal behavior, including human, in terms of survival strategies exploited by individuals within species. As things worked out at the Dahlem meeting, the term "naturalistic approach" in the conference task was effectively replaced by "sociobiology": the question, therefore, became, are moral norms simply part of a clever stratagem for getting us to behave in a way dictated by our genes?* New Scientist 12/15/77, p694 [**1975,** popularized by the book *Sociobiology: The New Synthesis* (1975) by the American zoologist Edward O. Wilson; the term was used earlier (OEDS 1943) in specialized contexts and later (about 1950) in the general sense of the study of society according to the concepts and methods of biology] ►In the current sense of the term, the apparent assumption that social behavior among all animals, including human beings, can be genetically transmitted and be subject to biological evolution, has stirred controversy. —**sociobiological,** *adj.: Sociobiological theories of altruism have been applied to primate behavior by Richard Alexander of the University of Michigan in Ann Arbor and by others.* Science 1/10/75, p50 —**sociobiologist,** *n.: Some sociobiologists go so far as to suggest that there may be human genes for such behavior as conformism, homosexuality and spite. Carried to an extreme, sociobiology holds that all forms of life exist solely to serve the purposes of DNA, the coded master molecule that determines the nature of all organisms and is the stuff of genes.* Time 8/1/77, p54

socioecology, *n.* social grouping or organization as related to or influenced by the environment. *The comparative study of the ecology and behaviour of pachyderms is not only interesting, but also instructive, because it can contribute to a broader understanding of mammalian socioecology in the same way that studies of other groups such as primates and antelopes have done.* New Scientist 9/15/77, p658 [**1972,** from *socio-* social, of society + *ecology*]

sociologese, *n.* the jargon of sociologists. *The outcome is about 200 tables, some of them positive cadenzas of sociologese, eg: "Attitudes towards university expansion by degree of apprehension, within categories of political position per cent."* Manchester Guardian Weekly 5/22/71, p13 [**1963,** from *sociology* + *-ese* language, jargon]

soda-pop wine, variant of POP WINE. *The cultural forces that produced this band of celebrants have lately included a merchandising milestone—the development of what are sometimes called "soda-pop wines."* New Yorker 5/20/72, p102 [**1972**]

soft-core, *adj.* simulating or suggesting sexual acts; not graphic or explicit in presenting erotic activity. Compare HARD-CORE.

It is soft-core pornography which represents the true degradation of sex. And also its maximum exploitation; since the teasing and the taunting is interminable, and because it never delivers the goods, the customers can be strung out for years, going to film after film, hoping this time to see a little more than the last time. Maclean's 7/74, p58 —*n.* Also spelled **soft core.** soft-core pornography. *Attempts to retract into soft-core, like Deep Throat II, in which the explicit scenes are all off-camera, have failed.* Time 5/13/74, p99 . . . *Dennis Hopper (Adult) Publications churn out soft-core for hard men.* New Statesman 7/4/75, p30 [**1966,** for adj.; **1973** for noun; patterned after *hard-core*]

soft-dock, *v.i.* to join orbiting spacecraft without a mechanical coupling, as by nylon line, etc. Compare HARD-DOCK. *The astronauts soft-docked with the station, took a dinner break and planned their method of attack.* Science News 6/2/73, p352 [**1973**]

soft drug, any drug that is not considered physically addictive, such as marijuana, mescaline, and various amphetamines. Compare HARD DRUG. *Although there was no doubt about the deleterious effects of hard drugs (heroin, morphine, etc.), there was much debate concerning the harmful effects of the softer drugs, such as marijuana.* 1971 Britannica Yearbook of Science and the Future, p233 [**1959**]

soft energy, energy derived from SOFT TECHNOLOGY. *Naturally enough, the book concentrates on soft energy technologies. There are sections on: tools, invention, solar, wind, transport, steam, biofuels, building, and integrated systems. Biofuels, for example, covers, among other things, methane makers and wood stoves.* New Scientist 10/12/78, pxviii [**1977**]

soft-land, *v.t.* to land (a spacecraft, instruments, etc.) slowly so as to avoid serious damage. *The four "feet" of the vehicle scheduled to soft-land two U.S. astronauts on the moon . . . received a patent from the U.S. Patent Office.* Science News Letter 4/17/65, p254 —*v.i.* to make a soft landing. *On May 30 the National Aeronautics and Space Administration (NASA) launched the Surveyor I spacecraft on a mission to soft-land on the moon and photograph its surface.* 1967 Compton Yearbook, p353 —*n.* a soft landing. *If instruments are to be soft-landed on Mars using parachutes, it is important that the density of the atmosphere is sufficient to allow the parachute to act. Soft-lands in bright areas—the lowlands—are therefore easier from an engineering point of view.* Times (London) 4/8/68, p7 [**1960,** back formation from *soft landing*]

soft-lander, *n.* a spacecraft designed to make a soft landing. Compare LANDER. *The same method applied to the lunar soft-lander Luna 9 enabled the Jodrell Bank observers to study its velocity changes during approach . . .* New Scientist 10/20/66, p73 *The calendar for unmanned flights seems set, though not all of the programs are funded. These include . . . two Mars soft landers . . .* Science News 7/25/70, p53 [**1962**]

soft landing, 1 a slow landing of a spacecraft to avoid damaging the spacecraft or its payload. *The flight came just "at the right time for lunar launches, consistent with other Soviet lunar launches for a soft landing or orbital mission" . . .* Science News 12/2/67, p535 **2** *U.S. Economics.* a slowing down of the rate of economic growth without causing a recession or high unemployment. *According to White House economists, it now looks as if the third-quarter real-growth rate of the gross national product will be almost exactly the 4 per cent a year that the Administration has been looking for. "That is right on the button for an at least temporary soft landing," said one.* Newsweek 10/15/73, p86 *Public Service Jobs—Going slow on those easily given commitments for federal funds to provide public service jobs at the local level as insurance for a "soft landing" against the recessionary consequences of the money squeeze would be prudent politically as well as fiscally.* Tuscaloosa News (Alabama) 9/15/74, p38 [**1958** for def. 1; **1973** for def. 2]

soft lens, a contact lens made of a porous plastic that becomes soft when it absorbs the moisture of the eyes. Also called HYDROPHILIC. *"I intend using the soft lenses on every patient I possibly can," said Dr. Mary Young, who maintains a 3,000-*

patient-a-year optometrical practice in Braintree, Mass. Time 5/31/71, p46 **[1964]**

soft line, a moderate, flexible attitude or policy, especially in politics. Compare HARD LINE. *The US, Britain and the Benelux trio tend to adopt a "hard" line, favouring the removal of the Atlantic Council from Paris, even though France has not requested this. But Canada, Norway, Denmark and Italy prefer a "soft" line and want to leave the Council where it is to minimise the rupture with France.* Sunday Times (London) 6/5/66, p4 **[1966]**

soft-liner, *n.* a person who adopts or follows a soft line. Compare HARD-LINER. *When a reporter asked Kissinger last week if he would characterize himself as a hard- or soft-liner, he replied: "I have tried to avoid labels like 'hard' or 'soft.'"* Time 12/13/68, p16 **[1967]**

soft path, the method or approach of SOFT TECHNOLOGY. *By following the soft path, a smooth transition would be made from the era of oil and gas to an era of renewable energy sources—sun, wind, tides, streams, and liquid fuels derived from vegetation.* Britannica Book of the Year 1978, p143 **[1977]**

soft porn, soft-core pornography. Compare HARD PORN. *The mystery deepens when it comes to the soft porn which sweeps in rivers of flesh along the edges of the pavements on a fine day.* New Statesman 3/21/75, p361 **[1974]**

soft rock, a low-keyed, rhythmically free, sophisticated form of rock music. *His songs delve ingeniously into hard and soft rock, blues, gospel, even country rock . . .* Time 1/11/71, p40 *Some soft-rock groups—the Association, the 5th Dimension, Simon & Garfunkel—have invaded the middle-of-the-road market themselves.* Harper's 9/69, p24 **[1969]**

soft science, any of the social or behavioral sciences, such as political science, economics, sociology, and psychology. Compare HARD SCIENCE. *One may define technology to mean political technique as well as nuts and bolts; that is, the soft sciences along with the hard.* Atlantic 10/71, p91 **[1966]**

soft sculpture, a sculpture made out of cloth, plastic, foam rubber, or other soft, pliable material. *The most noted creator of soft sculpture, Claes Oldenburg, was similarly honored* [with a retrospective] *at the Museum of Modern Art, New York.* Americana Annual 1970, p99 **[1969]**

soft technology, a form of technology that relies on solar power, wind power, and the like, instead of on large, costly machinery; APPROPRIATE TECHNOLOGY. *The term "soft technology" was coined amid the British counter-culture . . . Technology which is soft is gentle on its surroundings, responds to it, incorporates it, feeds it. A nuclear power-generation station doesn't qualify. A wooden windmill with cloth sails grinding local grain does.* Harper's 4/74, p6 *Another example would be underground architecture. I may be biased in being particularly interested in the innovative end of things. But it seems to be energy-saving, it seems to be material-saving, and these are things that supposedly make soft technology good.* Psychology Today 11/78, p73 **[1973]**

software, *n.* **1** the designs, instructions, routines, etc., required for the operation of a computer or the performance of particular tasks by a computer. Compare HARDWARE, FIRMWARE, WETWARE. *Software is the general term used to describe various levels of the language of computer instructions; it includes compilers and assemblers, as well as application programs in high-level languages such as FORTRAN.* McGraw-Hill Yearbook of Science and Technology 1971, p58 **2** the plans, fuel, etc., of a rocket, missile, or other space vehicle. *The US government . . . procures goods and services with sophisticated technological components (e.g. weapons, rocket boosters and analytical "software").* New Scientist 6/25/64, p800 **3** anything thought of as not directly related to some operation, principal function, or objective, such as the nonmechanized elements of a mechanized system. *Generally speaking, standardization means persuading the several services to buy identical "software"—that is, the thousand and one everyday housekeeping items ranging from paint brushes to belt buckles*

that aren't directly related to combat efficiency. Wall Street Journal 8/23/65, p1 **[1960]**

SoHo ('sou,hou), *n.* an area of New York City, in lower Manhattan, noted as a center of avant-garde art, music, film, and fashion. Compare NOHO. *A tour of SoHo, the bustling neighborhood in downtown Manhattan, is a must for visitors who want a firsthand look at New York's famous art community. Much livelier than the Establishment art scene to be found along upper Madison Avenue, SoHo has live-in artists, low-rise buildings and ground floor or walk-up galleries.* NY Times 7/9/76, pC22 **[1973**, from its being situated South of Houston Street; name probably influenced by the *Soho* district in the West End of London]

sol (sal), *n.* a Martian day, consisting of 24 hours, 37 minutes, and 22 seconds. *The squat little lander seemed to get through its first sol (as the Martian day . . . is called) without any problems. The temperature at night sinks to about −127°F but warms up to a more comfortable −5°F when the sun comes up.* Times (London) 7/22/76, p1 *On sol 8—the eighth sol, or day, after the first of the Viking landers had touched down on Chryse Planitia, a great basin in the northern hemisphere of Mars—the craft's sampler arm extended straight out and then dropped to the ground.* New Yorker 2/5/79, p41 **[1976**, from Latin *sōl* the sun, since a Martian day represents one rotation of the planet with respect to the sun]

solar cell, a cell that converts the energy of sunlight into electrical energy. *These* [thermoelectric] *generators also compete with solar cells, which are widely employed for supplying electricity from sunlight in space vehicles.* Scientific American 6/64, p70 **[1962]**

solar collector, any of various devices that catch and store radiation of the sun for use in heating, producing electric power, etc. Also shortened to COLLECTOR. See FLATPLATE COLLECTOR. *The solar collectors placed on the south side of the house at an angle of 48° cover an area of 20 sq.m. Each collector contains 18 evacuated glass tubes about 1 m long and 7 cm in diameter, equipped with integrated heat reflectors.* New Scientist 8/14/75, p382 **[1955]**

solar farm, a large area with solar collectors for storing heat and converting them to electric power. *One technique . . . involves spreading a "solar farm," consisting of piping containing a mixture of chemicals, over 25 sq.mi. of desert. Heated by the sun, the mix would be used to make steam, which would power turbines.* Time 5/7/73, p49 **[1972]**

solar panel, a panel of solar cells. *Electrical energy was derived from sunlight by two solar panels unfolded by the astronauts from either side of the device, and the seismic package began radioing data back to earth.* Americana Annual 1970, p32 **[1964]**

solar pond, any of various devices consisting of long, flat containers filled with water to absorb radiation of the sun and convert it into heat. *"Still another example is the solar ponds of Israel, which . . . consist of large containers about a meter deep with black bottoms. The bottom half of the pond is filled with salt water, the top half with fresh. The black bottom absorbs solar radiation and heats the adjacent salty water.* Scientific American 6/71, p127 *A solar pond acts as a collector. However, it differs from other collectors in that the pond can also store heat energy.* David Crabbe and Richard McBride, The World Energy Book, 1978, p164 **[1961**, from the resemblance of such a device to a *pond*]

solar wind, a stream of charged particles emitted into space from the corona of the sun. Compare STELLAR WIND. *The speed of the solar wind as it passes the earth has been measured at several hundred kilometers per second.* 1969 Britannica Yearbook of Science and the Future, p66 *Dust in space would be expected to soak up gases from the solar wind, and also it may have gases entrapped during its formation.* McGraw-Hill Yearbook of Science and Technology 1969, p209 **[1958]**

soldier, *n. U.S. Underworld Slang.* another name for BUTTON MAN. *The Luchese family . . . was suspected of being in the narcotics traffic and because it had a large number of low-*

ranking members, called soldiers or button men, who might be induced to talk. NY Times 12/23/67, p11 **[1963]**

solid-state, *adj.* of, relating to, or based upon solid-state physics; using the conductive and other properties of solid materials. *The availability of solid-state devices has resulted in the introduction of a new line of equipment which supersedes older vacuum-tube versions to provide improved performance, increased reliability, smaller size, and in some cases lower cost.* McGraw-Hill Yearbook of Science and Technology 1969, p213 *Epitaxy, the oriented overgrowth of one crystal upon another, is of particular interest to solid-state scientists.* New Scientist and Science Journal 4/22/71, p193 **[1959]**

solid-state physicist, a specialist in solid-state physics. *In his studies, the solid-state physicist must have some means of knowing what compounds are likely to be semi-conducting if he makes them.* New Scientist 6/4/64, p595 **[1964]**

solid-state physics, a branch of physics dealing with the physical properties of solid materials, such as crystals, glasses, and polymers. *From the beginning of solid-state physics, infrared, ultraviolet, and X-rays provided important methods of probing the properties in solids.* 1972 Britannica Yearbook of Science and the Future, p321 *A satisfactory quantitative explanation of the heat capacities of solids was one of the earliest successes of solid-state physics.* Encyclopedia Science Supplement (Grolier) 1965, p228 **[1953]**

soliton, *n. Physics.* a quantum unit for a solitary wave of energy caused by a single disturbance. *Solitons themselves appear when exact solutions of the classical field equations are quantised. They actually represent new "particle states," and carry a quantum number called soliton number. Solitons have actually been around in solid state physics for some years, in the guise of nondispersive waves.* New Scientist 2/16/78, p435 **[1965,** from *solit*ary + *-on* elementary unit or particle]

solution set, *Mathematics.* the set which contains all the solutions to a mathematical sentence. *In current terminology the "solution set" of a false statement is not the null set but an element (member) of the null set, and since the null set has no members the statement is true of nothing.* Scientific American 6/71, p123 **[1959]**

somatomedin (ˌsoʊmətə'miːdɪn), *n.* a hormone secreted by the liver which promotes the action of the growth hormone somatotropin. *Growth hormone does not act directly on growing cartilage. It causes the liver to secrete another hormone: somatomedin. The somatomedin molecule is much smaller than the growth hormone molecule, but its structure is not yet known.* Scientific American 9/73, p42 **[1971,** from *somato*tropin + Late Latin *mediārī* to intervene, mediate + English *-in* (chemical suffix); because it modifies the action of somatotropin]

somatostatin, *n.* a hormone produced primarily in the hypothalamus that inhibits the release of various other hormones, especially those regulating growth of the body and glucagon and insulin production. See BRAIN HORMONE. *Before somatostatin, diabetes was viewed as a disease in which one hormone, insulin, was important: diabetes was described as a disease characterized by a shortage of insulin. Now it is known that two hormones are involved in diabetes. The second hormone is glucagon, produced by the pituitary—and the production of glucagon is regulated by the brain hormone, somatostatin.* Sunday News (New York) 6/22/75, p74 *Biologists in California have recently succeeded in making a synthetic gene for the human brain hormone somatostatin and inserting it into bacteria, where the hormone has been produced in milligram quantities.* Times (London) 11/16/77, p24 **[1973,** from *somato*tropin the growth hormone affected by this + *-stat* combining form meaning regulating, controlling + *-in* (chemical suffix)]

something, *n.* **something else,** *U.S. Slang.* something special. *Buterakos beamed at me. "The sound effects are going to be something else.". . . "Wait 'til you hear that thing," Buterakos said. "It'll make the golfers jump into the next county."* Harper's 5/71, p62 *There is something about cathedral building that men like, Henry said . . . the awe is so thick you could cut*

it with a knife. *"You are something else, Henry,"* Perpetua said. New Yorker 6/12/71, p42 **[1957]**

SOMPA ('sɑmpə), *n. U.S.* acronym for *System of Multicultural Pluralistic Assessment,* a system for testing intelligence of children by comparing the scores of children from similar social and cultural backgrounds to eliminate the bias in I.Q. tests ascribed to cultural differences. *The SOMPA technique would remove the "retarded" stigma from many children but leaves them in a position where they still need special educational attention but do not qualify for any funds.* NY Times 2/18/76, p28 **[1976]**

son et lumière (ˌsɔ̃ ei lY'myer), a dramatic spectacle using light effects, recorded music, and narrative, often held at a historic site. Compare SOUND-AND-LIGHT. *In this bicentennial year of Napoleon's birth . . . more than 200,000 tourists went to Corsica in 1969 to see the balls, costume pageants, and* son et lumière *(sound and light) presentations that marked the event.* 1970 World Book Year Book, p263 . . . *we turned into Central Park south of the Metropolitan Museum, whose façade was floodlit as if for a performance of* son et lumière. New Yorker 8/17/68, p21 **[1957,** from French, sound and light]

sonicate, *v.t.* to break up or disperse (any substance) by means of ultrasonic waves. Compare INSONIFY. *Ten milliliters of the swollen gel pellet, containing 25 to 50 mg of DNA, were placed in a rosette flask cooled by an ice-brine bath and were sonicated with a Biosonik II sonicator.* Science 1/17/75, p174 **—n.** a particle of a substance that has been sonicated. *After specified periods of culture, cells were collected by centrifugation . . . and disrupted by sonication in 1 ml of buffer appropriate for each enzyme assay. Enzyme activities of the lymphocyte sonicates were determined by radioisotopic assay methods as previously described.* Nature 1/17/75, p214 **[1960** for verb, **1958** for noun; both from ultra*sonic* + *-ate*] **—sonication,** *n.: Cleaning these parts is a major branch of ultraclean technology involving . . . the use of 'sonication'—ultrasonic vibration—to jar the dirt loose . . .* Science Journal 4/70, p42 **—sonicator,** *n.: The cells were brought to a volume of 0.35 to 0.5 ml and then sonicated for 3 minutes in an Insonator model 1000 sonicator (Savant Instruments).* Science 3/9/73, p1001

sonic guide or **Sonicguide,** *n.* an ultrasonic transmitting and receiving device mounted on eyeglasses, similar to radar, and enabling blind persons to sense objects ahead of them. [The] *statement that electronic aids such as the sonic guide have not been popular with blind adults and that only 5 per cent can use them is misleading. The sonic guide was extensively evaluated during 1971-72 when professional mobility specialists in New Zealand, Australia, the US, and England trained over 100 blind people to use them. Some 78 per cent declared that the benefits they derived from the "glasses" made the considerable trouble and personal expense of being trained away from home worthwhile.* New Scientist 6/23/77, p709 **[1977]**

sonogram, *n.* short for ULTRASONOGRAM. *A mother can now see her child in her womb three months after conception. The black-and-white picture, which is translated from ultrasound waves and is called a sonogram, appears on a small screen of what looks like a television set.* New Yorker 8/11/80, p21 **[1978]**

sonograph, *n.* short for ULTRASONOGRAPH. *There is a sonograph, with computer-added color, showing a six-month-old human fetus in utero . . .* NY Times Book Review 11/13/83, p48 **[1978]**

sonographer, *n.* short for ULTRASONOGRAPHER. *"In the past, ultrasound equipment was used mostly in obstetrics, but now it is being used in all departments of the hospital so the demand is greater than ever before,"* said Marveen Craig, executive director of the Society of Diagnostic Medical Sonographers in Dallas. *"In the next 10 years, there will probably be 35,000 sonographers, an increase of 20,000 from today."* NY Times 3/28/82, pD3 **[1978]**

sopor or **soper** ('soupər), *n. U.S. Slang.* a sedative and hypnotic sold as a white tablet; QUAALUDE. Also spelled SOAPER. *Methaqualone—known on the street as sopor or quaalude—is a nonbarbiturate hypnotic downer.* Science News 3/10/73, p152 *Methaqualone has become the sixth best-selling sedative in the U.S. on the legal market; in addition, a huge supply of the drug has been diverted to campus and street pushers, who have found an apparently insatiable market for the "sopers" (catchall slang for the several brands of methaqualone) at 25 to 50 cents a pill.* Newsweek 2/12/73, p65 [**1972**, from *Sopor*, a trademark for this drug]

sortie lab, sortie can, or **sortie module,** variant names for SPACELAB. *The nations also agreed to develop a space laboratory sometimes called the sortie lab, which will be placed into earth orbit in the cargo bay of the space shuttle, now being built by NASA.* Science News 8/11/73, p87 *NASA has offered Europe the "sortie can"—a pressurised laboratory module that is to swing out from the cargo bay of the orbiting shuttle.* New Scientist 7/6/72, p3 *The main part of what remains is the so-called sortie module—a 12-man passenger compartment which fits into the cargo bay of the orbiter.* Times (London) 7/7/72, p17 [**1972**] ►The origin and usage of *sortie* as the first element in these compounds is discussed in the following quotation: *The Americans . . . call it the sortie-can or sortie-lab because it will go for excursions into space and return to Earth after a week or so. When the proposal came last year that Europe should tackle this integral package of the overall shuttle programme it was referred to as the sortie-lab. Objections arose at once. In French, it was pointed out,* sortie *means to leave with no suggestion of return. The name for the Europeans was duly changed to the over-used and colourless "spacelab." But this in turn prompted mutterings notably from the non-French majority of ESRO* [European Space Research Organization] *staff who were heard to say that an "ascenseur" in French did not change its name when it changed direction.* New Scientist 6/14/73, p702

sots, *n.* a form of dissident Soviet art that satirizes the style of socialist realism. *Others, done in a sort of pop-art style the artists called "sots," made fun of socialist realism, the officially imposed genre of heroic optimism that dominates everything from propaganda posters to landscapes.* NY Times 10/31/77, p2 [**1976**, from Russian, short for *sotsialist* socialist (realism)]

soul, *n.* short for SOUL MUSIC. *Soul is the pop music of the urban Negro community. It is a commercialized, stylized form of the blues, born in little bars and nightclubs on the wrong side of town. It is music to entertain, dance music; corporal, not cerebral. It relies on repetition, rhythm, vitality, and particularly bombast for its appeal.* Saturday Review 10/26/68, p91 *It was British groups like the Beatles and the Rolling Stones, with their heavy and acknowledged debt to American soul and blues, who revitalized rock by getting back to its roots.* Time 9/28/70, p51 —**adj. 1** characterized by a deeply felt emotional or spiritual quality found in black music, art, etc.; characteristic of black culture. . . . *Sonny Charles, the organist, took over, singing with a soul appeal that caught up even this predominantly white audience.* NY Times 6/17/68, p46 . . . *they listened to Bob Dylan, recorded the words of soul songs and classical blues, read poetry.* New Yorker 3/16/68, p168 *With Hollywood scrambling to exploit every current trend, "soul" movies were probably inevitable.* Time 7/6/70, p70 **2** belonging to or owned by black people; black. *Long before "black capitalism" became a politically popular catch phrase, Negro-owned "soul banks" started sprouting in ghetto areas.* Time 2/28/69, p60 [**1961** for noun from earlier sense referring to the quality inherent in such music (1946); **1962** for adj.]

soul brother, *U.S.* a fellow black man. *"Black is feeling you'll really be free when they cast a soul brother in a deodorant commercial."* Time 4/6/70, p77 [**1968**]

soul food, *U.S.* food typically eaten by blacks, especially in the South. *Soul food may be said to embrace all the food created or developed over the centuries by the Negro cooks of the South . . . It embraces such obvious dishes as fried chicken, spareribs, black-eyed peas, candied yams, mustard, turnip and collard greens cooked for hours with salt pork or fat back . . . To some minds, however, the dishes that might be termed the most basic soul food are those made from the nonluxury parts of animals, particularly pork. These were the lesser cuts not generally cov-*

eted for the white man's table—pigs' feet called trotters, neck bones, pigs' ears, pigs' tails, hog maw and, the soul food to beat all, chitterlings. NY Times Magazine 11/3/68, p102 [**1964**]

soul music, a blend of rhythm and blues and gospel music, developed and popularized by black singers. *As the greatest living exponent of gospel music, one of the main sources of the currently fashionable soul music, she* [Mahalia Jackson] *should be assured of a sell-out . . .* Punch 5/14/69, px [**1961**]

soul sister, *U.S.* a fellow black woman. . . . *plate glass in Negro-owned establishments remained intact and displayed the words, "Soul Brother" or "Soul Sister."* NY Times 6/17/68, p24 [**1967**]

sound, *v.i., v.t. U.S. Slang.* Usually, **sound on.** to engage (someone) in SOUNDING. *Somebody can "sound on" somebody else by referring to a ritualized attribute of that person.* Rappin' and Stylin' Out (edited by Thomas Kochman), 1972, p274 *The game begins when one youth "sounds" another to see if he will play. That is done either by "signifying" . . . or by "the dozens."* Peter Farb, Word Play, 1974, p122 [**1962**]

sound-alike, *n.* some person or thing that sounds just like another. *And to Monsieur D—and Auguste D—and the other sound-alikes, we should add the name of D—Hoffman who is as personally implicated in this critical narrative as Poe was in his stories and verses.* American Scholar, Autumn, 1972, p683 [**1970**, patterned after *look-alike* (OEDS 1947)]

sound-and-light, *adj.* involving the combined use of light effects and recorded sound. Compare SON ET LUMIÈRE. *Dr. Robert E. L. Masters, 40, and Dr. Jean Houston, 31, use a variety of non-drug stimuli—guided meditation, multisensory sound-and-light environments, electrical stimulation of the brain—to induce "altered states of consciousness . . ."* Time 10/5/70, p72 *In the midst of . . . East Village* [Manhattan] *stands a five-story neighborhood landmark . . . called Central Plaza. Other landmarks surround it: the Hebrew Actors Union, . . . an ancient Ukrainian church . . . antique shops, art galleries, sound-and-light discotheques . . .* Harper's 3/67, p141 [**1960**] ►Originally this term was a translation of SON ET LUMIÈRE, as in the following quotation: *A "Sound and Light" program, using controlled light and recorded stereophonic sound, narrative and dialogue to give a dramatic presentation of history, was inaugurated at Independence National Historical Park, Philadelphia, on July 4, 1962, the first such program presented in the U.S.* Britannica Book of the Year 1963, p589 *During the 1960's, as the son et lumière technique was extended to other forms of entertainment and other applications, the English term acquired a broader meaning which was not correspondingly imposed on the French phrase.*

sound bite, a small piece of film or videotape that captures the highlight of a speech, scene, or event. *Shot and edited on video . . . the nightly news reduces speakers to pithy sound bites.* Vanity Fair 7/88, p22 *Print journalists . . . like to sneer at television coverage as a collection of inconsequential, sensationalistic, sloganeering sound bites.* NY Times Magazine 11/13/88, p26 [**1988**]

sounding, *n. U.S. Slang.* another name for SIGNIFYING. *Sounding involves the exchange of usually obscene insults and invective which might well, in other circumstances, lead to violence: in sounding, however, one fights with words rather than with fists.* New Scientist 5/4/78, p280 [**1962**]

sound pollution, excessive noise of motor vehicles, jet planes, machinery, etc., considered harmful to the environment. Also called AUDIO POLLUTION. *Sound pollution has been gaining increased attention and new regulations limit the amount of noise to which workers and the general public can be subjected. But concern so far has been concentrated on the nuisance value of noise one actually hears.* Science News 12/8/73, p361 [**1970**]

soundscape, *n.* range of sounds; musical panorama. *Here, intimations of the dark progressions in the 'Munich' fugue of the Second Quartet and the icy, grinding dissonances of* A Child of Our Time *combine in a semi-palindromic wartime sound-*

scape of a blasted and tragic grandeur . . . Listener 11/11/71, p666 [**1968,** from *sound* + *-scape* view, landscape, vista]

sound sculpture, a sculptured work made of metal rods or other material that can emit pleasant sounds. Compare LIGHT-SCULPTURE. *The most recent artist to put the mall to work is Liz Phillips, a young woman who specializes in "sound sculpture." Miss Phillips calls the sound sculpture in the mall "City Flow," and its special trick—it is, by the way, genuinely tricky—is the ability to translate the human traffic in the mall into electronic sounds that the passers-through hear.* New Yorker 4/18/77, p31 [**1970**]

soup, *n.* **1** a mixture of basic chemical elements. Compare PRIMORDIAL SOUP. *By now all the vital molecular building blocks necessary for the accident of life to happen have been synthesized in the laboratory from stimulated "soups".* New Scientist 4/10/69, p66 *The proposed guidelines had indicated that life probably arose from "a soup of amino-acid-like molecules" some 3,000,000,000 years ago . . .* 1972 Britannica Yearbook of Science and the Future, p342 **2** *Surfing Slang.* the foam or froth formed by a wave breaking on the beach. *To the surfer each breaker has a "hook," or crest, a "shoulder," the calm portion behind the hook, and a "shore break," the final surge ending in the inevitable "soup," or foam.* NY Times 8/10/65, p31 [**1956** for def. 1; **1962** for def. 2]

source, *v.i.* in journalism, to provide or identify the source of a report or story. *Nouns continue to be overrun by the jargonaut: the New York* Times *demands stronger sourcing, meetings are preambled, situations are impacted.* Time 1/28/80, p90 *—v.t.* in manufacturing, to acquire (parts for a vehicle, etc.) from a particular source. Compare OUTSOURCE. *Ford works on stripped-down cars . . . that could be sourced and assembled anywhere in Asia.* Wall Street Journal 2/24/72, p1 [**1976** for verb intransitive; **1972** for verb transitive]

South, *n.* the less industrialized, technically, and economically advanced countries of the world. Compare NORTH. *The turbulent years of the 1970s have witnessed an uneasy confrontation between the North and the South, and a largely unresolved debate on a whole series of specific economic problems. The truth of the matter is that the fortunes of the developed and developing countries are more and more intertwined in our increasingly interdependent world.* Newsweek 11/19/79, p144 [**1975,** so called because most of the less industrialized countries lie in the southern latitudes]

sovereignty-association, *n.* an economic union between sovereign states based on a common currency and the free movement of people and goods. *. . . 59.5 percent of Quebeckers voting in a provincial referendum refused to grant his government a mandate to negotiate with Ottawa for sovereignty-association. Under such an arrangement, strongly advocated by Lévesque, Quebec would be politically independent but retain economic ties with Canada. Lévesque himself said after the referendum that the people had voted to give Canadian federalism one more chance.* 1981 Collier's Encyclopedia Year Book, p445 [**1978,** translation of Canadian French *souveraineté-association*]

Sovietologist, *n.* another name for KREMLINOLOGIST. *The great debate among Sovietologists is whether lust for power or divergence of policy is the main cause of the perennial quarreling in the Kremlin.* New Yorker 4/28/66, p21 [**1958**]

Sovietology, *n.* another name for KREMLINOLOGY. *The resulting figures will thus be rather like Soviet production statistics and will presumably need a science like Sovietology for their interpretation.* Times (London) 12/24/65, p7 [**1958**]

spa, *n. U.S.* **1** another name for HOT TUB. *Unless bathers get out of the hot tub and replace the lost fluid, they will feel tired. Sometimes they faint . . . Perhaps lulled by the too warm water and a bit of alcohol, they probably fell asleep minutes after settling into the spa.* Time 6/18/79, p62 *Because of their small size, spas do not require as much energy or money to keep the water hot. In California, approximately $10 to $15 is required to heat a spa for an entire month.* Today (New York) 9/20/79, pB-1 **2** short for HEALTH SPA. *The new spa . . . may offer a pool, steam room, sauna, exercise equipment, massage*

room, and the like. American Speech, Spring-Summer 1975, p29 [**1974,** extended sense of the term for a mineral spring used for cures (OED 1626) or a watering place having such a spring (1777)]

space, *n. Slang.* a person's position, attitude, or identity. *"Lucas is a good friend to me," she was telling us now, back on the track. "I was part of his space. For a while there, I really felt like the favorite . . ."* New Yorker 5/7/79, p45 *Finally, I would note the metaphorical use of the word* space *itself, meaning, well, where a person's at. "Kate wasn't really high on chest hair . . . but Leonard had a lot going for him otherwise, and Kate liked the space he was in."* The State of the Language (edited by Leonard Michaels and Christopher Ricks), 1980, p511 [**1976**]

spaceborne, *adj.* **1** carried in or through space. *Loss of the eight satellites, each of which cost $1.5 million, stalled Department of Defense plans to double its spaceborne network of radio relay stations.* Science News 9/10/66, p176 **2** carried out in space or using spaceborne instruments. *In spite of considerable lobbying to make optical astronomy a space-borne science, many practising observers show little enthusiasm for the idea.* New Scientist 3/28/68, p680 [**1953**]

space cadet, *U.S. Slang.* a flighty, light-headed person. *Sophie's talking to Lucas, when Marie-Carmen arrives—the new one, one of those long, tall Argentine women who wear alpaca all the time but a true space cadet at heart.* New Yorker 5/7/79, p47 [**1979,** extended sense (probably influenced by SPACY and SPACED) of the term for an astronaut-in-training (OEDS 1952)]

space club, *Informal.* the group of nations that have launched a rocket into space. *India Joins the Space Club. On July 18, 1980 India joined the ranks of space-launching nations. An Indian-built solid-fuel rocket, 21 meters (70 feet) long, boosted a 35-kilogram (76-pound) Indian-built scientific satellite, designated Robini Research Satellite 1, into orbit.* Encyclopedia Science Supplement (Grolier) 1982, p5 [**1961**]

space colony, a self-contained, self-supporting colony for human inhabitants to be established on a large artificial satellite in space, especially at any of various points where the gravitational fields of the earth and the moon balance each other. *A growing number of lawyers and others have been urging that more attention be paid to the specialized legal problems that are likely to arise with increasing activity in space, such as in the possibly quasi-independent domains of future "space colonies."* Science News 12/17/77, p409 *The fundamental ideas about space colonies that make them different from other talk about space is that they would involve large numbers of people in an essentially inside-out manufactured planet, and extraterrestrial materials would be used to build these environments.* Psychology Today 11/78, p78 [**1974**]

spaced, *adj. U.S. and Canadian Slang.* **1** stupefied or dazed by a narcotic. *Quite a few people came from the West Coast, mostly from Big Sur, bringing scores of children with them to New York . . . For years they had been living in the hills with little more than their own minds to look at, taking lots of psychedelics in vast, empty spaces. They were spaced.* Harper's 6/73, p32 **2** stupefied; dazed. [J.] *Fred* [Muggs, the chimpanzee] *looked really spaced. Roy and Buddy . . . said he hadn't slept a wink all night.* New Yorker 3/31/75, p26 [**1969,** shortened from SPACED-OUT. Compare SPACY.]

spaced-out, *adj. U.S. Slang.* stupefied by the use of narcotic drugs. *To a relieved public it seemed impossible that the police could have taken Kasabian under their wing and concocted a case against her group—the most spaced-out and helpless bunch of hippies available—but it did not seem so to me.* Harper's 11/70, p56 [**1965**]

spacefaring, *adj.* traveling in outer space; engaged in or having to do with space travel. *My own view when I first heard about pulsars was that they were perfect interstellar navigation beacons, the sort of markers that an interstellar spacefaring society would want to place throughout the galaxy for time-and-space fixes for their voyages.* Science News 11/3/73, p283 *—n.* the act or practice of traveling in outer space; space travel. *The shape of things to come in US spacefaring for the next genera-*

tion depends on the outcome of these trials. New Scientist 7/21/77, p142 *In spacefaring we have found, for the taking, new realms for the human imagination. In the exploration and exploitation of space, these new realms . . . may not be infinite.* NY Times Magazine 1/29/78, p29 **[1959,** patterned after *seafaring*] **—spacefarer,** *n.: Such an asteroid-ark might one day encounter spacefarers of another civilisation, members of an intellectual brotherhood between the stars that at this moment exists without our knowledge.* New Scientist 6/27/74, p772

spacelab, *n.* a scientific laboratory in space, especially **Spacelab** (an orbiting space facility transported by space shuttle in a project of the European Space Research Organization). Compare SKYLAB. *Spacelab is carried to orbit by the shuttle orbiter. When it reaches the desired orbit, the shuttle's cargo bay doors are opened, Spacelab is checked out and prepared for its planned series of experiments. The module is connected to the orbiter so that it is an extension of the somewhat confined cabin, and forms a working area for the Spacelab crew.* New Scientist 2/28/74, p551 **[1966,** short for *space laboratory* (1960)]

spacer, *n.* a segment of DNA that serves to separate genes of a specific type from one another. *Chemists from Moscow University have succeeded in synthesising a nucleotide complementary to a definite part of a small bacteriophage ("a virus" that infects bacteria), a part regarded as a spacer. The spacer is short, occupying a space between two of the three genes contained in the virus, and has a known sequence of nucleotides.* New Scientist 5/9/74, p329 *For the production of a small molecule of RNA that resides in ribosomes . . . there are no less than 20,000 identical genes separated from each other by an inert DNA "spacer."* New Scientist 4/1/76, p4 **[1970]**

Spaceship Earth or **spaceship earth,** the planet Earth and its inhabitants, conceived of as a spacecraft with its passengers who depend on its limited resources to survive. *What may happen between now and then is that the world will stop thinking in terms of superpowers and more in terms of Spaceship Earth. Perhaps the massive problem of cleaning up our seas and oceans will make the superpowers realize that the global political power game is being overtaken by events.* Newsweek 1/1/73, p23 *We also demonstrate our respect for "spaceship earth," the concept of accepting that there are limitations on the world's resources and that their use is a matter of common international concern. The more enlightened oil exporters, by the way, endorse "spaceship earth" themselves.* Manchester Guardian Weekly (Washington Post section) 5/8/77, p17 **[1966,** popularized by R. Buckminster Fuller, 1895-1983, American designer and author, in his book (1969) *Operating Manual for Spaceship Earth*]

space shuttle, a reusable space vehicle that is launched into orbit like a rocket and lands on earth like an aircraft. Also shortened to SHUTTLE. *Unlike the cone-shaped Apollo vehicles, which are not maneuverable in the atmosphere, the space shuttle will be capable of controlling where and how it lands.* Science News 4/4/70, p343 *The space shuttle, as envisioned in 1970, was to consist of a completely reusable rocket-powered vehicle consisting of an orbiter and booster.* 1971 Britannica Yearbook of Science and the Future, p128 **[1969]**

space telescope, a telescope housed in an artificial satellite in space. *But even though it will escape the distorting miasma of the atmosphere, the space telescope will offer no advance in resolving power because its mirror will be small compared with earthbound telescopes.* NY Times 9/23/86, pC3 **[1960]**

space tug, a space vehicle for servicing and linking orbiting spacecraft and space stations. See the quotation for details. *The space tug would consist of two parts: a propulsion module, which, as currently envisioned, would be approximately 22 feet in diameter and 25 feet long; and, attached to the propulsion module, a manned compartment with space for three to six people.* 1972 Britannica Yearbook of Science and the Future, p31 **[1970]**

spacewalk, *n.* the act of moving in space outside a spacecraft. *The perspiration that shortened Astronaut Eugene Cernan's Gemini 9 spacewalk by fogging his faceplate could have been*

due to nerves instead of the heat of his exertions alone. Science News 6/25/66, p509 **[1965]**

spacewalker, *n.* a person who takes a spacewalk. *Major White, who became the first American spacewalker, was protected by the regular rubberized air tight nylon suit reinforced by nine additional layers and two visors.* NY Times 6/4/65, p29 **[1965]**

spacewalking, *n.* the action of a spacewalker. *Spacewalking, although vitally important to orbiting space stations and any other missions that require outside repairs, will not be a part of the lunar flight.* Science News 3/26/66, p195 **[1965]**

spacewoman, *n.* a woman astronaut. Compare COSMONETTE. *Valentina [Tereshkova], history's first spacewoman, is inspiring proof of the distances women have advanced in the secular world of the last hundred years . . .* Maclean's 11/16/63, p84 **[1962]**

spacy or **spacey,** *adj. Slang.* **1** dazed; stupefied; dreamy. *A flautist was performing before a couple of hundred students . . . some giving merely spacy attention, some with acute professional eyes on a colleague.* Atlantic 11/72, p55 *The myopically spacey Timothy Bottoms plays such characters as the gentlest and least harmful of the representative Americans in "The White Dawn"; he's frazzled, out of it, ineffective.* New Yorker 11/8/76, p139 **2** unconventional; eccentric. *Fiona Dean is 21 and comes from Basingstoke and she does strangely unalarming spacey clothes which actually look forward rather than sideways or back.* Times (London) 7/4/72, p15 *Her* [Elizabeth Ray's] *former boy friends generally describe her as nutty, spacy, neurotic or dim.* Time 6/7/76, p12 *The solution to what Quebec really wants, it turns out, is a unique relationship with the rest of Canada to be known as "sovereignty-association." Even in a country where one of the major parties insists on calling itself both Progressive and Conservative, this spacey concept ranks high in the lexicon of political absurdities.* Maclean's 11/13/78, p3 **[1971,** from *space* + *-y* (adj. suffix); influenced by SPACED-OUT] **—spaciness,** *n.: I remember the . . . appreciations of intimate spaciness that might later be explain'd and followed as the Crazy Wisdom of Rinzai Zen.* Saturday Review 12/2/72, p63

spaghetti western, *U.S. Slang.* a western (cowboy film about the American West) produced by the Italian movie industry. *As a swaggering bad buy in spaghetti westerns, Berger began to command fees that ran his annual income into six figures.* Time 4/5/71, p38 **[1969]**

Spanglish, *n.* a blend of Spanish and English spoken in parts of the western United States and Latin America. *The Spanish-English potpourri is generally called Spanglish. Purists, damning "imported barbarisms," deplore the "mongrelization" of the language of Old Castile.* NY Times 12/18/67, p8 **[1967]**

Spansule, *n.* a trademark for a capsule of tiny grains of medicine with varying thickness of inert coating that dissolve at different times to maintain a constant infusion of medicine into the body over the dosage period (commonly spelled **spansule**). *He swallowed a fifteen-milligram dextro-amphetamine-sulphate spansule with his coffee, looked briefly at his watch, and calculated the time span of his awareness.* Atlantic 1/69, p90 **[1954,** from *span* + *capsule*]

spare-part surgery, a branch of surgery dealing with the replacement of damaged organs, such as the heart, lungs, kidneys, and liver, either by transplantation or by the grafting of manufactured devices. *What surgeons in all fields of spare-part surgery needed was some way of switching off the immune reaction against their grafts without at the same time lowering the body's defences against genuinely harmful foreigners.* Annual Register of World Events in 1967, p387 **[1963]**

spatio-perceptual, *adj.* relating to or involving perception of the spatial properties (position, direction, size, form, distance) of objects. Compare VISUOSPATIAL. *Both the left and right hemispheres of the brain have been found to have their own specialized forms of intellect. The left, which controls the right side of the body, is highly verbal and mathematical, performing with analytic, symbolic, computerlike logic. The right, by contrast . . . performs with a synthetic, spatio-perceptual, and* *mechanical kind of information processing that cannot yet be simulated by computers.* Encyclopedia Science Supplement (Grolier) 1976, p53 [**1973**, from *spatio-* spatial + *perceptual*]

–speak, *Informal.* a combining form meaning the typical language, jargon, or vocabulary of (something specified), used to create many nonce words, such as: —**artspeak,** *n.: An Arts Council handout on the Chilean-born painter, Matta, reads: "he remains a kind of escaped surrealist convinced of the necessity for a new system in which the solidarity, the organical creative spirit and not just the competitive spirit, would constitute a link between men to reach a social satisfaction." Phew, artspeak.* Times (London) 9/21/77, p14 —**discospeak,** *n.: One of the biggest-selling singles of the past two months is a funked-up, 12-incher called* Rapper's Delight, *which features the ribald discospeak of three New Jerseyites who call themselves the Sugarhill Gang.* Maclean's 2/11/80, p32 —**Freudspeak,** *n.: In the Freudspeak of Psychobabble, "you're paranoid about missing the train" means little more than that you are a nervous traveller; and, speaking loosely, "I'm quite schizophrenic about whether to wear the green or the blue."* Vogue 4/84, p134 —**Olympspeak,** *n.: Crowds at the venues have been sparse to medium ("venue" in ordinary English is something you try to change if you face a richly deserved conviction in a court case, but in Olympspeak it is a place where an athletic contest is held).* Time 2/25/80, p31 —**splitspeak,** *n.: People magazine discussed "splitspeak," the vocabulary of separation, quoting Hollywood composer David Shire about his "very positive and loving separation" from his wife, Talia.* NY Times Magazine 1/20/80, p10 [**1960**, abstracted from such terms as *doublespeak, Newspeak,* coined by the English writer George Orwell (1903-1950) in his novel *1984*]

speakerphone, *n.* a telephone receiver that need not be held in the hand. *The Yellow Pages extol the advantages of the speakerphone for "hands free" telephoning, a facility much prized in kitchen and bathroom.* Punch 6/23/65, p912 [**1955**]

spear carrier, 1 a person of secondary or minor importance; an underling. *His closest lieutenants, not to mention assorted spear carriers, have gone to jail or are about to stand trial for the same set of offenses of which Nixon is accused.* National Review 8/30/74, p956 *Many of Sheehy's findings were indeed reported earlier by academics; where she does cite experts they tend to be introduced as mere spear carriers in her own pageant.* Time 5/10/76, p69 **2** the most active and important leader of a movement, party, or the like; a standardbearer. *No one went so far as to say that Agnew, the spear-carrier of the fall campaign, was as good as dumped with Connally coming on board, but the sly winks and smiles suggested it.* Harper's 8/71, p30 *In Wisconsin on the same day Representative Morris Udall, the "liberal-progressive" spear carrier, will have to win to stay in the race.* Times (London) 3/18/76, p10 [**1960** for def. 1, figurative use originally in allusion to stage extras or members of a chorus holding spears in the background; **1967** for def. 2, figurative use probably alluding to a military leader wielding a spear to rally forces]

spearing, *n.* **1** the illegal ramming of an opponent with the helmet in American football. *New rules for high school football in Pennsylvania call for automatic ejection for spearing, but coaches and players say referees either rarely see spearing or else fail to enforce the rule.* Time 11/20/78, p8 **2** the illegal jabbing of an opponent with a hockey stick. *Leafs were shorthanded through a spearing penalty to Kent Douglas . . . Hull responded by taking a pass from Balfour and scoring on a quick slap-shot.* Globe and Mail (Toronto) 1/21/63, p16 [**1963**]

Special Drawing Rights, a monetary reserve of the International Monetary Fund from which member nations may draw credit in proportion to their contribution to the Fund. *Abbreviation:* S.D.R. or S.D.R.s Also called PAPER GOLD. *There are now four assets that are counted as official monetary reserves: gold, dollars, pounds sterling and IMF credit positions. With the creation of Special Drawing Rights on the IMF, there will be five.* NY Times 7/11/68, p36 *. . . the governors for the great powers turned more and more, as the meeting progressed,*

to an existing facility of the I.M.F. called Special Drawing Rights . . . New Yorker 10/23/71, p128 [**1967**]

speciesism (ˈspiːʃiːˌzizəm), *n.* discrimination practiced by people against certain species of animals; the misuse or exploitation of various animal species by human beings. *The antivivisectionists accuse the scientists of "speciesism," which means that the scientists are indifferent to the suffering of any species but humankind. Animals should have the same rights as humans to avoid suffering, the animal lovers say. The scientists reply that the real issue is human suffering and that the net effect of antivivisectionist success will be to slow efforts to help people live longer and healthier.* Daily News (New York) 5/27/79, p59 [**1975**, coined by Richard D. Ryder, an American psychologist and author, from *species* + *-ism,* patterned after *racism, sexism*] —**speciesist,** *adj., n.: Paradoxically, the public tends to be "speciesist" in its reaction to animal experimentation: For many people, a test is permissible when it inflicts pain on a "lower" animal like a hamster, but not when the victim is a dog.* NY Times Magazine 12/31/78, p21 *Sexists and racists have been superseded by speciesists. The humane side of the question is put in* Animal's rights: a symposium, *edited by David Paterson and Richard D. Ryder (Centaur Press, £6.50).* New Scientist 5/10/79, p465

speckle interferometry, *Optics, Astronomy.* a method of recording and measuring extremely small displacements of an object by analyzing a series of images obtained when speckles of light reflected from the target object are photographed and combined into a single image. *The technique, which is known as speckle interferometry, can also be used to map local deformations in stressed mechanical parts such as the components of telescope mountings, seismometers, optical benches and similar devices.* Scientific American 2/72, p106 *The use of speckle interferometry now makes it possible to observe binary stars with separations nearly 10 times smaller than any previously observed. That corresponds to an increase in the volume of available space and number of stars by a factor of 1000.* New Scientist 4/27/78, p239 [**1970**]—**speckle interferogram:** *Astronomers can now use speckle interferograms of stellar objects to reconstruct a complete image of a star system, even when this is complex and unsymmetrical.* New Scientist 12/21-28/78, p932

spectinomycin, *n.* an antibiotic derived from a species of actinomycete, used especially against certain strains of gonorrhea that resist treatment by penicillin. *The only cure so far for the new strain is spectinomycin, a drug four times as costly as penicillin and hence not widely applicable in the Far East. But health officials are also concerned that a spectinomycin-resistant strain may develop if the drug is overused.* Maclean's 2/7/77, p54 [**1964**, from (*Streptomyces*) *spect*abilis, the actinomycete (soil bacterium) from which the drug is derived + *acti-*nomycete + *-mycin* fungal substance (ultimately from Greek *mýkēs* fungus)]

spectrin, *n.* a protein found in the membranes of red blood cells. *The two heaviest polypeptide components, with molecular weights of 255,000 and 220,000, are collectively known as spectrin.* (Vincent T. Marchesi of the Yale University School of Medicine chose the name because he first isolated the components from "ghosts," the membranes of red blood cells that have been chemically deprived of their hemoglobin.) *Spectrin accounts for about a third of all the protein in the red-cell membrane.* Scientific American 3/74, p27 [**1968**, from *spectre* (from Latin *spectrum*) + *-in*]

spectroheliometer, *n.* an instrument which measures the wavelengths of spectra from the sun. *The spectroheliometer showed that they* [bright points, many as big as the earth] *extended up from the chromosphere, where the temperature averages about ten thousand degrees, into the transition region between the chromosphere and the corona, where the temperature averages around seven hundred thousand degrees.* New Yorker 9/6/76, p40 [**1973**, probably from *spectro*scope + *heliometer*]

speed, *n. Slang.* methamphetamine, a stimulant drug. Also called METH. *Workers in The Trailer in Toronto's Yorkville Village . . . studied amphetamine abusers for nine months and ran into not only freaks shooting every day, but "weekenders"* *(spasmodic drug-takers) who needed "speed" to get through school and personal crises.* Times (London) 2/23/70, pIV *The user tends to be nervous . . . His hands tremble and he constantly scratches his nose and licks his lips. This is because the "speed" dries up the membranes of the nose and mouth, leaving an uncomfortable, itchy feeling.* Maclean's 11/68, p62 **[1967]**

speedball, *v.i. Slang.* to take a mixture of cocaine and another narcotic drug. *The comedian Richard Pryor introduced the outer world to freebasing a couple of years ago, and John Belushi died after he speed-balled (mixed heroin and cocaine).* Time 11/8/82, p91 **[1982,** verb use of the slang noun meaning a mixture of cocaine and another narcotic drug (OEDS 1909)]

speed bump, a low ridge laid across a road to slow down vehicular traffic in a residential area or near a school. Also called *(British)* SLEEPING POLICEMAN. *Anyone who has driven on the Hackley Campus knows that our roads are narrow. Speed bumps have been put in at various places around the Campus to help limit speed.* News From Hackley (Tarrytown, N.Y.) 11/77, p3 **[1975]**

speed-read, *v.t.* to read rapidly by taking in several words, phrases, or sentences at a glance. *I speed-read a detective novel and fall asleep by midnight.* New Yorker 6/19/71, p24 **[1960]**

speed-reader, *n.* a person who speed-reads. *The Evelyn Wood Reading Dynamics Institute . . . teaches prospective speed-readers to see every word on the page—but to read three words at once, not one word out of three.* NY Times 6/5/65, p22 **[1965]**

speed-reading, *n.* the act or practice of reading rapidly by the assimilation of several words, phrases, or sentences at a glance. *Speed reading has been adopted by many harried business executives and government officials as a cure-all for paperwork pile-ups.* NY Times 6/5/65, p22 **[1965]**

sperm bank, a place for the storage of sperm to be used in artificial insemination. *Today, sperm banks have virtually revolutionized A.I.D. [Artificial Insemination by Donor] practice. Since semen can be kept frozen for years without loss of genetic quality, one of the clumsier aspects of A.I.D.—the synchronizing of donor-recipient appointments—has been eliminated.* NY Times Magazine 4/18/76, p17 **[1963,** patterned after the older term *semen bank* (OEDS 1954)] **—sperm banking:** *Biologist Mark Lappé of the Institute of Society, Ethics and Life Sciences in Hastings-on-Hudson, New York, is disturbed that commercial outfits are the first to introduce large-scale sperm banking. If it is worthwhile, he says, the government should be taking the lead.* Science 4/7/72, p32

SPF, abbreviation of *sun protection factor,* a classification of the U.S. Food and Drug Administration of the degree to which a sun block or sunscreen will protect the skin from sunburn. *Low numbers are only for those people who tan easily and these products have an SPF of three to eight. They are not really suitable for high altitude sunlight. A really effective sun block cream is best and this has an SPF of 10 to 15.* Financial Times 2/19/83, p11 **[1978]**

spider hole, *Military use.* a hole in the ground concealing a sniper. *Later I watched as Sheridan tanks crashed into the rubber trees to flush out Vietcong and North Vietnamese hiding in spider holes and bunkers.* Times (London) 5/7/70, p6 **[1967]**

spike, *v.t., v.i.* to slam the ball forcefully to the ground after a play in American football, especially after scoring a touchdown. *Says Assistant Coach Gary Bruch: "We're out there five days a week trying to teach high school kids to be good sports, working on the right ways to tackle and block. Then they go home and watch television, and what do they see? Pro players dancing in the end zone and spiking the ball to humiliate opponents, spearing, taking cheap shots."* Time 11/20/78, p8 **[1978,** transferred sense of the volleyball term meaning to slam (the ball) into the opponent's court at a sharp, downward angle]

spin, *v.t., v.i.* **spin down** or **spin up,** *Astronomy.* (of a star, planet, etc.) to decrease or increase in rotation. *There's an unusual pulsar that spins extremely slowly. . . . This pulsar is spinning down so slowly that when the effects of its motion across the*

sky on its apparent (to us) spin rate are considered, it may actually be spinning up from the point of view of someone riding along with it. Science News 10/30/76, p280 *The gist of their thesis is that hydrodynamical coupling between the outer layers of the Sun and its core would pretty soon "spin down" the core to the same rate as the exterior—or the latter would alternatively be "spun up" to match the former.* New Scientist 6/29/67, p751 **—**n. U.S. Informal. a way of regarding something; slant; angle. *The White House aides are growing concerned that there may indeed be a fight tomorrow over the budget resolution, and they won't rule out the possibility that they might lose; they are even beginning to try to figure out what "spin" to put on it for the press in that event.* New Yorker 1/15/79, p73 **[1967** for verb (see SPIN-DOWN, SPIN-UP); **1979** for noun]

spinar ('spin,ar), *n.* a rapidly spinning galactic body. *Current theories of explosive galaxies like NGC 1275 envision compact nuclear regions composed of millions of pulsar-like objects, or else a giant spinar containing a mass equivalent to 100 million stars and rotating with a period as short as days or months.* Science News 3/27/71, p209 **[1971,** from *spin*ning st*ar,* after *pulsar, quasar*]

spin doctor, *U.S. Slang.* a press agent hired to interpret news events for public presentation. *The spin doctors came out after Reykjavik; the spin doctors came out after the "Iranian connection."* American Speech 1988, p263 *You have just been massaged . . .—and maybe had—by some savvy movie publicists, the spin doctors of the entertainment industry.* Time 11/21/88, p144 **[1986]**

spin-down, *n.* **1** a decrease in the rotation of a star, planet, etc. *The D pulsars may not be so old as they appear; they may have started with small magnetic fields and thus suffered less spin-down from magnetic breaking.* Science News 7/24/71, p62 **2** angular momentum of an elementary particle in a direction opposite to that of spin-up. *In another "hybrid" technique, beta-ray spectroscopy has been combined with Mössbauer-effect spectroscopy to study the magnetic hyperfine field acting on an iron nucleus. With this technique, it is possible to calculate the difference between the spin-up and spin-down populations in each electron shell.* McGraw-Hill Yearbook of Science and Technology 1973, p287 **[1967** for def. 1; **1963** for def. 2]

spin-flip, *n.* a reversal in the direction of the spin of a nuclear particle or particles (often used attributively). *Neutral hydrogen atoms emit 21-cm radiation by a somewhat unusual "spin-flip" process in which the spins of the hydrogen nucleus and its attendant electron switch from being parallel to antiparallel.* New Scientist 1/22/76, p170 **[1955]**

spin-flip laser, a laser in which the spin-flip of electrons is used to produce a highly monochromatic output. *In the spin-flip laser a spin resonance in a semiconductor—indium antimonide, for example—is used to achieve stimulated emission that can be tuned over a limited frequency range by changing an external magnetic field.* Science 2/18/72, p740 **[1971]**

spinoff, *n.* a secondary product or result of some activity; byproduct. *The vaccine is the result of a new type of ultra high-speed centrifuge that is a spinoff from atomic weapons work conducted here by the Atomic Energy Commission.* NY Times 2/28/68, p18 *A hundred and one new technologies may have burgeoned in the laboratories and assembly plants of the Cape Kennedy subcontractors, but the spin-off in human terms—in consumer fashions and design, politics and industrial relations, entertainment, and the arts—has been very nearly nil.* Manchester Guardian Weekly 12/5/70, p19 *Water pollution is among the most undesirable spinoffs of heavy industrialization and technological progress.* Science News Yearbook 1969, p278 **[1959]**

spinout, *n.* a spin causing a car to run off the road, especially when rounding a corner at high speed. *Also popular: decorative features such as racing stripes, special identifying fender emblems and "spoilers"—vertical flaps that put pressure on the rear wheels to prevent spinouts but are largely nonfunctional at highway speeds.* Time 4/5/68, p38 **[1957]**

spin-up, *n.* **1** an increase in the rotation of a star, planet, etc. Compare SPIN-DOWN. *As these models accrete mass from outside they actually spin faster, explaining the otherwise very embarrassing observation that both Cen X-3 and Her X-1 are undergoing spin-up.* New Scientist 8/30/73, p486 **2** angular momentum of an elementary particle in a direction opposite to that of spin-down. *The exchange field causes the 3d electrons to be split into two energy bands depending on spin: the spin-down band comes out with slightly higher upper and lower limits than the spin-up band.* New Scientist 8/17/78, p468 [**1969** for def. 1; **1965** for def. 2]

spiroplasma (ˌspaɪrəˈplæzmə), *n.* any of a group of disease-causing microorganisms having a spiral shape and lacking a cell wall. *The organisms associated with corn stunt disease, and subsequently those associated with stubborn disease of citrus, have been shown to be unusual helical motile microorganisms now termed spiroplasmas.* McGraw-Hill Yearbook of Science and Technology 1975, p325 *A third possible spiroplasma has been found in natural populations of four closely related species of Drosophila. This agent, termed the sex ratio organism (SRO), is inherited maternally and associated with the absence of males in the progeny of infected females.* Nature 1/15/76, p118 [**1973,** from New Latin, from *spiro-* coil (as in *spirochete*) + *plasma* protoplasm]

splanch (splæntʃ), *n. U.S.* a house that combines features of split-level and ranch type architecture. *He is supervising the construction of Carriage House of Roslyn. It is a suburban subdivision of 104 colonials, ranches and "splanches," a splanch being a cross between a split-level and a ranch house. All 104 houses were spoken for within weeks of the opening of the models last March.* NY Times 1/20/78, pA15 [**1961,** from *split-level + ranch*]

splash, *v.i.* **splash down,** to land in water, especially in the ocean, after a space flight. *The mission will be over, however, when the Apollo spacecraft plunges back through the atmosphere to splash down in the Pacific Ocean north west of Hawaii.* NY Times 4/4/68, p10 *The dramatic recovery of Gemini 9 astronauts who splashed down within two miles of the USS Wasp was witnessed as it happened by millions of television viewers both in the United States and abroad.* Science News 6/18/66, p484 [**1962**]

splashdown, *n.* the splashing down of a spacecraft. *Gemini 11 is to end its three-day mission with a splashdown in the Atlantic tomorrow morning.* Times (London) 9/15/66, p1 *The spacecraft will later dive back into earth's atmosphere at a speed of 25,000 miles an hour, the same velocity it would reach on a return trip from the moon. Splashdown is expected in the Pacific Ocean northwest of Hawaii.* NY Times 4/3/68, p7 [**1961**]

splib (splɪb *or, occasionally,* splɪv), *n. U.S. (Black English) Slang.* a black person, especially a male. *Any other terms such as 'boy,' 'spook,' 'splib,' 'negro,' 'Uncle Tom,' 'nigra,' 'nigger,' or 'colored' carry connotations of prejudice and must be avoided.* Atlantic 1/70, p38 *"Boot". . . is often used as a nickname by blacks, and as a term which, like "blood," "brother," or "splib," refers to blacks in general.* Rappin' and Stylin' Out (edited by Thomas Kochman), 1972, p169 [**1964,** of unknown origin]

splice, *v.t. Molecular Biology.* **1** to join (a gene or DNA fragment of one organism) to that of another; recombine (strands of DNA molecules) from different organisms to form new genetic combinations. Compare ANNEAL. See also GENE-SPLICING. *The controversial research in question is a class of experiments that . . . include splicing the genes of a virus or bacteria to partially purified DNA from mammals or birds or lower animals known to produce potent toxins or pathogens.* Science News 1/29/77, p70 *Under favorable conditions, the resulting fragment of foreign DNA may be incorporated, or "spliced," into the gap in the plasmid, closing the circle to create a hybrid molecule. Then, after the linkage is sealed by another enzyme, called DNA ligase, the modified plasmid is introduced into a host cell, such as Escherichia coli, a common bacterium, where it reproduces itself.* 1978 Collier's Encyclopedia Year Book, p154 **2** to insert or transplant (a new or altered gene or DNA fragment obtained by the above means) into an

organism such as a bacterium, to introduce a new character or trait into the host. *One valuable product has already resulted from the work: human insulin, manufactured by splicing fragments of DNA that manufacture the hormone in humans into an intestinal bacterium, causing it to start producing insulin on its own.* Newsweek 6/4/79, p64 [**1975**]

split, *v.i. Slang.* **1** to go away; leave. *Another Pinkerton [guard] . . . said it was an easy night for the guards, because there were so few drunks. "I only do this part time," Chris told us . . . "Hey, thanks for the cigarette. I gotta split."* New Yorker 2/7/70, p22 **2** to run off; desert. *They [draftees] 'split' for different reasons—anything from personal problems to political resistance—but mainly go when they get Vietnam orders.* Listener 10/22/70, p539 [**1956**]

split-brain, *adj.* of, relating to, or subjected to the surgical separation of the hemispheres of the brain. Compare LEFT-BRAIN, RIGHT-BRAIN. *No one who has watched a split-brain patient performing complex visual discrimination and recognition tasks processed wholly by the right hemisphere could possibly doubt the presence of consciousness in the sense in which the term is ordinarily used.* Nature 1/11/74, p121 *The so-called split-brain operations . . . involved severing a bit of brain tissue, known as the corpus callosum, that serves as the principal direct link between the left and the right cerebral hemispheres. After this radical surgery, the patients had fewer epileptic seizures.* New Yorker 11/8/76, p36 [**1955**]

split end, an offensive player in American football who is separated a few yards from either end of the line of scrimmage so that he can immediately run downfield to catch passes. *Rather, a Michigan split end, carried the ball on an end around three times, once for a touchdown, in a 21-6 overrunning of Northwestern last month.* New Yorker 10/16/71, p166 [**1965**]

split gene, a gene with one or more intervening sequences that do not have a specific genetic code. *But although the idea of split genes was revolutionary, it was soon embraced wholeheartedly. Crick spoke for all molecular biologists when he wrote in the April 1979 issue of Science magazine, ". . . in September 1976, I had no idea that a typical gene might be split into several pieces and I doubt if anybody else had." He went on to note that, only two years later, the existence of split genes was universally accepted.* 1981 World Book Science Annual, p198 [**1980**]

Spodosol (ˈspɑdəˌsɔːl), *n.* (in U.S. soil taxonomy) any of a group of moist forest soils characterized by an ash-gray leached surface layer and an iron-rich layer beneath it. *The remaining broad groups of soils, the Alfisols, Entisols, Spodosols, and many Inceptisols, fall between the two extremes, both in nutrient losses during formation and in fertility levels. Mountainous regions, with their great variety of soils, also belong to this intermediate group. Collectively these occupy about 35% of the land surface.* McGraw-Hill Yearbook of Science and Technology 1972, p374 [**1960,** from Greek *spodós* ashes + English *-sol* (from Latin *solum* soil)]

spoiler, *n.* **1** *U.S.* a third political candidate who takes away enough votes to spoil another candidate's chances of winning. See also SPOILER PARTY. *It seems clear that William Buckley will poll enough votes to be a "spoiler," though it is not yet certain for whom.* NY Times 11/1/65, p40 **2** an airflow deflector on an automobile that helps reduce the danger of spinouts. *One of the Chaparrals has a high wing "spoiler," the other a more conventional spoiler rising from the rear deck. Spoilers are devices that catch the airflow over the car body and keep the rear wheels on the track.* NY Times 3/31/67, p41 [**1965** for def. 1; **1963** for def. 2]

spoiler party, *U.S.* a third political party formed especially to split one of the two regular parties so as to spoil its chances of winning in an election. . . . *the formation of a Third, or "spoiler" party is very much on the minds of peace activists, including dissident Democrats, as a rebuke to the Johnson administration for its conduct of the Vietnam war.* Maclean's 7/67, p2 [**1968**]

spokesperson, *n.* a person who speaks for another or others; a spokesman or spokeswoman. *That leaves as the crucial quali-*

ties required of a new president the humane gifts—sensitivity, awareness, appreciation, flexibility—that make for an effective spokesperson for higher education but have no practical consequence for the day-to-day running of an institution. Science 3/28/75, p1153 *The palace spokesperson immediately telephoned the man who should know about such things. He is Major-General Peter Gillett, the secretary of the Central Chancery of the Order of Knighthood. He didn't immediately know.* Manchester Guardian Weekly 1/11/76, p20 [**1972**, from *spokes*man (OED a1540) or *spokes*woman (OED 1654) + -PERSON] ►For the plural, the form **spokespeople** also occurs, as in the following quotations: *As the Boston Tea Party of December 16, 1773 was re-enacted . . . spokespeople for the Indians showed up to announce that the re-enactment would be degrading to Indians.* National Review 1/18/74, p69 . . . *the bizarre maunderings of those (usually anonymous), who, if they are, as they would claim, spokespeople for the "white British race" would leave one in grave doubts for the collective sanity of that august body.* New Scientist 12/7/78, p791

sponge, *n.* a contraceptive pessary saturated with a sperm-killing substance. *Physicians said the sponge proved to be about as effective as the diaphragm in tests on 2,000 women in several countries, including the United States. The diaphragm, which requires the application of spermicidal cream, has a failure rate of about 10 percent among all users, including women who fail to use it consistently or correctly.* NY Times 3/13/83, p25 [**1983**]

spork, *n. U.S.* a plastic spoon with blunt tines at the tip that can be used as a fork. *To eat the food, they frequently are crammed on benches at narrow tables as they try to cut meat, scoop up soup or wind up spaghetti with a spork.* NY Times 5/19/76, p1 [**1909, 1970** *Spork*, a trademark, blend of *spoon* and *fork*]

sports medicine, a branch of medicine dealing with the treatment and prevention of injuries or illnesses that result from engaging in sports. See GLASS ARM, HOLLOW FOOT, SURFER'S KNOB, TENNIS TOE. *Dr. Sheehan, a cardiologist and internist in Red Bank, New Jersey, is medical editor for* Runner's World *magazine and a leading authority on sports medicine.* Atlantic 8/75, p58 *Every coach who graduates from the Leipzig Institute . . . has been through a five-semester sports medicine course that begins with chemistry and physics, goes on to biomechanics and ends with an introduction to practical sports medicine.* NY Times 12/22/76, p24 [**1961**]

spread, *n. U.S. and Canada.* the number of points by which a stronger team may be expected to defeat a weaker team, used in betting, especially on football games. Compare LINE. *How does a bookie make money? He charges about 10% for handling the bets, a fee called "vigorish." And he manipulates the spread. Let us say Minnesota Vikings are favored by eight points over Green Bay Packers. If too much money is bet on Minnesota, the spread is increased to nine points, or 10 points, whatever it takes to achieve a balance.* Maclean's 10/3/77, p61 [**1967**, shortened from the earlier (1953) *point spread*]

spreadsheet, *n.* a computer program that displays an array of rows and columns into which a user may enter numbers, so that each time a member or variable is changed the program instantly recomputes all the figures affected. *Spreadsheet programs enable individuals to easily prepare tables. The users of such programs establish rules for handling large groups of numbers . . . Spreadsheets may be used for preparing budgets and financial plans, balancing a checkbook, or keeping track of personal investments.* 1986 World Book Year Book, p555 [**1982**]

sprint car, a fast medium-sized racing car used for racing over short distances. (*Our Maori guide took us to the speedway—he races sprint cars.*) New Yorker 5/4/87, p28 [**1954**]

spy satellite, an artificial satellite equipped with cameras and electronic sensing devices for ground surveillance. See EYE-IN-THE-SKY. *Costs would be high if western Europe tried to compete with the super powers, who launch spy satellites at the rate of about 30 a week during a crisis, but a far smaller number*

could conceivably provide all the information needed. New Scientist 11/1/73, p315 [**1960**]

square one, Usually in the phrase **back to square one.** the original starting point or same conditions (in allusion to board games in which certain conditions obligate a player to return to the starting point). *Within a year price increases and wage demands will again be out of control, and within two years we shall be back once again to square one.* Times (London) 1/15/68, p7 *The dilemma for the Kremlin is . . . thrown back to square one.* NY Times 6/18/67, pD1 *On balance we shall be back to square one with wages rising faster than productivity.* Punch 6/5/68, p798 [**1960**]

squaresville, *Slang.* —*n.* the world or society of squares or conventional people. *Leonard Hall* [former chairman of the Republican National Committee] *. . . gave the impression of an extraordinarily intelligent man, in appearance not unlike Jack E. Leonard* [a comedian] *doing a straight turn, as if all of Jack E. Leonard's hyper-acute intelligence had gone into the formidable bastions of Squaresville.* Harper's 11/68, p47 *If the book is intended to be the apotheosis of squaresville, I'm afraid Mr Cooper has proved to be a devil's advocate.* Sunday Times (London) 5/8/66, p34 —*adj.* not up-to-date or fashionable; conventional; square. . . . *they* [the students talking to me] *went away, more than ever convinced that the war between the generations was for real. And through the window there floated a querulous, puzzled voice. "A queer fish, real squaresville. You know something? I believe he really liked it that way."* Listener 7/11/68, p50 *On campus, where it once was squaresville to flip for the rock scene, it now is the wiggiest of kicks.* Time 5/21/65, p54 [**1956**; see -VILLE]

s quark, short for STRANGE QUARK. *In the quark model these particles are distinguished by the presence of an s quark or an $\bar{s}$ antiquark, which respectively carry strangeness quantum numbers of -1 and +1; the other quarks have zero strangeness.* Scientific American 10/77, p58 [**1976**]

squark, *n. Nuclear Physics.* the hypothetical counterpart of a quark in supersymmetry, differing from a quark by a one-half unit. Compare SELECTRON. *New experiments planned at the Stanford (CA) Linear Accelerator Center (SLAC), the European Center for Nuclear Research (CERN) in Geneva, and the Fermi National Accelerator (Fermilab) near Chicago should observe the hypothetical sleptons and squarks or determine that the masses are beyond the energy range of any existing accelerator.* Americana Annual 1987, p425 [**1987**, from *s*upersymmetric + QUARK]

squeaky-clean, *adj. Informal.* **1** spotlessly clean. *Starting with the important basic of squeaky-clean skin, she first applies a protective covering of moisturizer to keep the skin soft and fresh under make-up and to prepare the delicate tissues for the slap of the sun.* Tuscaloosa News (Alabama) 6/23/72, p9 **2** *Figurative use.* beyond reproach. *The Federal Election Commission is designed to keep financing squeaky-clean and consequently there is a mild irony in the fact that at the moment it is blemished by smudges of patronage.* NY Times 12/18/77, pD2 [**1972**]

squeal law or **squeal rule,** *U.S. Informal.* a proposed government regulation requiring Federally supported clinics to notify the parents of minors who ask for a prescription for contraceptives. *The so-called "squeal law" . . . would apply to girls 17 and under.* Daily News (New York) 2/15/83, p5 *The Reagan administration's "squeal rule" . . . did not survive its first court test.* News and Observer (Raleigh, N.C.) 2/25/83, p5A [**1982**]

squid, *n.* a very sensitive device for measuring weak magnetic fields, typically consisting of a thin film of superconducting niobium placed around a small quartz rod. Exposure to a magnetic field sets up a circulating current in the device. *Squids are proving useful in a number of studies where sensitivity to minute magnetic fields can yield information. Medicine, psychology, geophysics and metrology are especially active right now and physicists representative of those working in these fields were invited to discuss squids at the recent meeting of the American Physical Society in Chicago.* Science News 4/9/77, p234 [**1976**, originally (1967) spelled *SQUID*, acronym for *superconducting quantum interference device*]

SRAM, abbreviation of *short-range attack missile*, a rocket-propelled, air-to-surface, bomber-launched missile. *The new FB-111's would each carry 12 cruise missiles on their wings and four SRAM's in an internal rack.* 1978 Collier's Encyclopedia Year Book, p102 [**1970**]

Sri Lankan ('sri: 'lɑːŋkən), **1** a native or inhabitant of the Republic of Sri Lanka, the official name of Ceylon since 1972. *"A Sri Lankan works only every other day,"* complained Prime Minister Ranasinghe Premadasa recently, noting that between the abundance of Buddhist holidays and liberal trade-union work regulations, Sri Lankans work an average of only 178 days per year.* High Times 1/79, p111 **2** of or having to do with Sri Lanka. *China . . . agreed to export 200,000 tons of rice in exchange for 67,000 tons of Sri Lankan rubber.* Americana Annual 1977, p481 [**1973**, from Sanskrit *Sri Laṅkā*, from *Sri*, an honorific prefix + *Laṅkā* name of the island]

SRO, abbreviation of *sex-ratio organism*, a microorganism, believed to be a spiroplasma, that infects female fruit flies and causes the death of their male offspring. *Most attempts to understand why only the males die have dealt with manipulations of the chromosomes of flies carrying and transmitting the SRO. Hemolymph containing SROs was injected into females of a number of special stocks of* D. melanogaster. McGraw-Hill Yearbook of Science and Technology 1975, p361 [**1975**]

S.R.O. hotel or **S.R.O. building,** *U.S.* a welfare hotel for single occupants. *Peter Koenig made it appear that S.R.O. hotels are almost the only facilities available to chronic mental patients. There are others. One such facility is the adult foster home, which offers services and supervision for dependent adults who cannot manage alone but do not require skilled care.* NY Times Magazine 7/2/78, p39 *Queens has only one of New York's several hundred S.R.O. buildings . . .* New Yorker 6/27/77, p85 [**1967**, S.R.O. abbreviation of *single-room occupancy*]

SSBN, a naval designation for a nuclear-powered submarine capable of launching ballistic missiles. See SLBM. *The Navy provided the strategic deterrent of four SSBNs, each with 16 Polaris A-3 missiles with MRV, under independent British control.* Britannica Book of the Year 1976, p238 [**1972**, from SS (symbol for *submarine*), Ballistic, Nuclear]

S sleep, *n.* short for SYNCHRONIZED SLEEP. Compare D SLEEP. *Each sleeper spends about three-fourths of each cycle in S sleep (the S standing for synchronized delta waves, with from one to four peaks per second, that mark the deepest stages of this form) and the rest of the cycle in "paradoxical" D sleep.* Scientific American 5/74, p133 [**1974**]

SSPE, abbreviation of *subacute sclerosing panencephalitis*, a chronic brain disease chiefly affecting children, thought to be caused by the measles virus or by an unknown variety of slow virus. See SLOW INFECTION. *SSPE causes stiffness, jerkiness, mental deterioration and death in young people.* Science News 11/3/73, p286 *In contrast to kuru and CJD [Creutzfeldt-Jakob disease], SSPE raises some different problems. Measles is a common virus which most of us encounter in childhood. SSPE is a rare disease and yet the same virus seems to be involved. Here is a fascinating example of a virus undergoing two quite different types of interaction in the same host.* New Scientist 11/18/76, p382 [**1968**]

SST, abbreviation of SUPERSONIC TRANSPORT. *The industry argues that we must build SST's to retain the market which would otherwise go to the British-French Concorde.* NY Times Magazine 2/11/68, p22 [**1961**]

Stabex ('stei,beks), *n.* a system by which the European Economic Community compensates for any drop in the export earnings of developing countries in Africa, the Caribbean, and the Pacific. *On Stabex—the export stabilising mechanism, Ouko said the ACP had proposed that an additional 60 commodities be brought under the scheme.* Weekly Review (Nairobi) 7/27/79, p21 [**1975**, from *stabi*lize + *ex*ports]

stagflation, *n. British.* a stagnant economic condition marked by rising unemployment and spiraling inflation. *A lack of high competitiveness leads to stagflation, which tends to become a permanent feature of the economic system.* Manchester Guardian Weekly 8/21/71, p13 [**1965**, blend of *stagnation* and *inflation*] —**stagflationary,** *adj.: This was discussion of ways in which the antitrust movement could play a part in curing the stagflationary disease—the combination of rising prices and rising unemployment . . .* Sunday Times (London) 6/27/71, p54

staging, *n.* the jettisoning of a rocket stage. *The engines of the first stage began to cut off prior to staging (separation) and to ignition of the second-stage engines.* 1970 World Book Year Book, p66 [**1959**]

staging post, *British.* **1** a stopping place on a journey; stopover. *Although France is the principal staging post between the Orient and the United States in the opium chain, and secret laboratories for transforming it into heroin exist in the south, there is, according to the police, scarcely any drug problem.* Manchester Guardian Weekly 10/26/67, p9 **2** *Figurative use.* any major or significant preparatory stage. *If the politicians can resist the temptation to use the occasion as an opportunity for another footling slanging match, we may find that the controversy sparked off by Mr. Wedgwood Benn's attack on telepolitics becomes a staging-post in the development of TV.* Punch 10/30/68, p599 [**1959**, from the earlier (1952) military term for an assembly point for troops before an action or operation]

standard candle, *Astronomy.* a celestial object of known brightness used as a standard for measuring astronomical distances. *The titanic stellar explosions called supernovas can reach the luminosity of an entire galaxy for a short time, and they might make excellent "standard candles" for determining the distances of very remote objects.* 1987 Collier's Encyclopedia Year Book, p142 [**1959**, extended sense of the former term for a unit of luminous intensity (replaced by the *candela* in 1950)]

standard model or **Standard Model,** *Physics.* the prevailing theory of the basic constituents of matter, which treats all strong interactions in terms of gluons and quantum chromodynamics. *Subatomic, or particle, physics has been free of surprises for nearly a decade. All experiments have merely confirmed the Standard Model, the current concept of matter and forces . . . The Standard Model depicts matter as being made up of two kinds of building blocks:* leptons, including the electron, and quarks, *pointlike particles that make up protons and neutrons—which in turn make up atomic nuclei.* World Book Science Annual 1987, p300 [**1986**]

staplepuncture, *n.* a form of acupuncture in which small metal pieces are inserted into parts of the outer ear to enable a person to twist them at will when having pain, discomfort, etc. Compare ELECTROACUPUNCTURE. *The other fat fad to incur the displeasure of the A.M.A. is "staplepuncture," which is based on the theory—so far unconfirmed—that there are "obesity nerve endings" in the ear. Doctors who practice the art place surgical staples in their patients' ears and instruct them to wiggle the metal clips with their fingers whenever they feel like cheating on the 400-calorie-per-day diet that accompanies the treatment.* Time 12/16/74, p106 [**1974**]

stargaze, *v.i.* to watch famous actors or other celebrities as a fan does. *He [Christopher Porterfield] and his roommate, Dick Cavett, frequently got backstage at the Shubert Theater to stargaze at close range. "In those days," says Porterfield, "I regarded performers with a mixture of fascination and awe. Since then I've become more fascinated and less awed."* Time 9/25/72, p1 [**1970**, extended from the original meanings (1600's): (1) to study the stars; (2) to daydream] —**stargazer,** *n.: Stargazers could expect to see Jeanne Moreau, Jack Nicholson, Jane Fonda, Richard Burton and Marlon Brando, slated to close the festival with "Last Tango in Paris," directed by Italy's brilliant Bernardo Bertolucci.* Newsweek 10/9/72, p91 —**stargazing,** *n.: Nureyev and Bruhn danced the male lead roles. Although critical reception was generally poor, Raymon-*

da *offered a fine opportunity for stargazing.* 1976 World Book Year Book, p270

starquake, *n.* a series of rapid changes in the shape of a star or in the distribution of its matter, detected from sudden speed-ups in the star's pulse rate or radiation output. . . . *the Vela pulsar, which had been emitting sharp radio pulses almost precisely 11 times per second but which had been observed to be slowing down perceptibly, suddenly speeded up . . . What could have happened? One hypothesis is that the pulsars experienced a "starquake."* Scientific American 2/70, p44 *The favourite explanation that decreases in period, or "spin-ups", occur when starquakes take place in the deformed crust of the star seems to fall flat on its face when confronted with the discovery that the Crab pulsar, at least, also undergoes "spin-downs".* New Scientist and Science Journal 8/26/71, p452 [**1969,** from *star* + earth*quake*]

Star Wars, *Informal.* another name for SDI (Strategic Defense Initiative). . . . *I have not worked on a classified project in more than twenty years and do not have access to the classified aspects of Star Wars. I do have the impression that there is an attempt to revive the old idea of using artificially created Van Allen belts to stop missiles.* New Yorker 2/2/87, p58 [**1982,** from the title of a popular science-fiction motion picture (1977) directed by George Lucas]

stash, *n. U.S. Slang.* a mustache. . . . *his father swore "by Gibran and by his mustache" to renounce his lust for alcohol . . . Alas, the stash stayed but the vow did not.* NY Times Magazine 6/25/72, p28 [**1971,** clipped and altered form of *mustache*]

statement, *n.* the expression of an opinion, point of view, or attitude by means other than words. *Miss McGee added that she thought "Blacula"* [a motion picture] *makes a statement. "Blacula is a victim of circumstance, and any minority can relate to that. He was a black prince forced to deal with something he didn't know existed."* New Yorker 9/9/72, p30 *And finally, there are those whose idea of country is to erect an architect-designed home as a personal statement.* NY Times Magazine 4/19/87, p30 [**1953**]

state-of-the-art, *adj.* involving or using the latest or most advanced techniques in a field or product. *Position open in several areas for design of special purpose digital equipment related to high-speed, state-of-the-art, commercial computers.* NY Times 4/15/67, p36 *Certainly the absence of state-of-the-art claims or gadgets implies a growing realisation that the manufacturers need to shore up their tattered images in the eyes of customers who are used to late delivery, mediocre support, and software that is at least three years behind the hardware.* New Scientist and Science Journal 2/25/71, p425 [**1955,** adjective use of *state of the art* the current stage of development of a field or product (OEDS 1910)]

State of the State message, *U.S.* an annual speech by a governor to the state legislature, reviewing the state's development in the past year and outlining programs for the coming year. *Only 4 of the 39 governors who gave State of the State messages requested increases in sales or income taxes, the two major tax sources for the states.* 1973 World Book Year Book, p511 [**1967,** patterned after the yearly U.S. Presidential *State of the Union message* (1945)]

State of the World message, *U.S.* a report on American foreign policy sent by the President to Congress. *In his State of the World Message, issued just prior to his China trip, the President suggested that Taipei and Peking negotiate their differences.* NY Times Magazine 2/20/72, p47 [**1970,** originally a report by President Nixon in February 1970, and afterward applied to similar reports]

statesperson, *n.* a statesman or stateswoman. *Much of the credit for last year's record goes to Indian statesperson Indira Gandhi, who wearied of democracy and is now dabbling in dictatorship.* National Review 1/23/76, p17 *Ms Previn is not a political animal or, at least, not any more. She says she does not understand the very idea of someone being a politician. "I mean, to want to be a statesman, a statesperson, terrific. But a politician?"* Manchester Guardian Weekly 5/29/77, p21 [**1976**] ► The term is usually applied to a woman.

static, *n. U.S. Informal.* noisy criticism; loud arguments. *This is the most difficult decision that I have ever had to make and I have no misconceptions as to the pain it is going to cause others and . . . the static I am going to receive.* National Review 4/12/74, p417 *But the blond high jumper* [Dwight Stones] *fell short of setting yet another world mark. "I'm going to get a lot of static for this," he said after the meet.* Newsweek 3/10/75, p69 [**1953,** probably extended from the earlier (1920) sense "unpleasant interference in conversation, noisy chatter"]

status offender, *U.S.* a child or adolescent who, although not a delinquent, is placed under court jurisdiction because of habitual truancy, willful disobedience, and the like. *PINS are called status offenders because it is their state of being—their alleged "incorrigibility" or "unruliness," rather than any criminal offense—that brings them before the courts. Definitions of status offenders vary from state to state.* New Yorker 8/14/78, p56 [**1975**] —**status offense:** *The San Francisco law lost most of its muscle last year when California decriminalized all so-called status offenses—those acts, such as truancy, which would not be violations if committed by adults.* NY Times 1/6/78, pB6

STD[1], abbreviation of *Subscriber Trunk Dialling,* the British system enabling telephone callers to make long-distance calls directly from one region to another. Compare *U.S.* AREA CODE *The calls came from all over Britain, often by S.T.D.* Times (London) 11/21/66, p1 *When you're alone in the house on a dark wet evening . . . it's better than nothing to spot a crisp new STD code book, propped against the telephone by someone who hasn't thought its arrival worth mentioning.* Punch 12/11/68, p833 [**1958**]

STD[2] or **S.T.D.,** abbreviation of SEXUALLY TRANSMITTED DISEASE. *Venereal disease, . . . often called* VD *or sexually transmitted disease (STD), is any of several serious diseases spread almost entirely by sexual contact with an infected person.* World Book Encyclopedia (1988), Vol. 20, p315 [**1981**]

steady-state, *adj.* relatively stable; generally free from fluctuations. *X-ray still pictures of steady-state sounds, principally vowels, have been used for many years.* Language 3/71, p237 *A redistribution of wealth and a shorter working week would be sensible first steps in the replacement of growth economics by the steady state economics which is more realistic if the environment is to be considered.* New Scientist 2/3/72, p292 [**1965,** generalized sense of the term used in physics (OEDS 1885) to describe a system that is essentially constant]

steady-stater, *n.* a supporter of the theory that the universe is essentially unchanging, with new matter being continually created to compensate for the destruction of matter. Compare BIG BANGER. *As the galaxies move farther away from each other, steady-staters believe, new galaxies are constantly being formed out of hydrogen that is created and fill the gaps, keeping the expanding universe at a constant density.* Time 3/11/66, p51 [**1966,** from *steady-state* (OEDS 1948) + -*er*]

steamy, *n. U.S. Slang.* a pornographic motion picture. *The Rockne Theater aroused such ire when it began showing steamies that local matrons picketed in protest last summer.* Time 1/24/72, p8 [**1972,** noun use of the earlier adjective (1950's) in the sense of "sensual, erotic"]

steel-collar, *adj.* of or having to do with intelligent machines or robots as part of the labor force. *Eventually . . . they* [smart machines] *will make possible the full automation of many factories, displacing millions of blue-collar workers with a new "steel-collar" class.* Newsweek 6/30/80, p50 *Tomorrow's "steel-collar" workers should be able to react to their environment, combining sensing devices to "see" and "feel" and AI software to "think".* Christian Science Monitor 1/3/86, p14 [**1981,** patterned after *white-collar* (1928) and *blue-collar* (1950); compare GRAY-COLLAR, PINK-COLLAR]

steering, *n. U.S.* a practice in which real-estate agents steer or direct black clients to black or integrated communities without informing them of dwellings available for sale or rent in white ommunities. Compare REDLINING. *Presidential candidate Jimmy Carter's stand on "ethnic purity" of urban neighborhoods, to "maintain the homogeneity of neighborhoods if they have been established that way," is clear support for residential "steering" which is now being tested in the courts.* NY Times 4/13/76, p32 *The Supreme Court ruled 7-2 Tuesday that a village and residents of a target area within it have the right to sue realtors for alleged "steering" of home buyers on the basis of race.* Christian Science Monitor 4/18/79, p2 **[1976]**

stellarator (ˈstelə,reitər), *n.* a device in which plasma (highly ionized gas) is confined in an endless tube by means of an externally applied magnetic field, used to produce controlled thermonuclear power. *Medium-density plasma containers . . . include the stellarators, originally developed at the Princeton Plasma Physics Laboratory, and the tokamaks, originally developed at the I. V. Kurchatov Institute of Atomic Energy near Moscow.* Scientific American 2/71, p53 . . . *the Soviet plasma device called Tokamak exhibits a very low rate of diffusion even though it is likely to have the same fluctuations as similarly shaped devices such as Stellarators, which have much higher diffusion rates.* Science News 8/22/70, p168 **[1951,** coined about 1951 from *stellar* gener*ator;* so called from the fact that the device generates power by reactions similar to those produced in stars]

stellar wind, a stream of charged particles ejected from the corona of a star into space. Compare SOLAR WIND. *Such stars* [red giants] *may be steadily supplying heavy metals to the interstellar medium by blowing off material in the form of "stellar winds".* New Scientist 4/8/65, p107 **[1965]**

STEM (stem), *n.* acronym for *scanning transmission electron microscope,* an electron microscope that combines features of the scanning electron microscope (such as three-dimensional detail) with features of the transmission electron microscope (such as high-resolution power). *Albert Crewe and Michael Isaacson of the University of Chicago, while attempting to view biomolecular structures with a very-high-resolution STEM built in their own laboratory, instead obtained the first motion pictures of individual atoms.* 1978 Britannica Yearbook of Science and the Future, p277 **[1972]**

stem-winding, *adj. U.S.* extremely good, strong, etc.; first-rate. *. . . the Vice President drove from his home in Waverly, Minn., to Minneapolis, where he delivered a stem-winding, hard-line speech on the war and domestic violence.* Time 8/16/68, p18 *A stem-winding sermon by Reverend Cecil Todd called "Blue Print for Slavery" can be obtained by sending one dollar to Revival Fires in Joplin, Missouri . . .* Atlantic 9/66, p90 **[1966,** from *stem-winder* a first-rate person or thing (OED2, 1892) with the form influenced by *stem-winding* watch (one wound by turning the knob on the stem)]

Stepinfetchit (ˈstep,ənˈfetʃ,it), *n.* or **Stepin Fetchit,** *U.S. and Canada. Used attributively.* a stereotype of a shuffling, fawning black servant; *by extension,* any servile black man. *Mike Evans, who plays the young black neighbor Lionel, is obliged by his role to affect an occasional Stepinfetchit manner. It is the con act blacks sometimes employ to get what they want from whites.* NY Times Magazine 3/12/72, p125 *The driver, from a small town outside Houston, though white, seemed to have taken a course at the Stepin Fetchit school of etiquette. No matter what I said, or asked, his answer was the same: "Yassuh."* Maclean's 3/74, p70 **[1967,** from *Stepin Fetchit,* born 1902, stage name of a black American vaudeville actor who played the role of a shuffling, grinning, eye-rolling character in Hollywood films of the 1920's and 1930's, probably adopted from *Step-an'-fetch-it,* a nickname for any slow or lazy person]

stereology, *n.* the scientific study of the characteristics of three-dimensional objects that can be viewed only two-dimensionally. *Up to now it has not been easy to measure brain area but the rather new science of stereology, employing statistico-geometrical methods, now makes it possible to draw conclusions concerning three dimensional structures from flat images, such as cut sections.* Science Journal 3/68, p32 **[1963,** from *stereo-* three-dimensional + *-logy* study of]

sterile, *adj. U.S.* cleared for security purposes; screened to prevent access by enemy agents, etc. See STERILIZE. *The CIA had provided the plumbers with false identity papers, disguises, . . . two "safehouses" and a "sterile" telephone in Washington (permitting them to operate without being bugged or observed by rival spies from other government agencies).* Harper's 10/73, p79 *The so-called sterile concourse—the long airport corridor that only ticketed, searched travelers may enter—means that a passenger must be searched each time he changes planes and concourses.* Newsweek 5/7/73, p88 **[1973]**

sterilize, *v.t. U.S.* to clear for security purposes, especially by omitting any potentially damaging material from a government document; render harmless. *Only a select few persons who have been specially cleared, and who live under special controls, will have access to this information, and before passing it on to other officials who must make use of it they will "sterilize" it so that is contains only what is needed for the legitimate purposes at hand, and no more.* National Review 10/26/73, p1170 *Sterilize—To remove identification marks from material to be used in clandestine operations.* NY Times 4/27/76, p26 **[1973]**

stern drive, an inboard engine with an outboard drive unit. *When they appeared on the water about eight years ago, they looked like outboards with the power head sawed off. Closer examination revealed a drive shaft running through the transom, with an inboard engine on one end and an outboard-like lower unit on the other. Variously called stern drives, inboard-outboards, inboard-outdrives, or just plain "I-O's," they are one of the hottest items in recreational boating.* NY Times 2/9/68, p31 **[1968]**

stew, *n. U.S. Informal.* an airplane steward or stewardess. *Before moving on to airline desk jobs, however, male stews are learning to appreciate the occupational hazards of the job-long flights: screaming babies, jet lag and lecherous passengers.* Newsweek 3/19/73, p65 [Al] *Dellentash helps his stews aboard. Their outfits vary from shorts to long gowns, but pilot and co-pilot always wear uniforms.* Picture legend, People Weekly 10/9/78, p8 **[1970,** by shortening]

stick, *v.t.* to hit or drive with a hockey stick. *After a scoreless first period, Dennis Hull, Yvan Cournoyer and Paul Henderson sticked home shots that wiped out a 1-0 Russian lead.* Courier-Journal (Lexington, Ky.) 9/25/72, pB7 **[1972,** verb use of the noun; past tense *sticked* parallels baseball use of *flied* ("hit a fly")]

Stickey or **Stickie,** *n.* a nickname for a member of the official Irish Republican Army. See the first quotation for details. *"Stickeys" (as they are disparagingly tagged by the Provisional wing because of the sticky backs of their Easter seals) maintain close ties with the minor-league Irish Communist party.* NY Times Magazine 6/11/72, p64 *"Martin was our leadership— who else could have got the clubs stopping selling drinks at half eleven? Who'll stop the boys fighting with the stickies?"* Times (London) 8/21/72, p10 **[1972]**

sticky ends, ends of single strands of DNA molecules that complement each other in the sequence of their nucleotides and can be linked up or reconnected in the presence of the enzyme ligase. Restriction enzymes are used to produce sticky ends. *Lambda DNA is a double helix throughout most of its length, but one end of each polynucleotide chain extends for 12 nucleotides beyond the double helix. These two single-strand chains are complementary to each other and are called "sticky ends." Scientific American 12/76, p109 Sticky ends, indeed, have turned out to be of utmost importance for genetic engineering research. Clever biochemists now use them as connectors for tying foreign bits of DNA to other pieces of DNA, to other genes. This would resemble the way railroad cars are assembled into a long line to make up a whole train.* Robert Cooke, Improving on Nature, 1977, p50 **[1968]**

stimoceiver, *n.* a miniaturized radio device implanted in the scalp which through electrodes stimulates specific areas of the brain and transmits information from the brain to an outside receiver for study. Compare ESB, PACEMAKER. *She was referred to Dr. Vernon Mark and his colleagues, who theorized* that the trouble lay in epileptic disturbances of her amygdala, the "emotional thermostat of the brain." To prove their hypothesis, the neurosurgeons sought to induce a seizure artificially, using a stimoceiver, a remote-control device for sending and receiving electrical impulses. 1973 Collier's Encyclopedia Year Book, p79 [**1967**, from stimulate + connecting -o- + receiver]

sting, n. U.S. Slang. any scheme, trick, or operation designed to trap a suspected wrongdoer (often used attributively). *Most charges relate to the stolen goods unwittingly sold to police before hidden cameras and microphones, but "stings" also have led to arrests for murder, rape, bank robbery, arson, and other crimes,* . . . NY Times 9/8/77, pA5 *Congress's image was tarnished following reports that eight of its members had been implicated in an FBI "sting" operation called Abscam.* Britannica Book of the Year 1981, p696 [**1975**, originally underworld slang for a carefully planned and swiftly executed theft or swindle (OEDS 1930)]

stishovite ('stiʃə,vait), n. an extremely dense form of quartz produced under very high pressure (as by the impact of a meteorite). *Formula:* SiO_2 *The older craters have been identified thanks to the discovery that the explosive impacts in which they were formed left telltale transformations of the rock. These include tiny diamonds, greatly compressed forms of quartz (coesite and stishovite), shatter cones and minerals known as impactites.* NY Times 10/24/76, p26 [**1961**, named after S. M. *Stishov*, a Russian geochemist who produced it in a laboratory in 1961 + -ite (mineral suffix)]

stocker, n. U.S. a stock car, usually slightly modified, used in drag racing. *You simply can't believe the noise of these engines. Stockers, motorcycles, needle-nosed dragsters . . . tear the night apart for hours.* Harper's 1/76, p20 *Members of the National Association for Stock Car Auto Racing . . . rolled up to the "diplomatic entrance" in their Day-Glo colored "stockers."* Time 9/25/78, p88 [**1972**, from stock (car) + -er]

Stockholm syndrome, the desire of hostages to please their captors, to cooperate with them, and to condone or justify their action. *He had not succumbed psychologically. Rebhan had worried about the "Stockholm syndrome," the odd phenomenon whereby hostages begin to identify with their captors and even aid the very people who threaten their lives.* Reader's Digest 1/80, p142 [**1978**, named after an incident in which hostages were taken during a bank robbery in *Stockholm*, Sweden, in 1973, widely cited by social scientists to explain conversions among hostages]

stocking mask, a nylon stocking pulled over the head or wrapped around the face to conceal identity. *After three men in stocking masks raided Martins Bank in South Audley Street, W., the same day the £3,000 they stole was recovered from the boot of the escape car* . . . Times (London) 5/16/66, p10 [**1966**]

STOL (stɔːl), n. acronym for *short takeoff and landing.* Compare CTOL, VTOL, V/STOL. *The STOL plane tends to be slower than a conventional plane and much slower than a jet airliner but it is faster than a helicopter. It is able to use a field much smaller than the strip that a jetliner needs. But it needs more room than a helicopter* . . . NY Times 1/7/68, p68 [**1956**]

STOLport, n. an airfield for STOL aircraft. Compare VTOLport. *The STOLport, designed to handle aircraft using runways only about 1,000 feet long, would be built atop a 10-story building, 300 feet wide and seven blocks long.* Science News 2/22/69, p190 *Immediately, New York's proposed new heliport and stolport will be used to improve connections between Manhattan and its small outlying satellite fields* . . . Time 1/15/68, p25 [**1968**]

stonewall, v.i. to act in an obstructive or evasive manner. *He and his aides schemed to "stonewall," to make empty claims of "national security" and "executive privilege," to threaten the Speaker of the House, to maneuver prosecutors—all in order to keep the facts from coming out.* NY Times 5/20/74, p31 *Brezhnev's "nyet," however, put the Soviet Union on the defensive, and Moscow has since been working hard at trying to show it is not stonewalling on arms limitation.* Time 5/23/77, p31 —v.t. to resist, obstruct, or evade (an investiga-

tion, an opponent, etc.). *The President himself . . . served no tice that he would stonewall any further demands for tapes* the Watergate scandal. Newsweek 5/20/74, p23 *I had to d Ms. magazine and Clay Felker's been after me for years to a an interview. But I've stonewalled them.* Women's Wear Dail 8/9/74, p4 *When beleaguered by criticism in the generall liberal English-language press in the country, the Afrikane simply stonewall the issue.* Maclean's 11/14/77, p54 —n. Als spelled **stone wall.** an act or instance of stonewalling. *Ford re peated his view that the President's stone wall against th courts and Congress would produce an impeachment.* Harper' 8/74, p26 *Last fall . . . was a time when cries of "cover-up and "stonewall" reverberated along the Tory benches in th Commons, and the government squirmed under almost dail revelations of shenanigans.* Maclean's 4/17/78, p29 [**1914 1964**, but popularized during the Watergate hearings of 1973 74; extended from the term first used in Australian, and late British, political slang as a noun meaning Parliamentary ob struction (OED 1876) and as a verb, to use obstructive tactic in politics, especially by lengthy Parliamentary speeches; als a cricket term meaning to block balls persistently, to play solel on the defensive (OED 1889)]

stop, v. **stop out**, U.S. to interrupt one's education to pursu some other activity for a brief period. *The trend of stopping ou is growing, however, partly because the draft law now give young men with high lottery numbers a new freedom.* Tim 9/27/71, p47 [**1971**, patterned on *drop out*]

stop-go, British. —n. a government fiscal policy alternating be tween economic expansion and contraction. Also called GO STOP. *The victims of stop-go and unemployment are unio members.* Manchester Guardian Weekly 5/30/70, p12 [**1964** —adj. of or characterized by stop-go. *The "stop-go" cycle neve leaves time for the development of a satisfactory rate of eco nomic growth.* Manchester Guardian Weekly 8/22/70 p12 [**1962**]

stop-out, n. U.S. a student who interrupts his or her educatio to pursue some other activity for a brief period. *Still, man stop-outs do better academically than their less-seasoned class mates, if only because they are a year older.* Time 9/27/71 p47 [**1971**, from STOP OUT (see under STOP, v.)]

storage ring, *Nuclear Physics.* a device for storing a beam of ac celerated particles in a circular track and smashing it agains an opposing beam to produce the necessary energy for the cre ation of new particles. . . . *several storage rings for electron have been operated with electrons of energy in the range of 50(MeV* [million electron volts]. 1972 Britannica Yearbook of Sci ence and the Future, p314 [**1956**]

story art, a form of art which presents a concept, description or account by combining verbal and visual material. Also called NARRATIVE ART. *An increasingly popular form this year wa . . . story art—an offspring of conceptual art that sought tc convey a lighter level of information than its parent. Cap tioned photographs, videotapes, and live performances docu mented intimate aspects of people's lives that frequently were amusing as well.* 1976 Collier's Encyclopedia Year Book p135 [**1975**]

STP, abbreviation used as the name of a hallucinogenic drug (dimethoxy-methylamphetamine) chemically related to mesca line and amphetamine. . . . *there are chemists in laboratorie in Toronto, Montreal and Vancouver who produce amphet amines and psychedelic drugs, LSD, STP, DMT and other mo lecular variations.* Times (London) 2/23/70, pIV *In The People Next Door, LSD and STP users are said to require "a controlled environment indefinitely" following their initia tion, a situation that develops only rarely.* Time 2/15/71 p34 [**1967**, from *STP* (abbreviation of *Scientifically Treated Pe troleum*), a trade name for a gasoline additive]

straight, n. Slang. **1** a person who is straight; a conventional person, especially one who holds orthodox views; a square. *The silent majority, the broad group that includes blue and white collars, small businessmen, professionals, and assorted "straights" who are supposed to be susceptible to the social issue, were assiduously wooed by Nixon.* Time 11/16/70, p17 . . . *I do not believe the gay set is disproportionately large. An honest attempt is made by the straights, the otherwise and the police to keep the more flamboyant element under loose control.* NY Times 6/13/71, p4 **2** a heterosexual person. *But they* [homosexuals] *are gaining a degree of acceptance and even sympathy from heterosexuals, many of whom are still unsure how to deal with them, that neither straights nor gays would have thought possible just the day before yesterday.* Time 4/23/79, p72 [**1967,** noun use of the adjective meaning conventional, orthodox, heterosexual (OEDS 1941)]

straight-ahead, *adj. U.S.* (especially of popular music) simple; unadorned; pure. *I think a lot of artists who have gone in a fusion direction will realize that they don't have to do that exclusively, that they can play fusion music and make their money . . . and still play straight-ahead jazz, too.* NY Times Magazine 6/12/77, p87 [**1964,** from the earlier adjective sense meaning "straightforward" (OED 1836)]

straight arrow, *U.S.* a very proper, upright, straightforward person. *Smith* [the tennis player Stan Smith], *a wonderfully old-fashioned straight arrow, was right in character when, upon being asked if Tiriac's gamesmanship had bothered him, he said, "I don't call that gamesmanship. I call that rudeness."* New Yorker 10/11/69, p194 [**1969**]

straight-arrow, *adj. U.S.* very proper, upright, or straightforward. *The new eco-activists include groups as straight-arrow as the Girl Scouts, who last week campaigned for clean air in places ranging from Hartford, Conn., to smog-threatened Fairfax, Va.* Time 8/22/69, p43 [**1969**]

Strangelove, *n.* a militarist who plans or urges large-scale nuclear warfare and destruction. Also called DR. STRANGELOVE. *He displayed none of the usual fears about Strangeloves in disguise, no suppressed whiff of awe at the personified presence of the end of the world.* Harper's 3/78, p91 *That also was the period when everyone who believed that nuclear weapons should not be tossed into the sea except after the Soviet Union tossed theirs into the sea was labelled a Strangelove.* New York Post 4/12/79 (page not known) [**1966,** named for Dr. Strangelove, a fictional character who is a mad military nuclear-war strategist in a motion picture (1963) of the same name] **—Strangelovian** or **Strangelovean,** *adj.: Because it takes only about 100 warheads to kill 100 million people, both countries have long been able to rely on a Strangelovian strategic theory called "mutual assured destruction" (MAD) to deter a first strike by the other side.* Newsweek 7/8/74, p24 *Although the vocabulary is impenetrable, except to think-tank experts, and the concepts are often Strangelovean, the complex SALT negotiations may yet turn out to be the most important of the century.* Time 4/11/77, p13

strange quark, a type of quark (hypothetical nuclear particle) possessing a charge of $-\frac{1}{3}$ and a spin of $+\frac{1}{2}$. Also called S QUARK. *When Murray Gell-Mann and George Zweig of the California Institute of Technology in Pasadena formulated the quark theory, a third quark was required. It was dubbed a strange quark because the particles that contained it acted in a strange way. The existence of the psi particle requires at least a fourth quark.* World Book Science Annual 1977, p324 *The neutron and proton may be made with up and down quarks only, but the other members of the octet require the strange quark.* Science News 11/18/78, p341 [**1974,** from earlier *strange* in physics (1956)]

strap-on, *adj.* designed to be attached to a space vehicle or engine for additional thrust. *The vehicle seen on television appeared to have a two-stage core with four strap-on boosters, similar to those of the original* Sputnik-Voskhod *launcher.* New Scientist 10/31/68, p231 **—n.** a strap-on booster or engine. *Solid propellant strap-ons could be used to raise the Saturn V's orbital payload (now about 250,000 pounds) to as much as 427,000 pounds.* Science News 8/13/66, p107 [**1966**]

strategize, *v.i.* to devise a strategy or strategies; lay out careful plans. *The* [Alaskan] *ground was white, the brooks and rivers frozen. The people slept for the most part in tents. They strategized about the federal bureaucracy—how to oppose it, how to melt out of its way.* New Yorker 6/27/77, p66 *Men in dark*

suits and homburg hats will be commissioning think tanks to strategise, and calculating kill ratios in case the unthinkable should come to pass with the Internal Revenue Service. New Scientist 9/21/78, p873 [**1943, 1975,** from *strategy* + *-ize;* see the note under PRIORITIZE]

strategy, *n.* a behavior pattern evolved by an organism that enables it to survive and reproduce under adverse conditions. *Biologists Thomas Eisner, Karen Hicks, Maria Eisner, and Douglas Robson of Cornell University in Ithaca, N.Y., recently uncovered an instance of unusual insect strategy. They reported in February 1978 that the larva of the green lacewing uses a most extraordinary disguise to remain unnoticed among the woolly alder aphids upon which it feeds.* World Book Science Annual 1979, p349 [**1978**]

stratified-charge engine, an internal-combustion engine in which the cylinder is divided into two chambers, with a fuel-rich mixture used for ignition in one chamber and a lean mixture for main combustion in the other. *The stratified charge engine was invented in the United States and developed by Honda of Japan. This is a lean-burning engine (that is, one using a high air to fuel ratio that permits oxidation of HC and CO), and Honda says it can meet all the U.S. statutory standards right now.* Science 3/7/75, p822 *Fuel economy and reduced exhaust emissions can both be obtained in so-called stratified-charge engines.* Times (London) 2/13/76, p18 [**1972,** earlier *stratified charge* (1931)]

streak, *Slang. —v.i.* to dash in the nude through a public place, especially as a stunt or fad. *In the middle of the second Test between England and Australia at Lord's, this 24-year-old ship's cook took off all his clothes and 'streaked' across the pitch to win a £20 bet. Four months later, in Australia, three different men were doing the same thing in one afternoon of a Test match against West Indies.* Annual Register of World Events in 1975, p423 *There is something touchingly old-fashioned about the Athens campus; last spring, a few students were espied streaking.* New Yorker 2/6/78, p48 **—v.t.** to streak through (a public area, event, etc.). *"And I was the first to streak a play. I got sort of a double notoriety."* New York Post 3/1/74, p4 *They began drinking, and then they decided to streak the hotel lobby. So they did. They streaked the lobby.* Harper's 4/79, p63 **—n.** an act or instance of streaking. *"There were solo streaks, but no private streaks. After all the variations that were tried, there was no new way to attract attention."* NY Times 5/19/74, p35 [**1973,** from the sense "to move very fast"] **—streaker,** *n.: The* [Academy Awards] *festivities proceeded . . . as usual. No streakers, no scandals, no political filibusters.* New York Post 4/11/79, p54 **—streaking,** *n.: I was anywhere from six to eight months ahead of . . . jogging, streaking, therapeutic screaming, running like an idiot, and your other ridick things.* Saturday Review 6/23/79, p13

stream, *v.t. Chiefly British.* to divide (students) into separate classes according to level of intelligence or special interest. *Most of the schools streamed pupils into A, B, C, or D classes, about four out of five used some form of selection procedure, almost half were not getting a fair share of able pupils, and pupils from the working classes were over-represented.* Times (London) 10/22/68, p3 [**1957**]

streaming, *n. Chiefly British.* the division of students of a school into separate classes according to level of intelligence or special interest, as determined by examinations; homogeneous grouping. Also called TRACKING. *. . . there is far too little research evidence on the effects of streaming and other forms of in-school organization.* New Scientist 6/11/70, p521 [**1954**]

street, *adj.* bought, sold, or obtained on the illegal market; available only on the street, not in any commercial establishment. Compare STREET VALUE. *Because crack is . . . most popular as a "street" drug, few statistics on its use exist.* 1989 World Book Year Book, p64 [**1971**]

street academy, *U.S.* a school formed in a poor section of a city to help high-school dropouts continue their education. *Taxpayers are rebelling at the escalating costs of running the schools; many large systems face bankruptcy. Splinter groups—free schools, alternative schools, private schools, street academies—*

are springing up everywhere. Saturday Review 9/16/72, p67 [**1968**]

street Christian, *U.S.* one of the JESUS PEOPLE. *Jesus freaks. Evangelical hippies. Or, as many prefer to be called, street Christians. Under various names—and in rapidly increasing numbers—they are the latest incarnation of that oldest of Christian phenomena: footloose, passionate bearers of the Word, preaching the kingdom of heaven among the dispossessed of the earth.* Time 8/3/70, p31 [**1970**]

street people, a collective name for hippies, derelicts, vagrants, etc., usually living in city streets, in parks, and in other public places. *At Berkeley an angry confrontation erupted over the university's decision to fence in a two-block, off-campus area which radical elements and "street people" had turned into a people's park.* 1970 Collier's Encyclopedia Year Book, p220 *Moreover, the existence of a student society enables street people to live virtually free. Any young person is almost guaranteed a night's shelter in any university town. You only have to ask.* Manchester Guardian Weekly 4/3/71, p6 [**1967**]

street-smarts, *n. U.S. Slang.* practical knowledge and understanding about the ways of city streets. *Such young women* [who teach at a private school] *. . . refuse to live in New York as though it were the Peter and Paul Fortress and they were enemies of the Czar. To be free, however, requires street-smarts, the cunning of the survivor.* NY Times 8/9/76, p30 *They thought always about winning, and, one way or another, they almost always did win. Like the A's, these Yankees have street-smarts. They win.* New Yorker 11/20/78, p113 [**1972**, from *street* + SMARTS] **—street-smart**, *adj.: Norris also sought out local black leaders and followed their street-smart advice: Build a day care center for working mothers. Offer to put them on flexible hours, say, 8:30 a.m. to 2 p.m., or 1 to 5 p.m. Don't ask if the applicant has been arrested. Yes, many have been busted, but what difference does that make?* Time 4/3/78, p61

street theater, another term for GUERRILLA THEATER. *Earlier, 200 people watched an example of "street theatre", staged by the group, featuring United States marines versus Vietnamese peasants, in the main street of Newbury.* Times (London) 4/13/68, p1 [**1968**]

street value, the value of a narcotic on the illegal market. *Murphy called a news conference to announce that 57 pounds of heroin with an estimated street value of more than $10-million had been stolen.* NY Times 12/24/72, pD6 [**1972**]

streetwise, *adj. U.S.* familiar with local people and their problems; wise to the ways and needs of people on the street. *No mayor can function effectively unless he has around him competent and streetwise people who can assume much of his responsibility . . .* NY Times Magazine 2/25/68, p58 *. . . a* [social] *worker therefore had to be wary as well as trustful, be security-minded as well as loving, and be "street-wise" as well as compassionate.* New Yorker 3/27/65, p78 [**1965**]

streetworker, *n. U.S. and Canada.* a social worker who befriends and tries to help troubled or delinquent youngsters of a neighborhood. *Almost all of them have quit school. The streetworker has become so friendly with them that he can sometimes return stolen goods before the police are even aware of the theft.* Maclean's 1/25/64, p23 [**1964**]

stress test or **stress testing**, a heart examination in which a cardiogram is taken during or immediately after performing strenuous exercise in order to test the heart's ability to function under stress. *An exercise electrocardiogram, or stress test, is a valuable tool in the diagnosis of heart disease. By recording heart activity during exercise, often on a treadmill, it is possible for a trained clinician to detect many coronary abnormalities well ahead of time.* Joe Graedon, The People's Pharmacy, 1976, p272 *In any of 45 cardiac and pulmonary centers operated in 10 states . . . services include stress testing for potential heart-attack cases.* Herald Statesman (Yonkers, N.Y.) 3/19/75, p45 [**1973**]

stretch, *n. U.S. Informal.* a long limousine. *". . . this big Mercedes stretch pulls up with them sittin' in the back wavin' at me . . . That stretch, with the plush seats and the glass parti-*

tion, with the uniformed chauffeur in front and the bar and radio in back." NY Times Magazine 6/19/77, p70 [**1977**]

Strine (strain), *Slang.* —*n.* Australian English. *Anyone who goes to Australia thinking he speaks the Queen's English is in for a shock called "Strine," meaning Australian—the cockney-like vernacular that most Aussies spout.* Time 8/24/70, p60 *In the language I shall now always think of as "Strine," the man who says, "Dad'll ever never sprike tan the waze goane" means that his Dad'll have a nervous breakdown, the way he's going.* Punch 5/5/65, p656 **—adj.** Australian. *But Keneally's normal tone is tighter, and it suggests that here is a rarity—an Australian novelist who does not use his Strine literary context as a prop or an excuse, and thus remains sensitive to his actual and historical environment.* Times (London) 2/24/68, p21 [**1964**, a rendering of the Australian pronunciation of the word *Australian*]

string, *n.* **1** Also called **string bikini**, a very brief bikini. *Winter vacation time is coming and the string bikini is still with us . . . The string has come in for a lot of bad jokes but, actually, for a healthy, active woman, there is nothing immodest about it.* McCall's 11/74, p10 *Its tourist brochures may feature come-on close-ups of itty-bitty string bikinis, but the government of Brazil takes a somewhat different view of female sexuality when the subject is treated seriously.* Ms. 1/79, p98 [**1974**, probably influenced by *G string* (OEDS 1878)] **2** *Physics.* a hypothetical basic unit of matter consisting of a one-dimensional curve with zero thickness and a length of about 10^{-35} meter. *According to superstring theories, the strings are unimaginably short. The most likely length is about 10^{-35} meter—a decimal point followed by 34 zeroes and a 1. Strings come in three basic shapes. The graviton is a closed string—its ends joined to form a loop. All other messenger particles are open strings.* World Book Science Annual 1987, p190 [**1986**]

strip chart, a graphic representation of data in the form of a long strip of paper on which the course of something, such as a patient's fever, is charted. *. . . the computer recorded wave variations that often are undetectable to the eye of a physician using the traditional strip chart.* NY Times 2/3/66, p33 *Pressure transducers installed in the hydraulic braking system of each vehicle indicated fluid pressure on a two-channel stripchart recorder statically calibrated against pedal force.* New Scientist 10/29/70, p224 [**1950, 1961**]

strip city, *U.S.* a long, narrow stretch of urban development between two or more relatively distant cities. Compare SUPERCITY. *By 1980 or so, 80 per cent of us will live in cities, and the strip city—Boston to Washington, Los Angeles to San Diego, and Milwaukee to Cleveland—will have made its appearance.* Saturday Review 1/13/68, p68 [**1950, 1962**]

stroke, *U.S.* —*v.t.* **1** to enhance (a person's) self-esteem, as by praise or flattery; boost the ego of. *"You go to a party up there, and instead of people making real conversation they stop the proceedings so somebody can sing opera or play the piano or do a tap dance. It's Show Biz, man—a bunch a' egomaniacal people using a captive audience to stroke themselves."* Atlantic 3/75, p44 **2** to persuade, cajole, or otherwise influence or manipulate. *Then he talks about the most desirable legislative outcome and the fallback positions. He tells his client, "It's looking pretty good. We'll stay on top of it." This is what is known as "stroking" the client. The Washington influencer—the lobbyist, the lawyer, the representative of one of the infinite number of trade associations—not only must keep informed but must also convince his clients that he is informed, is on top of things. Part of his job is to calm the clients' anxieties, and he spends a lot of time on the telephone doing this.* New Yorker 1/9/78, p41 **—n. 1** something that enhances or reinforces self-esteem; approval or reward. *"The ability to give 'strokes' is a skill," says the public-relations specialist. (A "stroke" is a no-nonsense compliment, a bit of reinforcement. The women, instructed in its use, have been asking for, giving and getting "strokes" throughout the workshop.)* NY Times Magazine 5/29/77, p15 **2** power to persuade or cajole; ability to influence or manipulate. Transcript *P: What stroke have you got with Magruder . . .? E: I think the stroke Bob has with him is in the confrontation to say, "Jeb, you know that just isn't so,"* *and just stare him down on some of this stuff.* New Times 5/31/74, p29 [**1964:** verb and noun definitions 1 were popularized by use in transactional analysis]

stroke house, *U.S. Slang.* a theater where pornographic films are shown. *He would fly to New York once a week, ostensibly to "work on a deal." Actually, he would camp in the 42nd Street stroke houses and come back with tales of what they were getting away with now.* Atlantic 7/71, p52 [**1970,** from *stroke,* slang verb meaning to copulate]

strong force, the force that causes neutrons and protons to bind in the nucleus of an atom. It is stronger than any other known force. In quark theory, it is transmitted by gluons. Also called STRONG INTERACTION. Compare WEAK FORCE. *Knowledge of the internal structures of the proton and the neutron may provide the key to understanding the "strong" force that holds the atomic nucleus together and endows the universe with its stability. The strong force makes its presence known in the nuclear reactions that fuel the stars and that, on a more modest scale, provide the energy for nuclear power and nuclear explosives.* Scientific American 6/71, p61 [**1971**]

strong interaction, another name for STRONG FORCE. Compare WEAK INTERACTION. *When physicists first began to explore atomic nuclei, they found that the force that holds nuclei together is different from either the gravitational or the electromagnetic forces they were familiar with. Because it appeared much stronger than anything else, physicists called this new force the strong interaction.* Science News 8/21/71, p121 [**1954,** from the phrase *strong interaction,* used earlier in describing the force (1947)]

strontium-rubidium dating, variant of RUBIDIUM-STRONTIUM DATING. *The ironstone sediments were dated . . . within analytical error with a date of 3.70 billion ± 140 million years for granitic gneisses (igneous rocks) in the Isua area determined by strontium-rubidium dating.* Science News 10/6/73, p213 [**1973**]

structural gene, the part of the operon (a cluster of genes functioning as a unit) that determines the sequence of amino acids and the structure of the proteins. Compare OPERATOR. *The first known class consists of structural genes, which determine the amino acid sequence and three-dimensional shape of proteins; the second is regulatory genes, which specify whether [structural] genes will function and therefore control the rate of enzyme synthesis.* Science News Yearbook 1970, p103 [**1959**]

structurism, *n.* art that emphasizes basic structural forms or processes. [Charles] *Biederman himself, having grandly declared that both painting and sculpture were obsolete, arrived at what he has come to call "structurism"—reliefs that have the dimension of sculpture and the color of painting.* Time 1/26/70, p37 [**1963**]

structurist, *n.* an artist whose work emphasizes basic geometric forms or structures. [Reuben] *Nakian's sculpture, drawings, terra cotta statuettes and plaques are open on every level to a richly sensual interpretation, opposed to the compact, single-minded absolute sought by a younger generation of structurists.* NY Times 6/26/66, p15 —**adj.** of or characterized by structurism. *Biederman's "structurist" work developed from a study of Mondrian but differs from it in the clustered, projective nature of the relief elements and the saturated fields of colour against which they are seen.* Times (London) 3/17/67, p12 [**1958**]

structurize, *v.t.* to arrange in the form of an organized structure or series of patterns. *Research capacities are being structurized to the optimum in every single economic branch in order to meet the country's requirements of the scientific and technological revolution.* Times (London) 12/18/68, p9 [**1958**]

strung out, *U.S. Slang.* sick, weak, or disturbed, especially from drug addiction. *. . . songs are about a wild party, a girl who gets run over by a beach-cleaning truck, men hungry for women or strung out on dope and booze . . .* New Yorker 4/18/70, p159 *"These are very strung-out kids with individual*

hang-ups," said Jim Fouratt . . . describing the modern runaway. NY Times 8/18/67, p22 [**1959**]

student power, the control of a school, college, or university by members of the student body. *. . . the place* [the École des Beaux Arts in Paris] *is no longer under the direction of its professors, appointed by the state, but is operating under what is called "student power."* New Yorker 7/6/68, p62 *Some students call for student power—others shrink from the term because they have some sense of the arduous work, the sheer tedium, the high responsibilities that are always a part of administrative power.* NY Times 6/5/68, p32 *Student power means absolute student control—and that means teachers as well—over everything.* Times (London) 3/18/68, p2 [**1968**]

stuff, *n. U.S. Slang.* **1** marijuana. *. . . in the U.S. it is variously called the weed, stuff, Indian hay, grass, pot, tea, maryjane and other names.* Scientific American 12/69, p17 **2** heroin. *Heroin itself is a nightmare almost beyond description. By any of the names its users call it—scag, smack, the big H, horse, dope, junk, stuff—it is infamous as the hardest of drugs . . .* Time 3/16/70, p16 [**1965,** specialized senses of the earlier slang term for any narcotic drug or preparation (OEDS 1929)] —*v.t. U.S.* to throw, drop, or slam a basketball down through the basket. See SLAMDUNK. *But size is not quintessential. Alabama's Kent Looney, a 5-ft. 9 in., 141-lb. guard, went over a 7-ft. opponent to stuff a rebound.* Time 3/21/77, p61 [**1967**]

stun gas, an incapacitating gas that has the effect of causing temporary confusion and disorientation. *Police across the country have gratefully adopted Mace, a chemical stun gas in a pressurized can, as a means of coping with rioters and unruly suspects.* Time 5/17/68, p75 *Just to keep the record smug, here is a run-down of anti-crowd devices which other nations, notably America, are developing: . . . stun gas; gas which temporarily blinds; electrified water jets; and an electronic gadget said to produce "dynamic dysentery."* Punch 2/21/68, p253 [**1968**]

stun gun, 1 a long-barreled gun that fires a small bag containing sand, bird shot, etc. Compare BATON GUN. *Riot control in the United States is a field fast becoming strewn with gimmicks, but the stun gun has already been used effectively by the Alameda County Sheriff's Department who are called in whenever student riots at Berkeley become too much for the local police.* Sunday Times (London) 5/30/71, p5 *To maintain a constant level of effectiveness a regular stream of innovations is needed . . . These include nets which can be projected over demonstrators, and a stun-gun which fires a small sandbag.* New Scientist and Science Journal 8/12/71, p375 **2** a weapon designed to stun or temporarily immobilize a person with an electric shock. Compare TASER. *Promoted as a humane defensive weapon that will immobilize but normally not kill, the electric stun gun may be winning unwanted acceptance in the underworld as a sort of jailhouse insurance.* Tuscaloosa News (Alabama) 10/26/75, p10A [**1971**]

stylostatistics, *n.* the use of statistical methods to analyze the style of a writer. *There are two essays in stylo-statistics, those by Jiří Krámský and Jaroslav Peprink. Both are based on extensive corpora, and both show that frequency of items or classes of items can be shown to correlate with time and type of writing. The first-mentioned essay takes up frequency of verb forms; the second confines itself to a narrow class, the verbs that introduce quotations. Both essays prove their points quite neatly.* Language 6/71, p452 [**1956**]

subcompact, *n.* Also called **subcompact car.** a small, sporty, economically priced two-door car that is slightly smaller than a compact car. Compare INTERMEDIATE. *St. Thomas, Ontario: Ford has put its new subcompact car, the Pinto, into production here. It will be on sale September 11.* Times (London) 8/11/70, p18 *The subcompacts, though, are small and cheap enough to attract many motorists who might buy bigger U.S.-made cars if they felt more flush, but whose desire for economy has been sharpened by the bite of the 1970 recession and continuing inflation.* Time 3/1/71, p54 [**1967**]

subduct, *v.i., v.t. Geology.* to sink under the margin of a crustal plate; undergo or cause subduction. Compare OBDUCT. *When* an oceanic plate collides with a continental one, the oceanic plate usually dives toward the mantle and is subducted. That is because the continental plates are thicker and more buoyant. Scientific American 8/76, p53 *"The Juan de Fuca plate has been subducting," Riddihough says. "I see very little evidence that it has stopped now, so we have to assume that it still is."* Science News 11/26/77, p360 [**1970**] —**subduction,** *n.: When two plate margins converge, one plate undergoes subduction, which means that its leading edge buckles beneath the other plate and plunges diagonally downward into the earth's upper mantle to depths approaching 700 kilometers.* Britannica Book of the Year 1975, p64

subemployed, *adj.* insufficiently or inadequately employed; underemployed, as of a part-time worker, or unemployed. *Those now subemployed could provide the additional services by working as policemen and firemen, teachers' aides, health workers, or in conservation, transit, recreation and antipollution jobs.* NY Times Magazine 11/5/72, p56 [**1967**] —**subemployment,** *n.: In one study of low-income neighborhoods, the "sub-employment rate," including both unemployment and underemployment, was about 33 percent, or 8.8 times greater than the overall unemployment rate for all U.S. workers.* 1969 World Book Year Book, p547

sublimit, *n.* a limit somewhat lower than a maximum limit. *Now the United States is reported to have agreed to allow modernization of the Soviet force of about 300 heavy missiles, and Moscow has accepted limits of 800 to 850 land-based missiles with multiple warheads. This would be a "sublimit" within an overall ceiling of 1,320 ballistic missiles bearing multiple warheads.* NY Times 10/22/77, p3 [**1973**, perhaps shortening of earlier *sublimitation* (1781)]

subminiaturize, *v.t.* another word for MICROMINIATURIZE. *Moreover, the proliferation of transistorized and "subminiaturized" tape recording devices—many of them easily concealed or disguised—not only makes the activity more intriguing, but makes its proscription all but impossible to enforce.* Saturday Review 3/26/66, p55 [**1966**]

subnuclear, *adj.* of or relating to the particles or phenomena within the nuclei of atoms. *Consider the vast sums conned out of the US forces for laser developments by broad hints about death-rays, or the incredible amounts of money still happily sunk in the most far-out varieties of subnuclear physics because subnuclear research once delivered the military goods.* New Scientist 5/4/67, p293 [**1964**]

suboptimize, *v.i.* to make optimal use of parts or subdivisions of a system, process, etc. *In the . . . report the Sussex team says that "It is possible using the above scheme, however, to suboptimise across a set of projects and activities so that at least the adverse effects arising from these activities are more evenly distributed."* New Scientist 12/14/72, p638 [**1962**, from *sub-* subordinate + *optimize* to make as effective as possible] —**suboptimization,** *n.: Sub-optimization has a definite utility for certain situations but inherently it does not conform to the holistic idea that the total system is given meaning by the ways in which its components interact with each other when they are focussing on a given objective.* Ralph Parkman, The Cybernetic Society, 1972, p198 *Another source of human frustration with large technological systems is what systems experts call suboptimization (failure to perceive the relation of optimum smaller systems to the larger whole).* Britannica Book of the Year 1973, p30

subplate, *n.* Geology. a small crustal plate. . . . *the earth's crust in the intermountain West is divided into several subplates. Two of them, which they have named the Northern Rocky Mountain and Great Basin subplates, appear to be moving west with respect to the stable portion of the North American plate.* Science News 8/17/74, p105 [**1970**, from *sub-* secondary + (tectonic) *plate*]

subprofessional, *n.* another name for PARAPROFESSIONAL. *Dr. Gardner is training workers from the community, many of whom lack even high school diplomas, to act as therapists. The bulk of the therapeutic work is done by these subprofessionals . . .* Science News 10/5/68, p346 *The need is for a massive and*

innovative approach—from new procedures for teacher training and internship to the effective use of teachers' aides and other subprofessionals, preferably drawn from the schools' own neighborhoods. NY Times 3/16/67, p46 [**1967**]

subsatellite, *n.* an artificial satellite launched from a larger orbiting satellite. *The Command Module, piloted by Alfred Worden, will carry new equipment to map the Moon, and will eject for the first time, a sub-satellite carrying particle detectors and a magnetometer. Tracking this craft would provide improved lunar gravity profiles.* New Scientist 10/29/70, p212 [**1956**]

subsonic, *n.* an aircraft that flies at speeds less than the speed of sound; a subsonic aircraft. Compare SUPERSONIC. *Flight International (November 27, 1975) published noise footprints for Concorde and the leading subsonics.* Manchester Guardian Weekly 1/18/76, p2 *The subsonics will install new devices to reduce their noise to acceptable levels by 1985.* NY Times 9/28/77, p36 [**1970**, noun use of the adjective]

substorm, *n.* a disturbance in the earth's magnetosphere (region dominated by the magnetic field) in which magnetic energy accumulated in the tail of the magnetosphere is suddenly released and dissipated, manifesting itself as an aurora or other magnetic phenomenon. See MAGNETOTAIL. *Substorms occur either in isolated form once every several hours (sometimes days) or in a rapid sequence consisting of several events per hour, often as the result of an interplanetary compression or expansion shock wave, triggered by a solar flare, impinging on the magnetosphere. This latter event represents a magnetic storm (historically, this is the reason why substorms have been called* substorms). Science 1/11/74, p43 [**1961**, from *sub-* subordinate, secondary + (magnetic) *storm*]

subterrene, (ˌsəbtəˈriːn), *n.* a drill heated to melt the rock through which it bores. *Scientists predicted that eventually the drills, called subterrenes, would be used for large-scale projects such as highway and railroad tunnels.* 1973 Britannica Yearbook of Science and the Future, p336 [**1972**, from Latin *subterrēnus* under the earth, subterranean; perhaps influenced by earlier *subterrene, adj.* (OED 1610), noun (OED 1854)]

subtext, *n.* the underlying meaning of a literary or dramatic text. *"The Lodger" demonstrates a beautiful sense of subtext— of the gap between what people say and what is on their minds—which is rather an astonishing achievement in a silent picture.* New Yorker 9/11/71, p93 *Again in the kidnapping scene . . . you may recall* The Homecoming [a play by Harold Pinter]. *The resemblances are so strong that they suggest that the final solution lies somewhere in the subtext of Pinter's own allusive, enigmatic fantasies of persecution.* Listener 8/3/67, p156 [**1950, 1960**]

subtilisin, *n.* an enzyme that breaks down proteins, used especially in the study of protein synthesis. *These enzymes, and all but one of the others listed here, almost certainly have a common evolutionary origin. The exception is subtilisin, which has the same active site and catalytic function as trypsin but evolved independently.* Scientific American 7/74, p86 [**1953**, from New Latin (*Bacillus*) *subtilis,* a species of soil bacteria that was thought to produce it + English *-in* (chemical suffix)]

suction lipectomy, another name for LIPOSUCTION. *Fat farms and suction lipectomy will go the way of the Edsel.* NY Times Magazine 11/15/87, p22 [**1987**]

suction method, another name for VACUUM ASPIRATION. *It is something of a surprise to hear that they [the Women's Liberation movement] have now firmly launched a campaign for freely available abortions by the suction method—the so-called "lunch-time" abortion. This technique is about as difficult and traumatic as extracting a tooth and requires about the same amount of facilities and instrumentation.* New Scientist 5/11/72, p336 [**1972**]

sudden infant death syndrome, a technical name for CRIB DEATH. *This volume is the report of an international conference on the sudden infant death syndrome (SIDS in jargon) to which puzzles were brought by four groups of doctors: the epidemiologists, bearing thoughtfully tabulated numbers; the pathologists, with scalpel and lens, peering in their classic mode* *at the tiny dead; the physiologists, with electrocardiogram, blood-pressure record and respiratory chemistry, and the virologists, with their diagnostic tissue cultures in rapid growth.* Scientific American 3/71, p118 [**1970**]

sudser, *n. Especially U.S. Slang.* a soap opera. *Down to earth with* The Brothers, *the sudser with everything (BBC 1).* Listener 5/11/72, p631 *His plays are worthlessly "moving"—lyricized sudsers with stand-up-comic numbers, and synthetic to the core.* New Yorker 12/23/72, p52 [**1968,** from (soap) *suds* + *-er,* perhaps patterned after earlier slang *soaper* (1946)]

suedehead, *n.* a type of SKINHEAD (young British working-class tough). *The skinheads are lineal descendants of the rockers—with an added touch of mindless savagery. When their hair grows a trifle longer, they refer to themselves as suedeheads. Skins or suedes, they specialize in terrorising such menacing types as hippies and homosexuals, Pakistani immigrants and little old ladies.* Time 6/8/70, p37 [**1970**]

suffosion (sə'fouʒən), *n. Geology.* underground seepage of water into rock. Compare OBDUCT. *Headward extension will also be aided by sub-surface seepage or 'suffosion', helping to corrode the bedrock. It is evident that both suffosion processes and headcut migration will seek out weaknesses in the bedrock such as joint-planes, zones of fault-line debris or seams of clay between harder sediments.* Geographical Magazine 6/72, p602 [**1966,** from Latin *suffosio, -ōnis* a digging under, undermining, from *suffodere* to dig underneath] ▶This is apparently a reborrowing of an obsolete term, recorded in the OED as used in the general sense of the Latin word between 1623 and 1648.

suggestology, *n.* the study and use of suggestion, especially in teaching and psychotherapy. *Suggestology, the psychology of suggestion, has very wide application and it has achieved—according to Bulgarian scientists—striking results in the field of education, psychiatry, neurology and telepathy. It has nothing to do with hypnosis or sleep-teaching.* Times (London) 4/2/77, p14 [Dr. Georgi] *Lozanov began to develop his ideas concerning Suggestology several decades ago while involved in research on the stimulation of memory through hypnotic therapy . . . Lozanov's early research had to do with vocabulary learning in French and Greek, where students were shown to be able to acquire passive control over large numbers of words.* Linguistic Reporter 12/79, p7 [**1970,** from *suggestion* + *-ology* study of] **—suggestologic,** *adj.: His letter helpfully explains that, "apart from the specific suggestologic problems concerning the unconscious form of psychic interactions and the reserve capacities of the individual, . . . the symposium will also examine the problems of the place of suggestion in a number of spheres of psychological research."* New Scientist and Science Journal 2/18/71, p397

suggestopaedia, *n.* the application of suggestology to learning; teaching through suggestion. *In an hour-long presentation to the Interagency Language Round Table in Washington DC, Dr. Georgi Lozanov, a Bulgarian psychiatrist, sketched the major tenets of his philosophy of learning, Suggestology, and described some of the practical applications of these tenets in his method of language instruction, Suggestopaedia.* Linguistic Reporter 12/79, p7 [**1970,** from *suggestology* + Greek *paideía* instruction] **—suggestopaedics,** *n.: Since there are so many educational "wonder techniques" which eventually fizzle away, I asked Mr John E. Fobes, Unesco's deputy director-general to assess the Paris experiment with suggestopaedics.* Times (London) 4/2/77, p14

suicide seat, the seat next to the driver in an automobile, so called from the large incidence of fatality among those who occupy it in accidents. *I was in the mini-bus, in the suicide seat next to the driver.* Guardian (London) 5/24/72, p10 [**1954**]

suicidogenic, *adj.* producing or conducive to suicide. *As a sociologist he* [Emile Durkheim] *had two interests, in identifying the 'suicidogenic currents' whose variation caused observed variations in suicide rates, and in tracing the pathology of his own society, whose suicide rate was far too high to be normal.*

Listener 3/22/73, p383 [**1973,** from *suicide* + connecting *-o-* + *-genic* producing]

suicidology, *n.* the study of suicide and suicidal behavior. *Writing in the current issue of* Life-Threatening Behavior, *the new official journal of the American Association of Suicidology, Psychiatrist Blachly suggests that the suicidal person who wants to destroy his whole body may find an alternative in sacrificing just part of it.* Time 4/26/71, p56 [**1964**]

suitor, *n. U.S. Finance.* a person or group that seeks to acquire a company through a tender offer. *A suitor may be friendly or hostile. Once an offer has been made, the odds of eluding a suitor are about 1 to 4.* NY Times 8/30/81, pC3 [**1963**]

sulfinpyrazone (ˌsəlfin'pirəˌzoun), *n.* the generic name of ANTURANE. *The American research project was set up to test the theory that the risk of this further thrombosis might be reduced by treatment with a drug, sulfinpyrazone, which acts on the blood platelets, the small cells that start the process of thrombosis.* Times (London) 3/2/78, p16 [**1960,** from *sulfin*ic acid + *pyra*zole + *-one* (chemical suffix)]

Sullivan Principles, a set of principles under which American firms in South Africa pledge to follow nondiscriminatory employment practices. *I.B.M. has distributed the text of the Sullivan Principles to all its employees in South Africa.* New Yorker 5/14/79, p144 *Out of a sense of social responsibility or business prudence, more than 100 American companies have adopted the Sullivan Principles.* NY Times Magazine 6/3/79, p33 [**1977,** named after their author, Leon H. *Sullivan,* born 1923, an American Baptist clergyman and member of the board of directors of General Motors]

summit, *v.i.* to engage or participate in a summit meeting. *Prime Minister Indira Gandhi is willing to summit with the chap (probably at the end of the month).* Time 6/5/72, p40 *The presidential performance here continues to be played on a split screen, featuring . . . Nixon the President, summiting and clowning with the visiting Brezhnev, and Nixon, the suspect, seeking to elude the Watergate noose.* New Scientist 7/5/73, p30 [**1972,** verb use of the noun meaning summit meeting]

sumotori ('su:mou'touri:), *n., pl.* **-ris** or **-ri.** a practitioner of sumo, the Japanese form of wrestling. *Sumotori may look fat, says Jesse, "but anyone who [tries] socking a sumotori in the stomach will gladly go back to brick walls."* Newsweek 8/13/73, p92 *The most disappointing sumotori of the year was Wajima, who for the first time in four years failed to win a single title.* Britannica Book of the Year 1976, p198 [**1973,** from Japanese *sumōtori*]

Sunbelt, *n.* the southern region of the United States from Virginia to southern California (often used attributively). Compare SNOWBELT. *The most recent statistics for unemployment by area indeed show that joblessness is highest in the Northeast and lowest in the farm states, where there tend to be fewer major cities, and in the Sunbelt. However, in California and Florida, both part of the Sunbelt, unemployment has been higher than the national average.* NY Times 1/9/77, pC43 *An even larger triple-width size, already seizing a good part of the mobile home market in California and other "sunbelt" regions, is beginning to make an appearance in other states.* Ruth Rejnis, Her Home, 1980, p96 [**1969,** coined by the American writer Kevin P. Phillips as *Sun Belt;* patterned after *corn belt, Bible belt,* etc.]

sun block, a chemical substance, usually a cream, that protects the skin from sunburn. It provides more protection than a sunscreen. *There are various kinds of sun-tanning preparations which include differing combinations of these chemical sunscreens. These sun-tanning products are labeled in different ways according to the manufacturer. Products labeled as "sun blocks" usually screen out all, or almost all, damaging rays.* NY Times Magazine 5/21/78, p74 [**1977**]

sunchoke, *n.* the edible tuber of the Jerusalem artichoke. *Whether or not the sunchoke, formerly known as the Jerusalem artichoke, will ever make the big time is still unclear. There was a flurry of activity a few years ago when the vegetable was re-*

named and it can be found in some supermarkets today. But despite its delightful sweet, nutty taste and satisfying crisp texture, the sunchoke has yet to catch on in this country. NY Times 12/22/82, pC6 [**1982**]

Sun Day, a day in May set aside by advocates of solar power to dramatize the need for expanded research and interest in the sun as an alternative energy source. *Among other major spin-offs of Sun Day, Hayes described formation of two national organizations to promote a change in the political and social climate affecting solar energy development. The Solar Lobby, which should get underway within the next few months, will represent consumers on Capitol Hill.* Science News 5/13/78, p310 [**1978**]

sundown, *v.i.* to experience nighttime hallucinations because of strange surroundings. *During the day she was fine, if tired and dozing most of the time. But when darkness came she entered a shadowy world, a world seen only by her. In hospitals they call it "sundowning" and it is a common thing with old people when they are removed from a familiar environment and placed in the hospital. The darkness, the lack of familiar things around them, the strange sounds from the corridors cause a sort of sensory confusion which brings on hallucinations.* Atlantic 7/72, p75 [**1972,** verb use of the noun]

sunseeker, *n.* a person who seeks out places of sunshine and warmth to vacation in. *Sunseekers are beginning to look farther afield than the popular Spanish mainland.* Times (London) 12/31/70, pVII [**1970**]

sunset law, *U.S.* a law requiring that government agencies, commissions, or programs be reviewed to assess their usefulness. *The recently enacted "sunset law" requires the House and Senate to take a look at every department between now and 1980 and abolish any which cannot justify their continued operation.* Tuscaloosa News (Alabama) 9/26/76, p8D *A column on Colorado's "sunset law," which requires a yearly re-evaluation of spending programs, prompted legislators in eight other states to introduce similar measures.* Time 5/9/77, p49 [**1976,** from the figurative sense of *sunset* decline or close, because such laws terminate programs considered wasteful; influenced by SUNSHINE LAW]

sunshine law, *U.S.* a law which requires government bodies to conduct their regular sessions in public. *"Sunshine laws" are rapidly catching on in the states and cities and there are already cases where decision makers who have tried to settle things in private caucus have been hauled before the courts.* Manchester Guardian Weekly 8/1/76, p8 *Congress in 1976 passed the nation's first federal "sunshine law," a measure that would open the proceedings of some 50 government boards and agencies to the press.* Britannica Book of the Year 1977, p574 [**1972,** so called originally because it was first enacted in Florida (the "Sunshine State"), later equated with the idea of "letting the sunshine in," or meeting in open session]

sunshine pill, *U.S. Slang.* a yellow or orange tablet containing the hallucinogenic drug LSD. *The police . . . could often be induced to tell of green-speckled sunshine pills, little blue-and-black mini-bennies, caps of fake mescaline that looked like brown sugar, and other underground pharmaceuticals that kept turning up in all the worst pockets.* Harper's 5/74, p68 [**1970**]

superactinide series, a predicted series of superheavy chemical elements which is to follow the transactinide series in the periodic table. *Active searches are in progress for elements 110 and 114; scientists were already talking about elements up to 121; and Dr. [Glenn T.] Seaborg, for one, has predicted elements 122 to 153. He called this grouping the superactinide series.* Science News Yearbook 1970, p266 [**1970**]

superalloy, *n.* an alloy developed to resist high temperatures, stresses, and oxidation. *Superalloys such as nickel and cobalt-base alloys, even though some of them can withstand temperatures as high as 1,800 degrees F., will not hold up under the high-temperature requirements of upcoming jets, reactors and rockets.* Science News 1/24/70, p107 [**1953**]

superbaryon, *n.* a hypothetical elementary particle whose existence has been postulated to account for the development of the universe after the Big Bang. *In addition to the standard model of the big bang there is a very speculative new hypothesis* [which] *assumes that massive "superbaryons" formed just after the big bang. The superbaryons were approximately the same size as ordinary baryons, but their mass was as much as 10^{38} times greater.* Scientific American 5/74, p117 [**1972**]

superbolt, *n.* an unusually powerful bolt of lightning, releasing as much as 10 trillion watts of optical energy. *Winter storms over Japan, associated with a disproportionate share of the superbolts observed globally, have long been known for their anomalously intense lightning flashes. These are thought to occur between positively charged regions and the ground. This is in contrast to bolts derived from negatively charged regions as in a typical summer storm, or from upper level cloud to cloud discharges.* Science News 7/2/77, p15 [**1977**]

super-bug, *n.* a bacterium that consumes large amounts of petroleum, produced by splicing genes from several strains of bacteria of the same species that digest petroleum. *The oil-eating bacterium contains genes from four different strains of Pseudomonas bacteria. That "super-bug" digests petroleum several times faster than any of the individual strains. A spokesman for General Electric says the company will now reapply for the patent, but that the decision of the patent court may be appealed to the Supreme Court.* Science News 3/18/78, p175 [**1975**]

supercalifragilisticexpialidocious (ˌsuːpərˌkæləˌfrædʒəˌlistikˌekspiˌæləˈdouʃəs), *adj. Informal.* marvelous; fantastic; fabulous. *Enthusiastic supporters once erected a billboard to Lindsay in Midtown Manhattan: "Lindsay is supercalifragilisticexpialidocious."* Harper's 8/68, p44 *The tourist and construction surge in Florida, sparked largely by the Walt Disney amusement park, has . . . a suitable description: supercalifragilisticexpialidocious.* Time 12/11/72, p100 [**1964,** a nonsense word in a song popularized by the motion picture *Mary Poppins* (1964)]

supercell, *n. Meteorology.* a massive low-pressure center characterized by a very large cumulonimbus cloud and long-lasting thunderstorm, often producing thunder and violent tornadoes. *During the early 1960's, meteorologists noted that more violent tornadoes with wind speeds of 200 mph or more seemed to be associated with a massive, persistent type of thunderstorm called a supercell . . ., which expands to cover a vast area, lasts for six hours or longer. During its lifetime, a supercell can give rise to not one but many tornadoes.* World Book Science Annual 1986, p87 [**1985**]

superchip, *n.* a silicon chip having thousands of components and capable of processing large amounts of data at very high speed. *Japan still looks set to dominate the world computer market with a new 256k superchip that may be the key to the much-discussed "fifth generation" of computers, which will more closely resemble human brainpower.* Sunday Times (London) 7/3/83, p58 [**1978**]

superchurch, *n.* a large church formed by the unification of a group of separate churches. *. . . Episcopalians are potential participants in the proposed multichurch Protestant merger, the Church of Christ Uniting. Should the Episcopal Church join the new super-church, the questions of Episcopal belief, the Eucharist and ministerial orders could become more complicated yet.* Time 5/25/70, p76 [**1970**]

supercity, *n.* **1** a large urban area formed by the expansion and gradual coalescence of two or more relatively distant cities. Compare STRIP CITY. *I have the recurrent nightmare of the supercities that threaten us today, the titanic conurbations—already growing before our eyes—single vast towns from Boston to Baltimore, Pittsburgh to Chicago, London to Birmingham, each with thirty million people imprisoned in asphalt forever.* Manchester Guardian Weekly 10/10/70, p15 **2** a very large city; a megalopolis. *. . . daring solutions to the problems of urban design were offered by Paolo Soleri in exhibitions at the Corcoran Gallery, Washington, D.C., and the Whitney Museum in New York. He planned arcologies, gigan-*

tic supercities towering high in the air or floating on water, as a means of preventing man from destroying himself and his environment. Americana Annual 1971, p103 **[1970]**

supercluster, *n.* a very large cluster of galaxies. *Present data on the sizes of clusters of galaxies, and on possible "superclusters," are too sparse to enable us to assess the validity of theories that predict the mass spectrum of condensations.* Scientific American 6/70, p35 **[1958]**

supercoil, *n.* another name for SUPERHELIX. *They suggest that a single DNA double helix is wound up into a supercoil with diameter 100 angstroms and pitch 110 angstroms, with histones holding the whole thing rigid by bonding between different parts of the supercoil.* New Scientist 11/16/72, p378 **[1965]** —**supercoiled,** *adj.: The two strands of the DNA double helix are joined to form a duplex loop; these structures are "supercoiled," presumably so that the long DNA molecules can be fitted inside a cell. In the other kind only one of the DNA strands is joined; these molecules are not supercoiled. If a single break is made in one strand of a supercoiled molecule, the molecule loses its coils.* Scientific American 4/73, p21

supercontinent, *n.* any of several great land masses supposed to have once comprised the present continents. Also called PROTOCONTINENT. *The theory that Antarctica was once part of a supercontinent of all the major land masses has been reinforced by discovery of a fossil jawbone . . . near the South Pole.* NY Times 3/17/68, pD11 **[1963]**

supercrat, *n. U.S.* an official of high rank; a powerful bureaucrat. *Under the unconventional—sometimes downright confusing—new chain of command, administrative control . . . will be largely limited to five supercrats, each bearing the title of "assistant to the President."* Newsweek 1/15/73, p15 **[1972,** patterned after *bureaucrat]*

supercritical wing, an aircraft wing that maintains a supersonic flow of air over the upper wing surface to reduce drag by eliminating shock-induced separation of the boundary layer. *The supercritical wing, as it is called, was developed at NASA's Langley Research Center in Virginia under the direction of Dr. Richard T. Whitcomb.* Science News 11/14/70, p389 **[1969,** earlier *supercritical airfoil* (1967)]

superdense, *adj.* extremely dense or compact. *The quasar is composed of superdense material, especially in its central core. To obtain such densities the quasars would have to be composed purely of neutrons or other neutral particles.* Science Journal 5/68, p7 *Soviet scientists believe that there may be similar occurrences of super-dense water in areas deep inside the Earth, where conditions, as in the atmosphere, differ from those on the surface.* New Scientist 6/13/68, p590 **[1967]**

superfecta, *n. U.S.* a form of betting in horse races in which the bettor must pick the exact order of the first four horses to finish in a race. Compare TRIFECTA. *As for OTB* [off-track betting] *itself, the report recommends putting a five-percent tax on every wager (a $2 bet would cost $2.10) and channelling the play to gimmick betting—superfectas, exactas, and such.* New Yorker 3/24/73, p134 **[1971,** blend of *super-* and *perfecta* (in which the first two finishers are picked)]

superflare, *n. Astronomy.* a powerful stellar flare thought to be the source of gamma-ray bursts. *The superflare was part of an episode lasting more than two weeks, in which one or more "moderate-or-better" flares occurred almost every day. Ten such events were recorded on April 7 alone. If the more common, small flares are included, McIntosh says, the total during the two-week episode may have been as high as 200.* Science News 5/13/78, p309 **[1973]**

supergranular or **supergranulated,** *adj. Astronomy.* of, relating to, or forming supergranulations. *The result of the supergranular motions . . . is to spread the magnetic flux over very large areas of the solar surface, even to the poles of the sun.* Science 9/29/72, p1158 *Scientists see these supergranulated cells, as they are called, as the tops of convection bringing energy up from the center of the sun where it is generated by nuclear fusion.* World Book Science Annual 1975, p140 **[1967]**

supergranulation, *n. Astronomy.* any of a large number of gaseous cells of great density and heat that extend into the chromosphere from the deeper layers of the sun (often used attributively). *The supergranulation "cells," unlike the small convective granulations visible on the Sun's surface, are of the order of 15 000 to 30 000 km across . . . with a central upflow of material which then flows outward with a velocity of about 500 m/s and then down back into the body of the Sun.* New Scientist 1/13/77, p77 **[1962]**

supergravity, *n. Physics.* the gravitational force that arises from a symmetry used to explain the relationship of different classes of fundamental particles. See GRAVITINO, SUPERSYMMETRY. *The theory of supergravity suggests a new approach to unification. Supergravity is an extension of general relativity, and it makes the same predictions for the classical tests of Einstein's theory, such as the precession of planetary orbits . . .* Scientific American 2/78, p129 *Since supergravity incorporates standard general relativity in a very fundamental and unique way, it was hoped that the additional constraints imposed by the added symmetry would cause the unmanageable infinities to cancel each other. This indeed happens to the lowest order corrections, though it fails to work from the third order on.* Science News 5/12/79, p307 **[1976]**

supergroup, *n.* a rock'n'roll group made up of members or former members of other rock groups. *Rock groups disintegrated rapidly, the most dramatic split finally ending the Beatles. America's most successfull "supergroup," Crosby, Stills, Nash and Young, seemed to be fragmenting also.* Americana Annual 1971, p574 **[1970]**

superheavy, *adj.* **1** having a higher atomic number or greater atomic mass than those of the heaviest elements known. *Superheavy elements are generally created by accelerating heavy ions, such as argon, for interactions with heavier elements, such as uranium.* New Scientist 2/5/70, p249 **2** of or belonging to superheavy elements. *A heavy-ion accelerator is a machine especially designed to accelerate atomic nuclei that have been stripped of some or all of their attendant electrons . . . If such nuclei are struck against other heavy nuclei, they may fuse with them and form superheavy nuclei.* Science News 12/4/71, p373 —*n.* a superheavy element. *The superheavies are designated by the prefix eka, from eka-osmium to eka-lead, and each eka-element is expected to be identifiable in the chemical analysis along with its namesake.* Science News 2/20/71, p128 **[1955 for adj.; 1971 for noun]**

superhelix, *n.* a form of DNA consisting of a double helix coiled around itself. See GYRASE. *Recent neutron diffraction studies indicate that the DNA is wound in a superhelix around the outside of this histone core.* Nature 4/15/76, p577 *It is fairly clear that at the centre of this structure is a core of protein. Around the core is spun 1 ¾ turns of a helix of the double helix of DNA. The DNA is therefore said to be in a superhelix. That arrangement rather neatly explains most of the degradation products produced by the biochemists.* Times (London) 9/3/77, p14 **[1964]** —**superhelical,** *adj.: Normal, double-helix DNA is spiral, like a loosely coiled spring. But DNA has also been isolated from cells in a superhelical form in which the helix is twisted around itself. Gellert and his co-workers found that the enzyme they discovered changed normal DNA into superhelical DNA. They named the enzyme gyrase.* World Book Science Annual 1978, p251

superhero, *n.* **1** a person greatly admired for extraordinary talents in some field; an extremely popular or accomplished athlete, performer, etc. *The* [Grateful] *Dead's relaxation is something which Eric Clapton, former guitar superhero, is desperately trying to discover within his music.* Times (London) 9/12/70, p19 *At first base, the superhero Henry Aaron of Atlanta struck up a conversation.* NY Times Magazine 7/16/72, p18 **2** an imaginary character endowed with superhuman powers for fighting crime, injustice, etc. *If your young friends have the current zeal for health foods and comic-strip superheroes your list might be taken care of in a single trip to Pinch Penny Pick-A-Pocket, where . . . health foods—crunchy granola, for example—and all the up-to-the-minute superheroes have also been re-created with paint and glitter.* New

Yorker 11/26/73, p107 [**1965** for def. 1, from *super-* over, surpassing + *hero;* **1967** for def. 2, from *Superheroes,* title of a series of comic books about superhuman characters, a name influenced by *Superman,* comic-strip hero created in the 1930's] ►An isolated 1917 citation for *super-heroes* is recorded in the OEDS. —**superheroine,** *n.: Miss Comic Strip will be either male or female and selected for her originality of costume, ingenuity of stage presentation, and desirability as an imaginary superheroine.* Times (London) 12/22/70, p8 *A new series about teen-age superheroes, entitled "The Young Sentinels," will have among its principal characters a superheroine who is black.* NY Times 9/3/77, p31

superjet, *n.* a very large or fast jet aircraft. Compare JUMBO JET, MEGAJET. *A $100 million order by United Air Lines for five giant 747 superjets helped bring the company a total of $961 million in new commercial business over the past month, boosted its backlog to a staggering $5.6 billion.* Time 11/25/66, p66 *Shall we impose the hideous noise of super-jets on communities near airports, or impose the costs of limiting them on travellers?* New Scientist 5/2/68, p250 [**1958**]

supermultiplet, *n. Nuclear Physics.* a family or class of multiplets (related groups of nuclear particles). . . . *this led to a further grouping together of particles, in fact, to a 35-fold "supermultiplet".* Times (London) 1/23/65, p3 *These algebraic properties can be used to probe the problems of particle physics, especially to calculate many of the dynamical quantities . . . For this discussion it is assumed that all the masses within a supermultiplet are degenerate.* McGraw-Hill Yearbook of Science and Technology 1968, p141 [**1952**]

superovulate, *v.i.* to produce more than the normal number of eggs at one time. *Farm animals could be induced to superovulate, their fertilized eggs could be removed, and only embryos of the desired sex would then be put back into mother animals.* New Scientist 5/2/68, p220 [**1956**]

superpartner, *n. Nuclear Physics.* the hypothetical counterpart of any particle in supersymmetry, differing from that particle by a one-half unit. *Extensive but still exploratory searches for superpartners have been carried out in a variety of accelerator experiments.* McGraw-Hill Yearbook of Science and Technology 1988, p126 [**1987,** from *super*symmetric + *partner*]

superplastic, *adj.* **1** made out of a material capable of extreme plastic extension. *Superplastic cars should be quieter, and their scrap value far higher than that of steel cars.* Times (London) 12/18/68, p17 **2** characteristic of or relating to superplastic materials. *Some alloys, when deformed at certain rates and in certain temperature ranges, can stretch out like chewing gum and be tremendously deformed without breaking. This superplastic behavior is being studied to understand superplasticity and to put it to industrial use.* Americana Annual 1968, p437 [**1947, 1968**] —*n.* a plastic material, especially a metal that is unusually pliable at an elevated temperature. *The grain is so fine that atoms slip easily along crystal planes without cleavage. This metal, after treatment which reduces the grain size to about a micrometre, behaves like a superplastic at room temperature—it can be stretched by a factor of about 10 in one direction without breaking.* New Scientist 1/2/69, p22 [**1968**] —**superplastically,** *adv.: At one time, it was considered that superplastic metallic alloys were amorphous-like and for this reason behaved superplastically.* Science Journal 6/69, p75

superport, *n.* a very large port to accommodate megatankers and other large vessels, especially such a port built offshore. Compare MONOBUOY. . . . *Promoting construction of more domestic oil refineries and superports for oceangoing tankers through legislation that would give Federal agencies authority to select sites for such facilities.* Honolulu Star-Bulletin 2/12/73, pA21 [**1969**]

super rat, a hardy rat resistant to most poison, capable of passing on the immunity to its offspring. *This company [Sorex] has developed an anti-coagulant which is particularly effective against super rats . . ., which are already prevalent in the United States and are now being reported in Europe and Asia.*

These animals are resistant to all previously available poisons. New Scientist 4/28/77, p200 [**1974**]

Super Saver, *U.S.* a type of low-cost, domestic air fare for passengers who purchase tickets in advance of travel and do not return before a certain number of days. *On the other hand, the coast-to-coast Super Saver plan used by United, American and TWA has proved to be a profitable winner. Since April, on American alone, more than 450,000 passengers have taken advantage of the plan's discounts.* Time 2/13/78, p75 [**1978**]

super slurper, a material able to absorb large quantities of liquid at a rapid rate. It is a starch, such as corn flour, in the form of powder, flakes, or sheets copolymerized with acrylonitrile treated with a hot alkali. *The U.S. Department of Agriculture (USDA) increased the absorbability of its super slurper almost threefold. The newest modified version of this substance soaks up 5,000 times its weight of water. The material would be useful in such items as diapers or as a seed coating to promote germination.* World Book Science Annual 1978, p258 [**1976**]

supersonic, *n.* an aircraft that can fly at speeds greater than the speed of sound; a supersonic aircraft. *The supersonics are coming—as surely as tomorrow. You will be flying one version or another by 1980 and be trying to remember what the great debate was all about.* Time 6/1/70, p64 *The plane is no draw, and buyers aren't exactly falling over themselves to get to the factory. But they could make up their minds once the first results of employing the supersonic on a regular commercial run are known.* Manchester Guardian Weekly (Le Monde section) 2/10/73, p16 [**1947, 1962,** noun use of the adjective]

supersonic transport, a large jet aircraft designed to fly at speeds of 1200 to 1800 miles per hour, or twice to almost three times the speed of sound. *Abbreviation:* SST See also CONCORDE. . . . *supersonic transports might modify the stratosphere, globally . . . Present uncertainties about the engine emissions and their climatic consequences, must . . . be removed before supersonic transport goes commercial.* New Scientist 10/1/70, p12 [**1961**]

superspace, *n.* a theoretical mathematical expanse in which all three-dimensional spaces are points. [John A.] *Wheeler describes his field as "the chemistry of geometry," which takes place in* superspace *defined as "the arena within which the dynamics of space operate." In superspace there is no time. Time exists at a level less basic.* New Scientist and Science Journal 7/29/71, p242 [**1971**]

superstardom, *n.* the status of a superstar. *The laws that apply to ordinary writers should be suspended for Norman Mailer. Apparently, in the eyes of one dazzled by his own celebrity, and in the eyes of his dazzled admirers, superstardom puts a man above the law, whether writer or President.* Harper's 10/73, p111 *Singer and songwriter Dolly Parton aimed for superstardom by shifting from country to popular music and making more road tours.* 1978 World Book Year Book, p412 [**1968,** derived from *superstar* an exceptionally successful performer (OEDS 1925)]

superstore, *n. Chiefly British.* a large department store, usually situated in a suburban area. *Some of Carrefour's giant out-of-town superstores in France seem almost like temples dedicated to the belief that the private car is the central spirit of the consumer religion.* Listener 12/30/71, p919 *Superstores are not often built on High Streets. Rent and rates have grown so high that food would have to be sold at great speed to reach a turnover sufficient to cover costs. Moreover, superstores are designed for the car-borne shopper so that they need sites that will be bounded by their own customer car parks, not by double yellow lines.* Times (London) 5/5/78, pI [**1965**]

superstring theory, *Physics.* a gauge theory based on supersymmetry in which the basic units of matter are one-dimensional curves called strings. *A basic tenet of the new theory, known as superstring theory, states that the universe has not just three spatial dimensions, but nine. This may have a science-fiction ring to it, but it is nonetheless a perfectly sensible possibility in the context of a quantum superstring theory.* Encyclopedia Science Supplement (Grolier) 1987, p307 [**1986**]

supersymmetry, *n. Nuclear Physics.* a theory for unifying all the fundamental forces in nature by relating the symmetry of two broad classes of elementary particles, the fermions (such as protons and neutrons) and the bosons (such as photons and pions). *The symmetry operations of the hypothetical supersymmetry . . . assert that the fermions and bosons in a system of particles could be interchanged without substantially altering the system. Hence particles with integral spin and those with half-integral spin can be regarded as manifestations of a single underlying state of matter.* Scientific American 7/77, p59 *Studies of supersymmetry and exceptional groups have brought particle theory in contact with . . . new kinds of projective geometries.* McGraw-Hill Yearbook of Science and Technology 1978, p355 **[1974]** —**supersymmetric,** *adj.: Many supersymmetric theories that are sound mathematically have failed in at least one of two fundamental ways to describe physical reality . . .* 1986 World Book Year Book, p439

supertransuranic (ˌsuːpərˌtrænsyuˈrænik), *adj.* surpassing in mass the transuranic elements (those with atomic numbers higher than uranium); superheavy. *It appeared that supertransuranic nuclei might be made by the fusion of two fairly heavy nuclei that added up to the particular mass desired in the supertransuranic region or close to that mass.* 1970 Britannica Yearbook of Science and the Future, p378 —*n.* a supertransuranic element. *The heavy-ion accelerator facilities at Dubna were utilized during the past year in an intensive program aimed at direct production of the supertransuranics.* 1972 Britannica Yearbook of Science and the Future, p319 **[1968]**

supply-side, *adj.* of, relating to, or advocating an economic policy designed to stimulate the supply or production of goods and services, especially by such incentives as tax cuts. Compare DE-MAND-SIDE. *You've put your finger on the essence of the supply-side oriented strategy. If, putting it in the old colloquial expression, inflation is too many dollars chasing too few goods, we want to increase the supply of goods and services. Our objective is achieved not by pumping up demands but by increasing supply, by reducing unemployment and inflation simultaneously.* NY Times 4/19/81, pE3 **[1976]**

supply-sider, *n.* a supporter or advocate of supply-side economics. *The supply-siders . . . persuaded President Reagan to seek a balanced budget by cutting taxes.* Christian Science Monitor 9/7/81, p20 **[1980]**

suppressant, *n.* a substance used to suppress an effect, reaction, etc. *A material that is applied directly to the burning fuel to reduce the intensity or rate of burning is termed a suppressant. Chemicals known as wetting agents or surfactants may be added to water to increase its power to "wet" the surface of fuel and to penetrate fuel beds composed of duff and leaf litter.* McGraw-Hill Yearbook of Science and Technology 1968, p189 **[1958,** as in *appetite suppressant]*

suppressor T cell, a type of T cell that moderates the activity of helper T cells and killer T cells when they have destroyed viral, bacterial, and other foreign matter in the body. *T cells play an even more complex set of roles. Some, called helper T cells, bolster the activity of B cells. Others, called suppressor T cells, act to shut off that activity when it has gone far enough. The two are important in keeping the immune defense system in balance. When it gets out of balance the result can be serious disease.* NY Times 6/19/84, pC5 **[1972]**

supracellular, *adj.* of or having to do with living organisms above the level of the cell. *Supracellular biologists, he maintained, have made a far greater contribution to the progress of cancer therapy than molecular biologists.* Nature 12/1/72, p247 **[1972]**

supragenic, *adj.* of or having to do with heredity above the level of the gene. *The true function of heterochromatic DNA remained unknown; however, according to Hatch and J. A. Mazrimus of the Lawrence Livermore Laboratory, it seemed to be important for supragenic functions of the chromosome, such as recombination and translocation.* Britannica Book of the Year 1974, p420 **[1972]**

suprathermal ion detector, an instrument for recording the flux, quantity, density, velocity, and energy per unit charge of positive ions near the lunar surface. [Astronaut Edgar] *Mitchell struggled to loosen a dust-clogged fastener on the suprathermal ion detector that was designed to record the presence of any gases on the moon.* Time 2/15/71, p8 **[1969]**

supremo, *n. British.* a person who is highest in command or authority; the overall head or chief of one or several organizations. *For that reason Mr. Crossman becomes supremo of the social services, overlording the social security and health departments and perhaps, later, fragments broken off from the Home Office . . .* Times (London) 4/6/68, p1 *The creation of a national police Supremo, with greater power over Britain's police than anyone has had before, is under consideration by the Home Secretary, Mr. Roy Jenkins.* Sunday Times (London) 10/30/66, p1 **[1963,** transferred from the epithet applied in 1944 to Earl Mountbatten, who was then Supreme Allied Commander in South-East Asia, from Spanish, a military commander-in-chief, a generalissimo, from *supremo, adj.,* supreme]

surface-effect ship, *U.S.* an air cushion vehicle designed for travel over water. *The Department of Commerce and the Navy have announced a master plan for development of large, fast surface-effect ships. These are air-cushion vessels similar to the British Hovercraft.* NY Times 8/28/67, p61 . . . "*Surface Effect Ships." . . . were to be non-amphibious craft, driven by waterscrews and waterjets, respectively, and were expected to be operating by mid-1970.* Britannica Book of the Year 1970, p758 **[1962]**

surface structure, (in generative-transformational grammar) the formal structure or phonetic expression of a sentence. Compare DEEP STRUCTURE. *"John loves Mary" is the surface structure of the sentence. It constitutes the sort of "physical signal," or phonetic articulation, to which we can perfectly well apply the traditional syntax we have learned in school: noun, verb, object, and so on. But this surface structure tells us and obviously differs for every language.* New Yorker 11/15/69, p224 **[1964]**

surfer's knob, a lump or nodule that develops under the skin especially on the knee and upper part of the foot of a surfer at points of contact with the surfboard. See also SPORTS MEDICINE. *Another result of his research, he* [Dr. Christoph Wagner] *maintains, is confirmation that the recurrent inflammations of the hand and arm suffered by musicians are the result of overtaxing their native skills—a musical variation on tennis elbow, football knee and surfer's knob.* Time 12/25/72, p49 **[1972]**

surgical strike, a swift military attack, especially a limited air attack. *This electronic super technology lends itself to a specific type of offensive called 'surgical strike'. In a surgical strike, you wipe out your target with great precision, avoiding any damage to nearby non-military installations.* Listener 5/22/75, p666 *Even the language of the bureaucracy—the diminutive "nukes" for instruments that kill and mutilate millions of human beings, the "surgical strike" for chasing and mowing down peasants from the air by spraying them with 8,000 bullets a minute—takes the mystery, awe, and pain out of violence.* Harper's 11/71, p55 **[1965]**

surgicenter, *n. U.S.* a surgical unit or facility for operations that do not require hospitalization. *A trend toward development of more outpatient or ambulatory care services by hospitals was also evident in 1972. A noteworthy development was the emergence of "surgicenters" where minor surgery can be performed on an outpatient basis.* Americana Annual 1973, p450 *While the establishment has only recently begun to show a profit, it has spawned three satellite Surgicenters—in Sacramento and Palo Alto, Calif., and in Louisville—and inspired dozens of unaffiliated imitators in other cities.* Time 10/10/77, p96 **[1969** Surgicenter, the first such unit, established in Phoenix, Arizona, from *surgical center]*

surrogacy, *n.* the quality or condition of being a surrogate mother. *The Society's panel wants to discourage both types of surrogacy except when it is part of a research programme. Impregnation of a surrogate mother should take place under the* *supervision of a medical review board.* New Scientist 9/18/86, p25 [**1986,** from *surrogate* (*mother*) + -(*a*)*cy;* influenced by the earlier term (OED 1811) meaning the office or position of a surrogate]

surrogate, *n.* short for SURROGATE MOTHER. *It's all up for grabs, which means that Gregory and Kathleen Zaccanà and their surrogate, Lisa Spoor, are now entering the same legal limbo land in which the Sterns and Whiteheads have been writhing in that courtroom in New Jersey.* NY Times Magazine 3/29/87, p36 [**1978**]

surrogate mother, 1 a woman who gives birth to a child through artificial insemination by a man who is not her husband. *Suppose that early in the pregnancy the surrogate mother decides . . . to have an abortion. Can a contract with the biological father be an impediment?* Manchester Guardian Weekly 1/4/81, p2 **2** Also called **surrogate gestational mother.** a female who carries until birth the surgically implanted fertilized egg or embryo of another female. *The demand for surrogates remained strong. Keane says he has received a thousand letters from couples seeking volunteer mothers, simply because there are so few white babies available for adoption . . . As a result, despite potential legal problems, some have already opted for surrogate mothers.* Time 6/5/78, p59 [**1976**] **—surrogate motherhood:** *Yet today, surrogate motherhood is legal and flourishing.* Family Circle 9/1/81, p16

surround-sound, *n. Especially British.* high-fidelity sound reproduction having the effect of surrounding the listener (often used attributively). Compare AMBISONICS. *All of the systems are capable of giving a generally pleasing and spacious surround sound, with the direct program in the front and the ambience developed by means of signals in the rear channels.* McGraw-Hill Yearbook of Science and Technology 1973, p399 *The new surround-sound systems recognize that sound can come from literally any direction around the horizon, and they aim to convey this directional information in a smooth manner.* Times (London) 6/24/77, p19 [**1969**]

surveille, *v.t. U.S.* to keep under close watch. *In arguing the government's case before the high court, Griswold* [Solicitor General Erwin M. Griswold] *said the Army's practice of surveilling civilians "from my point of view . . . went too far. It was an absence of proper civilian control."* Courier-Journal (Louisville, Kentucky) 3/28/72, pA2 *If the U.S. Central Intelligence Agency is as adroit in surveilling others as it is in escaping surveillance of itself, the Republic can relax.* Harper's 10/66, p37 [**1960,** back formation from *surveillance*]

survival guilt or **survivor guilt,** a feeling of guilt often experienced by survivors of a war, flood, etc., where others died. See SURVIVOR SYNDROME. *Many residents also suffer from insomnia, crying spells, moodiness, and what has been called "survival guilt": unwarranted but painful self-reproach for having lived when others died.* Time 10/9/72, p43 *Psychologists say it is common for returning veterans to suffer some form of "survivor guilt."* NY Times Magazine 11/11/79, p139 [**1971**]

survivor syndrome, symptoms, ranging from survival guilt to severe traumatic neurosis, often exhibited by survivors of a war, flood, etc., where others died. *Many Jews who escaped the Nazi horrors of World War II were scarred for life by "survivor syndrome"—chronic anxiety, flattened emotions, depression, guilt and recurring nightmares. Now, says Israeli Psychiatrist Samai Davidson, similar symptoms are turning up in the children and grandchildren of Holocaust survivors.* Time 2/21/77, p48 *Psychologists call it the survivor syndrome. The survivor of some terrible ordeal, a concentration camp, for instance, or an earthquake, may pass several years in a state of apparently normal health, before entering a terrible depression and decline. It is as if the energy spent on readjustment gradually exhausts itself and the individual gives way to the trauma.* Manchester Guardian Weekly 11/5/78, p7 [**1968**]

suss, *v.t. British Slang.* Usually **suss out.** to figure out, as if by examination, study, or investigation. *Then there are those people who reckon they have got you all sussed out. "I know you really don't like too much help," they will yell, as you stand in the middle of Oxford Circus with traffic whipping all around you.* Listener 12/25/75 and 1/1/76, p853 *The tacky-chic room of Tanya McCallin's set . . . suggested that once again Miss McCallin had sussed out the characters of a play and placed them in the surroundings they deserved.* Times (London) 4/22/77, p11 [**1966,** originally (1953) a shortening and alteration of *suspect,* from earlier slang noun *sus, suss* suspicion, suspect (1936), both by shortening]

SU(3) symmetry, *Nuclear Physics.* another name for EIGHTFOLD WAY. *The A2 meson is an enigma. Until it came along high-energy physicists were smug in their belief that all the strongly interacting particles fit into a classification known as "SU(3) symmetry". The A2 meson stands out as a maverick among the 100 or more other "elementary" particles, because recent data indicate that it is really two particles of the same mass, or—even more inscrutable—that it is a new type of particle—a double resonance or a dipole. Neither of these possibilities can be explained by simple theories.* New Scientist 10/29/70, p211 [**1965,** abbreviation of Special Unitary (group in 3 dimensions) *symmetry*]

suture, *n. Geology.* the line or junction formed between crustal plates of the earth. *The Mid-Atlantic Ridge represents the suture, or master fracture, that separates several of the 20 giant plates that form the earth's outer shell.* 1975 World Book Year Book, p342 *The Vardar Zone is thought to include a line of "sutures" formed where two confidential blocks converged, sweeping up an intervening ocean floor.* NY Times 5/8/76, p8 [**1971**]

SVD, abbreviation of SWINE VESICULAR DISEASE. *SVD is confined to pigs—and pigs in Britain do not, as do many cattle, sheep, and deer, wander at large over vast areas of countryside.* New Scientist 3/8/73, p556 [**1972**]

SV40, abbreviation of *Simian Virus 40*, a virus that causes cancer in monkeys, widely used in genetic and medical research. *The possible use of polyoma and SV40 as vectors has caused some concern, particularly because SV40 can infect human cells and evidence of SV40 infections has been found in some cases of neurological and malignant diseases in humans. But scientists have not yet . . . demonstrated that SV40 can cause human disease.* World Book Science Annual 1978, p34 *SV40 carries its genetic blueprint on a single circular piece of DNA, the viral chromosome. So far five genes have been identified. The genetic instructions are encoded in the sequence of the chemical subunits (nucleotides) strung together to make the DNA molecule. It is the complete sequence of those nucleotides that has been determined by Professor Walter Fiers and his colleagues at Ghent, and, independently, by Dr S. M. Weissman and colleagues at Yale.* Times (London) 5/12/78, p18 [**1963**]

swap meet, *U.S.* a market or bazaar where cheap or used articles, especially of handcraft, are bartered or sold. *The latest way that Californians have discovered to use their golden hours is by going to what is called a "Swap Meet." (To be sure, there are swap meets in New Jersey, on Long Island, even in Georgia. Nobody, however, is interested in how people use up their lives in New Jersey, Long Island or Georgia.)* NY Times 1/17/76, p30 [**1973**]

SWAPO or **Swapo** ('swɑ:pou), *n.* acronym for *South-West Africa People's Organization*, a black independence movement in Namibia. *A settlement in Namibia is relevant only if it ends the guerrilla war in the north; but because SWAPO has been excluded from decision-making on the future of the territory, the guerrilla war is only beginning.* Manchester Guardian Weekly 1/2/77, p9 [**1962**]

SWAT or **S.W.A.T.** (swɑt), *n. Especially U.S.* a paramilitary police unit trained in the use of special weapons (often used attributively). *The flak-jacketed Special Weapons and Tactics teams had conducted themselves as in an exercise at Quantico or Benning, pouring 1,200 rounds into the target without bringing death or injury to anyone outside. Only twenty-three SWAT-schooled officers had actually engaged in the shooting.* Harper's 9/74, p32 *Policemen were all over the sidewalk. Many of them were wearing blue baseball caps, like the S.W.A.T. teams on TV.* New Yorker 8/7/78, p18 [**1968,** from the acronym for *Special Weapons and Tactics* (squad or team) or *Special Weapons Attack Team*]

sweat, *v.t. Slang.* to worry about (something). Often in the phrase **don't sweat it,** don't worry about it. *Mr. Quinn came a few days later and told him it was quite an accomplishment that he and his father made it alone in the world, and asked him to tell how they did things . . . told him to lay it on, that he was all ears, and not to sweat a thing because he was on their side . . .* New Yorker 4/10/71, p38 *"Don't sweat it. It'll all work—be over before we know it."* Margaret Truman, Murder At the FBI, 1985, p41 [**1963**]

sweat equity, *U.S.* a share or interest in a building earned by a tenant for contributing services to the building's maintenance or renovation. *A group of poor, racially mixed tenants took over a nearby city-owned tenement, stripped the shabby interiors and are building modern apartments to replace the narrow, cold-water flats . . . In return for their "sweat equity," the builder-residents will make payments as low as $80 per month and ultimately own the building as a cooperative.* Time 7/16/73, p43 *Today, after getting the loan and investing hundreds of thousands of hours of their own labor, called sweat equity, in the six-story building, the young people have shown what urban homesteaders can do in neighborhoods so decayed some people are ready to write them off as hopeless.* NY Times 10/7/77, p1 [**1968**]

sweet spot, the spot on the face of a racquet, bat, club, stick, etc., where a ball or puck is most effectively hit. *Many players swear by their new racquets. New Jersey Insurance Executive James Slote has bought five different racquets during the past two years and finally settled on the outsized Prince, which promises a sweet spot 3 ½ times that of normal racquets.* Time 12/27/76, p50 *Almost every player noticed a definite improvement in his game. 77% hit the sweetspot more often with it.* New Yorker 5/14/79, p125 [**1974**, originally used in reference to golf clubs]

swimming pool, a tank of water for cooling and temporarily storing low-level radioactive wastes from a nuclear power plant. *Next to each nuclear reactor core there is a "swimming pool" where burned up fuel elements are stored . . . The water cools the hot fuel and shields workers from its lethal radioactivity until it dies down in intensity.* Encyclopedia Science Supplement (Grolier) 1979, p185 [**1978**, from its resemblance to a pool]

swine vesicular disease, a virus disease of swine in which blisters develop on the tongue and hooves as they do in foot-and-mouth disease. It originally appeared in Italy in 1966 and first broke out in Great Britain in 1973. *Swine vesicular disease, which has already prompted the slaughter of about 30,000 pigs, and cost £½ million in compensation alone . . . is probably not spread to any great extent via the air; transmission is by contact with an infected animal or through infected feed.* New Scientist 3/8/73, p556 [**1972**]

swing, *v.i. Slang.* **1** to be fashionably lively and exciting. *Joy Carroll explores the bizarre boom in everything awful enough to be good, from buggy seats to Camp statues. Now your home swings if it's decorated with JUNK.* Maclean's 5/2/66, p13 *"This magazine has got to swing, like other magazines swing,"Ackerman had once said, and he had not meant simply that it should be fashionable but that it should be aware of the way society moved.* Harper's 12/69, p110 **2** to swap partners for sexual purposes. *During their investigation, the Bartells met hundreds of people interested in "swinging," an activity defined as "having sexual relations as a couple with at least one other individual." . . . As Gilbert Bartell discovered, getting started in swinging is easy. All that is required is a copy of* Kindred Spirits, Ecstasy, Swingers' Life, *or any one of 50 scruffy magazines filled with ads and advice on "The Etiquette of Swinging" and "How to Organize an Enjoyable Swinging Party."* Time 2/8/71, p36 [**1957** for def. 1; **1964** for def. 2]

swingaround, *n.* a spacecraft trajectory in which a planet's gravitational field is used to alter the direction of travel. Compare SLINGSHOT. *Physicist Harry Ruppe . . . envisions a wide range of solar missions using various techniques to get there*

such as planetary swing-arounds, auxiliary rockets and the space shuttle. Science News 8/3/74, p75 [**1974**]

swing-by, *n.* a planetary trajectory in which a spacecraft uses the planet's gravitational field to achieve the orbit necessary to change course for a more distant celestial body (often used attributively). *Venus swing-bys to Mercury can be accomplished in 1970 and 1973 but not again until the 1980s.* Science Journal 12/68, p77 [**1967**]

swinger, *n. Slang.* **1** a person who keeps up with the latest fashions in clothes, entertainment, the arts, etc., especially those considered youthful and lively. *"I was a swinger for half my life. Anything hip in outlook and idea at once captivated me."* New Yorker 2/28/70, p95 **2** a person who swaps partners for sexual purposes. *The Los Angeles* Free Press, *an underground paper, carries pages of ads for "swingers," couples or singles who want to trade bed partners . . .* Atlantic 9/69, p35 [**1964**]

swingle ('swiŋgəl), *n. Chiefly U.S. and Canadian Slang.* a sexually active single person. *At the same time, the sheer number of singles, meshed with the media's seductive imagery (singles who swing are jauntily dubbed "swingles"), is gradually revising society's view of its unwed members.* Newsweek 7/16/73, p53 *Let's look at the single girl's sex life from a practical point of view. All those how-tos, all that advice to swingles are still based on the old you-be-the-master-I'll-be-the-slave idea.* Maclean's 9/74, p40 [**1967**, blend of *swinging* and *single*]

swing-wing, *n.* **1** an aircraft wing that can be swung backward in flight to set the craft's motion for slow, intermediate, or supersonic speeds. Also called VARIABLE-SWEEP WING and VARIABLE GEOMETRY. *The "swing-wings" and low-pressure tyres will enable the F-111 to operate from small airstrips devoid of concrete runways.* New Scientist 1/27/66, p206 *2 an aircraft having a swing-wing. It was the third F-111 crash since a squadron of six of the $6,000,000 swing-wings made their combat debut in Viet Nam less than a month ago.* Time 5/3/68, p23 **—adj.** of, utilizing, or relating to a swing-wing. *The F-111, a controversial swing-wing fighter designed and made by General Dynamics, saw combat duty in Vietnam for the first time but had to be withdrawn after several accidents.* Britannica Book of the Year 1969, p411 [**1965**]

switch, *v.* **switch on,** *Slang.* **1** to have a hallucinogenic experience from taking narcotics. The more common expression is TURN ON (under TURN, v.). *After rumours that you could switch on with the help of the white fibre from the inside of a banana skin it became the great mystic symbol among the Greenwich Village hippies.* Manchester Guardian Weekly 5/9/68, p6 **2** to become fashionably up-to-date; follow the latest styles in music, fashion, etc. *Nor, in this respect, would local stations financed by advertising revenue be in a more advantageous position. I only pointed to a vast audience, millions strong, which does not listen to the B.B.C.; and, I submit, will continue to remain switched off to that institution till such time as the B.B.C., stimulated by competition, gets "switched on".* Times (London) 2/9/66, p13 [**1964**]

switched-on, *adj. Slang.* keeping up with the latest and brightest ideas, fashions, etc.; highly modern and sophisticated. *. . . such young London designers as Mary Quant and John Stephen began turning out styles for their switched-on friends.* Maclean's 8/20/66, p10 *It was this factor, as much as any other, that dictated the rejection of old, cloth-cap Socialism in favour of new, switched-on technology.* Sunday Times (London) 2/12/67, p11 [**1964**, from SWITCH ON (see under SWITCH, v.)]

switch selling, *British.* the selling of a more expensive item to customers than the one advertised at a much lower price. The equivalent U.S. term is *bait-and-switch selling.* See also BAIT-AND-SWITCH. *. . . all its salesmen are, and always have been, expressly forbidden to attempt 'switch selling'.* Sunday Times (London) 7/19/64, p12 [**1960**]

switch trading, international trading in commodities paid for by services, benefits, rare commodities, etc., instead of by currency. *The other principal method of barter involves a bilateral agreement, with a clearing mechanism, which is known as switch trading.* Times (London) 1/26/72, p19 *What Intertel* *does is . . . sanitize public images; shred red tape, monitor relevant government legislation, and lobby; advise on geopolitical "switch-trading" opportunities.*" Harper's 12/74, p54 [**1967**]

sword and sorcery, fantasy fiction involving knightly quests, magic and witchcraft, mythical creatures, and the like. *The Disney organization co-produced* Dragonslayer, *a dark slice of sword and sorcery that could have used some of Walt's old storytelling sense.* Newsweek 7/13/81, p2 *The college students chose these books themselves; but high school students—even college-bound high school students—do not, by and large, choose their own reading. There are exceptions: sword-and-sorcery purveyors like Piers Anthony, for instance, seem to have a voluntary, word-of-mouth following, often considered flaky by the other students.* NY Times Book Review 5/4/86, p50 [**1973**]

syli (ˈsili: *or* ˈsi:li:), *n.* the monetary unit of Guinea, which replaced the franc in 1972. *Finance. Monetary unit: syli, with an official rate (Sept. 22, 1975) of 20.46 sylis to U.S. $1 (free nominal rate of 42.40 sylis = £1 sterling). Budget (1972-73 est.) balanced at 4.5 billion sylis.* Britannica Book of the Year 1976, p373 [**1973**, from the Susu (West African language) word for elephant, the symbol of the Guinea Democratic Party]

syn-, a combining form meaning "synthetic," added to nouns. —**synjet**, *n.: In the long term, the choice must be between jet fuel derived from synthetic crude (synjet) or a wholly new type of fuel.* New Scientist 6/7/79, p818 —**synoil**, *n.: The future looks bright indeed—provided that coal can be economically turned into synthetic oil and natural gas. So far several plants have been . . . designed to turn 2,700 tons of high-sulfur Illinois coal into 22 million cu.ft. of "syngas" and 3,000 bbl. of "synoil" each day.* Time 3/1/76, p47 —**synroc**, *n.* [*syn-* + *rock*]: *The Australian National University has carried out tests that show that buried synroc will be more stable when it comes in contact with underground water than the products of either vitrification or the supercalcine method of disposing of nuclear wastes.* New Scientist 11/30/78, p669 —**Synthane**, *n.* [*syn-* + *methane*]: *Economical ways to make a high-heat gas from coal to rival natural gas is a goal of several projects. One such project, sponsored by the U.S. Bureau of Mines, uses a nickel-based catalyst. Even a pilot demonstration of this "Synthane" process is at least three or four years away, however, and no competing process seems nearer.* World Book Science Annual 1973, p307 —**synzyme**, *n.: It therefore comes as a considerable surprise to discover that a synthetic enzyme (or synzyme), put together in a chemical laboratory according to really rather simple reasoning and certainly very arbitrary design, actually outperforms the real thing.* New Scientist 9/21/72, p472 [**1971**, abstracted from *synthetic*] See also the main entries SYN-CRUDE, SYNFUEL, and SYNGAS.

synaptinemal complex or **synaptonemal complex** (si‚næptəˈni:məl), a threadlike protein structure present between chromosomes especially during the synaptic stage of meiosis. *Electron microscopy has revealed the presence of a tripartite structure (the synaptinemal complex) associated with meiotic chromosomes. Apparently restricted to germ cells, the complex is thought by some to represent the point-to-point pairing of homologs preparing for or undergoing exchange.* McGraw-Hill Yearbook of Science and Technology 1972, p134 *The dominant theme was the study by electron microscopy of the synaptonemal complex (SC), an organelle of remarkable uniform dimensions and appearance in a wide range of eukaryotes.* Nature 1/15/76, p82 [**1958**, from *synaptic* + connecting *-i-* or *-o-* + *-nemal* (from Greek *nêma* thread + English *-al*)]

synaptosome (siˈnæptə‚soum), *n.* a structure containing parts of nerve endings thought to represent the synapse. *The most remarkable feature of synaptosomes is that the attachment of the surface membranes of the two nerve cells (the synaptic junction) remains intact even though each of these membranes has been torn from its cell during the homogenisation. It is possible to isolate from synaptosomes the two synaptic membranes still joined by the intact synaptic junction, and it is this preparation which is used as a starting point for studies of the chemical structure of the junction itself.* New Scientist 1/8/76,

p57 [**1964**, from *synaptic* + connecting *-o-* + *-some* body] —**synaptosomal**, *adj.: For each analysis, the cerebral cortices of one control and one experimental mouse were homogenized gently in isotonic sucrose and crude synaptosomal fractions were prepared.* Science 1/18/74, p220

synchronized sleep, the form of sleep in which little or no dreaming occurs. Also called NREM SLEEP and S SLEEP. *Synchronized sleep . . . is characterized by slow brain waves, regular pulse and breathing, and the absence of rapid eye movements.* 1977 World Book Year Book, p112 [**1975**]

synchronous, *adj.* **1** orbiting the earth at the same rate as the earth moves; moving in a geostationary orbit. *This week could see a new development in marine communications with the fitting of a steerable receiver/aerial to the Cunard-Brocklebank liner* Atlantic Causeway *to make possible two-way ship-to-shore communications, through the NASA ATS-3 synchronous satellite.* New Scientist 7/2/70, p14 **2** of or relating to a synchronous satellite. *The basic idea of the communication satellite . . . is that an active radio repeater station high above the Earth can receive a radio transmission beamed to it and retransmit it to an area enormously greater than any ground station could reach. There are significant advantages in using satellites at the 'synchronous' altitude of about 36,000 km.* Science Journal 12/70, p64 [**1961**]

synchrotron radiation, a form of electromagnetic radiation produced by the spiraling motion of high-speed electrons around a magnetic field, as in a synchrotron (a type of particle accelerator) or in some galactic nebulae. . . . *Shklovsky suggested in 1953 that the radiation arises from electrons moving at relativistic speeds (that is, speeds near the speed of light) in a magnetic field inside the nebula; this type of radiation is called synchrotron radiation.* Scientific American 1/71, p59 [**1956**]

Syncom, *n.* any of a series of U.S. communications satellites relaying radio and telephone signals from a geostationary orbit. *This synchronous orbit, which is followed by such 'geostationary' satellites as the* Syncoms *and other communications relay stations, has an approximate height of 36,000 km.* Science Journal 8/68, p63 [**1968**, from *Syn*chronous *com*munications satellite]

syncrude, *n.* synthetic crude oil produced especially from low-grade (high-sulfur) coal. *Looking at the alternative power sources for private transport, the survey reckons that the most likely ones are a synthetic liquid fuel (such as methanol or syncrude) derived from coal, or electricity stored in batteries.* Times (London) 12/9/76, p27 [**1971**, from SYN- + *crude*]

syndrome, *n.* a distinctive pattern of behavior. *From the way the young man talked about his machine, Nicholi easily concluded that his patient was the victim of a hitherto unrecognized emotional ailment: the motorcycle syndrome.* Time 12/7/70, p65 *A student of mine explained Albuquerque's all-enveloping friendliness in terms of the Luke Short syndrome. Typically in a Luke Short novel, a cowboy, footsore and weary, comes into town carrying a saddle over his shoulders. Nobody asks any questions. Friendliness is simply his for the asking . . .* Harper's 2/65, p74 [**1955**, Aldous Huxley, extended sense of the medical term for a group of signs or symptoms characterizing a disease]

synectic, *adj.* of or relating to synectics. *I have come to the conclusion that there appears to be a problem-solving mechanism at work in the "mind" which can be stimulated to resolve problems adversely affecting survival, and which stimulates in a synectic fashion solutions to problems of a creative nature which enhance survival.* New Scientist 8/21/69, p395 [**1969**, formed in English as an adjective to earlier *synectics; synectic* used in the sense of immediate or continuous (1888) is a borrowing from Latin or Greek]

synectics, *n.* the free and unrestrained exchange of ideas among a group of thinkers, used as a method of developing new ideas, solving problems, and making discoveries. *A new philosophy, "synectics", which is said to liberate the creative instinct and so stimulate inventiveness, is gaining a following among big corporations.* Times (London) 8/11/65, p11 *The idea was produced by the International Synectics Foundation, a new* "think tank" at Westminster, British Columbia, of which Mr. Barry is a prominent member. NY Times 9/19/68, p48 [**1961**, probably from *syn-* together + dial*ectics*]

synergamy (si'nərgəmi:), *n.* communal marriage. *He* [Robert Rimmer] *calls this new form of marriage, in which one or both partners may be married to another person also, synergamy. But he thinks this kind of marriage won't work unless "you begin with reasonably happy monogamous marriages. You can't solve your neurotic problems in a group marriage; you just accentuate them."* New York Post 1/3/72, p7 [**1972**, from Greek *synergós* working together + English *-gamy* marriage, as in *polygamy*]

synergistic, *adj.* interacting or interdependent; mutually stimulating or responsive. *The synergistic action of these basic facets of our national economy—public information, public approval, public action—can be the difference between success and failure, survival and disintegration for the modern corporation.* Saturday Review 4/9/66, p71 . . . *we are convinced of the importance of the interdependence of science and the rest of society. This not only concerns the social implications of science, but the effects on science of decisions in Government, university councils, industry or wherever there is a synergistic or abrasive interface.* Science News 7/11/70, p28 [**1962**, extended sense of the biomedical term descriptive of the cooperative action between different drugs, muscles, organs, etc.]

synergistically, *adv.* in a synergistic manner. *By this he meant that science and technology had come to the point where the parts fed upon each other continuously and synergistically to enlarge the whole. This was accomplished by the direct application of rational technique and mathematics, of logic and experiment, to already existent invention, leading to multiplication and cascading of our power over the environment.* NY Times 1/8/68, p141 [**1968**, extended sense of the biomedical term]

synfuel, *n.* any synthetic fuel, such as SYNCRUDE or SYNGAS. *They note, in particular, that on an energy-equivalent basis a lot more CO_2 is released from production and combustion of synfuels than from the direct burning of coal.* Science 7/27/79, p376 [**1975**, from SYN- + *fuel*]

syngas, *n.* synthetic gas produced especially from low-grade coal. Compare BIOGAS. *Becoming a feedstock for "syngas" would open a major new potential for coal, especially the now stymied high-sulfur varieties.* Time 3/1/76, p47 [**1975**, from SYN- + *gas*]

syngeneic, *adj.* **1** of or involving an identity of genotype. *Mouse recipients of transplants are called "syngeneic" when the corresponding pair of genes in each host cell are identical with those of the homozygous tumor cells.* Science News Letter 3/5/66, p147 **2** of or involving similarity but not identity of genotype. *Successful transfers are more difficult with older recipients. This is consistent with Celada's report of a barrier to syngeneic transfer of immune cells which increased markedly with age.* Science 3/1/68, p995 *Our colleague, Dr Billington* (see *Nature* 202, 317, 1964), *found that pure-bred mouse eggs gave larger placentae when transferred to a genetically dissimilar foster mother than when transferred to the uterus of a mouse of similar (syngeneic) genotype.* Science Journal 2/68, p27 [**1961**, from Greek *syngéneia* kinship, relationship + English *-ic*]

synonym, *n.* a nucleotide triplet or codon in the genetic code that may be substituted for another to produce the same amino acid. *There are more than 60 translator RNA molecules, each corresponding to an RNA code word for one of the 20 amino acids. Because there are synonyms in the code, as many as six different translator RNA molecules may link to the same amino acid.* 1976 Britannica Yearbook of Science and the Future, p66 [**1975**]

synteny ('sintəni:), *n.* location of several genes on the same chromosomal strand. *Genes that are on the same chromosome will therefore usually be expressed together . . . Assaying a number of clones for various human enzymes therefore provides information on the synteny of genes.* Scientific American 7/74, p39 [**1971**, from *syn-* together + Latin *tenia* band] —**syntenic**, *adj.: The demonstration that two or more genes are syntenic . . . and the assignment of genes or groups of syntenic genes to particular chromosomes can be accomplished in three basic ways. The first and best-established method involves following the segregation of genetic markers in informative families.* McGraw-Hill Yearbook of Science and Technology 1975, p375

synthetic-aperture radar, a radar system that combines microwave signals reflected from the ground along the path of an aircraft or satellite to form an image of high resolution. *One of those sensors, however, does a job that is huge even on Seasat's scale: Called a synthetic-aperture radar (SAR), it carries a 2.1-by-10.7-meter antenna that works as the equivalent of a conventional radar antenna 14.8 kilometers long. Such a monster would span more than 160 football fields—nearly 36 New York World Trade Centers—laid end to end.* Science News 8/5/78, p89 [**1962**]

systems analysis, the scientific and mathematical analysis of systems to improve their efficiency, accuracy, or general performance. *RAND systems-analyses that Secretary Robert McNamara introduced into the Department of Defense are revolutionizing administration of far-flung enterprises outside of as well as within government.* Saturday Review 9/23/67, p94 [**1950**]

systems analyst, a specialist in systems analysis. *As a first step, the St Peter's group has employed a firm of systems analysts to analyse the flow of records in the hospitals and to suggest changes which could lead to computer handling of the data.* New Scientist 2/8/68, p312 [**1955**]

systems dynamics, the use of mathematical models to simulate the forces that produce a problem, trend, or development within a system or systems. *In demonstrating the usefulness of a "systems dynamics" approach to specific problems considered at a disaggregative level—as is done effectively in the papers on "DDT Movement in the Global Environment"; on "Mercury Contamination," and on "The Eutrophication of Lakes"—this objective may have been achieved.* New Scientist 3/22/73, p680 [**1972**] —**systems dynamicist:** *Securing a higher rate of industrial investment can, for instance, provide short-term gains for the economic well-being of many people. But the long-term result might be, say the systems dynamicists, an aggravation of the original problem.* Science News 3/25/72, p202

T

TA, abbreviation of TRANSACTIONAL ANALYSIS. *For the vast majority who use it, "TA"—as it is known—is neither panacea nor curse, but is one therapeutic comment among many that has both practical advantages and distinct limitations.* NY Times 2/29/76, p37 *TA . . . is a system of psychotherapy which encourages practitioners to give "strokes" or emotional rewards, like a kind word or a nice smile, to get desired responses.* Times (London) 4/13/77, p12 **[1972]**

tabbouleh (təˈbu:lə), *n.* a Middle Eastern salad made with chopped garden vegetables and cracked wheat. *Malca's tabbouleh is surprising: its major ingredients are parsley, tomatoes, and scallions with just a sprinkling of cracked wheat—rather than the other way around—and it is mixed with lemon juice and olive oil.* New Yorker 12/20/76, p91 **[1958,** from Arabic (in Lebanon and Syria) *tabbūla*]

TACAN (ˈtæˌkæn), *n.* acronym for *tactical air navigation,* an electronic system that provides an aircraft with a continuous reading of bearing and distance from a radio-transmitting station. *This tactical air navigation system is similar in principle to the omnidirectional range and distance measuring equipment now in use. It is reputed to be slightly more accurate than the omnirange. TACAN has a higher operating frequency than VOR, and the TACAN transmitter is more compact . . .* Encyclopedia Science Supplement (Grolier) 1967, p365 **[1955]**

tachyon (ˈtæki:ˌɑn), *n.* a hypothetical elementary particle with a speed greater than that of light, whose existence has been inferred mathematically from Einstein's special theory of relativity. . . . *tachyons, says Dr. Sudarshan, if they can exist, can go faster than light. They can go at any speed up to infinity and thus carry forces across any distance as fast as need be.* Science News 1/31/70, p126 **[1967,** coined by Gerald Feinberg, born 1933, an American physicist, from Greek *tachýs* swift + English *-on,* as in *electron, proton,* etc.]

tachyonic (ˌtæki:ˈɑnik), *adj.* of or having to do with tachyons. *A tachyonic electron would radiate all its energy . . . in about 10^{-19} seconds.* Nature 1/7/72, p11 *Large sums of money have already gone down the drain, the authors believe, in efforts to detect tachyons by methods that imply tachyonic communication.* Scientific American 5/74, p121 **[1970]**

TACV, abbreviation of *tracked air cushion vehicle,* a high-speed train that rides on a cushion of air over a concrete track. *The British developed their Hovertrain, the French their Aerotrain and the U.S. Federal Railroad Administration its TACV.* Scientific American 10/73, p18 **[1969]**

tadpole galaxy, any of a group of radio galaxies (sources of intense radio signals) having an elongated structure whose shape suggests a tadpole. *Tadpole galaxies appear to be an interesting variation on normal radio sources, one in which the familiar double structure is distorted by motion through the surrounding gas.* New Scientist 1/16/75, p118 **[1973]**

taekwondo (ˈtaiˌkwanˈdou), *n.* a method of self-defense developed in Korea, using powerful kicks and punches to disable an opponent. *Developed in Korea, tae kwon do is generally, except by Koreans, considered a style of karate. Like Japanese and Okinawan styles, it has origins traceable to China.* Esquire 8/73, p73 *Ford lunched with the troops and watched a taekwondo, the traditional Korean martial art, championship match between two divisions.* Time 12/2/74, p17 **[1966,** from Korean, from *tae* kick + *kwon* fist + *do* art, method]

tagari (təˈgɑ:ri:), *n.* a popular Greek shoulder bag, usually made of brightly patterned, coarse wool. *European stores still offer many bargains for the perspicacious visitor. . . Greece's hand-* woven shoulder bags, called tagari, are priced at only $7. Time 6/19/78, p79 **[1967,** from Modern Greek *tagári* peasant bag]

taggant, *n.* a chemical substance added to a substance to aid in detection and identification. *Proposed legislation would require taggants in all explosives (even gunpowder).* Science News 5/10/80, p247 **[1977,** from *tag, v.* + *-ant* (noun suffix)]

tagmemicist (tægˈmi:məsist), *n.* a linguist who specializes in the study of tagmemes (the smallest meaningful units of grammatical form). *In practice, a transformationalist concerns himself primarily with the formulation of rules* [of grammar] *and of universal constraints and conventions which govern those rules; the tagmemicist deals primarily with the identification and classification of basic patterns, and the formulation of procedures which are intended to yield the correct classifications.* Language 3/70, p186 **[1965,** from *tagmemics* (1947) the study of tagmemes, from *tagmeme* the smallest meaningful unit of grammatical form (1933), coined by the American linguist Leonard Bloomfield, 1887-1949, from Greek *tágma* order + English *-eme,* as in *phoneme:* "The tagmeme of exclamatory final-pitch occurs with any lexical form and gives it a grammatical meaning . . . which we may roughly describe, perhaps, as 'strong stimulus'." (Leonard Bloomfield, *Language* (1933), p 166)]

Tago-Sato-Kosaka (ˈtɑːgouˈsɑːtoukouˈsɑːkə), *n.* a comet discovered in October, 1969, named for the three Japanese amateur astronomers who first sighted it. Compare BENNETT. . . . *the substances found in Tago-Sato-Kosaka are typical of planetary atmospheres such as are found around the outer planets of the solar system.* Science News 2/7/70, p241 *NASA . . . claimed yet another "first"—the discovery of a big hydrogen cloud around the nucleus of the new bright comet Tago-Sato-Kosaka.* New Scientist 2/5/70, p247 **[1970]**

tag sale, a sale of old or used household belongings in which items for sale carry price tags. Compare GARAGE SALE, YARD SALE. . . . *a tag sale where the prices are within anyone's reach but the merchandise is mostly too shabby or useless to bother with.* Forbes 8/15/74, p103 **[1974]**

t'ai chi ch'uan (ˈtɑi dʒi: ˈtʃwaːn) or **t'ai chi** (ˈtɑi ˈdʒi:), a Chinese system of physical exercises resembling slow-motion shadowboxing. *Rise at six and you find Chinese young people exercising in parks, on the waterfront, on rooftops. They twist and spin, jerk and wheel, doing "hard" exercises (forms of karate), "soft" (forms of* T'ai Chi-ch'uan, *the snakelike, rhythmic art), and countless improvisations of their own.* Atlantic 11/71, p92 *Embrace Tiger and Return to Mountain it is called, this being the name of one exercise in T'ai-chi, a Chinese system of callisthenics claimed to produce pliability, health and peace of mind.* Times (London) 11/22/68, p9 **[1962,** from Chinese, from *t'ai* extreme + *chi* limit + *ch'uan* fist, boxing]

tailback, *n. British.* a long line of automobiles and trucks caused by an obstruction on the road. *On the northbound carriageway of the M1, there was a 12-mile tailback, while westbound drivers had long delays on the M4, aggravated by an accident between Slough and Maidenhead.* Times (London) 8/26/78, p1 **[1977]**

tailgating, *n. U.S.* a social gathering, especially of football fans outside a stadium, at which refreshments or a meal are served from the tailgate of a station wagon, the rear of a van, etc. *Tailgating started years ago at Ivy League games, where alumni would serve genteel picnics from the backs of their station wagons. Cold chicken and Chablis was a typical menu . . . The* *super bowl of tailgating occurs when the Green Bay Packers visit the Minnesota Vikings.* Time 10/15/73, p87 **[1973]**

taka ('tɑ:kə), *n.* the monetary unit of Bangladesh, introduced in 1972. *Mr.* [S.A.] *Karim is Political Secretary for the Ministry of Foreign Affairs in the new government. Like all Bengalis, he can draw a salary of no more than 2,000 takas, or about $275 a month.* National Geographic Magazine 9/72, p302 **[1972,** from Bengali *tākā]*

takeaway, *adj. British.* designating or dealing with food prepared to be eaten away from the premises. The equivalent U.S. term is TAKEOUT. . . . *so I said 'I'm gonna set a table under that Rembrandt.' So we did, and we got some white wine in, and we sent out to the Chinese restaurant for a Chinese takeaway curry and we brought it here.* Manchester Guardian Weekly 4/10/71, p15 *Mr Roger Masterman, general manager of a Liverpool chain of take-away chicken houses, said the local health authorities had not, so far asked him for chicken specimens.* Sunday Times (London) 2/16/69, p6 **[1964]**

takeout, *adj. U.S.* designating or dealing with food prepared to be eaten away from the premises. The equivalent British term is TAKEAWAY. *She* liked *canned chili and corned-beef hash, takeout pizza pies.* New Yorker 1/11/69, p29 *The Lily-Tulip Cup Corporation introduced yesterday a packaging system designed to provide leakproof take-out containers.* NY Times 6/29/65, p45 **[1962]**

tala ('tɑ:lə), *n.* the basic monetary unit of Western Samoa. *Western Samoa, a former territory of New Zealand, which recently became independent, will change its money system from the pound, shilling and pence to the tala (dollar) and sene (cent) July 10.* NY Times 2/3/67, p7 **[1967,** from Samoan, from English *dollar]*

talk-in, *n.* **1** a protest demonstration in which the participants take turns to speak up on the issues. *Last week 180 Free University students staged a 45-hour hunger strike and talk-in at a West Berlin Protestant Student Center to demand the release of a jailed anti-Shah demonstrator.* Time 6/30/67, p28 **2** an informal lecture or talk. *LeRoi Jones, poet, playwright and polemicist, sustained each aspect of his reputation Monday night, though in different degrees, at a reading at the Village Theater . . . It was the second in a series of talk-ins presented at that house.* NY Times 10/5/66, p46 . . . *Studs comes up with "Hard Times—an oral history of the Depression,". . . a talk-in on the psychology of remaining American, independent, and acquisitive, after laissez-fairing it to hell and back . . .* Manchester Guardian Weekly 10/3/70, p22 **3** a conference or discussion. *At the end of this month the insurance industry starts its talk-in with the Monopolies Commission over fire insurance.* Times (London) 9/7/70, p18 **[1966; see -IN]**

talking head, a person shown talking directly in close-up on a television or motion-picture screen. *Television often achieves its best effects by moving in close. 'Talking heads' can be superb television. I remember vividly, after more than a decade, A. J. P. Taylor's scintillating lectures on British prime ministers, delivered standing in a studio and looking straight into a camera from behind his floppy bow tie.* Listener 1/22/76, p70 *Len Maguire . . . is no glamorous figure—he probably wouldn't even get an audition as a television "talking head."* Daily News (New York) 5/30/79, p27 **[1968,** originally used (in television industry parlance) chiefly in the plural as a derogatory reference to an interview, documentary, etc., that lacks visual excitement or interest]

talk jockey, *U.S.* the host of a radio program which solicits telephone calls as part of the broadcast. Compare DISCO JOCKEY. *One of the most imitated and controversial new formats was the sex-oriented talk show in which female listeners discuss intimate details of their love lives by telephone with male "Talk Jockeys" (T.J.'s).* 1973 World Book Year Book, p479 **[1972,** patterned after *disk jockey* (1940's)]

talk line, another term for GAB LINE. *The use of nicknames is common on the talk lines, all of which have monitors who listen to, and sometimes direct, the conversation.* Philadelphia Inquirer 2/14/88, p16-A **[1988]**

talk radio, a kind of radio programming consisting of light talk or conversation, especially with listeners who call in on the telephone to make comments or ask questions of guests. *Talk radio's Eric Bogosian finds the real voice of America.* People Weekly 8/17/87, p99 **[1985]**

talk shop, *British.* a group or organization considered too weak or ineffectual to do anything more than engage in argument and discussion. *Sir Michael is opposed to any such council. In the first interview he has given to the press since taking office, he said: "I have said that if it does not have any power it is merely another talk shop, and if it does have power, it undermines the governors."* Times (London) 7/24/73, p4 **[1958,** used originally in the form *talking shop* (OEDS 1912), which about 1922 was applied contemptuously to the House of Commons; probably influenced by verb phrase *talk shop* (1850's)]

talk show, *Especially U.S.* a television or radio show in which guest celebrities are interviewed. A British equivalent is CHAT SHOW. *What with books, magazines and talk shows, no man today is considered complete without an expressed opinion on grass.* Time 1/26/70, p68 *Talk shows have never been more popular than they are now.* Harper's 3/70, p116 **[1965]**

tall ship, a square-rigged sailing vessel, used chiefly as a training ship for naval cadets. *The Tall Ships—the great sailing ships from around the world—captured the national imagination, and they seemed to do so simply because they did, not because we were told that they should.* New Yorker 9/20/76, p110 **[1976]** ►The spectacular procession of sailing ships during the U.S. Bicentennial celebrations in 1976 made this a popular term and substantially widened its usage beyond John Masefield's "Sea-Fever" (1902):

> *I must go down to the seas again, to*
> *the lonely sea and the sky,*
> *And all I ask is a tall ship and*
> *a star to steer her by . . .*

But the phrase precedes Masefield by three centuries (OED 1582).

tamarugo (ˌtɑ:mɑ:'ru:gou), *n.* a tree (*Prosapis tamarugo*) of Chile, related to the mesquite. *The tamarugo . . . grows in a part of Chile's desolate Atacama Desert where no rain falls in most years. Salt deposits, which are death to most plants, are so thick and widespread there that, except for the tamarugo groves, the area looks like a desolate moonscape. Chilean scientists have found that tamarugo leaves and pods are rich in protein, and large herds of sheep now graze on them . . . The tamarugo may also be useful in developing livestock industries in other salt desert regions.* World Book Science Annual 1977, p72 **[1972,** from Spanish, probably from Pampa del *Tamarugal,* name of plateau in the Atacama desert of northern Chile]

tambola (tæm'boulə), *n.* a unit of money in Malawi. *Malawi's decimal currency was to be introduced in March 1971; the new unit, the kwacha, is divided into 100 tambolas.* 1970 Compton Yearbook, p188 **[1970]**

tank top, *U.S.* an upper garment with wide shoulder straps, similar to the tops of one-piece bathing suits or men's underwear shirts. . . . *the staid Wall Street lawyer . . . turns Bloomingdale hippie in the evening, donning tie-dyed pants and tank top to weed the garden.* Time 6/29/70, p39 *Miss Farrell—a tall, pretty ballerina dressed in a purple tank top and baggy rubber warm-up pants—looked inquiringly at Mr. Martins . . .* New Yorker 1/27/68, p25 **[1968,** named after the so-called *tank suits* (1950's), one-piece bathing suits worn in the *tank* (swimming pool)]

tanning booth, a small enclosure fitted with ultraviolet lamps for producing a tan. *A man is much better off using a bronzer instead of a tanning booth during the winter months because of the skin hazards of ultraviolet radiation.* NY Times Magazine 9/7/80, p92 **[1980]**

tannoy ('tænɔi), *British.* —*n.* a public-address system. *A tannoy, droning out the while, is heard intoning "The major of Hackney."* Times (London) 7/28/73, p12 —*v.i.* to broadcast over such a system. *The Portuguese Socialist leader arrives behind a convoy of tannoying cars and almost bounces into the crowd.*

Times (London) 4/24/76, p4 [**1954** for noun, from *Tannoy* (1928) the trademark of such a system; **1966** for verb]

tape deck, another name for a TAPE PLAYER. *The simplest playback machine is the tape deck, which has to be plugged into one's own hi-fi equipment.* Harper's 8/65, p118 *Floodlights, sound equipment, tape-deck, and complete humourous script with blanks for personal and domestic references.* Punch 12/7/66, p856 [**1949, 1963**]

tape-delay, *n.* **1** a delay between recording on a tape recorder and the programming of the recording on a broadcast to eliminate possible unwanted material. *Most television people have treated the common public with great mistrust, filtering them through auditions, then through moderators, and then, as a final safeguard, through a tape-delay for blips, before allowing them to appear on the air.* Harper's 6/72, p92 **2** the tape recording of a segment of live music to play it back in order to create a fuller sound or the effect of an echo by combining the taped segment with the continued live performance. *The hallmarks of this style are well-known: asymmetrical riffs, cool-jazz harmonies, interlocking polymetric loops, striding tunes in octaves on fuzz bass and organ, tape-delay and wah-wah filtering effects.* Listener 7/26/73, p127 [**1966**]

tape player, a machine for playing back sound on magnetic tapes or in cassettes. Also called TAPE DECK. *Buttons, balloons and lollipops; bull horns, projectors and tape players; car rental through Hertz, Telex through Western Union—all these things and many more in handy catalogue . . .* NY Times 6/20/68, p72 *Starting this week is a £115,000 campaign for Philips car tape players.* Times (London) 5/6/70, p25 [**1961**]

TAPS (tæps), *n.* acronym for *Trans-Alaska Pipeline System. The start-up of the pipeline—known as TAPS—marks the virtual completion of a project which has cost eight of the world's biggest oil companies some $15 billions. In about four weeks' time that first oil will reach the pipeline's shipping terminal at Valdez on the southern Alaskan coast.* Manchester Guardian Weekly 6/26/77, p6 [**1970**]

taramasalata or **taramosalata** (ˌtarəməsəˈlɑːtə), *n.* a Greek appetizer consisting of a light creamy paste of fish roe mixed with bread crumbs or boiled potato, grated onion, dill, etc. *The Justin de Blank shop will have the same food as in Elizabeth Street—home-cured bacon from Wiltshire, quiches, kipper pate, taramasalata and so on.* Times (London) 3/10/72, p9 Taramosalata: *red fish-roe spread, usually made with carp.* Cue Magazine 1/22 thru 2/4/77, p11 [**1958,** from Modern Greek *taramasaláta,* from *taramâs* fish roe + *saláta* salad]

tardive dyskinesia (ˌdiskəˈniːʒə), a neuromuscular disorder marked by involuntary twitching of facial and other muscles, occurring as a complication of prolonged therapy with antipsychotic drugs. *Abbreviation:* TD *Scientists suspect that the cause of tardive dyskinesia is a lack of acetylcholine, which is depleted by years of using antipsychotic drugs.* Prevention 9/79, p182 [**1964,** *dyskinesia* from *dys-* bad, abnormal + *-kinesia* combining form meaning motion, movement, from Greek *kínēsis*]

tardyon (ˈtɑːrdiˌɑn), *n.* elementary particle that moves at a velocity less than the speed of light. Compare LUXON. *It is perfectly possible to convert a particle from one class to another. For example, an electron and a positron, both of which are tardyons, can combine to form gamma rays . . . There would seem, then, to be no theoretical objection to the conversion of tardyons to tachyons and back again, if the proper procedure could be found.* Saturday Review 7/8/72, p56 [**1969,** coined by Olexa-Myron Bilaniuk, an American physicist, patterned after *tachyon*]

target, *n.* **on target,** on the right track. *It is always a nerve-racking business, deciding when to make the upturn, but it is going all right. We are on target.* Times (London) 3/21/70, p1 *Diddy is sure he did it; yet a blind girl near by who hears all and who proves to be on target about everything else, says he never left his seat.* Time 8/18/67, p88 [**1963**]

targetable, *adj.* that can be aimed at a target. *That huge American advantage cannot be ended in a hurry, especially since the*

United States will in the next few years add to its arsenal missiles capable of putting into space a number of individually targetable warheads. NY Times 4/8/68, p46 [**1968**]

Tartan Turf, the trademark of an artificial surface resembling grass, used especially for playing fields. Compare ASTROTURF. *I stand behind the batting cage, watching in awe as Bobby Tolan, Joe Morgan, Pete Rose, Johnny Bench, and Tony Perez lace a rookie pitcher's fat deliveries far out into the unnaturally green reaches of the artificial Tartan Turf.* Saturday Review 11/11/72, p7 [**1966**]

Tasaday (ˌtɑːsɑːˈdɑi), *n., pl.* **-day** or **-days.** a member of a cave-dwelling forest people possibly of Stone-Age culture, discovered in 1971 (often used attributively). Compare ACHÉ, YANOMAMA. *The Tasaday are a . . . people recently discovered in the rain forests of the Philippines who may have had no contact with the outside world for centuries. Until this decade they were food gatherers; in other words they may exemplify the human state at a time when it had only just moved from the animal level.* Manchester Guardian Weekly 10/4/75, p21 [**1971,** named by their Filipino discoverers after a range of nearby mountains]

Taser, *n.* the trademark of a small gun-like device for firing electrified darts which temporarily immobilize a person. Also spelled **taser.** *The Montgomery County incident is not the first in which the Taser was used to commit a crime. Last September a Taser was used to hold up a gas station attendant in Miami.* New York Post 1/14/76, p24 —*v.t.* to immobilize with a Taser. *A powerful transformer within the Taser generates 50,000 volts when a trigger is pressed. This jolt, sent through the wires into the darts, which have been shot into the skin or clothing of the victim, cause him to become "Tasered."* NY Times Magazine 1/4/76, p13 [**1971** (patented in 1974), from Tele-Active Shock Electronic Repulsion; form influenced by *laser*]

tau, *n.* a weakly interacting elementary particle with a mass about three and a half thousand times that of the electron. *The tau joins the lepton group of particles, which interact only through the forces of the weak nuclear interaction responsible for the radioactive decay of nuclei and electromagnetism. The electron is the best known member of the family.* New Scientist 12/21-28/78, p935 *The number of massive leptons that exist limits the possible number of quark flavors. At the moment three massive leptons are known: the electron, the muon and the tau. If that is all the massive leptons there are, then quark flavors are limited to six. But there could be more massive leptons. They are limited by the number of possible neutrinos. (Neutrinos are leptons with zero mass.)* Science News 1/20/79, p43 [**1977,** from the Greek name of the first letter of Greek *tríton* third, adopted to indicate that the particle is the third charged lepton after the electron and the muon]

tax disc, *British.* a small, round sticker affixed to the windshield of a motor vehicle, indicating the date up to which the excise tax for that vehicle has been paid. *The Government yesterday acted against protests in Cornwall over road tax laws imposed by Westminster. More than 100 motorists have said they will not renew their tax discs. Instead, they want the ancient Cornish Stannary Parliament, which was revived in 1974 after a 222-year break, to issue discs of its own.* Times (London) 8/1/78, p4 [**1972**]

tax exile or **tax expatriate,** a person who leaves a country to avoid paying taxes. *Has Anthony Grey, Reuter's man lately in Peking, joined the ranks of the tax exiles?* Manchester Guardian Weekly 11/22/69, p11 *The American with a numbered account is likely to have children in one of the Swiss preparatory schools, or to be a genuine tax expatriate or one of that small group who like to keep 10 percent of their portfolios outside Wall Street. Except for the tax expatriate, these people are not trying to avoid taxes; good New York law firms have already shown them how to do so profitably at home.* Atlantic 7/65, p36 [**1965**]

taxi squad, *U.S.* a group of players on a football team who participate in practice sessions but do not play in the games. *Elsewhere, the Cincinnati Bengals cut Tommy Smith, the Olympic 200-meter champion in 1968 who had been on the taxi squad* or two years and was trying to make the club as a tight end. Tuscaloosa News (Alabama) 9/7/71, p6 [**1966**, originally a nickname given to a group of extra players which the owner of the Cleveland Browns during the 1940's, Arthur McBride, kept on the team by putting them on the payroll of a taxi company which he owned]

axmobile, n. U.S. a bus or other motor vehicle serving as a traveling tax-service facility. *"Taxmobiles" staffed with agents now trundle through back-country roads in Tennessee and into shopping centers in California bringing tax assistance to all who want it.* Time 3/12/73, p92 [**1973**, from *tax* + auto*mobile*, patterned after *artmobile, bloodmobile, bookmobile*]

ax revolt, U.S. a vote or lobbying effort to reduce taxes that are considered to be excessive. *That angry noise was the sound of a middle class tax revolt erupting, and its tremors are shaking public officials from Sacramento to Washington.* Time 6/19/78, p13 *The tax revolt of the middle 1970's coincided with the emergence of single-issue lobbying as a potent technique of legislative and electoral politics . . . This suggests that the tax revolt that burst into full bloom in 1978 may continue to gain breadth and momentum.* 1979 Collier's Encyclopedia Year Book, p579 [**1978**] ►The term became current with the passage in June 1978 of PROPOSITION 13, an amendment to the California state constitution which cut back the state's property taxes 57 per cent. The success of this popular initiative encouraged taxpayers throughout the country to put on the state ballots similar measures designed to reduce increasing government taxation.

ax shelter, an investment, allowance, etc., used as a means of reducing or avoiding liability to income tax. *. . . rapid-depreciation schedules on equipment . . . have hitherto made cable TV systems lucrative tax shelters.* Encyclopedia Science Supplement (Grolier) 1969, p381 *The other portions of the tax bill curtail some common abuses of foundations as tax shelters.* Science News 12/27/69, p591 [**1961**]

Tay-Sachs ('tei,sæks), n. a fatal hereditary disease of children characterized by degeneration of the cells of the central nervous system. It is caused by a deficiency of the enzyme hexaminidase. *A team of Montreal medical specialists has discovered Tay-Sachs in proportions never known before in the last place they might have looked—among non-Jewish French Canadians in the heartland of eastern Quebec.* Maclean's 4/19/76, p57 —adj. of or relating to this disease. *Tay-Sachs carriers—people who have the Tay-Sachs gene—are 10 times more prevalent among the Jewish population who have their ancestral origins in central and eastern Europe.* NY Times Magazine 9/12/79, p29 [**1976**, shortened from *Tay-Sachs disease* (1907), named after Warren *Tay*, 1843-1927, an English ophthalmologist, and Bernard *Sachs*, 1858-1944, an American neurologist, who independently described the disease in 1881 and 1887 respectively]

TCDD, abbreviation of *tetrachlorodibenzo-p-dioxin*, a very poisonous and persistent impurity present in herbicides, also known as dioxin. *TCDD is one of the most toxic substances known to man, and . . . Dow Chemical is the world's largest producer of the herbicide 2,4,5-T, which is contaminated with TCDD yet is used in spray operations affecting millions of acres of this country's forestlands, rangelands, pasturelands, and utility and railroad rights of way each year.* New Yorker 12/18/78, p27 [**1971**]

T cell or **T-cell**, n. a lymph cell that defends the body against disease and foreign matter. Also called T LYMPHOCYTE. *T cells are responsible, among other things, for the rejection of transplants, resistance to fungal infections and killing cells infected with viruses.* Times (London) 1/25/78, p11 *Back in the "Dark Ages" of immunological research—say five years ago—only two major kinds of white blood cells appeared to serve as immunological defenders of the body. These were B cells and T cells. T cells, however, have since been found to consist of at least three different subpopulations—killer T cells (credited with killing tumors and other "enemies"), helper T cells (henchmen to the killer T cells) and suppressor T cells (moderates that keep killer Ts from going overboard in slaying the* enemy). Science News 11/18/78, p342 [**1970**, from *t*hymus-derived *cell*]

tchotchke ('tʃɔtʃkə), n. U.S. Slang. a showy trifle or toy; trinket; gewgaw; bric-a-brac. Also spelled TSATSKE. *A New York, N.Y. Boutique, to the left of the entrance, [is] stocked with a careful selection of New York's best tchotchkes. These include thirteen-inch-long matchbooks . . . bronze Empire State Buildings with thermometers in them . . ., candles that look like bottles of Pepsi; and, naturally, candles that look like apples.* New Yorker 8/1/77, p14 [**1968**, from Yiddish *tshotshke*]

TD, abbreviation of TARDIVE DYSKINESIA. *TD is fairly common among chronic mental patients who have taken antipsychotic drugs for a substantial period of time. Scientists also believe that inadequate acetylcholine production may be linked to other ailments such as mania and memory loss.* Science News 2/11/78, p85 [**1976**]

T-dress, n. a T-shirt long enough to be worn as a dress. *Jackets, at $10, and T-dresses, at $21, were summer items and are where you can find them.* NY Times 9/18/76, p11 [**1967**, from *T*-shirt + *dress*]

teach-in, n. **1** a long meeting or session held by university teachers and students for the purpose of expressing dissenting or critical views on an important political or social issue. *Before the be-ins, hippies used the sit-in to desegregate Alabama lunchcounters, and the teach-in to get the Vietnam debate going at a time when the consensus was still intact.* Saturday Night (Canada) 8/67, p3 *Now shifting their targets to concern for the environment, students across the country are planning a massive ecological-environmental teach-in on university campuses . . .* Science News 12/20/69, p575 **2** any forum or seminar patterned on the university teach-in. *A series of "teach-ins" on drug addiction are to be held soon, the National Association on Drug Addiction announced on Saturday.* Times (London) 11/21/66, p10 *Parts are excellent, though, particularly editorial observations about the teach-in as a promising teaching device at the university level.* Saturday Review 8/19/67, p66 [**1965**]

teachware, n. audio-visual material used in teaching. *Audio-visual equipment exhibitors comprised the largest group of represented companies. Half the companies showing AV equipment came from outside Germany, mainly from the US and France. These two countries each provided another word for the audio-visual vocabulary; "teachware" from the Americans and the "videogramme" from the French.* New Scientist 5/11/72, p346 [**1972**, from *teach, v.* + -*ware*, as in *software*]

team handball, a combination of basketball and soccer in which two teams of seven players, each in a rectangular court, try to score by moving an inflated ball into each other's goal past a goalkeeper by passing, dribbling, and otherwise using only the hands. *Team handball: Very popular in Europe, almost unheard of in North America. Yugoslavia, Russia, Romania, Hungary, Poland: take your pick for gold, silver and bronze.* Maclean's 7/76, p40 [**1970**]

team-teach, v.i. U.S. and Canada. to practice or engage in team teaching. *Two answers to this problem . . . are to teach science ethics to college students by presenting them realistic case studies and to bring industrial scientists into the universities to team-teach.* Science News 2/28/76, p135 [**1976**, back formation from TEAM TEACHING]

team teaching, a method of classroom instruction in which two or more teachers skilled in separate subjects are jointly responsible for teaching a group of students. *Team teaching, in which a master teacher and several specially selected and prepared assistants approached a single classroom as a team . . .* NY Times 12/10/72, pD5 [**1960**]

techie ('teki:), n. Informal. **1** a technical institute or a student at such an institute. *Today, the presence of sophisticated universities determines where the corporations of the future will grow. Just as the spread of "aggie" schools throughout the Middle West in the 19th century increased the productivity of farms, so too would the spread of new "techie" schools revitalize Middle America.* NY Times 6/12/83, pE9 **2** a technician, especially in the field of computers. *"Microphone" is a breakthrough in communications software in that it supplies both simplicity of operation at the basic level and automation at the more complex level. It provides enough advanced features to keep most techies happy, while being accessible to the first-timer.* NY Times 8/19/86, pC4 [**1983**]

technetronic, *adj.* dominated or shaped by the impact of technology and electronic computers and communications. *The start of the second decade of jet air travel . . . has coincided in the final third of this century with the revolutionary emergence of communications satellites to mark the dawn of a technetronic era that will ultimately transform the Earth into a global village.* Saturday Review 10/24/70, p27 *And as one looks back over the curve he sees that space-time has begun to contract around us: before, cultural transformations occurred over hundreds of thousands of years in the Neolithic Revolution; then, over centuries in the Industrial Revolution; and now, in the Technetronic Revolution, the transformation is occurring over mere decades.* Harper's 12/71, p77 [**1967**, from Greek *téchnē* art, craft + English elec*tronic*]

technify, *v.t., v.i.* to provide with or adopt technical materials, methods, etc.; make or become technically efficient. *It relies on money and technology in unparalleled quantities. This method is designed to be effective against other industrial and technified countries, whose organisation can be so disrupted that they simply can no longer function.* Listener 5/18/72, p640 *They internalized their intelligence activities with headlong speed. They technified senselessly—charts, graphs, bugs, concealed cameras, dart guns, phone taps, the most expensive monitoring equipment ever to appear on any agent's expense voucher, where a single inside source and a few intelligent questions would have been enough.* Harper's 11/73, p82 [**1959**]

technism, *n.* excessive emphasis on practical results, technical methods, and procedures; that which relies too much on mechanical tools, etc. *In our highly developed technological society we have adopted, usually without knowing it, the implicit ideology called "technism," which places central value on what can be measured with numbers, assigns numbers to what cannot be measured, and redefines everything else as self-expression or entertainment.* NY Times 2/19/76, p35 [**1976**, probably alteration of earlier *technicism* (OEDS 1932)]

technologize, *v.t.* to make technological; change by technology. *Mailer accuses Millett of technologizing sex.* Time 2/22/71, p41 [**1960**]

technology assessment, the attempt to make advance assessments and predictions on the impact or effect of new technologies on society. *Technology assessment is a procedure designed to optimize the use of technology. Modern technology, which has brought social benefits and social costs, can also multiply societal options. It can do so through the enhanced capacity to perceive and predict unintended side effects by modern analytical methods reinforced by computers and through its capacity to design many alternative means to achieve a desired objective.* Scientific American 9/71, p192 *Particularly, may we urge that the added dimension of opinions from industry should be brought into contemplating the growing promise and popularity of "technology assessment."* NY Times 11/11/70, p44 [**1966**]

technology transfer, the transfer of new or advanced technological information, as from the developed to the less developed countries of the world or from the experimental laboratory to commercial use. *Technology transfer is sometimes used to describe information dissemination, but this is only a part of the technology transfer process.* Science 2/28/75, p713 *Regarding technology transfer, the . . . paper calls on the developed nations to "ensure full and free access to those technologies that are essential to [Third World] development, including advanced technologies." New technology should be supplied to the developing world on favourable terms, which were not spelt out.* New Scientist 6/7/79, p825 [**1969**]

technomania, *n.* undue interest in technology or excessive use of technology without regard to its consequences, especially

upon the environment. *The hostile reception of London "Westway" shows that we are at last moving out of the age c undiluted technomania. Even if a transport system is admira bly big, fast and expensive, it can yet be judged bad engineer ing.* New Scientist 8/13/70, p349 [**1969**]

technophobia, *n.* fear of the adverse effect of technology on so ciety or the environment. *Concerned actions of dissent group against the forthcoming nationwide census in the Netherland are forcing government officials, politicians and sociologists t consider changing their opinions about the psychosocial ef fects of technophobia.* New Scientist and Science Journa 2/25/71, p406 *People who had, in the past, suffered fron technophobia suffered even more. Others took other positions Things were not so bad. Things could be worse . . . The wors was yet to come.* New Yorker 6/13/70, p38 [**1965**]

technopolis, *n.* a society dominated by the results of technologi cal research and development. *"Technopolis"—the societ where our lives, thoughts and happiness are determined by th applications of a science and technology which often appear to be out of control, and where blame for the dangers and un pleasant consequences that may thus arise is often laid on th scientists and technologists themselves, instead of on the whole community, through their chosen political representatives* New Scientist 7/3/69, p38 *But there have also been several for mal surveys recently showing that all is far from well insid the white coats of technopolis.* New Scientist and Science Jour nal 3/11/71, p527 [**1965**, from *techno-* technology + *-polis,* a in *metropolis*]

technopolitan, *adj.* of or relating to technopolis. *Even the terri fying aspects of technopolitan society—its uncontrollednes and its assumption that "can" equals "should"—are measure of the human capacity for achievement.* Manchester Guardiar Weekly 6/19/71, p20 *For practical-minded technopolitar man, "life is a set of problems, not an unfathomable mystery. He is too engrossed in grappling with the realities of this lif to have much concern with those of the next.* Time 4/2/65 p34 [**1965**, from *technopolis,* after such pairs as *metropolis metropolitan*]

technopop, *n.* popular music played on synthesizers and othe electronic devices. *"Many musicians have become compute programmers who can digitally create virtually any musica sound and instruct the machine to play it in perfect time. Th technology has spawned pop bands—hence the phrase tech nopop—whose songs are heavy on perfect syncopation, mos notably Human League and the Eurythmics, whose first bir hit was "Sweet Dreams (Are Made of This)."* Daily News (New York) 7/25/84, p39 [**1984**]

technosphere, *n.* human technology; the technological activi ties of the human race. *It is encouraging to see so much evi dence of concrete results relevant to the urgent environmenta tasks of assisting the biosphere to hold out against the bruta impact of the technosphere.* New Scientist 12/13/73 p792 [**1969**]

technostructure, *n.* the people in control of a technology in a society. . . . *management is limited by the many kinds of spe cialists whose views must be consulted—the experts, whether ir marketing or in business-management methods, the whole class of people who occupy what Galbraith calls the "tech nostructure."* New Yorker 9/26/70, p54 *To an increasing ex tent, decisions intended to guide operations are made by the "technostructure", that combination of technical knowledge know-how and organizational capability which is the mos valuable asset of a modern enterprise.* Times (London) 3/4/70 p28 *"The reason is that the first kind of conflict affronts the industrial technostructure—the establishment."* New Scientist and Science Journal 2/18/71, p376 [**1967**]

tectonic plate, another term for PLATE. *Many geologists currently believe that the lithosphere is geographically divided into 6 major slablike sections, called tectonic plates, plus a number of smaller ones. These plates contain the continents and adjoining portions of the ocean floors.* Encyclopedia Science Supplement (Grolier) 1970, p130 [**1970**]

ectonomagnetism, *n.* anomalies in the earth's magnetic field aused by stresses in the earth's crust. *Tectonomagnetism . . . 's attracting increasing interest as a method of monitoring ocal changes in Earth stress.* Nature 12/8/72, p348 **[1972,** *rom tecton*ic (of the earth's crust) + connecting *-o-* + *magne-ism*] —**tectonomagnetic,** *adj.: Theory has it that stress in the arth's crust causes local anomalies in the magnetic field . . . f it could be quantified, the so-called tectonomagnetic effect ould provide a means of monitoring stress on faults and even-ually forecasting earthquakes.* Science News 12/23/72, p408

eeny, *n. Informal.* a young teen-ager. *Prince Andrew, the 16-year-old son of Queen Elizabeth, has proved the favorite mong royal visitors with many Canadians. "He's the biggest hing for teenies since Bjorn Borg,"* said one person. NY Times '/29/76, p26 **[1969,** from *teen* or *teen-*ager + *-y* diminutive uffix; or back formation from TEENY-BOPPER]

eeny-bopper, *n. Slang.* a girl (sometimes a boy) in the early eens who follows the current fashions and fads in clothing, nusic, etc. *Paris is a city for adults, and the eye moves past the microskirted teeny-bopper to the thirtyish lady in a Chanel uit and high heels . . .* Atlantic 1/70, p20 *Later on, O'Leary lucks the flower from his pants and unzips himself to the as-onished edification of the teeny-boppers milling around the stage.* Time 8/17/70, p66 **[1966,** from *teen* or *teen-*ager + *-y,* diminutive suffix (influenced by *teeny* small, tiny) + *bopper* ne that bops or hits]

TEFL ('tefəl), *n.* acronym for *teaching English as a foreign lan-guage. There is a growing awareness of the similarities of the various types of English teaching, as well as a recognition of the need for communication among teachers. Well-designed TESL or TEFL curricula, regardless of the type of program, share certain objectives and principles which emphasize the need for integration of the student into the target language community through carefully designed linguistic and cultural instruction.* Newsletter of the American Dialect Society 11/74, >45 **[1963]**

eh ch'i or **t'eh chi** ('te 'tʃi:), **1** a vibration detected by an ac-upuncturist when an acupuncture point is reached. *The tradi-tional Chinese doctors could tell whether a person was a likely andidate for acupuncture through a phenomenon called Teh Ch'i. Teh Ch'i is a vibration in the acupuncture needle that the doctor feels as he pushes through the surface layers of skin and begins twirling.* Rhodesia Herald 4/6/73, p27 **2** the sensation experienced by the patient when an acupuncture point is reached. *First, the correct point must be chosen in order to af-fect the required zone of the body; second, the needles give a correct point must elicit a special sensation called t'eh chi which has four qualities: heaviness, swelling and numbness, and soreness.* New Scientist 10/3/74, p34 **[1973,** from Chinese]

Teilhardian (te'yɑrdi:ən), *adj.* of or relating to the French theo-ogian Pierre Teilhard de Chardin, 1881-1955, or his theories. *Dr Doyle referred to the interest in meditation and mysticism mongst the young as one of the hopeful signs that Teilhard's optimism about the direction of social evolution was valid, but he seemed quite unaware that to most of the young in question, the whole emphasis of Teilhardian argument as displayed at the conference would be highly suspect.* New Scientist 10/22/70, p183 —*n.* a supporter or follower of Pierre Teilhard de Chardin or of his theories. *From the Teilhardians, the confi-dence that God, whoever he is, has something to do with the future and may yet meet man there.* Time 4/19/71, p34 **[1967]**

elecommute, *v.i.* to work at home while communicating with one's office or central workplace by computer, telephone, etc. *In any event, there is no way for me to telecommute down to the payroll department to vent my frustration, and all the tele-phone lines to that particular department seem to have been disconnected long ago.* NY Times 1/21/86, pC3 **[1974]**

eleconference, *n.* a conference of a group of people linked by long distance telephone. *Other specialized European satellite services envisaged include public data networks, private com-puter networks, remote printing, "teleconference" facilities and, in the longer term, videophone and electronic mail serv-*

ices. Times (London) 1/16/76, p19 **[1953,** from *tele-* long-distance + *conference*]

teleconsultation, *n.* a medical consultation made by means of long-distance telemetric equipment, closed-circuit television, etc. Compare TELEDIAGNOSIS. *Besides live seminars originat-ing at the National Medical Audiovisual Center in Atlanta, there will be computer-assisted instruction (the satellites also handle computer data), "tele-consultation," allowing the VA doctors to consult with specialists at teaching institutions, and even full patient-case presentations and diagnosis.* Science News 4/6/74, p227 **[1971]**

telecopier, *n.* a machine for transmitting and reproducing graphic material (such as written copy and drawings) over tele-phone lines. *The back of the plane looks more like a business office than like a campaign plane: a desk with two electric typewriters; . . . and a telecopier (which takes down copy that comes over a telephone).* New Yorker 1/10/77, p46 **[1967]**

telediagnosis, *n.* a long-distance diagnosis of an illness per-formed by means of electronic equipment and closed-circuit television linking the physician to the patient. Compare TELE-CONSULTATION. *Tele-diagnosis of physical ailments has been in progress for more than two years at a medical station just outside Boston which is connected by two-way television to the Massachusetts General Hospital in the city.* Times (London) 7/25/70, p12 **[1961,** from *tele-* television + *diagnosis*]

telefacsimile, *n.* a method of transmitting printed materials over a telephone circuit, as by an acoustic coupler. *. . . in 1965 a staff member of the library school of the University of New Mexico publicly advocated that libraries spend ninety per cent of their budgets on staff, telephones, copying, telefacsimiles, and the like, and only ten percent—a sort of tithe—on books and journals.* New Yorker 4/1/67, p61 **[1967,** from *tele-* tele-phone + *facsimile*]

telelecture, *n.* a lecture delivered by telephone to a classroom or other place equipped with special loudspeakers and facilities for two-way communication. *Colleges today are arranging ex-changes to increase their access to various competencies, pro-viding for temporary student sojourns elsewhere, enriching their troupe of visiting scholars, or piping the specialist's voice and face in by telelecture and television.* Saturday Review 2/17/68, p60 **[1968,** from *tele-* telephone + *lecture*]

telemarket, *v.t., v.i.* to sell or solicit sales by telephone. *Al Felly had a great way to telemarket his flowers and the good sense to trademark it. But when trucker Curt Jahn drew the winning phone number, petals began to fly.* Picture legend, Inc. 7/83, p51 *Some firms have gone even a step further in complaint handling, combining it with telemarketing.* Washington Post 10/14/84, pK1 **[1983]**

telematics, *n.* the machinery and processes for long-distance transmission of computerized information. *What is delaying greater use of telematics in libraries? High costs and limited communication capabilities.* Library Journal 10/1/82, p1812 **[1979,** from *tele*communications + infor*matics*]

telemedicine, *n.* the practice of medicine by means of telemet-ric, telephone, and television apparatus. See TELECONSULTA-TION, TELEDIAGNOSIS. *As well as these universally significant impacts, the video telephone will also play a part in . . . medi-cine ("decades hence, medical historians might write that telemedicine was only an easier way to deliver poorer quality health care").* New Scientist 9/20/73, p694 **[1970]**

teleonomic, *adj.* of or relating to teleonomy; governed or deter-mined by an overall purpose. *In the end you come to the con-clusion that teleonomic behaviour is a necessary defining characteristic of living beings.* Listener 8/3/72, p137 *C. S. Pit-tendrigh in Behaviour and Evolution, suggested that the word teleological should be reserved for cases where the idea of the end (goal) precedes the use of the means, and the word teleo-nomic for cases where the ends result from means that lack de-sign (intent)—as when adaptive traits are produced by random mutations and natural selection.* Nature 3/20/75, p176 **[1958]**

teleonomy, *n.* the quality or characteristic of being governed or determined by an overall purpose. *Teleonomy denotes the* characteristic "of being objects endowed with a purpose or project, which at the same time they exhibit in their structure and carry out through their performances". New Scientist and Science Journal 12/9/71, p112 *If the destructive forces accelerated by science can be brought under control before they have permanently damaged the planet, it will be because the new organic model of ecological association and self-organization (teleonomy and autonomy) which was first assembled by Darwin will have at last begun to prevail.* New Yorker 10/31/70, p88 [**1958**, from *teleo-* end, purpose + *-nomy* system of rules]

teleoperator, *n.* a robot or similar mechanical device that is operated by remote control. Compare AUGMENTOR. . . . *the choice of lunar exploration methods is not only between astronauts and automated spacecraft. There is a third alternative— use of remotely controlled devices with mobility, sensory and manipulative capabilities. Such devices are often referred to as "teleoperators."* NY Times 10/9/70, p36 [**1970**, from *tele-* long-distance + *operator*]

telephone bank, rows of telephones operated especially by volunteers to solicit votes, charitable contributions, etc. *The mobilization of labor . . . included . . . telephone banks in 638 localities, using 8,058 telephones, manned by 24,611 union men and women and their families.* National Review 8/2/74, p866 *One such recruit . . . worked telephone banks turning people out for ward conventions, the first step in the delegate selection process.* Time 6/28/76, p12 [**1972**]

telepresence, *n.* the feeling of the operator of a remote-control device that he or she is actually present at the site of the operation. *Another far-reaching technology to be developed along with the space station has the mystical-sounding name of telepresence. That means robot manipulators with TV stereo vision, other electronic senses, and dexterous arms and "hands" that enable remote operators to feel they are present and working at a distant site.* Christian Science Monitor 4/18/85, p20 [**1983**]

teletex, *n.* a communication system combining the use of teletype machines and word-processing equipment with a network of computer terminals. *"Teletex". . . is a far cry from teletext, the broadcast information service. Teletex is either a sophisticated form of telex or a standard [form] that allows computer terminals to communicate with each other.* Nature 5/27/82, p257 [**1979**, probably a blend of *telex* and *text*]

teletext, *n.* a communications system in which printed information transmitted by television is displayed on a screen by a special encoder attached to the set. *Viewdata and teletext, which allow a viewer to display a "page" of information from a choice of several hundred, will convert television sets into home terminals.* NY Times Magazine 9/23/79, p110 [**1974**, from *tele*vision + *text*]

televangelist, *n. U.S.* a television evangelist; preacher of an electronic church. *His* [Robert Schuller's] *syndicated Sunday morning TV service, The Hour of Power, reaches an audience of almost 3 million, placing him among the nation's top-rated televangelists.* Time 3/19/85, p70 [**1973, 1981**, blend of *television* and *evangelist*] —**televangelism**, *n.: The televangelists are also preparing a host of slick new programs for syndication . . . according to a recent Cable News Network report on televangelism by Jim Clancy.* Christian Science Monitor 9/24/81, pB6

telework, *n.* work done at one's home or other place away from an office or central work site. *The organization has a goal of seeing 12 percent of the office workers associated with state government jobs participating in some kind of telecommute or telework program by the year 2000. Telework is distinguished from telecommuting as work done at a remote location that doesn't necessarily involve or require computer equipment.* Infor-World 5/19/86, p43 [**1981**]

tell, *v.* **tell it like it is**, *U.S. Slang.* to tell the truth, no matter how unpleasant. *The* [TV] *series' intention, says* [Andy] *Griffith, is "to tell it like it is for the young people while remaining palatable to older audiences." The premiere involved a student who refused to pop "uppers" and "downers" like the rest of the kids. The comic relief, provided mostly by the school's bicep-brained*

athletic director (Jerry Van Dyke) was a downer. Time 9/28/70 p66 [**1964**]

Temin enzyme, an enzyme that causes the formation of DN (deoxyribonucleic acid) on a template or pattern of RNA (rib nucleic acid) in certain cancer-producing viruses, and that is re garded by some as essential to the ability of the virus to caus cancer. Also called REVERSE TRANSCRIPTASE. *No form of can cer in humans has yet been shown to be caused by a virus bu should this be the case, the Temin enzyme may offer an ur precedented chance of attacking the disease at its roots.* Time (London) 6/26/70, p6 [**1970**, named after Howard M. Temi its discoverer]

Teminism, *n.* the theory that the transmission of genetic infor mation is not an irreversible process always determined by th nucleic acid DNA, but that in certain cases RNA (ribonuclei acid) can act as a template or pattern for the formation of DNA The theory is based on the discovery that certain cance causing viruses whose genetic material is RNA contain an er zyme (the Temin enzyme) that causes the formation of DN to match the viral RNA. Compare CENTRAL DOGMA. . . . *D David Baltimore of the Massachusetts Institute of Technolog reported verification of Dr. Temin's theory, now being referre to as Teminism in scientific circles, from experiments with an other carcinogenic virus, the Rauscher leukemia virus, whic induces tumors in mice.* Science News 7/25/70, p54 . . . *per haps Teminism might lead to a way of preventing the replica tion of RNA tumour viruses by finding a block to th extraordinary reaction.* New Scientist 6/25/70, p614 [**1970**]

temp, *n.* a temporary employee, especially a typist or secretary *". . . I want to earn enough to drive about in my own ca Maybe I'd like to be a temp later on." She probably couldn have said anything more disastrous. The company would no be keen to train someone who was going to take off to becom a temp.* Manchester Guardian Weekly (Le Monde section 7/2/78, p19 —*v.i.* to work as a temporary employee. *Most c the students had given as their explanation for deciding t temp: "To gain office experience before taking up a permanen job."* Times (London) 10/2/78, pIII [**1965** for noun, **1973** fo verb; shortened from *temporary*] ►An isolated instance ap pears in 1932 in a list of words of "Speech in the Post Office, in American Speech, Vol. VII, no. 4, p. 278.

tempeh ('tempei), *n.* a food of Indonesia, made by fermentin, soaked, hulled soybeans with rhizopus fungus and frying then in deep fat. *A student researching in physics at the Australia National University believes that tempeh, a soya bean-base food used in Indonesia for 2000 years, could help to fill empt stomachs in underdeveloped areas.* Geographical 3/72 p428 [**1966**, from Indonesian *tempé*]

template, *n.* a molecule or molecules that serve as a pattern o blueprint which determines the order in which other mole cules are formed, especially such a molecule of DNA or RN in the synthesis of macromolecules of nucleic acids or protein: *Howard Temin at the University of Wisconsin and others hav shown that the normal processes of nucleic acid synthesis ca be reversed by certain RNA tumour viruses, so that DNA is syn thesized from an RNA template.* Science Journal 10/70 p8 [**1953**]

Ten, *n.* **1 the Ten,** the ten nations of the European Economi Community since 1981. *The Ten . . . intended to open a majo long-term review of the Community's budget system.* Britanni ca Book of the Year 1981, p376 **2** Usually written as **10,** *Infor mal.* someone or something scoring the highest on a scale fro one to ten. *"I don't think I am a 10, but other people say I an which is very flattering," says Derek, who checks in at 38-22 36.* Maclean's 9/3/79, p37 [**1981** for def. 1; **1979** for def. 2 (pop ularized by the motion picture *"10",* from the rating scale use in the Olympic Games)]

10-4 or **ten-four**, *interj. U.S. Slang.* a term meaning "messag received," "affirmative," "OK," used especially by citizer band radio operators. *"Aaay, we definitely thank you for tha info, good buddy. We'll back 'em down a hair. You a wes bound?" "Aaay, 10-4 on that. You got the Jack of Diamonds o this end, and we definitely westbound. How's it look over you* *shoulder, good buddy?"* NY Times Magazine 4/25/76, p64 *"Ten four old buddy, see you on the flip"* they yell as their trucks pass in a roar of spray and fumes. Manchester Guardian Weekly 5/30/76, p1 [**1963**] ▶The term was used earlier by police and other radio operators in the *ten code* to minimize air time: "leaving the air" (*10-7*), "repeat message" (*10-9*), and "trouble, emergency" (*10-34*). See the note under CB.

tennis toe, severe bruising of the toenails of tennis players, caused by abrupt stops which rupture small blood vessels in the toes. See also SPORTS MEDICINE. *Known for the severe throbbing pain it causes, tennis toe can be recognized by a swelling of the toe with a purple discoloration below the nail. According to the Podiatry Society of the State of New York, it can be prevented by wearing thick socks and well-fitted sneakers so that the foot doesn't slide inside the shoe.* New York Magazine 6/4/79, p9 [**1973**, patterned after *tennis elbow*]

TENS, *n.* acronym for *transcutaneous electrical nerve stimulator*, a small battery-operated device used to send stimulating impulses to the nerves through electrodes in order to block pain signals. *The TENS, when applied to the skin, creates tiny electrical impulses that are taken up by the underlying nerves to block signals from torn or overworked muscles—signals that the brain would otherwise interpret as pain.* NY Times Magazine 10/5/80, p49 [**1980**]

tensegrity (ten'segrəti:), *n. Architecture.* a three-dimensional structure in which contiguous members under tension are completely separated from members under compression that are noncontiguous. *The "tensegrity" geodesic sphere structure (originally coming from Buckminster Fuller's team) is one that is often discussed in connection with space habitats of the O'Neill colony type,* ... New Scientist 4/5/79, p56 [**1959**, from *tension* + *integrity;* coined by the American designer and architect R. Buckminster Fuller, 1895-1983]

tensiometric, *adj.* of or relating to tensiometry. ... *A tensiometric method utilizes a porous cup filled with water connected by a tube to a vacuum indicator. This approach measures the capillary potential or suction of soil water.* McGraw-Hill Yearbook of Science and Technology 1968, p351 [**1968**]

tensiometry, *n.* the branch of physics dealing with tension and tensile strength. *They [researchers of the Mining Institute of the Czechoslovak Academy of Sciences] claim that these models [of proposed mines] enable reliable forecasts of what will happen to the springs if this or that method of mining is adopted. Tensiometry, stereophotography, photogrammetry, isotope and ultrasound measurements play an important role in this work.* New Scientist 11/18/65, p497 [**1965**]

tensor light or **tensor lamp**, a high-intensity lamp with a hinged metal shaft that can be extended to various positions. *Thad and I had really nice offices with tensor lights all over the place.* James Dickey, Deliverance, 1970, p17 *The hall has ... fifteen dart boards along the walls, and tables and chairs in the middle. Each board has its own tensor lamp and a line taped eight feet in front of it.* Atlantic 8/73, p75 [**1970**, from *Tensor*, trademark (1962), from New Latin *tensor* thing that stretches, from Latin *tendere* to stretch]

tent trailer, a lightweight trailer that serves as a base for a canvas tent that unfolds for camping. *BOAC's latest holiday idea is worth mentioning here. Simply, the Landcruise holiday provides you with a motor-caravan or a car with a caravan or tent trailer and leaves you free to wander at will.* Times (London) 12/28/72, p11 [**1963**]

tenured, *adj. Especially U.S.* having a guaranteed tenure of office. *The popular image of the tenured professor is of a pipe-smoking highbrow who would rather be pushing back the frontiers of knowledge in the library or laboratory than guiding young minds in the classroom.* NY Times 7/9/78, p18E [**1968**]

tenure track, *U.S.* a career path, especially in education, carrying a guarantee of eventual tenure or permanent employment, usually within a given number of years (often used attributively). *Two-year appointment with the possibility of tenure track.* Nature 10/4/71, p xix *But even landing a "tenure-track" posi-*

tion is rarely the achievement of job security these days, because the young professors can find themselves off the track in a matter of months. NY Times Magazine 3/18/79, p58 [**1971**]

tequila sunrise, a mixed drink of tequila, orange or lemon juice, and grenadine. *The tequila boom was partly pushed by the Rolling Stones, who swigged the stuff on tour, and another rock group, the Eagles, who recorded a hit called* Tequila Sunrise *(named for the tequila potion made with orange juice and grenadine).* Time 1/26/76, p62 [**1965**]

ter, *n.* variant of TERR. *We have to drive very slowly on dirt roads so that we can watch out for land mines, which the ters [short for terrorists—the Rhodesians' term for the guerrillas] love planting. In fact, you aim the vehicle over existing tire tracks, and any disturbed soil has to be investigated.* National Review 3/30/79, p416 [**1976**]

tera-, a prefix meaning one million million (10^{12}) of any standard unit in the international meter-kilogram-second system of measurements (SI UNIT). *All these bodies unanimously recommend the use of the following prefixes: kilo to denote thousandfold, mega to denote millionfold, giga to denote thousand-millionfold, and tera to denote million-millionfold. They also unanimously recommend the abbreviations k, M, G and T respectively.* Times (London) 11/3/65, p13 [**1947, 1951** from Greek *téras* monster]

terabit ('terə,bit), *n.* a unit of information equivalent to one million million bits or binary digits. *The CG-100 computer is said to have a main memory capable of holding 10 million million bits (10 terabits) of information.* New Scientist and Science Journal 7/8/71, p80 [**1971**, from *tera-* + *bit*]

terahertz ('terə,hərts), *n. Physics.* one million million cycles per second; 10^{12} hertz. *Four scientists at the National Bureau of Standards' Boulder, Colo., laboratories found the absolute frequency of an emission from a helium-neon laser to be 88.376245 terahertz.* Science News 2/5/72, p85 [**1970**, from *tera-* one trillion + *hertz*]

teratogen ('terətədʒən), *n.* a drug or other agent that causes malformation of an embryo or fetus. *Rubella was the first clearly defined teratogen: an agent that causes developmental abnormalities.* Scientific American 7/66, p31 *Until German scientists reported in 1961 that 150 deformed infants—lacking developed arms and legs—had been born to women taking thalidomide during early pregnancy, the sedative was not a suspected teratogen.* Science News 7/1/67, p10 [**1959**, back formation from *teratogenic* producing deformed organisms (OED 1879), from Greek *téras, tératos* monster + English *-genic* producing]

teratogenicity (,terə,toudʒə'nisəti:), *n.* the tendency to cause malformations of the embryo or fetus. *Present safety regulations vary from agency to agency and country to country, but in general they demand standard levels of freedom from toxicity, teratogenicity, carcinogenicity, etc.* New Scientist and Science Journal 3/18/71, p601 [**1959**]

teravolt ('terə,voult), *n. Physics.* one million million electron volts. *For Fermilab, Congress will be asked to support a development program looking toward the creation of a proton beam of about 1,000 GeV, or one teravolt (TeV), in the present accelerator tunnel by adding a new doughnut-shaped vacuum tube fitted with superconducting magnets.* Scientific American 2/75, p40 [**1975**, short for *tera-electron-volt*]

terawatt ('terə,wɑt), *n. Physics.* one million million watts. *The Laboratory for Laser Energetics of the University of Rochester, recently dedicated its latest and largest piece of equipment, which will hit a target with six laser beams delivering a total of 3 or 4 terawatts of power.* Science News 11/4/78, p309 [**1969**]

Tercom, *n.* a computerized guidance system in a cruise missile that controls its flight path. *Tercom is one of the terminal-guidance techniques currently being developed in conjunction with the U.S. cruise-missile program. The system relies on a set of digital maps stored in the memory of the missile's on-board* *computer.* Scientific American 2/77, p28 [**1975**, acronym for *terrain contour matching*]

teriyaki (ˌteriˈyɑːkiː), *n.* a Japanese dish of fish or meat marinated in soy sauce and grilled or broiled. *The menu includes the usual tempura, sukiyaki, teriyaki . . . and it is good.* NY Times 6/23/67, p43 [**1962**, from Japanese, from *teri* glaze + *yaki* grilled]

terminal, *n.* a device connected to a computer for input or output of data. *Project MAC time-sharing system at the Massachusetts Institute of Technology has 160 terminals on the M.I.T. campus and nearby and is also available from distant terminals. As many as 30 terminals can be connected at one time, with each user carrying on a direct and in effect uninterrupted dialogue with the computer.* Scientific American 9/66, p129 [**1954**] —*adj.* **1** beyond saving; extreme. *Tom Bethell's article* ["Against Bilingual Education," February] *has succeeded in convincing me that the U.S. government is suffering from terminal insanity.* Harper's 4/79, p6 **2** ruinous or deadly; fatal. *He* [Canadian architect Arthur Erickson] *attacked the World Bank specifically, for founding . . . a three-thousand-room hotel development in Bali, "whose impact on that island will be terminal."* New Yorker 6/4/79, p44 [**1972**, figurative sense of the term (OED 1890's) applied to any condition resulting in death]

terminal sequencer, an electronic device which regulates by computer the final countdown before the launching of a rocket. *Then came Launch Control again, reporting that the cut-off was initiated automatically by the terminal sequencer, and that "safing" procedures were now being carried out by the astronauts while Launch Control itself tried to identify the cause of the cut-off.* New Scientist 12/14/72, p645 [**1972**]

terminator, *n.* the site on a segment of DNA where the formation of messenger RNA is terminated; a sequence of nucleotides that signal the end of transcription. *But to get the gene to work—to be transcribed—certain controlling base sequences had to be added at each end. One end had to have a "promoter" sequence so transcription could start; the other end had to have a "terminator" sequence to stop transcription. Neither the promoter nor terminator sequences were known.* World Book Science Annual 1978, p249 [**1969**]

terotechnology, *n.* the management and maintenance of the plant of a business or industry; maintenance engineering. *British Leyland won the award this year for applying terotechnology to reducing wear on its 30 miles of conveyor tracks at Longbridge for an estimated £250,000 annual saving.* Sunday Times (London) 12/14/75, p60 [**1970**, from Greek *tērein* care of + connecting *-o-* + English *technology*] —**terotechnologist,** *n.*: *Terotechnologists quote the case of breakdowns of waste heat boilers for 300 tonne oxygen steelmaking vessels.* New Scientist 4/12/73, p95

terr, *n. Slang.* (among whites in Rhodesia, later Zimbabwe) a black nationalist guerrilla. Also spelled TER. *A short time later, a helicopter rose out of the military garrison in town after reports that 25 "terrs" or Black guerrillas, had been sighted nearby.* Athens News (Greece) 11/12-13/78, p5 [**1976**, shortened from *terrorist*]

terrain-following radar, a radar system which automatically adjusts the altitude of an aircraft or missile in relation to the topography of the ground over which it is flying, allowing high-speed flight close to the ground. *The Tornado, which can fly at more than twice the speed of sound, is the first RAF aircraft to be equipped with Terrain Following Radar (TFR), which will enable low, high-speed penetration of enemy air space on missions against airfields, fuel dumps and troop concentrations. The aircraft could also be used against surface shipping in support of the Royal Navy.* Times (London) 8/15/78, p2 [**1970**]

Terran, *n.* an inhabitant of the planet earth; earthling. *Like our planet, we Terrans tend to be fat and slow or thin and quick.* New Scientist 1/23/69, p191 [**1953**, science fiction use, from Latin *terra* earth + English *-an*]

territorial imperative, *Anthropology.* the supposed innate character of vertebrate animals to regard areas possessively and defend them from encroachment. *And he* [Andrew M. Greeley] *keeps talking about "primordial" human urges to differentiate between a "we" and a "they," of the "territorial imperative," and of similar speculative and ahistorical notions, as if we all agreed on what is "primordial" and as if what is "primordial" had precedence over what is civilized.* New Yorker 11/20/71, p225 [**1966**]

tertiary recovery, any of various methods for extracting oil or gas when simpler methods have failed. Also called ENHANCED RECOVERY. *Oil companies are testing a number of tertiary recovery techniques to get at previously unrecoverable reserves. In places where the oil is too thick for waterflooding, it can be thinned by injecting steam into a well so that oil flows more freely. By injecting air into oil-bearing rocks, it is possible to ignite some of the oil, making the rest thin enough for waterflooding. A third method involves the pumping of surfactants into the rock. These compounds, which function like laundry detergents, remove oil droplets that would otherwise remain in the rock.* Encyclopedia Science Supplement (Grolier) 1975, p156 [**1975**, called *tertiary* because it is the next measure taken when *secondary recovery* (1953) proves inadequate]

TESL (ˈtesəl), *n.* acronym for *Teaching English as a Second Language. And though a major curriculum emphasis is developing fluency in the English language using the linguistic approach of TESL (Teaching English as a Second Language), the knowledge of Navaho is still essential to many jobs on the reservation as well as to communication with the older generation.* Saturday Review 9/16/67, p83 [**1967**]

tesla, *n.* the SI unit of measurement for magnetic flux density. *The earlier accelerator design had embodied a combined-function lattice structure—one using the same magnets for bending and focusing with a magnetic field limited to a flux density of 1.2 tesla (webers/sq.m).* New Scientist 6/18/70, p574 [**1960**, named after Nikola *Tesla,* 1856-1943, Croatian-born American electrical engineer]

TESOL (ˈtiːˌsɒl), *n.* acronym for *Teachers of English to Speakers of Other Languages* (an organization formed in the United States in 1966 to improve the teaching of English as a second language). *An initial objective of TESOL had its origin in two circumstances: the revelation that most ESL teachers lacked special preparation and the wide diversity in content and quality to be found in the multiplying graduate programs for ESL teacher preparation.* Current Trends in Linguistics, Vol. 10, 1973, p317 [**1966**]

test-tube baby, a baby conceived outside the womb by removing an egg from the mother, fertilizing it in a laboratory apparatus, and implanting the fertilized egg in the womb to develop normally. *The first "test-tube" baby to be apparently fertilised outside the mother's womb was born on 27 July to a British couple amid a flurry of scientific speculation on how the feat was achieved.* New Scientist 8/3/78, p325 *While the birth of the first "test-tube baby," in England last July, as a result of the experiments of Dr. Patrick C. Steptoe and Dr. Robert G. Edwards, has been widely publicized, the birth of the second "test-tube baby" has received little public attention, even in India.* New Yorker 11/20/78, p38 [**1974**] ►This term was formerly used in two other senses: (1) a baby produced through artificial insemination; (2) a baby of science fiction conceived and developed in a laboratory apparatus until birth.

tetrahydrocannabinol (ˌtetrəˌhaidrəˈkænəbəˌnɔːl), *n.* the active ingredient in marijuana and hashish, first synthesized in 1966 to study the drug more precisely and found to cause LSD-type psychotic hallucinations when administered in pure form to volunteers. *Abbreviation:* THC *On a weight basis, ethyl alcohol is thousands of times less potent than tetrahydrocannabinol, but in sufficient amounts it produces ill effects.* Scientific American 2/70, p6 [**1940, 1967**, from *tetrahydro-* combined with four hydrogen atoms + *cannabinol,* a phenol derived from the resin of Indian hemp]

tetrazzini (ˌtetrəˈziːniː), *adj.* served with cooked pasta covered with a cream sauce that has been seasoned with sherry and often nutmeg or cheese. *The maid brought in the turkey tetrazzini.* Atlantic 1/72, p81 [**1965**, named after Luisa *Tetrazzini*, 1874-1940, Italian opera singer]

Texas pterosaur, an extinct winged reptile of a previously unknown species, whose fossil bones were discovered in Big Bend National Park in west Texas in 1975. *Sheer size is not the only unusual feature of the Texas pterosaur. Most pterodactyls are thought to have subsisted on a diet of fish, which they snared by gliding over the surface of oceans and lakes, but* [Douglas A.] *Lawson suggests that the newly discovered creatures were meat eaters that scavenged the flesh of dead dinosaurs.* Newsweek 3/24/75, p80 [**1975**]

Tex-Mex, *adj. U.S.* of the Texas-Mexico border country; combining Texan and Mexican elements. *It is a mistake to come to Mexico and not try the local cuisine. It is not the Tex-Mex cooking that one is used to getting in the United States and much of it has no hot chili at all.* The News (Mexico City) (Vistas Supplement) 7/22/73, p7 *In their diversity, the Hispanics have brought some distinctive flavors to the American banquet: the thumping Tex-Mex music of the Southwest borderlands; the salsa dancers of urban discos* . . . Time 10/16/78, p50 **—n.** a variety of Mexican Spanish incorporating elements of English, spoken near the border of Texas and Mexico. *Born in Laredo, Mann spoke border Spanish—"Tex-Mex"—almost as soon as he spoke English and acquired a life-long fondness for the neighboring Mexicans and the Latin temperament.* Time 5/6/66, p15 [**1964** for adj., **1955** for noun; shortened from *Texan-Mexican*]

text-to-speech, *adj.* converting typewritten or printed text into speech as an aid to the blind. *Another computerized text-to-speech device is being developed by the Kurzweil Computer Products Company of Cambridge, Mass. It has a tiny camera attached to a computer that turns print images into a singsong type of mechanical speech.* 1977 World Book Year Book, p349 [**1976**]

textured vegetable protein, a protein derived from soybeans or other vegetables spun into fibers and flavored and used especially as a meat substitute or additive. *Abbreviation:* TVP *Textured vegetable proteins . . . got their first big start in 1971 when the Department of Agriculture approved their use in the national school-lunch program, which covers some 25 million children.* Reader's Digest 10/73, p119 *The soybean derivatives called textured vegetable proteins ("Now There's 'Meatless Meat,'" Feb. 1974) are being sold in more and more grocery stores.* Changing Times 5/74, p6 [**1968**]

T-group, *n.* **1** another name for ENCOUNTER GROUP. *As a psychologist he has reservations about experimental raptures like T-groups, and a considerable sympathy with the anxieties induced in people of established habits by the suggestion that they should review them.* Times (London) 11/30/70, p14 **2** any of various group seminars conducted by trained leaders to improve relations between people employed or working in corporations, government agencies, churches, and other institutions. *The T-group, an older method* [than the encounter group], *uses more verbal exercises and emphasizes the "here and now"—the relationship of each group member to what is happening in the group at that particular time. It allows the participant to know what others think of him* . . . Encyclopedia Science Supplement (Grolier) 1970, p79 [**1950**, from *T*raining *group*]

Thai stick, a thin twig or stick with a potent Asian variety of marijuana wrapped around it. Compare ACAPULCO GOLD, COLOMBIAN GOLD. *A customs and Excise officer, Mr Roderick Marr, said two parcels were opened at the overseas mail office and found to contain photograph albums packed with thai sticks, a form of cannabis.* Times (London) 8/14/76, p2 *Send us your Thai sticks . . . In the fertile heartlands of our broad nation they will soon flourish as American, the Beautiful!* High Times 1/79, p85 [**1976**, from its being produced especially in *Thai*land]

thalassochemical (ˌθæləsouˈkeməkəl), *adj.* of or relating to thalassochemistry. *Another useful abstraction is the "steady state" thalassochemical model. If the ocean composition does not change with time, it must be rigorously true that whatever*

is added by the rivers must be precipitated in marine sediments . . . Scientific American 11/70, p106 [**1970**]

thalassochemistry (ˌθæləsouˈkeməstri:), *n.* the chemistry of the sea. *The task is to persuade our engineers and business companies that working with sewage and junk is just as challenging as oceanography and thalassochemistry.* Scientific American 11/70, p115 [**1970**, from *thalasso-* sea (from Greek *thálassa*) + *chemistry*]

thanatology (ˌθænəˈtɑlədʒi:), *n.* the study of the psychological effects and treatment of approaching death. *There is even an emerging profession for the psychological treatment of the terminally ill. It's called thanatology and is in the human-services curriculum of several colleges.* NY Times Magazine 3/13/77, p90 [**1968**, from Greek *thánatos* death + *-logy* study of. The earlier sense of this word is "the scientific study of the phenomena of death."] **—thanatologist**, *n.: A basic tenet of the Hippocratic oath is preservation of life: yet thanatologists ask doctors also to help the terminal patient and his family to meet his own death.* New Scientist 3/2/72, p497 *Thanatologists claim to be experts in using the new tool of D & D (Death and Dying).* National Review 11/22/74, p1356

thankfully, *adv.* one is thankful (that). *Thankfully, he said, the kibbutzim had been able to show their mettle and resourcefulness in the face of government discrimination.* Jerusalem Post 5/6-12/79, p7 *Aldabra Island . . . where man "has thankfully failed to establish himself."* Times (London) 11/11/83, p2 [**1966**] ▶ The usage is old and well-established in English. It is found in such words as *surely, certainly,* etc., and was the subject of some discussion about *hopefully.* Some words have gone far beyond their usually adverbial meaning, such as *absolutely* with the established sense of 'yes'.

Thatcherism, *n.* the political and especially economic policies of the British Conservative political leader Margaret Thatcher, born 1925, who became Prime Minister in 1979. *The discrediting of monetarism by no means marked the ending of the experiment in Thatcherism.* Manchester Guardian Weekly 1/11/81, p4 [**1979**]

Thatcherite, *adj.* of, relating to, or characteristic of Margaret Thatcher or Thatcherism. *To some extent, but only to some extent, this will entail taking a leaf out of the Thatcherite book. The present Government is right in thinking that more decisions should be taken by the market, and fewer by the state.* Listener 6/26/80, p817 **—n.** a person who supports or advocates the policies of Margaret Thatcher. *Moreover, the free-market philosophy from which the Thatcherites drew such inspiration in opposition has already, in office, run into the hard economic and social reality of allowing the shipbuilding industry to go under.* Harper's 12/79, p28 [**1976**]

thaumatin (ˈθɔːmətən), *n.* a very sweet protein derived from the fruit of a tropical African plant. Compare MIRACULIN. *Robert Cagan of the University of Pennsylvania suggests that the two proteins—called monellin and thaumatin . . . should be termed chemostimulatory proteins because of their direct sensory effect. These proteins, which are at least 30,000 times sweeter than sucrose, could both turn out to be extremely useful tools in research into the taste mechanism.* New Scientist 7/12/73, p62 [**1972**, from New Latin *Thaumato*coccus danielli, the plant + English *-in*]

THC, abbreviation of TETRAHYDROCANNABINOL. *THC combined with morphine relieves pain more effectively than when THC or morphine is given separately.* Science News 9/11/71, p175 [**1968**]

theater, *n.* Used attributively to designate the nuclear weapons (or forces) in a theater of war, as distinguished from intercontinental or strategic nuclear weapons. *. . . to dispute which agency will head the arms control working groups on so-called theater missiles in Europe and on strategic arms limitation talks.* NY Times 6/28/81, pD5 *Attention within the alliance remained focused on the balance of theatre nuclear forces (TNF).* Britannica Book of the Year 1981, p284 *The modernisation of Soviet theatre nuclear weapons preceded, not followed,* *the NATO decision to install comparable weapons . . .* Manchester Guardian Weekly 8/30/81, p12 [**1977**]

theater of _____. The term THEATER OF THE ABSURD inspired the formation of a number of similar terms, such as the ones shown below. Two of the most widely used terms, THEATER OF CRUELTY and THEATER OF FACT, are separately entered and defined. **—Theater of Chance:** *Words must be used in an unprecedented way, if we are to hear them again, either radically out of sequence as in The Theater of Chance or as independent counters, made abstract by reiteration, as in* The Brig. Harper's 9/66, p79 **—theater of despair:** *Madame Duras is to me a dramatist whose importance is of the order of Beckett or of Ionesco, though her work has nothing to do either with the theatre of the absurd or the theatre of despair.* Sunday Times (London) 6/12/66, p25 **—Theater of Involvement:** *At the moment, the theater is the vanguard. Its use as a revolutionary medium, deliberately intended to shock and flout the middle-class standards of order, decency, and entertainment, has a name: the Theater of Involvement.* 1969 World Book Year Book, p52 **—theater of protest:** *None of this was felt immediately in Britain, although the Twenties did produce a modest theatre of protest which continued to weaken accepted ideas.* Sunday Times (London) 5/28/67, p25 **—Theater of the Mind:** *The Theater of the Mind might lead to something beyond the pleasure principle, in fact, if its proponents could get past the fad of the pseudo-psychedelic, of trying to fake trips for stay-at-homes.* NY Times 9/15/68, pB24 **—Theater of the Obscure:** *Make way, please, Eugene Ionesco, Samuel Beckett and Pinter, H. Charles Wood has arrived to join you in the Theatre of the Obscure.* Times (London) 8/7/72, p8 **—Theater of the Streets:** *Sheffer said that the idea of getting political cabaret "out of history, out of the Berlin cafés of the twenties, and into New York City in the spring of 1968" was just as exciting, potentially, as the recent experiments in Guerrilla Theatre and the Theatre of the Streets, which lean toward direct confrontation with the Establishment. . .* New Yorker 4/27/68, p36 **—theater of the ridiculous:** *But there is. . . a clear connection between the sensibility that Sontag defined and the sensibility behind the theatre of the ridiculous. Both are playful, anti-serious, and wholly aesthetic. . .* New Yorker 11/15/76, p86 **—theater of violence:** *In the midst of one performance of the theater-of-violence satire Roda Viva, a whistle blew and men armed with clubs, pistols and boxing gloves rose on signal . . .* Time 10/25/68, p44

theater of cruelty, a form of theater based on the theories of the French actor and poet Antonin Artaud, 1896-1948, in which dialogue, plot, and character are subordinated to a representation of harsh physical and sensual rituals. The audience is deliberately involved and the action is intended to provide a shocking or abrasive personal experience to all the participants. *Pierre Clementi stars as a young drama teacher in Rome whose twin aims in life are to carry the Theatre of Cruelty to its logical conclusion (revolution) and to seduce his professor's delectable daughter.* Manchester Guardian Weekly 10/10/70, p21 *On the one hand, the violence doesn't bother the heads, because they don't take it for real—it's a trip, a fantasy experience, separate from day-to-day living. On the other hand, the violence is what blows their minds. Devices from the theatre of cruelty are used to set off kicky fantasies. The cruelty becomes delectable, like the gore.* New Yorker 11/20/71, p218 [**1954**, translation of French *théâtre de la cruauté*]

theater of fact, a form of theater that draws its subjects from events of recent history, often utilizing excerpts from actual speeches, articles, books, etc., to convey realism. *Murderous Angels is another example of The Theatre of Fact. [Conor] O'Brien has subtitled his play "A political tragedy and comedy in black and white", and the two main characters are Dag Hammarskjold and Patrice Lumumba.* Times (London) 2/9/70, p5 [**1966**]

theater of the absurd, a form of theater that stresses the absurdity of the human condition and the futility of man's attempts to cope with it. See also THE ABSURD (under ABSURD). . . . *theater-of-the-absurd plays such as* Zoo Story *and* The Bald Soprano, *and next year selections from* The Deputy. Time 9/4/64, p46 . . . *these little tid-bits, more from the theater of the ludicrous than the theater of the absurd, have only the pretentious*

smell of red herring about them. NY Times 1/11/68, p41 [**1961**]

thebe (ˈθeibei), *n.* a monetary unit in Botswana. See the quotation. *The new unit—the pula, which will be divided into 100 thebe—will have the same value, however, as the rand, which ceases to become legal tender in this country as of Aug. 23.* NY Times 8/15/76, p6 [**1976,** from Setswana, literally, shield]

theme park, an amusement park whose features and attractions are organized around one or several unifying ideas, such as wildlife, fairy tales, or space travel. *The number of Americans who visit the theme parks which now dot the U.S. landscape from coast to coast has soared from about 16 million in 1964 to more than 54 million in 1973 and will reach 73 million by 1976, the industry forecasts.* New York Post 5/30/74, p30 [**1960**]

theology of liberation, variant name of LIBERATION THEOLOGY. *Jesuits are at loggerheads in Latin America over a Christian-Marxist synthesis known as the "theology of liberation." . . . But longtime Political Activist Roger Vekemans, a Belgian Jesuit who has spent years backing Christian social democracy in Latin America (most particularly Chile's former President Frei), decries the theology of liberation as simplistic and totalitarian.* Time 4/23/73, p42 *Alienation is a useful word that no longer belongs exclusively to Marxists; and liberation illuminated by the so-called theology of liberation, adds to our understanding of human relationships at personal, political and religious levels.* Times (London) 1/7/74, p12 [**1969**]

therapeutic community, a mental-health group, clinic, or institution in which various techniques of group psychotherapy are used, especially to rehabilitate drug addicts. . . . *not widely known outside the mental health profession, has been the development of a method of treatment that is called the therapeutic community. The term describes a way of operating a small psychiatric unit in a hospital. Ideally a unit will have between 20 and 40 patients; a large hospital may have more than one therapeutic community.* Scientific American 3/71, p34 [**1964**]

thermal breeder, a breeder reactor (atomic power plant able to produce its own fuel as well as generate power with almost no loss of fissionable material) that uses relatively slow neutrons to produce fissionable material. *Two different breeder systems are involved, depending on which raw material is being transmuted. The thermal breeder, employing slow neutrons, operates best on the thorium 232-uranium 233 cycle (usually called the thorium cycle). The fast breeder, employing more energetic neutrons, operates best on the uranium 238-plutonium 239 cycle (the uranium cycle).* Scientific American 11/70, p13 [**1970**]

thermal pollution, pollution by the discharge of heat into water or air, often with other waste liquids or gases, by nuclear power plants, factories, refineries, etc. Also called CALEFACTION. *Hot water pollution, often called thermal pollution, may act the same way as overfertilization . . . Warm water, even water heated by only 5 to 10 degrees F., can promote the growth of certain algae over certain others, just as sewage does, with adverse consequences for existing food chains.* Science News Yearbook 1970, p300 [**1970**]

thermoform (ˈθərməˌfɔrm), *n.* a process for shaping plastic by the application of heat. *A fairly new development, concentrated at Yate, . . . is the thermoform process whereby thin plastic film, made at Yate, is moulded into such objects as the subdivided holders in biscuit and chocolate boxes, and lightweight trays for serving meals in aircraft.* Times (London) 3/20/70, pII **—v.t., v.i.** to shape (plastic substances) into desired forms by the application of heat. *To exploit the full potential of thermoformed materials in packaging and to gain extra marketing power in a sector now being staked out by major combines.* Sunday Times (London) 11/7/71, p64 [**1958**]

thermogram, *n.* a photograph or image produced by infrared rays emitted by the body, which shows differences in temperature between normal and abnormal tissue. *Blood flows are heat flows in the human body, and if the blood supply to a surface area has been destroyed, this will appear cooler in a thermo-*

gram of the body—some 3°C cooler than adjacent healthy areas, in fact. New Scientist 2/26/70, p407 [**1957**]

thermoluminescent dating or **thermoluminescence dating**, a method of determining the age of an archaeological or geological specimen by measuring the intensity of the light given off by the specimen when heated at a controlled rate. Also called TL DATING. *Forged Hui Hsien Chinese pottery widely bought by collectors and museums 25 years ago has been unmasked by the Oxford Research Laboratory for Archaeology and the History of Art. Thermoluminescent dating established that the pottery was only 30 years old, not 2300 years old as claimed.* New Scientist 8/10/72, p296 [**1962**]

thermolysin (θərˈmɑləsən), *n.* a calcium-dependent enzyme that breaks down peptides, found in bacteria which require high temperature for growth. *Complete molecular structures of enzymes are being determined by X-ray crystallography so rapidly now that the publication of a new structure is no longer worthy of comment in itself. But the recent analysis of the structure of thermolysin by a group at the University of Oregon is noteworthy because the enzyme is remarkably stable to heat.* New Scientist 12/14/72, p624 [**1965**, from *thermo-* heat + *lys-* dissolution + *-in* suffix meaning protein]

thermophysical, *adj.* of or relating to the physical characteristics of substances under high temperature or increasing temperature. *More than two years in the making, this encyclopedic and unique reference work is specifically designed to give you easy access to all the thermophysical properties data presently available.* Scientific American 9/67, p297 [**1957**]

theta pinch, the rapid compression of a magnetic field surrounding plasma (highly ionized gas) to produce a controlled fusion reaction. *The high-density devices are pulsed because of the means they use to heat high-density plasma quickly. One such method is by the shock and compression of a magnetic implosion, called a theta pinch.* Science News 10/17/70, p321 *The simplicity of the theta pinch as a means of achieving that sought-after goal of power from thermonuclear reactions has led to considerable studies of its real effectiveness in confining and heating up a plasma.* New Scientist 11/9/67, p369 [**1959**]

thick film, a relatively thick, multimolecular layer of material used in integrated circuits and in making electronic components (often used attributively). Compare THIN FILM. *Thick film materials are generally deposited onto a flat substrate by a screen printing process. Materials to produce resistors, capacitors, conductors and insulating layers are supplied in the form of an ink.* New Scientist 10/15/70, p8 [**1967**]

thin film, a very thin layer of material used in various processes and devices, especially in electronics (often used attributively). Compare THICK FILM. *Optical interference in a thin film can be explained in terms of the wave theory of light.* Scientific American 12/70, p59 *Assignment—Develop advance thin-film processes and materials, improve photoetching techniques, and process thin-film components.* NY Times 7/12/67, p54 [**1956**]

thing, *n. Slang.* that which one likes best or does best (used especially in the phrases **do one's thing** or **do one's own thing**). [What] *I admire about Robbins is that he's making a lot of money. That's just his thing. He's doing his own thing.* New Yorker 11/29/69, p48 *"My life-style revolves around my work—photography. I* [Chet Morrison] *don't advocate anybody else's doing what I've done or thinking what I'm thinking. Everybody ought to do his own thing."* Time 11/30/70, p14 *Quite a few people prefer to do their own thing on holiday, of course.* Sunday Times (London) 4/11/71, p41 [**1968**]

thingism, *n.* emphasis on or concern with physical objects and details in literature and art. *The aim is not solely to mock materialism: Godard is also influenced, reportedly, by the poetry of Francis Ponge, which is concerned with "Thingism," the seeming life and effect of "things."* New Republic 5/9/70, p24 [**1961**, translation of French *chosisme*, from *chose* thing + *-isme* -ism]

think-in, *n. Informal.* any conference or symposium. *The Social Democratic and Labour Party is to have a major "think-in" this weekend to prepare the party and its supporters for the White Paper.* Belfast Telegraph 2/23/73, p4 *Between May 31 and June 11, some 2,000 delegates from more than 140 nations will meet in Vancouver for a multimillion-dollar think-in entitled Habitat, or more formally the United Nations Conference on Human Settlements.* Maclean's 5/31/76, p21 [**1972**, originally (1965) applied to a university forum or seminar to discuss important political or social issues, formed on the model of *teach-in* (1965)]

think tank, a center or institute for theoretical studies, especially of the problems of culture and society, and research in science and technology. *The 'think tanks', the oldest and most important being the RAND Corporation, have had much influence on developments.* Science Journal 3/69, p90 *The Urban Institute was set up by the Johnson Administration as a private, nonprofit corporation to serve as the Government's "think tank" for research into city problems.* NY Times 9/11/68, p24 [**1959**]

think-tanker, *n.* a member of a think tank. *Throughout this century think-tankers have been confidently predicting the imminent exploitation (an appropriate term) of the seas.* New Scientist and Science Journal 9/2/71, p536 [**1971**]

thin-layer chromatography, a method of analyzing the chemical substances of a mixture by passing it through a thin layer of filtering material. *Sperling analyzed a series of hallucinogenic tryptamines by gas and thin-layer chromatography.* McGraw-Hill Yearbook of Science and Technology 1971, p360 [**1957**]

thioridazine (ˌθɑiəˈridəˌziːn), *n.* a drug used as a tranquilizer in the treatment of schizophrenia and senility, and in the study of learning capacity. *Tranquilizers such as thioridazine forestall behavioral disorganization in schizophrenics and make them less excitable. But recent findings by Dr. Michael J. Goldstein of the University of California at Los Angeles indicate that some schizophrenics may do better without tranquilizers.* Science News 6/26/71, p430 [**1959**, from *thio-* sulfur + *piperidine* a blood vessel dilator + *-az* nitrogen + *-ine* (chemical suffix)]

third age, the years after middle age; old age. *"We have devised a package deal for elderly people from the Continent,"* Mr [Peter] *Bedford said. "We are attempting to attract some Belgian old age pensioners. In Belgium it is called the third age."* Times (London) 3/16/72, p13 [**1972**, translation of French *troisième âge*] **—third ager:** *When the Third Agers first arrived on campus there was a bit of snickering from the younger students.* Time 3/11/74, p75

third kingdom, a proposed division of living organisms comprising the ARCHAEBACTERIA, as distinguished from the animal and plant kingdoms. *Scientists studying the evolution of primitive organisms reported in late 1977 the existence of a separate form of life that is hard to find in nature. They described it as a "third kingdom" of living material, not plant or animal. The organisms in the third kingdom are composed of ancestral cells that abhor oxygen, digest carbon dioxide, and produce methane.* Encyclopedia Science Supplement (Grolier) 1979, p68 [**1977**]

third-level carrier, *U.S.* an airline that makes short flights between cities and towns. *Now the CAB is trying a different approach to serve smaller communities: strengthening the nation's 3,200 "third-level" carriers—the air taxis and commuter lines that usually fly smaller planes—Cessnas, Pipers, Beechcraft and the like.* Time 2/28/72, p74 [**1969**]

third market, *U.S.* the market in listed stocks not traded on a stock exchange; over-the-counter trading in listed stocks, as distinguished from trading on a national exchange or in unlisted stocks. *Unable to get discounts on the Big Board, mutual funds, pension funds and other institutional investors are channeling a growing share of their business to regional exchanges and the so-called third market, where brokers arrange private trades of listed stocks.* Time 11/30/70, p73 [**1964**]

Third World or **third world, 1** the group of underdeveloped countries, especially of Africa and Asia, that receive aid from both the Communist world and the non-Communist world and therefore cannot be aligned with either. *Europeans are quite as anxious as Canadians about American policing of nationalist revolutions throughout the emerging "third world".* Saturday Night (Canada) 11/66, p15 . . . *western techniques, unadapted, cannot be grafted on to Third World economies without some transitional period in which the new skills and attitudes needed can be learnt.* New Scientist 10/29/70, p227 **2** the underdeveloped countries of the world, especially those of Africa, Asia, and Latin America, without regard to their political alignment. *The world was now divided into three. The First World was that of the two superpowers, the Second was that of the other developed countries and the Third was that of the developing countries. China was a socialist country belonging to the Third World. The Third World was described as the motive force propelling history forward in the world today.* Annual Register of World Events in 1974, p318 **3** *Attributive use* (often in allusion to the racial composition of peoples in the Third World). *"The law penalized the poor and third-world woman who has no other options than prostitution if they want to pay the rent. The law does not hit the wealthy call girl—just the one on the street who is most deprived."* NY Times 4/18/76, p21 [**1963**, translation of French *tiers monde*, based on the eighteenth-century *tiers état*, the Third Estate]

Third Worlder, one belonging to the Third World, especially an African or Asian. *Skills which the average 16-year-old western youth would have little difficulty in mastering apparently pose almost insoluble problems for the average Third Worlder.* New Scientist 10/29/70, p227 [**1970**]

Third Worldism, a movement supporting the Third World; sympathy and support for the aspirations of Third Worlders. *This allows a comfortable slide from the pragmatic what's-in-it-for-me attitude toward neutrality that dominates the adult population to the revolutionary Third Worldism of large sections of Sweden's politically active youth and intellectuals.* New Yorker 12/26/70, p46 [**1970**]

tholin ('θoulin), *n.* a sticky solid substance containing organic compounds, found in interstellar space. *On the basis of this research the Cornell group proposed that the interstellar solid grains are composed of tholins and that the more complex interstellar gas molecules are their degradation products. The grains, Sagan maintained, were ejected from solar nebulae by radiation pressure and by stellar winds from cool stars during their early evolution.* 1980 Britannica Yearbook of Science and the Future, p258 [**1979**, from Greek *tholós* mud + English *-in* (chemical suffix)]

thong, *n.* a bathing suit consisting of a narrow strip of material running between the thighs to a cord around the waist. *Thong bathing suits, swimsuits that expose the derriere, aren't considered appropriate attire in . . . Myrtle Beach and the Isle of Palms, S.C. Thongs are OK on Hilton Head . . .* Herald-Statesman (Yonkers, N.Y.) 6/18/89, p8 [**1989**]

threatened, *adj.* (of a wildlife species) facing serious, but not immediate, danger of extinction. *Seven hundred and sixty-one plants were designated as "endangered," meaning their survival was in doubt, twelve hundred and thirty-eight were listed as "threatened" and an even one hundred were declared extinct—at least in the wild.* New Yorker 1/12/76, p58 [**1960**]

3HO ('θri:'eitʃ'ou), *n.* a form of Sikhism (a kind of monotheistic Hinduism including elements of Islam) practiced in North America that sometimes incorporates elements of yoga and vegetarianism, founded by the Indian Sikh Yogi Bhajan in 1969. *The 3HO Sikhs lead a life that combines asceticism and idealism with rigorous exercise and entrepreneurial ventures.* Maclean's 4/18/77, p74 *Neighbors are nervous about 3HO's expensive land purchases in the area. Less visible than the cymbal-clanging Hare Krishnas, the 3HO disciples rival them in devotion. Men and women alike follow the Sikh traditions of not cutting their hair and bearing symbolic daggers, combs and bracelets.* Time 9/5/77, p70 [**1971**, from the abbreviation of *Happy, Healthy, Holy Organization*, its name]

three-martini lunch (or **luncheon**), *U.S.* a lavish lunch, especially one deducted as a business expense. *Other reforms that the President proposed would further restrict certain tax shelters for well-off people . . . and cut in half permitted deductions for business meals—an attack on the by now fabled three-martini lunch.* Time 1/30/78, p21 *A small band of us devoted an entire three-martini luncheon to the problem the other day.* New York Post 3/22/79, p25 [**1972**] ▶ According to *Safire's Political Dictionary* (William Safire, 1978), the term was first used by Senator George McGovern during the national election campaign of 1972.

threshold, *British.* —*adj.* of or having to do with an agreement in which wage increases depend upon the cost-of-living index reaching a predetermined figure. *The threshold idea, which ties pay to the cost of living and automatically compensates workers when prices rise above an agreed figure, originated with the unions. They suggested it in the National Economic Development Council some two years ago, but the Government was unimpressed.* Times (London) 7/23/73, p1 *From the second quarter of 1974 the rate of increase of money wages accelerated sharply. This was partly due to "threshold agreements," which permitted addition to wages of £0.40 per week for every 1 percentage point rise of the cost-of-living index above its level of October 1973.* Britannica Book of the Year 1975, p271 —*n.* a threshold agreement. *Thresholds are giving about 10 million workers supplements of up to £2.80 a week and a further two payments would bring the total to £3.60.* Manchester Guardian Weekly 10/19/74, p4 [**1967**]

thrombosthenin (ˌθrɑmˈbɑsθənin), *n.* a contractile protein found in human blood platelets. *Investigators . . . at the National Institutes of Health in Bethesda, Md., isolated actin and myosin-like proteins from thrombosthenin—a group of contractile proteins in human blood platelets. It is probably involved in coagulation.* World Book Science Annual 1973, p276 [**1961**, from *thrombo-* blood platelet (from Greek *thrómbos* clot) + *sthen-* strength (from Greek *sthénos*) + *-in* (protein) substance]

thromboxane (θrɑmˈbɑkˌsein), *n.* a hormonelike substance that stimulates the aggregation of blood platelets and the constriction of blood vessels. *A Swedish research team discovered that platelets can convert prostaglandins into previously unknown compounds, called thromboxanes, which not only encourage the platelets to stick to one another but also cause arteries to contract. That combined action can result in thrombosis and therefore needs to be suppressed. The mechanism of that suppression, it turns out, involves another new compound, probably a prostaglandin.* Times (London) 10/21/76, p16 [**1975**, from *thrombosis* (from Greek *thrómbos* clot) + *oxygen* + *-ane* (chemical suffix)]

through-deck cruiser, a British lightweight, nuclear-powered aircraft carrier. *The Kiev and her sisters, at about 40,000 tons displacement, fit neatly between the US Navy's carriers of twice the size and the Harrier-equipped 18,000 ton vessels such as the Royal Navy's through-deck cruisers and the US Navy's Guam.* New Scientist 8/19/76, p394 [**1970**, so called from its having the flat deck of a carrier and the displacement of a cruiser]

throughput, *n.* the amount of data put through a computer; a computer's input and output collectively. . . . *time sharing (or multi-programming) is already well established as a means of increasing the throughput and utilization of a computer.* New Scientist 6/24/65, p883 [**1965**, transferred from the original sense of the amount of oil, ore, etc., processed by a plant (OEDS 1915)]

throwaway, *adj.* casual; offhand; understated. *His* [Georges Brassens, a French singer] *songs give a better idea of the man than the few throwaway remarks he will volunteer about himself.* Manchester Guardian Weekly 12/13/69, p20 . . . *here is an author who is refreshingly gentle and sympathetic; a comic leg-pull or shrewd aside is his most lethal weapon; he has a beguiling throw-away humour.* Punch 6/10/64, p873 [**1955**, figurative use of the earlier sense of "disposable" (OEDS 1928), from the noun meaning any disposable item (1922), from the verb phrase *throw away*]

throw weight, the maximum weight in megatons which a nuclear missile can deliver on a target. *The U.S. has placed a higher priority on the accuracy of its missiles, while the Soviet Union has emphasized higher firepower or "throw weight." Each side would be free to change that emphasis if it desired.* Time 12/9/74, p16 *The powerful throw-weight of the Soviet missiles means that they can carry more warheads. As a result, the explosions they cause would be larger, and they would not have to be aimed so precisely at their targets.* New York Review of Books 3/22/79, p36 [**1969**]

thrust chamber, the chamber of a rocket in which the expansion of gases produces enough thrust for takeoff. *Bacchus* [a rocket] *would have an enlarged first stage—Octavie—with four long tanks and eight thrust chambers, supporting two further liquid propellant stages, Diane and Mirible.* New Scientist 5/9/68, p270 [**1962**]

thruster or **thrustor**, *n.* any of various small engines for producing thrust, as for maneuvering a spacecraft. *The* Glomar Challenger *is placed in position over the drilling pipe by extra side propulsion propellers called thrusters, which are controlled by computers.* Encyclopedia Science Supplement (Grolier) 1970, p153 *At 6:00 a.m. on the second day in orbit, Conrad reported to ground control in Houston that No. 8 thrustor (out of 16) was "not up to snuff."* Science News 9/24/66, p223 [**1962**]

thrust stage, a stage extending into the auditorium, with seats on three sides of the stage. *"Hedda Gabler" was not meant for anything but a proscenium stage. Putting it on the thrust-stage was like entering a vintage Rolls for the Mille Miglia.* Manchester Guardian Weekly 12/19/70, p17 *The Fine Arts Theatre . . . is a compact, multipurpose amphitheater seating 600, which can be utilized for conventional theatricals, as a thrust stage, or even—with the built-in pit—for musicals and intimate opera.* Saturday Review 6/1/68, p22 [**1968**]

thumb piano, any of various small African musical instruments consisting of a wooden box with tuned metal or wooden strips inserted along it lengthwise that vibrate when played with the thumbs. *He might have added that this instrument is usually called a thumb piano, that its most common African name is zanza, and that you can buy a kit to make one in American novelty shops.* Natural History 12/72, p92 [**1952**]

thumper, *n.* a device for producing a shallow seismic wave to test structural properties of the earth, lunar surface, etc. *This time, they* [astronauts] *will also have brought along a variety of ordnance to make different types of explosions for the benefit of the seismometer—a sort of walking stick called a "thumper," which sets off a small charge whenever it is tapped against the ground, and a mortar, which will fire charges to varying distances.* New Yorker 1/9/71, p70 [**1962**]

thunderboat, *n.* another name for UNLIMITED HYDROPLANE. *In 1973 unlimited hydroplane championship was not settled until the last race on the U.S. circuit, when an innovative, tail-winged thunderboat nailed down the title.* Britannica Book of the Year 1974, p494 [**1965**, so called from the noise made by its powerful engine]

thylakoid ('θailəˌkɔid), *n. Botany.* one of the membranous structures in a chloroplast which contains most of the pigment molecules needed for photosynthesis. *Zooxanthellae possess four conspicuous organelles. The chloroplast is single-lobed and peripheral, and its lamellae exhibit a three-thylakoid arrangement.* McGraw-Hill Yearbook of Science and Technology 1974, p403 [**1962**, from Greek *thýlax, -akos* sack + *-oid* thing resembling]

thymosin, *n.* a hormone produced by the thymus gland, believed to be associated with the development of T cells. *Thymosin treatment has raised the T-cell count in more than 75 per cent of the cancer patients receiving it either alone or along with chemical and radiation therapy.* World Book Science Annual 1978, p298 [**1966**, from Greek *thýmos* thymus gland + English *-in* (chemical suffix)]

thyristor, *n.* a transistor or semiconductor that forms an open circuit until signaled to switch to the conducting state by a controlling electrode. *If thyristors are used to control the motor of*

an electric car, the vehicle moves smoothly but with poor efficiency at low speeds. New Scientist 3/12/70, p510 [**1958**, from Greek *thýrā* door + English trans*istor*]

thyrocalcitonin (ˌθairouˌkælsəˈtounən), *n.* another name for CALCITONIN. *. . . three hormones, calciferol, thyrocalcitonin and the parathyroid hormone are linked together in the delicate control of the level of calcium in the blood.* Scientific American 12/70, p89 [**1963**]

TIA ('tiːˈaiˈei), abbreviation of *transient ischemic attack*, a temporary or minor cerebrovascular accident or mild stroke. *Temporary symptoms caused by poor blood flow (ischemia) to the brain, TIA's precede about 10% of all strokes.* 1980 Britannica Yearbook of Science and the Future, p352 [**1978**]

ticky-tacky, *Especially U.S.* —*n.* cheap or inferior material, especially that used in building rows of uniform small houses. *The real point is, will . . . Watchung Pharmaceutical get those 250 unspoiled acres around Howard's tree farm which have been zoned for a park, there to produce more poppable pills and sprinkle company ticky-tacky over the landscape?* Newsweek 7/30/73, p71 —*adj.* made of ticky-tacky. *A part-time social worker sits in a tent waiting for the victims of bad acid trips to reel in. 'Look, they're young, they're still free, they really love love and they hate materialism. They've got maybe two years before they join their own little nuclear families and live in ticky-tacky mortgaged houses.'* Listener 9/6/73, p305 [**1962** for noun, coined by the American folk-song writer Malvina Reynolds, 1900-1978, probably by reduplication of *tacky, adj.* shabby, dowdy (1880's); **1969** for adj.]

tie-break, *n. Especially British.* **1** a system for breaking a tie in tennis in which the player winning five points out of nine takes the set. *In principle, the tie-break is an undesirable expedient, but there is a case for it in indoor tournaments confined to one court.* Times (London) 3/5/70, p13 *It was the first time that a tie-break system had been used, and though confusing at first it eventually served its purpose of getting matches finished in reasonable order.* Manchester Guardian Weekly 11/21/70, p23 **2** any system for choosing a winner out of several who have tied. *Nigel . . . failed in a tie-break to win the British chess championship . . .* Daily Telegraph 12/19/79, p1 [**1970**]

tie-dye, *n.* a tie-dyed garment. *. . . the stars fussed with their see-through dresses, tie-dyes and black ties and then paraded up a red-carpeted walkway.* Time 4/20/70, p72 [**1956**, noun use of the earlier verb (OEDS 1904)]

tight end, an offensive end in American football who lines up close to the tackle. *By way of celebration, a number of Colts crowd into a tavern near the practice field . . . linebacker Ted (The Mad Stork) Hendricks, tight end Tom Mitchell, guard Dan Sullivan, tackle Fred Miller.* Atlantic 1/72, p74 [**1963**]

tilt, *U.S.* —*v.i.* to tend or incline (toward one side and against another); have a slant or bias. *A widespread belief that the balance of effective nuclear power was tilting against the United States might encourage the Soviets to adopt more adventurous policies—for example, in the Middle East.* Atlantic 6/72, p12 *Mr. Nixon disclosed that he "tilted toward" a proposal to bomb several North Korean military airfields in April 1969 to retaliate for the downing of an unarmed American reconnaissance plane.* NY Times 9/4/77, p25 —*n.* inclination (toward or against); slant; bias. *The contribution to the American language of other cultures has long been acknowledged . . . but it is unscholarly to insist on a "tilt" toward minority contribution to satisfy resentment over past neglect.* NY Times Book Review 5/11/75, p14 *The pro-Soviet tilt of the new rulers in Kabul, the Afghan capital, is already stirring some recriminations in Washington.* Time 12/18/78, p40 [**1967** for verb, figurative use of *tilt, v.i.*, to slope, slant (OED 1626); **1975** for noun]

time frame, the limits of time for any given situation or event. *The time frame envisaged as necessary for significant change is, as in the Prince Edward Island Plan, fifteen years.* Geographical 7/72, p679 *This trial, like most trials, has created jargon all of its own. Witnesses speak, for instance not of dates on the calendar as May or June, say, but as "time frames," which was a holdover from the Senate Watergate hearings.* NY

Times 4/28/74, p51 [**1964**, originally used in aerospace and computer technology]

timeline, *n.* a schedule detailing the times and sequence of activities of the crew of a space flight. *When at last Carr and Pogue came upon the camera on the floor of the workshop, they were well behind the timeline, for the ground had allotted only ten minutes to move from one experiment to the next.* New Yorker 8/30/76, p59 [**1967**]

time reversal, a principle in physics which postulates that if the time in which a sequence of operations occurs is reversed, the same sequence will occur again but in the reverse order (often used attributively). *Another symmetry consideration is that of "time reversal." This notion says in effect that a motion-picture film of any process should show the system appearing to obey the same laws of physics whether the film is run forward or backward.* Scientific American 7/66, p75 *Time-reversal invariance refers to the principle that the direction of the flow of time should have no effect on the validity of physical laws.* Americana Annual 1970, p546 [**1955**]

time-shared, *adj.* of or relating to time-sharing. *Display unit designed by John Ward and Robert Stotz has access to the large time-shared central computer at the Massachusetts Institute of Technology.* Scientific American 6/66, p52 *Although this concept was not new, it was not until 1969 that time-shared systems began to flourish.* 1971 Britannica Yearbook of Science and the Future, p170 [**1966**]

time-sharing, *n.* **1** the use by many persons at remote locations of a single central computer whose speed in processing data is greater than the combined speed of all the users. *Time sharing allows the user access to a much more powerful computer than he could afford to buy. This is because he is one of a large group of users who share the computer's time, and hence its cost, from individual terminals.* Science Journal 10/70, p69 *Time-sharing is generally described as simultaneous access by multiple users to a single large computer. In reality, the machine moves swiftly from user to user, processing programs both sequentially and independently.* NY Times 1/9/67, p137 [**1953**] **2** an arrangement in which a person shares the cost of a furnished vacation dwelling by buying a percentage of the unit at a set price for a fixed limited time each year (often used attributively). *Under time-sharing plans, participants pay anywhere from $800 to $8,000 for bargain-rate accommodations in a certain condominium or vacation resort for a given number of weeks in a particular season each year, usually for at least twelve years and in some cases indefinitely. In exchange for guaranteed occupancy over an extended period, time-sharing resorts offer low prices, luxury suites usually equipped with kitchens, and discounts on the use of entertainment facilities.* Time 8/30/76, p67 [**1976**] —**time-share**, *n.: A time-share can be very inexpensive, though, certainly compared to hotel costs in that location. Generally, 1979 prices ran from $5,000 to $9,000 or so for two weeks for however many years you like at a two-bedroom two-bath luxury condominium unit that might cost you $90,000 to purchase.* Ruth Rejnis, Her Home, 1980, p73

time-symmetric, *adj.* moving both forward and backward in time. Compare ARROW OF TIME. *This finding . . . suggests that the universe is not ever-expanding but rather is "time-symmetric" (that is, alternately expanding and contracting).* Scientific American 10/73, p50 [**1972**]

time warp, an imaginary discontinuity or distortion in the flow of time. *Science-fiction writers, stymied by the laws of physics, turn to such literary devices as time warps to make interstellar travel possible.* Time 9/11/72, p47 *The other dominant subject is science's latest fad (and it may be no more than that)— black holes, the suspected but so far unverified regions of the cosmos that constitute tunnels in space and might even turn out to be the long dreamed-of space and time warps capable of providing instantaneous passage across the universe.* Maclean's 8/22/77, p56 [**1954**, patterned after *space warp* (1947)] —**time-space warp**: *There have been about half a dozen successful books on the Bermuda Triangle . . . they have encountered a time-space warp and been carried into another dimension.* Listener 2/19/76, p199 —**time-warped**, *adj.: Splendidly mali-*

cious fables about the exaggerated elaborations of the astronaut Tichy, who meets himself in time-warped multitude and who, as Earth's delegate to United Planets, has a most difficult time explaining why the human race should be admitted to the organization. Times (London) 11/11/76, p14

timolol ('timəlɔːl), *n.* a beta-blocking agent used in treating high blood pressure, also used to reduce fluid pressure within the eyeball in the treatment of glaucoma. *Formula:* $C_{13}H_{24}N_4O_3S$ *One of a class of substances called beta-adrenergic blocking agents, timolol blocks the actions of hormones that affect heart action and blood pressure by making the heart beat more slowly. Researchers suggest timolol may thus protect a damaged heart by reducing its demand for the oxygen and other substances in the blood.* NY Times 4/5/81, p8E [**1973**, origin uncertain]

tin parachute, *U.S.* a contract guaranteeing continued wages and benefits to the rank and file after control of the company is transferred to new owners. Compare GOLDEN PARACHUTE. *Unlike golden parachutes for executives, which must be disclosed publicly, tin parachutes are often kept secret—at least until a hostile bidder appears on the scene.* NY Times 3/19/87, pD8 [**1987**]

Tio Taco ('tiːouˈtɑːkou), *U.S. Slang (derogatory use).* a Mexican American who adopts the culture and values of white American society. *California's only Mexican-American congressman depends on Anglo suburbs for more than half his support, and in the state legislature the gerrymandering is even more effective; there was in 1971 only one Mexican assemblyman and no state senator. It was a system that placed high premium on the Tio Taco, or Uncle Tom.* Atlantic 6/71, p45 [**1969**, from Spanish, literally, Uncle Taco]

tipee or **tippee**, *n.* a person who receives inside information about a company's status and uses it to profit on its stocks and shares. *What about so called "tipees"—people who come by price sensitive information often because of a breakdown in security by a professional adviser or within the company? The CSI feels it is ethically wrong for anyone who receives from an insider information which he believes to be price sensitive and then deals on it.* Times (London) 10/12/78, p29 [**1961**, from *tip* to give secret information to + *-ee*]

tissue plasminogen activator, a protein substance in the cells that catalyzes the conversion of plasminogen to plasmin, produced synthetically as a drug capable of rapidly dissolving blood clots in the arteries. *Abbreviation:* TPA or T-PA *Tissue plasminogen activator. . . acts only at clots, whereas streptokinase acts throughout the bloodstream and can cause excess bleeding.* Science News 4/13/85, p229 [**1978**]

tissue-type, *v.t.* to determine the compatibility of the tissues of. *. . . this would enable donors and recipients to be tissue-typed on an international basis.* Times (London) 11/7/68, p3 [**1968**]

tissue typing, a procedure for determining the compatibility of tissues, used especially before an organ transplant by having a computer match the tissue of a donor with those of several potential recipients to select the recipient most compatible with the donor's tissue. *Tissue-typing, we now know, is essential in the transplantation of any organ in contact with the bloodstream.* Sunday Times (London) 12/10/67, p46 *. . . the improvement in tissue typing (to match the tissue of donor and recipient) and a better understanding of how to control rejection had resulted in a success rate in most centers of 80% for kidney transplants between living relatives and of 50% for cadaver kidney transplants.* 1971 Britannica Yearbook of Science and the Future, p236 [**1965**]

t.j. or **T.J.**, abbreviation of TALK JOCKEY. *Some of the new talk jockeys—or t.j.s—still play music, but it is always subordinate to their dialogue with listeners.* Time 5/22/72, p76 [**1972**, patterned after *D.J.* for disc jockey]

TL dating, short for THERMOLUMINESCENT (or THERMOLUMINESCENCE) DATING. *TL-dating was developed in the 1960s for dating pottery and other fired materials from archaeological sites; it has not been without its difficulties, as with the Glozel forgeries . . . but recent results on pottery have generally* *been archaeologically acceptable.* Times (London) 11/11/78, p3 **[1972]**

TLP, abbreviation of *transient lunar phenomena. Sudden local increases in brightness in certain regions of the Moon have been puzzling astronomers for centuries. Herschel reported events of this kind, known as Transient Lunar Phenomena (TLPs), in 1787.* Times (London) 1/8/72, p16 **[1971]**

T lymphocyte, another name for T CELL. *In seeking the answer, Dr. Good found that there are two kinds of mature lymphocytes. One kind is called the T lymphocyte; the other, the B lymphocyte.* Reader's Digest 10/76, p267 *In the mid-1960's, research revealed that the lymphocyte controls the immune defenses and that there are two basic types of lymphocytes, T lymphocytes and B lymphocytes, each controlling different parts of the immune system.* NY Times Magazine 4/2/78, p64 **[1976]**

TM, abbreviation of TRANSCENDENTAL MEDITATION. *Although transcendental meditation or TM as it has come to be called, appears to be an effective method of mental relaxation, it probably has no advantages over any other meditative techniques, whether they be zen or yoga or what-have-you.* Joe Graedon, The People's Pharmacy, 1976, p262 **[1967]**

TMer (ˌtiːˈemər), *n. U.S.* an adherent or practitioner of transcendental meditation. *Sure they keep repeating their mantra—so do insurance salesmen, housewives and millions of other T.M.'ers (though I grant you with less ardor and frequency). Other people say rosary beads.* NY Times Magazine 5/1/77, p42 **[1972,** from *TM* + *-er*]

T-mycoplasma, *n.* a viruslike microorganism (mycoplasma) that coats and distorts the bodies of sperm cells, possibly causing infertility. *Another possible new approach to birth control arose from research on microorganisms called T-mycoplasmas . . . These microorganisms can trigger certain cases of reproductive failure among men, apparently by inhibiting the movement of sperm up the female vaginal tract.* 1977 Collier's Encyclopedia Year Book, p356 **[1976,** perhaps from its resemblance to the letter *T*]

T.N.F. or **TNF**, abbreviation of *theater nuclear forces. Indeed, while the Soviets have more than 250 new SS-20s within striking range of Europe, NATO as yet has no weapons with a reciprocal capability. The original 1979 decision to deploy the U.S.-built T.N.F. was intended to offset precisely that advantage.* Time 11/16/81, p39 **[1980]**

toaster oven, a small oven for toasting and baking. *Two . . . couches had been delivered, along with a small refrigerator, hot plate, and toaster oven.* Margaret Truman, Murder at the FBI, 1985, p35 **[1961]**

tobaccophobe, *n.* a person who hates tobacco smoke, especially one who opposes smoking in public places and supports the enactment of anti-smoking laws. *While many tobaccophobes maintain that their aim is to "educate" smokers, they have not in the past been noticeably successful—as witness a turn-of-the-century campaign to censor a nursery rhyme because Old King Cole "called for his pipe."* Time 1/12/76, p36 **[1975,** from *tobacco* + *-phobe* one who hates or has a phobia about (something)]

TOEFL (ˈtoufəl), *n.* acronym for *Testing of English as a Foreign Language. It is of primary importance that all such materials, like all TOEFL materials, take the student's native language (here, dialect) into full account.* J. L. Dillard, Black English, 1972, p272 **[1962]**

toe sock, a sock with a separate place for each toe or for the big toe. Compare TUBE SOCK. *By far the best seller in the socks scene is a style known as the "toe sock" or "wiggler," which fits, glovelike, in between the toes.* Time 2/3/75, p56 **[1975]**

togavirus (ˈtougəˌvairəs), *n.* any of a group of viruses containing RNA and enveloped in a layer of lipid. *Although viral taxonomists initially wished to confine the term arbovirus to those that were physiochemically characterized as cuboid, RNA, lipid-enveloped viruses, thus including some, such as rubella, known not to be arthropod-transmitted and excluding others,*

such as vesicular stomatitis, that are, agreement has been reached that many so characterized will be classified as togaviruses, leaving arboviruses to a biological definition. Science 10/19/73, p273 **[1970,** from Latin *toga* layered robe or cloak + *virus*]

together, *U.S. Slang. —adj.* free of confusion, anxiety, etc.: mentally and emotionally stable. *Crockett is "just about the most together brother on the bench," says Ken Cockrell, a black activist lawyer in Detroit.* Time 4/6/70, p60 *"People don't realize that a young lady of twenty-two who's been through what Twiggy has been through has got to be a very together person to survive," Justin said.* New Yorker 12/18/71, p31 **—get it all together,** to become free of confusion, anxiety, etc.; assume a sound, positive, stable attitude or outlook on life. *For him, Deborah had thrown out all her posters, and with him she had moved from Hesse and Alan Watts to Mann and Kierkegaard. "Let's face it, babe, they've got more to say. I mean, they've really got it all together."* New Yorker 5/22/71, p41 **[1968]**

tokamak (ˈtoukəˌmæk), *n.* a device for producing controlled thermonuclear power, in which plasma (highly ionized gas) is confined in an endless tube by magnetic fields produced by currents outside the tube and inside the plasma itself. *Stellarators and tokamaks are two varieties of toroidal or doughnut-shaped chambers in which physicists are trying to achieve controlled thermonuclear fusion. Recently the tokamaks have produced plasmas nearer to fusion conditions than any other devices have been able to do . . .* Science News 2/20/71, p129 **[1969,** from Russian *tokamák*, an acronym for *toroidál-naya kámera s magnítnym pólem* (toroidal chamber with a magnetic field)]

toke (touk), *U.S. Slang. —n.* a puff or smoke on a cigarette or pipe containing marijuana, hashish, or other narcotic. *. . . he [a pothead] sits down on the steps in front of the sheriff's place, lights up, and takes a few tokes.* New Yorker 7/19/69, p20 **[1968,** apparently from earlier *toke, v.,* to smoke or puff on a cigarette (1952), of uncertain origin] **—v.i.** to smoke or puff on a cigarette or pipe containing marijuana, hashish, etc. *Bill Buckley says he went "outside the 3-mile limit—I'm a law-and-order advocate, you know"—to toke up, but neglects to mention where he got the stuff.* Newsweek 1/1/73, p4 **[1970,** verb use of the noun]

token economy, a method used in behavior modification to reinforce desirable behavior by rewards of token money that can be exchanged for predetermined items of value, such as food or free time. *The goals of the token economy, as with other contingency management procedures, are to promote behaviors necessary for effective personal functioning, not only in an institutional or school environment, but also in natural settings.* McGraw-Hill Yearbook of Science and Technology 1976, p53 **[1968]**

tokenism, *n.* a policy or practice of attempting to fulfill one's obligations with token efforts or gestures, especially to minority groups or women. *On the drive to the campus, Powell asked how many blacks attended the school, and the student said there were about fifteen. "Fifteen!" Powell fumed in mock-anger. "Why, that's tokenism, sheer tokenism!"* Harper's 4/71, p53 *When I subsequently said some critical things about the planning of the programme I was told, "Oh well, it was a good piece of tokenism."* Watch out. *"Tokenism" is a new vogue word of the communicators.* Times (London) 12/10/71, p13 **[1962]**

tolley, *n. British.* a marble used to shoot at marbles; a taw or shooter. *Playing marbles requires a player to bend double to flick the tolley and we feel that ladies in this position are open to ridicule at the very least.* Times (London) 2/18/70, p2 **[1970,** variant of *taw-alley* (in English Dialect Dictionary)]

Tom, *U.S. Slang (derogatory use). —n.* an Uncle Tom (a black who is servile or ingratiating to whites). *The late William Dawson was the only other Negro in Congress when Powell arrived, and together they represented the two available alternatives, the Tom and the Bad Nigger, the one meekly accepting the system on its own terms, the other staging fake confrontations with it which produced a measure of vicarious revenge for* *black people but few real gains.* Harper's 4/71, p59 . . . *"This building is not integrated. No Whites, Black ONLY. Police not pass this door. Black, white or toms."* Manchester Guardian Weekly 12/12/70, p5 —v.i. Often in the phrase **Tom it,** to be or act like an Uncle Tom. *"She* [the singer Bessie Smith] *was an absolutely direct black woman. No Tomming, not a shade of the phony to her."* New Yorker 11/6/71, p172 *In Mr. Wright's view, the whole gamut of Negro behavior . . . involves one form or another of "Tomming it:" being like Uncle Tom.* NY Times 3/5/66, p25 [**1959** for noun, **1963** for verb; both shortened from earlier *Uncle Tom* (1922 noun, 1947 verb)]

Tomism, *n. U.S.* the behavior of an Uncle Tom. . . . *the extremist group that captured control of Wayne State University's student newspaper last year and turned it into a black separatist organ . . . Recently, on vague grounds, it condemned one Hamtramck labor-relations aide for "Tomism and treason to his black brothers."* Time 4/11/69, p58 [**1969,** short for *Uncle Tomism* (OEDS 1937)]

tonfa ('tɑnfə), *n.* a long wooden or plastic stick with a projecting handle, used as a weapon in martial arts and sometimes by police. *A cop trained in using the tonfa can employ about eight different "locking and pinning" holds on an unruly suspect—something one can't do with a nightstick, he says.* New York Post 12/17/82, p14 [**1982,** from Japanese]

ton-up ('tən,əp), *adj. British Slang.* that rides a motorcycle at high speeds; that does "a ton" (a speed of 100 miles an hour). *Sunning themselves by the warm walls were all varieties of layabouts and modern youth beatniks, mods, and ton-up boys . . .* Manchester Guardian Weekly 4/22/65, p6 [**1961**]

toot, *U.S. and Canadian Slang.* —*n.* **1** cocaine. *A couple from Flushing, Queens, New York, was busted on Miami street corner in possession of nine pounds of toot.* High Times 1/79, p33 *20 little white plastic spoons . . . ringed a brass bowl. Each man dipped a spoon into the white powder and got his toot the same way.* Daily News (New York) 9/23/79, p5 **2** a snort of cocaine. *The possibility of a jail sentence is enough to make most of Vancouver's professional people ultra discreet about their use of the drug, while they slink into some of the finer furnished bathrooms of the city for a quick toot.* Maclean's 5/2/77, p24 —*v.t.* to inhale (cocaine) through the nostrils. *The connoisseur's choice. You'll feel better knowing that what you toot is cut with the original Italian Mannite Conoscenti.* Advertisement in High Times 1/79, p52 [**1977,** origin unknown]

topless, *adj.* **1** without a top or upper garment to cover the breasts. *It was the silly season. And the 'topless' dress (for wearing which three young women appeared briefly at Bow Street on 21 August) was much in the news.* Annual Register of World Events in 1964, p29 . . . *we did demand a few brief deletions of visual material, including the topless bathing suit, a striptease scene, and a magazine cover with the title "Jazz Me, Baby!"* Harper's 5/65, p128 **2** wearing a topless garment; exposing the breasts. *One evening a couple of weeks ago the CBC's National News . . . flashed a picture of a topless dancer across the nation's TV screens.* Maclean's 9/17/66, p4 **3** employing or featuring waitresses, dancers, or others wearing topless garments. . . . *the evidence mounted that a topless bar no more incites to lust and criminality than a swimming pool or a bust of the Venus de Milo.* Manchester Guardian Weekly 3/7/70, p5 —*n.* **1** a topless waitress, dancer, etc. *He advertised for "College Topless Queens," "Put Yourself Through College by Becoming a Topless!" he shouted, intimating that a high IQ was no hindrance if other vital statistics were in evidence . . .* Saturday Review 4/22/67, p80 **2** a topless dress, bathing suit, etc. . . . *even his critics grant that Rudi's topless was only an incident in his rapid rise to leadership as the most way-out, far-ahead designer in the U.S.* Time 12/1/67, p34 **3** a bar, restaurant, nightclub, etc., featuring topless waitresses or performers. *"I hope you don't have toplesses in Toronto. We stopped it here. Soon as one has it, then the other guy across the street has to have it . . .* Saturday Night (Canada) 9/67, p24 [**1964** for adj.; **1967** for noun] ►Use is recorded as early as 1937, but in reference to bathing suits for males.

topless radio, *U.S.* radio programming which solicits telephone calls to discuss the caller's sexual problems with the host as part of the broadcast. See TALK JOCKEY. *No phone-in programme I have heard sounds quite like the master of the Los Angeles air-waves, Bill Ballance. He pioneered what is now known as 'topless radio' in the United States. For five hours every day on station KGBS, he delved into the psyche of Californian women and collected confessional erotica from them.* Listener 12/5/74, p730 [**1973**]

top-of-the-line, *adj.* of or being the best or most advanced of a line of products. *The difference in quality is attributable in large part to the application by the Japanese of "top-of-the-line" computer-controlled processing equipment . . .* Scientific American 7/87, p36 [**1963**]

toponium (tɑ'pouni:əm), *n. Nuclear Physics.* a hypothetical subatomic particle consisting of a top quark and its antiparticle. *About two years ago, the upsilon particles were discovered. These are generally held to be bottomonium (bottom-antibottom combinations), evidence for the existence of the bottom quark. So far the corresponding toponium has not appeared. The next question is whether these "new" quarks have families of particles analogous to those associated with the up, down, and strange.* Science News 1/12/80, p24 [**1978,** from TOP (QUARK) + *-onium,* as in CHARMONIUM]

top quark, a hypothetical quark that may have a mass 13 times that of the proton. Compare BOTTOM QUARK. *Dr. Samuel Ting of M.I.T., who shared a Nobel Prize for discovery of the J/Psi particle, says that he and other scientists . . . have been working toward collision energies of 40 billion electron volts, more than they expect is needed to detect the top quark.* NY Times 2/13/79, pC2 [**1977**]

torque, *v.t., v.i.* to give a turning or twisting force to an axle, bolt, wheel, etc.; apply torque. *During high altitude chamber experiments on man's ability to work in a near vacuum, Lockheed's Lou Testaguzza performed simple tasks of threading nuts, torquing bolts and connecting electrical cables on an adjustable panel.* Science News 9/24/66, p222 *Electronic circuitry translates the displacement of the accelerometer's pendulum into an electrical signal, which is amplified and sent to a torquing device on the pivot axis of the pendulum.* Scientific American 3/70, p82 [**1954,** verb use of the noun]

toss, *U.S. Slang.* —*v.t.* to search (a person), especially for narcotics; frisk. *The dissenters were also worried about "the possibility that a police officer . . . will use a traffic arrest as a pretext to conduct a search." In fact, some do already; if they "toss" the suspect and find nothing, they may not even bother with the traffic arrest.* Time 12/24/73, p74 —*n.* an act or instance of tossing; a frisk. *A toss is no funny business, and the risks for a cop are enormous at all times, and for this reason he has mastered some extremely impressive techniques.* NY Times Magazine 11/19/72, p106 [**1939, 1969,** so called from the manner in which suspects are often handled by the police]

total, *U.S. Slang.* —*v.t.* to wreck beyond repair; destroy totally. *An accident serious enough to "total" a car generally "totals" the occupants as well.* Scientific American 4/68, p90 *And, oh, yes: Townshend did total his instrument during his last song.* New Yorker 8/28/71, p81 —*v.i.* to be totaled. . . . *yes, there it is, the beautiful movie, wandering off among far-away drive-ins at the intersections of numbered highways. Glimpsing a frame or two, motorists will total and die.* Atlantic 6/71, p64 [**1954,** verb use of the noun] ►OED2 cites an earlier but isolated use recorded in a word list of East Anglian vocabulary (1895).

total fertility rate, the number of offspring born per woman during a lifetime of childbearing, used as a measure of the fertility of a population. *The total fertility rate of 1.5 births per woman in West Germany is unquestionably the lowest in the world.* Scientific American 9/74, p112 *The total fertility rate, an index used by demographers to measure the birth rate in any given year, in fact dropped from 2.9 children per woman of childbearing age (18 to 40) in 1964 to 2.1 a decade later and 1.9 last year. It's the lowest peacetime rate recorded in French* *demographic history.* Manchester Guardian Weekly (Le Monde section) 2/15/76, p12 **[1974]**

total history, historical writing that includes many of the significant aspects of human endeavor in a particular time. *The book has been acclaimed as a masterpiece of 'total history'. What does this mean? It is an attempt to depict a society in all its aspects embracing economic, social, cultural, religious and political developments all at once.* Listener 1/29/76, p123 **[1972]**

touch dancing, dancing in which the partners hold each other, especially ballroom dancing. Also called BODY DANCING. *A few lessons are more important than ever now that real dancing is back,* touch *dancing—that exciting contact-to-music that brings out feelings no other kind of dancing ever did.* Advertisement in Newsweek 9/24/73, p56 *TV dance programs, such as an updated American Bandstand and Soul Train, now feature teen touch dancing.* Harper's Bazaar 2/74, p131 **[1972,** so called to distinguish it from rock'n'roll dances in which partners do not touch] ►As interest in the "old" form of social dancing was revived, the term *touch dancing* developed to fill the need for a distinction between closely coordinated ballroom dancing and the individual style of rock'n'roll dancing.

touch tablet, a computer input device in the form of a tablet or pad operated by touch. *Atari took the spotlight . . . for graphics-input devices. Its light pen ($125) lets you draw lines on the computer's display or select menu options by touch. The touch tablet* (price not available) *performs a similar function except that you touch an electronic pad rather than the screen, giving higher resolution and allowing the use of templates.* Popular Computing 11/83, p236 **[1983]**

touch-tone, *adj.* involving the use of push buttons to transmit electronically coded signals. *The touch-tone telephone allows the user to put numeric data into a system via telephone lines without introducing the problem of voice recognition.* New Scientist 5/28/70, p430 *The Touch-Tone dial meets the needs of most motion-handicapped individuals. Those unable to operate it with a finger or a prosthesis can usually dial with a mouth stick.* McGraw-Hill Yearbook of Science and Technology 1971, p412 **[1962,** as trademark *Touch-Tone*]

Tourette's syndrome (tu'rets) or **Tourette syndrome** (tu'ret), a nervous disorder characterized by spasms of the facial muscles, shoulders, and extremities accompanied by grunts and other noises. It usually begins in late childhood and is found mostly in males. *. . . it was* Tourette's Syndrome *that made Johnson's life a misery. He had the classic symptoms. Apart from involuntary movements and repetitive speech patterns, he had a compulsion to touch things, such as every lamp post along a street. If he missed one, he'd go back and touch it. Not being a conformist in other things, Johnson managed to refrain from expressing one trait of the syndrome: compulsive, involuntary swearing.* Maclean's 4/13/78, p66 **[1972,** named after Gilles de la *Tourette,* 1857-1904, a French neurologist who first described it]

touriste (tu:'ri:st), *n. Canadian Slang.* traveler's diarrhea acquired in French Canada. *The Queen brings her own drinking water, out of concern for* touriste. Maclean's 9/73, p72 **[1973,** from Canadian French, literally, tourist] ►The doublet *turista* (from Spanish) has been applied since about 1959 to this condition when contracted in Mexico.

tout (taut), *n. Slang.* (in Northern Ireland) an informer. *Corrigan and Williams, who plan to take their campaign throughout Northern Ireland, have also received death threats and obscene letters branding them "touts."* Time 9/6/76, p27 **[1959,** probably extended from the earlier slang meaning (OED 1718) "a thieves' scout or watchman," ultimately from the Middle English verb *tuten* to peep]

TOW (tou), *n.* or **TOW missile,** an antitank missile guided to its target by signals sent over a wire connected to the missile during flight. See WIRE-GUIDED. *The U.S. is allowing the export of the remote-controlled TOW, perhaps the world's deadliest antitank weapon, to Israel, South Viet Nam, Lebanon and Jordan.* Time 3/3/75, p34 *The TOW missile can be used offensively from jeeps or armed cars when accompanying armor and in-*

fantry on attack. NY Times 3/28/76, p1 **[1969,** acronym for *tube-launched, optically tracked, wire-guided]*

towaway, *U.S. —adj.* of or involving the towing away and impounding of an illegally parked car. *If a man living in the New York area decides to take his wife out to dinner and a Broadway play he had better be ready to shell-out . . . the $25 towaway charge for illegal parking.* Saturday Review 6/3/67, p8 **—n.** the towing away and impounding of an illegally parked car. *On a weekday basis—despite the published warnings about illegal parking—towaways averaged close to 200 cars daily during February.* NY Times 3/5/67, p75 **[1956,** for adj.; **1967** for noun]

tower block, *British,* a tall residential or office building. *Modern "industralized" methods of building tall tower blocks increase productivity, but present the designer with new stability problems.* New Scientist 5/23/68, p388 *Tower blocks can be accused of leading to eardrum degeneration, owing to constant use of high-speed elevators, without any risk of a return to lots of little low-built homes in gardens.* Atlantic 10/66, p127 **[1966]**

town house, *U.S. and Canada.* an attached one-family house; row house. The equivalent British term is *terrace house. . . . people will move into "townhouses" and semidetached houses, which have less privacy than single family houses, but still provide private yards and a feeling of separateness from the next-door neighbors.* NY Times Magazine 1/7/68, p85 *The younger Mr. Plumer had got wind of a developer who was looking around the neighborhood for a site on which to build small town houses for rent and was thought to be considering an abandoned school nearby and a certain parking lot.* New Yorker 8/5/67, p38 **[1965]**

toxicoid, *n.* any poisonous chemical substance. *The process which must be controlled is the voiding of morbid material: anything which will taint, poison, or reduce the fecundity of any member of the food web to the detriment of the marine resource. This includes toxicoids (heavy metals, pesticides), oil, detergents, emulsifiers and hot water.* New Scientist 4/13/72, p77 **[1972,** noun use of the adjective (1890's) meaning resembling poison, from Latin *toxicum* poison + English *-oid* resembling]

toxic shock syndrome, an acute and sometimes fatal bacterial infection accompanied by high fever, vomiting, diarrhea, and a sharp drop in blood pressure. It is thought to be especially stimulated by use of vaginal tampons. *The highly invasive bacterium* Staphylococcus aureus, *responsible for such diverse maladies as pimples, food poisoning, blood poisoning, cystitis, endocarditis, pneumonia, severe infections and toxic shock syndrome, may spread through the body in the same way that metastasizing cancer cells do.* S. aureus's *capacity to bind to a molecule found in the matrix between cells may allow the bacterium to move in and out of the bloodstream by slipping through vascular walls and into tissues . . .* Science News 7/20/85, p39 **[1978]**

TPA or **t-PA,** abbreviation of TISSUE PLASMINOGEN ACTIVATOR. *. . . t-PA may be useful in preventing brain damage in human stroke patients if it is given quickly after the first symptoms of stroke appear.* World Book Science Annual 1987, p286 **[1978]**

t quark, short for TOP QUARK. *Theory right now envisions six, and to those four it adds a t quark (prosaically called "top," but the more philosophically inclined say "truth") and a b quark ("bottom" or "beauty").* Science News 6/3/78, p357 **[1977]**

tracker dog, a bloodhound or other trained dog used to track fugitives. *Police with tracker dogs search the area in Epping Forest where the body of a murdered woman was found.* Times (London) 3/31/66, p5 **[1962]**

tracking, *n. U.S.* another name for STREAMING. See also TRACK SYSTEM. *Tracking can be a useful educational device if tests are frequently administered and if movement from one track to another is made easy.* NY Times 6/23/67, p36 *. . . on the secondary level, till very recently, most teachers resisted community demands for an end to tracking.* Saturday Review

12/21/68, p49 [**1967**, from *track* a class or course of study arranged by homogeneous grouping of students (1959) + *-ing*]

track lighting, lighting by means of a metal strip or track along which light fixtures can be inserted, moved and adjusted to the desired position. *For all their versatility, track-lighting systems do have disadvantages over conventional floor and table lamps. Installation of the track on the ceiling is tricky, and, in most instances, involves hiding the wires from the ceiling to the light switch. Special bulbs are usually required.* NY Times Magazine 8/15/76, p47 [**1972**] —**track light:** *Walls and floors are lit with ellipses of color from track lights.* NY Times Magazine 5/14/78, p74

track record, the record of performance made by a person, business, etc., in a particular field or endeavor. *In sum, your endorsement of four Democrats—in one by ignoring the issues and in two others by placing rhetoric over commendable track records—gives credence to the belief that you have ceased your role as an independent newspaper to take up one as spokesman for the Democratic National Committee.* NY Times 10/29/70, p42 *A modern university president is expected to have practical vision, a good track record in administration, and national prominence as a scholar.* Atlantic 4/71, p40 [**1965**, figurative sense from the racing term (1940's) for the record of speed set by a horse at a particular distance and track]

track suit, a suit used by athletes (originally track athletes) to keep warm. *At which point, the one remaining member of the British Olympics Team (all the rest having fainted from the altitude) took off his tracksuit . . .* Punch 2/28/68, p294 *. . . I met a group of astonishingly tall men and women in track suits. Their eyes radiated Olympic health.* NY Times 6/18/71, p39 [**1955**]

track system, U.S. an educational system in which students are grouped according to ability or aptitude as shown in standardized tests. Compare STREAMING. [Carl F.] *Hansen's track system, which became a focal point for criticism of the schools, was the prime example of a well meant idea that the former superintendent* [of schools in the District of Columbia] *was not flexible enough to adapt to changing educational needs.* Saturday Review 11/18/67, p73 [**1959**]

tractorcade, *n.* a procession of tractors. *Turned-over tractors were parked on highway overpasses, tractorcades drove through the streets of county seats and state capitals, and bright orange strike stickers glowed over the cigar counter of every small-town café.* Harper's 5/78, p33 [**1977**, from *tractor* + *-cade* combining form meaning procession, as in *motorcade*]

tradecraft, *n.* the craft of espionage and intelligence work. *Howard learned the "tradecraft" of intelligence, practicing the recruitment of agents and the use of "dead drops" to pass messages . . .* NY Times Magazine 11/2/86, p22 [**1961**]

trade-off, *n.* a balanced exchange; compromise; bargain. *But now that the U.S. industrial and social system is delivering such "disproducts" as pollution and racial tension and no longer seems to be supplying the compensating efficiency, many Americans feel they have been swindled in the trade-off.* Time 3/23/70, p75 *Trade-offs between apparently unrelated topics are a classic feature of international diplomacy.* Listener 10/15/70, p506 [**1961**]

trailable, *adj.* (of a boat) able to be carried on and launched from a trailer pulled by an automobile. *As slip and mooring space become more difficult to find, the trailable boat represents an alternative—it can be dry sailed from a boatyard or moored at home.* NY Times 9/5/76, pE11 [**1976**, probably alteration of *trailerable* (1971, used in advertisements), from TRAILER, *v.* + *-able*]

trail bike, a lightweight, rugged motorcycle for use on rough terrain. *Anyone hoping to escape the filth and din of cities for the quiet beauty of our woods, mountains or deserts is in for a rude shock. He is greeted by the rattling snarl of trail bikes, dune buggies and the like.* Time 9/12/69, p17 [**1969**]

trailer, *v.t.* **1** U.S. and Australia. to transport on a trailer. *In the past three years we have trailered and sailed our small sloop.* NY Times 1/11/76, pE11 **2** to publicize in advance by means

of trailers (excerpts from films, etc.). *Those resonant gatherings, once trailered earnestly and extravagantly . . .* Times (London) 7/8/78, p12 —**v.i.** to travel by or in a trailer. *I just returned from an enjoyable two-month trailering tour of Mexico . . .* National Review 3/2/73, p234 [**1970** for verb transitive def. 1, **1965** for def. 2; **1973** for verb intransitive]

trail mix, a mixture of nuts, seeds, and dried fruits, used as a snack by hikers and campers; GORP. *There was some trail mix, but no other food. ("If I carry a lot of food in the airplane, I just eat it. I carry trail mix the way some people carry chewing tobacco.")* New Yorker 11/26/84, p49 [**1977**]

trank, *n.* U.S. and Canada, Informal. a tranquilizing drug. *The Canadian Medical Association has officially expressed "alarm" about over-prescriptions of minor tranks, and their abuse by consumers.* Maclean's 3/22/76, p58 [**1967**, by shortening and alteration of *tranquilizer*]

trannie or **tranny**, *n.* British Informal. a transistor radio. *Take a piece of tin foil and rotate it round a really cheap "trannie" turned to a blank part of the dial, volume at maximum. If the foil obstructs a micro-wave source the radio static will become louder.* Manchester Guardian Weekly 8/14/77, p20 *You do better by sticking in London and keeping your ear glued to the tranny. These news programmes they have on all the time are a right godsend and better still there's police radio.* Punch 3/26/75, p523 [**1969**, shortening and alteration of *transistor*]

tranquillityite (træn'kwiliti:ˌɑit), *n.* a mineral discovered in moon rock samples, consisting of a compound of titanium, iron, and magnesium. *A few minerals that are unknown on earth were found in the mare basalts. These include armalcolite, whose name is derived from the first syllables of the names of the Apollo 11 astronauts (Armstrong, Aldrin and Collins), and tranquillityite, named for Mare Tranquillitatis, where it was found.* Encyclopedia Science Supplement (Grolier) 1974, p19 [**1970**, from Sea of *Tranquillity* + *-ite*]

transactinide series, a predicted series of heavy chemical elements which is to follow the actinide series (ending with element 103 or lawrencium) in the periodic table. Compare SUPERACTINIDE SERIES. *The element 104 begins a new series. Dr. Glenn T. Seaborg, head of the Atomic Energy Commission and Nobelist in chemistry for discovery of transuranian elements, called the new element the first of the transactinide series. This series should extend from 104 to 112.* Science News Yearbook 1970, p265 [**1970**]

transaction, *n.* (in transactional analysis) any exchange or interaction between persons involving the ego-states of the participants. *Steps of the transaction are shown by drawing arrows from one circle to another. Let us imagine a married couple, John and Barbara. These two adults (but not at the moment, in T. A. vocabulary, Adults) are having fun at a party. The transaction of having fun together involves the Child ego-state on both sides.* NY Times Magazine 11/19/72, p130 [**1961**]

transactional analysis, a method of psychotherapy in which interpersonal relationships are analyzed in terms of confrontations between three ego-states (Parent, Adult, and Child) whose misplacement in the individual's personality is supposed to be responsible for most neurotic behavior. It was developed by the Canadian-born psychiatrist Eric Berne, 1910-1970. Abbreviation: TA *In the 1960s it was encounter groups. In the 1970s it is transactional analysis, or T.A., the pop-psychological path to happiness charted by Sacramento Psychiatrist Thomas A. Harris in his bestseller* I'm OK—You're OK. *T.A., or close facsimiles of it, is now practiced by some 3,000 psychiatrists, psychologists, social workers and ministers in the U.S. and 14 foreign countries.* Time 8/20/73, p44 *Roman Catholics leave the priesthood to marry; and Protestants leave the ministry to conduct encounter groups and workshops in transactional analysis.* Atlantic 3/75, p90 [**1961**] —**transactional analyst:** *"What we have are competing systems of belief. The scream therapist says, 'We are better than the transactional analyst,' who says, 'We are better than the group therapist,' who says, 'We are better than the sex therapist,' and so on."* New Yorker 5/15/78, p78 transactivate, *v.t.* to cause (a cell) to undergo transactivation. *HTLV-I causes some forms of human leukemia and lymphoma. HTLV-II, found originally in a human cancer, has not yet been proved to cause any disease. The newly identified regulatory system common to these viruses has been named transactivation by Dr. William A. Haseltine, of Dana-Farber Cancer Institute and Harvard Medical School. He said transactivation might also have counterparts in other organisms. The products of transactivating viral genes appear to force the cells they infect into an abnormally high state of growth and reproductive activity. Under this influence they make abnormally large numbers of the virus particles, or of the products of any other genes that come under the influence of the system.* NY Times 6/28/85, pA14 **[1983]**

transactivation, *n. Genetics.* a process by which a viral gene causes the host cell to transcribe a protein which in turn induces the cell to reproduce large amounts of the virus's components. *Finally, within the past year, a novel transactivation mechanism known for certain DNA tumor viruses has been proposed for [a] retrovirus without oncogene sequences, the human T-cell leukemia-lymphoma virus. These viruses (and others such as BLV and HTLV-III as well) apparently bring about cellular transformation (or cytopathic effects—HTLV-III) through a transactivation mechanism via a transactivating protein.* Journal of the National Cancer Institute 4/86, p769 **[1983]**

transbus, *n. U.S.* a bus of advanced design with such features as extra length, reduced noise level, and lower floors to facilitate access by the elderly and handicapped. See KNEELING BUS. *He [David Duffy] prefers specially constructed vans, which already provide door-to-door service in Dade County for more than 800 people a day, but he expects that the high cost of the transbuses (as much as $50,000 more than a regular bus) will halt the expansion of the special van service.* Time 12/5/77, p34 **[1973, from *trans*- beyond + *bus*, because the improved design transcends the quality of service offered by conventional bus service]**

transcendental meditation, a method of meditation that is supposed to help the mind transcend all thought to bring about a blissful state of pure consciousness through complete physical and mental relaxation induced by such techniques as repetition of a secret personal incantation. It was developed by the Hindu guru Maharishi Mahesh Yogi, born about 1911. *Transcendental meditation (TM) has been found to produce definite physiological changes in respiration, brain wave and heart rate. Just exactly how these changes affect behavior is still not clear but psychologists have found personality differences in persons before and after they began using TM.* Science News 9/8/73, p152 *It was not long after this startling discovery that Dr. Benson applied the techniques of transcendental meditation to a group of hypertensive patients. By recording their blood pressure weeks before they learned how to meditate, he was able to establish baseline blood pressure levels.* Joe Graedon, The People's Pharmacy, 1976, p261 **[1966]**

transcribe, *v.t. Genetics.* to form or synthesize (a molecule of messenger RNA) from the genetic information imparted by DNA. Compare TRANSLATE. *The latest research . . . suggests that, in its action against viruses, rifampicin blocks protein synthesis late in the virus growth cycle and that it does not interfere with the synthesis of the enzyme essential for transcribing RNA from DNA.* Science Journal 2/70, p16 **[1962]**

transcriptase, *n.* short for REVERSE TRANSCRIPTASE. *The transcription processes, and the replication of DNA and of viral RNA, could be understood in terms of three distinctive enzymes: DNA-replicase, transcriptase, and RNA-replicase.* 1972 Britannica Yearbook of Science and the Future, p306 **[1963]**

transcription, *n.* the process by which messenger RNA is formed from DNA. Compare TRANSLATION. *Gene transcription, whereby enzyme reactions mediate the synthesis of RNA molecules from DNA templates, has been investigated mostly in microbial organisms . . .* Nature 3/30/68, p1286 *The discovery in 1970 that RNA tumor viruses contain certain enzyme (polymerase) activities capable of reversing the familiar direction of genetic transcription—that is, using RNA as a template*

(model) *for the formation of DNA, the genetic coding material—promised an extraordinarily rich harvest for cancer researchers.* 1972 Britannica Yearbook of Science and the Future, p292 **[1961]**

transearth, *adj.* in or toward the direction of the earth, especially of a spacecraft returning to earth. *Then, at 12:10 A.M. Christmas Day, came the crucial moment—ignition of the SPS [Service Propulsion System] to boost Apollo VIII out of lunar orbit on the transearth trajectory.* 1969 World Book Year Book, p48 **[1965]**

transfect, *v.t.* to infect (a bacterial cell) with nucleic acid of viruses. *Scientists employed the DNA from an animal virus, vaccinia, to transfect competent cells of B[acillus] subtilis. They obtained evidence for the production of new infective viruses within the cytoplasm of the bacterial cells.* McGraw-Hill Yearbook of Science and Technology 1968, p120 **[1964, from *trans*-through + in*fect*]** —transfection, *n.: For certain phage the presence of . . . DNase in recipient cells reduces the efficiency of transfection, which involves introduction of intact purified phage DNA.* Nature 1/10/75, p140

transfer cell, a specialized plant cell which exchanges dissolved substances with its surroundings and transfers them across the plant membranes. *In flowering plants, transfer cells are found where the embryo sac (a gametophyte) comes into contact with its host (a sporophyte) or, later, where the embryo absorbs from nutritive tissues such as the endosperm.* McGraw-Hill Yearbook of Science and Technology 1971, p420 **[1971]**

transfer factor, a substance that may transfer cellular immunity from one organism to another. It has been isolated from white blood cells and is smaller than an antibody or protein cell. *Another possible way around the problem [of organ rejection] is not to transplant cells at all, but instead to use a very mysterious molecule known as transfer factor. Transfer factor . . . can apparently, when given to people suffering from immune deficiency diseases, transfer to them the immunological status of the donor.* New Scientist and Science Journal 5/13/71, p396 **[1956]**

transfer RNA, a special form of RNA (ribonucleic acid) which attaches itself to specific amino acids and transports them to their proper site in the protein chain. *Abbreviation:* tRNA Compare MESSENGER RNA. *Each transfer RNA is a relatively small molecule with less than 100 nucleotides in its chain, and all of the transfer RNA's have a similar sequence of nucleotides at the two ends of the chain. They are unique in that they contain certain unusual purines and pyrimidines—that is, ones other than adenine, guanine, cytosine, and uridine.* 1969 Collier's Encyclopedia Year Book, p136 **[1961]**

transformation, *n.* any of various rules for deriving different types of grammatical sentences from more basic underlying ones. *We have a considerable knowledge about universal (that is, expected) features of language: which segments are probable in any phonological system; which unusual and therefore possibly valuable for determining genetic relationship; which kinds of transformation (like those that delete identical noun phrases in constructions such as relative clauses) have close to universal status, making them a weak source of support for genetic relationship.* Language 6/70, p488 **[1955]**

transformational grammar, a grammatical system in which sentence structures are derived by transformation. Compare GENERATIVE-TRANSFORMATIONAL GRAMMAR, PHRASE-STRUCTURE GRAMMAR. *"Now, the fundamental idea of transformational grammar is that the bracketed and labelled representation of a sentence is its surface structure, and associated with each sentence is a long sequence of more and more abstract representations of the sentence—we transformationalists call them phrase markers—of which surface structure is only the first" . . .* New Yorker 5/8/71, p53 **[1961]**

transformationalism, *n.* the linguistic theory or study concerned with transformations and transformational grammar. *He frequently contrasts his position with that of proliferating Bloomfieldians busily at work on linguistic theory, with no mention of some schools of thought which were very evident in 1968—though there are three or four brief mentions of transformationalism (which the reader is told is recent, p.1).* Language 9/70, p672 [**1969**]

transformationalist, *n.* a follower or advocate of transformationalism. Compare GENERATIVIST. . . . *the school of transformationalists contends that language is an innate, instinctively acquired facility; the study of it should start with sentences, then try to discern the rules by which a sentence conveys its meaning.* Time 2/16/68, p46 *The second example is from phrase-structure grammar (which some of the more condescending transformationalists are already calling "classical linguistics"). The interconnected boxes are a graphic device to show how the sentence, "What do you advise me to give my wife for Christmas?" is analyzed. To do this, you peel the grammatical construction apart by orderly stages, much as a mechanic disassembles an automobile . . . on to the ultimate constituents.* Harper's 10/64, p83 [**1964**]

transform fault, *Geology.* a deep fault forming a steplike pattern on the edge of a plate and indicating the path of the plate. *Global analysis has established that the big shears called transform faults are the zones along which crustal plates glide as they separate.* New Scientist and Science Journal 8/26/71, p450 [**1965**]

transgenic, *adj.* of, produced by, or containing genes transferred from one species to another by means of genetic engineering. *Another very promising tool in molecular genetics is a . . . technique that leads to the creation of transgenic mice: mice that contain single genes or groups of genes from humans.* Scientific American 8/87, p60 [**1982**, from *trans-* across + *genic* of genes]

translate, *v.t. Genetics.* to form or synthesize (an amino-acid molecule) from the genetic information imparted by messenger RNA. Compare TRANSCRIBE. *In this way, the transfer-RNA molecules act as "translating devices," translating a codon at one end into an amino acid at the other end.* World Book Science Annual 1965, p150 [**1961**]

translation, *n. Genetics.* the formation of amino acids based on the messenger RNA template. Compare TRANSCRIPTION. *Translation is the process whereby the genetic information contained in m-RNA determines the linear sequence of amino acids in the course of protein synthesis. Translation occurs on ribosomes, complex particles in the cytoplasm.* 1971 Britannica Yearbook of Science and the Future, p241 [**1963**]

translunar, *adj.* in or toward the direction of the moon, used especially of a spacecraft traveling to the moon. *Once satisfied with the tests, the craft will set off towards the Moon—the translunar coast* [coasting toward the moon]. New Scientist 10/26/67, p235 [**1965**]

transmission electron microscope, an electron microscope that transmits electrons through a specimen so that all the illuminated points of the image are produced at the same time. *Two different types of electron microscope are currently in use. The transmission electron microscope is analogous to a conventional light microscope. The scanning electron microscope employs a flying spot of electrons to scan the object, producing a television-like image.* Scientific American 4/71, p26 [**1969**]

transmodality, *n.* the integration of different modes of transportation. *Movement in containers, bulk and unit loads, and by roll-on/roll-off services can involve one continuous transport process by road, rail, sea, and inland waterway—the word transmodality was coined to describe it—and new facilities and handling equipment were being provided on an increasing scale to cope with it.* Britannica Book of the Year 1973, p687 [**1972**]

transnational, *n.* another name for MULTINATIONAL. *In these circumstances there is no free market: the transnationals are buying and selling to themselves in a closed circuit. Typically, a raw material is extracted by a transnational in a developing country and sold to the same transnational in an industrialised country, where it is processed, manufactured and distributed.* New Scientist 9/4/75, p529 [**1969**, noun use of the adjective (OEDS 1921), but abstracted from *transnational company* or *corporation* (1968)] —**transnationalism**, *n.: Energy relation-*

ships, for instance, are being taken out of the hands of multinational companies and becoming the direct concern of governments . . . Yet the reality of transnationalism, at any rate in the non-Communist world, simply cannot be denied. Listener 12/20/73, p845

transpersonal psychology, a method of psychotherapy that postulates various levels of consciousness and is concerned especially with extrasensory perception. *Many humanistic psychologists have gone into transpersonal psychology, with its emphasis on the suprapersonal or mystical experiences.* Britannica Book of the Year 1973, p11 [**1968**]

transphasor, *n.* a semiconductor crystal, resembling a transistor in function, in which one beam of (laser) light can be modulated by another. *In recent years, computer research scientists have designed an "optical switch" called a* transphasor *through which multiple light beams pass simultaneously. Whereas more than a single current flowing through a transistor simultaneously is virtually impossible, it is the "interference" between two streams of photons that creates the switching action in the transphasor.* Encyclopedia Science Supplement (Grolier) 1987, p105 *Once an optical transistor has been constructed, the assembly of the prototype of a logic gate is a straightforward procedure. Indeed, a single transphasor could serve as either an* AND *gate or an* OR *gate depending on the beams supplied to it.* Scientific American 2/83, p92 [**1979**, from *trans-* (as in *transistor*) + *phasor* (OEDS 1944)]

transposon, *n.* a segment of chromosomal or plasmid DNA that is capable of undergoing transfer to a new position within the same or another chromosome or plasmid. Also called JUMPING GENE, MOBILE GENETIC ELEMENT. *What makes this phenomenon so important is that many plasmid genes which confer resistance to antimicrobial agents—including penicillin, and sulfonamide, streptomycin, chloramphenicol, and tetracycline—reside upon transposons.* 1979 Britannica Yearbook of Science and the Future, p125 [**1974**, from *transposition* + *-on* unit of genetic material, as in *operon*]

transputer, *n.* a silicon chip that incorporates all the functions of a standard computer. *A system for scheduling tasks is wired into the transputer; this allows it to switch quickly between jobs. (Most processors waste time because they use software to control their internal schedules.)* Economist 3/2/85, p86 [**1978**, from *trans-* beyond + com*puter*]

transracial, *adj.* across racial boundaries. *The Merediths' decision is part of a growing phenomenon known in sociologists' jargon as transracial adoption.* Time 8/16/71, p46 [**1971**]

transsexual, *n.* **1** a person who wishes to have the anatomical characteristics of the opposite sex. *The Gender Identity Clinic of the Johns Hopkins Hospital has performed sexual adjustment operations on 14 male transsexuals as part of a pilot study to determine the effects of such surgical changes. The results so far do not show any major psychological changes following the operations . . .* Science News 5/23/70, p506 **2** a person who has undergone surgery to make sexual organs resemble those of the opposite sex. *Britain's state-run health service has started a night school for transsexuals where men who have changed their sex can learn to face the world as women.* Washington Post 1/26/76, pA2 —*adj.* of or relating to transsexuals or transsexualism. *As probably everyone in the world but a few Tibetan monks know by now, the story* ["Myra Breckinridge"] *concerns a Myron who becomes a Myra after a transsexual operation. He-she determines to conquer Hollywood and devastate mankind.* Time 7/6/70, p70 [**1957**]

transsexualism, *n.* the condition of being a transsexual. *One of the specialists, who has been working in the area of transsexualism for more than 20 years, said yesterday: "Those who have the operations are seriously disturbed people."* Times (London) 12/21/70, p2 [**1953**]

transuranic, *n.* a chemical element whose atomic number is higher than that of uranium; a transuranic element. *The new elements are called transuranic because uranium number 92 is the heaviest to occur naturally on earth. There is debate over whether the transuranics can and do exist naturally in the universe outside earth, but from a provincial terrestrial point of* *view they can truly be called manufactured elements.* Science News 9/14/74, p164 [**1969**, noun use of the adjective (OEDS 1935), abstracted from *transuranic element*]

trash, *Colloquial.* —*v.i., v.t.* **1** to destroy willfully and at random, especially as a symbol of rebellion; vandalize. *A Harvard senior argued that "one just should be here, not to trash or fight but to be on the right side."* Time 5/11/70, p24 *The Times, too, has likened the American left to the Nazi movement, saying in a recent editorial that "it is not surprising that the new breed of campus revolutionaries intent on destroying all freedom except their own are now turning to what they call 'trashing'—the setting of fires, hurling of rocks, smashing of windows—ominously reminiscent of the shattered storefronts with which the Nazis sought to intimidate their political opponents of a generation ago."* New Yorker 6/27/70, p25 *Backstage at Comes a Day he got drunk and trashed his dressing room . . .* Time 3/22/71, p26 **2** *Figurative use.* to slight or belittle; deprecate. *In Hollywood, the writer is an underling who is trashed . . .* New Yorker 5/12/75, p114 —*n.* an act of trashing. *In Baltimore last week an American Weatherman told Martin Walker how the system is supposed to work: "Look, even when we lose we win. We know how the Man is. The Man is repressive. The Man is Fascist . . . Every trash we do, every bomb we plant, is forcing the Man to repress that much more and that much more visibly."* Manchester Guardian Weekly 11/7/70, p1 [**1970**]

trasher, *n. Colloquial.* a person who trashes. . . . *current revisionist efforts . . . give cachet to today's radical anarchists and mindless "trashers" by comparing them favorably with our Colonial rebels.* NY Times 10/13/70, p44 [**1970**]

trash sports, *U.S.* competitive sports events featuring celebrities and shown on television as entertainment. *Trash Sports—those hokey, hyped-up, pseudo sports—have clogged the airwaves for months, diminishing the impact of legitimate athletics with every broadcast.* New York Post 5/11/78, p54 [**1978**]

travelator or **travellator,** *n. British.* a moving platform or sidewalk operating like a conveyor belt to carry pedestrians between certain points. . . . *the suburban traffic of the two lines should be concentrated on either a rebuilt King's Cross or a new station on the site of Somers Town goods depot, linked, perhaps, by a travelator . . .* Manchester Guardian Weekly 9/15/66, p16 *The scheme, linked by travellator to Sheperds Bush Underground station, also includes four 20-storey blocks of flats . . .* Times (London) 8/10/70, p12 [**1957**, alteration (influenced by *travel*) of the trademark *Travolator* (1955), patterned after *escalator*]

tree diagram, (in generative-transformational grammar) a diagram of a sentence or phrase in which the components are shown as subdividing branches of the main structure. *If we want to show deep structure with a tree diagram, it will often be necessary to reorder the morphemes of a sentence so that those elements that are closely connected in meaning are grouped together. Just as* leave a light on *has a deep structure that groups its morphemes in a fashion not suggested by the linear sequence, namely* (leave . . . on) *plus* (a light), *so do other expressions . . .* Thomas Pyles and John Algeo, English: An Introduction to Language, 1972, p139 [**1965**]

Trekkie, *n. Especially U.S.* a fan of the science-fiction television series "Star Trek." *"Of course, I didn't know George was a Trekkie when I married him."* Cartoon legend, New Yorker 2/16/76, p39 *At a cost of $15 million, the movie remake of the late '60s television show will reunite the original cast of the Starship Enterprise, hoping to cash in on the Trekkies craze which has spawned 371 fan clubs, annual conventions, more than 50 books and 431 fan publications.* Maclean's 1/15/79, p35 [**1976**] ►This name is not acceptable to fans who generally prefer *Trekker,* according to Patricia Byrd (University of Florida), in "Star Trek Lives: Trekker Slang" (*American Speech,* Spring 1978, pp 54-58). See also ZINE.

tremblant, *adj.* set on springs to make a trembling or vibrating motion. . . . *a very fine diamond tremblant brooch in the*

shape of a five petalled flower brought the same price. Times (London) 3/26/70, p12 [**1970**]

trendily, *adv. British.* fashionably. *Hans Christiansen, director of the Royal Greenland Trading Company . . . plans to sell what he trendily calls "pre-pollution" ice to clink in the glasses of comfort-loving stay-at-homes.* New Scientist 4/30/70, p253 [**1967**]

trendiness, *n.* fashionableness; up-to-dateness. *They start up in a blaze of glory as a "hot shop" and attract advertising directors anxious to show their trendiness.* Sunday Times (London) 9/14/69, p26 [**1966**]

trendsetter, *n.* a person or thing that helps establish a new fashion or trend. *Model girls are accepted trendsetters in the fashionable world.* Times (London) 2/27/68, p7 *Last week . . . the 19-year-old Jacob Riis public-housing project on Manhattan's Lower East Side . . . dedicated a new three-acre open space that is likely to be a trend setter for cities across the nation.* Time 6/3/66, p44 [**1960**]

trendsetting, *adj.* capable of setting a trend or fashion. *This collection is not trendsetting nor is it haute couture in the traditional sense; the sole consistency is in skirt length.* Times (London) 7/21/70, p7 *The two parks, models of excellent design, are like a small electric charge of new ideas that could change New York's park and playground program from moribund to trend-setting.* NY Times 2/2/66, p29 [**1960**]

trendy, —*adj.* fashionable; stylish. *Would not a trendy karate jacket encourage more clients?* New Scientist 10/8/70, p61 *Like any topical issue, eco-theology has yielded its share of trendy superficiality.* Time 6/8/70, p49 *The country must return to nationalism and decency, which the "trendy intellectuals" had been trying very hard to rub out.* Daily Telegraph (London) 6/6/72, p30 —*n.* a person who keeps up with the latest trends and fashions; a fashion plate. *These are stock characters going through familiar contortions—doing their thing, as we middle-aged trendies are only too inclined to say, tapping away so remuneratively in our pad.* Manchester Guardian Weekly 5/22/71, p19 *Up here among us trendies, it's Christmas red in tooth and claw, friends, and don't you forget it . . .* Punch 12/17/69, p989 [**1962** for adj.; **1968** for noun]

TRF or **TRH,** abbreviation of *thyrotropin-releasing factor* (or *hormone*), a hormone produced in the hypothalamus that causes the release of the thyroid-stimulating hormone thyrotropin. Compare LRF. *After processing some 270,000 sheep hypothalami they had obtained a 1 mg sample of thyrotropin-releasing factor (TRF), the hormone with which the brain directs the pituitary's control of the thyroid gland. Their sample was pure enough to allow two conclusions to be drawn. First, the sheep TRF molecule consisted of three amino acids, glutamate, histidine, and proline.* New Scientist 5/4/78, p301 *The first hypothalamic hormone to be discovered is called TRH for thyrotropin-releasing hormone. TRH causes the pituitary gland to release a substance called thyrotropin, which, in turn, causes the thyroid gland to release thyroid hormone.* Encyclopedia Science Supplement (Grolier) 1979, p95 [**1970**]

triad, *n.* **1** the strategic nuclear force of the United States, consisting of land-based missiles, submarine-launched missiles, and long-range bombers. *The President . . . confirmed the continuing commitment to the three-legged "triad" (air- and sea-launched and land-based strategic missiles) of the American nuclear deterrent.* Time 3/27/78, p16 **2** Attributive use: *The so-called "triad composition" of our strategic forces—the distribution of warheads in silos, submarines, and bombers—was designed to reduce the threat of a Soviet first strike aimed at our land-based missiles.* New York Review of Books 3/22/79, p36 [**1978**, specialized use of the sense "group or set of three" (OED 1546)]

triage (tri:'ɑːʒ *or* 'tri:ɑːʒ), *n.* the principle or policy of allocating limited resources, such as food, on the basis of urgency or expediency rather than according to humanitarian or other moral principles. Compare LIFEBOAT ETHIC. *In the West, there is increasing talk of triage, a common-sense if callous concept that teaches that when resources are scarce, they must be used where* *they will do most good.* Time 11/11/74, p80 *Finally, and most significantly, one cannot talk about triage without addressing its ethical implications. What does it mean to countries too poor to make the "aid list"? And what does it mean to those in affluent societies who are in a position to help?* Natural History 6/75, p6 *Triage is one thing more: it is* racist, *for triagelike categories follow not only economic but racial lines as well. The upper economic third is composed mainly of the white race, the middle one of the yellow, and the bottom of the brown and black.* Albert J. Fritsch, et al., Environmental Ethics, 1980, p285 [**1974** extended sense of the World War I military term for the emergency sorting of wounded on the battlefield, from French, from *trier* to sort] ► In the original sense, *triage* meant dividing the wounded into three groups. In the current sense, triage would apportion the world's resources in an analogous order of priority.

triathlon (traɪˈæθlən), *n.* an athletic contest, modeled on the biathlon, combining swimming, bicycling, and running. *They have* [a new challenge]. *It is the triathlon, a contest that combines successive excesses of swimming, bicycling and running. To complete Hawaii's triathlon, appropriately named the Ironman, a competitor must swim 2.4 miles in the ocean, race the 112 miles around Oahu island on a bicycle, and then run a full 26.2-mile marathon.* Wall Street Journal 9/15/82, p1 [**1973**, from *tri-* three + b*iathlon*]

tribological, *adj.* of or relating to tribology. . . . *although a spot of oil can work wonders on a squeaking hinge, a relatively smaller spot of catalyst will liven up a chemical reaction. To an extent the effect of catalyst is proportional to its quantity, which is not true of lubricant. And lubricants will work the tribological oracle for many sorts of rubbing surface: a substance which is a catalyst for reaction A may leave reactions B to Z unmoved.* New Scientist 9/10/70, p545 [**1966**]

tribology, *n.* the study of interacting surfaces, dealing especially with the problems of friction, wear, etc., in technology. *Leeds University and the University College of Swansea, for example, have centres concentrating on tribology—the science of lubrication and wear.* Science Journal 3/70, p75 *The fact that it was recently thought necessary to introduce a new word into the English language, tribology, is a sign of both the previous unsatisfactory state of lubrication awareness and the rapid progress now being made.* Times (London) 4/3/68, pI [**1966**, suggested in 1965 by a group of British engineers in consultation with Robert Burchfield, editor of the *Oxford English Dictionary Supplement*, in a word coined by C. G. Hardie from Greek *tríbos* rubbing (from *tríbein* to rub) + English *-logy* study of]

Tribunite, *n. British.* one of a group of Labourites holding extreme left-wing views. Compare MONDAY CLUBBER. *The Prime Minister decided that the rebellion had to be put down instantly, if only to prove to the outside world that he still controlled what happened at Westminster, and that his Government was not to be brought down by a mere 37 Tribunites. He called for a vote of confidence and got it after a debate.* Manchester Guardian Weekly 3/21/76, p4 [**1970**, from *Tribune* (group), named after the *Tribune*, the group's weekly journal]

Tricap (ˈtraɪˌkæp), *n.* a division of the United States Army, introduced in 1971, in which tanks, mechanized light infantry, and mobile air support are coordinated to protect one another (often used attributively). *Within the continental U.S., the main active unit was the Strategic Reserve of one Tricap* (triple-capable) *division, one infantry, one air-mobile, and one airborne division, though most of these units were not at full strength.* Britannica Book of the Year 1974, p234 [**1971**, short for *Tri*ple-*cap*able division]

trick, *v.i. U.S. and Canadian Slang.* to engage in casual sex with someone, especially for money. *One of the largest selling disco groups of 1979, The Village People, wear archetypal gay clothing and shout lyrics celebrating the gay lifestyle as embodied in . . . tricking at the YMCA and joining the navy to cruise sailors.* Maclean's 2/18/80, p47 [**1965**, verb use of the noun meaning a casual sexual act with someone, especially for money (OEDS 1926)]

trickle-irrigate, *v.t.* to irrigate by TRICKLE IRRIGATION. *Vast areas in the Negev Desert of Israel are now trickle-irrigated.* World Book Science Annual 1972, p255 [**1971**]

trickle irrigation, a method of irrigation involving the slow application of water at regulated intervals by small-diameter perforated hoses placed on top of the soil. *The concept, which is now called drip irrigation or trickle irrigation, has gained wide acceptance, proving to be particularly valuable in areas that are arid and have high labor costs. An unforeseen benefit is that the system works well with water that is highly saline, as water in arid regions often is.* Scientific American 11/77, p62 [**1969**]

tricyclic, *n.* any of a class of antidepressant drugs that prevent the breakdown of serotonin, a chemical transmitter of nerve impulses believed to be involved in depression. *Tricyclics antidepressants help the people who get to sleep, but wake up at about three, seeing everything as a disaster: their mortgage is going to fall in, they're going to lose their job, their daughter's going to marry the wrong man, their wife's going to leave them . . . You want to give them tricyclics at night sufficient to stop this early-morning waking, this early-morning panic.* Listener 10/18/73, p515 [**1966**; so called from the drugs being tricyclic compounds (having a three-ringed molecular structure)]

Trident, *n.* **1** a large, nuclear-powered United States submarine, capable of carrying up to twenty-four ballistic missiles. *The rush to develop a fleet of new submarines, called Tridents, is even harder to justify. They are designed to fire missiles with a longer range than those fitted into our present Polaris and Poseidon submarines; consequently the Tridents could roam around a wider area of the ocean and thus make it harder for an enemy to find them.* Harper's 9/73, p20 **2** a ballistic missile designed to be carried on and launched from this submarine. *A new submarine-launched ballistic missile (SLBM), the Trident, entered the flight test phase January 18, and by September the navy had launched six more, all of them successfully. Trident is expected to carry ten multiple independently targetable reentry vehicles (MIRV's) to distances of 4,600 to 6,700 miles.* 1978 Collier's Encyclopedia Year Book, p102 [**1972**]

trifecta (traɪˈfɛktə), *n. U.S.* **1** a form of betting in horse races in which the bettor must pick the first three horses to finish in the exact order in a given race. Also called TRIPLE. *The money that is bet on gimmick races like the trifecta is placed in a separate pool from the straight win, place, and show wagering.* Daily News (New York) 2/6/74, p46 **2** this form of betting used in the game of jai alai. *For the trifecta, more recently introduced, you have to pick teams to win, place and show—in order. It usually pays off in four figures.* NY Times Magazine 9/19/76, p82 [**1974**, from *tri-* + per*fecta* (in which the first two finishers are picked)]

triffid, *n.* (in science fiction) a huge walking plant that attacks human beings. *This system has now grown like a menacing forest of triffids to the stage where it threatens to strangle the people who invented it.* New Scientist 8/30/73, p513 [**1963**, from the name of the imaginary plant in the science-fiction novel *The Day of the Triffids* (1951), by the English writer John Wyndham, 1903-1969, perhaps formed by alteration of *trifid* three-cleft (plant or animal)]

trigger price, *U.S.* a minimum price set by the government below which an imported product, such as steel, may not be sold without an investigation by the Treasury Department. *President Jimmy Carter announced a government assistance program . . . to reinstate "trigger prices" to provide limited protection against low-priced imports by setting minimum prices for foreign steel and allowing domestic steel companies to delay reducing air and water pollution.* 1981 World Book Year Book, p490 [**1978**; so called because it is designed to trigger automatically an investigation]

trijet, *n.* an aircraft with three jet engines. *Originally designed for shorter-range routes than the 747, the trijets are now being offered in stretched intercontinental versions as the two manufacturers compete for orders.* Time 1/19/70, p44 —*adj.* having three jet engines. *The Soviets have developed . . . the Tu-154 trijet airbus with a 250-passenger capacity . . .* 1970 Collier's

Encyclopedia Year Book, p83 [**1968**, from *tri-* three + *jet* (engine)]

trilateralism, *n.* a policy of fostering close ties and cooperation among the industrialized countries of North America, Western Europe, and Japan. *The United States must widen its relationship beyond western Europe and Japan. The present trilateralism was not enough. That was why the President had visited key countries such as Nigeria, Iran and Saudi Arabia.* Times (London) 7/13/78, p16 [**1976**, from the *Trilateral (Commission)*, a group organized in 1973 to promote such a policy + *-ism*]—**trilateralist**, *n.*: *Among the other Trilateralists, a band of half a hundred elitists from politics, government, business, labor and academia, were Harold Brown . . . Cyrus R. Vance . . . Walter F. Mondale . . . and Zbigniew Brzezinski.* NY Times 1/6/77, p41

trimethoprim, *n.* an antibiotic used in combination with a sulfonamide to destroy or inhibit the growth of various bacteria. *Formula:* $C_{14}H_{18}N_4O_3$ *A remarkably potent combination of two antibiotics—trimethoprim, a folate antagonist, and sulfamethoxazole, a slow-acting sulfonamide—was approved by the FDA. These two drugs act synergistically against a wide variety of organisms, particularly the gram negative bacilli, a common cause of urinary tract infections. This drug combination is also effective against typhoid fever.* 1975 Collier's Encyclopedia Year Book, p338 [**1962**, from *trimetho*xybenzyl-*py*ri*m*idine, part of the chemical name]

trimuon, *n. Nuclear Physics.* a triplet of muons that are products of the decay of particles governed by the interactions of neutrinos at high energy. *Events with three muons (trimuons) have not yet been observed, even though the efficiency of detection of trimuons is comparable to that for dimuons.* McGraw-Hill Yearbook of Science and Technology 1977, p211 *The new events are rare. Corrected for detection efficiencies the group have found a rate of 3×10^{-3} for dimuons . . . and 1×10^{-4} for trimuons.* New Scientist 3/24/77, p697 [**1975**, from *tri-* three + *muon*]

trip, *Colloquial.* —*n.* **1** the hallucinatory experience produced by taking LSD or another psychedelic drug. *One girl was taking LSD for the first time and during the midst of the trip suddenly—it was like a flash of insight came over her—she started almost screaming ecstatically: "I found the secret."* Listener 12/19/68, p825 *He* [the Rev. James E. Smith, of the United Church of Canada] *has returned more than a few teenyboppers to their distraught parents. He's seen youngsters suffer through bad drug "trips."* Maclean's 8/68, p2 **2** any stimulating experience. *The psychiatrist looked at him and said, "You're high, aren't you?" The guy said yes, he sure was, and the psychiatrist signed something and then looked up at the fellow and said, "You'll like the army. It's a good trip."* Atlantic 3/68, p48 *Part of the message is in the drug argot that he* [Southern Baptist Arthur Blessitt] *raps out to his street audiences: "You don't need no pills. Jes' drop a little Matthew, Mark, Luke, and John. Christ is the ultimate, eternal trip."* Time 8/3/70, p32 **3** any obsessive course of action, state of mind, etc., on which one embarks or in which one is involved for a time. *"Most of the groups in the city are fragmented into their own trips," says Woods, "whether it's women's groups, teen-agers, immigrants, you name it . . ."* Maclean's 4/74, p16 —*v.i.* Often, **trip out.** to experience the hallucinatory effects of LSD or other psychedelic drug. *They went to the seedy suburb of Haight Ashbury, the capital of the hippies, to smoke a little (pot), to love a little (sex), to trip a little (LSD) . . .* Manchester Guardian Weekly 5/2/70, p16 *Somebody slipped some acid* [LSD] *into the potato and corn chips at a swinging singles party in the Marina del Rey section of Los Angeles, and nearly 40 of the 200 guests tripped out.* Time 4/20/70, p8 [**1959** for noun def. 1, **1966** for defs. 2 and 3; **1966** for verb]

triple, *n.* another name for TRIFECTA (def. 1). *For, ah, tax reasons, each bet was placed in the name of a different member of the group. They had hit on a triple (picking the first three horses in the right order), and it was the young woman's turn to collect.* NY Times 8/21/76, p22 [**1972**]

triple-digit, *adj. Especially U.S.* equaling or exceeding a rate of 100 per cent (up to a possible 999 per cent). *Last week the* [Israeli] *government conceded that the cost of living for April had jumped a shocking 8.7%, more than 100% if projected over the entire year. The admission provoked howls of alarm that the country could be heading toward uncontrollable triple-digit inflation.* Time 5/28/79, p22 [**1976**, patterned after DOUBLE-DIGIT]

triple witching hour, *U.S. Finance.* the final hour of trading on a stock market on four specified Fridays of the year when contracts on stock options, futures, and options on futures expire simultaneously. *That 60-minute period has become known as "the triple witching hour" because . . . traders are frantically buying or selling stocks in the final hour to offset expiring futures or options.* Business Week 9/23/85, p84 [**1985**]

trippy, *adj. U.S. and Canadian Slang.* of, relating to, or characteristic of a hallucinatory or psychedelic trip. *In my trippy daze, dope was the filter for the movie camera in my mind, the regulator of my psychic jets.* Harper's 6/75, p9 *The trippy optimism of the '60s lent importance to such things as creativity and communication, which in the '70s have given way to matters of a homelier urgency.* Maclean's 11/13/78, p78 [**1969**] —**trippiness**, *n.*: *Robert Wise directed with tame, impersonal good taste; there's none of the blissful trippiness of being carried in the belly of a zeppelin, and none of the carnival vulgarity of the recent disaster thrillers.* New Yorker 1/19/76, p48

triumphalism, *n.* the doctrine or belief that the teachings of a particular faith are eternal and indestructible. *Wayne H. Cowan, managing editor of the liberal Protestant journal, Christianity and Crisis, said the pastoral "mutes the triumphalism of the past, but still places great emphasis on the mystery and infallibility of the church."* NY Times 1/12/68, p25 *Without the nostalgia for the pre-Conciliar years of exclusivity and triumphalism, the Teilhard approach makes a perfect sense of the present and even a sense of joy at the prospect of the future.* Catholic Herald 6/9/72, p4 [**1964**]▶ *Triumphalism* and *triumphalist* are usually used in a pejorative way.

triumphalist, *n.* a follower of triumphalism. *The favourite sport of the triumphalist was heretic hunting.* Times (London) 4/22/67, p12 —*adj.* of or relating to triumphalism. *The Mexican hierarchy's triumphalist view that the Church had never erred, and had nothing to learn or be sorry for, epitomized the traditionalists' resistance to ecumenism . . .* New Yorker 4/25/70, p56 [**1967**]

trivia, *n.* a quiz game involving little-known or trivial facts. *"Trivia," long a favorite of the camp set, became a parlor pastime across the country in 1966. It was a question-and-answer game based upon such inconsequential information as the names of the horses that cowboy stars rode.* 1967 Compton Yearbook, p249 [**1966**]

tRNA, abbreviation of TRANSFER RNA. *Busby and Hele have managed to show that the tRNA of the livers of laying hens is 25 per cent more active in the formation of lysyl-tRNA than in those of immature controls.* New Scientist and Science Journal 3/18/71, p598 [**1962**]

troika, *n.* a group of three administrators or rulers; a triumvirate (also used attributively). *Dynamic as the innovate Government-university-industry troika is, it has raised some questions about the role of the university as an academic institution and of the professor as a teacher of students.* NY Times 1/8/68, p139 *. . . he* [President Lyndon B. Johnson] *reorganized the District government, replacing the old troika Commission with a single Commissioner—Walter E. Washington . . .* New Yorker 9/23/67, p168 [**1954**, from Russian *troika* a three-horse team or sled; any group of three; popularized in this latter sense by the Soviet proposal in 1961, after the death of the U.N. Secretary General Dag Hammarskjold, to replace the vacant office with a *troika* of three Secretaries General, one from each side of the Iron Curtain and one from the neutral countries]

Trojan horse, any set of unauthorized instructions inserted in a computer program to perform some illegal operation. *One form of Trojan horse, called "a logic bomb," is designed to release voluminous amounts of sensitive data to open terminals at a given time in the future.* Progressive 11/80, p21 [**1974**, from *Trojan horse* a person or thing that subverts or undermines from within (OEDS 1837), figurative use of the name of the legendary wooden horse in which the Greeks concealed soldiers to enter Troy]

troopie, *n. Slang.* a soldier of the lowest rank in Zimbabwe (Rhodesia) and South Africa. *Whether tracking guerrillas by day or setting up ambush positions at night, the "troopies" communicate by hand signals as they search out foot and boot prints, bowed grass, broken camps or other varieties of "terr spoor," army slang for terrorist tracks.* Time 2/27/78, p38 [**1972,** probably diminutive from *troop* or *trooper*] ►The term is also reported in the *Dictionary of South African English* (Jean Branford, 1978) with the spelling *troepie* (from Afrikaans and Dutch *troep* troop).

tropocollagen (ˌtroupouˈkɑlədʒən), *n.* a protein from which the collagen fibers of connective tissue, bone, etc., are formed. *The implant materials—air, saline, preserved vitreous, hyaluronic acid, and tropocollagen—are used to reform the globe, restore normal tension, and push the detached retina back against the choroid.* Americana Annual 1974, p375 [**1954,** from *tropo-* a turning, change (from Greek *trópos*) + *collagen*]

tropoelastin (ˌtroupouiˈlæstən), *n.* a substance from which elastin, the basic unit of elastic tissue, is formed. . . . *Dr. Sandberg reports isolation of the precursor molecules, subunits of elastic tissue. Called tropoelastin, each subunit is built of 800 amino acid molecules that may constitute a spherical protein.* Science News 4/25/70, p416 *Tropoelastin has an amino acid composition much like that of elastin, with two significant exceptions: it contains no desmosine and has a much higher content of lysine than elastin does.* Scientific American 6/71, p51 [**1970,** from *tropo-* tendency toward + *elastin*]

troponin (ˈtroupənin), *n.* a protein in muscle tissue regulated by calcium ions, important in muscle contraction. Compare ACTININ. *Troponin, a protein intimately associated with actin, inhibits the interaction that produces movement if calcium ions are present. As a result of its presence the contraction of muscle becomes sensitive to fluxes of calcium ions and its regulation by the nervous system possible.* New Scientist 1/27/72, p199 [**1966,** from *tropo-* turning + *-nin,* perhaps as in *actinin*]

Trot, *n. Informal.* a Trotskyite. *The Alliance sent over a delegation. But having resisted a Communist Party takeover in its early days, it is now definite on the fact that it has no "Trots" on the Council.* Manchester Guardian Weekly 5/30/68, p5 [**1962**]

trouble, *n.* **the troubles,** a euphemism for the riots, bombings, and continued violence in Northern Ireland during the 1970's and 1980's. *Four years ago, when the troubles in Ulster were just becoming serious there were signs of growing nationalism in both Scotland and Wales.* Listener 4/28/73, p533 *For the first time since the troubles began six years ago, the British army will actively attempt to seek out and destroy the terrorists.* Time 1/19/76, p41 *Although nearly everyone in Northern Ireland knows of a mixed marriage somewhere in his own family, it is assumed that fewer mixed marriages are occurring than before the Troubles, particularly among working-class people, because of the hardening of ghetto frontiers and the greater dangers involved.* New Yorker 5/8/78, p56 [**1973,** a new application of the phrase formerly used to describe violence in Ireland during the 1920's, and earlier (1880) in reference to the rebellion of 1641]

truck, *v.i. U.S. Slang.* to move ahead; go or march forward (especially in the catch phrase of encouragement or approval **keep on truckin').** *One poster taped on the wall at YVP's Los Angeles headquarters on Wilshire Boulevard shows the famous R. Crumb cartoon characters and bears the caption: "Let's Keep On Truckin'. . ."* Saturday Review 10/28/72, p12 [**1972,** originally (1930's) Black English (especially jazz) slang meaning to go, walk, stroll; phrase probably influenced by the strolling, shuffling dance of the 1930's called *trucking,* but also found earlier (1925) in the sense of to go, move, proceed, either by truck or by foot]

truck cap, *U.S.* a plastic and aluminum shelter mounted over the bed of a pickup truck to convert it into a camper. *The truck*

cap . . . offers a place to get in out of the weather and eliminates the need of pitching a tent at every stop. Since it adds very little weight and bulk to a truck, it is popular with hunters, fishermen, and others who get far off the beaten path. Americana Annual 1972, p56 [**1972**]

truth, *n.* the property of a type of quark called TOP QUARK. *The new quarks will apparently be called "top" and "bottom," the names being meant to suggest properties surpassing those of the up and down quarks found in ordinary matter. If the two new quarks do exist, there must also be two new properties of matter, which some physicists have taken to calling "truth" and "beauty."* Scientific American 10/77, p74 [**1977,** named on the models of BEAUTY, CHARM]

tsatske (ˈtsɑtskə), *n.* variant of TCHOTCHKE. *"Décor doesn't add to the glamour of a suit," an owner pointed out. "You're not buying the rugs or the lamps or the tsatskes."* NY Times 7/12/74, p31 [**1964,** from Yiddish]

tsutsumu (tsuˈtsuːmuː), *n.* the Japanese art of wrapping articles in bamboo sheaths, paper, etc., so that the packages harmonize with and enhance their contents. *Each of the 300 packages in the show (called "Tsutsumu, The Art of the Japanese Package") was purchased in 1974 in Japan, where an object's wrapping can be as important as the object itself.* NY Times Magazine 2/9/75, p56 [**1975,** from Japanese, to wrap]

tube, *n.* **1** Usually, **the tube.** *U.S. Slang.* television. Compare BOOB TUBE, BOX. *Viewers were inundated by an avalanche of campaign commercials this year. Probably more money was spent in 1970 to reach voters through the tube than in any other off-year election.* 1971 Collier's Encyclopedia Year Book, p534 *As the reader may recall, my last column nattered at some length on the perennially reliable theme that the arts are in a dire way; and it gave warning that in future I might be obliged to turn for material to the tube.* Harper's 4/70, p112 [**1959, 1965,** from the picture *tube* (cathode ray tube) which reproduces the images on the television screen] **2** *Surfing Slang.* the hollow space formed by the curling of a breaking wave. See CURL. *Hollow plungers are the most challenging waves for surfers because their steepness makes for a very fast ride, and it is often possible for surfers to crouch under the falling crest—to be "locked in the tube."* Encyclopedia Science Supplement (Grolier) 1976, p159 *Shootin' the tube, a surfer threads the eye of a breaker off Little Avalon, northeast of Sydney.* National Geographic Magazine 2/79, p235 [**1962**] **3 go down the tube** (or **tubes**), *Slang.* to be lost or finished; go down the drain. *Dumping the Vice President simply made no political sense . . . Said one aide: "Let's face it; if Agnew goes down the tube, that rubs off on the old man too."* Time 10/1/73, p15 *One of the Senate's most powerful unknown men, Republican Milton Young, is about to go down the tubes here.* New Times 10/4/74, p11 *"I really think the Supreme Court will realize that they did take the wrong step. The death penalty will be so narrowly defined that it will go down the tubes. But it's going to be a lot of bloody years before that comes to pass."* Manchester Guardian Weekly (Washington Post section) 12/12/76, p15 [**1963**]

tube sock, an elasticized sock shaped like a tube with no heel, used especially for sport and casual wear. *Now a young man and woman in turtlenecks and Earth shoes wheel up a grocery cart full of comic books, cotton hats, incense, and tube socks.* New Yorker 7/3/78, p52 [**1976**]

tube top, a close-fitting elasticized top worn by women and girls over the upper body from under the arms usually to the waist. *There were other fashion innovations that never made it far from the runway. Women loved the bare-shouldered look of strapless tube tops or evening camisoles.* 1981 Collier's Encyclopedia Year Book, p242 [**1974**]

tubing, *n.* the sport of sliding on an automobile inner tube downhill on snow. *But the big rage of the ski year—and the most painful—is a pastime called "tubing." For experts, the idea is to take a running start and then execute a belly-flop onto an ordinary inflated inner tube. The tube is almost impossible to control and it can reach speeds of 40 mph.* Newsweek 2/3/75, p69 [**1975**] ►This is a new application of the sport of *tubing* known since the 1950's, which consists of riding or floating down a stream on an inner tube.

tubulin, *n.* the protein from which microtubules are formed. *Osborn and Weber have for some time been developing methods for studying the . . . network of fibres (microtubules) extending from the nucleus and running through the cytoplasm. These fibres can be isolated and shown to contain one main protein component which has been named tubulin. By purifying tubulin and raising antibodies against it Osborn and Weber have been able to study the distribution of tubulin, and hence of microtubules in whole cells.* New Scientist 11/2/78, p356 [**1968,** from micro*tubule* + *-in* (chemical suffix)]

tuition tax credit, an allowance that may be deducted from taxable income for the cost of tuition. *Congressional supporters of tuition tax credits found the issue to be widely popular among the middle class, whose spokespersons argued that the rich have enough money to pay high tuitions and that the poor have access to extensive federal stipend and loan programs. But for the middle class, the argument went, there is nothing.* 1979 Collier's Encyclopedia Year Book, p235 [**1978**]

tumesce (tu:'mes), *v.i.*, *v.t.* to experience or cause to have tumescence. *Peter Miller was tooling along in his Jaguar XK 150 S on the Hamburg autobahn . . . savoring memories of a glorious night spent tumescing and detumescing with Sigi, a smart stripper with a heart of eighteen-karat gold.* National Review 11/24/72, p1311 *I'd never heard, from Athene or the several accounts of fellow-heroes which I'd studied in the past decade, of erections in Elysium, whereas the Olympians seemed as permanently tumesced as the mount they dwelt on.* Harper's 10/72, p81 [**1966,** back formation from *tumescence*]

tumorgenic, *adj.* producing tumors. *In animal model systems the loss of contact inhibition induced by SV40 is clearly associated with the development of tumorgenic potential by the cells.* McGraw-Hill Yearbook of Science and Technology 1971, p421 [**1965,** alteration of earlier (1948) *tumorigenic*]

tumorigenicity or **tumorgenicity,** *n.* tumor-producing tendency or capacity. *By refined methods of collection and extraction, the TRC [Tobacco Research Council] workers were able to show that rather more than 50 per cent of the tumorigenicity of 24-hour condensate (an extract made and applied to the mice within 24 hours of smoking the cigarettes), was due to stable, non-volatile carcinogens.* New Scientist 5/25/67, p478 *To his delight he found the new cells to have a dramatically reduced malignancy—only one in 10⁶ produced a tumour in mice compared with almost 100 per cent tumourgenicity shown by Ehrlich cells.* New Scientist and Science Journal 6/24/71, p732 [**1967**]

tumorogenesis, *n.* the formation or production of a tumor or tumors. *Hot particles produce a disrupted tissue mass and the description of such lesions suggests an incipient tumorogenic response. We have proposed that the tumorogenesis involves an injury mediated mechanism.* New Scientist 5/29/75, p499 [**1973,** alteration of earlier (1948) *tumorigenesis*]

tunnel vision, a very narrow perspective or point of view. *The answer is to expand our tunnel vision beyond the parks themselves to what they are a small fragment of, the nation's total of recreational resources, and to relate these to the nation's total of recreational needs.* Saturday Review 1/1/72, p56 *Discussing his analysis of the tunnel vision of some American intellectuals lurching along their fellow-travelling trips with totalitarian socialism, Wolfe remarks with genuine bewilderment: "Some critics called me Fascist for that article. I see myself as a real democrat."* Maclean's 11/6/78, p6 [**1967,** figurative use of the term for an eye disorder characterized by a lack of peripheral vision] —**tunnel-visioned,** *adj.*: ". . . research that scrupulously involves informed consent and full explanation and avoids coercion to the satisfaction of all but the most tunnel-visioned doctrinaire". . . Science News 4/9/77, p230

Tupamaro (,tu:pə'ma:rou), *n.* a member of an extreme left-wing guerrilla organization in Uruguay, known for their acts of terrorism. *Uruguay's Tupamaros take their name from Tupac Amaru, a Peruvian Indian who led a revolt against the Spanish*

in Peru in the 18th century. Sunday Times Magazine (London) 9/26/71, p11 [**1969**]

turboliner, *n.* a high-speed, lightweight passenger train driven by a gas turbine engine built into one or more of the cars. Compare TURBOTRAIN. *The new trains to be maintained at Rensselaer are American-built versions of the French turboliners now operated by Amtrak between Chicago and Milwaukee, Chicago and Port Huron, Mich., and Chicago and Detroit. On good track they are capable of 125 miles an hour.* NY Times 6/8/76, p35 [**1970**] ▶ This term was used earlier (1952) to refer to a passenger airplane powered by turboprop engines.

turbotrain, *n.* a train powered by turbine engines, capable of speeds up to 170 mph. . . . *it* [Canadian National Railways] *has now ordered five of the turbotrains developed by the U.S.'s United Aircraft Corp. Even without roadbed improvements, these lightweight, low-slung, turbojet-powered whiz-bangs should be able to clip nearly an hour off the present five-hour Montreal-Toronto run.* Time 5/27/66, p52 *The French Railways are interested only in their "turbotrain" and are openly hostile to the privately owned "aerotrain."* New Scientist 7/23/70, p187 [**1966**]

turf, *n.* a sphere of influence or activity; territory; domain. *The Irish . . . will give their hearts to any politician ambitious enough to guard his turf properly.* New Yorker 2/19/72, p56 *Its* [The Los Angeles Times'] *metropolitan staff of 96 has problems making sense of its turf—4,800 sq. mi. of overlapping municipal governments that constitute a city editor's nightmare.* Time 1/21/74, p59 *For months he has watched impatiently as Congress encroached upon his diplomatic turf.* Newsweek 1/20/75, p29 [**1970,** from the earlier (1953) slang sense of a gang's exclusive territory]

turn, *v.i.*, *v.t. Colloquial.* In the phrases: —**turn off,** to lose or cause to lose interest, liking, or enthusiasm; the opposite of *turn on.* "*We were sympathetic to the problems of the young and found ourselves increasingly turned off by friends who kept mouthing the same old clichés.*" Time 11/30/70, p13 *This gratuitous, incestuous plugging of its own mini-personalities which Radio-1 is for ever indulging in is what really turns one off.* Listener 3/28/68, p419 [**1965**] —**turn on, a.** to be or cause to be stimulated by drugs; to get high on narcotics. Also, SWITCH ON (under SWITCH, v.). . . . *he regularly turned on with marijuana or blew his mind with LSD.* NY Times 3/21/66, p1 *People at pot parties "turn on" together; an LSD guru "turns on" his congregation.* Saturday Night (Canada) 6/67, p24 [**1953**] **b** to cause to become interested, aroused, or enthusiastic; to stimulate or excite. "*Sometimes hundreds of people walk out of our performances but we will reach some people. If we turn on one or two people each night, that's enough for us.*" NY Times 9/8/68, pB5 *Terry Scott is another funny man who is still looking for the writers who can turn him on.* Listener 1/4/68, p27 [**1903, 1965**] —**turn around,** to change for the better; bring from a bad to a good condition. *At Mendocino State Hospital in California . . . children (ages 13-17) with severe behavioral problems (drug abuse, runaways, stealing) are treated in a "family" situation with hospital staff members as surrogate parents. An innovative school program helps "turn youngsters around."* Science News 2/13/71, p108 *In fairness, figuring out what can be done to improve the lot of farmers must seem comfortingly simple to most members of Congress compared with the desperate riddle of what, if anything, can be done to turn around the South Bronx.* New Yorker 9/4/78, p82 [**1945, 1965,** but earlier *turn round* in the sense "change to the opposite opinion, course, etc." (1830)]

turnkey, *adj.* supplying a complete product or service ready for immediate use. *The company unwisely signed some "turnkey" contracts to supply complete plants at a fixed fee.* Time 1/31/69, p52 *There is tremendous scope here for developing—and exporting—complete fishing "turnkey systems", with fishing vessels, refrigeration plant, factory and mother ships as parts of an integrated package.* Times (London) 4/22/68, p25 *Enable the city to use the "turnkey" program under which the Housing Authority would buy a completed building from a private builder rather than build it itself.* NY Times 3/1/68, p26 [**1958,** abstracted from *turn-key job* (1930's), a term used

, in the building trades to indicate that on the day the contractor will complete the job the owner merely need turn the key of the door]

turn-off, *n.* **1** a turning off or stopping of an action, process, etc. *Hicks attributed Kleindienst's unusual turn-off of the investigation to the 'love affair' between Fitzsimmons and Nixon.* S. Brill, Teamsters, 1978, p104 [**1967**] **2** *Colloquial.* something that causes loss of interest, liking, or enthusiasm. *At first impression, this uneasy blend of piano quintet and violin sonata . . . was a gigantic four-square turn-off.* Listener 12/23-30/82, p48 [**1975**]

turn-on, *n. Colloquial.* excitement; stimulation. *He also offers a large number of lubricious case studies, thus providing shopgirls too shy to read Harold Robbins in public with the kind of mild turn-ons they seem to crave . . .* Harper's 2/70, p122 [**1969**]

tush (tuʃ) or **tushy** (ˈtuʃiː), *n. Especially U.S. Slang.* the backside or buttocks. *I mean, there were 1,100 people there, looking at me with a fork up my tush!* NY Times 6/10/73, pB1 *This lawyer . . . tells me there's a distinct possibility he could do something through Immigration to get Moreno's temporary work permit lifted and have his* tushy *kicked back to Panama.* New Yorker 7/12/69, p30 [**1962**, alteration of Yiddish *tokhes*, from Hebrew *taḥat* beneath]

TV (ˈtiːˈviː), *n. Slang.* a transvestite. *Gradually I learned the swingers' lingo: "TVs" meant transvestites; "toys" meant anything from vibrators to whips; . . . "uncut" meant uncircumcised, and "well-end" an abbreviation of "endowed."* Maclean's 7/74, p25 [**1965**]

TVP, 1 abbreviation of TEXTURED VEGETABLE PROTEIN. *The most stunning fact about TVPs is that they are made from beans. And whereas the tradition of mass carnivorousness is new, pulses have formed a key component of great cuisines for thousands of years.* New Scientist 2/19/76, p403 **2** a trademark for a brand of textured vegetable protein. *Because TVP is a registered trademark it should not be used interchangeably with the generic names textured vegetable protein or textured vegetable product, but used only when it is identified as the trademark of Archer Daniels Midland Company.* Atlantic 4/75, p30 [**1968**]

T-W (ˌtiːˈdəbəlyuː), *n. U.S. Informal.* a three-wheeled motorcycle with balloon tires which allow it to traverse rough or soft terrain. *The three-wheelers' serious uses include farm haulage, tending vineyards, construction work and herding cattle. But the T-Ws' principal allure is recreational.* Time 11/9/81, p111 [**1981**, abbreviation of *three-wheeler*]

two cultures, Usually, **the two cultures.** the arts and humanities, or social sciences, on the one hand, and the physical sciences and engineering technology on the other, viewed as two distinct and often conflicting cultures dominating the thinking of modern society. *The conference called on UNESCO to convene a world-wide conference that might be instrumental in narrowing the gap between the two cultures.* New Scientist 7/2/70, p3 *To the scientists who gathered in Chicago this week for the annual jamboree of the American Association for the Advancement of Science, it must have seemed that Snow's model of the*

two cultures had some deep validity. Science News 1/2/71, p5 [**1961**, from *The Two Cultures and the Scientific Revolution*, title of a celebrated lecture delivered by the English writer C. P. Snow in 1959 at Cambridge University, in which Snow expressed his concern over the lack of communication between the scientific and the literary-scholarly community]

two-digit, *adj.* variant of DOUBLE-DIGIT. *"In recent months we've had a two-digit inflation with the rise in consumer price index 10.2 per cent above the year before levels."* National Observer 6/15/74, p6 [**1974**]

tylectomy, *n.* another name for LUMPECTOMY. *For example, at Guy's Hospital in London, a 10-year study of 370 women with breast cancer has been made. Half the women had radical surgery, and the other half had what is termed a tylectomy: removal of the lump and about an inch of surrounding tissue.* Encyclopedia Science Supplement (Grolier) 1973, p270 [**1972**, from Greek *týlē* lump + English *-ectomy* surgical removal]

tylosin (ˈtailəsən), *n.* an antibiotic derived from a species of streptomyces, used in the treatment of animal diseases. *Formula:* $C_{46}H_{77}NO_{17}$ *Tylosin is not used in human medicine, and to that extent its use in animals could be reasonable.* New Scientist 10/5/67, p35 *Antibiotics (including synthetic antibacterial agents) which have been used as feed additives, and which are now classified as 'therapeutic', are penicillin, tetracyclines, tylosin, sulphonamides and nitrofurans.* Science Journal 3/70, p4 [**1961**, perhaps from *tylosis*, the name of several diseases (from Greek *týlōsis* formation of a callus) + *-in* (chemical suffix)]

Type A, 1 a behavior pattern characterized by tenseness, impatience, and competitive drive, associated with a tendency to develop coronary heart disease (often used attributively). *What is a Type A personality? According to the originators of the theory, a Type A person is highly competitive and aggressive, totally involved in her or his job, and constantly striving for achievement. This kind of behavior is characterized by haste, impatience, restlessness, hyperalertness, hard-driving conscientiousness, and forceful expression. A Type A person will have "hurry sickness"—he or she never seems to have enough time to do all the things that he feels must be accomplished each day.* Joe Graedon, The People's Pharmacy, 1976, p275 **2** a person exhibiting such a behavior pattern. *We have met some Type A's so severely afflicted that they almost never enjoy a moment of tranquility. One sees the darting, hateful, belligerent sparks escaping from their eyes even when they are merely asking the time of day.* Maclean's 6/74, p82 [**1972**, coined by Meyer Friedman and Roy H. Rosenman, American cardiologists] ► *Type A* is often contrasted with an easygoing, relaxed behavior pattern designated as *Type B: Type A is an obsessive striver, has an excessive sense of urgency, fights constantly against deadlines and has an extra dose of hostility and aggression. Type B is the opposite.* NY Times Magazine 11/20/77, p50

type C virus, variant of C-TYPE VIRUS. *Some human leukemia cells, and possibly other human cells, contain a type C virus that is in a dormant state or is defective—that is, with incomplete genetic information. Also, the virus is related to the tumor viruses isolated from some primates.* World Book Science Annual 1977, p300 [**1975**]

U

U, a symbol used in Great Britain to designate motion pictures recommended for general audiences. The equivalent U.S. symbol is *G*. *At the Classic, Hendon, a piece from Israel,* The Policeman *(director Ephraim Kishon; U), a comedy about a kindhearted, butter-fingered Jaffa cop.* Sunday Times (London) 2/10/74, p30 [**1970**, for *U*niversal or *U*nrestricted Exhibition]

Überfremdung, (ˌyɐrˈfremduŋ), *n. German.* See the quotations for the meaning. *Nowhere in Europe have relations between guest and host become more acrimonious than in Switzerland.* Überfremdung *(over-foreignization) has been a battle cry of the far right for the past five years.* Time 6/8/70, p39 *The issue of* Überfremdung *("over-alienation"; i.e., the high percentage of foreign workers in Switzerland) continued to make news.* Britannica Book of the Year 1969, p709 [**1965**]

ubiquitin (yuːˈbikwətin), *n.* any of a group of small, stable proteins found in all living cells except those of bacteria, whose function is to tag abnormal, harmful, or other designated proteins so that they are broken down chemically. *The ubiquitins from barley, yeast, and mammalian species differ only in two or three amino acids. Ubiquitin . . . really does occur ubiquitously and exhibits a high order of conservation.* McGraw-Hill Yearbook of Science and Technology 1988, p469 [**1986**, from *ubiquitous* + *-in*]

UDAG (ˈyuːˌdæg), *n. U.S.* a government program granting federal funds for projects to revitalize and develop poor or older sections of a city. *Most UDAG projects have been initiated by city governments or agencies, but about one-fifth have been proposed by private developers, with lesser numbers proposed by nonprofit corporations, banks or financial institutions, and citizens' groups.* 1980 Collier's Encyclopedia Year Book, p215 [**1977**, acronym for *Urban Development Action Grant*]

UDI or **U.D.I.**, abbreviation of *Unilateral Declaration of Independence* (originally referring to the declaration of independence from Great Britain issued by the premier of Southern Rhodesia, Ian Smith, on November 11, 1965). *The British often 'lean over backwards' in their determination to do justice to George Washington and the other U.D.I. heroes.* Listener 2/17/66, p251 *Support for a U D I is growing after the continued refusal of the T G W U's* [Transport and General Workers' Union's] *No. 1 Docks Groups to allow work to start on the terminal until a wage agreement is made for all London's enclosed docks.* Sunday Times (London) 11/23/69, p25 [**1965**]

ufological, *adj.* of or relating to the study or tracking of unidentified flying objects. *As for 1966, it has got off to a very promising start with the U.F.O. flap in Michigan. The ufological definition of a flap is a concentration of sightings in a small area within a short period. The Michigan flap is either a remarkable case of mass hysteria or a U.F.O. classic.* New Yorker 4/9/66, p32 [**1966**, from *ufology* + *-ical*]

ufologist, *n.* a person who studies or keeps track of unidentified flying objects. *Saucer buffs, or "ufologists," point out that the Air Force's Project Blue Book, the best source of saucer statistics, has recently published a list of eight hundred and eighty-six sightings for 1965.* New Yorker 4/9/66, p32 *. . . these civilizations* [supposedly advanced civilizations in the Milky Way] *are probably separated from one another by anywhere from 300 to 1,000 light-years, Sagan estimates (a light-year is the equivalent of 6 trillion miles). This deflates the argument of UFOlogists that saucers have begun observing the earth because of man's recent technological strides.* Time 8/4/67, p33 [**1963**]

ufology, *n.* the study or tracking of unidentified flying objects, often called UFOs or flying saucers. *This principle, that it is not the UFO which is studied but the UFO report, is a basic law of ufology . . .* New Scientist 10/25/79, p296 *UFOlogy, like all sciences, has its frustrations.* NY Times Book Review 5/20/79, p22 [**1959**, from *UFO*, abbreviation of *Unidentified Flying Object* (1950) + *-logy* study of]

ugly American, an American living abroad who presents an unflattering image of Americans, especially by acting offensively or insensitively towards the natives and their culture. *. . . he can spring before us a host of odd and funny foreigners: bogus Russian counts, semi-aristocratic Slavic ladies, German officers, and an early type of the ugly American abroad.* Atlantic 5/65, p152 *I don't think we were Ugly Americans; perhaps just Unaware, or Unlettered.* Saturday Review 3/9/68, p76 [**1965**, from *The Ugly American*, a book of stories about Americans in southeastern Asia, written by Eugene Burdick and William Lederer and published in 1958]

ujamaa (ˌuːdʒɑːˈmɑːɑː), *n.* a form of socialism in Tanzania that develops local cooperatives, collective farming, and self-help projects, based on traditional African concepts of the extended family and kinship responsibility. *Again, the* ujamaa—*literally "family"—cooperative system is a way of coping with a specifically African problem, the fact that the majority of the 14 million people in the vast rural Tanzanian mainland are scattered in small units.* Times (London) 10/18/72, p16 *Ujamaa means "familyhood," and the purpose is to build upon the old African kinship customs, with handicapped citizens or the unemployed from the city put back into the care of their hometowns.* Harper's 8/76, p67 [**1962**, from Swahili, from *u-*, prefix meaning state or quality of + *jamaa* family (from Arabic *jamā'a* community)] ▶Introduced by President Julius K. Nyerere, in *Ujamaa: The Basis of African Socialism* (1962), the term avoids negative connotations of *socialism*, and stresses an approach rooted in traditional African tribal concepts.

ULCC, a petroleum supertanker with a capacity of over 400,000 tons. Compare VLCC. *The incredible ULCC . . . will be able to deliver 3.5 million barrels of oil from a foreign land to an American port in a single journey.* Advertisement by Tenneco Inc., Houston, Tex. Time 10/14/74, p59 [**1973**, abbreviation of *ultra-large crude carrier*]

ulcerogenic, *adj.* producing an ulcer or ulcers. *By studying a group of such related compounds, he has been able to determine that the ulcerogenic activity of a toxic substance is "mostly but not exclusively" related to a two-carbon group bearing a reactive radical such as cyanide, nitrile, or sulfhydril.* Science News 9/7/74, p155 [**1959**, from *ulcer* + connecting *-o-* + *-genic* producing]

ULMS, a ballistic missile with a range of 4500 to 6000 miles, developed to be launched from a submarine. *The ULMS will have a greater range than either Polaris or Poseidon and in its most sophisticated form would need a new class of submarine, the Trident.* New Scientist 8/30/73, p483 [**1970**, abbreviation of *underwater long-range missile system*]

Ultimate, *n.* short for ULTIMATE FRISBEE. *In the fast-moving game of Ultimate, players dive, jump, stall and leap, but mostly they run. Always they pursue what they call "the disk" or "plastic." Most Ultimate players avoid using the term "Frisbee," which is a registered trademark.* NY Times 5/8/83, pK22 [**1983**]

ultimate Frisbee, a game in which two teams of seven players each try to move a plastic disk, by passing, up a field 120 yards long by 40 yards wide) to score a goal worth one point. Also called AIRBORNE SOCCER or shortened to ULTIMATE. *In ultimate Frisbee . . . Points are scored when the Frisbee is caught* *beyond the opponent's goal line, similar to the end-zone catch in football* . . . American Speech 49 (1974), p301 *"Ultimate skate frisbee is totally incredible," he said. "It's playing frisbee on skates. It's exactly like ultimate frisbee but the rules are changed a little because of the roller skating factor involved.* Indiana Daily Student 10/7/80, p7 **[1972]**

Ultisol ('əltə,sɔ:l), *n.* (in U.S. soil taxonomy) any of a group of highly weathered and leached yellow-to-red soils found chiefly in old land surfaces of humid tropical or temperate climates (as in the southeastern United States and in Asia). *Oxisols and Ultisols . . . constitute approximately one-third of the world's potentially arable land. Accordingly, they represent a vast resource for expansion of food production in developing countries, and studies on their mineralogical nature will be of aid in development of agronomic techniques suitable to their efficient utilization.* McGraw-Hill Yearbook of Science and Technology 1973, p379 **[1960,** probably from Latin *ulti*mus final, ultimate + *-sol* (from Latin *solum* soil)]

ultraclean, *adj.* maintaining a high level of cleanliness, especially under germ-free conditions, as by the use of sterilized laboratories and instruments, isolation techniques, and the like. *Ultraclean technology can reduce rejection rates, increase reliability and make possible new products and procedures that otherwise would be unachievable.* Science Journal 4/70, p41 **[1963]**

ultradian, *adj.* of or relating to biological rhythms or cycles that recur more than once per day. Compare INFRADIAN. *Every month,* Psychology Today *(circ. 1.1 million) tells Americans all they might want to know about sex, psychosurgery, biofeedback, insomnia, ultradian rhythms—indeed the whole galaxy of behavioral phenomena, from alienation to Zen.* Time 5/17/76, p78 *The cyclic pattern of biological life, however, does not stop with the obvious 24-hour cycle. Scientists are finding increasing evidence for a 90-minute cycle, named the ultradian rhythm . . . Ultradian rhythms were first suspected more than 20 years ago when researchers discovered that rapid eye movement or REM sleep occurs in cycles of 90 to 100 minutes.* Science News 4/12/75, p244 **[1961,** from *ultra-* beyond + Latin *diēs* day + English *-an*]

ultraelementary particle, a constituent of an elementary particle; a subatomic or subnuclear particle. *The subparticles . . . were tentatively named "partons" to avoid identification with the ultraelementary "quark" particles predicted by theory but not yet surely discovered despite eight years of search.* 1971 Compton Yearbook, p389 **[1969]**

ultrafiche ('əltrə,fi:ʃ), *n.* a microfilm card containing highly reduced frames of printed matter. *Ultrafiches of the photochronic microimage process store up to 4,000 pages on a 4in by 6in film and provide complete industrial data compilations on a pocket scale.* Times (London) 12/1/72, pII *In this new process, for example, 1,800 large, highly detailed maps covering a continuous area of 775 square miles are reduced to a single, continuous ultrafiche of standard 4-by-6-inch size.* Encyclopedia Science Supplement (Grolier) 1973, p411 **[1971,** by shortening from *ultra-* beyond + micro-*fiche* (micro) card]
▶A *microfiche* (1953) and an *ultrafiche* are usually the same size card, but microfiche contains about 100 microfilmed pages of a book, while an ultrafiche may contain several thousand pages.

ultralight, *n.* a small, usually open airplane constructed of an aluminum frame with sailcloth wings and a small motor. *On October 4, 1982, rules came into effect stating that an ultralight may not weigh more than 254 pounds (115 kilos), fly faster than 55 knots (63 miles an hour), or stall at more than 24 knots (27 miles an hour). It may not carry more than five gallons of fuel, must stay out of controlled airspace, and may not fly at night. Operators do not need a pilot's license.* National Geographic Magazine 8/83, p213 **[1974]**

ultramarathon, *n.* a long distance race greater than a marathon (26 miles, 385 yards), especially a foot race of 36 miles or more. *As other runners begin to find that small is beautiful, one option is the ultra-marathon. The week before the New York marathon last fall, Dannon sponsored a 36-miler in Washington.*

About 140 runners showed up. Washington Post 3/2/80, pB14 **[1977]**

ultramicrofiche (,əltrə'maikrə,fi:ʃ), *n.* another name for ULTRAFICHE. *Ultramicrofiche achieves a reduction ratio of more than 200 and puts up to 8,000 pages on a single film, each page so miniaturized that it is barely visible to the naked eye.* Encyclopedia Science Supplement (Grolier) 1973, p409 **[1967,** from *ultra-* beyond + *microfiche*]

ultramilitant, *adj.* militant to an extreme. *Panthers and members of the ultramilitant white Weathermen brought dynamite into the city . . .* Time 5/11/70, p25 *M. Nicoud first gained attention last spring as one of the leaders of a new, ultra-militant shopkeepers' organization . . .* Times (London) 3/11/70, p6 **[1970]**

ultraminiature, *adj.* extremely small. *Key elements in the device, an ultraminiature vacuum pump and a mass spectrometer, will be worn directly under the astronaut's chin, in a unit about one inch in diameter and four inches long.* Science News 12/7/68, p573 **[1963]**

ultraminiaturized, *adj.* reduced to an extremely small size. . . . *using a multitude of ICs* [integrated circuits], *ultraminiaturized, working in parallel, together with functional circuits, he may build electronic devices tomorrow that seem like impossible dreams even today.* World Book Science Annual 1968, p215 **[1968]**

ultrasonogram, *n.* a recording or tracing made by an ultrasonograph. Also shortened to SONOGRAM. *During 1970, the use of these "ultrasonograms" in the diagnosis of brain tumors and eye disorders remained largely experimental and was nowhere in routine clinical use, but the technique was attracting increasing interest and was being successfully extended to such fields as cardiology, abdominal exploration (kidney stones show up particularly clearly), and obstetrics and gynecology . . .* 1972 Britannica Yearbook of Science and the Future, p242 **[1958]**

ultrasonograph, *n.* an instrument using ultrasonic waves (those of a frequency of 15 to 20 megahertz) to penetrate tissue and make recordings of abnormalities. Also shortened to SONOGRAPH. *Clearly, then, obstetric diagnosis has benefited enormously from the application of ultrasonics. Where to from here? Donald's group at Glasgow have recently been experimenting with a newly developed, more powerful ultrasonograph. He hopes that this will mark the beginning of really sophisticated foetal medicine.* New Scientist and Science Journal 9/2/71, p523 **[1971]**

ultrasonographer, *n.* a specialist in ultrasonography. Also shortened to SONOGRAPHER. *All the necessary parts and players had been assembled: . . . Dr. Thomas Brown, a neurosurgeon; Dr. Rudy Sabbagha, an obstetrician and ultrasonographer; and Nancy Reedy, a certified nurse midwife.* NY Times Magazine 2/28/82, p21 **[1978]**

ultrasonography, *n.* the use of ultrasonic devices in detecting abnormalities in the body. . . . *a research team at Bristol General Hospital . . . hope that they will soon be using ultrasonography for routine diagnosis of disease affecting the mitral valve of the heart.* New Scientist 11/16/67, p404 **[1960]**

ultrasonologist, *n.* another word for ULTRASONOGRAPHER. *Another reason ultrasonics is gaining acceptance in obstetrics is that it is offering ever greater accuracy in recording events in the womb. Four kinds of diagnoses made on 521 pregnant women gave an accurate reading 96 to 100 percent of the time,* Ross Brown, ultrasonologist *at the University of Oklahoma Medical Center, reported . . .* Science News 12/25/71, p424 **[1971]**

Ultrasuède, *n.* a trademark for a washable fabric that resembles suède, made of polyester and nonfibrous polyurethane. *Halston hasn't forgotten the fabric he helped launch around the world, Ultrasuède. This time, he matches it up exactly to beige* (Ultrasuède *jacket over scoop-neck dress) or pink jersey.* NY Times 1/14/77, pB4 *One Ultrasuede safari-type beige jacket with pocketless khaki pants worn by a gentleman with a reced-*

ing hairline and brown horn-rimmed glasses. New Yorker 9/25/78, p35 [**1973,** from *ultra-* beyond + *suède*]

ultraviolence, *n.* extreme or unrelenting violence. *The film* [A Clockwork Orange] *showed how a young hoodlum (Malcolm McDowell), homicidal in his employment of "ultraviolence" (a term that immediately entered the language), was subjected to brainwashing by government scientists.* 1973 Collier's Encyclopedia Year Book, p393 [**1972**]

ultraviolet astronomy, the study of stars and nebulae in the ultraviolet region of the spectrum, conducted especially by means of orbiting artificial satellites. *Most wavelengths of ultraviolet light cannot get through the earth's atmosphere. So ultraviolet astronomy has to be done from above the atmosphere. Systematic scans of the sky in ultraviolet had to await a satellite.* Science News 6/16/73, p391 [**1971**]

umbilical, *n.* **1** short for UMBILICAL CABLE. *Bacchus* [an underwater habitat] *will receive its breathing mixture either by means of an umbilical from the surface or from high pressure storage bottles situated in the capsule itself.* New Scientist 2/27/69, p458 **2** *Figurative.* a connection; link. *Hamlets living on beer and thatch would have been abandoned centuries ago—and perhaps never existed at all—if there had been no twisting lanes to give them perspective and act as an umbilical to the outside world.* Manchester Guardian Weekly 2/14/70, p11 [**1969**]

umbilical cable, a long cable by which a person or thing remains connected to a ship, the ground, etc. *The operators, working under normal atmospheric pressure, will travel in the capsule to a compartment fitted permanently over the wellhead on the ocean floor. The mobile capsule is powered and serviced by an umbilical cable, running from a support ship.* New Scientist 7/16/70, p133 [**1970**]

unbundle, *v.t., v.i.* to separate (the costs of different products, services, etc.) into separate transactions. *The industry giant, International Business Machines Corp. (IBM), faced with several antitrust suits . . ., decided in response to "unbundle" or separate the costs of computer software and hardware, previously offered as a package deal.* Britannica Book of the Year 1970, p321 [**1969**]

uncharmed, *adj.* (of a quark) lacking the property of CHARM. *The new particle, designated upsilon* [is] *three times as heavy as any known uncharmed particle, and one and a half times as heavy as any previously discovered charmed particle. Its lifetime may be less than 10^{-18} seconds.* Science News 2/14/76, p100 [**1972,** from *un-* not + CHARMED]

Uncle Tomahawk, *U.S.* a derogatory name for an American Indian who works within the white establishment or adopts the culture and values of white society. Also called APPLE. *President Charlie Vigil has a future some place, perhaps working for the B.I.A. If the tribal constitution permitted it, he would prefer to remain in office rather than join the wandering bureaucrats some call Uncle Tomahawks.* NY Times Magazine 2/13/72, p46 [**1971,** blend of *Uncle Tom* a servile black man and *tomahawk* a light axe used by North American Indians]

unconstructed, *adj.* (of clothes) not shaped with interfacings or paddings and therefore pliant or supple in design. *The classic, unconstructed jacket with lapels and one, two, or three buttons can be adapted to many uses, many occasions.* Daily News (New York) 7/26/75, p12 [**1973**]

uncool, *adj. Slang.* unpleasant, troublesome, or disturbing; lacking self-control or sophistication; not cool. *On occasion, the subject turned to drugs. It was uncool in a state whose government likes to see its grass mowed, not smoked.* Time 2/16/70, p62 *"There are some very uncool people here—cats who come because they like a fight, and when I suspected this I really thought about packing up.* Sunday Times (London) 9/21/69, p3 *We didn't talk politics—that would have been uncool.* New Yorker 11/6/71, p72 [**1953**]

uncorrectable, *adj.* irremediable; irreparable. . . . . *a regularly scheduled airliner bound for Boston radioed the Logan tower to report a sudden failure of all navigational and directional instruments, as well as an undiagnosed and uncorrectable loss*

of power. New Yorker 5/30/70, p26 *For many years, facial paralysis has been uncorrectable. Lately, however, surgeons have been experiencing success with several new operations.* Time 9/21/70, p57 [**1970**]

uncorrectably, *adv.* irredeemably; hopelessly. *In outline, Skelton's life there in the caravan on the edge of the high meadow over the lake, in a place that must be uncorrectably gloomy during the wet rains of winter, seemed cagelike and hopeless to me—unacceptably lonely.* Atlantic 1/70, p45 [**1970**]

underabundant, *adj.* less than abundant; not as abundant as should be. *The production and abundance of nitrogen is very sensitively dependent on the availability of these heavier elements in the interstellar medium and should they be underabundant an extreme deficiency of nitrogen is possible.* Nature 5/5/72, p28 [**1971,** patterned after *overabundant*]

underboss, *n. U.S. Underworld Slang.* a member of a Mafia family next below the head (capo) in rank. *In the restructured family on which Joe Colombo solidified his hold as boss, another tantalizing figure emerged, Charles (Charlie Lemons) Mineo . . . Mineo has become a unique kind of underboss, one who is virtually inactive. According to some reports he was enjoying the fruits of retirement when Colombo elevated him to the No. 2 spot in the family.* NY Times Magazine 6/4/72, p95 [**1964**]

undercast, *v.t.* **1** to cast (an actor or performer) in a secondary or minor role. *Rossellini deliberately undercasts him, as he does everyone else. Colbert is made to look uninteresting and rather bourgeois.* New Yorker 8/22/70, p59 *Ridderbush, a light-voiced brass-baritone, is an instance of undercasting.* Saturday Review 12/2/72, p91 **2** to cast (a play, film, etc.) with secondary actors or minor performers. *Porter had done a dull job in the staging, and the play was woefully undercast. James Valentine—who seemed successfully concerned with giving a moderately accurate impersonation of John Gielgud as Jack Worthing—probably had the best of it.* Times (London) 7/9/77, p10 [**1964**] ► Recorded in literature of theater circles as early as 1827, in the meaning of def. 2, the word is not recorded in general publications before the mass interest in the arts after World War II.

undercharacterization, *n.* too little development of the characters in a novel, short story, drama, etc., or the themes in a piece of music. *Couples* [a novel] *is flawed by overwriting and undercharacterization, but the charge of irrelevance will no longer stand up.* Time 4/26/68, p50 [**1968**]

undercharacterize, *v.t.* to fail to develop the characters enough in a novel, short story, drama, etc., or the themes in a piece of music. *But in the wry second movement (taken fast) the players needed more detailed help with phrasing, and the work as a whole was undercharacterized.* Times (London) 12/16/70, p11 [**1960**]

underclass, *n.* the class of people who remain on the lowest economic level. *But he* [Martin Luther King] *could not, states Williams, relate to the black underclass or understand its impatience with a system that refused to recognize its legitimate demands.* Time 8/17/70, p12 *"Social scientists have a great deal to tell us about the life styles of various class groupings . . . but the larger societal mechanisms that produce the underclass have been largely ignored."* Manchester Guardian Weekly 4/24/71, p18 [**1963,** from Swedish *underklass;* popularized by the writings of Gunnar Myrdal, though recorded as early as 1918]

undercount, *n.* a count that is too low (especially of a census); an incomplete count. *Today's arithmetic lesson involves vocabulary. As the process of counting 222 million Americans begins, the besetting problem of the Census is something called the undercount, and the remedy prescribed with increasing frequency is called adjustment. Undercount means just what it says—the number of people not counted, with consequences for the distribution of representatives in Congress and of billions in Federal aid.* NY Times 3/30/80, pD20 —*v.t.* to make an undercount of. *The second concern about the census arises because federal funds are distributed according to population. Minority groups argue that they have not been receiving their* *fair share because they were undercounted in the last census.* Time 1/14/80, p36 [**1955**]

underdevelop, *v.i.* to become less developed and fail to remain economically self-sufficient by losing or wasting capital, resources, etc. *But on closer inspection, there is something very radically wrong with Uruguay. Its GNP regularly declines from year to year. It is a developed country that is underdeveloping at speed.* Manchester Guardian Weekly 8/15/70, p4 —*v.t.* to cause to underdevelop. *"For 20 years we have been underdeveloping ourselves. We have missed our last chance. The country* [Czechoslovakia] *is ruined."* Times (London) 12/31/68, p9 [**1968**, back formation from *underdeveloped, adj.* (OEDS 1949)]

underdogger, *n.* a person who supports the underdog in a fight or contest. *But hopelessness springs eternal on Rhode Island Sound. After three crushing defeats,* Australia's [a boat] *loyal underdoggers were busy recalling all the old familiar whiny excuses, among them the "She can only move in light air" ploy.* Time 10/3/77, p54 [**1970**]

underfund, *v.t.* to fund inadequately; to fail to provide with sufficient funds. *All of these old programs can help at least some institutions carry out at least some of their educational missions. Most of them, however, have been woefully underfunded in recent years, and now they must compete for funds with the costly new higher education programs.* Saturday Review 7/22/72, p39 [**1967**]

underground, *n.* any group, organization, or movement whose activities are outside the traditions or values of the established society or culture. Compare COUNTERCULTURE. . . . *so-called undergrounds—the hippie communes, the drug subcultures, the anti-Establishment press—actually are about as clandestine as a circus parade. . .* Harper's 2/70, p12 *What these film makers, who proudly identify themselves as the "underground," profess to want is the freedom to create motion pictures in accordance with their own, intensely personal artistic visions, untrammeled by anything that has gone before.* 1969 World Book Year Book, p120 *The Catholic "underground" has removed worship from the sanctuary entirely and transferred it to private homes.* NY Times 5/26/68, pD4 *The Underground is comprised of artists whose concepts reflect highly specialized, distilled styles.* Saturday Review 10/26/68, p88 —*adj.* of or belonging to an underground. *The lot of underground newspapers anywhere in the U.S. is a hard one, inasmuch as the papers often reflect a zest for rebellion and four-letter words.* Time 3/23/70, p38 . . . *"There were underground filmmakers coming out of the wall all over the neighborhood. I saw some of their work and thought I could do as well."* New Yorker 1/13/68, p20 *The Paris café theatres, an underground movement for 18 months now, providing valuable experience for writers and performers, are just now beginning to bear fruit.* Times (London) 3/11/68, p6 [**1959** for noun, extended from the earlier figurative sense of a secret revolutionary or antigovernment political group (OEDS 1946); **1953** for adjective]

underground church, a church that functions outside of an established or organized religious denomination. *Divine Disobedience is divided into three long sections. The first, and sketchiest, is an account of the communal lifestyle of East Harlem's Emmaus House, a prototype for countless so-called "underground churches." When Francine* [Francine du Plessix Gray] *began her project, Emmaus House was a hotbed of zealous ecumaniacs, bent on building a new kind of parish with home rule and spontaneous liturgies.* Time 7/27/70, p73 [**1968**]

underground economy, an unregulated sector of the economy in which income is not reported in order to avoid paying taxes. *Often working independently and surreptitiously, many Americans have established an "underground economy" in the face of high inflation and taxation. It consists of barter arrangements between professionals, nonrecorded tips, under-the-table cash payments for services, and black-market activities—all designed to elude the tax collector.* Britannica Book of the Year 1981, p141 [**1978**]

underground press, the unconventional newspapers and periodicals published by those who consider themselves to be outside the established society or culture. *A wave of parajournalistic publications, the so-called underground press, was mounting a serious challenge to established dailies.* Americana Annual 1970, p503 [**1968**]

underkill, *n.* **1** an inability to defeat an enemy. *As for the nation's nuclear forces, Mr McNamara cited a 200 per cent increase "in the number of nuclear warheads and total megatonnage in the strategic alert forces" . . . Obviously, Goldwater's fears that America was lapsing into a state of "underkill" were groundless.* New Scientist 3/10/66, p618 **2** something that causes far less harm than one could reasonably inflict. *Noting that "our legal tradition has special repugnance toward prior restraint," Harvard's Paul A. Freund maintained that "risk for risk, the law has opted for underkill in duels over publication."* Time 7/5/71, p13 [**1964**, patterned after *overkill*]

underoccupied, *adj.* **1** having fewer occupants than there is room for. *To find room in this way for the elderly and others needing small homes would release seriously underoccupied large houses for bigger families.* Times (London) 3/23/70, p5 **2** having little to do; not sufficiently employed. *Its* [Mexico City's] *street scenes off the massive dual carriageways have an impressive shabbiness—that stained and damaged identity of overoccupied housing and underoccupied people.* Manchester Guardian Weekly 6/6/70, p5 [**1961**]

underreact, *v.i.* to react with less force or intensity than the circumstances require. *The police, taken unawares and unprepared, took their response from a page of the riot manual of the early '60's. First they underreacted, allowing the march to become a mob and the mob to become milling looters.* Time 5/25/70, p25 [**1965**, patterned after *overreact*]—**underreaction**, *n.: The difference is in the creases of your suit, in the way tension is replaced by boredom and over-reaction with the danger of under-reaction.* Times (London) 1/13/72, pI

understand, *v.t.* (of a computer) to follow programming instructions. *Acorn's Atom microcomputers use a "dialect" of BASIC; and, unfortunately, virtually no other microcomputer can understand it. Acorn has agreed to modify substantially the BASIC used by its current range of machines, called Atoms, so that other microcomputers can understand the language as well.* New Scientist 3/12/81, p662 [**1981**]

undertax, *v.t., v.i.* to tax insufficiently or inadequately. *Ralph Nader has added the reform of property taxes to his roster of causes, charging that so much business and industrial real estate is undertaxed as to constitute "a national scandal of corruption, illegalities and incompetence."* Time 5/3/71, p49 *"The root causes of our trouble are not mysterious," Mr. Rockefeller said in his text. "We are overspending. And we are undertaxing."* NY Times 5/23/68, p23 [**1964**, patterned after *overtax*] —**undertaxation**, *n.: . . . the undertaxation of land helps speculators hold property out of use while they wait for a city's growth to raise its price.* Time 4/4/69, p56

underwhelm, *v.t.* to create a feeling of indifference in; fail to excite or arouse enthusiasm. *It was very nice of him and I suppose I should be duly grateful. But I am bound to say, churlish though it may seem, that I am distinctly underwhelmed by his generosity.* Times (London) 10/30/70, p11 *Rockefeller's long, prepared speeches in more formal settings often underwhelm his audiences, but his peppy little talks followed by question periods show a perky platform style.* Time 5/17/68, p15 [**1956**, from *under* + *overwhelm*]

undock, *v.i., v.t.* to disconnect (orbiting spacecraft), especially a lunar module from the command craft. *Cosmos 212 and 213 docked, coasted and undocked in orbit automatically . . .* Science News 5/18/68, p473 *Engineers at Houston . . . were planning alternate ways to undock the command module.* Science News 6/2/73, p353 [**1966**]

UNDP, abbreviation of *United Nations Development Program,* an organ of the UN that oversees funds for aiding needy or developing countries. *This project* [reporting of locust migration between countries] *which lasted six years and involved 30 or* *so countries . . . was the biggest single scheme ever financed by the UNDP.* Science Journal 1/70, p66 [**1966**]

UNEP ('yu:nep), *n.* acronym for *United Nations Environment Program,* an agency created in 1972 to initiate and coordinate global efforts to protect the earth's environment. It was originally charged with operating the EARTHWATCH system. *Work supported by UNEP, an agency with headquarters in Nairobi, ranges from formation of a world network of information for action against poisonous chemicals to research projects intended to improve living conditions in towns and rural areas.* Times (London) 3/23/76, p7 [**1973**]

uneven bars, parallel wooden bars, one about 7½ feet high, the other about 5 feet high, used in women's gymnastic events. *Whether doing backflips on the beam or rocketing herself around the uneven bars, the deceptively frail-looking sprite . . . was so much in her element that the audience had no more fear of her falling than of a fish drowning.* Time 8/6/76, p47 [**1972**]

unflappability, *n.* calmness; composure; self-possession. *All the young Americans seem to respond to Mark Satin. His enthusiasm for the job and general air of unflappability seem catching.* Saturday Night (Canada) 9/67, p22 [**1959**]

unflappable, *adj.* not disturbed or agitated; unruffled; calm. Compare FLAPPABLE. *The United States Government, in the words of Chairman Arthur M. Okun of the Council of Economic Advisers, remained "unflappable," even though the rush cost it more of its dwindling supply of gold.* NY Times 3/10/68, pD6 [**1958,** from *un-* not + *flap* confusion, excitement (especially in the phrase *in a flap*) + *-able;* originally applied to Harold Macmillan, British Prime Minister from 1957 to 1963]

unflappably, *adv.* calmly. *Particularly if the City unflappably sticks to its bowlers in astrakhan weather.* Sunday Times (London) 4/20/69, p25 [**1966**]

Unification Church, an evangelistic sect combining Christian and Buddhist elements, founded in South Korea by the Reverend Sun Myung Moon. See MOONIE and MOONISM. *The Unification Church . . . moved its headquarters to the United States in the 1960's. It says that it has about 10,000 members in the United States, out of a total of 500,000 worldwide.* NY Times 1/5/77, pA12 *Parents who attack the Unification Church are called "Satanic." The top secret 120-day training manual instructs members to have contact with parents "before they start to investigate the UC," so that they "feel peaceful . . ."* Times (London) 12/14/77, p5 [**1973**]

Unionism, *n.* the principles and practices of the Unionist Party (the ruling Protestant political party) of Northern Ireland. *The solution was a Protestant alliance with Unionism in the North, to match that between Catholicism and Irish Nationalism.* Listener 12/21/72, p854 [**1969,** from *Unionist, adj., n.* (1953)]

unisex, *adj.* designed or suitable for both sexes; not distinguishing or discriminating between males and females. *"Unisex" clothes were advertised from the walls of London's subway, and the psychological implications of unisex were eagerly discussed.* Britannica Book of the Year 1970, p341 *Garbed in loose-fitting tunics and trousers, the Chinese have a unisex look.* NY Times 6/26/71, p8 *Twenty-six angry women, representing 120,000 female workers, were urged that the time had come for "unisex" jobs to be accepted.* Times (London) 3/19/70, p22 —*n.* integration or equalization of the sexes in work, sports, fashions, etc. *To Charles Winick, professor of anthropology and sociology at the City University of New York, the rise of "unisex" in the U.S. has ominous connotations for the future of the nation. In a survey of 2,000 different cultures, Winick found that some 55 were characterized by sexual ambiguity. Not one of those cultures has survived.* Time 10/12/70, p57 *Drug addiction, drag and unisex are now much more fashionable subjects for the popular press.* Manchester Guardian Weekly 8/21/69, p9 [**1968,** from *uni-* one + *sex*]

unisexed, *adj.* not distinguishable by sex. *In the background busy young men and women, sartorially unisexed, were laying out the ground plans . . .* Punch 9/3/69, p381 [**1969**]

unisexual, *adj.* of or relating to unisex or unisexuality. *"It astounds me that we have progressed so far in sexuality that ultimately* [fashion designer] *Rudi Gernreich's unisexual concept should be as asexual as the Virgin birth . . . It's ending up to be the same bag."* Time 2/23/70, p36 [**1970**]

unisexuality, *n.* unisex look or appearance. *In ballet, adults adore the unisexuality of Nureyev; in books, children prefer easy-to-read real-life adventures to fairy tales with their "idealized, romantic role-models of the masculine and feminine."* Time 10/12/70, p57 *If it works in the Village, it won't be long before unisexuality starts creeping uptown—and over the Atlantic?* Manchester Guardian Weekly 11/21/68, p4 [**1968**]

UNISIST or **Unisist,** *n.* a system for international exchange of scientific and technical information, sponsored by the International Council of Scientific Unions and UNESCO. *The object of the system, to be known as UNISIST, would be to help scientists and engineers to get easier access to about 2 million articles published every year in some 70,000 specialized scientific journals.* Annual Register of World Events in 1971, p343 [**1971,** acronym for *United Nations Intergovernmental System of Information in Science and Technology*]

UNITA or **Unita** ('yu:nita:), *n.* a guerrilla organization in Angola. See the quotation. *Secretary of State Cyrus Vance . . . defeated a move by President Carter's national security advisor, Zbigniew Brzezinski, proposing the covert sending of arms to UNITA guerrillas fighting in Angola against the Marxist Government of President Agostinho Neto.* Manchester Guardian Weekly 7/2/78, p6 [**1967,** from the Portuguese acronym for National Union for the Total Independence of Angola]

unitard, *n.* a leotard covering the torso and legs and, usually, the feet. Also called **unitards.** *Red headbands and black eyepatches, track pants, silver lamé jackets and flashing neon lapel pins are the order of the night here. Girls boogie by in the shortest of shorts and one woman, dressed in unitards and a wide gold sash, bounces dull-eyed in the center of the room.* NY Times 2/2/79, pC16 [**1978,** from *uni-* one (probably a reference to *one-piece*) + *leotard*] ►The word *Unitard* was formerly (1961) a registered trademark in the United States for a one-piece garment with sleeves, covering the body from neck to feet.

unitarity, *n. Nuclear Physics.* a principle that states, if a particle can decay by several modes, the sum of the fractions taking each mode should add up to one. *For a long time, unsuccessful attempts to discover the radioactive decay of K^0L (pronounced K-zero-long) mesons into a pair of muons made particle physicists very nervous. Among all the processes particle physicists have to deal with, the decay of K into two muons may seem a small thing to cause consternation, but its nonappearance indicated a possible violation of a fundamental law, the principle of unitarity.* Science News 2/28/76, p130 [**1971,** from *unitary* + *-ity*]

unitholder, *n. British.* a stockholder in a unit trust (a mutual fund). *The recent unit trust management mergers raise the interesting question: what are a unitholder's rights when a management company changes hands?* Times (London) 3/28/70, p21 [**1965**]

unit pricing, the pricing of commodities by the pound, ounce, or other standard unit together with the overall price. . . . *unit pricing of grocery items . . . permits instant comparison of relative costs of different brands and sizes.* NY Times 7/8/70, p42 *Essentially, unit pricing means that shoppers will find two prices on the food items they select—the total price and the price per standard unit of measurement. Thus, a 7½-ounce box of detergent might be labeled 65 cents, or 8²/₃ cents an ounce.* 1971 Collier's Encyclopedia Year Book, p239 [**1970**]

unit train, *U.S. and Canada.* a freight train which operates as a permanent unit, without uncoupling and reassembly of cars, in transporting goods from one fixed point to another. . . . *the most important innovation came in 1962 with the introduction* *of the "unit train," that is, a train that shuttles constantly back and forth between the mine and the power station, thereby achieving optimum equipment utilization.* Scientific American 2/68, p27 . . . *the competition of river barges has spurred the railroads to introduce massive, low-cost "unit" trains and to cut rates to the bone on everything from steel to fertilizer for river valley deliveries.* Harper's 4/67, p67 **[1967]**

Universal Coordinated Time, standard time measured by atomic clocks at several timekeeping stations. It is equivalent to Greenwich Mean Time but corrected periodically to match the earth's rotation. Also called COORDINATED UNIVERSAL TIME. *M. Guinot's Bureau International de l'Heure was empowered to proclaim the addition or subtraction of a second to or from Universal Coordinated Time at the halfway point or the end of any year. Thus the two leap seconds of 1972. Just before the first one was added, on June 30th, atomic time was seventenths of a second behind earth time; on December 31st it was lagging by two-tenths of a second.* New Yorker 8/27/73, p56 **[1973]**

Universal Product Code, *U.S.* a coded series of lines, spaces, and numbers printed on a package for an optical scanner to identify the product at a store's checkout counter. *Abbreviation:* UPC See BAR CODE. *The computer system has no need for the usual price markings on packages. The checkout clerk merely moves any packaged product past an electronic scanner at the checkout counter and drops it in the bag. The machine does the rest: It reads a special code on the package (those now familiar bar symbols, called the Universal Product Code), flashes the product's price on a viewer for the shopper to glimpse, prints the product's name and price on the register slip, and, finally, prints the total bill on the receipt.* Consumer Reports 2/76, p65 *The assumption underlying these laws is the consumer's basic right to information and equity in transactions. Proposed legislation to further safeguard this right included a bill that would require unit and item price disclosure in conjunction with a universal product code.* Americana Annual 1976, p198 **[1974]**

unk-unks, *n.pl. U.S. Slang.* a series of unknowns, especially of inexplicable calamaties. *Lately the industry has suffered a succession of blows: a slow-down in space exploration, a $6.9 billion cutback in Washington's defense budget, and a fall-off in orders for commercial aircraft. As a result, aerospacemen have come down with a severe case of what they call the "unkunks"—the "unknown unknowns."* Time 3/9/70, p63 *"Unk Unks"—aerospace jargon for "unknowns"—are the villains favoured by Lockheed to explain the extraordinary series of financial disasters that has led it to the verge of bankruptcy.* Manchester Guardian Weekly 8/1/70, p24 **[1970,** duplication of *unk-* (in *unknown*) + plural suffix *-s]*

unleaded, *adj.* another word for NONLEADED. *Performance is improved when cars burn gas without lead, which tends to clog pollution control gadgets. In February, Henry Ford sent an open letter to the presidents of 19 oil companies, demanding that they speed their marketing of unleaded gas.* Time 7/20/70, p65 **[1965]** ▶The preferred term now is *unleaded.*

unlib, *adj.* short for UNLIBERATED. Ms. . . . *is the feminist magazine, the one with Gloria Steinem, with slick paper, full-color, full-page Chevrolet ads . . . Ms. seems to be to women's lib what* Vogue *is to the unlib.* National Review 5/24/74, p579 **[1971]**

unliberated, *adj.* submitting to a passive or secondary role in society; not liberated. *More likely, dearie, you'll hold down two jobs—'cause when you get home from that executive job in the sky, there ain't gonna be no unliberated woman left (and certainly no man) to do your grub work.* Time 3/20/72, p11 **[1970]**

unlimited, *n.* short for UNLIMITED HYDROPLANE. *For one thing, unlimiteds, those manta-ray-shaped thunderboats that have hit over 200 mph on straightaways, had been . . . attracting hundreds of thousands of devotees on both sides of the river.* 1972 Collier's Encyclopedia Year Book, p521 **[1956, 1965,** earlier used in *unlimited engine displacement* (1953)]

unlimited hydroplane, the largest type of hydroplane, powered by an inboard aircraft engine of unlimited displacement. Also called THUNDERBOAT. *The national championship series for unlimited hydroplanes consisted of 10 races with $350,000 in purses.* 1976 World Book Year Book, p218 **[1959]**

unnil- (‚yu:nil-), a combining form of Latin *ūnus* + *nil* nothing, zero, used in chemistry and physics for names of the transuranic elements following element 103 (lawrencium). For example: —**unnilquadium** (-'kweidi:əm) = ELEMENT 104. [Latin *quadri-* four] —**unnilpentium** (-'penti:əm) = ELEMENT 105. [Greek *pénte* five] —**unnilhexium** (-'heksi:əm) = ELEMENT 106. [Greek *héx* six] —**unnilseptium** (-'septi:əm) = ELEMENT 107. [Latin *septem* seven] —**unniloctium** (-'akti:əm) = ELEMENT 108. [Latin *octō* eight] —**unnilnonium** (-'nani:əm) = ELEMENT 109. [Latin *nōn-* nine] **[1976]**

unpeople, *n.* **1** people lacking the semblance of humanity or individuality. *People on foot on a hot road in the country walking from nowhere to nowhere, a suitcase on their head. Tired people. Unpeople.* Manchester Guardian Weekly 3/21/70, p6 **2** unpersons collectively. *They are so devoid of romance or passion they're like the un-people at the end of "1984."* New Yorker 10/25/69, p177 **[1962]**

unperson, *n.* a political or other public figure who has lost importance or influence and has been relegated to an inferior or inconsequential status. . . . *Molotov, too, is an unperson, dead politically if not corporally.* NY Times 11/6/67, p46 —*v.t.* to cause to become an unperson. *What is of greatest value is not only the account of the indictment of Khrushchev and his "unpersoning," but the sketch of the careers and personalities of Brezhnev and Kosygin . . .* Manchester Guardian Weekly 3/31/66, p11 . . . *The Fierce and Beautiful World, by Andrei Platonov, unpersoned under Stalin.* Manchester Guardian Weekly 1/16/71, p19 **[1954,** originally used in George Orwell's novel *1984* to describe people eliminated from official existence by the eradication of their names from all documents, newspapers, etc.; **1966** for verb]

unsocial hours, *British.* working hours outside the normal or usual times. *The Department of Employment said: "Any supplementary allowance for unsocial hours, overtime or bonuses can under the policy continue to be paid. But the criteria for calculating them cannot be altered. This claim would contravene the policy."* Times (London) 1/24/76, p3 **[1973,** so called because the time does not conform to the standard social hours (time spent with family and friends) of most workers]

Untermensch ('untər‚menʃ), *n., pl.* **Untermenschen** ('untər‚menʃən). *German.* a person regarded as less than human; a subhuman. *In Britain, only a century ago, the workers were widely regarded as Untermenschen, sub-species fortunate to live in their hovels, to eat bread and enjoy long hours in foul mines, mills and factories.* Punch 4/24/68, p587 *To the Germans, Lithuanians were* Untermenschen, *a second-class people to be exploited and, when politically expedient, enslaved.* Saturday Review 3/26/66, p34 **[1964]**

untogether, *adj. U.S. Slang.* confused; disorganized. *The labels have been stuck so fast for so many years it's hard tearin' 'em away. Lots of ofays still think we all play boogie woogie and shine shoes, but I'll tell you, the most prejudiced, jivest, complex, untogether race in the world is blacks. There are so many divisions, so many gradations of color, that's why it's taken us so long to get anywhere; all those years black, brown, high yeller shovin' each other to get closer to the front of the bus. Survival. Mm-hmm.* Harper's 10/72, p50 **[1972]**

unwindase (ən'wain‚deis), *n. Molecular Biology.* an enzyme that unwinds the double-stranded DNA molecule and aligns the template strands before the DNA polymerase replicates the molecule. Also called UNWINDING PROTEIN. *The functions of the products of genes 32 and 43 have, of course, been determined; they specify a DNA unwindase and T4 DNA polymerase.* Nature 10/6/72, p310 **[1972,** from *unwind* + *-ase* enzyme]

unwinding protein, another name for UNWINDASE. *An interesting class of proteins was discovered by B. Alberts (Princeton) and called unwinding proteins . . . These proteins serve to de-*

nature or unwind the double-stranded DNA molecule. Britannica Book of the Year 1972, p422 **[1972]**

up, *Especially U.S. Slang.* —*adj.* cheerful; happy; upbeat. *Although Alec Wilder responds to a wide range of styles, he prefers ballads to up tunes; he prizes suavity and finesse more than drive and vigor.* NY Times Book Review 4/23/72, p6 *Your friend has wide personality swings which are a symptom of mental illness. When she's "up" she's friendly. When she's "down" she's cool and distant.* The News (Mexico City) 4/22/73, p16 —*v.i.* to take uppers (stimulant drugs). *Amphetamines and barbiturates also have two faces. They are a familiar item in the doctor's armamentarium and, as such, reassuring. And yet excessive "upping" or "downing" can cause severe psychic dislocation, certainly as damaging as any of the effects of LSD.* Norman E. Zinberg and John A. Robertson, Drugs and the Public, 1972, p49 —*n.* another word for UPPER. *In Hollywood, a boy of eleven . . . has been pushing "ups" (amphetamine and methedrine pills) and "downs" (barbiturates, tranquilizers) since he was nine . . .* Time 2/16/70, p36 **[1969]**

UPC or **U.P.C.,** *U.S.* abbreviation of UNIVERSAL PRODUCT CODE. *UPC is a series of thin black bars on a label that has ten numbers right below the bars. The first five numbers represent the manufacturer or distributor, and the last five numbers represent the specific product and package which carries that number.* Americana Annual 1975, p196 **[1974]**

upconvert, *v.t.* to change by means of an upconverter. . . . *a laser beam can be used to upconvert infrared light to visible light . . .* New Yorker 4/11/70, p34 **[1968]**

upconverter, *n.* a device for converting radiant energy to a higher frequency. *A new system called an upconverter . . . can produce a three-dimensional color image from infrared waves. Basically, the system is composed of a crystalline material, such as potassium dihydrogen phosphate, into which are beamed and mixed the infrared waves and laser light, explains Dr. Arthur H. Firester. The laser beam pumps the infrared photons into visible light. The system, successful in the laboratory stage, has worked as far as 10 microns into the far infrared region.* Science News 4/4/70, p345 **[1958]**

update, *n.* the most recent or up-to-date information available. *. . . I'm going to pass you general procedures for the reentry, you'll get the 63-1 updates and the general details on your next pass . . .* NY Times 6/8/65, p22 *Update Pad: information on spacecraft attitudes, and other data, transmitted to the crew in standard format; e.g. manoeuvre update, navigation check, landmark tracking, entry update, etc.* Sunday Times (London) 7/13/69, p13 **[1967,** noun use of the verb (OEDS 1948)]

up-front, *adj. U.S. Informal.* **1** straightforward; open; frank; uninhibited. *All the double-edged kidding and up-front aggressiveness stand in some contrast to the cool, measured and often affectless characters Nicholson has played so well on the screen.* Time 8/12/74, p47 *But what, several asked, can we hope to learn from Ron Ziegler? "He can't be a worthwhile speaker 'cause he won't be honest and up-front."* National Review 2/28/75, p224 **2** of or in the forefront; foremost, leading, or important. *Integration has become a back-burner issue, by choice or hard political realism. The up-front concern now is to improve economic and social conditions for blacks in the urban ghettos and the rural backwaters—where most blacks are.* Newsweek 2/19/73, p33 *As another up-front New York office building, it is the perfect object for vague aesthetic discussion about architecture with all socially responsible or even utilitarian questions left out.* Harper's 1/77, p91 **3** of or belonging to the management of a business or other organization. *Colson sees his ministry to crowds as a religious duty. "I never liked to give speeches. I was not an up-front guy—that's why I never saw you people of the press. I was a back-room guy."* NY Times Magazine 8/1/76, p49 **4** made or coming in advance. *The condominium . . . makes possible multimillion-dollar housing communities with expensive amenities requiring heavy "up-front" outlays for heavy-cost investments such as pools, recreational buildings, sewer-treatment plants, and*

roads. NY Times 2/1/76, pH1 **[1967,** from the phrase (to be) *up front*] See UP FRONT (under FRONT, n.).

uplink, *n.* transmission of data, signals, etc., from the ground to a spacecraft or satellite (often used attributively). *Problems were uncovered, Mr. Martin said of the simulation, but nothing major. The computer program had to be redesigned to facilitate "uplink commands" to the spacecraft cameras.* NY Times 3/4/76, p32 —*v.t.* to transmit from the ground to a spacecraft or satellite. *Deiterich, who felt he was beginning to run out of time, passed to Russell, the GUIDO, some of the reëntry information that would have to be up-linked to the spacecraft computer; however, he asked Russell to hold off sending it, because some of the data might have to be changed.* New Yorker 11/18/72, p159 **[1968** for noun; **1972** for verb] Compare DOWN-LINK.

upmanship, *n.* the art or practice of scoring an advantage or being one-up on someone. *Nifty for cocktail parties and upmanship: While everyone discusses plot and character, you talk of plasticity of space, electricity of motion, and the director as creator.* Saturday Review 12/17/66, p37 *"Well, what's your price?" Morgan asked . . . John D. Jr. said, "I did not come here to sell. I understood you wished to buy." Honors evened in upmanship.* NY Times 5/25/65, p39 **[1962,** short for *one-upmanship.* See the etymology under ONE-UP.]

up-market, *Especially British.* —*adj.* of or for the high-income consumer; of higher grade or quality. *Faced with the need to cut their motoring costs, car owners appear to be choosing a solution which is least painful to the ego as well as to the pocket—to buy a car which is slightly more up-market than they would previously have done, look after it better and keep it longer.* Sunday Times (London) 4/13/75, p23 *The object of this growing wrath on the part of many conservative Winnipeggers, for whom caution is almost as precious as a block heater, is an up-market women's clothing store opened last December by 32-year-old psychologist Kimie McIvor.* Maclean's 6/27/77, p18 —*adv.* in or into the up-market field. *It is possible that Chrysler could still move upmarket, but it will need less conservative management from the US parent.* New Scientist 1/1/76, p2 *Mr Barber was identified with a strategy designed to move Leyland "up market" by concentrating on more profitable specialist cars whereas Turnbull, a life-long "production" man, wanted to see an expansion of the high volume cars produced by the Austin Morris division.* Manchester Guardian Weekly 1/14/79, p4 —*v.t., v.i.* to place or go into a high-income or higher-income consumer market. *Mathew Clark wants to upmarket Noilly Dry French, plugging heavily the drink's provenance compared with that of the Italian Martini and Cinzano (although to be strictly correct, Cinzano Dry comes from France as well).* Times (London) 8/25/72, p17 *In the United States, the hi-fi industry has breathlessly watched its sales soar . . . as customers have upmarketed continuously from monaural to stereo equipment and now to quadraphonic.* New Scientist 1/11/73, p78 **[1972]** Compare DOWN-MARKET, UPSCALE.

upper, *n. U.S. Slang.* **1** a stimulant drug. Also called UP. Compare DOWNER. *It was a glorious cruise, save for . . . one major misunderstanding in 1962 when Atlanta police charged him with being in the company of an excessive number of amphetamine tablets and assorted other "uppers" . . .* Harper's 9/70, p54 **2** *Figurative.* something stimulating; a pleasant experience. *Your story "The Pleasures of Dying" [Dec. 4] was unbelievably absurd. A morbid comment on human curiosity . . . Once you've made the jump, you're gone. Granted, it certainly is a relief to know that State 2 is an upper; but by that time, who cares?* Time 1/1/73, pK2 **[1968]**

up quark, a type of quark (hypothetical nuclear particle) possessing a charge of $+2/3$ and a spin of $+ 1/2$. Also called U QUARK. *It was possible to distinguish between two types of quarks on the basis of their different masses and electric charges. These were called "up quarks" and "down quarks." The two kinds of quarks were sufficient to construct neutrons and protons. According to this conjecture, everything in the workaday world is made up exclusively of these two kinds of quarks, along with electrons.* Encyclopedia Science Supplement (Grolier) 1977, p318 [**1976**, so called in reference to the upward spin it is supposed to exhibit]

uprate, *v.t.* to increase in rating, especially rating of power; upgrade; improve. *Missing power machines, in which only part of the power supplies and accelerating equipment are built at the first stage, . . . can be uprated comparatively cheaply.* Science Journal 9/70, p60 [**1965**]

upscale ('əp,skeil), *adj. U.S.* in the upper levels of income, education, and social standing; belonging to a higher-than-average economic and social stratum. *Its* [Smithsonian magazine] *affluent readership constitutes what one magazine-industry spokesman calls "one of the most up-scale demographics in the business."* Newsweek 8/27/73, p76 *The size and character— young and "upscale"—of the Python audience inevitably attracted the interest of the commercial networks.* New Yorker 3/29/76, p70 [**1966**]

upsilon, *n.* any of a group of extremely heavy, short-lived subatomic particles produced by bombarding beryllium nuclei with high-energy protons. *Symbol:* ʏ. *The existence of upsilon can also be taken to mean that a quark whose existence had been theoretically postulated, but for which there had not been any experimental evidence, does exist. This would bring the number of experimentally observed quarks to five.* 1978 Collier's Encyclopedia Year Book, p450 *The impact of the upsilon has already been far-reaching. It has prompted searches for other heavy particles in hitherto unexplored ranges of mass, and it has shed light on the inscrutable strong force. This force, which binds quarks together into hadrons and hadrons together into atomic nuclei, is too powerful to investigate by conventional scattering and collision techniques.* Scientific American 10/78, p79 [**1977**, from the name of the 20th letter of the Greek alphabet]

upstream, *adj., adv.* **1** of, relating to, or for the discovery, extraction, and transportation of oil and gas to the port of shipment. Compare DOWNSTREAM. *The most natural way the oil producers can spend their vast wealth, however, is in developing the industry itself. Huge investment is needed "upstream" . . . Until now most of the oil companies' profits have been upstream.* Auckland Star (N.Z.) 2/10/73, p18 **2** *Molecular Biology.* in or toward the starting point of a genetic segment of transcription. Compare DOWNSTREAM. *If the prion includes a small piece of nucleic acid, that could be the trigger for gene activation. This hypothetical small prion nucleic acid might be inserted into a host-cell chromosome just "upstream" of the PrP gene, or in other words just ahead of the point at which transcription of the gene begins. The inserted sequence could then serve as a promoter or enhancer of gene expression.* Scientific American 10/84, p58 [**1965** for def. 1; **1980** for def. 2]

uptick, *n. U.S.* an upward turn or trend, especially in business; upswing. *A recent uptick in applications, following a massive publicity campaign, apparently persuaded the President that his postwar "act of mercy" was finally working.* Newsweek 2/10/75, p20 *Less cheering was an uptick in the unemployment rate, which had earlier been inching down.* Time 7/18/77, p66 [**1970**, extended from the original sense (1957) of a sale of stocks made at a price higher than the immediately preceding one]

uptight, *adj. Slang.* **1** very uneasy or apprehensive; anxious. *. . . sometimes you can get so uptight about your disadvantages that you ignore your advantages.* Atlantic 12/70, p60 **2** nervous; tense; irritable. *I'm getting a little uptight, just about washing my hands, because I can't find the soap, which somebody has used and not put back in the soap dish, all of which is extremely irritating . . .* New Yorker 3/7/70, p35 *When Mia Farrow left New York for India she was hassled and really uptight.* Maclean's 6/68, p47 **3** strait-laced or conventional; stiff; formal. *"Nobody gives you a ride or takes you in for a night. I tell you the French people are—" "Uptight?" I offered. She nodded.* Saturday Review 10/10/70, p42 *Who would have thought that an uptight institution like the august Oxford University Press would have done a thing like this? Here is a . . . spirited and spiritous piece of autobiography and served up as a book, a book by a genuine Oxford mandarin, an*

historical Fellow of Balliol. Manchester Guardian Weekly 8/28/69, p18 [**1966**]

uptime, *n.* the time in which a machine, department, or the like is working or active. *Not only can the robot work three shifts a day, but it takes no coffee breaks, does not call in sick on Mondays, does not become bored, does not take vacations or qualify for pensions—and does not leave Coca-Cola cans rattling around inside the products it has helped assemble. Its "uptime" on the job averages around 95% (the figure for the average blue-collar worker is about 75%).* Time 12/8/80, p73 [**1958**]

upwardly mobile, tending or seeking to rise from a lower to a higher economic or social class. *Not all of them were born and educated in Toronto but they have the Toronto manner. That is, they're clearly recognizable as members of the upwardly mobile, forward marching, Anglophone-Canadian middle class who give that city its predominant tone.* Maclean's 10/74, p38 *There are class differences in women's headgear. The upwardly mobile class wears knitted caps or fur hats; the nonmobile, the timeless Slavic shawl, folded in the timeless Slavic manner.* National Review 2/20/76, p160 [**1964**]

upward-mobile, *adj.* characterized by upward mobility. *Mrs. Johnson divides all Christmas cards into three groups: (1) reciprocals, (2) sent but not received and (3) received but not sent . . . For a typical upward-mobile professional couple in their thirties or forties (such as the Johnsons) the three groups of cards may be about equal.* Scientific American 3/71, p48 [**1969**]

upward mobility, the ability or tendency to rise from a lower to a higher economic or social class. *Upward mobility is an unfortunate drive in one who hopes to be an artist.* New Yorker 3/13/71, p89 [**1964**]

u quark, short for UP QUARK. *The proton is a particle with spin 1/2, charge + 1, and strangeness 0. It can be constructed with two* u *quarks and one* d *quark.* 1977 Britannica Yearbook of Science and the Future, p157 [**1976**]

ur- (ur-), a prefix taken from German, meaning "original" or "earliest," used especially in music and the arts. **—ur-instrument**, *n.: . . . the Purcell-Bach-Handel age is "in," and with it an exaggerated interest in the historical instruments of the period. Purists insist not only on the ur-text but on the ur-instruments as well . . .* Atlantic 3/64, p176 **—ur-performance**, *n.: The BBC . . . are offering the symphonies in urtext and (as far as may be) in ur-performance—that is, with original mistakes uncorrected (or original strokes of inspiration restored?), and with an orchestra of the size and proportions that might have been used in original performances.* Manchester Guardian Weekly 4/18/70, p20 **—ur-racialism**, *n.: If you will turn to page 314 of your Oxford Book of Ballads, you will fall upon a nugget of ur-racialism which, in its social, sexual and political implications might have wept from the pen of J. Baldwin.* Punch 8/18/65, p227 **—ur-tank**, *n.: Above is Leonardo da Vinci's design for an ur-tank, and left, a model made from his plans, illustration in Leonardo da Vinci by Jay Williams.* Picture legend, Punch 11/9/66, p718

urb (ərb), *n. U.S. and Canada.* an urban or metropolitan area. *". . . The City is obsolete. Ask the computer. It is to the urb what LSD is to the electronic yokel; that is, it ends all goals and objectives and points of view."* Manchester Guardian Weekly 6/20/70, p18 *What is all this space, space, space? How do I get out of here? The urb has been Renewed by an Expert.* Harper's 5/69, p48 *The growth of American suburbia, fed by the yearning for a home of one's own, raises problems for urb and suburb alike . . .* NY Times Magazine 1/7/68, p25 [**1965**, partly abstracted from *urban* and *suburb;* partly back formation from Latin *urbs* city, taken as an English plural]

urban anthropology, a branch of cultural anthropology dealing with the subcultures of people living in urban communities. *Urban anthropology . . . focused research on a variety of populations including the urban and rural, migrant labourers, women, the young and the elderly, the ill and the handi-*

capped, as well as all ethnic and racial minorities. Britannica Book of the Year 1973, p82 [**1972**]

urban guerrilla, 1 a revolutionary who uses guerrilla tactics in the cities to spread terror and undermine the government. *The terrorist activity is worldwide, and most of it is carried out by a new type in the history of political warfare: the urban guerrilla.* Time 11/2/70, p19 **2** an organized band of urban guerrillas. *In Guatemala the peasant-based groups of Cesar Montes and Yon Sosa were bombed and cajoled out of the countryside in 1967 and have been operating ever since as an urban guerrilla, effective at kidnaping diplomats . . .* Listener 10/1/70, p438 [**1967**]

urban homesteading, *U.S.* a federal program sponsoring the reoccupation and renovation of abandoned buildings by tenants who obtain in return an equity ownership in the restored property. Also shortened to HOMESTEADING. *You read all about urban homesteading when local governments began early in the 1970s to sell or offer through a lottery vacant city properties they acquired through transfer from HUD. The houses, many of them tumbledown shells, were sold for token sums, sometimes as little as $1.00 to individuals or families who would make repairs to meet minimum standards before moving in.* Ruth Rejnis, Her Home, 1980, p22 [**1975**, from the *Urban Homestead* Act of 1973] **—urban homesteader:** *Several score "urban homesteaders" have taken title to dilapidated row houses for a dollar each on condition that they restore them and live in them for three years.* NY Times Magazine 5/9/76, p18

urbanoid, *adj.* having the characteristics of a large city. *I use "kakotopia" [kakos = bad] as the opposite of "utopia," to describe a misplanned and ugly urbanoid place.* New Yorker 10/10/70, p100 [**1970**]

urbanologist, *n.* a social scientist who specializes in the study of cities and their problems. . . . *they are the "Establishment" and "silk-stocking" suburban types who make their livings as "research directors, associate professors, social workers, educational consultants, urbanologists . . ."* Harper's 5/70, p49 *In another essay urbanologist Daniel Moynihan restates his now well-known conclusion that "the streets of the Negro slums contain the wreckage of a generation of good intentions on the part of the American liberals."* Saturday Review 8/10/68, p32 [**1968**]

urbanology, *n.* the study of cities and their problems. *Just as the word urbanology is a cross between Latin and Greek, the science—or is it an art?—is a mélange of many disciplines.* Time 7/28/67, p11 *Levine believes the Center will . . . bring together many existing talents within the University to provide an interdisciplinary approach to solving the problems of the nation's cities. "Urbanology," as some have called the field, has far more questions than answers today.* Johns Hopkins Journal 12/68, p1 [**1967**]

urban ore, discarded tin cans, bottles, and other solid refuse buried in urban landfills, held to be a rich source of raw material. *One can consider MSW [municipal solid waste] as an "urban ore" and follow its assay from location to location and also for a long time period during which its composition may change. These changes may be caused either by the purchasing tastes of the public, which can alter the composition of MSW, or by the choice of disposal techniques, which might concentrate given materials in an area where special beneficiation methods are warranted.* Science 2/20/76, p671 [**1971**]

urban renewal, a program for replacing slums and inadequate housing in a city, by either renovation or rebuilding. *The heart of downtown Denver has been torn out in the name of urban renewal, with one old-fashioned block of Larimer Street left to preserve its memory . . .* NY Times 8/28/70, p30 *Angry black teen-agers then led a charge across the Penn Central tracks into the fringe of the white business district. The litany of their grievances was reproachfully familiar: too little urban renewal, too few jobs, inadequate play areas, inadequate communications between black and white leaders.* Time 7/20/70, p13 [**1955**]

urban sprawl, the uncontrolled growth of a city over the countryside. *We see nineteenth-century urban sprawl as the trams reach out to Highgate . . .* New Yorker 5/23/70, p140 *The automobile has brought another consequence that tends to be overlooked but is no less serious: by fostering "urban sprawl" it has in effect isolated much of the population.* Scientific American 7/69, p19 [**1958**]

urbicide, *n.* the destruction of a city, usually by altering its appearance with building projects that destroy existing architecture or disregard land use in surrounding areas. *It does no good to speculate at what point real estate becomes art, or history, or a talisman of place. When it does, it enters the public domain. To destroy it is an act of urbicide.* NY Times 10/15/72, pD14 [**1966**, coined by Wolf Von Eckardt, American architectural critic, from *urbi-* (from Latin *urbs* city) + *-cide* a killing]

urgicenter, *n.* a medical facility that provides immediate care in emergencies or for minor injuries or complaints. *The chains are buying into another phenomenon: the "urgicenters," "surgicenters" and "quick care centers" that have sprung up in business districts and shopping centers. There are 2,500 such mini-clinics—sometimes dubbed "McDoctors"—today, 1,400 more than there were a year ago.* Washington Post 4/3/85, p12 [**1984**, from *urgent* + *center;* patterned after *surgicenter*]

urokinase (ˌyurouˈkaiˌneis), *n.* a protein enzyme that dissolves blood clots. *From this research has come a wealth of fundamental data and substances such as streptokinase and urokinase, with which the clot, once formed, may be dissolved, have recently been discovered.* New Scientist and Science Journal 9/16/71, p620 [**1952, 1967** from *uro-* urine + *kinase* an enzyme that catalyzes inactive enzymes]

use immunity, *U.S. Law.* a form of immunity which protects witnesses compelled to testify from subsequent prosecution based solely on evidence revealed in their testimony. *To get around the Fifth Amendment privilege against self-incrimination, the act gives the government the right to offer "use immunity"—a guarantee that the witness's testimony will not be used against him.* Newsweek 10/29/73, p68 *The Federal law, which was immediately copied by half the states, grants a witness "use" immunity, which blocks prosecutors from the later use of what the witness has specifically testified to.* NY Times 4/15/76, p39 [**1972**]

user-friendly, *adj.* designed to be easy to use. *Computer artist Paul Jablonka has written several minicomputer graphics programs his colleagues have hailed as user-friendly. "But even with those systems," says Jablonka, "I usually have to stand over the artist's shoulder the first time through to make sure the person doesn't hit keys that'll make the program crash."* Popular Computing 11/83, p105 [**1977**] **—user-friendliness,** *n.: Not until 1980 and 1981, when the Apple IIe and the IBM PC were introduced, did the idea that the computer could become a commodity for the masses take hold. Dramatically lowered costs were largely the reason for the change, but so was the blossoming idea of "user friendliness": that computer hardware and software could be designed specifically for nonprogrammers.* Encyclopedia Science Supplement (Grolier) 1988, p119

U-value, *n. British.* a measure of the resistance to heat flow through a wall, roof, or floor, especially as provided by insulating material. A low U-value corresponds to a high level of insulating effectiveness. Compare R-VALUE. *Clearly it is a good idea to exceed the current Regulations. Our improved semi has the following U-values—roof and ceiling 0.40 watts/sq.m/°C; external walls (excluding the windows) 0.51 watts/sq.m/°C; external walls (overall) 0.97 watts/sq.m/°C. These values are all considerably better than the current statutory maxima.* New Scientist 1/29/76, p227 [**1958**, from British Thermal *U*nit, a unit for measuring heat]

Uzi (ˈuːziː), *n.* a highly accurate and rapid-firing submachine gun made in Israel. *Thwarting at least five attempted holdups, so far, the Uzis have been heavily used in controlling a massive crime wave which, since the middle of 1977, has netted the IRA more than $5 million in some 1,300 separate armed robberies.* Maclean's 2/19/79, p30 *But parents are sometimes complicit,* too, Kramer says, ignoring the problem because "the rent gets paid and there's a new TV in the living room." When they do get alarmed, Kramer adds, it may be too late. "The time to start disciplining a youngster is not when he's 15 or 16 years old and

carrying an Uzi." People Weekly 5/2/88, p46   [**1959**, from Modern Hebrew, named after *Uzi*el Gal, an Israeli army officer in the Sinai Campaign of 1956]

V

vacancy decontrol, *U.S.* the legal removal of rent control from an apartment or other dwelling unit after it has been vacated. *Another innovation of this period was vacancy decontrol. This was a great victory for the landlords . . . Vacancy decontrol meant higher rents for new tenants at a time when recession and inflation were hitting people badly, particularly the old and/or poor.* NY Times Magazine 4/18/76, p24 **[1971]**

vaccinate, *v.t.* to protect (a computer or its operating system) from a computer virus by means of a vaccination program. *Researchers have taken several approaches to block virus entry or "vaccinate" computers so that users are notified when a virus is at work.* NY Times 5/30/89, pC9 **[1989]**

vaccination program or **vaccine program,** a computer program designed to detect computer viruses and prevent them from destroying or altering data by triggering an alarm, interrupting the operation, and the like. Also called VACCINE. *At least 14 vaccination programs designed to protect computer disks . . . are now available.* Philadelphia Inquirer 3/27/88 (page not known) *Virus experts suggest that vaccine programs may actually compound the problem by offering an intellectual challenge to rogue programmers.* NY Times 5/30/89, pC9 **[1988]**

vaccine, *n.* another term for VACCINATION PROGRAM. *Other vaccines screen the commands that programs send to the computer's operating system. If an illicit command is issued, the vaccine interrupts operation, alerting the user.* NY Times 5/30/89, pC1 **[1989]**

vaccinee (ˌvæksəˈniː), *n.* a person who has been vaccinated. . . . *it was of cardinal importance to show that the* [rubella] *virus does not spread from vaccinees to pregnant women . . .* 1970 Britannica Yearbook of Science and the Future, p276 **[1969]**

vacuum aspiration, a method of abortion, performed within the first 10 to 12 weeks of pregnancy, in which a specially designed tube is inserted into the uterus to draw out the contents by suction. Also called SUCTION METHOD, LUNCHTIME ABORTION. *Induced abortion is performed on request, usually in very early pregnancy . . . The procedure is almost always done by vacuum aspiration conducted by nurses, midwives or barefoot doctors and the rate of complications is said to be very low.* Scientific American 11/72, p50 **[1967]**

vacuum cleaner, any of various suction-producing devices. See the quotations. *16 "vacuum cleaners" sucking at an overhead rail lift it* [a train] *off its supports. Riding on air, the train accelerates to 30 mph in seconds, without a sound; when the current is reversed, it decelerates equally rapidly and silently.* 1971 Britannica Yearbook of Science and the Future, p281 *The vacuum cleaner is actually a hydraulic pump designed to lift as much as 400 tons of material from the sea floor daily.* World Book Science Annual 1972, p342 **[1970,** transferred sense of the term (OED 1903) meaning a suction device for cleaning carpets, rugs, etc.]

V-agent, *n.* any of a class of extremely toxic nerve gases, including GB and VX. *Today, as the world knows well, the V-agents that resulted from this British research and development programme, lie stockpiled in the US, partially in ready-to-fire munitions in quantities estimated at tens, if not hundreds, of thousands of tonnes.* Science Journal 12/70, p9 **[1964]**

Val, *n.* short for VALLEYSPEAK. *"Val" is really a sort of satire of slang, a goof on language and on the dreamily dumb and self-regarding suburban kids who may actually talk like that.* Time 11/8/82, p91 **[1982]**

valinomycin (ˌvælənouˈmaisən), *n.* an antibiotic derived from soil bacteria that activates the movement of ions in cells. *There is no significant difference in permeability between the alkali metal ions, but by incorporating certain cyclic polypeptides (for example, Valinomycin) into the liposomes, they can be made permeable to K^+ and Rb^+ but not to Na^+ or Li^+.* New Scientist 1/14/71, p64 **[1955,** from *valine* an amino acid $\pm$ *-mycin* a soil bacteria derivative, as in *actinomycin*]

Valium (ˈveiliːəm), *n.* Also popularly spelled **valium.** a trademark for DIAZEPAM. *His dose of Valium, to contain his agitation, was reduced.* Atlantic 3/70, p53 *Federal officials said that vials of dexedrine, valium and compazine were found in her luggage when she arrived at Cleveland Hopkins International airport on a flight from Toronto.* Times (London) 11/4/70, p8 **[1961]**

valley of the dolls, a condition of excessive dependence on stimulant and depressant drugs. See DOLL. *Like the Bogart and Garland cults, today's Monroemania has its far-out fringe—the masochists who identify with suffering and the parlor psychoanalysts who hone their Freudian clichés on her Dickensian childhood, failed marriages and miscarriages . . . and her almost preordained plunge into the valley of the dolls.* Newsweek 10/16/72, p80 *When I asked if she liked him she replied "No—he's beyond the valley of the dolls."* Bulletin (Sydney, Australia) 8/7/76 (page not known) **[1972,** from the novel *Valley of the Dolls* (1966) by the American author Jacqueline Susann, 1921-1974]

Valleyspeak, *n. U.S.* a kind of slang used by teenagers of the San Fernando Valley in southern California. Also shortened to VAL. . . . *Valleyspeak struck a responsive chord. Jennifer Jones and Halley Finkelstein, two students at the National Cathedral School, use words such as "massive" to express delight, as in "a massive guy". . . . "Like, it's tenacious."* Washington Post Magazine 1/23/83, p8 **[1982]**

valproate (vælˈproueit), *n.* an anticonvulsive drug effective against petit mal. *Formula:* $C_8H_{15}NaO_2$ *The drug, valproate, has been available in Europe for a decade. It will benefit more than 560,000 patients a year, the Epilepsy Foundation predicts.* Science News 3/11/78, p151 **[1974,** from *valeric* acid + *propyl* + *-ate* salt]

Valspeak, *n.* another word for VALLEYSPEAK. *Valspeak, as a special language confined to the San Fernando Valley, is a media myth, but its dissemination is typical of our language.* R. McCrum, W. Cran, and R. MacNeil, The Story of English, 1986, p349 **[1982]**

vanity plate, *U.S.* an automobile license plate with a distinctive combination of letters or numbers chosen by the purchaser, usually at extra cost. *The Assembly—not without a few hoots and whistles—passed a bill imposing $15 fee for legislators, newsmen and physicians wishing special license plates identifying their work . . . The bill also would raise the regular $5 charge for non-specialized "vanity plates" to $15.* NY Times 5/6/76, p21 **[1967]**

vanner, *n. U.S. and Canada.* an owner or operator of a van, especially one used for recreation. *Semiprofessional vanners go through about a van a year, selling at a tidy profit and starting from scratch again. But it's creativity not profit that motivates the true vanner.* Maclean's 12/13/76, p72 *Vanners themselves, or at least the zealots, seem as much a cult as a fellowship. They have formed hundreds of societies. Many drive hundreds or even thousands of miles to converge with other vanners at picnicky socials that are held all over the country.* Time 9/5/77, p55 **[1973]** ►In the 1800's the term was used for a horse pulling a small van.

vanpool, *U.S.* —*n.* an arrangement in which a group of people share commuting costs by using a large passenger van. *Federal money was made available for as much as 90 percent of the start-up costs of a vanpool, including the purchase or leasing of the vehicle, and the department said that a dozen states had taken advantage of the program . . . The energy saving in a vanpool was high, officials said, and the projects were operated and coordinated on state levels.* NY Times 1/17/78, p2 —*v.i.* to join or take part in a vanpool. *By making commuters aware of the costs of driving alone . . ., it is hoped that more commuters who presently drive alone will carpool or vanpool.* U.S. Department of Transportation, 1978, p1 **[1976]**

varactor (vəˈræktər), *n.* a diode semiconductor in which the capacitance can be varied with the voltage (often used attributively). *The varactor—a special type of semiconductor diode that has a voltage-variable capacitance—serves the same purpose as the conventional mechanically variable capacitor in the tuning circuit. The use of a varactor eliminates complex mechanical linkages inside the tuner and makes remote control much simpler.* Americana Annual 1969, p575 **[1959,** from *vari*able re*actor*]

variable geometry, another name for SWING-WING (often used attributively). *The Boeing Company, competing with Lockheed to build the American plane, uses a radically different approach—a "variable geometry" or "swing-wing" that can be set at three positions for slow, intermediate or supersonic speeds.* NY Times 11/20/66, pL13 *The French variable geometry aircraft, the Mirage G, made its first flight today at the Melun-Villaroche military airfield near Paris.* Times (London) 10/19/67, p1 **[1957]**

variable life insurance, a form of life insurance in which the face value of the policy varies with an equity index or some other variable factor. *The variable life insurance policy concept has been employed for years in Britain, and such policies have been offered in recent years in Canada. No such policies are now available in the United States.* NY Times 2/4/76, p46 **[1972]**

variable rate mortgage, *U.S.* a mortgage on which the interest rate rises or falls with the interest rate on the money market. *Variable rate mortgages (VRMs) are in use at savings and loan associations in about a dozen states. The VRM is usually offered at half a percentage point below the going interest rate, but after five years it fluctuates, depending on such factors as the long-term federal bond rate.* Ruth Rejnis, Her Home, 1980, p25 **[1979]**

variable-sweep wing, another name for SWING-WING. *The X-5 was the first aircraft to incorporate variable-sweep wings, a feature now part of the F-111 fighter and Boeing's supersonic transport.* Science News 2/24/68, p188 **[1965]**

variomatic, *adj. British.* of or relating to a belt-driven automatic transmission. *Careful design at the planning stage could make optional variations for the disabled cheap to incorporate . . . variomatic drive (now common in many cars) eliminates the difficulties of changing gear.* New Scientist 7/22/76, p162 **[1973,** from *vari*able + aut*omatic*]

varoom, *v.i. U.S.* to travel or take off with a roar, as that made by the motor of a racing car. See also VROOM. *The way the show tells it, there are these four really neat-looking southern-California guys whose job it is to raise the very Ned with boring old Rommel's boring supply lines and how they do it is to go varooming all over the desert in a couple of jeeps in search of the thousands of comical Germans . . .* New Yorker 1/21/67, p76 **[1967,** imitative of the roaring sound]

VASCAR or **Vascar** (ˈvæsˌkɑr), *n.* a trademark for a computer-controlled electronic device for clocking the speed of motorists. *There are 9000 VASCARs currently in use in all but three states. It works on all kinds of roads and in most weather conditions (except when visibility is severely reduced).* New Scientist 8/23/73, p446 *Vascar . . . measures the time a vehicle takes to travel between two "reference points" fixed by the operator. It measures the distance between the points and works out the vehicle's average speed over that distance.* Times (London)

11/22/73, p4 **[1966,** acronym for *Visual Average Speed Computer And Recorder*]

vasoactive (ˌvæsouˈæktiv), *adj.* acting on the blood vessels, as by constricting or dilating them. *A vasoactive peptide, perhaps responsible for the local swellings, has been isolated from plasma from* [angioneurotic edema] *patients during attacks . . .* McGraw-Hill Yearbook of Science and Technology 1971, p156 **[1958,** from *vaso*- vessel, blood vessel + *active*]

vasoligate (ˌvæsouˈlɑigeit), *v.t.* to tie off the vasa deferentia or sperm-carrying tubes of (a person or animal) in order to produce sterility; to subject to vasoligation. *They got together three groups of young rats, each containing about thirty animals. One group were vasectomised, the second vasoligated, and the last were controls.* New Scientist 1/25/73, p172 **[1973,** back formation from *vasoligation* (1926) surgical ligation of the vasa deferentia]

VAT (væt), *n.* acronym for *value-added tax,* a sales tax levied on a product in such a way that manufacturers, wholesalers, retailers, etc., are taxed for that part of the sales price which represents the value added at their particular stage of the production and distribution process. Also called ADDED-VALUE TAX. *The Shadow Cabinet was . . . unable to decide whether a VAT (excluding food) would be more satisfactory than a combination of purchase tax and excise duties on goods which might come under the new tax.* Manchester Guardian Weekly 2/7/70, p9 *The remaining 700m will come from vat, which the state will not be retaining at all this year.* Times (London) 1/13/72, p15 **[1966]**

Vaticanologist, *n.* a student of the policies, leaders, and practices of the Vatican. *As the Cardinals entered their carefully sealed sanctum, most Vaticanologists anticipated a wide-open race but, paradoxically, a relatively brief conclave.* Time 9/4/78, p65 **[1974,** from *Vatican* + *-ologist* student of]

Vaticanology, *n.* the study of the policies, practices, etc., of the Vatican. *It is high time that Vaticanology was recognized as a serious field of historical inquiry.* Times Literary Supplement 2/12/82, p154 **[1976]**

Vatican roulette, *Informal.* the rhythm method of birth control. *This controversial encyclical was issued by Paul VI in July 1968. It forbade the world's 600 million Catholics to use any artificial methods of birth control; it gave its approval only to the rhythm method (mockingly dubbed "Vatican Roulette").* Maclean's 9/5/77, p23 **[1962,** patterned after *Russian roulette* (OEDS 1937)]

VC, abbreviation of *Vietcong* (the former pro-Communist guerrilla force in South Vietnam). *The VC had recently captured two Americans, a captain and a sergeant, and had committed appalling atrocities against them, which was unusual because in the past atrocities had been used regularly against the South Vietnamese, but not against the Americans.* Harper's 2/71, p64 **[1964]**

VCR, abbreviation of VIDEOCASSETTE RECORDER. *Most VCRs have a pause-control button so the viewer can edit out commercials while recording. The tapes are reusable; the VCR simply erases the old program as it records the new one.* Reader's Digest 2/79, p142 **[1971]**

VDT, abbreviation of VIDEO (or VISUAL) DISPLAY TERMINAL. *The VDT, a more elaborate device, is changing editing methods. By tapping out a code at the VDT keyboard, an editor can call back any story from computer storage for display on the screen. He can make desired changes by using the keyboard and pressing a button to send the edited story back to the computer, which digests the changes and readies the copy for the photocomposition machine.* 1976 Collier's Encyclopedia Year Book, p375 **[1973]**

VDU, abbreviation of VISUAL (or VIDEO) DISPLAY UNIT. *The computer programs . . . involve the patient sitting down in front of the screen and answering either yes, no, or "don't understand" to questions displayed on the VDU. All the information captured will be printed out and given to the doctor, who* will then question patients more closely on the relevant aspects of their health. New Scientist 8/3/78, p345 [**1968**]

vector, *v.t.* to carry or direct toward a particular point or on a particular course. *Decades ago Wegener proposed that the drift of the continents was vectored by forces he termed Westwanderung* (*westward drift*) *and Polarfluchtkraft* (*flight from the poles*). *Although real, these forces are minuscule and not likely to be the underlying cause of drift.* Scientific American 10/70, p41 [**1958**, from Latin *vector* carrier, but influenced in meaning by various modern technical uses of the noun]

vedutista (ˌveduˈtistə), *n.*, *pl.* **vedutisti** (ˌveduˈtisti:). an artist who paints or draws panoramic views of places, usually towns and cities. *Another school which has risen dramatically in popular esteem in recent years is that of the Venetian vedutisti of the eighteenth century.* Times (London) 5/9/70, p19 . . . *an exhibition of drawings by an eighteenth-century Florentine named Giuseppe Zocchi, who rendered the world around him exactly as he saw it. Zocchi was a vedutista, or depicter of views, and the eighteenth century was a time of viewmaking.* New Yorker 5/18/68, p32 [**1962**, from Italian, from *veduta* a painting or drawing of a place, (literally) a view + *-ista* -ist; *veduta* has been in English use since about 1900]

veejay, *n. Slang.* another word for VIDEO JOCKEY. . . . *a video jockey—or "veejay," a cross between a disc jockey and a TV emcee* . . . NY Times 7/4/82, pC17 [**1982**, from the pronunciation of V.J.]

veer, *n.* a type of offense in American football, using a variation of the T-formation, in which the quarterback pitches the ball to a running back or runs with it himself. Compare WISHBONE. *"We feel we have the personnel to run the veer," says Jordan. "Our quarterbacks are able to read defenses and they can execute the option."* Southeastern Football (Nashville, Tenn.) Pre-Season Ed., 1974, p20 [**1974**, transferred sense of a shift in direction, because the quarterback usually runs laterally before pitching the ball back or running upfield]

veganist (ˈviːgənist), *n. Especially British.* a person who practices vegetarianism in which no animals or animal products are used; strict vegetarian. Compare OVOLACTARIAN. *I like, too, his* [John Hawthorn's] *swipe at the veganists whose diet in Britain "is a form of slow but certain suicide unless* [it] *is supplemented with vitamin B12."* New Scientist 2/3/72, p287 [**1972**, from earlier *veganism* and *vegan* (1944), from *vegetable* + *-an*]

vegetablize, *v.t.* to turn into lifeless, inert creatures. *They charged that the Establishment's scheme for dealing with heroin addicts . . . was to vegetablize them, give them their junk, keep them passive and on the nod.* NY Times Magazine 7/2/72, p7 —*v.i.* to be or live like a vegetable; lead a monotonous existence; vegetate. *She doesn't want children: "I think I'm a bit frightened by the whole childbearing thing and the effect I've seen it have on my friends—sort of vegetablizing while it's going on."* Times (London) 7/20/70, p5 [**1970**, from *vegetable* a person who is like a vegetable (OEDS 1921) + *-ize*] ►This verb was used in the 1800's in the transitive form as a technical term meaning to convert to a vegetable substance. —**vegetablization**, *n.*: . . . *another phrase common in psychiatric circles, namely "the social breakdown syndrome"—the vegetablization of patients whose hospital doors not only don't revolve, but never open at all.* NY Times Magazine 4/30/72, p48

veggies or **vegies** (ˈvedʒiːz), *n.pl. Informal.* vegetables. *They wash and chop veggies and hand them out at the right time to the right people.* New Yorker 3/8/76, p28 *He pushes away his cole slaw. "You should eat it," I say. "No no; can't eat vegies," he says.* Harper's 2/72, p80 [**1955**, by shortening and alteration of *vegetables*]

Velcro, *n.* Also popularly spelled **velcro**. a trade name for a nylon fabric used as a fastener, having two strips with tiny hooks and loops that fasten on being pressed together. *They also considered covering both the floor and the soles of the shoes with Velcro, the material that clings to itself by microscopic hooks in its fibres, but since Velcro, which holds very well against any vertical pull, gives way when it is peeled sidewise, they found that an astronaut in Velcro shoes would come unhooked if he leaned over.* New Yorker 2/27/71, p33 *The*

proofed poplin coat has a zip-up front for cold weather wear; a quick-fasten velcro strip for brief sorties to feed the meter or dive into a restaurant. Times (London) 2/23/68, p12 [**1960**, from French *Velours croché* hooked velvet]

verbal, *n.* a verbal confession introduced as evidence at a trial. *. . . in criminal cases, upwards of three quarters of convictions secured at trial are the result of confessions or "verbals," alleged admissions by the defendant at time of arrest, put in evidence by the police. Many barristers believe that verbals are all too often invented by the police.* Atlantic 2/70, p22 [**1963**]

verkrampte (fərˈkrɑːmptə), *n.* the name given in South Africa to a person holding narrow-minded or ultraconservative views, especially in favoring rigid policies toward black Africans (often used attributively). *After Vorster dropped him from the Cabinet in 1968, Hertzog became leader of South Africa's* verkramptes (*narrow-minded ones*), *in opposition to Vorster's* verligtes (*enlightened ones*). Time 10/24/69, p38 [**1967**, from Afrikaans, literally, cramped (one)]

verligte (fərˈlixtə), *n.* the name given in South Africa to a person holding broad-minded or progressive views, especially in favoring moderate policies toward black Africans (often used attributively). *If the verkramptes of Louis Stoffberg and Dr Herzog win the day, against Mr Vorster's* verligtes *and their good neighbour policy towards black Africa, it will be a useful gain for Peking.* Manchester Guardian Weekly 7/24/69, p14 *The campaign is being fought largely in the press and, apparently, behind the scenes in Afrikaner political circles as a further manifestation of the "verkrampte" (reactionary) versus "verligte" (enlightened) factions in the ruling Nationalist Party.* Times (London) 8/5/68, p4 [**1967**, from Afrikaans, literally, enlightened (one)]

vernier rocket, a small auxiliary rocket engine used for minute adjustments in velocity or trajectory, as before a spacecraft softlands or docks. *On Jan. 9, 1968, following a 66-hour flight, a large retrorocket and three smaller vernier rockets slowed Surveyor VII from 6,000 to 3 mph.* World Book Science Annual 1968, p42 [**1958**, from *vernier* a scale or device used for making fine adjustments in a mechanism or equipment (named after French mathematician *Vernier*, 1580-1637)]

vertical divestiture, the disposal of a company's holdings in related operations or businesses whose control allows it to regulate activities in a market or business. Compare HORIZONTAL DIVESTITURE. *Proponents of the effort call it vertical divestiture, by which they mean forcing the largest oil companies to pick one activity—production or refining or transportation/marketing—and sell off the other parts of the action. As it is today, a company like Exxon is vertically integrated in its operations in such a way that it controls everything from the oil well to the retail pump.* NY Times Magazine 10/3/75, p15 [**1975**]

vertical proliferation, increase in the number of nuclear weapons among nations. Compare HORIZONTAL PROLIFERATION. *Two questions dominate the argument about the threat to mankind from nuclear weapons. One ("vertical proliferation," which can equally well be called upward spread) is the size of the arsenals already possessed by the six countries, including India, which have carried out nuclear tests and especially the size of the American and Russian arsenals.* Manchester Guardian Weekly 1/29/78, p10 [**1966**]

vertiport, *n.* a landing and takeoff area for VTOL aircraft. Also called VTOLPORT. *The major part of the Southampton team's survey . . . has been concerned with possible sites for 'vertiports' in or near the city centres of these candidate towns.* Science Journal 3/70, p6 [**1963**, from *vertical* takeoff and landing + air*port*]

Vertisol, *n.* (in U.S. soil taxonomy) any of a group of soils having a large proportion of clay forming deep surface cracks, found in regions with one or more dry seasons. *Dark, cracking tropical clays, that is, vertisols, are characteristic of . . . the restricted clay plugs and back swamps of the Omo Floodplain.* Nature 5/2/70, p429 [**1960**, from *vertical* + *-sol* (from Latin *solum* soil)]

vestibulectomy, *n.* surgical removal of the sensors of equilibrium in the vestibule of the inner ear. *Another mechanism contributing to the remarkable recovery in the coordination of the eye-head movements that occurs within the first two to three months following vestibulectomy entails a "recalibration" of saccadic eye movements with respect to visual input.* Scientific American 10/74, p106 [**1974,** from *vestibule* + *-ectomy* surgical removal]

veto-proof, *adj. U.S.* (of a legislature or legislation) protected or safe from a veto or vetoes, especially by the President. *There is even an outside chance that the election could produce a "veto-proof Congress," with the Democrats controlling two-thirds of both the House and the Senate.* Time 10/14/74, p13 [**1957**]

vexillologist, *n.* a student of flags. *Vexillology sounds rather like an obscure branch of tropical medicine, which for the vexillologists of the world must be rather vexing. But the almost universal ignorance of the discipline is understandable, since it is so new. Vexillology, the study of flags, has only just fluttered into the dictionaries.* Time 10/1/73, p44 [**1961**]

vexillology, *n.* the study of flags. *Vexillology is not normally a very vexed subject. It concerns the design, making and history of flags.* Daily Telegraph (London) 11/19/71, p13 [**1959,** from Latin *vexillum* a flag or banner + English *-ology* study of]

V gene, a gene that codes for the variable portion of an immunoglobulin (protein antibody). *An individual mammal can make in its lifetime an astonishing variety of antibodies that differ in amino-acid composition. These differences in structure appear in a variable part of the immunoglobulin molecule, which is otherwise constant. The variable part is under the control of one or only a few V genes.* 1976 Britannica Yearbook of Science and the Future, p343 [**1970,** short for *variable gene*]

vibes, *n.pl. Slang.* an intuitive feeling about a person or thing. *"The vibes were bad," he said affably. "On Friday night, they were beautiful. You couldn't walk twenty-five feet up on the hill without someone smiling at you. But things began going bad yesterday afternoon."* New Yorker 7/17/71, p80 *"We're not getting the right vibes," I said.* Sunday Times (London) 10/1/67, p10 [**1967,** short for *vibrations* (figurative use, 1899)]

vibriocidal (ˌvibriˈəˈsaidəl), *adj.* destroying vibrios (a genus of bacteria, a species of which causes cholera); vibrio-killing. *The vaccine now in use (killed V. cholerae) elicits formation of vibriocidal antibody, which reacts with the somatic, or cell-wall, antigen of the organism. In contrast, the antibody produced in response to pure toxin (or pure toxoid) is an antitoxin that inactivates toxin but has no vibriocidal activity.* Science 2/9/73, p554 [**1962,** from *vibrio* (OEDS 1850) + *-cidal* destroying, killing (from *-cide* killer, killing + *-al*, adj. suffix)]

Vibroseis (ˈvaibrouˌsaiz), *n.* the trademark of a system for locating oil or gas underground without the use of explosives by measuring reflected sound waves produced by a large vibrator that strikes the ground repeatedly. *Then four 22-ton trucks, the thumpers or vibrators, lined up nose-to-tail like a train of circus elephants. Each truck was equipped with a mechanism, called Vibroseis, that presses a steel plate to the ground, vibrates it, and sends tremors of seismic waves deep below the surface.* Encyclopedia Science Supplement (Grolier) 1982, p181 [**1968,** from *vibra*tor + connecting *-o-* + *seis*mic]

vicariance, *n.* the geographical separation of similar species of plants or animals by barriers such as mountain ranges and oceans resulting from massive displacements of the earth's crust. *Dr. Niles Eldridge, an American Museum paleontologist, said at the opening session that "the debate here is whether a certain pattern of species distribution was caused by dispersal or vicariance."* NY Times 5/8/79, pC2 [**1957,** from earlier *vicariant* that evolved from a common stock in areas separated by geographical barriers (1952), from German *vikarirend,* Latin *vicārius* that takes the place of another (used in the broad sense of being placed in widely separated areas)]

victimless, *adj. Especially U.S.* (of legal offenses) not having or involving a victim. *Drug offenses are on the whole "victimless"*

crimes. Possessing or using a drug is usually a private act. Even drug sales occur in private with other consenting persons. Drug offenses seldom impinge so forcefully on others that they feel impelled to notify the police. Norman E. Zinberg and John A. Robertson, Drugs and the Public, 1972, p219 *"Victimless sex laws," said Marilyn Haft, director of the Sexual Privacy Project of the American Civil Liberties Union, "are just a way of one group imposing their morality upon another group. They are used as a weapon against 'undesirables,' like hippies, homosexuals. Sex is something most people do, but only a select few are prosecuted for."* New York Post 6/21/75, p23 *Over the dissent of one member, a federally financed advisory committee has urged state legislatures to go slow in decriminalizing or legalizing so-called victimless crimes such as gambling, prostitution and pornography.* NY Times 12/26/76, p39 [**1965**]

victimologist, *n.* a specialist in victimology. *There is less consensus about the role of the victim in rape cases. Some victimologists contend that rape victims invite attack. But Amir believes that fewer than 20% of rapes are precipitated by the woman's being "negligent or reckless or seductive."* Time 7/5/71, p46 [**1971**]

victimology, *n.* the study of victims and their roles in the crimes committed against them. *For the first time in the U.S. three courses in victimology are being offered, one at the University of California, the others at Northeastern University and at Boston University Law School.* Time 7/5/71, p46 [**1958**]

Victor Charlie, *U.S. Military Slang.* **1** a Vietcong guerrilla. Also shortened to CHARLIE. *Nobody can hear Westmoreland talk about Vietnam with the military cliché of "real estate," or hear his men say they have to get them one "Victor Charlie," without being aware that the American killer-boy scout is one of the more brutal dangers to be unleashed on this sad, sad world.* Saturday Night (Canada) 8/68, p15 **2** the Vietcong. *He asked the young man where he had acquired all this erudition, and was told about being shot out of a helicopter by Victor Charlie and about relieving eight months of hospital tedium by reading science.* New Yorker 6/18/66, p135 [**1966,** from *Victor Charlie,* the communications code name for *VC,* abbreviation of *Vietcong*]

vidarabine (vidˈærəˌbin), *n.* another name for ARA-A. *An infectable drug, Vidarabine, that successfully treats herpes simplex virus encephalitis, a rare but often deadly viral infection, was approved for use by the Federal Drug Administration.* World Book Science Annual 1980, p268 [**1977,** from Latin *vidēre* to see (because the drug is often used to treat viral infections of the eye) + *arab*inose + aden*ine*]

video, *n.* a videotaped recording, as of a motion picture or a dramatization of a popular song. *More and more, hits were made in dance-rock clubs, both through records being played there and through custom-made videos much like those shown on Britain's Top of the Pops show.* 1982 Collier's Encyclopedia Year Book, p361 [**1968,** short for VIDEOTAPE]

video art, a form of art utilizing videotapes to produce abstract or representational works; art that uses or stresses the visual effects of television. *The video art of Nam June Paik, Bruce Nauman, and Vito Acconci provided occasion for thought rather than compelling forms for the eye, but engineers continue to extend the possibilities for richer visual experience.* Americana Annual 1975, p105 *The video world is much larger than the art world, and people who eventually wind up making video art can have very diverse backgrounds in the medium. Consequently, the term "video art" does not describe any single unified style; it indicates a shared medium.* RF Illustrated 3/76, p9 [**1972**] —**video artist:** *Mr. Gillette, whose new work is part of a 12-piece cycle with an ecological theme, is one of a growing breed of video artists, for whom the TV screen has become an esthetic medium.* NY Times 4/14/75, p33

videocassette, *n.* a cassette containing a videotape for showing on a television screen. *The major issue at stake was whether performers would share in profits from the growing market of cable and pay television, videocassettes, and videodisks.* 1981 Collier's Encyclopedia Year Book, p349 [**1970**]

videocassette recorder, a machine for playing videotapes and for recording television programs from a television set onto videotape cassettes. *Abbreviation:* VCR *The video-cassette recorder was introduced* [into the mass market] *in 1975. It boasted, correctly, that the owner could watch one channel while recording another.* 1978 World Book Year Book, p52 *The introduction of video cassette recorders, which allow us to record television programs we can't be home to watch, . . . type us as busy, working, afraid-to-miss-anything people.* NY Times 5/3/79, pC14 **[1971]** —**videocassette recording:** *Allied Artists . . . plans to offer videocassette recordings of all future movie releases.* Reader's Digest 2/79, p142

videoconference, *n.* a teleconference in which the participants can see each other on television screens. *Whether a face-to-face meeting is in any sense 'better' than a videoconference is a different question.* Times (London) 6/25/83, p8 —**v.i.** to communicate by videoconference. *More general communications activities—like telephone facsimile, and videoconferencing—also benefit from high rates of data transfer . . .* New Scientist 1/8/81, p74 **[1977]**

videodisk or **videodisc**, *n.* a disk for recording information, especially images, in digital form. *Thin flexible video discs which can be played through an ordinary domestic TV set have been developed . . . The necessary reproduction equipment is far cheaper than that required for the various cassette systems more generally favoured at present.* Science Journal 10/70, p16 *The amount of information a single videodisk can hold is truly staggering. A videodisk can store two gigabytes on a side, for a total of four gigabytes, or four billion characters.* NY Times 6/7/83, pC2 **[1967]**

video display terminal or **visual display terminal**, a computer terminal with a display screen and a keyboard. *Abbreviation:* VDT *A V.D.T., or Video Display Terminal, is a machine that combines a television screen with a typewriter keyboard and is connected to what Dr. Strangelove might call a "gigantic network of computers"; words are typed onto the screen, before finding their way to paper.* New Yorker 3/1/76, p23 *The news agency DPA (Deutsche Presse Agentur) has introduced computers and "screens" (visual display terminals or VDTS) without industrial strife and without a single redundancy.* New Scientist 4/12/79, p116 **[1970]**

video game, a game played by manipulating points of light on a television screen or other display screen by means of an electronic or computerized control device. Compare COMPUTER GAME. *There are two types of video games. The cheaper, "dedicated" type is designed to provide a number of "ball-and-paddle" games—usually tennis or ping-pong, hockey, squash or handball (some models refer to it as jai alai), and a practice game that one person can play alone. A few models also have simple target games . . . The second type is the programmable video game. It relies on a microprocessor, a small computer-like device, to provide the potential for an almost unlimited variety of games. Some programmable models come with a few games built right in.* Consumer Reports 11/77, p630 **[1973]**

videogram, *n.* a videotaped motion picture, especially one that is not a copy of a cinematographic film. *A pointer to the future is a scheme to be launched by IPC of its MirrorVision project of videograms, which will give the best known of writers a new medium to work in.* Times (London) 1/25/80, p1 **[1972]**

videographer, *n.* a person who produces videograms. *Composer Richard Feliciano collaborated with videographer Stephen Beck in January 1971 on* Point of Inflection, *a high geometric work in which diamonds re-form as squares, and periodic waves interrupt the screen.* Harper's 6/72, p90 **[1972]**

video jockey, an announcer for a program of video recordings of popular music. *Abbreviation:* V.J. *"Many of the dance clubs that young singles go to now have installed videocassette recorders and large screens. Kids dance to promotional clips from record companies, music videos by performers like Michael Jackson, Culture Club and Prince. In some clubs there are video jockeys. Instead of turntables, you have two Advent screens."* NY Times 6/4/83, p15 **[1982]**

videophile, *n.* a lover or devotee of television, ⟨⟩ visual aspects or components. *One interesting ⟨⟩ video technology, which has thus far been ⟨⟩ videophiles, is the growing selection of accessories.⟨⟩* Magazine 9/27/81, p74 **[1976]**

videophone, *n.* a telephone combined with a televisio⟨⟩ and screen so people talking on the telephone can ⟨⟩ other. Also called VIDEOTELEPHONE and VIEWPHONE.⟨⟩ *personal communication side, apart from videophones⟨⟩ diotelephones small enough to be carried in the pocket, ⟨⟩ the main trend as being towards far greater communicati⟨⟩ tween the ordinary person and computers of all kinds.* Su⟨⟩ Times (London) 9/24/67, p2 **[1955, 1967]**

videoplayer, *n.* another name for VIDEOCASSETTE RECORD⟨⟩ *In October 1969, Sony Corporation announced it would m⟨⟩ ket a videoplayer that uses cassettes similar to those used ⟨⟩ tape recorders. An adapter will permit home recording in bla⟨⟩ and white or color on the cassettes.* Encyclopedia Science Sup⟨⟩ plement (Grolier) 1970, p358 **[1970]**

videoporn, *n. Informal.* pornographic movies on videocassettes ⟨⟩ or cable television. *The traveller meets mattresses of all kinds. ⟨⟩ Touring in the US he can even find rooms with waterbeds and ⟨⟩ video-porn.* Sunday Times (London) 4/12/81, p21 **[1979]**

video-record, *v.t. Especially British.* to record on videotape; to videotape. *The National Archives at Washington DC are video-recording news programmes off the air for preservation, and there are, throughout the world, at least a dozen other archives known to the International Film and Television Council of UNESCO which collect television material.* Listener 2/26/76, p244 **[1961]**

videot, *n. U.S. Slang.* a person who watches too much television. *"I went to see him as a seer of the post-McLuhan age, . . . frightened at the rapid change television has effected on the collective psyche of America—a country he described in the mid-seventies as a nation of 'videots.' " The average American graduate student will have spent 18,000 hours watching television by the time he graduates.* Listener 3/28/85 (page not known) **[1977**, blend of *video* the television medium (OEDS 1941) and *idiot;* or alteration of earlier (1966) *vidiot*]

videotape, *n.* a length of magnetic tape on which television or motion-picture images and sounds are recorded for showing on a display screen. *Mr. Williams's encounters with the sheik weren't the only damaging videotapes shown at the trial.* NY Times 5/3/81, pD2 —**v.t.** to record on videotape. *After the lesson Carter ran through the speech and watched a videotaped replay . . .* Time 7/30/79, p12 **[1960 for noun; 1963 for verb]**

videotelephone, *n.* another name for VIDEOPHONE. *You need not leave home from one day to another, and you will have your wife for company because she can browse through the shops on her screen, order the goods on her keyboard, and see Mother on videotelephone.* New Scientist and Science Journal 12/23/71, p232 **[1964]**

videotext or **videotex**, *n.* any system providing computerized information by the use of television, such as viewdata or teletext. *The British pioneered viewdata (now known as videotext according to international standards) with Prestel . . .* New Scientist 7/3/80, p49 *TELIDON is Canada's own videotex (video plus text) system, basically just a new way to pipe in information, using a keyboard to call up messages and illustrations on the TV screen.* Maclean's 1/7/80, p30 **[1978]**

Vidifont, *n.* a trademark for an electronic device that displays letters and numbers on a television screen by means of a keyboard. *165 people . . . will appear on home screens; twenty-one cameras, 16 of them the full-size "hard" variety, three handheld, one in a helicopter and one in the Goodyear blimp, five slow-motion "discs" for replays, and a vidifont, a computer-like machine that can instantaneously cough up players' names and statistics.* Time 1/10/77, p28 **[1972**, from *vidi-* visual (ultimately from Latin *vidēre*) + *font* set of type]

Viet (vyet), *U.S.* —*n.* a Vietnamese. *'No-one' said the GI 'sees the Viets as real people".* Sunday Times (London) 11/23/69, p13 *They were Viets, all 15 of them . . . asking me the question*

rican? American? Ameri-
tnamese. Said Ralph Com-
.pporting a government that
.sts. We don't have the support
.1/69, p21 [**1958,** short for *Viet-*

.ent of U.S. involvement in the war
.CENIK. *I would rather trust the deci-*
of 200 million Americans and 10 mil-
the noisy utterances of irresponsible
.itelligentsia and even well-intentioned
/15/66, p64 [**1965,** from *Viet*nam + -NIK]

.ystem or network providing computerized
.nking television sets to a computer and dis-
.ntout on the television screen. See PRESTEL,
.JEOTEXT. *UK Post Office engineers travelled to*
.iis week to investigate new German proposals on
.ng viewdata characters which could defuse a nasty
.ion between Britain and France. New Scientist
., p522 In education, Viewdata makes possible a sort
.vay Sesame Street *for handicapped children who need*
dually paced instruction in the home; in politics, it offers
.tional poll on issues of the moment; and at income tax
.e, it can do everything from providing data on laws and
.ocedures to making the calculations and delivering the re-
.urns to the revenue department. It even offers an elegant solu-
tion to postal paralysis; electronic mail. Maclean's 1/9/78,
p55 *The Federal Communications Commission is working on*
technical standards for viewdata right now. NY Times Magazine 9/23/79, p110 [**1975**]

viewership, *n.* the number of people who watch television or
a particular television program; the audience of viewers. *The*
book will receive not only a wide readership (it is already a se-
lection of the Book-of-the-Month Club) but also a wide viewer-
ship. The BBC has filmed The Age of Uncertainty *as a 13-part*
TV series. Time 4/4/77, p85 *Media freaks here may have read*
that television-viewership in the US declined in 1977, for the
first year since the Creation. Listener 6/22/78, p802 [**1954,**
patterned after *listenership* (1940's)]

viewphone, *n.* another name for VIDEOPHONE. *In association*
with the "viewphone", access could be gained, on demand, to
a wide range of information sources for local visual display on
the customer's screen. New Scientist 7/16/70, p22 [**1964**]

villagization, *n.* (in parts of Africa and Asia) the placement of
land under the control of villages. *But the nomadic use of the*
remaining area needs study; "villagization" in the Kenya sense
is unlikely to be the answer. Times (London) 3/31/67, p13 . . .
the majority of land-owners in more than 140,000 Indian vil-
lages have declared themselves in favour of Gramadan (gift of
village), a more radical concept which involves the principle of
villagisation (as distinct from nationalisation) of land. Manchester Guardian Weekly 8/22/70, p2 [**1963**]

-ville (-vil), a chiefly U.S. slang suffix used to form nouns (and
sometimes adjectives) denoting a state or condition characterizing a place, person, or thing. Typically an *-s* is added to the
root form together with *-ville.* The suffix often carries with it
the suggestion of smallness, backwardness, dullness, etc. The
place name suffix is not entirely unknown in Great Britain (e.g.
Perkinsville in County Durham, England), but it is rare. The
following is a selection of uses of *-ville* in the 1960's and 1970's:
—**Bananasville,** *n.:* . . . *a disparagement of a lazy tropical*
town, a world apart from "Bananasville," that frantic city
across the river from Shrinksville. NY Times Magazine
12/2/79, p18 —**doomsville,** *n.: The only sure-fire attractions?*
"Country-and-western music. If you brought Barbra Streisand
here, it would be doomsville." Maclean's 3/68, p19 —**for**
keepsville: *Or, as London sales chief Roy Kirkdorfer puts it,*
"When you sign on with Bernie, it's for keepsville." Sunday
Times (London) 6/5/66, p7 —**Nowheresville,** *n.: Sitting con-*
tentedly on the banks of the Illinois River in the very heartland
of America; Peoria has for years been the butt of jokes, the
gagman's tag for Nowheresville. Time 10/21/66, p26
—**Splitsville,** *n.: WASHINGTON—Oh, it started out as a bliss-*
ful romance. And now it looks as if it's headed for Splitsville.

Manchester Guardian Weekly (Washington Post section)
1/8/78, p15 —**Thinsville,** *n.: And there we are on the ship com-*
ing over. Look at you in the G.I. togs and look at me. Thinsvil-
le." New Yorker 1/20/73, p50 —**weirdsville,** *n.: Yorkville*
Village does measure up to the East Village in New York or
Haight Ashbury in San Francisco. It's an area that reads hippie
weirdsville to the old folks, refuge to runaway teenyboppers
and a place to play for rock musicians. Maclean's 2/68,
p39 See also the main entries DRAGSVILLE, DULLSVILLE, ENDS-
VILLE, and SQUARESVILLE.

vinblastine (vin'blæs,ti:n), *n.* an alkaloid derivative of the red
periwinkle of Madagascar, used in the treatment of leukemia
and lymphoma. . . . *actinomycin D and vinblastine . . . in-*
duce temporary remissions in certain types of cancer. 1971 Britannica Yearbook of Science and the Future, p224 [**1962,** from
Vinca rosea (the Latin name of the red periwinkle) +
leuko*blast* a budding white blood cell + *-ine* (chemical suffix)]

vincaleukoblastine (,viŋkə,lu:kou'blæs,ti:n), *n.* another name for
VINBLASTINE. *Of the alkaloids isolated some eight years ago*
from the periwinkle plant (Vinca), *experience has shown that*
two, vincristine and vincaleukoblastine, have therapeutic
value. Vincristine, combined with steroids, is proving useful in
treating acute leukemia of children . . . Vincaleukoblastine is
most useful in the treatment of conditions like Hodgkin's dis-
ease. Britannica Book of the Year 1969, p498 [**1962**]

vincristine (vin'kristi:n), *n.* an alkaloid derived from the periwinkle of Madagascar, used to treat acute leukemia. *Formula:*
$C_{46}H_{56}N_4O_{10}$ *Vincristine can cause constipation and is usually*
given in conjunction with a laxative or stool-softener. About
half the time, vincristine also causes children to lose their hair
temporarily. At the end of this initial four weeks, however,
about 90 to 95 percent of children have achieved a state called
remission. NY Times Magazine 12/10/78, p161 [**1962,** from
New Latin *Vinca,* the genus name of the periwinkle + Latin
crista crest + English *-ine*]

vinify, *v.t.* to make wine from; to convert the juice of (grapes,
etc.) into wine by fermentation. *They [Californians] like to*
drink wine, and despise New York State winemakers for trying
to vinify table grapes. Manchester Guardian Weekly 7/10/69,
p19 [**1969,** from Latin *vīnum* wine + English *-ify,* as in *fructi-*
fy, acidify, etc.]

Virazole ('vairə,zoul), *n.* a trademark for RIBA-VIRIN. *Medical*
scientists are finding or designing drugs that attack viruses se-
lectively, that is, by largely or even totally sparing the cells
that house them. Two of these drugs look especially promising
in the treatment of more serious viral diseases, those that strike
the body internally. One is Virazole. It has successfully coun-
tered flu in both animals and humans. Science News 8/20/77,
p116 [**1972,** from *virus* + *azole*]

virginiamycin (vər,dʒinyə'maisən), *n.* an antibacterial substance
derived from a species of streptomyces. Compare FLAVOMY-
CIN. *Only three true antibiotics may now be used in animal*
feeds without prescription. One is virginiamycin which . . .
significantly enhances rabbit growth over six- or eight-week
periods—and does not depress growth during the first two
weeks of feeding. New Scientist 1/6/72, p5 [**1969,** from (*Strep-*
tomyces) *virginiae,* the species from which the substance is derived + *-mycin* fungal substance]

viridian (və'ridi:ən), *adj.* green; verdant. . . . *I was uneasy, op-*
pressed by the viridian hills flecked with black, unmoving cat-
tle. New Yorker 6/13/70, p30 . . . *a geometrical forest scene*
drawn in vigorous triangular forms of yellow ochre, Venetian
red and black, and it is inhabited by three viridian nudes who
are clearly related to Cézanne's 'Bathers'. Listener 1/30/64,
p200 [**1950,** from Latin *viridis* green + English *-ian*]

virion, *n.* the mature, infective form of a virus, consisting of
RNA enclosed in a protein shell. . . . *in certain tumour-*
producing viruses the first two steps may be reversed and it is
RNA from the virus chromosome or virion which makes DNA.
Science Journal 9/70, p19 *We decided . . . to fractionate a*
number of virions, or virus particles, and to try to find a com-

ponent or components responsible for inducing interferon. Scientific American 7/71, p28 [1959]

virogene ('vairə,dʒi:n), *n.* a viral gene, especially one able, under certain conditions, to produce a carcinogenic virus within a normal cell. See C-TYPE VIRUS. *Endogenous viruses are postulated to be produced by a gene, known as a virogene, which may be part of the genetic complement of each member of a species.* Science 1/31/75, p336 *Tricks for getting the virogenes to express themselves as infectious viruses in cultured cells were discovered some time ago. But the viruses produced in this way are generally not very good at reproducing themselves in the animal, and seldom cause tumours, although they belong to the C-type cancer-causing group of viruses.* New Scientist 9/14/78, p768 [1969]

viroid, *n.* any of a group of infectious particles of RNA, smaller than any known viruses, that have been identified as the cause of various plant diseases. *Named a viroid, the infectious particle causes potato spindle tuber. . . The discovery may have implications in the elusive nature of some human diseases, such as multiple sclerosis, infectious hepatitis, and some types of cancer. Many plant and animal diseases whose causes have eluded scientists may also be caused by viroids.* Americana Annual 1972, p80 *Viroids have been identified by T. O. Diener as the smallest known agents of infectious disease. The molecular weight of viroids is estimated to be as little as 7.5-8.5 × 10⁴ daltons, in marked contrast to the conventional plant virus genomes, which have molecular weights of approximately 2 × 10⁶ daltons.* McGraw-Hill Yearbook of Science and Technology 1977, p417 [1971, coined by Theodor O. Diener of the U.S. Dept. of Agriculture, from *virus* + *-oid* one like] ▶In the 1940's and 1950's this term was used to describe a hypothetical viruslike organism capable of infecting a host cell or mutating into a virus.

virtual memory or **virtual storage**, a method of computer programming that permits the temporary transfer of internally stored programs to less expensive external memory devices, such as magnetic disks, making the computer's main memory or storage capacity appear to be much larger. *Virtual memory . . . provided for the efficient transfer of programs between the computer's main memory and auxiliary storage units. It is an exciting idea which hardly anyone in the business has ever been able to carry out effectively. RCA decided to concentrate its energies on developing a virtual memory system which would surpass the most advanced efforts of IBM.* Atlantic 5/72, p37 *Virtual storage is a combination of hardware and software that permits a programmer to ignore the physical capacity of the computer's memory; what spills over is kept on a disk or drum and retrieved automatically as needed.* Britannica Book of the Year 1973, p192 [1959, *virtual memory;* 1966 *virtual storage*]

virus, *n.* short for COMPUTER VIRUS. *Aldus officials said the virus contaminated a master program disk and had inadvertently been widely distributed as part of a three-day production run of the program . . .* NY Times 3/17/88, pD7 *In many cases, viruses spread through the illegal copying of software sold on diskettes. Industry experts believe, however, that viruses are transmitted mainly through electronic bulletin boards—public forums run by commercial database services.* World Book Science Annual 1989, p247 [1988, so called from the resemblance of its action to the behavior of biological viruses infiltrating cells]

visagiste (vi:za'ʒi:st), *n.* an expert in applying facial cosmetics; a makeup artist. *The crop-eared look is a natural for a new hair style and just imagine what the visagistes will be able to do recreating a historical Cromwell makeup, warts and all.* Times (London) 5/5/70, p9 [1958, from French, from *visage* face, visage + *-iste* -ist]

visceral learning, the faculty of acquiring control over involuntary bodily processes. *Psychologists were astounded when New York researchers demonstrated that humans and experimental animals could alter their heart rate, apparently at will. The nature of the phenomenon—known as visceral learning—is now*

being questioned because of data from recent new experiments. New Scientist 1/31/74, p269 [1970]

vision-mix, *v.i.* to combine film shots in motion pictures or camera views in television. *He* [Mike Leckebusch, a television director in Germany] *also vision mixes himself. In England and elsewhere it is the practice to employ vision mixers, the director shouting the appropriate shot numbers to him.* Times (London) 8/19/70, p11 *As a director, I* [Rollo Gamble, a BBC television director] *prefer light entertainment. I believe it really can be an art form, as television. It's great fun, vision-mixing. You have cameramen roaming around the studio, ad libbing shots within an overall plan, and you see something you like on the monitors and cut from one to another.* Punch 10/6/65, p508 [1961]

VISTA ('vistə), *n.* acronym for *Volunteers in Service to America,* a U.S. government agency providing programs of food distribution, employment, housing, etc., for low-income people. . . . *VISTA, the domestic Peace Corps.* Harper's 12/65, p44 [1964]

visual, *n.* Often, **visuals**, *pl.* Especially *U.S.* **1** a photograph, film, videotape, or other visual display. *"Today's children are exposed to extremely well-done visuals—on television and in printed media," the Zaner-Bloser series explains.* NY Times Magazine 5/23/76, p68 **2** a picture or film for promotion. *So today is farm day in the Carter campaign, and the Presidential candidate, in pursuit of the sort of "visual" that every Presidential candidate seeks, has come to Hans Sieverding's farm.* New Yorker 1/10/77, p43 [1961, originally (1950's) used in the plural to refer to the visual or soundless part of a motion picture]

visual artist, a person engaged in any of the visual arts, such as painting, photography, sculpture, and architecture. *The plight of the visual artist is described as deplorable, most having to resort to part-time jobs to supplement meagre earnings. The number and level of bursaries and fellowships should be increased, more artists-in-residence schemes encouraged and more public bodies should employ artists. Visual artists should also be paid for lending their work for exhibition in public and commercial galleries.* Times (London) 9/9/77, p3 [1974]

visual capture, the dominance of sight over the other senses when visual input conflicts with input perceived by any of the other senses. *A person wearing distorting spectacles tends to rely completely on vision for localising an object in space, even when other stimuli, for example sound from a loudspeaker, provide truer information. Psychologists call this "visual capture" and have assumed that it occurs because most of our spatial information is received through the eyes so the brain is in some way set to respond such that "seeing is believing."* New Scientist 5/6/76, p291 [1967]

visual display unit or **video display unit**, any device for displaying data from a computer, tape, etc., on a screen. *Abbreviation:* VDU *Visual display units equipped with microprocessors—designed at Warwick University—enabled Braille typists to produce small quantities of useful documents such as menus and knitting patterns quickly and cheaply in Braille, and to type music in Braille.* 1979 Annual Register, p386 *Engineers have at their disposal newly developed hardware and software, with modern distributed control systems using computer interface and video display units.* Engineering and Mining Journal 5/83, p99 [1968]

visual literacy, the ability to understand or appreciate things perceived through the sense of sight. See GRAPHICACY, ORACY. *In Nashville, Tennessee, next month, a conference on 'Visual Literacy' is being held—a subject not too remote from the language of dance and the language of sport.* Listener 2/26/76, p238 [1972]

visuospatial ('viʒuou'speiʃəl), *adj.* relating to or involving the field of vision, especially as it involves the relationships of space and configuration of objects seen. Compare SPATIO-PERCEPTUAL. *Psychological testing has repeatedly shown that girls are in general better at verbal skills, whereas boys are better at visuo-spatial skills (such as jigsaw puzzles).* Times (London) 5/5/76, p18 *About 60 percent of left-handed individuals have language functions in the left hemisphere and visuospa-*

tial functions in the right (the same as right-handed individuals). Science News 10/16/76, p247 [**1962**]

vitamin B₁₇, another name for LAETRILE. *Still a third assertion by Laetrile proponents is that Laetrile is a vitamin—vitamin B₁₇—and thus a nutritional substance rather than a drug . . . In contrast [Thomas H.] Jukes declares that Laetrile has "not the slightest resemblance to a vitamin. The crucial property of a vitamin is that its absence from the diet produces a specific deficiency disease in vertebrate animals. The cyanogenetic glycosides do not have this property."* Science News 8/6/77, p94 [**1976**]

vitrectomy, *n.* the surgical operation of removing a clouded or damaged vitreous humor from the eye and replacing it with a clear saline solution. *Vitrectomy works like a mini-vacuum cleaner, sucking blood and clots out of the vitreous and replacing their volume with clear saline. This scavenging restores optical clarity and prevents new retinal deformations.* Encyclopedia Science Supplement (Grolier) 1981, p230 [**1968**, from *vitreous* (humor) + *-ectomy* surgical removal]

v.j. or **V.J.,** abbreviation of VIDEO JOCKEY. *A "v.j.," short for "video jockey," is a person who appears between segments of video music to announce the names of rock groups and songs, give news reports on the pop music industry and, at times, conduct interviews with major performers.* NY Times 12/18/83, pB39 [**1983**]

VLA, abbreviation of *Very Large Array,* a system of radio telescopes coordinated to function as a unit in the U.S. National Radio Astronomy Observatory. *The VLA will consist of 27 radio reflectors, each one a fully steerable dish 82 feet in diameter. Arranged in a 39-mile-long, Y-shaped pattern, it will be built on the Plains of San Agustin, west of Socorro, N. Mex.* World Book Science Annual 1973, p269 [**1972**]

VLBI, abbreviation of *very long baseline interferometry,* a method used in radio astronomy for measuring signals from a radio source by matching tape recordings of the signals received simultaneously at widely separated radio telescopes. Compare APERTURE SYNTHESIS. *VLBI . . . gives a signal that can discern finer detail in the source than any single telescope could.* Science News 4/14/73, p239 [**1969**]

VLCC, abbreviation of *very large crude carrier,* a petroleum supertanker with a capacity of over 300,000 tons. Compare ULCC. *The present boom in ordering of VLCCs . . . has consolidated the position of 300,000 ton vessels, so that ships of this size can no longer be regarded as outside freaks.* Times (London) 7/17/73, pIV [**1968**]

VLDL, abbreviation of *very low-density lipoprotein,* a lipoprotein containing a very large proportion of lipids to protein, thought to carry most cholesterol from the liver to the tissues. Compare HDL and LDL. *VLDLs . . . are primarily responsible for transporting triglycerides, which result from dietary excesses of carbohydrates and calories, from the liver to the fatty deposits throughout the body.* NY Times 1/18/77, p13 [**1977**]

VLSI, abbreviation of *very large scale integration,* a microminiaturization technique for fabricating hundreds of thousands of integrated circuits as a unit on a single silicon chip. *Many experts believe that VLSI will make it possible, perhaps within five years, to compress the number-handling prowess of a modern, large computer into a single part about the size of a match head . . . In addition, products already given some electronic intelligence by LSI chips—ovens, clocks, traffic lights, to name a few—will become smarter with VLSI. Thus, the electric office typewriter, which became the electronic typewriter with the addition of a few memory chips, could be transformed by a superchip into a complete word-processing system allowing a user to edit substantial quantities of text before putting the final version on paper.* Wall Street Journal 4/27/79, p1 [**1976**]

voice-over, *n.* the voice of a narrator, commentator, or announcer speaking offscreen in a motion-picture film, television commercial, etc. (often used attributively). *The voiceover during the 60-second spot has been saying right along: "Cigarette smoke contains some interesting elements: carbon monoxide,*

formaldehyde, benzopyrene, hydrogen cyanide." Time 11/15/68, p58 *One hears [Henry] Miller's prose as one reads him . . . But when that same prose is used in the film as a voice-over narration, it doesn't have the drive of common speech, it has the static fake poetry of cultivated literary language.* New Yorker 3/7/70, p97 —**adv.** in a voice-over; speaking without being seen. *More cheers. A band started playing. Mr. Nixon stepped away from the ramp. "And now Mr. Nixon is plunging into the crowd," Mike Wallace said, voice-over.* New Yorker 11/16/68, p51 . . . *it's all done voice-over, except for the flashbacks before the war.* New Yorker 8/7/71, p65 [**1966** for noun, **1968** for adv.; extended from earlier noun sense of a narration spoken off screen (OEDS 1947)]

voiceprint, *n.* a graph of the patterns of pitch, juncture, etc., in a person's speech, produced on a sound spectrograph and regarded by some as sufficiently distinctive to be used for the purpose of individual identification. . . . *the assumed analogy between fingerprints and voiceprints is false: finding a similarity between fingerprints involves the objective study of anatomical evidence but finding a similarity between voiceprints is a matter of subjective judgment on the observer's part.* Scientific American 12/69, p54 . . . *unless the protagonists of voiceprints can come up with a far more rigorous proof of the technique's validity than they have provided hitherto, its use in courts of law is more likely to hinder the course of justice than aid it.* New Scientist 4/30/70, p216 [**1962**]

voiceprinter, *n.* an apparatus for producing voiceprints. *Another major protagonist [of The First Circle, a novel by Aleksandr Solzhenitsyn] is Lev Rubin, the philologist who develops the voiceprinter.* Time 9/27/68, p26 [**1966**]

voiceprinting, *n.* the method of identification based on voiceprints. *One of the most interesting examples involved the identification of Nasser and Hussein as the speakers in a radio conversation conspiring to blame the United States and Great Britain for the Arab failure in the Middle East war, a use of voiceprinting which was widely publicized.* Encyclopedia Science Supplement (Grolier) 1968, p352 [**1962**]

volcaniclastic (vɑlˌkænəˈklæstik), *adj.* consisting of volcanic fragments or sediments. *The only close-up of an outcrop of welded tuff (plate 168A) is a highly atypical example. A geologist who seeks guidance in distinguishing between the various kinds of volcaniclastic rock will be disappointed.* Nature 8/4/72, p294 —**n.** a volcaniclastic rock. *The major detrital sources were nearby granitic batholiths and andesitic lava flows, all of late Mesozoic age, rhyolitic volcaniclastics of Cenozoic age, and uplifted sedimentary rocks of all ages.* Science 11/3/72, p503 [**1961**, blend of *volcanic* and *clastic*]

volcanogenic (ˌvɑlkænəˈdʒenik), *adj.* originating in or produced by volcanoes. *In the Indian Ocean gaps in the sedimentary record have been encountered in a broad spectrum of terrigenous, pelagic, biogenic and volcanogenic sediments encompassing late Mesozoic and Cainozoic time.* Nature 1/3/75, p15 [**1965**, from *volcano* + *-genic* produced by]

volunteerism, *n.* U.S. and Canada. action or service by volunteers, especially in social welfare. *This is a government with a commitment to volunteerism, and letting people do more things for themselves.* Maclean's 9/10/79, p24 *That was the Democratic style for nearly a half-century of dominance in American politics, and indeed it replaced and made largely irrelevant the personal ward politics of a Plunkitt. Whether a modernized Republican version, dubbed volunteerism, will help bring things full circle is anybody's guess.* NY Times 4/19/81, pD2 [**1977**]

voucher plan or **voucher system,** *U.S.* a system for allotting tax revenues in the form of redeemable certificates which a parent can apply as tuition in a private school. *On the national level the alternative receiving the most attention was the voucher plan, which would permit parents to decide whether they wanted to send a child to the public schools or to some private or church school.* Britannica Book of the Year 1972, p271 *A voucher system, he [John E. Coons] contends, would improve education by eliminating the monopoly that the public schools* *now have, in a system . . . in which the rich get choice and deductions, and the poor get sent.* NY Times 12/4/79, pC5 **[1970]**

vox pop, *British Informal.* an opinion on some current topic given by a person who is stopped in the street and questioned by a television or radio reporter. *A few days ago, a BBC camera crew went round Washington collecting vox pops—close-ups of men in the street saying pithily what they think of things.* Listener 2/8/68, p164 *"You find a different class of people in England", we are assured by one vox pop.* Times (London) 11/20/68, p9 **[1964,** shortened from Latin *vōx populi* the voice of the people, the expressed general opinion (attested in the *OED* since about 1550). "The Latin maxim *Vox Populi vox Dei* 'the voice of the people is the voice of God', is frequently cited or alluded to in English works from the 15th cent. onwards" (*OED*).]

VRM, abbreviation of VARIABLE RATE MORTGAGE. *After VRMs were introduced in California in 1975 by some savings and loan companies, two of the largest of these made 80 percent of all their new mortgage loans in the form of VRMs. This was great for the savings and loan associations because they were insulating themselves from the usual money squeeze that banking institutions feel when rates rise.* Alix Granger, Don't Bank on It, 1981, p178 **[1979]**

vroom, *n. U.S.* the roaring sound of a racing-car or motorcycle engine. See also VAROOM. *The trooper lies on his back, drinking a Pepsi-Cola and reading* Hot Rod *magazine, hearing the vroom-vroom of engines, seeing the open highway in the mind's eye.* Atlantic 10/70, p75 *They* ["Nam's Angels"] *are not satisfied, however, with their Hondas, which are underpowered for the workout they get on a patrol through the boondocks . . . The foursome would prefer tough scramblers, "with big drive sprockets, knobby wheels—and more vroom."* Time 5/2/69, p33 **[1968,** imitative of the sound]

V/STOL (ˈviːˌstoul), *n.* acronym for *vertical* or *short takeoff and landing,* a cover-all term for VTOL and STOL. *Technical and operating problems have hampered the growth of V/STOL (vertical or short takeoff and landing) aircraft, light airplanes, and helicopters in serving the market for transporting travelers to major airports from home or office.* Americana Annual 1967, p29 **[1961]**

VTOL (ˈviːˌtoul), *n.* acronym for *vertical takeoff and landing,* used to describe an aircraft other than a helicopter that can take off and land vertically. *In another two or three years these new crossbreeds between a small plane and a helicopter, the VTOL fans believe, will take us from tiny landing fields or even rooftops anywhere in our metropolitan areas to airports or nearby cities. Perhaps. Those VTOLs will be hellishly noisy and sound no more pleasant than their name.* Harper's 3/67, p75 **[1955]**

VTOLport, *n.* another name for VERTIPORT. Compare STOL-PORT. *The reason, it said, was the need for less land area for VTOLports and for fewer planes because VTOL planes spend less time on the ground.* NY Times 3/26/67, p54 **[1967]**

vulcanist, *n.* another name for HOT MOONER. *The moon remains a puzzle, and there is still no solution to the question about crater origin. At the moment, vulcanists remain vulcanists and impact supporters remain impact supporters.* New Scientist and Science Journal 1/28/71, p185 **[1971]**

VX, symbol for a very lethal nerve gas. *The chemical formula of VX is still a secret, although the WHO* [World Health Organization] *report suggests that the agent is ethyl S-dimethylaminoethyl methylphosphonothiolate . . . Also a liquid but several times more toxic than Sarin and much less volatile. VX is lethal either when inhaled or deposited on the skin.* Scientific American 5/70, p18 **[1966]**

W

wacko, *Chiefly U.S. Slang.* —*adj.* crazy; eccentric; wacky. *Gizmo! - A cheerful* ʁ*etrospective documentary about old-time amateur inventors and wacko performers (Americans, for the most part) and their feats, as recorded in many dozens of old newsreel clips and publicity films dating back forty or fifty years or more. Take the children.* New Yorker 3/17/80, p24 —*n.* a crazy or eccentric person. *Most of the involuntary pedestrians' responses were polite, and on the few occasions when someone gave him some back talk he* [Mayor E. Koch] *simply dismissed the troublemaker as "a wacko."* New Yorker 4/28/80, p108 [**1977**, from *wacky* crazy (OEDS 1935) + *-o*, as in *blotto, socko, weirdo,* etc.]

wafer, *n.* a small, thin disk of silicon or other semiconductor containing one or more integrated circuits. Wafers are usually 3 to 5 inches in diameter. Compare CHIP. *By suitable masking and "doping" techniques, which selectively altered the electrical behavior of small regions, several score transistors could be created on each wafer.* Scientific American 2/70, p22 [**1956**]

wafer chip, a wafer-sized silicon chip provided with a circuitry equal to the power of a hundred or more microchips. *Because processing video images takes so much memory and computer power, image processing could be the main near-term market for wafer chips, says Bernd K.F. Koenemann, a senior engineering fellow at Honeywell. For example, the key to the wrist-watch-size TV set recently introduced by Japan's NTT is a "miniwafer" memory chip.* Business Week 11/12/84, p154J [**1981**]

wage drift, an upward movement of wages resulting in an increase in average earnings over the official average wage rates of a country. *What the report revealed was this—"wage drift," or the addition to workers' earnings that local bargaining adds to national wage agreements, has been running at a rate of 4 per cent., a year, and not the 2 per cent., that has been officially estimated.* Sunday Times (London) 5/19/68, p34 [**1963**]

wage-push inflation, the cost-push resulting from inflationary wage increases. *Wage-push inflation got its strongest nudge in construction; union craftsmen wrung out raises averaging 17 ½ %.* Time 12/28/70, p53 [**1968**]

wage-stop, *v.t.* British. to limit the government benefits of (an unemployed person) to the level received while working. *Ninety per cent of the people wage-stopped under the NJC* [National Joint Council] *ruling would be lifted back to full benefit, and the total number of wage-stop cases would be halved.* Sunday Times (London) 8/8/71, p9 [**1963**]

waitron, *n.* U.S. a waiter or waitress (used to eliminate the reference to the subject's sex). *Sandwiches are larger and reasonable . . . The waitrons are efficient and friendly—and not in that forced, chatty way that seems like someone just pulled a string at the base of their necks.* Washington Post 11/11/83, p7 [**1980**, blend of *waiter* or *waitress* and *-tron,* as in *neutron* (to suggest, perhaps jocularly, a *neuter* gender)]

walk, *n.* the slow orbiting of a spacecraft around a celestial body. *The three drifting "walks" by the orbiters have been particularly valuable to the radio team in refining the shape of the Martian gravitational field.* Science News 11/20/76, p326 —*v.i.* to follow a slow orbit. *Because the pathway of Viking 2 "walks" around the planet every nine days or so, it can study different regions at different times of day.* NY Times 8/10/76, p12 [**1976**]

Walk, *n.* a dance usually done by several people in a line to disco music. It is characterized by steps similar to walking but also includes kicks and turns. *The new Walk, just to make things difficult, is an anathema to all this talk of returning ro-*

manticism, because you do it alone, without touching. You needn't even look at the person next to you. It does have style though, and it's friendly; you can hardly be a wallflower if you can Walk. Perhaps . . . the Walk is "a copout for people who can't Hustle."* New York Post 12/27/75, p23 —*v.i.* to dance the Walk. *There is no shortage here of glittering clubs in which to hustle, walk, bump or samba the night away.* NY Times 1/3/76, p10 [**1975**, earlier applied to other dance steps, such as the Walk (1937), Lambeth Walk (1937), camel walk (1921), cake-walk (1902 dance, 1879 competition)]

walking catfish, a species of catfish that can crawl over ground by means of its spiny fins and live on land for extended periods by taking in air through its auxiliary breathing apparatus. *An example of an imported species that became a dangerous threat to the freshwater ecology of the subtropical United States in less than two years is* Clarias batrachus, the *"walking catfish." It was imported by tropical-fish dealers from Southeast Asia; a few specimens escaped from aquariums into Florida waters.* 1970 Compton Yearbook, p119 [**1968**]

walking machine, a mechanical or robotic device attached to a person to serve as an extension or enlargement of the body, enabling the operator to climb large obstacles, cover a greater distance in walking, etc. Compare MAN AMPLIFIER. *A four-legged "walking machine" mimics and amplifies the movements of its human operator. The right front leg of the machine is controlled by the operator's right arm, the left front leg by his left arm, the right rear leg by his right leg, and the left rear leg by his left leg.* 1973 Britannica Yearbook of Science and the Future, p102 [**1971**]

walk-on, *n.* U.S. Sports. a team player who has not been drafted, scouted, etc.; a minor or unimportant member of a team. *. . . Martínez has had to make do with New Mexico talent, including one player who did not even come to Highlands on a basketball scholarship—a category of athlete known in the trade as "walk-ons."* New Yorker 3/3/80, p80 [**1974**, extended sense of the theatrical term meaning an actor who has a walk-on part (OEDS 1946)]

wall, *n.* **1 the Wall,** the 26-mile long wall dividing East and West Berlin. *. . . he is a photographer in a small town near Hamburg, she is a nurse in East Berlin. They meet casually and arrange to see each other again. Then the Wall separates them.* Atlantic 1/67, p117 [**1961**] **2 jump** (or **leap**) **over the wall,** to leave the church or a religious order. *No one knows exactly how many religious have jumped over the wall—partly because it is so easy today for a priest, nun or brother simply to take a leave of absence and never return.* Time 2/23/70, p51 *Mr. Vizzard was a Jesuit seminarian who yearned for the world, leapt over the wall, and found what he was looking for in Hollywood.* Harper's 4/70, p110 [**1970**] ▶The expression *leap over the wall* may have been popularized by the book *I Leap Over the Wall,* 1949, by Monica Baldwin (the niece of former British Prime Minister Stanley Baldwin), written after she left an enclosed religious order to which she had belonged from 1914 to 1941. **3 off the wall,** *U.S. Slang.* unconventional; unusual; out of the ordinary. See OFF-THE-WALL. *It's been suggested that when Kiss* [a rock group] *began, some of the boys didn't even know how to play instruments. "That is absolutely not true," says Delaney. "Kiss was so off the wall the rock critics didn't know what to say, so they dumped on them, talking about their 'three-chord knee-jerk' music and stuff like that."* NY Times Magazine 6/19/77, p69 *"Our meetings on the Guild business were right off the wall,"* he said to me afterward.

"Murdoch had his hit list, and he was highly emotional about it." New Yorker 1/22/79, p56 **[1968]**

wall-attachment effect, another name for COANDA EFFECT.... *the "wall-attachment" effect (a preference for moving along a wall rather than through an open space—one of the fundamentals of fluidics component design).* New Scientist 5/16/68, p350 **[1968]**

wallbanger, *n. U.S.* a cocktail consisting of vodka or gin with orange juice, and sometimes with rose hip tea or cinnamon. *"A wallbanger is . . . much the same as what they call an orange blossom, but the name of a wallbanger goes down better with the men when they're at a function. The vodka gives you a lift, you know."* New Yorker 9/30/72, p41 **[1970]**

wall cloud, another name for EYEWALL. *The eye* [of a hurricane] *is bounded by so-called "wall clouds," which are towering thunderstorm clouds that extend to great altitudes.* 1972 Britannica Yearbook of Science and the Future, p122 **[1966]**

wallcovering, *n.* a covering of plastic, fabric, etc., usually with ornamental designs, for pasting on interior walls. *The wallcovering on three walls is glossy yellow p.v.c.* [polyvinyl chloride] *by Nairn of Lancaster and the remaining wall surface is finished in plain white emulsion paint.* Times (London) 12/11/70, p16 **[1970]**

wallpaper music, *British.* recorded music piped into an office, restaurant, etc., through a public-address system; background music. *"It's the 'wallpaper music' I'm against—the plastic, bland pop stuff that churns out as a comfy background you don't really have to notice," says John Peel.* Sunday Times (London) 9/22/68, p3 **[1966]**

wallposter, *n.* a bulletin or newspaper written in large characters and containing political propaganda or information, posted on walls in public places in China. Also called DAZIBAO. *Wallposters have appeared at Shanghai University criticising senior Vice-Premier Teng Hsiao-ping as "China's new Khrushchev."* Manchester Guardian Weekly 2/22/76, p6 **[1966,** translation of Chinese (Pinyin) *dazubao* big-character poster]

wall system, a set of shelves, cabinets, and other modules designed to be mounted on or set against a wall in various ways. *Wall systems are the fastest-growing category of furnishings.* Christian Science Monitor 12/4/80, p17 **[1978]**

wall-to-wall, *adj. Chiefly U.S.* extending from one end or extreme to the other. *The only way you could counter their Mediterranean ships is with enough ships that there wouldn't be room for theirs—wall-to-wall ships.* Atlantic 5/70, p20 . . . *he made a highly successful series of wall-to-wall mood-music recordings with Jackie Gleason* . . . New Yorker 11/25/67, p222 **[1967,** figurative use of the term applied to carpeting covering an entire floor (OED 1953)]

wallyball, *n. U.S.* volleyball played in a walled court. *Wallyball, which its founders claim is the fastest growing indoor sport in the country, was designed by a Californian. But when the 1986 Inaugural Wallyball Tournament was held last weekend in Westerville, Ohio, teams from Brooklyn won five of the seven titles.* [. . . The sport was founded by Joe Garcia of Los Angeles in 1979.] Daily News (New York) 2/9/86, pB7 **[1985,** blend of *wall* and *volleyball*] —**wallyballer**, *n.:* . . . . *she organizes leagues for scores of regular players—and is a devoted wallyballer herself.* Newsweek 7/8/85, p63

waltz, *n. Slang.* a thing accomplished with ease; something simple; a breeze. . . . *his bold putt from twenty-five feet hit the back of the cup, jumped up in the air, landed outside the cup, and toppled in. After that, it was a waltz.* New Yorker 8/1/70, p62 *Though Dancer eased him up at the end, Nevele Pride won in a waltz.* Time 7/5/68, p38 **[1968,** from the slang verb phrase to *waltz through* something, meaning to do easily, breeze through it (OED 1887)]

Wankel engine (ˈwɑːŋkəl *or* ˈvɑːŋkəl), Often shortened to **Wankel**, *n.* an internal-combustion engine in which nearly triangular rotating pistons spin in one direction in a chamber without the reciprocating movement of a conventional engine. *Compared to the like-rated conventional engines, the Wankel is 30-*

50% *lighter and smaller, has 40% fewer parts, operates on non-leaded fuel, and is very responsive to antipollution devices.* 1972 Britannica Yearbook of Science and the Future, p332 **[1961,** named for Felix *Wankel*, born 1902, the German engineer who invented it]

wantable, *adj.* desirable; attractive. *This collection is not trend-setting nor is it haute couture in the traditional sense; the sole consistency is in skirt length. But it is extremely pretty, wantable and smart in a personal private way.* Times (London) 7/21/70, p7 **[1970]**

warden, *v.i.* to guard or protect as a game warden. *The flight of one young bird represented the culmination of many weeks' continuous wardening by the Nature Conservancy and the Royal Society for the Protection of Birds* . . . Times (London) 8/1/70, p3 **[1962,** verb use of the noun]

warehouse, *U.S.* (used disparagingly). —*n.* any large and impersonal public facility for the care of the mentally ill, the aged, the poor, etc. *But for most of Willowbrook's residents, the institution is a warehouse, a place capable of providing only shelter and the barest essentials, for those whose families are either unwilling or unable to care for them.* Time 2/14/72, p67 *We ought to protect our families from the emotional and material burden of such diseased individuals, and from the misery of their simply "existing"* (not living) *in a nearby "warehouse" or public institution.* Joseph Fletcher, The Ethics of Genetic Control, 1974, p157 —*v.t.* to commit to a place of this kind. . . . *large custodial institutions where people are warehoused and where they are denied the opportunity to develop their full potential* . . . Tuscaloosa News (Alabama) 2/22/72, p1 *California's shift from the "warehousing of the mentally ill" in large state mental institutions has become a model for the nation.* National Review 12/7/73, p1259 **[1970]**

warfighting, *n.* combat between ballistic missiles; warfare conducted by using missiles to attack or intercept enemy missiles (often used attributively). *He* [General Brown] *agreed that the American-Soviet balance currently remained in "rough equivalence"* . . . *His formal report declared: "I now believe the Soviets are striving to achieve warfighting capabilities which, if war occurred, could leave them in the better relative position."* Times (London) 1/26/77, p6 **[1965,** probably from *war*head + *fighting*]

war-game, *v.t.* to examine or test (a plan, strategy, etc.) by means of a war game (simulated military confrontation). *At one point Nixon told Kissinger: "Let's you and me war-game this," and they worked the plans over to see, as Nixon put it, "where the weak points might be."* Time 10/5/70, p13 —*v.i.* to engage in or play a war game. *War-gaming is the preoccupation of tens of thousands of mini-generals round the world.* Time 1/4/71, p48 **[1970,** back formation from *war-gaming* the playing of war games (1954), from *war game* (OEDS 1910)]

war-gamer, *n.* one who engages in war games. *The collector of lead toy soldiers is not the same as the war-gamer. And the collector of miniature military models will mount a one-man cavalry charge if the ignorant call his pieces "toys."* Manchester Guardian Weekly 1/9/71, p17 **[1967]**

wargasm (ˈwɔːrˌgæzəm), *n. U.S.* **1** the sudden outbreak of total war. *But if an all-out exchange—"wargasm," in the jargon—were to take place, it would end, in Mr. Rusk's words, "with a handful of miserable survivors contemplating the folly of man."* New Yorker 1/9/71, p54 **2** a crisis that could lead to the outbreak of total war. *Goodman had found much to displease him then, and kept referring to the "wargasms" of the Kennedy Administration, which wargasms he attached with no excessive intellectual jugglery to the existential and Reichian notions of the orgasm which Mailer had promulgated in his piece* The White Negro. Harper's 3/68, p55 **[1968,** blend of *war* and *orgasm*]

washeteria, *n.* **1** a self-service laundry. . . . *the expansion of washeterias and the contraction of the average British kitchen will eventually make all but the family with small children unwilling to pay even £56 for a washing machine.* Sunday Times (London) 1/26/69, p29 **2** Usually, **car washeteria.** a self-service car wash. . . . *I have long grown accustomed to a cafete-*

ria but I now clean my car at a car washeteria. Times (London) 12/24/70, p9 [**1959** for def. 1, **1965** for def. 2; patterned after *cafeteria*]

Washingtonologist, *n.* a student of the policies, leaders, and practices of the United States government. *One of the rules of Kremlinology is that if two contradictory views are expressed in the Soviet press, then the Kremlin itself is probably divided on the issue. This impression is strengthened by some of the questions which the Kremlin's own Washingtonologists have lately been asking.* Manchester Guardian Weekly 9/19/76, p8 [**1974**, from *Washington, D.C. + -ologist* student of]

Wasp or **WASP** (wɑsp), *n.* a person belonging to the group of middle- and upper-class Americans descended from British and northern European settlers who espouse and represent the cultural and religious traditions of their ancestors (often used attributively). Compare ASP. *"Mr. Plimpton is the quintessential Wasp," Johnston has said. "He's the most intense embodiment of the Wasp I can imagine. I have an immense respect for him."* New Yorker 12/4/71, p74 [On the Cairo television] *I watch something new to me called "Jet Jackson—World Commando." It consists of the hero, a straight, clean-limbed young WASP with a private jet fighter, punching coloured villains in the face.* Manchester Guardian Weekly 3/17/66, p14 [**1962**, acronym (used especially in statistical and sociological studies of American ethnic groups) formed from the initials of *White, Anglo-Saxon, Protestant*]

Waspdom or **WASPdom,** *n.* the characteristics, beliefs, attitudes, etc., of the Wasps. *Thus Roman Catholics like William Buckley, Sargent Shriver and Ted Kennedy are pushed toward Waspdom by their associations, professions and life styles.* Time 1/17/69, p21 *The foundation of WASP dominance in national politics and culture rested on the supposition that WASPdom was the true America . . .* Harper's 4/70, p86 [**1969**]

Waspish or **WASPish,** *adj.* belonging to or typical of Wasps. *She says that she hated the Waspish ambience of the school, but she had got a scholarship at the end of her freshman year, and she wanted to keep it.* New Yorker 11/28/70, p129 *He was a Harvard Business School graduate, WASPish, attractive, crisp, alert, and formidably informed.* Atlantic 4/71, p41 [**1968**]

Waspy or **WASPy,** *adj.* of, belonging to, or characteristic of Wasps as a group. *Lydia Kingswell Commander regards "the ballot as the best cure for race-suicide."* Women's Suffrage *washes whiter and Waspier.* Times Literary Supplement 2/18/72, p180 *In one historic suburb an open-admissions class . . . ends up anyway with the same sort of membership as Mrs. Exeter's—"kind of WASPy but fun."* NY Times Magazine 12/19/76, p96 [**1968**]

waste, *v.t. U.S. (originally military) Slang.* to destroy; kill. *Then somebody said "What do we do with them?" A GI answered "Waste them." Suddenly there was a burst of automatic fire from many guns.* Harper's 5/70, p69 [**1964**, probably from the idiom *to lay waste*]

wastemaker, *n.* a person, company, industry, etc., that produces an excessive amount of waste, especially by using goods made to last briefly and become waste. Compare PLANNED OBSOLESCENCE. *New York generates three times as much waste per capita as London; Americans are "the wastemakers."* NY Times 12/23/70, p27 *And as we succeed in raising the standard of living so we shall become increasingly preoccupied with man's activities as a waste-maker.* Manchester Guardian Weekly 2/27/71, p13 [**1961**, from *The Wastemakers*, a book, 1960, by Vance Packard, critical of the product-design field. A formation echoic of LOSSMAKER.]

wasteplex, *n.* an industrial complex for recycling wastes. *The laboratory will analyze the raw materials entering the area and the refuse leaving it. Then "wasteplexes"—recycling centres feeding city wastes back to cities as new raw materials— will be designed specifically for local needs.* New Scientist 3/7/74, p614 [**1974**, from *waste + complex*]

-watcher, a combining form meaning "a habitual observer or student of _____; a close follower of the activities of _____."

The form became widespread during the 1970's, probably influenced by the political term *China-watcher* (1966), which may have been adapted from *bird watcher* (OEDS 1905). Some uses appear below: **—celebrity-watcher:** *The men accompanying the women who were lovely escorted them as in a ballet . . . It was a celebrity-watchers' paradise.* New Yorker 12/20/76, p29 **—court-watcher:** *Some court-watchers are expecting a reversal by "Nixon's Court," if only because of a series of recent retreats from the liberalism of the years under the now retired chief justice Earl Warren.* Maclean's 4/19/76, p18 **—Iran-watcher:** *. . . Ramazani, an Iran-watcher at the University of Virginia, suggests that Khomeini still has a tenacious hold on the people . . .* Time 9/14/81, p45 **—Peking-watcher:** *To be a real "Peking-watcher," do not wear bright Western clothes; try to dress Chinese-style, in dark blues or whites.* NY Times Magazine 1/11/76, p21 **—people-watcher:** *The scribe, a full-time people-watcher, had opened the day by watching Pierre Trudeau . . .* Maclean's 10/29/79, p64 **—Washington-watcher:** *The Soviet leaders would hardly have taken such a calculated risk in Angola without first consulting Mr Arbatov and his Washington-watchers on probable United States reaction.* Times (London) 3/23/76, p14

-watching, a combining form meaning "the act of a habitual observer or student of (a particular person, country, group, object, etc.). See -WATCHER. **—man-watching:** *Part of the mythology of the new pastime of man-watching is that people exert an enormous degree of unconscious (yet precise) control over one another's movements . . .* New Scientist 3/20/80, p920 **—spy-watching:** *All of this spy activity requires a lot of spy-watching.* Saturday Review 5/26/79, p14

watchlist, *n. U.S.* a list of items that require close scrutiny or surveillance. *Many institutions had gotten into difficulty during the recession from bad loans, particularly those involving real estate. The so-called watchlists maintained by the Federal Reserve Board, the Comptroller of the Currency, the Federal Deposit Insurance Corporation, and the Federal Home Loan Bank Board swelled to or approached record levels.* Americana Annual 1977, p114 [**1973**]

water bed or **waterbed,** *n.* a bed with a mattress consisting of a water-filled vinyl bag and usually equipped with a temperature-control device. *But his efforts to improve it led him* [designer Charles Prior Hall] *to a much splashier creation, which is now making an appearance—and creating a sensation—in department stores across the nation. It is the water bed, the bounciest bedroom invention since the innerspring mattress.* Time 9/7/70, p42 *And the waterbed ("ideal for pregnant women"), a kind of gigantic hot water bottle, must surely be the ultimate in nocturnal comfort.* New Scientist and Science Journal 3/4/71, p515 [**1970**, earlier a mattress filled with water for an invalid (1844)]

water cannon, a large nozzle usually mounted on a truck to shoot water at high pressure. *At one point police used water cannons to stop the demonstrators when they tried to storm the center court.* NY Times 5/4/68, p50 *In the fighting which followed several people were batoned by police and a number of marchers and bystanders were hosed down by water-cannon.* Manchester Guardian Weekly 10/9/71, p9 [**1964**]

water farm, *U.S.* a tract of land purchased by a city or state to draw from the water table beneath it. *The future this so-called "water farming" portends for outlying regions is being studied by the legislature; meanwhile some private developers have begun purchasing their own water farms.* NY Times Magazine 11/1/87, p58 [**1987**]

Watergate, *n.* **1** a major political scandal in the administration of President Richard M. Nixon, including attempts to conceal illegal activities of the participants (often used attributively). *So many other crimes and malpractices came to light that the word Watergate became a generic term for the many abuses of power that made up this complex and explosive political scandal.* Annual Register of World Events in 1973, p61 *Napoleon had his Waterloo and Nixon had his Watergate.* New York Post 5/22/74, p80 **2** any scandal, especially one that involves an attempt to conceal damaging information or illegal activities. *Do we need a dental Watergate? The worldwide evidence for and*

against fluoridation is now in. NY Times Book Review 4/27/75, p29 If the jockeys really did know something in advance, we'd have a horse-racing Watergate. Esquire 6/76, p11 The pro-laetrile movement responds in like fashion, accusing the US medical establishment of a cover-up. "It's a medical Watergate," said one. New Scientist 6/30/77, p766 The easiest refuge in dull times is to hype a story—to make every major or minor shenanigan a Watergate (as in Koreagate, Lancegate and Hollywoodgate). Time 6/12/78, p102 —v.t. to involve in scandal; charge with wrongdoings. "Why are they Watergating her [Marilyn Monroe]?" he asks. "Why can't they let her rest in peace. She was a bedeviled, fatherless young woman, torn between being a waif one minute and a princess the next . . ." Week-end Star (Kingston, Jamaica) 9/21/73, p27 [1972, from the Watergate, a building in Washington, D.C., where the Democratic National Committee had headquarters. An attempt to break into and take documents from the headquarters by men associated with reelection efforts of President Nixon led to an investigation and a scandal.] ▶The Watergate affair left a strong imprint on the language of the 1970's. The word spawned various coinages and the combining form -gate, used to denote scandal or corruption (see the entry -GATE). The following quotations illustrate some of the derivatives:
—Watergateana, n.: In all the immense outpouring of Watergateana . . . it has been next to impossible to form any clear notion of what actually happened. Esquire 9/74, p58
—Watergater, n.: Having sentenced 17 Watergaters to prison terms, Sirica was ruling on petitions for leniency from the only ones who are still imprisoned. Time 10/17/77, p19
—Watergatese, n.: Translations of a famous passage of Churchill's not into Basic English but into Watergatese: At no previous point of time in a conflict situation personnelwise has global indebtedness to an occupational minority group been operative in the same ball-court. Times (London) 9/26/73, p14 —Watergatish, adj.: Even more 'Watergatish' is the fact that these tapes are never made public; they are only there in case there is a legal disagreement. Listener 1/29/76, p100
—Watergatism, n.: His critics say he was knowingly helping Nixon "stonewall it," to use a Watergatism. NY Times Magazine 8/8/76, p49 —Watergatologist, n.: Hawkeyed Watergatologists will note a new fact in the film of All the President's Men which is not in the book. Times (London) 5/4/76, p6

water hole or waterhole, n. a part of the electromagnetic spectrum that is comparatively free of radio noise, considered as the most likely frequency band to be used by extraterrestrial beings trying to make contact with earth. See SETI. Between the hydrogen and hydroxyl (OH) bands, for example, lies the "water hole," the emission frequency of H_2O, which is not only a basic constituent of life as even most exobiologists can envision it, but also offers a frequency less drowned in deep-space static, or "sky noise." Science News 2/28/76, p132 The waterhole is freer from radio noise than any other band, and aliens, presumably, would broadcast on it for just that reason. However, portions of the band are now available by international agreement, for satellite communications. NY Times 9/4/77, pD7 [1976, so called because interstellar hydrogen and oxygen (the elements forming water) radiate on this band of frequencies]

water pick, an electric device for cleaning the teeth by aiming a pulsed jet of water at them. The film . . . shows that a beetle's spray is actually a series of pulses, as from a "water pick". . . . Science News 5/19/79, p331 [1971, alteration of Water Pik, a trademark for such a device, patented in 1963]

Watson-Crick, adj. of or relating to various genetic concepts and hypotheses, such as the double helix and the central dogma, postulated by the American biologist James D. Watson, born 1928, and the English biologist Francis H. C. Crick, born 1916. . . . the so-called Watson-Crick Theory, which holds that all genetic traits are basically derived from the structure of a kind of master molecule in the chromosomes called deoxyribonucleic acid, or DNA. NY Times 4/2/68, p52 The implication here is that most of this particular fragment of messenger RNA associates with itself to form a double-helical structure like the Watson-Crick spiral of DNA. New Scientist 5/8/69, p278 [1964]

watusi (wɑ:'tu:si:) or watutsi (wɑ:'tutsi:), n. Also Watusi or Watutsi. a dance in two-beat rhythm popular in the 1960's, characterized by jerky movements of the arms and head. Behind the church . . . a handful of young Indians were dancing the frug, the watusi, and variations thereof. Saturday Review 9/2/67, p41 —v.i. to dance the watusi. . . . they fed on lotus and daiquiri, they frugged and watutsied . . . Punch 7/20/66, p116 [1963, from Watusi, name of a tall people of Rwanda and Burundi, having a tribal dance characterized by high jumping movement]

wave, n. U.S. make waves, to cause disturbance; upset a normal course or routine. Something of a hard-nose with an Irish talent for hot-headedness, but never one to make waves, to rock the boat. Harper's 9/71, p72 This is the kind of broker you love to have working for you . . . He makes no waves, runs up no extensive phone bills, keeps his major account supplied with gifts of wine, dinners, and tickets. Atlantic 6/71, p48 [1962]

wave cloud, a lens-shaped cloud held stationary by a high point of the wave motion of air, used as an indicator of air waves by glider pilots. Wave clouds from the Alleghenies often appear over Washington, D.C., and over the New Jersey coast. Seen from Black Forest, wave clouds over the Rockies appear and disappear, very small fish in the vast sky; but the effect is electric: there she blows, the wave! Harper's 11/71, p125 [1959]

wave power, energy derived from the motion of waves and converted or put to useful work. Recent inventions utilizing wave power are the RUSSELL RECTIFIER and the SALTER DUCK. The new solar-power programme came after similar research commitments on wave power and on geothermal energy, and other alternative sources of energy were being examined. Times (London) 2/18/77, p2 Says Alexander Eadie, Britain's Under Secretary for Energy: "Wave power is not just a boffin's pipe-dream. It is a credible proposition." The British government has doubled spending on wave-power research this year, to $5.5 million . . . Time 10/16/78, p92 [1973] —wave-powered, adj.: Wave-powered buoys and small lighthouses have been used in the past, but tapping Japan's sea potential in a big way is just beginning. Science News 6/24/78, p402

wax, n. the whole ball of wax, U.S. Slang. the whole matter or thing; everything. . . . the Soviets are also getting "very sophisticated robotics technology from Japan," says one Washington source. "Japan is selling them the whole ball of wax—hardware, software, and technical data packages." Business Week 5/30/83, p49 [1976, but compare BALL OF WAX (1969)]

way, n. no way, Informal. under no circumstances. . . . none of these conditions will ever get any better. ("No way," as they keep saying . . .) New Yorker 12/25/71, p50 [1968]

way-out, Slang. —adj. far removed from the conventional or the ordinary; far-out. This could be followed up by other practical steps such as a pooling of research in the "way out" field of nuclear fusion . . . Times (London) 4/13/67, p23 This way-out West German virtuoso puts on a razzle-dazzle performance of expressionistic stunts. Time 1/31/64, pNY8 —n. a person who holds very unconventional or radical views. The change was well expressed by a participant in a 1969 conference sponsored by the conservationist Sierra Club: "The years ago we were considered way-outs. Nobody knew what conservation meant." Encyclopedia Science Supplement (Grolier) 1970, p158 [1958 for adj.; 1968 for noun]

weak force, the force that governs the interaction of neutrinos. It is probably interactive in fermion coupling and causes radioactive decay. Its hypothetical quantum is the W particle. Also called WEAK INTERACTION. Compare STRONG FORCE. Physicists distinguish four different kinds of force by which objects in the universe act upon each other: the strong nuclear force, the weak force, electromagnetism and gravity. Science News 8/21/71, p121 The intermediate boson was originally postulated by theoretical physicists as the quantum of the weak force, in analogy to the pion (the quantum of the nuclear force), the photon (the quantum of the electromagnetic force) and the graviton (the proposed quantum of gravity). Scientific American 10/71, p42 [**1967**; compare WEAK INTERACTION for earlier date, and also found earlier (1953) contrasted with *strong* in physics]

weak interaction, another name for WEAK FORCE. *This weak interaction, as its name implies, is very much weaker than the strong interaction. Its main effect is to govern certain long-lived modes of radioactive decay for certain particles. Historically it first showed up in nuclear beta decay.* Science News Yearbook 1969, p154 [**1954**]

weakon, *n.* another name for the W PARTICLE. *The quantum of gravitation is the graviton, and the strong force between quarks is transmitted by the particles called gluons. For the weak force the mediating particle is the intermediate vector boson, now also known as the weakon; it comes in three charge states, designated* W^+, W^-, *and* Z°. *Whereas the photon, the graviton and presumably the gluons are all massless, the weakon is expected to be very heavy.* Scientific American 1/80, p44 [**1980**, from *weak* (*force* or *interaction*) + -*on* (suffix of elementary particles), as in *boson*]

wealth tax, an annual tax on all of an individual's assets above a specified minimum, whether they produce income or not. *A Wealth Tax . . . has the disadvantage of being extremely difficult to collect, as it is administratively equivalent to the imposition of Estate Duty on all wealthy people once a year.* Times (London) 6/11/70, p11 [**1963**]

weatherize, *v.t. U.S.* to provide (a dwelling) with new or improved insulation or other materials and devices to keep heating and cooling costs down. *Last year Mr. Ballou, who . . . lives on Social Security and Supplemental Security Income, spent about one-third of his income for heat. His house is now weatherized and already he's noticed a difference.* NY Times 11/7/76, p55 [**1946, 1976**, from *weather* + -*ize;* patterned after *winterize*] —**weatherization**, *n.*: *Criteria for Retrofit Materials and Products for Weatherization of Residences. This booklet identifies and lists criteria for materials and products considered eligible under the Department of Energy Weatherization Assistance Program. The materials included are insulation and vapor barriers, storm windows and doors, caulking and weatherstripping, clock thermostats, replacement windows, and replacement glazing.* Selected U.S. Government Publications 1/79, Vol. 8, No. 1, p11 ▶ *Weatherize* was occasionally used in the past in the restricted sense (applied to leather, cloth, etc.) "to make weatherproof." The new use gained currency as an energy-conservation measure to counteract the shortage and rising cost of fuel.

Weatherman, *n.* a member of a militant revolutionary youth organization in the United States that split off from the politically radical but less extreme SDS (Students for a Democratic Society). . . . *the alleged bias for "activists" typically meant that delegates were presidents of youth organizations or youth members of town councils, not Weathermen or Panthers as the word suggests.* Harper's 8/71, p26 [**1970**, from a line in the song *Subterranean Homesick Blues,* by the American folk singer and composer Bob Dylan, born 1941: *"You don't need a weatherman To know which way the wind blows."*]

wedel ('veidəl), *v.i.* to ski by performing Wedeln. *They wedeled down the 1,200-ft. slope or slammed through the slalom course.* Time 11/15/68, p49 [**1963**, back formation from English *wedeln*]

wedeln or **Wedeln** ('veidəln), *n. sing.* or *pl.* a skiing maneuver consisting of quick, short swiveling movements down a sloping course. *"Like* Wedeln,*" I said. "What's that?" said a greatniece. "Useful word," I said. "It's a series, really, of short rhythmic parallel turns in the fall line, characterised by fluid continuity minimal upper body movement."* Punch 2/19/69, p256 *Down he goes, anyway, his Wedeln so crisp he never seems to care at all for the configuration of the snow . . .* New Yorker 2/2/63, p37 [**1957**, from German *Wedeln,* from *wedeln, v.,* to wag the tail, from *Wedel* tail]

wedge, *n.* a woman's short hairdo that falls over the forehead and forms a triangle in the back. *There are many variations on the new wedge. Stylists at the Paul McGregor shops in New York and Los Angeles have shaped the back of the cut into three inverted pyramids.* Time 4/19/76, p69 [**1976**]

weeknightly, *adj.* occurring on weeknights. . . . *one real innovation in television news, a half-hour each night confined to exploring one timely topic. This is the special achievement of public television's weeknightly MacNeil-Lehrer Report, now seen in some 200 cities.* Time 12/20/76, p69 [**1976**, from *weeknight* a night of the week other than Saturday or Sunday (OED 1859) + -*ly* (adjective suffix)]

weeny-bopper, *n. Slang.* a preadolescent girl (sometimes a boy) who follows the latest fashions and fads in dress, music, etc. Compare TEENY-BOPPER. *Two groups of young Americans, the Osmonds and the Jackson Five, have brought the Weenyboppers out in strength.* Week-end Star (Kingston, Jamaica) 7/20/73, p22 *My fairly concentrated listening so far shows a pattern of middle-of-the-road pop during the day: screaming weeny-bopper pop at night; and then, after midnight, a succession of those meandering songs sung sotto voce by breathy young ladies.* Listener 11/7/74, p644 [**1973**, from *weeny* very small + -*bopper*, as in *teeny-bopper*]

weight-watcher, *n.* a person who tries to lose weight, especially by dieting. *Weight-watchers and manufacturers of diet foods in the United States may perhaps be excused if they have had the feeling this past year of being treated like yoyos.* Science Journal 11/70, p6 *Italians are not exactly the keenest weight-watchers in the world and hardly let a day go by without forking into the pasta.* Sunday Times (London) 11/10/68, p35 [**1966**, from *Weight Watchers, Inc.*, an organization of dieters (registered 1960)]

Weinberg-Salam theory or **model**, *Physics.* a theory uniting weak and electromagnetic interactions and predicting the existence of the neutral current. *The Weinberg-Salam theory . . . hypothesized that electromagnetism and the weak force would be found to behave in the same way, in that a neutral current, analogous to electromagnetic currents, would be detected in reactions involving the weak force.* 1980 Collier's Encyclopedia Year Book, p398 *The modern unified field theory, often called the Weinberg-Salam model . . . begins with the weak and electromagnetic interactions. An experiment recently done at the Stanford Linear Accelerator Center has confirmed some key predictions of the Weinberg-Salam model, suggesting that there are not four forces in nature but three: gravity, the strong interaction and the one for which there is no name yet, the weak interaction* cum *electromagnetism.* Science News 7/8/78, p20 [**1976**, named after Steven *Weinberg*, born 1933, an American physicist, and Abdus *Salam*, born 1926, a Pakistani physicist, who independently developed the theory in the 1960's]

weirdo, *Especially U.S. Slang.* —*n.* an odd or eccentric person. . . . *this lunatic commotion* ["Cul-de-Sac"] *in which an American thug confines a pair of married weirdoes for about 24 hours in an 11th-century castle on the coast of northern England . . .* NY Times 11/8/66, p44 *Considered a weirdo because he believed in the oath of office he'd sworn to, he began to act the weirdo.* New Yorker 12/17/73, p107 —*adj.* odd; eccentric; queer. *He is being blackmailed by a weirdo youth who carries out the pretense of being his son . . .* Time 2/16/68, p36 [**1955** for noun; **1962** for adj.]

welfare hotel, a hotel in which people on welfare are housed, usually until permanent quarters are found for them. Compare S.R.O. HOTEL. *A year ago, conditions in the welfare hotels were a scandal.* Times (London) 3/7/72, p6 *Few Outsiders venture into welfare hotels. Mothers picking up their children at P.S. 75 across the street steer clear of the hotel's entrance. Pedestrians pass hurriedly by.* NY Times Magazine 5/21/78, p17 [**1971**]

welfare mother, *U.S.* a woman who is on relief because she has small children and no husband to support them. *The needs of the working man . . . the jobless veteran, the pressured pensioner, the welfare mother, and the harried commuter in our cities involve the whole range of vital urban services—police,* *fire, sanitation, health, education, jobs, and recreation.* NY Times 6/9/71, p43 **[1969]**

welfarist, *n.* an advocate of welfare programs such as public relief for the poor, unemployment insurance, social security, etc.; one who believes in the principles of the welfare state (often used attributively). *"Much of the black militant talk these days is actually in terms far closer to the doctrines of free enterprise than to those of the welfarist of the 30's . . .* Atlantic 7/68, p7 *. . . once electricity disappears so do most distinguishing features of our affluent, industrial, welfarist society.* New Statesman 11/14/75, p610 **[1968]**

welfarite, *n.* U.S. (*used disparagingly*). a person supported by public welfare; person on relief. *(The doctor who had written the report specialized in welfarites and mentioned that this patient would be coming to him for a substantial amount of treatment.) The welfare department, fearing legal suits if they made the man work and it turned out that he really was ill, decided to classify him unemployable.* National Review 1/18/74, p78 **[1974]**

West Banker, a native or inhabitant of the West Bank of the Jordan River, a region held by Jordan from 1948 until 1967, and since then occupied by Israel. *Israelis point out that West Bankers choose their own mayors. The West Bank's standard of living has improved dramatically, and more than 40,000 Palestinians work in Israel. As might be expected, there are differing opinions between Israelis and West Bankers on what the occupation has meant economically to the region.* Time 6/19/78, p39 **[1968]**

Western blot, a test for confirming the presence of the AIDS virus in blood by detecting antibodies in a blood serum sample spread on a special paper and sizing the antibodies to ascertain that they are known antibodies to AIDS. . . . *the existing combination of antibody tests—the so-called Elisa test, backed by the Western blot—will continue to be the best tool for large-scale testing.* NY Times 6/9/87, pC14 **[1985]**

Westpolitik ('vestpouli,ti:k), *n.* a policy, especially of a Communist country, of establishing normal diplomatic and trade relations with Western countries. Compare OSTPOLITIK. *Once his Westpolitik was launched, Brandt began a complex series of diplomatic maneuvers with the East.* Time 1/4/71, p14 **[1970,** from German, Western policy]

wet, *n.* **1** U.S. Informal. an illegal Mexican immigrant who swims or wades across the Rio Grande; wetback. . . . *a group of "wets," or "undocumented workers," as official jargon calls them.* Time 10/8/79, p33 **2** British Informal. a moderately conservative politician, especially one belonging to the Conservative party and opposed to Prime Minister Margaret Thatcher's policies. *Mrs Thatcher defiantly reinforced the right-wing of her Government on Monday when she dropped three "wets" from her Cabinet, brought in three loyalists and exiled Mr James Prior to Stormont Castle.* Manchester Guardian Weekly 9/20/81, p3 **[1973** for def. 1; **1980** for def. 2, short for *wetback* (OEDS 1929)]

wet bar, U.S. and Canada. a bar with running water and a sink, used for mixing and serving alcoholic drinks in a house, apartment, etc. *Mr. and Mrs. Mim's dream house would recapitulate a catalogue of status hardware: a room-to-room intercom, a "wet bar" in the "game room," an "in-ground" swimming pool and a "full" sprinkler system for the lawn.* Time 10/2/78, p95 *Capacity seating for hockey exceeds 19,000, and that doesn't include 61 luxury penthouse suites with "closed-circuit color TV and wet-bar availability."* Maclean's 2/11/80, p40 **[1968]**

wet-dog shakes, *Slang.* violent trembling during withdrawal from drug or alcohol addiction. *The effects of these very similar chemicals can be quite different. (What they all do, however, greatly to the amazement of Bloom and his collaborators, is to produce . . . the "wet-dog shakes" characteristic of morphine withdrawal—quite unexpected in a drug which is supposed to imitate morphine.) New Scientist 11/11/76, p332 . . . after a while the rodents became so addicted that they exhibited all the symptoms of alcoholism, including a rodent version of delirium tremens (DTs) characterized by whisker-twitching, jerk-*

ing movements and "wet-dog" shakes. Time 5/9/77, p56 **[1973]**

wet look, a chemical finish given to fabrics, furniture, and other products to make them look shiny and wet (often used attributively). *Other good buys: wet-look stackable plastic chairs and chrome-base table, $79.95.* Woman's Day 4/73, p101 **[1968]**

wet thumb, ability or success in raising fish in aquariums, fish farms, etc. Compare BROWN THUMB. *Possession of a "wet thumb" is still the most important attribute for any fish keeper, be he professional fish culturist or pet fish fancier.* Natural History 11/72, p60 **[1972,** patterned after *green thumb* (1943)]

wetware, *n.* the brain, as compared with the computer in its ability to perform mathematical and logical operations. *The human brain in some circles is now referred to as wetware.* Time 11/8/82, p92 **[1975,** from *wet* + *-ware,* as in *hardware* and *software*]

whacked-out, *adj. Slang.* **1** crazy; mad. *"The Peacock, the Peacock," the director says, and as he explains to the cameraman why the shot is a problem, it begins to dawn on everybody in the control room that this whacked-out, insane-looking bird has become for all of us, a peacock.* Harper's 8/72, p112 **2** intoxicated with alcohol or narcotics. *A Blake Edwards slapstic specialty—a party—ensues at the house in the evening, ending in whacked-out debauchery with a highway patrolman having his legs shaven.* Maclean's 7/6/81, p52 **[1968]**

wheeler-dealer, *v.i. Chiefly U.S. Slang.* to wheel and deal; trade or scheme shrewdly. *LBJ wheeler-dealered in his ornate Capitol suite of crystal chandeliers and gold-embossed doorknobs . . .* Harper's 4/70, p38 **[1970,** verb use of the U.S. slang term *wheeler-dealer, n.* one who trades or schemes shrewdly (DAS 1960), from the verb phrase *wheel and deal,* in which *wheel* literally means to act as a "wheel" or "big wheel" (slang for an important or influential person, a leader)]

wheeler-dealing, *n. Chiefly U.S. Slang.* shrewd scheming or trading. *The men in New York kept . . . wondering what wheeler-dealing was going on over telephone lines among the various managements.* NY Times 2/1/68, p42 *In the event, all the arm-squeezing and whispered wheeler-dealing along the corridors had its intended effect.* Times (London) 4/8/68, p2 **[1968]**

wheelie, *n.* a stunt in which a lightweight vehicle is made to stand for a moment on one or two of its wheels. *A popular sport for young bicycle riders is "doing a wheelie." This means lifting the front wheel off the ground and balancing on the rear wheel alone.* NY Times 11/12/66, p45 *Then he discovered a way to turn his motorcycling skill into real money, by becoming a stunt rider. "I started out with simple things—wheelies, crashing through fire walls . . ."* Sunday Times Magazine (London) 6/27/71, p41 **[1966]**

wheels, *n.pl. Slang.* a car. *"Bread" and "wheels" (money and car) are the high value-symbols for unimpeded movement to where the action is. "Wheels," a synecdoche for car, while not embodying a kinetic element per se, has an obvious potential for movement.* Thomas Kochman, Rappin' and Stylin' Out, 1972, p162 **[1959]**

where, *adv.* **where it's at,** U.S. Slang. **a** the place where the most important activity, current development or fashion, etc., is going on. *"Since you instinctively rap with those who are Now, you will always be more or less where it's at and should readily find your bag."* Cartoon legend, New Yorker 10/25/69, p61 **b** the true state of affairs; the essential nature of a situation. *"This crazy Katz knows where it's at, if it's anywhere," he said poetically.* Saturday Review 10/10/70, p34 *I . . . see in this the final proof that Eliot* [the central character in C. P. Snow's novels] *is the ultimate square. As they said only yesterday, he just doesn't know where it's at.* Atlantic 9/70, p114 **[1965]**

whiffleball, *n.* a lightweight, hollow, plastic ball with openings or holes to catch the air and reduce its speed and distance of travel. Originally developed for golf practice in a confined area, whiffleballs are made like a softball and are used by children to play baseball or some variation of it. Also spelled WIFFLE BALL. . . . *they were mingling with the other occupants of* the Sheep Meadow—picnickers, folk singers, kids playing with whiffleballs and baseballs . . . New Yorker 7/11/70, p20 [1965]

whipcord, adj. taut, tough, or sinewy. He [René Belbenoit] was deeply tanned, middle-aged, and he had the whipcord conditioning of an athlete. Saturday Review 10/24/70, p70 Many experts believed that [Ferdinand Lewis] Alcindor, with his size, reach, long legs with whipcord muscles . . . might become basketball's greatest attraction. Britannica Book of the Year 1969, p140 [1963, figurative sense of whipcord, n., a thin, tightly twisted cord used for whips] ►An isolated meaning "tough as whipcord" is recorded in OED2 (1879).

whistleblower, n. Chiefly U.S. Slang. a person who exposes, denounces, or informs against another. From the testimony of . . . a young "whistleblower" who had written segments of the Interior report and then resigned in protest over the Department's final decision, a pattern of startling administrative ineptness and short-sightedness emerged. Harper's 11/72, p30 Whistleblowers are people in government departments or other bodies who give confidential information to journalists on the ground that the disclosure is in the public interest. Sunday Times (London) 1/5/80, p3 [1970, from the idiom blow the whistle (on someone)]

whistleblowing, n. Chiefly U.S. Slang. the act or practice of a whistleblower. Further, the Code [of Good Conduct of The British Computer Society] contains secrecy clauses that effectively prohibit Nader style whistle-blowing to call public attention to harmful practices. New Scientist and Science Journal 12/9/71, p69 What would recent American history have been, for example, without those grand panjandrums of whistle-blowing, Daniel Ellsberg, who Xeroxed the Pentagon Papers, and Victor Marchetti, the first to tell us how the C.I.A. really works. NY Times Magazine 10/30/77, p52 [1971]

white backlash, another term for BACKLASH (def. 1). The so-called "white backlash," fearful resentment among white property-owners over the economic and territorial advance of Negroes . . . NY Times 10/23/66, pD3 [1964]

white-bread, adj. U.S. and Canada, Informal. of, belonging to, or reflecting the values of North American white society. The contrast between his white-bread liberalism and the boys' ghetto wit is the basis of all the comedy in Diff'rent strokes. TV Guide 1/13/79, p30 "This cast! A real Canadian mosaic. Four blondes, five WASPs, all white-bread." Maclean's 3/24/80, p53 [1968, in allusion to the whiteness and bland quality of white bread (made with white flour) as a metaphor of the smoothly agreeable and self-satisfied attitude of many whites]

white-collar criminal, a person in a business or profession who breaks the law, as by committing embezzlement or fraud, or engaging in tax evasion, bribery, patent infringement, misrepresentation in advertising, and the like. Strong disapproval of lenient sentences for white-collar criminals has been voiced by a top Federal prosecutor, who said that substantial prison terms could deter businessmen from committing crimes. NY Times 8/1/76, p25 The percentage of prisoners who are nonviolent felons—burglars, auto thieves, and larcenists—has declined, as has the percentage who are "white-collar" criminals (embezzlers, forgers, and defrauders). Harper's 11/77, p20 [1972, derived from white-collar crime (1952), a term anticipated by such formations as white-color criminaloid (1934)]

White English, English as spoken by white Americans in contrast to Black English. Intonation patterns of Black English were studied and compared with those occurring in White English and formal Black English. It was found that: (1) the Black English corpus was characterized by a wider pitch range, extending into higher pitch levels than either the White vernacular or the formal Black English of the adult information. Newsletter of the American Dialect Society, Vol. 6, No. 3, 11/74, p44 [1974]

white flight, Chiefly U.S. the movement of urban whites, especially middle-class whites, to the suburbs to avoid consequences of living in a city, such as increased danger from a high rate of crime, racial integration, high taxation, etc. Previous studies of this so-called "white flight" phenomenon have been criticized

for not taking into account the type of desegregation involved and for ignoring other factors that might have induced white families to leave the central city anyway. Armor tries to correct these deficiencies by comparing white flight under court-ordered busing to that under voluntary integration plans . . . Science News 9/23/78, p216 [1974]

white hole, Astronomy. a hypothetical object in space which expands outwards from a singularity. See WORMHOLE. Recent speculation suggests that matter in our universe is disappearing into the fantastic gravitational wells of black holes, only to appear in other universes through what appear to be "white holes." Our white holes may be the quasars, whose prodigious energies we are currently at a loss to explain. Natural History 4/72, p44 Asimov . . . suggests that a network of black holes interlacing the universe may have, through all eternity, been sucking matter in at one end and expelling it through "white holes" at the other end to "create a closed circuit, sending matter back into a more contracted past to begin expansion all over" again—an idea that sounds suspiciously like a new version of Hoyle's discredited Steady State and brings the complex and confusing debate over the origins and future of the universe neatly full circle. Maclean's 8/22/77, p59 [1971, patterned after BLACK HOLE]

white knight, 1 a political reformer or champion of a cause. The Italian Communist Party . . . will take its members into the regional election campaign next month as white knights dealing with the joint evils of corruption and reaction. Times (London) 4/23/70, p7 . . . unlike other political white knights, Lindsay [Mayor John Lindsay of New York] has curiously escaped a major journalistic unhorsing. Time 6/29/70, p60 **2** U.S. Finance. a friendly bidder sought by a company to outbid a hostile company that has made a tender offer for its control. In late 1985, Dallas investor Harold Simmons began acquiring Sea-Land Stock in a hostile takeover bid, prompting Sea-Land to search for a so-called white knight—a corporation to offer better terms than the original bidder. 1987 Collier's Encyclopedia Year Book, p514 [1970 for def 1; 1978 for def. 2]

white market, legal or officially sanctioned trade in ration coupons, etc., to discourage illegal transactions or the emergence of a black market. The Administration presented a new proposal for standby gasoline rationing that . . . would permit motorists to sell their rationing coupons to others in a "white market." NY Times 12/9/79, p1E [1972] ►This is a revival of a term used in the 1940's, especially in the sense of the legal market in currencies existing at that time in Europe.

white meter, British. an electric meter that registers off-peak consumption of electricity. The consumer has to compare white meter costs himself, Which? says. A typical family in the North-east using 1.050 units a quarter and paying 10.67 on the standard domestic tariff, would have to use well over 300 units at night to benefit from going onto the white meter, it claims. Times (London) 10/11/73, p6 [1972, so called from its color, to distinguish it from the ordinary gray meter]

white noise, an overlay of nondescript sound to cover up distracting or annoying noises. Also called ACOUSTIC PERFUME. The most widely used of the noisemakers produce a mild form of radio static called "white noise" by engineers. Turned down to a discreet volume, the static masks distracting outside noises and disturbing interior echoes. Time 5/4/70, p92 [1970, extended sense of the technical term (OEDS 1943) for a sound covering the range of audible frequencies, such as the sound of a jet engine]

white-shoe, adj. Especially U.S. Informal. of or associated with individuals thought of as having special rank and privilege in society and considered the best people; belonging to the privileged, moneyed, or upper class; elitist. Her other son was now at Yale, going very white-shoe. Harper's 5/67, p96 With the use of Mr. Milken's junk bonds, the debt instrument once derided by the white-shoe Wall Street firms, many corporations that could not get bank financing suddenly had access to huge pools of capital. NY Times 4/3/89, pD4 [1957; so called from the casual white shoes worn in the summer by Ivy League students]

white tea commune, a commune in China which is impoverished because of its poor agricultural resources or its distance from city markets. *One may legitimately ask how long peasants in "white tea" communes will accept the idea of "learning from Tachia" (the model "self-reliance" brigade) as it becomes clear that nothing except direct Government help will lift the poorer units to the level of the richer?* Manchester Guardian Weekly 11/28/76, p7 [**1976**, so called from the commune's drinking of hot water instead of real tea]

whitey, *n. Chiefly Black English, Slang* (used as a common noun). a white person. *The confrontation began after six youths from the camp taunted six park policemen chanting: "Going to get me a whitey!" and "Going to get me a honky!"* NY Times 6/21/68, p24 [**1942, 1964**, from use especially as a proper noun meaning white people collectively, white society (1828)]

whiz kid or **whizz kid**, *Informal*. an exceptionally intelligent or successful person. *The disenchantment is all the more profound because Giscard swept into office after Pompidou's death in 1974 as the candidate of change, as a debonair whiz-kid . . .* Maclean's 5/11/81, p37 *It is clear that Dr David Owen (December 18) has been reading the Communist Party's revised British Road to Socialism and is frightened of its implications. I'm not surprised—the last thing a whizz kid like Dr Owen wants is for someone to breathe the word "socialism" ever so softly in his ear.* Manchester Guardian Weekly 1/1/78, p2 [**1962**, originally applied to the team of young executives brought to the Department of Defense in 1961 by Secretary Robert McNamara, who had himself been a member of a group of ten young former army statisticians hired in 1946 by the Ford Motor Company and known informally as the "Whiz Kids," probably associated with the "Quiz Kids" who answered questions of fact on a national radio show of the 1940's]

wholefood, *n. British*. any food grown organically and prepared without artificial additives or preservatives. *Those attending the festival will live in a geodesic domed village, enjoying solar heated showers, eat wholefoods prepared at a vegetarian kitchen, and take part in discussions.* Times (London) 8/23/77, p12 [**1960**]

whydunit (ˌhwaiˈdənˌit), *n.* a mystery novel, play, or motion picture which deals primarily with the motivation for the crime. *Psychological whydunnit, with Dame Peggy Ashcroft wonderfully piteous as the naughty butcher.* Manchester Guardian Weekly 8/7/71, p19 *Connery takes over the interrogation and in the process beats the man to death. This much we know almost from the beginning, so the film is less of a whodunit than a whydunit.* Time 6/4/73, p99 [**1968**, patterned after *whodunit* (OEDS 1930)]

Wicca or **wicca** (ˈwikə), *n.* the practice or cult of witchcraft. *Witches call their religion Wicca, from the Anglo-Saxon word meaning wisdom, which is the root of such words as witch, wizard and wicked. They practice a rite similar in form to Baptism in which infants are accepted into the faith.* Sunday Post-Herald (Hong Kong) 7/22/73, p22 *The ancient rites of the wicca, as witchcraft is known to its serious practitioners, were practiced in 1971 with no one knows what degree of success by no one knows how many witches in the United States.* 1972 Collier's Encyclopedia Year Book, p10 [**1970**, from Old English *wicca* (masculine) wizard] —**Wiccadom**, *n.: The most important fertility rites in all Wiccadom occur in spring. It is the time to worship fervently in the coven of one's choice.* Time 4/27/70, p98 —**Wiccan**, *adj.: Witches do not . . . torture animals or kill them for pleasure. Such perverted practices are the antithesis of all Wiccan teachings.* New York Post 8/22/79, p26

wide-body, *adj.* having a wide fuselage. . . . *the introduction of quieter wide-body turbo-fan aircraft is unfortunately not only still remote, but totally inadequate.* Times (London) 5/3/73, p18 *The new planes are needed to modernize the United Fleet, largest in the free world, to improve fuel efficiency and to expand operation of wide body jets.* New Yorker 12/11/78, p120 —**n.** a wide-body aircraft. *"Tomorrow, son, I am flying a widebody to L.A."* New Yorker 2/18/80, p47 [**1968**]

wide-out, *n.* another name for WIDE RECEIVER. *The surprising thing is not that the "wide-out" is the N.F.L.'s new hero, but that for so long he seemed an antihero, a shadowy figure with a name like a stereo component, an incidental appendage to the glory of the quarterback and running back.* NY Times Magazine 11/25/79, p63 [**1976**]

wide receiver, a pass receiver in American football who stands a few yards to the side of the rest of the team to enable him to get quickly downfield without having to run through the opposing team's line. Also called WIDE-OUT. *Holtz lost his five best running backs through defections, trades and retirement. He lost his best wide receiver and his best defensive lineman through injuries.* NY Times Magazine 12/12/76, p65 [**1968**]

widow's mandate, *U.S.* the election or appointment of a widow to the political office held by her husband, usually to complete his unexpired term. *Among the widows who were elected to office on the basis of "widow's mandate" were many who developed distinct political reputation and won terms in their own right.* NY Times 8/27/76, pB4 [**1976**]

Wiffle ball, a variant of WHIFFLEBALL. *He [David Eisenhower] had to settle for passing the afternoon playing Wiffle ball on the south lawn of his father-in-law's White House.* Time 5/25/70, p43 [**1970**, earlier *Wiffle* (1957)]

wig, *v.i. U.S. Slang*. **wig out, 1** to get high or light-headed on or as if on narcotic drugs. *Astonishing supermarket full of senior citizens who all look stoned out of their minds. Wigging out on the gherkins.* Atlantic 2/68, p123 **2** to get very excited or enthusiastic. . . . *a "teen-age R & R nut who wears $3.98 boots, a transistor at the ear and who wigs out over the Stones, the Turtles, the Beatles, and anything else with a concussive 4/4 beat."* NY Times 12/27/65, p20 [**1955**, from *wig, n.*, U.S. slang (especially jazz) term for the head or mind, and initially (1930's) a person's hair, ultimately from *wig* hairpiece]

wiggle seat, a lie detector fitted into a chair to measure physiological changes and movement of the occupant. *In addition to the 50-year-old polygraph, which measured blood pressure, respiration rate, and galvanic skin response, several new lie detectors are now available. These include the "wiggle seat," which registers body temperature and minute muscle movements; a device which records changes in the size of the pupil of the eye; and the Psychological Stress Evaluator.* Encyclopedia Science Supplement (Grolier) 1976, p345 [**1976**]

wiglet, *n.* a small hairpiece added to a woman's hair to make it longer or higher, to frame the face, etc. *Wiglets set in long loopy curls were attached to the crown of the head, while separate curls were used to cascade down the back in more elaborate evening styles.* 1968 Collier's Encyclopedia Year Book, p250 *In her salon she has a very wide selection of wigs, "almost" wigs, braids, wiglets, chignons and postiches.* NY Times 2/24/65, p44 [**1964**]

wild-card, *adj. U.S.* (of a sports team) qualifying for championship play-offs by winning an arbitrary play-off among second-place teams or by winning the most games among teams that did not qualify for play-offs. *The Cowboys locked up the National Conference's "wild card" slot Saturday as they defeated the East Division champion Washington Redskins 34-24.* Tuscaloosa News (Alabama) 12/10/72, p8B *This would entail the establishment of three geographical divisions within each league, and a playoff season that would stretch over several weeks, involving three regional winners in each league plus a "wild card" team.* New Yorker 11/20/78, p57 [**1970**, so called from the supposed resemblance of such a team to a *wild card*, a playing card of arbitrary denomination, from *wild* applied to cards in auction bridge (1927)]

wilding, *n.* the act of rampaging through the streets as a gang and randomly attacking passers-by, usually to rob, beat, or rape them. *They were a gang, out for a night of "wilding." They had beaten people, with fists and a 12-inch length of lead pipe wrapped in black tape. Now, they were ready for more.* Daily News (New York) 4/23/89, p5 [**1989**, apparently from the slang phrase *go wilding* to go on a wild rampage, from *wild, adj.* + *-ing* (noun suffix), a use anticipated by *wilding, n.* a wild person or thing, as in "The air of the fireside withers out all the fine wildings of the husband's heart," R. L. Stevenson (1881)]

wildlifer, *n.* a person who advocates the protection of wildlife. *It none the less ill becomes the Wildlifers to aid and abet so aggressive and systematic a piece of pollution promotion.* Times (London) 11/18/70, p12 *There will of course be carping critics of a Grand Canyon Dam . . . do-gooders, conservationists, starry-eyed liberals and wild-lifers.* Harper's 8/65, p63 **[1963]**

wild-track, *adj.* that is recorded with sound or voicing separate or different from the action shown on film off-screen. *Another humanising technique is to explain the idea in a 'wild-track' . . . commentary while showing film of people going about their business in easily recognisable and vaguely apposite ways.* Listener 10/15/70, p506 *A simple, straightforward commentary and some "wild track" recording of music and dialogue (one wonders if the dialogue actually relates to the scenes one is witnessing) add to the realism of the visuals.* New Scientist 2/2/67, p284 **[1964,** from *wild track,* n. (1940)]

wildwater, *n.* water with strong currents; the turbulent part of a stream (often used attributively). *Evans had beaten the man who was acknowledged to be the best wild-water boater in southern California . . .* New Yorker 3/21/70, p133 **[1963]**

Wilson cycle, the pattern of appearance and disappearance of oceans in geologic time. *The sites of old hot spots have proved readily recognizable, and during 1974 it was shown that hot spots have formed a distinctive feature of the Wilson cycle throughout the last 2,000,000,000 years.* McGraw-Hill Yearbook of Science and Technology 1975, p168 **[1975,** named after John Tuzo *Wilson,* born 1908, a Canadian geologist]

WIMP, *n. Nuclear Physics.* any of a class of weakly interacting massive particles thought to be present in the sun's core and strongly affecting the amount of energy found there. *Applying GUT and other theories, physicists predict that an abundance of exotic dark elementary particles must have been created in the Big Bang. Theorists give them names like photinos, axions, and gravitinos. Collectively, they are known as weakly interactive massive particles, or (of course) WIMPs.* Encyclopedia Science Supplement (Grolier) 1987, p28 **[1985,** acronym for *weakly interactive massive particle*]

wimpiness or **wimpishness,** *n. Slang.* wimpy character or behavior; feebleness; unassertiveness. *Ling-Ling's previous headaches were blamed on Hsing-Hsing's all-round wimpiness and a previous suitor's clumsiness, but this time the fault may be human.* NY Times 3/26/82, pA26 *If Michael Straight is a wimp . . . as some people allege, the wimpishness is not immediately apparent.* Times (London) 3/9/83, p10 **[1982** for *wimpiness,* from *wimpy;* **1978** for *wimpishness,* from *wimpish* (OEDS 1925)]

wimpy, *adj. Slang.* of or resembling a wimp; unassertive; feeble; ineffectual. *Since coming-of-age movies are, for obvious reasons, almost always about writers, . . . people must come away from these movies wondering if all wimpy kids grow up to be writers.* New Yorker 9/29/80, p142 **[1967,** from *wimp* a weakling (OEDS 1920), of unknown origin]

WIN¹, *n., v. U.S.* acronym for *Whip Inflation Now,* a slogan promoted under the administration of President Gerald R. Ford (1974-76). *Richard Nixon tried mandatory wage-price controls, Gerald Ford tried the WIN button, Jimmy Carter tried voluntary guidelines.* Newsweek 11/19/79, p89 **[1974]**

WIN², *n. U.S.* acronym for *Work Incentive,* a federal program designed to provide jobs for people on welfare, instituted by a 1967 amendment to the Social Security Act. *The number of "slots" WIN was able to offer for training was always exceeded by the number of persons voluntarily seeking training.* New Yorker 1/20/73, p67 **[1970]**

Winchester, *adj.* of, relating to, or designating a computer storage system that incorporates tightly sealed hard disks with large capacities and rapid access. *It is now known generically as Winchester technology, that being the code name under which the device was developed at IBM. A Winchester disk*

memory has one or more rigid disks . . . Scientific American 8/80, p117 **[1973]**

wind¹, *n.* **twist in the wind,** to experience great uncertainty or endure painful suspense. *There were those who felt that for one who had sat on the ducking stool, and been tarred and feathered in addition, I had suffered enough. But the inquisitors thought otherwise. For ten months I was left hanging there, twisting in the wind.* Harper's 10/74, p76 *Everybody, or a lot of the press, has taken it that, in fact, the Government was jolly well making you wait for the money; it was keeping you twisting in the wind, I think is the phrase.* Listener 2/13/75, p201 **[1974]** ►The expression *twist (slowly) in the wind* became current during the Watergate affair (1972-74). In *Safire's Political Dictionary* (William Safire, 1978), the origin of the phrase is attributed to John Ehrlichman, President Nixon's assistant for domestic affairs; however a similar phrase *hang in the wind* in the sense of remain in suspension is known from about 1531.

wind² (waind), *v.* **wind down,** to reduce gradually so as to bring or come to an end; de-escalate; phase down. *The enemy might prefer gradually to 'wind down' the level of combat step by step.* Manchester Guardian Weekly 8/5/69, p2 *With the headquarters offices empty, the war—in that theater, anyhow—would soon wind down, and we could all go home.* Harper's 3/70, p28 **[1952, 1969]**

wind-down ('waind,daun), *n.* a winding down; a gradual reduction; de-escalation. *. . . the campaign heralds the official wind-down of the Cultural Revolution, a finale that is to climax in "all-round victory."* Time 2/21/69, p29 *The dispirited ones say that the US lead in technology has now gone for ever and, as proof, point to the reduction in the number of students enrolling for engineering courses, the cutback in government research and development spending, the cancellation of the SST, the wind-down of space exploration . . .* New Scientist and Science Journal 7/8/71, p95 **[1969]**

windfall profits tax, *U.S.* a tax levied on unexpectedly large profits. *Carter forecast that his windfall profits tax on crude oil will finance energy programs that will amount to "one of the biggest construction projects in world history—on a scale comparable to building our interstate highway system."* Time 10/22/79, p40 **[1973,** from earlier *windfall profit* (1951), but also influenced by *excess profits tax* (OEDS 1915)]

window, *n.* **1** short for LAUNCH WINDOW. *Between February and April next year the 'window' will be open for launchings to Mars and there is the chance of sending craft on fly-by, orbital or lander missions.* Science Journal 12/68, p17 **2** *Figurative.* **a** a period considered to be the most favorable or advantageous for any undertaking. *Hitherto there has been an age "window" for* [papal] *candidates, ranging from the early 60s to the mid-70s, mainly because Cardinals feared having a Pope in office for more than ten or 15 years.* Time 10/9/78, p80 *Officials reckon that there is "a three-day window" for a new PM* [prime minister] *to decide on the nature of his ministry before sharing power with its members.* Maclean's 2/25/80, p17 **b** any period of time (favorable or unfavorable). *. . . the United States was reaching what the military terms a "window of vulnerability" to Soviet missiles, that he thought for the Soviets "it's a window of opportunity". . .* New Yorker 6/23/80, p71 **3** a computer display screen. *In computer jargon the screen is described as a "window," the visible part of a "scroll;" as with a scroll, when one part is uncovered, another is covered.* ACLS Newsletter Winter/Spring 1984, p23 **[1965** for def. 1; **1978** for def. 2; **1966** for def. 3]

windsurfer, *n.* **1** a person who engages in windsurfing. Also called SAILBOARDER. *From Nov. 15 to 20 in the Bahamas, 400 or so windsurfers will be . . . participating in the 1976 World Championships of Windsurfing.* NY Times 10/31/76, pJ5 **2 Windsurfer.** the trademark for a kind of sailboard. *You can't imagine a simpler craft than a Windsurfer. There is no rudder and no ropes: the mast is supported and controlled by the sailor, and the 'boat' is steered by moving the body.* Sunday Times Magazine (London) 12/21/75, p3 **[1969]**

windsurfing, *n.* the sport of riding a SAILBOARD. Also called SAILBOARDING. *For recreation, she likes windsurfing and tennis, though windsurfing is something more than a pastime since she teaches this burgeoning sport. It involves standing on a surf board and allowing a hand-held sail, once laboriously hauled from the water by strength of arm, to propel the craft along. It requires exceptional balance, too . . .* Times (London) 12/8/77, p9 **[1969]**

wing, *v.* **wing it,** *Chiefly U.S. Slang.* to improvise. Cox: *The resistance put up against us dictates* [our] *strategy.* Bernstein (lounging in an armchair in tartan slacks): *You mean you've got to wing it . . . I dig absolutely.* Time 1/26/70, p12 **[1970,** from earlier theater slang *wing it* to refresh one's memory for each scene in the wings before going on to play it (OED 1933), in the same sense, *to wing* (1885)]

winless, *adj.* without a single win or victory in a series of sports contests. *This winless finale could happen again in 1979, given all the Rams' injuries. The team has had an incredibly unlucky year.* NY Times Magazine 12/23/79, p22 **[1966]**

winterim, *adj. U.S.* of, relating to, or occurring during the winter intersession. *Interscholastic and recreational sports—On and off campus Winterim.* NY Times Magazine 9/30/79, p91 **[1972,** blend of *winter* and *interim*]

wipe-out, *n. U.S. Slang.* **1** a fall from an upright position on a surfboard, motorcycle, skis, etc. *Like a practiced surfer, he was balanced carefully in the curl, in control of his board and in no apparent danger of a wipe-out.* Time 8/15/69, p11 *Knievel* [motorcyclist Evel Knievel] *still limps because of a severe wipe-out in Las Vegas three years ago, when he jumped the fountains at Caesars Palace.* New Yorker 7/24/71, p23 **2** total defeat or annihilation. *The idea that the United States, capable of the final human wipe-out, could possibly lose to the Republic of North Korea . . . was too patently nonsensical.* NY Times 5/12/70, p38 **[1962** for def. 1; **1968** for def. 2]

wire-guided, *adj.* guided to a target by electrical impulses transmitted through a wire connecting the weapon and the operator. See TOW. *More than 130 Israeli tanks had been killed by Russian-made Saggar antitank missiles: 25-pound wire-guided rockets carried by lightly armored vehicles, widely deployed since 1965 by the Warsaw Pact forces and others.* Scientific American 10/78, p57 **[1958,** earlier in the sense of any electrical signals transmitted by wire (1922)]

wireman, *n. U.S.* an expert in wiretapping. *. . . never before have there been so many "spooks" abroad in the land, so many spies and counterspies, clandestine analysts, secret movers, shakers, agents, operatives, wiremen, and gumshoes.* Harper's 12/74, p51 *Among the practitioners of his craft, Frank Chin, 48, was a pro. He had been one of the most sought-after "wiremen," or electronic eavesdroppers, in the East, supplying bugging and recording devices to clients on both sides of the law.* Time 2/21/77, p19 **[1973,** from *wire*tap + *man*]

wishbone, *n.* or **wishbone T,** an offensive formation in American football, a variant of the T-formation, in which the fullback is lined up ahead of the two halfbacks in an alignment resembling a wishbone (often used attributively). Compare VEER. *. . . Alabama's incredibly fast wishbone attack also proved somewhat erratic.* Newsweek 1/14/74, p70 *. . . Penn's wishbone offense has ground out 1,118 yards in four league games, far better than any other team.* NY Times 10/28/77, pA20 **[1970]**

Wiskott-Aldrich syndrome ('wɪs,kɑt'ɔːl,drɪtʃ), a genetic disorder characterized especially by a decrease in white blood cells and platelets, chronic eczema, and recurrent infections. *Fifteen-month-old Tony Olivo of Dallas was reported to have spent his entire short life in a special germ-free room in a hospital; he had been born a victim of the Wiskott-Aldrich syndrome: having virtually no resistance to any infection, he could not survive outside a sterile environment.* Harper's 8/78, p21 **[1968,** named after R. A. *Aldrich,* a 20th-century American pediatrician; origin of the name *Wiskott* is not known]

witch's cradle or **witches' cradle,** a metal platform or cage, suspended several inches above the ground in a darkened, sound-proof room, in which a subject of parapsychological experiments is placed to undergo various altered states of consciousness. *The "witch's cradle," or suspended sensory isolation cradle, is one prop they use to produce an ASC.* Science News 11/10/73, p300 *ESP* [extrasensory perception] *scores also appear to be enhanced when extraneous sensory input is reduced. Experiments supporting this point have been done with subjects strapped into a "witches' cradle," in which sight and sound are blocked off as one swings slowly through the air in a metal frame.* Britannica Book of the Year 1975, p77 **[1973,** probably named after an old, cradlelike device into which suspected witches were strapped to punish or isolate them]

with-it, *adj. Slang.* fashionably up-to-date. *. . . . his* [Pierre Trudeau's] *managers created a new image of him as the youthful, debonaire, "with-it" man of the jet-set age.* Americana Annual 1970, p694 *The papier-mâché toe rings are very simple and very with-it.* Maclean's 10/1/66, p15 *Hooper Bolton must have one of the most "with-it" collections of jewelry in London.* Times (London) 7/22/65, p12 **[1962,** from the slang phrases *be with it* (1931), *get with it* (1961) to be or get smart, alert, etc., originally meaning to be within an exclusive set (*not be with it* = be an outsider)]

with-it-ness, *n. Slang.* the quality or character of keeping up with the latest trends; up-to-date-ness. *It is extremely well served by its staff of editors . . . who radiate a youthful enthusiasm and with-it-ness.* Punch 9/10/69, p434 *. . . modernity . . . can now just as often be caution in the cinema, with film after film chasing with-it-ness and looking more and more conventional.* New Yorker 7/18/70, p45 **[1963]**

wok (wɑk), *n.* a traditional Chinese cooking utensil shaped somewhat like a bowl. *. . . it is no longer necessary to trek down to Chinatown for woks. Macy's has them, made of stainless steel and with black hard-plastic handles.* New Yorker 11/28/70, p163 **[1969,** from Cantonese; earlier *wock* (1952)]

woman, *n.* ►The movement to eliminate sexism in language led during the 1970's to an increasing avoidance of words and phrases that refer to women in a patronizing or disparaging way or in needless typing by sex. Also regarded as sexist and proscribed by many of the new style guides of publishing houses, newspapers, and magazines, were references to women, such as "the fair sex" and "busy housewife and mother".

Similar guidelines have been issued and popularized to deal with the use of *man* in the generic sense of "any human being," equalizing the sexes in language with the use of *person* as a neutral designation.

In the quotations below, *woman* is used to replace or supplement *man* in words and phrases.—**one's own woman** [formed after *one's own man,* but known as early as 1605, though labeled "obsolete" in OED 2]: *Thank heaven I have graduated from the "girl who cain't say no." I'm my own woman now. I don't belong to the party, nor the people.* Maclean's 7/74, p4 —**woman-year,** *n.* [formed after *man-year*]: *The pill's failure rate as a contraceptive is miniscule—0.34 per hundred woman-years.* Manchester Guardian Weekly 5/25/74, p8

womb-envy, *n.* a masculine envy of the female capacity to give birth. *In these men one saw a real womb-envy, a feeling that their women, however they treated them, had a direct line to the Lord through their wombs.* NY Times Magazine 12/25/77, p13 **[1972,** patterned after *penis envy* (OEDS 1924)]

womb-to-tomb, *adj. Informal.* from birth to death; spanning a lifetime. *His principal monument is Britain's National Health Service, still the model of womb-to-tomb medical care.* Time 1/28/74, pK6 *Along with work and community involvement we need "life-cycle education"—a womb-to-tomb activity covering the human life span.* Maggie Kuhn, "New Life for the Elderly: Liberation from 'Ageism'," in The New Old: Struggling for Decent Aging, 1978, p301 **[1964,** from the phrase *from womb to tomb;* compare *cradle-to-grave* (OEDS 1943)] ►Strictly, *womb-to-tomb* medical care includes prenatal care of the mother-to-be as well as monitoring the fetus before its birth.

Women's Lib, a militant movement of women calling for liberation from sexism and all other forms of male domination. Also called WOMEN'S LIBERATION, FEM LIB. *While some fear that Women's Lib is a threat to the family, many experts believe that its more sensible goals could strengthen it.* Time 12/28/70, p38 *I personally don't believe in Women's Lib for black women, as we have always been liberated to work—many times at menial jobs.* NY Times 6/27/71, p31 [**1969**]

Women's-Libber, *n.* another name for WOMEN'S LIBERATIONIST. *Women's-Libbers, both of them (it was too bad that the linesman in question was a woman), they said that they didn't care what happened to the prize money . . .* Time 10/11/71, p44 *A batch of Pain Parlors and guillotines that had already been delivered to the stores . . . provoked an angry delegation of women's-libbers to picket Nabisco's embarrassed Park Avenue headquarters last month with signs blaming the rise in juvenile crime on their monster kits.* New Yorker 12/11/71, p109 [**1971**]

Women's Liberation, another name for WOMEN'S LIB. . . . *the editors of Harper's wish to reassert our belief that Women's Liberation is a development of possibly very great significance to the future of American Society . . .* Harper's 3/71, p4 [**1966**]

Women's Liberationist, a member, follower, or supporter of Women's Lib; a militant feminist. Also called WOMEN'S-LIBBER. *Construction workers waving their flags, Women's Liberationists waving their bras—these threaten to become the unsmiling faces of the '70s.* Time 7/20/70, p30 *The demands of the women's movements, at least those demands that can be brought to socioeconomic focus, are transparently just. So much so that to some people, including the more fanatical Women's Liberationists, they also seem a little dull.* Harper's 12/70, p110 [**1969**]

women's movement or **Women's Movement,** the Women's Liberation Movement. Also called the MOVEMENT. *Because of the women's movement, men must now take seriously inquiries about the female condition, and women must also.* American Scholar, Autumn 1972, p621 *Before the Women's Movement you either, if you were married, popped pills which your sympathetic shrink prescribed (for anxiety about "frigidity") . . . or, if unmarried, got involved in work and periodically swore off men in a fit of disgust and self-reproach.* Maclean's 11/74, p19 *By 1979, pornography had done what a million abortions a year had done: it had given the "women's movement" doubts about the dogma that sexual mores are none of the law's business.* Newsweek 11/19/79, p59 [**1972**] ►This term was probably influenced by the 19th-century term *woman movement* (OEDS 1883) and its variant *woman's movement* (OEDS 1894), defined in the OED as "the movement for the emancipation of women, or the recognition and extension of women's rights." The plural form *women's movement* is first recorded in 1902 in the sense of the women's suffrage movement. The present-day use is in part a revival of the earlier use, and in part a shortening of *Women's Liberation Movement.*

women's studies, a program of courses dealing with the role of women in history and culture. *"Women's studies" was nearly unknown before 1970; now 78 institutions have complete women's studies programs, and some 2,000 courses are offered on another 500 campuses.* Newsweek 12/10/73, p124 [**1972**]

wonk, *n. U.S. Slang.* a person who is too bookish; bookworm. *At Harvard the excessively studious student is derided as a 'wonk,' which Amy Berman, Harvard '79, fancifully suggests may be 'know' spelled backward.* NY Times Magazine 7/20/80, p8 [**1962**, of uncertain origin]

Woodstock, *n.* an American rock-music festival where hundreds of thousands of young people converged in August, 1969 (usually used allusively). *The film of the Off Broadway smash called "Godspell" is a version of the Gospels designed to be read as show-biz literature by the Woodstock generation.* New Yorker 4/7/73, p134 *The most exciting part of the Second World Black and African Festival of Arts and Culture is . . . the nightly parties and jam sessions taking place at Festac Village, a barracks-style housing development for 22,000 people six miles out of town that has become an African Woodstock.* NY Times 1/29/77, p6 [**1970**, so called because the festival was held near *Woodstock, N.Y.*] —**Woodstockian,** *adj.:* This sum-

mer Miami will be swamped with conventioneers grappling with the dilemma of picking a candidate and finding a place in the sun . . . *During that time, Miami will affect a Woodstockian aura.* Saturday Review 5/20/72, p24 —**Woodstock Nation:** *High days for the Woodstock Nation, when . . . a generation of youth could skip the work force and join a children's crusade that rejected materialism and set forth to the East, seeking experience, drugs, ultimate truth and gurus in India.* NY Times Book Review 12/9/79, p12

woofing or **woofin',** *n. U.S. (Black English) Slang.* an aggressive or emphatic way of asserting oneself verbally and by stance or gesture, especially to intimidate another person. Compare the DOZENS, SHUCKING AND JIVING, SIGNIFYING, SOUNDING. *Woofing is a style of bragging and boasting about how "bad" one is and is sometimes used by males and females when rapping to each other. This would be a sincere self-image, and the attitude is very emphatic, as "I'm bad and I know I'm bad!"* ["Bad" means excellent.] Rappin' and Stylin' Out, 1972, p45 *In colleges, woofin' is usually used for personal or group gain. In some rare cases, woofin' has actually been used to procure an undergraduate degree in mostly independent study. Assuredly, some of the woofin' has been precipitated by Whites trying to hustle Blacks out of goods and materials which have been promised or which are rightfully theirs.* Today's Education, Sept./Oct. 1975, p54 [**1942, 1969,** back formation from *woof, v.* to talk much and loudly (OEDS 1934), probably from *woof* to bark like a dog]

word, *n.* any of the three-letter combinations (such as UGA for the sequence uracil-guanine-adenine) that represent the nucleotide triplets or codons in the genetic code. Compare SYNONYM. See also EXPRESSION, SENTENCE. *The genetic code, which is the same for all living beings from viruses to men, is written in three-letter "words" (codons) made of different combinations of the four chemical building blocks that make DNA. Each codon specifies one of the 20 amino acids that go into the making of protein chains.* Scientific American 11/6/76, p16 *In two regions of phiX174, a stretch of DNA codes for two completely different proteins. The overlapping genes begin at different "start" signals so they group nucleotide "letters" into different three-letter "words" and thus code for different amino acid parts of a protein.* Encyclopedia Science Supplement (Grolier) 1979, p67 [**1968,** probably short for CODE WORD (def. 2)]

word processing, the use of high-speed, computerized typewriters and other office equipment to produce letters, reports, memoranda, etc. *Abbreviation:* WP *The vague, catch-all term, "word processing," describes the use of a computer's ability to store and process electronic information in composing and producing the paperwork of an office: letters, contracts, reports, statistical tables and the like.* NY Times 1/1/77, p21 *The keyboard of the word-processing typewriter, which has already made its appearance in some of the most modern offices, is standard but typing on it produces not only a paper copy but also a magnetic recording which can be automatically searched and edited.* Times (London) 9/12/77, p5 [**1970**] —**word processor:** *Word processors call up documents, page by page and line by line, on cathode ray screens for editing. They print out finished versions automatically or send them via telephone lines to distant points. Similar systems are penetrating the newspaper business rapidly.* NY Times 1/1/77, p22 *The name "word processor" can be confusing. Basically it is any machine that handles paperwork electronically—at its simplest this embraces typing, data recording, dictating and transcribing, etc. The most straightforward word processor is an automatic typewriter of the type that first appeared in the early 1960s.* New Scientist 6/15/78, p747

workaholic, *n.* a person who has a strong urge to work constantly, especially preferring work to leisure activities. *The workaholic "drops out of the human community," Oates says, and "eats, drinks and sleeps his job." . . . How does a workaholic know that he is one? Sometimes he finds out only when he suffers a heart attack . . .* Time 7/5/71, p46 [**1968,** coined from *work* + *alcoholic* by Wayne Oates, an American pastoral counselor; see -AHOLIC]

workaholism, *n.* a strong urge to work constantly, especially in preference to leisure activities. *The story goes that he was conservative and inclined to workaholism, while she converted from Bendel's to the barricades.* New York Magazine 11/4/74, p50 *Many officers have left First Chicago because Abboud has a short fuse—befitting a man who is 5 ft. 6 in. and expects everybody to share his own I-made-it-the-hard-way workaholism.* Time 8/21/78, p58 [**1968,** from WORKAHOLIC + *-ism*]

workaround, *n. Aerospace.* an alternative method available in the event a plan or mechanism fails to work as expected (often used attributively). *Finally, at 12.15 am, Launch Control announced that everyone was happy with the "workaround" solution devised at Huntsville and the count was resumed at 12.25.* New Scientist 12/14/72, p645 *"We may never have dreamed that an oxygen bottle would blow and do the sort of damage that one did, but we designed and built the total spacecraft in such a way that there were always 'workarounds'—different ways of getting around a problem—so that we wouldn't be left hanging by our thumbs if something unexpected did crop up."* NY Times Magazine 6/20/76, p46 [**1972,** from the verb phrase *work around* (a problem, etc.)]

worker-director, *n. Especially British.* a company employee selected to serve on the company's board of directors. *The worker-directors, who will continue to do their own jobs, will participate in a four-tier system of management. On the main board will be the chairman, Sir Brian Morton, five executive directors and the five employee representatives.* Times (London) 4/1/76, p1 *In Britain, action was never taken on a 1977 government recommendation to require worker directors in all companies with more than 2,000 employees.* U.S. News and World Report 11/19/79, p85 [**1968**]

worker participation, a system in which employees take part in the management of the company they work for, as by helping to formulate policies dealing with production and workers' benefits. Also called COMANAGEMENT, COSUPERVISION. *Worker participation is a catch-all description of widely varied efforts all over Europe to give employees a greater say in how they do their jobs and how their companies are run. At the extreme, it means wresting all control of industry from the stockholders and turning it over to the workers.* NY Times 9/9/76, p57 *I believe that worker-participation will be accepted as an essential part of the proper management of industry throughout Europe and beyond Europe before very long.* Times (London) 9/10/76, p4 [**1971**]

work ethic, a set of values that stresses the virtuous aspects of hard work, diligence, and industry. Compare PROTESTANT ETHIC. *From the first, it was understood that a guaranteed income could come about only if it was accompanied by some assurance that the nation was not abandoning what is, in truth, a potent and deeply believed "work ethic."* New Yorker 1/20/73, p72 *Because of these values, which include a religious respect for the work ethic, welfare comes under savage criticism in New Brunswick. Welfare "bums," "freeloaders," and "chiselers" are favorite targets for the writers of letters to the editor.* Maclean's 7/74, p54 *One institution that seemed in particular peril from these political, economic, and social upheavals was the work ethic, foundation stone of the American industrial system.* 1978 World Book Year Book, p143 [**1959**]

workfare, *n.* a welfare program in which recipients of public welfare payments are required to work at assigned jobs or to enlist in job training. *The new law will take 18 months to set up and, at that, is expected to increase the number of recipients registered for workfare by no more than 30,000.* Time 12/27/71, p26 *Just as in the domestic welfare reform programme, Nixon calls for work-fare instead of welfare, so in foreign policy the "do-it-yourself" principle will be applied.* Sunday Times (London) 1/25/70, p8 [**1968,** from *work* + *welfare*]

work-in, *n.* a form of protest demonstration in which a group of people report to work or study but disregard the rules and procedures they normally follow. *Last summer more than 3,000 city welfare employees staged a "work-in," during which they showed up at the office but refused to process cases.* Time 8/23/68, p50 *Several hundred students decided yesterday to* hold an all-night "work-in" in their library after the principal had refused to call an emergency meeting of the university court. Times (London) 3/6/70, p2 [**1968;** see -IN]

work island. See the quotation for the meaning. *Other labor innovations that have been hailed in Germany and Scandinavia . . . include "flextime," whereby workers set their own hours, usually within specified limits, and assembly lines are replaced by "work islands"—autonomous groups of workers assigned to work together on an entire section of a project.* NY Times 1/25/76, pC44 [**1976**]

workover, *n.* a maintenance procedure on an oil rig to repair or replace dull or fouled equipment by forcing oil back into its underground reservoir and sealing the well. *One of the prime reasons for deciding to recover the platform was that corrosion in the steel tubing of the well system itself had meant that the whole structure needed a "workover"—offshore terminology for a major refit.* New Scientist 12/14/78, p842 [**1976,** noun use of the verb phrase *work over* to subject to thorough treatment]

work-release, *adj.* of or designed for the part-time release of prisoners to permit them to engage in normal work or continue in their regular jobs. *The defendants . . . will be eligible for "work-release" programs. That means they could report to their offices by day but would have to spend their nights locked up.* Time 12/13/76, p65 [**1957**]

work-to-contract, *n. British.* a form of job slowdown in which employees refuse to fulfill any tasks except those specified in their contract. *So the question . . . is whether the Government feels able to approve an award to hospital doctors who, by their work-to-contract, are causing delays in admission and limiting the number of patients treated.* Manchester Guardian Weekly 4/5/75, p4 [**1969,** patterned after WORK-TO-RULE]

work-to-rule, *n.* a job action marked by vigorous observance and literal interpretation of every regulation for a job. It is often used by workers as a form of protest or to force concessions from management (often used attributively). *Hospital consultants began a work-to-rule on 2 January, in protest against the new contract they had been offered.* Annual Register of World Events in 1975, p37 *The work-to-rules and goslows by Spanish air traffic controllers have already led to an admission by the Ministry of Aviation in Madrid that there were "technical difficulties and difficulties in some equipment" at some of the country's civil airports.* Manchester Guardian Weekly 4/3/77, p6 [**1950,** from the verb phrase *work to rule* (OEDS 1940)]

workwear, *n.* **1** clothes made for workers; working clothes. *The replacement of cotton by Terylene workwear was found to reduce considerably the amount of dust which entered the workers' breathing zone.* New Scientist 1/15/70, p122 **2** a style of clothing fashioned after working clothes. *Blue jeans continued to be the most popular single fashion garment, and denim skirts, coats, tunics and overblouses were introduced, often designed as Chinese 'workwear', a new term introduced to describe loose garments fastened with strings or toggles.* Annual Register of World Events in 1975, p418 [**1970**]

World Beat, popular dance music combining traditional African rhythms with elements of jazz and rock. *The proliferation of radio programs offering World Beat indicates that a growing minority of listeners wants to hear something exotic.* Arizona Republic 9/4/88, p1 [**1988**]

world car, an economical automobile assembled from parts made in several countries and sold throughout the world. *Both Ford and GM will introduce front-wheel drive, so-called world cars, which may be the industry's best prospect for future profits.* Time 4/28/80, p42 [**1968**]

world-class, *adj.* of international note or quality. . . . *Granados was in glorious voice and in total sympathy with Ashkenazy, who showed himself a world-class accompanist.* Manchester Guardian Weekly 7/18/70, p21 *It is now widely known that Fisons claims to have pulled a potentially world-class drug, Intal, out of its rag-bag of health food and proprietary pharmaceuticals interests.* Sunday Times (London) 11/23/69, p26 [**1969,** originally applied to boxers of world champion caliber (1950), later to other types of athletes]

wormery, *n.* a place for breeding worms, especially to be sold as fishing bait. *The Manitoba Department of Agriculture has lent Main $10,000 to expand his wormery into a large-scale business with 100 work pits and 7.5 million wriggling workmen.* Maclean's 2/9/76, p48 [**1952, 1972,** patterned after *fishery*]

wormhole, *n. Astronomy.* a hypothetical passageway in space connecting a black hole and a white hole. See EVENT HORIZON, SINGULARITY, WHITE HOLE. *Perhaps because of a philosophical or psychological reluctance to accept the finality of black holes, some scientists speculate that matter going down these drains may not always be destroyed. On the contrary, under special circumstances the matter might be conducted by a rapidly rotating black hole through space and time via passages dubbed wormholes. It would reemerge in a different part of the universe or perhaps in another universe entirely.* Time 9/4/78, p54 *Particularly appealing to science-fiction writers is the concept of "wormholes," which tunnel through the contorted space-time geometry of black holes into other universes—or emerge into our own universe at some other time and place. If a star went through such a wormhole it might, according to one hypothesis, burst forth far away, in space-time dimensions, radiating intense energy.* Walter Sullivan, Black Holes, 1979, p197 [**1957, 1978,** figurative use of the noun meaning the thin burrow of a worm]

worry beads, a string of beads played with for relaxation or distraction, derived from rosary-like beads used in the Middle East. *Worry beads and clunky ball-bearings are two traditional office diversions for nervy captains of industry . . .* Times (London) 11/7/70, p12 *Top brass relaxation rooms should also be provided, plentifully equipped with worry beads . . .* New Scientist and Science Journal 12/9/71, p105 [**1964**]

worst-case, *adj.* designed to include or provide for the most unfavorable conditions or circumstances possible. Compare BEST-CASE. *In a limited war, with the wind blowing south, one in every 11 Canadians could be killed or injured. In a worst-case scenario with a stiff breeze driving the fallout on to Canada instead of away, half the population could be lost in a day.* Maclean's 5/29/78, p22 *San Francisco Mayor George Moscone was studying a worst-case budget: the $84.9 million to operate city buses, trolleys and cable cars would be more than halved, the street-cleaning fund would drop from $783,000 to $90,000, and the city's human rights commission (scheduled to spend $332,101) would get no money at all.* Time 6/19/78, p14 *Also included in the Sandia study was a "worst case" projection that a massive accident or act of sabotage that succeeded in breaching the cask of a shipment of elements carried by truck in mid-city could afflict more than 3,300 New Yorkers with fatal radiation doses or radiation-induced fatal cancers. (An even worse worst-case projection would involve rail shipments.)* New Yorker 11/13/78, p146 [**1964**]

WP, abbreviation of WORD PROCESSING. *The basic hardware in WP systems is the typewriter with a memory. Text which is stored on discs, tapes or cards can be reproduced quickly and stored information can easily be edited and revised. Like the development of the computer, WP combines a specific type of technology and an economic requirement for the best use of the technology.* Times (London) 10/2/78, pIII [**1974**]

W particle, a subatomic particle with either a positive or a negative charge, held to be a carrier, or quantum, of the weak force. It has a mass about 86 times that of the proton. Also called INTERMEDIATE VECTOR BOSON and WEAKON. Compare Z PARTICLE. *Evidence of the existence of a hitherto hypothetical subatomic particle—the intermediate boson, or W particle—has been found in an abandoned silver mine in Utah. The finding, made by a group of physicists from the University of Utah led by Jack W. Keuffel and Haven E. Bergeson, was reported recently at the 12th International Conference on Cosmic-Ray Physics, held in Tasmania.* Scientific American 10/71, p42 [**1971,** but referred to earlier as *W* (1960)]

wrap, *n.* the end of a session of filming or videotaping. *The director says: "Cut! Thank you, Ben, that's a wrap—there is no more filming."* Listener 6/23/83, p18 [**1974**]

wraparound, *adj.* **1** completely encircling or surrounding. *The Volkswagen is the German's ideal image of space: it's a wraparound, secure little thing . . .* Maclean's 9/67, p14 [**1957,** from the meaning of extending around a corner of edge (1954)] **2** *Figurative.* all-inclusive; all-embracing. *The social issue, the wraparound inphrase of the year, covering dissatisfaction with protest, fear of crime, and disgust with drugs, promiscuity and pornography, had less universal impact than initially assumed.* Time 11/16/70, p17 [**1964**] **3** of or designating letterpress printing adapted to a flexible plate for a rotary press, as opposed to a flat-bed press, thus gaining the advantage of speedy reproduction. *Wraparound letterpress printing is the direct transfer of ink to paper from a thin, flexible relief plate which is wrapped around the cylinder of a rotary press.* McGraw-Hill Yearbook of Science and Technology 1969, p284 [**1959**] **4** having lenses that extend around the sides of the head. *He wore wraparound sunglasses and white perforated shoes.* New Yorker 7/9/79, p34 [**1957**] ►The term was originally applied to a garment wrapped around the body (OED 1887)]

wristwrestling, *n.* a variety of Indian wrestling in which the contenders lock right thumbs instead of hands in trying to force down each other's arm. *It seems perfectly natural for a wristwrestling championship to be held in Timmins, wristwrestling being a backwoods barroom sport and Timmins being a backwoods barroom mining town in Northern Ontario. No dazzling footwork here; you put his arm down or he puts yours down. Brawn, pure brawn. Timmins has hosted the World Wristwrestling Championships for eight years.* Maclean's 6/12/78, p62 [**1973**]

wu shu or **wushu** (ˈwuːˈʃuː), *n.* the Chinese martial arts. See KUNG FU. *With a history going back more than 2,000 years, "Wu shu"—meaning "traditional Chinese sports"—was once the pastime of exclusive sects organized into elaborate hierarchies of masters and disciples.* Newsweek 7/15/74, p52 [**1973,** from Chinese, literally, military art]

X

X, a symbol meaning "not for children; restricted to adults." *If county Board of Legislators Chairman Andrew O'Rourke has his way, Westchester "head shops" will be rated "X"—for adults only. O'Rourke . . . is launching a campaign to either outlaw or restrict to adults the sale of rolling paper, cocaine spoons, and other drug-related paraphernalia.* Metro (Westchester, N.Y.) 5/2/79, pA9 [**1970**, originally (1950's) applied to motion pictures; see X-RATED]

xanthan ('zænthən), *n.* or **xanthan gum**, a water-soluble gum made from polysaccharides produced by certain bacteria in sugar solutions. It is used as a thickener and stabilizer especially in the food industry, medicine, and pharmacy. *A new gum called xanthan was developed on a commercial scale in 1974. In the food industry it serves as an emulsion stabilizer in salad dressings and enhances certain starch products. When xanthan is used in gluten-free bread dough, it is possible to enrich the product with soybean protein, thereby greatly increasing the nutritional qualities of the bread.* Americana Annual 1975, p382 *A thickener called xanthan gum is being used with detergents to help free oil that clings to underground rock formations and resists recovery by conventional methods. Once injected into a well, the thickener restricts the detergent to where it will do the most good, keeping it from running all over the place.* NY Times Magazine 2/6/77, p41 [**1964**, from *Xanth(omonas campestris)* a species of bacteria cultivated to produce this gum + *-an* (chemical suffix)]

X-C skiing, *U.S. and Canada.* another name for SKI TOURING. *Appreciated the rundown (Travel Notes, Dec. 12) of spectator-participant events for the cross-country ski enthusiast. Finally, X-C skiing is being appreciated for the "total" sport it has become with multitudes of adherents.* NY Times 1/2/77, pJ11 [**1972**, *X-C* from *X* (for *cross*) + *C*, abbreviation of *country*]

xenobiotic, *n.* a foreign substance capable of harming or affecting a living organism. *Groups of exposed women (smokers) and controls (nonsmokers) were readily available. "Nicotine can be a model for other xenobiotics—for a broad spectrum of foreign substances," Castagnoli explains. In other experiments, Petrakis and colleagues observed barbiturates and foreign fatty acids secreted into breast fluids.* Science News 1/21/78, p39 [**1965**, from *xeno-* foreign + *-biotic* relating to life]

xenocurrency, *n.* currency circulating outside its country of origin. See also ASIADOLLAR. *International bankers are adding a new word to their jargon: "xenocurrency." . . . Schmidt and Miller made a point of referring to "xenocurrency" markets [and] argued that Eurodollars and Eurocurrency are misnomers when applied to the billions of dollars and marks now circulating in Hong Kong, Singapore, the Bahamas and other non-European money markets.* Newsweek 10/15/79, p37 [**1979**, from *xeno-* foreign + *currency*]

xenogeneic, *adj.* (of transplanted tissues) deriving from an organism of a different species. Compare ALLOGENEIC. *The survival of these grafts, as compared with similar grafts on females inoculated with female rat lymph node cells, indicated whether the xenogeneic male cell inoculum had sensitized the recipients with respect to H-Y antigen.* Science 8/10/73, p571 [**1961**, from *xeno-* foreign + *-geneic*, as in *syngeneic* of the same origin]

xenograft, *n.* a graft of tissue taken from an individual of another species. *A xenograft, formerly heterograft, is one in which there is interspecific difference between donor and recipient, as between a man and a monkey.* 1969 Britannica Yearbook of Science and the Future, p177 *If the donor and recipient are non-identical members of the same species, the graft is called an allograft or homograft; if they belong to different species, the graft is called a xenograft or heterograft.* New Scientist 11/9/67, p364 [**1961**, from *xeno-* foreign (from Greek *xénos*) + *graft*]

xenotropic, *adj.* (of a virus) inactive in a host species and replicating only in cells foreign to the host. *Although it has the murine leukaemia virus (MLV) gs-1 antigen and reverse transcriptase, it cannot be propagated in mouse cells. It is only infectious for cells foreign to the host species and has been termed xenotropic.* Nature 1/10/75, p140 [**1973**] —**xenotropism**, *n.: Another example of xenotropism is the endogenous feline virus which when activated replicates in human cells.* Nature 3/22/78, p279

xerography, *n.* a xerographic process used in medicine for producing an image of internal parts of the body on a sheet of opaque, plastic-coated paper. *Simple X-ray procedures are often helpful in finding breast cancer. So is a new technique called xerography, which uses a charged electric plate and a photoelectric system to build an image on paper.* Americana Annual 1975, p371 [**1968**, extended sense of the term for a dry photographic printing process (1948)]

xeroradiograph, *v.t.* to make an X-ray picture of by using an electrically charged metal plate; to photograph or record by means of xeroradiography. *After X-raying and xeroradiographing the mummy, the pathologists cut the stiff wrapping lengthwise, to open up the specimen like a violin case.* New Scientist 4/19/73, p169 [**1973**, verb use of the noun (1955) meaning an X-ray picture made by *xeroradiography* (1950)]

xerox, *v.t., v.i.* to make copies of graphic material by a xerographic or dry photocopying process. *In view of the sentiments expressed at the meeting, I thought that the affluent gr up would be more likely to spend their money on xeroxing Foxe's Book of Martyrs, but I was wrong.* New Scientist 12/31/70, p604 *Morning coffee, in-box, out-box, Xeroxing, and other matters were handled by staff services.* Harper's 3/70, p87 [**1965**, from *Xerox*, trademark for a xerographic process and machine patented in 1952]

X-ogen ('eksədʒən), *n.* an interstellar molecule detected through radio emissions from several galactic sources. Compare Y-OGEN. *X-ogen was first noticed about three years ago. The latest report on the subject . . . shows that it is found in at least eight locations in the sky: W3(OH), Orion, Sagittarius A, W51, W3(companion), NGC 2024, NGC 6334N and K3-50.* Science News 4/27/73, p258 [**1970**, coined by the American astronomers David Buhl and Lewis Snyder from *X* for unknown (from the uncertainty of its structure until 1976) + *-ogen* as in *hydrogen* and *nitrogen*]

X-rated, *adj.* **1a** that is sexually explicit or prurient; pornographic. Compare ADULT. *"Phaedra" (1962), which has also been revived, is taken much more seriously than it deserves to be. It's Graham's X-rated treatment of Euripides; Noguchi provided the peep-show scenery.* New Yorker 6/13/77, p104 *The mass production of indifferent or plainly bad X-rated films persisted, notably in Japan, West Germany, Italy and America.* Annual Register of World Events in 1973, p436 **b** featuring nude performers or performances, as in a burlesque show. *BUMP AND GRIND REVUE: The Colonial Tavern . . . Hot Tamale and her breathtaking Fire Dance accompanied by X-rated live shows. Exotic dancers perform noon to 1 a.m.* Globe and Mail (Toronto) 3/29/79, p16 **2** vulgar; obscene. *His communicators at the same time kept insisting improbably that the transcripts actually clear the President of any crime more grievous than using X-rated language and* *thinking unsavory thoughts.* Newsweek 5/20/74, p23 [**1970**, from the symbol *X*, used in the United States and Great Britain since the 1950's to rate motion pictures dealing with subjects or using language suitable only for adults]

X-ray astronomer, a specialist in X-ray astronomy. *The group of X-ray astronomers at Massachusetts Institute of Technology have made a speciality of studying X-rays emanating from the centre of our Galaxy.* New Scientist and Science Journal 3/11/71, p534 [**1969**]

X-ray astronomy, the astronomical study of X-ray stars. *The young field of X-ray astronomy has found another mystery: a second pulsating X-ray star quite different from the only other one known.* Science News 4/3/71, p239 [**1963**]

X-ray burst, one of the periodic bursts emitted by an X-ray burster. Compare GAMMA-RAY BURST. *The cooperative observations are being arranged as a result of the first detection of light bursts coincident with X-ray bursts by the 150-centimeter telescope at the Cerro Tololo Inter-American Observatory in Chile on June 2. The source was MXB1735-44. Two optical bursts were recorded. There are no X-ray data for the time of the first burst, but SAS 3 recorded an X-ray burst coincident with the second.* Science News 6/24/78, p405 [**1976**]

X-ray burster, a celestial body that is the source of powerful periodic bursts of X rays. Also shortened to BURSTER. *The new X-ray bursters, as they are being colloquially called, flare up and die again in only a few seconds, which has so far made them more difficult to detect. "X-ray bursts are going to be the big story of 1976," predicted Leicester University's Professor Ken Pounds.* New Scientist 3/25/76, p676 [**1976**]

X-ray laser, a device similar in function to a laser, which amplifies X-rays by stimulated emission to produce a beam of great penetrating power. Compare GAMMA-RAY LASER. *During the year development of an X-ray laser, which would have particular application to crystallography and medical holography, progressed along two separate routes.* Britannica Book of the Year 1978, p584 [**1967**]

X-ray nova, a nova (type of star that suddenly becomes very bright and then fades) that emits X rays. *Meanwhile, the second example of an 'X-ray nova' was reported during the summer of 1969, based on observations from two US Vela satellites built to monitor man-made nuclear explosions in space.* Science Journal 4/70, p64 [**1970**]

X-ray pulsar, a pulsar that is the source of powerful X-ray emissions. *One of the most remarkable developments of X-ray astronomy was the Mar. 13, 1969, discovery of an X-ray pulsar in the Crab Nebula. Pulsars, celestial objects which emit vast amounts of power in brief intense bursts with extremely precise periodicity, were first observed in the radio region.* McGraw-Hill Yearbook of Science and Technology 1971, p441 [**1969**]

X-ray star or **X-ray source**, an astronomical source of X rays concentrated at a point; a celestial body that emits X rays. *New discoveries would shed light on the relationship between pulsars and other kinds of X-ray stars . . .* New Scientist 12/3/70, p364 *Most of the known discrete X-ray sources lie close to the Milky Way and therefore very probably belong to the local galaxy.* Science Journal 4/70, p61 [**1964**]

X-ray telescope, a telescope used in X-ray astronomy, consisting of mirrors focused on a gas-filled X-ray scintillation counter, which is attached to a rocket and telemeters X-ray emissions to earth. *X-ray telescopes using confocal paraboloidal-hyperboloidal mirrors have been fabricated and flown on Aerobee rockets to obtain photographs of the Sun in the soft x-ray region.* McGraw-Hill Yearbook of Science and Technology 1971, p439 [**1963**]

XYY syndrome, a congenital disorder of males resulting from the presence of an extra male chromosome (XYY instead of XY) in the cells, and thought by some to be characterized by aggressive behavior and social inadequacy. *The XYY syndrome, a defect in sexual chromosomes, has, for instance, been linked to criminal behavior in some men.* Science News 10/19/68, p388 *The judge, however, ruled that there was insufficient evidence to prove that there was any relationship between the XYY syndrome and human behaviour . . .* Science Journal 12/70, p8 [**1968**]

Y

Y, symbol for UPSILON. *Designated upsilon (Y), the new particle points to the existence of a fifth quark, one more massive than any of the others . . . Its existence appears to be a mixed blessing for the quark hypothesis.* Scientific American 10/78, p22 [**1977,** from the Greek letter upsilon]

yachtie, *n. Informal.* a person who owns or sails a boat, especially a yacht. *Less familiar, because less conspicuous, are the ones who do it by sea—shoals of them, from Mr Saunders's account, bumming around the world in little boats. There is even a word for them: yachties.* Listener 2/13/75, p221 [**1965,** from *yacht* + *-ie* (diminutive suffix)] ▶A variant spelling *yachty* appears in "English As It Is Spoken In New Zealand," by J. A. W. Bennett, *American Speech*, April, 1943.

YAG (yæg), *n.* acronym for *yttrium aluminum garnet,* a synthetic crystal of aluminum oxide used to generate laser beams. Compare YIG. . . . *the neodymium doped YAG laser operating in the second harmonic mode provides hundreds of kilowatts at a wavelength of 0.53 microns. It can be operated at pulse rates of up to 10 Hz.* New Scientist 4/17/69, p123 [**1964**]

yakitori (ˌyaːkiˈtɔriː), *n.* a Japanese dish of grilled or skewered chicken, usually boneless and served with soy sauce. *To stop him [the cook] from frying, simply hold up your hand. A similar technique, both of cooking and eating, applies in the hundreds of* yakitori *(chicken) restaurants scattered round Tokyo . . .* Times (London) 6/17/70, pVII [**1962,** from Japanese, from *yaki* grilling + *tori* fowl]

yakow (ˈyækaʊ), *n.* any of a breed of beef cattle developed in Great Britain by crossbreeding yaks and Highland cows. *Roast Yakow could be Britain's answer to American beefalo—offering cheaper, leaner Sunday joints. But whereas the Beefalo (a cross between the American Buffalo and a beef cow) has been bred to produce meat from warm grassland, the Yakow should be better adapted to our cool wet higher land.* Sunday Times (London) 11/23/75, p15 [**1975,** blend of *yak* and *cow*]

yakuza (ˈyaːkuˌzaː), *n. sing.* or *pl.* a Japanese hoodlum or gangster. Compare YAMAGUCHI-GUMI. *The yakuza are Japanese mobsters, and one of the items in their "code" is that you can show penitence for an offence against the mob chieftain by slicing off your little finger and presenting it to him. Robert Mitchum plays an American private eye who goes to Japan to rescue an American girl kidnapped by yakuza; he enlists the aid of a "retired" yakuza, a master-teacher of swordsmanship (Takakura Ken), and they fight side by side, the gun and the sword.* New Yorker 2/23/76, p25 [**1964,** from Japanese, a good-for-nothing, literally, an eight-nine-three (the worst hand at a card game), from *ya* eight + *ku* nine + *za* three]

Yamaguchi-gumi (ˌyaːmaːˈguːtʃiːˈguːmiː), *n.* a large organization of criminals in Japan. Also **Yamaguchi.** Compare YAKUZA. *Yamaguchi-gumi is a veritable army of 10,000 men. Under the command of Japan's top mobster, Kazuo Taoka, 60, police say that Yamaguchi-gumi has become a criminal conglomerate that controls more than 50 corporations, ranging from restaurants and bars to trucking companies and talent agencies.* Time 2/26/73, p31 *"We are linked by a spiritual bond," says Oda, unabashedly reiterating the precept of public and personal honor inculcated among the Yamaguchi's 11,000 members, unquestionably the largest, most tightly knit band of gamblers, extortionists, pimps and general hoodlums-about-town in modern times.* NY Times Magazine 12/12/76, p61 [**1973,** from Japanese, literally, Yamaguchi-gang, from Harukichi *Yamaguchi,* the organization's original leader + *-gumi* gang]

Yanomama (ˌyaːnoumaːˈmaː) or **Yanomamo** (ˌyaːnoumaːˈmou), *n.* a member of a primitive, warlike people of northern Brazil and southern Venezuela, who have been the subject of numerous studies since contact was established with them in the late 1960's (often used attributively). Compare ACHE and TASADAY. *As the Yanomama population grew and new villages were founded, the blood protein differences and linguistic differences between Yanomama groups grew at about the same rate, indicating that biological and cultural change rates correspond closely.* 1975 World Book Year Book, p197 *Among the Yanomamo tribes population is controlled by warfare, feuding and infanticide.* Times (London) 11/1/72, p10 [**1967**]

yard, *n.* **the whole nine yards,** *Informal.* the whole thing; everything; the works. *While returning from a weekend visit to the Shenandoah Valley, [they] passed a 1983 Lincoln on Interstate 66. It had "smoked windows, antennas, the whole nine yards."* Washington Post 10/12/83, pE22 [**1983**]

Yard (yard), *n.* another name for MONTAGNARD. *From the beginning, the Americans, unlike the Vietnamese, got along well with the "Yards."* Time 7/19/68, p31 [**1968,** from the pronunciation of the final syllable of *Montagnard*]

yard sale, *U.S.* a sale of old or used household belongings, held on the front or backyard or lawn of a house. Compare GARAGE SALE. *A man never realizes how ruthless a wife can be until she holds a yard sale. Nothing is sacred. A set of Hardy Boys in mint condition, a Turkish water pipe, a rowing machine . . . She said the whole point of a yard sale was to get rid of stuff.* Reader's Digest 5/79, p150 [**1976**]

YAVIS, *n. U.S.* acronym for *Young, Attractive, Verbal, Intelligent, and Successful. From its inception, psychoanalysis has been plagued by an elitist image . . . Analysts say that the treatment works best for the YAVIS.* Time 4/2/79, p79 [**1976**]

yecch, *interj. Especially U.S. Slang.* variant of YUCK. *"And lunches. We have terrible lunches. Yecch!"* Time 2/14/72, p45 *"You ask a guy today how the economy will be in three weeks and he'll say 'Yecch!' " a Ford official said last week.* Newsweek 3/24/75, p72 [**1969**]

yecchy, *adj. Especially U.S. Slang.* variant of YUCKY. *The disgusted "yecchy," with its comic-strip origins, fades, but the equally disgusted gross (ugly, objectionable, and sometimes used admiringly) shows staying power.* NY Times Magazine 3/21/76, p111 [**1969**]

yellow card, *Soccer.* a card of a yellow color raised by a referee as a warning to a player who has violated a rule. *Den Haag were, understandably, bitterly disappointed and their frustration was shown in the cautions administered to Mansveld for arguing and Kila for a foul on Robson. Jennings was also shown the yellow card, for kicking the ball away after yet another offside decision.* Times (London) 3/18/76, p19 [**1976**]

yellow flu, *U.S.* an organized absence of students from schools to which they are bused, on the pretext of sickness but actually as a protest against compulsory BUSING. *The Community had reacted strongly to an earlier plan which required busing between the suburbs and the central city . . . In an allusion to the buses that transport students, two groups called for an epidemic of "yellow flu," but absenteeism was only slightly greater last week than what is considered normal for the first week of a new school term.* NY Times 2/1/76, pD2 [**1976,** so called from the yellow color of school buses]

Yellow Pages, *U.S.* a classified directory of businesses, services, professions, or products in any field. *A "Yellow Pages" of technology is how Control Data Corp. describes Technotec, its com-*

puter-based technology-exchange service. Users interested in a particular technology need only search, for an average charge of $8 or $10, the listings stored in a $1 billion computer network via a Telex, . . . telephone or computer-terminal connection. Science News 9/3/77, p152 [**1966**, transferred sense of the term for the classified directory of a telephone book, usually printed on pages of a yellow color (OEDS 1956)]

yellow rain. See the quotation for the meaning. *The nature of "yellow rain"—a supposedly toxic powder observed in battle areas of southeast Asia, Afghanistan, and Iraq—remained a mystery. The U.S. government has suggested that yellow rain represents a new sort of chemical warfare, involving compounds called tricothecene mycotoxins. . . But a 28-nation scientific conference was unable to resolve a contradictory theory that the powder could be of natural origin, such as bee droppings.* Encyclopedia Science Supplement (Grolier) 1986, p197 [**1979**; so called from the color of the powder; found earlier (1891) referring to the pollen from fir trees]

yenbond, *n.* a Japanese government or corporation bond (often used attributively). *There was some future possibility of a yen-bond market for the financing of international direct investment, said Mr. Iwasa.* Times (London) 10/5/70, p19 [**1970**, from *yen* the Japanese monetary unit + *bond*]

Yerkish, *n.* an artificial language in which geometric symbols represent words, designed for communication between chimpanzees and humans or computers (also used attributively). *In order to teach Lana to communicate, a special language, Yerkish, had to be designed. It is made up of nine simple geometric figures that can be superimposed on each other to form lexigrams that stand for various concepts.* Science News 6/2/73, p360 *A parrot that asks for a cracker is only mimicking a human or another parrot. But a chimpanzee who can "speak" in Ameslan (American sign language) or Yerkish by striking combinations on a keyboard of color-coded symbols seems to be creating syntax, a property of human language. It is not the voice but the process that is critical.* Time 6/26/78, p75 [**1973**, coined by the American psychologist Duane M. Rumbaugh from *Yerkes* Regional Primate Center, Georgia (named after Robert M. Yerkes, 1876-1956, American primatologist), where the language was devised and applied + *-ish*, as in *English*]

yersiniosis (yər,sini:'ousis), *n.* an intestinal disease with symptoms resembling those of appendicitis, caused by a highly contagious type of bacteria. *Surgeons also performed three or four emergency appendectomies on children at City Hospital in nearby Rome, according to a hospital pathologist who declined to be identified. He said the hospital's laboratory later isolated yersiniosis bacteria in the patients' stools.* NY Times 10/21/76, p35 [**1971**, from New Latin *Yersinia*, the genus name of the bacteria (from Alexandre *Yersin*, 1863-1943, Swiss bacteriologist) + *-osis* diseased condition]

yé-yé ('yei,yei), *adj.* of or relating to the mod style of music, clothes, etc., in France, especially during the 1960's. *The jet screechings, like a thousand pieces of chalk rubbed on a thousand blackboards and then amplified like yé-yé music, will blow out the frontal lobes of those waiting at the gate . . .* Saturday Review 3/4/67, p49 **—n.** the yé-yé style of music, clothes, etc. *Turning back to business, Régine disclosed that the orchestra Chez Régine will play anything "from yé-yé to regular music, which is combing back."* NY Times 7/3/68, p30 [**1960**, from French slang *yé-yé*, from English *yeah, yeah*, interjection used in the songs of some rock groups, especially the Beatles]

YIG (yig), *n.* acronym for *yttrium iron garnet*, a synthetic crystal of iron oxide with versatile magnetic properties, used especially in laser modulation. Compare YAG. *Gas lasers offer some advantages in infrared gas analysis as selective sources, and their potential is now being helped by the development of yttrium-iron-garnet (YIG) modulators capable of working out to 3.5 micrometres.* Times (London) 5/13/68, pIV [**1959**]

Yinglish, *n.* English containing many Yiddish words and expressions. *Relying not on my memory alone (that is, my memory of grandparents' and parents' conversations in English, Yiddish, and Yinglish) but also on Leo Rosten's* The Joys of Yid-

dish, *I present the following old joke as explanation: "The schlemozzle is the guy who the schlemiel spills the soup on."* Saturday Review 9/9/72, p27 [**1951**, blend of *Yiddish* and *English*] ►This word was popularized by the American writer Leo Rosten in his book *The Joys of Yiddish* (1968), where he used it primarily to designate Yiddish words, such as *bagel* and *chutzpah*, that have become part of colloquial English. In the sense of "a Yiddish-English mixture" the term was occasionally used in the 1950's, as in the title of an article by H. J. Gans in *American Quarterly*, 21 (1953): "The 'Yinglish' Music of Mickey Katz." The coinage of this word apparently preceded the parallel terms *Spanglish, Japlish,* and *Hinglish,* all hybrids of English with another language.

yip, *n. U.S.* short for YIPPIE. *After swallowing and, at times, choking on an unending diet of . . . the gappy generation, with-it, hung-up, love-in, way-out, freak-out, out of sight, uptight, trips, hips, yips, drugs, thugs, dig, groove, swing and all the power the LOVE can bring, I wish to protest . . .* Time 2/16/70, p4 [**1967**, from *YIP*; see YIPPIE]

yippie ('yipi:), *n.* Also frequently spelled **Yippie.** *U.S.* any of a group of politically active, radical hippies. Also shortened to YIP. *In Anaheim, Calif., about 300 garishly garbed Yippies "liberated" Disneyland. Before the cops arrived, the raiders hoisted a Viet Cong flag atop a fort on Tom Sawyer's Island and yowled slogans like "Free Mickey Mouse!"* Time 8/17/70, p35 [**1968**, formed from *YIP* (abbreviation of *Youth International Party,* the professed name of the yippie group) + hip*pie*]

Y-ogen ('wɑiəd͡ʒən), *n.* an unidentified interstellar molecule detected through radio emission in the region of the constellation Sagittarius. *The H¹³C¹⁶O⁺ line in Sagittarius B2 is contaminated with yet another new molecule nearly overlapping in frequency . . . Thus no sooner is the X-ogen mystery laid to rest than Y-ogen springs up to fox radio astronomers. Will Y-ogen prove as elusive?* New Scientist 10/28/76, p212 [**1976**, patterned after X-OGEN]

yokozuna (,youkə'zu:nə), *n.* a grand champion sumo wrestler; a wrestler of the highest rank in sumo. Compare OZEKI. See also BASHO. *To be yokozuna in Japan is to be a Babe Ruth or Willie Mays, and here, as almost everywhere, fame brings fortune.* NY Times 1/6/74, pJ1 [**1966**, from Japanese]

yordim (yɔr'di:m), *n.pl.* Israeli citizens who emigrate to another country, especially the United States. Compare CHOZRIM. *Those who stay call those who leave yordim (from the Hebrew verb meaning to descend) and look down on them as deserters . . . Some of the yordim reply that they have left for one reason only: greater opportunity.* Time 1/12/76, p24 [**1966**, from Hebrew, literally, those who descend, patterned after OLIM immigrants to Israel, (literally) those who ascend]

Young Lord, *U.S.* a member of the *Young Lords,* a radical organization of young Spanish-speaking Americans, chiefly of Puerto Rican descent, seeking to gain political and economic power for Latin-Americans in the United States. *Then there were the Young Lords . . . who seized the First Spanish Methodist Church in East Harlem. Religion, you understand, is the oppressor, unresponsive to the needs of the community, an arm of the Establishment, and so on, and the Young Lords went about the work of the Revolution by sitting in, and seizing, the First Spanish Methodist Church.* Harper's 11/70, p62 [**1970**]

youthcult, *n.* another name for YOUTH CULTURE. *Clifford Adelman, who has taught at CCNY and Yale, "wished to verify the extent to which the equation of the youthcult with the multifarious spirits of counter culture and counter politics was justified."* Saturday Review 9/2/72, p58 [**1968**, contraction of YOUTH CULTURE]

youth culture, the values and mores of the generation under thirty viewed as a distinctive culture. *A great many people, especially the better educated, take it for granted that today's "youth culture" is the wave of the future. They assume that as the present generation of college students become the young adults of tomorrow, their new life-styles will come to dominate American society and our economy.* Harper's 7/71, p35 [**1958**]

youthquake, *n.* the widespread agitation caused by student up-risings and other expressions of rebellion and radicalism among the youth during the 1960's and 1970's. *Play Power, his* [Richard Neville's] *exploration of the . . . youthquake, is at once spirited, informative, and clearly the work of an engaging and concerned man.* Manchester Guardian Weekly 2/28/70, p18 *He was an Aquarian, yet not of this Aquarian Age of psychedelic blast-offs and amplified youthquakes.* Time 1/11/71, p54 [**1968,** from *youth* + *earth*quake]

yo-yo, *adj.* going up and down; fluctuating. *Dr. Sacks spoke of a "Yo-Yo effect" in which some patients* [treated with L-Dopa] *alternate between sudden restless excitements and a reversion to their original immobility.* Encyclopedia Science Supplement (Grolier) 1970, p213 *Certainly it is not a quickie device which destabilizes the tax system. Congress has come to object to "yo-yo" tax devices.* NY Times 12/16/70, p47 —*v.i.* to waver or fluctuate. *There is plenty of room for debate on this point, because the Supreme Court has yoyoed on the issue of the right to travel.* NY Times 12/17/67, pD12 *But its profits have yoyoed up from £28,200 to £97,100 through 1958/67, which must leave the Berger Jenson parent wondering what might have been if the accent had been on "service."* Sunday Times (London) 3/9/69, p29 —*n. U.S. Slang.* a stupid person, probably so called from the comparison of a yo-yo's motion to a "jerk" (a fool). *Upon catching their attention, he would leer, and categorize them in a loud, mocking voice. ("Weirdo" was one of his favorite appellations; also "Freak," "Yo-Yo," and "Creep.")* New Yorker 11/28/70, p40 [**1960** for adj., **1967** for verb, **1970** for noun; from *yo-yo,* a toy spun up and down on a string (OEDS 1915)]

YSO, abbreviation of *young stellar object,* a protostar, especially a faint star with a high degree of irregularity in its emission spectrum. *The most logical regions to search for YSOs were the dark interstellar clouds. Before the late 1960s, searches of stellar birthplaces could only be made at optical wavelengths. Three major classes of YSOs were isolated from such searches.* 1977 Britannica Yearbook of Science and the Future, p78 [**1976**]

yuck or **yuk,** *Slang.* —*interj.* an exclamation of strong distaste or disgust. Also spelled YECCH. *In one seminar I attended, a personnel-placement specialist . . . tried to demonstrate how perspectives have to be broadened by asking one young woman in the audience how she would react to the name of the Chase Manhattan Bank. "You'd say it sounds awful, wouldn't you?" he said. "Yuck! Who wants to work in a bank!"* New Yorker 3/7/77, p90 *Expand your thinking about meats. Too many people say 'yuk' to liver because they have never tasted it cooked well. Kidneys and liver combine beautifully with wine and spices.* New York Post 1/23/79, p24 —*n.* something distasteful or disgusting. *'The offices now are so ugly and so*

standard, such standardized urban yuk . . .' Times (London) 10/17/77, p12 [**1966,** perhaps imitative of the sound of retching]

yucky or **yukky,** *adj. Slang.* disgusting; repugnant; repulsive. Also spelled YECCHY. *"Mmmm," purred an ecstatic Zero Mostel, dipping his tongue into a lemon meringue pie topped with whipped cream. Then his face congealed in horror: "I never eat this glop," he growled. Picky-Eater Mostel was not indulging a fad: he was acting first "yummy" and then "yucky" for Poet/Novelist George Mendoza's* The Sesame Street Book of Opposites, *a picture book.* Time 1/21/74, p42 *"It's a nice street, there's a good community spirit and I like the mixture of old and new residents. But from an architectural point of view, it's yukky."* Sunday Times (London) 3/30/75, p41 [**1970**]

yuppie ('yəpi:), *n. Especially U.S.* a young urban professional, especially one who is highly career-minded and lives in a conspicuously affluent manner. *Who are all those upwardly mobile folk with designer water, running shoes, pickled parquet floors and $450,000 condos in semislum buildings? Yuppies, of course, . . . and the one true guide to their carefully hectic lifestyle is* The Yuppie Handbook *. . .* Time 1/9/84, p66 *With "Thirtysomething," ABC makes a play for the* Quiche-and-Condo Crowd. *It's a show about the yuppies' favorite subject—themselves.* American Film 11/87, p49 [**1984,** from the initials of *y*oung *u*rban *p*rofessional + -*ie,* diminutive suffix; patterned after HIPPIE and YIPPIE]

yusho ('yu:ʃou), *n.* a diseased condition caused by ingestion of polychlorinated biphenyl (PCB), characterized by skin eruptions, swollen eyelids, swelling of joints, palsy, etc. (often used attributively). *Even today, almost nine years after eating tiny quantities of PCB's—and long after all traces have passed from their bodies—the symptoms of many* Yusho *victims persist. Recently, a Japanese researcher told a cancer conference at Cold Spring Harbor that the incidence of liver cancer among Yusho patients now appears to be as high as 15 times the normal rate.* NY Times Magazine 10/24/76, p26 [**1969,** from Japanese *yushō,* literally, oil disease (from *yu* oil + *shō* disease), so called from its occurrence in Japan in 1968 among thousands of people who consumed rice oil that had been accidentally contaminated with PCB]

Yvette (i:'vet), *n. Canadian Slang.* an old-fashioned French Canadian woman or girl. *"We didn't go along with bra-burning and other excesses of women's liberation. We won't go along with the excesses of sovereignty-association," exults an Yvette as she introduces Madeleine Ryan.* Maclean's 5/12/80, p4 [**1980,** from the name of such a character in Quebec school primers] ►This usage was popularized by Lise Payette, a Parti Québecois cabinet minister, during the campaign preceding the May 1980 referendum on SOVEREIGNTY-ASSOCIATION between Canada and an independent Quebec.

Z

za (tsɑ:), *n. U.S. Slang.* short for *pizza. Nothing that can't be set to rights by nuking a little frozen za, of course.* Fairfax Journal (VA) 9/7/88, pA10 [**1968**]

zaikai (ˈzɑiˌkai), *n.* commercial groups or financial circles of Japan. *Only now, as industry and business come to be seen as major suspects for rocketing prices and rampant pollution, has a wider spectrum of Japanese begun to scrutinize the* zaikai *and how it works.* Times (London) 7/10/73, pIX *Some top* zaikai *(business community) leaders have sought to explain Lockheed not as a product of a corrupt system but as an aberration caused by overly ambitious, vulgar and greedy men.* NY Times Magazine 11/21/76, p112 [**1968**, from Japanese, from *zai* money, wealth + *-kai* community, world, domain]

zaire (zɑːˈir), *n., pl.* **zaires** or **zaire.** the basic unit of money in Zaire (the former Democratic Republic of the Congo), equal to 100 makuta. *A little over a year ago, the Government, with International Monetary Fund advice, performed a drastic 3-for-1 currency devaluation, replacing the inflation-riddled franc with a new currency, the zaire, worth about $2.* NY Times 7/9/68, p2 [**1967**]

Zairean or **Zairian** (zɑːˈiriːən), *n.* a native or inhabitant of Zaire, the name since 1971 of the former Democratic Republic of the Congo (capital, Kinshasa). *All Zaireans may keep their present first names or opt for local ones until the party congress next May decides whether people should be identified by their surnames or their first names.* Times (London) 1/13/72, p6 —*adj.* of or having to do with Zaire. *A new nationality bill . . . required all Zairean nationals having a Zairean mother and a foreign father to adopt their mother's name in place of that of their father.* Britannica Book of the Year 1973, p735 *The target of the authenticity programme is Zairian control and administration of Zairian resources.* Times (London) 11/24/72, pI [**1972**]

Zambian, *n.* a native or inhabitant of Zambia, the name since 1964 of the former Northern Rhodesia. *The Zambians . . . are probably more anti-white-Rhodesian at heart than any other people of the Commonwealth of whatever colour.* Listener 12/15/66, p879 —*adj.* of or having to do with Zambia. *The Zambian authorities have coordinated youth programs with their rural-development plans . . .* NY Times 4/30/71, p14 [**1964**]

Zamboni (zæmˈbouni:), *n.* the trademark for a small tractorlike vehicle used to smooth the surface of ice-skating or ice-hockey rinks. *The basketball court, the Zamboni ice-making machine and other gear normally stored in the building, will be taken out, and, according to Deputy Mayor Stanley M. Friedman, will be stored free in city warehouses.* NY Times 2/16/76, p30 —*v.t.* to smooth (ice) with such a vehicle. *At the conclusion of each skating session, a crew of a half-dozen city employees— all of them skating guards at Lasker—take to the ice and skim the worn surface with broad-bladed shovels . . . Following that, the ice receives a light spray of hot water, which leaves the surface almost as slick as if it had been mechanically Zambonied.* New Yorker 2/6/78, p25 [**1965**, named after Frank J. Zamboni, its inventor]

ZANU (ˈzɑːnu:), *n.* acronym for *Zimbabwe African National Union*, a black nationalist guerrilla organization formed in Zimbabwe (Rhodesia) in 1963. Compare ZAPU. See also PATRIOTIC FRONT. *Serious problems developed as a result between the estimated 12,000 ZANU guerrillas and the local population, who often were forced to yield their crops and cattle to the insurgents. The Mozambique peasantry made little secret of their distaste for ZANU, a feeling which was reflected by several Frelimo officials who also had a poor opinion of the disci-*

pline and politicisation of their guerrilla guests. Manchester Guardian Weekly 1/1/79, p11 [**1963**]

zap, *Chiefly U.S. Slang.* —*v.t.* **1** to shoot; hit. *". . . I worry about my own son getting hit by a sniper because of that damn long hair. It's dangerous to walk around looking hairy, man. You could get zapped."* Harper's 9/70, p61 **2** to beat; defeat. *"No police force can stop a riot," a captain said. "They'll need the Army to zap those hoodlums, just like in Detroit."* NY Times 5/1/68, p14 **3** to engage in a confrontation or attack verbally. *They* [homosexuals] *have also made it a practice to "trash" (wreck) restaurants, publishing houses, and other businesses that discriminate against the third world of sex; "dump on" (heckle) religious leaders, such as Billy Graham, who don't like them; and "zap" (confront) politicians until they express themselves one way or the other on equal housing and employment rights for homosexuals.* Saturday Review 2/12/72, p24 **4** to move or make quickly. *For quick acceleration . . . the nickel-cadmium batteries would cut in briefly, could zap the car from a standstill to 50 m.p.h. in 20 seconds.* Time 12/22/67, p56 *Nobody except his grandmother thought he'd live overnight, for he* [the jockey Willie Shoemaker] *weighed only two and a half pounds, but she zapped up an incubator for him—a cardboard box lined with cotton wool, which she put in the oven of the kitchen stove. And it did the trick.* New Yorker 9/19/70, p131 **5** Also, **zap out.** *U.S.* to switch off (commercials or other unwanted parts of a television program or videotape) by using a remote control unit or by fast-forwarding the videotape. *VCRs also have the ability to zap out commercials, they complain, thus attacking the revenue base of commercial television. Advertisers will insist on paying less for commercial time.* Christian Science Monitor 5/12/82, p11 *I've been manually and remotely zapping commercials, network promos and newsbreaks for some time. Now I've developed a microprocessor-based signal analyzer that does it for me automatically. It's able to identify commercials by the electronic codes that are broadcast before them. On Saturday mornings the automatic zapper switches to an "empty" channel during the ads., giving my kids about three minutes of quiet every so often to wander off.* Fortune 2/18/85, p15 —*v.i.* to go quickly; move fast. *Nothing is quite as sad as watching Lynn watching Lightfoot zap off out of a parking lot. I wondered how she'd get back. "By bus, or hooking a ride with someone," Lightfoot said.* Maclean's 9/68, p55 —*n.* **1** vitality; force; zip. *. . . when the heat's too much and the gin's lost its zap (gin rummy, of course), tranquilize your jangled nerves with the Swinging Wonder.* NY Times 8/2/68, p3 **2** a confrontation or attack by opponents. *Despite six zaps, New York's Mayor Lindsay has consistently refused to meet with any homosexual delegation. However, last May he did declare: "Antihomosexual policies are arbitrary victimization."* Saturday Review 2/12/72, p26 —*interj.* imitative of the sound, speed, suddenness, etc. of a hard blow. *Bang! Zap! Pow! With flashing laser beams and cracking doomsday machines, the deadly-serious superheroes swarmed out . . .* Maclean's 3/68, p77 [**1942, 1965** for verb; **1968** for noun; **1929, 1962** for interj.]

Zapata mustache, a mustache that slants sharply down on each side. *Lip gloss, hair spray, three-tone streaks, cocoa-butter tans, insecure Zapata mustaches and wine red crushed velvet tuxedos: the women looked like tennis club matrons and their escorts like croupiers.* Time 4/12/76, p61 [**1968**, named after the Mexican revolutionist Emiliano *Zapata*, c1880-1919, probably from his portrayal in the motion picture *Viva Zapata!* (1952) by the American actor Marlon Brando]

zapper, *n. U.S.* **1** a device for directing microwave or other radiation against a target, especially insects, weeds, and other pests. *One particularly promising application, making use of small portable zappers, is for greenhouses and other horticultural enterprises.* Scientific American 9/73, p74 *Although various alternatives are promising, there is no magic 'insect zapper'. . . to replace chemical poisons in the near future.* Nature 2/12/76, p441 **2** *Figurative use.* **a** a forceful attacker or critic. *The* [Alice Cooper] *group was so weird that it naturally came to the attention of that master zapper of the Establishment Frank Zappa, who released Alice's first LP (Pretties for You) on his own Straight label.* Time 5/28/73, p83 **b** a forceful attack or criticism. *He* [Mr. Rockefeller] *titillated his audience with such zappers as: "Today, New York City has neither an effective, citywide, oldline political organization . . . nor does it have true community or neighborhood elective government with the power to be either responsive to the people or accountable to them in meeting their needs."* NY Times 1/23/72, pD3 [**1969,** from ZAP, *v.* + *-er*]

zapping, *n. Chiefly U.S. Slang.* the practice of switching off commercials or other unwanted parts of a television program or videotape by using a remote control unit or by fast-forwarding the videotape. *It's difficult for advertising agencies to stay in business making commercials that people won't watch. So zapping has become, in the words of a handout that J. Walter Thompson issued to financial analysts in November, "unquestionably the topic of the year."* Fortune 1/21/85, p68 [**1983**]

zap pit, a microscopic depression on the surface of lunar rocks, caused by the impact of micrometeorites, particles of cosmic dust, etc. *Measurements of micrometeorite impact pits ("zap" pits) on surfaces dated by particle track techniques have led to the suggestion that the present flux of micrometeorites is about tenfold higher than the average value during the last several million years.* McGraw-Hill Yearbook of Science and Technology 1974, p327 [**1973,** from ZAP interjection used to indicate a sudden blow or impact]

zappy, *adj. Informal.* full of vitality; lively; energetic. *The style is De Vries's customarily zappy, pun-a-minute stuff.* Listener 9/13/73, p352 *The method: Zappy brochures, massive repetitive mailings, fund-raising kaffeeklatches.* Maclean's 1/10/77, p54 [**1969,** from *zap* force, vitality + *-y* (adj. suffix)]

ZAPU ('zɑ:pu:), *n.* acronym for *Zimbabwe African People's Union,* a black nationalist guerrilla organization formed in Zimbabwe (Rhodesia) in 1961. Compare ZANU. See also PATRIOTIC FRONT. *The slogans shouted at the meeting described what is on the minds of ZAPU officials and all nationalist politicians these days. First the speaker shouts, "Z," and the thunderous reply is "Zimbabwe," the nationalist name for Rhodesia. Next, he cries out, "ZAPU," and the refrain is Puza, a rearrangement of the group's initials. Finally, the climax comes: "Nkomo," bellows the speaker. "P-O-W-E-R," roars back the crowd.* Manchester Guardian Weekly (Washington Post section) 7/30/78, p17 [**1961**]

ZBB or **Z.B.B.,** abbreviation of ZERO-BASED BUDGETING. *ZBB is just the latest of many management science ideas to sweep through business and government. Perhaps their ultimate value is that in the name of novelty they prod organizations to do what common sense would dictate anyway.* Maclean's 5/30/77, p51 [**1976**]

Z disk or **Z disc,** a thin, dark disk of fibrous protein that passes through striated muscle fiber and marks the boundaries of contiguous contractile units. *Skeletal muscles contract by way of thick protein rods sliding between thin rods. The muscle is given strength, and its speed of contraction increased, by intermittent cross-walls known as Z discs. These appear as narrow stripes under the microscope—one reason why skeletal muscle is often called "striped" muscle. But because of those Z-discs, contraction is limited; the contracted length of a skeletal muscle is only 40 per cent of the extended length.* New Scientist 5/31/73, p533 [**1972,** translation of German *Z-Scheibe,* abbreviated form of *Zwischenscheibe* intermediate disk] ►Earlier names (still used) of this structure are *Z line* (1916) and *Z band* (1950).

zeatin ('zi:ətin), *n.* a naturally occurring plant hormone that stimulates cell division (cytokinin), originally isolated from young maize kernels. *Zeatin, dihydrozeatin (zeatin's counterpart with the saturated double bond) and the ribosides of these compounds have been isolated from extracts of plant tissues.* McGraw-Hill Yearbook of Science and Technology 1970, p302 [**1963,** coined by D. S. Letham, researcher for the New Zealand Department of Scientific and Industrial Research, from New Latin *Zea (mays)* the maize plant + English kine*tin* a synthetic type of cytokinin]

zebra, *n. U.S. Slang.* a referee, linesman, or other official in a football game. *This year's Super Bowl zebras will, as always, be an all-star cast, chosen by N.F.L.* [National Football League] *Supervisor of Officials Art McNally and his staff after watching game films and grading performances.* Time 1/16/78, p70 [**1978,** from the striped shirts worn by officials]

zedonk ('zi:,dɔŋk), *n.* the offspring of a male zebra and a female donkey. Also called ZONKEY. *Melbourne, Australia—A local donkey breeding farm claims to have mated a zebra with a donkey and produced a zedonk named Zarebba . . . Mrs. Finnigan said she knows of only three zedonks in the world, two in England and one in Canada. "The two in England don't have the same markings and look more like donkeys," she said.* New York Post 9/3/76, p4 [**1971,** from ze*bra* + *donkey*]

ZEG or **Z.E.G.,** abbreviation of ZERO ECONOMIC GROWTH. *A third view is that there is very little relationship between Z.P.G.* [zero population growth] *and Z.E.G. Sociologist Lincoln Day believes that "there is nothing in a stationary population itself that would inevitably be productive of any particular economic change or condition."* Time 9/16/74, p63 [**1972**]

zeitgeber or **Zeitgeber** ('tsaɪt,geibər), *n. sing.* or *pl.* any of various time indicators, such as light, dark, or temperature, that influence the workings of the biological clock. *Still, the circannual clock itself is not an adequate regulator. As we have seen, it is never set at exactly 365 days. If the natural environment played no part, the clock and the animal's rhythm would become increasingly out of phase with the natural seasons. Hence the animal still must depend on Zeitgeber, or cues from the environment, to correct the clock and thus entrain its rhythm each year.* Scientific American 4/71, p79 *The question of biological clock master key aside, most scientists of either school concur that external or geophysical factors can reset the clock or throw it out of phase. Light is considered by many researchers to be the most critical external timer or zeitgeber.* Science News 9/11/71, p179 [**1964,** from German *Zeitgeber,* literally, time giver]

zek, *n.* an inmate of a Soviet prison or forced labor camp. See also GULAG. *In a system based on mistrust and espionage, they . . . intrigued among themselves, but were united against the rabble. The newly arrived zek soon learned, as in an army, to hide his skills and watch his chance.* New Statesman 12/5/75, p716 *A web of concentration camps had developed around Rubtsovsk, and shifts of prisoners, or zeks, as the Russians called them, were trucked in to keep the industries going 24 hours a day.* Reader's Digest 1/80, p192 [**1964,** from Russian prison slang, probably from the pronunciation of *z/k,* abbreviation of Russian *zaklyuchennyi* prisoner; popularized by the Russian author Aleksandr Solzhenitsyn, born 1918]

zendo, *n.* a Zen Buddhist center for meditation and study. *We gather in silence outside the zendo and do our best, with various forms of yoga and calisthenics, to stretch out our backs and legs.* NY Times Magazine 10/10/76, p64 [**1959,** from Japanese *zendō*]

zener diode ('zi:nər), a silicon semiconductor used as a voltage stabilizer. *The Zener diode is in effect a variable resistor that automatically maintains fixed voltage in a circuit.* Scientific American 5/70, p132 [**1957,** named after Clarence M. *Zener,* born 1905, an American physicist]

zero-based budgeting or **zero-base budgeting,** *U.S. and Canada.* a method of preparing a budget by reviewing the basis of all expenditures of a department, agency, etc., rather than calculating the necessary percentage of increase or decrease in spending from the budget of the previous year. *Abbreviation:* ZBB *In Georgia Mr. McIntyre pushed zero-base budgeting, a tougher justification process for money than the budget office is now applying to the more than 100 Federal agencies.* NY Times 9/7/77, p48 [**1976** for *zero-based;* **1970** for *zero-base*]

zero economic growth, a condition in which a nation's per capita income shows no appreciable increase. *Abbreviation:* ZEG *There is a real crisis . . . in the shape of the looming recession, and the prospect of zero economic growth next year. That will mean a double crunch, political and economic; the first duty will be survival once again.* Listener 12/27/73, p871 [**1965**]

zero growth, 1 short for *zero population growth* (the condition in which the size of a population remains constant). *Several European countries—Austria, East and West Germany and Luxembourg—have already gone beyond zero growth: they have more deaths than births each year. The United Kingdom is right at the balance point, with births and deaths about equal. If current trends in fertility continue, Belgium, Czechoslovakia, Denmark, Hungary, Norway and Sweden will reach or fall below zero growth in a few years.* Scientific American 12/78, p51 **2** short for ZERO ECONOMIC GROWTH. *In 1965, the Oxford undergraduate economics exam asked, "Can economies have simultaneously zero growth, rapid inflation, substantial unemployment, and a balance of payments deficit?" The acceptable answer back then was that this combination could occur only in an underdeveloped country.* Atlantic 1/76, p4 **3** a policy of preventing expansion or development. *This community of 1,500 [Bolinas] is not an incorporated township, but power to stop new construction is wielded through the five-man water board of the Public Utility District, a majority of which is dedicated to zero growth. They keep out developers by refusing to issue new water meters.* NY Times Magazine 7/4/76, p73 [**1967** for defs. 1 and 3; **1965** for def. 2]

zero norm, *British.* another name for NIL NORM. *In principle at least, this type of operation does not need to use a zero norm—as the 1966 freeze did. It would be possible for wages to be semifrozen, with maximum increases of 2%, or 4%, or whatever.* Sunday Times (London) 6/18/72, p62 [**1966**]

zero population growth, the condition in which a population ceases to grow and a balance is reached in the average number of births and deaths. *Abbreviation:* ZPG *If winter* [in Alaska] *is unusually long, a whole species* [of migratory birds] *may achieve zero population growth because it lacks time to hatch and rear its young before the ice begins to return in late August.* Time 7/27/70, p49 *Transition from a time in which babies were the thing to an era of zero population growth must have profound consequences on the relations between men and women and on the structure of society.* Science 1/14/72, p127 [**1967**]

zero-rate, *v.t. British.* to exempt from payment of a value-added tax. See ADDED VALUE and VAT. *The structure of the value added tax, which zero-rates half—the most important half—of family expenditure, can be shown to be in many respects progressive rather than regressive.* Manchester Guardian Weekly 12/12/76, p3 [**1972**] —**zero-rating,** *n.: There would also probably be fewer anomalies between items which were zero-rated and items which were positively rated, because the broad blocks of expenditure which had been relieved by zero-rating were clearly defined.* Times (London) 5/11/72, p10

zero tillage, another name for NO-TILLAGE. *Zero tillage, a technique for growing crops, enables grain farmers to reduce fuel consumption by 50 percent while protecting the soil from erosion, according to Elmer Stobbe, a plant scientist . . . Zero tillage, which means no cultivation, involves seeding directly into untilled soil with minimum disturbance of the soil.* NY Times 8/14/79, pC3 [**1971**]

zetz, *U.S. Slang. Often figurative.* —*n.* a punch, blow, or slap. *The actor had come to tape "The Phil Donahue Show," to talk about his new movie, "The Big Fix," and maybe even to get a little zetz going with Donahue, whose political barbs during interviews had impressed him.* Rolling Stone 1/11/79, p85 —*v.t.* to strike, throw, or deliver. *We said we hadn't quite got his last remark. "That's glyph for 'Mein Gott im̄ Himmel,'"* he

said. *"I like to zetz in a little glyph now and then."* New Yorker 12/25/78, p21 [**1968**, from Yiddish *zets*, ultimately from *zetsn* to set, put]

Zhdanovian (ʒdɑːˈnouviːən), **Zhdanovite** (ˈʒdɑːnəˌvait), or **Zhdanovist** (ˈʒdɑːnəvist), *adj.* of or relating to the policy or practice of Zhdanovism. *It is, indeed, a Leninist principle to make what is usable in non-socialist culture contribute to socialist culture, though this has been forgotten because of the indiscriminateness with which Zhdanovian aesthetics were applied.* Listener 10/22/70, p557 *Four times last year, before the Central Committee suppressed it altogether in a fit of Zhdanovite rage, the union's weekly,* Literarni Noviny, *was forced to accept a different editor.* Harper's 8/68, p68 *Then in 1948, along with other political events, all Czechoslovak cultural life fell under the powerful influence of Zhdanovist esthetics and Stalinist practices.* Saturday Review 12/23/67, p11 [**1957** *Zhdanovite,* **1966** *Zhdanovist,* **1970** *Zhdanovian*]

Zhdanovism (ˈʒdɑːnəˌvizəm), *n.* the strict political control of writers and other intellectuals in the Soviet Union fostered under Stalin by the Communist leader and general Andrei Z. Zhdanov, 1896-1948. *Ehrenburg at last ventured on criticism of Zhdanovism and made an open plea for greater artistic freedom in Russia.* Annual Register of World Events in 1967, p520 [George] *Lukacs . . . has been one of the very few theoretically educated adherents of 'socialist realism', perhaps the only important expounder of the so-called 'aesthetic ideal' of Zhdanovism.* Listener 11/3/66, p659 [**1958**]

zidovudine (ˌzaidəvuˈdiːn), *n.* another name for AZIDOTHYMIDINE. *Recently renamed zidovudine, AZT slows viral replication and currently is the only federally approved AIDS treatment.* Science News 9/12/87, p165 [**1987**]

zilch, *n. U.S. Slang.* nil; nothing; zero. *"Seventy-five percent of our alcoholics eventually return to work, but our record of drug rehabilitation is zilch."* Time 6/29/70, p70 [**1966**, from earlier *Mr. Zilch,* a humorous indefinite name (OEDS 1931)]

zills (zilz), *n.pl.* a pair of round metal pieces attached by loops to the thumb and second finger and struck together for percussion and rhythm in belly dancing. *As the mid-eastern music starts to wail . . . the dancers begin to acquire some semblance of the right movement while finger cymbals (called zills) start tinkling out a dance rhythm.* NY Times 11/24/74, p39 [**1973**, from Turkish *zill* cymbal, handbell]

Zimbabwean (zimˈbɑːbwiːən), *n.* a native or inhabitant of Zimbabwe, the black African nationalist name of Rhodesia since 1961, and the official name since 1980. *Once the Namibians and Zimbabweans have got their independence, the great black majority in South Africa is going to move to change the Republic into the state of Azania.* Times (London) 5/4/76, p12 —*adj.* of or having to do with Zimbabwe. *A guerrilla war would radicalize the Zimbabwean situation in the manner of Angola and Mozambique.* Britannica Book of the Year 1977, p10 [**1967**]

zine (ziːn), *n. U.S.* a magazine or newsletter produced by a science-fiction fan or group of fans. *Devra Langsam, one of our hard-working crew, was editor of* Spockanalia, *the very first "Star Trek" zine and still one of the best.* Joan Winston, The Making of the Trek Conventions, 1977, p19 [**1965**, back formation from *fanzine* (1949), from *fan* + *magazine*] ►This form is frequently used by science-fiction fans to create compounds such as *newszine, letterzine, book-a-zine.* For other examples, see "Star Trek Lives: Trekker Slang," by Patricia Byrd, in *American Speech,* Spring 1978, pp 52-54.

zing, *Slang.* —*v.i.* to move or act in a lively or energetic manner. . . . *put her in front of a camera and she starts to zing.* NY Times 3/30/65, p41 *Fishermen arrive in force, . . . zinging along in snowmobiles.* Time 2/16/81, p6 —*v.t.* **1** Usually, **zing up.** to give life or zest to; enliven. *Charles Revson is the philosopher-king of the cosmetic world . . . He claims to know by instinct how to "zing up" a face . . .* New Yorker 11/14/70, p154 **2** *U.S.* to attack verbally; criticize. *The all-time male chauvinist, never missing a chance to zing the women tennis pros . . .* The News (Mexico City) 8/26/73, p33 **3** *U.S.* to deliver or throw in a speedy or lively manner. . . . *we zing in a cou-*

ple of great production numbers with lots of pizzazz . . . New Yorker 5/16/64, p45 . . . her usual practice of zinging brash, hostile questions at world leaders. Time 1/10/77, p26 [**1961**, extended use of "to travel rapidly making a sharp whining sound" (OED2, 1940), and verb use of the slang noun *zing* liveliness, zest (OED2 1918), originally imitative of a sharp, high-pitched ringing sound (OED2, 1911)]

zinger ('ziŋər), *n. Chiefly U.S. Slang.* **1** one who has spirit or vitality; a peppy person. *A stunning blonde zinger from North Carolina, Mrs. Howar, 36, got her social start as a Johnson campaign volunteer in 1964 and as the wife of a rich Washington builder . . .* Time 11/30/70, p32 **2** something that hits the mark, such as a witty retort, or the like. *. . . you had to get right in there with Williams, stand eyeball to eyeball, and plant the zinger on him, bang . . .* Harper's 6/69, p74 *Ann-Margret is giving him a hard time on the home front, too, cooking lousy dinners, casting aspersions on his sexual prowess, and tossing out little zingers about his advancing age like "Flab is reality."* Time 10/12/70, p7 **3** something outstandingly good. *"I think every actress needs one zinger of a part early in her career."* Times (London) 5/30/68, p10 [**1970** for def. 1; **1969** for def. 2; **1955** for def. 3]

zip¹, *U.S. Slang. —n.* zero; nothing (often referring to a score in sports). *"Here are your facts," he said. "I think I've got everything here. Armed robbery. Zip to ten. Second offense. That's you, isn't it?"* John Cheever, Falconer, 1975, p67 *In that span, folks, the Milwaukee Bucks did not score a basket. None. Zip. Zero.* New York Post 2/11/76, p88 *A reliance on black culture, they say . . . may make you feel good, and it may be something you feel in your bones and on weekends and when the beat thumps, but it goes for zip in the real world.* NY Times Magazine 12/3/78, p150 *—v.t.* to beat (a team) without allowing it to score; shut out. *The Adams Division leaders zipped Los Angeles, 4-0.* Picture legend, Daily News (New York) 1/16/76, p82 [**1972**, originally dialectal use (*c*1900) meaning a mark or grade of zero]

zip², *n.* short for ZIP CODE. *The salesgirl carefully wrote down some details of the complicated address, which was in Dhahran, Saudi Arabia, and then . . . asked earnestly, "Would you by any chance know the zip?"* New Yorker 3/25/72, p32 [**1969**]

zip code, *U.S.* a five-digit number used to identify a mail-delivery zone in the United States. The corresponding system in Great Britain is called POSTCODE. Also shortened to ZIP. *The first three digits of the familiar five-digit zip code system identify sectional centers, and the last two indicate the particular post office.* NY Times 1/2/68, p23 [**1963**, from *ZIP*, acronym for *Zone Improvement Plan*, the U.S. Postal Service system of coding by zones for faster mail sorting and delivery, introduced on July 1, 1963, + *code*]

zip-code, *v.t. U.S.* to provide with the zip code. *Third-class bulk mailers earn their lower postage rates by zip-coding every address, sorting the mail in numerical sequence, facing it and tieing it in bundles, placing it in properly tagged sacks and delivering it to the Post Office . . .* NY Times 4/27/70, p32 [**1966**]

zipless, *adj. Slang.* sexually uninhibited; openly erotic. *A year after the unanticipated success of* Fear of Flying, *Erica Jong . . . had already programmed her next zipless book, "How to Save Your Own Life."* Britannica Book of the Year 1978, p514 [**1973**, from *zip* a zipper (OEDS 1928) + *-less*]

zip-top, *adj.* having a top that may be removed by pulling a strip around its rim. Compare POP-TOP. *Easy opening devices are undergoing considerable development—and ring-pull and zip-top cans are already available.* Times (London) 2/16/70, pIII [**1970**]

zircalloy or **zircaloy** ('zərkə,lɔi), *n.* an alloy of zirconium and other metals, widely used for its heat-resistant and corrosion-resistant properties, especially in reactors to separate the fuel from the coolant. *It will have a capacity of 125 tons per year of uranium oxide, and 50 tons of zircalloy products from Indian zircon, to be used for containing uranium oxide in fuel elements and structural elements in reactor assemblies.* Science

News 8/10/68, p146 *This* [clad metal] *may be aluminum, stainless steel or zirconium (usually a zirconium alloy called zircaloy).* Encyclopedia Science Supplement (Grolier) 1968, p218 [**1956**, from *zirconium alloy*]

zit, *n. U.S. Slang.* **1** a pimple. *The characters in the commercial are usually a young girl talking breathlessly about "blemishes" to a friend, or a girl and her brother "telling it like it is" by referring to their affliction as "zits."* NY Times Magazine 4/15/79, p69 **2** Transferred use: *One splendid effort in 1971 featured districts that looked like giant chickens . . . and districts with remarkable pimples in their boundary lines, zits that popped up to include the home of one liberal incumbent in the district of another liberal incumbent.* Atlantic 3/75, p51 [**1966**, of unknown origin]

ziti ('zi:ti:), *n.* pasta in the form of short, slightly curved tubes. *One of the great revelations to come about within the past few years is the awakening in the American public's consciousness that pasta in all its multifarious forms—spaghetti, linguine, ziti and so on—need not invariably be served with tomato sauce, meat sauce or meatballs.* NY Times Magazine 8/5/79, p60 [**1964**, from Italian; *zita* (1845)]

zizzy, *adj. Slang.* **1** showy in dress or manner. *My wife said I should wear a dark suit but I did risk a particularly zizzy tie. Everyone else seemed to be in deepest mourning.* Times (London) 10/4/76, p27 **2** that is boisterous and often clownish. *You have to let this Mel Brooks comedy do everything for you, because that's the only way it works. If you accept the silly, zizzy obviousness, it can make you laugh helplessly.* New Yorker 5/17/76, p69 [**1966**, from *zizz* humming sound (as of a bee), buzz + *-y* (adj. suffix)]

Zollinger-Ellison syndrome, a condition of excessive secretion and hyperacidity of gastric juices resulting in the formation of peptic ulcers and tumors in cells of the pancreas. *The F.D.A.'s approval was . . . limited to the prescribing of Tagamet for up to eight-week treatments of duodenal ulcers and possibly longer periods for treatments of one of a complex of diseases known collectively by the forbidding eponym of Zollinger-Ellison syndrome.* NY Times Magazine 11/6/77, p76 [**1956**, named after R. M. *Zollinger*, born 1903, and E. H. *Ellison*, 1918-1970, American surgeons who first described it]

zone melting, another name for ZONE REFINING. *William G. Pfann . . . invented zone melting, a purification process for metals, semiconductors, and other materials. This technique led to the large-scale manufacture of transistors, diodes, and integrated circuits.* 1969 Britannica Yearbook of Science and the Future, p258 [**1952**]

zone refining, a method of purifying metal in which a high-temperature heat source is passed along the metal, carrying off impurities and concentrating them at one or both ends of the treated metal. Also called ZONE MELTING. *Germanium was produced which contained less than one atom of impurity per trillion atoms of germanium. This is comparable to one grain of salt in a carload of sugar. The material was prepared by zone refining where a heat source is moved along an ingot of metal, and a seed crystal, added to the melt, triggers crystallization. A typical crystal thus formed is from 1 to 1.5 inches thick and 6 inches long.* Americana Annual 1971, p199 [**1952**]

zonk, *v.i., v.t. Slang.* to lose consciousness; fall deeply asleep. *The day had been a long one, exhausting, and he had just, as he put it, "zonked," when Hubert Humphrey was on the phone, waking him . . .* Atlantic 9/72, p6 **—zonk out. 1** to fall deeply asleep. *If mothers zonk out at three in the afternoon, they may continue that pattern after it's no longer necessary.* NY News Magazine 3/18/84, p18 **2** to stupefy or intoxicate with drugs. *. . . connivers who have baffled their Selective Service boards by zonking themselves out on speed . . .* Saturday Review 11/18/72, p41 [**1968**, from earlier slang *zonk* to hit or knock (1950), ultimately imitative of the sound of a blow]

zonked, *adj. Slang.* stupefied or intoxicated by narcotics or alcohol. *. . . . "Guys are always stoned. Either they're high from pills to keep them awake or they're zonked on a joint they had on a break."* Time 6/29/70, p70 *It seems to me that most of the drivers one meets should not be allowed to take charge of a car* *when sober—let alone when three-parts zonked.* New Scientist 11/19/67, p185 [**1959**, probably from *zonk!*, an interjection imitative of the sound of a stunning blow on the head]

zonkey, *n.* another name for ZEDONK. *"Eleven, eleven, eleven,"* he chants, peddling a zonkey, an exotic cross between a zebra and a donkey.* Time 1/19/81, p8 [**1953, 1973,** from zebra + donkey]

zonky, *adj. Slang.* queer; weird. *"I tried the State Employment Office and all the guy does there is show you unemployment figures for the country and shakes his head. Makes you feel very zonky."* New Yorker 4/18/77, p48 [**1971**, probably from *zonked* + *-y* (adj. suffix)]

zoo, *n. Slang.* the large number and variety of nuclear particles discovered or proposed as a result of research in high-energy physics. *No one has yet seen a quark on its own—but the relevant categories of particles in the high energy physics zoo can now be fairly easily labelled by the number and type of quarks that make them up.* New Scientist 9/21/78, p838 [**1972**, from a comparison to animals in a zoo]

zoo event, an astronomical event of no known source or cause. *. . . the flash was a "zoo event," a signal of unknown origin, possibly caused by the impact of a small meteoroid on the satellite. No supporting evidence, such as radioactive debris, could be found to confirm a nuclear explosion.* Science News 2/28/81, p134 [**1980**; so called from a comparison of the variety of possible sources of the event to the variety of animals found in a zoo]

zoomer, *n.* a camera lens that can zoom in or out for wide-angle or close-up shoots; a zoom lens. *So he edges close to the television crew and waits for their whoop of delight as the zoomer sweeps the horizon and zeros in on the parachutes.* Manchester Guardian Weekly 4/25/70, p5 [**1966**, respelling of *Zoomar, zoomar* tradename of a telescopic lens (1946)]

zoomy, *adj.* by means of a zoom lens; using a zoomer. *. . . what Angus Wilson has called "the mysterious bond that ties gentleness to brutality, a bond that has made our times at once so shocking and so hopeful." Instead, we've been getting glib "statements" and cheap sex jokes, the zoomy shooting and shock cutting of TV commercials . . .* New Yorker 10/3/70, p78 [**1970**]

zoo plane, *U.S.* a plane carrying members of the news media assigned to follow a candidate during a campaign. *The atmosphere on the Zoo Plane became crazier and crazier as the atmosphere on the Dakota Queen became more reserved and somber. The kinkier members of the press tended to drift onto the Zoo Plane. The atmosphere was more comfortable. There were tremendous amounts of cocaine, for instance . . . What happened was that the press took over the Zoo Plane—totally.* Hunter S. Thompson, Fear and Loathing: On the Campaign Trail '72, 1973, p424 [**1972**]

zoosemiotics (ˌzouəˌsiˈmiˈɑtiks), *n.* the study of communication between animals. *In a collection of papers written by various experts in the field of . . . "zoosemiotics"—in other words, animal communication—each writer tries valiantly to define what he means by the term, and, if no two of them actually agree on a definition, at least they provide a most stimulating lot of theories.* New Yorker 4/17/78, p78 [**1963**, coined by the American linguist Thomas A. Sebeok, born 1920, from *zoo-* combining form meaning animal + *semiotics* study of signs and symbols]

zootoxin (ˌzouəˈtɑksən), *n.* any of various poisons produced by animals. *Zootoxins can be divided into: (1) oral poisons, those poisonous when eaten; (2) parenteral poisons or venoms . . . and (3) crinotoxins.* 1977 Britannica Yearbook of Science and the Future, p229 [**1976**]

zouk (zu:k), *n.* a lively form of Caribbean music with a strong beat that originated in Guadeloupe and Martinique and combines elements of highlife, soca, salsa, funk, and disco music, played with a synthesizer and other electronic instruments. *What's missing from zouk . . . is much verbal content . . . But zouk, like Nigerian juju and the best dub reggae, tells a story*

through music itself. NY Times 5/29/88, pC23 [**1988**, from West Indies Creole, probably from English *juke*]

Z particle, a subatomic particle with a neutral charge and a mass about 100 times that of the proton, held to be a carrier, or quantum, of the weak force. Also called Z-ZERO. Compare W PARTICLE. *They want to check the standard model. That includes studying the newly discovered W and Z particles, to find out, for example, what other kinds of particles are made with them and what particles they turn into. It involves looking for the Higgs particles, which play an important role in the standard model.* Science News 9/28/85, p203 [**1967**]

ZPG, abbreviation of ZERO POPULATION GROWTH. *Reaching this situation, defined by demographers as NRR (Net Reproductive Rate) = 1.0, would not lead to zero population growth (ZPG) at once, because of persons still living who were born when the NRR exceeded 1.0.* Saturday Review 10/3/70, p58 [**1970**]

Z-therapy, *n.* a form of psychotherapy in which the patient is held down by a group of people, interrogated sharply, and compelled by rough prodding or tickling to release pent-up emotions supposedly leading to a catharsis. *The controversial 'Z therapy' . . . may benefit nonpsychotic children who have severe antisocial personality disorders, Dr. Foster W. Cline said at the annual meeting of the American Association for the Advancement of Science . . . 'Z therapy' is based on the assumption that children who are unable to love because they were unloved must have love forced on them before they can develop other loving attachments.* Thomas Szasz, The Myth of Psychotherapy, 1979, p206, quoting Clinical Psychiatry News (June, 1977), p. 50 [**1973**, from Robert W. Zaslow, an American psychologist, who developed it + *therapy*]

Zugunruhe (ˈtsu:kunˌru:ə; *Anglicized* ˈzu:gənˌru: *or* -ˌru:ə), *n.* the migratory drive in animals, especially birds. *The behavior of the four groups was studied in terms of signs of Zugunruhe, or migratory urge, as shown by night activity and by the molt of feathers (which normally occurs during the winter after migration to the wintering area).* Scientific American 4/71, p76 *There have been several reports in the literature of extraretinally mediated effects of light on avian circadian and reproductive cycles, for example, Zugunruhe, fat deposition, and testicular growth.* Science 5/18/73, p753 [**1950, 1967,** from German, from *Zug* travel + *Unruhe* unrest]

Zulu, *n.* the aeronautical name for Greenwich Mean Time. *On the walls, digital clocks told the time at Greenwich, England—Zulu it is called—at major radar stations.* NY Times 1/29/78, p8 *At 1750 hours Zulu, about three in the afternoon local time, the Double Eagle II climbed to 10,000 feet, but it was still difficult to maintain altitude.* Reader's Digest 11/79, p283 [**1960**, from the present radio code name for the letter *z* (replacing the older name *Zebra,* as in *Zebra time* and *Z Time*) to represent *zero* degrees, the longitude at Greenwich, England]

zveno (zveˈnou), *n.* an experimental type of collective or state farm in the Soviet Union. See the quotation for details. *I strongly suspect that one reason for inefficiency is the very large size of the farms . . . This is a matter of serious concern to Soviet specialists. Some of them advocate the use of small groups of peasants (the zveno system); five or six peasants, members of a collective or state farm, are allocated land, animals, and machines and left free to work at their own pace, their income depending on what they produce.* Manchester Guardian Weekly 11/28/70, p6 [**1970**, from Russian, literally, link (of a chain)]

Zwicky galaxy or **Zwicky object,** any of a group of compact galaxies whose luminosity is concentrated in a small area. *Along with a small army of research students he has . . . circulated several lists of compact galaxies (now called Zwicky galaxies).* New Scientist 3/2/72, p501 [E.E.] *Khachikyan says that it is now clear that the Markarian galaxies, under their broad umbrella of excess ultraviolet, contain many different types: Seyferts, Zwicky objects, . . . many giant galaxies, many dwarf galaxies, distant galaxies and close galaxies; even quasars might be numbered among them.* Science News 8/18-25/73, p117 [**1969**, named for Fritz *Zwicky*, 1898-1974, a Bulgarian-born American astronomer and inventor, who catalogued them]

Zydeco or **zydeco** ('zɑidəkou), *n. U.S.* a style of country music developed in Louisiana, similar to bluegrass but with elements of rock, blues, and Latin-American music. *It is this concoction of musical styles that has helped make Zydeco popular, . . . with a big following in Europe. Another sign that Zydeco's time has come was the 1982 Grammy Award for best eth-nic/folk album.* Daily Argus (Mount Vernon, N.Y.) 10/2/83, pE1 [**1960,** from Louisiana French, probably from the Creole pronunciation of *Les Haricots* the beans, from a dance of this name popular among the Cajuns]

zymogram ('zɑimə,græm), *n.* a diagram or other representation of the different molecular forms of an enzyme, obtained by electrophoresis. *Most varieties have consistent patterns of iso-zymes (variants of the esterase enzymes) . . . The isozyme dis-tribution can be summarised in a zymogram, which provides the basis for identifying the variety of the seedling. But the identification is not a "finger-printing"—some varieties can-not be distinguished from each other.* New Scientist 4/4/74, p26 [**1957,** from *zymo-* combining form meaning enzyme + *-gram* something drawn]

Z-zero, *n.* another name for the Z PARTICLE. *An international team of 126 researchers at CERN, the European Laboratory for Particle Physics near Geneva, appears to have detected the last of the three particles that theorists believe transmit the so-called weak force in subatomic reactions. Only one particle of the new type has been observed so far. Known as the Z-zero, it would be the heaviest—more properly, the most massive—ever detected, roughly 100 times the mass of the proton, which forms the nucleus of hydrogen atoms.* NY Times 5/12/83, pA13 [**1977**]